Contents

The MILEPOST®
All-The-North Travel Guide®

Introduction

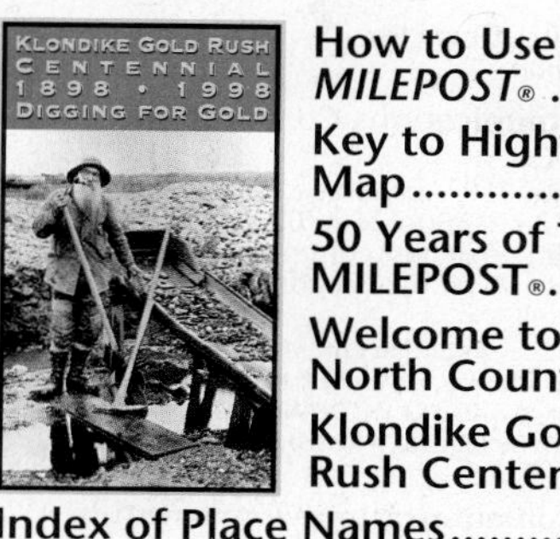

Major Attractions

Highways

Railroads

Marine Access Routes

Travel Planning

Watson Lake Signpost Forest. (© Chris Sharp)

Managing Editor, Kris Valencia Graef. **Associate Editor**, Wendy McLeod. **Editorial Assistance**, Mick Alberts, Debbie Brickman, Eleanore Cole. **Field Editors and Advertising Representatives:** Earl L. Brown, Lynn Owen, Jerrianne Lowther, Judy Parkin. **Production Manager**, Barton R. Vernon. **Advertising and Production Coordinator**, Miyuki Zybura. **Advertising Design**, Elizabeth A. Hackett. **Production Staff**, Jennifer Ring, Trevor Vernon. **Art Director**, David L. Ranta. **Page Designer**, Pam Smith. **Pre-press Supervisor**, Glen Jasmer. **Fulfillment Manager**, Tina L. Boyle. **Fulfillment Assistance**, Lisa Knight, Mary Waldrum, Molly Munro. **Associate Publisher**, Michele Andrus Dill.

ISSN 0361-1361 ISBN 1-878425-30-7
Key title: The Milepost
Printed in U.S.A.

COVER: Two sub-adult brown bears (*Ursus arctos*) rest in the green grass of Kodiak Island. *(© Howie Garber/Ken Graham Agency)*
COVER INSETS: Upper left: Gold stampeder in Nome, AK. *(Courtesy of Alaska State Library, Skinner, #44-11-3)*
Center of anniversary seal: RV travels south on the Seward Highway along Turnagain Arm. *(© Ken Graham/Ken Graham Agency)*
Cover Design, David L. Ranta
Additional photo credits (column insets): Earl L. Brown, pages 1, 52, 54, 114, 116, 118, 140, 233, 237, 288, 301; Blake Hanna, pages 43, 69; Jerrianne Lowther, pages 176, 524, 666; Judy Parkin, pages 44, 60, 68, 248, 273

Editorial and Advertising Offices:
The MILEPOST®
4220 B St., Suite 210, Anchorage, AK 99503
Until April 1, 1998: (425) 827-9900
After April 1,1998: (907) 561-4772, Fax (907) 561-5669

Book Orders and Customer Service:
The MILEPOST®
3000 Northup Way, Suite 200, Bellevue, WA 98004
Phone 1-800-726-4707
E-mail: books@themilepost.com
Internet address: www.themilepost.com

Publishers of The MILEPOST® since 1949:

Alaska Highway Research Co.
William A. Wallace

Alaska Northwest Publishing Co.
Robert A. Henning

Alaska Northwest Books
A Division of GTE Discovery Publications Inc.

Vernon Publications Inc.
Geoffrey P. Vernon

Morris Communications Corporation
The MILEPOST®
4220 B St., Suite 210, Anchorage, AK 99503
(907) 561-4772 • 1-800-726-4707
E-mail: books@themilepost.com
Internet address: www.themilepost.com

Publishers of:
The MILEPOST® • ALASKA A to Z • NORTHWEST MILEPOSTS® • The ALASKA WILDERNESS GUIDE • The MILEPOST® Souvenir Logbook • Alaska Roadhouse Recipes

Morris Communications Corporation
William S. Morris III, Chairman & CEO
Matthew H. Brown, Publisher

How to Use The MILEPOST®

The MILEPOST® provides mile-by-mile descriptions of all major highways and roads in Alaska and northwestern Canada; detailed information on all major destinations (cities, communities, national parks and other attractions) in the North; and how-to help for various modes of transportation (air, ferry, railroads, etc.). Refer to the Contents page and Index for subjects and destinations.

The MILEPOST® will work for you regardless of how you plan to travel—whether by car, by plane, on a tour bus, or by bicycle. It will help you plan your trip, as well as acting as a valuable guide during your trip.

The backbone of *The MILEPOST®* is the highway logs. The Key to Highways map on page 4 shows you what highways are covered in *The MILEPOST®*. In these mile-by-mile descriptions of the highways and byways of the North, you will find campgrounds; businesses offering food, gas, lodging and other services; attractions; fishing spots; road conditions; descriptions of the geography and history of the land and communities; and much more.

To the right is an abbreviated version of part of the Parks Highway log, keyed to help you understand how to read all highway logs in *The MILEPOST®*.

1. A boldface paragraph appears at the beginning of each highway log in *The MILEPOST®* that explains what beginning and ending destinations are used, and what boldface letters represent those destinations. In this log **A** represents **Anchorage**, **F** is **Fairbanks.**

2. The boldface numbers represent the distance in miles from the beginning and ending destinations, and the lightface numbers are the metric equivalent in kilometers (unless otherwise noted). For example, the entrance to Denali National Park and Preserve is 237.3 miles, or 381.9 kilometers, from Anchorage.

3. References to other sections in *The MILEPOST®* are always uppercased. In this example, the DENALI NATIONAL PARK section is referenced. Refer to the Contents page to quickly find other sections.

4. "Log" advertisements are classified-type advertisements that appear in the text. These are identified by the boldface name of the business at the beginning of the entry and "[ADVERTISEMENT]" at the end. These log advertisements are written by the advertisers.

5. Display advertisements are keyed in the log by a boldface entry at their highway locations, followed by the words "See display ad." Their advertisement will appear near this entry or a page or section will be referenced.

It may also help you to know how our field editors log the highways. *The MILEPOST®* field editors drive each highway, taking notes on facilities, features and attractions along the way and noting the mile at which they appear. Mileages are measured from the beginning of the highway, which is generally at a junction or the city limits, to the end of the highway, also usually a junction or city limits. Most highways in *The MILEPOST®* are logged either south to north or east to west. If you are traveling the opposite direction of the log, you will read the log back to front.

To determine driving distance between 2 points, simply subtract the first mileage figures. For example, the distance from Crabb's Crossing at **Milepost A 231.3** to the park entrance at **Milepost A 237.3** is 6 miles.

Look for these symbols throughout *The MILEPOST®*:

▲ Campground
Fishing
♿ Wheelchair accessible
MP On-line advertiser; visit www.themilepost.com for more information.

Parks Highway Log

ALASKA ROUTE 1 ❶
Distance from Anchorage (A) is followed by distance from Fairbanks (F).

A 231.3 (372.2 km) **F 126.7** (203.9 km) Crabb's Crossing, second bridge northbound over the Nenana River. At the north end of this bridge is the boundary of Denali National Park and Preserve.

A 233.1 (375.1 km) **F 124.9** (201 km) Gravel turnout to east.

A 234.1 (376.7 km) **F 123.9** (199.4 km) Double-ended turnout with litter barrels to east; scenic viewpoint. No overnight parking or camping. Mount Fellows (elev. 4,476 feet/1,364m) to the east.

A 235.1 (378.4 km) **F 122.9** (197.8 km) *CAUTION: Railroad crossing.*

A 237.2 (381.7 km) **F 120.8** (194.4 km) Riley Creek bridge.

❷ **A 237.3** (381.9 km) **F 120.7** (194.2 km) Entrance to Denali National Park and Preserve (formerly Mount McKinley National Park) to west. Fresh water fill-up hose and dump station 0.2 mile/0.3 km from junction on Park Road; Visitor Center is 0.5 mile/0.8 km from the highway junction. See DENALI NATIONAL PARK section for details. ❸

A 238 (383 km) **F 120** (193.4 km) Third bridge northbound over the Nenana River.

❹ **A 238.1** (383.2 km) **F 119.9** (193 km) **Denali Raft Adventures.** Come with the original Nenana River rafters! Paddleboats too! Age 5 or older welcome, 7 departures daily. Whitewater or scenic floats. Get awayto untouched wilderness! 2-hour, 4-hour, full-day and overnight trips are available. See display ad in DENALI NATIONAL PARK section. Phone (907) 683-2234. Internet: www.alaskaone.com/denraft. VISA, Master Card accepted. [ADVERTISMENT]

A 238.4 (383.6 km) **F 119.6** (192.5 km) **Denali Bluffs Hotel.** See display ad in the DENALI NATIONAL PARK section. ❺

The introduction to each highway logged in *The MILEPOST®* includes a chart of mileages between major points (see below).

Maps also accompany each highway logged in *The MILEPOST®*. Consult the map key for an explanation of abbreviations (see example at bottom). Mileage boxes at communities and junctions on the highway map reflect the rounded off mileage in the highway log at the corresponding point.

	Anchorage	Denali Park	Fairbanks	Talkeetna	Wasilla
Anchorage		237	358	113	42
Denali Park	237		121	153	195
Fairbanks	358	121		245	316
Talkeetna	113	153	245		71
Wasilla	42	195	316	71	

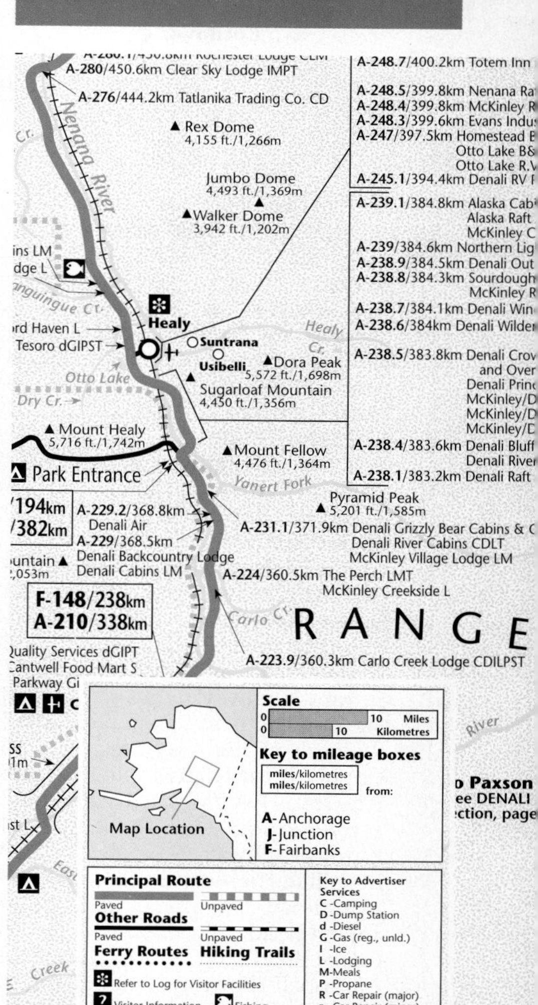

Key to Highways in *The MILEPOST*®

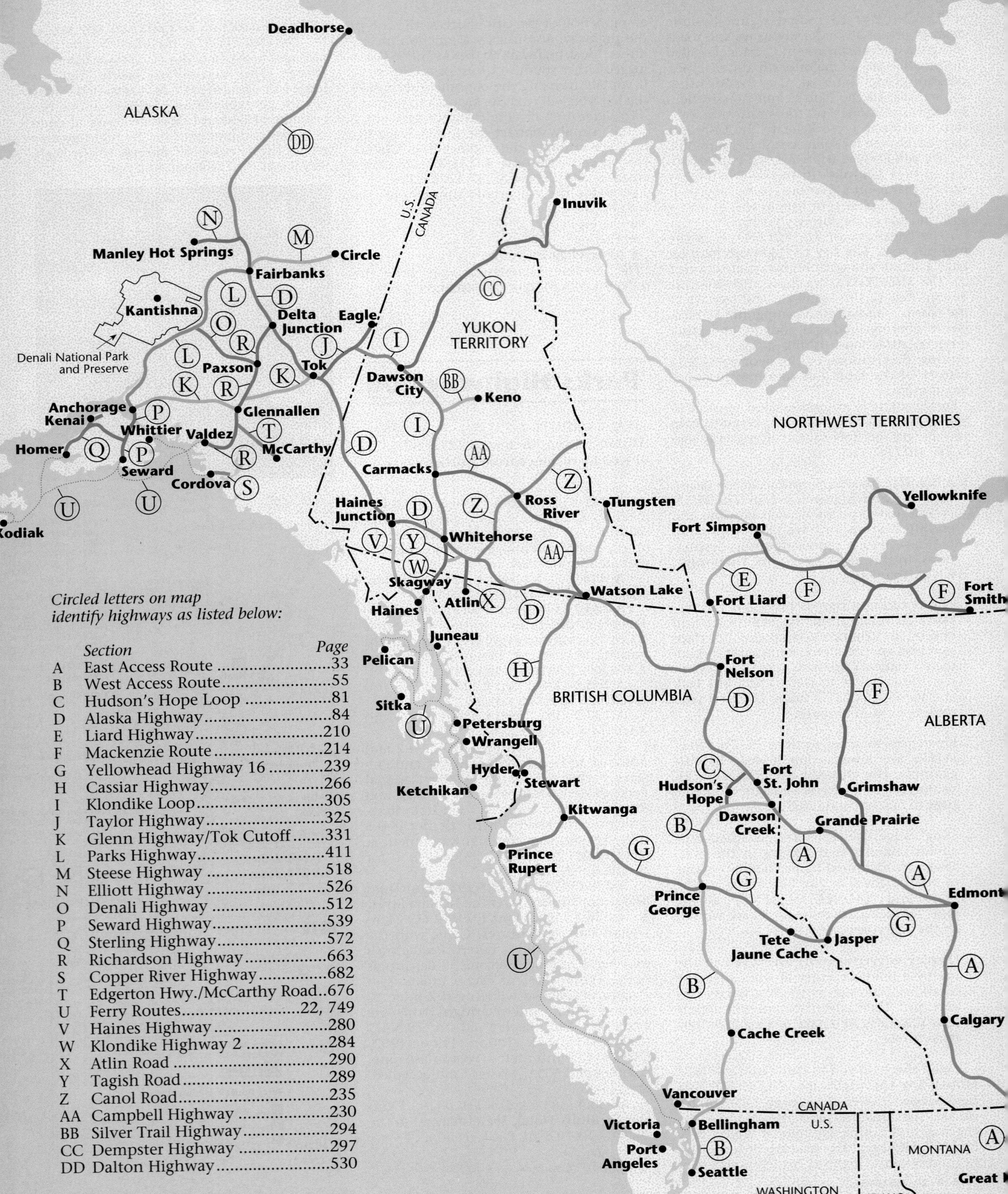

CELEBRATING 50 YEARS OF THE MILEPOST®

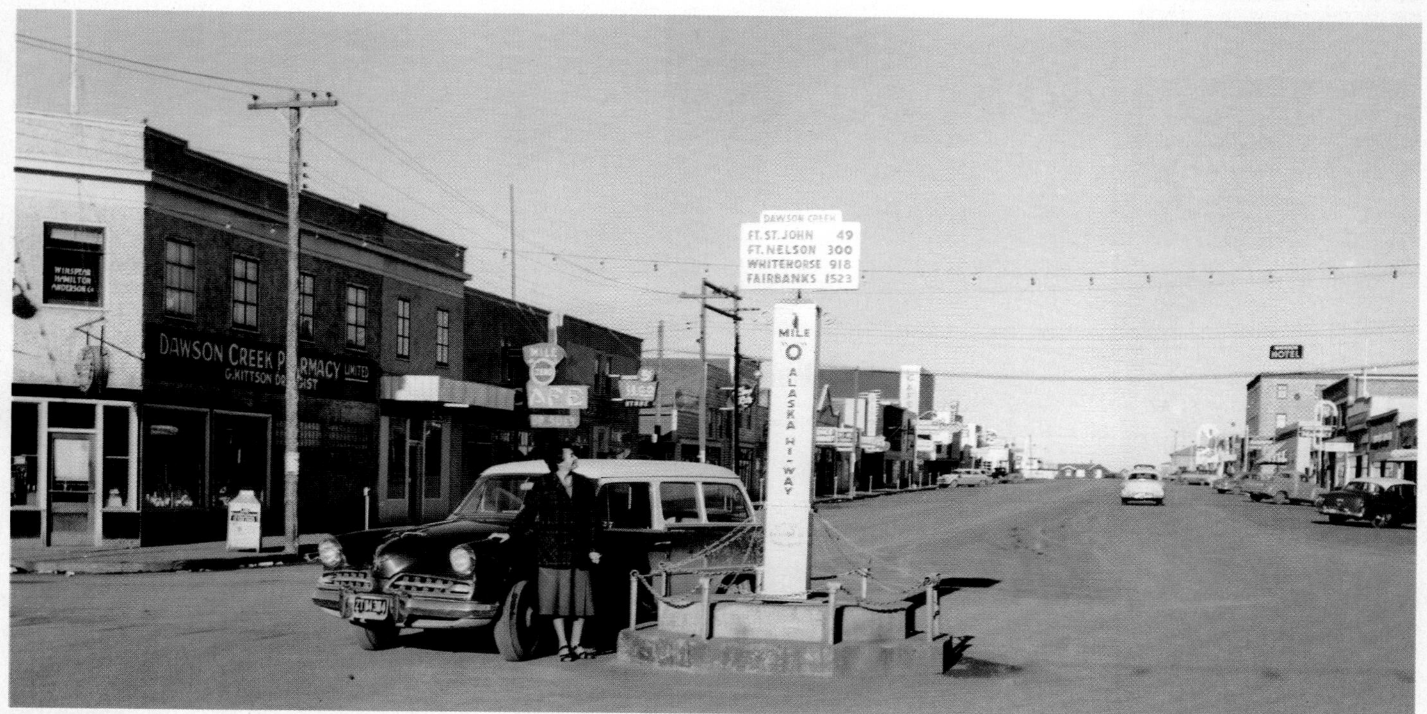

Milepost 0 in Dawson Creek, BC. The original post was erected in 1946. This photo appeared in the 1955 edition of The MILEPOST®. *(Bill Wallace)*

The Alaska Highway was a rugged road when it opened for tourist traffic in 1948. Facilities along the highway were few and far apart. There was not a single garage for 600 miles between Fort Nelson, BC, and Whitehorse, YT, or between Whitehorse and Fairbanks, AK. On such a road, a reliable guidebook was essential, and in 1949, *The MILEPOST®* was published. This year marks our 50th edition, and we celebrate it with a look back at those early editions of *The MILEPOST®* in the following pages and in our special history pages in Whitehorse (page 153), Anchorage (page 389), Fairbanks (page 469) and the Inside Passage (page 692).

The first edition of *The MILEPOST®* was a 72-page, 5¼ x 8¼-inch saddle-stitched booklet, and it sold for $1.00. It was filled with facts and practical information gathered by its publisher, William A. "Bill" Wallace, during his many trips up and down the highway, designed "especially for those who travel over the Alaska Highway and the highways of Alaska." Wallace had named his guidebook after the mileage location posts "that filled such a vital need along the wilderness road."

Wallace's interest in an Alaska Highway guide began during WWII when he was working for the Interior Department's Alaska Fire Control Service at Tanacross, AK. In 1944, Wallace published his first Alaska highway map for the agency. It was a crudely drawn sketch, on a tiny brochure, of Alaska's highway system, and marked the locations of fire stations, as well as a few other services. In 1948, Wallace formed the Alaska Research Company and published a large fold-out map. In 1949, he published *The MILEPOST®* with the help of Anchorage newspaper publisher, Bob Atwood.

In 1949, there were about 1,000 miles of connected road in Alaska (public road mileage in Alaska today—including all city streets—is about 14,400 miles), and a few small, recently established highway businesses. The first edition of *The MILEPOST®* noted: "There are many fine lodges and roadhouses offering every comfort and modern convenience. There are numerous other establishments, which though primitive when judged by the stricter standards of more settled country, are deserving of patronage. Desperate shortages of materials, difficulties of transportation, and long hard winters have been the common lot. If this is borne in mind during your trip—then the spirit of hospitality and friendly helpfulness common to these pioneers will more than compensate for those imperfections of facilities and accommodations encountered along the way."

Since 1949, *The MILEPOST®* has grown from 72 pages to 768 pages. Editorial coverage has expanded from 8 highways to 88 highways and roads; from 2 steamship lines to 42 cruise ships and 2 major ferry systems; from one Plan-A-Trip map to 100 city, highway and vicinity maps, as well as the Plan-A-Trip map.

Much has changed since the early editions of *The MILEPOST®*, although you'll find a remarkable number of businesses have persevered at the same spot for all these years (with a change in owners and decor since 1949), and the land—mountains, glaciers, forests, rivers and lakes—hasn't changed that much. The cities have changed. They are much bigger. *The MILEPOST®* is bigger too. But what hasn't changed is our sincere wish to guide you safely over Northern roads, making sure you don't miss anything except the potholes. Have a good trip!

40's

50's

60's

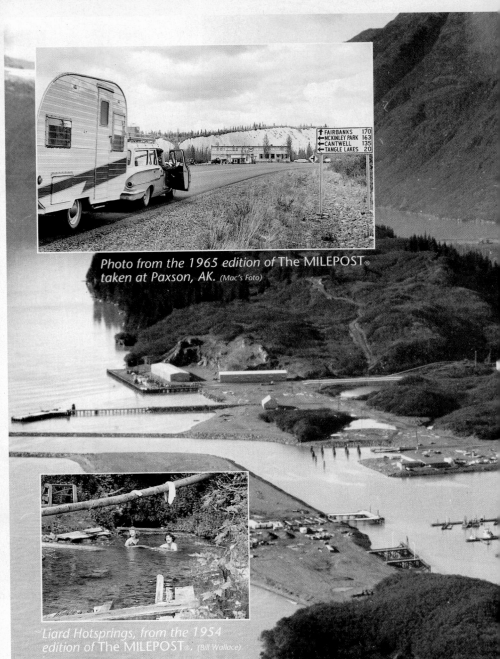

Photo from the 1965 edition of The MILEPOST® taken at Paxson, AK. (Mac's Foto)

Liard Hotsprings, from the 1954 edition of The MILEPOST®. (Bill Wallace)

THUNDERBIRD MOTEL - "We sell 99% sleep!"

HAINES, ALASKA—BOX 12 • PHONE 76-6-4431

ALL NEW & ULTRA-MODERN

City center, 1 block north of U.S. Customs. Automatic washing & drying facilities available. Singles, doubles, triples, twins & family units. Optional fully equipped kitchenettes. All 80 inch beds. All private baths. Thermostat controlled radiant base-board heating.

RATES FROM $7 SINGLE & $11 DOUBLE • FAMILY RATES

Wilma & Bill Jahn—Owners & Managers

CLUB WHITE SWAN

MILEPOST 10 HAINES HIWAY

One of Alaska's Finest Steak Houses
Delicious Steaks • Seafoods • Cocktails
Overnight Cabins - Liquor Store

15 MINUTE DRIVE FROM HAINES (PAVED HIWAY)

Dick & Bertha Bush—Owners, Mgrs.

Some examples of early advertisements that appeared in The MILEPOST®.

Original hand-drawn map of the Alaska Highway system published by Bill Wallace in 1944.

"New" Valdez townsite and harbor in 1966, 2 years after the Good Friday earthquake. (William A. Wallace Collection)

70's

80's

Anchorage Philatelic Society • 46th APEX—February 20-22, 1998

The MILEPOST®

50th Anniversary

The MILEPOST®

TRIP PLANNER FOR ALASKA, YUKON TERRITORY, BRITISH COLUMBIA, ALBERTA & NORTHWEST TERRITORIES

"The quintessential reference." — Associated Press

50th Edition Spring '98-Spring '99

Mile-by-mile logs and detailed maps of all Northern highways, including the famous Alaska Highway

Ferries and Cruise ships including Alaska State Ferry schedules and the Inside Passage

FREE 21"x31" fold-out map ($5.95 value!)

Anchorage Philatelic Society issued a cachet in 1998 marking The MILEPOST®'s 50th anniversary. Send $2.50 plus self-addressed envelope to P.O. Box 10-2214, Anchorage, AK 99510, to order.

Watson Lake Signpost Forest in the 1950s. Begun during Alaska Highway construction in 1942, the signs now number more than 37,000. (Bill Wallace)

Welcome to the North Country

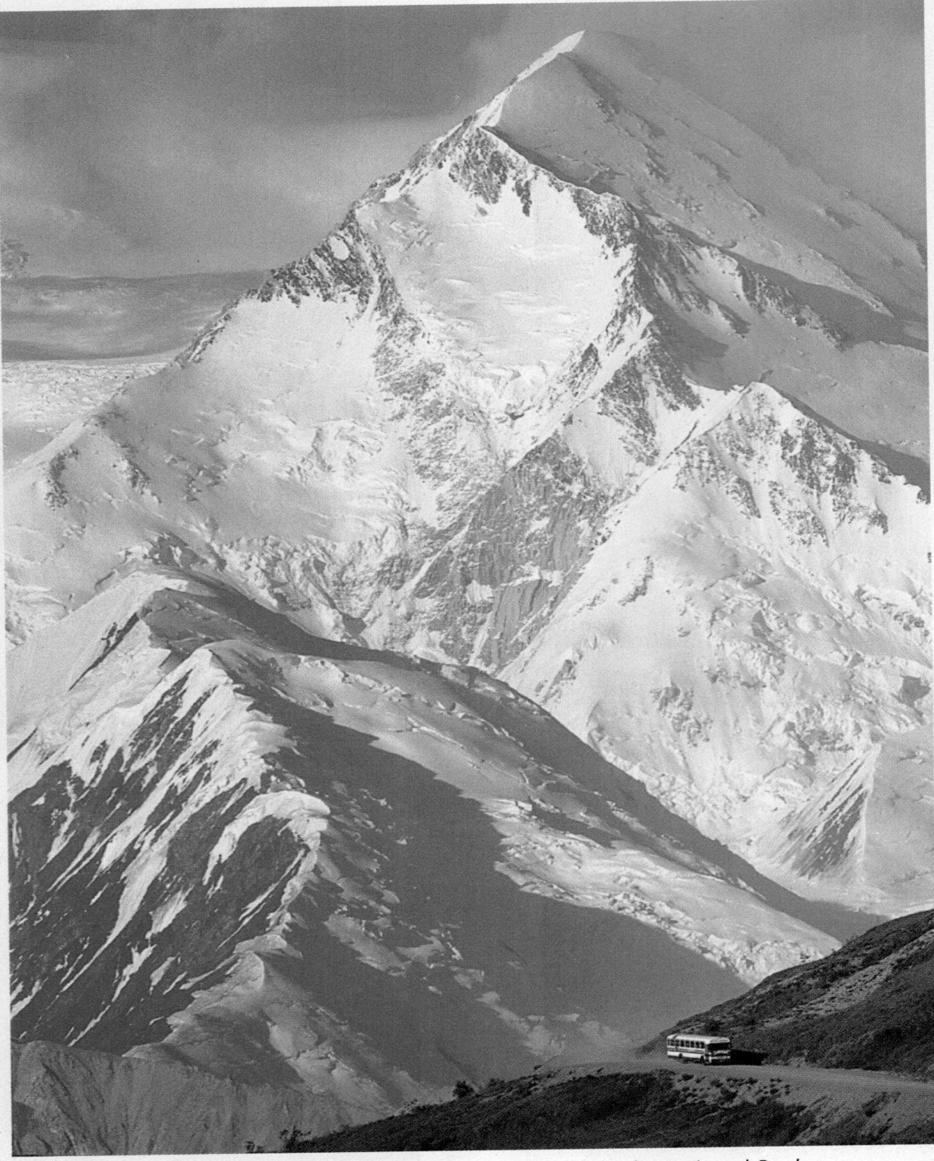

Tour bus is dwarfed by Mount McKinley massif in Denali National Park.

(© Roy Corral)

The North Country is the land north of 51° 16' latitude. Geographically, it encompasses Alaska, Yukon Territory, western Northwest Territories, northern British Columbia and Alberta. Following are some facts and figures about each of these areas.

Alaska

Population: 606,000
Capital: Juneau
Largest City: Anchorage
Area: 587,878 square miles/ 1,522,596 square km
Highest Point: Mount McKinley, 20,320 feet/6,095m
Lowest Point: Pacific Ocean, sea level
State Flower: Forget-me-not
State Tree: Sitka spruce
State Bird: Willow ptarmigan
State Motto: "North to the Future"
Major Industries: Tourism, petroleum, fishing, lumber
Drinking age: 21. The sale and/or importation of alcoholic beverages is prohibited in some 70 bush communities.

Top Ten Attractions:

1. Inside Passage
2. Portage Glacier
3. Mendenhall Glacier
4. Ketchikan Totems
5. Denali/McKinley
6. Skagway Historic Gold Rush District
7. Glacier Bay
8. Anchorage Museum of History and Art
9. Trans-Alaska Pipeline
10. Sitka's Russian Church and Dancers

Fish & Game: Alaska Dept. of Fish and Game, Box 25526, Juneau, AK 99802; phone (907) 465-4180, fax (907) 465-2772; Internet www.state.ak.us/local/akpages/FISH.GAME/adfghome.htm
Visitor Information: Alaska Division of Tourism, Box 110801, Juneau, AK 99811-0801; phone (907) 465-2010; Internet www.travelalaska.com and www.state.ak.us/tourism

Alaska was purchased by the U.S. from Russia in 1867. It became the 49th state on January 3, 1959. Alaska is the largest state in the union in area (twice the size of Texas), but ranks 49th in population, based on the 1990 census. (Only Wyoming has fewer residents.) Approximately 15 percent of the population is Native: Eskimo, Aleut and Indian (Athabascan, Tlingit, Haida, Tsimshian).

Alaska has 17 of the 20 highest mountains in the United States, including the highest peak in North America—Mount McKinley (Denali). Geographically, the state falls into roughly 6 distinct natural regions: Southeastern, Southcentral, the Interior, Southwestern, Western and the Brooks Range/Arctic.

Southeastern Alaska is a moist, luxuriantly forested panhandle extending some 500 miles/805 km from Dixon Entrance south of Ketchikan to Icy Bay on the Gulf of Alaska coast. This narrow strip of coast, separated from the mainland and Canada by the Coast Mountains, and the hundreds of islands of the Alexander Archipelago, form the Inside Passage water route used by ships and ferries. Cruise ships bring thousands of passengers through the Inside Passage each summer.

The Southcentral region of Alaska curves 650 miles/1,046 km north and west from the Gulf of Alaska coast to the Alaska Range. This region's tremendous geographic variety includes the Matanuska–Susitna river valleys, the Chugach and Wrangell–St. Elias mountain ranges, the Kenai Peninsula and the glaciers of Prince William Sound. Anchorage, the state's largest city, is the hub of Southcentral.

Interior Alaska lies cradled between the Brooks Range to the north and the Alaska Range to the south, a vast area that drains the Yukon River and its tributaries. It is a climate of extremes, holding both the record high (100°F at Fort Yukon) and the record low (-80°F at Prospect Creek). Fairbanks is the hub of the Interior and a jump-off point for bush communities in both the Interior and Arctic.

Southwestern Alaska takes in Kodiak Island, the Alaska Peninsula and Aleutian Islands. Kodiak, less than an hour's flight from Anchorage and about 10 hours by ferry from Homer, is the largest island in Alaska. Kodiak was Russian Alaska's first capital city. Brown bear viewing is an attraction on Kodiak and at Katmai National Park and Preserve near King Salmon. The Southwest ferry system provides service from Kodiak to Unalaska/ Dutch Harbor.

Western Alaska stretches from the head of Bristol Bay north along the Bering Sea coast to the Seward Peninsula near the Arctic Circle. This region extends inland from the coast to encompass the Yukon–Kuskokwim Delta. Nome is perhaps one of the best known destinations in Western Alaska.

Arctic Alaska lies above the Arctic Circle (latitude 66°33′), between the Brooks Range to the south and the Arctic sea coast to the north, and from the Canadian border to the east westward to Kotzebue. Day and overnight trips to Kotzebue, Barrow and Prudhoe Bay are popular packages offered out of both Anchorage and Fairbanks.

If you include the Marine Highway, all regions of Alaska are connected by highway with the exception of Western Alaska. And that region's hub cities—Bethel and Nome—are less than 2 hours from Anchorage by air.

Bush travel in all regions of Alaska is covered in detail in our companion book, *The Alaska Wilderness Guide*.

Yukon Territory

Population: 27,800
Capital: Whitehorse
Largest City: Whitehorse
Area: 186,661 square miles/ 483,450 square km
Highest Point: Mount Logan, 19,545 feet/5,959m
Lowest Point: Beaufort Sea, sea level
Territorial Flower: Fireweed
Territorial Bird: Raven
Drinking age: 19. Packaged liquor, beer and wine are sold in government liquor stores.
Major Industries: Tourism, mining

Top Ten Attractions:
1. SS *Klondike*, Whitehorse
2. MacBride Museum, Whitehorse
3. Northern Lights Centre, Watson Lake
4. Diamond Tooth Gerties, Dawson City
5. Palace Grand Theatre, Dawson City
6. Beringia Interpretive Centre, Whitehorse
7. Dredge #4, Dawson City
8. Kluane National Park
9. Whitehorse Fish Ladder
10. Robert Service Cabin, Dawson City

Fish & Game: Yukon Government, Dept. of Renewable Resources, Fish and Wildlife Branch, Box 2703, Whitehorse, YT Y1A 2C6, phone (867) 667-5221
Visitor Information: Tourism Yukon, Box 2703, Whitehorse, YT Y1A 2C6; phone (867) 667-5340; Internet www.touryukon.com; E-mail info@touryukon.com

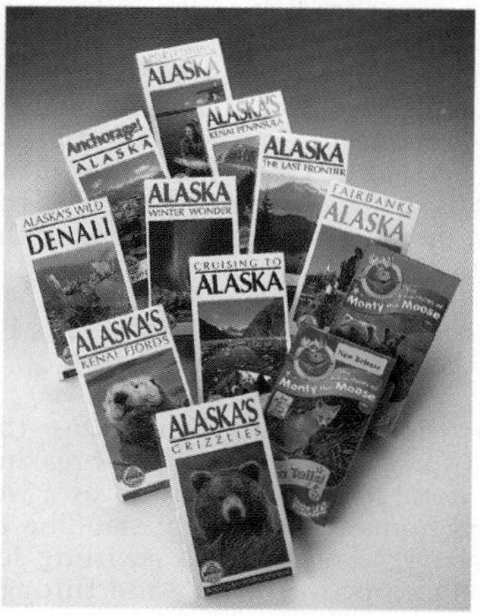

Shaped somewhat like a right triangle, Yukon Territory is bordered on the west by Alaska at 141° longitude; on the north by the Beaufort Sea/Arctic Ocean; on the south by British Columbia at latitude 60°; and on the east by the western Northwest Territories.

Yukon Territory is larger than all the New England states combined. Canada's highest peak, Mount Logan (elev. 19,524 feet/5,951m), is located in Yukon's St. Elias Mountains.

First Nations peoples of the Yukon belong to the Athapaskan and Tlingit language families. These are Gwitchin, Han, Northern Tutchone, Southern Tutchone,

(Continues on page 12)

KLONDIKE GOLD RUSH CENTENNIAL 1898-1998

The Klondike Gold Rush Centennial, celebrated throughout the North this year, commemorates the people and events of those few heady years a century ago. If 1896 was the year of discovery, and 1897 the year of the stampede, then 1898 was the year of digging for gold and striking it rich–at least for the lucky few who managed to stake a rich claim.

By early June of 1898, gold production was at an all-time high. Prospectors' 500-foot claims were staked and registered along 230 miles of the rivers and streams in the Klondike. And at that time, the big influx hadn't even arrived! But they were on their way. Dawson City was about to be inundated by throngs of would-be miners—15,000 to 20,000 that season alone. Few of these newcomers knew much about mining, building a cabin or surviving the sub-zero temperatures. That, however, wasn't the issue. They believed their own histories would soon mirror the get-rich tales so widely publicized about others.

First Avenue in Dawson City, YT, photographed at midnight June 10, 1904.

(Adams & Co. Photo)

Contrary to those dreams, few miners left the Klondike with pockets full of gold. Even fewer held onto their wealth. The Canadian historian Pierre Berton estimates about 100,000 headed for the gold fields between 1897 and 1899. About one-third made it; probably half of them actually mined for gold. Of those, only a few hundred struck it rich. One of the places that seemed lined with gold was Eldorado, a tiny tributary of Bonanza Creek—another source of riches. It was the stories of these places and the people who found wealth there that created the fever of '98—the fever that convinced so many to pack up for the far-away Klondike.

One wealthy baron, well-known in Seattle and San Francisco, was Clarence Berry, owner of one of the largest Klondike fortunes. The average person could identify with him. He was an ex-fruit farmer who lost everything in the Panic of 1893; who, prior to his big find, tended bar. If he could take $1.5 million out of Eldorado, anyone could. But he was not an ordinary man. Berry had the Midas touch, even outside the Klondike. He hit pay dirt in Alaska, and later oil in California.

Charlie Anderson was another who had a head start. As it turned out, a fateful start. After a night of drinking, he realized he had spent every last nugget of gold he owned for an untried claim. Since he couldn't get his $800 of gold back, he tried to reclaim it from his new stake. It was on the Eldorado—and it was rich with gold. Soon he became the million dollar miner, the man called the "Lucky Swede." What the gold stampeders of 1898 didn't know was that when Charlie began his cold and lonely burn-to-bedrock operation, he was broke, had to buy beans and bacon on credit, and didn't even have a cabin to live in. His road to riches was paved with hardships the newcomers couldn't imagine.

Big Alex McDonald's struggle ended when he bought half interest in No. 30 on the Eldorado (the purchase price was flour and bacon). Then he hired 2 men to work his plot for half of the stake. With his percentage, Alex invested in more and more claims—all 40 or so on gold-producing creeks. Though he arrived with no money, he amassed a fortune so large, it's said he didn't know how many millions he was worth. Probably the reason he was known as the "King of the Klondike."

The Goldfields: Dirty, Wet and in the Middle of Nowhere

For those who did own claims, the search for gold was hard, back-breaking labor done by hand. Mining was a wet process from start to finish: standing in chilly rivers and streams, swirling icy water in pans, in rockers, and through sluice boxes. The climate didn't offer a warm welcome either. On average, the area had only 90 frost-free days per year. Hordes of mosquitoes were ever-present during those "good months," too.

When winter came, all the miners could do was set fires to melt the ground. Then, with pick and shovel, they'd loosen and scrape whatever earth they could, repeating the process again and again. As they neared bedrock, the miner had to work alone in a smokey hole, on hands and knees, filling bucket after bucket with gravel. If he didn't have a partner aboveground cranking a windlass to lift the buckets to the surface, the man would leave the warmth of the hole and enter the frigid air above to work the windlass himself. When the loose gravel did reach the ground, it froze once again—and stayed that way until spring. That's when the payoff came. It was what the miners called "spring cleaning." As soon as the creeks ran freely, they'd shovel winter's hard-fought-for gravel into the sluice box and harvest the gold. The work—and the wait—paid off for many.

Early on, it was the small-time hopefuls like Charlie Anderson or Clarence Berry going after the gold. Or people like Dick Lowe, who came upon his fortune when he worked as a surveyor. In fact, he acquired the richest piece of land staked during the Gold Rush—a plot just 86 feet wide and worth $500,000. Later, Klondike gold attracted big American capitalists like the Rothschilds and Guggenheims. In between, the mechanics of mining changed from labor-intensive work done by hand to machinery-driven mining.

What triggered the change? Money for one—and lots of it. Money to finance more efficient means of tapping the limited amounts of ore still in the ground. The rich deposits taken by the hand-miners were nearly exhausted. That left low-grade ore which was profitable to mine only if done by machine—and on a massive scale. Enter the government. To ease the way for capitalist expansion and to stimulate the sagging economy, the bureaucrats created leases for huge parcels. One concession was for 40 square miles of the Klondike River valley. Despite the miners' resistance to this and other leases, mining had entered a new phase.

View of Dawson City from the Dome, taken at midnight in June 1901.
(Adams & Larkin Photo)

Klondike Gold Rush commemorative stamp issued in 1998 by the U.S. Postal Service.

As methods changed so did the men of the Klondike. By 1899, the boom-time miners were nearing obsolescence. The new dynamics cut manpower needs dramatically. Besides leasing whole blocks of claims, the big mining interests in New York and London invested millions in hydraulic and dredging machinery.

The first dredge in the area came in 1901. It had huge buckets which dug up the earth and moved it back into the dredge, where the material was washed and rotated, separating out the gold. The amount of gravel 2 old-style miners could process in an entire winter now took just one afternoon. With dredges on the scene, miners began to leave—some to join the stampede to Fairbanks, others to give up gold altogether.

By 1905, large-scale dredging of Bear Creek was underway with an enormous 500-ton machine, driven by its own wood-fired power plant. Simultaneously, another powerhouse entered the picture—the hydraulic monitor. It blasted the hillsides with water, washing the gravel into sluice boxes. With adequate water pressure, one monitor replaced dozens of hand-miners.

Socially, Dawson City changed, too. In 1898 it became the capital of Yukon Territory, home to bureaucrats and other new arrivals, including women and children. By 1901, with the mining community no longer dominant, new social morés and laws took over. For Klondike Kate, who made up to $750 a night entertaining the miners, it was the beginning of the end. As Kate Rockwell, part-owner of the Orpheum, respecting the laws was the end of profits and her life in Dawson City. She retired to Oregon.

Even with all the money and mechanization the new century brought, gold production declined until 1908, when it bottomed out at $3.6 million. Since then it's had ups and downs, but never the frenzy of the late 19th century.

Dawson City in 1998

One hundred years later, gold remains the main attraction and the major topic of conversation in Dawson City. Large-scale mining operations exist to this day—one on Bonanza Road. Authentic small-time miners still come in search of a late 20th century find. Others come to recapture the boom days and retrace the steps of the gold rush pioneers, part of the reason Dawson City's year-round population of about 2,000 swells to about 5,000 in the summer. Many buildings of the gold rush era are gone, but other historical monuments stand to remind visitors of turn-of-the-century life.

Today's highways pass through gold rush territory where dredges and their after-effects dot the landscape. In Alaska, the Taylor Highway goes into the historic Fortymile Mining District, past active mining sites and one of the first bucket-line dredges used in the area. The Steese Highway travels through the still-active Circle Mining District, past Gold Dredge No. 8, Chatanika Camp and the Davidson Ditch, on its way to Circle City on the Yukon River.

Communities throughout the region, from Dawson City, YT, to Skagway, AK, plan to look into the rearview mirror of history on this important 100-year anniversary. Photo exhibits are everywhere. The Dyea to Dawson, a race in which 2-person teams mimic the gold rush trip over the Chilkoot Trail to Lake Bennett, then canoe the 400 miles to Dawson, sets off in June. Sled dog races, gold panning and other events fill the 1998 calendar.

For a current rundown on Klondike Gold Rush Centennial events, contact the Yukon Anniversaries Commission at (867) 648-8665; the Klondike Visitors Association (867) 993-5575, or the Alaska Division of Tourism (907) 465-2010.

(Continued from page 9)
Kaska, Tagish, Tlingit and Upper Tanana.

The Yukon was made a district of the Northwest Territories in 1895, and became a separate territory in June of 1898. The territory's first capital was Dawson City, site of the great Klondike gold rush, which brought thousands of gold seekers to the Yukon and Alaska in 1897–98. The Klondike gold rush began celebrating its centennial in 1996—marking the discovery of gold on Bonanza Creek on August 16, 1896—and continues the celebration in 1998 (see pages 10–11).

At the height of the gold rush, an estimated 40,000 people lived in Dawson City. By 1903, as other gold stampedes drew off much of Dawson's population, the city's boom days were over, although mining continued to support the community for many years. On March 31, 1953, Whitehorse—on the railway and the highway, with a large airport—replaced Dawson City as capital.

Western Northwest Territories

Population: 57,600
Capital: Yellowknife (until 1999)
Largest City: Yellowknife
Area: 550,000 square miles/1.4 million square km
Highest Point: Cirque of the Unclimbables Mountain, 9,062 feet/2,762m
Lowest Point: Beaufort Sea, sea level
Territorial Flower: Mountain avens
Drinking age: 19. Packaged liquor, beer and wine are sold in government liquor stores. Sale and possession of alcohol is prohibited in several communities.
Major Industries: Mining, manufacturing, fishing

Top Ten Attractions:
1. Nahanni National Park Reserve
2. Wood Buffalo National Park
3. Canol Heritage Trail Park Reserve
4. Dempster Highway
5. Pingos (cone-shaped hills) of the Tuktoyaktuk Peninsula
6. Roman Catholic "Igloo" Church, Inuvik
7. Twin Falls Gorge Territorial Park
8. Prince of Wales Northern Heritage Center, Yellowknife
9. Northwest Territories Legislative Assembly Building, Yellowknife
10. Wildcat Cafe, Yellowknife

Fish & Game: Dept. of Economic Development and Tourism, Tourism Development and Marketing, Box 1320, Yellowknife, NT X1A 2L9; phone (800) 661-0788
Visitor Information: Dept. of Economic Development and Tourism, Tourism Development and Marketing, Box 1320, Yellowknife, NT X1A 2L9; phone (800) 661-0788; Internet www.nwttravel.nt.ca

On April 1, 1999, Northwest Territories will be divided into 2 territories. Passed by popular vote in 1982 and approved by the Canadian Parliament in 1993, this division will create Nunavut and its capital, Iqaluit on Baffin Island, in what is now the eastern half of Northwest Territories.

Northwest Territories comprises about a third of Canada. Western Northwest Territories is about the size of Alaska. Western Northwest Territories' Wood Buffalo National Park is the second largest national park in the world.

A majority of the population of Northwest Territories is Native. Aboriginal groups are the Dene, Inuvialuit, Inuit, Gwich'in, Dogrib and Metis.

Access to western Northwest Territories is from Alberta via the Mackenzie Highway system, from British Columbia via the Liard Highway, and from Yukon Territory via the Dempster Highway. A major road-building project in the 1960s constructed most of the highway system in western Northwest Territories. Road improvement is ongoing, with paving under way on much of the remaining gravel road.

British Columbia

Population: 3,764,200
Capital: Victoria
Largest City: Vancouver
Area: 365,900 square miles/947,800 square km
Highest Point: Mount Fairweather, 15,295 feet/4,663m
Lowest Point: Pacific Ocean, sea level
Provincial Flower: Pacific dogwood
Provincial Tree: Western red cedar
Provincial Bird: Settler's jay
Provincial Motto: *Splendor Sine Occasu* (Splendour Without Diminishment)
Drinking age: 19. Packaged liquor, beer and wine are sold in government liquor stores.
Major Industries: Forestry, mining and energy, tourism, agriculture, seafood products, food

Top Attractions:
1. Royal BC Museum, Victoria
2. Butchart Gardens, Victoria
3. Vancouver Aquarium
4. Capilano Suspension Bridge, North Vancouver
5. Barkerville Historic Town
6. Fort Steele Heritage Town
7. Grist Mill and Gardens, Keremeos
8. Grouse Mountain, North Vancouver
9. Ksan Historical Indian Village Museum, Hazelton

Fish & Game: Fish and Wildlife Branch, Ministry of Environment, Parliament Buildings, Victoria, BC V8V 1X4
Visitor Information: Tourism British Columbia, Dept. TG, Box 9830, Stn. Prov. Govt., Victoria, B.C. V8W 9W5 Canada; phone (800) 663-6000; Internet www.travel.bc.ca

Canada's most westerly—and 3rd largest—province, British Columbia stretches 813 miles/1,300 km from its southern border with the United States to the north boundary with Yukon Territory. It is bounded on the east by Alberta and on the west by the Pacific Ocean. The province encompasses the Queen Charlotte Islands and Vancouver Island, site of the capital city of Victoria. Approximately half the province's population resides in the Victoria–Vancouver area.

British Columbia entered the Dominion of Canada on July 20, 1871, as the 6th province. The region was important in early fur trade, and expansion of the province came with the 1860s Cariboo gold rush, followed by the completion of Canada's first transcontinental railway—the Canadian Pacific.

The cities of Vancouver and Victoria are popular tourist areas, as are Vancouver Island and the Gulf and San Juan island groups. The Sunshine Coast, along the shores of British Columbia facing Vancouver Island, is popular for its scenic drives, parks and beaches. The region's national parks, including Glacier, Mt. Revelstoke, Kootenay and Yoho, are among the most spectacular in North America.

Mile Zero of the Alaska Highway is located in Dawson Creek, BC (not to be confused with Dawson City, YT), in the northeastern corner of the province.

Alberta

Population: 2,545,600
Capital: Edmonton
Largest City: Calgary
Area: 255,287 square miles/661,190 square km
Highest Point: Mount Columbia, 12,293 feet/3,747m
Lowest Point: Salt River at the border with Northwest Territories, 600 feet/183m
Drinking age: 18. Liquor, beer and wine are sold in private liquor stores.
Major Industries: Petrochemicals, plastics, forest products, computer and business services, processed foods, electronics, tourism

Top Ten Attractions:
1. Calgary Zoo
2. Glenbow Museum, Calgary
3. Heritage Park, Calgary
4. Alberta Legislature Building, Edmonton
5. Fort Edmonton Park, Edmonton
6. Muttart Conservatory, Edmonton
7. Provincial Museum of Alberta, Edmonton
8. Storyland Valley Zoo, Edmonton
9. Royal Tyrrell Museum of Palaeontology, Drumheller
10. Edmonton Space and Science Centre

Fish & Game: Environmental Protection Branch, Information Centre, 9920 108 St., Edmonton, AB T5K 2M4
Visitor Information: Travel Alberta, 3rd floor, Commerce Place, 10155 102 St., Edmonton, AB T5J 4G8; phone (800) 661-8888; Internet www.atp.ab.ca

The Province of Alberta is bounded to the west by British Columbia, to the south by Montana, to the east by Saskatchewan and to the north by the Northwest Territories. Among the dramatic features of this geographically fascinating area are a stretch of the Rocky Mountains and the Columbia Icefield—source of the Athabasca, Columbia and Saskatchewan glaciers—along the British Columbia border, and the bizarre rock formations of the badlands to the west along the Red Deer River.

Native inhabitants included Assiniboine, Blackfoot, Cree and Sarcee Indians. The first European settlers—fur traders—arrived in the mid-18th century. In 1875 Alberta became a province of Canada. Discoveries of oil and natural gas deposits in the 1930s caused economic growth, and in the 1970s and 1980s these same deposits brought new industries to the area and a resulting rise in population.

Edmonton in central Alberta and Calgary to the south are popular areas. The national parks—Banff and Jasper along the British Columbia border, Waterton Lakes in the southwest corner and Wood Buffalo far in the north—are also major attractions.

Air Mileage Between Major Points In Alaska

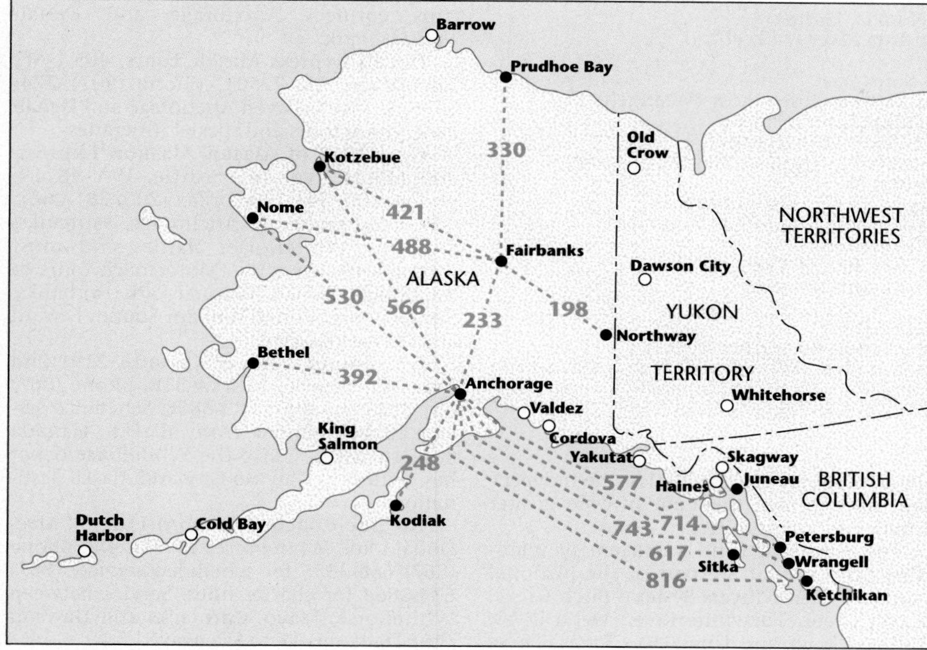

Air Travel

Slightly more than half of all visitors to Alaska arrive by air. Air travel is also one of the most common forms of transportation in the North. You can fly just about anywhere. If there is no scheduled service, you can charter a plane.

About 10 domestic airlines and 2 dozen small scheduled carriers provide scheduled service within Alaska. In addition to scheduled air service, there are more than 200 certified charter/air taxi operators in Alaska.

Air taxi operators conduct their business from a specific base of operations, primarily through the charter of aircraft, and offer a wide variety of options: drop-off and pickup for hunters, sport fisherman and river runners; photo safaris to see wildlife or glaciers; round-trip flights to remote communities which may include an overnight.

Check the advertisements for scheduled and charter air service in the communities covered in *The MILEPOST®*. There are many to choose from.

Air taxi rates may vary from carrier to carrier. Most operators charge an hourly rate either per plane load or per passenger; others may charge on a per-mile basis. Flightseeing trips to area attractions are often available at a fixed price per passenger.

Sample per-hour fares for charter planes with varied wheel, float and ski capabilities (luggage space limited and dependent on number of passengers): Piper Archer (3 passengers), $175; Piper Cherokee 6 (5 passengers), $230; Islander (9 passengers), $430; Chieftain (9 passengers), $650.

Any pilot flying for hire is required to hold a commercial or airline transport pilot certificate. The customer can and should be protected by having the pilot show his/her credentials. A pilot with the necessary credentials will be glad to show them. Do not fly with a pilot who cannot produce certification.

The MILEPOST® highway logs include the location of most airstrips along the highways and in the communities in Alaska and northwestern Canada. Aircraft symbols corresponding to airstrip locations are included on the highway strip maps. The map symbols are a white plane for airports with scheduled service, and a black plane for airstrips with no scheduled service and limited facilities.

Private aircraft information in these logs includes only the name and location of the airstrip, the elevation, length and surface material of the longest runway and the availability of fuel. Many Northland pilots fly jet craft. Jet and other fuel is available at many airports. Fuel sold in Alaska and Canada is almost exclusively 100LL; 80 octane fuel is no longer available, though some airports offer car gasoline. *NOTE: The brief description of airstrips given in* The MILEPOST® *is in no way intended as a guide.* For a packet of free brochures including *Flight Tips for Pilots in Alaska*, write the Federal Aviation Administration, 222 W. 7th Ave., Anchorage, AK 99513.

Pilots may also get in touch with the Alaska Airmen's Assoc., Inc., P.O. Box 241185, Anchorage, AK 99524-1184, phone (907) 272-1251, fax (907) 274-2788 to buy a copy of the *Alaska Airmen's Logbook for Alaska, Northwest Canada and Russia.*

Two free Canadian publications of interest are *Air Tourist Information—Canada* (TP771) and *Flying the Alaska Highway in Canada* (TP2168). Both are available from the Civil Aviation Publications Office, phone (800) 305-2059.

Boating

Whether traveling by sailboat, cruiser, rowboat, canoe, inflatable raft or kayak, the North offers thousands of miles of challenging and scenic waterways.

For marine sailors, the Inside Passage and Southcentral Alaska's Prince William Sound provide scenic recreational boating and a sheltered transportation route. There are numerous marine charter services (most skippered, some bare-boat) along the Inside

FLIGHT TIMES BETWEEN SELECTED CITIES

Between	Time	Between	Time	Between	Time
Anchorage—Bethel	1 hr. 15 min.	Anchorage—Valdez	40 min.	Juneau—Haines	35 min.
Anchorage—Cordova	45 min.	Anchorage—Wrangell	2 hrs. 20 min.	Juneau—Ketchikan	50 min.
Anchorage—Dutch Harbor	2 hrs. 5 min.	Fairbanks—Barrow	1 hr. 20 min.	Juneau—Seattle, WA	2 hrs. 10 min.
Anchorage—Fairbanks	50 min.	Fairbanks—Delta Junction	35 min.	Juneau—Sitka	35 min.
Anchorage—Juneau	1 hr. 35 min.	Fairbanks—Kotzebue	2 hrs. 10 min.	Juneau—Skagway	45 min.
Anchorage—King Salmon	1 hr.	Fairbanks—Nome	2 hrs. 20 min.	Juneau—Whitehorse, YT	1 hr.
Anchorage—Kodiak	55 min.	Fairbanks—Northway	1 hr.	Juneau—Yakutat	45 min.
Anchorage—Kotzebue	1 hr. 30 min.	Fairbanks—Prudhoe Bay	1 hr. 25 min.	Ketchikan—Sitka	50 min.
Anchorage—Nome	1 hr. 30 min.	Fairbanks—Whitehorse, YT	3 hrs. 35 min.	Nome—Kotzebue	40 min.
Anchorage—Petersburg	2 hrs.	(1 stop in Dawson City)		Whitehorse—Dawson City	1 hr. 40 min.
Anchorage—Seattle, WA	3 hrs. 15 min.	Juneau—Glacier Bay	25 min.	Yakutat—Cordova	45 min.

Day Cruises

Visitors and residents alike enjoy sightseeing by boat on inland and coastal waterways in the North. Most day cruises are designed for viewing wildlife and glaciers, seeing Northern history, or experiencing Bush living and Native culture. There are many of these scheduled day cruises to choose from. Check the advertisements in *The MILEPOST*® for cruise tour operators to the following destinations (listed alphabetically by country and region) out of the communities that are listed here. Keep in mind that you can charter a boat or rent a kayak in many communities and go exploring on your own.

ALASKA
—Interior
Chena and Tanana rivers (Fairbanks)
Yukon River (Eagle, Fairbanks)

—Southcentral
Barren Islands (Homer)
Chiswell Islands (Seward, Anchorage)
Halibut Cove (Homer)
Kachemak Bay (Homer)
Kenai Fjords (Anchorage, Seward)
Portage Glacier (Anchorage)
Prince William Sound—Columbia Glacier, College Fjord, Meares Glacier, Shoup Glacier and others (Anchorage, Whittier and Valdez)
Seldovia (Homer)
Susitna River (Talkeetna)

—Southeast
Anan Bear Observatory (Wrangell)
Chilkat River (Haines)
Chilkoot Lake (Haines)
Glacier Bay (Juneau, Haines, Skagway, Gustavus)
Icy Strait (Juneau, Gustavus)
Misty Fiords National Monument (Ketchikan)
Stikine River (Wrangell)
Tracy Arm (Juneau)

CANADA
Mackenzie River (Inuvik, NT)
Yukon River (Whitehorse, Minto, Dawson City , YT)

Passage from Prince Rupert, BC, to Haines and Skagway, AK, and in Southcentral Alaska ports. See the advertisements appearing in the communities. Marine facilities and transient moorage are also noted in the community descriptions.

Sea kayaking is popular in many coastal communities in Alaska. Rentals and/or guided kayak tours are available out of the following ports: Homer (for Kachemak Bay); Seward (Resurrection Bay, Kenai Fjords National Park); Valdez and Whittier (Prince William Sound); and in Southeastern Alaska out of Juneau, Sitka and Ketchikan. Southeast has hundreds of miles of sheltered waterways that are ideal for sea kayaking. Favorite destinations include: Gastineau Channel and Tracy Arm (out of Juneau); Glacier Bay National Park and Preserve; Point Adolphus in Icy Strait (out of Hoonah); Misty Fiords (out of Ketchikan); Sitka Sound and Outer Chichagof Island (from Sitka); Tebenkof Bay and Kuiu Island (from Kake); Yakutat Bay and Russell Fiord (from Yakutat); and Seymour Canal on Admiralty Island (from Juneau).

Outstanding sea kayaking opportunities are also available on the west coast of Prince of Wales Island. Canoe trails have been established on Prince of Wales Island along the Honker Divide and at Sarkar Lakes. Contact Craig Ranger District, Tongass National Forest, Box 145, Craig, AK 99921, phone (907) 826-3271. For maps and information contact the Thorne Bay Ranger District, Tongass National Forest, Box 19001, Thorne Bay, AK 99919, phone (907) 828-3304.

Inland boaters will find hundreds of river and lake systems suitable for traveling by boat, raft, kayak or canoe. In Alaska and Yukon Territory, the Yukon River system provides many of these waterways. In western Northwest Territories, it is the Mackenzie River system.

Guided float trips are found on most major runnable rivers in the North, and many of these operators advertise in *The MILEPOST*®. Some of those with scheduled daily departures are: the Kenai River (Cooper Landing); Nenana River (Denali National Park entrance area, Parks Highway); and the Mendenhall River (Juneau). For the independent river runner, there are an even greater number of opportunities.

The Bureau of Land Management maintains 6 rivers that are part of the National Wild and Scenic Rivers System: Birch Creek, Beaver Creek, Fortymile River, Delta River, Gulkana River and Unalakleet River. These rivers offer a variety of float trips. The Fortymile River is accessible from the Taylor Highway; the Gulkana River is accessible from the Richardson and the Denali highways. The BLM offers brochures on the river trails, including access points, portages and scale of difficulty. Write the Bureau of Land Management, 1150 University Ave., Fairbanks, AK 99709-3899; phone (907) 474-2251.

Canoeing on the Kenai Peninsula's Swan Lake and Swanson River canoe trails starts about late May and continues until late October. For details on the trails write the Refuge Manager, Kenai National Wildlife Refuge, Box 2139, Soldotna, AK 99669. These canoe trails are accessable from the Swanson River road off the Sterling Highway.

Northern rivers pass through wild country and help is a long way off. Follow safety guidelines and prepare a float plan. For more information on Alaska's wild rivers, see *The Alaska Wilderness Guide*, available from *The MILEPOST*®.

Bus Lines

Independent travelers wishing to travel by public bus within Alaska and Yukon Territory will generally find routes and services much more limited than in the Lower 48. Scheduled bus service is available within Alaska and Yukon Territory, but scheduled direct bus service to Alaska from the Lower 48 is not available, unless you wish to join an escorted motorcoach tour. If your schedule allows, you can travel from the Lower 48 to Alaska via public bus service by using several carriers. Most scheduled bus service in the North is seasonal.

Contact the following companies for current schedules:

Alaska Direct Bus Line, 2191 2nd Ave., Whitehorse, YT Y1A 2E3, phone (800) 770-6652 or (867) 668-4833. Service from Anchorage to Fairbanks, Tok, Whitehorse, Dawson City, Skagway and Denali.

Alaska Sightseeing/Cruise West, 4th and Battery Building, Suite 700, Seattle, WA 98121, phone (800) 426-7702. Motorcoach trips connect Anchorage and Denali National Park.

Denali Express Alaska Tours, 405 L St., Anchorage, AK 99501, phone (907) 274-0696. Service between Anchorage and Denali Park; group tours and special itineraries.

Gray Line of Alaska/Alaskon Express, 300 Elliott Ave. W., Seattle, WA 98119, phone (800) 544-2206 or fax (206) 281-0621. Scheduled service to Anchorage, Fairbanks, Skagway, Whitehorse, Haines and most communities en route. Motorcoach tours to Anchorage, Denali National Park, Fairbanks, Prudhoe Bay, Prince William Sound, Seward and Portage Glacier.

Greyhound Lines of Canada, 2191 2nd Ave., Whitehorse, YT Y1A 3T8, phone (867) 667-2223, fax (867) 633-6858. Scheduled service to Whitehorse from all U.S.–Canada border crossings; also the Whitehorse depot has carriers to Dawson City and Alaska destinations.

Norline Coaches (Yukon) Ltd., 34 MacDonald Rd., Whitehorse, YT Y1A 4I2, phone (867) 668-3355 for scheduled service, (867) 633-3864 for charter lines. Service between Whitehorse, Mayo, Carmacks and Dawson City. Daily service to Skagway.

Parks Highway Express, Box 82884, Fairbanks, AK 99708, phone (907) 479-3065, (888) 600-6001. Service between Anchorage, Denali Park and Fairbanks.

Princess Tours®, 2815 2nd Ave., Suite 400, Seattle, WA 98121, phone 1-800-835-8907. Motorcoach tours include the Klondike in Canada's Yukon, Anchorage, the Kenai Peninsula, Denali National Park, Fairbanks and Prudhoe Bay.

Seward Bus Line, Box 1338, Seward, AK 99664, phone (907) 224-3608, fax (907) 244-7237. Daily, year-round service between Anchorage and Seward.

Calendar of Events

Travelers may wish to take into account some of the North's major celebrations when planning their visit. Following are some of these events listed by month and by place. Additional events are detailed under Attractions for the communities covered in the highway logs. In 1998, watch for events throughout the North that celebrate the centennial of the Klondike Gold Rush.

FEBRUARY

Anchorage—Fur Rendezvous. **Cordova**—Iceworm Festival. **Fairbanks/Whitehorse, YT**—Yukon Quest Sled Dog Race; Yukon Sourdough Rendezvous. **Nenana**—Tripod Raising Festival. **Whitehorse, YT**—Sourdough Rendezvous.

MARCH

Anchorage—Iditarod Trail Sled Dog Race. **Bethel**—Camai Native Dance Festival. **Dawson City, YT**—Thaw-Di-Graw Spring Carnival. **Fairbanks**—Winter Carnival; North American Sled Dog Championships. **Nome**—Bering Sea Ice Classic Golf Tournament; month of Iditarod events. **North Pole**—Winter Carnival. **Valdez**—Winter Carnival.

APRIL

Girdwood—Alyeska Spring Carnival. **Juneau**—Alaska Folk Festival. **Whitehorse, YT**—Rotary Music Festival. **Valdez**—Extreme Skiing Championships, Mountain Man Snowmachine Hill Climb.

MAY

This month is a busy one for fishing derbies for halibut (Homer, Seldovia and Valdez) and salmon (Ketchikan, Petersburg, Seldovia and Sitka). **Dawson City, YT**—International Gold Show. **Delta Junction**—Buffalo Wallow Square Dance Jamboree. **Kodiak**—Crab Festival. **Nome**—Polar Bear Swim. **Petersburg**—Little Norway Festival. **Talkeetna**—Miners Day Festival.

JUNE

Anchorage—Mayor's Midnight Sun Marathon. **Fairbanks**—Midnight Sun Baseball Game. **Haines Junction, YT**—Alsek Music Festival. **Nenana**—River Daze. **Nome**—Midnight Sun Festival. **Palmer**—Colony Days. **Sitka**—Summer Music Festival. **Whitehorse, YT**—Yukon International Storytelling Festival.

JULY

Chugiak/Eagle River—Bear Paw Festival. **Dawson City, YT**—Canadian Airlines International Midnight Dome Race; Dawson City Music Festival; Yukon Gold Panning Championships. **Delta Junction**—Deltana Fair. **Fairbanks**—Golden Days; World Eskimo-Indian Olympics. **Seward**—Mount Marathon Race. **Soldotna**—Progress Days. **Talkeetna**—Moose Dropping Festival. **Watson Lake, YT**—Watson Lake Rodeo.

AUGUST

Dawson City and Watson Lake, YT—Discovery Days. **Fairbanks**—Tanana Valley State Fair. **Haines**—Southeast Alaska State Fair. **Kodiak**—State Fair and Rodeo. **Ninilchik**—Kenai Peninsula State Fair. **Palmer**—Alaska State Fair. **Seward**—Silver Salmon Derby. **Whitehorse/Dawson City, YT**—Annual Sourdough Rendezvous Gold-Rush Bathtub Race; Klondyke Harvest Fair.

SEPTEMBER

Dawson City, YT—Great Klondike Outhouse Race and Bathroom Wall Limerick Contest. **Fairbanks**—Equinox Marathon. **Nome**—Great Bathtub Race. **Seldovia**—Blueberry Festival. **Skagway**—Klondike Trail of '98 Road Relay to Whitehorse, YT. **Whitehorse, YT,** —Klondike Trail of '98 International Road Relay to Skagway, AK.

OCTOBER

Anchorage—Oktoberfest. **Sitka**—Alaska Day Festival.

NOVEMBER

Anchorage—Great Alaska Shootout.

Camping

Alaska and Canada offer both government and private campgrounds. With few exceptions, government and private campgrounds are located along the road system and most roadside campgrounds accommodate both tents and RVs. Wilderness camping is also available in most state, federal and provincial parklands. *The MILEPOST®* logs all public roadside campgrounds and includes facilities (water, firewood, etc.) and camping fees, length of vehicle or length of stay limits. *The MILEPOST®* highway logs also include private campgrounds. Keep in mind that government campgrounds do not maintain dump stations (except some British Columbia provincial parks) and few offer electrical hookups. Season dates for most campgrounds in the North depend on weather.

NOTE: Campers are urged to use established campgrounds. Overnighting in rest areas and turnouts is illegal unless otherwise posted, and may be unsafe.

The MILEPOST® indicates both private and public campgrounds with ▲ tent symbols in the highway logs and on the strip maps.

ALASKA

Federal agencies offering recreational campsites are the Bureau of Land Management (BLM), the National Park Service (NPS), the U.S. Forest Service (USFS) and the U.S. Fish and Wildlife Service (USF&WS). Alaska State Parks, the largest state park system in the United States, maintains more than 3,000 campsites within its 120-unit park system.

Camping is available at 40 state recreation sites, 5 state parks (Chugach, Denali, Chilkat, Kachemak Bay and Wood-Tikchik), 14 state recreation sites and a state historic park. Reservations are not accepted at any state campgrounds. Camping rates (subject to change) range from $6 to $15. An annual pass, good for unlimited camping in a calendar year, is available for $75 for Alaska residents and $200 for nonresidents. The pass is a windshield decal and is not transferable. There is a day-use parking fee of $3 or $5 per vehicle at a small number of state park facilities, including some picnic sites, trailheads and fishing access sites. A full-year parking pass may be purchased for $25. To obtain camping or parking passes, send check or money order payable to the State of Alaska. Mail to Alaska Camping Pass, Division of Parks and Outdoor Recreation, 3601 C Street, Suite 200, Anchorage, AK 99503-5929.

BLM maintains about 12 campgrounds; fees are charged at some. Unless otherwise posted, all undeveloped BLM public lands are open to free camping, usually for a maximum of 14 days per stay. Write the Bureau of Land Management, 1150 University Ave., Fairbanks, AK 99709-3899, phone (907) 474-2251.

The National Park Service maintains 7 campgrounds in Denali National Park and Preserve (see DENALI NATIONAL PARK section). There are established hike-in campgrounds at Glacier Bay and Katmai national parks and preserves, and wilderness camping in other national parks and preserves in Alaska. For more information, contact any of the Alaska Public Lands Information Centers or access on-line information for the national parks (see "National Parks" on page 28).

Most USFS campgrounds charge a fee of under $10 per night depending on facilities. There is a 14-day limit at most campgrounds; this regulation is enforced. For further information write the Office of Information, USDA Forest Service, Box 21628, Juneau, AK 99802.

U.S. Fish & Wildlife Service manages sev-

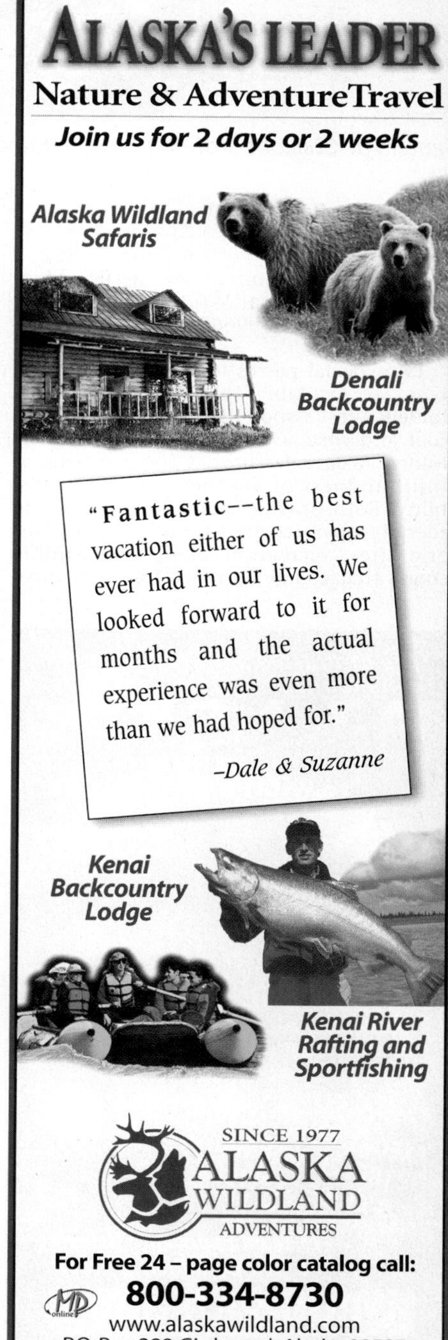

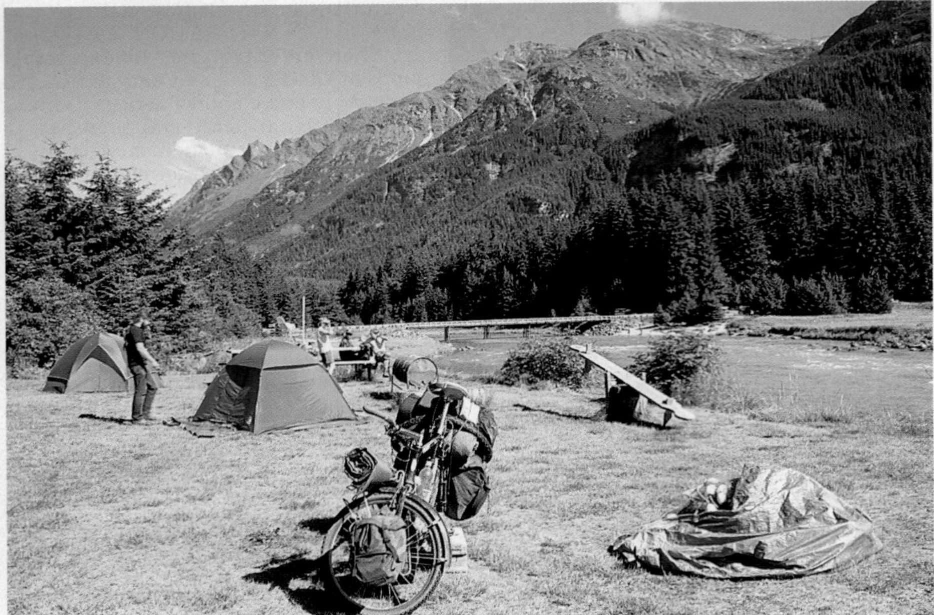

Tenters at Chilkoot State Park near Haines, AK. (© Ruth von Spalding)

eral camping areas within Kenai National Wildlife Refuge. Contact the Refuge Manager, Kenai National Wildlife Refuge, Box 2139, Soldotna, AK 99669, phone (907) 262-7021.

Two special passes for federal recreation areas are available to U.S. citizens. The Golden Age Passport is for persons 62 and older and costs a one time fee of $10. The Golden Access Passport is free for persons with blindness or another permanent disability. Both provide lifetime admittance to federally operated parks, monuments, historic sites, recreation areas and wildlife refuges that charge entrance fees. Accompanying passengers in a private car enter without charge as well. The passport bearer also receives a 50 percent discount on federal use fees charged for facilities and services such as camping, boat launching and parking (exceptions to the 50 percent discount may apply in government facilities operated by concessionaires, such as the Russian River ferry). These passes must be obtained in person by showing proof of age for a Golden Age Passport, or proof of being medically diagnosed with blindness or another permanent disability for the Golden Access Passport. The passports are available at most of the federal recreation areas where they may be used, so travelers do not need to obtain them in advance. They also can be obtained at Alaska Public Lands Information Centers in Anchorage and Fairbanks.

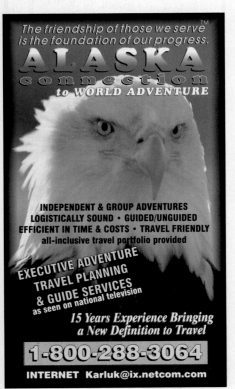

CANADA

Territorial campgrounds in Northwest Territories charge $12 or $15 per night, depending upon the site, in attended campgrounds and parks with facilities. Campground-use firewood is available for a fee.

Yukon Territory has 43 Yukon government campgrounds located along its road system. There is a per night fee of $8 charged for nonresidents. These well-maintained campgrounds often have kitchen shelters (which may not be used as sleeping accommodations) and free firewood for use at the campground. There is a 14-day limit.

Provincial park campgrounds and private campgrounds are readily available along Alaska Highway connecting routes in British Columbia and Alberta. Provincial park camping fees range from $10 to $20 a night depending on facilities.

National park campgrounds in Canada generally have a per-night fee ranging from $12 for a tent site to $25 for a full-hookup site. A park motor-license sticker is required for motorists staying overnight in the national parks. Electrical service is standard 60 cycle. Wood for campfires is supplied free to all camping and picnicking grounds. Bring your own ax to split kindling. "Serviced" campgrounds have caretakers.

Crossing the Border

Travel between the United States and Canada is usually a fairly straightforward procedure. However, travelers are reminded that all persons and their vehicles are subject to search and seizure at the border according to the laws of whichever country they are entering. Vehicles may be searched at the discretion of the customs officials, whether or not the traveler feels that he or she has complied with customs requirements.

Customs agents in both Canada and the U.S. are charged with enforcing a daunting number of regulations pertaining to agricultural products, commercial goods, alcohol, tobacco and firearms. Canada vigorously enforces its firearms importation laws, and border officials may—at their discretion—search any vehicle for handguns.

Certain items, mainly crafts and souvenirs made from parts of wild animals, have caused some problems for travelers to the North in recent years. An item which may be purchased legally in Alaska, for example carved ivory, can be brought back into the Lower 48 but may not be permitted transit through Canada without a permit. Some items which may be purchased legally in parts of Canada may not be allowed into the United States. For example, a seal-fur doll purchased in Inuvik, NWYT, would be confiscated by the U.S. Fish and Wildlife Service or U.S. customs because the import of seal products is prohibited except by special permit.

For information on Canadian customs, contact Customs Border Services, Regional Information Unit, 333 Dunsmuir St., Main Floor, Vancouver, BC V6B 5R4; phone (604) 666-0545; Internet address: http://www.revcan.ca.

For further U.S. customs information, contact the nearest U.S. customs office or write U.S. Customs Service, P.O. Box 7407, Washington, DC 20044. In Seattle, WA, phone (206) 553-4676.

Following are the locations and hours of operation for highway customs offices located along the southern border of Alberta and British Columbia. Stations are open year-round unless otherwise noted.

Border Crossing	Open
Aden, AB–Whitlash, MT	9 A.M.–5 P.M.
Aldergrove, BC–Lynden, WA	8 A.M.–midnight
Boundary Bay, BC–Point Roberts, WA	24 hours
Carson, BC–Danville, WA	8 A.M.–midnight
Carway, AB–Piegan, MT	7 A.M.–11 p.m.
Cascade, BC–Laurier, WA	8 A.M.–midnight
Chief Mountain, AB–MT (June 1–Sept. 22)	7 A.M.–10 P.M.
Chopaka, BC–Nighthawk, WA	9 A.M.–5 P.M.
Coutts, AB–Sweetgrass, MT	24 hours
Del Bonita, AB–MT (Sept. 16–May 31)	9 A.M.–6 P.M.
Douglas, BC–Blaine, WA	24 hours
Flathead, BC–Trail Creek, MT (June 1–Oct. 31)	9 A.M.–5 P.M.
Huntingdon, BC–Sumas, WA	24 hours
Kingsgate, BC–Eastport, ID	24 hours
Midway, BC–Ferry, WA	9 A.M.–5 P.M.
Nelway, BC–Boundary Dam, WA	8 A.M.–midnight
Osoyoos, BC–Oroville, WA	24 hours
Pacific Highway	24 hours

Paterson, BC–Frontier, WA	24 hours
Roosville, BC–Port of Roosville, MT	24 hours
Rykerts, BC–Porthill, ID	
(October–April)	8 A.M.–midnight
(May–September)	7 A.M.–midnight
Waneta, BC–Boundary, WA	9 A.M.–5 P.M.
Wildhorse, AB–MT	
(October–May 14)	8 A.M.–5 P.M.
(May 15–September)	8 A.M.–9 P.M.

Entry into Canada from the U.S. (non-residents)

Identification: Citizens or permanent residents of the United States do not require passports or visas to enter Canada. However, native-born U.S. citizens should carry some identifying paper that shows their citizenship, in case they are asked for it. This could include a driver's license and voter's registration (together), passport with photo, or some employment cards with description and photo. Social security cards or driver's licenses alone are not positive identification. Birth certificates of children are sometimes required. Proof of residence may also be required. Naturalized U.S. citizens should carry a naturalization certificate or some other evidence of citizenship. Permanent residents of the United States who are not U.S. citizens are advised to have their Resident Alien Card (U.S. Form 1-151 or Form 1-551).

Officials at Canadian customs are concerned about child abductions. If you are traveling with children, remember to bring identification for them. A divorced parent traveling with his or her young child may find a copy of the divorce/custody papers helpful. When traveling with children who are not your own, have proper identification *and* written permission from a parent or guardian.

Persons under 18 years of age who are not accompanied by an adult should bring a letter with them from a parent or guardian giving them permission to travel into Canada. Proof of sufficient funds to travel within—and back out of—Canada may be required.

Motorists: U.S. motorists are advised to obtain a Canadian Nonresident Interprovincial Motor Vehicle Liability Insurance Card, which provides evidence of financial responsibility. This card is available only in the United States through U.S. insurance companies or their agents. All provinces in Canada require visiting motorists to produce evidence of financial responsibility should they be involved in an accident. Financial responsibility limits vary by province.

All national driver's licenses are valid in Canada. (See also Driving Information this section.)

Entry by private boat or plane: Report to Canada Customs by phoning (888) 226-7277. Provide the names, dates of birth and citizenships of all people on board, the purpose of trip, and declare any firearms or other goods. You will then be given a reporting number for your records. Upon arriving at the designated customs reporting site, you must call Canada Customs a second time to be advised either to wait for a customs officer or to proceed with your travels.

Baggage: The necessary wearing apparel and personal effects in use by the visitor are admitted free of duty. Up to 50 cigars, 200 cigarettes (1 carton) and 14 ounces of manufactured tobacco, 200 tobacco sticks, and up to 40 ounces of spiritous liquor or wine or 24 12-ounce cans or bottles of beer or ale may be allowed entry in this manner. Additional quantities of alcoholic beverages up to a maximum of 2 gallons may be imported into Canada (except the Northwest Territories) on payment of duty and taxes plus charges for a provincial permit at port of entry. To import tobacco products a person must be 18 years of age or over, and to import alcoholic beverages the importer must have reached the legal age established by authorities of the province or territory into which the alcoholic beverages are being entered.

Gifts: Be prepared to provide receipts for gifts, in case you are asked to show the dollar value. Gifts are duty- and tax-free when each gift is valued at $60 (Canadian) or less. If the value of a gift exceeds $60, you may have to pay duties and taxes on the excess amount.

Firearms: Firearms are divided into 3 categories—prohibited, restricted and long guns. The *only* category of gun a U.S. visitor may bring into Canada is a long gun, which is a regular hunting rifle or shotgun with a barrel at least 18½ inches/47 cm, and an overall length of 26 inches/66 cm, and which does not fall into the category of a prohibited or restricted firearm. Non-restricted firearms may be imported only for sporting or hunting use while in Canada, for use in competitons, for in-transit movement through Canada or for a person's protection against wildlife in remote regions of Canada (excluding national parks) as long as the customs officer is satisfied that the circumstances warrent the importation of the firearm. Restricted weapons may only be imported for the purpose of attending an approved shooting competition in Canada. A temporary permit to carry is required.

Nonresidents arriving at a Canada customs port must declare all their firearms, including long guns. Anyone who illegally carries a firearm into Canada is subject to a number of penalties, including seizure of the weapon and the vehicle in which it is carried. It is against the law for visitors to bring handguns into Canada. Personal protection devices such as stun-guns, mace or pepper spray are also prohibited. Specific questions on importing guns should be directed to the Regional Information Unit at (604) 666-0545 or Automated Customs Information Service at (800) 461-9999.

Plants, fruit and vegetables: House plants may be imported without a permit. Some fruits and vegetables may be restricted or prohibited entry into Canada and all are subject to inspection at the border.

Meat and dairy products: You can import some meat and dairy products from the United States. There are limits on the quantity or dollar value of certain food products you can bring into Canada at the low rates of duty or that you can include in your personal exemption. If you bring in quanitities of these products over and above the limits, you will have to pay a high rate of duty (from 150 to 350 percent). You may also need an agricultural inspection certificate.

Animals: Dogs and cats (over 3 months of age) from the United States must be accompanied by a certificate issued by a licensed veterinarian of Canada or the United States certifying that the animal has been vaccinated against rabies during the preceding 36 months; such a certificate shall describe the animal and date of vaccination and shall be initialed by inspectors and returned to the owner.

Up to 2 pet birds per family may be imported into Canada. Birds of the parrot family and song birds may be admitted when accompanied by the owner, if the owner certifies in writing that, upon entering the country, the birds have not been in contact with any other birds during the preceding 90 days and have been in the owner's possession for the entire period. All birds of the parrot family, except budgies, cockatiels and Rose-ringed parakeets, are on the CITES endangered species list and require special permits.

GST Refund: You can claim a Goods and Services Tax (GST) refund of the GST paid on most goods and on accommodation of less than one month. For more information, phone (800) 668-4748 when in Canada.

Re-entry into the U.S. (residents)

It is the responsibility of the traveler to satisfy U.S. immigration authorities of his right to re-enter the United States. Canadian immigration officers may caution persons entering from the United States if they may have difficulty in returning.

Re-entry to the United States can be simplified if you list all your purchases before you reach the border, keep sales receipts and invoices handy, and pack purchases separately.

Within 48 hours: Residents of the United States visiting Canada for less than 48 hours may bring in for personal or household use merchandise to the fair retail value of $200, free of U.S. duty and tax. Any or all of the following may be included, as long as the total value does not exceed $200: 50 cigarettes, 10 cigars (non-Cuban in origin), 4 ounces/150 ml of alcoholic beverages or alcoholic perfume.

If any article brought back is subject to duty or tax, or if the total value of all articles exceeds $200, no article may be exempted from duty or tax. Members of a family household are not permitted to combine the value of their purchases under this exception.

Persons crossing the international boundary at one point and re-entering the United States in order to travel to another part of Canada should inquire at U.S. customs regarding special exemption requirements.

After more than 48 hours: Residents may bring back, once every 30 days, merchandise for personal or household use to the value of $400 free of U.S. duty and tax. The exemption will be based on the fair retail value of the article acquired and goods must accompany the resident upon arrival in the United States. Members of a family household traveling together may combine their personal exemptions—thus a family of 5 could be entitled to a total exemption of $2,000. Up to 100 cigars (non-Cuban in origin) per person may be imported into the United States by U.S. residents, and up to 200 cigarettes, and 1 liter of alcoholic beverages if the resident has reached the age of 21 years.

Animals: Your pets, including those taken out of the country and being returned, must have a valid veterinarian health certificate. Particularly, dogs must have proof of rabies vaccination. If you are traveling with pet birds, check with customs about specific requirements. Wildlife and fish are subject to certain import and export restrictions, prohibitions, permits or certificates, and quarantine requirments. Endangered species of wildlife and products made from them are generally prohibited from being imported or exported.

Trademarked items: Foreign-made trademarked items may be limited as to the quantity which can be brought into the U.S. The types of items usually of interest to tourists are lenses, cameras, binoculars, optical goods, tape recorders, musical instruments, jewelry, precious metal-ware, perfumes, watches and clocks. Returning residents are allowed an exemption, usually one article of a type bearing a protected trademark. The item must be for your personal use and not for sale.

Plants: Plants, cuttings, seeds, unprocessed plant products and certain endangered species either require an import permit or are prohibited from entering the U.S. Every single plant or plant product must be declared to the customs officer. Call Quarantines at (303) 436-8645 for information on current plants and import permits.

Entry into the U.S. from Canada (non-residents)

Exemptions: Non-residents of the U.S. may bring in for personal or household use merchandise to the fair retail value of $200, free of U.S. duty and tax. In addition to $200 in items, some articles may be brought in free of duty and tax. They must be for your personal use and not for others or for sale. These exemptions include personal effects (wearing apparel, articles of personal adornment, toilet articles, hunting, fishing and photographic equipment); one liter of alcoholic beverages (wine, beer or liquor) if you are an adult non-resident; 200 cigarettes, or 50 cigars, or 2 kilograms (4.4 lb.) of smoking tobacco, or proportionate amounts of each; and vehicles for personal use if imported in connection with your arrival.

Gifts: Articles up to $100 in total value for use as bona fide gifts to other persons may be brought in free of duty and tax, if you will be in the U.S. for at least 72 hours and have not claimed this gift exemption in the past 6 months. This gift exemption may include up to 100 cigars.

Restricted or Prohibited Items: Some items must meet certain requirements, require a license or permit, or may be prohibited entry. Among these are: liquor-filled candy (prohibited); fruits, plants and endangered species of plants, vegetables and their products; firearms and ammunition, if not intended for legitimate hunting or lawful sporting purposes; hazardous articles (fireworks, dangerous toys, toxic or poisonous substances); lottery tickets; meats, poultry and products (sausage, pate); narcotics and dangerous drugs; pets (cats, dogs and birds); pornographic articles and publications; switchblade knives; trademarked items (certain cameras, watches, perfumes, musical instruments, jewelry and metal flatware); vehicles and motorcycles not equipped to comply with U.S. safety or clean air emission standards if your visit is for more than one year; wildlife (birds, fish, mammals, animals) and endangered species, including any part or product (pheasants, articles from reptile skins, whalebone or ivory, mounted specimens and trophies, feathers or skins of wild birds).

If you require medicine containing habit-forming drugs, carry only the quantity normally needed and properly identified, and have a prescription or written statement from your personal physician that the medicine is necessary for your physical well-being. Other pharmaceuticals and/or medicinal devices other than for the personal use of the traveler must be approved by the U.S. Food and Drug Administration.

Re-entry into Canada (residents)

When returning to Canada, residents must declare all of the goods they acquired abroad and are bringing back, as purchases, gifts, prizes or awards. Residents need to include goods still in their possession that they bought at a Canadian or foreign duty-free shop. They must also declare any repairs or modifications made to their vehicle, vessel or aircraft while they were out of the country. If unsure about whether an article is admissible or if it should be declared, residents should always declare it first and then ask a customs officer.

Absence of 24 hours or more: Residents can claim goods worth up to $50 as a personal exemption. This does not apply to tobacco products and alcoholic beverages. Residents may have to make a written declaration. If the goods they bring in are worth more than $50, they cannot claim this exemption and must pay duties on the full value.

Absence of 48 hours or more: Residents can claim goods worth up to $200 in total. These goods can include tobacco products and alcoholic beverages. They may have to make written declaration.

After any trip of 48 hours or longer, you are entitled to a special duty rate on goods worth up to $300 more than your personal exemption. The current special duty rate under the United States Tariff treatment, when combined with GST, is 8 percent.

Absence of 7 days or more: Residents can

claim goods up to $500 in total. These goods can include tobacco products and alcoholic beverages. Residents may have to make a written declaration.

To claim tobacco products and alcoholic beverages, residents must meet the age requirements set by the province or territory where they enter Canada. Tobacco products may include up to 200 cigarettes, 50 cigars or cigarillos, 200 tobacco sticks and 200 grams of manufactured tobacco. Alcoholic beverages may include up to 1.14 litres (40 ounces) of wine or liquor, or 24 355 ml (12-ounce) cans or bottles (8.5 liters) of beer or ale. If you bring in more than the free allowance, the cost may be high, since you will have to pay both customs and provincial or territorial assessments.

Gifts: Under certain conditions, residents may send gifts from outside Canada duty- and tax-free to friends in Canada. Each gift must be worth $60 or less and cannot be an alcoholic beverage, a tobacco product or advertising matter. If the gift is worth more than $60, the recipient will have to pay regular duties on the excess amount. It is always a good idea to include a gift card to avoid any misunderstanding. Gifts brought back with the resident do not qualify for the gift exemption.

In most cases, you have to pay regular duties on prizes and awards you receive outside Canada. ♿

Cruise Ship Travel

Cruises to Alaska are primarily available from May through September on board more than 30 ships—ranging from large luxury cruise ships to small explorer-class ships. Most ships depart from Vancouver, BC (some from San Francisco and Seattle) and cruise to Alaska via the Inside Passage.

The Inside Passage is the route north along the coast of British Columbia and through southeastern Alaska that uses the protected waterways between the islands and the mainland. (Inside Passage is also commonly used to refer to Southeast Alaska and its communities, which are the ports of call for the cruise ships.) The water passage travels along hundreds of miles of forested coastline, passing deep fjords and the steep, snow-capped peaks of the Coast Range. Other ports of call include:

College Fjord, an 18-mile-long estuary that extends northeast off Port Wells, another estuary, in the northwest corner of Prince William Sound, near Whittier. Glaciers cascade down the west side of College Fjord. At the north end of College Fjord, where a large black island of rock divides Harvard Arm from Yale Arm, are the "twin" tidewater glaciers— named Yale Glacier and Harvard Glacier by members of the Harriman Alaska Expedition in 1899.

Hubbard Glacier, about 34 miles northeast of Yakutat, has become a popular port of call with cruise ships crossing the Gulf of Alaska between Southeast Alaska's Inside Passage and Southcentral Alaska's Prince William Sound. Framed by snow-covered mountains, Hubbard Glacier rolls toward the sea like a blue-white breaking wave. The glacier made headlines in June 1986, when it surged, damming Russell Fiord. The ice dam eventually weakened and broke..

Misty Fiords, a national monument encompassing more than 2 million acres of Southeast Alaska. Large cruise ships sail Behm Canal, a more than 100-mile-long, deepwater canal that is the major waterway through the monument. The scenery is dramatic: thick rainforest, vertical granite cliffs and snowy peaks. Waterfalls plunge to salt water along the steep-walled waterways, fed by lakes and streams which absorb an annual rainfall in excess of 14 feet.

Tracy Arm, and adjoining *Endicott Arm*, both long, deep, narrow fjords that extend more than 30 miles into the heavily glaciated Coast Mountain Range, about 50 miles southeast of Juneau. At the head of each arm are active tidewater glaciers, which continually calve icebergs into the fjords: Sawyer and South Sawyer glaciers at the head of Tracy Arm; Dawes Glacier at the head of Endicott Arm.

Cruise Lines

Following is a list of cruise lines serving Alaska in 1998. Included are the names of the line's ships (passenger capacity is shown in parentheses) and proposed Alaska ports of call. Not all ships have the same itinerary. Contact the cruise line directly or your travel agent for more details.

There's a bewildering array of travel options connected with cruise ship travel. Both round-trip and one-way cruises are available, or a cruise may be sold as part of a packaged tour that includes air, rail and/or motorcoach transportation. Various shore excursions may be included in the cruise price or offered to passengers for added cost. Ports of call may depend on length of cruise, which ship you choose, time of sailing or debarkation point. Because of the wide variety of cruise trips available, it is wise to work with your travel agent.

Alaska Sightseeing/Cruise West, 4th & Battery Bldg., Suite 700, Seattle, WA 98121-1438; phone 1-800-426-7702 or (206) 441-8687, fax (206) 441-4757. *Spirit of Glacier Bay* (58 passengers); *Sheltered Seas* (80 passengers, no cabin space); *Spirit of Alaska* (82 passengers); *Spirit of Discovery* (84 passengers); *Spirit of '98* (101 passengers); and *Spirit of Endeavor* (107 passengers). Ports of call: Anchorage, Cordova, Glacier Bay, Haines, Juneau, Ketchikan, Misty Fiords, Petersburg, Sitka, Skagway, Tracy Arm, Valdez, Wrangell.

Carnival Cruise Line, Carnival Place, 3655 NW 87th Ave., Miami, FL 33178-2428; phone (305) 599-2600. *Jubilee* (1,486 passengers). Ports of call: College Fjord, Haines, Hubbard Glacier, Juneau, Ketchikan, Seward, Sitka, Skagway, Tracy Arm, Valdez.

Celebrity Cruises, Inc., 5201 Blue Lagoon Dr., Miami, FL 33126; phone (305) 262-6677. *Mercury* (1,870 passengers) and *Galaxy* (1,870 passengers). Ports of call: College Fjord, Glacier Bay, Haines, Hubbard Glacier, Inside Passage, Juneau, Ketchikan, Misty Fiords, Seward, Sitka, Skagway, Valdez.

Clipper Cruise Lines, Windsor Bldg., 7711 Bonhomme Ave., St. Louis, MO 63105-1956; phone 1-800-325-0010 or (314) 727-2929, fax (314) 727-6576. *Yorktown Clipper* (138 passengers). Ports of call: Glacier Bay, Haines, Juneau, Ketchikan, Misty Fiords, Petersburg, Sitka, Skagway, Tracy Arm, Wrangell.

Crystal Cruises, 2121 Avenue of the Stars, Los Angeles, CA 90067; phone 1-800-446-6620, (310) 785-9300. *Crystal Harmony (960 passengers)* and *Crystal Symphony* (960 passengers). Ports of call: Glacier Bay, Hubbard Glacier, Juneau, Ketchikan, Misty Fiords, Seward, Sitka, Skagway, Tracy Arm.

Glacier Bay Tours & Cruises, 520 Pike St., Suite 1400, Seattle, WA 98101; phone 1-800-451-5952 or (206) 623-2417, fax (206) 623-7809; Internet: www.glacierbaytours.com. *Executive Explorer* (49 passengers), *Wilderness Discoverer* (86 passengers), *Wilderness Explorer* (36 passengers) and the *Wilderness Adventure* (74 passengers). Glacier Bay, Haines, Juneau, Kake, Ketchikan, Misty Fiords, Tracy Arm, Sitka, Skagway.

Hanseatic Cruises GmbH, Nagelsweg 55, 20097 Hamburg, Germany; phone 49-40-231603. *Hanseatic*. Ports of call: College Fjord, Glacier Bay, Haines, Juneau, Ketchikan, Misty Fiords, Seward, Sitka, Skagway, Tracy Arm, Wrangell.

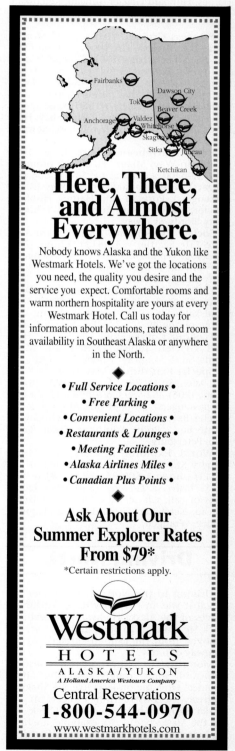

Holland America Westours, 300 Elliot Ave. W., Seattle, WA 98119; phone (206) 281-3535, fax (206) 281-0351; Internet: www.hollandamerica.com. *Statendam* (1,266 passengers), *Nieuw Amsterdam* (1,214 passengers), *Noordam* (1,214 passengers), *Ryndam* (1,266 passengers), *Maasdam* (1,266 passengers) and *Westerdam* (1,494 passengers). Ports of call: College Fjord, Glacier Bay, Hubbard Glacier, Skagway, Juneau, Ketchikan, Seward, Sitka, Valdez.

Norwegian Cruise Lines, 95 Merrick Way, Coral Gables, FL 33134; phone 1-800-327-7030, (305) 436-4000. *Windward* (1,246 passengers) and *Norwegian Dynasty* (800 passengers). Ports of call: Cordova, Glacier Bay, Haines, Hubbard Glacier, Juneau, Ketchikan, Prince William Sound, Seward, Sitka, Skagway.

Princess Cruises, 10100 Santa Monica Blvd., Los Angeles, CA 90067; phone (310) 553-1770, fax (310) 277-6175. *Regal Princess* and *Crown Princess* (1,590 passengers), *Star Princess* (1,490 passengers), *Golden Princess* (830 passengers), *Sky Princess* (1,200 passengers) and *Sun Princess* (1,950 passengers). Ports of call: College Fjord, Glacier Bay, Hubbard Glacier, Juneau, Ketchikan, Seward, Sitka, Skagway.

Royal Caribbean Cruise Line, 1050 Caribbean Way, Miami, FL 33132; phone 1-800-327-6700. *Legend of the Seas* (1,808 passengers), and *Rhapsody of the Seas* (2,400 passengers). Ports of call: Haines, Hubbard Glacier, Glacier Bay, Juneau, Ketchikan, Misty Fiords, Skagway.

Society Expeditions, 2001 Western Ave., Suite 710, Seattle, WA 98121; phone (206) 728-9400. *World Discoverer* (138 passengers). Ports of call: College Fjord, Hubbard Glacier, Misty Fiords, Seward, Sitka, Tracy Arm.

Unicom Management Services, Oasis Center, 2nd Floor, Gladstone and Karaiskakis Sts., P.O. Box 6674, Bonn, Germany; phone 49-228-726280. *Maxim Gorkiy*. Ports of call: College Fjord, Glacier Bay, Hubbard Glacier, Juneau, Ketchikan, Misty Fiords, Sitka, Skagway, Valdez, Wrangell.

Special Expeditions Marine, 1415 Western Ave., Suite 700, Seattle, WA 98101; phone (206) 382-9593. *Sea Bird* and *Sea Lion* (70 passengers). Ports of call: Althorp Rocks, Glacier Bay, Haines, Juneau, Ketchikan, Le Conte Bay, Point Adolphus, Sitka, Tracy Arm, Petersburg.

World Explorer Cruises, 555 Montgomery St., Suite 1400, San Francisco, CA 94111; phone 1-800-854-3835, (415) 393-1565. *Universe Explorer* (550 passengers). Ports of call: Glacier Bay, Hubbard Glacier, Juneau, Ketchikan, Seward, Sitka, Skagway, Valdez, Wrangell.

Driving North

Driving to the North is no longer the ordeal it was in the early days. Those old images of the Alaska Highway with vehicles stuck in mud up to their hubcaps are far removed from the asphalt-surfaced Alaska Highway of today.

Motorists can still expect road construction and some rough road, but have patience! Ongoing projects like the Shakwak Highway Reconstruction Project on the Alaska Highway between Beaver Creek, YT, and the Alaska border, for example, are helping to improve severely deteriorated sections of road.

Roads in the North range from multi-lane freeways to 1-lane dirt and gravel roads. The more remote roads are gravel. Motorists are much farther from assistance and more preparation is required for these roads.

Major highways in Alaska are paved with the exception of the following highways that are at least partially gravel: Steese Highway (Alaska Route 6), Taylor Highway (Alaska Route 5), Elliott Highway (Alaska Route 2), Dalton Highway (Alaska Route 11) and Denali Highway (Alaska Route 8).

In Yukon Territory, the Alaska Highway, the Haines Highway and the Klondike Highway from Skagway to Dawson City are asphalt-surfaced. All other roads are gravel.

Major routes through Alberta and British Columbia are paved, with the exception of the Cassiar Highway (BC Highway 37).

Highways within western Northwest Territories are mostly gravel roads, although paving continues on many routes. Paving is almost completed on NWT Highway 3 to Yellowknife, and NWT Highway 1 is paved from its junction with Highway 3 to the Alberta border.

RV owners should be aware of the height of their vehicles in metric measurements, as bridge heights in Canada are noted in meters.

Know your vehicle and its limitations. Some Northern roads may not be suitable for a large motorhome or trailer, but most roads will present no problem to a motorist who allots adequate time and uses common sense.

Also safeguard against theft while at campgrounds, rest stops or in the cities. Always lock your vehicle, be sure valuables are out of sight in an unattended vehicle and report any thefts to the authorities.

NOTE: Driving with the headlights on at all times is the law in Yukon Territory and on posted roads in Alaska.

ROAD CONDITIONS

General road conditions are noted in the introduction to each highway in *The MILEPOST®*. Specific areas of concern are also called out in the log.

Keep in mind the variable nature of road conditions. Some sections of road may be in poor condition because of current construction or recent bad weather. Other highways—particularly gravel roads closed in winter—may be very rough or very smooth, depending on when maintenance crews last worked on the road.

Asphalt surfacing for most Northern roads is Bituminous Surface Treatment (BST), an alternative to hot-mix pavement which involves application of aggregates and emulsified asphalt. Also known as "chip seal," recently applied or repaired BST is as smooth as any Lower 48 superhighway. However, weather and other factors can lead to failures in the surfacing which include potholes and loss of aggregate.

Also watch for "frost heaves" caused by subsidence of the ground under the road.

Many gravel roads in the North (such as the Dalton Highway) are treated with calcium chloride as a dust-control measure. Because calcium chloride tends to eat into paint and metal parts on your vehicle, be sure to thoroughly wash your vehicle.

PLANNING YOUR TRIP

Depending on where you want to stop and how much time you have to spend, you can count on driving anywhere from 150 to 500 miles a day. On most roads in the North, you can figure on comfortably driving 250 to 300 miles a day.

Log mileages are keyed on the highway strip maps which accompany each highway section in *The MILEPOST®*. Use the mileage boxes on these maps to calculate mileages between points (or refer to the mileage box at the beginning of the highway).

Once you have figured the number of driving miles in your itinerary, you can calculate approximate gas cost using the Gas Price Averages chart. (Keep in mind that 1998 prices may vary from 1997 summer averages.) U.S. motorists factor in the exchange rate for Canadian prices using the accompanying conversion chart.

Normally, May through October is the best time to drive to Alaska. A severe winter or wet spring may affect road conditions and there may be some rough road until road maintenance crews get out to upgrade and repair. Motels, hotels, gas stations and restaurants are open year-round in the cities and on many highways. On more remote routes, such as the Cassiar Highway, not all businesses are open year-round. Check ahead for accommodations and gas if traveling these roads in winter.

VEHICLE PREPARATION

There are some simple preparations that motorists can make for their trip North to make driving easier. First make sure your vehicle and tires are in good condition. An inexpensive and widely available item to include is a set of clear plastic headlight covers (or black metal matte screens). These protect your headlights from flying rocks and gravel. You might also consider a wire-mesh screen across the front of your vehicle to protect paint, grill and radiator from flying rocks. The finer the mesh, the more protection from flying gravel. For those hauling trailers, a piece of quarter-inch plywood fitted over the front of your trailer offers protection.

There is practically no way to protect the windshield, although some motorists have experimented with screen shields that do not seriously impair their vision. These are not recommended nor do you see many of them in the North, but it is, of course, up to the individual motorist whether these are worthwhile.

Crankcases are seldom damaged, but gas tanks can be harmed on rough gravel roads. Sometimes rocks work their way in between the plate and gas tank, wearing a hole in the tank. However, drivers maintaining safe speeds should have no problems with punctured gas tanks. A high vehicle clearance is best for some of the rougher gravel roads.

Also keep in mind the simple precautions that make driving easier. A visor or tinted glass helps when you're driving into the sun. Good windshield wipers and a full windshield washer (or a bottle of wash and a squeegee) make life easier. Many motorists also find bug screens to be a wise investment.

Dust and mud are generally not a major problem on Northern roads, though you may run into both. Heavy rains combined with a gravel road or roadbed torn up for construction make mud. Mud flaps are suggested. Dust can seep into everything and it's difficult if not impossible to keep it out. Remember to close the windows on your trailer or camper when on a dusty road. It also helps to keep clothes, food and bedding in sealed plastic bags. Also check your air filter periodically.

Driving at slow, safe speeds not only keeps down the dust for drivers behind you, it also helps prevent you from spraying other vehicles with gravel.

Drive with your headlights on at all times. This allows you to be seen easier, especially in dusty conditions, or when approaching vehicles are driving into the sun. It is also the law in the Yukon and posted roads in Alaska.

NOTE: If driving on a paved surface, it is still necessary to observe "Loose Gravel" signs. Drive slowly.

Although auto shops in Northern communities are generally well-stocked with parts, carry the following for emergencies and on-the-spot repairs: flares; first-aid kit; trailer bearings; bumper jack with lug wrench; electrician's tape; assortment of nuts and bolts; fan belt; 1 or 2 spare tires (2 spares for remote roads); and a tool set including crescent wrenches, socket and/or open-end wrenches, hammer, screwdrivers, pliers, wire, and prybar for changing the fan belt.

If you are driving a vehicle which may require parts not readily available up North, add whatever you think necessary. You may wish to carry an extra few gallons of gas, water, and fluid for brakes, power steering and automatic transmissions.

If your vehicle should break down on the highway and tow truck service is needed, normally you will be able to flag down a passing motorist. Travelers in the North are generally helpful in such situations (traditionally, the etiquette of the country requires one to stop and provide assistance). If you are the only person traveling in the disabled vehicle, be sure to leave a note on your windshield indicating when you left the vehicle and in what direction you planned to travel.

GASOLINE

Unleaded gas is widely available in Alaska and is the rule in Canada. Diesel fuel is also commonly available. Good advice for Northern travelers: gas-up whenever possible.

In the North, as elsewhere, gas prices vary (see chart at right). Generally, gas prices are slightly higher in Canada and Alaska than the Lower 48, but this is not a hard and fast rule. You may find gas in Anchorage or elsewhere at the same price—or even lower—than at home. A general rule of thumb is the more remote the gas station, the higher the price. Gas prices may vary considerably from service station to service station within the same community.

It is a good idea to carry cash, since some gas stations in Alaska are independents and do not accept credit cards. Most Chevron, Texaco and Tesoro stations will accept VISA or MasterCard. Also watch for posted gas prices that are for *cash,* but not noted as such. Besides double-checking the posted price before filling up, also ask the attendant which pump is for unleaded, regular or diesel, depending on what you want.

Keep in mind that Canadian gas stations have converted to the metric system; quantity and price are based on liters (see Gas Cost in U.S. Funds Per Gallon chart below). There are 3.785 liters per U.S. gallon, 4.5 liters per imperial gallon. See also Liters to U.S. Gallons conversion chart.

INSURANCE

Auto insurance is mandatory in all Canadian provinces and territories. Drivers should carry adequate car insurance before entering the country. Visiting motorists are required to produce evidence of financial responsibility should they be involved in an accident. There is an automatic fine if visitors are involved in an accident and found to be uninsured. Your car could be impounded for this. Your insurance company should be able to provide you with proof of insurance coverage (request a Canadian Nonresident Interprovincial Motor Vehicle Liability Insurance Card) that would be accepted as evidence of financial responsibility.

The minimum liability insurance requirement in Canada is $200,000 Canadian, except in the Province of Quebec where the limit is $50,000 Canadian. Further information regarding automobile insurance in Canada may be obtained from The Insurance Bureau of Canada, 151 Young St., 18th floor, Toronto, ON M5C 2W7; phone (416) 362-2031 or fax (416) 361-5952.

TIRES

On gravel, the faster you drive, the faster your tires will wear out. So take it easy and you should have no tire problems, provided you have the right size for your vehicle, with the right pressure, not overloaded, and not already overly worn. Belted bias or radial ply tires are recommended for gravel roads.

Carry 1 good spare. Consider 2 spares if you are traveling remote gravel roads such as the Dempster or Dalton highways. The space-saver doughnut spare tires found in some passenger cars are not adequate for travel on gravel roads.

GAS PRICE AVERAGES SUMMER 1997

Alaska Location	Per Gallon U.S. Funds	Canada Location	Per Liter Canadian Funds*
Anchorage	$1.32	Atlin, BC	$.77
Big Lake	1.35	Contact Creek, BC	.68
Chitina	1.75	Dawson City, YT	.79
Cordova	1.72	Dawson Creek, BC	.60
Eagle	1.72	Destruction Bay, YT	.73
Fairbanks	1.40	Fort Nelson, BC	.68
Glennallen	1.65	Fort St. John, BC	.60
Soldotna	1.40	Grande Prairie, AB	.56
Tok	1.60	Teslin, YT	.69
Valdez	1.49	Watson Lake, YT	.70
		Whitehorse, YT	.69

*See chart below for equivalent cost in U.S. funds for 1 gallon

LITERS TO U.S. GALLONS

Liters	Gallons	Liters	Gallons	Liters	Gallons
1	.3	21	5.5	41	10.8
2	.5	22	5.8	42	11.1
3	.8	23	6.1	43	11.4
4	1.1	24	6.3	44	11.6
5	1.3	25	6.6	45	11.9
6	1.6	26	6.9	46	12.2
7	1.8	27	7.1	47	12.4
8	2.1	28	7.4	48	12.7
9	2.4	29	7.7	49	12.9
10	2.6	30	7.9	50	13.2
11	2.9	31	8.2	51	13.5
12	3.2	32	8.5	52	13.7
13	3.4	33	8.7	53	14.0
14	3.7	34	9.0	54	14.3
15	4.0	35	9.2	55	14.5
16	4.2	36	9.5	56	14.8
17	4.5	37	9.8	57	15.0
18	4.8	38	10.0	58	15.3
19	5.0	39	10.3	59	15.6
20	5.3	40	10.6	60	15.9

For more precise conversion: 1 liter equals .2642 gallons; 1 gallon equals 3.785 liters.

GAS COST IN U.S. FUNDS PER GALLON

If the Canadian Exchange rate is: $1.00 U.S. equals Canadian funds:		25% $1.25	30% $1.30	35% $1.35	40% $1.40	45% $1.45
	$.56	$1.70	$1.63	$1.57	$1.51	$1.46
	.57	1.73	1.66	1.60	1.54	1.49
	.58	1.76	1.69	1.63	1.57	1.51
	.59	1.79	1.72	1.65	1.60	1.54
	.60	1.82	1.75	1.68	1.62	1.57
Canadian	.61	1.85	1.78	1.71	1.65	1.59
Price	.62	1.88	1.81	1.74	1.68	1.62
Per Liter	.63	1.91	1.83	1.77	1.70	1.64
	.64	1.94	1.86	1.79	1.73	1.67
	.65	1.97	1.89	1.82	1.76	1.70
	.66	2.00	1.92	1.85	1.78	1.72
	.67	2.03	1.95	1.88	1.81	1.75
	.68	2.06	1.98	1.91	1.84	1.78
	.69	2.09	2.01	1.93	1.87	1.80
	.70	2.12	2.04	1.96	1.89	1.83

For example: If gas costs $0.60 Canadian per liter and the current exchange rate is 30% ($1.00 U.S. equals $1.30 Canadian), using the above chart, the equivalent to 1 U.S. gallon of gas costs $1.75 U.S. Or cost per liter X 3.785 divided by exchange rate (1.30)=U.S. cost per gallon.

WINTER DRIVING

In addition to the usual precautions taken when driving in winter, such as keeping the windshield clear of ice, checking antifreeze and reducing driving speeds on icy pavement, equip your vehicle with the following survival gear: traction material (ashes, kitty litter, wood chips); chains (even with snow tires); first-aid kit; shovel, ice scraper, flashlight, flares; fire extinguisher; extra warm clothing (including gloves and extra socks), blankets or sleeping bags; food; tools; and an extension cord to plug car into block heater. Other items which may be added to your survival gear are a tow rope or cable, ax, jumper cables and extra gas.

Extremely low temperatures occur in the North. A motorist may start out in -35° to -40°F weather and hit cold pockets along the road where temperatures drop to -60°F or more. If you do become stranded in weather like this, do not leave your vehicle; wait for aid. DO NOT attempt to drive unmaintained secondary roads or highways in winter (i.e. Denali Highway, Top of the World Highway), even if the roads look clear of snow.

Call ahead for road conditions and weather reports.

RULES AND REGULATIONS

Regulations common to Alaska, Alberta, British Columbia, Northwest Territories and Yukon Territory include: Right turn on red permitted after complete stop, unless prohibited by sign; transporting open alcoholic beverage containers within a motor vehicle is prohibited.

Following are rules and regulations in effect in Alaska and northwestern Canada at our presstime:

ALASKA

Division of Motor Vehicles, Dept. of Public Safety, 5700 E. Tudor Rd., Anchorage, AK 99507; phone (907) 269-5551.

Road Condition Report: For summer road construction advisories, phone 24-hour recorded daily reports hot line (907) 273-6037 for Anchorage and Southcentral Alaska; phone (907) 456-7623 for Fairbanks, Tok and Valdez areas. Or toll-free (in Alaska) 1-800-478-7675. Or visit the Alaska Dept. of Transportation home page at http://www.dot.state.ak.us. "Navigator" reports on road construction are available from visitor centers; also check local newspapers.

Headlight use: One-half hour after sunset to one-half hour before sunrise. Driving with headlights on during all hours of the day is permitted. Headlights required at all times on designated roadways where speed is in excess of 45 mph.

Minimum driver's age: 16 years; 14 with driver's permit if accompanied by a licensed driver 19 years or older.

Rest area camping: Permitted as posted.

Seat belts: Seat belts are mandatory for all drivers and passengers. Child restraints are mandatory for children under 7 years. Applies to out-of-state drivers.

Studded tires: Permitted from Sept. 15 to May 1 (Sept. 30 to April 15 south of 60°N).

Motorcycles: Protective glasses, goggles or windscreen required. Reflectorized helmet required if under 19 and for passenger.

CB Radio: The following channels may be monitored: 2,9,11,14,19, 21 and 22.

Firearms: Permitted. Unlawful to discharge firearm on, from or across the driveable portion of any roadway including roadway shoulders.

Trailers: Independent braking system not required for trailers where gross weight is less than 3,000 lbs. Riding in trailer is prohibited, but riding in pickup/camper is permitted.

ALBERTA

Alberta Registries, Municipal Affairs, 9th floor, 10365 97th St., Edmonton, AB T5J 3W7; phone (403) 427-4095.

Road Condition Report: 1-800-642-3810 (in Alberta).

Headlight use: When light conditions restrict visibility to 500 feet/150m or less. Driving with headlights on during all hours of the day is permitted.

Minimum driver's age: 16 years; 14 to receive learner's permit.

Rest area camping: Prohibited unless otherwise designated.

Seat belts: Seat belts are mandatory for all drivers. Child restraints are mandatory for children under 6 years or 18kg (40 lbs.). Applies to out-of-province drivers.

Studded tires: Permitted year-round but only where marked or posted within federal parks.

Motorcycles: Safety helmet required.

CB Radio: Channel 9 is monitored for emergencies.

Firearms: Rifles must be unloaded and safely stored in trunk. Pistols must be carried in a secure storage box, unloaded, trigger locked and safely stored in trunk.

Trailers: Independent braking system not required for trailers where gross weight is less than 909 kg (2,000 lbs.) and is less than half that of towing vehicle. Riding in trailer prohibited.

BRITISH COLUMBIA

Licensing Operations Insurance Corp. of British Columbia, 2631 Douglas St., Victoria, BC V8T 5A3; phone (250) 387-3140 or (800) 950-1498.

Road Condition Report: Province-wide operator information (604) 660-9770; province-wide recorded information, 75¢/minute (VISA or Mastercard) 1-800-550-4997; province-wide recorded information, 75¢/min. (900) 565-4997; Vancouver-area recorded information, 75¢/min. (604) 420-4997; province-wide recorded information from the U.S., $1/min. (900) 288-4997. Free cellular call at *4997. Or call Talking Yellow Pages in Victoria (250) 953-9000 ext. 7623; Vancouver (604) 299-9000 ext. 7623. Internet address: www.th.gov.bc.ca/bchighways.

Minimum driver's age: Driver's license divided into 6 classes—age 19 for class 1, 2 and 4; 18 for class 3; 16 for classes 5 and 6.

Rest area camping: Prohibited.

Seat belts: Seat belts are mandatory for driver and all passengers. Child restraints are mandatory for children under 6 years. Applies to out-of-province drivers.

Studded tires: Permitted from Oct. 1 to April 30.

Motorcycles: Safety helmet required.

CB Radio: Not monitored for emergencies.

Firearms: All rifles and shotguns must be declared at the border. Pistols are prohibited; strictly enforced.

Trailers: Independent braking system not required for trailers where gross weight is less than 2,000 kg (4,400 lbs.) and is less than 40 percent of licensed weight of towing vehicle. Riding in trailer prohibited.

NORTHWEST TERRITORIES

Motor Vehicle Division, P.O. Box 1320, Yellowknife, X1A 2L9; phone (867) 873-7406, fax (867) 873-0120.

Road Condition Report: For the South Mackenzie, phone 1-800-661-0750 in NWT; for the North Mackenzie, 1-800-661-0752 in NWT.

Minimum driver's age: 16 years, 15 with learner's permit.

Rest area camping: Prohibited.

Seat belts: Seat belts are mandatory for driver and all passengers. Child restraints are mandatory for children less than 18 kg (40 lbs.). Applies to out-of-territory drivers.

Studded tires: Tires that are manufactured as studded tires are permitted year-round for passenger vehicles.

Motorcycles: Safety helmet required for driver and passenger.

CB Radio: Channel 9 or 19 is monitored for emergencies.

Firearms: Contact the Canadian Firearms Centre, phone 1-800-731-4000.

Trailers: Independent braking system not required for trailers where gross weight is less than 1,360 kg (2,992 lbs.) and is less than half of licensed weight of towing vehicle. Riding in trailer prohibited, but riding in pickup/camper is permitted.

YUKON TERRITORY

Dept. of Motor Vehicles, Box 2703, Whitehorse, YT Y1A 2C6; phone (867) 667-5315, fax (867) 393-6220.

Road Condition Report: (867) 667-8215. Internet: www.yukonweb.wis.net/tourism/roads.html.

Minimum driver's age: 16 years, 15 with learner's permit.

Rest area camping: Prohibited.

Seat belts: Seat belts are mandatory for driver and all passengers. Child restraints are mandatory for children 6 and under weighing less than 18 kg (40 lbs.). Applies to out-of-territory drivers.

Studded Tires: No restrictions.

Motorcycles: Safety helmet required.

CB Radio: Channel 9 may be monitored for emergencies.

Firearms: No regulations on firearms in vehicles.

Trailers: Independent braking system not required for trailers where gross weight is less than 910 kg (2002 lbs.) and is less than half of licensed wieght of towing vehicle. Riding in trailer prohibited.

Ferry Travel

Ferry travel to and within Alaska is provided by the Alaska Marine Highway, which is the name of the Alaska state ferry system and also refers to the water route the ferries follow from Bellingham, WA, up the Inside Passage to Skagway, AK.

The Inside Passage is the route north along the coast of British Columbia and through southeastern Alaska that uses the protected waterways between the islands and the mainland. (Inside Passage is also commonly used to refer to Southeast Alaska and its communities; see page 685.)

BC Ferries also serves the Inside Passage, providing marine transportation for passengers and vehicles between Port Hardy and Prince Rupert, BC. Port Hardy is located at the north end of Vancouver Island. Prince Rupert is the western terminus of Yellowhead Highway 16 and the southern port for 3 Alaska

(Continues on page 25)

FERRY ROUTES *Washington and British Columbia from Puget Sound to Hecate Strait*

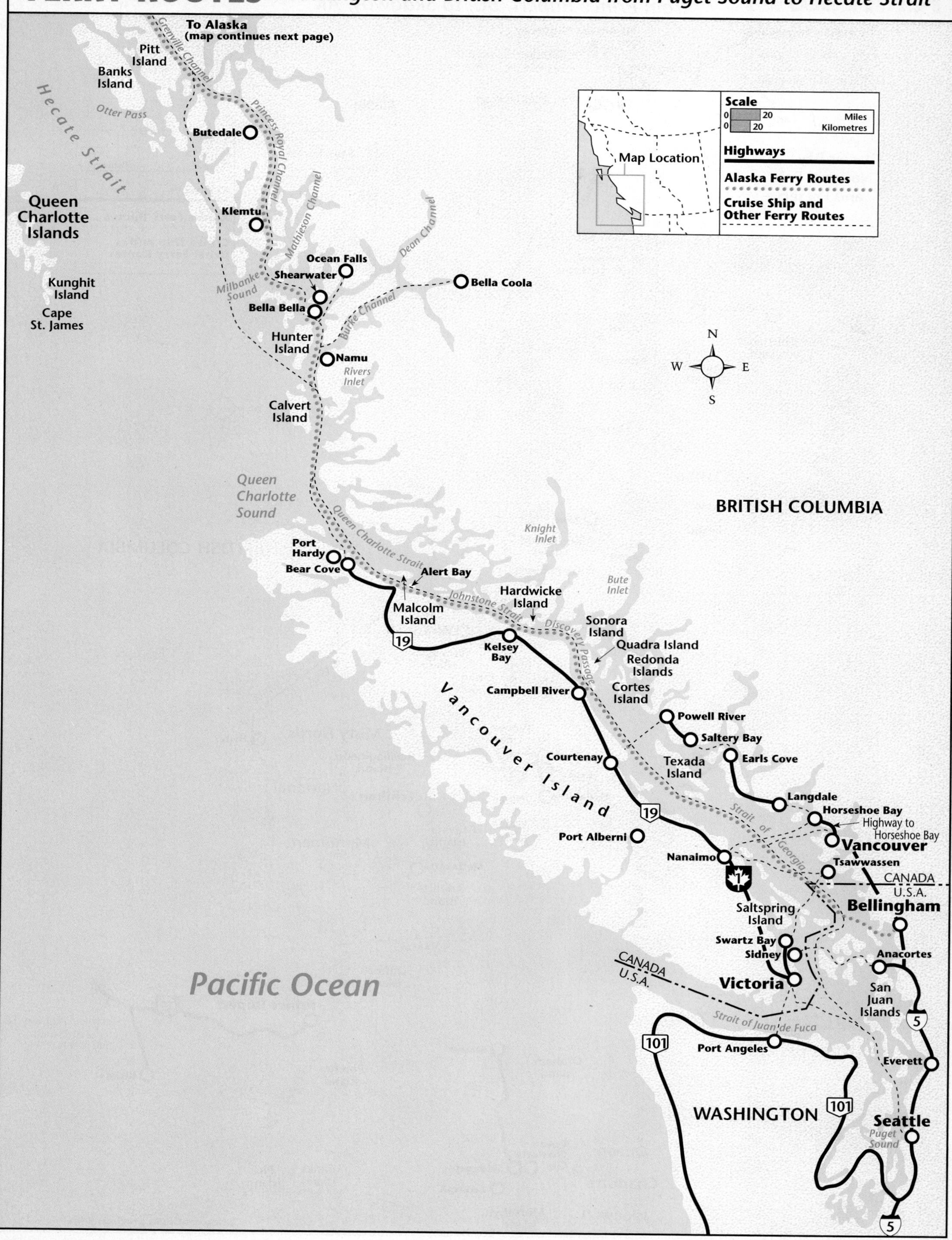

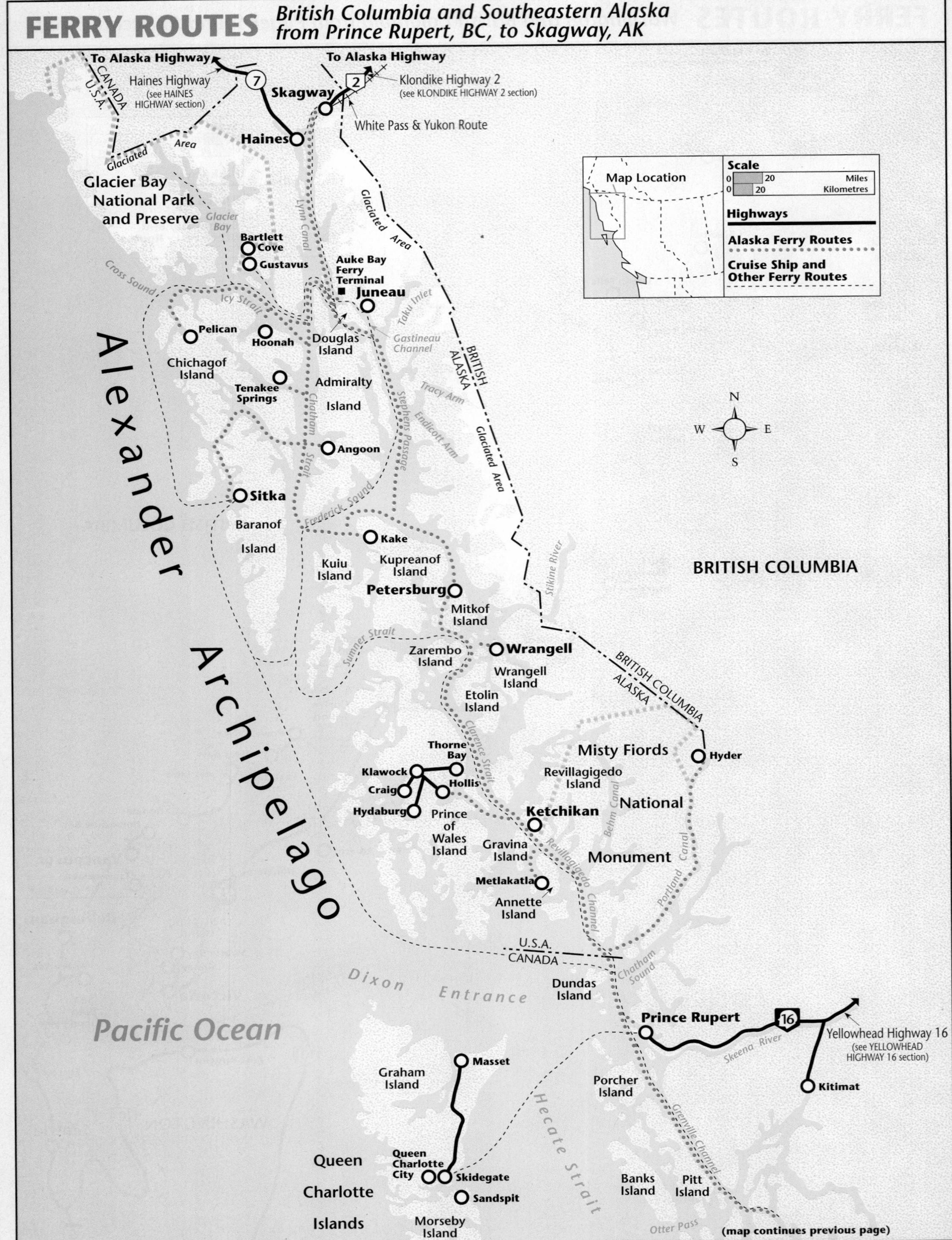

FERRY ROUTES British Columbia and Southeastern Alaska from Prince Rupert, BC, to Skagway, AK
To Alaska Highway
To Alaska Highway
Haines Highway (see HAINES HIGHWAY section)
CANADA
U.S.A.
7
2
Klondike Highway 2 (see KLONDIKE HIGHWAY 2 section)
Skagway
White Pass & Yukon Route
Haines
Glaciated Area
Glacier Bay National Park and Preserve
Glacier Bay
Lynn Canal
Glaciated Area
Map Location
Scale
0 20 Miles
0 20 Kilometres
Highways
Alaska Ferry Routes
Cruise Ship and Other Ferry Routes
Bartlett Cove
Gustavus
Auke Bay Ferry Terminal
Juneau
Cross Sound
Icy Strait
Taku Inlet
Pelican
Hoonah
Douglas Island
Gastineau Channel
Chichagof Island
BRITISH
ALASKA
Tenakee Springs
Admiralty Island
Tracy Arm
Chatham Strait
Stephens Passage
Endicott Arm
N
W
E
S
Angoon
Glaciated Area
Alexander Archipelago
Sitka
Baranof Island
Frederick Sound
Kake
Kuiu Island
Kupreanof Island
Stikine River
BRITISH COLUMBIA
Petersburg
Mitkof Island
Sumner Strait
Zarembo Island
Wrangell
Wrangell Island
BRITISH COLUMBIA
ALASKA
Etolin Island
Thorne Bay
Klawock
Craig
Hollis
Hydaburg
Clarence Strait
Misty Fiords
Revillagigedo Island
National
Monument
Hyder
Behm Canal
Prince of Wales Island
Ketchikan
Gravina Island
Revillagigedo Channel
Portland Canal
Metlakatla
Annette Island
U.S.A.
CANADA
Chatham Sound
Dixon Entrance
Dundas Island
Pacific Ocean
Prince Rupert
16
Yellowhead Highway 16 (see YELLOWHEAD HIGHWAY 16 section)
Skeena River
Masset
Graham Island
Porcher Island
Kitimat
Hecate Strait
Grenville Channel
Queen Charlotte City
Skidegate
Sandspit
Queen Charlotte Islands
Morseby Island
Banks Island
Pitt Island
Otter Pass
(map continues previous page)

SOUTHCENTRAL/SOUTHWEST FERRY ROUTES

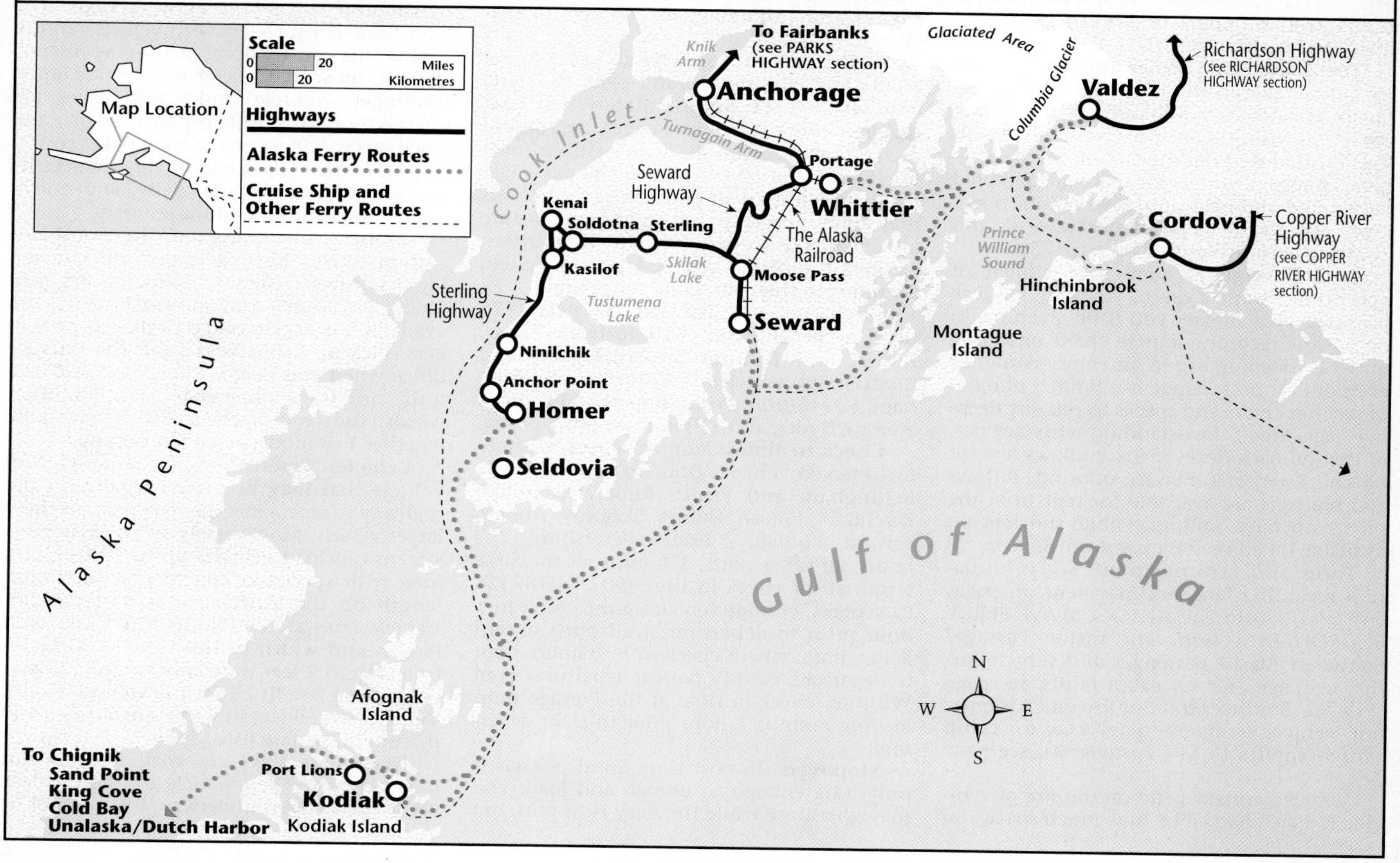

(Continued from page 22)
state ferries serving southeastern Alaska. Prince Rupert is also the farthest north of the 46 ports served by BC Ferries.

If traveling to Alaska by ferry, visitors may make their way up the Inside Passage to any Southeast Alaska community via the Inside Passage/Southeast ferry system. Motorists often use the Alaska Marine Highway northbound or southbound as an alternative to driving all of the Alaska Highway and its access routes. By using the Alaska state ferry one way to transport themselves and their vehicles between Bellingham or Prince Rupert and Skagway or Haines, travelers can eliminate between 700 and 1,700 miles of highway driving (depending on their itinerary), avoid covering the same ground twice, and have the opportunity to take in the magnificent scenery and picturesque communities of the Inside Passage. (The new *Kennicott* route can spare travelers additional highway mileage, though it sails only once monthly and only in summer.)

The Alaska Marine Highway also provides marine access for passengers and vehicles to various communities in Southcentral/Southwest Alaska. Complete details on the Alaska state ferry system are given here. See also the ALASKA STATE FERRY SCHEDULES beginning on page 749.

Alaska State Ferries

The main office of the Alaska Marine Highway is in Juneau. Write P.O. Box 25535, Juneau, AK 99802-5535; phone toll free 1-800-642-0066, TDD 1-800-764-3779; fax (907) 277-4829. Local reservation numbers in Juneau (907/465-3941) and in Anchorage (907/272-7116). Or via Internet: www.dot.state.ak.us/external/amhs/home.html.

The Alaska Marine Highway actually operates 2 ferry systems, one in Southeast Alaska and one in Southcentral/Southwest Alaska. A new (1998) vessel, the MV *Kennicott*, will connect the 2 systems with once a month service in summer.

The Alaska state ferries on the Southeast system depart from Bellingham, WA (85 miles north of Seattle on Interstate 5, Exit 250), or Prince Rupert, BC (450 miles/724 km west of Prince George, BC, or approximately 1,000 miles/1,609 km by highway from Seattle, WA) for Southeast Alaska communities.

Bellingham is accessible by Amtrak and bus. Fairhaven Station transportation center, next to the Bellingham Cruise Terminal at 401 Harris Ave. in south Bellingham, provides a central location for rail, bus, airporter, taxi and ferry services.

Motorists should keep in mind that only 2 major Southeast communities are connected to the Alaska Highway: Haines, via the Haines Highway; and Skagway, via Klondike Highway 2. (See the HAINES HIGHWAY and KLONDIKE HIGHWAY 2 sections.)

The Southeast system also includes feeder service between Ketchikan and Stewart/Hyder; Ketchikan and Hollis; Ketchikan and Metlakatla; and Juneau and Pelican. See Inside Passage/Southeast Alaska schedules.

The Southcentral/Southwest ferry system of the Alaska Marine Highway serves coastal communities from Prince William Sound to the Aleutian Islands. Southcentral communities on the ferry system that are also accessible by highway are Valdez, Seward and Homer. Southcentral communities accessible only by ferry are Cordova, Seldovia and Kodiak. Whittier is accessible only via shuttle train (see "Railroads" this section). All communities on the Southwest system are accessible only by ferry or by air.

Travel on the Alaska state ferries is at a leisurely pace, with observation decks, food service (hot meals, snacks and beverages) and vehicle decks on all ferries. Cabins are available only on 5 Southeast ferries and 1 Southwest ferry.

Keep in mind that the state ferries are not cruise ships: They do not have beauty salons, gift shops, deck games, telephones and the like. The small stores on the larger ferries are open limited hours and sell a limited selection of items.

It's a good idea to bring your own snacks, books, games and toiletries, since these are not always available on board.

Season: The Alaska ferry system has 2 seasons—May 1 to Sept. 30 (summer), when sailings are most frequent, and Oct. 1 to April 30 (fall/winter/spring), when departures are somewhat less frequent. Proposed summer schedules for 1998 appear in the ALASKA STATE FERRY SCHEDULES beginning on page 749. Contact the Alaska Marine Highway office for fall/winter/spring schedules, fares and information.

Reservations: Required on all vessels for passengers, vehicles and cabins. For reservations write the Alaska Marine Highway, P.O.

Box 25535, Juneau, AK 99802-5535; phone toll free 1-800-642-0066, or fax (907) 277-4829; TDD 1-800-764-3779. Phone local reservation numbers in Juneau (907/465-3941) and Anchorage (907/272-7116).

The Alaska state ferries are very popular in summer. Reservations should be made as far in advance as possible to get the sailing dates you wish. Cabin space on summer sailings is often sold out quickly on the Bellingham sailings. Requests for space are accepted year-round and held until reservations open. (See also "Call or Fax Reservations" and "Getting on our Waitlist" on page 750.)

Deck Passage: If cabin space is filled, or you do not want a cabin, you may go deck passage. This means you'll be sleeping in one of the reclining lounge chairs or rolling out your sleeping bag in an empty corner or even out on deck. There is a limited number of recliner chairs and spaces to roll out sleeping bags. Small, free-standing tents are permitted on back decks if space allows (except on the *Kennicott*). Beware of wind. Pillows and blankets are available for rent from the purser on most sailings. Public showers are available on all vessels except the *Bartlett*.

Fares and fare payment: See information regarding fares and payment on pages 749 and 750 in the ALASKA STATE FERRY SCHEDULES section. For Inside Passage/Southeast Alaska passenger and vehicle tariffs, see page 762; for cabin tariffs, see page 763. For Southcentral/Southwest passenger and vehicle tariffs, see page 766; for cabin tariffs (applies to MV *Tustumena*), see page 764.

Vehicle tariffs depend on the size of vehicle. You are charged by how much space you take up, so a car with trailer is measured from the front of the car to the end of the trailer, including hitch space. Bicycles, kayaks and inflatables are charged a surcharge.

Passenger tariffs are charged as follows: adults and children 12 and over, full fare; children 2 to 11, approximately half fare; children under 2, free. Passenger fares do not include cabins or meals. Senior citizen (over 65) discount of 50 percent off the passenger fare between Alaskan ports only; restrictions may apply. Special passes and travel rates are also available to persons with disabilities. Contact the Alaska Marine Highway System for more on these fares and restrictions.

Surcharges are assessed on pets ($25 to/from Bellingham, $10 to/from Prince Rupert and to/from Stewart/Hyder) and unattended vehicles ($50 to/from Bellingham, $20 to/from Prince Rupert and to/from Stewart/Hyder, and $10 to/from other ports).

Check-in times: Summer check-in times for reserved vehicles prior to departure are: Bellingham and Prince Rupert, 3 hours; Ketchikan, Juneau, Haines, Skagway, Homer, Seward, Kodiak, 2 hours; Petersburg, $1^1/_2$ hours; all other ports, 1 hour. Call the Sitka terminal for check-in time (907/747-8737). Passengers without vehicles must check in 1 hour prior to departure at all ports except Bellingham, where check-in is 2 hours prior to departure. For MV *Bartlett* departures from Whittier, check-in time at the Portage train loading ramp is 1 hour prior to train departure.

Stopovers: In-port time on all vessels is only long enough to unload and load. You may go ashore while the ferry is in port, but you must have your ticket receipt with you to reboard. A stopover is getting off at any port between your point of origin and final destination and taking another vessel at a later time. For travelers with vehicles and/or cabins this can be done as long as reservations to do so have been made in advance. Passenger, vehicle and cabin fares are charged on a point-to-point basis, and stopovers will increase the total ticket cost.

NOTE: Check the schedules carefully. Ferries do *NOT* stop at all ports daily, and northbound and southbound routes vary.

Cabins: All cabins on the Southeast system ferries have a toilet and shower. Linens (towels, sheets, blankets) are provided. Restrooms and shower facilities are available for deck-passage (walk-on) passengers. Pick up cabin keys from the purser's office when you board. Cabins are sold as a unit, not on a per berth basis. In other words, the cost of the cabin is the same whether 1 or more passengers occupy it.

Vehicles: Reservations are required. Any vehicle that may be driven legally on the highway is acceptable for transport on the 4 larger vessels. Most vessels on the Southeast system can load vehicles up to 70 feet/21m long with special arrangements. Maximum length on the *Tustumena* is 40 feet/12m. Vehicle fares are determined by the overall length and width of the vehicle. Vehicles from $8^1/_2$ to 9 feet wide are charged 125 percent of the fare listed for the vehicle length. Vehicles over 9 feet in width are charged 150 percent of the fare listed for vehicle length.

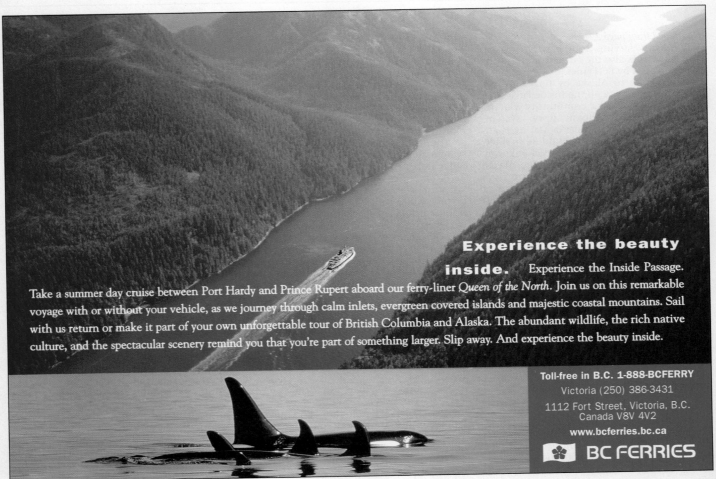

Passengers traveling with RVs do not have access to their vehicle on the car deck while the vessel is underway. RVs can not be used as dining or sleeping facilities while on the ferries.

Hazardous materials may not be transported on the ferries. Bottled gas containers must be turned off. Portable containers of fuel are permitted but must be stored with vessel personnel while en route.

The state assumes no responsibility for the loading and unloading of unattended vehicles.

Food Service: Food service varies from vessel to vessel. There's dining room service on the *Columbia*, *Tustumena* and *Bartlett*. The *Columbia* also has a 24-hour snack bar. Cafeteria service is available on all other ferries. Alcoholic beverages are available on some vessels. The cost of meals is not included in passenger, cabin or vehicle fares.

Luggage: You are responsible for your own luggage! Foot passengers may bring hand luggage only (not to exceed 100 lbs.). There is no limit on luggage carried in a vehicle. Coin-operated storage lockers are available aboard most ships, and baggage carts are furnished on the car deck. Baggage handling is NOT provided by the Marine Highway.

Vehicle deck restrictions: U.S. Coast Guard regulations prohibit passenger access to the vehicle deck while under way, so plan on bringing up items you will need for the voyage soon after boarding the vessel. Passengers can gain access to their vehicle by applying to the purser's desk for an escort. Regulations prohibit sleeping in your vehicle while the vessel is under way.

Pet policy: Dogs and other pets are not allowed in cabins and must be transported on the vehicle deck only—*NO EXCEPTIONS.* (There are special accommodations for animals aiding disabled passengers. Proper paperwork is required.) Animals and pets are to be transported inside a vehicle or in suitable containers furnished by the passenger. Animals and pets must be cared for by the owner. Passengers who must visit pets or animals en route should apply to the purser's office for an escort to the vehicle deck. (On long sailings the purser periodically announces "cardeck calls.") You may walk your pet at port stops. Keep in mind that some port stops are very brief and that sailing time between some ports will be as long as 36 hours (Bellingham to Ketchikan).

BC Ferries

BC Ferries provides year-round service on 25 routes throughout coastal British Columbia, with a fleet of 40 passenger- and vehicle-carrying ferries. BC Ferries' "Inside Passage" service between Port Hardy and Prince Rupert offers Alaska-bound travelers a convenient connection with the Alaska Marine Highway at Prince Rupert.

Port Hardy is approximately 307 miles/494 km north of Victoria via Trans-Canada Highway 1 and BC Highway 19. From Nanaimo it is 236 miles/380 km—or about 5 hours' driving time—to Port Hardy. If you are driving from Victoria, allow at least 8 hours (the route is almost all 2-lane highway between Victoria and Campbell River). The Port Hardy ferry terminal is located at Bear Cove, 4 miles/7 km south of downtown Port Hardy.

Prince Rupert is located 450 miles/724 km west of Prince George via the Yellowhead Highway (see YELLOWHEAD HIGHWAY 16 section).

Summer service between Port Hardy and Prince Rupert is aboard the *Queen of the North,* which carries 750 passengers and 157 vehicles. The ferry has a cafeteria, buffet dining room, news/gift shop, elevator, facilities for passengers with special needs, video arcade, licensed and view lounges, children's playroom, day cabins and staterooms (for round-trip use). Summer service (May 19 to Oct. 17, 1998) on this route is during daylight hours to make the most of the scenery, so cabins are not necessary. Fall/winter/spring service is an overnight trip on the *Queen of Prince Rupert.*

Or travel the Discovery Coast Passage, a new route between Port Hardy and Bella Coola. Summer service only from June 3 to Sept. 30, 1998. The *Queen of Chilliwack* features a cafeteria, gift shop, licensed lounge, reclining seats, showers and a lively and sociable atmosphere.

Reservations: Strongly recommended for passengers and required for vehicles on the Inside Passage and Discovery Coast Passage routes. For reservations (7 A.M. to 10 P.M. daily) and recorded schedule information (24-hours) phone (888) BC-FERRY or (250) 386-3431 in Victoria; and 1-888-223-3779 elsewhere in British Columbia. Or fax (250) 381-5452. Reservations may also be made on-line at www.bcferries.bc.ca. The Internet site also has rates, schedules and fleet profiles. Or contact BC Ferries at 1112 Fort St., Victoria, BC V8V 4V2.

Schedules and fares: The 1998 Inside Passage sailing schedule is shown here. Schedules are subject to change without notice. Rates current at time of printing (subject to change) are as follows (1-way, in Canadian funds): Adult passenger, $104; child (5 to 11 years), $52; car, $214; camper/RV (up to 20 feet in length, over 6 feet 8 inches in height), $356; additional length, $17.80 per foot; motorcycle, $107; bicycle, $6.50. Service during the fall, winter and spring is less frequent and fares are reduced. Contact BC Ferries for details.

Check-in time is 1 hour before sailing. Cancellations made less than 30 days prior to departure are subject to a cancellation fee.

BC FERRIES 1998 INSIDE PASSAGE SCHEDULE

PORT HARDY TO PRINCE RUPERT

NORTHBOUND	SOUTHBOUND
Departs: Port Hardy 7:30 A.M.	**Departs:** Prince Rupert 7:30 A.M.
Arrives: Prince Rupert 10:30 P.M.	**Arrives:** Port Hardy 10:30 P.M.
Dates: May 19, 21, 23, 25, 27, 29, 31 only.	**Dates:** May 20, 22, 24, 26, 28, 30 only.
June, July, September (even-numbered days)	June, July, September (odd-numbered days)
August (odd-numbered days)	August (even-numbered days)
October 2, 4, 6, 8, 10, 12, 14, 16, only.	October 1, 3, 5, 7, 9, 11, 13, 15, 17 only

Fishing

The biggest challenge for fishermen visiting Alaska and northwestern Canada is the sheer number and variety of fishing opportunities available. The following information is designed to help figure out the what, when, where and how of your fishing trip.

Fishermen are advised to first identify whether they want to fish fresh water or salt water and their desired species. Salmon are the most popular sport fish in Alaska, with all 5 species of Pacific salmon found here: King (chinook), silver (coho), pink (humpy), chum (dog) and red (sockeye). Salmon are anadromous, spawning in fresh water and maturing in the sea. King salmon fishing in Southeast is restricted to salt water. Silver and pink salmon can be taken in fresh water and salt water. Reds are taken in freshwater streams. Large landlocked lakes have populations of kokanee (landlocked red salmon).

Other sport fish include halibut, rainbow trout and steelhead, Dolly Varden and Arctic char, cutthroat and brook trout, northern pike, and lake trout.

Halibut, a saltwater fish that can weigh more than 300 pounds, is the largest fish in Alaska that a fisherman is likely to catch. The Pacific halibut is also the best known member of the "bottomfish" family, a catch-all term for non-salmon fish that includes lingcod, rockfish and a variety of other species.

Rainbows are a freshwater trout, the sea-run of which is the steelhead. Cutthroat are common on the mainland and every major island in Southeastern Alaska, occuring in both fresh water (nono-seagoing) and salt water (sea-going). Dolly Varden and Arctic char also both have populations that go to sea and do not, which spawn in streams and migrate to sea in the spring to feed, may be either a saltwater or freshwater sportfish. Eastern brook trout is an introduced species to freshwater lakes.

Northern pike (also called pike, jack fish and pickeral) are widely distributed throughout most of Alaska except southeastern. The northern pike is the most sought-after indigenous sport fish in Interior Alaska after the Arctic grayling. Alaska's Interior also has the largest Arctic grayling fishery in North America. These popular game fish are the main sport fish species in the Tanana River drainage.

If you know what kind of fish you want, that may also determine when to go. Although most fishing enthusiasts focus their trips between April and October, when the weather is generally more mild, the fish have something to say about timing. The Alaska Dept. of Fish and Game Sportfish Division gives a run timing for all fisheries by region.

Where to fish is probably the most difficult choice, with the number of fishing destinations available well beyond the capability of most anglers to visit. The list of possible fishing spots is also beyond our capability to list here, although many favorite fishing spots are mentioned under Area Fishing in the Attractions section of each community covered in *The MILEPOST*®. The Alaska Dept. of Fish and Game is the source for much of this information, and they have literally hundreds of pamphlets on fishing regional waters. Particularly helpful is their "Sportfishing Alaska" brochure, which shows run times and also lists area office phone numbers. Or write the Sport Fish Division, Box 25526, Juneau, AK 99802-5526; phone (907) 465-4180; Internet address: www.state.ak.us/local/akpages/FISH.GAME/adfghome.htm.

While you may fish any body of water with fish in it, local knowledge greatly increases your chances of success. Many fishing guides and charter operators advertise in *The MILEPOST*®. It is possible to fly out of almost any Alaskan community, fish a remote body of water, and fly back to town, all within 3 hours. Charter planes charge an hourly rate, either per plane load or per passenger, or may offer a fixed-rate fishing charter that may or may not include guide services and fishing gear. Fly-in fishing operators may offer lodge accommodations or only provide drop-off and pickup service, with the client either camping or overnighting at a U.S. Forest Service cabin. (Many of these cabins are located on fishing lakes with skiffs available.)

Charter boats are available for half-, full- or multi-day fishing trips out of most Southcentral, Southeast and Southwestern Alaska port communities. Multi-day fishing boat charters may overnight on board yachts or in floating lodges. Boat charters for saltwater sportfishing average $185 per person per day, based on a shared charter boat. Rates often include gear, license, bait, fish processing and land transportation, but ask ahead of time. Clients may have a destination in mind, or depend on the charter boat operator for guiding services.

There are also numerous fishing lodges in the North. Full-service lodges generally offer food and lodging, guide service, boats for saltwater fishing and daily fly-outs for freshwater fishing. Rates range anywhere from $300 to $800 per person per day, and include transportation to the lodge, accommodations, meals, guide services, fishing license and equipment, and fish processing. Refreshments, gratuities and personal items are extra.

When, where and how you fish requires some careful thought and planning, but the rewards are well worth it. Throughout *The MILEPOST*® you will find this friendly little symbol. Wherever you see one, you will find a description of the fishing at that point.

Contact fish and game offices (listed in the "Welcome to the North Country" section) for current license fees and regulations.

Hiking

Alaska State Parks, the U.S. Forest Service, and Bureau of Land Management maintain most of the established trails within Alaska. *The MILEPOST*® notes all trailheads along roads and highways in the highway logs, and popular hiking trails accessible from a major city are usually noted under Attractions in that community. Check trail conditions locally before hiking.

Within the Alaska state park system, Chugach State Park outside of Anchorage has the most extensive trail system, with more than 200 miles of hiking trails (see page 408 in the ANCHORAGE section). Kachemak Bay State Park, across the water from Homer, also has a fairly extensive trail system.

Tongass National Forest in Southeast Alaska has almost 600 miles of trails.

Chugach National Forest offers some 200 miles of trail, including an extensive system of hiking trails on the Kenai Peninsula, maintained by the Glacier and Seward Ranger districts. The most popular trail is the Resurrection Pass trail, a 38.6-mile/62.1-km trail that follows Resurrection Creek from Hope up Resurrection Pass then down Juneau Creek to the Sterling Highway.

Other popular Kenai Peninsula trails are Johnson Pass USFS Trail (which follows a portion of the Iditarod National Historic Trail), Crow Pass (a Chugach State Park trail that also follows a portion of the Iditarod National Historic Trail), Russian Lakes and Ptarmigan Creek USFS trails. There are USFS public-use cabins along many of the trails; these must be reserved in advance. See the STERLING HIGHWAY and SEWARD HIGHWAY for trailhead locations.

The Alaska Public Lands Information Center, 605 W. 4th, Anchorage, AK 99501, has general information on hiking in all public lands in Alaska. The USDA Forest Service Supervisor and District Ranger offices have trail maps and detailed information on hiking trails in Tongass and Chugach national forests.

Most national parklands in Alaska have no established trail systems, instead offering cross-country hiking or—depending on the terrain—bushwacking. An exception is the 33-mile Chilkoot Trail out of Skagway, managed by the National Park Service. See "National Parks" this page.

The BLM's White Mountains National Recreation Area north of Fairbanks has more than 200 miles of winter trails and 20 miles of summer hiking trails. The BLM also manages the 27-mile Pinnell Mountain National Recreation Trail—the first national recreation trail established in the state—located within Steese National Conservation Area outside Fairbanks. See both the ELLIOTT HIGHWAY and STEESE HIGHWAY sections.

Yukon Territory has established wilderness trails, too. Information about hiking in Kluane National Park Reserve is available from Parks Canada, Canadian Heritage, 300 Main St., Room 105, Whitehorse, YT Y1A 2B5. For other hiking trails in the Yukon, contact Tourism Yukon, Box 2703, Whitehorse, YT Y1A 2C6, phone (867) 667-5340.

Holidays

The following list of observed holidays for 1998 in Alaska and Canada can help you plan your trip. Keep in mind that banks and other agencies may be closed on these holidays and traffic may be heavier.

ALASKA

New Year's Day	Jan. 1
Martin Luther King Day	Jan. 19
Presidents' Day	Feb. 16
Seward's Day	Last Monday in March
Easter Sunday	April 12
Memorial Day	May 25
Independence Day	July 4
Labor Day	Sept. 7
Columbus Day	Oct. 12
Alaska Day	Oct. 18
Veterans Day	Nov. 11
Thanksgiving Day	Nov. 26
Christmas Day	Dec. 25

CANADA

New Year's Day	Jan. 1
Good Friday	April 10
Easter Monday	April 13
Victoria Day	May 18
Canada Day	July 1
British Columbia Day	First Monday in Aug.
Labour Day	Sept. 7
Thanksgiving Day	Oct. 12
Remembrance Day	Nov. 11
Christmas Day	Dec. 25
Boxing Day	Dec. 26

National Parks

Denali National Park and Preserve is one of 15 national park units in Alaska. Parklands range from the remote Bering Land Bridge National Preserve on the Bering Sea to Skagway's Klondike Gold Rush National Historical Park, one of the state's most visited attractions.

The MILEPOST® has detailed information on Denali National Park (see page 491) and Glacier Bay National Park (see page 729). Road-accessible national parks in Alaska also covered in *The MILEPOST*® include Wrangell-St. Elias National Park (see page 681 in the EDGERTON HIGHWAY/McCARTHY ROAD section), Kenai Fjords National Park (see the description under Seward Attractions in the SEWARD HIGHWAY section); Sitka National Historical Park (see Sitka on page 712 in the INSIDE PASSAGE section); and Klondike Gold Rush National Historial Park (see Skagway on page 742 in the INSIDE PASSAGE section). There's also a description of Yukon–Charley Rivers National Park, accessible via the Yukon River from Eagle (see page 330 in the TAYLOR HIGHWAY section).

On-line information is available on the National Park Service's World Wide Web pages (www.nps.gov) for the following national parks in Alaska: Aniakchak (/ania); Bering Land Bridge (/bela); Cape Krusenstern (/cakr); Denali (/dena); Gates of the Arctic (/gaar); Glacier Bay (/glba); Katmai (/katm); Kenai Fjords (/kefj)/ Klondike Gold Rush (/klgo); Kobuk Valley (/kobu); Lake Clark (/lacl); Noatak (/noat); Sitka (/sitk); Wrangell-St. Elias (/wrst) and Yukon–Charley Rivers (/yuch).

Or contact the Alaska Public Lands Information Centers in Anchorage, AK at 605 W. 4th Ave., Suite 105, Anchorage 99510, phone (907) 271-2737; Fairbanks, AK at 250 Cushman St., Suite 1A, Fairbanks 99701, phone (907) 456-0527; or Ketchikan at 50 Main St., Ketchikan, AK 99901, phone (907) 228-6214.

Railroads

Although no railroads connect Alaska or the Yukon with the Lower 48, there are 2 railroads in the North: the Alaska Railroad and the White Pass & Yukon Route.

The Alaska Railroad

The Alaska Railroad operates year-round passenger and freight service between Anchorage, Fairbanks, Portage and Whittier. In summer, passenger service is available daily between Anchorage and Fairbanks via Talkeetna and Denali Park; Portage and Whittier; Anchorage and Whittier; and between Anchorage and Seward. For more information on the Alaska Railroad, write Passenger Services Dept., Box 107500, Anchorage 99510. Phone 1-800-544-0552 or (907) 265-2494; fax 265-2323. Homepage: http://www.alaska.net/~akrr.

Construction of the railroad began in 1915 under Pres. Woodrow Wilson. On July 15, 1923, Pres. Warren G. Harding drove the golden spike at Nenana, signifying completion of the railroad. The main line extends from Seward to Fairbanks, approximately 470 miles/756 km.

The Alaska Railroad accommodates visitors with disabilities. Six coaches feature wheelchair lifts. Coaches have provisions for occupied wheelchairs, and restrooms are accessible. With advance notice, sign language interpreters are available. ♿

Following are services, schedules and fares available on Alaska Railroad routes. Keep in mind that schedules and fares are subject to change without notice.

Anchorage–Talkeetna–Denali–Fairbanks: Passenger service between Anchorage, Talkeetna, Denali Park and Fairbanks is offered daily on the *Denali Star* from May 16 to Sept. 13, 1998. The express service operates with full-service dining, a vista-dome for all passengers to share and coaches with comfortable reclining seats. Travel along the 350-mile/560-km route between Anchorage and Fairbanks is at a leisurely pace with comfortable window seats and good views of the countryside. Packages including sightseeing tours, hotels, river rafting, hiking and flightseeing are available in Talkeetna, Denali, Fairbanks and Anchorage from Alaska Railroad Scenic Tours.

Luxury railcars are available on the Anchorage–Denali Park–Fairbanks route through Gray Line of Alaska (Holland America Lines/Westours) and Princess Tours. These tour companies operate (respectively) the *McKinley Explorer* and *Midnight Sun Express*. These luxury railcars, which are coupled onto the end of the regular Alaska Railroad train, are glass-domed and offer gourmet cuisine along with other amenities. Tickets are priced higher than those for the regular Alaska Railroad cars, and are sold on a space-available basis. Packages with a Denali Park overnight are also available. Phone Princess Tours at (800) 835-8907, or Gray Line of Alaska at (800) 544-2206 for details.

During the summer, Northbound express trains depart Anchorage at 8:15 A.M., arrive Talkeetna at 11:25 A.M., arrive Denali Park at 3:45 P.M., and arrive Fairbanks at 8:15 P.M. Southbound express trains depart Fairbanks at 8:15 A.M., arrive Denali Park at noon, and arrive Anchorage at 8:15 P.M.

One-way fares are as follows: Anchorage–Denali Park, $99; Anchorage–Talkeetna, $59; Fairbanks–Denali Park, $53; Anchorage–Fairbanks, $149. Children ages 2 through 11 ride for 75 percent of adult fare; under 2 ride free.

During fall, winter and spring, weekend-only rail service is provided between Anchorage and Fairbanks on the *Aurora*. The train travels from Anchorage to Fairbanks on Saturday and returns on Sunday. The *Aurora* is a "flag stop" train and will stop wherever people want to get on or off.

Reservations should be made more than 40 days prior to travel. Include the dates you plan to travel, points of departure and destination, the number of people in your party and your home phone number. Tickets may be purchased in advance by mail if you desire. Checks, Visa, MasterCard, Discover and Diners Club are accepted.

Each adult is allowed 2 pieces of luggage to a maximum combined weight of 100 lbs. Children are allowed 2 pieces of baggage to a maximum combined weight of 75 lbs. Excess baggage may be checked for a nominal fee. Bicycles are accepted for a charge of $20 per station, on a space-available basis on the day of travel. Keep in mind that baggage, including backpacks, must be checked before boarding, and it is not accessible during the trip. Canoes, motors, motorcycles, items weighing over 150 lbs., etc., are not accepted for transportation on passenger trains. These items are shipped via freight train.

Local Service: Local rural service between Talkeetna and Hurricane Gulch operates Thursday, Friday, Saturday and Sunday each week between May 16 and Sept. 13, 1998. This 1-day trip aboard the *Hurricane* takes you past breathtaking views of Mount McKinley into some remote areas and provides an opportunity to meet local residents who use the train for access. Local service uses self-propelled rail diesel cars and provides vending-machine snacks. The *Hurricane* is a "flag stop" train and will stop wherever people want to get on or off.

Portage–Whittier: The Portage–Whittier shuttle train carries passengers and vehicles between Portage on the Seward Highway and Whittier on Prince William Sound. Portage, which has no facilities other than the railroad's vehicle loading ramp, is 47 miles/75 km south of Anchorage at **Milepost S 80.3** on the Seward Highway. Whittier, on Prince William Sound, is port to the Alaska Marine Highway's ferry MV *Bartlett,* which provides passenger and vehicle service to Cordova and Valdez. The Portage–Whittier railway line is 12.4 miles/20 km long, includes 2 tunnels (one 13,090 feet/3,990m long, the other 4,910 feet/1,497m long). Called the Whittier Cutoff, the line was constructed in 1942–43 as a safeguard for the flow of military supplies. It is a 35-minute train ride.

The shuttle makes several round trips daily between Portage and Whittier, from mid-May through mid-September, connecting with Alaska Marine Highway ferry sailings and other vessels which operate between Whittier and Valdez. (Remember that ferry tickets are purchased separately from train tickets.)

Train tickets for the Whittier shuttle may be purchased from ticket sellers at Portage. Reservations are not accepted for the shuttle train, although passengers with confirmed ferry connections are given priority boarding on the 1:20 P.M. shuttle between Portage and Whittier, if vehicles are at Portage by no later than 12:30 P.M. Standard vehicles under 24 feet/7m in length are charged $72, round-trip, between Portage and Whittier; this includes driver fare. Other adult passengers in the vehicle are charged $20 round-trip; children (2 through 11 years of age) pay $10 round-trip. Vehicle rates are based upon length. Some height and width restrictions apply.

During fall, winter and spring, service to Whittier is provided on Wednesday, Friday, Saturday and Sunday.

Anchorage–Seward: Rail passenger service between Anchorage and Seward operates daily on the *Coastal Classic* between May 16 and Sept. 7, 1998. (Weekend service to Seward is available May 9–10 and Sept. 12–13.) The 230-mile/370-km round-trip excursion follows Turnagain Arm south from Anchorage and passes through some of the most beautiful scenery to be found along the railroad. Travel is aboard classic passenger coaches. Food service is available in the bar/deli car. Departs Anchorage at 6:45 A.M., arrives Seward at 11:05 A.M. The return trip departs Seward at 6 P.M., arriving Anchorage at 10:25 P.M. Reservations are recommended. The round-trip fare is $86 for adults; 75 percent fare for children 2 through 11. Overnight tours which include hotel and Resurrection Bay boat excursions, Exit Glacier and Alaska SeaLife Center are available from the railroad ticket office.

Anchorage–Whittier: Rail passenger service between Anchorage and Whittier operates daily on the *Glacier Discovery* between May 16 and Sept. 13, 1998. The 50-mile/80-km excursion follows the Turnagain Arm of the Cook Inlet, passes through 2 tunnels, and arrives in Whittier, located on the Prince William Sound. Food service is available in the bar/deli car. Departs Anchorage at 9 A.M. and arrives Whittier at 11:30 A.M. The return trip departs Whittier at 5:45 P.M. and arrives Anchorage at 8:15 P.M. Reservations are recommended. The round-trip fare is $49 for adults; children ages 2-11 pay 75 percent of adult fare. Tours are available, including one-day connecting cruises of Prince William Sound and cruises offering overnight accommodations.

White Pass & Yukon Route

The White Pass & Yukon Route (WP&YR) is a narrow-gauge (36-inch) privately owned railroad built in 1898 at the height of the Klondike Gold Rush. Between 1900 and 1982, the WP&YR provided passenger and freight service between Skagway, AK, and Whitehorse, YT. The WP&YR no longer offers rail service the entire way to Whitehorse.

The WP&YR now operates a 3-hour round-trip train excursion between Skagway and the White Pass Summit, an 8-hour steam excursion between Skagway and Lake Bennett, and a combination train and bus trip between Skagway and Whitehorse.

Construction of the WP&YR began in May 1898. The railroad reached White Pass in February 1899 and Whitehorse in July 1900. It was the first railroad in Alaska and at the time the most northern of any railroad in North America. The White Pass & Yukon Route was declared an International Historic Civil Engineering Landmark, one of only 22 in the world, in 1994.

The railroad follows the old White Pass trail. The upper section of the old "Deadhorse" trail near the summit (Mile 19 on the WP&YR railway) is visible beside the tracks. During the Klondike Gold Rush, thousands of men took the 40-mile/64-km White Pass trail from Skagway to Lake Bennett, where they built boats to float down the Yukon River to Dawson City and the goldfields.

The WP&YR has one of the steepest railroad grades in North America. From sea level at Skagway the railroad climbs to 2,885 feet/879m at White Pass in only 20 miles/32 km of track. Currently, the railroad offers daily train service between Skagway and Fraser, BC, mid-May to mid-September, and a limited number of rail trips to Carcross and steam trips to Lake Bennett in summer.

Following are services, schedules and fares (U.S. funds) for White Pass & Yukon Route in 1998. All times indicated in schedules are local times (Skagway is on Alaska Time, which is 1 hour earlier than Whitehorse, which is on Pacific Time.) Children 12 and under ride for half fare when accompanied by an adult. Children under 2 years ride free if not occupying a seat; half fare for separate seat. Reservations are required. (Tuesdays, Wednesdays and Thursdays are especially busy days.) For reservations and information, contact the White Pass & Yukon Route, Box 435, Skagway, AK 99840. Phone toll free in the U.S. and Canada (800) 343-7373 or (907) 983-2217 in Skagway. Internet: www.whitepassrailroad.com.

Summit Excursion: This approximately 3-hour round-trip excursion features the most spectacular part of the WP&YR railway, including the steep climb to White Pass Summit, Bridal Veil Falls, Inspiration Point and Dead Horse Gulch. Offered twice daily from May 12 to Sept. 24, 1998; the morning train departs Skagway at 8:30 A.M. and returns at 11:45 A.M.; the afternoon train departs Skagway at 1 P.M. and returns at 4:15 P.M. Fares are $78 for adults and $39 for children 12 and under.

Skagway to Whitehorse: Through-service between Skagway, AK, and Whitehorse, YT, is offered daily from May 21 to Sept. 14, 1998. Through passengers travel 28 miles/45km by train between Skagway, AK, and Fraser, BC, and then 87 miles/140 km by bus between Fraser and Whitehorse, YT. The train portion of this trip takes passengers over historic White Pass Summit. Northbound service departs Skagway at 12:40 P.M. and arrives Whitehorse at 5:30 P.M. Southbound service departs Whitehorse at 8 A.M. and arrives Skagway at noon. One-way fares are $95 for adults and $47.50 for children 12 and under.

Special Steam Excursions: Steam travel returns to the White Pass & Yukon Route with limited summer runs to beautiful Lake Bennett. This 80-mile/128.7-km round-trip takes 8 hours and includes a layover at a restored 1903 station. St. Andrews Presbyterian Church, built in 1898, is an easy visit from the station. Steam trips are scheduled for June 13 and 27, July 11 and 25, and August 8 and 22, 1998. Departs Skagway at 8 A.M. Fares are $156 for adults and $78 for children 12 and under; includes lunch.

Yukon Territory Adventure: This is White Pass and Yukon Route's longest rail journey, traveling 67 miles/107 km beyond Bennett to Carcross, YT. Departs 8 A.M.; stopover in Bennett and Carcross; bus back to Skagway; every Sunday in June, July and August. Fares are $128 for adults, $64 for children 12 and under; includes lunch.

Lake Bennett Adventure: Travel 20 miles/32 km beyond the Summit to historic Bennett, BC, the end of the Chilkoot Trail. A two-hour layover allows time to explore the area and tour historic displays in the restored 1903 station. The 8 1/2-hour, 80-mile/128km round-trip is every Monday, Thursday, Friday and Saturday, in June, July and August. Fares are $128 for adults and $64 for children 12 and under; includes lunch.

Chilkoot Trail Hikers Service: Service between Bennett and Fraser, BC, offered on Mondays, Thursdays, Fridays and Saturdays in June, July and August. Hikers who have completed the 33-mile Chilkoot Trail can be picked up at Lake Bennett twice daily and transported back to Skagway, or with bus connections on to Whitehorse. $25 to Fraser, BC; $65 to Skagway.

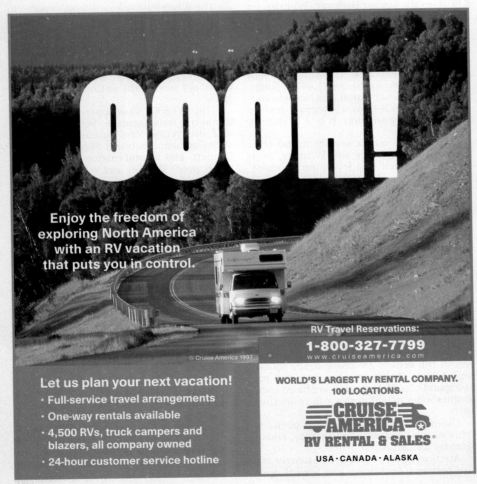

Renting An RV

An increasingly popular way to explore Alaska and northwestern Canada is through the big, wide windows of an RV. The good news is you don't have to own an RV to take an RV vacation. You can rent one!

Across the North, dealers offer every type of rig, from modest tent trailers to top-of-the-line self-contained motorhomes. In between, you have a choice of trailers, converted vans or truck campers. Amenities vary from luxurious to utilitarian, and some dealers have specially-equipped wheelchair-accessible units. Many RV rental companies advertise in *The MILEPOST®*. Check advertisements in Anchorage, Fairbanks and other cities.

How do you decide what to rent? The most popular are Class C units, measuring 20 to 29 feet in length. Laura Bly of "USA Today," in an article on her RV rental experience, wrote: "When estimating how much space you'll need, err on the liberal side. In our case, a 29-footer for a family of 3. What had initially seemed like a palace grew smaller with each passing mile, and I was grateful we didn't need to fold the dinette table into an extra bed each evening." And she and her family were gone only 3 nights.

Further evidence of that point comes from the Recreational Vehicle Renters Association (www.rvamerica.com): "Most families will want the space and comfort of a full-size motorhome. Smaller units are ideal for smaller parties or those who want to 'rough it'."

Inside a Class C, you'll find almost every convenience of home. Some larger units include 2 queen-size beds, air conditioning, a microwave, dinette seating 4, even a bathroom with a shower stall. On the other hand, you can choose a trimmed-down RV for much less money and still have your shower by using the campground facilities.

What will it cost? The basic rule is: The more space, privacy and comfort you want, the more the RV costs to rent. How much depends on the size of the RV you rent and the length of your vacation. Depending on the season, motorhomes generally rent from about $70 to $170 per day plus mileage. Truck campers and travel trailers average $50 to $120 per day. Weekly rates offer a savings over daily rates. Keep in mind that some RVs come fully equipped with all the necessities so you need only your personal items. Others provide linens and kitchen gear, but for an additional charge. Or you can pack your own bedding (sleeping bags work well) and cooking supplies. Ask what your RV rental includes.

The "early bird gets the worm" adage applies here, so make reservations as soon as possible. That way you get exactly the model and size you want. One experienced renter suggests getting the reservation in writing, so you won't encounter any last-minute disappointments. He had nothing on paper, nothing to show confirmation. As a result, he ended up with a smaller unit than he requested.

What's more, you need to know exactly what's inside the unit before you confirm. Are kitchen supplies (cookware, dinnerware, utensils) included? Bed and bath linens? Maps? Are airport transfers provided? At a charge or no charge? Be sure to know the fee for dropping the RV at a destination other than your pick-up point. Fees can be extremely high.

If you see a sign that states a small unit sleeps 6, be advised that even the larger ones claim sleeping room for no more than 6 or 7 people. Also find out when seasonal rates change. You could save a significant amount of money or rent a larger vehicle for about the same price just by scheduling your trip to coincide with the off-season. Many consider May off-season, June peak time, which means mid-to-late May could be an ideal time for your holiday.

A deposit of about $200 holds your reservation. The majority of rental agencies accept major credit cards, cash or traveler's checks. As a rule, they don't take personal checks. The reservationist will inform you of payment options.

You don't need a special license to rent an RV, yet it is a bit more complicated than renting a car. Most dealers include comprehensive insurance coverage, but with a high deductible. To lower it, some offer a waiver for a daily fee. Talk to your own insurance agent; your policy may or may not cover rentals.

You may be eager to get on the road right away, but take the advice of some renters who regretted they didn't learn more about their new traveling companion before driving off. Here are some things to remember:

When the dealer demonstrates how to operate the rental, pay close attention. This is for your safety and convenience. Ask questions. For example, how to extinguish the propane pilot light (necessary when you add gas) and how to re-ignite it. Critical areas are maintenance and operation: filling fresh water tanks, emptying waste, using appliances, hooking up. The more you know about your home on wheels, the more likely you'll enjoy a trouble-free trip.

On your rental agreement, note any dents, rips or other damage you see in or on the RV. Keep a log of anything that goes wrong with the RV which is not your fault. You may be able to negotiate a discount at the end of your trip.

Make a backup set of keys if the dealer doesn't give you one.

Ask for a written statement about the fee structure. Will your reservation deposit be applied to your total charges? Are you required to prepay the rental including mileage charges? Does the rental agency require a security deposit? Is it refundable? Is there a prep charge? Are you required to fill the gas tank to avoid additional charges? Propane? How much do additional days and miles cost? Will you be charged if you don't clean the interior and/or wash the exterior?

Know exactly what procedures to follow if you encounter mechanical problems or an emergency. What if you get a ding in the windshield? Is the unit equipped with a spare tire? Write down emergency phone numbers and be sure you have a thorough understanding of all of the agency's policies.

Ask the dealer about any restrictions for RV travel due to the size or weight of the vehicle, or conditions of the roads you plan to travel. Don't overload the RV. Factor in full gas, water and waste tanks to allowable load.

Be sure you understand the papers required should you cross the border between Alaska and Canada.

Know what time the vehicle must be returned to avoid another day's charge.

Shipping

Whether you are moving to Alaska, or plan to ship your vehicle North rather than drive one or both ways, there is a shipper to accommodate your needs.

Vehicles: Carriers that will ship cars, campers, trailers and motorhomes from Anchorage to Seattle include: Alaska Railroad, Box 107500, Anchorage, AK 99510-7500, phone (907) 265-2490; Alaska Vehicle Transport, Inc., phone 1-800-422-7925; Sea–Land Freight Service, Inc., 1717 Tidewater Ave., Anchorage, AK 99501, phone 1-800-478-2671 or (907) 274-2671; and Totem Ocean Trailer Express (TOTE), 2511 Tidewater, Anchorage, AK 99501, phone (907) 276-5868 or toll free 1-800-234-8683.

In the Seattle, WA, area, contact A.A.D.A. Systems, Box 2323, Auburn 98071, phone (206) 762-7840 or 1-800-929-2773; Alaska Railroad, 2203 Airport Way S., Suite 215, Seattle, WA 98134, phone (206) 624-4234; Sea–Land Service, Inc., 3600 Port of Tacoma Road, 4th floor, Tacoma, WA 98424, phone (206) 593-8100 or 1-800-426-4512 (outside the Tacoma area); or Totem Ocean Trailer Express (TOTE), 500 Alexander Ave., Tacoma, WA 98421, phone (206) 628-9280 or 1-800-426-0074.

Vehicle shipment between southeastern Alaska and Seattle is provided by Alaska Marine Lines, 5615 W. Marginal Way SW, Seattle, WA 98106, phone (206) 763-4244 or toll free (800) 950-4AML or (800) 326-8346 (direct service to Ketchikan, Wrangell, Prince of Wales Island, Kake, Petersburg, Sitka, Juneau, Haines, Skagway, Yakutat, Excursion Inlet and Hawk Inlet). Boyer Alaska Barge Line, 7318 4th Ave. S., Seattle, WA 98108, phone (206) 763-8575 (serves Ketchikan, Metlakatla, Prince of Wales Island and Wrangell).

Persons shipping vehicles between Seattle/Tacoma and Anchorage are advised to shop around for the carrier that offers the services and rates most suited to the shipper's needs. Not all carriers offer year-round service, and freight charges vary greatly depending upon the carrier and the length and height of the vehicle. Rates increase frequently and the potential shipper is cautioned to call carriers' rate departments for those rates in effect at shipping time. An approximate sample fare from Seattle/Tacoma to Anchorage to ship a 4-door sedan one-way is $1,141; for a truck, you might pay $1,332. From Anchorage to Seattle/Tacoma, it is approximately $738 for a vehicle and $919 to ship a truck.

Not all carriers accept rented moving trucks and trailers, and a few of those that do, require authorization from the rental company to carry its equipment to Alaska. Check with the carrier and your rental company before booking service.

Book your reservation at least 2 weeks in advance and 3 weeks during summer months, and prepare to have the vehicle at the carrier's loading facility 2 days prior to sailing. Carriers differ on what non-vehicle items they allow to travel inside, from nothing at all to goods packaged and addressed separately. Coast Guard regulations forbid the transport of vehicles holding more than one-quarter tank of gas, and none of the carriers listed above allow owners to accompany their vehicles in transit. Remember to have fresh antifreeze installed in your car or truck prior to sailing!

Household Goods and Personal Effects: Most moving van lines have service to and from Alaska through their agency connections in most Alaska and Lower 48 cities. To initiate service contact the van line agents nearest your origin point.

Northbound goods are shipped to Seattle and transferred through a port agent to a water vessel for carriage to Alaska. Few shipments go over the road to Alaska. Southbound shipments are processed in a like manner through Alaska ports to Seattle, then on to destination.

U-Haul provides service into the North Country for those who prefer to move their goods themselves. There are 53 U-Haul dealerships in Alaska and northwestern Canada for over-the-road service. In Alaska, there are 8 dealerships in Anchorage, 6 in Fairbanks, 2 in Soldotna and Juneau and 1 in each of the following communities: Eagle River, Glennallen, Homer, Ketchikan, Delta Junction, Kenai, Palmer, Petersburg, Seward, Tok, Valdez, Wasilla, Sitka and North Pole. In Canada, there are dealerships and ready stations in Dawson City (summer only), Fort St. John, Fort Nelson, Whitehorse and at other locations along the Alaska Highway. There are also breakdown stations for service of U-Haul vehicles in Beaver Creek, Swift River and the Kluane Wilderness Area.

It's also possible to ship a rented truck or trailer into southeastern Alaska aboard the water carriers that accept privately owned vehicles (see Shipping Vehicles). A few of the water carriers sailing between Seattle and Anchorage also carry rented equipment. However, shop around for this service, for this has not been common practice in the past, and rates can be very high if the carrier does not yet have a specific tariff established for this type of shipment. You will not be allowed to accompany the rented equipment. Be aware, however, that U-Haul allows its equipment to be shipped on TOTE or Sea-Land, resulting in a 30 percent savings over the price of driving it between Seattle and Anchorage.

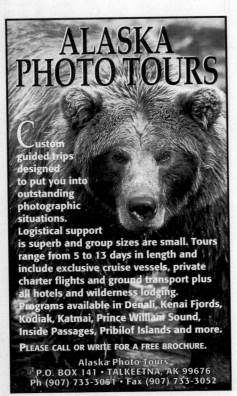

When to go

One of the most often asked questions is "when is the best time to travel?" The high season is June through August, generally the warmest and sunniest months in the North, although July is often one of the wettest months in some regions. The weather is as variable and unpredictable in the North as anywhere else. Go prepared for sunny hot days and cold rainy days. Waterproof footwear is always a good idea, as are a warm coat and rain gear. Generally, dress is casual. Comfortable shoes and easy-care clothes are best. There are stores in the North—just like at home—where you can buy whatever you forgot to bring along. There are laundromats (some with showers) in most communities and dry cleaners in the major cities and some smaller towns.

Because most people travel in the summer, filling up hotels, motels, campgrounds and ferries, you might consider an early spring (April or May) or fall (late August into October) trip. There's usually more room at the lodges and campgrounds and on the ferries in these shoulder seasons. The weather can also be quite beautiful in early spring and in the fall. Keep in mind that some tours, attractions, lodges and other businesses operate seasonally. Check the advertisements in *The MILEPOST®* for details on months of operation or call ahead if in doubt.

While June through August are the warmest months, weather can be quite beautiful—clear, sunny and mild—in spring and fall. Record highs are generally in the 90s with record lows to minus 60 degrees. Precipitation is normally heaviest in August and September in Anchorage; July and August in Fairbanks; and September and October in Juneau. But you can have a dry summer or a wet summer, depending on El Niño.

The landscape usually doesn't "green up" until June, which is also the month with the longest day (21 hours and 49 minutes of daylight in Fairbanks). Wildflowers peak in July. The trees and tundra are especially colorful in the fall; they start turning in late August. The days are short in winter (3 hours and 42 minutes of daylight is the winter minimum in Fairbanks), but people who live in the North feel that the winter has a special beauty all its own, and there are some popular events in winter (Fur Rendezvous and the Iditarod, for example).

The following numbers provide recorded weather information: Anchorage, (907) 936-2525; Fairbanks, (907) 452-3553; Alaska Highway in BC, (250) 774-6461; Alaska Highway in Yukon Territory, (867) 668-6061; Dawson Creek, BC, (250) 784-2244. The Alaska region National Weather Service Internet address is www.alaska.net/~nwsar/.

Wildlife

The opportunity to observe and photograph birds and mammals is a major attraction for visitors to the North. *The MILEPOST®* road logs point out wildlife viewing spots along the highways where travelers have a good chance of seeing dall sheep, moose, caribou, mountain goats, eagles, sandhill cranes, and other mammals and birds.

Besides the chance encounter with wildlife along the roads or in the parks, Alaska offers several opportunities for planned wildlife viewing, such as bear observatories, bird festivals (Copper River Delta Shorebird Festival in Cordova, and Kachemak Bay Shorebird Festival in Homer; both in May), custom bird-watching trips, and sightseeing cruises.

The privately-operated summer sightseeing cruises to view Alaska's glaciated coastline provide a great opportunity to see wildlife: sea otters, Steller sea lions, dolphins, harbor seals, Dall porpoises, whales (minke, gray, fin, humpback), puffins, eagles, black-legged kittiwakes, common murres, cormorants, parakeet and rhinoceros auklets, among others. See "Day Cruises" on page 14 for a list of some of these popular destinations—as well as inland lake and river cruises that also offer an opportunity to see wildlife.

There are 3 types of bears found in Alaska: the black bear, brown/grizzly bear and polar bear. Black bears range throughout most of the state, with highest densities in Southeast, Prince William Sound and Southcentral. Black bears can be brown in color, and may be confused with a grizzly, although they are normally smaller than a grizzly, with a more pointed head. Brown/grizzly bears range in color from black to blond, and range over most of the state. Alaska's coastal brown/grizzly bear is the world's largest carnivorous land mammal. (While polar bears are as large or larger, they actually live at sea on the ice, rather than on land.) Grizzlies have a distinct shoulder hump and larger head than black bears.

Formal bear viewing areas include: Pack Creek bear observatory on Admiralty Island (permit required, fly-in or boat-in from Sitka or Juneau); Anan Bear Observatory (fly-in or boat-in from Wrangell); McNeil River State Game Sanctuary (permit required, fly-in from Homer or Anchorage); and Brooks Falls/Katmai National Park (fly-in from Homer and Anchorage). Visitors are most likely to see brown/grizzly bears in Denali National Park and on Kodiak Island.

Visitors to Alaska may not see the largest rodent in North America while traveling around, but they will likely see its work. Beaver dams reaching 15 feet in height and hundreds of feet in length are not uncommon.

Much more visible are 2 members of the squirrel familiy: the arctic ground squirrel and the hoary marmot. There's also a good chance of seeing snowshoe hare, especially during cyclical population highs.

Moose and caribou are commonly spotted from the road. Moose can be aggressive; never approach them.

Best rules for observing all wildlife, but especially the larger mammals: Do not feed them and keep your distance.

Alaska Highway via

EAST ACCESS ROUTE

15 2 3 4 34 43

Connects: Great Falls, MT, to Dawson Creek, BC **Length:** 866 miles
Road Surface: Paved **Season:** Open all year
Major Attractions: Waterton Lakes National Park, Head-Smashed-In Buffalo Jump, Royal Tyrrell Museum, Fort Edmonton Park

(See maps, pages 34–35)

	Calgary	Dawson Creek	Edmonton	Great Falls	Lethbridge	Valleyview
Calgary		548	181	318	140	395
Dawson Creek	548		367	866	688	153
Edmonton	181	367		499	321	214
Great Falls	318	866	499		178	713
Lethbridge	140	688	321	178		535
Valleyview	395	153	214	713	535	

Dinosaur model outside entrance to Royal Tyrrell Museum in Drumheller.
(Blake Hanna, staff)

The East Access Route is logged in *The MILEPOST®* as one of the 2 major access routes (the other is the West Access Route) to the Alaska Highway.

When the Alaska Highway opened to civilian traffic in 1948, this was the only access route to Dawson Creek, BC, the start of the highway. At that time the route led from Great Falls, MT, through Alberta to Edmonton. From Edmonton, it continued north through the province to Clyde and from there to Athabasca via Highway 2 or Smith via Highway 44. At Triangle, the junction of Highways 2 and 2A (then Highway 34), motorists either headed north to McLennan and Peace River, or south via Valleyview to Grande Prairie, AB. In late 1955, Highway 43 was completed connecting Edmonton and Valleyview via Whitecourt.

Highways on this route are all paved primary routes, with visitor services readily available along the way. Total driving distance from Great Falls, MT, to Dawson Creek, BC, is 867 miles/1,394 km.

INTERSTATE HIGHWAY 15

The East Access Route begins in **GREAT FALLS** (pop. 55,097; elev. 3,333 feet/1,016m), Montana's second largest city. Head north through northcentral Montana

(Continues on page 36)

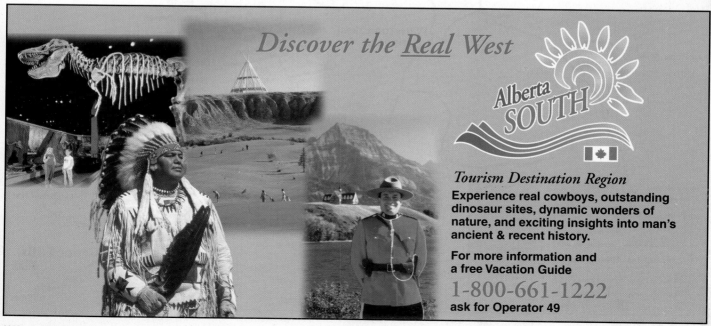

EAST ACCESS ROUTE *Great Falls, MT, to Edmonton, AB*

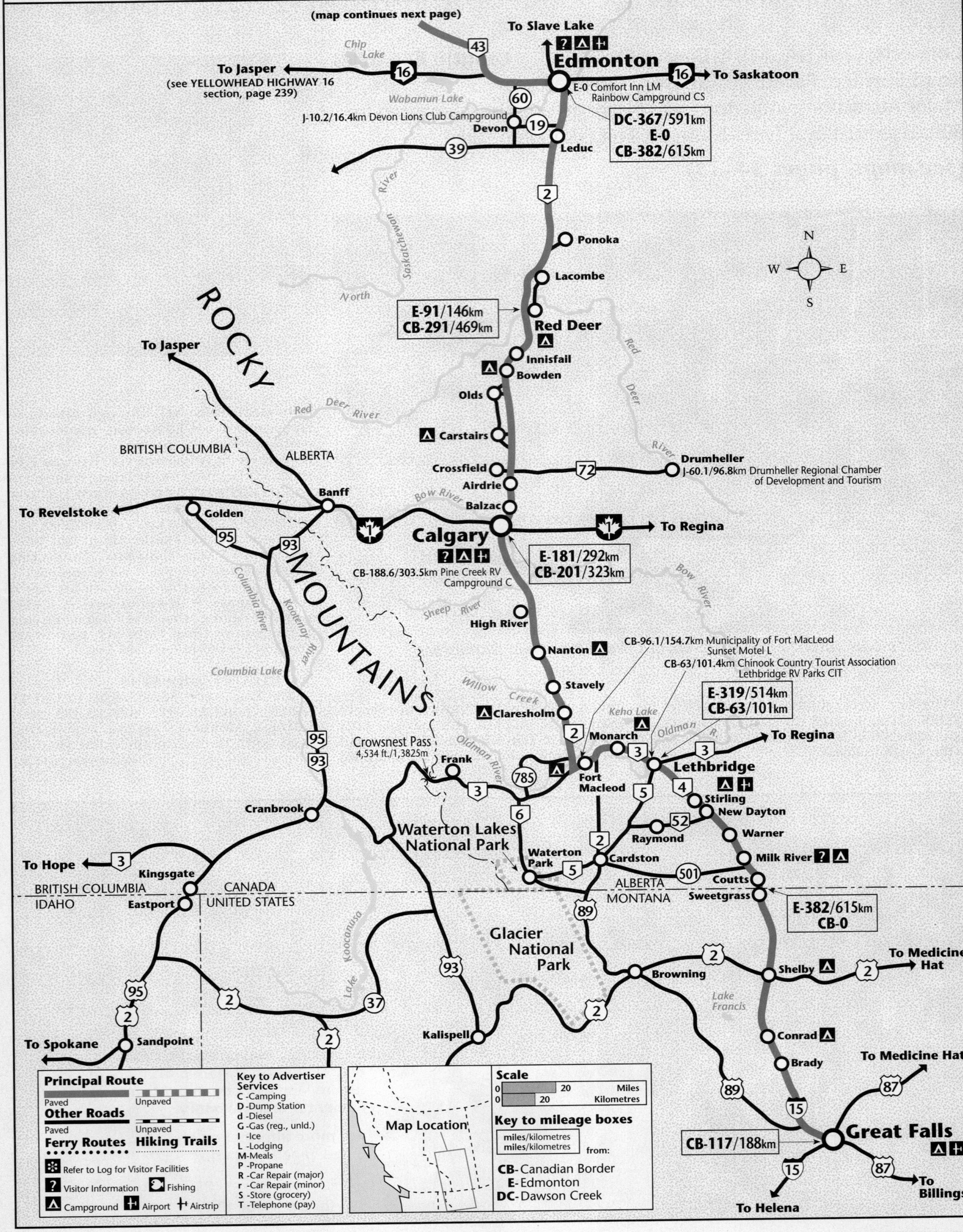

(map continues next page)

To Slave Lake

Edmonton

E-0 Comfort Inn LM
Rainbow Campground CS

DC-367/591km
E-0
CB-382/615km

To Jasper
(see YELLOWHEAD HIGHWAY 16 section, page 239)

To Saskatoon

Chip Lake

Wabamun Lake

J-10.2/16.4km Devon Lions Club Campground

Devon

Leduc

North Saskatchewan River

Ponoka

Lacombe

E-91/146km
CB-291/469km

Red Deer

Innisfail

Bowden

Olds

Carstairs

Crossfield

Airdrie

Balzac

Drumheller
J-60.1/96.8km Drumheller Regional Chamber of Development and Tourism

Red Deer River

ROCKY MOUNTAINS

To Jasper

BRITISH COLUMBIA

ALBERTA

Banff

Bow River

To Revelstoke

Golden

Calgary

E-181/292km
CB-201/323km

CB-188.6/303.5km Pine Creek RV Campground C

To Regina

Bow River

Columbia River

Kootenay River

Columbia Lake

Sheep River

High River

Nanton

CB-96.1/154.7km Municipality of Fort MacLeod
Sunset Motel L

CB-63/101.4km Chinook Country Tourist Association
Lethbridge RV Parks CIT

E-319/514km
CB-63/101km

Stavely

Willow Creek

Claresholm

Keho Lake

Oldman R.

Monarch

To Regina

Crowsnest Pass
4,534 ft./1,3825m

Frank

Oldman River

Fort Macleod

Lethbridge

Stirling

New Dayton

Warner

Raymond

Milk River

Cranbrook

Waterton Lakes National Park

Waterton Park

Cardston

To Hope

Kingsgate

ALBERTA
MONTANA

Coutts

Sweetgrass

E-382/615km
CB-0

BRITISH COLUMBIA
IDAHO

CANADA
UNITED STATES

Eastport

Lake Koocanusa

Glacier National Park

Browning

Shelby

To Medicine Hat

Lake Francis

Conrad

Brady

To Medicine Hat

To Spokane

Sandpoint

Kalispell

Great Falls

CB-117/188km

To Helena

To Billings

N
W E
S

Principal Route
Paved
Unpaved

Other Roads
Paved
Unpaved

Ferry Routes

Hiking Trails

Refer to Log for Visitor Facilities
Visitor Information
Fishing
Campground
Airport
Airstrip

Key to Advertiser Services
C -Camping
D -Dump Station
d -Diesel
G -Gas (reg., unld.)
I -Ice
L -Lodging
M -Meals
P -Propane
R -Car Repair (major)
r -Car Repair (minor)
S -Store (grocery)
T -Telephone (pay)

Map Location

Scale
0 20 Miles
0 20 Kilometres

Key to mileage boxes
miles/kilometres
miles/kilometres
from:

CB-Canadian Border
E-Edmonton
DC-Dawson Creek

EAST ACCESS ROUTE *Edmonton, AB, to Dawson Creek, BC*

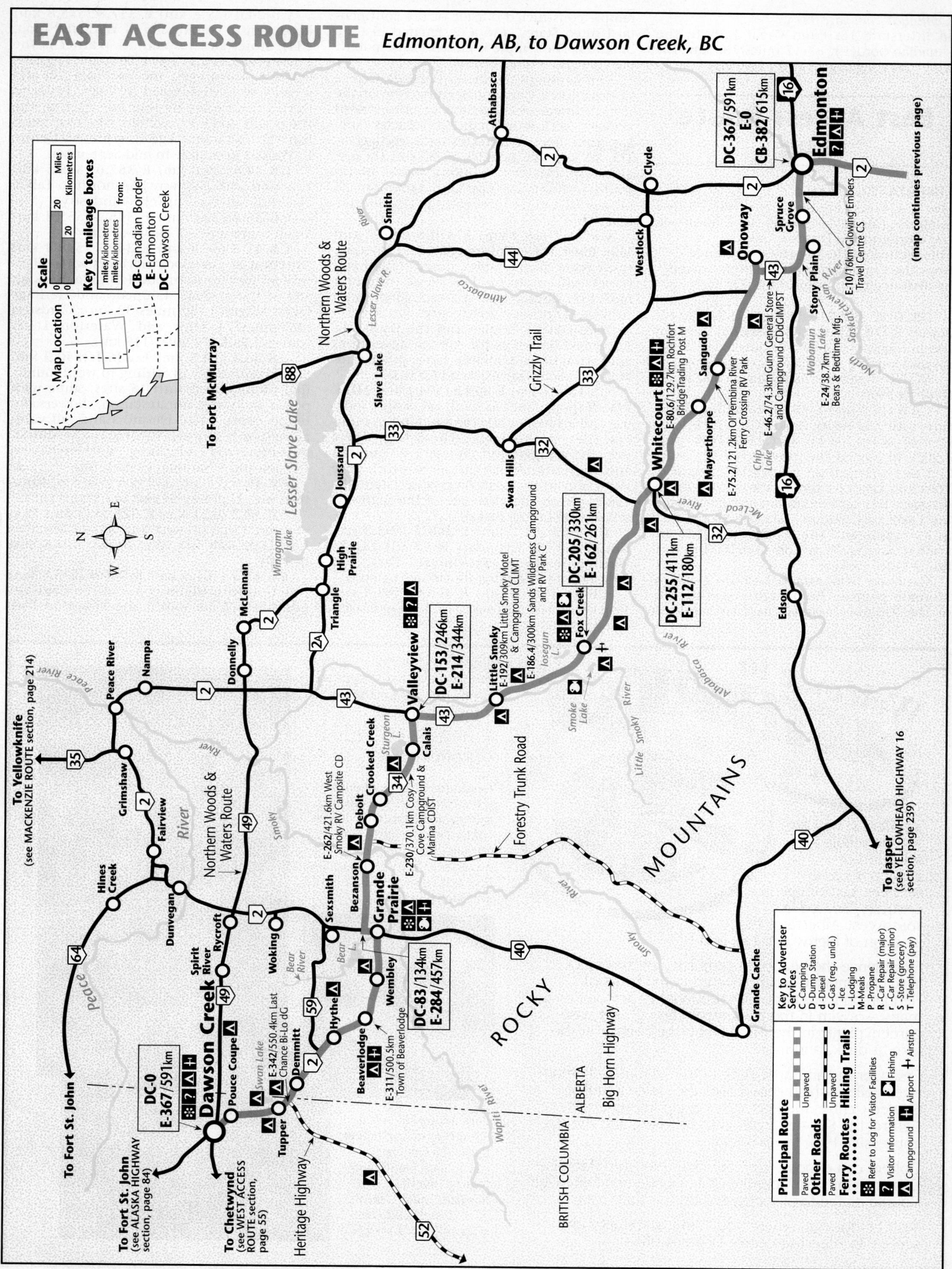

(Continued from page 33)
on Interstate 15. From Great Falls to the Canadian border it is 117 miles/188 km. *The MILEPOST®* log begins at the border.

East Access Route Log

ALBERTA HIGHWAY 4
The East Access Route log is divided into 2 sections: Canadian border to Edmonton, and Edmonton to Dawson Creek.
This section of the log shows distance from the Canadian border (CB) followed by distance from Edmonton (E).

CB 0 E 382.2 (615 km) U.S.–Canada border, **COUTTS** border crossing; customs and immigration open 24 hours a day. Food, gas and lodging at border. Duty-free shop.

NOTE: Watch for road construction at the border in 1998.

CB 8 (12.9 km) **E 374.2** (602.1 km) **Junction** with Secondary Road 501, which leads west 67 miles/108 km to **CARDSTON** (pop. 3,502), located at the **junction** of Highways 2, 5 and 501, just 25 miles/40.2 km east of Waterton Lakes National Park. Known for its dramatic lake and mountain scenery, Waterton Lakes Park adjoins Glacier National Park in Montana, and the 2 parks together are known as the Waterton–Glacier International Peace Park.

Cardston was established in 1887 by Mormon pioneers from Utah and is the site of the Alberta Temple, the first Mormon temple constructed outside of the continental United States, and a designated historic building. The temple is closed to the public, but there is a visitor centre.

The Remington–Alberta Carriage Centre in downtown Cardston features one of the world's foremost collections of horse-drawn vehicles, with more than 200 vehicles ranging from elegant carriages to stagecoaches. The 20-acre site includes an 80-seat theatre, gift shop, cafeteria, working stable, blacksmith/restoration shop and tackroom. A provincial tourist infocentre is also located here.

CB 11.7 (18.9 km) **E 370.5** (596.2 km) Milk River Travel Information and Interpretive Centre; picnic tables, dump station and travel information. The large dinosaur model on display here makes a good photo subject. Dinosaur fossil sites in Alberta include Devil's Coulee and the Badlands. Advanced bookings for Alberta adventures and attractions available here, open mid-May to Labour Day weekend for tickets.

CB 13 (21 km) **E 369.2** (594.1 km) **MILK RIVER** (pop. 926) has food, gas, stores, lodging and a small public campground (6 informal sites; no hookups). The 8 flags flying over the campground represent 7 countries and the Hudson's Bay Co., all of which once laid claim to the Milk River area. Grain elevators are on the west side of the highway, services are on the east side. ▲

CB 13.5 (21.7 km) **E 368.7** (593.3 km) **Junction** with Secondary Road 501 east to Writing-on-Stone Provincial Park, 26 miles/42 km; camping, Indian petroglyphs.

CB 16.3 (26.3 km) **E 365.9** (588.8 km) Stop of interest sign about Milk River Ridge.

CB 24.4 (39.2 km) **E 357.8** (575.8 km) Road west to community of **WARNER** (pop. 434); store, gas, restaurant. Warner is the gateway to Devil's Coulee Dinosaur Egg Site, where dinosaur eggs, and fossilized fish and reptiles were discovered in 1987. Visits to Devil's Coulee are by tour bus only, as the site is still under excavation. The tour buses leave the Dinosaur Egg Interpretive Centre in Warner from June to mid-September.

CB 24.6 (39.6 km) **E 357.6** (575.5 km) **Junction** with Highway 36A north to Taber, centre of Alberta's sugar beet industry.

CB 36.8 (59.2 km) **E 345.4** (555.8 km) Small community of New Dayton.

CB 41.5 (66.8 km) **E 340.7** (548.3 km) **Junction** at Craddock elevators with Highway 52 west to Raymond (10 miles/16 km), site of the annual Stampede and Heritage Days; Magrath (20 miles/32 km); Cardston (46 miles/74 km); and Waterton Lakes National Park (74 miles/119 km).

CB 46.1 (74.2 km) **E 336.1** (540.9 km) Small community of Stirling to west; municipal campground with 15 sites, some with power and water, dump station, showers and tennis court. Grain elevators and rail yards alongside highway. Stirling is the oldest, best-preserved Mormon settlement in Canada and a National Historic Site. ▲

CB 46.6 (75 km) **E 335.6** (540 km) **Junction** with Highway 61 east to Cypress Hills.

CB 57.2 (92.1 km) **E 325** (523 km) Stop of interest sign on west side of road describes how large-scale irrigation began in this area in 1901.

CB 62.9 (101.3 km) **E 319.3** (513.8 km) **Junction** with Highway 5 south to Cardston (48 miles/77 km south) and Waterton Park in Waterton Lakes National Park. Mayor Magrath Drive to north provides access to Lethbridge motels, hotels and Henderson Lake Park (see city description following). Continue west on Scenic Drive for access to Indian Battle Park (via Whoop-Up Drive) and junction with Crowsnest Highway 3.

Alberta's Waterton Lakes National Park (also accessible from **Milepost CB 0.8**) is actually one large lake broken into 3 sections—Lower, Middle and Upper Waterton lakes. Lower Waterton Lake extends down into Montana. Waterton Park townsite, the tourist centre for the park, is approximately 81 miles/131 km from this junction.

Chinook Country Tourist Information Centre, on the north side of the intersection of Highways 4, 5 and Mayor Magrath Drive, has RV parking, restrooms, picnic shelter, dump station and dumpster; open year-round.

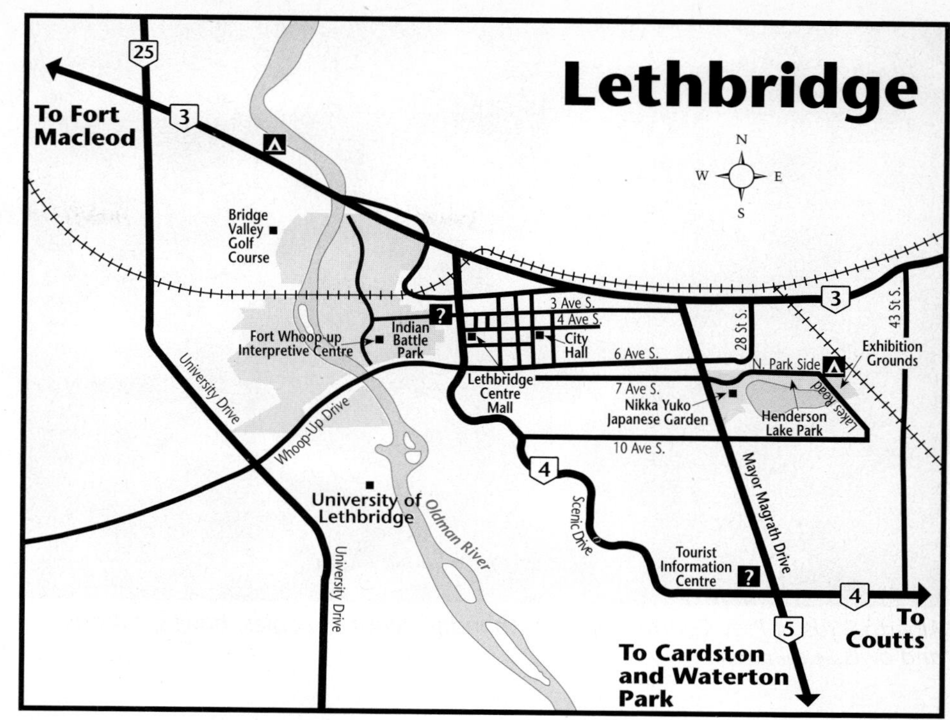

Lethbridge

CB 63 (101.4 km) **E 319.2** (513.7 km) At junction of Highways 3, 4 and 5. **Population:** 66,000. **Elevation:** 3,048 feet/929m. **Emergency Services:** Phone 911 for police, ambulance and fire department. **Hospital:** Lethbridge Regional Hospital, phone (403) 382-6111.

Visitor Information: Chinook Country Tourist Association, on the north side of the intersection of Highways 4, 5 and Mayor Magrath Drive, has souvenirs, RV parking, restrooms, picnic shelter, dump station and dumpster; open year-round. Phone (800) 661-1222 and ask for operator 48 (while in the area call 320-1222) for information on attractions and facilities in southwest Alberta. A tourist information centre is also located at Highway 3 at the west entrance to the city next to the Brewery Gardens; open March 1 to Oct. 31. **Newspaper:** *The Lethbridge Herald* (daily).

Private Aircraft: Airport 4 miles/6.4 km southeast; elev. 3,047 feet/929m; length 6,500 feet/1,981m; paved, fuel 100, jet. FSS.

The Lethbridge region was home to 3 Indian nations: the Sik-si-kah (Blackfoot), Kai'nah (Many Chiefs, now called Bloods), and Pi-ku'ni (Scabby Robes, now called Peigans). Collectively, they formed the Sow-ki'tapi (Prairie People). Because European fur traders along the North Saskatchewan River first came into contact with the Blackfoot, that tribal name came to be applied to the entire confederacy.

In 1869, the American Army decided to stop trade in alcohol with Indians on reservations across Montana. In December 1869, 2 American traders, John Jerome Healy and Alfred Baker Hamilton, built a trading post at the junction of the St. Mary and Belly (now Oldman) rivers, near the future site of Lethbridge. The post became known as Fort Whoop-Up, the most notorious of some 44 trading posts built in southern Alberta from 1869 to 1874. An important trade commodity was "whiskey," a concoction of 9 parts river water to 1 part pure alcohol, to which was added a plug of chewing tobacco for colour and a can of lye for more taste. The mixture was boiled to bring out its full flavour, and well deserved the Indian name "firewater."

Alarmed by the activities of the whiskey traders, Prime Minister Sir John A. Macdonald formed the North West Mounted Police (NWMP), now the Royal Canadian Mounted Police, to bring law and order to the West. The NWMP reached Fort Whoop-Up on Oct. 9, 1874, and immediately put a stop to the whiskey trade.

Early development of Lethbridge commenced in 1874 with the arrival of Nicholas Sheran in search of gold. The gold, in fact, turned out to be black gold—coal—and by the late 1870s a steady coal market and permanent settlement had developed. Elliot Galt, working with his father, Sir Alexander Galt, helped pioneer coal shipments on the Oldman River and later a narrow-gauge railway that connected to the mainline of the Canadian Pacific Railway.

The climax of the early development of Lethbridge came with the CPR construction in 1909 of the high level rail bridge that today carries freight shipments by rail westward through Crowsnest Pass to Vancouver, and onward by ship to the Pacific Rim. The "Bridge"—with a mile-long span and 300-foot elevation—is still the longest and highest bridge of its kind in the world.

Today, Lethbridge is Alberta's third largest city. It has a strong agricultural economy. In late June and early July, bright yellow fields of canola surround the highways leading into the city. Other fields, both irrigated and dryland, produce wheat, sugar beets, potatoes, corn and a variety of other crops.

Lethbridge is southwest Alberta's service and shopping centre, with several malls and a variety of retail businesses. There are a wide choice of restaurants, hotel/motel accommodations, and bed and breakfasts.

There are 2 campgrounds in the city: Henderson Lake campground and Bridgeview campground. ▲

Henderson Lake Park also holds several of the city's attractions, including the Nikka Yuko Japanese Garden, a golf course, swimming pool, picnic area and rose gardens. The Lethbridge Black Diamonds professional baseball team also plays at the park.

An extensive trail system leads to Indian Battle Park in the beautiful Oldman River valley. Indian Battle Park showcases a replica of Fort Whoop-Up, the Helen Schuler Coulee Centre, the Sir Alexander Galt Museum and the High Level Bridge.

Lethbridge hosts the Ag–Expo in March and the Lethbridge International Airshow and Whoop-Up Days in August.

There are a wealth of attractions located within a short drive from the city. The Alberta Birds of Prey Centre, a 10-minute drive east of Lethbridge, is a 70-acre working conservation centre featuring hawks, fal-

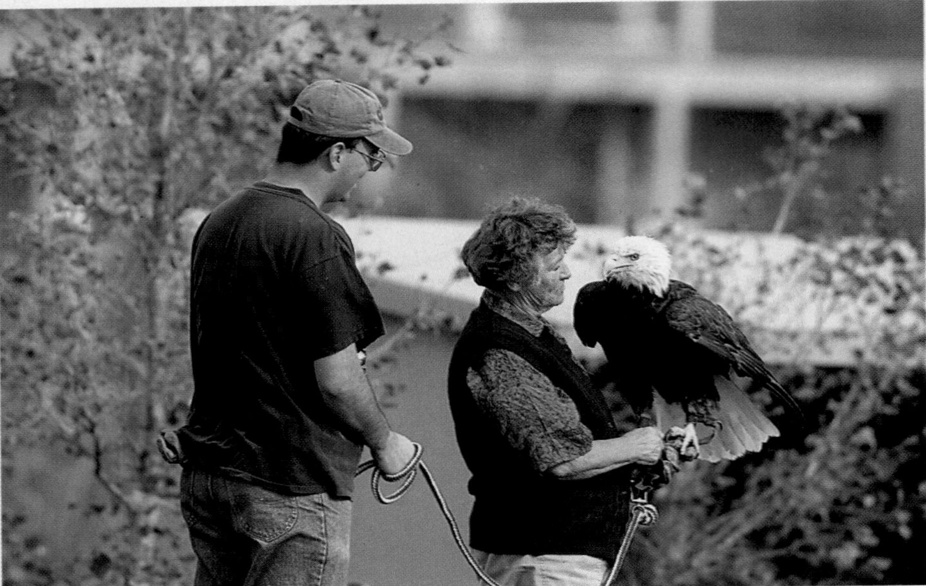

Alberta Birds of Prey Centre, east of Lethbridge, features eagles, hawks, falcons and owls. (© Beth Davidow)

cons, eagles and owls from around the world. Live flying shows with hawks and falcons are presented, weather permitting. Open May 1 to early October, 10:30 A.M. to 5 P.M.; admission fee charged.

Waterton Lakes National Park, a UNESCO World Heritage Site, is located about an hour's drive away in the Rocky Mountains and offers spectacular scenery and recreation opportunities. Another UNESCO World Heritage Site is Head-Smashed-In Buffalo Jump Interpretive Centre located outside of Fort Macleod (see **Milepost CB 100.4**).

Other sites of interest in southern Alberta include the Remington–Alberta Carriage Centre and Alberta Temple in Cardston (see **Milepost CB 0.8**) and the Frank Slide Interpretive Centre at Crowsnest Pass (see **Milepost CB 99**).

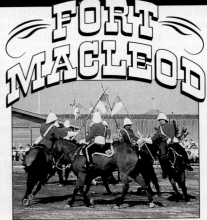

Chinook Country Tourist Association. See display ad this section.

Lethbridge R.V. Parks. Lethbridge has 2 beautiful RV parks. Bridgeview, on the banks of the Oldman River, has 100 serviced sites, a brand new 10,000-square-foot clubhouse which includes a registration office, large laundromat and bright, clean washrooms. A new Olympic-sized heated pool, lots of pull-throughs, shade and easy access from Highway 3. Phone (403) 381-2357. Henderson Lake RV Park is centrally located in the city, has 100 sites, close to shopping, restaurants, golf. Phone (403) 328-5452. At both parks you will receive a sampling of friendly Alberta hospitality. See display ad this section. [ADVERTISEMENT] ▲

East Access Route Log

(continued)

CB 66.6 (107.2 km) **E 315.6** (507.9 km) **Junction** with Crowsnest Highway 3. Tourist information centre beside Brewery Gardens.

CROWSNEST HIGHWAY 3

CB 69.5 (111.8 km) **E 312.7** (503.2 km) **Junction** with Highway 25. Access to **Park Lake** Provincial Park (9 miles/14 km north);

53 campsites, swimming, boat launch, fishing, playground. ▲

CB 72 (115.9 km) **E 310.2** (499.2 km) Community of Coalhurst just north of highway; gas station.

CB 73.5 (118.3 km) **E 308.7** (496.8 km) CPR marshalling yards at Kipp.

CB 80.3 (129.2 km) **E 301.9** (485.8 km) **Junction** with Highway 23 north. Continue west on Highway 3 for Fort Macleod.

CB 81.5 (131.2 km) **E 300.7** (483.9 km) Community of Monarch; hotel, gas.

Westbound, the highway enters Oldman River valley. Good view west of the Rockies on a clear day.

CB 96.1 (154.7 km) **E 286.1** (460.4 km) **Junction** with Highway 2 south to the U.S. border and access to Waterton Lakes and Glacier national parks.

Highway 3 continues through **FORT MACLEOD** (pop. 3,100; elev. 3,300 feet/1,006m). Fort Macleod, built in 1874, was the first outpost of the North West Mounted Police (later the RCMP) in western Canada.

There are several hotels and motels, campgrounds, restaurants, shopping facilities and gas stations. This community's Main Street is a designated historic site; walking tours are offered. The main attraction in Fort Macleod is the Fort Museum, which features the history of the Mounted Police, local Native cultures and early pioneers, in a fort setting. During July and August, the museum features a local re-creation of the official RCMP Musical Ride: Youth in NWMP uniforms execute drills on horseback in a colorful display. The museum is open daily from May to mid-October; open weekdays the rest of the year (closed Dec. 24 to March 1). ▲

Municipality of Fort Macleod. See display ad this section.

The Sunset Motel, winner of 10 Alberta Tourism Housekeeping Awards, 2 Diamond AAA/CAA rated, and an Alberta Best property, emphasizes clean, comfortable rooms, friendly service and reasonable prices. They offer air-conditioned 1-, 2-, and 3-room units, free toast and coffee, refrigerators, kitchenettes, remote control cable televisions, free movies, direct dial touch-tone phones, free local calls and Native crafts shop. Laundromat, convenience store, gas and fast food adjacent. Full U.S. exchange. Off-season rates Oct. 1 to May 15. 104 Highway 3 West. Phone (403) 553-4448. [ADVERTISEMENT]

CB 99 (159.4 km) **E 283.2** (455.8 km) **Junction** with Highway 2 north to Calgary and Edmonton.

Highway 3 (Crowsnest) continues 600 miles/965.6 km west to Hope, BC. The highway takes its name from Crowsnest Pass (elev. 4,534 feet/1,382m), one of the lowest passes in the Rockies, which Highway 3 crosses 65.5 miles/105.5 km west of here. East of the pass (52.8 miles/85 km west of Fort Macleod) is the Frank Slide Interpretive Centre. The centre features the history of the Crowsnest Pass coal mining industry, the railway, and the catastrophic rock slide, which killed 70 people in April 1903, when millions of tons of limestone from Turtle Mountain engulfed the coal mining town of Frank.

ALBERTA HIGHWAY 2

CB 100 (160.8 km) **E 282.2** (454.1 km) **Oldman River** bridge. Alberta government campground to southwest with 10 campsites, dump station, playground, fishing and swimming. North of the river is the largest turkey farm in Alberta. ▲

CB 100.4 (161.6 km) **E 281.8** (453.5 km) **Junction** with Highway 785, which leads 10 miles/16 km to Head-Smashed-In Buffalo Jump, a UNESCO World Heritage Site. The 1,000-foot/305-m-long cliff, where Plains peoples stampeded buffalo to their deaths for nearly 6,000 years, is one of the world's oldest, largest and best-preserved buffalo jumps. The site was named, according to legend, for a young brave whose skull was crushed when he tried to watch the stampede from under a protective ledge which gave way. An interpretive centre houses artifacts and displays describing the buffalo hunting culture. First Nations interpretive guides available on site. Guided walks available twice daily during July and August. Open year-round; 9 A.M. to 7 P.M., June 1 to Labour Day; 9 A.M. to 5 P.M., Labour Day through May; closed major holidays. Admission fee charged.

CB 111.2 (179 km) **E 271** (436.1 km) Road east to Granum, a small settlement dominated by grain elevators. Recreation park with 41 campsites in town . ▲

CB 116.2 (187 km) **E 266** (428 km) Community of Woodhouse.

CB 121.8 (196 km) **E 260.4** (419.1 km) **CLARESHOLM** (pop. 3,297), a prosperous ranching centre with all visitor facilities. The old railway station houses a museum and tourist infocentre. Camping at Centennial Park; 17 sites, dump station, playground. ▲

CB 125.9 (202.6 km) **E 256.3** (412.5 km) Stop of interest sign commemorating The Leavings, a stopping place on the Fort Macleod–Calgary trail in 1870.

CB 131.3 (211.3 km) **E 250.9** (403.8 km) Community of Stavely to the east.

CB 132.1 (212.6 km) **E 250.1** (402.5 km) Access road west to **Willow Creek** Provincial Park; 150 campsites, swimming, fishing. ▲

CB 138.4 (222.8 km) **E 243.8** (392.3 km) Small settlement of Parkland.

CB 145.9 (234.8 km) **E 236.3** (380.3 km) Nanton campground (75 sites) at **junction** with Secondary Road 533, which leads west to Chain Lakes Provincial Park. ▲

CB 146.8 (236.3 km) **E 235.4** (378.8 km) **NANTON** (pop. 1,612); all visitor facilities. Nanton is famous for its springwater, which is piped from Big Spring in the Porcupine Hills, 6 miles/10 km west of town, to a large tap located in town centre. Springwater tap operates mid-May to September. WWII Lancaster bomber on display at Centennial Park.

CB 151.1 (243.2 km) **E 231.1** (371.9 km) **Junction** with Highway 2A, which parallels Highway 2 northbound.

CB 162.8 (262 km) **E 219.4** (353.1 km) **Junction** with Highway 23 west to **HIGH RIVER** (pop. 6,893) located on Highway 2A. All visitor facilities. Once the centre of a harness-making industry, High River has elegant sandstone buildings and the Museum of the Highwood (open in summer).

CB 164 (264 km) **E 218.2** (351.1 km) Stop of interest commemorating Spitzee Post, built in 1869.

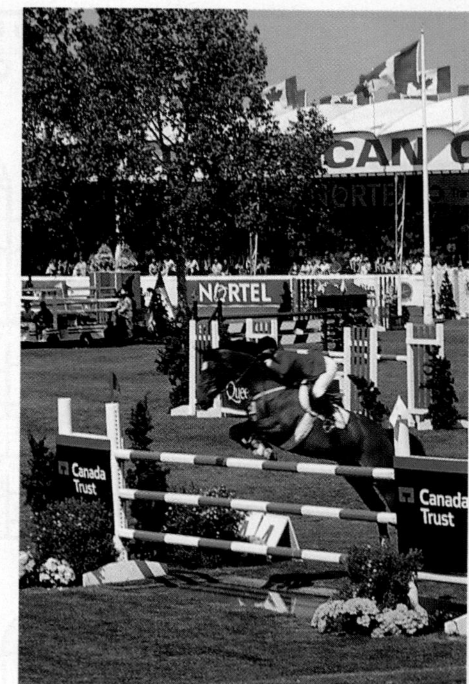

Spruce Meadows Equestrian Center near Okotoks hosts major competitions. *(Blake Hanna, staff)*

CB 170 (273.6 km) **E 212.2** (341.5 km) Stop of interest sign about cattle brands.

CB 171.6 (276.1 km) **E 210.6** (338.9 km) **Junction** at Aldersyde with Highways 2A and 7 to Okotoks, Black Diamond and Turner Valley (18.5 miles/30 km). Stop of interest commemorating the Turner Valley oil fields.

CB 173.3 (278.9 km) **E 208.9** (336.2 km) Sheep Creek bridge. **Sheep Creek** Provincial Park has a picnic area, playground, swimming and fishing.

CB 183 (294.5 km) **E 199.2** (320.6 km) **Junction** with Highway 2A to **OKOTOKS** (5 miles/8 km west), which has a general store, RV repair and a tea room. Near Okotoks is Spruce Meadows Equestrian Center, which hosts the International Horse Show, June to September; phone (403) 974-4200.

CB 184.6 (297.2 km) **E 197.6** (318 km) Gas station to east with diesel and propane.

CB 188.6 (303.5 km) **E 193.6** (311.6 km) Calgary southern city limits. Private RV park to east. ▲

Pine Creek R.V. Campground. See display ad this section. ▲

NOTE: To bypass downtown Calgary, exit at Marquis of Lorne Trail and continue to Highway 2 (Deerfoot Trail) north.

CB 196.5 (316.2 km) **E 185.7** (298.8 km) Exit for Glenmore Trail, the southwest bypass route that connects with Trans-Canada Highway 1 west to Banff and Vancouver, BC.

Calgary

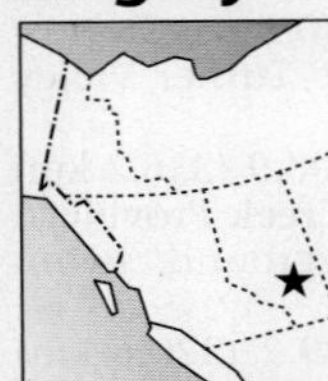

CB 200.8 (323.1 km) **E 181.4** (291.9 km) Located at the confluence of the Bow and Elbow rivers. **Population:** 767,059. **Elevation:** 3,440 feet/ 1,049m. **Emergency Services:** Phone 911 for emergency services. **Hospitals:** Bow Valley Centre, 841 Centre Ave. NE; Foothills, 1403 29th St. NW; Rockyview, 7007 14th St. SW; Peter Lougheed Center, 3500 26th Ave. NE.

Visitor Information: In the downtown area at the base of Calgary Tower, and at the Calgary Airport; both are open year-round. A visitor centre at Canada Olympic Park is open in summer only. Or call Calgary Convention & Visitors Bureau at (403) 263-8510 or (800) 661-1678 (toll-free in North America).

Private Aircraft: Calgary International Airport, 4 miles/6.4 km northeast; elev. 3,557 feet/1,084m; 3 runways. See Canadian Flight Supplement.

This bustling city is one of Alberta's 2 major population and business centres. A great influx of homesteaders came to Calgary with the completion of the Canadian Pacific Railway in 1883. It grew as a trading centre for surrounding farms and ranches. Oil and gas discovered south of the city in 1914 contributed to more growth.

Perhaps the city's best-known attraction is the annual Calgary Stampede, which takes place at the Exhibition Grounds, July 3–12, 1998. The 10-day event includes a parade and daily rodeo; phone (800) 661-1260 for Stampede information and tickets.

Some other major attractions are: Calgary Science Centre, 11th Street and 7th Avenue; the Glenbow Museum, which presents a lively journey into the heritage of the Canadian West, 130 9th Avenue SE; the Eau Claire Market, adjacent to Prince's Island in the downtown area; the Calgary Chinese Cultural Centre, 197 1st St. SW; the Energeum, at the Energy Resources Bldg., 640 5th Ave. SW; Fort Calgary Interpretive Centre, 750 9th Ave. SE; Calgary Zoo Botanical Garden and Prehistoric Park, off Memorial Drive, featuring a prehistoric park with life-sized replicas of dinosaurs; and Heritage Park, west of 14th Street and Heritage Drive SW, a re-creation of Calgary's pioneer eras. Visitors may recognize the distinctive Saddledome, located at the Exhibition Grounds, which was the site of the 1988 Winter Olympics skating and hockey events. Canada Olympic Park (site of ski jumping, luge and bobsled) is on Trans-Canada Highway 1, west of Sarcee Trail.

Calgary has large shopping malls, department stores, restaurants, and many hotels and motels. Most lodging is downtown or on Highway 2 south (Macleod Trail), Trans-Canada Highway 1 north (16th Avenue) and Alternate 1A (Motel Village). There are several campgrounds in and around the city. ▲

East Access Route Log

(continued)

CB 211.3 (340 km) **E 170.9** (275 km) Calgary northern city limits.

Highway 2 from Calgary to Edmonton bypasses most communities. Except for a few service centres built specially for freeway traffic, motorists must exit the freeway for communities and gas, food or lodging.

CB 211.9 (341 km) **E 170.3** (273 km) Exit to community of **BALZAC**. Private RV park with dump station. ▲

CB 217.9 (350.7 km) **E 164.3** (264.4 km) Road west to **AIRDRIE** (pop. 14,506). Visitor facilities include hotels and motels.

CB 225 (362 km) **E 157.2** (253 km) Dickson–Stephensson Stopping House on Old Calgary Trail; rest area, tourist information.

CB 232.2 (373.6 km) **E 150** (241.4 km) **Junction** with Highway 2A west to Crossfield and Highway 72 east to Drumheller, 60 miles/97 km, site of Alberta's Badlands. The Badlands are famous for the dinosaur fossils found there. Fossil displays at world-renowned Tyrrell Museum of Paleontology in Drumheller. See "Side Trip to Alberta's Badlands" this page.

CB 232.6 (374.4 km) **E 149.6** (240.7 km) Stop of interest sign about the buffalo that once darkened the prairies here. Gas and restaurant at turnout.

CB 235.1 (378.3 km) **E 147.1** (236.7 km) Exit to **CROSSFIELD**; gas, hotel, food.

CB 243.1 (391.2 km) **E 139.1** (223.9 km) Exit west for **CARSTAIRS** (pop. 1,796), a farm and service community with tourist information centre and campground. The campground has 28 sites, electric hookups, hot showers and dump station. Services here include groceries, liquor store, banks, a motel, propane and gas stations. ▲

CB 252.7 (406.6 km) **E 129.5** (208.4 km) **Junction** with Highway 27 west to **OLDS** (pop. 5,542); all visitor facilities, museum and information booth.

CB 268.8 (432.5 km) **E 113.4** (182.5 km) **Junction** with highway west to Bowden and Red Lodge Provincial Park (8.5 miles/14 km); 110 campsites, playground, swimming and fishing. **BOWDEN** (pop. 936) is the site of a large oil refinery and Alberta Nurseries and Seeds Ltd., a major employer. Most visitor services available. Heritage rest area with 24 campsites, dump station and tourist information booth at junction. ▲

CB 276 (444 km) **E 106.2** (171 km) **Junction** with Highway 54 west to **INNISFAIL** (pop. 6,064); all visitor facilities. South of Innisfail 3 miles/5 km is the RCMP Dog Training Centre, the only one in Canada; open to the public daily year-round from 9 A.M. to 4 P.M.

CB 278.8 (448.7 km) **E 103.4** (166.4 km) Stop of interest sign about explorer Anthony Henday.

CB 290 (466.8 km) **E 92.2** (148.3 km) Tourist service area with gas stations and

Side Trip to Alberta's Badlands

Alberta Highways 72 and 9 lead 60 miles/97 km east to Drumheller in Alberta's Badlands—a region characterized by scanty vegetation and intricate erosional features. Besides its fantastic scenery, the Badlands is also famous for its dinosaurs. It is one of the best places in the world to recover the fossilized remains of dinosaurs, many of which are displayed at the world-famous Tyrrell Museum of Paleontology in Drumheller. **Distance from Highway 2 junction (J) is shown.**

J 0 Junction with Alberta Highway 2 at **Milepost CB 232.2** (approximately 31 miles/50 km north of Calgary).

J 7.5 (12.1 km) **Junction** with Highway 791, which leads to the Fairview Colony.

J 13.8 (22.2 km) Rosebud River.

J 14 (22.6 km) Beiseker Colony.

J 20.7 (33.4 km) **BEISEKER** (pop. 640); all services available. Highway 72 becomes Highway 9 eastbound.

J 33.2 (53.5 km) **Junction** with Highway 21 to Three Hills and Trans-Canada Highway 1.

J 37.3 (60.1 km) **Junction** with Highway 836. Food and gas available.

J 50.6 (81.5 km) Horseshoe Canyon Viewpoint; restrooms and picnic tables. Canyon tours available.

J 45.1 (72.6 km) **Junction** with Highway 840 to Rosebud and Standard.

J 60.1 (96.8 km) **DRUMHELLER** (pop. 6,277); all visitor facilities available, including bed and breakfasts, motels, campgrounds, restaurants and gas. **Visitor Information:** Drumheller Regional Chamber of Development and Tourism, Box 999, Alberta T0J 0Y0; phone (403) 823-8100.

The first dinosaur fossil found in the badlands was an Albertosaurus (a slightly smaller version of the Tyrannosaurus), unearthed in 1884 by Joseph Burr Tyrrell, just east of what is today Drumheller. His find sparked the "Great Canadian Dinosaur Rush," as famous fossil hunters Barnum Brown, Joseph Sternberg and others vied for trophies. Today, the major attraction in Drumhbeller is the Tyrrell Museum of Paleontology, located in Midland Provincial Park just outside the city limits. The museum boasts an outstanding fossil collection presented in stunning displays. More than 30 complete dinosaur skeletons, as well as flying reptiles, prehistoric mammals and marine invertebrates, are displayed in a huge walk-through diorama exhibit. A tropical plant conservatory with more than 100 species of plants simulates the botanical world of the dinosaurs. A viewing window in the main laboratory allows visitors a watch scientists at work. Park rangers lead visitors on 90-minute interpretive hikes into the badlands around the museum, and there are special programs for children. The museum has a restaurant and gift shop. Summer hours are 9 A.M. to 9 P.M. daily. Admission is free. For more information, contact the museum at Box 7500, Drumheller, AB T0J 0Y0; phone (403) 823-7707; fax (403) 823-7131; e-mail: rtmp@dns.magtech.ab.ca.

Scenic drives in the area include the Dinosaur Trail and East Coulee Drive. Highlights along the Dinosaur Trail, a 30-mile/50-km driving loop through the Red Deer River Valley from Drumheller, include the Dinosaur Burial Grounds; the Homestead Antique Museum; the West Drumheller Oil Field; Horse Thief Canyon; and Midland Mine office in Midland Provincial Park. The East Coulee Drive includes the much-photographed hoodoos; the swinging bridge at Rosedale; East Coulee School Museum and Tea Room; and the Atlas Coal Mine.

Drumheller Regional Chamber of Development and Tourism. See display ad this section.

Return to Milepost CB 232.2 East Access Route

restaurants.

CB 291.4 (468.9 km) **E 90.8** (146.1 km) **Junction** with Highway 2A (Gaetz Avenue) east to **RED DEER** (pop. 59,834). **Emergency Services:** Phone 911. **Visitor Information:** At Heritage Ranch, adjacent Highway 2 at **Milepost CB 295** (watch for signs). Heritage Ranch has a staffed visitor centre (open daily year-round) with a gift shop and snack bar, ample parking and access to Waskasoo Park. Phone (800) 215-8946 or (403) 346-0180.

Private Aircraft: Airport 6 miles/9.6 km southwest; elev. 2,968 feet/905m; length 5,528 feet/1,685m; fuel 100, jet. FSS.

Located midway between Edmonton and Calgary, Red Deer is in the centre of cattle ranching and grain growing, with a burgeoning oil and gas industry and nearby ethylene plants.

Red Deer is often called the "city within a park," referring to the extensive Waskasoo Park system that stretches through the city along the banks of the Red Deer River. The park has more than 46.5 miles/75 km of walking and cycling trails connecting a variety of popular attractions.

The major annual event in Red Deer is Westerner Days in mid-July.

All visitor facilities available, including major chain motels and retail outlets. Camping at Lions Municipal Campground on Riverside Drive; from Highway 2 exit to 67th Street or 32nd Street. Open May to September, 127 sites (88 full-service), dump station, laundry, picnic area, playground. ▲

CB 298 (479.6 km) **E 84.2** (135.5 km) **Junction** with Highway 11 to Sylvan Lake (10 miles/16 km), a popular watersports destination for Red Deer residents, with swimming beach and marina. Sylvan Lake Provincial Park has picnicking and swimming. Private campgrounds and waterslide nearby. ▲

CB 302.5 (486.8 km) **E 80.2** (129.1 km) Access road east to community of **BLACKFALDS** (pop. 1,769). Tourist services and accommodations.

CB 309.1 (497.4 km) **E 73.1** (117.6 km) **Junction** with Highway 12. Exit east for **LACOMBE** (pop. 7,580); all visitor facilities. Camping at Michener Park; 21 sites. Site of the Federal Agricultural Research Station; open to the public weekdays, 8 A.M. to 4:30 P.M. Exit west on Highway 12 for Aspen Beach Provincial Park at Gull Lake (6 miles/10 km); camping, swimming. ▲

CB 325 (524.7 km) **E 56.2** (90.4 km) **Junction** with Highway 53 east to **PONOKA** (pop. 5,861); all visitor facilities. Camping at Ponoka Stampede Trailer Park, May to October. Ponoka's Stampede is held June 29 to July 3 at Stampede Park. ▲

CB 340.7 (548.3 km) **E 41.5** (66.8 km) Northbound-only access to Wetaskiwin rest area with picnic tables and information centre (open May to September); restrooms, gas service and groceries.

CB 345.3 (555.7 km) **E 36.9** (59.4 km) **Junction** of Highway 13 east to Wetaskiwin, site of the Reynolds–Alberta Museum and Aviation Hall of Fame.

CB 356 (572.9 km) **E 26.2** (42.2 km) Turnout to east with litter barrels and pay phone.

CB 366 (589 km) **E 16.2** (26.1 km) Exit to **LEDUC** (pop. 14,117); all visitor facilities. Founded and named for the Leduc oil field. The Leduc well was drilled on Feb. 13, 1947, before an invited asssembly of businesspeople, government officials and reporters. It was the 134th try for Imperial Oil after drilling 133 dry wells, and it was wildly successful. The 200-million barrel Leduc oil field was the first in a series of post-war oil and natural gas finds that changed the economy of Alberta.

CB 372 (598.6 km) **E 10.2** (16.4 km) **Junction** with Highway 19 west and Edmonton Bypass route (see DEVONIAN WAY BYPASS log this page). Access to Leduc No. 1 well historic site.

NOTE: Northbound motorists wishing to avoid heavy traffic through Edmonton may exit west on Highway 19 (Devonian Way) for Devon Bypass route. Drive 8.2 miles/13.2 km west on Highway 19, then 14.5 miles/23.3 km north on

Devonian Way Bypass

This bypass route circles the southwest edge of Edmonton, connecting Highway 2 and Highway 16 via Secondary Highway 19 (Devonian Way) and Highway 60. **Distance from Highway 2 and Devonian Way junction (J) is shown.**

J 0 Junction with Highway 19, Devonian Way, at **Milepost CB 372**. Follow Devonian Way west.

J 0.4 (0.7 km) Rest area to south.

J 2.1 (3.4 km) Capital Raceway to south, Amerlea Meadows equestrian facility to north.

J 5.2 (8.3 km) Rabbit Hill Ski area to west.

J 8.2 (13.2 km) **Junction** with Highway 60 (Edmonton truck bypass). Turn north on Highway 60 for Devon and Yellowhead Highway; turn south at intersection and drive 0.6 mile/1 km for Leduc No. 1 well historic site. A 174-foot/53-m derrick marks the site at which oil was struck on February 13, 1947, making Edmonton the "Oil Capital of Canada." Visitors may climb to the drilling floor to view drilling equipment and tools.

J 9.2 (14.8 km) Dump station.

J 10.2 (16.4 km) Turn east on Athabasca Avenue for downtown **DEVON**; all visitor services. Camping at Devon Lions Club Campground, 180 sites on North Saskatchewan River; follow signs for Patrick O'Brien Memorial Park. The campground is adjacent to Devon Golf & Country Club.

Devon Lions Club Campground. See display ad this section. ▲

J 10.6 (17 km) Bridge over North Saskatchewan River.

J 13.8 (22.2 km) University of Alberta Devonian Botanic Garden; alpine garden, 5-acre Kurimoto Japanese Garden, and other special collections gardens set in natural landscape. Live exotic butterfly showhouse with 30 species of butterflies. Open daily, 10 A.M. to 7 P.M. in summer, shorter hours rest of year. Fee charged.

J 16.9 (27.2 km) **Junction** with Secondary Highway 627; turn east for Edmonton.

J 22.7 (36.6 km) **Junction** with Yellowhead Highway 16; turn to **Milepost E 10**.

Return to Milepost E 10 or CB 372 East Access Route

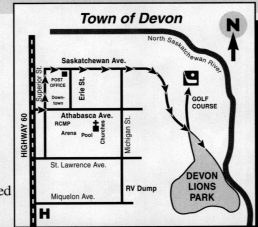

Highway 60 to junction with Yellowhead Highway 16, 10 miles/16 km west of Edmonton (see ***Milepost E 10*** *this section).*

Highway 2 northbound becomes Calgary Trail. Access to Edmonton International Airport.

CB 377.9 (608.2 km) **E 4.3** (6.9 km) Stoplight at Ellerslie (grain elevator). Access to golf course and private campground; follow Ellerslie west to 127th and turn south to 41st Avenue SW. ▲

CB 382.2 (615 km) **E 0 Junction** with Whitemud Drive. Turn east for Highway 16 East, turn west for Highway 16 West (see YELLOWHEAD HIGHWAY 16 section). Continue north for Edmonton city centre (description follows).

Whitemud Drive west continues as Highway 2, crossing the North Saskatchewan River, then turns north to become 170 Street. Access to West Edmonton Mall on 170 Street.

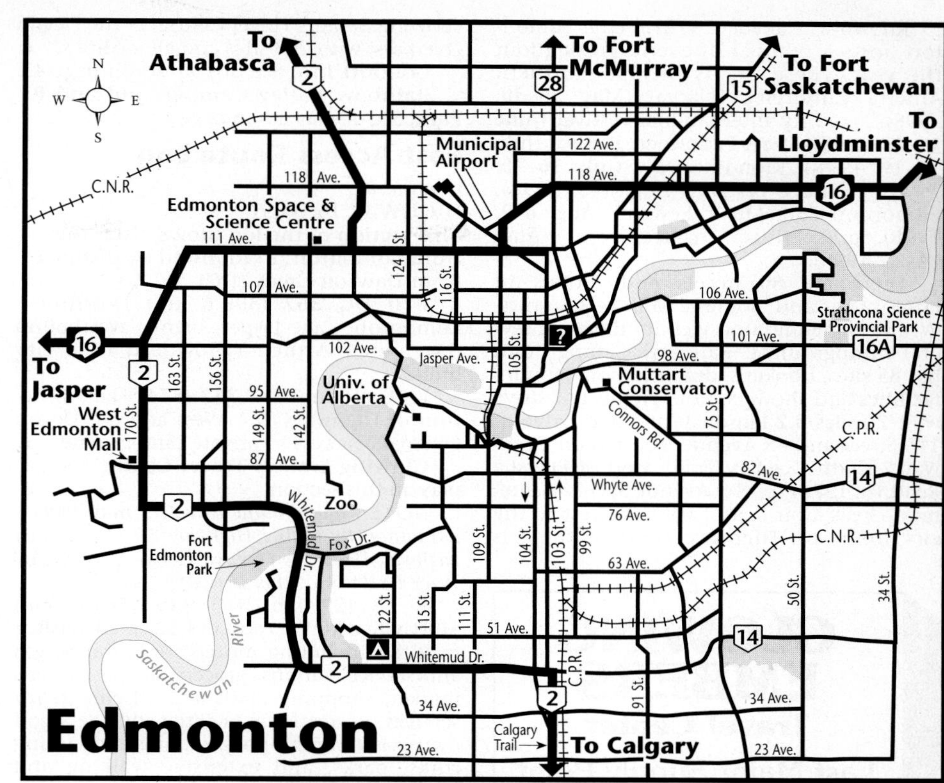

Edmonton

E 0 DC 367 (590.6 km) Capital of Alberta, 1,853 miles/2,982 km from Fairbanks, AK. **Population:** 627,000; area 890,000. **Elevation:** 2,182 feet/668m. **Emergency Services:** Phone 911 for all emergency services. **Hospitals:** Grey Nun's, 34th Avenue and 66th Street; Misericordia, 16940 87th Ave.; Royal Alexandra, 10240 Kingsway Ave.; University, 84th Avenue and 112th Street.

Visitor Information: Edmonton Tourism operates visitor information centres downtown and on Highway 2 south. Or write Edmonton Tourism, Dept. MI 98, 9797 Jasper Ave. #104, Edmonton, AB T5J 1N9; phone (403) 496-8400 or (800) 463-4667 for information.

Private Aircraft: Edmonton International Airport 14 miles/22.5 km southwest and Edmonton City Centre north side of downtown. See Canadian Flight Supplement.

The North Saskatchewan River winds through the centre of Edmonton, its banks

lined with public parks. Edmonton Coliseum is home to the Edmonton Oilers NHL hockey team. The Edmonton Trappers baseball team play at Telus Field. Major attractions include the Edmonton Space & Science Centre; Muttart Conservatory; Alberta Legislature Building; the Provincial Museum of Alberta, with its Aboriginal Peoples Gallery; and Fort Edmonton Park, Canada's largest living history park.

Fort Edmonton Park features more than 60 period buildings on 158 acres. Costumed interpreters bring history to life on 1885 Street, 1905 Street, 1920 Street and in the Hudson's Bay Co. fort (1846). The original fort was established in 1795 as part of the westward expansion of the fur trade, and by 1846 its main function was to prepare the pemmican and build the York boats necessary to make the journey to York Factory on the Hudson Bay to bring out furs and return with trade goods each summer.

Activities and attractions at the park include a steam train ride, stagecoach and streetcar rides; blacksmithing and rope-making demonstrations; retail shops and food outlets. Plenty of hands-on activities for the whole family. Open 10 A.M. daily, May to September; special events year-round. Contact Fort Edmonton Park, Box 2359, Edmonton, AB T5J 2R7; phone (403) 496-8787.

Also on the list of major attractions for visitors to Edmonton is the world's largest shopping mall—West Edmonton Mall. The mall features some 800 stores and services, a waterpark, ice arena, aquariums and some 90 eating establishments. Located on 87 Avenue at 170 Street, the shopping mall is open 7 days a week.

Known as Canada's festival city, Edmonton hosts a number of events throughout the year. These events include Northern Alberta Children's Festival (May 26–30, 1998); Jazz City International Festival (June 19–28, 1998); Street Performers Festival (July 10–19, 1998); Klondike Days (July 16–25, 1998); Heritage Festival (Aug. 1–3, 1998); Edmonton Folk Music Festival (Aug. 6–9, 1998); and Fringe Theatre Event (Aug. 14–23, 1998).

There are 80 hotels and motels in Edmonton and some 2,000 restaurants. Within the Edmonton vicinity there are several campgrounds. Rainbow Campground has 85 sites, hookups, dump station, laundry facilities and showers; from Highway 2 drive west 2 miles/3.2 km on Whitemud Drive to 119 Street and 45 Avenue. Located off Highway 2 south (Calgary Trail), west of Ellerslie Road via 127th to 41st Avenue SW, is Whitemud Creek Golf & RV Park. Just west of the city limits off Highway 16 West there is Glowing Embers Travel Centre, at the Devon Overpass, with 273 sites and all facilities. ▲

Comfort Inn. See display ad on page 43.

Rainbow Valley Campground and RV Park. See display ad on page 43.

East Access Route Log

(continued)

HIGHWAY 16 WEST

This section of the log shows distance from Edmonton (E) followed by distance from Dawson Creek (DC).

E 0 DC 367 (590.6 km) Downtown Edmonton. Take Jasper Avenue westbound (becomes 16A then Yellowhead 16 at city limits).

E 10 (16 km) **DC 357** (574.5 km) **Junction** of Highways 16A West and 60 (Devon Overpass); access to private campground. ▲

Glowing Embers Travel Centre. See display ad this section. ▲

NOTE: Southbound travelers may bypass Edmonton by taking Highway 60 south, then Highway 19 east to Highway 2 (see DEVONIAN WAY BYPASS log this section).

E 18 (29 km) **DC 349** (561.6 km) **SPRUCE GROVE** (pop. 14,123). All visitor facilities including motels, restaurants, gas and service stations, grocery stores, farmer's market, shopping malls and all emergency services. Recreational facilities include a golf course, swimming pool, skating and curling rinks, parks, and extensive walking and cycling trails. The chamber of commerce tourist information booth, located on Highway 16A, is open year-round; phone (403) 962-2561.

E 24 (38.7 km) **DC 345** (555.2 km) **STONY PLAIN** (pop. 7,405). All visitor facilities including hotels, restaurants, supermarkets, shopping mall and gas stations with major repair service; RCMP and hospital; outdoor swimming pool, tennis courts and 18-hole golf course. The Multicultural Heritage Centre here has historical archives, a craft shop and home-cooked meals. Other attractions include 16 outdoor murals; Oppertshauser Art Gallery; the Andrew Wolf Winery; and the Pioneer Museum at Exhibition Park. Visitor information centre at Rotary Park rest area. Camping at Lions RV Park and Campground; 26 sites. ▲

Bears and Bedtime Mfg. features handmade, limited-edition collectable teddy bears, bear-making supplies, teddy bear books, Cherished Teddies, Boyd's Bearstones, Beanie Babies and other gift items. Hours: Monday–Friday 9 A.M.–6 P.M., Saturday 10 A.M.–6 P.M. Visit our website at www.bearsandbedtime.com. Phone 1-800-461-BEAR(2327). See ad in the YELLOWHEAD HIGHWAY section. [ADVERTISEMENT]

E 25.6 (41.2 km) **DC 341.4** (549.4 km) Edmonton Beach turnoff to south; campground. ▲

E 26.1 (42 km) **DC 340.9** (548.6 km) Hubbles Lake turnoff to north.

E 27.2 (43.8 km) **DC 339.8** (546.8 km) Restaurant, gas station and store to north.

E 27.7 (44.6 km) **DC 339.3** (546 km) Andrew Wolf Wine Cellars; visitors welcome.

E 28 (45 km) **DC 339** (545.6 km) Multicultural Heritage Centre, a regional museum, with restaurant and crafts shop. Open daily.

E 31 (49.9 km) **DC 336** (540.7 km) **Junction** of Yellowhead Highway 16 and Highway 43. Turn north onto Highway 43. (If you are continuing west on Yellowhead Highway 16 for Prince George or Prince Rupert, BC, turn to **Milepost E 25** in the YELLOWHEAD HIGHWAY section.)

HIGHWAY 43

E 37.3 (60 km) **DC 329.7** (530.6 km) Turnout to east with litter barrel and historical information sign about construction of the Alaska Highway.

E 38.7 (62.3 km) **DC 328.3** (528.3 km) Gas station to east.

E 39.2 (63.1 km) **DC 327.8** (527.5 km) Highway 633 west to Alberta Beach Recreation Area on Lac Ste. Anne. Facilities include a municipal campground (open May 15 to Sept. 15) with 115 sites. ▲

E 41.6 (66.9 km) **DC 325.4** (523.7 km) **ONOWAY** (pop. 681) has a medical clinic, dentist and veterinary clinic. Other services include gas, propane, banks and bank machine, grocery stores, laundromat, restaurants, motel, car wash, post office, pharmacy, RV park with hookups and dump station. Information booth and Elks campground with 8 sites. ▲

E 45.6 (73.4 km) **DC 321.4** (517.2 km) **Junction** of Highways 43 and 33 (Grizzly Trail). Continue on Highway 43.

Alberta government campground with dump station, water, toilets and stoves. ▲

E 46.2 (74.3 km) **DC 320.8** (516.3 km) Restaurant and gas station.

Gunn General Store & Campground. See display ad this section. ▲

E 48 (77.2 km) **DC 318.9** (513.2 km) **Lessard Lake** county campground; water, stoves, boat launch, fishing for pike and perch. Golf course to west. ▲

E 63.7 (102.5 km) **DC 303.3** (488.1 km) Gas station.

E 72 (115.8 km) **DC 295** (474.8 km) **SANGUDO** (pop. 405) is on a 0.3-mile/0.4-km side road. Restaurants, motel and hotel accommodations; gas station with garage open 7 days a week; grocery, clothing and liquor stores; antique shop; banks, post office, pharmacy, laundromat and car wash. Oval race car track with racing in summer; shale baseball diamonds; elk farm tours. A public campground with 14 sites, showers and flush toilets, is located at the sportsground. ▲

E 74.4 (119.7 km) **DC 292.6** (470.9 km) Pembina River bridge.

E 75.2 (121.2 km) **DC 291.8** (469.4 km) **Ol' Pembina River Ferry Crossing RV Park.** "Peaceful camping along the Pembina River, where history surrounds the RV park." Walking/history trails. Old ferry site. Community firepit. Water and power sites. Pull-throughs, sewer dump, shower and flush toilet, coin washer and dryer. 1 km off Highway 43, turn south at RV park sign, flying 3 flags. Phone (403) 785-3243. [ADVERTISEMENT] ▲

E 75.4 (121.3 km) **DC 291.6** (469.3 km) Gas station and restaurant to south.

E 79.5 (128 km) **DC 287.5** (462.7 km) Second longest wooden railway trestle in the world crosses highway and Paddle River. The C.N.R. Rochfort Bridge trestle is 2,414 feet/736m long and was originally built in 1914.

E 80.6 (129.7 km) **DC 286.4** (460.9 km) **ROCHFORT BRIDGE.** Trading post (open daily, year-round) with gas, convenience store, gift shop, restaurant and Lac Ste. Anne Pioneer Museum. Camping. ▲

Rochfort Bridge Trading Post—A fun stop. Fresh bread and pies baked from scratch: rhubarb, saskatoon berries, sourcream and raisin pies, and more. Home-style meals. Licensed. Verandah. One of the largest all-Canadian gift stores. Distinctive items, including rare First Nations art: birch bark biting, fish scale art and moose tufting. Par 3 golf course with rentals. And you can photograph our cute donkeys. See display ad this section. [ADVERTISEMENT]

E 83.1 (133.7 km) **DC 283.9** (456.1 km) Paved turnouts with litter barrels both sides of highway.

E 85 (136.8 km) **DC 282** (453.8 km) **MAYERTHORPE** (pop. 1,692). One mile/1.6 km from the highway on a paved access road. Hotel, motel, restaurant, grocery store, gas stations with repair service, car wash, hospital, laundromat, post office, RCMP and banks. A public campground with 30 sites (no hookups, pit toilets) and 9-hole golf course are located 1 mile/1.6 km south of town. Airstrip located 2 miles/3.2 km southwest of town; no services. (Most northbound air travelers use Whitecourt airport, which has fuel.) ▲

E 87 (140 km) **DC 280** (450.6 km) Gas station and restaurant at junction with Highway 658 north to Goose Lake.

E 109 (175.4 km) **DC 258** (415.2 km) Lions Club Campground; 74 sites, flush toilets, showers, water, tables and firepits. Fee charged. ▲

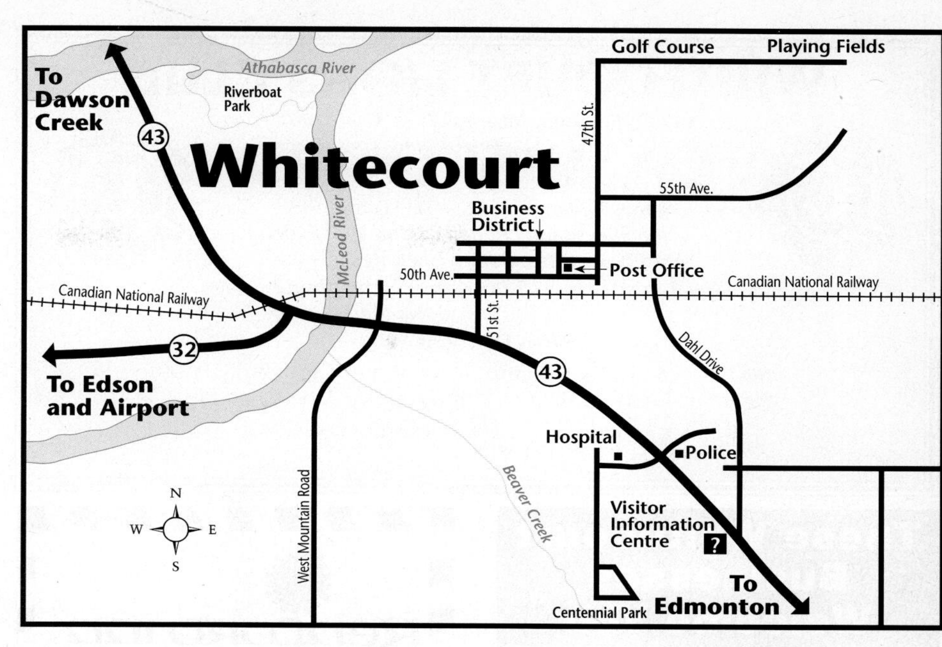

Whitecourt

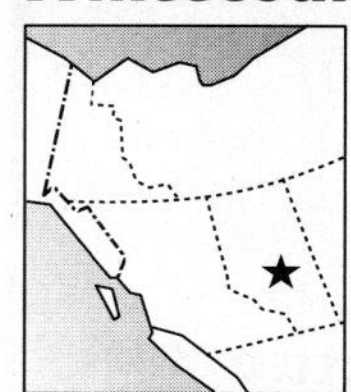

E 111.8 (179.9 km) **DC 255.2** (410.7 km). Located two hours from Edmonton. **Population:** 7,800. **Emergency Services: Police,** phone (403) 778-5454. **Fire Department,** phone (403) 778-2311. **Hospital** located on Hilltop, phone (403) 778-2285. Ambulance service available.

Visitor Information: Tourist information booth on Highway 43 west at the traffic lights. The helpful staff will assist with travel plans and directions to Whitecourt sights and activities. The booth is fully stocked with pamphlets and brochures. Open daily, 9 A.M. to 6 P.M., May 1 to Sept. 1; weekdays only, 9 A.M. to 5 P.M., September through April. Free dump station and freshwater fill-up adjacent tourist booth. Information is also available from the Chamber of Commerce, P.O. Box 1011, Whitecourt, AB T7S 1N9; phone (403) 778-5363, fax 778-2351.

Elevation: 2,567 feet/782m. **Radio:** 96.7 CJYR-FM, 107.5 SKUA-FM. **Television:** 10 channels. **Newspaper:** *Whitecourt Star* (weekly); *Whitecourt Advertiser* (biweekly).

Private Aircraft: Airport 4 miles/6.4 km south on Highway 32; elev. 2,567 feet/782m; length 5,800 feet/1,768m; paved; fuel 80, 100, jet (24-hour, self-serve). Aircraft maintenance, 24-hour flight service station, all-

WHITECOURT ADVERTISERS

Gateway Esso	Hwy. 43
Glenview Motel	Ph. (403) 778-2276
McDonald's	Hwy. 43
Quality Inn	Ph. (800) 228-5151
Renford Inn	Ph. (403) 778-3133
Sagitawah Tourist Park	Ph. (403) 778-3734
Tags Food & Gas/A&W	3711 Highway St.
White Kaps Motel & RV Parking	Ph. (403) 778-2246
Whitecourt Lions Club Campground	Hwy. 43

Alberta was named for Queen Victoria's daughter, Princess Louise Alberta.

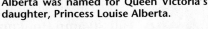

weather facility.

Transportation: Air—Local charter air service available; helicopter and fixed-wing aircraft. **Bus**—Greyhound service to Edmonton, Grande Prairie, Peace River and points north.

Located at the junction of Highways 43 and 32, Whitecourt dubs itself the "Gateway to the Alaska Highway and the fabulous North." Established as a small trading, trapping and forestry centre, Whitecourt became an important stop for Alaska Highway travelers when a 106-mile section of Highway 43 connecting Whitecourt and Valleyview was completed in October 1955. This new route was 72 miles shorter than the old Edmonton to Dawson Creek route via Slave Lake.

Several major forest industries operating in and around Whitecourt offer tours. Visitors may observe state-of-the-art technologies at sawmills, medium-density fiberboard production and pulp plants. Check with the tourist information booth or chamber of commerce for tour times.

The Eric S. Huestis Demonstration Forest, northwest of town on Highway 32 (see **Milepost E 117.1**), has 4.3 miles/7 km of self-guided trails with interpretive sites and information signs describing forest management techniques and the forest life-cycle; phone (403) 778-7165.

Recreational activities include an excellent 18-hole public golf course and fishing in area creeks, rivers and lakes (boat rentals at Carson–Pegasus Provincial Park). Swimming, in-line skating, tennis, gold panning, walking trails, beach volleyball and river boating are also enjoyed in summer. In the fall, big game hunting is very popular. During the winter there is ice fishing, snowmobiling and cross-country skiing on area trails, downhill skiing at a local facility, skating and curling, bowling and swimming at the indoor pool.

There are 14 hotels/motels, a bed and breakfast, 23 restaurants, 14 gas stations, several laundromats, 2 malls, 6 liquor stores and 5 banks. Most services are located on the highway or 2 blocks north in the downtown business district. Some gas stations and restaurants are open 24 hours.

This full-service community also supports a library and 7 churches. The Legion, located in the business district, is open year-round. Service clubs (Lions, Kinsmen) and community organizations (Masons, Knights of Columbus) welcome visitors.

A popular wilderness area nearby is Carson–Pegasus Provincial Park, located 14.6 miles/23.5 km west and north of town on Highway 32 (paved). The park has 182 campsites, electrical hookups, dump station, boat launch, boat rentals, concession, convenience store, hot showers and laundry facilities. Powered sites and showers are open year-round. There are 2 lakes at the park:

McLeod (Carson) Lake, stocked with rainbow trout, has a speed limit of 12 kmph for boaters; **Little McLeod (Pegasus) Lake** has northern pike and whitefish, electric motors and canoes only. Eagle River Outfitting (phone 403/778-3251), located 7 miles/11.3 km south of town via Highway 32, offers camping and wilderness activities.

East Access Route Log

(continued)

E 111.9 (180.1 km) **DC 255.1** (410.5 km) Beaver Creek bridge.

CAUTION: The highway between Whitecourt and Valleyview is known locally as "Moose Row" and "Moose Alley." Several moose–vehicle accidents occur yearly. Northbound travelers, watch for moose on road, especially at dusk and at night.

E 112.4 (180.9 km) **DC 254.6** (409.7 km) McLeod River.

E 112.6 (181.2 km) **DC 254.4** (409.4 km) Railroad crossing.

E 112.7 (181.4 km) **DC 254.3** (409.2 km) **Junction** with Highway 32 South (paved). Access to Eagle River Outfitting, 7 miles/11.3 km south; camping, wilderness activities. Highway 32 leads 42 miles/68 km to Yellowhead Highway 16 (see **Milepost E 97.5** in the YELLOWHEAD HIGHWAY section).

E 112.9 (181.7 km) **DC 254.1** (408.9 km) Gas stations both sides of highway.

E 113.4 (182.5 km) **DC 253.6** (408.1 km) Turnoff to north for Sagitawah Tourist Park (RV camping) and Riverboat Park, both at the confluence of the McLeod and Athabasca rivers. Riverboat Park has a boat launch, picnic area and toilets.

E 113.6 (182.8 km) **DC 253.4** (407.8 km) Athabasca River bridge.

E 115.6 (186 km) **DC 251.4** (404.6 km) Vehicle inspection station to north.

E 117.1 (188.4 km) **DC 249.9** (402.2 km) **Junction** with Highway 32 North (paved). Access to Eric S. Huestis Demonstration Forest (self-guided trails and information signs on forest life-cycle) and Carson–Pegasus Provincial Park. The provincial park, 9.3 miles/15 km north, has 182 campsites, electrical hookups, group camping area, tables, flush toilets, showers, water, dump station, firewood, store, laundromat and playground. (Powered sites and showers open year-round.) Boat launch, boat rentals and rainbow trout fishing are available.

E 117.6 (189.2 km) **DC 249.4** (401.4 km) Alberta Newsprint Co. to south.

E 122 (196.3 km) **DC 245** (394.3 km) Turnout with litter barrel.

E 122.5 (197.1 km) **DC 244.5** (393.5 km) Chickadee Creek government campground; 7 sites, pit toilets, water, tables and firepits.

E 124.3 (200 km) **DC 242.7** (390.6 km) Chickadee Creek.

E 131.8 (212.1 km) **DC 235.2** (378.5 km) Turnouts with litter barrels both sides of highway.

E 140.5 (226.1 km) **DC 226.5** (364.5 km) Two Creeks government campground; 8 campsites, pit toilets, water, picnic tables and firepits.

E 142.5 (229.3 km) **DC 224.5** (361.3 km) Turnout with litter barrel to south.

E 143 (230.1 km) **DC 224** (360.5 km) Turnout with litter barrel to north.

E 152 (244.6 km) **DC 215** (346 km) Iosegun Creek government campground; 12 sites, pit toilets, water, tables and firepits.

E 159 (255.9 km) **DC 208** (334.7 km) Fox Creek airport.

Fox Creek

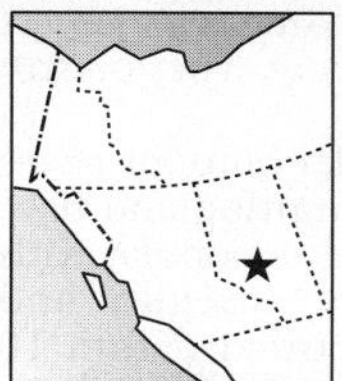

E 162 (260.7 km) **DC 205** (329.9 km) **Population:** 2,600. **Elevation:** 2,800 feet/853m. **Emergency Services: RCMP,** phone (403) 622-3740. **Ambulance,** phone (403) 622-3000. **Hospital,** phone (403) 622-3545. **Visitor Information:** Tourist Information Centre at the Rig Earth Resource Park, open in summer; gift shop, coffee area and selection of informational videos to view; phone (403) 622-2000. Off-season contact the Town Office at (403) 622-3896 for information.

Private Aircraft: Fox Creek airport, 3 miles/4.8 km south on Highway 43; elev. 2,840 feet/866m; length, 2,950 feet/899m; paved; no fuel. Unattended.

All visitor facilities including 2 hotels, 3

A 150-foot/46m drilling rig marks Fox Creek's visitor information centre.

(Earl L. Brown, staff)

FOX CREEK ADVERTISERS

Alaskan Motel, The ....Ph. (403) 622-3073
Ernie O's Restaurant ....Ph. (403) 778-4844
Fox Creek R.V. Campground ....Ph. (403) 622-3896
Guest House, The ....Ph. (403) 778-4844
Regal Motor Inn ....Ph. (403) 622-3333

motels and gas stations with repair service. Grocery store open daily until midnight. Convenience stores, pharmacy, laundromats, liquor stores, restaurants, banks and bank machines.

Recreation facilities include a 9-hole golf course with grass greens and driving range; outdoor swimming pool; tennis courts; and ice arena with 4 sheet curling rink.

A popular winter activity is snowmobiling. Snowmobile enthusiasts can ride for miles on the "Golden Triangle" that links the communities of Swan Hills, Whitecourt and Fox Creek.

Municipal campground with 17 sites, full hookups, showers and dump station ▲

Fox Creek is in the centre of oil and gas exploration and production. (A Jomax 4, 150-foot/46m drilling rig is on display at Rig Earth Resource Park.) North America's largest known natural gas field is here. The forestry industry is also prominent.

Fox Creek is also a popular outdoor recreation area, with plenty of hunting and fishing in summer. Two local lakes popular with residents and visitors are **Iosegun** and **Smoke lakes**, which are located within 10 miles/16 km on either side of the townsite on good gravel road. Camping, boat launch and fishing for northern pike, perch and pickerel are favorites for this area. ▲

East Access Route Log

(continued)

E 167 (268.7 km) **DC 200** (321.9 km) Turnout with litter barrel.

E 169.5 (272.8 km) **DC 197.5** (317.8 km) Turnouts with litter barrels both sides of highway.

E 172 (276.8 km) **DC 195** (313.8 km) Pines government campground; 25 sites, shelter, firewood, pump water, tables and pit toilets. ▲

E 182.1 (293 km) **DC 184.9** (297.6 km) Turnout with litter barrel.

E 186.4 (300 km) **DC 180.6** (290.6 km) **Sands Wilderness Campground & R.V. Park.** 24-hour security campground. Power and unserviced sites, tenting area. Spacious pull-throughs with power. Water fill-up and dump station. Laundromat, showers. Concession; hot and cold snacks. Horseshoe pits and mini-golf. Hiking trail. Children's playground. Free firewood. Guests have said, "One of the nicest campgrounds in Canada." Outdoor adventures—trail rides and raft trips. Your host—"Wild Bill" Sands, Box 511, Valleyview, AB T0H 3N0. Phone/fax: (403) 524-3757. [ADVERTISEMENT] ▲

E 192 (309 km) **DC 175** (281.6 km) **LITTLE SMOKY** (pop. about 50). Motel, RV park, tea house, gift shop, pay phone, propane, grocery store, service station and post office. ▲

Little Smoky Motel & Campground. See display ad this section. ▲

E 192.2 (309.3 km) **DC 174.8** (281.3 km) Little Smoky River bridge.

E 193.5 (311.4 km) **DC 173.5** (279.2 km) Waskahigan (House) River bridge at confluence with Smoky River. Government campground with 24 sites, pit toilets, water, tables and firepits. ▲

E 197 (317 km) **DC 170** (273.6 km) Turnout.

E 206.7 (332.6 km) **DC 160.3** (258 km) Turnout with litter barrel.

E 208.5 (335.5 km) **DC 158.5** (255.1 km) Peace pipeline storage tanks.

E 210.8 (339.2 km) **DC 156.2** (251.4 km) Valleyview Riverside golf course.

E 213.2 (343.1 km) **DC 153.8** (247.5 km) Valleyview tourist information centre (phone 403/524-2410); pay phone, postal service, souvenirs, picnic tables, flush toilets. Open daily in summer, 8 A.M. to 8 P.M.

E 213.4 (343.4 km) **DC 153.6** (247.2 km) Valleyview airport to west.

Private Aircraft: Valleyview airport; elev. 2,434 feet/742m; length, 3,300 feet/1,006m; paved; no fuel. Unattended.

CAUTION: The highway between Valleyview and Whitecourt is known locally as "Moose Row" and "Moose Alley." Several moose–vehicle accidents occur yearly. Southbound travelers, watch for moose on road, especially at dusk and at night.

Valleyview

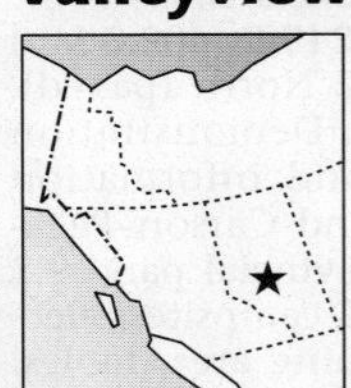

E 214.1 (344.4 km) **DC 152.9** (246.1 km) **Junction** of Highways 43 and 34, approximately 4 hours drive time from Edmonton. **Population:** 1,906. **Emergency Services: RCMP**, phone (403) 524-3343. **Fire Department**, phone (403) 524-3211. **Ambulance**, phone (403) 524-3916. **Hospital**, Valleyview General, 45 beds, phone (403) 524-3356.

Visitor Information: Major tourist information centre and rest stop located 0.9 mile/1.5 km south of Valleyview on Highway 43. Open daily, 8 A.M. to 8 P.M. from May through Labour Day weekend; phone (403) 524-2410, fax (403) 524-2727, e-mail valvadm@vvw-TEQ.Net. Postal service, souvenirs and refreshments, as well as regional travel and community events and services information. For information on small business opportunities, contact the Valleyview Regional Economic Development Board office at (403) 524-5051.

Elevation: 2,400 feet/732m. **Newspaper:** *Valley Views* (weekly). **Transportation: Air**—Airport 0.7 mile/1.1 km south (see **Milepost**

VALLEYVIEW ADVERTISERS

Horizon Motel, Restaurant & Gift Shop..................Ph. (403) 524-3904
Sherk's R.V. Park..............Ph. (403) 524-4949
Town of Valleyview..........Ph. (403) 524-5150
Valleyview Esso Service....Ph. (403) 524-3504

E 213.4). **Bus**—Greyhound.

Valleyview, known as the "Portal to the Peace Country" of northwestern Alberta, is located at the junction of Highways 43 and 34. From Valleyview, Highway 34 leads west to Grande Prairie and Dawson Creek. Highway 43 continues north to Peace River. From Peace River, travelers may follow the Mackenzie Highway to Northwest Territories (see the MACKENZIE ROUTE section for details).

Highway 43 also connects with Highway 2 east to Athabasca, the Slave Lake route from Edmonton used by Alaska Highway travelers until 1955, when Highway 43 was completed to Whitecourt.

Originally called Red Willow Creek when it was homesteaded in 1916, Valleyview boomed with the discovery of oil and gas in the 1950s, and services grew along with the population. Today, Valleyview's economy has diversified to include the oil and gas industry, forestry, tourism, agriculture and government services. Farming consists mainly of grain, oilseed, beef cattle and forage production.

The community has a full range of services including banks, automatic teller machines, post office, a library, several churches and a veterinary clinic.

All visitor facilities available, including 5 motels and hotels, several restaurants, gas stations (many with major repair service, propane and diesel), laundromat, grocery, liquor store, clothing and hardware stores, a bakery, gift shops and a golf course. Some gas stations and restaurants open 24 hours a day.

The area boasts many lakes and streams, abundant wildlife, and lush vegetation, including berries. Summer travelers can take advantage of the long summer days here by attending local rodeos, fairs and festivals; playing a round of golf on one of the local golf courses; visiting one of the provincial parks along Sturgeon Lake; taking a dip in the outdoor swimming pool in town; or exploring the wilderness by all-terrain vehicle, horse, canoe or hiking trail.

Lion's Den Campground, west end of town, has 19 sites with hookups, tables, showers and toilets. Full-service private campground (Sherk's RV Park) with 56 sites, close to town. ▲

East Access Route Log

(continued)

E 216 (347.6 km) **DC 151** (243 km) Highway 43 continues north 86 miles/138.4 km to **PEACE RIVER** (pop. 6,690). Highway 43 **junctions** with the Mackenzie Highway 12 miles/19 km west of Peace River. See the MACKENZIE ROUTE section for a description of Peace River and the log of the Mackenzie Highway to western Northwest Territories.

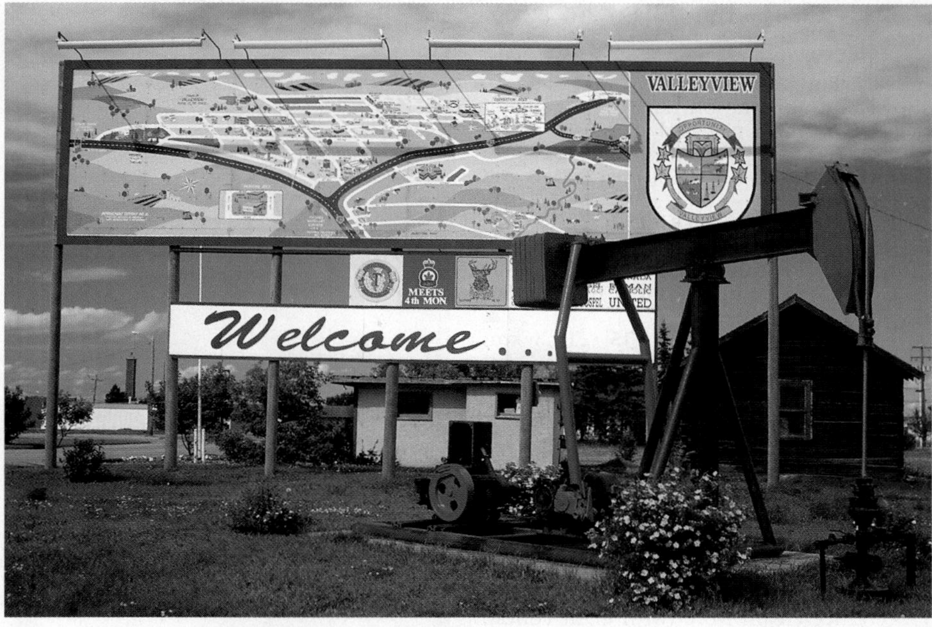

Located at a major highway junction, Valleyview is a popular stop for tourists.
(© Wes Bergen, DIARAMA)

Highway 34 begins westbound from Valleyview; continue west on Highway 34.

ALBERTA HIGHWAY 34

E 222.6 (358.2 km) **DC 144.4** (232.4 km) 24-hour convenience store and gas.

E 224.7 (361.6 km) **DC 142.3** (229 km) Access north to **Sturgeon Lake**; fishing and camping. Williamson Provincial Park (1.2 miles/2 km); 60 campsites, boat launch, showers, dump station. Fishing for perch, pickerel, northern pike and whitefish.

E 227 (365.3 km) **DC 140** (225.3 km) **CALAIS** (pop. about 550); post office and grocery store.

E 230 (370.1 km) **DC 137** (220.5 km) Private campground and marina on **Sturgeon Lake**; fishing, boat rentals.

Cosy Cove Campground & Marina. See display ad this section.

E 232 (373.3 km) **DC 135** (217.3 km) Sturgeon Heights. Turnoff for Youngs Point Provincial Park, 6 miles/10 km northeast; 97 campsites (some with electrical hookups), firewood, showers, playground, hiking trails, dump station, boat launch, fish cleaning station, beach, fishing in **Sturgeon Lake.**

E 235 (378.2 km) **DC 132** (212.4 km) Turnouts both sides of highway; historic marker.

E 240 (386.2 km) **DC 127** (204.4 km) **CROOKED CREEK** (pop. 10); gas station, grocery, ice cream store (with giant cones), post office and pay phone.

E 246 (395.9 km) **DC 121** (194.7 km) **DeBOLT**, a small farming community north of highway with a general store and district museum. Garage with gas on highway.

E 253.8 (408.7 km) **DC 113.2** (181.9 km) **Junction.** Forestry Trunk Road leads 632 miles/1,017 km south, intersecting Yellowhead Highway 16 and Trans-Canada Highway 1, to Highway 3.

E 255.2 (410.7 km) **DC 111.8** (179.9 km) Microwave towers to east.

E 259.5 (417.6 km) **DC 107.5** (173 km) Smoky River bridge and government campground; 30 sites, shelter, firepits, firewood, tables, pit toilets, water pump and boat launch.

E 262 (421.6km) **DC 105** (169 km) **West Smoky RV Campsites.** You will find us on the west side of Smoky River. (New—1996.) Pull-through sites, power, fresh water, washrooms, showers, laundromat, dumping station, picnic tables, firepits, free wood, mini-golf, horseshoes and play area. 5 minutes from food store, gas, restaurant. 20 minutes from Grande Prairie major shopping and services. Owners Cliff and Berniece Sydbo. Phone/fax (403) 538-3024. [ADVERTISEMENT]

E 264 (424.9 km) **DC 103** (165.7 km) **BEZANSON.** Post office, gas station with diesel, cafe, liquor store, grocery, general store, propane.

E 269 (432.9 km) **DC 98** (157.7 km) Kleskun Hills Park to north 3 miles/5 km. The park features an ancient sea bottom with fossils of dinosaurs and marine life.

Bright yellow canola fields along the highway near Grande Prairie.

(© Roger Pickenpaugh)

E 270.6 (435.5 km) **DC 96.4** (155.1 km) Turnout to north with historical sign about the Kleskun Hills.

E 283.5 (456.2 km) **DC 83.5** (134.4 km) Weigh scales to north.

E 283.8 (456.7 km) **DC 83.2** (133.9 km) Railroad crossing.

E 284 (457 km) **DC 83** (133.6 km) **Junction**, Highways 34 and 2. Westbound travelers turn south for Grande Prairie and Highway 2 to Dawson Creek (log follows). Turn north on Highway 2 for Sexsmith (8.5 miles/13.7 km), site of the Sexsmith Blacksmith Shop, Sexsmith Municipal campground and Grimshaw (105 miles/169 km), Mile 0 of the Mackenzie Highway to Northwest Territories (see MACKENZIE ROUTE section).

ALBERTA HIGHWAY 2

From its junction with Highway 34, Highway 2 leads south into Grande Prairie (description follows). To reach Grande Prairie city centre, keep straight ahead on Highway 2 (Clairmont Road) as it becomes 100th Street and follow it downtown. To skirt the downtown area, take the Highway 2 Bypass. Highway 2 becomes 100th Avenue (Richmond Avenue) on the west side of Grande Prairie.

NOTE: Bighorn Highway 40 (paved) connects Grande Prairie with Grande Cache and Yellowhead Highway 16. To reach the Bighorn Highway, follow Wapiti Road (108th Street) south from Highway 2 on the west side of Grande Prairie. See BIGHORN HIGHWAY log page 52.

Grande Prairie

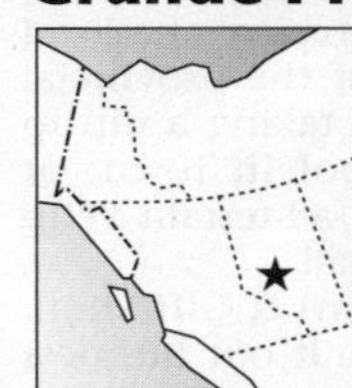

E 288 (463.5 km) **DC 79** (127.1 km). Located at **junction** of Highways 2 and 34. **Population:** 32,000. **Emergency Services: RCMP**, phone (403) 538-5700. **Fire Department**, phone (403) 532-2100. **Ambulance**, phone (403) 532-9511. **Hospital**, Queen Elizabeth, 10409 98th St., phone (403) 538-7100.

Visitor Information: Chamber of Commerce office at 10632 102nd Ave, T8V 6J8; open weekdays 8:30 A.M. to 8:30 P.M. Visitor service center located off Highway 2 Bypass on 106th Street at Bear Creek Reservoir, open 9 A.M. to 9 P.M. in July and August, shorter hours in June. The Grande Prairie Rotary Club operates a free bus tour of the city Monday, Tuesday and Thursday at 7 P.M.

Check with the infocentre for details.

Private Aircraft: Airport 3 miles/4.8 km west; elev. 2,195 feet/669m; length 6,500 feet/1,981m; paved; fuel 80, 100, jet. 24-hour flight service station.

Elevation: 2,198 feet/670m. **Transportation: Air**—Scheduled air service to Vancouver, BC, Edmonton, Calgary, and points north. **Bus**—Greyhound.

Grande Prairie was first incorporated as a village in 1914, as a town in 1919, and as a city in 1958, by which time its population had reached nearly 8,000.

With a strong and diverse economy based on agriculture (cereal grains, fescue, honey, livestock), forestry (a bleached kraft pulp mill, sawmill and oriented strand board plant), and oil and gas, Grande Prairie is a regional centre for much of northwestern Alberta and northeastern British Columbia. The trumpeter swan is the symbol of Grande Prairie and is featured throughout the city.

A variety of shopping is available at 2 major malls, several strip malls and a well-developed downtown area. Visitor facilities include several restaurants, hotels, motels, and bed and breakfasts. Recreation facilities include 2 swimming pools, 3 18-hole golf courses, a par 3 golf course, ball diamonds, amusement park, tennis courts, public library, a public art gallery and 3 private galleries. Churches representing almost every denomination are located in Grande Prairie. There are several public schools and a regional college.

Area attractions include Muskoseepi Park, which follows the Bear Creek corridor. The park includes 9 miles/15 km of paved walking and biking trails, a bird sanctuary at Crystal Lake, picnic areas, swimming pool, lawn bowling, mini-golf, a stocked pool, playground and canoe, paddleboat and bike rentals. Visitor services are available in the Pavilion. Nearby is the Grande Prairie Museum & Pioneer Village and the Regional College, a unique circular facility designed by Douglas Cardinal. Several of the downtown buildings have murals by local artists.

Weyerhaeuser offers tours of their pulp mill and sawmill in summer; phone (403) 539-8213 for details.

The area has prime hunting for both migratory birds and big game. Area lakes are the nesting sites of the trumpeter swan. Hiking, camping and fishing are popular outdoor activities.

Annual events include the Stompede the first weekend in June, several smaller rodeos, Canada Games, Highland Games, pari-mutuel racing during July, the County Fair, Heritage Day and the Dinosaur Festival. Contact the visitor information centre for more information.

Three campsites within the city limits offer showers and full hookups. Rotary Park

(Continues on page 53)

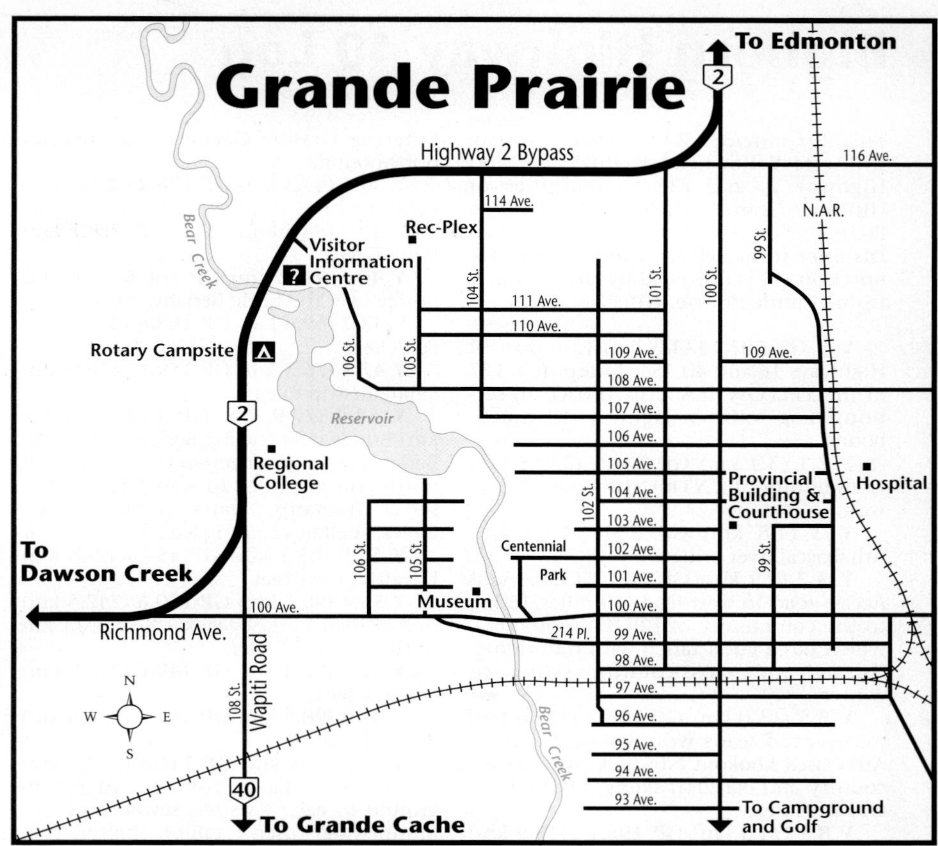

GRANDE PRAIRIE ADVERTISERS

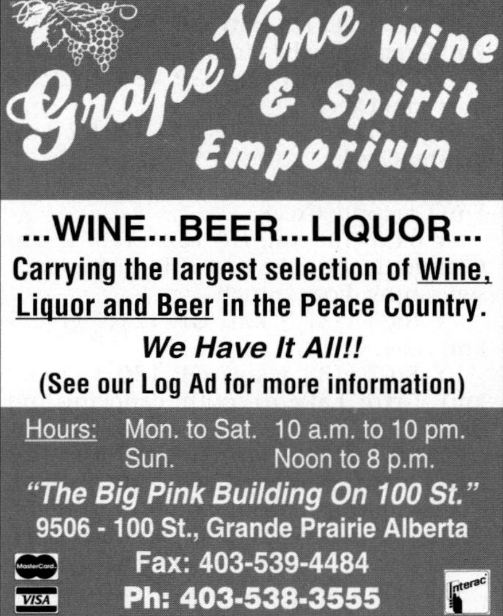

Welcome to the North Country!

Bighorn Highway 40 Log

This 207-mile/333.2-km paved highway connects Yellowhead Highway 16 and Highway 2, and the communities of Hinton, Grande Cache and Grande Prairie.

Distance from Yellowhead Highway 16 junction (Y) is followed by the distance from Grande Prairie (GP).

Y 0 GP 207 (333.2 km) **Junction** of Highways 16 and 40. (See **Milepost E 177** in the YELLOWHEAD HIGHWAY 16 section.) Log follows Highway 40 northbound.

Y 2.1 (3.4 km) **GP 204.9** (329.8 km) Community of ENTRANCE (pop. 79) to west.

Y 3 (4.8 km) **GP 204** (328.4 km) Athabasca River bridge.

Y 3.7 (5.9 km) **GP 203.3** (327.3 km) Access road to west leads 10 miles/16 km to the community of **BRULE** (pop. 161), which has a guest ranch with trail riding, fishing and cross-country skiing in winter.

Y 8.5 (13.6 km) **GP 198.5** (319.6 km) Access road leads west 4 miles/7 km to Athabasca Lookout Nordic Centre; cross-country and biathlon skiing, hiking trails and day lodge.

Y 8.9 (14.3 km) **GP 198.1** (318.9 km) Turnout to east with litter barrels and information sign about William A. Switzer Provincial Park.

Y 9.8 (15.8 km) **GP 197.2** (317.4 km) Access road leads east to Jarvis Lake day-use area; pump water, public phone, beach and boat launch.

Y 12.8 (20.5 km) **GP 194.2** (312.7 km) Kelley's Bathtub day-use area to west; hiking trail, public phone, swimming.

Y 15.2 (24.5 km) **GP 191.8** (308.7 km) Winter Creek.

Y 15.3 (24.7 km) **GP 191.7** (308.5 km) Side road to east leads 1.2 miles/2 km to Cache Lake and 2.4 miles/4 km to Graveyard Lake. Cache Lake campground has 14 sites, sewer hookups, water pump, picnic tables, shelter, children's playground, camping fee $9. Graveyard campground has 16 sites, sewer hookups, water available at Cache Lake campground, camping fee $9. ▲

Y 16.8 (27 km) **GP 190.3** (306.2 km) Access road to east leads to **Gregg Lake** day-use area and campground; 164 sites, sewer hookups, tap water, picnic tables, shelter, children's playground, fish-cleaning stand, beach, hiking trails, public phone. Camping fee $13. ▲

Y 17.6 (28.4 km) **GP 189.4** (304.8 km) Turnout to west with litter barrels and information sign about William A. Switzer Provincial Park for southbound travelers.

Y 22.9 (36.9 km) **GP 184.1** (296.3 km) Wildhay River bridge.

Y 25.6 (41.2 km) **GP 181.4** (292 km) Side road to west leads 20 miles/32 km to Rock Lake campground on Rock Lake; 96 sites, sewer hookups, water pump, picnic tables, shelter, hiking trails, boat launch, camping fee $9. ▲

Y 28.9 (46.5 km) **GP 178.1** (286.7 km) Entering Grande Cache ranger district northbound.

Y 30.6 (49.3 km) **GP 176.4** (283.9 km) Fred Creek.

Y 36.3 (58.5 km) **GP 170.7** (274.7 km) Pinto Creek.

Y 40.5 (65.2 km) **GP 166.5** (268 km) Bridge over the Little Berland River.

Y 43.2 (69.6 km) **GP 163.8** (263.6 km) Fox Creek.

Y 47.4 (76.3 km) **GP 159.6** (256.9 km) Small airstrip to east.

Y 48.4 (77.9 km) **GP 158.6** (255.3 km) Bridge over the Big Berland River. Big Berland River government campground at north end of bridge to west has 12 sites, sewer hookups, water pump, picnic tables, shelter, camping fee $9. ▲

Y 52.9 (85.2 km) **GP 154.1** (248 km) Hendrickson Creek.

Y 56.4 (90.7 km) **GP 150.6** (242.5 km) Access road to east leads 1.8 miles/3 km to Hucklebury Tower.

Y 57.4 (92.3 km) **GP 149.6** (240.9 km) Shand Creek.

Y 61.3 (98.6 km) **GP 145.7** (234.6 km) Burleigh Creek.

Y 65.2 (105 km) **GP 141.8** (228.2 km) Pierre Grey's Lakes government campground to east; 83 sites, sewer hookups, pump water, picnic tables, shelter, fireplaces, firewood (for sale), hiking trails, boat launch, camping fee $9. ▲

Y 66.1 (106.4 km) **GP 140.9** (226.8 km) Entering **MUSKEG RIVER** (pop. 22) northbound; pay phone.

Y 67.9 (109.3 km) **GP 139.1** (223.9 km) **Junction** with Highway 734 (Forestry Trunk Road, gravel) which leads north 116 miles/187 km to Highway 34. There are no services along the highway.

Y 69.4 (111.7 km) **GP 137.6** (221.5 km) Turnout to south.

Y 70 (112.6 km) **GP 137** (220.6 km) Veronique River bridge.

Y 74.1 (119.3 km) **GP 132.9** (213.9 km) Muskeg River bridge.

Y 74.9 (120.6 km) **GP 132.1** (212.6 km) Mason Creek day-use area; picnic facilities and hiking trail to the Muskeg River.

Y 75.1 (120.8 km) **GP 131.9** (212.3 km) Mason Creek.

Y 75.7 (121.8 km) **GP 131.3** (211.4 km) Grande Cache airport to south.

Y 80.8 (130.1 km) **GP 126.2** (203.1 km) Susa Creek.

Y 82 (132 km) **GP 125** (201.2 km) Washy Creek.

Y 84.1 (135.3 km) **GP 122.9** (197.9 km) Carconte Creek.

Y 84.5 (136 km) **GP 122.5** (197.2 km) Grande Cache Lake to south; picnic area, swimming, boat launch.

Y 85.3 (137.3 km) **GP 121.7** (195.9 km) Allen Creek.

Y 86.7 (139.5 km) **GP 120.3** (193.7 km) **Victor Lake** to south; canoeing and fishing.

Y 88.1 (141.7 km) **GP 118.9** (191.5 km) Entering Grande Cache northbound. Visitor information and interpretive centre to east. Wildlife displays, rest area, the Bighorn Gallery and souvenirs.

Grande Cache

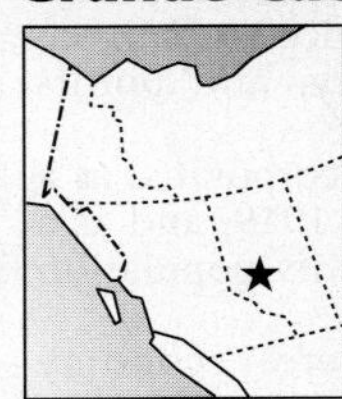

Y 88.2 (142 km) **GP 118.8** (191.2 km) Located 116 miles/188 km south of Grande Prairie. **Population:** 5,000. **Emergency services: RCMP**, phone (403) 827-2222. **Hospital**, phone (403) 827-3701. **Ambulance**, phone (403) 827-3600. **Fire department**, phone (403) 827-3600.

Visitor information: Tourist information centre is located on 100th Street (Highway 40) at the south entrance into town, open 9 A.M. to 7 P.M. daily, May–September; 9 A.M. to 5 P.M. Monday–Friday the rest of the year. Phone (888) 827-3790.

Elevation: 4,200 feet/1,280m. **Private Aircraft:** Grande Cache airport, 12 miles/19 km east on Highway 40; elev. 4,117 feet/1,255m; length 5,000 feet/1,524m; asphalt; no fuel available.

Grande Cache was established in 1969 in conjunction with resource development by McIntyre Porcupine Coal Ltd. In 1980 a sawmill was constructed by British Columbia Forest Products Ltd. and in 1984 a medium security correctional centre was built.

Historically, the location was used as a staging area for fur trappers and Natives prior to their departure to trap lines in the valleys and mountain ranges now known as Willmore Wilderness Park. Upon their return, they stored large caches of furs while waiting for transportation opportunities to trading posts.

Today Grande Cache, nestled on the leeward side of the Rocky Mountains, is a picturesque and vibrant community. Visitor facilities include hotel, bed and breakfast, 4 motels, 2 banks, restaurants, laundromats, service stations with repair facilities, car washes and a library. Shopping facilities include several small shopping centres, 2 supermarkets, a bakery, sporting goods store and department store.

Recreational facilities include a recreation centre which houses a curling rink, swimming pool, skating rink, fitness rooms and saunas. Grande Cache Golf and Country Club, located in the northeast part of town, has 9 holes, grass greens, clubhouse and pro shop.

Camping at Marv Moore municipal campground on the south side of the highway, at the north end of town just past the golf course. There are 55 sites, full hookups, showers, flush toilets, public phone, children's playground. Camping fee from $10 (dry camping) to $15 (hookups). ▲

Big Horn Highway Log

(continued)

Y 88.7 (142.7 km) **GP 118.3** (190.5 km) Highway 40 descends northbound to the Smoky River.

Y 91.3 (146.9 km) **GP 115.7** (186.3 km) Smoky River campground to south has 22 sites, sewer hookups, no water, shelters, firewood, firepits, tables, pit toilets, boat launch. Camping fee $8. Trail access to Willmore Wilderness Park. ▲

Y 91.5 (147.2 km) **GP 115.5** (186 km) **Smoky River** bridge, fishing for arctic grayling, Dolly Varden and whitefish.

Y 92.3 (148.6 km) **GP 114.7** (184.6 km) Turnoff to south for Willmore Wilderness Park and Hell's Gate campground (4 miles/6.4 km south) with 10 sites, sewer hookups, horse holding areas, camping fee $8. ▲

Y 95.3 (153.4 km) **GP 111.7** (179.8 km) Grande Cache gun range to east. Northbound, the highway parallels the Northern Alberta Resource Railroad and the Smoky River.

Y 100.8 (162.2 km) **GP 106.2** (171 km) Turnout to east overlooks Smoky River Coal Ltd. and H.R. Milner Generating Station.

Y 104.8 (168.7 km) **GP 102.2** (164.5 km) Entering Grande Prairie Forest northbound, entering Edson Forest southbound.

Y 106.7 (171.7 km) **GP 100.3** (161.5 km) Turnoff to east for Sheep Creek day-use area; shaded picnic tables, water pump, firepits, firewood, litter barrels, outhouses and gravel parking areas. Boat launch on the Smoky River.

Y 107.1 (172.4 km) **GP 99.9** (160.8 km) Sheep Creek. Sheep Creek campground to east; 9 sites, sewer hookups, water pump, camping fee $8. ▲

Y 108.4 (174.5 km) **GP 98.6** (158.7 km) Entering Game Country Tourist Zone northbound, Evergreen Tourist Zone southbound.

Y 110.1 (177.2 km) **GP 96.9** (156 km) Wayandie Road. Highway ascends steep hill northbound, some sections of 7 percent grade.

Y 115.9 (186.5 km) **GP 91.1** (146.7 km) Small turnout to east.

Y 125.1 (201.3 km) **GP 81.9** (131.9 km) Southview recreation area to east; gravel parking area, shaded picnic tables, litter barrels, outhouses, highbush cranberries in season.

Y 128.5 (206.8 km) **GP 78.5** (126.4 km) *CAUTION: logging trucks next 36 miles/60 km northbound.*

Y 130.4 (209.8 km) **GP 76.6** (123.4 km) 16th base line sign marks north–south hunting boundary.

Y 142 (228.6 km) **GP 65** (104.6 km) Distance marker indicates Grande Prairie 62 miles/100 km.

Y 145.6 (234.3 km) **GP 61.4** (98.9 km) Kakwa River bridge.

Y 145.9 (234.8 km) **GP 61.1** (98.4 km) Turnoff for **Kakwa River** campground and day-use area; 14 sites, sewer hookups, picnic tables, firewood, firepits, water pump, litter barrels, outhouses, gravel parking area. Camping fee $5.50. Fishing for arctic grayling. ▲

Y 155.2 (249.7 km) **GP 51.8** (83.5 km) Side road to west leads 7 miles/11 km to Unocal oil field office.

Y 159.1 (256.1 km) **GP 47.9** (77.1 km) Access road to east leads 3.6 miles/6 km to **Musreau Lake** campground and day-use area. There are 50 picnic sites, 69 campsites, sewer hookups, picnic tables, firewood, firepits, water pump, litter barrels, outhouses, equestrian trails, boat launch and fishing. ▲

Y 161.8 (260.4 km) **GP 45.2** (72.8 km) Sheep Creek.

Y 164.3 (264.4 km) **GP 42.7** (68.8 km) Cutbank River bridge. River access at north end of bridge. Area historic sites and museums sign.

Y 165.6 (266.5 km) **GP 41.4** (66.7 km) Elk Creek.

Y 165.8 (266.8 km) **GP 41.2** (66.4 km) *CAUTION: Logging trucks next 36 miles/60 km southbound.*

Y 172.2 (277.1 km) **GP 34.8** (56.1 km) Distance marker indicates Grande Prairie 31 miles/50 km.

Y 179.5 (288.9 km) **GP 27.5** (44.3 km) Canfor Road leads east to Gold Creek Gas Plant and Highway 734.

Y 180.9 (291.1 km) **GP 26.1** (42.1 km) Big Mountain Creek.

Y 182.8 (294.1 km) **GP 24.2** (39.1 km) Bald Mountain Creek.

Y 189.4 (304.5 km) **GP 17.6** (28.5 km) Access road leads west 0.1 mile/0.2 km to picnic area and 7 miles/11 km to Grovedale.

Y 191.1 (307.5 km) **GP 15.9** (25.7 km) Bent Pipe Creek.

Y 194.1 (312.4 km) **GP 12.9** (20.8 km) Ainsworth O.S.B. Plant.

Y 199.7 (321.3 km) **GP 7.3** (11.8 km) **Junction** with Highway 666 which leads southwest to O'Brien Provincial Park and day-use area; water pump, firewood, playground, hiking trails. Also access to Nitehawk ski resort, which has a 460-foot/140-m rise, 3 runs, ski lifts and food service. Highway 666 continues from this junction 5 miles/8 km to Grovedale. ▲

Y 199.8 (321.5 km) **GP 7.2** (11.6 km) Wapiti River bridge.

Y 200.1 (322 km) **GP 6.9** (11.1 km) Entering Grovedale ranger district southbound.

Y 201.6 (324.4 km) **GP 5.4** (8.7 km) Access road leads east 15 miles/25 km to the Dunes golf and winter club; 18 holes, grass greens, driving range, pro shop.

Y 204.7 (329.4 km) **GP 2.3** (3.7 km) Access to Dunvegan Garden and Old Barn Tea House and Gift Shop to west.

Y 207 (333.2 km) **GP 0 Junction** of Highways 40 and 2 at Grande Prairie.

Return to Milepost E 284
East Access Route

(Continued from page 51)
public campground is located off the Highway 2 Bypass at the northwest edge of town near the college. Wee Links Golf and Campground and the South Bear Creek Campground are located at the south end on 100 Avenue. ▲

East Access Route Log

(continued)

HIGHWAY 2 WEST

E 298 (479.6 km) **DC 69** (111 km) Saskatoon Island Provincial Park is 1.9 miles/3 km north on park road; 96 campsites, dump station, boat launch, swimming, playground; Saskatoon berry picking in July; game preserve for trumpeter swans. ▲

E 299 (481.2 km) **DC 68** (109.4 km) **WEMBLEY** (pop. 1,463) has a hotel (banking service and liquor store at hotel), post office, grocery store, gas stop, car wash and restaurants. Picnicking and camping at Sunset Lake Park in town (dumpstation). Camping May 1 to Oct. 15 at Pipestone Creek County Park, 9 miles/14.5 km south; 99 sites, showers, flush toilets, dump station, boat launch, firewood, fishing, playground, fossil display and an 18-hole golf course with grass greens nearby. Bird watching is good here for red-winged blackbirds and yellow-headed blackbirds. ▲

Beaverlodge

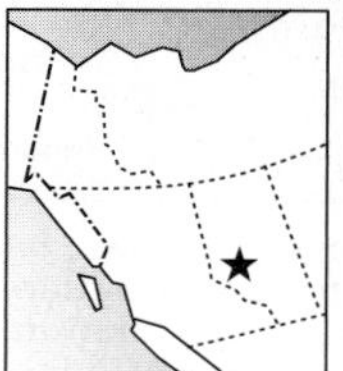

E 311 (500.5 km) **DC 56** (90.1 km) **Population:** 1,997. **Elevation:** 2,419 feet/737m. **Emergency Services: RCMP**, phone 911. **Ambulance**, phone 911. **Hospital**, Beaverlodge Municipal Hospital, phone (403) 354-2136.

Visitor Information: Located in the restored Lower Beaver Lodge School at Pioneer Campsite on the north side of Highway 2 at the west end of town.

Private Aircraft: DeWit Airpark 2 miles/3.2 km south; elev. 2,289 feet/1,698m; length 3,000 feet/914m; paved; no fuel.

Beaverlodge is a service centre for the area with RCMP, hospital, medical and dental clinic. There are 9 churches, schools, a swimming pool and tennis courts.

Visitor services include 3 motels, 8 restaurants and gas stations. There are supermarkets, banks, a drugstore, car wash and sporting goods store. Beaverlodge Area Cultural Centre, at the south end of town, features local arts and crafts as well as a tea room. South Peace Centennial Museum is west of town (see **Milepost E 312**). Camping is available at the municipal Pioneer Campsite (19 sites, showers, dump station, electrical hookups, tourist information). The Beaverlodge Airpark, 2 miles/3.2 km south of town, is becoming a popular stopover on the flying route to Alaska. ▲

Beaverlodge is the gateway to Monkman Pass and Kinuseo Falls. Beaverlodge is also home to Canada's most northerly Agricultural Research Station (open to the public), and serves as regional centre for grain transportation, seed cleaning and seed production. Cereal grains, such as wheat, barley and oats, are the main crops in the area. The PRT Alberta Inc. reforestation nursery here, visible from the highway as you enter town, grows about 8 million seedlings a year. Tours are available; phone (403) 354-2288.

Town of Beaverlodge. See display ad this section.

East Access Route Log

(continued)

E 312 (502.1 km) **DC 55** (88.5 km) South Peace Centennial Museum to east, open daily in summer; phone (403) 354-8869. Well worth a stop, the museum features vintage vehicles and working steam-powered farm equipment from the early 1900s. Open 10 A.M. to 8 P.M., mid-May through mid-October. The annual Pioneer Day celebration, held here the third Sunday in July, attracts several thousand visitors.

E 312.4 (502.7 km) **DC 54.6** (87.9 km) Turnoff for Driftwood Ranch Wildlife Haven, 14.3 miles/23 km west, a private collection of exotic and endangered animals. Opens May 1 for season; phone (403) 356-3769 for more information.

E 314.3 (505.8 km) **DC 52.6** (84.8 km) Golf course. This joint project of Hythe and Beaverlodge residents has a clubhouse that was once an NAR station. The 9-hole par 35 course has grass greens. Visitors are welcome; rentals available.

E 320 (515 km) **DC 47** (75.6 km) **HYTHE** (pop. 623) is an agricultural service community and processing center for fruit and berry crops, especially saskatoon berries. Canola is also a major crop. The town has a motel, a bed and breakfast, restaurant, laundromat, gas station, tire repair, car wash, outdoor covered heated swimming pool, complete shopping facilities and a hospital. Municipal campground in town with 17 sites, showers, dump station and playground. The information centre is housed in the Tags Food and Gas store. Inquire locally for directions to Riverside Bison Ranch. An old 1910 tack shop, staffed by volunteers in summer, is located between the highway and railroad tracks. ▲

E 329 (529.4 km) **DC 38** (61.1 km) **Junction** with Highway 59 east to Sexsmith.

E 337 (542.3 km) **DC 30** (48.3 km) **DEMMITT**, an older settlement, site of a sawmill (worth a visit), postal service, cafe and gas.

E 340 (547.2 km) **DC 27** (43.4 km) Railway crossing.

E 341 (548.8 km) **DC 26** (41.8 km) Public campground to east; 15 sites, shelter, firewood, tables, pit toilets, pump water and playground. ▲

E 341.3 (549.2 km) **DC 25.7** (41.3 km) Vehicle inspection station to west.

E 342 (550.4 km) **DC 25** (40.2 km) Gas, diesel and convenience store.

Last Chance Bi-Lo. See display ad this section.

E 343.3 (552.5 km) **DC 23.7** (38.1 km) Alberta–British Columbia border. Turnout with litter barrels and pay phone.

TIME ZONE CHANGE: Alberta is on Mountain time; most of British Columbia is on Pacific time.

E 345.1 (555.4 km) **DC 21.9** (35.2 km) **Junction** with Heritage Highway 52 (gravel surface) which leads 18.5 miles/30 km south to **One Island Lake** Provincial Park (30 campsites, fee charged, rainbow and brook trout fishing) and 92 miles/148 km southwest from Highway 2 to Tumbler Ridge townsite, built in conjunction with the North East Coal development. Monkman Provincial Park, site of spectacular Kinuseo Falls, lies south of Tumbler Ridge. A campground with viewing platform of falls is accessible via a 25-mile/40-km road from Tumbler Ridge. Heritage Highway loops north 59.5 miles/96 km from Tumbler Ridge to join Highway 97 just west of Dawson Creek (see **Milepost PG 237.7** in the WEST ACCESS ROUTE section).

E 345.7 (556.3 km) **DC 21.3** (34.3 km) Tupper Creek bridge.

E 347 (558.5 km) **DC 20** (32.1 km) Swan Lake Provincial Park, with 41 campsites, picnic area, playground and boat launch, is 1.2 miles/2 km north of the tiny hamlet of **TUPPER**, which has a general store. ▲

E 347.9 (559.9 km) **DC 19.1** (30.7 km) Sudeten Provincial Park day-use area; 8 picnic tables. Plaque tells of immigration to this valley of displaced residents of Sudetenland in 1938–39.

E 348.9 (561.5 km) **DC 18.1** (29.1 km) Tate Creek bridge.

E 349.7 (562.7 km) **DC 17.3** (27.8 km) Side road west to community of Tomslake.

E 356.3 (573.4 km) **DC 10.7** (17.2 km) Turnout to east with litter barrel.

E 358 (576.1 km) **DC 9** (14.5 km) Historic sign tells of Pouce Coupe Prairie.

E 359.4 (578.4 km) **7.6** (12.2 km) Railway crossing.

E 360 (579.3 km) **DC 7** (11.2 km) Weigh scales to east.

E 360.4 (580 km) **DC 6.6** (10.6 km) Bissett Creek bridge. Regional park located at south end of bridge.

E 361 (581 km) **DC 6** (9.6 km) **POUCE COUPE** (pop. 904; elev. 2,118 feet/646m). **Visitor Information:** Tourist Bureau Office located in Pouce Coupe Museum, 5006 49th Ave. (1 block south of Highway 2). Open 8 A.M. to 5 P.M., May 15 to Sept. 15. Phone (250) 786-5555.

The Pouce Coupe area was first settled in 1898 by a French Canadian, Hector Tremblay, who set up a trading post in 1908. The Edson Trail, completed in 1911, brought in the main influx of settlers from Edmonton in 1912. Historical artifacts are displayed at the Pouce Coupe Museum, located in the old NAR railroad station. 1998 marks the 100th anniversary of Tremblay's arrival and the 25th anniversary of the museum.

The village has a motel, hotel, restaurant, post office, gas station, dump station, car wash, municipal office, library, schools and food store. Camping at Regional Park, open May to September; hookups. ▲

E 364.5 (586.6 km) **DC 2.5** (4 km) Dawson Creek airport.

E 367 (590.6 km) **DC 0 DAWSON CREEK**, the beginning of the Alaska Highway. Turn to the ALASKA HIGHWAY section, page 84.

Alaska Highway via

WEST ACCESS ROUTE

  97

Connects: Seattle, WA, to Dawson Creek, BC **Length:** 817 miles
Road Surface: Paved **Season:** Open all year
Highest Summit: Pine Pass, 3,068 feet
Major Attractions: Fraser River Canyon/Hell's Gate, Barkerville

(See maps, pages 56–57)

	Cache Creek	Dawson Creek	Prince George	Seattle
Cache Creek		527	277	290
Dawson Creek	527		250	817
Prince George	277	250		567
Seattle	290	817	567	

Scenic Thompson River north of Lytton. *(© Eero Sorila)*

The West Access Route links Interstate 5, Trans-Canada Highway 1 and BC Highway 97 to form the most direct route to Dawson Creek, BC, for West Coast motorists. This has been the major western route to the start of the Alaska Highway since 1952, when the John Hart Highway connecting Prince George and Dawson Creek was completed.

The West Access Route junctions with Yellowhead Highway 16 at Prince George. This east–west highway connects with the Alaska State Ferry System and BC Ferries at Prince Rupert, and with the East Access Route to the Alaska Highway at Edmonton. Turn to the YELLOWHEAD HIGHWAY 16 section for a complete log of that route.

INTERSTATE HIGHWAY 5

The West Access Route begins in the city of **SEATTLE, WA** (pop. 532,900; greater metropolitan, 2,183,200), the Alaska gateway city since the Klondike Gold Rush days, when it became the major staging and departure point for most of the gold seekers. Seattle was also southern terminus of the Alaska Marine Highway System until 1989, when the Alaska state ferries moved to the Fairhaven Terminal at Bellingham, WA (I-5, Exit 250). Seattle–Tacoma International Airport is the departure point for jet flights to Alaska. The air terminal is located 10 miles/16 km south of city center via Interstate 5 (Exit 154).

Like most interstate routes in the United States, I-5 has physical mileposts along its route and corresponding numbered exits. Exit numbers and physical mileposts reflect distance from Mile 0 at the OR–WA border. I-5 in Oregon and Washington is logged in *Northwest Mileposts®*, available from Vernon Publications Inc.; phone (800) 726-4707.

From Seattle, drive 92 miles north on I-5 to Bellingham and turn off onto Highway 539 north (Exit 256), which goes north 12 miles to Highway 546, which will take you another 13 miles to Highway 9 and Sumas, WA, at the U.S.–Canada border (customs open 24 hours a day). Then follow BC Highway 11 a short distance north from the Huntingdon, BC, border crossing to Abbotsford. This route is a scenic drive through rural Whatcom County via 2-lane highways. *The MILEPOST®* log begins on Trans-Canada Highway 1 near Abbotsford.

Travelers may also continue on I-5 to the international border at Blaine (22 miles/35.4 km beyond Exit 256), the more direct route if you are bound for Vancouver, BC.

From Seattle to Abbotsford via Sumas it is 120 miles. From Abbotsford to Cache Creek, it is 170 miles; from Cache Creek to Prince George, 277 miles; and from Prince George to Dawson Creek it is 250 miles.

West Access Route Log

TRANS-CANADA HIGHWAY 1

The West Access Route log is divided into 3 sections: Abbotsford to Cache Creek; Cache Creek to Prince George; and Prince George to Dawson Creek.

This section of the log shows distance from Abbotsford (A) followed by distance from Cache Creek (CC).

A 0 CC 170 (273.6 km) Exit 92. **Junction** of Trans-Canada Highway 1 and Highway 11 south to the international border crossing at Sumas–Huntingdon. Highway 11 north to **ABBOTSFORD** (pop. 105,403), all visitor services. Abbotsford is the "Raspberry Capital of Canada" and is the home of the Abbotsford International Airshow in August. **Visitor Information:** Abbotsford Chamber of Commerce, 2462 McCallum Road; phone (604) 859-9651.

Highway 11 north crosses the bridge over the Fraser River to Mission (7.2 miles/11.9 km north), and connects with Highway 7 to Harrison Hot Springs (41 miles/66 km). This 2-lane highway traverses the rural farmland on the north side of the Fraser River, rejoining Trans-Canada Highway 1 at Hope (56 miles/90 km).

A 1.9 (3 km) **CC 168.1** (270.5 km) Exit 95 to Whatcom Road and westbound exit to Sumas River rest area. Access to Sumas Mountain Provincial Park; hiking.

A 5.3 (8.5 km) **CC 164.7** (265.1 km) Exit 99 to Sumas River rest area (eastbound only); tables, toilet, pay phones.

A 8.8 (14.2 km) **CC 161.2** (259.4 km) Exit 104 to small farming community of Yarrow and road to Cultus Lake. The Lower Fraser Valley is prime agricultural land.

CAUTION: Watch for farm vehicles crossing freeway.

A 15 (24.1 km) **CC 155** (249.4 km) Exit

WEST ACCESS ROUTE *Seattle, WA, to Lac La Hache, BC*

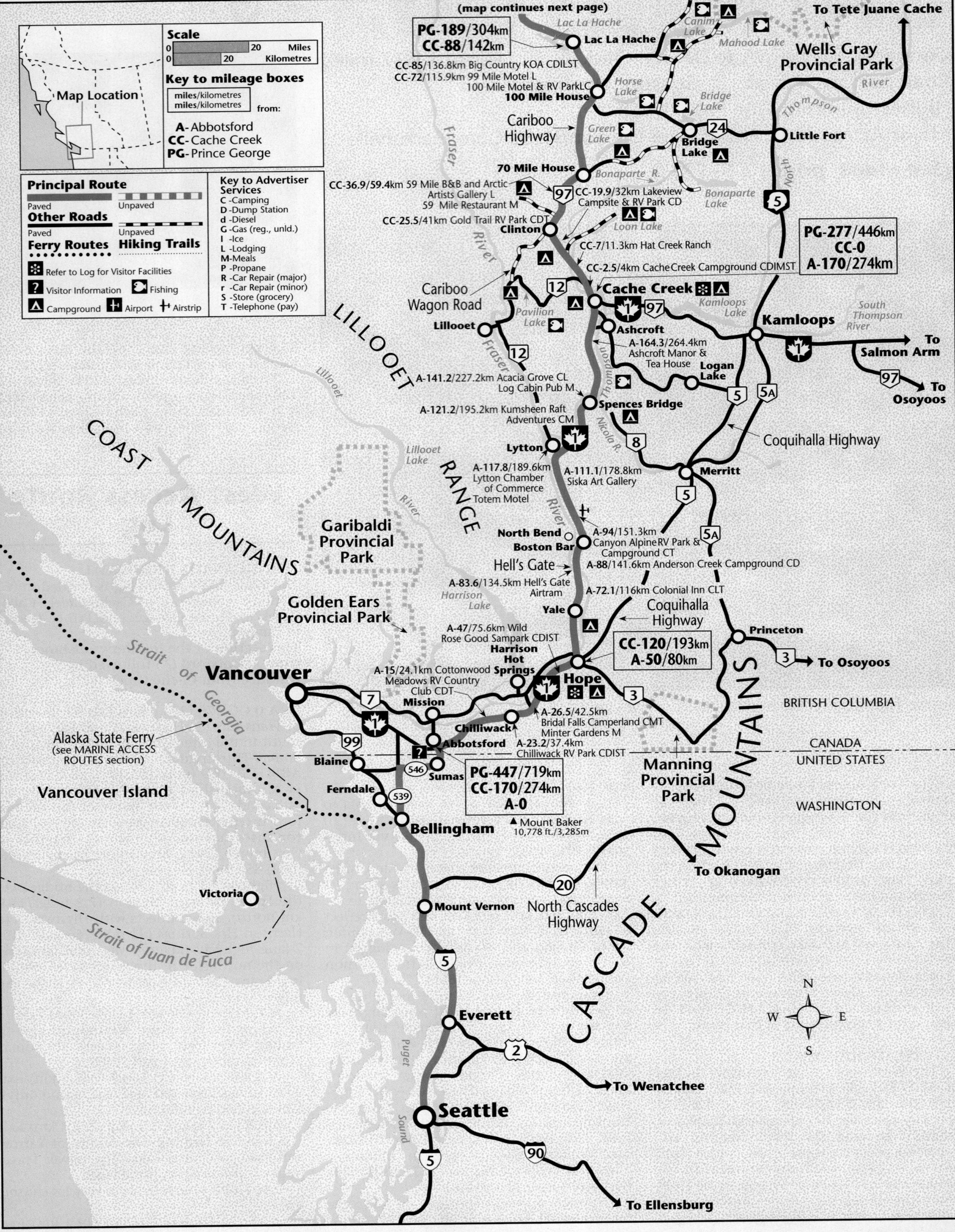

(map continues next page)

Map Location

Scale
0 20 Miles
0 20 Kilometres

Key to mileage boxes
miles/kilometres
miles/kilometres
from:
A- Abbotsford
CC- Cache Creek
PG- Prince George

Principal Route
Paved
Other Roads
Paved
Unpaved
Unpaved
Ferry Routes
Hiking Trails
Refer to Log for Visitor Facilities
Visitor Information
Fishing
Campground
Airport
Airstrip

Key to Advertiser Services
C -Camping
D -Dump Station
d -Diesel
G -Gas (reg., unld.)
I -Ice
L -Lodging
M-Meals
P -Propane
R -Car Repair (major)
r -Car Repair (minor)
S -Store (grocery)
T -Telephone (pay)

Lac La Hache
PG-189/304km
CC-88/142km
Lac La Hache
Canim Lake
Mahood Lake
To Tete Jaune Cache
Wells Gray Provincial Park
River
CC-85/136.8km Big Country KOA CDILST
CC-72/115.9km 99 Mile Motel L
100 Mile Motel & RV ParkLC
100 Mile House
Horse Lake
Bridge Lake
Thompson
Fraser
Cariboo Highway
Green Lake
24
Bridge Lake
Little Fort
North
70 Mile House
Bonaparte R.
CC-36.9/59.4km 59 Mile B&B and Arctic Artists Gallery L
59 Mile Restaurant M
97
CC-19.9/32km Lakeview Campsite & RV Park CD
Bonaparte Lake
CC-25.5/41km Gold Trail RV Park CDT
Clinton
Loon Lake
5
PG-277/446km
CC-0
A-170/274km
CC-7/11.3km Hat Creek Ranch
River
CC-2.5/4km CacheCreek Campground CDIMST
Cariboo Wagon Road
12
Cache Creek
1
97
Kamloops Lake
South Thompson River
Kamloops
Pavilion Lake
Lillooet
Ashcroft
To Salmon Arm
LILLOOET
Fraser
12
A-164.3/264.4km Ashcroft Manor & Tea House
Logan Lake
Thompson
97
To Osoyoos
Lillooet
A-141.2/227.2km Acacia Grove CL
Log Cabin Pub M
5
5A
Spences Bridge
A-121.2/195.2km Kumsheen Raft Adventures CM
Nicola R.
COAST
Coquihalla Highway
8
Lytton
1
Lillooet Lake
RANGE
A-117.8/189.6km Lytton Chamber of Commerce
Totem Motel
A-111.1/178.8km Siska Art Gallery
Merritt
MOUNTAINS
River
River
5
Garibaldi Provincial Park
North Bend
Boston Bar
A-94/151.3km Canyon AlpineRV Park & Campground CT
5A
Hell's Gate
A-88/141.6km Anderson Creek Campground CD
A-83.6/134.5km Hell's Gate Airtram
Harrison Lake
A-72.1/116km Colonial Inn CLT
Golden Ears Provincial Park
Yale
Coquihalla Highway
Princeton
A-47/75.6km Wild Rose Good Sampark CDIST
Strait of Georgia
Vancouver
Harrison Hot Springs
CC-120/193km
A-50/80km
A-15/24.1km Cottonwood Meadows RV Country Club CDT
Hope
3
To Osoyoos
7
Mission
3
BRITISH COLUMBIA
1
A-26.5/42.5km Bridal Falls Camperland CMT
Minter Gardens M
Chilliwack
A-23.2/37.4km Chilliwack RV Park CDIST
Alaska State Ferry (see MARINE ACCESS ROUTES section)
99
Abbotsford
CANADA
UNITED STATES
Blaine
546
Sumas
PG-447/719km
CC-170/274km
A-0
Manning Provincial Park
Vancouver Island
Ferndale
539
WASHINGTON
Bellingham
Mount Baker 10,778 ft./3,285m
To Okanogan
MOUNTAINS
Victoria
20
Mount Vernon
North Cascades Highway
Strait of Juan de Fuca
CASCADE
5
N
W
E
S
Everett
Puget Sound
2
To Wenatchee
Seattle
90
5
To Ellensburg

WEST ACCESS ROUTE *Lac La Hache, BC, to Dawson Creek, BC*

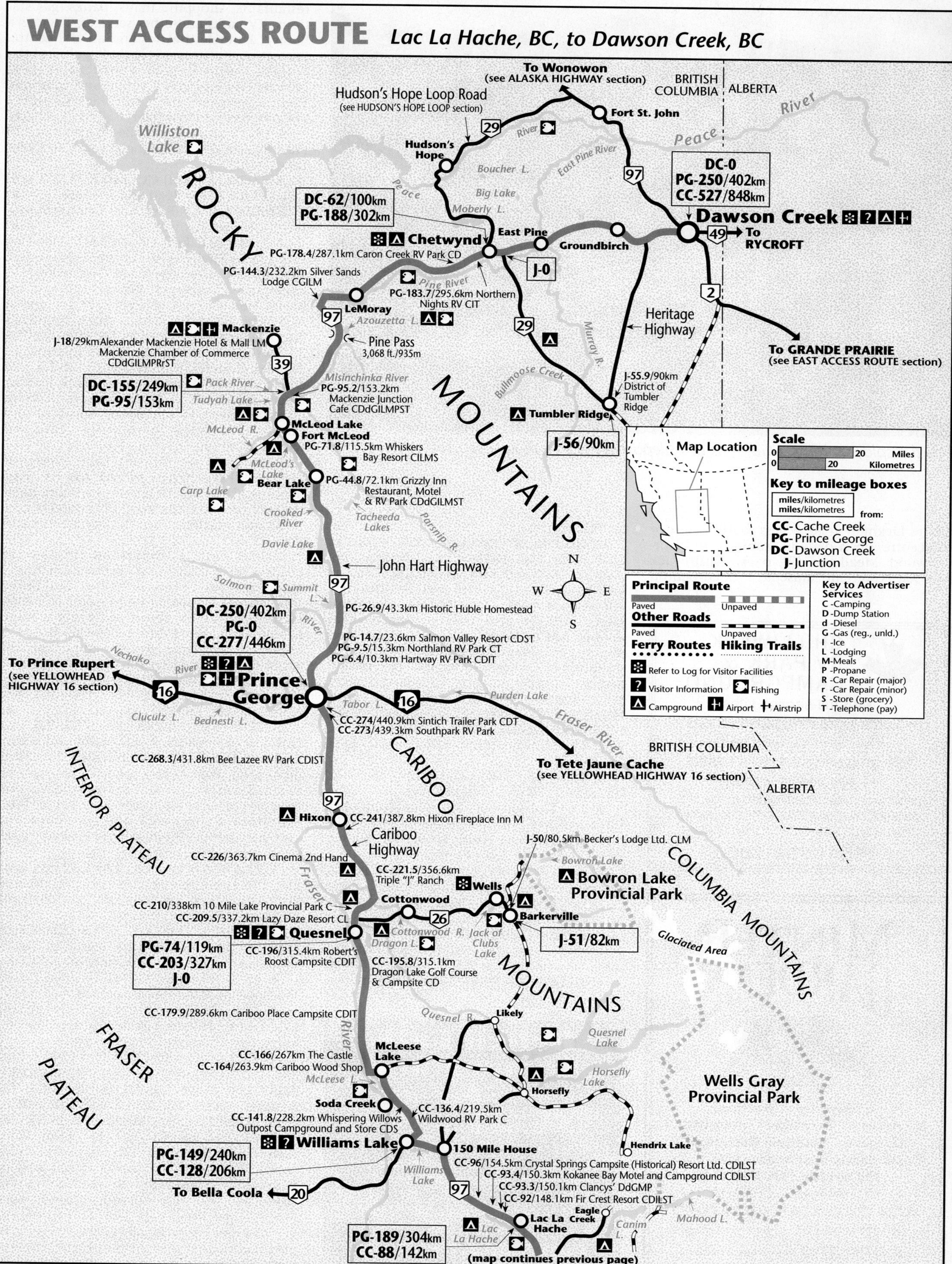

Floral display at Minter Gardens at Milepost A 26.5. (© Wes Bergen, DIARAMA)

116 to Lickman Road; access south to Visitor Infocentre, open daily in summer, and Cottonwood Meadows RV park. Chilliwack Antique Powerland museum located behind the infocentre. ▲

A 16.8 (27.1 km) **CC 153.2** (246.5 km) Highway 119B to Chilliwack Airport.

A 17 (27.4 km) **CC 153** (246.2 km) Exit 119 north to Chilliwack (all services, description follows) and south to Sardis (all services) and Cultus Lake Provincial Park.

Cultus Lake Provincial Park has 300 campsites; water, flush and pit toilets, showers, firewood, water, boat launch, swimming, fishing, canoeing, kayaking, and hiking and walking trails. Cultus Lake resort area also offers water slides, go-carts and other activities. ▲

CHILLIWACK (pop. 60,186) has motels, restaurants, shopping malls, banks, gas stations, RV parks and other services. There is a library, 2 movie theatres and an arts centre. Recreational attractions include golf and the popular Cultus Lake area with water park, boat rentals, horseback riding and camping. **Visitor Information:** Chilliwack Chamber of Commerce, phone (604) 858-8121. ▲

A 18 (29 km) **CC 152** (244.6 km) Exit 123 Prest Road north to Rosedale, south to Ryder Lake.

A 23.2 (37.4 km) **CC 146.8** (236.2 km) Exit 129 for Annis Road and RV park. ▲

Chilliwack RV Park and Campground. See display ad this section. ▲

A 26.5 (42.5 km) **CC 143.5** (230.9 km) Exit 135 to Highway 9 east to Harrison Hot Springs and alternate route Highway 7 to Hope and Vancouver. Westbound exit for Bridal Veil Falls. Also exit here for access to Minter Gardens, which rivals Victoria's famous Butchart Gardens for beauty. The 27 acres of floral displays feature 11 themed gardens, topiary figures and a rare collection of Chinese Penjing Rock Bonsai. Opens 9 A.M. daily, April through October. Entertainment is scheduled Sundays and holidays, weather permitting. Internet: www.minter.org.

Exit north for Cheam Lake Wetlands Regional Park. Once mined for its marl deposits, Cheam Lake is now a wildlife habitat; interpretive trails, good bird watching.

Minter Gardens. See display ad this section.

A 27.3 (43.9 km) **CC 142.7** (229.6 km) Exit 138 to Popkum Road. Eastbound access to Bridal Veil Falls Provincial Park to south; picnicking, trail to base of falls. Also access to small community of Popkum and various roadside attractions, including water slide, Sandstone Gallery rock and gem museum, and prehistoric-themed amusement park. Food, gas and lodging.

A 34.5 (55.5 km) **CC 135.5** (218.1 km) Exit 146 Herrling Island, a cottonwood tree farm (no access or services), visible from highway.

A 40.5 (65.2 km) **CC 129.5** (208.4 km) Exit 153 to Laidlaw and access to Jones (Wahleach) Lake. Country store on Laidlaw.

A 42.5 (68.4 km) **CC 127.5** (205.2 km) Truck weigh scales; public phone.

A 44.7 (71.9 km) **CC 125.3** (201.6 km) Exit 160 to Hunter Creek rest area; tables, toilet, pay phone, information kiosk.

A 45.5 (73.2 km) **CC 124.5** (200.4 km) Exit 165 to Flood/Hope Road. Access to RV parks and Hope airport (glider rides on summer weekends). Also access this exit to Silver Skagit Road (see **Milepost A 48.5**). ▲

A 47 (75.6 km) **CC 123** (197.9 km) **Wild Rose Good Sampark.** On Highway 1 east (from Vancouver) 4.8 km (3 miles) west of Hope; take Flood–Hope Road exit 165. On Highway 1 west (from Hope) take Flood–Hope Road exit 168. Full hookups, 15–30 amps, tenting, level grassy sites in parklike setting, 60-foot pull-throughs, free cable TV, free hot showers, laundry, playground, clubroom, horseshoes, firepits, picnic tables, a limited store. Ice, wood, pay phone, sani-station, near restaurant. Senior citizen discount, weekly rates, MasterCard, VISA. Small pets. Cancellation policy—two days. Open April 1 to Oct. 1. Phone (604) 869-9842, fax 869-3171. Toll-free reservations in Canada and U.S.A. Phone (800) 463-7999. [ADVERTISEMENT] ▲

A 48.5 (78.1 km) **CC 121.5** (195.5 km) Exit 168 to Silverhope Creek. Access to RV park. Also access to Silver Skagit Road, which leads south 37 miles/60 km through the Skagit Valley past Silver Lake Provincial Park and Skagit Valley Provincial Park. ▲

A 48.7 (78.4 km) **CC 121.3** (195.2 km) Silver Creek, Flood–Hope Road exit.

A 50 (80.5 km) **CC 120** (193.1 km) **Junction** of Trans-Canada Highway 1, Highway 3 (Crowsnest Highway) and Highway 5 (Coquihalla Highway). Use Exit 170 northbound for Trans-Canada Highway 1 to Hope.

Hope

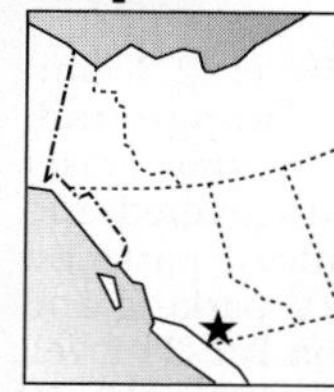

A 50.2 (80.8 km) CC 119.8 (192.8 km) **Population:** 6,247. **Elevation:** 140 feet/43m. **Emergency Services: RCMP, Fire Department, Ambulance,** phone 911. **Hospital,** 1275 7th Ave., phone (604) 869-5656. **Visitor Information:** Visitor InfoCentre and museum building, corner of Hudson Bay Street and Water Avenue, on the right northbound as you enter town. Open daily 8 A.M. to 8 P.M. in July and August, 9 A.M. to 5 P.M. in May, June and September; weekdays only, 10 A.M. to 4 P.M., rest of the year.

Hope is on a bend of the Fraser River where it flows through a picturesque gap in the forested Coast Mountains near Mount Hope (elev. 6,000 feet/1,289m). It is a popular tourist stop with complete services. About 30 motels and resorts are in Hope or just outside town on Trans-Canada Highway 1 and on Highway 3. Other facilities include auto body shops, service stations, department stores, restaurants and grocery stores.

Hope is rapidly becoming known for its collection of locally crafted chain saw carvings. There are approximately 25 of these large wooden carvings throughout the downtown area. Ask at the Visitor InfoCentre for directions to see all the carvings.

The major attraction in the Hope area is the Coquihalla Canyon Provincial Recreation Area, the focus of which is the Othello Quintette Tunnels. The 5 rock tunnels which cut through the tortuous canyon were part of the Kettle Valley Railway. This stretch of railway has been restored as a walking trail through the tunnels and across bridges. The tunnels are accessible from downtown Hope via Kawkawa Lake Road and Othello Road, about a 10-minute drive.

Other Hope attractions include the Rainbow Junction Community Art Centre, the Japanese Friendship Garden, miles of mountain biking and hiking trails, and many summer festivals.

The Coquihalla Highway, completed in 1987, connects Hope with the Trans-Canada Highway just west of Kamloops, a distance of 118 miles/190 km. This is a 4-lane divided highway; toll charged.

There are private campgrounds on all roads into town. The municipal campground on Kawkawa Lake Road has 31 RV sites, 81 tent sites, coin showers and sani-station. ▲

Hell's Gate airtram at Milepost A 83.6 carries passengers across the Fraser River to a complex on the west side. (Judy Parkin, staff)

West Access Route Log
(continued)

A 50.7 (81.6 km) **CC 119.3** (191.9 km) Bridge over Fraser River. Turnout at north end, access to pedestrian bridge across the Fraser.

A 51.5 (82.8 km) **CC 118.5** (190.7 km) **Junction** with Highway 7, which leads west to Harrison Hot Springs (22.5 miles/36 km) and Vancouver.

A 53.1 (85.5 km) **CC 116.9** (188.1 km) Rest area (westbound access only) with picnic tables to west by Lake of the Woods.

A 60.8 (97.8 km) **CC 109.2** (175.7 km) Easy-to-miss turnoff (watch for sign 1,320 feet/400m before turn) for Emory Creek Provincial Park east of highway; 34 level gravel sites in trees, water, fire rings, picnic tables, firewood, flush and pit toilets, and litter barrels. Camping fee April to October. Hiking and walking trails. Gold panning and fishing in **Fraser River.** ▲

Very much in evidence between Hope and Cache Creek are the tracks of the Canadian National and Canadian Pacific railways. Construction of the CPR—Canada's first transcontinental railway—played a significant role in the history of the Fraser and Thompson river valleys. Begun in 1880, the CPR line between Kamloops and Port Moody was contracted to Andrew Onderdonk.

A 64.8 (104.3 km) **CC 105.2** (169.3 km) **YALE** (pop. 500; elev. 250 feet/76m). **Emergency Services: Police, Fire Department, Ambulance,** phone 911. **Visitor Information:** In the museum, phone (604) 863-2324. Visitor facilities include motels, stores, gas stations and restaurants.

Yale was the head of navigation for the Lower Fraser River and the beginning of the overland gold rush trail to British Columbia's goldfields. The Anglican Church of Saint John the Divine here was built for the miners in 1859 and is the oldest church still on its original foundation in mainland British Columbia. Next to the church is Yale Museum and a bronze plaque honouring Chinese construction workers who helped build the Canadian Pacific Railway. Walking around town, look for the several plaques relating Yale's history. Daily guided walking tours of historic Yale are offered in summer; fee charged, includes admission to museum and church. Phone (604) 863-2428 for more information.

A 65.6 (105.5 km) **CC 104.5** (168.2 km) Entering Fraser Canyon northbound. The Fraser River and canyon were named for Simon Fraser (1776–1862), the first white man to descend the river in 1808. This is the dry forest region of British Columbia, and it can be a hot drive in summer. The scenic Fraser Canyon travelers drive through today was a formidable obstacle for railroad engineers in 1881.

A 66 (106.2 km) **CC 104** (167.4 km) Yale Tunnel, first of several northbound through the Fraser Canyon.

A 67.3 (108.3 km) **CC 102.7** (165.2 km) Turnout to east with plaque about the Cariboo Waggon Road, which connected Yale with the Cariboo goldfields near Barkerville. Built between 1861 and 1863 by the Royal Engineers, it replaced an earlier route to the goldfields—also called the Cariboo Waggon Road—which started from Lillooet.

A 68.4 (110.1 km) **CC 101.6** (163.5 km) Saddle Rock Tunnel. This 480-foot-/146-m-long tunnel was constructed from 1957–58.

A 72.1 (116 km) **CC 97.9** (157.5 km) **Colonial Inn & RVs.** In scenic Fraser Canyon. See the hummingbirds mid-April to mid-July. Cabin-style sleeping and kitchen units with showers and satellite TV. Pay phones. Picnic area with barbecues. Mountain views. Campground with full hookups and showers. For reservations phone (604) 863-2277 or write RR #1, Yale, BC V0K 2S0. [ADVERTISEMENT] ▲

A 72.3 (116.3 km) **CC 97.7** (157.2 km) Sailor Bar Tunnel, nearly 984 feet/300m long. There were dozens of bar claims along the Fraser River in the 1850s bearing colourful names such as Sailor Bar.

A 76.5 (123.1 km) **CC 93.5** (150.5 km) Spuzzum (unincorporated), gas station and food.

A 77.1 (124.1 km) **CC 92.9** (149.5 km) Stop of interest at south end of Alexandra Bridge, built in 1962, the second largest fixed arch span in the world at more than 1,640 feet/500m in length.

A 77.5 (124.8 km) **CC 92.5** (148.9 km) Alexandra Bridge Provincial Park, picnic areas and interpretive displays on both sides of highway. Hiking trail down to the old Alexandra Bridge, still intact. This suspension bridge was built in 1926, replacing the original built in 1863.

A 77.8 (125.2 km) **CC 92.2** (148.4 km) Historic Alexandra Lodge (closed), is the last surviving original roadhouse on the Cariboo Waggon Road.

A 79.5 (128 km) **CC 90.5** (145.6 km) Alexandra Tunnel.

A 80.5 (129.5 km) **CC 89.5** (144 km) Rest area by Copper Creek to east.

A 82.6 (133 km) **CC 87.4** (140.7 km) Hells Gate Tunnel (328 feet/100m long).

A 83.3 (134 km) **CC 86.7** (139.5 km) Ferrabee Tunnel (328 feet/100m long).

A 83.6 (134.5 km) **CC 86.4** (139 km) Hells Gate, the narrowest point on the Fraser River and a popular attraction. (Northbound traffic park at lot immediately south of attraction on east side of road; southbound traffic park on west side of road at attraction.) Two 25-passenger airtrams take visitors some 500 feet down across the river to a restaurant and shop complex. Footbridge across river to view fishways through which some 2 million salmon pass each year. A display details the life cycle of the salmon, the construction of the International Fishways and the history of Hells Gate. Trams operate daily, April 9 to Oct. 31, 1998. There is also a steep trail down to the fishways; strenuous hike.

Hells Gate was well named. It was by far the most difficult terrain for construction of both the highway and the railway. To haul supplies for the railway upstream of Hells Gate, Andrew Onderdonk built the sternwheel steamer *Skuzzy*. The *Skuzzy* made its way upstream through Hells Gate in 1882, hauled by ropes attached to the canyon walls by bolts.

Hell's Gate Airtram. See display ad this section.

A 83.8 (134.9 km) **CC 86.2** (138.7 km) Hells Gate turnaround for travelers who miss the Hells Gate parking lot.

A 85.7 (137.9 km) **CC 84.3** (135.7 km) China Bar Tunnel, built in 1960. It is almost 2,300 feet/700m long, one of the longest tunnels in North America. Point of interest sign at south end about Simon Fraser.

A 88 (141.6 km) **CC 82** (132 km) **Anderson Creek Campground.** Quiet, secluded, some riverfront locations. Try fishing or view the rafters. Easy turnaround at bottom of hill. Pull-throughs, shaded parking, washrooms and free hot showers. 30-amp service, sani-station, reasonable rates. In season, help yourself to fresh fruit off the old orchard trees. Phone (604) 867-9125. [ADVERTISEMENT] ▲

A 91 (146.5 km) **CC 79** (127.1 km) **BOSTON BAR** (pop. 885; elev. 400 feet/122m). **Emergency Services: Police, Fire Department, Ambulance**, phone 911. Services include gas stations, cafes, grocery stores, motels and private RV parks. Site of the J.S. Jones Timber Mill; tours may be available in summer, phone (604) 867-9214 for information. Boston Bar was the southern landing for the steamer *Skuzzy*, which plied the Fraser River between here and Lytton during construction of the CPR.

North Bend, located across the river from Boston Bar, is a former railway community. Old cable cage from the aerial car ferry that once served North Bend is on display at the CN station in Boston Bar.

North Bend is the access point for the Nahatlatch River and lakes via a logging road. River rafting trips are available on the Nahatlatch River.

A 94 (151.3 km) **CC 76** (122.3 km) **Canyon Alpine RV Park & Campground.** Still the best-kept secret in the Fraser Canyon, but quickly being discovered and described as "...one of the nicest parks on the Alaskan route." Secure RV parking and tenting 3 miles north of Boston Bar. 31 level, pull-through sites, fully serviced with 30 amp, water, sewer and cable TV. Easy access and turnarounds for rigs over 35 feet. 14-foot entrance gate clearance. Away from traffic noise and railroads. Clean washrooms. Hot showers. Shaded sites. Fire rings. Free firewood. 50 yards south of restaurant, store, laundromat and telephones. Pets on leash welcome. 10 minutes from world-famous Hell's Gate Airtram. Open April 15 to Oct. 15. 50490 Trans-Canada Highway. Toll free (800) 644-PARK. Your friendly hosts, Jane and John. See display ad this section. [ADVERTISEMENT] ▲

A 101 (162.5 km) **CC 69** (111 km) Turnoff for Blue Lake, 0.6 mile/1 km gravel road.

A 111.1 (178.8 km) **CC 58.9** (94.8 km): **Siska Art Gallery.** See display ad this section.

A 112.8 (181.5 km) **CC 57.2** (92.1 km) Viewpoint to west overlooking the Fraser River.

A 113.6 (182.9 km) **CC 56.4** (90.7 km) Canadian National and Canadian Pacific railways cross over the Fraser River here; a favorite spot for photos. Gravel turnout to east.

A 114.6 (184.5 km) **CC 55.4** (89.2 km) Skupper rest area (northbound only); toilets, tables, litter barrels.

A 117.8 (189.6 km) **CC 52.2** (84 km) **Junction** with Highway 12 to Lillooet. Turn

Whitewater rafting is popular on the Fraser and Thompson rivers.
(Judy Parkin, staff)

west here for community of Lytton (description follows).

LYTTON (pop. 322; elev. 561 feet/171m). **Emergency Services: RCMP**, phone (250) 455-2225. **Fire Department**, phone (250) 455-2333. **Ambulance**, phone (250) 374-5937. **Hospital**, St. Bartholomew's, phone (250) 455-2221. **Visitor Information**: Visitor Infocentre, 400 Fraser St., phone (250) 455-2523. Located at the confluence of the Thompson and Fraser rivers, Lytton acts as headquarters for river raft trips. All visitor facilities are available. Sand bars at Lytton yielded much gold, and river frontage has been set aside for recreational gold panning. Lytton has recorded the highest temperature in British Columbia, 111°F/44°C.

A 121.2 (195.2 km) **CC 48.8** (78.4 km) Rafting centre. Watch for rafters in the river during the summer months.

A 122.8 (197.6 km) **CC 47.2** (76 km) Skihist Provincial Park to east; 58 campsites on east side of highway with water, flush and pit toilets, firewood and dump station. Picnic area on west side of highway (good place to watch the trains go by); wheelchair-accessible restrooms. ♿▲

A 134.7 (216.8 km) **CC 35.3** (56.8 km) Goldpan Provincial Park to west alongside river; 14 campsites, picnic area, water, firewood, canoeing, kayaking, fishing. ▲

A 136 (218.9 km) **CC 34** (54.7 km) In summer, watch for fruit stands selling locally grown produce along the highway. Watch for bighorn sheep on the hillsides in the fall.

A 137 (220.5 km) **CC 33** (53.1 km) **BIG HORN**; trading post, fuel, tire shop and 24-hour towing.

A 140 (225.3 km) **CC 30** (48.3 km) **Junction** with Highway 8 to Merritt and south access to Spences Bridge. Plaque here about the great landslide of 1905.

A 141.2 (227.2 km) **CC 28.8** (46.3 km) North access to **SPENCES BRIDGE** (pop. 300; elev. 760 feet/231m) located at the confluence of the Thompson and Nicola rivers. Services include lodging, camping, restaurant, pub and grocery with tackle and fishing licenses. A record 30-lb., 5-oz. steelhead was caught in the Thompson River in 1984. Look for an osprey nest atop the hydroelectric pole on the east side of the river. ▲

A 153.4 (246.9 km) **CC 16.6** (26.7 km) Viewpoint overlooking Thompson River with plaque about the Canadian Northern Pacific (now the Canadian National Railway), Canada's third transcontinental railway, completed in 1915.

A 158.4 (255 km) **CC 11.6** (18.7 km) Red Hill rest area to east; tables, toilets, litter barrels, pay phone.

A 164.3 (264.4 km) **CC 5.7** (9.2 km) Stop of interest sign to east describes Ashcroft Manor, a roadhouse on the Cariboo Waggon Road. Summer temperatures in this dry and desert-like region typically reach the high 80s and 90s (26°C to 32°C).

Ashcroft Manor & Tea House. See display ad this section.

Fields under black plastic mesh tarps—which may be seen as the highway descends northbound—are ginseng, an Asian medicinal root crop. The world supply of North American ginseng, which takes 4 years to mature, is grown in the southern Cariboo.

A 164.5 (264.7 km) **CC 5.5** (8.9 km) **Junction** with road to **ASHCROFT**, a small village on the Thompson River with full tourist facilities just east of the highway. Historic Ashcroft supplanted Yale as gateway to the Cariboo with the arrival of the Canadian Pacific Railway in 1885. There are a number of original buildings with distinctive architectural details. Ashcroft Museum houses a fine collection of artifacts tracing the history of the region. Logan Lake, east of Ashcroft, is the site of the second largest open-pit copper mine in North America (tours available).

Also **junction** with Highway 97C to Logan Lake and Merritt.

A 168.2 (270.7 km) **CC 1.8** (2.9 km) Second turnoff northbound for Ashcroft and road to Logan Lake.

Cache Creek

A 170 (273.6 km) PG 277 (445.8 km) Located at the junction of Trans-Canada Highway 1 and Highway 97. **Population:** 1,115. **Elevation:** 1,508 feet/460m. **Emergency Services: RCMP,** phone (250) 453-2216. **Ambulance,** phone (250)-374-5937. **Hospital,** phone (250) 453-5306.

Visitor Information: Write Box 460, Cache Creek, BC V0K 1H0; fax (250) 457-9669.

Cache Creek has ample facilities for the traveler (most located on or just off the main highways), including motels, restaurants, service stations and grocery store. Private campgrounds are available east of Cache Creek on Trans-Canada Highway 1 (across from the golf course) and just north of town on Highway 97.

A post office and bus depot are on Todd Road. Nearby, Cariboo Jade Shoppe offers free stone-cutting demonstrations in summer. On display out front is a 2,850-lb. jade boulder. Public park and swimming pool on the Bonaparte River, east off Highway 97 at the north edge of town.

The settlement grew up around the confluence of the creek and the Bonaparte River. The Hudson's Bay Co. opened a store here, and Cache Creek became a major supply point on the Cariboo Waggon Road. Today, hay and cattle ranching, ginseng farming, mining, logging and tourism support the community. Area soils are dry but fertile. Residents claim that with irrigation nearly anything can be grown here.

From the junction, Highway 97 leads north 277 miles/445.8 km to Prince George. Kamloops is 52 miles/83.7 km east via Trans-Canada Highway 1. Traveling north from Cache Creek the highway generally follows the historic route to the Cariboo goldfields.

Brookside Campsite. 1 km east of Cache Creek on Highway 1, full (30 amp) and

Gold panner in Cache Creek represents gold rush history of this region.
(© Eero Sorila)

partial hookups, pull-throughs, tent sites, super- clean heated wash and laundry rooms, free showers, sani-stations, store, playground, nature path, heated pool, golf course adjacent, pets on leash, pay phones. VISA, MasterCard, C.P. two days. Good Sam. Box 737, Cache Creek, BC V0K 1H0. Phone/fax: (250) 457-6633. [ADVERTISEMENT] ▲

West Access Route Log

(continued)

BC HIGHWAY 97/CARIBOO HIGHWAY

From Cache Creek, continue north on BC Highway 97 for Dawson Creek. Kilometre-posts on this section of highway are located on the east side of the highway facing west, so that they may be seen by traffic traveling in either direction. Highway 97 between Cache Creek and Prince George is called the Cariboo Highway, and the region is locally referred to as "Super, Natural Cariboo Country." Contact the Cariboo Tourist Assoc., P.O. Box 4900, Williams Lake, BC V2G 2V8; phone toll free (800) 663-5885.

This section of the log shows distance from Cache Creek (CC) followed by distance from Prince George (PG).

CC 0 PG 277 (445.8 km) Cache Creek, **junction** of Trans-Canada Highway 1 and Highway 97.

CC 2.5 (4 km) **PG 274.5** (441.8 km) **Cache Creek Campground**, 3 km north of Cache Creek on Highway 97 north. Full hookups, pull-throughs and tenting, sani-station, store, country kitchen restaurant, laundromat, coin showers, heated wash-rooms. Outdoor pool and whirlpool (no charge). 18-hole mini-golf, horseshoes, seasonal river swimming and fishing. P.O. Box 127, Cache Creek, BC V0K 1H0. For reservations, phone (250) 457-6414. See display ad this section. [ADVERTISEMENT] ▲

CC 7 (11.3 km) **PG 270** (434.5 km) **Junction** with Highway 99 west to Lillooet (46.5 miles/75 km) and Vancouver (209 miles/336.5 km) via Whistler and Blackcombe ski areas. Formerly Highway 12, this route was designated as part of Highway 99 when the logging road between Lillooet and Pemberton was paved, making it possible to drive to the Cariboo from Vancouver via Squamish. Highway 99, promoted as the "Sea to Sky Highway," is logged in *Northwest Mileposts®*, available from Vernon Publications Inc.; phone (800) 726-4707.

Drive 0.4 mile/0.7 km west on Highway 99 for Hat Creek Heritage Ranch, a restored Cariboo Trail roadhouse and farm with reconstructed barn, working blacksmith shop, wagon and trail rides and tours. Open daily 10 A.M. to 6 P.M., mid-May to mid-October. Phone (800) 782-0922 for current information.

Hat Creek Ranch. See display ad this section.

Marble Canyon Provincial Park, 17.5 miles/28 km west on Highway 99, has 34 campsites, picnicking, swimming and hiking trails. ▲

CC 10 (16 km) **PG 267** (430 km) Gravel turnout with plaque about the BX stage-coaches that once served Barkerville. Formally known as the BC Express Company, the BX served the Cariboo for 50 years.

CC 13.6 (21.9 km) **PG 263.4** (423.9 km) Paved road leads east to **Loon Lake**, rainbow fishing, boat launch. Camping at Loon Lake Provincial Park (16 miles/26 km); 14 sites, water, pit toilets, firewood. ▲

CC 16.6 (26.7 km) **PG 260.4** (419.1 km) Carguile rest area.

CC 19.9 (32 km) **PG 257.1** (413.7 km) **Lakeview Campsite & RV Park**. See display ad this section. ▲

CC 25 (40.2 km) **PG 252** (405.5 km) **Junction** with Pavilion Mountain Road west to Pavilion via Kelly Lake. Camping at Downing Provincial Park (11 miles/18 km); 25 sites, swimming, fishing. ▲

CC 25.5 (41 km) **PG 251.5** (404.7 km) **CLINTON** (pop. 729, area 4,000; elev. 2,911 feet/887m). **Visitor Information:** Available at various local businesses; look for signs. All visitor facilities are available, including 3 motels, campground, gas stations, 24-hour towing and stores. Originally the site of 47 Mile Roadhouse, a gold-rush settlement on the Cariboo Waggon Road from Lillooet, today Clinton is called the "guest ranch capital of British Columbia." The museum, housed in a building of local, handmade red brick that once served as a courthouse, has fine displays of pioneer tools and items from the gold rush days, and a scale model of the Clinton Hotel. Clinton pioneer cemetery just north of town. Clinton boasts the oldest continuously held event in the province, the Clinton Ball (in May the weekend following Victoria Day), an annual event since 1868.

Clinton has its own sign forest. Visitors may sign a wooden slab (donated by the local sawmill) and add it to the sign forest.

Gold Trail RV Park. Fully serviced sites, 30-amp power. Pull-throughs. Immaculate. Washrooms with flush toilets, handicap-equipped. Free hot showers for guests. On highway in town; easy walking to all amenities. Well-lit level sites. Grassed and landscaped. Sani-station. 1640 Cariboo Highway North, Clinton, BC V0K 1K0. Phone (250) 459-2519. [ADVERTISEMENT] ▲

CC 31 (49.9 km) **PG 246** (395.9 km) Dirt and gravel road leads 21 miles/34 km west to **Big Bar Lake** Provincial Park; 33 campsites, water, pit toilets, firewood, swimming, fishing and boat launch. ▲

Clinton Lookout and Big Bar rest area to east just north of turnoff; toilets, tables, litter barrels.

CC 35 (56.3 km) **PG 242** (389.5 km) Loop road leads east 3 miles/5 km to Painted Chasm geological site and Chasm Provincial Park picnic area. This 1-mile/1.6-km-long bedrock box canyon was cut by glacial melt-waters.

CC 36.9 (59.4 km) **PG 240.1** (408.9 km) **59 Mile Bed & Breakfast and Arctic Artists Gallery.** Original Eskimo art by award-winning carver Iyak. Visit this fine gallery and meet the artist. Iyak uses soapstone, whale-bone, muskox horn and cariboo antler. Also available are paintings by arctic artist Lyle R. Trimble. Iyak, Laurie and family offer a warm and friendly bed and breakfast. Come and stay with this Eskimo family and relax and enjoy the Gallery. Phone/Fax (250) 459-7076. P.O. Box 518, Clinton, BC V0K 1K0. [ADVERTISEMENT]

59 Mile Restaurant. The place where the German and Canadian homestyle cooking is at home in a great and cozy western atmosphere. We use only fresh, in-season vegetables and fruits. Try our daily specials or vegetarian meals. We also bake our own pies, cakes, and buns. The restaurant is on

100 Mile House visitor centre features a pair of 39-foot-/12-m-long skis.

(© Fred Chapman, DIARAMA)

Highway 97 with easy RV access and also fully handicap accessible. Open year round from Tuesday to Sunday, 7 A.M.–10 P.M. Group bookings welcome. Phone (250) 459-7750. [ADVERTISEMENT]

CC 45 (72.4 km) **PG 232** (373.4 km) **70 MILE HOUSE** (unincorporated), originally a stage stop named for its distance from Lillooet, Mile 0. General store, post office, restaurant, motel, gas station with diesel and bus depot.

North Bonaparte Road leads east 7.5 miles/12 km to Green Lake Provincial Park; 121 campsites, water, toilets, firewood, dump station, swimming and boat launch. Rainbow and kokanee fishing at **Green Lake**. Paved road leads north to Watch Lake, east to Bonaparte Lake, and northeast to join Highway 24 at Bridge Lake.

CC 58.8 (94.7 km) **PG 218.2** (351.1 km) **83 MILE HOUSE**; restaurant, gas, propane, store, public phone. Turnoff for Green Lake (7 miles/11 km).

CC 60 (96 km) **PG 217** (347.2 km) Lookout Road to forestry tower on summit of Mount Begbie (elev. 4,186 feet/1,276m); great views.

CC 66 (106.2 km) **PG 211** (339.6 km) **Junction** with Highway 24 East to Lone Butte Bridge Lake and Little Fort (60 miles/96.5 km) on Yellowhead Highway 5. Highway 24 provides access to numerous fishing lakes and resorts, including **Bridge Lake** Provincial Park (31 miles/50 km east) with 20 campsites.

100 Mile House

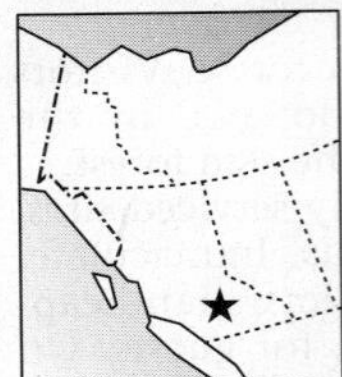

CC 72 (115.9 km) **PG 205** (329.9 km) **Population:** 2,600. **Elevation:** 3,050 feet/930m. **Emergency Services: Police,** phone (250) 395-2456. **Ambulance,** phone (250) 395-3288. **Hospital,** phone (250) 395-2202. **Visitor Information:** At the log cabin by 100 Mile House Marsh (a bird sanctuary at the south edge of town); phone (250) 395-5353, fax 395-4085. Look for the 39-foot-/12-m-long skis! Or contact the Cariboo Tourist Assoc., P.O. Box 4900, Williams Lake, BC V2G 2VB; phone toll free (800) 663-5885. Also the South Cariboo Chamber of Commerce, Box 2312, 100 Mile House, BC V0K 2E0; phone (250) 395-5353; Internet: www.netshop.net/-100mile/sccofc.html.

This large, bustling town was once a stop for fur traders and later a post house on the Cariboo Waggon Road to the goldfields. In 1930, the Marquess of Exeter established the 15,000-acre Bridge Creek Ranch here. Today, 100 Mile House is the site of 2 lumber mills, and an extensive log home building industry.

Visitor services include restaurants, motels, a campground, gas stations with repair service, stores, a post office, 2 golf courses, a government liquor store, 2 supermarkets and banks. Shopping malls and the downtown area are located east of the highway. Centennial Park in town has picnic sites and walking trails.

100 Mile House is a popular destination for snowmobiling and cross-country skiing in winter. It is also the jumping-off point for fishermen headed for Canim Lake and Mahood Lake in Wells Gray Provincial Park. Well-known for its spectacular waterfalls, including 460-foot/140-m Helmcken Falls, 4th largest in Canada, Wells Gray main entrance is from Yellowhead Highway 5 at Clearwater. Yellowhead Highway 5 is logged in *Northwest Mileposts®*, available from Vernon Publications Inc.; phone (800) 726-4707.

Horse Lake Road leads east from 100 Mile House to **Horse Lake** (kokanee) and other fishing lakes of the high plateau.

99 Mile Motel. Air-conditioned sleeping and housekeeping units. Fridges in all units, housekeeping units with microwave ovens. DD touchtone phones, remote control cable TV, super channel and TSN, courtesy in-room coffee and tea. Carports, winter plug-ins, freezer available for guests, bowling, legion; supermarket and cross-country ski trails. Senior citizens discount, commercial rates, partially wheelchair accessible, small dogs only. Highway 97, 100 Mile House, BC V0K 2E0. (250) 395-2255 (call collect), or fax (250) 395-2243. [ADVERTISEMENT]

100 Mile Motel and RV Park. 310 Highway 97. Centrally located. Ground-level sleeping and housekeeping units. DD phones, cable TV. RV park and campground, quiet setting, pull-throughs with 30-amp service, showers, flush toilets, cable TV (mid-April to end of October), close to all amenities. Your hosts, Mark and Teresa Livingston. 100 Mile House, BC. Phone (250) 395-2234. See display ad this section. [ADVERTISEMENT]

West Access Route Log

(continued)

CC 74 (119 km) **PG 203** (326.7 km) **Junction** with road east to **Ruth, Canim** and **Mahood lakes**; resorts and fishing. Camping at Canim Beach Provincial Park (27 miles/43 km); 16 sites, water, pit toilets, swimming. Access to Canim Falls.

CC 78.2 (125.8 km) **PG 198.8** (319.9 km) 108 Mile Ranch, a recreational community built in the 1970s, was once a cattle ranch. Motel and golf course.

CC 80.5 (129.5 km) **PG 196.5** (316.2 km) Rest area to west beside 108 Mile Lake. Alongside is 108 Heritage Site with some of the original log buildings from 108 Mile Ranch, and others relocated from 105 Mile. Guided tours; open May to early September.

CC 85 (136.8 km) **PG 192** (309 km) **Big Country KOA.** Located on 60 acres of rolling ranchland 3 miles south of Lac La Hache. Heated swimming pool, free showers, store, gift shop, laundromat, games room. Extra-long shady pull-throughs; shaded grassy tent sites; camping cabin. Full hookup facilities, sani-dump, phone. Pets welcome. VISA, MasterCard. (250) 396-4181. Box 68, Lac La Hache, BC V0K 1T0. [ADVERTISEMENT]

CC 88 (141.6 km) **PG 189** (304.2 km) **LAC LA HACHE** (pop. 400; elev. 2,749 feet/838m); motels, stores, gas stations and a museum. The community holds a fishing derby in July and a winter carnival in mid-February. Lac La Hache is French for "Ax Lake." There are many stories of how the lake got its name, but local historian Molly Forbes says it was named by a French–Canadian *coureur de bois* (voyageur) "because of a small ax he found on its shores."

Lac La Hache, lake char, rainbow and kokanee; good fishing summer and winter (great ice fishing).

CC 92 (148.1 km) **PG 185** (297.7 km) **Fir Crest Resort** (Good Sam). Quiet parklike setting just two minutes from Highway 97, but away from traffic noise. Full hookups including pull-throughs, camping and cabins on the lakeshore. Sandy beach, swimming, games room, groceries, sani-dump, laundromat. Full marina with boat, motor, canoe and tackle rentals. Show this ad for a 10 percent discount. Phone (250) 396-7337. [ADVERTISEMENT]

CC 93.3 (150.1 km) **PG 183.7** (295.6 km) **Clancys'** restaurant, truck stop (full-serve gas, diesel, propane), convenience store and gifts. Open 7 A.M.–12 A.M. 2 acres, paved parking, air-conditioned, licensed with home cooking and homemade desserts. Very easy access to pumps for any length of vehicle. American exchange. Clancys', located Mile 122, Highway 97 at Kokanee Bay. [ADVERTISEMENT]

CC 93.4 (150.3 km) **PG 183.6** (295.4 km) **Kokanee Bay Motel and Campground.** Relaxation at its finest right on the lakeshore. Fish for kokanee and char or take a refreshing dip. We have a modern, comfortable motel, cabins. Full trailer hookups, grassy tenting area, hot showers, laundromat. Aquabike, boat and canoe rentals. Fishing tackle and ice. Phone (250) 396-7345. Fax (250) 396-4990. [ADVERTISEMENT] ▲

CC 96 (154.5 km) **PG 181** (291.3 km) **Crystal Springs (Historical) Resort Ltd.** Visit the Cariboo's best. We honour Good Sam, AAA and are a Good Neighbor Park, senior rates. 8 miles north of Lac La Hache. Parklike setting on lakeshore. Showers, flush toilets, laundromat, full (20- and 30-amp pull-throughs) and partial hookups, boat rentals. New chalets. Groceries, tackle, camping supplies, handicrafts. Games room, playground, picnic shelter. Pets on leash. Public beach and boat launch adjacent, fishing. Your hosts, Doug and Lorraine Whitesell. Phone (250) 396-4497. [ADVERTISEMENT] ♿▲

CC 96 (154.5 km) **PG 181** (291.3 km) **Lac La Hache** Provincial Park; 83 campsites, lakeshore picnic area, water, flush and pit toilets, firewood, dump station, boat launch, swimming, hiking trail and fishing. Camping on east side of highway, picnicking and boat launch on west side of highway. ▲

CC 97 (156.1 km) **PG 180** (289.7 km) San Jose River parallels highway to west. Canadian artist A.Y. Jackson painted in this valley.

CC 104.4 (168 km) **PG 172.6** (277.7 km) Stop of interest sign commemorating the miners, traders and adventurers who came this way to the Cariboo goldfields in the 1860s.

CC 116.6 (187.6 km) **PG 160.4** (258.1 km) 148 Mile Ducks Unlimited conservation area. This is an important waterfowl breeding area in Canada and offers good bird watching for bald eagles, osprey, great horned owls, American kestrels and pileated woodpeckers.

CC 118.5 (190.7 km) **PG 158.5** (255.1 km) **150 MILE HOUSE,** so named because it was 150 miles from Lillooet on the old Cariboo Waggon Road. The post office, which serves about 1,200 people in the area, was established in 1871. Hotel, restaurant, pub, gas station with repair service and a store open daily. Hunting and fishing licenses available at the store.

CC 119.1 (191.7 km) **PG 157.9** (254.1 km) **Junction** with road to **Quesnel** and **Horsefly lakes.** Horsefly Lake Provincial Park (40 miles/65 km) has 22 campsites. Fishing for rainbow and lake trout. ▲

Fall colours on McLeese Lake. (© Fred Chapman, DIARAMA)

Williams Lake

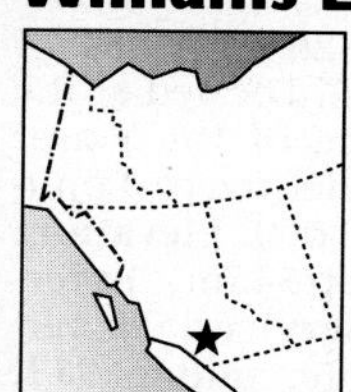

CC 128 (206 km) **PG 149** (239.8 km) Located at the junction of Highway 97 and Highway 20 to Bella Coola. **Population:** 36,737. **Elevation:** 1,922 feet/586m. **Emergency Services: Police,** phone (250) 392-6211. **Hospital,** phone (250) 392-4411. **Ambulance,** phone (250) 392-5402.

Visitor Information: Visitor Infocentre located on east side of highway just south of the junction of Highways 97 and 20, open year-round; phone (250) 392-5025, fax (250) 392-4214. Write 1148 S. Broadway, Williams Lake, BC V2G 1A2. Or contact the Cariboo Tourism Association, P.O. Box 4900, Williams Lake, BC V2G 2V8; phone toll free (800) 663-5885.

The administrative and transportation hub of the Cariboo–Chilcotin region, Williams Lake has complete services, including hotels/motels, restaurants, an 18-hole golf course and par-3 golf course, a twin sheet arena and pool complex. Highway 97 northbound bypasses the business and shopping districts of downtown Williams Lake, which are situated to the west of the highway. Motels, gas stations and fast-food restaurants are located on frontage roads paralleling Highway 97 on the south side of town.

A museum featuring the ranching and rodeo history of the region is located downtown at the corner of 4th Avenue and Borland; open year-round.

The airport, 7 miles/11 km north of town on Highway 97, is served by daily flights to Vancouver and other interior communities.

Located on the shore of the lake of the same name, it was named for Shuswap Indian Chief Willyum. The town grew rapidly with the advent of the Pacific Great Eastern Railway (now B.C. Railway) in 1919, to become a major cattle marketing and shipping centre for the Cariboo–Chilcotin. Today the city has the largest and most active cattleyards in the province. Lumber and mining for copper–molybdenum are the mainstays of the economy.

The famous Williams Lake Stampede, British Columbia's premier rodeo, is held here annually on the July 1 holiday. The 4-day event draws contestants from all over Canada and the United States. The rodeo grounds are located in the city.

At the north end of Williams Lake is Scout Island Nature Center. This island is reached by a causeway, with boardwalks providing access to the marshes. A nature house is open May to August.

Highway 20, the Chilcotin Highway, heads west from Williams Lake 282 miles/454 km (paved and gravel) to Bella Coola, giving access to the Chilcotin country's excellent fishing, Tweedsmuir Provincial Park, and the remote central coast. At Heckman Pass (elev. 5,000 feet/1,524m), 218.5 miles/352 km west of Williams Lake, the highway descends a section of narrow, switchbacked road with an 18 percent grade for 5.4 miles/9 km. Highway 20 is logged in *Northwest Mileposts®* (Vernon Publications Inc.; phone 800/726-4707).

Fraser Inn. See display ad this section.

West Access Route Log
(continued)

CC 136.4 (219.5 km) **PG 140.6** (226.3 km) Wildwood Road; gas station, store, access to private campground. ▲

Wildwood RV Park. See display ad this section. ▲

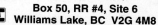

C 141.3 (227.3 km) **PG 135.7** (218.4 km) Turnout with litter barrel.

CC 141.8 (228.2 km) **PG 135.2** (217.6 km) **Whispering Willows Outpost Campground and Store.** RV pull-throughs, sani-dump. Power and water hookups, free hot showers, flush toilets. Level, spacious treed area for camping. Safe firepits, wood available. Teepee for rent. Play area. Confectionary store. Pets and horse trailers welcome, corrals available. Deep Creek runs by Whispering Willows Campground, RR 4, Site 12, Comp. 46, Williams Lake, BC V2G 4M8. (250) 989-0359. [ADVERTISEMENT] ▲

CC 145.3 (233.9 km) **PG 131.7** (211.9 km) Turnout with litter barrel.

CC 147.8 (237.9 km) **PG 129.2** (207.9 km) Replica of a turn-of-the-century roadhouse (current status of services unknown) at junction with side road which leads west 2.5 miles/4.5km to the tiny settlement of **SODA CREEK**. The original wagon road to the goldfields ended here and miners went the rest of the way to Quesnel by river steamboats. Soda Creek became an important transfer point for men and supplies until the railway went through in 1920. Soda Creek was so named because the creek bed is carbonate of lime and the water bubbles like soda water.

CC 155 (249.4 km) **PG 122** (196.4 km) **McLEESE LAKE,** small community with gas stations, cafe, post office, store, pub, private campground and motel on McLeese Lake. The lake was named for a Fraser River steamboat skipper. **McLeese Lake**, rainbow to 2 lbs., troll using a flasher, worms or flatfish lure. ▲

Junction with road to Beaver Lake and on to Likely. Historic Quesnelle Forks, a heritage site with a Forestry campsite, is located near Likely. Travelers may continue north from Likely to Barkerville and rejoin Highway 97 at Quesnel.

CC 155.5 (250.2 km) **PG 121.5** (195.5 km) Rest area to west overlooking McLeese Lake.

CC 160 (257.5 km) **PG 117** (188.3 km) Turnout with litter barrel to west with plaque about Fraser River paddle-wheelers.

CC 164 (263.9 km) **PG 113** (181.8 km) **Cariboo Wood Shop**. Specializing in Canadiana gifts, custom wood working on premises, hand-carved faces, unique custom wood boxes. Pottery, wheat weaving, souvenirs, toys and puzzles. Music tapes and CDs. Fresh fudge, 24 varieties; ask about our seasonal special! Easy access drive-through loop for RVs. Open 7 days a week 9:30 A.M.–5:30 P.M. Groups welcome. Phone (800) 986-WOOD. [ADVERTISEMENT]

CC 166 (267 km) **PG 111** (178.6 km) Glass sculpture museum and rock shop.

Cornish waterwheel used in gold mines is displayed at Quesnel's Riverfront Park.
(© Fred Chapman, DIARAMA)

the Castle. See display ad this section.

CC 166.5 (267.9 km) **PG 110.5** (177.8 km) Marguerite rest area. View upriver to Marguerite reaction cable ferry across the Fraser River. Ferry crossing takes 10 minutes, operates 7 A.M. to 6:45 P.M.; 2 cars and 10 passengers, no charge.

CC 168.5 (271.2 km) **PG 108.5** (174.6 km) Basalt columns to east create a formation known as the Devil's Palisades. Cliff swallows nest in the columns.

CC 169.8 (273.2 km) **PG 107.2** (172.5 km) Stone cairn commemorates Fort Alexandria, the last North West Co. fur-trading post established west of the Rockies, built in 1821. The actual site of the fort is across the river. Cairn also marks the approximate farthest point reached by Alexander Mackenzie in his descent of the Fraser in 1793.

CC 179.9 (289.6 km) **PG 97.1** (156.2 km) **Cariboo Place Campsite**. We have the Cariboo in the palm of our hands. Beautiful natural park setting. A convenient and delightful stop, just off Highway 97. Pull-through bays for large units, tenters welcome. Exceptionally clean showers and washrooms. Laundromat. Picnic tables and firepits. Sani-dump station. Electrical and water hookups. Pets welcome but must be leashed. Rates $13–$15 plus tax. Electrical and water extra. Open 24 hours. [ADVERTISEMENT] ▲

CC 180 (289.7 km) **PG 97** (156.1 km) Australian rest area to west with toilets, tables and litter barrels. Private campground to east. ▲

CC 188.5 (303.4 km) **PG 88.5** (142.4 km) Kersley (unincorporated), gas and food.

CC 188.6 (303.6 km) **PG 88.4** (142.3 km) Restaurant, gas and private campground. ▲

CC 195.8 (315.1 km) **PG 81.2** (130.6 km) **Dragon Lake Golf Course & Campsite.** Situated on edge of Dragon Lake. RV and campsites at $10 per night. Flush toilets, showers, sani-dump, wharf, trout fishing. Located off Hwy 97 just 10 minutes south of city centre. 9-hole golf course with driving range. Snack bar, lounge. Campers register at golf club pro shop. Phone (250) 747-1358. 1692 Flint Avenue, Quesnel, BC, V2J 2M6. [ADVERTISEMENT] ▲

CC 196 (315.4 km) **PG 81** (130.4 km) South end of loop road east to **Dragon Lake,** a small, shallow lake popular with Quesnel families. Camping and fishing for rainbow. ▲

CC 196 (315.4 km) **PG 81** (130.4 km) **Robert's Roost Campsite** located 6 km south of Quesnel and 2 km east of Highway 97 in a parklike setting on beautiful Dragon Lake. Grass sites, both partial and fully serviced. 15- and 30-amp service. Sani-dump, fishing, boat rental, swimming, horseshoes, playground, coin-operated showers, flush toilets and laundromat. Can accommodate any length unit. Limited accommodation. Ask about our e-mail access. Approved by Tourism BC. Hosts: Bob and Vivian Wurm, 3121 Gook Road, Quesnel, BC V2J 4K7. Phone (250) 747-2015 or (888) 227-8877. [ADVERTISEMENT] ▲

CC 197.5 (317.8 km) **PG 79.5** (127.9 km) **Valhalla Motel.** Quietly situated at the top of Dragon Hill. All rooms have air conditioning, individual electric heat, colour televisions, direct dial telephones, queen beds, refrigerators. Nonsmoking rooms available. Complimentary coffee. Guest laundry. Winter plug-ins. Close to fairgrounds, recreation centre, racing oval, shopping centre. Senior discount. Pets welcome. Major credit cards. 2010 Valhalla Rd., Quesnel, BC V2J 4C1. (250) 747-1111. See display ad this section. [ADVERTISEMENT]

Quesnel

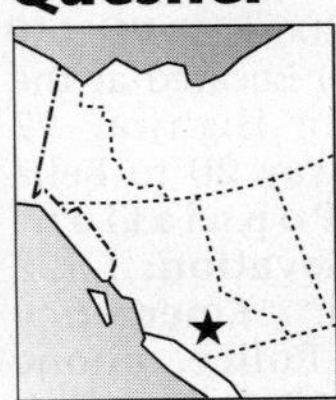

CC 203 (326.7 km) **PG 74** (119.1 km). Located at the confluence of the Fraser and Quesnel rivers. **Population:** 10,000. **Elevation:** 1,789 feet/545m. **Emergency Services:** Emergency only, phone 911. **RCMP**, phone (250) 992-9211. **Ambulance**, phone (250) 992-3211. **Hospital,** phone (250) 992-2181.

Visitor Information: Located on the

west side of the highway just north of Quesnel River bridge, in LeBourdais Park. Open year-round. Write Quesnel Visitor Infocentre, Stn. A, 703 Carson Ave., Quesnel, BC V2J 2B6; phone (250) 992-8716, or toll free (800) 992-4922. For information on the Cariboo Tourist Region, contact the Cariboo Tourist Assoc., P.O. Box 4900 Williams Lake, BC V2G 2V8; phone toll free (800) 663-5885.

Quesnel (kwe NEL) began as a supply town for the miners in the gold rush of the 1860s. The city was named after the Quesnel River, which in turn was named after fur trader Jules Maurice Quesnel, a member of Simon Fraser's 1808 expedition down the Fraser River and later a political figure in Quebec. Today, forestry is the dominant economic force in Quesnel, with 2 pulp mills, a plywood plant, and 5 sawmills and planer mills. Check with the Tourist Infocentre about tours.

Accommodations include 4 hotels, 15 motels, 5 bed and breakfasts and 8 campgrounds. There are gas stations (with diesel and propane), 2 shopping malls and 45 restaurants offering everything from fast food to fine dining. Golf and a recreation centre with pool are available.

Visitors can take a walking tour of the city along the Riverfront Park trail system. The 3.1-mile/5-km north Quesnel trail starts at Ceal Tingley Park at the confluence of the Fraser and Quesnel rivers. The west Quesnel trail is a 2.7-mile/4.3-km walk through a residential area. Trail information is available at the Visitor Infocentre.

Local attractions include the Quesnel and District Museum and Archives, located adjacent the Tourist Infocentre. It has been noted as one of the best community museums in the province, and boasts the largest collection of Chinese artifacts west of Ottawa.

There are some interesting hoodoo formations and scenic canyon views at Pinnacles Provincial Park, 5 miles/8 km west of Highway 97; picnicking. It is a 1.1-mile/1.8-km walk round-trip from the parking area to the pinnacle viewpoints.

Quesnel offers gold panning tours, guided hiking tours and Voyager canoe trips on the Fraser River. Boat tours are also available on other area rivers. Contact the Visitor Infocentre for more information.

A worthwhile side trip is Highway 26, which intersects Highway 97 at **Milepost CC 206.** This 51-mile/82-km paved highway leads to Wells, Bowron Lake and Barkerville Provincial Historic Park, a reconstructed and restored Cariboo gold rush town. (See HIGHWAY 26 side road log pages 68-69.) Gold Pan City Stage Lines offers charter and scheduled tours of Barkerville and surrounding area from Quesnel.

Billy Barker Days, a 4-day event held the third full weekend in July, commemorates the discovery of gold at Barkerville in 1862. Held in conjunction with the Quesnel Rodeo, Billy Barker Days is the third largest outdoor family festival in the province. For more information, write Box 4441, Quesnel, BC V2J 3J4. The Barlow Creek Music Festival takes place on Highway 26 the weekend after Billy Barker Days.

QUESNEL ADVERTISERS

Cariboo Tourist Assoc. .....Ph. (800) 663-5885
Heritage House Restaurant ....Ph. (250) 992-2700
Talisman Inn ....Ph. (250) 992-7247
Valhalla Motel ....Ph. (250) 747-1111

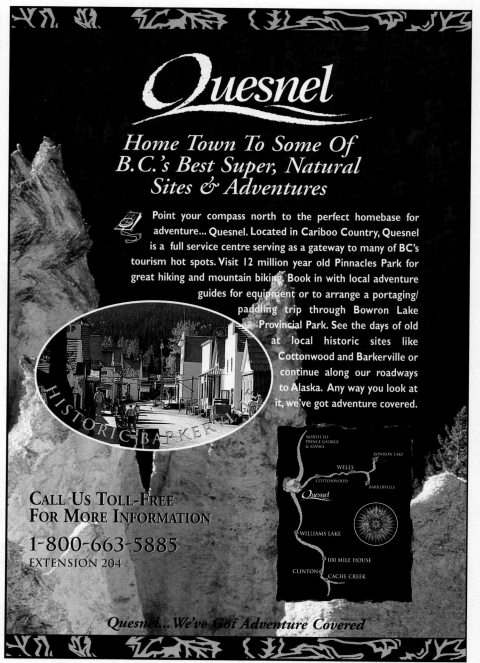

Highway 26 Log

This 51-mile/82-km paved road leads to Barkerville Historic Town in the historic Cariboo gold fields (active mining under way). Gas available in Wells.

The Barkerville gold strike was made in 1861. Today, Highway 16 follows the route of the original Cariboo wagon road built to serve the boom towns.

Distance from Highway 97 junction (J) is shown.

J **0 Junction** with Highway 97 at **Milepost CC 206.** Visitor Infocentre on southeast side of junction.

J 0.8 (1.3 km) Barlow Creek residential area; grocery, food and fuel. Eastbound, Highway 26 accesses local roads. Watch for deer.

J 13 (21 km) Rest area and interpretive trails to south. Wooden rail "snake" and wire fences with wooden top rail allow deer and moose to safely jump them, while penning domestic livestock.

J 15.2 (24.5 km) Cottonwood River bridge. The river is named for the black cottonwood trees growing alongside it.

J 16.7 (26.9 km) Cottonwood House Historic Site, a restored and furnished log roadhouse built in 1864. Gift shop, coffee shop, picnicking and guided tours by costumed docents. Open May to September.

J 20.1 (32.4 km) Swift River Forest Road leads 0.2 mile/0.3 km to Lightning Creek Forest Service recreation site (first turn on left); free camping, 14-day limit. *CAUTION: Active logging road, drive with headlights on.* ▲

J 21.4 (34.5 km) Lover's Leap viewpoint and Mexican Hill Summit, one of the steepest grades on the original Cariboo Waggon Road, to the south.

J 27.1 (43.6 km) Historical stop of interest marker for Charles Morgan Blessing's grave. Blessing, from Ohio, was murdered on his way to Barkerville in 1866. His killer, John Barry, was caught when he gave Blessing's keepsake gold nugget stickpin, in the shape of a skull, to a Barkerville dance-hall girl. John Barry was the only white man hanged in the Cariboo during the gold rush.

J 37.3 (60.1 km) Stanley Road and Boulder Gold Mines (active claim). Stanley Road is a 1.9-mile/3-km loop road that leads past the gold-rush ghost towns of Stanley and VanWinkle, the old Lightning Hotel, and gold rush-era gravesites. A worthwhile sidetrip.

J 38.6 (62.2 km) Stanley (Loop) Road, Chisholm Creek. Remnants of Stanley townsite and cemetery dating back to 1800's. The authentic Stanley Trail leads from the townsite through the remnants of Van Winkle, ending at the Richfield Courthouse in Barkerville.

J 40.2 (64.7 km) Devil's Canyon paved turnout on south. This was the highest point on the Cariboo Waggon Road.

J 42.9 (69 km) Slough Creek, site of much hydraulic mining activity after Joe Shaw discovered gold here in 1870.

J 44.9 (72.2 km) Paved turnout to litter barrel to south. **Jack o' Clubs Lake**; fishing for rainbows, lake trout and Dolly Varden.

J 45.2 (72.7 km) Rest area on peninsula to south with picnic tables, pit toilets and boat launch.

J 45.7 (73.6 km) Paved turnout with litter barrels to south.

J 46.1 (74.2 km) Lakeshore turnout with area information sign.

J 46.7 (75.2 km) **WELLS** (pop. 300, elevation 4,200 feet/1280m) offers all visitor facilities, including motels, restaurants, liquor outlet, groceries, gas, fishing and hunting licenses, 24-hour towing and mechanics, art schools, laundromat and full-service RV park. The closest banking facilities are in Quesnel. Wells dates to the 1930s when the Cariboo Gold Quartz Mine, promoted and developed by Fred Wells, brought hundreds of workers to this valley. The mine closed in 1967, but the town has continued as a service centre and attraction for tourists. There are numerous art galleries and gift shops, some housed in refurbished buildings from the 1930s. Guided and self-guided tours of the town are available. A museum with displays of local mining history is open daily from June to September.

Recreation in the area is centered around some 30 miles/50 km of marked trails leading into alpine country. Summer activities include hiking historical trails, mountain biking (rentals available), gold panning, llama trekking and fishing. In winter, trails are groomed for skiing, snowmobiling and dogsledding.

The local Legion hosts horseshoes and bocci tournaments, has a pub and offers potluck suppers throughout the year. Winter events include: Yamafest in November; the Gold Rush Dogsled races in January; Snowarama in February; and the Great Canadian Hillclimb in March.

Merchants of Wells. See display ad this section.

The Wells Hotel. See display ad this section.

J 49.6 (79.8 km) Barkerville Provincial Park Forest Rose Campground to north. Lowhee Campground to south; 170 campsites, picnic areas and dump stations. ▲

J 50 (80.5 km) Gravel road leads north 18 miles/29 km to **Bowron Lakes** Provincial Park, noted for its interconnecting chain of lakes and the resulting 72-mile/116-km canoe circuit which takes from 7 to 10 days to complete. Visitor information available at registration centre next to main parking lot where canoeists must register and pay circuit fees. Reservations recommended in July and August (required for 7 or more people); phone (250) 992-3111.

Airfield at junction with 2,500-foot/762-m paved runway, elev. 4,180 feet/1,274m.

There are 2 private lodges at the north end of the lake with restaurants, camping (at Becker's Lodge), a general store and canoe rentals. Provincial park campground has 25 sites, water, pit toilets, firewood and a boat launch. Swimming, fishing, canoeing, kayaking and hiking. ▲

Becker's Lodge. Overlooking Bowron Lake and the snowcapped Cariboo Mountains from our beautifully restored lodge restaurant, open for breakfast, lunch and dinner. We also offer cabins, chalets and bungalows, campsites with firepits and picnic tables. Hot showers, flush toilets, coin laundry. Licensed canoe outfitter for the Bowron Lake Wilderness Park. Canoe/kayak day-rentals. Store. Reservations: (800) 808-4761. Local calls: (250) 992-8864. [ADVERTISEMENT] ▲

J 50.1 (80.7 km) Entrance to Barkerville; admission charged. Admission fees in 1997 for a 2-day pass were: Adults, $5.50; youth and seniors, $3.25; children, $1; and families, $10.75.

J 50.3 (81.7 km) Former site of Cameronton, named for John A. "Cariboo" Cameron who found gold in this area. Also in this area is Williams Creek, the richest gold-producing creek during the gold rush.

J 50.9 (81.9 km) Turnoff on 1.8-mile/2.9-km side road for gold rush cemetery and Government Hill Campground (0.2 mile/0.4 km), New Barkerville (0.4 mile/0.7 km) and Grubstake Store (0.7 mile/1.1 km). ▲

J 51 (82.1 km) **BARKERVILLE**, a provincial historic town; open year-round, phone (604) 994-3332. Visitor information at Reception Centre.

Barkerville was named for miner Billy Barker, who struck gold on Williams Creek. The resulting gold rush in 1862 created Barkerville. Virtually a ghost town when the provincial government began restoration in 1958, today Barkerville's buildings and boardwalks are faithful restorations or reconstructions from the town's heyday. Visitors can pan for gold, shop at the old-time general store, watch a blacksmith at work, or take in a show at the Theatre Royal. Restaurants and food service available. It is best to visit between June 1 and Labour Day, when the Theatre Royal offers performances and all exhibits are open.

The Theatre Royal is extremely popular with visitors. The half-hour spring show plays daily (except Saturdays) from 12:45 to 1:15 P.M. between May and June. Regular season begins mid-June and continues until Labour Day. Admission is charged at all shows.

History comes alive at Barkerville thanks to interpreters and street performers who represent actual citizens of the town in 1870, discuss "current" events with visitors, conduct tours and stage daily dramas throughout the summer.

Beyond Main Street, the Cariboo Waggon Road leads on (for pedestrians only) to Richfield, 1 mile/1.6 km, to the courthouse of "Hanging" Judge Begbie.

Return to Milepost CC 206
West Access Route

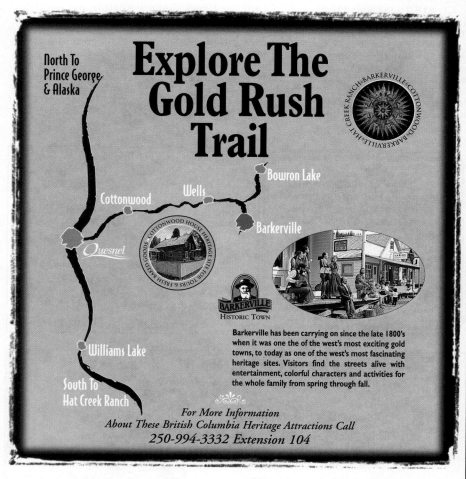

West Access Route Log

(continued)

CC 206 (331.5 km) **PG 71** (114.3 km) Quesnel airport. **Junction** with Highway 26 to Barkerville and Bowron Lake. See HIGHWAY 26 side road log this section.

CC 209.5 (337.2 km) **PG 67.5** (108.6 km) **Lazy Daze Resort.** RV sites, cabins and tenting only 3 minutes off highway. Pull-throughs, hookups. 30 amp service. Free hot showers for guests. Located on Ten Mile Lake; boat rentals, convenience store, laundry, play area and picnic shelter. Toll free (888) 992-9872 or (250) 992-3282. RR8, Box 29, Best site, Quesnel, BC, V2J 5E6. [ADVERTISEMENT] ▲

CC 210 (338 km) **PG 67** (107.8 km) **Ten Mile Lake** Provincial Park; 142 campsites, flush toilets, picnic area, boat launch, good swimming beach, nature trails, dump station. Self-guided trail to beaver colony, good bird watching (pileated woodpeckers, warblers, snowy owls). Good fishing for rainbow to 3 lbs. ▲

10 Mile Lake Provincial Park—Clean, friendly park, one paved kilometer from Highway 97. Quiet, treed sites with table and firepit. Some pull-throughs available. Coin-operated hot showers. Security gates closed 11 P.M.–7 A.M. 30 kms of hiking and maintained mountain bike trails. Playground. Ask about our park naturalist programs and special events. Only one hour to Barkerville. [ADVERTISEMENT] ▲

CC 214.2 (344.7 km) **PG 62.8** (101.1 km) Cottonwood River bridge. Turnout with litter barrels and stop-of-interest sign at south end of bridge describing railway bridge seen upriver.

CC 218.7 (352 km) **PG 58.3** (93.8 km) Hush Lake rest area to west; toilets, tables, litter barrels.

CC 221.5 (356.6 km) **PG 55.5** (89.3 km) **Triple "J" Ranch.** Free rustic overnight RV parking or camping with purchase of minimum 2-hour trail ride. We offer hourly, daily and overnight horseback trips. Pony rides, petting zoo, souvenir and gift shop, snack shack. Come ride with us for that real cowboy experience on our working ranch. Phone (250) 998-4746. [ADVERTISEMENT]

CC 226 (363.7 km) **PG 51** (82 km) **Cinema 2nd Hand.** General store, groceries. Movie rentals, souvenirs. Local artwork, circle drive. 9 A.M.–9 P.M. every day. Free camping, picnic tables, firepits and wood, toilet, some long pull-throughs, some shady sites, fireworks, phone. Welcome to friendly Cinema, BC. Vic and Theresa Olson, RR 1 Box 1, Site 10, Hixon, BC V0K 1S0. (250) 998-4774. [ADVERTISEMENT] ▲

CC 229.6 (369.5 km) **PG 47.4** (76.3 km) Strathnaver (unincorporated), no services.

CC 241 (387.8 km) **PG 36** (58 km) **HIXON** (pop. 1,500) has a post office, 2 motels, gas stations, grocery stores, 2 restaurants (1 with licensed premises), a pub and private campground. Hixon is the Cariboo's most northerly community. Extensive placer mining took place here in the early 1900s. Southbound motorists watch for roadside display about points of interest in the Cariboo region located just north of Hixon. ▲

Hixon Fireplace Inn. Excellent cuisine. Food preparation on the premises. Soups and chowders. In-season specialties. Try our delicious pies. Easy RV access, ample parking. Monday to Saturday 7 A.M. to 8 P.M., Sunday noon to 8 P.M. Your hosts, Dave and Fran Krieger. Most major credit cards, Interac. Wir spechen Deutch. (250) 998-4518. [ADVERTISEMENT]

CC 247.6 (398.5 km) **PG 29.4** (47.3 km) Woodpecker rest area to west; toilets, tables, litter barrels.

CC 257.7 (414.7 km) **PG 19.3** (31 km) Stoner (unincorporated), no services.

CC 261.8 (421.3 km) **PG 15.2** (24.5 km) Red Rock (unincorporated); ice; gas station with diesel; pay phone.

CC 268.3 (431.8 km) **PG 8.7** (14 km) **Bee Lazee RV Park, Campground & Honey Farm.** See display ad this section. ▲

CC 270.6 (435.5 km) **PG 6.4** (10.3 km) **Junction** with bypass road to Yellowhead 16 East. Keep left for Prince George; continue straight ahead for Jasper and Edmonton. If you are headed east on Yellowhead Highway 16 for Jasper or Edmonton, turn to **Milepost E 450** in the YELLOWHEAD HIGHWAY 16 section and read the log back to front.

CC 273 (439.3 km) **PG 4** (6.4 km) **Southpark RV Park.** See display ad this section. ▲

CC 273.4 (440 km) **PG 3.6** (5.8 km) Access to Prince George airport to east.

CC 274 (440.9 km) **PG 3** (4.8 km) **Sintich Trailer Park.** See display ad this section. ▲

CC 275.2 (442.8 km) **PG 1.8** (2.8 km) Bridge over the Fraser River. Turn right at north end of bridge then left at stop sign for city centre via Queensway. This is the easiest access for Fort George Park; follow Queensway to 20th Avenue and turn east.

Continue straight ahead for Highway 16 entrance to city.

CC 276 (444.1 km) **PG 1** (1.6 km) **Junction** of Highway 97 with Yellowhead 16 West. Description of Prince George follows. If you are headed west on Yellowhead Highway 16 for Prince Rupert, turn to **Milepost PG 0** in the YELLOWHEAD HIGHWAY 16 section. Prince Rupert is port of call for Alaska state ferries and BC Ferries.

Prince George

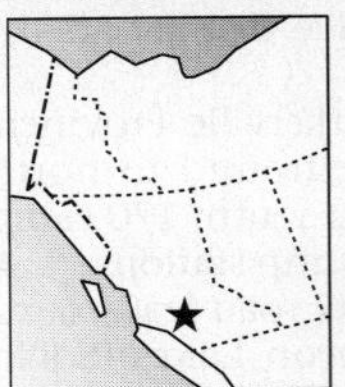

CC 277 (445.8 km) **Population:** 76,500, area 160,000. **Emergency Services: RCMP**, phone (250) 562-3371, emergency only, phone 911. **Fire Department**, phone 911. **Ambulance**, 24-hour service, phone 911. **Poison Control Centre**, phone (250) 565-2442. **Hospital**, Prince George Regional, phone (250) 565-2000; emergency, phone (250) 565-2444.

Visitor Information: Tourism Prince George, Dept. MP, 1198 Victoria St., phone (250) 562-3700 or fax 563-3584, or toll free (800) 668-7646. Open year-round, 8:30 A.M. to 5 P.M. weekdays Monday through Saturday. Visitor centre, junction Yellowhead 16

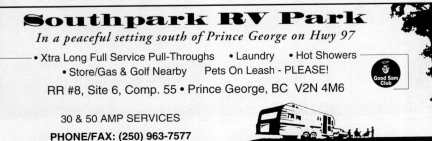

Canada is on the metric system: 1 gallon=3.785 liters; 1 liter=.2642 gallons; 1 mile=1.609 kilometres; 80 kmph=50 mph; 100 kmph=62 mph

PRINCE GEORGE

~ BC's Northern Capital ~

Dutch Maid Laundromat

☞ Shower ☞ 100% Soft Water
☞ Drop Off Laundry Service
☞ Open 8 am; last wash @ 8:45 pm

2930 5th Avenue (5th & Harper)
Prince George, BC Phone 564-1260
(3 BLOCKS OFF HIGHWAY 97)

6777 Hart Highway *(Playplace)*	3338 - 8th Avenue *(Playplace)*
3250 Massey Drive *(Playplace)*	5099 Domano Blvd. *(Express)*
2001 Victoria Street *(Playplace)*	Parkwood Place *(Express)*

Grama's Inn Ltd.

An Annex of Esther's Inn

901 Central Street, Prince George, BC
Canada V2M 3C8

• 62 Air Conditioned Units
• Family Restaurant • Cable TV
• Centrally Located

Ph:(250) 563-7174 Fax: (250) 563-7147

Steak.

In a word, that's what we do best.
Great steak, seafood, ribs, chicken salad bar and good friends.
See you tonight!

THE KEG®

582 George St. (Downtown)
Open from 4pm nightly

563-1768

PRINCE GEORGE RAILWAY & FORESTRY MUSEUM

Box 2048, Prince George
BC V2N 2S6
Ph: (250) 563-7351
Fax: (250) 563-7337

The Museum site is open from May 'till September. Besides the large collection of rolling stock and static displays, the museum is also home to an old firehall, telephone and telegraph display.

A Tropical Oasis in Northern BC

Esther's Inn

LOUNGE • DINING ROOM
COFFEE GARDEN • SWIMMING POOL
Jacuzzis • Sauna • Waterslides
132 Air Conditioned Units
Health and Fitness Club
In-House Movies

1151 Commercial Drive
Prince George, BC V2M 6W6
Toll Free 1-800-663-6844
Phone: 250-562-4131 Fax: 250-562-4145
Located at 10th Avenue off Highway 97

Prince George Native Art Gallery

TRADITIONAL & CONTEMPORARY NATIVE ARTS

carvings - prints & original works of art - handcrafted leather work - silver & gold jewellery

- CUSTOM ORDERS TAKEN -
(250) 562-7385
1600 - 3rd Avenue

Prince George ART GALLERY

Local Regional and National Artists

Call (250) 563-6447 or 1-888-221-1155 for special events and exhibitions.
2820-15th Avenue, Prince George
e-mail pgag@vortex.netbistro.com

northwood
pulp and timber limited

Pulpmill, Sawmill and Plywood Mill Tours
Presented by ...
Tourism Prince George at
(250) 562-3700

ANCO MOTEL

• 65 comfortable rooms
• kitchenettes • affordable rates
• free phones • Cable TV
• fully licensed restaurant
• heated pool (seasonal)
• movie channels • laundry

Call (250) 563-3671 **1630 Central Street**
1-800-663-3290 (BC only) **(on Hwy 97)**

DOWNTOWN MOTEL

• 45 Comfortable Rooms • Air Conditioning
• Cable TV W/Remote • Movies
• Direct Dial Phones • Winter Plug-ins
Phone (250) 563-9241
BC Toll Free 1-800-663-5729
650 Dominion St., Prince George, BC V2L 1T8

Econo Lodge

1915 Third Avenue,
Prince George, BC V2M 1G6
Phone: 250-563-7106
Fax: 250-561-7216
1-800-55-ECONO

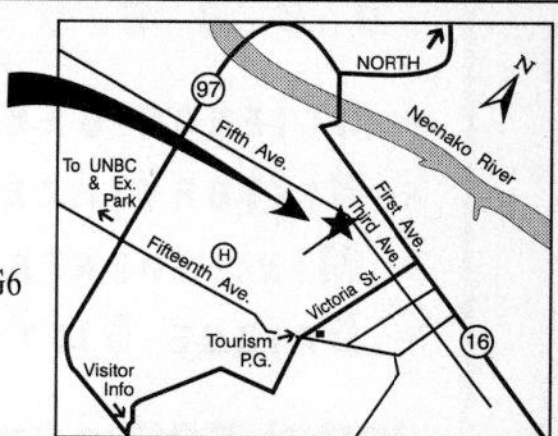

For Information Contact: Tourism Prince George, 1198 Victoria Street, Prince George, BC V2L 2L2
Phone: (250) 562-3700 Fax: (250) 563-3584 1-800-668-7646 e-mail: information@tourismpg.bc.ca

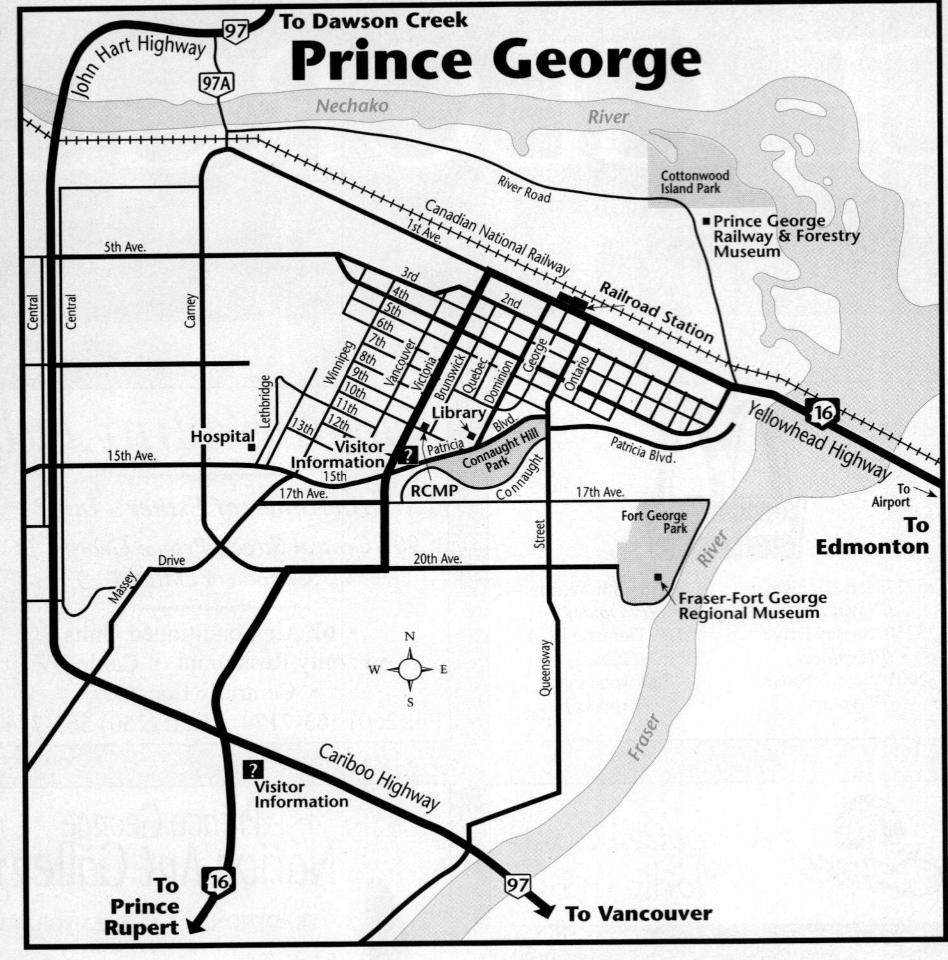

and Highway 97; open daily late-May to Labour Day, phone (250) 563-5493.

Elevation: 1,868 feet/569m. **Climate:** The inland location is tempered by the protection of mountains. The average annual frost-free period is 85 days, with 1,793 hours of bright sunshine. Dry in summer; chinooks off and on during winter which, accompanied by a western flow of air, break up the cold weather. Summer temperatures average 72°F/22°C with lows to 46°F/8°C. **Radio:** CKPG 550, CJCI 620, BC-FM 94.3, CBC-FM 91.5, C-101 FM. **Television:** 36 channels via cable. **Newspaper:** *The Citizen* (daily except Sunday); *Prince George This Week* (Sunday); *Free Press* (Thursday and Sunday).

Prince George is located at the confluence of the Nechako and Fraser rivers, near the geographical centre of British Columbia. It is the fourth largest city in British Columbia. Hub of the trade and travel routes of the province, Prince George is located at the junction of Yellowhead Highway 16—linking Prince Rupert on the west coast with the Interior of Canada—and Highway 97, which runs south to Vancouver and north to Dawson Creek.

In the early 1800s, Simon Fraser of the North West Trading Co. erected a post here which he named Fort George in honour of the reigning English monarch. In 1906, survey parties for the transcontinental Grand Trunk Pacific Railway (later Canadian National Railways) passed through the area, and with the building of the railroad a great land boom took place. The city was incorporated in 1915 under the name Prince George. Old Fort George is now a park and picnic spot and the site of Fort George Museum.

Prince George is primarily an industrial centre, fairly dependent on the lumber industry, with 3 pulp mills, sawmills, planers, dry kilns, a plywood plant and 2 chemical plants to serve the pulp mills. Oil refining, mining and heavy construction are other major area industries. The Prince George Forest Region is the largest in the province.

Prince George is the focal point of the central Interior for financial and professional services, equipment and wholesale firms, machine shops and many services for the timber industry. Canada's newest university opened here in the fall of 1994. The campus of the University of Northern British Columbia is located at the top of Cranbrook Hill.

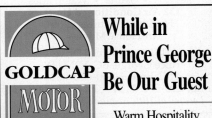

PRINCE GEORGE ADVERTISERS

Anco Motel ....Ph. (250) 563-3671
Arctic RV Service Centre...Ph. (250) 962-9631
Bed & Breakfast Assn. of Prince George..............Ph. (250) 964-2603
Blue Spruce RV Park & Campground ....Ph. (250) 964-7272
Celeste's R.V. Center Ltd. .Ph. (250) 962-2049
Downtown Motel ....Ph. (250) 563-9241
Dutch Maid Laundromat ..Ph. (250) 564-1260
Econo Lodge ....Ph. (250) 563- 7106
Esther's Inn ....Ph. (250) 562-4131
Fraser-Fort George Regional Museum.......Ph. (250) 562-1612
Goldcap Motor Inn..........Ph. (250) 563-0666
Grama's Inn ....Ph. (250) 563-7174
Inland Spring and Axle Ltd. ....Ph. (250) 562-9090
Keg, The...........................Ph. (250) 563-1768
McDonald's ....See ad for locations
Northwood Pulp and Timber Limited...................Tours available
Pine Centre Mall ....Ph. (250) 563-3681
P.G. Hi-Way Motel..................1737 20th Ave.
Prince George Art Gallery ....Ph. (250) 563-6447
Prince George Native Art Gallery ....Ph. (250) 562-7385
Prince George Railway & Forestry Museum.........Ph. (250) 563-7351
Ricky's Pancakes & Family Restaurant ....Ph. (250) 564-8114
Tourism Prince George.....Ph. (250) 562-3700

Agriculture in central British Columbia is basically a forage-livestock business, for which the climate and soils are well suited. Dairying and beef are the major livestock enterprises, with minor production in sheep and poultry.

ACCOMMODATIONS/VISITOR SERVICES

Prince George offers 5 hotels, 17 motels, 9 RV parks, and more than 3 dozen bed and breakfasts. Most accommodations are within easy reach of the business district. There are more than 80 restaurants in the city. Most stores are open 7 days a week. The usual hours of operation are: Sunday, noon to 5 P.M.; Saturday and Monday through Wednesday, 9:30 A.M. to 6 P.M.; Thursday and Friday, 9:30 A.M. to 9 P.M.

TRANSPORTATION

Air: Prince George airport is southeast of the city, serviced by Canadian Airlines International, Air BC and Central Mountain Air. Limousine service to and from the airport.

Railroad: VIA Rail connects Prince George with Prince Rupert and Jasper, AB. Passenger service south to Vancouver via British Columbia Railway 3 days a week.

Bus: Greyhound. City bus service by Prince George Transit & Charter Ltd.

ATTRACTIONS

City View: Follow Connaught Drive to the viewpoint at Connaught Hill Park for a panoramic view of the city.

City Landmarks: Centennial Fountain at the corner of 7th Avenue and Dominion Street depicts the early history of Prince George in mosaic tile. A cairn at Fort George Park commemorates Sir Alexander Mackenzie.

Fort George Park is the largest park in Prince George and a good stop for travelers with its playgrounds, picnic tables, barbecue facilities and museum. The Fort George Rail-

Unique stairway at Prince George's University of Northern British Columbia.
(© Judy Parkin, staff)

way operates on weekends and holidays at the park from a railway building patterned after the original Grand Trunk Pacific stations.

Fraser Fort George Regional Museum. Located in Fort George Park at 333 20th Avenue, the museum includes an explorations gallery focusing on the region's natural history and environment. A history hall provides an overview of the area's developmental history and includes an interactive multimedia film display. Open daily in summer, 10 A.M. to 5 P.M. Wheelchair accessible. Admission fee charged. For more information phone (250) 562-1612. ♿

Giscome Portage Regional Park, next to the scenic Fraser River, includes the Huble Homestead, which dates from 1912. These original and reconstructed buildings are surrounded by grazing land and forest. Picnic tables and snackbar. Guided interpretive tours during peak season; admission free. Located north of Prince George on Highway 97; turn east off the highway at **Milepost PG 26.9** and drive 3.7 miles/ 6 km.

Cottonwood Island Park, located on the Nechako River (see city map), has picnic facilities and extensive nature trails.

Prince George Railway and Forestry Museum features a dozen original railway buildings, including 2 stations. Among the 50 pieces of rolling stock are 5 locomotives, a 1903 snow plow, a 1913 100-ton steam wrecking crane and a 90-foot 100-ton turntable. Items from 8 past and present railway companies are displayed. There is also a small collection of forestry, mining and agricultural machinery. Located at 850 River Road next to Cottonwood Island Nature Park. Open May to September daily from 9:30 A.M. to 5 P.M. For more information phone (250) 563-7351.

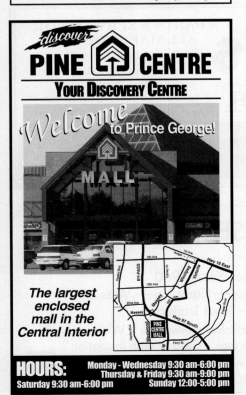

Golf Courses. Aspen Grove Golf Club is 9 miles/14.5 km south of the city; Yellowhead Grove Golf Club, Pine Valley Golf Club, and Prince George Golf and Curling Club are on Yellowhead Highway 16 West.

Swimming. Four Seasons Swimming Pool at the corner of 7th Avenue and Dominion Street has a pool, water slide, diving tank and fitness centre. Open to the public afternoons and evenings.

Rockhounding. The hills and river valleys in the area provide abundant caches of Omineca agate and Schmoos. For more information, contact Prince George Rock and Gem Club, phone (250) 562-4526; or Spruce City Rock and Gem Club, phone (250) 562-1013.

Tennis Courts. A total of 20 courts currently available to the public at 3 places: 20th Avenue near the entrance to Fort George Park; at Massey Drive in Carrie Jane Gray Park; and on Ospika Boulevard in the Lakewood Secondary School complex.

Industrial Tours are available from mid-May through August by contacting Tourism Prince George at (250) 562-3700. Tours, which are on weekdays only, include Northwood Pulp and Timber, Prince George Sawmill and North Central Plywoods. Tours of Prince George Pulp and Intercon Pulp are available June–August, Monday–Friday; reservations required.

Tours of the Pacific Western Brewery are available; reservations required. Phone (250) 562-2424 or (800) 663-8002, Monday through Friday.

Special Events: Elks May Day celebration; Prince George Regional Forest Exhibition in May (even years); Folkfest on July 1, Canada Day; Prince George Live, Sunday through Thursday during July and August; International Food Festival in August; Annual Sandblast Skiing in August; Prince George Airshow in July; Prince George Exhibition in August; Oktoberfest in October; and the winter Mardi Gras Festival in mid-February. Details on these and other events are available from Tourism Prince George; phone (250) 562-3700.

Side Trips: Prince George is the starting point for some of the finest holiday country in the province. There are numerous lakes and resorts nearby, among them: Bednesti Lake, 30 miles/48 km west of Prince George; Cluculz Lake, 44 miles/71 km west; Purden Lake, 42 miles/68 km east; and Tabor Lake, 6 miles/10 km east.

AREA FISHING: Highways 16 and 97 are the ideal routes for the sportsman, with year-round fishing and easy access to lakes and rivers. Hunters and fishermen stop over in Prince George as the jumping-off place for some of North America's finest big game hunting and fishing. For more information contact Fish & Wildlife at (250) 565-6145, or Tourism Prince George, phone (250) 562-3700.

West Access Route Log

(continued)

BC HIGHWAY 97/HART HIGHWAY

The John Hart Highway, completed in 1952, was named for the former B.C. premier who sponsored its construction. The highway is a 2-lane paved highway with both straight stretches and winding stretches.

This section of the log shows distance from Prince George (PG) followed by distance from Dawson Creek (DC).

PG 0 DC 250 (402.3 km) John Hart Bridge over the Nechako River. The 4-lane highway extends 6.5 miles/10.5 km northbound through the commercial and residential suburbs of Prince George.

PG 1.5 (2.4 km) **DC 248.5** (399.9 km) Truck weigh scales. 24-hour gas station with diesel and propane; lube and oil service.

PG 2.5 (4 km) **DC 247.5** (398.3 km) RV service centre.

PG 6.4 (10.3 km) **DC 243.6** (392 km) **Hartway RV Park.** Shaded, fully-serviced sites. Pull-throughs. Free hot showers, laundromat, 30-amp, cable TV. Groceries nearby.

Phone. On-site antique and gift shop. On south Kelly Road adjacent to highway. Access at stop light (Handlen Road Junction); south of RV park. 7729 South Kelly Rd., Prince George, BC V2K 3H5. Phone (250) 962-9724. [ADVERTISEMENT] ▲

PG 6.5 (10.5 km) **DC 243.5** (391.9 km) Two-lane highway (with passing lanes) begins abruptly northbound.

PG 9.5 (15.3 km) **DC 240.5** (387 km) **Northland RV Park.** Park-like setting with extra-wide, long sites; level, grassy pull-throughs. Full service sites with 20/30/50 amp service. For guests: Free hot showers and firewood. Pay phone. Pets on leash. Flush toilets. Cooking shelters. Easy access off highway. R.R. #2, Site 9, Comp. 1, Prince George, BC V2N 2H9. Phone/fax (250) 962-5010. [ADVERTISEMENT] ▲

PG 14.6 (23.5 km) **DC 235.4** (378.8 km) Salmon River bridge. Litter barrel and river access to west at north end of bridge.

PG 14.7 (23.6 km) **DC 235.3** (378.7 km) **Salmon Valley RV Park and Campground** and convenience store, on over 27 acres along the scenic Salmon River. All facilities are wheelchair accessible, including showers. 50 treed sites, 12 pull-throughs, all with fire

rings, tables, laundry. Limited water and power 15–30 amp. Swimming and camping on the Salmon that's second to none. Fair fishing for rainbows, grayling and spring salmon. "Home of the Happy Camper." Phone (250) 971-2212. Fax (250) 971-2229. Good Sam discounts. [ADVERTISEMENT] ♿▲

PG 16.4 (26.4 km) **DC 233.6** (375.9 km) Highway overpass crosses railroad tracks.

PG 22 (35.4 km) **DC 228** (366.9 km) Gravel turnouts both sides of highway.

PG 26.5 (42.6 km) **DC 223.5** (359.7 km) Paved turnout to east with litter barrels and point-of-interest sign about Crooked River Forest Recreation Area.

PG 26.9 (43.3 km) **DC 223.1** (359 km) Access east 3.7 miles/6 km to Giscome Portage regional park via Mitchell Road. Site of historic Huble Homestead; guided tours, picnicking. Free admission.

Historic Huble Homestead. Relax and visit a historic Northern BC settlement. Scenic location next to the mighty Fraser River. Original furnished log buildings. Includes the Huble's house—the oldest home in the region. Farm animals. Numerous picnic tables. Guided interpretive tours. Free admission. Just 6 km east of Highway 97. Phone (250) 960-4400. [ADVERTISEMENT]

PG 28.2 (45.4 km) **DC 221.8** (356.9 km) Turnoff to west for **Summit Lake**, a resort area popular with Prince George residents; lake char and rainbow fishing spring and fall.

PG 29.3 (47.2 km) **DC 220.7** (355.2 km) Westcoast Energy compressor station.

PG 30.7 (49.4 km) **DC 219.3** (352.9 km) Second turnoff to west for Summit Lake.

PG 36.6 (58.9 km) **DC 213.4** (343.4 km) Cottonwood Creek.

PG 38.8 (62.4 km) **DC 211.2** (339.9 km) Paved turnout with litter barrel.

PG 40.6 (65.3 km) **DC 209.4** (337 km) Railroad crossing.

PG 42 (67.6 km) **DC 208** (334.7 km) Slow down for sharp turn across railroad tracks.

PG 43.9 (70.6 km) **DC 206.1** (331.7 km) Turnoff to west for Crooked River Provincial Park; 90 campsites, picnic area, flush toilets, tables, firepits, dump station. Camping fee charged. Also horseshoe pits, volleyball, playground, trails, swimming and paddle-boat rentals. Powerboats prohibited. Picnic shelter with wood stove. **Crooked River** and area lakes have fair fishing for rainbow, Dolly Varden, grayling and whitefish. ▲

Highway 97 follows the Crooked River north to McLeod Lake.

PG 44.8 (72.1 km) **DC 205.2** (330.1 km) **BEAR LAKE** (unincorporated). Population 300; gas, diesel, propane, grocery, restaurant, motel, RV park, gift shop, post office and ambulance station. Highway maintenance camp. ▲

The 2 lumber mills in town are the main industry of the area, employing approximately two-thirds of the community. Information on area fishing, hiking, hunting and swimming may be obtained from the Bear Lake Community Commission; phone (250) 972-4488, or write general delivery, Bear Lake, BC V0J 3G0.

Grizzly Inn, Restaurant, Motel & RV Park. See display ad this section. ▲

PG 50.7 (81.6 km) **DC 199.3** (320.7 km) Angusmac Creek.

PG 54.2 (87.2 km) **DC 195.8** (315.1 km) Tumbler Ridge branch line British Columbia Railway connects Tumbler Ridge with the B.C. Railway and Canadian National Railway, allowing for shipments of coal from Tumbler Ridge to Ridley Island near Prince Rupert.

PG 55.6 (89.5 km) **DC 194.4** (312.8 km) Large gravel turnout with litter barrel to west.

PG 56.1 (90.3 km) **DC 193.9** (312 km) Large gravel turnout with litter barrel to west.

PG 57 (91.7 km) **DC 193** (310.6 km) Large gravel turnout with litter barrel to west.

PG 60.8 (97.8 km) **DC 189.2** (304.5 km) Turnout with litter barrel to east.

PG 62.4 (100.4 km) **DC 187.6** (301.9 km) Large gravel turnout with litter barrel to east.

PG 65.2 (104.9 km) **DC 184.8** (297.4 km) Lomas Creek.

PG 67.9 (109.3 km) **DC 182.1** (293 km) Large, double-ended, paved rest area to west beside small lake; litter barrels, picnic tables and pit toilets.

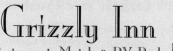

Interpretive guide tours the 1912 Huble Homestead, located east of Milepost PG 26.9. (Judy Parkin, staff)

PG 68.8 (110.7 km) **DC 181.2** (291.6 km) 42 Mile Creek.

PG 71.8 (115.5 km) **DC 178.2** (286.8 km) **Whiskers Bay Resort** has beautiful lakeside camping spots on a quiet bay, some with electricity and water. Hot showers. Cabins with showers, fridges and cooking facilities. Fishing is right off our dock or in the many surrounding lakes. Sunsets are sensational and hummingbirds are bountiful. The cafe offers breakfast, lunch, wonderful burgers, homemade pies, soups, the best coffee on the highway and real northern hospitality. Come visit us! [ADVERTISEMENT] ▲

PG 76.6 (123.3 km) **DC 173.4** (279.1 km) First view northbound of McLeod Lake and view of Whisker's Point.

PG 77.7 (125 km) **DC 172.3** (277.3 km) Turnoff to west for Whisker's Point Provincial Park on McLeod Lake. This is an exceptionally nice campground with a paved loop road, 69 level gravel sites, a dump station, tap water, flush toilets, boat ramp, fire rings, firewood and picnic tables. Also horseshoe pits, volleyball, playground and picnic shelter. Camping fee charged. Boat launch, swimming, sandy beach and fishing. ▲

McLeod Lake has fair fishing for rainbow, lake char and Dolly Varden, spring and fall, trolling is best.

PG 81.4 (131 km) **DC 168.6** (271.3 km) Lodge (closed).

PG 84 (135.2 km) **DC 166** (267.1 km) Food, gas, camping and lodging. ▲

PG 84.5 (136 km) **DC 165.5** (266.3 km) **FORT McLEOD** (unincorporated) has a gas station, grocery, motel and cafe. A monument here commemorates the founding of Fort McLeod, oldest permanent settlement west of the Rockies and north of San Francisco. Founded in 1805 by Simon Fraser as a trading post for the North West Trading Co., the post was named by Fraser for Archie McLeod.

PG 84.7 (136.3 km) **DC 165.3** (266 km) **McLEOD LAKE** (unincorporated), post office, store, lodging and liquor store.

PG 85 (136.8 km) **DC 165** (265.5 km) Turnoff for Carp Lake Provincial Park, 20 miles/32 km west via a gravel road; 105 campsites on Carp and War lakes, limited island camping, picnic tables, firepits, boat launch, fishing and swimming. Also tap water, dump station, horseshoe pits, playground and picnic shelter with wood stove. Ten-minute walk to scenic War Falls. Camping fee charged. Park access road follows the McLeod River to Carp Lake. **Carp Lake**, rainbow June through September; special restrictions in effect, check current posted information. **McLeod River**, rainbow from July, fly-fishing only. ▲

PG 85.6 (137.8 km) **DC 164.4** (264.6 km) Paved turnout with litter barrel to west.

PG 87.6 (141 km) **DC 162.4** (261.4 km) Westcoast Energy compressor station and McLeod Lake school.

PG 89.8 (144.5 km) **DC 160.2** (257.8 km) Turnoff to west for Tudyah Lake Provincial Park; 36 campsites, picnic tables, fire rings, firewood, pit toilets, drinking water. Also swimming, boat ramp, fishing. Camping fee charged. ▲

Tudyah Lake, shore access, rainbow, Dolly Varden and some grayling in summer and late fall. **Pack River** (flows into Tudyah Lake), fishing for grayling (catch-and-release only), June 1 to July 1; rainbow, June 10 to November; large Dolly Varden, Sept. 15 to Oct. 10, spinning.

PG 89.9 (144.7 km) **DC 160.1** (257.6 km) Bear Creek bridge.

PG 93.9 (151.1 km) **DC 156.1** (251.2 km) Gas, food and lodging (open year-round).

PG 94.7 (152.4 km) **DC 155.3** (249.9 km) Parsnip River bridge. This is the Rocky Mountain Trench, marking the western boundary of the Rocky Mountains. Northbound motorists begin gradual climb through the Misinchinka then Hart ranges of the Rocky Mountains.

Parsnip River, good fishing for grayling and Dolly Varden, some rainbow, best from August to October; a boat is necessary.

PG 95.2 (153.2 km) **DC 154.8** (249.1 km) **Junction** with Highway 39 (paved), which leads 18 miles/29 km to the community of Mackenzie (description follows). Food, gas, lodging, camping and tourist information at junction. Signed trailheads along Highway 39 are part of the Mackenzie Demonstration Forest. There are 8 self-guiding trails in the demonstration forest, each focusing on an aspect of forest management. Interpretive signs are posted along each trail.

Mackenzie Junction Cafe. See display ad this section. ▲

Mackenzie

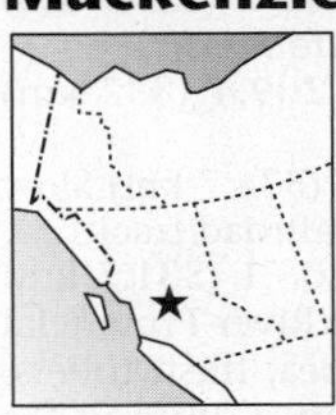

J 18 (29 km) Located 18 miles/29 km northwest of the John Hart Highway 97 via Highway 39. **Population:** 6,000. **Emergency Services:** Emergency only, phone 911. **RCMP**, phone (250) 997-3288. **Hospital**, 12 beds. **Ambulance**, phone 911.

Visitor Information: Visitor/tourist information booth in the railway caboose located at the junction of Highways 97 and 39. Or write the Chamber of Commerce, Box 880, Mackenzie, BC V0J 2C0; phone (250) 997-5459.

Elevation: 2,300 feet/701m. **Radio:** CKMK 1240, CKPG 1240; CBC-FM 990. **Television:** Channels 3, 13 and cable.

A large, modern, planned community, Mackenzie was built in 1965. The city was named after Alexander Mackenzie, early explorer. It lies at the south end of Williston Lake, the largest manmade reservoir on the continent. Construction of the new town in what had been just wilderness was sparked by the Peace River Dam project and the need to attract skilled employees for industrial growth. Mackenzie was incorporated in May 1966 under "instant town" legislation; the first residents moved here in July 1966. Industry here includes mining and forestry, with 4 sawmills, a paper mill and 2 pulp mills. Inquire about mill tours at the Infocentre.

On display in Mackenzie is the "world's largest tree crusher." The 56-foot-long electrically powered Le Tourneau G175 tree crusher was used in clearing land at the Peace River Power Project in the mid-1960s.

Attractions include swimming, waterskiing, fishing and boating at Morfee Lake, a 10-minute walk from town. There are boat launches on both Morfee Lake and Williston Lake reservoir. Good view of Mackenzie and Williston Lake reservoir from the top of Morfee Mountain (elev. 5,961 feet/1,817m); check with Infocentre for directions. There are self-guided hiking trails at John Dahl Regional Park, located behind the recreation centre. Check at the infocentre for additional hiking information. Local businesses offer llama trekking.

The Mackenzie and District Museum, located at the Ernie Bodin Community Centre, offers exhibits on early settlers, area wildlife and lakes, and the birth of the town; phone (250) 997-3021. The Mackenzie Community Arts Council displays new shows of local artists monthly at the Mountain Gifts and Gallery, (250) 997-5818, located at the Mackenzie Arts Centre in the Ernie Bodin Bldg.

Mackenzie has all visitor facilities, including motels, restaurants, shopping malls, gas stations, swimming pool, tennis courts, 9-hole golf course and other recreation facilities. There is also a paved 5,000-foot/1,524-m airstrip.

There is a municipal RV park with 20 sites, flush toilets, showers and sani-dump. Fee only for electrical hookups ($10–$16). Fishing for rainbow, Dolly Varden, arctic char and grayling in **Williston Lake.**

Alexander Mackenzie Hotel & Mall. See display ad this section.

District of Mackenzie. See display ad this section.

West Access Route Log

(continued)

PG 95.2 (153.2 km) **DC 154.8** (249.1 km) **Junction** with Highway 39 to Mackenzie; food, gas, lodging and tourist booth.

PG 95.5 (153.7 km) **DC 154.5** (248.6 km) Highway crosses railroad tracks.

PG 98.9 (158.2 km) **DC 151.1** (243.2 km) Gravel turnout with litter barrel to east.

PG 106 (170.6 km) **DC 144** (231.7 km) Turnout with litter barrel to east.

PG 108.4 (174.4 km) **DC 141.6** (227.9 km) Highway maintenance yard.

PG 108.5 (174.6 km) **DC 141.5** (227.7 km) Bridge over Honeymoon Creek.

PG 109.6 (176.4 km) **DC 140.4** (225.9 km) Powerlines crossing highway carry electricity south from hydro dams in the Hudson's Hope area. (See HUDSON'S HOPE LOOP section.)

PG 110.5 (177.8 km) **DC 139.5** (224.5 km) Slow down for sharp curve across railroad tracks.

PG 112.3 (180.7 km) **DC 137.7** (221.6 km) Bridge over Rolston Creek; dirt turnout by small falls to west.

PG 115.3 (185.6 km) **DC 134.7** (216.8 km) Bijoux Falls Provincial Park; pleasant picnic area adjacent falls on west side of highway. This day-use area has paved parking for 50 cars, pit toilets and picnic tables. Good photo opportunity.

Misinchinka River, southeast of the highway; fishing for grayling, whitefish and Dolly Varden.

PG 116.3 (187.2 km) **DC 133.7** (215.2 km) Highway crosses under railroad.

PG 119.3 (191.8 km) **DC 130.8** (210.5 km) Crossing Pine Pass (elev. 3,068 feet/935m), the highest point on the John Hart-Peace River Highway. Beautiful view of the Rockies to the northeast. Good highway over pass; steep grade southbound.

PG 119.4 (192.2 km) **DC 130.6** (210.2 km) Turnoff to Powder King Ski Village. Skiing November to late April; chalet with ski shop, cafeteria, restaurant and lounge, hostel-style hotel. This area receives an annual average snowfall of 495 inches.

PG 121.4 (195.4 km) **DC 128.6** (207 km) Viewpoint to east with point-of-interest sign about Pine Pass and view of Azouzetta Lake. Pit toilet and litter barrels.

PG 122.4 (197 km) **DC 127.6** (205.3 km) Pine Valley Park, open year-round; cafe, lodge, campground on **Azouzetta Lake.** Very scenic spot. Spectacular hiking on Murray Mountain Trail; inquire at lodge for details. A scuba diving school operates at Azouzetta Lake in summer. Fishing for rainbow (stocked lake) to 1½ lbs., flies or lures, July to October. Boat launch.

PG 125.5 (202 km) **DC 124.5** (200.3 km) Microwave station and receiving dish to west.

PG 125.7 (202.3 km) **DC 124.3** (200 km) Westcoast Energy compressor station.

PG 128.7 (207.1 km) **DC 121.3** (195.2 km) Power lines cross highway.

PG 131.1 (211 km) **DC 118.9** (191.3 km) Turnout with litter barrel. Watch for moose northbound.

PG 140.6 (226.3 km) **DC 109.4** (176.1 km) Bridge over Link Creek.

PG 141.4 (227.5 km) **DC 108.6** (174.8 km) Gravel turnout with litter barrels.

PG 142.3 (229 km) **DC 107.7** (173.3 km) Bridge over West Pine River.

PG 142.8 (229.8 km) **DC 107.2** (172.5 km) Bridge over West Pine River.

PG 143 (230.1 km) **DC 107** (172.2 km) Paved rest area with litter barrels and pit toilets beside Pine River.

PG 143.4 (230.8 km) **DC 106.6** (171.6 km) Bridge over West Pine River, B.C. Railway overpass. Private RV park.

PG 144.3 (232.2 km) **DC 105.7** (170.1 km) Food, gas, towing, lodging and camping; autotel 784-9443.

Silver Sands Lodge. See display ad this section.

PG 146.1 (235.1 km) **DC 103.9** (167.2 km) Cairns Creek.

PG 146.9 (236.4 km) **DC 103.1** (165.9 km) Gravel access road to Pine River to south.

PG 148.2 (238.5 km) **DC 101.8** (163.8 km) LeMoray (unincorporated). Lodge to north of highway was closed in 1997, current status unknown. Highway maintenance camp.

PG 148.3 (238.7 km) **DC 101.7** (163.7 km) Gravel turnout to south.

PG 148.8 (239.5 km) **DC 101.2** (162.9 km) Lillico Creek.

PG 149.7 (240.9 km) **DC 100.3** (161.4 km) Marten Creek.

PG 150.4 (242 km) **DC 99.6** (160.3 km) Big Boulder Creek.

PG 156.2 (251.4 km) **DC 93.8** (151 km) Fisher Creek.

PG 156.9 (252.5 km) **DC 93.1** (149.8 km) Large gravel turnout with litter barrel to south beside Pine River.

PG 159.9 (257.3 km) **DC 90.1** (145 km) Crassier Creek. Watch for moose in area, especially at dusk and night.

PG 161.7 (260.2 km) **DC 88.3** (142.1 km) Westcoast Energy compressor station.

PG 163.6 (263.3 km) **DC 86.4** (139 km) Pine Valley rest areas, both sides of highway, with picnic tables and pit toilets. View of Pine River to south.

PG 169.5 (272.8 km) **DC 80.5** (129.5 km) Turnout with picnic tables, pit toilets and litter barrel to south overlooking the beautiful Pine River valley.

PG 172.4 (277.4 km) **DC 77.6** (124.9 km) Westcoast Energy (natural gas), Pine River plant. View of the Rocky Mountain foothills to the south and west.

PG 177.4 (285.5 km) **DC 72.6** (116.8 km) Turnout with litter barrel.

PG 178.4 (287.1 km) **DC 71.6** (115.2 km) **Caron Creek RV Park.** See display ad this section.

PG 181.9 (292.7 km) **DC 68.1** (109.6 km) Bissett Creek.

PG 183.6 (295.5 km) **DC 66.4** (106.9 km) Turnout with litter barrels at Wildmare Creek.

PG 183.7 (295.6 km) **DC 66.3** (106.7 km) **Northern Nights R.V.** 50 sites. 32 long pull-throughs, back-ins, with full hookups, firepits and picnic tables. Tent sites. Quiet, beautifully treed with easy access to and from the highway. Hot showers, flush toilets and pay phone. 3 miles west of Chetwynd on Highway 97. Phone (250) 788-2747. Box 42, Chetwynd, BC V0C 1J0. [ADVERTISEMENT] ▲

PG 184.1 (296.3 km) **DC 65.9** (106 km) Truck stop; gas, diesel, food and lodging.

PG 187 (300.9 km) **DC 63** (101.4 km) Forestry Interpretive Centre.

PG 187.2 (301.3 km) **DC 62.8** (101.1 km) Little Prairie Heritage Museum. Features the region's pioneer days, and is well worth a visit. The museum is open from the first Tuesday in July to the last Saturday in August. Phone (250) 788-3358.

Chetwynd

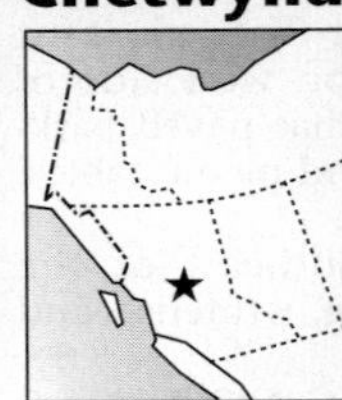

PG 187.6 (301.9 km) **DC 62.4** (100.4 km) Located on Highway 97 at the junction with Highway 29 north to the Alaska Highway via Hudson's Hope, and south to Tumbler Ridge. **Population:** 3,200, area 8,000. **Emergency Services:** RCMP, phone (250) 788-9221. **Hospital, Poison Control Centre** and **Ambulance**, phone (250) 788-3522. **Fire Department**, phone (250) 788-2345.

Visitor Information: Chetwynd Infocentre is located on the North Access Road adjacent to Highway 97 in town by the traffic lights, welcome to Chetwynd sign and bear sculpture.Chamber of Commerce, open 8 a.m. to 5 p.m. July 1 to Labour Day weekend; open 9 a.m. to 4 p.m. rest of year. Write Box 1000, Chetwynd V0C 1J0, or phone (250) 788-3345 or 788-3655; fax 788-7843.

Elevation: 2,017 feet/615m. **Radio:** CFGP 105, CISN-FM 103.9, CJDC 890, CKNL 560, CBC 1170, CFMI-FM 102, CHET-FM 94.5. **Television:** 7 channels (includes CBC, BCTV, ABC, CBS and NBC) plus pay cable.

The town was formerly known as Little Prairie and is a division point on the British Columbia Railway. The name was changed to honour the late British Columbia Minister of Railways, Ralph Chetwynd, who was instrumental in the northward extension of the province-owned railway. In recent years, Chetwynd's collection of chain saw sculptures has earned it the title, "Chain Saw Sculpture Capital of the World." The Infocentre has a map showing locations of the 2 dozen sculptures in town.

Chetwynd lies at the northern end of one of the largest known coal deposits on earth. Access from Chetwynd south to Tumbler Ridge and the resource development known as the North East Coal is via Highway 29 south, a 56-mile/90-km paved road (see HIGHWAY 29 SOUTH side road log this section). Forestry, mining, natural gas processing, ranching and farming are the main industries in Chetwynd. Louisiana Pacific has a modern non-polluting pulp mill here.

Chetwynd is a fast-growing community with several large motels, fast-food outlets, restaurants, banks and 4 bank machines, post office, 2 laundromats, gas stations,

One of Chetwynd's many chainsaw sculptures. (Earl L. Brown, staff)

CHETWYND ADVERTISERS

District of Chetwynd ....Ph. (250) 788-2281
Pine Cone Motor Inn ....Ph. (800) 663-8082
Robert's Towing ....Ph. (250) 788-9194
Swiss Inn
Restaurant, The....0.5 mile E. of traffic light
Westwind RV Park ....Ph. (250) 788-2199

supermarkets and 2 9-hole golf courses. Good traveler's stop with easy access to all services. (Heavy commercial and industrial traffic often fill up local motels and campgrounds; reserve ahead.) Chetwynd & District Leisure Pool has a wave machine, whirlpool, sauna and weight room; open daily 6 A.M. to 10 P.M., visitors welcome. A skate park is located at the city recreation centre.

Chetwynd has established a 30-mile/50-km scenic trail system for hiking and mountain biking. Contact the Visitor Infocentre for more details.

There's a dump station at the 51st Avenue car/truck wash. There are private RV parks in town and on Highway 97. Moberly Lake Provincial Park is 12 miles/19.3 km north of Chetwynd via Highway 29 north (see **Milepost PG 187.9**) and 1.9 miles/3 km west via a gravel road. The park has 109 campsites, beach, picnic area, playground, nature trail, boat launch and a private marina next door with boat rental and concession. There's good swimming at huge Moberly Lake on a warm summer day. Worth the drive. ▲

West Access Route Log

(continued)

PG 187.8 (302.2 km) **DC 62.2** (100.1 km) Highway crosses railroad tracks.

PG 187.9 (302.4 km) **DC 62.1** (99.9 km)

Highway 29 South Log

Highway 29 South is a paved road that leads 55.9 miles/90 km from **Milepost PG 189.4** to the community of Tumbler Ridge. Travelers may return to Highway 97 via Highway 29, or via the Heritage Highway, a paved road that leads 59.5 miles/95 km from Tumbler Ridge to junction with Highway 97 at **Milepost PG 237.7.**

Distance from Highway 97 junction (J) is shown.

J 0 Junction with Highway 97 at **Milepost PG 189.4.**

J 0.1 (0.2 km) Turnout with litter barrels to east.

Highway 29 climbs next 2.3 miles/3.7 km southbound.

J 1.9 (3.1 km) Distance marker indicates Tumbler Ridge 88 km.

J 2.8 (4.5 km) Sign: Trucks check brakes, steep hill ahead.

J 3 (4.8 km) Large gravel turnouts with litter barrels both sides of highway.

J 5.5 (8.8 km) Twidwell Bend bridge.

J 5.6 (9 km) Access road east to Long Prairie (8 miles/12.9 km).

J 6.6 (10.6 km) Highway parallels Sukunka River to west.

J 8.2 (13.2 km) Zonnebeke Creek.

J 8.5 (13.7 km) Natural Springs Resort; 9-hole golf course.

J 9 (14.5 km) Kilometrepost 15.

J 10.6 (17 km) Bridge over Dickebush Creek.

J 11 (17.7 km) Sanctuary River.

J 13.7 (22 km) **Junction** with Sukunka Forest Road, which leads west 11 miles/17.7 km to Sukunka Falls. *NOTE: Radio-controlled road, travelers must monitor channel 151.325 MHz.*

J 13.8 (22.2 km) Highway climbs next 3 miles/4.8 km southbound.

J 16.7 (26.9 km) Turnouts with litter barrels both sides of highway.

J 21.6 (34.8 km) Turnout with litter barrels to east.

J 26.9 (43.3 km) Turnouts with litter barrels both sides of highway.

J 28.4 (45.7 km) Paved road leads east 1.2 miles/1.9 km to **Gwillim Lake** Provincial Park (gate closed 11 P.M. to 7 A.M.); 49 campsites, picnic tables, firewood and firepits. Day-use area and boat launch. Fishing for lake trout, grayling and pike. Camping fee $7 to $12. ▲

J 40.8 (65.6 km) Access road leads west 9 miles/14.5 km to Bullmoose Mountain and mine. Mine tours may be available; phone (250) 242-5221 for current information.

J 41.1 (66.1 km) Turnout to east.

J 41.5 (66.8 km) Bridge over Bullmoose Flats River.

J 46.1 (74.2 km) Turnout with litter barrels to east. Phillips Way Summit, elev. 3,695 feet/1,126m.

J 51.4 (82.7 km) Bullmoose Creek bridge.

J 52.6 (84.3 km) Wolverine River bridge.

J 54.1 (87 km) Murray River bridge.

J 54.8 (88.2 km) Flatbed Creek bridge.

J 54.9 (88.3 km) Flatbed Creek Campground; 28 sites, hookups, water, flush toilets, showers, dump station, picnic tables and playground. Camping fee $10. ▲

J 55.9 (90 km) Turnoff for community of Tumbler Ridge (description follows).

Tumbler Ridge

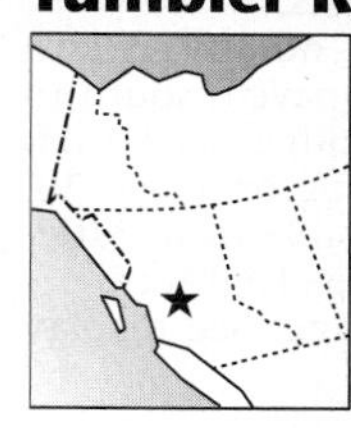

Located 116.5 miles/187.5 km southwest of Dawson Creek via Highways 97 and 29. **Population:** 3,775. **Emergency Services:** **RCMP**, phone (250) 242-5252. **Medical Centre**, phone (250) 242-5271. **Ambulance**, phone (800) 461-9911. **Fire Department**, phone (250) 242-5555.

Visitor Information: Located in town at Southgate Road and Front Street, across from the hospital. Open year-round. Write the Chamber of Commerce, Box 606, Tumbler Ridge, BC V0C 2W0, or phone (250) 242-4702, fax 242-5159.

Elevation: 3,000 feet/914m. **Private Aircraft**: 9 miles/15 km south; elev. 3,150 feet/960m, length 4,000 feet/ 1,218m; asphalt; fuel 80, 100, Jet B.

Tumbler Ridge was built in conjunction with development of the North East Coal resource. Construction of the townsite began in 1981. It is British Columbia's newest community, incorporated June 1, 1984.

Visitor facilities include a motel, restaurants, retail and grocery outlets, service stations with major repairs and propane and a car wash. Camping at Flatbed Creek Campground just outside of town and at Monkman RV Park in town. Recreational facilities include a community centre with arena, curling rink, weight room, indoor pool and a library. Outdoor facilities include tennis courts and a 9-hole golf course. ▲

The Visitor Infocentre provides a free slide presentation on Tumbler Ridge history and development. The Grizzly Valley Days Maritime West Festival, held Aug. 18–24, 1998, includes a parade, cod barrel race, Mr. Grizzly Valley contest, craft fair, lobster boil and other activities for the whole family.

Major attraction in the area is Monkman Provincial Park, site of spectacular 225-foot/69-m Kinuseo (keh-NEW-see-oh or Keh-NEW-soh) Falls. The falls and a 42-site campground are accessible from Tumbler Ridge via a 37-mile/60-km dirt road (watch for trucks) south from town. Viewing platform of falls is a short walk from the campground. For more information on the park, contact BC Parks in Fort St. John, phone (250) 787-3407.

The Quintette Mine is the World's largest computerized open pit mine. Coal mine tours are available at Quintette Mine south of town and at Bullmoose Mine (see **Milepost J 40.7** on Highway 29).

District of Tumbler Ridge. See display ad on page 80.

Return to Milepost PG 189.4
West Access Route

Junction with Highway 29 north, which leads 12 miles/19.3 km to Moberly Lake, 36.5 miles/58.7 km to Peace River Provincial Recreation Area and Peace Canyon dam, and 40.4 miles/64.9 km to community of Hudson's Hope and access to W.A.C. Bennett Dam; Highway 29 north connects with the Alaska Highway 53.7 miles/86.4 km north of Dawson Creek. (See HUDSON'S HOPE LOOP section for details.)

Highway climbs next 12 miles/19 km for Dawson Creek-bound motorists.

PG 189.4 (304.8 km) **DC 60.6** (97.5 km) **Junction** with Highway 29 (paved) south to Gwillim Lake and Tumbler Ridge (see HIGHWAY 29 SOUTH side road log on page 79). Tumbler Ridge is also accessible from **Milepost PG 237.7** via the Heritage Highway.

District of Tumbler Ridge. See display ad this section.

PG 199.3 (320.7 km) **DC 50.7** (81.6 km) Gravel turnouts with litter barrels both sides of highway.

PG 201.2 (323.8 km) **DC 48.8** (78.5 km) Slow down for sharp curve across railroad tracks.

PG 204.3 (328.8km) **DC 45.7** (73.5km) Access to Louisianna Pacific Pulp Mill to north.

PG 205.6 (330.9 km) **DC 44.4** (71.5 km) Turnout with litter barrel and a commanding view of the East Pine River valley to the south.

PG 206.5 (332.3 km) **DC 43.5** (70 km) Sharp curves approximately next 2 miles/3.2 km as highway descends toward Dawson Creek. View of Table Mountain.

PG 207.9 (334.6 km) **DC 42.1** (67.7 km) Highway crosses under railroad.

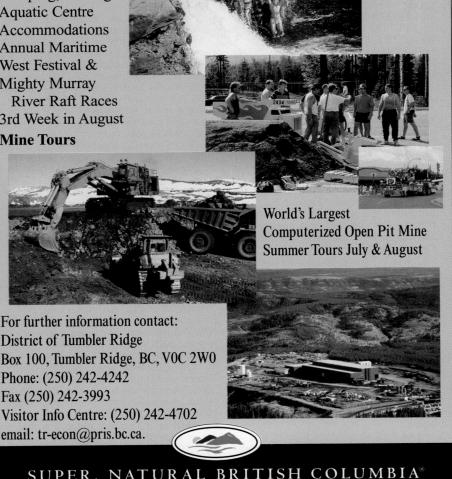

PG 208.1 (334.9 km) **DC 41.9** (67.4 km) Sharp turn to south at west end of bridge for East Pine Provincial Park (0.5 mile on gravel road); picnicking and boat launch on Pine River. Turnout with litter barrel at park entrance.

From East Pine Provincial Park, canoeists may make a 2-day canoe trip down the Pine River to the Peace River; take-out at Taylor Landing Provincial Park (at **Milepost DC 34** on the Alaska Highway).

PG 208.2 (335.1 km) **DC 41.8** (67.3 km) Bridge across East Pine River. Railroad also crosses river here.

PG 208.3 (335.2 km) **DC 41.7** (67.1 km) Turnout with litter barrel to south.

PG 209.8 (337.6 km) **DC 40.2** (64.7 km) East Pine (unincorporated) has a store and gas station.

PG 211.7 (340.7 km) **DC 38.3** (61.6 km) Turnout with litter barrel to north. Westbound brake-check area.

PG 221.5 (356.5 km) **DC 28.5** (45.9 km) Turnouts with litter barrels both sides of highway.

PG 222 (357.3 km) **DC 28** (45 km) Groundbirch (unincorporated); store, liquor outlet, gas, propane, diesel, post office and camping. ▲

PG 230.7 (371.3 km) **DC 19.3** (31.1 km) Progress (unincorporated), highway maintenance yard, cairn and pay phone.

PG 234.4 (377.2 km) **DC 15.6** (25.1 km) Turnout with litter barrels to north.

PG 237.7 (382.5 km) **DC 12.3** (19.8 km) **Junction** with Heritage Highway, which leads 59.5 miles/96 km (paved) south to the community of Tumbler Ridge and access roads to the North East Coal Development. (Tumbler Ridge is also accessible via Highway 29 south from Chetwynd. See side road log this section.)

From Tumbler Ridge, the Heritage Highway continues 92 miles/148 km east and north to connect with Highway 2 southeast of Dawson Creek. Inquire locally about road conditions.

PG 238 (383 km) **DC 12** (19.3 km) Kiskatinaw River bridge.

PG 240.7 (387.4 km) **DC 9.3** (15 km) Arras (unincorporated), cafe and gas station.

PG 247.9 (398.9 km) **DC 2.1** (3.4 km) Small turnout with litter barrel and point of interest sign to south.

PG 248 (399.1 km) **DC 2** (3.2 km) Private RV Park. ▲

PG 249.9 (402.2 km) **DC 0.1** (0.2 km) Entering Dawson Creek. Private campground on south side of highway; Rotary Lake Park and camping on north side of highway. ▲

PG 250 (402.3 km) **DC 0 Junction** of the Hart Highway and Alaska Highway; turn right for downtown Dawson Creek, Mile Zero of the Alaska Highway. See the description of Dawson Creek in the ALASKA HIGHWAY section.

HUDSON'S HOPE LOOP 29

Connects: Chetwynd, BC, to Alaska Hwy. **Length:** 87 miles
Road Surface: Paved **Season:** Open all year
Steepest Grade: 10 percent
Major Attraction: W.A.C. Bennett and Peace Canyon Dams

(See map, page 82)

	Alaska Hwy	Chetwynd	Hudson's Hope
Alaska Hwy		87	47
Chetwynd	87		40
Hudson's Hope	47	40	

Peace Canyon Dam, at Milepost C 36.5, has self-guided tours.
(Earl L. Brown, staff)

The Hudson's Hope Loop links the John Hart Highway (Highway 97) with the Alaska Highway (also Highway 97). This 86.9-mile/139.8-km paved loop road provides year-round access to the town of Hudson's Hope, W.A.C. Bennett Dam, Peace Canyon Dam and Moberly Lake. As a shortcut bypassing Dawson Creek, the Hudson's Hope Loop saves 28.9 miles/46.5 km. Highway 29 is a good, scenic 2-lane road but is steep and winding in places.

A popular side trip with Alaska Highway travelers today, and an alternate access route to the Alaska Highway, Highway 29 was only a 53-mile/85.3-km side road to the Hudson Hope Coal Mines in the 1950s. In the 1960s, with construction of the W.A.C. Bennett Dam under way, Alaska Highway travelers drove the side road to see the Peace River dam site. The highway was completed to Chetwynd in 1968.

Hudson's Hope Loop Log

Distance from Chetwynd (C) is followed by distance from Alaska Highway junction (AH).

C 0 AH 86.9 (139.8 km) **Junction** of Highways 29 and 97 at Chetwynd (see **Milepost PG 187.6** in the WEST ACCESS ROUTE section for description of Chetwynd).

C **0.5** (0.8 km) **AH 86.4** (139 km) Truck weigh scales to west. Highway climbs next 4.3 miles/7 km westbound.

C **2.3** (3.7 km) **AH 84.6** (136.1 km) Jackfish Road to east.

C **5** (8 km) **AH 81.9** (131.8 km) Turnout with litter barrel to west.

C **12** (19.3 km) **AH 74.9** (120.5 km) Gravel access road leads 2 miles/3.2 km west to **Moberly Lake** Provincial Park on south shore; 109 campsites, swimming, waterskiing, picnicking, drinking water, dump station, boat launch, $9.50 camping fee. This beautiful 9-mile-/14.5-km-long lake drains at its east end into Moberly River, which in turn runs into the Peace River. Fishing for lake trout, Dolly Varden and whitefish. ▲

Moberly Lake Marina & Resort. See display ad this section.

C **12.2** (19.6 km) **AH 74.7** (120.2 km) Moberly River bridge; parking area with litter barrel at south end.

C **15.9** (25.6 km) **AH 71** (114.3 km) Highway cairn is memorial to John Moberly, fur trader and explorer who first landed here in 1865.

C **16.4** (26.4 km) **AH 70.5** (113.5 km) Spencer Tuck Regional Park; picnic tables, swimming, fishing and boat launch.

C **17.4** (28 km) **AH 69.5** (111.8 km) **Harv's Resort**, on the north shore of beautiful Moberly Lake. Treed picnic sites, large grass picnic field, cabins, campsites, 40 full-service 30-amp hookups. Swimming, fishing, pay phone, laundromat and showers. Store, restaurant. Gas, oils, propane, hunting and fishing licenses. Dock. Boat launch and golf course nearby. Your hosts, Harvey and Darlene Evans. Open till 10 P.M. daily. VISA, MasterCard and Interac. Phone (250) 788-9145. [ADVERTISEMENT] ▲

C **18.3** (29.5 km) **AH 68.6** (110.4 km) **MOBERLY LAKE.** Post office, cafe, store and pay phone.

C **18.5** (29.8 km) **AH 68.4** (110.1 km) Moberly Lake and District Golf Club, 0.7 mile/1.1 km from highway; 9 holes, grass greens, rentals, clubhouse, licensed lounge. Open May to September.

C **25.4** (40.9 km) **AH 61.5** (99 km) Cameron Lake camping area; tables, water, toilets, firewood, playground, horseshoe pits, boat launch (no motorboats) and swimming. Camping fee by donation. ▲

C **30.7** (49.4 km) **AH 56.2** (90.4 km) Gravel turnout with litter barrel to east. Highway descends northbound to Hudson's Hope.

C **35.9** (57.8 km) **AH 51** (82.1 km) Suspension bridge over Peace River; paved turnouts at both ends of bridge with concrete totem pole sculptures. View of Peace Canyon Dam.

C **36.5** (58.7 km) **AH 50.4** (81.1 km) Turnoff to west for Dinosaur Lake Campground and B.C. Hydro Peace Canyon Dam.

HUDSON'S HOPE LOOP *Chetwynd, BC, to Milepost DC 53.7 Alaska Highway*

To Fort Nelson (see ALASKA HIGHWAY section)
C-87/140km AH-0
Fort St. John
C-74.2/119.4km Pine Ridge Campground C
C-40/65km AH-47/75km
Hudson's Hope
W.A.C. Bennett Dam
Williston Lake
Peace Canyon Dam
Boucher Lake
Moberly Lake
C-17.4/28km Harv's Resort CDGIMPST
C-12/19.3km Moberly Lake Marina & Resort CILST
C-0 AH-87/140km
Chetwynd
ROCKY MOUNTAINS
To Prince George (see WEST ACCESS ROUTE section)
To Tumbler Ridge (see WEST ACCESS ROUTE section)
John Hart Highway (see WEST ACCESS ROUTE section)
Alaska Highway (see ALASKA HIGHWAY section)
Dawson Creek
To Spirit River
To Grande Prairie (see EAST ACCESS ROUTE section)
BRITISH COLUMBIA
ALBERTA

Scale: 10 Miles; 10 Kilometres

Key to mileage boxes: miles/kilometres from: C-Chetwynd, AH-Alaska Highway

Map Location

Principal Route: Paved, Unpaved. Other Roads: Paved, Unpaved. Ferry Routes. Hiking Trails.
Refer to Log for Visitor Facilities; Visitor Information; Fishing; Campground; Airport; Airstrip

Key to Advertiser Services: C-Camping; D-Dump Station; d-Diesel; G-Gas (reg., unld.); I-Ice; L-Lodging; M-Meals; P-Propane; R-Car Repair (major); r-Car Repair (minor); S-Store (grocery); T-Telephone (pay)

The dam's visitor centre, 0.6 mile/1 km on paved access road, is open from 8 A.M. to 4 P.M. daily from late May through Labour Day; Monday through Friday the rest of the year (closed holidays). Self-guided tour includes a full-scale model of duck-billed dinosaurs (hadrosaurs), a tableau portraying Alexander Mackenzie's discovery of the Peace River canyon and a section on local pioneering. A pictorial display traces the construction of the Peace Canyon Dam. You may view the dam spillway from the visitor centre. Get permission before walking across top of dam. Phone (250) 783-5211 for a guided tour (groups of 8 or more).

Dinosaur Lake Campground, on Dinosaur Lake, has 30 campsites with firepits, water, toilets and tables. Boat launch and swimming area. Camping fee by donation.▲

C 38.3 (61.6 km) **AH 48.6** (78.2 km) Alwin Holland Memorial Park (0.5 mile/0.8 km east of highway) is named for the first teacher in Hudson's Hope, who willed his property, known locally as The Glen, to be used as a public park. There are 17 campsites, picnic grounds, barbecues and water. Camping fee by donation. ▲

C 38.9 (62.6 km) **AH 48** (77.2 km) Welcome to Hudson's Hope sign.

C 39 (62.8 km) **AH 47.9** (77.1 km) King Gething Park; small campground with 15 grassy sites, picnic tables, cookhouse, flush toilets, showers and dump station east side of highway. Camping fee by donation. ▲

Hudson's Hope

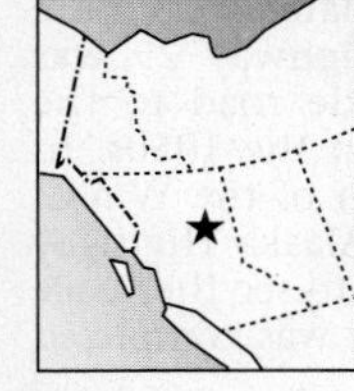

C 40.4 (65 km) **AH 46.5** (74.8 km) **Population:** 1,122. **Emergency Services: RCMP,** phone (250) 783-5241. **Fire Department,** phone (250) 783-5700. **Ambulance,** phone (800) 461-9911. **Medical Clinic,** phone (250) 783-9991.

Visitor Information: A log building houses the tourist information booth at Beattie Park, across from the museum and St. Peter's Anglican United Church. Open daily mid-May to the end of August, hours are 8 A.M. to 5:30 P.M. Phone (250) 783-9154 or write Box 330, Hudson's Hope, BC V0C 1V0. (Off-season, phone the District Office at 250/783-9901.)

Elevation: 1,707 feet/520m. **Climate:** Summer temperatures range from 60°F/16°C to 90°F/32°C, with an average of 135 frost-free days annually. **Radio:** CBC, CKNL 560, CJDC 870. **Television:** Channels 2, 5, 8, 11 and cable.

Private Aircraft: Hudson's Hope airstrip, 3.7 miles/6 km west; elev. 2,200 feet/671m; length 5,200 feet/1,585m; asphalt.

Hudson's Hope is the third oldest permanently settled community in British Columbia. The site was first visited in 1793 by Alexander Mackenzie. In 1805 a Hudson's Bay trading post was established here by Simon Fraser. In 1916, after the fur-trading days were over, a major influx of settlers arrived in the area. It was the head of navigation for steamboats on the lower Peace River until 1936, the year of the last scheduled steamboat run. Area coal mines supplied Alaska Highway maintenance camps during the 1940s.

Modern development of Hudson's Hope was spurred by construction of the Peace Power project in the 1960s. Today the area's principal claim to fame is the 600-foot-/ 183-m-high W.A.C. Bennett Dam at the upper end of the Peace River canyon, 15 miles/24.1 km west of Hudson's Hope. The 100-million-ton dam is one of the largest earth-fill structures in the world, and Williston Lake, behind it, is the largest body of fresh water in British Columbia. The dam provides about 20 percent of British Columbia's hydroelectricity. Tours of the Gordon M. Shrum generating station are available daily from mid-May to the end of September, weekdays only the remainder of the year (closed holidays). Phone (250) 783-5211 for information. Tours are available each hour on the half hour from 9:30 A.M. to 4:30 P.M. Self-guided tours are available at the Peace Canyon Dam.

Also of interest is the Hudson's Hope Museum on Highway 29 in town. The museum has a fine collection of artifacts and dinosaur fossils from the Peace District. It offers hands-on paleontology and dinosaur activities, and is well worth a visit. Souvenir shop in the museum; (250) 783-5735; admission by donation. The active congregation of the log-constructed St. Peter's Anglican United Church (next to the museum) welcomes visitors to look inside.

Several hiking trails have been developed in the area. Descriptions and a map are available at the Hudson's Hope tourist information booth.

Visitor services in Hudson's Hope include a motel, hotel, 2 bed and breakfasts, 3 restaurants, 2 service stations, a laundromat, supermarket, bakery, and convenience and hardware stores. There are also a bank, post office, fitness centre, liquor store, community hall, library, swimming pool, tennis courts, and numerous parks and playgrounds. Sightseeing and flightseeing tours are available locally. The main business district is along Highway 29 and adjoining streets. The RCMP office is on 99th Street.

Hudson's Hope Loop Log

(continued)

C 41.2 (66.3 km) **AH 45.7** (73.5 km) Turnout to north with Hudson's Hope visitor map.

CAUTION: Watch for deer between here and the Alaska Highway, especially at dusk and at night.

C 44 (70.8 km) **AH 42.9** (69 km) Lynx Creek bridge.

C 48.4 (77.9 km) **AH 38.5** (62 km) Turnout to south for view of the Peace River.

C 50.9 (81.9 km) **AH 36** (57.9 km) Farrell Creek bridge and picnic site.

C 56.6 (91.1 km) **AH 30.3** (48.8 km) Pull-through turnout with litter barrels. View of Peace River valley. *CAUTION: Watch for frost heaves and rough spots next 10 miles/16 km.*

C 57.1 (91.9 km) **AH 29.8** (48 km) Turnout to south with litter barrels and view of Peace River valley.

C 59.3 (95.4 km) **AH 27.6** (44.4 km) Turnout to south with litter barrels.

C 64.7 (104.1 km) **AH 22.2** (35.7 km) Halfway River.

C 67.2 (108.1 km) **AH 19.7** (31.7 km) Rest area to south with point of interest sign, litter barrel and toilet. A slide occurred here on May 26, 1973, involving an estimated 10 million to 15 million cubic yards of overburden. Slide debris completely blocked the river channel for some 12 hours, backing up the river an estimated 24 feet/7.3m above normal level.

C 68.4 (110.1 km) **AH 18.5** (29.8 km) Milepost 19.

C 71.1 (114.4 km) **AH 15.8** (25.4 km) Turnout to north.

C 71.4 (114.9 km) **AH 15.5** (24.9 km) Milepost 16.

C 73.5 (118.3 km) **AH 13.4** (21.6 km) Beaver dam to north.

C 74.2 (119.4 km) **AH 12.7** (20.4 km) ▲

C 74.6 (120.1 km) **AH 12.3** (19.8 km) Cache Creek 1-lane bridge. Turnout to north at east end of bridge for picnic area with litter barrels.

C 76.6 (123.3 km) **AH 10.3** (16.6 km) Turnout with litter barrel to north overlooking Bear Flat in the Peace River valley. Highway begins climb eastbound. *CAUTION: Switchbacks.*

C 78.1 (125.7 km) **AH 8.8** (14.2 km) Highest point on Highway 29 (2,750 feet/838m) overlooking Peace River Plateau. Highway descends on a 10 percent grade westbound. *CAUTION: Switchbacks.*

C 86.9 (139.8 km) **AH 0 Junction** with the Alaska Highway, 6.7 miles/10.8 km north of Fort St. John (see **Milepost DC 53.7** in the ALASKA HIGHWAY section). Truck stop at junction with gas, diesel, propane, tire repair, restaurant and convenience store.

CAUTION: Watch for deer on the highway between here and Hudson's Hope, especially at dusk and at night.

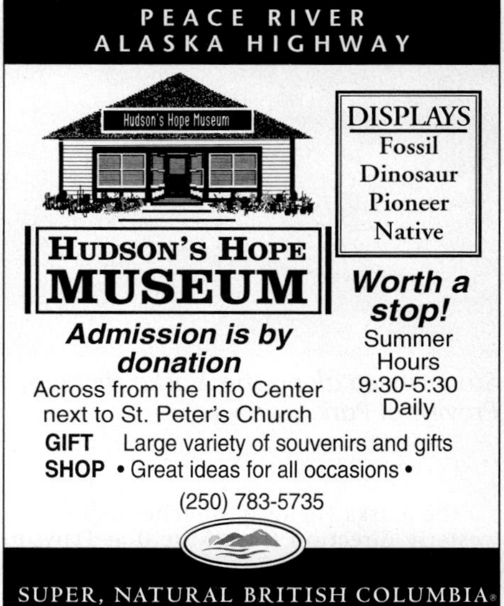

ALASKA HIGHWAY 97 1 2

Connects: Dawson Creek, BC, to Fairbanks, AK **Length:** 1,488 miles
Road Surface: Paved **Season:** Open all year
Highest Summit: Summit Lake 4,250 feet
Major Attractions: Muncho Lake, Liard Hotsprings, Watson Lake Signforest, SS *Klondike*, Kluane Lake, Trans-Alaska Pipeline Crossing

(See maps, pages 85–89)

	Dawson Cr.	Delta Jct.	Fairbanks	Ft. Nelson	Haines Jct.	Tok	Watson Lk.	Whitehorse
Dawson Cr.		1390	1488	283	985	1282	613	895
Delta Jct.	1390		98	1107	405	108	777	495
Fairbanks	1488	98		1205	593	206	875	593
Ft. Nelson	283	1107	1205		702	999	330	612
Haines Jct.	985	405	593	702		297	372	90
Tok	1282	108	206	999	297		669	387
Watson Lk.	613	777	875	330	372	669		282
Whitehorse	895	495	593	612	90	387	282	

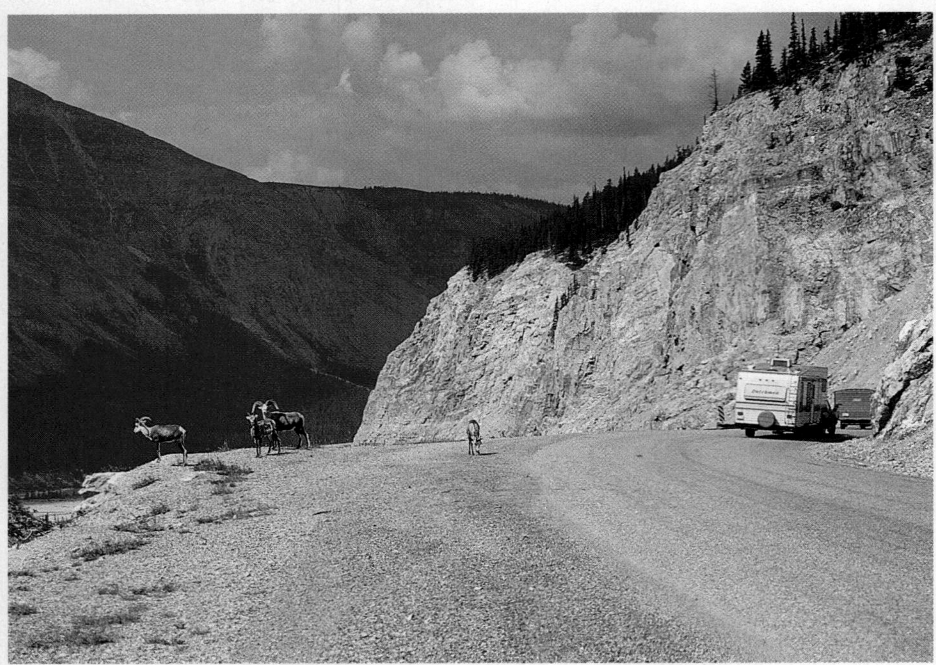

Stone sheep along the Alaska Highway in British Columbia's Stone Mountain Provincial Park. (Earl L. Brown, staff)

The Alaska Highway stretches in a northwesterly direction from Mile 0 at Dawson Creek, BC, through Yukon Territory to Mile 1520 at Fairbanks, AK. Actual driving distance is 1,488 miles/2,394.6 km. Although the Alaska Highway does not compare with highways in the Lower 48, it is no longer a wilderness road but rather a road through the wilderness. The Alaska Highway is driven by thousands of people each year in all sorts of vehicles. The highway is open and maintained year-round.

For more information, contact Peace River Alaska Highway Tourist Assoc., P.O. Box 6850M, Fort St. John, BC V1J 4J3; phone toll free (888) 785-2544 or (250) 785-2544, fax 785-4424.

Road Conditions

All of the Alaska Highway between Dawson Creek, BC, and Fairbanks, AK, is asphalt surfaced. Repaving and highway improvement continue. Surfacing of the Alaska Highway ranges from poor to excellent.

There are still some stretches of poor surfacing with many chuckholes, gravel breaks (sections of gravel ranging from a few feet to several miles), hardtop with loose gravel, deteriorated shoulders and bumps. On the northern portion of the highway—in Yukon Territory and on into Alaska—watch for frost heaves. This rippling effect in the pavement is caused by the freezing and thawing of the ground. Drive slowly in sections of frost heaves to avoid breaking an axle or trailer hitch.

Surfacing on much of the highway is fair, with older patched pavement and a minimum of gravel breaks and chuckholes. There are also sections of excellent surfacing where highway maintenance crews have recently upgraded the road.

Loose gravel patches are common on the Alaska Highway and are often signed. *CAUTION: Slow down for loose gravel! Excessive speeds can lead to loss of control of your vehicle.*

Travelers should keep in mind that road conditions are subject to change! Weather and traffic may cause deterioration of newer pavement, while construction may improve older sections. Always be alert for bumps and holes in the road and for abrupt changes in highway surfacing. There are stretches of narrow, winding road without shoulders. Also watch for soft shoulders.

Always watch for construction crews along the Alaska Highway. Extensive road construction may require a detour, or travelers may be delayed while waiting for a pilot car to guide them through the construction. Motorists may encounter rough driving at construction areas, and muddy roadway if there are heavy rains while the roadbed is torn up.

For current road conditions, contact sources listed in Driving Information in the TRAVEL PLANNING section of this book.

Detailed weather information for the Canadian portion of the Alaska Highway is available from Atmospheric Environment Service of Environment Canada. For 24-hour recorded weather information between Dawson Creek and Sikanni Chief, phone (250) 784-2244 or (250) 785-7669; for detailed weather information, phone the weather office at (250) 785-4304 between 6:15 A.M. and 4:45 P.M.; or for weather broadcasts, tune to 580 AM. Between Sikanni Chief and the BC–YT border, phone (250) 774-6461 for 24-hour recorded message; for detailed weather information phone (250) 774-2302 between 3 A.M. and 6:15 P.M.; or tune your radio to 590 AM for weather broadcasts. Between the BC–YT border and the YT–AK border, phone (867) 668-6061 for 24-hour recorded message; for detailed weather information phone (867) 667-8464 (24 hours a day); or tune your radio to CBC Yukon (570 AM) for weather broadcasts. Regional weather forecasts are also supplied to local visitor information centres, local hotels and motels, and lodges along the highway.

Road conditions along the Alaska Highway may be summarized as follows. Good pavement first 300 miles/483 km (through Fort Nelson) with recent resurfacing improving some sections. Watch for surface changes and continued construction in some areas. Between Fort Nelson and the BC–YT border, the Alaska Highway crosses the Rocky Mountains, so be prepared for narrow, winding road and some rough spots in surfacing due to deterioration from weather and traffic. Also watch for construction projects on this stretch. Between the BC–YT border and Haines Junction, expect fair to excellent road with a few rough spots

(Continues on page 90)

ALASKA HIGHWAY Dawson Creek, BC, to Milepost DC 409

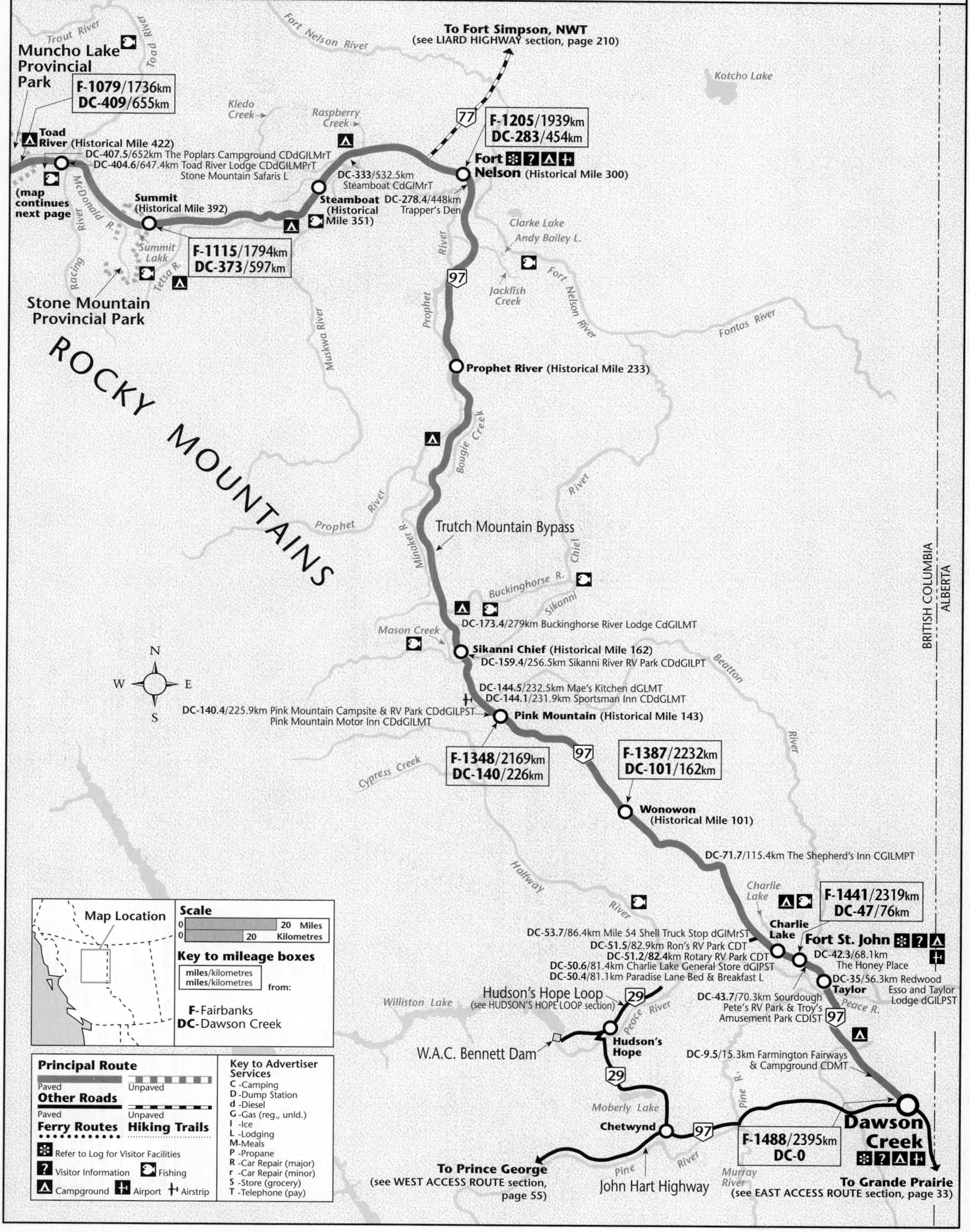

To Fort Simpson, NWT
(see LIARD HIGHWAY section, page 210)

Trout River
Toad River
Fort Nelson River
Kotcho Lake
Muncho Lake Provincial Park
F-1079/1736km
DC-409/655km
Kledo Creek
Raspberry Creek
77
F-1205/1939km
DC-283/454km
Toad River (Historical Mile 422)
DC-407.5/652km The Poplars Campground CDdGILMrT
DC-404.6/647.4km Toad River Lodge CDdGILMPrT
Stone Mountain Safaris L
(map continues next page)
Fort Nelson (Historical Mile 300)
DC-333/532.5km
Steamboat CdGIMrT
Steamboat (Historical Mile 351)
DC-278.4/448km
Trapper's Den
Summit (Historical Mile 392)
McDonald R.
Racing River
Summit Lake
Tetsa R.
F-1115/1794km
DC-373/597km
Stone Mountain Provincial Park
Clarke Lake
Andy Bailey L.
Jackfish Creek
Fort Nelson River
Prophet River
97
Fontas River
Muskwa River

ROCKY MOUNTAINS

Prophet River (Historical Mile 233)
Bougie Creek
Prophet River
River
Trutch Mountain Bypass
Minaker R.
Chief
Buckinghorse R.
Sikanni
DC-173.4/279km Buckinghorse River Lodge CdGILMT
Mason Creek
Sikanni Chief (Historical Mile 162)
DC-159.4/256.5km Sikanni River RV Park CDdGILPT
Beatton River
DC-144.5/232.5km Mae's Kitchen dGLMT
DC-144.1/231.9km Sportsman Inn CDdGLMT
DC-140.4/225.9km Pink Mountain Campsite & RV Park CDdGILPST
Pink Mountain Motor Inn CDdGILMT
Pink Mountain (Historical Mile 143)
N
W
E
S
F-1348/2169km
DC-140/226km
97
F-1387/2232km
DC-101/162km
Cypress Creek
Wonowon (Historical Mile 101)
BRITISH COLUMBIA
ALBERTA
DC-71.7/115.4km The Shepherd's Inn CGILMPT
Halfway River
Charlie Lake
F-1441/2319km
DC-47/76km
Charlie Lake
Fort St. John
DC-53.7/86.4km Mile 54 Shell Truck Stop dGIMrST
DC-51.5/82.9km Ron's RV Park CDT
DC-51.2/82.4km Rotary RV Park CDT
DC-50.6/81.4km Charlie Lake General Store dGIPST
DC-50.4/81.1km Paradise Lane Bed & Breakfast L
DC-42.3/68.1km
The Honey Place
DC-35/56.3km Redwood Esso and Taylor Lodge dGILPST
Taylor
Peace R.
Hudson's Hope Loop
(see HUDSON'S HOPE LOOP section)
29
Peace River
Williston Lake
DC-43.7/70.3km Sourdough Pete's RV Park & Troy's Amusement Park CDIST
97
Hudson's Hope
W.A.C. Bennett Dam
DC-9.5/15.3km Farmington Fairways & Campground CDMT
29
Moberly Lake
Pine R.
Chetwynd
97
Dawson Creek
F-1488/2395km
DC-0
To Prince George
(see WEST ACCESS ROUTE section, page 55)
Pine River
John Hart Highway
Murray River
To Grande Prairie
(see EAST ACCESS ROUTE section, page 33)

Map Location

Scale
0 20 Miles
0 20 Kilometres

Key to mileage boxes
miles/kilometres
miles/kilometres
from:
F-Fairbanks
DC-Dawson Creek

Principal Route
Paved
Unpaved
Other Roads
Paved
Unpaved
Ferry Routes
Hiking Trails
Refer to Log for Visitor Facilities
Visitor Information
Fishing
Campground
Airport
Airstrip

Key to Advertiser Services
C -Camping
D -Dump Station
d -Diesel
G -Gas (reg., unld.)
I -Ice
L -Lodging
M-Meals
P -Propane
R -Car Repair (major)
r -Car Repair (minor)
S -Store (grocery)
T -Telephone (pay)

ALASKA HIGHWAY *Milepost DC 409 to Teslin, YT*

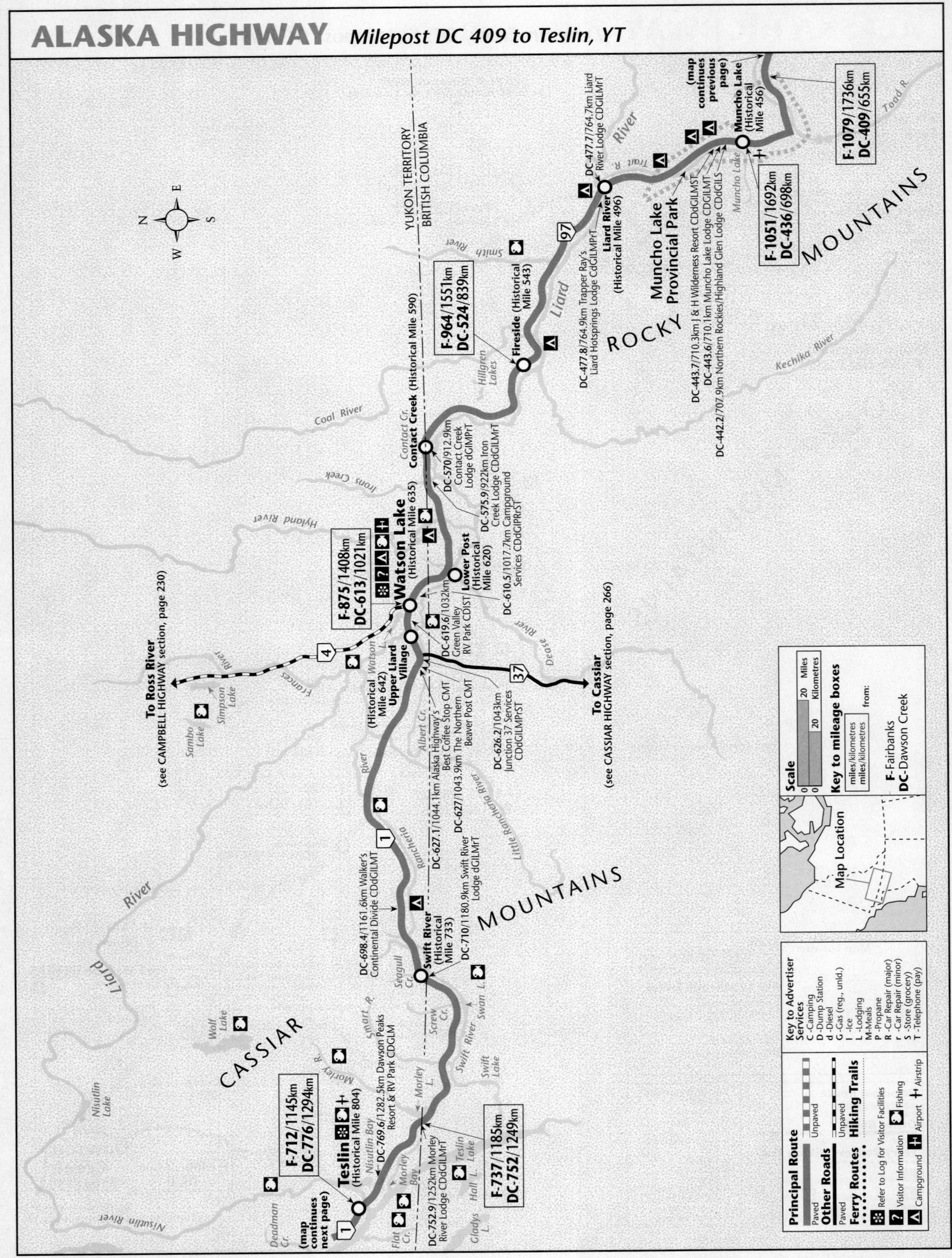

ALASKA HIGHWAY *Teslin, YT, to Milepost DC 1136*

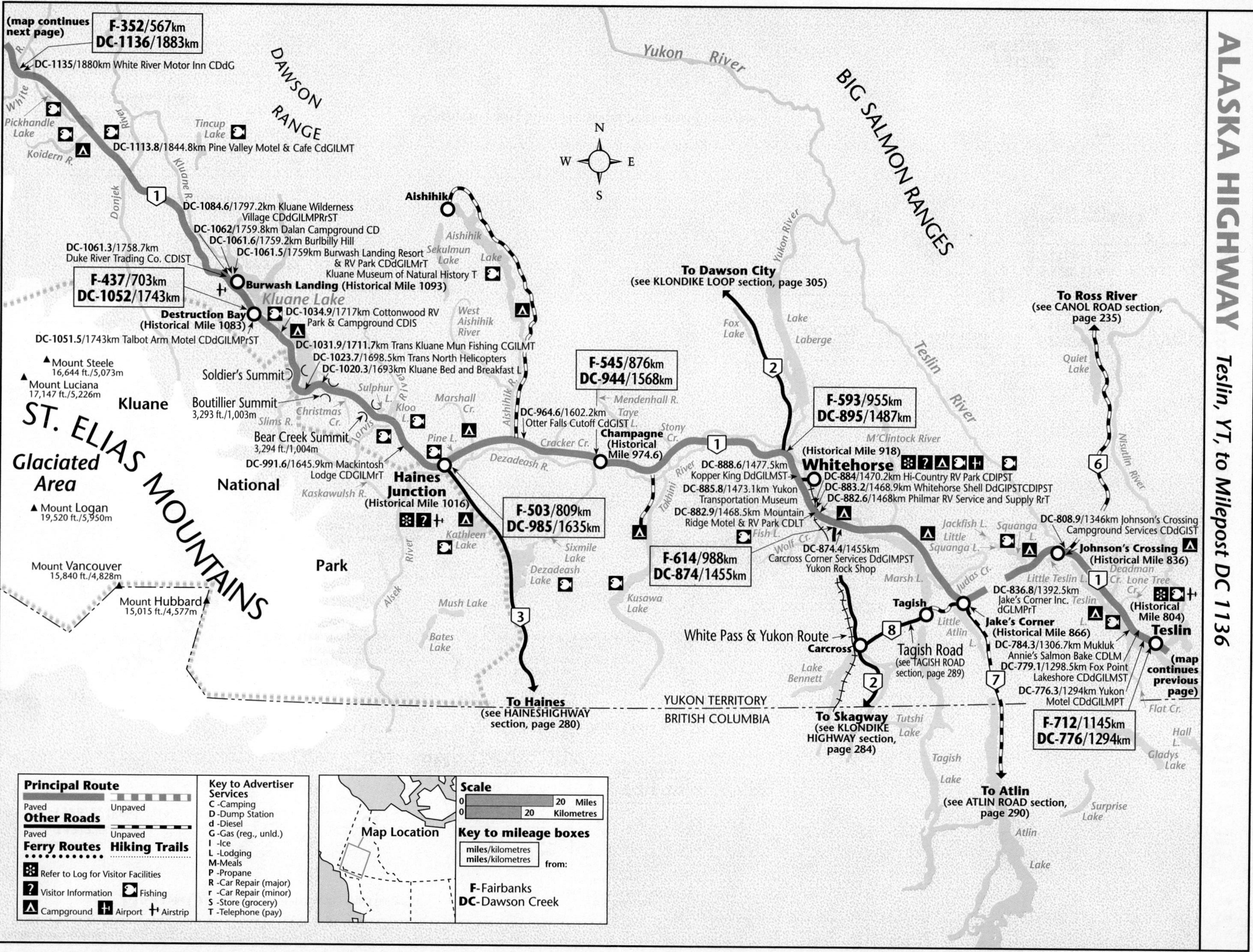

ALASKA HIGHWAY *Milepost DC 1136 to Milepost DC 1378*

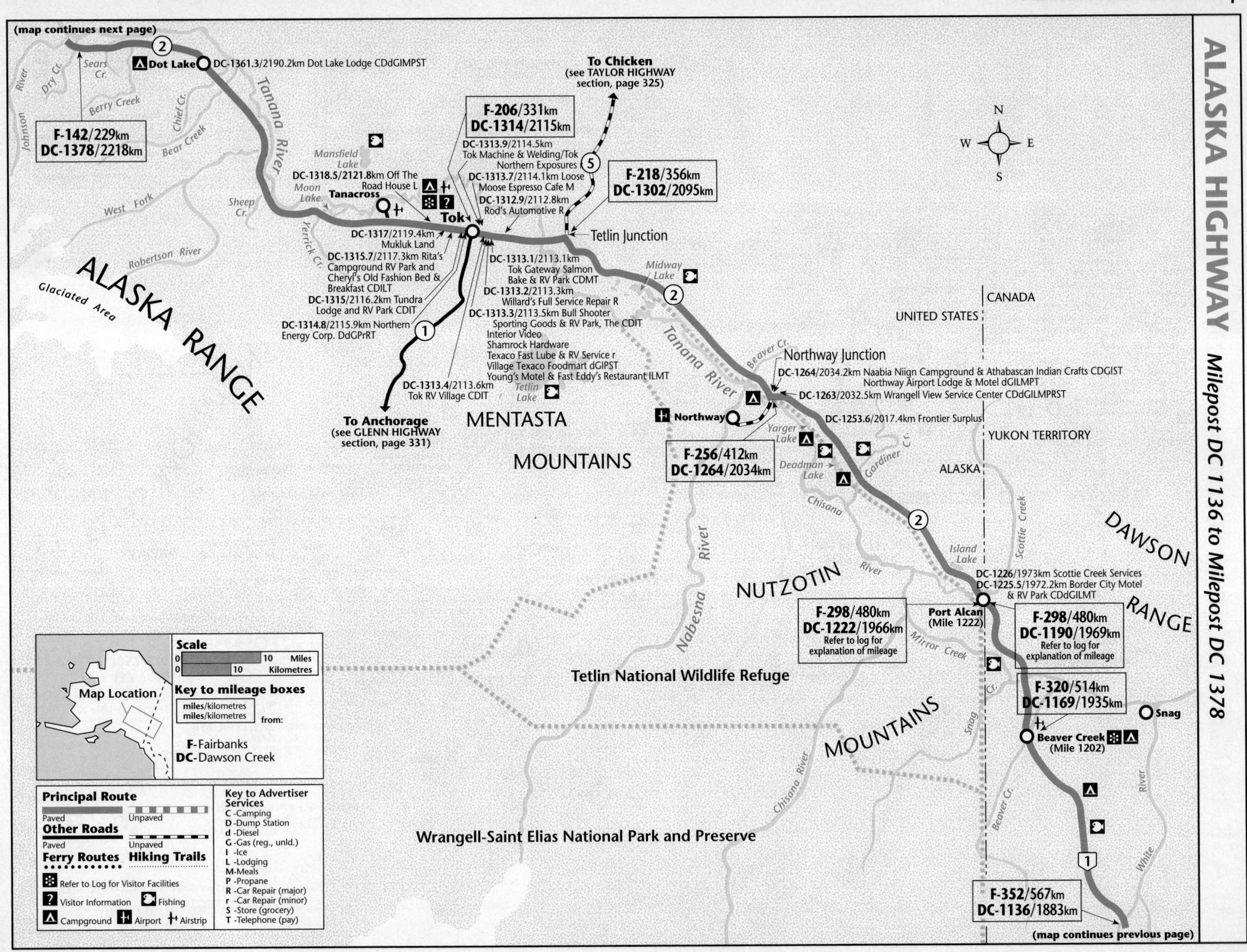

ALASKA HIGHWAY *Milepost DC 1378 to Fairbanks, AK*

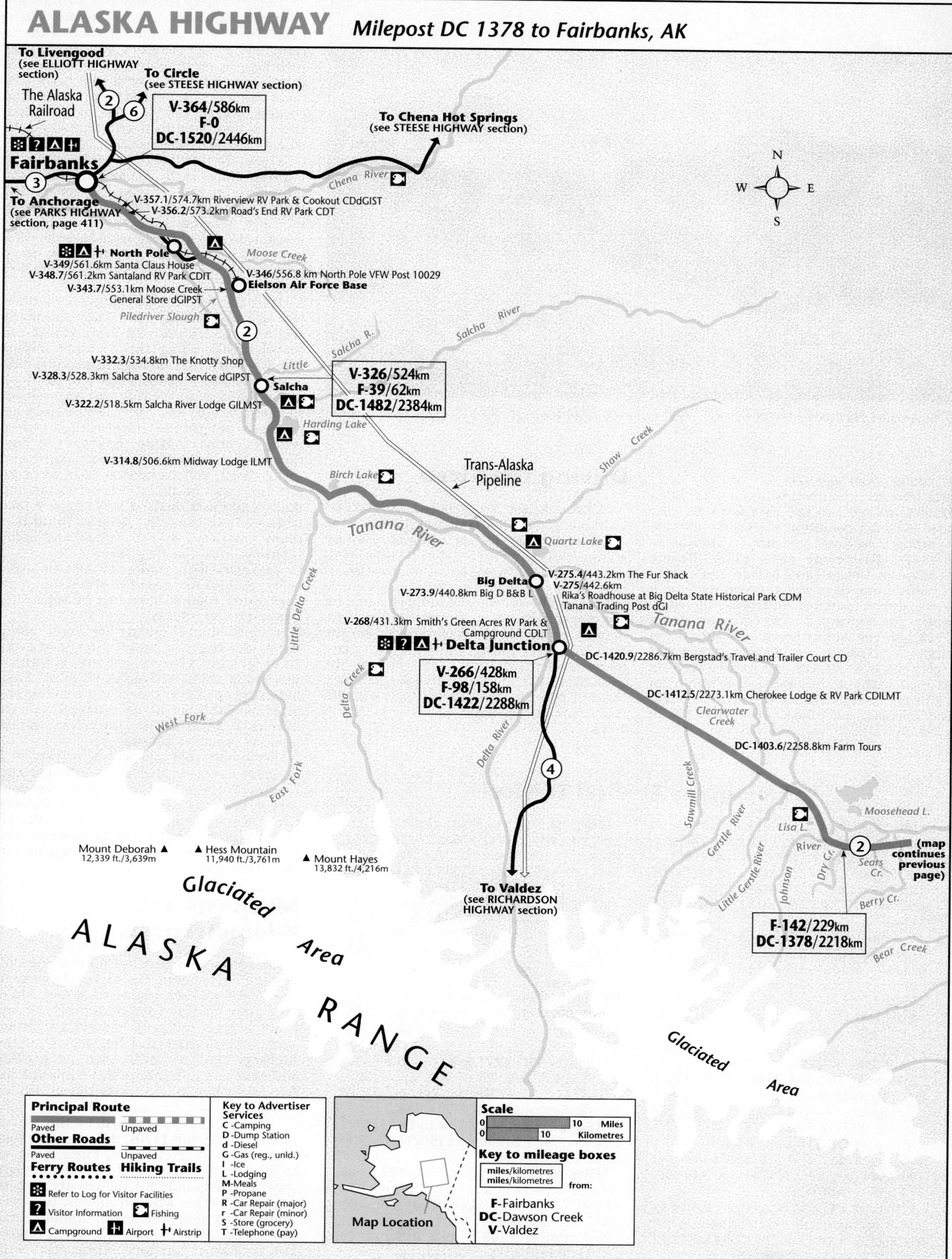

The Alaska Highway skirts Rocky Crest Lake at Milepost DC 375.9. (Earl L. Brown, staff)

(Continued from page 84)
and sections of narrow, winding road. From Haines Junction to the YT–AK border, the road is in fair condition with some narrow, winding sections without shoulders. Between **Historical Mile 1118** (Kluane Wilderness Village) and Beaver Creek there is both improved road and rough road, with some gravel patches and winding road; watch for continued road construction in 1998. On the Alaska portion of the Alaska Highway, expect fair to good surfacing, but watch for frost heaves and narrow sections of road without shoulders. Also watch for continued road construction on the highway between the YT–AK border and Tok in 1998.

Driving the Alcan

Although not really called the ALCAN anymore, quite a few people still refer to the Alaska Highway by its original military acronym. What visitors don't know—and what some Northerners may remember—is that ALCAN (which stood for Alaska-Canada military highway) was the military name for the pioneer road at its completion in 1942. Because civilian traffic was restricted on the new highway during the war years, and many residents did not take kindly to the restriction, the military name for the road was not popular. The pioneer road was officially named the Alaska Highway in March 1943.

Emergency Medical Services

Milepost DC 0 Dawson Creek to **DC 47** Fort St. John. Dawson Creek ambulance (250) 782-2211; RCMP (250) 782-5211.

Milepost DC 47 Fort St. John to **DC 222.3** Bougie Creek bridge. Fort St. John ambulance (250) 785-2079; RCMP (250) 785-6617.

Milepost DC 222.3 Bougie Creek bridge to **DC 373.3** Summit Lake Lodge. Fort Nelson ambulance (250) 774-2344, hospital (250) 774-6916; RCMP (250) 774-2777.

Milepost DC 373.3 Summit Lake Lodge to **DC 605.1** BC–YT border. Toad River ambulance (250) 232-5351; Fort Nelson RCMP (250) 774-2777.

Milepost DC 605.1 BC–YT border to **DC 710** Swift River. Watson Lake ambulance (867) 536-4444; RCMP (867) 536-5555 or (867) 667-5555.

Milepost DC 710 Swift River to **DC 821** Squanga Lake. Teslin ambulance (867) 390-4444 or (867) 667-3333; RCMP (867) 390-5555 or (867) 667-5555.

Milepost DC 821 Squanga Lake to **DC 936.8** Mendenhall River bridge. Whitehorse ambulance (867) 667-3333; RCMP (867) 667-5555.

Milepost DC 936.8 Mendenhall River bridge to **DC 1023.7** Kluane Lake Lodge. Haines Junction ambulance (867) 634-4444 or (867) 667-3333; RCMP (867) 634-5555 or (867) 667-5555.

Milepost DC 1023.7 Kluane Lake Lodge to **DC 1122.7** Longs Creek. Destruction Bay ambulance (867) 841-3333 or (867) 667-3333; RCMP (867) 634-5555 or (867) 667-5555.

Milepost DC 1122.7 Longs Creek to **DC 1189.8** YT–AK border. Beaver Creek RCMP (867) 862-5555 or (867) 667-5555; Ambulance (867) 862-3333 or (867) 667-3333.

Milepost DC 1221.8 YT–AK border to **DC 1314.2** Tok. Northway EMS (907) 778-2211. Port Alcan Rescue Team (Alaska Customs) (907) 774-2252.

Milepost DC 1314.2 Tok to **DC 1361.3** Dot Lake. Tok ambulance (907) 883-2300 or 911.

Milepost DC 1361.3 to **DC 1422** Delta Junction. Delta Rescue Squad phone 911 or (907) 895-4600; Alaska State Troopers (907) 895-4800.

Milepost DC 1422 Delta Junction to **DC 1520** Fairbanks. Dial 911.

Today's Alaska Highway is a 2-lane highway that winds and rolls across the wilderness. There are sections of road with no centerline and stretches of narrow highway with little or no shoulder. The best advice is to take your time; drive with your headlights on at all times; keep to the right on hills and corners; watch for wildlife on the road; and—as you would on any highway anywhere else—drive defensively.

There are relatively few steep grades or high summits on the Alaska Highway, with most occuring as the Alaska Highway crosses the Rocky Mountains between Fort Nelson, BC, and Watson Lake, YT. The highest summit on the highway is at Summit Lake, elev. 4,250 feet/1,295m. The few steep grades are generally short stretches from 6 to 10 percent.

Dust and mud are generally only a problem in construction areas. There are many sections of hardtop with loose gravel and gravel breaks along the highway. Flying gravel—which may damage headlights, radiators, gas tanks, windshields and paint—is still a problem. Side roads and access roads to campgrounds and other destinations are generally not paved. Gravel road is treated with calcium chloride to keep the dust down. This substance corrodes paint and metal; Wash your vehicle as soon as possible. In heavy rains, calcium chloride and mud combine to make a very slippery road surface; drive carefully! Keep in mind that many highways in the Yukon and some highways in Alaska are gravel.

Travelers with trailers should be especially cautious in areas of frost heaving. This corrugated road surface can be especially hard on trailer hitches.

Gas, food and lodging are found along the Alaska Highway on an average of every 20 to 50 miles. (The longest stretch without services is about 100 miles.) Not all businesses are open year-round, nor are most services available 24 hours a day. There are dozens of government and private campgrounds along the highway.

Remember that you will be driving in 2 different countries that use 2 different currencies: For the best rate, exchange your money at a bank. There are banks in Dawson Creek, Fort St. John, Fort Nelson, Watson Lake, Whitehorse, Tok, Delta Junction and Fairbanks. Haines Junction has banking service at the general store.

Mileposts and Kilometreposts

Mileposts were first put up at communities and lodges along the Alaska Highway in the 1940s to help motorists know where they were in this vast wilderness. Today, those original mileposts remain a tradition with communities and businesses on the highway and are still used as mailing addresses and reference points, although the figures no longer accurately reflect driving distance.

When Canada switched to the metric system in the mid-1970s, the mileposts were replaced by kilometreposts. These posts are located on the right-hand side of the highway (Alaska-bound). Kilometreposts, consisting of reflective white numerals on green signs, are up along the British Columbia portion of the Alaska Highway every 3 miles/5 km. In Yukon Territory, white posts with black numerals are up along the highway every 1.2 miles/2 km. There are stretches of straightened and improved highway where kilometreposts are missing.

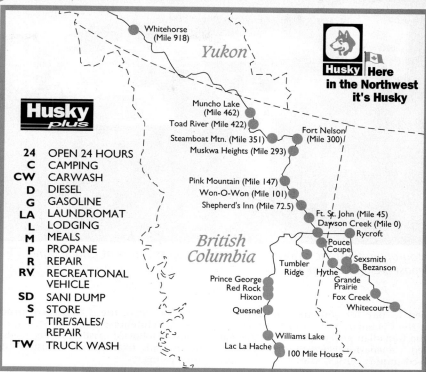

The kilometerage of the British Columbia portion of the Alaska Highway was recalibrated by the government in the fall of 1990, with kilometreposts corrected to reflect current driving distances. As of our press time, kilometreposts along the Yukon Territory portion of the Alaska Highway still reflected the metric equivalent of the historical mileposts. Thus, at the BC–YT border **(Historical Mile 627)** the kilometerage from Dawson Creek is given as 967.6 km on the BC side and 1009 km on the YT side.

The MILEPOST® log of the Alaska Highway gives distance from Dawson Creek to the AK–YT border as actual driving distance in miles from Dawson Creek followed by kilometre distance based on the kilometreposts. Use our mileage figure from Dawson Creek to figure correct distance between points on the Alaska Highway in Canada. Use our kilometre figure from Dawson Creek to pinpoint location in reference to physical kilometreposts on the Alaska Highway in Canada. On the Alaska portion of the highway, mileposts are based on historical miles, so distance from Dawson Creek in the log is given according to the mileposts up along the road. This figure is followed by the metric equivalent in kilometres.

NOTE: Due to road reconstruction, many kilometreposts have been removed.

Traditional milepost figures in Canada are indicated in the text as **Historical Mile**. Where the governments of British Columbia, Yukon and Alaska have installed commemorative mileposts, the text reads **Historic Milepost**. Restored in 1992 to commemorate the 50th anniversary of the construction of the Alaska Highway, many of these historic markers are accompanied by signs and interpretive panels. These mileposts reflect the original or traditional mileage and do not reflect actual driving distance.

A Brief History of the Alaska Highway

Construction of the Alaska Highway officially began on March 9, 1942, and ended eight months and 12 days later on Oct. 25, 1942. But an overland link between Alaska and the Lower 48 had been studied as early as 1930 under President Herbert Hoover's authorization. It was not until the bombing of Pearl Harbor in December 1941 that construction of the highway was deemed a military necessity. Alaska was considered vulnerable to a Japanese invasion. On Feb. 6, 1942, approval for the Alaska Highway was given by the Chief of Staff, U.S. Army. On Feb. 11, President Roosevelt authorized construction of the pioneer road.

The general route of the highway, determined by the War Department, was along a line of existing airfields from Edmonton, AB, to Fairbanks, AK. This chain of airfields was known as the Northwest Staging Route, and was used to ferry more than 8,000 war planes from Great Falls, MT, to Ladd Air Force Base in Fairbanks, AK, as part of the Russian–American Lend Lease Program. The planes were flown from Fairbanks to Nome, then on to Russia.

In March 1942, rights-of-way through Canada were secured by formal agreement between the 2 countries. The Americans

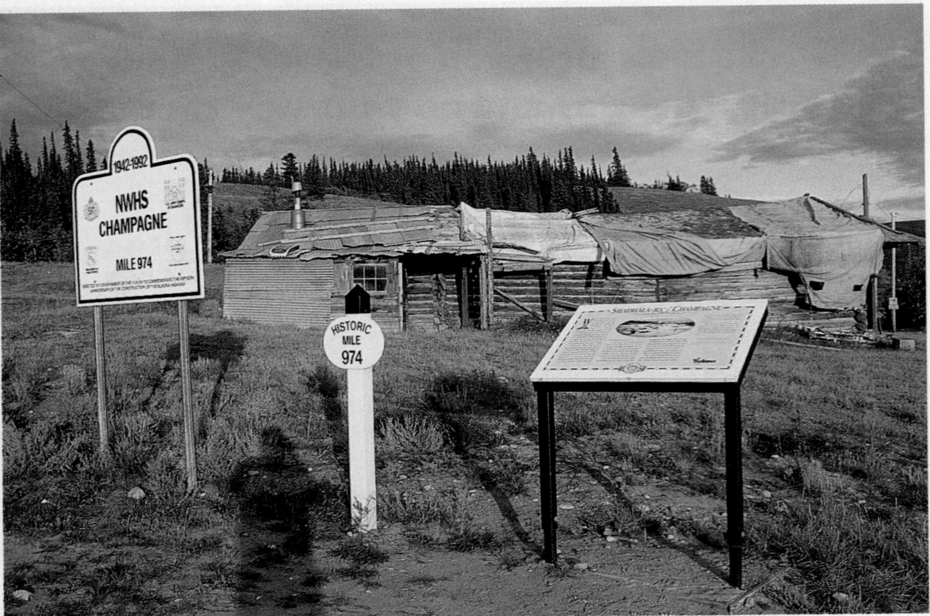

Photographing historic highway markers and log structure at Champagne, YT, Milepost DC 943.5. (Earl L. Brown, staff)

agreed to pay for construction and turn over the Canadian portion of the highway to the Canadian government after the war ended. Canada furnished the right-of-way, waived import duties, sales taxes, income taxes and immigration regulations, and provided construction materials along the route.

A massive mobilization of men and equipment began. Regiments of the U.S. Army Corps of Engineers were moved north to work on the highway. By June, more than 10,000 American troops had poured into the Canadian North. The Public Roads Administration tackled the task of organizing civilian engineers and equipment. Trucks, road-building equipment, office furniture, food, tents and other supplies all had to be located and then shipped north.

Road work began in April, with crews working out of the 2 largest construction camps, Whitehorse and Fort St. John. The highway followed existing winter roads, old Indian trails, rivers and, on occasion, "sight" engineering.

For the soldiers and civilian workers, it was a hard life. Working 7 days a week, they endured mosquitoes and black flies in summer, and below zero temperatures in winter. Weeks would pass with no communication between headquarters and field parties. According to one senior officer with the Public Roads Administration, "Equipment was always a critical problem. There never was enough."

In June 1942, the Japanese invaded Attu and Kiska islands in the Aleutians, adding a new sense of urgency to completion of the road. Crews working from east and west connected at Contact Creek on Sept. 25. By October, it was possible for vehicles to travel the entire length of the highway. The official opening of the Alaska Highway was a ribbon-cutting ceremony held Nov. 20, 1942, on Soldier's Summit at Kluane Lake. (A rededication ceremony was held Nov. 20, 1992, as part of the 50th anniversary celebration of the Alaska Highway.) The Alaska Highway was named an International Historical Engineering Landmark in 1996.

Dawson Creek

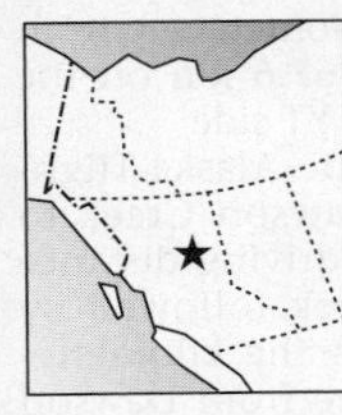

Milepost 0 of the Alaska Highway. **Population:** 11,125, area 66,500. **Emergency Services:** **RCMP**, phone (250) 782-5211. **Fire Department**, phone (250) 782-5000. **Ambulance**, phone (250) 782-2211. **Hospital and Poison Centre**, Dawson Creek and District Hospital, 11000 13th St., phone (250) 782-8501.

Visitor Information: At NAR (Northern Alberta Railway) Park on Alaska Avenue at 10th Street (one block west of the traffic circle), in the building behind the railway car. Open year-round, 8 A.M. to 7 P.M. daily in summer, 10 A.M. to 4 P.M. Tuesday through Saturday in winter. Phone (250) 782-9595, or e-mail dawsoncrk@pris.bc.ca. Trained visitor-information counselors can answer questions about weather and road conditions, local events and attractions. Plenty of public parking in front of the refurbished grain elevator that houses the Dawson Creek Art Gallery and Museum.

Elevation: 2,186 feet/666m. **Climate**: Average temperature in January is 0°F/-18°C; in July it is 60°F/15°C. The average annual snowfall is 72 inches with the average depth of snow in midwinter at 19.7 inches. Frost-free days total 97, with the first frost of the year occurring about the first week of September. **Radio**: CJDC 890. **Television**: 13 channels via cable including pay TV. **Newspapers**: *Peace River Block News* (daily); *The Mirror* (weekly).

Private Aircraft: Dawson Creek airport, 2 miles/3.2 km southeast; elev. 2,148 feet/655m; length 5,000 feet/1,524m;

asphalt; fuel 100, jet. Floatplane base parallels runway.

Dawson Creek lies 367 miles/591 km northwest of Edmonton, AB, and 250 miles/402 km northeast of Prince George, BC.

Dawson Creek (like Dawson City in the Yukon Territory) was named for George Mercer Dawson of the Geological Survey of Canada, whose geodetic surveys of this region in 1879 helped lead to its development as an agricultural settlement. The open, level townsite is surrounded by rolling farmland, part of the government-designated Peace River Block.

The Peace River Block consists of 3.5 million acres of arable land in northeastern British Columbia, which the province gave to the Dominion Government in 1883 in return for financial aid toward construction of the Canadian Pacific Railway. (While a route through the Peace River country was surveyed by CPR in 1878, the railroad was eventually routed west from Calgary through Kicking Horse Pass.) The Peace River

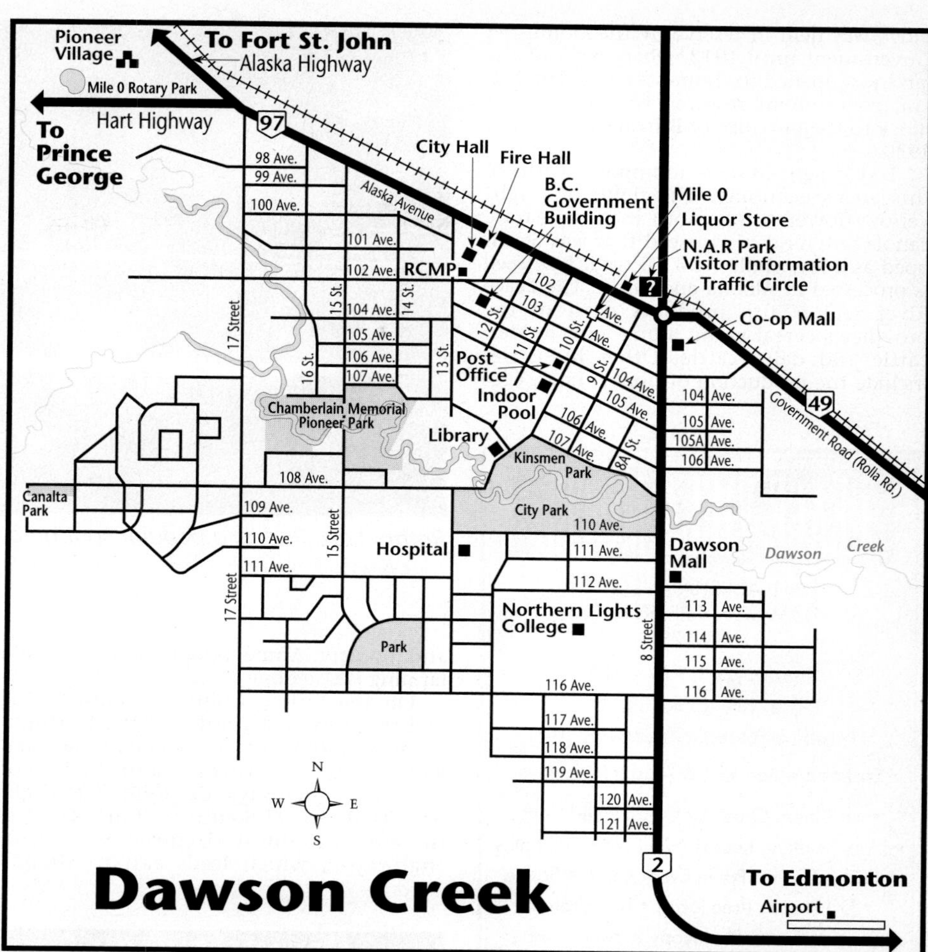

DAWSON CREEK ADVERTISERS

Alahart RV Park.................Ph. (250) 782-4702
Alaska Hotel Cafe & Dew Drop Inn Pub ....55 paces south of Mile 0 Post
Dawson Creek Art Gallery ....NAR Park
Dawson Creek Coin Laundry Ltd.........5 blocks S. of traffic circle
Dawson Creek Tourist Information Bureau.....Ph. (250) 782-9595
Farmington Fairways & Campground ....Ph. (250) 843-7774
Handy Crafters Corner Co-op..........................Ph. (250) 782-6470
Joy Propane.......................Ph. (888) 782-6008
Kim's Yarn Barn................Ph. (250) 782-8994
King Koin Laundromat.....Ph. (250) 782-2590
Lodge Motor Inn, The......Ph. (250) 782-4837
Mile 0 RV Park & Campsite.....Adjacent Walter Wright Pioneer Village
Northern Lights RV Park Ltd.........1 mile from Alaska Hwy. Jct. on Hwy. 97 S.
Northwinds Lodge.........1 block E. Co-op Mall
Organic Farms Bakery.......Ph. (250) 782-6533
Peace Villa Motel..................1641 Alaska Ave.
Rowland House Bed & Breakfast...........Ph. (250) 782-5654
Seto's Avenue A Studio..........................Ph. (250) 782-4501
TLC Car Wash................Across from Northern Lights College
Trail Inn, The...................Ph. (250) 782-8595
Treasure House Imports..........10109 10th St.
Tubby's RV Park.....................1913 Hart Hwy.
United Spring & Brake Ltd.........Directly behind McDonald's

Drive with your headlights on.

Block was held in reserve by the Dominion Government until 1912, when some of the land was opened for homesteading. The federal government restored the Peace River Block to the province of British Columbia in 1930.

Today, agriculture is an important part of this area's economy. The fields of bright yellow flowers (in season) in the area are canola, a hybrid of rapeseed that was developed as a low cholesterol oil seed. Raw seed is processed in Alberta and Japan. The Peace River region also produces most of the province's cereal grain, along with fodder, cattle and dairy cattle. Other industries include the production of honey, hogs, eggs and poultry. Some potato and vegetable farming is also done here.

Rotary Lake Park is a popular spot on a warm, sunny day in Dawson Creek, BC.
(Earl L. Brown, staff)

On the British Columbia Railway line and the western terminus of the Northern Alberta Railway (now Canadian National Railway), Dawson Creek is also the hub of four major highways: the John Hart Highway (Highway 97 South) to Prince George; the Alaska Highway (Highway 97 North); Highway 2, which leads east to Grande Prairie, AB; and Highway 49, which leads east to Spirit River and Donnelly.

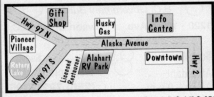

The Northern Alberta Railway reached Dawson Creek in 1931. As a railhead, Dawson Creek was an important funnel for supplies and equipment during construction of the Alaska Highway in 1942. Some 600 carloads arrived by rail within a period of five weeks in preparation for the construction program, according to a report by the Public Roads Administration in 1942. A "rutted provincial road" linked Dawson Creek with Fort St. John, affording the only approach to the southern base of operations. Field headquarters were established at Fort St. John and Whitehorse. Meanwhile, men and machines continued to arrive at Dawson Creek. By May of 1942, 4,720 carloads of equipment had arrived by rail at Dawson Creek for dispersement to troops and civilian engineers to the north.

With the completion of the Alaska Highway in 1942 (and opening to the public in 1948) and the John Hart Highway in 1952, Dawson Creek expanded both as a distribution centre and tourist destination. Dawson Creek was incorporated as a city in 1958.

The development of oil and natural gas exploration in northeastern British Columbia, and related industries such as pipeline construction and oil storage, has contributed to the economic expansion of Dawson Creek. The city is also one of the major supply centres for the massive resource development known as North East Coal, southwest of Dawson Creek. Access to the coal development and the town of Tumbler Ridge is via the Heritage Highway, which branches off the John Hart Highway just west of Dawson Creek and also branches off Highway 2 southeast of the city. Highway 29 extends south from Chetwynd to Tumbler Ridge.

Provincial government offices and social services for the South Peace region are located in Dawson Creek. The city has a modern 100-bed hospital, a public library and a college (Northern Lights, associated with the University of Northern BC in Prince George). There are also an indoor swimming pool, 2 skating arenas, a curling rink, bowling alley, golf course, art gallery, museum, tennis and racquetball courts. There are numerous churches in Dawson Creek. (Check at the Visitor Infocentre for location and hours of worship.)

ACCOMMODATIONS/VISITOR SERVICES

There are 14 hotels/motels, several bed and breakfasts, and dozens of restaurants. Department stores, banks, grocery, an organic bakery, drug and hardware stores, and many specialty shops are located both downtown and in the 2 shopping centres, Co-op Mall and Dawson Mall. Visitors will also find laundromats, car washes, gas stations and automotive repair shops. The

For details on customs requirements, see the TRAVEL PLANNING section.

liquor store is adjacent the NAR Visitor Infocentre on Alaska Avenue.

There are 4 campgrounds in Dawson Creek, 2 located on either side of the Hart Highway at its junction with the Alaska Highway and 2 located on Alaska Avenue. There is a private campground on the Hart Highway, 2 miles/3.2 km west from the Alaska Highway junction. There are also campgrounds (both private and provincial) north of Dawson Creek on the Alaska Highway. ▲

The Alaska Hotel Cafe & Dew Drop Inn Pub combines the spirit of Northern Adventure with Old World charm. Where to Eat in Canada, which lists the 500 top restaurants, suggests, "It is a good idea to start out on the Alaska Highway with a good meal under your belt, and there's no better place than the Alaska Cafe." The cafe also holds membership in World Famous Restaurants International. The pub features live entertainment nightly, a hot spot in town. The building, having 15 "rooms with charm," provides a perfect backdrop for the Kux-Kardos collection of antiques and works of art (tours available). At the Alaska, our philosophy is Deluxe Evolutionary ... "Always changing for the better." Phone (250) 782-7998 to reserve. Pets welcome. Located 55 paces south of the mile "0" post. A definite must to experience. [ADVERTISEMENT]

Northern Lights RV Park welcomes you! Enjoy peaceful surroundings just 1.5 miles from Dawson Creek. Spacious, level pull-throughs with your own lawn and picnic table. Check out our souvenir shop or try fly fishing in our trout pond. Come to see the attractions in our area? Day trips to the WAC Bennett Dam, Kinuseo Falls and the Kiskatinaw Bridge all offer gorgeous scenery and abundant wildlife. Or, just sit back and relax while we pamper you and your rig to prepare you for your Alaska Highway adventure! Your hosts—the Bates Family. Phone (250) 782-9433. E-mail: lbates@pris.bc.ca. Internet address: www.pris.bc.ca\rvpark\. [ADVERTISEMENT] ▲

Organic Farms Bakery. Using grain crops from our family farm, 100 percent certified organic stoneground flour. Specializing in German-style rye, spelt and whole wheat breads, buns, pretzels and delicious pastries. Flours and spelt pastas. Taste the difference! 1425 97th Ave., Dawson Creek (look for our colourful bakery), just off Alaska Ave. Phone (250) 782-6533. [ADVERTISEMENT]

TRANSPORTATION

Air: Scheduled service from Dawson Creek airport to Prince George, Vancouver, Edmonton, Grande Prairie and Calgary via Air BC. The airport is located 2 miles/3.2 km south of the Alaska Avenue traffic circle via 8th Street/Highway 2; there is a small terminal at the airport. There is also a floatplane base.

Railroad: Canadian National Railroad and British Columbia Railway provide freight service only. B.C. Railway provides passenger service from Vancouver to Prince George.

Bus: Greyhound service to Prince George and Vancouver, BC; Edmonton, AB; and Whitehorse, YT. Dawson Creek also has a city bus transit system.

ATTRACTIONS

NAR Park, on Alaska Avenue at 10th Street (near the traffic circle), is the site of the Visitor Infocentre, which is housed in a restored railway station; phone (250) 782-9595. The Visitor Infocentre offers a self-guided historical walking tour with descriptions of Dawson Creek in the early 1940s during construction of the Alaska Highway.

Also at the station is the Dawson Creek Station Museum, operated by the South Peace Historical Society, which contains pioneer artifacts and wildlife displays. Be sure to leave enough time to view the hour-long video about the building of the Alaska Highway. Souvenirs and restrooms at the museum.

In front of the station is a 1903 railway car, called "The Blue Goose Caboose." Adja-

DAWSON
CREEK
FT ST. JOHN 48
FORT NELSON 300
WHITEHORSE 918
FAIRBANKS 1523

MILE "0" ALASKA HIGHWAY

For further information contact
Dawson Creek Visitor Information Bureau
Department MP
900 Alaska Avenue
Dawson Creek, BC V1G 4T6

Tel (250) 782-9595
Fax (250) 782-9538

SUPER, NATURAL BRITISH COLUMBIA®

Walter Wright Pioneer Village features a collection of local pioneer buildings and northern gardens. (Earl L. Brown, staff)

cent to the station is a huge wooden grain elevator, which has been refurbished; its annex now houses an art gallery with art shows throughout the summer; admission by donation. Good display of Alaska Highway construction photos; restroom, gift shop. The last of Dawson Creek's old elevators, it was bought and moved to its present location through the efforts of community organizations. Every Saturday in summer there is an outdoor farmer's market featuring flowers, produce, baked goods and crafts for sale.

Inquire at the Visitor Infocentre for the location of Bear Mountain Community Forest. This Ministry of Forests recreation area features interpretive trails on the flora and fauna of the area. It is located 6 miles/10 km south of the city.

Recreational facilities in Dawson Creek include a bowling alley, miniature golf, indoor pool, 2 ice arenas, curling rink, 18-hole golf course, tennis courts and an outdoor pool at Rotary Lake Park.

Walter Wright Pioneer Village and Mile 0 Rotary Park. The entrance to the village is highlighted by Gardens North, consisting of 9 separate gardens, including a memorial rose garden. Bring a camera to capture the amazing variety of perennials and annuals that grow in the North. The pioneer village contains an impressive collection of local pioneer buildings, including a teahouse; antiques and collectibles shop; and a general store. Souvenirs and Gardens North seeds are available. Admission is $1. Food service available at the Mile 1 Cafe. Check at the infocentre for summer tours of the gardens.

Adjacent to the village is the Sudeten Memorial Hall. "A Mile Zero Welcome," a presentation about Dawson Creek, then and now, by Marilyn Croutch, is held either in Sudeten Hall or the old Dawson School in summer; phone (250) 782-7144. Check with the Visitor Infocentre for details on entertainment offerings. Also located here is Rotary Lake, an outdoor man-made swimming facility; restrooms and picnic areas are found throughout Rotary Park.

Special Events. Mile Zero Celebration Days held in May. July 4th festivities take place at Sudeten Hall. The Fall Fair and Stampede in August features the largest amateur rodeo in North America.

Tumbler Ridge Side Trip. To reach Tumbler Ridge, drive west from Dawson Creek 12 miles/20 km on Highway 97 to junction with the Heritage Highway (see **Milepost PG 237.7** in the WEST ACCESS ROUTE section), or drive west 60.6 miles/97.5 km to junction with Highway 29 South (see **Milepost PG 189.4** in the WEST ACCESS ROUTE section). Heritage Highway 52 (paved) leads south 59.5 miles/96 km to the community of Tumbler Ridge. Highway 29 South is a paved maintained road all the way to Tumbler Ridge. Tumbler Ridge is the townsite for Quintette Coal Limited's large-scale surface mines, and also serves workers of the Bullmoose Mine. Tours of Quintette and Bullmoose mines are available; inquire at the Visitor Infocentre in Tumbler Ridge. The huge coal processing plant and overhead conveyor are visible from the road. Monkman Provincial Park, site of spectacular 225-foot/69-m Kinuseo (Keh-NEW-see-oh) Falls, lies south of Tumbler Ridge. Contact BC Parks in Fort St. John (phone 250/787-

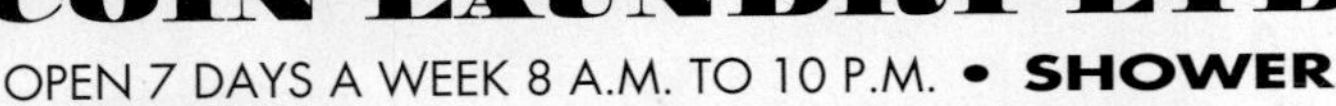

3407) or Tumbler Ridge Infocentre (250/242-4702) for more information.

At Tumbler Ridge, motorists have a choice: return to Highway 97 via Highway 52; return to Highway 97 via Highway 29 South to Chetwynd; or continue on the Heritage Highway loop, 76 miles/123 km via all-gravel road and 16 miles/25 km via paved road, to Highway 2 southeast of Dawson Creek. (Highway 29 South offers the best road surface.) There are no services on the Heritage Highway except at Tumbler Ridge, which has a motel, campgrounds, restaurants, a bank and shopping. On gravel stretches of the road, watch for poor road conditions in wet weather.

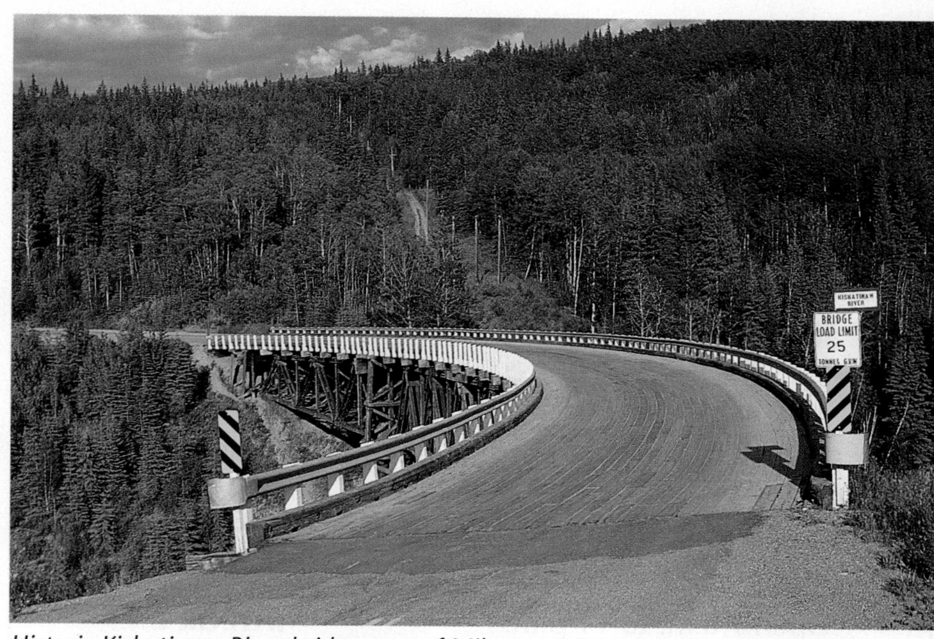

Historic Kiskatinaw River bridge east of Milepost DC 17.3 is the only surviving original timber bridge built on the Alaska Highway. (Earl L. Brown, staff)

Alaska Highway Log

BC HIGHWAY 97
Distance* from Dawson Creek (DC) is followed by distance from Fairbanks (F). Original mileposts are indicated in the text as Historical Mile.

*Mileages from Dawson Creek are based on actual driving distance. Kilometres from Dawson Creek are based on physical kilometreposts. Read Mileposts and Kilometreposts in the introduction on page 90 for an explanation of how this highway is logged.

DC 0 F 1488 (2394.6 km) **Mile 0** marker of the Alaska Highway on 10th Street in downtown Dawson Creek.

Northbound: Good pavement approximately next 284 miles/457 km (through Fort Nelson). Watch for road construction and surface changes from Pink Mountain north.

DC 1.2 (1.9 km) **F 1486.8** (2392.7 km) **Junction** of the Alaska Highway and John Hart Highway.

Prince George-bound travelers turn to the end of the WEST ACCESS ROUTE section and read log back to front. Alaska-bound travelers continue with this log.

DC 1.5 (2.4 km) **F 1486.5** (2392.2 km) Mile 0 Rotary Park, Walter Wright Pioneer Village and Mile 0 Campground to west. ▲

DC 1.7 (2.7 km) **F 1486.3** (2391.9 km) **Historic Milepost 2.** Sign about Cantel Repeater Station. Cantel telephone–teletype lines stretched from Alberta to Fairbanks, AK, making it one of the world's longest open-wire toll circuits at the time.

DC 2 (3.2 km) **F 1486** (2391.4 km) Recreation centre and golf course to west. Louisiana Pacific waferboard plant to east.

DC 2.7 (4.3 km) **F 1485.3** (2390.3 km) Truck scales and public phone to east. Truck stop to west; gas, cafe.

DC 2.9 (4.7 km) **F 1485.1** (2390 km) Northern Alberta Railway (NAR) tracks.

DC 3.3 (5.3 km) **F 1484.7** (2389.3 km) Turnout with litter barrel to east. **Historic Milepost 3;** historic sign marks Curan & Briggs Ltd. Construction Camp, U.S. Army Traffic Control Centre.

DC 3.4 (5.5 km) **F 1484.6** (2389.2 km) **Historical Mile 3.** The Trading Post to east.

DC 9.5 (15.3 km) **F 1478.5** (2379.3 km) Golf course, driving range and RV park. ▲

DC 11.2 (18 km) **F 1476.8** (2376.6 km) Turnout with litter barrels to west.

DC 11.5 (18.5 km) **F 1476.5** (2376.1 km) Turnout with litter barrels to east.

DC 13.1 (21.1 km) **F 1474.9** (2373.5 km) **Historic Milepost 13** "Start of Storms Contracting Co. Ltd. contract."

DC 14.8 (24 km) **F 1473.2** (2370.8 km) Farmington (unincorporated).

DC 15.8 (25.4 km) **F 1472.2** (2369.2 km) Farmington store to west; gas, groceries, phone.

DC 17.3 (27.8 km) **F 1470.7** (2366.8 km) Exit east for loop road to Kiskatinaw Provincial Park. Follow good 2-lane paved road (old Alaska Highway) 2.5 miles/4 km for Kiskatinaw Provincial Park. This interesting side road gives travelers the opportunity to drive the original old Alaska Highway and to cross the historic curved wooden Kiskatinaw River bridge. Sign at bridge notes that this 531-foot-/162-m-long structure is the only original timber bridge built along the Alaska Highway that is still in use today. The provincial park has 28 campsites, drinking water, firewood, picnic tables, fire rings, outhouses and garbage containers. Camping fee $7 to $12. ▲

DC 17.5 (28.2 km) **F 1470.5** (2366.5 km) Distance marker indicates Fort St. John 29 miles/47 km.

DC 19.4 (31.2 km) **F 1468.6** (2363.4 km) Large turnout to east.

DC 19.8 (31.9 km) **F 1468.2** (2362.8 km) Highway descends northbound to Kiskatinaw River.

DC 20.9 (33.6 km) **F 1467.1** (2361 km) Kiskatinaw River bridge. *CAUTION: Strong crosswinds on bridge.* Turnout with litter barrel and picnic tables to east at north end of bridge. View of unique bridge support.

DC 21.6 (34.5 km) **F 1466.4** (2359 km) Loop road to Kiskatinaw Provincial Park and Kiskatinaw River bridge (see **Milepost DC 17.3**).

DC 25.4 (41 km) **F 1462.6** (2353.8 km) NorthwesTel microwave tower to east. Alaska Highway travelers will be seeing many of these towers as they drive north. The Northwest Communications System was constructed by the U.S. Army in 1942–43. This land line was replaced in 1963 with the construction of 42 microwave relay stations by Canadian National Telecommunications (Cantel, now NorthwesTel) between Grande Prairie, AB, and the YT–AK border.

DC 30.5 (49.1 km) **F 1457.5** (2345.5 km) Turnout to east with litter barrels. Turnout to west with litter barrels, pit toilet and historical marker about explorer Alexander Mackenzie.

Highway begins steep winding descent northbound to the Peace River bridge. *CAUTION: Trucks check your brakes.* Good views to northeast of Peace River valley and industrial community of Taylor. Some wide gravel shoulder next 4 miles/6.4 km for northbound traffic to pull off.

DC 32.1 (51.6 km) **F 1455.9** (2343 km) Large turnout with litter barrels. Viewpoint with information panel.

DC 33.8 (54.4 km) **F 1454.2** (2340.2 km) Pingle Creek.

DC 34 (54.7 km) **F 1454** (2339.9 km) Access to Taylor Landing Provincial Park; boat launch, parking and fishing. Jet boat outfitter. Also access to Peace Island Regional Park, 0.5 mile/0.8 km west of the highway, situated on an island in the **Peace River** connected to the south shore by a causeway. Peace Island has 35 shaded campsites with gravel pads, firewood, fire rings, picnic tables, picnic shelter, toilets, potable water, playground and horseshoe pits. There are also 4 large picnic areas and a tenting area. Camping fee. Open Memorial Day to Labour Day. Nature trail, good bird watching and good fishing in clear water. Boaters should use caution on the Peace River since both parks are downstream from the W.A.C. Bennett and Peace Canyon dams and water levels may fluctuate rapidly. ▲

DC 34.4 (55.4 km) **F 1453.6** (2339.3 km) Peace River bridge. Gas pipeline bridge visible to east.

Bridging the Peace was one of the first goals of Alaska Highway engineers in 1942. Traffic moving north from Dawson Creek was limited by the Peace River crossing, where 2 ferries with a capacity of 10 trucks per hour were operating in May. Three different pile trestles were constructed across the Peace River, only to be washed out by high water. Work on the permanent 2,130-foot suspension bridge began in December 1942 and was completed in July 1943. One of 2 suspension bridges on the Alaska Highway, the Peace River bridge collapsed in 1957 after erosion undermined the north anchor block of the bridge. The cantilever and truss-type bridge that crosses the Peace River today was completed in 1960.

DC 35 (56.3 km) **F 1453** (2338.3 km) **Historic Milepost 35** at **TAYLOR** (pop. 1,031; elev. 1,804 feet/550m), located on the north bank of the Peace River. **Visitor Information**: On left northbound (10114 100 St.); phone (250) 789-9015. Inquire here about industrial tours of Canadian Forest Products, Fiberco Pulpmill and Greenhouse Complex. Taylor is an industrial community clustered around a Westcoast Energy Inc. gas-processing plant and large sawmill. Established in 1955 with the discovery and development of a natural gas field in the area, Taylor is the site of a pulp mill and plants that handle sulfur processing, gas compressing, high-octane aviation gas production and other byproducts of natural gas. The Westcoast Energy natural gas pipeline reaches from here to Vancouver, BC, with a branch to western Washington.

The fertile Taylor Flats area has several market gardens and roadside stands in summer. A hotel, motels, cafes, grocery store, private RV park, gas station and post office are located here. Free municipal dump station and potable water located behind the North Taylor Inn. Recreation facilities include an 18-hole golf course, a motorcross track and a recreation complex with swimming pool, curling rink and district ice centre for skating (open year-round). Gold Panning Championship held in August. ▲

Redwood Esso and Taylor Lodge. See display ad this section.

DC 36.3 (58.4 km) **F 1451.7** (2336.2 km) Railroad tracks.

DC 40 (64.5 km) **F 1448** (2330.3 km) **Historical Mile 41**. Post office; private campground. ▲

DC 40.3 (64.9 km) **F 1447.7** (2329.8 km) Exit east for Fort St. John airport.

DC 40.4 (65 km) **F 1447.6** (2329.6 km) B.C. Railway overhead tracks.

DC 40.9 (65.8 km) **F 1447.1** (2328.8 km) **Historic Milepost 42** Access Road to Fort St. John Airport.

DC 42.3 (68.1 km) **F 1445.7** (2326.6 km) World's largest glass beehive at the Honey Place to west.

The Honey Place. See display ad this section.

DC 43.7 (70.3 km) **F 1444.3** (2324.3 km) Miniature golf, driving range and RV park. ▲

Sourdough Pete's RV Park and Troy's Amusement Park. See display ad this section. ▲

DC 44.6 (71.7 km) **F 1443.4** (2322.9 km) Access to Fort St. John via 86th Street.

Private RV park. ▲

DC 45.7 (73.5 km) **F 1442.3** (2321.1 km) **Historic Milepost 47**, Fort St. John/"Camp Alcan" sign. In 1942, Fort St. John "exploded." What had been home to 200 became a temporary base for more than 6,000.

DC 45.8 (73.7 km) **F 1442.2** (2320.9 km) South access to Fort St. John via 100th Street. Exit east for Visitor Infocentre and downtown Fort St. John.

DC 47 (75.6 km) **F 1441** (2319 km) **Historical Mile 48.** North access to Fort St. John via 100th Avenue to downtown. Truck stop with 24-hour gas and food.

Fort St. John

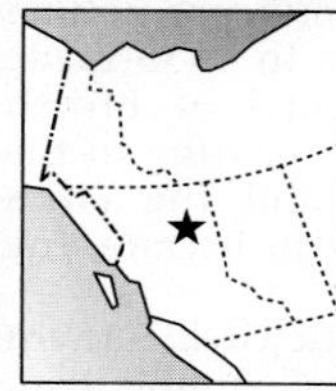

DC 47 (75.6 km) **F 1441** (2319 km) Located approximately 236 miles/380 km south of Fort Nelson. **Population:** 15,021; area 40,000. **Emergency Services: RCMP**, phone (250) 787-8100. **Fire Department**, phone (250) 785-2323. **Ambulance**, phone (250) 785-2079. **Hospital**, on 100th Avenue and 96th Street, phone (250) 785-6611.

Visitor Information: Visitor Infocentre is located beside Centennial Park and next to the leisure pool, in the same building as the chamber of commerce and the Peace River Alaska Highway Tourist Assoc. (PRAHTA) at, 9923 96th Ave., Fort St. John, BC V1J 4K9; phone (250) 785-3033. Open year-round: 8 A.M. to 8 P.M. in summer, 8:30 A.M. to 5 P.M. the rest of the year. Visitors may also contact the Ministry of Envi-

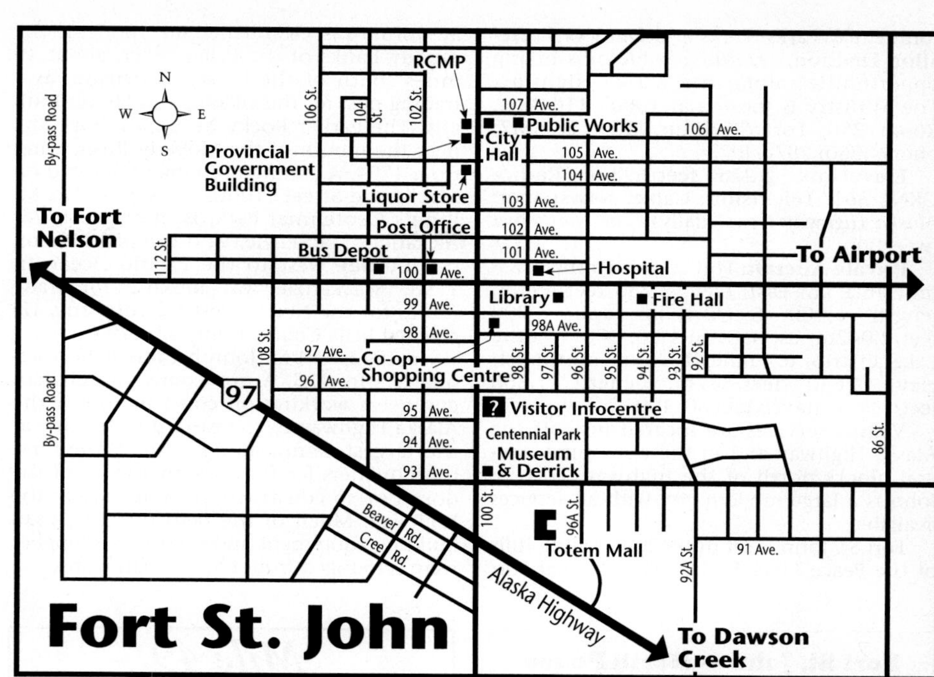

FORT ST. JOHN ADVERTISERS

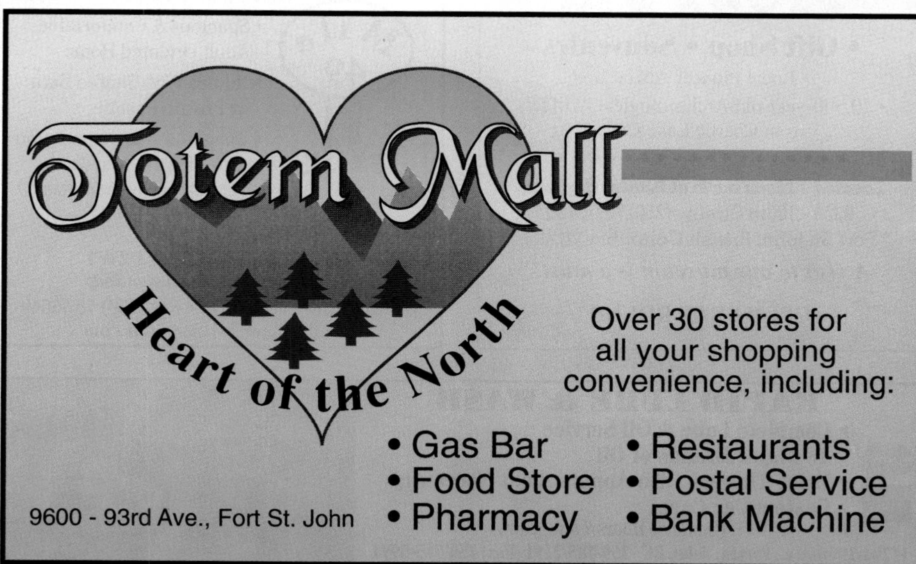

ronment & Parks, Parks and Outdoor Recreation Division, regarding wilderness hiking opportunities along the Alaska Highway. The Ministry is located at 10003 110 Ave., Room 250, Fort St. John, BC V1J 6M7; phone (250) 787-3407.

Elevation: 2,275 feet/693m. **Radio**: CKNL 560. **Television**: Cable. **Newspaper**: *Alaska Highway News* (daily), *The Northerner* (weekly).

Private Aircraft: Fort St. John airport, 3.8 miles/6.1 km east; elev. 2,280 feet/695m; length 6,900 feet/2,103m and 6,700 feet/2,042m; asphalt; fuel 80, 100. Charlie Lake airstrip, 6.7 miles/10.8 km northwest; elev. 2,680 feet/817m; length 1,800 feet/549m; gravel; fuel 80, 100.

Visitor services are located just off the Alaska Highway and in the city centre, several blocks north of the highway. Fort St. John is a large modern city with all services available.

Fort St. John is set in the low, rolling hills of the Peace River Valley. The original Fort St. John was established in 1806 on the muddy banks of the Peace River, about 10 miles south of the present townsite, as a trading post for the Sikanni and Beaver Indians. The earlier Rocky Mountain Fort site, near the mouth of the Moberly River, dates from 1794. A granite monument, located on Mackenzie Street (100th Street) in Fort St. John's Centennial Park, is inscribed to Sir Alexander Mackenzie, who camped here on his journey west to the Pacific Ocean in 1793. Mackenzie was looking for trade routes for the North West fur company. He reached Bella Coola on July 22, 1793.

In 1942, Fort St. John became field headquarters for U.S. Army troops and civilian engineers working on construction of the Alaska Highway in the eastern sector. It was the largest camp, along with Whitehorse (headquarters for the western sector), of the dozen or so construction camps along the highway. Much of the field housing, road building equipment and even office supplies were scrounged from old Civilian Conservation Corps camps and the Work Projects Administration.

As reported by Theodore A. Huntley of the Public Roads Administration, "A narrow winter road from Fort St. John to Fort Nelson, 256 miles north, provided the only access to the forest itself. From Fort St. John north and west for almost 1,500 miles the wilderness was broken only by dog and pack trails or short stretches of winter road, serviceable only until made impassable by the spring thaw. Within 6 months the first vehicle to travel overland to Alaska would roll into Fairbanks. Thus was a highway born."

The Alaska Highway was opened to the traveling public in 1948, attracting vacationers and homesteaders. An immense natural oil and gas field discovered in 1955 made Fort St. John the oil capital of British Columbia. "Energetic City," referring to the natural energy resources and the city's potential for positive growth, became the slogan for the region.

An extension of the Pacific Great Eastern Railway, now called British Columbia Railway, from Prince George in 1958 (continued to Fort Nelson in 1971), gave Fort St. John a link with the rail yards and docks at North Vancouver.

Today, Fort St. John is the hot spot in North America for natural gas, but it also depends on other industries, including forestry and agriculture. Farms in the North Peace region raise grain and livestock, such as sheep and cattle. Bison are also raised locally. The fields of clover and alfalfa have also attracted bees, and honey is produced for both local markets and export.

TRANSPORTATION

Air: Canadian Regional Airlines and Central Mountain Air to Fort Nelson, Whitehorse, Vancouver, Grande Prairie, Edmonton and Prince George. **Bus:** Coachways service to Prince George, Vancouver, Edmonton and Whitehorse; depot at 10355 101st Ave., phone (250) 785-6695.

ACCOMMODATIONS/VISITOR SERVICES

Numerous major motels, hotels, bed and breakfasts, restaurants, fast-food outlets and full-service gas stations are located on the Alaska Highway and in town. Other services include supermarkets, laundromats, several banks (automatic teller machines at Totem Mall and downtown at Charter Banks), a car wash and shops. The Totem Mall is located on the Alaska Highway. Indoor leisure pool, with waterslide, wave pool and children's play area at North Peace Recreation Centre; phone (250) 785-6148 for schedule. The North Peace Cultural Centre has a library, a 413-seat theatre, a gallery/gift shop and cafe. Open 6 days a week, 9 A.M. to 3 P.M.

Fresh water fill-up and dump station located at the northwest corner of 86th Street and the Alaska Highway. Camping north of the city at Beatton and Charlie Lake provincial parks, and at private and Rotary campgrounds at Charlie Lake. ▲

ATTRACTIONS

Centennial Park, located on 100th Street, has a museum and the Visitor Infocentre. The Fort St. John–North Peace Museum houses more than 6,000 artifacts from the region, including items from Finch's Store (the first store in Fort St. John), an 1806 Fort St. John post, a trapper's cabin and early-day schoolroom. The museum gift shop offers a good selection of local and Northwest books. Inquire at the Visitor Infocentre about local hiking trails, fishing, boat tours, trail rides and the lily farm. The tourist centre is open 8 A.M. to 8 P.M. daily in summer.

Directly in front of the museum is a 150-foot oil derrick, presented to the North Peace Historical Society and the people of Fort St. John. Check with the North Peace Museum at (250) 787-0430 about summer entertainment at the derrick.

Play golf. Fort St. John's only in-town golf course is Links Golf Course, just off the Bypass Road at 86 Street; 9 holes, pro shop and lounge. Phone (250) 785-9995. The Lakepoint Golf Course, on Golf Course Road at Charlie Lake, is rated one of the nicest courses in British Columbia. Open 8 A.M. to 9 P.M. daily; 18 holes, pro shop, lounge and restaurant. Phone (250) 785-5566.

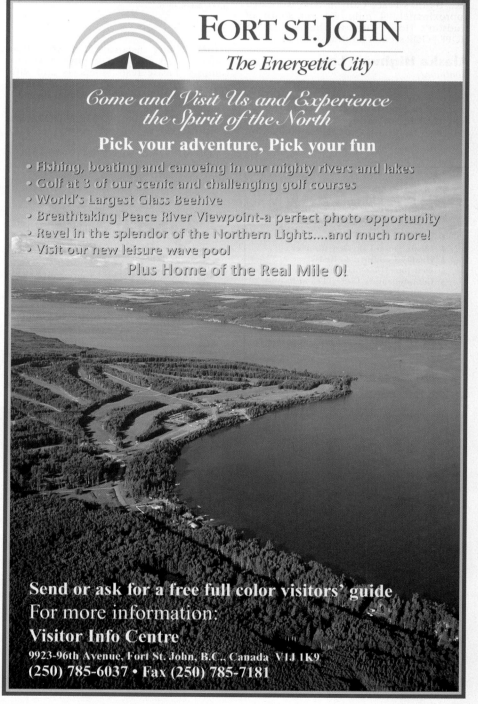

Industry and agriculture of the area are showcased for the public at various places. Check with the Infocentre for directions and details. Canada Forest Products offers tours of their mills, phone (250) 785-8906 for details. The Honey Place, just south of town on the Alaska Highway, offers guided tours, fresh honey for sale, and the world's largest glass beehive for viewing year-round; phone (250) 785-4808.

Fish Creek Community Forest, adjacent Northern Lights College, has 3 interpretive trails to view forest management activities and learn more about the forest. Cross-country ski trails in winter. From the Alaska Highway follow 100th Street north 1.2 miles/2 km to parking area at college.

W.A.C. Bennett Dam is a major attraction in the area. For an interesting side trip, drive north from Fort St. John on the Alaska Highway to **Milepost DC 53.7** and take Highway 29 west 46.5 miles/74.8 km to Hudson's Hope. Highway 29 follows the original Canadian government telegraph trail of 1918. Hudson's Hope, formerly a pioneer community established in 1805 by explorer Simon Fraser, grew with construction of the W.A.C. Bennett Dam, which is located 13.5 miles/21.7 km west of town. B.C. Hydro's Peace Canyon dam is located approximately 4 miles/6.4 km south of Hudson's Hope. Turn to the HUDSON'S HOPE LOOP section for more information.

Fort St. John Visitor Infocentre at 9923 96th Ave., adjacent Centennial Park.
(Earl L. Brown, staff)

Alaska Highway Log

(continued)

Distance* from Dawson Creek (DC) is followed by distance from Fairbanks (F). Original mileposts are indicated in the text as Historical Mile.

*Mileages from Dawson Creek are based on actual driving distance. Kilometres from Dawson Creek are based on physical kilometreposts. Please read Mileposts and Kilometreposts in the introduction for an explanation of how this highway is logged.

DC 45.8 (73.7 km) **F 1442.2** (2320.9 km) South access to Fort St. John via 100th Street.

DC 47 (75.6 km) **F 1441** (2319 km) **Historical Mile 48.** North access to Fort St. John via 100th Avenue.

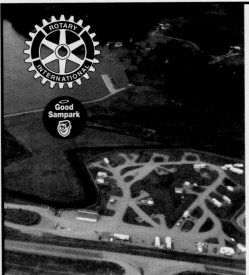

DC 48.6 (78.2 km) **F 1439.4** (2316.4 km) **Historic Milepost 49** commemorates "Camp Alcan."

DC 49.5 (79.6 km) **F 1438.5** (2315 km) Exit for Beatton Provincial Park, 5 miles/8 km east via paved road; 37 campsites, picnic shelter, wood stove, horseshoe pits, volleyball net, playground, baseball field, sandy beach, swimming and boat launch. Camping fee $7 to $12. Fishing for northern pike, walleye (July best) and yellow perch in **Charlie Lake.** ▲

DC 50.4 (81.1 km) **F 1437.6** (2313.5 km) **Paradise Lane Bed and Breakfast.** See display ad this section.

DC 50.6 (81.4 km) **F 1437.4** (2313.2 km) **CHARLIE LAKE** (unincorporated), gas, diesel and propane, grocery, pub, post office, bed and breakfast, private RV parks and Ministry of Energy, Mines and Petroleum. Access to lakeshore east side of highway; boat launch, no parking. At one time during construction of the Alaska Highway, Charlie Lake was designated Mile 0, as there was already a road between the railhead at Dawson Creek and Fort St. John, the eastern sector headquarters for troops and engineers.

Charlie Lake General Store. See display ad this section.

DC 51.2 (82.4 km) **F 1436.8** (2312.2 km) **Historic Milepost 52.** Charlie Lake Mile 0 Army Tote Road. Site of a major distribution camp for workers and supplies heading north. 12 American soldiers also drowned here in 1942 while crossing the lake aboard pontoon barges.

Rotary R.V. Park. See display ad this section. ♿▲

DC 51.5 (82.9 km) **F 1436.5** (2311.7 km) **Ron's R.V. Park. Historical Mile 52.** Treed sites with complete RV hookups, shaded lawned tenting areas, picnic tables, firepits, firewood provided. Walking trails, playground, flush toilets, hot showers, laundromat, pay phone, ice. Shaded full-hookup pull-throughs, good drinking water. Large boat launching facilities nearby. Boat rentals. Quiet location away from hectic city confusion. Post office, golf course, fishing licenses, Red Barn Pub nearby. Charlie Lake, world famous for walleye and northern pike fishing. Phone (250) 787-1569. [ADVERTISEMENT] ▲

DC 52 (83.7 km) **F 1436** (2311 km) Exit east on Charlie Lake Road for lakeshore picnicking.

DC 53.6 (86.3 km) **F 1434.4** (2308.4 km) Truck weigh scales east side of highway.

DC 53.7 (86.4 km) **F 1434.3** (2308.2 km) **Junction** with Highway 29 and truck stop with restaurant, gas and diesel (open year-round). Highway 29 leads west 47 miles/75.6 km to Hudson's Hope and the W.A.C. Bennett Dam, then south to connect with the Hart Highway at Chetwynd (see HUDSON'S HOPE LOOP section).

Mile 54 Shell Truck Stop. See display ad this section.

Turn east for Charlie Lake Provincial Park, just off highway; paved loop road (with speed bumps) leads through campground. There are 58 shaded sites, picnic tables, kitchen shelter with wood stove, firepits, firewood, outhouses, dump station, water and garbage. Level gravel sites, some will accommodate 2 large RVs. Camping fee $7 to $12. Playfield, playground, horseshoe pits, volleyball net and a 1.2-mile/2-km hiking trail down to lake. Watch for wildflowers. Because of the wide variety of plants here, including some that may not be seen elsewhere along the Alaska Highway, Verna E. Pratt's *Wildflowers Along the Alaska Highway* includes a special list of species for this park. Fishing in **Charlie Lake** for walleye, northern pike and yellow perch. Access to the lake for vehicles and boats is from the Alaska Highway just east of the park entrance. Boat launch and picnic area at lake. ▲

DC 63.6 (102 km) **F 1424.4** (2292.3 km) Microwave tower to east.

DC 65.4 (105 km) **F 1422.6** (2289.4 km) Turnout with litter barrel to west.

DC 71.7 (115.4 km) **F 1416.3** (2279.3 km) **Historical Mile 72.** Food, gas, camping, lodging and crafts store. ▲

DC 72.8 (117.1 km) **F 1415.2** (2277.5 km) **Historic Milepost 73** commemorates Beatton River Flight Strip, 1 of 4 gravel airstrips built for American military aircraft during WWII. Road to Prespetu and Buick Creek.

DC 79.1 (127.3 km) **F 1408.9** (2267.3 km) **Historical Mile 80** paved rest area to west with litter barrels, picnic tables, water and flush toilets. Information panel on Alaska Highway parks.

DC 91.4 (147.1 km) **F 1396.6** (2247.5 km) **Historical Mile 92.** Westcoast Energy compressor station to west.

DC 94.6 (152.2 km) **F 1393.4** (2242.4 km) Oil pump east of highway behind trees.

DC 101 (161.7 km) **F 1387** (2232.1 km) **Historic Milepost 101. WONOWON** (pop. 150), unincorporated, has 3 gas stations (gas, diesel, propane), 3 restaurants, 2 motels, camping, a food store, pub and post office. Formerly known as Blueberry, Wonowon was the site of an official traffic control gate during WWII. Wonowon Horse Club holds an annual race meet and gymkhana at the track beside the highway, where the community club holds its annual snowmobile rally in February. ▲

The historic sign and interpretive panel here commemorate Blueberry Control Station, "site of the Blueberry Control Gate, a 24-hour military checkpoint operated by U.S. Army personnel through the war years."

The Alaska Highway follows the Blueberry and Prophet river drainages north to Fort Nelson. The Blueberry River, not visible

The Alaska Highway rolls across northern British Columbia. (© Beth Davidow)

from the highway, lies a few miles east of Wonowon.

DC 101.5 (163.3 km) **F 1386.5** (2231.3 km) Food, diesel, gas, camping and lodging to east; open year-round. ▲

DC 103.5 (166.5 km) **1384.5** (2228.1 km) **Historic Milepost 104** marks start of Adolphson, Huseth, Layer & Welch contract during Alaska Highway construction.

DC 114 (183.2 km) **F 1374** (2211.2 km) Paved turnout with litter barrel to east.

DC 124.3 (200 km) **F 1363.7** (2194.6 km) The Cut (highway goes through a small rock cut). Relatively few rock cuts were necessary during construction of the Alaska Highway in 1942–43. However, rock excavation was often made outside of the roadway to obtain gravel fill for the new roadbed.

DC 135.3 (217.7 km) **F 1352.7** (2176.9 km) Gravel turnout to east.

CAUTION: Northbound travelers watch for moose next 15 miles/24 km, especially at dusk and at night.

DC 140.4 (225.9 km) **F 1347.6** (2168.7 km) **Historical Mile 143. PINK MOUNTAIN** (pop. 99, area 300; elev. 3,600 feet/1,097m). Post office, grocery, motels, restaurant, campgrounds, gas stations (gas, diesel, propane) with minor repair service. Bus depot at Pink Mountain Motor Inn east side of highway. Pink Mountain is home to Darryl Mills, Canadian champion bullrider. ▲

Pink Mountain Campsite & R.V. Park, on the left northbound. Take it easy folks, you've arrived at one of the nicest campgrounds on the highway ... coffee's always on. Unleaded Tempo gas, diesel, metered propane for RVs and auto. Post office, general store, liquor store, fishing and hunting licenses. Souvenirs—you'll like our prices. Shaded campsites, picnic tables, firepits and firewood. Tents and RVs welcome. Full hookups, power hookups, water and sani-

dump. Pull-throughs. Something for everyone. Cabins starting at $20 (weekly rates available). Laundromat and clean showers. Open year-round. VISA and MasterCard. Phone and fax (250) 772-5133. Your hosts, Ron and Pat. [ADVERTISEMENT] ▲

Pink Mountain Motor Inn. Mile 143, a welcome stopping point for all travelers. 34 rooms, gift shop, and licensed restaurant with pies and pastries and home-cooked meals. The perfect lunch break stop for bus tours. For RVs, electric hookups, gravel sites. Treed camping and picnic tables. Water, hot showers, laundromat. Dump station. Caravans welcome, reservations recommended. Full line of Esso products. Fax (250) 774-1071. Phone (250) 772-3234. Your hosts, Jimmy and Grace. [ADVERTISEMENT] ▲

DC 144.1 (231.9 km) **F 1343.9** (2162.7 km) **Historical Mile 147. Sportsman Inn.** See display ad this section. ▲

DC 144.5 (232.5 km) **F 1343.5** (2162.1 km) **Historical Mile 147. Mae's Kitchen**. See display ad this section.

DC 144.7 (232.9 km) **F 1343.3** (2161.8 km) **Historic Milepost 148** commemorates Suicide Hill, one of the most treacherous hills on the original highway, noted for its ominous greeting: "Prepare to meet thy maker." Beatton River bridge. The Beatton River was named for Frank Beatton, a Hudson's Bay Co. employee. The Beatton River flows east and then south into the Peace River system.

DC 146 (234 km) **F 1342** (2159.7 km) **Private Aircraft**: Sikanni Chief flight strip to east; elev. 3,258 feet/993m; length, 6,000 feet/1,829m; current status unknown. Well-known local pilot Jimmy "Midnight" Anderson used the Sikanni Chief airstrip.

DC 150.3 (241.9 km) **F 1337.7** (2152.8 km) *CAUTION: Southbound travelers watch for moose next 15 miles/24 km, especially at dusk and at night.*

DC 155.6 (250.4 km) **F 1332.4** (2144.2 km) Large double-ended, gravel turnout with litter barrels. *CAUTION: Slow down! Watch for loose gravel.*

DC 156.6 (252 km) **F 1331.4** (2142.6 km) Sikanni Hill. *CAUTION: Slow down for hill.*

DC 159.2 (256.2 km) **F 1328.8** (2138.4 km) Sikanni Chief River bridge (elev. 2,662 feet/811m). To the west you may see steel stanchions, all that remains of the historic wooden Sikanni bridge, which was destroyed by arson July 10, 1992. The original timber truss bridge built across the Sikanni Chief River in the spring of 1943 was the first permanent structure completed on the Alaska Highway. Highway construction crews rerouted much of the pioneer road built in 1942 and replaced temporary bridges with permanent structures in 1943. The Sikanni Chief River flows east and then north into the Fort Nelson River, which flows into the Liard River and on to the Mackenzie River, which empties into the Arctic Ocean. Check at the lodge for information on Sikanni River Falls (see **Milepost DC 168.5**).

Sikanni Chief River, fair fishing at mouth of tributaries in summer for pike; grayling to 2½ lbs.; whitefish to 2 lbs.

DC 159.4 (256.5 km) **F 1328.6** (2138.1 km) **Historical Mile 162. SIKANNI CHIEF.** Food, gas, lodging and camping.

Sikanni River RV Park. This riverside RV park offers a beautiful, natural setting for your enjoyment, with easy access to well

graveled, long sites. Its reputation for both cleanliness and beauty has made it a popular destination. Make it a must on your list. Reservations recommended. Resident owners. Clean, safe, secure. Recommended as a fueling stop in "Alaska Highway—An Insiders Guide" for 6 years. Located at the bottom of Sikanni River Hill. Phone (250) 774-1028. [ADVERTISEMENT] ▲

DC 160 (257.5 km) **F 1328** (2137.2 km) "Drunken forest" on hillside to west is shallow-rooted black spruce trees growing in unstable clay-based soil that is subject to slide activity in wet weather.

DC 160.4 (258.1 km) **F 1327.6** (2136.5 km) Section of the old Alaska Highway is visible to east; no access.

DC 168.5 (271.2 km) **F 1319.5** (2123.5 km) Gravel road west to Sikanni River Falls. This private road is signed "Travel at own risk." Drive in 10.5 miles/16.9 km to parking area with picnic tables at B.C. Forest Service trailhead; 10-minute hike in on well-marked trail to view falls. Gravel access road has some steep hills and a single-lane bridge. *CAUTION: Do not travel in wet weather. Not recommended for vehicles with trailers.*

IMPORTANT: Watch for moose on highway northbound to ***Milepost DC 200****, especially at dusk. Drive carefully!*

DC 172.5 (277.6 km) **F 1315.5** (2117 km)

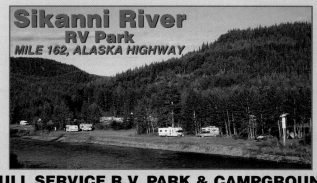

Polka Dot Creek.

DC 173.1 (278.6 km) **F 1314.9** (2116 km) Buckinghorse River bridge; access to river at north end of bridge.

DC 173.2 (278.7 km) **F 1314.8** (2115.9 km) **Historical Mile 175**. Inn with gas and camping to east at north end of bridge. Also turnoff east for Buckinghorse River Provincial Park. Follow the narrow gravel road past the gravel pit 0.7 mile/1.1 km along river to camping and picnic area. Camping fee $7 to $12. The park has 30 picnic tables, side-by-side camper parking, firewood, fire rings, water pump, outhouses and garbage containers. Fishing for grayling in **Buckinghorse River**. Swimming in downstream pools.

DC 173.4 (279 km) **F 1314.6** (2115.6 km) **Historical Mile 175. Buckinghorse River Lodge**, on left northbound. Motel, cafe with home cooking, hard ice cream and ice cream novelties. Bed and breakfast available. Service station, large parking area, free camping. Pets welcome, corrals available. Look forward to our friendly atmosphere. Picnic tables and beautiful scenery. A great spot to take a break for fishing or walking. Phone (250) 773-6468. [ADVERTISEMENT]

DC 176 (283.2 km) **F 1312** (2111.4 km) South end of 27-mile/43-km Trutch Mountain bypass. Completed in 1987, this section of road rerouted the Alaska Highway around Trutch Mountain, eliminating the steep, winding climb up to Trutch Summit (and the views). Named for Joseph W. Trutch, civil engineer and first governor of British Columbia, Trutch Mountain was the second highest summit on the Alaska Highway, with an elevation of 4,134 feet/1,260m. The new roadbed cuts a wide swath through the flat Minaker River valley. The river, not visible to motorists, is west of the highway; it was named for local trapper George Minaker. Trutch Mountain is to the east of the highway. Motorists can see part of the old highway on Trutch Mountain.

DC 182.8 (294.2 km) **F 1305.2** (2100.4 km) Large gravel turnout with litter barrel to west.

DC 199.1 (320 km) **F 1288.9** (2074.2 km) Large gravel turnout with litter barrels.

DC 202.5 (325.5 km) **F 1285.5** (2068.8 km) Turnout with litter barrels at north end of Trutch Mountain bypass (see **Milepost DC 176**).

CAUTION: Southbound travelers watch for moose on highway, especially at dusk, to Sikanni Chief. Drive carefully!

DC 204.2 (328 km) **F 1283.8** (2066 km) **Beaver Creek**; fishing for grayling to 2½ lbs.

DC 217.2 (349.3 km) **F 1270.8** (2045.1 km) Turnoff to west for Prophet River Provincial Park, 0.4 mile/0.6 km via gravel road. Side-by-side camper parking (36 sites, some pull-throughs available), picnic tables, firewood, fire rings, water pump, outhouses and garbage containers. Camping fee $7 to $12. The park access road crosses an airstrip (originally an emergency airstrip on the Northwest Air Staging Route) and part of the old Alaska Highway (the Alcan). This provincial park is also the first stop on the self-guided Forest Ecology Tours (Ecotours) established by the Fort Nelson Forest District. A pamphlet, available from their office in Fort Nelson (phone 250/774-3936), describes the forests at various sites along the Alaska Highway. This Ecotour stop is noted for its trembling aspen stands and mature white spruce.

Approaching Fort Nelson at Historical Mile 300 on the Alaska Highway.

(Earl L. Brown, staff)

The Alaska Highway roughly parallels the Prophet River from here north to the Muskwa River south of Fort Nelson.

Private Aircraft: Prophet River emergency airstrip; elev. 1,954 feet/596m; length 6,000 feet/1,829m; gravel.

DC 218.2 (350.7 km) **F 1269.8** (2043.5 km) View of Prophet River to west.

DC 222.3 (357.2 km) **F 1265.7** (2036.9 km) Bougie Creek bridge; turnout with litter barrel beside creek at south end of bridge. At this Ecotour stop, note the typical climax white spruce stand and trees of a variety of ages.

CAUTION: Watch for rough road approaching Bougie Creek bridge from either direction.

DC 224.8 (360.6 km) **F 1263.2** (2032.8 km) Microwave tower to east.

DC 226.2 (363.4 km) **F 1261.8** (2030.6 km) Prophet River Indian Reserve to east.

DC 226.5 (363.9 km) **F 1261.5** (2030.1 km) St. Paul's Roman Catholic Church to east.

DC 227 (364.7 km) **F 1261** (2029.3 km) **Historical Mile 233. PROPHET RIVER**, gas, diesel, propane, food, camping and lodging. Prophet River Services is on the left northbound; Prophet River Inn on right. Southbound travelers note: Next service 68 miles/109 km.

DC 227.6 (366.3 km) **F 1260.4** (2028.4 km) **Historic Milepost 234**, Adsett Creek Highway Realignment. This major rerouting eliminated 132 curves on the stretch of highway that originally ran between Miles 234 and 275. Turnout with litter barrels.

DC 227.7 (366.4 km) **F 1260.3** (2028.2 km) Adsett Creek.

DC 230.7 (371.3 km) **F 1257.3** (2023.3 km) Natural gas pipeline crosses beneath highway.

DC 232.9 (374.8 km) **F 1255.1** (2019.8 km) Turnout to west with litter barrels.

DC 235.5 (378.4 km) **F 1252.5** (2015.6 km) Mesa-like topography to the east is Mount Yakatchie.

DC 241.5 (388 km) **F 1246.5** (2006 km) Parker Creek.

DC 245.9 (395.7 km) **F 1242.1** (1998.9 km) Gravel turnout with litter barrels.

DC 261.1 (420.2 km) **F 1226.9** (1974.4 km) Turnout with litter barrels to east.

DC 264.6 (425.2 km) **F 1223.4** (1968.8 km) Jackfish Creek bridge. Ecotour stop; note the variety of trembling aspen stands and the white spruce seedlings under them.

DC 265.5 (426.5 km) **F 1222.5** (1967.4 km) Turnoff to east for Andy Bailey Lake Provincial Park (day use only) via 6.8-mile/11-km dirt and gravel access road. (Large RVs and trailers note: only turnaround space on access road is approximately halfway in.) The park is located on **Andy Bailey Lake** (formerly Jackfish Lake); picnic tables, fire rings, firewood, water, outhouses, garbage containers, boat launch (no powerboats), swimming and fair fishing for northern pike. Bring insect repellent!

DC 270.8 (435.1 km) **F 1217.2** (1958.8 km) Gas pipeline crosses highway overhead.

DC 271 (435.4 km) **F 1217** (1958.5 km) Westcoast Energy gas processing plant to east. Petrosul (sulfur processing) to west.

DC 272.4 (437.6 km) **F 1215.6** (1956.3

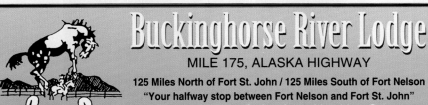

km) Access to downhill skiing to east.

DC 276.2 (443.8 km) **F 1211.8** (1950 km) Rodeo grounds to west. The rodeo is held in August.

DC 276.7 (444.6 km) **F 1211.3** (1949.3 km) Railroad tracks. Microwave tower.

DC 277.5 (446.2 km) **F 1210.5** (1948 km) Muskwa Heights (unincorporated), an industrial area with rail yard, plywood plant, sawmill and bulk fuel outlet.

DC 277.9 (447.2 km) **F 1210.1** (1947.4 km) Truck stop with gas, restaurant and RV campground. ▲

DC 278.1 (447.5 km) **F 1209.9** (1947.1 km) Truck scales to west.

DC 278.4 (448 km) **F 1209.6** (1946.6 km) **Trapper's Den. Historic Mile 293.** Owned and operated by a local trapping family. Moose horns, diamond willow, Northern novelties, books, artwork. Fur hats, headbands, earmuffs. Birchbark baskets, moosehair tuftings. Mukluks, moccasins, mits and gloves. Professionally tanned furs. See our

"Muskwa River Pearls." Photographers welcome. Located 1/2 mile north of Husky 5th Wheel RV Park on the Alaska Highway. VISA, MasterCard. Mail orders. Open 10 A.M. to 6 P.M. daily or phone for appointment. John, Cindy and Mandy Wells. Box 1164, Fort Nelson, BC V0C 1R0. (250) 774-3400. Recommended. [ADVERTISEMENT]

DC 279 (448.6 km) **F 1209** (1945.6 km) Site of oriented strand board plant processing aspen and balsam poplar. This 400,000-square-foot building is the largest industrial building of its kind in the province.

DC 281 (451.4 km) **F 1207** (1942.4 km) **Muskwa River** bridge, lowest point on the Alaska Highway (elev. 1,000 feet/305m). The Muskwa River flows to the Fort Nelson River. Fair fishing at the mouth of tributaries for northern pike; some goldeye. The Fort Nelson River is too muddy for fishing. The Muskwa River valley exhibits typical river-bottom balsam poplar and white spruce stands, according to the Fort Nelson Forest District's Forest Ecology Tours pamphlet.

The Alaska Highway swings west at Fort Nelson above the Muskwa River, winding southwest then northwest through the Canadian Rockies.

DC 283 (454.3 km) **F 1205** (1939.2 km) Entering Fort Nelson northbound. Fort Nelson's central business district extends along the highway from the private campground at the east end of the city to the private campground at the west end. Businesses and services are located both north and south of the highway.

Fort Nelson

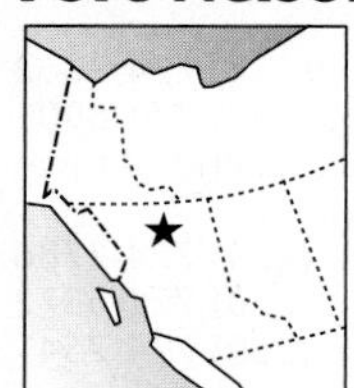

DC 283 (454.3 km) **F 1205** (1939.2 km) **Historical Mile 300. Population:** 4,401; area 5,856. **Emergency Services: RCMP**, phone (250) 774-2777. **Fire Department**, phone (250) 774-2222. **Hospital**, 35 beds, phone (250) 774-6916. **Ambulance**, phone (250) 774-2344. Medical, dental and optometric clinics. Visiting veterinarians and chiropractors.

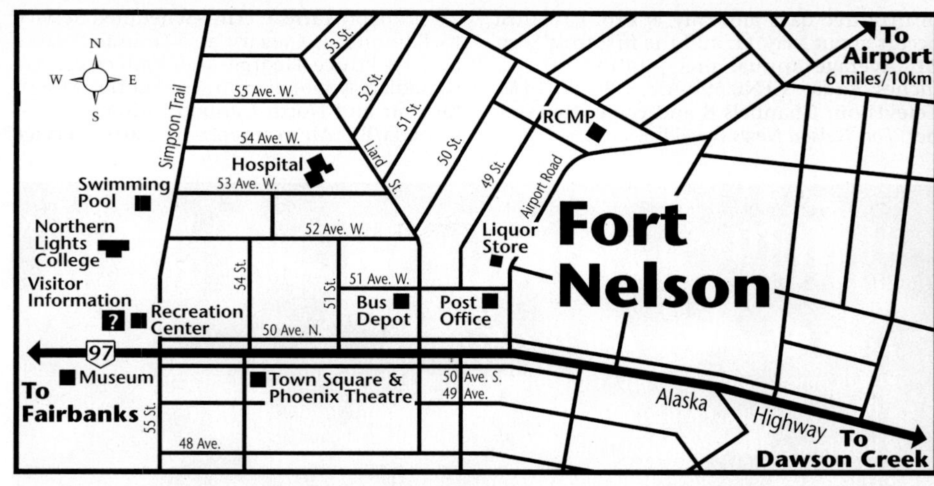

Visitor Information: Located in the Recreation Centre at the west end of town, open 8 A.M. to 8 P.M. Inquire here about local attractions, industrial tours and information about the Liard Highway. Fort Nelson Heritage Museum across the highway from the Infocentre. Contact the Town of Fort Nelson by writing Bag Service 399M, Fort Nelson, BC V0C 1R0; phone (250) 774-6400 (seasonal) or (250) 774-2541 (all year).

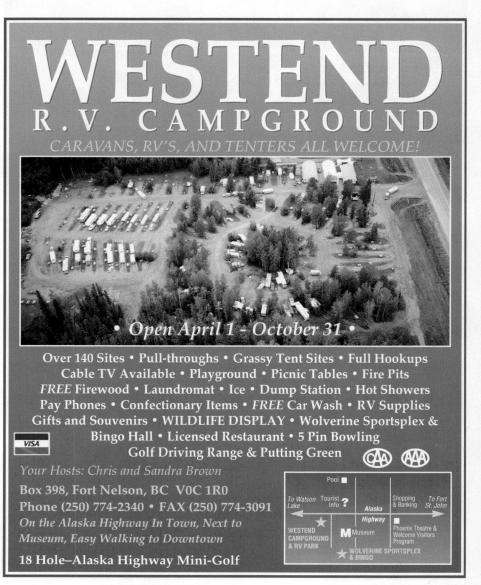

Elevation: 1,383 feet/422m. **Climate**: Winters are cold with short days. Summers are hot and the days are long. In mid-June (summer solstice), twilight continues throughout the night. The average number

of frost-free days annually is 116. Last frost occurs about May 11, and the first frost Sept. 21. Average annual precipitation of 17.7 inches. **Radio**: CFNL 590-AM, CBC 88.3-FM. **Television**: Channels 8 and cable. **Newspaper**: *Fort Nelson News* (weekly).

Transportation: **Air**—Scheduled service to Edmonton, Calgary and Grande Prairie, and to Prince George and Vancouver via Canadian Regional Airlines, Central Mountain Air and North Cariboo Airlines, an Air Canada/BC Air connector. Charter service available. **Bus**—Greyhound service. **Railroad**—B.C. Railway (freight service only).

Private Aircraft: Fort Nelson airport, 3.8 air miles/6.1 km east-northeast; elev. 1,253 feet/382m; length 6,400 feet/1,950m; asphalt; fuel 80, 100, Jet B. Gordon Field, 4 miles/6.4 km west; elev. 1,625 feet/495m approximately; length 2,000 feet/610m; turf; fuel 80.

Fort Nelson is located in the lee of the Rocky Mountains, surrounded by the Muskwa, Fort Nelson and Prophet rivers. The area is heavily forested with white spruce, poplar and aspen. Geographically, the town is located about 59° north latitude and 122° west longitude.

Flowing east and north, the Muskwa, Prophet and Sikanni Chief rivers converge to form the Fort Nelson River, which flows into the Liard River, then on to the Mackenzie River, which empties into the Arctic Ocean. Rivers provided the only means of transportation in both summer and winter in this isolated region until 1922, when the Godsell Trail opened, connecting Fort Nelson with Fort St. John. The Alaska Highway linked Fort Nelson with the Outside in 1942.

In the spring, the Muskwa River frequently floods the low country around Fort Nelson and can rise more than 20 feet/6m. At an elevation of 1,000 feet/305m, the Muskwa (which means "bear") is the lowest point on the Alaska Highway. There was a danger of the Muskwa River bridge washing out every June during spring runoff until 1970, when a higher bridge—with piers arranged to prevent log jams—was built.

Fort Nelson's existence was originally based on the fur trade. In the 1920s, trap-

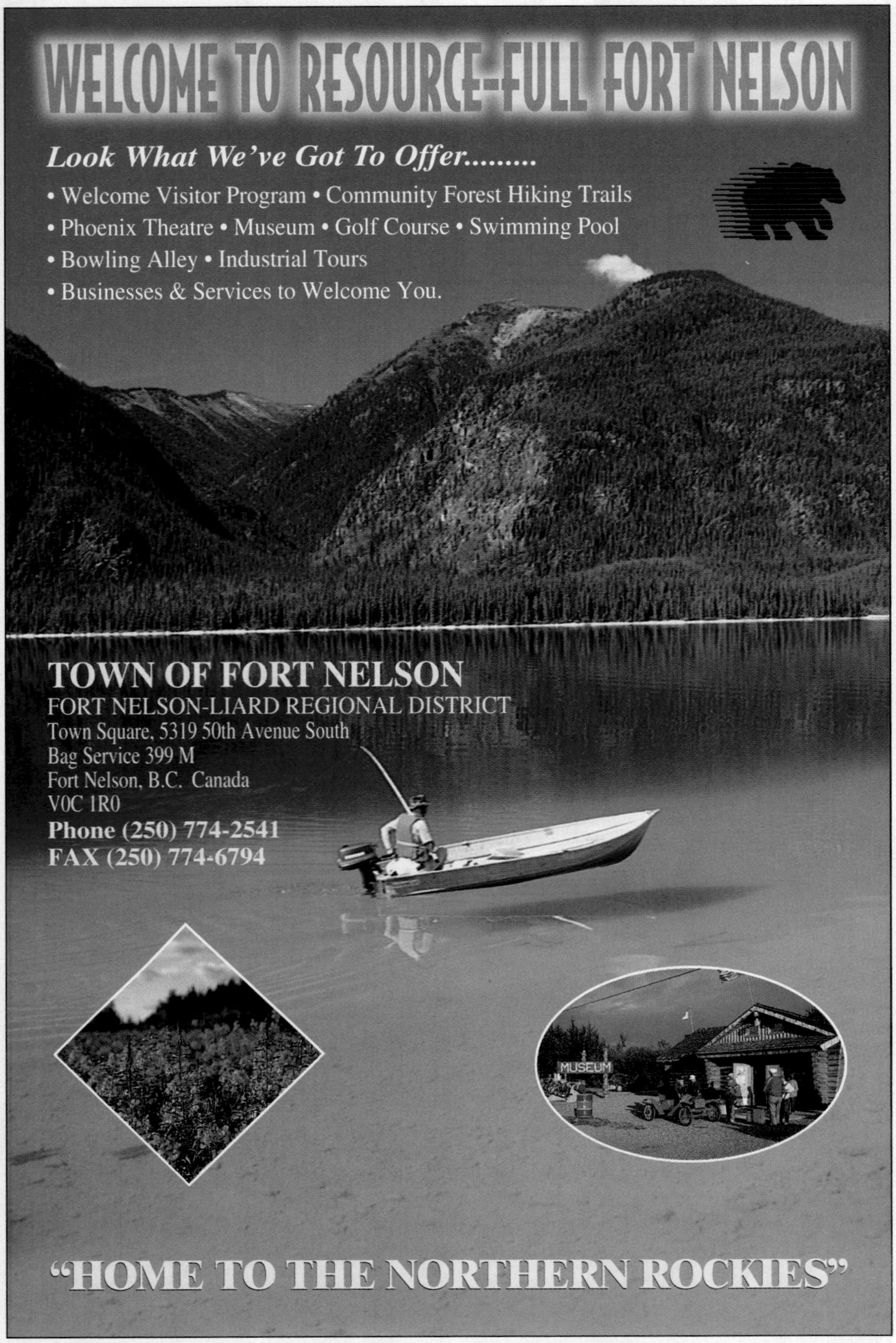

FORT NELSON ADVERTISERS

Ardendale
Bed & Breakfast..........Ph. (250) 774-2433
Best Western
Woodlands Inn..........Ph. (250) 774-6669
Bluebell Inn, The..............Ph. (800) 663-5267
Coachouse Inn..............Ph. (250) 774-3911
Dan's Neighborhood Pub.........S. end of town
Dixie Lee........................Ph. (250) 774-6226
Donovan & Co.................Ph. (250) 774-6869
Fabric Fun......................New Landmark Plaza
Fort Nelson Bed &
Breakfast.......................Ph. (250) 774-6050
Fort Nelson Heritage
Museum........Across from Travel Infocentre
Fort Nelson Hotel............Ph. (250) 774-6971
Fort Nelson
Service Centre............Ph. (250) 774-7950
KaCee's Koin Kleaners..Next to IGA Foodstore
Mini-Price Inn..................Ph. (250) 774-2136
Northern Husky...........................Downtown
Northern Lights Deli.........Ph. (250) 774-3311
Northern Rockies Lodge...Ph. (800) 663-5269
Northern Vision Health
Foods.........................New Landmark Plaza
Pioneer Motel..................Ph. (250) 774-6459
Poplar Hills Golf &
Country Club..............Ph. (250) 774-3862
Provincial Motel................Ph. (250) 774-6901
Red Rose Convenience Store...S. end of town
Sukhi's Coin-Op
Laundromat................Ph. (250) 774-7786
Tirecraft..........................Ph. (250) 774-6372
Town of Fort Nelson.........Ph. (250) 774-2541
Westend R.V. Campground
and Mini-Golf..............Ph. (250) 774-2340

ping was the main business in this isolated pioneer community populated with less than 200 Indians and a few white men. Trappers still harvest beaver, wolverine, weasel, wolf, fox, lynx, mink, muskrat and marten. Other area wildlife includes black bear, which are plentiful, some deer, caribou and a few grizzly bears. Moose remains an important food source for the Indians.

Fort Nelson aboriginal people are mostly Slave (slay-vee), who arrived here about 1775 from the Great Slave Lake area and speak an Athabascan dialect.

Fort Nelson was first established in 1805 by the North West Fur Trading Co. The post, believed to have been located about 80 miles/129 km south of Nelson Forks, was named for Lord Horatio Nelson, the English admiral who won the Battle of Trafalgar.

A second Fort Nelson was later located south of the first fort, but was destroyed by fire in 1813 after Indians massacred its 8 residents. A third Fort Nelson was established in 1865 on the Fort Nelson River's west bank (1 mile from the present Fort Nelson airport) by W. Cornwallis King, a Hudson's Bay Co. clerk. This trading post was built to keep out the free traders who were filtering in from the Mackenzie River and Fort St. John areas.

The free traders' higher fur prices were a threat to the Hudson's Bay Co., which in 1821 had absorbed the rival North West Fur Trading Co. and gained a monopoly on the fur trade in Canada.

This Hudson's Bay Co. trading post was destroyed by a flood in 1890 and a fourth Fort Nelson was established on higher ground upstream and across the river, which is now known as Old Fort Nelson. The present town of Fort Nelson is the fifth site.

Fort Nelson saw its first mail service in 1936. Scheduled air service to Fort Nelson—by ski- and floatplane—also was begun in the 1930s by Yukon Southern Air (which was later absorbed by CPAir, now Canadian Airlines International and Canadian Regional Airlines). The Canadian government began construction of an airport in 1941 as part of the Northwest Air Staging Route, and this was followed by perhaps the biggest boom to Fort Nelson—the construction of the Alaska Highway in 1942. About 2,000 soldiers were bivouacked in Fort Nelson, which they referred to as Zero, as it was the beginning of a road to Whitehorse and another road to Fort Simpson. Later Dawson Creek became Mile 0 and Fort Nelson Mile 300.

Fort Nelson expanded in the 1940s and 1950s as people came here to work for the government or to start their own small businesses: trucking, barging, aviation, construction, garages, stores, cafes, motels and sawmills. It is surprising to consider that as recently as the 1950s Fort Nelson was still a pioneer community without power, phones, running water, refrigerators or doctors. Interesting recollections of Fort Nelson's early days may be found in Gerri Young's book *The Fort Nelson Story*, available at the museum.

Fort Nelson was an unorganized territory until 1957 when it was declared an Improvement District. Fort Nelson took on village status in 1971 and town status in 1987.

Forestry is a major industry here with a veneer plant, plywood plant, oriented strand board plant and sawmill complex. Check with the Infocentre about scheduled industrial tours.

Forestry products are shipped south by truck and rail. Fort Nelson became a railhead in 1971 with the completion of a 250-mile extension of the Pacific Great Eastern Railway (now British Columbia Railway) from Fort St. John.

Agriculture is under development here with the establishment of the 55,000-acre McConachie Creek agricultural subdivision.

Northeastern British Columbia is the only sedimentary area in the province currently producing oil and gas. Oil seeps in the Fort Nelson area were noted by early residents. Major gas discoveries were made in the 1960s when the Clarke Lake, Yoyo/Kotcho, Beaver River and Pointed Mountain gas reserves were developed. The Westcoast Energy natural gas processing plant at Fort Nelson, the largest in North America, was constructed in 1964. This plant purifies the gas before sending it south through the 800-mile-long pipeline that connects the Fort Nelson area with the British Columbia lower mainland. Sulfur, a byproduct of natural gas processing, is processed in a recovery plant and shipped to outside markets in pellet form.

In 1997, the BC government set aside more than 4.4 million hectares of Northern Rockies wilderness near Fort Nelson. The Muskwa–Kechika area preserves critical wildlife habitat while allowing logging, mining, oil and gas exploration, and is designed to balance resource management with conservation. For more information contact the Land Use Coordination Office; phone (250) 953-3471, www.luco.gov.bc.ca.

Fort Nelson Heritage Museum in summer. See winter view next page. (Earl L. Brown, staff)

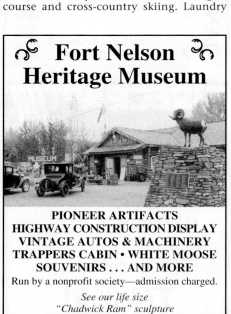

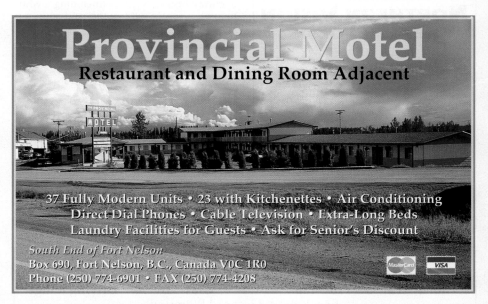

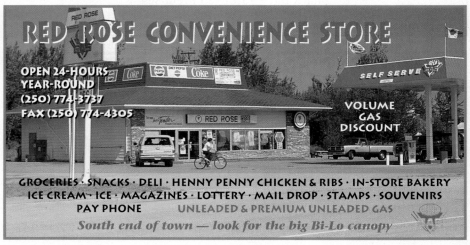

ACCOMMODATIONS/VISITOR SERVICES

Fort Nelson has 10 hotels/motels, 4 bed and breakfasts, several gas stations and restaurants, a pub, fast food, deli and health food outlets; laundromat; an auto supply store, department stores and other services, most located north and south just off the Alaska Highway. The post office and liquor store are on Airport Drive. There are 2 banks, both with bank machines, on the business frontage road north of the highway. Fresh water fill-up and free municipal dump station adjacent the blue chalet near the museum. Inquire at the Infocentre for location of local churches and their hours of worship.

Ardendale Bed & Breakfast. Welcome to our large log home overlooking a beautiful view. Very comfortable rooms, 2 with ensuite bathrooms and one with private bath. Spa available to guests. Cable TV in guest lounge. Excellent breakfast of your choice. Sleigh, buggy and wagon rides available. Our hobby farm is close to the golf course and cross-country skiing. Laundry facilities. Smoking outdoors on deck. Phone (250) 774-2433. Fax (250) 774-2436. VISA. Lot 7635, Old Alaska Highway. Frank and Gail Parker, Box 427, Fort Nelson, BC V0C 1R0. [ADVERTISEMENT]

Fort Nelson Bed & Breakfast. (Nonsmoking). For your convenience and privacy, our B&B is a self-contained unit on one side of our duplex. En suite bathrooms. Home-style breakfast. Laundry facilities. Cable TV. "Come and be spoiled." Your hosts, Doug and Renee. Box 58, Fort Nelson, BC V0C 1R0. (250) 774-6050. VISA. Open year-round. (Member—Northern Network of B&B's.) [ADVERTISEMENT]

Fort Nelson has 3 campgrounds: one is

located at the north (or west) end of town near the museum; one is at the south (or east) end of town; and one is at Muskwa Heights area south of Fort Nelson. ▲

Westend RV Campground and Mini Golf welcomes RVs, caravans and tenters. Located in town next to the Museum, only a few minutes from stores and downtown. Over 130 sites, lots of shade, full hookups, pull-throughs. Town water, coin-op showers

and laundry, playground. Free RV wash and firewood. Open April 1–November 1. We invite you to see our beautiful wildlife display. Nearby, the Wolverine Sportsplex with golf driving range, putting green, bowling, bingo, restaurant and more. We hope you enjoy our northern hospitality. Phone (250) 774-2340. [ADVERTISEMENT] ♿▲

ATTRACTIONS

Fort Nelson offers travelers a free "Welcome Visitor Program" on summer evenings (Monday through Thursday in 1998) at 6:45 P.M. at the Phoenix Theatre. These interesting and entertaining presentations are put on by local residents and range from slide shows to talks on items of local interest. Check with the Visitor Infocentre or at the Town Square for details.

The Fort Nelson Heritage Museum, across the highway from the Travel Infocentre, has excellent displays of pioneer artifacts, Alaska Highway history, wildlife (including a white moose), a spruce bark canoe, and souvenirs and books for sale. Outside the museum is the Chadwick Ram, a bronze sculpture by Rick Taylor. The statue commemorates the

world record stone sheep taken in the Muskwa Valley area in 1936. This nonprofit museum charges a modest admission fee. Native crafts are displayed at the Fort Nelson–Liard Native Friendship Centre, located on 49th Avenue.

The recreation centre, across from the museum, has tennis courts; hockey and curling arena for winter sports. There is also a sportsplex with bowling alley. Swimming pool, swirl pool, sauna and gym located in the Aqua Centre on Simpson Trail. For golfers, the Poplar Hills Golf and Country Club, just north of town on the Old Alaska Highway, has grass greens; open daily.

A community demonstration forest is open to the public. There is a forest trail (0.6 mile/1 km, half-hour walk), a silviculture trail (1.9 miles/3 km, 45-minute walk) and a Native trail. Located off the Simpson Trail via Mountainview Drive; check at the Infocentre for trail guide.

Fort Nelson hosts a number of annual benefits, dances, tournaments and exhibits. Check locally for details and dates on all events. Summer events include a rodeo in August. Winter events include a big cash prize curling bon spiel in February, Trapper's Rendezvous in March and the Canadian Open Sled Dog Races in December (with local racers from the well-known Streeper Kennels). Terry Streeper is a four-time World Champion (Anchorage) and also an Open North American Champion (Fairbanks) sled dog racer, and won more than 30 major races in 6 countries during the 1990s. Streeper Kennels is located on Radar Road.

Alaska Highway Log

(continued)

Distance* from Dawson Creek (DC) is followed by distance from Fairbanks (F). Original mileposts are indicated in the text as Historical Mile.

*Mileages from Dawson Creek are based on actual driving distance. Kilometres from Dawson Creek are based on physical kilometreposts. Please read Mileposts and Kilometreposts in the introduction for an explanation of how this highway is logged.

DC 284 (456.4 km) **F 1204** (1937.6 km) **Historic Milepost 300**, historic sign and interpretive panel at west end of Fort Nelson. Visitor information in the Recreation Centre north side of highway, log museum south side of highway. Private campground adjacent museum. ▲

Northbound: Watch for sections of rough, narrow, winding road and breaks in surfacing between Fort Nelson and the BC–YT border (approximately next 321 miles/516.5 km). Road reconstruction may still be underway at Steamboat Mountain in summer 1998.

Southbound: Good pavement, wider road, next 284 miles/457 km (to Dawson Creek).

DC 284.5 (457.5 km) **F 1203.5** (1936.8 km) Fort Nelson Forest District Office to north provides a pamphlet of self-guided Forest Ecology Tours on the Alaska and Liard highways; phone (250) 774-3936.

DC 284.7 (458.2 km) **F 1203.3** (1936.5 km) **Junction** with south end of Old Alaska Highway (**Mile 301–308**). The Muskwa Valley bypass between Mile 301 and 308 opened in 1992.

DC 287.9 (462.6 km) **F 1200.1** (1931.3 km) Access to Poplar Hills Golf and Country Club, located on Old Alaska Highway; 9-hole golf course, driving range, grass greens, clubhouse (licensed), golf club rentals. Open 8 A.M. to dusk, May to October.

DC 291 (467.6 km) **F 1197** (1926.3 km) Parker Lake Road. **Junction** with north end of Old Alaska Highway (**Mile 308–301**).

DC 292 (469.9 km) **F 1196** (1924.7 km) Private airstrip alongside highway; status unknown.

DC 301 (483.5 km) **F 1187** (1910.2 km) **Junction** with Liard Highway (BC Highway 77) north to Fort Liard, Fort Simpson and other Northwest Territories destinations. See LIARD HIGHWAY section.

DC 304.1 (489.4 km) **F 1183.9** (1905.3 km) **Historic Milepost 320**. Sign marks start of Reese & Olson contract during construction of the Alaska Highway.

DC 308.2 (495.3 km) **F 1179.8** (1898.7 km) Raspberry Creek. Turnout with litter barrels to south.

DC 316.6 (506.2 km) **F 1171.4** (1885.1 km) Turnout with litter barrel to south.

DC 318.4 (509.1 km) **F 1169.6** (1882.2 km) Kledo Creek bridge.

DC 318.7 (509.5 km) **F 1169.3** (1881.8 km) Kledo Creek wayside rest area to north (unmaintained).

DC 322.7 (516 km) **F 1165.3** (1875.3 km) Steamboat Creek bridge. Highway begins climb northbound up Steamboat Mountain; some 10 percent grades.

DC 329 (526.1 km) **F 1159** (1865.2 km) Pull-through turnout with litter barrel to south.

DC 333 (532.5 km) **F 1155** (1858.7 km) **Historic Milepost 351. STEAMBOAT** (unincorporated), lodge with food, gas, diesel and camping to south; open year-round. Historical sign marks start of Curran & Briggs Ltd. contract during construction of the Alaska Highway. ▲

Steamboat at **Historical Mile 351**. Cafe with fresh-baked bread, pies and pastry. Husky gas, diesel and oil products. Level pull-throughs, RV parking with a view. Public phone. Picnic area (pets on a leash, please). Ice, souvenirs and handicrafts. Your hosts, Willa and Ken MacRae and family. Open year-round. Phone (250) 774-3388. [ADVERTISEMENT] ▲

DC 333.7 (533.5 km) **F 1154.3** (1857.6 km) Winding road ascends Steamboat Mountain westbound. Views of the Muskwa River valley and Rocky Mountains to the southwest from summit of 3,500-foot/1,067-m Steamboat Mountain, named because of its resemblance to a steamship. *CAUTION: Narrow road; watch for sharp curves and rough spots. Watch for road construction in 1998.*

DC 334.3 (534.5 km) **F 1153.7** (1856.6 km) Turnout with view and dumpster to south.

DC 336.7 (538.5 km) **F 1151.3** (1852.8 km) Turnout to south with dumpster and pit toilets. Highway descends for westbound travelers.

DC 337.5 (540 km) **F1150.5** (1851.5 km) *NOTE: Watch for road construction and expect possible delays next 9.3 miles/15 km northbound in 1998.*

DC 339.1 (542.5 km) **F 1148.9** (1848.9 km) Drinking water to north. *CAUTION: Hairpin curve!*

DC 342.8 (548 km) **F 1145.2** (1843 km) View of Indian Head Mountain, a high crag resembling the classic Indian profile.

DC 343.4 (549 km) **F 1144.6** (1842 km) Turnout with litter barrel, outhouse and point of interest sign to south.

IMPORTANT: DO NOT FEED BEARS!

DC 345 (551.5 km) **F 1143** (1839.4 km) Scenic Teetering Rock viewpoint with litter barrel and outhouses to north. Teetering Rock is in the distance on the horizon. Fort Nelson Forest District (phone 250/774-3936) has developed a 7.6-mile-/12.3-km-long trail to Teetering Rock; steep climbs. Stay on well-marked trails, keep pets on leash; it is easy to get lost in this country.

DC 346.4 (553.9 km) **F 1141.6** (1837.2 km) Mill Creek, which flows into the Tetsa River. The highway follows the Tetsa River westbound. The Tetsa heads near Summit Lake in the northern Canadian Rockies.

Tetsa River, good fishing for grayling to 4 lbs., average 1½ lbs., flies or spin cast with lures; Dolly Varden to 7 lbs., average 3 lbs., spin cast or black gnat, coachman, Red Devils, flies; whitefish, small but plentiful, use flies or eggs, summer.

DC 346.5 (554 km) **F 1141.5** (1837 km) Turnoff to south for Tetsa River Provincial Park, 1.2 miles/1.9 km via gravel road. Grass tenting area, 25 level gravel sites in trees, picnic tables, fire rings, firewood, outhouses, water and garbage containers. Camping fee $7 to $12. ▲

DC 351 (561.2 km) **F 1137** (1829.8 km) *CAUTION: Slow down, dangerous curve! Watch for road construction next mile northbound in 1998.*

DC 357.5 (571.5 km) **F 1130.5** (1819.3 km) **Historical Mile 375.** Gas, store, cabins and private campground. ▲

DC 358.6 (573.3 km) **F 1129.4** (1817.5 km) Highway follows Tetsa River westbound. Turnouts next 0.2 mile/0.3 km south to river.

DC 360.2 (575.9 km) **F 1127.8** (1815 km) Turnout with dumpster, picnic site. Ecotour stop: Note the aspen-dominated slopes on the north side of the Tetsa River, and the white spruce on the south side.

DC 364.4 (582.6 km) **F 1123.6** (1808.2 km) Gravel turnout to south.

DC 365.6 (584.6 km) **F 1122.4** (1806.3 km) Tetsa River bridge No. 1, clearance 17 feet/5.2m.

DC 366 (585.4 km) **F 1122** (1805.6 km) Pull-through turnout with litter barrel to north.

DC 367.3 (587.3 km) **F 1120.7** (1803.5 km) Tetsa River bridge No. 2.

The high bare peaks of the central Canadian Rockies are visible ahead westbound.

DC 371.5 (594.2 km) **F 1116.5** (1796.8 km) South boundary of Stone Mountain Provincial Park. Stone sheep are indigenous to the mountains of northern British Columbia and southern Yukon Territory. They are darker and somewhat slighter than the bighorn sheep found in the Rocky Mountains. Dall or white sheep are found in the mountains of Yukon, Alaska and Northwest Territories.

CAUTION: Northbound, watch for caribou and stone sheep along the highway. DO NOT FEED WILDLIFE. DO NOT STOP VEHICLES ON THE HIGHWAY TO TAKE PHOTOS; use shoulders or turnouts. You are now in bear country ... a fed bear is a dead bear—don't feed bears!

DC 372.7 (596 km) **F 1115.3** (1794.9 km) Pull-through turnout with dumpster to north.

DC 373.3 (597 km) **F 1114.7** (1793.9 km) **Historical Mile 392. SUMMIT LAKE** (unincorporated), lodge with gas, diesel, propane, cafe, camping and lodging. The peak behind Summit Lake is Mount St. George (elev. 7,419 feet/2,261m) in the Stone Mountain range. The Summit area is known for dramatic and sudden weather changes. ▲

DC 373.5 (597.4 km) **F 1114.5** (1793.5 km) Rough gravel side road leads 1.5 miles/2.5 km to Flower Springs Lake trailhead, 4.3 miles/7 km to microwave tower viewpoint. Not suitable for motorhomes, trailers or low clearance vehicles. (This road was closed beyond Flower Springs Lake in 1997; current status unknown.)

DC 373.6 (597.6 km) **F 1114.4** (1793.4 km) Gravel turnout and **Summit Lake** provincial campground to south at east end of lake. **Historic Milepost 392** sign and interpretive panel mark the highest summit on the Alaska Highway, elev. 4,250 feet/1,295m. A very beautiful area of bare rocky peaks (which can be snow-covered anytime of the year). The provincial campground has 28 level gravel sites; camping fee $7 to $12; picnic tables; water and garbage containers; information shelter; boat launch. Hiking trails to Flower Springs Lake and Summit Peak. Fair fishing for lake trout, whitefish and rainbows. ▲

DC 375.6 (600.8 km) **F 1112.4** (1790.2 km) Turnout to north.

DC 375.9 (601.3 km) **F 1112.1** (1789.7 km) Picnic site to south with tables and dumpster on Rocky Crest Lake. Nice spot for photos; good reflections in lake when calm.

DC 376 (601.5 km) **F 1112** (1789.5 km) Erosion pillars north of highway (0.6-mile/1-km hike north); watch for caribou. Northbound, the highway winds through a rocky limestone gorge before descending into the wide and picturesque MacDonald River valley. Turnouts next 2.5 miles/4 km northbound with views of the valley. Watch for Stone sheep along rock cut.

DC 378.2 (605.1) **F 1109.8** (1786 km) Baba Canyon to north. Popular with hikers (strenuous).

DC 378.6 (605.7 km) **F 1109.4** (1785.4 km) **Historical Mile 397.** Rocky Mountain Lodge to south; gas, lodging, store and camping. ▲

DC 379.7 (607.4 km) **F 1108.3** (1783.6 km) Turnout to south.

DC 380.7 (609 km) **F 1107.3** (1782 km) North boundary of Stone Mountain Provincial Park. *CAUTION: Southbound, watch for wildlife alongside and on the road. DO NOT FEED WILDLIFE.*

DC 381.2 (611.2 km) **F 1106.8** (1781.2 km) Highway winds along above the wide rocky valley of MacDonald Creek. MacDonald Creek and river were named for Charlie McDonald, a Cree Indian credited with helping Alaska Highway survey crews locate the best route for the pioneer road.

DC 382.2 (612.8 km) **F 1105.8** (1779.5 km) Trail access via abandoned Churchill Mines Road (4-wheel drive only beyond river) to Wokkpash Recreation Area, located 12 miles/20 km south of the highway, which adjoins the southwest boundary of Stone Mountain Provincial Park. This remote area features extensive hoodoos (erosion pillars) in Wokkpash Gorge, and the scenic Forlorn Gorge and Stepped Lakes. Contact the Parks District Office in Fort St. John before venturing into this area; phone (250) 787-3407.

DC 383.3 (614.6 km) **F 1104.7** (1777.8 km) 113 Creek. The creek was named during construction of the Alaska Highway for its distance from Mile 0 at Fort Nelson. While Dawson Creek was to become Mile 0 on the completed pioneer road, clearing crews began their work at Fort Nelson, since a rough winter road already existed between Dawson Creek and Fort Nelson. Stone Range to the northeast and Muskwa Ranges of the Rocky Mountains to the west.

DC 384.2 (615.4 km) **F 1103.8** (1776.3 km) 115 Creek provincial campground to southwest, adjacent highway; double-ended entrance. Side-by-side camper parking (8 sites), water, garbage containers, picnic tables. Camping fee $7 to $12. Access to the riverbank of 115 Creek and **MacDonald Creek.** Beaver dams nearby. Fishing for grayling and Dolly Varden. ▲

DC 385.4 (616.6 km) **F 1102.6** (1774.4 km) 115 Creek bridge. Turnout to south at east end of bridge with tables and dumpster. Like 113 Creek, 115 Creek was named during construction of the pioneer road for its distance from Fort Nelson, Mile 0 for clearing crews.

DC 390.5 (624.8 km) **F 1097.5** (1766.2 km) **Historical Mile 408.** MacDonald River Services (closed in 1997; current status unknown).

DC 392.5 (627.8 km) **F 1095.5** (1763 km) MacDonald River bridge, clearance 17 feet/5.2m. Highway winds through narrow valley.

MacDonald River, fair fishing from May to July for Dolly Varden and grayling.

DC 394.8 (631.8 km) **F 1093.2** (1759.3 km) Turnout with litter barrel to east.

DC 396.1 (633.8 km) **F 1091.9** (1757.2 km) Folding rock formations on mountain face to west. The Racing River forms the boundary between the Sentinel Range and the Stone Range, both of which are composed of folded and sedimentary rock.

DC 399.1 (638.6 km) **F 1088.9** (1752.4 km) Stringer Creek.

DC 400.7 (641.1 km) **F 1087.3** (1749.8 km) Racing River bridge, clearance 17 feet/5.2m. River access to north at east end of bridge. Ecotour stop: Note the open south-facing slopes on the north side of the river that are used as winter range by stone sheep, elk and deer. Periodic controlled burns encourage the growth of forage grasses and shrubs, and also allow chinook winds to clear snow from grazing grounds in winter.

Racing River, grayling to 16 inches; Dolly Varden to 2 lbs., use flies, July through September.

DC 404.6 (647.4 km) **F 1083.4** (1743.5 km) **Historical Mile 422. TOAD RIVER** (unincorporated), situated in a picturesque valley. Popular artist Trish Croal makes her home here. Highway maintenance camp, school and private residences on north side of highway. Toad River Lodge on south side of highway with cafe, gas, tire repair, propane, camping and lodging. Ambulance service. Toad River Lodge is open year-round. The lodge is known for its collection of hats, which numbers more than 4,000. Also, inquire at the lodge about good wildlife viewing locations nearby. ▲

Toad River Lodge. See display ad this section. ▲

Stone Mountain Safaris. New 4-bedroom cedar log lodge with queen bed and single bed per room. Two shared baths. Hot tub, snooker table, wildlife displays. Experience our bed and breakfast or our "all inclusive" package. Horseback rides and adventure trips available. Mountain views and wildlife viewing. Located halfway between Dawson Creek and Whitehorse. So why not get off the highway and experience our quiet, private ranch setting. From Toad River go west 6 miles on Alaska Highway and turn right for 1 mile, then right again for 2 miles. Reservations required. Your hosts Dave and Ellie Wiens, Box 7870, Toad River, B.C. V0C 2X0. Fax/Phone (250) 232-5469. [ADVERTISEMENT]

Private Aircraft: Emergency gravel airstrip; elev. 2,400 feet/732m; length 2,300 feet/701m. Unattended; no fuel.

DC 405.5 (648.8 km) **F 1082.5** (1742.1 km) Turnout to south with **Historic Milepost 422.** Sign and interpretive panel commemorate Toad River/Camp 138 Jupp Construction.

DC 406.3 (650.1 km) **F 1081.7** (1740.8 km) Turnout with dumpster to north.

DC 407.5 (652 km) **F 1080.5** (1738.8 km) **Historical Mile 426.** Food, gas, propane, tire repair, cabins and camping south side of highway. Inquire here about local hiking trails and riverboat tours. ▲

The Poplars Campground. See display ad this section. ▲

DC 409.2 (654.6 km) **F 1078.8** (1736.1 km) South boundary of Muncho Lake Provincial Park.

DC 410.6 (656.8 km) **F 1077.4** (1733.9 km) Turnout with information panel on area geology. Impressive rock folding formation on mountain face, known as Folded Mountain.

DC 411 (657.4 km) **F 1077** (1733.2 km) Beautiful turquoise-coloured Toad River to north. The highway now follows the Toad River westbound.

Toad River, grayling to 16 inches; Dolly Varden to 10 lbs., use flies, July through September.

DC 415.5 (664.7 km) **F 1072.5** (1726 km) 150 Creek bridge. Creek access to south at east end of bridge.

DC 417.6 (668.2 km) **F 1070.4** (1722.6 km) Centennial Falls to south.

DC 419.8 (671.7 km) **F 1068.2** (1719 km) **Toad River** bridge. Turnout with dumpster to south at west end of bridge; fishing.

DC 422.6 (676.2 km) **F 1065.4** (1714.5 km) Watch for moose in pond to north; morning or evening best.

DC 423 (676.8 km) **F 1065** (1713.9 km) Double-ended turnout with litter barrel to north. Excellent wildlife viewing area; watch for Stone sheep, caribou, bear and moose.

CAUTION: Watch for Stone sheep along the highway (or standing in the middle of the highway). DO NOT FEED WILDLIFE. Do not stop vehicles on the highway to take photos; use shoulders or turnouts.

DC 423.1 (677 km) **F 1064.9** (1713.7 km) The highway swings north for Alaska-bound travelers. Highway climbs next 6 miles/9.7 km northbound. For Dawson Creek-bound travelers, the highway follows an easterly direction.

DC 424.1 (678.7 km) **F 1063.9** (1712.1 km) **Historic Milepost 443** at Peterson Creek No. 1 bridge. The creek was named for local trapper Pete Peterson, who helped Alaska Highway construction crews select a route through this area. Historic sign marks start of Campbell Construction Co. Ltd. contract during construction of the Alaska Highway.

DC 424.3 (679 km) **F 1063.7** (1711.8 km) The Village; gas, snacks and camping. ▲

DC 429.5 (688.9 km) **F 1058.5** (1703.4 km) Viewpoint to east with information shelter and dumpster. Information panel on geology of "Sawtooth Mountains."

DC 436.5 (698.5 km) **F 1051.5** (1692.2 km) **Historic Milepost 456.** Entering **MUNCHO LAKE** (pop. 26; elev. 2,700 feet/823m). Muncho Lake businesses extend from here north along the east shore of Muncho Lake to approximately **Milepost DC 443.7**. Businesses in Muncho Lake include 4 lodges, gas stations with towing and repair, restaurants, cafes and campgrounds. The post office is located at Double G Service; open year-round. ▲

A historic sign and interpretive panel mark Muncho Lake/Refueling Stop, Checkpoint during Alaska Highway construction. The road around the lake was a particular challenge. Workers had to cut their way through the lake's rocky banks. Horses were used to haul away the rock. The Muncho

Lake area offers hiking in the summer and cross-country skiing in the winter. Boat rentals are available from J&H Wilderness Resort and Northern Rockies Lodge. Flightseeing and fly-in fishing service available at Northern Rockies Lodge. An annual lake trout derby is held in June; inquire locally for dates.

CAUTION: Watch for Stone sheep and caribou on the highway north of here. Please DO NOT FEED WILDLIFE. Please do not stop on the highway to take photos; use shoulders or turnouts.

DC 436.9 (699.2 km) **F 1051.1** (1691.5 km) Gravel airstrip to west; length 1,200 feet/366m. View of Muncho Lake ahead northbound. The highway along Muncho Lake required considerable rock excavation by the Army in 1942. The original route went along the top of the cliffs, which proved particularly hazardous. (Portions of this hair-raising road can be seen high above the lake.) The Army relocated the road by benching into the cliffs a few feet above lake level.

Muncho Lake, known for its beautiful deep green and blue waters, is 7 miles/11 km in length, and 1 mile/1.6 km in width; elevation of the lake is 2,680 feet/817m. The colours are attributed to copper oxide leaching into the lake. Deepest point has been reported to be 730 feet/223m, although recent government tests have not located any point deeper than 400 feet/122m. The lake drains the Sentinel Range to the east and the Terminal Range to the west, feeding the raging Trout River in its 1,000-foot/305-m drop to the mighty Liard River. The mountains surrounding the lake are approximately 7,000 feet/2,134m high.

Muncho Lake, fishing for Dolly Varden; some grayling; whitefish to 12 inches; lake trout (record to 50 lbs.), use spoons, spinners, diving plug or weighted spoons, June and July best. The lake trout quota is 3 trout per person; minimum size 15 3/4 inches. Make sure you have a current British Columbia fishing license and a copy of the current regulations. Also rainbow trout.

DC 437.7 (700.5 km) **F 1050.3** (1690.2 km) Strawberry Flats Campground, Muncho Lake Provincial Park; 15 sites on rocky lakeshore, picnic tables, outhouses, garbage containers. Camping fee $7 to $12. ▲

CAUTION: Watch for bears in area.

DC 442.2 (707.9 km) **F 1045.8** (1683 km) **Historical Mile 462.** Northern Rockies/Highland Glen Lodge (open year-round) with lodging, restaurant, gas and camping west side of highway. Flying service for sightseeing and fly-in fishing. ▲

Northern Rockies/Highland Glen Lodge, Mile 462, Muncho Lake, BC. Toll-free reservation line: (800) 663-5269. Phone (250) 776-3481, fax (250) 776-3482. New hotel, lakeshore chalets and motel rooms. The newest and largest log building in BC. Featuring a 45-foot-high fireplace in open-ceiling dining room. Restaurant with European-trained chef and bakery. Spacious lakeshore RV sites, power and water hookups, dump station for guests. Children's playground. Fly-in fishing trips into the Arctic and Pacific watersheds for arctic grayling, Dolly Varden, rainbow trout, lake trout, northern pike and walleye. Outpost fishing cabins. Air taxi service, glacier and Muncho Lake local sightseeing flights. [ADVERTISEMENT] ▲

DC 442.9 (709 km) **F 1045.1** (1681.9 km) Turnoff to west for MacDonald campground, Muncho Lake Provincial Park; 15 level gravel sites, firewood, picnic tables, outhouses, boat launch, information shelter, pump water, on Muncho Lake. Camping fee $7 to $12. *CAUTION: Watch for bears in area.* ▲

DC 443.6 (710.1 km) **F 1044.4** (1680.8 km) **Historical Mile 463.** Muncho Lake Lodge; gas, propane, food, camping and lodging. ▲

Muncho Lake Lodge. See display ad this section. ▲

DC 443.7 (710.3 km) **F 1044.3** (1680.6 km) **Historical Mile 463.1.** J&H Wilderness Resort; food, gas, store, boat rentals, tackle,

Moose crossing boardwalk trail at Liard Hotsprings Provincial Park.
(Earl L. Brown, staff)

lodging and camping available. Muncho Lake businesses extend south to **Milepost DC 436.5.** ▲

J&H Wilderness Resort. See display ad this section. ▲

DC 444.9 (712.2 km) **F 1043.1** (1678.7 km) Muncho Lake viewpoint to west with information panel, large parking area, picnic tables, litter barrels and outhouses. View of Peterson Mountain at south end of lake.

NOTE: Watch for Stone sheep on highway next 10 miles/16 km northbound.

DC 453.3 (725.6 km) **F 1034.7** (1665.1 km) Turnout with litter barrel to east.

NOTE: Watch for Stone sheep on highway next 10 miles/16 km southbound.

DC 454 (726.7 km) **F 1034** (1664 km) Mineral lick; watch for Stone sheep. There is a trailhead 0.2 mile/0.3 km off the highway; a 5- to 10-minute loop hike takes you to viewpoints overlooking the Trout River valley and the steep mineral-laden banks frequented by sheep, goats, caribou and elk. Good photo opportunities, early morning best. *CAUTION: Steep banks, slippery when wet. Bring insect repellent.*

DC 455.5 (729.2 km) **F 1032.5** (1661.6 km) Turnout with litter barrel and message board to west.

DC 457.7 (732.7 km) **F 1030.3** (1658.1 km) Trout River bridge. The Trout River drains into the Liard River. The highway follows the Trout River north for several miles.

Trout River, grayling to 18 inches; whitefish to 12 inches, flies, spinners, May, June and August best.

DC 458.9 (734.6 km) **F 1029.1** (1656.1 km) Gravel turnout to east.

DC 460.7 (737.4 km) **F 1027.3** (1653.2 km) Prochniak Creek bridge. The creek was named for a member of Company A, 648th Engineers Topographic Battalion, during construction of the Alaska Highway. North boundary of Muncho Lake Provincial Park.

DC 463.3 (741.6 km) **F 1024.7** (1649 km) Watch for curves next 0.6 mile/1 km northbound.

DC 465.6 (745.3 km) **F 1022.4** (1645.3 km) Turnout with dumpster to east.

DC 466.3 (746.3 km) **F 1021.7** (1644.2 km) *CAUTION: Dangerous curves next 3 miles/5 km northbound.*

DC 468.9 (749.5 km) **F 1019.1** (1640 km) Pull-through turnout with dumpster to east. This Ecotour stop shows the extent of the 1959 fire that swept across the valley bottom. Lodgepole pine, trembling aspen and paper birch are the dominant species re-establishing this area.

DC 471 (754.1 km) **F 1017** (1636.7 km) First glimpse of the mighty Liard River for northbound travelers. Named by French-Canadian voyageurs for the poplar ("liard") that line the banks of the lower river. The Alaska Highway parallels the Liard River from here north to Watson Lake. The river offered engineers a natural line to follow during routing and construction of the Alaska Highway in 1942.

DC 472.2 (756 km) **F 1015.8** (1634.7 km) Washout Creek.

DC 474.3 (759.5 km) **F 1013.7** (1631.3 km) Turnout with dumpster to west.

DC 476.7 (763 km) **F 1011.3** (1627.5 km) Lower Liard River bridge. This is the only remaining suspension bridge on the Alaska Highway. The 1,143-foot suspension bridge was built by the American Bridge Co. and McNamara Construction Co. of Toronto in 1943.

The **Liard River** flows eastward toward the Fort Nelson River and parallels the Alaska Highway from the Lower Liard River bridge to the BC–YT border. The scenic Grand Canyon of the Liard is to the east and not visible from the highway. Good fishing for Dolly Varden, grayling, northern pike and whitefish.

DC 477.1 (763.8 km) **F 1010.9** (1626.8 km) **Historical Mile 496. LIARD RIVER** (unincorporated), lodge with gas, store, pay phone, food, camping and lodging to west; open year-round. ▲

Liard River Lodge. See display ad this section. ▲

DC 477.7 (764.7 km) **F 1010.3** (1625.9 km) **Historic Milepost 496.** Turnoff to north for Liard River Hotsprings Provincial Park, long a favorite stop for Alaska Highway travelers. The park has become so popular in recent years that the campground fills up very early each day in summer. Overflow day-parking area across highway from park entrance. The park is open year-round. This well-developed provincial park has 53 large, shaded, level gravel sites (some will accommodate 2 RVs), picnic tables, picnic shelter, water, garbage containers, firewood, fire rings, playground and heated restrooms at the hot springs with wheelchair-accessible toilet. Camping fees to $15.50. Pay phone at park entrance. ♿▲

Excellent interpretive programs and nature walks in summer; check schedule posted at park entrance and at information shelter near trailhead. Emergency phone at park headquarters. *CAUTION: BEWARE OF BEARS!*

A boardwalk leads to the pools, crossing a wetlands environment that supports more than 250 boreal forest plants, including 14 orchid species and 14 plants that survive at this latitude because of the hot springs. Also watch for moose feeding in the pools. There are 2 hot springs pools with water temperatures ranging from 108° to 126°F/42° to 52°C. Nearest is the Alpha pool with a children's wading area. Beyond the Alpha pool is Beta pool, which is larger and deeper.

Both have changing rooms. Beta pool is about a 0.4-mile/0.6-km walk. Plenty of parking at trailhead.

DC 477.8 (764.9 km) **F 1010.2** (1625.7 km) **Historical Mile 497.** Liard Hotsprings Lodge (open year-round) with food, gas, lodging and camping. Fishing, sightseeing charter trips and jetboat tours available. ▲

Trapper Ray's Liard Hotsprings Lodge. See display ad this section. ▲

DC 482.8 (772.9 km) **F 1005.2** (1617.7 km) Teeter Creek. A footpath leads upstream; 10-minute walk to falls. Grayling fishing.

DC 484.1 (775 km) **F 1003.9** (1615.6 km) *NOTE Watch for road construction next 5 miles/8 km northbound in 1998.*

DC 485.4 (777 km) **F 1002.6** (1613.5 km) Small turnout overlooking the Liard River.

DC 489 (783.6 km) **F 999** (1607.7 km) **Private Aircraft:** Liard River airstrip; elev. 1,400 feet/427m; length 4,000 feet/1,219m; gravel.

DC 495 (792.3 km) **F 993** (1598 km) **Historic Milepost 514. Smith River** bridge, clearance 17 feet/5.2m. Access to Smith River Falls via 1.6-mile/2.6-km gravel road; not recommended for large RVs or trailers or in wet weather. There is a hiking trail down to 2-tiered Smith River Falls from the parking area. Grayling fishing.

The historic sign here commemorates Smith River Airport Road. The old airstrip, part of the Northwest Staging Route, is located in a burned-over area about 25 miles/40 km from the highway (accessible by 4-wheel drive only).

DC 509.4 (815.6 km) **F 978.6** (1574.9 km) Large turnout with dumpster to east.

DC 513.9 (822.8 km) **F 974.1** (1567.6 km) **Historical Mile 533. COAL RIVER,** lodge with gas, diesel, food, camping and lodging. ▲

DC 514.2 (823.2 km) **F 973.8** (1567.1 km) **Historical Mile 533.2.** Coal River bridge. The Coal River flows into the Liard River south of the bridge.

DC 519.5 (831.4 km) **F 968.5** (1558.6 km) Sharp easy-to-miss turnoff to west for undeveloped "do-it-yourself campsite" (watch for sign). Small gravel parking area with outhouse, dumpster, and beautiful view of the Liard River (not visible from the highway). Although signed "Whirlpool Canyon," this scenic stretch of the Liard River has been identified by one astute reader as Mountain Portage Rapids, with Whirlpool Canyon being located farther downriver. ▲

DC 524.2 (839.2 km) **F 963.8** (1551 km) **Historical Mile 543. FIRESIDE** (unincorporated). Highway maintenance camp and truck stop with services and RV park. Sign reads: *Please keep pets in vehicles.* This community was partially destroyed by fire in the summer of 1982. Evidence of the fire can be seen from south of Fireside north to Lower Post. The 1982 burn, known as the Eg fire, was the second largest fire in British Columbia history, destroying more than 400,000 acres. ▲

DC 524.7 (840 km) **F 963.3** (1550.2 km) Good view of Liard River and Cranberry Rapids to west.

DC 530 (848.7 km) **F 958** (1541.7 km) Gravel turnout with dumpster to south.

DC 540.4 (865.3 km) **F 947.6** (1525 km) North end of rerouting of Alaska Highway (see **Milepost DC 527.7**).

DC 545.9 (874.2 km) **F 942.1** (1516.1 km) Turnout with litter barrel to west overlooking the Liard River.

DC 550.9 (882.2 km) **F 937.1** (1508 km) **Historical Mile 570.** Allen's Lookout; very large pull-through turnout with picnic tables, outhouse and dumpster to west overlooking the Liard River. Goat Mountain to west. Legend has it that a band of outlaws took advantage of this sweeping view of the Liard River to attack and rob riverboats.

DC 555 (888.8 km) **F 933** (1501.5 km) Good berry picking in July among roadside raspberry bushes; watch for bears.

DC 556 (890.4 km) **F 932** (1499.9 km) Highway swings west for Alaska-bound travelers.

DC 562.5 (900.8 km) **F 925.5** (1489.4 km) Large gravel turnout with dumpster.

Smith River Falls is 1.6 miles/2.6 km off the Alaska Highway at Milepost DC 495.

(Earl L. Brown, Staff)

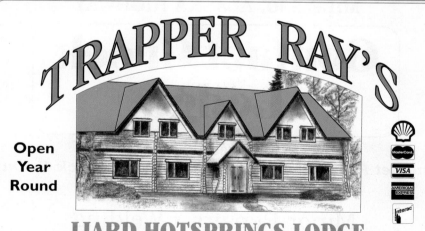

DC 565.7 (906 km) **F 922.3** (1484.3 km) *NOTE: Watch for road construction next 10 miles/16 km northbound in 1998.*

DC 567.9 (909.4 km) **F 920.1** (1480.7 km) **Historic Milepost 588.** Contact Creek bridge. Turnout to south at east end of bridge with tables, toilets, litter barrels and information shelter. Contact Creek was named by soldiers of the 35th Regiment from the south and the 340th Regiment from the north who met here Sept. 24, 1942, completing the southern sector of the Alaska Highway. Historic sign and interpretive panel.

DC 568.3 (910.2 km) **F 919.7** (1480.1 km) First of 7 crossings of the BC–YT border. Large gravel turnout to north with point of interest sign about the Yukon Territory. "The Yukon Territory takes its name from the Indian word *Youcon,* meaning 'big river.' It was first explored in the 1840s by the Hudson's Bay Co., which established several trading posts. The territory, which was then considered a district of the Northwest Territories, remained largely untouched until the Klondike Gold Rush, when thousands of people flooded into the country and communities sprang up almost overnight. This sudden expansion led to the official formation of the Yukon Territory on June 13, 1898."

DC 570 (912.9 km) **F 918** (1477.3 km) **Historical Mile 590. CONTACT CREEK,** lodge open year-round; food, gas, diesel, car repair, towing and pay phone.

Contact Creek Lodge. See display ad this section.

DC 573.9 (918.9 km) **F 914.1** (1471.1 km) Irons Creek bridge. Turnout with litter barrel to south at east end of bridge. According to the folks at Iron Creek Lodge, Irons Creek was named during construction of the Alaska Highway for the trucks that stopped here to put on tire irons (chains) in order to make it up the hill.

DC 575.9 (922 km) **F 912.1** (1467.8 km) **Historical Mile 596.** Iron Creek Lodge; food, gas, diesel, dump station, lodging, camping and fishing at private stocked lake.

Iron Creek Lodge. See display ad this section.

DC 582 (931.8 km) **F 906** (1458 km) NorthwesTel microwave tower.

DC 585 (937 km) **F 903** (1453.2 km) **Hyland River** bridge; good fishing for rainbow, Dolly Varden and grayling.

NOTE: Watch for logging trucks northbound to Watson Lake.

DC 585.3 (937.2 km) **F 902.7** (1452.7 km) **Historical Mile 605.9.** Hyland River bridge. The Hyland River is a tributary of the Liard River. The river was named for Frank Hyland, an early-day trader at Telegraph Creek on the Stikine River. Hyland operated trading posts throughout northern British Columbia, competing successfully with the Hudson's Bay Co., and at one time printing his own currency.

DC 598.7 (957.5 km) **F 889.3** (1431.2 km) Access to **LOWER POST** (unincorporated), at **Historical Mile 620,** via short gravel road; cafe and store. A B.C. Forest Service field office is located here. This British Columbia settlement is a historic Hudson's Bay Co. trading post and the site of an Indian village. The Liard and Dease rivers meet near here. The Dease River, named for Peter Warren Dease, a fur trader for the Hudson's Bay Co., heads in Dease Lake to the southwest on the Cassiar Highway.

DC 605.1 (967.6 km) **F 882.9** (1420.8 km) **Historic Milepost 627** marks official BC–YT border; Welcome to the Yukon sign. Monitor CB Channel 9 for police. The Alaska Highway (Yukon Highway 1) dips back into British Columbia several times before making its final crossing into the Yukon Territory near Morley Lake (**Milepost DC 751.5**).

NOTE: Kilometreposts on the Yukon Territory portion of the highway reflect historical mileposts. Kilometreposts on the British Columbia portion of the highway reflect actual driving distance. There is approximately a 40-kilometre difference at the BC–YT border between these measurements.

Northbound: Good paved highway with wide shoulders next 380 miles/611.5 km to Haines Junction, with the exception of some short sections of narrow road and occasional gravel breaks.

Southbound: Watch for rough, narrow, winding road and breaks in surfacing between border and Fort Nelson (approximately 321 miles/516.6 km).

DC 606.9 (1011.9 km) **F 881.1** (1418 km) Lucky Lake picnic area to south; ball diamond and 1.2-mile/2-km hiking trail to Liard River Canyon (watch for signs), observation platform with information panels at river. **Lucky Lake** is a popular local swimming hole for Watson Lake residents, who installed a water slide here. Relatively shallow, the lake warms up quickly in summer, making it one of the few area lakes where swimming is possible. Stocked with rainbow trout.

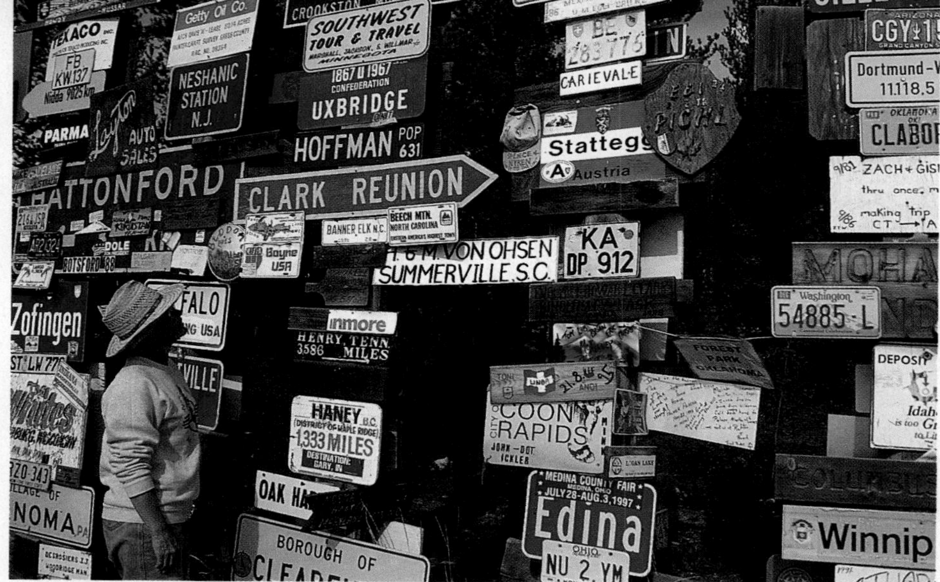

A favorite pastime for travelers: reading the signs at Watson Lake Signpost Forest.

(© Roger Holden)

According to R. Coutts in *Yukon Places & Names*, Lucky Lake was named by American Army Engineer troops working on construction of the Alaska Highway in 1942: "A young woman set up a tent business and clients there referred to transactions as 'a change of luck.'"

DC 609.2 (1015.5 km) **F 878.8** (1414.3 km) Paved drive-through rest area with litter barrel and outhouses to north.

DC 610.4 (1017.5 km) **F 877.6** (1412.3 km) Weigh station.

DC 610.5 (1017.7 km) **F 877.5** (1412.2 km) **Mile 632.5. Campground Services** at Mile 632.5 is the largest and best equipped RV park in Watson Lake, the gateway to the Yukon. The park features 140 full or partial hookups and pull-throughs, tent sites, playground, firepits and a screened kitchen.

Coin-op showers, laundry and car wash. Good Sam Park. A food market stocks groceries, "chester fried" chicken, convenience items, movie rentals, fishing tackle, licenses and ice. Gasoline and diesel and ICG propane are available at the self-serve pumps. A licensed mechanic is available for repairs, alignments, tire changes, etc. Agents for Western Union money transfers. Open for business year-round, serving the traveler's needs for over 25 years! Phone (867) 536-7448. [ADVERTISEMENT] ▲

Watson Lake

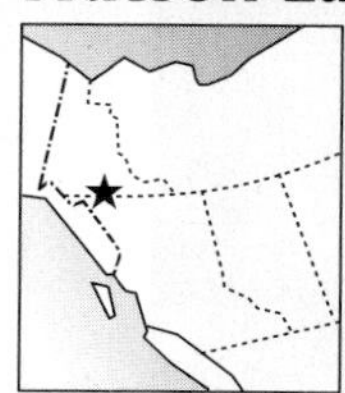

DC 612.9 (1021 km) **F 875.1** (1408.3 km) **Historic Milepost 635.** "Gateway to the Yukon," located 330 miles/531 km from Fort Nelson, 275 miles/443 km from Whitehorse. **Population:** 1,794. **Emergency Services: RCMP**, phone (867) 536-5555 (if no answer call toll-free (867) 667-5555). **Fire Department**, phone (867) 536-2222. **Ambulance**, phone (867) 536-4444. **Hospital**, phone (867) 536-4444.

Visitor Information: Located in the Alaska Highway Interpretive Centre behind the Signpost Forest, north of the Alaska Highway; access to the centre is from the Campbell Highway. Phone (867) 536-7469. The town of Watson Lake provides a toll-free number (Lower 48 only) for information on local attractions; phone (800) 663-5248.

Elevation: 2,265 feet/690m. **Climate:** Average temperature in January is -15°F/-26°C, in July 57°F/14°C. Record high temperature 93°F/34°C in June 1950, record low -74°F/-59°C in January 1947. Annual snowfall is 90.6 inches. Driest month is April, wettest month is September. Average date of last spring frost is June 2; average date of first fall frost is Sept. 14. **Radio:** CBC 990, CKYN-FM 96.1 (Visitor Radio CKYN is broadcast from the visitor information centre from mid-May to mid-September). **Television:** Channel 8 and cable.

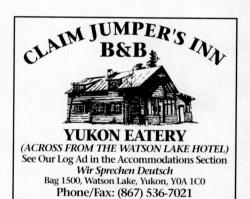

Private Aircraft: Watson Lake airport, 8 miles/12.9 km north of Campbell Highway; elev. 2,262 feet/689m; length 5,500 feet/1,676m and 3,530 feet/1,076m; asphalt; fuel 100, jet. Heliport and floatplane bases also located here. The Watson Lake airport terminal building was built in 1942. The log structure has been designated a Heritage Building.

In the late 1800s, Watson Lake was known as Fish Lake. The lake was later renamed Watson, for Frank Watson of Yorkshire, England. He gave up on the gold rush in 1898 to settle here on its shores with his Indian wife. Today, Watson Lake is an important service stop on the Alaska and Campbell highways (Campbell Highway travelers, fill your gas tanks here!); a communication and distribution centre for the southern Yukon; a base for trappers, hunters and fishermen; and a supply point for area

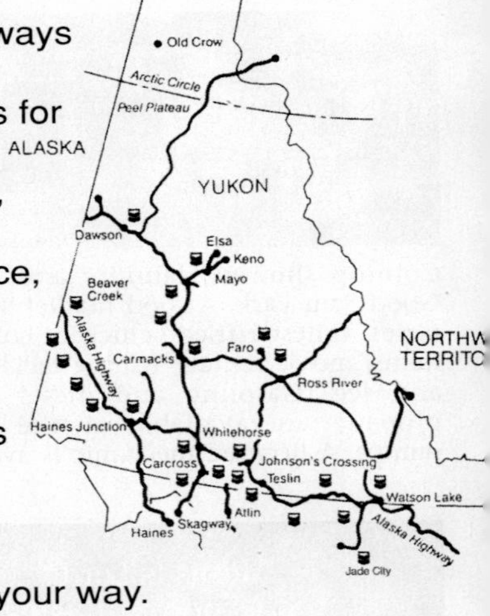

mining and mineral exploration.

Watson Lake businesses are located along either side of the Alaska Highway. The lake itself is not visible from the Alaska Highway. Access to the lake, airport, hospital and Mount Maichen ski hill is via the Campbell Highway (locally referred to as Airport Road). The ski area is about 4 miles/6.4 km out the Campbell Highway from town.

Watson Lake was an important point during construction of the Alaska Highway in 1942. The airport, built in 1941, was one of the major refueling stops along the Northwest Staging Route, the system of airfields through Canada to ferry supplies to Alaska and later lend-lease aircraft to Russia. Of the nearly 8,000 aircraft ferried through Canada, 2,618 were Bell P–39 Airacobras. A full-scale replica of the P–39 Airacobra is displayed at the Alaska Highway Interpretive Centre by the Signpost Forest.

The Alaska Highway helped bring both people and commerce to this once isolated settlement. A post office opened here in July 1942. The economy of Watson Lake is based on services and also the forest products industry. White spruce and lodgepole pine are the two principal trees of the Yukon and provide a forest industry for the territory. White spruce grows straight and fast wherever adequate water is available, and it will grow to extreme old age without showing decay. The lodgepole pine developed from the northern pine and can withstand extreme cold, grow at high elevations and take full advantage of the almost 24-hour summer sunlight of a short growing season.

ACCOMMODATIONS/VISITOR SERVICES

There are several hotels/motels, a bed and breakfast, restaurants and gas stations with unleaded, diesel and propane, automotive and tire repair. Dump stations available at local campgrounds and service stations. There are department, variety, grocery and hardware stores. The RCMP office is east of town centre on the Alaska Highway. There is 1 bank in Watson Lake—Canadian Imperial Bank of Commerce; it is open Monday through Thursday from 10 A.M. to 3 P.M., Friday 10 A.M. to 6 P.M., closed holidays. Automatic teller machine available 24 hours. Check at the Visitor Information Centre for locations of local churches. Dennis Ball Memorial Swimming Pool is open weekdays in summer. Lucky Lake waterslide is open on

WATSON LAKE ADVERTISERS

As You Wish V&S Department Store ....Ph. (867) 536-2550
Belvedere Motor Hotel.....Ph. (867) 536-7712
Big Horn Hotel ....Ph. (867) 536-2020
Campground Services ....E. edge of town
Cedar Lodge Motel...........Ph. (867) 536-7406
Claim Jumper's Inn B&B ...Ph. (867) 536-7021
Downtown R.V. Park ....Ph. (867) 536-2646
Gateway Motor Inn..........Ph. (867) 536-7744
Green Valley RV Park...................Kmpost 1032 Alaska Hwy.
Hougen's Department Store ....Alaska Hwy.
Northern Lights Centre ....Ph. (867) 536-STAR
Napa Auto Parts ....Ph. (867) 536-2521
O'Neill Repairs........1 blk. S. of Signpost Forest
Totem Oil..........................Ph. (800) 661-0550
Watson Lake Hotel ....Ph. (867) 536-7781
Watson Lake Rodeo..........Ph. (867) 536-2272

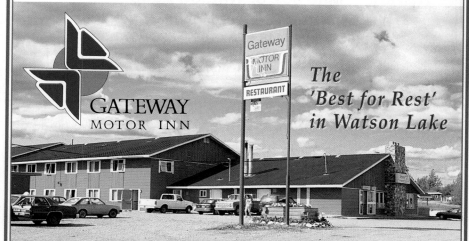

weekends in summer from 1–4 P.M.

Belvedere Motor Hotel, located in the centre of town, is Watson Lake's newest and finest hotel. It offers such luxuries as Jacuzzi tubs in the rooms, waterbeds and cable TV, and all at competitive prices. Dining is excellent, whether you decide to try the superb dining room menu or the coffee shop menu. Phone (867) 536-7712, fax (867) 536-7563. [ADVERTISEMENT]

Big Horn Hotel. New in 1993. 29 beautiful rooms. Centrally located on the Alaska Highway in downtown Watson Lake, YT. Our rooms are quiet, spacious, clean and they boast queen-size beds and complimentary coffee. You get quality at a reasonable price. Available to you are king-size motionless waterbeds, Jacuzzi rooms, kitchenette suites. We know you'll enjoy staying with us. Book ahead. Phone (867) 536-2020, fax (867) 536-2021. [ADVERTISEMENT]

Claim Jumper's Inn. Built in 1948, the two-story, log Claim Jumper's Inn is the oldest house in Watson Lake. Extensively restored, this historic home is now a unique B & B and eatery. We offer clean, cozy rooms, with shared or private bath, at the most reasonable rates in the Yukon. Our public dining room (under construction in 1998) features all-you-can-eat sourdough pancake and bannock breakfasts, light lunches, Yukon afternoon tea, wild game and salmon barbecues and our Innkeeper's Dinner. We invite all travelers to join us for our nightly campfire with music, storytelling and Robert Service recitals by Gascan Larry. Bring an instrument and join the fun! Phone/fax (867) 536-7021. See display ad. [ADVERTISEMENT]

Watson Lake Hotel. The historic Watson Lake Hotel. We're right in the heart of Watson Lake's historical Signpost Forest. Enjoy northern hospitality at its finest. Ample parking on our 6 acres of property. Quiet outside modern units (renovated May 1993), boardwalk gift shops and espresso bar. Senior, government, military and corporate discounts. Phone for reservations (867) 536-7781; fax (867) 536-2724. [ADVERTISEMENT]

The turnoff for Watson Lake Yukon government campground is 2.4 miles/3.9 km west of the Signpost Forest via the Alaska Highway; see description at **Milepost DC 615.3.** There is a private campground at **Milepost DC 619.6**, 4.3 miles/6.9 km past the turnoff for the government campground; a private campground 2.4 miles/3.9 km east of the Signpost Forest on the Alaska Highway (see **Milepost DC 610.5**); and an RV park located downtown. ▲

Downtown R.V. Park, situated in the centre of town. 71 full-hookup stalls, 19 with pull-through parking; showers; laundromat. Free truck/trailer, motorhome wash with overnight stay. Easy walking distance to stores, garages, hotels, restaurants, liquor store, banking, churches, information centre and the world-famous Signpost Forest. Just across the street from Wye Lake Park. Excellent hiking trails. Phone (867) 536-2646 in summer, 536-2224 in winter. [ADVERTISEMENT] ▲

TRANSPORTATION

Air: Scheduled service to Whitehorse via Alkan Air; to Prince George, Vancouver, Victoria, Smithers and Dease Lake via Central Mountain Air. Helicopter charters available from Frontier Helicopters and Trans North Helicopters.

Bus: Scheduled service to Edmonton and Whitehorse via Coachways.

Taxi and **Car Rental:** Available.

ATTRACTIONS

The **Alaska Highway Interpretive Centre**, operated by Tourism Yukon, is well worth a visit. Located behind the Signpost Forest, north of the Alaska Highway. Excellent slide presentation and displays, including photographs taken in the mid-1940s showing the construction of the Alaska Highway in this area, and a brief Alaska Highway video. Full-scale reproduction of a P–39 Airacobra fighter plane on display just outside the centre. The centre is open daily, May to mid-September. Free admission. Phone (867) 536-7469.

Northern Lights Centre. The only planetarium in North America featuring the myth and science of the northern lights. Using advanced video and laser technology, the new (1997) centre offers 2 different presentations on the aurora borealis inside a 110-seat "Electric Sky" theatre environment. Also interactive displays. Afternoon and evening showings daily from May to September. Admission charged. Located across from the Signpost Forest. Phone (867) 536-STAR; Internet www.yukon.net/northernlights.

The Watson Lake Signpost Forest, seen at the north end of town at the junction of the Alaska and Robert Campbell highways, was started by Carl K. Lindley of Danville, IL, a U.S. Army soldier in Company D, 341st Engineers, working on the construction of the Alaska Highway in 1942. Travelers are still adding signs to the collection, which numbers well over 37,000. Visitors are encouraged to add a sign to the Signpost

Forest. **Historic Milepost 635** is located at the Signpost Forest.

Special Events. The 5th annual Watson Lake Rodeo (NRA-approved) will be held at Lucky Lake July 4–5, 1998. A parade, 8 main events and junior events will be featured.

Wye Lake Park offers a picnic area and boardwalk trails for viewing birds. There is also a bandshell, kitchen shelter and wheelchair-accessible restrooms. The lake attracts both migrating birds (spring and fall) and resident species, such as nesting grebes. Native plants and flowers are identified by plaques. The development of this park was initiated by a local citizens group.

St. John the Baptist Anglican Church has a memorial stained-glass window designed by Yukon artist Kathy Spalding. Titled "Our Land of Plenty," the window features a scene just north of Watson Lake off the Campbell Highway.

Drive the Campbell Highway. This good gravel road offers an excellent wilderness highway experience. Motorists can travel the entire 373 miles/600 km of the Campbell Highway, stopping at Ross River and Faro en route, to junction with the Klondike Highway at Carmacks. Or drive north 52 miles/83 km from Watson Lake to Simpson Lake for picnicking, fishing and camping. (See CAMPBELL HIGHWAY section for details.)

Play golf at Upper Liard, 6 miles/9.6 km north of Watson Lake on the Alaska Highway. The 9-hole, par-35 course has grass greens and is open daily May through September. Phone (867) 536-2477.

Explore the area. Take time to fish, canoe a lake, take a wilderness trek or sightsee by helicopter. Outfitters in the area offer guided fishing trips to area lakes. Trips can be arranged by the day or by the week. Check with the visitor information centre.

AREA FISHING: **Watson Lake** has grayling, trout and pike. **McKinnon Lake** (walk-in only), 20 miles/32 km west of Watson Lake, pike 5 to 10 lbs. **Toobally Lake**, string of lakes 14 miles/23 km long, 90 air miles/145 km east, lake trout 8 to 10 lbs.; pike 5 to 10 lbs.; grayling 1 to 3 lbs. **Stewart Lake,** 45 air miles/72 km north northeast; lake trout, grayling.

Alaska Highway Log

(continued)

YUKON HIGHWAY 1

Distance* from Dawson Creek (DC) is followed by distance from Fairbanks (F). Original mileposts are indicated in the text as Historical Mile.

*Mileages from Dawson Creek are based on actual driving distance. Kilometres from Dawson Creek are based on physical kilometreposts. Please read Mileposts and Kilometreposts on page 90.

DC 612.9 (1021 km) **F 875.1** (1408.3 km) Watson Lake Signpost Forest at the **junction** of the Campbell Highway (Yukon Route 4) and Alaska Highway. The Campbell Highway leads north to Ross River and Faro (see CAMPBELL HIGHWAY section), to junction with the Klondike Highway to Dawson City. Campbell Highway travelers should fill gas tanks in Watson Lake. The first 6 miles/9.7 km of the Campbell Highway is known locally as Airport Road; turn here for access to visitor information (in the Alaska Highway Interpretive Centre), airport, hospital and ski hill.

DC 615.3 (1025 km) **F 872.7** (1404.4 km) Turnoff to north for Watson Lake Recreation Park. Drive in approximately 2 miles/3 km for Watson Lake Yukon government campground; 55 gravel sites, most level, some pull-through, drinking water, kitchen shelters, outhouses, firepits, firewood and litter barrels. Camping fee $8.

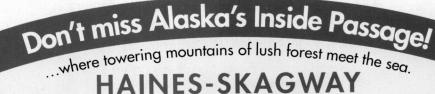

There is a separate group camping area and also a day-use area (boat launch, swimming, picnicking at Watson Lake). Follow signs at fork in access road. Trails connect all areas.

DC 618.5 (1030 km) **F 869.5** (1399.3 km) Watch for livestock.

DC 619.6 (1032 km) **F 868.4** (1397.5 km) **Green Valley R.V. Park.** Phone (867) 536-2276. Just 7 miles west of Watson Lake, quiet greenbelt area along Liard River. Friendly service, clean facilities. Pay phone. Serviced and unserviced sites, dump station, grassy tent sites, riverside camping, firepits, car wash, laundry, showers, grocery, coffee, pastries, ice, souvenirs, free gold panning, game room, fishing licenses and tackle. Fish for grayling and dollies. Pick wild strawberries and raspberries in season. Cold beer and off sales. Bikers welcome. Your hosts: Ralph and Marion Bjorkman. [ADVERTISEMENT] ▲

DC 620 (1032.4 km) **F 868** (1396.9 km) Upper Liard River bridge. The Liard River heads in the St. Cyr Range in southcentral Yukon Territory and flows southeast into British Columbia, then turns east and north to join the Mackenzie River at Fort Simpson, NWT.

Liard River, grayling, lake trout, whitefish and northern pike.

DC 620.2 (1032.7 km) **F 867.8** (1396.5 km) **Historical Mile 642. UPPER LIARD VILLAGE**, site of Our Lady of the Yukon Church. Gas, food, lodging and camping. ▲

DC 620.3 (1033 km) **F 867.7** (1396.4 km) Greenway's Greens golf course to south with 9 holes, par 35, grass greens, open daily in summer.

DC 620.8 (1033.7 km) **F 867.2** (1395.6 km) Albert Creek bridge. Turnout with litter barrel to north at east end of bridge. A sign near here marks the first tree planting project in the Yukon. Approximately 200,000 white spruce seedlings were planted in the Albert Creek area in 1993.

DC 626.2 (1043 km) **F 861.8** (1386.9 km) **Historic Milepost 649. Junction** with the Cassiar Highway, which leads south to Yellowhead Highway 16 (see CASSIAR HIGHWAY section). Services here include towing, gas, store with souvenirs, propane, car repair, car wash, laundromat, cafe, camping and lodging. ▲

Junction 37 Services. See display ad this section.

DC 627 (1043.9 km) **F 861** (1385.6 km) **Alaska Highway's Best Coffee Stop.** See display ad this section.

The Northern Beaver Post. Historical Mile 649.9. As with trading posts of the past, The Northern Beaver Post is an essential stop for any traveler. Here you will find unique, quality items which are often as useful as they are decorative. In the friendly atmosphere of the Post, discover a fine selection of Native crafts, jewellery, gold, jade, authentic Eskimo carvings, furs, woolens, northern art, tufting, sweat shirts and tees, cards, gifts and more. Show us this editorial and receive 10 percent off your purchase of a Beaver Post T-shirt or sweat shirt. Open May to October, 7 days a week, extended summer hours until 10 P.M. Caravans and bus tours welcome. Limited free overnight RV parking. Clean rustic cabins available. Largest inventoried family-owned gift shop on the highway. Quality Northern items—90 percent Canadian made. Take home a truly unique souvenir ... The Northern Beaver Post's own album with Elvis Presley "Still Living" Yukon-written Yukon songs. Buses and caravans phone ahead to arrange for early morning openings. Don't miss "Alaska Highway's Best Coffee Stop" next door—fresh home baking. VISA, MasterCard, Discover. Shipping and mail order available. Phone (867) 536-2307, fax (867) 536-7667. [ADVERTISEMENT]

DC 627.3 (1044.5 km) **F 860.7** (1385.1 km) Large gravel turnout and rest area with litter barrels, pit toilets and Watson Lake community map.

DC 630 (1050.8 km) **F 858** (1380.8 km) Several hundred rock messages are spelled out along the highway here. The rock messages were started in summer 1990 by a Fort Nelson swim team.

DC 633 (1055.6 km) **F 855** (1375.9 km) Gravel turnout to north.

DC 637.8 (1063.3 km) **F 850.2** (1368.2 km) Microwave tower access road.

DC 639.8 (1066.5 km) **F 848.2** (1365 km) Hill and sharp curve.

DC 647.2 (1078.5 km) **F 840.8** (1353.1 km) Turnout with litter barrel on Little Rancheria Creek to north.

DC 647.4 (1079 km) **F 840.6** (1352.8 km) Little Rancheria Creek bridge. Northbound winter travelers put on chains here.

DC 650.6 (1084 km) **F 837.4** (1347.6 km) Highway descends westbound to Big Creek.

DC 651.1 (1084.8 km) **F 836.9** (1346.8 km) Big Creek bridge, clearance 17.7 feet/5.4m. Turnout at east end of bridge.

DC 651.2 (1085 km) **F 836.8** (1346.7 km) Turnoff to north for Big Creek Yukon government day-use area, adjacent highway on Big Creek; gravel loop road, outhouses, firewood, kitchen shelter, litter barrels, picnic tables, drinking water.

DC 652.5 (1087.3 km) **F 835.5** (1344.6 km) Sign reads: "Northbound winter travelers chains may be removed."

NOTE: Watch for road construction northbound between kilometreposts 1089 and 1102 in 1998.

DC 658.4 (1096.7 km) **F 829.6** (1335.1 km) Pull-through turnout south side of highway.

DC 662.3 (1102.9 km) **F 825.7** (1328.8 km) NorthwesTel microwave tower road to north.

NOTE: Recent highway reconstruction and straightening in this area has resulted in the displacement of many kilometreposts.

DC 664.1 (1105.8 km) **F 823.9** (1325.9 km) Double-ended turnout to north to Lower Rancheria River.

DC 664.3 (1106.2 km) **F 823.7** (1325.6 km) Bridge over Lower Rancheria River. For northbound travelers, the highway closely follows the Rancheria River west from here to the Swift River. Northern bush pilot Les Cook was credited with helping find the best route for the Alaska Highway between Watson Lake and Whitehorse. Cook's Rancheria River route saved engineers hundreds of miles of highway construction.

Rancheria River, fishing for Dolly Varden and grayling.

DC 665.1 (1110.4 km) **F 822.9** (1324.3 km) Scenic viewpoint.

DC 667.2 (1113.7 km) **F 820.8** (1320.9 km) Turnout to south.

DC 667.6 (1114.3 km) **F 820.4** (1320.2 km) Large double-ended turnout with litter barrel to south.

DC 671.9 (1118.7 km) **F 816.1** (1313.3 km) Spencer Creek.

DC 673.4 (1121 km) **F 814.6** (1310.9 km) Improved highway and view of Cassiar Mountains westbound.

DC 677 (1126.9 km) **F 811** (1305.1 km) Turnout with litter barrel to south overlooking the Rancheria River. Trail down to river.

According to R.C. Coutts, author of *Yukon: Places & Names,* the Rancheria River was named by Cassiar miners working Sayyea Creek in 1875, site of a minor gold rush at the time. Rancheria is an old Californian or Mexican miners' term from the Spanish, meaning a native village or settlement. It is pronounced Ran-che-RI-ah.

DC 678.5 (1129.3 km) **F 809.5** (1302.7 km) George's Gorge, culvert.

DC 683.2 (1137 km) **F 804.8** (1295.2 km) NorthwesTel microwave tower to south.

DC 684 (1138.4 km) **F 804** (1293.9 km) Turnout with litter barrel overlooking Rancheria River. *CAUTION: Watch for livestock on or near highway in this area.*

DC 687.2 (1143.8 km) **F 800.8** (1288.7 km) **Historic Milepost 710.** Rancheria Hotel–Motel to south; gas, food, camping and lodging. Open year-round. Historic sign and interpretive panel on highway lodges. ▲

DC 687.4 (1143.9 km) **F 800.6** (1288.4 km) Turnoff to south for private campground (formerly Rancheria Yukon government campground) adjacent highway overlooking Rancheria River. The Rancheria is a tributary of the Liard River. ▲

DC 689.2 (1146.6 km) **F 798.8** (1285.5 km) Canyon Creek.

DC 690 (1148 km) **F 798** (1284.2 km) Highway follows the Rancheria River.

DC 692.5 (1152 km) **F 795.5** (1280.2 km) Young Creek.

DC 694.2 (1155 km) **F 793.8** (1277.5 km) **Historical Mile 717.5.** Abandoned building.

DC 695.2 (1156.5 km) **F 792.8** (1275.8 km) Rancheria Falls recreation site has a good gravel and boardwalk trail to the falls; easy 10-minute walk. Large parking area with toilets and litter barrels at trailhead.

DC 697.4 (1160 km) **F 790.6** (1272.3 km) Beautiful view of the Cassiar Mountains.

DC 698.4 (1161.6 km) **F 789.6** (1270.7 km) **Historical Mile 721.** Walker's Continental Divide; gas, food, camping and lodging. ▲

Walker's Continental Divide. Fresh baking daily, mouth-watering cinnamon rolls, rhubarb pie, muffins and tarts. Breakfast served all day—try our sourdough pancakes. Gift shop, hard ice cream. Motel with clean, comfortable, cozy rooms. Proposed for 1998—full-service RV park with laundromat, showers and trailer dump. Clean washrooms. Hospitality spoken here, free of charge. Phone (867) 851-6451. [ADVERTISEMENT] ▲

DC 698.7 (1162 km) **F 789.3** (1270.2 km) Upper Rancheria River bridge, clearance 17.7 feet/5.4m. For northbound travelers, the

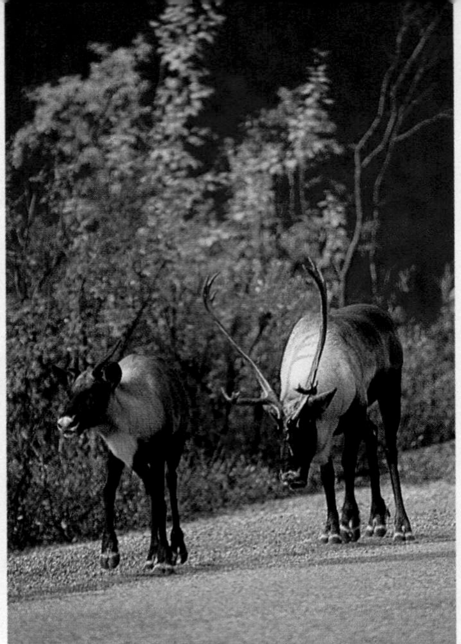
Wildlife seen along the Alaska Highway includes caribou. (Earl L. Brown, staff)

highway leaves the Rancheria River.

DC 699.1 (1162.8 km) **F 788.9** (1269.6 km) Large gravel turnout to north with point of interest signs, outhouses and litter barrels. This marks the Continental Divide, the water divide between rivers that drain into the Arctic Ocean via the Mackenzie River system and those that drain into the Pacific Ocean via the Yukon River system. All rivers crossed by the Alaska Highway between here and Fairbanks, AK, drain into the Yukon River system.

DC 699.6 (1163.3 km) **F 788.4** (1268.8 km) **Historic Milepost 722.** Pine Lake airstrip to north (status unknown).

DC 702.2 (1168 km) **F 785.8** (1264.6 km) Swift River bridge. For northbound travelers, the highway now follows the Swift River west to the Morley River.

DC 706.2 (1174.5 km) **F 781.8** (1258.2 km) Steep hill for westbound travelers.

DC 709.7 (1180 km) **F 778.3** (1252.5 km) Seagull Creek.

DC 710 (1180.9 km) **F 778** (1252 km) **Historic Milepost 733, SWIFT RIVER.** Lodge with food, gas, lodging, car repair, pay phone and highway maintenance camp. Open year-round.

DC 710.5 (1181.5 km) **F 777.5** (1251.2 km) **Historical Mile 733.5.** The highway re-enters British Columbia for approximately 42 miles/68 km northbound.

DC 712.7 (1185 km) **F 775.3** (1247.7 km) Partridge Creek.

DC 716 (1190.3 km) **F 772** (1242.4 km) Gravel turnout with litter barrels.

DC 718.5 (1194.2 km) **F 769.5** (1238.3 km) Screw Creek.

DC 719.6 (1196 km) **F 768.4** (1236.6 km) **Historical Mile 743.** Turnout with litter barrel to south on **Swan Lake.** Fishing for trout and whitefish. The pyramid-shaped mountain to south is Simpson Peak.

DC 724.2 (1203.7 km) **F 763.8** (1229.2 km) Pull-through turnout to south.

DC 727.9 (1209.5 km) **F 760.1** (1223.2 km) Logjam Creek.

DC 735.8 (1222.5 km) **F 752.2** (1210.5 km) Smart River bridge. The Smart River flows south into the Cassiar Mountains in British Columbia. The river was originally called Smarch, after the Indian family of that name who lived and trapped in this area. The Smarch family currently includes well-known artists Keith and Jack Smarch.

DC 741.4 (1231.7 km) **F 746.6** (1201.5 km) Microwave tower access road to north.

DC 744.1 (1236 km) **F 743.9** (1197.2 km) Upper Hazel Creek.

DC 745.2 (1238 km) **F 742.8** (1195.4 km) Lower Hazel Creek.

DC 746.9 (1240.7 km) **F 741.1** (1192.6 km) Turnouts both sides of highway; litter barrel at south turnout.

DC 749 (1245 km) **F 739** (1189.3 km) Andrew Creek.

DC 751.5 (1249.2 km) **F 736.5** (1185.2 km) Morley Lake to north. The Alaska Highway re-enters the Yukon Territory northbound. This is the last of 7 crossings of the YT–BC border.

DC 752 (1250 km) **F 736** (1184.4 km) Sharp turnoff to north for **Morley River** Yukon government day-use area; large gravel parking area, picnic tables, kitchen shelter, water, litter barrels and outhouses. Fishing.

DC 752.3 (1251 km) **F 735.7** (1184 km) Morley River bridge; turnout with litter barrel to north at east end of bridge. Morley River flows into the southeast corner of Teslin Lake. The river, lake and Morley Bay (on Teslin Lake) were named for W. Morley Ogilvie, assistant to Arthur St. Cyr on the 1897 survey of the Telegraph Creek–Teslin Lake route.

Morley Bay and **River,** good fishing near mouth of river for northern pike 6 to 8 lbs., best June to August, use small Red Devils; grayling 3 to 5 lbs., in May and August, use small spinner; lake trout 6 to 8 lbs., June to August, use large spoon.

Travelers take a break at a turnout in the Rancheria River valley.
(Earl L. Brown, staff)

DC 752.9 (1252 km) **F 735.1** (1183 km) **Historic Milepost 777.7.** Morley River Lodge, food, gas, diesel, towing, tires, camping and lodging. Open year-round. ▲

Morley River Lodge. See display ad this section. ▲

DC 754.8 (1256 km) **F 733.2** (1179.9 km) *CAUTION: Watch for livestock on highway.*

DC 757.9 (1261 km) **F 730.1** (1174.9 km) Small marker to south (no turnout) reads: "In memory of Max Richardson 39163467, Corporal Co. F 340th Eng. Army of the United States; born Oct. 10, 1918, died Oct. 17, 1942. Faith is the victory."

DC 761.5 (1267.9 km) **F 726.5** (1169.1 km) Strawberry Creek.

DC 764.1 (1273.7 km) **F 723.9** (1165 km) Hayes Creek.

DC 769.6 (1282.5 km) **F 718.4** (1156.1 km) **Historical Mile 797.** Food, lodging and camping. ▲

Dawson Peaks Resort & RV Park. Slow down folks! No need to drive any farther. Fishing's good, coffee's on, camping is easy and the rhubarb pie can't be beat. Couple that with our renowned Yukon hospitality and you'll have one of the best experiences on your trip. We're looking forward to seeing you this summer. [ADVERTISEMENT] ▲

DC 769.9 (1283 km) **F 718.1** (1155.6 km) Food, gas and bar.

DC 776 (1292 km) **F 712** (1145.8 km) Nisutlin Bay (Nisutlin River) bridge, longest water span on the Alaska Highway at 1,917 feet/584m. The Nisutlin River flows into Teslin Lake here. Good view northbound of the village of Teslin and Teslin Lake. Teslin Lake straddles the BC–YT border; it is 86 miles/138 km long, averages 2 miles/3.2 km across, and has an average depth of 194 feet/59m. The name is taken from the Indian name for the lake—Teslintoo ("long, narrow water").

Turnout with litter barrel and point of interest sign at south end of bridge, east side of highway.

Historic Milepost 804 at the north end of the bridge, west side of the highway; historic sign and interpretive panel, parking area, marina and day-use area with picnic tables and boat ramp. Turn west on side road here for access to Teslin village (description follows).

DC 776.3 (1294 km) **F 711.7** (1145.3 km) Entering Teslin **(Historic Milepost 804)** at north end of bridge. Gas, food, camping and lodging along highway.

Yukon Motel, just right (northbound) on the north side of Nisutlin Bridge. An excellent stop for a fresh lake trout dinner (or full menu), accompanied by good and friendly service topped off with a piece of fantastic rhubarb and strawberry pie (lots of fresh baking). Soft ice cream. Recently renovated. New for 1998 ... visit our Yukon wildlife display. Three satellite TV channels. Open year-round, summer hours 6 A.M.–11 P.M. New lakeshore RV park (mosquito control area), 70 sites, full and partial hookups. "Good Sam Park"—washhouse rated TL 9.5. A real home away from home on the shore of beautiful Nisutlin Bay. Phone (867) 390-2575. [ADVERTISEMENT] ▲

Nisutlin Bay bridge crosses the Nisutlin River at Teslin. It is the longest water span on the Alaska Highway. (Earl L. Brown, staff)

Teslin

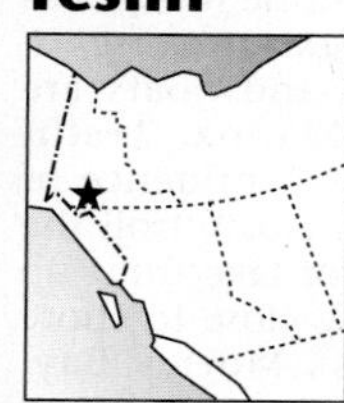

Located at **Historic Milepost 804,** 111 miles/179 km southeast of Whitehorse, 163 miles/263 km northwest of Watson Lake. **Population:** 482. **Emergency Services: RCMP,** phone (867) 390-5555 (if no answer call toll free 867/667-5555). **Fire Department,** phone (867) 390-2222. **Nurse,** phone (867) 390-4444.

Elevation: 2,239 feet/682.4m. **Climate:** Average temperature in January, -7°F/-22°C, in July 57°F/14°C. Annual snowfall 66.2 inches/168.2 cm. Driest month April, wettest month July. Average date of last spring frost is June 19; first fall frost Aug. 19. **Radio:** CBC 940; CHONFM 90.5; CKRW 98.7. **Television:** Channel 13.

The village of Teslin, situated on a point of land at the confluence of the Nisutlin River and Teslin Lake, began as a trading post in 1903. Today the community consists of a trading post, Catholic church, health centre and post office. There is a 3-sheet regulation curling rink and a skating rink.

Teslin has one of the largest Native populations in Yukon Territory and much of the community's livelihood revolves around traditional hunting, trapping and fishing. In addition, some Tlingit residents are involved in the development of Native woodworking crafts (canoes, snowshoes and sleds); traditional sewn art and craft items (moccasins, mitts, moose hair tufting, gun cases); and the tanning of moose hides.

George Johnston Museum is located on the left side of the highway heading north. The museum, operated by the Teslin Historical Museum Society (phone 867/390-2550), is open daily, 9 A.M. to 7 P.M. in summer; minimal admission fee, wheelchair accessible. The museum displays items from gold rush days and the pioneer mode of living, Indian artifacts and many items of Tlingit culture. A Tlingit Indian, George Johnston (1884–1972) was an innovative individual,

TESLIN ADVERTISERS

George Johnston Museum ....Ph. (867) 390-2550
Nisutlin Trading Post ....Ph. (867) 390-2521
Yukon Motel ....Ph. (867) 390-2575

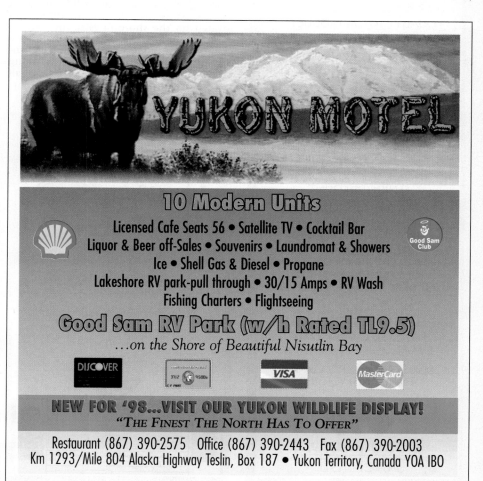

known for his trapping as well as his photography. With his camera he captured the life of the inland Tlingit people of Teslin and Atlin between 1910 and 1940. Johnston also brought the first car to Teslin, a 1928 Chevrolet. Since the Alaska Highway had not been built yet, George built a 3-mile road for his "Teslin taxi." In winter, he put chains on the car and drove it on frozen Teslin Lake. The '28 Chevy has been restored and is now on permanent display at the museum. ♿

Teslin is located west of the Alaska Highway, accessible via a short side road from the north end of Nisutlin Bay bridge. Nisutlin Trading Post in the village has groceries and general merchandise. Gas, diesel and propane, car repair, gift shop, restaurants and motels are found along the Alaska Highway.

Kayakers on the bank of the Teslin River at Johnson's Crossing. (© Beth Davidow)

There is 1 bank, located in the Tlingit Band office building; open Monday, Wednesday, Thursday and Friday, 11 A.M. to 2 P.M., in summer. The Teslin area has an air charter service, boat rentals and houseboat tours.

Nisutlin Trading Post, on short loop road, left northbound in Teslin Village. A pioneer store established in 1928, and located on the shore of Nisutlin Bay, an "arm" of Teslin Lake. This store handles a complete line of groceries, general merchandise including clothing, hardware, fishing tackle and licenses. Lottery tickets. Open all year 9 A.M. to 5:30 P.M. Closed Sunday. Founded by the late R. McCleery, Teslin pioneer, the trading post is now operated by Mr. and Mrs. Bob Hassard. Phone (867) 390-2521, fax 390-2103. [ADVERTISEMENT]

AREA FISHING: Guides and boats are available at Nisutlin Bay Marina. **Teslin Lake's Nisutlin Bay** (at the confluence of the Nisutlin River and Teslin Lake), troll the mud line in May and June for lake trout up to 25 lbs.; **Eagle Bay**, casting close to shore for northern pike to 15 lbs.; **Morley Bay**, excellent fishing for lake trout at south end of the bay's mouth, good fishing at the bay's shallow east side for northern pike to 10 lbs. **Morley River**, excellent fly fishing for grayling to 4 lbs. near river mouth and upriver several miles (by boat), fish deep water.

Alaska Highway Log

(continued)

Distance* from Dawson Creek (DC) is followed by distance from Fairbanks (F). Original mileposts are indicated in the text as Historical Mile.

*Mileages from Dawson Creek are based on actual driving distance. Kilometres from Dawson Creek are based on physical kilometreposts. Please read Mileposts and Kilometreposts in the introduction for an explanation of how this highway is logged.

DC 777 (1295 km) **F 711** (1144.2 km) **Historic Milepost 805. Private Aircraft:** Teslin airstrip to east; elev. 2,313 feet/705m; length 5,500 feet/1,676m; gravel; fuel 100, jet. Runway may be unusable during spring breakup.

DC 779.1 (1298.5 km) **F 708.9** (1140.8 km) **Historical Mile 807. Fox Point Lakeshore Resort.** See display ad this section. ▲

DC 779.5 (1299 km) **F 708.5** (1140.2 km) Fox Creek.

DC 784.3 (1306.7 km) **F 703.7** (1132.5 km) **Historical Mile 812.** Mukluk Annie's; food, lodging and camping. ▲

Mukluk Annie's Salmon Bake. See display ad this section. ▲

DC 785.2 (1308 km) **F 702.8** (1131 km) **Historical Mile 813.** Teslin Lake Yukon government campground to west; 27 sites (some level) in trees on **Teslin Lake,** water pump, litter barrels, kitchen shelter, firewood, firepits, picnic tables. Camping fee $8. Fishing. Boat launch 0.3 mile/0.5 km north of campground. ▲

DC 785.3 (1308.2 km) **F 702.7** (1130.8 km) Tenmile Creek.

DC 788.9 (1314 km) **F 699.1** (1125 km) Lone Tree Creek.

DC 794.6 (1323 km) **F 693.4** (1115.9 km) Deadman's Creek.

DC 800.8 (1333.3 km) **F 687.2** (1105.9 km) Robertson Creek.

DC 801.6 (1334.4 km) **F 686.4** (1104.6 km) **Historic Milepost 829.** Brooks' Brook. According to R.C. Coutts in *Yukon: Places & Names,* this stream was named by black Army engineers, who completed this section of road in 1942, for their company officer, Lieutenant Brooks.

DC 808.2 (1345 km) **F 679.8** (1094 km) **Junction** with the Canol Road (Yukon Highway 6) which leads northeast to the Campbell Highway. (See the CANOL ROAD section for details.) Historic sign and interpretive panel about the Canol Project.

The Canol (Canadian Oil) Road was built in 1942–44 to provide access to oil fields at Norman Wells, NWT. Conceived by the U.S. War Dept., the $134 million project was abandoned soon after the war ended in 1945. Canol truck "graveyard" nearby.

DC 808.6 (1345.6 km) **F 679.4** (1093.3 km) Teslin River bridge, third longest water span on the highway (1,770 feet/539m), was constructed with a very high clearance above the river to permit steamers of the British Yukon Navigation Co. to pass under it en route from Whitehorse to Teslin. River steamers ceased operation on the Teslin River in 1942. Before the construction of the Alaska Highway, all freight and supplies for Teslin traveled this water route from Whitehorse.

DC 808.9 (1346 km) **F 679.1** (1092.9 km) **Historic Milepost 836. JOHNSON'S CROSSING** to east at north end of bridge; store, food and camping. One of the original lodges on the Alaska Highway, the history of Johnson's Crossing is related in Ellen Davignon's *The Cinnamon Mine.* Access to Teslin River; boat launch, no camping on riverbank. ▲

Johnson's Crossing Campground Services. Located across the Teslin River bridge, home of the "world famous cinnamon buns," including a small store with a full array of mouth-watering baked goods, souvenirs and groceries. Full-service RV campground facilities include treed pull-throughs, complete laundry and washhouse facilities, Chevron gasoline products, cold beer and ice, and great fishing. Treat yourselves to the historically scenic Km 1346 (Mile 836) Alaska Highway, YT Y1A 9Z0. Phone (867) 390-2607. [ADVERTISEMENT] ▲

Teslin River, excellent grayling fishing from spring to late fall, 10 to 15 inches, use spinner or red-and-white spoons for spinning or black gnat for fly-fishing. King salmon in August.

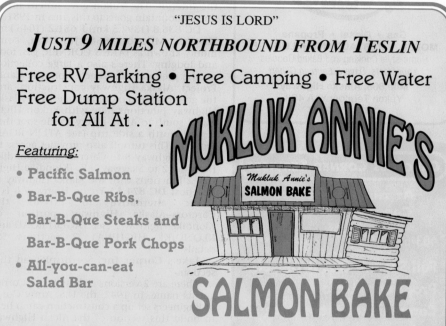

Canoeists report that the Teslin River is wide and slow, but with gravel, rocks and weeds. Adequate camping sites on numerous sand bars; boil drinking water. Abundant wildlife—muskrat, porcupine, moose, eagles and wolves—also bugs and rain. Watch for bear. The Teslin enters the Yukon River at Hootalinqua, an old steamboat landing and supply point (under restoration). Roaring Bull rapids: choppy water. Pull out at Carmacks. Inquire locally about river conditions before setting out.

DC 809.1 (1346.5 km) **F 678.9** (1092.5 km) Access road east to the Teslin River. The Big Salmon Range, also to the east, parallels the Teslin. For Alaska-bound travelers, the highway now swings west.

DC 812.8 (1352.5 km) **F 675.2** (1086.6 km) Little Teslin Lake on south side of highway.

DC 819.8 (1364 km) **F 668.2** (1075.3 km) In mid-June, the roadside is a profusion of purple Jacob's ladder and yellow dandelions.

DC 820.3 (1364.8 km) **F 667.7** (1074.5 km) Seaforth Creek bridge.

DC 820.4 (1365 km) **F 667.6** (1074.4 km) Large turnout to south; picnic area.

DC 820.6 (1365.3 km) **F 667.4** (1074 km) Squanga Lake to northwest. Named Squanga by Indians for a type of whitefish of the same name found in the lake. Watch for **Historic Milepost 843,** with historic sign about Squanga Lake flightstrip. Look for the eagle's nest in the old observation tower.

DC 821 (1366 km) **F 667** (1073.4 km) Turnoff to northwest to **Squanga Lake** Yukon government campground: 13 sites, kitchen shelter, drinking water. Small boat launch. Fishing for northern pike, grayling, whitefish, rainbow and burbot.

DC 827.5 (1376.8 km) **F 660.5** (1062.9 km) White Mountain, to the southeast, was named by William Ogilvie during his 1887 survey, for Thomas White, then Minister of the Interior. The Yukon government introduced mountain goats to this area in 1981.

DC 836.8 (1392.5 km) **F 651.2** (1048 km) **Historic Milepost 866. Junction,** commonly known as **JAKE'S CORNER;** gas, food and lodging. There's also a large collection on the premises of artifacts from the Canol Project, Alaska Highway construction, and the gold rush and other antiques. The Alaska Highway junctions here with Yukon Highway 7 south to Atlin, a very scenic spot that is well worth a side trip (see ATLIN ROAD section). This turnoff also provides access to Yukon Highway 8 to Carcross and Klondike Highway 2 to Skagway, AK. (Klondike Highway 2 junctions with the Alaska Highway at **Milepost DC 874.4.**) Yukon Highway 8 is a scenic alternative to driving the Carcross–Alaska Highway portion of Klondike Highway 2 (see TAGISH ROAD and KLONDIKE HIGHWAY 2 sections for details).

Jake's Corner Inc. See display ad this section.

There are 2 versions of how Jake's Corner got its name. In 1942, the U.S. Army Corps of Engineers set up a construction camp here to build this section of the Alcan Highway and the Tagish Road cutoff to Carcross for the Canol pipeline. (The highway south to Atlin, BC, was not constructed until 1949–50.) The camp was under the command of Captain Jacobson, thus Jake's Corner. However, another version that predates the Alcan construction is that Jake's Corner was named for Jake Jackson, a Teslin Indian who camped in this area on his way to Carcross. Roman "Jake" Chaykowsky (1900–1995) operated Jake's Corner Service here for many years. It was known locally as The Crystal Palace, after the first lodge Chaykowsky had owned at Judas Creek, just up the road.

DC 843.2 (1402.7 km) **F 644.8** (1037.7 km) Judas Creek bridge.

DC 850 (1413.5 km) **F 638** (1026.7 km) Turnoff to west for Lakeview Resort on Marsh Lake; camping, lodging, restaurant, boat rentals and boat launch. ▲

Marsh Lake, excellent fishing for grayling and northern pike.

DC 851.6 (1416 km) **F 636.4** (1024.1 km) Several access roads along here which lead to summer cottages. Marsh Lake is a popular recreation area for Whitehorse residents.

DC 852.7 (1417.8 km) **F 635.3** (1022.4 km) Good view of Marsh Lake to west. The highway parallels this beautiful lake for several miles. Marsh Lake (elev. 2,152 feet/656m) is part of the Yukon River system. It is approximately 20 miles/32 km long and was named in 1883 by Lt. Frederick Schwatka, U.S. Army, for Yale professor Othniel Charles Marsh.

DC 854.4 (1421 km) **F 633.6** (1019.6 km) **Historic Milepost 883,** Marsh Lake Camp historic sign. Boat ramp turnoff to west.

DC 854.8 (1421.2 km) **F 633.2** (1019 km) Caribou Road leads northwest to Airplane Lake; hiking trail, good skiing and snowmachining in winter. This road was bulldozed out to get men and equipment into a small lake where an airplane had made an emergency landing.

DC 859.9 (1432 km) **F 628.1** (1010.8 km) **Historical Mile 890.** Turnoff to west for Marsh Lake Yukon government campground via 0.4-mile/0.6-km gravel loop road: 47 sites, most level, some pull-through; outhouses, firewood, firepits, litter barrels, picnic tables, kitchen shelter, water pump. Camping fee $8. ▲

For group camping and day-use area, follow signs near campground entrance. Day-use area includes sandy beach, change house, picnic area, playground, kitchen shelter and boat launch.

DC 861.1 (1433.9 km) **F 626.9** (1008.9 km) M'Clintock River, named by Lieutenant Schwatka for Arctic explorer Sir Francis M'Clintock. This river flows into the north end of Marsh Lake. Boat ramp turnoff to west at north end of bridge. M'Clintock River is narrow, winding and silty with thick brush along shoreline. However, it is a good river for boat trips, especially in late fall.

DC 864.3 (1437 km) **F 623.7** (1003.7 km) Bridge over Kettley's Canyon.

DC 867.3 (1441.8 km) **F 620.7** (998.9 km) **Historic Milepost 897.** Yukon River bridge. Turnout to north for day-use area and boat launch on **Yukon River** at Marsh Lake bridge near Northern Canada Power Commission (NCPC) control gate. Point of interest sign and litter barrels. From here (elev. 2,150 feet/645m) the Yukon River flows 1,980 miles/3,186 km to the Bering Sea. Good fishing for grayling, jackfish and some trout.

DC 873.5 (1453.3 km) **F 614.5** (988.9 km) **Historical Mile 904.** Sourdough Country Campsite to east. ▲

DC 874.4 (1455 km) **F 613.6** (987.5 km) **Historical Mile 905. Junction** with Klondike Highway 2 (Carcross Road) which leads south to Carcross and Skagway. (See KLONDIKE HIGHWAY 2 section.) Restaurant, convenience store, gas, diesel, propane, car repair and rock shop here.

Carcross Corner Services. See display ad this section.

Yukon Rock Shop. See display ad this section.

Examining the archaeological excavation at Canyon City, reached by hiking trail from Miles Canyon bridge. (Earl L. Brown, staff)

DC 874.6 (1455.3 km) **F 613.4** (987.1 km) Whitehorse city limits. Incorporated June 1, 1950, Whitehorse expanded in 1974 from its original 2.7 square miles/6.9 square kilometres to 162 square miles/421 square kilometres.

DC 875.6 (1456.9 km) **F 612.4** (985.5 km) Kara Speedway to west.

DC 875.9 (1457.4 km) **F 612.1** (985 km) Cowley Creek.

DC 876.8 (1459 km) **F 611.2** (983.6 km) **Historical Mile 906.** Wolf Creek Yukon government campground to east. An 0.8-mile/1.3-km gravel loop road leads through this campground: 49 sites, most level, some pull-through; kitchen shelters, water pumps, picnic tables, firepits, firewood, outhouses, litter barrels, playground. Wolf Creek self-guiding trail; varied and abundant plant life, views of and access to Yukon River. Camping fee $8. Fishing in **Wolf Creek** for grayling. ▲

DC 879.4 (1463 km) **F 608.6** (979.4 km) Highway crosses abandoned railroad tracks of the White Pass & Yukon Route (WP&YR) narrow-gauge railroad. Construction of the WP&YR began in May 1898 at the height of the Klondike Gold Rush. Completion of the railway in 1900 linked the port of Skagway, AK, with Whitehorse, YT, providing passenger and freight service for thousands of gold seekers. The WP&YR ceased operation in 1982, but started limited service again in 1988 between Skagway and Fraser.

DC 879.6 (1463.3 km) **F 608.4** (979.1 km) Point of interest sign about 135th meridian to east; small turnout. Gas station.

DC 879.8 (1463.7 km) **F 608.2** (978.8 km) **Historic Milepost 910.** Historic sign reads: "McCrae originated in 1900 as a flag stop on the newly-constructed White Pass & Yukon Railway. During WWII, this area served as a major service and supply depot, a major construction camp and a recreation centre." McCrae truck stop to east.

DC 880.4 (1464.5 km) **F 607.6** (977.8 km) Turnoff to west for Whitehorse Copper Mines (closed). Road to east leads to Yukon River.

DC 881 (1465.5 km) **F 607** (976.8 km) **Historic Milepost 911.** Site of Utah Construction Co. Camp. Pioneer RV Park, store and self-serve gas to east. ▲

DC 881.3 (1466 km) **F 606.7** (976.4 km) White Pass & Yukon Route's Utah siding to east. This was also the site of an Army camp where thousands of soldiers were stationed during construction of the Alaska Highway.

DC 881.7 (1466.6 km) **F 606.3** (975.7 km) Sharp turnoff to east (watch for camera viewpoint sign) to see Miles Canyon. Drive down side road 0.3 mile/0.5 km to fork. The right fork leads to Miles Canyon parking lot. From the parking area it is a short walk to the Miles Canyon bridge; good photo spot. Cross bridge for easy hiking trails overlooking Yukon River. A 1.1-mile/1.7-km hiking trail from the bridge leads to the historic site of **CANYON CITY**, a gold rush settlement that existed from 1897 to 1900 as a portage point around Miles Canyon and Whitehorse Rapids. Two tramways, each several miles long, transported goods along the east and west sides of the river. Completion of the White Pass & Yukon Route in 1900 made the trams obsolete, and the settlement was abandoned. Canyon City is currently undergoing archaeological excavation. Interpreter on site weekdays in July and part of August. No restrooms or litter barrels available at site; plan accordingly.

The left fork on this side road leads to Schwatka Lake Road, which follows the lake and intersects the South Access Road into Whitehorse. Turnouts along road overlook Miles Canyon.

DC 881.9 (1466.9 km) **F 606.1** (975.4 km) Riding stable with daily trail rides in summer.

DC 882.6 (1468 km) **F 605.4** (974.3 km) **Historical Mile 912. Philmar RV Service and Supply.** See display ad this section.

DC 882.9 (1468.5 km) **F 605.1** (973.8 km) **Mountain Ridge Motel & RV Park.** See display ad this section. ▲

DC 883.2 (1468.9 km) **F 604.8** (973.3 km) **Historical Mile 913. Whitehorse Shell.** See display ad this section.

DC 883.7 (1469.7 km) **F 604.3** (972.5 km) Turnout to east with litter barrel, out-

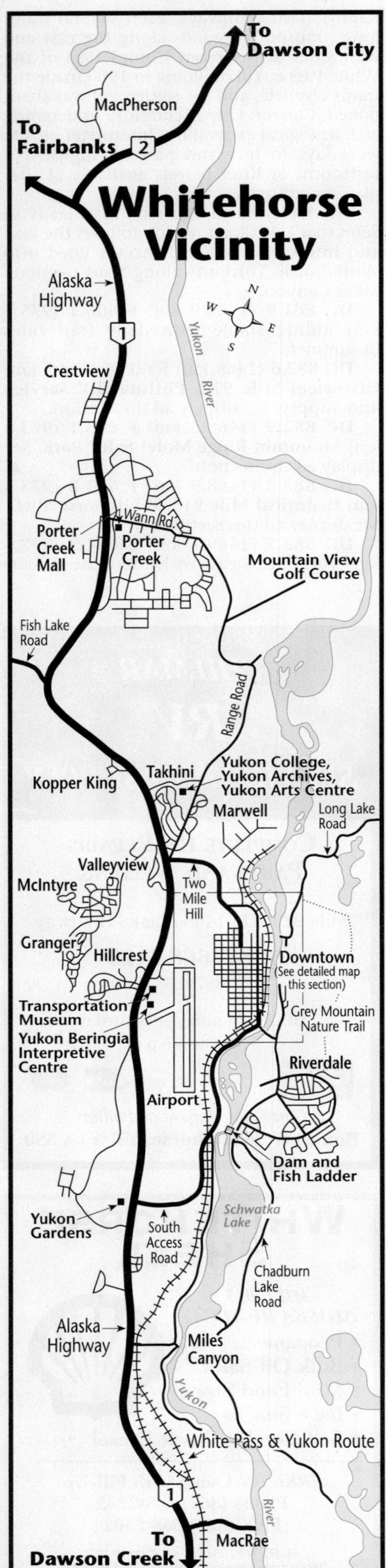

houses and information sign.

DC 884 (1470.2 km) **F 604** (972 km) **Hi-Country R.V. Park.** Good Sam. New facilities to serve the traveler. Large wooded

sites, 30-amp electric and water hookups, dump station, hot clean showers, some serviced sites. Picnic tables and firepits, gift shop with wildlife display. Conveniently located on the highway at the south access to Whitehorse. Just 2 minutes by vehicle to Miles Canyon, the Beringia Centre and the Transportation Museum. Mile 913.4 Alaska Highway. P.O. Box 6081, Whitehorse, YT Y1A 5L7; phone (867) 667-7445, fax (867) 668-6342. See display ad this section. [ADVERTISEMENT] ▲

DC 884 (1470.2 km) **F 604** (972 km). First exit northbound for Whitehorse. Exit east for Robert Service Way (also known as South Access Road) to Whitehorse via 4th Avenue and 2nd Avenue. At the turnoff is Yukon Gardens botanical exhibit. At Mile 1.4/2.3 km on this access road is the side road to Miles Canyon and Schwatka Lake; at Mile 1.6/2.6 km is Robert Service Campground (tent camping only) with a picnic area for day use; at Mile 2.6/4.2 km is the SS *Klondike* National Historic Site, turn left for downtown Whitehorse. ▲

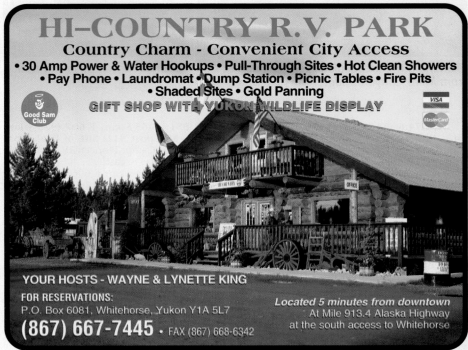

DC 884.5 (1471.1 km) **F 603.5** (971.2 km) Government weigh scale and vehicle

inspection station to west.

DC 885.7 (1472.9 km) **F 602.3** (969.3 km) Site of the new (1997) Yukon Beringia Interpretive Centre. The centre displays Ice Age artifacts, including a cast of the largest woolly mammoth skeleton ever recovered. Open daily late May to mid-September. Phone (867) 667-8895, fax (867) 667-8844.

DC 885.8 (1473.1 km) **F 602.2** (969.1 km) Yukon Transportation Museum features exhibits on all forms of transportation in the North (see Attractions in the WHITEHORSE section for more details). A mural on the front of the museum depicts the methods of transportation used in construction of the Alaska Highway in 1942. The 16-by-60-foot/5-by-8-m mural was painted by members of the Yukon Art Society. Open mid-May to mid-September. Admission fee.

Cairns in front of the museum commemorate 18 years of service on the Alaska Highway (1946–64) by the Corps of Royal Canadian Engineers. Near this site, the U.S. Army officially handed over the Alaska Highway to the Canadian Army on April 1, 1946.

Yukon Transportation Museum. See display ad this section.

DC 886.2 (1473.8 km) **F 601.8** (968.5 km) Turnoff to east for Whitehorse International Airport. Built for and used by both U.S. and Canadian forces during WWII. Watch for the DC–3 weathervane (see Attractions in the WHITEHORSE section for details).

DC 887.4 (1475.6 km) **F 600.6** (966.5 km) Second (and last) exit northbound for Whitehorse. North access road to Whitehorse (exit east) is via Two-Mile Hill and 4th Avenue. Access to private RV park. At Mile 1.2/1.9 km on this access road is Qwanlin Mall.

Alaska Highway log continues on page 159. Description of Whitehorse follows.

Whitehorse

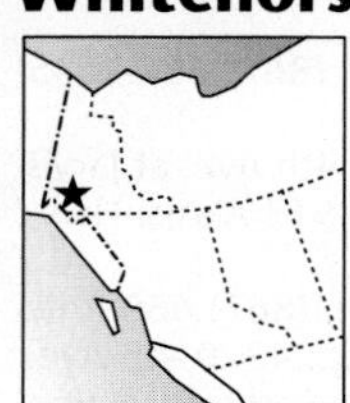

Historic Milepost 918. Located on the upper reaches of the Yukon River in Canada's subarctic at latitude 61°N. Whitehorse is 100 miles/160 km from Haines Junction; 109 miles/175 km from Skagway, AK; 250 miles/241 km from Haines, AK; and 396 miles/637 km from Tok, AK. **Population:** 23,474. **Emergency Services: RCMP, Fire Department, Ambulance, Hospital,** phone 911.

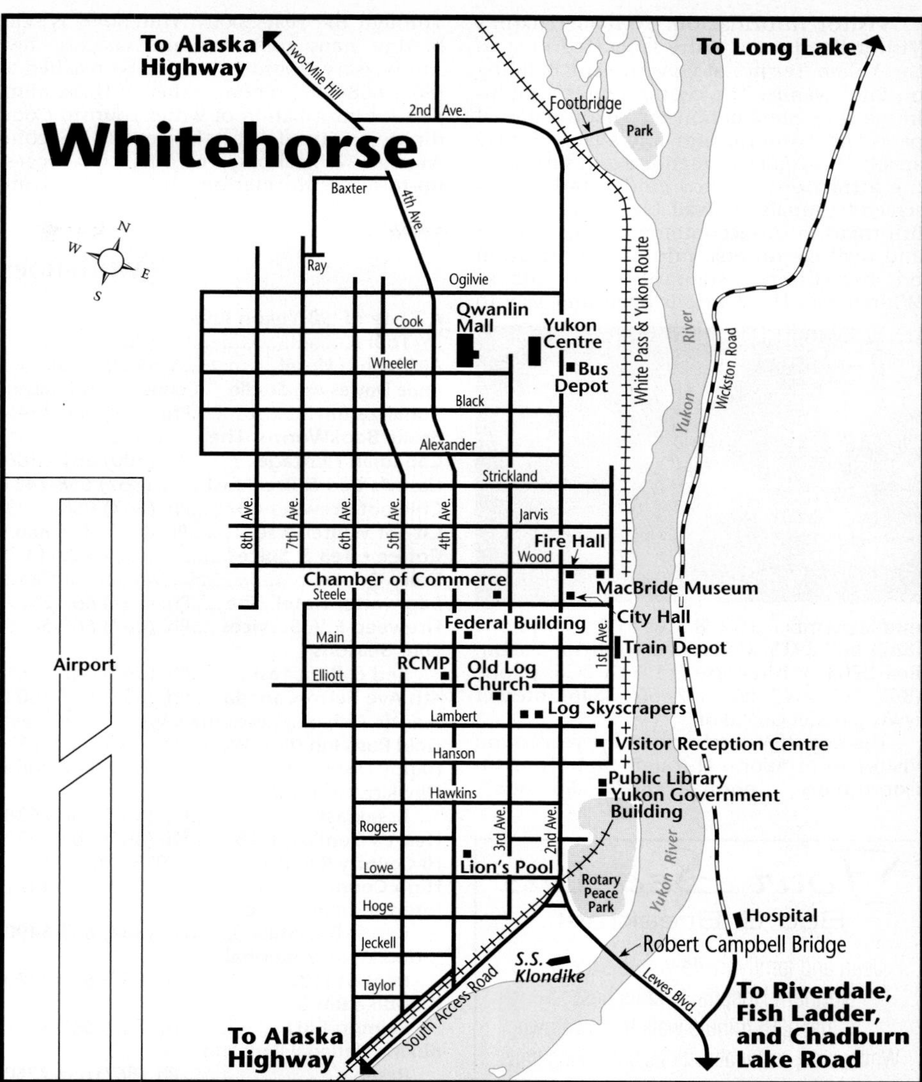

Whitehorse replaced Dawson City as capital of Yukon Territory in 1953.

Visitor Information: Tourism Yukon's Visitor Reception Centre is located next to the Yukon Territorial Government Building on 2nd Avenue. The centre houses a multi-image slide presentation on Yukon national parks and historical sites, and a large display area that includes Whitehorse and surrounding attractions. Visitor guides and touch-screen terminals are available; daily, updated information on accommodations, weather and road conditions; printout information on attractions, restaurants or events in Whitehorse. The centre is open mid-May to

mid-September daily 8 A.M. to 8 P.M.; phone (867) 667-2915. Or contact Tourism Yukon, Box 2703, Whitehorse, YT Y1A 2C6; phone (867) 667-5340; fax (867) 667-3546; Internet www.parallel.ca/Yukon.

The city of Whitehorse offers year-round visitor information through their Tourism Coordinator; phone (867) 668-8687. Through the year 2000, Whitehorse is celebrating many gold rush anniversaries; their Anniversary Coordinator can be reached at (867) 668-8665. Phone either of these numbers for information or write: Tourism Coordinator, City of Whitehorse, 2121 Second Avenue, Whitehorse, YT Y1A 1C2. Access up-to-date information on events, accommodations and attractions on the City of Whitehorse Internet web page at www.City.Whitehorse.YK.ca.

Whitehorse Visitor Radio, CKYN "Yukon Gold" 96.1 FM, broadcasts current events as well as heritage and Gold Rush anniversary event information. Tune in at the City Limits for approximately 30 minutes of driv-

WHITEHORSE ADVERTISERS

A Taste of '98 Yukon River Tours ....Ph. (867) 633-4767
Airline Inn Hotel ....Across from airport
Anne Doyles Art Studio ....Corner 2nd & Lambert
Bonanza Inn ....Ph. (867) 668-4545
Broke BookWorms, The ....210B Ogilvie St.
Canadian Heritage ....Ph. (800) 661-0486
Casey's Bed & Breakfast ....Ph. (867) 668-7481
Chilkoot Brewing Co. ....Ph. (867) 668-4183
City of Whitehorse ....Ph. (867) 668-8665
Coffee • Tea & Spice ....Qwanlin Mall
Dairy Queen ....2nd Ave. at Elliott
Edgewater Hotel, The ....Ph. (867) 667-2572
Fireweed R.V. Services ....Ph. (867) 668-5046
Four Seasons Bed & Breakfast ....Ph. (867) 667-2161
4th Ave Petro-Canada ....Ph. (867) 667-4003
Frantic Follies ....Westmark Whitehorse Hotel
Gold Rush Inn (Best Western) ....411 Main St.
Happy Daze R.V. Center ....Ph. (867) 667-7069
Hawkins House Bed & Breakfast ....Ph. (867) 668-7638
Heart's Content B&B ....Ph. (867) 667-4972
Hi-Country R.V. Park ....Mile 913.4 Alaska Hwy.
High Country Inn ....Ph. (800) 554-4471
International House Bed & Breakfast ....Ph. (867) 633-5490
Klondike Recreational Rentals Ltd. ....Ph. (867) 668-2200
Klondike Rib & Salmon BBQ ....Ph. (867) 667-7554
Kluane National Park and Reserve ....Ph. (867) 634-7250
Learning to Fly Fly Shop ....Ph. (867) 668-FLYS
MacBride Museum ....Ph. (867) 667-2709
MacKenzie's RV Park ....Km 1484 Alaska Hwy.
Mac's Fireweed Books ....203 Main St.
Midnight Sun Gallery & Gifts ....205C Main St.
Mohawk Gas Bar ....Mile 916 Alaska Hwy.
Murdoch's ....207 Main St.
1940's Canteen Show ....see ad this section
Norcan Car and Truck Rentals ....Ph. (867) 668-2137
North West Company Trading Post, The ....Next to bus depot
NorthwesTel ....see ad for locations
Pioneer RV Park ....Ph. (867) 668-5944
Pizza Hut ....Ph. (867) 667-6766
Pot O' Gold ....4th Ave. & Wood
Qwanlin Mall, The ....4th Ave. & Ogilvie
river view Hotel ....Ph. (867) 677-7801
Sandor's Main Man ....at the Qwanlin Mall
SkyJacker Lounge ....Ph. (867) 668-4410
Special Discoveries. ....Ph. (867) 667-6765
Spring Shop, The ....Mile 922 Alaska Hwy.
S.S. *Klondike* National Historical Site ....Ph. (867) 634-7250
Stop In Family Hotel ....Ph. (867) 668-5558
Stratford Motel ....Ph. (867) 667-4243
Sourdough Country Campsite ....Ph. (867) 668-2961
Tagish Wilderness Lodge ....Tagish Rd.
Takhini Hot Springs ....Takhini Hot Springs Rd.
Thomas Cook ....Ph. (867) 668-2867
Three Beans Natural Foods ....Ph. (867) 668-4908
Tirecraft ....Ph. (867) 667-4251
Totem Oil ....Ph. (800) 661-0550
Town & Mountain Hotel, The ....Ph. (867) 668-7644
Trail of '98 RV Park ....Ph. (867) 668-3768
Trails North Car & Truck Stop Ltd. ....Mile 922 Alaska Hwy.
Up North Bed & Breakfast, Boat & Canoe Rentals ....Ph. (867) 667-7905
Wharf on Fourth, The ....Ph. (867) 667-7473
Westmark Klondike Inn ....Ph. (800) 544-0970
Westmark Whitehorse ....Ph. (800) 544-0970
Whitehorse Chamber of Commerce ....Ph. (867) 667-7545
Whitehorse Performance Centre ....4th Ave. at Jarvis
Whitehorse Shell ....Mile 913 Alaska Hwy.
White Pass & Yukon Route ....Ph. (867) 668-RAIL
Yukon Inn, The ....4220 4th Ave.
Yukon Mining Co. ....see ad this section
Yukon Radiator ....108 Industrial Rd.
Yukon Tire Centre Ltd. ....107 Industrial Rd.
Yukon Transportation Museum ....Ph. (867) 668-4792

Yukon became a territory on June 13, 1898.

ing and listening before reaching the downtown Visitor Reception Centre.

SS *Klondike* greets the visitor arriving in Whitehorse from the South. This site, operated by Parks Canada, has a visitor centre with helpful information for tourists.

Elevation: 2,305 feet/703m. **Climate:** Wide variations are the theme here with no two winters alike. The lowest recorded temperature is -62°F/-52°C and the warmest 94°F/35°C. Mean temperature for month of January is -6°F/-21°C and for July 57°F/14°C. Annual precipitation is 10.3 inches, equal parts snow and rain. On June 21 Whitehorse enjoys 19 hours, 11 minutes of daylight and on Dec. 21 only 5 hours, 37 minutes. **Radio:** CFWH 570, CBC network with repeaters throughout territory; CBC Montreal; CKRW 610, local; CKYN-FM 96.1, summer visitor information station "Yukon Gold" broadcasts mid-May to mid-September; CHON-FM 98.1. **Television:** CBC–TV live, colour via ANIK satellite, Canadian network; WHTV, NADR (First Nation issues), local cable; CanCom stations via satellite, many channels. **Newspapers:** *Whitehorse Star* (weekdays); *Yukon News* (twice-weekly).

Private Aircraft: Whitehorse International Airport, 3 runways; has approach over city and an abrupt escarpment; elev. 2,305 feet/703m; main runway length 7,200 feet/2,195m; surfaced; fuel 80, 100, jet fuel available. Customs clearance available.

Floatplane base on Schwatka Lake above

Whitehorse Welcomes you!

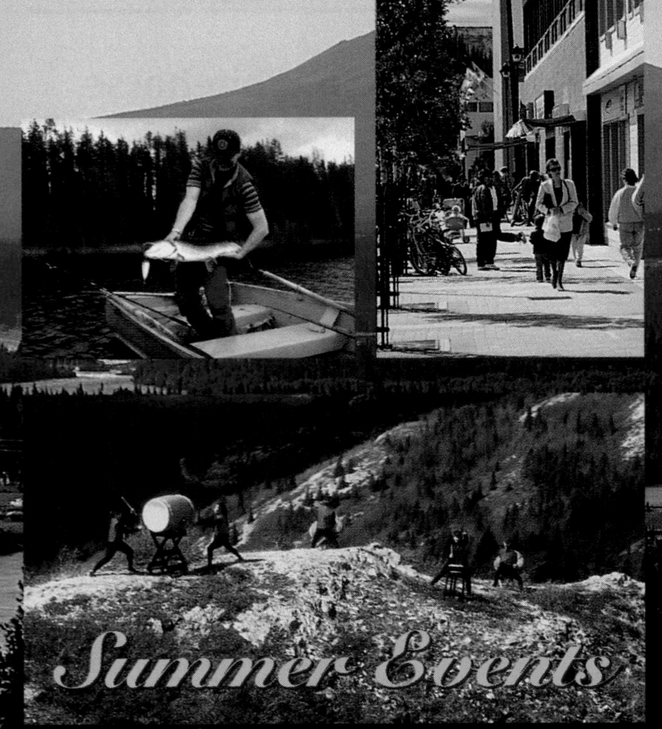

This is your year to visit the Yukon!

Summer Events

May to August
"Summer Arts in the Park"
LePage Park.

May 1-3
Yukon Trade Show.

June 18-21
Yukon International
Storytelling Festival

June 21
Summer Solstice.

June 26-28
1998 Gathering of the Clans

June 28-July 4
Canadian National Rifle
Silhouette Championship

July to August
British Klondikers
Commemorative
Expedition: Trail of '98

July 1
Canada Day
Event of the summer!
Parade, all day and
evening entertainment.
Too much fun! All

July 1-5
Alaska State Square and Round
Dance Festival

Over 400 dancers from Canada
and U.S. participate.

July 1
Great Canadian Rubber Ducky
Race

July 5-18
Follow the Gold Rush Stampede
- Girl Guides of Canada

July 10-12
Yukon Rodeo

July 17/18
Go for Gold Sister Cities Golf
Tournament

August 2-8
Scouts Gold Rush Jamboree

August 6-9
Trail of 98 Orienteering Festival

August 14-17
Sourdough Yukon Bathtub Race

August 15
2nd Annual Discovery Days
Celebration

Pancake breakfast, Dance,
entertainment all day

August 21-23
Klondike Harvest Fair

September 11/12
Klondike Trail of 98
International Road Relay -
Skagway to Whitehorse. Huge
event with teams from Canada
and U.S.

Whitehorse welcomes visitors travelling the Alaska Highway. Take time to stay in the Capital of Yukon and enjoy some of our warm Yukon hospitality. There is lots to see and do in Whitehorse and the surrounding areas: great Fishing, beautiful Hotsprings, trips on the historic Yukon River, a walking tour of our downtown, great shopping, exciting entertainment from Vaudeville to Bach, an interpreted River Walk, Golf under the midnight sun, wildlife viewing, restaurants both casual and chic, tons of summer events and Goldrush celebrations, and a gorgeous new Visitor Reception Centre with easy access RV Parking.

Whitehorse provides RV Parking, at the waterfront and throughout the city core. We have some of the best RV Campgrounds surrounding us, with the nicest hosts you would wish to meet. Please take your time to enjoy us for a few days. Stop in at the City Hall for more information, sign our guest book and collect your city pin. Call or write ahead to

Tourism,
City of Whitehorse,
2121, 2nd Avenue
Whitehorse, Yukon
(867) 668-8687

Places to see

SS Klondike Sternwheeler
Mac Bride Museum
Yukon Transportation Museum
Yukon Arts Centre Gallery
Yukon Berengia Interpretive Centre
Miles Canyon
Canyon City
Whitehorse Fishway
Old Log Church
LePage Park, Heritage walking tour
The Visitor Reception Centre and film
The Yukon River by boat
All the great nightly entertainment

Day Trips

Skagway and the Whitepass and Yukon Route Railway, Kukatsoon Lake, the Hot Springs, Ibex Valley, Marsh Lake and Swan Haven wildlife viewing, Atlin, Fox Lake, Carcross and the smallest dessert in the world

Rotary Peace Park hosts a number of special events, such as the Yukon International Storytelling Festival shown here. (Earl L. Brown, staff)

Whitehorse Dam (take the South Access Road from Alaska Highway and turn on road by the railroad tracks).

DESCRIPTION

Whitehorse has been the capital of Yukon Territory since 1953, and serves as the centre for transportation, communications and supplies for Yukon Territory and the Northwest Territories.

The downtown business section of Whitehorse lies on the west bank of the Yukon River. The Riverdale subdivision is on the east side. The low mountains rising behind Riverdale are dominated by Canyon Mountain, known locally as Grey Mountain. Wolf Creek, Hillcrest and Granger subdivisions lie south of the city; McIntyre subdivision is to the west; and Porter Creek, Takhini and Crestview subdivisions are north of the city. The Takhini area is the location of the Yukon College campus.

Downtown Whitehorse is flat and marked at its western limit by a rising escarpment dominated by the Whitehorse International Airport. Originally a woodcutter's lot, the airstrip was first cleared in 1920 to accommodate 4 U.S. Army planes on a test flight from New York to Nome. Access to the city is by Two-Mile Hill from the north and by Robert Service Way (South Access Road) from the south; both connect with the Alaska Highway.

In 1974, the city limits of Whitehorse were expanded from the original 2.7 square miles/6.9 square kilometres to 162 square miles/421 square kilometres, making Whitehorse at one time the largest metropolitan area in Canada. More than two-thirds of the population of Yukon Territory live in the city. Whitehorse is the hub of a network of about 2,664 miles/4,287 km of all-weather roads serving Yukon Territory.

HISTORY, ECONOMY

When the White Pass & Yukon Route railway was completed in July 1900, connecting Skagway with the Yukon River, Whitehorse came into being as the northern terminus. Here the famed river steamers connected the railhead to Dawson City, and some of these boats made the trip all the way to St. Michael, a small outfitting point on Alaska's Bering Sea coast.

Klondike stampeders landed at Whitehorse to dry out and repack their supplies after running the famous Whitehorse Rapids. (The name Whitehorse was in common use by the late 1800s; it is believed that the first miners in the area thought that the foaming rapids resembled white horses' manes and so named the river rapids.) The rapids are no longer visible since construction of the Yukon Energy Corporation's hydroelectric dam on the river. This dam created man-made Schwatka Lake, named in honour of U.S. Army Lt. Frederick Schwatka, who named many of the points along the Yukon River during his 1883 exploration of the region.

The gold rush brought stampeders and the railroad. The community grew as a transportation centre and trans-shipment point for freight from the Skagway–Whitehorse railroad and the stern-wheelers plying the Yukon River to Dawson City. The river was the only highway until WWII, when military expediency built the Alaska Highway in 1942.

Whitehorse was headquarters for the western sector during construction of the Alaska Highway. Fort St. John was headquarters for the eastern sector. Both were the largest construction camps on the highway.

The first survey parties of U.S. Army engineers reached Whitehorse in April of 1942. By the end of August, they had constructed a pioneer road from Whitehorse west to White River, largely by following an existing winter trail between Whitehorse and Kluane Lake. November brought the final breakthrough on the western end of the highway, marking completion of the pioneer road.

During the height of the construction of the Alaska Highway, thousands of American military and civilian workers were employed in the Canadian North. It was the second boom period for Whitehorse.

There was an economic lull following the war, but the new highway was then opened to civilian travel, encouraging new development. Mineral exploration and the development of new mines had a profound effect on the economy of the region, as did the steady growth of tourism. The Whitehorse Copper Mine, located a few miles south of the city in the historic Whitehorse copper belt, is now closed. The Grum Mine site north of Faro produced lead, silver and zinc concentrates for Cyprus–Anvil (1969– 1982), Curragh Resources (1986–1992) and Anvil Range Mining Corp. (1994–present). Stop by the Yukon Chamber of Mines office on Main Street for information on mining and rockhounding in Yukon Territory. The Chamber of Mines log building also houses a mineral display.

Because of its accessibility, Whitehorse became capital of the Yukon Territory (replacing Dawson City in that role) on March 31, 1953.

Bridges built along the highway to Dawson City, after Whitehorse became capital of the territory, were too low to accommodate the old river steamers, and by 1955 all steamers had been beached. After her last run in 1960, the SS *Keno* was berthed on the riverbank in Dawson City where she became a national historic site in 1962. The SS *Klondike* was moved through the streets of Whitehorse in 1966 to its final resting place as a riverboat museum beside the Robert Campbell bridge.

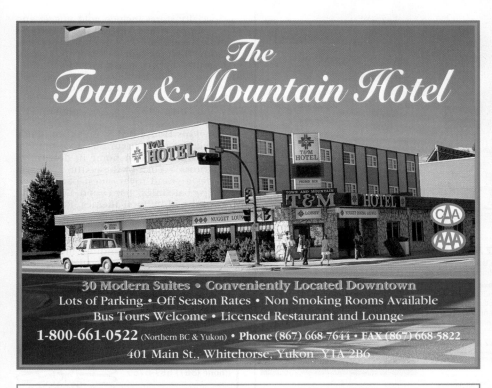

ACCOMMODATIONS/VISITOR SERVICES

Whitehorse offers 22 hotels and motels for a total of about 840 rooms. Several hotels include conference facilities; most have cocktail lounges, licensed dining rooms and taverns. Rates range from $60 to $150 for a double room with bath. Bed-and-breakfast accommodations are also available.

The city has 31 restaurants downtown and in surrounding residential subdivisions that serve meals ranging from French cuisine to fast food; 14 have liquor licenses.

Whitehorse has a downtown shopping district stretching along Main Street. The Qwanlin Mall at 4th Avenue and Ogilvie has a supermarket and a variety of shops. The Yukon Centre Mall on 2nd Avenue has a liquor store. The Riverdale Mall is located on the east side of the river in the Riverdale subdivision. Another shopping mall is located in the Porter Creek subdivision north of the city on the Alaska Highway.

In addition to numerous supermarkets, garages and service stations, there are churches, movie houses, beauty salons and a covered swimming pool. Whitehorse also has several banks with automatic teller machines. (Many businesses in Whitehorse participate in the Fair Exchange Program, which guarantees an exchange rate within 4 percent of the bank rate set once a week on Mondays. Participating businesses display the Fair Exchange logo.)

NOTE: There is no central post office in Whitehorse. Postal services are available in Qwanlin Mall at Coffee • Tea & Spice; The Hougen Centre on Main Street (lower floor below Shoppers Drugs); and in Riverdale and Porter Creek subdivisions. Stamps are available at several locations. General delivery pickup at corner of 3rd Avenue and Wood Street.

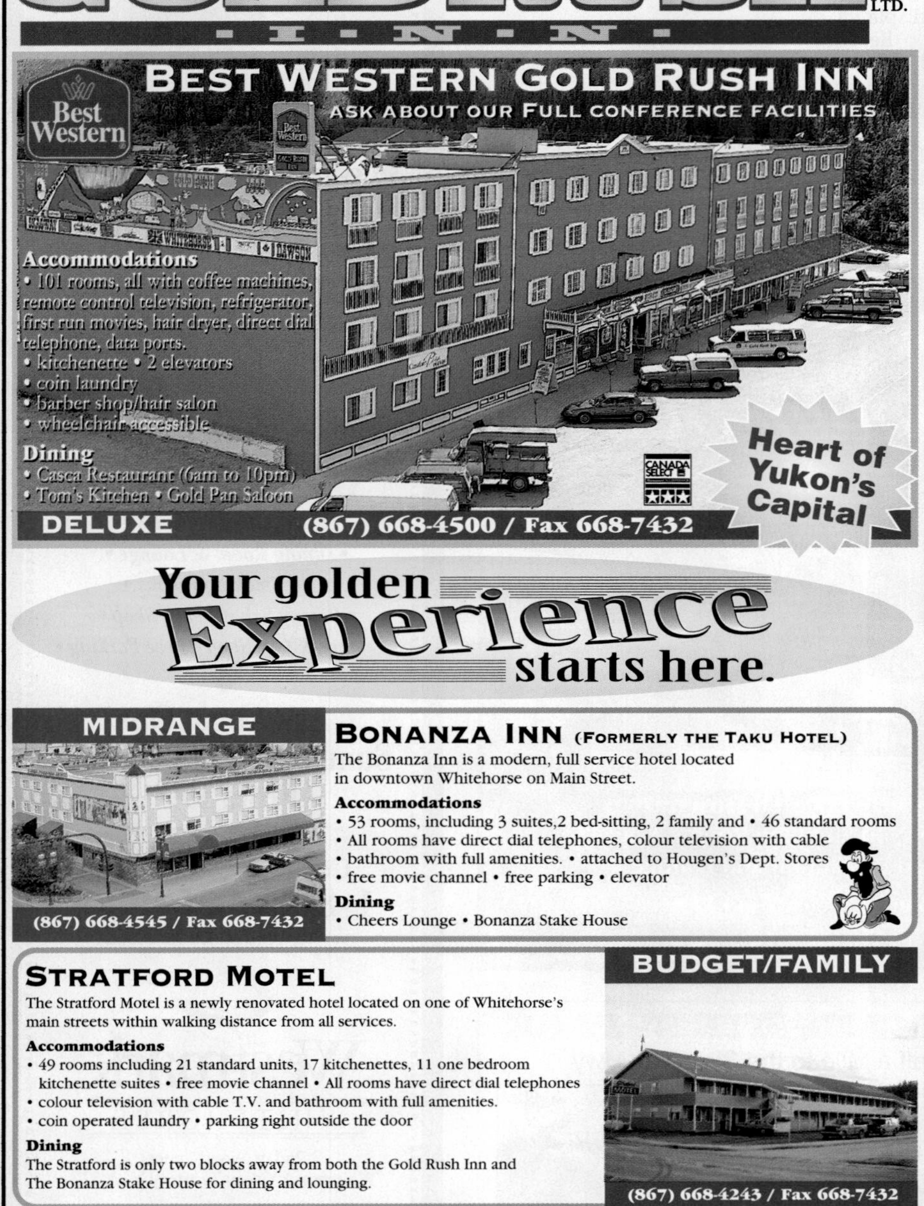

Woolly mammoth skeleton is on display in the Yukon Beringia Interpretive Centre at Whitehorse. (Earl L. Brown, staff)

Specialty stores include gold nugget and ivory shops where distinctive jewelry is manufactured, and Indian craft shops specializing in moose hide jackets, parkas, vests, moccasins, slippers, mukluks and gauntlets. Inuit and Indian handicrafts from Canada's Arctic regions are featured in some stores. Whitehorse area maps are available at Jim's Toy and Gifts; 4137 4th Ave., phone (867) 667-2606.

Hawkins House Bed & Breakfast. Enjoy the Yukon's most luxurious accommodations in our Victorian home in downtown Whitehorse. Turn-of-the-century charm includes a grand foyer, guest parlor, high ceilings, balconies, hardwood floors, and historical and cultural themes. Rooms feature private bath, telephone, cable TV and VCR, bar sink and fridge, quality beds, soundproofing and a great view of the downtown and surrounding mountains. Jacuzzis® and claw foot tub available. Enjoy a 5-minute walk to Main Street shops and restaurants. Non-smoking. Open year-round. Français, Deutsch. Phone (867) 668-7638, fax (867) 668-7632, or write 303 Hawkins

St., Whitehorse, YT, Canada Y1A 1X5. [ADVERTISEMENT]

High Country Inn. During your stay in Whitehorse, relax and enjoy "Country Inn" atmosphere and great Northern hospitality. We offer 100 rooms from executive and Jacuzzi suites to deluxe double rooms. Located downtown, great views, elevators, guest laundry, exercise room, colour TV, coffee maker, etc. AAA approved (3 stars, reservations recommended). Phone (800) 554-4471 or (403) 667-4471, fax (403) 667-6457. See our display advertisement. [ADVERTISEMENT]

International House Bed & Breakfast. Enjoy a clean, quiet, cozy country-style home of charm and hospitality. Lots of great food, full breakfast, home baked goodies at night. Quiet neighborhood, walking and cross-country skiing, on bus route, 2 short blocks off Alaska Highway. Pickup available. Non-smoking. Enjoy one of the finest bed and breakfasts anywhere. Your hosts Al and Ann Dibbs. Open year-round. VISA, MasterCard. (867) 633-5490. Fax (867) 668-4751. [ADVERTISEMENT]

Klondike Rib & Salmon BBQ. Located in 2 of the oldest buildings in Whitehorse at Second and Steele, across from the Frantic Follies and Westmark Hotel. A delicious salmon BBQ, and Texas BBQ ribs, English-style fish and chips, and specialty northern food like bison burgers, caribou, musk-ox, arctic char and fresh bannock. Just some of the mouthwatering fare served in a unique historic Klondike Airways building with historical exhibits as part of the fascinating decor. (867) 667-7554. [ADVERTISEMENT]

Yukon Mining Company. Join us for "Barbecue" on the deck at the most popular 'Eatery' in Whitehorse. Try wild game, including buffalo and caribou steaks and burgers, chicken and ribs, pasta, great seafood and local brewed beer, including our very own "Grizzly Beer"—the best beer in the North! Meet local folk and enjoy great food and the friendliest staff in the north. (See our display ad for more detail.) [ADVERTISEMENT]

Tent camping only is available at Robert Service Park on Robert Service Way (South Access Road). There are 4 private campgrounds south of downtown Whitehorse on the Alaska Highway (see **Mileposts DC 873.5**, **881**, **882.9** and **883.7** in the highway log), and 1 private campground 6 miles/9.6 km north of the city on the highway (see **Milepost DC 891.9**). Wolf Creek Yukon government campground is 7 miles/11 km south of Whitehorse on the Alaska Highway. A private campground and Yukon government campground are located at Marsh Lake. Takhini Hot Springs on the Klondike Loop is also a popular camping spot (1/2-hour drive from Whitehorse). ▲

IMPORTANT: RV caravans should contact

private campground operators well in advance of arrival regarding camping arrangements. At our press time, there was no designated RV parking in downtown Whitehorse.

TRANSPORTATION

Air: Service by Canadian Airlines International and Alkan Air daily to major cities and Yukon communities. Air North to Dawson City, Old Crow, Juneau and Fairbanks, AK. (Air North offers a 21-day Klondike Explorer's Pass between Juneau, Old Crow, Fairbanks, Whitehorse and Dawson City). Royal Airlines and N.W.T. Air offer summer service with connections to major Canadian and U.S. cities. Whitehorse International Airport is reached from the Alaska Highway.

Seaplane dock on Schwatka Lake just above the Whitehorse Dam (take Robert Service Way from Alaska Highway and turn right on road by the railroad tracks to reach the base). Flightseeing tours available.

Trans North Air offers helicopter sightseeing tours from the airport.

Bus: Whitehorse Transit offers downtown and rural service. See also Bus Lines in the TRAVEL PLANNING section.

Railroad: Arrangements for White Pass & Yukon Route rail trips may be made by phoning WP&YR in Whitehorse at (867) 668-RAIL, or contacting local travel agencies.

Taxi: 5 taxi companies operate in Whitehorse.

Car, Truck, Motorhome and Camper Rentals: Several local and national agencies are located in Whitehorse.

A variety of craft ply the Yukon River. Sightseeing cruises are available in Whitehorse. (Earl L. Brown, staff)

ATTRACTIONS

The **SS *Klondike* National Historic Site** is hard to miss. This grand old stern-wheeler sits beside the Yukon River near the Robert Campbell bridge. After carrying cargo and passengers between Whitehorse and Dawson City from 1937 until the 1950s, the SS *Klondike* went into permanent retirement on the bank of the Yukon River, donated to the people of Canada by the White Pass & Yukon Route. Refurbished by Parks Canada, the stern-wheeler is open to the public. Built by British Yukon Navigation Co., the SS *Klondike* is 210 feet/64m long and 41.9 feet/12.5m wide. Visitor information centre, gift shop and public parking at the site. A film on the history of riverboats is shown continuously in a tent theatre adjacent the boat. Tours of the stern-wheeler leave on the half hour. The 20-minute film is shown prior to each tour. Admission fee charged. Large groups are advised to book tours in advance. Contact Canadian Identity, 300

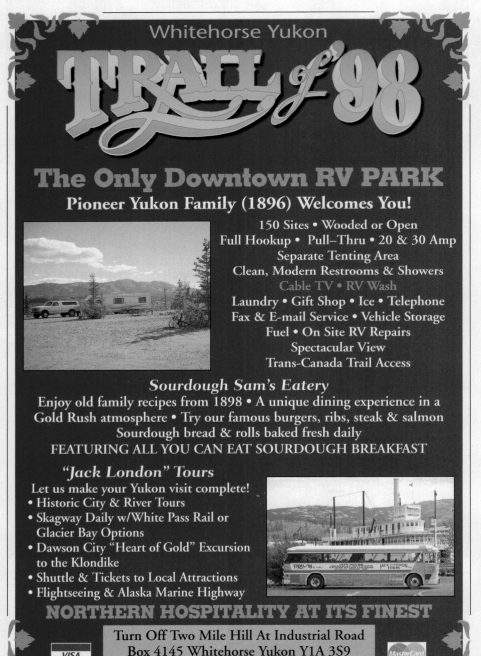

Main St., Room 205, Whitehorse, YT Y1A 2B5; phone (867) 667-3970, fax (867) 398-6701. The SS *Klondike* visitor centre and stern-wheeler are open from mid-May to mid-September.

Live Shows. Frantic Follies, a very popular vaudeville stage show, is held nightly mid-May through mid-September at the Westmark Whitehorse Hotel. 1998 marks the 29th season for this 1½-hour show which features a chorus line, rousing music and hilarious skits from Robert W. Service ballads. Visitors are advised to get tickets in advance; available at the box office in the Westmark or phone (867) 668-2042.

The Canteen Show is a light-hearted revue of 1940s Whitehorse and the construction of the Alaska Highway. Inquire at the Yukon Inn.

1940's Canteen Show. Serendipity unfolds for those attending this outstanding production. Joyous music performed on stage in a fun-filled comedy with a look at the lighter side of the war years during the construction of the Alaska Highway. The 1940's Canteen Show should not be missed! 8 P.M. nightly at the Yukon Inn. 12th season. Box office (867) 667-2527. E-mail: canteen@yknet.yr.ca. Web site: www.hyperborean-webcom/canteen/. [ADVERTISEMENT]

Special Events. Whitehorse has a full schedule of events throughout 1998. Visitors can attend the Rotary Music Festival (April 13–19, 1998); the Celebration of Swans (trumpeter and tundra) returning to M'Clintock Bay (mid April); the Square Dance Jamboree (July 1–5, 1998); and the Yukon International Storytelling Festival, held at Rotary Peace Park on June 18–21, 1998. Also in June is the National Aboriginal Day Festivities, June 21, 1998. Canada Day kicks off July 1, 1998, with a parade and celebrations at Rotary Peace Park. There are many Gold Rush Centennial celebrations scheduled for 1998. Visit the Website for more information: www.yukonweb.com.

Take a hike with the Yukon Conservation Society (YCS). Every summer the society offers free guided nature walks, ranging in difficulty from easy to strenuous, from July to late August. Trips are 1 to 6 hours in length and informative guides explain the local flora, fauna, geology and history along the trails. The YCS conducts interpretive walks at Canyon City (see **Milepost DC 881.7**) during the summer on a regular basis, including evenings and weekends. For a schedule of hikes, contact the Yukon Conservation Society, at 302 Hawkins St.; phone (867) 668-5678.

World's largest weathervane. Located in front of the Whitehorse International Airport is the world's largest weathervane—a

Douglas DC–3. This vintage plane (registration number CF–CPY) flew for several Yukon airlines from 1946 until 1970, when it blew an engine during takeoff. The plane was restored by Joe Muff with the help of

© Ruth Fairall

the Yukon Flying Club and the Whitehorse community. It is now owned and managed by the Yukon Transportation Museum. The restored plane was mounted on a rotating pedestal in 1981 and now acts as a weathervane, pointing its nose into the wind.

The Yukon Transportation Museum, located on the Alaska Highway adjacent to the Whitehorse Airport (see **Milepost DC 885.8**), features exhibits on all forms of transportation in the North. Displays inside include the full-size replica of the *Queen of the Yukon* Ryan monoplane, sister ship to Lindbergh's *Spirit of St. Louis;* railway rolling stock; Alaska Highway vintage vehicles, dogsleds and stagecoaches. Also featured are the Chilkoot Trail, the Canol Highway and bush pilots of the North. The museum includes video theatres and a gift shop. Plenty of parking. Admission charged. Open daily, 9 A.M. to 6 P.M., mid-May to mid-September. Write P.O. Box 5867, Whitehorse, YT Y1A 5L6 or phone (867) 668-4792, fax 633-5547.

Historical walking tours of Whitehorse are conducted by the Yukon Historical & Museums Association. Tour guides wear period costumes for these walks that take in the city's heritage buildings. Meet at the Donnenworth House, 3126 3rd Ave.; phone 667-4704. Fee charged. There are tours Monday through Saturday from June to the end of August. For self-guided tours, *A Walking Tour of Yukon's Capital* or *Exploring Old Whitehorse* are available from local stores or from the Yukon Historical & Museums Assoc., Box 4357, Whitehorse, YT Y1A 3T5.

MacBride Museum, on 1st Avenue between Steele and Wood streets, showcases Yukon's cultural and natural history in 4 indoor galleries featuring gold rush exhibits and outdoor displays featuring Sam McGee's cabin. The Museum Shop features books, local arts and crafts and northern souvenirs. Admission charged. Open daily, 10 A.M. to 6 P.M., June, July and August; phone for seasonal hours, (867) 667-2709, fax 633-6607 or write Box 4037, Whitehorse, YT Y1A 3S9. Phone for winter hours. ♿

Old Log Church Museum, 1 block off Main on Elliott at 3rd. Built in 1900 by Rev. R.J. Bowen for the Church of England, this recently restored log church and rectory have been declared the first territorial historic sites in the Yukon. The museum, located in the log church, displays relics of pioneer northern missions. Open to the public June to September; admission fee.

Yukon Government Building, 2nd Avenue and Hawkins, open 9 A.M. to 5 P.M. Administrative and Legislative headquarters of Yukon Territory, the building contains some notable artworks. On the main floor mall is an acrylic resin mural, 120 feet/37m long, which portrays the historical evolution of the Yukon. The 24 panels, each measuring 4 by 5 feet/1.2 by 1.5m, highlight events such as the arrival of Sir John Franklin at Herschel Island in 1825, the Klondike Gold

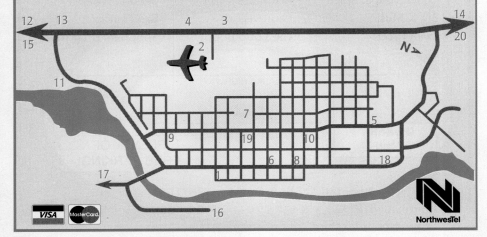

Whitehorse Rapids Fishway has interpretive displays and viewing decks. (Earl L. Brown, staff)

Rush, and the coming of the automobile. The mural was created by Vancouver, BC, artist David MacLagen.

In the Legislative Chamber, an 18-by-12-foot/5-by-4m tapestry is an abstraction of the fireweed plant, Yukon's floral emblem. The Yukon Women's Tapestry, 5 panels each 7-by-13-feet/2-by-4m, hangs in the legislative library lounge. The wool panels portray the role of women in the development of the territory, depicting the 5 seasons of the North; spring, summer, autumn, winter and "survival," the cold gray season between winter and spring and fall and winter. Begun by the Whitehorse Branch of the Canadian Federation of Business and Professional Women in 1976 to mark International Women's Year, the wall hangings were stitched by some 2,500 Yukoners.

A Taste of '98 Yukon River Tours. The best 3-hour river tour in the Yukon. Experience gold rush history first hand, and discover the abundant wildlife of the Whitehorse area on motorized steel pontoon river craft. Tours, as well as the unique craft, were designed to enhance your Yukon experience and the thrill of discovery. Just $36 per person (group rates available). Daily at 12 noon, 3:30 P.M. and 7 P.M. Phone (867) 633-4767. [ADVERTISEMENT]

WHITEHORSE
CELEBRATING 50 YEARS OF THE MILEPOST®

WHITEHORSE SERVICES & BUSINESSES
Catering to Visitors and Vacationists

PHOTOGRAPHERS—CAMERA "FANS"—Please note: You will wish to long remember the beautiful scenery encountered along the highway, and those "back home" can share it if it is recorded on film. For those without cameras, a wide selection of color slides and scenic folders are carried by **HOUGEN'S VARIETY STORE** (at the turn going up Main St.) The largest stock of photographic supplies in the Yukon, also souvenirs and fishing tackle. Leave film here for quick service, then you can check to see if any of the best highway "shots" have been missed. You'll enjoy shopping at Hougen's, open 9 a.m. to 9 p.m.

YUKON TIRE SHOP—Next to Regina Hotel on First Ave. This business, which has been serving the public since 1926, operates the only completely equipped tire shop in the Yukon, and carries the largest stock of new tires in the Territory. For the best in service follow the signs to this shop with ALL your tire troubles. Owner, Ernest Lortie.

MAC'S NEWS STAND
Centrally located in the business district, across from Whitehorse Inn. Open from 9 a.m. to 10 p.m. weekdays and 10 a.m. to 10 p.m. Sundays. All current U.S., Canadian & foreign magazines, periodicals & pocket books. Newspapers, guide books, maps, ice cream, confectionery, soft drinks, cigarettes, cigars & tobacco, film, novelties, greeting cards, post cards & souvenirs. BIRDS—TROPICAL FISH & PET SUPPLIES. All are welcome—Mac's, your friendly store. Rosina C. Anker, proprietor.

THE MOST WIDELY KNOWN HOSTELRY IN YUKON, CANADA

The WHITEHORSE INN

Phone 6363—In The Heart Of Business District—Main At 2nd Avenue
MODERN HOTEL ROOMS, DOUBLE OR TWIN BEDS, TUB OR SHOWER BATHS
Large & Modern Cafe In Connection—Booth & Counter Service
Attractive Cocktail Lounge—"The Rainbow Room"
"Bowladrome" for Your Recreation
BURNIE'S EXCLUSIVE APPAREL SHOP—BEAUTY SHOP—PAN AMERICAN AIRWAYS
TAXI & SIGHTSEEING SERVICE
WHITEHORSE HOTELS, LTD.—T. C. RICHARDS, PRESIDENT & DIRECTOR

LOG OF THE ALASKA HIGHWAY

R. Hougen, Whitehorse, Y. T. Can.

Whitehorse and Yukon River Steamers

MILEPOST 919. Whitehorse. This thriving frontier town, which had a prewar population of 300, has been greatly benefited by the advent of the Alaska Highway, and the activity of war time construction. Established during Klondike gold-rush days, the town has long been known as a colorful tourist center, and the point where The Yukon and White Pass Railroad from Skagway, Alaska, connects with the river steamers which ply between here and Dawson. As the chief and central supply point for construction of the highway and the movement of war material, Whitehorse experienced an unprecedented boom during 1942, and the many abandoned warehouses in the vicinity, built for wartime needs, give an impression of recession which is far from the actuality. True, the feverish activity of the war period is gone, but a new life and substantiality has come to the community with the revival of tourist travel, and the ever-growing traffic over the Alaska Highway. With the renewed and greatly increased interest in the North, and with the Alaska Highway trip a "must" on the programs of motorists for years to come, Whitehorse has a future as assured and economically sound as that of the great northland of which it is a vital part. Here the traveler will find good hotels, modern stores, specialty and souvenir shops, a theater, schools and churches. It is a hub for interesting side trips and excursions for sight-seers, including the nearby Whitehorse Rapids and Miles Canyon, the Robert W. Service memorial cabin, the trip by river steamship to Dawson in the Klondike, and the rail trip over the narrow gauge to Carcross to connect with the boat trip on the lovely West Taku Arm of Tagish Lake.

—25—

Yukon Gardens, located at the junction of the Alaska Highway and Robert Service Way (South Access Road), is the only formal northern botanical garden. The 22-acre site features more than 100,000 wild and domestic flowers; vegetables, herbs and fruits; scenic pathways and floral displays; a children's "Old MacDonald's farm"; gift shop; and fresh produce in summer. Open daily in summer. Admission charged.

Whitehorse Rapids Fishway. The fish ladder was built in 1959 to provide access for chinook (king) salmon and other species above the Yukon Energy Corporation hydroelectric dam. Located at the end of Nisutlin Drive in the Riverdale suburb. Open daily, 9 A.M. to 5 P.M. from May 25 to July 1, 8 A.M. to 10 P.M. from July to September. Interpretive displays and viewing decks.

Mountain View Public Golf Course, located in Porter Creek subdivision on the Yukon River, is accessible via the Porter Creek exit off the Alaska Highway or from Range Road; 18 holes, grass greens; green fees. Midnight Sun Golf Tournament June 21–22, 1998.

Picnic in a park. Picnicking on a small island in the Yukon River, accessible via footbridge from 2nd Avenue, north of the railroad tracks. Picnic facilities are also available at Robert Service Campground, located on Robert Service Way into Whitehorse. Rotary Peace Park is central to downtown and a popular picnic spot.

Whitehorse Public Library, part of the Yukon Government Building on 2nd Avenue, has a room with art displays and books about the Yukon and the gold rush. It

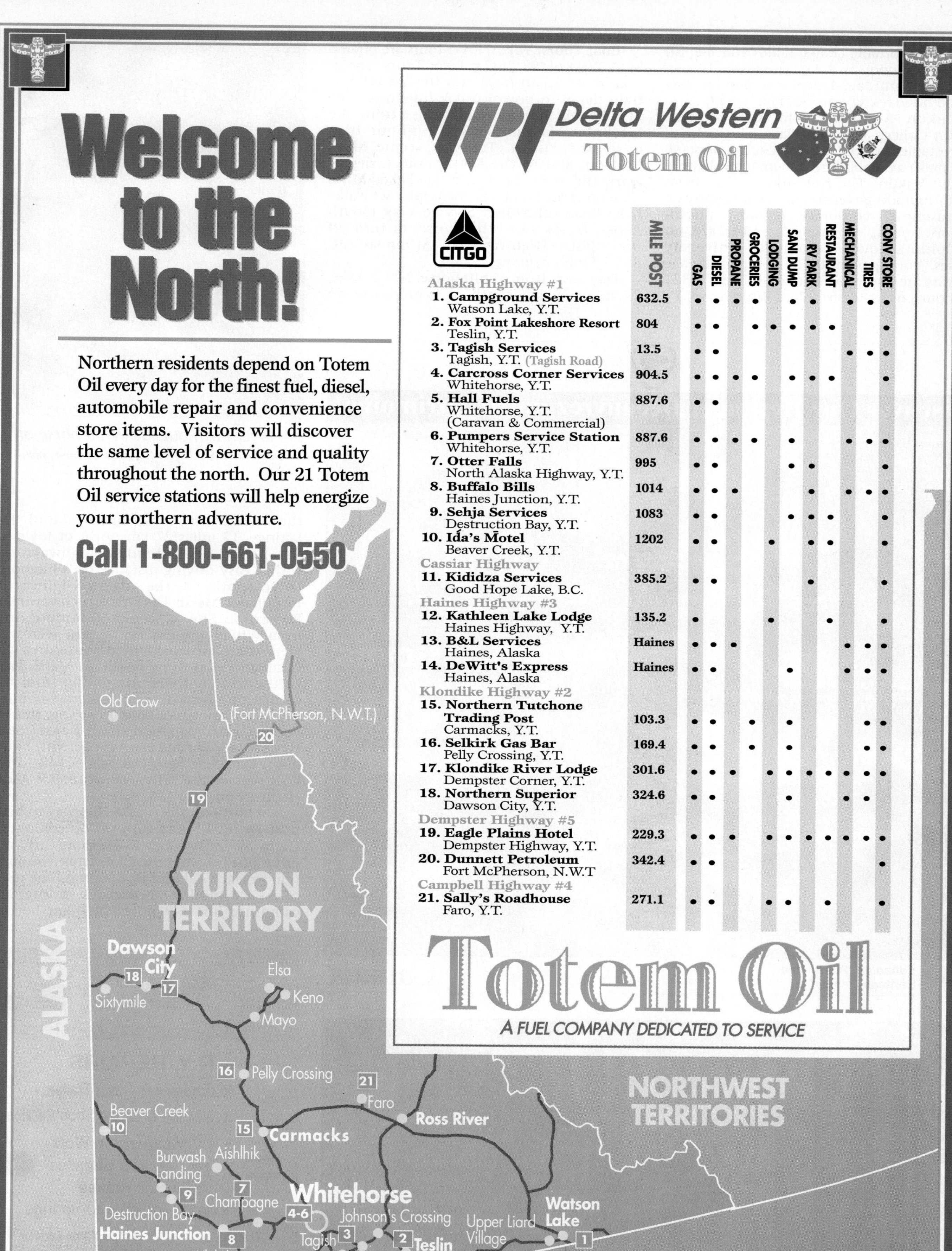

	MILE POST	GAS	DIESEL	PROPANE	GROCERIES	LODGING	SANI DUMP	RV PARK	RESTAURANT	MECHANICAL	TIRES	CONV STORE
Alaska Highway #1												
1. Campground Services Watson Lake, Y.T.	632.5	•	•	•	•		•	•		•	•	•
2. Fox Point Lakeshore Resort Teslin, Y.T.	804	•	•		•	•	•	•	•			•
3. Tagish Services Tagish, Y.T. (Tagish Road)	13.5	•	•							•	•	•
4. Carcross Corner Services Whitehorse, Y.T.	904.5	•	•	•	•		•	•	•			•
5. Hall Fuels Whitehorse, Y.T. (Caravan & Commercial)	887.6	•	•									
6. Pumpers Service Station Whitehorse, Y.T.	887.6	•	•	•	•		•			•	•	•
7. Otter Falls North Alaska Highway, Y.T.	995	•	•				•	•				•
8. Buffalo Bills Haines Junction, Y.T.	1014	•	•	•				•		•	•	•
9. Sehja Services Destruction Bay, Y.T.	1083	•	•				•	•	•			•
10. Ida's Motel Beaver Creek, Y.T.	1202	•	•			•		•	•			•
Cassiar Highway												
11. Kididza Services Good Hope Lake, B.C.	385.2	•	•					•				•
Haines Highway #3												
12. Kathleen Lake Lodge Haines Highway, Y.T.	135.2	•				•			•			•
13. B&L Services Haines, Alaska	Haines	•	•	•						•	•	•
14. DeWitt's Express Haines, Alaska	Haines	•	•				•			•	•	•
Klondike Highway #2												
15. Northern Tutchone Trading Post Carmacks, Y.T.	103.3	•	•		•		•				•	•
16. Selkirk Gas Bar Pelly Crossing, Y.T.	169.4	•	•		•		•				•	•
17. Klondike River Lodge Dempster Corner, Y.T.	301.6	•	•	•		•	•	•	•	•	•	•
18. Northern Superior Dawson City, Y.T.	324.6	•	•				•			•	•	
Dempster Highway #5												
19. Eagle Plains Hotel Dempster Highway, Y.T.	229.3	•	•	•		•	•	•	•	•	•	•
20. Dunnett Petroleum Fort McPherson, N.W.T	342.4	•	•									•
Campbell Highway #4												
21. Sally's Roadhouse Faro, Y.T.	271.1	•	•			•	•		•			•

features a large stone and copper double fireplace, comfortable chairs, tables and helpful staff. Open noon to 9 P.M. weekdays, 10 A.M. to 6 P.M. Saturday, 1 to 9 P.M. Sunday and closed holidays. Phone (867) 667-5239.

Yukon Archives is located adjacent Yukon College at Yukon Place. The archives was established in 1972 to acquire, preserve and make available the documented history of the Yukon. The holdings, dating from 1845, include government records, private manuscripts, corporate records, photographs, maps, newspapers (most are on microfilm), sound recordings, university theses, books, pamphlets and periodicals. Visitors are welcome. Phone (867) 667-5321 for hours, or write Box 2703, Whitehorse, YT Y1A 2C6, for more information.

Boat Tours. Yukon River tours are offered by A Taste of '98 Yukon River Tours. The 3-hour tours depart from near the old WP&YR train depot in downtown Whitehorse. The MV *Youcon Kat*, docked across from the MacBride Museum, offers 2 1/2-hour trips down the Yukon. Tours of scenic Miles Canyon, aboard the MV *Schwatka*, depart from the dock on Schwatka Lake. Miles Canyon is accessible by road: take Schwatka Lake Road off Robert Service Way (South Access Road) into Whitehorse, or turn off the Alaska Highway (see **Milepost DC 881.7**); follow signs.

Day trips from Whitehorse. Marsh Lake, 24 miles/39 km south of Whitehorse on the Alaska Highway, and Takhini Hot Springs, 17 miles/27 km north of town via the Alaska and Klondike highways, are within easy driving distance of Whitehorse. Drive south on the Alaska Highway to turnoff for Marsh Lake Yukon Government Recreation Site, a scenic 30-minute drive from Whitehorse city centre. The recreation area offers an excellent day-use area and campground at Army Beach on Marsh Lake. In the winter, trails originating from this recreation site are used for cross-country skiing and snowmobiling. In spring, this is a popular swan migration viewing area. "Swan Haven" viewing site is equipped with binoculars. Lakeview Resort at Marsh Lake offers boat rentals. See **Milepost DC 859.9** Alaska Highway on page 136.

Go north on the Alaska Highway to **Milepost DC 894.8** and turn off onto Klondike Highway 2 (the road to Dawson City) and drive just 3.8 miles/6.1 km from the junction to reach Takhini Hot Springs. The resort offers swimming, horseback riding and camping. Just 6.9 miles/11.1 km beyond

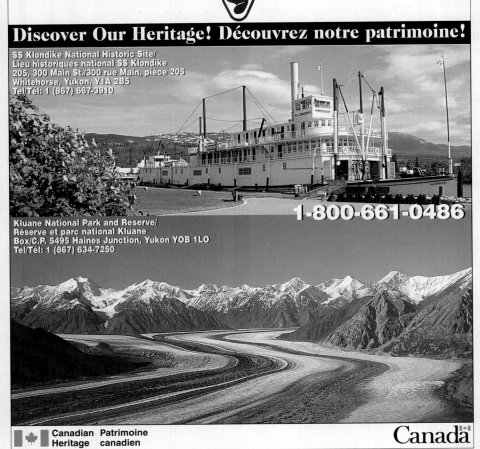

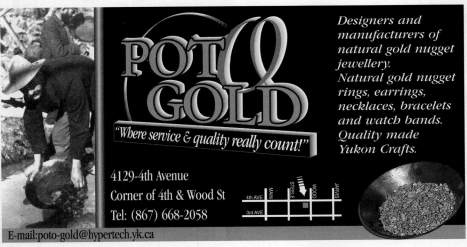

Reindeer farm outside Whitehorse on the Klondike Highway. (Earl. L. Brown, staff)

Takhini Hot Springs is Northern Splendour Reindeer Farm. See **Mileposts J 3.8** and **J 10.7** on page 307 in the KLONDIKE LOOP section for details.

Longer trips (which you may want to extend to an overnight) are to Atlin, about 2½ hours by car, and Skagway, 3 hours by car. Skagway is an old gold rush town and port of call for both the Alaska state ferries and cruise ships. Skagway is also home to the famed White Pass & Yukon Route Railway, said to be the most scenic railway in the world as it climbs through beautiful mountain terrain to White Pass summit. Book ahead for the trip. Complete your Skagway visit with a trip to Dyea, a short drive from downtown, to see the start of the Chilkoot Trail and a gold rush graveyard. Atlin, which also dates from 1898, is known for its spectacular scenery. Visitors heading for Skagway should call ahead for accommodations if they expect to overnight. You may make a circle tour, driving down to Skagway then turning off onto the Tagish Road on your way back and continuing on to Atlin via the Atlin Road.

Rockhounding and Mining. A wide variety of minerals can be found in the Whitehorse area. Sources of information for rock hounds and gold panners include the Yukon Rock Shop, at the junction of the Alaska Highway and Klondike Highway 2 (Carcross Road), which has mineral samples, gold pans and nuggets, and Murdoch's gem shop on Main Street, which displays gold nugget jewellery and gold rush artifacts and photos.

The following rockhounding location is suggested by Fred Dorward of the Whitehorse Gem & Mineral Club (26 Sunset Dr. N., Whitehorse, YT Y1A 4M8). Drive north on the Alaska Highway to the Fish Lake Road turnoff (**Milepost DC 889.4**), located 2 miles/3.2 km from the north entrance to Whitehorse. About 0.5 mile/0.8 km in on Fish Lake Road, park and walk across McIntyre Creek to the old Copper King mine workings. Excellent but small specimens of brown garnet, also serpentine.

IMPORTANT: Rock hounds should exercise extreme caution when exploring. Do not enter old mine workings. Please respect No Trespassing signs.

Canoe, Raft or Boat to Dawson City. Canoe rentals by the day, week or month, and guide services are available in Whitehorse. From the Yukon River's outlet at Marsh Lake south of Whitehorse to the Alaska border it is 530 river miles/853 km; from Whitehorse to Dawson City it is 410 river miles/660 km. There is a boat launch at Rotary Peace Park, behind the Yukon Government Bldg. You may also launch at Deep Creek Campground on Lake Laberge. Contact Up North Canoe Rentals, phone (867) 667-7905.

NOTE: Before leaving on any river or other wilderness trip, for your own protection, report your plans and itinerary to the RCMP. Be guided by the advice in government publications regarding travel on the Yukon's rivers and lakes. Do not attempt the Five Finger Rapids on the Yukon River without qualified advice.

For more information on wilderness travel, contact Tourism Yukon office, located between 2nd and 3rd on Hawkins; phone (867) 667-5340. Hikers planning to do the Chilkoot Trail should check with Parks Canada, in the Federal Building at 4th and Main; phone (867) 668-2116. The Chilkoot Trail fee is $35 for adults ($17.50 for children under 14).

Mount McIntyre Recreation Centre, 0.9 mile/1.5 km west of the Alaska Highway (see **Milepost DC 887.6**), has 70 kilometres of groomed cross-country ski trails (open for hiking, running and mountain biking in summer). Contact Whitehorse Cross-Country Ski Club, P.O. Box 4639, Whitehorse, YT Y1A 3Y7.

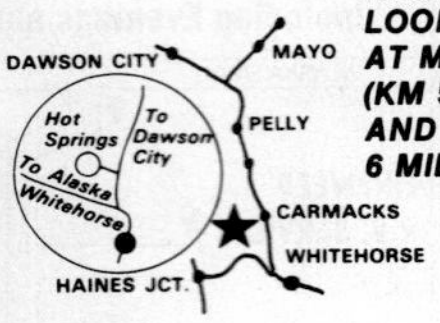

Sportsmen can obtain complete information on fishing and hunting in the Whitehorse area by writing Tourism Yukon, Box 2703, Whitehorse, YT Y1A 2C6. They will provide lists of guides and advise what licenses are required.

AREA FISHING: Fish for rainbow and coho salmon in the following lakes: **Hidden, Scout, Long, Jackson** and **McLean.** Inquire locally for directions. Nearby fly-in fishing lakes are accessible by charter plane; see advertisements in this section. **Yukon River,** fish for grayling below the dam and bridge. Fishing below the dam prohibited in August during the salmon run.

Alaska Highway Log

(continued from page 139)

Distance* from Dawson Creek (DC) is followed by distance from Fairbanks (F). Original mileposts are indicated in the text as Historical Mile.

*Mileages from Dawson Creek are based on actual driving distance. Kilometres from Dawson Creek are based on physical kilometreposts. Please read Mileposts and Kilometreposts in the introduction for an explanation of how this highway is logged.

DC 887.4 (1475.6 km) **F 600.6** (966.5 km) First exit southbound for Whitehorse. North access road to Whitehorse (exit east) is via Two-Mile Hill and 4th Avenue.

DC 887.6 (1476 km) **F 600.4** (966.2 km) Turnoff to west on Hamilton Boulevard for Mount McIntyre Recreation Centre (0.9 mile/1.5 km); 70 kilometres of cross-country ski trails (summer hiking and biking), chalet for indoor waxing, curling and bonspiels. Truck weigh scales west side of highway.

DC 888.6 (1477.5 km) **F 599.4** (964.6 km) **Historical Mile 918.3. Kopper King Services.** See display ad this section.

DC 889.3 (1478.6 km) **F 598.7** (963.5 km) McIntyre Creek.

DC 889.4 (1478.8 km) **F 598.6** (963.3 km) Fish Lake Road to west. Located only 9.3 miles/15 km from Whitehorse, Fish Lake and adjacent Bonneville Lakes were the site of a Kwanlin Dun First Nations archaeology project documenting the long history of habitation in this area.

DC 890.1 (1479.9 km) **F 597.9** (962.2 km) Rabbit's Foot Canyon.

DC 890.5 (1480.6 km) **F 597.5** (961.6 km) Turnoff to Porter Creek to east.

DC 891 (1481.4 km) **F 597** (960.8 km) Porter Creek grocery.

DC 891.3 (1482 km) **F 596.7** (960.3 km) **Historical Mile 921,** laundromat, gas and other businesses.

Log skyscrapers are a Whitehorse landmark. (© Eero Sorila)

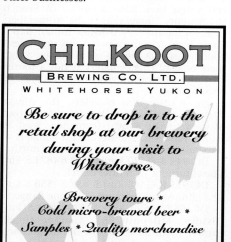

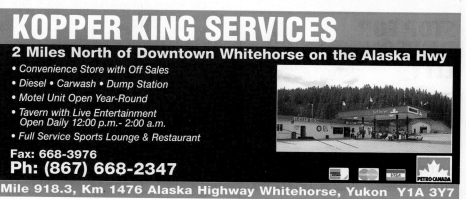

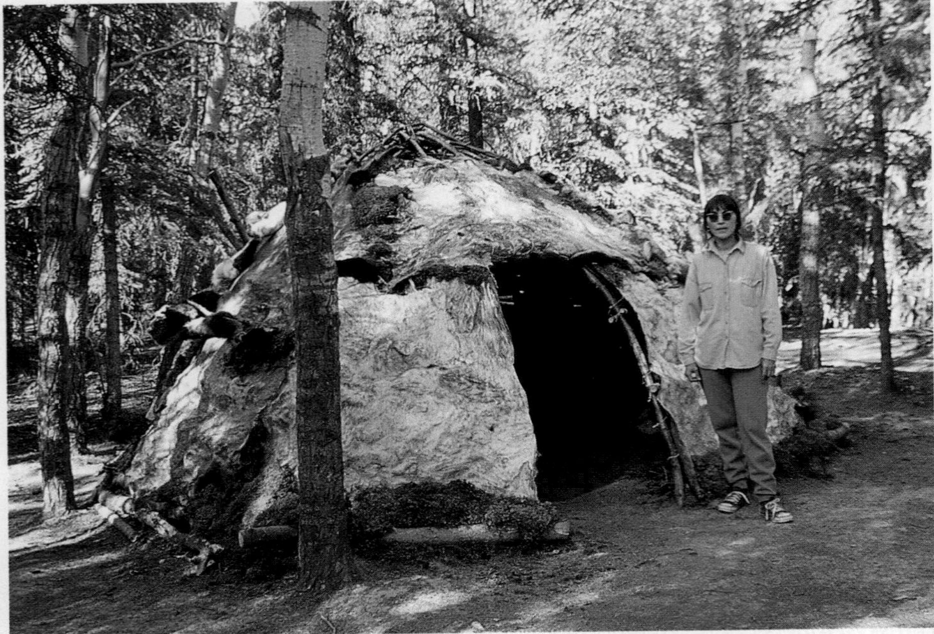

A Native traditional camp is an interpretive exhibit at Milepost DC 942.2.

(Earl L. Brown, staff)

DC 891.5 (1482.3 km) **F 596.5** (959.9 km) Clyde Wann Road and Porter Creek subdivision, a residential suburb of Whitehorse. Access to Range Road and Mountain View Golf Course (18 holes).

DC 891.6 (1482.4 km) **F 596.4** (959.8 km) **Historical Mile 922.** Trails North Car & Truck Stop, and Tamarack Welding and Spring Shop are located here.

DC 891.8 (1482.5 km) **F 596.2** (959.5 km) MacDonald Road to north; auto repair.

DC 891.9 (1484 km) **F 596.1** (959.3 km) **Historical Mile 922.5.** Azure Road. Access to MacKenzie's RV Park. ▲

DC 894.3 (1486.4 km) **F 593.7** (955.4 km) Turnoff east to Cousins dirt airstrip.

DC 894.5 (1486.7 km) **F 593.5** (955.1 km) Rest area to west with litter barrels, outhouses, information sign and pay phone.

DC 894.8 (1487.2 km) **F 593.2** (954.6 km) **Junction** with Klondike Highway 2 to Dawson City (see KLONDIKE LOOP section). Turn off on Klondike Highway 2 for Takhini Hot Springs (swimming, camping), 3.8 miles/6.1 km north. ▲

For Alaska-bound travelers, the highway now swings west.

DC 895.5 (1488.3 km) **F 592.5** (953.5 km) Turnoff to south for Haeckel Hill. Not recommended for hiking as this area is used for target practice.

STOP FOR DAWSON CITY
STOP
1998
THE JOURNEY BEGINS
TAKE THE KLONDIKE HIGHWAY JUST NORTH OF WHITEHORSE

DC 899.1 (1495.4 km) **F 588.9** (947.7 km) Turnoff for 3-mile/4.8-km loop drive on old section of Alaska Highway. Access to stocked lake.

DC 901.6 (1499.3 km) **F 586.4** (943.7 km) Turnoff to north to sled dog track.

DC 905.4 (1507.1 km) **F 582.6** (937.6 km) **Historic Milepost 937.** Camera viewpoint turnout to north with point of interest sign about the old Dawson Trail. There were at least 50 stopping places along the old Dawson Trail winter stagecoach route between Whitehorse and Dawson City, and from 1 to 3 roadhouses at each stop. At this point, the stagecoach route crossed the Takhini River. This route was discontinued in 1950 when the Mayo–Dawson Road (now Klondike Highway 2) was constructed.

DC 908.7 (1512.4 km) **F 579.3** (932.3 km) Private farm and windmill; good example of Yukon agriculture. Facilities for overnighting large livestock.

DC 914.7 (1525 km) **F 573.3** (922.6 km) Takhini River bridge. According to R. Coutts in *Yukon: Places & Names,* the name Takhini derives from the Tagish Indian *tahk,* meaning mosquito, and *heena,* meaning river.

DC 922.7 (1535 km) **F 565.3** (909.7 km) Watch for horses and other livestock grazing on open range near highway.

DC 924.5 (1538.4 km) **F 563.5** (906.8 km) Stoney Creek.

DC 924.7 (1538.7 km) **F 563.3** (906.5 km) View of Mount Bratnober.

DC 926 (1540.8 km) **F 562** (904.4 km) Turnout to south with litter barrels and information panels on Takhini River valley, Kusawa Lake, and the changing landscape and wildlife of the area. Point of interest sign about 1958 burns; more than 1.5 million acres/629,058 hectares of Yukon forest lands were burned in 1958. Campfires were responsible for most of these fires.

DC 927.3 (1542.9 km) **F 560.7** (902.3 km) Turnoff to south for viewpoint (1.9 miles/3 km) and Kusawa Lake Yukon government campground (15 miles/24 km). Access road to campground is a narrow, winding gravel road, very slippery when wet; not recommended for long trailers or heavily loaded vehicles. ▲

Day-use area with sandy beach, boat dock, kitchen shelter and drinking water; boat launch 0.6 mile/1 km south. Campground at north end of lake has 48 sites, kitchen shelter, firepits and drinking water. Camping fee $8.

Kusawa Lake (formerly Arkell Lake), located in the Coast Mountains, is 45 miles/72 km long and averages 2 miles/3.2 km wide, with a shoreline perimeter of 125 miles/200 km. An access road to the lake was first constructed by the U.S. Army in 1945 to obtain bridge timbers for Alaska Highway construction.

Kusawa Lake, lake trout to 20 lbs., good to excellent; also grayling and pike.

DC 936.8 (1558 km) **F 551.2** (887 km) Mendenhall River bridge. A tributary of the Takhini River, the Mendenhall River—like the Mendenhall Glacier outside Juneau, AK—was named for Thomas Corwin Mendenhall (1841–1924), superintendent of the U.S. Coast & Geodetic Survey.

DC 939.5 (1562.3 km) **F 548.5** (882.7 km) View of 3 prominent mountains northbound (from left to right): Mount Kelvin; center mountain unnamed; and Mount Bratnober.

DC 942.2 (1565.5 km) **F 545.8** (878.4 km) Native traditional camp, Kwaday Dan Kenji, featuring Native crafts in a replica traditional First Nation camp interpretive site. Fee charged, open daily 9 A.M. to 7:30 P.M. May to October. Dry camping available. Phone (867) 667-6375. ▲

DC 942.8 (1567.6 km) **F 545.2** (877.4 km) NorthwesTel microwave tower to south.

DC 943.5 (1568.5 km) **F 544.5** (876.3 km) **Historic Milepost 974.** Historic sign and interpretive panel about **CHAMPAGNE.** Originally a camping spot on the Dalton Trail to Dawson City, established by Jack Dalton in the late 1800s. In 1902, Harlow "Shorty" Chambers built a roadhouse and trading post here, and it became a supply centre for first the Bullion Creek rush and later the Burwash Creek gold rush in 1904. The origin of the name is uncertain, although one account is that Dalton's men—after successfully negotiating a herd of cattle through the first part of the trail—celebrated here with a bottle of French champagne. Today, it is home to members of the Champagne–Aishihik Indian Band. There is an Indian cemetery on right westbound, just past the log cabin homes; a sign there reads: "This cemetery is not a tourist attraction. Please respect our privacy as we respect yours."

For northbound travelers, the Alaska Highway parallels the Dezadeash River (out of view to the south) from here west to Haines Junction. The Dezadeash Range is to the south and the Ruby Range to the north.

DC 944.4 (1570 km) **F 543.6** (874.8 km) Gravel turnout with litter barrel.

DC 955.8 (1588 km) **F 532.2** (856.5 km) First glimpse northbound of Kluane Range.

DC 957 (1590 km) **F 531** (854.5 km) **Historic Milepost 987.** Cracker Creek. Former roadhouse site on old stagecoach trail. Watch for "Old Man Mountain" on right northbound (the rocky crags look like a face, particularly in evening light).

DC 964.6 (1602.2 km) **F 523.4** (842.3 km) **Historical Mile 995.** Otter Falls Cutoff, **junction** with Aishihik Road. Gas station, store and camping to south, Aishihik Road turnoff to north. Bird-watching trails. ▲

Otter Falls Cutoff. See display ad this section. ▲

Aishihik Road leads 84 miles/135 km north to the old Indian village of Aishihik (AYSH-ee-ak, means high place). Northern Canada Power Commission built a 32-megawatt dam at the foot of Aishihik Lake in 1976 to supply power principally to the mining industry. Flow hours for the Otter Falls hydro project are given at the start of Aishihik Road. This is a narrow, gravel road, maintained for summer travel only to the government campground. Aishihik Road is not recommended for large RVs and trailers.

There is a day-use recreation site at Otter Falls, 18.6 miles/30 km distance; picnic shelter, tables, outhouses and boat ramp.

The Yukon government Aishihik Lake Campground is located at the south end of Aishihik Lake, approximately 26 miles/41.8 km distance; 13 sites, drinking water, picnic tables, firepits, kitchen shelter, boat launch and playground. Camping fee $8. ▲

Aishihik Lake, fishing for lake trout and grayling. As with most large Yukon lakes, ice is not out until late June. Low water levels may make boat launching difficult. *WARNING: Winds can come up suddenly on this lake.* **Pole Cat Lake,** just before the Aishihik weather station; fishing for pike.

CAUTION: Bears in area. Other wildlife includes eagles, moose and caribou.

DC 965.6 (1603.8 km) **F 522.4** (840.7 km) **Historic Milepost 996.** Turnoff to north at east end of Aishihik River bridge (watch for camera viewpoint sign) to see Canyon Creek bridge. The original bridge was built about 1920 by the Jacquot brothers to move freight and passengers across the Aishihik River to Silver City on Kluane Lake, and from there by boat to Burwash Landing. The bridge was reconstructed in 1942 by Army Corps of Engineers during construction of the Alaska Highway. It was rebuilt again in 1987.

DC 965.7 (1604 km) **F 522.3** (840.5 km) Aishihik River bridge.

DC 966.3 (1605 km) **F 521.7** (839.6 km) View of impressive Kluane Range ice fields straight ahead northbound between Kilometreposts 1604 and 1616.

DC 974.9 (1619 km) **F 513.1** (825.7 km) Turnout to south on Marshall Creek.

DC 977.1 (1622.4 km) **F 510.9** (822.2 km) The rugged snowcapped peaks of the Kluane Icefield Ranges and the outer portion of the St. Elias Mountains are visible to the west, straight ahead northbound.

The Kluane National Park Icefield Ranges are Canada's highest and the world's largest nonpolar alpine ice field, forming the interior wilderness of the park. In clear weather, Mount Kennedy and Mount Hubbard, 2 peaks that are twice as high as the front ranges seen before you, are visible from here.

DC 979.3 (1626 km) **F 508.7** (818.6 km) Between Kilometreposts 1626 and 1628, look for the NorthwesTel microwave repeater station on top of Paint Mountain. The station was installed with the aid of helicopters and supplied by the tramline carried by high towers, which is also visible from here.

DC 980.8 (1628.4 km) **F 507.2** (816.2 km) Turnoff to north for Yukon government Pine Lake recreation park and campground. Day-use area has sandy beach, boat launch and dock, group firepits, drinking water and 7 tent sites near beach. A 3.5-mile/6-km walking and biking trail begins at the campground entrance and ends at Haines Junction. The campground, adjacent **Pine Lake** with a view of the St. Elias Mountains, has 33 sites, outhouses, firewood, litter barrels, kitchen shelter, playground and drinking water. Camping fee $8. Fishing is good for lake trout, northern pike and grayling. There is a half-mile interpretive trail along the lakeshore featuring wildlife displays. ▲

DC 980.9 (1628.5 km) **F 507.1** (816.1 km) Access road to floatplane dock.

DC 982.2 (1630.8 km) **F 505.8** (814 km) Turnoff to north for Haines Junction airport. Flightseeing tours of glaciers, fly-in fishing and air charters available; fixed-wing aircraft or helicopters. **Private Aircraft:** Haines Junction airstrip; elev. 2,150 feet/655m; length 5,000 feet/1,524m; gravel. Fuel sales (100L) from Sifton Air.

Highway swings to south for last few miles into Haines Junction, offering a panoramic, close-up view of the Auriol Range straight ahead.

DC 984.8 (1635 km) **F 503.2** (809.8 km) Northbound travelers turn right (southbound travelers turn left) on Kluane Street for Kluane National Park Visitor Centre.

DC 985 (1635.3 km) **F 503** (809.5 km) **Historic Milepost 1016, junction** of Alaska Highway and Haines Highway (Haines Road).

IMPORTANT: THIS JUNCTION CAN BE CONFUSING; CHOOSE YOUR ROUTE CAREFULLY! Fairbanks- and Anchorage-bound travelers TURN RIGHT at this junction for

Flightseeing tours of the glaciated Kluane Range are available in Haines Junction, at Milepost DC 1023.7, and in Destruction Bay and Burwash Landing. (Earl L. Brown, staff)

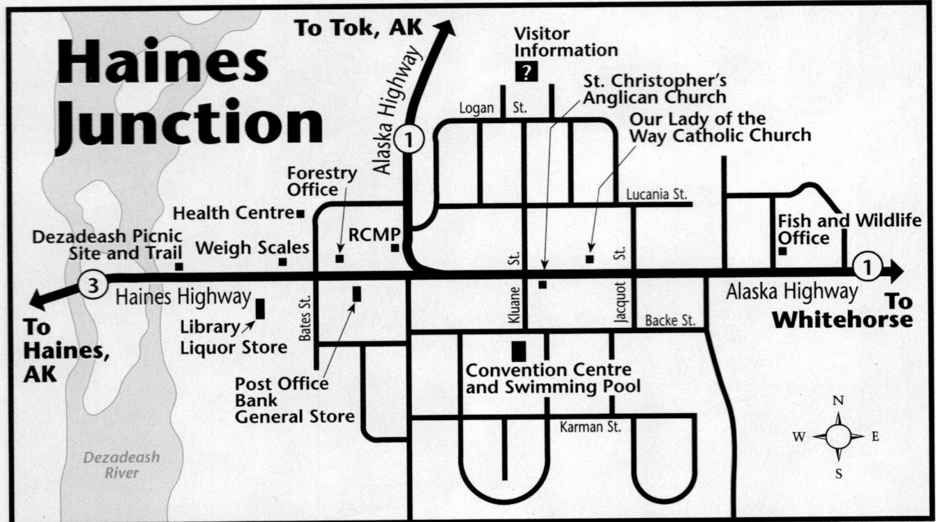

continuation of Alaska Highway (Yukon Highway 1); highway log follows description of Haines Junction, YT. Continue straight ahead (south) on the Haines Highway (Yukon Highway 3) for port of Haines, AK; see HAINES HIGHWAY section. (Haines-bound motorists note: It is a good idea to fill up with gas in Haines Junction. Gas is available en route only at Kathleen Lake Lodge and 33 Mile Roadhouse.)

Haines Junction

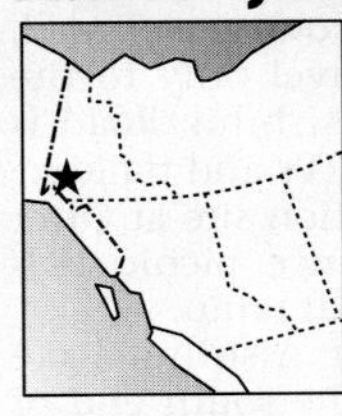

DC 985 (1635.3 km) **F 503** (809.5 km) **Historic Milepost 1016,** at the **junction** of the Alaska Highway (Yukon Highway 1) and the Haines Highway (Yukon Highway 3, also known as the Haines Road). Driving distance to Whitehorse, 100 miles/161 km; YT–AK border, 205 miles/330 km; Tok, 296 miles/476 km; and Haines, 150.5 miles/242 km. **Population:** 811. **Elevation:** 1,956 feet/596m. **Emergency Services: RCMP,** phone (867) 634-5555 or (867) 667-5555 **Fire Department,** phone (867) 634-2222. **Nursing Centre,** phone (867) 634-4444. **Radio:** 106.1 FM, 103.5 FM, CKRW 98.7 FM, CHON 90.5 FM, visitor radio 96.1 FM.

Visitor Information: At the Kluane National Park and Yukon government visitor information centre, 0.2 mile/0.3 km east of the junction just off the Alaska Highway. Phone (867) 634-2345. Interpretive exhibits, displays and an outstanding multi-image slide presentation are featured. The centre is open 8 A.M. to 8 P.M. daily from May to September, Monday through Friday the rest of the year.

Haines Junction was established in 1942 during construction of the Alaska Highway. The first buildings here were Army barracks for the U.S. Army Corps of Engineers. The engineers were to build a new branch road connecting the Alaska Highway with the port of Haines on Lynn Canal. The branch road—today's Haines Highway—was completed in 1943.

The Our Lady of the Way Catholic mission in Haines Junction was built in 1954, using parts from an old Army hut left from highway construction days. The octagonal log St. Christopher's Anglican Church was built in 1987, replacing a 1955 structure built from an old garage used in the pipeline project.

Haines Junction is still an important stop for travelers on the Alaska and Haines highways. Services are located along both highways, and clustered around Village Square at the junction, where a 24-foot monument depicts area wildlife.

Haines Junction offers an excellent range of accommodations. Visitor services include motels, 5 bed and breakfasts, restaurants, gas stations, garage services, groceries, souvenirs and a bakery. Gourmet dining at The Raven. There is a full-facility indoor heated swimming pool with showers available; open daily from May to late-August, fee charged. Also here are a RCMP office, Lands and Forest District Office and health centre. The post office and bank are located in Madley's General Store. (Banking service weekday afternoons; extended hours on Fridays.) The Commissioner James Smith Administration Building, at Kilometre 255.6 Haines Road, 0.2 mile/0.3 km south from the Alaska Highway junction, contains the government liquor store and public library. The airport is located on the Alaska Highway just east of

A 1st of July (Canada Day) parade in Haines Junction, YT. (Earl L. Brown, staff)

HAINES JUNCTION ADVERTISERS

Cozy Corner Motel & Restaurant ....Ph. (867) 634-2511
Frosty Freeze........Ph. (867) 634-2674
Gateway Motel and Lounge ....Ph. (867) 634-2371
Kluane Park Adventure Center........Ph. (867) 634-2313
Kluane Park Inn Ltd. ....Ph. (867) 634-2261
Kluane R.V. Kampground........Mile 985.3 Alaska Hwy.
Madley's General Store ....Ph. (867) 634-2200
Mountain View Motor Inn ....Ph. (867) 634-2646
North Country RV Park.....Ph. (867) 634-2505
Raven, The ....Ph. (867) 634-2500
Stardust Motel........Ph. (867) 634-2591
Trans North Helicopters........At the airport
Triple S Service Station.....Ph. (867) 634-2915
Village Bakery ....Next to visitor centre
Village of Haines Junction ....Ph. (867) 634-2291

town (see **Milepost DC 982.2**).

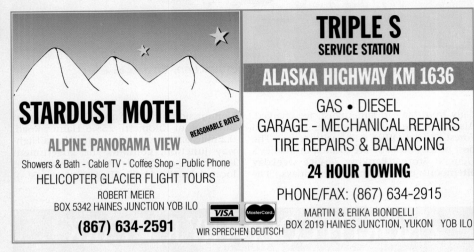

Haines Junction is on the eastern boundary of Kluane National Park Reserve. Administration offices and the visitor centre for the park are located north of town along with the park warden and general works station. Kluane (pronounced kloo-WA-nee) National Park Reserve encompasses extensive ice fields, mountains and wilderness. There is one campground, Kathleen Lake, located 16 miles/27 km south of town on the Haines Highway. There are numerous hiking trails of varying degrees of difficulty; check with the park visitor centre or see Vivien Lougheed's *Kluane Park Hiking Guide* (1992). Flightseeing the park by fixed-wing aircraft or helicopter from Haines Junction is a popular way to see Kluane's scenery; check with charter services at the airport.

The park was first suggested in 1942, and in 1943 land was set aside and designated the Kluane Game Sanctuary. A formal park region was established in 1972 and the national park boundaries were official in 1976. In 1980, Kluane National Park Reserve, along with Wrangell–St. Elias National Park in Alaska, became a joint UNESCO World Heritage Site. Kluane has become a world-class wilderness destination among outdoor recreation enthusiasts. Hikers note: There is mandatory registration for overnight trips into the park. Nightly or annual wilderness permits may be purchased. Bear resistant food canisters are mandatory on some overnight hikes ($150 deposit required).

For more information on Kluane National Park Reserve, stop by the excellent visitor centre and see the exhibits and the award-winning multi-image slide presentation; shown on the hour and half hour, fee charged. Also check at the visitor centre for a schedule of guided hikes, walks and campfire talks. These interpretive programs are available daily from the third week in June through August; fee charged. Contact Kluane National Park at Box 5495, Haines Junction, YT Y0B 1L0, or phone (867) 634-7209, fax (867) 634-7208.

Haines Junction is also headquarters for the new Tatshenshini–Alsek Wilderness Park. Created in 1993, the park protects the magnificent Tatshenshini and Alsek rivers area in Canada, where the 2 rivers join and flow (as the Alsek) to the Gulf of Alaska at Dry Bay. Known to riverrunners as "the Tat," the Tatshenshini is famous for its whitewater rafting, stunning scenery and wildlife. Due to a dramatic increase in river traffic in recent years, permits are required from the park agencies (the National Park Service in Alaska and B.C. Parks in Canada). Locally, Kluane Park Adventure Center (867/634-2313) offers rafting trips to the Tatshenshini. Contact Access Kluane Tours and Information at (867) 634-2816. For more information about the park, contact Tatshenshini–Alsek Wilderness Park, Box 5495, Haines Junction, YT Y0B 1L0; phone (867) 634-7209, fax (867) 634-7208.

Picnicking available at day-use area on the Dezadeash River, located at the west edge of town on the Haines Highway, which also has a wheelchair-accessible trail. Other outdoor recreation available locally includes guided fishing and boating (canoe and boat rentals available). ♿

RV camping available at several campgrounds in and near town. Dump stations and water are also available at local service station and campgrounds. Yukon government campground located 4.2 miles/6.7 km east of junction on the Alaska Highway at Pine Lake. ▲

Special events in Haines Junction include the Alsek Music Festival held June 12–14, 1998, and the Pine Lake Regatta in July (see **Milepost DC 980.8**). Also remember that July 1st is Canada Day (the anniversary of Canada's confederation) and is celebrated with parades, barbecue and flags. Kluane Mountain Festival May 8–10, 1998.

Bicycling offers several events, including the Trail of '42 Road Race (May 30, 1998) and the Kluane to Chilkat International Bike Relay (June 20, 1998), which attracted 950 cyclists last year. *IMPORTANT: Watch for cyclists on the Alaska and Haines highways during these events.*

Alaska Highway Log

(continued)

Distance* from Dawson Creek (DC) is followed by distance from Fairbanks (F). Original mileposts are indicated in the text as Historical Mile.

*Mileages from Dawson Creek are based on actual driving distance. Kilometres from Dawson Creek are based on physical kilometreposts. Please read Mileposts and Kilometreposts in the introduction for an explanation of how this highway is logged.

DC 985 (1635.3 km) **F 503** (809.5 km) **Junction** of the Alaska Highway (Yukon Highway 1) and the Haines Highway (Yukon Highway 3). Markers indicate distance to Destruction Bay 67 miles/108 km, Beaver Creek 186 miles/299 km.

Northbound: From Haines Junction to the YT–AK border, the Alaska Highway is in fair to good condition but narrow, often without shoulders. Watch for frost heaves north from Destruction Bay to Beaver Creek.

Southbound: Good paved highway with wide shoulders next 380 miles/611.5 km (from here to Watson Lake) with the exception of some short sections of narrow road and occasional gravel breaks. *NOTE: This junction can be confusing; choose your route carefully!* Whitehorse-bound travelers TURN LEFT at junction for continuation of Alaska Highway (Yukon Highway 1); highway log follows description of Haines Junction. TURN RIGHT for the Haines Highway (Yukon Highway 3) to the port of Haines, AK; see HAINES HIGHWAY section for log. (Haines-bound motorists note: Between Haines Junction, YT, and Haines, AK, a distance of 151.6 miles/246 km, gas is available only at Kathleen Lake Lodge, summers only, and 33 Mile Roadhouse.)

DC 985.3 (1635.9 km) **F 502.7** (809 km) Kluane RV Kampground; RV and tent camping, gas, diesel, dump station, pay phone. ▲

DC 985.8 (1636.5 km) **F 502.2** (808.2 km) **Historical Mile 1017.** Alcan Fuels; gas, diesel, propane, auto repair and towing. Open daily, year-round.

DC 985.9 (1636.7 km) **F 502.1** (808 km) Stardust Motel and Triple S Service Station.

DC 986.6 (1637.8 km) **F 501.4** (806.9 km) Highway follows the Kluane Ranges which are to the west.

DC 987.8 (1639.8 km) **F 500.2** (805 km) **Historical Mile 1019.** Kluane National Park warden headquarters. (Visitor information in Haines Junction at the visitor centre.)

DC 988.3 (1640.6 km) **F 499.7** (804.1 km) Rest area to west with pit toilets.

DC 991.4 (1645.6 km) **F 496.6** (799.1 km) Highway climbs next 9 miles/14.5 km northbound to Bear Creek Summit.

DC 991.6 (1645.9 km) **F 496.4** (798.9 km) **Historic Milepost 1022**, Mackintosh Trading Post historic sign. Lodge to east; food, gas, lodging and camping. Helicopter flightseeing service across from lodge. Trailhead to west for Alsek Pass trail; 18 miles/29 km long, suitable for shorter day hikes, mountain bikes permitted. ▲

Mackintosh Lodge offers something for everyone, from our delicious homemade meals and fresh baking from "Gramma's Kitchen" to our comfy rooms with handmade quilts. A favorite stopping spot for Alaskan travelers. Across from the lodge, the Alsek Trail leads to Kluane National Park, a world heritage site. "Majestic mountains make for Mackintosh miracles." [ADVERTISEMENT]

DC 1000.1 (1660 km) **F 487.9** (785.2 km) Bear Creek Summit (elev. 3,294 feet/1,004m), highest point on the Alaska Highway between Whitehorse and Fairbanks.

Silver City at Milepost DC 1020.3 was a trading post with roadhouse and NWMP barracks. (Earl L. Brown, staff)

Glimpse of Kloo Lake to north of highway between Kilometreposts 1660 and 1662.

DC 1003.5 (1665.4 km) **F 484.5** (779.7 km) Jarvis Creek.

DC 1003.6 (1665.6 km) **F 484.4** (779.5 km) **Historic Milepost 1035.** Turnout to west next to Jarvis Creek. Pretty spot for a picnic. Trail rides may be available here with Ruby Range Trail Rides.

Jarvis Creek, poor to fair fishing for grayling 8 to 16 inches all summer; Dolly Varden 8 to 10 inches, early summer.

DC 1013.6 (1682 km) **F 474.4** (763.5 km) Beautiful view to west of the snow-covered Kluane Ranges. For northbound travelers, the Alaska Highway parallels the Kluane Ranges from Haines Junction to Koidern, presenting a nearly unbroken chain of 7,000- to 8,000-foot/2,134- to 2,438-m summits interrupted only by a few large valleys cut by glacier-fed rivers and streams. West of the Kluane Ranges is the Duke Depression (not visible from the highway), a narrow trough separating the Kluane Ranges from the St. Elias Mountains. Major peaks in the St. Elias (not visible from the highway) are: Mount Logan, Canada's highest peak, at 19,545 feet/5,959m (recalculated in 1992 from 19,520 feet by a scientific expedition); Mount St. Elias, 18,008 feet/5,489m; Mount Lucania, 17,147 feet/5,226m; King Peak, 16,971 feet/5,173m; Mount Wood, Mount Vancouver, Mount Hubbard and Mount Steele, all over 15,000 feet/4,572m. Mount Steele (16,664 feet/5,079m) was named for Superintendent Sam Steele of the North West Mounted Police. As commanding officer of the NWMP in the Yukon in 1898, Steele established permanent detachments at the summits of the White and Chilkoot passes to ensure not only that gold stampeders obeyed Canadian laws, but also had sufficient supplies to carry them through to the gold fields.

DC 1016.5 (1686.7 km) **F 471.5** (758.8 km) Turnout to west with view of Kluane Ranges.

DC 1017.2 (1687.8 km) **F 470.8** (757.7 km) Christmas Creek.

DC 1019.8 (1692 km) **F 468.2** (753.5 km) First glimpse of Kluane Lake for northbound travelers at Boutillier Summit (elev. 3,293 feet/1,003m), second highest point on the highway between Whitehorse and Fairbanks.

DC 1020 (1692.5 km) **F 468** (753.2 km) Turnout to east with information plaques on area history and geography.

DC 1020.3 (1693 km) **F 467.7** (752.7 km) **Historic Milepost 1053.** Historic sign and interpretive panel at turnoff for Silver City. Access to a bed and breakfast. Follow dirt and gravel road east 3.1 miles/5 km to ruins of Silver City. This old trading post, with roadhouse and North West Mounted Police barracks, was on the wagon road from Whitehorse to the placer goldfields of Kluane Lake (1904–24). Good photo opportunities.

DC 1020.9 (1694 km) **F 467.1** (751.7 km) Silver Creek.

DC 1022.5 (1696.5 km) **F 465.5** (749.1 km) Turnout to east for Kluane Lake Research Station; station and airstrip are 0.9 mile/1.4 km via a straight gravel road. This research station is sponsored by the Arctic Institute of North America, University of Calgary.

Highway follows west shore of Kluane Lake next 39 miles/63 km northbound to Burwash Landing.

DC 1023.7 (1698.5 km) **F 464.3** (747.2 km) **Historical Mile 1056.** Kluane Camp commemorative plaque. Kluane Lake Lodge (closed). Trans North helicopter base operates here, offering flightseeing trips in summer. These highly recommended flightseeing trips offer spectacular views of the Slims River Valley and Kaskawulsh Glacier.

Trans North Helicopters. See display ad this section.

DC 1026.8 (1703.4 km) **F 461.2** (742.2 km) Slim's River East trail turnoff (2-mile/3.3-km access road, not recommended for motorhomes); parking at trailhead. This 12.4-mile/20-km trail is rated "easy" by the *Kluane Hiking Guide.*

DC 1027.8 (1705 km) **F 460.2** (740.6 km) Slim's River bridge (clearance 17.7 feet/5.4m). Slim's River, which flows into Kluane Lake, was named for a packhorse that drowned here during the 1903 Kluane gold rush. Sheep Mountain is directly ahead

Aerial view of Slim's River bridge area on Kluane Lake. (Earl L. Brown, staff)

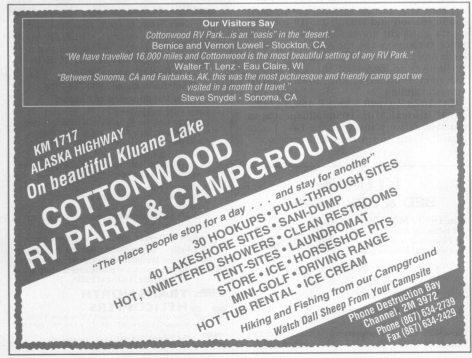

for northbound travelers. The highway winds along Kluane Lake: Drive carefully!

DC 1028.8 (1706.6 km) **F 459.2** (739 km) Sheep Mountain visitor information centre. Excellent interpretive programs, laser disc information videos, parking and outhouses are available. Open mid-May to mid-September. Hours are 9 A.M. to 5 P.M. June through August, 9:30 A.M. to 5 P.M. in May and September. Stop here for information on Kluane National Park's flora and fauna. A viewing telescope is set up to look for sheep on Sheep Mountain. This is the sheep's winter range; best chance to see them is late August and September, good chance in late May to early June. Register at the Sheep Mountain Centre for hiking in the park. *NOTE: The face of Sheep Mountain has been designated a special preservation zone. Check with the centre for designated hiking areas.*

DC 1029 (1706.9 km) **F 459** (738.7 km) Slim's River West trail; trailhead adjacent visitor information centre.

The small white cross on the side of Sheep Mountain marks the grave of Alexander Clark Fisher, a prospector who came into this area about 1906.

DC 1030.7 (1709.5 km) **F 457.3** (735.9 km) **Historic Milepost 1061.** Soldier's Summit. The Alaska Canada Military Highway was officially opened with a ribbon-cutting ceremony here on blizzardy Nov. 20, 1942. A rededication ceremony was held Nov. 20, 1992, commemorating the 50th anniversary of the highway. A trail leads up to the original dedication site from the parking area.

Several turnouts overlooking Kluane Lake next mile northbound. This beautiful lake is the largest in Yukon Territory, covering approximately 154 square miles/400 square km. The Ruby Range lies on the east side of the lake. Boat rentals are available at Destruction Bay and Burwash Landing.

Kluane Lake, excellent fishing for lake trout, northern pike and grayling.

DC 1031.9 (1711.7 km) **F 456.1** (734 km) **Kluane Mun Fishing.** "Fish Place" in southern Tutchone. Luxuriate in our lakeside hot tub, enjoy the view while savoring a delicious meal. Stay in one of our country-style rooms. Enjoy guided-fishing, fly-fishing and wilderness river trips, while your First Nations guide narrates the history and culture of the indigenous peoples. Phone (867) 841-4551. [ADVERTISEMENT]

DC 1034.5 (1715.8 km) **F 453.5** (729.8 km) Williscroft Creek.

DC 1034.9 (1717 km) **F 453.1** (729.2 km) **Historical Mile 1067. Cottonwood RV Park and Campground.** See display ad this section. ▲

DC 1039.7 (1724.7 km) **F 448.3** (721.4 km) Congdon Creek trailhead to west; 16-mile/26-km hike to Sheep Mountain.

DC 1039.9 (1725 km) **F 448.1** (721.1 km) **Historical Mile 1072.** Turnoff to east for Congdon Creek Yukon government campground on Kluane Lake. Drive in 0.4 mile/0.6 km via gravel loop road; tenting area, 77 level sites (some pull-through), outhouses, kitchen shelters, water pump, firewood, firepits, picnic tables, sandy beach, interpretive talks, playground, boat launch. Camping fee $8. ▲

DC 1040.4 (1725.6 km) **F 447.6** (720.3 km) Congdon Creek. According to R. Coutts, *Yukon: Places & Names,* Congdon Creek is believed to have been named by a miner after Frederick Tennyson Congdon. A lawyer from Nova Scotia, Congdon came to the

Yukon in 1898 and held various political posts until 1911.

DC 1046.9 (1735.3 km) **F 441.1** (709.9 km) Nines Creek. Turnout to east.

DC 1047.3 (1736.2 km) **F 440.7** (709.2 km) Mines Creek.

DC 1048.9 (1739 km) **F 439.1** (706.6 km) Bock's Brook.

DC 1051.5 (1743 km) **F 436.5** (702.5 km) **Historic Milepost 1083. DESTRUCTION BAY** (pop. less than 100). **Emergency Services: Health clinic,** phone (867) 841-4444; **Ambulance,** phone (867) 841-3333; **Fire Department,** phone (867) 841-2221. Located on the shore of Kluane Lake, Destruction Bay is one of several towns that grew out of the building of the Alaska Highway. It earned its name when a storm destroyed buildings and materials here. Destruction Bay was one of the many relay stations spaced at 100-mile intervals to give truck drivers a break and a chance to repair their vehicles. Historic sign adjacent historic milepost. A highway maintenance camp is located here. Destruction Bay has camping, boat launch, boat rentals and guided fishing tours. A fishing derby is held first weekend in July. Food, gas, camping and lodging available at the Talbot Arm (open year-round) and Sehja Services. Glacier flightseeing trips available.

Talbot Arm Motel in Destruction Bay at historic Mile 1083 Alaska Highway has been offering Yukon visitors a modern, clean and friendly stop since 1967. Built and managed by the Van der Veen family, Talbot Arm has been setting the standard for rural lodges. In 1988 we were recognized by our peers for our efforts by winning the Sourdough Award from Tourism Industry Association, and Customers Service Award from Chevron. Recently we have added 2 attractions to our list of services: Ruby Range Airways Ltd. is headquartered at Talbot Arm and is offering glacier flights in Kluane National Park and surrounding area. Enjoy a scenic flight over the largest non-polar icefield in the world and Canada's most majestic peaks in a Cessna 182P piloted by Neil Hardy. Talbot Arm Fishing Tours are also

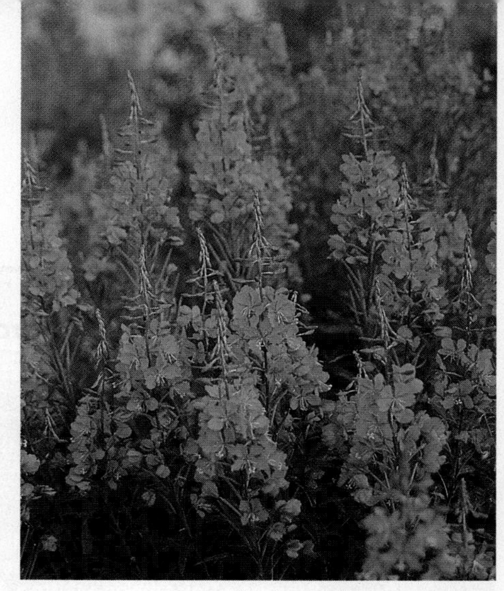

Fireweed, named for its ability to thrive in fire-ravaged areas, is the Yukon territorial flower. (Earl L. Brown, staff)

arranged at the lodge. Our 3 available guides have over 50 years total experience hunting the huge Kluane Lake trout. A day in a boat on our crystal clear waters in the best scenery in the Yukon won't soon be forgotten. [ADVERTISEMENT]

DC 1051.7 (1743.3 km) **F 436.3** (702.1 km) Gas, meals, lodging and camping. ▲

DC 1051.9 (1743.6 km) **F 436.1** (701.8 km) Rest area with litter barrels and toilet.

DC 1055.1 (1748.8 km) **F 432.9** (696.7 km) Lewes Creek.

World's largest gold pan is next to Kluane Museum in Burwash Landing.

(© Beth Davidow)

DC 1058.3 (1753.9 km) **F 429.7** (691.5 km) Halfbreed (Copper Joe) Creek trailhead.

DC 1061.3 (1758.7 km) **F 426.7** (686.7 km) Store, post office, RV park and snack bar.

Duke River Trading Co. See display ad this section. ▲

DC 1061.5 (1759 km) **F 426.5** (686.4 km) **Historic Milepost 1093.** Kluane Museum and turnoff to east for **BURWASH LANDING,** (pop. 84) a village with post office, community hall, church and 24-hour gas, food, camping and lodging on Kluane Lake. Boat rentals and Kluane Lake fishing trips available. Helicopter flightseeing trips of Kluane National Park are also available out of Burwash Landing.

Burwash Landing is known for its black spruce burl bowls. Burls start as an irritation or infection in the spruce. The tree sends extra sap as healant, which creates a growth or burl. After the tree dies, the burl is cut out and smoothed into a bowl. Check out Burlbilly Hill at **Milepost DC 1061.6.**

The highly recommended Kluane Museum of Natural History is located on the east side of the highway at the turnoff; open 9 A.M. to 9 P.M. in summer; phone (867) 841-5561. The museum features a video room with Northern interest videos; wildlife, minerals and other natural history exhibits; and has a souvenir shop displaying locally made handicrafts. Admission is charged. Next to the museum is the world's largest gold pan, measuring 28 feet/ 8m high.

Burwash Landing was settled in 1904 by the Jacquot brothers, Louis and Eugene, as a supply centre for local miners. The log mission here, Our Lady of the Holy Rosary, was built in 1944. The historic sign here reads: "After months of rough camp life, American soldiers were surprised and delighted when they reached this prosperous little settlement which seemed like an oasis in the wilderness. Burwash also became the home of Father Eusebe Morisset, an Oblate Missionary, who served as an auxiliary chaplain with the American Army."

Burwash Landing Resort & RV Park. See display ad this section. ▲

Kluane Museum of Natural History. See display ad this section.

DC 1061.6 (1759.2 km) **F 426.4** (686.2 km) **Burlbilly Hill.** The most unique stop at Mile 1093 is "Burlbilly Hill," 200 feet north of the museum. The visitor will see rows of "burly logs" on the hill. Another surprise is a small woodshop with its variety of finely finished burl products, "burl bowls" and "diamond willow canes." Come and watch Obie and Dubie at work. Wir sprechen deutsch! Phone (867) 841-4607. [ADVERTISEMENT]

DC 1062 (1759.8 km) **F 426** (685.5 km) **Dalan Campground.** Turn off north, to Dalan Campground, 1 km off the Alaska Highway on the shores of beautiful Kluane Lake, "largest lake in the Yukon." Owned and operated by Kluane First Nation, this campground offers 25 individual private campsites, RVs welcome! Firewood, water pump, picnic tables, firepits and dump station are available. New for 1998 in Burwash—community recreation centre with library, weight room, kitchen and hall rental. Laudromat and showers adjacent. For additional information, call (867) 841-4274. [ADVERTISEMENT] ▲

Spruce burls on display along the Alaska Highway. The burls start as an irritation or infection in the spruce, with extra sap creating the growth. (© Roger Holden)

DC 1062.7 (1761 km) **F 425.3** (684.4 km) **Historic Milepost 1094. Private Aircraft:** Burwash Yukon government airstrip to north; elev. 2,643 feet/806m; length 6,000 feet/1,829m; gravel, no fuel.

DC 1067 (1768.8 km) **F 421** (677.5 km) Duke River bridge (clearance 17.7 feet/5.4m). The Duke River flows into Kluane Lake; named for George Duke, an early prospector.

DC 1071.9 (1776.5 km) **F 416.1** (669.6 km) Turnout to north. Burwash Creek, named for Lachlin Taylor Burwash, a mining recorder at Silver City in 1903.

DC 1076.7 (1784.1 km) **F 411.3** (661.9 km) Sakiw Creek.

DC 1077.3 (1785.1 km) **F 410.4** (660.5 km) Rest area with information panels and observation platform overlooking Kluane River.

DC 1078.5 (1787 km) **F 409.5** (659 km) Buildings to west belong to Hudson Bay Mining and Smelting Co.'s Wellgreen Nickel Mines, named for Wellington Bridgeman Green, the prospector who discovered the mineral showing in 1952. During the mine's operation, from May 1972 to July 1973, three shiploads of concentrates (averaging 13,000 tons each) were trucked to Haines, AK. The material proved to be too insufficient to be economical. No facilities or services.

DC 1079.4 (1788.5 km) **F 408.6** (657.6 km) Quill Creek.

DC 1080.9 (1791 km) **F 407.1** (655.1 km) Glacier Creek. Kluane River to east of highway.

DC 1083.5 (1795.5 km) **F 404.5** (651 km) **Historic Milepost 1117.** Turnout. Sign commemorates 1st Lt. Roland Small, of the 18th Engineers Regiment, who died in a jeep accident near this site during construction of the Alaska Highway in 1942. Short road to Kluane River; no turnaround.

DC 1084.6 (1797.2 km) **F 403.4** (649.2 km) **Historical Mile 1118.** Kluane Wilderness Village; gas, restaurant, saloon with burl bar; camping and lodging. Open year-round. Viewing platform of Mount Kennedy, Mount Logan and Mount Lucania. Halfway mark between Whitehorse and Tok. ▲

DC 1086.6 (1799.5 km) **F 401.4** (646 km) Swede Johnson Creek. Turnout to east.

DC 1091.3 (1808 km) **F 396.7** (638.4 km) Buildings to east are a dormant pump station once used to pressure up fuel being transferred from Haines to Fairbanks.

DC 1095 (1814 km) **F 393** (632.4 km) NorthwesTel microwave tower visible ahead northbound.

DC 1095.4 (1814.6 km) **F 392.6** (631.8 km) Abandoned Mountain View Lodge. View of Donjek River Valley.

Alaska Highway workers faced one of their toughest construction jobs during completion of the Alaska Highway in 1943 from the Donjek River to the Alaska border. Swampy ground underlain by permafrost, numerous creeks, lakes and rivers, plus a thick insulating ground cover made this section particularly difficult for road builders.

DC 1096.3 (1816 km) **F 391.7** (630.4 km) Turnout to west with view of Donjek River Valley and the Icefield Ranges of the St. Elias Mountains. Interpretive display.

DC 1099.7 (1819.5 km) **F 388.3** (624.9 km) **Historic Milepost 1130.** Turnout with interpretive panel on the Donjek River bridge. Sign reads: "Glacial rivers, like the Donjek, posed a unique problem for the builders of the Alaska Highway. These braided mountain streams would flood after a heavy rainfall or rapid glacial melt, altering the waters' course and often leaving bridges crossing dry ground."

DC 1100 (1820 km) **F 388** (624.4 km) Donjek River bridge (clearance 17.4 feet/5.3m). Access to river at north end of bridge on west side of highway. This wide silty river is a major tributary of the White River. According to R. Coutts, *Yukon: Places & Names,* the Donjek is believed to have been named by Charles Willard Hayes in 1891 from the Indian word for a peavine that grows in the area.

DC 1113.5 (1844.4 km) **F 374.5** (602.7 km) **Edith Creek** bridge, turnout to west. Try your hand at gold panning here; "colours" have been found. Grayling fishing, June through September.

DC 1113.8 (1844.8 km) **F 374.2** (602.2 km) **Historical Mile 1147. Pine Valley Motel and Cafe.**

DC 1118.3 (1852.2 km) **F 369.7** (595 km) Koidern River bridge No. 1.

DC 1118.8 (1853 km) **F 369.2** (594.2 km) **Historical Mile 1152.** Lake Creek Yukon government campground just west of highway; 30 large level sites (6 pull-through), water pump, litter barrels, firewood, firepits, picnic tables, kitchen shelter and outhouses. Camping fee $8. ▲

DC 1122.7 (1859.5 km) **F 365.3** (587.9 km) **Historical Mile 1156.** Longs Creek.

DC 1125 (1863.5 km) **F 363** (584.2 km) Turnout to east with litter barrel.

DC 1125.7 (1864.7 km) **F 362.3** (583 km) **Pickhandle Lake** to west; interpretive panels on native trading routes, pond life and muskrats. Good fishing from boat for northern pike all summer; also grayling, whitefish and lingcod.

DC 1127.8 (1868 km) **F 360.2** (579.7 km) *CAUTION: Watch for road construction next 2.5 miles/4 km northbound in 1998.*

DC 1128 (1868.4 km) **F 360** (579.3 km) Aptly named Reflection Lake to west mirrors the Kluane Ranges. The highway parallels this range between Koidern and Haines Junction.

DC 1130.6 (1872.6 km) **F 357.4** (575.2 km) **Historical Mile 1164.** Lodge.

DC 1130.7 (1872.8 km) **F 357.3** (575 km) Koidern River bridge No. 2.

DC 1133.7 (1877.6 km) **F 354.3** (570.2 km) **Historic Milepost 1167.** Bear Flats Lodge (closed in 1997, current status unknown).

DC 1135 (1880 km) **F 353** (568 km) **Historical Mile 1169.** White River Motor Inn; food, gas, lodging and camping. Open year-round. ▲

White River Motor Inn. See display ad this section. ▲

DC 1135.6 (1881 km) **F 352.4** (567.1 km) White River bridge, clearance 17.1 feet/5.2m. The White River, a major tributary of the Yukon River, was named by Hudson's Bay Co. explorer Robert Campbell for its white colour, caused by the volcanic ash in the water. *This river is considered very dangerous; not recommended for boating.*

CAUTION: Slow down for sharp turn in road at north end of bridge.

DC 1141.5 (1890.5 km) **F 346.5** (557.6 km) **Moose Lake** to west, grayling to 18 inches, use dry flies and small spinners, midsummer. Boat needed for lake.

DC 1144.3 (1895 km) **F 343.7** (553.1 km) Sanpete Creek, named by an early prospector after Sanpete County in Utah.

DC 1147.5 (1900.3 km) **F 340.5** (548 km) Dry Creek No. 1. Turnout to east.

DC 1150.3 (1904.5 km) **F 337.7** (543.5 km) **Historical Mile 1184.** Dry Creek No. 2. Historical marker to west about the Chrisna gold rush.

DC 1155 (1911.8 km) **F 333** (535.9 km) Small Lake to east.

DC 1155.2 (1913 km) **F 332.8** (535.6 km) **Historical Mile 1188.** Turnoff for Snag Junction Yukon government campground, 0.4 mile/0.6 km in on gravel loop road. There are 15 tent and vehicle sites (some level), a kitchen shelter, outhouses, picnic tables, firewood, firepits and litter barrels. Camping fee $8. Small-boat launch. Swimming in Small Lake. A dirt road (status unknown) connects the Alaska Highway here with the abandoned airfield and Indian village at Snag to the northeast. ▲

DC 1162.1 (1924.5 km) **F 325.9** (524.5 km) Inger Creek.

DC 1165.7 (1930 km) **F 322.3** (518.7 km) View of Nutzotin Mountains to northwest, Kluane Ranges to southwest. On a clear day you should be able to see the snow-clad Wrangell Mountains in the distance to the west.

DC 1167.2 (1932.4 km) **F 320.8** (516.3 km) Beaver Creek plank bridge, clearance 17.1 feet/5.2m.

Beaver Creek

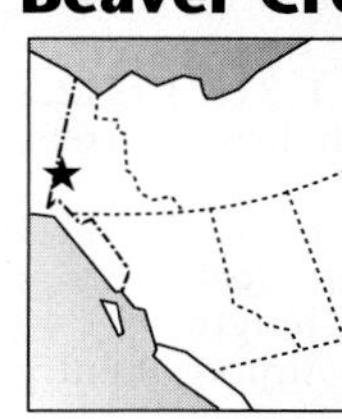

DC 1168.5 (1934.5 km) **F 319.5** (514.2 km) **Historic Milepost 1202.** Driving distance to Haines Junction, 184 miles/295 km; to Tok, 113 miles/182 km; to Haines, 334 miles/537.5 km. **Population:** 140. **Emergency Services: RCMP**, phone (867) 862-5555. **Ambulance**, phone (867) 862-3333. **Nursing Station:** (867) 862-4444. **Visitor Information:** Yukon government visitor information centre, open daily late May through mid-September. Phone (867) 862-7321. The visitor centre has a book of dried Yukon wildflowers for those interested in the flora of the territory.

Site of the old Canadian customs station. Local residents were pleased to see customs relocated north of town in 1983, having long endured the flashing lights and screaming sirens set off whenever a tourist forgot to stop.

Beaver Creek is 1 of 2 sites where Alaska Highway construction crews working from opposite directions connected the highway. In October 1942, Alaska Highway construction operations were being rushed to conclusion as winter set in. Eastern and western sector construction crews (the 97th and 18th Engineers) pushed through to meet at a

BEAVER CREEK ADVERTISERS

Beaver Creek Motor Inn ....Ph. (867) 862-7600
Ida's Motel & Restaurant ....Ph. (867) 862-7223
Westmark Beaver Creek................Ph. (800) 544-0970

junction on Beaver Creek on Oct. 28., thus making it possible for the first time for vehicles to travel the entire length of the highway. East–west crews had connected at Contact Creek on Sept. 24, 1942.

Motels, gas stations with repair service, a post office and licensed restaurants are located here. Beaver Creek is also an overnight stop for bus travelers. Private RV park with hookups, hot showers, store, laundry and dump station. Informational panels on the Yukon Centennial are located throughout the city. ▲

The interesting looking church here is Our Lady of Grace mission. Built in 1961, it is 1 of 3 Catholic missions on the north Alaska Highway (the others are in Burwash Landing and Haines Junction). Services from the last Sunday of May to first Sunday of September. There is a public swimming pool beside the community club. Check with the information centre about the live stage show at the Westmark Inn, evenings in summer; admission charged.

Alaska Highway Log

(continued)

Distance* from Dawson Creek (DC) is followed by distance from Fairbanks (F). Original mileposts are indicated in the text as Historical Mile.

*Mileages from Dawson Creek are based on actual driving distance. Kilometres from Dawson Creek are based on physical kilometreposts. Please read Mileposts and Kilometreposts in the introduction for an explanation of how this highway is logged.

DC 1169.7 (1936.3 km) **F 318.3** (512.2 km) Rest area to west with litter barrels, picnic tables and outhouses.

DC 1170.3 (1937.3 km) **F 317.7** (511.3 km) **Private Aircraft:** Beaver Creek airstrip; elev. 2,129 feet/649m; length 3,740 feet/1,140m; gravel; no fuel. Airport of entry for Canada customs.

DC 1170.5 (1937.6 km) **F 317.5** (511 km) Beaver Creek Canada customs station; phone (403) 862-7230. Open 24 hours a day year-round. All traffic entering Canada must stop here for clearance.

Canada–U.S. international boundary.

(© Bruce M. Herman)

NOTE: Narrow winding road northbound from here to border (next 19.4 miles/31.2 km). Road reconstruction has improved this stretch of highway over past years.

DC 1175.4 (1945.5 km) **F 312.6** (503.1 km) Snag Creek plank bridge.

DC 1176.3 (1946.9 km) **F 311.7** (501.6 km) Mirror Creek.

DC 1178.3 (1952 km) **F 309.7** (498.4 km) Lake to east, turnout to west.

DC 1186 (1963 km) **F 302** (486 km) Little Scottie Creek.

DC 1189.5 (1967.5 km) **F 298.5** (480.4 km) **Historic Milepost 1221.** Turnout with plaque and other markers at Canada–U.S. international border. Litter barrels. From the viewing decks, note the narrow clearing marking the border. This is part of the 20-foot-/6-m-wide swath cut by surveyors from 1904 to 1920 along the 141st meridian (from Demarcation Point on the Arctic Ocean south 600 miles/966 km to Mount St. Elias in the Wrangell Mountains) to mark the Alaska–Canada border. This swath continues south to mark the boundary between southeastern Alaska and Canada. Portions of the swath are cleared periodically by the International Boundary Commission.

TIME ZONE CHANGE: Alaska observes Alaska time; Yukon Territory observes Pacific time.

DC 1189.8 (1968 km) **F 298.2** (479.9 km) **Historical Mile 1221.8.** U.S. customs border station.

IMPORTANT: *The MILEPOST®* log now switches to physical mileposts for northbound travelers. For southbound travelers, the log is based on actual driving distance. The Alaska Highway is approximately 32 miles/51 km shorter than the traditional figure of 1,221.8 miles between Dawson Creek and the YT–AK border. Please read the information on Mileposts and Kilometre posts in the introduction to the Alaska Highway.

Northbound: Fair to good pavement to Fairbanks. Watch for frost heaves, potholes and pavement breaks next 40 miles/64 km.

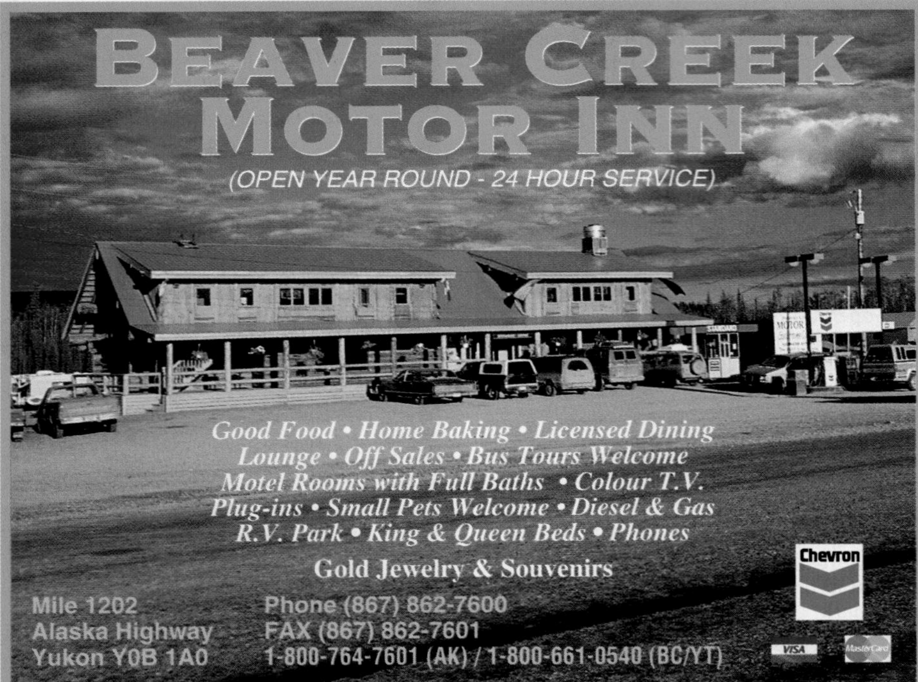

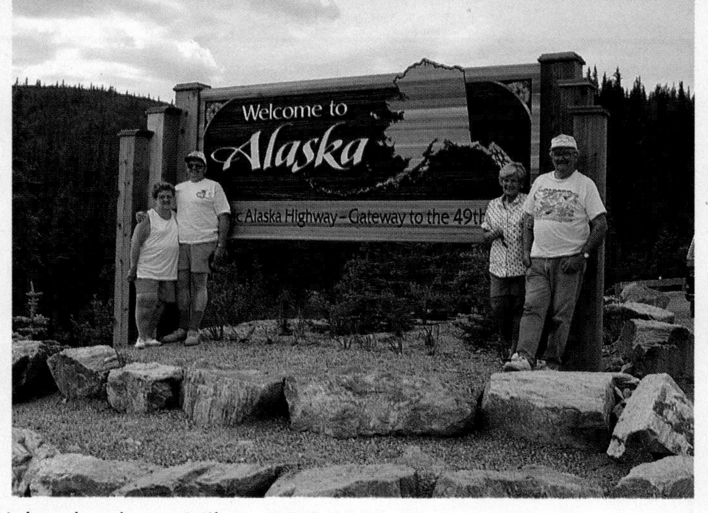

Travelers take advantage of photo opportunities at the Alaska–Yukon border at Milepost DC 1189.5. (*Earl L. Brown, staff*)

NOTE: Watch for road construction northbound to Tok.

Southbound: Narrow, winding road to Haines Junction. Improved highway to Beaver Creek, fair to good pavement to Haines Junction. Watch for frost heaves, rough spots, gravel breaks and road construction.

ALASKA ROUTE 2

Distance* from Dawson Creek (DC) is followed by distance from Fairbanks (F).

*Mileages from Dawson Creek and Fairbanks are based on physical mileposts in Alaska. Kilometres given are the metric equivalents of these mileages. Read Mileposts and Kilometreposts on page 90 for more detail.

DC 1221.8 (1966.3 km) **F 298.2** (479.9 km) Port Alcan U.S. Customs and Immigration Service border station, open 24 hours a day year-round; pay phone (credit card and collect calls only) and restrooms. All traffic entering Alaska must stop for clearance. Phone (907) 774-2242; emergencies, (907) 774-2252.

Border Branch U.S. post office is located here (ZIP 99764); ask for directions at the customs office.

DC 1222.5 (1967.4 km) **F 297.5** (478.8 km) Tetlin National Wildlife Refuge boundary sign to west.

DC 1223.4 (1968.9 km) **F 296.6** (477.3 km) Scotty Creek bridge.

DC 1224.6 (1970.7 km) **F 295.4** (475.4 km) Double-ended gravel turnout to southwest at Highway Lake with USF&WS interpretive sign on wetlands. Beaver lodges southwest side of highway.

DC 1225.4 (1972 km) **F 294.6** (474.1 km) USF&WS Desper Creek parking area and canoe launch.

DC 1225.5 (1972.2 km) **F 294.5** (473.9

km) **Border City Motel & RV Park.** See display ad this section. ▲

DC 1226 (1973 km) **F 294** (473.1 km) **Scottie Creek Services.** See display ad this section.

DC 1227.8 (1975.9 km) **F 292.2** (470.2 km) Large double-ended paved parking area to southwest with USF&WS interpretive sign on migratory birds and area geography. View to south of lakes in Chisana (SHOE-sanna) River valley along Scotty Creek and west to the Nutzotin Mountains. The Chisana gold rush took place in 1913. A mining camp was established on Cross Creek near the Chisana River, 38 miles southeast of Nabesna in the Wrangell Mountains. The settlement's population peaked at 148 in 1920.

DC 1229 (1977.8 km) **F 291** (468.3 km) USF&WS log cabin visitor center to south. Viewing deck and outdoor displays on wildlife and other subjects. Indoor wildlife

displays and mounts. Deckside nature talks given daily. Restrooms (wheelchair accessible). Open 7 A.M. to 7 P.M. Memorial Day to Labor Day. Current highway conditions and fishing information posted on bulletin board. ♿

CAUTION: Watch for frost heaves, patches and potholes northbound and southbound.

DC 1230.9 (1980.9 km) **F 289.1** (465.3 km) View of Island Lake.

DC 1233.3 (1984.7 km) **F 286.7** (461.4 km) Large paved double-ended parking area to northeast on old alignment. Watch for bears and frost heaves.

DC 1237 (1990.7 km) **F 283** (455.4 km) Trail to **Hidden Lake** (1 mile/1.6 km); rainbow fishing. USF&WS interpretive signs on rainbow trout and permafrost.

DC 1240 (1995.5 km) **F 280** (450.6 km) Turnout to west; no easy turnaround. Access to **Willow Lake** for fishing (stocked with trout every other year).

DC 1240.3 (1996 km) **F 279.7** (450.1 km) Vertical culverts on either side of highway are an experiment to keep ground from thawing and thus prevent frost heaves.

DC 1243.6 (2001.3 km) **F 276.4** (444.8 km) Paved turnout. Scenic viewpoint to south on loop road has USF&WS interpretive signs on fire management and the effects of forest fires on the natural history of area. Sand dunes.

DC 1246.6 (2006.1 km) **F 273.4** (440 km) **Historic Milepost 1248. Gardiner Creek** bridge; parking to west at south end of bridge. Grayling fishing.

DC 1247.6 (2007.8 km) **F 272.4** (438.4 km) Paved double-ended viewpoint to east.

DC 1249.3 (2010.5 km) **F 270.7** (435.6 km) **Historic Milepost 1254. Deadman Lake** USF&WS campground, 1.2 miles/1.9 km in on dirt road. Turnout at highway junction with campground access road. The campground has 18 sites on long loop road, firepits, toilets, picnic tables, no drinking water, boat ramp, interpretive signs, information board and self-guided nature trail. Occasional evening programs offered. Wheelchair accessible. Scenic spot. Swimming and fishing. Northern pike average 2 feet, but skinny (local residents call them "snakes"); use wobbling lures or spinners.

DC 1250.1 (2011.8 km) **F 269.9** (434.3 km) Rest area to west. Double-ended paved parking area, 4 picnic tables, concrete fireplaces, no water or toilets.

DC 1252.2 (2015.2 km) **F 267.8** (431 km) Double-ended gravel turnout to southwest with USF&WS interpretive sign on solar basins (warm ponds and shallow marshes) and scenic viewpoint.

DC 1253 (2016.5 km) **F 267** (429.7 km) Views of lakes and muskeg in Chisana River valley.

DC 1253.6 (2017.4 km) **F 266.4** (428.7 km) **Frontier Surplus.** Military surplus goods. Clothing, sleeping bags, extreme cold weather "bunny boots," military tents, ammunition, tanned furs. Alaska T-shirts and caps. Local crafts, shed moose and caribou antlers. Antler products, belt buckles,

bolo ties, hat racks, handmade ulus. "Moosquitoes," diamond willow lamps and canes, finished or unfinished. Used Alaska license plates, cold pop. Open late every day. Motorhome and RV loop. Phone (907) 778-2274. [ADVERTISEMENT]

DC 1256.3 (2021.7 km) **F 263.7** (424.4 km) Northway state highway maintenance camp; no services.

DC 1256.7 (2022.5 km) **F 263.3** (423.7 km) Lakeview USF&WS campground on beautiful Yarger Lake; 8 sites, tables, toilets, firepits, firewood, no drinking water, occasional evening programs offered. Wheelchair accessible. Interpretive signs. *NOTE: No turnaround space. Not recommended for trailers, 5th wheels or RVs over 30 feet. (Large vehicles use Deadman Lake Campground at **Milepost DC 1249.3**.)*

This is a good place to view ducks and loons. Look for the Nutzotin Mountains to the south and Mentasta Mountains to the west.

Roadside wildflowers include sweet pea, pale yellow Indian paintbrush, yarrow and Labrador tea.

DC 1260.2 (2028 km) **F 259.8** (418.1 km) 1260 Inn roadhouse (closed in 1997, current status unknown).

DC 1263 (2032.5 km) **F 257** (413.6 km) **Wrangell View Service Center.** See display ad this section.

DC 1263.5 (2033.4 km) **F 256.5** (412.8 km) Chisana River parallels the highway to the southwest. This is the land of a thousand ponds, most unnamed. Good trapping country. In early June, travelers may note numerous cottony white seeds blowing in the wind; these seeds are from willow and poplars.

DC 1264 (2034.2 km) **F 256** (412 km) **Northway Junction.** Campground, gas, laundromat, store, and Native arts and crafts shop located at junction. An Alaska State Trooper is also stationed here.

Caribou foraging along the Alaska Highway near Northway. Northway is located within Tetlin National Wildlife Refuge. (© Ruth Fairall)

Naabia Niign Campground & Athabascan Indian Crafts. See display ad this section. ▲

A 7-mile/11.3-km side road leads south across the Chisana River bridge to the community of Northway (description follows). A boat launch at Chisana River bridge is one of 3 boat access points to Tetlin National Wildlife Refuge.

Northway

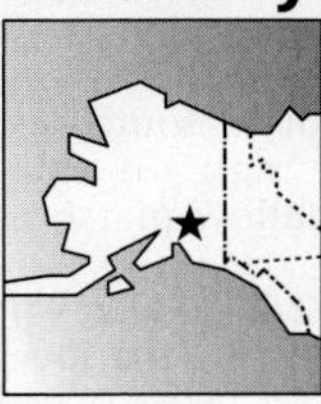

Located 7 miles/11.3 km south of the Alaska Highway via a side road. **Population:** 364 (area). **Emergency Services: Alaska State Troopers,** phone (907) 778-2245. **EMS,** phone (907) 778-2211. **Fire Department,** emergency phone, (907) 778-2211. **Clinic,** phone (907) 778-2283.

Elevation: 1,710 feet/521m. **Climate:** Mean monthly temperature in July, 58.5°F/15°C. In January, -21°F/-30°C. Record high 91°F/33°C in June 1969; record low -72°F/-58°C in January 1952.

Private Aircraft: Northway airport, adjacent south; elev. 1,716 feet/523m; length 5,147 feet/1,569m; asphalt; fuel 100LL, Jet B, MOGAS; customs available.

Northway has a community hall, post office and modern school. FAA station and customs office are at the airport. Visitor services include motels, liquor store, propane, gas stations and air taxi service.

Historically occupied by Athabascan Indians, Northway was named to honor the village chief who adopted the name of a riverboat captain in the early 1900s. (Chief Walter Northway died in 1993. He was thought to be 117 years old.) The rich Athabascan traditions of dancing, crafts, and hunting and trapping continue today in Northway Village. Local Athabascan handicrafts available for purchase include birchbark baskets, beadwork accessories, and moose hide and fur items such as moccasins, mukluks, mittens and hats.

Northway's airport was built in the 1940s as part of the Northwest Staging Route. This cooperative project of the United States and Canada was a chain of air bases from Edmonton, AB, through Whitehorse, YT, to Fairbanks. This chain of air bases helped build up and supply Alaska defense during WWII and also was used during construction of the Alcan and the Canol project. Lend-lease aircraft bound for Russia were flown up this route to Ladd Field (now Fort Wainwright) in Fairbanks. Northway is still an important port of entry for air traffic to Alaska, and a busy one.

Northway is located within **Tetlin National Wildlife Refuge.** Established in 1980, the 730,000-acre refuge stretches south from the Alaska Highway and west from the Canadian border. The major physical features include rolling hills, hundreds of small lakes and 2 glacial rivers (the Nabesna and Chisana) which combine to form the Tanana River. The refuge has a very high density of nesting waterfowl. Annual duck production in favorable years exceeds 50,000. Among the larger birds using the refuge are trumpeter swans, sandhill cranes, Pacific and common loons, osprey, bald eagles and ptarmigan. Other wildlife includes moose, black and grizzly bear, wolf, coyote, beaver, red fox, lynx and caribou. Activities allowed on the refuge include wildlife observation, hunting, fishing, camping, hiking and trapping. Check with refuge personnel at the USF&WS office in Tok prior to your visit for more detailed information. Write Refuge Manager, Tetlin National Wildlife Refuge, Box 779, Tok, AK 99780; or phone (907) 883-5312. Information on the refuge is also available at the USF&WS visitor center at **Milepost DC 1229** on the Alaska Highway.

Confluence of Moose Creek and Chisana River, about 0.8 mile/1.3 km downstream from Chisana River bridge on Northway Road, south side of river, northern pike to 15 lbs., use red-and-white spoon, spring or fall. **Chisana River**, downstream from bridge, lingcod (burbot) to 8 lbs., use chunks of liver or meat, spring. **Nabesna Slough**, south end of runway, grayling to 3 lbs., use spinner or gold flies, late May.

Northway Airport Lodge & Motel. See display ad this section.

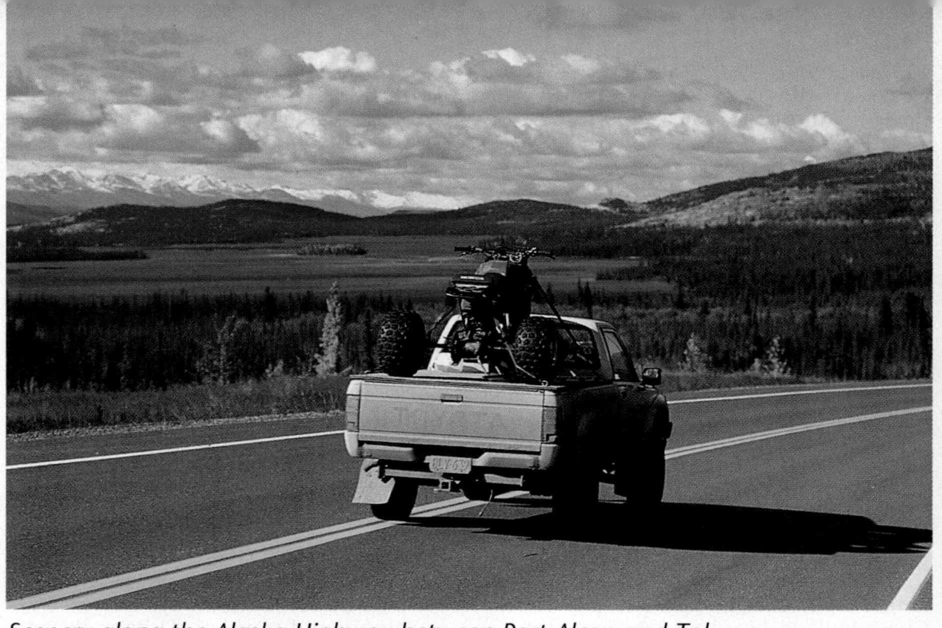
Scenery along the Alaska Highway between Port Alcan and Tok. (© Ruth von Spalding)

Alaska Highway Log

(continued)

DC 1267.4 (2039.6 km) **F 252.6** (406.5 km) Wonderful view of the Tanana River at Beaver Slide.

DC 1268.1 (2040.8 km) **F 251.9** (405.4 km) Beaver Creek bridge. The tea-colored water flowing in the creek is the result of tannins absorbed by the water as it flows through muskeg. This phenomenon may be observed in other Northern creeks.

DC 1269 (2042.2 km) **F 251** (403.9 km) **Historic Milepost 1271.** Scenic viewpoint. Double-ended gravel turnout to west has a litter barrel and USF&WS interpretive sign about the Tanana River, largest tributary of the Yukon River.

DC 1272.7 (2048.2 km) **F 247.3** (398 km) Scenic viewpoint. Double-ended paved turnout to west with USF&WS interpretive sign on pond ecology and mosquitoes.

To the northwest the Tanana River flows near the highway; beyond, the Kalukna River snakes its way through plain and marshland. Mentasta Mountains are visible to the southwest.

DC 1273.9 (2050.1 km) **F 246.1** (396 km) Paved parking area to west by Tanana River.

In June, wild sweet peas create thick borders along the highway. This is rolling country, with aspen, birch, cottonwood, willow and white spruce.

DC 1275.5 (2052.7 km) **F 244.5** (393.5 km) Slide area next 0.3 mile/0.5 km northbound.

DC 1279 (2058.3 km) **F 241** (387.8 km) Highway cuts through sand dune stabilized by aspen and spruce trees.

DC 1281 (2061.5 km) **F 239** (384.6 km) Rough road, pavement cracks.

DC 1284.6 (2067.3 km) **F 235.4** (378.8 km) Large double-ended paved turnout to east.

DC 1285.7 (2069.1 km) **F 234.3** (377.1 km) Granite intrusion in older metamorphosed rock is exposed by road cut.

DC 1289 (2074.4 km) **F 231** (371.7 km) First view northbound of 3.4-mile-/5.5-km-long Midway Lake.

DC 1289.4 (2075 km) **F 230.6** (371.1 km) **Historic Milepost 1292.** Turnout uphill on east side of highway, view of Midway Lake and the Wrangell Mountains. USF&WS interpretive signs on Wrangell–St. Elias National Park and Native peoples.

NOTE: Difficult access for large vehicles and trailers, easier access from southbound lane.

DC 1290 (2076 km) **F 230** (370.1 km) Beautiful view of Midway Lake southbound.

DC 1291 (2077.6 km) **F 229** (368.5 km) Watch for frost heaves.

DC 1292.4 (2079.8 km) **F 227.6** (366.3 km) Paved turnout west side.

DC 1293.7 (2081.9 km) **F 226.3** (364.2 km) Paved turnout west side.

DC 1294.3 (2082.9 km) **F 225.7** (363.2 km) Bad pavement break.

DC 1301.7 (2094.8 km) **F 218.3** (351.3 km) **Historic Milepost 1306. Tetlin Junction**, Alaska Highway and Taylor Highway (Alaska Route 5) junction. 40 Mile Roadhouse; status of services unknown. The Taylor Highway (gravel, open summer only) heads northeast via Jack Wade Junction to Eagle (see TAYLOR HIGHWAY section) and to Yukon Highway 9 (Top of the World Highway) to Dawson City. (See KLONDIKE LOOP section for log of Yukon Highway 9 and description of Dawson City.)

NOTE: If you are traveling to Dawson City, keep in mind that both the Canada and U.S. customs stations are closed at night; you CANNOT cross the border unless customs stations are open. Customs hours in summer have been 8 A.M. to 8 P.M. Alaska time, 9 A.M. to 9 P.M. Pacific time on the Canadian side. Travelers are advised to check for current information at Alaska Public Lands Information Center, (907) 883-5667.

DC 1302.7 (2096.4 km) **F 217.3** (349.7 km) Scenic viewpoint at paved turnout to southwest.

DC 1303.4 (2097.5 km) **F 216.6** (348.6 km) Tanana River bridge. Informal parking area and boat launch to east at north end of bridge. Tanana (TAN-uh-naw), an Indian name, was first reported by the Western Union Telegraph Expedition of 1886. According to William Henry Dall, chief scientist of the expedition, the name means "mountain river." The Tanana is the largest tributary of the Yukon River in Alaska. From here the highway parallels the Tanana to Fairbanks. The Alaska Range looms in the distance.

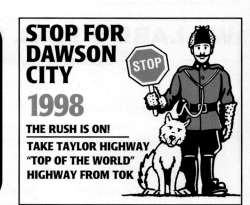

DC 1304.6 (2099.5 km) **F 215.4** (346.6 km) Evidence of 1990 burn from here north to Tok. The Tok River fire occurred in July of

1990 and burned 97,352 acres. The fire closed the Alaska and Glenn highways at times and threatened the town of Tok.

DC 1306.6 (2102.7 km) **F 213.4** (343.4 km) Road east to lake.

DC 1308.5 (2105.7 km) **F 211.5** (340.4 km) Weigh station and turnoff to U.S. Coast Guard loran-C station and signal towers.

This loran (long range navigation) station is 1 of 7 in Alaska. A series of four 700-foot/213-m towers suspends a multi-element wire antenna used to transmit navigation signals. These signals may be used by air, land and sea navigators as an aid in determining their position. This station is located here as necessary for good geometry with 2 Gulf of Alaska loran transmitting stations.

DC 1308.8 (2106.3 km) **F 211.2** (339.9 km) Paved turnout to west.

DC 1309.2 (2106.9 km) **F 210.8** (339.2 km) Tok River State Recreation Site; 25 campsites, overflow parking, tables, firepits, toilets (wheelchair accessible), litter barrels, nature trail, boat launch and pay phone. Check bulletin board for schedule of interpretive programs. Camping fee $10/night or annual pass. *CAUTION: Swift water.* ♿▲

Annual passes good for unlimited camping at all Alaska state parks within a calendar year are available for $75 for Alaska residents and $200 for nonresidents. Annual daily parking pass is $25, annual boat launch pass is $50. Super Pass (camping, boat launch and parking) is available to Alaska residents only for $135. Passes may be purchased at the Alaska Public Lands Information Center in Tok.

DC 1309.4 (2107.2 km) **F 210.6** (338.9 km) Tok River bridge.

DC 1312.7 (2112.5 km) **F 207.3** (333.6 km) Tok community limits. Mountain views ahead northbound.

DC 1312.8 (2112.7 km) **F 207.2** (333.4 km) Tok Dog Mushers Assoc. track and buildings. Paved bike trail from Tok ends here.

DC 1312.9 (2112.8 km) **F 207.1** (333.3 km) **Rod's Automotive.** All automotive work. RVs, light trucks and towing. Estimates given first. Come in and have some coffee with us. Open Monday–Saturday 9 A.M.–6 P.M. Phone (907) 883-2886. [ADVERTISEMENT]

DC 1313 (2113 km) **F 207** (333.1 km) Airstrip. See Private Aircraft information in Tok section. Entering Tok (northbound), description follows. Tok is located at the junction of the Alaska Highway and Tok Cutoff (Glenn Highway). Anchorage-bound travelers turn west on the Tok Cutoff (see the TOK CUTOFF/GLENN HIGHWAY section). Fairbanks-bound travelers continue north on the Alaska Highway.

Southbound travelers: Driving distance from Tok to Beaver Creek is 113 miles/182 km; Haines Junction 296 miles/476 km; Haines (departure point for Alaska state ferries) 446.5 miles/718.5 km; and Whitehorse 396 miles/637 km.

DC 1313.1 (2113.1 km) **F 206.9** (332.9 km) **Tok Gateway Salmon Bake and RV Park.** Rated, *Alaska's Best Places*, Tok's Gateway Salmon Bake, features outdoor flame-grilled Alaska king salmon, halibut, ribs and reindeer sausage. Buffalo burgers. Chowder. Good food, friendly people; casual dining at

its best. Open 11 A.M. to 9 P.M., except Sunday 4 P.M. to 9 P.M. Free shuttle bus service from local hotels and RV parks. Wooded RV and tent sites with tables, clean restrooms, dump station and water. Free dry camping with dinner. Phone/fax (907) 883-5555. Internet www.tokalaska.com/toksamon.shtml. [ADVERTISEMENT] ▲

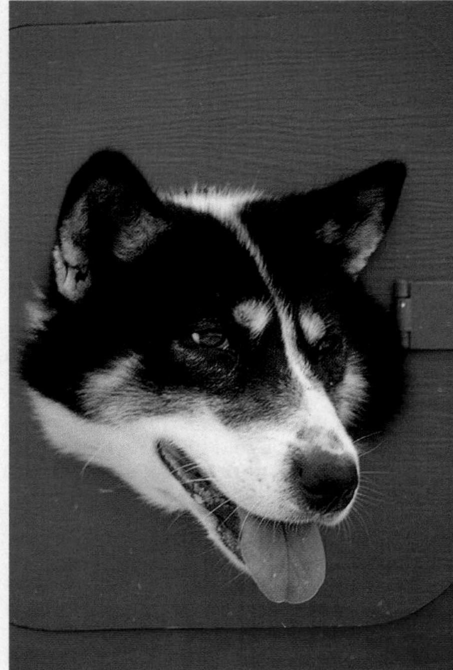

Dog mushing is the official state sport of Alaska. (© Barbara Willard)

DC 1313.2 (2113.3 km) **F 206.8** (332.8 km) **Willard's Full Service Repair.** See display ad this section.

DC 1313.3 (2113.5 km) **F 206.7** (332.6 km) **Interior Video.** On the left northbound. Home of frozen yogurt and premium quality hand-dipped Alaskan ice cream. Check out our movies, video games, popcorn, candy, pop and "Hex" tanning unit. Copy and fax service available. Phone (907) 883-5343. Fax (907) 883-5344. [ADVERTISEMENT]

DC 1313.3 (2113.5 km) **F 206.7** (332.6 km) **Village Texaco Foodmart.** Filtered unleaded and premium gas and diesel. Lubricants and propane. Automatic teller machine, laundromat, phone cards, pay phones and clean restrooms. Deli chicken, burritos, mojos, snacks, pop, ice, milk shakes, ice cream and espresso. RV supplies. Alaskan souvenirs. Across highway from Tok RV Village. See display ad this section. [ADVERTISEMENT]

DC 1313.3 (2113.5 km) **F 206.7** (332.6 km) **Young's Motel and Fast Eddy's Restaurant.** A touch of Alaskana in a modern setting. Affordable, clean and spacious. We cater to the independent highway traveler. Open year-round with all the amenities: telephones, private baths, satellite TV,

ample parking. Nonsmoking rooms available. Check in at Fast Eddy's full-service restaurant, open 6 A.M. to midnight. Reserve early! P.O. Box 482, Tok, AK 99780. (907) 883-

4411; fax (907) 883-5023. [ADVERTISEMENT] MP

DC 1313.3 (2113.5 km) F 206.7 (332.6 km) **The Bull Shooter Sporting Goods & RV Park**. Fishing and hunting licenses. Sporting goods. Fishing tackle. Camping supplies. Guns, ammo. Plan to stay at the Bull Shooter's RV park. 30 spaces, 24 pull-throughs. Full or partial hookups, 30-amp electric, dump station. Non-metered showers, restrooms, ice, phone. VISA, MasterCard. On the left coming into Tok. P.O. Box 553, Tok, AK 99780. Reservations: (907) 883-5625. See display ad in Tok section. [ADVERTISEMENT] ▲

DC 1313.3 (2113.5 km) F 206.7 (332.6 km) **Shamrock Hardware**. See display ad this section.

DC 1313.4 (2113.6 km) F 206.6 (332.5 km) **Tok RV Village.** Alaska's finest. Good Sam or KOA cards honored. Convenient pull-through spaces with 20-30-50 amp. Full and partial hookups, clean restrooms and showers, dump station, laundry, vehicle wash, picnic tables, public phones, e-mail terminals. Gift shop. RV supplies, ice. MasterCard, VISA and Discover. Located across highway from Village Texaco Food-mart. Restaurants, liquor store, night club, hardware store, oil change and lube service nearby. See display ad this section. [ADVERTISEMENT] ▲

DC1313.7 (2114.1 km) F 206.3 (332 km) **Loose Moose Espresso Cafe**. Breakfast omelettes. Lunch and dinner specials. Home-style cooking. Mostly vegetarian and other wholesome dishes. Fresh homemade baked goods. Sourdough waffles, cinnamon rolls, homemade cheesecake, fruit pies. Soups, quiches, tacos on Friday. Espresso drinks, fresh roasted bulk coffee. Natural

Fish & Game Headquarters
Mainstreet Visitor Center, Alaska Public Lands Information Center
State Troopers, Public Health Clinic
Alaska Highway
To Fairbanks
Alaska Highway
To Canada
Post Office
Center St.
USF&W Office
N
W E
S
Tok Cutoff (Glenn Highway)
Tok
To Anchorage

vanilla ice cream. Sack lunches. Open summers. (907) 883-5282 (JAVA). [ADVERTISEMENT]

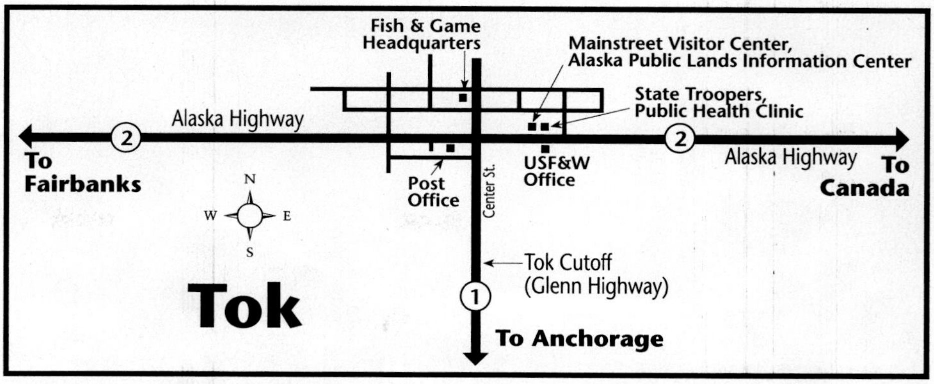

DC 1313.9 (2114.5 km) F 206.1 (331.7 km) **Tok Machine & Welding/Tok Northern Exposures 1-Hour Photo.** Your one stop in Tok for RV repair needs. Machine shop and certified welder; oil change; lubrication; (907) 883-5670. Get your film developed next door and have your "olde tyme" portrait taken. Film, batteries, albums, frames, gifts; (907) 883-5424. On your left northbound. See display ad. [ADVERTISEMENT]

DC 1314.1 (2114.8 km) F 205.9 (331.3 km) Tok Civic Center; Alaska Public Lands Information Center and Tok Mainstreet Visitor Center.

Tok

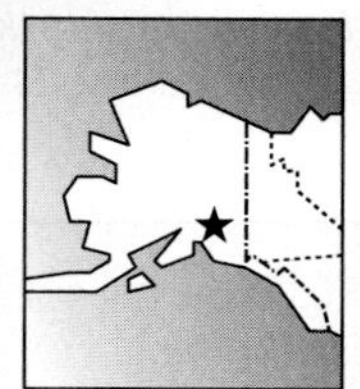

DC 1314.2 (2115 km) **F 205.8** (331.2 km) At the junction of the Alaska Highway and Tok Cutoff (Glenn Highway) between the Tanana River to the north and the Alaska Range to the southwest. **Population:** 1,405. **Emergency Services: Alaska State Troopers,** phone (907) 883-5111. **Fire Department,** phone (907) 883-2333. **Community Clinic,**

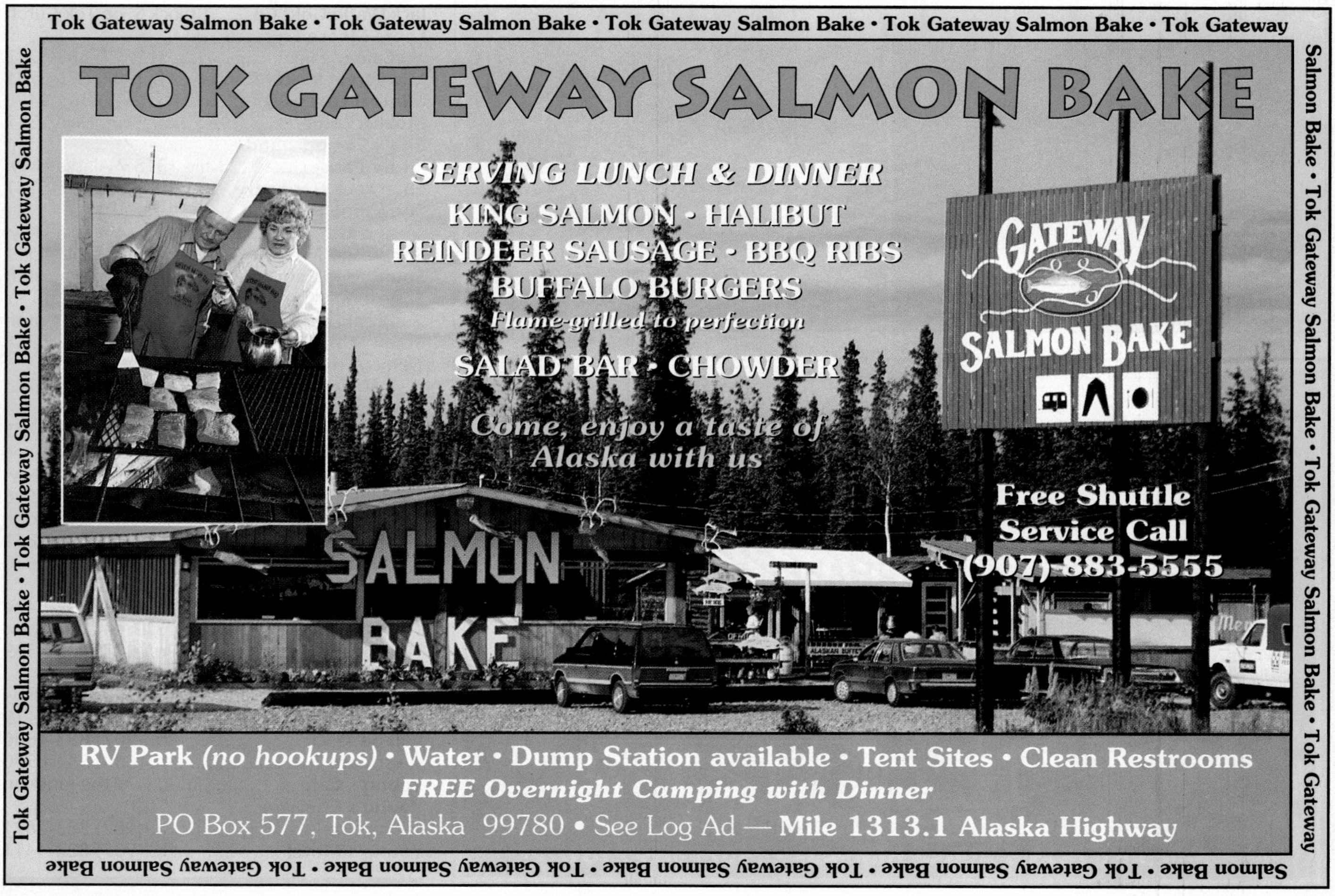

Tok Civic Center, at junction of the Alaska Highway and Tok Cutoff, houses visitor information and natural history exhibits. (Jerrianne Lowther, staff)

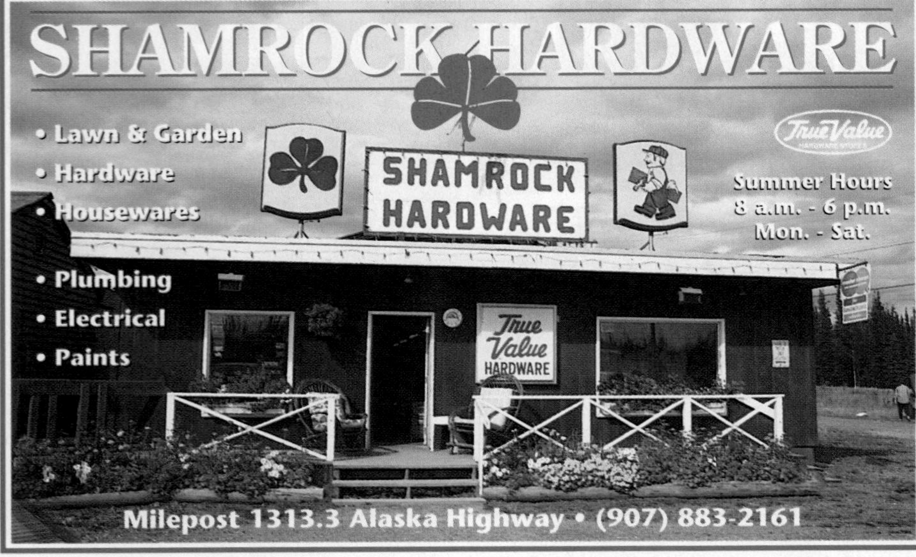

across from the fire hall on the Tok Cutoff, phone (907) 883-5855 during business hours. **Ambulance**, phone (907) 883-2300 or 911. EMT squad and air medivac available. **Public Health Clinic**, next to the Alaska State Troopers at **Milepost 1314.1**, phone (907) 883-4101.

Visitor Information: Operated by Alaska Public Lands Information Center and housing the Tok Chamber of Commerce, the Tok Civic Center is located at the junction of the Alaska Highway and Tok Cutoff. This huge log building is a center for local and state information, trip planning, art exhibits and shows. They sell Alaska State Parks annual

TOK ADVERTISERS

"A Tent in Tok" ....P.O. Box 110
A WinterCabin B & B ....Ph. (907) 883-5655
Alaska Biking Adventures ....Ph. (907) 883-4219
All Alaska Gifts & Crafts ....N. corner of junction
Bull Shooter Sporting Goods & RV Park, The ....Mile 1313.3 Alaska Hwy.
Burnt Paw ....Adjacent post office
Cabins Outback B&B ....Ph. (907) 883-4121
Cleft of the Rock B&B ....Ph. (907) 883-4219
Denali State Bank ....Ph. (907) 883-2265
Faith Chapel ....First & Center
Fast Eddy's Restaurant ....Mile 1313.3 Alaska Hwy.
40 Mile Air Flightseeing Tours ....Ph. (907) 883-5191
Golden Bear Motel, Restaurant, RV Park ....Ph. (888) 252-2123
Grizzly Auto Repair ....1 mile S. on Tok Cutoff
Hayner's Trading Post ....Mile 1.7 Tok Cutoff
Jack Wade Gold Co. ....1 block S. on Tok Cutoff
Loose Moose Espresso Cafe ....Ph. (907) 883-5282
Mainstreet Visitor Center ....Ph. (907) 883-5775
Mineral Lakes B&B ....Ph. (970) 883-5498
Mukluk Land ....Mile 1317
Rita's Campground/ RV Park ....Mile 1315.7 Alaska Hwy.
Shamrock Hardware ....Ph. (907) 883-2161
Snowshoe Fine Arts and Gifts ....Mile 1314 Alaska Hwy.
Snowshoe Motel ....Ph. (907) 883-4511
Sourdough Campground ....Mile 1.7 Tok Cutoff
Sourdough Campground's Pancake Breakfast ....Mile 1.7 Tok Cutoff
Stage Stop, The ....Ph. (907) 883-5338
Texaco Fast Lube & R.V. Service ....Next to Village Texaco
Tok Chamber of Commerce ....Ph. (907) 883-5775
Tok Gateway Salmon Bake ....Mile 1313.1 Alaska Hwy.
Tok Line Camp B&B ....Ph. (907) 883-5506
Tok Liquor & Mini-Mart ....Adjacent Tok Lodge
Tok Lodge ....Ph. (907) 883-2851
Tok Machine & Welding ....Ph. (907) 883-5670
Tok Northern Exposures 1-Hour Photo ....Ph. (907) 883-5424
Tok RV Village ....Mile 1313.4 Alaska Hwy.
Tok Saveway ....Ph. (907) 883-5389
Tundra Lodge and RV Park ....Mile 1315 Alaska Hwy.
Ulu Factory, The ....Ph. (800) 478-3119
Village Texaco ....Ph. (907) 883-4660
Westmark Tok ....Ph. (800) 544-0970
Young's Cafe ....At the junction
Young's Chevron Service ....Ph. (907) 883-2821
Young's Motel ....Ph. (907) 883-4411

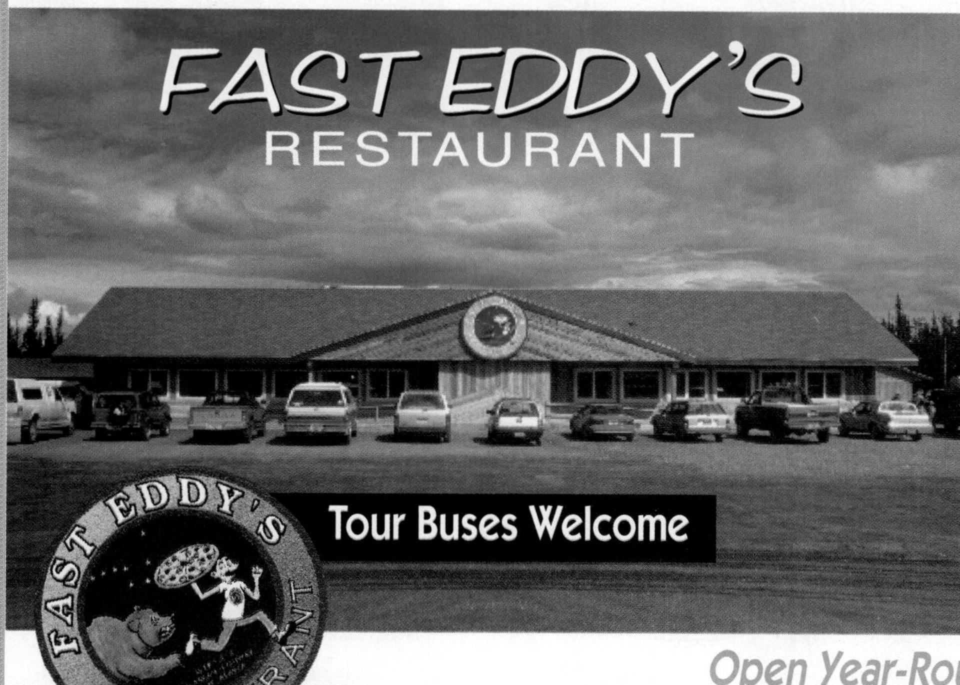

(907) 883-4411

Breakfast • Lunch • Dinner
Steaks • Seafood
Pasta • Burgers
• Sandwiches •
Fresh Salad Bar
Pies • Ice Cream
Milk Shakes

Entire Menu Available To Go

Open Year-Round • 6am to Midnight

(907) 883-4411

YOUNG'S MOTEL

43 Large,
Clean, Modern Rooms
Non-Smoking Rooms
Private Baths
with Tubs & Showers
Satellite TV • Private,
In-Room Telephones

Ample Parking

YOUNG'S MOTEL
TOK, ALASKA

When You Visit Tok, Enjoy the Comfort!

Office and Motel Check-In Inside Fast Eddy's Restaurant

(907) 883-4411 • fax (907) 883-5023

Box 482, Tok, Alaska 99780

See our log ad at Mile 1313.3 Alaska Highway

3/4 mile from the Junction

Village TEXACO

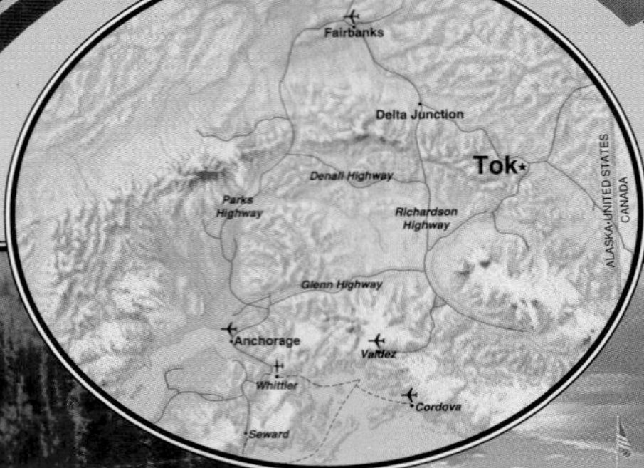

Mile 1313.3 Alaska Highway
P.O. Box 739
Tok, Alaska 99780
Phone (907) 883-4660

Foodmart
Laundromat
Deli
Alaskan Souvenirs
Clean Restrooms
Gas • Diesel • Propane
ATM Machine • Phone Cards

TOK RV VILLAGE

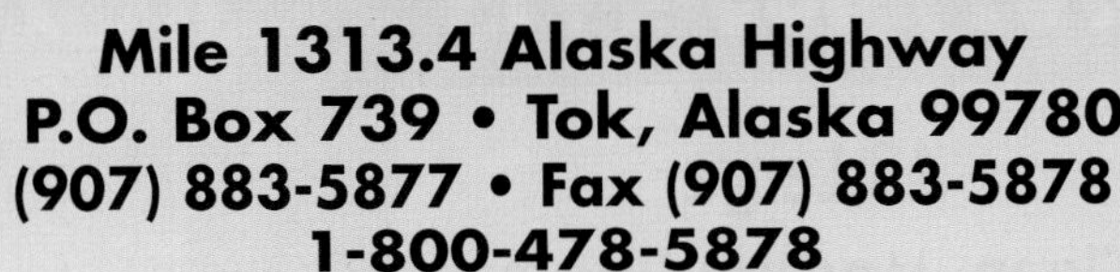

Mile 1313.4 Alaska Highway
P.O. Box 739 • Tok, Alaska 99780
(907) 883-5877 • Fax (907) 883-5878
1-800-478-5878
Toll Free in Alaska Reservations Accepted

95 Sites • Full & Partial Hookups
Pull Thrus • Tent Sites • 30-50 Amp.
Dump Station • Vehicle Wash Facility
Gift Shop • Hunting & Fishing Licenses
Clean Restrooms & Showers • Laundry
RV Supplies • Good Sam or KOA Discounts
• E-mail Terminals

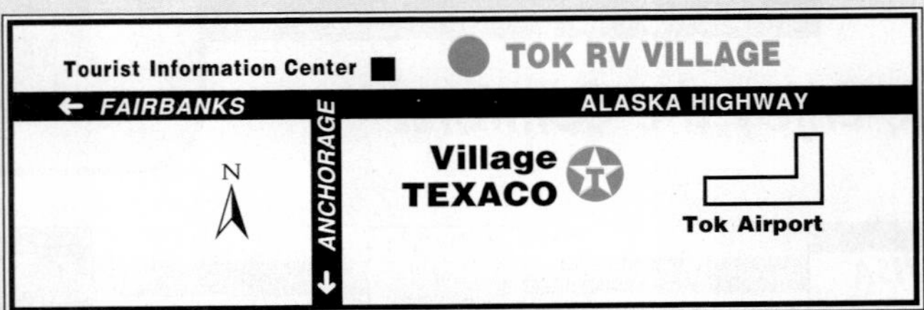

We thank all of you wonderful customers who help to make our business such a great success.

The Jernigan Family

COMCHEK TCHEK NTS CCIS CCC

Come visit the

TOK RV VILLAGE GIFT SHOP

A small gift shop full of surprises

T-shirts • Sweatshirts
Hats • Videos
Postcards • Jewelry
Alaskan Made Crafts

Quality Gifts at Reasonable Prices

Mention This Ad and Receive:

5¢ Per Gallon Fuel Discount

Limit 1 Discount Per Customer
Present before paying

passes and also book Alaska Marine Highway reservations; phone (907) 883-3259. The center offers free coffee, public telephones, restrooms and a message board. It is open daily 8 A.M. to 8 P.M. Memorial Day to Labor Day. Write P.O. Box 359, Tok, Alaska 99780; phone (907) 883-5667 or 883-5666.

The U.S. Fish & Wildlife Service office is located at **Milepost DC 1314.1** next to the grocery store, directly across the highway from the State Troopers. Visitors are welcome. Stop in for information regarding Tetlin National Wildlife Refuge. Office hours are 8 A.M. to noon and 1 P.M. to 4:30 P.M., weekdays. Write Box 155, Tok, AK 99780, or phone (907) 883-5312.

Elevation: 1,635 feet/498m. **Climate:** Mean monthly temperature in January, -19° F/-29°C; in July 59°F/14°C. Record low was -71°F/-57°C in January 1965; record high, 96°F/36°C in June 1969. **Radio:** FM stations are 90.5, 91.1 (KUAC-FM, University of Alaska–Fairbanks) and 101.5. **Television:** Satellite channel 13. **Newspaper:** *Mukluk News* (twice monthly).

Private Aircraft: Tok Junction, 1 mile/1.6 km east; elev. 1,630 feet/497m; length 2,510 feet/765m; asphalt; fuel 100 LL; unattended. Tok airstrip, 2 miles/3.2 km south; elev. 1,670 feet/509m; length 1,690 feet/515m; gravel; no fuel, unattended. Tok NR 2 airstrip across the highway to the west of Tok airstrip is private.

Tok had its beginnings as a construction camp on the Alcan Highway in 1942. Highway engineer C.G. Polk was sent to Fairbanks in May of 1942 to take charge of Alaskan construction and start work on the road between Tok Junction and Big Delta. Work was also under way on the Gulkana–Slana–Tok Junction road (now the Tok Cutoff on the Glenn Highway to Anchorage). But on June 7, 1942, a Japanese task force invaded Attu and Kiska islands in the Aleutians, and the Alcan took priority over the Slana cutoff.

The name Tok (rhymes with poke) was long believed to be derived from Tokyo Camp, patriotically shortened during WWII to Tok. There exist at least three other versions of how Tok got its name. According to local author Donna Blasor–Bernhardt in *Tok, the Real Story* (1996), Tok was named for a young husky pup during construction of the Alaska Highway in 1942.

Because Tok is the major overland point of entry to Alaska, it is primarily a trade and service center for all types of transportation, especially for summer travelers coming up the Alaska Highway. A stopover here is a good opportunity to meet other travelers and swap experiences. Tok is the only town in Alaska that the highway traveler must pass through twice—once when arriving in the state and again on leaving the state. The governor proclaimed Tok "Mainstreet Alaska" in 1991. Townspeople are proud of this designation and work hard to make visitors happy.

Tok's central business district is at the junction of the Alaska Highway and Tok Cutoff (Glenn Highway). From the junction, homes and businesses spread out along both highways on flat terrain dotted with densely timbered stands of black spruce.

Tok has 13 churches, a public library, an elementary school, a 4-year accredited high school and a University of Alaska extension program. Local clubs include the Lions, Disabled American Veterans, Veterans of Foreign Wars and Chamber of Commerce.

Rock ptarmigan in summer plumage. The willow ptarmigan, also common in Alaska, is the state bird. (© Bill Sherwonit)

ACCOMMODATIONS/VISITOR SERVICES

There are 8 hotels/motels, a variety of restaurants and several gas stations, as well as bed and breakfasts in Tok, just north of Tok Junction along the Alaska Highway and south on the Glenn Highway (Tok Cutoff). Grocery, hardware and sporting goods stores, bakery, beauty shop, gift shops, liquor stores, auto repair and auto parts stores, wrecker service, laundromats and a post office are also available. The bank is located across the highway from the Public Lands Information Center. There is an automatic teller machine at Village Texaco.

Tok AYH youth hostel is located on Pringle Road, 0.8 mile/1.3 km south of **Milepost DC 1322.6**; phone (907) 883-3745.

There are several private RV parks in Tok. Nearby state campgrounds include: Tok River State Recreation Site at **Milepost DC 1309.2** and Moon Lake State Recreation Site at **Milepost DC 1331.9** Alaska Highway; and Eagle Trail State Recreation Site at **Milepost GJ 109.3** Tok Cutoff (Glenn Highway) 16 miles/25 km west. ▲

A WinterCabin Bed & Breakfast. New, individual log cabins each with peaceful surroundings, sun porch, picnic table, barbecue, microwave, breakfast-stocked refrigerator, excellent beds, fully carpeted. Special feature: Alaskan-size tub/shower in modern, separate, shared bath house. No pets. Nonsmoking. Reservations advised. Built on original site of the "Tent In Tok." Reservations/brochure—P.O. Box 61, Tok, AK 99780. Phone (970) 883-5655. Internet: www.polarnet.com/~wntrcabn/Donna.html. E-mail: wntrcabn@polarnet.com. [ADVERTISEMENT]

Golden Bear Motel. Quiet location, 62 deluxe units, RV park with wooded pull-through sites, heated bathhouse, laundry; fine restaurant. Open 6 A.M. to 11 P.M. Our gift shop carries an extensive selection of Alaskana, jewelry, T-shirts and souvenirs. The friendly atmosphere you came to Alaska to find! Phone (888) 252-2123. Internet: www.tokalaska.com/gol. See display ad this section. [ADVERTISEMENT] MP ▲

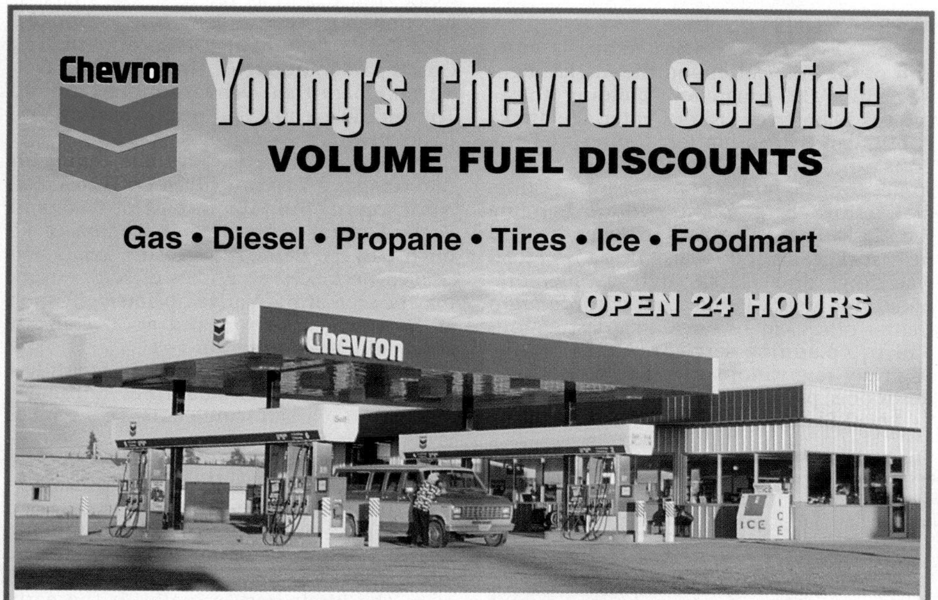

Sourdough Campground's Pancake Breakfast, served 7–11 A.M. (June, July, August). Genuine "Sourdough!" Full and

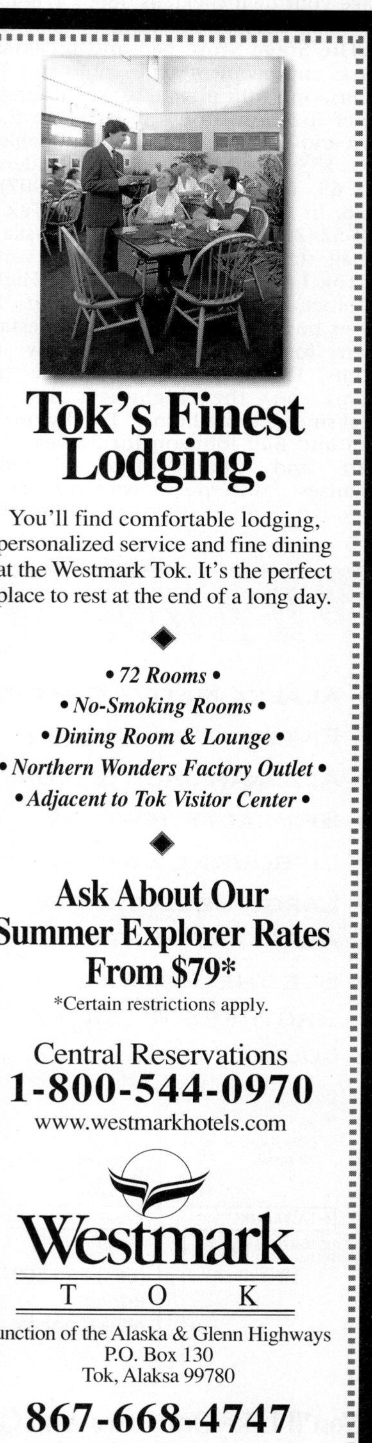

partial RV hookups. Dry campsites. Showers included. Guaranteed clean restrooms. High-pressure car wash. Open-air museum with gold rush memorabilia. Free evening video program. Located 1.7 miles from the junction toward Anchorage on Tok Cutoff (Glenn Highway). See display ad this section. [ADVERTISEMENT] MP ▲

Snowshoe Motel. 24 units with private baths. Excellent accommodations for families or 2 couples traveling together. In-room phones, satellite TV. Free continental breakfast served summers only. Our guests are invited to enjoy panoramic mountain views and sunsets from our Midnight Sun Room. We provide barbecue facilities and a place to make your own cocktails. (800) 478-4511 or (907) 883-4511. [ADVERTISEMENT]

The Stage Stop, bed and breakfast for horses and people. Private cabin and 3 large rooms, one with private bath. Full breakfast. Quiet location Mile 1.7 Tok Cutoff. New barn and corrals for horses. Reasonable rates from $35. Open all year. Mary Underwood, Box 69, Tok, AK 99780. Phone (907) 883-5338. In Alaska, (800) 478-5369. Fax (907) 883-5242. Internet: www.tokalaska.com. E-mail: stagestop@tokalaska.com. [ADVERTISEMENT]

Tok Lodge, located on Glenn Highway, 1 block from junction. Alcan Room serves buses, leaving full-service restaurant open for car traffic. 36 new motel rooms. Common comments are “nicest rooms on the highway” and “best meal since leaving home.” Locally owned by Pam and Bud Johnson for 22 years. Mini-Mart and liquor store located on premises. Internet: www.alaskan.com/toklodge. E-mail: toklodge@polarnet.com. See display ad this section. [ADVERTISEMENT] MP

Tundra Lodge & RV Park. Spacious, tree-shaded camping sites. Full and partial hookups; 20-, 30-, 50-amp power. Tent sites. Pull-throughs. Clean restrooms and showers included in price. Picnic tables, fire rings and wood. Dump station. Laundromat. Vehicle wash. Pay phone. Ice. Cocktail lounge and meeting room. Internet: www.tokalaska.com/tundra. E-mail: tundra@polarnet.com. See display ad **Milepost 1315** Alaska Highway. [ADVERTISEMENT] MP ▲

TRANSPORTATION

Air: Charter air service available; inquire at Tok state airstrip (**Milepost DC 1313**). Charter flightseeing and fly-in fishing trips available. Scheduled passenger and freight service between Tok, Delta Junction and Fairbanks 4 days a week via 40-Mile Air.

ATTRACTIONS

Tok Civic Center. Located at the junction of the Tok Cutoff and the Alaska Highway, this 7,000-square-foot building houses the Tok Mainstreet Visitor Center, the Alaska Public Lands Information Center and the Tok Community Library. Huge natural spruce logs support an open-beamed, cathedral ceiling. Large picture windows frame the Alaska Range. Displays include: the gold rush; rock, gems and fossils; Alaskan wildlife; waterfowl; and Alaska Highway memorabilia. The Alaska Public Lands Information Center offers videos on Alaska destinations and trip-planning services. Alaska Marine Highway reservations may be booked here. Restrooms, pay phone and message board.

Local Events: There is a variety of things to do in Tok, thanks to local individuals, businesses and clubs. Local campgrounds offer slide shows, movies, gold panning, a salmon bake, miniature golf and sourdough pancake breakfasts. Sled dog demonstrations are given at Burnt Paw gift shop and at the Westmark.

Other local events include bingo games and softball games at the local field. Visitors are welcome at the senior citizens center. The Tok Triathlon (12 miles of biking, 10 of canoeing and 5 of jogging) and Tok Trot are both held annually. Tok's Fourth of July celebration is a major event, complete with a parade, picnic and games. Check at the Mainstreet Visitor Center for more information on these local events.

Bike Trail: A wide paved bike trail extends southeast from Tok on the Alaska Highway as far east as the Dog Mushers Assoc. track, and as far west as Tanacross Junction; approximate length is 13.2 miles/21.2 km. You may also bike out the Tok Cutoff past Sourdough Campground. Travelers may park their vehicles in and around Tok and find a bike trail nearby leading into or out of Tok.

Native Crafts: Tok is a trade center for the Athabascan Native villages of Tanacross, Northway, Tetlin, Mentasta, Dot Lake and Eagle. Several of the Native women make birch baskets, beaded moccasins, boots and beaded necklaces. Examples of Native work may be seen at the Native-operated gift shop at Northway junction and at several gift shops and other outlets in Tok.

The state of Alaska has a crafts identification program which identifies authentic Native and Alaskan handicrafts. This symbol is of a polar bear.

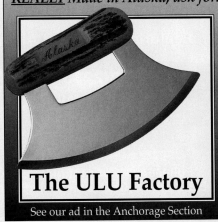

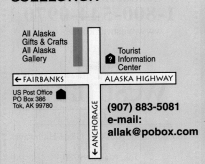

Birch baskets were once used in the Native camps and villages. Traditionally they had folded corners, which held water, and were even used for cooking by dropping heated stones into the liquid in the baskets. The baskets are made by peeling the bark from the birch trees, usually in the early summer months. The bark is easiest to work with when moist and pliable. It is cut into shape and sewn together with strips of spruce root dug out of the ground and split. If the root is too dry it is soaked until it is manageable. Holes are put in the birch bark with a punch or screwdriver, and the spruce root is laced in and out. Native women dye the spruce root with food coloring, watercolors or berry juice. A few Natives also make birch canoes and birch baby carriers.

Many of the moccasins and mukluks for sale in Tok are made with moose hide that has the "Native tan." This means moose hide tanned by the Native. First the excess fat and meat is scraped off the hide, then it is soaked in a soap solution (some use a mixture of brains and ashes). After soaking, all the moisture is taken out by constant scraping with a dull knife or scraper. The hide is then scraped again and rubbed together to soften it. Next it is often smoke-cured in rotted spruce wood smoke. The tanning process takes from a few days to a week.

Beading can be a slow and tedious process. Most women say if they work steadily all day they can put the beading on one moccasin, but usually they do their beadwork over a period of several days, alternating it with other activities.

Snowshoe Fine Arts and Gifts invites you to come browse and shop in our gift store. See our gallery of art prints, figurines,

Watch for moose crossing the highway at any time during the year. (© Bill Sherwonit)

Alaska Native-made carvings, masks, dolls, birch and grass baskets, and beadwork. Jewelry made of natural Alaska gemstones, ivory

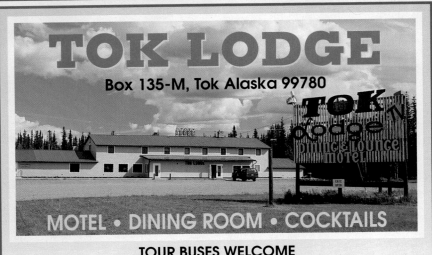

and gold nugget. Lots of caps, T-shirts and sweatshirts. Souvenir items and Alaska-made products. Phone (907) 883-4181. [ADVERTISEMENT]

Sled Dog Breeding and Training: Dog mushing is Alaska's official state sport, and Tok has become known as the "Sled Dog Capital of Alaska," with at least 1 out of every 3 people in town involved in some way with raising dogs. Kennels range in size from 100 dogs to a single family pet. Visitors who come to Tok seeking either a pet or a racing sled dog will probably find what they are looking for here.

The Siberian husky is the most popular sled dog and oftentimes has distinctive blue eyes. The Alaskan malamute is much larger than the Siberian and is used for hauling heavy loads at a slower pace. Both breeds are AKC recognized. The Alaskan husky (or husky) is a catchall term for any of the arctic breeds or northern types of dogs and is usually a cross. Sled dogs may be any registered breed or crossbreed, since mushers look for conformation, attitude and speed when putting together a working team rather than pedigrees. Common strains in racing dogs have included Irish setter, Labrador and wolf, among others.

Sled Dog Trails and Races: Tok boasts a well-known and long-established dog mushing trail, which draws many world-class and recreational mushers. The 20.5-mile/33-km trail begins at the rustic log Tok Dog Mushers Assoc. building at **Milepost DC 1312.8** on the Alaska Highway. The trail is a favorite with spectators because it affords many miles of viewing from along the Alaska Highway.

Racing begins in late November and extends through the end of March. Junior mushers include 1-, 2-, 3- and 5-dog classes; junior adult mushers include 5- and 8-dog classes. Open (unlimited) classes can run as many as 16 dogs.

The biggest race of the season in Tok is the Race of Champions, held in late March, which also has the largest entry of any sprint race in Alaska. Begun in 1954 as a bet between 2 roadhouse proprietors, today the Race of Champions includes over 100 teams in 3 classes competing for prize money and trophies. It is considered to be the third leg of sled dog racing's "triple crown," following the Fur Rendezvous in Anchorage and the

Fairbanks North American Championship. Visitors are also welcome to attend the Tok Native Assoc.'s potlatch, held the same weekend as the race, in the Tok school gym.

AREA FISHING: Fly-in fishing to area lakes for northern pike, grayling and lake trout; inquire at Tok state airstrip. There are 43 lakes in the Delta–Tok area that are stocked by the Alaska Dept. of Fish and Game. Lakes are stocked primarily with rainbow trout; other stocked species include arctic grayling, lake trout, arctic char and king salmon. Most of these lakes are located close to the road system, but there are walk-in lakes available as well. Most easily accessible are **North Twin**, **South Twin** and **Mark lakes**. There is a trailhead 0.5 mile/0.8 km east of the Gerstle River bridge for **Big Donna Lake** (3.5-mile/5.6-km hike) and **Little Donna Lake** (4.5 miles/7.2 km). **Quartz Lake**, north of Delta Junction, is a popular spot for rainbow trout and silver salmon. Consult ADF&G offices in Tok or Delta Junction for other locations.

Alaska Highway Log

(continued)

DC 1314.8 (2115.9 km) **F 205.2** (330.2 km) **Northern Energy Corp.** See display ad on page 191.

DC 1315 (2116.2 km) **F 205** (329.9 km) **Tundra Lodge and RV Park.** See display ad this section. ▲

DC 1315.7 (2117.3 km) **F 204.3** (328.8 km) **Rita's Campground RV Park & Cheryl's Old Fashion Bed & Breakfast Cabin.** See display ad this section. ▲

DC 1316.6 (2118.8 km) **F 203.4** (327.3 km) Scoby Road, Sundog Trail. Access to bed and breakfasts.

DC 1317 (2119.4 km) **F 203** (326.7 km)

Mukluk Land. See display ad this section.

DC 1318.5 (2121.8 km) **F 201.5** (324.3 km) **Off The Road House.** See display ad this section.

DC 1322.6 (2128.5 km) **F 197.4** (317.7 km) Pringle Road. Tok youth hostel, housed in a wall tent, is located 0.8 mile/1.3 km south; 10 beds, tent space available.

DC 1324.6 (2131.7 km) **F 195.4** (314.5 km) Tanacross fireguard station.

DC 1324.7 (2131.8 km) **F 195.3** (314.3 km) Gravel access road to Tanacross airstrip. (See also **Milepost DC 1325.7.**)

DC 1325.6 (2133.3 km) **F 194.4** (312.8 km) **Historic Milepost 1328.**

DC 1325.7 (2133.4 km) **F 194.3** (312.7 km) **Tanacross Junction.** End of paved bike trail from Tok and access to Tanacross.

Drive in 1.2 miles/1.9 km on gravel road to junction, turn left for village of **TANACROSS** (pop. 106), home of the once numerous branch of the Tanah, or Tinneh, Indians. This village of colorful modern houses is built on a short 0.7-mile/1.1-km loop road. Turn right at junction and drive 0.2 mile/0.3 km for access road to airstrip, or 0.3 mile/0.5 km to reach Tanana River and view across river of the white church steeple in the old village of Tanacross which burned down in 1979. Road eventually dead ends in residential area.

Private Aircraft: Tanacross airstrip; elev. 1,549 feet/472m; 2 runways, length 5,000 feet/1,524m and 5,100 feet/1,554m; asphalt; unattended.

DC 1327.4 (2136.2 km) **F 192.6** (310 km) Parking area at lake to north.

DC 1330.1 (2140.5 km) **F 189.9** (305.6 km) Paved turnout to east. View of Alaska Range to the west.

DC 1330.7 (2141.5 km) **F 189.3** (304.6 km) Paved turnout to east.

DC 1331.9 (2143.5 km) **F 188.1** (302.7 km) Moon Lake State Recreation Site, 0.2 mile/0.3 km north off highway; 15 campsites, toilets, tables, water, firepits, swimming (watch for floatplanes). Camping fee $10/night or annual pass. ▲

DC 1333.6 (2146.2 km) **F 186.4** (300 km) **Historic Milepost 1339**. Yerrick Creek bridge.

DC 1335 (2148.4 km) **F 185** (297.7 km) Watch for moose.

DC 1338.2 (2153.5 km) **F 181.8** (292.6 km) Highway crosses Cathedral Creeks 3 times between here and **Milepost DC 1339.**

DC 1342.2 (2160 km) **F 177.8** (286.1 km) Sheep Creek culvert.

DC 1344.5 (2163.8 km) **F 175.5** (282.4 km) **Historic Milepost 1352.** Double-ended paved parking area to east. Interpretive panel on the "father of the international highway," Donald MacDonald. Alaska Range to the south. Good photo stop.

Look for sandhill cranes in fields in the spring. (© Loren Taft, Alaskan Images)

DC 1347.2 (2168 km) **F 172.8** (278 km) **Forest Lake** trailhead; 6 mile/9.6 km ATV trail (not easy access) to lake stocked with rainbow trout.

DC 1347.3 (2168.2 km) **F 172.7** (277.9 km) Entering Game Management Unit 20D northbound, Unit 12 southbound.

DC 1347.5 (2168.5 km) **F 172.5** (277.6 km) Robertson River bridge. The river was named by Lt. Henry T. Allen for a member of his 1885 expedition.

DC 1348 (2169.3 km) **F 172** (276.8 km) Bad frost heaves.

DC 1348.1 (2169.5 km) **F 171.9** (276.6 km) Side road west to parking lot at old Haines pipeline right-of-way. Hike in 0.3 mile/0.5 km for **Robertson No. 2 Lake**; rainbow fishing.

DC 1348.8 (2170.6 km) **F 171.2** (275.5 km) *CAUTION*: Very bad frost heaves.

DC 1350.5 (2173.3 km) **F 169.5** (272.8 km) Double-ended paved turnout to west. Rough road next mile northbound.

DC 1353.7 (2178.5 km) **F 166.3** (267.6 km) Jan Lake Road. Drive in 0.5 mile/0.8 km to parking area with boat launch and toilets. No overnight camping, carry out garbage.

Gerstle River Black Veterans Recognition bridge at Milepost DC 1392.7.

(© Bruce M. Herman)

Jan Lake is stocked with rainbow; use spinners, flies, or salmon eggs with bobber. Dot Lake Native Corp. land, limited public access.

DC 1357.3 (2184.4 km) **F 162.7** (261.8 km) Bear Creek bridge. Paved turnout to west.

DC 1358.7 (2186.6 km) **F 161.3** (259.6 km) Chief Creek bridge. Paved turnout to west at north end of bridge.

DC 1361.3 (2190.2 km) **F 158.7** (255.4 km) **DOT LAKE** (pop. 70). Lodge with gas, groceries, restaurant, car wash, motel, camping and post office. Headquarters for the Dot Lake (Athabascan) Indian Corp. Homesteaded in the 1940s, a school was established here in 1952. Dot Lake's historic chapel was built in 1949. ▲

Dot Lake Lodge. See display ad on page 193. ▲

DC 1361.6 (2191 km) **F 158.4** (254.9 km) **Historic Milepost 1368.** Gravel turnout by lake to east. Rough narrow road northbound. Wild blue irises bloom in roadside ditches in June.

DC 1370.2 (2205.1 km) **F 149.8** (241.1 km) Double-ended paved parking area to east.

DC 1370.5 (2205.4 km) **F 149.5** (240.6 km) **Historic Milepost 1376.** Alaska Highway interpretive panel on "the Crooked Road."

DC 1371.5 (2207.2 km) **F 148.5** (239 km) Berry Creek bridge. Parking area to west.

DC 1374.2 (2211.5 km) **F 145.8** (234.6 km) Sears Creek bridge. Parking area to west.

DC 1376 (2214.4 km) **F 144** (231.7 km) Entering Tok Management Area, Tanana State Forest southbound.

DC 1378 (2217.6 km) **F 142** (228.5 km) Bridge over Dry Creek. Evidence of forest fire next mile northbound.

DC 1379 (2219.2 km) **F 141** (226.9 km) Double-ended paved turnout with mountain views to west.

DC 1380.5 (2221.6 km) **F 139.5** (224.5 km) Johnson River bridge. A tributary of the Tanana River, the Johnson River was named by Lt. Henry T. Allen in 1887 for Peder Johnson, a Swedish miner and member of his party.

DC 1381.1 (2222.6 km) **F 138.9** (223.5 km) Paved turnout to west. Access road to **Lisa Lake** (stocked).

DC 1383.9 (2227.1 km) **F 136.1** (219 km) **Craig Lake** access west side of highway via 0.5-mile/0.8-km trail; rainbow trout fishing.

DC 1385 (2228.9 km) **F 135** (217.3 km) Double-ended gravel turnout. Tanana River access.

*CAUTION: Watch for major road construction between **Mileposts DC 1386 and 1398** in 1998.*

DC 1388.4 (2234.4 km) **F 131.6** (211.8 km) Little Gerstle River bridge (to be replaced in 1998).

DC 1391.9 (2240 km) **F 128.1** (206.2 km) Trailhead to **Big Donna Lake**, 3.5 miles/5.6 km, and **Little Donna Lake**, 4.5 miles/7.2 km; stocked with rainbow.

DC 1392.3 (2240.6 km) **F 127.7** (205.5 km) Cummings Road through Delta barley project. *CAUTION: Watch for buffalo (bison) on highway between here and Delta Junction.*

On the southwest side of the Alaska Highway approaching Delta Junction is the Bison Sanctuary. This range provides the bison herd with autumn and winter grazing on over 3,000 acres of grassland. It was developed to reduce agricultural crop depredation by bison.

DC 1392.7 (2241.3 km) **F 127.3** (204.9 km) Gerstle River Black Veterans Recognition bridge. The river was named for Lewis Gerstle, president of the Alaska Commercial Co., by Lt. Henry T. Allen, whose 1885 expedition explored the Copper, Tanana and Koyukuk river regions for the U.S. Army Dept. of the Columbia.

Rest area on north side of bridge, overnight RV parking and camping permitted; toilets, tables and firepits. ▲

DC 1395.2 (2245.3 km) **124.8** (200.8 km) Scenic view of the "largest farm in Alaska."

DC 1398 (2249.8 km) **F 122** (196.5 km) Watch for bison next 15 miles/24 km northbound.

CAUTION: Watch for major road construction next 12 miles/19 km southbound in 1998.

DC 1401.2 (2255 km) **F 118.8** (191.2 km) Double-ended gravel turnout to northeast.

DC 1403.6 (2258.8 km) **F 116.4** (187.3 km) Sawmill Creek Road to northeast. This rough gravel road goes through the heart of the Delta barley fields. A sign just off the highway explains the barley project. Visiting farmers are welcome to talk with local farmers along the road, except during planting (May) and harvesting (August or September) when they are too busy. Commercial farm tours available.

Farm Tours. See display ad this section.

DC 1403.9 (2259.3 km) **F 116.1** (186.8 km) Sawmill Creek bridge.

DC 1408 (2265.9 km) **F 112** (180.2 km) Access to University of Alaska Agricultural and Forestry Experiment Station. Major research at this facility concentrates on agricultural cropping, fertilization and tillage management.

DC 1410 (2269.1 km) **F 110** (177 km) Access road north to Delta barley project.

DC 1411 (2270.7 km) **F 109** (175.4 km) Look for wild irises in roadside ditches in June.

DC 1411.7 (2271.8 km) **F 108.3** (174.3 km) Double-ended gravel turnout. Scenic view of Alaska Range to south.

DC 1412.5 (2273.1 km) **F 107.5** (173 km) **Cherokee Lodge and RV Park.** See display ad this section. ▲

DC 1413.3 (2274.4 km) **F 106.7** (171.7 km) Grain storage facility.

DC 1414.9 (2277 km) **F 105.1** (169.1 km) Clearwater Road leads north past farmlands to Clearwater State Recreation Site campground and junctions with Remington Road. Stay on pavement leading to Jack Warren Road, which goes west to the Richardson Highway at **Milepost DC 1424.3 (V 268.3).** Good opportunity to see area agriculture; see Delta Vicinity map this page.

To reach the state campground, follow Clearwater Road 5.2 miles/8.4 km north to junction with Remington Road; turn right and drive 2.8 miles/4.5 km east for Clearwater state campground, situated on the bank of Clearwater Creek. There are 15 campsites, toilets, tables, firepits, water and boat ramp. Camping fee $8/night or annual pass. ▲

Delta–Clearwater River (local reference; stream is actually Clearwater Creek, which flows northwest to the Tanana River), boat needed for best fishing; beautiful spring-fed stream; grayling and whitefish; silver salmon spawn here in October. **Goodpaster River,** accessible by boat via Delta–Clearwater and Tanana rivers; excellent grayling fishing.

DC 1415.4 (2277.8 km) **F 104.6** (168.3 km) Dorshorst Road; access to homestead farm and private museum, open to public June 1 to Sept. 15, admission charged.

DC 1420.7 (2286.3 km) **F 99.3** (159.8 km) Alaska State Troopers.

DC 1420.9 (2286.7 km) **F 99.1** (159.5 km) **Bergstad's Travel and Trailer Court.** See display ad this section. ▲

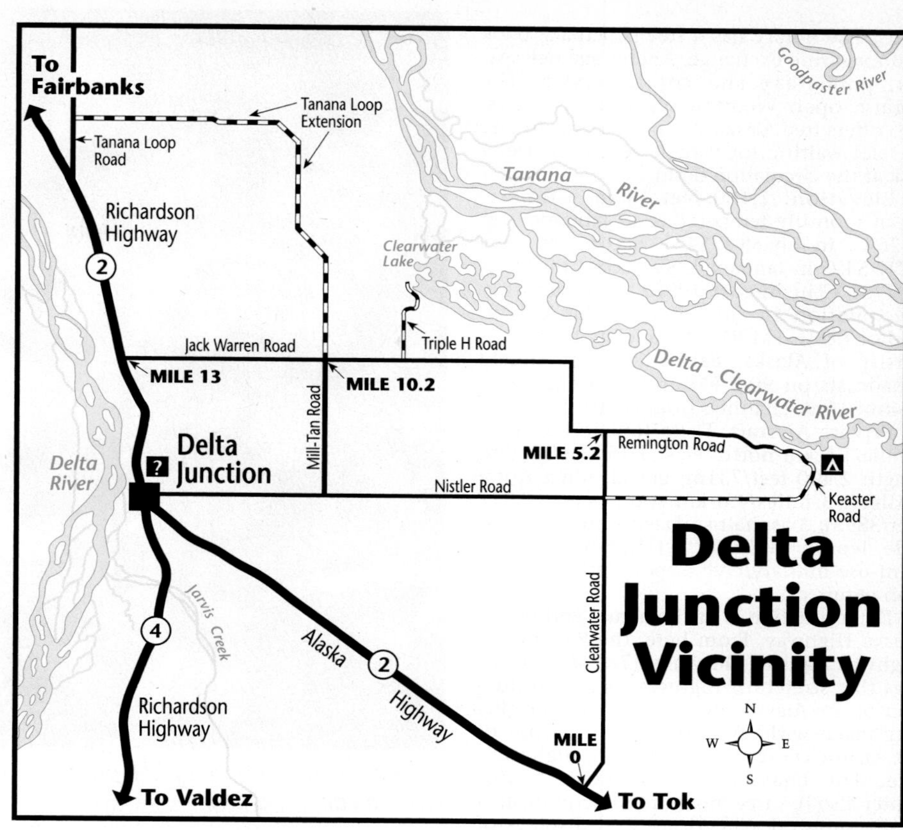

Delta Junction

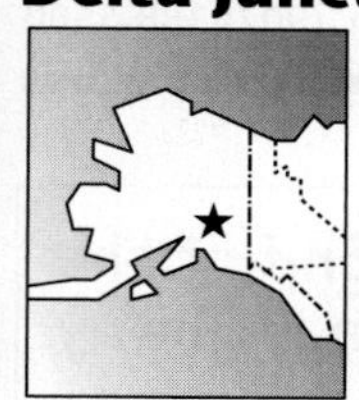

DC 1422 (2288.4 km) **F 98** (157.7 km) **V 266** (428.1 km). Located at the junction of the Alaska and Richardson highways. **Population:** 657. **Emergency Services:** Emergencies only phone 911. **Alaska State Troopers,** in the Jarvis Office Center at **Milepost DC 1420.7**, phone (907) 895-4800. **Fire Department** and **Ambulance Service**, emergency only phone 911. **Clinics,** Two doctors and 2 dentists in private practice at Family Medical Center.

Visitor Information: Visitor Center junction of Alaska and Richardson highways, open daily 8 A.M. to 7:30 P.M., May to mid-September; phone (907) 895-9941 or (907) 895-5069. The visitor center has historical and wildflower displays and a pay phone. Highway information, phone (907) 451-2207. Dept. of Fish and Game at north edge of town, **Milepost DC 1422.8**; phone (907) 895-4632.

City Hall and the Delta Junction Library, located at **Milepost V 266.5**, are also good sources of information. City Hall, open 2 P.M. to 5 P.M. weekdays, has a pay phone, public restrooms and can give local direc-

Alaska became the 49th state on Jan. 3, 1959, under President Dwight D. Eisenhower.
— ALASKA A TO Z

tions. The library has a free paperback book and magazine exchange, Anchorage newspaper, public fax and copier service. The library, open Wednesdays and Saturdays, also offers free Alaska video programs to any traveler waiting for vehicle repairs in Delta (ask at the circulation desk).

Elevation: 1,180 feet/360m. **Climate:** Mean monthly temperature in January, -15°F/-26°C; in July 58°F/14°C. Record low was -66°F/-54°C in January 1989; record high was 88°F/31°C in August 1990. Mean monthly precipitation in July, 2.57 inches/6.5cm. **Radio:** KUAC-FM 91.7 broadcasts from University of Alaska, Fairbanks; Fort Greely broadcasts on 90.5 FM and 93.5 FM. **Television:** Three channels from Fairbanks.

Private Aircraft: Delta Junction airstrip, 1 mile/1.6 km north; elev. 1,150 feet/350m; length 2,400 feet/731m; gravel. Allen Army Airfield, 3 miles/4.8 km south; elev. 1,277 feet/389m; 3 asphalt-surfaced runways available, length to 7,500 feet/2,286m; fuel J4; joint-use military/civil airport (prior permission required).

Delta Junction is at the actual end of the Alaska Highway. From here, the Richardson Highway leads to Fairbanks. (*The MILEPOST®* logs this stretch of highway as a continuation of the Alaska Highway.) Have your picture taken with the monument in front of the visitor center that marks the highway's end. The chamber of commerce visitor center also has free brochures describing area businesses and attractions, and displays of Alaska wildflowers, mounted animals and furs to touch. Travelers may also purchase certificates here, certifying that they have reached the end of the Alaska Highway.

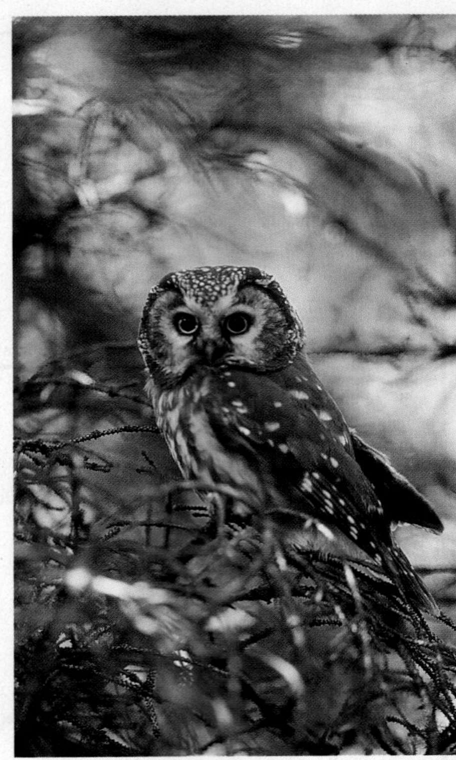

Boreal owl has a ringing bell and whistle call. (© Mike Jones)

Delta Junction is also the first view of the trans-Alaska pipeline for travelers coming up

End of the ALASKA HIGHWAY . . .

Delta Junction, Alaska

End of the Alaska Highway certificates available, $1

"Make Your First Stop in Delta the Visitor Center at the Junction of the Alaska and Richardson Highways."

photo courtesy Sheryl L. Mills

ANNUAL EVENTS:

- Delta Deep Freeze Classic
- Memorial Day Buffalo Wallow Square Dance
- July 4th Buffalo Barbecue
- Deltana Fair, July 31-August 2, 1998
- Summer Mud Bog Races

ACTIVITIES:

- Spectacular Mountain Views
- Pipeline Pump Station Tours
- Agricultural, Scenic and Wildlife Tours
- Historical Sites/Museums
- Great fishing, hunting in season
- Hiking throughout the season
- Quartz Lake: fishing, hiking, camping, picnics
- Largest free-roaming bison herd in Alaska

photo courtesy Nanci Ruthschild-Kennedy

SERVICES:

- Fine Dining, Motels and Bed & Breakfasts
- Four State campgrounds
- Several private RV parks with full hookups
- Groceries/Gifts
- Several Service Stations

Alaska's Friendly Frontier

For further information contact:

Delta Chamber of Commerce

PO Box 987MP

Delta Junction, AK 99737

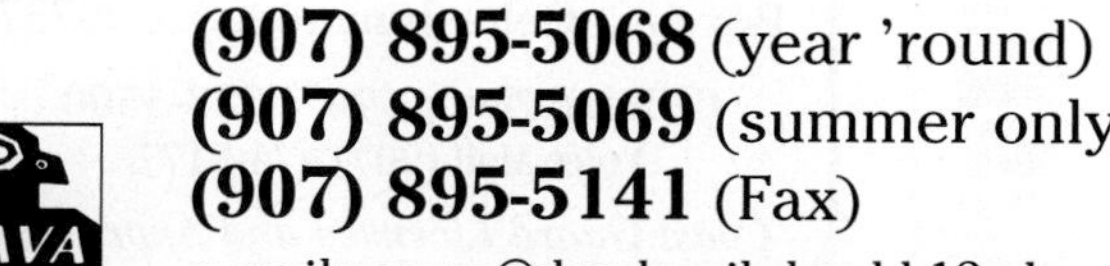

(907) 895-5068 (year 'round)

(907) 895-5069 (summer only)

(907) 895-5141 (Fax)

e-mail: npsm@dgsdmail.dgsd.k12.ak.us

AVA

photo courtesy Mike Kingston

Gardens at Rika's Roadhouse, Big Delta State Park. (Jerrianne Lowther, staff)

the Alaska Highway from Canada. A good spot to see and photograph the pipeline is at **Milepost V 275.4**, 9.5 miles/15.3 km north of town, where the pipeline crosses the Tanana River. Pump station No. 9, accessible from **Milepost V 258.3** Richardson Highway, offers tours daily from June to August; stop by or phone (907) 869-3270. There is also an interesting display of pipe used in 3 Alaska pipeline projects outside the visitor center in Delta Junction.

Named after the nearby Delta River, Delta Junction began as a construction camp on the Richardson Highway in 1919. (It was first known as Buffalo Center because of the American bison that were transplanted here in the 1920s.)

The Richardson Highway, connecting Valdez at tidewater with Fairbanks in the Interior, predates the Alaska Highway by 20 years. The Richardson was already a wagon road in 1910, and was updated to automobile standards in the 1920s by the Alaska Road Commission (ARC).

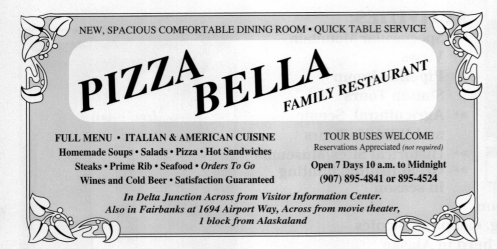

Since the late 1970s, the state has encouraged development of the agricultural industry in the Delta area. They have conducted local land disposal programs involving more than 112,000 acres. These programs generated 37 farms averaging 2,310 acres and 169 small farms averaging 161 acres.

In 1996, nearly 40,000 acres were in some form of agricultural use (including production of barley, oats, wheat, forage, pasture, grass seed, canola, potatoes, field peas, forage brassicas) and conservation use. Barley is the major feed grain grown in Delta. It is an excellent energy feed for cattle, hogs and sheep. Production acreages are determined by the anticipated in-state demand for barley.

Delta barley is stored on farms or in a local co-op elevator, sold on the open market or used to feed livestock. Small-scale farming of vegetables, 3 commercial potato farms, 5 active dairies, a dairy processing center, 6 beef producers, 2 beef feedlots, 3 swine producers, 3 bison ranches, 1 red-meat processing plant and 4 commercial greenhouses all contribute to Delta Junction's agriculture.

ACCOMMODATIONS/VISITOR SERVICES

Delta Junction has 3 motels, several bed and breakfasts, restaurants, gas stations, a coin-operated car wash, a shopping center, post office, gift shops, RV park, bank with automated banking machine and other businesses. There are several churches. Delta Community Park, on Kimball Street one block off the highway, has softball and soccer fields and playground.

There are private RV parks just south and just north of town. Three public campgrounds are located nearby: Delta state campground at **Milepost V 267.1**, and Clearwater state campground on Remington Road (see **Milepost DC 1414.9** and **V 268.3**) and Quartz Lake campground. ▲

TRANSPORTATION

Air: Scheduled service via 40-Mile Air from Tok to Fairbanks; Delta stop on request. Local air service available.

ATTRACTIONS

Buffalo Herd. American bison were transplanted into the Delta Junction area in the 1920s. Because the bison have become costly pests to many farmers in the Delta area, the 90,000-acre Delta Bison Sanctuary was created south of the Alaska Highway in 1980. However, keeping the bison on their refuge and out of the barley fields is a continuing problem. Summer visitors who wish to look at the bison are advised to visit the viewpoint at **Milepost V 241.3** on the Richardson Highway; use binoculars. The herd contained 482 bison in 1992 when the last census was taken by the ADF&G.

Special Events: Delta Junction celebrates a traditional Fourth of July with a Buffalo Barbecue. Buffalo Wallow, a 4-day square dance festival hosted by Buffalo Squares, is held every Memorial Day weekend. The Buffalo Squares also sponsors a campout and dance at Delta state campground the second Saturday in July.

The Deltana Fair is held in late July. The fair includes a barbecue, Lions' pancake breakfast, local handicrafts, horse show, livestock display and show, games, concessions, contests and a parade. A highlight of the fair is the Great Alaska Outhouse Race, held on Sunday, in which 4 pushers and 1 sitter compete for the coveted "Golden Throne" award.

A Festival of Lights is held each February in Delta Junction. This special event, designed to break up the monotony of long winter nights, features a parade of lights where the local citizenry builds and decorates floats with lights. There are also dog races, fireworks, square dancing, ice sculpting and more. It was -40°F/-40°C for the 1994 festival—an evening to remember, according to residents!

Area Museums. Alaska Homestead & Historical Museum, located approximately 6 miles/9.6 km east of town at **Milepost DC 1415.4** Alaska Highway, offers guided tours of an authentic Alaska homestead farm. There's also a large collection of historical farming equipment. Open June 1 to Sept. 15, daily 10 A.M. to 7 P.M.

North of town about 8 miles/12.9 km at **Milepost V 275** Richardson–Alaska Highway is Rika's Roadhouse at Big Delta State Historical Park. This restored roadhouse was built in 1910. Open daily in summer.

The Sullivan Roadhouse, relocated across from the visitor center, was originally built in 1906. It is one of the last remaining roadhouses from Valdez to Fairbanks. Open daily in summer as a walk-through museum.

Tour the agriculture of the area by driving Sawmill Creek Road (turn off at **Milepost DC 1403.6** Alaska Highway) and Clearwater Road (see **Milepost DC 1414.9**). Sawmill Creek Road goes through the heart of the grain-producing Delta Ag Project. Local farmers welcome visiting farmers' questions in between planting and harvesting. Commercial farm tours are available at the Hollenback farm on Sawmill Creek Road. Along Clearwater and Remington roads you may view the older farms, which produce forage crops and livestock. Tanana Loop Road (**Milepost V 271.7**), Tanana Loop Extension and Mill–Tan Road also go past many farms. The visitor information center in downtown Delta Junction can answer many questions on local agriculture. The Alaska Bureau–Delta Chamber sponsor an annual farm tour through the Delta agricultural district July 10, 1998. It's an all-day bus tour. Contact the Alaska Cooperative Extension for more information; phone (907) 895-4215.

Alaska Range Adventures. Flightseeing. Unique "Bush" fly-in culinary adventures, backpacking and nature tours; fly-in camping. One-hour flightseeing tours of the local wildlife and glaciers. "The real Alaskan 'Bush' experienced by air." It's the same view the eagle has. Phone Jack Morris or Bob Gibson, (907) 895-4876. [ADVERTISEMENT]

AREA FISHING: Delta–Clearwater River, grayling and whitefish; silver salmon spawn here in October. Access via Clearwater Road or Jack Warren Road (see Delta Vicinity map). (Although USGS topographic maps show this tributary of the Tanana River as Clearwater Creek, local residents refer to the stream as the Delta–Clearwater River.) **Goodpaster River**, accessible by boat via Delta–Clearwater and Tanana rivers; excellent grayling fishing.

There are 43 lakes in the Delta–Tok area that are stocked by the Alaska Dept. of Fish and Game. Lakes are stocked primarily with rainbow trout, and also with arctic grayling, lake trout, arctic char and king salmon. Most of these lakes are located close to the road

On the banks of the Tanana River at ***BIG DELTA STATE HISTORICAL PARK***, enjoy

RIKA'S ROADHOUSE & LANDING

"Best food in all 1,488 miles of the Alaska Highway . . ." *Seattle Times-Seattle Post-Intelligencer*

. . . a Roadhouse & Historical Buildings clustered in 10-acre Park

RATED #1 ON THE ALASKA HIGHWAY BY MAJOR TOUR COMPANIES

Hours
Park 8–8 Daily
Roadhouse &
Restaurant 9–5 Daily

TOUR BUSES WELCOME
FREE ADMISSION,
PARKING AND TOURS

Call (907) 895-4201 or
(907) 895-4938 Anytime
WORLDWIDE
POSTAL SERVICE

THE ROADHOUSE GIFT SHOP
Specializing in Alaskan-made gifts of
Gold Nugget Jewelry, Wood Puzzles,
Diamond Willow Walking Sticks,
Clocks, Tables and Fur Accessories

WHITESTONE FURS OF ALASKA
features Fur & Leather Coats, Jackets,
Stoles, Flings, Clings & Collars,
Hats, Hand Muffs & Earmuffs,
Slippers & Mittens
Fur Items Made To Order

Mile 275
chardson/Alaska Highway
P.O. Box 1229
Delta Jct., Alaska 99737
Just 1/4 mile from the
Trans-Alaska Pipeline
Tanana River Crossing

PACKHOUSE RESTAURANT
- Serving Breakfast & Lunch
- Seating for over 150
- Homemade Soups
- Fresh Salads & Sandwiches
- Fresh Baked Pies, Breads, Cookies & the Famous Bear Claw,

all from **The Alaska Baking Company**

View of Trans-Alaska pipeline Tanana River crossing at Milepost V 275.4

(© Tom Culkin)

system, but there are walk-in lakes available as well. **Quartz Lake**, at **Milepost V 277.7** north of Delta Junction, one of the most popular fishing lakes in the Delta area, is also the largest and most easily accessed of area lakes; angler success is excellent. Consult ADF&G offices in Delta or Tok for other locations.

Richardson–Alaska Highway Log

Although logged here as a natural extension of the Alaska Highway, the highway between Delta Junction and Fairbanks is designated as part of the Richardson Highway, with existing mileposts showing distance from Valdez.

Distance from Valdez (V) is followed by distance from Dawson Creek (DC) and distance from Fairbanks (F).

V 266 (428 km) **DC 1422** (2288.5 km) **F 98** (157.7 km) Delta Junction visitor information center sits at the junction of the Alaska and Richardson highways. Turn south for Valdez (see RICHARDSON HIGHWAY section). Continue north for Fairbanks.

V 266.3 (428.6 km) **DC 1422.3** (2289 km) **F 97.7** (157.2 km) Delta Junction post office.

V 266.5 (428.9 km) **DC 1422.5** (2289.2 km) **F 97.5** (156.9 km) Delta Junction library and city hall. Library hours are 11 A.M. to 6 P.M. Monday through Thursday and 11 A.M. to 4 P.M. Friday and Saturday; free paperback book and magazine exchange, Alaska videos, public fax and copier service. City Hall is open 9 A.M. to 5 P.M. weekdays; pay phone and public restrooms.

V 266.8 (429.4 km) **DC 1422.8** (2289.7 km) **F 97.2** (156.4 km) Alaska Dept. of Fish and Game office.

V 267 (429.7 km) **DC 1423** (2290 km) **F 97** (156.1 km) BLM airstrip; current status unknown.

V 267.1 (429.8 km) **DC 1423.1** (2290.2 km) **F 96.9** (155.9 km) Delta state campground to east; 24 sites, water, tables, shelter with covered tables, toilets, $8 nightly fee or annual pass. Large turnout at campground entrance. Turnout on west side of highway on bank of the Delta River offers excellent views of the Alaska Range. ▲

V 267.2 (430 km) **DC 1423.2** (2290.4 km) **F 96.8** (155.7 km) Alaska Division of Forestry office.

V 267.3 (430.2 km) **DC 1423.3** (2290.5 km) **F 96.7** (155.6 km) Medical clinic.

V 268 (431.3 km) **DC 1424** (2291.6 km) **F 96** (154.5 km) **Smith's Green Acres RV Park & Campground & Nightly Lodging.** Avoid the rush and the crowds, stay with us. One of Alaska's finest RV parks. 9.5 Good Sam rating. From a guest: "One of the best we've seen in Alaska." Nightly wildlife tours available. Great trout and grayling fishing nearby. See display ad. [ADVERTISEMENT] ▲

V 268.3 (431.7 km) **DC 1424.3** (2292.1 km) **F 95.7** (154 km) **Junction** with Jack Warren Road (see Delta Vicinity map this section). Turn here for access to Clearwater state campground (10.5 miles/16.9 km). Clearwater campground has toilets, tables, water and boat launch; pleasant campsites on bank of river. Camping fee $8/night or annual pass. ▲

Driving this loop is a good opportunity to see local homesteads. Note that mileposts on these paved side roads run backward from Mile 13 at this junction to Mile 0 at the junction of Clearwater Road and the Alaska Highway.

V 270.3 (435 km) **DC 1426.3** (2295.3 km) **F 93.7** (150.8 km) Alaska 7 Motel.

V 271.7 (437.2 km) **DC 1427.7** (2297.6 km) **F 92.3** (148.5 km) Tanana Loop Road. Turn here for Delta Junction youth hostel. To make a loop drive through farmlands, follow Tanana Loop Road approximately 1 mile/1.6 km, turn right on Tanana Loop Extension, which connects with Jack Warren Road. Turn west on Jack Warren Road to return to highway.

V 272.1 (437.9 km) **DC 1428** (2298 km) **F 92** (148 km) Fire station.

V 273.9 (440.8 km) **DC 1429.8** (2301 km) **F 90.2** (145.2 km) **Big D B&B.** See display ad this section.

V 275 (442.6 km) **DC 1431** (2303.9 km) **F 89** (143.2 km) **The Tanana Trading Post.** See display ad this section.

V 275 (442.6 km) **DC 1431** (2303.9 km) **F 89** (143.2 km) **Rika's Roadhouse at Big Delta State Historical Park.** Turn northeast at Rika's Road for Rika's Roadhouse and Landing on the banks of the Tanana River. Tour buses welcome. Parking areas with restrooms at both park entrances. The newly renovated Rika's Roadhouse offers worldwide postal service and gift shop specializing in fox furs, gold, diamond willow and interlocking wood puzzles. Visit the barn, Signal Corp station, sod-roofed museum and other historic structures. Live farm animals. Guides are available to walk with you through the history of this important crossroads on the Valdez–Fairbanks trail. Meals

served 9 A.M. to 5 P.M. in our Packhouse Restaurant, home of the Alaska Baking Co. Try our famous bear claws and homemade

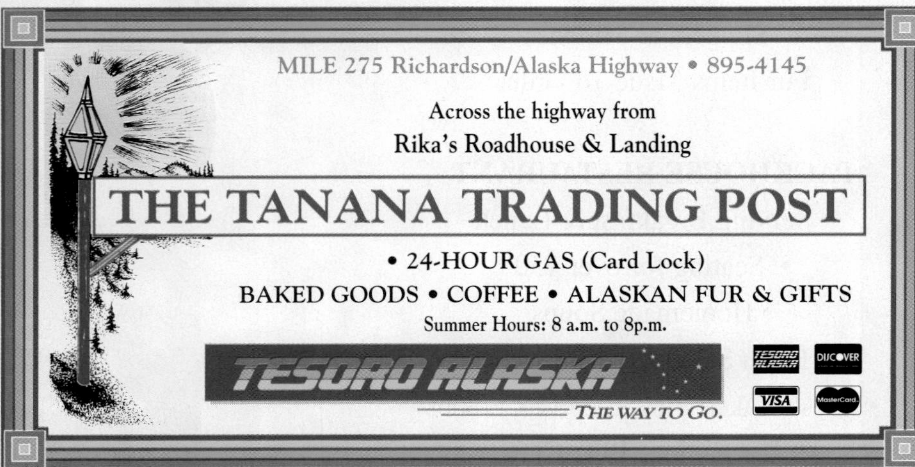

muffins. The Packhouse Restaurant also offers homemade soups, fresh salads and sandwiches. Guests love our homemade pies: strawberry–rhubarb, blueberry, apple, pecan and chocolate truffle. Overnight RV parking and dump station. After the dust of the highway, the green gardens of the 10-acre park are a welcome haven. Brochure available. P.O. Box 1229, Delta Junction, AK 99737. Phone (907) 895-4201 or 895-4938 anytime. Free admission. Handicapped access. See display ad this section. [ADVERTISEMENT] ♿▲

Rika's Roadhouse was built in 1910 by John Hajdukovich. In 1923, Hajdukovich sold it to Rika Wallen, a Swedish immigrant who had managed the roadhouse since 1917. Rika ran the roadhouse into the late 1940s and lived there until her death in 1969. Big Delta State Historical Park campground; camping fee $8/vehicle, dump station ($3). ▲

V 275.4 (443.2 km) **DC 1431.4** (2304.5 km) **F 88.6** (142.6 km) Big Delta Bridge across the Tanana River; spectacular view of pipeline suspended across river. Slow down for parking area at south end of bridge with litter barrels and interpretive sign about pipeline.

From here to Fairbanks there are views of the Tanana River and the Alaska Range to the south. Farming community of **BIG DELTA** (pop. 400); gas, store, 2 bars, a church, Kenner Sawmill and Tanana River boat landing.

The Fur Shack. See display ad this section.

V 277.7 (446.9 km) **DC 1433.7** (2307.2 km) **F 86.3** (138.9 km) Turnoff to east for Quartz Lake Recreation Area. Drive in 2.5 miles/4 km on gravel road to intersection: turn left for Lost Lake, continue straight ahead for Quartz Lake (another 0.3 mile/0.5 km). Lost Lake, 0.2 mile/0.3 km from intersection, has 8 campsites with picnic tables, toilet, and a large parking area with tables and litter barrels. A shallow, picturesque lake with no fish. Quartz Lake has more developed campsites on good loop road, firepits, water, tables, toilet and 2 boat launches. Boat launch fee $3 or annual boat launch pass. Camping fees at both campgrounds: $8/night or annual pass. A trail connects Lost Lake and Quartz Lake camping areas. ▲

Private cabins are scattered along the northern and eastern shorelines of Quartz Lake. About half the land along the lake is undeveloped and there is no road access beyond the campground. The lake covers 1,500 acres, more than 80 percent of which are less than 15 feet/5m deep. Maximum depth is 40 feet/12m. Aquatic vegetation covers most of the lake surface, hampering swimmers and waterskiers. Boat and motor rentals available from Black Spruce Lodge. **Quartz Lake** offers excellent fishing for stocked rainbow to 18 inches, silver salmon to 13 inches and Arctic char; use spinners, plugs and artificial flies. Ice fishing in winter. For more information phone the ADF&G office in Delta at (907) 895-4632.

V 277.9 (447.2 km) **DC 1433.9** (2307.5 km) **F 86.1** (138.6 km) Former U.S. Army petroleum station, now closed. Pay phone beside highway.

V 278.2 (447.7 km) **DC 1434.2** (2308 km) **F 85.8** (138.1 km) South end of long double-ended turnout to west. Several of these long turnouts northbound are old sections of the Alaska Highway.

V 280.3 (451.1 km) **DC 1436.3** (2311.4 km) **F 83.7** (134.7 km) Gravel turnout to east.

V 282 (453.8 km) **DC 1438** (2314.2 km) **F 82** (132 km) Watch for frost cracking.

V 284 (457 km) **DC 1440** (2317.4 km) **F 80** (128.7 km) Watch for moose.

V 286.6 (461.2 km) **DC 1442.6** (2321.6 km) **F 77.4** (124.6 km) Shaw Creek bridge; boat launch and snack shop. Excellent wildflower displays of sweet peas blooming in June.

V 286.7 (461.4 km) **DC 1442.7** (2321.7 km) **F 77.3** (124.4 km) **Shaw Creek** road. Good to excellent early spring and fall grayling fishing; subject to closure (check locally). Good view northbound of Tanana River which parallels the highway. Fireweed, pale oxytrope, sweet peas bloom along roadside.

V 287.2 (462.2 km) **DC 1443.2** (2322.5 km) **F 76.8** (123.6 km) Turnout and road to slough to east. Birch trees are thick along this stretch of highway.

V 288 (463.5 km) **DC 1444** (2323.8 km) **F 76** (122.3 km) Panoramic view to the south with vistas of 3 great peaks of the Alaska Range: Mount Hayes, elev. 13,832 feet/4,216m, almost due south; Hess Mountain, elev. 11,940 feet/3,639m, to the west (right) of Mount Hayes; and Mount Deborah, elev. 12,339 feet/3,761m, to the west (right) of Hess Mountain. Mount Hayes is named for Charles Hayes, an early member of the U.S. Geological Survey. Mount Deborah was named in 1907 by the famous Alaskan Judge Wickersham for his wife.

V 289.8 (466.4 km) **DC 1445.8** (2326.7 km) **F 74.2** (119.4 km) Paved double-ended turnout to east.

V 291.8 (469.6 km) **DC 1447.8** (2329.9 km) **F 72.2** (116.2 km) Northbound truck lane begins.

V 292.8 (471.2 km) **DC 1448.8** (2331.5 km) **F 71.2** (114.6 km) Truck lane ends. View of Tanana River valley.

V 294 (473.1 km) **DC 1450** (2333.5 km) **F 70** (112.7 km) Paved double-ended turnout.

V 294.2 (473.5 km) **DC 1450.2** (2333.8 km) **F 69.8** (112.3 km) Southbound truck lane begins.

V 294.9 (474.6 km) **DC 1450.9** (2334.9 km) **F 69.1** (111.2 km) Game Management Unit boundary between 20B and 20D. Entering Fairbanks North Star borough northbound.

V 295 (474.7 km) **DC 1451** (2335.1 km) **F 69** (111 km) Site of the original old Richardson Roadhouse, which burned down in December 1982.

V 295.4 (475.4 km) **DC 1451.4** (2335.7 km) **F 68.6** (110.4 km) Banner Creek bridge; historic placer gold stream.

V 296.4 (477 km) **DC 1452.4** (2337.3 km) **F 67.6** (108.8 km) Paved turnout to west; view of Alaska Range and Tanana River to south.

V 297.7 (479.1 km) **DC 1453.7** (2339.4 km) **F 66.3** (106.7 km) Large gravel parking area to west below highway; good scenic viewpoint. Paved access road to Tanana River.

V 298.2 (479.9 km) **DC 1454.2** (2340.2 km) **F 65.8** (105.9 km) Scenic viewpoint; paved double-ended turnout to west. Watch for frost heaves and dips.

V 301.7 (485.5 km) **DC 1457.7** (2345.9 km) **F 62.3** (100.3 km) South end of long double-ended turnout to west.

V 304.3 (489.7 km) **DC 1460.3** (2350 km) **F 59.7** (96.1 km) Small paved turnout to east.

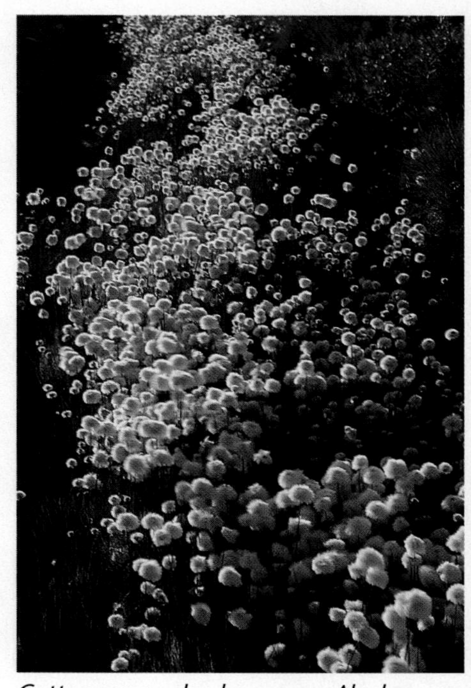

Cottongrass, also known as Alaska cotton. The stem bases are edible.

(© Harry M. Walker Photo)

V 305.2 (491.2 km) **DC 1461.2** (2351.5 km) **F 58.8** (94.6 km) Birch Lake Road to east; access to military recreation area (restricted).

V 306 (492.4 km) **DC 1462** (2352.8 km) **F 58** (93.3 km) Large parking area to east overlooking **Birch Lake**; unimproved gravel boat launch and beach; fish from shore in spring, from boat in summer, for rainbow and silver salmon. Many Fairbanks residents have summer homes at Birch Lake.

V 306.1 (492.6 km) **DC 1462.1** (2352.9 km) **F 57.9** (93.2 km) Turnoff to west for **Lost Lake**. Drive in 0.7 mile/1.1 km on dirt road; silver salmon fishing.

V 307.2 (494.3 km) **DC 1463.2** (2354.7 km) **F 56.8** (91.4 km) Birch Lake highway maintenance station.

V 308.4 (496.3 km) **DC 1464.4** (2356.6

Adult common loon in summer plumage has all black head and broken white collar. (© Mike Jones)

km) **F 55.6** (89.5 km) South end of long double-ended turnout to east.

V 310 (498.9 km) **DC 1466** (2359.2 km) **F 54** (86.9 km) Double-ended paved parking area to west.

V 313 (503.7 km) **DC 1469** (2364 km) **F 51** (82.1 km) Paved double-ended turnout to west. Access to **Silver Fox Pond**; stocked with arctic char.

V 314.8 (506.6 km) **DC 1470.8** (2366.9 km) **F 49.2** (79.2 km) **Midway Lodge** is open 7 A.M. to 11 P.M. daily. Bar open till ? Breakfast anytime, famous homemade chili, royal ½-pound hamburgers, fresh pies. Clean rooms starting at $35. Showers. Gifts. We are a family-oriented stop on the Alaska Highway and welcome your visit. 11191 Richardson Highway, Salcha, AK 99714. Phone (907) 488-2939. [ADVERTISEMENT]

V 317.9 (511.6 km) **DC 1473.9** (2371.9 km) **F 45.4** (73.1 km) Double-ended gravel turnout to west.

V 319.3 (513.8 km) **DC 1475.3** (2374.2 km) **F 44.7** (71.9 km) Access road leads east to Harding Lake summer homes.

V 319.8 (514.7 km) **DC 1475.8** (2375 km) **F 44.2** (71.1 km) Second access road northbound leads east to Harding Lake summer homes. Access to **Little Harding Lake**, king salmon fishing.

V 321.5 (517.4 km) **DC 1477.5** (2377.8 km) **F 42.5** (68.4 km) **Harding Lake** State Recreation Area turnoff; drive east 1.5 miles/2.4 km on paved road to campground. Park headquarters, drinking water fill-up and dump station ($3 charge) at campground entrance. Picnic grounds on lakeshore, swimming, boat ramp ($5 launch fee or annual boat launch pass), ball fields and about 80 campsites. Camping fee $8/night or annual pass. Fishing for lake trout, arctic char, burbot, northern pike and salmon. Lake is reported to be "hard to fish." Worth the drive! *Bring your insect repellent. You may need it!*

V 322.2 (518.5 km) **DC 1478.2** (2378.9 km) **F 41.8** (67.3 km) Salcha post office and Salcha River Lodge; food, gas and lodging.

Salcha River Lodge. Alaskan hospitality. Gas, diesel, propane, clean showers, modern motel, groceries, restaurant, gift shop, post office. Ice cream cones, shakes, sundaes, homemade pie. Close to rivers and lakes; excellent fishing. 9162 Richardson Highway, Salcha, AK 99714. Phone (907) 488-2233. [ADVERTISEMENT]

V 323.1 (520 km) **DC 1479.1** (2380.3 km) **F 40.9** (65.8 km) **Salcha River** State Recreation Site; large parking area with 75 sites, boat ramp ($3 launch fee or annual boat launch pass), picnic area, toilets and water. Camping fee $8/night per vehicle or annual pass. Fishing for king and chum salmon, grayling, sheefish, northern pike and burbot.

V 323.4 (520.4 km) **DC 1479.4** (2380.8 km) **F 40.6** (65.3 km) Salcha River bridge.

V 324 (521.4 km) **DC 1480** (2381.7 km) **F 40** (64.4 km) Clear Creek bridge.

V 324.6 (522.4 km) **DC 1480.6** (2382.7 km) **F 39.4** (63.4 km) Double-ended gravel turnout to east.

V 324.8 (522.7 km) **DC 1480.8** (2383 km) **F 39.2** (63.1 km) Munsons Slough bridge.

V 325.5 (523.8 km) **DC 1481.5** (2384.2 km) **F 38.5** (62 km) The community of **SALCHA** (pop. 354) stretches along the highway in both directions. The elementary school is located here. The post office (ZIP 99714) is at **Milepost V 322.2.**

V 326.4 (525.3 km) **DC 1482.4** (2385.6 km) **F 37.6** (60.5 km) Salcha Baptist log church to west.

V 327 (526.2 km) **DC 1483** (2386.6 km) **F 37** (59.5 km) Picturesque log home to west.

V 327.7 (527.4 km) **DC 1483.7** (2387.7 km) **F 36.3** (58.4 km) Little Salcha River bridge.

V 328.3 (528.3 km) **DC 1484.3** (2388.7 km) **F 35.7** (57.4 km) **Salcha Store and Service.** See display ad this section.

V 330.4 (531.7 km) **DC 1486.4** (2392.1 km) **F 33.6** (54.1 km) Johnson Road. Access to Pump Station 8.

V 331.7 (533.8 km) **DC 1487.7** (2394.2 km) **F 32.3** (52 km) Salcha Fairgrounds.

V 332.2 (534.6 km) **DC 1488.2** (2395 km) **F 31.8** (51.2 km) Access east to **31-Mile Pond**; stocked with arctic char.

V 332.3 (534.8 km) **DC 1488.3** (2395.1 km) **F 31.7** (51 km) **The Knotty Shop.** Stop and be impressed by a truly unique Alaskan gift shop and wildlife museum. Jim and

Paula have attempted to maintain a genuine Alaskan flavor—from the unusual burl construction to the Alaskan wildlife displayed in a natural setting to the handcrafted Alaskan gifts. Don't miss the opportunity to stop and browse. See display ad this section. Show us *The MILEPOST®* advertisement for a free small ice cream cone. [ADVERTISEMENT]

V 334.5 (538.3 km) **DC 1490.5** (2398.7 km) **F 29.5** (47.5 km) Public dumpster at gravel pit.

V 334.7 (538.6 km) **DC 1490.7** (2399 km) **F 29.3** (47.2 km) South boundary of Eielson AFB. Watch for various military aircraft taking off and landing to the east. Aircraft include Air Force F-16s, F-15s, KC-135s, C-130s, C-141s, OA-10s, Navy A-6s, F-14s and others.

V 335.1 (539.3 km) **DC 1491.1** (2399.6 km) **F 28.9** (46.5 km) Access east to **28-Mile Pond;** stocked with rainbow and silver salmon.

V 340.7 (548.3 km) **DC 1496.7** (2408.6 km) **F 23.3** (37.5 km) Divided highway begins for northbound traffic. *CAUTION: Watch for heavy traffic southbound turning east into the base, 7–8 A.M., and merging northbound traffic, 3:45–5:30 P.M., weekdays.*

V 341 (548.8 km) **DC 1497** (2409.1 km) **F 23** (37 km) Entrance to **EIELSON AIR FORCE BASE,** constructed in 1943 and named for Carl Ben Eielson, a famous Alaskan bush pilot. A weekly tour is offered for groups of 10 or more. Phone the Public Affairs office at (907) 377-1410 for reservations and more information.

V 343.7 (553.1 km) **DC 1499.7** (2413.5 km) **F 20.3** (32.7 km) Moose Creek Road and general store; diesel, gas, propane.

Moose Creek General Store. See display ad this section.

Piledriver Slough parallels the highway from here north, flowing into the Tanana River. It is stocked with rainbow trout. Check with general store for access and fishing information. **Bathing Beauty Pond,** stocked with rainbow, arctic char and grayling, is accessible via Eielson Farm Road off Moose Creek Road.

V 344.7 (554.7 km) **DC 1500.7** (2415 km) **F 19.3** (31.1 km) Moose Creek bridge.

V 345.5 (556 km) **DC 1501.5** (2416.4 km) **F 18.5** (29.8 km) *CAUTION: Highway crosses Alaska Railroad tracks.*

V 346 (556.8 km) **DC 1502** (2417.2 km) **F 17.9** (28.8 km) Chena Flood Channel bridge. Upstream dam is part of flood control project initiated after the Chena River left its banks and flooded Fairbanks in 1967.

V 346.7 (558 km) **DC 1502.7** (2418.4 km) **F 17.3** (27.8 km) Laurance Road.

North Pole VFW Post. See display ad this section.

Harding Lake state recreation area at Milepost V 321.5 offers camping, picnicking and fishing. (© Tom Culkin)

Turn east for Chena Lakes Recreation Area (follow signs, 2.2 miles/3.5 km to entrance). Constructed by the Army Corps of Engineers and run by Fairbanks North Star Borough, the recreation area has 80 campsites, 92 picnic sites (some with wheelchair access), pump water, volleyball courts and a 250-acre lake with swimming beach. **Chena Lake** is stocked with silver salmon, arctic char, grayling and rainbow trout. Nonmotorized boats may be rented from a concessionaire. The **Chena River**

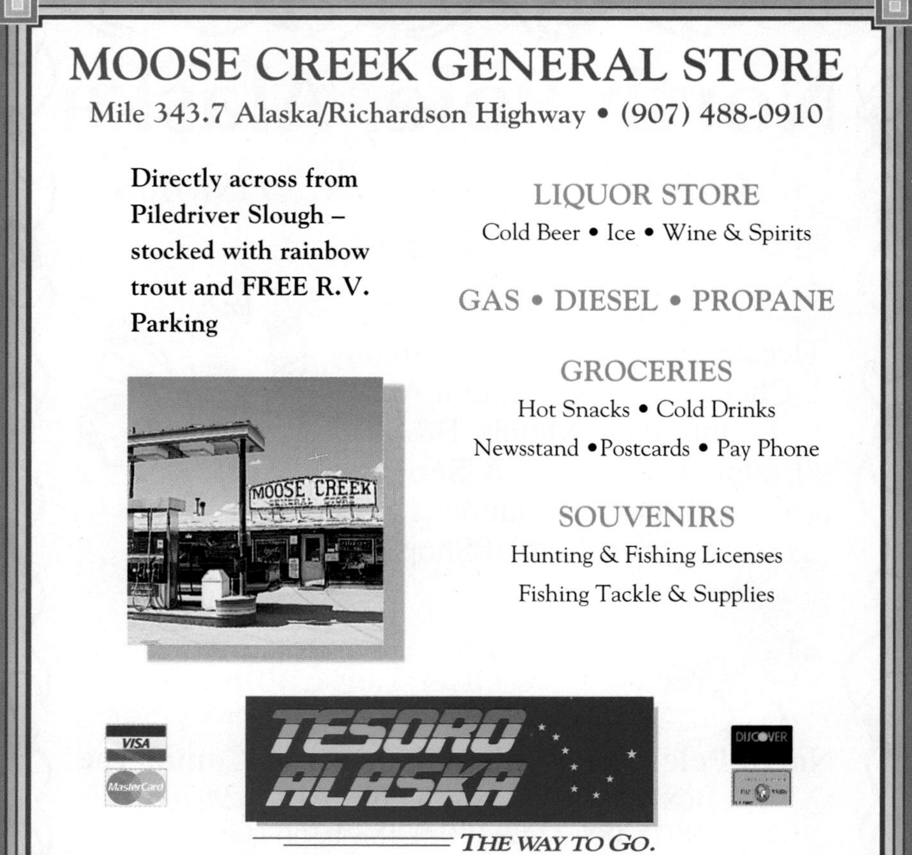

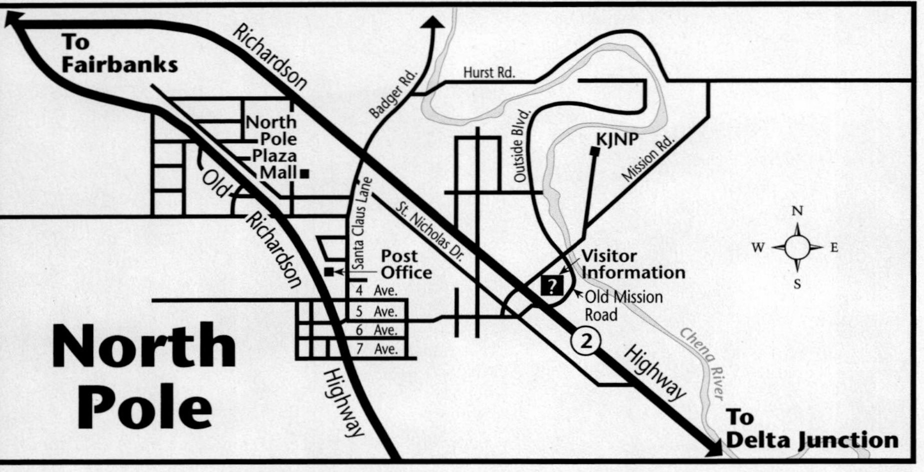

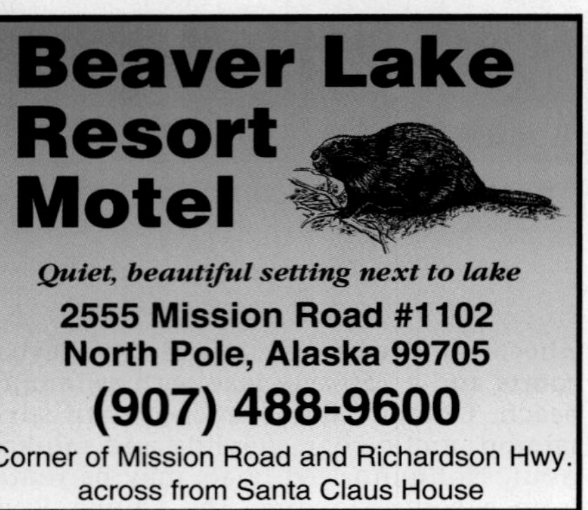

flows through part of the recreation area and offers good grayling fishing and also northern pike, whitefish and burbot. Hiking and self-guiding nature trails. Open year-round. Fee charged Memorial Day to Labor Day; day use $3 per vehicle, camping $6 per day. ▲

V 347.1 (558.6 km) **DC 1503.1** (2419 km) **F 16.9** (27.2 km) Newby Road.

V 347.7 (559.6 km) **DC 1503.7** (2419.9 km) **F 16.3** (26.2 km) Exit west for St. Nicholas Drive, east for Dawson Road.

V 348.7 (561.2 km) **DC 1504.7** (2421.5 km) **F 15.3** (24.6 km) North Pole Visitor Information Center; open 8 A.M. to 7 P.M. daily, Memorial Day to mid-September. Turn right on Mission Road for radio station KJNP, turn left northbound for 5th Avenue businesses, RV park and Santa Claus House.

Santaland RV Park. Good Sampark. Center of North Pole, next to Santa Claus House, home of Dancer and Prancer, North Pole's resident reindeer. City water, full service pull-throughs, car wash. Free private showers, laundry, pay phones. Handicapped accessible. Tour sales and reservations. Daily shuttle bus to Fairbanks points of interest. See display ad, or call (888) 488-9123 or (907) 488-9123. [ADVERTISEMENT] ▲

V 349 (561.6 km) **DC 1505** (2422 km) **F 15** (24.1 km) **Santa Claus House.** In 1949, Con Miller began wearing a Santa Claus suit on business trips throughout the territory, bringing the spirit of St. Nicholas to hundreds of children for the first time. Here, the Miller family continues this tradition. Ask about Santa's Christmas letter. Mail your cards and letters here for authentic North Pole postmark. Enjoy the unique gift shop and exhibits. Summer hours: 8 A.M.–8 P.M. daily, Memorial Day through Labor Day. Ride the Snowy River Railroad daily except Sunday, summers only. Visit with Santa Claus summers and Christmas season only. Santa's reindeer, Dancer and Prancer, live on the grounds all summer long. Santa Claus House winter hours: 10 A.M.–6 P.M. (closed January and February for Santa's annual vacation). See display ad this section. [ADVERTISEMENT]

V 349.5 (562.3 km) **DC 1505.5** (2422.8 km) **F 14.5** (23.3 km) North Pole and North Pole Plaza to the left northbound via Santa Claus Lane; Badger Road to the right. Truck stop with diesel, 2 small shopping malls, motel and other businesses are located on Badger Road. Santa Claus Lane has several businesses along it, and connects with 5th Avenue, which loops back to the highway at **Milepost V 348.6**. Badger Road is a loop road leading 12 miles/19.3 km along Badger Slough and providing access to an RV park, salmon bake, convenience store with gas, and several bed and breakfasts. It also junctions with Nordale Road to Chena Hot Springs Road. It re-enters the Alaska Highway 7 miles/11.3 km outside of Fairbanks at **Milepost V 357.1**.

North Pole

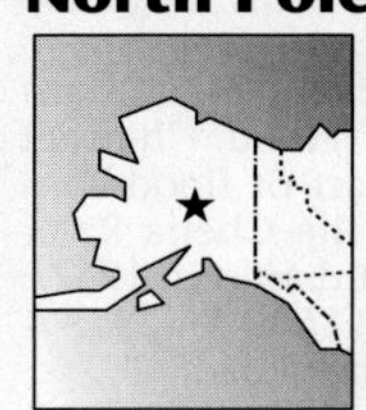

V 349.5 (562.3 km) **DC 1505.5** (2422.8 km) **F 14.5** (23.3 km) West of the Alaska Highway. **Population:** 1,598. **Emergency Services:** Emergencies only phone 911. **Police,** phone (907) 488-6902. **Alaska State Troopers,** phone (907) 452-2114. **Fire Department,** phone (907) 488-2232.

Visitor Information: At **Milepost V 348.7**. Open 8 A.M. to 7 P.M. daily, Memorial Day to mid-September.

Elevation: 500 feet/152m. **Radio:** KJNP-AM 1170, KJNP-FM 100.3; also Fairbanks stations.

Private Aircraft: Bradley Sky Ranch, 0.9

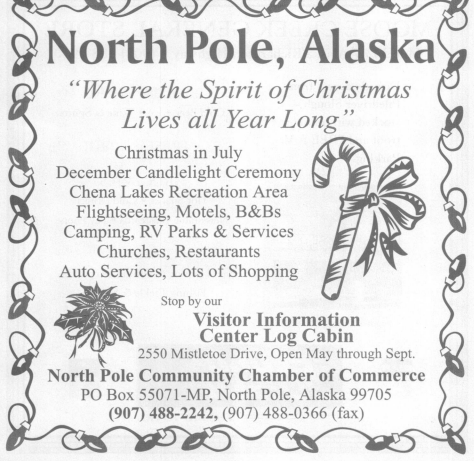

SANTA CLAUS HOUSE
"Where It's Christmas Every Day"
The North Pole Story
It's Christmas every day at Santa Claus House, where Santa lives year round. Our "Santa Claus" is Con Miller, and to the children responsible for the "Santa" nickname, Con Miller is indeed *the* "Kris Kringle."
In 1949, Con and Nellie Miller found a red Santa Claus suit among the merchandise in their Fairbanks trading post. Each summer Con had trekked into interior Alaska trading for furs and other items of barter. For his first Christmas in the Territory of Alaska, Miller donned the red suit and brought the spirit of Saint Nicholas to hundreds of Alaska Native children. He has been "Santa" to young and old of many villages ever since.
Soon after, the Millers moved their business to North Pole, then just a scattering of buildings 14 miles south of Fairbanks.
In 1952, as Miller and his sons struggled to erect the spruce log building, a truckload of youngsters drove by and called, "Hi, Santa Claus! Are you building a new house?" The Millers' new business immediately became known as "Santa Claus House."
When the state rerouted the highway in 1970, by-passing North Pole and Santa Claus House, Con and Nellie built a new Santa Claus House on the four-lane highway. Nestled among towering spruce trees, Santa Claus House has gained international recognition.
When you visit Santa Claus House, you'll likely catch a glimpse of Mr. and Mrs. Claus busily answering letters from boys and girls around the world. But they'll never be too busy to wish you a very Merry Christmas.
Mile 349 Alaska-Richardson Highway
between the two North Pole exits
Interior Alaska's Largest Gift Shop
Alaskan Gifts & Jewelry
Collectibles • Christmas Shop
Santa's Toy Cache • Coffee Cache
Espresso & Brewed Coffee
Soft Drinks & Snacks
Ride the Snowy River Railroad
NORTH POLE Santa's Official Mail ALASKA
Home of the Original "Letter From Santa." Place your order when you visit or write us.
Mail your cards & letters from Santa Claus House for an authentic North Pole postmark
Phone (907) 488-2200 • Fax (907) 488-5601
Santa Claus House, 101 St. Nicholas Drive, North Pole, AK 99705
See log ad at Mile 349 Alaska-Richardson Highway

As street signs indicate, North Pole takes its name seriously.

(© Ruth von Spalding)

mile/1.4 km northwest; elev. 483 feet/147m; length 4,100 feet/1,250m; gravel; fuel 100.

North Pole has most visitor facilities including restaurants, a motel, bed and breakfasts, campgrounds, laundromats, car wash, grocery and gas stops, gift stores, library, churches, a public park, pharmacy and supermarket. The post office is on Santa Claus Lane.

North Pole has an annual Winter Carnival with sled dog races, carnival games, food booths and other activities. There's a big summer festival weekend celebration with carnival rides, food booths, arts and crafts booths, and a parade.

In 1944 Bon V. Davis homesteaded this area. Dahl and Gaske Development Co. bought the Davis homestead, subdivided it and named it North Pole, hoping to attract a toy manufacturer who could advertise products as being made in North Pole.

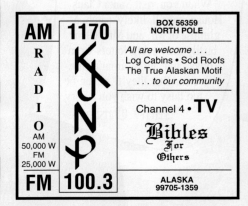

North Pole is the home of many Fairbanks commuters. It has an oil refinery that produces heating fuel, jet fuel and other products. Eielson and Wainwright military bases are nearby.

Radio station KJNP, operated by Calvary's Northern Lights Mission, broadcasts music and religious programs on 1170 AM and 100.3 FM. They also operate television station KJNP Channel 4. Visitors are welcome between 8 A.M. and 10 P.M.; tours may be arranged. KJNP is located on Mission Road about 0.6 mile/1 km northeast of the Alaska Highway. The missionary project includes a dozen hand-hewn, sod-roofed homes and other buildings constructed of spruce logs.

Full-service campgrounds at Santaland RV Park downtown, Road's End RV Park at **Milepost V 356.2** and Riverview RV Park at **Milepost V 357.1** Alaska–Richardson Highway. North Pole Public Park, on 5th Avenue, has tent sites in the trees along a narrow dirt road; no camping fee. Dump station available at North Pole Plaza. ▲

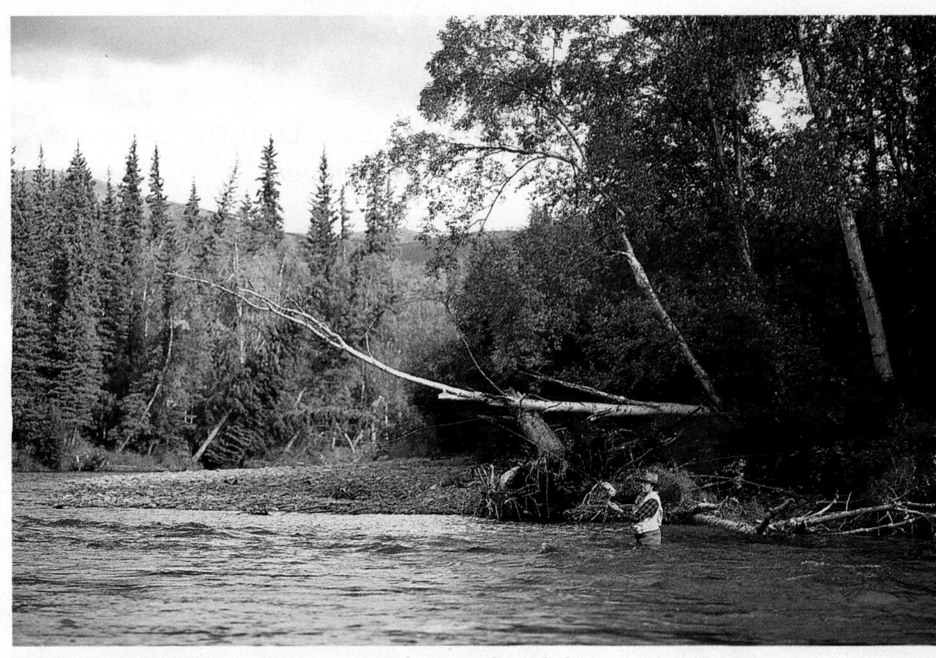

Fly-fishing the Chena River, a popular grayling fishery. (© Robin Brandt)

Richardson–Alaska Highway Log

(continued)

V 350.2 (563.6 km) **DC 1506.2** (2423.9 km) **F 13.8** (22.2 km) Peridot Street.

V 350.6 (564.2 km) **DC 1506.6** (2424.6 km) **F 13.4** (21.6 km) *CAUTION: Highway crosses Alaska Railroad tracks.*

V 351 (564.9 km) **DC 1507** (2425.3 km) **F 13** (20.9 km) Twelvemile Village exit. Greenhouse with floral displays.

V 354.4 (570.3 km) **DC 1510.4** (2430.7 km) **F 9.6** (15.4 km) Old Richardson Highway exit.

V 356.2 (573.2 km) **DC 1512.2** (2433.6 km) **F 7.8** (12.6 km) **Road's End RV Park.** Just 6.5 miles south of Fairbanks on the Richardson–Alaska Highway. Halfway between North Pole and Fairbanks. Full and partial hookups, tent camping, showers, laundry, pay phone, good water. Easy access. Reasonable rates. Weekly and monthly rates available. VISA/MasterCard accepted. Cash discounts given. Phone/fax: (907) 488-0295. [ADVERTISEMENT] ▲

V 357.1 (574.7 km) **DC 1513.1** (2435 km) **F 6.9** (11.1 km) Badger Road. This loop road connects with the Alaska Highway again at North Pole. Motel, RV park, salmon bake, bed and breakfasts, and other businesses are located on Badger Road. Badger Road also junctions with Nordale Road to Chena Hot Springs Road and access to the Chena River.

Riverview RV Park. See display ad this section.

V 357.6 (575.5 km) **DC 1513.6** (2435.8 km) **F 6.4** (10.3 km) Weigh stations both sides of highway.

V 358.6 (577.1 km) **DC 1514.6** (2437.4 km) **F 5.4** (8.7 km) Entrance to Fort Wainwright.

V 359.2 (578.1 km) **DC 1515.2** (2438.4 km) **F 4.8** (7.7 km) *CAUTION: Highway crosses Alaska Railroad tracks.*

V 359.6 (578.7 km) **DC 1515.6** (2439.1 km) **F 4.4** (7.1 km) West truck route (Old Richardson Highway) exit for westbound traffic only. Access to motels, restaurants and Cushman Street business area.

V 360.6 (580.3 km) **DC 1516.6** (2440.7 km) **F 3.4** (5.5 km) Denali Park/Parks Highway (Alaska Route 3) exit northbound to bypass Fairbanks via the Robert J. Mitchell expressway. Hospital this exit.

V 361 (581 km) **DC 1517** (2441.4 km) **F 3** (4.8 km) Exit via 30th Avenue to Big Bend business area for east- and westbound traffic. Access to motels, restaurants, Old Richardson Highway, Van Horn Road, Cushman Street and downtown Fairbanks.

V 361.3 (581.4 km) **DC 1517.3** (2441.8 km) **F 2.7** (4.3 km) 30th Avenue overpass; exits both sides of highway. A heart-shaped picture created from plantings of yellow flowers represents the Golden Heart of Fairbanks.

V 363 (584.2 km) **DC 1519** (2444.6 km) **F 1** (1.6 km) Turn right on Gaffney Road for Fort Wainwright; left on Airport Way for downtown Fairbanks, University of Alaska, Alaskaland and Parks Highway (Alaska Route 3). Follow city center signs to downtown Fairbanks and visitor information center. Go straight ahead on the Steese Expressway for Gavora Mall, Bentley Mall, Fox, Steese and Elliott highways, and Chena Hot Springs Road.

V 363.3 (584.7 km) **DC 1519.3** (2445 km) **F 0.7** (1.1 km) 10th Avenue exit to Fairbanks.

V 363.6 (585.1 km) **DC 1519.6** (2445.6 km) **F 0.4** (0.6 km) Steese Expressway crosses Chena River.

V 363.9 (585.6 km) **DC 1519.9** (2446 km) **F 0.1** (0.2 km) 3rd Street exit. Gavora Mall.

V 364 (585.8 km) **DC 1520** (2446.2 km) **F 0 FAIRBANKS.** College Road exit route to University of Alaska, Bentley Mall and city center (turn left). For details see FAIRBANKS section.

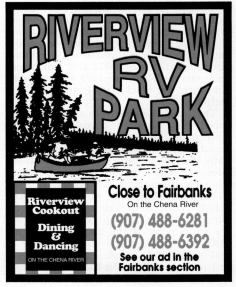

LIARD HIGHWAY 77 7

Connects: Alaska Hwy. to Mackenzie Hwy. **Length:** 244 miles
Road Surface: Gravel **Season:** Open all year
Steepest Grade: 10 percent
Major Attraction: Nahanni National Park

Junction of the Liard Highway with the Mackenzie Highway to Fort Simpson.
(© Lyn Hancock)

	Fort Liard	Fort Nelson	Fort Simpson
Fort Liard		126	176
Fort Nelson	126		302
Fort Simpson	176	302	

The Liard Highway, also called the Liard Trail or "Moose Highway" (after the road sign logo), is named for the Liard River Valley through which it runs for most of its length. The Liard Highway begins about 17 miles/27 km north of Fort Nelson on the Alaska Highway and leads northeast through British Columbia and Northwest Territories for 244.4 miles/393.4 km to junction with the Mackenzie Highway (NWT Highway 1).

The Liard is a relatively straight 2-lane gravel road through boreal forest and muskeg. In French, Liard means "black poplar," and this wilderness highway (officially opened in June 1984) is a corridor through a forest of white and black spruce, trembling aspen and balsam poplar.

The road can be dusty when dry and very muddy when wet. Poor road conditions (potholes, lack of grading) were reported on the BC portion of the Liard Highway in 1997. The NWT portion of the highway is well-maintained. Travelers may check current road conditions on the BC section of the highway (first 85 miles/136.8 km of road) by inquiring at the Visitor Infocentre in Fort Nelson, BC. Travel information for the Northwest Territories is available from Northwest Territories Tourism; phone toll free weekdays (800) 661-0788. Food, gas and lodging are available at Fort Liard. Gas and accommodations are also available at the Mackenzie Highway junction. It is a good idea to fill up in Fort Nelson.

Although the Northwest Territories portion of the Liard Highway parallels the Liard River, there is little access to the river. Travelers may enhance their trip by visiting Blackstone Territorial Park and exploring Nahanni National Park by air charter out of Fort Liard, Fort Simpson or Fort Nelson. Blackstone Territorial Park is accessible by road. Along the highway, travelers may walk the cut lines, drive to abandoned construction camps, swim in the borrow pits and bird watch at the barge landings. Remember to bring along lots of insect repellent!

Fishing the highway streams is only fair, but watch for wildlife such as moose, black bear, wood bison and grouse.

Liard Highway Log

Physical kilometreposts are up on the British Columbia portion of the highway about every 5 kilometres, starting with Km 0 at the Alaska Highway junction and ending at the BC–NWT border. Kilometreposts are up about every 2 kilometres on the Northwest Territories portion of the highway, starting with Km 0 at the BC–NWT border and ending at the junction with the Mackenzie Highway.

Distance from the junction with the Alaska Highway (A) is followed by distance from the Mackenzie Highway junction (M).

A 0 M 244.4 (393.4 km) **Junction** with the Alaska Highway.

A 6.2 (10.1 km) **M 238.2** (383.3 km) Beaver Creek.

A 6.4 (10.3 km) **M 238** (383.1 km) Short side road east to Beaver Lake recreation site; 2 picnic tables, litter barrels, pit toilets, firewood, turnaround space. Short hike downhill through brush to floating dock; limited lake access.

A 14.3 (23.1 km) **M 230.1** (370.3 km) Stanolind Creek. Beaver dams to west.

A 15.6 (25.2 km) **M 228.8** (368.2 km) Gravel pit to west.

A 17.5 (28.2 km) **M 226.9** (365.2 km) Pond to west and cut line through trees shows Cat access in summer, ice road in winter.

A 21.1 (34 km) **M 223.3** (359.4 km) Westcoast Transmission Pipeline crossing. Pipeline transports natural gas from Pointed Mountain near Fort Liard to the company's gas plant on the Alaska Highway just south of Fort Nelson.

A 23.9 (38.4 km) **M 220.5** (355 km) Gravel pit to west.

A 24.2 (38.9 km) **M 220.2** (354.5 km) Road begins descent northbound to Fort Nelson River.

A 26.4 (42.5 km) **M 218** (350.9 km) Fort Nelson River bridge, single lane, reduce speed. The Nelson bridge is the longest Acrow bridge in the world at 1,410 feet/430m. It is 14 feet/4m wide, with a span of 230 feet/70m from pier to pier. The Acrow bridge, formerly called the Bailey bridge after its designer Sir Donald Bailey, is designed of interchangeable steel panels coupled with pins for rapid construction.

A 26.6 (42.9 km) **M 217.8** (350.5 km) Turnout at north end of bridge with pit toilet, table and garbage container.

A 39.7 (63.9 km) **M 204.7** (329.5 km)

Tsinhia Creek, grayling run for about 2 weeks in spring.

A 43.4 (69.8 km) **M 201** (323.5 km) Trapper's cabin to east.

A 51.8 (83.3 km) **M 192.6** (310.1 km) Side road leads west 1.9 miles/3 km to Tsinhia Lake and dead-ends in soft sandy track. A recreation site is planned at Tsinhia Lake.

A 59.2 (95.3 km) **M 185.2** (298.1 km) There are several winter roads in this area used by the forest, oil and gas industries. To most summer travelers these roads look like long cut lines or corridors through the Bush.

The Liard Highway replaced the old Fort Simpson winter road that joined Fort Nelson and Fort Simpson. The original Simpson Trail was first blazed in November 1942 by Alaska Highway engineers, including the 648th, Company A detachment.

A 69.4 (111.7 km) **M 175** (281.7 km) Bridge over d'Easum Creek. Good bird-watching area.

A 71.4 (115 km) **M 173** (278.4 km) Access to Maxhamish Lake via 8-mile/13-km winter road accessible in summer by all-terrain vehicles only. A recreation site is planned for Maxhamish Lake.

A 74 (119.1 km) **M 170.4** (274.3 km) Wide unnamed creek flows into Emile Creek to east. Good bird-watching area, beaver pond.

A 75.4 (121.4 km) **M 169** (272 km) Highway emerges from trees northbound; view west of Mount Martin (elev. 4,460 feet/1,360m) and the Kotaneelee Range.

A 80.6 (129.7 km) **M 163.8** (263.7 km) View northwest of mountain ranges in Northwest Territories.

A 81.2 (130.7 km) **M 163.2** (262.6 km) Highway begins descent (7 percent grade) northbound to Petitot River.

A 82.8 (133.2 km) **M 161.6** (260.2 km) Petitot River bridge. The **Petitot River** is reputed to have the warmest swimming water in British Columbia (70°F/21°C). A 9-hour canoe trip to Fort Liard is possible from here (some sheer rock canyons and rapids en route). Good bird-watching area. Also freshwater clams, pike and pickerel; short grayling run in spring.

The Petitot River was named for Father Petitot, an Oblate missionary who came to this area from France in the 1860s.

The Petitot River bridge was the site of the official opening of the Liard Highway on June 23, 1984. The ceremony was marked by an unusual ribbon-cutting: A 1926 Model T Ford, carrying dignitaries, was driven through the ribbon (which stretched for about 20 feet before snapping) while a guard of kilted pipers from Yellowknife played. The Model T, driven by Marl Brown of Fort Nelson, had been across this route in March 1975 just weeks after the bush road had been punched through by Cats and seismic equipment. This earlier trip, in which Mr. Brown was accompanied by Mickey Hempler, took 44 hours from Fort Nelson to Fort Simpson.

A 84.1 (135.4 km) **M 160.3** (258 km) Crest of Petitot River hill (10 percent grade).

A 85 (136.8 km) **M 159.4** (256.6 km) BC–NWT border. TIME ZONE CHANGE: British Columbia observes Pacific time, Northwest Territories observes Mountain time.

Northwest Territories restricts liquor importation as follows: 1 40-oz. hard liquor, 1 40-oz. wine or 1 dozen bottles of beer per person.

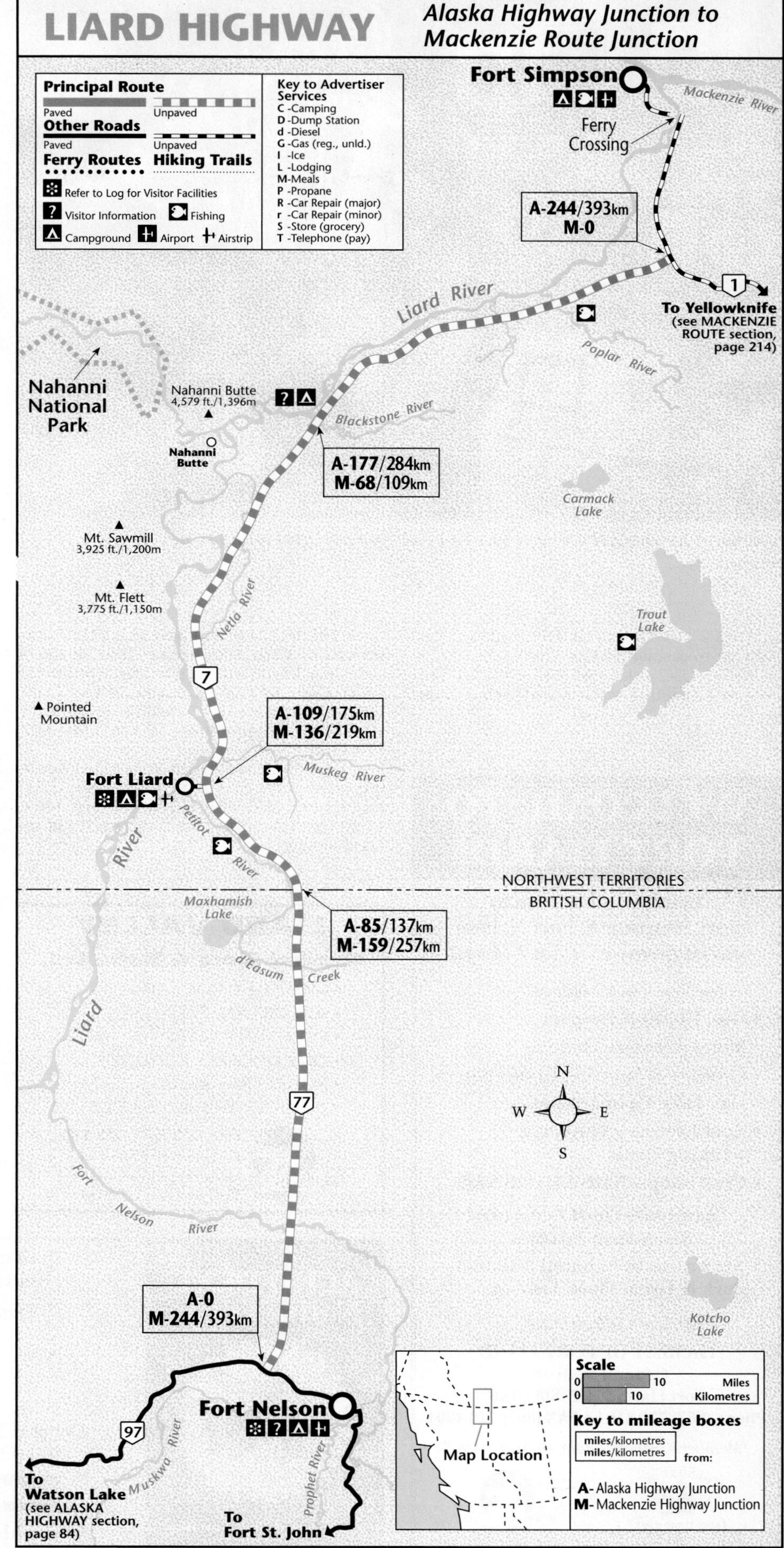

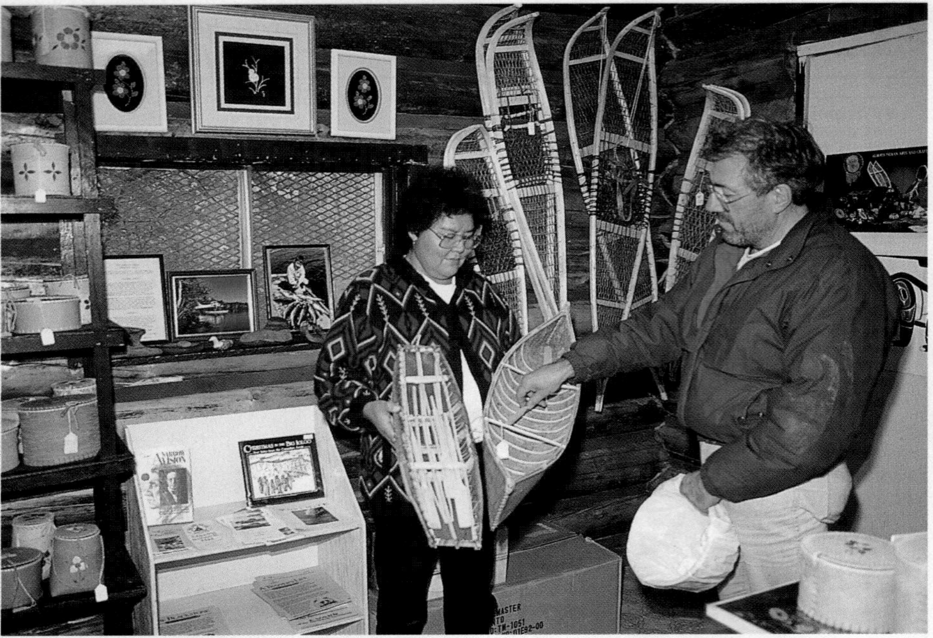

Shopping for moosehide and spruce boats in Fort Liard crafts store.

(© Lyn Hancock)

A 85.2 (137.1 km) **M 159.2** (256.2 km) Turnout to east with litter barrels.

A 107 (172.2 km) **M 137.4** (221.1 km) Vehicle inspection station and weigh scales to east.

A 108.6 (174.8 km) **M 135.8** (218.5 km) **Junction** with side road that leads 4 miles/6.4 km to Fort Liard (description follows). Gas and diesel available in Fort Liard. Tourist information is available at the Acho Craft Shop; phone (867) 770-4161; fax (867) 770-4160.

Views from road into Fort Liard across the Liard River of Mount Coty (elev. 2,715 feet/830m) and Pointed Mountain (elev. 4,610 feet/1,405m) at the southern tip of the Liard Range.

Fort Liard

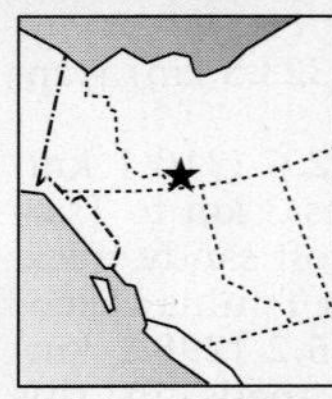

Located on the south bank of the Liard River near its confluence with the Petitot River (known locally as Black River because of its colour), about 50 miles/80 km south of Nahanni Butte. **Population:** 500. **Emergency Services: RCMP**, phone (867) 770-4221. **Fire Department**, phone (867) 770-2222. **Nursing Station**, phone (867) 770-4301.

Elevation: 700 feet/213m. **Climate:** There is no permafrost here. Good soil and water, a long summer season with long hours of daylight, and comparatively mild climate considering Fort Liard's geographical location. Several luxuriant local gardens. The Liard River here is approximately 1,500 feet/450m wide, fairly swift and subject to occasional flooding. **Radio** and **Television:** CBC radio (microwave), a Native language station from Yellowknife and a community radio station; 4 channels plus CBC Television (Anik), TVNC and private satellite receivers. Canadian Aerodrome Radio Station (CARS) operates Monday through Friday 8 A.M. to 7 P.M.

Private Aircraft: Fort Liard airstrip; elev. 700 feet/213m; length 2,950 feet/899m; gravel; fuel 100/130 (obtain from Deh Cho Air Ltd.).

Transportation: Air—Charter service year-round via Deh Cho Air. **Barge**—Nonscheduled barge service in summer. Scheduled and charter taxi service available.

This small, well-laid-out settlement of traditional log homes and new modern housing is located among tall poplar, spruce and birch trees on the south bank of the Liard River. The residents live a comparatively traditional life of hunting, trapping, fishing and making handicrafts, although there are more people taking jobs in construction and highway maintenance. Fort Liard residents are well known for the high quality of their birch-bark baskets and porcupine quill workmanship.

Recreation and sightseeing in the area include swimming and fishing (for pike, pickerel, goldeye and spring grayling) at the confluence of the Liard and Petitot rivers; air

FORT LIARD ADVERTISERS

Acho Dene Native Crafts ....Ph. (867) 770-4161
Deh Cho Air Ltd. ....Ph. (867) 770-4103
Hamlet of Fort Liard ....Ph. (867) 770-4104
Liard Valley General Store & Motel Ltd. ....Ph. (867) 770-4441

charter or canoe trip to Trout Lake, Bovie Lake, Fisherman's Lake, 300-foot/91-m-high Virginia Falls in Nahanni National Park, Tlogotsho Plateau, or scenic Liard and Kotaneelee mountain ranges. Good viewing for Dall sheep, grizzly bear and caribou. Canoe rentals available from Deh Cho Air Ltd. The traditional Dene settlement of **TROUT LAKE** (pop. 60) is also accessible by air from Fort Liard.

The North West Co. established a trading post near here at the confluence of the Liard and Petitot rivers called Riviere aux Liards in 1805. The post was abandoned after the massacre of more than a dozen residents by Indians. It was re-established in 1820, then taken over by the Hudson's Bay Co. in 1821 when the 2 companies merged. The well-known geologist Charles Camsell was born at Fort Liard in 1876.

Facilities here include 2 motels (reservations suggested), 2 general stores, playground, outdoor rink, craft shop (open 1–5 P.M. weekdays, extended hours in summer), snack bar, restaurant, the modern Acho Dene School and a Roman Catholic mission. There is no bank in Fort Liard. Gas, diesel and propane fuel available.

Community-run Hay Lake Campground located just off the access road into Fort Liard; campsites, picnic tables, toilets and floating dock. Campground road may be slippery when wet. ▲

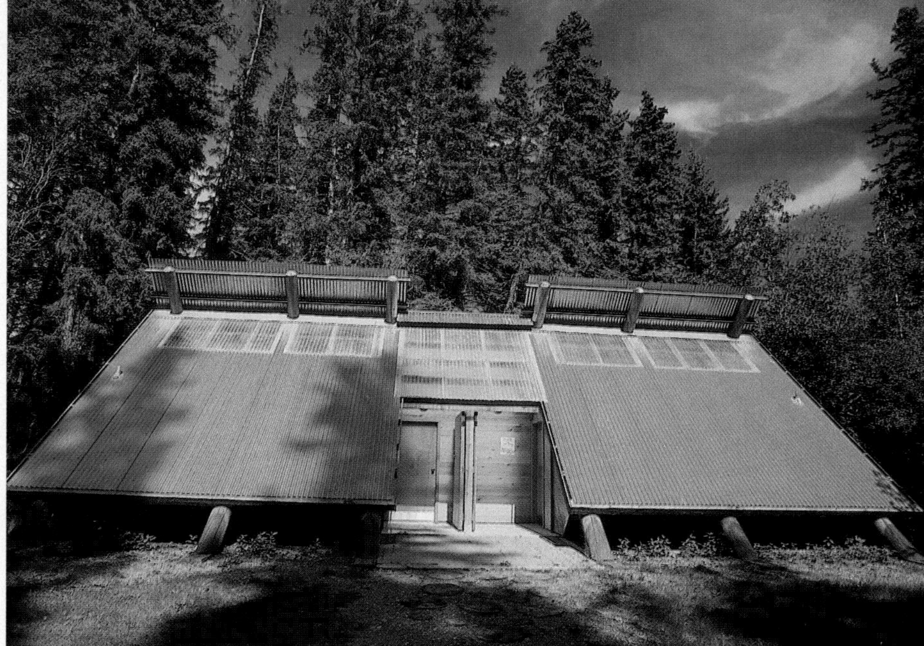

One of the most interesting buildings along the Liard Highway is the state-of-the-art restroom at Blackstone Territorial Park. (© Lyn Hancock)

Liard Highway Log

(continued)

A 113.3 (182.4 km) **M 131.1** (211 km) **Muskeg River** bridge; turnout at north end. Gravel bars on the river make a good rest area. Trapper's cabin on left. Fishing for pike, pickerel and freshwater clams. The Muskeg River is the local swimming hole for Fort Liard residents.

A 124.9 (201 km) **M 119.5** (192.4 km) Rabbit Creek bridge. Highway now runs close to the Liard River with good views of Liard Range to the west and northwest for the next 13 miles/21 km northbound.

A 128 (206 km) **M 116.4** (187.4 km) Kilometrepost 70.

A 131.1 (211 km) **M 113.3** (182.4 km) Good view of Mount Flett (elev. 3,775 feet/1,150m) ahead northbound.

A 136.7 (220 km) **M 107.7** (173.4 km) Access to Liard River (15-minute hike) via Paramount Mine winter road, an abandoned exploration road across the Liard River into the Liard Range.

A 146.9 (236.4 km) **M 97.5** (157 km) Short road west to locally named Whissel Landing on the Liard River, where road construction materials were brought in by barge during construction of the Liard Highway.

A 147.3 (237 km) **M 97.1** (156.4 km) Road widens for an emergency airstrip.

A 157.8 (253.9 km) **M 86.6** (139.5 km) Netla River bridge. The Netla River Delta is an important waterfowl breeding habitat, and Indian fishing and hunting area.

A 163.7 (263.4 km) **M 80.7** (130 km) Road widens for an emergency airstrip.

A 165.9 (267 km) **M 78.5** (126.4 km) Turnoff to west for winter ice road that leads 13.8 miles/22.3 km to the Dene settlement of **NAHANNI BUTTE** (pop. 87), at the confluence of the South Nahanni and Liard rivers. Summer access by boat or floatplane.

A 171.8 (276.5 km) **M 72.6** (116.8 km) Creek Bridge, once called Scotty's Creek after an old trapper who had a cabin upstream. There are many such cabins in this area that once belonged (and still belong) to prospectors and trappers, but they are not visible to the motorist. Stands of white spruce, white birch and balsam poplar along highway.

A 176.3 (283.7 km) **M 68.1** (109.7 km) Bridge over Upper Blackstone River. Picnic day-use area on riverbank with tables, firewood, firepits and garbage containers.

A 176.6 (284.2 km) **M 67.8** (109.2 km) Blackstone River bridge.

A 179.1 (288.3 km) **M 65.3** (105.1 km) Entrance to Blackstone Territorial Park; 19 campsites with tables and firepits; firewood, water and garbage containers, boat dock and state-of-the-art restroom. The boat launch is usable only in high water early in the season; use boat launch at Cadillac Landing, **Milepost A 182.9**, during low water. The visitor information building, built with local logs, is located on the bank of the Liard River with superb views of Nahanni Butte (elev. 4,579 feet/1,396m). The centre is open mid-May to mid-September. ▲

A 180.9 (291.2 km) **M 63.5** (102.2 km) Entrance to Lindberg Landing, the homestead of Liard River pioneers Edwin and Sue Lindberg. The Lindbergs offer a bed and breakfast; rustic accommodations, bring your own sleeping bag. By appointment only. Contact Mobile Telephone JR36644 Arrowhead Channel, or write Sue and Edwin Lindberg, Box 28, Fort Simpson, NWT XOE ONO.

Blackstone Aviation operates floatplane flightseeing trips of Nahanni National Park from here. (See description of Nahanni National Park under Fort Simpson attractions in the MACKENZIE ROUTE section.)

A 182.9 (294.3 km) **M 61.5** (99.1 km) Barge landing once used to service Cadillac Mine and bring in construction materials. Access to river via 0.6-mile/0.9-km road (muddy when wet).

A 192.8 (310.3 km) **M 51.6** (83.1 km) Road widens for emergency airstrip.

A 197.8 (318.4 km) **M 46.6** (75 km) Kilometrepost 180.

A 211.3 (340.1 km) **M 33.1** (53.3 km) Bridge over Birch River.

A 216.7 (348.8 km) **M 27.7** (44.6 km) Kilometrepost 210.

A 222.8 (358.5 km) **M 21.6** (34.9 km) Good grayling and pike fishing in **Poplar River** culverts.

A 223 (358.8 km) **M 21.4** (34.6 km) Dirt road on left northbound leads 4 miles/6.4 km to Liard River; 4-wheel drive recommended. Wide beach, good spot for viewing wildlife.

A 228.1 (367.1 km) **M 16.3** (26.3 km) Microwave tower to east. Vegetation changes northbound to muskeg with black spruce, tamarack and jackpine.

A 235.6 (379.2 km) **M 8.8** (14.2 km) Kilometrepost 240.

A 244.2 (393 km) **M 0.2** (0.4 km) Road maintenance camp.

A 244.4 (393.4 km) **M 0 Junction** with the Mackenzie Highway (NWT 1). "Checkpoint": gas, diesel, propane; licensed restaurant and 4-room motel. Phone (867) 695-2953. Turn right (south) for Hay River and Yellowknife; turn left (north) for Fort Simpson. See **Milepost G 550.6** on the Mackenzie Highway, page 222 in the MACKENZIE ROUTE section, for log.

MACKENZIE ROUTE

35 1 2 3 4 5 6

Connects: Grimshaw, AB to Western NWT **Length:** 1,231 miles
Road Surface: 47% paved, 53% gravel **Season:** Open all year
Major Attractions: Nahanni National Park; Wood Buffalo National Park

(See maps, pages 215–216)

	Ft. Resolution	Ft. Simpson	Ft. Smith	Valleyview	Yellowknife
Ft. Resolution		358	185	560	391
Ft. Simpson	358		431	692	393
Ft. Smith	185	431		633	464
Valleyview	560	692	633		725
Yellowknife	391	393	464	725	

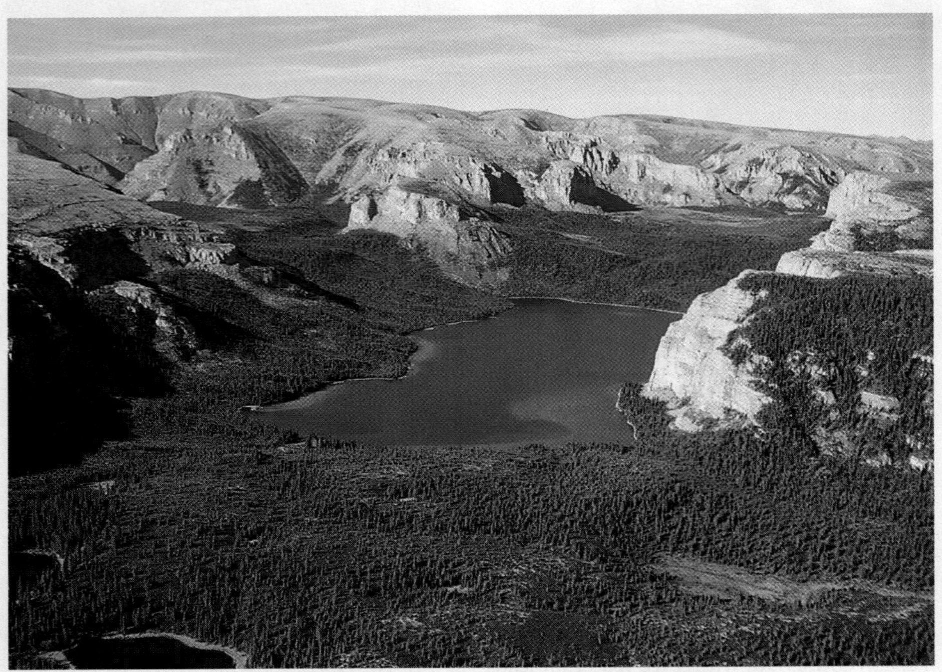

Flightseeing Ram Canyon country west of Fort Simpson in the Mackenzie Mountains. (© Lyn Hancock)

Named for explorer Alexander Mackenzie, who in 1779 navigated Great Slave Lake and sailed to the mouth of the Mackenzie River seeking a trade route for the Hudson's Bay Co., the Mackenzie Route is an adventure for modern explorers. It is not a trip for the impulsive. While there are accommodations, gas stations and other services in cities and settlements along the highways, long distances require that motorists plan in advance.

The Mackenzie Route covers the following highways: Alberta Highway 35 and NWT Highway 1 to Fort Simpson (Mackenzie Highway) and the extension to Wrigley; Highway 2 to Hay River; Highway 3 to Yellowknife; Highway 4 (Ingraham Trail); Highway 5 to Fort Smith; and Highway 6 to Fort Resolution. NWT Highway 7, the Liard Highway, connecting the Mackenzie Highway with the Alaska Highway north of Fort Nelson, is covered in the LIARD HIGHWAY section. The Dempster Highway (NWT Highway 8) to Inuvik is covered in the DEMPSTER HIGHWAY section.

Allow at least 2 weeks to travel the entire route. For general information on travel in the Northwest Territories, phone Northwest Territories Tourism toll free at (800) 661-0788 during business hours on weekdays.

Northwest Territories highways are both paved and gravel. Asphalt chip seal surfacing is under way on the remaining gravel portions of Highways 1 (Mackenzie Highway) and 3 (Yellowknife Highway). Gravel road is treated with calcium chloride to control the dust; wash your vehicle when possible. For road conditions, phone (800) 661-0750.

In summer, the Northwest Territories government provides free ferry service for cars and passengers across the Mackenzie River to Fort Providence, across the Liard River to Fort Simpson and across the Mackenzie River to Wrigley. In winter, traffic crosses on the ice. For current ferry information call (867) 873-7799 in Yellowknife, or (800) 661-0751.

The Mackenzie Highway begins at Grimshaw, AB. There are several routes to Grimshaw to choose from (see map). *The MILEPOST®* logs the Valleyview–Peace River route to the Mackenzie Highway via Highways 43 and 2.

Log of the Valleyview–Peace River Route to the Mackenzie Highway

Distance from Valleyview (V) is followed by distance from Mackenzie Highway (MH).

ALBERTA HIGHWAY 43

V 0 MH 101.1 (162.7 km) **Junction** of Highways 34 and 43. Follow Highway 43 north.

V 0.6 (1 km) **MH 100.5** (161.6 km) Turnoff to west for downtown Valleyview (see description of Valleyview in the EAST ACCESS ROUTE section).

V 2.2 (3.5 km) **MH 98.9** (159.3 km) **Junction** with Secondary Road 669 which leads east 20 miles/32 km to Sunset House Community Campground on Snipe Lake; 20 sites, firewood, playground, boat launch, camping fee. ▲

V 4 (6.4 km) **MH 97.1** (156.3 km) Sturgeon Creek.

V 18 (29 km) **MH 83.1** (133.7 km) East Dollar Lake to west.

V 23.1 (37.2 km) **MH 78** (125.6 km) Entering Midnight Twilight Tourist Zone northbound, entering Game Country Tourist Zone southbound.

V 25.1 (40.4 km) **MH 76** (122.3 km) **Junction** with Secondary Road 676 to Whitemud Creek, 14 miles/22 km west.

V 28.3 (45.6 km) **MH 72.8** (117.3 km) Entering Grande Prairie Forest southbound.

V 29.1 (46.8 km) **MH 72** (115.8 km) Little Smokey River bridge. Little Smokey River provincial recreation area to west on south bank of river; 12 sites, shelters, picnic tables, camping fee. ▲

V 30.3 (48.8 km) **MH 70.8** (114 km) **Junction** with Highway 2A east, a spur road which leads 17 miles/27 km to junction with Highway 2.

V 31.3 (50.4 km) **MH 69.8** (112.3 km) Turnout with litter barrels to east.

V 32.4 (52.1 km) **MH 68.7** (110.6 km) Entering Peace River Forest northbound.

V 36.4 (58.6 km) **MH 64.7** (104.2 km) Community of **GUY** (pop. 57) to east; pay phone. Access road leads west 7 miles/11 km to Five Star Golf Course; 9 holes, grass greens, pro shop.

V 40.5 (65.2 km) **MH 60.6** (97.5 km) **Junction** with Secondary Road 679 to Highway 2 and Winigami Lake Provincial Park (19 miles/30.5 km east).

V 48.7 (78.4 km) **MH 52.4** (84.4 km) **Donnelly Corners, junction** of Highways 2 and 49. **DONNELLY** (pop. 450) has a hotel, restaurants, stores, service stations with repair facilities and a library. Historic site 3 miles/5 km south of town features a fully operational 1904 Case Steam Engine. High-

MACKENZIE ROUTE *Valleyview, AB, to Steen River, AB*

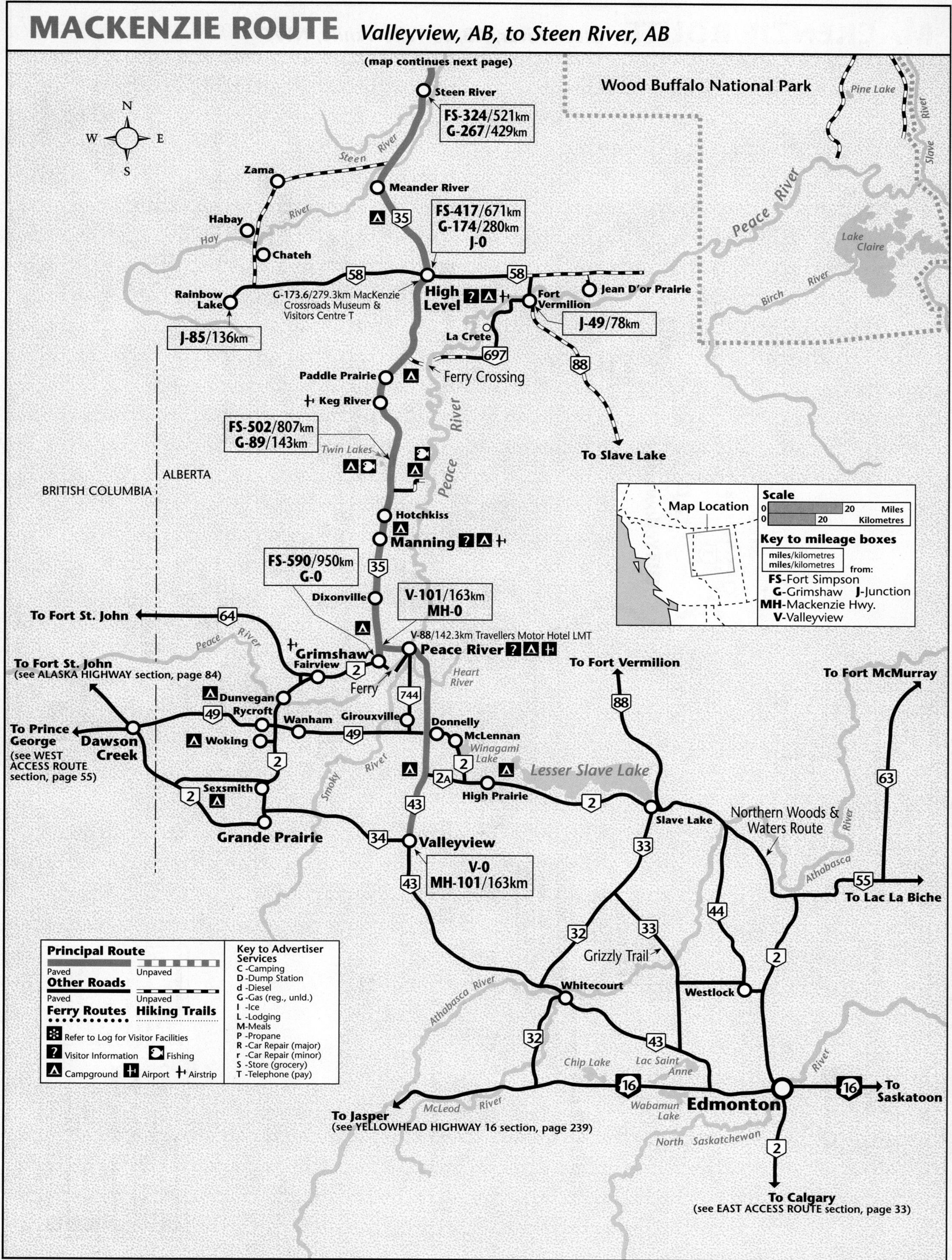

MACKENZIE ROUTE *Steen River, AB, to Yellowknife, NWT*

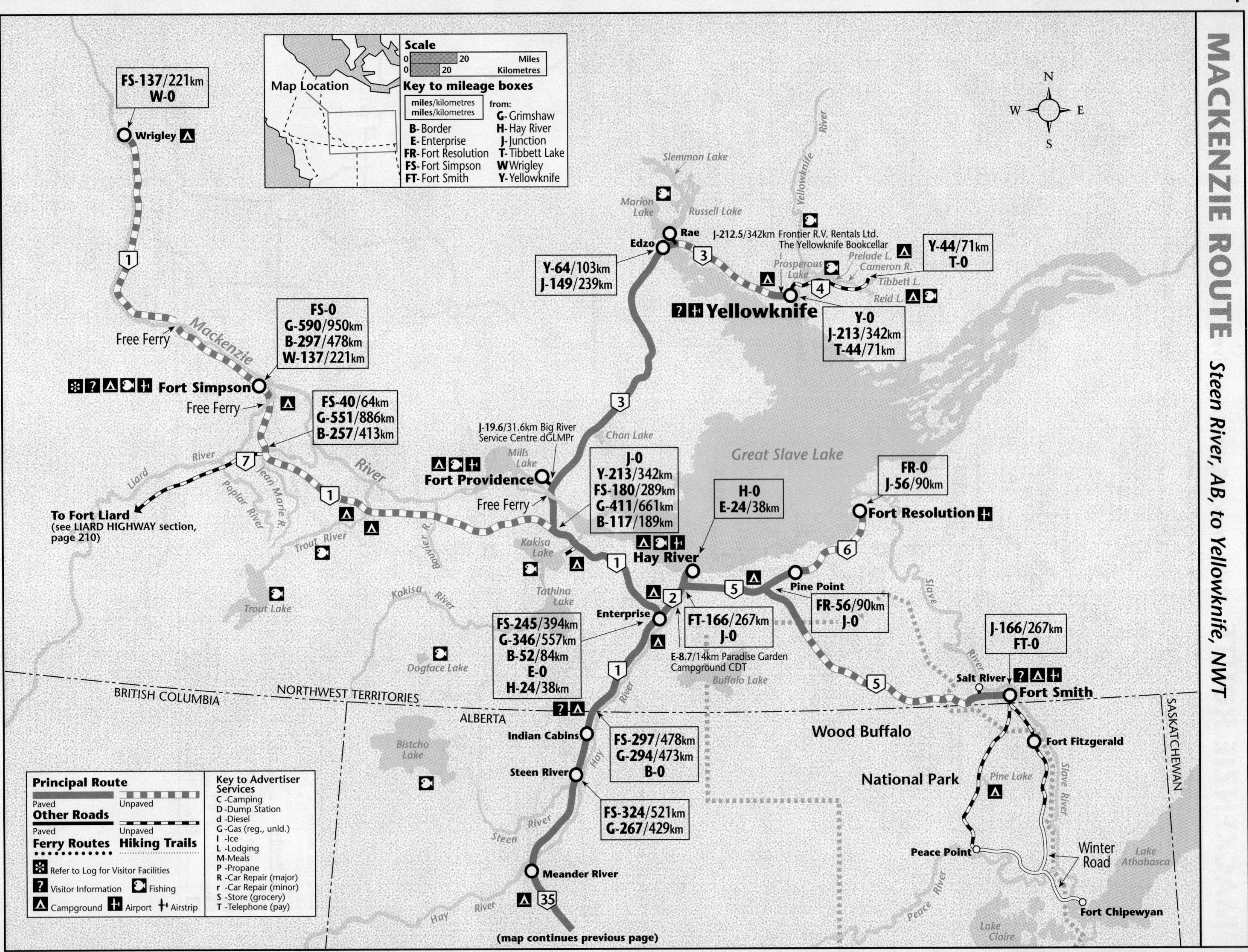

way 43 ends northbound. Continue on Highway 2 North.

ALBERTA HIGHWAY 2

V 61 (98.1 km) **MH 40.1** (64.5 km) Access leads west 7 miles/11 km to **JEAN COTE** (pop. 65), and 18 miles/28 km to Rainbow Trout Park and Campground; 55 sites, hookups, picnic tables, shelter, firewood, playground, rental cabins, mini-golf, horseshoe pits. Camping fee $9. ▲

V 66.1 (106.5 km) **MH 35** (56.3 km) Entering Land of the Mighty Peace Tourist Zone northbound, Midnight Twilight Tourist Zone southbound.

V 67.2 (108.1 km) **MH 33.9** (54.6 km) Access road leads east 5.5 miles/9 km to Reno.

V 70.7 (113.8 km) **MH 30.4** (49 km) Nampa visitor centre and museum to west. **NAMPA** (pop. 500) was founded in 1917 when the East Dunvegan and BC Railway Company built a line through the area. Visitor facilities include a hotel, motel, restaurants, grocery and retail stores, service stations with repair facilities and a library. Recreational facilities include a curling rink, ball diamonds and tennis courts. Heart River Golf Club, 5 miles/8 km northeast, has 9 holes. Camping at Mill Brown Memorial Park. ▲

V 71.3 (114.7 km) **MH 29.8** (48 km) **Junction** with Secondary Road 683 which leads west 6 miles/10 km to Secondary Road 744 to Marie Reine.

V 72.1 (116 km) **MH 29** (46.6 km) Heart River bridge.

V 73.4 (118.1 km) **MH 27.7** (44.6 km) South Harmon Road east to Harmon Valley Fairgrounds (14 miles/23 km).

V 73.5 (118.3 km) **MH 27.6** (44.4 km) Access road leads east 3 miles/5 km to Harmon Valley Golf Course.

V 75.3 (121.2 km) **MH 25.8** (41.6 km) Grain storage equipment on both sides of highway.

V 79.6 (128.1 km) **MH 21.5** (34.6 km) North Harmon Valley Road east to Harmon Valley Fairgrounds (12 miles/20 km).

V 84.3 (135.7 km) **MH 16.8** (27 km) **Junction** with Secondary Road 688 (Three Creeks Road) which leads east 5 miles/8 km to **ST. ISIDORE** (pop. 180); gas station, pay phone and library.

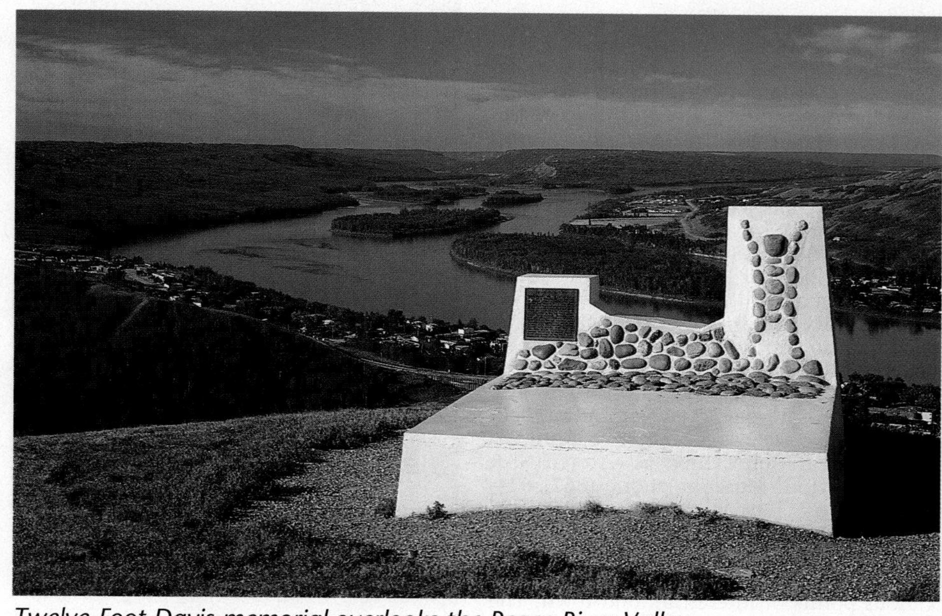

Twelve-Foot Davis memorial overlooks the Peace River Valley. (© Wes Bergen, DIARAMA)

V 85 (136.8 km) **MH 16.1** (25.9 km) Highway begins descent northbound into Peace River Valley.

V 87.6 (141 km) **MH 13.5** (21.7 km) Turnout to east with information sign about Peace River.

Peace River

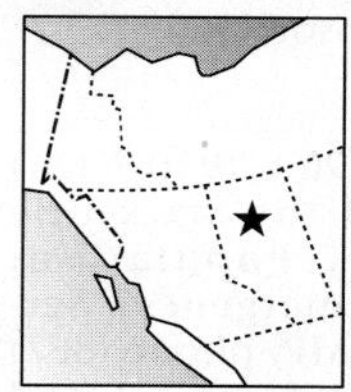

V 88.4 (142.3 km) **MH 12.7** (20.5 km). Located on the banks of the Peace River, 15 miles/24 km northeast of Grimshaw (Mile 0 of the Mackenzie Highway). **Population:** 6,700. **Emergency Services: RCMP**, phone (867) 624-6611. **Hospital**, phone (867) 624-7500. **Ambulance** and **Fire Department**, phone (867) 624-3911.

Visitor Information: Tourist Information located in the NAR station at the first right after the railway trestle at the east entrance to downtown; phone (867) 624-2044. Open mid-May to mid-September, 9 A.M. to 9 P.M. The Mighty Peace Tourist Association, at the north end of Main Street in the restored railway station, also has information on northern Alberta destinations; phone (867) 624-4042.

Elevation: 1,066 feet/325m. **Private Aircraft:** Peace River airport, 7 miles/11.2 km west; elev. 1,873 feet/571m; length 5,000 feet/1,524m; asphalt; fuel 80, 100, Jet B.

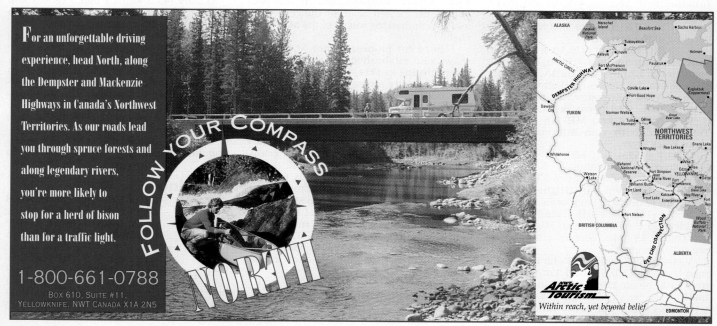

An important transportation centre on the Peace River, the town of Peace River was incorporated in 1919, 3 years after the railroad reached Peace River Crossing. Today, Peace River is a centre for government services in the region. Area industry includes Peace River Pulp, Shell Canada and farming.

Visitor facilities include 3 hotels, a motel and many restaurants. Camping at Lions Club Campground on the west side of the river; 85 sites, hookups, restrooms, dump station and laundry. ▲

There are 9 campgrounds along the Peace River. For details, contact the Peace Valley Conservation, Recreation and Tourism Society, phone (867) 835-2616 or fax 835-3131.

The Centennial Museum (on the south side of town along the river) houses archives and exhibits on Sir Alexander Mackenzie, the fur trade and local history. Historical re-enactments in summer. Open 9 A.M. to 5 P.M. Monday to Wednesday, noon to 8 P.M. Thursday to Saturday. (May 1 to Aug. 31); 9 A.M. to 5 P.M. weekdays Sept. 1 to April 31. Rail transportation exhibit at restored NAR railway station. Museum phone (867) 624-4261.

Visitors can take the Historic Mackenzie Moose Walking Trail by following the moose tracks from the Centennial Museum to various points of interest around town. The tour includes the statue of Twelve-Foot Davis, a gold miner who struck it rich on a 12-foot strip of land between 2 larger claims in the Cariboo gold fields. He invested his $15,000 in gold in a string of trading posts along the Peace. He is buried on Grouard Hill overlooking the Peace River Valley; a stone memorial marks the spot.

Log of Valleyview–Peace River Route

(continued)

V 89.2 (143.5 km) **MH 11.9** (19.1 km) Peace River bridge.

V 90 (144.8 km) **MH 11.1** (17.9 km) **Junction** with Secondary Road 684 which leads southwest 15 miles/24 km to Secondary Road 740 and the Shaftsbury Ferry Crossing of the Peace River.

V 90.8 (146.1 km) **MH 10.3** (16.5 km) **Junction** with Secondary Road 743 which leads north 10 miles/16 km to Secondary Road 686 to the Mackenzie Highway. Access to Peace View golf course, 2.5 miles/4 km north; 9 holes, sand greens, pro shop.

V 91.6 (147.4 km) **MH 9.5** (15.3 km) Turnout to south with information sign about Peace River.

V 94.7 (152.4 km) **MH 6.4** (10.3 km) Peace River airport to south.

V 96 (154.5 km) **MH 5.1** (8.2 km) **Roma Junction, junction** with Highway 2A to Grimshaw (7 miles/12 km southwest).

V 97.1 (156.3 km) **MH 4** (6.5 km) Access road leads 1.2 miles/2 km to Mighty Peace golf course; 18 holes, licensed dining room, pro shop, camping.

V 99.1 (159.5 km) **MH 2** (3.2 km) Access road leads south 0.6 mile/1 km to Wilderness Park; picnic tables, outhouses, hiking trails.

V 101.1 (162.7 km) **MH 0 Junction** with Highway 35 (Mackenzie Highway).

Twelve-Foot Davis statue in Peace River.
(Earl L. Brown, staff)

Mackenzie Highway Log

ALBERTA HIGHWAY 35
Distance from Grimshaw (G) is followed by distance from Fort Simpson (FS).

Grimshaw

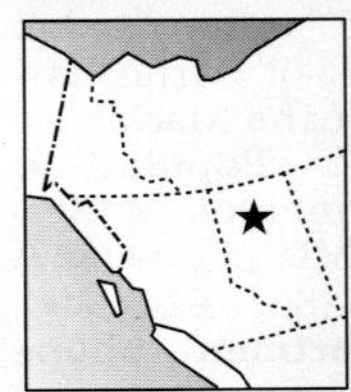

G 0 FS 590.4 (950.2 km) Mile 0 of the Mackenzie Highway. **Population:** 2,812. **Emergency Services: RCMP**, phone (867) 332-4666. **Hospital** and **Ambulance**, phone (867) 332-1155. **Fire Department**, phone (867) 332-4430. **Visitor Information:** In the NAR railway car located adjacent the centennial monument marking Mile 0 of the Mackenzie Highway.

Named for pioneer doctor M.E. Grimshaw, who established a practice at Peace River Crossing in 1914, Grimshaw developed as a community centre for area farmers and as a shipping point with the arrival of the railroad in 1921. Scheduled air service from Edmonton and High Level to Peace River airport, 8 miles/12.8 km east.

Grimshaw became a town in February 1953. Local resources are wheat and grains, livestock, gravel, lumber, gas and oil.

Grimshaw has 1 motel, 2 hotels, 6 service stations, 2 car washes, a laundromat and all other visitor facilities. RV dump station and drinking water located south of the Mile 0 marker and 2 blocks east. Camping just north of town (see **Milepost G 1.9**). There are also an outdoor swimming pool, tennis courts, golf course and seasonal market garden located here.

Mackenzie Highway Log

(continued)

G 0.2 (0.4 km) **FS 590.2** (949.8 km) **Private Aircraft**: Airstrip to west; elev. 2,050 feet/625m; length, 3,000 feet/914m; turf; fuel 80, 100.

G 1.9 (3 km) **FS 588.5** (947.2 km) Grimshaw provincial campsite and Queen Elizabeth Provincial Park to west. Grimshaw campsite has 20 sites, picnic shelter, firepits, firewood, tables, outhouses, water pump and no camping fee. Queen Elizabeth park (located 3 miles/5 km west) on Lac Cardinal has 56 campsites, picnic shelter, firewood, firepits, toilets, playground and swimming. ▲

G 2.8 (4.6 km) **FS 587.6** (945.6 km) **Junction** of Highways 35 and 2 East.

G 3.4 (5.5 km) **FS 587** (944.7 km) Sign about construction of the Mackenzie Highway.

G 4.1 (6.6 km) **FS 586.3** (943.6 km) Turnout to east with litter barrels.

G 5 (8 km) **FS 585.4** (942.1 km) **Junction** with Chinook Valley Road to east.

G 6.9 (11.1 km) **FS 583.5** (939.1 km) Truck scales to west.

G 7.8 (12.5 km) **FS 582.6** (937.6 km) Bear Creek Drive and Bear Creek golf course to west; 9 holes, sand greens, clubhouse.

G 8.6 (13.8 km) **FS 581.8** (936.3 km) **Junction** with Secondary Road 737 (Warrensville) to west.

G 12.3 (19.8 km) **FS 578.1** (930.3 km) Road widens to 4 lanes northbound.

G 12.6 (20.3 km) **FS 577.8** (929.8 km) **Junction** with Secondary Road 686 to east.

G 13 (20.9 km) **FS 577.4** (929.2 km) Road narrows to 2 lanes northbound.

G 19 (30.6 km) **FS 571.4** (919.5 km) Entering Manning Ranger District northbound.

G 20.8 (33.5 km) **FS 569.6** (916.7 km) Chinook Valley to east; cafe, pay phone and 24-hour gas station with tire repair.

G 21 (33.8 km) **FS 569.4** (916.3 km) Chinook Valley Road to east.

G 23 (37 km) **FS 567.4** (913.1 km) Whitemud River.

G 25.1 (40.4 km) **FS 565.3** (909.8 km) **DIXONVILLE** (pop. 200) has a post office, gas station, souvenir shop, museum, store and cafe. Sulphur Lake provincial campground is located 34 miles/55 km west via Highway 689 (the first 14 miles/22.5 km are paved, the remainder is gravel to the campground).

G 26.9 (43.3 km) **FS 563.5** (906.8 km) Sulphur Lake Road leads west to junction with Highway 689 from Dixonville.

G 38.4 (61.8 km) **FS 552** (888.4 km) **Junction** with Secondary Road 690 east to Deadwood (6.8 miles/11 km). There is a private exotic bird farm located 2 miles/3.2 km east then 1 mile/1.6 km south. The Bradshaws have geese, peacocks, turkeys, pheasants and other birds; visitors welcome.

G 44.4 (71.5 km) **FS 546** (878.7 km) Buchanan Creek.

G 46.8 (75.4 km) **FS 543.6** (874.8 km) Community of **NORTH STAR** (pop. 52) to east.

Manning

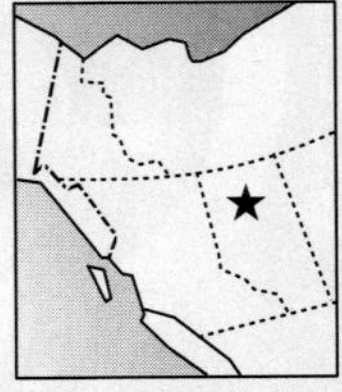

G 50.6 (81.4 km) **FS 539.8** (868.8 km) Located on the Notikewin River at the junction of Highways 35 and 691. **Population:** 1,260. **Emergency Services: RCMP**, phone (867) 836-3007. **Hospital** and **Ambulance**, phone (867) 836-3391. **Fire Department**, phone (867) 836-3000.

Visitor Information: In the information centre. There is a playground adjacent the centre and a dump station across the street.

Named for an Alberta premier, Manning was established in 1947. The railway from Roma, AB, to Pine Point, NWT, reached Manning in September 1962. Today, Manning is a service centre and jumping-off point for hunters and fishers.

Manning has 5 restaurants, 3 hotel/motels, a pharmacy, food market, golf course, swimming pool and ice rink. Attractions here include the Battle River Pioneer Museum, located on the grounds of the Battle River Agricultural Society, 0.6 mile/1 km east via Highway 691. The museum, which features tools and machinery from the pioneer days, is open daily 1–5 P.M., from June 1 to mid-September. A small ski hill is located 12.5 miles/20 km northeast of town via Highways 691 and 741; 1 T-lift and 3 runs.

Turn east at the information centre for Manning municipal campground; 14 sites on the banks of the Notikewin River, fireplaces, tables, water and flush toilets. ▲

NOTE: Last sizable community with all facilities for the next 123 miles/198 km northbound.

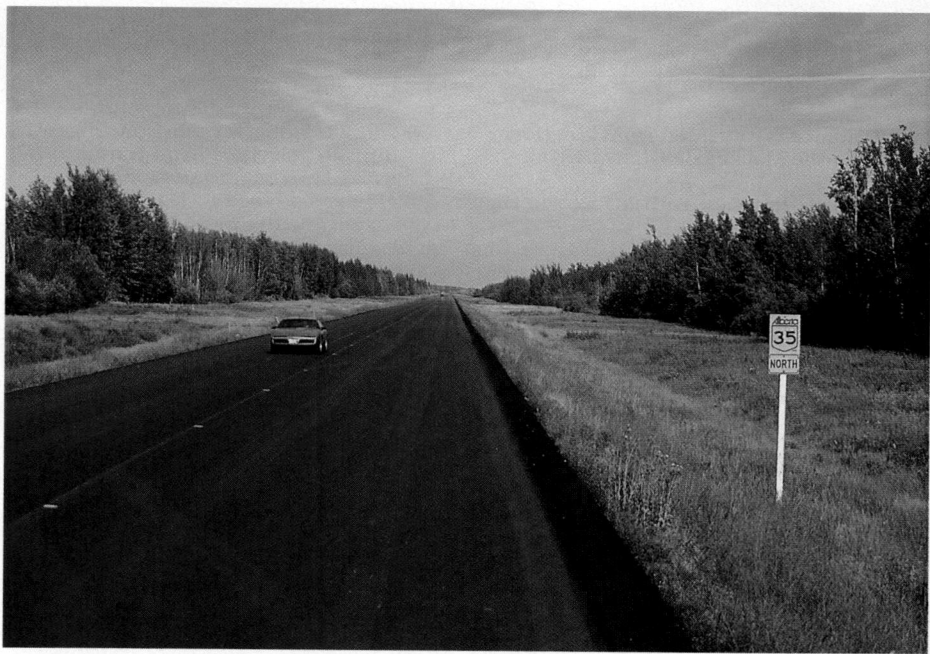

Alberta Highway 35 cuts a straight path through the northern half of the province. (Earl L. Brown, staff)

Mackenzie Highway Log

(continued)

G 50.7 (81.6 km) **FS 539.7** (868.5 km) Downtown Manning; bridge over the Notikewin River.

G 52.9 (85.1 km) **FS 537.5** (865.1 km) **Private Aircraft**: Manning airstrip to west; elev. 1,611 feet/491m; length 5,577 feet/1,700m; asphalt; fuel 100/130, Jet B.

G 53.2 (85.6 km) **FS 537.2** (864.5 km) Hotel, restaurant and service station to west.

G 54.6 (87.8 km) **FS 535.8** (862.4 km) Community of Notikewin to west.

G 60.6 (97.6 km) **FS 529.8** (852.6 km) Hotchkiss River bridge.

G 60.8 (97.8 km) **FS 529.6** (852.4 km) Hotchkiss Provincial Park to east; 10 sites, no fee, picnic shelter, tables, firepits, fishing, outhouses and water pump. ▲

G 61.3 (98.6 km) **FS 529.1** (851.6 km) Community of **HOTCHKISS** to east, golf course to west. Hotchkiss has a post office, service station, pay phone, coffee bar, grocery, and fuel and propane available. Condy Meadow golf course; 9 holes, grass greens, pro shop.

G 63.3 (101.8 km) **FS 527.1** (848.3 km) Large lumber plant to west.

G 66.9 (107.6 km) **FS 523.5** (842.6 km) Meikle River bridge.

G 71.2 (114.6 km) **FS 519.2** (835.5 km) Turnout with litter barrel to west.

G 74.3 (119.5 km) **FS 516.1** (830.7 km) **Junction** with Highway 692 and access to Notikewin Provincial Park (18.6 miles/30 km) on the Notikewin and Peace rivers. Highway 692 is fairly straight with pavement for the first 8 miles/13 km followed by good gravel surface to the park, although the road narrows and the surfacing may be muddy in wet weather as you approach the park. Just past the entrance to the park is the Top of Hill trailer drop-off site; 10 campsites with tables, toilets, water pump and garbage container. The park road then winds down the hill for 1.4 miles/2.2 km (not recommended for trailers, slippery when wet) to the riverside campground and day-use area; 19 campsites on the **Notikewin River** and 6 picnic sites on the **Peace River**; facilities include tables, water pump, pit toilets, garbage containers, firepits, boat launch and fishing. *CAUTION: Bears in area.* ▲

G 88.4 (142.3 km) **FS 502** (807.9 km) Twin Lakes Lodge to east; gas, food, lodging, pay phone and fishing supplies.

G 88.9 (143 km) **FS 501.5** (807.2 km) Twin Lakes Campground to west; 30 shaded sites, picnic shelter, fireplaces, firewood, tables, outhouses, water; beach, boat launch (no gas motors). No camping fee. **Twin Lakes** is stocked with rainbow; good fishing June to September. ▲

G 95.8 (154.1 km) **FS 494.6** (796.1 km) Turnout to west.

G 102.9 (165.6 km) **FS 487.5** (784.6 km) Kemp Creek.

G 111.2 (179 km) **FS 479.2** (771.2 km) **Junction** with Highway 695 East which leads 24 miles/38 km to community of **CARCAJOU** (pop. 50). Access to Keg River airstrip 0.4 mile/0.6 km east. **Private Aircraft**: Keg River airstrip; elev. 1,350 feet/410m; approximate length 2,700 feet/832m; turf; emergency only.

G 112.3 (180.8 km) **FS 478.1** (769.4 km) Keg River bridge. The community of **KEG RIVER** (area pop. 400) just north of the bridge has a gas station, post office, grocery, cafe, motel, pay phone and airstrip.

G 115.6 (186 km) **FS 474.8** (764 km) **Junction** with Secondary Road 695 West. This paved road leads 9 miles/14.5 km to Keg River Post.

G 124 (199.6 km) **FS 466.4** (750.6 km) Boyer River bridge.

G 129.5 (208.4 km) **FS 460.9** (741.8 km) **PADDLE PRAIRIE** (pop. 164) has a gas station, grocery store and cafe. Paddle Prairie is a Metis settlement. The Metis culture, a combination of French and Amerindian, played a key role in the fur trade and development of northwestern Canada.

G 134.2 (216 km) **FS 456.2** (734.2 km) Turnout to west with litter barrels.

G 135.1 (217.4 km) **FS 455.3** (732.7 km) Boyer River Campground to east; 8 sites, tables, firewood, firepits, picnic shelter, toilets and water pump. ▲

G 136.2 (219.2 km) **FS 454.2** (731 km) **Junction** with Secondary Road 697, which leads northeast 75 miles/121 km to junction with Highway 88 near Fort Vermilion (see description of Fort Vermilion in the HIGHWAY 58 EAST side road log on page 220). This is a 2-lane, mostly paved road with a ferry crossing of the Peace River at Tompkin's Landing, 11 miles/18 km east from here. The ferry operates 24 hours a day, except in heavy fog, and carries 6 cars or 4 trucks.

Highway 697 provides access to **BUFFALO HEAD PRAIRIE** (pop. 453), 43.6 miles/70.2 km east, which has a small store and gas. Highway 697 also accesses **LA CRETE** (pop. 902), 53.8 miles/86.6 km east and north, Canada's most northerly agricultural community. La Crete has a motel, 3 restaurants, service stations with repair facilities, car wash, grocery, hardware and retail stores, a laundromat and bank. Recreation facilities include a golf course and a sports complex with hockey, curling and bowling.

G 141 (226.9 km) **FS 449.4** (723.2 km) Entering High Level Ranger District northbound.

G 146.3 (235.4 km) **FS 444.1** (714.7 km) Chuckegg Creek.

G 153.5 (247 km) **FS 436.9** (703.2 km) Turnout with litter barrel to west. Watch for waterfowl in small lakes along highway.

G 161.2 (259.4 km) **FS 429.2** (690.7 km) Bede Creek.

G 161.9 (260.5 km) **FS 428.5** (689.6 km) Parma Creek.

G 165.5 (266.3 km) **FS 424.9** (683.9 km) Melito Creek.

G 170.6 (274.6 km) **FS 419.8** (675.6 km) Turnout with litter barrel to west.

G 171.9 (276.7 km) **FS 418.5** (673.5 km) Private campground with hot showers and electrical hookups. ▲

G 173.3 (278.9 km) **FS 417.1** (671.3 km) **Junction** with Highway 58 West, which leads 84.5 miles/136 km to Rainbow Lake. See side road log of HIGHWAY 58 WEST on page 221.

Highway 58 East Log

Distance is measured from junction with the Mackenzie Highway (J).

J 0 Junction with Mackenzie Highway at High Level.

J 0.2 (0.4 km) High Level Lions Club Campground to south; 33 sites, no camping fee, picnic shelter, stoves, firewood, tables, toilets, water pump. ▲

J 0.4 (0.6 km) High Level rodeo grounds to north.

J 1.5 (2.5 km) Bushe River bridge.

J 2.4 (3.8 km) Small grocery and gas pumps to north.

J 15.3 (24.7 km) Turnoff to south for Machesis Lake Campground, 16 miles/27 km via gravel road; 21 sites, picnic shelter, firepits, firewood, tables, toilets, water. Fishing for rainbows in **Machesis Lake.** ▲

J 20.3 (32.7 km) Turn south for Eleske Shrine (5 miles/8 km), Child Lake Reserve Native church and burial grounds. The Eleske Shrine, on the banks of the Boyer River, was built in 1950 and dedicated to St. Bernadette in hopes that the grotto would cure a tuberculosis epidemic in the community.

J 22.3 (35.9 km) Entering Fort Vermilion Ranger District eastbound.

J 27 (43.5 km) Turnout with litter barrels to north.

J 28 (45 km) Ponton River bridge.

J 35.4 (57 km) **Junction** of Highways 58 and 88. From this junction, Highway 58 turns to gravel road and continues 37 miles/59 km east to junction with a 5-mile/8-km side road to Jean D'Or Prairie (no services). Highway 88 (renumbered and renamed the Bicentennial Highway to commemorate the 200th anniversary of Fort Vermilion in 1988) leads south to Fort Vermilion (log follows), then continues 255 miles/410 km to Slave Lake. Highway 88 is paved to Fort Vermilion; the 150-mile/242-km section to Red Earth Creek is gravel; the remaining 105 miles/168 km to Slave Lake are paved. There are no services along the road south of Fort Vermilion, and travel is not recommended on the gravel portion in wet weather.

HIGHWAY 88

J 40 (64.3 km) Boyer River bridge.

J 42.6 (68.5 km) Side road leads west 8.5 miles/14 km to Rocky Lane.

J 43.1 (69.3 km) Historical sign about Fort Vermilion and access to Fort Vermilion provincial campground (0.1 mile/0.2 km east); 16 sites, picnic shelter, fireplace, firewood, tables, toilets, water, no camping fee. ▲

J 43.4 (69.8 km) Fort Vermilion Bridge over the Peace River.

J 45.2 (72.7 km) **Junction** with Secondary Road 697 which leads south to Le Crete (21.5 miles/34.6 km) and rejoins the Mackenzie Highway at **Milepost G 136.2** (75.3 miles/121.2 km from here).

J 48 (77.2 km) **Junction** with Highway 88 south to Red Earth and Slave Lake (255miles/410 km). Continue straight ahead for Fort Vermilion (description follows).

J 48.5 (78 km) **FORT VERMILION** (pop. 850), located on the Peace River. **Emergency Services: RCMP**, phone (403) 927-3258. **Hospital**, St. Theresa, phone (403) 927-3761. A trading post was established near here by the North West Co. in 1786. By 1831, the Hudson's Bay Co. had established a prosperous trading enterprise at Fort Vermilion. The area's farming potential gained attention when Fort Vermilion's wheat took top prize at the 1893 Chicago World's Fair. Transportation to the community was by riverboat until the Mackenzie Highway was built in the 1950s. The Peace River bridge was completed in 1974.

Visitor facilities include a hotel, motel, 3 restaurants, service stations, bank, laundromat and liquor store. The airport is located just east of town. Attractions include historic homes and buildings dating back to the mid-1800s. Pick up a walking tour brochure from the visitor centre; phone (867) 927-3216.

Return to Milepost G 174
Mackenzie Highway

High Level

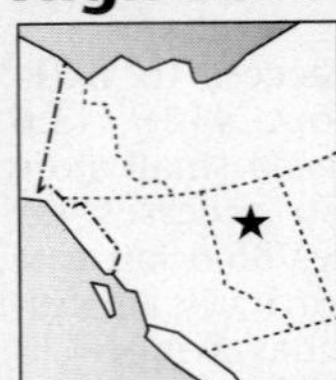

G 173.6 (279.3 km) **FS 416.8** (670.9 km) Located at the junction of Highways 35 and 58. **Population:** 3,093. **Emergency Services: RCMP**, phone (867) 926-2226. **Hospital**, 25 beds, 6 doctors, phone (867) 926-3791. **Ambulance**, phone (867) 926-2545. **Fire Department**, phone (867) 926-3141.

Visitor Information: The visitors centre and Mackenzie Crossroads Museum are located at the south end of town; displays, souvenirs and rest area. Open year-round; 9 A.M. to 9 P.M. daily in summer. Internet address is www.town.highlevel.ab.ca. **Radio:** 530 AM, 89.9, 104.1-FM.

Begun as a small settlement on the Mackenzie Highway after WWII, High Level grew with the oil boom of the 1960s and completion of the railroad to Pine Point. High Level has a strong agricultural economy and boasts the most northerly grain elevators in Canada. The community is also supported by a sawmill complex and serves as a transportation centre for the northwestern Peace River region. There is scheduled air service to Edmonton daily.

Visitor facilities include 7 motels, restaurants and service stations with major repair. RV dump located at the Shell station. There are also an ice arena and curling rink, golf course, swimming pool, playgrounds, banks, schools and churches. Recreation includes hunting (moose, caribou, deer) and fishing for northern pike, perch, walleye, whitefish, goldeye and grayling.

There is a private campground at the south edge of town. A campground operated by the local Lions Club is located just east of town on Highway 58. ▲

Mackenzie Highway Log

(continued)

G 173.6 (279.3 km) **FS 416.8** (670.9 km) Downtown High Level.

G 174 (280 km) **FS 416.4** (670.2 km) **Junction** with Highway 58 East to Jean D'Or Prairie and Highway 88 to Fort Vermilion. See side road log of HIGHWAY 58 EAST this section.

G 176.2 (283.5 km) **FS 414.2** (666.7 km) High Level golf and country club to east. Open daily, May 1 to first snow, until midnight. Clubhouse, grass greens and 9 holes.

G 181.1 (291.5 km) **FS 409.3** (658.7 km) **Private Aircraft**: High Level airport; elev. 1,110 feet/338m; length 5,000 feet/1,524m; asphalt; fuel 80, 100, Jet B. Floatplane base at Footner Lake, 0.6 mile/1 km west.

G 193.4 (311.2 km) **FS 397** (639 km) Turnoff to west for Hutch Lake Recreation Area; parking, 8 picnic sites with tables and firepits, toilets. Short path leads down to lake. Bring mosquito repellent.

G 196 (315.5 km) **FS 394.4** (634.7 km) Hutch Lake provincial campground, 2.9 miles/4.6 km west; 12 sites, firepits, firewood, tables, toilets. Beach and boat launch on Hutch Lake. Hiking trails. Good spot for bird watchers. Camping fee $7.50. ▲

G 196.8 (316.7 km) **FS 393.6** (633.5 km) Turnouts with litter barrels both sides of highway.

G 207.3 (333.6 km) **FS 383.1** (616.6 km) Wooden railway bridge to east.

G 219.3 (352.9 km) **FS 371.1** (597.3 km) **MEANDER RIVER** (pop. 340) has a post office, gas, grocery store and confectionary with pay phone. *NOTE: Last gas northbound until Enterprise at **Milepost G 345.8**, 126.5 miles/203.6 km from here.*

G 221.5 (356.4 km) **FS 368.9** (593.7 km) Mission Creek.

G 223.8 (360.1 km) **FS 366.6** (590.1 km) The Mackenzie Highway crosses the Hay River here and follows it north into Northwest Territories.

G 227.5 (366.2 km) **FS 362.9** (584 km) Railway bridge over Hay River to east. Construction of the Great Slave Lake Railway (now part of Canadian National Railway's Peace River Division) was one of the largest railway construction projects since the boom of the first transcontinental railway lines in the late 1800s and early 1900s in Canada. The line extends 377 miles/607 km from Roma Junction near Peace River, AB, to Hay River, NWT, on the shore of Great Slave Lake. (A 54-mile/87-km branch line extended the line to the now-defunct lead–zinc mine at Pine Point, NWT.) Opened for traffic in 1964, the line carries mining shipments south and supplies north to Hay River.

G 228.1 (367.1 km) **FS 362.3** (583.1 km) Gravel road leads west 39 miles/63 km to **ZAMA** (pop. 200), an oil field community. Drilling and related operations take place at Zama in winter. Zama is the southern terminal of the interprovincial pipeline, carrying Norman Wells crude to Edmonton refineries.

G 231.5 (372.5 km) **FS 358.9** (577.6 km) Slavey Creek.

G 241.2 (388.2 km) **FS 349.3** (562 km) Rough patch in pavement. Watch for frost heaves north to NWT border.

G 243.5 (391.9 km) **FS 346.9** (558.3 km) Paved turnout with litter barrels to west.

G 250.2 (402.6 km) **FS 340.2** (547.5 km) Lutose Creek.

G 263.3 (423.7 km) **FS 327.1** (526.5 km) Steen River bridge.

G 266.7 (429.2 km) **FS 323.7** (521 km) **STEEN RIVER** (pop. 25) to east; no services.

G 266.9 (429.5 km) **FS 323.5** (520.7 km) Steen River Forestry Tanker Base to west. Grass airstrip.

G 268.1 (431.5 km) **FS 322.3** (518.7 km) Sam's Creek.

G 270.1 (434.7 km) **FS 320.3** (515.4 km) Jackpot Creek.

G 276.2 (444.5 km) **FS 314.2** (505.6 km) Bannock Creek.

G 283.3 (455.9 km) **FS 307.1** (494.2 km) Indian Cabins Creek.

G 284 (457 km) **FS 306.4** (493.2 km) **INDIAN CABINS** (pop. 10); no services, historic log church. The old Indian cabins that gave this settlement its name are gone, but nearby is an Indian cemetery with spirit houses.

G 285.3 (459.1 km) **FS 305.1** (491 km) Delphin Creek.

G 293.7 (472.7 km) **FS 296.7** (477.5 km) 60th parallel. Border between Alberta and Northwest Territories. The Mackenzie Highway now changes from Alberta Highway 35 to NWT Highway 1.

Highway 58 West Log

Distance is measured from junction with the Mackenzie Highway (J).

J 0 Junction with Mackenzie Highway at High Level.

J 6.1 (9.8 km) High Level Sporting Assoc. and Gun Club to north.

J 27.2 (43.8 km) Paved turnout with litter barrels to south.

J 31.2 (50.2 km) Entering Rainbow Lake Ranger District westbound.

J 44.2 (71.1 km) Bridge over Chinchaga River.

J 46.3 (74.5 km) Large turnout and gravel stockpiles to south.

J 50 (80.5 km) Bridge over East Sousa Creek.

J 56.5 (90.9 km) Bridge over West Sousa Creek.

J 56.9 (91.6 km) **Junction** with secondary road north to communities of Chateh, Habay and Zama.

J 59.7 (96.1 km) North Canadian Oils Ltd. wells and equipment to north.

J 60.7 (97.7 km) Oil pumping station to north.

J 63.3 (101.8 km) Paved turnout with litter barrel to north.

J 65.3 (105.1 km) Power station to north.

J 70.3 (113.1 km) Side road leads north to the Zama Tower.

J 70.7 (113.8 km) Esso Resources Canada oil production plant to north.

J 71.5 (115 km) Rainbow Lake Field Office to north.

J 76.8 (123.6 km) Side road leads north to Rainbow Lake gas plant.

J 80.5 (129.5 km) Oil station to south. Side road leads south to Rainbow Processing Plant.

J 82.5 (132.8 km) Turnout with picnic table to south.

J 84.5 (136 km) **RAINBOW LAKE** (pop. 1,146). **Emergency Services: RCMP**, phone (867) 321-3753. **Nursing Station**, phone (867) 356-3646. **Fire Department**, phone (867) 956-3934. **Radio:** 103.7-FM.

Private Aircraft: Rainbow Lake airport 0.8 mile/1.3 km west, 0.5 mile/0.8 km south on Frontage Road; elev. 1,100 feet/335m; length 4,550 feet/1,390m; asphalt; fuel 80, 100, Jet B.

A service community for oil and natural gas development in the region. The first oil well was brought in by Banff Oil and Gas in 1965 at the Rainbow field. (The Zama field was discovered in 1967.)

Visitor facilities include a hotel, motel with licensed restaurant, 3 gas stations and a bank. The community also supports a school, 3 churches, 2 car washes, a grocery store, gift shop, laundromat and a 9-hole golf course. Rainbow Lake Campground is located 14 miles/24 km south of town via a secondary road.

Return to Milepost G 173.3 Mackenzie Highway

NWT HIGHWAY 1

Highway 1 begins its own series of kilometre markers, starting with Kilometre 0 at the border, which appear about every 2 kilometres.

Distance from Grimshaw (G) is followed by distance from Fort Simpson (FS) and distance from the AB–NWT border (B).

G 293.7 (472.7 km) **FS 296.7** (477.5 km) **B 0** AB–NWT border, 60th Parallel. A government visitor information centre here has brochures, maps, fishing licenses, camping permits, a dump station and emergency radiophone. Dene (Indian) arts and crafts are on display. Also check here on road and ferry conditions before proceeding. The visitor centre is open May 15 to Sept. 15 from 8 A.M. to 10 P.M.

60th Parallel Campground and picnic area adjacent visitor centre. Facilities include 12 campsites, 5 picnic sites, kitchen shelter and drinking water. The park overlooks the Hay River and canoeists may launch here. Information on canoeing the river can be obtained at the visitor centre. ▲

Driving distances from the border to destinations in Northwest Territories are as follows (see individual highway logs this section for details): Hay River 76 miles/122 km; Fort Simpson 297 miles/478 km; Wrigley 430 miles/694 km; Fort Providence 140 miles/225 km; Yellowknife 330 miles/531 km; Fort Smith 238 miles/383 km.

G 295.5 (475.6 km) **FS 294.9** (474.6 km) **B 1.8** (2.9 km) Reindeer Creek.

G 318.5 (512.6 km) **FS 271.9** (437.6 km) **B 24.8** (39.9 km) Grumbler Rapids, just off highway, is audible during low water periods in late summer.

G 319.1 (513.5 km) **FS 271.3** (436.6 km) **B 25.4** (40.8 km) Swede Creek.

G 319.8 (514.6 km) **FS 270.6** (435.5 km) **B 26.1** (42 km) Large turnout and gravel stockpile to west.

G 334.2 (537.8 km) **FS 256.2** (412.4 km) **B 40.5** (65.1 km) Mink Creek.

G 335.5 (539.9 km) **FS 254.9** (410.2 km) **B 41.8** (67.3 km) Large turnout and gravel stockpile to west.

G 338.8 (545.3 km) **FS 251.6** (404.9 km) **B 45.1** (72.6 km) Twin Falls Gorge Territorial Park; Alexandra Falls picnic area to east. Paved parking area and gravel walkway to falls viewpoint, overlooking the Hay River, which plunges 109 feet/33m to form Alexandra Falls. Excellent photo opportunities; easy hike down to top of falls. A walking trail connects with Louise Falls.

G 340.3 (547.6 km) **FS 250.1** (402.6 km) **B 46.6** (74.9 km) Turnoff to east for Louise Falls picnic area and campground, now part of Twin Falls Gorge Territorial Park; 18 campsites, 6 picnic sites, kitchen shelters, tables, toilets, firepits, firewood, water. Hiking trails to viewpoint overlooking 3-tiered Louise Falls, which drops 50 feet/15m. (It is not advisable to walk down to the water.) Hike along bluff 3 miles/5 km for Alexandra Falls. ▲

G 341.9 (550.2 km) **FS 248.5** (400 km) **B 48.2** (77.5 km) Escarpment Creek picnic area; tables, shelter, toilets, firepits, garbage container, water pump. Spectacular series of waterfalls downstream.

G 342.1 (550.5 km) **FS 248.3** (399.7 km) **B 48.4** (77.8 km) Highway crosses Escarpment Creek.

G 345.4 (555.9 km) **FS 245** (394.3 km) **B 51.7** (83.2 km) Truck weigh scales to east, service station to west. Entering Enterprise northbound.

G 345.8 (556.5 km) **FS 244.6** (393.7 km) **B 52.1** (83.8 km) **Junction** of Highway 1 and Highway 2. Highway 2 leads 23.6 miles/38 km from here to **HAY RIVER** (pop. 2,891), the hub for transportation on Great Slave Lake and a major service centre with all visitor facilities (see HAY RIVER HIGHWAY log this section for details on Hay River). Continue on Highway 1 for Enterprise (description follows) and Fort Simpson.

ENTERPRISE (pop. 56), a highway community with food, grocery store, gas, diesel

Jean Marie River, a Slavey community, is accessible by all-weather road.

(© Lyn Hancock)

and lodging. Pay phone. It is a good idea to fill up gas tanks here. View of Hay River Gorge just east of the highway.

*NOTE: Last gas southbound until Meander River at **Milepost G 219.3**, 126.5 miles/203.6 km from here.*

G 369.3 (594.3 km) **FS 221.1** (355.8 km) **B 75.6** (121.6 km) Turnout to north with view of McNally Creek Falls.

Highway crosses McNally Creek northbound.

G 370.5 (596.2 km) **FS 219.9** (353.9 km) **B 76.8** (123.6 km) Large paved turnout to north with litter barrels and scenic view.

G 374.7 (603 km) **FS 215.7** (347.2 km) **B 81** (130.3 km) Easy-to-miss Hart Lake Fire Tower access road turnoff leads 0.5 mile/0.8 km to picnic area and forest fire lookout tower. Panoramic view over more than 100 square miles/259 square km of forest to Great Slave Lake and Mackenzie River. Path to ancient coral reef. *CAUTION: Keep the fly repellent handy and stay away from the edge of escarpment.*

G 378.9 (609.8 km) **FS 211.5** (340.4 km) **B 85.2** (137.1 km) Crooked Creek.

G 379.4 (610.5 km) **FS 211** (339.7 km) **B 85.7** (137.8 km) Trapper's cabin to north.

G 385.6 (620.5 km) **FS 204.8** (329.6 km) **B 91.9** (147.9 km) Side road to highway maintenance camp.

G 391.7 (630.3 km) **FS 198.7** (319.9 km) **B 98** (157.6 km) Turnout with litter barrels.

G 398.2 (640.8 km) **FS 192.2** (309.3 km) **B 104.5** (168.2 km) Highway maintenance camp and stockpiles to north.

G 398.7 (641.7 km) **FS 191.7** (308.5 km) **B 105** (169 km) Access road leads south 4.5 miles/7.2 km to Lady Evelyn Falls where the Kakisa River drops 49 feet/15m over an escarpment. Staircase down to viewing platform. Hiking trail to base of falls; swimming and wading. Ample parking, interpretive display, territorial campground with 10 tent sites, 18 RV sites and 5 picnic sites; tables, firepits, firewood, garbage containers, water pump, kitchen shelters. At end of road, 4 miles/6.4 km past campground, is Slavey Indian village and **Kakisa Lake**; fair fishing for walleye, pike and grayling.

G 399.6 (643.1 km) **FS 190.8** (307.1 km) **B 105.9** (170.4 km) Kakisa River bridge.

G 399.8 (643.4 km) **FS 190.6** (306.8 km) **B 106.1** (170.7 km) Kakisa River bridge picnic area with 10 sites, tables, fireplaces and firewood. Hiking trails along river lead upstream to Lady Evelyn Falls. Fair fishing in **Kakisa River** for grayling.

G 410.5 (660.6 km) **FS 179.9** (289.5 km) **B 116.8** (187.9 km) Turnout with litter barrels, log cabin, outhouse, picnic tables and map display on Highways 1 and 3.

G 410.9 (661.2 km) **FS 179.5** (289 km) **B 117.2** (188.5 km) **Junction** of Highway 1 and Highway 3. Highway 3 (paved and gravel) leads 212.5 miles/342 km north to Yellowknife, capital of Northwest Territories (see YELLOWKNIFE HIGHWAY log section). Highway 1 (gravel) leads west 179.5 miles/289 km to Fort Simpson. Continue with this log for Fort Simpson.

G 438.4 (705.5 km) **FS 152** (244.7 km) **B 144.7** (232.8 km) Emergency survival cabin and turnout with litter barrels and outhouse to south.

G 450.5 (725 km) **FS 139.9** (225.1 km) **B 158.6** (255.3 km) Turnout to north with parking and scenic view.

G 466.2 (750.3 km) **FS 124.2** (199.9 km) **B 172.5** (277.6 km) Bouvier River.

G 467.2 (751.9 km) **FS 123.2** (198.3 km) **B 173.5** (279.2 km) Emergency survival cabin and turnout with litter barrels to south.

G 471.9 (759.5 km) **FS 118.5** (190.7 km) **B 180.1** (289.8 km) Turnout to north.

G 473.9 (762.6 km) **FS 116.5** (187.6 km) **B 180.2** (289.9 km) Wallace Creek. Scenic canyon to north.

G 477 (767.6 km) **FS 113.4** (182.6 km) **B 183.3** (294.9 km) Highway maintenance camp to south.

G 477.6 (768.6 km) **FS 112.8** (181.6 km) **B 183.9** (295.9 km) Redknife River.

G 488.7 (786.4 km) **FS 101.7** (163.8 km) **B 195** (313.7 km) Morrissey Creek.

G 491.7 (791.8 km) **FS 98.7** (158.8 km) **B 199.8** (321.6 km) Winter ice road leads south 78 miles/126 km to **TROUT LAKE** (pop. 66), a Dene settlement.

G 494.1 (795.3 km) **FS 96.3** (155 km) **B 202** (325.1 km) Trout River bridge.

G 495 (796.3 km) **FS 95.4** (153.5 km) **B 202.8** (326.4 km) Turnout to south with litter barrels.

G 495.7 (797.8 km) **FS 94.7** (152.4 km) **B 203.5** (327.9 km) Whittaker Falls (Sambaa Deh) Territorial Park, overlooking the **Trout River canyon** *(CAUTION: Stay away from edge)*. There are 3 picnic sites, 8 campsites, tables, litter barrels, showers, kitchen shelter, firepits and firewood. Walk along the river to view large deposits of shale and limestone. Grayling fishing, use dry flies in deep pools. Hike to Coral Falls.

G 498.1 (801.6 km) **FS 92.3** (148.5 km) **B 206.1** (331.7 km) Emergency survival cabin and turnout with litter barrels to north.

G 523.7 (842.8 km) **FS 66.7** (107.3 km) **B 229.9** (370 km) **Ekali Lake** access; pike and pickerel fishing.

G 527.4 (848.7 km) **FS 63** (101.4 km) **B 233.6** (376 km) All-weather road leads 17 miles/27 km to **JEAN MARIE RIVER** (pop. 67), a traditional Slavey community known for its hand-crafted moose hide clothing decorated with moose tufting, porcupine quilling and embroidery. Also accessible by boat from Fort Simpson.

G 530.5 (853.7 km) **FS 59.9** (96.5 km) **B 236.8** (381 km) Emergency survival cabin and turnout to north with outhouse and litter barrels.

G 534.8 (860.7 km) **FS 55.6** (89.5 km) **B 241.1** (388 km) I.P.L. pipeline camp and pump station to north. Highway crosses pipeline.

G 536.3 (863 km) **FS 54.1** (87 km) **B 242.6** (390.4 km) Microwave tower to south.

G 550.4 (885.8 km) **FS 40** (64.4 km) **B 256.7** (413.1 km) Jean Marie Creek bridge.

G 550.5 (885.9 km) **FS 39.9** (64.3 km) **B 256.8** (413.2 km) "Checkpoint"; 24-hour gas, diesel, propane, licensed restaurant and accommodations. Phone (403) 695-2953. Open year-round.

G 550.6 (886.1 km) **FS 39.8** (64.1 km) **B 256.9** (413.4 km) **Junction** with the Liard Highway (NWT Highway 7), which leads south to Fort Liard and junctions with the Alaska Highway near Fort Nelson. See the LIARD HIGHWAY section for details.

G 552 (888.4 km) **FS 38.4** (61.8 km) **B 258.3** (415.7 km) Turnout to east.

G 563.7 (907.1 km) **FS 26.7** (43.1 km) **B 270** (434.4 km) Emergency survival cabin and turnout with litter barrels and outhouse to west.

G 577.8 (929.8 km) **FS 12.6** (20.4 km) **B 284.1** (457.1 km) Highway crests hill; view of Liard River ahead. Ferry landing 3,280 feet/1,000m.

G 578.2 (930.5 km) **FS 12.2** (19.7 km) **B 284.5** (457.8 km) Liard River Campground to accommodate travelers who miss the last ferry at night, has 5 sites, tables, firepits, water, outhouse and garbage container.

G 578.5 (930.9 km) **FS 11.9** (19.3 km) **B 284.8** (458.2 km) Free government-operated Liard River ferry operates daily May through October from 8 A.M. to 11:40 P.M., 7 days a week. Crossing time is 6 minutes. Capacity is 8 cars or 2 trucks, with a maximum total weight of 130,000 lbs./59,090 kg. An ice bridge opens for light vehicles in late November and heavier vehicles as ice thickens. *NOTE: No crossing possible during breakup (about mid-April to mid-May) and freezeup (mid-October to mid-November).* For ferry information phone (867) 873-7799 or (800) 661-0751.

G 580.7 (934.6 km) **FS 9.7** (15.6 km) **B 287** (461.9 km) Fort Simpson airport. See Private Aircraft information in Fort Simpson.

G 588.1 (946.4 km) **FS 2.3** (3.8 km) **B 294.4** (473.7 km) **Junction** with Fort Simpson access road which leads 2.3 miles/3.8 km to Fort Simpson (description follows). The extension of NWT Highway 1 to Wrigley was completed in 1994; see WRIGLEY EXTENSION log this section.

G 589.7 (949 km) **FS 0.7** (1.2 km) **B 296** (476.3 km) Causeway to Fort Simpson Island.

G 590.1 (949.6 km) **FS 0.3** (0.6 km) **B 296.4** (476.9 km) Turnoff for village campground.

Fort Simpson

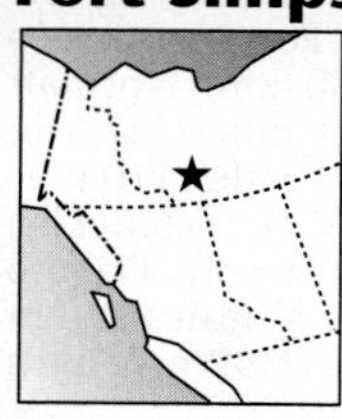

G 590.4 (950.2 km) **FS 0 B 296.7** (477.5 km) Located on an island at the confluence of the Mackenzie and Liard rivers. **Population:** 1,450. **Emergency Services: RCMP**, phone (403) 695-3111. **Hospital** (12 beds), for medical emergency phone (403) 695-2291. **Fire Department** (volunteer), phone (403) 695-2222.

Visitor Information: Village office operates a visitor booth June through August and has a photo exhibit and films. The visitor information centre is open until 8 P.M., 7 days a week in summer; closed Sundays in winter. Nahanni National Park information centre is open 8:30 A.M. to 5 P.M., 7 days a week in July and August, weekdays the rest of the year.

Television: Channels 2, 4, 6, 7, 9, 11. **Transportation:** Scheduled service to Yellowknife and Whitehorse, YT via First Air. Fixed wing and helicopter charters available. **Rental cars**—Available. **Taxi service**—Available.

Private Aircraft: Fort Simpson airport; elev. 554 feet/169m; length 6,000 feet/1,829m; asphalt; fuel 100, Jet B. Fort Simpson Island; elev. 405 feet/123m; length 3,000 feet/914m; gravel; fuel 100, Jet B.

Fort Simpson is a full-service community. There is a motel with kitchenettes, 2 bed and breakfasts and a hotel; dining at the hotel (licensed premises) and 2 restaurants in town; gas stations with repair service (unleaded, diesel and propane available); 2 grocery stores, department store, hardware store, a bank, laundromat, post office, crafts shop and sports shop. Small engine repair shop and mechanics available. Fort Simpson has grade schools, churches (Anglican, Catholic and Pentecostal), the Stanley Isaiah Senior Citizen's Centre, and various territorial and federal offices. Recreational facilities include an arena, curling rink, gym, ball diamond, tennis, small indoor pool, golf course and a boat launch at government wharf. A number of community activities are held at the Papal Site, a large field with a cross, log tepee and stone monument commemorating Pope John Paul II's visit here in 1987.

Public campground at edge of town in wooded area has 30 campsites and 4 picnic

FORT SIMPSON ADVERTISERS

Fort Simpson Tourism & Visitor Services ....Ph. (867) 695-3192
Maroda Motel, The...........Ph. (867) 695-2602
Wolverine Air Ltd.............Ph. (867) 695-2263

sites. ▲

Fort Simpson is the oldest continuously occupied site on the Mackenzie River, dating from 1804 when the North West Co. established its Fort of the Forks. There is a historical marker on the bank of the Mackenzie. The Hudson's Bay Co. began its post here in 1821. At that time the fort was renamed after Sir George Simpson, one of the first governors of the combined North West Co. and Hudson's Bay Co. Fort Simpson served as the Mackenzie District headquarters for the Hudson's Bay Co. fur-trading operation. Its key location on the Mackenzie River also made Fort Simpson an important transportation centre. Anglican and Catholic missions were established here in 1858 and 1894.

Fort Simpson continues to be an important centre for the Northwest Territories water transport system. Visitors may walk along the high banks of the Mackenzie River and watch the boat traffic and floatplanes.

© Lyn Hancock

One of the easiest places to get down to the water is by Alfred Faille's cabin on Mackenzie Drive. Faille was a well-known Fort Simpson pioneer and prospector.

For visitors, Fort Simpson has Slavey crafts, such as birch-bark baskets and beadwork. Fort Simpson is also the jumping-off point for jet boat trips on the North Nahanni River; Mackenzie River traffic; and fly-in trips to Nahanni National Park.

The 4,766-square-km **NAHANNI NATIONAL PARK**, listed as a unique geological area on the UNESCO world heritage site list, is accessible only by nonpowered boat or aircraft. Located southwest of Fort Simpson near the Yukon border, the park has day-trip flightseeing tours that may be arranged in Fort Simpson, Fort Liard and Yellowknife, and from Fort Nelson, BC, and Watson Lake, YT. Highlights include the spectacular Virginia Falls (300 feet/90m, twice as high as Niagara Falls). One of the most popular attractions in the park is running the South Nahanni River or its tributary, the Flat River. The South Nahanni River route stretches about 186 miles/300 km from Rabbitkettle Lake to the eastern park boundary. Rabbitkettle Hot Springs, a major feature on the upper section of the river, is reached by trail (restricted access, hikers must be guided by park staff). Near the east park boundary is Kraus Hot Springs, on the remains of the old Kraus homestead. The Flat River route stretches 80 miles/128 km from Seaplane Lake to the confluence with the South Nahanni. Charter air service for canoe drop-offs is available in Fort Simpson.

In order to evenly distribute visitor use and maintain ecological integrity within Nahanni National Park Reserve, the park has implemented a mandatory reservation system for overnight use. Twelve guided and 12 non-guided visitors are allowed to camp at Virginia Falls each day. The maximum length of stay at Virginia Falls is 2 nights. Reservations may be made by telephone or fax. User fees are charged. The seasonal overnight-use fee is $100, payable by VISA or MasterCard at the time a reservation is made. (Seasonal user fees are transferable to any national park in Northwest Territories.) A day-use fee of $10 per person is charged to those visitors flying into Virginia Falls for a day trip. Reservations are not required for day trips. Contact Nahanni National Park Reserve, Box 348, Fort Simpson, NT X0E 0N0; phone (867) 695-3151, fax 695-2446.

AREA FISHING: **Willow, Dogface** and **Trout lakes** accessible by air. Good fishing for trout and grayling. Inquire locally.

Mackenzie Highway Log

(continued)

WRIGLEY EXTENSION

Improved to all-weather road standards, this former trail to Wrigley officially opened in 1994 as part of Highway 1 (although it's still referred to locally as the "road to Wrigley"). Slippery when wet. Use caution approaching all bridges. Driving time is approximately 3 hours between Fort Simpson and Wrigley. Allow at least 2 hours from Wrigley to the Camsell ferry crossing.

Distance from Fort Simpson (FS) is followed by distance from Wrigley (W).

FS 0 W 137 (220.5 km) **Junction** with Fort Simpson access road.

FS 9.5 (15.3 km) **W 127.5** (205.2 km) Single-lane bridge over Martin River. *CAUTION: Slow down for steep descent to bridge.*

FS 17.9 (28.8 km) **W 119.1** (191.7 km) Creek crossing. *CAUTION: Slow down, steep drop-offs and no guardrails.*

FS 33.4 (53.7 km) **W 103.6** (166.7 km) Single-lane bridge over Shale Creek.

FS 34 (54.7 km) **W 103** (165.8 km) Turnout to east.

FS 46.6 (75 km) **W 90.4** (145.5 km) Ferry crossing of the Mackenzie River at Camsell Bend (Ndulee Crossing). Ferry operates daily, 9 to 11 A.M. and 2 to 8 P.M. Capacity is 6 cars or 4 trucks. *NOTE: There are no overnight facilities for anyone missing the ferry. Ferry does not operate in fog. Be prepared to wait.*

FS 71 (114.3 km) **W 66** (106.2 km) Mackenzie Mountains come into view to the west, northbound.

FS 73.5 (118.3 km) **W 63.5** (102.2 km) Highway maintenance camp to east.

FS 94.2 (151.6 km) **W 42.8** (68.9 km) Willowlake River bridge, longest bridge in the Northwest Territories.

FS 95.2 (153.2 km) **W 41.8** (67.3 km) Highway climbs steep hill northbound.

FS 97.7 (157.2 km) **W 39.3** (63.2 km) Turnout to west at top of hill with litter barrels and scenic view of the Mackenzie River.

FS 110.9 (178.5 km) **W 26.1** (42 km) Single-lane wooden bridge over the "River Between Two Mountains."

FS 112.6 (181.2 km) **W 24.4** (39.3 km) Scenic view of the Mackenzie River to west.

FS 121.5 (195.5 km) **W 15.5** (25.1 km) Wrigley interprovincial pipeline pump station and radio tower to east.

FS 128.9 (207.4 km) **W 8.1** (13 km) Single-lane bridge over Smith's Creek.

FS 131.1 (211 km) **W 5.9** (9.5 km) Highway maintenance camp to west.

FS 132.2 (212.7 km) **W 4.8** (7.7 km) **Junction** with winter ice road to east which leads north to Fort Norman, Norman Wells, Fort Franklin and Fort Good Hope. Winter road mileages are as follows: Wrigley to Fort Norman, 148 miles/238 km; Fort Norman to Norman Wells, 50 miles/80 km; Norman Wells to Fort Good Hope, 91 miles/147 km; Norman Wells to Franklin, 68 miles/110 km.

FS 132.9 (213.9 km) **W 4.1** (6.6 km) Turnoff to west for Wrigley airport. **Private Aircraft:** Wrigley airport, 4 miles/7 km south of town; elev. 493 feet/142m; length 3,500 feet/1,148m; gravel; fuel 80.

FS 136.8 (220.1 km) **W 0.2** (0.4 km) Airport Lake, Wrigley community campground; 12 sites, firepits and washrooms. Suitable for RVs; located on high, dry ground in mostly birch and white spruce trees. ▲

FS 137 (220.5 km) **W 0 WRIGLEY** (pop. 200; 90 percent Dene ancestry). **Emergency Services: RCMP,** station manned intermittently. **Nursing Station,** with full-time nurse, phone (867) 587-3441.

Visitor Information: Visitor Information Centre manned by knowledgeable young people, open daily in summer; local crafts.

The Hudson's Bay Co. built a trading post here in 1870 called Fort Wrigley. The fort was abandoned in 1910 due to disease and famine, and the inhabitants moved down river. Although a church and school were built at that site in 1957, the community decided to move to higher ground in 1965. 15 homes were built at the "new" townsite of present-day Wrigley. The church, school and other buildings were moved from the old townsite by boat. Wrigley is the home of the Pehdzeh Ki First Nation.

Visitor facilities here include the Petanea Hotel and restaurant; co-op store and craft shop; Ed's Mobile Mechanical Service; a convenience store; and a government gas station operating 9 A.M. to 6 P.M. weekdays and 1 to 6 P.M. weekends. There is also a community-built, walk-in campground with washrooms and fireplaces along the bank of the Mackenzie River, with picturesque, bug-free views of the Mackenzie Mountains. ▲

Hay River Highway Log

NWT HIGHWAY 2

Highway 2 is paved from Enterprise to Hay River; watch for rough spots in the surfacing. Kilometreposts along the highway reflect distance from Enterprise.

Distance from Enterprise (E) is followed by distance from Hay River (H).

E 0 H 23.6 (38 km) **Junction** of Highways 1 and 2.

E 8.7 (14 km) **H 14.9** (24 km) Private campground, 0.7 mile/1.1 km east, with large organic gardens. ▲

Paradise Garden Campground. See display ad this section. ▲

E 11.6 (18.6 km) **H 12** (19.4 km) Sawmill Road to east.

E 16 (25.7 km) **H 7.6** (12.3 km) Gravel road leads east 0.6 mile/1 km to Hay River golf course; large log clubhouse, driving range, 9 holes (par 36), artificial greens. Site of the NWT Open every second year in late August.

E 20 (32.3 km) **H 3.6** (5.7 km) **Junction** with Highway 5 to Fort Smith (see Fort Smith Highway Log this section).

E 22.4 (36 km) **H 1.2** (2 km) Chamber of Commerce Welcome to Hay River sign. Parking area to east.

Hay River

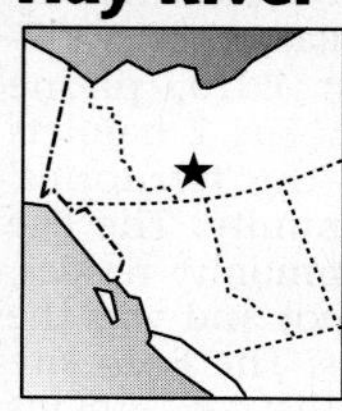

E 23.6 (38 km) **H 0** Located on the south shore of Great Slave Lake at the mouth of the Hay River, on both the mainland and Vale Island. **Population:** 3,800 **Emergency Services: Police,** phone (867) 874-6555. **Fire Department,** phone (867) 874-2222. **Hospital,** phone (867) 874-6512.

Visitor Information: Visitor information centre, just east of the highway, is housed in a 2-story brown structure. The centre is open daily, late May to early September; 9 A.M. to 9 P.M. There is a dump station located here. Write the Chamber of Commerce at 10K Gagnler St., Hay River, NWT X0E 1G1; phone (867) 874-2565, fax (867) 874-3255.

Radio: CKHR-FM 107.3, 93.7, 100.1-FM. **Television:** Channels 2 through 13 via satellite. **Newspaper:** *The Hub* (weekly). **Transportation: Air**—Canadian Regional Airline, First Air, Landa Aviation, Carter Air and Buffalo Airways. **Bus**—Coachways. **Rental cars**—Available.

Private Aircraft: Hay River airport; elev. 543 feet/165m; length 6,000 feet/1,830m, paved; 4,000 feet/1,219m, gravel; fuel 100, Jet B.

Hay River was established in 1868 with the building of a Hudson's Bay Co. post. Today's economy combines transportation, communications, commercial fishing and service industries.

The community is the transfer point from highway and rail to barges on Great Slave Lake bound for arctic and subarctic communities. Hay River harbour is also home port of the Mackenzie River barge fleet that plies the river in summer.

The airstrip was built in 1942 on Vale Island by the U.S. Army Corps of Engineers. Vale Island was the townsite until floods in 1951 and 1963 forced evacuation of the population to the mainland townsite, where most of the community is now concentrated. Vale Island, referred to as "Old Town," is bounded by Great Slave Lake and the west and east channels of the Hay River.

The town boasts the tallest building in the Northwest Territories—a 17-story apartment high-rise that can be seen for miles around— and a purple high school designed by Douglas Cardinal. Hay River also has Paradise Gardens, the largest market-gardening operation in Northwest Territories, and Perron's Funny Farm, one of the few livestock producers in the territories.

There are 10 restaurants, gas stations with unleaded gas, propane and repair service, and grocery stores. Reservations are a must at the town's 5 hotels/motels; lodgings may be heavily booked in the busy summer season. There is also a bed and breakfast. Other facilities include 2 banks, a laundromat, and a variety of gift and arts and crafts shops.

Hay River has schools, churches, a civic centre with a swimming pool (1 of only 2 year-round swimming pools in Northwest Territories), curling sheets, hockey arena and dance hall. Northwest Territories Centennial Library headquarters is located here. There is a public boat launch at Porritt Landing on Vale Island.

There is a public campground, Hay River Centennial Park, on Vale Island (follow the signs; it is about 6 miles/10 km past the information centre). There are 21 sites (4 with electrical hookups), showers, firewood and firepits, picnic area, playground and horseshoe pit. Camping fee is $15 per night. Open mid-May to mid-September. Paradise Garden Campground, 14.9 miles/24 km south of Hay River on Highway 2, has dry campsites and hookups (electrical and water), a dump station, playground and organic gardens. ▲

Great sportfishing area with fly-in fishing camps (check with the chamber of commerce). Boat rentals on nearby **Great Slave Lake**, where northern pike up to 40 lbs. are not unusual. Inconnu (sheefish), pickerel and grayling also found here.

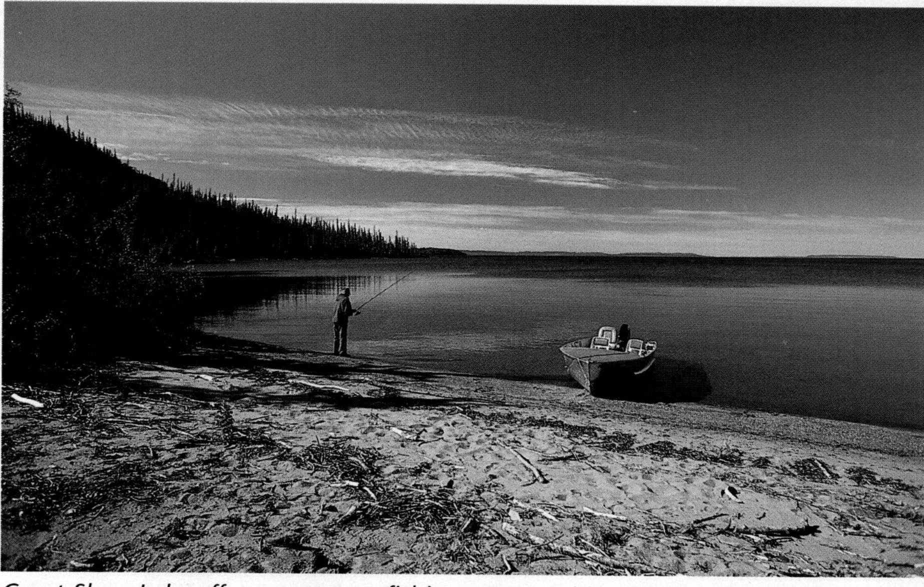

Great Slave Lake offers great sportfishing opportunities. (© Lyn Hancock)

Yellowknife Highway Log

NWT HIGHWAY 3
Distance from the junction of Highways 1 and 3 (J) is followed by distance from Yellowknife (Y).

J 0 Y 212.5 (342 km) **Junction** of Highways 1 and 3. Turn right northbound for Fort Providence, Rae–Edzo and Yellowknife.

The first 152.3 miles/245.1 km of Highway 3 are paved. There is one remaining stretch of gravel— 56.2 miles/90.4 km—between Edzo and Yellowknife. Plans call for continued paving of this highway over the next several years.

J 4.8 (7.7 km) **Y 207.7** (334.3 km) Chikilee Creek.

J 4.9 (7.9 km) **Y 207.6** (334.1 km) Wolf Skull Creek.

J 9.1 (14.7 km) **Y 203.4** (327.3 km) Dory Point maintenance camp to west.

J 10.6 (17 km) **Y 201.9** (324.9 km) Turnoff for winter ice crossing to east.

J 13.2 (21.2 km) **Y 199.3** (320.8 km) Dory Point picnic area to east with 5 sites and kitchen shelter, no drinking water; overlooking Mackenzie River with view of passing riverboats.

J 13.9 (22.4 km) **Y 198.6** (319.6 km) Campground with hookups, service station with regular, unleaded and diesel, and restaurant. ▲

J 14.5 (23.3 km) **Y 198** (318.6 km) Dory Point marine access camp to west.

J 15.1 (24.3 km) **Y 197.4** (317.7 km) Free government-operated Mackenzie River ferry operates daily May through October or November from 6 A.M. to midnight. Crossing time is 8 minutes. Capacity is 10 cars or 4 trucks, with a maximum total weight of 220,000 lbs./100,000 kg. An ice bridge opens for light vehicles in December and heavier vehicles as ice thickens. *NOTE: No crossing possible during breakup (about April to mid-May).* Ice-breaking procedures now keep the channel open for the ferry during freezeup while an ice bridge is being constructed. For ferry information phone (867) 873-7799 or (800) 661-0751.

J 15.9 (25.6 km) **Y 196.6** (316.4 km) Sign indicates Mackenzie Wood Bison Sanctuary. The wood bison are not often seen along the highway; however, sandhill cranes, squirrels, spruce grouse and ptarmigan may be seen in season.

J 19.4 (31.2 km) **Y 193.1** (310.8 km) Motel, restaurant and service station with unleaded, diesel and propane. Pay phone.

J 19.6 (31.6 km) **Y 192.9** (310.4 km) **Junction** with access road which leads 2.8 miles/4.5 km west to Fort Providence (description follows). Motel, restaurant, lounge; Native crafts; gas station with unleaded, diesel, propane and tire repair. There is an airstrip located 0.4 mile/0.6 km west on the access road. *NOTE: It is a good* *idea to fill gas tanks here if you are bound for Yellowknife. Next gas available is in Rae–Edzo.*

Big River Service Centre. See display ad this section.

Fort Providence territorial campground is located 0.7 mile/1.1 km west of the highway on the access road; 30 sites, tables, firewood, kitchen shelter, garbage container, pump water and dump station. Situated on the banks of the Mackenzie River. Rental boats, boat launch and fishing nearby. ▲

Entering Mackenzie Bison Sanctuary northbound.

Fort Providence

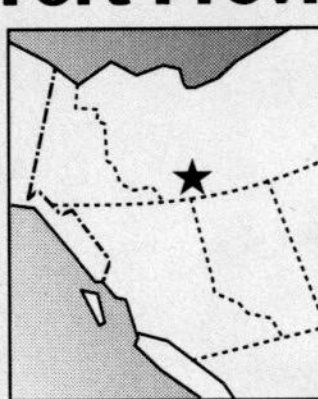

Located on the Mackenzie River, 2.8 miles/4.5 km northwest of Highway 3. **Population:** 688. **Emergency Services: Police,** phone (867) 699-3291. **Fire Department,** phone (867) 699-4222. **Nursing station,** phone (867) 699-4311. **Elevation:** 550 feet/168m. **Radio:** 1230. **Television:** Channels 6 and 13 (CBC). **Transportation: Air**—Air Providence and charter service. **Bus**—Coachways.

Private Aircraft: Fort Providence airstrip; elev. 530 feet/162m; length 3,000 feet/915m; gravel; fuel emergency only.

Facilities include 2 motels, 2 restaurants, gas stations with minor repair service, grocery and general stores.

A Roman Catholic mission was established here in 1861. Although noted for its early agricultural endeavors, Fort Providence is traditionally a trapping community. Three historical markers in the community commemorate the roles of the church and explorer Alexander Mackenzie in settling the area.

Unique and popular with northern collectors is the moose hair embroidery found in local gift shops. Local craftswomen are also noted for their porcupine quill work. Along with seeing the crafts, visitors may cruise the Mackenzie River. Spectacular photo opportunities here for sunsets on the Mackenzie.

Good to excellent fishing in **Mackenzie River;** guides and cabins available, also boats and air charter trips. Northern pike to 30 lbs., May 30 to September, use large Red Devils; grayling and pickerel from 1 to 6 lbs., June to September, use anything (small Red Devils will do).

Yellowknife Highway Log
(continued)

J 26.4 (42.5 km) **Y 186.1** (299.5 km) Side road west to highway maintenance camp and stockpiles.

J 27.5 (44.3 km) **Y 185** (297.7 km) Bluefish Creek.

J 37 (59.5 km) **Y 175.5** (282.4 km) Large turnout to east at sand and gravel stockpiles.

J 38.7 (62.3 km) **Y 173.8** (279.7 km) Small gravel turnout to east.

J 42.3 (68.1 km) **Y 170.2** (273.9 km) Turnout to east with litter barrels and sign about Mackenzie Bison Sanctuary.

J 51.7 (83.2 km) **Y 160.8** (258.8 km) Turnout to west.

J 59.2 (95.3 km) **Y 153.3** (246.7 km) Telecommunications building to east.

J 75.6 (121.6 km) **Y 136.9** (220.4 km) Chan Lake picnic area to east with kitchen shelter, tables, firepits and firewood. No drinking water. Watch for waterfowl.

J 76.1 (122.5 km) **Y 136.4** (219.5 km) Turnout with litter barrels to east.

100 (160.9 km) **Y 112.5** (181.1 km) Turnout with litter barrels, outhouse and highway map sign to east. Watch for buffalo.

J 104.4 (168 km) **Y 108.1** (174 km) Telecommunications building to east.

J 124.7 (200.7 km) **Y 87.8** (141.3 km) Entering Yellowknife District northbound.

J 129.7 (208.8 km) **Y 82.8** (133.2 km) Turnout with litter barrels to east. Northbound travelers may notice the trees are getting shorter as you move farther north.

J 140.2 (225.7 km) **Y 72.3** (116.3 km) Turnout to east. Highway descends northbound to Mosquito Creek.

J 141.2 (227.3 km) **Y 71.3** (114.7 km) Highway crosses **Mosquito Creek**. Fishing for pickerel and whitefish, May and June.

J 144.2 (232 km) **Y 68.3** (110 km) North Arm Territorial Park on the shores of Great Slave Lake. Picnic area with kitchen shelter, tables, toilets, firewood and firepits. Lowbush cranberries and other berries in area. *Beware of bears.*

J 148.3 (238.6 km) **Y 64.2** (103.3 km) **Junction** with winter ice road north to communities of Lac La Marte and Rae Lakes.

J 148.5 (239 km) **Y 64** (103 km) **Junction** with access road west to community of Edzo (see description at **Milepost J 152.2**).

J 148.8 (239.5 km) **Y 63.7** (102.5 km) Picnic area to west. Pickerel fishing in **West Channel** in spring.

J 149.3 (240.2 km) **Y 63.2** (101.8 km) West Channel.

J 151.5 (243.8 km) **Y 61** (98.2 km) Bridge over **Frank Channel**, which extends from the head of the North Arm of Great Slave Lake to the Indian village of Rae. Watch for turnoff to Rabesca's Bear Healing Rock; lodging, mud baths, boating and fishing for whitefish.

© Lyn Hancock

J 152.2 (245 km) **Y 60.3** (97 km) **Junction** with road which leads west 7 miles/11.2 km to community of Rae (description follows).

RAE–EDZO (pop. about 2,000). **Emergency Services: RCMP,** in Rae, phone 392-6181. **Nursing station** in Edzo, phone 371-3551. **Radio:** 105.9-FM. The 2 hamlets of Rae and Edzo contain the territories' largest Dene (Indian) community. The Rae area, where most of the community resides, is an old Indian hunting spot and was the site of 2 early trading posts. The Edzo site was developed in 1965 by the government to provide schools and an adequate sanitation system. Rae has grocery stores, a post office, Native crafts shop, 2 hotels, food service and gas stations with regular, unleaded and diesel. Pay phones are located at the community sports centre and at the cafe.

J 152.3 (245.1 km) **Y 60.2** (96.9 km) Pavement ends, gravel begins, eastbound.

J 159.8 (257.2 km) **Y 52.7** (84.8 km) Stagg River bridge. After crossing the North Arm of Great Slave Lake, the highway swings southeast toward Yellowknife. Winding road to Yellowknife, good opportunities to see waterfowl in the many small lakes.

J 160.4 (258.1 km) **Y 52.1** (83.9 km) Turnout with litter barrels to south.

J 189.2 (304.5 km) **Y 23.3** (37.5 km) Turnout with litter barrels to north.

J 189.5 (304.9 km) **Y 23** (37.1 km) Boundary Creek.

J 203.8 (328 km) **Y 8.7** (14 km) Yellowknife city limits.

J 208.5 (335.5 km) **Y 4** (6.5 km) Gravel ends, pavement begins, eastbound.

J 208.7 (335.8 km) **Y 3.8** (6.2 km) Yellowknife Golf Club to north; 9 holes, sand greens, pro shop, licensed clubhouse. Built on the Canadian Shield, the course is mostly sand and bedrock. Each player gets a small piece of carpet to take along on the round as their own portable turf. Site of the June 21 Midnight Tournament. Some modified rules have been adopted by this Far North golf course, among them: "No penalty assessed when ball carried off by raven."

J 209.8 (337.7 km) **Y 2.7** (4.3 km) Yellowknife airport to south.

J 210 (338 km) **Y 2.5** (4 km) Fred Henne Territorial Park on Long Lake. Attractive public campground with 82 sites, water, firewood, firepits, picnic area, boat launch, snack bar, showers and pay phone. Daily and seasonal rates available; open from mid-May to mid-September. Sandy beach and swimming in Long Lake. Interpretive trail. ▲

J 210.5 (338.7 km) **Y 2** (3.3 km) Old Airport Road access to Yellowknife. Just past the turnoff is the Welcome to Yellowknife sign and the hard-to-miss Wardair Bristol freighter to the south. A historical plaque commemorates the Bristol freighter, which was the first wheel-equipped aircraft to land at the North Pole. Picnic sites nearby.

J 211.4 (340.2 km) **Y 1.1** (1.8 km) Stock Lake to south.

J 211.7 (340.7 km) **Y 0.8** (1.3 km) **Junction** of Highway 3 and Highway 4 (Ingraham Trail); see log this section.

Yellowknife

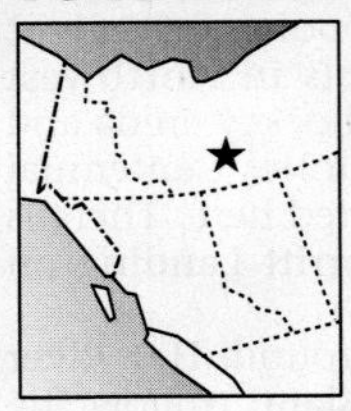

J 212.5 (342 km) **Y 0** On the north shore of Great Slave Lake, approximately 940 miles/1,513 km from Edmonton, AB. **Population:** 17,500. **Emergency Services: RCMP,** phone (867) 920-8311. **Fire Department** and **Ambulance,** phone (867) 873-3434 or 873-2222. **Hospital,** Stanton Yellowknife, phone (867)

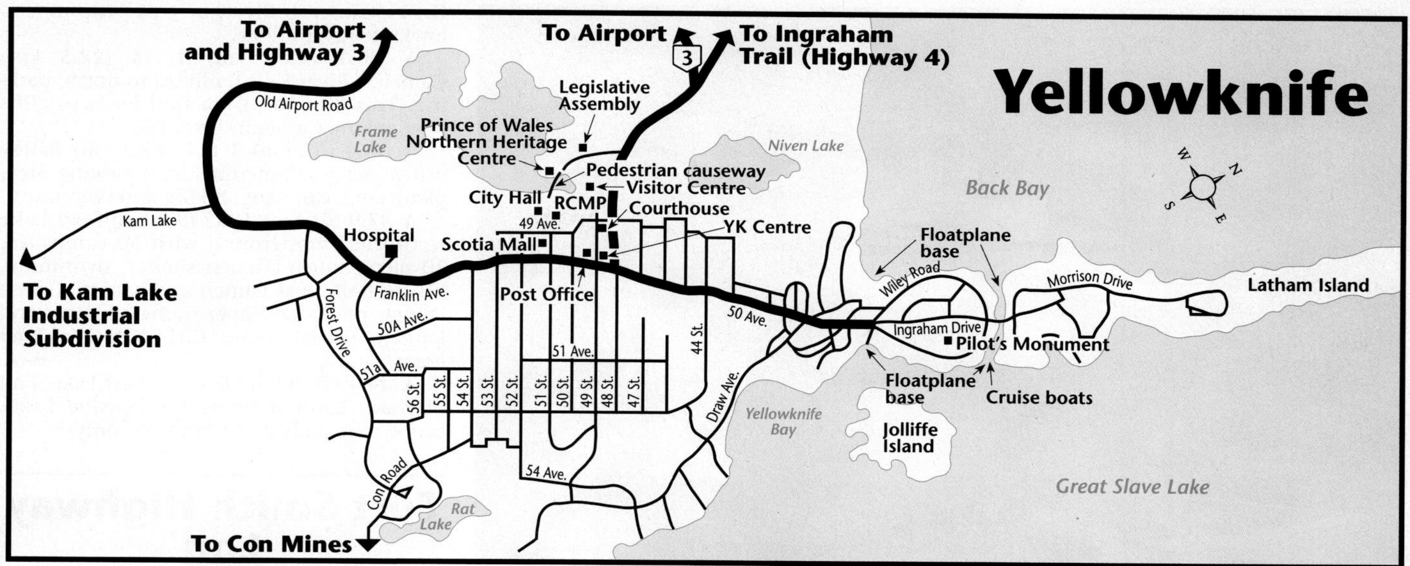

920-4111.

Visitor Information: Northern Frontier Regional Visitors Centre, showcasing the culture and crafts of the area, is located at 4807 49th St. Reservation desk for booking tours. Open daily year-round; summer hours 8 A.M. to 8 P.M. Phone (867) 873-4262. Information also available from Northwest Territories Tourism, P.O. Box 1320, Yellowknife, NT X1A 2L9. Phone (800) 661-0788 or (867) 873-7200. Or write the Chamber of Commerce, No. 6, 4807 49th St. (MP), Yellowknife, NWT X1A 3T5; phone (867) 920-4944.

Radio: 1240, 1340, 101.1-FM. **Television:** Channel 8; 15 cable channels. **Newspapers:** *News/North* (weekly); *Yellowknifer* (twice weekly).

Private Aircraft: Yellowknife airport; elev. 674 feet/205m; length 7,500 feet/2,286m; asphalt; fuel 100/130, Jet B. Floatplane bases located at East Bay and West Bay of Latham Island.

Yellowknife, capital of Northwest Territories and considered the only "city" in Northwest Territories, is a relatively new community. White settlers arrived in the 1930s with the discovery of gold in the area and radium at Great Bear Lake.

Cominco poured its first gold brick in 1938. WWII intervened and gold mining was halted until Giant Yellowknife Mines began milling on May 12, 1948. It was not until 1960 that the road connecting the city with the provinces was completed. Yellowknife became capital of the Northwest Territories in 1967.

The most recent mining boom in Yellowknife was the discovery of diamonds north of Yellowknife at Lac de Gras in 1992. The find set off a rush of claim stakers. An estimated 150 companies have staked claims in an area stretching from north of Yellowknife to the Arctic coast, and east from the North Arm of Great Slave Lake to Hudson Bay.

For 2 to 6 weeks each spring, vehicle traffic to Yellowknife is cut off during breakup on the Mackenzie River crossing near Fort Providence. All fresh meat, produce and urgent supplies must be airlifted during this period, resulting in higher prices.

Yellowknife has continued to develop as a mining, transportation and government administrative centre for the territories.

ACCOMMODATIONS/VISITOR SERVICES

Accommodations at 3 hotels, 3 motels, 14 bed and breakfasts, and the YWCA (coed). There are 47 restaurants, 7 dining lounges (no minors), 18 cocktail lounges and several shopping malls. Northern handicraft shops for fur parkas and other Native crafts are a specialty here, and there are shops specializing in Northern art.

TRANSPORTATION

Air: Scheduled air service to Edmonton via NWT Airways and Canadian Airlines International; Winnipeg via NWT Airways. Carriers serving Yellowknife and Arctic communities are NWT Airways, Canadian Airlines International, Ptarmigan Airways, Simpson Air, Air Providence and First Air. Charter service available. **Bus:** Greyhound from Edmonton with connections at Enterprise. **Rentals:** Several major car rental agencies; boat, canoe and houseboat rentals.

ATTRACTIONS

Northern Frontier Regional Visitors Centre. (MP5) No. 4, 4807 49th St., Yellowknife, Northwest Territories X1A 3T5. Featuring interpretive displays, exhibits and a bush plane elevator ride. Information on things to see and do. A tour reservation desk operates during the summer. Open year-round, 7 days a week (8 A.M. to 6 P.M. summer hours). Phone (867) 873-4262, fax 873-3654.

Prince of Wales Northern Heritage Centre was built to collect, preserve, document, exhibit, study and interpret the North's natural and cultural history. For visitors there are a variety of temporary exhibits ranging from Inuit stone sculpture to historical photographs, and permanent exhibits in the galleries. The orientation gallery gives general background on the Northwest Territories; the south gallery tells the story of the land and the Dene and Inuit people; the north gallery shows the arrival of the Euro–Canadians. The centre is located on Frame Lake, accessible via 48th Street or by way of a pedestrian causeway behind City Hall.

Yellowknife's City Hall and Prince of Wales Northern Heritage Centre sit across from each other on Frame Lake. (© Lyn Hancock)

Tours. There are a variety of local tours offered. Public tours of the Legislative Assembly are available by calling the Coordinator of Public Information at (867) 669-2230. Visitors may take a 2- or 3-hour tour of the city or a 2-hour cruise on Great Slave Lake. Local tour operators also offer tours out to Ingraham Trail (NWT Highway 4) and to a traditional Dene Camp in Ndilo's Rainbow Valley.

Explore Yellowknife. Walk along the popular Frame Lake Trail with its views of Yellowknife's skyline, including the Armed Forces Northern Headquarters and Legislative Assembly buildings. The trail is a favorite with dog walkers, bicyclists, birdwatchers and commuters. Niven Lake Trail is excellent for bird-watching. Drive or walk down the hill and around the "Rock" where the original town sprang up on Yellowknife Bay and where there are now barges, fishing boats and a large floatplane base; climb steps to the cairn on top of the rock, a tribute to early-day bush pilots who opened up this country in the 1930s and 1940s. The log Wildcat Cafe at the bottom of the rock is open May to September. Drive out to Old Town on Latham Island to see some of the creative solutions builders have found to the problem of building on solid rock.

Frontier R.V. Rentals Ltd. See display ad this section.

The Yellowknife Bookcellar. See display ad this section.

Ingraham Trail Log

NWT HIGHWAY 4

NWT Highway 4 begins in Yellowknife and extends 44 miles/71 km along an almost continuous chain of lakes and streams, ending at Tibbett Lake. In winter, this highway is used as part of the 380-mile/612-km ice road to Lupin gold mine. The winter road also serves Lac de Gras, heart of the diamond rush.

Distance from Yellowknife (Y) is followed by distance from Tibbett Lake (T).

Y 0 T 44.1 (70.9 km) **Junction** of Highways 3 and 4.

Y 1.9 (3.1 km) **T 42.2** (67.9 km) Giant Yellowknife Mines main office. The mine has been operating since 1947.

Y 3.1 (5 km) **T 41** (66 km) Side road leads north 3 miles/5 km to Vee Lake.

Y 4.7 (7.5 km) **T 39.4** (63.4 km) Single-lane bridge across the **Yellowknife River.** Historical sign at north end of bridge about the Ingraham Trail. Picnic area with tables and boat launch. Good fishing for northern pike, lake trout and grayling.

Y 6.1 (9.8 km) **T 38** (61.2 km) Turnoff to south by 2 transmission towers for 7-mile/11-km road to Detah Indian village; no services.

Y 11.9 (19.2 km) **T 32.2** (51.7 km) **Prosperous Lake** picnic area and boat launch to north. Fishing for northern pike, whitefish and lake trout.

Y 14.9 (24 km) **T 29.2** (46.9 km) **Madeline Lake.** Boat launch to north. Fishing for northern pike, whitefish, cisco and yellow perch.

Y 16.4 (26.4 km) **T 27.7** (44.5 km) **Pontoon Lake** picnic area and boat launch to south. Fishing for northern pike, whitefish, cisco and suckers.

Y 17.5 (28.2 km) **T 26.6** (42.7 km) Side road leads north 1 mile/1.6 km to Prelude Lake territorial campground with 45 campsites, 20 picnic sites, boat launch and swimming. Prelude Wildlife Trail is a 1½-hour walk. The trail has 15 interpretive stations showing the adaptations and relationships of wildlife in the North. Boat rentals, cabins and a restaurant located here. ▲

Fishing in **Prelude Lake** for lake trout, grayling, whitefish, cisco, burbot, suckers and northern pike.

Good views of Prelude Lake from the highway next 10 miles/16 km eastbound.

Y 28.6 (46 km) **T 15.5** (24.9 km) Powder Point on Prelude Lake to north; parking area. Boat launch for canoeists doing the route into Hidden Lake Territorial Park, Lower Cameron River, or 4-day trip to Yellowknife River bridge.

Y 30.1 (48.4 km) **T 14** (22.5 km) Cameron River Falls trailhead to north; parking. This 0.6-mile/1-km trail leads to cliffs overlooking Cameron River Falls.

Y 35.4 (57 km) **T 8.7** (13.9 km) Bailey bridge across Cameron River; parking area, picnicking, canoeing, hiking and swimming.

Y 37.9 (61 km) **T 6.2** (9.9 km) **Reid Lake** territorial campground with 50 campsites, 10 picnic sites, kitchen shelter, swimming, hiking trail, boat launch and fishing. Canoe launch point for Upper Cameron River and Jennejohn Lake routes. *CAUTION: Watch for bears.* ▲

Y 44.1 (70.9 km) **T 0** Tibbett Lake. End of road. Launch point for Pensive Lakes canoe route (advanced canoeists only).

Fort Smith Highway Log

NWT HIGHWAY 5

Distance from Highway 2 junction (J) followed by distance from Fort Smith (FT).

J 0 FT 166 (267.2 km) Highway 5 begins its own series of markers giving distances in kilometres.

J 1.3 (2.2 km) **FT 164.7** (265 km) Railroad and auto bridge crosses Hay River.

J 1.5 (2.5 km) **FT 164.5** (264.7 km) Access road leads north 3.7 miles/5.9 km to Hay River reserve.

The first 37.7 miles/60.8 km of Highway 5 are paved. Watch for construction and rough spots in surfacing. There are no services or gas available until Fort Smith.

J 5.4 (8.8 km) **FT 160.6** (258.4 km) Highway crosses Sandy Creek.

J 11 (17.7 km) **FT 155** (249.5 km) Highway maintenance yard to south.

J 17.3 (27.9 km) **FT 148.7** (239.3 km) Birch Creek bridge.

J 23.7 (38.2 km) **FT 142.3** (229 km) Highway crosses Twin Creek.

J 30.3 (48.8 km) **FT 135.7** (218.4 km) Good gravel road leads 1 mile/1.6 km north to **Polar Lake.** Lake is stocked with rainbow; no motorboats allowed. Good bird watching.

J 33.8 (54.4 km) **FT 132.2** (212.7 km) Buffalo River bridge.

J 34.1 (55 km) **FT 131.9** (212.2 km) Turnout to north with litter barrel and map.

J 37.3 (60 km) **FT 128.7** (207.1 km) **Junction** with Highway 6 east to Pine Point and Fort Resolution (see log this section). Highway 5 turns south for Fort Smith (continue with this log). Highway maintenance camp.

J 54 (87 km) **FT 112** (180.2 km) Turnoff for **Sandy Lake,** 8 miles/13 km south; swimming, sandy beach, fishing for northern pike.

J 54.2 (87.2 km) **FT 111.8** (180 km) Pavement ends, gravel begins, southbound.

J 59.6 (96 km) **FT 106.4** (171.2 km) Entrance to Wood Buffalo National Park. Established in 1922 to protect Canada's only remaining herd of wood bison, **WOOD BUFFALO NATIONAL PARK** (a UNESCO world heritage site) is a vast wilderness area of 44,800 square kilometres with the greater portion located in the northeast corner of Alberta. Park headquarters and Visitor Reception Centre are located in Fort Smith and Fort Chipewyan; excellent audio-video presentations, exhibits and visitor information are available. Or write Wood Buffalo National Park, Box 750, Fort Smith, NT X0E 0P0; or phone (867) 872-7900 Fort Smith or (867) 697-3662 Fort Chipewyan.

The wood bison, a slightly larger and darker northern relative of the Plains bison, numbered about 1,500 in the area at the time the park was established, representing the largest free-roaming herd in Canada. Soon after this, more than 6,600 Plains bison were moved from southern Alberta to the park. Today's herd of about 3,500 bison is considered to be mostly hybrids.

Also found within the park are many species of waterfowl and the world's only remaining natural nesting grounds of the endangered whooping crane.

The park is open year-round. Check the schedule of events at the park office.

J 63.8 (102.7 km) **FT 102.2** (164.4 km) Paralleling most of the highway to Fort Smith are hydro transmission power lines carrying power that is generated at the Taltson Dam in the Canadian Shield north of the Slave River to Fort Smith, Pine Point and Fort Resolution .

Much of the flora along this stretch of highway is new growth following the devastating forest fires of 1981. *NOTE: To report a forest fire, call the operator toll free and ask for Zenith 5555.*

J 66 (106.2 km) **FT 100** (160.9 km) Picnic area with tables to north at Angus Fire Tower. The sinkhole seen here is an example of karst topography. Sinkholes are formed when the roofs of caves (formed by underground water dissolving bedrock) collapse.

Buffalo wallow beside highway from here to approximately **Milepost J 98.9.**

J 74 (119.2 km) **FT 92** (148 km) Highway crosses Nyarling River, which runs underground beneath the dry creekbed.

J 74.2 (119.4 km) **FT 91.8** (147.7 km) Turnout to south with litter barrel.

J 98.9 (159.2 km) **FT 67.1** (108 km) Highway maintenance building to north.

J 110.8 (178.4 km) **FT 55.2** (88.8 km) Highway crosses Sass River. Shallow lakes from here south to Preble Creek provide nesting areas for whooping cranes.

J 116.2 (187 km) **FT 49.8** (80.1 km) Highway crosses Preble Creek.

J 121.2 (195 km) **FT 44.8** (72.1 km) Wetlands pull off with litter barrel and interpretive signs.

J 130.5 (210 km) **FT 35.5** (57.1 km) The highway leaves and reenters Wood Buffalo National Park several times southbound.

J 131 (211 km) **FT 34.9** (56.1 km) Little Buffalo River bridge. Day-use picnic area with picturesque waterfall.

J 142.5 (229.4 km) **FT 23.5** (37.8 km) Turnoff for Parsons Lake Road (narrow gravel) which leads south 8 miles/13 km to Salt Plains overlook. Interpretive exhibit and viewing telescope. Springs at the edge of a high escarpment bring salt to the surface and spread it across the huge flat plain; only plants adapted to high salinity can grow here. Fine view of a unique environment. Gravel parking area with tables, firepits and toilets at overlook; hiking trail down to Salt Plains (bring boots). *CAUTION: Parsons Lake Road beyond the overlook may be impassable in wet weather.*

J 144.7 (232.8 km) **FT 21.4** (34.4 km) Turnout to south and gravel stockpile.

J 147.3 (237 km) **FT 18.7** (30.1 km) Pavement begins eastbound into Fort Smith.

J 147.9 (238 km) **FT 18.1** (29.1 km) Salt River bridge.

J 151.6 (244 km) **FT 14.4** (23.2 km) Thebacha (Salt River) private campground and picnic area 10 miles/16 km north via good gravel road. Located on the **Salt River;** 8 sites, toilets, parking, small-boat launch (cruise down to Slave River), and fishing for pike, walleye, inconnu and goldeye. ▲

J 163.4 (263 km) **FT 2.6** (4.2 km) Turnoff to north for Fort Smith airport and Queen Elizabeth Park campground with 19 campsites, 15 picnic sites, water, kitchen shelter, showers and dump station. Short hike from campground to bluff overlooking Rapids of the Drowned on the Slave River; look for pelicans feeding here. ▲

Fort Smith

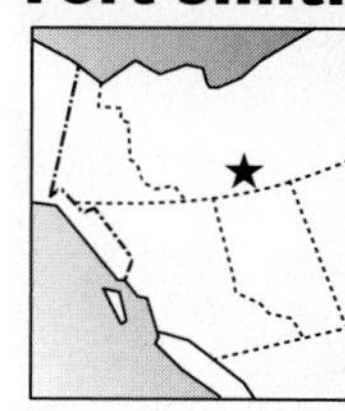

J 166 (267.2 km) **FT 0 Population:** 2,460. **Emergency Services: RCMP,** phone (867) 872-2107. **Fire Department,** phone (867) 872-6111. **Health Centre,** phone (867) 872-2713. **Visitor Information:** Chamber of commerce information centre in Conibear Park, open June to September phone (867) 872-2515. For general information on the area, contact the Economic Development and Tourism Office, Box 390, Fort Smith, NT X0E 0P0.

Climate: Mean high temperature in July 75°F/24°C; mean low 48°F/9°C. **Radio:** 860, 101.9-FM. **Television:** Channels 12 (local) and 5 (CBC) plus 15 cable channels. **Newspaper:** *Slave River Journal.*

Transportation: Air—Canadian Regional Airlines and Northwestern Air Lease provide scheduled service; there are also 3 charter air services here. **Bus**—Available. **Rental cars**—Available.

Private Aircraft: Fort Smith airport; elev. 666 feet/203m; length, 6,000 feet/1,829m; asphalt; fuel 80, 100.

Fort Smith began as a trading post at a favorite campsite of the portagers traveling the 1,600-mile/2575-km water passage from Fort McMurray to the Arctic Ocean. The 4 sets of rapids, named (south to north) Cassette, Pelican, Mountain and the Rapids of the Drowned, separate the Northwest Territories from Alberta. In 1874 Hudson's Bay Co. established a permanent post, and the Roman Catholic mission was transferred here in 1876. By 1911 the settlement had become a major trading post for the area.

There are a 2 hotels, a motel, several bed and breakfast establishments, 2 groceries, a takeout outlet, 4 restaurants, 3 bars, 2 convenience stores, and gas stations with unleaded gas and repair service. Recreation includes a swimming pool, ice arena (open in summer for rollerblading), curling rink and cross-country ski and walking trails.

Wood Buffalo National Park headquarters is located in the Federal Building on McDougal Road, which also houses the post office. The multi-image presentation here is highly recommended. Exhibit area and trip planning assistance available at the visitor reception area. You can drive from Fort Smith to Peace Point via an all-weather gravel road. There are several hiking trails off the road, a picnic area at the Salt River, and a 36-site campground at Pine Lake, 38 miles/61 km south of Fort Smith. There is also a good opportunity for seeing bison on the road between Pine Lake and Peace Point. Contact the park office, phone (867) 872-7900.

Other attractions in Fort Smith include Northern Life Museum, which features a comprehensive view of the area's Native culture and life of the white settlers since the mid-19th century.

Fort Resolution Highway Log

NWT HIGHWAY 6
Distance from junction with Highway 5 (J) is followed by distance from Fort Resolution (FR).

J 0 FR 55.9 (90 km) **Junction** of Highways 5 and 6. The first 14.7 miles/23.7 km of the highway is paved; the rest is gravel to Fort Resolution. Narrow shoulders.

J 13.2 (21.3 km) **FR 42.7** (68.7 km) Main access road north to **PINE POINT;** no services. A mining town, Pine Point was built in the 1960s by Cominco Ltd. The open-pit lead–zinc mine shut down in 1987. The town was once a community of almost 2,000 residents, but most people moved out in 1988, and houses and structures have been moved or destroyed. The Great Slave Lake Railway (now CNR) was constructed in 1961 from Roma, AB, to Pine Point to transport the lead–zinc ore to market.

J 14.6 (23.6 km) **FR 41.3** (66.4 km) Secondary access road to Pine Point.

J 14.7 (23.7 km) **FR 41.2** (66.3 km) Pavement ends, gravel begins, eastbound. Dust-free zone to Fort Resolution.

J 15.8 (25.5 km) **FR 40.1** (64.5 km) Pine Point airport to north, microwave and satellite dish to south.

J 24.6 (39.6 km) **FR 31.3** (50.3 km) Tailing piles from open-pit mining to south.

J 32.3 (52 km) **FR 23.6** (38 km) Turnoff to north for Dawson Landing viewpoint on Great Slave Lake, accessible via a 25-mile/40-km bush road (not recommended in wet weather).

J 36.5 (58.8 km) **FR 19.4** (31.2 km) Turnout to north with litter barrel.

J 37.8 (60.8 km) **FR 18.1** (29.1 km) Glimpse of Great Slave Lake to north.

J 41.4 (66.7 km) **FR 14.5** (23.3 km) Bridge over **Little Buffalo River.** Good fishing for northern pike and walleye.

J 42.4 (68.3 km) **FR 13.5** (21.7 km) Access road to Little Buffalo River Indian village.

J 54.5 (87.7 km) **FR 1.4** (2.2 km) Campground to west; 5 gravel sites, outhouses, tables and firepits. ▲

J 55.9 (90 km) **FR 0 FORT RESOLUTION** (pop. 447), located on the south shore of Great Slave Lake on Resolution Bay. **Emergency Services: RCMP,** phone (867) 394-4111. This historic community grew up around a Hudson's Bay Co. post established in 1786, and was named Fort Resolution in 1821 when the Hudson's Bay Co. and North West Co. united. Missionaries settled in the area in 1852, establishing a school and hospital to serve the largely Chipewyan population. Walking tours through the village may be arranged. The road connecting Fort Resolution with Pine Point was built in the 1960s.

Today's economy is based on trapping, and a logging and sawmill operation. There are a small motel, 2 general stores, a gas station with minor repair service, a post office and cafe. Meals are also available at the community hall.

CAMPBELL HIGHWAY (4)

Connects: Watson Lake, YT, to Klondike Hwy. **Length:** 373 miles
Road Surface: 85% gravel, 15% paved **Season:** Open all year
Major Attraction: Faro Mine

	Carmacks	Dawson City	Faro	Ross River	Watson Lake
Carmacks		225	115	150	375
Dawson City	225		338	373	598
Faro	115	338		32	271
Ross River	150	373	32		239
Watson Lake	375	598	271	239	

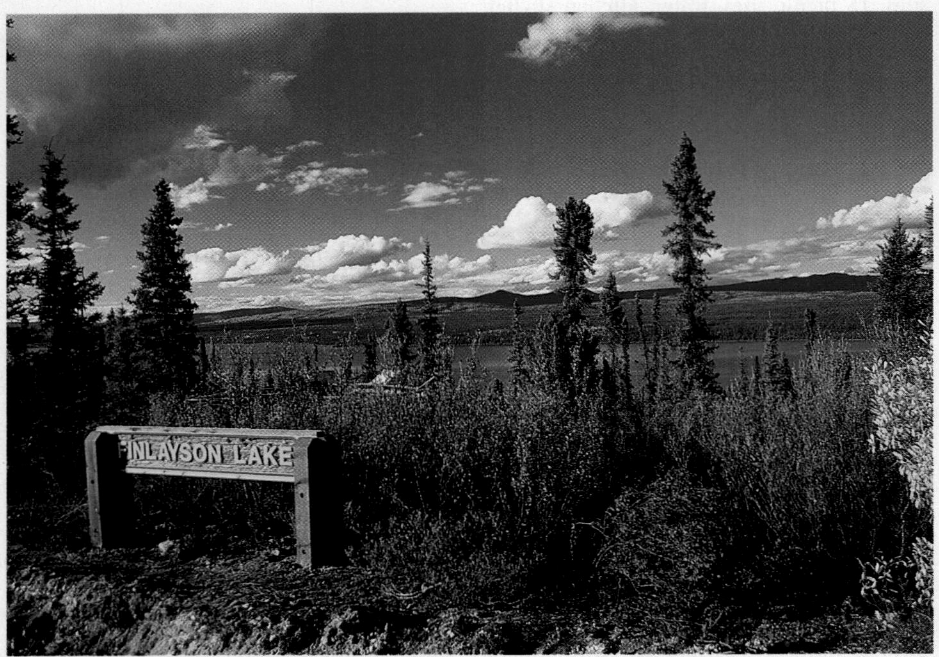

View of Finlayson Lake, Milepost WL 148.1 (*Earl L. Brown, staff*)

Named for Robert Campbell, the first white man to penetrate what is now known as Yukon Territory, this all-weather, mostly gravel road leads 373 miles/600.2 km northwest from the Alaska Highway at Watson Lake, to junction with the Klondike Highway 2 miles/3.2 km north of Carmacks (see the KLONDIKE LOOP section). Gas is available at Watson Lake, Ross River, Faro and Carmacks.

The highway is gravel with the exception of stretches of pavement at Watson Lake, Ross River and the Klondike Highway junction (see map). There is a working mine at Faro; watch for large ore trucks between Faro and Carmacks. Drive with your headlights on at all times.

The Campbell Highway is an alternative route to Dawson City. It is about 20 miles/32 km shorter than driving the Alaska Highway through to Whitehorse, then driving up the Klondike Highway to Dawson City.

The Robert Campbell Highway was completed in 1968 and closely follows sections of the fur trade route established by Robert Campbell. Campbell was a Hudson's Bay Co. trader who was sent into the region in the 1840s to find a route west into the unexplored regions of central Yukon. Traveling from the southeast, he followed the Liard and Frances rivers, building a chain of posts along the way. His major discovery came in 1843, when he reached the Yukon River, which was to become the major transportation route within the Yukon.

Emergency medical services: Phone the RCMP or ambulance in Watson Lake, Ross River or Carmacks. Or phone toll free, Yukon-wide, the RCMP at (867) 667-5555, or the ambulance at (867) 667-3333.

Campbell Highway Log

YUKON HIGHWAY 4
Mileages reflect the location of physical kilometreposts; driving distance may vary from log.
Distance from Watson Lake (WL) is followed by distance from junction with the Klondike Highway just north of Carmacks (J).

WL 0 J 373 (600.2 km) **Junction** of the Campbell Highway with the Alaska Highway at Watson Lake (see description of Watson Lake beginning on page 123 in the ALASKA HIGHWAY section). The famous sign forest is located at this junction. In the parking area off the Campbell Highway (also called Airport Road) is a point of interest sign relating the highway's history. Also located at this junction is the Alaska Highway Interpretive Centre and visitor information.

WL 0.6 (1 km) **J 372.4** (599.3 km) Hospital on right northbound.

WL 4.3 (6.9 km) **J 368.7** (593.3 km) Access road on right northbound to Mount Maichen ski hill.

WL 6.3 (10.1 km) **J 366.7** (590.1 km) Airport Road left to Watson Lake airport.

WL 6.7 (10.8 km) **J 366.3** (589.5 km) Watson Creek. The highway begins to climb to a heavily timbered plateau and then heads north following the east bank of the Frances River. Tamarack is rare in Yukon, but this northern type of larch can be seen along here. Although a member of the pine family, it sheds its needles in the fall.

WL 10.4 (16.7 km) **J 362.6** (583.5 km) MacDonald Creek.

WL 22.5 (36.2 km) **J 350.5** (564.1 km) Tom Creek, named after an Indian trapper whose cabin is at the mouth of the stream.

WL 27.3 (44 km) **J 345.7** (556.3 km) Sa Dena Hes Mine access.

WL 36.1 (58.1 km) **J 336.9** (542.2 km) Frances River bridge. Turnout at north end of bridge; picnic spot. The highway crosses to west bank and follows the river northward. Named by Robert Campbell for the wife of Sir George Simpson, governor of the Hudson's Bay Co. for 40 years, the Frances River is a tributary of the Liard River. Robert Campbell ascended the Liard River to the Frances River and then went on to Frances Lake and the Pelly River. The Frances River was part of Hudson's Bay Co.'s route into central Yukon for many years before being abandoned because of its dangerous rapids and canyons.

WL 47.2 (76 km) **J 325.8** (524.3 km) Lucky Creek.

WL 49.6 (79.8 km) **J 323.4** (520.4 km) Simpson Creek.

WL 51.8 (83.4 km) **J 321.2** (516.9 km) Access road leads west 1 mile/1.6 km to **Simpson Lake** Yukon government campground: 10 campsites, $8 fee, boat launch, dock, swimming beach, playground, kitchen shelter and drinking water (boil water). Excellent fishing for lake trout, arctic grayling and northern pike.

WL 58.5 (94.2 km) **J 314.5** (506.1 km) Large turnout with litter barrels.

WL 58.7 (94.5 km) **J 314.3** (505.8 km) Access road west to Simpson Lake.

WL 68.5 (110.2 km) **J 304.5** (490 km) **Miner's Junction**, junction with Nahanni Range Road (formerly known as Cantung Junction); no services. Nahanni Range Road leads 125 miles/201 km northeast to Tungsten; see NAHANNI RANGE ROAD log on page 232. The road is not maintained and is not recommended for tourist traffic.

WL 70.3 (113.2 km) **J 302.7** (487.1 km) Yukon government Tuchitua River mainte-

CAMPBELL HIGHWAY *Watson Lake, YT, to Junction with Klondike Loop (includes Nahanni Range Road)*

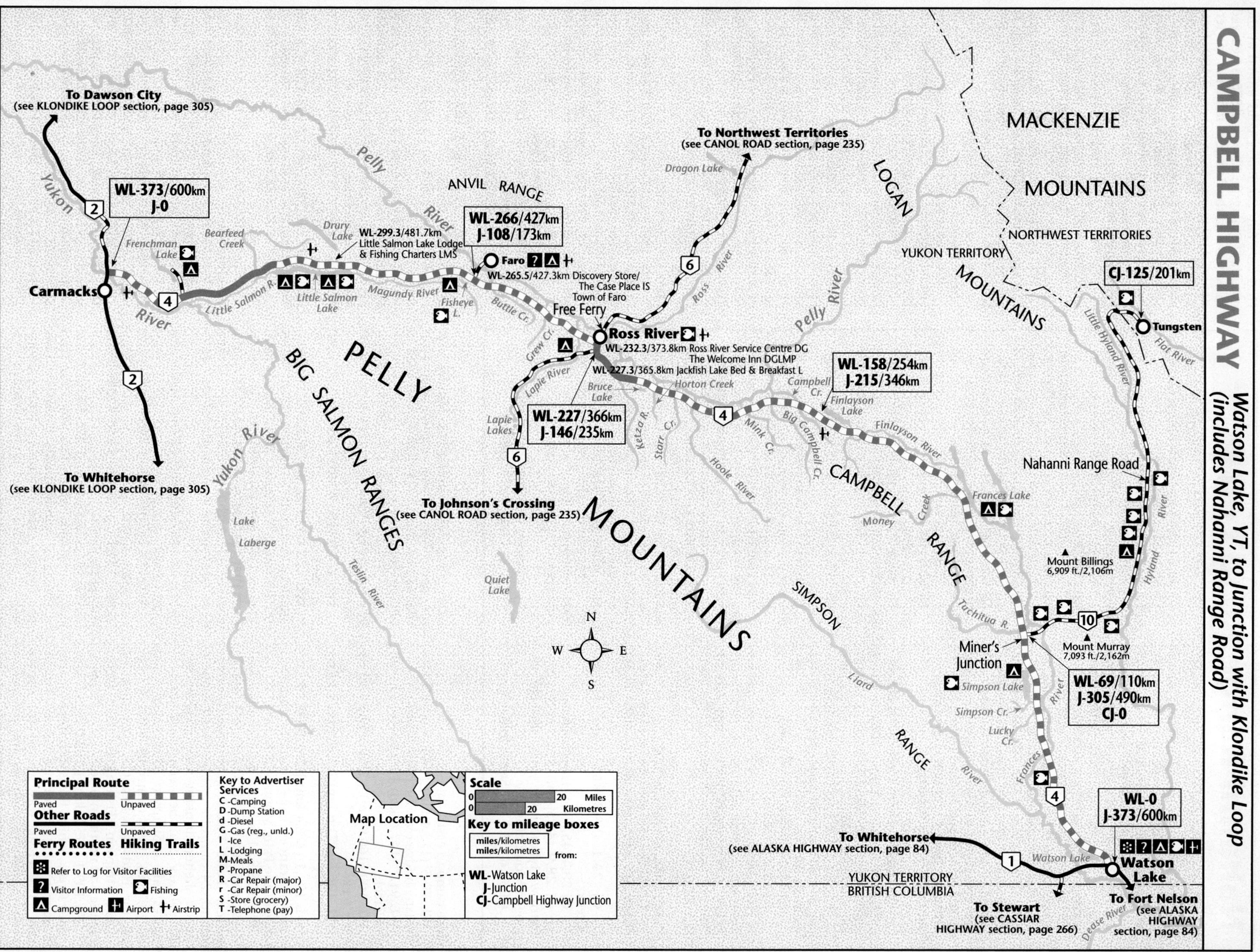

To Dawson City
(see KLONDIKE LOOP section, page 305)
Yukon
WL-373/600km
J-0
Frenchman Lake
Bearfeed Creek
Carmacks
River
Little Salmon R.
Little Salmon Lake
Drury Lake
WL-299.3/481.7km
Little Salmon Lake Lodge
& Fishing Charters LMS
Magundy River
Fisheye L.
Pelly
ANVIL RANGE
River
WL-266/427km
J-108/173km
Faro
WL-265.5/427.3km Discovery Store/
The Case Place IS
Town of Faro
Buttle Cr.
Free Ferry
Ross River
WL-232.3/373.8km Ross River Service Centre DG
The Welcome Inn DGLMP
WL-227.3/365.8km Jackfish Lake Bed & Breakfast L
Grew Cr.
Lapie River
Lapie Lakes
Bruce Lake
WL-227/366km
J-146/235km
To Whitehorse
(see KLONDIKE LOOP section, page 305)
PELLY
BIG SALMON RANGES
Yukon River
Lake Laberge
Teslin River
To Johnson's Crossing
(see CANOL ROAD section, page 235)
MOUNTAINS
Quiet Lake
To Northwest Territories
(see CANOL ROAD section, page 235)
Dragon Lake
Ross River
Pelly River
LOGAN
Horton Creek
Ketza R.
Starr Cr.
Hoole River
Mink Cr.
Big Campbell Cr.
Campbell Cr.
Finlayson Lake
WL-158/254km
J-215/346km
Finlayson River
CAMPBELL
RANGE
Money
Creek
Frances Lake
SIMPSON
RANGE
Liard
River
MACKENZIE
MOUNTAINS
NORTHWEST TERRITORIES
YUKON TERRITORY
MOUNTAINS
CJ-125/201km
Tungsten
Little Hyland River
Flat River
Nahanni Range Road
Hyland River
Mount Billings 6,909 ft./2,106m
Mount Murray 7,093 ft./2,162m
Tuchitua R.
Miner's Junction
Simpson Lake
Simpson Cr.
Lucky Cr.
Frances River
WL-69/110km
J-305/490km
CJ-0
WL-0
J-373/600km
Watson Lake
Watson Lake
To Whitehorse
(see ALASKA HIGHWAY section, page 84)
YUKON TERRITORY
BRITISH COLUMBIA
To Stewart
(see CASSIAR HIGHWAY section, page 266)
To Fort Nelson
(see ALASKA HIGHWAY section, page 84)
Dease River
N
W
E
S
Principal Route
Paved
Unpaved
Other Roads
Paved
Unpaved
Ferry Routes
Hiking Trails
Refer to Log for Visitor Facilities
Visitor Information
Fishing
Campground
Airport
Airstrip
Key to Advertiser Services
C -Camping
D -Dump Station
d -Diesel
G -Gas (reg., unld.)
I -Ice
L -Lodging
M-Meals
P -Propane
R -Car Repair (major)
r -Car Repair (minor)
S -Store (grocery)
T -Telephone (pay)
Map Location
Scale
0 20 Miles
0 20 Kilometres
Key to mileage boxes
miles/kilometres
miles/kilometres
from:
WL-Watson Lake
J-Junction
CJ-Campbell Highway Junction

Nahanni Range Road Log

The Nahanni Range (Tungsten) Road branches off the Campbell Highway at **Milepost WL 68.5** and leads 125 miles/201.2 km northeast to the former mining town of Tungsten, NWT. The road is gravel surfaced with some washouts and soft steep shoulders. *CAUTION: The Yukon government does not recommend this road for tourist travel due to lack of services and maintenance.*

Construction of the Nahanni Range Road was begun in 1961 to provide access to the mining property. The road was completed in 1963 with the bridging of the Frances and Hyland rivers.

Distance from Campbell Highway junction (CJ) is shown.

CJ 0 Junction with Campbell Highway.

CJ 5.1 (8.2 km) **Upper Frances River** bridge; good grayling fishing in stream on southeast side.

CJ 7.4 (11.9 km) Good grayling fishing at confluence of **Sequence Creek** and **Frances River.**

CJ 11.8 (19 km) Queen Creek.

CJ 13.1 (21.1 km) King Creek.

CJ 14.2 (22.8 km) Road passes between Mount Billings to the north (elev. 6,909 feet/2,106m) and Mount Murray to the south (elev. 7,093 feet/2,162m).

CJ 20.3 (32.7 km) Short access road to **Long Lake**, grayling fishing.

CJ 21.5 (34.6 km) Long Lake Creek. There are a few private log cabins along here.

CJ 24.1 (38.8 km) Dolly Varden Creek.

CJ 28.4 (45.7 km) French Creek.

CJ 28.9 (46.5 km) Road enters the narrow Hyland River valley through the Logan Mountains.

CJ 32.6 (52.4 km) South Bridge Creek.

CJ 33.2 (53.4 km) North Bridge Creek.

CJ 38.1 (61.3 km) Jackpine Creek.

CJ 40.6 (65.3 km) **Spruce Creek**, good glides and broken pools upstream for grayling fishing.

CJ 42.8 (68.9 km) Short access road to Hyland River.

CJ 45.8 (73.7 km) **Conglomerate Creek**, scenic spot to picnic. Good grayling fishing near small waterfall.

CJ 48 (77.2 km) Mining road to west.

CJ 52.1 (83.8 km) South Moose Creek.

CJ 52.2 (84 km) Yukon government campground (unmaintained); 10 sites, kitchen shelter, picnic tables. ▲

CJ 52.5 (84.5 km) North Moose Creek.

CJ 62.4 (100.4 km) **Flood Creek**, good grayling fishing.

CJ 68.4 (110.1 km) Hyland River bridge; turnout with litter barrel.

CJ 71 (114.2 km) Emergency airstrip to west.

CJ 75.9 (122.1 km) Ostensibility Creek.

CJ 82 (132 km) **Piggott Creek**, good grayling fishing. Outhouse.

CJ 116.8 (188 km) YT–NWT border.

CJ 125 (201.2 km) **TUNGSTEN**, which was the company town for one of the richest mines in the world and Canada's only tungsten producer, was originally called Cantung (Canada Tungsten Mining Corp. Ltd.). Open-pit mining began here in the early 1960s with the discovery of scheelite in the Flat River area. Scheelite is an ore of tungsten, an oxide used for hardening steel and making white gold. The mine shut down in 1986, and the population of 500 moved out. Only a security staff remains. Hot springs in area.

Return to Milepost WL 68.5 Campbell Highway

nance camp to east.

WL 70.5 (113.4 km) **J 302.5** (486.8 km) One-lane bridge over Tuchitua River.

WL 91.7 (147.6 km) **J 281.3** (452.7 km) Jules Creek.

WL 100 (160.9 km) **J 273** (439.3 km) 99 Mile Creek.

WL 106.6 (171.6 km) **J 266.4** (428.7 km) Caesar Creek.

WL 107.1 (172.4 km) **J 265.9** (427.9 km) View of Frances Lake to east, Campbell Range of the Pelly Mountains to west.

WL 108.9 (175.3 km) **J 264.1** (425 km) Access road east leads 0.6 mile/1 km to **Frances Lake** Yukon government campground: 24 campsites, $8 fee, boat launch, kitchen shelter, drinking water (boil water). The solitary peak between the 2 arms of Frances Lake is Simpson Tower (elev. 5,500 feet/1,676m). It was named by Robert Campbell for Hudson's Bay Co. Governor Sir George Simpson. Fishing for lake trout, grayling and northern pike. ▲

WL 109.1 (175.5 km) **J 263.9** (424.7 km) Money Creek, which flows into the west arm of Frances Lake, one of the Yukon's largest lakes. The creek was named for Anton Money, a mining engineer and prospector who found and mined placer gold in this area between 1929 and 1946. Money later operated "The Village" service station at Mile 442 on the Alaska Highway. He died in 1993, in Santa Barbara, CA.

WL 109.4 (176 km) **J 263.6** (424.2 km) Gravel turnout. View southbound of Frances Lake.

WL 113.8 (183.2 km) **J 259.2** (417.1 km) Dick Creek.

WL 123.8 (199.2 km) **J 249.2** (401 km) Highway descends Finlayson River valley northbound, swinging west away from Frances Lake and following the Finlayson River that may be seen occasionally to the east for about the next 20 miles/32 km. Mountains to the west are part of the Campbell Range.

WL 126.4 (203.5 km) **J 246.6** (396.9 km) Light Creek.

WL 129.1 (207.7 km) **J 243.9** (392.5 km) Van Bibber Creek.

WL 134.1 (215.8 km) **J 238.9** (384.5 km) Wolverine Creek.

WL 147.5 (237.4 km) **J 225.5** (362.9 km) Finlayson Creek, which flows into the river of the same name, drains Finlayson Lake into Frances Lake. Named by Robert Campbell in 1840 for Chief Factor Duncan Finlayson, who later became director of the Hudson's Bay Co. Placer gold mined at the mouth of Finlayson River in 1875 is believed to be some of the first gold mined in the territory. Finlayson Lake (elev. 3,100 feet/945m), on the Continental Divide, separates watersheds of Mackenzie and Yukon rivers.

WL 148.1 (238.4 km) **J 224.9** (361.9 km) Access road north to Finlayson Lake picnic area; litter barrels. To the southwest are the Pelly Mountains.

WL 149 (239.8 km) **J 224** (360.5 km) Turnout with observation platform and information panel on Finlayson caribou herd.

WL 158.1 (254.5 km) **J 214.9** (345.8 km) **Private Aircraft:** Finlayson Lake airstrip to south; elev. 3,300 feet/1,006m; length 2,100 feet/640m; gravel. No services.

WL 163.7 (263.5 km) **J 209.3** (336.8 km) Nancy J. Creek.

WL 164.4 (264.5 km) **J 208.6** (335.7 km) Little Campbell Creek. Robert Campbell followed this creek to the Pelly River in 1840.

WL 170.4 (274.2 km) **J 202.6** (326 km) Bridge over Big Campbell Creek, which flows into Pelly River at Pelly Banks. Robert Campbell named the river and banks after Hudson's Bay Co. Governor Sir John Henry Pelly. Campbell built a trading post here in 1846; never successful, it burned down in 1849. Isaac Taylor and William S. Drury later operated a trading post at Pelly Banks, one of a string of successful posts established by their firm in remote spots throughout the Yukon from 1899 on.

The highway follows the Pelly River for the next 90 miles/145 km.

WL 179 (288.1 km) **J 194** (312.2 km) Mink Creek culvert.

WL 193.9 (312 km) **J 179.1** (288.2 km) Bridge over Hoole Canyon; turnout to north. Confluence of the Hoole and Pelly rivers. Campbell named the Hoole River after his interpreter, Francis Hoole, a half-Iroquois and half-French Canadian employed by the Hudson's Bay Co. Dig out your gold pan—this river once yielded gold.

WL 199.8 (321.6 km) **J 173.2** (278.7 km) Starr Creek culvert.

WL 206.5 (332.3 km) **J 166.5** (267.9 km) Horton Creek.

WL 210.7 (339 km) **J 162.3** (261.2 km) Bruce Lake to south.

WL 211.8 (340.8 km) **J 161.2** (259.4 km) Bruce Creek.

WL 215.4 (346.6 km) **J 157.6** (253.6 km) Private side road leads south 27.3 miles/44 km to Ketza River Project. The first gold bar was poured at Ketza River mine in 1988. The Ketza River hard-rock gold deposit was first discovered in 1947. No visitor facilities.

WL 217.9 (350.7 km) **J 155.1** (249.6 km) Ketza River. St. Cyr Range to southwest.

WL 219.4 (353 km) **J 153.6** (247.2 km) Ketza Creek.

WL 221.4 (356.3 km) **J 151.6** (244 km) Beautiful Creek culvert.

WL 224.8 (361.8 km) **J 148.2** (238.5 km) **Coffee Lake** to south; local swimming hole, picnic tables, trout fishing (stocked).

WL 227.3 (365.8 km) **J 145.7** (234.5 km) **Junction** with South Canol Road (see CANOL ROAD section) which leads south 129 miles/207 km to Johnson's Crossing and the Alaska Highway. Ross River Flying Service; floatplane base on Jackfish Lake here.

Jackfish Lake Bed and Breakfast. See display ad this section.

WL 227.5 (366.1 km) **J 145.5** (234.1 km) Unmaintained side road on right westbound is continuation of Canol Road to Ross River.

Use the main Ross River access road next milepost.

WL 232.3 (373.8 km) **J 140.7** (226.4 km) Access road leads 7 miles/11.2 km to Ross River (description follows). Rest area with toilets on highway just north of this turnoff.

Ross River

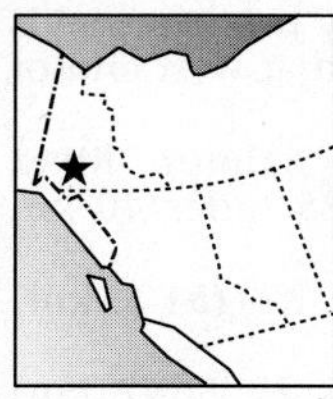

Located on the southwest bank of the Pelly River. **Population:** about 352. **Emergency Services: RCMP**, phone (867) 969-5555. **Hospital**, phone (867) 969-2222. **Radio:** CBC 990, local FM station. **Transportation:** Scheduled air service via Trans North Air.

Private Aircraft: Ross River airstrip; elev. 2,408 feet/734m; length 5,500 feet/1,676m; gravel; fuel 40.

A point of interest sign on the way into Ross River relates that in 1843, Robert Campbell named Ross River for Chief Trader Donald Ross of the Hudson's Bay Co. From 1903, a trading post called Nahanni House (established by Tom Smith and later owned by the Whitehorse firm of Taylor and Drury) located at the confluence of the Ross and Pelly rivers supplied the Indians of the area for nearly 50 years. With the building of the Canol pipeline service road in WWII and the completion of the Robert Campbell Highway in 1968, the community was linked to the rest of the territory by road. Originally situated on the north side of the Pelly River, the town has been in its present location since 1964. Today, Ross River is a supply and communication base for prospectors testing and mining mineral bodies in this region.

Ross River has gas stations with diesel, mechanical and tire repair, grocery stores, 2 motels with dining, and a bed and breakfast. The nearest campground is Lapie Canyon (see **Milepost WL 233.5**). Self-contained RVs may overnight at the gravel parking lot at the end of the pedestrian suspension bridge on the Ross River side.

Ross River is also a jumping-off point for big game hunters and canoeists. There are 2 registered hunting outfitters here. Canoeists traveling the Pelly River can launch just downriver from the ferry crossing. Experienced canoeists recommend camping on the Pelly's many gravel bars and islets to avoid bears, bugs and the danger of accidentally setting tundra fires. The Pelly has many sweepers, sleepers and gravel shallows, some gravel shoals, and extensive channeling. There are 2 sets of rapids between Ross River and the mouth of the Pelly: Fish Hook and Granite Canyon. Water is potable (boil), firewood available and wildlife plentiful. Inquire locally about river conditions before setting out.

Rock hounds check Pelly River gravels for jaspers and the occasional agate.

The suspension footbridge at Ross River leads across the Pelly River to the site of an abandoned Indian village 1 mile/1.6 km upstream at the mouth of the Ross River.

A government ferry crosses the Pelly River daily in summer, from 8 A.M. to noon and 1–5 P.M. Across the river, the North Canol Road leads 144 miles/232 km to Macmillan Pass at the Northwest Territories border. See the CANOL ROAD section for details.

Ross River Service Centre Ltd. See display ad this section.

The Welcome Inn. See display ad this section.

Campbell Highway Log

(continued)

WL 232.3 (373.8 km) **J 140.7** (226.4 km) Access road leads 7 miles/11.2 km to Ross River (see preceding description).

WL 232.5 (374.2 km) **J 140.5** (226.1 km) Rest area with toilets.

WL 233.4 (375.6 km) **J 139.6** (224.6 km) Lapie River bridge crosses deep gorge of Lapie River, which flows into the Pelly River from Lapie Lakes on the South Canol Road. Highway continues to follow the Pelly River and Pelly Mountains.

WL 233.5 (375.8 km) **J 139.5** (224.5 km) Turnoff to left (south) to Lapie Canyon Yukon government campground adjacent Lapie River: short scenic trails, viewpoint, picturesque canyon; kitchen shelters, firewood, group firepit and picnic area; walk-in tent sites, 18 campsites, $8 fee, drinking water (boil water); boat launch. ▲

WL 236.3 (380.3 km) **J 136.7** (220 km) Danger Creek. In 1905, naturalist Charles Sheldon named this creek after his horse, Danger.

WL 239.9 (386 km) **J 133.1** (214.2 km) Panoramic view of the Pelly River valley just ahead westbound.

WL 243.6 (392 km) **J 129.4** (208.2 km) *CAUTION: Hill and bad corner.*

WL 244.2 (393 km) **J 128.8** (207.3 km) Highway narrows over Grew Creek, no guide rails. This creek was named for Hudson's Bay Co. trader Jim Grew, who trapped this area for many years before his death in 1906.

WL 251 (404 km) **J 122** (196.3 km) Turnout to north.

WL 260.4 (419 km) **J 112.6** (181.2 km) Buttle Creek, named for Roy Buttle, a trapper, prospector and trader who lived here in the early 1900s and at one time owned a trading post at Ross River.

WL 264.7 (426 km) **J 108.3** (174.3 km) Across the wide Pelly River valley to the north is a view of the mining community of Faro.

WL 265.5 (427.3 km) **J 107.5** (173 km) Access road on right westbound leads 5.6 miles/9 km to Faro. Point of interest sign about Faro at intersection. Rest area with toilets and litter barrels to south just west of this junction.

Faro

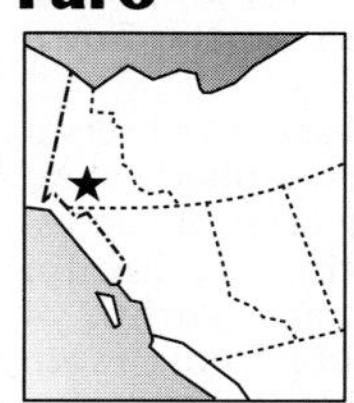

Located in east-central Yukon Territory, 220 road miles/354 km from Whitehorse. **Population:** 1,261. **Emergency Services: RCMP**, phone (867) 994-5555. **Fire Department**, phone (867) 994-2222. **Hospital**, phone (867) 994-4444.

Visitor Information: Centre at the municipal-operated John Connelly RV Park, open June through August. For information on wildlife viewing, hiking, biking, horseback trails, town facilities and services, special events and individual businesses, phone (867) 994-2288 (seasonal). Or contact the Faro Town Office, phone (867) 994-3154; e-mail townof@yknet.yk.ca. The Campbell Region Interpretive Tourist Information Centre, located directly across from John Connelly RV Park, has historical displays on the Yukon centennial; phone (867) 994-2728.

Climate: Temperatures range from -51°F/-46°C in winter to a summer maximum of 84°F/29°C. **Radio:** CBC-FM 105.1, CKRW-FM 98.7. **Television:** CBC and 7 cable channels. **Transportation:** Scheduled air service to Whitehorse and Ross River via Alcan Air. Floatplane service from Horizons North.

Private Aircraft: Faro airstrip; 1.5 miles/2.4 km south; elev. 2,351 feet/717m; length 3,000 feet/914m; gravel; fuel 100.

The town of Faro lies on a series of benches or terraces on the northern escarpment of the Tintina Trench. Many places in town offer a commanding view of the Pelly River.

There are 3 restaurants in town: the Faro Hotel, Redmond's (known locally as Cranky Frank's) and Sally's Road House. Both Redmond's and Sally's Road House offer motel accommodations. RV camping and dump station at municipal and private campgrounds. The service station has gas, diesel, propane and full garage services. The area offers excellent fly-in fishing. Other services in town include a large grocery, liquor store, video rental, post office, public library, art

gallery, movie theatre and recreation centre with indoor swimming pool, squash courts and outdoor tennis courts. Catholic and Protestant Sunday services are available. ▲

Faro is named after the card game. The Cyprus Anvil mining and milling operation began producing lead–silver and zinc concentrates in 1969; operation was shut down in 1982 because of depressed metal prices

and a poor economic market. Mothballing of the mine began in the spring of 1985, but the mine was reopened in 1986 by Curragh Resources Inc. It closed down again in 1993 and was purchased in June 1994 by Anvil Range Mining Corp. Reopened in 1995, the Faro mine is one of the western world's largest producers of lead and zinc concentrates. Tours are available, contact John Connelly RV Park (867/994-2288) or the Town Office (867/994-3154).

Attractions include an all-season observation cabin and isolated photographer's blind for wildlife viewing. Viewing areas are accessible via a gravel road skirting the Fannin sheep grazing area and are within 4 miles/6.4 km of town. A public boat ramp and canoe rentals are available for exploring

the Pelly River.

Discovery Store/The Case Place. See display ad this section.

Town of Faro. See display ad this section.

Campbell Highway Log

(continued)

WL 268.4 (432 km) **J 104.6** (168.3 km) Johnson Lake Yukon government campground; 15 sites (7 pull-throughs), $8 fee, toilets, water pump, firewood, picnic shelter, boat launch. ▲

Westbound, the Campbell Highway follows the Magundy River. There are several turnouts.

WL 285.8 (460 km) **J 87.2** (140.3 km) Magundy River airstrip to north; summer use only. Watch for livestock.

WL 288.1 (463.7 km) **J 84.9** (136.6 km) First glimpse of 22-mile-/35-km-long Little Salmon Lake westbound.

WL 299.3 (481.7 km) **J 73.7** (118.6 km) East end of **Little Salmon Lake.** Highway follows north shore. Lodge with meals, groceries, fishing licenses, guided fishing charters and boat rentals. Fishing for northern pike, grayling, lake trout.

Little Salmon Lake Lodge & Fishing Charters. Featuring home-cooked meals and bakery items, licensed dining, off sales, gifts and groceries. (Emergency fuel available.) Open year-round. Guided fishing charters and boat rentals, half- and full-day tours on beautiful Little Salmon Lake. Fish for northern pike, lake trout and arctic grayling. Complete fishing, meals and accommodation packages available. Contact Little Salmon Lake Lodge & Fishing Charters, General Delivery, Faro, YT Y0B 1K0. (Mobile radio 2M5172, on the Salmon Channel.) [ADVERTISEMENT]

WL 300.1 (483 km) **J 72.9** (117.3 km) Short access road south to Drury Creek Yukon government campground, situated on the creek at the east end of **Little Salmon Lake:** boat launch, fish filleting table, kitchen shelter, group firepit, 6 campsites, $8 fee, drinking water. Good fishing for northern pike, grayling, whitefish, lake trout 2 to 5 lbs., June 15 through July. ▲

WL 300.4 (483.5 km) **J 72.6** (116.8 km) Turnout at east end Drury Creek bridge. Yukon government maintenance camp to north.

WL 308.2 (496 km) **J 64.8** (104.3 km) Turnout overlooking lake.

WL 311.3 (501 km) **J 61.7** (99.3 km) *CAUTION: Slow down for curves.* Highway follows lakeshore; no guide rails. Turnouts overlooking Little Salmon Lake next 8.5 miles/13.6 km westbound.

WL 316.9 (510 km) **J 56.1** (90.3 km) **Private Aircraft**: Little Salmon airstrip; elev. 2,200 feet/671m; length 1,800 feet/549m; sand and silt.

WL 321.4 (517.3 km) **J 51.6** (83 km) Steep, narrow, winding road south leads to Yukon government **Little Salmon Lake** campground; boat launch, fishing, 15 campsites, $8 fee, drinking water, picnic tables, outhouses, firepits and kitchen shelter. ▲

WL 324.7 (522.6 km) **J 48.3** (77.7 km) Bearfeed Creek, a tributary of Little Salmon River, named because of the abundance of bears attracted to the berry patches in this area. Access to creek to north at west end of bridge.

Highway follows Little Salmon River (seen to south) for about 25 miles/40 km westbound.

WL 341 (548.7 km) **J 32** (51.5 km) *CAUTION: Slow down for hill.*

WL 343.8 (553.2 km) **J 29.2** (47 km) Picnic spot on Little Salmon River, which flows into the Yukon River.

WL 347.3 (559 km) **J 25.7** (41.4 km) Access road leads 4.9 miles/8 km north to **Frenchman Lake** Yukon government campground (10 sites), 5.6 miles/9 km to photo viewpoint of lake, and 9.3 miles/15 km to Nunatak Yukon government campground (10 sites, $8 fee). Access road narrows and surface deteriorates beyond Frenchman Lake Campground. South end of this 12-mile/19-km-long lake offers good fishing for trout, pike and grayling. ▲

WL 349.5 (562.4 km) **J 23.5** (37.8 km) Turnoff to south for 0.9-mile/1.4-km gravel road to Little Salmon Indian village near confluence of Little Salmon River and Yukon River. There are some inhabited cabins in the area and some subsistence fishing. Private lands, no trespassing.

WL 356.2 (573.2 km) **J 16.8** (27 km) Turnout with point of interest sign overlooking Eagles Nest Bluff (formerly called Eagle Rock), well-known marker for river travelers. One of the worst steamboat disasters on the Yukon River occurred near here when the paddle-wheeler *Columbian* blew up and burned after a crew member accidentally fired a shot into a cargo of gunpowder. The accident, in which 6 men died, took place Sept. 25, 1906.

WL 356.7 (574 km) **J 16.3** (26.2 km) View of the Yukon River. At this point Whitehorse is about 160 miles/258 km upstream and Dawson City is about 300 miles/483 km downriver.

WL 360.4 (580 km) **J 12.6** (20.3 km) Northern Canada Power Commission's transmission poles and lines can be seen along highway. Power is transmitted from Aishihik dam site via Whitehorse dam and on to Cyprus Anvil mine and Faro. Orange balls mark lines where they cross river as a hazard to aircraft.

WL 370 (595.4 km) **J 3** (4.8 km) **Private Aircraft**: Carmacks airstrip to south; elev. 1,770 feet/539m; length 5,200 feet/1,585m; gravel.

WL 370.7 (596.5 km) **J 2.3** (3.7 km) Tantalus Butte coal mine on hill to north overlooking junction of Campbell and Klondike highways. The butte was named by U.S. Army Lt. Frederick Schwatka in 1883 because of the tantalizing appearance of the formation around many bends of the river before it is reached.

WL 373 (600.2 km) **J 0 Junction** with the Klondike Highway (Yukon Highway 2) at **Milepost J 104.4.** Turn south on the Klondike Highway for Carmacks (2 miles/3.2 km) and Whitehorse (115 miles/184 km); turn north for Dawson City (223 miles/357 km). Turn to page 309 the KLONDIKE LOOP section for highway log.

CANOL ROAD ⑥

Connects: Alaska Hwy. to NWT Border **Length:** 286 miles
Road Surface: Gravel **Season:** Closed in winter
Highest Summit: Big Salmon Summit 4,000 feet
Major Attraction: Canol Heritage Trail

(See map, page 236)

	Alaska Hwy. Jct.	Ross River	NWT Border
Alaska Hwy. Jct.		142	286
Ross River	142		144
NWT Border	286	144	

South Canol Road winds its way north to Ross River. *(Earl L. Brown, staff)*

The 513-mile-/825-km-long Canol Road (Yukon Highway 6) was built to provide access to oil fields at Norman Wells, NWT, on the Mackenzie River. Conceived by the U.S. War Dept. to help fuel Alaska and protect it from a Japanese invasion, the Canol (Canadian Oil) Road and a 4-inch-diameter pipeline were constructed from Norman Wells, NWT, through Macmillan Pass, past Ross River, to Johnson's Crossing on the Alaska Highway. From there the pipeline carried oil to a refinery at Whitehorse.

Begun in 1942 and completed in 1944, the Canol Project included the road, pipeline, a telephone line, the refinery, airfields, pumping stations, tank farms, wells and camps. Only about 1 million barrels of oil were pumped to Whitehorse before the war ended in 1945 and the $134 million Canol Project was abandoned. (Today, Norman Wells, pop. 757, is still a major supplier of oil with a pipeline to Zama, AB, built in 1985.) The Canol Road was declared a National Historic Site in 1990.

Since 1958, the Canol Road between Johnson's Crossing on the Alaska Highway and Ross River on the Campbell Highway (referred to as the South Canol Road) and between Ross River and the YT–NWT border (referred to as the North Canol Road) has been rebuilt and is open to summer traffic. It is maintained to minimum standards.

The 136.8-mile/220.2-km South Canol Road is a narrow winding road which crests the Big Salmon Range and threads its way above Lapie Canyon via a difficult but scenic stretch of road. Reconstruction on the South Canol has replaced many old bridges with culverts, but there are still a few 1-lane wooden bridges. Driving time is about 4 hours one way. Watch for steep hills and bad corners. There are no facilities along the South Canol Road, and it is definitely not recommended for large RVs or trailers. Not recommended for any size vehicle in wet weather. Inquiries on current road conditions should be made locally or with the Yukon Dept. of Highways in Whitehorse (867/667-8215) before driving this road.

The 144.2-mile/232-km North Canol Road is also a narrow, winding road which some motorists have compared to a roller coaster. All bridges on the North Canol are 1-lane, and the road surface can be very slippery when wet. Not recommended during wet weather and not recommended for large RVs or trailers. If mining is under way along the North Canol, watch for large transport trucks. *NOTE: Drive with headlights on at all times!*

Our log of the North Canol ends at the YT–NWT border, where vehicles may turn around. Road washouts prohibit travel beyond this point. From the border to Norman Wells it is 230 miles/372 km of unusable road that has been designated the Canol Heritage Trail by the NWT government. Northwest Territories Tourism recommends contacting the Norman Wells Historical Centre (phone 867/587-2415, fax 867/587-2469) for current description of trail conditions and recommended precautions.

WARNING: The only facilities on the Canol Road are at Ross River and at Johnson's Crossing on the Alaska Highway.

Emergency medical services: In Ross River, phone (867) 969-2222; or phone the RCMP, (867) 969-5555, or (867) 667-5555.

South Canol Road Log

YUKON HIGHWAY 6

Kilometre figures in the log from the Alaska Highway junction reflect the location of physical kilometreposts when they occur. **Distance from the junction with the Alaska Highway (J) is followed by distance from the Campbell Highway junction (C).**

J 0 C 136.8 (220.2 km) **Junction** of the Canol Road (Yukon Highway 6) with the Alaska Highway. Food, gas and camping at Johnson's Crossing at the southwest end of the Teslin River bridge, 0.7 mile/1.1 km from Canol Road turnoff.

J 0.2 (0.3 km) **C 136.6** (219.8 km) Information panel on the history and construction of Canol Road. A short, dirt road (on left, northbound) leads to an auto "boneyard" that includes several WWII Canol Project trucks (all have been significantly cannibalized). Limited turnaround area, not suitable for trailers. Not recommended for any vehicle in wet weather.

J 3.9 (6.2 km) **C 132.9** (213.8 km) Fourmile Creek. Road begins ascent across the Big Salmon Range to the summit (elev. about 4,000 feet/1,219m). Snow possible at summit early October to late spring.

J 6.2 (10 km) **C 130.6** (210.1 km) Beaver Creek.

J 13.9 (22.4 km) **C 122.9** (197.8 km) Moose Creek. Small gravel turnout with litter barrels.

J 17.2 (27.6 km) **C 119.6** (192.4 km) Seventeenmile Creek.

J 19.4 (31.2 km) **C 117.4** (188.9 km) Murphy Creek.

J 19.8 (32 km) **C 117** (188.3 km) Pelly Mountains can be seen in distance northbound.

J 27 (43.4 km) **C 109.8** (176.7 km) One-lane wooden bridge over Evelyn Creek.

J 28.7 (46.2 km) **C 108.1** (174 km) Two-lane bridge over Sidney Creek.

CANOL ROAD *Alaska Highway Junction, YT, to NWT Border*

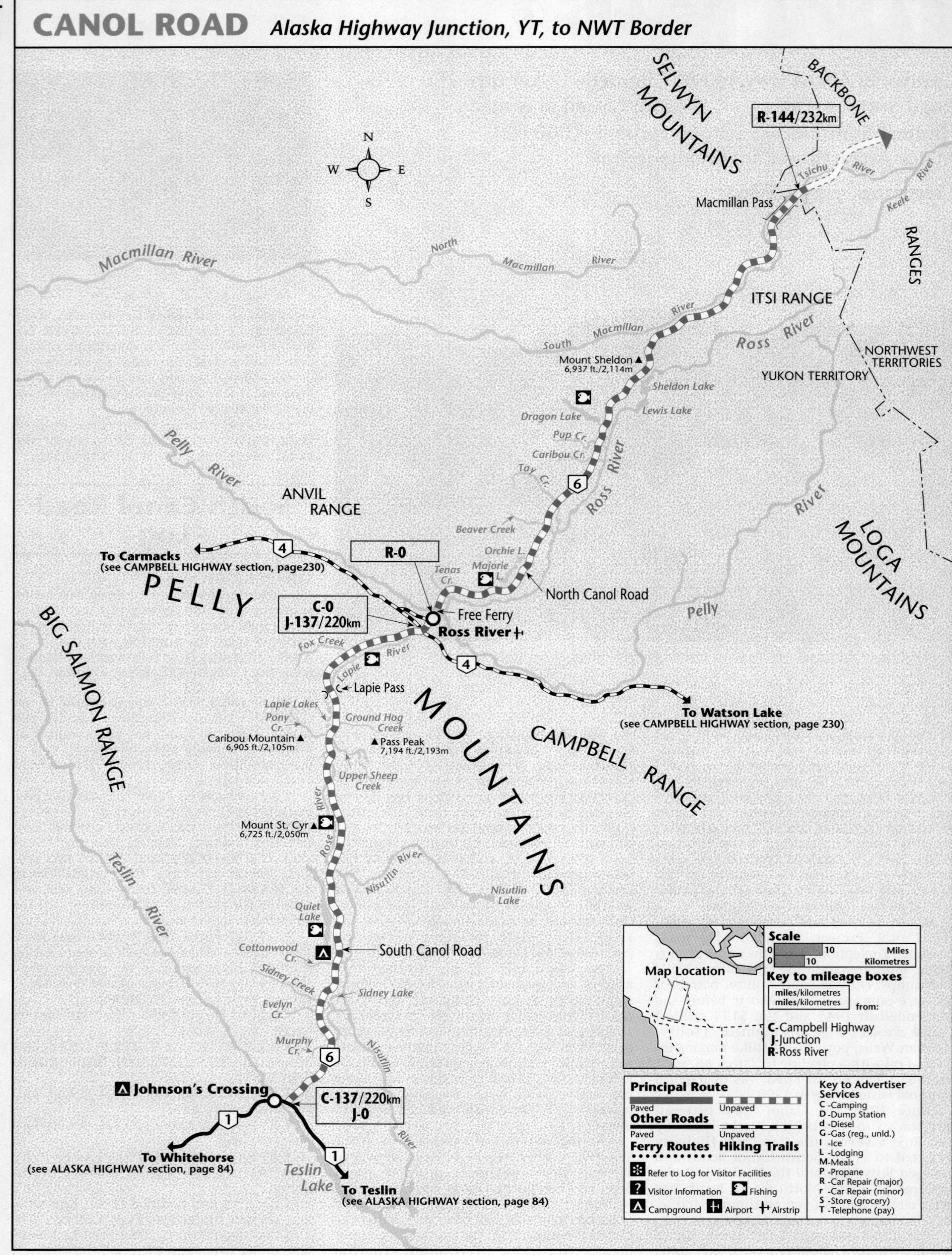

SELWYN MOUNTAINS
BACKBONE
R-144/232km
Tsichu River
Keele River
RANGES
Macmillan Pass
Macmillan River
North Macmillan River
South Macmillan River
ITSI RANGE
Ross River
NORTHWEST TERRITORIES
YUKON TERRITORY
Mount Sheldon
6,937 ft./2,114m
Sheldon Lake
Lewis Lake
Dragon Lake
Pup Cr.
Caribou Cr.
Tay Cr.
Pelly River
ANVIL RANGE
Beaver Creek
Orchie L.
Majorie L.
Tenas Cr.
LOGA MOUNTAINS
To Carmacks
(see CAMPBELL HIGHWAY section, page230)
R-0
North Canol Road
PELLY
C-0
J-137/220km
Free Ferry
Ross River
Pelly
BIG SALMON RANGE
Fox Creek
Lapie River
Lapie Pass
Lapie Lakes
Pony Cr.
Ground Hog Creek
MOUNTAINS
CAMPBELL RANGE
To Watson Lake
(see CAMPBELL HIGHWAY section, page 230)
Caribou Mountain
6,905 ft./2,105m
Pass Peak
7,194 ft./2,193m
Upper Sheep Creek
Mount St. Cyr
6,725 ft./2,050m
Rose River
Teslin River
Nisutlin River
Nisutlin Lake
Quiet Lake
Cottonwood Cr.
South Canol Road
Sidney Creek
Sidney Lake
Evelyn Cr.
Murphy Cr.
Johnson's Crossing
C-137/220km
J-0
To Whitehorse
(see ALASKA HIGHWAY section, page 84)
Teslin Lake
To Teslin
(see ALASKA HIGHWAY section, page 84)
Map Location
Scale
0 10 Miles
0 10 Kilometres
Key to mileage boxes
miles/kilometres
miles/kilometres
from:
C-Campbell Highway
J-Junction
R-Ross River
Principal Route
Paved
Unpaved
Other Roads
Paved
Unpaved
Ferry Routes
Hiking Trails
Refer to Log for Visitor Facilities
Visitor Information
Fishing
Campground
Airport
Airstrip
Key to Advertiser Services
C -Camping
D -Dump Station
d -Diesel
G -Gas (reg., unld.)
I -Ice
L -Lodging
M -Meals
P -Propane
R -Car Repair (major)
r -Car Repair (minor)
S -Store (grocery)
T -Telephone (pay)

J 30.6 (49.2 km) **C 106.2** (170.9 km) Access road on right northbound leads to Sidney Lake. Nice little lake and good place to camp.

From here northbound the South Canol follows the Nisutlin River, which is to the east and can be seen from the road the next 30 miles/48 km until the road crosses the Rose River beyond Quiet Lake.

J 30.9 (49.7 km) **C 105.9** (170.4 km) Turnout with litter barrel to east.

J 36.7 (59 km) **C 100.1** (161.1 km) Coyote Creek, culverts.

J 39.1 (62.9 km) **C 97.7** (157.2 km) Good view of Pelly Mountains ahead. Road crosses Cottonwood Creek.

J 42 (67.6 km) **C 94.8** (152.5 km) Access road on right northbound leads 0.4 mile/0.6 km to Nisutlin River. Good place to camp with tables and outhouse. ▲

J 47.8 (76.9 km) **C 89** (143.2 km) Quiet Lake Yukon government campground; 20 sites, $8 fee, boat launch, picnic tables, kitchen shelter, firewood. Watch for steep hills northbound to Quiet Lake. ▲

J 54.7 (88 km) **C 82.1** (132.1 km) Lake Creek. Road now follows **Quiet Lake** to west; good fishing for lake trout, northern pike and arctic grayling.

J 56 (90.1 km) **C 80.8** (130 km) Turnout with litter barrels and point of interest sign overlooking Quiet Lake. This is the largest of 3 lakes that form the headwaters of the Big Salmon River system. The 17-mile-/28-km-long lake was named in 1887 by John McCormack, 1 of 4 miners who prospected the Big Salmon River from its mouth on the Yukon River to its source. Although they did find some gold, the river and lakes have become better known for their good fishing and fine scenery. Until the completion of the South Canol Road in the 1940s, this area was reached mainly by boating and portaging hundreds of miles up the Teslin and Nisutlin rivers.

J 61.2 (98.5 km) **C 75.6** (121.6 km) Turnoff on left northbound (west) for **Quiet Lake**, day-use area with picnic sites, water, boat launch and fishing. Entry point for canoeists on the Big Salmon River.

J 61.5 (99 km) **C 75.3** (121.2 km) Yukon government Quiet Lake maintenance camp on left northbound. A vintage Canol Project dump truck and pull grader is on display in front of the camp.

J 62.6 (100.7 km) **C 74.2** (119.4 km) Distance marker indicates Ross River 126 km.

J 63.7 (102 km) **C 73.1** (117.6 km) Steep hill and panoramic view of mountains and valley.

J 65.5 (105.4 km) **C 71.3** (114.7 km) One-lane Bailey bridge across Rose River No. 1. The road now follows the valley of the Rose River into Lapie Pass northbound. According to R.C. Coutts in "Yukon Places and Names," Oliver Rose prospected extensively in this area in the early 1900s. He came to the Yukon from Quebec, and was known as a hard-working, solitary and respected man.

J 70.4 (113.3 km) **C 66.4** (106.8 km) Canol Creek culvert.

J 71.9 (115.7 km) **C 64.9** (104.4 km) Deer Creek.

J 75.7 (121.8 km) **C 61.1** (98.3 km) Gravel Creek culvert.

J 81.1 (130 km) **C 55.7** (89.6 km) Road crosses creek (name unknown) in culvert.

J 83.7 (134 km) **C 53.1** (85.4 km) Dodge Creek culvert.

J 87.1 (140 km) **C 49.7** (80 km) Rose River No. 2 culvert.

J 89.7 (144.3 km) **C 47.1** (75.8 km) Rose River No. 3 culverts.

J 91.5 (147.2 km) **C 45.3** (72.9 km) Rose River No. 4 culverts.

J 93.8 (151 km) **C 43** (69.2 km) Rose River No. 5 culverts.

J 94.1 (151.4 km) **C 42.7** (68.7 km) Distance marker indicates Ross River 76 km.

J 95.1 (153 km) **C 41.7** (67.1 km) Upper Sheep Creek joins the Rose River here. To the east is Pass Peak (elev. 7,194 feet/2,193m).

J 96.4 (155.1 km) **C 40.4** (65 km) Rose River No. 6.

J 97.1 (156.2 km) **C 39.7** (63.9 km) Rose Lake to east.

J 97.5 (156.9 km) **C 39.3** (63.2 km) Pony Creek. Caribou Mountain (elev. 6,905 feet/2,105m) to west.

J 101.1 (162.7 km) **C 35.7** (57.4 km) Lakes to west are part of Lapie Lakes chain, headwaters of the Lapie River. These features were named by Dr. George M. Dawson of the Geological Survey of Canada in 1887 for Lapie, an Iroquois Indian companion and canoeman of Robert Campbell, who was the first to explore the Pelly River area in 1843 for the Hudson's Bay Co.

A short dirt road provides access to the lake shore. Watch for grazing moose. Unmaintained camping area and boat launch. ▲

J 101.2 (162.8 km) **C 35.6** (57.3 km) Ground Hog Creek.

J 102.5 (165 km) **C 34.3** (55.2 km) Access road on left northbound leads west a short distance to Lapie Lakes. Good place to camp.

J 107.4 (172.8 km) **C 29.4** (47.3 km) Lapie River No. 1 culverts. Ponds reported good for grayling fishing. Watch for horses on the road.

J 107.5 (173 km) **C 29.3** (47.1 km) Ahead northbound is Barite Mountain (elev. about 6,500 feet/1,981m).

J 110 (177 km) **C 26.8** (43.1 km) Gold Creek.

J 111.4 (179.2 km) **C 25.4** (40.8 km) Bacon Creek.

J 113.4 (182.5 km) **C 23.4** (37.6 km) Boulder Creek.

J 115.6 (186 km) **C 21.2** (34.1 km) Road runs to the east side of Barite Mountain.

J 120.2 (193.4 km) **C 16.6** (26.7 km) Fox Creek culverts.

J 120.7 (194.2 km) **C 16.1** (25.9 km) The road follows the Lapie River Canyon for about the next 11 miles/18 km, climbing to an elevation of about 500 feet/152m above the river. Narrow road, watch for rocks.

J 123.3 (198.4 km) **C 13.5** (21.7 km) Kilometrepost 200. Distance marker indicates Ross River 26 km. Lapie River runs to right side of road northbound.

J 124.7 (200.6 km) **C 12.1** (19.4 km) Glacier Creek.

J 126.3 (203.2 km) **C 10.5** (16.9 km) Turnouts on right side of road northbound overlooking Lapie River Canyon.

J 132.3 (212.9 km) **C 4.5** (7.2 km) Narrow 1-lane bridge over Lapie River No. 2. Point of interest sign on north end of bridge about the Lapie River Canyon. Approximately 100 million years ago, flat horizontal layers of rock were buried several kilometres below the surface of the earth. Movement by rigid plates of the earth's crust subjected the rock to massive compression and strain, and it was deformed into folds. Over millions of years, the rocks rose, exposing the folds in the canyon wall.

J 133 (214 km) **C 3.8** (6.1 km) Erosional features called hoodoos can be seen in the clay banks rising above the road.

J 133.3 (214.5 km) **C 3.5** (5.6 km) Ash layer can be seen in clay bank on right side of road.

J 135.6 (218.2 km) **C 1.2** (1.9 km) Jackfish Lake, below on left northbound, is used for docking floatplanes.

J 136.8 (220 km) **C 0 Junction** of South Canol Road with the Campbell Highway. Approximately straight ahead northbound, across the Campbell Highway, a poorly maintained section of the Canol Road continues to Ross River. Motorists bound for Ross River or the North Canol Road are advised to turn left (west) on the Campbell Highway from the South Canol and drive about 5 miles/8 km to the main Ross River access road (see map).

North Canol Road Log

The North Canol Road leads 144.2 miles/232 km to the NWT border. Physical kilometreposts along the North Canol Road reflect distance from the Alaska Highway junction. *WARNING: There are no services along this road.*

Distance from Ross River (R) is shown.

R 0 ROSS RIVER (see page 233 for description). Yukon government Ross River ferry (free) crosses the Pelly River. Ferry operates from 8 A.M. to noon and 1–5 P.M. daily from late May to mid-October. Those who

miss the last ferry crossing of the day may leave their vehicles on the opposite side of the river and use the footbridge to walk into Ross River; vehicles can be brought over in the morning.

R 0.4 (0.6 km) Stockpile to west is barite from the Yukon Barite Mine.

R 0.6 (1 km) Road to east leads to original site of Ross River and Indian village.

R 0.9 (1.4 km) Second access road east to old Ross River and Indian village. Canol Road follows the Ross River.

R 2.1 (3.4 km) *CAUTION: Slide area, watch for falling rocks.*

R 4.7 (7.6 km) Raspberry patch. Good pickings.

R 6.8 (10.9 km) One-lane bridge over Tenas Creek.

R 10.6 (17 km) Gravel pit to west.

R 17 (27.3 km) Deep Creek.

R 20.9 (33.6 km) **Marjorie Creek.** Locals report good grayling fishing.

R 21 (33.8 km) Access road to west leads to Marjorie Lake. Access road not recommended for large RVs.

R 21.7 (34.9 km) Marjorie Lake to west.

R 27 (43.4 km) Unnamed lake to east.

R 28.1 (45.2 km) Boat launch on Orchie Lake to west.

R 29.8 (48 km) Distance marker indicates NWT border 195 km, Ross River 50 km.

R 31.9 (51.3 km) One-lane bridge over Gravel Creek. The next 15 miles/24 km are excellent moose country.

R 33.4 (53.7 km) One-lane bridge over Flat Creek.

R 37 (59.5 km) One-lane bridge over Beaver Creek.

R 41.8 (67.2 km) One-lane bridge over 180 Mile Creek.

R 43.9 (70.6 km) One-lane bridge over Tay Creek.

R 46.3 (74.5 km) One-lane bridge over Blue Creek.

R 48.1 (77.4 km) Kilometrepost 306. Flood Creek culvert.

R 57.6 (92.7 km) Clifford's Slough to the east.

R 58.6 (94.3 km) Steep hill to 1-lane bridge over Caribou Creek.

R 61.1 (98.3 km) Distance marker indicates NWT border 145 km, Ross River 100 km.

R 61.8 (99.4 km) **B 82.4** (132.6 km) One-lane bridge over Pup Creek.

R 64.8 (104.3 km) Turnout to west. Steep hill.

R 65.1 (104.7 km) Turnout to **Dragon Lake**; overnight parking, litter barrels. Locals report that early spring is an excellent time for pike and trout in the inlet. Rock hounds check roadsides and borrow pits for colorful chert, which can be worked into jewelry.

R 65.4 (105.2 km) Kilometrepost 334. Large, level gravel turnout to west overlooking Dragon Lake; boat launch.

R 69.6 (112 km) Wreckage of Twin Pioneer aircraft to west. WWII remnants can be found in this area.

R 69.9 (112.5 km) Road to Twin Creek.

R 70.8 (113.9 km) Airstrip.

R 71 (114.2 km) One-lane bridge over Twin Creek No. 1. Yukon government maintenance camp.

R 71.1 (114.4 km) One-lane bridge over Twin Creek No. 2. Good views of Mount Sheldon.

R 75.1 (120.8 km) Kilometrepost 350. Mount Sheldon ahead, located 3 miles/4.8 km north of Sheldon Lake; a very beautiful and distinguishable feature on the Canol Road (elev. 6,937 feet/2,114m). In 1900, Poole Field and Clement Lewis, who were fans of writer Rudyard Kipling, named this peak Kipling Mountain and the lake at its base Rudyard. In 1907, Joseph Keele of the Geological Survey of Canada renamed them after Charles Sheldon, a well-known sheep hunter and naturalist who came to the area to collect Stone sheep specimens for the Chicago Natural History Museum in 1905.

R 76.4 (123 km) Kilometrepost 352. Of the 3-lake chain, Sheldon Lake is farthest north, then Field Lake and Lewis Lake, which is just visible from here. Lewis Lake is closest to the confluence of the Ross and Prevost rivers.

Field Lake and Lewis Lake were named in 1907 by Joseph Keele of the Geological Survey of Canada after Poole Field and Clement Lewis. The 2 partners, who had prospected this country, ran a trading post called Nahanni House at the mouth of the Ross River in 1905.

R 77.6 (124.9 km) Kilometrepost 354. One-lane bridge over Riddell Creek. Tip of Mount Riddell (elev. 6,101 feet/1,859m) can be seen to the west.

R 78.8 (126.8 km) View of Sheldon Lake ahead, Field Lake to right northbound.

R 79.8 (128.4 km) Access road east to Sheldon Lake.

R 82.7 (133.1 km) One-lane bridge over Sheldon Creek. Road climbs, leaving Ross River valley and entering Macmillan Valley northbound.

R 89.3 (143.7 km) Height of land before starting descent northbound into South Macmillan River system.

R 89.7 (144.3 km) Steep hill. Road may wash out during heavy rains. Deep ditches along roadside help channel water.

R 91.4 (147.1 km) One-lane bridge over Moose Creek.

R 91.6 (147.4 km) **B 52.6** (84.6 km) Milepost 230.

R 92.3 (148.5 km) Kilometrepost 378. Peaks of the Itsi Range ahead. Rugged, spectacular scenery northbound.

R 92.7 (149.1 km) Distance marker indicates NWT border 95 km, Ross River 150 km.

R 93.8 (151 km) First of several WWII vehicle dumps to west. To the east is a wannigan, or skid shack, used as living quarters by Canol Road workers during construction of the road. It was too far to return to base camp; these small buildings were strategically located along the route so the workers had a place to eat and sleep at night.

R 94 (151.3 km) To east are remains of a maintenance depot where heavy equipment was repaired. Concrete foundations to west. First glimpse of the South Macmillan River northbound.

R 94.7 (152.4 km) Kilometrepost 382. Another Canol project equipment dump to explore. Watch ditches for old pieces of pipeline.

R 97.8 (157.4 km) One-lane bridge over Boulder Creek.

R 98.5 (158.5 km) Access road west to South Macmillan River where boats can be launched. Locals advise launching boats here rather than from the bridge at **Milepost R 113.6**, which washes out periodically and leaves dangerous debris in the river.

R 100.8 (162.5 km) Kilometrepost 392. Itsi Range comes into view ahead northbound. Itsi is said to be an Indian word meaning "wind" and was first given as a name to Itsi Lakes, headwaters of the Ross River. The road dips down and crosses an unnamed creek.

R 104.5 (168.2 km) Kilometrepost 398. View of the South Macmillan River from here.

R 105.3 (169.4 km) View of Selwyn Mountains, named in 1901 by Joseph Keele of the Geological Survey of Canada for Dr. Alfred Richard Selwyn (1824–1902), a distinguished geologist in England. Dr. Selwyn later became director of the Geological Survey of Australia and then director of the Geological Survey of Canada from 1869 until his retirement in 1895.

R 111 (178.6 km) One-lane bridge over Itsi Creek.

R 112.2 (180.5 km) One-lane bridge over Wagon Creek.

R 113.6 (182.8 km) Turnout to east on South Macmillan River. Good place for a picnic but not recommended as a boat launch. One-lane Bailey bridge over South Macmillan River No. 1.

Robert Campbell, a Hudson's Bay Co. explorer on a journey down the Pelly River in 1843, named this major tributary of the Pelly after Chief Factor James McMillan, who had sponsored Campbell's employment with the company.

R 115.1 (185.2 km) Access road on left northbound leads about 7 miles/11 km to Yukon Barite Mine. Barite is a soft mineral that requires only crushing and bagging before being shipped over the Dempster Highway to the Beaufort Sea oil and gas wells, where it is used as a lubricant known as drilling mud.

R 117.2 (188.6 km) Access road on right northbound to gravel pit.

R 118.8 (191.2 km) Dept. of Public Works maintenance camp; status unknown.

R 118.9 (191.3 km) One-lane bridge over Jeff Creek.

R 121.2 (195 km) One-lane bridge over Hess Creek. Bears in area.

R 123.2 (198.3 km) Gravel turnout on left northbound with RCMP trailer. Distance marker indicates NWT border 45 km, Ross River 200 km. One-lane bridge over Dewhurst Creek.

R 127.5 (205.2 km) Entering Macmillan Pass. At "Mac Pass," the road climbs to elevations above 4,480 feet/1,366m.

R 129.4 (208.2 km) One-lane bridge over Macmillan River No. 2.

R 129.5 (208.4 km) Abandoned Army vehicles from the Canol Project on left northbound.

R 129.6 (208.6 km) Abandoned Army vehicles from the Canol Project on right northbound.

R 133.6 (215 km) To the west is Cordilleran Engineering camp, managers of the mining development of Ogilvie Joint Venture's Jason Project. The Jason deposit is a zinc, lead, silver, barite property.

One-lane bridge over Sekie Creek No. 1.

R 134.4 (216.3 km) Fuel tanks on left northbound.

R 136.3 (219.3 km) Sekie Creek No. 2 culvert.

R 136.4 (219.5 km) Access to Macmillan airstrip on left northbound. Access road to right to Hudson Bay Mining & Smelting's Tom lead–zinc mineral claims. The Tom is a stratabound silver–lead–zinc deposit and the size is yet to be determined. At one time it was considered to be 9 million tons of 16 percent combined lead–zinc.

R 137.7 (221.6 km) One-lane bridge over Macmillan River No. 3.

R 141.8 (228.2 km) One-lane bridge over Macmillan River No. 4.

R 142.9 (230 km) One-lane bridge over Macmillan River No. 5.

R 144.1 (231.9 km) One-lane bridge over Macmillan River No. 6.

R 144.2 (232 km) YT–NWT border. Sign cautions motorists to proceed at their own risk. The road is not maintained and bridges are not safe beyond this point. Vehicles turn around here.

Ahead is the Tsichu River valley and the Selwyn Mountains. The abandoned North Canol Road continues another 230 miles/372 km from the YT–NWT border to Norman Wells, NWT. Designated the Canol Heritage Trail, and set aside as a territorial park reserve, the trail is currently under development. Some river crossings required; large stretches deemed dangerous and arduous. It passes through mountains, tundra and forest, and past many relics of the Canol Project. The Historical Centre museum in Norman Wells features the history of the Canol Project and has outdoor displays of Canol vehicles Phone (867) 587-2415; fax (867) 587-2469.

YELLOWHEAD HIGHWAY 16

Connects: Edmonton, AB, to Prince Rupert, BC **Length:** 898 miles
Road Surface: Paved **Season:** Open all year
Highest Summit: Obed Summit, 3,819 feet
Major Attractions: Jasper National Park, Mt. Robson, Fort St. James

(See maps, pages 240–242)

	Edmonton	Jasper	Prince George	Prince Rupert	Terrace
Edmonton		216	450	898	807
Jasper	216		234	682	591
Prince George	450	234		448	357
Prince Rupert	898	682	448		91
Terrace	807	591	357	91	

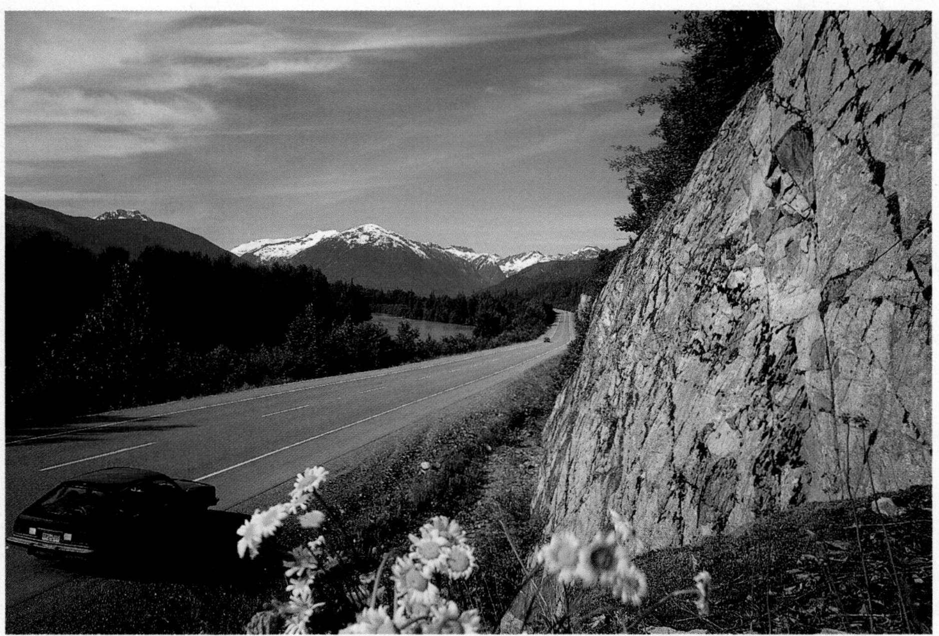

Yellowhead Highway 16 follows the Skeena River east of Prince Rupert, BC.
(© Eero Sorila)

Yellowhead Highway 16 is a paved trans-Canada highway extending from Winnipeg, MB, through Saskatchewan, Alberta, and British Columbia to the coastal city of Prince Rupert. (The highway connecting Masset and Queen Charlotte on Graham Island has also been designated as part of Yellowhead Highway 16.) *The MILEPOST®* logs Yellowhead Highway 16 from Edmonton, AB, to Prince Rupert, BC, a distance of 898 miles/1,444 km.

Yellowhead Highway 16 terminates at Prince Rupert, BC, where you may connect with the Alaska Marine Highway System to southeastern Alaska cities, and the British Columbia ferry system to Port Hardy on Vancouver Island and Skidegate in the Queen Charlotte Islands.

This is a major east–west route, providing access to a number of attractions in Alberta and British Columbia. Yellowhead Highway 16 is also a very scenic highway, passing through mountains, forest and farmland. Visitor services are readily available in towns along the way, and campsites may be found in towns and along the highway at both private and provincial park campgrounds. (It is unsafe and illegal to overnight in rest areas.)

Yellowhead Highway 16 Log

The Yellowhead Highway log is divided into 2 sections: Edmonton to Prince George, and Prince George to Prince Rupert. Kilometreposts on Yellowhead reflect distances within highway maintenance districts; *The MILEPOST®* periodically notes these physical posts as reference points.

This section of the log shows distance from Edmonton (E) followed by distance from Prince George (PG).

E 0 PG 450 (724.2 km) **EDMONTON** city limit. See page 43 in the EAST ACCESS ROUTE section for description of city.

E 4 (6.4 km) **PG 446** (717.8 km) **Junction** of Highways 16 West and 60 (Devon Overpass); access to Glowing Embers Travel Centre campground with 273 sites. ▲

E 12 (19.3 km) **PG 438** (704.9 km) **SPRUCE GROVE** (pop. 13,076). All visitor facilities including motels, restaurants, gas and service stations, grocery stores, farmer's market, shopping malls and all emergency services. Recreational facilities include a golf course, swimming pool, 2 ice skating rinks, a curling rink, and extensive walking and cycling trails. The chamber of commerce tourist information booth, located on Highway 16, is open year-round; phone (403) 962-2561.

E 18.1 (29.1 km) **PG 431.9** (695.1 km) **STONY PLAIN** (pop. 7,800). All visitor facilities including hotels, restaurants, supermarkets, shopping mall and gas stations with major repair service; RCMP and hospital; outdoor swimming pool and 18-hole golf course. The Multicultural Heritage Centre nearby (see **Milepost E 22**) has historical archives, a craft shop and home-cooked meals. Other attractions include 16 outdoor murals; a teahouse; Oppertshauser Art Gallery; the Andrew Wolf Winery; and the Pioneer Museum at Exhibition Park. Visitor information centres at Rotary Park and rest area. Camping at Lions RV Park and Campground; 26 sites. ▲

Bears & Bedtime. See display ad this section.

Stony Plain Highway Inn. See display

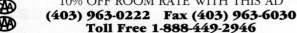

YELLOWHEAD HIGHWAY 16 *Edmonton, AB, to Prince George, BC*

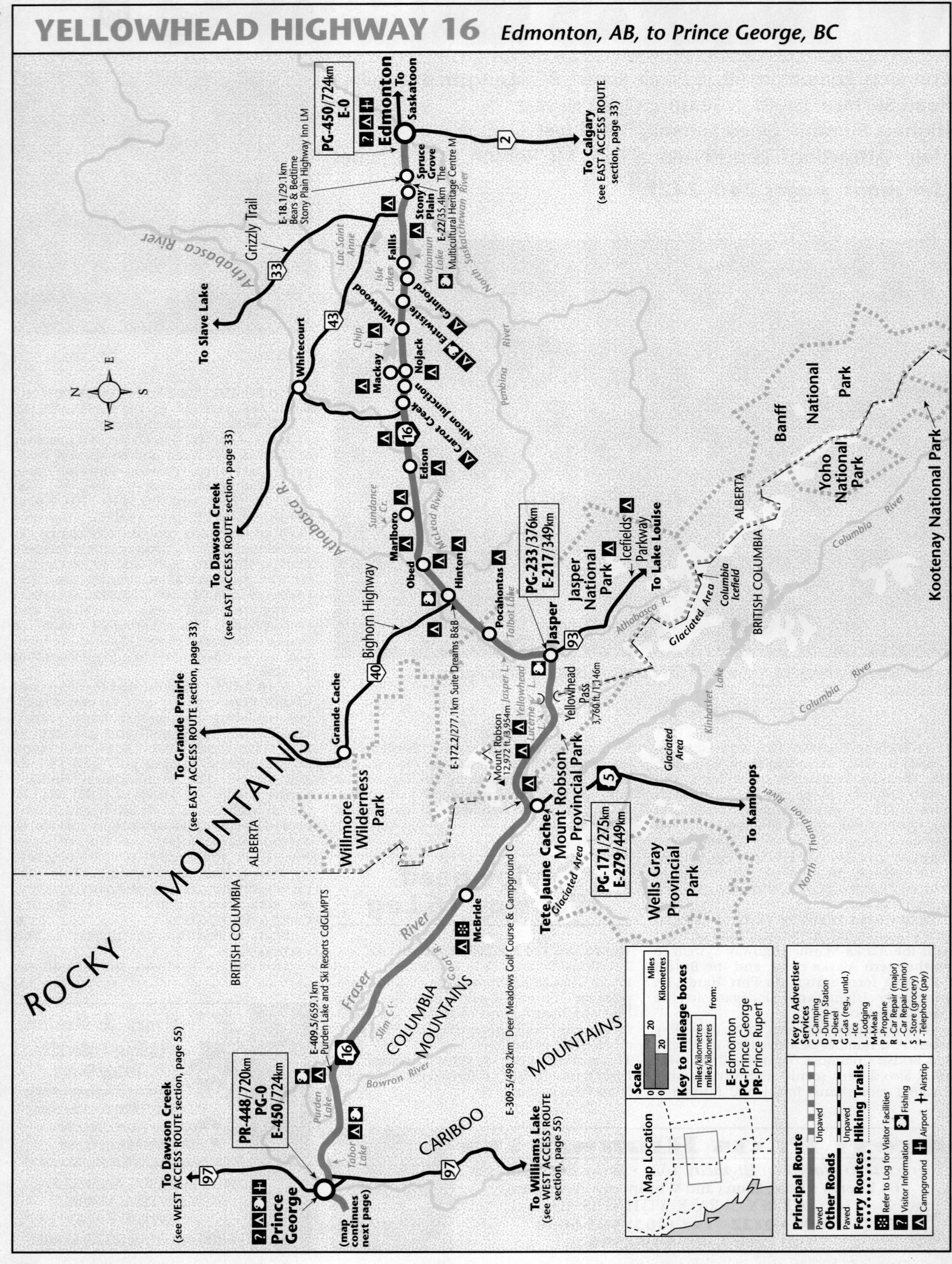

YELLOWHEAD HIGHWAY 16 *Prince George, BC, to Topley, BC*

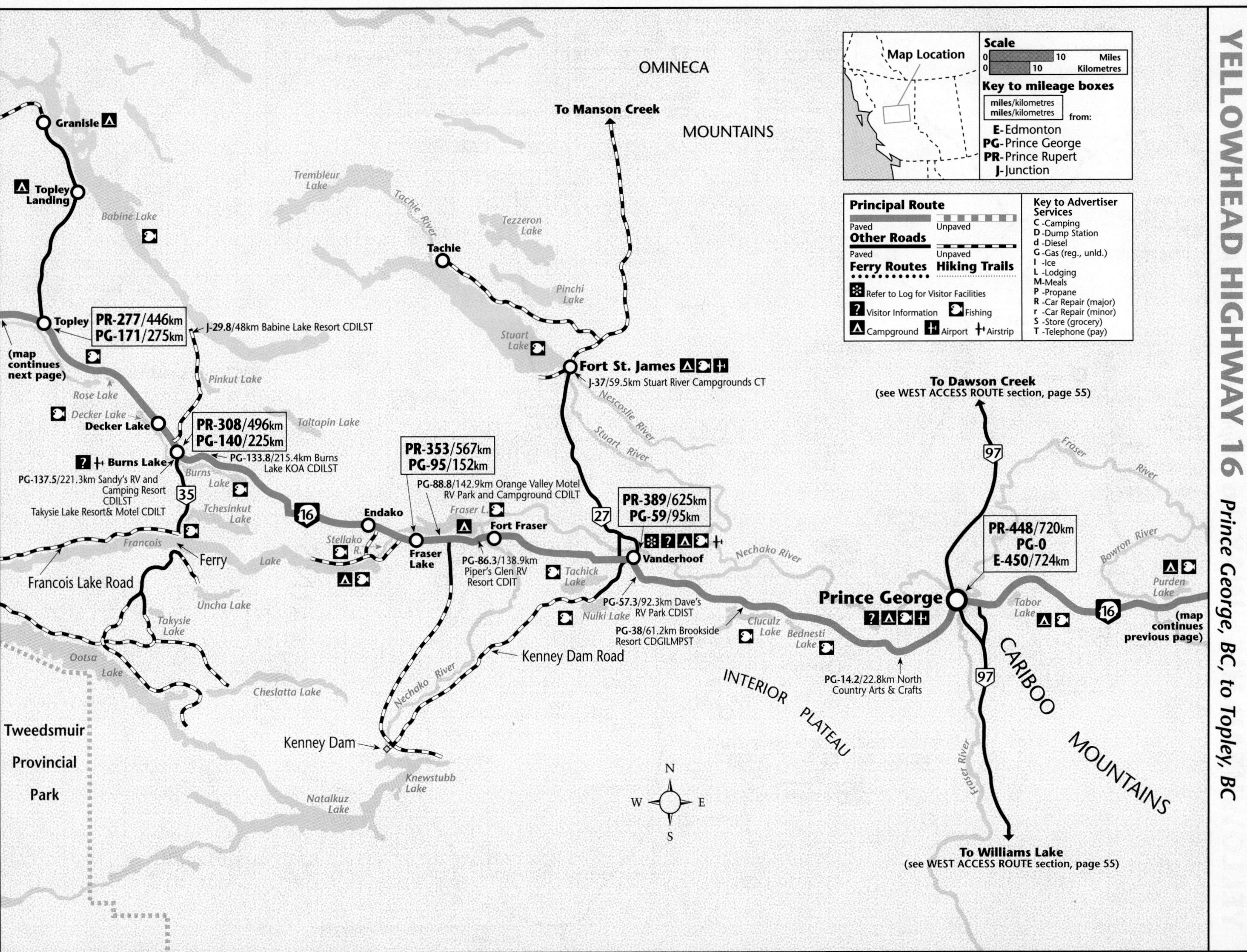

YELLOWHEAD HIGHWAY 16 *Topley, BC, to Prince Rupert, BC*

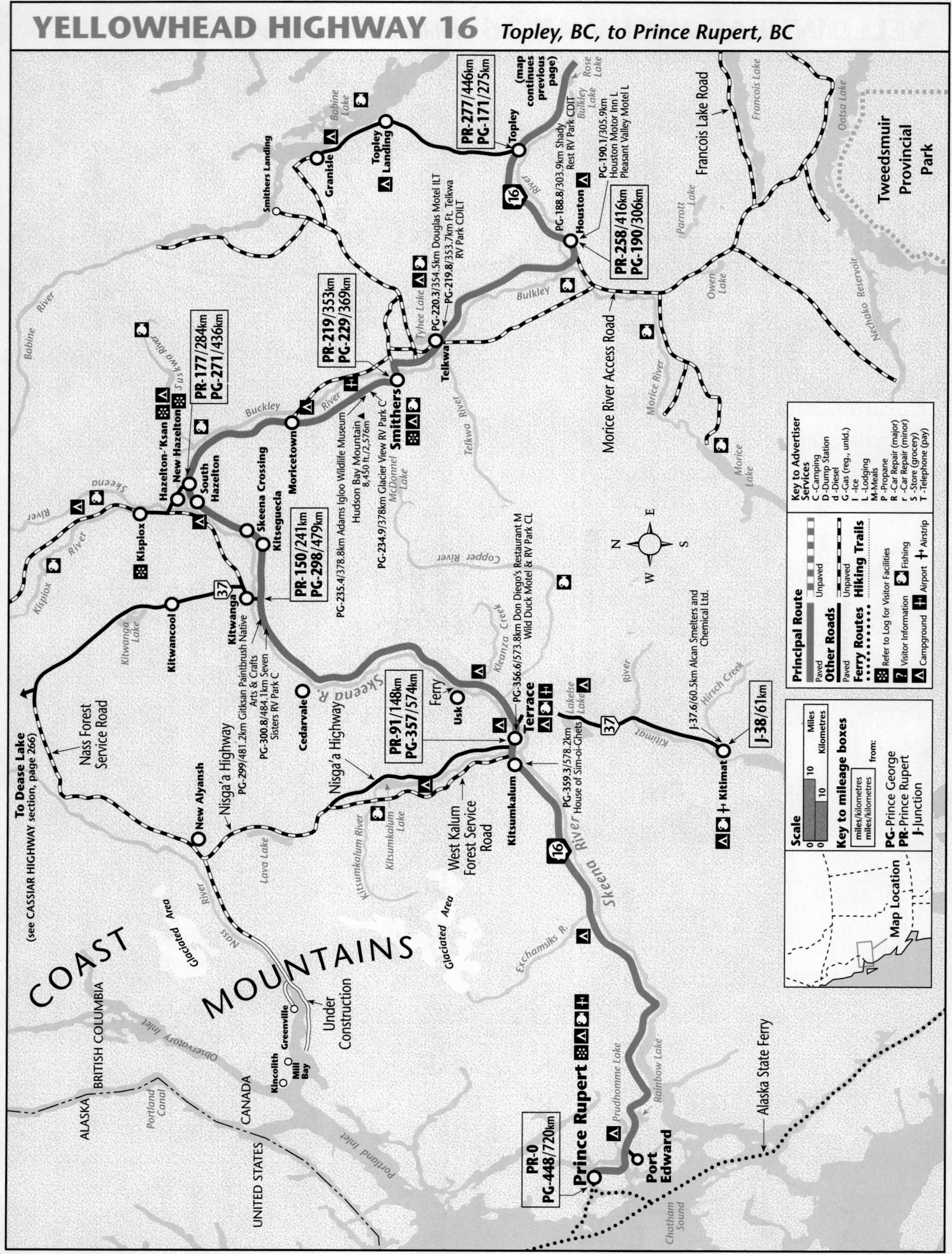

ad this section.

E 19.6 (31.5 km) **PG 430.4** (692.7 km) Turnoff to south for Edmonton Beach and campground. ▲

E 20.1 (32.3 km) **PG 429.9** (691.9 km) Hubbles Lake turnoff to north.

E 21.2 (34.1 km) **PG 428.8** (690.1 km) Restaurant, gas station and store to north.

E 21.7 (35 km) **PG 428.3** (689.2 km) Andrew Wolf Winery; visitors welcome.

E 22 (35.4 km) **PG 428** (688.8 km) **The Multicultural Heritage Centre.** Features a regional museum, unique restaurant, a public art gallery featuring Canadian artists, as well as both local and imported craft shops. Award-winning grounds and historically significant buildings complete this rewarding experience. Open Monday to Saturday 10 A.M. to 4 P.M., Sunday 10 A.M. to 6:30 P.M. Phone (403) 963-2777. Address: 5411–51 St. [ADVERTISEMENT]

E 25 (40.2 km) **PG 425** (684 km) **Junction** with Highway 43. Turn north for access to Alaska Highway (see the EAST ACCESS ROUTE section) and Northwest Territories (see MACKENZIE ROUTE section). Continue west for Prince George.

E 25.5 (41 km) **PG 424.5** (683.2 km) Hubbles Lake to north.

E 30.3 (48.8 km) **PG 419.7** (675.4 km) Gas and groceries south side of road at junction.

E 30.9 (49.8 km) **PG 419.1** (674.4 km) Sign: Watch for moose.

E 33 (53.1 km) **PG 417** (671.1 km) **Wabamun Lake** Provincial Park, 1 mile/1.6 km south on access road; 288 campsites, fishing, boating and swimming. ▲

E 34.7 (55.9 km) **PG 415.3** (668.3 km) Village of **WABAMUN** with gas, convenience store, car wash, laundromat, dump station, hotel and post office. Park with shelter, tables, litter barrels, washroom and flush toilets. Also located here is Trans Alta Utilities generating station, which generates electricity from coal.

E 38.5 (61.9 km) **PG 411.5** (662.3 km) Emergency phone to south. Propane, fuel and groceries.

E 42.5 (68.4 km) **PG 407.5** (655.8 km) **FALLIS** (pop. 190); no services. Strip mining of coal on north side of highway.

E 46.2 (74.4 km) **PG 403.8** (649.8 km) Private campground/RV park, open year-round. ▲

E 48.7 (78.3 km) **PG 401.3** (645.9 km) **GAINFORD** (pop. 205). Cafe, hotel and post office. Free public campground at west end of town with 8 sites, firewood, tables, pit toilets and water. ▲

E 56.6 (91.1 km) **PG 393.4** (633.1 km) **ENTWISTLE** (pop. 477). Restaurants, gas station, 2 motels, post office, swimming pool and grocery store. **Pembina River** Provincial Park, 1.9 miles/3.1 km north; 129 campsites, firewood, tables, pit toilets, water and dump station. Camping fee $11. Fishing, swimming, playground and phone. ▲

E 66.2 (106.5 km) **PG 383.8** (617.7 km) **WILDWOOD** (pop. 375), the "Bingo Capital of Canada." Post office, hotel, gas station, restaurants and shops. Campground at **Chip Lake** with 14 sites, tables, firewood, pit toilets, water, fishing, swimming and boat launch. ▲

E 68.7 (110.6 km) **PG 381.3** (613.6 km) View of Chip Lake to north.

E 81.5 (131.1 km) **PG 368.5** (593.1 km) **NOJACK** and **MACKAY** (pop. 250). Grocery, post office, restaurant and gas station with towing, diesel and major repair service.

Visitor information centre at Edson, AB, Milepost E 114.9. (© Wes Bergen, DIARAMA)

Mackay is 1.9 miles/3.1 km north of Nojack on a gravel road. Campgrounds 1 mile/1.6 km and 3 miles/4.8 km west of town on Highway 16. ▲

E 81.6 (131.4 km) **PG 368.4** (592.8 km) Emergency phone.

E 84.6 (136.1 km) **PG 365.4** (588.1 km) Private campground to north. ▲

E 89.5 (144 km) **PG 360.5** (580.2 km) **NITON JUNCTION.** Hamlet has 2 gas stations with tires and parts, diesel, propane, car wash, pay phone, groceries, post office, 2 restaurants, lounge, motel. Private campground with full hookups. ▲

E 93.7 (150.8 km) **PG 356.3** (573.4 km) **CARROT CREEK.** Post office, grocery store, gas station, car wash and phone.

E 97.5 (157 km) **PG 352.5** (567.2 km) **Junction** with Highway 32 which leads to Whitecourt and Highway 43, 42 miles/67.6 km north on paved road. (See **Milepost E 112.7** in the EAST ACCESS ROUTE section.)

E 102.1 (164.4 km) **PG 347.9** (559.8 km) Wolf Lake public campground, 33 miles/53 km south on gravel road; 14 sites, pit toilets, tables, litter barrels. ▲

E 105 (169 km) **PG 345** (555.2 km) Edson rest area to south with flush toilets, water, tables, shelter, phone and sani-dump.

E 106 (170.6 km) **PG 344** (553.6 km) Rosevear Road; eastbound access to Edson rest area.

E 110 (177.1 km) **PG 340** (547.1 km) Private campground with full hookups to south, open May to Oct. ▲

E 113.1 (182 km) **PG 336.9** (542.2 km) McLeod River bridge.

E 114.9 (185 km) **PG 335.1** (539.2 km) **EDSON** (pop. 7,323). **Emergency Services: Hospital** and RCMP post **Visitor Information:** South on 55th Street. Edson's economy is based on coal mining, forestry, oil, natural gas and manufacturing. Edson is a large highway community with 14 motels, many restaurants and gas stations; 18-hole golf course and indoor pool. Camping at Lions Club Campground east of town (42 sites), and at Willmore Recreation Park, 3.7 miles/6 km south of town on the McLeod River. ▲

E 123.2 (198.3 km) **PG 326.8** (525.9 km) Food, gas, lodging and phone.

E 128 (206 km) **PG 322** (518.2 km) Government campground to north adjacent to highway. ▲

E 133 (214 km) **PG 317** (510.2 km) Small community of Marlboro to north. First view of Canadian Rockies westbound.

E 140.8 (226.6 km) **PG 309.2** (497.6 km) Westbound-only turnout with picnic tables, pit toilets and litter barrels; generous, paved parking area.

E 142.7 (229.6 km) **PG 307.3** (494.6 km) Eastbound-only turnout with litter barrels.

E 148.1 (238.3 km) **PG 301.9** (485.9 km) Obed Lake public campground to north; 13 sites, firewood, tables, pit toilets, water. ▲

E 150.3 (241.9 km) **PG 299.7** (482.3 km) **OBED**. Phone, gas and groceries.

E 156.4 (251.8 km) **PG 293.6** (472.4 km) Obed Summit, highest elevation on the Yellowhead Highway at 3,819 feet/1,164m. Paved turnout with picnic tables, toilets and litter barrels; good view of the Rockies, weather permitting.

E 157.7 (253.9 km) **PG 292.3** (470.3 km) Treed roadside turnout; generous parking area, picnic tables, toilets and litter barrels.

E 160.8 (258.8 km) **PG 289.2** (465.4 km) Motel to south.

E 166.7 (268.3 km) **PG 283.3** (455.9 km) **HINTON** (pop. 8,537). All visitor facilities including hotels and motels, golf course, hospital, dentist, RCMP and recreation complex with indoor pool. Campground with 50 sites, hookups and dump station. Site of St. Regis (Alberta) Ltd. pulp mill; tours of mill complex may be arranged. ▲

E 171 (275.3 km) **PG 279** (448.9 km) South **junction** with Highway 40.

E 172.2 (277.1 km) **PG 277.8** (447.1 km) **Junction** with Bighorn Highway 40, which leads north 90 miles/145 km (paved) to Grande Cache then another 117 miles/188 km (gravel) to Grande Prairie. See BIG HORN HIGHWAY log on page 52. William A. Switzer Provincial Park 16.8 miles/27 km north; camping, picnicking, fishing. ▲

Visitor Infocentre at viewpoint of Mount Robson, Milepost E 268.8. (© Dan Skillman)

Suite Dreams Bed & Breakfast. See display ad on page 243.

E **176.8** (284.5 km) **PG 273.2** (439.7 km) Maskuta Creek picnic area with tables, shelter, toilets and litter barrels.

E **177.8** (286.2 km) **PG 272.2** (438 km) Weigh scales and pay phone.

E **179** (288.1 km) **PG 271** (436.1 km) Public campground 3.1 miles/5 km north. ▲

E **181.5** (292.2 km) **PG 268.5** (432 km) Private campground, pay phone. ▲

E **182.4** (293.6 km) **PG 267.6** (430.6 km) Point of interest sign about Athabasca River to north.

E **182.9** (294.4 km) **PG 267.1** (429.8 km) Resort with lodging to north.

E **184.2** (296.5 km) **PG 265.8** (427.7 km) East entrance to Jasper National Park; public phones. Park fees charged on a per-person basis and must be paid by all visitors using facilities in Rocky Mountain national parks.

Highway 16 has restricted speed zones where wildlife sightings are frequent. Drive carefully and watch out for moose, elk, white-tailed and mule deer, mountain goats, bighorn sheep, and black and grizzly bears. *NOTE: It is illegal to feed, touch, disturb or hunt wildlife in the national park. All plants and natural objects are also protected and may not be removed or destroyed.*

E **185.6** (298.8 km) **PG 264.4** (425.4 km) Fiddle River bridge.

E **187.6** (302 km) **PG 262.4** (422.2 km) Weather permitting, layering in mountains is quite apparent. It is speculated that the Rockies were once part of a sea bed that was lifted from the water and folded. The visible layers are sedimentary deposits laid on the bottom of the sea.

E **189** (304.2 km) **PG 261** (420 km) **POCAHONTAS.** Grocery, motel, cafe and gas station with minor-repair service. **Junction** with Miette Hot Springs Road, which leads 0.6 mile/1 km south to Park Service campground (140 sites) and 11 miles/17.7 km south to Miette Hot Springs and resort. There are 2 thermal pools; towels and bathing suits for rent; admission fee. Beautiful setting, look for mountain goats. ▲

E **192** (309 km) **PG 258** (415.2 km) Turnout with cairn to south. Mineral lick here is frequented by goats and sheep. Watch for wildlife, especially at dawn and dusk. Many turnouts next 25 miles/40 km westbound.

E **193** (310.6 km) **PG 257** (413.6 km) First Rocky River bridge westbound.

E **194.3** (312.7 km) **PG 255.7** (411.5 km) Second Rocky River bridge westbound.

E **203** (326.7 km) **PG 247** (397.5 km) Two bridges spanning the Athabasca River. Watch for elk and stone sheep.

E **205.1** (330.1 km) **PG 244.9** (394.1 km) Snaring River bridge.

E **206.7** (332.7 km) **PG 243.3** (391.5 km) Jasper airfield to south.

E **208.1** (335 km) **PG 241.9** (389.2 km) Snaring overflow camping south. ▲

E **208.4** (335.4 km) **PG 241.6** (388.8 km) Snaring rest area to south.

E **208.8** (336 km) **PG 241.2** (388.2 km) Palisades picnic area.

E **212.9** (342.6 km) **PG 237.1** (381.6 km) Access road to Jasper Park Lodge, Maligne Lake and park office. The area is home to a large population of harlequin ducks, endangered elsewhere.

E **215.8** (347.3 km) **PG 234.2** (376.9 km) **Junction** with Highway 93A. Lodging and restaurant to south.

E **216.6** (348.6 km) **PG 233.4** (375.6 km) Access to Jasper and **junction** with Highway 93, the scenic Icefields Parkway, south to Banff past Columbia Icefield.

Many residents in this area maintain hummingbird feeders. The 2 species of hummingbirds found in the Canadian Rockies are the Rufous and the Calliope.

Jasper is also in elk territory. Elk can be dangerous during calving (May through June) and mating (August through October), so stay back at least 40 paces.

NOTE: No fuel next 62.5 miles/100.6 km westbound.

E **217.1** (349.5 km) **PG 232.9** (374.7 km) Miette River.

E **222.2** (357.6 km) **PG 227.8** (366.6 km) Paved turnout to north with outhouses, litter barrels and interpretive sign about Yellowhead Pass. Many turnouts next 25 miles/40 km eastbound.

E **223.2** (359.3 km) **PG 226.8** (364.9 km) Meadow Creek.

E **223.4** (359.5 km) **PG 226.6** (364.7 km) Trailhead for Virl Lake, Dorothy Lake and Christine Lake.

E **226.1** (363.9 km) **PG 223.9** (360.3 km) Clairvaux Creek.

E **229.4** (369.3 km) **PG 220.6** (354.9 km) West entrance to Jasper National Park; park fee must be paid by all visitors using facilities in Rocky Mountain national parks.

E **231.6** (372.7 km) **PG 218.4** (351.5 km) Yellowhead Pass (elev. 3,760 feet/1,146m), Alberta–British Columbia border. Named for an Iroquois trapper and guide who worked for the Hudson's Bay Co. in the early 1800s. His light-colored hair earned him the name Tete Jaune ("yellow head") from the French voyageurs.

East entrance to Mount Robson Provincial Park. Portal Lake picnic area with tables, toilets, information board and hiking trail.

TIME ZONE CHANGE: Alberta observes Mountain standard time. Most of British Columbia observes Pacific standard time. Both observe daylight saving time.

E **232.8** (374.7 km) **PG 217.2** (349.5 km) Kilometrepost 75. Kilometreposts on Yellowhead Highway 16 reflect distances within highway maintenance districts; *The MILEPOST®* periodically notes these physical posts as reference points.

E **235.8** (379.6 km) **PG 214.2** (344.6 km) Rockingham Creek.

E **236.2** (380.1 km) **PG 213.8** (344.1 km) **Yellowhead Lake**; picnic tables, viewpoint, boat launch and fishing.

E **238** (383 km) **PG 212** (341.2 km) Lucerne Campground; 32 sites, picnic tables, drinking water, firewood and swimming; camping fee charged. ▲

E **239.3** (385.2 km) **PG 210.7** (339 km) Fraser Crossing rest area to south; litter barrels and toilets.

E **239.4** (385.3 km) **PG 210.6** (338.9 km) Fraser River bridge No. 1.

E **242.4** (390.1 km) **PG 207.6** (334.1 km) Fraser River bridge No. 2.

E **245.2** (394.6 km) **PG 204.8** (329.6 km) Kilometrepost 55.

E **246.2** (396.2 km) **PG 203.8** (328 km) Grant Brook Creek.

E **249** (400.8 km) **PG 201** (323.4 km) Moose Creek bridge.

E **251.1** (404.2 km) **PG 198.9** (320 km) Turnout at east end of Moose Lake; information kiosk, tables, litter barrels, toilet and boat launch.

E **255.5** (411.2 km) **PG 194.5** (313 km) Turnout with litter barrels.

E **257.5** (414.4 km) **PG 192.5** (309.8 km) Kilometrepost 35.

E **263.7** (424.4 km) **PG 186.3** (299.8 km) Paved turnout with litter barrels.

E **268** (431.3 km) **PG 182** (292.9 km) Overlander Falls rest area to south; pit toilets and litter barrels. Hiking trail to Overlander Falls, about 30 minutes round-trip.

E **268.8** (432.7 km) **PG 181.2** (291.4 km) Viewpoint of Mount Robson (elev. 12,972 feet/3,954m), highest peak in the Canadian Rockies, and Visitor Infocentre. Parking, picnic tables, restrooms, litter barrels, gas and restaurant. Berg Lake trailhead; hike-in campgrounds. Private campground north of highway. Robson Meadows government campground south of highway with 125 sites, dump station, showers, pay phone, interpretive programs, tables, firewood, flush toilets, water and horseshoe pits; group camping; camping fee charged. ▲

E 269.4 (433.6 km) **PG 180.6** (290.6 km) Robson River government campground to north with 19 sites (some wheelchair-accessible), tables, firewood, pit toilets, showers, water and horseshoe pits; camping fee charged. ♿▲

E 269.8 (434.3 km) **PG 180.2** (289.9 km) Kilometrepost 15.

E 269.9 (434.4 km) **PG 180.1** (289.8 km) Robson River bridge. Look for Indian paintbrush June through August. The bracts are orange-red while the petals are green.

E 270.3 (435.1 km) **PG 179.7** (289.1 km) West entrance to Mount Robson Provincial Park. Turnout with litter barrels and statue.

E 270.5 (435.3 km) **PG 179.5** (288.9 km) Gravel turnout to south.

E 271.4 (436.8 km) **PG 178.6** (287.4 km) Swift Current Creek.

E 274.4 (441.7 km) **PG 175.6** (282.5 km) Mount Terry Fox Provincial Park picnic area with tables, restrooms and viewing telescope. The information board here points out the location of Mount Terry Fox in the Selwyn Range of the Rocky Mountains. The peak was named in 1981 to honour cancer victim Terry Fox, who, before his death from the disease, raised some $25 million for cancer research during his attempt to run across Canada.

E 276.3 (444.7 km) **PG 173.7** (280.5 km) Gravel turnout to north with Yellowhead Highway information sign.

E 276.4 (444.9 km) **PG 173.6** (280.3 km) Rearguard Falls Provincial Park picnic area. Easy half-hour round-trip to falls viewpoint. Upper limit of 800-mile/1,300-km migration of Pacific salmon; look for chinook in late summer.

E 277.8 (447.1 km) **PG 172.2** (277.1 km) Gravel turnout to south overlooking Fraser River.

E 278.2 (447.8 km) **PG 171.8** (276.4 km) Weigh scales.

E 278.7 (448.6 km) **PG 171.3** (275.6 km) Tete Jaune Cache rest area with tables, litter barrels and toilets.

E 279 (449.1 km) **PG 171** (275.1 km) **Junction** with Yellowhead Highway 5 to the small community of **TETE JAUNE CACHE** (0.5 mile/0.8 km south of junction) and Kamloops (208 miles/335 km south), British Columbia's fourth largest settlement. Food, gas and lodging just west of the junction. Yellowhead Highway 5 opened in 1969. A year earlier, construction of the section of the highway east from Prince George to Tete Jaune Cache had connected Highway 16 with a rough road east to Jasper National Park. The final link in Northern Trans-provincial Highway 16 (now Yellowhead Highway 16)—between Prince George and Edmonton—officially opened in 1969.

E 279.1 (449.2 km) **PG 170.9** (275 km) Turnoff for gas, general store and deli, camping and lodging.

NOTE: No fuel eastbound next 62.5 miles/100.6 km.

E 279.6 (450.1 km) **PG 170.4** (274.1 km) Private lodging, restaurants.

E 283.1 (455.7 km) **PG 166.9** (268.5 km) Spittal Creek Interpretive Forest; hiking trails, tables, litter barrels and toilets. Kilometrepost 140.

E 288.2 (463.8 km) **PG 161.8** (260.4 km) Private resort. Lodging, restaurant.

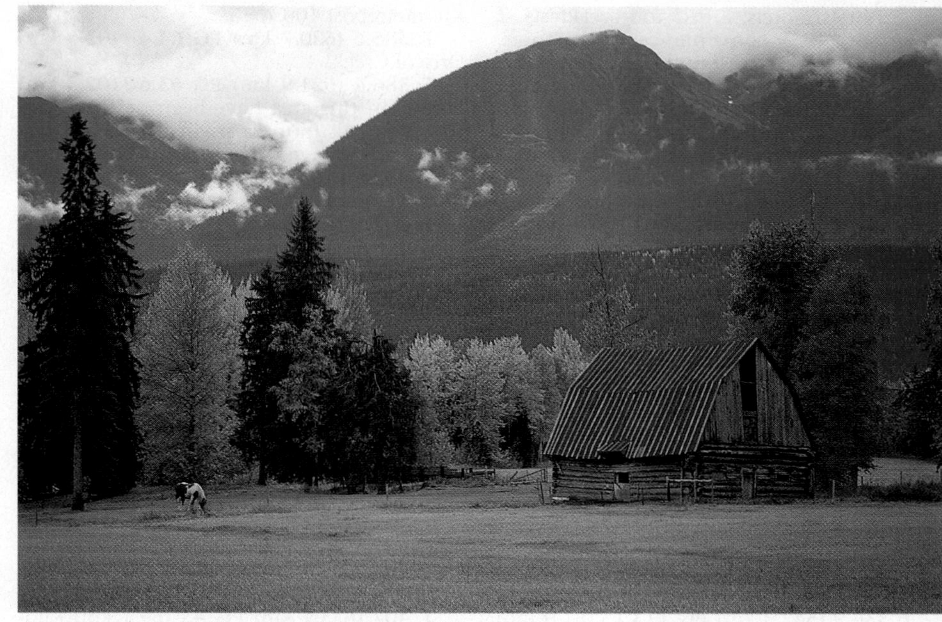

Scenery along Yellowhead Highway 16 near Tete Jaune Cache, BC. (© Rick Driskell)

E 289.1 (465.3 km) **PG 160.9** (258.9 km) Small River rest area by stream with tables, toilets and litter barrels.

E 293.6 (472.5 km) **PG 156.4** (251.7 km) Horsey Creek.

E 295.4 (475.5 km) **PG 154.6** (248.7 km) Kilometrepost 120.

E 300 (482.9 km) **PG 150** (241.3 km) Turnoff to south for settlement of Dunster; gas and general store.

E 303.8 (489 km) **PG 146.2** (235.2 km) Holiday Creek rest area with toilets, picnic tables, litter barrel and hiking trails.

E 304.3 (489.7 km) **PG 145.7** (234.5 km) Baker Creek rest area with tables, litter barrels and toilets.

E 308.5 (496.6 km) **PG 141.5** (227.6 km) Kilometrepost 100.

E 308.9 (497.2 km) **PG 141.1** (227 km) Nevin Creek.

E 309.5 (498.2) **PG 140.5** (226 km) **Deer Meadows Golf Course & Campground.** 16 scenic sites adjacent to golf course. Quiet location away from the crowds. Easy access pull-throughs with hookups. Open, grassed sites with tables. Washrooms. Course open 8 A.M.–10 P.M.; club and cart rentals available. Reservations: P.O. Box 337, McBride, BC V0J 2E0. (250) 569-3383. [ADVERTISEMENT] ▲

E 312 (502.1 km) **PG 138** (222.1 km) Turnouts at both ends of Holmes River bridge.

E 317.9 (511.6 km) **PG 132.1** (212.6 km) Fraser River bridge. A forest fire swept through the Robson Valley in 1912. As you look at the sides of the mountain to the north of the highway, it is possible to distinguish the new growth which has taken place in the last 81 years.

E 318.2 (512.1 km) **PG 131.8** (212.1 km) Turnout to north with litter barrels.

E 318.8 (513.1 km) **PG 131.2** (211.1 km) **McBRIDE** (pop. 700; elev. 2,369 feet/722.1m), located in the Robson Valley by the Fraser River. The Park Ranges of the Rocky Mountains are to the northeast and the Cariboo Mountains are to the southeast. A road leads to Teare Mountain lookout for a spectacular view of countryside. The village of McBride was established in 1913 as a divisional point on the railroad and was named for Richard McBride, then premier of British Columbia. Forest products are a major industry here today.

Visitor Information: Visitor Infocentre located in railcar on south side of Highway 16. Look for the carved grizzly bear family in front. When the Infocentre isn't open, try the McBride Village Office. Located beside the railcar in the same parking lot, it is open 9 A.M. to 5 P.M.

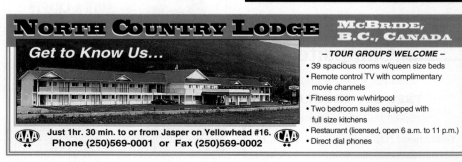

McBride has all visitor facilities, including 5 hotels/motels, 2 bed and breakfasts, 2 supermarkets, 2 convenience/video stores, clothing stores, restaurants, pharmacy, hospital and gas stations. A library, museum and neighborhood pub are 1.9 miles/3 km from town. There is a private campground just east of town. Dump station located at the gas station. ▲

While in McBride, watch wood ducks, scoters, teals and more at the Horseshoe Lake Bird Watch. In late summer, see the salmon run in the Holmes River. In winter, go cross-country skiing on developed trails and snowmobiling in the backcountry. Helicopter service available for fly-in skiing and hiking.

NOTE: Next gas westbound is 90.7 miles/146 km from here (Purden Lake).

E 321.9 (518.1 km) **PG 128.1** (206.1 km) Dore River bridge.

E 326.7 (525.8 km) **PG 123.3** (198.4 km) Macintosh Creek.

E 328.8 (529.2 km) **PG 121.2** (195 km) Clyde Creek.

E 333.1 (536.2 km) **PG 116.9** (188 km) Kilometrepost 60.

E 336.9 (542.3 km) **PG 113.1** (181.9 km) West Twin Creek bridge.

E 343.6 (553.1 km) **PG 106.4** (171.1 km) Goat River bridge. Paved rest area to north with tables, toilets and litter barrels.

E 346.7 (558 km) **PG 103.3** (166.2 km) Little LaSalle Recreation Area and BC Forest Service site. Small lake, small wharf, toilet.

E 351.2 (565.2 km) **PG 98.8** (159 km) Snowshoe Creek.

E 351.8 (566.2 km) **PG 98.2** (158 km) Kilometrepost 30.

E 354.9 (571.2 km) **PG 95.1** (153 km) Catfish Creek.

E 360.7 (580.6 km) **PG 89.3** (143.6 km) Ptarmigan Creek bridge.

E 363.8 (585.6 km) **PG 86.2** (138.6 km) Turnout with litter barrels to north.

E 369.2 (594.1 km) **PG 80.8** (130.1 km) Dome Creek.

E 371.5 (597.9 km) **PG 78.5** (126.3 km) Food, phone.

E 373.3 (600.8 km) **PG 76.7** (123.4 km) Slim Creek paved rest area to south with information kiosk, tables, playground, litter barrels and wheelchair-accessible toilets. Watch for bears. ♿

E 373.4 (601 km) **PG 76.6** (123.2 km) Ministry of Highways camp.

E 374.1 (602.1 km) **PG 75.9** (122.1 km) Slim Creek bridge.

E 382.5 (615.6 km) **PG 67.5** (108.6 km) Kilometrepost 100.

E 385.6 (620.7 km) **PG 64.4** (103.5 km) Driscol Creek.

E 386.4 (621.9 km) **PG 63.6** (102.3 km) Forests in this area have been destroyed by the hemlock looper, an insect which has killed or damaged over 45.9 million cubic feet/1.3 million cubic metres of wood in British Columbia.

E 387.6 (623.9 km) **PG 62.4** (100.3 km) Gravel turnout with litter barrel to north.

E 388.9 (626 km) **PG 61.1** (98.2 km) Lunate Creek.

E 391.8 (630.6 km) **PG 58.2** (93.6 km) Grizzly hiking trail to south.

E 392 (630.9 km) **PG 58** (93.3 km) Hungary Creek. Watch for Ministry of Forests signs indicating the year in which a logged area was replanted. Wildflowers include fireweed, mid-July through August.

E 394.8 (635.4 km) **PG 55.2** (88.8 km) Kilometrepost 80.

E 395.8 (637 km) **PG 54.2** (87.2 km) Sugarbowl Creek.

E 400.5 (644.6 km) **PG 49.5** (79.6 km) Paved turnout with litter barrel to north.

E 407 (655.1 km) **PG 43** (69.1 km) Kilometrepost 60.

E 408.2 (657 km) **PG 41.8** (67.2 km) Kenneth Creek.

E 408.4 (657.4 km) **PG 41.6** (66.8 km) Purden Mountain ski resort.

E 409.5 (659.1 km) **PG 40.5** (65.1 km) Purden Lake resort with gas, phone, lodging and camping. ▲

NOTE: Next gas eastbound is 90.7 miles/146 km from here (McBride).

E 411.2 (661.9 km) **PG 38.8** (62.3 km) **Purden Lake** Provincial Park, 1.9 miles/3 km from highway; 78 campsites, 48 picnic tables, water, dump station, firewood, playground and horseshoe pits. This recreation area offers a sandy beach, change houses, swimming, walking trails, waterskiing and boat launch. Good rainbow fishing to 4 lbs. Camping fee charged. ▲

E 412.6 (664.1 km) **PG 37.4** (60.1 km) Bowron River bridge. Paved rest area to north beside river, on west side of bridge; toilets, tables and litter barrels. Entrance on curve; use care.

E 420.7 (677.1 km) **PG 29.3** (47.1 km) Kilometrepost 40.

E 421 (677.6 km) **PG 29** (46.6 km) Vama Vama Creek.

E 424 (682.4 km) **PG 26** (41.8 km) Wansa Creek.

E 427.1 (687.4 km) **PG 22.9** (36.8 km) Willow River bridge. Rest area at west end of bridge beside river; tables, litter barrels, toilets and nature trail. The 1.2-mile-/1.9-km-long Willow River Forest Interpretation Trail is an easy 45-minute walk.

E 429.5 (691.3 km) **PG 20.5** (32.9 km) Bowes Creek.

E 429.7 (691.6 km) **PG 20.3** (32.6 km) Turnout to north with litter barrels and information board on 1961 forest fire and moose habitat. Circle trail to moose observation site.

E 433 (697 km) **PG 17** (27.2 km) Kilometrepost 20.

E 435.2 (700.5 km) **PG 14.8** (23.7 km) Tabor Mountain ski hill.

E 435.4 (700.8 km) **PG 14.6** (23.4 km) Gravel turnout to north with litter barrels.

E 437.6 (704.3 km) **PG 12.4** (19.9 km) Access to **Tabor Lake**; good fishing for rainbow in spring. ▲

E 444.8 (715.9 km) **PG 5.2** (8.3 km) **Junction**, Highway 16B with Highway 97 south bypass. See the WEST ACCESS ROUTE section for log of Highway 97 South.

E 450 (724.2 km) **PG 0 PRINCE GEORGE** (see description on pages 70–74). **Junction** with Highway 97 north to Dawson Creek and the beginning of the Alaska Highway.

Turn to the WEST ACCESS ROUTE section for the log of Highway 97 North. Continue west on Yellowhead Highway 16 for Prince Rupert (log follows).

Yellowhead Highway 16 Log

(continued)

Physical kilometreposts west from here are up along Highway 16 about every 5 km and reflect distance from Prince Rupert. Because the posts do not always accurately reflect driving distance, mileages from Prince Rupert are based on actual driving distance while the kilometre conversion is based on physical kilometreposts as they occurred in summer 1997.

This section of the log shows distance from Prince George (PG) followed by distance from Prince Rupert (PR).

PG 0 PR 447.7 (720 km) **Junction** of Highways 16 and 97 (Central Avenue/Cariboo Highway) in Prince George. From Prince George to Prince Rupert, Highway 16 is a 2-lane highway with 3-lane passing stretches. Fairly straight, with no high summits, the highway follows the valleys of the Nechako, Bulkley and Skeena rivers, paralleling the Canadian National Railway route. There are few services between towns.

PG 0.2 (0.4 km) **PR 447.5** (719.6 km) Prince George Golf and Curling Club.

PG 0.6 (1 km) **PR 447.1** (719 km) Ferry Avenue.

PG 1.2 (1.9 km) **PR 446.5** (718.1 km) **Junction** with Vince–Cowart/Domano Blvd.; access to the University of Northern B.C.

PG 2.9 (4.6 km) **PR 444.8** (715.4 km) Blue Spruce RV Park and Campground to north. ▲

PG 3.3 (5.3 km) **PR 444.4** (714.6 km) Tyner Blvd.

PG 4.7 (7.6 km) **PR 443** (712.3 km) **West**

Vanderhoof's Heritage Village contains relocated pioneer structures from the Nechako Valley. (© Eero Sorila)

Lake Provincial Park 8 miles/12.9 km south; day-use area with picnic shelter, swimming, fishing and boat launch.

PG 6.5 (10.4 km) **PR 441.2** (707.2 km) Western Road.

PG 11.5 (18.5 km) **PR 436.2** (699.6 km) Chilko Road.

PG 14.2 (22.8 km) **PR 433.5** (696.1 km) **North Country Arts & Crafts.** See display ad this section.

PG 26.9 (43.3 km) **PR 420.8** (676.4 km) Tamarac Lake to south.

PG 29.4 (47.4 km) **PR 418.3** (672.2 km) Access to lakeside resort and fishing at **Cluculz Lake** (not visible from highway). Rainbow to 3³/₄ lbs. by trolling, use snell hook and worms; kokanee to 1¹/₂ lbs., troll with snell hook and worms in spring; char to 57 lbs., use large flatfish, spoons, plugs and weights, early spring and late fall; whitefish to 5 lbs., year-round. Very good fishing in spring; ice goes out about the first week of May. Good ice fishing December to March. In September kokanee are at their peak. *Lake gets rough when windy.*

PG 36.4 (58.6 km) **PR 411.3** (661 km) Food and lodging.

PG 37.6 (60.5 km) **PR 410.1** (659.1 km) Cluculz rest area to south with flush toilets (summer only), picnic tables and litter barrels.

PG 38 (61.2 km) **PR 409.7** (658.4 km) **Brookside Resort.** Stay in a quiet pine forest next to Cluculz Creek. Serviced and unserviced sites. 30-amp spacious, shaded, level pull-throughs. Tent and camper sites with tables. Clean washrooms. Free hot showers

for registered guests. Sani-dump, laundromat, convenience store, restaurant, driving range, gift shops. Ice, propane, gasoline and boat gas. Phone. VISA and MasterCard. R.R. #1, Site 16, Comp 78, Vanderhoof, BC V0J 3A0. (888) 441-0035. [ADVERTISEMENT]

PG 40.2 (64.7 km) **PR 407.5** (654.9 km) Cluculz Lake campground to south.

PG 57.3 (92.3 km) **PR 390.4** (627.1km) **Dave's R.V. Park.** 2 miles east of downtown Vanderhoof, 1/2 mile down paved Derksen Road. Quiet, clean, rural setting. Washrooms, free hot showers for guests. Laundry. Cable TV available. Public telephone. Full and partial hookups. Level graveled pads, each with grass site. 48 sites, 22 extra-long (65 feet) pull-throughs. Sani-dump. Tent sites. Convenience store. Pets on leash. VISA, MasterCard. Box 1512, Vanderhoof, BC V0J 3A0; (250) 567-3161. [ADVERTISEMENT]

Vanderhoof

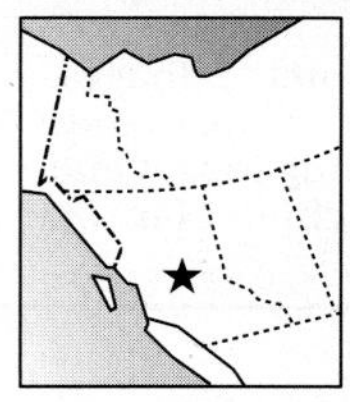

PG 58.7 (94.5 km) **PR 389** (624.8 km). Stoplight at junction with Highway 27; turnoff to downtown Vanderhoof. **Population:** 4,400; area 12,000. **Emergency Services: Police,** phone (250) 567-2222. **Fire Department**, phone (250) 567-2345. **Ambulance**, phone (800) 461-9911. **Hospital**, St. John's, Northside District, phone (250) 567-2211.

Visitor Information: Visitor Infocentre downtown on Burrard Avenue, 1 block off Highway 16. Write Vanderhoof & District Chamber of Commerce, Box 126-MP, Vanderhoof, BC V0J 3A0; phone (250) 567-2124.

Elevation: 2,225 feet/667.5m. **Radio:** CJCI 620, CFPR-FM 96.7, CKPG 550, CIVH 1340, CIRX-FM 95.9. **Television:** Channels 2, 4, 5, 6, 8. **Newspapers:** *Omineca Express–Bugle* (weekly). **Transportation: Air**—Vanderhoof airport, 2 miles/3.2 km from intersection of Highways 16 and 27; 5,000-foot/1,524-m paved runway. Seaplane landings on Nechako River at corner of View Street and Boundary Avenue. **Railroad**—VIA Rail, station at 2222 Church Ave. **Bus**—Greyhound.

Vanderhoof is the geographical centre of British Columbia. The city was named for Chicago publisher Herbert Vanderhoof, who founded the village in 1914 when he was associated with the Grand Trunk Development Co. Today, Vanderhoof is the supply and distribution centre for a large agricultural, lumbering and mining area.

The community's history is preserved at Vanderhoof Heritage Village Museum, just off Highway 16. Relocated pioneer structures furnished with period artifacts recall the early days of the Nechako Valley.

Located on the Nechako River, Vanderhoof is a stopping place in April and September for thousands of migrating waterfowl. The river flats upstream of the bridge are a bird sanctuary. Pelicans have been spotted feeding at Tachick Lake south of town.

There are 7 hotels and motels and 17 restaurants in the town. All shopping facilities and several gas stations. Dump station at Dave's R.V. Park and Riverside Campsite. Municipal campground is on Burrard Avenue close to downtown. An 18-hole golf course is located 1.9 miles/3.1 km north of town.

Riverside Campsite. Overlooking Nechako River with bird-watching tower and groomed walking trails. Private sites, some with 30-/50-amp service; some with hook-ups. Firepits and firewood. Flush toilets and free hot showers for guests. Public phone. Sani-dump. Pets welcome. Attendant on duty 24 hours. Gates open 7 A.M. to 10 P.M. 3100 Burrard Avenue, P.O. Box 380, Vanderhoof, BC V0J 3A0. Phone (250) 567-4710. [ADVERTISEMENT]

Area attractions include Fort St. James (see description on page 248), Tachick Lake and Kenney Dam. Follow the gravel road southwest from Vanderhoof 42 miles/67.6 km to Kenney Dam. At the time of its construction in 1951, it was North America's largest earth-filled dam. Near the dam site are Cheslatta Falls and Nechako River canyon (good area for rockhounding). Beautiful Tachick Lake (18 miles/29 km south)

VANDERHOOF ADVERTISERS

Fort St. James

Fort St. James

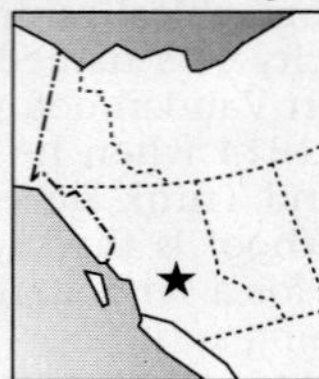

Located 37 miles/59.5 km north of Vanderhoof on Highway 27. **Population:** 2,146. **Emergency Services: Police**, phone (250) 996-8269. **Ambulance:** phone 1-562-7241. **Elevation:** 2,208 feet/673m. **Radio:** CKPG 550, CJCI 1480; CBC-FM 107.0.

Fort St. James is the home of **FORT ST. JAMES NATIONAL HISTORIC SITE.** Established in 1806 by Simon Fraser as a fur trading post for the Northwest Co., Fort St. James served throughout the 19th century as headquarters for the Hudson's Bay Co.'s New Caledonia fur trade district. The fur warehouse, fish cache, men's house, officers' dwelling and trade store have been restored in 1896-style and are open to the public. Check with the Visitor Infocentre regarding program information.

From mid-May through September, visitors may experience "living history." staff members, dressed in period costumes, play out historic scenarios, demonstrate old-time skills and provide interesting facts about fur trade history. Hours are 9 A.M. to 5 P.M. daily. For the remainder of the year, the site is closed. Admission fee.

The historic site and village are located on Stuart Lake. Named for John Stuart, the man who succeeded Simon Fraser as head of the New Caledonia district, the 59-mile-/95-km-long lake is the southernmost in a 3-lake chain which provides hundreds of miles of boating and fishing. Fort St. James also boasts the Nation Lakes, a chain of 4 lakes (Tsayta, Indata, Tchentlo and Chuchi) connected by the Nation River.

Attractions include the Our Lady of Good Hope Catholic Church and the Chief Kwah burial site. The recently renovated church is one of the oldest in British Columbia. Open for summer evening services only, check schedule. Chief Kwah was one of the first Carrier Indian chiefs to confront early white explorers. His burial site is located on the Nak'azdli Indian Reserve at the mouth of the Stuart River. At Cottonwood Park on the shore of Lake Stuart, look for a model of a Junkers airplane, which depicts the Fort's major role in early bush flying in Northern British Columbia.

Fort St. James has a hotel, 2 lodges, resort, 4 motels, 3 private campgrounds and a number of surrounding lodges and settlements, such as Tachie, Manson Creek and Germansen Landing in the Omineca Mountains. Other services in Fort St. James include 3 gas stations, 4 dump stations, a government marina, 2 private marinas and several restaurants. The district also has a theatre and 2 shopping centres. Picnicking and swimming at Cottonwood Park on Stuart Lake. A 9-hole golf course overlooks Stuart Lake; rentals available. Murray Ridge ski area, a 20-minute drive from town, has 21 downhill ski runs and 18.5 miles/30 km of cross-country ski trails. ▲

Camping is also available at **Paarens Beach** Provincial Park, located 6.8 miles/10.9 km off Highway 27 on Sowchea Bay Road; 36 campsites, picnic shelter, picnic tables, toilets, water, firepits, firewood, boat launch and swimming; camping fee. Sowchea Bay Provincial Park, located 10.6 miles/17.1 km off Highway 27 on Sowchea Bay Road, has 30 campsites, camping fee, picnic tables, toilets, water, firepits, firewood, boat launch and swimming. ▲

Good fishing in **Stuart Lake** for rainbow and char (to trophy size), kokanee and Dolly Varden.

Return to Milepost PG 58.7 or PG 63.2 Yellowhead Highway 16

has a modern log building fishing resort and a lodge which serves European food. Also access to Sai' Kuz Park on Nulki Lake, with annual fishing derby, Native dancers, Native crafts and gambling; phone (250) 567-4916. Kenney Dam Road turnoff is at the Kwik-Save gas station on Highway 16.

Nulki Lake, 10 miles/16 km west on Kenney Dam Road, rainbow to 6 or 7 lbs., average 2 lbs., use worms, year-round. **Tachick Lake**, 18 miles/29 km south on Kenney Dam Road, rainbow 2 to 7 lbs. year-round, largest fish in the area were taken from this lake; several small lakes in the area abound with rainbow and kokanee. Fishing charters available at Vanderhoof airport.

Yellowhead Highway 16 Log

(continued)

PG 58.7 (94.5 km) **PR 389** (624.8 km) First **junction** westbound with Highway 27, which extends north from Vanderhoof several hundred miles. The 37 miles/60 km to Fort St. James are fully paved; see description this page.

PG 59.2 (95.2 km) **PR 388.5** (624.1 km) Vanderhoof Historical Museum to south.

PG 63.2 (101.7 km) **PR 384.5** (617.6 km) Second **junction** westbound with Highway 27 (see description at **Milepost PG 58.7**). This route skirts Vanderhoof. Truck weigh scales to north.

PG 72.3 (116.3 km) **PR 375.4** (602.9 km) Plateau Division Sawmill to south.

PG 81.5 (131.1 km) **PR 366.2** (588 km) Turnout to south with view of Nechako River. The Grand Trunk Pacific Railway was completed near this site in 1914. The railroad (later the Canadian National) linked Prince Rupert, a deep-water port, with interior British Columbia. Entering Lakes District. This high country has over 300 freshwater lakes.

PG 81.8 (131.6 km) **PR 365.9** (587.5 km) **FORT FRASER** (pop. 600). **Radio:** CBC-FM 102.9. Small community with food, gas, propane, lodging and first-aid station. Gas station with hot showers, convenience store and restaurant. Named for Simon Fraser, who established a trading post here in 1806. Now a supply centre for surrounding farms and sawmills. The last spike of the Grand Trunk Railway was driven here on April 7, 1914.

PG 82.6 (133 km) **PR 365.1** (586.1 km) Nechako River bridge. Turnout to south with parking, litter barrels and access to **Nechako River**; fishing for rainbow and Dolly Varden, June to fall. At the east end of Fraser Lake, the Nautley River—less than a mile long—drains into the Nechako River.

PG 84.1 (135.4 km) **PR 363.6** (583.7 km) Nautley Road. Beaumont Provincial Park, on beautiful **Fraser Lake**, north side of highway; site of original Fort Fraser. Boat launch, swimming, hiking, fishing, 49 campsites, picnic tables, firewood, flush toilets, water, playground, horseshoe pits, dump station. Fishing for rainbow and lake trout, burbot, sturgeon and Dolly Varden. ▲

PG 85.9 (138.3 km) **PR 361.8** (580.8 km) View of Fraser Lake to north.

PG 86.3 (138.9 km) **PR 361.7** (580.5 km) **Pipers Glen RV Resort**. See display ad this section. ▲

PG 87.9 (141.4 km) **PR 359.8** (578 km)

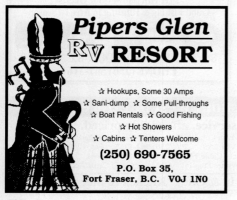

Dry William Lake rest area to south with picnic tables, toilets and litter barrels.

PG 88.8 (142.9 km) **PR 358.9** (577.4 km) **Orange Valley Motel, RV Park and Campground.** Easy access featuring level sites, large pull-throughs, electricity, water, some with sewer. Free showers, flush toilets, sani-dump, treed shaded sites with picnic tables. Firepits, firewood available; freezer space available. Quiet relaxed setting. Pay phone, hiking trails, beaver dam. Phone (250) 699-6350. [ADVERTISEMENT] ▲

PG 89.7 (144.4 km) **PR 358** (575 km) View of Mouse Mountain to northwest.

PG 90.9 (146.3 km) **PR 356.8** (573 km) Fraser Lake sawmill to north.

PG 91.3 (147 km) **PR 356.4** (572.3 km) Gas and diesel.

PG 94.5 (152.1 km) **PR 353.2** (567.2 km) **FRASER LAKE** (pop. 1,400; elev. 2,580 feet/786m). **Visitor Information:** Fraser Lake Museum and Visitor Infocentre in log building. **Radio:** CJCI 1450. Small community with all facilities. Created by Endako Mines Ltd. in 1964 on an older townsite; named after the explorer Simon Fraser. Endako Mines Ltd. began operating in 1965 and was Canada's largest molybdenum mine until production slowed in 1982. Mining resumed in 1986. Mine tours are available on Wednesdays; check with the Visitor Infocentre for reservations. Also located here is Fraser Lake Sawmills, the town's largest employer.

PG 96.9 (156 km) **PR 350.8** (563.3 km) **Junction** with main access road south to scenic Francois Lake; also accessible via roads from Burns Lake to Houston. Francois Lake Road (chip seal surfacing) leads south 7 miles/11 km to the east end of Francois Lake (where the Stellako River flows from the lake) and back to Highway 16 at Endako. (It does not link up to the Francois Lake Ferry, south of Burns Lake.) Golf course and several resorts with camping, cabins and boats are located on this scenic rural road along the lake through the Glenannan area. ▲

Francois Lake, good fishing for rainbow to 5 lbs., May to October; kokanee to 3/4 lb., use flashers, willow leaf, flashers with worms, flatfish or spinners, August and September; char to 30 lbs., use large flatfish or spoon, June and July. **Stellako River** is considered one of British Columbia's better fly-fishing streams with rainbow over 2 lbs., all summer; whitefish averaging 1 lb., year-round.

PG 97.6 (157.1 km) **PR 350.1** (562.2 km) Bridge over Stellako River. Highway passes through the Stellako Indian Reserve. Slenyah Indian village to north.

PG 102.5 (164.9 km) **PR 345.2** (554.3 km) Endako Mine (molybdenum) Road and Four Mile Creek.

PG 103 (165.8 km) **PR 344.7** (553.4 km) **ENDAKO**, a small highway community. A log home construction company is located here. Several private campgrounds are located along Francois Lake Road to the south in the Glenannan area. ▲

PG 103.8 (167.1 km) **PR 343.9** (552 km) CNR Bunkhouse.

Watch for moose next 10 miles/16 km westbound.

PG 105.5 (169.8 km) **PR 342.2** (549.3 km) Endako River bridge.

PG 109.1 (175.6 km) **PR 338.6** (543.5 km) Savory rest area to north beside Watskin Creek.

PG 109.8 (176.8 km) **PR 337.9** (542.3 km) Restaurant to north.

Burns Lake Heritage Centre has a museum and visitor information.

(Judy Parkin, staff)

PG 112 (180.3 km) **PR 335.7** (538.8 km) Ross Creek.

PG 112.9 (181.7 km) **PR 334.8** (537.4 km) Tschinkut Creek and moose flats.

PG 120.4 (193.8 km) **PR 327.3** (525.2 km) Moose meadow to south.

PG 121 (194.7 km) **PR 326.6** (524.3 km) Paved turnout to south with litter barrel.

PG 125 (201.1 km) **PR 322.7** (517.8 km) Babine Forest Products sawmill to south.

PG 128.3 (206.4 km) **PR 319.4** (512.5 km) View of Burns Lake to south.

PG 130.1 (209.4 km) **PR 317.6** (509.5 km) Tintagel Creek.

PG 130.2 (209.6 km) **PR 317.5** (509.3 km) Rest area to south with toilet, tables, litter barrels and Tintagel Cairn point of interest.

PG 133.8 (215.4 km) **PR 313.8** (503.4 km) **Burns Lake K.O.A.**, a day's drive from Prince Rupert ferry. Cabins, tenting to full hookups, store, heated showers, laundromat, game room, playground. Mini-golf, lake swimming. Open May 1 to Sept. 30. Pay phone. Your host, Ed Brown, Box 491, Burns Lake, BC V0J 1E0. Phone (250) 692-3105, (800) 562-0905. [ADVERTISEMENT] ▲

PG 136.7 (220 km) **PR 311** (498.9 km) Motel.

PG 137.5 (221.3 km) **PR 310.2** (497.5 km) Welcome to Burns Lake sign.

Junction with scenic Highway 35 (paved) south 18 miles/29 km past **Tchesinkut Lake** to **Francois Lake** ferry landing. A free 36-car ferry departs from the south shore on the hour, from the north shore on the half-hour. From the south shore of Francois Lake, Highway 35 continues to **Takysie Lake** and **Ootsa Lake,** with access to a number of other fishing lakes. Another of the Yellowhead's popular fishing areas with a variety of family-owned camping and cabin resorts. Gas stations, stores and food service are also available. ▲

Sandy's RV and Camping Resort. Over 50 full-service, easy-access sites along the shores of Francois Lake. Hot showers, laundromat, boat rentals, launch, marina, cabins and more. Enjoy northern hospitality; only 18 paved miles south of Burns Lake on Highway 35; located on a true fishing lake. Rainbow, kokanee and lake trout. Pets welcome. VISA, MasterCard. May 15–Oct. 1. Phone/fax (250) 695-6321. Box 42, Burns Lake, BC V0J 1E0. [ADVERTISEMENT] ▲

Takysie Lake Resort & Motel. See display ad this section.

Burns Lake

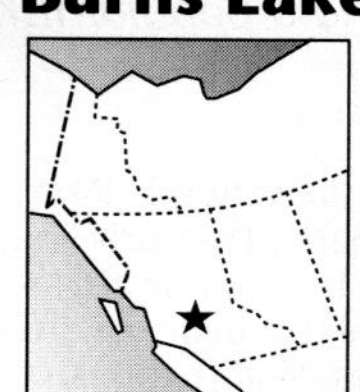

PG 139.9 (225.1 km) **PR 307.8** (496.3 km) **Junction** with road to Babine Lake. **Population:** 2,500; area 10,000. **Visitor Information:** At Burns Lake Heritage Centre on Highway 16. Chamber of Commerce, Box 339, Burns Lake, BC V0J 1E0; phone (250) 692-3773; fax (250) 692-3493.

Elevation: 2,320 feet/707m. **Radio:** CFLD 730, CJFW-FM 92.9, CBC-FM 99.1. **Transportation:** Greyhound Bus, VIA Rail.

The village of Burns Lake had its modest beginnings in 1911, as the site of railway construction. Forestry is the mainstay of the economy, along with ranching and tourism.

Burns Lake has 5 motels, 7 bed and breakfasts, 14 restaurants, 3 shopping centres and a golf course. Overnight camping is available at the municipal campground at Radley Beach; washrooms, playground, picnic tables and swimming area. Winter recreation includes snowmobiling, curling, hockey, figure skating, ringette, broomball and cross-country skiing. ▲

Area attractions include Cheslatta Falls, Pinkut Creek spawning area, Skins Lake Dam, Nourse Creek Falls and a llama ranch. Rockhounds can visit the Eagle Creek Agate and Opal Beds, a short drive south of Burns Lake. Two trails lead into the beds: the opal trail is a challenging 45-minute hike, and the Agate trail is recommended for experienced hikers only. Burns Lake is also the

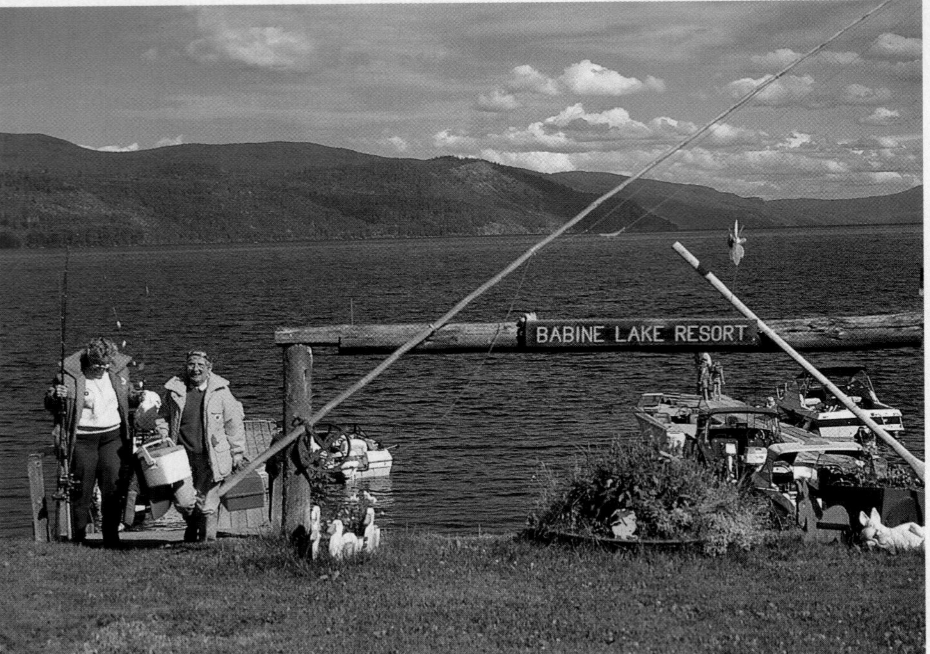

Babine Lake, 30 miles/48 km north of Burns Lake, is British Columbia's largest natural body of water and a popular fishing and boating destination. (Judy Parkin, staff)

gateway to Tweedsmuir Provincial Park, British Columbia's largest park. This pristine wilderness area is accessible by boat or air.

Burns Lake is situated in the heart of the Lakes District, which boasts "3000 miles of fishing." Species include kokanee, rainbow trout, char and salmon. Small family-owned campgrounds and fishing resorts, offering lodging, camping and boat rentals, are tucked along these lakes.

From Burns Lake, a side road leads north to **Babine Lake**, the longest natural lake in the province. One of British Columbia's most important salmon producing lakes, Babine Lake drains into the Skeena River. Excellent fishing for char and trout in summer. At Mile 15/Km 24.1 on this road is Ethel F. Wilson Provincial Park on **Pinkut Lake**; 10 campsites, fishing, swimming, drinking water, toilets, firewood, picnic tables, boat launch. Tours of nearby Pinkut Fish Hatchery available. Look for pictographs on cliffs across from hatchery. Pendleton Bay Provincial Park on Babine Lake, open May to October, offers 20 campsites, picnic tables, fishing, swimming and boat launch. Resorts with cabins and camping on Babine Lake.

Yellowhead Highway 16 Log

(continued)

PG 143.9 (231.5 km) **PR 303.8** (489.9 km) Small community of **DECKER LAKE**.

Decker Lake, good char and trout fishing; fly-fishing in **Endako River**, which joins Decker and Burns lakes.

PG 149.3 (240.3 km) **PR 298.4** (481.2 km) Golf course.

PG 150.9 (242.8 km) **PR 296.8** (478.7 km) Palling rest area with picnic tables, toilets and litter barrels.

PG 153.2 (246.5 km) **PR 294.5** (475 km) Baker Lake airstrip to south is used by firefighting tankers. Weather station. Emergency telephone.

PG 158 (254.2 km) **PR 289.7** (467.3 km) Rose Lake to south.

PG 161.7 (260.3 km) **PR 286** (461.2 km) **Broman Lake**, rainbow and char to 4 lbs., use white-winged flies, spring and summer. Dyncan Lake Indian band. Broman Lake Fuel.

PG 164.7 (265.1 km) **PR 283** (456.4 km) Six Mile Summit (elev. 4,669 feet/1,423m) to west. China Nose Mountain, with steep west-facing cliff, is visible to the south.

PG 165 (265.5 km) **PR 282.7** (456 km) Turnout with litter barrel to south.

PG 166.3 (267.7 km) **PR 281.4** (453.7 km) Turnout to south.

PG 171 (275.3 km) **PR 276.7** (446.1 km) **TOPLEY** (pop. 300). Grocery, post office, cafe, motel and gas station. Turn north here for **Babine Lake** Recreation Area. This paved side road leads north to Topley Landing and Granisle on Babine Lake (descriptions follow). From its junction with the highway at Topley, mileages are as follows: Mile 23.6/38 km, private lodge; Mile 24.4/39.3 km, turnoff to village of Topley Landing; Mile 28.8/46.3 km, Fulton River spawning channel; Mile 28/45.1 km, Red Bluff Provincial Park with 43 campsites, picnicking and day-use facilities, boat launch, drinking water, toilets, firewood, swimming, fishing and hiking; Mile 30.6/49 km, Lions Beach Park with 16 campsites, picnicking and day-use facilities, boat launch, dock, toilets, firewood, swimming and fishing; Mile 31.4/50.5 km, Granisle; Mile 33.4/53.8 km, begin 16-mile/25.7-km gravel road to Smithers Landing Road, which connects Smithers Landing and Smithers. *CAUTION: Watch for moose along road.*

TOPLEY LANDING has several resorts and an unmaintained provincial park. It is also the home of the restored, historic Church of Angels; open June through September. This rustic log church has a collage of angels, a museum and gift shop.

The government-operated Fulton River spawning channel has 2 major spawning channels on the river that connect Fulton Lake and Babine Lake. Babine Lake, which flows into the Skeena River, is one of the largest freshwater habitats for sockeye salmon. The salmon enhancement project at Fulton River produces about 95 million sockeye fry annually. The sockeye run takes place in August and September. Tours may be available at hatchery office.

GRANISLE (pop. 400) was established in 1965 as a company town for the Granisle Copper Mine. In 1972, Noranda Bell Mines Copper Division went into operation. Granisle Copper was closed in 1982 and the Noranda mine was closed in 1992. During mining excavations, a mammoth skeleton was unearthed. The fossilized remains were donated to the Museum of Civilization in Ottawa–Hull. Granisle has become a retirement community and remains a resort area for fishing, boating, waterskiing and camping on Babine Lake. Facilities at Granisle include a convenience store, liquor outlet, hotel with licensed restaurant, resort condominiums, post office, museum, boat rentals, marina and tackle shop. Dump station, showers, laundromat and fresh water available at the Visitor Infocentre.

Babine Lake, rainbow 6 to 8 lbs.; lake trout to 40 lbs., use spoons, flashers and red-and-white spoons, May through November. When fishing early in the year, use a short troll.

PG 172.3 (277.3 km) **PR 275.4** (444 km) Rest area to south with view of mountains.

PG 176.9 (284.7 km) **PR 270.8** (437.8 km) Byman Creek.

PG 178.7 (287.6 km) **PR 269** (434.9 km) Motel, laundromat and restaurant.

PG 180.1 (289.9 km) **PR 267.6** (432.5 km) Turnout to north.

PG 186.5 (300.1 km) **PR 261.2** (422.2 km) Golf course to south.

PG 188.8 (303.9 km) **PR 258.9** (418.4 km) **Shady Rest RV Park**. See display ad this section.

Houston

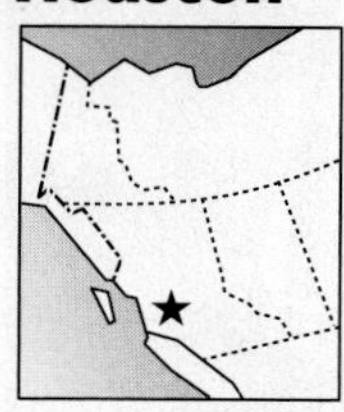

PG 190.1 (305.9 km) **PR 257.6** (416.4 km) Houston Infocentre. **Population:** 3,960. **Emergency Services: Police**, phone (250) 845-2204. **Ambulance**, phone 112-562-7241. **Visitor Information:** Visitor Infocentre in log building on Highway 16 across from the mall; open year-round. Write Houston Visitor Infocentre, Box 396, Houston, BC V0J 1Z0, or phone (250) 845-7640.

Elevation: 1,949 feet/594m. **Radio:** CFBV 1450, CFPR-FM 102.1, CJFW-FM 105.5. **Transportation:** Greyhound bus, VIA Rail.

Established in the early 1900s, Houston was a tie-cutting centre during construction of the Grand Trunk Pacific Railway in 1912. It was named for Prince Rupert newspaperman John Houston, the former mayor of Nelson, BC. Logging continued to support the local economy with the rapid growth of mills and planer mills in the 1940s and 1950s. Houston was incorporated as a village in 1957.

The Equity Silver Mine began production in 1980. Production ceased in January 1994 and equipment was dismantled.

Today, the main industry in Houston is forest products. The 2 large sawmills here, Houston Forest Products and Northwood Pulp and Timber, offer forestry-awareness tours. The Chamber of Commerce and Visitor Infocentre arrange tours of the sawmills and also offer a day-long tour through the area's forests to provide a first-hand look at the forest industry.

Hunting, canoeing, cross-country skiing and especially sportfishing are major attractions here with the Bulkley River, nearby Morice River and several lakes. Look for the World's Largest Fly Fishing Rod on display at the Visitor Infocentre. The 60-foot-long anodized aluminum fly rod was designed by a local avid fly fisherman and built by local volunteers. (The 21-inch fly is a fluorescent "Skykomish Sunrise.")

Houston has all visitor facilities, including motels, campgrounds, restaurants, gas stations, a shopping centre and golf courses. ▲

Houston Motor Inn. See display ad this section.

Pleasant Valley Motel. 52 newly renovated rooms with good beds. Some non-smoking and kitchenette units. Handicap access. Cable TV. Public telephone. Guest laundromat. Full-service restaurant, well known for homestyle cooking and generous portions. For reservations call collect (250) 845-2246, fax (250) 845-3065. 3030 Hwy. 16, Houston, BC V0J 1Z0. [ADVERTISEMENT]

A 60-foot-long fly rod is displayed at Houston's visitor infocentre. (© Beth Davidow)

Yellowhead Highway 16 Log

(continued)

PG 192.6 (310 km) **PR 255.1** (412.2 km) **Junction** with the Morice River access road which extends 52 miles/84 km south to Morice Lake. Approximately 20 miles/32 km along the Morice River Road you can turn east on a gravel road which leads past Owen Lake and Nadina River Road to Francois Lake. From Francois Lake ferry landing Highway 35 leads north to Burns Lake.

The 2 famous salmon and steelhead streams, **Morice** and **Bulkley**, unite near Houston, and it is possible to fish scores of pools all along the Morice River. *NOTE: Special requirements apply to fishing these streams; check with Fish and Game office.*

PG 193 (310.7 km) **PR 254.7** (411.5 km) Bulkley River bridge and rest area; tables, litter barrel and toilets.

PG 196.7 (316.5 km) **PR 251** (405.7 km) Barrett Station Airport. View of Barrett's Hat northbound.

PG 200.5 (322.6 km) **PR 247.2** (399.6 km) Hungry Hill Summit (elev. 2,769 feet/844m). To the north are the snow-capped peaks of the Babine Mountains, to the west is the Hudson Bay Range.

PG 203.3 (327.2 km) **PR 244.4** (394.9 km) Bulkley View paved rest area with picnic tables, toilets and litter barrels.

PG 208.1 (334.9 km) **PR 239.6** (387 km) Deep Creek.

PG 210.4 (338.7 km) **PR 237.2** (383.2 km) Quick Road East. Original telegraph cabin.

PG 211.4 (340.2 km) **PR 236.3** (381.7 km) Garage.

PG 213.3 (343.3 km) **PR 234.4** (378.6 km) Quick Road West.

PG 216.8 (348.9 km) **PR 230.9** (373 km) Bulkley field and river.

PG 217.1 (349.4 km) **PR 230.6** (372.5 km) Rest area to west overlooking the Bulkley River.

PG 219.8 (353.7 km) **PR 227.9** (368.1 km) **Ft. Telkwa R.V. Park.** See display ad this section. ▲

PG 220.3 (354.5 km) **PR 227.4** (367.3 km) **TELKWA** (pop. 959). A pleasant village at the confluence of the Telkwa and Bulkley rivers (you can fish from Riverside Street or the riverbanks). Visitor Infocentre at the village office and museum. Facilities include a grocery, post office and a gas station with auto repair. Lodging at Douglas Motel, dining at 3 restaurants. A unique shop found here is Horsfield Leather, which specializes in handmade fishing rod cases, leather water bottles and other leather goods. Fishing and hunting information, licenses and supplies available at the general store. Kinsmen Barbecue is held over Labour Day weekend; games, contests and demolition derby. Eddy Park, on the western edge of town beside the Bulkley River, is a good spot for picnicking (look for the wishing well). St. Stephen's Anglican Church was built in 1911 and the bell and English gate added in 1921. Other Heritage buildings date back to 1908.

Douglas Motel beside beautiful Bulkley River. Riverview units, suites, log cabin with fireplace in relaxing resort atmosphere. Hot pool, sauna complex, kitchens, cablevision, queen beds, electric heat, summer ceiling fans, picnic area, firepit, barbecues, horseshoe pitch, summer outdoor sports equipment. Salmon and steelhead fishing. Walking distance to stores, restaurants and lake. VISA and MasterCard. Douglas Family, (250) 846-5679. [ADVERTISEMENT]

PG 220.7 (355.3 km) **PR 227** (366.5 km) Turnoff to north for **Tyhee Lake** Provincial Park; 55 campsites, 20 picnic tables, dump station, hiking trails, fishing, swimming, boat launch. Seaplane base at lake; charter fly-in fishing. ▲

Also turnoff here on the Telkwa High Road, which intersects with Babine Lake access road (gravel), which leads 46 miles/74 km north to Smithers Landing on Babine Lake and 56 miles/90 km to Granisle.

Tyhee Lake, rainbow and lake trout to 2 lbs., June through August; Kamloops trout to 2 lbs. **Babine River,** steelhead to 40 lbs., late fall. **Telkwa River,** spring and coho salmon to 24 lbs., summer to fall.

PG 221.1 (355.9 km) **PR 226.6** (365.9 km) Gas station.

PG 225.5 (362.9 km) **PR 222.2** (358.8 km) Second turnoff westbound for Babine Lake.

PG 227.2 (365.7 km) **PR 220.5** (356 km) Riverside Recreation Centre; golf, restaurant and campground.

PG 227.5 (366.1 km) **PR 220.2** (355.7 km) Turnoff to north on gravel road for Driftwood Canyon Provincial Park; picnic area and toilets. Fossil beds in shale outcroppings along creekbank. This gravel side road continues north to Smithers Landing.

PG 227.7 (366.4 km) **PR 220** (355.3 km) Bridge over Bulkley River.

Smithers

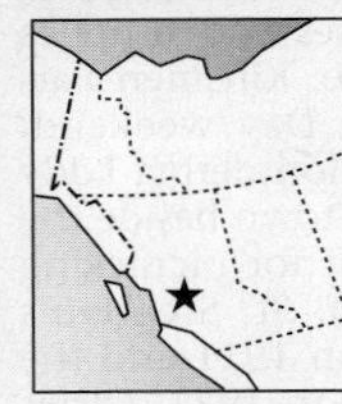

PG 229.2 (368.8 km) PR 218.5 (352.6 km). Smithers infocentre. **Population:** 6,000; area 30,000. **Emergency Services: Police,** phone (250)847-3233. **Hospital and Poison Centre,** 3950 8th Ave., phone (250) 847-2611. **Ambulance,** phone 1-562-7241. **Visitor Information:** Visitor Infocentre and Chamber of Commerce are located above the museum in the Central Park Bldg., open year-round. Also at Cantrek Tours, 1285 Main Street; phone (250) 847-2797.

Elevation: 1,621 feet/494m. **Climate:** Relatively warmer and drier than mountainous areas to the west; average temperature in July is 58°F/14°C, in January 14°F/-10°C; annual precipitation, 13 inches. **Radio:** CFBV 1230, CFPR-FM 97.5. **Television:** Channels 5, 13 and cable. **Newspaper:** *Interior News* (weekly).

Transportation: Air—Scheduled service to Vancouver and Terrace via Canadian Airlines International. Daily flights to Prince George and Terrace via Central Mountain Air. **Railroad**—VIA Rail. **Bus**—Greyhound. **Car Rentals**—Available.

Sitting amidst rugged mountains, the town has been enhanced by Swiss-style storefronts that have been added to many of the buildings. Reconstructed in 1979, Main Street offers many shops and restaurants. Incorporated as a village in 1921, Smithers officially became a town in Canada's centennial year, 1967. The original site was chosen in 1913 by construction crews working on the Grand Trunk Pacific Railway (the town was named for one-time chairman of the railway A.W. Smithers). Today it is a distribution and supply centre for farms, mills and mines in the area.

Smithers is the largest town in the Bulkley Valley and the site of Hudson Bay Mountain, a popular ski area (skiing from November to mid-April).

Smithers has several motels, gas stations, restaurants, laundromat/car wash and good shopping. Government liquor store located on Queen Street at Broadway Avenue. There are 2 18-hole golf courses, both with rentals and clubhouses.

Town clock in Smithers. This Bulkley Valley town has several Swiss-style storefronts. (© Wes Bergen, DIARAMA)

There is a municipal campground with security and firewood (no hookups) at Riverside Park on the Bulkley River; turn north at the museum across from Main Street and drive up the hill about a mile and watch for sign. There are private campgrounds located east and west of town; see highway log. ▲

Special events include the Bulkley Valley Fall Fair, held on the last weekend in August each year, one of the largest agricultural exhibitions in the province. The Midsummer Music Festival in June features local, regional and national artists.

Smithers offers a number of scenic drives. Hudson Bay Mountain (elev. 8,700 feet/2,652m) is a 14-mile/23-km drive from Highway 16; the plateau above timberline at the ski area is a good spot for summer hikes. In the winter months, Smithers boasts one of the largest ski hills in northern British Columbia. A 6,000-foot/1,829-m triple chair and 2 T-bars climb the 1,750-foot/533-m vertical, offering skiers 18 different runs.

Fossil hunters should drive to Driftwood Canyon Provincial Park; turn off Highway 16 just east of the Bulkley River bridge (travelers are advised to stop first at the Visitor Infocentre in town for a map and directions). A display at the park illustrates the fossils, such as metasequoia, a type of redwood which occurs in the shale formation.

Adams Igloo Wildlife Museum, just west of town on Highway 16, has an excellent display of mammals found in British Columbia.

A beautiful spot not to be missed is Twin Falls and Glacier Gulch. Take the 4-mile-/6.4-km-long gravel road (steep in places) from Highway 16 on the western edge of town.

A 2.2-mile-/3.5-km-long interpretive nature trail with native wildlife and plant species is 10 miles/16 km west of Smithers on the Hudson Bay Mountain Ski Hill road in Smithers Community Forest. This trail can also be used in winter for cross-country skiing, and connects to other cross-country ski trails. Detailed maps of the area showing all hiking trails are available at the infocentre.

An extensive list of lake and river fishing spots in the area, with information on boat launches and boat rentals, is available from the Smithers District Chamber of Commerce, Box 2379, Smithers, BC V0J 2N0; phone (250) 847-9854; or ask at the Visitor Infocentre.

Moose, mule deer, grizzly and black bears, mountain goats and caribou are found in the area, and guides and outfitters are available locally. All species of grouse can be hunted in the Bulkley Valley during the fall. Information is available from the Fish and Wildlife Branch office in Smithers.

Cantrek Tours Inc. New information service center, 1285 Main Street, Smithers. A "travelers" haven. Ultimate lodging, recreation and adventure. Discover our playground. "We'll fit you in—Get you set up!" Meet our people. Great selection of local and native art. Phone (250) 847-2797. North America (888) VIP-5456. Fax (250) 847-2757. E-mail: cantrek@mail.netshop.net. Internet: sss.sd54.bc.ca/tech/cantrek/cantrek.htm. [ADVERTISEMENT]

Yellowhead Highway 16 Log

(continued)

PG 230.6 (371.1 km) **PR 217.1** (350.1 km) Smithers golf club.

PG 231.7 (372.8 km) **PR 216** (348.4 km) Paved access road to Lake Kathlyn. There is a municipal park with small beach and boat launch located here. Powerboats not permitted. Closed to waterfowl hunting. Side road continues 4 miles/6.4 km (gravel) to Twin Falls and Glacier Gulch.

PG 232.7 (374.5 km) **PR 215** (346.7 km) Road to north leads to Smithers airport.

PG 234 (376.6 km) **PR 213.7** (344.6 km) Lake Kathlyn Road to west.

PG 234.9 (378 km) **PR 212.8** (343.6 km) **Glacier View RV Park.** Wake up to a panoramic view of the Hudson Bay Glacier. Eight level gravel sites with 15-/30-amp service and water hookups. Dry pull-throughs up to 55 feet. Pit toilets. Walking distance to Wildlife Museum. Easy access. Reservations: RR 1, S 9 C 31, Smithers, BC V0J 2N0, (250) 847-3961. [ADVERTISEMENT] ▲

PG 235.1 (378.3 km) **PR 212.6** (342.9 km) Hudson Bay rest area to west with picnic tables, toilets and litter barrels. Beautiful view of Hudson Bay Mountain.

PG 235.4 (378.8 km) **PR 212.3** (342.4 km) **Adams Igloo Wildlife Museum.** The finest collection of big game animals, furbearers and birds native to British Columbia, mounted life-size and displayed in their natural habitat. The inside mural, painted by leading wildlife artist Tom Sander, gives a 3-dimensional impression for realism. Stop at the White Dome, 6 miles west of Smithers beside one of the highway's most beautiful viewpoints. Fur rugs and souvenirs for sale. Ted Moon, Curator. [ADVERTISEMENT]

Black bear cub. Black bears range throughout British Columbia.

(© Beth Davidow)

PG 238.4 (383.6 km) **PR 209.3** (337.6 km) Tobogan Creek Fish Hatchery.

PG 243.1 (391.3 km) **PR 204.6** (329.8 km) Trout Creek bridge. Store with groceries, post office and phone; fishing licenses available.

PG 248.7 (400.3 km) **PR 199** (320.7 km) Turnout to north with picnic tables and view of Bulkley River and Moricetown Canyon; good photo stop.

PG 248.9 (400.6 km) **PR 198.8** (320.4 km) Telkwa High Road is a short side road on the north side of the highway leading to Moricetown Canyon and Falls on the Bulkley River and Moricetown campground. For centuries a famous First Nation's fishing spot, Aboriginal people may still be seen here gaffing, jigging and netting salmon in July and August. A worthwhile stop. ▲

PG 249.2 (401.1 km) **PR 198.5** (319.9 km) **MORICETOWN** (pop. 680; elev. 1,341 feet/409m). **Radio:** CBC-FM 96.5. Moricetown has a gas station with minor repair service and diesel fuel. There is a handicraft store. A campground is located in Moricetown Canyon (turnoff at **Milepost PG 255.7**). Moricetown is a First Nations reserve and village, the oldest settlement in the Bulkley Valley. Traditionally, the Native people (Wet'su-wet'en) took advantage of the narrow canyon to trap salmon. The centuries-old settlement ('Kyah Wiget) is now named after Father A.G. Morice, a Roman Catholic missionary. Born in France, Father Morice came to British Columbia in 1880 and worked with the Aboriginals of northern British Columbia from 1885 to 1904. He achieved world recognition for his writings in anthropology, ethnology and history.

PG 253.8 (408.5 km) **PR 193.9** (312.4 km) Chicken Creek.

PG 255.9 (411.9 km) **PR 191.8** (306.6 km) East Boulder Creek.

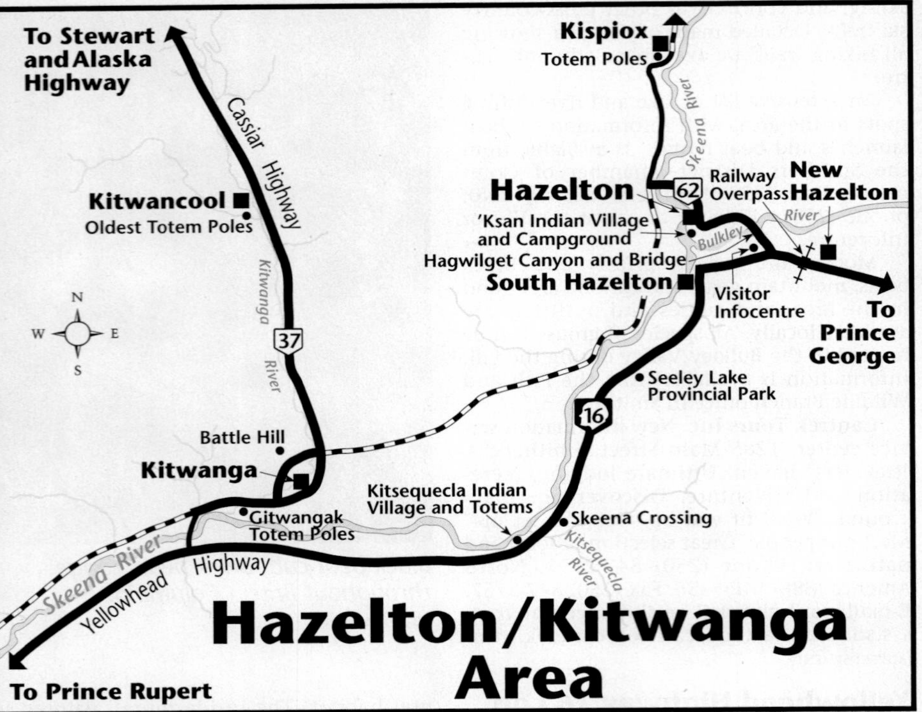

PG 258.9 (416.6 km) **PR 188.8** (304.3 km) Paved turnout.

PG 260.7 (419.5 km) **PR 187** (301.4 km) Paved turnout with picnic tables and litter barrels.

PR 260.9 (419.9 km) **PR 186.8** (300.9 km) View of Bulkley River.

PG 261.5 (420.9 km) **PR 186.2** (299.9 km) Paved turnout.

PG 263.9 (424.8 km) **PR 183.8** (296 km) Turnoff to north for Forest Service campsite (7.5 miles/12.1 km) with pit toilets, tables and litter barrels. Fishing in **Suskwa River;** coho salmon to 10 lbs., use tee-spinners in July; steelhead to 20 lbs., use Kitamat #32 and soft bobbers in late fall.

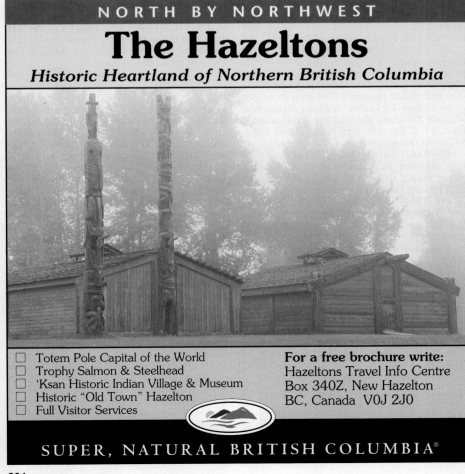

PG 269.1 (433.1 km) **PR 178.6** (287.6 km) Turnoff to north for **Ross Lake** Provincial Park; 25 picnic sites, boat launch (no powerboats), swimming. Fishing for rainbow to 4 lbs.

PG 270.5 (435.3 km) **PR 177.2** (285.4 km) Entering New Hazelton, the first of 3 communities westbound sharing the name Hazelton (the others are Hazelton and South Hazelton), known collectively as The Hazeltons; description follows.

New Hazelton

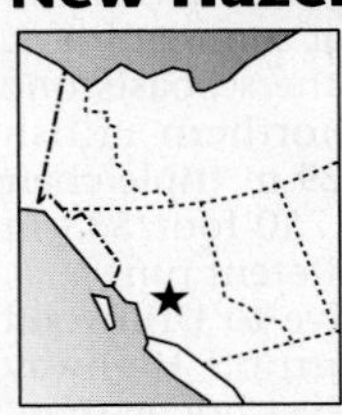

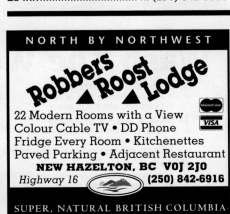

PG 271.1 (436.3 km) **PR 176.6** (284.4 km) **Junction** of Highway 16 with Highway 62 to Hazelton, 'Ksan and Kispiox (descriptions follow). The turnoff for Highway 62 is located just west of the railway overpass in New Hazelton. The easy-to-miss turn is on the north side (right for westbound travelers) of Highway 16 between the overpass and the Visitor Infocentre at the base of the hill. **Population:** area 1,300. **Emergency Services: Police,** phone (250) 842-5244.

Visitor Information: Visitor Infocentre in 2-story log building at the junction. Look for the 3 statues representing the gold rush packer Cataline, the Northwest miner, and the Upper Skeena logger. Museum located in Infocentre.

Elevation: 1,150 feet/351m. **Radio:** CBC 1170. **Transportation:** VIA Rail. Greyhound bus.

This small highway community has gas stations, major auto repair, restaurants, cafes, post office, general store, a hotel and a motel. Laundromat, propane, sporting goods, and hunting and fishing licenses available in town. An ATM is located at the Chevron station in New Hazelton and at the mall on the highway.

Attractions here include historic Hazelton, the Indian village of 'Ksan and sportfishing the Bulkley and Kispiox rivers

First Nations canoe on display at 'Ksan Historical Village. *(Judy Parkin, staff)*

(descriptions follow). Mount Rocher Deboule, elev. 8,000 feet/2,438m, towers behind the town.

HAZELTON. Situated at the confluence of the Skeena and Bulkley rivers, Hazelton grew up at "The Forks" as a trans-shipping point at the head of navigation on the Skeena and a wintering place for miners and prospectors from the rigorous Interior. Thomas Hankin established a Hudson's Bay Co. trading post here in 1868. The name Hazelton comes from the numerous hazelnut bushes growing on the flats.

Cataline, famous pioneer packer and traveler, is buried near here in an unmarked grave at Pioneer Cemetery. Jean Caux (his real name) was a Basque who, from 1852 to 1912, with loaded mules plodding 12 miles/19 km a day, supplied mining and construction camps from Yale and Ashcroft northward through Hazelton, where he often wintered. His mule trails became roads; his exploits are legends.

For some years, before the arrival of the railroad and highways, supplies for trading posts at Bear and Babine lakes and the Omineca goldfields moved by riverboat from the coast to Hazelton and from there over trails to the backcountry. Some of the Yukon gold rushers passed through Hazelton on their way to the Klondike, pack trains having made the trip from Hazelton to Telegraph Creek over the old Telegraph Trail as early as 1874.

This community has reconstructed much of what the town was like in the 1890s. Look for the antique machinery downtown. The history of the Hazelton area can be traced by car on the Hand of History tour. Pick up a brochure from the Visitor Infocentre showing the location of the 19 historic sites on the driving tour.

'KSAN HISTORICAL VILLAGE and Museum, a replica Gitksan Indian village, is 4.5 miles/7.2 km from Highway 16. It is a reconstruction of the traditional Gitksan Village, which has stood at this site for centuries. It is located at the confluence of the Bulkley and Skeena rivers by the 'Ksan Assoc. There are 7 communal houses, totem poles and dugout canoes. At the carving shed, carvers produce First Nation's arts and crafts which can be purchased. Food service is available on site.

For a nominal charge from May to September, you can join a guided tour of the communal houses. Performances of traditional song and dance are presented every Friday evening during July and August in the Wolf House. Admission to grounds is $2, children under 6 are free. Guided tours of the grounds run $7 for adults, $6 for students. The site is open year-round, hours vary. Open daily April 15–Oct. 15. Tours are available mid-April to late September. Phone (250) 842-5544.

A well-maintained full-service trailer park and campground on the banks of the Skeena and Bulkley rivers is operated by the Gitanmaax Indian Band from the Gitanmaax Reserve.

KISPIOX (pop. 825) Indian village and 3 fishing resorts are 20 miles/32 km north on a good paved road at the confluence of the Skeena and Kispiox rivers. Kispiox is noted for its stand of totems close to the river. There is a market garden (fresh vegetables) located approximately 7 miles/11 km north on the Kispiox Road (about 2 miles/ 3.2 km before the Kispiox totem poles). Camping, cabins and fishing at lodges and campgrounds in the valley. Valley residents host the Kispiox Rodeo the first weekend of June. This excellent event has run annually since 1952.

Kispiox River Resort & Campground. Beautiful location on banks of Kispiox River in peaceful valley setting. Excellent fishing throughout the year including spring salmon, cutthroat and rainbow trout, Dolly Varden and steelhead. Campground. Housekeeping cabins. Showers. Laundry. Tenters welcome. Fishing licenses. Guides. Tackle. 26 miles from Highway 16. Kispiox Valley Road. RR 1, Hazelton, BC V0J 1Y0. (250) 842-6182. [ADVERTISEMENT]

Bulkley River, Dolly Varden to 5 lbs.; spring salmon, mid-July to mid-August; coho salmon 4 to 12 lbs., Aug. 15 through September, flies, spoons and spinners; steelhead to 20 lbs., July through November, flies, Kitamats, weighted spoons and soft bobbers. **Kispiox River** is famous for its trophy-sized steelhead. Check on regulations and obtain a fishing license before your arrival. Fishing is done with single-hook only, with catch-release for steelhead between Aug. 15 and Sept. 30. Season is July 1 to Nov. 30 for salmon, trout and steelhead. Excellent fly-fishing waters: spring salmon, July to early August; coho salmon, late August to early September; steelhead from September until freezeup. Sizable Dolly Vardens and cutthroat. Steelhead average 20 lbs., with some catches over 30 lbs.

Yellowhead Highway 16 Log

(continued)

PG 273.3 (439.9 km) **PR 174.4** (280.8 km) Turnoff to north for 2-mile/3.2-km loop road through small community of **SOUTH HAZELTON**; restaurant, general store, gas station with minor repair, lodging.

PG 277.1 (445.9 km) **PR 170.6** (274.8 km) **Seeley Lake** Provincial Park; 20 campsites, drinking water, pit toilets, firewood, sani-dump, day-use area with picnic tables, swimming, fishing.

PG 278.8 (448.8 km) **PR 168.8** (271.8 km) Restaurant.

PG 282.4 (454.5 km) **PR 165.3** (266.1 km) Carnaby Sawmill.

PG 286.6 (461.2 km) **PR 161.1** (259.3 km) Skeena Crossing. Historic Canadian National Railways bridge (see plaque at Kitseguecla).

PG 287.4 (462.5 km) **PR 160.3** (258 km) **KITSEGUECLA,** First Nation's village. Totem poles throughout village are classic examples, still in original locations. Historical plaque about Skeena Crossing.

PG 287.7 (463 km) **PR 160** (257.6 km) Sheep's Rapids.

PG 292.5 (470.7 km) **PR 155.2** (250 km) Road winds along edge of river.

CAUTION: Watch for falling rock next 32 miles/51.5 km.

PG 297.7 (479.1 km) **PR 150** (241.4 km) Gas station and cafe at **junction** with Cassiar Highway (BC Highway 37). Bridge across Skeena River to Kitwanga and Cassiar Highway to Stewart, Hyder, AK, and Alaska Highway. See CASSIAR HIGHWAY section page 266.

Highway passes Seven Sisters peaks; the highest is 9,140 feet/2,786m.

PG 299 (481.2 km) **PR 148.7** (239.4 km) **Gitksan Paintbrush Native Arts & Crafts.** Silver and gold jewelry: rings, earrings, bracelets. Limited edition prints and originals. Smoked moosehide moccasins, beaded leatherwork. Wood carvings, cedar baskets.

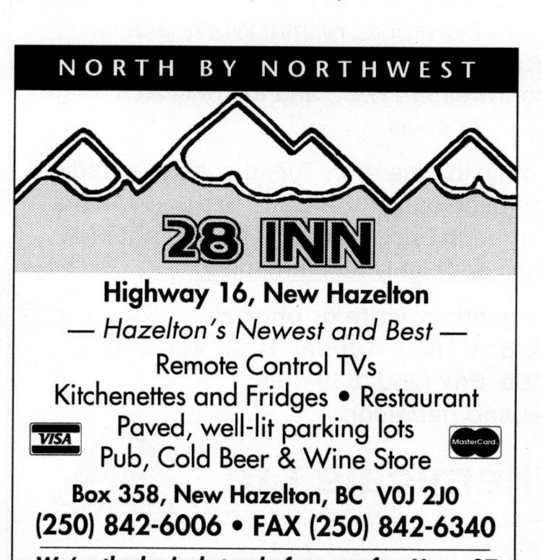

Highway 37 South Log

Distance is measured from the junction with Yellowhead Highway 16 (J).

J 0 Junction with Yellowhead Highway 16 at **Milepost PG 354.7** (east exit to Terrace).

J 0.9 (1.4 km) Krumm Road. Turn east for golf course.

J 3.1 (5 km) Terrace–Kitimat airport access road.

J 7.9 (12.7 km) Lakelse Lake Provincial Park parking area and trail to Gruchy's Beach.

J 8.7 (14 km) Lakelse Lake Provincial Park parking areas and picnic area; tables, toilets, showers, changehouses and beach. Park headquarters located here.

J 10.6 (17.1 km) Waterlily Bay; food, lodging, boat launch.

J 11.4 (18.3 km) Lakelse Lake Provincial Park Furlong Bay campground and picnic area; 156 vehicle and tent campsites, nature trails, swimming, sandy beach, flush toilets, showers, dump station, boat launch, drinking water, wheelchair access, firewood and interpretive programs.

J 13.8 (22.2 km) Onion Lake hiking and ski trails to west.

J 20.6 (33.2 km) Access to Kitimat River.

J 27.4 (44.1 km) Kitimat Airpark landing strip for small planes.

J 34.8 (56 km) Hirsch Creek Park to west; picnic area, camping, fishing and hiking.

J 35 (56.3 km) Hirsch Creek bridge.

J 35.8 (57.6 km) Kitimat Travel Infocentre to east.

J 36.2 (58.3 km) Minette Bay Road leads east to MK Bay Marina.

J 36.6 (58.9 km) Viewpoint of Douglas Channel and city map. Picnic tables, garden.

Kitimat

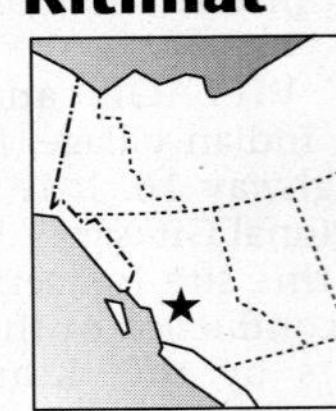

J 37.6 (60.5 km) Located at the head of Douglas Channel. **Population:** 12,000. **Emergency Services: RCMP**, phone (250) 632-7111. **Fire Department**, phone (250) 639-9111. **Ambulance**, phone (250) 632-5433. **Hospital**, phone (250) 632-2121. **Radio:** CKTK 1230; CBC-FM 101.1, CJFW-FM 103.1. **Newspaper:** *The News Advertiser* (weekly); *Northern Sentinel* (weekly).

This community was planned and built in the early 1950s when the B.C. government attracted Alcan (Aluminum Co. of Canada) to establish a smelter here. Today, Kitimat is a major port and home to several industries. Free tours are available (primarily in summer, reservations recommended) at Alcan, (250) 639-8259; Eurocan Pulp and Paper, (250) 639-3597; Methanex Corp., (250) 639-9292; and Kitimat fish hatchery, (250) 639-9616. Tour Mike's Wildlife Museum to see over 100 mounts; admission fee; (250) 632-7083.

Paved Highway 37 south of Terrace.
(© Fred Chapman, DIARAMA)

Kitimat's location at the head of Douglas Channel makes it a popular boating, fishing and scuba diving destination. There are several charter operators.

Kitimat has all visitor facilities, including a modern shopping mall, restaurants and motels; library, theatre, swimming pool and gym; and an 18-hole golf course. Many scenic hiking trails are available. A free guide to area day hikes is available at the Visitor Infocentre. The Centennial Museum is located at city centre. Information on local Native art, canoe trips and heli-adventures available at the Chamber of Commerce, Box 214 (M), Kitimat, BC V8C 2G7; phone (800 664-6554 or (250) 632-6294; fax (250) 632-4685; e-mail gguise@kitimat.sno.net.

There is camping at Radley Park in town; electrical hookups, showers, fishing, toilets, playground and dump station. (Radley Park—on the other side of the river—is also the site of a 500-year-old, 165-foot/50-m Sitka spruce, one of the largest of its kind in the province.) There is also camping at Hirsch Creek Park on the edge of town and private campgrounds.

Local fishermen line the banks of the **Kitimat River** in May for the steelhead run. Chinook salmon run in June and July. Coho run from August into September.

Kitimat also offers many winter activities, including cross-country skiing and indoor ice rinks. Downhill skiing at nearby Terrace and Smithers.

Alcan Smelters and Chemical Ltd. See display ad this section.

Return to Milepost PG 354.7
Yellowhead Highway 16

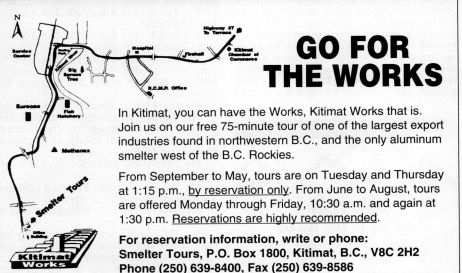

Clothing and souvenirs. Quality merchandise, most from local artists. Excellent prices. Easy access. Summer hours 9 A.M.–7 P.M. P.O. Box 97, Kitwanga, BC V0J 2A0. Phone or fax (250) 849-5085. [ADVERTISEMENT]

PG 300.8 (484.1 km) **PR 146.9** (236.5 km) **Seven Sisters RV Park and Campground.** Outstanding value. Beautiful park-like setting. Many treed sites. Fresh water, sani-dump, picnic tables at every site, flush toilets, shower, firepits with free firewood, all for $9. Excellent salmon fishing close by. Tenters and cyclists welcome. (250) 849-5489 for reservations. Box 338, Kitwanga, BC V0J 2A0. [ADVERTISEMENT] ▲

PG 303.4 (488.2 km) **PR 144.3** (232.4 km) Boulder Creek rest area; parking for large vehicles; toilets, litter barrels and picnic tables.

PG 306.6 (493.4 km) **PR 141.1** (227.3 km) Whiskey Creek.

PG 307.6 (495 km) **PR 140.1** (225.8 km) Gravel turnout to north with litter barrel.

PG 308 (495.6 km) **PR 139.7** (225.2 km) Gull Creek.

PG 309.1 (497.4 km) **PR 138.6** (223.4 km) **CEDARVALE,** cafe. Loop road through rural setting. Historical plaque about Holy City.

PG 309.2 (497.6 km) **PR 138.5** (223.2 km) Hand of History sign about "Holy City."

Watch for bears fishing the river for salmon in late July and early August.

PG 312.5 (502.9 km) **PR 135.2** (218 km) Gravel turnout to north with litter barrel.

PG 313.6 (504.6 km) **PR 134.1** (216.4 km) Watch for fallen rock on this stretch of highway.

PG 315.3 (507.4 km) **PR 132.4** (213.6 km) Flint Creek.

PG 318.5 (512.6 km) **PR 129.2** (208.5 km) Turnout with historical plaque about Skeena River Boats: "From 1889, sternwheelers and smaller craft fought their way through the Coast Mountains, churning past such awesome places as 'The Devil's Elbow' and 'The Hornet's Nest.' Men and supplies were freighted upstream, furs and gold downstream. A quarter century of colour and excitement began to fade in 1912, as the Grand Trunk Pacific neared completion."

PG 322.4 (518.8 km) **PR 125.2** (202.4 km) Gravel turnout to north.

PG 323.2 (520.1 km) **PR 124.5** (201.1 km) Gravel turnout to south with litter barrel.

PG 332 (534.3 km) **PR 115.7** (187.3 km) Legate Creek.

PG 335.7 (540.2 km) **PR 112** (181.5 km) Rest area on river with water pump, picnic tables, toilets and litter barrels.

PG 336 (540.7 km) **PR 111.7** (181 km) Skeena Cellulose bridge (private) crosses Skeena River to access tree farms on north side.

PG 336.9 (542.1 km) **PR 110.8** (179.6 km) St. Croix Creek.

PG 340.3 (547.7 km) **PR 107.4** (173.9 km) Chindemash Creek.

PG 342.8 (551.6 km) **PR 104.9** (170 km) Tiny chapel to south serves small community of **USK;** the village is reached via the reaction ferry seen to north. The nondenominational chapel is a replica of the pioneer church that stood in Usk until 1936, when the Skeena River flooded, sweeping away the village and the church. The only item from the church to survive was the Bible, which was found floating atop a small pine table.

PG 345 (555.2 km) **PR 102.7** (166.4 km) Entrance to Kitselas Canyon (1 mile/1.6 km).

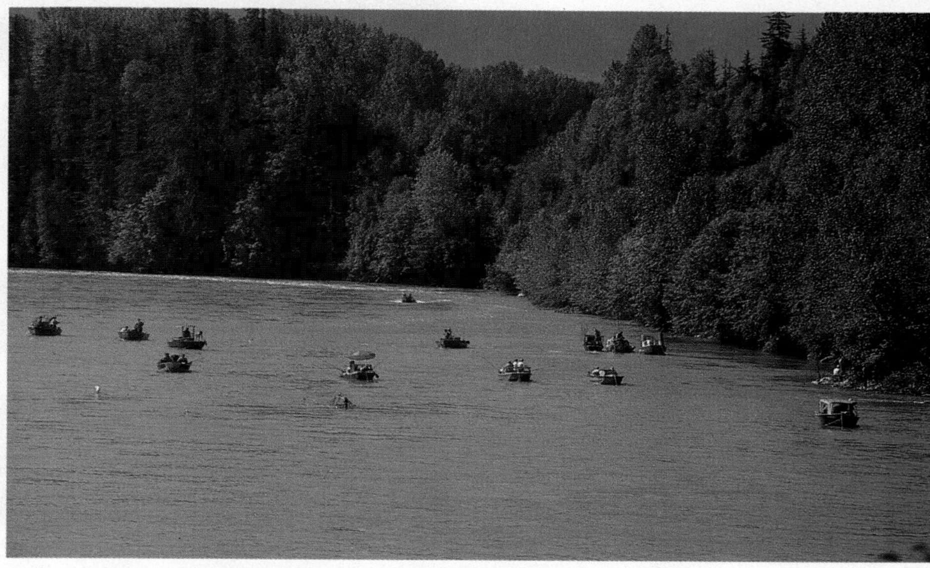

Salmon fishing on the Skeena River near Terrace. (Judy Parkin, staff)

PG 345.2 (555.6 km) **PR 102.4** (166 km) Side road leads 0.5 mile/0.8 km south to **Kleanza Creek** Provincial Park; 21 campsites, 25 picnic sites, fishing, drinking water, toilets, firewood, wheelchair access. Short trail to remains from Cassiar Hydraulic Mining Co. gold-sluicing operations here (1911–14). ♿ 🐟 ▲

PG 345.4 (555.9 km) **PR 102.3** (165.7 km) Kleanza Bridge.

PG 346.9 (558.3 km) **PR 100.8** (163.3 km) Gravel turnout to north.

PG 349.7 (562.8 km) **PR 98** (158.7 km) Fishing lodge.

PG 350.5 (564.1 km) **PR 97.2** (157.4 km) Gas and lodging. **Copper (Zymoetz) River,** can be fished from Highway 16 or follow local maps. Coho salmon to 10 lbs., use tee-spinners in July; steelhead to 20 lbs., check locally for season and restrictions. 🐟

PG 352 (566.5 km) **PR 95.7** (155 km) Turnout to north with tourist information sign and area map.

PG 352.2 (566.8 km) **PR 95.5** (154.7 km) Motel and gas.

PG 352.9 (568 km) **PR 94.8** (153.5 km) Motel.

PG 354.3 (570.2 km) **PR 93.4** (151.3 km) Old Lakelse Lake Road.

PG 354.7 (570.8 km) **PR 93** (150.7 km) Four-way stop; east access to Terrace and **junction** with Highway 37 south to Kitimat. For access to downtown Terrace, turn north here and continue over 1-lane bridge. For west access to Terrace and continuation of Yellowhead Highway 16 westbound, go straight at intersection. Turn off for Kitimat, 37 miles/60 km south via Highway 37.

Kitimat is a major port and home to several industries. (See log of HIGHWAY 37 SOUTH opposite page.)

PG 354.9 (571.1 km) **PR 92.8** (150.4 km) First bridge westbound over **Skeena River.** "Skeen" means "River of the mist" in First Nation's language.

PG 355.2 (571.7 km) **PR 92.5** (149.8 km) Ferry Island municipal campground; 68 sites, some electrical hookups. Covered picnic shelters, barbecues, walking trails and a fishing bar are also available. 🐟 ▲

PG 355.3 (571.8 km) **PR 92.4** (149.7 km) Second westbound Skeena River Bridge.

PG 355.7 (572.4 km) **PR 92** (149.1 km) Terrace Chamber of Commerce Visitor Infocentre.

PG 356.6 (573.8 km) **PR 91.1** (147.7 km) Stoplight; west access to Terrace. Turn north at intersection for downtown.

Continue through intersection on Highway 16 westbound for Prince Rupert, eastbound for Prince George.

CAUTION: No gas or services available between Terrace and Prince Rupert.

Terrace

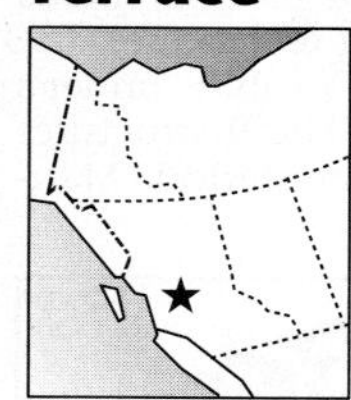

Located on the Skeena River. City centre is located north of Highway 16: Exit at **PG 356.6** or at Highway 37 junction (**PG 354.7**). **Population:** 13,000; area 21,500. **Emergency Services:** Police, fire and ambulance located at intersection of Eby Street and Highway 16. **Police,** phone (250) 635-4911. **Fire Department,** phone (250) 638-8121. **Ambulance,** phone (250) 638-1102. **Hospital,** phone (250) 635-2211.

Visitor Information: Visitor Infocentre located in the chamber of commerce log building at **Milepost PG 355.7** Open daily in summer, 9 A.M. to 8 P.M.; weekdays in winter, 8 A.M. to 4:30 P.M. Write 4511 Keith Ave, Terrace, BC V8G 1K1; phone (250) 635-2063. Information also available from Municipal Hall, #5-3215 Eby St.; open weekdays, phone (250) 635-6311.

Elevation: 220 feet/67m. **Climate:** Average summer temperature is 69°F/21°C; average annual rainfall 44 inches/112 cm, snowfall 129 inches/327 cm. **Radio:** CFTK 590; CFPR-FM 95.3, CFNR 92.1. **Television:**

13 channels (cable). **Newspapers:** *Terrace Standard* (weekly) *Terrace Times* (weekly).

Transportation: Air—Canadian Airlines International, Air BC and Central Mountain Air from Terrace-Kitimat airport on Highway 37 South. **Railroad**—VIA Rail, 4531 Railway Ave. **Bus**—Farwest Bus Lines, Greyhound and Seaport Limousine with connection between Terrace and Stewart/Hyder. **Car Rentals**—Available.

Terrace was once a port of call for Skeena River stern-wheelers. The first farmer in the area, George Little, gave land to the community that became a port of call and post office in 1905. Originally it was known as Little Town, and later was named Terrace because of the natural terraces cut by the river. The village site was laid out in 1910 and the Grand Trunk Pacific Railway reached Terrace in 1914. The municipality was incorporated in 1927.

There are 17 motels/hotels, 35 restaurants and 2 shopping centres. The government liquor store is at 3250 Eby St. There are 5 laundromats. The community has a library and art gallery, indoor swimming pool, tennis courts, a golf course, bingo parlor, bowling alley, theatre and billiards.

Terrace has private campgrounds (see advertisements this section) and a public campground located at Ferry Island (see **Milepost PG 355.2**). Lakelse Lake Provincial Park at Furlong Bay, 11.4 miles/18.3 km south of Highway 16 on Highway 37, offers campsites and day-use facilities, restrooms, changing rooms, showers, boat launch, sandy beaches, swimming, nature trails and interpretive forestry programs. ▲

Major attractions in Terrace include Heritage Park, a collection of original log buildings from this region. Chosen to represent both the different aspects of pioneer life as well as different log building techniques, the structures include a trapper's cabin, miner's cabin and lineman's cabin. The 9 structures also house artifacts from the period. Managed by the Terrace Regional Museum Society; guided tours available in summer, admission charged.

House of Sim-oi-Ghets crafts center west of Terrace. (© Wes Bergen, DIARAMA)

Recreation includes hiking, biking, rock-climbing, canoeing, kayaking and snowmobiling. Hiking trails in the Terrace area range from easy to moderate. Terrace Mountain Nature Trail is a 3.2-mile/5.1-km uphill hike which offers good views of the area; it begins at Halliwell and Anderson streets. Check with the Visitor Infocentre for details on other area trails.

Special events in Terrace include the Skeena Valley Fall Fair, Labour Day weekend; River Boat Days, B.C. Day weekend; and the Terrace Trade Show in late April.

Nisga'a Lava Memorial Park lava beds are 42 miles/67 km north of Terrace via the Nisga'a Highway (see NISGA'A HIGHWAY/NASS ROAD log this section). Limited picnic spots; limited camping; interesting hikes. Canada's youngest volcano last erupted approximately 250 years ago, burying 2 Indian villages. Guided hikes into the cones are available; phone (250) 798-2277.

Terrace is ideally situated for sportfishing, with easy access to the **Skeena, Copper, Kalum, Kitimat** and **Lakelse rivers.** Cutthroat, Dolly Varden and rainbow are found in all lakes and streams; salmon (king and coho) from May to late autumn. Kings average 40 to 70 lbs.; coho 14 to 20 lbs. Check locally for season and restrictions on steelhead. Information and fishing licenses are available from B.C. Government Access Centre, 3220 Eby St., Terrace (phone 250/638-6515), and at most sporting goods stores.

Don Diego's Mexican Restaurant. See display ad this section.

Wild Duck Motel & RV Park. See display ad this section. ▲

Yellowhead Highway 16 Log

(continued)

PG 356.6 (573.8 km) **PR 91.1** (147.7 km) Stoplight; west access to Terrace. Turn north at intersection for downtown. Continue through intersection eastbound for Prince George, westbound for Prince Rupert.

PG 357.5 (575.4 km) **PR 90.2** (146.1 km) **Junction** with Nisga'a Highway (Kalum Lake Road) to New Aiyansh. Beyond the Nass Road junction, the Nisga'a Highway is a narrow gravel and pavement road used by logging trucks. See NISGA'A HIGHWAY/NASS ROAD log opposite page.

The Cassiar Highway junctions with the Yellowhead Highway at Kitwanga, **Milepost PG 306.6**; see the CASSIAR HIGHWAY section.

PG 357.9 (576 km) **PR 89.8** (145.5 km) West Fraser Sawmill.

PG 359 (377.8 km) **PR 88.7** (143.7 km) Kalum Bridge.

PG 359.2 (578 km) **PR 88.5** (143.5 km) Access road to boat launch (fee charged) on the Kitsumkalum River downstream from Highway 16 bridge; RV parking.

Leaving Terrace, Highway 16 is in good condition westbound although the few straightaways are interrupted by some amazing 70-degree zigzags as the highway crosses the railroad tracks. The highway along the Skeena River is spectacular, with waterfalls cascading down the steep rock faces.

PG 359.3 (578.2 km) **PR 88.4** (143.3 km) **KITSUMKALUM.** Grocery store and Native craft centre. House of Sim-oi-Ghets handles only authentic arts and crafts such as totem poles, leather goods and local carvings.

House of Sim-oi-Ghets. See display ad this section.

This is also the **junction** with West Kalum Forest Service Road, which leads north to Kitsumkalum Provincial Park (15 miles/24 km), with 20 campsites, and to Red Sand Demonstration Forest, with 14 campsites. West Kalum Road junctions with the Nisga'a Highway. ▲

PG 359.7 (578.8 km) **PR 88** (142.7 km) Turnout to south.

PG 360 (579.4 km) **PR 87.7** (142.1 km) Paved turnout to south.

PG 363.1 (584.4 km) **PR 84.6** (137 km) Zimacord Bridge.

PG 366.1 (589.2 km) **PR 81.6** (132.1 km) Turnout to south.

PG 368.7 (589.2 km) **PR 79** (127.9 km) Delta Creek.

PG 371.3 (597.5 km) **PR 76.4** (123.7 km) Shames River.

PG 371.4 (597.7 km) **PR 76.3** (123.5 km) Shames Mountain Ski Area.

PG 377.2 (607.1 km) **PR 70.5** (113.8 km) Rest area on left westbound with picnic

Nisga'a Highway/Nass Road Log

The Nisga'a Highway/Nass Forest Service Road junctions with Yellowhead Highway 16 west of Terrace at **Milepost PG 357.5** and travels north to join the Cassiar Highway at **Milepost J 44.9.** Total driving distance is 98.6 miles/158.7 km and the first 39.3 miles/63.2 km are paved; the remainder is gravel. Services along this route are limited. Grading on the gravel sections often turns up sharp rocks, especially in the lava sections, and travelers are advised to carry a spare tire. Portions of the road are narrow and winding, and there are many 1-lane bridges. Fuel is available at New Aiyansh, which is the major settlement on this route. Limited campsites are available.

There is active logging in the area and travelers share the route with logging and local traffic. Motorists are advised to exercise caution and drive with headlights on. Between New Aiyansh and the Cassiar Highway, there are a number of Y-intersections and, in most instances, the route is signed; however, if in doubt, follow the hydro lines.

Yellow kilometre markers begin at **Milepost J 58.5** and continue to the Cassiar Highway. These markers are used by loggers when reporting their road positions and marker '0' is at the Ginlulak log dump near Greenville. During winter, depending on logging activity, the eastern portion of the road may not be maintained (plowed).

Distance is measured from junction (J) with Yellowhead Highway 16.

J 0 Junction with Yellowhead Highway 16 at **Milepost PG 357.5.**

J 7 (11.2 km) Finlay Lake to west.

J 13.7 (22 km) Kitsumkalum River to west.

J 17.4 (28 km) View of Kitsumkalum Lake to west.

J 19.8 (31.9 km) Paved turnout to west overlooking Kitsumkalum Lake.

J 23 (37 km) Rosswood settlement at the head of the lake, named for Annie Ross, who homesteaded here with her 4 children at the turn of the century.

J 25.8 (41.5 km) Rosswood General Store; groceries, fishing tackle (open year-round).

J 30.4 (48.9 km) Entering Skeena Cellulose Tree Farm License #1. Twenty-five year tree farm licenses are issued by the Crown and define the terms of timber harvest, including taxation, reforestation and long-term planning requirements.

J 31.4 (50.5 km) One-lane bridge crosses Cedar River.

J 37 (59.6 km) Sand Lake, marshy area to south. Watch for wildlife.

J 39.3 (63.2 km) Pavement ends, gravel begins, northbound. **Junction** with West Kalum Road.

J 39.5 (63.6 km) Gainor Lake west.

J 42.2 (67.9 km) Southern park boundary for Nisga'a Memorial Lava Bed Park. Lava Lake to west. Narrow winding road next 6.2 miles/10 km northbound. *Note: Removal of lava prohibited; stay on designated trails and roads.*

Lava beds along the Nisga'a Highway in Nisga'a Memorial Lava Bed Park.
(© Lyn Hancock)

The flow is thought to be the most recent volcanic eruption in Canada (approximately 300 years ago). It covers an area approximately 6.3 miles/10 km long and 1.8 miles/3 km wide and was created by a volcano less than 361 feet/100m high. The eruption produced little ash or cinder, but large quantities of basalt. The eruption destroyed 2 villages and killed more than 2,000 people.

The flow entered the Tseax Valley, filling it to depths of more than 98 feet/30m, and blocking the upper section of the valley. Waters from the surrounding drainage filled the valley to form the 180 foot-/55m-deep Lava Lake, which in turn drains into the permeable lava flow and reappears approximately 1.2 miles/2 km downstream as the Tseax River and Vetter Creek.

J 46 (74.1 km) Access to Lava Lake on west side of road.

J 48.3 (77.8 km) North end of Lava Lake. Sil Tax picnic site; toilets, litter barrels, tables, park information. No overnight camping.

J 48.7 (78.4 km) Lava flow to east. Interpretive sign, trail (0.6 mile/1 km) and photo viewpoint.

J 50.1 (80.6 km) One-lane wooden bridge.

J 54.7 (88 km) Beaupre Falls trail (10 minutes round trip).

J 56.2 (90.5 km) Vetter Falls viewpoint and "phantom fish." Near Vetter Falls the Tseax River divides; the western channel flows into the Nass River. The eastern channel flows over Vetter Falls to join Vetter Creek. Just east of the Vetter Falls campsite, the runoff sinks into channels below the lava. Often, steelhead spawning in the Tseax River return to the ocean; occasionally the fish take the eastern channel and go over the falls, becoming trapped in this section of the river. They starve and become "snake-like" in appearance. Locals refer to them as "phantom fish."

J 58.5 (94.1 km) **Junction** with road to Gitwinksihlkw (Canyon City) and Greenville. Information sign. Turn east (right). Road presently ends at Greenville. Vetter Falls campsite to northwest; tables, fire rings, and toilets. Water from creek; recommend boiling. ▲

Nisga'a Enterprises operates a fishing lodge at Nass Harbour with good fishing and ocean kayaking.

J 59.6 (95.9 km) Northern boundary for Nisga'a Memorial Lava Bed Park; information, toilets, viewpoint. Turnout by creek to south. One-lane bridge.

J 60.1 (96.7 km) RCMP station to north.

J 60.2 (96.9 km) Village of **NEW AIYANSH** to south is the major settlement on the Nisga'a Highway. Repairs, gas, grocery and convenience stores, community hall with Native design, a school, post office, first aid, fire and police stations, post office and gift shop are available. Area bed and breakfast and lodge operators offer meals and accommodation. Limited campsites are available. ▲

J 67.7 (109 km) Northbound: Highway becomes Nass Forest Service Road at Y-intersection. Keep left for Nass Camp/Bill-Nor Tillicum Lodge (all visitor services), keep right for Cassiar Highway.

J 71.3 (114.7 km) BC Forest Recreation Site on Dragon Lake. A medium, semi-open, user-maintained site with good water and broad access; mixed forest; boat launch. ▲

J 73.7 (118.6 km) Y-intersection: Keep to right for Cassiar Highway, left for Alice Arm/Kitsault. Follow hydro lines.

J 80.5 (129.5 km) One-lane wooden bridge with turnouts at each end. Leaving Skeena Tree Fall License #1 northbound.

J 94.8 (152.5 km) Y-intersection: Follow yellow kilometreposts on right side of road for Cassiar Highway.

J 98.6 (158.7 km) **Junction** with Cassiar Highway 37 (see Cassiar Highway section).

Return to Milepost PG 357.5 Yellowhead Highway or J 46.8 Cassiar Highway

Camping along the Exchamsiks River, 58 miles east of Prince Rupert.

(Judy Parkin, staff)

tables, toilets and water pump.

PG 378.2 (608.7 km) **PR 69.5** (112.4 km) Exstew River.

PG 383 (616.4 km) **PR 64.7** (104.9 km) *CAUTION! Highway turns sharply across railroad tracks.*

PG 385.3 (620.1 km) **PR 62.4** (100.9 km) *CAUTION: Carwash Rock overhangs highway. Water cascades down mountain and onto highway during heavy rains.*

PG 385.8 (620.8 km) **PR 61.9** (100.2 km) Sharp curves and falling rocks approximately next mile westbound. *CAUTION: Slow down for sharp curve and steep grade.*

PG 389.6 (627 km) **PR 58.1** (94 km) **Exchamsiks River** Provincial Park; 20 campsites and 20 picnic sites among old-growth Sitka spruce. Open May to October, camping fee, water and pit toilets. Good salmon fishing in Exchamsiks River. Access to Gitnadoix River canoeing area across Skeena River.

PG 389.8 (627.3 km) **PR 57.9** (93.7 km) Very pleasant rest area north side of road at west end of Exchamsiks bridge; boat launch on Exchamsiks River. Toilets, tables and litter barrels.

PG 390 (627.7 km) **PR 57.7** (93.3 km) Boat launch.

PG 390.2 (628 km) **PR 57.5** (93 km) *CAUTION: Very narrow road next to railway.*

PG 391.3 (629.7 km) **PR 56.4** (91.3 km) Conspicuous example of Sitka spruce on north side of highway. Aboriginal people ate its inner bark fresh or dried in cakes, served with berries. As you travel west, the vegetation becomes increasingly influenced by the maritime climate.

PG 394.1 (634.2 km) **PR 53.6** (86.8 km) Kasiks River and view of mountains.

PG 394.8 (635.3 km) **PR 52.9** (85.7 km) Kasiks River; boat launch.

PG 394.9 (635.5 km) **PR 52.8** (85.5 km) River access at the west end of bridge.

PG 396 (637.3 km) **PR 51.7** (83.7 km) Bridal Falls.

PG 399.9 (643.5 km) **PR 47.8** (77.4 km) Boat launch.

PG 401.1 (645.6 km) **PR 46.6** (75.3 km) Hanging Valley and Blackwater Creek.

PG 404.8 (651.4 km) **PR 42.9** (69.5 km) Kwinitsa River bridge and boat launch. No public moorage.

PG 409.3 (658.7 km) **PR 38.4** (62.1 km) Telegraph Point rest area to south on bank of Skeena River; paved turnout with outhouses, picnic tables, litter barrels and water pump. Watch for seals and sea lions in spring and during salmon season.

PG 413.3 (665.1 km) **PR 34.4** (55.7 km) Paved turnout with litter barrel.

PG 415.5 (668.7 km) **PR 32.2** (52.1 km) Basalt Creek rest area to south with picnic tables.

PG 416.3 (669.9 km) **PR 31.4** (50.8 km) Khyex River bridge. Remains of old sawmill visible at west end of bridge to south.

PG 420.2 (676.2 km) **PR 27.5** (44.5 km) Turnout to south.

PG 422.5 (680 km) **PR 25.2** (39.8 km) Watch for pictograph, visible from the road for eastbound traffic only, possibly a boundary marker for Chief Legaic over 150 years ago. It was rediscovered in the early 1950s by Dan Lippett of Prince Rupert.

PG 423.7 (681.8 km) **PR 24** (38 km) Scenic viewpoint to south with litter barrels and historical plaque about Skeena River. Highway leaves Skeena River westbound. Abandoned townsite of Port Essington visible on opposite side of river.

PG 424.6 (683.3 km) **PR 23.1** (37.4 km) Green River Forest Service road.

PG 427.5 (688 km) **PR 20.2** (32.7 km) Rainbow Summit, elev. 528 feet/161m.

PG 430 (692 km) **PR 17.7** (28.7 km) Side road south to Rainbow Lake Reservoir; boat launch. The reservoir water is used by the pulp mill on Watson Island.

PG 432.5 (695.9 km) **PR 15.2** (24.7 km) **Prudhomme Lake** Provincial Park; 24 campsites, well water, toilets, firewood, fishing, camping fee.

PG 432.9 (696.6 km) **PR 14.8** (24 km) Turnout to north with litter barrel.

PG 433.4 (697.5 km) **PR 14.3** (23.1 km) Turnoff for Diana Lake Provincial Park, 1.5 miles/2.4 km south via single-lane gravel road (use turnouts). Day-use facility. Very pleasant grassy picnic area on lakeshore with 50 picnic tables, kitchen shelter, firewood, grills, wheelchair access, outhouses, water pump and garbage cans. Parking for 229 vehicles. The only freshwater swimming beach in the Prince Rupert area. Fish viewing at Diana Creek on the way into the lake; 2 hiking trails.

PG 438 (704.9 km) **PR 9.7** (15.6 km) **Junction.** Turnoff for **PORT EDWARD**, pulp mill and historic cannery. The North Pacific Cannery Village and Fishing Museum at Port Edward is open daily in summer. Built in 1889, this is the oldest cannery village on the north coast. Phone (250) 628-3538 for more information.

PG 438.3 (705.3 km) **PR 9.4** (15.2 km) Galloway Rapids rest area to south with litter barrels, picnic tables and visitor information sign. View of Watson Island pulp mill.

PG 439.1 (706.6 km) **PR 8.6** (13.9 km) Miller Bay Hill campground.

PG 439.5 (707.3 km) **PR 8.2** (13.2 km) Ridley Island access road. Ridley Island is the site of terminals used for the transfer of coal and grain—from, respectively, the North East Coal resource near Dawson Creek and Canada's prairies—to ships

PG 440.2 (708.5 km) **PR 7.5** (12 km) Oliver Lake rest area to south just off highway; picnic tables, grills, firewood. Point of interest sign about bogs.

PG 441.2 (710 km) **PR 6.5** (10.5 km) Shoe Tree or Tree of Lost Soles to east. Tongue-in-cheek local attraction which has grown over years. Worn-out footwear is hung from trees in this local shrine to shoes.

PG 442.3 (711.8 km) **PR 5.4** (8.7 km) Butze Rapids viewpoint.

PG 442.7 (712.4 km) **PR 5** (8.1 km) Prince Rupert industrial park on the outskirts of Prince Rupert. Yellowhead Highway 16 becomes McBride Street as you enter the city centre.

PG 443.4 (713.7 km) **PR 4.2** (6.8 km) Frederick Street junction.

PG 447 (719.3 km) **PR 0.7** (1.2 km) Park Avenue campground.

PG 447.7 (720 km) **PR 0** Ferry terminal for B.C. Ferries and Alaska state ferries. Airport ferry terminal. End of Highway 16.

CAUTION: No gas or services available eastbound between Prince Rupert and Terrace.

Prince Rupert

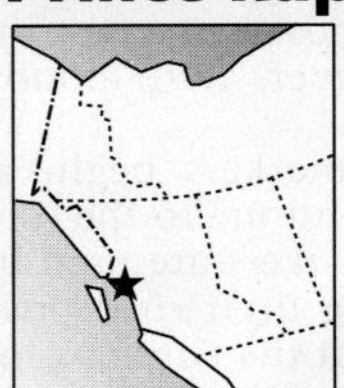

Located on Kaien Island near the mouth of the Skeena River, 90 miles/145 km by air or water (6-hour ferry ride) south of Ketchikan, AK. **Population:** 17,500; area 25,000. **Emergency Services:** Phone 911 for **Police, Ambulance** and **Fire Department. RCMP**, 6th Avenue and McBride Street, non-emergency phone (250) 627-0700. **Hospital,**

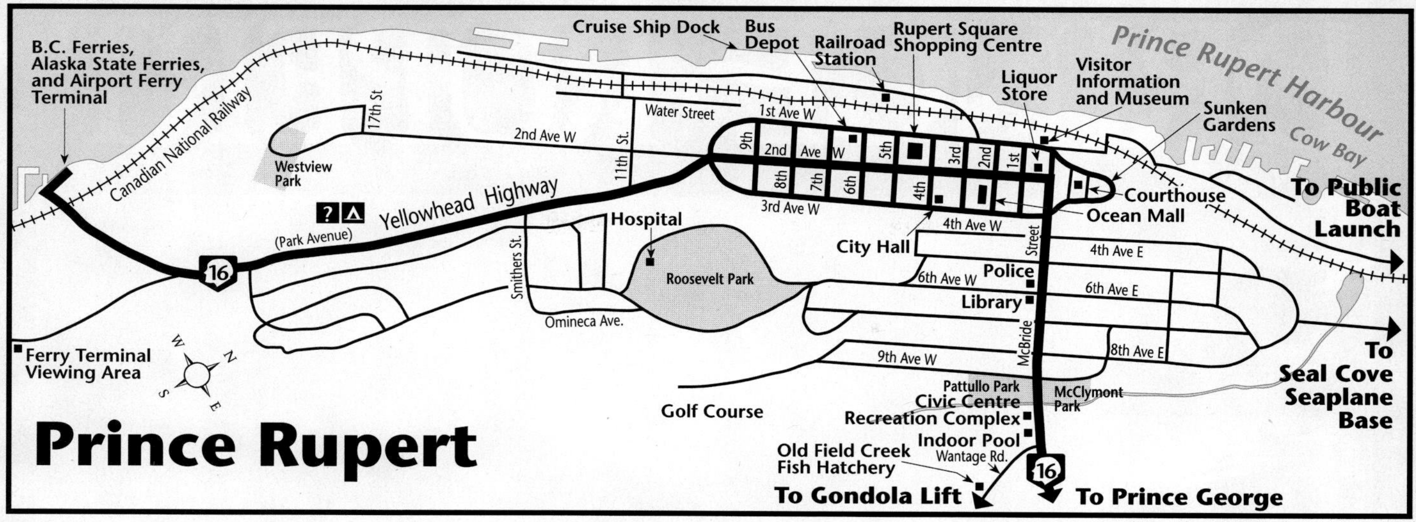

Prince Rupert Regional, phone (250) 624-2171.

Visitor Information: Visitor Infocentre at 1st Avenue and McBride Street. Open daily in summer, 9 A.M. to 9 P.M. Travel information is also available at the Park Avenue Campground; open daily in summer, 9 A.M. to 8 P.M., and until midnight for B.C. Ferry arrivals. Write Box 669-MP, Prince Rupert, BC V8J 3S1, phone (800) 667-1994 and (250) 624-5637, fax (250) 627-8009.

Elevation: Sea level. **Climate:** Temperate with mild winters. Annual precipitation 95.4 inches. **Radio:** CHTK 560, CBC 860; CJFW-FM 101.9. **Television:** 31 channels, cable. **Newspaper:** *The Prince Rupert Daily News, Prince Rupert This Week* (weekly).

Prince Rupert, "Gateway to Alaska," was surveyed prior to 1905 by the Grand Trunk Pacific Railway (later Canadian National Railways) as the terminus for Canada's second transcontinental railroad.

Twelve thousand miles/19,300 km of survey lines were studied before a final route along the Skeena River was chosen. Some 833 miles/1,340 km had to be blasted from solid rock, 50 men drowned and costs rose to $105,000 a mile (the final cost of $300 million was comparable to Panama Canal construction) before the last spike was driven near Fraser Lake on April 7, 1914. Financial problems continued to plague the company, forcing it to amalgamate to become part of the Canadian National Railways system in 1923.

Charles M. Hays, president of the company, was an enthusiastic promoter of the new terminus, which was named by competition from 12,000 entries. While "Port Rupert" had been submitted by two contestants, "Prince Rupert" (from Miss Eleanor M. Macdonald of Winnipeg) called to mind the dashing soldier–explorer, cousin to Charles II of England and first governor of the Hudson's Bay Co., who had traded on the coast rivers for years. Three first prizes of $250 were awarded and Prince Rupert was officially named in 1906.

Prince Rupert's proposed port and adjacent waters were surveyed by G. Blanchard Dodge of the Hydrographic branch of the Marine Dept. in 1906, and in May the little steamer *Constance* carried settlers from the village of Metlakatla to clear the first ground on Kaien Island. Its post office opened Nov. 23, 1906, and Prince Rupert, with a tent-town population of 200, began an association with communities on the Queen Charlotte Islands, with Stewart served by Union steamships and Canadian Pacific Railways boats, and with Hazelton 200 miles/322 km up the Skeena River on which the stern-wheelers of the Grand Trunk Pacific and the Hudson's Bay Co. traveled.

Incorporated as a city March 10, 1910,

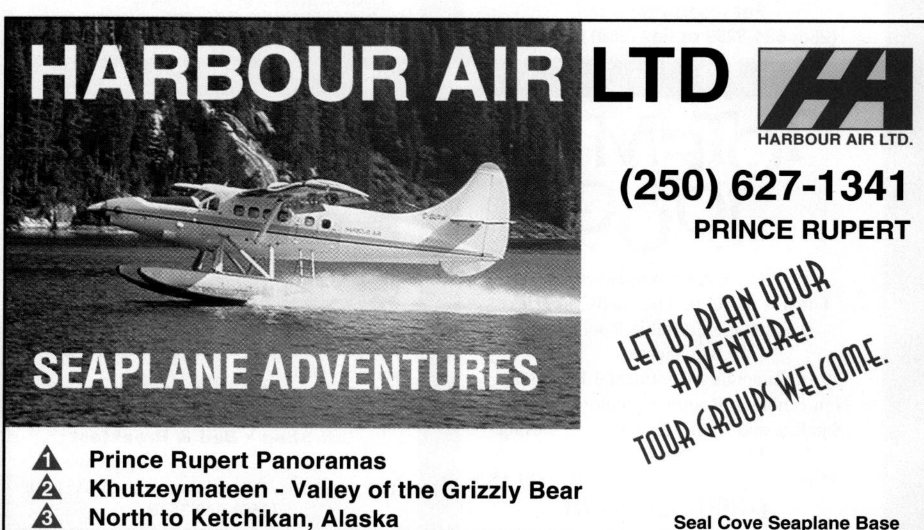

PRINCE RUPERT

Ocean View Hotel

950 First Avenue West, V8J 1A9

Single & double accommodation available, from budget priced rooms (with shared bathroom facilities) to deluxe, ocean view rooms, beautifully appointed to suit your every need. Visit the "Knox Bar & Grill" to relax and enjoy a delicious meal and the nightly entertainers.

For reservations call
(250) 624-6259 or Fax (250) 624-6162

The Museum of Northern British Columbia

100 - 1st. Avenue West, Prince Rupert, B.C.
Tel (250) 624-3207

Celebrate our natural splendour and history
• harbour tours • walking tours • drama
special activities • events • exhibits • art shows
Don't miss historic Kwinitsa Station and the superb Museum Gift Shop.

Newly Renovated
•76 Spacious, comfortable rooms
• Downtown location • Covered parking
• 3 Minutes to ferries
909 West Third Avenue
Prince Rupert, B.C. V8J 1M9
Phone (250) 627-1711

TOTEM LODGE

CAA/AAA Approved
Closest motel to Alaska/BC Ferries

31 Quiet Comfortable Rooms with Kitchenettes
Complimentary Continental Breakfast
Non-Smoking Rooms • Laundry Facilities
Satellite and Cable TV • Vehicle Storage
Phone (250) 624-6761
1335 Park Ave., Prince Rupert, BC V8J 1K3
1-800-550-0178

B.C.'s Oldest Cannery Village

Built in 1889 - Ongoing Restoration Project. Visit North Pacific's diverse exhibits in original cannery buildings.

Summer Tours & Live Shows
Scenery • Wildlife • Great Food
Gift Shop • Bed & Breakfast

North Pacific Cannery Village Museum
P.O. Box 1104, Port Edward, B.C. V0V 1G0
(250) 628-3538

SEAFOOD HOUSE

The most popular restaurant on the North Coast.

Featuring mouth-watering seafood specialties like halibut, black cod, salmon, crab, prawns, shrimp and oysters. Also, charbroiled steaks, chicken, lamb and duck. Something on the menu for everyone!

Reservations Recommended
624-9309
Major Credit Cards Accepted

PRINCE RUPERT'S
COW BAY
MUNICH
NEW YORK

Prince Rupert attracted settlers responding to the enthusiasm of Hays, with his dreams of a population of 50,000 and world markets supplied by his railroad. Both the city and the railway suffered a great loss with the death of Charles M. Hays when the *Titanic* went down in April 1912. Even so, work went ahead on the Grand Trunk Pacific. Two years later the first train arrived at Prince Rupert, linking the western port with the rest of Canada. Since then, the city has progressed through 2 world wars and economic ups and downs to its present period of growth and expansion, not only as a busy port but as a visitor centre.

During WWII, more than a million tons of freight and 73,000 people, both military and civilian, passed through Prince Rupert on their way to military operations in Alaska and the South Pacific.

Prince Rupert's City Hall building originally housed the post office.

(© Gladys Blyth)

Construction of the pulp operations on Watson Island in 1951 greatly increased the economic and industrial potential of the area. The operations include a pulp mill and a kraft mill.

With the start of the Alaska State Ferry System in 1963, and the British Columbia Ferry System in 1966, Prince Rupert's place as an important visitor centre and terminal point for highway, rail and marine transportation was assured.

Prince Rupert is the second major deep-sea port on Canada's west coast, exporting grain, pulp, lumber and other resources to Europe and Asia. Prince Rupert has also become a major coal and grain port with facilities on Ridley Island. Other industries include fishing and fish processing, and the manufacture of forest products.

Prince Rupert is underlaid by muskeg (a deep bog common to Northwest Canada and Alaska) over solid rock, which makes for a difficult foundation to build on. Many sites are economically unfeasible for development as they would require pilings 70 feet/21m or more into the muskeg to provide a firm foundation. Some of the older buildings have sagged slightly as a result of unstable foundations.

ACCOMMODATIONS/VISITOR SERVICES

More than a dozen hotels and motels accommodate the influx of ferry passengers each summer. Many restaurants feature fresh local seafood in season.

Modern supermarkets, shopping centres and a hospital are available. Government liquor store is at the corner of 2nd Avenue and Highway 16. There are 5 main banks, the Civic Centre Recreation Complex, 18-hole golf course, racquet centre, bowling alley, a swimming pool and tennis courts.

Park Avenue Campground on Highway 16 in the city has 87 campsites with hookups, unserviced sites, restrooms with hot showers, coin-operated laundry facilities, children's play area and picnic shelters. There are 24 campsites at Prudhomme Lake Provincial Park, 12.5 miles/20.1 km east on Highway 16. A private RV park on McBride Street offers camper and trailer parking. ▲

TRANSPORTATION

Air: Harbour Air and Inland Air Charter to outlying villages and Queen Charlotte Islands; Canadian Airlines International and Air BC offer daily jet service to Terrace and Vancouver; Taquan Air daily floatplane service in summer to Ketchikan, AK (weekly air services in winter).

Prince Rupert airport is located on Digby Island, which is connected by city-operated ferry to Prince Rupert. There is a small terminal at the airport. The airport ferry leaves from the Fairview dock, next to the Alaska state ferry dock; fare is charged for the 20-minute ride. Check with the Canadian Airlines International office at the downtown Rupert Mall (office is open for passenger check-in only when planes are arriving or departing). Air BC check-in at corner of 6th Street and 1st Avenue West. Bus service to airport from airline check-in areas.

There is a seaplane base at Seal Cove with airline and helicopter charter services.

Ferries: British Columbia Ferry System, Fairview dock, phone (250) 624-9627, provides automobile and passenger service from Prince Rupert to Port Hardy, and between Prince Rupert and Skidegate in the Queen Charlotte Islands.

Alaska Marine Highway System, Fairview dock, phone (250) 627-1744 or (800) 642-0066, provides automobile and passenger service to southeastern Alaska.

NOTE: Vehicle storage is available; inquire at the Information Centre.

Car Rentals: Tilden, phone (250) 624-5318, and Budget, phone (250) 627-7400.

Taxi: Available. Prince Rupert taxi cabs are powered by LNG (liquefied natural gas); phone (250) 624-2185.

Railroad: VIA Rail, in British Columbia, phone (800) 561-8630 (from Manitoba west to British Columbia) or (800) 561-3949 (from the United States).

Mariner's Park on the waterfront in Prince Rupert. (© Gladys Blyth)

Bus: Greyhound, phone (250) 624-5090. Farwest Bus Lines, phone (250) 624-6400. Charter sightseeing tours available.

ATTRACTIONS

Take a Tour. Tour the city's historic and scenic points of interest. Maps are available at the Visitor Infocentre. Scattered throughout the city are 18 large cedar totem poles, each with its own story. Most are reproductions by Native craftsmen of the original Tsimshian (SHIM shian) poles from the mainland and the Haida (HI duh) carvings from the Queen Charlotte Islands. The originals are now in the British Columbia Provincial Museum in Victoria. Several totem poles may be seen at Service Park, near 3rd Avenue W. and Fulton.

Check with the Museum of Northern British Columbia (1st and McBride) about tours of area archaeological sites. Included is a stop at "Old" Metlakatla in Prince Rupert harbour ("new" Metlakatla is located on Annette Island near Ketchikan, AK; see METLAKATLA section).

Cannery Tour. North Pacific Cannery Village Museum at Port Edward (turn off Highway 16 at **Milepost PG 438**). Built in 1889, this restored heritage site has dozens of displays on this once-major regional industry. A live performance highlights the history of the cannery. Open daily in summer, closed Mondays and Tuesdays October through April; admission charged. Phone (250) 628-3538.

Watch the Seaplanes. From McBride Street, head north on 6th Avenue E. (watch for signs to seaplane base); drive a few miles to Solly's Pub, then turn right to Seal Cove seaplane base. Visitors can spend a fascinating hour here watching seaplanes loading, taking off and landing. Helicopter and seaplane tours of the area are available at Seal Cove.

Visit the Queen Charlotte Islands. Ferry service is available between Prince Rupert and Skidegate on Graham Island, largest of the 150 islands and islets that form the Queen Charlotte Islands. Located west of Prince Rupert—a 6- to 8-hour ferry ride—Graham Island's paved road system connects Skidegate with Masset, the largest town in the Queen Charlottes. Scheduled flights from Prince Rupert to Sandspit and Masset are available. Island attractions include wild beaches, Haida culture, flora and fauna. For more information, contact the Visitor Infocentre in Queen Charlotte; phone (250) 559-8316.

Kwinitsa Station Railway Museum. Built in 1911, Kwinitsa Station was one of nearly 400 identical stations along the Grand Trunk Pacific Railway line. In 1985 the station was moved to the Prince Rupert waterfront park. Restored rooms, exhibits and videos tell the story of early Prince Rupert and the role the railroad played in the city's development. Open daily in summer; contact the Museum of British Columbia for more information.

New Museum of Northern British Columbia/Art Gallery, situated in an award-winning Chatham Village Longhouse, displays an outstanding collection of artifacts depicting the settlement history of British Columbia's north coast. Traveling art collections are displayed in the gallery, and works by local artists are available for purchase. Centrally located at 1st Avenue and McBride Street, marked by several tall totem poles. Summer hours 9 A.M. to 8 P.M. Monday through Saturday; 9 A.M. to 5 P.M. Sunday. Winter hours 10 A.M. to 5 P.M. Monday through Saturday. Phone (250) 624-3207. Admission fee.

Performing Arts Centre offers both professional and amateur theatre, with productions for children, and classical and contemporary plays presented. The 700-seat facility may be toured in summer; phone (250) 627-8888.

Special Events. Seafest is a 4-day celebration, held the second weekend in June, which includes a parade and water-jousting competition. Indian Culture Days, a 2-day event held during Seafest, features Native food, traditional dance, and arts and crafts. The All Native Basketball Tournament, held in February, is the largest event of its kind in Canada.

The Civic Centre Recreation Complex located on McBride Street (Highway 16) welcomes visitors. Activities include fitness gym, squash, basketball and volleyball. Supervised children's activities during summer. Ice skating and roller skating rinks also located at the centre. Phone (250) 624-6707 for more information.

Swim at Diana Lake. This provincial park, about 13 miles/21 km from downtown on Highway 16, offers the only freshwater swimming in the Prince Rupert area. Picnic tables, kitchen shelter, parking and beach.

Swim at Earl Mah Aquatic Centre, located next to the Civic Centre Recreation Complex. There is an indoor swimming pool, tot pool, weight room, saunas, showers, whirlpool, slides and diving boards. Access for persons with disabilities. Phone (250) 627-7946. Admission charged.

Golf Course includes 18-hole course, resident pro, equipment rental, clubhouse and restaurant. Entrance on 9th Avenue W.

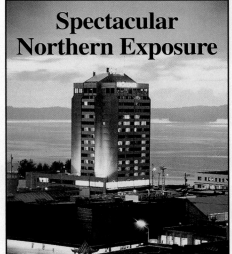

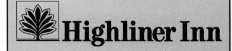

Go Fishing. Numerous freshwater fishing areas are available near Prince Rupert. For information on bait, locations, regulations and licensing, contact local sporting goods stores or the Visitor Infocentre. This area abounds in all species of salmon, steelhead, crab and shrimp. Public boat launch facility is located at Rushbrook Public Floats at the north end of the waterfront. Public floats are also available at Fairview, past the Alaska state ferry terminal near the breakwater.

Harbour Tours and Fishing Charters are available. For information, contact the Prince Rupert Infocentre at (800) 667-1994.

CASSIAR HIGHWAY 37

Connects: Yellowhead Hwy. 16 to Alaska Hwy. **Length:** 446 miles
Road Surface: 65% paved, 35% gravel **Season:** Open all year
Highest Summit: Gnat Pass 4,072 feet
Major Attractions: Bear and Salmon glaciers, Stikine River

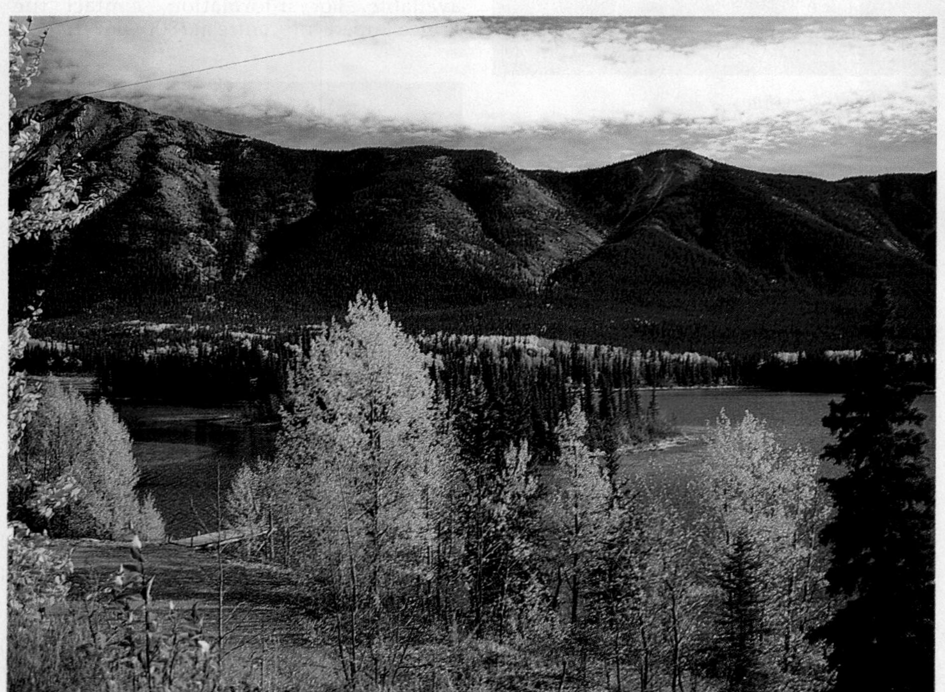

The Cassiar Highway offers outstanding scenery. (© Rick Driskell)

	Alaska Hwy.	Dease Lake	Iskut	Stewart/Hyder	Yellowhead Hwy.	Watson Lake
Alaska Hwy.		145	196	390	446	14
Dease Lake	145		51	245	301	159
Iskut	196	51		194	250	210
Stewart/Hyder	390	245	194		136	404
Yellowhead Hwy.	446	301	250	136		460
Watson Lake	14	159	210	404	460	

The Cassiar Highway junctions with Yellowhead Highway 16 at the Skeena River bridge (**Milepost PG 297.7** in the YELLOWHEAD HIGHWAY 16 section) and travels north to the Stewart, BC–Hyder, AK, access road, Telegraph Creek access road and Dease Lake, ending at the Alaska Highway 13.3 miles/21.4 km west of Watson Lake, YT. Total driving distance is 446.1 miles/718 km. Travelers driving between Prince George and the junction of the Alaska and Cassiar highways will save 132.4 miles/213 km by taking the Cassiar Highway. (Yellowhead–Cassiar route is 743.8 miles/1,197 km; Alaska Highway route is 876.2 miles/1,410.1 km.) The Cassiar Highway, which was completed in 1972, is a rougher road and has fewer facilities than the Alaska Highway, but it does offer outstanding scenery.

In summer 1997, the highway was paved from **Milepost J 0 to J 116** (Bell I). From Bell I to Iskut, 65 percent of the highway was gravel with intermittent seal coat From Iskut north to the Alaska Highway, there were 2 short sections of gravel. There were several complaints from readers about road conditions on the Cassiar in 1997—principally between Bell I and Iskut— with reports of rough surface, rocks, mud and potholes between Bell I and Dease Lake. According to the Ministry of Transportation and Highways, the extreme road conditions travellers experienced in 1997 were unusual and are not anticipated in 1998. Inquire locally for current road conditions. For a recorded message on road conditions on the Cassiar Highway, phone (800) 663-4997 in Canada. Current road conditions are also available by phoning the Highways Maintenance Contractor at (250) 771-3000 (if no answer, contact the District Highways office at 250/771-4511). If north of 60° only call (900) 565-4997 within Canada; (900) 288-4997 in USA; or on the Internet http://www.th.gov.bc.ca/bchighways/.

In 1998, travelers are advised to watch for bridge construction at Rescue Creek, and to anticipate road construction between Bell I and Iskut. There will be some gravel work between Dease Lake and Jade City, and seal coating is planned in the Good Hope Lake area in early spring.

On gravel stretches watch for washboard and potholes. Gravel road may be dusty in dry weather and muddy in wet weather. The calcium chloride, which is used for dust control and to stabilize the road base, results in the road surface becoming muddy and rough in wet weather. (Wash calcium chloride off your vehicle as soon as possible.) Seal coat is subject to deterioration from weather and traffic. A few bridges are still single lane. Watch for potholes at bridge ends and slippery bridge decks. There are several 8 percent grades. Drive with your headlights on at all times.

Watch for logging and freight trucks on the highway. *WARNING: Exercise extreme caution when passing or being passed by these trucks; reduce speed and allow trucks adequate clearance.*

The Cassiar also provides access to Hyder and Stewart. These communities are described in detail in this section beginning on page 271. Watch for bears with cubs along the highway (especially in spring); cariboo at Gnat Pass (spring and fall); and Dall sheep south of Good Hope.

Food, gas and lodging are available along the Cassiar Highway, but check the highway log for distances between services. Be sure your vehicle is mechanically sound with good tires. It is a good idea to carry a spare tire and extra fuel, especially in the off-season. In case of emergency, motorists are advised to flag down trucks to radio for help. It is unlawful to camp overnight in turnouts and rest areas unless otherwise posted. Camp at private campgrounds or in provincial park campgrounds.

According to the Ministry of Highways, litter barrels on the Cassiar Highway are often moved to areas which are being used more frequently. Litter barrels may not be in the same location from season to season. *The MILEPOST®* log indicates their location as of summer 1997.

Cassiar Highway Log

BC HIGHWAY 37

Kilometreposts are along the Cassiar Highway every 5 km. Because the posts do not always accurately reflect driving distance, mileages from the Yellowhead Highway 16 junction are based on actual driving distance while the kilometre conversion is based on physical kilometreposts as they occurred in summer 1997.

Distance from junction with the Yellowhead Highway (J) is followed by distance from Alaska Highway (AH).

J 0 AH 446.1 (718 km) **Junction** with Yellowhead Highway 16 (see **Milepost PG 297.7** on page 255 in the YELLOWHEAD HIGHWAY 16 section). Gas station. Bridge across Skeena River from Yellowhead Highway 16 to start of Cassiar Highway.

CASSIAR HIGHWAY *Yellowhead Highway Junction to Alaska Highway Junction*

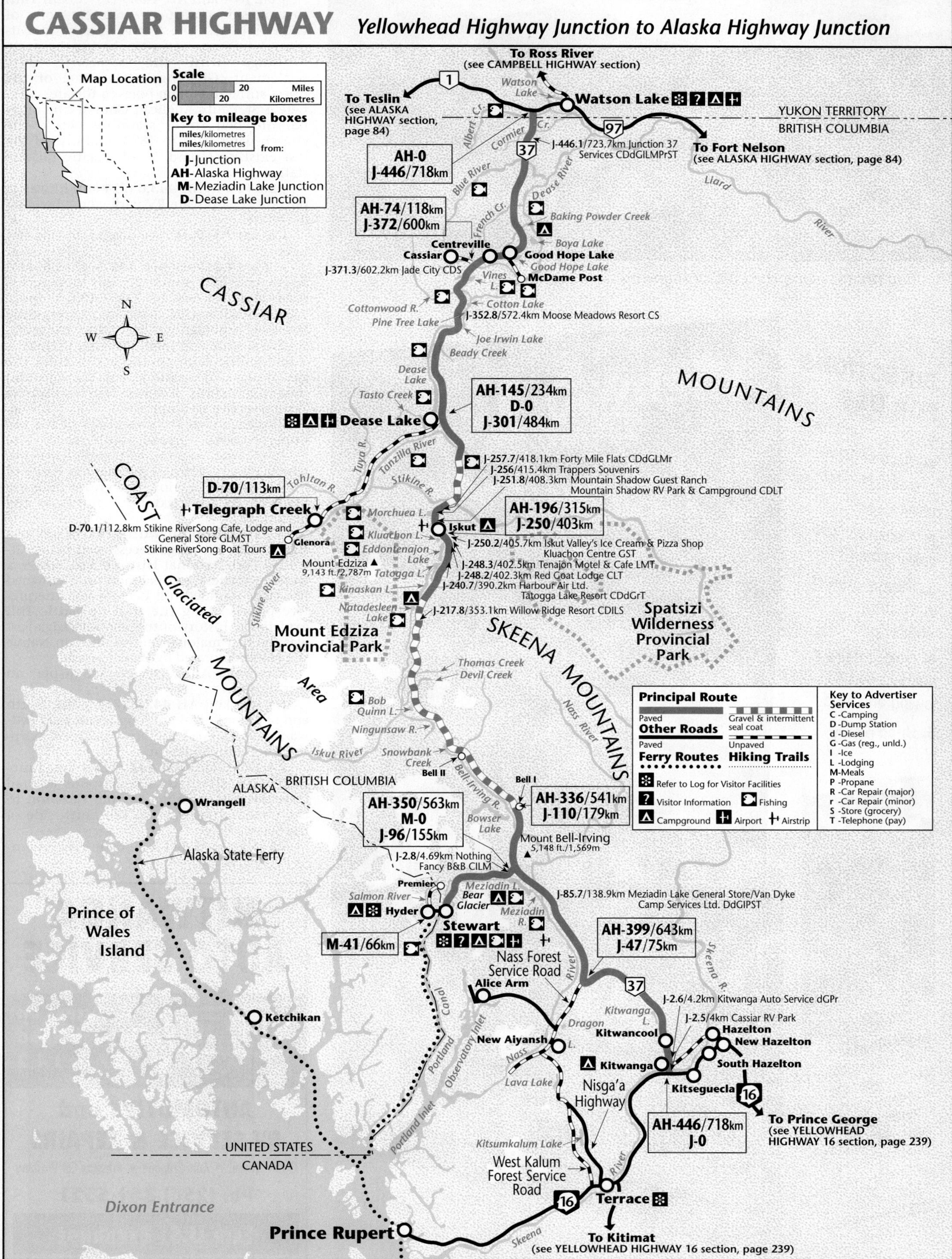

Map Location
Scale
20 Miles
20 Kilometres
Key to mileage boxes
miles/kilometres
miles/kilometres
from:
J-Junction
AH-Alaska Highway
M-Meziadin Lake Junction
D-Dease Lake Junction
To Ross River
(see CAMPBELL HIGHWAY section)
To Teslin
(see ALASKA HIGHWAY section, page 84)
Watson Lake
YUKON TERRITORY
BRITISH COLUMBIA
To Fort Nelson
(see ALASKA HIGHWAY section, page 84)
AH-0
J-446/718km
J-446.1/723.7km Junction 37 Services CDdGILMPrST
AH-74/118km
J-372/600km
Baking Powder Creek
Boya Lake
Centreville
Cassiar
Good Hope Lake
McDame Post
J-371.3/602.2km Jade City CDS
Cotton Lake
J-352.8/572.4km Moose Meadows Resort CS
Pine Tree Lake
Joe Irwin Lake
Beady Creek
CASSIAR
MOUNTAINS
AH-145/234km
D-0
J-301/484km
Dease Lake
J-257.7/418.1km Forty Mile Flats CDdGLMr
J-256/415.4km Trappers Souvenirs
J-251.8/408.3km Mountain Shadow Guest Ranch
Mountain Shadow RV Park & Campground CDLT
D-70/113km
Telegraph Creek
D-70.1/112.8km Stikine RiverSong Cafe, Lodge and General Store GLMST
Stikine RiverSong Boat Tours
Glenora
AH-196/315km
J-250/403km
Iskut
J-250.2/405.7km Iskut Valley's Ice Cream & Pizza Shop
Kluachon Centre GST
J-248.3/402.5km Tenajon Motel & Cafe LMT
J-248.2/402.3km Red Goat Lodge CLT
J-240.7/390.2km Harbour Air Ltd.
Tatogga Lake Resort CDdGrT
J-217.8/353.1km Willow Ridge Resort CDILS
Mount Edziza 9,143 ft./2,787m
Mount Edziza Provincial Park
Spatsizi Wilderness Provincial Park
SKEENA MOUNTAINS
COAST MOUNTAINS
Glaciated Area
ALASKA
BRITISH COLUMBIA
Wrangell
Alaska State Ferry
AH-350/563km
M-0
J-96/155km
AH-336/541km
J-110/179km
Bell I
Bell II
Mount Bell-Irving 5,148 ft./1,569m
J-2.8/4.69km Nothing Fancy B&B CILM
Premier
Hyder
Stewart
J-85.7/138.9km Meziadin Lake General Store/Van Dyke Camp Services Ltd. DdGIPST
M-41/66km
AH-399/643km
J-47/75km
Nass Forest Service Road
Alice Arm
Prince of Wales Island
Ketchikan
J-2.6/4.2km Kitwanga Auto Service dGPr
J-2.5/4km Cassiar RV Park
Kitwancool
Hazelton
New Hazelton
South Hazelton
Kitwanga
Kitsegueclа
New Aiyansh
Nisga'a Highway
AH-446/718km
J-0
To Prince George
(see YELLOWHEAD HIGHWAY 16 section, page 239)
UNITED STATES
CANADA
West Kalum Forest Service Road
Terrace
Dixon Entrance
Prince Rupert
To Kitimat
(see YELLOWHEAD HIGHWAY 16 section, page 239)
Principal Route
Paved
Gravel & intermittent seal coat
Other Roads
Paved
Unpaved
Ferry Routes
Hiking Trails
Refer to Log for Visitor Facilities
Visitor Information
Fishing
Campground
Airport
Airstrip
Key to Advertiser Services
C -Camping
D -Dump Station
d -Diesel
G -Gas (reg., unld.)
I -Ice
L -Lodging
M -Meals
P -Propane
R -Car Repair (major)
r -Car Repair (minor)
S -Store (grocery)
T -Telephone (pay)

Shooting photos along the Cassiar Highway. (© Eero Sorila)

J 0.2 (0.4 km) **AH 445.9** (717.6 km) Turn east on side road to view totem poles of **GITWANGAK.** The Native reserve of Gitwangak was renamed after sharing the name Kitwanga with the adjacent white settlement. Gitwangak has some of the finest authentic totem poles in the area. Also here is St. Paul's Anglican Church (the original old bell tower standing beside the church dates back to 1893) and one of the last existing Grand Trunk Pacific railway stations.

J 2.5 (4 km) **AH 443.6** (714 km) Kitwanga post office, a private RV park, and a bed and breakfast. ▲

Cassiar RV Park. See display ad this section. ▲

J 2.6 (4.2 km) **AH 443.5** (713.8 km) South end of 1.6-mile/2.5-km loop access road which leads to **KITWANGA** (pop. 1,200). **Radio:** CBC 630 AM. **Emergency Services:** Ambulance. Gas station, car wash, a general store and small restaurant. There is a free public campground across from the gas station. (Donations for campground upkeep gratefully accepted at the Kitwanga Tempo service station.) ▲

Kitwanga is at the crossroads of the old upper Skeena "grease trail" trade. The "grease" was eulachon (candlefish) oil, which was a trading staple among tribes of the Coast and Interior. The grease trails are believed to have extended north to the Bering Sea.

A paved turnout with litter barrel and sign on the Kitwanga access road mark Kitwanga Fort National Historic Site, where a wooden fortress and palisade once crowned the large rounded hill here. Seven interpretive panels along the trail up Battle Hill explain the history of the site. Kitwanga Fort was the first major western Canadian Native site commemorated by Parks Canada.

Kitwanga Auto Service. See display ad this section.

J 4 (6.5 km) **AH 442.1** (711.5 km) North end of 1.6-mile/2.6-km loop access road (Kitwanga North Road) to Kitwanga; see description preceding milepost.

J 4.1 (6.6 km) **AH 442** (711.4 km) **Junction** with alternate access route (signed Hazelton–Kitwanga Road) from Hazelton to the Cassiar Highway via the north side of the Skeena River.

J 5 (8 km) **AH 441.1** (710 km) The mountain chain of Seven Sisters is visible to southwest (weather permitting) next 4 miles/6.4 km northbound.

J 12.5 (20.2 km) **AH 433.6** (697.9 km) Turnout with litter barrels to west.

J 12.6 (20.3 km) **AH 433.5** (697.7 km) Highway follows Kitwanga River and former grease trail route.

J 13 (21 km) **AH 433.1** (697.1 km) South access to **KITWANCOOL** (2 miles/3.3 km from highway) is a small Indian village with many fine old totems, some recently restored. Guided tours of the totem poles may be available; inquire at the Visitor Infocentre. A Native craft shop in the village sells local art. The village of Kitwancool was originally called Gitanyow, meaning place of many people, but was renamed Kitwancool, meaning place of reduced number, after many of its inhabitants were killed in raids.

J 16.1 (26.1 km) **AH 430** (692.1 km) North access to Kitwancool.

J 18.8 (30.4 km) **AH 427.3** (687.8 km) Bridge over Moonlit Creek.

J 18.9 (30.7 km) **AH 427.2** (687.5 km) Rest area north of creek, east of road, with tables, toilets and litter barrels. Road west is the old highway and access to **Kitwanga Lake.** Fishing, camping and boat launch spots on lake. Old highway may be in poor condition; drive carefully. It rejoins the main highway at Mile 24.1. Access to the lake is strictly from the old highway.

J 19.9 (32.2 km) **AH 426.2** (686 km) Access to Kitwanga Lake.

J 21.3 (34.5 km) **AH 424.8** (683.7 km) Good views of Kitwanga Lake to west; old highway visible, below west, winding along lakeshore.

J 26.1 (42.2 km) **AH 420** (676 km) Kitwancool Forest Road to west.

J 38.8 (62.9 km) **AH 407.3** (655.5 km) **Cranberry River** bridge No. 1. A favorite salmon stream in summer; consult fishing regulations.

J 46.5 (75.3 km) **AH 399.6** (643.2 km) Paved turnout to west.

J 46.8 (75.9 km) **AH 399.3** (642.6 km) **Junction** with the Nass Forest Service Road to New Aiyansh (38.4 miles/61.8 km) and Terrace. *NOTE: This intersection is easy to miss.* See NISGA'A HIGHWAY/NASS ROAD log on page 299. A B.C. Forest Service campsite is 27 miles/44 km west at Dragon Lake; room for 10 to 12 vehicles, cartop boat launch. Bed and breakfast at New Aiyansh.

J 47.1 (76.3 km) **AH 399** (642.2 km) Cranberry River bridge No. 2. Turnout with toilets, tables and litter barrels.

J 53.1 (86 km) **AH 393** (632.6 km) BC Hydro power line crosses and parallels highway. Completed in 1990, this line links Stewart to the BC Hydro power grid. Previously, Stewart's power was generated by diesel fuel.

Entering Kalum Forest District northbound. Watch for signs telling dates of logging activity, and observe patterns of regrowth.

J 58.6 (94.9 km) **AH 387.5** (623.7 km) Kelly Lake rest area at north end of lake on west side of highway, with tables, toilet and litter barrels. First view northbound of Nass River.

J 64.1 (103.8 km) **AH 382** (614.9 km) Paved turnout.

J 65.6 (106.4 km) **AH 380.5** (612.4 km) View of Nass River to west. The Nass River is one of the province's prime producers of sockeye salmon.

J 66.4 (107.7 km) **AH 379.7** (611.1 km) Views northbound (weather permitting) of the Coast Mountains to the west. Cambrian ice field to west.

J 70.1 (113.6 km) **AH 376** (605.2 km) Paved turnout with litter barrel to west.

J 78.7 (127.4 km) **AH 367.4** (591.3 km) Paved turnout with litter barrel.

J 85 (137.8 km) **AH 361.1** (581.2 km) Paved turnout with litter barrels to west.

J 85.7 (138.9 km)**AH 360.4** (580.1 km) Elsworth logging camp and Van Dyke camp services (Meziadin Lake General Store), open to public; fuel, groceries, dump station, hunting and fishing licenses, emergency phone. Private airstrip.

Meziadin Lake General Store/VanDyke Camp Services. See display ad this section.

J 87.9 (142.4 km) **AH 358.2** (576.6 km) *CAUTION: 1-lane bridge over Nass River.* Paved rest area with picnic tables, toilets and litter barrel to east at south end of bridge. A plaque at the north end commemorates bridge opening in 1972 that joined roads to form Highway 37. The gorge is almost 400 feet/122m wide; main span of bridge is 186 feet/57m. Bridge decking is 130

Picnicking alongside Bear Glacier, 14.4 miles/23.2 km west of the Cassiar Highway on the Stewart/Hyder access road. (© Beth Davidow)

feet/40m above the riverbed.

J 89.4 (145 km) **AH 356.7** (574.1 km) Tintina Logging Road.

J 93.1 (151 km) **AH 353** (568.1 km) Tintina Creek. Along with Hanna Creek, this stream produces 40 percent of the sockeye salmon spawning in the Meziadin Lake watershed.

J 94.3 (152.8 km) **AH 351.8** (566.3 km) Large gravel turnout to west with litter barrels.

J 94.4 (153 km) **AH 351.7** (566 km) Bridge over Hanna Creek South. Sockeye salmon spawn here in autumn and can be observed from creek banks and bridge deck. It is illegal to fish for or harass these fish. *CAUTION: Watch for bears.*

J 95.6 (155.3 km) **AH 350.5** (564.2 km) **Meziadin Lake** Provincial Park; 46 campsites (many on lake), drinking water, toilets, wheelchair access, swimming, firewood, bear-proof garbage containers, boat launch. The lake has a significant fish population, including rainbow trout, mountain whitefish and Dolly Varden. Fishing is especially good at the mouths of small streams draining into Meziadin Lake.

Four species of salmon spawn in the lake. This is one of only 3 areas in the province where salmon spawn in the bays and inlets of a lake. *CAUTION: Watch for bears. The hills around the lake are prime bear habitat.*

J 96.2 (156.4 km) **AH 349.9** (563.1 km) **Meziadin Junction** (Mezy-AD-in); Cassiar Highway junctions with the access road to Stewart, BC, and Hyder, AK. Fuel, propane, minor car repair, food, laundry, RV parking and dump station. See the STEWART, BC–HYDER, AK, ACCESS ROAD this section. *NOTE: This junction can be confusing. Choose your route carefully.*

J 97.5 (158.5 km) **AH 348.6** (561.1 km) Travelers will notice large areas of clear-cut along the southern half of the Cassiar Highway. Bark beetle infestation necessitated the harvest of timber along this particular stretch of highway. After logging, it was reforested.

J 100.8 (164.8 km) **AH 345.3** (555.8 km) Hanna Creek North river and bridge. Gravel turnout at north end of bridge on west side of road with litter barrel.

J 104.1 (169.2km) **AH 342** (550.5 km) Large paved turnout to west with litter barrels.

J 109.8 (178.5 km) **AH 336.3** (541.3 km) Pavement ends, gravel begins northbound.

NOTE: There was construction/maintenance work northbound to the Bell–Irving River bridge in 1997. Driving distance over this stretch may vary from log due to detours. Project is scheduled for completion in summer 1998.

J 116 (189.2 km) **AH 330.1** (531.3 km) Bell I crossing of Bell-Irving River. Rest area at north end of Bell–Irving bridge with picnic tables, pit toilets and litter barrels.

J 118.2 (192.2 km) **AH 327.9** (527.7 km) Spruce Creek bridge.

J 122.8 (198.9 km) **AH 323.3** (520.3 km) Bell–Irving River parallels highway.

J 125.1 (202.5 km) **AH 321** (516.7 km) Cousins Creek.

J 126.7 (205.2 km) **AH 319.4** (514.1 km) Ritchie Creek bridge, wooden-decked, slippery when wet.

J 130.4 (211.2 km) **AH 315.7** (508.1 km) Taft Creek bridge, wooden-decked, slippery when wet.

J 136.1 (220.4 km) **AH 310** (499 km) Deltaic Creek.

J 141.5 (229.2 km) **AH 304.6** (490.3 km) Glacier Creek.

J 142 (230 km) **AH 304.1** (489.5 km) Seal coat begins, gravel ends northbound.

J 143.6 (232.7 km) **AH 302.5** (486.8 km) Skowill Creek Bridge.

J 145.1 (235 km) **AH 301** (484.5 km) Large gravel turnout with litter barrels.

J 148.1 (239.8 km) **AH 298** (479.7 km) Oweegee Creek.

J 152.1 (246.2 km) **AH 294** (473.2 km) Provincial rest area by **Hodder Lake**; information kiosk, tables, litter barrels, pit toilets, cartop boat launch. Fly or troll for small rainbows.

J 153.6 (248.8 km) **AH 292.5** (470.7 km) Bell II Crossing; food, gas, diesel, propane, pay phone and lodging just south of second crossing (northbound) of Bell-Irving River.

J 153.8 (249.3 km) **AH 292.3** (470.5 km) Bridge crosses Bell–Irving River.

NOTE: In 1998, watch for road work from here north to Iskut.

J 156.8 (254.2 km) **AH 289.3** (465.6 km) Large gravel turnout with litter barrel.

J 159.2 (258.1 km) **AH 286.9** (461.7 km) Snowbank Creek.

J 161.2 (261.1 km) **AH 284.9** (458.6 km) Avalanche area: No stopping in winter or spring. Avalanche chutes are visible on slopes to west in summer. Highway serves as emergency airstrip. Watch for aircraft landing or taking off; keep to side of road!

J 161.6 (261.8 km) **AH 284.5** (457.9 km) Redflat Creek.

J 164.1 (266 km) **AH 282** (453.8 km) Revision Creek.

J 165.1 (267.6 km) **AH 281** (452.2 km) Fan Creek.

J 167.3 (271 km) **AH 278.8** (448.7 km) Avalanche area. No stopping.

J 168.7 (273.2 km) **AH 277.4** (446.5 km) Turnout with litter barrels to east overlooking large moose pasture, beaver lodge.

J 169.6 (274.9 km) **AH 276.5** (445 km) Ningunsaw Pass (elev. 1,530 feet/466m). Nass–Stikine water divide; turnout with litter barrels to west beside **Ningunsaw River**. Mountain whitefish and Dolly Varden. The highway parallels the Ningunsaw northbound. Watch for fallen rock on road through the canyon. The Ningunsaw is a tributary of the Stikine watershed.

J 169.9 (275.4 km) **AH 276.2** (444.5 km) Beaverpond Creek Bridge.

J 170.3 (276 km) **AH 275.8** (443.9 km) Liz Creek Bridge.

J 172.7 (279.9 km) **AH 273.4** (440 km) Alger Creek. The massive piles of logs and debris in this creek are from a 1989 avalanche. Avalanche chutes visible to west.

J 173 (280.3 km) **AH 273.1** (439.5 km) Large gravel turnout to east with litter barrel.

J 174.8 (283.2 km) **AH 271.3** (436.7 km) Bend Creek.

J 175.6 (284.5 km) **AH 270.5** (435.4 km) Gamma Creek.

J 176.9 (286.9 km) **AH 269.2** (433.2 km) Ogilvie Creek.

J 177.8 (288.2 km) **AH 268.3** (431.9 km) Point of interest sign about Yukon Telegraph line. The 1,900-mile/3,057-km Dominion Telegraph line linked Dawson City with Vancouver. Built from 1899–1901, the line was a route for prospectors and trappers headed to Atlin, BC; it was replaced by radio in the 1930s.

J 178 (288.6 km) **AH 268.1** (431.5 km) Echo Lake. Flooded telegraph cabins are visible in the lake below. Good view of Coast Mountains to west. Spectacular cliffs seen to the east are part of the Skeena Mountains (Bowser Basin).

J 181 (293.7 km) **AH 265.1** (426.6 km) Bob Quinn Forest Service Road, under construction as the Iskut Mining Road, will provide year-round access to goldfields west of the Ningunsaw River. The road will follow the Iskut River Valley toward the Stikine River, with a side branch to Eskay Creek gold deposit. *CAUTION: Watch for turning trucks.*

J 181.5 (294.4 km) **AH 264.6** (425.9 km) **Little Bob Quinn Lake**, rainbow and Dolly Varden, summer and fall. Access to Bob

(Continues on page 274)

Stewart, BC–Hyder, AK, Access Road Log

HIGHWAY 37A
Distance is measured from Meziadin Lake Junction (M).

M 0 Junction with Cassiar Highway at **Milepost J 96.2**. Visitor information cabin, status unconfirmed at press time.

M 2.8 (4.6 km) **Nothing Fancy.** RV, camping, lodging and cafe in beautiful lake setting. Extra-long, level, lakeside sites. Full services with 20-amp electrical. Tenting area. Shower and laundry facilities. Simple bunkhouse-style bed and breakfast with shared bathroom. Cafe with tasty home cooking. Open year-round. (250) 636-9171. P.O. Box 42, Stewart, BC V0T 1W0. [ADVERTISEMENT] ▲

M 7.7 (12.4 km) Surprise Creek bridge.

M 10.1 (16.3 km) Turnout to north with view of hanging glaciers.

M 10.4 (16.7 km) Turnout to south with view of hanging glaciers.

M 11.5 (18.5 km) Windy Point bridge.

M 12.5 (20.1 km) Cornice Creek bridge.

M 13.5 (21.7 km) Strohn Creek bridge.

M 14.4 (23.2 km) Rest area with litter barrels, view of Bear Glacier.

M 15.4 (24.8 km) Turnouts along lake into which Bear Glacier calves its icebergs. Watch for falling rock from slopes above road in spring. Morning light is best for photographing spectacular Bear Glacier. At one time the glacier reached this side of the valley; the old highway can be seen hundreds of feet above the present road.

M 17.5 (28.8 km) Cullen River bridge.

M 19.8 (31.9 km) Huge delta of accumulated avalanche snow. Little shoulder; no stopping.

M 21 (33.8 km) Argyle Creek.

M 22.4 (36.1 km) Narrow, steep-walled Bear River canyon. Watch for rocks on road.

M 23.9 (38.5 km) Turnout with litter barrel to north.

M 24.3 (39.1 km) Bear River bridge. Trailer court and RV park. ▲

M 28.9 (46.5 km) Turnout with litter barrel to south.

M 29.4 (47.4 km) Bitter Creek bridge.

M 31.8 (51.2 km) Wards Pass cemetery. The straight stretch of road along here is the former railbed from Stewart.

M 36.1 (58.1 km) Bear River bridge and welcome portal to Stewart.

M 37.8 (60.8 km) Highway joins main street of Stewart (description follows).

M 40.1 (64.4 km) U.S.–Canada border. Hyder (description follows).

TIME ZONE CHANGE: Stewart observes Pacific time, Hyder observes Alaska time.

Stewart, BC–Hyder, AK

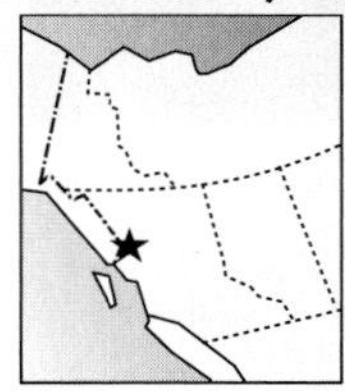

Stewart is at the head of Portland Canal on the AK–BC border. **Hyder** is 2.3 miles/3.7 km beyond Stewart. **Population: Stewart** about 1,000; **Hyder** 102. **Emergency Services:** In Stewart, **RCMP**, phone (250) 636-2233. EMS personnel and Medivac helicopter in Hyder. **Fire Department,** phone (250) 636-2345. **Hospital** and **Ambulance,** Stewart Health Care Facility (3 beds), phone (250) 636-2221.

Visitor Information: Stewart Visitor Infocentre (Box 306, Stewart, BC V0T 1W0), located in Chamber of Commerce/Infocentre Building on 5th Avenue; phone (250) 636-9224 or fax (250) 636-2199. Limited off-season hours. Hyder Information Center and Museum is located on the right as you drive into Hyder.

Elevation: Sea level. **Climate:** Maritime, with warm winters and cool rainy

STEWART ADVERTISERS

Bear River Trailer Court Ltd.........Hwy. 37A
Bitter Creek Cafe and
Marmot Bay Trading ....5th Ave.
Granmac Services Ltd...Ph. (250) 636-2307
King Edward Motel/
Hotel ....5th & Columbia
Lions Rainey Creek Municipal
Campground...........Ph. (250) 636-2537
Nothing Fancy Bed &
Breakfast ....Ph. (250) 636-9171

Stewart, BC–Hyder, AK, Access Road Log

Stewart yacht club. The harbor is Canada's most northerly ice-free port.
(© Wes Bergen, DIARAMA)

summers. Summer temperatures range from 41°F/5°C to 57°F/14°C; winter temperatures range from 25°F/-4°C to 43°F/6°C. Average temperature in January is 27°F/-3°C; in July, 67°F/19°C. Reported record high 89°F/32°C, record low -18°F/-28°C. Slightly less summer rain than other Northwest communities, but heavy snowfall in winter. **Radio:** CFPR 1450, CJFW-FM 92.9, CFMI-FM 101. **Television:** Cable, 15 channels.

Private Aircraft: Stewart airport, on 5th Street; elev. 10 feet/3m; length 3,900 feet/1,189m; asphalt; fuel 80, 100.

Stewart and Hyder are on a spur of the Cassiar Highway, at the head of Portland Canal, a narrow saltwater fjord approximately 90 miles/145 km long. The fjord forms a natural boundary between Alaska and Canada. Stewart has a deep harbour and boasts of being Canada's most northerly ice-free port.

Prior to the coming of the white man, Nass River Indians knew the head of Portland Canal as *Skam-A-Kounst,* meaning safe place, probably referring to the place as a retreat from the harassment of the coastal Haidas. The Nass came here annually to hunt birds and pick berries. Little evidence of their presence remains.

In 1896, Captain D.D. Gaillard (after whom the Gaillard Cut in the Panama Canal was later named) explored Portland Canal for the U.S. Army Corps of Engineers. Two years after Gaillard's visit, the first prospectors and settlers arrived. Among them was D.J. Raine, for whom a creek and mountain in the area were named. The Stewart brothers arrived in 1902 and in 1905 Robert M. Stewart, the first postmaster, named the town Stewart. Hyder was first called Portland City. It was then renamed Hyder, after Canadian mining engineer Frederick B. Hyder, when the U.S. Postal Authority told residents there were already too many cities named Portland.

Gold and silver mining dominated the early economy. Hyder boomed with the discovery of rich silver veins in the upper Salmon River basin in 1917–18. Hundreds of pilings, which supported struc-

HYDER ADVERTISERS

Bear Country Gifts ......Ph. (250) 636-2593
Camp Run–A–Muck.....Ph. (604) 636-2486
Grand View Inn, The...Ph. (250) 636-9174
Hyder Community Assoc. ....Ph. (250) 636-9148
Sealaska Inn ....Ph. (604) 636-2486
Taquan Air ....Ph. (800) 770-8800
This-N-That Shop ....Premier Ave.

tures during this boom period, are visible on the tidal flats at Hyder.

Hyder became an access and supply point for the mines, while Stewart served as the centre for Canadian mining activity. Mining ceased in 1956, with the exception of the Granduc copper mine, which operated until 1984. Currently, Westmin Resources Ltd. operates a gold and silver mine. Today the economy is driven by forestry, mining and tourism.

ACCOMMODATIONS/VISITOR SERVICES

Stewart: 3 hotels/motels, 3 restaurants, 1 grocery store, 4 churches, service stations, laundromat, pharmacy, post office, a bank (open Monday, Wednesday and Friday), ATM, liquor store and other shops. Camping at 3 campgrounds/RV parks with washrooms, showers and hookups. ▲

Hyder: 2 groceries, 4 gift shops, a post office, 3 cafes, a Baptist church, 2 motels and 2 bars. Boat launch at salt water, tenting area and RV park with TV reception. Visitor infocentre and museum. Laundromat, public restroom and showers. There is no bank in Hyder. There is an automatic teller machine in Stewart/Hyder. ▲

TRANSPORTATION

Air: Taquan Air; scheduled service from Hyder to Ketchikan. **Bus:** Limousine service to Terrace with connections to Greyhound and airlines. **Ferry:** Service between Ketchikan and Hyder. *IMPORTANT: Check ferry departure times carefully!*

ATTRACTIONS

Historic Buildings: In Stewart, the former fire hall at 6th and Columbia streets built in 1910, which now houses the Historical Society Museum; the Empress Hotel (now occupied by a hardware store) on 4th Street; and St. Mark's Church (built in 1910) on 9th Street at Columbia. On the border at Eagle Point is the stone storehouse built by Captain D.D. Gaillard of the U.S. Army Corps of Engineers in 1896. This is the oldest masonry building in Alaska. Originally 4 of these buildings were built to hold exploration supplies. This one was subsequently used as a cobbler shop and jail. Storehouses Nos. 3 and 4 are included on the (U.S.) National Register of Historic Places.

Stewart Historical Society Museum, in the fire hall, has a wildlife exhibit on the main floor and an exhibit of historical items on the top floor. Included is a display on movies filmed here: "Bear Island" (1978), John Carpenter's "The Thing" (1981), and "The Ice Man" (1982).

Hyder's night life is well-known, and has helped Hyder earn the reputation and town motto of "The Friendliest Little Ghost Town in Alaska."

Recreation in Stewart includes winter sports at the indoor skating rink; an outdoor tennis court; ball parks; hiking trails; and a self-guided historical walking tour.

Sightseeing tours of the area take in active and abandoned mine sites, such as Granduc, and glaciers, including the spectacular Salmon Glacier. Other sights include nearby Fish Creek and Summit Lake at the toe of Salmon Glacier. Once a year, usually in August, the ice dam holding back Summit Lake breaks, and the force of the meltwater results in a spectacular flooding of the Salmon River valley at Hyder. Chum and pink salmon are seen in their spawning colors in Fish Creek during August; they ascend the streams and rivers in great numbers to spawn. Visitors may photograph feeding bald eagles and black bears which are drawn to the streams by the salmon.

Visit the old mines. A 30-mile-/48-km-long road leads to movie locations and former mine sites. *CAUTION: The road is narrow and winding.* Access to Premier Mine, Big Missouri Mine and Salmon Glacier. Inquire at the Stewart Infocentre for more information.

International Days. Fourth of July begins July 1 as Stewart and Hyder celebrate Canada Day and Independence Day. Parade and fireworks.

International Rodeo. The Seward–Hyder International Rodeo is held the second weekend in June.

Charter trips by small boat on Portland Canal and vicinity available for sightseeing and fishing. Flightseeing air tours available.

AREA FISHING: Portland Canal, salmon to 50 lbs., use herring, spring and late fall; coho to 12 lbs. in fall, fly-fishing. *(NOTE: Alaska or British Columbia fishing license required, depending on whether you fish U.S. or Canadian waters in Portland Canal.)* **Fish Creek,** up the Salmon River road from Hyder, Dolly Varden 2 to 3 lbs., use salmon eggs and lures, best in summer. Fish Creek is a fall spawning ground for some of the world's largest chum salmon; it is illegal to kill chum in fresh water in British Columbia. It is legal to harvest chum from both salt and fresh water in Alaska.

Return to Milepost J 96.2 on the Cassiar Highway

(Continued from page 270)
Quinn Lake at **Milepost J 183.3.**

J 182.2 (295.3 km) **AH 263.9** (424.7 km) Bob Quinn flight airstrip. This is a staging site for supplies headed for the Stikine/Iskut goldfields. Paved rest area with litter barrels, picnic tables and toilet.

J 183.3 (297 km) **AH 262.8** (423 km) Bob Quinn highway maintenance camp; helicopter base. Emergency assistance. Access to Bob Quinn Lake; toilet, picnic table, cartop boat launch.

J 187 (303.1 km) **AH 259.1** (417 km) Gravel turnout with litter barrels on both sides of road.

J 188.3 (305.2 km) **AH 257.8** (415 km) Old kilometrepost 150, which reflects distance from Meziadin Junction.

J 190.2 (308.4 km) **AH 255.9** (411.8 km) Devil Creek Canyon bridge.

J 191.1 (309.7 km) **AH 255** (410.5 km) Gravel turnout with litter barrel to west.

J 191.6 (310.7 km) **AH 254.5** (409.6 km) Devil Creek Forest Service Road.

J 193.6 (313.9 km) **AH 252.5** (406.4 km) Thomas Creek and Thomas Creek Forest Service Road.

Highway passes through Iskut burn, where fire destroyed 78,000 acres in 1958. This is also British Columbia's largest huckleberry patch.

Northbound, the vegetation begins to change to northern boreal white and black spruce. This zone has cold, long winters and low forest productivity. Look for trembling aspen and lodgepole pine.

Southbound, the vegetation changes to become part of the interior cedar–hemlock zone. Cool wet winters and long dry summers produce a variety of tree species including western hemlock and red cedar, hybrid white spruce and subalpine fir.

CAUTION: Watch for turning trucks.

J 196.3 (318.1 km) **AH 249.8** (402 km) Large gravel turnout with litter barrel to west.

J 197.3 (319.6 km) **AH 248.8** (400.5 km) Slate Creek.

J 198.4 (321.5 km) **AH 247.7** (398.6 km) Gravel turnout with litter barrels to east.

J 199 (322.6 km) **AH 247.1** (397.7 km) Brake-check pullout.

J 199.7 (323.7 km) **AH 246.4** (396.6 km) Durham Creek.

J 203.7 (330.2 km) **AH 242.4** (390.1 km) Gravel begins, seal coat ends northbound.

J 204 (330.6 km) **AH 242.1** (389.7 km) Gravel turnout with litter barrels to west.

J 205.1 (332.4 km) **AH 241** (387.9 km) Single-lane bridge crosses Burrage River, northbound traffic yields. Note the rock pinnacle upstream to east.

J 205.5 (333 km) **AH 240.6** (387.2 km) Iskut River to west.

J 206.8 (335 km) **AH 239.3** (385.2 km) Gravel turnout to west.

J 207.8 (336.6 km) **AH 238.3** (383.6 km) Emergency airstrip crosses road; no stopping, watch for aircraft.

J 213 (345.4 km) **AH 233.1** (375.1 km) Rest area by Eastman Creek; picnic tables, outhouses, litter barrels, and information sign with map and list of services in Iskut Lakes Recreation Area. The creek was named for George Eastman (of Eastman Kodak fame), who hunted big game in this area before the highway was built.

J 216 (350.2 km) **AH 230.1** (370.3 km) Slow down for 1-lane bridge across Rescue Creek, northbound traffic yields. *NOTE: Watch for bridge construction here in 1998.*

J 217.7 (352.9 km) **AH 228.4** (367.6 km) Slow down for 1-lane bridge over Willow Creek, northbound traffic yields.

J 217.8 (353.1 km) **AH 228.3** (367.4 km) **Willow Ridge Resort**. See display ad this section.

J 218.3 (353.9 km) **AH 227.8** (366.6 km) Willow Creek Forest Service Road. *CAUTION: Watch for turning trucks.*

J 219.9 (356.6 km) **AH 226.2** (364 km) Gravel turnout with litter barrels to east.

J 220.6 (357.7 km) **AH 225.5** (362.9 km) Natadesleen Lake trailhead to west; toilets and litter barrel. Hike 0.6 mile/1 km west to lake.

J 222.6 (360.9 km) **AH 223.5** (359.7 km) Gravel turnout to west.

J 223.9 (362.9 km) **AH 222.2** (357.7 km) Snapper Creek.

J 225.1 (365 km) **AH 221** (355.7 km) Entrance to Kinaskan campground with 50 sites, outhouses, firewood, picnic and day-use area, wheelchair access, swimming, 2 hiking trails, drinking water and boat launch on **Kinaskan Lake**; rainbow fishing, July and August. Start of 15-mile/24.1-km hiking trail to Mowdade Lake in Mount Edziza Provincial Park.

J 230.1 (373.1 km) **AH 216** (347.6 km) Turnout with litter barrel and view of Kinaskan Lake to west.

J 231.1 (374.6 km) **AH 215** (346.1 km) Small lake to east.

J 233.1 (377.9 km) **AH 213** (342.8 km) Gravel turnout with litter barrels to east.

J 233.4 (378.4 km) **AH 212.7** (342.3 km) Todagin Creek 1-lane bridge, northbound traffic yields.

J 239.4 (388.1 km) **AH 206.7** (332.7 km) Gravel turnout to west.

J 240.7 (390.2 km) **AH 205.4** (330.6 km) **Harbour Air Ltd.** See display ad this section.

Tatogga Lake Resort. See display ad this section.

J 241.3 (391.1 km) **AH 204.8** (329.7 km) Coyote Creek.

J 241.9 (392.1 km) **AH 204.2** (328.7 km) Ealue Lake (EE-lu-eh) turnoff. Small B.C. Forest Service recreation area, 7.5 miles/12 km off highway on gravel access road. Rustic sites, picnic tables, rock fire rings (bring own firewood), user-maintained, no fee.

J 244.5 (396.4 km) **AH 201.6** (324.5 km) Turnout with litter barrel.

J 244.6 (396.6 km) **AH 201.5** (324.3 km) Spatsizi trailhead to east. Turnout with litter barrel beside **Eddontenajon Lake** (Ed-don-TEN-ajon). It is unlawful to camp overnight at turnouts. People drink from the lake; be careful not to contaminate it. Use dump stations. Breakup in late May; freezeup early Nov. Rainbow fishing July and August.

J 248.2 (402.3 km) **AH 197.9** (318.6 km) **Red Goat Lodge.** Lovely treed lakeshore setting with power and water hookups for RVs and tents, and bed and breakfast with unparalleled reputation. Coin showers, laundry, phone. Canoe and fishing boat rentals. Fishing is excellent from shore. Choose Red Goat for a special vacation experience. AAA approved and undoubtedly one of the finest facilities on Highway 37. Open year-round. Jacquie and Mitch Cunningham, P.O. Box 101, Iskut, BC V0J 1K0. Phone/fax (250) 234-3261. [ADVERTISEMENT] ▲

J 248.3 (402.5 km) **AH 197.8** (318.4 km) **Tenajon Motel & Cafe**. See display ad this section.

J 250 (405.4 km) **AH 196.1** (315.6 km) Zetu Creek. B.C. Hydro generating plant, supplies power for Iskut area.

J 250.2 (405.7 km) **AH 195.9** (315.3 km) **ISKUT** (pop. 300). Small Tahltan Native community with post office in the Kluachon Centre on the highway, grocery store, public phone, motel and gas station. Quality leather goods available locally. Camping and cabins available at local lodges and guest ranches. Horse trips, canoe rentals and river rafting may be available; inquire at local lodges and resorts. Clinic: Phone (250) 234-3511. ▲

Iskut Valley's Ice Cream & Pizza. See display ad this section.

Kluachon Centre. See display ad this section.

Private Aircraft: Eddontenajon airstrip, 0.6 mile/1 km north of Iskut; elev. 3,100 feet/945m; length 3,000 feet/914m; gravel; fuel available at Trans-Provincial Airlines base south on Eddontenajon Lake.

NOTE: Southbound travelers watch for road work from here to Bell II in 1998.

J 251.8 (408.3 km) **AH 194.3** (312.7 km) **Mountain Shadow.** 50 miles south of Dease Lake. A quiet, secluded, park-like setting with spectacular mountain vistas and lake views. Set away from highway noise and traffic for a restful stopover or extended stay. Short nature walk for exclusive access to Kluachon Lake with excellent fishing. Wilderness trails, bird and wildlife viewing. A unique, private and breathtaking wilderness setting. [ADVERTISEMENT] ▲

J 256 (415.4 km) **AH 190.1** (306 km) **Trapper's Souvenirs**. See display ad this section.

J 257.6 (418 km) **AH 188.5** (303.4 km) Tsaybahe Creek. Watch for beaver lodges which are visible from the highway.

J 257.7 (418.1 km) **AH 188.4** (303.3 km) **Forty Mile Flats.** See display ad this section. ▲

J 260.6 (423 km) **AH 185.5** (298.5 km) Turnout with litter barrels to west. From here the dormant volcano of Mount Edziza (elev. 9,143 feet/2,787m) and its adjunct cinder cone can be seen to the southwest. The park, not accessible by road, is a rugged wilderness with a glacier, cinder cones, craters and lava flows. Panoramic view of Skeena and Cassiar mountains for next several miles northbound. Information signs.

J 261.8 (424.9 km) **AH 184.3** (296.6 km) Turnoff to Morchuea Lake B.C. Forest Service campsite. Rustic, some tables, rock fire rings (bring firewood), no fee. ▲

J 264 (428.4 km) **AH 182.1** (293.1 km) Entering Stikine River Recreation Area.

J 266.3 (432.1 km) **AH 179.8** (289.4 km) Steep grade. Winding road next 1.2 miles/2 km northbound.

J 267.2 (433.6 km) **AH 178.9** (287.9 km) Hairpin turn: Keep to right. Highway descends to Stikine River in switchbacks.

J 269 (436.6 km) **AH 177.1** (285 km) Turnout with litter barrels and toilets to south. Tourist map and services directory for area located here.

J 269.5 (437.3 km) **AH 176.6** (284.3 km) Stikine River bridge. Turnout at north end of bridge.

J 271.3 (440.2 km) **AH 174.8** (281.4 km) Turnout to east with litter barrel.

J 273.4 (443.6 km) **AH 172.7** (278 km) Leaving Stikine River Recreation Area northbound.

J 277.3 (450 km) **AH 168.8** (271.6 km) Turnout on Upper Gnat Lake; tables, toilets, litter barrels. Long scar across Gnat Pass valley to east is grading preparation for B.C. Railway's proposed Dease Lake extension from Prince George. Construction was halted in 1977. Grade is visible for several miles northbound.

J 279 (452.7 km) **AH 167.1** (268.9 km) Large gravel turnout with litter barrel to east at Tees Creek.

J 282 (457.6 km) **AH 164.1** (264.1 km) Gravel turnout with litter barrel to east.

J 283.9 (460.7 km) **AH 162.2** (261.1 km) Gravel turnout to east.

J 284.2 (461.3 km) **AH 161.9** (260.5 km) Upper Gnat Rest Area.

J 284.5 (461.7 km) **AH 161.6** (260.1 km)

Telegraph Creek Road Log

Built in 1922, this was the first road in the Cassiar area of northern British Columbia. The scenery is remarkable and the town of Telegraph Creek is a picture from the turn of the century. Many of the original buildings remain from the gold rush days.

CAUTION: Telegraph Creek Road has some steep narrow sections and several sets of steep switchbacks; it is not recommended for trailers or large RVs. Car and camper drivers who are familiar with mountain driving should have no difficulty, although some motorists consider it a challenging drive even for the experienced. DRIVE CAREFULLY! Use caution when road is wet or icy. Watch for rocks and mud. There are no visitor facilities en route. Allow a minimum of 2 hours driving time with good conditions. Check road conditions at highway maintenance camp or RCMP office in Dease Lake before starting the 70.1 miles/112.8 km to Telegraph Creek. Phone the Stikine RiverSong Cafe (250) 235-3196 for weather and road conditions.

Distance from Dease Lake junction (D) on the Cassiar Highway is shown.

D 0 Dease Lake junction, Milepost J 300.9 Cassiar Highway.

D 0.9 (1.4 km) **Junction** with road to Dease Lake. Turn left for Telegraph Creek.

D 1.4 (2.3 km) Entrance to airport.

D 3.1 (5 km) Pavement ends, gravel begins westbound.

D 5 (8 km) Entering Tanzilla Plateau.

D 7.2 (11.6 km) Tatsho Creek (Eightmile).

D 15.9 (25.6 km) 16 Mile Creek.

D 17.1 (27.5 km) Augustchilde Creek, 1-lane bridge.

D 18.8 (30.3 km) 19 Mile Creek.

D 20.2 (32.5 km) 22 Mile Creek. Turnout with litter barrels south.

D 22.4 (36 km) Tanzilla River to south.

D 35.7 (57.5 km) Cariboo Meadows. Entering old burn area for 12 miles/19.3 km.

D 36.7 (59.1 km) Entering Stikine River Recreation Area. Tuya River valley viewpoint to north; turnout with litter barrels. Short walk uphill for good views and photographs.

Stikine River Canyon near Telegraph Creek. (© Wes Bergen, DIARAMA)

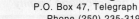

D 37.7 (60.6 km) Approximate halfway point to Telegraph Creek from Dease Lake. Turnout with litter barrels to north. Excellent view of Mount Edziza on clear days.

D 45.5 (73.2 km) Begin 18 percent grade as road descends canyon; steep and narrow with switchbacks.

D 46 (74.1 km) Turnout with litter barrels to south.

D 47.2 (76 km) Tuya River bridge.

D 47.7 (76.8 km) End of burn area.

D 49 (78.9 km) Road makes Y-intersection. Old road to left; keep right for newer section.

D 50.4 (81.1 km) Old road rejoins newly constructed section.

D 50.8 (81.7 km) Golden Bear Mine access road. Private.

D 51.1 (82.2 km) Twenty percent downhill grade for approximately 0.6 mile/1 km. Day's Ranch on left.

D 54.2 (87.3 km) Rest area with table, toilet and litter barrel; overlooks river gorge.

D 55.7 (89.7 km) Road runs through lava beds, on narrow promontory about 150 feet/51m wide, dropping 400 feet/122m on each side to Tahltan and Stikine rivers. Sudden 180-degree right turn begins steep descent to Tahltan River and Indian fishing camps. Excellent views of the Grand Canyon of the Stikine and Tahltan Canyon can be seen by walking a short distance across lava beds to promontory point. Best views of the river canyon are by flightseeing trip. The Stikine River canyon is only 8 feet/2.4 m wide at its narrowest point.

D 56.1 (90.3 km) Sudden 180-degree turn begins 18 percent downhill grade to Tahltan River.

D 56.5 (90.9 km) Tahltan River bridge. Turnout with litter barrel south, on north side of bridge. Traditional communal Indian smokehouses adjacent to road at bridge. Smokehouse on north side of bridge is operated by a commercial fisherman; fresh and smoked salmon sold. There is a commercial inland fishery on the Stikine River, one of only a few such licensed operations in Canada.

D 57.5 (92.6 km) Start of very narrow road on ledge rising steeply up the wall of the Stikine Canyon for 3 miles/4.8 km, rising to 400 feet/122m above the river.

D 60 (96.6 km) Ninemile Creek.

D 60.1 (96.7 km) Old Tahltan Indian community above road. Private property: No trespassing! Former home of Tahltan bear dogs. The Tahltan bear dog, believed to be extinct, was only about a foot high and weighed about 15 pounds. Short-haired, with oversize ears and shaving-brush tail, the breed was recognized by the Canadian Kennel Club. First seen by explorer Samuel Black in 1824, the dogs were used to hunt bears.

D 61.8 (99.5 km) Eightmile Creek bridge. Spectacular falls into canyon on left below. Opposite the gravel pit at the top of the hill there is a trailhead and parking on the west side of the creek.

D 63.1 (101.5 km) Turnout. Good photos of Stikine Canyon to east.

D 69.1 (111.2 km) Indian community. Road follows steep winding descent into old town, crossing a deep narrow canyon via a short bridge. Excellent picture spot 0.2 mile/0.3 km from bridge. Glenora Road **junction** on right.

D 70.1 (112.8 km) **TELEGRAPH CREEK** (pop. 300; elev. 1,100 feet/335m). Former head of navigation on the Stikine and once a telegraph communication terminal. During the gold rush, an estimated 5,000 stampeders set off from Telegraph Creek to attempt the Stikine–Teslin Trail to the goldfields in Atlin and the Klondike.

There are a cafe, lodge, general store, post office, and a public school and nursing station here. Gas, minor auto and tire repair are available. Stikine River trips and charter flights are available. Anglican church services held weekly; Roman Catholic services held every-other week.

Residents make their living fishing commercially for salmon, doing local construction work and guiding visitors on hunting, fishing and river trips. Telegraph Creek is becoming a jumping-off point for wilderness hikers headed for Mount Edziza Provincial Park.

The scenic view along the main street bordering the river has scarcely changed since gold rush days. The 1898 Hudson's Bay Co. post, which now houses the RiverSong Cafe, is a recognized Heritage Building. Historic St. Aidan's Church (Anglican) and several other buildings pre-dating 1930 are also located here.

A 12-mile/19.3-km road continues west to Glenora, site of attempted railroad route to the Yukon and limit of larger riverboat navigation. There are 2 primitive B.C. Forest Service campsites on the road to Glenora. Several spur roads lead to the Stikine River and to Native fish camps. ▲

Return to Milepost J 300.9
Cassiar Highway

Wilderness trail rides.

J 285.8 (463.8 km) **AH 160.3** (258 km) Turnout overlooking **Lower Gnat Lake,** abundant rainbow.

J 287.9 (467.1 km) **AH 158.2** (254.7 km) Turnout with litter barrel.

J 290.6 (467.7 km) **AH 155.5** (250.2 km) Gnat Pass Summit, elev. 4,072 feet/1,241m. Watch for cariboo in spring.

J 291.7 (473.3 km) **AH 154.4** (248.5 km) Steep grade, 8 percent downhill.

J 295.2 (479.1 km) **AH 150.9** (242.8 km) **Tanzilla River** bridge. Pleasant rest area with picnic tables and outhouses at north end of bridge beside river. Fishing for grayling to 16 inches, June and July; use flies.

J 296.5 (481.2 km) **AH 149.6** (240.7 km) Dalby Creek.

J 298.4 (484.1 km) **AH 147.7** (237.8 km) Turnout with litter barrel to west.

J 300.2 (487.1 km) **AH 145.9** (234.9 km) Divide (elev. 2,690 feet/820m) between Pacific and Arctic ocean watersheds.

J 300.9 (488.3 km) **AH 145.2** (233.7 km) **Junction** with Telegraph Creek Road and access to Dease Lake (description follows). See TELEGRAPH CREEK ROAD this section.

Dease Lake

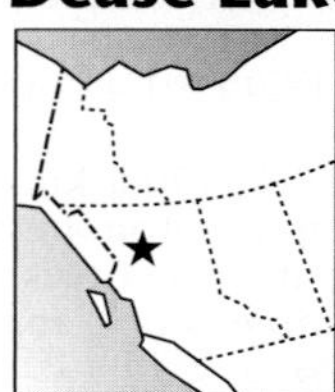

Located just west of the Cassiar Highway. **Emergency Services: RCMP** detachment. **Private Aircraft:** Dease Lake airstrip, 1.5 miles/2.4 km south; elev. 2,600 feet/792m; length 6,000 feet/1,829m; asphalt; fuel JP4, 100. **Visitor Information:** Write Dease Lake and Tahltan District Chamber of Commerce, Box 338, Dease Lake, BC V0C 1L0; phone (250) 771-3900.

Dease Lake has motels, gas stations (with regular, unleaded, diesel, propane and minor repairs), food stores, restaurant, a post office, hardware/sporting goods, highway maintenance centre and government offices. Charter flights and regular air service to Terrace

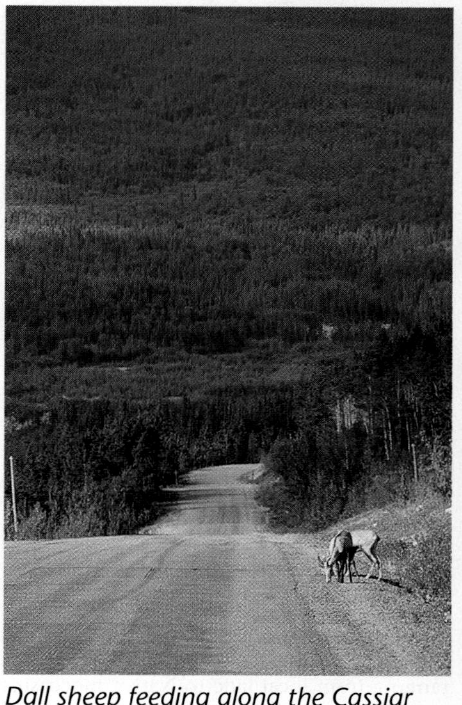

Dall sheep feeding along the Cassiar Highway. *(© Dan Skillman)*

and Smithers with interprovincial connections. Information kiosks at south entrance to town. ▲

A Hudson's Bay Co. post was established by Robert Campbell at Dease Lake in 1838, but abandoned a year later. The lake was named in 1834 by John McLeod of the Hudson's Bay Co. for Chief Factor Peter Warren Dease. Laketon, on the west side of the lake (see **Milepost J 327.7**), was a centre for boat building during the Cassiar gold rush of 1872–80. In 1874, William Moore, following an old Indian trail, cut a trail from Telegraph Creek on the Stikine River to the gold rush settlement on Dease Lake. This trail became Telegraph Creek Road, which was used in 1941 to haul supplies for Alaska Highway construction and Watson Lake Airport to Dease Lake. The supplies were then ferried down the Dease River.

Today, Dease Lake is a government centre and supply point for the district. The community has dubbed itself the "jade capital of the world." Jade is available locally. It is a popular point from which to fly-in, hike-in, or pack-in by horse to Mount Edziza and Spatsizi wilderness parks.

Cassiar Highway Log

(continued)

J 300.9 (488.3 km) **AH 145.2** (233.7 km) **Dease Lake Junction.** Junction with access road to Dease Lake and Telegraph Creek Road (see log page 276).

*NOTE: Watch for road work from here north to Jade City (**Milepost J 371.1**) in 1998.*

J 301.7 (489.6 km) **AH 144.4** (232.4 km) Hotel Creek.

J 308.8 (501.3 km) **AH 137.3** (220.9 km) Turnout with litter barrel to west.

J 309.6 (502.5 km) **AH 136.5** (219.7 km) Serpentine Creek.

J 313.5 (508.7 km) **AH 132.6** (213.5 km) Gravel turnout to west with litter barrel.

J 314.1 (509.8 km) **AH 132** (212.4 km) Good views of Dease Lake, limited access to lake shore.

J 315.7 (512.3 km) **AH 130.4** (209.9 km) Gravel turnout to west.

J 316.3 (513.3 km) **AH 129.8** (208.9 km) Halfmoon Creek.

J 318.8 (517.4 km) **AH 127.3** (204.9 km) Rabid Grizzly rest area with picnic tables, travel information signs, litter barrels and outhouses. View of Dease Lake.

J 322.1 (522.8 km) **AH 124** (199.5 km) Gravel turnout to west.

J 324.2 (526.1 km) **AH 121.9** (196.2 km) Black Creek.

J 326.3 (529.5 km) **AH 119.8** (192.8 km) Sawmill Point Recreation Site to west; side road leads to **Dease Lake** for fishing. Lake trout to 30 lbs., use spoons, plugs, spinners, June to October, deep trolling in summer, spin casting in fall.

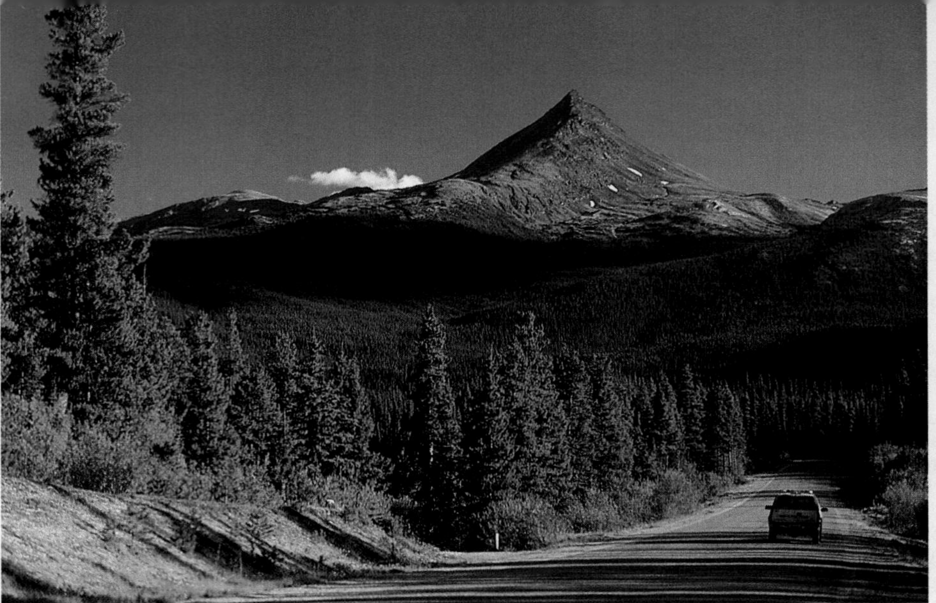

View of aptly-named Needlenose Mountain, southbound on the Cassiar Highway at Milepost J 353.7. (© Lyn Hancock)

J 327.2 (531.2 km) **AH 118.9** (191.4 km) Dorothy Creek.

J 327.7 (532 km) **AH 118.4** (190.5 km) The site of the ghost town Laketon lies across the lake at the mouth of Dease Creek. Laketon was the administrative centre for the district during the Cassiar gold rush (1872–80). Boat building was a major activity along the lake during the gold rush years, with miners heading up various creeks and rivers off the lake in search of gold. Today's miners ford the lake when the water is low to reach claims on the northwest side.

J 330.2 (535.9 km) **AH 115.9** (186.5 km) Beady Creek. Entering the Cassiar Mountains northbound.

J 333.5 (541.1 km) **AH 112.6** (181.3 km) Turnout to west with litter barrels.

J 333.8 (541.7 km) **AH 112.3** (180.7 km) Turnout with litter barrel to west. **Dease River** parallels the highway. Grayling to 17 inches; Dolly Varden and lake trout to 15 lbs.; northern pike 8 to 10 lbs., May through September.

Marshy areas to west; good moose pasture. Watch for wildlife, especially at dawn and dusk.

J 334.4 (542.7 km) **AH 111.7** (179.7 km) Packer Tom Creek, named for a well-known Indian who lived in this area.

J 336.1 (545.4 km) **AH 110** (177 km) Elbow Lake.

J 342 (554.7 km) **AH 104.1** (167.5 km) Pyramid Creek.

J 342.4 (555.6 km) **AH 103.7** (166.9 km) Dease River 2-lane concrete bridge.

J 343.9 (558 km) **AH 102.2** (164.5 km) Beale Creek.

J 348.7 (561.1 km) **AH 97.4** (156.7 km) Road widens. Generous paved pullout to east overlooking Pine Tree Lake.

J 350.9 (563.4 km) **AH 95.2** (153.2 km) Turnout beside **Pine Tree Lake.** Good grayling and lake char fishing.

J 351 (569.5 km) **AH 95.1** (153.1 km) Burn area. An abandoned campfire started the fire in July 1982.

J 352.8 (572.4 km) **AH 93.3** (150.2 km) **Moose Meadows,** (formerly Mighty Moe's).

J 353.7 (573.9 km) **AH 92.4** (148.7 km) Gravel turnout with litter barrels to east. Views of Needlenose Mountain southbound.

J 357.9 (580.9 km) **AH 88.2** (141.9 km) **Cottonwood River** bridge; rest area 0.4 mile/0.6 km west on old highway on south side of river. Fishing for grayling and whitefish. Early summer runs of Dolly Varden.

J 358.7 (582 km) **AH 87.4** (140.7 km) Cottonwood River rest area No. 2 is 0.5 mile/0.8 km west on old highway on north side of river.

J 363.6 (589.8 km) **AH 82.5** (132.8 km) Turnout to west beside **Simmons Lake;** information kiosk, picnic tables, picnic shelter, toilets, small beach and dock. Fishing for lake trout.

J 365.3 (592.7 km) **AH 80.8** (130 km) Road runs on causeway between Twin Lakes.

J 365.8 (593.5 km) **AH 80.3** (129.2 km) **Vines Lake,** named for bush pilot Lionel Vines; fishing for lake trout.

J 366.9 (595.3 km) **AH 79.2** (127.4 km) Limestone Creek.

J 367.3 (595.9 km) **AH 78.8** (126.8 km) Lang Lake and creek. Needlepoint Mountain visible straight ahead southbound.

J 369.8 (599.9 km) **AH 76.3** (122.8 km) Cusak gold mine visible on slopes to east. Gold mined on the far side of the mountain is processed in the mill here.

J 370.1 (600.3 km) **AH 76** (122.3 km) Side road east leads to McDame Lake.

J 370.9 (601.6 km) **AH 75.2** (121 km) Trout Line Creek.

J 371.1 (601.9 km) **AH 75** (120.7 km) **JADE CITY** (pop. 12), named for the jade deposits found to the east of the highway community. The huge jade boulders that visitors can see being cut here are from the Princess Jade Mine, 82 miles/132 km east, one of the largest jade claims in the world.

NOTE: Southbound travelers watch for road work from here to Dease Lake in 1998.

J 371.3 (602.2 km) **AH 74.8** (120.4 km) Jade store and RV park. ▲

Jade City. World famous jade capital. Extensive selection of raw jade, jade jewellery and carvings crafted from local Cassiar and Princess jade. Best jade and jewellery prices in the North. Rock hounds will appreciate the extensive selection of raw Canadian gemstones and jewellery. See display ad this section. Jesus is Lord. [ADVERTISEMENT]

J 372.5 (604.1 km) **AH 73.6** (118.5 km) **Cassiar junction.** Cassiar Road to west leads 9.7 miles/15.6 km to the former Cassiar townsite and Cassiar Asbestos Mine. Continue straight ahead for Alaska Highway.

CASSIAR (pop. 25) was the company town of Cassiar Mining Corp. Much of the world's high-grade chrysotile asbestos came from Cassiar. The mine closed in March 1992, and the site is closed to visitors. It is now the site of a B.C. Chrysotile Corp. reclamation project. No services available.

J 372.7 (604.4 km) **AH 73.4** (118.2 km) Snow Creek.

J 372.8 (605.6 km) **AH 73.3** (117.9 km) Gravel turnout with litter barrel to east.

J 373.5 (606.1 km) **AH 72.6** (116.8 km) Deep Creek.

J 377.4 (612.2 km) **AH 68.7** (110.6 km) No. 3 North Fork Creek.

J 378.4 (613.9 km) **AH 67.7** (108.9 km) No. 2 North Fork Creek. Small gold mining operations may be visible to east.

J 381 (618 km) **AH 65.1** (104.7 km) Historic plaque about Cassiar gold.

CENTREVILLE (pop. 2; elev. 2,600 feet/792m), a former gold rush town of 3,000. The only evidence of Centreville along the highway today is the town name painted on an old piece of mining equipment parked on the east side of the road. Centreville was founded and named by miners for its central location between Sylvester's Landing (later McDame Post) at the junction of McDame Creek with the Dease River, and Quartzrock Creek, the upstream limit of pay gravel on McDame Creek. A miner named Alfred Freeman washed out the biggest all-gold (no quartz) nugget ever found in British Columbia on a claim near Centreville in 1877; it weighed 72 ounces. Active mining in area.

J 381.1 (618.2 km) **AH 65** (104.6 km) No. 1 North Fork Creek.

J 383 (621.3 km) **AH 63.1** (101.5 km) Watch for Dall sheep in this area.

J 385.2 (625 km) **AH 60.9** (98 km) **GOOD HOPE LAKE** (pop. 100), Indian village with limited services; fuel may be available.

Turn east on Bush Road and drive 9 miles/14.5 km for **McDAME POST**, an early Hudson's Bay post, at the **confluence of Dease River and McDame Creek.** Good fishing and hunting here.

NOTE: Watch for seal-coating work here in 1998.

J 386.9 (627.7 km) **AH 59.2** (95.3 km) Turnout to east alongside Aeroplane Lake.

J 387.7 (629 km) **AH 58.4** (94 km) Dry Creek.

J 389.5 (631.9 km) **AH 56.6** (91.1 km) Mud Lake to east.

J 393.6 (638.5 km) **AH 52.5** (84.5 km) Turnout with litter barrels at entrance to **Boya Lake** Provincial Park. The park is 1.6 miles/2.6 km east of highway; 45 campsites, picnic area on lakeshore, boat launch, toilets, wheelchair access, walking trails, drinking water, firewood and swimming. Fishing for lake char, whitefish and burbot. Attendant on duty during summer. ▲

J 393.7 (638.6 km) **AH 52.4** (84.4 km) Turnout. Horseranch Range may be seen on the eastern horizon northbound. These mountains date back to the Cambrian period, or earlier, and are the oldest in northern British Columbia. According to the Canadian Geological Survey, this area contains numerous permatites with crystals of tourmaline, garnet, feldspar, quartz and beryl. Road crosses Baking Powder Creek and then follows Dease River.

J 397.9 (645.4 km) **AH 48.2** (77.6 km) Camp Creek.

J 399.4 (648 km) **AH 46.7** (75.1 km) Beaver Dam Creek.

J 400.3 (649.4 km) **AH 45.8** (73.7 km) Beaver Dam rest area with visitor information sign to west.

J 400.6 (649.8 km) **AH 45.5** (73.3 km) Leaving Cassiar Mountains, entering Yukon Plateau, northbound.

J 402.5 (652.9 km) **AH 43.6** (70.2 km) Baking Powder Creek.

J 410.9 (666.5km) **AH 35.2** (56.7 km) Gravel access road to French Creek B.C. Forest Service campsite 0.6 miles/1 km from highway. Rustic. Tables, rock fire ring (bring firewood), small boat launch into Dease River, no fee. ▲

J 411.2 (667 km) **AH 34.9** (56.1 km) French Creek 2-lane concrete bridge.

J 417.5 (677.2 km) **AH 28.6** (46.1 km) Twentyeight Mile Creek. Cassiar Mountains rise to south.

J 420.2 (681.8 km) **AH 25.9** (41.6 km) Wheeler Lake to west.

J 422.9 (686.1 km) **AH 23.2** (37.3 km) Blue River Forest Service Road to east.

J 426.3 (691.5 km) **AH 19.8** (31.9 km) Blue River 2-lane concrete bridge.

J 429.7 (697.1 km) **AH 16.4** (26.4 km) Turnout at **Blue Lakes;** litter barrels, picnic tables and fishing for pike and grayling.

J 431.5 (700 km) **AH 14.6** (23.5 km) Mud Hill Creek.

J 436 707.4 km) **AH 10.1** (16.2 km) Old Faddy Forest Service Road.

J 440.1 (714 km) **AH 6** (9.6 km) Turnout with litter barrels beside Cormier Creek.

J 441.3 (718.5 km) **AH 4.8** (7.7 km) High Lake to east.

J 444 (720.3 km) **AH 2.1** (3.4 km) Turnout to west at BC–YT border, 60th parallel. Information sign. Yukon Territory's flag consists of 3 vertical panels of colour: blue, representing the rivers and lakes; green symbolizing forests; and white signifying snow. The Yukon coat of arms appears on the central panel, framed by 2 stems of fireweed, the territory's floral emblem. The flag was chosen from a design competition sponsored in 1967. Yukon Territory was made a district of Northwest Territories in 1895 and became a separate territory in June 1898, at the height of the Klondike Gold Rush. *NOTE: Drive with headlights on at all times in Yukon Territory.*

J 445.3 (722.5 km) **AH 0.8** (1.2 km) **Albert Creek.** Good grayling fishing. Yukon Territory fishing license required.

J 446.1 (723.7 km) **AH 0 Junction** of Cassiar Highway with Alaska Highway. Gas, store, campground and RV park, cafe, souvenirs, laundromat, camp-style motel, saloon, propane, towing and car repair at junction. Turn left for Whitehorse, right for Watson Lake, 13.3 miles/21.4 km southeast. Watson Lake is the nearest major community. ▲

Junction 37 Services. See display ad this section.

Turn to **Milepost DC 626.2** on page 129 in the ALASKA HIGHWAY section for log of Alaska Highway from this junction.

HAINES HIGHWAY   (3)

Connects: Haines, AK, to Haines Junction, YT **Length:** 152 miles
Road Surface: Paved **Season:** Open all year
Highest Summit: Chilkat Pass 3,493 feet
Major Attraction: Chilkat Bald Eagle Preserve

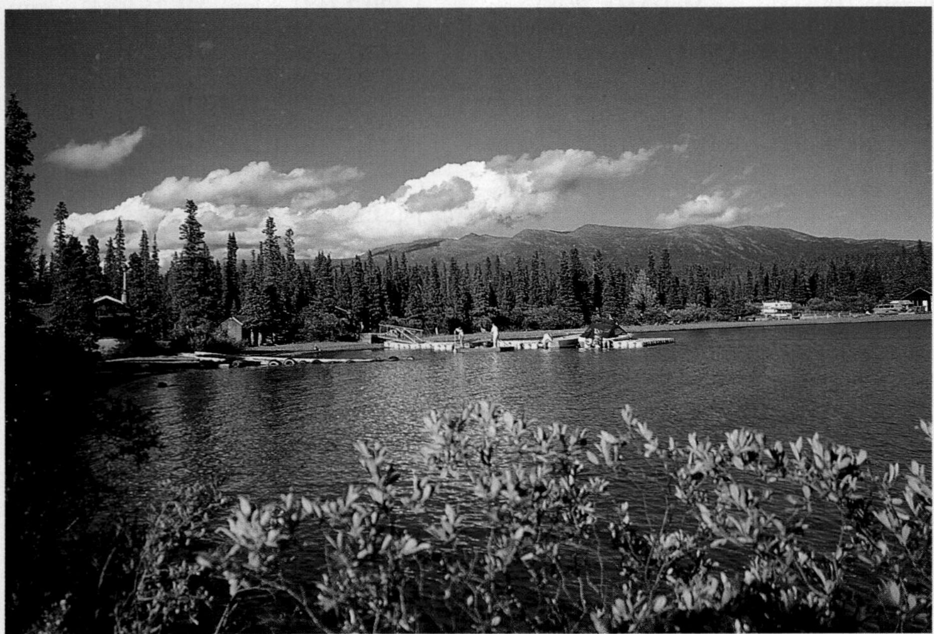

Camping at glacier-fed Kathleen Lake, Milepost H 134.8 Haines Highway.

(Earl L. Brown, staff)

	Beaver Creek	Haines	Haines Jct.	Tok	Whitehorse
Beaver Creek		335	184	113	283
Haines	335		152	449	252
Haines Jct.	184	152		297	100
Tok	113	449	297		396
Whitehorse	283	252	100	396	

The paved 151.6-mile-/244-km-long Haines Highway connects Haines, AK (on the state ferry route), at the head of Lynn Canal with the Alaska Highway at Haines Junction, YT. The highway is open year-round. Allow about 4 hours driving time. Watch for logging and fuel trucks. *NOTE: In summer, gas is available along the highway only at 33 Mile Roadhouse and at Kathleen Lake Lodge,* ***Milepost H 135.2.***

Noted for the grandeur and variety of its alpine scenery, the highway leads from coastal forests near Haines through the Chilkat Eagle Preserve up over the backbone of the St. Elias Mountains, skirting Tatshenshini–Alsek Wilderness Provincial Park, and running along the eastern border of Kluane National Park Reserve and down into the valleys of the Yukon basin. Information on Kluane National Park Reserve is available in Haines Junction, YT.

Part of what is now the Haines Highway was originally a "grease trail" used by the coastal Chilkat Indians trading eulachon oil for furs from the Interior. In the late 1880s, Jack Dalton developed a packhorse trail to the Klondike goldfields along the old trading route. The present road was built in 1943 as a military access highway during WWII to provide an alternative route from the Pacific tidewater into Yukon Territory.

This historic corridor is celebrated each year during Dalton Trail Days, July 1–4. Watch for bikes on the highway during the annual Kluane/Chilkat International Bike Race (June 20, 1998). Some 950 cyclists participated in 1997.

U.S. and Canada customs stations are located about 40 miles/64 km north of Haines. U.S. customs is open from 7 A.M. to 11 P.M. (Alaska time); Canada customs is open from 8 A.M. to midnight (Pacific time). There are no facilities or accommodations at the border. All travelers must stop.

A valid Alaska fishing license is required for fishing along the highway between Haines and the international border at **Milepost H 40.7.** The highway then crosses the northern tip of British Columbia into Yukon Territory. You must have valid fishing licenses for both British Columbia and Yukon Territory if you fish these areas, and a national park fishing license if you fish waters in Kluane National Park.

If you plan to drive the Haines Highway in winter, check road conditions before starting out. In Haines Junction, the maintenance garage (867/634-2227) or weigh scale station (867/634-2228) can help if they are in. (Flashing lights at the Haines Junction weigh scales indicate hazardous winter road conditions; travel not recommended.) Or phone (867) 667-8215 for the daily recorded road condition report.

Emergency medical services: Between Haines and the U.S.–Canada border at **Milepost H 40.7**, phone 911. Between the U.S.–Canada border and Haines Junction, phone the RCMP at (867) 634-5555.

Haines Highway Log

ALASKA ROUTE 7

Driving distance is measured in miles from Haines, AK. Mileposts are up along the Alaska portion of the highway. The kilometre figures on the Canadian portion of the highway reflect the physical kilometre-posts and are not an accurate metric conversion of the mileage figure.

Distance from Haines (H) is followed by distance from Haines Junction (HJ).

H 0 HJ 151.6 (244 km) **HAINES.** See HAINES section for accommodations and facilities.

H 0.2 (0.3 km) **HJ 151.4** (243.7 km) Front Street.

H 0.4 (0.6 km) **HJ 151.2** (243.4 km) Second Street. Turn right northbound (left southbound) for visitor information center and downtown Haines.

H 0.5 (0.8 km) **HJ 151.1** (243.2 km) Third Street. Turn right northbound (left southbound) for downtown Haines.

H 1 (1.6 km) **HJ 150.6** (242.4 km) Haines Hitch-Up RV Park. ▲

H 1.2 (1.9 km) **HJ 150.4** (242.1 km) Main Street Y. If southbound, turn right to Fort William H. Seward, left to downtown Haines.

H 1.3 (2.1 km) **HJ 150.3** (241.9 km) Eagle's Nest Motel.

H 3.3 (5.3 km) **HJ 148.3** (238.7 km) Indian graveyard on the right northbound.

H 3.5 (5.6 km) **HJ 148.1** (238.3 km) **Private Aircraft:** Haines airport; elev. 16 feet/5m; length 3,000 feet/914m; asphalt; fuel 100; unattended.

The Chilkat River estuary, which the highway parallels for the next 15 miles/24 km, flows into Chilkat Inlet of Lynn Canal, a massive fjord about 60 miles/96.5 km long. Lynn Canal was named by English explorer Captain Vancouver for his birthplace (King's Lynn) in England. The yellow signs along the highway indicate mileages on the U.S. Army oil pipeline. The pipeline formerly pumped oil from Haines over the St. Elias Mountains to the Alaska Highway at Haines Junction, YT. These signs were used for aerial checking and monitoring of the line.

H 4.3 (6.9 km) **HJ 147.3** (237 km) Turnout along river.

H 6 (9.6 km) **HJ 145.6** (234.3 km) Picnic

HAINES HIGHWAY *Haines, AK, to Haines Junction, YT*

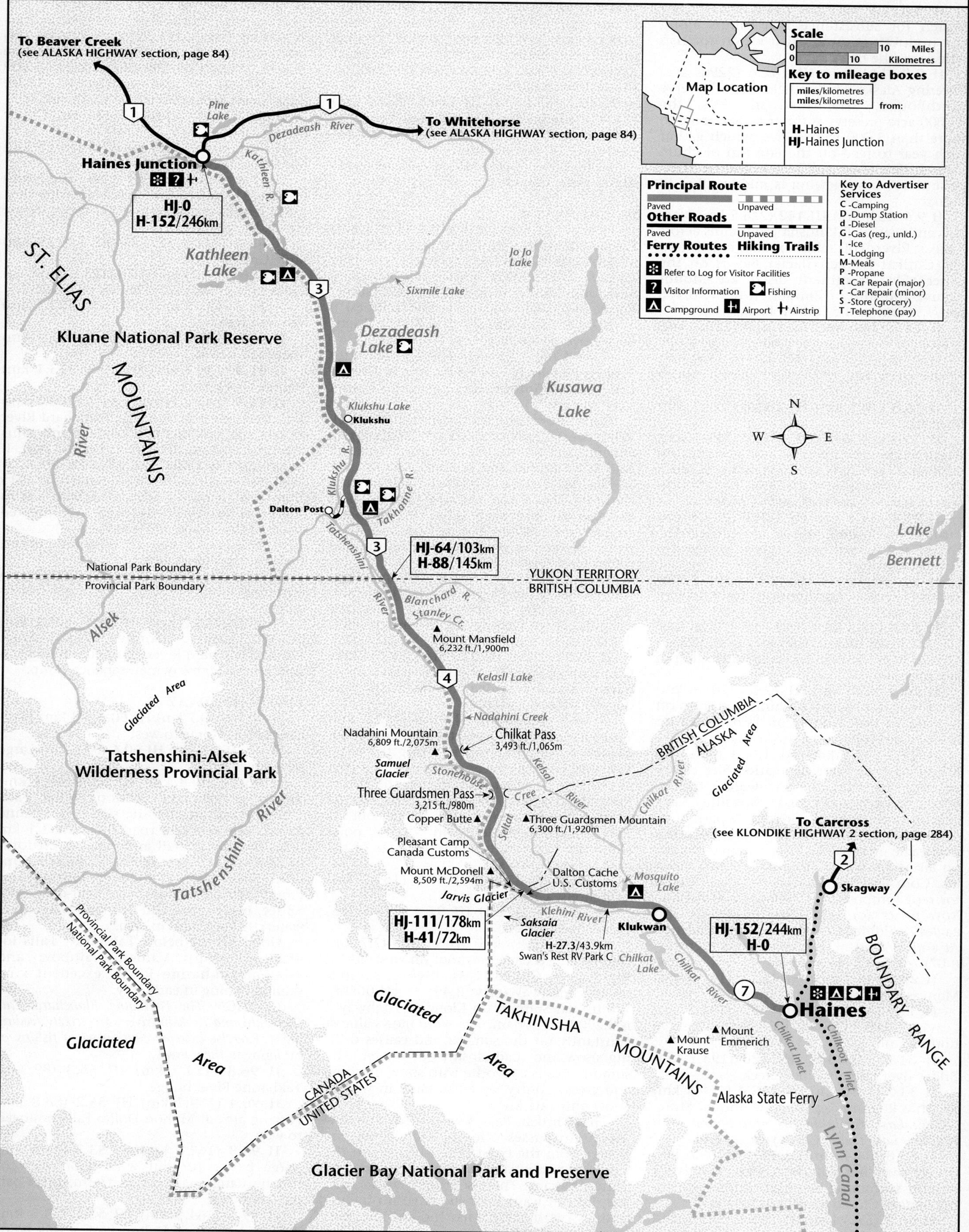

To Beaver Creek
(see ALASKA HIGHWAY section, page 84)
To Whitehorse
(see ALASKA HIGHWAY section, page 84)
Pine Lake
Dezadeash River
Haines Junction
HJ-0
H-152/246km
Kathleen R.
Kathleen Lake
ST. ELIAS
MOUNTAINS
Kluane National Park Reserve
Dezadeash Lake
Sixmile Lake
Jo Jo Lake
Kusawa Lake
Klukshu Lake
Klukshu
Klukshu R.
Takhanne R.
Dalton Post
Tatshenshini River
HJ-64/103km
H-88/145km
National Park Boundary
Provincial Park Boundary
YUKON TERRITORY
BRITISH COLUMBIA
Lake Bennett
Blanchard R.
Stanley Cr.
Mount Mansfield
6,232 ft./1,900m
Alsek River
Kelasll Lake
Nadahini Creek
Glaciated Area
Nadahini Mountain
6,809 ft./2,075m
Chilkat Pass
3,493 ft./1,065m
Samuel Glacier
Stonehouse
Tatshenshini-Alsek
Wilderness Provincial Park
Three Guardsmen Pass
3,215 ft./980m
Cree
Kelsal River
Copper Butte
Seltat
Three Guardsmen Mountain
6,300 ft./1,920m
BRITISH COLUMBIA
ALASKA
Chilkat River
Glaciated Area
Pleasant Camp
Canada Customs
Mount McDonell
8,509 ft./2,594m
Jarvis Glacier
Dalton Cache
U.S. Customs
Mosquito Lake
Klehini River
Klukwan
HJ-111/178km
H-41/72km
Saksaia Glacier
H-27.3/43.9km
Swan's Rest RV Park C
Chilkat Lake
Chilkat River
To Carcross
(see KLONDIKE HIGHWAY 2 section, page 284)
Skagway
HJ-152/244km
H-0
Haines
BOUNDARY RANGE
Provincial Park Boundary
National Park Boundary
Glaciated Area
Glaciated Area
TAKHINSHA MOUNTAINS
Mount Krause
Mount Emmerich
Chilkat Inlet
Chilkoot Inlet
Alaska State Ferry
CANADA
UNITED STATES
Lynn Canal
Glacier Bay National Park and Preserve
N
S
E
W
Scale
0 10 Miles
0 10 Kilometres
Map Location
Key to mileage boxes
miles/kilometres
miles/kilometres
from:
H-Haines
HJ-Haines Junction
Principal Route
Paved
Unpaved
Other Roads
Paved
Unpaved
Ferry Routes
Hiking Trails
Refer to Log for Visitor Facilities
Visitor Information
Fishing
Campground
Airport
Airstrip
Key to Advertiser Services
C -Camping
D -Dump Station
d -Diesel
G -Gas (reg., unld.)
I -Ice
L -Lodging
M-Meals
P -Propane
R -Car Repair (major)
r -Car Repair (minor)
S -Store (grocery)
T -Telephone (pay)

spot next to Chilkat River and a clear creek.

H 6.6 (10.6 km) **HJ 145** (233.3 km) Mount Ripinski trailhead.

H 8 (12.8 km) **HJ 143.6** (231.1 km) Watch for subsistence fish camps along the highway in June. Also watch for fish wheels on the river.

H 9.2 (14.8 km) **HJ 142.4** (229.2 km) Entering Alaska Chilkat Bald Eagle Preserve northbound. Established in 1982, the 48,000-acre preserve is the seasonal home to more than 3,000 bald eagles, which gather each year to feed on the late run of chum salmon. Eagle-viewing area begins at **Milepost H 19**; best viewing is mid-October to January.

H 9.6 (15.4 km) **HJ 142** (228.5 km) Magnificent view of Takhinsha Mountains across Chilkat River. This range extends north from the Chilkat Range; Glacier Bay is on the other side. Prominent peaks are Mount Krause and Mount Emmerich (elev. 6,405 feet/1,952m) in the Chilkat Range.

H 14.7 (23.6 km) **HJ 136.9** (220.3 km) Watch for mountain goats on the ridges.

H 17.6 (28.3 km) **HJ 134** (215.6 km) Rustic barn and old cabins. Good photo shots.

H 18.8 (30.3 km) **HJ 132.8** (213.7 km) Slide area.

H 19 (30.6 km) **HJ 132.6** (213.4 km) Begin eagle viewing area (northbound) on Chilkat River flats. Best viewing is mid-October to January. *CAUTION: Eagle watchers, use turnouts and park well off highway!*

H 21.4 (34.4 km) **HJ 130.2** (209.5 km) Turnoff to Indian village of **KLUKWAN**. Gravel access road dead ends at village. No visitor facilities.

H 22 (35.4 km) **HJ 129.6** (208.5 km) Second access northbound to Klukwan (steep grade).

H 23.8 (38.3 km) **HJ 127.8** (205.6 km) Chilkat River bridge. Highway now follows Klehini River. Watch for eagles beginning in late summer.

H 26.3 (42.3 km) **HJ 125.3** (201.6 km) Road west leads across Klehini River; turn off here for jet boat landing on Tsirku River for Birch Island Lodge on Chilkat Lake.

H 27.3 (43.9 km) **HJ 124.3** (200 km) Mosquito Lake State Recreation Site campground; 10 sites, tables, water, toilets, $6/night or annual pass. Mosquito Lake general store. Access to private RV park. ▲

H 28.8 (46.3 km) **HJ 122.8** (197.6 km) Muncaster Creek bridge.

H 30.9 (49.7 km) **HJ 120.7** (194.2 km) Leaving Alaska Chilkat Bald Eagle Preserve northbound.

H 31.6 (50.9 km) **HJ 120** (193.1 km) Bridge over Little Boulder Creek.

H 33.2 (53.4 km) **HJ 118.4** (190.5 km) 33 Mile Roadhouse; gas and phone. Store. *NOTE: Last available gas northbound until Kathleen Lake Lodge. Check your gas tank.*

H 33.8 (54.4 km) **HJ 117.8** (189.6 km) Bridge over Big Boulder Creek. Watch for salmon swimming upstream during spawning season. Closed to salmon fishing.

H 36.2 (58.3 km) **HJ 115.4** (185.7 km) View of Saksaia Glacier.

H 40.4 (65 km) **HJ 111.2** (179 km) U.S. customs, Dalton Cache station. All travelers entering United States MUST STOP. Open year-round 7 A.M. to 11 P.M., Alaska time. Phone (907) 767-5511. Restrooms, large parking area. Jarvis Glacier moraine is visible from the old Dalton Cache (on the National Register of Historic Places), located behind the customs building.

H 40.7 (65.5 km) **HJ 110.9** (178.5 km) U.S.–Canada border. Last milepost marker is Mile 40, first kilometrepost marker is Kilometrepost 74, northbound.

TIME ZONE CHANGE: Alaska observes Alaska time, Canada observes Pacific time.

BC HIGHWAY 4

H 40.8 (71.8 km) **HJ 110.8** (178.3 km) Canada Customs and Immigration office at Pleasant Camp. All travelers entering Canada MUST STOP. Office is open daily year-round, 8 A.M. to midnight, Pacific time. Phone (907) 767-5540. No public facilities.

H 44.9 (78.5 km) **HJ 106.7** (171.7 km) Bridge over Fivemile Creek.

H 49.4 (80.3 km) **HJ 102.2** (164.5 km) Large gravel double-ended turnout at **Historical Mile 48**; information panels on Haines Road history.

Good viewpoint for Tatshenshini–Alsek Wilderness Provincial Park. This park encompasses the rugged northwest corner of British Columbia and is dominated by the St. Elias Mountains. It is also habitat for grizzly bears, Dall sheep, the rare "glacier" bear and also rare birds such as the king eider and Stellar's eider. The Tatshenshini and Alsek rivers are famous for their river rafting and sightseeing opportunities.

H 49.7 (86 km) **HJ 101.9** (164 km) Highway crosses Seltat Creek. This is eagle country; watch for them soaring over the uplands. Three Guardsmen Mountain (elev. 6,300 feet/1,920m) to the east.

H 53.9 (92 km) **HJ 97.7** (157.2 km) Three Guardsmen Lake to the east. Glave Peak, part of Three Guardsmen Mountain, rises directly behind the lake.

H 55.1 (94.6 km) **HJ 96.5** (155.3 km) Three Guardsmen Pass to the northeast, hidden by low hummocks along the road. Stonehouse Creek meanders through a pass at the base of Seltat Peak to join the Kelsall River about 6 miles/10 km to the east. To the north is the Kusawak Range; to the south is Three Guardsmen Mountain. The tall poles along the highway indicate the edge of the road for snowplows.

H 55.8 (95.8 km) **HJ 95.8** (154.2 km) Stonehouse Creek culvert.

H 56.2 (96.3 km) **HJ 95.4** (153.5 km) Clear Creek culvert.

H 59.8 (102.1 km) **HJ 91.8** (147.7 km) Double-ended paved turnout on west side of highway at Chilkat Pass, highest summit on this highway (elev. 3,493 feet/1,065m). White Pass Summit on Klondike Highway 2 is 3,290 feet/1,003m. The wind blows almost constantly on the summit and causes drifting snow and road closures in winter. The summit area is a favorite with snow machine and cross-country ski enthusiasts in winter. Snow until late May.

The Chilkat Pass was one of the few mountain passes offering access into the Yukon from the coast. The Chilkat and the Chilkoot passes were tenaciously guarded by Tlingit Indians. These southern Yukon Indians did not want their lucrative fur-trading business with the coastal Indians and Russians jeopardized by white strangers. But the gold rush of 1898, which brought thousands of white people inland, finally opened Chilkat Pass, forever altering the lifestyle of the Interior Natives.

From the Chilkat Pass over Glacier Flats to Stanley Creek, the highway crosses silt-laden streams flowing from the Crestline Glacier. Nadahini Mountain (elev. 6,809 feet/2,075m) to the northwest. Three Guardsmen Mountain to the southeast.

H 63 (107 km) **HJ 88.6** (142.6 km) Chuck Creek culvert.

H 64.4 (109.3 km) **HJ 87.2** (140.3 km) Nadahini River culvert.

H 67.8 (114.7 km) **HJ 83.8** (134.8 km) **Private Aircraft:** Mule Creek airstrip; elev. 2,900 feet/884m; length 4,000 feet/1,219m; gravel. No services.

H 68.9 (116.4 km) **HJ 82.7** (133 km) Mule Creek.

H 73.6 (124.2 km) **HJ 78** (125.5 km) Goat Creek bridge. Watch for horses on road.

H 75.7 (127.3 km) **HJ 75.9** (122.1 km) Holum Creek.

H 80.1 (128.9 km) **HJ 71.5** (115.1 km) Mansfield Creek.

H 81.3 (136.3 km) **HJ 70.3** (113.1 km) Stanley Creek bridge.

H 86.5 (143.6 km) **HJ 65.1** (104.8 km) Blanchard River bridge. The Blanchard River crosses the Yukon–BC boundary and joins the Tatshenshini River near Dalton Post. It was originally called the Kleheela River by local Native tribes. It was re-named in 1915 after G. Blanchard Dodge, DLS, who was in charge of survey parties which delineated much of the Yukon–BC boundary.

H 87.1 (144.5 km) **HJ 64.5** (103.8 km) Welcome to Yukon sign.

H 87.4 (145 km) **HJ 64.2** (103.3 km) Entering Kluane Game Sanctuary northbound.

H 87.5 (145.2 km) **HJ 64.1** (103.1 km) BC–YT border. Former U.S. Army Alaska–Blanchard River Petroleum pump station, now a highway maintenance camp.

YUKON HIGHWAY 3

H 90.7 (150.7 km) **HJ 60.9** (98 km) Blanchard River Gorge to west.

H 91 (151.2 km) **HJ 60.6** (97.5 km) Large paved turnout.

H 96.2 (159.4 km) **HJ 55.4** (89.1 km) Yukon government Million Dollar Falls Campground on opposite side of Takhanne River; follow access road 0.7 mile/1.1 km west. Boardwalk trail and viewing platform of scenic falls. View of the St. Elias Mountains. Two kitchen shelters, tenting and group firepit, 27 campsites, 8 tent-only sites, $8 fee, playground and drinking water (boil water). Hiking trails in area. ▲

Good fishing below **Takhanne Falls** for grayling, Dolly Varden, rainbow and salmon. **Takhanne River**, excellent king salmon fishing in early July.

CAUTION: The Takhanne, Blanchard, Tatshenshini and Klukshu rivers are grizzly feeding areas. Exercise extreme caution when fishing or exploring in these areas.

H 96.3 (159.5 km) **HJ 55.3** (89 km) Takhanne River bridge.

H 96.4 (159.7 km) **HJ 55.2** (88.8 km) Parking area at Million Dollar Falls trailhead to west.

H 98.3 (162.6 km) **HJ 53.3** (85.8 km) Large paved turnout with good view of Kluane Range; viewing platform, litter barrels, outhouse.

H 99.5 (164.5 km) **HJ 52.1** (83.8 km) Turnoff to historic Dalton Post, a way point

Eagle feeds on chum salmon carcass, as gull and magpie watch, in Alaska Chilkat Bald Eagle Preserve. (© Bill Sherwonit)

on the Dalton Trail. Steep, narrow, winding access road; four-wheel drive recommended in wet weather. Road not recommended for large RVs or trailers at any time. Several old abandoned log cabins and buildings are located here. Indians once formed a human barricade at Dalton Post to harvest the Klukshu River's run of coho salmon. The river system here hosts seasonal runs of chinook, sockeye and coho salmon. Chinook are most visible in July, coho in late September and October, and sockeye from August to October. In fall, grizzly bears come here to feast on the fish. *Be alert to their presence.*

Fishing for chinook, coho, sockeye salmon in **Village Creek**. Grayling, Dolly Varden and salmon in **Klukshu River.** Fishing restrictions posted. *CAUTION: Watch for bears.*

H 103.4 (169.7 km) **HJ 48.2** (77.5 km) Viewpoint with information sign to west. Alsek Range and Tatshenshini River to southwest.

H 104 (170.7 km) **HJ 47.6** (76.6 km) Motheral Creek culvert.

H 106.1 (174 km) **HJ 45.5** (73.2 km) Vand Creek.

H 110.8 (181.6 km) **HJ 40.8** (65.6 km) Klukshu Creek.

H 111.6 (183 km) **HJ 40** (64.4 km) Turnoff for **KLUKSHU**, an Indian village, located 0.5 mile/0.8 km off the highway via a gravel road. This summer fish camp and village on the banks of the Klukshu River is a handful of log cabins, meat caches and traditional fish traps. Steelhead, king, sockeye and coho salmon are taken here. Each autumn, families return for the annual catch. The site is on the old Dalton Trail and offers good photo possibilities. Museum, picnic spot, souvenirs for sale. Information panels on First Nations heritage and traditional fishing techniques.

Kluane National Park Reserve borders the highway to the west from here to Haines Junction (the visitor centre there has information on the park). Watch for signs for hiking trails, which are posted 3.1 miles/5 km before trailheads. For more information on the park, contact Kluane National Park Reserve, Parks Canada, Box 5495, Haines Junction, YT Y0B 1L0, phone (867) 634-7209, fax (867) 634-7208. Also visit the park information centre in Haines Junction. Open daily, May to September, the centre has excellent interpretive displays.

H 112.8 (185 km) **HJ 38.8** (62.4 km) Gribbles Gulch.

H 114 (187 km) **HJ 37.6** (60.5 km) Parking area at St. Elias Lake trailhead (4.5-mile/7.2-km round-trip). Novice and intermediate hiking trail winds through subalpine meadow. Watch for mountain goats.

H 117.8 (193 km) **HJ 33.8** (54.4 km) Dezadeash Lodge (closed in 1997, current status unknown). Historically, this spot was known as Beloud Post and is still noted as such on some maps. Mush Lake trail (13.4 miles/21.6 km long) begins behind lodge. It is an old mining road.

NOTE: Watch for horses on highway.

H 119.3 (195 km) **HJ 32.3** (52 km) Turnout along Dezadeash Lake, one of the earliest known features in the Yukon, which parallels the highway for 9 miles/14.5 km northbound, and Dezadeash mountain range. Dezadeash (pronounced DEZ-dee-ash) is said to be the Indian word describing their fishing method. In the spring, the Indians built small fires around the bases of large birch trees, peeled the heat-loosened bark and placed it, shiny white side up, on the bottom of the lake near shore, weighted with stones. From log wharfs built over the white bark, Indians waited with spears for lake trout to cross the light area. Another interpretation of Dezadeash relates that Chilkat Indians referred to it as *Dasar-ee-ASH,* meaning "Lake of the Big Winds." Entire tribes were annihilated during mid-19th century Indian wars here.

Dezadeash Lake offers good trolling, also fly-fishing along the shore where feeder streams flow into the lake. There are northern pike, lake trout and grayling in Dezadeash Lake. *CAUTION: This is a mountain lake and storms come up quickly.*

H 119.7 (195.7 km) **HJ 31.9** (51.3 km) Entrance to Yukon government Dezadeash Lake Campground; 20 campsites, $8 fee, kitchen shelter, picnic area, boat launch, no drinking water, pit toilets. ▲

H 123.9 (202.3 km) **HJ 27.7** (44.6 km) Rock Glacier trailhead to west; short 0.5-mile/0.8-km self-guiding trail, partially boardwalk. Interesting walk, some steep sections. Parking area and viewpoint.

H 126.2 (206.9 km) **HJ 25.4** (40.8 km) Dalton Trail Lodge to east with food, lodging and boat rentals.

H 134.7 (216.8 km) **HJ 16.9** (27.2 km) Access to bed and breakfast.

H 134.8 (219 km) **HJ 16.8** (27 km) Access road west to Kathleen Lake, a glacier-fed turquoise-blue lake, nearly 400 feet/122m deep. Access to Kathleen Lake Campground, the only established campground within Kluane National Park; 42 sites and a kitchen area; day-use area with boat launch at lake; campfire programs by park staff. Fees charged for camping ($10). Campfire talks and backcountry registration. The 53-mile/85-km Cottonwood loop trail begins here. ▲

NOTE: National parks fishing license required. **Kathleen Lake** lake trout average 10 lbs., use lures, June and July; kokanee average 2 lbs., June best; grayling to 18 inches, use flies, June to September. **Kathleen River** rainbow to 17 inches, June to September; grayling to 18 inches, July and August; lake trout average 2 lbs., best in September.

H 135.2 (220.3 km) **HJ 16.4** (26.4 km) Kathleen Lake Lodge; food, gas and lodging.

NOTE: Last available gas southbound for next 102 miles. Check your gas tank.

H 135.8 (220.5 km) **HJ 15.8** (25.4 km) **Kathleen River** bridge; a popular spot for rainbow, lake trout and grayling fishing. Some kokanee. A turnout on the east side of the road provides access to Kathleen River. From here, you can canoe to Lower Kathleen Lake and Rainbow Lake. This is an easy half-day paddle, but do not attempt to go further on Kathleen River, as there are many falls. Waterfowl in this area include harlequins, northern pintails and American wigeon. Lesser yellowlegs, spotted sandpiper, western wood-pewee and common yellowthroat are also present.

H 139.2 (227 km) **HJ 12.4** (20 km) Turnout to west. Good view of Kathleen Lake. Information plaque on Kluane and Wrangell–St. Elias national parks.

H 143.4 (233.5 km) **HJ 8.2** (13.2 km) Quill Creek trailhead to west (7-mile/11-km trail).

H 147.1 (239.1 km) **HJ 4.5** (7.2 km) Parking area to west at Auriol trailhead (9.3-mile/15-km loop trail); skiing and hiking.

H 148.8 (241.1 km) **HJ 2.8** (4.5 km) Rest stop to east with litter barrels and pit toilets. View of community of Haines Junction and Shakwak Valley.

H 151 (245 km) **HJ 0.6** (1 km) Bridges over Dezadeash River. This river is part of the headwaters system of the Alsek River, which flows into the Pacific near Yakutat, AK.

H 151.6 (246 km) **HJ 0 HAINES JUNCTION,** turn left for Alaska, keep straight ahead for Whitehorse. Turn to Haines Junction in the ALASKA HIGHWAY section for description of town and highway log. Whitehorse-bound travelers read log back to front, Alaska-bound travelers read log front to back.

Approximate driving distances from Haines Junction are: Whitehorse 100 miles/161 km; Tok 297 miles/475 km; Fairbanks 503 miles/805 km; and Anchorage 625 miles/1000 km.

KLONDIKE HIGHWAY 2

Connects: Skagway, AK, to Alaska Hwy., YT **Length:** 99 miles
Road Surface: Paved **Season:** Open all year
Highest Summit: White Pass 3,290 feet
Major Attraction: Klondike Gold Rush National Historical Park

(See map, page 285)

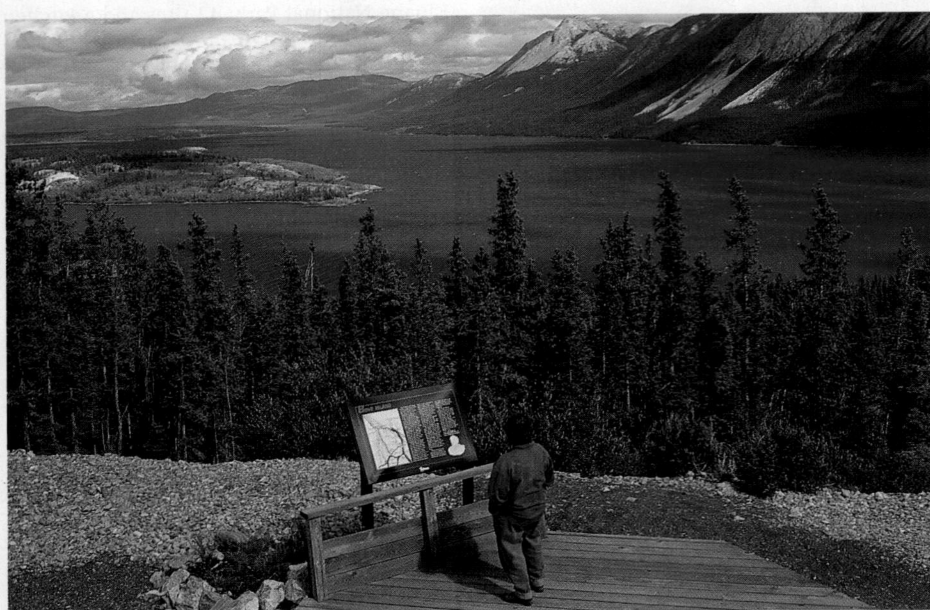

Turnout with historic information sign about Bove Island at Milepost S 59.5.

(© Harry M. Walker Photo)

	Alaska Hwy. Jct.	Atlin	Carcross	Skagway	Whitehorse
Alaska Hwy. Jct.		125	33	99	10
Atlin	125		92	158	81
Carcross	33	92		66	43
Skagway	99	158	66		109
Whitehorse	10	81	43	109	

The 98.8-mile-/159-km-long Klondike Highway 2 (also known as the Skagway–Carcross Road and South Klondike Highway) connects Skagway, AK, with the Alaska Highway at **Milepost 874.4** south of Whitehorse. The highway between Skagway and Carcross (referred to locally as the Skagway Road) was built in 1978 and formally dedicated on May 23, 1981. The highway connecting Carcross with the Alaska Highway (referred to locally as the Carcross Road) was built by the U.S. Army in late 1942 to lay the gas pipeline from Skagway to Whitehorse.

Klondike Highway 2 is a 2-lane, asphalt-surfaced road, open year-round. The road has been improved in recent years and is fairly wide. There is a steep 11.5-mile/18.5-km grade between Skagway and White Pass.

IMPORTANT: If you plan to cross the border between midnight and 8 A.M., inquire locally regarding customs stations' hours of operation or phone (907) 983-3144.

Klondike Highway 2 is one of the two highways connecting ferry travelers with the Alaska Highway; the other is the Haines Highway out of Haines. Klondike Highway 2 offers some spectacular scenery and adds only about 55 miles/89 km to the trip for Alaska-bound motorists, as compared to the Haines Highway. (The distance from Haines to Tok, AK, is approximately 445 miles/716 km; the distance from Skagway to Tok is 500 miles/805 km.) Klondike Highway 2, like the Haines Highway, crosses from Alaska into British Columbia, then into Yukon Territory.

Klondike Highway 2 continues north of Whitehorse, turning off the Alaska Highway to Dawson City. See the KLONDIKE LOOP section for the log of Klondike Highway 2 between the Alaska Highway and Dawson City.

CAUTION: Watch for ore trucks, 85-foot-long, 8-axle vehicles carrying up to 50 tons of lead–zinc concentrates from Faro mine on the Campbell Highway to Skagway.

Emergency medical services: Between Skagway and the BC–YT border, phone the Skagway Fire Department at (907) 983-2300. Between the border and the Alaska Highway, phone the Whitehorse ambulance at (867) 667-3333, RCMP at (867) 667-5555. Police monitor CB Channel 9.

Klondike Highway 2 Log

Mileposts in Alaska and kilometreposts in Canada reflect distance from Skagway. The kilometre distance from Skagway in *The MILEPOST®* log reflects the location of the physical kilometreposts, and is not necessarily an accurate conversion of the mileage figure.

Distance from Skagway (S) is followed by distance from Alaska Highway (AH).

S 0 AH 98.8 (159 km) Ferry terminal in **SKAGWAY**, northern terminus of the Alaska Marine Highway. Skagway owes its birth to the Klondike Gold Rush; see the description of Skagway in the INSIDE PASSAGE section.

S 1.6 (2.6 km) **AH 97.2** (156.4 km) Skagway River bridge.

S 2.3 (3.7 km) **AH 96.5** (155.3 km) **Junction** with Dyea Road.

S 2.6 (4.2 km) **AH 96.2** (154.8 km) Highway maintenance camp.

S 2.8 (4.5 km) **AH 96** (154.5 km) Plaque to east honoring men and women of the Klondike Gold Rush, and access to parklike area along Skagway River.

S 2.9 (4.7 km) **AH 95.9** (154.3 km) Access road east to Skagway River. Highway begins steep 11.5-mile/18.5-km ascent northbound from sea level to 3,290 feet/1,003m at White Pass.

S 4.7 (7.6 km) **AH 94.1** (151.4 km) Turnout to west.

S 5 (8 km) **AH 93.8** (151 km) Turnout to east with view across canyon of White Pass & Yukon Route railway tracks and bridge. The narrow-gauge WP&YR railway was completed in 1900.

S 5.5 (8.8 km) **AH 93.3** (150.1 km) Turnout to west with historical information signs.

S 6 (9.6 km) **AH 92.8** (149.3 km) Turnout to east.

S 6.8 (10.9 km) **AH 92** (148 km) U.S. customs station; open 24 hours in summer (manned 8 A.M. to midnight, video camera reporting midnight to 8 A.M.). Phone (907) 983-3144 for border crossing (immigration); phone (907) 983-2325 for customs in Skagway. All travelers entering the United States must stop. Have identification ready. Residents of North America must present birth certificate, driver's license or voter registration. All other foreign visitors must have a passport. Identification is also required for children.

S 7.4 (11.9 km) **AH 91.4** (147.1 km) View to east of WP&YR railway line.

S 7.7 (12.4 km) **AH 91.1** (146.6 km) Good photo stop for Pitchfork Falls, visible across the canyon. Pitchfork Falls flows from Goat Lake.

S 8.1 (13 km) **AH 90.7** (146 km) Turnout to east.

S 9.1 (14.6 km) **AH 89.7** (144.4 km) Paved turnout to east with historical interest signs about the Klondike Gold Rush trail.

KLONDIKE HIGHWAY 2

Skagway, AK, to Junction with Alaska Highway (includes Tagish and Atlin Roads)

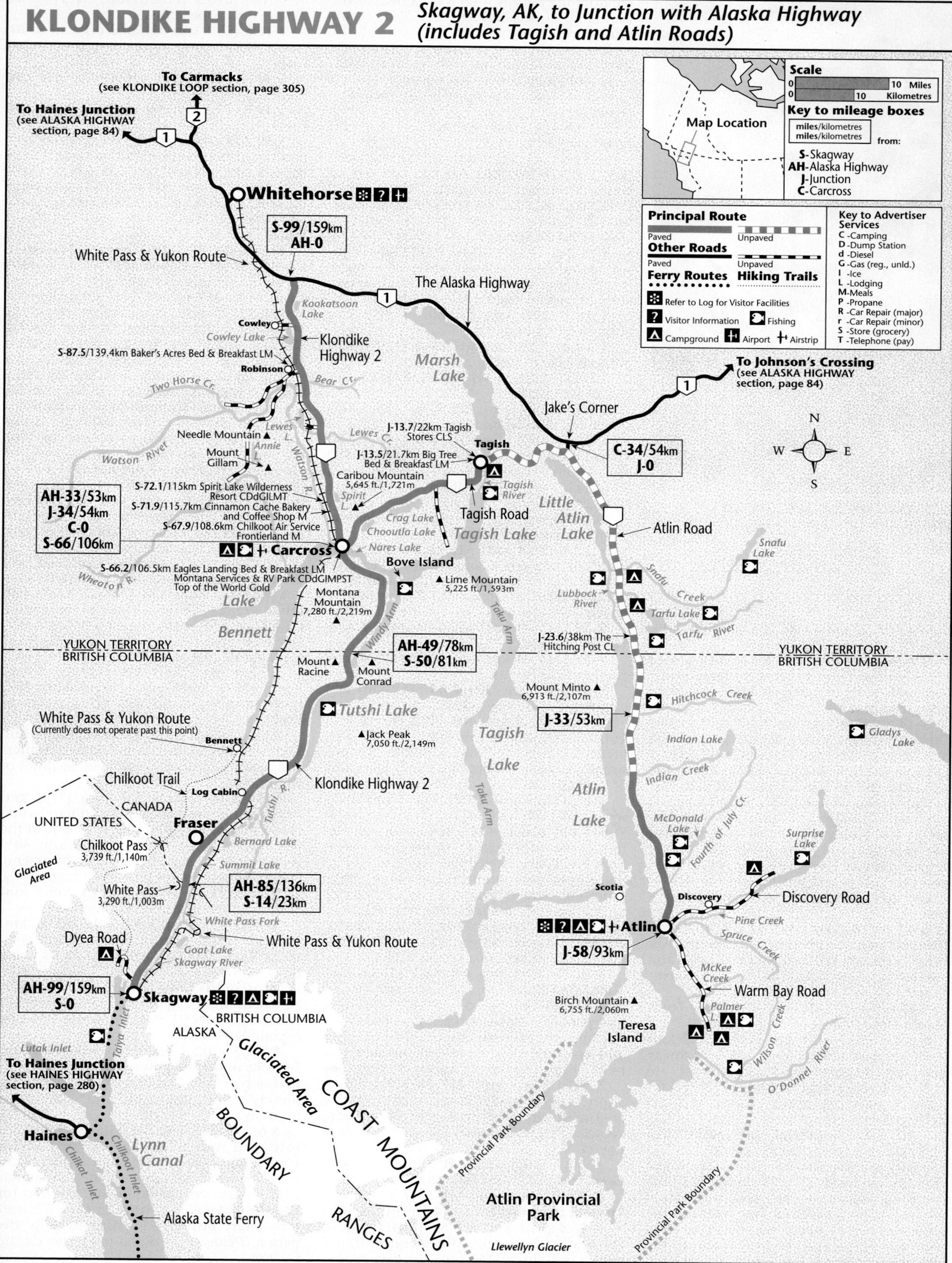

To Carmacks
(see KLONDIKE LOOP section, page 305)
To Haines Junction
(see ALASKA HIGHWAY section, page 84)
Whitehorse
S-99/159km
AH-0
White Pass & Yukon Route
The Alaska Highway
Kookatsoon Lake
Cowley
Cowley Lake
Klondike Highway 2
S-87.5/139.4km Baker's Acres Bed & Breakfast LM
Robinson
Marsh Lake
Two Horse Cr.
Bear Cr.
To Johnson's Crossing
(see ALASKA HIGHWAY section, page 84)
Jake's Corner
Needle Mountain
Lewes L.
Lewes Cr.
J-13.7/22km Tagish Stores CLS
Tagish
C-34/54km
J-0
Mount Gillam
Annie L.
Watson River
Watson R.
J-13.5/21.7km Big Tree Bed & Breakfast LM
Caribou Mountain
5,645 ft./1,721m
Tagish River
S-72.1/115km Spirit Lake Wilderness Resort CDdGILMT
S-71.9/115.7km Cinnamon Cache Bakery and Coffee Shop M
S-67.9/108.6km Chilkoot Air Service Frontierland M
AH-33/53km
J-34/54km
C-0
S-66/106km
Spirit L.
Crag Lake
Chooutla Lake
Nares Lake
Tagish Road
Tagish Lake
Little Atlin Lake
Atlin Road
Carcross
Bove Island
S-66.2/106.5km Eagles Landing Bed & Breakfast LM
Montana Services & RV Park CDdGIMPST
Top of the World Gold
Wheaton R.
Lime Mountain
5,225 ft./1,593m
Snafu Lake
Snafu Creek
Lubbock River
Montana Mountain
7,280 ft./2,219m
Lake Bennett
Windy Arm
Taku Arm
Tarfu Lake
Tarfu River
J-23.6/38km The Hitching Post CL
YUKON TERRITORY
BRITISH COLUMBIA
AH-49/78km
S-50/81km
Mount Racine
Mount Conrad
Mount Minto
6,913 ft./2,107m
Tutshi Lake
Hitchcock Creek
J-33/53km
White Pass & Yukon Route
(Currently does not operate past this point)
Bennett
Jack Peak
7,050 ft./2,149m
Tagish Lake
Indian Lake
Gladys Lake
Klondike Highway 2
Chilkoot Trail
Log Cabin
Indian Creek
CANADA
UNITED STATES
Fraser
Tutshi R.
Atlin Lake
McDonald Lake
Fourth of July Cr.
Surprise Lake
Glaciated Area
Chilkoot Pass
3,739 ft./1,140m
Bernard Lake
Summit Lake
White Pass
3,290 ft./1,003m
AH-85/136km
S-14/23km
Scotia
Discovery
Discovery Road
White Pass Fork
Atlin
Pine Creek
Dyea Road
White Pass & Yukon Route
Spruce Creek
Goat Lake
Skagway River
J-58/93km
AH-99/159km
S-0
Skagway
McKee Creek
Warm Bay Road
Taiya Inlet
BRITISH COLUMBIA
ALASKA
Birch Mountain
6,755 ft./2,060m
Palmer L.
Wilson Creek
Teresa Island
Lutak Inlet
To Haines Junction
(see HAINES HIGHWAY section, page 280)
Glaciated Area
COAST MOUNTAINS
O'Donnel River
Provincial Park Boundary
Haines
Lynn Canal
Chilkoot Inlet
Chilkat Inlet
BOUNDARY
RANGES
Alaska State Ferry
Atlin Provincial Park
Provincial Park Boundary
Llewellyn Glacier
Map Location
Scale
0 10 Miles
0 10 Kilometres
Key to mileage boxes
miles/kilometres
miles/kilometres
from:
S-Skagway
AH-Alaska Highway
J-Junction
C-Carcross
Principal Route
Paved
Unpaved
Other Roads
Paved
Unpaved
Ferry Routes
Hiking Trails
Refer to Log for Visitor Facilities
Visitor Information
Fishing
Campground
Airport
Airstrip
Key to Advertiser Services
C -Camping
D -Dump Station
d -Diesel
G -Gas (reg., unld.)
I -Ice
L -Lodging
M-Meals
P -Propane
R -Car Repair (major)
r -Car Repair (minor)
S -Store (grocery)
T -Telephone (pay)
N
W
E
S

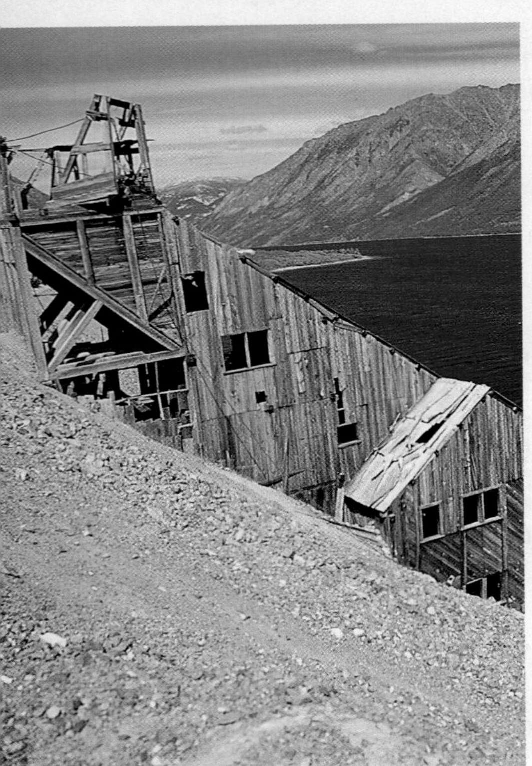

Old Venus mining structure on Windy Arm on Klondike Highway 2.

(Earl L. Brown, staff)

Viewpoint looks across the gorge to the WP&YR railway tracks.

S 9.9 (15.9 km) **AH 88.9** (143.1 km) Truck runout ramp to west for large transport units that may lose air brakes on steep descent southbound.

S 11.1 (17.9 km) **AH 87.7** (141.1 km) Captain William Moore Bridge. This unique cantilever bridge over Moore Creek spans a 110-foot-/34-m-wide gorge. Just north of the bridge to the west is a large waterfall. The bridge is named for Capt. Billy Moore, a riverboat captain and pilot, prospector, packer and trader, who played an important role in settling the town of Skagway. Moore helped pioneer this route over White Pass into the Yukon and was among the first to realize the potential of a railroad across the pass.

S 11.6 (18.7 km) **AH 87.2** (140.3 km) Turnouts to east with view of Skagway River gorge, Captain William Moore Bridge and waterfalls, next 0.1 mile/0.2 km northbound.

S 12 (19.3 km) **AH 86.8** (139.7 km) Truck runout ramp to west.

S 12.6 (20.3 km) **AH 86.2** (138.7 km) Posts on east side of road mark highway shoulders and guide rails for snowplows.

S 14.4 (23.2 km) **AH 84.4** (135.8 km) White Pass Summit (elev. 3,290 feet/1,003m). Turnout to west.

CAUTION: Southbound traffic begins steep 11.5-mile/18.5-km descent to Skagway.

Many stampeders on their way to the Klondike goldfields in 1898 chose the White Pass route because it was lower in elevation than the famous Chilkoot Pass trail, and the grade was not as steep. But the White Pass route was longer and the final ascent to the summit treacherous. Dead Horse Gulch (visible from the railway line) was named for the thousands of pack animals that died on this route during the gold rush.

The North West Mounted Police were stationed at the summit to meet every stampeder entering Canada and ensure that each carried at least a year's provisions (weighing about a ton).

S 14.5 (23.3 km) **AH 84.3** (135.7 km) Paved turnout to west.

S 14.9 (24 km) **AH 84** (135.2 km) U.S.–Canada (AK–BC) border. Turnout to west. Monument to east. TIME ZONE CHANGE: Alaska observes Alaska time; British Columbia and Yukon Territory observe Pacific time.

S 16.2 (26.1 km) **AH 82.6** (133 km) Highway winds through rocky valley of Summit Lake (visible to east). Several small gravel turnouts next 6 miles/9.6 km northbound.

S 18.1 (29.1 km) **AH 80.7** (129.9 km) Summit Creek bridge.

S 18.4 (29.6 km) **AH 80.4** (129.4 km) Summit Lake to east.

S 19.3 (31.1 km) **AH 79.5** (128 km) North end of Summit Lake.

S 21.4 (34.4 km) **AH 77.4** (124.5 km) Creek and railroad bridge to east.

S 22.5 (36.2 km) **AH 76.3** (122.8 km) Canada customs at **FRASER** (elev. 2,400 feet/732m), open 24 hours; phone (867) 821-4111. Pay phone. All travelers entering Canada must stop.

Old railroad water tower to east, highway maintenance camp to west.

S 22.6 (36.4 km) **AH 76.2** (122.7 km) Beautiful deep-green Bernard Lake to east.

S 22.8 (36.7 km) **AH 76** (122.3 km) Large double-ended turnout with 2 interpretive panels on area attractions and the WP&YR.

S 24.2 (38.9 km) **AH 74.6** (120.1 km) Turnout to east.

S 25.1 (40.4 km) **AH 73.7** (118.6 km) Shallow Lake to east.

S 25.5 (41 km) **AH 73.3** (118 km) Old cabins and buildings to east.

S 26.6 (42.8 km) **AH 72.2** (116.2 km) Turnout to east. Beautiful view of Tormented Valley, a rocky desolate "moonscape" of stunted trees and small lakes east of the highway.

S 27.3 (43.9 km) **AH 71.5** (115 km) Highway crosses tracks of the White Pass & Yukon Route at **LOG CABIN**. With completion of the railway in 1900, the North West Mounted Police moved their customs checkpoint from the summit to Log Cabin. There is nothing here today.

NOTE: There are numerous turnouts along the highway between here and Carcross. Turnouts may be designated for either commercial ore trucks or passenger vehicles.

S 30.7 (49.4 km) **AH 68.1** (109.6 km) Tutshi (too-shy) River visible to east.

S 31.1 (50 km) **AH 67.7** (108.9 km) Highway parallels **Tutshi Lake** for several miles northbound. Excellent fishing for lake trout and grayling early in season. Be sure you have a British Columbia fishing license.

S 40.1 (64.5 km) **AH 58.7** (94.5 km) Short, narrow gravel access road to picnic area with pit toilet on Tutshi Lake. Large vehicles check turnaround space before driving in.

S 40.7 (65.5 km) **AH 58.1** (93.5 km) Good views of Tutshi Lake along here.

S 43.7 (70.5 km) **AH 55.1** (88.7 km) Turnout to east with view of Tutshi Lake.

S 46.4 (75.1 km) **AH 52.4** (84.3 km) To the east is the Venus Mines concentrator, with a capacity of 150 tons per day. A drop in silver prices caused the Venus mill's closure in October 1981.

S 48.5 (78.1 km) **AH 50.3** (81 km) South end of Windy Arm, an extension of Tagish Lake.

S 49.2 (79.2 km) **AH 49.6** (79.9 km) Viewpoint to east.

S 49.9 (80.5 km) **AH 48.9** (78.7 km) Dall Creek.

S 50.2 (81 km) **AH 48.6** (78.2 km) BC–YT border. Turnout with picnic table and litter barrel to east overlooking Windy Arm.

S 51.9 (83.5 km) **AH 46.9** (75.5 km) Large turnout to east with litter barrel, picnic table and historical information sign about Venus Mines.

The first claim on Montana Mountain was staked by W.R. Young in 1899. By 1904 all of the mountain's gold veins had been claimed. In 1905, New York financier Col. Joseph H. Conrad acquired most of the Montana Mountain claims, formed Conrad Consolidated Mines, and began exploration and mining. A town of about 300 people sprang up along Windy Arm and an aerial tramway was built from the Conrad townsite up the side of Montana Mountain to the Mountain Hero adit. (This tramline, visible from the highway, was completed in 1906 but was never used to ship ore because the Mountain Hero tunnel did not find a vein.) More tramways and a mill were constructed, but by 1911 Conrad was forced into bankruptcy: The ore was not as rich as estimated and only a small quantity of ore was milled before operations ceased.

Small mining operations continued over the years, with unsuccessful startups by various mining interests. United Keno Hill Mines (Venus Division) acquired the mining claims in 1979, constructed a 100-ton-per-day mill and rehabilitated the old mine workings in 1980.

S 52.9 (85.1 km) **AH 45.9** (73.8 km) Pooly Creek and canyon, named for J.M. Pooly, who staked the first Venus claims in 1901.

Access road east to Pooly Point and Venus Mines maintenance garage, trailers and security station. No services, facilities or admittance.

S 54.2 (87.2 km) **AH 44.6** (71.8 km) Venus Mines ore storage bin and foundation of old mill to east. The mill was built in the late 1960s, then disassembled and sold about 1970. A sign here warns of arsenic being present: Do not pick or eat berries.

S 55.7 (89.6 km) **AH 43.1** (69.4 km) Tramline support just east of highway.

S 59.5 (95.8 km) **AH 39.3** (63.3 km) Turnout with historic information sign about Bove Island. Magnificent views along here of Windy Arm and its islands (the larger island is Bove Island). Windy Arm is an extension of Tagish Lake. Lime Mountain (elev. 5,225 feet/1,593m) rises to the east beyond Bove Island.

S 63.5 (102.2 km) **AH 35.3** (56.8 km) Sections of the old government wagon roads that once linked Carcross, Conrad and other mining claims, visible on either side of the highway.

S 65.3 (105.1 km) **AH 33.5** (53.9 km) Private road west to homes, Carcross Tagish First Nation's Band office and Carcross cemetery. Buried at the cemetery are the famous gold discoverers Skookum Jim, Dawson (or Tagish) Charlie and Kate Carmack; pioneer missionary Bishop Bompas; and Polly the parrot. (Cemetery is closed to visitors during services.)

S 65.8 (104.3 km) **AH 33** (53.6 km) Small Native-operated convenience store.

S 65.9 (106 km) **AH 32.9** (52.9 km) Access road west to Montana Mountain.

S 66 (106.2 km) **AH 32.8** (52.7 km) Nares Bridge crosses the narrows between Lake Bennett to the west and Tagish Lake to the east. Nares Lake remains open most winters, despite air temperatures that drop well below -40°F/-40°C. The larger lakes freeze to an ice depth of more than 3 feet/1m.

Caribou Mountain (elev. 5,645 feet/ 1,721m) is visible to the east.

S 66.2 (106.5 km) **AH 32.6** (52.4 km) Turnoff west for Carcross (description follows).

Carcross

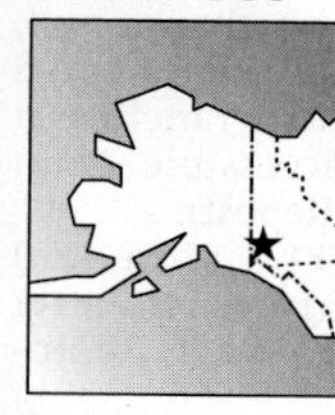

On the shore of Lake Bennett, 44 miles/71 km southeast of Whitehorse. **Population:** 277. **Emergency Services: Police,** phone (867) 821-5555. **Fire Department,** phone (867) 821-2222. **Ambulance,** phone (867) 821-3333. **Health Centre,** phone (867) 821-4444.

Visitor Information: Carcross Visitor Reception Centre, operated by Tourism Yukon, is located in the old White Pass & Yukon Route train station. Model train and lifeboat display. The centre operates daily from 8 A.M. to 8 P.M., mid-May to mid-September; phone (867) 821-4431. Ferry schedules, maps and information on Yukon, British Columbia and Alaska available. Yukon attractions may be previewed on laser disc.

Elevation: 2,175 feet/663m. **Climate:** Average temperature in January, -4.2°F/ -20.1°C; in July, 55.4°F/13°C. Annual rainfall 11 inches, snowfall 2 to 3 feet. Driest month is April, wettest month August. **Radio:** 590-AM, CHON-FM 90.5, CKRW, CKYN-FM 96.1 visitor information station. **Television:** CBC. **Transportation: Bus**—Scheduled bus service by Atlin Express Service, between Atlin and Whitehorse via Tagish and Carcross, 3 times weekly.

Private Aircraft: Carcross airstrip, 0.3 mile/0.5 km north of town via highway; elev. 2,161 feet/659m; length 2,000 feet/ 610m.

There are a hotel, general store, gift shops with Native handicrafts, snack bar and RV park. Gas station with gifts, groceries and cafe located on the highway by the airstrip. ▲

Carcross was formerly known as Caribou Crossing because of the large numbers of caribou that traversed the narrows here between Bennett and Nares lakes. In 1903 Bishop Bompas, who had established a school here for Native children in 1901, petitioned the government to change the name of the community to Carcross because of confusion in mail services due to duplicate names in Alaska, British Columbia and the Klondike. The post office made the change official the following year, but it took the WP&YR until 1916 to change the name of its station.

Carcross became a stopping place for gold stampeders on their way to the Klondike goldfields. It was a major stop on the White Pass & Yukon Route railroad from 1900 until 1982, when the railroad ceased operation. Passengers and freight transferred from rail to stern-wheelers at Carcross. One of these stern-wheelers, the SS *Tutshi* (too-shy), was a historic site here in town until it burned down in July 1990.

A cairn beside the railroad station marks the site where construction crews laying track for the White Pass & Yukon Route from Skagway met the crew from Whitehorse. The golden spike was set in place when the last rail was laid at Carcross on July 29, 1900. The construction project had begun May 27, 1898, during the height of the Klondike Gold Rush.

Other visitor attractions include St. Saviour's Anglican Church, built in 1902; the Royal Mail Carriage; and the little locomotive *Duchess,* which once hauled coal on Vancouver Island. Frontierland, 2 miles/ 3.2 km north of town on the highway, is also a popular attraction. On sunny days you may sunbathe and picnic at Sandy Beach on Lake Bennett. Behind the post office there is a footbridge across Natasaheenie River. This small body of water joins Lake Bennett and Nares Lake. Check locally for boat tours and boat service on Bennett Lake.

Fishing in **Lake Bennett** for lake trout, northern pike, arctic grayling, whitefish and cisco.

Klondike Highway 2 Log

(continued)

S 66.4 (106.9 km) **AH 32.4** (52.1 km) Airstrip to east. Turn on access road directly north of airstrip for Carcross Yukon government campground; 14 sites, picnic tables, firewood, drinking water, outhouses, camping fee. ▲

S 66.5 (107 km) **AH 32.3** (52 km) **Junction** with Yukon Highway 8, which leads east to Tagish, Atlin Road and the Alaska Highway at Jake's Corner (see TAGISH ROAD section on page 289). Turn east here for alternate access to Alaska Highway and for Yukon government campground on Tagish Road.

S 67.3 (108.3 km) **AH 31.5** (50.7 km) Turnout with point of interest sign about Carcross desert. This unusual desert area of sand dunes, seen east of the highway between Kilometreposts 108 and 110, is the world's smallest desert and an International Biophysical Programme site for ecological studies. The desert is composed of sandy lake-bottom material left behind by a large glacial lake. Strong winds off Lake Bennett have made it difficult for vegetation to take hold here; only lodgepole pine, spruce and

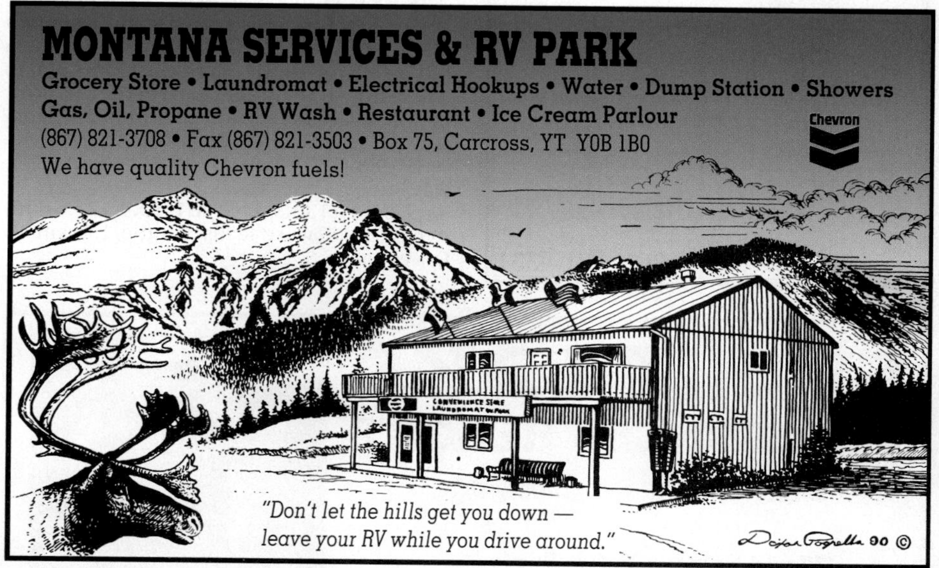

kinnikinnick survive. (Kinnikinnick is a low trailing evergreen with small leathery leaves; used for tea.)

S 67.9 (108.6 km) **AH 30.9** (49.7 km) Frontierland (formerly the Museum of Yukon Natural History) features a Yukon wildlife museum, gift shop and coffee house. Displays include a saber-toothed tiger and the world's largest mounted bear—a polar bear. Flightseeing tours of Chilkoot Trail, glaciers and wildlife are available from Chilkoot Air Service.

Chilkoot Air Services. See display ad this section.

Frontierland. See display ad on page 287.

S 70.3 (112.3 km) **AH 28.5** (45.9 km) Dry Creek.

S 71.2 (113.8 km) **AH 27.6** (44.4 km) Carl's Creek.

S 71.9 (115.7 km) **AH 26.9** (43.3 km) **Cinnamon Cache Bakery Coffee Shop.** See display ad this section.

S 72.1 (115 km) **AH 26.7** (43 km) Spirit Lake Wilderness Resort east side of road with food, gas, propane, repairs, lodging, camping and ice cream. Access road east to public-use area on Spirit Lake. ▲

Spirit Lake Wilderness Resort. See display ad this section. ▲

S 73.2 (116.8 km) **AH 25.6** (41.2 km) Spirit Lake is visible to the east.

S 73.5 (117.3 km) **AH 25.3** (40.7 km) Large turnout with point of interest sign to west overlooking beautiful Emerald Lake,

also called Rainbow Lake by Yukoners. (Good view of lake by climbing the hill across from the turnout.) The rainbowlike colors of the lake result from blue-green light waves reflecting off the white sediment of the lake bottom. This white sediment, called marl, consists of fragments of decomposed shell mixed with clay; it is usually found in shallow, freshwater lakes that have low oxygen levels during the summer months.

S 75.4 (120.3 km) **AH 23.4** (37.7 km) Highway follows base of Caribou Mountain (elev. 5,645 feet/1,721m). View of Montana Mountain to south, Caribou Mountain to east and Gray Ridge Range to the west between Kilometreposts 122 and 128. Flora consists of jack and lodgepole pine.

S 79.8 (127.1 km) **AH 19** (30.6 km) Highway crosses Lewes Creek.

S 85.4 (136.3 km) **AH 13.4** (21.6 km) Access road west leads 1 mile/1.6 km to Lewes Lake.

S 85.6 (136.5 km) **AH 13.2** (21.2 km) Rat Lake to west.

S 86.7 (138.2 km) **AH 12.1** (19.4 km) Bear Creek.

S 87 (140 km) **AH 11.8** (19 km) Access to bed and breakfast and Bear Creek Dog Sled Kennels.

S 87.3 (139.1 km) **AH 11.5** (18.5 km) Access road west to large gravel pull-through with historic information sign about Robinson and view of Robinson. In 1899, the White Pass & Yukon Route built a railroad siding at Robinson (named for Stikine Bill Robinson). Gold was discovered nearby in the early 1900s and a townsite was surveyed. A few buildings were constructed and a post office—manned by Charlie McConnell—operated from 1909 to 1915. Low mineral yields caused Robinson to be abandoned, but postmaster Charlie McConnell stayed and established one of the first ranches in the Yukon. Robinson is accessible from Annie Lake Road (see next milepost).

S 87.5 (139.4 km) **AH 11.3** (18.2 km) Road west to Annie Lake (turn left after crossing the railroad tracks to reach Robinson).

Annie Lake Road (can be rough) leads 0.8 mile/1.4 km to Annie Lake golf course (18 holes, wilderness setting), 1.9 miles/3.1 km to McConnell Lake and 11 miles/17.7 km to Annie Lake. Beyond Annie Lake the road crosses the Wheaton River. The Wheaton Valley–Mount Skukum area has seen a surge of mineral exploration by private prospectors and mining companies in recent years. For the adventuresome, this is beautiful and interesting country. There are no facilities along Annie Lake Road. *CAUTION: Annie Lake Road can be very muddy during spring breakup or during rain.*

Baker's Acres Bed & Breakfast. See display ad this section.

S 93 (148.5 km) **AH 5.8** (9.4 km) Turnoff west for Cowley and for access to Cowley Lake (1.6 miles/2.6 km).

S 95.5 (154.2 km) **AH 3.3** (5.3 km) Turnoff east for Kookatsoon Lake. There is a Yukon government picnic area at Kookatsoon Lake (day use only). The lake is shallow and usually warm enough for swimming in summer. Picnic tables, firepits and pit toilets. Canoe launch.

S 98.4 (156.5 km) **AH 0.4** (0.7 km) Rock shop on east side of road.

S 98.8 (157.1 km) **AH 0 Junction** with the Alaska Highway. Turn left (north) for Whitehorse, right (south) for Watson Lake. Turn to **Milepost DC 874.4** on page 136 in the ALASKA HIGHWAY section: Whitehorse-bound travelers continue with that log; travelers heading south down the Alaska Highway read that log back to front.

TAGISH ROAD

Connects: Alaska Hwy. to Carcross, YT **Length:** 34 miles
Road Surface: 40% gravel, 60% paved **Season:** Open all year
(See map, page 285)

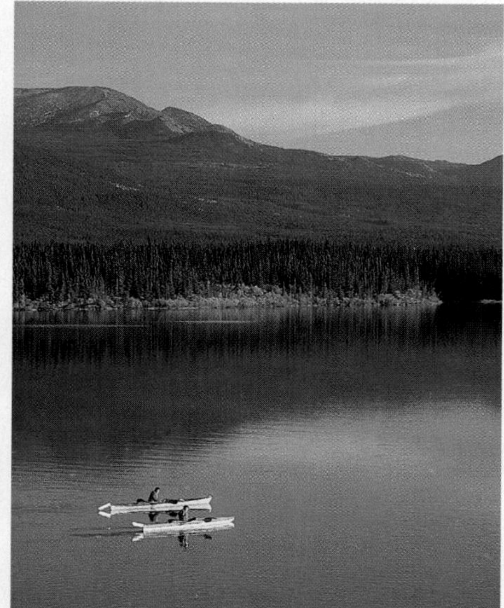
Kayaking the Tagish River.
(Rollo Pool photo)

The Tagish Road was built in 1942 to lay a gas pipeline. It leads south from the Alaska Highway junction at Jake's Corner (**Milepost DC 836.8**) through the settlement of Tagish to Carcross. This was the original route of the Alaska Highway in 1942. This 33.8-mile/54.4-km road connects the Alaska Highway with Klondike Highway 2. The road is good gravel from the Alaska Highway junction to Tagish, asphalt-surfaced between Tagish and Carcross.

If you are traveling Klondike Highway 2 between Skagway and Whitehorse, Tagish Road provides access to Atlin Road and also makes a pleasant side trip. Travelers may wish to use Tagish Road as an alternate route if there is road construction on Klondike Highway 2 between Carcross and the Alaska Highway. This is also a very beautiful drive in the fall; good photo opportunities.

Emergency medical services: Phone the RCMP, (867) 667-5555; ambulance, phone (867) 667-3333.

Tagish Road Log

Kilometreposts measure east to west from Alaska Highway junction to Carcross turn-off; posts are up about every 2 kilometres. **Distance from the junction (J) is followed by distance from Carcross (C).**

J 0 C 33.8 (54.4 km) **Junction** with the Alaska Highway at Jake's Corner, **Milepost DC 836.8** (see the ALASKA HIGHWAY section). Drive south 1.1 miles/1.8 km to junction of Tagish Road and Atlin Road (Highway 7).

J 1.1 (1.8 km) **C 32.7** (52.6 km) **Junction** of Tagish and Atlin roads. Turn southeast for Atlin, BC (see ATLIN ROAD section); head west for Tagish and Carcross.

J 8.8 (14.2 km) **C 25** (40.2 km) For several miles, travelers may see the NorthwesTel microwave tower on Jubilee Mountain (elev. 5,950 feet/ 1,814m) to the south between Little Atlin Lake and Tagish River. Jubilee Mountain was named by Dr. G.M. Dawson in 1887 in honor of Queen Victoria's Jubilee.

J 12.8 (20.6 km) **C 21** (33.8 km) Tagish Yukon government campground, on **Six Mile River** between Marsh Lake to the north and Tagish Lake to the south. Good fishing, boatlaunch, picnic area, playground, kitchen shelter, 28 campsites with firepits and tables, drinking water and toilets. Camping fee $8. *CAUTION: Watch for black bears.*

J 13 (20.9 km) **C 20.8** (33.5 km) Gas, oil, minor repairs, snacks and post office. Pay phone on road. Marina on north side of road at east end of Tagish bridge has bait, tackle, fishing licenses, boat rental.

J 13.1 (21 km) **C 20.7** (33.3 km) Tagish bridge. Good fishing is a tradition here; Tagish bridge has an anglers' walkway on the north side. **Tagish River**, lake trout, arctic grayling, northern pike, whitefish and cisco.

West end of bridge has a day-use area with parking, 4 picnic sites and water pump. Gravel ends, pavement begins, westbound.

J 13.5 (21.7 km) **C 20.3** (32.6 km) Improved gravel road leads through parklike area to settlement of **TAGISH** (pop. about 134) on Tagish River between Marsh and Tagish lakes. Express bus service between Atlin and Whitehorse stops here and in Carcross 3 times weekly. Tagish means "fish trap" in the local Indian dialect. It was traditionally an Indian meeting place in the spring on the way to set up fish camps and again in the fall to celebrate the catch. Post office at Tagish Service at east end of Tagish bridge. Wilderness lodge on Taku Arm of Tagish Lake.

Two miles/3.2 km south of Tagish on the Tagish River is **TAGISH POST**, originally named Fort Sifton, the Canadian customs post established in 1897. Two of the original 5 buildings still stand. The North West Mounted Police and Canadian customs collected duties on thousands of tons of freight carried by stampeders on their way to the Klondike goldfields between September 1897 and February 1898.

J 13.7 (22 km) **C 20.1** (32.3 km) **Tagish Stores, Cafe, Motel, RV**, built 1996–97, is located in the greenbelt of the Tagish Road Km 22. The store offers groceries, non-food, hardware, gifts and movies. Cafe: breakfast, lunch, ice cream. Motel: 6 units, showers and luxury king-size beds. RV: 11 sites, 15-/30-amps, water, sani-dump and shower house. Phone/fax (867) 399-3344. [ADVERTISEMENT]

J 16.3 (26.2 km) **C 17.5** (28.1 km) Side road leads 1.2 miles/2 km to Tagish Lake and homes.

Tagish Lake, fishing for trout, pike and grayling.

J 23 (37 km) **C 10.8** (17.4 km) Bryden Creek.

J 24.7 (39.7 km) **C 9.1** (14.6 km) Eagles Landing B&B. Phone (867) 667-1057.

J 24.8 (39.9 km) **C 9** (14.4 km) Crag Lake. Road now enters more mountainous region westbound. Caribou Mountain (elev. 5,645 feet/1,721m) on right.

J 27.2 (43.8 km) **C 6.6** (10.6 km) Porcupine Creek.

J 27.5 (44.3 km) **C 6.3** (10.1 km) **Historic Milepost 7.**

J 28.4 (45.7 km) **C 5.4** (8.7 km) Pain Creek.

J 30.2 (48.6 km) **C 3.6** (5.8 km) Side road to Chooutla Lake.

J 31 (49.9 km) **C 2.8** (4.5 km) First glimpse westbound of Montana Mountain (elev. 7,230 feet/2,204m) across narrows at Carcross.

J 33.8 (54.4 km) **C 0 Junction** with Klondike Highway 2. Westbound travelers turn left for Carcross (see description on page 287), right for Whitehorse. See **Milepost S 66.5** in the KLONDIKE HIGHWAY 2 section.

ATLIN ROAD

Connects: Tagish Road Jct. to Atlin, BC **Length:** 58 miles
Road Surface: 60% gravel, 40% paved **Season:** Open all year
Major Attraction: Atlin Lake

(See map, page 285)

	Atlin	Carcross	Jake's Corner	Skagway	Whitehorse
Atlin		92	59	158	106
Carcross	92		35	66	43
Jake's Corner	59	35		101	47
Skagway	158	66	101		109
Whitehorse	106	43	47	109	

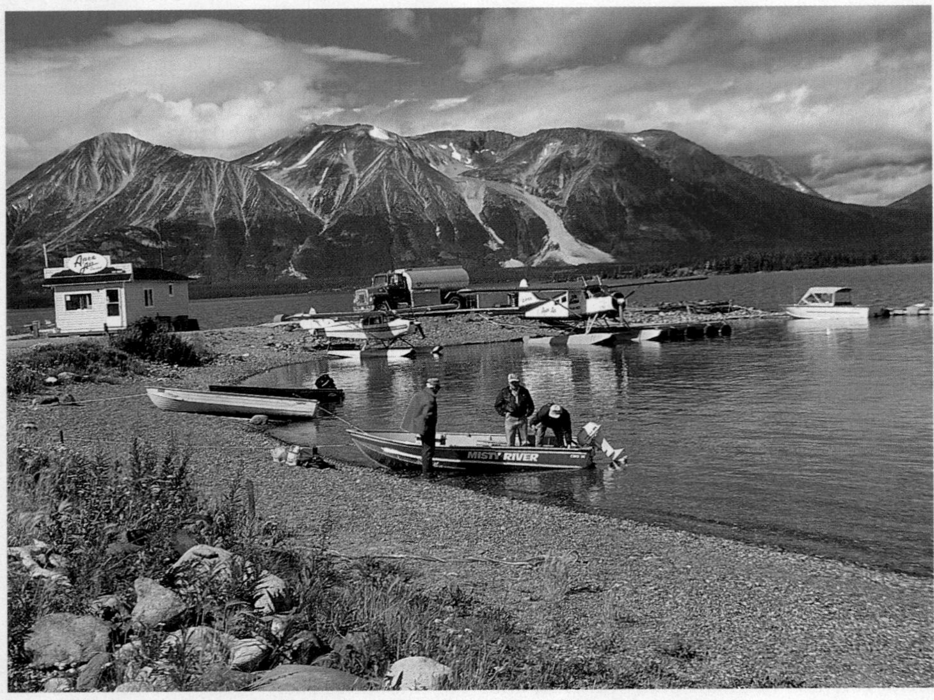

Floatplanes and boats along the waterfront at Atlin. (Earl L. Brown, staff)

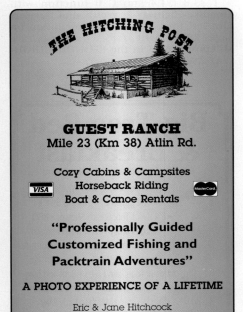

This 58-mile/93.3-km all-weather road leads south to the pioneer gold mining town of Atlin. Built in 1949 by the Canadian Army Engineers, Atlin Road is a good road, usually in excellent condition, with some winding sections. The first 40 miles/64.4 km are gravel, with the remaining 18 miles/29 km into Atlin paved. Watch for slippery spots in wet weather.

To reach Atlin Road, turn south at Jake's Corner, **Milepost DC 836.8** on the Alaska Highway; drive 1.1 miles/1.8 km to the junction of Atlin Road (Highway 7) and Tagish Road (Highway 8); turn left (south) for Atlin.

It is about a 2½-hour drive to Atlin from Whitehorse, and the lake scenery from the village is well worth the trip. For more information contact the Atlin Visitors Assoc., Box 365-M, Atlin, BC V0W 1A0; fax (250) 651-7721. Or phone the Atlin museum at (250) 651-7522 for visitor information.

Atlin Road Log

Physical kilometreposts in Yukon Territory and mileposts in British Columbia show distance from Tagish Road junction.
Distance from Tagish Road junction (J) is shown.

J 0 Junction of Tagish and Atlin roads.

J 1.4 (2.3 km) Fish Creek crossing. The road is bordered by many low-lying, boggy areas brilliant green with horsetail *(equisetium).*

J 1.8 (2.9 km) Side road west to Little Atlin Lake. Atlin Road descends along east shoreline of Little Atlin Lake approximately 7.6 miles/12.2 km southbound. During midsummer, the roadsides are ablaze with fireweed and wild roses.

J 2.4 (3.9 km) Large turnout to west on Little Atlin Lake; informal boat launch and camping area. Mount Minto (elev. 6,913 feet/2,107m) can be seen to the southwest. Road climbs southbound.

J 2.8 (4.5 km) Turnout to west. Watch for bald eagles.

J 5 (8 km) Information sign to east about 1983–84 mountain goat transplant. The 12 goats were brought from Kluane National Park. They may be observed on the mountainsides.

J 7.8 (12.6 km) Private campground, cabins and boat rentals.

J 8.1 (13 km) Greenhouse and farm, roadside vegetable stand in season. Haunka Creek. Turnout to west.

J 8.9 (14.3 km) Good view of Mount Minto ahead southbound.

J 13.8 (22.2 km) Unmarked side road leads 2.4 miles/3.9 km to **Lubbock River,** which connects Little Atlin Lake with Atlin Lake. Excellent for grayling from breakup to mid-September.

J 15.5 (24.9 km) Snafu Creek. Turnout to west, north of bridge. According to R. Coutts, author of "Yukon Places & Names," the creek name is an acronym bestowed by army crews who built the road. It stands for Situation Normal—All Fouled Up. (Mr. Coutts resides in Atlin.)

J 16.4 (26 km) Access road leads 0.7 mile/1.1 km to **Snafu Lake** Yukon government campground; 4 sites, $8 camping fee, pit toilets, tables, gravel boat ramp, good fishing.

J 18.6 (29.9 km) Tarfu Creek. Small turnout to east, north of bridge. Creek name is another army acronym. This one stands for Things Are Really Fouled Up.

J 18.7 (30 km) Abandoned cabin and turnout to west.

J 20.4 (32.8 km) Turnoff to east for **Tarfu Lake** Yukon government campground via 2.4-mile/3.8-km side road; 6 sites, $8 camping fee, pit toilets, fishing. Steep grade near campground; not recommended for large RVs or trailers.

J 20.5 (33 km) Short narrow side road leads east to Marcella Lake; good lake for canoeing.

J 21.8 (35.1 km) Turnout to west with view of Atlin Lake, which covers 307 square miles/798 square km and is the largest natural lake in British Columbia. Coast Mountains to the southwest.

J 23.6 (38 km) **The Hitching Post Guest Ranch**. See display ad this section.

J 25.8 (41.5 km) BC–YT border. Road follows east shoreline of Atlin Lake into Atlin.

J 27 (43.5 km) Mount Minto to west, Black Mountain to east, and Halcro Peak (elev. 5,856 feet/1,785m) to the southeast.

J 28.5 (45.8 km) Slow down for sharp curve.

J 32 (51.5 km) Excellent views of Coast Mountains, southwest across Atlin Lake, next 6 miles/9.7 km southbound.

J 32.7 (52.6 km) **Hitchcock Creek**, grayling to 2 lbs.

J 32.8 (52.7 km) Campground on Atlin Lake; 6 sites, pit toilets, tables, ramp for small boats.

J 36.3 (58.4 km) Turnout with litter barrel to west. Base Camp Creek.

J 36.8 (59.2 km) **Historic Milepost 38.**

J 40 (64.4 km) Indian River. Pull-through turnout south of creek. Highway is paved from here to Atlin.

J 40.2 (64.7 km) Big-game outfitter/guest ranch to east. Watch for horses.

J 45.3 (72.9 km) Turnout to west.

J 49.8 (80.1 km) Burnt Creek.

J 49.9 (80.3 km) Davie Hall Lake and turnout to west. Waterfowl are plentiful on lake.

J 51.6 (83 km) Ruffner Mine Road leads east 40 miles/64.4 km. Access to **MacDonald Lake**, 2 miles/3.2 km east; bird watching and lake trout fishing from spit.

J 52.8 (85 km) Fourth of July Creek.

J 53.4 (85.9 km) Spruce Mountain (elev. 5,141 feet/1,567m) to west.

J 55.1 (88.7 km) Road skirts east shore of Como Lake next 0.6 mile/1 km southbound.

J 55.2 (88.8 km) Turnout with litter barrel to west on **Como Lake**; good lake for canoeing, also used by floatplanes. Stocked with rainbow.

J 55.7 (89.6 km) South end of Como Lake; boat ramp.

J 57.1 (91.9 km) Atlin city limits.

J 58 (93.3 km) **Junction** of Atlin Road with Discovery Road. Turn right (west) on Discovery Avenue for town of Atlin; description follows. Turn left (east) for Discovery Road and Warm Bay Road (see logs this section).

Atlin

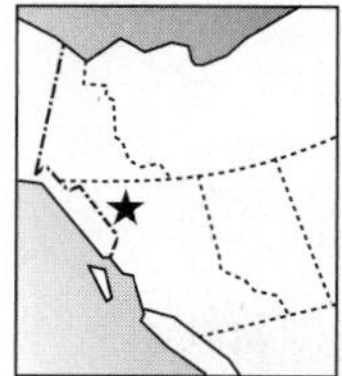

The most northwesterly town in British Columbia, located about 112 miles/180 km southeast of Whitehorse, YT. **Population:** 500. **Emergency Services: Police**, phone (250) 651-7511. **Fire Department**, phone (250) 651-7666. **Ambulance**, phone (250) 651-7700. Red Cross outpost clinic, phone (250) 651-7677.

Visitor Information: Contact the Atlin Visitors Assoc., P.O. Box 365-M, Atlin, BC V0W 1A0, fax (250) 651-7721, phone (250) 651-7522, (250) 651-7522.

Elevation: 2,240 feet/683m. **Radio:** CBC on FM-band. **Television:** 3 channels (CBC, BCTV and the Knowledge Network).

Private Aircraft: Peterson Field, 1 mile/1.6 km northeast; elev. 2,348 feet/716m; length 3,950 feet/1,204m; gravel.

Transportation: Air—Regular service from Juneau via Summit Air, Apex Air and Tuchone Air. **Bus**—Service from Whitehorse 3 times a week.

Referred to by some visitors as Shangri-la, the village of Atlin overlooks the crystal clear water of 90-mile/145-km-long Atlin Lake and is surrounded by spectacular mountains. On Teresa Island in Atlin Lake is Birch Mountain (elev. 6,755 feet/2,060m), the highest point in fresh water in the world.

Atlin was founded in 1898. The name was taken from the Indian dialect and means Big Water. The Atlin Lake area was one of the richest gold strikes made during the great rush to the Klondike in 1897–98. The first claims were registered here on July 30, 1898, by Fritz Miller and Kenneth McLaren.

ATLIN ADVERTISERS

Apex Air Charters Ltd.	Ph. (250) 651-0025
Atlin General Store	Ph. (250) 651-7555
Atlin Inn, The	Ph. (250) 651-7546
Fireweed Inn, The	Ph. (250) 651-7729
Kirkwood Cottages	Ph. (250) 651-7546
Noland House, The	Ph. (250) 651-7585
Norseman Adventures	Ph. (250) 651-7535
Northern Place, The	Ph. (250) 651-7503
Pine Tree Services	Ph. (250) 651-7636
Quilts & Comforts	Ph. (250) 651-7476
Simply Gold	Ph. (250) 651-7708

Guided tour of old mining equipment, Atlin Historical Museum. (Earl L. Brown, staff)

VISITOR SERVICES/ACCOMMODATIONS

The village has a hotel, inns, cottages, bed and breakfasts, laundromat (with showers), restaurants, gas stations (propane, diesel and unleaded available), grocery, government liquor store and general stores, and a post office. Atlin branch of Bank of Montreal located at Government Agents Office on 3rd Street; open weekdays 10 A.M. to noon and 1–3 P.M. Dump station at Mile 2.3 Discovery Road. The museum and several shops feature local gold nugget jewelry, arts and crafts, and other souvenirs. Air charter service for glacier tours and fly-in fishing trips. Charter boats and fishing charters available. Bus tours are welcome, but phone ahead so this small community can accommodate you.

The Noland House. This historic home has been restored to provide luxurious accommodations for 4 guests. Host residence is next door. Private baths and sitting rooms, complimentary wine and snacks, fully equipped kitchen, lake and mountain views, airport and floatplane dock pickup. Single $85, double $95, open May–October. Box 135, Atlin, BC V0W 1A0. Phone/fax: (250) 651-7585. [ADVERTISEMENT]

RV park with electric and water hookups, showers and laundry, pay phone and boat moorage downtown on lake. There are several camping areas on Atlin Road, Discovery Road and Warm Bay Road (see logs this section). Atlin community operates the Pine Creek campground at **Milepost J 1.6** Warm Bay Road; 14 sites, $5 fee (pay at any downtown business or at the museum). ▲

ATTRACTIONS

The MV *Tarahne* (Tah-ron) sits on the lakeshore in the middle of town. Tours daily in summer at 3 P.M.; admission by donation. Sunday brunch is served aboard the MV *Tarahne*. Built at Atlin in 1916 by White Pass & Yukon Route, she carried passengers and freight from Atlin to Scotia Bay until 1936. (Scotia Bay is across the lake from Atlin and slightly north.) A 2-mile/3.2-km railway connected Scotia Bay on Atlin Lake to Taku Landing on Tagish Lake, where passengers arrived by boat from Carcross, YT. The *Tarahne* was the first gas-driven boat in the White Pass fleet. After she was lengthened by 30 feet in 1927, she could carry up to 198 passengers. In recent years, Atlin residents have launched a drive to restore the boat; they hope to eventually refloat the vessel and offer tours of Atlin Lake.

Atlin Historical Museum, open weekends during June and September, daily July through August. Located in Atlin's original 1-room schoolhouse, the museum has mining artifacts and photo exhibits of the Atlin gold rush. Gift shop features the work of local artisans. Walking-tour guide of Atlin available here. Admission fee; phone (250) 651-7522.

Visit the mineral springs at the north end of town, where you may have a drink of sparkling cold mineral water. The gazebo-like structure over the springs was built by White Pass in 1922. Picnic area nearby.

The Pioneer Cemetery, located at **Milepost J 1.1** Discovery Road, contains the weathered grave markers of early gold seekers, including Fritz Miller and Kenneth McLaren, who made the first gold discovery in the Atlin area in July 1898. Also buried here is Walter Gladstone Sweet, reputed to have been a card dealer for Soapy Smith in Skagway.

Public Gold Panning Area has been set aside on Spruce Creek. Turn off Discovery Road at **Milepost J 3.6.** Check at the museum for details. Gold pans available locally for rent or purchase.

Take a Hike. At **Milepost J 2.3** Warm Bay Road are 2 trails: the 3-mile/4.8-km Monarch trail and the short, easy Beach trail. The Monarch trail is a moderately strenuous hike with a steep climb at the end to a bird's-eye view of the area.

Weekend guided nature walks are available at Warm Bay and Warm Springs, late May to early September. Fee charged. Inquire locally for details.

Tours and Rentals. Motorbike rentals, houseboat rentals, boat tours of Atlin and Tagish lakes, guided fishing trips and marine gas are available. Helicopter service, floatplanes for charter hunting and fishing trips and flightseeing trips of Llewellyn Glacier and the Atlin area are also available.

Atlin Provincial Park, accessible by boat or plane only (charters available in Atlin). Spectacular wilderness area; varied topography; exceptional wildlife habitat.

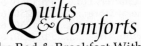

Take a Drive. 13-mile/21-km Discovery Road and 16.5-mile/26.5-km Warm Bay Road are both suitable for passenger cars and RVs, and both offer sightseeing and recreation. See side road logs this section for details.

Atlin Art Centre, located at **Milepost J 2** Warm Bay Road, offers alpine hiking, boating and canoeing adventures to the general public from June to September. The centre is also a summer school and retreat for artists and students, run by Gernot Dick. The centre is designed to allow participants to distance themselves from urban distractions and focus on the creative process. Contact Atlin Art Centre, Monarch Mountain, Atlin, BC V0W 1A0; (800) 651-8882 for more information. Currently, a number of talented artists, authors and other creative people make their home in Atlin.

AREA FISHING: The Atlin area is well known for its good fishing. Fly-in fishing for salmon, steelhead and rainbow, or troll locally for lake trout. Grayling can be caught at the mouths of most creeks and streams or off Atlin docks. Public boat launch on Atlin Lake, south of the MV *Tarahne*. Boat charters available. For information on fishing in the area, contact local businesses. British Columbia fishing licenses are available from the government agent and local outlets. Fresh and smoked salmon may be available for purchase locally in the summer. Annual fishing derby held in June.

Discovery Road Log

Discovery Road begins 0.4 mile/0.6 km from Atlin's business district at junction with Atlin Road and leads east 13 miles/20.9 km. This is a good, wide gravel road, bumpy in spots. Posted speed limit is 50 mph/80 kmph, but 40 mph/60 kmph or less is recommended. There is active gold mining under way along the road; watch for large trucks. Beyond Surprise Lake Dam bridge, the road becomes steep and winding for 1.2 miles/1.9 km to road end (large RVs use caution).

Distance is measured from junction with Atlin Road (J).

J 0 Junction of Atlin Road and Discovery Avenue.

J 0.3 (0.5 km) **Junction** with Warm Bay Road.

J 1.1 (1.8 km) Atlin airport to east. Pioneer cemetery to west contains grave markers and monuments to many of Atlin's historical figures.

J 2.3 (3.7 km) Dump station to south.

J 3.5 (5.6 km) Turnout to south with view of Pine Creek and falls.

J 3.6 (5.8 km) Spruce Creek Road leads south 0.9 mile/1.4 km to designated public recreational gold panning area and 1.5 miles/2.4 km to active gold mining on Spruce Creek (no tours but operations can be photographed from the road). This side road is signed as rough and narrow; suitable for cars, vans and pickups.

J 3.9 (6.3 km) Winding road next 1 mile/1.6 km.

J 5.4 (8.7 km) Former townsite of Discovery, originally called Pine Creek, now a ghost town. In its boom days, the town supplied miners working in the area.

J 7 (11.2 km) Active gold mining operation to south can be photographed from the road.

J 8.6 (13.8 km) Slow down for Pine Creek 1-lane bridge. Road follows creek drainage from here to Surprise Lake.

J 9.2 (14.8 km) Small lake to east usually has waterfowl.

J 10.7 (17.2 km) View west of mining road switchbacks on mountainside.

J 11.2 (18 km) Road forks: bear to left. Small lake to west.

J 11.8 (19 km) Surprise Lake Dam bridge. Turnout east side of bridge with litter barrel and view of Surprise Lake.

CAUTION: Steep and winding road next 1.2 miles/1.9 km eastbound to road end.

J 12 (19.3 km) **Surprise Lake** recreation site. One campsite near main road. Steep, bumpy access road leads to more campsites near lake. Pit toilets, picnic tables, firepits. Boat launch for cartop boats and canoes. A gold mining operation is visible across the lake. Fishing for arctic grayling.

View of Pine Creek Falls at Mile 3.5 Discovery Road. *(Earl L. Brown, staff)*

J 13 (20.9 km) Road forks and both forks dead end along Boulder Creek. Ample turnaround space for vehicles.

Warm Bay Road Log

Warm Bay Road leads south 16.5 miles/26.5 km to numerous points of interest and 5 camping areas. Warm Bay Road begins at **Milepost J 0.3** Discovery Road, 0.7 mile/1.1 km east of Atlin business district.

Distance is measured from junction with Discovery Road (J).

J 0 Junction with Discovery Road.

J 0.3 (0.5 km) Atlin School.

J 1.5 (2.4 km) Pine Creek 1-lane bridge.

J 1.6 (2.6 km) Pine Creek Campground and picnic area; 14 campsites, tenting area, pit toilets, picnic tables, firepits, some firewood and water. Camping fee $5; pay at any Atlin business. Short trail to Pine Creek and Pine Creek Falls.

J 2 (3.2 km) Atlin Art Centre (see Attractions in Atlin).

J 2.3 (3.7 km) Trailheads either side of road. Monarch trail is a moderately strenuous 3-mile/4.8-km hike through meadows to scenic vista of Atlin area. Some steep sections; summit of Monarch Mountain at elev. 4,723 feet/1,439m. Beach trail is short and easy.

J 2.5 (4 km) Drinking water from pipe beside road.

J 5.7 (9.2 km) Lina Creek.

J 7 (11.2 km) Viewpoint with litter barrel. Llewellyn Glacier and Atlin Lake are to the southwest. Good photo spot.

J 7.3 (11.7 km) Bed and breakfast, canoe rentals.

J 9.5 (15.3 km) McKee Creek 1-lane bridge. The McKee Creek area has been mined since the 1890s. In July 1981, 2 area miners found what has been dubbed the "Atlin nugget," a 36.86-troy-ounce, hand-sized piece of gold.

J 11.3 (18.2 km) Palmer Lake to east.

J 11.9 (19.1 km) **Palmer Lake** recreation site to east; camping, fishing, picnic tables, pit toilets. No camping fee.

J 13.9 (22.3 km) Warm Bay recreation site on **Atlin Lake**; camping, fishing, picnic tables, pit toilets. No camping fee. Boat launch for small boats.

J 14.4 (23.2 km) Warm Springs to north. This is a small and shallow spring, good for soaking road-weary bones. Large grassy camping area, pit toilet. No camping fee. The meadow streams are lined with watercress. Guided nature walks available; inquire locally for details.

J 16.3 (26.2 km) Grotto recreation site; 2 campsites, picnic tables, pit toilets, firepits, litter barrel.

J 16.4 (26.4 km) "The Grotto" to north. Large turnaround. Water flows through a hole in the rocks from an underground stream. Locals report this is a good place to obtain drinking water.

J 16.5 (26.5 km) Maintained road ends. Steep, bumpy and narrow road continues beyond this point; not recommended for travel.

SILVER TRAIL HIGHWAY (11)

Connects: Klondike Hwy. to Keno City, YT **Length:** 69 miles
Road Surface: 50% paved, 50% gravel
Season: Open all year to Mayo and Keno City
Major Attraction: Keno City Mining Museum

	Keno City	Klondike Hwy. Jct.	Mayo
Keno City		69	37
Klondike Hwy. Jct.	69		32
Mayo	37	32	

MILEPOST® field editor Earl Brown poses next to milepost sign atop Keno Hill, elev. 6,065 feet/1,849m. (© Alisha A. Brown)

The Silver Trail leads northeast from the Klondike Highway (see **Milepost J 214.4** on page 312 in the KLONDIKE LOOP section) to Mayo, Elsa and Keno City. From its junction with the Klondike Highway (Yukon Highway 2), the Silver Trail (Yukon Highway 11) leads 31.9 miles/51.3 km to Mayo; 60.3 miles/97 km to Elsa; and 69.1 miles/111.2 km to Keno City. The Silver Trail also provides access to Duncan Creek Road, the original Silver Trail. It is approximately 140 miles/225 km round-trip to Keno City and an easy day trip for motorists. The road is asphalt-surfaced to Mayo, hard-packed gravel from Mayo to Keno. Watch for soft shoulders, especially in wet weather. The highway is open all year to Mayo; maintained winter road to Keno City. Gas is available only at Mayo and at Stewart Crossing.

There is an information kiosk on the Klondike Highway at the south end of Stewart River bridge. Stop at the kiosk for information on the Silver Trail, or visit Binet House in Mayo. Or write Silver Trail Tourism, Box 268, Mayo, YT Y0B 1M0; phone (in summer) (867) 996-2926, fax (867) 995-2409, winter phone (867) 996-2290. Information on the Silver Trail is also available from a 5-minute recorded broadcast on 93.3-FM near Stewart Crossing on the Klondike Highway.

The Silver Trail to Mayo follows the Stewart River through what has been one of the richest silver mining regions in Canada. The Silver Trail region encompasses the traditional lands of the Na Cho N'y'ak Dun First Nations.

Emergency medical services: In Mayo, phone (867) 996-4444; or phone the RCMP toll free, Yukon-wide, at (867) 667-5555.

Silver Trail Log

Distance is measured from the junction with the Klondike Highway (J).

J 0 Junction of Silver Trail (Yukon Highway 11) and Klondike Highway (Yukon Highway 2) at **Milepost J 214.4** Klondike Highway (see page 312 in the KLONDIKE LOOP section).

J 0.2 (0.3 km) Marker shows distance to Mayo 51 km, Elsa 97 km, Keno 110 km.

J 1.2 (2 km) Stewart River to the south.

J 3 (4.8 km) Bad curve. Turnout to south.

J 9.6 (15.4 km) Large gravel pit turnout to south.

J 12 (19.2 km) Large double-ended turnout with litter barrels overlooking the Stewart River.

J 27.4 (44.1 km) Pull-through rest area; outhouses, litter barrel, picnic tables.

J 30.7 (49.5 km) Winding descent for northeast-bound traffic; good view of valley.

J 31.2 (50.2 km) McIntyre Park picnic area to south on banks of the Mayo River; 9 picnic sites and a shelter.

J 31.3 (50.3 km) **Mayo River** bridge. Good fishing from bridge for grayling.

J 31.9 (51.3 km) **Junction** with access road to Mayo (description follows). Turn right (south) for Mayo, keep left (north) for road to Elsa and Keno City.

Mayo

Located on the bank of the Stewart River near its confluence with the Mayo River. **Population:** 500. **Emergency Services: RCMP**, phone (867) 996-5555. **Fire Dept.**, phone (867) 996-2222. **Nursing Station**, phone (867) 996-2345. **Ambulance**, phone (867) 996-4444.

Visitor Information: At Binet House Interpretive Centre, open 10 A.M. to 6 P.M.

SILVER TRAIL HIGHWAY *Klondike Highway Junction to Keno City, YT*

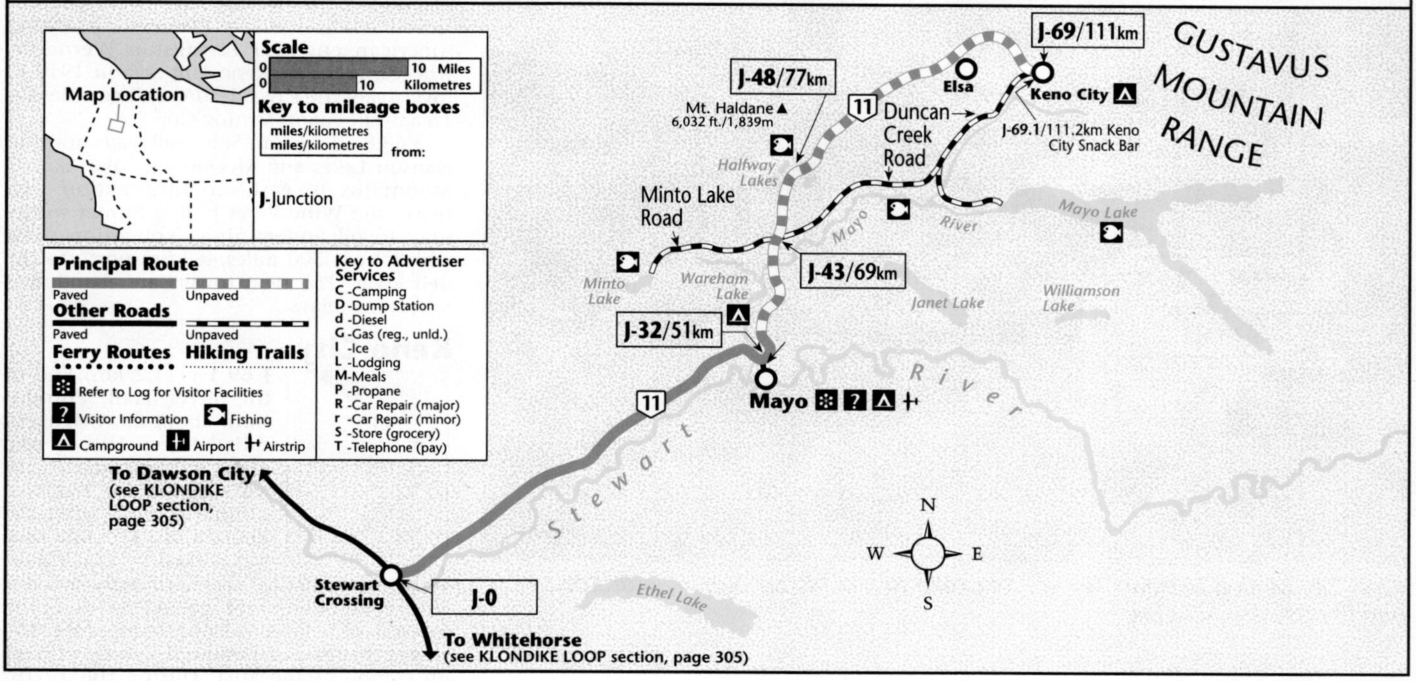

Map Location

Scale
0 10 Miles
0 10 Kilometres

Key to mileage boxes
miles/kilometres
miles/kilometres
from:
J-Junction

Principal Route
Paved Unpaved
Other Roads
Paved Unpaved
Ferry Routes **Hiking Trails**
Refer to Log for Visitor Facilities
Visitor Information
Fishing
Campground
Airport
Airstrip

Key to Advertiser Services
C -Camping
D -Dump Station
d -Diesel
G -Gas (reg., unld.)
I -Ice
L -Lodging
M -Meals
P -Propane
R -Car Repair (major)
r -Car Repair (minor)
S -Store (grocery)
T -Telephone (pay)

GUSTAVUS MOUNTAIN RANGE
J-69/111km
J-48/77km
Mt. Haldane 6,032 ft./1,839m
Elsa
Keno City
Duncan Creek Road
J-69.1/111.2km Keno City Snack Bar
Halfway Lakes
Minto Lake Road
Mayo River
Mayo Lake
Minto Lake
Wareham Lake
J-43/69km
Janet Lake
Williamson Lake
J-32/51km
Mayo
Stewart River
To Dawson City (see KLONDIKE LOOP section, page 305)
Stewart Crossing
J-0
Ethel Lake
To Whitehorse (see KLONDIKE LOOP section, page 305)

daily from late June through first week in September; phone (867) 996-2926. Exhibits include floral and mineral displays, silver and galena samples, and information panels on mining and geology. **Elevation:** 1,650 feet/503m.**Climate:** Residents claim it's the coldest and hottest spot in Yukon. Record low, -80°F/-62.2°C (February 1947); record high, 97°F/36.1°C (June 1969). **Radio:** CBC 1230, CHON-FM 98.5 CKRN 98-FM. **Television:** CBC Anik, Channel 7, BCTV, TVNC, ITV, WDIV. **Transportation:** Charter floatplane and helicopter service available. Scheduled bus service.

Private Aircraft: Mayo airstrip, 4 miles/6.5 km north; elev. 1,653 feet/504m; length 4,850 feet/1,478m; gravel; fuel 100, Jet B.

Mayo has most traveler facilities including overnight accommodations at Bedrock Motel and bed and breakfasts; food service at motel, Chinese restaurant and a cafe; laundromat; full-service gas and diesel, fishing licenses and snack at Heartland Services–Mayo Chevron; hardware, grocery and variety stores (closed Sunday). Tire repair and minor vehicle repair are available. Post office, liquor store and library located in the Territorial Building. Bank service available 10 A.M. to 2 P.M., Tuesday, Thursday and Friday.

Mayo was formerly known as Mayo Landing and began as a river settlement and port for silver ore shipments to Whitehorse. (A walking tour brochure of May's historic sites is available.) Today, Mayo is a service centre for mineral exploration in the area. Yukon Electrical Co. Ltd. operates a hydro-electric project here. Canoeists can put in at Mayo on the Stewart River for a paddle to Stewart Crossing or Dawson City.

MAYO ADVERTISERS

Bedrock Motel ....Ph. (867) 996-2290
Heartland Services............Ph. (867) 996-2329
Silver Trail Tourism Association..................Ph. (867) 996-2926

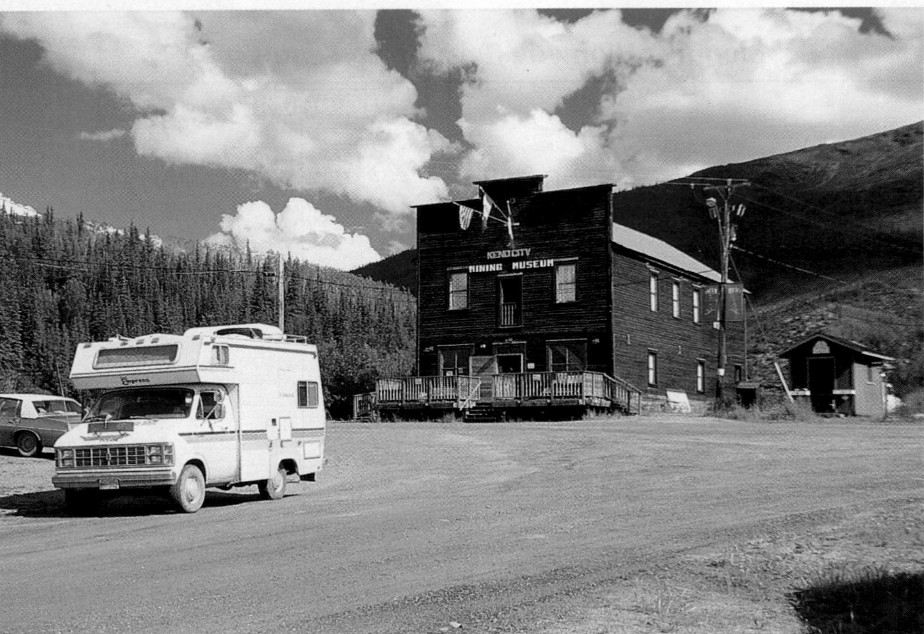

Keno City Mining Museum has a great collection of historical mining artifacts and photos. (Earl L. Brown, staff)

Silver Trail Log

(continued)

J 32.8 (52.8 km) Mayo airport, built in 1928 by the Treadwell Mining Co.

J 34.9 (56.2 km) Side road to Mayo hydro dam, built in 1951 and completed in 1952.

J 35.8 (57.6 km) Turnoff to west for Five Mile Lake Yukon government campground; 20 sites, boat launch, picnic tables, firepits. ▲

J 36.1 (58.1 km) Five Mile Lake day-use area. Pavement ends, gravel begins, northbound.

J 37.6 (60.5 km) Wareham Lake to east, created by the Mayo River power project.

J 38.2 (61.4 km) Survival shelter to east.

J 42.9 (69 km) **Junction** of Yukon Highway 11 with Minto Lake Road and Duncan Creek Road. Turn west (left) and drive 12 miles/19 km for **Minto Lake;** good fishing for lake trout and grayling. Also access to Highet Creek.

Turn east (right) at junction for Duncan Creek Road, which leads to Mayo Lake and Keno City. The original Silver Trail, Duncan Creek Road was used by Treadwell Yukon during the 1930s to haul silver ore from Keno into Mayo, where it was loaded onto riverboats.

This 25-mile/40-km back road is mostly good hard-packed gravel. Motorists note, however, that the last 10 miles/16 km into Keno City via Duncan Creek Road are narrow and winding, slippery when wet and not recommended for large vehicles or trailers. Heading northeast on Duncan Creek Road, travelers will see the site of Fields Creek Roadhouse at Mile 5, and Stones Roadhouse at Mile 11. At Mile 14 Duncan Creek Road junctions with a 6-mile/10-km side road which leads to **Mayo Lake;** there is good fishing along the **Mayo River** to the dam at the west end of Mayo Lake. At Mile 14.2 there is a private gold mine. The Duncan Creek Golddusters offer gold panning and a guided placer mine tour for about $11 per person (less for seniors and groups; children under 12 free). At Mile 18 are the remains of the Van Cleaves Roadhouse. At Mile 25 Duncan Creek Road junctions with highway 11 at Keno City.

J 47.1 (77 km) Watch for turnoff for Mount Haldane trail; follow gravel road 2 miles/3.2 km to trailhead. This 4-mile-/6.4-km-long walking trail leads to the summit of Mount Haldane, elev. 6,023 feet/1,836m, and offers sweeping views of the McQuesten River valley and the towns of Elsa and Mayo. A brochure on the trail suggests anyone in average physical condition can make the round-trip in 6 hours (including an hour for lunch at the top). The switch-backed trail is visible on the south face of Mount Haldane. The trail was cut by a mining company in the 1970s.

J 48 (77.2 km) **Halfway Lakes;** fishing for northern pike. Silver Trail Inn; food and lodging in summer.

J 49 (78.8 km) Mount Haldane Lions survival shelter.

J 54.9 (88.3 km) South McQuesten River Road.

J 60.3 (97 km) **ELSA** (pop. 10) was a company town for United Keno Hill Mines, formerly one of the largest silver mines in North America and one of the Yukon's oldest continuously operating hardrock mines until its closure in 1989. The Elsa claim is a well-mineralized silver vein, located on Galena Hill and named for the sister of prospector Charlie Brefalt, who received $250,000 for Treadwell Yukon's richest mine. A plaque here commemorates American engineer Livingston Wernecke, who came to the Keno Hill area in 1919 to investigate the silver–lead ore discoveries for Treadwell–Yukon Mining Co.

J 63.8 (102.6 km) Side road leads north to Hanson Lakes and McQuesten Lake. Galena Mountains to east. An information sign marks the Wind River trail, a former winter road to oil and mining exploration sites, which leads 300 miles/483 km north to the Bell River. The twin towers are abandoned telephone relays.

Keno City

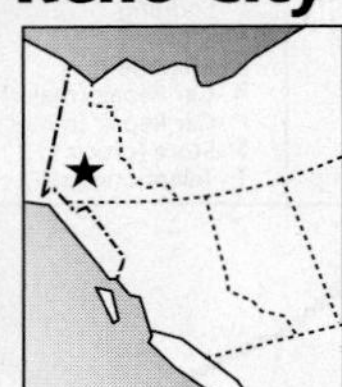

J 69.1 (111.2 km) End of the Silver Trail. **Population:** about 25. Originally called Sheep Hill by the early miners, Keno City was renamed Keno—a gambling game—after the Keno mining claim that was staked by Louis Bouvette in July 1919. This enormously rich discovery of silver and galena sparked the interest of 2 large mining companies, the Guggenheims and Treadwell Yukon, who set up camps in the area. During the 1920s, Keno City was a boom town.

Keno has the Keno City Hotel, with a unique bar (no food service available), and a snack bar. Washers, dryers and showers available for the public at the recreation hall. There is a city campground on Lightning Creek; 17 sites, water, firewood and firepits. ▲

Well worth a visit here is the Keno Mining Museum, phone (867) 995-2792, fax (867) 395-2730. Photographs and tools recall the mining history of the area. It is open 10 A.M. to 6 P.M. in summer.

There are a number of hiking trails in the Keno area; inquire at the museum. The Summit trail (can be driven) leads 6.5 miles/10.5 km to the milepost sign on top of Keno Hill, elev. 6,065 feet/1,849m. *NOTE: Before driving up to the summit, check at the Keno City Museum or the Keno City Snack Bar for current road conditions.*

Keno City Snack Bar. See display ad this section.

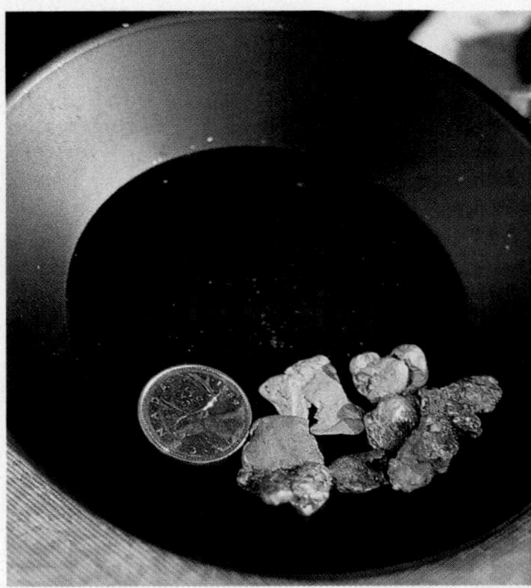

Gold nuggets from Duncan Creek Golddusters. (Earl L. Brown, staff)

DEMPSTER HIGHWAY (5) (8)

Connects: Klondike Hwy. to Inuvik, NWT **Length:** 456 miles
Road Surface: Gravel **Season:** Open all year
Highest Summit: North Fork Pass 4,265 feet
Major Attractions: Lost Patrol Gravesite, Mackenzie River Delta

	Dawson City	Ft. McPherson	Inuvik	Klondike Hwy.
Dawson City		367	481	25
Ft. McPherson	367		114	342
Inuvik	481	114		456
Klondike Hwy.	25	342	456	

Some snow remains along the banks of the Blackstone River in July.
(Earl L. Brown, staff)

The Dempster Highway (Yukon Highway 5, NWT Highway 8) begins 25 miles/40.2 km east of Dawson City, YT, at its junction with Klondike Highway 2 (see **Milepost J 301.6** on page 313 in the KLONDIKE LOOP section), and leads 456.3 miles/734.3 km northeast to Inuvik, NWT.

Construction of the Dempster Highway began in 1959, under the Road to Resources program, and was completed in 1978. A 5-year major reconstruction and surfacing program on the highway concluded in 1988, although freezing weather and heavy truck traffic may erode both road base and surfacing in areas. Calcium chloride is used in some areas to reduce dust and as a bonding agent; wash your vehicle as soon as practical.

The Dempster is a gravel road. There are stretches of clay surface that can be slippery in wet weather. Summer driving conditions on the Dempster vary depending on weather and maintenance. Generally, road conditions range from fair to excellent, with highway speeds attainable on some sections.

Facilities are still few and far between on the Dempster. Full auto services are available at Klondike River Lodge at the Dempster Highway turnoff on Klondike Highway 2. Gas, propane, food and lodging, and car repair are also available at Eagle Plains Hotel, located at about the halfway point on the Dempster. Gas, food and lodging are also available in Fort McPherson. Gas up whenever possible.

The Dempster is open year-round. The highway is fairly well-traveled in summer: A driver may not see another car for an hour, and then pass 4 cars in a row. Locals say the highway is smoother and easier to drive in winter, but precautions should be taken against cold weather, high winds and poor visibility; check road conditions before proceeding in winter. It is strongly recommended motorists carry at least 2 spare tires while traveling the Dempster. DRIVE WITH YOUR HEADLIGHTS ON!

There are 2 ferry crossings on the Dempster, at **Milepost J 334.9** (Peel River crossing) and **J 377.9** (Mackenzie River and Arctic Red River crossings). Free government ferry service is available 15 hours a day (9 A.M. to 1 A.M. Northwest Territories time, 8 A.M. to midnight Yukon time) during summer (from about June to mid-October). Cross by ice bridge in winter.

General information on Northwest Territories is available by calling the Arctic Hotline at (800) 661-0788. For recorded messages on ferry service, road and weather conditions, phone (800) 661-0752. If you are in Dawson City, the Western Arctic Visitor Centre has information on Northwest Territories and the Dempster Highway. Located in the B.Y.N. Building on Front Street, across from the Yukon Visitor Centre, it is open 9 A.M. to 9 P.M., June to September; phone (867) 993-6167. Or write the Western Arctic Tourism Assoc., Box 2600MP, Inuvik, NT X0E 0T0; phone (867) 777-4321, fax (867) 777-2434 for more information.

The MILEPOST© expresses its appreciation to the Yukon Dept. of Renewable Resources, Parks and Recreation for its assistance with information in this highway log.

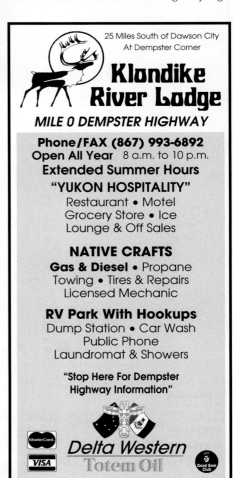

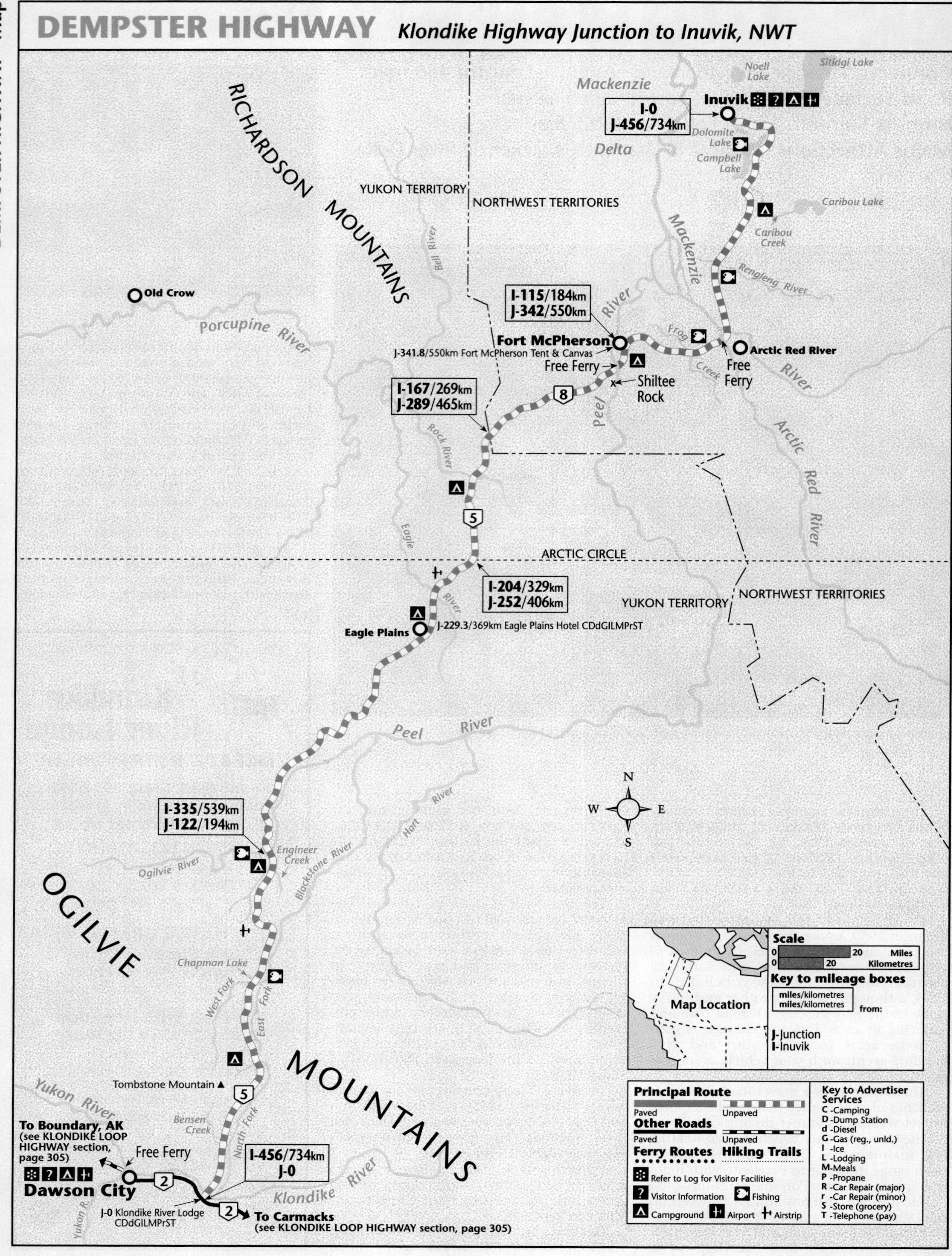
DEMPSTER HIGHWAY
Klondike Highway Junction to Inuvik, NWT
Inuvik
I-0
J-456/734km
Mackenzie
Delta
Noell Lake
Sitidgi Lake
Dolomite Lake
Campbell Lake
Caribou Lake
Caribou Creek
RICHARDSON MOUNTAINS
YUKON TERRITORY
NORTHWEST TERRITORIES
Bell River
Mackenzie
Rengleng River
Old Crow
Porcupine River
I-115/184km
J-342/550km
Fort McPherson
J-341.8/550km Fort McPherson Tent & Canvas
Free Ferry
Shiltee Rock
Peel River
Frog Creek
Arctic Red River
Free Ferry
I-167/269km
J-289/465km
Rock River
Arctic Red River
Eagle River
ARCTIC CIRCLE
I-204/329km
J-252/406km
YUKON TERRITORY
NORTHWEST TERRITORIES
Eagle Plains
J-229.3/369km Eagle Plains Hotel CDdGILMPrST
Peel River
Hart River
N
W
E
S
I-335/539km
J-122/194km
Engineer Creek
Ogilvie River
Blackstone River
OGILVIE
MOUNTAINS
Chapman Lake
West Fork
East Fork
Tombstone Mountain
Yukon River
Bensen Creek
North Fork
To Boundary, AK
(see KLONDIKE LOOP HIGHWAY section, page 305)
Free Ferry
Dawson City
I-456/734km
J-0
Yukon R.
J-0 Klondike River Lodge CDdGILMPrST
Klondike River
To Carmacks
(see KLONDIKE LOOP HIGHWAY section, page 305)
Map Location
Scale
0 20 Miles
0 20 Kilometres
Key to mileage boxes
miles/kilometres
miles/kilometres
from:
J-Junction
I-Inuvik
Principal Route
Paved
Unpaved
Other Roads
Paved
Unpaved
Ferry Routes
Hiking Trails
Refer to Log for Visitor Facilities
Visitor Information
Fishing
Campground
Airport
Airstrip
Key to Advertiser Services
C -Camping
D -Dump Station
d -Diesel
G -Gas (reg., unld.)
I -Ice
L -Lodging
M -Meals
P -Propane
R -Car Repair (major)
r -Car Repair (minor)
S -Store (grocery)
T -Telephone (pay)

Dempster Highway Log

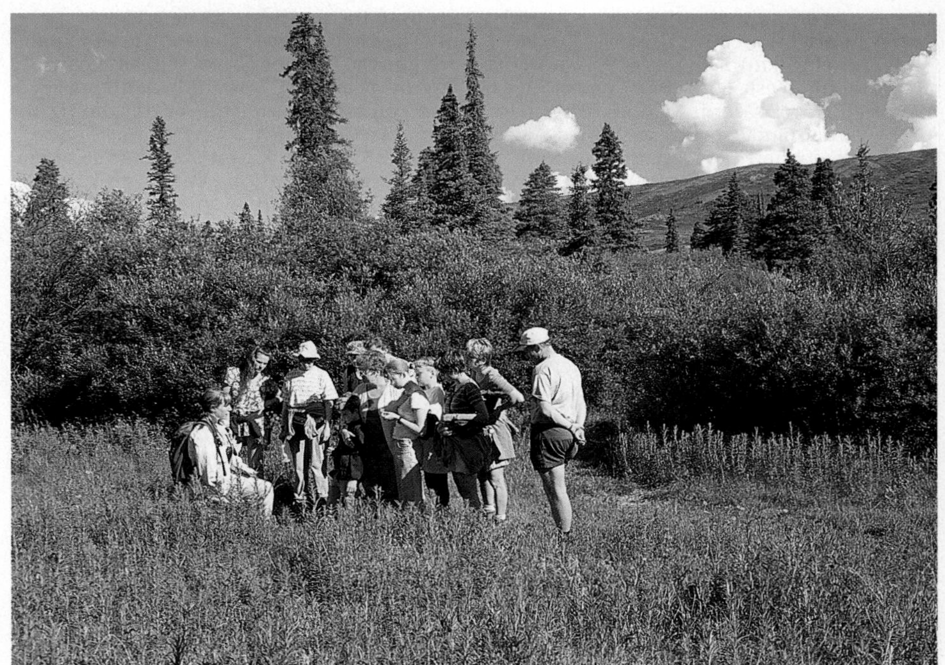

Guided nature walk at Tombstone Mountain Yukon government campground, Milepost J 44.4. (Earl L. Brown, staff)

YUKON HIGHWAY 5

Driving distance is measured in miles. The kilometre figure on the Yukon portion of the highway reflects the physical kilometreposts and is not necessarily an accurate metric conversion of the mileage figure. Kilometreposts are green with white lettering and are located on the right-hand side of the highway, northbound.

Distance from junction with Klondike Highway 2 (J) is followed by distance from Inuvik (I).

J 0 I 456.3 (734.3 km) **Junction** of Yukon Highways 2 and 5, 25 miles/40.2 km east of Dawson City, also known as Dempster Corner. Klondike River Lodge (open all year); food, gas, propane, lodging, camping, and tire repair and sales.

Klondike River Lodge. See display ad this section. ▲

J 0.1 (0.2 km) **I 456.2** (734.2 km) Dempster Highway monument with information panels on history and culture, wildlife, ecology and driving tips.

J 0.2 (0.3 km) **I 456.1** (734 km) One-lane wood-planked bridge over Klondike River. The road follows the wooded (spruce and poplar) North Klondike River valley.

J 0.9 (1.4 km) **I 455.4** (732.9 km) Distance marker shows Eagle Plains 363 km (226 miles), Inuvik 735 km (457 miles).

J 3 (5 km) **I 453.3** (729.5 km) Burn area from 1991 fire that burned 5,189 acres/2,100 hectares.

J 4 (6.4 km) **I 452.3** (727.9 km) The North Fork Ditch channeled water from the North Klondike River to a power plant 15.5 miles/25 km farther west for nearly 60 years, until the 1960s, and it helped to provide electricity and water for huge gold-dredging operations farther down the valley. Watch for salmon migrating upstream from late July through August.

J 4.8 (7.7 km) **I 451.5** (726.6 km) Turnoff for Viceroy Brewery Creek Gold Mine (private road). Inquire locally about tours.

J 6.5 (10.5 km) **I 449.8** (723.9 km) Antimony Mountain (elev. 6,693 feet/2,040m) about 18.5 miles/30 km away, is one peak of the Ogilvie Mountains and part of the Snowy Range.

J 12.4 (20 km) **I 443.9** (714.4 km) North Klondike Range, Ogilvie Mountains to the west of the highway lead toward the rugged, interior Tombstone Range. These mountains were glaciated during the Ice Age.

J 15.4 (24.5 km) **I 440.9** (709.5 km) Glacier Creek.

J 16.6 (26.7 km) **I 439.7** (707.6 km) Pullout to west.

J 18.1 (29 km) **I 438.2** (705.2 km) Bensen Creek.

J 25.6 (41 km) **I 430.7** (693.1 km) Pea Soup Creek.

J 29.8 (48 km) **I 426.5** (686.4 km) Scout Car Creek.

J 31.7 (51 km) **I 424.6** (683.3 km) Wolf Creek. Private cabin beside creek.

J 34.7 (55.8 km) **I 421.6** (678.5 km) Highway follows North Fork Klondike River.

J 36.6 (58.9 km) **I 419.7** (675.4 km) Grizzly Creek. Mount Robert Service to right northbound.

J 39.6 (63.7 km) **I 416.7** (670.6 km) Mike and Art Creek.

J 40.4 (65 km) **I 415.9** (669.3 km) Klondike Camp Yukon government highway maintenance station. No visitor services but may provide help in an emergency.

J 41.8 (67.3 km) **I 414.5** (667.1 km) First crossing of the North Fork Klondike River. The highway now moves above tree line and on to tundra northbound. At an elevation of approximately 4,003 feet/1,220m, you'll cross the watershed between the Yukon and Mackenzie basins.

J 43 (69.2 km) **I 413.3** (665.2 km) Spectacular first view of Tombstone Range northbound.

J 44.4 (71.5 km) **I 411.9** (662.9 km) Tombstone Mountain Yukon government campground (3,392 feet/1,034m above sea level) with 31 sites, $8 fee, shelter, fireplaces, water from the river, tables, pit toilets. Designated cyclist camping area with bear-proof food cache available. Dempster Interpretive Centre located at campground, open 10 A.M. to 10 P.M., mid-June to early September; fossil displays, resource library, handouts with area information, campfire talks and nature walks. Good hiking trail begins past the outhouses and leads toward the headwaters of the North Fork Klondike River. ▲

J 46 (74 km) **I 410.3** (660.3 km) Large double-ended viewpoint. Good views of North Fork Pass and river. To the southwest is the needle-like peak of Tombstone Mountain (7,195 feet/2,193m), which forms the centrepoint in a panorama of ragged ridges and lush green tundra slopes. To the north is the East Fork Blackstone River valley; on each side are the Ogilvie Mountains, which rise to elevations of 6,890 feet/2,100m. Watch for Dall sheep, grizzlies, hoary marmots and ptarmigan. The Tombstone, Cloudy and Blackstone mountain ranges are identified as a Special Management Area by the Yukon government and will eventually become a Yukon Territorial Park.

Day hikes up the North Klondike River valley and 4-day wilderness hikes to Tombstone Mountain are popular. There are no established trails. The staff at the Dempster Interpretive Centre at Tombstone Campground can provide maps and suggest itineraries. Hikers should be well prepared for rough terrain, drastic weather changes and potential wildlife encounters, as well as practicing "leave-no-trace" camping. For more information on the Tombstone region, call Yukon Dept. of Renewable Resources, Parks & Outdoor Recreation Branch at (867) 667-8299 or e-mail <jack.schick@gov.yk.ca>.

Outstanding aerial view of the mountain available through flightseeing trip out of Dawson City.

J 48.4 (77.9 km) **I 407.9** (656.4 km) Blackstone River culvert. Tundra in the region indicates permafrost.

J 51 (82 km) **I 405.3** (652.2 km) North Fork Pass Summit, elev. 4,265 feet/1,300m, is the highest point on the Dempster Highway. Wildflowers abundant late June–early July. Descent to the Blackstone River. Good birdwatching area. A hike up to the lower knoll to the right of the main mountain increases chances of seeing pika and marmots.

J 52.2 (84 km) **I 404.1** (650.3 km) Anglecomb Peak (also called Sheep Mountain) is a lambing and nursery habitat for Dall sheep during May and June, as well as a frequent nesting area for a pair of golden eagles.

J 54.2 (87.2 km) **I 402.1** (647.1 km) First crossing of East Fork Blackstone River.

J 56.5 (91 km) **I 399.8** (643.4 km) The Blackstone Uplands, stretching from North Fork Pass to Chapman Lake, are a rich area for birdlife (long-tailed jaegers, gyrfalcons, peregrine falcons, red-throated loons, Whimbrels, upland sandpipers and oldsquaw ducks) and big game hunting for Dall sheep and grizzly bear.

J 63.4 (102 km) **I 392.9** (632.3 km) Distance marker shows Eagle Plains 261 km (162 miles), Inuvik 633 km (393 miles), Dawson 142 km (88 miles), Whitehorse 600 km (373 miles).

J 66.9 (107.6 km) **I 389.4** (626.7 km)

Large gravel pullout with litter barrels. Access to Blackstone River.

J 71.5 (115 km) **I 384.8** (619.3 km) First crossing of West Fork Blackstone River. Watch for arctic terns. Good fishing for Dolly Varden and grayling a short distance downstream where the west and east forks of the Blackstone join to form the **Blackstone River**, which the road now follows. After the river crossing, 2 low, cone-shaped mounds called pingos are visible upriver about 5 miles/8 km.

J 72.1 (116 km) **I 384.2** (618.3 km) Commemorative road sign about sled dog patrols of the Royal North West Mounted Police. Also a sign: Watch for horses. View over Chapman Lake, one of the few lakes close to the highway that is large enough to permit floatplane operations. Porcupine caribou herd sometimes crosses the highway in this area in mid-October.

J 77.3 (124.4 km) **I 379** (609.9 km) **Private Aircraft:** Government airstrip (road is part of the strip); elev. 3,100 feet/945m; length 3,000 feet/914m.

J 96 (154.5 km) **I 360.3** (579.8 km) Northbound, highway passes through barren gray hills of Windy Pass. The mountain ridges are the breeding habitat for some species of butterflies and moths not known to exist anywhere else.

J 106 (169.7 km) **I 350.3** (563.7 km) Creek culvert is red from iron oxide. Sulfurous smell is from nearby sulfur springs. Watch for interesting geological features in hills along road.

J 108.1 (173 km) **I 348.2** (560.4 km) Views of red-coloured Engineer Creek, and also erosion pillars and red rock of nearby hills between here and Kilometrepost 182.

J 121.7 (194 km) **I 334.6** (538.5 km) Sapper Hill, named in 1971 in honour of the 3rd Royal Canadian Engineers who built the Ogilvie River bridge. "Sapper" is a nickname for an army engineer. **Engineer Creek** Yukon government campground; 15 sites, $8 fee, fireplaces, water, tables, pit toilets. Grayling fishing.

J 122.9 (195.7 km) **I 333.4** (536.5 km) The 360-foot/110-m Jeckell Bridge spans the Ogilvie River here. Built by the Canadian Armed Forces Engineers as a training exercise, it is named in honour of Allan Jeckell, controller of the Yukon from 1932 to 1946. Fossil coral may be visible in limestone outcrops to the northeast of the bridge.

The Ogilvie River and Ogilvie Mountains were named in honour of William Ogilvie, a highly respected Dominion land surveyor and commissioner of the Yukon during the Klondike Gold Rush.

J 123 (195.8 km) **I 333.3** (536.4 km) Ogilvie grader station, Yukon government maintenance camp is on north side of the river.

For the next 25 miles/40 km, the highway follows the narrow valley of the Ogilvie River. For the first 12 miles/20 km, talus slopes edge the road, and game trails are evident along their precipitous sides.

J 124.3 (197.7 km) **I 332** (534.3 km) View of castlelike outcroppings of rock, known as tors, on mountaintops to north.

J 131.9 (209.5 km) **I 324.4** (522.1 km) Between here and Kilometrepost 216, watch for bird nests in the shale embankments along the highway and unusual rock outcroppings and erosion pillars in surrounding hills. Highway crosses rolling plateau country near Kilometrepost 218.

J 137.5 (221.2 km) **I 318.8** (513 km) Small turnout with litter barrels. Easy access to **Ogilvie River**. Good grayling fishing. Elephant Rock may be viewed from right side of road northbound. Fascinating mountain of broken rock and shale near Kilometrepost 224.

J 137.6 (221.5 km) **I 318.7** (512.9 km) Davies Creek.

J 149.1 (235.8 km) **I 307.2** (494.4 km) Ogilvie airstrip, status unknown. The great gray owl, one of Canada's largest, is known to nest as far north as this area.

J 154.4 (244 km) **I 301.9** (485.8 km) Highway climbs away from the Ogilvie River, following a high ridge to the Eagle Plains plateau. One of the few unglaciated areas in Canada, this country is shaped by wind and water erosion rather than by ice. Views of Mount Cronkhite and Mount McCullum to the east.

Seismic lines next 62 miles/100 km provide hiking paths across the tundra. This was the major area of oil and gas exploration activity for which the road was originally built. In season, fields of cotton grass and varieties of tundra plants make good photo subjects. The road continues to follow a high ridge (elev. 1,969 feet/600m) with broad sweeps and easy grades.

J 160.9 (259 km) **I 295.4** (475.4 km) Large double-ended turnout. Panoramic Ogilvie–Peel viewpoint. Lowbush cranberries in August. Outhouse, litter barrels.

J 171.7 (270.6 km) **I 284.6** (458 km) Highway begins descent northbound and crosses fabulous high rolling country above tree line.

J 175.6 (276.7 km) **I 280.7** (451.7 km) Gravel pit full of old oil drums.

J 187.7 (302 km) **I 268.6** (432.3 km) Forest fire burn area; 13,590 acres/5,500 hectares burned in July–August 1991.

J 204.5 (321 km) **I 256.3** (412.5 km) Road widens to become part of an airstrip.

J 215.6 (347 km) **I 240.7** (387.4 km) Richardson Mountains to the northeast. The thick blanket of rock and gravel that makes up the roadbed ahead is designed to prevent the underlying permafrost from melting. The roadbed conducts heat more than the surrounding vegetation does and must be extra thick to compensate. Much of the highway was built in winter.

J 229.3 (369 km) **I 227** (365.3 km) **Milepost 231. EAGLE PLAINS;** hotel, phone (867) 993-2453; food, gas, propane, aviation fuel, diesel, lodging and camping. Open year-round.

Built in 1978, just before completion of the Dempster Highway, the hotel here was an engineering challenge. Engineers considered the permafrost in the area and found a place where the bedrock was at the surface. The hotel was built on this natural pad, thus avoiding the costly process of building on pilings as was done at Inuvik.

J 234.8 (377.8 km) **I 221.5** (356.5 km) Short side road to picnic site with information sign about Albert Johnson, "The Mad Trapper of Rat River." Something of a mystery man, Johnson killed one mounted policeman and wounded another in 2 separate incidents involving complaints that Johnson was tampering with Native trap lines. The ensuing manhunt became famous in the North, as Johnson eluded Mounties for 48 days during the winter of 1931–32. Johnson was killed in a shoot-out on Feb. 17, 1932. He was buried at Aklavik, a community located 36 miles/58 km west of Inuvik by air.

Dick North, author of 2 books on Johnson (and also author of *The Lost Patrol*), was quoted in the *New York Times* (June 3, 1990) as being 95 percent certain that Johnson, whose true identity has not been known, was a Norwegian–American bank robber named Johnny Johnson.

J 234.9 (378 km) **I 221.4** (356.3 km) **Eagle River** bridge. Like the Ogilvie bridge, it was built by the Dept. of National Defense as a training exercise. In contrast to the other rivers seen from the Dempster, the Eagle is a more sluggish, silt-laden stream with unstable banks. It is the main drainage channel for the western slopes of the Richardson Mountains. It and its tributaries provide good grayling fishing. Canoeists leave here bound for Alaska via the Porcupine and Yukon rivers.

J 239.4 (385.3 km) **I 216.9** (349.1 km) Views of the Richardson Mountains (elev. 3,937 feet/1,200m) ahead. Named for Sir John Richardson, surgeon and naturalist on both of Sir John Franklin's overland expeditions to the Arctic Ocean.

J 241.7 (389 km) **I 214.6** (345.4 km) **Private Aircraft:** Emergency airstrip; elev. 2,365 feet/721m; length 2,500 feet/762m; gravel. Used regularly by aircraft hauling freight to Old Crow, a Kutchin Indian settlement on the Porcupine River and Yukon's most northerly community.

J 252 (405.5 km) **I 204.3** (328.8 km) Large double-ended turnout. On June 21, the sun does not fall below the horizon for 24 hours at this latitude. Picnic tables, litter barrels, outhouses nearby. Sign marks Arctic Circle crossing, 66°33′N. Highway crosses arctic tundra on an elevated berm beside the Richardson Mountains; sweeping views.

J 277 (445.8 km) **I 179.3** (288.5 km) Rock River Yukon government campground; 18 sites, $8 fee, tables, kitchen shelter, water, firepits, outhouses. Black flies prevalent; bring repellent.

J 280.1 (450.8 km) **I 176.2** (283.6 km) Turnout. Northbound, the highway winds toward the Richardson Mountains, crossing them at George's Gap near the YT–NWT border. Good hiking area and excellent photo possibilities.

J 288 (463.5 km) **I 168.3** (270.8 km) Turnout; good overnight spot for self-contained vehicles.

J 288.5 (464.3 km) **I 167.8** (270 km) Plaque about Wright Pass, named for Al Wright, a highway engineer with Public Works Canada who was responsible for the routing of the Dempster Highway.

J 288.9 (465 km) **I 167.4** (269.4 km) YT-NWT border. Historical marker. Continental Divide in the Richardson Mountains: West of here, water flows to the Pacific Ocean. East of here, water flows to the Arctic Ocean. Good photo spot.

TIME ZONE CHANGE: Yukon Territory observes Pacific standard time; Northwest Territories is on Mountain time.

NWT HIGHWAY 8

IMPORTANT: Kilometreposts northbound (with white letters on a blue background) indicate distance from YT–NWT border and are indicated at intervals in our log. Highway descends, road narrows, northbound.

J 297.6 (479 km) **I 158.7** (255.4 km) Kilometrepost 14. **James Creek;** good fishing. Highway maintenance camp. Good spot to park overnight.

J 299 (481.2 km) **I 157.3** (253.1 km) Sign advises no passing next 4.3 miles/7 km; climb to Wright Pass summit.

J 303.7 (488.7 km) **I 152.6** (245.6 km) Wright Pass Summit. From here northbound, the Dempster Highway descends 2,300 feet/853m to the Peel River crossing, 32 miles/51 km away.

J 316.3 (509 km) **I 140** (225.3 km) Kilometrepost 44. Side road leads down to Midway Lake.

J 319.4 (514 km) **I 136.9** (220.3 km) **Private Aircraft:** Highway widens to form Midway airstrip; length 3,000 feet/914m.

J 329.3 (530 km) **I 127** (204.4 km) View of Peel River Valley and Fort McPherson to north. Litter barrels.

J 332.4 (535 km) **I 123.9** (199.4 km) Kilometrepost 70. Highway begins descent northbound to Peel River.

J 334.9 (539 km) **I 121.4** (195.4 km) Peel River crossing, locally called Eightmile because it is situated 8 miles/12.8 km south of Fort McPherson. Free government ferry service 15 hours a day during summer (from about early or mid-June to mid-October). Double-ended cable ferry: Drive on, drive off. Light vehicles cross by ice bridge in late November; heavier vehicles cross as ice thickens. *No crossing possible during freezeup or breakup.* Phone toll free (800) 661-0752 for information on ferry crossings, road conditions and weather.

The level of the Peel River changes rapidly in spring and summer in response to meltwater from the mountains and ice jams on the Mackenzie River. The alluvial flood plain is covered by muskeg on the flats, and scrubby alder and stunted black spruce on the valley sides.

Indians from Fort McPherson have summer tent camps on the Peel River. The Indians net whitefish and sheefish (inconnu) then dry them on racks or in smokehouses for the winter.

About 4 miles/6.4 km south upstream is a trail leading to Shiltee Rock, which gives excellent views of the Peel River and the southern end of the Mackenzie.

J 335.9 (540.6 km) **I 120.4** (193.8 km) Nitainilall territorial campground with 20 sites. (Campground name is from the Gwich'in term *Noo-til-ee,* meaning "fast flowing waters." Information centre open daily June to September. Camping permits, potable water, firewood, pit toilets and kitchen shelter available. ▲

J 337.4 (543 km) **I 118.9** (191.3 km) Kilometrepost 78.

J 340.4 (547.8 km) **I 115.9** (186.5 km) Access road right to Fort McPherson airport.

J 341.8 (550 km) **I 114.5** (184.3 km) Side road on left to Fort McPherson (description follows).

Fort McPherson

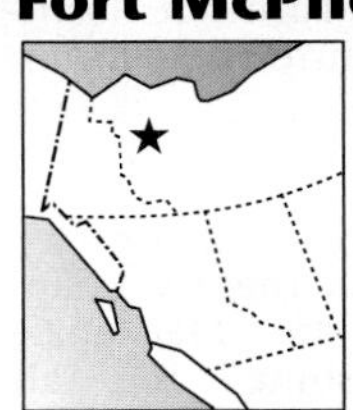

Located on a flat-topped hill about 100 feet/30m above the Peel River, 24 miles/38 km from its junction with the Mackenzie River; 100 miles/160 km southwest of Aklavik by boat along Peel Channel, 31 miles/50 km directly east of the Richardson Mountains. **Population**: 632. **Emergency Services: RCMP**, phone (867) 952-2551. **Health Center**, phone (867) 952-2586.

Visitor Information: Located in a restored log house, the former home of elder Annie G. Robert; open daily, early June through mid-September, 9 A.M. to 9 P.M. **Radio**: CBC 680.

Transportation: Air—Aklak Air provides scheduled air service from Inuvik.

Private Aircraft: Fort McPherson airstrip; 67°24'N 134°51'W; elev. 142 feet/43m; length 3,500 feet/1,067m; gravel.

This Déné Indian settlement has a public phone, cafe, bed and breakfast, 2 general stores and 2 service stations (1 with tire repair). A co-op hotel here offers 8 rooms and a restaurant. Arts and crafts include beadwork and hide garments. Wildlife watching, adventure tours and canoe trips are popular along the Peel River.

Fort McPherson was named in 1848 for Murdoch McPherson, chief trader of the Hudson's Bay Co., which had established its first posts in the area 8 years before. Between 1849 and 1859 there were frequent feuds with neighboring Inuit, who later moved farther north to the Aklavik area, where they established a fur-trading post.

In addition to subsistence fishing and hunting, income is earned from trapping (mostly muskrat and mink), handicrafts, government employment, and commercial enterprises such as Fort McPherson Tent and Canvas factory, which specializes in travel bags, tents and tepees. Tours during business hours, 9 A.M. to 5 P.M. weekdays; (867) 952-2179, fax (867) 952-2718.

Photos and artifacts depicting the history and way of life of the community are displayed in the Chief Julius School. Buried in the cemetery outside the Anglican church are Inspector Francis J. Fitzgerald and 3 men from the ill-fated North West Mounted Police patrol of 1910–1911 between Fort McPherson and Dawson.

Inspector Fitzgerald and the men had left Fort McPherson on Dec. 21, 1910, carrying mail and dispatches to Dawson City. By Feb. 20, 1911, the men had not yet arrived in Dawson, nearly a month overdue. A search party led by Corporal W.J.D. Dempster was sent to look for the missing patrol. On March 22, 1911, Dempster discovered their frozen bodies only 26 miles from where they had started. Lack of knowledge of the trail, coupled with too few rations, had doomed the 4-man patrol. One of the last entries in Fitzgerald's diary, quoted in Dick North's *The Lost Patrol*, an account of their journey, read: "We have now only 10 pounds of flour and 8 pounds of bacon and some dried fish. My last hope is gone. ... We have been a week looking for a river to take us over the divide, but there are dozens of rivers, and I am at a loss."

Dempster Highway Log

(continued)

J 342.4 (551 km) **I 113.9** (183.3 km) Kilometrepost 86.

J 365.1 (587.6 km) **I 91.2** (146.8 km) **Frog Creek.** Grayling and pike. Road on right northbound leads to picnic area.

J 377.1 (606.8 km) **I 79.2** (127.5 km) Mackenzie River wayside area.

J 377.9 (608.2 km) **I 78.4** (126.2 km) Mackenzie River crossing. Free government ferry service available 15 hours a day during summer (from about early or mid-June to early October). Double-ended ferry: Drive on, drive off. Light vehicles may cross by ice bridge in late November; heavier vehicles can cross as ice thickens. *No crossing possible during freezeup and breakup.*

The ferry travels between landings on either side of the Mackenzie River and also provides access to **TSIIGEHTCHIC (formerly ARCTIC RED RIVER)**, a small Athapaskan community (pop. 140) located at the confluence of the Mackenzie and Arctic Red rivers. Tsiigehtchic has a community-owned grocery store and cafe. The Sunshine Inn provides accommodations for up to 8 people. Boat tours are available through the Band Store or local operators. For more information on lodging or tours call (867) 953-3003 or fax (867) 953-3906.

Tsiigehtchic, which means "mouth of iron river," is one of 4 communities in the Gwich'in Settlement Area. The residents speak a dialect of Gwich'in, one of the Athapaskan languages. They refer to themselves as the Gwichya Gwich'in or "People of the flat land." The Gwich'in Social & Cultural Institute here was formed at an annual assembly in Fort McPherson in 1992 in response to people's concern about the loss of their culture and language.

The Arctic Red River (Tsiigehnjik) was declared a Canadian Heritage River in 1993. Tsiigehnjik, the Gwich'in name for the river, winds it way out of the Mackenzie Mountains and flows into the Mackenzie River at Tsiigehtchic. The Gwichya Gwich'in have long used and traveled the river for fishing, hunting and trapping.

J 399.6 (643 km) **I 56.7** (91.2 km) **Rengling River**, grayling fishing.

J 404.4 (650.8 km) **I 51.9** (83.5 km) Beginning of 13-mile/21-km straight stretch.

J 409.7 (659.3 km) **I 46.6** (75 km) Distance marker shows Inuvik 75 km.

J 426.3 (686 km) **I 30** (48.3 km) Vadzaih Van Tshik picnic and camping area. ▲

J 431.4 (694.3 km) **I 24.9** (40.1 km) Campbell Lake and Campbell escarpment ahead northbound. Good place to glass for peregrine falcons.

J 440.6 (709 km) **I 15.7** (25.3 km) Ehjuu Njk picnic spot; pit toilets.

J 442.4 (712 km) **I 13.9** (22.4 km) Nihtak campground picnic area; pit toilets. Good fishing for pike and whitefish, some sheefish (inconnu). Creek leads a short distance to Campbell Lake. Boat launch. Bring mosquito repellent.

J 449.9 (724 km) **I 6.4** (10.3 km) Airport Road turnoff; pavement begins.

J 451 (725.8 km) **I 5.3** (8.5 km) Food, gas and lodging.

J 451.7 (727 km) **I 4.6** (7.4 km) Kilometrepost 262.

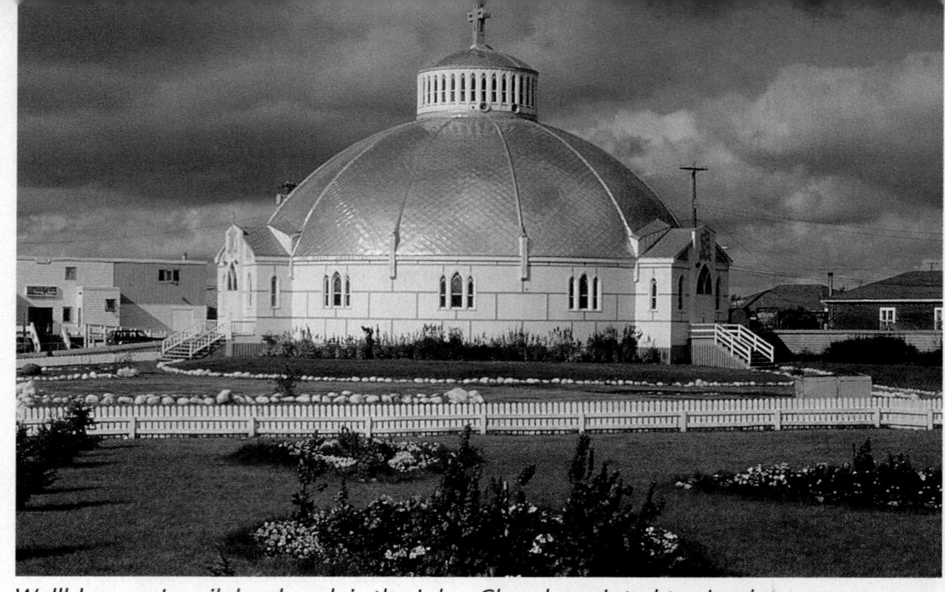

Welll-known Inuvik landmark is the Igloo Church, painted to simulate snow blocks. (© Lyn Hancock)

J 454 (730.6 km) **I 2.3** (3.7 km) Chuk Park territorial campground; 38 campsites, 20 pull-through, electric hookups, firewood, water, showers, $15 fee. Lookout tower. Interpretive information available. ▲

J 456.3 (734.3 km) **I 0** Turn left northbound for Inuvik town centre (description follows).

Inuvik

Situated on a flat wooded plateau on the east channel of the Mackenzie River, some 60 air miles/96 km south of the Beaufort Sea, 36 air miles/58 km and 70 water miles/113 km from Aklavik on the western edge of the delta. **Population:** 3,206, Déné, White and Inuvialuit.

Emergency Services: RCMP, phone (867) 777-2935. **Hospital**, Inuvik General, phone (867) 777-2955.

Visitor Information: Western Arctic Regional Visitors Centre is located on Mackenzie Road across from the hospital. The centre is open mid-May to mid-September and features interactive displays, excellent wildlife displays, clean restrooms and knowledgeable staff. A must visit in Inuvik. A green and white Cessna 170 is mounted as a weather vane at the centre and rotates to face into the wind. Phone (867) 777-4727. Or contact the Western Arctic Trade & Tourism Assoc., Box 2600MP, Inuvik, NT X0E 0T0, phone (867) 777-4321, fax (867) 777-2434. Or on the internet: http://www.inuvik.net. Visitors are also welcome to stop by the Ingamo Hall Friendship Centre.

Elevation: 224 feet/68m. **Climate:** Weather information available by calling (867) 979-4381. May 24 marks 57 days of midnight sun. The sun begins to set on July 19; on Dec. 6, the sun sets and does not rise until Jan. 6. Average annual precipitation 4 inches rainfall, 69 inches snowfall. July mean high 67°F/19°C, mean low 45°F/7°C. January mean high -11°F/-24°C, mean low is -30°F/-35°C. **Radio and Television:** CBC and local. **Newspaper:** *The Drum* (weekly).

Private Aircraft: Inuvik airstrip; elev. 224 feet/68m; length 6,000 feet/1,829m; asphalt; fuel 80, 100. Townsite airstrip; elev. 10 feet/3m; length 1,800 feet/549m; gravel; fuel 80, 100, Jet B, F40. High pressure refueling.

Inuvik, meaning "The Place of Man," is the largest Canadian community north of

INUVIK ADVERTISERS

Aklak Air .... Ph. (867) 777-3777
Arctic Chalet B&B .... Ph. (867) 777-3535
Arctic Nature Tours .... Ph. (867) 777-3300
Beaufort/Delta Tours .... Ph. (867) 777-2333
Blue Moon Bistro .... Ph. (867) 777-2020
Boreal Books .... Ph. (867) 777-3748
Eskimo Inn Ltd. .... Ph. (867) 777-2801
Great Northern Arts Festival, The .... Ph. (867) 777-3536
Inuvik Shirt Co. .... Ph. (867) 777-4829
Mackenzie Hotel, The .... Ph. (867) 777-2861
Oopik Tours & Adventures Ltd. .... Ph. (867) 977-2170
Originals on Mackenzie ... Ph. (867) 777-2433
Peppermill Restaurant ..... Ph. (867) 777-2999
Saunatuk Fishing Lodge Ltd. .... Ph. (867) 977-2348
Western Arctic Trade & Tourism Assoc. .... Ph. (867) 777-4321

SET YOUR SIGHTS A LITTLE HIGHER

Travel to Canada's Western Arctic

Drive Our Northernmost
Road

From Dawson City Yukon, drive one of the world's spectacular wilderness routes. Watch for wildlife as you skirt the peaks of the Richardson range, cross the Arctic Circle, and head for Inuvik, in the heart of the Mackenzie River delta.

Visit Our Northernmost
Town

To experience Inuvik, YOU have to be there!

All necessary services available. **http://www.inuvik.net**

• Banking • Post office • Restaurants • Hospital • Churches
• Tours • Automotive • Hotels • Campgrounds • Markets
• Dental • Shopping • Fuel/propane • Crafts

BLUE MOON *Bistro*

Chinese & Western Cuisine
The Bistro Pizza
(867) 777-2020
Open Daily 11am ➡ after midnight
175 Mackenzie Rd. Inuvik NWT

Ookpik Tours & Adventures Ltd.

James & Maureen Pokiak

- ***Community Cultural Tours***
- ***Guided Canoe Trips***
- ***Booking Agency for Big Game Hunts***

Box 131, Tuktoyaktuk NWT X0E 1C0
Phone (867) 977-2170 • Fax (867) 977-2399

The Mackenzie Hotel

Inuvik's First Hotel

First Class Lodging
2° North of Arctic Circle

Large Rooms & Suites, Cafe, Fine Dining, Pub
Cocktail Lounge, Cable TV, Laundry Facilities

Box 1618, Inuvik, NT Tel. (867) 777-2861 Fax (867) 777-3317 Parking: Car/Bus
e-mail: mack@permafrost.com

Peppermill Restaurant

Air Conditioned

Sundays we feature a buffet style brunch from 11:00 a.m to 2:00 p.m.

Welcomes you to Inuvik

Enjoy Northern hospitality by joining us for a scrumptious breakfast or lunch

– OUR DINNER MENU INCLUDES –
· Continental Dishes · Pastas
· Northern specialties such as musk ox, caribou, Arctic char & Lake Trout

For reservations call: (867) 777-2999
We are located at the Flinto Motor Inn, 288 Mackenzie Rd • Inuvik, NT

Beaufort/Delta Tours

Explore the Beaufort and Delta region with the people that know it Best.

Providing tours to Herschel Island, Richardson Mts., Tuktoyaktuk, Territorial Parks.
Cultural Tours, Photo Safaris, Eco Tourism, Sport Hunting, and Sport Fishing. Customized tours also available.

1-3 Council Crescent, Box 2040, Inuvik, NT., Canada X0E 0T0
Phone: (867) 777-2333 • Fax: (867) 777-3758

Looking for the perfect Northern Treasure?

Come and visit us. . .

Originals on Mackenzie
171 Mackenzie Rd., Box 1130
Inuvik, N.T. X0E 0T0
Ph: (867) 777-2433
Fax: (867) 777-2762

Saunatuk
Fishing Lodge Ltd.

– World class fishing –

• Lake Trout • Arctic Grayling • Guided fishing tours with local Inuit
• fully modern • up to 16 guests • ideal for couples and groups

Contact: James or Sharon Gruben P.O. Box 266 Tuktoyaktuk, NT X0E 1C0
Phone (867) 977-2348 Fax (867) 977-2257

Arctic Nature Tours

. . .Beyond the Arctic Circle

- **Arctic Coast, Herschel Island, Mackenzie Delta, Dempster Highway and much more.**
- **Write or call for free catalogue.**

Arctic Nature Tours Ltd. Box 1530 (MP) Inuvik, NT X0E 0T0
Phone (867) 777-3300 Fax (867) 777-3400

For a free copy of the Western Arctic Vacation Planner, contact

Western Arctic Trade & Tourism Box 2600 (MP), Inuvik, NT, X0E 0T0
Phone: (867) 777-4321 Fax: (867) 777-2434

Arctic coast in June at Tuktoyaktuk. Scheduled air service is available to "Tuk," as the community is commonly called. (© Eero Sorila)

the Arctic Circle, and the major government, transportation and communication centre for Canada's western arctic. Construction of the town began in 1955 and was completed in 1961. It was the main supply base for the petrochemical exploration of the delta until Tuktoyaktuk took over that role as activity centered in the Beaufort Sea. In Inuvik some hunting, fishing and trapping is done, but most people earn wages in government and private enterprises, particularly in transportation and construction. As the delta is one of the richest muskrat areas in the world, Inuvik is the western centre for shipping furs south.

The town's official monument says, in part, that Inuvik was "the first community north of the Arctic Circle built to provide the normal facilities of a Canadian town."

TRANSPORTATION

Air: Aklak Air provides scheduled service between Inuvik and Tuktoyaktuk, Sachs Harbour, Fort McPherson and Paulatuk. Scheduled service to Whitehorse and Old Crow, YT, via Alkan Air. Scheduled service to Edmonton, AB, and to Yellowknife, NWT, via NWT Air and Canadian Airlines International. Scheduled service to Aklavik and Tuktoyaktuk via Arctic Wings. Several air charter services operate out of Inuvik, offering flights to delta communities and charter service for hunting, fishing and camping trips.

Highways: Dempster Highway from Dawson City. Winter roads (December into April) to Aklavik and Tuktoyaktuk.

Bus: Service from Dawson City to Inuvik by charter service via Arctic Tour Co., phone (867) 777-4100.

Taxi and **rental cars:** Available.

ACCOMMODATIONS/VISITOR SERVICES

Visitors will find most facilities available, although accommodations should be reserved in advance. Inuvik has 3 hotels, all with dining lounges, and bed and breakfasts. There are also a laundry, post office, territorial liquor store, banks and churches. There are 3 gas stations and a car wash; propane, auto repair and towing are available. Hardware, grocery and general stores, and gift shops are here.

Happy Valley territorial campground; 38 RV sites, electrical hookups, 10 tent pads, hot showers, firewood, water, dump station, fee. Chuk Park territorial campground; 36 sites, electrical hookups, firewood, water, showers, $10 fee. ▲

Arctic Chalet B&B. Lakeside country setting on edge of town. 7 rooms and private cabins with private or shared bath. Clean, comfortable, non-smoking rooms with single, double and queen beds. Laundry facility. Complimentary canoes. A hearty breakfast included in rates. $80–$100. VISA, MasterCard accepted. Phone (867) 777-3535; fax (867) 777-4443. [ADVERTISEMENT]

ATTRACTIONS

Igloo Church, painted white with lines to simulate snow blocks, is on Mackenzie Road as you drive into Inuvik. Inside the church is Inuit painter Mona Thrasher's interpretation of the Stations of the Cross. Visitors are welcome.

Visitors are encouraged to stop by the town office (2 First St.) to sign the guest book and pick up an "Order of the Arctic" adventures certificate. Phone (867) 777-2607 for more information.

Ingamo Hall is a 2-story log community hall that serves the social and recreational needs of Native families. Visitors are welcome. The hall was built by Allan Crich over a 3-year period, using some 1,020 logs that were cut from white spruce trees in the southern part of the Mackenzie River valley and floated down the river to Inuvik.

Tour Western Arctic Communities: Air charter service is available to **AKLAVIK** (pop. 800), an important centre for muskrat harvesting; **TUKTOYAKTUK** (pop. 950), an Inuit village on the Arctic coast and site of oil development; **SACHS HARBOUR** (pop. 158) on Banks Island, an Inuit settlement supported by trapping and some big game outfitters; **PAULATUK** (pop. 255), an Inuit settlement supported by hunting, fishing, sealing and trapping; and **HOLMAN** (pop. 360), an Inuit community on the west coast of Victoria Island, famous for its printmaking. Scheduled air service is also available to **OLD CROW** (pop. 267), an Indian settlement on the Porcupine River in Yukon Territory.

The **Mackenzie River delta**, one of the largest deltas in North America and an important wildlife corridor to the Arctic, is 40 miles/64 km wide and 60 miles/97 km long. A maze of lakes, channels and islands, the delta supports a variety of bird life, fish and muskrats. Boat tours of the Mackenzie River are available.

Boreal Books carries a full range of northern books on history, Native studies, exploration and wildlife. Full selection of area postcards, northern posters and local music. Authorized agent for topo maps, marine charts and air charts. Heritage books. Catalogue available. Mail orders welcome. Open all week. Phone (867) 777-3748, fax (867) 777-4429. [ADVERTISEMENT]

Special Events. The annual Northern Games are held in Inuvik or other western Arctic communities in summer. Visitors are welcome to watch participants compete in traditional Inuit and Déné sports; dances, and crafts are also part of the festival. For information, write Northern Games Assoc., Box 1184, Inuvik, NT X0E 0T0.

KLONDIKE LOOP

Connects: Alaska Hwy. to Taylor Hwy. **Length:** 406 miles
Road Surface: 80% paved, 20% gravel
Season: Hwy. 2 open all year, Hwy. 9 closed in winter
Major Attraction: Dawson City

(See maps, pages 306–307)

	Alaska Hwy. Jct.	Carmacks	Dawson City	Taylor Hwy Jct.	Whitehorse
Alaska Hwy Jct.		103	327	406	10
Carmacks	103		225	303	113
Dawson City	327	225		79	337
Taylor Hwy Jct.	406	303	79		416
Whitehorse	10	113	337	416	

View of Dawson City and a parasailer from the top of the Dome.

(Earl L. Brown, staff)

The "Klondike Loop" refers to the 327-mile/527-km-long stretch of Yukon Highway 2 (the North Klondike Highway, also sometimes called the "Mayo Road"), from its junction with the Alaska Highway north of Whitehorse to Dawson City; the 79-mile/127-km Top of the World Highway (Yukon Highway 9); and the 96 miles/154 kms of the Taylor Highway (Alaska Route 5) that connect with the Alaska Highway near Tok. The North Klondike Highway and Top of the World Highway are logged in this section. The Taylor Highway is logged in the TAYLOR HIGHWAY section following.

Alaska-bound motorists turn off the Alaska Highway north of Whitehorse (**Milepost DC 894.8**); follow the Klondike Highway to Dawson City; ferry from there across the Yukon River; drive west via the Top of the World Highway into Alaska; then take the Taylor Highway south back to the Alaska Highway near Tok (**Milepost DC 1301.7**). Total driving distance is 501 miles/806 km. (Driving distance from Whitehorse to Tok via the Alaska Highway is approximately 396 miles/637 km.)

All of the Klondike Highway between the Alaska Highway junction and Dawson City is asphalt-surfaced. Watch for Yukon Alaska Transport trucks, each carrying up to 50 tons of lead–zinc concentrates, operating between Faro on the Campbell Highway and the port of Skagway on the south Klondike Highway. The trucks are 8½ feet wide and 85 feet long. *Drive with your headlights on at all times.*

Watch for road construction on the Top of the World Highway (Yukon Highway 9). This is a gravel and seal-coated road with some hills. A truly scenic route, but slippery in wet weather with some steep grades and winding sections. The first 19 miles/30 km of the Top of the World Highway is scheduled for new seal coating in 1998, between Kilometreposts 0 and 30 on the Canadian side. Check with the Dawson City Visitor Centre for current road and weather conditions; phone (867) 993-5566. The Taylor Highway (Alaska Route 5) is a narrow gravel road with some steep, winding sections and washboard (see the TAYLOR HIGHWAY section). Both the Taylor and Top of the World highways are not maintained from mid-October to April and the arrival of snow effectively closes the roads for winter. Yukon Highway 2 is open year-round.

Travelers should be aware that the Top of the World Highway (reached by ferry from Dawson City) may not open until late spring. In heavy traffic, there may be a wait of 3 hours or longer for the Yukon River ferry at Dawson City during peak hours. Customs stations are open in summer only, 12 hours a day: 9 A.M. to 9 P.M. (Pacific time). There are no restrooms, services or currency exchanges available at the border.

The highway between Skagway and the Alaska Highway, sometimes referred to as the South Klondike, is also designated Klondike Highway 2 (see KLONDIKE HIGHWAY 2 section for log of that road).

Kilometreposts along the highway to Dawson City reflect distance from Skagway. Our log's driving distances were measured in miles from the junction of the Alaska Highway to Dawson City by our field editor. These mileages were converted into kilometres with the exception of the kilometre distance following Skagway (**S**). That figure reflects the physical location of the kilometrepost and is not necessarily an accurate conversion of the mileage figure.

The route from Whitehorse to Dawson City began as a trail, used first by Natives, trappers and prospectors, and then by stampeders during the Klondike Gold Rush of 1897–98. Steamships also provided passenger service between Whitehorse and Dawson City. A road was built connecting the Alaska Highway with the United Keno Hill Mine at Mayo in 1950. By 1955, the Mayo Road had been upgraded for automobile traffic and extended to Dawson City. In 1960, the last of 3 steel bridges, crossing the Yukon, Pelly and Stewart rivers, was completed. The only ferry crossing remaining is the Yukon River crossing at Dawson City. Mayo Road (Yukon Highway 11) from Stewart Crossing to Mayo, Elsa and Keno was redesignated the Silver Trail in 1985 (see SILVER TRAIL section for road log).

Emergency Medical Services: On Yukon Highway 2 from **Milepost J 0** to **J 55.6** (Whitehorse to Braeburn Lodge), phone Whitehorse Ambulance toll free 1-667-3333 or RCMP 1-667-3333. From **Milepost J 55.6** to **J 169.4** (Braeburn Lodge to Pelly Crossing), phone Carmacks Medical Emergency (867) 863-4444 or RCMP (867) 863-5555. From **Milepost J 169.4** to **J 242.9** (Pelly Crossing to McQuesten River Lodge), phone Mayo Medical Emergency (867) 996-4444 or RCMP (867) 996-5555. From **Milepost J 242.9** to **J 327.2** and on Yukon Highway 9 from **Milepost D 0** to **D 66.1** (McQuesten River Lodge to Dawson City to Alaska border), phone Dawson City Medical Emergency (867) 993-4444 or RCMP (867) 993-5555. From **Milepost D 66.1** to **D 78.8** (Alaska border to Taylor Highway), phone

KLONDIKE LOOP *Milepost J 0 to Milepost J 296*

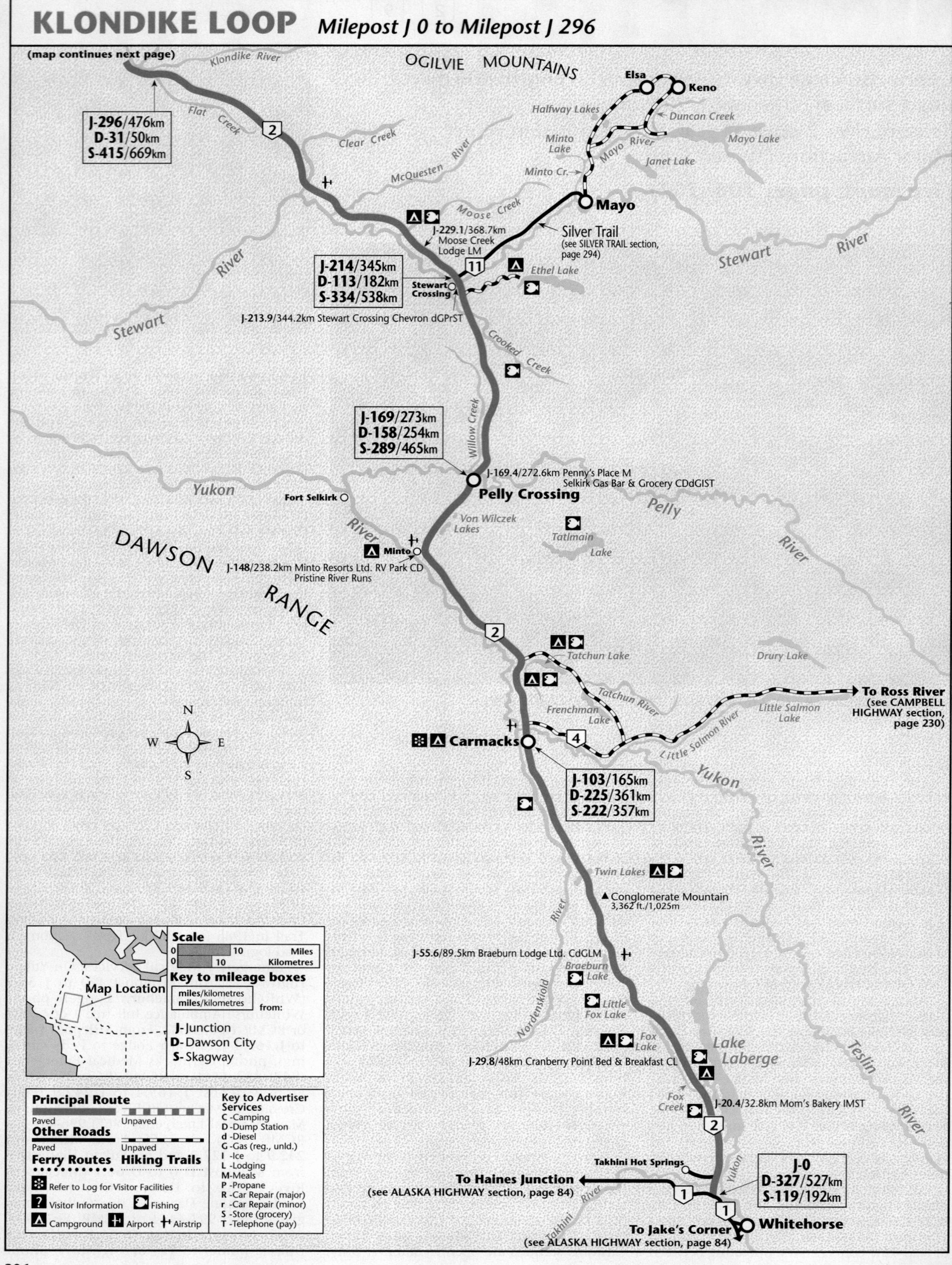

KLONDIKE LOOP *Milepost J 296 to Tetlin Junction, Alaska Highway (includes Taylor Highway)*

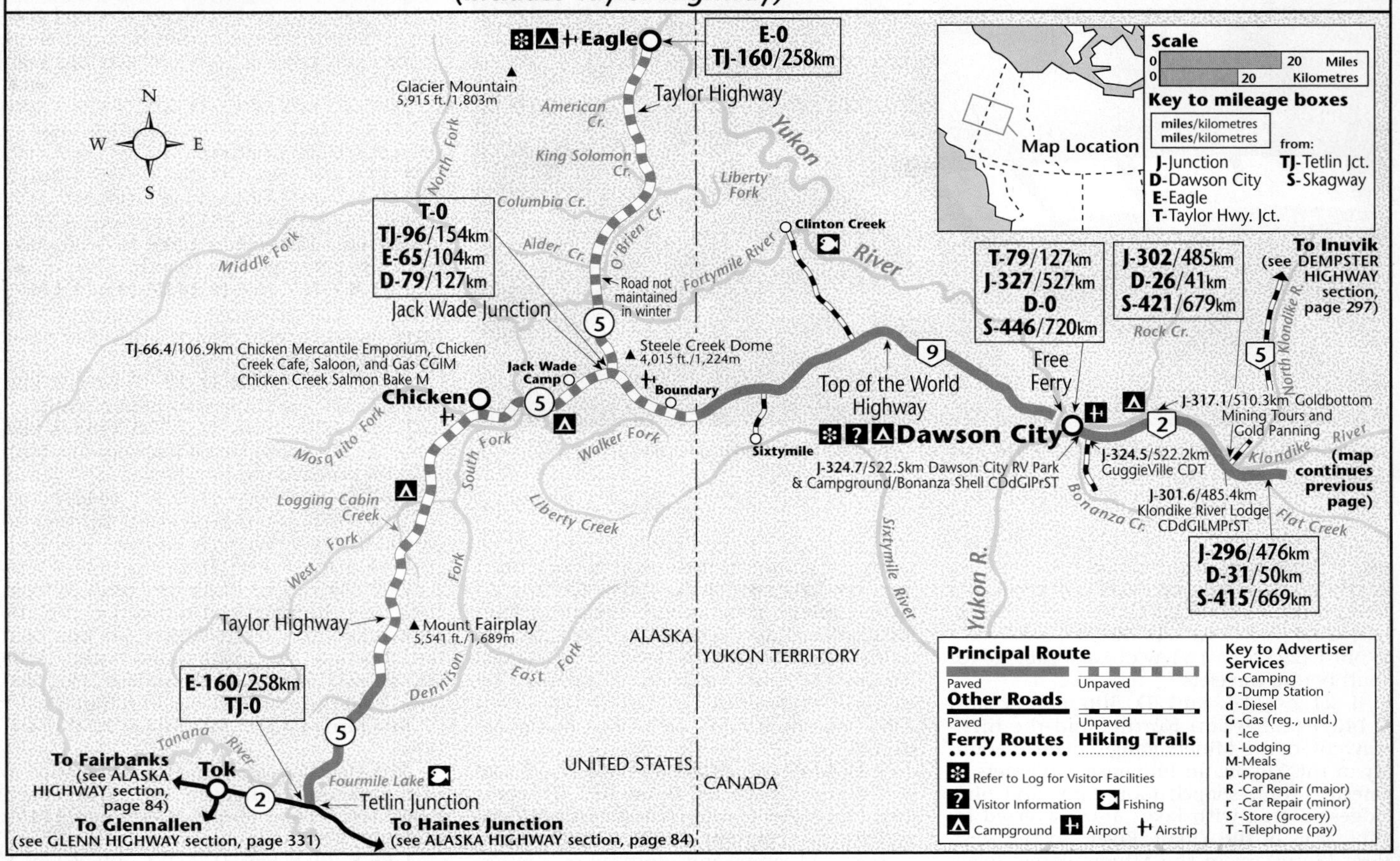

Tok Area EMS at 911 or (907) 883-5111.

Klondike Loop Log

YUKON HIGHWAY 2
This section of the log shows distance from junction with the Alaska Highway (J) followed by distance from Dawson City (D) and distance from Skagway (S). Physical kilometreposts show distance from Skagway.

J 0 D 327.2 (526.6 km) **S 119.2** (191.8 km) **Junction** with the Alaska Highway (**Milepost DC 894.8**).

J 0.6 (1 km) **D 326.6** (525.6 km) **S 119.8** (192.8 km) Road west leads to McPherson subdivision.

J 1 (1.6 km) **D 326.2** (525 km) **S 120.2** (193.4 km) Ranches, farms and livestock next 20 miles/32 km northbound.

J 2.3 (3.7 km) **D 324.9** (522.9 km) **S 121.5** (195.5 km) Takhini River bridge. The Takhini flows into the Yukon River.

J 3.8 (6.1 km) **D 323.4** (520.4 km) **S 123** (197.9 km) Takhini Hot Springs Road. Drive west 6 miles/9.7 km via paved road for Takhini Hot Springs; bed and breakfasts, camping, cafe, trail rides, ski trails in winter. The source of the springs maintains a constant 117°F/47°C temperature and flows at 86 gallons a minute. The hot springs pool averages 100°F/38°C year-round. The water contains no sulfur. The chief minerals present are calcium, magnesium and iron. ▲

Trappers and Indians used these springs around the turn of the century, arriving by way of the Takhini River or the old Dawson Trail. During construction of the Alaska Highway in the early 1940s, the U.S. Army maintained greenhouses in the area and reported remarkable growth regardless of the season.

J 6.7 (10.8 km) **D 320.5** (515.8 km) **S 125.9** (202.6 km) Start odometer test section next 5 km northbound.

J 7 (11.3 km) **D 320.2** (515.3 km) **S 126.2** (203.1 km) Whitehorse rodeo grounds to west. Yukon Rodeo scheduled for July 11–12, 1998.

J 9.4 (15.1 km) **D 317.8** (511.4 km) **S 128.6** (207 km) Sawmill to west.

J 10.7 (17.2 km) **D 316.5** (509.3 km) **S 129.9** (209 km) Shallow Bay Road. Access to Northern Splendor Reindeer Farm. This reindeer farm is 0.8 mile/1.3 km east. The farm is open to visitors in summer from 7 A.M. to 6 P.M.; there is an admission charge. Pull-through drive for big rigs.

J 12.7 (20.4 km) **D 314.5** (506.1 km) **S 131.9** (212.2 km) Horse Creek Road leads east to Lower Laberge Indian village and lakeshore cottages. **Horse Creek**; good grayling fishing from road.

J 15.1 (24.3 km) **D 312.1** (502.3 km) **S 134.3** (216.1 km) Access to bed and breakfast, 0.9 miles/1.5 km west.

J 15.8 (25.4 km) **D 311.4** (501.1 km) **S 135** (217.2 km) Microwave site near road.

J 16.8 (27 km) **D 310.4** (499.5 km) **S 136** (219.1 km) Large turnout to west.

J 17.4 (28 km) **D 309.8** (498.6 km) **S 136.6** (220 km) Lake Laberge to east. The Yukon River widens to form this 40-mile-/64-km-long lake. Lake Laberge was made famous by Robert W. Service with the lines: "The Northern Lights have seen queer sights. But the queerest they ever did see, was that night on the marge of Lake Lebarge I cremated Sam McGee," (from his poem "The Cremation of Sam McGee").

J 18.2 (29.3 km) **D 309** (497.3 km) **S 137.4** (221.1 km) Gravel pit turnout to east.

J 20.3 (32.7 km) **D 306.9** (493.9 km) **S 139.5** (224.5 km) Deep Creek.

J 20.4 (32.8 km) **D 306.8** (493.7 km) **S 139.6** (224.6 km) Turnoff for Lake Laberge Yukon government campground. On the campground road are a small store, bakery, canoe rentals, emergency phone and message post. The campground is situated 1.8 miles/2.9 km east on Lake Laberge next to Deep Creek (see description following).

Lake Laberge Yukon government campground has 22 RV sites, $8 camping fee, resident campground host, group camping area, kitchen shelter, water, boat launch, and fishing for lake trout, grayling and northern pike. Interpretive panels located lakeside at the campground highlight the 30-mile Heritage River. *CAUTION: Storms can blow up quickly and without warning on Lake Laberge, as on other northern lakes. Canoes and small craft stay to the west side of the lake, where the shoreline offers safe refuges. The east side of the*

Interpretive display at Lake Laberge Yukon government campground at Milepost J 20.4. (Earl L. Brown, staff)

lake is lined with high rocky bluffs, and there are few places to pull out. Small craft should not navigate the middle of the lake.

J 20.9 (33.6 km) **D 306.3** (492.9 km) **S 140.1** (225.5 km) View of Lake Laberge for southbound travelers.

J 21.2 (34.1 km) **D 306** (492.4 km) **S 140.4** (225.9 km) Northbound the highway enters the Miners Range, plateau country of the Yukon, an immense wilderness of forested dome-shaped mountains and high ridges, dotted with lakes and traversed by tributaries of the Yukon River. To the west, Pilot Mountain in the Miners Range (elev. 6,739 feet/2,054m) is visible.

J 22.8 (36.7 km) **D 304.4** (489.9 km) **S 142** (228.5 km) **Fox Creek**; grayling, excellent in June and July.

J 23.5 (37.8 km) **D 303.7** (488.7 km) **S 142.7** (229.8 km) Marker shows distance to Dawson City 486 km.

J 26.9 (43.3 km) **D 300.3** (483.3 km) **S 146.1** (235.1 km) Gravel pit turnout to east.

J 28.8 (46.3 km) **D 298.4** (480.2 km) **S 148** (238.2 km) Highway now follows the east shoreline of Fox Lake northbound.

J 29.4 (47.3 km) **D 297.8** (479.2 km) **S 148.6** (239.1 km) Turnout to west on Fox Lake. Sign reads: "In 1883, U.S. Army Lt. Frederick Schwatka completed a survey of the entire length of the Yukon River. One of many geographical features that he named was Fox Lake, which he called Richthofen Lake, after geographer Freiherr Von Richthofen. Known locally as Fox Lake, the name was adopted in 1957. The Miners Range to the west was named by geologist/explorer George Mercer Dawson in 1887 'for the miners met by us along the river.'"

J 29.8 (48 km) **D 297.4** (478.6 km) **S 149** (239.8 km) **Cranberry Point Bed & Breakfast.** Open year-round. Wonderful northern wilderness experience with sauna, gravity showers, oil lamps and sanitized outhouses. Right on beautiful Fox Lake. Woodstove

cooking, full breakfast, other meals arranged! Comfortable guest-room and cabin. Limited dry camping. Radio phone Whitehorse mobile operator, JJ3-9257 Fox Lake Channel. Km 240 Klondike Hwy., Site 15, #91, Whitehorse, YT Y1A 5W8. [ADVERTISEMENT]

J 34.8 (56 km) **D 292.4** (470.6 km) **S 154** (247.8 km) Turnoff west for **Fox Lake** Yukon government campground; 30 RV and 3 tent-only sites, $8 camping fee, kitchen shelter, drinking water and boat launch. Good fishing for lake trout and burbot from the shore at the campground; excellent grayling year-round.

J 35.2 (56.6 km) **D 292** (469.9 km) **S 154.4** (248.5 km) Turnout with view of Fox Lake. Good photo spot.

J 39.8 (64.1 km) **D 287.4** (462.5 km) **S 159** (255.8 km) North end of Fox Lake.

J 42 (67.6 km) **D 285.2** (459 km) **S 161.2** (259.4 km) **Little Fox Lake** to west; lake trout 3 to 8 lbs., fish the islands.

J 43.8 (70.5 km) **D 283.4** (456.1 km) **S 163** (262.1 km) Double-ended turnout with litter barrel to west beside Little Fox Lake. Small boat launch.

J 49.5 (79.7 km) **D 277.7** (446.9 km) **S 168.7** (271.5 km) Large turnout to west.

J 50.1 (80.6 km) **D 277.1** (445.9 km) **S 169.3** (272.4 km) First glimpse of Braeburn Lake for northbound travelers.

J 52.5 (84.5 km) **D 274.7** (442.1 km) **S 171.7** (276.3 km) Gravel pit turnout to east. *CAUTION: Watch for elk along highway.*

J 55.6 (89.5 km) **D 271.6** (437.1 km) **S 174.8** (281.5 km) Braeburn Lodge to west; food, gas, lodging and minor car repairs. One Braeburn Lodge cinnamon bun will feed 4 people. The lodge is also home of the 200-mile/320-km "Cinnamon Bun" Dog Sled Race, held the first weekend in February.

Braeburn Lodge. See display ad this section.

Private Aircraft: Braeburn airstrip to east, dubbed Cinnamon Bun Strip; elev. 2,350 feet/716m; length 3,000 feet/914m; dirt strip; wind sock.

J 55.8 (89.8 km) **D 271.4** (436.8 km) **S 175.1** (281.8 km) Side road to Braeburn Lake.

J 66.3 (106.7 km) **D 260.9** (419.9 km) **S 185.5** (298.5 km) Photo stop; pull-through turnout on east side of highway with information sign about Conglomerate Mountain (elev. 3,361 feet/1,024m). Sign reads: "The Laberge Series was formed at the leading edge of volcanic mud flows some 185 million years ago (Early Jurassic). These flows solidified into sheets several kilometres long and about 1 km wide and 100m thick. This particular series of sheets stretches from Atlin, BC, to north of Carmacks, a distance of about 350 km. Other conglomerates of this series form Five Finger Rapids."

Rock hounds can find pieces of conglomerate in almost any borrow pit along this stretch of highway.

J 71.6 (115.2 km) **D 255.6** (411.3 km) **S 190.8** (307 km) Turnouts on both sides of highway between Twin Lakes. These 2 small lakes, 1 on either side of the road, are known for their beauty and colour.

J 72.3 (116.4 km) **D 254.9** (410.2 km) **S 191.5** (308.2 km) Turnoff to west for **Twin Lakes** Yukon government campground; 8 sites, $8 camping fee, drinking water, boat launch. Lake is stocked. Large parking area with informational panels on the Nordenskiold River. Enjoyable fishing for lake trout, grayling and pike. Good swimming for the *hardy!*

J 81.4 (131 km) **D 245.8** (395.6 km) **S 200.6** (323 km) Large turnout with litter barrel to east at remains of Montague House, a typical early-day roadhouse which offered lodging and meals on the stagecoach route between Whitehorse and Dawson City. A total of 52 stopping places along this route were listed in the Jan. 16, 1901, edition of the *Whitehorse Star* under "On the Winter Trail between White Horse and Dawson Good Accommodations for Travellers." Montague House was listed at Mile 99. Good photo stop.

J 87.4 (140.7 km) **D 239.8** (385.9 km) **S 206.6** (332.5 km) Small lake to west.

J 93.7 (150.8 km) **D 233.5** (375.8 km) **S 212.9** (343.9 km) Plume Trail Agate Road to east, information sign about agate deposits.

J 100.1 (161.1 km) **D 227.1** (365.5 km) **S 219.3** (352.9 km) Carmacks town limits.

J 101.3 (163 km) **D 225.9** (363.5 km) **S 220.5** (354.8 km) **Nordenskiold River** to west was named by Lt. Frederick Schwatka, U.S. Army, for Swedish arctic explorer Erik Nordenskiold. Good grayling and pike fishing all summer. This river, which parallels the highway for several miles, flows into the Yukon River at Carmacks.

J 101.5 (163.3 km) **D 225.7** (363.2 km) **S 220.7** (355.2 km) Pull-through rest area to east with large mural of *Moment at Tantalus Butte*. Litter barrels and outhouses.

Carmacks

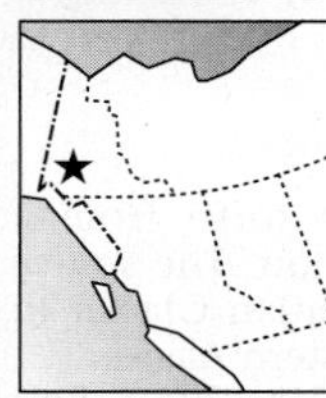

J 102.7 (165.3 km) **D 224.5** (361.3 km) **S 221.9** (357.1 km). Located on the banks of the Yukon River, Carmacks is the only highway crossing of the Yukon River between Whitehorse and Dawson City. **Population:** 489. **Emergency Services: RCMP**, phone (867) 863-5555. **Fire Department**, phone (867) 863-2222. **Nurse**, phone (867) 863-4444. **Ambulance**, phone (867) 863-4444. **Forest Fire Control**, (867) 863-5271.

Private Aircraft: Carmacks airstrip; elev. 1,770 feet/539m; length 5,200 feet/1,585m; gravel; no fuel.

Carmacks was once an important stop for Yukon River steamers traveling between Dawson City and Whitehorse, and it continues as a supply point today for modern river travelers. Carmacks has survived—while other river ports have not—as a service centre for highway traffic and mining interests. Carmacks was also a major stopping point on the old Whitehorse to Dawson Trail.

Carmacks was named for George Carmack, who established a trading post here in the 1890s. Carmack had come North in 1885, hoping to strike it rich. He spent the next 10 years prospecting without success. In 1896, when the trading post went bankrupt, Carmack moved his family to Fortymile, where he could fish to eat and cut timber to sell. That summer, Carmack's remarkable persistence paid off—he unearthed a 5-dollar pan of coarse gold, during a time when a 10-cent pan was considered a good find. That same winter, he extracted more than a ton of gold from the creek, which he renamed Bonanza Creek, and its tributary, Eldorado. When word of Carmack's discovery reached the outside world the following spring, it set off the Klondike Gold Rush.

Traveler facilities include a hotel, motel, bed and breakfast, the village-operated Tantalus Campground on the bank of the Yukon River; restaurant, gas bar, general store (with groceries, bakery and hardware) and laundromat at Hotel Carmacks; post office and bank (both with limited hours), general store, gas bar and dump station at Northern Tutchone Trading Post. The trading post also has some Native crafts for sale. There are also churches, a school, swimming pool, service centre, cafe and a community library. A 1.2-mile/2-km interpretive boardwalk makes it possible to enjoy a stroll along the Yukon River; beautiful view of countryside and Tantalus Butte, gazebo and park at end of trail. Wheelchair accessible.

The Northern Tutchone First Nations Interpretive Centre features archaeological displays on Native life in a series of indoor and outdoor exhibits, and marked interpretive trails.

Carmacks is also an excellent area for rock hounds. There are 5 agate trails in the area, which can double as good, short hiking trails.

Check locally for boat tours to Five Finger and Rink rapids and Fort Selkirk. Fort Selkirk was an important trading post and subsequent RCMP post (see **Milepost J 148.6**). Helicopter service and local canoe and hiking tours available. Abundant fishing in area rivers and lakes: salmon, grayling, northern pike, lake and rainbow trout, whitefish and ling cod.

Klondike Loop Log

(continued)

J 103.2 (166.1 km) **D 224** (360.5 km) **S 222.4** (357.9 km) Yukon River bridge. Turnout and parking area at south end of bridge; 2.3-mile-/3.7-km-long trail to Coal Mine Lake.

J 103.3 (166.2 km) **D 223.9** (360.3 km) **S 222.5** (358.1 km) Northern Tutchone Trading Post with store, gas and diesel, vehicle repair and post office at north end of Yukon River bridge. Fishing tackle and licenses available. Interpretive centre.

J 104.4 (168 km) **D 222.8** (358.6 km) **S 223.6** (359.8 km) **Junction** with Campbell Highway (Yukon Highway 4), also known as Watson Lake–Carmacks Road, which leads east and south to Faro, Ross River and Watson Lake. See CAMPBELL HIGHWAY section.

J 105.1 (169.1 km) **D 222.1** (357.4 km) **S 224.3** (361 km) Side road east to Tantalus Butte Coal Mine; the coal was used in

CARMACKS ADVERTISERS

Hotel Carmacks	Ph. (867) 863-5221
Northern Tutchone Interpretive Centre	Ph. (867) 863-5576
Northern Tutchone Trading Post	Ph. (867) 863-5381
Tantalus Campground	Ph. (867) 863-6271

Cyprus Anvil Mine's mill near Faro for drying concentrates. The butte was named by Lt. Frederick Schwatka because it is seen many times before it is actually reached.

J 105.4 (169.6 km) **D 221.8** (356.9 km) **S 224.6** (361.4 km) Turnout to west with litter barrels, information sign, view of Yukon River Valley.

J 108 (173.8 km) **D 219.2** (352.8 km) **S 227.2** (365.3 km) Side road west to agate site for rock hounds.

J 110 (177 km) **D 217.2** (349.5 km) **S 229.2** (368.8 km) Small lake to west.

J 117.5 (189.1 km) **D 209.7** (337.5 km) **S 236.7** (378.5 km) Pull-through rest area to west with toilets, litter barrels and viewing platform for Five Finger Rapids. Information sign here reads: "Five Finger Rapids named by early miners for the 5 channels, or fingers, formed by the rock pillars. They are a navigational hazard. The safest passage is through the nearest, or east, passage." Stairs (219 steps) and a trail lead down to a closer view of the rapids.

J 118.9 (191.3 km) **D 208.3** (335.2 km) **S 238.1** (380.6 km) Tatchun Creek. Side road to Five Finger Rapids boat-tour operator.

J 119 (191.5 km) **D 208.2** (335.1 km) **S 238.2** (380.8 km) First turnoff (northbound) to east for **Tatchun Creek** Yukon government campground; 12 sites, $8 camping fee, kitchen shelter and drinking water. Good fishing for grayling, June through September; salmon, July through August.

J 119.1 (191.7 km) **D 208.1** (334.9 km) **S 238.3** (380.9 km) Second turnoff (northbound) east for Tatchun Creek Yukon government campground.

J 119.6 (192.5 km) **D 207.6** (334.1 km) **S 238.8** (381.8 km) Side road leads east to **Tatchun Lake.** Follow side road 4.3 miles/6.9 km east to boat launch and pit toilets. Continue past boat launch 1.1 miles/1.8 km for Tatchun Lake Yukon government campground with 20 sites, $8 camping fee, pit toilets, firewood, litter barrels and picnic tables. Fishing for northern pike, best in spring or fall.

This maintained side road continues east past Tatchun Lake to Frenchman Lake, then loops south to the Campbell Highway, approximately 25 miles/40 km distance. The main access to Frenchman Lake is from the Campbell Highway.

Fort Selkirk, reached by boat tour from Milepost J 148.6, was originally a trading post for the Hudson's Bay Co. *(Earl L. Brown, staff)*

J 121.8 (196 km) **D 205.4** (330.6 km) **S 241** (388 km) Tatchun Hill.

J 126.6 (203.7 km) **D 200.6** (322.8 km) **S 245.8** (395.8 km) Large turnout overlooking Yukon River.

J 126.9 (204.2 km) **D 200.3** (322.3 km) **S 246.1** (396.3 km) Highway descends hill, northbound. Watch for falling rocks.

J 132 (212.4 km) **D 195.2** (314.1 km) **S 251.2** (404.5 km) McGregor Creek.

J 135 (217.3 km) **D 192.2** (309.3 km) **S 254.2** (409.4 km) Northbound, first evidence of burn. The June 1995 fire consumed 325,000 acres of forest.

J 136.6 (219.8 km) **D 190.6** (306.7 km) **S 255.8** (411.9 km) Good representation of White River ash layer for approximately one mile northbound. About 1,250 years ago a layer of white volcanic ash coated a third of the southern Yukon, or some 125,000 square miles/323,725 square km, and it is easily visible along many roadcuts. This distinct line conveniently provides a division used by archaeologists for dating artifacts: Materials found below this major stratigraphic marker are considered to have been deposited before A.D. 700, while those found above the ash layer are postdated A.D. 700. The small amount of data available does not support volcanic activity in the White River area during the same period. One theory is that the ash could have spewn forth from a single violent volcanic eruption. The source may be buried under the Klutlan Glacier in the St. Elias Mountains in eastern Alaska.

J 144 (231.7 km) **D 183.2** (294.8 km) **S 263.2** (423.8 km) McCabe Creek.

J 148 (238.2 km) **D 179.2** (288.4 km) **S 267.2** (430.4 km) Private RV park and boat tours. Trees along this portion of highway were burned in a 1995 forest fire. Amazingly, the businesses in the immediate surrounding area were spared.

Pristine River Runs. See display ad this section.

Minto Resorts Ltd. R.V. Park. 1,400-foot Yukon River frontage. Halfway between Whitehorse and Dawson City on the Old Stage Road, Minto was once a steamboat landing and trading post. 27 sites, wide easy access, picnic tables, firepits, souvenirs, fishing licenses, ice, snacks, pop. Coin-op showers and laundry, clean restrooms, dump station and water. Bus tour buffet, reservation only. Caravans welcome. Wildlife viewing opportunities. Try fishing the river. Owned and operated by Yukoners. Come and visit us! See display ad this section. [ADVERTISEMENT]

J 148.6 (239.1 km) **D 178.6** (287.4 km) **S 267.8** (431.4 km) Minto Road, a short loop road, leads west to location of the former riverboat landing and trading post of **MINTO.** Check with Pristine River Runs about river tours to Sheep Mountain and Fort Selkirk leaving daily from Minto Resorts.

FORT SELKIRK, 25 river miles/40 km from here, was established by Robert Campbell in 1848 for the Hudson's Bay Co. In 1852, the fort was destroyed by Chilkat Indians, who had dominated the fur trade of central Yukon—trading here with the Northern Tutchone people (Selkirk First Nation), who used the area as a seasonal home and exchanged furs for the Chilkats' coastal goods—until the arrival of the Hudson's Bay Co. The site was occupied sporadically by traders, missionaries and the RCMP until the 1950s. About 40 buildings—dating from

1892 to 1940—still stand in good repair. A river trip to Fort Selkirk lets travelers see the fort virtually unchanged since the turn of the century. A highly recommended side trip, if time permits. Government preservation and interpretation staff are available on site.

Private Aircraft: Minto airstrip; elev. 1,550 feet/472m; length 5,000 feet/1,524m; gravel.

J 160.3 (258 km) **D 166.9** (268.6 km) **S 279.5** (450.5 km) Side road east to Von Wilczek Lakes.

J 162.8 (262 km) **D 164.4** (264.6 km) **S 282** (454.5 km) Northern limits of damage from 1995 fires.

J 163.4 (263 km) **D 163.8** (263.6 km) **S 282.6** (455.5 km) Rock Island Lake to east.

J 164.2 (264.2 km) **D 163** (262.3 km) **S 283.4** (456.8 km) Turnout. Small lake to west.

J 168.7 (271.5 km) **D 158.5** (255.1 km) **S 287.9** (464 km) Road west to garbage dump.

J 169.4 (272.6 km) **D 157.8** (253.9 km) **S 288.6** (465 km) Side road to **PELLY CROSSING** (pop. about 350). **Emergency Services:** RCMP, phone (867) 537-5555; Nurse, phone (867) 537-4444. Located on the banks of the Pelly River, traveler facilities include take-out food, grocery store, gas, minor vehicle repairs, campground, post office and a bank. There is a school, curling rink, baseball field, swimming pool and church. ▲

Private Aircraft: Pelly Airstrip, elev. 1,870 feet/570m; length 3,000 feet/914m; gravel; no services.

Pelly Crossing became a settlement when the Klondike Highway was put through in 1950. A ferry transported people and vehicles across the Pelly River, where the road eventually continued to Dawson City. Most inhabitants of Pelly Crossing came from historic Fort Selkirk. Today, the restored Fort Selkirk can be visited by boat from Pelly Crossing.

This Selkirk Indian community attracted residents from Minto when the highway to Dawson City was built. School, mission and sawmill located near the big bridge. The local economy is based on hunting, trapping, fishing and guiding. The Selkirk Indian Band has erected signs near the bridge on the history and culture of the Selkirk people.

The Selkirk Heritage Centre, located adjacent to the Selkirk Gas Bar, is a replica of the Big Jonathon House at Fort Selkirk. The centre will offer a self-guided tour of First Nation heritage.

Selkirk Gas Bar. See display ad this section. ▲

Penny's Place. A unique and cozy oasis in the middle of Yukon's vast wilderness, a "must" visit on your travels North. Stop by for your favourite ice cream, a delicious burger, a cold drink while enjoying this quaint spot. Groups reserve for fully catered service. So who is Penny anyhow? Drop by and find out. Wilderness tour packages also available. Phone (867) 537-3011. [ADVERTISEMENT]

J 169.7 (273.1 km) **D 157.5** (253.5 km) **S 288.9** (465.5 km) Pelly River bridge.

J 170.4 (274.2 km) **D 156.8** (252.3 km) **S 289.6** (467 km) Turnout with litter barrel to east. View of Pelly Crossing and river valley. A historical marker here honours the Canadian Centennial (1867–1967). The Pelly River was named in 1840 by explorer Robert Campbell for Sir John Henry Pelly, governor of the Hudson's Bay Co. The Pelly heads near the Northwest Territories border and flows approximately 375 miles/603 km to the Yukon River.

J 171.5 (276 km) **D 155.7** (250.6 km) **S 290.7** (468.6 km) **Private Aircraft:** Airstrip to east; elev. 1,870 feet/570m; length 3,000 feet/914m; gravel. No services.

J 179.6 (289 km) **D 147.6** (237.5 km) **S 298.8** (481.7 km) Pull-through turnout to east.

J 180.9 (291.1 km) **D 146.3** (235.4 km) **S 300.1** (483.8 km) Small lake to west.

J 183.8 (295.8 km) **D 143.4** (230.8 km) **S 303** (488.6 km) Large turnout to west. Bridge over Willow Creek.

J 185.5 (298.5 km) **D 141.7** (228 km) **S 304.7** (491.3 km) Side road west to Jackfish Lake.

J 195.6 (314.8 km) **D 131.6** (211.8 km) **S 314.8** (506.6 km) Access road west to **Wrong Lake** (stocked); fishing.

J 197.4 (317.7 km) **D 129.8** (208.9 km) **S 316.6** (511 km) Turnout with litter barrel to west. Winding descent begins for northbound traffic.

J 203.6 (327.7 km) **D 123.6** (198.9 km) **S 322.8** (521 km) Pull-through turnout to east.

J 205.9 (331.4 km) **D 121.3** (195.2 km) **S 325.1** (524.6 km) **Crooked Creek**; pike; grayling, use flies, summer best.

J 207.2 (333.4 km) **D 120** (193.1 km) **S 326.4** (526.7 km) Pull-through turnout with litter barrel to east at turnoff for **Ethel Lake** Yukon government campground. Drive in 16.6 miles/26.7 km on narrow and winding side road (not recommended for large RVs) for campground; 12 sites, boat launch, fishing. Camping fee $8. ▲

J 213.8 (344.1 km) **D 113.4** (182.5 km) **S 333** (537.3 km) Stewart Crossing government maintenance camp to east.

J 213.9 (344.2 km) **D 113.3** (182.3 km) **S 333.1** (537.5 km) Stewart Crossing Chevron (camping, food), private RV park and campground, and gas station with towing, tires and minor repair, east side of highway. Turnout with information sign west side of highway; Silver Trail information booth (unmanned) contains information on the Silver Trail, or listen to a 5-minute message on the radio at 93.3 FM.▲

In 1886 **STEWART CROSSING** was the site of a trading post established by Arthur Harper, Alfred Mayo and Jack McQuesten to support gold mining in the area. Later a roadhouse was built here as part of the Whitehorse to Dawson overland stage route. Stewart Crossing also functioned as a fuel stop for the riverboats and during the 1930s was a transfer point for the silver ore barges from Mayo. Harper, Mayo and McQuesten are 3 prominent names in Yukon history.

Stewart River bridge at Stewart Crossing. The Stewart River flows into the Yukon River. (Earl L. Brown, staff)

Harper, an Irish immigrant, was one of the first white men to prospect in the Yukon, although he never struck it rich. He died in 1898 in Arizona. (His son, Walter Harper, was on the first complete ascent of Mount McKinley in 1913. Walter died in 1918 in the SS *Princess Sophia* disaster off Juneau.)

Mayo, a native of Maine, explored, prospected and traded in the Yukon until his death in 1924.

McQuesten, like Harper, worked his way north from the California goldfields. Often referred to as the "Father of the Yukon" and a founding member of the Yukon order of Pioneers, Jack Leroy Napoleon McQuesten ended his trading and prospecting days in 1898 when he moved to California. He died in 1909 while in Seattle for the Alaska–Yukon–Pacific Exposition.

Stewart Crossing Chevron. See display ad this section.

J 214.3 (344.9 km) **D 112.9** (181.7 km) **S 333.5** (538 km) Stewart River bridge. The Stewart River flows into the Yukon River upstream from Dawson City.

J 214.4 (345 km) **D 112.8** (181.5 km) **S 333.6** (538.2 km) **Silver Trail (Stewart Crossing) Junction** at north end of Stewart River bridge. Marker shows distance to Dawson 182 km. The Silver Trail Information Centre is located in the restored Binet House in Mayo; phone (867) 996-2926 in summer. The Silver Trail (Yukon Highway 11) leads northeast to Mayo, Elsa and Keno; see SILVER TRAIL section.

J 214.8 (345.7 km) **D 112.4** (180.9 km) **S 334** (538.8 km) View to west of Stewart River and mountains as highway climbs northbound.

J 220.8 (355.3 km) **D 106.4** (171.2 km) **S 340** (545.1 km) Dry Creek.

J 224.4 (361.1 km) **D 102.8** (165.4 km) **S 343.6** (556.2 km) Access to Stewart River to west. Historical information sign about Stewart River. A major tributary of the Yukon River, the Stewart River was named for James G. Stewart, who discovered it in 1849. Stewart was assistant to Robert Campbell of the Hudson's Bay Co.

J 229.1 (368.7 km) **D 98.1** (157.9 km) **S 348.3** (561.9 km) **Moose Creek Lodge**. A must for Yukon travelers! An authentic trapper's cabin and a large selection of Northern books, souvenirs and crafts. In our cozy cafe, enjoy a hearty sourdough pancake breakfast, our scrumptious cinnamon buns, homebaked sourdough bread. Hearty homemade soups, delicious belt-bustin' sandwiches and burgers, mouth-watering homebaked pies. Try our Triple Berry Crumble or Chocolate Heaven ice cream dessert. Meet Max the Mosquito and Murray the Moose! Smokehouse. Cozy rustic economical log cabins. For reservations, phone (867) 667-1324; fax (867) 996-2139; or write Bag 1, Mayo, YT Y0B 1M0. Moose Creek is also serving group tours in their beautiful open-air gazebo, reservations a must. VISA and MasterCard. Your hosts, the Lefler family. [ADVERTISEMENT]

J 229.2 (368.9 km) **D 98** (157.7 km) **S 348.4** (562 km) Moose Creek bridge.

J 229.5 (369.3 km) **D 97.7** (157.2 km) **S 348.7** (562.4 km) Turnout to west at turnoff for Moose Creek Yukon government campground adjacent to **Moose Creek** and Stewart River; good picnic spot. There are 30 RV sites, 6 tent-only sites, kitchen shelter, playground and playfield. Camping fee \$8. Short trail to Stewart River. Good fishing for grayling, 1 to 1¼ lbs.

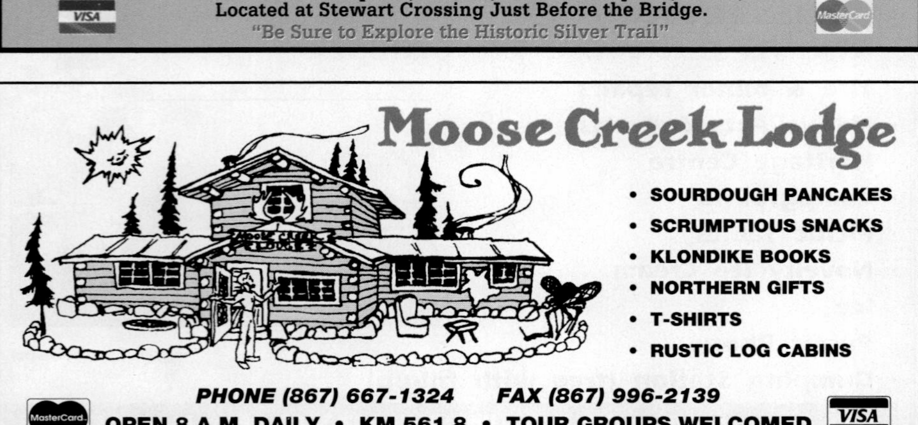

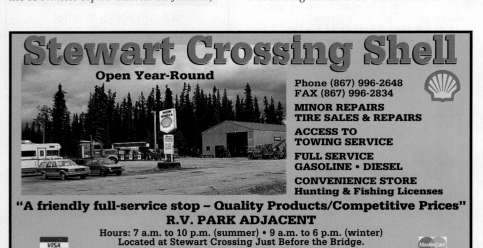

J 242.7 (390.6 km) **D 84.5** (136 km) **S 361.9** (583.7 km) McQuesten River, a tributary of the Stewart River, named for Jack (Leroy Napoleon) McQuesten.

J 242.9 (390.9 km) **D 84.3** (135.7 km) **S 362.1** (584 km) McQuesten, a lodge with cafe, cabins and RV sites. Site of Old McQuesten River Lodge to east. ▲

J 247.5 (398.3 km) **D 79.7** (128.3 km) **S 366.7** (590.1 km) Partridge Creek Farm. Organic vegetables in season.

J 249.3 (401.2 km) **D 77.9** (125.4 km) **S 368.5** (594 km) **Private Aircraft:** McQuesten airstrip 1.2 miles/1.9 km west; elev. 1,500 feet/457m; length 5,000 feet/1,524m; gravel and turf. No services.

J 251.3 (404.4 km) **D 75.9** (122.1 km) **S 370.5** (596.5 km) Clear Creek, access via side road west.

J 260.4 (419.1 km) **D 66.8** (107.5 km) **S 379.6** (612 km) Barlow Lake, access via 0.6-mile-/1-km-long side road west.

J 263.7 (424.4 km) **D 63.5** (102.2 km) **S 382.9** (617.2 km) Beaver Dam Creek.

J 266 (428.1 km) **D 61.2** (98.5 km) **S 385.2** (621 km) Willow Creek.

J 268.5 (432.1 km) **D 58.7** (94.5 km) **S 387.7** (625 km) Flat Hill.

J 268.8 (432.6 km) **D 58.4** (94 km) **S 388** (625.5 km) Gravel Lake to east.

J 272.1 (437.9 km) **D 55.1** (88.7 km) **S 391.3** (630.8 km) Meadow Creek.

J 272.5 (438.5 km) **D 54.7** (88 km) **S 391.7** (631.4 km) Rest area with litter barrel to south.

J 276.5 (445 km) **D 50.7** (81.6 km) **S 395.7** (637.9 km) French Creek.

J 279.7 (450.1 km) **D 47.5** (76.4 km) **S 398.9** (643.1 km) Stone Boat Creek.

J 288.9 (464.9 km) **D 38.3** (61.6 km) **S 408.1** (657.9 km) Rest area.

J 289.3 (465.6 km) **D 37.9** (61 km) **S 408.5** (658.5 km) Geologic point of interest turnout, with information sign, to east overlooking Tintina Trench. This geologic feature, which extends hundreds of miles across Yukon and Alaska, provides visible proof of plate tectonics.

J 295.1 (474.9 km) **D 32.1** (51.7 km) **S 414.3** (667.8 km) Flat Creek.

J 295.9 (476.2 km) **D 31.3** (50.4 km) **S 415.1** (669 km) Klondike River to east.

J 297.6 (478.9 km) **D 29.6** (47.6 km) **S 416.8** (671.9 km) Large turnout to east with historic sign about Klondike River and information sign on Dempster Highway.

J 298 (479.6 km) **D 29.2** (47 km) **S 417.2** (672.5 km) Watch for livestock.

J 301.6 (485.4 km) **D 25.6** (41.2 km) **S 420.8** (678.5 km) **Dempster Corner, junction** of Klondike Highway and the Dempster Highway (Yukon Highway 5). Klondike River Lodge east side of highway just north of the junction; open year-round, food, lodging, camping, gas, diesel and propane. The Dempster Highway leads northeast to Inuvik, NWT. See DEMPSTER HIGHWAY section for log of that road. (Details on the Dempster are also available from the Western Arctic Information Centre in Dawson City.) ▲

Klondike River Lodge. See display ad this section.

J 307.3 (494.5 km) **D 19.9** (32 km) **S 426.5** (687.4 km) Goring Creek.

J 308.4 (496.3 km) **D 18.8** (30.3 km) **S 427.6** (689.2 km) Turnout to north for Rock Creek subdivision and Klondike River access.

J 315.2 (507.3 km) **D 12** (19.3 km) **S 434.4** (700 km) Turnoff to north for Klondike River Yukon government campground, located on Rock Creek near the Klondike River; 38 sites, kitchen shelter, drinking water, playground. Camping fee $8. ▲

J 315.7 (508.1 km) **D 11.5** (18.5 km) **S 434.9** (700.8 km) Dawson City airport to south. **Private Aircraft:** Runway 02-20; elev. 1,211 feet/369m; length 5,000 feet/1,524m; gravel; fuel 80 (in drums at Dawson City), 100, JP4. Flightseeing trips and air charters available.

J 317.1 (510.3 km) **D 10.1** (16.3 km) **S 436.3** (703.4 km) Hunker Creek Road to south. Access to Goldbottom Mining Tours, 9 miles/15km south, a family-run placer mine offering tours, cabins and gold panning; fee charged.

Goldbottom Mining Tours and Gold Panning. See display ad this section.

J 318.4 (512.4 km) **D 8.8** (14.2 km) **S 437.6** (705.4 km) Turnout to south with point of interest sign about Hunker Creek. Albert Hunker staked the first claim on Hunker Creek Sept. 11, 1896. George Carmack made the big discovery on Bonanza Creek on Aug. 17, 1896. Hunker Creek is 16 miles/26 km long, of which 13 miles/21 km was dredged between 1906 and 1966.

J 318.9 (513.2 km) **D 8.3** (13.4 km) **S 438.1** (706.1 km) Bear Creek Road leads to subdivision.

J 319.6 (514.3 km) **D 7.6** (12.2 km) **S 438.8** (707.2 km) Turnout with historic sign about the Yukon Ditch and tailings to north. To the south is Bear Creek historical site, operated by Parks Canada. Open daily in summer, with scheduled tours. Admission: adults $5, youth $2.50, family $12.50, children 12 and under free. Multi-tour program pass available. This 62-acre compound of the Yukon Consolidated Gold Corp. features blacksmith and machinery shops and Gold Room.

J 323.3 (520.3 km) **D 3.9** (6.3 km) **S 442.5** (712 km) Callison industrial area; charter helicopter service, mini-storage, bulk fuel plant and heavy equipment repairs. Restaurant.

J 324.5 (522.2 km) **D 2.7** (4.3 km) **S 443.7** (714 km) Bonanza Creek Road to Discovery Claim and historic Dredge No. 4, largest wooden hull dredge in North America. Restoration of the dredge is under way. Interpretive centre on site; scheduled tours daily June through August. Admission: adults $2.25, children 12 and under free. Multi-tour pass available. Bonanza Creek Road is maintained for 10 miles/16.1 km. Commercial RV park and gold panning at junction. ▲

GuggieVille. Good Sam. This clean, attractive campground is built on dredge tailings at the former site of the Guggenheim's mining camp. 72 RV sites with water and electricity, 28 unserviced sites,

public showers ($2 each). Car wash, dump station and laundromat are available. A mining display is open to the public free of charge. Gold panning discount for those staying at GuggieVille. Phone (867) 993-5008. Fax (867) 993-5006. Winter phone/fax (250) 558-3334. [ADVERTISEMENT] ▲

J 324.7 (522.5 km) **D 2.5** (4 km) **S 443.9** (715.3 km) Campground, gas station and store. ▲

Dawson City R.V. Park & Campground

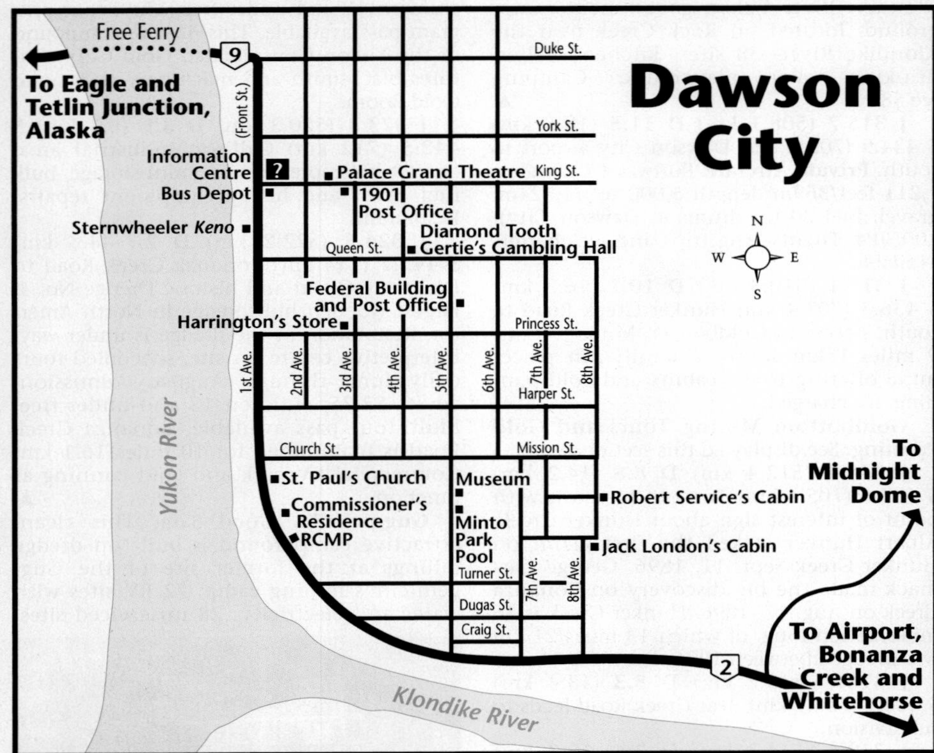

and **Bonanza Shell.** See display ad this section. ▲

J 324.8 (522.7 km) **D 2.4** (3.9 km) **S 444** (715.5 km) Klondike River bridge.

J 325.3 (523.5 km) **D 1.9** (3.1 km) **S 444.5** (716.4 km) Large turnout with information sign and map.

J 325.8 (524.3 km) **D 1.4** (2.3 km) **S 445** (717.2 km) Dome Road to north leads 4.5 miles/7.2 km to Dome Mountain (elev. 2,911 feet/887m), which offers views of Dawson City, the Yukon and Klondike rivers, Bonanza Creek and the Ogilvie Mountains.

J 325.9 (524.5 km) **D 1.3** (2.1 km) **S 445.1** (717.4 km) Trans North Helicopter base on left northbound; Klondike goldfield tours. Rock face on right northbound is known locally as Crocus Bluff; short, interpretive foot trail leads to viewpoint overlooking Klondike River and Dawson City.

J 326.1 (524.8 km) **D 1.1** (1.8 km) **S 445.3** (717.7 km) Fifth Avenue. Turnout with sign about the Klondike River to south: "With headwaters in the Ogilvie Mountains, the Klondike River and its tributaries gave birth to the world's greatest gold rush—the Klondike Gold Rush of '98."

J 327.2 (526.6 km) **D 0 S 446.4** (719.5 km) Dawson City, ferry at Yukon River. *Description of Dawson City follows. Log of Klondike Loop continues on page 324.*

Dawson City

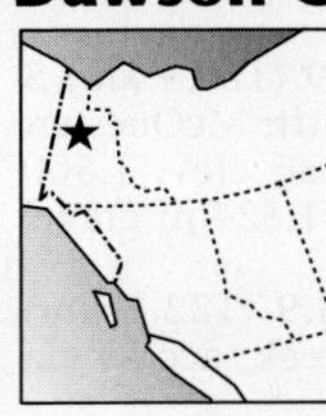

J 327.2 (526.6 km) **D 0 S 446.4** (719.5 km) Located 165 miles/266 km south of the Arctic Circle on the Yukon River at its junction with the Klondike River. **Population:** 2,019. **Emergency Services:** RCMP, 1st Avenue S., phone (867) 993-5555. **Fire Department,** phone (867) 993-2222. **Nursing station,** phone (867) 993-4444. **Ambulance,** phone (867) 993-4444.

Visitor Information: Visitor Reception Centre, operated by Tourism Yukon and Parks Canada, at Front and King streets, is housed in a replica of the 1897 Alaska Commercial Co. store. Accommodation information and a Dawson City street map are available. Video disks on a variety of subjects, particularly Dawson attractions and history. Walking tours are part of the daily schedule. Open daily, 8 A.M. to 8 P.M. mid-May to mid-September, phone (867) 993-5566, fax (867) 993-6449. Dawson City has lots to do and see. If you want to take it all in, plan for 3 days to cover most of the attractions.

The Dempster Highway and Northwest

DAWSON CITY

"THE HEART OF THE KLONDIKE GOLD RUSH!"

Diamond Tooth Gerties
Canada's Only Northern Casino

Discover the delights of Diamond Tooth Gerties gambling hall, Canada's oldest and most unique casino. Meet Diamond Tooth Gertie and The Gold Rush Can Can girls while trying a hand at blackjack, roulette, slot machines, and poker. Shows nightly at 8:30, 10:30 & 12:30 mid May to September. Admission $5.00.

Outstanding Tours & Exhibits
Take a step back in time!

Join us for the Klondike Goldrush Centennial celebrations! 1998 brings a year full of unique activities, commemorating an event that SHOOK THE WORLD. Thrill to the excitement of rich, living history around every corner. National historic treasures and a museum & informative guided tours without equal.

Palace Grand Theatre
Gaslight Follies Revue

There is no theatre like the Palace Grand anywhere in the North. The Gaslight Follies show is written to reflect the lavish and exciting times of the gold rush era. It is two hours of high energy, musical comedy, performed in one of the most magnificent theatres ever built! It's a must see!

DON'T MISS WHAT TRAVELLERS CALL...
"The best part of our northern vacation... it takes a week to see it all!"

Send for your Dawson City Information Package today!
P.O.Box 389M, Dawson City, Yukon, Canada Y0B 1G0
Tel: (867) 993-5575 Fax: (867) 993-6415
e mail: KVA@Dawson.net web: http://www.DawsonCity.com

ACCOMMODATIONS

DAWSON CITY

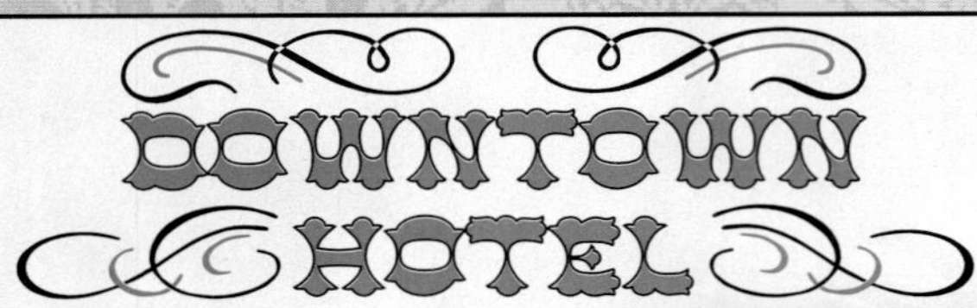

- Modern Comfortable Rooms
- Jacuzzi • Plug-ins
- Telephones • Cable TV
- Complimentary Airport Transfers
- Grace's Gift Shop
- Sterndeck BBQ
- Locally Owned & Operated by Yukoners

PROUD SUPPORTER

Box 780, Dawson City, Yukon Canada Y0B 1G0 Ph: (867) 993-5346 Fax: (867) 993-5076

RESERVATIONS ONLY: 1-800-661-0514

Major Credit Cards Accepted

E-mail: downtown@yknet.yk.ca Homepage: www.yukonweb.com/tourism/downtown

• Owned & Operated year-round by Yukoners •

Sluice Box Lounge
Air Conditioned

Bonanza Dining Room
Featuring northern specialties
Pleasant surroundings, excellent service

We are northern hospitality!

Open Year-Round • All Modern Rooms • Suites • Kitchenettes
Phones • Color TV • Laundry • Winter Plug-Ins
All Major Credit Cards Accepted

3rd Avenue & Princess Street P.O. Box 338 Dawson City, Yukon Y0B 1G0
FOR RESERVATIONS CALL (867) 993-5451 • Fax 993-5256
Northern B.C. & Yukon 1-800-661-0518 Ak. 1-800-764-ELDO

DAWSON CITY

TRIPLE JJJ HOTEL

- Hotel Rooms • Executive Suite
- Cabins with Kitchenettes/Full Baths
- Air-Conditioned Lounge & Restaurant
- Licensed Outdoor Patio
- Coin Laundry, Satellite TV
- Complimentary Airport Limo

Ak: 1-800-764-3555 • B.C./YT 1-800-661-0405 • E-mail: JJJ@dawson.net

5th AVE & QUEEN, BOX 359, DAWSON CITY, Y0B 1G0 • PH: (867) 993-5323 • FAX: (867) 993-5030

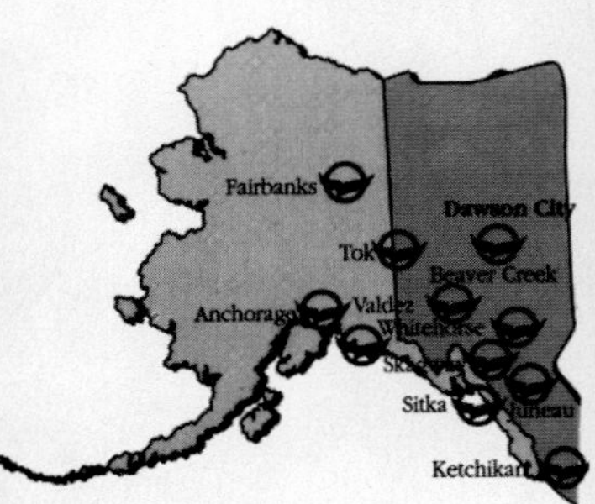

In Dawson City & Almost Everywhere Else.

Nobody knows the Yukon and Alaska like Westmark Hotels. We've got the locations like Dawson City, the quality you desire and the service you expect. Comfortable rooms and warm northern hospitality are yours at every Westmark Hotel. Call us today for information about locations, rates and room availability in the Yukon or anywhere in Alaska.

- Full Service Locations
- Free Parking
- Convenient Locations
- Restaurants & Lounges
- Meeting Facilities
- Alaska Airlines Miles
- Guest Rewards Points

Ask About Our Summer Explorer Rates

DAWSON CITY

Fifth & Harper Streets
P.O. Box 420
Dawson City, Yukon Territory Y0B1G0

867-993-5542

Central Reservations
1-800-544-0970
www.westmarkhotels.com

ACCOMMODATIONS

DAWSON CITY

GOLD CITY TOURS

Sightseeing Tours
Dawson City
Klondike Goldfields
Midnight Dome
993-5175

"Locally owned & operated"
Open year-round

Tickets & Reservations
All Airlines & Hotels
Alaska & B.C. Ferries
Cruises & Car Rentals
993-6424

GOLD CITY TRAVEL

DEMPSTER HIGHWAY VAN & BUS CHARTERS, CROSSING THE ARCTIC CIRCLE

P.O. Box 960, Dawson City, Yukon Y0B 1G0 • FAX 993-5261
Located on Front Street, Across from the Steamship "Keno"

THE ROBERT SERVICE SHOW

starring
TOM BYRNE

AUTOGRAPHED TAPES & VIDEOS AVAILABLE

"Storytelling at its best"

This unique show is an absolute must see for all lovers of Robert Service works and will be a highlight of your trip.

Robert Service Cabin on 8th Avenue

Dates and Showtimes Available at the Visitors Reception Centre

Admission tickets available at site. $7.00 tax included, $3.00 for children.

Top of the World Golf Course

Across the Yukon River on the Top of the World Highway
5 miles from Dawson City

COME TEE OFF AT MIDNIGHT ON CANADA'S MOST NORTHERN GOLF COURSE WITH GRASS GREENS

• Public 9 holes • Driving Range • Power Cart & Equipment Rentals
• Pro Shop • Licensed Lounge • Snack Bar
• Unserviced Overnight RV Parking for Golfers
• Shuttle Service Available

Located in the scenic Yukon River Valley with its strategically placed bunkers & water hazards. It's challenging & enjoyable for all levels of golfers.

Box 189, Dawson City, YT Y0B 1G0 **Tel (867) 667-1472**

Grilled Smoked Salmon

Yukon River Cruise

For reservations: FRONT STREET BIRCH CABIN
Box 859, Dawson City, Yukon Y0B 1G0
Ph: (867) 993-5482 Winter: (907) 883-3292

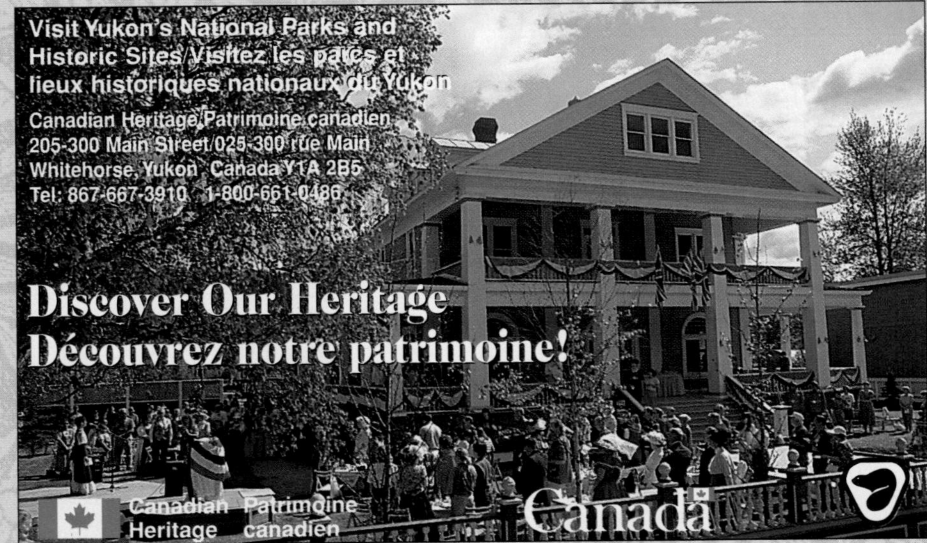

Visit Yukon's National Parks and Historic Sites/Visitez les parcs et lieux historiques nationaux du Yukon
Canadian Heritage/Patrimoine canadien
205-300 Main Street/025-300 rue Main
Whitehorse, Yukon Canada Y1A 2B5
Tel: 867-667-3910 1-800-661-0486
Discover Our Heritage
Découvrez notre patrimoine!
Canadian Heritage
Patrimoine canadien
Canada

Fishwheel
CHARTER
Daily 2 Hour Boat Tours
Tea & Bannock
Fishwheels • Area History
Han Culture • Adventure
Historic Sites • Wildlife
Tickets at the Trading Post and On-Site
4 trips per day.
993-6857
E-mail:
fishwheel@dawsoncity.net
Box 891, Dawson City
YT, Canada Y0B 1G0

ATTRACTIONS • SHOPPING • SERVICES

When in town visit the . . .

DAWSON CITY MUSEUM

Open 10 a.m. - 6 p.m.
Victoria Day - Labour Day

KINGS OF THE KLONDIKE GALLERY
City Life Gallery - Visible Storage
Movies - Demonstrations
"Meet a Klondike Character"
Gift Shop
Resource Library
Historic Train Collection

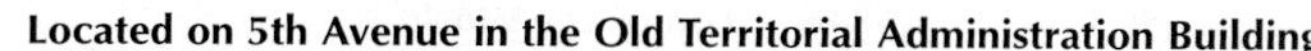

Located on 5th Avenue in the Old Territorial Administration Building
Ph: (867) 993-5291 • FAX: (867) 993-5839 • email: dcmuseum@yknet.yk.ca
P.O. Box 303, Dawson City, Yukon Y0B 1GO

KLONDIKE NUGGET AND IVORY SHOP LTD.

Dawson City's Oldest Jewellery Store, Established 1904.

Phone: 867•993•5432

Corner of Front & Queen St.
Box 250, Dawson City, Yukon Y0B 1G0

Nugget Jewellery handcrafted on premises, gifts, fine china, carvings, mammoth ivory jewellery.
Open year-round.
Mail orders gladly accepted.
Visa, M/C, American Express

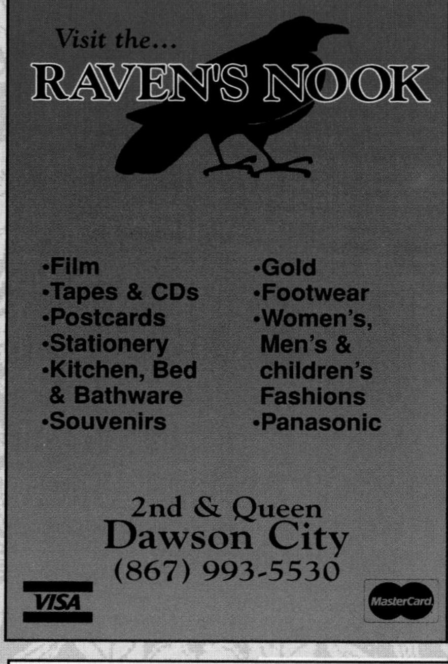

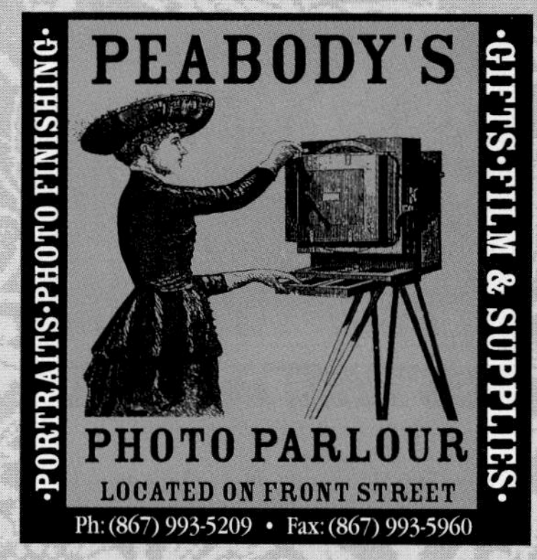

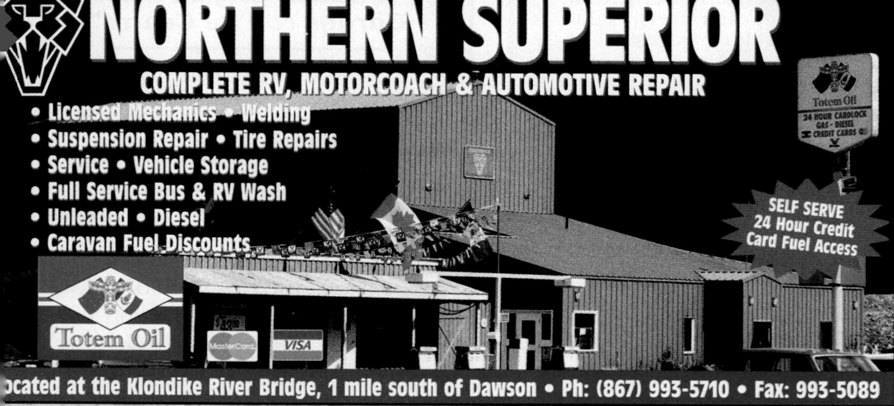

DAWSON CITY ADVERTISERS

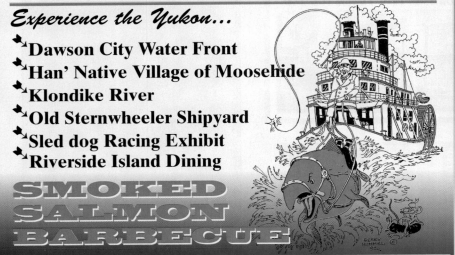

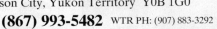

At the height of the Klondike Gold Rush, Dawson City's population fluctuated between 30,000 and 40,000 people.

Territories Information Centre is located in the B.Y.N. (British Yukon Navigation) Building on Front Street, across from the Yukon visitor centre; open 9 A.M. to 8 P.M., June to September. Information on Northwest Territories and the Dempster Highway. Phone (867) 993-6167, fax 993-6334.

Elevation: 1,050 feet/320m. **Climate:** There are 20.9 hours of daylight June 21, 3.8 hours of daylight on Dec. 21. Mean high in July, 72°F/22.2°C. Mean low in January, -30.5°F/-34.7°C. First fall frost end of August, last spring frost end of May. Annual snowfall 59.8 inches. **Radio:** CBC 560; CFYT-FM 106, CKYN-FM 96.1 (summer visitor station). **Television:** CBC Anik Channel 7 and 14 other channels via cable. **Newspaper:** *Klondike Sun* (semi-monthly) and *Dawson City Insider* (weekly).

Private Aircraft: Dawson City airport located 11.5 miles/18.5 km southeast (see **Milepost J 315.7**). Customs available.

Historically, Dawson City dates from the discovery of gold on a Klondike River tributary (Rabbit Creek, renamed Bonanza Creek) in 1896. Previously, the site had been a Native fish camp. There were several hundred prospectors in the Fortymile area before the big strike, and most of them swarmed over the Klondike creeks, staking claims long before stampeders began trickling into the country the following year.

Dawson City was Yukon's first capital, when the Yukon became a separate territory in 1898. But by 1953, Whitehorse—on the railway and the highway, and with a large airport—was so much the hub of activity that the federal government moved the capital from Dawson City, along with 800 civil servants, and years of tradition and pride. Some recompense was offered in the form of a road linking Whitehorse with the mining at Mayo and Dawson City. With its completion, White Pass trucks replaced White Pass river steamers.

New government buildings were built in Dawson, including a fire hall. In 1962 the federal government reconstructed the Palace Grand Theatre for a gold rush festival that featured the Broadway musical *Foxy,* with Bert Lahr. A museum was established in the Administration Building and tours and entertainments were begun.

Dawson City was declared a national historic site in the early 1960s. Parks Canada is

Restored historical structures house Dawson City businesses. (© Eero Sorila)

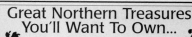

currently involved with 35 properties in Dawson City. Many buildings have been restored, some reconstructed and others stabilized. Parks Canada offers an interpretive program each summer for visitors to this historic city.

Dawson City is hosting a "Decade of Centennials" to 2002. Highlights include the Klondike Gold Rush Centennial and the completion of the White Pass and Yukon Route Railway. For further information on events, contact the Klondike Centennial Society, Bag 1996, Dawson City, YT Y0B 1G0.

ACCOMMODATIONS/VISITOR SERVICES

Accustomed to a summer influx of visitors, Dawson has modern hotels and motels (rates average $75 and up) and several bed and breakfasts. The community has a bank, automatic teller machine (cash advances on MasterCard and VISA are also available at Diamon Tooth Gerties Casino), restaurants, 4 laundromats (3 with showers), 2 grocery stores (with bakeries), deli/grocery store, general stores, souvenir shops, churches, art gallery, post office, government offices, government liquor store, nursing station and doctor services, information centre, hostel, swimming pool, tennis, basketball and plenty of entertainment. Many Dawson City merchants abide by the Fair Exchange Policy, offering travelers an exchange rate within 4 percent of the banks'. Dawson City's hotels and motels fill up early, especially at times of special events. Reservations are a must from June through August.

Bear Creek Bed & Bannock. First Nation family offers "a touch of culture." This 4 bedroom, full facility bed and breakfast is separate from the main home. We offer a continental breakfast with fresh bannock. Elder and family discounts in a quiet, natural setting 10 minutes from town. Handicap accessible. Reservations recommended. (867) 993-6765 or (867) 993-5605 or fax (867) 993-6532. VISA/ MasterCard. [ADVERTISEMENT] ♿

5th Avenue Bed and Breakfast. Located adjacent to the museum overlooking Victory Gardens. A modern home with a historic finish, serving a hearty, healthy, all-you-can-eat breakfast. We guarantee comfort, cleanliness and courteous service along with the

most convenient location in town. VISA. Call or write Larry and Pat Vezina, Box 722, Dawson City, YT Y0B 1G0. Phone (867) 993-5941. [ADVERTISEMENT]

Klondike Kate's Cabins and Restaurant. We offer you charming, clean and affordable accommodations with private bath. Located near all major attractions. Enjoy the friendly atmosphere of our restaurant, set in a 1904 historic building. Dine inside or on our outdoor patio. Full-service, fully licensed restaurant with Canadian and ethnic foods. Espresso coffees. Box 417, Dawson City, YT Y0B 1G0. Phone (867) 993-6527. Fax (867) 993-6044. [ADVERTISEMENT]

White Ram Manor Bed & Breakfast. Look for the pink house at 7th and Harper.

Centrally located. A clean, comfortable, friendly home-away-from-home. Full breakfast. Laundry. Guest kitchen. Barbecue/ picnic sun deck area. Hot tub. Our guarantee: If there is a room in Dawson, we'll find it for you. (Reservations recommended.) VISA, MasterCard. Box 302, Dawson City, YT Y0B 1G0. Phone (867) 993-5772. Fax (867) 993-6509. Internet: www.dawson.net/ whiteram. [ADVERTISEMENT]

There are 2 Yukon government (YTG) campgrounds in the Dawson area. Yukon

Dawson City Museum, housed in the renovated Territorial Administration Building on 5th Avenue. (Earl L. Brown, staff)

River YTG campground is across the Yukon River (by ferry) from town, adjacent to the west-side ferry approach (see **Milepost D 0.2** on Top of the World Highway log, following Dawson City section). Klondike River YTG campground is southeast of town near the airport (see **Milepost J 315.2**). Private RV parks in the Dawson area include Gold Rush Campground, downtown at 5th and York; GuggieVille, east of town at **Milepost J 324.5**; and Dawson City R.V. Park and Campground at **Milepost J 324.7**. ▲

TRANSPORTATION

Air: Dawson City airport is 11.5 miles/18.5 km southeast of the city. Alkan Air provides scheduled service to Inuvik, NWT, Old Crow, Mayo and Whitehorse. Air North connects Dawson City with Whitehorse (daily service in summer); with Old Crow and Juneau (3 times weekly in summer); and Fairbanks (4 times weekly in summer). Charter and flightseeing tours available from Bonanza Aviation. Helicopter tours from Trans North Air and Fireweed.

Ferry: The Yukon government operates a free ferry, the *George Black,* across the Yukon River from about the third week in May to mid-October (depending upon breakup and freezeup). The ferry operates 24 hours a day (except for Wednesdays, 5–7 A.M. when it is shut down for servicing), and departs Dawson City on demand. The ferry carries vehicles and passengers across to the public campground and is the only connection to the Top of the World Highway (Yukon Highway 9). Be prepared to wait 3 hours or more during peak traffic periods (7–11 A.M. and 4–7 P.M. daily). Shut off all propane appliances and follow directions from ferry personnel when loading and unloading. Tour bus traffic has priority 6–9 A.M. and 5–9 P.M.; fuel truck traffic has priority 7 P.M. to 6 A.M. Phone (867) 993-5441 or 993-5344 for more information.

Bus: Service between Whitehorse and Dawson City by Norline coaches; 3 times weekly June through September. Service between Inuvik, NWT, and Dawson City available by charter only, contact Gold City Tours. Service from Whitehorse via Dawson City to Tok, AK, by Alaska Direct Buslines; weekly. Phone (800) 770-6652.

Taxi: Airport taxi service available from downtown hotels and bed and breakfasts. Scheduled and charter limo service available from Gold City Tours.

Rental Car: Car and truck rentals at Norcan, located in the Northern Superior Bldg., and Budget Rent-A-Car, located on Craig Street.

Boat: Service to Eagle, AK, on the *Yukon Queen.* Canoe rentals available from Dawson Trading Post and at the hostel across the river.

ATTRACTIONS

Take a Walking Tour. Town-core tours leave the Visitor Reception Centre 2 times daily in summer. The Fort Herchmer Northwest Mounted Police walking tour starts outside the restored Commissioner's Residence on Front Street. This handsome building was once the residence of Hon. George Black, M.P., Speaker of the House of Commons, and his famous wife, Martha Louise, who walked to Dawson City via the Trail of '98 and stayed to become the First Lady of the Yukon. Pierre Berton's boyhood home has also been restored. Berton is the author of *Klondike Lost*, an account of the Klondike Gold Rush. Pick up a schedule of daily events at the Visitor Reception Centre.

Take a Bus Tour. Motorcoach and van tours of Klondike creeks, goldfields and Dawson City are available; inquire at Gold City Tours (ask about step-on guide service, too). For a panoramic view of Dawson City, the Klondike River, Bonanza Creek and Yukon River, take the bus or drive the 5 miles/8 km to the top of Dome Mountain (elev. 2,911 feet/887m).

Take a River Tour: Yukon River Cruises offers tours aboard the miniature stern-wheeler launch *Yukon Lou,* leaving the dock behind Birch Cabin booking office near SS *Keno* at 1 P.M. daily in summer and traveling to Pleasure Island and the stern-wheeler graveyard. Cruise takes $1^1/_2$ hours. Fishwheel Charter offers guided 2-hour river tours 4 times a day; tickets at the Trading Post. Westours (Grayline Yukon) operates the *Yukon Queen* on the Yukon River between Dawson City and Eagle, AK; check with the Grayline Yukon office about tickets. One-way and round-trip passage is sold on a space-available basis. The trip takes 4 hours downstream to Eagle, and 6 hours back to Dawson.

Ancient Voices Wilderness Camp. Let your adventurous spirit soar as you discover nature's splendor in an authentic First Nation's camp. Three northern Native cultures share their traditional way of life in a wilderness setting along the banks of the mighty Yukon River. Rustic cabins, wall tents, meals and cultural activities provided. Day, overnight or package trips available from Dawson City, transportation provided via our Ancient Voices *"River Dancer"* boats. Tickets sold locally at the Trading Post on 5th Ave. Canoe travelers from Whitehorse to Dawson have enthusiastically remarked, "We have discovered an oasis in the Yukon!" Group discounts. VISA, MasterCard accepted. Mailing address: Box 679, Dawson City, YK Y0B 1G0. Phone (867) 993-5605. Fax (867) 993-6532. Internet: www.yukon.net/avw-camp. [ADVERTISEMENT]

Cruise the Yukon River. Cruise from Dawson City down the famous Yukon River to Eagle, Alaska, aboard the MV *Yukon Queen.* Retrace the old stern-wheeler route of this historic Gold Rush area as you cruise past abandoned settlements among the forested hills. A hearty prospector's meal is included. Daily departures. Roundtrip fare is $135 U.S. per person. Prices subject to change. Phone (867) 993-5599. [ADVERTISEMENT]

Pleasure Island Restaurant. Don't miss the riverboat cruise on the MV *Yukon Lou* (refurbished 1996). See the old stern-wheeler shipyard, historic Native village of Moosehide and stop in at Pleasure Island for an all-you-can-eat smoked salmon barbecue.

Dinner includes garden fresh salad and slow-baked potatoes, topped off by homemade chocolate cake. Steak available on request. Lunch cruises include a soup and salad buffet. This is a "must" when in Dawson City. For reservations phone (867) 993-5482 or (907) 883-3292 (September–May). Group rates. [ADVERTISEMENT]

Fishwheel Charter Services. A tour with a personal touch! Don't miss your chance to hear about the peoples of the area and of course the majestic Yukon River. The historic sites, salmon runs and stories gone by. Come and relax, laugh, and take home an experience that will last a lifetime. Contact FCS (867) 993-6857. E-mail: fishwheel@dawsoncity.net. [ADVERTISEMENT]

Visit the Palace Grand Theatre. This magnificently reconstructed theatre, now a national historic site, is home to the "Gaslight Follies," a turn-of-the-century entertainment. Performances nightly except

Tuesday, from mid-May to mid-September. Arizona Charlie Meadows opened the Palace Grand in 1899, and today's visitors, sitting in the curtained boxes around the balcony, will succumb to the charm of this beautiful theatre. Tours of the building are conducted once daily by Parks Canada, June through September. Films and presentations daily in summer.

Diamond Tooth Gertie's Casino, open daily 7 P.M. to 2 A.M. mid-May to mid-September, has Klondike gambling tables (specially licensed in Yukon), 56 "Vegas-style" slot machines, bar service and floor shows nightly. You may have a soft drink if you prefer, and still see the cancan girls present their floor show. Persons under 19 not admitted. Gertie's hosts Yukon Talent Night in August.

Visit the Dawson City Museum. Housed in the renovated Territorial Administration Building on 5th Avenue, the museum is open daily from 10 A.M. to 6 P.M., mid-May through early September; by appointment year-round. Featured are the Kings of the Klondike and City Life Galleries, hourly audiovisual and dramatic presentations, and the museum's collection of narrow-gauge locomotives, including a Vauclain-type Baldwin engine, the last one in existence in Canada. Weekly lecture series during summer; check for schedule. The films "City of Gold" and "The Yukoner" are shown daily. A selection of silent film serials, news and documentary reels from 1903 to 1929 is shown in the gallery. Also take part in the "Meet a Klondike Character" show and explore the "Klondike Gold" CD Rom.

The museum has a gift shop, wheelchair ramp, resource library, genealogy service and an extensive photography collection. A nominal admission fee is charged. For more information write the museum at Box 303, Dawson City, YT Y0B 1G0; phone (867) 993-5291, fax 993-5839. ♿

SS *Keno* National Historic Site. The SS *Keno* was the last steamer to run the Yukon River when she sailed from Whitehorse in 1960 to her present berth on the riverbank next to the bank. Although she is closed to the public, an interpretive display is set up beside the site.

Visit Robert Service's Cabin. Highly recommended. On the hillside on 8th Avenue, the author–bank clerk's cabin has been restored by Parks Canada. Stories and poetry recitals are offered daily in summer. Photographers are welcomed, but no videotaping. Visitors come from every part of the world to sign the guest book on the rickety desk where Service wrote his famous poems, including "The Shooting of Dan McGrew" and "The Cremation of Sam McGee." Open daily. Admission charged.

Visit the Historic Post Office, where you may buy stamps; all first-class mail sent from here receives the old hand-cancellation stamp. Open daily.

Fire Fighters Museum, located at the fire hall at 5th Avenue and King Street, is open Tuesday through Sunday, 12:30 to 5:30 P.M.

Visit the Jack London Interpretive Centre: Along 8th Avenue and past Service's home is Jack London's cabin, built from half of the logs saved from the original cabin in the Bush where the writer stayed on his way to the Klondike. Also at the site are a cache for perishables and a museum with photos and memorabilia. Interpretation daily at noon and 2:15 P.M. mid-May to mid-September. No admission charged. Dick North, author of *Cabin Fever—the Story of Jack London in Alaska and Yukon,* is curator and consultant at the cabin.

Pierre Berton Residence, located on 8th Avenue, was once home of the famous Canadian author. Now used for a writer-in-residence program. View the grounds and interpretive signage placed by the Klondike Visitors Association.

Special Events. Dawson City hosts a number of unique and unusual celebrations during the year. 1998 brings a wealth of activity centered around the 100th anniversary of the Great Klondike Gold Rush.

The Commissioner's Ball is held June 13, 1998. This gala event, commemorating Yukon becoming a territory in 1898, features turn-of-the-century fashion. June 13–16, 1998, is the Dyea-to-Dawson Centennial Race to the Klondike. The Yukon Gold Panning Championship is held July 1 each year in Dawson City, along with a celebration of Canada Day to Independence Day (July 1–4, 1998). Then on July 18, 1998, it's the Canadian Airlines International Dome Race, which attracts more than 200 runners each year from all over the world. The 4.6-mile/7.4-km course rises a total elevation of 1,850 feet/564m.

The 20th Annual Dawson City Music Festival, July 14–19, 1998, features entertainers and artists from Canada and the United States, free workshops, dances and dinners. Tickets and information from the Music Festival Assoc., Box 456, Dawson City, YT Y0B 1G0. Phone (867) 993-5584.

If you are near Dawson Aug. 11–17, 1998, be sure to join the Discovery Days Festival fun when Yukon Order of Pioneers stages its annual parade. This event is a Yukon holiday commemorating the Klondike gold discovery of Aug. 17, 1896.

The Great Klondike International Outhouse Race, held the Sunday of Labour Day weekend, is a race of outhouses (on wheels) over a 1.9 mile/3-km course through the streets of Dawson City; before the race, all contestants must recite original limericks.

Other Dawson City summer events include the International Gold Show, May 15–16, 1998; Gertie's International Dart Tournament, May 22–24, 1998; and the Yukon Talent Night, Sept. 25, 1998.

See the Midnight Sun: If you are in Dawson City on June 21, be sure to make it to the top of the Dome by midnight, when the sun barely dips behind the 6,000-foot/1,829-m Ogilvie Mountains to the north—the picture of a lifetime. There's quite a local celebration on the Dome on June 21, so for those who don't like crowds, a visit before or after summer solstice will also afford fine views and photos. Turnoff for Dome Mountain is at **Milepost J 325.8;** it's about a 5-mile/8-km drive.

Pan for Gold: The chief attraction for most visitors is panning for gold. There are several mining operations set up to permit you to actually pan for your own "colours" under friendly guidance. Take Bonanza Creek Road from **Milepost J 324.5** up famous Bonanza Creek, past Dredge No. 4, Discovery Claim and miles of gravel tailings worked over 2 and 3 times in the continuing search for gold. The Klondike Visitors Assoc. sponsors a public panning area at No. 6 above Discovery, 13 miles/21 km from Dawson City on Bonanza Creek Road. Check with the Visitor Reception Centre for more information.

Bear Creek Camp, (see **Milepost J 319.6** on the Klondike Highway), was operated by Yukon Consolidated Gold Corp. until 1966. Tours are conducted by Parks Canada interpreters; check with the Visitor Reception Centre for current tour schedule. The compound features the Gold Room, where the gold was melted and poured into bricks, complete blacksmith and machinery shops, and other well-preserved structures. Open 9:30 A.M. to 5 P.M. from mid-June to late August. Admission: adults \$3, children 12 and under free.

Hike the historic Ridge Road. Originally built in 1899 to move mining supplies along Bonanza Creek, the Ridge Road was abandoned by 1902. The road was restored in 1996 into a 20-mile/32-km historic hiking trail. Travel time is 1 1/2 to 2 days by foot

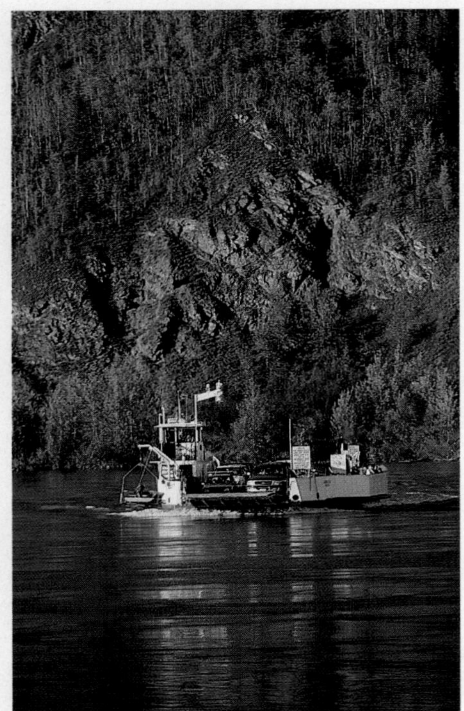

Government ferry George Black *crosses Yukon River to Top of World Highway.*

(© Joe Prax)

(or 4–6 hours by mountain bike), and interpretive signs and building remnants are along the route. There are 2 tent campgrounds on the trail, at Mile 6.8/Km 11 and Mile 13.1/Km 21, with firepits and running water.

Klondike Loop Log

(continued from page 314)

YUKON HIGHWAY 9

The Top of the World Highway (Yukon Highway 9) connects Dawson City with the Taylor Highway (Alaska Route 5). A free ferry carries passengers and vehicles from Dawson City across the Yukon River to the beginning of the Top of the World Highway. NOTE: The ferry wait in heavy traffic may be 3 hours or longer during peak times. The Alaska Highway is 174.5 miles/280.8 km from here; Eagle, AK, is 143.4 miles/230.8 km from here. Allow plenty of time for this drive; average speed for this road is 25 to 40 mph/40 to 64 kmph. DRIVE WITH YOUR HEADLIGHTS ON! Yukon Highway 9 and the Taylor Highway (Alaska Route 5) in Alaska are not maintained from mid-October to April, and the arrival of snow effectively closes the roads for winter.

CAUTION: Road conditions on some sections of the Alaska portion of this road were rough in 1997. The Top of the World Highway is also scheduled for seal coating in 1998 between the ferry landing and Kilometrepost 30 on the Canadian side. Check with the Dawson City Visitor Reception Centre for current road and weather conditions; phone (867) 993-5566.

*IMPORTANT: U.S. and Canada customs are open from about May 15 to Sept. 15. In summer 1997, customs was open 7 days a week, 9 A.M. to 8 P.M. (Pacific time) on the Canadian side; 8 A.M. to 9 P.M. (Alaska time) on the U.S. side. Check with the RCMP or Visitor Reception Centre in Dawson City to make certain the border crossing at **Milepost D 66.1** will be open. Serious fines are levied for crossing the border without clearing customs! There are no restrooms, services or currency exchanges available at the border.*

This section of the log shows distance from Dawson City (D) followed by distance from junction with the Taylor Highway (T) at Jack Wade Junction. Physical kilometreposts show distance from Dawson City.

D 0 T 78.8 (126.8 km) **DAWSON CITY.** Free ferry crosses the Yukon River daily in summer. See TRANSPORTATION page 322.

D 0.2 (0.3 km) **T 78.6** (126.5 km) **Yukon River** government campground on riverbank opposite Dawson City; 74 RV sites, 24 tent-only sites, 2 kitchen shelters, playground and drinking water. Camping fee $8. Within walking distance of stern-wheeler graveyard. Put in and takeout spot for Yukon River travelers. ▲

D 2.7 (4.4 km) **T 76.1** (122.5 km) Access to 9-hole golf course via 3.2-mile/5.1-km gravel road; rentals.

D 2.9 (4.6 km) **T 75.9** (122.1 km) Turnout for viewpoint overlooking Dawson City and the Yukon and Klondike rivers.

D 3.2 (5 km) **T 75.6** (121.7 km) Turnout with good view of Yukon River and river valley farms.

D 8.7 (11.9 km) **T 70.1** (112.8 km) Interpretive displays about the Fortymile caribou herd.

D 9 (12.4 km) **T 69.8** (112.3 km) Rest area with pit toilets, picnic tables, litter barrels and information sign about Top of the World Highway (also has ferry information for travelers to Dawson City).

D 11 (15.6 km) **T 67.8** (109.1 km) "Top of the world" view as highway climbs above tree line.

D 16.4 (26.2 km) **T 62.4** (100.4 km) Snow fence along highway next 8 miles/13 km westbound.

D 18.4 (29.4 km) **T 60.4** (97.2 km) Large turnout on left.

D 29.2 (47 km) **T 49.6** (79.8 km) Evidence of 1989 burn.

D 32.1 (51.2 km) **T 46.7** (75.2 km) First outcropping (westbound) of Castle Rock. Turnout to south with panoramic view of countryside.

D 33.1 (52.8 km) **T 45.7** (73.5 km) Distance marker shows customs 52 km, Dawson City 53 km.

D 35.2 (56 km) **T 43.6** (70.2 km) Main outcropping of Castle Rock; lesser formations are also found along this stretch. Centuries of erosion have created these formations. Turnout on left westbound.

D 37.4 (59 km) **T 41.4** (66.6 km) Unmaintained road leads 25 miles/40 km to the former settlement of Clinton Creek, which served the Cassiar Asbestos Mine from 1967–79. There are no facilities or services available there. Distance marker shows U.S. border 43 km.

The confluence of the Yukon and Fortymile rivers is 3 miles/4.8 km below the former townsite of Clinton Creek. Clinton Creek bridge is an access point on the Fortymile River National Wild and Scenic River system, managed by the Bureau of Land Management. The Fortymile River offers intermediate and advanced canoeists over 100 miles/160 km of challenging water.

Yukon River, near Clinton Creek, grayling to 3 lbs. in April; chum salmon to 12 lbs. in August; king salmon to 40 lbs., July and August. **Fortymile River**, near Clinton Creek, grayling to 3 lbs. during spring breakup and fall freezeup; inconnu (sheefish) to 10 lbs. in July and August.

D 54 (85.6 km) **T 24.8** (39.9 km) Old sod-roofed cabin on right westbound, originally a supply and stopping place for the McCormick Transportation Co.

D 54.3 (86.1 km) **T 24.5** (39.4 km) Road forks left westbound to old mine workings at Sixtymile, which have been reactivated by Cogasa Mining Co. Keep to right for Alaska. The road winds above timberline for many miles. The lack of fuel for warmth and shelter made this a perilous trip for the early sourdoughs.

D 64.1(101.9 km) **T 14.7** (23.7 km) Large gravel turnout. Information sign about Top of the World Highway viewpoint.

D 65.2 (103.7 km) **T 13.6** (21.9 km) Pull-through rest area with toilet and litter barrels; good viewpoint. Just across the highway, short hike to cairn, excellent viewpoint. Highest point on Top of the World Highway (elev. 4,515 feet/1,376 m).

D 66.1 (105.1 km) **T 12.7** (20.4 km) U.S.–Canada border (elev. 4,127 feet/1,258m). Customs only; no public facilities available.

Canada Customs and Immigration Little Gold Creek office is open 9 A.M. to 9 P.M. (Pacific time) from about May 15 to Sept. 15. All traffic entering Canada must stop here. The U.S. border station Poker Creek office, just past the Canadian station, is open 8 A.M. to 8 P.M. (Alaska time) from about May 15 to Sept. 15. All traffic entering the United States must stop here. Both stations are closed in winter. A short hike up the hill behind U.S. border station provides good viewpoint. *NOTE: Customs hours of operation subject to change.*

TIME ZONE CHANGE: Alaska observes Alaska time; Yukon Territory observes Pacific time.

D 67.1 (108 km) **T 11.7** (18.8 km) Double-ended turnout to north with viewing platform to see mountains; toilet, litter barrel, aluminum can recycling bin.

D 69.2 (111.4 km) **T 9.6** (15.4 km) **BOUNDARY.** Boundary Lodge was one of the first roadhouses in Alaska; food, gas, lodging, diesel, tire repair, emergency phone.

Watch your gas supply. Between here and Tetlin Junction on the Alaska Highway, gas is available again only at Chicken, **Milepost TJ 66.5.** From here to Eagle, gas may be available at O'Brien Creek Lodge, **Milepost TJ 125.4.** Gas is available in Eagle.

Private Aircraft: Boundary airstrip; elev. 2,940 feet/896m; length 2,100 feet/640m; earth and gravel; fuel 80; unattended.

D 78 (125.6 km) **T 0.8** (1.3 km) Viewpoint.

D 78.8 (126.9 km) **T 0 Jack Wade Junction, Milepost TJ 95.7** on the Taylor Highway. The Taylor Highway (Alaska Route 5), also known as the Eagle Road or Eagle Cutoff, leads north 64.6 miles/104 km to Eagle, AK, or south 95.7 miles/154 km to Tetlin Junction, just east of Tok, on the Alaska Highway. *CAUTION: The Taylor Highway is a narrow, winding, mountain road. Drive carefully!*

*NOTE: Eagle-bound and Alaska Highway-bound travelers turn to **Milepost TJ 95.7** on page 328 in the TAYLOR HIGHWAY section to continue log. Eagle-bound travelers continue with log forward from **Milepost TJ 95.7**. Alaska Highway-bound travelers read log backward from **Milepost TJ 95.7**.*

TAYLOR HIGHWAY ⑤

Connects: Alaska Hwy. (Tetlin Jct.) to Eagle, AK **Length:** 160 miles
Road Surface: Gravel **Season:** Closed in winter
Steepest Grade: 9 percent
Major Attraction: Fort Egbert

(See map, page 307)

	Chicken	Dawson City	Eagle	Tok
Chicken		109	94	78
Dawson City	109		144	187
Eagle	94	144		172
Tok	78	187	172	

Sunset on the Yukon River at Eagle Bluff, end of the Taylor Highway.
(Jerrianne Lowther, staff)

The 160.3-mile/258-km Taylor Highway (Alaska Route 5) begins at Tetlin Junction on the Alaska Highway and ends at the small town of Eagle on the Yukon River. This is a beautiful "top of the world" drive, and Eagle is well worth a visit. Construction of the Taylor Highway began in 1946, and was completed to Eagle in late 1953, providing access to the historic Fortymile Mining District.

The Taylor Highway is a narrow, winding, mountain road with many steep hills and some hairpin curves. Allow plenty of time to drive its length. The road surface is mostly gravel, with sporadic soft spots during breakup or after heavy rains. Road surface ranges from very poor to good depending on maintenance. Shoulders are narrow and may be unstable. Large RVs and trailers especially should use caution in driving this road. Watch for large tanker trucks, some with double trailers, hauling fuel between Tetlin Junction and Boundary. (Your best defense is to pull over and stop, if possible.) The Taylor Highway is not maintained from mid-October to April, and the arrival of snow effectively closes the road for winter.

The Taylor is the shortest route to Dawson City, YT, from Alaska. Drive 95.7 miles/154 km north on the Taylor Highway to Jack Wade Junction, and turn east on the Top of the World Highway (Yukon Highway 9) for Dawson City. (See end of KLONDIKE LOOP section for log of Yukon Highway 9.)

Dawson City-bound travelers keep in mind that gas is available only at Chicken and at Boundary Lodge. Also, the U.S. and Canadian customs offices at the border are open from about mid-May to mid-September. Probable customs hours for summer 1998 are 8 A.M. to 8 P.M. Alaska time; 9 A.M. to 9 P.M. Pacific time on the Canadian side. Check for current information with Alaska Public Lands Information Center; (907) 883-5667. There are no restrooms, services or currency exchanges available at the border.

IMPORTANT: You cannot cross the border unless the customs office for the country you are entering is open. Severe fines are levied for crossing without clearing customs. Officials at Canadian customs are concerned about child abductions. If you are traveling with children, remember to bring identification for them.

NOTE: All gold-bearing ground in area is claimed. Do not pan in streams.

The highway also provides river runners with access to the Fortymile River National Wild and Scenic River system. A brochure on access points and float times is available from the Bureau of Land Management, 1150 University Ave., Fairbanks, AK 99709-3844; phone (907) 474-2350.

The Fortymile Mining District is home range for the Fortymile caribou herd. Once a massive herd of 500,000 animals, the herd is now stable at about 23,000 caribou. The herd moves east across the highway in late fall for the winter, and returns again in spring for calving. During the summer, small bands of caribou can sometimes be seen in the high country above timberline. The Fortymile Caribou Planning Team, a group of Alaskan and Yukon residents, was created to develop a strategy for restoring the caribou herd and other area wildlife. State, federal and territorial agencies sponsored the effort and provide logistical support.

Emergency medical services: Between Tetlin Junction and O'Brien Creek bridge at **Milepost TJ 113.2**, phone the Tok Area EMS at 911 or (907) 883-5111. Between O'Brien Creek bridge and Eagle, phone the Eagle EMS at (907) 547-2300 or (907) 547-2211. Use CB channel 21.

Taylor Highway Log

Distance from Tetlin Junction (TJ) is followed by distance from Eagle (E).

TJ 0 E 160.3 (258 km) **Tetlin Junction. Junction** with the Alaska Highway at **Milepost DC 1301.7** (see page 179 in the ALASKA HIGHWAY section). 40 Mile Roadhouse; current status of services unknown.

Begin 9 miles/14.5 km of winding road up out of the Tanana River valley. Highway

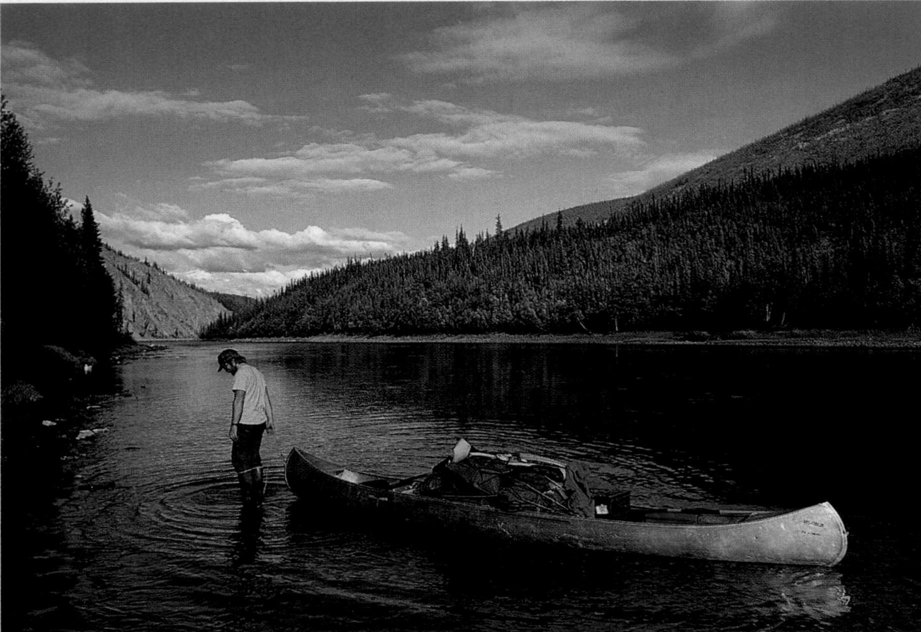

The Taylor Highway provides access to the Fortymile River canoe trail.

(© George Wuerthner)

traverses stabilized sand dunes first 5 miles/8 km.

TJ 0.9 (1.4 km) **E 159.4** (256.5 km) Double-ended turnout to east.

TJ 2.7 (4.3 km) **E 157.6** (253.6 km) Double-ended turnout to east.

TJ 4.5 (7.2 km) **E 155.8** (250.7 km) Gravel turnout to east. A 0.7-mile/1.1-km trail leads to **Four Mile Lake**; rainbow trout and sheefish.

TJ 5.4 (8.7 km) **E 154.9** (249.3 km) Evidence of 1990 forest fire known as the Porcupine burn.

TJ 5.9 (9.5 km) **E 154.4** (248.5 km) Entering Tok Management Area, Tanana Valley State Forest, northbound.

TJ 6 (9.7 km) **E 154.3** (248.3 km) Double-ended turnout to east, easy for trailers.

Wildflowers along the highway include arnica, chiming bells, wild roses and Labrador tea. As the name suggests, Labrador tea leaves (and flowers) may be steeped in boiling water to make tea. However, according to Janice Scofield, author of *Discovering Wild Plants*, Labrador tea contains a narcotic toxin that can cause ill effects if used too frequently or in high concentrations.

NOTE: Winding road northbound. Watch for ruts and soft spots and for loose gravel on curves. Watch for frost heaves.

TJ 9.4 (15.1 km) **E 150.9** (242.8 km) Entering Game Management Unit 20E northbound; entering GMU 12 southbound. Road begins gradual climb of Mount Fairplay for northbound travelers.

TJ 10 (16 km) **E 150.3** (240.5 km) Double-ended turnout to east.

TJ 12.1 (19.5 km) **E 148.2** (238.5 km) Entering Tok Management Area, Tanana State Forest, southbound.

TJ 14.6 (23.5 km) **E 145.7** (234.5 km) Small turnout to west. Blueberries in season.

TJ 16 (25.7 km) **E 144.3** (232.2 km) Parking at one of Mount Fairplay's several summits.

TJ 18.9 (30.2 km) **E 141.4** (226.2 km) Double-ended turnout to west.

TJ 21.2 (34.1 km) **E 139.1** (223.9 km) Long descent northbound from true summit of Mount Fairplay.

TJ 22.1 (35.4 km) **E 138.2** (221.1 km) Double-ended turnout to east.

TJ 22.4 (35.8 km) **E 137.9** (220.6 km) Double-ended turnout to east.

TJ 23 (37 km) **E 137.3** (219.4 km) Scenic views, Alaska Range to west.

TJ 28.3 (45.5 km) **E 132** (212.4 km) Turnout with view to west.

TJ 32.8 (52.8 km) **E 127.5** (205.2 km) Turnout to west.

TJ 34.4 (55.4 km) **E 125.9** (202.6 km) Double-ended turnout with view to west. Nine-percent downgrade northbound.

TJ 35.1 (56.5 km) **E 125.2** (201.5 km) Entering Fortymile Mining District northbound. The second-oldest mining district in Alaska, it first yielded gold in 1886. Claims were filed in both Canada and Alaska due to boundary uncertainties.

Double-ended turnout to east near summit of Mount Fairplay (elev. 5,541 feet/1,689m). Interpretive sign, viewing platform, litter barrels, aluminum recycling, toilet, wheelchair accessible.

Highway descends a 9-percent grade northbound. Southbound, the road descends for the next 25 miles/40 km from Mount Fairplay's summit, winding through heavily forested terrain. Panoramic views of the Fortymile River forks' valleys. Views of the Alaska Range to the southwest.

TJ 39.1 (62.9 km) **E 121.2** (195 km) Large turnout to west, no easy turnaround.

TJ 41 (65.6 km) **E 119.3** (190.9 km) Watch for soft shoulders.

TJ 43 (69.2 km) **E 117.3** (188.8 km) Logging Cabin Creek bridge (abrupt edge on bridge); small turnout to west at south end of bridge. Side road to creek. This is the south end of the Fortymile River National Wild and Scenic River system managed by BLM. Evidence of old forest fire.

TJ 49 (78.9 km) **E 111.3** (179.1 km) Loop roads through BLM West Fork Recreation Site; 25 sites (7 pull-through sites), tables, firepits, no water, covered tables, toilets, dumpsters. Access point of Fortymile River canoe trail. Improved campground. ▲

TJ 49.3 (79.3 km) **E 111** (178.6 km) Bridge over West Fork of the Dennison Fork of the Fortymile River. Access point for Fortymile River National Wild and Scenic River system.

TJ 50.5 (81.3 km) **E 109.8** (176.7 km) Taylor Creek bridge. Watch for potholes and rough road at bridge approaches (abrupt edge on bridge). All-terrain vehicle trail to Taylor and Kechumstuk mountains; heavily used in hunting season.

TJ 57 (91.7 km) **E 103.3** (166.2 km) Scenic viewpoint turnout to east, no easy turnaround.

TJ 58.9 (94.8 km) **E 101.4** (163.2 km) Scenic viewpoint turnout to east.

TJ 62.5 (100.6 km) **E 97.8** (157.4 km) Turnout to west. Drive-in, no easy turnaround.

TJ 63.2 (101.7 km) **E 97.1** (156.3 km) View of Chicken.

TJ 63.3 (101.9 km) **E 97** (156.1 km) Turnout to west. Drive-in, no easy turnaround.

TJ 63.7 (102.5 km) **E 96.6** (155.5 km) Steep descent northbound to Mosquito Fork.

TJ 64.1 (103.2 km) **E 96.2** (154.8 km) Well-traveled road leads to private buildings, not into Chicken.

TJ 64.3 (103.5 km) **E 96** (154.5 km) Bridge over Mosquito Fork of the Fortymile River; day-use area with table, toilet and litter barrel at north end of bridge. The Mosquito Fork is a favorite access point for the Fortymile National Wild and Scenic River system, according to the BLM.

TJ 66 (106.2 km) **E 94.3** (151.8 km) Entering **CHICKEN** (pop. 37), northbound. *(NOTE: Driving distance between **Mileposts TJ 66 and 67** is 0.7 mile.)* This is the newer commercial settlement of Chicken. The original mining camp (abandoned, private property) is north of Chicken Creek (see **Milepost TJ 67**). Chicken is a common name in the North for ptarmigan. One story has it that the early miners wanted to name their camp ptarmigan, but were unable to spell it and settled for Chicken. Access point for the Fortymile River canoe trail is below Chicken airstrip.

Fuel is available in Chicken. Gas is also available at O'Brien Creek Lodge, en route to Eagle, **Milepost TJ 125.4**; in Boundary, en route to Canada (Top of the World Highway, **Milepost D 69.2**); or in Tok.

TJ 66.3 (106.7 km) **E 94** (151.3 km) Chicken post office (ZIP code 99732) located on hill beside the road. The late Ann Purdy lived in this area. The book *Tisha* is based on her experiences as a young schoolteacher in the Alaska Bush.

© Ruth von Spalding

TJ 66.4 (106.9 km) **E 93.9** (151.1 km) Airport Road. Access to Chicken airstrip and "downtown" Chicken. Combination grocery

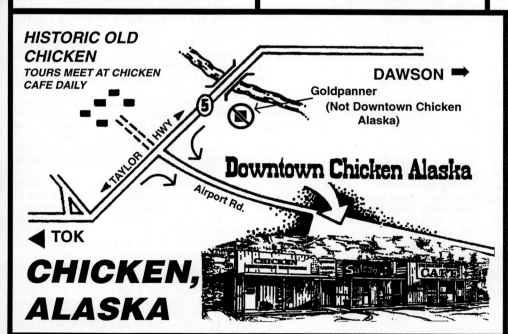

store, restaurant, bar and gas station located here.

Private Aircraft: Chicken airstrip, adjacent southwest; elev. 1,640 feet/500m; length 2,500 feet/762m; gravel; maintained year-round.

TJ 66.6 (107.2 km) **E 93.7** (150.8 km) Chicken Creek bridge.

TJ 67 (107.8 km) **E 93.3** (150.1 km) View of abandoned old townsite of Chicken. The road in is blocked off, and the dozen or so old buildings are owned by a mining company. Private property, do not trespass. Guided walking tours available; inquire at Chicken Creek Cafe. Look upstream (northwest) on Chicken Creek to see the old gold dredge, which was shut down in the 1960s.

TJ 68.2 (109.8 km) **E 92.1** (148.2 km) BLM Chicken field station; information and emergency communications. Trailhead for Mosquito Fork Dredge trail (3 miles/4.8 km round-trip). *NOTE: Watch for potholes and soft spots.*

TJ 68.9 (110.9 km) **E 91.4** (147.1 km) Lost Chicken Creek. Site of Lost Chicken Hill Mine, established in 1895. Mining was under way in this area several years before the Klondike Gold Rush of 1897–98. The first major placer gold strike was in 1886 at Franklin Gulch, a tributary of the Fortymile. Hydraulic mining operations in the creek.

TJ 70 (112.7 km) **E 90.3** (145.3 km) Turnouts at gravel pits on both sides of road.

CAUTION: Watch for hairpin turns.

TJ 71.7 (115.4 km) **E 88.6** (142.6 km) Steep descent northbound as road switchbacks down to South Fork. Watch for June wildflowers: pink wild roses, blue lupine, chiming bells and white Labrador tea.

TJ 74.4 (119.7 km) **E 85.9** (138.2 km) South Fork River access road.

TJ 74.5 (119.9 km) **E 85.8** (138.1 km) South Fork DOT/PF state highway maintenance station.

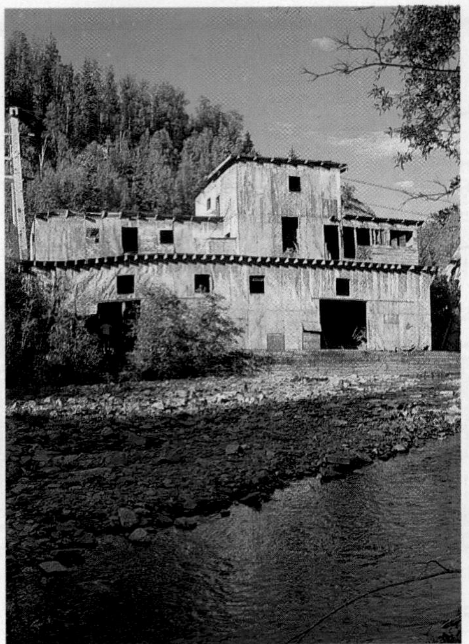

Jack Wade No. 1 gold dredge at Milepost TJ 86.1. (Earl L. Brown, staff)

TJ 75.3 (121.2 km) **E 85** (136.8 km) South Fork bridge. Day-use area with toilet and litter barrels at south end of bridge, west side of road. Access point for the Fortymile River National Wild and Scenic River system. The muddy, bumpy road leading into the brush is used by miners.

TJ 76.8 (123.6 km) **E 83.5** (134.4 km) Turnout to west. View of oxbow lakes in South Fork valley.

CAUTION: Watch for rough road.

TJ 78.5 (126.3 km) **E 81.8** (131.6 km) Views of Fortymile River valley northbound to **Milepost TJ 82.**

TJ 78.8 (126.8 km) **E 81.5** (131.2 km) Steep descent northbound.

TJ 81.9 (131.8 km) **E 78.4** (126.2 km) Walker Fork bridge.

TJ 82.1 (132.1 km) **E 78.2** (125.8 km) Walker Fork BLM campground; 16 campsites, picnic sites with covered tables, fee charged. ▲

TJ 86.1 (138.6 km) **E 74.2** (119.4 km) Old Jack Wade No. 1 dredge in creek next to road. Turnout to east. This is actually the Butte Creek Dredge, installed in 1934 below the mouth of Butte Creek and eventually moved to Wade Creek. This was one of the first bucketline dredges used in the area, according to the BLM.

TJ 88.3 (142.1 km) **E 72** (115.9 km) Mining camp. Active mining is under way in this area. *Do not trespass on mining claims.* Road width varies from here to Eagle. *NOTE: Large vehicles use turnouts when meeting oncoming vehicles.*

CAUTION: Section of 1-lane road here in 1997 due to washout; check for current status.

TJ 90 (144.8 km) **E 70.3** (113.1 km) Jack Wade, an old mining camp that operated until 1940.

TJ 91.9 (147.9 km) **E 68.4** (110.1 km) Turnout to east. Primitive campsite by stream.

TJ 93.5 (150.5 km) **E 66.8** (107.5 km) *Slow down for hairpin curve.* Road climbs northbound.

TJ 95.7 (154 km) **E 64.6** (104 km) **Jack Wade Junction.** Continue north on the Taylor Highway for Eagle. Turn east for Boundary Lodge and the Alaska–Canada border. Dawson City is 78.8 miles/126.8 km east via the Top of the World Highway. The Top of the World Highway (Yukon Highway 9) is a winding gravel road with some steep grades. Slippery in wet weather, closed by snow. Drive carefully.

NOTE: *Dawson City-bound travelers turn to the end of the KLONDIKE LOOP section on page 324 and read the Top of the World Highway log back to front. Eagle-bound travelers continue with this log.*

TJ 96 (154.5 km) **E 64.3** (103.5 km) Turnout. Lupine and chiming bells bloom in June. View to the north-northeast of Canada's Ogilvie Mountains in the distance.

TJ 99.5 (160.1 km) **E 60.8** (97.8 km) Road winds around the summit of Steele Creek Dome (elev. 4,015 feet/1,224m) visible directly above the road to the east. *CAUTION: Road is slippery when wet.*

TJ 99.6 (160.3 km) **E 60.7** (97.7 km) *CAUTION: Slow down for hairpin curve.*

TJ 105.5 (169.8 km) **E 54.8** (88.2 km) Scenic viewpoint to east. The road descends next 7 miles/11.3 km northbound to the valley of the Fortymile River, so named because its mouth was 40 miles below Fort Reliance, an old trading post near the confluence of the Yukon and Klondike rivers. Along the road are abandoned cabins, tailings and dredges.

TJ 108.5 (174.6 km) **E 51.8** (83.4 km) *CAUTION: Slow down for hairpin curve!*

TJ 109 (175.4 km) **E 51.3** (82.6 km) *CAUTION: Steep, narrow, winding road northbound. Slow down!* Frequent small turnouts and breathtaking views to north and west. Watch for arctic poppies and lupine along the highway in June.

TJ 112.6 (181.2 km) **E 47.7** (76.8 km) Fortymile River bridge; parking area at south end of bridge, toilet, canoe launch, trash cans. No camping. Active mining in area. Nearly vertical beds of white marble can be seen on the northeast side of the river. Access to the Fortymile River National Wild and Scenic River system.

TJ 112.8 (181.5 km) **E 47.5** (76.4 km) Private home and mining camp.

TJ 113.1 (182 km) **E 47.2** (76 km) O'Brien Creek DOT/PF highway maintenance camp located here.

TJ 113.2 (182.2 km) **E 47.1** (75.8 km) O'Brien Creek bridge. Access to creek.

TJ 114.2 (183.8 km) **E 46.8** (75.3 km) Winding road northbound with rock slide areas to **Milepost TJ 116**; highway parallels O'Brien Creek to Liberty Fork; several turnouts. Road narrows northbound: Watch for falling rock next 1.5 miles/2.4 km northbound.

CAUTION: Watch for small aircraft using road as runway. Section of 1-lane road here in 1997 due to washout; check for current status.

TJ 117.2 (188.6 km) **E 43.1** (69.4 km) Alder Creek bridge.

TJ 119.7 (192.6 km) **E 40.6** (65.3 km) Slide area, watch for rocks.

TJ 124.6 (200.5 km) **E 35.7** (57.5 km) Columbia Creek bridge.

TJ 125.4 (201.8 km) **E 34.9** (56.2 km) O'Brien Creek Lodge; gas. Nearest gas stations in Eagle, Chicken and Boundary.

TJ 130.5 (208.8 km) **E 29.8** (47.7 km) Turnout to east.

TJ 131.5 (211.6 km) **E 28.8** (46.3 km) King Solomon Creek bridge. Highway follows King Solomon Creek next 0.5 mile/0.8 km northbound. (The creek has a tributary named Queen of Sheba.)

TJ 135.7 (218.4 km) **E 24.6** (39.6 km) *CAUTION: Slow down for hairpin curve.*

TJ 135.8 (218.5 km) **E 24.5** (39.4 km) North Fork Solomon Creek bridge.

TJ 141 (226.9 km) **E 19.3** (31.1 km) Glacier Mountain management area; walk-in hunting only. Top of the world views to west.

TJ 143.2 (230.5 km) **E 17.1** (27.5 km) Turnout on summit. Top of the world views. Road begins winding descent northbound to Yukon River.

TJ 148 (236.8 km) **E 12.3** (19.7 km) Two small turnouts.

TJ 149.1 (239.9 km) **E 11.2** (18 km) Bridge over Discovery Fork. Turnout to east by creek.

TJ 150.7 (242.5 km) **E 9.6** (15.4 km) Old cabin by creek to west is a local landmark. Private property.

TJ 151.8 (244.3 km) **E 8.5** (13.7 km) American Creek bridge No. 1. Outcroppings of asbestos, greenish or gray with white, and serpentine along creekbank. Doyon Ltd. claims ownership of surface and mineral estates on these lands; do not trespass.

TJ 152.5 (245.4 km) **E 7.8** (12.6 km) Bridge No. 2 over American Creek.

TJ 153.2 (246.5 km) **E 7.1** (11.4 km) Small turnout. Springwater piped to road.

TJ 153.6 (247.2 km) **E 6.7** (10.8 km) Small turnout. Springwater piped to road.

TJ 159.3 (256.4 km) **E 1** (1.6 km) Gas station.

TJ 159.7 (257 km) **E 0.6** (1 km) Historical sign about the settlement of Eagle.

TJ 160.3 (258 km) **E 0** Fourth Avenue, Eagle (description follows). Eagle school to east. Side road to west leads 1 mile/1.6 km to Fort Egbert mule barn, officers' quarters and parade ground. The U.S. Army established Fort Egbert in 1899, then abandoned it in 1911. From here a road leads 0.8 mile/1.3 km to Eagle BLM Campground; 13 sites, fee charged. ▲

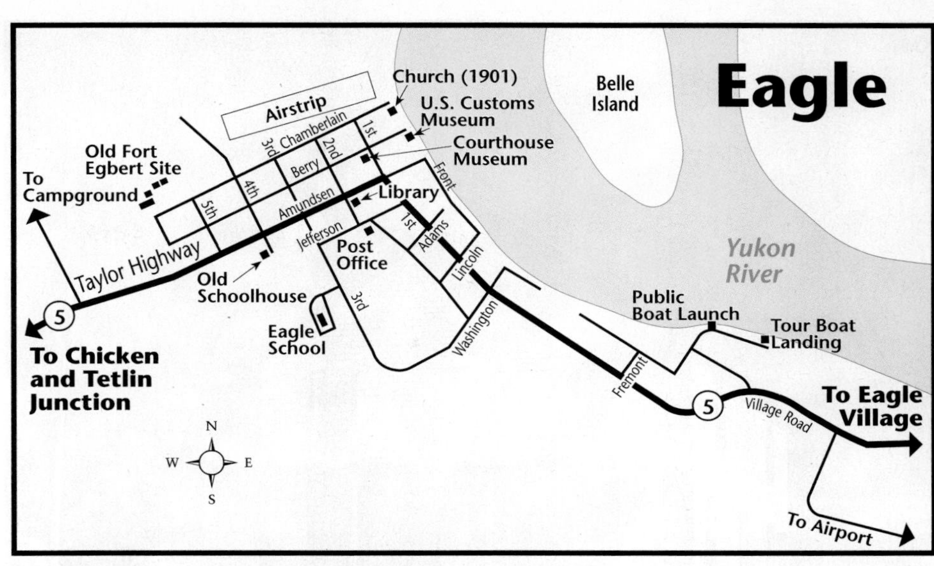

Eagle

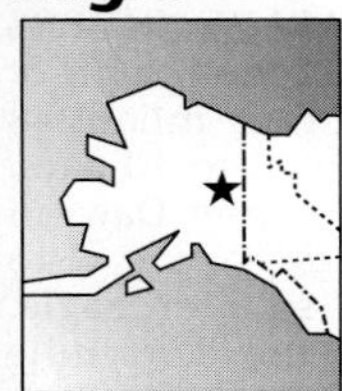

Population: 146. **Emergency Services:** Eagle EMS (907) 547-2300 or (907) 547-2211; use CB channel 21; Eagle health clinic. **Visitor Information:** Contact the Eagle Historical Society and Museums (Box 23, Eagle, 99738; phone 907/547-2325; fax 907/547-2232) for information on area tours, museums and events. Archives and photo collection on display for history buffs and geologists. The museum store offers books on local subjects and unique handcrafts.

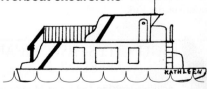

The National Park Service office, headquarters for Yukon–Charley Rivers National Preserve, is located on the banks of the Yukon River at the base of Fort Egbert. Reference library available to the public. Office hours are 8 A.M. to 5 P.M. weekdays. The National Park Service Visitor Center offers maps and books for sale. Also a video on the preserve is shown on request. Informal talks and interpretive programs available. Visitor

Historic Wickersham Courthouse is included on the Eagle Historical Society walking tour. (© Tom Culkin)

center hours are 8 A.M. to 5 P.M. daily in summer (Memorial Day weekend through Labor Day weekend). Check at the visitor center for information on the Yukon River, Yukon–Charley Rivers National Preserve and other parklands in Alaska. (Write them at Box 167, Eagle 99738, or phone 907/547-2233.)

Elevation: 820 feet/250m. **Climate:** Mean monthly temperature in July 59°F/15°C; in January -13°F/-25°C. Record low -71°F/-57°C in January 1952; record high 95°F/35°C in July 1925. July also has the greatest mean number of days (21) with temperatures above 70°F/21°C. Mean precipitation in July, 1.94 inches; in December, 10.1 inches. Record snow depth 42 inches in April 1948.

Transportation: By road via the Taylor Highway (closed by snow October to April); air taxi, scheduled air service; dog team and snow machine in winter. Eagle is also accessible via the Yukon River. U.S. customs available at post office for persons entering Alaska via the Yukon River or by air.

Private Aircraft: Eagle airstrip, 2 miles/3.2 km east; elev. 880 feet/268m; length 3,500 feet/1,067m; gravel; unattended.

This small community was once the supply and transportation center for miners working the upper Yukon and its tributaries. Francois Mercier established his Belle Isle trading post here in 1874. With the establishment of Fort Egbert in 1889, Eagle became the military center for the upper Yukon. By 1898, Eagle's population was 1,700. Gold strikes in Fairbanks and Nome lured away many, and by 1910, the population had dwindled to 178.

In the center of town stands a windmill and wellhouse (hand-dug in 1903); the well still provides water for over half the town's population. There are gas stations, restaurants, gift shops, museum store, post office, showers, laundromat, hardware store and mechanic shop with tire repair. Groceries and sundries are available. Fax service is available at both stores. Overnight accommodations at the motel, rental cabins and bed and breakfasts. RV parking with hookups is available or stay at Eagle BLM campground just outside town (turn left on 4th Avenue and left again along airstrip at Fort Egbert). Eagle Village, an Athabascan settlement, is 3 miles/4.8 km from Eagle. ▲

Eagle, perched on the south bank of the Yukon River below Eagle Bluff (elev. 1000 feet/305m), remains relatively untouched. Locals still practice traditional subsistence activities—fishing with nets, gathering berries, gardening and handcrafting necessities—and many of the town's original cabins, over 100 years old, are used today.

In celebration of the Eagle Gold Rush Centennial, Eagle is hosting its own centennial festivities in early July, 1998. Contact the Eagle Historical Society and Museums; phone (907) 547-2325, fax (907) 547-2232 for more information.

Eagle also boasts the largest museum system in the state. Walking tours, offered by the Eagle Historical Society and Museums, include the Wickersham Courthouse, Waterfront Customs House and the Mule Barn, Water Wagon Shed and NCO quarters at Fort Egbert. Tours are guided by long-time Eagle residents and begin at 9 a.m. daily (from the courtroom upstairs in the courthouse), Memorial Day through mid-September; cost is $5, members of Eagle Historical Society and Museums and children under 12 free (annual society membership: $10 individual, $15 family). Special tours may be arranged. Books, maps and gifts available at the museum store in the courthouse. For more information, contact the Eagle Historical Society and Museums (Box 23, Eagle 99738; phone 907/547-2325; fax 907/547-2232). Fort Egbert, renovated and restored by the Bureau of Land Management, has an interpretive exhibit and a photo display showing the stages of reconstruction. Videos of the Eagle area, art demonstrations, educational programs and readings by local authors are conducted every Monday at 7 P.M. in the public library (June 15 through Labor Day).

Historically an important riverboat landing, Eagle is still a popular jumping-off point for Yukon River travelers. Most popular is a summer float trip from Eagle downriver through the **YUKON–CHARLEY RIVERS NATIONAL PRESERVE** to Circle. Length of the Eagle–Circle trip is 154 river miles/248 km, with most trips averaging 5 to 10 days. Float trips may also be made from Dawson City, YT, to Circle (252 miles/406 km, 7 to 10 days) with a halfway stop at Eagle. Boaters also often float the Fortymile River to the Yukon River, then continue to the boat landing at Eagle to take out. Commercial boat trips are also available. Westours (Gray Line Yukon) operates the Yukon Queen daily boat service between Eagle and Dawson City, YT. Breakup on the Yukon is in May; freezeup in October. For details on weather, clothing, gear and precautions, contact the National Park Service, Box 167, Eagle 99738; phone (907) 547-2233.

GLENN HIGHWAY/TOK CUTOFF 

Connects: Tok to Anchorage, AK **Length:** 328 miles
Road Surface: Paved **Season:** Open all year
Highest Summit: Eureka Summit 3,322 feet
Major Attractions: Matanuska Glacier, Palmer State Fair

(See maps, pages 332–333)

	Anchorage	Glennallen	Palmer	Tok	Valdez
Anchorage		189	42	328	304
Glennallen	189		147	139	115
Palmer	42	147		286	262
Tok	328	139	286		254
Valdez	304	115	262	254	

View of King Mountain and the Matanuska River in autumn. (© Tom Bol Photography)

The Glenn Highway/Tok Cutoff (Alaska Route 1) is the principal access route from the Alaska Highway west to Anchorage, a distance of 328 miles/527.8 km. This route includes the 125-mile/201-km Tok Cutoff, between Tok and the Richardson Highway junction; a 14-mile/22.5-km link via the Richardson Highway; and the 189-mile/304-km Glenn Highway, between the Richardson Highway and Anchorage.

It is a full day's drive between Tok and Anchorage on this paved all-weather highway. There is some spectacular scenery along the Glenn Highway with mountain peaks to the north and south. Road conditions are generally good. The highway between Tok and Glennallen has some very narrow sections with no shoulders. There is also winding road without shoulders between Matanuska Glacier and Palmer. Watch for frost heaves and pavement breaks along the entire highway. Slow down at signs saying Bump—they mean it!

NOTE: In 1998, watch for road construction between ***Milepost A 97*** *and* ***A 105*** *(Matanuska Glacier area) and between* ***A 109*** *and* ***A 118*** *(west of Tahneta Pass).*

Four side roads are logged in this section: the Nabesna Road to the old Nabesna Mine, which also provides access to Wrangell–St. Elias National Park and Preserve; Lake Louise Road to Lake Louise Recreation Area; the Hatcher Pass Road, connecting the Glenn and Parks highways to Independence Mine State Historical Park; and the Old Glenn Highway, an alternate route between Palmer and Anchorage.

Emergency medical services: Between Tok and Duffy's Roadhouse at **Milepost GJ 63**, phone the Alaska State Troopers at 911 or (907) 883-5111. Between Duffy's and Gakona Junction, phone the Copper River EMS at Glennallen at (907) 822-3203 or 911. From Gakona Junction to Anchorage phone 911. CB channel 9 between **Milepost A 30.8** and Anchorage.

Tok Cutoff Log

ALASKA ROUTE 1
Physical mileposts read from **Milepost 125** at Tok to **Milepost 0** at Gakona Junction, the north junction with the Richardson Highway.
Distance from Gakona Junction (GJ) is followed by distance from Anchorage (A) and distance from Tok (T).

GJ 125 (201.2 km) **A 328** (527.8 km) **T 0** Tok (see description beginning on page 181 in the ALASKA HIGHWAY section).

GJ 124.2 (199.9 km) **A 327.2** (526.6 km) **T 0.8** (1.3 km) Tok Community Center.

GJ 124.1 (199.7 km) **A 327.1** (526.4 km) **T 0.9** (1.4 km) Tok Community Clinic, Tok Fire Station.

GJ 124 (199.6 km) **A 327** (526.2 km) **T 1** (1.6 km) Dept. of Natural Resources.

GJ 123.9 (199.4 km) **A 326.9** (526.1 km) **T 1.1** (1.8 km) Dept. of Transportation and Public Facilities, Tok Station.

GJ 123.7 (199.1 km) **A 326.7** (525.8 km) **T 1.3** (2.1 km) Borealis Avenue. Road narrows westbound.

GJ 123.3 (198.4 km) **A 326.3** (525.1 km) **T 1.7** (2.7 km) **Hayner's Trading Post.** Alaskan handmade jewelry and gifts, beads and supplies, greeting and note cards. Sporting goods and black powder supplies. Custom leather work and repairs. Free coffee and tea. Open year-round. Summer hours 10 A.M. to 8 P.M. Rocky and Sue Hayner, owners. (907) 883-5536. See display ad in Tok in the ALASKA HIGHWAY section. [ADVERTISEMENT]

GJ 122.8 (197.6 km) **A 325.8** (524.3 km) **T 2.2** (3.5 km) **Sourdough Campground's Pancake Breakfast** served 7–11 A.M. June,

GLENN HIGHWAY *Tok Cutoff (GJ-125 to GJ-0) to Milepost A 160*

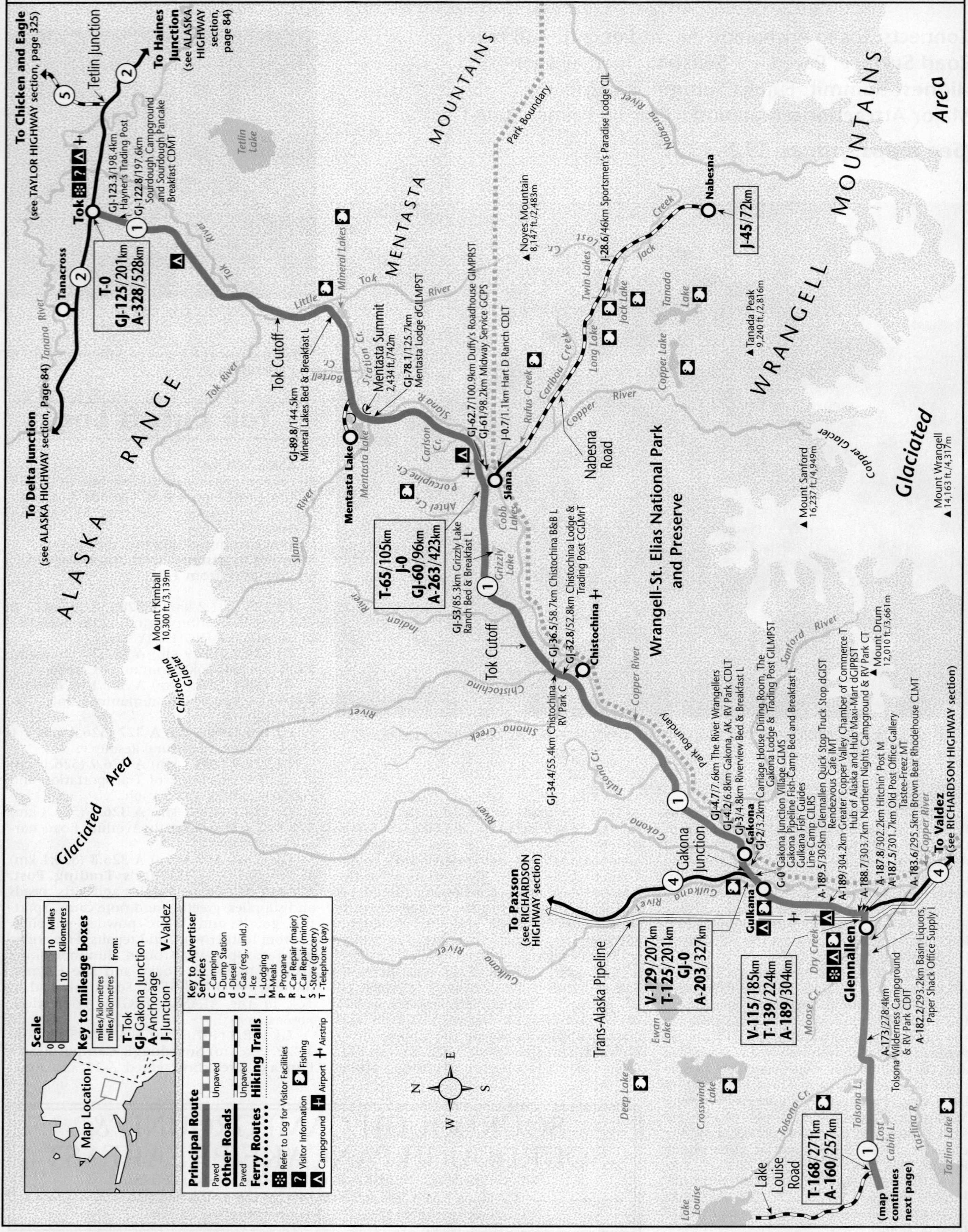

To Chicken and Eagle (see TAYLOR HIGHWAY section, page 325)

Tetlin Junction

To Haines Junction (see ALASKA HIGHWAY section, page 84)

GJ-123.3/198.4km Hayner's Trading Post

GJ-122.8/197.6km Sourdough Campground and Sourdough Pancake Breakfast CDMT

Tok

Tetlin Lake

Tanacross

T-0
GJ-125/201km
A-328/528km

To Delta Junction (see ALASKA HIGHWAY section, Page 84)

Tanana River

Tok River

Mineral Lakes

Little Tok River

MENTASTA MOUNTAINS

Park Boundary

Noyes Mountain 8,147 ft./2,483m

J-28.6/46km Sportsmen's Paradise Lodge CIL

Nabesna River

Nabesna

J-45/72km

Lost Cr.

Jack Creek

Twin Lakes

Jack Lake

Tanada Lake

Tanada Peak 9,240 ft./2,816m

WRANGELL MOUNTAINS

Glaciated Area

ALASKA RANGE

Tok Cutoff

Mentasta Summit 2,434 ft./742m

GJ-78.1/125.7km Mentasta Lodge dGILMPST

GJ-89.8/144.5km Mineral Lakes Bed & Breakfast L

Station Cr.

Bartell Cr.

Tok River

Mentasta Lake

Slana R.

Carlson Cr.

GJ-62.7/100.9km Duffy's Roadhouse GIMPRST

GJ-61/98.2km Midway Service GCPS

J-0.7/1.1km Hart D Ranch CDLT

Rufus Creek

Caribou Creek

Long Lake

Copper Lake

Copper River

Nabesna Road

Slana

Porcupine Cr.

Ahtel Cr.

Slana River

Cobb Lakes

T-65/105km
J-0
GJ-60/96km
A-263/423km

GJ-53/85.3km Grizzly Lake Ranch Bed & Breakfast L

Grizzly Lake

Mount Kimball 10,300 ft./3,139m

Indian River

Wrangell-St. Elias National Park and Preserve

Copper Glacier

Mount Sanford 16,237 ft./4,949m

Mount Wrangell 14,163 ft./4,317m

GJ-36.5/58.7km Chistochina B&B L

GJ-32.8/52.8km Chistochina Lodge & Trading Post CGLMrT

Chistochina

Chistochina Glacier

Chistochina River

GJ-34.4/55.4km Chistochina RV Park C

Sinona Creek

Tulsona Cr.

Copper River

Park Boundary

Sanford River

Mount Drum 12,010 ft./3,661m

GJ-4.7/7.6km The River Wrangellers

GJ-4.2/6.8km Gakona, AK. RV Park CDLT

GJ-3/4.8km Riverview Bed & Breakfast L

GJ-2/3.2km Carriage House Dining Room, The Gakona Lodge & Trading Post GILMPST

Gakona

Gakona River

Gakona Junction

G-0 Gakona Junction Village GLMS
Gakona Pipeline Fish-Camp Bed and Breakfast L
Gulkana Fish Guides
Line Camp CILRS

A-189.5/305km Glennallen Quick Stop Truck Stop dGIST
Rendezvous Cafe IMT

A-189/304.2km Greater Copper Valley Chamber of Commerce T
Hub of Alaska and Hub Maxi-Mart dGIPRST

A-188.7/303.7km Northern Nights Campground & RV Park CT

A-187.8/302.2km Hitchin' Post M

A-187.5/301.7km Old Post Office Gallery
Tastee-Freez MT

A-183.6/295.5km Brown Bear Rhodehouse CLMT

To Valdez (see RICHARDSON HIGHWAY section)

Glaciated Area

To Paxson (see RICHARDSON HIGHWAY section)

Gulkana River

Gulkana

V-129/207km
T-125/201km
GJ-0
A-203/327km

Trans-Alaska Pipeline

Glennallen

V-115/185km
T-139/224km
A-189/304km

Dry Creek

Moose Cr.

Ewan Lake

Deep Lake

Crosswind Lake

A-173/278.4km Tolsona Wilderness Campground & RV Park CDIT

A-182.2/293.2km Basin Liquors, Paper Shack Office Supply I

Tazlina R.

Tazlina Lake

Tolsona Cr.

Tolsona L.

Lost Cabin L.

Lake Louise

Lake Louise Road

T-168/271km
A-160/257km

(map continues next page)

Map Location

Scale
0 — 10 Miles
0 — 10 Kilometres

Key to mileage boxes
miles/kilometres
miles/kilometres
from:
T-Tok
GJ-Gakona Junction
A-Anchorage
J-Junction
V-Valdez

Principal Route
Paved
Other Roads
Paved
Unpaved
Ferry Routes
Hiking Trails
Unpaved

Refer to Log for Visitor Facilities
Visitor Information
Fishing
Campground
Airport
Airstrip

Key to Advertiser Services
C -Camping
D -Dump Station
d -Diesel
G -Gas (reg., unld.)
I -Ice
L -Lodging
M -Meals
P -Propane
R -Car Repair (major)
r -Car Repair (minor)
S -Store (grocery)
T -Telephone (pay)

N E S W

GLENN HIGHWAY *Milepost A 160 to Anchorage, AK*

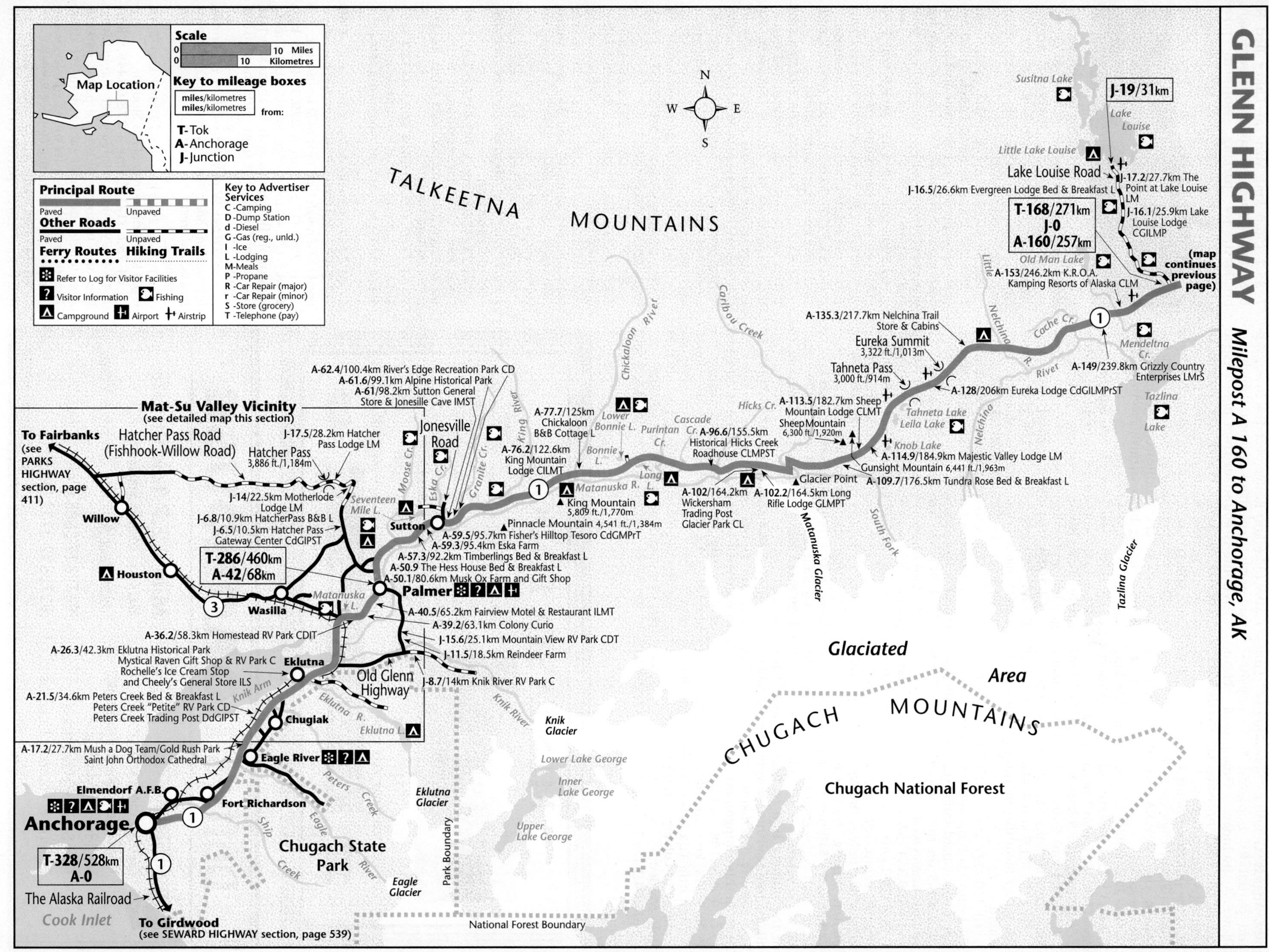

July, August. Genuine "Sourdoughs." Full and partial RV hookups. Dry campsites. Showers included. Guaranteed clean restrooms. High-pressure car wash. Free evening video program. Located 1.7 miles from the junction toward Anchorage on Tok Cutoff (Glenn Highway). See display ad in Tok in the ALASKA HIGHWAY section. [ADVERTISEMENT] ▲

GJ 122.6 (197.3 km) **A 325.6** (524 km) **T 2.4** (3.9 km) Bayless and Roberts Airport. Paved bike trail from Tok ends here.

GJ 116.7 (187.8 km) **A 319.7** (514.5 km) **T 8.3** (13.4 km) Entering Tok Management Area, Tanana Valley State Forest, westbound.

GJ 113 (181.9 km) **A 316** (508.5 km) **T 12** (19.3 km) Beautiful mountain views westbound.

GJ 110 (177 km) **A 313** (503.7 km) **T 15** (24.1 km) Flashing lights to north are from U.S. Coast Guard loran station at **Milepost DC 1308.5** on the Alaska Highway. Watch for frost heaves westbound.

GJ 109.3 (175.9 km) **A 312.3** (502.6 km) **T 15.7** (25.3 km) Eagle Trail State Recreation Site; 40 campsites, 15-day limit, 4 picnic sites, water, toilets, firepits, pay phone, rain shelter, hiking trail, Clearwater Creek. Camping fee $10/night or annual pass. The access road is designed with several loops to aid larger vehicles. A 0.9-mile/1.4-km section of the pioneer trail to Eagle is signed for hikers; trailhead near covered picnic tables. The historic Tok–Slana Cutoff road goes through this campground. ▲

GJ 104.5 (168.2 km) **A 307.5** (494.9 km) **T 20.5** (33 km) Small paved turnout to north. **Little Tok River** overflow runs under highway in culvert; fishing for grayling and Dolly Varden.

GJ 104.1 (167.5 km) **A 307.1** (494.2 km) **T 20.9** (33.6 km) Bridge over Tok River, side road north to riverbank and boat launch.

Wildlife is abundant from here west to Mentasta Summit. Watch for moose in roadside ponds, bears on gravel bars and Dall sheep on mountainsides. For best wildlife viewing, stop at turnouts and use good binoculars. Wildflowers include sweet peas, chiming bells, arnica, oxytrope and lupine.

GJ 103.5 (166.6 km) **A 306.5** (493.3 km) **T 21.5** (34.6 km) Paved turnout to north. **Little Tok River** overflow; fishing for grayling and Dolly Varden.

GJ 102.4 (164.8 km) **A 305.4** (491.5 km) **T 22.6** (36.4 km) Entering Tok Management Area, Tanana Valley State Forest, eastbound.

GJ 99.3 (159.8 km) **A 302.3** (486.5 km) **T 25.7** (41.4 km) Rest area; paved double-ended turnout to north. Cranberries may be found in late summer.

GJ 98 (157.7 km) **A 301** (484.4 km) **T 27** (43.5 km) Bridge over Little Tok River, which parallels highway. Parking at end of bridge.

GJ 97.7 (157.2 km) **A 300.7** (483.9 km) **T 27.3** (43.9 km) *CAUTION: Watch for sections of narrow highway (no shoulders), bumps, dips and pavement breaks and frost heaves next 20 miles/32.2 km westbound.*

GJ 95.2 (153.2 km) **A 298.2** (479.9 km) **T 29.8** (48 km) Rest area; paved turnout to south.

GJ 91 (146.4 km) **A 294** (473.1 km) **T 34** (54.7 km) Gravel turnout to north. Side road to east with bridge (weight limit 20 tons) across **Little Tok River;** good fishing for grayling, 12 to 14 inches, use small spinner.

GJ 90 (144.8 km) **A 293** (471.5 km) **T 35** (56.3 km) Small paved turnout to south.

GJ 89.8 (144.5 km) **A 292.8** (471.2 km) **T 35.2** (56.6 km) **Mineral Lakes Bed & Breakfast.** Cabins on lake with sourdough breakfast. RV parking. Northern pike

fishing trips, boating, fishing licenses, tackle; gift shop. Come relax—an Alaskan rural getaway. Your hosts, Gary, Patty and Ashley Stender. HC72, Box 830, Tok, AK 99780-9410. Phone (907) 883-5498. Reservations welcome. [ADVERTISEMENT]

GJ 89.5 (144 km) **A 292.5** (470.7 km) **T 35.5** (57.1 km) **Mineral Lakes.** These are sloughs of the Little Tok River and provide both moose habitat and a breeding place for waterfowl. Good fishing for northern pike and grayling.

GJ 89 (143.2 km) **A 292** (469.9 km) **T 36** (57.9 km) Small paved turnout to south.

GJ 86.7 (139.5 km) **A 289.7** (466.2 km) **T 38.3** (61.6 km) Good place to spot moose.

GJ 85.7 (137.9 km) **A 288.7** (464.6 km) **T 39.3** (63.2 km) Turnout to north.

GJ 83.2 (133.9 km) **A 286.2** (460.6 km) **T 41.8** (67.3 km) Bridge over Bartell Creek. Just beyond is the divide between the drainage of the Tanana River, tributary of the Yukon River system flowing into the Bering Sea, and the Copper River system, emptying into the North Pacific near Cordova.

GJ 81 (130.4 km) **A 284** (457 km) **T 44** (70.8 km) Access road to **MENTASTA LAKE** (pop. 72), a Native village.

GJ 79.4 (127.8 km) **A 282.4** (454.5 km) **T 45.6** (73.4 km) Mentasta Summit (elev. 2,434 feet/742m). Watch for Dall sheep on mountainsides. Boundary between Game Management Units 12 and 13C and Sport-fish Management Units 8 and 2. Mountain views westbound.

GJ 78.1 (125.7 km) **A 281.1** (452.4 km) **T 46.9** (75.5 km) **Mentasta Lodge**. See display ad this section.

GJ 78 (125.5 km) **A 281** (452.2 km) **T 47** (75.6 km) View for westbound traffic of snow-covered Mount Sanford (elev. 16,237 feet/4,949m).

GJ 77.9 (125.4 km) **A 280.9** (452.1 km) **T 47.1** (75.8 km) Paved turnout to north by Slana Slough; salmon spawning area in August. Watch for beavers.

GJ 77 (123.9 km) **A 280** (450.6 km) **T 48** (77.2 km) *CAUTION: Watch for pavement breaks and rough road next mile westbound.*

GJ 76.3 (122.8 km) **A 279.3** (449.5 km) **T 48.7** (78.4 km) Bridge over Mabel Creek. Mastodon flowers (marsh fleabane) in late July; very large (to 4 feet) with showy seed heads.

CAUTION: Watch for sections of narrow highway (no shoulders), bumps, dips, pavement breaks and frost heaves next 20 miles/32.2 km eastbound.

GJ 76 (122.3 km) **A 279** (449 km) **T 49** (78.8 km) Bridge over Slana Slough.

GJ 75.6 (121.7 km) **A 278.6** (448.3 km) **T 49.4** (79.5 km) Bridge over Slana River. Rest area to south with large paved parking area, toilets and picnic tables along the river. This river flows from its source glaciers some 55 miles/88.5 km to the Copper River.

GJ 74 (119.1 km) **A 277** (445.8 km) **T 51** (82.1 km) Large paved turnout to south

overlooking Slana River.

GJ 69 (111 km) **A 272** (437.7 km) **T 56** (90.1 km) Turnout to north.

GJ 68 (109.4 km) **A 271** (436.1 km) **T 57** (91.7 km) Carlson Creek bridge. Paved turnout to south at west end of bridge.

GJ 65.5 (105.4 km) **A 268.5** (432.1 km) **T 59.5** (95.8 km) Paved turnout to south; viewpoint.

GJ 64.2 (103.3 km) **A 267.2** (430 km) **T 60.8** (97.8 km) Bridge over **Porcupine Creek** State Recreation Site 0.2 mile/0.3 km from highway; 12 forested campsites on loop road, 15-day limit, $10 nightly fee (concessionaire-operated, annual state park pass not accepted), drinking water, firepits, toilets, picnic tables and fishing (wood and charcoal available from concessionaire at Hart D Ranch, Mile 0.7 Nabesna Road). Low-bush cranberries in fall. *CAUTION: Watch for bears.* ▲

GJ 63 (101.4 km) **A 266** (428 km) **T 62** (99.8 km) Scenic viewpoint with view of Wrangell Mountains. The dominant peak to the southwest is Mount Sanford, a dormant volcano; the pinnacles of Capital Mountain can be seen against its lower slopes. Mount Jarvis (elev. 13,421 feet/4,091m) is visible to the south behind Mount Sanford; Tanada Peak (elev. 9,240 feet/2,816m) is more to the south. (Tanada Peak is sometimes mistaken for Noyes Mountain.)

Walk up the gravel hill to view Noyes Mountain (elev. 8,147 feet/2,483m), named for U.S. Army Brig. Gen. John Rutherford Noyes, a one-time commissioner of roads in the territory of Alaska. Appointed adjutant general of the Alaska National Guard in 1953, he died in 1956 from injuries and frostbite after his plane crashed near Nome.

GJ 62.7 (100.9 km) **A 265.7** (427.6 km) **T 62.3** (100.3 km) **Duffy's Roadhouse.** See display ad this section.

Private Aircraft: Duffy's Tavern airstrip; elev. 2,420 feet/737m; length 1,800 feet/548m; gravel; unmaintained.

GJ 61 (98.2 km) **A 264** (424.9 km) **T 64** (103 km) **Midway Service.** See display ad this section. ▲

GJ 60.8 (97.8 km) **A 263.8** (424.6 km) **T 64.2** (103.3 km) Bridge over **Ahtell Creek;** grayling. Parking area to north at east end of bridge. This stream drains a mountain area of igneous rock, where several gold and silver-lead claims are located.

GJ 59.8 (96.2 km) **A 262.8** (422.9 km) **T 65.2** (104.9 km) **Junction** with Nabesna Road. See NABESNA ROAD log page 336.

GJ 59.7 (96.1 km) **A 262.7** (422.8 km) **T 65.3** (105.1 km) View of Tanada Peak, Mount Sanford, Mount Blackburn and Mount Drum to the south and southwest. The Mentasta Mountains are to the east.

GJ 58.6 (94.3 km) **A 261.6** (421 km) **T 66.4** (106.9 km) Ahtell Creek trailhead.

GJ 57 (91.7 km) **A 260** (418.4 km) **T 68** (109.4 km) Scenic viewpoint overlooking Cobb Lakes.

GJ 55.2 (88.8 km) **A 258.2** (415.5 km) **T 69.8** (112.3 km) Tanada Peak viewpoint; gravel turnout to south.

GJ 53 (85.3 km) **A 256** (412 km) **T 72** (115.9 km) Grizzly Lake; lodging, camping, trail rides. Watch for horses on road.

Grizzly Lake Ranch Bed & Breakfast. See display ad this section. ▲

GJ 47 (75.6 km) **A 250** (402.3 km) **T 78** (125.5 km) Indian Creek trailhead to north.

GJ 44.6 (71.8 km) **A 247.6** (398.5 km) **T 80.4** (129.4 km) Turnout to north. Eagle Trail access (not marked).

Glenn Highway/Tok Cutoff offers views of Mt. Sanford, Mt. Drum and Mt. Wrangell. (Jerrianne Lowther, staff)

GJ 43.8 (70.5 km) **A 246.8** (397.1 km) **T 81.2** (130.6 km) Bridge over Indian River. This is a salmon spawning stream, usually late-June through July. Picnic site to south at west end of bridge with tables, 2 firepits, toilets.

GJ 43.4 (69.8 km) **A 246.4** (396.5 km) **T 81.6** (131.3 km) Double-ended gravel turnout to south.

GJ 41.2 (66.3 km) **A 244.2** (393 km) **T 83.8** (134.8 km) Long, double-ended turnout overlooking pond.

GJ 40.1 (64.5 km) **A 243.1** (391.2 km) **T 84.9** (136.6 km) Fish Creek in culvert. Small paved turnout to south. Fish Creek BLM trailhead at end of former alignment.

GJ 39 (62.8 km) **A 242** (389.5 km) **T 86** (138.4 km) Views of the Copper River valley and Wrangell Mountains. Looking south, peak on left is Mount Sanford and on right is Mount Drum (elev. 12,010 feet/3,661m).

Look for cotton grass and mastodon flowers in late July and August.

CAUTION: Rough road next 2 miles/3.2 km eastbound.

GJ 38.7 (62.2 km) **A 241.7** (389 km) **T 86.3** (138.8 km) Paved turnout to north. Mankoman Lake trail.

GJ 38 (61.2 km) **A 241** (387.8 km) **T 87** (140 km) *CAUTION: Road narrows westbound.*

GJ 36.5 (58.7 km) **A 239.5** (385.4 km) **T 88.5** (142.4 km) **Chistochina B&B.** See display ad this section.

GJ 35.5 (57.1 km) **A 238.5** (383.8 km) **T 89.5** (144 km) Chistochina River Bridge No. 2. Mount Sanford is first large mountain to the southeast, then Mount Drum.

GJ 35.4 (57 km) **A 238.4** (383.7 km) **T 89.6** (144.2 km) Chistochina River Bridge No. 1; parking at west end. Chistochina River trailhead. This river heads in the Chis-

(Continues on page 337)

Nabesna Road Log

Upper Skolai Valley in Wrangell–St. Elias National Park. Slana NPS ranger station on Nabesna Road has information on access to this enormous park.

(© Bill Sherwonit)

The Nabesna Road leads 45 miles/72.4 km southeast from **Milepost GJ 59.8** Glenn Highway (Tok Cutoff) to the old mining community of Nabesna. This side trip can be enjoyable for campers; there are no formal public campgrounds but there are plenty of beautiful spots to camp and a private campground at Mile 0.7/1.1 km. The area also offers good fishing. Horses are permitted on all trails. Off-road vehicles must have permits from the National Park Service. The Nabesna Road provides access to the northwest corner of Wrangell–St. Elias National Park and Preserve. The National Park Service ranger station at Slana has information on current Nabesna Road conditions and on backcountry travel in the park. (The Wrangell–St. Elias National Park visitor center is near Copper Center on the old Richardson Highway.)

The first 4 miles/6.4 km of road is chip seal surface; the remainder is gravel. Beyond **Milepost J 28.6** the road becomes rough and crosses several creeks which may be difficult to ford. The state-maintained road ends at Mile 42; vehicles are not recommended beyond this point. **Distance is measured from the junction with the Glenn Highway (J).**

J 0.1 (0.2 km) Slana highway maintenance station.

J 0.2 (0.3 km) Slana NPS ranger station; information on road conditions and on Wrangell–St. Elias National Park and Preserve. Open 8 A.M. to 5 P.M. daily, June 1 through September. USGS maps and natural history books for sale. Phone (907) 882-5238. For more information contact: Superintendent, Wrangell–St. Elias National Park and Preserve, P.O. Box 439, Copper Center, AK 99573; phone (907) 822-5234.

J 0.7 (1.1 km) Slana post office and Hart D Ranch complex. The picturesque ranch is the home and studio of sculptor Mary Frances DeHart. The ranch offers RV and tent camping, an art gallery, bed and breakfast accommodations, pay phone and dog kennels (DeHart raises Affenpincscher dogs).

Hart D Ranch. See display ad this section. ♿▲

J 1 (1.6 km) **SLANA** (pop. 39), once an Indian village on the north bank of the Slana River, now refers to this general area. Besides the Indian settlement, Slana boasted a popular roadhouse, now a private home. Slana elementary school is located here.

J 1.5 (2.4 km) Slana River Bridge; undeveloped camping area. Boundary between Game Management Units 11 and 13C.

J 2 (3.2 km) BLM homestead area next 2 miles/3.2 km southbound. Blueberries in the fall; grouse are seen in this area.

J 3.9 (6.2 km) Entering Wrangell–St. Elias National Park and Preserve. The Glenn Highway follows the northern boundary of the preserve between Slana and Gakona Junction; Nabesna Road provides access to the northwest corner of the park.

J 4 (6.4 km) Turnouts. Hard surface ends, gravel begins, southbound.

J 7 (11.3 km) Road crosses **Rufus Creek** culvert. Dolly Varden to 8 inches, June to October. Watch out for bears, especially during berry season.

J 8.9 (14.3 km) Rough turnout.

J 11 (17.7 km) Suslota Lake trailhead No. 1 to north.

J 11.4 (18.3 km) Gravel pit, room to park or camp.

J 12.2 (19.6 km) Road crosses Caribou Creek culvert.

J 12.5 (20.1 km) Turnout to southeast; Copper Lake trailhead.

J 13.1 (21.1 km) Suslota Lake trailhead No. 2 to north.

J 15 (24.1 km) Turnout.

J 15.4 (24.8 km) Beautiful views of Mount Sanford and Tanada Peak in the Wrangell Mountains, across the great plain of the Copper River.

J 16 (25.7 km) Turnout to northeast.

J 16.6 (26.7 km) Turnout to southwest.

J 16.9 (27.2 km) Turnout by large lake which reflects Mount Sanford.

J 18 (29 km) Pond to northeast. The highly mineralized Mentasta Mountains are visible to the north. This is sparsely timbered high country.

J 18.8 (30.3 km) Caribou Creek culvert.

J 19.3 (31.1 km) Turnout at gravel pit to northwest. Look for poppies, lupine, arnica and chiming bells in season.

J 19.7 (31.7 km) Hiking trail to north.

J 21.2 (34.1 km) Turnout at gravel pit to northwest.

J 21.8 (35.1 km) Rock Creek culvert.

J 22.3 (35.9 km) Rock Lake; turnouts both sides of road.

J 22.9 (36.8 km) Long Lake.

J 23.4 (37.7 km) Turnout. Floatplane landing.

J 24.4 (39.3 km) Turnout to southwest with view of Wrangell Mountains. Tanada Lake trail.

J 25.2 (40.6 km) Boundary between Sportfish Areas C and K, and Game Management Areas 11 and 12.

J 25.5 (41 km) Lodge. Glimpse of Tanada Lake beneath Tanada Peak to the south.

J 25.9 (41.7 km) Little Jack Creek.

J 26.1 (42 km) Access road to private campground and floatplane service at Jack Lake; no turnaround. ▲

J 27 (43.5 km) Turnouts to north and south.

J 28.2 (45.4 km) Turnouts at Twin Lakes; primitive campsite, good place to observe waterfowl. Wildflowers in June include Lapland rosebay, lupine and 8-petalled mountain avens.

AREA FISHING: Twin Lakes, grayling 10 to 18 inches, mid-May to October, flies or small spinner; also burbot. **Copper Lake** (fly in from Long Lake or Jack Lake), lake trout 10 to 12 lbs., mid-June to September, use red-and-white spoon; kokanee 10 to 12 inches, mid-June to July, use small spinner; grayling 12 to 20 inches, July through September; also burbot. **Long** and **Jack lakes,** grayling fishing. **Tanada Lake** (fly in from Long Lake or Jack Lake), grayling and lake trout.

J 28.6 (46 km) **Sportsmen's Paradise Lodge** is located 28.6 miles from the

Glenn Highway on the Nabesna Gold Mine Road. Miles of magnificent views on this old road to the former Nabesna Gold Mine. Free camper parking, sandwiches, bar, air taxi service, fishing, boating, hunting. A side trip not to miss. Fly-in fishing to Copper Lake, boats, motors, light-housekeeping cabins available. Dick and Lucille Frederick, your hosts. Phone (907) 822-5288 (radiophone). [ADVERTISEMENT] ▲

J 28.6 (46 km) The road deteriorates beyond this point and you may have to ford several creeks. Inquire at lodge here or Slana Ranger Station about road conditions.

J 29.6 (47.6 km) Trail Creek crosses road; no culvert but road has gravel base here. Easy to drive through creek, especially in fall. Overnight hikers may hike up Lost Creek and return via Trail Creek.

J 31.4 (50.5 km) Road crosses Lost Creek, a very wide expanse of water in spring, and may remain difficult to cross well into summer. Loose gravel makes it easy to get stuck in creek if you spin your wheels. Scout it out first. If you hesitate once in the creek, wheels may dig in. The road crosses several more creeks beyond here; these may also be difficult to ford.

J 31.6 (50.9 km) Boyden Creek (may have to ford after rain or during spring melt). Trailhead to north.

J 32.4 (52.1 km) Chalk Creek culvert.

J 33 (53.1 km) Big Grayling Lake hiking trail. Horses allowed.

J 34.1 (54.9 km) Radiator Creek culvert.

J 35 (56.3 km) Creek (must ford).

J 36 (57.9 km) Jack Creek Bridge.

J 36.1 (58.1 km) Informal campsites with picnic tables (1 north, 2 south). The road crosses 5 creeks the next 4.3 miles/6.9 km southbound. Watch for loose gravel in creekbeds.

J 41 (66 km) A marked trail, approximately 5 miles/8 km long, leads to Nabesna River and old Reeves Field airstrip, once used to fly gold out of and supplies in to mining camps. Devil's Mountain is to the left of the trail. The trail on the river also leads to the old Indian village of Khiltat.

J 41.4 (66.6 km) Skookum Creek in culvert.

J 42 (67.6 km) Devil's Mountain Lodge (private property). State-maintained road ends. Hiking only recommended beyond this point. Bed and breakfast, trail rides, flightseeing and showers available.

J 45 (72.4 km) **NABESNA** (area pop. less than 25; elev. 3,000 feet/914m). No facilities. This region has copper reserves, as well as gold in the streams and rivers, silver, molybdenum and iron ore deposits. Tailings deposits here are currently closed to the public. Nabesna gold mine is located here. Area residents subsist on caribou, Dall sheep, moose, bear, fish and small game. Fire fighting and trapping also provide some income. Big game hunting is popular in this area; registered guides and several outfitters have headquarters along Nabesna Road.

Return to Milepost GJ 59.8
Glenn Highway (Tok Cutoff)

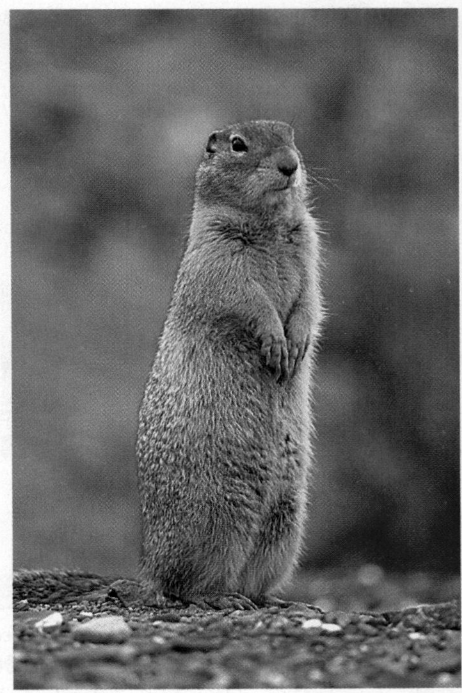

Arctic ground squirrels are abundant in tundra areas throughout Alaska.
(© Craig Brandt)

tochina Glacier on Mount Kimball (elev. 10,300 feet/3,139m). Chistochina is thought to mean marmot creek.

GJ 34.7 (55.8 km) **A 237.7** (382.5 km) **T 90.3** (145.3 km) Posty's Sinona Creek Trading Post (current status unknown).

GJ 34.6 (55.7 km) **A 237.6** (382.4 km) **T 90.4** (145.5 km) Bridge over Sinona Creek. Sinona is said to mean place of the many burls, and there are indeed many burls on area spruce trees.

GJ 34.4 (55.4 km) **A 237.4** (382 km) **T 90.6** (145.8 km) **Chistochina RV Park.** See display ad this section. ▲

GJ 34.1 (54.9 km) **A 237.1** (381.6 km) **T 90.9** (146.3 km) Chistochina ball fields.

GJ 32.9 (52.9 km) **A 235.9** (379.6 km) **T 92.1** (148.2 km) Road access to Native village of **CHISTOCHINA** (pop. 43).

Private Aircraft: Barnhart airstrip, 3 miles/4.8 km north; elev. 1,930 feet/588m; length 2,500 feet/762m; earth; unattended. Chistochina airstrip, adjacent southwest; elev. 1,850 feet/564m; length 2,000 feet/610m; turf and gravel.

GJ **32.8** (52.8 km) A **235.8** (379.5 km) T **92.2** (148.4 km) **Chistochina Lodge.** National Historic Site. Family restaurant specializing in sourdough pancakes, caribou sausage and steaks. Rooms, cabins and

bunkhouse. RV hookups. Hike the Eagle–Valdez trail. Learn of area gold mining. Fish, hunt or sightsee. Family-owned, operated and occupied. Summer and winter entertainment headquarters. "A place to feel at home." See display ad. [ADVERTISEMENT] ▲

GJ **30.1** (48.4 km) A **233.1** (375.1 km) T **94.9** (152.7 km) Paved turnout to south.

CAUTION: Road narrows eastbound; no shoulders. Watch for frost heaves.

GJ **28.1** (45.2 km) A **231.1** (371.9 km) T **96.9** (155.9 km) Double-ended paved parking area to south with a marker on the Alaska Road Commission. The ARC was established in 1905, the same year the first automobile arrived in Alaska at Skagway. The ARC operated for 51 years, building roads, airfields, trails and other transportation facilities. It was replaced by the Bureau of Public Roads (referred to by some Alaskans at the time as the Bureau of Parallel Ruts) in 1956. In 1960 the Bureau of Public Roads was replaced by the Dept. of Public Works.

GJ **24** (38.6 km) A **227** (365.3 km) T **101** (162.5 km) Large rest area to south with paved double-ended parking area, toilets, picnic tables and firepits on grass under trees; paths lead to Copper River. Mount Sanford is to the southeast, Mount Drum to the south.

GJ **20.9** (33.6 km) A **223.9** (360.3 km) T **104.1** (167.5 km) Turnout to Buster Gene trailhead to south.

GJ **17.8** (28.6 km) A **220.8** (355.3 km) T **107.2** (172.5 km) **Tulsona Creek** bridge. Good grayling fishing.

GJ **14.4** (23.2 km) A **217.4** (349.9 km) T **110.6** (178 km) *CAUTION: Watch for rough road next 7 miles eastbound.*

GJ **13** (20.9 km) A **216** (347.6 km) T **112** (180.2 km) Wide paved shoulder north. View of Mount Sanford.

GJ **11.6** (18.7 km) A **214.6** (345.4 km) T **113.4** (182.5 km) Yellow pond lily *(Nuphar polysepalum)* in ponds along highway.

GJ **9.4** (15.1 km) A **212.4** (341.8 km) T **115.6** (186 km) Paved turnout to north by lake. Fox Lake BLM trailhead.

GJ **8.8** (14.2 km) A **211.8** (340.8 km) T **116.2** (187 km) Paved turnout to north. BLM trailhead.

GJ **6.3** (10.1 km) A **209.3** (336.8 km) T **118.7** (191 km) Paved turnout to southeast.

GJ **4.7** (7.6 km) A **207.7** (334.3 km) T **120.3** (193.6 km) **The River Wrangellers.** See display ad this section.

GJ **4.2** (6.8 km) A **207.2** (333.4 km) T **120.8** (194.4 km) **Gakona, Alaska R.V. Park.** See display ad this section. ▲

GJ **3** (4.8 km) A **206** (331.5 km) T **122** (196.3 km) **Riverview Bed & Breakfast.** See display ad this section.

GJ **2.7** (4.3 km) A **205.7** (331 km) T **122.3** (196.8 km) **GAKONA** (area pop. 200). The village of Gakona lies between the Gakona and Copper rivers. (Gakona is Athabascan for "rabbit".) Originally Gakona was a Native wood and fish camp, and fish wheels are still common. The post office is

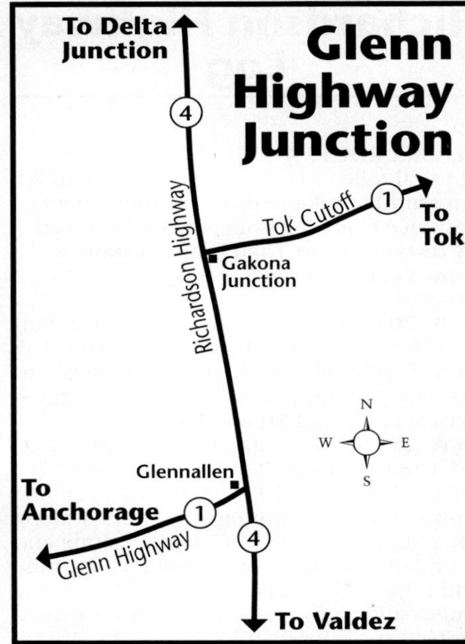

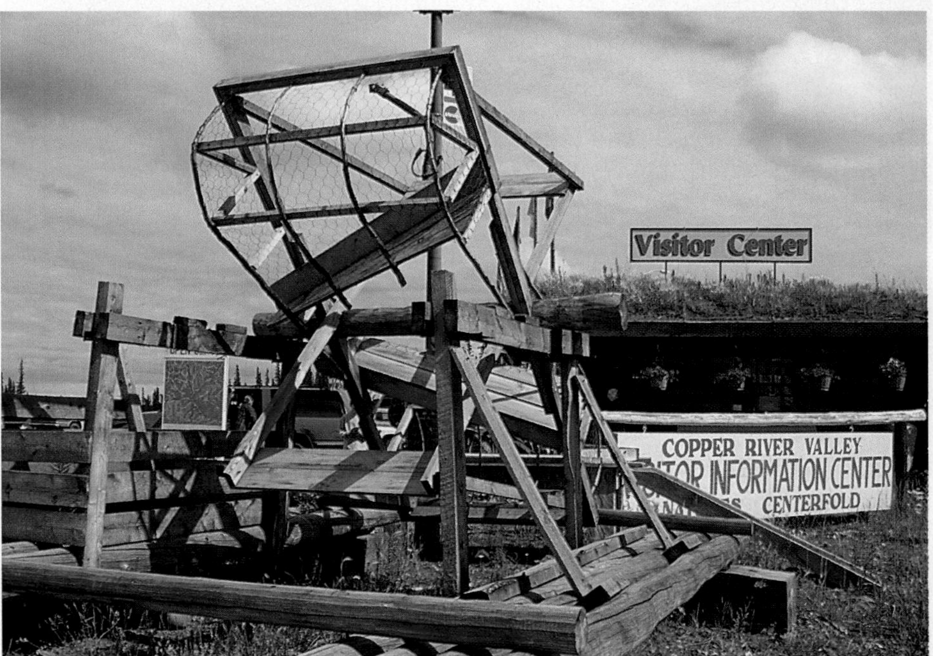

Fish wheel is displayed at Copper River Valley Visitor Center. Fish wheels are widely used for subsistence salmon fishing. (© Bruce M. Herman)

located on the highway here.

GJ 2 (3.2 km) **A 205** (330 km) **T 123** (198 km) Gakona Lodge, entered on the National Register of Historic Places in 1977. Originally one of several roadhouses providing essential food and lodging for travelers, it opened in 1905 and was first called Doyle's Ranch. The original carriage house is now a restaurant.

Gakona Lodge & Trading Post and **The Carriage House Dining Room.** See display ad this section.

GJ 1.8 (2.9 km) **A 204.8** (329.6 km) **T 123.2** (198.3 km) Bridge over Gakona River. Entering Game Management Unit 13B westbound and 13C eastbound. The highway climbs a short hill and joins the Richardson Highway 1.8 miles/2.9 km from this bridge. From the hill there is a fine view of the many channels where the Gakona and Copper rivers join.

GJ 1 (1.6 km) **A 204** (328.3 km) **T 124** (200 km) Rest area to south has paved turnout overlooking the valley of the Gakona and Copper rivers; picnic tables. View of Mount Drum and Mount Sanford. Good photo stop.

GJ 0 A 203 (326.7 km) **T 125** (201.2 km) **Gakona Junction.** Lodge, gas, fishing guide services, store, camping and bed and breakfasts at **junction** of Tok Cutoff (Alaska Route 1) with the Richardson Highway (Alaska Route 4). The 2 roads share a common alignment for the next 14 miles/22.5 km westbound.

Turn north here for Delta Junction via the Richardson Highway (see **Milepost V 128.6** in the RICHARDSON HIGHWAY section). Turn south for Anchorage or Valdez. *NOTE: This junction can be confusing. Choose your route carefully.*

Gakona Junction Village. See display ad this section.

Gakona Pipeline Fish-Camp Bed and Breakfast. Clean, comfortable rooms for budget-minded travelers. Rooms from $49.95 (including breakfast), lowest in Copper Valley. Gakona Stop 'n Shop, Gakona Texaco and Gulkana Fish Guides, at the same location, provide one-stop shopping for highway visitors. Reservations: Phone (907) 822-3664; Fax (907) 822-3696; e-mail: gakona@alaska.net. Internet connection: www.akpub.com/akbbrv/gakon.html. [ADVERTISEMENT]

Gulkana Fish Guides operates from Gakona Junction Village. Fish for king salmon in Gulkana and Klutina Rivers. Half-day and full-day trips. All gear provided. We filet, freeze and ship. Bed and breakfast, Texaco and groceries. Dress for the weather. We do the rest. Reservations phone (907) 822-3664; fax (907) 822-3696; e-mail gakona@alaska.net; Internet www.akpub.com/fhwag/gulka.html. [ADVERTISEMENT]

Line Camp (at junction with Tok Cutoff). Groceries, ice, sporting goods, minor repairs, welding, 2 bed and breakfast units (2 bedrooms and kitchen in each). RV parking. Tourist information, guided king salmon on the Gulkana River. Specialized tours available. Phone (907) 822-3508 or (907) 822-5723; P.O. Box 255, Glennallen, AK 99588. [ADVERTISEMENT]

The highway community of Glennallen is 187 miles east of Anchorage and 141 miles west of Tok. (© Tom Culkin)

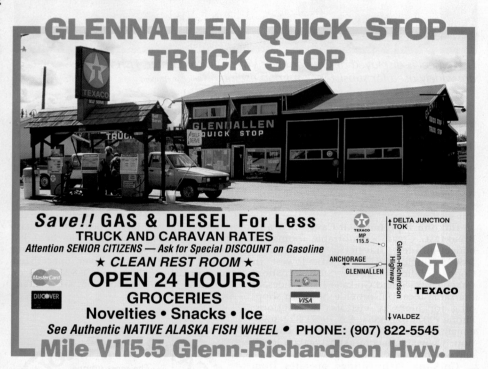

Richardson Highway Log

ALASKA ROUTE 4
Physical mileposts for the next 14 miles/22.5 km southbound give distance from Valdez. **Distance from Anchorage (A) is followed by distance from Tok (T) and distance from Valdez (V).**

A 203 (326.7 km) **T 125** (201.2 km) **V 128.6** (207 km) **Junction** of the Tok Cutoff with the Richardson Highway at Gakona Junction. Watch for frost heaves between here and **Milepost V 124.**

A 201 (323.5 km) **T 127** (204.4 km) **V 126.9** (204.2 km) Access road to **GULKANA** (pop. 100) on the bank of the Gulkana River. Camping is permitted along the river by the bridge. Grayling fishing and good king and sockeye salmon fishing (June and July) in the **Gulkana River.** Most of the Gulkana River frontage in this area is owned by Gulkana village and managed by Ahtna, Inc. Ahtna lands are closed to the public for hunting, fishing and trapping. ▲

A 200.9 (323.3 km) **T 127.1** (204.5 km) **V 126.8** (204 km) Gulkana River Bridge. Entering Game Management Unit 13B eastbound, 13A westbound.

A 200.3 (322.3 km) **T 127.7** (205.5 km) **V 126.2** (203.1 km) Inn.

A 200.1 (322 km) **T 127.9** (205.8 km) **V 126** (202.8 km) Paved double-ended turnout to north.

A 197.3 (317.5 km) **T 130.7** (210.3 km) **V 123.2** (198.3 km) Large paved turnout to south.

A 192.1 (309.1 km) **T 135.9** (218.7 km) **V 118.1** (190 km) **Private Aircraft:** Gulkana airstrip; elev. 1,578 feet/481m; length 5,000 feet/1,524m; asphalt; fuel 100. Flying service located here.

A 192 (309 km) **T 136** (218.9 km) **V 118** (189.9 km) Dry Creek State Recreation Site; 58 campsites, 15-day limit, $10 nightly fee or annual pass, 4 picnic sites, toilets, picnic shelter. *Bring mosquito repellent!* ▲

A 189.5 (305 km) **T 138.5** (222.9 km) **V 115.5** (185.9 km) **Glennallen Quick Stop Truck Stop.** Stop for friendly family service, gas, diesel, convenience store with ice, pop, snacks, postcards, ice cream, specialty items, pay phone and free coffee. Truck, caravan, senior citizen discounts. Several interesting items on display, including an authentic Native Alaskan fish wheel. Full-service restaurant adjacent. See display ad this section. [ADVERTISEMENT]

A 189.5 (305 km) **T 138.5** (222.9 km) **V 115.5** (185.9 km) **Rendezvous Cafe.** See display ad this section.

A 189 (304.2 km) **T 139** (223.7 km) **V 115** (185.1 km) **Junction** of the Richardson Highway (Alaska Route 4) with the Glenn Highway (Alaska Route 1). Turn south here on the Richardson Highway for Valdez (see **Milepost V 115** in the RICHARDSON HIGHWAY section). Continue west on the Glenn Highway for Anchorage. *NOTE: This junction can be confusing. Choose your route carefully. See map page 339.*

Greater Copper Valley Chamber of Commerce Visitor Information center, convenience store with automatic teller machine and gas station. Alaska State Troopers, Dept. of Motor Vehicles, Fish and Wildlife Protection and courthouse located on east side of highway.

Greater Copper Valley Chamber of Commerce Visitor Center in log cabin; open 8 A.M. to 7 P.M. daily in summer. There's also a convenience grocery and a gas station (with diesel) at junction.

The Greater Copper Valley Chamber of Commerce. See display ad this section.

The Hub of Alaska and **Hub Maxi-Mart.** See display ad this section.

Glenn Highway Log

ALASKA ROUTE 1
Physical mileposts between Glennallen and Anchorage show distance from Anchorage. **Distance from Anchorage (A) is followed by distance from Tok (T).**

A 188.7 (303.7 km) **T 139.3** (224.2 km) **Northern Nights Campground RV Park.** See display ad this section. ▲

A 188.3 (303 km) **T 139.7** (224.8 km) Trans–Alaska pipeline passes under the highway.

A 187.8 (302.2 km) **T 140.2** (225.6 km) **The Hitchin' Post.** Serving breakfast, lunch and dinner. Open at 6 A.M. It's *THE* place for breakfast among locals, with a $2.99 special! Quaint dining room, drive-through window and clean outdoor tables. Hand-scooped gourmet ice creams, famous fries, Mexican fare, old-fashioned burgers. Look for the yellow place across from the car wash! [ADVERTISEMENT]

A 187.5 (301.7 km) **T 140.5** (226.1 km) **Tastee–Freez.** This popular spot features an excellent menu of fast food, including breakfast, with some of the lowest prices on the highway. We satisfy appetites of all sizes, from a quick taco to double cheeseburgers, cooked fresh and fast. Our comfortable dining room displays a selection of the finest original drawings and handmade gifts. Plan to stop! See display ad on page 343. [ADVERTISEMENT]

Old Post Office Gallery. Owner and resident artist Jean Rene´ invites you to explore an appealing array of fine art and one-of-a-kind gifts. Here you will find original paintings, limited edition prints, Alaska Native crafts, photography, Alaskan books and more. Stop by for a memorable experience. See display ad page 344. [ADVERTISEMENT]

A 187.2 (301.3 km) **T 140.8** (226.6 km) National Bank of Alaska; 24-hour automatic teller machine. Post office a block north of highway. Description of Glennallen follows.

Glennallen

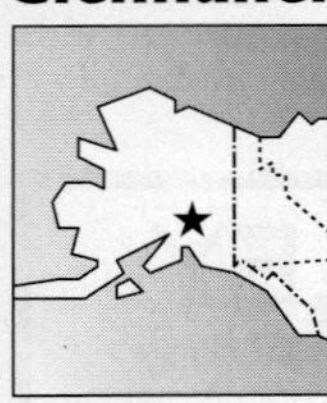

A 187 (300.9 km) **T 141** (226.9 km) Near the south junction of Glenn and Richardson highways. **Population**: 928. **Emergency Services: Alaska State Troopers, Milepost A 189**, phone (907) 822-3263. **Fire Department**, phone 911. **Ambulance**, Copper River EMS, phone (907) 822-3203 or 911. **Clinic, Milepost A 186.6**, phone (907) 822-3203. **Road Conditions**, phone (907) 822-5511.

Visitor Information: The Greater Copper Valley Chamber of Commerce Visitor Center is located in the log cabin at the junction of the Glenn and Richardson highways. **Milepost A 189**; open 8 A.M. to 7 P.M. daily in summer, phone (907) 822-5555 or write Box 469MP, Glennallen, AK 99588. The Alaska Dept. of Fish and Game office is located at **Milepost A 186.2** on the Glenn Highway, open weekdays 8 A.M. to 5 P.M.; phone (907) 822-3309.

Elevation: 1,460 feet/445m. **Climate:** Mean monthly temperature in January, -10°F/-23°C; in July, 56°F/13°C. Record low was -61°F/-52°C in January 1975; record high, 90°F/32°C in June 1969. Mean precipitation in July, 1.53 inches/3.9cm. Mean precipitation (snow/sleet) in December, 11.4 inches/29cm. **Radio:** KCAM 790, KOOL 107.1, KUAC-FM 92.1. **Television:** KYUK (Bethel) and Wrangell Mountain TV Club via satellite; Public Broadcasting System.

Private Aircraft: Gulkana airstrip, 4.3 miles/6.9 km northeast of Glennallen at **Milepost A 192.1**; elev. 1,578 feet/481m; length 5,000 feet/1,524m; asphalt; fuel 100. Parking with tie downs. Mechanic available.

The name Glennallen is derived from the combined last names of Capt. Edwin F. Glenn and Lt. Henry T. Allen, both leaders in the early exploration of the Copper River region.

Glennallen lies at the western edge of the huge Wrangell–St. Elias National Park and Preserve. It is a gateway to the Wrangell Mountains and the service center for the Copper River basin. Glennallen is also a fly-in base for several guides and outfitters.

Four prominent peaks of the majestic Wrangell Mountains are to the east; from left they are Mounts Sanford, Drum, Wrangell and Blackburn. The best views are on crisp winter days at sunset. The rest of the countryside is relatively flat.

The main business district is 1.5 miles/2.4 km west of the south junction of the Glenn and Richardson highways. There are also several businesses located at the south junction. About two-thirds of the area's residents are employed by trade/service firms; the balance hold various government positions. Offices for the Bureau of Land Management, the Alaska State Troopers and Dept. of Fish and Game are located here. There are several small farms in the area. There is a substantial Native population in the area, and the Native-owned Ahtna Corp. has its headquarters in Glennallen at the junction of the Glenn and Richardson highways.

Also headquartered here is KCAM radio, which broadcasts on station 790. KCAM broadcasts area road condition reports daily and also airs the popular "Caribou Clatter," which will broadcast personal messages. Radio messages are still a popular form of communication in Alaska and a necessary one in the Bush. Similar radio programs

GLENNALLEN ADVERTISERS

Bishop's RV Park & Car Wash ....Downtown
Brown Bear Rhodehouse ....Mile 183.6 Glenn Hwy.
Caribou Cafe Family Restaurant ....Ph. (907) 822-3656
Copper Valley Cellular ......Ph. (800) 235-5414
Glennallen Chevron ....Ph. (907) 822-3303
KCAM Radio ....Ph. (907) 822-3434
Mechanix Warehouse Auto Parts ....Ph. (907) 822-3444
Moose Horn RV Park ....Mile 187.7 Glenn Hwy
New Caribou Hotel, Gift Shop and Restaurant ....Ph. (907) 822-3302
Northern Nights Campground & RV Park ....Ph. (907) 822-3199
Old Post Office Gallery ..Adjacent Tastee-Freez
Park's Place Supermarket ....Ph. (907) 822-3334
Tastee-Freez ....Downtown
Tolsona Wilderness Campground ....Mile 173 Glenn Hwy.

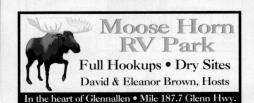

throughout the state are KJNP's "Trapline Chatter"; KYAK's "Bush Pipeline"; KHAR's "Northwinds"; and KIAK's "Pipeline of the North."

ACCOMMODATIONS/VISITOR SERVICES

Because of its strategic location, most traveler services are available. During summer months reservations are advised for visitor accommodations. Glennallen has several lodges and motels and a variety of restaurants. Auto parts, groceries, gift shops, clothing, propane, sporting goods and other supplies are available at local stores. Services include a bank and automatic teller machine, a dentist, several churches, a chiropractic center, a laundromat, gas stations and major auto repair.

New Caribou Hotel, Gift Shop and Restaurant. The New Caribou Hotel in downtown Glennallen, on the edge of the largest national park in America, was completed fall of 1990. This 55-unit modern facility features custom-built furniture, state-of-the-art color coordinated Alaskan decor, 6 rooms with 2-person whirlpool baths, 2-bedroom, fully furnished suites with kitchens and cooking facilities. Alaskan art, handicap facilities, conference rooms, phones and fax lines, satellite TV. Large full menu restaurant with banquet room, unique Alaskan gift shop (a must stop in your travels). All major credit cards accepted. Tour buses welcome. Airport transportation. Ask us for travel and visitor information. Open year-round. Phone (907) 822-3302. Toll free in Alaska phone (800) 478-3302, fax (907) 822-3711. [ADVERTISEMENT] ♿

There are private campgrounds west of

View of Tazlina Glacier and Lake from Lake Louise Road west of Glennallen.
(Jerrianne Lowther, staff)

town on the Glenn Highway (see **Milepost A 183.6, A 173** and **A 170.5**) and east of town at **Milepost A 188.7**. There are 2 private RV parks in Glennallen and at **Milepost V 110.5** Richardson Highway (4.5 m/7.2 km south of the junction). Northeast of Glennallen 5 miles/8 km is Dry Creek state campground (see **Milepost A 192**). ▲

TRANSPORTATION

Bus: Scheduled service between Anchorage and Whitehorse via Glennallen. Bus service between Glennallen and McCarthy via Copper Center and Chitina in summer.

ATTRACTIONS

Fourth of July weekend is a major event in Glennallen. Activities include the Ahtna Arts and Crafts Fair, a music festival, raft race, parade and salmon bake.

Recreational opportunities in the Glennallen area include hiking, flightseeing, hunting, river running, bird watching and fishing. According to the ADF&G, approximately 50 lakes in the Glennallen area are stocked with grayling, rainbow trout and coho salmon. A complete list of lakes, locations and species is available at the Copper River Valley Visitor Center at **Milepost A 189**, or from the ADF&G office at **Milepost A 186.2.** Locally, there is good grayling fishing in **Moose Creek; Tulsona Creek** to the east at **Milepost GJ 17.5;** west on the Glenn Highway at **Tolsona Creek, Milepost A 173;** and **Mendeltna Creek, Milepost A 152.8. Lake Louise**, approximately 27 miles/43 km west and 16 miles/25.7 km north from Glennallen, offers excellent grayling and lake trout fishing.

Many fly-in lakes are located in the Copper River basin and Chugach Mountains near Glennallen. **Crosswind Lake,** large lake trout, whitefish and grayling, early June to early July. **Deep Lake,** all summer for lake trout to 30 inches. **High Lake,** lake trout to 22 inches, June and early July with small spoons; some rainbow, fly-fishing; cabin, boat and motor rental. **Tebay Lakes,** excellent rainbow fishing, 12 to 15 inches, all summer, small spinners; cabin, boat and motor rental. **Jan Lake,** 12- to 14-inch silver salmon, June, spinners; also rainbow. **Hanagita Lake,** excellent grayling fishing all summer; also lake trout and steelhead in September. **Minnesota Lake,** lake trout to 30 inches, all summer; boat only, no cabins.

Glenn Highway Log

(continued)

A 186.6 (300.3 km) **T 141.4** (227.6 km) Cross Road Medical Center clinic. Alaska Bible College, the state's only accredited resident 4-year bible college, is located behind the clinic.

A 186.4 (300 km) **T 141.6** (227.9 km) Bureau of Land Management district office; phone (907) 822-3217.

A 186.2 (299.7 km) **T 141.8** (228.2 km) Alaska State Dept. of Fish and Game; phone (907) 822-3309.

A 186.1 (299.5 km) **T 141.9** (228.4 km) Copper Valley library.

A 186 (299.3 km) **T 142** (228.5 km) **Moose Creek** culvert; good grayling fishing in spring.

CAUTION: Watch for frost heaves.

A 183.6 (295.5 km) **T 144.4** (232.4 km) **Brown Bear Rhodehouse.** Because of the excellent food, reasonable prices and Alaskan hospitality, this famous old lodge is a favorite eating and gathering place for local people and travelers alike. If eating in the Glennallen area, we recommend stopping here, and if coming from south it is well worth the extra few minutes' wait. Superb steaks and seafood are the specialties, along with broasted chicken and the widest sandwich selection in the area. Your hosts, Doug and Cindy Rhodes, have managed to take one of the largest grizzly brown bear photograph collections anywhere. So, if not dining, you will enjoy just stopping and looking at the many photographs that cover the walls or listening to a few bear tales in the lounge. This is the only place in the area where you have a campground, camping cabins, motel, restaurant and bar at one stop. This is also the only place on the highway to get a bucket of golden brown broasted chicken to go. Phone (907) 822-3663. [ADVERTISEMENT]

A 183 (294.5 km) **T 145** (233.3 km) *CAUTION: Watch for frost heaves.*

A 182.2 (293.2 km) **T 145.8** (234.6 km) **Basin Liquors, Paper Shack Office Supply.**

Liquor store opens 8 A.M., 7 days a week, 365 days a year. Liquor, snacks, ice, cigarettes. We invite you to take a break; walk around in one of the most beautiful yards on the Glenn Highway, longtime home of pioneer resident "Gramma Ole" Hanson. [ADVERTISEMENT]

A 176.6 (284.2 km) **T 151.4** (243.6 km) Paved turnout to south with interpretive sign about the Wrangell Mountains and view east across the Copper River valley to Mount Drum. Northeast of Mount Drum is Mount Sanford and southeast is Mount Wrangell (elev. 14,163 feet/4,317m), a semi-active volcano. Mount Wrangell last erupted in 1912 when lava flowed to its base and ash fell as far west as this point.

Wildflowers growing along the roadside include lupine, cinquefoil, oxytrope, Jacob's ladder and sweet pea.

A 174.7 (281.1 km) **T 153.3** (246.7 km) Double-ended paved turnout to south.

A 173 (278.4 km) **T 155** (249.4 km) **Tolsona Wilderness Campground & RV Park.** AAA approved, Good Sam Park. This beautiful campground, located three-quarter mile north of the highway, is surrounded on 3 sides by untouched wilderness. All 80 campsites are situated beside sparkling Tolsona Creek and are complete with table, litter barrel and fireplace. It is a full-service campground with tent sites, restrooms,

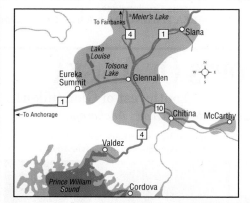

dump station, hot showers, laundromat, water and electric hookups for RVs. Internet access available. Browse through the extensive turn-of-the-century antique display. Hiking trail and public phone. Open from May 20 through Sept. 10. $12 to $18 per night. Phone (907) 822-3865. E-mail: twcg@alaska.net. See display ad in Glennallen section. [ADVERTISEMENT]

Tolsona Creek, grayling to 16 inches, use mosquito flies in still, clear pools behind obstructions, June, July and August. Best fishing 1.5 miles/2.4 km upstream from highway. **Tolsona** and **Moose lakes,** rainbow trout, burbot, grayling to 16 inches, all summer; good ice fishing for burbot in winter; boats, food and lodging.

A 170.5 (274.4 km) **T 157.5** (253.5 km) **Tolsona Lake,** grayling to 16 inches, burbot, rainbow. **Crosswind Lake,** 18 miles/29 km north by floatplane, excellent fishing for lake trout, grayling and whitefish.

A 169.3 (272.3 km) **T 158.7** (255.4 km) **Mae West Lake** trail. Paved double-ended turnout to south. The long narrow lake, fed by Little Woods Creek, is a little less than 1 mile/1.6 km away. Grayling fishing.

CAUTION: Watch for frost heaves and rough pavement next several miles westbound.

A 168 (270.4 km) **T 160** (257.5 km) Soup Lake to north. Trumpeter swans can sometimes be seen in lakes and ponds along this section of highway. In June and July look for wildflowers such as sweet pea, fireweed, lupine, cinquefoil, oxytrope, Jacob's ladder and milk-vetch.

A 166.1 (267.3 km) **T 161.9** (260.5 km) Atlasta House, a local landmark, was named by the homesteader who was happy to have a real house at last.

A 166 (267.2 km) **T 162** (260.7 km) Tolsona Mountain (elev. 2,974 feet/906m), a prominent ridge just north of highway, is a landmark for miles in both directions. This area is popular with berry-pickers in late summer and early fall. Varieties of wild berries include blueberries, lowbush cranberries and raspberries.

A 165.9 (267 km) **T 162.1** (260.9 km) Paved double-ended turnout to south and 2-mile/3.2-km hiking trail to **Lost Cabin Lake;** grayling fishing.

A 162.3 (261.2 km) **T 165.7** (266.7 km) Paved turnout to south. Wildflowers include Jacob's ladder, tundra rose, paintbrush, yarrow, dwarf fireweed and lupine.

A 162 (260.7 km) **T 166** (267.1 km) **Tex Smith Lake** to north; stocked with rainbow.

A 161 (259 km) **T 167** (268.7 km) *CAUTION: Bad frost heaves next 0.4 mile/0.6 km eastbound.*

A 159.8 (257.2 km) **T 168.2** (270.7 km) **Junction** with 19.3-mile/31-km Lake Louise Road (gravel) to Lake Louise Recreation Area. See LAKE LOUISE ROAD log on opposite page.

A 159.6 (256.8 km) **T 168.4** (271 km) **Little Junction Lake** trailhead, 0.3-mile/0.4-km hike south; grayling.

A 157 (252.6 km) **T 171** (275.2 km) *CAUTION: Watch for bumps in pavement and frost heaves westbound to* ***Milepost A 135.***

A 156.9 (252.5 km) **T 171.1** (275.3 km) Trails to south to **DJ Lake** 0.5 mile/0.8 km (rainbow fishing) and **Sucker Lake** 4 miles/6.4 km (grayling and burbot).

A 156.4 (251.7 km) **T 171.6** (276.1 km) Views of Tazlina Glacier in the distance, eastbound as the highway crests hills. The glacier feeds into 20-mile/32-km-long Tazlina Lake at its foot.

A 156.3 (251.5 km) **T 171.7** (276.3 km) **Buffalo Lake;** stocked with rainbow.

A 156.2 (251.4 km) **T 171.8** (276.5 km) Tazlina Glacier Lodge.

A 156 (251 km) **T 172** (276.8 km) **Private Aircraft:** Tazlina airstrip; elev. 2,450 feet/747m; length 1,200 feet/366m; gravel; unattended.

A 155.8 (250.7 km) **T 172.2** (277.2 km) **Arizona Lake** to south; fishing for grayling.

A 155.6 (250.4 km) **T 172.4** (277.4 km) Paved turnout to south.

A 155.2 (249.8 km) **T 172.8** (278.1 km) **Gergie Lake** 1.3 mile/2.1 km to south; fishing for grayling and rainbow.

A 153 (246.2 km) **T 175** (281.6 km) **K.R.O.A. Kamping Resorts of Alaska** on the Little Mendeltna, a natural spring-fed stream. Excellent fishing for grayling, whitefish and others. Many lakes nearby. Fishing, hunting guides available. Gateway to Tazlina Lake and Glacier. Skiing, hiking, snow machine trails. Modern hookups. Pull-throughs. Laundromat. Hot showers. Can handle any size caravan. Rustic cabins. Brick-oven fresh dough pizza. Homemade cinnamon rolls. Museum of Alaska's Drunken Forest, a large collection of unusual and artistic natural designs of trees. Minerals. Artifacts of Alaska's drunken forest. Free. [ADVERTISEMENT]

A 152.8 (245.9 km) **T 175.2** (282 km) Mendeltna Creek bridge.

AREA FISHING: Mendeltna Creek, good fishing north to Old Man Lake; watch for bears. (The Mendeltna Creek drainage is closed to the taking of salmon.) Excellent fishing for grayling to 17½ inches and whitefish to 16 inches, May to November, use spinners and flies. Walk or boat away from the bridge.

A 152.7 (245.7 km) **T 175.3** (282.1 km) Paved double-ended rest area to north with picnic tables, dumpster and toilets. Rough road.

A 150 (241.4 km) **T 178** (286.4 km) Eastbound view of Mount Sanford and Mount Drum straight ahead.

A 149 (239.8 km) **T 179** (288.1 km) Food, lodging and towing. **Ryan Lake;** fishing for grayling and rainbow.

Grizzly Country Enterprises. Browse in our gift shop, find that specially made Alaskan gift. Our grocery store has what you need at reasonable prices. A cozy cabin awaits you in our breathtaking Alaskan wilderness, where wildlife is abundant. Miles of trails nearby for snowmachines and hikers. Don't forget our coffee and ice cream shop. RVs welcome. Our towing company is known for our fair prices, fast and friendly

(Continues on page 348)

Salmonberries, related to the raspberry, are common in woods and along roadsides. (© Lee Foster)

Lake Louise Road Log

This scenic gravel road leads north 19.3 miles/31 km from **Milepost A 159.8** Glenn Highway to Lake Louise Recreation Area. It is open year-round. Lake Louise is known for its lake trout fishing; ice fishing in winter. Excellent cross-country skiing. Many turnouts and parking areas along the road; views of Tazlina Glacier and Lake; berry picking for wild strawberries and blueberries (July and August), and cranberries (September).

Distance is measured from the junction with the Glenn Highway (J).

J 0.2 (0.3 km) **Junction Lake** to east; grayling fishing.

J 1.1 (1.8 km) Turnout with view of Tazlina Glacier and Crater Lake.

J 1.2 (1.9 km) Double-ended turnout to west. Just north is the road west to **Crater Lake.** There are a number of small lakes along the road with good fishing for grayling.

J 5.2 (8.4 km) **Old Road Lake and Round Lake** trails to east; rainbow fishing.

J 6 (9.7 km) **Mendeltna Creek** trail to west (0.5 mile/0.8 km); grayling fishing.

J 7 (11.2 km) **Forgotten Lake** trail to east (0.1 mile/0.2 km); grayling fishing.

J 9.4 (15.1 km) Beautiful pothole lakes. First view of Lake Louise northbound.

J 11 (17.7 km) Good view on clear days of the Alaska Range and Susitna River valley.

J 11.5 (18.5 km) Road west to **Caribou Lake;** grayling fishing. Turnout to east by Elbow Lake.

J 14 (22.5 km) Boundary of Matanuska–Susitna Borough.

J 15.5 (24.9 km) Gas station, public dumpster.

J 16 (25.7 km) **North and South Jan's Lakes** trails to north (0.4 mile/0.6 km); fishing.

J 16.1 (25.9 km) **Lake Louise Lodge.** See display ad this section.

J 16.5 (26.6 km) **Evergreen Lodge Bed & Breakfast.** See display ad this section.

J 16.8 (27 km) **Conner Lake,** rainbow and grayling fishing.

J 17.2 (27.7 km) Side road to lodge and Lake Louise State Recreation Area's Army Point and Lake Louise campgrounds; 52 campsites on 2 loop roads, firepits, toilets (wheelchair accessible), covered picnic tables at lakeshore and a boat launch. Well water. Camping fee $10/night or annual pass. Swimming in Lake Louise. Winter ski trail access.

J 17.2 (27.7 km) **The Point Lodge at Lake Louise.** See display ad this section.

J 17.6 (28.3 km) Turnout to west. Winter ski trail access.

J 18.8 (30.3 km) Airport road to west. **Private Aircraft:** Lake Louise airstrip; elev. 2,450 feet/747m; length 2,000 feet/610m; gravel. Seaplane base adjacent.

J 19.3 (31 km) Road ends at Lake Louise rest area; picnic tables, fireplaces, toilets, parking, boat launch.

Lake Louise, excellent grayling and lake trout fishing; lake trout 20 to 30 lbs., average 10 lbs., good year-round, best spring through July, then again in late September; early season use herring or whitefish bait, cast from boat; later (warmer water) troll with #16 red-and-white spoon, silver Alaskan plug or large silver flatfish; grayling 10 to 12 inches, casting flies or small spinners, June, July and August; in winter jig for lake trout.

Susitna Lake can be reached by boat across Lake Louise; burbot, excellent lake trout and grayling fishing. Both lakes can be rough; under-powered boats not recommended. **Dinty Lake,** access by boat across Lake Louise; grayling and lake trout fishing.

Return to Milepost A 159.8 Glenn Highway

River rafters at Little Nelchina River state recreation site, Milepost A 137.6.
(© Tom Culkin)

service. VISA and MasterCard. Open 8 A.M.–10 P.M. Towing and Recovery 24 hours. (907) 822-3700. [ADVERTISEMENT]

A 147.3 (237.1 km) **T 180.7** (290.8 km) **Cache Creek** culvert. Grayling in late May and June. Trail leading from parking area to lake, approximately 0.5 mile/0.8 km. Small picnic area on east side of highway. Steep approach.

A 147 (236.6 km) **T 181** (291.3 km) *CAUTION: Very bad frost heaves next 0.7 mile/1.1 km westbound.*

A 144.9 (233.2 km) **T 183.1** (294.7 km) Lottie Sparks (Nelchina) Elementary School.

A 141.2 (227.2 km) **T 186.8** (300.6 km) Nelchina state highway maintenance station. Slide Mountain trailhead located behind station.

A 137.6 (221.4 km) **T 190.4** (306.4 km) Little Nelchina State Recreation Site 0.3 mile/0.5 km from highway; 11 campsites, 15-day limit, no camping fee, no drinking water, tables, firepits, toilet, boat launch. Watch for moose and bear. ▲

A 137.5 (221.3 km) **T 190.5** (306.6 km) Little Nelchina River bridge.

A 137 (220.5 km) **T 191** (307.4 km) Boundary of Matanuska–Susitna Borough.

A 135.7 (218.4 km) **T 192.3** (309.5 km) Small paved turnout. Highway widens eastbound. Truck lane next 2.3 miles/3.7 km westbound.

A 135.3 (217.7 km) **T 192.7** (310.1 km) **Nelchina Trail Store & Cabins.** See display ad this section.

A 134.8 (216.9 km) **T 193.2** (310.9 km) Watch for livestock on highway.

A 133 (214 km) **T 195** (313.8 km) Paved turnout to north.

A 132.1 (212.6 km) **T 195.9** (315.2 km) Caribou crossing. Gravel turnout to north. View of Mount Sanford eastbound. Caribou and moose seen in this area in winter. (The Nelchina caribou herd travels through here October through November.)

A 131.8 (212.1 km) **T 196.2** (315.7 km) Snow poles along roadside guide snow plows in winter.

A 131 (210.8 km) **T 197** (317 km) View west to the notch of Gunsight Mountain. From here to Eureka Summit there are views of the Wrangell and Chugach mountains.

A 130.3 (209.7 km) **T 197.7** (318.2 km) Old Man Creek trailhead parking to north. Old Man Creek 2 miles/3 km; Crooked Creek 9 miles/14.5 km; Nelchina Town 14.5 miles/23 km. Established trails west from here to Palmer are part of the Chickaloon–Knik–Nelchina trail system.

A 129.3 (208.1 km) **T 198.7** (319.8 km) Eureka Summit (elev. 3,322 feet/1,013m). Highest point on the Glenn Highway, near timberline, with unobstructed views south toward the Chugach Mountains. The Nelchina Glacier winds downward through a cleft in the mountains. To the northwest are the peaks of the Talkeetnas, and to the west the highway descends through river valleys which separate these 2 mountain ranges. This is the divide of 3 big river systems: Susitna, Matanuska and Copper.

A 128 (206 km) **T 200** (321.9 km) Site of the first lodge on the Glenn Highway, the Eureka Roadhouse, which was opened in 1937 by Paul Waverly and has operated continuously ever since. The original log building is next to Eureka Lodge.

Eureka Lodge. See display ad this section.

Private Aircraft: Skelton airstrip; elev. 3,289 feet/1,002m; length 2,400 feet/732m; gravel; fuel mogas; unattended.

A 127 (204.4 km) **T 201** (323.4 km) Gravel turnout to south.

A 126.4 (203.4 km) **T 201.6** (324.4 km) Watch closely for turnout to Belanger Creek–Nelchina River trailhead parking to south. Eureka Creek 1.5 miles/2.4 km; Goober Lake 8 miles/13 km; Nelchina River 9 miles/14.5 km.

A 125 (201.2 km) **T 203** (326.7 km) Gunsight Mountain (elev. 6,441 feet/1,963m) is visible to the west for the next few miles to those approaching from Glennallen. The notch or "gunsight" is plain if one looks closely. Eastbound views of snow-covered Mount Sanford (weather permitting), Mount Drum, Mount Wrangell and Mount Blackburn.

A 123.3 (198.4 km) **T 204.7** (329.4 km) Belanger Pass trailhead: Belanger Pass 3 miles/5 km; Alfred Creek 6.5 miles/10.5 km; Albert Creek 8 miles/13 km.

A 123.1 (198.1 km) **T 204.9** (329.8 km) Old Tahneta Inn (closed).

Private Aircraft: Tahneta Pass airstrip; elev. 2,960 feet/902m; length 1,100 feet/335m; gravel/dirt. Floatplanes land on Tahneta Lake.

A 122.9 (197.8 km) **T 205.1** (330 km) Gunsight Mountain Lodge (current status unknown).

A 122 (196.3 km) **T 206** (331.5 km) Tahneta Pass (elev. 3,000 feet/914m). Double-ended paved turnout to north. **Leila Lake** trailhead (unsigned) on old alignment to north; grayling 8 to 14 inches abundant through summer, best fishing June and July. Burbot, success spotty for 12 to 18 inches in fall and winter.

A 120.8 (194.4 km) **T 207.2** (333.4 km) Boundary of Sportfish Management Area 2 and Sheep Mountain Closed Area.

A 120.3 (193.6 km) **T 207.7** (334.3 km) View eastbound overlooks Tahneta Pass. The largest lake is Leila Lake; in the distance is Tahneta Lake. Drive carefully along the southern part of Tahneta Pass.

*NOTE: Watch for road construction westbound to **Milepost A 109** in 1998.*

A 118.6 (190.9 km) **T 209.4** (337 km) Double-ended gravel turnout to south.

A 118.5 (190.7 km) **T 209.5** (337.1 km) FAA road south to communication towers.

A 118.3 (190.4 km) **T 209.7** (337.5 km) Large gravel turnout to south.

A 117.8 (189.5 km) **T 210.2** (338.2 km) Turnout with viewpoint. Looking southeast of the highway, a tip of a glacier can be seen coming down South Fork Canyon. Knob Lake and the "knob" (elev. 3,000 feet/914m) can be seen to the northeast.

A 117.6 (189.3 km) **T 210.4** (338.6 km) Squaw Creek trailhead: Squaw Creek 3.5 miles/5.6 km; Caribou Creek 9.5 miles/15 km; Alfred Creek 13 miles/21 km; Sheep Creek 15 miles/24 km.

A 115 (185 km) **T 213** (342.8 km) Between **Mileposts A 115** and **116** there are 3 turnouts with views of mineralized Sheep Mountain and Matanuska Glacier area.

A 114.9 (184.9 km) **T 213.1** (342.9 km) **Majestic Valley Lodge** combines the rustic charm of a quaint mountain lodge with modern conveniences to cater to the individual 4 seasons of the year. Enjoy hiking treks, viewing Dall sheep and other wildlife in the Gunsight Reserve, blueberry picking, glacier walks, cross-country skiing and snowmobiling. Gourmet meals, wood-stove sauna and an imposing view top off a relaxing day in the mountains. Rooms include private baths, quilted coverings and use of the large viewing lounge. (907) 746-2930; fax 746-2931; e-mail: MVWL@pobox.alaska.net. See display ad this section. [ADVERTISEMENT]

A 114.5 (184.3 km) **T 213.5** (343.6 km) In season, on slopes adjacent the highway and along old creek beds back from the road, are many kinds of flowers, including lupine, Labrador tea, bluebells, fireweed, chiming bells and large patches of forget-me-nots, Alaska's state flower.

A 114.3 (183.9 km) **T 213.7** (343.9 km) For Anchorage-bound travelers a vista of incomparable beauty as the road descends in a long straightaway toward Glacier Point, also known as the Lion Head, an oddly formed rocky dome.

A 113.5 (182.7 km) **T 214.5** (345.2 km) **Sheep Mountain Lodge.** Our charming log lodge, established in 1946, has been serving travelers for half a century. We're famous for our wholesome homemade food, fresh baked breads, pastries and desserts. Our comfortable guest cabins, all with private bathrooms, boast spectacular mountain views. We also have RV hookups, full bar, liquor store and Alaskan gifts. You can watch Dall Sheep through our telescope and relax in the hot tub or sauna after a day of traveling or hiking. HC03 Box 8490, Palmer, AK 99645. Phone (907) 745-5121; fax (907) 745-5120. E-mail: sheepmtl@alaska.net. Internet: www.alaska.net/~sheepmtl. See display ad this section. [ADVERTISEMENT]

Private Aircraft: Sheep Mountain airstrip; elev. 2,750 feet/838m; length 2,300 feet/701m; gravel/dirt; unattended.

A 113.5 (182.7 km) **T 214.5** (345.2 km) As the highway descends westbound into the valley of the Matanuska River, there is a view of the great glacier which is the main headwater source and gives the water its milky color.

A 113 (181.9 km) **T 215** (346 km) Gravel turnout to Sheep Mountain airstrip.

A 112.5 (181.1 km) **T 215.5** (346.8 km) View to north of Sheep Mountain (elev.

View westbound of the Lion Head, also known as Glacier Point. (Jerrianne Lowther, staff)

6,300 feet/1,920m) for 11 miles/17.7 km between Tahneta Pass and Caribou Creek. Sheep are often seen high up these slopes. The area surrounding Sheep Mountain is closed to the taking of mountain sheep.

A 112 (180.2 km) **T 216** (347.6 km) Gravel turnout by creek. View westbound of Lion Head and first view of Matanuska Glacier.

A 111 (178.6 km) **T 217** (349.2 km) Sharp curves and falling rocks for the next mile westbound.

A 110.3 (177.5 km) **T 217.7** (350.3 km) Watch for mountain sheep.

A 109.7 (176.5 km) **T 218.3** (351.3 km) Paved turnout to south. Access to bed and breakfast.

Tundra Rose Bed & Breakfast. See display ad this section.

A 109.5 (176.2 km) **T 218.5** (351.6 km) Paved turnout to south.

A 109 ((175.4 km) **T 219** (352.4 km) *NOTE: Watch for road construction eastbound to **Milepost A 118** in 1998.*

A 108.4 (174.4 km) **T 219.6** (353.4 km) Large gravel turnout to south. Winding road, long stretches without shoulders, watch for rocks and frost heaves westbound between here and Palmer.

A 107.8 (173.5 km) **T 220.2** (354.4 km) Turnout with view of Glacier Point (Lion Head) and Matanuska Glacier. Exceptional picture stop.

A 107.1 (172.4 km) **T 220.9** (355.5 km) Large gravel turnouts to south, viewpoint.

A 106.8 (171.9 km) **T 221.2** (356 km) Caribou Creek Bridge and Caribou Creek trailhead. Hiking distances: Squaw Creek 9 miles/14.5 km; Alfred Creek 13 miles/21 km; Sheep Creek 15 miles/24 km; and Squaw Creek trailhead 18.5 miles/30 km. Caribou Creek trail zigzags up the mountainside between the highway and the creek and leads back behind Sheep Mountain. A pleasant hike for good walkers.

Highway makes a steep descent (from both directions) down to Caribou Creek. The banks of this stream provide good rockhounding, particularly after mountain storms. There are turnouts on both sides of the highway here. Fortress Ridge (elev. 5,000 feet/1,524m) above the highway to the north. Sheep Mountain reserve boundary.

A 106 (170.6 km) **T 222** (357.3 km) Large gravel turnout overlooking Caribou Creek canyon. Steep descent eastbound.

A 105.8 (170.3 km) **T 222.2** (357.6 km) Road (closed to public) to FAA station on flank of Glacier Point. Mountain sheep occasionally are seen on the upper slopes.

A 105.5 (169.8 km) **T 222.5** (358.1 km) Gravel turnout to south.

A 105.3 (169.4 km) **T 222.7** (358.4 km) Turnout with views of Matanuska Glacier and the FAA station on Glacier Point.

A 105 (169 km) **T 223** (358.9 km) *NOTE: Watch for road construction westbound to **Mile A 97** in 1998.*

A 104.1 (167.5 km) **T 223.9** (360.3 km) Access to Glacier View School, which overlooks Matanuska Glacier.

A 104 (167.4 km) **T 224** (360.5 km) From here to **Milepost A 98** several kinds of wild orchids and other wildflowers may be found along the trails into the roadside brush.

A 102.8 (165.4 km) **T 225.2** (362.4 km) Paved turnout to south with view of Matanuska Glacier.

A 102.2 (164.5 km) **T 225.8** (363.4 km) **Long Rifle Lodge**. Welcome to Alaska's most fabulous dining view of the Matanuska Glacier. We offer a complete breakfast, lunch and dinner menu, specializing in home-cooked meals. Twenty-five wildlife mounts make our lodge a "must see" for all ages. Numerous hiking, cross-country skiing and snowmobile trails surround the area. In addition, we have motel rooms, gasoline, 24-hour wrecker service, gift shop and a full-service lounge. Phone (800) 770-5151. Fax (907) 745-5153. E-mail: lrl@matnet.com. See display ad this section. [ADVERTISEMENT] MP

A 102 (164.2 km) **T 226** (363.7 km) Access to foot of Matanuska Glacier via Glacier Park Resort. Admission fee charged.

Wickersham Trading Post. See display ad this section.

Glacier Park. We would like to invite you to experience the Matanuska Glacier at Glacier Park of Alaska. A 540-acre private resort located at the terminus of the Matanuska Glacier, in the heart of the Chugach Mountains. This is a great addition to your vacation. We offer glacier tours, hiking, backcountry adventures, recreation camping, tent camping, gift shop, rooms, laundry, showers, liquor store, film, snack foods, picnic area, snow machining, cross-country skiing. Flightseeing with Glacier Air. Motorcoaches and tours welcome. Open all year. Access at Milepost 102 Glenn Highway. HC03 Box 8449, Palmer, AK 99645. Phone (907) 745-2534. See display ad this section. [ADVERTISEMENT] ▲

A 101.7 (163.7 km) **T 226.3** (364.2 km) Paved turnout with good view of Matanuska Glacier, which heads in the Chugach Mountains and trends northwest 27 miles/43.5 km. Some 18,000 years ago the glacier reached all the way to the Palmer area. The glacier's average width is 2 miles/3.2 km; at its terminus it is 4 miles/6.4 km wide. The glacier has remained fairly stable the past 400 years. At the glacier terminus meltwater drains into a stream which flows into the Matanuska River.

A 101 (162.5 km) **T 227** (365.3 km) Matanuska Glacier State Recreation Site; 12 campsites on loop drive, 15-day limit, $10, nightly fee or annual pass, wheelchair accessible, water and toilets. Excellent views of the glacier from hiking trails along the bluff. (Use caution when walking near edge of bluff.) Wildflowers here in late July include fireweed, yarrow and sweet peas. ♿▲

A 100.8 (162.2 km) **T 227.2** (365.6 km) Large gravel turnout to south.

A 99.2 (159.6 km) **T 228.8** (368.2 km) Gravel turnout to south, with viewpoint. Pinochle–Hicks Creek trail. Winding road

Red-fruited bunchberries (dwarf dogwood) in autumn, near Long Lake. (© Nancy Faville)

with steep grades westbound.

A 97 (156 km) **T 231** (371.7 km) Gravel turnout to north. *NOTE: Watch for road construction eastbound to **Mile A 105** in 1998.*

A 96.6 (155.5 km) **T 231.4** (372.4 km) Private campground, lodge and store. Hicks Creek was named by Captain Glenn in 1898 for H.H. Hicks, the guide of his expedition. Ridges back from here, right side Anchorage-bound, are good rockhound areas. Anthracite Ridge has jasper, rosy-banded agate, petrified wood and rock crystal. Difficult to reach on foot.

Historical Hicks Creek Roadhouse. See display ad this section. ▲

A 96.5 (155.3 km) **T 231.5** (372.6 km) Bridge over Hicks Creek.

A 96.4 (155.1 km) **T 231.6** (372.7 km) Small gravel turnout to south.

A 94.9 (152.7 km) **T 233.1** (375.1 km) Victory Road. Slide area. Look for lupine and wild sweet pea.

A 93.4 (150.3 km) **T 234.6** (377.5 km) Cascade state highway maintenance camp.

A 93 (149.7 km) **T 235** (378.2 km) Gravel turnouts both sides of highway. Views of Amulet Peak and Monument Glacier and Valley.

A 91.3 (146.9 km) **T 236.7** (380.9 km) Cascade Creek culvert.

A 91 (146.4 km) **T 237** (381.4 km) First view eastbound of Matanuska Glacier.

A 90.6 (145.8 km) **T 237.4** (382 km) Paved turnout to south.

A 90.1 (145 km) **T 237.9** (382.9 km) Turnout to south gives access to Purinton Creek trailhead and parking.

A 89 (143.2 km) **T 239** (384.6 km) Purinton Creek trailhead. Bridge over Purinton Creek. Good blueberry patches in season if you can beat the bears to them. The stream heads on Anthracite Ridge and flows into the Matanuska River. Westbound, watch for coal seams along the highway.

A 87.8 (141.3 km) **T 240.2** (386.5 km) Two small gravel turnouts to south.

A 87.6 (141 km) **T 240.4** (386.9 km) Large gravel turnout above Weiner Lake.

A 87.5 (140.8 km) **T 240.5** (387 km) Turnout with water.

A 87.4 (140.6 km) **T 240.6** (387.2 km) **Weiner Lake** access; fishing for rainbow and grayling.

A 87.3 (140.5 km) **T 240.7** (387.4 km) Turnout. Highway descends eastbound.

A 86.8 (139.7 km) **T 241.2** (388.2 km) Slide area: Watch for falling rock.

A 86.5 (139.2 km) **T 241.5** (388.6 km) Good gravel turnout overlooking Long Lake to south.

A 85.3 (137.3 km) **T 242.7** (390.6 km) **Long Lake**, in a narrow canyon below the highway, is a favorite fishing spot for Anchorage residents. Fair for grayling to 18 inches, spring through fall; fish deeper as the water warms in summer. Good ice fishing in winter for burbot, average 12 inches. Long Lake State Recreation Site has 9 campsites, 15-day limit, no camping fee, no water, tables, firepits and toilets. Wildflowers include roses, sweet pea, paintbrush and lupine. Long upgrade begins eastbound. ▲

A 84.6 (136.1 km) **T 243.4** (391.7 km) There are several gravel turnouts westbound.

A 84.3 (135.7 km) **T 243.7** (392.2 km) Large double-ended turnout. View of Matanuska River and unnamed mountains.

A 84.1 (135.3 km) **T 243.9** (392.5 km) Large double-ended gravel turnout.

CAUTION: Watch for road equipment in slide areas next 4 miles/6.4 km eastbound.

A 83.2 (133.9 km) **T 244.8** (394 km) Narrow gravel road to Ravine and Lower Bonnie lakes. (Side road not signed.) Drive in 0.8 mile/1.3 km on side road to reach **Ravine Lake**; fishing from shore for rainbow. **Lower Bonnie Lake** is a 2-mile/3.2-km drive from the highway; Bonnie Lake State Recreation Site has 8 campsites, 15-day limit, no camping fee, no water, toilets and boat launch. Fishing for grayling and rainbow. Steep and winding road beyond Ravine Lake is not recommended for large vehicles or trailers; during rainy season this side road is not recommended for any vehicle. ▲

A 82 (132 km) **T 246** (395.9 km) Pyramid-shaped King Mountain is to the right (westbound) of the milepost as you look across the canyon. Several small gravel turnouts westbound. Highway ascends steeply eastbound.

A 80.8 (130 km) **T 247.2** (397.8 km) Entering Matanuska Valley Moose Range westbound. Large gravel turnout to south.

A 79.5 (127.9 km) **T 248.5** (399.9 km) Views of King Mountain (elev. 5,809 feet/1,770m).

A 79.1 (127.3 km) **T 248.9** (400.6 km) Gravel turnout to south.

A 78.2 (125.8 km) **T 249.8** (402 km) Gravel turnout with view of King Mountain and Matanuska River.

A 77.7 (125 km) **T 250.3** (402.8 km) Chickaloon River bridge. Gravel turnout. Boundary between Game Management Units 13 and 14. Chickaloon River Road winds upstream a short distance. Access to bed and breakfast and Matanuska Valley Moose Range. Watch for no trespassing and private property signs. Inquire locally about public access beyond the old railroad bridge at Mile 0.2 and about Chickaloon River access.

Chickaloon B&B Cottage. See display ad this section.

A 77.5 (124.7 km) **T 250.5** (403.1 km)

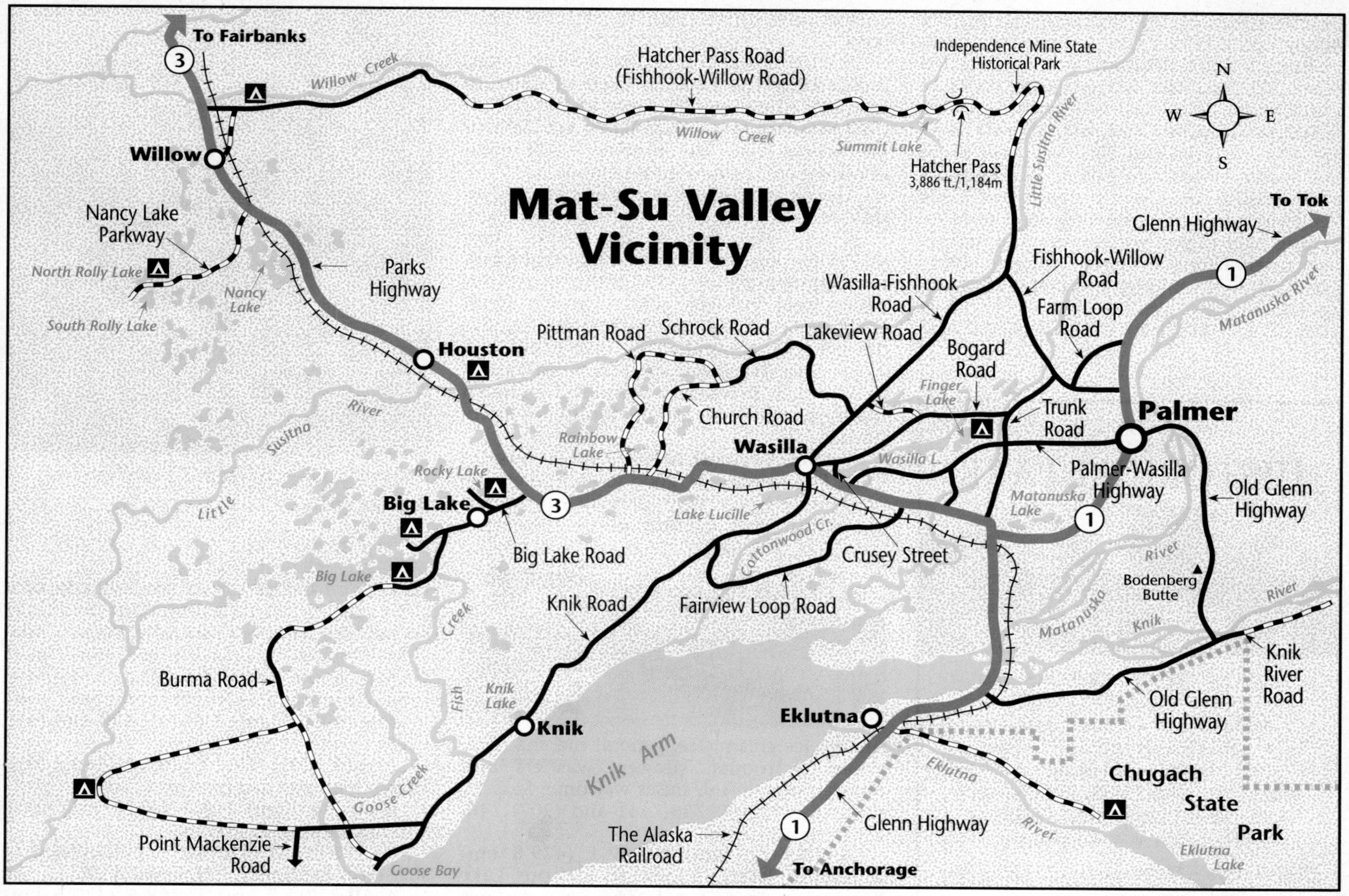

Mat-Su Valley Vicinity

To Fairbanks
Hatcher Pass Road (Fishhook-Willow Road)
Independence Mine State Historical Park
Willow Creek
Willow
Summit Lake
Hatcher Pass 3,886 ft./1,184m
Little Susitna River
To Tok
Glenn Highway
Nancy Lake Parkway
North Rolly Lake
Nancy Lake
South Rolly Lake
Parks Highway
Fishhook-Willow Road
Wasilla-Fishhook Road
Farm Loop Road
Matanuska River
Pittman Road
Schrock Road
Lakeview Road
Bogard Road
Houston
Finger Lake
Trunk Road
Palmer
Church Road
Rainbow Lake
Wasilla
Wasilla L.
Palmer-Wasilla Highway
Old Glenn Highway
Rocky Lake
Big Lake
Little Susitna River
Matanuska Lake
Lake Lucille
Cottonwood Cr.
Crusey Street
Big Lake Road
Bodenberg Butte
Big Lake
Knik Road
Fairview Loop Road
Knik River
Burma Road
Fish Creek
Knik Lake
Knik River Road
Old Glenn Highway
Knik
Eklutna
Knik Arm
Chugach State Park
Eklutna River
Goose Creek
Point Mackenzie Road
The Alaska Railroad
Glenn Highway
Goose Bay
To Anchorage
Eklutna Lake

Gravel turnout to south. Steep ascent eastbound. Highway parallels Matanuska River.

A 76.5 (123.1 km) **T 251.5** (404.7 km) **CHICKALOON** (pop. 145); lodge, cafe, cabins, camping, general store, gas station and river rafting office. ▲

A 76.2 (122.6 km) **T 251.8** (405.2 km) **King Mountain Lodge,** established 1947, oldest continuously operated lodge on the Glenn Highway, with its own resident ghost. Authentic Alaskan atmosphere in the plank-floor bar ("Chickaloon Performing Arts Center") dates from coal mining days. Stay in a real miner's cabin or camp free along the Matanuska River. All cooking from scratch. Famous sausage gravy, musk ox or buffalo burgers. Home of the King Mountain Burger, the most bodacious burger of all. [ADVERTISEMENT] ▲

A 76.1 (122.5 km) **T 251.9** (405.4 km) King Mountain State Recreation Site. Pleasant campground on the banks of the Matanuska River with 22 campsites, 2 picnic sites, fireplaces, picnic tables, water, toilets. Camping fee $10/night or annual pass; 15-day limit. King Mountain to the southeast.▲

CAUTION: Watch for road equipment in slide areas westbound to ***Milepost A 60.***

A 73 (117.5 km) **T 255** (410.4 km) Ida Lake/Fish Lake subdivision. Chickaloon River loop road.

A 72.3 (116.4 km) **T 255.7** (411.5 km) Ida Lake is visible to the west through trees.

A 71.2 (114.6 km) **T 256.8** (413.3 km) End slide area. Beaver pond to north.

A 71 (114.3 km) **T 257** (413.6 km) Turnouts to south by Matanuska River.

A 70.6 (113.6 km) **T 257.4** (414.2 km) Access to Matanuska River to south.

A 69.7 (112.2 km) **T 258.3** (415.7 km) Chickaloon post office (ZIP code 99674). Private campground (closed in 1997, current status unknown).

A 68.6 (110.4 km) **T 259.4** (417.5 km) Slide areas. Highway winds along bank of the Matanuska River. Several gravel turnouts; watch for soft shoulders along highway.

A 68 (109.4 km) **T 260** (418.4 km) Pinnacle Mountain (elev. 4,541 feet/1,384m) rises directly southeast of the highway—easy to identify by its unusual top. Cottonwoods and aspen along the highway. Talkeetna Mountains to the north.

A 66.8 (107.5 km) **T 261.2** (420 km) Large turnout by lake.

A 66.5 (107 km) **T 261.5** (420.8 km) King River bridge. Turnouts both sides of road.

AREA FISHING: King River (Milepost A 66.5), trout, early summer best, use eggs. **Granite Creek (Milepost A 62.4),** small Dolly Varden and trout, spring or early summer, use flies or single eggs. **Seventeenmile Lake (Milepost A 57.9** or **60.9),** small grayling, early spring, use flies or spinners; trout, early spring, use eggs. **Eska Creek (Milepost A 60.8),** small Dolly Varden, spring, use flies or single eggs; silver salmon, August or September, use eggs. **Moose Creek (Milepost A 54.6),** trout and Dolly Varden, summer, use eggs.

A 66.4 (106.8 km) **T 261.6** (421 km) King River trailhead (no sign in 1997); King River Crossing 5 miles/8 km.

A 62.7 (100.9 km) **T 265.3** (426.9 km) Large gravel turnout with interpretive sign to south along Matanuska River. Dwarf fireweed and sweet pea in June.

A 62.4 (100.4 km) **T 265.6** (427.4 km)

Maximum summer daylight in Southcentral Alaska is 19 hours and 21 minutes.
—ALASKA A TO Z

Granite Creek bridge and access to private campground. ▲

River's Edge Recreation Park. Nestled between 2 mountain ranges on the banks of a clearwater creek, our campground offers secluded campsites with picnic tables and fire pits for tents and RVs. We have fresh well water, restrooms, private hot showers with dressing room, dump station and a few electrical hookups. Spawning king salmon, nesting bald eagles, wildflowers and berries. Site reservations accepted, phone (907) 746-2267. Open mid-May to mid-September. [ADVERTISEMENT] ♿▲

A **62.2** (100.1 km) T **265.8** (427.7 km) Sutton post office. Sign in at their guest book.

A **61.6** (99.1 km) T **266.4** (428.7 km) Alpine Historical Park, an open-air museum featuring the concrete ruins of the Sutton Coal Washery (1920–22). Access via Elementary School Road. The museum is still under development. Donations accepted.

Alpine Historical park. See display ad this section.

A **61** (98.2 km) T **267** (429.7 km) **SUTTON** (pop. 340) was established as a railroad siding in about 1918 for the once-flourishing coal industry and is now a small highway community. Sutton has a fire department, general store, post office and gas station. Fossilized shells and leaves can be found in this area 1.7 miles/2.7 km up the Jonesville Road. Inquire locally for directions.

Sutton General Store and Jonesville Cafe. Full line menu, good food, homemade pies, orders to go. We supply all your camping, fishing and cooking needs. Groceries,

snacks, ice cream, ice, general merchandise. Clean restrooms, shower, washers and dryers, phone. Tour buses welcome. Stop by and see us! (907) 746-7461 and (907) 746-7561. [ADVERTISEMENT]

A **60.9** (98 km) T **267.1** (429.8 km) Jonesville Road. Access to Coyote Lake Recreation Area (3 miles/4.8 km); day-use area with pavilion, covered picnic tables, toilets, fireplaces, trails and swimming. Also access to Seventeenmile Lake (for recommended access see **Milepost A 57.9**). Drive north 1.7 miles/2.7 km to end of pavement; continue straight ahead for residential area and old Jonesville and Eska coal mines; turn left where pavement ends for Seventeenmile Lake. From the turnoff on Jonesville Road it is 3.1 miles/5 km via a rough dirt road (may be muddy) to **Seventeenmile Lake;** undeveloped parking area on lakeshore, boat launch, good grayling fishing. Inquire at local businesses about road conditions.

A **60.8** (97.8 km) T **267.2** (430 km) Eska Creek bridge.

A **60.7** (97.7 km) T **267.3** (430.2 km) Paved double-ended turnout to south.

A **60** (96.6 km) T **268** (431.3 km) Long winding descent eastbound.

*CAUTION: Watch for road equipment in slide areas eastbound to **Milepost A 76.***

A **59.5** (95.7 km) T **268.5** (430.5 km) **Fisher's Hilltop Tesoro**. See display ad this section.

A **58.6** (94.3 km) T **269.4** (433.5 km) Small gravel turnout to south. View of Matanuska River.

A **57.9** (93.2 km) T **270.1** (434.7 km) 58 Mile Road. Access to Palmer Correctional Center. Alternate access (see also **A 60.9**) to Seventeenmile Lake. Drive north 0.5 mile/0.8 km; turn right and drive 1.7 miles/2.7 km; turn left, drive 0.3 mile/0.5 km; turn right, drive 0.2 mile/0.3 km; turn right again and drive 0.2 mile/0.3 km to

(Continues on page 356)

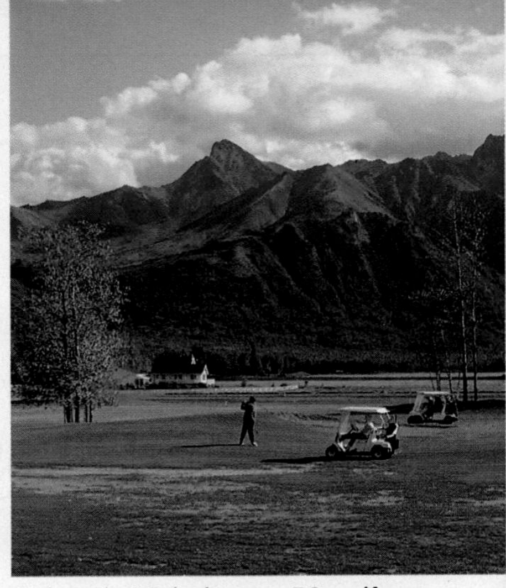

Palmer's 18-hole, par 72 golf course.
(© Barbara Willard)

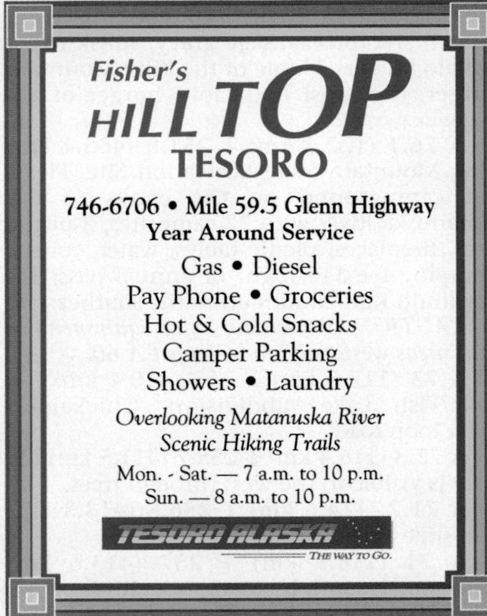

Hatcher Pass Road Log

The 49-mile-/79-km-long Hatcher Pass (Fishhook–Willow) Road leads north and west from **Milepost A 49.5** on the Glenn Highway to **Milepost A 71.2** on the Parks Highway, providing access to Independence Mine State Historical Park (see Mat–Su Valley Vicinity map on page 353). It is a mostly gravel road, not recommended for large RVs or trailers beyond **Milepost J 14.** The road usually does not open until late June or early July and snow may close the pass in September. The road stays open to the historical park and to Hatcher Pass Lodge, a popular winter sports area for snowmobiling and cross-country skiing, in winter.

Distance from junction with the Glenn Highway (J) is followed by distance from junction with the Parks Highway (P).

J 0 P 49.1 (79 km) **Junction** with the Glenn Highway at **Milepost A 49.5.** Fishhook–Willow Road heads west through farm country.

J 1.4 (2.3 km) **P 47.7** (76.8 km) **Junction** with Farm Loop Road.

J 2.4 (3.9 km) **P 46.7** (75.2 km) **Junction** with Trunk Road.

J 6.5 (10.5 km) **P 42.5** (68.4 km) **Hatcher Pass Gateway Center.** See display ad this section.

J 6.8 (10.9 km) **P 42.3** (68.1 km) **Junction** with Wasilla–Fishhook Road.

Hatcher Pass Bed and Breakfast. See display ad this section.

J 7.2 (11.6 km) **P 41.9** (67.4 km) Edgerton Parks Road to Wasilla.

J 8.1 (13 km) **P 41** (66 km) Hatcher Pass Management Area boundary.

J 8.5 (13.7 km) **P 40.6** (65.3 km) Little Susitna River bridge. Pavement ends, gravel begins, northbound. Road parallels river; turnouts westbound.

J 9 (14.5 km) **P 40.1** (64.5 km) Entering Hatcher Pass public-use area westbound. No flower picking or plant removal without a permit.

J 14 (22.5 km) **P 35.1** (56.5 km) Side road to lodges and access to mine and trails. Trailhead parking for Gold Mint and Arkose Ridge trails.

Motherlode Lodge. See display ad on page 357.

Hatcher Pass Road begins climb to Hatcher Pass via a series of switchbacks. There are several turnouts the next 2.4 miles/3.9 km westbound.

J 14.6 (23.5 km) **P 34.5** (55.5 km) Archangel Valley Road to Mabel and Fern mines and Reed Lakes. Road crosses private property (do not trespass). Winter trails (snowmobiles prohibited east of Archangel Road). Reed Lakes Trail access.

J 16.4 (26.4 km) **P 32.7** (52.6 km) Parking lot to east, snowmobile trail to west.

J 17.3 (27.8 km) **P 31.8** (51.2 km) Gold Cord Road provides year-round access to lodge and Independence Mine State Historical Park (1.5 miles/2.4 km). The 271-acre **INDEPENDENCE MINE STATE HISTORICAL PARK** includes several buildings and old mining machinery.

Independence Gold Mine State Historical Park includes old mine buildings and mining machinery. (© Susan Cole Kelly)

Park visitor center is housed in the red-roofed building, which was built in 1939 to house the mine manager. The visitor center and assay office are open 11 A.M. to 7 P.M. daily from June through Labor Day; weekends the rest of the year. (Hours and days may vary.) Guided tours of the bunkhouse, mess hall and warehouse are given from June to Labor Day (weather permitting) for a nominal fee; phone visitor center at (907) 745-2827 or phone 745-3975 in Palmer for current information. Groups of 20 or more call ahead for tours. Office hours and tour

Hatcher Pass Road (continued)

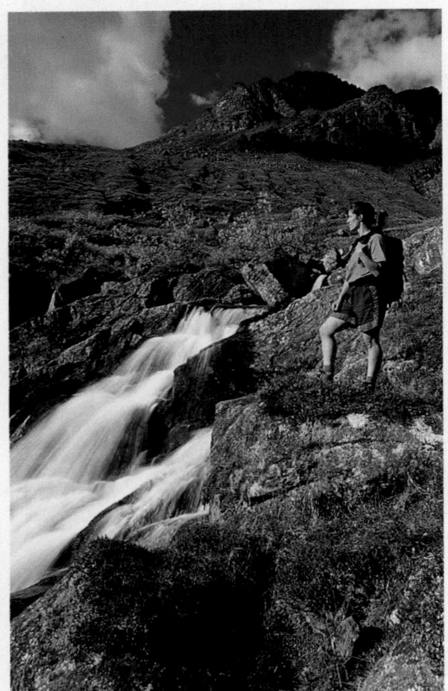

Hiker pauses on Reed Lakes Trail. Access is from Milepost J 14.6 Hatcher Pass Road. (© Michael DeYoung)

times may vary, but visitors are always welcome to explore on their own.

Alaska Pacific Consolidated Mine Co., one of the largest gold producers in the Willow Creek mining district, operated here from 1938 through 1941. The Gold Cord Mine buildings (private property) are visible on the hill above and to the north of Independence Mine.

Recreational gold panning is permitted in the park. Some pans are available for loan at the visitor center.

Snowmobiling is prohibited in the park.

J 17.5 (28.2 km) **P 31.6** (50.8 km) **Hatcher Pass Lodge.** See display ad this section.

J 18.7 (30.1 km) **P 30.4** (48.9 km) Entering Summit Lake State Recreation Site; no ground fires permitted.

J 18.9 (30.4 km) **P 30.1** (48.4 km) Hatcher Pass Summit (elev. 3,886 feet/1,184m). Several turnouts westbound.

J 19.2 (30.9 km) **P 29.8** (48 km) Summit Lake, headwaters of Willow Creek. Summit Lake State Recreation Site under development. The road follows Willow Creek from here to the Parks Highway.

J 20.4 (32.8 km) **P 28.6** (46 km) Upper Willow Creek Valley Road to mine.

J 23.8 (38.3 km) **P 25.3** (40.7 km) Craigie Creek Road (very rough) leads to mine sites. Remains of historic Lucky Shot and War Baby mines on hillside are visible on hillside ahead westbound.

J 24.3 (39.1 km) **P 24.8** (39.9 km) Beaver lodges and dams.

J 25.6 (41.2 km) **P 23.5** (37.8 km) View of Beaver Ponds to west; mine site visible to south below road. Road begins descent westbound into Little Willow Creek valley; numerous turnouts.

J 30.3 (48.8 km) **P 18.7** (30.1 km) Leaving Hatcher Pass public-use area westbound.

J 34.2 (55 km) **P 14.9** (24 km) Little Willow Creek bridge; large parking area.

J 38.9 (62.6 km) **P 10.2** (16.4 km) Gravel ends, pavement begins, westbound.

J 47.9 (77.1 km) **P 1.2** (1.9 km) Willow Creek State Recreation Area Deception Creek Campground; 7 campsites, 15-day limit, $10 nightly fee per vehicle or annual pass, covered picnic tables, water, toilets (wheelchair accessible). ♿▲

J 48 (77.2 km) **P 1.1** (1.8 km) Deception Creek Bridge.

J 48.2 (77.5 km) **P 0.9** (1.4 km) Deception Creek picnic area. Back road into Willow from here.

J 48.5 (78.1 km) **P 0.6** (1 km) Road crosses Alaska Railroad tracks.

J 49.1 (79 km) **P 0 Junction** with Parks Highway at **Milepost A 71.2.** (Turn to the PARKS HIGHWAY section.)

Return to Milepost A 49.5 Glenn Highway or Milepost A 71.2 Parks Highway

lake. Undeveloped camping on lakeshore.

A 57.3 (92.2 km) **T 270.7** (435.6 km) **Timberlings Bed and Breakfast.** A treasure among B&Bs. Log house on 150 acres of

wooded hills with panoramic mountain views. Fantastic breakfast, gracious artist hosts, exotic birds, friendly dogs. In-room TV, VCR. One guest room, shared bath. Call ahead: (907) 745-4445. Buz and Alma Blum, P.O. Box 732, Palmer, AK 99645. [ADVERTISEMENT]

A 56.7 (91.2 km) **T 271.3** (436.6 km) Entering Matanuska Valley Moose Range eastbound.

A 54.6 (87.9 km) **T 273.4** (440 km) Bridge over Moose Creek. Highway ascends steeply from creek in both directions. Look for fossils in the road bank on the west side of the highway.

A 54 (86.9 km) **T 274** (440.9 km) Truck lane starts westbound.

A 53.6 (86.3 km) **T 274.4** (441.6 km) Truck lane ends westbound.

A 53 (85.3 km) **T 275** (442.6 km) Side road to Buffalo Coal Mine. Access to Wishbone Lake 4-wheel-drive trail. Wild rose, geranium and chiming bells bloom along this section of highway.

A 52.3 (84.2 km) **T 275.7** (443.7 km) Soapstone Road. Wild geraniums in June.

A 51.2 (82.4 km) **T 276.8** (445.5 km) Fire station.

A 50.9 (81.9 km) **T 277.1** (445.9 km) Farm Loop Road, a 3-mile/4.8-km loop road connecting with Fishhook–Willow Road.

The Hess House Bed and Breakfast. Part of the original agricultural colony founded in the Matanuska Valley in the 1930s, we are located in the quiet countryside just 5 minutes from Palmer. Stay in our summer bedroom or our private 1918 log cabin. Enjoy a breakfast including homemade pie! Nearby attractions: Musk Ox Farm, Hatcher Pass and scenic Matanuska Glacier. Turn onto Fishhook road, drive 1.4 miles; turn right on Farm Loop; drive 1 mile. HC03 Box 9576, Palmer, AK 99645-9507. Phone (907) 745-1376. [ADVERTISEMENT]

A 50.1 (80.6 km) **T 277.9** (447.2 km) **Musk Ox Farm and Gift Shop.** The world's only domestic musk-oxen farm. The

animals are combed for the precious qiviut, which is then hand-knit by Eskimos in isolated villages, aiding the Arctic economy. During the farm tours in the summer, you can see these shaggy ice age survivors romping in beautiful pastures with Pioneer Peak as a backdrop. Open May to September.

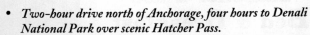

Phone (907) 745-4151. P.O. Box 587, Palmer, AK 99645. [ADVERTISEMENT]

A 50 (80.5 km) **T 278** (447.4 km) Matanuska River viewpoint. Double-ended turnout with walkway. Road narrows eastbound.

A 49.5 (79.7 km) **T 278.5** (448.2 km) **Junction** with Hatcher Pass (Fishhook–Willow) Road which leads west and north over Hatcher Pass to connect with the Parks Highway at **Milepost A 71.2** north of Willow. Trail rides at Mile 5.2. See HATCHER PASS ROAD log this section.

A 49 (78.9 km) **T 279** (449 km) Entering Palmer, which extends to **Milepost A 41.** Actual driving distance between **Milepost 49** and **42** is 1 mile/1.6 km. Just beyond here the highway emerges on a hill overlooking the Matanuska Valley, a view of the farms and homes of one of Alaska's agricultural areas, and the business center of Palmer.

A 42.1 (67.8 km) **T 285.9** (460.1 km) Arctic Avenue leads east through Palmer to the Old Glenn Highway, a scenic alternate route to Anchorage that rejoins the highway at **Milepost A 29.6.**

Highlights along the old Glenn Highway include the original Matanuska Colony Farms, U-pick vegetable farms, campgrounds and salmon-spawning viewing areas. See OLD GLENN HIGHWAY log on page 360 (Anchorage-bound travelers read log back to front). Access to Palmer High School west at this junction.

Palmer

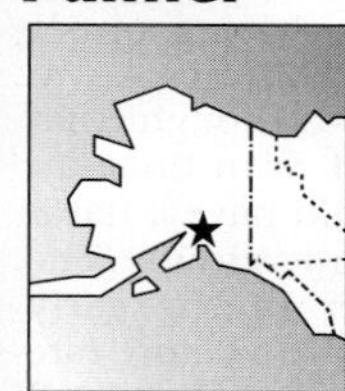

A 42 (67.6 km) **T 286** (460.3 km) In the Matanuska Valley northeast of Anchorage. The city extends from about **Milepost A 49** to **A 41**, an actual driving distance of 2.1 miles/3.4 km. **Population:** 4,100. **Emergency Services:** Phone 911. **Alaska State Troopers,** phone (907) 745-2131. **City Police,** phone (907) 745-4811. **Fire Department** and **Ambulance,** phone (907) 745-3271. **Valley Hospital,** 515 E. Dahlia, phone (907) 745-4813.

Visitor Information: Visitor center in log cabin across the railroad tracks on South Valley Way at East Fireweed Avenue. Pick up a brochure and map of downtown Palmer's historic buildings. Open daily 8 A.M. to 7 P.M. May to Sept. 15; weekdays 9 A.M. to 4 P.M. mid-September to May. Pay phone. Small museum in basement; Alaskan-made gifts may be for sale on main floor. Mailing address: Chamber of Commerce, P.O. Box 45, Palmer, AK 99645. Matanuska Valley Agricultural Showcase adjacent visitor center

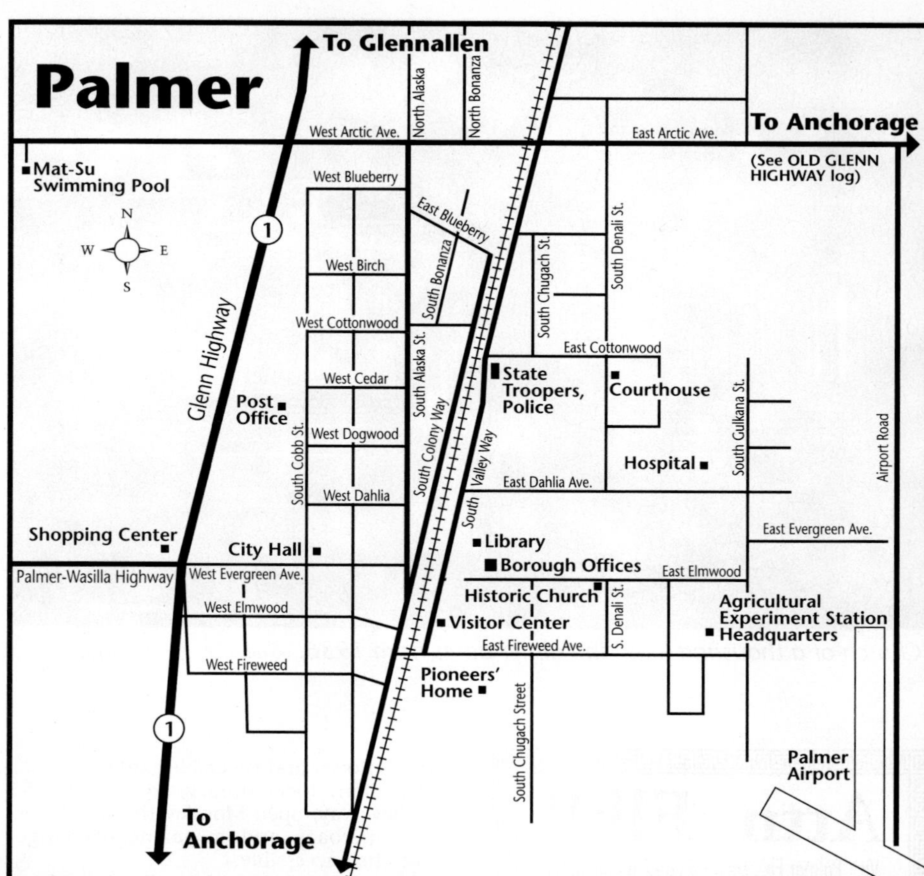

"Church of a thousand logs" in Palmer dates from 1936. *(© Loren Taft, Alaskan Images)*

features flower and vegetable gardens.

Excellent local library, located at 655 S. Valley Way; open Monday through Saturday. Paperback and magazine exchange. Wheelchair accessible. ♿

Elevation: 240 feet/74m. **Climate:** Temperatures range from 4° to 21°F/-16° to -6°C in January and December, with a mean monthly snowfall of 8 to 10 inches. Record low was -40°F/-40°C in January 1975. Temperatures range from 44° to 68°F/7° to 20°C in June and July, with a mean monthly precipitation of 2 inches. Record high was 89°F/32°C in June 1969. Mean annual rainfall is 15.5 inches, with 50.7 inches of snow. **Radio:** Anchorage stations; KMBQ (Wasilla). **Television:** Anchorage channels and cable. **Newspaper:** *The Frontiersman* (twice weekly).

Private Aircraft: Palmer Municipal Airport, adjacent southeast; elev. 232 feet/71m; length 6,000 feet/1,829m; asphalt; fuel 100LL, Jet A1, B. Butte Municipal, 6 miles/9.7 km southeast; elev. 64 feet/19m; length 1,800 feet/549m; gravel; unattended. Seaplane base on Finger Lake.

Palmer is a commercial center for the Matanuska and Susitna valleys (collectively referred to as the Mat–Su valleys). The town was established about 1916 as a railway station on the Matanuska branch of the Alaska Railroad.

In 1935, Palmer became the site of one of the most unusual experiments in American history: the Matanuska Valley Colony. The Federal Emergency Relief Administration, one of the many New Deal relief agencies created during Franklin Roosevelt's first year in office, planned an agricultural colony in Alaska to utilize the great agricultural potential in the Matanuska–Susitna valleys, and to get some American farm families—struck by first the dust bowl, then the Great Depression—off the dole. Social workers picked 203 families, mostly from the northern counties of Michigan, Wisconsin and Minnesota, to join the colony, because it was thought that the many hardy farmers of Scandinavian descent in those 3 states would have a natural advantage over other ethnic groups. The colonists arrived in Palmer in the early summer of 1935, and though the failure rate was high, many of their descendants still live in the Matanuska Valley. Palmer gradually became the unofficial capital of the Matanuska Valley, acting as headquarters for a farmers cooperative marketing organization and as the business and social center for the state's most productive farming region.

Palmer is Alaska's only community that developed primarily from an agricultural economy. (Real estate now takes a close second to agriculture.) The growing season averages 80 to 110 days a year, with long hours of sunshine. The University of Alaska–Fairbanks has an Agricultural and Forestry Experiment Station Office and a district Cooperative Extension Service Office here. The university also operates its Matanuska Research Farm, located on Trunk Road off the Parks Highway, about a 7-mile/11.3-km drive from Palmer. The university farm conducts research in agronomy, horticulture, soil science and animal science.

The community has a hospital, the Mat–Su College (University of Alaska), a library, banks, the Mat–Su Borough offices, borough school district, and several other state and federal agency offices. Palmer has churches representing most denominations. The United Protestant Church in Palmer, the "church of a thousand logs," dates from Matanuska Colony days and is one of the oldest churches in Alaska still holding services. It is included in the National Register of Historic Places.

ACCOMMODATIONS/VISITOR SERVICES

Palmer has all visitor facilities including 3

PALMER ADVERTISERS

B–J's Services Inc. ....Ph. (907) 745-3050
City of Palmer ....231 W. Evergreen Ave.
Colony Inn ....325 Elmwood St.
Farm Country Bed & Breakfast...........Ph. (907) 745-1234
Gold Miner's Hotel ....Ph. (800) 725-2752
Iditarod House Bed & Breakfast......................Ph. (907) 745-4348
Motherlode Lodge............Ph. (907) 746-1464
Mountain View RV Park....Off Old Glenn Hwy.
Musk Ox Farm & Gift Shop ....Mile 50.1 Glenn Hwy.
Palmer Elks Lodge.............Ph. (907) 745-3950
Pioneer Motel & Apt. ....Ph. (907) 745-3425
Pollen's Bed & Breakfast...Ph. (907) 745-8920
Prickly Rose Garden Inn B&B.............................Ph. (907) 745-0532
Tara Dells Bed & Breakfast......................Ph. (907) 745-0407
Valley Hotel...........................606 S. Alaska St.

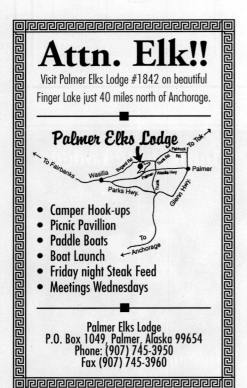

hotels, 2 motels, bed and breakfasts, gas stations, grocery stores, laundromat, auto repair and parts, and shopping. The Matanuska Valley region has several lake resorts offering boat rentals, golf, fly-in fishing, hunting and horseback riding.

There is a private RV park on Smith Road off the Old Glenn Highway. There are also private campgrounds on the Glenn Highway a few miles west of Palmer. The Mat–Su Borough operates Matanuska River Park, located 1.1 miles/1.8 km south of town at Mile 17.5 Old Glenn Highway; 80 campsites for tents or RVs, picnic area, water, dump station (fee charged), firewood for sale, flush toilets, hot showers, camping fee. **Finger Lake** State Recreation Site, about 6 miles/9.7 km northwest of Palmer just off Bogard Road, has 69 campsites, 7-day limit, toilets, water, trails, boating and fishing. Camping fee $10/night. To reach Finger Lake, take Palmer–Wasilla Highway north 4 miles/6.4 km from **Milepost A 41.8** to Trunk Road, then follow Trunk Road to Bogard Road.

Farm Country Bed & Breakfast. Clean, comfortable, quiet atmosphere, 2 miles from Palmer, near the state fairgrounds. Country-style home or bed and breakfast cabin. Plenty of room to accommodate 9–12 people. Lodging packages available for groups or families. Mountain and glacier views. Farm animals to view. Cable TV. "If you have a little country in ya, you'll love our hospitality." Open year-round. Reservations suggested. Phone (907) 745-1234 or (907) 746-0243. Fax (907) 745-1234. HC 5 Box 9782, Palmer, AK 99645. E-mail: zello@alaska.net. Internet: www.alaska.net/~zello/farmcountrybb. [ADVERTISEMENT]

Iditarod House Bed and Breakfast. Hosted by two-time Iditarod racer and 1980 Iditarod "Rookie of the Year" Donna (Gentry) Massay. Convenient, quiet, country acreage with scenic mountain view. Newly finished with queen beds, private baths, private entrance, kitchenette. Wheelchair accessible. Healthy continental breakfast at your leisure. Open year-round. Reasonable rates. An excellent location for exploring the Mat–Su Valley and Anchorage. P.O. Box 3096, Palmer, AK 99645. Phone/fax (907) 745-4348. [ADVERTISEMENT]

Mountain View RV Park offers breathtaking views of the Matanuska mountains.

Watch wildlife from your door. Full hookups, hot showers included. New bathrooms and laundromat, dump station. Good Sam Park. Half-day scenic airboat tours on Knik River. Call (907) 745-5747 for reservations. Mail forwarding. Write P.O. Box 2521, Palmer, AK 99745. From Mile A 42.1 Glenn Highway (Arctic), follow Old Glenn Highway 2.8 miles. Turn east on Smith Road, drive 0.6 mile, turn right (0.3 mile). We're 3.7 miles from the Glenn Highway. See display ad this section. [ADVERTISEMENT]

Pollen's Bed & Breakfast. One mile from Palmer. Spacious, modern, smoke-free home. Sleep on firm queen beds. Private/shared baths, full hot breakfasts, china cups and cloth napkins. Genuine hospitality from lifelong Alaskans. Since 1986. Rates $60-$70. HC01 Box 6005D, Palmer, AK 99645. Phone (907) 745-8920. Daytime fax (907) 745-7665. [ADVERTISEMENT]

Prickly Rose Garden B&B. Country retreat on 6 acres features hiking and nature trails, gardens, sun room, suite with private bath, homemade baked goods, close to Hatcher Pass, Independence Gold Mine and the Musk Ox Farm. Groomed cross-country ski trails in winter. Private cabin also available. Hosts: Robert and Laura Irlbeck, (907) 745-0532. [ADVERTISEMENT]

TRANSPORTATION

Air: No scheduled service, but the local airport has a number of charter operators.

ATTRACTIONS

Go Swimming: The 80-foot/25m swimming pool is open to the public 6 days a week (closed Sundays)—$4 for adults, showers available. The pool is located at Palmer High School; phone (907) 745-5091.

Get Acquainted: Stop at the visitor information center, a log building just off the "main drag" (across the railroad tracks at the intersection of East Fireweed Avenue and South Valley Way). The center includes a museum, artifacts, a gift shop and agricultural showcase garden.

Visit the Musk Ox Farm. Located east of Palmer on the Glenn Highway at **Milepost 50.1**, the Musk Ox Farm is open May to September; admission charged. Hunted to near extinction in Alaska in 1865, the species was reintroduced in the 1930s.

Visit a Reindeer Farm, located 8.1 miles/11.5 km south of Palmer via the Old Glenn Highway to Bodenburg Loop Road. This commercial reindeer farm is open daily in summer; admission is charged.

Play Golf. Palmer links golf course has 18 holes (par 72, USGA rated), rental carts

(Continues on page 361)

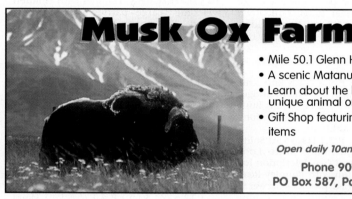

Old Glenn Highway (Palmer Alternate) Log

This 18.6-mile/29.9-km paved road is a scenic alternate route between Palmer and Anchorage, exiting the Glenn Highway at **Milepost A 29.6** and rejoining the Glenn Highway at **Milepost A 42.1**. The Old Glenn Highway goes through the heart of the original Matanuska Colony agricultural lands.

Distance from south junction with the Glenn Highway (J) is followed by distance from Palmer (P).

J 0 P 18.6 (29.9 km) Exit from Glenn Highway at **Milepost A 29.6.**

J 6.1 (9.8 km) **P 12.3** (19.8 km) Goat Creek Bridge.

J 7.2 (11.6 km) **P 11.4** (18.3 km) View of Bodenburg Butte across Knik River.

J 8.7 (14 km) **P 9.9** (15.9 km) **Junction** with Knik River Road, a gravel side road that leads to an RV park and a view of Knik Glacier. Pioneer Ridge/Knik River trailhead 3.6 miles/5.8 km from bridge. Knik River Road dead ends 11.4 miles/18.3 km from here.

Knik River RV Park. See display ad this section. ▲

J 8.8 (14.2 km) **P 9.8** (15.8 km) Knik River bridge; parking at east end of bridge.

J 11.4 (18.3 km) **P 7.2** (11.6 km) Butte branch U.S. post office. Pioneer Peak dominates the skyline southbound.

J 11.5 (18.5 km) **P 7.1** (11.4 km) South **junction** with Bodenburg Butte Loop Road which leads west (see description following), and **junction** with Plumley Road to east. Plumley Road provides access to **Jim Creek** trail off Caudill Road; fishing for Dolly Varden, silver and red salmon.

The 5.8-mile/9.3-km Bodenburg Butte Road rejoins the Old Glenn Highway opposite Dack Acres Road (**Milepost J 12.6**). The **BODENBURG BUTTE** area (pop. 1,232) has original Matanuska Colony farms and a commercial reindeer farm (visitors welcome, fee charged).

Reindeer Farm. Commercial reindeer farm and zoological park on Bodenburg Butte Loop Road 0.8 mile off Old Glenn Highway (turn at **Mile J 11.5** at the flashing light). View tame reindeer and famous Pioneer Peak. Hand feed reindeer,

moose, black-tailed deer, elk. Guided horseback trail rides. Bring camera. Hours 10 A.M.-6 P.M. daily. Families with children welcome. Large parties please phone ahead. Fee charged. (907) 745-4000, e-mail: reindeer@corecom.net, Internet site: www.corecom.net/~reindeer/tours. [ADVERTISEMENT] MP

J 12.6 (20.3 km) **P 6** (9.7 km) **Junction** with Dack Acres Road, north end of Bodenburg Butte Loop Road (see **Milepost J 11.5**).

J 13.3 (21.4 km) **P 5.3** (8.5 km) Turnout to west. Bodenburg Creek parallels highway next 0.7 mile/1.1 km northbound; red and pink salmon spawn here from late August through September. Eagles nest across the creek. *CAUTION: Use turnouts and watch for heavy traffic.*

J 14.5 (23.3 km) **P 4.1** (6.6 km) Maud Road. Access to **Mud Lake** (4 miles/6.4 km); fishing for Dolly Varden.

J 15.6 (25.1 km) **P 3** (4.8 km) **Junction** with Smith Road. Access to private campground. Trail rides may be available at a nearby ranch.

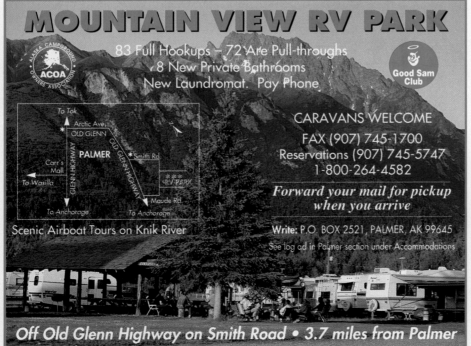

Matanuska Valley farm on Bodenburg Butte Loop Road.
(© Susan Cole Kelly)

Mountain View RV Park. See display ad this section. ▲

J 16.1 (25.9 km) **P 2.5** (4 km) Clark–Wolverine Road; access to Lazy Mountain recreation area hiking trails. Drive in 0.7 mile/1.1 km; turn right on Huntly Road at T; drive 1 mile/1.6 km on gravel road and take right fork to recreation area and overlook. Picnic tables, toilets, berry picking.

J 16.8 (27 km) **P 1.8** (2.9 km) Matanuska River bridge. Access to river.

J 17.5 (28.2 km) **P 1.1** (1.8 km) Matanuska River Park; 51 campsites, picnic area, some pull-through sites, water, fireplaces, dump station, flush toilets, hot showers. Camping, shower and dump station fees charged. ▲

J 17.7 (28.5 km) **P 0.9** (1.4 km) Palmer airport.

J 18.6 (29.9 km) **P 0 Junction** of Old Glenn Highway (Arctic Avenue) at Palmer, **Milepost A 42.1** Glenn Highway.

Return to Milepost A 42.1 or A 29.6 Glenn Highway

(Continued from page 359)
and clubs, driving range and clubhouse. Phone (907) 745-4653.

Enjoy Water Sports. Fishing, boating, waterskiing and other water sports are popular in summer at Finger Lake west of Palmer. Kepler–Bradley Lakes State Recreation Area on Matanuska Lake has canoe rentals; turn off the Glenn Highway at **Milepost A 36.4.**

The Alaska State Fair, an 11-day annual event ending on Labor Day, has agricultural exhibits from farms throughout Alaska. There are also food booths, games and rides. This is a very popular event, and fairgoers from Anchorage can tie up traffic. But it's worth the drive just to see the huge vegetables. Phone (907) 745-4827.

Visit Scenic Hatcher Pass: A 6- to 8-hour drive from **Milepost A 49.5** near Palmer that climbs through the beautiful Hatcher Pass Recreation Area and connects with the Parks Highway at **Milepost A 71.2.** Access to Independence Mine State Historical Park. See HATCHER PASS ROAD this section.

See the Matanuska Glacier: Drive 50 miles/80 km east on the Glenn Highway from Palmer to visit this spectacular 27-mile/43.5-km-long glacier, one of the few you can drive to and explore on foot. Access to the foot of the glacier is through a private campground at **Milepost A 102**; admission charged. If you're not interested in getting close, there are several vantage points along the highway and from trails at Matanuska Glacier Campground, **Milepost A 101.**

Glenn Highway Log

(continued)

A 41.8 (67.3 km) **T 286.2** (460.6 km) **Junction** with Palmer–Wasilla Highway. Gas station and shopping mall. West Evergreen Avenue access to downtown Palmer.

Carrs Pioneer Square shopping mall, located at this junction, is the site of a bronze sculpture by Jacques and Mary Regat dedicated to the Matanuska Valley pioneers.

Palmer–Wasilla Highway (see log on page 416) leads northwest 10 miles/16 km to the Parks Highway. It provides access to a car wash, several other businesses, Mat–Su College, Finger Lake State Recreation Site (via Trunk and Bogard roads) and Wolf Lake State Recreation Site. At Mile 1.9 on the Palmer–Wasilla Highway is the Crevasse Moraine trailhead; parking, picnic tables, fireplaces and access to 5 loop hiking trails.

A 41.6 (66.9 km) **T 286.4** (460.9 km) Gas station.

A 41.2 (66.3 km) **T 286.8** (461.5 km) First access road to Palmer business district for eastbound travelers.

A 40.5 (65.2 km) **T 287.5** (462.7 km) **Fairview Motel & Restaurant.** See display ad this section.

A 40.2 (64.7 km) **T 287.8** (463.2 km) Main entrance to fairgrounds (site of Alaska State Fair) and Herman Field (home of the Mat–Su Miners baseball team). Alaska State Fair is held the end of August to Labor Day.

A 39.2 (63.1 km) **T 288.8** (464.8 km) Outer Springer Loop. Gift shop. Short, steep trail to **Meiers Lake**; grayling fishing.

Colony Curio. A unique Alaskan gift shop with something for everyone. Our

shop carries a broad selection of made-in-Alaska products, with a large variety of Native and local crafts. Located next to the gift shop are 2 Matanuska colony homes, on

Palmer hosts the Alaska State Fair the end of August to Labor Day.
(© Barbara Willard)

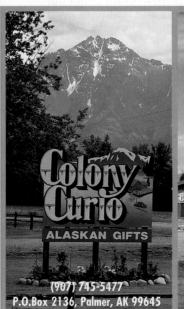

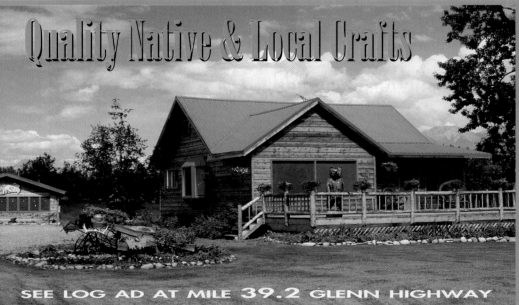

the original Meiers' homestead. See authentic farm equipment, a true Alaskan garden and our 10-foot carved bear. Stop in for the friendly atmosphere you came to Alaska to find. See display ad this section. [ADVERTISEMENT]

A 37.4 (60.2 km) **T 290.6** (467.7 km) Kepler Drive; access to private campground and lake. ▲

A 37.2 (59.9 km) **T 290.8** (468 km) **Echo Lake** turnout; parking and trail to lake. Fishing for landlocked salmon and rainbow.

A 37 (59.5 km) **T 291** (468.3 km) Echo Lake Road.

A 36.4 (58.6 km) **T 291.6** (469.3 km) Kepler–Bradley Lakes State Recreation Area on Matanuska Lake; day-use area with water, toilets, parking, picnic tables, canoe rentals, fishing and hiking. Wheelchair-accessible trail to lake. The lakes are **Matanuska Lake, Canoe Lake, Irene Lake** and **Long Lake.**

A 36.2 (58.3 km) **T 291.8** (469.6 km) **The Homestead RV Park.** Beautiful, wooded setting overlooking the scenic Matanuska Valley. Good Sam, AAA, 64 sites, pull-throughs to 70 feet, tent sites. Very clean restrooms and showers. Electric and water hookups; dump station; also on-site portable dumping. Laundry. Picnic tables, pay phone. Enclosed pavilion and Matanuska Amphitheatre, home of the musical narrative "Cream Puff Pioneers." Area tours, evening entertainment. Square dancing Thursday nights. Walking and jogging trails, trout fishing nearby. Handicap access. Commuting distance to Anchorage. Caravans welcome. Phone (907) 745-6005. Toll free in Alaska (800) 478-3570. See display ad this section. [ADVERTISEMENT] ▲

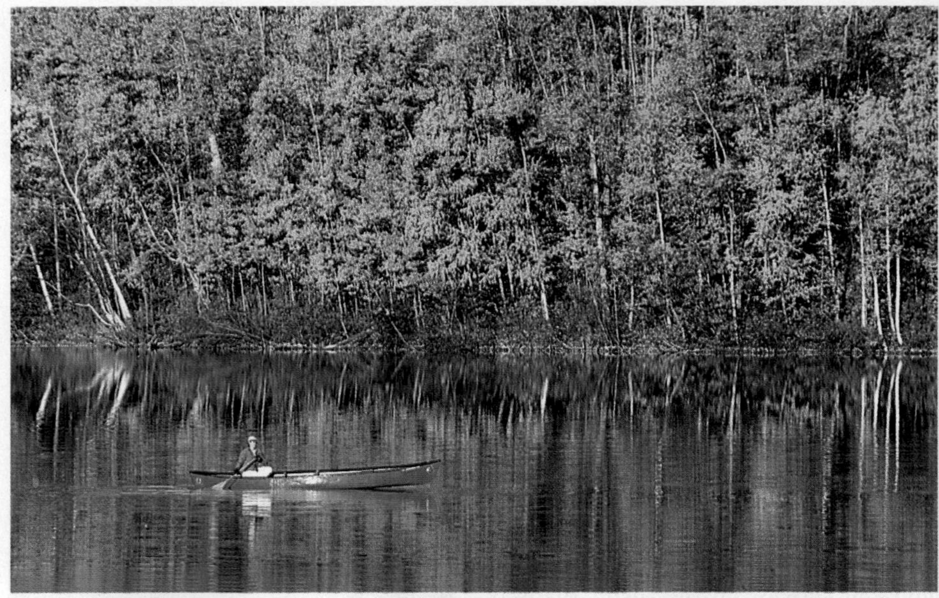

Canoeing on a bright fall day at Kepler–Bradley Lakes SRA, Milepost A 36.4.
(© Tom Bol Photography)

A 35.3 (56.8 km) **T 292.7** (471.1 km) *CAUTION: Traffic signal at busy* ***junction*** *of the Glenn Highway and Parks Highway (Alaska Route 3), which form a common highway into Anchorage.* If headed for Fairbanks or Mount McKinley turn north on the Parks Highway. See **Milepost A 35** PARKS HIGHWAY section for details.

A 34.9 (56.2 km) **T 293.1** (471.7 km) *CAUTION: Highway crosses the Alaska Railroad tracks.*

A 34 (54.7 km) **T 294** (473.1 km) Paved double-ended turnout west side of highway. Rabbit Slough.

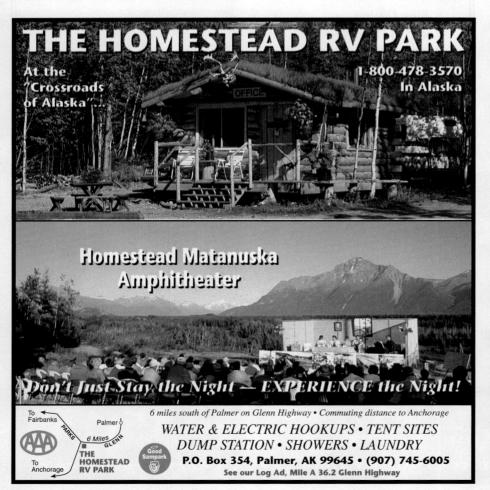

A 32.4 (52.1 km) **T 295.6** (475.7 km) Palmer Hay Flats state game refuge. According to the ADF&G, this is the most heavily utilized waterfowl hunting area in Alaska. Access to the refuge is via Fairview Loop Road off the Parks Highway.

A 31.5 (50.7 km) **T 296.5** (477.2 km) Bridge over the Matanuska River, which is fed by the Matanuska Glacier.

A 30.8 (49.6 km) **T 297.5** (478.8 km) There are 2 Knik River bridges. Exits to parking areas below highway between the bridges. The Knik River comes down from the Knik Glacier to the east and splits into several branches as it approaches Knik Arm. Game Management Unit 14C boundary. Also boundary of Matanuska–Susitna Borough.

Moose winter in this area, and the cows and calves may be seen early in the morning and in the evening as late as early July. In winter, watch for moose on the road between here and Anchorage.

A 29.6 (47.6 km) **T 298.4** (480.2 km) Exit to the Old Glenn Highway (Palmer Alternate). See OLD GLENN HIGHWAY log page 360.

A 27.3 (43.9 km) **T 300.7** (483.9 km) The highway crosses a swampy area known locally as Eklutna Flats. These flats are a protected wildflower area (picking flowers is strictly prohibited). Look for wild iris, shooting star, chocolate lily and wild rose in early June.

A 26.8 (43.1 km) **T 301.2** (484.7 km) Highway crosses Alaska Railroad via overpass.

A 26.3 (42.3 km) **T 301.7** (485.5 km) Eklutna overpass, exits both sides of highway. Access to Eklutna Road (description follows), the village of Eklutna and also access to Thunderbird Falls (see **Milepost A 25.3**) for Anchorage-bound travelers. West of the highway is the Indian village of **EKLUTNA** (pop. 25), site of Eklutna Historical Park, which preserves the heritage and traditions of the Athabascan Alaska Natives. Attractions include the Eklutna Heritage Museum, the historic St. Nicholas Russian Orthodox Church and a hand-built Siberian prayer chapel. Admission fee charged. Open daily mid-May to mid-September. The bright little grave houses or spirit houses in the cemetery are painted in the family's traditional colors.

Eklutna Historical Park. See display ad this section.

Eklutna Road leads east 10 miles/16.1 km to Eklutna Lake Recreation Area in Chugach State Park. General store at Mile 9. The recreation area has a campground, picnic area and hiking trails. The campground has 50 sites, drinking water, pit toilets and a 15-day limit. Camping fee $10/night or annual pass. The 32-unit picnic area is located at the trailhead parking lot, which will accommodate 80 cars and has a boat launch for hand-carried boats. Three trails branch off the trailhead: Twin Peaks, Lakeside and Bold Ridge. The Lakeside trail skirts Eklutna Lake and gives access to Eklutna Glacier (12.7 miles/20.4 km). **Eklutna Lake** is the largest lake in Chugach State Park, measuring approximately 7 miles long by a mile wide. Fed by Eklutna Glacier, it offers fair fishing for Dolly Varden. *CAUTION: Afternoon winds can make the lake dangerous for boaters.* Interpretive displays on wildlife and a telescope for viewing Dall sheep, eagles and other wildlife are located at the trailhead. ▲

Eklutna Historical Park at Milepost A 26.3 preserves Russian Orthodox Church and Athabascan spirit houses. (© Susan Cole Kelly)

Mystical Raven Gift Shop & RV Park. Exit east at Eklutna overpass. Planned to open spring 1998: 40 space RV park without hookups. Conveniently located near historical site and 2 state recreational parks. City bus within walking distance. Authentic Alaska Native gifts. Phone (907) 688-0570, fax (907) 688-0574. P.O. Box 671886, Chugiak, AK 99567-1886. [ADVERTISEMENT] ▲

Rochelle's Ice Cream Stop and Cheely's General Store. Best milkshakes, old fashioned banana splits, espresso, fishing licenses, ice, groceries, picnic supplies, Eklutna Lake posters, and mountain bikes for rent. Cabins for rent—located within Chugach State Park wildlife viewing area. Shower and laundry available. Phone (907) 688-6201, fax (907) 688-6150. In Alaska (800) 764-6201. [ADVERTISEMENT]

A 25.7 (41.3 km) **T 302.3** (486.5 km) Highway crosses Eklutna River.

A 25.3 (40.7 km) **T 302.7** (487.1 km) Thunderbird Falls exit (northbound traffic only) and northbound access to Eklutna Road (see **Milepost A 26.3** for description). Drive about 0.3 mile/0.5 km to parking area. Thunderbird Falls is about 1 mile/1.6 km from the highway. The scenic trail to the falls winds through private property on a 25-foot right-of-way and follows a hillside down to Thunderbird Creek. The falls are just upstream. *CAUTION: Do not climb the steep cliffs overhanging the falls!*

A 24.5 (39.4 km) **T 303.5** (488.4 km) Southbound exit to Edmonds Lake residential area and Mirror Lake picnic wayside. The shallow 73-acre **Mirror Lake** is located at the foot of Mount Eklutna; rainbow.

A 23.6 (38 km) **T 304.4** (489.9 km) Access to Mirror Lake picnic wayside for northbound traffic only.

A 23 (37 km) **T 305** (490.8 km) North Peters Creek overpass, exits both sides of highway.

A 21.5 (34.6 km) **T 306.5** (493.3 km) South Peters Creek underpass, exits both sides of highway. Access to Peters Creek and portion of the Old Glenn Highway, which parallels the newer highway south to Eagle River and provides access to a number of local services. **PETERS CREEK** services include gas stations, grocery, car wash, body repair shop and restaurant.

Peters Creek Bed & Breakfast. Located on the north shore of Peters Creek only 0.8 mile from exit. Wheelchair accessible; open year-round. Rooms have private baths, cable TV, VCR, refrigerator; full Alaskan breakfast. Lovely new home, wooded setting, smoke-free environment, major credit cards accepted. Phone (888) 688-3465, (907) 688-3465, fax (907) 688-3466. [ADVERTISEMENT]

Peters Creek "Petite" RV Park. See display ad this section. ▲

Peters Creek Trading Post. See display ad this section.

A 21.2 (34.1 km) **T 306.8** (493.7 km) Peters Creek bridge.

A 20.9 (33.6 km) **T 306.9** (493.9 km)

The Chugiak–Eagle River area has a full range of businesses. (© Barbara Willard)

North Birchwood Loop Road underpass, exits both sides of highway; turn east for community of **CHUGIAK** and for portion of Old Glenn Highway, which leads south to Eagle River and north to Peters Creek. There are many services and attractions in the Peters Creek–Chugiak–Eagle River area.

A 20.4 (32.8 km) **T 307.6** (495 km) Exit for North Birchwood Loop Road, Chugiak post office, senior center and services.

A 17.2 (27.7 km) **T 310.8** (500.2 km) South Birchwood Loop Road underpass, exits both sides of highway. Access to St. John Orthodox Cathedral, sled dog demonstrations, Chugiak High School and Old Glenn Highway.

Mush A Dog Team/Gold Rush Park. Year-round—a must see! Experience Alaska's living history—sled dog rides, gold panning, antiques at Pioneer Village on creek. Open daily, closed Sunday. Turn at South Birchwood exit. Drive $^3/_4$ mile past High School. Signs on left. Phone (907) 688-1391. Internet: mushing@alaska.net. [ADVERTISEMENT]

Saint John Orthodox Cathedral. Take a peaceful break from your travels. Visit this unique, geodesic-dome cathedral with birch ceiling and beautiful icons. Discover how

this church connects to the early church and how Christianity came to Alaska 200 years ago. Bookstore. Monastery Drive off Old Glenn. (907) 696-2002. [ADVERTISEMENT]

A 15.3 (24.6 km) **T 312.7** (503.2 km) Exits for Fire Lake residential area, Old Glenn Highway and Eagle River.

A 13.4 (21.6 km) **T 314.6** (506.3 km) Eagle River overpass. Exit east for community of Eagle River (all visitor services), the North Anchorage Visitor Information Center and Eagle River Road to Chugach State Park Nature Center (a highly recommended stop); descriptions follow.

Eagle River

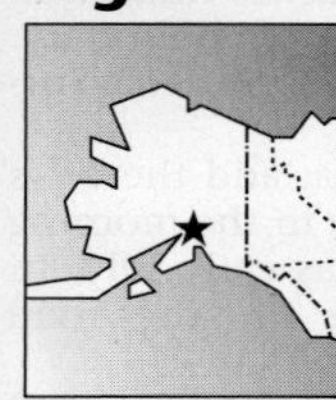

A 13.4 (21.6 km) **T 314.6** (506.3 km) **Population:** Area 18,040. **Emergency Services: Clinic,** phone (907) 694-2807. **Visitor Information:** The Anchorage Convention and Visitors Bureau North Anchorage Visitor Information Center is located in the Parkgate Building, along with the Southcentral Alaska Museum of Natural History, in downtown Eagle River. Stop by for information on Anchorage events, parking maps and brochures, or phone (907) 696-4636. For information on Eagle River/Chugiak, contact the Chugiak–Eagle River Chamber of Commerce, P.O. Box 770353, Eagle River, AK 99577; phone (907) 694-4702. You can also visit the Chamber office at 11401 Old Glenn Highway, Ste. 110A, in the Eagle River Shopping Center.

The Chugiak–Eagle River area was homesteaded after WWII when the new Glenn Highway opened this rural area northeast of Anchorage. Today, the Eagle River community offers a full range of businesses, most located near or on Business Boulevard and the Old Glenn Highway east off the Glenn Highway. There are motels, restaurants,

EAGLE RIVER ADVERTISERS

Alaska Limited Editions.....Ph. (907) 688-3627
Alaska Museum of Natural History.....Ph. (907) 694-0819
Boondock Sporting Goods & Outfitters.....Eagle River Loop Rd.
C–Alaska Motorhome Rental.....Ph. (907) 696-RENT
Chugiak-Eagle River Chamber of Commerce.....Ph. (907) 694-4702
Eagle River Car Wash and Duck Pond.....Old Glenn Hwy.
Eagle River Motel/Hotel...Ph. (907) 694-5000
Hidden Haven RV Park.....Ph. (907) 694-7275
Laundry Basket, The.....Business Blvd.
Tips Bar & Cafe.....Old Glenn Hwy.

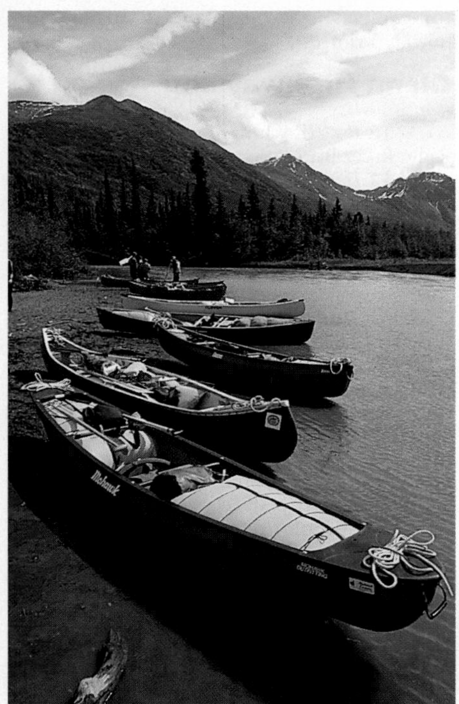

Canoes line a gravel bar of the Eagle River, a popular day trip.
(© Michael DeYoung)

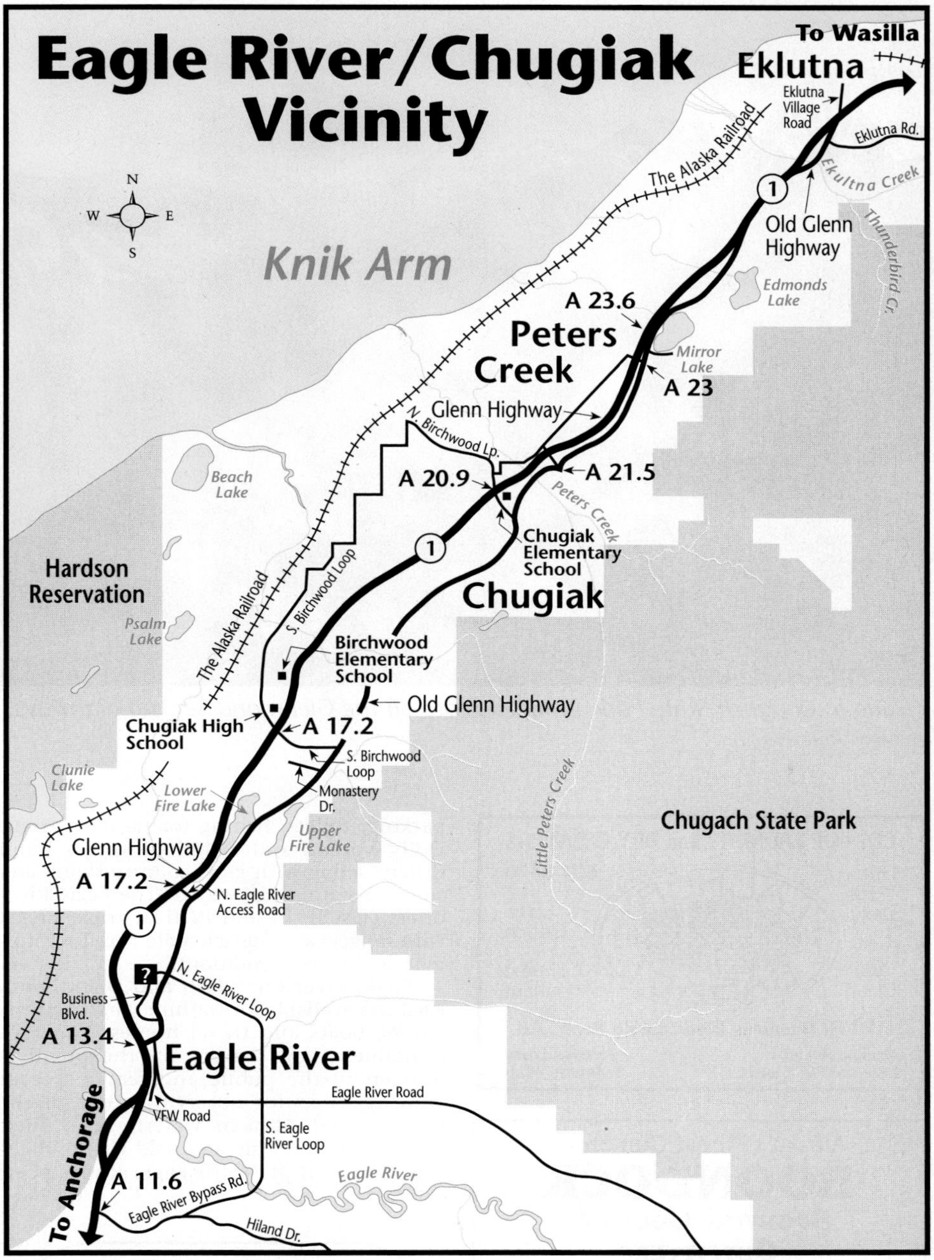

Eagle River/Chugiak Vicinity
To Wasilla
Eklutna
Eklutna Village Road
Eklutna Rd.
Eklutna Creek
The Alaska Railroad
Old Glenn Highway
Thunderbird C.
Knik Arm
Edmonds Lake
A 23.6
Peters Creek
Mirror Lake
A 23
Glenn Highway
N. Birchwood Lp.
A 20.9
A 21.5
Beach Lake
Peters Creek
Chugiak Elementary School
Hardson Reservation
Chugiak
S. Birchwood Loop
The Alaska Railroad
Psalm Lake
Birchwood Elementary School
Old Glenn Highway
Chugiak High School
A 17.2
S. Birchwood Loop
Clunie Lake
Monastery Dr.
Lower Fire Lake
Upper Fire Lake
Little Peters Creek
Chugach State Park
Glenn Highway
A 17.2
N. Eagle River Access Road
N. Eagle River Loop
Business Blvd.
A 13.4
Eagle River
Eagle River Road
VFW Road
S. Eagle River Loop
Eagle River
To Anchorage
A 11.6
Eagle River Bypass Rd.
Hiland Dr.
N
W
E
S

supermarkets, laundromat, post office, gas stations and shopping center. Eagle River also has 30 churches, 10 public schools, a library, movie theaters, bowling alley and recreation center.

Attractions in Eagle River include artist Jon Van Zyle's studio and the Southcentral Alaska Museum of Natural History. The museum features 20 exhibits on Cook Inlet, dioramas of local ecosystems, and a duck-billed dinosaur skeleton. Located across from McDonald's at the corner of Easy Street and Old Glenn Highway; phone (907) 694-0819 for hours. Boondock Sporting Goods store on Eagle River Loop Road has an antique gun display and also rents fishing tackle.

From downtown Eagle River, follow scenic Eagle River Road (paved) 12.7 miles/20.4 km to reach the Chugach State Park Nature Center. Beautiful views of the Chugach Mountains from the center's veranda; telescopes are set up for viewing Dall sheep and other wildlife. The center has a pay phone and restrooms, and is the trailhead for the Old Iditarod–Crow Pass trail. There are also short hiking trails from the center and guided hikes and naturalist programs. The center is staffed, but hours vary in summer and winter. Phone (907) 694-2108 for current information.

Kayaks, rafts and canoes can put in at Mile 7.5 Eagle River Road at the **North Fork Eagle River** access/day-use area with paved

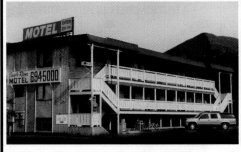

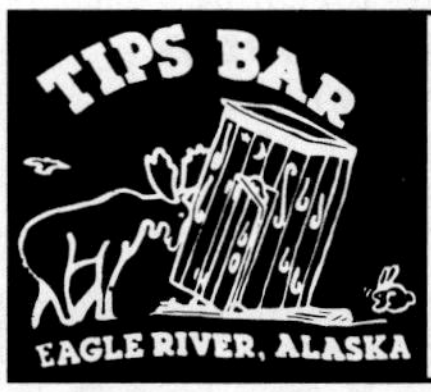

Hiking in Chugach State Park. Trailheads are off the Glenn and Seward highways.
(© Tom Bol Photography)

parking, toilets, fishing for rainbow trout, Dolly Varden and a limited king salmon fishery, along with cross-country skiing and snow machining in winter. The Eagle River offers class II, III and IV float trips. Check with rangers at Chugach State Park for information on river conditions.

Eagle River Car Wash and Duck Pond. Facilities available for washing cars, campers, trucks, boats and travel homes. Vacuums available. A duck pond on the premises is open to the public and features cedar viewing decks for observing some of the natural wild Alaskan waterfowl in their natural habitat. Mile 15.5 Old Glenn Highway. Turn off at North Eagle River access for car wash. See display ad this section. [ADVERTISEMENT]

Glenn Highway Log
(continued)

A 12.8 (20.6 km) **T 315.2** (507.3 km) Eagle River Bridge.

A 11.6 (18.7 km) **T 316.4** (509.2 km) Hiland Road exit. Access to Alaska State Forest Nursery and Eagle River Campground in Chugach State Park. The nursery welcomes visitors; phone (907) 694-5880 for tours.

Eagle River Campground, 1.4 miles/2.3 km from the highway, has 58 campsites, walk-in tent camping, a 4-day camping limit, picnic shelter (may be reserved in advance), dump station, pay phones, flush toilets and drinking water. Camping fee $15/night. Day-use fee $3. Canoe/kayak staging area. This is one of the most popular campgrounds in the state. Phone the state park office at (907) 345-5014 for information. ▲

A 10.6 (17.1 km) **T 317.4** (510.8 km) Truck weigh stations on both sides of highway. Pay phones.

The last 9 miles/14.5 km of the Glenn Highway has been designated the Veterans' Memorial Parkway.

NOTE: Watch for off-ramp construction.

A 7.5 (12.1 km) **T 320.5** (515.8 km) Southbound exit to **FORT RICHARDSON** and Arctic Valley road. *CAUTION: Watch for moose.*

A 6.1 (9.8 km) **T 321.9** (518 km) Northbound exit to Fort Richardson and Arctic Valley Road. Road to Arctic Valley Ski Area is steep and winding but offers spectacular views of Anchorage and Cook Inlet. It is approximately 7.5 miles/12 km to the ski area. Alpine wildflowers in spring, good berry picking in late summer. Not recommended for large vehicles.

A 6 (9.7 km) **T 322** (518.2 km) Ship Creek.

A 4.4 (7.1 km) **T 323.6** (520.8 km) Muldoon Road overpass. (Exit here to connect with Seward Highway via Muldoon and Tudor roads bypass.) Exit north to Oilwell Road for Anchorage RV Park; 195 hookup sites, dump station. Exit south on Muldoon Road for Centennial Park municipal campground. To reach the campground, go south on Muldoon to first left (Boundary); go about 100 yards then make a second left; continue about quarter-mile to campground entrance. There is a bicycle trail from Muldoon Road to Mirror Lake, **Milepost** A 23.6. ▲

A 3 (4.8 km) **T 325** (523 km) Boniface Parkway; access to businesses. Russian Jack Springs city campground is located south of the Glenn Highway on Boniface Parkway just north of DeBarr. Turn north for Elmendorf AFB. ▲

A 1.8 (2.9 km) **T 326.2** (525 km) Bragaw Street.

A 0.7 (1.1 km) **T 327.3** (526.7 km) Reeve Boulevard; access to **ELMENDORF AFB.**

A 0.3 (0.5 km) **T 327.7** (527.4 km) Concrete Street. Access to Elmendorf AFB.

A 0 T 328 (527.9 km) The Glenn Highway ends at Medfra Street. Continue straight ahead on 5th Avenue (one way westbound) to downtown Anchorage. Turn left at Gambell Street (one way southbound) for the Seward Highway and Kenai Peninsula. See ANCHORAGE section following for description of city.

NOTE: Watch for road construction on 5th and 6th Avenues in 1998.

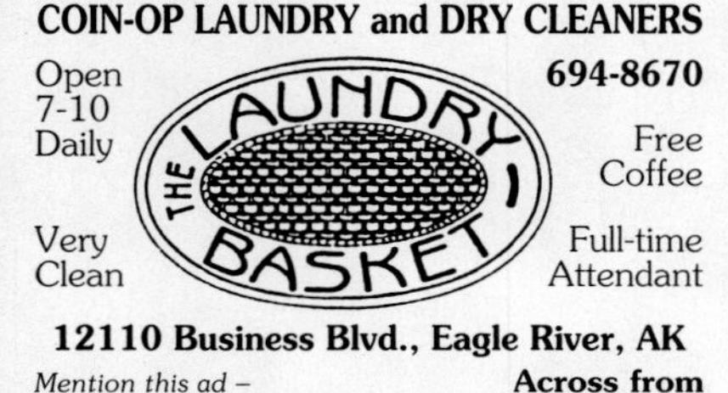

Chugach State Park has more than 200 miles of established hiking trails. —ALASKA A TO Z

ANCHORAGE

(See maps, pages 368 and 370)

Seasonal views of the Log Cabin Visitor Information Center on 4th Avenue in Anchorage. Summer view (above left) and a winter view photographed in January.

(Photo above left: © Susan Cole Kelly. Photo above right: © James D. Ronan, Jr.)

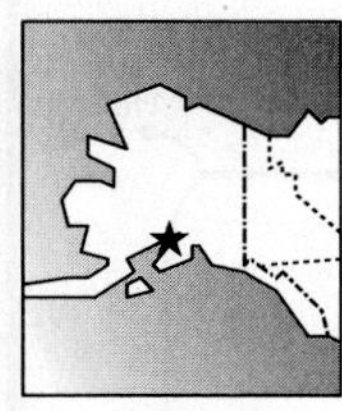

Located on the upper shores of Cook Inlet, at 61° north latitude and 150° west longitude, Anchorage is in the heart of Alaska's southcentral gulf coast. The townsite is on a low-lying alluvial plain bordered by mountains, dense forests of spruce, birch and aspen, and water. Cook Inlet's Turnagain Arm and Knik Arm define the broad peninsula on which the city lies. Anchorage is situated 358 miles/576 km south of Fairbanks via the Parks Highway; 304 miles/489 km from Valdez, southern terminus of the trans-Alaska pipeline, via the Glenn and Richardson highways; 2,459 driving miles/3,957 km via the West Access Route, Alaska Highway and Glenn Highway/Tok Cutoff; 1,644 nautical miles/2,646 km, and 3 hours flying time from Seattle. Anchorage has been called the "Air Crossroads of the World." In terms of nonstop air mileages, Anchorage is the following distance from each of these cities: Amsterdam, 4,475/7,202 km; Chicago, 2,839/4,569 km; Copenhagen, 4,313/6,941 km; Hamburg, 4,430/7,129 km; Honolulu, 2,780/4,474 km; London, 4,487/7,221 km; Paris, 4,683/7,536 km; San Francisco, 2,015/3,243 km; Seattle, 1,445/2,325 km; Tokyo, 3,460/5,568 km.

Population: Anchorage Municipality, 257,780. **Emergency Services: Police, Fire Department, Ambulance** and **Search & Rescue**, phone 911, CB Channel 9. **Police**, phone (907) 786-8500. **Alaska State Troopers**, phone (907) 269-5511. **Hospitals:** Alaska Regional Hospital, phone (907) 276-1131; Alaska Native Medical Center, phone (907) 279-6661; Providence, Alaska Medical Center, phone (907) 562-2211; Elmendorf Air Force Base emergency room, phone (907) 552-5555. **Dental Emergencies**, phone (907) 279-9144 (24-hour service). **Emergency Management**, phone (907) 267-4904. **Suicide Intervention**, phone (907) 563-3200 (24-hour service). **Rape & Assault**, phone (907) 276-7273. **Battered Women**, phone (907) 272-0100. **Pet Emergency**, phone (907) 274-5636. **Poison Control**, phone (907) 261-3193. **Road Conditions**, statewide, phone (800) 478-7675 or (907) 273-6037.

Visitor Information: Log Cabin Visitor Information Center, operated by the Anchorage Convention and Visitors Bureau, is at 4th Avenue and F Street; open daily, year-round. Hours are 7:30 A.M. to 7 P.M. June through August; 8 A.M. to 6 P.M. in May and September; and 9 A.M. to 4 P.M. the remainder of the year. The cabin offers a wide assortment of free brochures and maps. Write 524 W. 4th Ave., Anchorage 99501; phone (907) 274-3531; Internet, www.alaska.net/~acvb.; e-mail at acvb@alaska.net. The bureau also operates a year-round visitor information phone with a recorded message of the day's special events and attractions, including films, plays, sports events and gallery openings, and it produces several publications including 2 visitor guides, a restaurant directory, a fall/winter discount book and a monthly calendar of events; phone (907) 276-3200. Additional visitor information centers are open daily at Anchorage International Airport, one on the lower level for passengers arriving on domestic flights; another in the customs-secured area of the international concourse; and a third in the lobby of the international terminal. The North Anchorage Visitor Information Center is located in the Parkgate Building, just off the Glenn Highway at 11723 Old Glenn Highway. The Anchorage Convention and Visitors Bureau offers information on community events, phone (907) 276-4118.

The Alaska Public Lands Information Center, 605 W. 4th, in the historic Old Federal Building, has extensive displays and information on outdoor recreation lands in Alaska; phone (907) 271-2737. (See detailed description under Attractions, this section.)

Elevation: 38 to 120 feet/16 to 37m. **Climate:** Anchorage has a climate closely resembling that of the Rocky Mountains area. Shielded from excess Pacific moisture by the Kenai Mountains to the south, the city has an annual average of only 15.9 inches of precipitation. Winter snowfall averages about 70 inches per year, with snow on the ground typically from October to April. Anchorage is in a transition zone between the moderating influence of the Pacific Ocean and the extreme temperatures found in interior Alaska. The average temperature in January (coldest month) is 15°F/-9°C; in July (warmest month), 58°F/14°C. A record 40 days of 70°F/21°C temperatures or higher was set in 1936, according to the National Weather Service. Record high was 85°F/29°C in June of 1969. Record low was -34°F/-37°C in January 1975. The growing season in the area is 100 to 120 days and typically extends from late May to early September. Anchorage has a daily maximum of 19 hours, 21 minutes of daylight in summer, and 5 hours, 28 minutes in winter. Prevailing wind direction is north.

Radio: KENI 550, KHAR 590, KYAK 650, KBYR 700, KFQD 750, KLEF 98.1, KFFR 1020, KKSD 1080, KRUA-FM 88.1, KATB-FM 89.3, KSKA-FM 91.1, KJMM-FM 94.5, KEAG-FM 97.3, KYMG-FM 98.9, KBFX-FM 100.5, KGOT-FM 101.3, KKRD-FM 102.1, KMXS-FM 103.1, KBRJ-FM 104.1, KNIK-FM 105.3, KWHL-FM 106.5, KASH-FM 107.5 and KNBA 90.3-FM. **Television:** KTUU (NBC), Channel 2; KTBY (Fox), Channel 4; KYES (independent), Channel 5; KAKM (PBS), Channel 7;

(Continues on page 372)

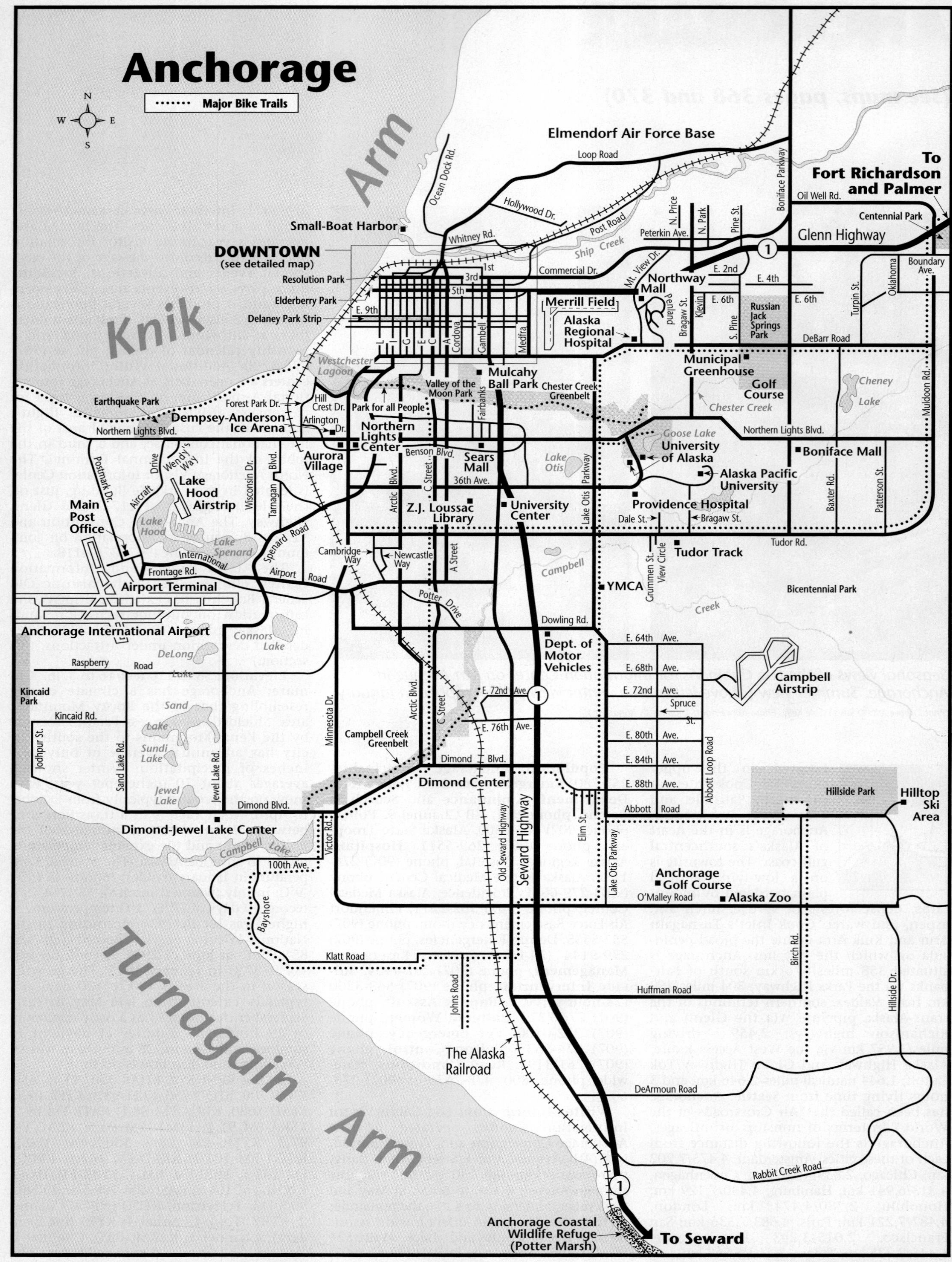
Anchorage
Major Bike Trails
N
S
E
W
Elmendorf Air Force Base
Loop Road
To Fort Richardson and Palmer
Oil Well Rd.
Centennial Park
Glenn Highway
Boundary Ave.
Ocean Dock Rd.
Hollywood Dr.
Post Road
Whitney Rd.
Ship Creek
Small-Boat Harbor
DOWNTOWN
(see detailed map)
Resolution Park
Elderberry Park
Delaney Park Strip
E. 9th
3rd
1st
5th
Commercial Dr.
Peterkin Ave.
N. Price
N. Park
Pine St.
Boniface Parkway
Mt. View Dr.
Northway Mall
E. 2nd
E. 4th
E. 6th
Merrill Field
Alaska Regional Hospital
Russian Jack Springs Park
DeBarr Road
Turpin St.
Oklahoma
Bragaw St.
Klevin
S. Pine
Knik
Arm
Westchester Lagoon
Cordova
Gambell
Medfra
Municipal Greenhouse
Golf Course
Cheney Lake
Chester Creek
Muldoon Rd.
Earthquake Park
Forest Park Dr.
Hill Crest Dr.
Dempsey-Anderson Ice Arena
Arlington Dr.
Park for all People
Valley of the Moon Park
Mulcahy Ball Park
Chester Creek Greenbelt
Northern Lights Blvd.
Northern Lights Center
Aurora Village
Benson Blvd.
Sears Mall
Fairbanks
Lake Otis
Goose Lake
University of Alaska
Boniface Mall
Alaska Pacific University
Postmark Dr.
Aircraft Drive
Wendy's Way
Lake Hood Airstrip
Wisconsin Dr.
Tarnagan Blvd.
Arctic Blvd.
C Street
36th Ave.
Lake Otis Parkway
Providence Hospital
Baxter Rd.
Patterson St.
Main Post Office
Lake Hood
Lake Spenard
Z.J. Loussac Library
University Center
Dale St.
Bragaw St.
Spenard Road
International
Cambridge Way
Newcastle Way
A Street
Tudor Rd.
Tudor Track
Grummen St.
View Circle
Frontage Rd.
Airport Road
Airport Terminal
Campbell
YMCA
Bicentennial Park
Creek
Potter Drive
Anchorage International Airport
Connors Lake
DeLong Lake
Raspberry Road
Dowling Rd.
Dept. of Motor Vehicles
E. 64th Ave.
E. 68th Ave.
E. 72nd Ave.
Campbell Airstrip
Spruce St.
E. 76th Ave.
E. 80th Ave.
E. 84th Ave.
E. 88th Ave.
Kincaid Park
Kincaid Rd.
Sand Lake
Sundi Lake
Jewel Lake
Jodhpur St.
Sand Lake Rd.
Jewel Lake Rd.
Minnesota Dr.
Campbell Creek Greenbelt
Dimond Blvd.
Dimond Center
Abbott Road
Abbott Loop Road
Hillside Park
Hilltop Ski Area
Dimond-Jewel Lake Center
Campbell Lake
100th Ave.
Victor Rd.
Old Seward Highway
Seward Highway
Elim St.
Lake Otis Parkway
Anchorage Golf Course
O'Malley Road
Alaska Zoo
Bayshore
Turnagain
Klatt Road
Johns Road
Huffman Road
Birch Rd.
Hillside Dr.
The Alaska Railroad
DeArmoun Road
Arm
Rabbit Creek Road
1
Anchorage Coastal Wildlife Refuge (Potter Marsh)
To Seward

Alaska
Please circle No.10 on the reader service card
Apone's T-Shirt Cache
BIGGEST and BEST selection of T-SHIRTS
& SWEATSHIRTS in the Universe (we've checked)
436W 4TH AVE
ANCHORAGE, AK
99501-2364
FREE
Catalogue
1-800-770-1007
PH 907 272-1007
FAX 907-272-1019
Alaska
Alaska
TUNDRA
UNSUCCESSFUL BUSINESS VENTURES
OF THE FAR NORTH
ESKIMO BOB'S
DRIVE - THRU
DOG SLED WASH
FROM ALASKA . . . THE LAST FRONTIER
ALASKA FLY FISHING

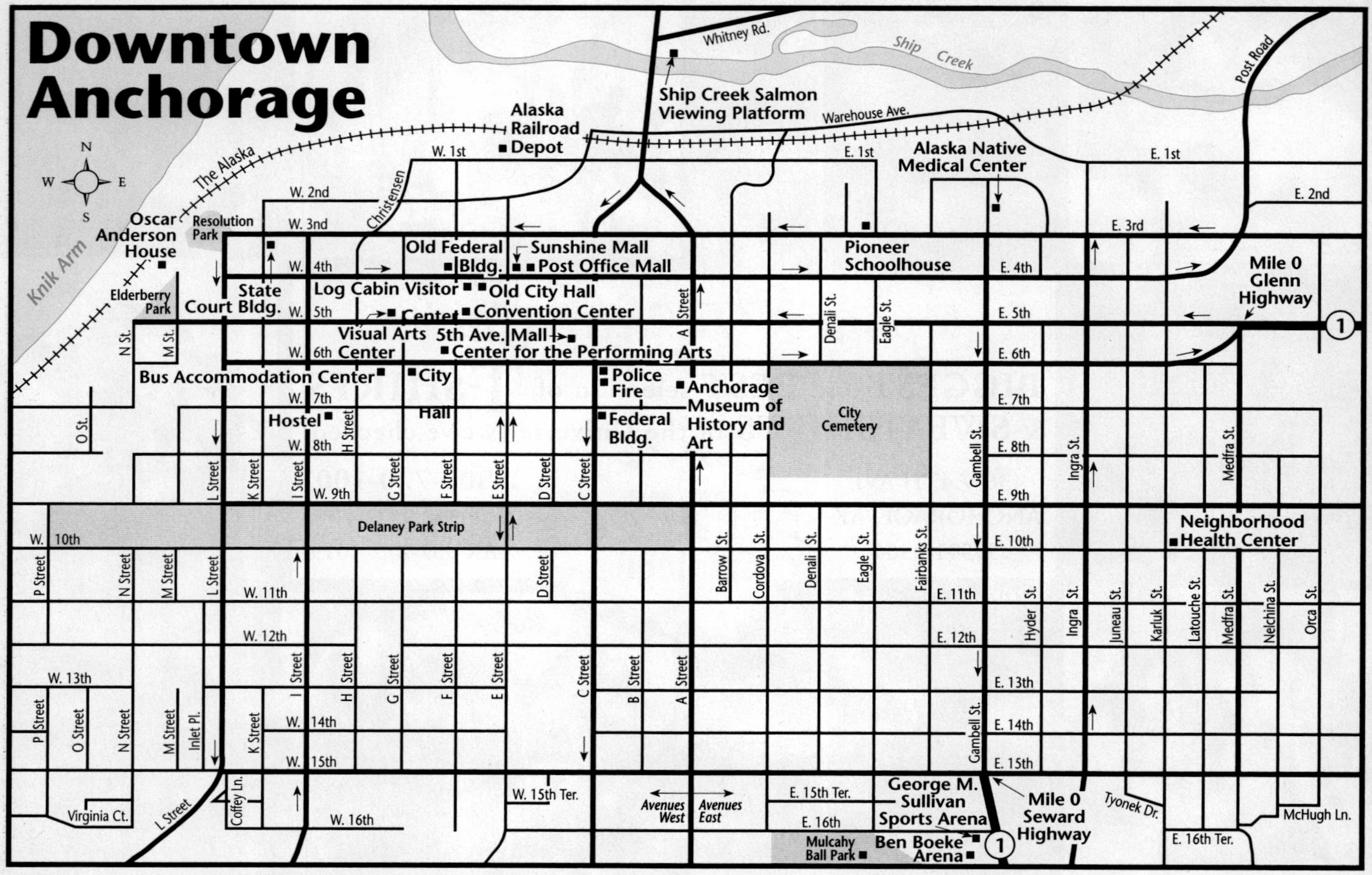

Downtown Anchorage

Whitney Rd. · Ship Creek · Post Road · Ship Creek Salmon Viewing Platform · Warehouse Ave. · Alaska Railroad Depot · The Alaska (Railroad) · Knik Arm · W. 1st · E. 1st · Alaska Native Medical Center · W. 2nd · E. 2nd · W. 3rd · E. 3rd · Christensen · Oscar Anderson House · Resolution Park · Elderberry Park · Old Federal Bldg. · Sunshine Mall · Post Office Mall · Pioneer Schoolhouse · W. 4th · E. 4th · Mile 0 Glenn Highway · State Court Bldg. · Log Cabin Visitor Center · Old City Hall · Convention Center · W. 5th · E. 5th · Visual Arts Center · 5th Ave. Mall · Center for the Performing Arts · W. 6th · E. 6th · Bus Accommodation Center · City Hall · Police Fire · Anchorage Museum of History and Art · W. 7th · E. 7th · Hostel · Federal Bldg. · City Cemetery · W. 8th · E. 8th · W. 9th · E. 9th · Delaney Park Strip · W. 10th · E. 10th · Neighborhood Health Center · W. 11th · E. 11th · W. 12th · E. 12th · W. 13th · E. 13th · W. 14th · E. 14th · W. 15th · E. 15th · W. 15th Ter. · E. 15th Ter. · George M. Sullivan Sports Arena · Mile 0 Seward Highway · Tyonek Dr. · McHugh Ln. · Virginia Ct. · L Street · Coffey Ln. · W. 16th · E. 16th · E. 16th Ter. · Avenues West · Avenues East · Mulcahy Ball Park · Ben Boeke Arena · P Street · O Street · N Street · M Street · L Street · K Street · Inlet Pl. · I Street · H Street · G Street · F Street · E Street · D Street · C Street · B Street · A Street · Barrow St. · Cordova St. · Denali St. · Eagle St. · Fairbanks St. · Gambell St. · Hyder St. · Ingra St. · Juneau St. · Karluk St. · Latouche St. · Medfra St. · Nelchina St. · Orca St.

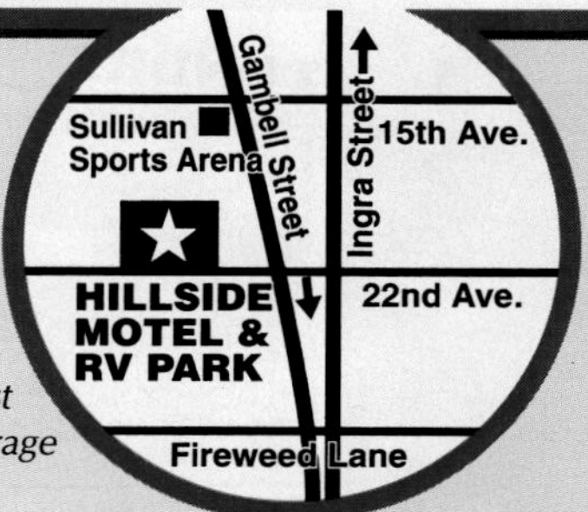

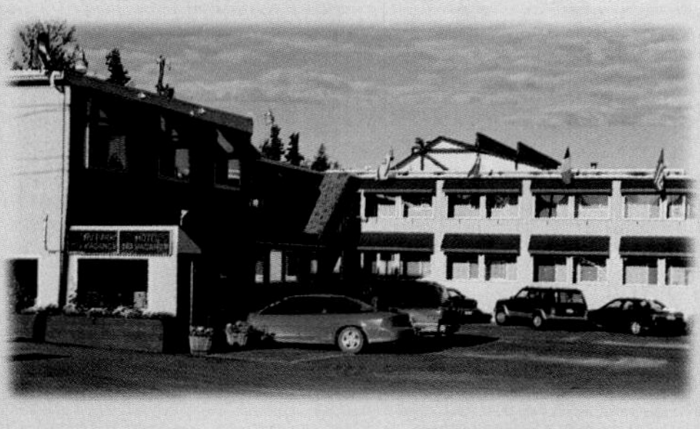

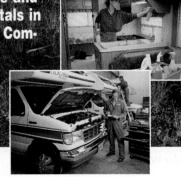

(Continued from page 367)
KTVA (CBS), Channel 11; KIMO (ABC), Channel 13; KDMD TV 20; and UHF channels. Pay cable television is also available. **Newspapers:** *Anchorage Daily News* (daily); *Alaska Journal of Commerce, Anchorage Press* (weekly); *Chugiak-Eagle River Star* (semi-weekly).

Private Aircraft: Anchorage airports provide facilities and services to accommodate all types of aircraft. Consult the *Alaska Supplement,* the *Anchorage VFR Terminal Area Chart* and *Terminal Alaska Book* for the following airports: Anchorage International, Merrill Field, Campbell airstrip, and Lake Hood seaplane and strip.

HISTORY AND ECONOMY

In 1914 Congress authorized the building of a railroad linking an ocean port with the interior river shipping routes. The anchorage at the mouth of Ship Creek was chosen as the construction camp and headquarters for the Alaskan Engineering Commission. By the summer of 1915 the camp's population, housed mainly in tents, had grown to about 2,000.

The name Anchorage (earlier names included Woodrow, Ship Creek, Ship Creek Landing and Knik Anchorage) was chosen by the federal government when the first post office opened in May 1915. A few months later the bluff south of the creek was cleared and surveyed, and 655 lots, on 347 acres, were auctioned off by the General Land Office for $148,000. The intersection of 4th Avenue and C Street was regarded as the center of the business district, and by late summer about 100 wooden structures had been built. Anchorage continued to prosper and was incorporated in 1920.

Anchorage's growth has been in spurts, propelled by: (1) construction of the Alaska Railroad and the transfer of its headquarters from Seward to Anchorage in 1917; (2) colonization of the Matanuska Valley, a farming region 45 miles/72 km to the north, in 1935; (3) construction of Fort Richardson and Elmendorf Field in 1940; (4) oil discoveries between 1957 and 1961 in Cook Inlet; and (5) the development of North Slope oil fields and the construction of the trans-Alaska pipeline—all since 1968.

The earthquake of March 27, 1964, which caused millions of dollars in damage, resulted in a flurry of new construction. Government relief funds (in the form of Small Business Administration loans) were offered to those who wished to rebuild. Most did, and a distinctly new Anchorage began to emerge.

In the 1970s and 1980s, Anchorage underwent a population and construction boom tied to oil production. Oil companies located their headquarters in Anchorage. ARCO completed its 21-story office tower in 1983. The decline in oil prices in recent years has brought about a slower economy than was enjoyed in those "boom" years. Today, Anchorage is a center of commerce and distribution for the rest of Alaska.

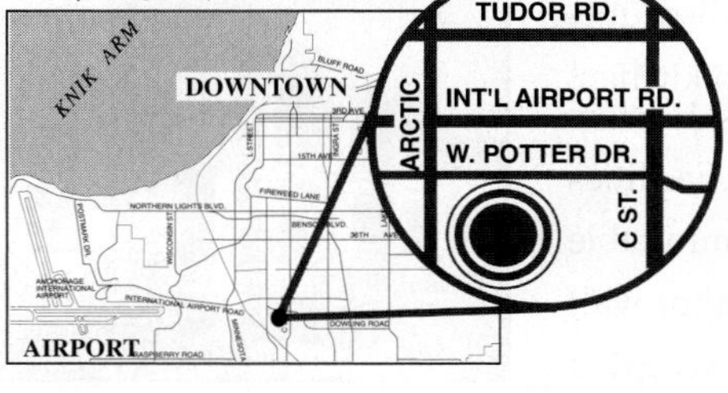

DESCRIPTION

Anchorage is a sprawling city, bordered

Anchorage skyline above Westchester Lagoon in September.
(© James D. Ronan, Jr.)

on the east by the stunningly beautiful Chugach Mountain Range and on the west by Knik Arm of Cook Inlet. On a clear day, you can catch a tantalizing glimpse of Mount McKinley, 135 miles/217 km to the north.

Many new buildings dot the Anchorage skyline. Millions of dollars were allocated by the legislature for Project 80s, the largest construction program in Anchorage's history. Perhaps best known is the Alaska Center for the Performing Arts, located at the corner of 5th Avenue and F Street. Construction costs on the center grew from an original estimate of $22 million to more than $70 million. Visitors may notice the fences on the center's roof: these had to be added to prevent snow from sliding off the

steep pitch of the roof and onto pedestrians below. Other completed projects include the George M. Sullivan Sports Arena, William A. Egan Civic and Convention Center, Z.J. Loussac Public Library, and a major expansion and renovation of the Anchorage Museum of History and Art.

With its curious mixture of the old frontier and the jet age, Anchorage is truly a unique place. In profile, the town has:

• About 80 schools, including special education and alternative public programs and a number of privately operated schools, and also the University of Alaska, Alaska Pacific University and Alaska Business College.

• More than 200 churches and temples.

• Z.J. Loussac Public Library, plus 4 branch libraries, National Bank of Alaska Heritage Library Museum, Dept. of the Interior's Alaska Resource Library, the Oil Spill Public Information Center, Alaska State Library Services for the Blind and the University of Alaska Library.

• Municipal bus service and 7 taxi services.

• In the arts—**Dance:** Alaska Center for Performing Arts; Alaska Dance Theatre; Anchorage Concert Assoc.; Anchorage Opera; Ballet Alaska. **Music:** Alaska Airlines Autumn Classics; Anchorage Concert Chorus; Anchorage Community Concert Band; Anchorage Concert Assoc.; Anchorage Children's Choir; Anchorage Symphony Orchestra; Anchorage Festival of Music; Sweet Adelines (Cheechako and Sourdough chapters); University of Alaska Anchorage Singers; Young People's Concerts. **Theater:** Out North Theater Company; Alaska Junior Theater; Alaska Theatre of Youth; Anchorage Community Theatre; Alaska Stage Company; Valley Performing Arts; UAA Theatre; Alaska Festival Theatre; Cyrano's Off Center Playhouse. **Art:** About 20 art galleries.

• An award-winning trail system, including 75 miles of summer hiking trails, 120 miles of paved bike trails and 105 miles of maintained ski trails.

ACCOMMODATIONS/VISITOR SERVICES

There are more than 70 motels and hotels in the Anchorage area with prices for a double room ranging from \$50 to \$70 and up. Reservations are a must. Bed-and-breakfast accommodations are also available in more than 100 private residences.

Hosteling International–Anchorage is located at 700 H St., 1 block from the People Mover Transit Center in downtown Anchorage. The hostel is open 8 A.M. to noon and 1 P.M. to 11 P.M. June through October; 8:30 A.M. to noon and 5 P.M. to 11 P.M., October through May. Cost for members is \$15 per night, nonmembers \$18. American Youth Hostel cards available at the hostel or by mail. The hostel has dormitory rooms with bunkbeds, kitchen facilities, common rooms, laundry room and TV room. For information or to make reservations no less than 1 day in advance with VISA or MasterCard, phone (907) 276-3635, or write for reservations (prepayment required): 700 H St., Anchorage 99501.

Spenard Hostel International is a nonaffiliated hostel located on the bus line at 2845 W. 42nd Place. Cost is $12–$15 per night. For more information or to make reservations, phone (907) 248-5036; fax (907) 248-5063; e-mail hostel@alaskalife.net.

Restaurants number more than 600, with many major fast-food chains, formal dining rooms and specialty establishments including Italian, Japanese, Korean, Chinese (Cantonese and Mandarin), Mexican, Polynesian, Greek, German, Sicilian, Thai, soul food, seafood, smorgasbord and vegetarian.

Alaskan Frontier Gardens Bed and Breakfast. Elegant Alaska hillside estate on peaceful scenic 3 acres by Chugach State Park, 20 minutes from downtown. Spacious luxury suites with big Jacuzzi, sauna, and fireplace, laundry facility. Getaway for honeymooners. Gourmet breakfast, museum-like environment with Alaskan hospitality and exceptional comfort. Truly Alaska's finest. Year-round service. Credit cards accepted. P.O. Box 241881, Anchorage, AK 99524-1881. (907) 345-6556 or 345-6562. Fax (907) 562-2923. [ADVERTISEMENT]

Anchorage Homestead Inn. (907) 561-3138; toll free: (888) 488-1800. E-mail: homesteadinn@corecom.net. Quiet, clean rooms conveniently located near airport, Lake Hood and downtown. Low rates—$39/night and up. Open year-round. Free HBO, coffee, phone use. Kitchen, laundry and freezer facilities available. Walking distance from restaurants and shops. 4215 Spenard Rd., Anchorage, AK 99517. [ADVERTISEMENT]

Arctic Fox Bed & Breakfast Inn. 326 E. 2nd Ct., Anchorage, AK 99501. Phone (907) 272-4818, fax 272-4819. Quiet downtown location with some inlet views. Tastefully decorated rooms and suites with moderate summer rates, low winter rates. Near downtown hotels, restaurants, museum, bike trail, train and Ship Creek. Laundry. Private baths, TV and phone in room. [ADVERTISEMENT]

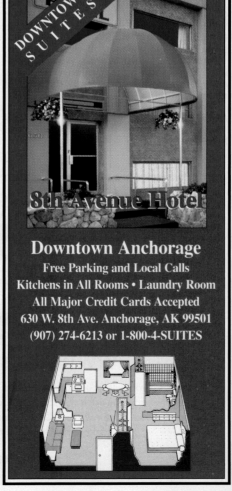

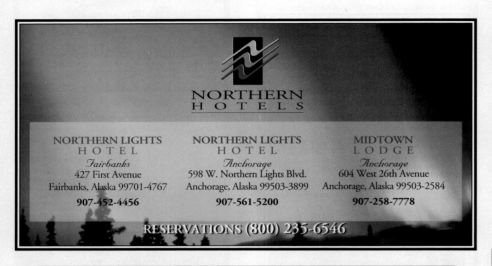

The Aurora Winds. Anchorage's exceptional bed and breakfast resort is situated on 2 meticulously landscaped acres and features 5 suites, all with private bath, TV, VCR and phone. The "McKinley Suite" also has a fireplace, wide-screen TV, double Jacuzzi and a habitat-environment chamber. The atmosphere is one of quiet elegance: contemporary, with an Alaskan home-style atmosphere where breakfast is a gourmet delight, and the staff strives to satisfy your every need. Take advantage of the full gym, billiard room, sauna, theater room, 10-person outdoor hot tub, or one of the 4 fireplaces. "Our recommendation for Anchorage's best bed and breakfast, the Aurora Winds B & B Resort." For information, phone (800) 642-9640, (907) 347-2533, or e-mail awbnb@alaska.net. [ADVERTISEMENT]

Bed and Breakfast Association of Alaska. Stay where real Alaskans stay, in their homes! A new directory is available representing our members throughout Alaska. All types of accommodations, from homestays to inns, from luxurious B&B's to cabins, from cities to the bush. Licensed, insured and many inspected. BBAA, P.O. Box 202663, Anchorage, AK 99501; phone (907) 566-2627 or fax (907) 272-1899. [ADVERTISEMENT]

Caribou Inn. 501 L Street, Anchorage, AK 99501. Clean, comfortable rooms in an excellent downtown Anchorage location. Shared or private bath, some with kitchenettes. Major credit cards accepted. Free shuttle to airport and train station. (907) 272-0444 or fax (907) 274-4828. Toll free (800) 272-5875. E-mail: caribou@alaska.net. [ADVERTISEMENT]

Chugach Bed & Breakfast. Serene adult setting in a quiet neighborhood nestled at the foot of the beautiful Chugach Mountains. Easy access to airport, city, wilderness. A full breakfast and other amenities too numerous to mention. Your hosts of 35 years plus. 3901 Laron Lane, Anchorage, AK 99504-4652; phone (907) 333-4615, fax (907) 337-6095. [ADVERTISEMENT]

Coastal Trail Bed & Breakfast invites you to warm Alaskan-style hospitality with a home-style breakfast and a comfortable bed. A beautiful home in an excellent neighborhood, conveniently located near airport and downtown. Adjoins scenic urban trail. Private baths, phone, TV, amenities. Business travelers welcome. Year round. (907) 243-5809; fax (907) 248-9010; e-mail coastaltrail@alaskana.com. [ADVERTISEMENT]

Downtown Bed & Breakfast. (907) 279-5293. Please stop in when you arrive in Anchorage and we'll help you find a place to stay. We're also home to Downtown Bicycle Rental. For more information, write us: 245 W. 5th Ave. #6, Corner 5th and C, Anchorage, AK 99501. Fax (907) 279-8338. [ADVERTISEMENT]

Glacier Way Bed & Breakfast. 2051 Glacier St., Anchorage, Alaska. Five luxurious rooms, hilltop setting, quiet, close to town. Stay includes: Jacuzzi, Habitat, pool, table tennis at no extra charge. Backyard accesses 180 miles of bike trails, ski trails. $70 single, $80 doubles, private bath $90 and special rates for off-season. Phone (907)

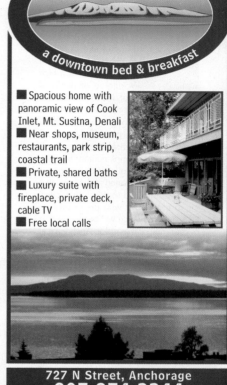

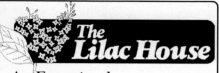

337-5201, (907) 244-7148 or fax (907) 337-5308. [ADVERTISEMENT]

"K" Street Bed & Breakfast. Downtown, 2 blocks to coastal trail, market, dining and bus line. Near airport, railroad and shopping. Healthy breakfast, gourmet coffee, teas. Private or shared bath with sitting areas. Secure area, ample parking, smoke-free. Hostess 21-year resident. Fully licensed. Phone/fax (907) 279-1443. 1443 "K" Street, Anchorage, AK 99501. E-mail: kstbb@alaska.net. Toll free (888) KST-BANB. [ADVERTISEMENT]

North Country Castle Bed & Breakfast. Luxuriate in our spacious, sunny, warm Victorian home! Relax on any of 4 decks with sparkling mountain and Cook Inlet views. Explore moose trails on our forested acreage or amble down our country road to nearby hiking paths. Only minutes from major Anchorage attractions and the wilds of Alaska. Bounteous breakfasts. Year-round. Credit cards accepted. P.O. Box 111876, Anchorage, AK 99511. (907) 345-7296. [ADVERTISEMENT]

Puffin Inn. Experience comfortable, quality accommodations and exceptional service at reasonable rates. Our friendly Alaskan hospitality includes complimentary coffee, muffin and daily newspaper. Located near Lake Hood floatplane airport with courtesy airport shuttle, nonsmoking rooms, cable TV and freezer space for your hunting and fishing needs. Handicap accessible. 4400 Spenard Rd., Anchorage, AK 99517. Phone (907) 243-4044. Fax (907) 248-6853. (800) 4PU-FFIN. [ADVERTISEMENT] ♿

Puffin Place Studios & Suites. Relax and enjoy 1 of our 38 attractively furnished studios and 1-bedroom suites featuring fully equipped kitchens with microwaves. Within walking distance of restaurants, shopping and Tony Knowles Coastal Trail. Our amenities include: courtesy airport shuttle, nonsmoking rooms, laundry facility, freezer space, cable TV. Weekly and monthly rates offered October–May. 1058 W. 27th, Anchorage, AK 99503, (907) 279-1058. Fax (907) 257-9595. (800) 71-PLACE. [ADVERTISEMENT]

Snowshoe Inn. 826 K Street, Anchorage, AK 99501. Phone (907) 258-7669. Fax (907) 258-7463. Convenient downtown location, private lodging, smoke-free environment, quiet, beautifully decorated rooms/suites with private and shared bath, TV and phone in each room. Amenities: laundry, freezer space, free parking. Open year-round. [ADVERTISEMENT]

Susie's Lake View Bed & Breakfast. Enjoy the quiet setting overlooking scenic

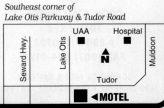

Captain Cook statue in Resolution Park overlooking Cook Inlet. (©Tom Culkin)

Campbell Lake. Unwind with a leisure tour of our quaint garden setting. The large deck areas offer comfortable privacy for an individual but are big enough for a family barbecue. Start or end your day with a steamy hot tub—available 24 hours a day and located where it should be ... outside. Continental or traditional breakfast. Business travelers welcome. Located only 11 minutes from the airport. VISA and MasterCard accepted. 9256 Campbell Terrace, Anchorage, AK 99515. Phone (907) 243-4624. [ADVERTISEMENT]

The Teddy Bear House Bed & Breakfast. Experience a traditional home stay in our uniquely decorated home in a quiet south Anchorage neighborhood, 15 minutes from airport and downtown. Close to Anchorage Zoo and shopping. Twin or queen beds. Private and shared bath. Continental or traditional breakfast. Large deck for your relaxation. Open year-round. No smoking. P.O. Box 190265, Anchorage, AK 99519; (907) 344-3111. [ADVERTISEMENT]

12th & L Bed and Breakfast. Downtown Anchorage. Private baths, cable TV. Free phone and laundry. Convenient, casual, comfortable, congenial and clean. Flexible check in/check out. Low winter rates. Informative brochure. (907) 276-1225. Fax (907) 276-1224. Web address www.customcpu.com/commercial/twelfth/default.htm. [ADVERTISEMENT]

Anchorage has 2 public campgrounds: Centennial Park, open from May through September, and Lions Camper Park, open July and part of August on an as-needed basis. Fees are $13 for non-Alaskans and $11 for Alaska residents. To reach Centennial Park, take the Muldoon Road exit south off the Glenn Highway, take the first left onto Boundary, take the next left and follow the signs. Lions Camper Park is located at 5800 Boniface Parkway, half a mile south of the Glenn Highway. Centennial, recommended for large RVs, has 90 RV sites and 40 tent sites. Lions has 50 tent sites. Both feature barracks-type showers, flush toilets, water and dump stations and no hookups. Between May and September, phone (907) 333-9711 for details on either park. In the off-season, phone (907) 343-6397.

Chugach State Park has campgrounds located near Anchorage at Bird Creek (Seward Highway), and at Eagle River and Eklutna Lake (Glenn Highway). Anchorage also has several private campgrounds. ▲

Anchorage RV Park. Visit Alaska's premier RV park. Wooded setting, minutes from downtown Anchorage. 195 full-hookup spaces, beautiful main lodge with laundry, restrooms and showers, camp store and community room, paved streets. Easy access off Glenn Highway, next to bike trails. Alaska Native owned and operated. Season: mid-May through September. To make reservations call (800) 400-7275, (907) 338-7275, 7300 Oilwell Rd., Anchorage, AK 99504. [ADVERTISEMENT] ▲

Highlander Camper Park. 42 full hook-up spaces, free showers, clean restrooms. Located across from the Sears Mall. A quiet location within walking distance of grocery store, beauty salons, bank, restaurants and more. 2704 Fairbanks Street, Anchorage, AK 99503. Reservations (907) 277-2407. [ADVERTISEMENT] ▲

TRANSPORTATION

Air: More than a dozen international and domestic air carriers and numerous intrastate airlines serve Anchorage International Airport, located 6.5 miles/10.5 km from downtown. Limousine service to and from major downtown hotels is available.

Ferry: There is no ferry service to Anchorage. The nearest port is Whittier on Prince William Sound, served by Alaska state ferry from Cordova and Valdez. Whittier is accessible by train from either Anchorage or Portage on the Seward Highway.

Railroad: The Alaska Railroad offers daily passenger service in summer from Anchorage to Seward and to Fairbanks via Denali National Park. Reduced service in winter. Summer rail service is also available between Anchorage and Whittier, with optional connections to Prince William Sound cruises. In addition, a shuttle train for foot passengers and vehicles operates daily in summer between Portage and Whittier, connecting with the state ferry to Valdez and Cordova. Contact Passenger Services Dept., Box 107500, Anchorage 99510-7500; phone (800) 544-0552 or (907) 265-2494, fax 265-2323 or 265-2509.

The Alaska Railroad depot is located on 1st Avenue, within easy walking distance of downtown.

Bus: Local service via People Mover, which serves most of the Anchorage bowl from Peters Creek to Oceanview. Fares are $1 for adults, 50¢ for youth 5 to 18, 25¢ for senior citizens and disabled citizens with transit identification. Monthly passes are sold at the Transit Center (6th Avenue and H Street), the Dimond Transit Center and municipal libraries. Day passes are also available for $2.50 at the Transit Center, Dimond Transit Center and 7–11 stores. For bus route information, phone the Rideline at (907) 343-6543.

Taxi: There are 7 taxi companies.

Car and Camper Rentals: There are more than 2 dozen car rental agencies located at the airport and downtown. There are also several RV rental agencies (see advertisements this section).

RV Parking: The Anchorage Parking Authority offers a lot with spaces for oversized vehicles (motorcoaches, campers, large trucks) at 3rd Avenue, north of the Holiday Inn, between A and C streets. Parking is $5 per space, per day. For more information, phone (907) 276-PARK or (800) 770-ACAR.

Highway: Anchorage can be reached via the Glenn Highway and the Seward Highway. See GLENN HIGHWAY and SEWARD HIGHWAY sections for details.

ATTRACTIONS

Get Acquainted: Stop by the Log Cabin Visitor Information Center at 4th Avenue and F Street, open 7:30 A.M. to 7 P.M. June through August; 8 A.M. to 6 P.M. in May and September; and 9 A.M. to 4 P.M. the remainder of the year; phone (907) 274-3531. Free visitor guidebooks.

Take a Historic Walking Tour: Start at the Log Cabin Visitor Information Center at 4th Avenue and F Street. The Anchorage Convention and Visitors Bureau's *Anchorage Visitors Guide* suggests an excellent downtown walking tour.

Take a Tour: Several tour operators offer

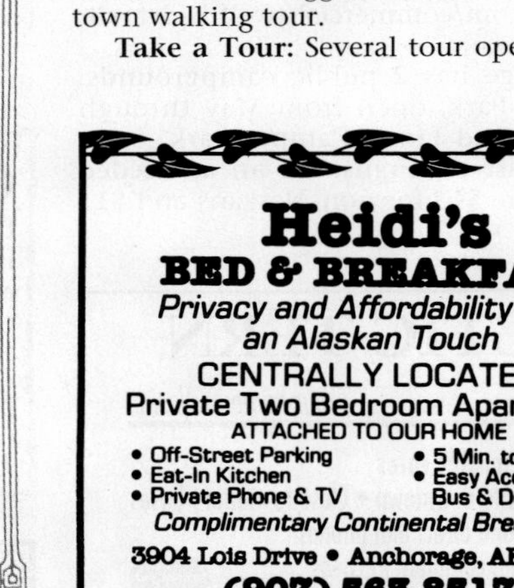

local and area sightseeing tours. These range from a 1-hour narrated trolley tour of Anchorage to full-day tours of area attractions such as Portage Glacier and Alyeska Resort. Two-day or longer excursions by motorcoach, rail, ferry and air to nearby attractions such as Prince William Sound or remote areas are also available. Inquire at your hotel, see ads this section, or contact a travel agent.

Anchorage City Trolley Tours. It's fun. It's 1-hour. It's only $10. A lively, informative tour of Alaska's largest city. Located on Fourth Avenue between F and G streets.

Departs hourly. 9 A.M.–6 P.M. P.O. Box 102299, Anchorage, AK 99510. Phone (907) 276-5603. [ADVERTISEMENT]

The Alaska Public Lands Information Center, located in the historic Old Federal Building on 4th Avenue and F Street, offers a wide variety of information on all of Alaska's state and federal parks, forests and wildlife refuges. Displays, video programs and computers permit self-help trip-planning. Expert staff provide additional assistance and supply maps, brochures and other aids. Federal passports (Golden Age, Eagle and Access) and state park passes are available. Reservations may be made here (in person or by mail only) for Kenai Fjords National Park cabins. The center is open year-round. Summer hours (Memorial Day to Labor Day) are 9 A.M. to 5:30 P.M. daily; open in winter 10 A.M. to 5:30 P.M. Monday through Friday, closed weekends and holidays. Phone (907) 271-2737 or write the center at 605 W. 4th Ave., Suite 105, Anchorage 99501, for more information.

The Anchorage Museum of History and Art, located at 121 W. 7th Ave., is a must stop. One of the most visited attractions in Anchorage, the museum features permanent displays of Alaska's cultural heritage and artifacts from its history. The 15,000-square-foot/1,400-square-meter Alaska Gallery on the second floor is the museum's showcase, presenting Alaska Native cultures—Aleut, Eskimo and Indian—and displays about the Russians, New England whalers, as well as gold rush, WWII, statehood and Alaska today. Displays include full-scale dwellings and detailed miniature dioramas. The gallery contains some 300 photographs, more than 1,000 artifacts, 33 maps, and specially made ship and aircraft models. The main floor of the museum consists of 6 connecting galleries displaying Alaska art, such as works by Sydney Laurence. Also on the 1st floor are a Children's Gallery and 3 temporary exhibition galleries. The museum has a reference library and archives, a free film series and public tours (daily in summer), the Museum Shop and a cafe in the atrium. Admission is $5 for adults, $4.50 for seniors, under 18 free. Open 9 A.M. to 6 P.M. daily, May 8 to Sept. 20, 1998, 10 A.M. to 6 P.M. Tuesday through Saturday, and 1–5 P.M. Sunday, in winter (closed Monday and holidays). Phone (907) 343-6173 for recorded information about special shows, or (907) 343-4326 during business hours for more information.

Visit the Oscar Anderson House

Museum, one of the city's first wood-frame houses. Built in 1915, it was home to Oscar Anderson, a Swedish immigrant and early Anchorage pioneer and businessman. Now on the National Register of Historic Places, it has been beautifully restored and is well worth a visit. Located in the north corner of Elderberry Park, at the west end of 5th Avenue, 420 M St. Open mid-May to mid-September for guided tours. Hours are 11 A.M. to 4 P.M., Tuesday through Saturday. Swedish Christmas tour, first 2 weekends in December. Adults, $3; seniors over 65, $2; children 5 to 12, $1. Group tours may be arranged year-round by appointment. Phone (907) 274-2336; fax (907) 274-3600.

Tracy Anna Bader Design Studio/ Denali Wear. "Original Art to Wear Outdoors.™" Visit this contemporary Alaskan artist, working in her colorful storefront studio, creating exclusive coats, novelty jackets, vests, blankets and accessories. Custom orders a specialty. For hours phone/fax (907) ART-WEAR (278-9327). Look for the beautiful flower box downtown at 416 G Street. [ADVERTISEMENT]

The Knitting Frenzy Store. Best source for yarn, fiber, books, patterns, supplies for use in knitting, weaving, spinning, crochet and tatting. Largest Alaskan inventory. Choose a project for the road! Open Monday through Saturday 10–6. Day phone (907) 563-2717. In Alaska, (800) 478-8322. 4240 Old Seward Hwy. #18, corner of Old Seward and Tudor. Fax (907) 563-1081. E-mail: frenzy@alaska.net. [ADVERTISEMENT]

Laura Wright Alaskan Parkys. Known worldwide for beautiful Eskimo-style summer and winter parkas. Off the rack or custom-made. Started by Laura Wright in Fairbanks in 1947; continuing the tradition is granddaughter Sheila Ezelle. Purchase "Wearable Alaskan Art" for the whole family at 343 W. 5th Ave., Anchorage, AK 99501. Phone (907) 274-4215. Bank cards welcome. Mail and phone orders accepted. We airmail worldwide. [ADVERTISEMENT]

Oomingmak, Musk Ox Producers' Co-operative, is a Native-owned co-operative specializing in knitted masterpieces. Using Qiviut, the soft and rare fiber from the arctic Musk Oxen, our 250 Native Alaskan knitters create hats and scarves in a variety of traditional patterns from their culture. Since 1969, this co-operative organization has provided the opportunity for Native women to

earn a supplementary income while still pursuing their subsistence lifestyle. For over 25 years, the exquisite items the co-op members make on their knitting needles have been worn with pride and enjoyment by satisfied customers from around the world. We invite you to visit us in downtown Anchorage at the little brown house with the Musk Ox mural on the corner of 6th and H streets. (907) 272-9225, 604 H Street, Anchorage, AK 99501. [ADVERTISEMENT]

Exercise Your Imagination: Visit the Imaginarium, 737 W. 5th Ave., Suite 140

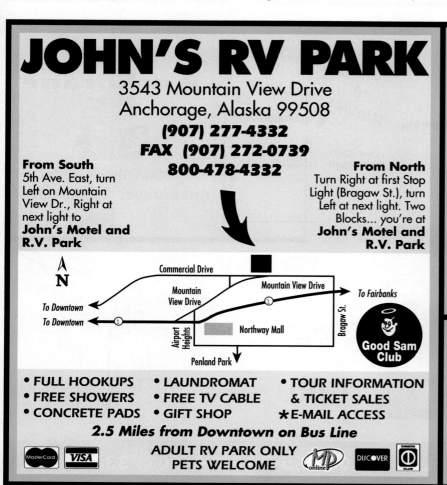

(across from the Westmark Hotel), a hands-on science discovery center offering unique insights into the wonders of nature, science and technology. Open daily year-round Monday through Saturday 10 A.M. to 5 P.M., Thursday open until 8 P.M., Sunday noon to 5 P.M., closed Mondays and major holidays. Adults, $5; seniors, $4; children 2 to 12, $4. Wheelchair accessible. Phone (907) 276-3179. ♿

Tour a Campus: Two colleges are located in Anchorage: the University of Alaska–Anchorage at 3211 Providence Dr. and Alaska Pacific (formerly Alaska Methodist) University at 4101 University Dr.

Alaska Pacific University was dedicated June 29, 1959, the same year that Alaska became the 49th state, and is now the state's largest private 4-year university. APU's first students were enrolled in the fall of 1960. The university offers liberal arts-based educational programs for all ages, including an annual Elderhostel. The APU campus is located on 270 forested acres, featuring the 3-tiered Atwood Fountain, Waldron Carillon Bell Tower and the Jim Mahaffey Trail System for skiers, runners, hikers and mountain bikers. Phone (907) 561-1266 or (800) 252-7528 for tours or information about university programs, or access the university on the Internet at www.alaska.net/~apu.

The University of Alaska–Anchorage is 1 of 3 regional institutions in the state's university system (the others are in Fairbanks and Southeast Alaska). For information on

tours of the UA campus in Anchorage, phone (907) 786-1529.

Go to the Zoo: The Alaska Zoo is located on 25 acres of wooded land and displays more than 85 species of Alaskan wildlife, including glacier bears, polar bears, brown and black bears, reindeer, moose, Dall sheep, otters, wolves, foxes, Bactrian camels, musk-oxen and wolverines. Be sure to stop in at the gift shop, located on your right as you enter. The zoo is open 9 A.M. to 6 P.M. daily from May 1 to Oct. 1; 10 A.M. to 5 P.M. the remainder of the year. Drive south from the downtown area on the Seward Highway to **Milepost S 120.8.** Take O'Malley exit, turn left on O'Malley Road and proceed 2 miles/3.2 km to the zoo, which will be on your left. Admission $6 for adults, $5 for seniors, $4 for students 13 to 18, and $3 for children 3 to 12. Family passes $45. Free admission for children under 3. Handicap parking, wheelchair accessible. Phone (907) 346-3242 for details. ♿

See Alaskan Wildlife: Fort Richardson Alaskan Fish and Wildlife Center, located in Building 600 on Fort Richardson Military Reservation, has a display of approximately 250 mounts and trophies of Alaskan sport fish, birds and mammals, including a world-record Dall sheep. Open weekdays year-round 9 A.M.–4:30 P.M. (closed 11:30 A.M.–1 P.M. for lunch), free admission. Phone (907) 384-0431 for hours. Elmendorf Air Force Base Wildlife Museum is open year-round Monday–Thursday 3 P.M.–4:45 P.M.; Friday noon–4:45 P.M.; Saturday 3 P.M.–4:45 P.M.; and closed on Sunday. Displays include more than 200 native Alaskan species, from big game to small birds and fish. Wheelchair access but not to restroom. Enter the base from the intersection of Boniface Parkway and the Glenn Highway. Ask guards for directions to Building 4-803. Phone (907) 552-2282 for details. ♿

See an Old Schoolhouse: The Pioneer Schoolhouse at 3rd Avenue and Eagle Street is a 2-story memorial to the late Ben Crawford, an Anchorage banker. It was the first school in Anchorage. The interior is not open to the public.

Visit the Library, City Hall, Federal Building, Post Office: The city hall offices are at 6th Avenue and G Street. The Z.J. Loussac Public Library is located at 36th Avenue and Denali Street. The Federal Building, located at 7th Avenue and C Street, is one of the largest and most modern office buildings in Anchorage. The lobby features a multimedia collection of artwork, and the cafeteria is open to the public. In downtown Anchorage, the U.S. Post Office is located on the lower level of the Post Office Mall at 4th Avenue and D Street. The main post office, located near the airport, offers all services, 24 hours a day. Smaller postal stations are located throughout the city.

"Whaling Wall": Stop by D Street between 5th and 6th avenues for a sight of the 400-foot long, 5-story airbrushed mural of beluga whales, bowhead whales and seals by artist Wyland covering the west wall of J.C. Penney.

Visit Wolf Song of Alaska, at the corner

of 6th Avenue and C Street in downtown Anchorage. Features over 4,000 square feet of educational exhibits and displays focusing on the wolf's natural history, its historical relation to humans, and its role as a major symbol in human folklore, art and religion. Also in the education center are wildlife dioramas, wolf photography and art, and a gift shop that includes educational books, tapes and videos. Open daily in summer; hours vary in winter. Parking is available on the street and at garages at 6th Avenue and E Street, or 5th Avenue and C Street. RV parking is available 3 blocks north of the center at 3rd Avenue and C Street. For more information about "experiencing the wolf," phone (907) 274-WOLF or (907) 346-3073.

4th Avenue Theatre. Built in 1947 by Alaska millionaire "Cap" Lathrop, this Anchorage landmark has been refurbished and now operates as a gift shop, cafe, museum exhibit and live entertainment center. Much of the original art-deco design has been preserved and the trademarks of the theater have been restored, including the ceiling lights marking the Big Dipper and the bas-relief gold leaf murals. There is no admission fee to the theater. The 4th Avenue Theatre is located a half block from the visitor center. Open year-round 8 A.M.–10 P.M. summers, 9 A.M.–6 P.M. winters. For more information phone (907) 257-5650.

Visit the Saturday Market. Located at the Lower Bowl parking lot, corner of Third and E Street, this open-air market is held Saturdays from Memorial Day weekend to Labor Day weekend. Hours are approximately 10 A.M. to 6 P.M. (subject to change). There is no admission fee. The market features Alaska products, fresh produce, fish, arts and crafts, antiques, food and entertainment. There are also garage-sale and used-car-sale areas. For more information, contact the Anchorage Parking Authority at (907) 276-7275 or the Downtown Anchorage Assoc. at (907) 276-5015.

Visit the Port of Anchorage: The Anchorage waterfront, with its huge cargo cranes off-loading supplies from container ships, makes an interesting stop, especially in winter when ice floes drift eerily past the dock on the fast-moving tide. Visitors may watch activity on the dock from a viewing platform on the 3rd floor of the port office building. To get there, drive north from the downtown area on A Street, take the Port off-ramp and follow Ocean Dock Road to the office about 1.5 miles/2.4 km from downtown. A good viewpoint of the port for downtown walkers is at the northeast corner of 3rd Avenue and Christensen Drive.

Heritage Library Museum, in the National Bank of Alaska, Northern Lights

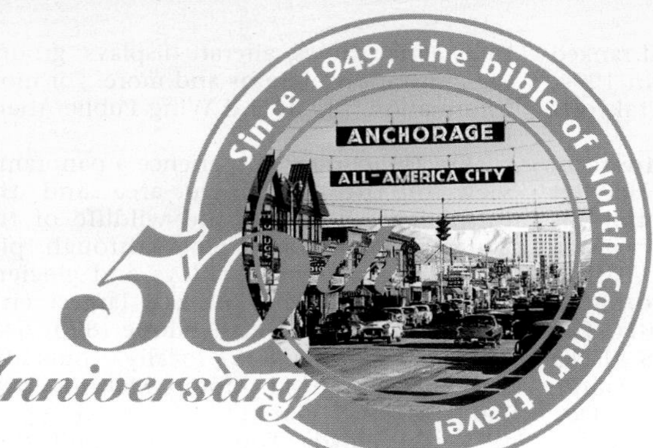

ANCHORAGE
CELEBRATING 50 YEARS OF THE MILEPOST®

Mac's Foto

TRAILER COURTS—ANCHORAGE & VICINITY

LOG OF THE PALMER HIGHWAY

MILEPOST 0. Anchorage, located on an excellent level townsite, on the south shore of Knik Arm, at the head of Cook Inlet. Founded in 1914, and known as a small-boat "anchorage" at the mouth of Ship Creek, it sprang into importance in 1915 as a construction center and headquarters for the Alaska Railroad. Before the recent war the population was over 3500, and with the advent of the tremendous activity of war-time construction and army installations, has leaped to an estimated 15,000 and is still growing. Shortages and high cost of building materials, shipping strikes and the sudden increase in population combined to create a severe housing shortage, the results of which are plainly manifest in the numerous little cabins and makeshift shelters which are in evidence on the fringes of the city. New and permanent construction is slowly but steadily alleviating this condition, and the visitor will find many modern homes, apartment buildings and hotels, most of them of very recent construction. The flood of new residents constantly pouring into the city has caused crowding in the schools and has severely overtaxed city utilities, the post office, and all civic services. Remedial measures are rapidly gaining headway and in time this community, which is already by far the largest city in Alaska will become a full-fledged modern metropolis.

It is the hub of the airlines serving the North, with daily plane service to the U.S. and thrice weekly schedules to the Orient. It is the key distribution center for all of peninsular Alaska and is the focal point of commerce by air, rail, steamship and commercial trucking. Here will be found most of the attributes of cities of many times the size elsewhere, including three radio broadcasting stations, theaters, a large modern hospital, office buildings, night clubs, motels and trailer courts, department stores and specialty shops, two daily and two weekly newspapers, churches of every denomination, excellent cafes and an efficient city transit system.

The geographic setting of Anchorage is remarkably beautiful. It is surrounded by snowcapped mountains, dense spruce forest, and overlooks both Turnagain and Knik Arms and Cook Inlet. The climate is moderate and healthful, with just under 15 inches of annual precipitation and average temperatures of from 11.6 degrees above zero in January ,(coldest month) to 57 degrees above in July, (warmest month). Maximum temperature recorded is 92 degrees, and minimum -36 degrees. The location makes this city the logical outfitting center for big game hunting on the nearby Kenai Peninsula, soon to be connected with Anchorage by a new highway. The numerous lakes and streams near the city give the angler many and varied opportunities to try his skill, and winter sports, particularly skiing and skating are immensely popular because of the ideal conditions existing and the comparatively mild winter climate.

—55—

Hewitt's Photo Shop

Boulevard and C Street, has an excellent collection of historical artifacts, Native tools, clothing and weapons, paintings by Alaskan artists and a research library. Free admission. Open weekdays noon to 5 P.M. between Memorial Day and Labor Day, noon to 4 P.M. at other times of the year. Phone (907) 265-2834.

Charter a Plane: Dozens of air taxi operators are based in Anchorage. Fixed-wheel (skis in winter) planes or floatplanes may be chartered for flightseeing trips to Mount McKinley and Prince William Sound, for fly-in hunting and fishing or just for transportation. Scheduled flightseeing trips by helicopter are also available.

Watch Small Planes: Drive out to Merrill Field, Lake Hood or Lake Spenard for an afternoon of plane watching. Lake Hood is the world's largest and busiest seaplane base, with more than 800 takeoffs and landings on a peak summer day. Merrill Field ranked 74th busiest airport in the nation in 1994, with a monthly average of 1,460 takeoffs and landings.

Alaska Aviation Heritage Museum, located on the south shore of Lake Hood at 4721 Aircraft Dr., preserves the colorful history of Alaska's pioneer bush pilots. Included are rare historical films of Alaska's pioneer aviators and an extensive photo exhibit of pioneer pilot memorabilia. The museum features a collection of 28 Alaska bush planes. RV parking. Open year-round, May 1 to Sept. 15, 9 A.M. to 6 P.M. daily; Oct. 1 to April 30, 10 A.M. to 4 P.M. Tuesday through Saturday; phone (907) 248-5325. Adults, $5.75, seniors and active military, $4.50, children 7 to 12, $2.75, children 6 and under, free. Wheelchair accessible.

Elmendorf Air Force Base Open House. This annual, day-long summer event features aerial shows, aircraft displays, ground demonstrations, booths and more. For more information, phone 3rd Wing Public Affairs (907) 552-8151.

Era Helicopters. Experience a panoramic view of the Anchorage area and the unspoiled wilderness and wildlife of the Chugach Mountains. Soar through picturesque mountains, valleys and glaciers, minutes away from Alaska's largest city. One- and 2-hour tours. Phone (800) 843-1947 or (907) 266-8351 locally. Tours also available in Juneau, Mount McKinley and Valdez. [ADVERTISEMENT]

Kenai Fjords Tours Ltd. Don't miss Kenai Fjords National Park with its abundant wildlife and glaciers. "Alaska's #1 Wildlife and Glacier Cruise" departs daily from Seward and has a convenient reservation office in downtown Anchorage. Located in the Hilton Hotel, Kenai Fjords Tours is at 536 W. 3rd Ave. Phone (970) 276-6249 or (800) 468-8068. Convenient one-day transportation packages are available from Anchorage. This is the original Kenai Fjords National Park cruise you've been looking for. [ADVERTISEMENT] MP

Major Marine Glacier Tours. At Major Marine Tours, we don't try to see every glacier in Prince William Sound ... just the best glaciers. Our relaxing, 6-hour cruise takes you to see the active tidewater glaciers in Blackstone Bay. We stop the boat, turn off the engines, and drift in front of the glaciers, watching the wildlife and spectacular calving. Every passenger on board is assigned table seating in our comfortable heated cabin. Our outside viewing decks are perfect for spotting otters, eagles, seals and the large bird colonies on our route. A freshly prepared all-you-can-eat salmon and roasted chicken buffet is available for only $10. Complete tours cost only $89 and depart daily from Whittier's boat harbor early May to mid-September. Convenient rail and bus packages are available from Anchorage. Why rush around Prince William Sound when you can relax and see the best of Alaska at a more leisurely pace? Major Marine Tours ... always your best value in Prince William Sound. For reservations or free brochure, phone: (800) 764-7300 or (907) 274-7300. Major Marine Tours, 411 West 4th, Anchorage, AK 99501. Internet address: www.majormarine.com. [ADVERTISEMENT]

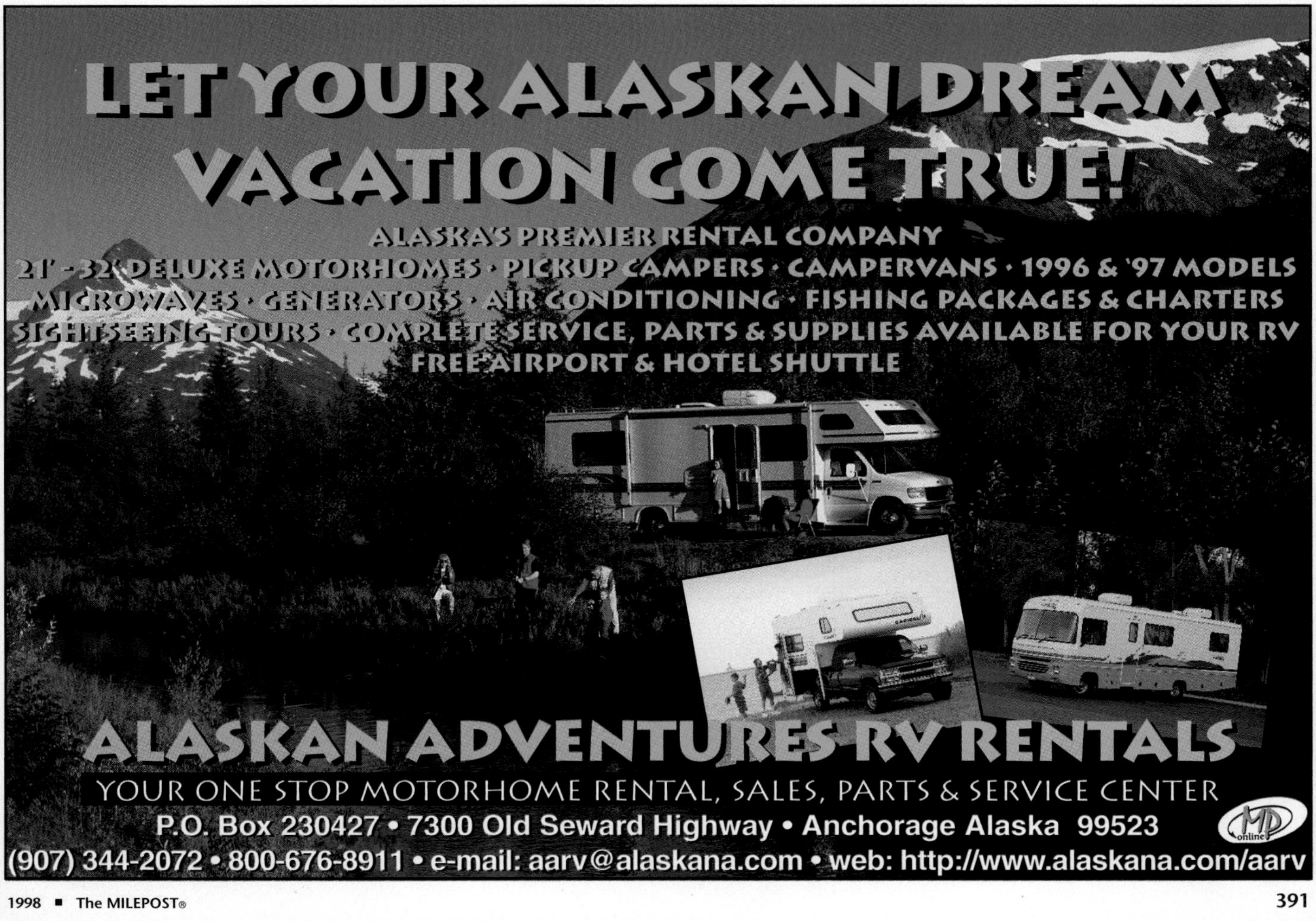

Philips' Cruises & Tours. Enjoy Alaska's most popular one-day glacier and wildlife adventure through the calm and protected waters of the Prince William Sound. it's a perfect one-day tour from Anchorage. Watch for sea otters, seals, whales and bird life that inhabit Prince William Sound on this fully narrated 5-hour cruise aboard a 420-passenger deluxe catamaran. Departs from Whittier, mid-May - mid-September. Sales office: 519 W. 4th Avenue, Suite 100, Anchorage, AK 99501-2211. (907) 276-8023; 1-800-544-0529; Fax (907) 265-5890. [ADVERTISEMENT]

Portage Glacier Cruise. See Alaska's most popular attraction, up close from the deck of the MV *Ptarmigan*. This Gray Line of Alaska cruise takes you right to the face of imposing 10-story-high Portage Glacier. An incredible experience. Tours depart Anchorage twice daily or you may drive to Portage Glacier and board the MV *Ptarmigan* for the cruise-only portion. Tour price is $60 per person; cruise-only price is $25 per person. Prices subject to change. Phone (907) 277-5581. [ADVERTISEMENT]

Prince William Sound Cruise. Experience the spectacular beauty of Prince William Sound aboard the *MV Nunatac*. This Gray Line of Alaska tour cruises past Columbia Glacier, the largest glacier in Prince William Sound. Watch for abundant marine life as you travel to picturesque Valdez. Return to Anchorage via the scenic Matanuska Valley. Two days, 1 night from $275 ppdo. Prices subject to change. Tour departs Anchorage daily. Phone (907) 277-5581. [ADVERTISEMENT]

Train to Denali. Ride the luxurious private, domed railcars of the *McKinley Explorer* to Denali National Park from either Anchorage or Fairbanks. Overnight packages in Denali with roundtrip train service are

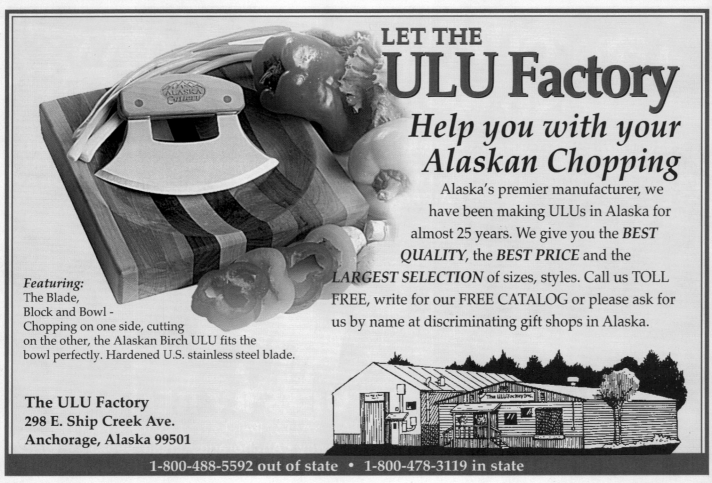

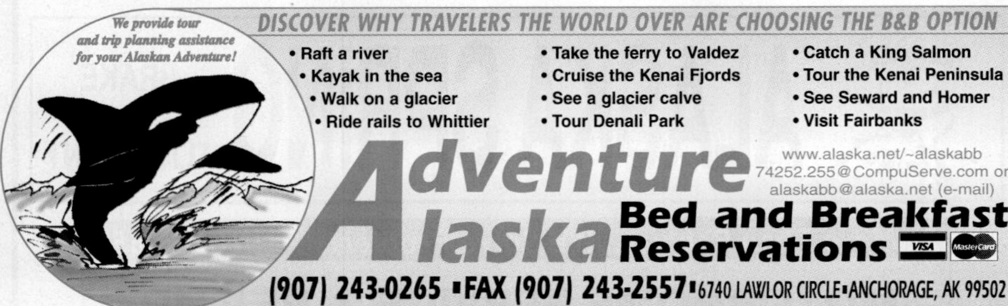

available from only $285 ppdo. Prices subject to change. Phone Gray Line of Alaska at (907) 277-5581 for train and package tour options. [ADVERTISEMENT]

Take in an Alaska Film: Alaska films can be seen at the Anchorage Museum of History and Art, 121 W. 7th Ave., at 3 P.M., daily during summer. Alaska Experience Center, located at 6th Avenue and G Street, offers "Alaska the Great Land," a 70mm film presented on a 180-degree domed screen, and a film and exhibit on the 1964 earthquake. Admission fee charged; open year-round. Call (907) 276-3730 for recorded information.

Watch the Tide Come In: With frequent tidal ranges of 30 feet/9m within 6 hours, and some approaching 40 feet/12m, one of Anchorage's best nature shows is the rise and fall of the tides in both the Knik and Turnagain arms of upper Cook Inlet. Among the better vantage points along Knik Arm are Earthquake Park, Elderberry Park (at the west end of 5th Avenue), Resolution Park (near the corner of 3rd Avenue and L Street) and the Anchorage small-boat harbor.

A good overlook for the tides in Turnagain Arm is Bird Creek State Recreation Site south of Anchorage at **Milepost S 101.2** on the Seward Highway. With good timing you might see a tidal bore, an interesting phenomenon you probably won't see elsewhere. A bore tide is a foaming wall of tidal water, up to 6 feet/2m in height, formed by a flood tide surging into a constricted inlet such as Knik or Turnagain Arm.

CAUTION: In many places the mud flats of Knik and Turnagain arms are like quicksand. Don't go wading!

Play Golf: The Municipality of Anchorage maintains a 9-hole golf course at Russian Jack Springs Park, Debarr Road and Boniface Parkway, featuring artificial turf greens. It is open from mid-May through September; phone (907) 333-8338 or (907) 343-4474 off-season (October–April). Alyeska Resort maintains the Anchorage Golf Course, 3651 O'Malley Road, an all-grass, 18-hole course open from mid-May through mid-September; phone (907) 522-3363 for more information. Two military courses are open to civilians. Eagle Glen Golf Course, an 18-hole par-72 course, is located on Elmendorf Air Force Base, near the Post Road gate. Open mid-May through September. Phone (907)

Bore tide in Turnagain Arm. (© Tom Culkin)

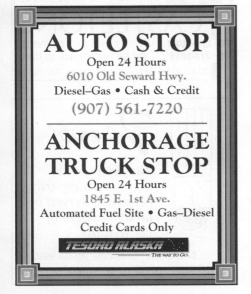

552-2773 for tee times; rentals available. Fort Richardson's 18-hole Moose Run Golf Course is the oldest golf course in Alaska. The course is accessible from Arctic Valley Road (**Milepost A 6.1** on the Glenn Highway) and is open May through September. Rentals available. Phone (907) 428-0056 for tee times. All golf course hours depend on the amount of sunlight.

Play Tennis: The Municipality of Anchorage maintains 58 tennis courts, including those in Eagle River and Girdwood. In addition, private clubs offer year-round indoor courts.

Picnic at a Park. Anchorage has several parks for picnicking. Chester Creek Green Belt, which stretches from Westchester Lagoon to Goose Lake, has a number of public parks along it, and a paved bike trail (also popular with joggers) runs the length of the greenbelt. The greenbelt is accessible from several streets; Spenard Road leads to Westchester Lagoon and E Street leads to Valley of the Moon Park. For picnic reservations, phone (907) 343-4474. Municipality of Anchorage Web page: www.ci.anchorage.ak.us.

Elderberry Park, at the foot of 5th

Avenue, overlooks Knik Arm. Nearby Resolution Park, at 3rd Avenue and L Street, where a statue of Capt. James Cook stands, has terraced decks overlooking Knik Arm. The Capt. James Cook statue was dedicated in 1976 as a bicentennial project.

Tour Anchorage by Bicycle: The municipality has about 120 miles/193 km of paved bike trails (including trails in Eagle River and Girdwood) paralleling many major traffic arteries and also passing through some of the city's most beautiful greenbelt areas. Maps of the trail system are available at Anchorage Parks & Recreation, 120 South Bragaw St. Offering an especially unique experience is the 11-mile/17.7-km Tony Knowles Coastal Trail, which begins at 3rd Avenue and Christensen Drive, and follows the coast around Point Woronzof to Point Campbell and Kincaid Park. One of the most popular trails in the city, it is used by bicyclists, joggers and walkers who are treated to close-up views of Knik Arm (watch for beluga whales) and on clear days a beautiful view of the Alaska Range.

Another popular bike route for families is the Chester Creek Bike Trail from Westchester Lagoon, at 15th Avenue and U Street, to Russian Jack Springs Park. The 6.5-mile/10.5-km trail traverses the heart of Anchorage, following Chester Creek past Goose Lake, a favorite summer swimming beach.

Downtown Bicycle Rental. Bike the Coastal Trail. Lowest rates in town. Located downtown at 5th and C. Open every day. Stay at I Street B&B or 12th & L B&B and receive bikes for half-price. Please phone for more information, (907) 279-5293, fax (907) 279-8338. [ADVERTISEMENT]

Watch Birds: There are some surprisingly

good bird-watching spots within the city limits. Lakes Hood and Spenard, for instance, are teeming with seaplanes but also, during the summer, are nesting areas for grebes and arctic loons. Also seen are wigeons, arctic terns, mew gulls, green-winged teals and sandpipers.

Another great spot is the Potter Point State Game Refuge, south of downtown on the Seward Highway at **Milepost S 117.4.** Early July evenings are best, according to local bird watchers. Forests surrounding Anchorage also are good for warblers, juncos, robins, white-crowned sparrows, varied thrushes and other species.

The Park for All People in the Chester Creek Green Belt on W. 19th Avenue near Spenard Road has a nature trail through a bird-nesting area.

Go for a Hike. Hiking trails in the Anchorage area are found in Chugach State Park and in Municipality of Anchorage parks. Three popular hikes in Chugach State Park's Hillside Trail System, accessed from the Glen Alps trailhead, are Flattop Mountain, Powerline Trail and Williwaw Lakes. To reach the trailhead, take the Seward Highway south to the O'Malley exit and go east to Hillside Drive; take a right on Hillside then a left at the trailhead sign and continue to Glen Alps parking lot. The hike up Flattop Mountain begins here; elevation gain is 1,550 feet/472m in 3.5 miles/5.6 km, hiking time is 3 to 5 hours. Also accessible from Glen Alps is the Powerline trail; total length 11 miles/18 km, elevation gain 1,300 feet/396m. Williwaw Lakes trail branches off Powerline trail to several small alpine lakes; round-trip is 13 miles/21 km with a 742-foot/226-m elevation gain. For more information phone Chugach State Park at (907) 345-5014.

Hilltop Ski Area, 4 miles/6 km east of the Seward Highway at Dimond, is the trailhead for summer hiking, biking and horseback riding on trails in Bicentennial and Hillside municipal parks. The trails range in length from an easy mile walk to a strenuous 16-mile/26-km hike. For more information phone Hilltop Ski Area at (907) 346-1446.

Other Anchorage parks offering hiking, jogging or biking include Kincaid Park, Russian Jack Springs Park and Far North Bicentennial Park. For more information phone Anchorage Parks and Recreation at (907) 343-4474.

Summer Solstice. Alaskans celebrate the longest day of the year with a variety of special events. In Anchorage, there's the annual Mayor's Midnight Sun Marathon, a 26-mile/42-km, 385-yard run through the city. This event is usually scheduled on the Saturday nearest summer solstice (June 20 or 21).

See a Baseball Game: Some fine semi-pro baseball is played in Anchorage. Every summer some of the nation's top college players play for the Anchorage Glacier Pilots and Anchorage Bucs, the Peninsula Oilers, the Mat–Su Miners and the Fairbanks Goldpanners. Anchorage games are played at Mulcahy Ball Park, Cordova Street and E. 16th Avenue. Check local newspapers for schedules or call the Anchor-

Minimum winter daylight hours in Anchorage is 5 hours and 28 minutes.—ALASKA A TO Z

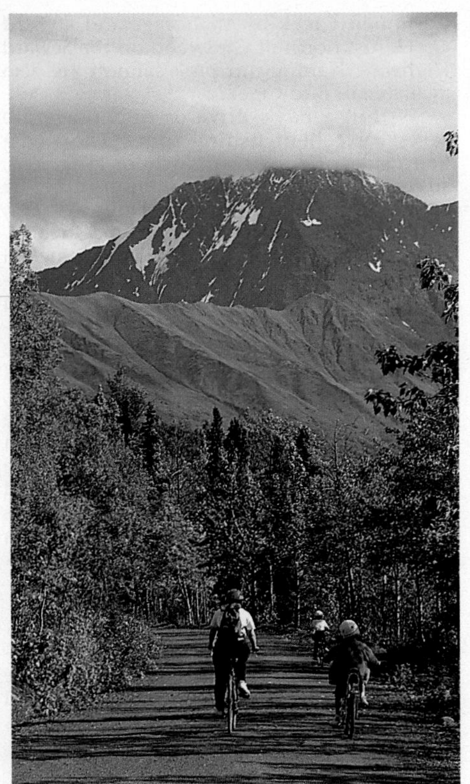

The municipality of Anchorage has about 120 miles of bike trails.

(© George Wuerthner)

age Bucs, (907) 561-2827, or the Glacier Pilots, (907) 344-5444.

Watch Salmon: King, coho, pink and a few chum salmon swim up Ship Creek and can be seen jumping a spillway in the dam just east of Ocean Dock Road. Watch for kings from early June until mid-July and for other species from mid-August until September. A fine wooden viewing platform has been built to make salmon watching easy.

Watch an Equestrian Event. The William Clark Chamberlin Equestrian Center in 530-acre Ruth Arcand Park hosts a variety of equestrian events every weekend from late-May through August. This public facility is open from 11 A.M. to 9 P.M. Phone (907) 522-1552.

Kayaking, Canoeing, Rafting: All are available in or near Anchorage. Guided tours from 1 to 14 days run on several rivers within 100 miles/160 km of Anchorage, including the Chulitna, Susitna, Little Susitna, Matanuska and Kenai rivers. Information on guided raft and canoe trips is available through travel agencies, local sporting goods stores and in the free *Visitors Guide* available from the Log Cabin Visitor Information Center.

Several flying services provide unguided float trips. The service flies customers to a remote river, then picks them up at a predetermined time and place downriver.

Several streams in the area make excellent canoeing and kayaking paths. Information on the Swanson River and Swan Lake canoe trails on the Kenai Peninsula is available from the Kenai National Wildlife Refuge Manager, Box 2139, Soldotna, AK 99669-2139; phone (907) 262-7021. Nancy Lake State Recreation Area, 67 miles north of Anchorage, offers a popular canoe trail system. Contact the Alaska State Parks, Mat–Su/Valdez–Copper River Area, H.C. 32, Box 6706, Wasilla, AK 99654-9719; phone (907) 745-3975.

Sailing in the Anchorage area is limited to freshwater lakes and lagoons (usually ice free by May).

Mirror Lake, 24.5 miles/39.4 km north of Anchorage on the Glenn Highway, and Big Lake, 52.3 miles/84.2 km north of Anchorage on the Parks Highway, are also popular spots for small sailboats.

Motorboating: Big Lake and Lake Lucille along the Parks Highway offer motorboating. Several rivers, including the Susitna, offer riverboating, but the shallowness and shifting bottoms of most of Alaska's rivers mean a jet-equipped, flat-bottom boat is almost required.

Cruises on larger boats are available from Whittier into Prince William Sound, from Homer Spit into Kachemak Bay and Cook Inlet, and from Seward into Resurrection Bay and Kenai Fjords National Park. Venturing into those areas in small boats without a local guide with knowledge of the area can be dangerous.

Cook Inlet waters around Anchorage are only for the experienced because of powerful bore tides, unpredictable weather, dangerous mud flats and icy, silty waters. Turnagain Arm is strictly off-limits for any boat, and Knik Arm and most of the north end of Cook Inlet is the domain of large ships and experienced skiff and dory operators.

Swimming: Anchorage Parks and Recreation can answer questions about aquatics; phone (907) 343-4476.

Goose Lake is open daily, June through August, from 10:30 A.M. to 5:30 P.M.; lifeguards, bathhouse and picnic area. It is located 3 miles/4.8 km east from downtown Anchorage on UAA Drive.

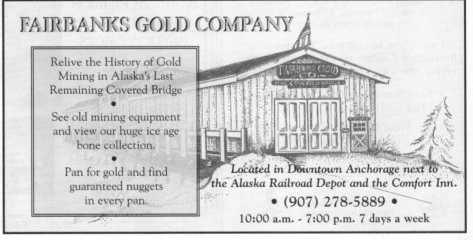

Jewel Lake, 6.5 miles/10.4 km from downtown Anchorage on W. 88th Avenue off Jewel Lake Road, is open daily June through August, from 10:30 A.M. to 5:30 P.M.; lifeguards, restrooms and covered picnic area.

Spenard Lake is open daily, June through August, from 10:30 A.M. to 5:30 P.M.; lifeguards, restrooms, picnic area. Located 3 miles/4.8 km southwest of downtown Anchorage on Spenard Road, then west on Wisconsin Street to Lakeshore Drive.

CAUTION: Do not even consider swimming in Cook Inlet! Soft mud, swift tides and icy water make this extremely dangerous!

The YMCA, 5353 Lake Otis Parkway, offers discounts to outside members with YMCA identification. Phone (907) 563-3211 for pool schedule and information on other facilities.

The following pools are also open to the public: Service High School pool, 5577 Abbott Road, phone (907) 346-3040; Bartlett

High School pool, 25-500 Muldoon Road, phone (907) 337-6375; West High School pool, 1700 Hillcrest Dr., phone (907) 274-5161; East High School pool, 4025 E. 24th Ave., phone (907) 278-9761; Dimond High School pool, 2909 W. 88th Ave., phone (907) 249-0356; Chugiak High School pool, South Birchwood Loop Road, off the Glenn Highway north of Anchorage, phone (907) 696-2010; and University of Alaska pool, Providence Drive, phone (907) 786-1233.

Charter Boats: Visitors must drive south to the Kenai Peninsula for charter boats. Sightseeing and fishing charters are available at Whittier, Seward and Homer.

Fishing: The Alaska Dept. of Fish and Game annually stocks about 28 lakes in the Anchorage area with rainbow trout, landlocked chinook (king) salmon, grayling and arctic char. Approximately 103,000 6- to 8-inch rainbow trout are released each year along with about 50,000 salmon. All lakes are open to the public. In addition, salmon-viewing areas and limited salmon fishing are available in the immediate Anchorage area. For specific information, check the Alaska fishing regulations book, call the agency at (907) 267-2218, or phone (907) 349-4687 for a recorded message. Urban salmon fisheries have been developed recently by the Alaska Dept. of Fish and Game in several Anchorage-area streams. King and coho salmon can be caught in **Ship Creek** in downtown Anchorage through July as well as in **Eagle River** just north of town. Coho salmon fisheries opened for the first time in 1993 in **Campbell Creek** in Anchorage and at **Bird Creek** just north of Girdwood on the Seward Highway. Natural-run pink salmon are also available in Bird Creek.

Within a day's drive of Anchorage are several excellent fishing spots. The Kenai Peninsula offers streams where king, red, silver, pink and chum salmon may be caught during the season. Dolly Varden and steelhead also run in peninsula streams. Several lakes contain trout and landlocked salmon. In-season saltwater fishing for halibut, rockfish and several species of salmon is excellent at many spots along the peninsula and out of Whittier, Homer and Seward. For specific fishing spots both north and south of Anchorage see the Seward, Sterling, Glenn and Parks highways sections. Because of the importance of fishing to Alaska both commercially and for sport, regulations are strictly enforced. Regulations are updated yearly by the state, often after *The MILEPOST®* deadline, so it is wise to obtain a current regulations book.

WINTER ATTRACTIONS

Alyeska Resort. Located in the community of Girdwood, Alyeska Resort is a 45-mile/65-km drive south from Anchorage along scenic Turnagain Arm via the Seward Highway. Judged by *Conde Nast Traveler* as

DAZZLE YOUR SENSES

One of Alaska's Top Visitor Attractions

Explore with us "Alaska the Greatland" in a dazzling OMNI THEATER motion picture experience.

Our unique 180-degree wrap-around screen unfolds the majesty of Alaska's wildlife, scenery and people before your eyes.

Filmed from helicopters, trains and river rafts, this new technology projects 70mm film onto a huge domed screen, bringing Alaska alive in a three-dimensional illusion above you!

"Alaska the Greatland" packs a lifetime of adventure into an unforgettable forty-minute experience.

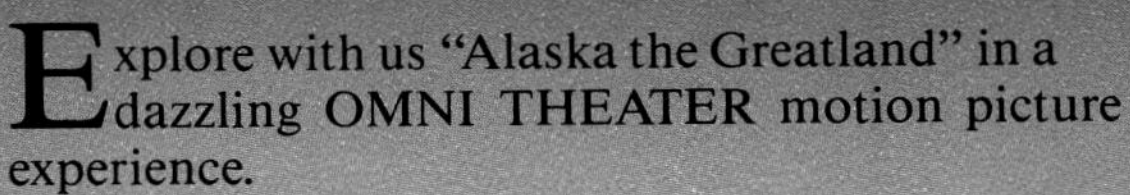

Alaska's cataclysmic earthquake of 1964 was as powerful as 2,000 nuclear explosions.

Now, YOU can explore the causes and effects of earth's most mysterious force in our unique *Alaska Earthquake Exhibit.*

Tour the inter-active displays that demonstrate the Richter Scale, the massive slide of Earthquake Park and the Tsunami Warning Center.

Feel the ground actually shake and rumble beneath your feet in our "safequake" room, as you relive history through our movie presentation of the great Alaska earthquake!

It's an experience you won't soon forget.

THE ALASKA EARTHQUAKE EXHIBIT

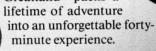

The Alaska Experience Center

TWO great attractions at ONE convenient downtown location near all major hotels — corner of 6th and G.
Alaska Experience Theatre — shows begin on the hour
Earthquake Exhibit — shows continuously
For admission prices and showtimes call 24-hr. recorded message at
276-3730
Anchorage, Alaska

Gift Shop

Don't miss Alaska's finest gift shop in our lobby. Featuring more than 150 T-shirt styles, plus an outstanding selection of Alaskan souvenirs and gifts.

having the "best view" of any U.S. ski resort, Alyeska Resort is Alaska's largest ski resort, with snow from early November to the middle of April. Night skiing is available during holiday periods in December and on Fridays and Saturdays from January through March. Ski facilities include a high-speed detachable bubble quad, 2 fixed grip quads, 3 double chair lifts and 2 pony tows. Chair 7, a fixed grip quad, added 20 acres of beginner and intermediate ski terrain to the resort's existing terrain. A 60-passenger aerial tram takes sightseers and skiers from the mountain's base at 250 feet/76m to a mountaintop facility at the 2,300-foot/701-m level. This facility, open year-round and accessible by wheelchair, features a large viewing deck, a cafeteria-style restaurant and a fine dining restaurant and lounge. Centerpiece for the resort is the 307-room, chateau-style Westin Alyeska Prince Hotel. The hotel features a fitness facility with indoor swimming pool and 16-person whirlpool, 4 restaurants and 2 lounges. For more information, phone (907) 754-1111 or (800) 880-3880. ♿

Alpenglow at Arctic Valley: East of downtown Anchorage in the Chugach Mountains, Alpenglow Ski Area has a 4,500-foot/1,372-m double chair lift, a 2,200-foot/671-m double chair lift, a 2,800-foot/873-m T-bar platter lift combination and a 700-foot/213-m rope tow for beginners. There is a day lodge with full cafeteria and ski shop. Cross-country skiing is available, but trails are not maintained. The ski area operates from about late October until early May. Hours are 1–9 P.M. Wednesday and

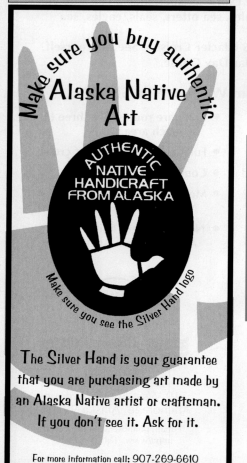

Thursday, 10 A.M. to 9 P.M. Friday, Saturday and all school holidays, and 10 A.M. to 6 P.M. Sunday. Drive northeast from downtown on the Glenn Highway. Just beyond Ship Creek, turn right on Arctic Valley Road and follow the main road 7.5 miles/12 km to the ski area. For more information, phone (907) 563-2524.

Hilltop Ski Area: Located 15 minutes from downtown Anchorage 4 miles/6.4 km east of the Seward Highway at Dimond, Hilltop has 2 miles/3.2 km of lighted slopes classified as beginner to intermediate. Ski facilities include a double chair lift; a beginner rope tow; 15m, 40m and 60m jumps; and certified snowboard half-pipe. Ski rentals (Alpine, Nordic and snowboards), ski school, gift shop and restaurant. The area is open daily with complete night lighting. Hours are 3–9 P.M. Monday through Friday, and 9 A.M. to 9 P.M. weekends. There are also 9 miles/15 km of cross-country ski trails in adjoining Hillside and Bicentennial parks, with 5 miles/8 km offering night lighting. For more information, phone (907) 346-1446.

Chugach State Park: Although the entire park is open to cross-country skiers, most maintained ski trails are found in the Hillside Trail System/Campbell Creek area, accessible via Upper Huffman Road and Upper O'Malley Road. Skiers are encouraged to use established trails as most of Chugach State Park is prime avalanche country.

Five major areas in the park are open to snowmobiling when snow levels are deep enough: Eklutna Lake Valley, reached from the Glenn Highway via Eklutna Road; Eagle River valley, also accessible from the Glenn Highway; Bird Creek, **Milepost S 101.2** Seward Highway; Peters Creek Valley and Little Peters Creek, accessible from the Glenn Highway; and portions of the Hillside/Campbell Creek area, accessible from Upper Huffman Road. A 24–hour recorded message giving the status of all snowmobile areas is available at (907) 694-6391.

Ski trail maps and snowmobiling information are available at the trailheads or from the park office, phone (907) 345-5014.

Russian Jack Springs: Located at DeBarr Road and Boniface Parkway. This ski area has a chalet, a ski rope tow and 8 miles/13 km of cross-country ski trails, 3 miles/5 km of which are lighted. The ski area is maintained by the Municipality of Anchorage. Ski trail maps are available at Anchorage Parks and Recreation, phone (907) 343-4474.

Far North Bicentennial/Hillside Parks: Best access to this 5,000-acre tract in the eastern portion of the Anchorage bowl is via Hilltop Ski Area on Abbott Road. There are 13.7 miles/22 km of groomed cross-country ski trails, 3.9 miles/6.3 km of which are lighted. There are also 6 miles/9.7 km of multi-use trails. Cross-country skiing is allowed anywhere in the area except on dogsled trails. For further information, phone Anchorage Parks and Recreation, (907) 343-4474.

Beach Lake Park: 10.5 miles/16.9 km of groomed cross-country ski trails with 3 miles/4.8 km lighted. There are approximately 20 miles/32 km of dog mushing trail. Wheelchair-accessible lodge and cabins available for a minimal user fee. Outstanding views of lake and wildlife from lodge

Day Trips From Anchorage

Several interesting and memorable sights may be taken in on a day's drive from Anchorage by heading either south of downtown on the Seward Highway or north on the Glenn or Parks highways. Following are some of the points of interest along these roads. Follow the mile-by-mile logs given in the related highway sections in *The MILEPOST®*. Keep in mind that several companies offer motorcoach tours to many of these same attractions and that you can see a great many attractions in a short amount of time by taking a flightseeing trip out of Anchorage; there's even a 1-day trip to Kotzebue from Anchorage.

South from Anchorage, the Seward Highway offers some spectacular views of Turnagain Arm less than 10 miles/16 km from downtown. Stop at one of the scenic viewpoints for photos. Other stops close to Anchorage include Potter Marsh for bird watching and the Potter Section House, which serves as the Chugach State Park Visitor Center and features displays of railroad history.

Continue south to **Milepost S 90** (37 miles/59.5 km from Anchorage) for the Girdwood/Alyeska Road turnoff. About 2 miles/3.2 km up this road, a gravel road forks to the left and leads 3.1 miles/5 km to Crow Creek Mine, a historic 1898 mining camp where visitors can pan for gold and tour the camp's old buildings. Returning from the mine to the main road, continue about another mile for Alyeska Resort.

Back out on the Seward Highway, continue south 11 miles/17.7 km to **Milepost S 79.1** and the Portage Glacier Access Road. On the 5-mile/8-km drive to the glacier, watch for salmon spawning at Williwaw Creek and look for the hanging Explorer Glacier. The Begich, Boggs Visitor Center at Portage Glacier has interpretive displays on glaciers, regular showings of films of interest and Forest Service naturalists available to answer your questions. You can stand on the shore of Portage Lake or take a tour boat for a close-up view of Portage Glacier.

Return to the Seward Highway. Depending on your time, you may wish to head back up the highway to Anchorage (which would add up to about 114 miles/183 km total driving distance), or extend your trip farther south to take in the old gold mining town of Hope.

North from Anchorage, the Glenn and Parks highways offer many attractions. Drive out on the Glenn Highway from downtown Anchorage to Palmer, 42 miles/67.6 km. Heart of the Matanuska–Susitna Valley, the Palmer–Wasilla area has the Alaska State Fair, Colony Village, a musk-oxen farm, Knik Museum and Mushers' Hall of Fame, Wasilla Museum and Frontier Village, and the Iditarod Trail headquarters visitor center. Drive 59 miles/95 km east on the Glenn Highway from Palmer to see the spectacular Matanuska Glacier. Several lakes in the area offer picnicking and water sports. Largest is Big Lake, a year-round recreation area accessible from Big Lake Road off the Parks Highway, 52 miles/84 km from Anchorage. Kepler–Bradley State Recreation Area on Matanuska Lake, at **Milepost A 36.4** Glenn Highway, has canoe rentals.

You may wish to stop off at Eklutna Lake or the Eagle River Visitor Center. Also, take the Eklutna Road exit for Eklutna Village Historical Park, which features 350 years of Athabascan culture. The park includes St. Nicholas Russian Orthodox Church and spirit houses. It is open daily, 9 A.M. to 9 P.M., from the end of May to mid-September; admission charged.

deck and cabins. Contact Eagle River Parks and Recreation, phone (907) 694-2011. ♿

Campbell Creek Green Belt: The municipality maintains approximately 3 miles/4.8 km of multi-use ski trails in south Anchorage.

Centennial Park: 3 miles/4.8 km of wooded cross-country ski trails over some hilly terrain, and located near Glenn Highway and Muldoon Road. Contact Anchorage Parks and Recreation (907) 333-8338 or (907) 343-4474 off season (October–April).

Chester Creek Green Belt: Located in the heart of Anchorage, the municipality maintains more than 6.2 miles/10 km of

Chugach State Park

This 495,000-acre park, flanking Anchorage to the north, east and south, offers wilderness opportunities for all seasons: hiking, wildlife viewing, camping, berry picking, skiing and snowmobiling. Information about the park is available from Chugach State Park, H.C. 52, Box 8999, Indian, AK 99540; phone (907) 345-5014. The Chugach State Park office, located in Potter Section House on the Seward Highway, has maps showing access to the park's recreation areas.

Between June and September, park staff offer guided nature walks and more strenuous hikes on the weekends to various points of interest in the park. The nature walks, which last about 2 hours, focus on some aspect of natural history, such as wildflower identification or bird watching. The longer hikes last approximately 4 hours. Phone (907) 694-6391 for a recorded message.

There are several access points to Chugach State Park attractions from Anchorage. North from downtown on the Glenn Highway take the Eklutna Road exit (**Milepost A 26.3**) and drive in 10 miles/16 km to reach Eklutna Lake Recreation Area. Eklutna Lake is the largest lake in Chugach State Park. The recreation area has a campground, picnic area and hiking trails. Cross-country skiing and snowmobiling in winter.

You may also reach Eagle River Nature Center for Chugach State Park by driving north on the Glenn Highway and taking the Eagle River exit (**Milepost A 13.4**). Follow Eagle River Road 12.7 miles/20.4 km to reach this beautifully situated visitor center with its views of the Chugach Mountains. Excellent wildlife displays, a nature trail, Dall sheep viewing and other summer activities make this a worthwhile stop. Cross-country skiing and snowmobiling in winter. Phone (907) 694-2108 for more information.

Another park area easily accessible from downtown is Arctic Valley. Turn off the Glenn Highway at Arctic Valley Road, **Milepost A 6.1**, and drive in 7.5 miles/12 km. Spectacular views of Anchorage and Cook Inlet. Good berry picking and hiking in summer; downhill and cross-country skiing in winter.

The park's hillside trailheads may be reached by driving south from downtown to the O'Malley Road exit at **Milepost S 120.8** on the Seward Highway. Follow O'Malley Road east for 4 miles/6.4 km until Hillside Drive enters from the right; turn on Hillside and proceed about 1.5 miles/2.4 km to the intersection of Upper Huffman Road and Hillside Drive. Turn left on Upper Huffman Road and continue 4 miles/6.4 km to the Glen Alps trailhead. Hiking in summer, cross-country skiing and snowmobiling in winter.

The Seward Highway south from Anchorage gives access to several Chugach State Park hiking trails.

cross-country ski trails.

Connors Lake Park: A popular site to learn skijoring, run in conjunction with the local skijoring club. Over 4.8 miles/7.7 km of multi-use trails.

Kincaid Park: 31 miles/50 km of cross-country ski trails are marked and maintained for novice, intermediate and expert skiers by the municipality. There are 16.5 miles/26.5 km of lighted trails and a warm-up chalet. Access is from the west end of Raspberry Road. Ski trail maps are available at Anchorage Parks and Recreation, phone (907) 343-4474; or Kincaid Park, phone (907) 343-6397.

Turnagain Pass: On the Seward Highway, about 59 miles/95 km south of downtown Anchorage. Turnagain Pass (elev. 988 feet/301m) is a popular winter recreation area in the Chugach National Forest. The west side of the pass is open to snowmobiling as soon as snow cover permits; the east side is reserved for skiers. Snow depths in this pass often exceed 12 feet/4m.

Dog Mushing begins in December. Dog mushing organizations in the Montana Creek area, Knik, Chugiak, Palmer and Anchorage sponsor races every weekend. Anchorage races usually begin in January at the Tozier Track and continue through the end of February. In addition, some of the clubs offer instruction in the sport. Several of the races are considered preliminaries to the World Championship races held during the Anchorage Fur Rendezvous.

The annual Iditarod Trail Sled Dog Race, 1,049 miles/1688.2 km to Nome, takes place in March. The race begins on 4th Avenue in downtown Anchorage, and mushers on the trail can be seen along the Glenn Highway, in the Knik Bridge area about 30 miles/48 km north of Anchorage and at Knik on the west side of Knik Arm.

To find a race, watch local newspapers

Prince William Sound

Glaciers, Wildlife, Waterfalls and the Great Taste of Alaska

Join Major Marine Tours for a memorable 6-hour glacier cruise in Alaska's famous Prince William Sound. Once aboard the 100-foot Emerald Sea you'll encounter eagles, otters, porpoises, seals, and massive bird rookeries. Cruise past towering mountains and hundreds of waterfalls as you head toward the awe-inspiring glaciers in Blackstone Bay. We slow down and pull up close to these massive tidewater glaciers as they calve off huge chunks of ice. The photo opportunities are tremendous. As we cruise take advantage of our all-you-can-eat Alaska salmon and chicken dinner with all the trimmings. For your comfort, the boat offers full bar service, heated cabins, reserved table seating, restrooms and a knowledgeable staff. The cruise departs daily from Whittier, which can be accessed via Alaska Railroad service out of Anchorage or Portage. Active travelers love our convenient day cruises, which sail May to mid-September. Witness the magnificence of Alaska like never before with Major Marine Tours...always your best cruise value in Prince William Sound.

Major MARINE TOURS

World-Class Wildlife & Glacier Cruises

Reservations/Free Brochure

907-274-7300

(Anchorage area)

800-764-7300

(Nationwide, except Anchorage)

411 West 4th Ave. • Anchorage, AK 99501 • Visit us at www.majormarine.com. Ticket offices located in Anchorage, Portage and Seward. All major credit cards accepted.

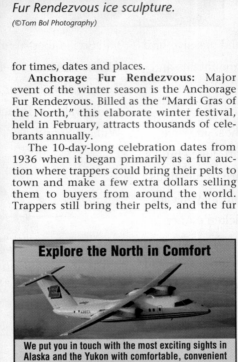

Fur Rendezvous ice sculpture.
(©Tom Bol Photography)

for times, dates and places.

Anchorage Fur Rendezvous: Major event of the winter season is the Anchorage Fur Rendezvous. Billed as the "Mardi Gras of the North," this elaborate winter festival, held in February, attracts thousands of celebrants annually.

The 10-day-long celebration dates from 1936 when it began primarily as a fur auction where trappers could bring their pelts to town and make a few extra dollars selling them to buyers from around the world. Trappers still bring their pelts, and the fur auction still attracts many buyers.

Alaskans shake off cabin fever during "Rondy" (the local term for the Fur Rendezvous). There are arts and crafts exhibits, a parade, the Miners' and Trappers' Ball, a blanket toss, a carnival and pet shows. And Rondy competitions are unique: a beard-growing contest, a waiter and waitress race, an ice and snow sculpturing contest and a home-brew competition.

During the first weekend of the Fur Rendezvous, the Annual World Championship Dog Weight Pulling Contest attracts several thousand spectators at Mulcahy Park, located at E. 16th Avenue and Cordova Street.

The highlight of the Fur Rendezvous, however, is dog mushing. The World Championship Sled Dog Race, held during the final 3 days, attracts dozens of mushers from Alaska, Canada and the Lower 48. Thousands of spectators line the 25-mile/40-km race course, which begins and ends on 4th Avenue in downtown Anchorage. *(CAUTION: Leave pets and flashbulbs home, as they'll distract the dog teams.)* The musher with the best total elapsed time in 3 heats over 3 days is declared the winner. The women's and junior world championship sled dog races are held at Tozier Track the first weekend of the Fur Rendezvous. For more information, phone (907) 277-8615.

Ice Skating: Three municipal facilities, Ben Boeke Ice Arena (334 E. 16th Ave., phone 907/274-2767), Dempsey-Anderson Ice Arena (1741 W. Northern Lights, phone 907/277-7571) and Harry J. McDonald Center (13701 Old Glenn Highway in Eagle River, phone 907/696-0051) offer a total of 4 indoor rinks for spectator as well as participatory uses. The University of Alaska also has 1 indoor rink as does the Dimond Center shopping mall. Outdoor ice-skating areas include Cheney Lake, Chester Creek Sports Complex, Delaney Recreation Area, Goose Lake, Jewel Lake Park, Spenard Lake, Delong Lake, Tikishla Park and Westchester Lagoon.

Sledding: Popular sledding hills are at Balto Seppala Park, Centennial Park, Conifer Park, Kincaid Park, Nunaka Valley Park, Sitka Street Park, Sunset Park, Service High School and Alaska Pacific University.

Snowshoeing: Muldoon Park, Far North Bicentennial Park and Campbell Creek Green Belt are used for snowshoeing, as are backcountry areas of Chugach National Forest and Chugach State Park.

Winter Basketball. Anchorage hosts 2 major collegiate basketball events. The Great Alaska Shootout, held every Thanksgiving weekend, features 8 major college basketball teams in this well-known invitational tournament. The Northern Lights Invitational showcases women's collegiate basketball with 8 teams in a 3-day playoff the last weekend in February.

Ice Fishing: Countless lakes in the Anchorage and the Matanuska–Susitna Valley areas offer excellent ice fishing. Ice fishing is especially good in the early winter in Southcentral. Some Anchorage lakes are stocked each year with landlocked king salmon or rainbow trout. Among them: **Beach Lake, Cheney Lake, Delong Lake, Jewel Lake, Little Campbell Lake** in Kincaid Park and **Sand Lake.** For more information contact the Alaska Dept. of Fish and Game at (907) 344-0541; for a recorded message on fishing and ice conditions, phone (907) 349-4687.

PARKS HIGHWAY ① ③

Connects: Anchorage to Fairbanks, AK **Length:** 358 miles
Road Surface: Paved **Season:** Open all year
Highest Summit: Broad Pass 2,300 feet
Major Attraction: Denali National Park

(See maps, pages 412–413)

	Anchorage	Denali Park	Fairbanks	Talkeetna	Wasilla
Anchorage		237	358	113	42
Denali Park	237		121	153	195
Fairbanks	358	121		245	316
Talkeetna	113	153	245		71
Wasilla	42	195	316	71	

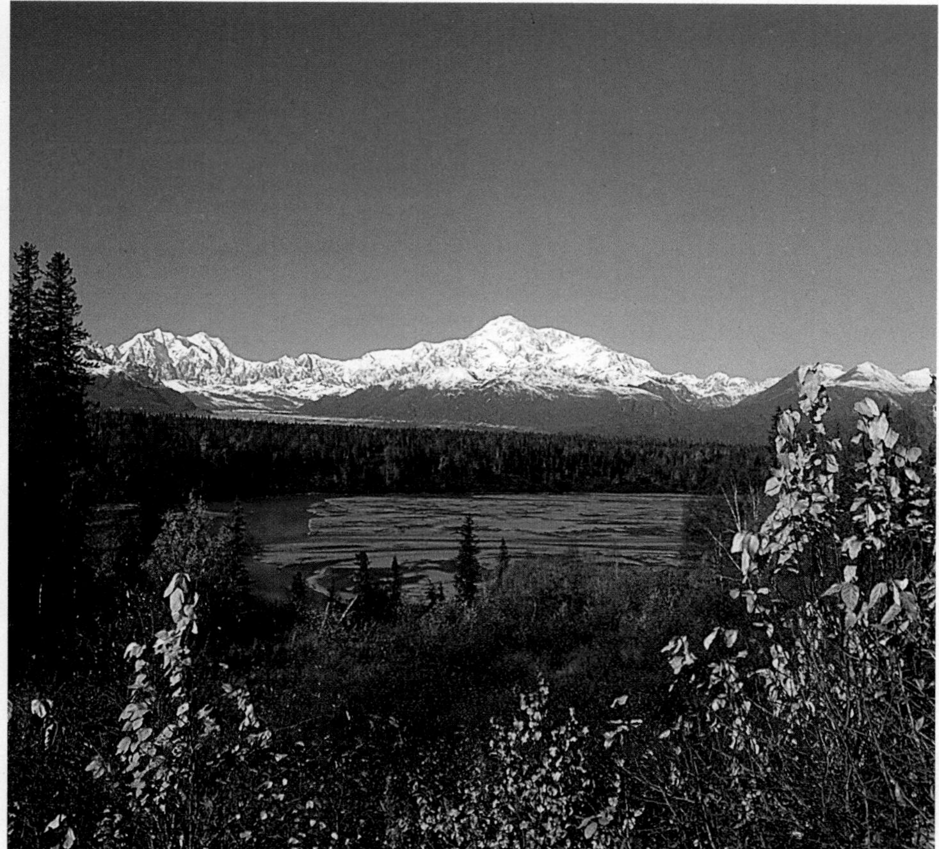

Viewpoint at Milepost A 135.2 offers spectacular view of Mount McKinley.
(© Barbara Willard)

The Parks Highway was called the Anchorage–Fairbanks Highway after its completion in 1971, and renamed in July 1975, in honor of George A. Parks (1883–1984), the territorial governor from 1925 to 1933. The Parks Highway (Alaska Route 3) junctions with the Glenn Highway (Alaska Route 1) 35 miles/56.3 km from Anchorage and leads 323 miles/520 km north to Fairbanks. Together, these highways connect Alaska's largest population centers.

The entire route runs 358 miles/576 km through some of the grandest scenery that Alaska has to offer. The paved highway, maintained year-round, is mostly in good condition with some pavement breaks and frost heaves. *NOTE: In 1998, expect road construction along Big Lake Road and on the Park Road in Denali National Park.*

Motorists who plan to drive the highway during the winter (roughly from Oct. 1 to June 1) should check highway conditions before proceeding. Severe winter storms and extremely low temperatures can create hazardous driving conditions. Some facilities along the highway north of the Talkeetna turnoff (**Milepost A 98.7**) and south of Nenana (**Milepost A 304.5**) are open in summer only.

The Parks Highway provides the most direct highway access to Denali National Park and Preserve (formerly Mount McKinley National Park) from either Anchorage or Fairbanks. Driving distance to the park entrance is 237.3 miles/381.9 km from Anchorage and 120.7 miles/194.2 km from Fairbanks. Mount McKinley—also called Denali—(elev. 20,320 feet/6,194m) is visible from the highway, weather permitting, and there are several viewing turnouts. Formal turnouts with interpretive signage are located at **Milepost A 135.2** and **A 162.7** on the Parks Highway, and at Mile J 13 on the Talkeetna Spur Road. See DENALI NATIONAL PARK section for details on the park.

Emergency medical services: Between the Glenn Highway junction and **Milepost A 202.1**, phone 911. Between **Milepost A 174** at Hurricane Gulch bridge and **Milepost A 224** at Carlo Creek bridge, phone the Cantwell ambulance at 768-2982 or the state troopers at 768-2202. Between **Milepost A 224** and Fairbanks, phone 911.

Parks Highway Log

ALASKA ROUTE 1
Distance from Anchorage (A) is followed by distance from Fairbanks (F).

A 0 F 358 (576.1 km) **ANCHORAGE.** Follow the Glenn Highway (Alaska Route 1) north 35 miles/56.3 km to junction with the Parks Highway. (Turn to the end of the GLENN HIGHWAY section on page 366 and read log back to front from Anchorage to junction with the Parks Highway.)

ALASKA ROUTE 3
A 35 (56.3 km) **F 323** (519.8 km) Traffic light at **junction** of the Parks Highway (Alaska Route 3) and the Glenn Highway (Alaska Route 1).

A 35.4 (57 km) **F 322.6** (519.2 km) Trunk Road. Turn right, northbound, for Mat–Su College and the University of Alaska Fairbanks' Matanuska Research Farm. The Matanuska Research Farm conducts research

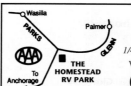

PARKS HIGHWAY *Anchorage, AK, to Milepost A 169*

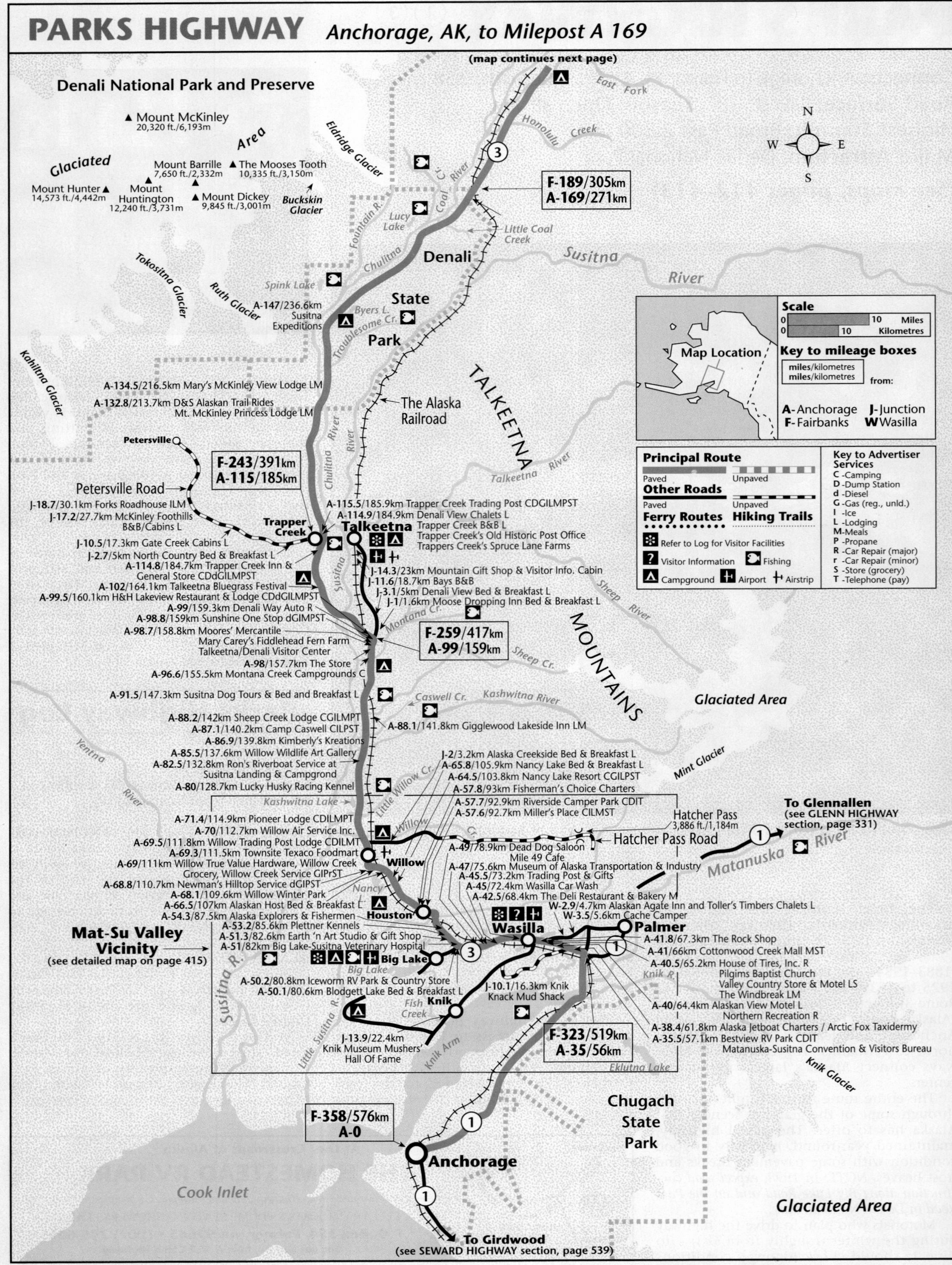

PARKS HIGHWAY Milepost A 169 to Fairbanks, AK

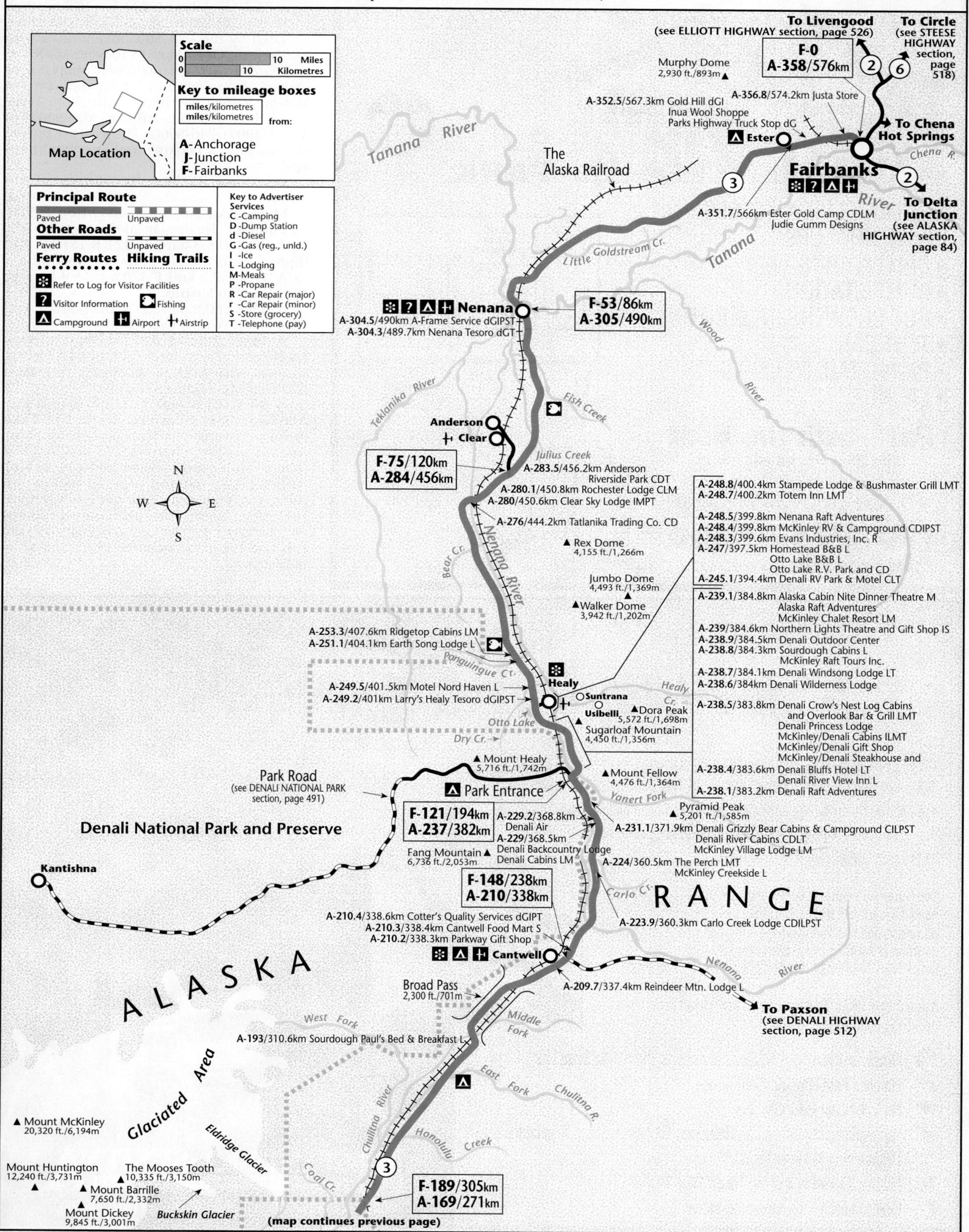

in agronomy, horticulture, soil science and animal science. No formal tours are conducted.

A **35.5** (57.1 km) F **322.5** (519 km) Welcome Way; access to Mat–Su Visitors Center, operated by the Mat–Su Convention & Visitors Bureau. Open May 15 to Sept. 15, 8 A.M. to 6 P.M. daily. This large center offers a wide variety of displays and information on the Mat–Su Valley; pay phone, gift shop. Write HC01, Box 6166J21, Palmer, AK 99645; or phone (907) 746-5000. The visitors bureau also operates a booking and reservation service.

Best View RV Park. See display ad this section. ▲

Matanuska–Susitna Convention & Visitors Bureau. See display ad this section.

A **36.2** (58.3 km) F **321.8** (517.9 km) Highway narrows to 2 lanes northbound.

A **37.4** (60.2 km) F **320.6** (515.9 km) Air Road; road to airstrip.

A **37.8** (60.8 km) F **320.2** (515.3 km) Hyer Road. Wasilla Creek bridge. Turnout.

A **38** (61.2 km) F **320** (515 km) Fairview Loop Road to west leads 11 miles/17.7 km to connect with Knik Road. Access to Palmer Hay Flats State Game Refuge.

A **38.4** (61.8 km) F **319.6** (514.3 km) **Alaska Jetboat Charters, Arctic Fox Taxidermy.** Fishing charters, taxidermy shop, Alaska Jetboat Charters (907) 376-4776. Offers guided full-day or half-day fishing trips for king salmon May 25 to July 14; silver, red, pink and chum salmon July 15 to September. Arctic Fox Taxidermy, a full service taxidermy shop, specializes in Alaskan fish and big game mounts. (907) 376-4776. [ADVERTISEMENT]

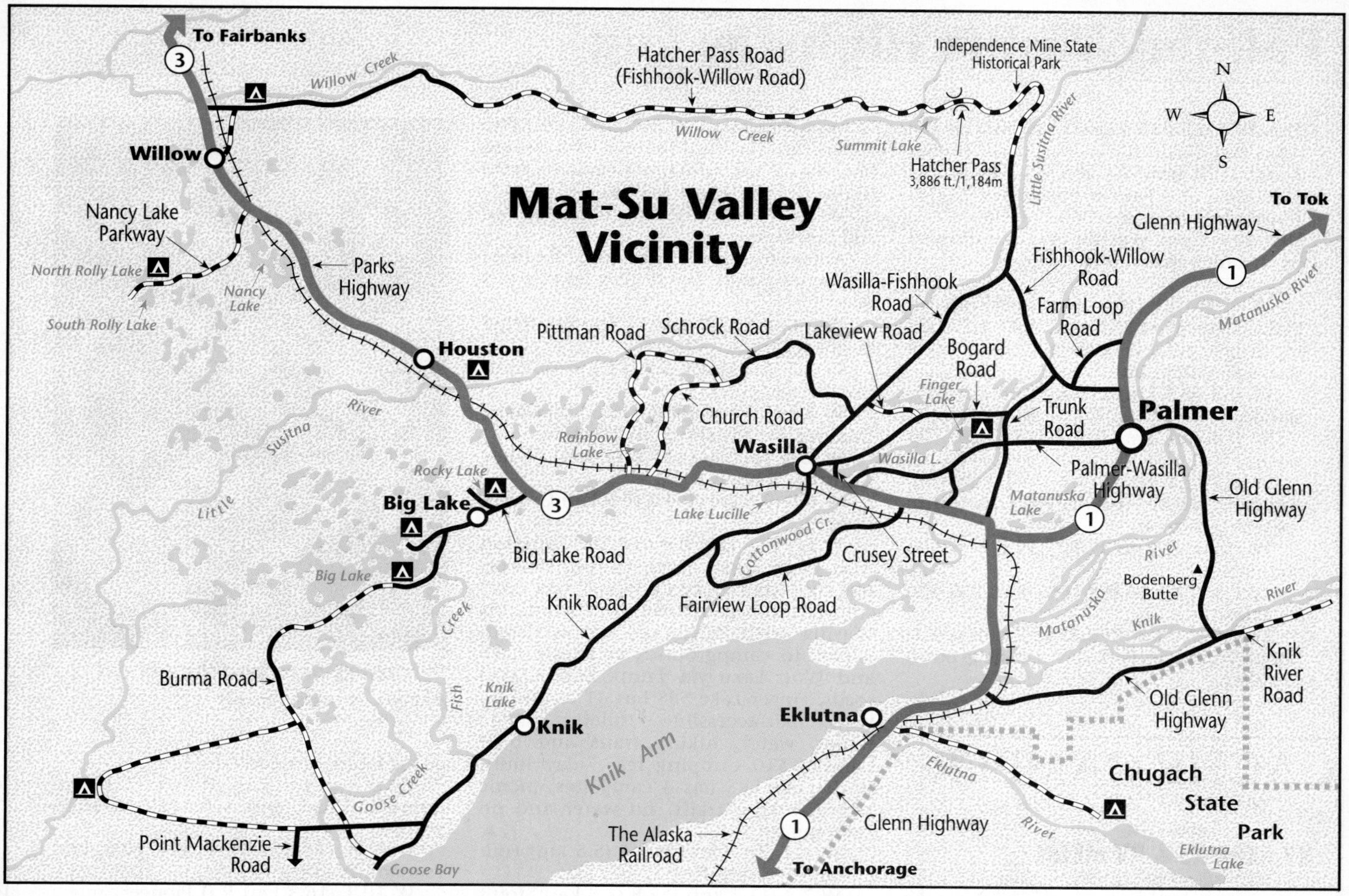

Mat-Su Valley Vicinity

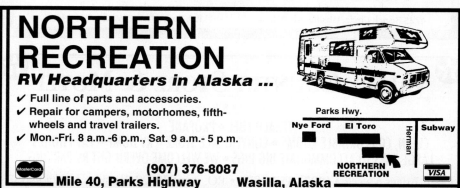

A 39.4 (63.4 km) **F 318.6** (512.7 km) Seward Meridian Road, which junctions with the Palmer–Wasilla Highway, which leads east to Palmer and provides access to Finger Lake State Recreation Site (see **Milepost A 41.1**). Shopping center.

A 39.5 (63.6 km) **F 318.5** (512.6 km) Wasilla city limits; medical clinic (376-1276). Wasilla shopping, services and attractions are located along the highway (from here north to **Milepost A 45**) and at Main Street in Wasilla city center.

A 40 (64.4 km) **F 318** (511.8 km) **Alaskan View Motel.** We proudly present Wasilla's newest motel. This beautiful Alaskan log motel, complete with Alaskan decor, features a breathtaking mountain and inlet view from each of our 24 rooms. Minutes from fine dining, entertainment, shopping and theater. Welcome! Phone (907) 376-6787. [ADVERTISEMENT]

Northern Recreation. See display ad this section.

A 40.5 (65.2 km) **F 317.5** (511 km) Tire and auto repair, church, hotel, cafe and lounge.

House of Tires, Inc. See display ad this section.

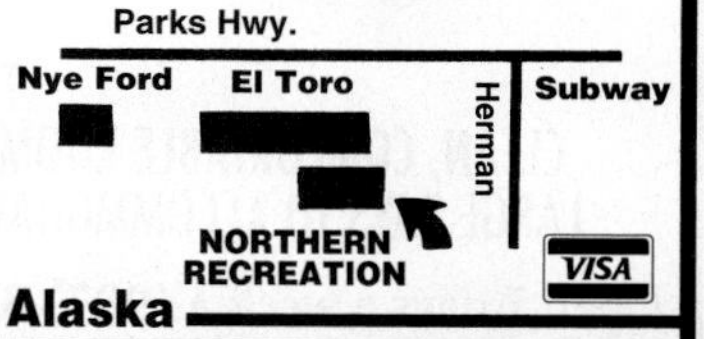

Palmer-Wasilla Highway Log

This 10.1 mile/16.3 km road connects the Parks and Glenn highways (Alaska Routes 3 and 1). It provides access to a number of Wasilla and Palmer businesses. *NOTE: Watch for road construction in 1998.*

Distance from Wasilla (W) is followed by distance from Palmer (P).

W 0 P 10.1 (16.3 km) **Junction** with Parks Highway at **Milepost A 41.1.** Access to drugstore, gas stations, auto body shops and other businesses.

W 0.3 (0.5 km) **P 9.8** (15.8 km) Gas station.

W 0.4 (0.6 km) **P 9.7** (15.6 km) Car wash.

W 0.7 (1.1 km) **P 9.4** (15.1 km) Cottonwood Creek; fish viewing platform; spawning salmon.

W 0.9 (1.4 km) **P 9.2** (14.8 km) Gas station.

W 1.1 (1.8 km) **P 9** (14.5 km) Bed and breakfast.

W 1.6 (2.6 km) **P 8.5** (13.7 km) Cottle Loop; Volunteer Park day-use area; bowling alley.

W 1.9 (3.1 km) **P 8.2** (13.2 km) Fire station, gas station. **Junction** with Seward Meridian Road, which connects to Parks Highway at **Milepost A 39.4.**

W 2.9 (4.7 km) **P 7.2** (11.6 km) Bed and breakfast.

Alaskan Agate Inn and Tollers' Timbers Chalets. See display ad this section.

W 3 (4.8 km) **P 7.1** (11.4 km) Hatcher Business Park.

W 3.2 (5.1 km) **P 6.9** (11.1 km) Brentwood Plaza.

W 3.5 (5.6 km) **P 6.6** (10.6 km) **Cache Camper.** See display ad this section.

W 5.1 (8.2 km) **P 5** (8 km) Valley Christian Schools.

W 5.9 (9.5 km) **P 4.2** (6.8 km) Grocery store.

W 6.1 (9.8 km) **P 4** (6.4 km) **Junction** with Trunk Road; access to Four Corners Mat–Su Community College. Trunk Road connects to Bogard Road, which connects Wasilla with Fishhook–Willow Road. Access to campgrounds at Finger Lake and Wolf Lake via Trunk and Bogard roads. Finger Lake SRS has 41 campsites, wheelchair-accessible toilets, picnic tables, water, hiking trails and boat launch, $10 camping fee, 7-day limit. Wolf Lake SRS has 4 campsites, picnic tables, hiking trails, no water and no camping fee. ♿▲

W 6.7 (10.8 km) **P 3.4** (5.5 km) Four Corners Business Park.

W 7.3 (11.7 km) **P 2.8** (4.5 km) Moffit Road; access to 49th Street, middle school and refuse dump.

W 7.9 (12.7 km) **P 2.2** (3.5 km) Colony Plaza; pizza, chiropractor and Eagle View Car Wash.

W 8.1 (13 km) **P 2** (3.2 km) Loma Prieta Road. Access to Crevasse–Moraine trailhead (5-mile/8-km loop); parking, picnic tables, fireplaces.

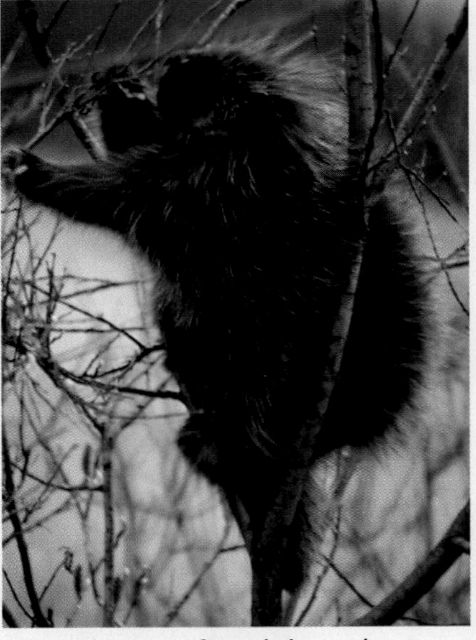

Porcupines are found throughout Alaska. (© Corinne Smith/RKI)

W 9.2 (14.8 km) **P 0.9** (1.4 km) Hemmer Road; access to Palmer High School.

W 9.7 (15.6 km) **P 0.4** (0.6 km) Tsunami Warning Center.

W 10.1 (16.3 km) **P 0** Pioneer Square (Carr's Mall). **Junction** with Glenn Highway at **Milepost A 41.8** in Palmer (see GLENN HIGHWAY section).

Return to Milepost A 41.1 Parks Highway or A 41.8 Glenn Highway

A 40.5 (65.2 km) **F 317.5** (511 km) **Pilgrims Baptist Church.** See display ad this section.

Valley Country Store & Motel. See display ad this section.

The Windbreak. See display ad this section.

A 41 (66 km) **F 317** (510.1 km) Cottonwood Creek bridge.

Cottonwood Creek Mall. The area's only enclosed mall is located in Wasilla! Ample, free parking—RVs welcome! We offer 24-

hour grocery; a drugstore and pharmacy; banking; sporting goods, apparel, hair, nail and health shops; gifts, entertainment, dining. Hours: Monday–Friday 10 A.M.–9 P.M.; Saturday 10 A.M.–6 P.M.; Sunday 12–5 P.M. (907) 376-6802. See our advertisement in this section. [ADVERTISEMENT]

A 41.1 (66.1 km) **F 316.9** (510 km) **Junction** with Palmer–Wasilla Highway, which leads east 10 miles/16 km to the Glenn Highway at Palmer. It provides access to several businesses, Finger Lake state recreation site and a day-use area with picnic sites and playground. See PALMER–WASILLA HIGHWAY side road log opposite page.

A 41.7 (67 km) **F 316.3** (509 km) Park with picnic shelter, restrooms, playground and swimming beach on Wasilla Lake; limited parking. Monument to George Parks.

A 41.8 (67.3 km) **F 316.2** (508.9 km) Crusey Street, access to Bogard Road, a resort with motel and dining, and Finger Lake state recreation site. Turn right (northbound) and drive 3.7 miles/6 km via Crusey Street and Bogard Road to reach Finger Lake. (The recreation site is also accessible from Palmer–Wasilla Highway, or turn east at **Milepost A 42.2** and drive 0.3 mile/0.5 km to intersection of Wasilla–Fishhook and Bogard roads, then follow Bogard Road 4.1 miles/6.6 km to Finger Lake.) Finger Lake has picnic tables, campsites, water, toilets and a boat launch. Camping fee $10. Also access to Wolf Lake state recreation site, off Bogard Road, which has picnic sites, toilets and hiking trail. ▲

The Rock Shop. Rough rock to finished gemstones. Handmade Alaskan jewelry. Original and custom designs. Native art and artifacts. Huge bead selection. Leather, feathers, furs. Hours Monday–Friday 10 A.M.–7 P.M., Saturday 10 A.M.–6 P.M. Day phone (907) 373-3094. Turn at Crusey Street and follow the blue highway signs off Parks Highway. [ADVERTISEMENT]

A 42 (67.6 km) **F 316** (508.5 km) Art gallery and food market.

A 42.1 (67.8 km) **F 315.9** (508.4 km) Boundary Street, Lake Lucille Park.

A 42.2 (67.9 km) **F 315.8** (508.2 km) Wasilla's Main Street; visitor center and museum 1 block north; post office 2 blocks north (ZIP code 99687). Access to Hatcher Pass and Knik from this intersection. Turn south across railroad tracks for Knik Road to Knik, the "Dog Mushing Center of the World" (see KNIK ROAD log on page 418). Turn north on Wasilla's Main Street for downtown Wasilla and Hatcher Pass. Description of Wasilla follows.

Wasilla–Fishhook Road leads northeast about 10 miles/16 km to junction with the Hatcher Pass (Fishhook–Willow) Road to Independence Mine State Historical Park; turn to the Hatcher Pass side road log on page 355 in the GLENN HIGHWAY section for a description of the road to Hatcher Pass from this junction (**J 6.8** in that log). See also the map on page 415. The 49-mile/79-km Hatcher Pass Road junctions with the Parks Highway at **Milepost A 71.2.**

Wasilla

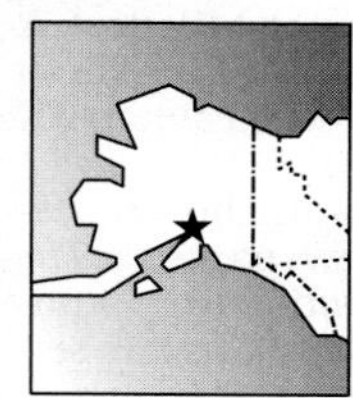

A 42.2 (67.9 km) **F 315.8** (508.2 km). Located between Wasilla and Lucille lakes in the Susitna Valley, about an hour's drive from Anchorage. **Population:** 5,119. **Emergency Services: City Police,** phone (907) 745-2131, emergency only phone 911. **Fire Department** and **Ambulance,** phone (907) 376-5320, emergency only phone 911. **Hospital,** in Palmer. **Doctor** on Seward Meridian Road, **Milepost A 39.5,** phone (907) 376-1276, and at West Valley Medical Center, E. Bogard Road, phone (907) 376-5028. Chiropractic clinics, phone (907) 373-2022.

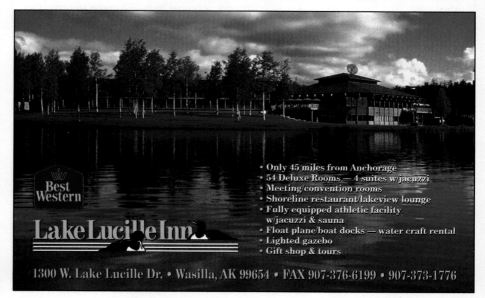

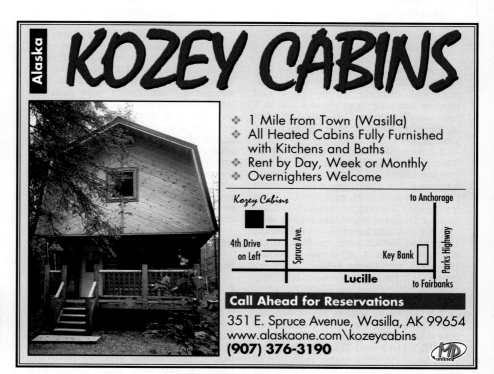

Visitor Information: At the Dorothy G. Page Museum and Old Wasilla Town Site Park on Main Street just off the Parks Highway, phone (907) 373-9071, fax 373-9072. Or contact the chamber of commerce, Box 871826, Wasilla 99687, phone (907) 376-1299. Mat-Su Visitors Center at **Milepost A 35.5**, write Mat-Su Convention & Visitors Bureau, HC 01, Box 6166J21-MP, Palmer, AK 99645; phone (907) 746-5000.

Radio and Television via Anchorage stations; KNBZ-FM 99.7. **Newspapers:** *The Valley Sun* (weekly); *The Frontiersman* (semi-weekly). **Transportation: Air**—Charter service available. **Railroad**—Alaska Railroad. **Bus**—Matanuska Valley commuter to Anchorage.

Private Aircraft: Wasilla municipal airport, 4.8 miles/7.7 km north on Neuser Drive; elev. 348 feet/ 106m; length 3,700 feet/1,128m; gravel; unattended. Wasilla Lake seaplane base, 0.9 mile/1.4 km east; elev. 330 feet/100m. Numerous private airstrips and lakes in vicinity.

Wasilla is one of the Matanuska–Susitna Valley's pioneer communities, supplying mines and farms in the area. Long before the Parks Highway was built, local residents and visitors bound for Lake Lucille, Wasilla Lake, Big Lake and Knik drove over the valley roads from Palmer to the village of Wasilla. Wasilla became a station on the Alaska Railroad about 1916.

Today, Wasilla is the largest community on the Parks Highway between Anchorage and Fairbanks. Shopping malls and businesses here offer a wide assortment of services. *NOTE: There are no banks between Wasilla and Fairbanks, but automatic teller machines are available and noted in the log.*

ACCOMMODATIONS/VISITOR SERVICES

All visitor facilities are available here,

Knik Road Log

Distance is measured from the junction (J) with Parks Highway.

J 0 Junction with Parks Highway, **Milepost A 42.2.**

J 0.1 (0.2 km) *CAUTION: Road crosses railroad tracks.*

J 0.2 (0.3 km) VFW Post No. 9365.

J 0.7 (1.1 km) Glenwood Avenue, senior center.

J 1.5 (2.4 km) Gas station.

J 2.1 (3.4 km) Smith ball fields.

J 2.2 (3.5 km) Iditarod Trail Sled Dog Race® headquarters and visitor center; historical displays, films, dogs and musher, souvenir shop. Open 8 A.M. to 5 P.M., daily in summer, weekdays the rest of the year. Adjacent Lake Lucille campground.

J 2.3 (3.7 km) **Lake Lucille** Mat–Su Borough Park Campground and day-use area 0.6 mile/1 km north via gravel road; 64 campsites, pavilion with covered picnic tables, firepits, parking. Camping fee charged. Fishing for landlocked silver salmon. Non-motorized lake access.

J 4.1 (6.6 km) **Junction** with Fairview Loop Road, which joins the Parks Highway at **Milepost A 38**; access to Palmer Hay Flats State Game Refuge. Shopping center with gas and groceries at this junction.

J 7 (11.3 km) Knik fire hall.

J 8 (12.9 km) Settlers Bay, a housing development built around a lodge; golf course and stables.

J 10.1 (16.3 km) Turnoff for Homestead Museum, with a large collection of early Alaskan memorabilia, and gift shop.

Knik Knack Mud Shack. See display ad this section.

J 11.1 (17.9 km) Laurence airport.

J 13 (20.9 km) Knik Kennels.

J 13.3 (21.4 km) **KNIK** (area pop. 462) on **Knik Lake.** There is a bar here with a pay phone, a liquor store, gas station and private campground. Lake fishing for rainbow; inquire at the Knik Bar. Knik is a checkpoint on the Iditarod Trail Sled Dog Race® route and is often called the "Dog Mushing Center of the World"; many famous Alaskan dog mushers live in this area.

J 13.9 (22.4 km) Knik Museum and Sled Dog Mushers' Hall of Fame, open noon to 5 P.M. Wednesday through Sunday, from June 1 through Aug. 31. The museum is housed in 1 of 2 buildings remaining from Knik's gold rush era (1898–1916). Regional memorabilia, artifacts, archives, dog mushing equipment, mushers' portraits and historical displays on the Iditarod Trail. Admission fee $2 for adults, $1.50 for seniors, free for children under 18. Phone (907) 376-7755, from September through May call 376-2005.

Traditional Athabascan graveyard with fenced graves and spirit houses next to Knik Museum. The gravesite can be observed from the Iditarod Trail.

Knik Museum and Sled Dog Mushers' Hall of Fame. See display ad this section.

J 16.1 (25.9 km) **Fish Creek** bridge; parking, fishing for silver salmon.

J 17.2 (27.7 km) Goose Bay Point Road to Little Susitna River public-use facility at Susitna Flats State Game Refuge (12 miles/19.3 km); 83 parking spaces, 65 campsites, boat ramps, dump station, water, tables, toilets. Also access to Point Mackenzie. Daily parking $5; boat launch, $5 (includes parking); overnight camping, $10. State parks annual pass not accepted here. For more information phone (907) 745-3975.

Acord Guide Service. See display ad on page 420.

J 18.5 (29.8 km) Pavement ends at small bar beside road. Road continues into rural area.

Return to Milepost A 42.2
Parks Highway

WASILLA ADVERTISERS

Advertiser	Contact
Acord Guide Service	Ph. (907) 376-0692
B & B Association of Alaska	Ph. (800) 401-7444
Cottonwood Creek Mall	Ph. (907) 376-6802
Dorothy G. Page Museum & Visitors Information Center	Ph. (907) 373-9071
Evergreen Acres Bed and Breakfast	Ph. (907) 376-2608
Iditarod Trail Sled Dog Race®	Mile 2.2 Knik Rd.
Inlet View	Ph. (907) 376-9675
Kozey Cabins	Ph. (907) 376-3190
Lake Lucille Inn	Ph. (907) 373-1776
Mat-Su Resort	Ph. (907) 376-3328
Mr. Lube	See ad
North Star Adventures B&B Locations	Ph. (907) 822-5110
Shady Acres Inn Bed & Breakfast	Ph. (907) 376-3177
Six Robblees	Mile 40.5 Parks Hwy.
Tesoro 7-Eleven	See ad
Town Square Art Gallery	Ph. (907) 376-0123
Valley Chiropractic Clinic Inc.	Ph. (907) 373-2022
Valley River Charters	Ph. (907) 376-6581
Veterans of Foreign Wars Post #9365	Mile 0.2 Knik Rd.
Wasilla Home Style Laundry	Wasilla Shopping Center
Wasilla One-Hour Photo	Wasilla Shopping Center

including sporting goods stores, post office, gas stations, tire and RV repair, laundromats and other services. Mat–Su Ice Arena, at Bogard Road and Crusey Street, has ice skating, picnic area and fitness court. Swimming and showers are available at Wasilla High School.

Alaska Kozey Cabins & RV Rental. Modern, hand-crafted log cabins set in the state's No. 1 recreation area. Cabins feature queen and full beds, fully equipped kitchens, bath and living rooms. Cross-country skiing, snow machining, hiking, fishing, and hunting abound. Near the official Iditarod restart. Open year-round. Phone (907) 376-3190. See display ad this section. [ADVERTISEMENT]

Lake Lucille Inn. Located 45 miles north of Anchorage on the shores of beautiful Lake Lucille. 54 deluxe rooms, suites with Jacuzzi, health club with sauna and hot tub. Boat and float plane dock, water craft rentals and lighted gazebo. Winter activities include lighted ice rink. Fine dining restaurant and lounge with pristine view. Convention and meeting facilities. [ADVERTISEMENT]

Valley Chiropractic Clinic Inc. Phone (907) 373-2022. 24-hour emergency service. Complete modern facility, same-day emergency care. Reasonable fees with VISA and MasterCard accepted. We're accustomed to treating travelers' needs. We're located at 400 N. Main St., in Wasilla. Turn north on to Main Street from the Parks Highway and go up 2 blocks on the left, directly across the street from the post office. [ADVERTISEMENT]

Jet skiing on Wasilla Lake. A public park on the lake is located at Milepost A 41.7 Parks Highway. (© Barbara Willard)

ATTRACTIONS

On the town's Main Street, north of the Parks Highway, are the Dorothy G. Page Museum and Visitors Information Center, the library and the post office. The museum is open daily year-round, 10 A.M. to 6 P.M. in summer, 8 A.M. to 5 P.M. in winter; admission fees are $3 adults, $2.50 senior citizens; under 18 years free. Included in the price of admission to the museum is entrance to the Old Wasilla Town Site Park, located behind the museum. Picnic tables and museum shop on site. Local Farmer's Market on Wednesdays in summer. The historical park has 7 renovated buildings from before, during and after Wasilla's pioneer days, including Wasilla's first schoolhouse (built in 1917). Adjacent to the park is the Herning/Teeland Country Store, which is currently under restoration. The log museum building, school, store and nearby railroad depot are on the National Register of Historic Sites.

Wasilla is home to the **Iditarod Trail Sled Dog Race® Headquarters**. The internationally known 1,150-mile Iditarod Trail Sled Dog Race® between Anchorage and Nome takes place in March. The Iditarod Headquarters and Visitors Center is located at Mile 2.2 Knik Road. The center has historical displays on the Iditarod, videos, an Iditarod musher and dog team, and a gift shop with unique souvenirs. Open daily in summer, weekdays in winter, from 8 A.M. to 7 P.M. Large tours are welcome, phone (907) 376-5155 in advance. Circular drive for buses and motorhomes, camping at adjacent Lake Lucille campground. No fee for museum or film. Fee charged for rides on wheeled dogsled.

Historical displays on Alaskan mushers and sled-dog trails can be found at the Knik Museum at Mile 13.9 Knik Road (see KNIK

ROAD log this section). The museum is open from noon to 5 P.M. daily except Monday and Tuesday in summer. Admission fee $2 adults.

Iditarod Days is held in conjunction with the Iditarod Race in March. Other area winter events include ice golf at Mat–Su Resort and ice bowling at Big Lake. Check with the chamber of commerce about summer events.

Town Square Art Gallery. Representing the best of Alaskan and national artists—prints and originals distinctively custom framed. Local jewelry, pottery, basketry, Native dolls and masks. Unique gifts, porcelain collectibles, plates, books, cards. Open Monday–Friday 10 A.M.–6 P.M., Saturday 10 A.M.–5 P.M., seasonally Sundays 12–4 P.M. We pack, ship and welcome credit cards. Carrs Mall. (907) 376-0123. [ADVERTISEMENT]

Parks Highway Log

(continued)

A 42.5 (68.4 km) **F 315.5** (507.7 km) **The Deli Restaurant & Bakery.** See display ad this section.

A 42.7 (68.7 km) **F 315.3** (507.4 km) Airport Drive; food and shopping.

A 43.5 (70 km) **F 314.5** (506.1 km) Lucas Road; Hallea Lane access to Lake Lucille.

A 44.2 (71.1 km) **F 313.8** (505 km) Divided highway ends northbound.

A 44.4 (71.4 km) **F 313.6** (504.7 km) Church Road. *NOTE: In 1998, watch for road construction at this intersection and on Church Road.*

A 45 (72.4 km) **F 313** (503.7 km) Wasilla city limits. Shopping and services are located along the highway to **Milepost A 39.5** and at Main Street in Wasilla city center.

Wasilla Car Wash. See display ad this section.

A 45.5 (73.2 km) **F 312.5** (502.9 km) **Trading Post & Gifts.** Mile 45.5 Parks Highway, (907) 376-1327 or (907) 376-2327. Blue building with moose, bears and sheep in front. Safe bear encounters in our wildlife studio with your camera or ours. 9 A.M.–7 P.M. or appointment. Group discounts and prices available. Gifts, ice cream, espresso and more. Taxidermist available. [ADVERTISEMENT]

A 46.7 (75.2 km) **F 311.3** (501 km) Highway crosses over the Alaska Railroad.

A 47 (75.6 km) **F 311** (500.5 km) Neuser Drive. Turnoff for Wasilla municipal airport and the Museum of Alaska Transportation and Industry. The museum features historic aircraft, railroad equipment, old farm machinery and heavy equipment. Steam train rides on selected Saturdays. Admission fees in summer are $5 adults, $12 families. Group tours by arrangement.

Museum of Alaska Transportation & Industry. See display ad this section.

A 48.8 (78.5 km) **F 309.2** (497.6 km) Turnoff on Pittman Road to Rainbow Lake. Medical center, convenience store, gas station, cafe and Meadow Lakes post office.

A 49 (78.9 km) **F 309** (497.3 km) **Dead Dog Saloon.** See display ad this section.

Big Lake Road Log

The 6.5-mile/10.5-km Big Lake Road leads south from the Parks Highway junction at **Milepost A 52.3** to **BIG LAKE** (pop. 2,333), a recreation area with swimming, camping, boating, fishing, jet skiing and tour boat rides in summer. Winter sports include snow machining. Businesses are found along Big Lake Road and along North Shore Drive, which forks off Big Lake Road at **Mile J 3.6**. Evidence of the June 1996 Big Lake wildfire, which began on Millers Reach Road, is visible from the road. Many Big Lake businesses and facilities escaped the fire, while some were partially burned or destroyed; many have rebuilt.

Note: Watch for road construction along Big Lake Road in 1998–99.

Distance is measured from the junction (J) with the Parks Highway.

J 0 Junction with Parks Highway. Meadowood Mall and gas station; automatic teller machine.

J 3.4 (5.5 km) Beaver Lake Road turnoff. Turn right here for public and private campgrounds. Drive 0.5 mile/0.8 km on Beaver Lake Road (gravel) for Rocky Lake state recreation site; 10 campsites, $10 nightly fee or annual pass, toilets, firepits, water and boat launch. ▲

J 3.5 (5.6 km) Gas station with automatic teller machine.

Feeding future Iditarod champs.

(© Roger Pickenpaugh)

J 3.6 (5.8 km) Fisher's Y; gas station and Big Lake post office (ZIP code 99652). Big Lake Road forks here: Go straight ahead for North Shore Drive (description follows); keep to left for south Big Lake Road businesses and Big Lake South state recreation site (continue with this log).

North Shore Drive provides access to Klondike Inn and restaurant (1.4 miles/2.3 km) and Big Lake North state recreation site (1.6 miles/2.6 km), which has parking for 120 vehicles, overnight RV parking, tent sites, $10 nightly fee per vehicle or annual pass, covered picnic tables, water, toilets, dumpsters, boat launch ($5 fee) and sandy beach. Day-use parking $2. Pay phone. ▲

J 3.7 (6 km) Shopping mall.

J 3.9 (6.3 km) Big Lake fire station.

J 4 (6.4 km) East Lake Mall; visitor information center, restaurant and grocery.

J 4.7 (7.6 km) Aero Drive and Big Lake airport. Big Lake is a 15-minute flight from Anchorage.

Private Aircraft: 1 mile/1.6 km southeast; elev. 150 feet/46m; length 2,400 feet/732m; gravel; fuel 100LL.

J 5 (8 km) Big Lake Motel. Bridge over Fish Creek. Fish Creek park picnic area; fish weir with salmon spawning view area. Fishing prohibited.

J 5.2 (8.4 km) Big Lake South state recreation site; 13 campsites, 6 picnic sites, toilets, water, dumpsters, boat ramp ($5 fee). Camping fee $10/night per vehicle or annual pass. Day-use fee $2. ▲

J 5.3 (8.5 km) Double-ended turnout with picnic tables and water.

J 5.7 (9.2 km) Gravel turnout, Echo Lake Road. Dog mushers' race track.

J 6.5 (10.5 km) Pavement ends. Burma Road continues into rural area, providing access to the south Big Lake area, former Point MacKenzie dairy project and the Little Susitna River public-use facility at Susitna Flats State Game Refuge (also accessible via Knik Road); parking, camping, boat ramps. Fee charged, state parks annual pass not accepted. See description and fee schedule at **Milepost J 17.2** Knik Road this section. ▲

Big Lake is connected with smaller lakes by dredged waterways. It is possible to boat for several miles in the complex. Fish in Big Lake include lake trout, Dolly Varden, rainbow, red and coho salmon, and burbot.

Return to Milepost A 52.3 Parks Highway

BIG LAKE ADVERTISERS

Paddling the canoe trail at Nancy Lake Recreation Area, Milepost A 67.2.
(© Michael DeYoung)

A 49 (78.9 km) **F 309** (497.3 km) **Mile 49 Cafe.** See display ad this section.

A 50.1 (80.6 km) **F 307.9** (495.5 km) **Blodgett Lake B & B.** See display ad this section.

A 50.2 (80.8 km) **F 307.8** (495.3 km) **Ice Worm RV Park & Country Store.** See display ad this section. ▲

A 51 (82 km) **F 307** (494 km) **Big Lake–Susitna Veterinary Hospital.** See display ad this section.

A 51.3 (82.6 km) **F 306.7** (493.6 km) **Earth'n Art Studio and Gift Shop.** Located 1 block east of the Parks Highway on Spring Drive you will find the workshop of Michael Stanelle, craftsman, ceramist and master mold maker. Michael creates individually handcrafted "Down to Earth" wind chimes and displays them in his showroom. Manufactured on site. Other local artists are also featured in this unique, quality gift shop. Open year-round. Easy RV access. VISA and MasterCard accepted. (907) 892-7516. [ADVERTISEMENT]

A 52.3 (84.2 km) **F 305.7** (492 km) **Junction** with Big Lake Road. Meadowood shopping mall located here with a service station, hardware store, automatic teller machine, grocery and emergency phone (dial 911). See BIG LAKE ROAD log opposite page.

A 53.2 (85.6 km) **F 304.8** (490.5 km) **Plettner Kennels.** A full-service Iditarod sled dog training facility. Two blocks off the Parks Highway on Hawk Lane, next to Houston High School. Summer and winter sled dog rides, guided kennel tours; play with puppies, learn to mush dogs; sled shop and more. RV, tour bus and wheelchair accessible. P.O. Box 878586, Wasilla, AK 99687, (907) 892-6944. [ADVERTISEMENT] ♿

A 53.3 (85.8 km) **F 304.7** (490.4 km) Houston High School and Wasilla Senior Center. Turnout to west with map and information sign.

A 54.3 (87.5 km) **F 303.7** (488.7 km) **Alaska Explorers & Fisherman.** See display ad this section.

A 56.1 (90.3 km) **F 301.9** (485.8 km) Miller's Reach Road. Alaska's most destructive wildfire began here in June 1996. The Big Lake wildfire burned some 37,000 acres and more than 350 homes.

A 56.4 (90.8 km) **F 301.6** (485.4 km) *CAUTION: Railroad crossing.*

A 57.1 (91.9 km) **F 300.9** (484.2 km) Bridge over the Little Susitna River; turnouts either side; toilets. This river heads at Mint Glacier in the Talkeetna Mountains to the northeast and flows 110 miles/177 km into Upper Cook Inlet.

A 57.3 (92.4 km) **F 300.7** (483.9 km) Turnoff to Houston City Hall, fire station, emergency phone and city-operated Little Susitna River Campground. Large, well-maintained campground with 86 sites (many wide, level gravel sites); camping fee, water, restrooms, covered picnic area, 10-day limit. Off-road parking lot near river with access to river. Follow signs to camping and river. Day-use area with water and toilets west side of highway. ▲

The **Little Susitna River** has a tremendous king salmon run and one of the largest silver salmon runs in southcentral Alaska. Kings to 30 lbs. enter the river in late May and June; use large red spinners or salmon eggs. Silvers to 15 lbs. come in late July and August, with the biggest run in August; use small weighted spoons or fresh salmon roe. Artificials are required during the early weeks of the fishery in the first part of August. Also red salmon to 10 lbs.; in mid-July, use coho flies or salmon eggs. Charter boats nearby. 🐟

A 57.5 (92.5 km) **F 300.5** (483.6 km) **HOUSTON** (pop. 874) has a grocery store, restaurant (open daily), laundromat, gift shop, inn with food, lodging and pay phone, a campground and gas station. Post office located in the grocery store. Fishing charter operators and marine service are located here. Emergency phone at Houston fire station. ▲

Homesteaded in the 1950s, incorporated as a city in 1966. Houston is a popular fishing center for anglers on the Little Susitna

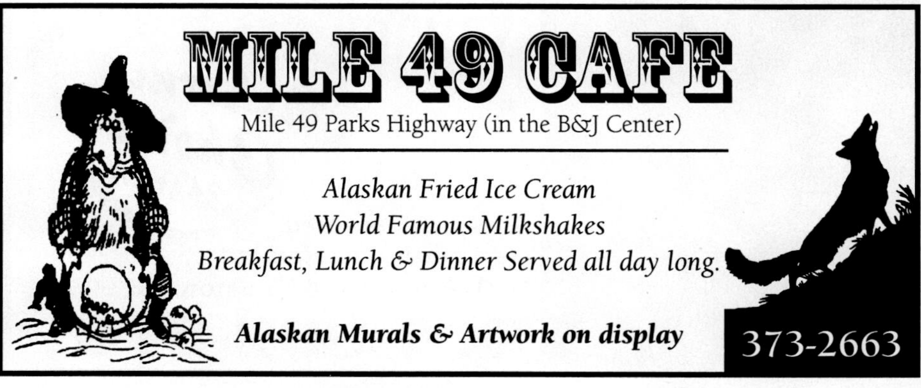

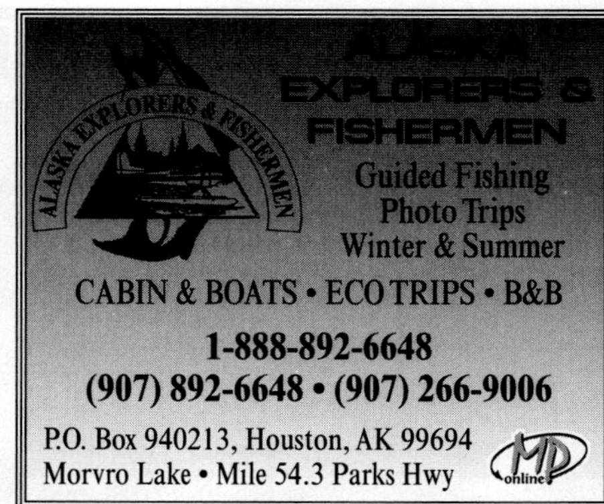

River.

A 57.6 (92.7 km) **F 300.4** (483.4 km) **Miller's Place.** Don't miss this stop! Groceries, post office, laundry, RV parking, cabin rentals, tenting on riverbank. Gift shop, fishing tackle and licenses, fresh salmon eggs. Ice, sporting goods sales and rental, pay phone. Fishing charters available; full day only $45. Probably the best soft ice cream and hamburgers in Alaska. Clean restrooms. Visitor information experts. Family-run Christian business. Gary and Debbie Miller. (907) 892-6129. [ADVERTISEMENT] ▲

A 57.7 (92.9 km) **F 300.3** (483.3 km) **Riverside Camper Park.** See display ad this section. ▲

A 57.8 (93 km) **F 300.2** (483.1 km) **Fisherman's Choice Charters.** Guided trips on the Little Susitna and Talkeetna Rivers. Trophy kings, silvers, reds and rainbow trout. Drop-offs available. May through September. Reservations, information: (800) 989-8707. Box 940276, Houston, AK 99694. E-mail: fish@matnet.com. Internet: www.alaskan.com/fishermanschoice. See display ad. [ADVERTISEMENT]

A 61.2 (98.5 km) **F 296.8** (477.6 km) View of 1996 forest fire damage.

A 64.5 (103.8 km) **F 293.5** (472.3 km) **Nancy Lake Resort.** See display ad this section.

A 65.8 (105.9 km) **F 292.2** (470.2 km) **Nancy Lake Bed & Breakfast.** Great full breakfast or Continental style. Two rooms with private baths. Single, double or family welcome. Meet our Siberian husky sled dog team. Visiting dog teams welcome. Mushing,

cross-country skiing, snow machining, hiking, fishing, canoeing. Open year-round. Swiss Canadian American hosts Romano and Maureen Conzett, Box 67, Willow, AK 99688. Phone/fax (907) 495-5845. [ADVERTISEMENT]

A 66.5 (107 km) **F 291.5** (469.1 km) **Alaskan Host Bed & Breakfast.** See display ad this section.

A 66.7 (107.3 km) **F 291.3** (468.8 km) Turnoff (not well marked) for Nancy Lake state recreation site; 30 campsites, 30 picnic sites, toilets, boat launch, horseshoe pits. Camping fee $10/night or annual pass. ▲

CAUTION: Highway crosses Alaska Railroad tracks.

A 67.2 (108.1 km) **F 290.8** (468 km) Wide gravel road into Nancy Lake Recreation Area in the mixed birch and spruce forest of the Susitna River valley (good mushroom hunting area). At Mile 2.5/4 km on the access road there is a well-marked nature trail, toilets and parking area. At Mile 4.7/7.6 km there is a canoe launch, toilet and parking area. At Mile 5.7/9.2 km a hiking trail leads 3 miles/4.8 km to Chicken Lake, 5.5 miles/8.9 km to Red Shirt Lake. At Mile 6.2/10 km is South Rolly Lake overlook (day use only) with barbecues, 11 picnic tables, litter barrels and toilets. There are 106 campsites at South Rolly Lake Campground, at Mile 6.6/10.6 km, with firepits, toilets, water, canoe rentals and boat launch; firewood sometimes is provided. Camping fee $10/night or annual pass. ▲

South Rolly Lake, small population of rainbow, 12 to 14 inches.

A 68.1 (109.6 km) **F 289.9** (466.5 km) **Willow Winter Park Bed & Breakfast.** Overlooking peaceful Winter Park Lake, 1/2 mile off Parks Highway. Beautiful smoke-free rooms decorated with flannel sheets and antiques. Laundry facilities, barbecue, hot tub. Lakefront cabins also available. Great for families. Paddleboating. Hiking, biking, cross-country skiing and snowmobile trails.

Winter snowmobile and dog sled tours. A great place to stop and relax going to or from Mount McKinley. Phone (907) 495-7547; fax (907) 495-7638; e-mail: winterpark@matnet.com. See display ad. [ADVERTISEMENT] MP

A 68.8 (110.7 km) **F 289.2** (465.4 km) Miner's Last Stand Museum of Hatcher Pass, gas, diesel and gift shop.

Newman's Hilltop Service. See display ad this section.

A 69 (111 km) **F 289** (465.1 km) **WILLOW** (pop. 368). Visitor facilities include 2 gas stations, grocery, hardware and notions store, air taxi service, lodges, RV parks, video rental and restaurants. The Willow civic organization sponsors an annual Winter Carnival in January.

Willow extends about 2.5 miles/4 km north along the Parks Highway. The community is also a stop on the Alaska Railroad. Willow had its start about 1897, when gold was discovered in the area. In the early 1940s, mining in the nearby Talkeetna Mountains slacked off, leaving Willow a virtual ghost town. The community made a comeback upon completion of the Parks Highway in 1972. In 1976, Alaska voters selected the Willow area for their new capital site. However, funding for the capital move from Juneau to Willow was defeated in the November 1982 election.

Willow True Value Hardware, Willow Creek Grocery and **Willow Creek Service.** See display ad this section.

A 69.2 (111.4 km) **F 288.8** (464.8 km) Long Lake Road. Alternate access to Deshka Landing Cafe.

A 69.3 (111.5 km) **F 288.7** (464.6 km) **Townsite Texaco Foodmart.** See display ad this section.

A 69.4 (111.7 km) **F 288.6** (464.4 km) Gas station, convenience store.

A 69.5 (111.8 km) **288.5** (464.3 km) Short road to Willow post office, lodge, trading post with cabins and camper spaces, and Alaska Railroad depot. ▲

Willow Trading Post Lodge. See display

ad this section. ▲

A 69.6 (112 km) **F 288.4** (464.1 km) Willow elementary school.

A 69.7 (112.2 km) **F 288.3** (464 km) Willow Community Center, open daily, has a large parking area, commercial kitchen, showers, covered picnic pavilion, grills, ball court, boat launch and pay phone. (Available for rent to groups, 500-person capacity; phone 907/495-6633). Willow library.

A 69.9 (112.5 km) **F 288.1** (463.6 km) Fire station.

A 70 (112.7 km) **F 288** (463.5 km) **Private Aircraft:** Willow airport; elev. 220 feet/67m; length 4,200 feet/1,280m; gravel; fuel 100LL.

Willow Air Service Inc. See display ad this section.

A 70.8 (113.9 km) **F 287.2** (462.2 km) Willow Creek Parkway (**Susitna River** access road) to Willow Creek state recreation area (4 miles/6.4 km); camping $10/night, parking, litter barrels, water, toilets, dump station, trail to mouth of creek. Access to Deshka Landing boat launch. Fishing for king and silver salmon, rainbow trout. ▲

A 71 (114.3 km) **F 287** (461.9 km) Willow DOT/PF highway maintenance station.

A 71.2 (114.6 km) **F 286.8** (461.5 km) **Junction** with Hatcher Pass (Fishhook–Willow) Road. This road leads east and south across Hatcher Pass 49 miles/79 km to junction with the Glenn Highway. Independence Mine State Historical Park is 31.8 miles/51.2 km from here. Access to Willow Creek state recreation area via Hatcher Pass Road. Deception Creek main campground, with 17 campsites, is located 1.2 miles/1.9 km from this junction via Hatcher Pass Road. Additional campsites and a picnic area are located 0.8 mile/1.3 km east. Both sites have tables, firepits and toilets. Camping fee $10/night or annual pass. Bed and breakfast located 2 miles/3.2 km east of highway past the campground. ▲

Alaska Creekside Bed & Breakfast. See display ad this section.

Turn to the Hatcher Pass side road log one page 355 in the GLENN HIGHWAY section for log of this road. (Parks Highway travelers should read that log back to front.) See also the Mat–Su Valley Vicinity map page 415. Hatcher Pass Road is mostly gravel with some steep, narrow, winding sections.

A 71.4 (114.9 km) **F 286.6** (461.2 km) Lodge. Bridge over **Willow Creek.** This stream heads in Summit Lake, west of Hatcher Pass on the Hatcher Pass Road, and is a favorite launch site for airboat enthusiasts. Excellent king salmon fishing; also silvers, rainbow. Inquire at either lodge or resort for information. Entering Game Management Subunit 14B northbound, 14A southbound. From here to Denali National Park and Preserve watch for views of the Alaska Range to the east of the highway.

Pioneer Lodge. One of Alaska's oldest original log lodges. Restaurant with full bar overlooking Willow Creek. Liquor store. Full RV hookups $12, campground—tent sites $8, showers, laundromat, dump station. Rooms. Fishing, hunting charters, drop offs, wilderness tours, fly-ins, bank fishing—4 types of salmon, rainbows, grayling. Hiking trails. Boat launch. Bait, tackle, fishing

rentals. Licenses, ice, gift shop. Phone (907) 495-1000. See display ad. [ADVERTISEMENT]

A 74.7 (120.2 km) **F 283.3** (455.9 km) Bridge over **Little Willow Creek.** Parking on either side of creek; fishing for salmon and trout.

A 76.4 (122.9 km) **F 281.6** (453.2 km) Paved double-ended turnout to west by **Kashwitna Lake.** Stocked with rainbow trout. Small planes land on lake. Good camera viewpoints of lake and Mount McKinley (weather permitting).

A 80 (128.7 km) **F 278** (447.4 km) **Lucky Husky Racing Kennel.** Experience a true Alaskan lifestyle. Take an exciting summer dogsled ride! Meet the Lucky Husky family. Get dressed in original musher's clothes at the Iditarod checkpoint display. Take pictures with your favorite husky. Individuals and groups are welcome. Wir sprechen Deutsch. May–September: Open daily 10 A.M.–6 P.M. November–March: Reservation only. See display ad this section. [ADVERTISEMENT]

A 81.3 (130.8 km) **F 276.7** (445.3 km) **Grey's Creek**, gravel turnouts both sides of highway. Fishing for salmon and trout.

A 82.5 (132.8 km) **F 275.5** (443.4 km) Susitna Landing, 1 mile/1.6 km on side road; boat launch, camping, wheelchair-accessible restrooms, bank fishing, riverboat service. Concessionaire-operated (ADF&G land) boat launch on **Kashwitna River**, just upstream of the **Susitna River**; access to both rivers on

Susitna River with—from left to right—Mt. Russell, Mt. Foraker and Mt. McKinley in background. (© W. Wright-Diamond Photo)

site. The Susitna River heads at Susitna Glacier in the Alaska Range to the northeast and flows west then south for 260 miles/418 km to Cook Inlet.

Ron's Riverboat Service at Susitna Landing & Campground. See display ad this section.

A 83.2 (133.9 km) **F 274.8** (442.2 km) Bridge over the **Kashwitna River**; parking areas located at both ends of bridge. Salmon and trout fishing. The river heads in a glacier in the Talkeetna Mountains and flows westward 60 miles/ 96.5 km to enter the Susitna River 12 miles/19 km north of Willow.

A 84.1 (135.3 km) **F 273.9** (440.8 km) Large paved turnout to west.

A 84.3 (135.7 km) **F 273.7** (440.5 km) Gravel turnout to west. Walk-in for fishing at **Caswell Creek;** kings, silvers, pinks and rainbow.

A 85.1 (137 km) **F 272.9** (439.2 km) Caswell Creek, large, steep gravel turnout.

A 85.5 (137.6 km) **F 272.5** (438.5 km) Gift shop and art gallery.

Willow Wildlife Art Gallery. Features Alaskan wildlife and sled dog art, as well as locally handcrafted gifts. Meet artist Dave

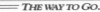

Totten in his home studio/gallery. "From Anchorage to Fairbanks ... best gallery," Jerry Griswold, *L.A. Times,* Aug. 1, 1993. Free coffee and wildberry muffins. Phone (907) 495-1090. Open all year. [ADVERTISEMENT]

A 86 (138.4 km) **F 272** (437.7 km) Public access road leads 1.3 miles/2.1 km to mouth of Sheep Creek public boat launch and Bluffs on Susitna. **Sheep Creek** has parking, toilets, dumpster and wheelchair-accessible trail to mouth of creek; fishing for kings, silvers, pinks and rainbow.

A 86.9 (139.8 km) **F 271.1** (436.3 km) **Kimberly's Kreations/ Kiana of Alaska.** Stop in and see one of Alaska's largest manufacturers. Specializing in Native arts, crafts and cultured marble. Visit our unique gift shop in a beautiful log cabin atmosphere. Alaskan Native owned and operated. Easy horseshoe driveway. Large parking area. Open daily 9 A.M.–9 P.M. Phone (907) 495-8008. [ADVERTISEMENT]

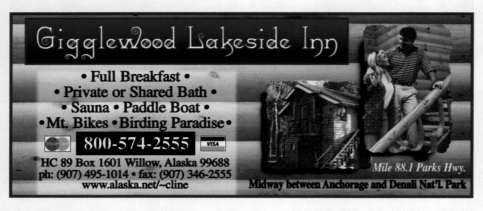

A 87.1 (140.2 km) **F 270.9** (436 km) **Camp Caswell RV Park.** Open year-round. Located in the heart of Alaska's finest fishing and winter sports. We offer secluded RV and tent sites, parking, cabins, pull-throughs, hookups, propane, fishing tackle, snacks, ice, firewood, winter snowmachining, phone and information. Free coffee and Alaska friendly! Phone (907) 495-7829. P.O. Box 333, Willow, AK 99688. [ADVERTISEMENT]

A 88.1 (141.8 km) **F 269.9** (434.4 km) **Gigglewood Lakeside Inn.** See display ad this section.

A 88.2 (142 km) **F 269.8** (434.2 km) **Sheep Creek Lodge.** Beautiful log lodge, built with Alaskan white spruce logs, some over 200 years old. Fine dining, cocktail lounge, serving breakfast, lunch and dinner. Warm cozy cabins, creekside RV parking or camping. Excellent salmon and trout fishing within walking distance of lodge. Package liquor store, ice, fuel and propane. Gift shop featuring unique local Alaskan gifts, many Alaskan wildlife mounts and local tour information. Open year-round with winter activities including cross-country skiing, marked snow machine trails, ice fishing and dog mushing. Phone (907) 495-6227. Internet: www.sheepcreeklodge.com. [ADVERTISEMENT]

A 88.6 (142.6 km) **F 269.4** (433.5 km) Bridge over **Sheep Creek.** Unimproved picnic area on west side below bridge by creek. Fishing for salmon and trout.

A 89 (143.2 km) **F 269** (432.9 km) Gravel turnouts both sides of highway.

A 91.5 (147.3 km) **F 266.5** (428.9 km) **Susitna Dog Tours & Bed and Breakfast.** Easy access to newly built log home offering a unique blend of Alaskan living and wilderness sled dog mushing or just a peaceful night's rest. Hot showers, sauna. Trails and seminars available for cross-country skiing, skijoring, dog mushing. Located within striking distance of Talkeetna and Denali National Park. Your hosts: Iditarod Veterans Bill and Rhodi Davidson and 50 sled dogs. Open year-round. Phone (907) 495-6324; e-mail: susdog@matnet.com. [ADVERTISEMENT]

A 91.7 (147.6 km) **F 266.3** (428.5 km) *CAUTION: Railroad crossing.*

A 93.4 (150.3 km) **F 264.6** (425.8 km) Gravel turnouts both sides of highway.

A 93.5 (150.5 km) **F 264.5** (425.7 km) **Goose Creek** culvert; gravel turnout. Fishing.

A 93.6 (150.6 km) **F 264.4** (425.5 km) Goose Creek community center; park pavilion, picnic tables, grills, litter barrels.

A 95.1 (153 km) **F 262.9** (423.1 km) **Private Aircraft:** Montana Creek airstrip; elev. 250 feet/76m; length 2,400 feet/731m; gravel; fuel 80, 100.

A 96.6 (155.5 km) **F 261.4** (420.7 km) Bridge over **Montana Creek.** Homesteaders settled in the area surrounding this creek in the 1950s. Today, about 200 families live in the area. Camping and picnic areas on both sides of Montana Creek (operated by concessionaire, state park annual pass not accepted). Water and parking. Excellent king salmon fishing, also silvers, pinks (even-numbered years), grayling, rainbow and Dolly Varden.

Montana Creek Campgrounds. Located on the south side of Montana Creek, all

Avoid bear encounters: let bears know you are coming by making lots of noise!

campsites in these private campgrounds are scenic, with some overlooking one of Alaska's best salmon and trout fishing streams. Picnic tables, campfires, toilets, tackle shop, tackle rentals and snacks. Only a short walk to the Susitna River. Conveniently located within 3 miles of grocery store, cafe, laundromat and showers. [ADVERTISEMENT] ▲

A 97.8 (157.4 km) **F 260.2** (418.7 km) Alaska State Troopers post (phone 907/733-2556 or 911 for emergencies).

A 98 (157.7 km) **F 260** (418.4 km) For weather information, tune your radio to 830-AM (99.7-FM).

The Store. See display ad this section.

A 98.4 (158.3 km) **F 259.6** (417.8 km) Susitna Valley High School; 3.1-mile/5-km trail for running in summer, cross-country skiing in winter. Senior Center.

A 98.7 (158.8 km) **F 259.3** (417.3 km) **Talkeetna junction.** Junction with Talkeetna Spur Road; 2 visitor information cabins. Access to hardware, lumber and feed store with automatic teller machine. Turn right northbound on paved spur road that leads 14.5 miles/23.3 km to community of Talkeetna, an interesting side trip (description begins on page 431). See TALKEETNA SPUR ROAD log this section. Continue straight ahead on the Parks Highway for Fairbanks.

Mary Carey's Fiddlehead Fern Farm. See display ad this section.

Moores' Mercantile. See display ad this section.

Talkeetna/Denali Visitor Center. Staffed by knowledgeable local residents. Information and bookings of area recreational activities, including fishing, flightseeing, rafting,

lodging and Denali Park. Statewide brochures and information. Large garden and picnic area. Public restrooms. Parks Highway at Talkeetna Junction. Write Box 688, Talkeetna, AK 99676. Phone (800) 660-2688 or (907) 733-2688. [ADVERTISEMENT]

A 98.8 (159 km) **F 259.2** (417.1 km) **Sunshine One Stop/Tesoro Alaska.** See display ad this section.

A 99 (159.3 km) **F 259** (416.8 km) **Denali Way Auto.** See display ad this section.

A 99.3 (159.8 km) **F 258.7** (416.3 km) **Montana and Little Montana lakes** on opposite sides of highway, stocked with rain-

Five species of Pacific salmon are found in Alaska: pink, chum, sockeye (red), silver and chinook (king).

bow. Watch for floatplanes. Double-ended gravel turnout to west.

A 99.5 (160.1 km) **F 258.5** (416 km) **H&H Lakeview Restaurant & Lodge**, serving travelers since 1965. Feast your senses in our

spacious lakeside dining room, hidden away from the busy highway by a birch grove. You'll love our omelettes. Great hamburgers and steaks. Prime rib and seafood too. Our bread pudding is famous statewide. Take home a taste of Alaska in jellies from our gift shop. We make the jellies from Alaska berries, each with its own distinct flavor. Lakeside RV parking and camping. Hear the loons and watch beavers from your motorhome. Gerald and Sherry Berryman, proprietors since 1977. See display ad for details. [ADVERTISEMENT] ▲

A 99.8 (160.6 km) **F 258.2** (415.5 km) Access road to YMCA camp on Peggy Lake.

A 100.4 (161.6 km) **F 257.6** (414.6 km) *CAUTION: Railroad crossing.*

A 101.4 (163.2 km) **F 256.6** (412.9 km) Beaver lodge; watch for swans.

A 102 (164.1 km) **F 256** (412 km) Large, paved double-ended turnout to east. Lakes both sides of highway.

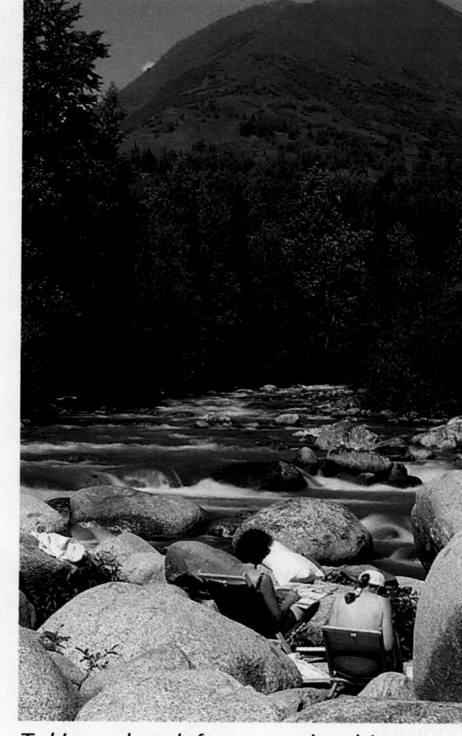

Taking a break for some sketching along a stream. (© Loren Taft, Alaskan Images)

Talkeetna Blue Grass Festival, Aug. 6, 7, 8, 9, 1998. Alaska's greatest musicians, arts, crafts and food. Good roads, outhouses, RV parking, no hookups. Great family weekend camping. Bring camping gear and cushions. $25 fee. Seniors and children 12 and under are free. No carry-in alcohol please. For information, phone (907) 495-6718. [ADVERTISEMENT]

A 102.6 (165.1 km) **F 255.4** (411 km) Turnout at Sunshine Road; access to **Sunshine Creek** for fishing via dirt road.

A 104.2 (167.7 km) **F 253.8** (408.4 km) Entering Game Management Unit 16A, northbound, Unit 14B southbound.

A 104.3 (167.8 km) **F 253.7** (408.3 km) Bridge over Big Susitna River. State rest area to west on south bank of river; loop road, parking area, tables, firepits, toilets, no drinking water. ▲

Some of the finest stands of white birch in Alaska may be seen for several miles on both sides of the river. This area is also noted for its fiddlehead ferns. The ferns (lady fern, ostrich fern and shield fern) are harvested in the spring, when their young shoots are tightly coiled, resembling a fiddle's head. Fiddleheads should be cooked before consumption.

A 104.6 (168.3 km) **F 253.4** (407.8 km) Rabideaux Creek access; parking, 0.3 mile/0.5 km trail to mouth of creek. Watch for seasonal flooding.

A 104.8 (168.7 km) **F 253.2** (407.5 km) Double-ended turnout to west.

A 105.9 (170.4 km) **F 252.1** (405.7 km) Rabideaux Creek access and bridge.

A 107.6 (173.2 km) **F 250.4** (403 km) View of Mount McKinley for northbound travelers.

A 114.8 (184.7 km) **F 243.2** (391.4 km) Cluster of businesses serving highway travelers and Trapper Creek the next mile north-

(Continues on page 437)

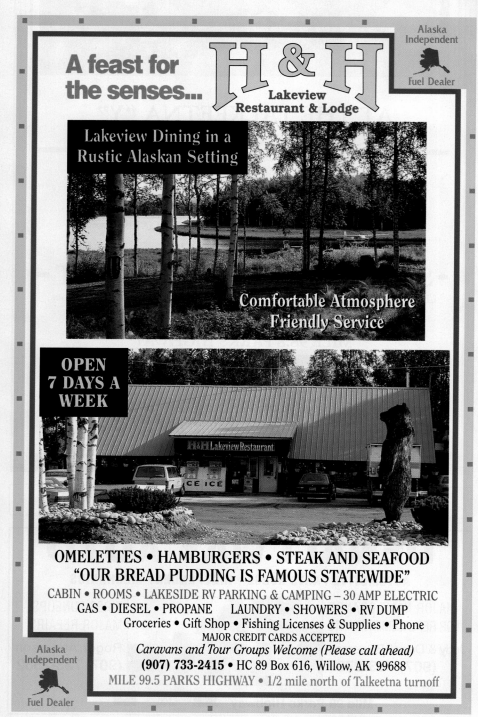

Talkeetna Spur Road Log

Distance from Parks Highway junction (J) at Milepost A 98.7 is shown.

J 0 Junction with the Parks Highway; visitor center.

J 1 (1.6 km) Fiddlehead fern farm and lodging.

Moose Dropping Inn Bed & Breakfast. See display ad this section.

J 3.1 (5 km) Turn west on Jubilee Road for bed and breakfast. Turn east on Yoder Road for Benka Lake (private).

Denali View B&B. (Turn on Jubilee, St. Johns and Coffee roads.) Cozy cedar home offers hunting and fishing motif, antiques, great homemade breakfasts. Private baths. Located 12 miles south of Talkeetna, midway between Anchorage

and Denali Park. View of Denali. Lush gardens. Wonderful, friendly atmosphere. Let us book your Talkeetna experience. Book early; deposit required. Resident hosts, long-time Alaskans LesLee and Norm Solberg. HC 89 Box 8360, Talkeetna, AK 99676. Phone or fax (907) 733-2778. Internet: www.alaskaone.com/denview. [ADVERTISEMENT]

J 5.3 (8.5 km) Answer Creek. Sunshine Community Health Center.

J 7.1 (11.4 km) Question Lake.

J 7.8 (12.6 km) Paradise Cabins.

J 9.2 (14.8 km) Fish Lake private floatplane base.

J 11.6 (18.7 km) **Bays B&B.** See display ad this section.

J 12 (19.3 km) Turn east on paved Comsat Road (unmarked) for Christianson Lake; drive in 0.7 mile/1.1 km on Comsat Road, turn left at Christianson Lake Road sign onto gravel road and drive 0.7 mile/1.1 km, turn right and follow signs to floatplane base. Fishing for silvers and rainbow. Good place to observe loons and waterfowl. Also access to Alascom Earth Station (no tours). The dish-shaped antenna stands 98 feet/32m and can rotate 1 degree per second to receive satellite signals.

J 13 (20.9 km) Large gravel double-ended turnout with interpretive sign and viewpoint at crest of hill. Splendid views of Mount McKinley, Mount Foraker and the Alaska Range above the Susitna River. A must photo stop when the mountains are out. *CAUTION: Watch for traffic and construction vehicles entering highway.*

J 13.3 (21.4 km) *CAUTION: Alaska Railroad crossing.*

J 13.5 (21.7 km) Talkeetna public library. Gas station.

J 13.8 (22.2 km) Restaurant and motel. VFW Post No. 3836 is 2 blocks west.

J 14 (22.5 km) East Talkeetna Road leads to state airport, municipal campground and boat launch on Talkeetna River and businesses. ▲

J 14.2 (22.9 km) Talkeetna post office (ZIP code 99676).

J 14.3 (23 km) "Welcome to Beautiful Downtown Talkeetna" sign and Talkeetna Historical Society visitor center log cabin; walking tour brochures available. (Description of Talkeetna follows.)

Mountain Gift Shop/Visitor Information Cabin. Near the famous "Welcome to Beautiful Downtown Talkeetna" sign. Enjoy shopping for mountain theme items: books, maps, posters, T-shirts, flags, colorful gemstone necklaces and quill jewelry handmade in Alaska. Moose nugget items our specialty. Open summer 10–5:30. Free town map. Information, reservation (907) 733-1686. [ADVERTISEMENT]

J 14.5 (23.3 km) Talkeetna Spur Road ends at Talkeetna River Park.

Talkeetna

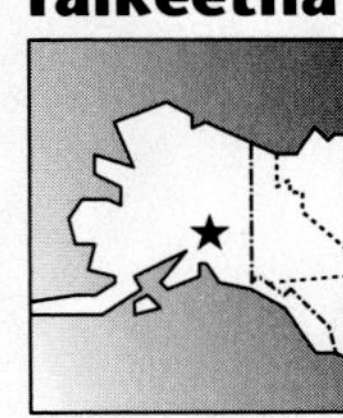

Located on a spur road, north of **Milepost A 98.7** Parks Highway. **Population:** 441. **Emergency Services: Alaska State Troopers, Fire Department** and **Ambulance**, phone 911 or 733-2556. **Doctor**, phone 733-2708.

Visitor Information: Stop by the Talkeetna Historical Society Museum one block off Main Street opposite the Fairview Inn. Visitor information also available at the Mountain Gift Shop and the Visitor Information Cabin entering Talkeetna, and at 2 log cabins on either side of the junction of Parks Highway and Spur Road. Or write the Chamber of Commerce, P.O. Box 334, Talkeetna, AK 99676.

The National Park Service maintains a ranger station that is staffed full time from mid-April through mid-September and intermittently during the winter. Mountaineering rangers provide information on Denali National Park and climbing within the Alaska Range. A reference library and video program are available to climbers. Mountaineering regulations and information may be obtained from Talkeetna Ranger Station, P.O. Box 588, Talkeetna, AK 99676; phone (907) 733-2231.

Talkeetna Spur Road Log (continued)

Moose rack decorates the side of a Talkeetna home.
(© W. Wright-Diamond Photo)

Elevation: 346 feet/105m. **Radio:** KSKA-FM (PBS). **Television:** Channels 4, 6, 9.

Private Aircraft: Talkeetna airstrip (state airport), adjacent east; elev. 358 feet/109m; length 3,500 feet/1,067m; paved; fuel 100LL, Jet B. Talkeetna village airstrip on Main Street; elev. 346 feet/105m; length 1,200 feet/366m; gravel; village airstrip not recommended for transient aircraft or helicopters (watch for closures and poor conditions).

A "Welcome to Beautiful Downtown Talkeetna" sign is posted at the town park as you enter Talkeetna's old-fashioned Main Street, the only paved street in town. Log cabins and clapboard homes and businesses line Main Street, which dead-ends at the Susitna River.

Talkeetna is the jumping-off point for many climbing expeditions to Mount McKinley. Most climbing expeditions use the West Buttress route, pioneered by Bradford Washburn, flying in specially

TALKEETNA ADVERTISERS

Back Door B & B	Ph. (907) 733-1032
Chinook Winds Cabins	Ph. (907) 733-1899
Crowley Guide Service	Ph. (907) 733-1279
Denali Dry Goods	Main St.
Denali Floats	Ph. (907) 733-2384
Doug Geeting Aviation	Ph. (907) 733-2366
ERA Helicopters	Ph. (800) 843-1947
Fitzgerald Guide Service	Ph. (907) 733-2704
Hudson Air Service, Inc.	Ph. (907) 733-2321
K2 Aviation	Ph. (800) 764-2291
Latitude 62° Lodge/Motel	Ph. (907) 733-2262
Mahay's Riverboat Service	Ph. (907) 733-2223
McKinley Air Service	State Airport
Moose's Tooth	Ph. (907) 258-7952
Mountain Gift Shop/Visitor Information Cabin	Main St.
Museum of Northern Adventure	Mile J 14.3
Nagley's Store	Ph. (907) 733-3663
Peak Dodger Flight Tours	Main St.
Swiss–Alaska Inn	Ph. (907) 733-2424
Talkeetna & Beyond Bed & Breakfast	Ph. (907) 733-3050
Talkeetna Air Taxi	Ph. (907) 733-2218
Talkeetna Gifts and Collectables	Mile J 14.3
Talkeetna Motel	Ph. (907) 733-2323
Talkeetna River Adventures	Ph. (907) 733-2604
Talkeetna River Guides	Main St.
Talkeetna Riverboat Service	Main St.
Talkeetna Roadhouse	Main St.
Three Rivers Accommodations	Ph. (907) 733-2741
Three Rivers Tesoro	Main St.
Trapper John's Bed & Breakfast	Ph. (907) 733-2354
Village Arts & Crafts	Ph. (907) 733-2281

equipped ski-wheel aircraft to Kahiltna Glacier. The actual climb on Mount McKinley is made from about 7,000 feet/2,134m (where the planes land) to the summit of the South Peak (elev. 20,320 feet/6,194m). Several air services based in Talkeetna specialize in the glacier landings necessary to ferry climbers and their equipment to and from the mountain. The climb via the West Buttress route usually takes 18 to 20 days. Flightseeing the mountain is also popular (and easier!).

ACCOMMODATIONS/VISITOR SERVICES

Talkeetna has 5 motels/hotels, several bed and breakfasts, 6 restaurants, 2 gas stations, laundromats, gift and clothing shops, grocery and general stores. A dump station is located at Three Rivers Tesoro.

There is a campground with toilets and shelters at the public boat launch (fee charged) just beyond the Swiss Alaska Inn; take East Talkeetna Road (a right turn at Mile 14 on the Spur Road as you approach Talkeetna). Limited RV and tent camping at River Park (located at the end of main street) is planned for 1998; operated by the Talkeetna Chamber of Commerce, fee charged. ▲

Talkeetna Motel, Restaurant and Lounge. Built in 1964 by "Evil Alice" and Sherm Powell, the "Tee-Pee" (nicknamed by oldtimers) became known for its excellent food, fast service and sincere Alaskan hospitality. Today, we also offer private baths, color TV in rooms and lounge, full menu for casual and fine dining. MasterCard/VISA welcome. See display ad this section. [ADVERTISEMENT]

Talkeetna Roadhouse. Located on the edge of wilderness in a living pioneer village, the Talkeetna Roadhouse (Frank Lee cabin, circa 1917) has served the territory since early gold rush days. Still family owned and operated, this historic restaurant, lodge and bakery featuring 1902 sourdough is known worldwide for its fine home-style cooking, cinnamon rolls, and frontier hospitality. Slow down to "Talkeetna time," relax amidst the rustic charm and listen to the stories these old walls have to tell! Rooms start at $45, bunk spaces $21. Restaurant features classic roadhouse breakfast, daily soup and sandwich menu. Locally home-brewed beers on tap. Phone (907) 733-1351, fax (907) 733-1353. E-mail: rdhouse@alaska.net. Internet: www.alaska.net/~rdhouse. [ADVERTISEMENT] MP

TRANSPORTATION

Air: There are several air taxi services in Talkeetna. Charter service, flightseeing and glacier landings are available. See ads this section.

Railroad: The Alaska Railroad.

Highway: At the end of a 14.5-mile/23.3-km spur road off the Parks Highway (Alaska Route 3).

ATTRACTIONS

Museums. Talkeetna boasts two museums, including a privately operated wax museum.

The Talkeetna Historical Society Museum is located 1 block off Main Street opposite the Fairview Inn. The original 1-room schoolhouse, built in 1936, exhibits historical items, local art, a historical library and a display on the late Don Sheldon, famous Alaskan bush pilot. In the Railroad Section House see the impressive 12-foot-by-12-foot scale model of Mount McKinley (Denali) with photographs by Bradford Washburn. A mountaineering display features pioneer and recent climbs of Mount McKinley. The Ole Dahl cabin, an early

Talkeetna Spur Road Log (continued)

trapper/miner's cabin located on the museum grounds, is furnished with period items. Admission: $1 adult, under 12 free. Pick up a walking tour map of Talkeetna's historic sites here. Picnic area adjacent museum. Museum buildings open 10 A.M. to 5 P.M. daily in summer. Reduced hours other seasons. Phone (907) 733-2487. Privately operated guided history tours.

Miners Day. Held the weekend before Memorial Day, this family event has a trade and craft fair, local cancan dancers, softball tournament, a thrilling outhouse race, street dance and parade.

The Talkeetna Gold Dust Dancers perform at the pavilion in the park, next to the "Welcome to Beautiful Downtown Talkeetna" sign, in summer. Check locally for schedule.

Annual Moose Dropping Festival is held the second Saturday in July as a fund-raising project for the museum. Activities include a 5-km run and walk, a parade, entertainment, music, barbecue, food and game booths, and, of course, a moose dropping throwing contest.

Riverboat tours up Talkeetna Canyon, Devils Canyon, Chulitna River and Tokositna River are available. Several guides also offer riverboat fishing trips from Talkeetna. Commercial float trips and raft tours offer another popular way of exploring the roadless wilderness. Talkeetna is located at the confluence of the Susitna, Talkeetna and Chulitna rivers. Inquire locally for details and see ads this section.

Crowley Guide Service. Main Street, Talkeetna. Guided fishing for salmon, rainbow trout and arctic grayling. River transportation and camp support. Scenic and wildlife charters. Mountain biking, rentals, sales and tours. Mount McKinley scenic flights and river rafting. International expeditions. Personalized service at reasonable rates. VISA, MasterCard. P.O. Box 431, Talkeetna, AK 99676. Phone (907) 733-1279; fax (907) 733-1278. [ADVERTISEMENT]

ERA Helicopters. Lift off over the banks of the Chulitna River and see the numerous glaciers covering the high mountain peaks and the vast south slope of Denali, known as "The Great One." Located at Milepost 134. May to September. For reservations phone (800) 843-1947. Tours also available in Juneau, Anchorage, Valdez and Denali Park. [ADVERTISEMENT]

Hudson Air Service, Inc. is Talkeetna's "senior" air taxi; 50 years of experience and knowledge of Mount McKinley will make your flightseeing tour the highlight of your Alaskan adventure! Visit with pioneer aviator Cliff Hudson and fly with second generation Hudson pilots as you tour Denali National Park while enjoying narratives on the natural and local history. Fly over the Kahiltna Glacier and view base camp as climbers from all over the world prepare to ascend "The Great One." Includes a landing on either the Ruth or

Kahiltna Glacier for an experience you will never forget. We offer summit flights, wildlife tours (bear, moose, caribou and sheep) and remote fly-in hunting/fishing. 1998 is our 50th anniversary—celebrate with us! Open year-round. Hudson Air Service Inc. is a National Park Service concessionaire. Office at Talkeetna State Airport. P.O. Box 648, Talkeetna, AK 99676. Phone (907) 733-2321, fax (907) 733-2333, e-mail: hasi@customcpu.com. Web site: www.alaskan.com/husonair/. See display ad in DENALI NATIONAL PARK section. [ADVERTISEMENT]

Mahay's Riverboat Service. Fish clear-water streams for all 5 species of Pacific salmon and trout. Custom-designed jet boats allow access to over 200 miles of prime fishing territory. Guided fishing charters include all equipment needed. Fishing packages are also available that include accommodations, meals and all the "extras." Spend the afternoon exploring an authentic trapper's cabin, viewing nesting bald eagles and sightseeing on the McKinley View River Cruise. Drop-off fishing also available at reasonable rates. Credit cards accepted. (907) 733-2223, fax (907) 733-2712. In Alaska, (800) 736-2210. [ADVERTISEMENT]

Museum of Northern Adventure. Highlighting Alaska's exciting history in 24 realistic dioramas, featuring life-sized figures and sounds. Entertaining and educational for all ages. Meander through the historic railroad building, experiencing Alaskana at every turn: homesteading, prospecting, wildlife, famous characters and more. Open daily year-round with special group/family rates. Clean restrooms. Gift shop featuring Eskimo dolls and totems. Carved grizzly and prospector outside to greet you. Main Street, Talkeetna. (907) 733-3999. Handicap accessible. [ADVERTISEMENT] ♿

Peak Dodger Flight Tours. Experience a flight with renowned glacier and flying expert Doug Geeting, who knows the climbers and all the lore and legend

of Denali (the great one). You can experience a glacier landing and look up at 5,000-foot walls of ice and rock that will astound the most world-weary traveler. This flight will definitely be the high point of all your Alaska adventures! Intercom-equipped. Group rates available. Accommodations available, $65 per night. Fly-in fishing cabins. Open year-round. For reservations and prices write or call Doug Geeting Aviation, Box 42

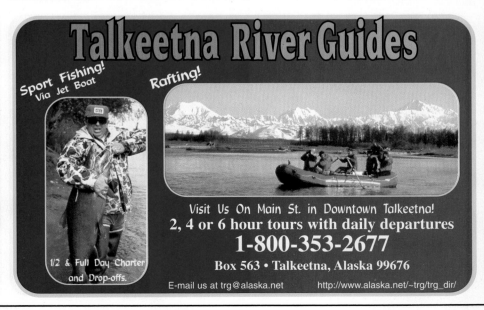

Talkeetna Spur Road Log (continued)

MP, Talkeetna, AK 99676; (800) 770-2366 or (907) 733-2366. Fax (907) 733-1000. See display ad in the DENALI NATIONAL PARK section. [ADVERTISEMENT]

Talkeetna Air Taxi. The ultimate Denali experience. Fly Mount McKinley. Glacier landing, wildlife tours, aerial photography. Remote backpacking. In business since 1947. Office in log building at state airport. Write Box 73-MP, Talkeetna, AK 99676. For information, reservations, call ahead (800) 533-2219 or (907) 733-2218. See display ad. [ADVERTISEMENT]

Talkeetna Gifts & Collectables. "One of the nicest and most complete gift shops in Alaska," located in a spacious log building with handmade keepsakes, souvenirs, jewelry, books, Alaskana, birch bowls, quilts and other treasures. Fur slippers/accessories, beautiful sweatshirts, sweaters, plush toys, puppets and huggable Eskimo dolls. Alaskan foods and sourdough. Suzy's exclusive "Alaska Map" cross-stitch pattern. Quality merchandise with friendly service. We mail purchases. Goldpanning, with gold guaranteed! Open daily year-round. Main Street, Talkeetna. (907) 733-2710. [ADVERTISEMENT]

Talkeetna River Guides. Fish with a recognized leader for salmon and trout in our exciting, area streams and rivers. Guided charters start at $119 and include all equipment and use of our specialized jet boats. Drop-off fishing available as well. Also, join us on a wildlife, natural history float trip. 2-, 4- and 6-hour tours available daily. 1-800-353-2677. See display ad. [ADVERTISEMENT]

Fishing. A Calico (chum) Salmon Derby is held the first 3 weeks of August. The **Susitna River** basin offers many top fishing streams and lakes, either accessible by road, plane or riverboat.

Return to Milepost A 98.7 Parks Highway

Alascom Earth Station on Comsat Road. (© W. Wright-Diamond Photo)

(Continued from page 430)
bound include: lodges with groceries, gift shops, gas and restaurants; RV park; laundromats; and flightseeing service. ▲

Trapper Creek Inn & General Store. Gateway to Denali visitors information center. Tesoro gas, diesel, deluxe lodging with Mount McKinley view, large RV campground, full hookups, dump station, large barbecue/picnic pavilion, ATM, propane, showers, restrooms, laundry, pay phone, deli, espresso, groceries, coffee, ice, etc. Fishing and hunting licenses, supplies and charters. Flightseeing Mount McKinley. Major credit cards accepted. Phone (907) 733-2302. Fax (907) 733-1002. E-mail: innmaster @juno.com. Tour buses welcome. See large display ad this section. [ADVERTISEMENT]

A 114.9 (184.9 km) **F 243.1** (391.2 km) **TRAPPER CREEK** (area pop. about 700), at **junction** with Petersville Road. Trapper Creek post office (ZIP code 99683). Miners built the Petersville Road in the 1920s and federal homesteading began here in 1948, with settlement continuing through the 1950s and 1960s. Today it is the southern gateway to Denali Park and the Alaska Range, with access via the Petersville Road (description follows). Trapper Creek businesses are located along the Parks Highway and up Petersville Road.

Petersville Road leads west and north from Trapper Creek approximately 40 miles/64 km (no winter maintenance beyond Mile 14). This scenic gravel road (with excellent views of Mount McKinley) goes through a homestead and gold mining area that also contains some new subdivisions. Berry picking in season. Lodging available at Mile 2.7, 10.5, 17.2 and 18.7. Turn down the right fork for the former mining camp of Petersville (4-wheel drive recommended). *Please respect private property.* The left fork leads 0.2 mile/0.3 km to **Peters Creek** stream. Fishing for salmon and trout. The road to Petersville is rough and used primarily by miners and trappers beyond The Forks Roadhouse at Mile 18.7. ▲

Denali View Chalets. Mile 2 Petersville Road. Private, secluded, modern chalets with spectacular views of Mount McKinley and the Alaska Range. Open year-round

with access by paved road. Fully furnished with kitchenettes, microwave, gas grills and 2 twin and 2 double beds. Lots of area activities. The wilderness at your doorstep. Reasonable rates. E-mail address: denaliview@polarnet.com. Homepage address: www.polarnet.com/~denalivw. P.O. Box 13245, Trapper Creek, AK 99683. Phone (907) 733-1333. [ADVERTISEMENT]

North Country Bed and Breakfast (Mile 2.7 Petersville Road). Nestled on a lake with a spectacular view of Mount McKinley. Five first-class rooms with private bathrooms and private entries. Mount McKinley flightseeing trips available at the lake by appointment. Bird watching, wildlife, paddleboating and horseshoes available. Open year-round. Your hosts—Mike and Sheryl Uher. Phone (907) 733-3981. [ADVERTISEMENT]

Gate Creek Cabins. Modern log cabins, equipped for comfortable stay of day, week or longer. Located Mile 10.5 on historic Petersville Road, with year-round access. Fur-

nished with linens, dishes, utensils, stove, refrigerator, TV, VCR, showers, sauna, BBQ grill. Bring your personal items, food and recreation equipment. Fishing, mountain viewing, hiking, biking, photography,

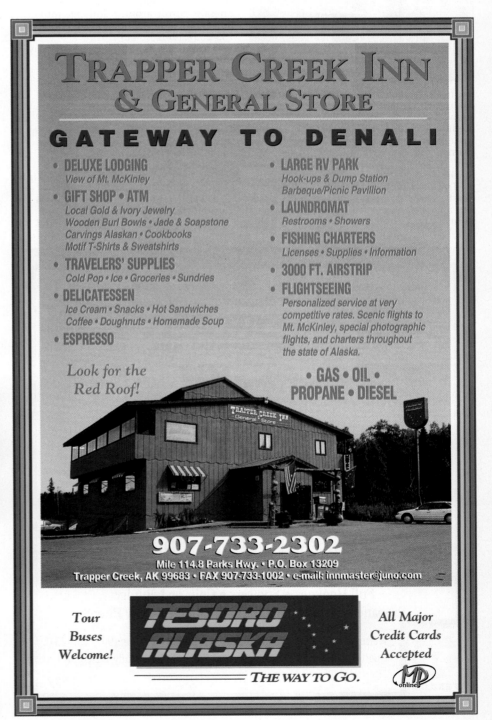

berry picking, canoeing, paddle boating on our small lake; cross-country skiing, snowmobiling, with rentals and guided tours available. Rates: $38/person/night, children 12 and under free, 5 percent bed tax. Weekly rate. Family pets welcome. Your hosts, Gary and Dorothy Rawie, reservations phone (907) 733-1393 (cabins), (907) 248-2765 (Anchorage). [ADVERTISEMENT]

McKinley Foothills B&B/Cabins. Off Mile 17.2 Petersville Road. Furnished, secluded log cabins, kitchenettes. Full breakfast. Great food, Alaskan hospitality. Great Mount McKinley views. Summer: gold

panning tours, fishing nearby, birding, hiking, mountain biking. Winter: skiing, snow machining, dog mushing tours. Major credit cards. Homepage: www.matnet.com/mckinley. E-mail: mckinley@matnet.com. Phone/fax (907) 733-1454. P.O. Box 13089, Trapper Creek, AK 99683. [ADVERTISEMENT]

Trapper Creek B & B. Mile 0.3 Petersville Road. You will enjoy your stay with hosts Jim and Susan in a truly friendly Alaskan home. Clean rooms, hot showers, wholesome food and cedar sauna. Tent camping welcome. Safe area for walkabout. Excellent fishing, hunting, snowmachining and cross country skiing area. Open year-round. Phone (907) 733-2234. [ADVERTISEMENT]

Trapper Creek's Old Historic Post Office. Come visit and bring your camera. See Alaskan artifacts and collectables you'll see nowhere else. Historian Mike Carpenter to greet you with 39 years of Alaskan tales. Some are true! Truly romantic Alaskan visitors center you can tell the folks back home about. Phone (907) 733-2637. [ADVERTISEMENT]

Trapper Creek's Spruce Lane Farms Museum and Gifts. (Mile 0.7 Petersville Road.) Visit historic homestead log cabin museum in view of Mount McKinley. Relive the local area's mining, trapping and homesteading eras, while browsing through local arts, crafts and authentic historic collectables on sale. Stroll around and pet miniature horses raised on the homestead. Phone (907) 733-2557. [ADVERTISEMENT]

The Forks Roadhouse. See display ad this section.

Parks Highway Log

A 115.2 (185.4 km) **F 242.8** (390.7 km) Trapper Creek community park.

A 115.5 (185.9 km) **F 242.5** (390.2 km) **Trapper Creek Trading Post.** See display ad this section. ▲

A 115.6 (186 km) **F 242.4** (390.1 km) Highway crosses Trapper Creek.

Excellent views of Mount McKinley (weather permitting) northbound.

A 117.3 (188.8 km) **F 240.7** (387.4 km) Turnout east; vehicle weighing.

A 121.1 (194.9 km) **F 236.9** (381.2 km) Chulitna highway maintenance camp.

A 121.5 (195.5 km) **F 236.5** (380.6 km) Easy-to-miss large paved double-ended rest area to east with tables, firepits, drinking water, toilet and interpretive bulletin board. Shade trees; cow parsnip grows lush here.

A 123.4 (198.6 km) **F 234.6** (377.5 km) Wooded area with many dead trees covered with "conks" (a term applied to a type of bracket fungus).

A 126.6 (203.7 km) **F 231.4** (372.4 km) Large paved turnout to east.

A 126.8 (204.1 km) **F 231.2** (372.1 km) Large unpaved turnout to west.

A 128.4 (206.6 km) **F 229.6** (369.5 km) Undeveloped parking area below highway by creek.

A 132 (212.4 km) **F 226** (363.7 km) Boundary of Denali State Park (see description next milepost).

A 132.7 (213.6 km) **F 225.3** (362.6 km) Denali State Park entrance sign. This 325,460-acre state park has 48 miles/77.2 km of hiking trails. Camping at Troublesome Creek (**Milepost A 137.3**), Byers Lake (**Milepost A 147**) and Denali View North (**Milepost A 162.7**). Hunting is permitted in the park, but discharge of firearms is prohibited within 0.3 mile of highway, 0.5 mile of a developed facility or 0.5 mile of trail around Byers Lake. ▲

A 132.8 (213.7 km) **F 225.2** (362.4 km) **Chulitna River** bridge. Fishing for grayling, rainbow. Game Management Unit 13E, leaving unit 16A, northbound.

Mt. McKinley Princess Lodge. A stylish, cozy riverside retreat bordering the south side of Denali National Park featuring incredible views of Mount McKinley and the Alaska Range, expansive main lodge, finely appointed guest rooms, array of dining options, tour desk, gift shop. Open mid-May through mid-September. Phone (800) 426-0500 year round. [ADVERTISEMENT]

D & S Alaskan Trail Rides, open mid-

May through mid-September, offers 1 1/2- to

Alaska Veterans Memorial at Milepost A 147.2 honors the armed forces.

(© Bruce M. Herman)

8-hour nature trail rides with majestic views of Mount McKinley and Ruth Glacier. You can only discover these views by riding the best horses and mules in Alaska. It's the ride of a lifetime! Ride our horse-drawn wagon to view Mount McKinley, pan for gold and see reindeer. Summer phone (907) 733-2207; winter (907) 243-2589; fax (907) 243-7951. [ADVERTISEMENT]

A 134.5 (216.5 km) **F 223.5** (359.7 km) **Mary's McKinley View Lodge.** Located on Mary Carey's original homestead. Spectacular view of McKinley from every room, especially the glass-walled restaurant. Mary, famous for Alaskan books, homesteaded before the state park was created. She fought for highway completion to share her magnificent view with travelers. Enjoy dining, browse the gift shop or spend a pleasant night in the modern rooms. Call (907) 733-1555. See display ad this page. [ADVERTISEMENT]

A 134.8 (216.9 km) **F 223.2** (359.2 km) Small turnout to east. Springwater piped to road. *CAUTION: Spring water is not treated. Use at own risk.*

A 135.2 (217.6 km) **F 222.8** (358.6 km) Large paved turnout with toilet and view of 20,320-foot/6,194-m Mount McKinley; a display board here points out peaks. From here northbound for many miles there are views of glaciers on the southern slopes of the Alaska Range to the west. Ruth, Buckskin and Eldridge glaciers are the most conspicuous.

Ruth Glacier trends southeast through the Great Gorge for 31 miles/50 km. The glacier was named in 1903 by F.A. Cook for his daughter. The Great Gorge was named by mountain climbers in the late 1940s. Peaks on either side of the gorge tower up to 5,000 feet/1,500m above Ruth Glacier. The gorge, nicknamed the Grand Canyon of Alaska, opens into Don Sheldon Amphitheater at the head of Ruth Glacier, where the Don Sheldon mountain house sits. Donald E. Sheldon (1921–75) was a well-known bush pilot who helped map, patrol, and aid search and rescue efforts in this area.

Flightseeing trips can be arranged that take you close to Mount McKinley, into the Don Sheldon Amphitheater, through the Great Gorge and beneath the peak of The Mooses Tooth. Inquire at Trapper Creek Inn, **Milepost A 114.8**, or with air taxi operators in Talkeetna and in the national park.

Peaks to be sighted, left to right, along the next 20 miles/32.2 km to the west are: Mount Hunter (elev. 14,573 feet/4,442m); Mount Huntington (elev. 12,240 feet/3,731m); Mount Barrille (elev. 7,650 feet/2,332m); and Mount Dickey (elev. 9,845 feet/3,001m).

A 137.3 (221 km) **F 220.7** (355.1 km) Troublesome Creek bridge. Lower Troublesome Creek state recreation site has 10 campsites, $6/night camping fee per vehicle or annual pass, day-use area with sheltered picnic sites, toilets, water and litter barrels. Lower Troublesome Creek trailhead. This is usually a clear runoff stream, not silted by glacial flour. The stream heads in a lake and flows 14 miles/22.5 km to the Chulitna River. ▲

Troublesome Creek, rainbow, grayling and salmon (king salmon fishing prohibited); June through September.

A 137.6 (221.4 km) **F 220.4** (354.7 km) Upper Troublesome Creek trailhead and parking area. Trails to Byers Lake (15 miles/24 km) and Tarn Point, elev. 2,881 feet/878m (10.8 miles/17.3 km). *NOTE: Trailhead and trail to Mile 5.5 closed from mid-July to Sept. 1 due to the high concentration of bears feeding on spawning salmon.*

A 139.9 (225.1 km) **F 218.1** (351 km) Paved turnout to west.

A 143.9 (231.6 km) **F 214.1** (344.6 km) Bridge over Byers Creek.

A 145.7 (234.5 km) **F 212.3** (341.6 km) Paved turnout to west.

A 147 (236.6 km) **F 211** (339.6 km) **Byers Lake** state campground with 66 sites, $12/night camping fee or annual pass, picnic tables, firepits, water, toilets (wheelchair accessible) and access to Byers Lake (electric motors permitted). Fishing for grayling, burbot, rainbow, lake trout and whitefish. Remote campsite 1.8-mile/2.9-km hike from campground (see directions posted on bulletin board). Hiking trail to Curry Ridge and south to Troublesome Creek. *CAUTION: Bears frequent campground. Keep a clean camp.* ♿▲

Susitna Expeditions offers canoe, kayak and boat rentals in Denali State Park. We also offer guided hiking, kayak and mountain bike tours, firewood bundles and visitor information. Experience Alaska with lifelong Alaskans Kay and Toby Riddell. Our office is located at Byers Lake Campground. Phone (800) 891-6916. [ADVERTISEMENT]

A 147.2 (236.9 km) **F 210.8** (339.2 km) Alaska Veterans Memorial turnoff. This concrete memorial honoring the armed forces includes a park store, spotting scopes, viewing deck, visitor contact station, interpretive kiosk, picnic area and restrooms. Wheelchair accessible. The store is open 9 A.M. to 6 P.M. daily, Memorial Day to Labor Day. ♿

A 155.6 (250.4 km) **F 202.4** (325.7 km) For the next mile northbound, there are views of Eldridge Glacier to the left. The face of the glacier is 6 miles/9.7 km from the road. The Fountain River heads at the terminus of the glacier and flows into the Chulitna.

A 157.7 (253.8 km) **F 200.3** (322.3 km) Small paved turnout to west.

A 159.4 (256.5 km) **F 198.6** (319.6 km) Double-ended paved turnout to west.

A 159.9 (257.3 km) **F 198.1** (318.8 km) Parking area east side of highway by Horseshoe Creek.

A 160.8 (258.8 km) **F 197.2** (317.4 km) The highway makes a steep descent northbound with moderate S-curves to Little Coal Creek.

A 161 (259.1 km) **F 197** (317 km) Large gravel turnout to east.

A 162.4 (261.4 km) **F 195.6** (314.8 km) Large paved turnout to west; Mount McKinley viewpoint.

A 162.7 (261.8 km) **F 195.3** (314.3 km)

Rainbow photographed near Broad Pass, Milepost A 201.3. (Jerrianne Lowther, staff)

Denali View North campground; 20 sites, $10/night, day-use parking, toilets (wheelchair accessible), water, interpretive kiosks, spotting scope, short loop trail. Overlooks Chulitna River. Views of Denali, Mooses Tooth, Mount Huntington and Alaska Range peaks above Hidden River valley.

A 162.8 (262 km) **F 195.2** (314.1 km) Small paved turnout to east. Watch for beaver pond to west northbound. Denali view to north.

A 163.1 (262.5 km) **F 194.9** (313.6 km) Large double-ended paved turnout to west.

A 163.2 (262.6 km) **F 194.8** (313.5 km) Bridge over Little Coal Creek.

Coal Creek; rainbow, grayling and salmon, July through September.

A 163.8 (263.6 km) **F 194.2** (312.5 km) Little Coal Creek trailhead and parking area. According to park rangers, this trail offers easy access (1½-hour hike) to alpine country. It is a 27-mile/43.5-km hike to Byers Lake via Kesugi Ridge.

A 165.6 (266.5 km) **F 192.4** (309.6 km) A small stream passes under the road; paved turnouts on both sides of highway. Good berry picking in the fall.

A 168.5 (271.2 km) **F 189.5** (305 km) Denali State Park boundary sign.

A 169 (272 km) **F 189** (304.2 km) *CAUTION: Railroad crossing.* A solar collector here helps power the warning signals.

Denali State Park boundary (leaving park northbound, entering park southbound).

A 170.3 (274 km) **F 187.7** (302.1 km) Paved viewpoint area to west.

A 171 (275.2 km) **F 187** (300.9 km) There are several small turnouts next 5 miles/8 km northbound.

A 174 (280 km) **F 184** (296.1 km) Bridge over Hurricane Gulch; rest area. From the south end of the bridge, scramble through alders up the east bank of the gulch to find photographers' trail (unmarked). A 0.3-mile/0.4-km trail along edge of Hurricane Gulch offers good views of the bridge span and gulch. A pleasant walk, good berry picking in the fall. *Do not go too near the edge.* Parking areas at both ends of bridge.

Construction costs for the bridge were approximately $1.2 million. The 550-foot/168m deck of the bridge is 260 feet/79m above Hurricane Creek, not as high as the railroad bridge that spans the gulch near the Chulitna River. From this bridge the highway begins a gradual descent northbound to Honolulu Creek.

A 176 (283.2 km) **F 182** (292.9 km) Paved turnout to east. There are several small turnouts next 5 miles/8 km southbound.

A 176.5 (284 km) **F 181.5** (292.1 km) Double-ended gravel turnout to west with view of the Alaska Range. Highway descends long grade northbound.

A 177.8 (286.1 km) **F 180.2** (290 km) Paved turnout and view of eroded bluffs to west.

A 178.1 (286.6 km) **F 179.9** (289.5 km) Bridge over Honolulu Creek. The highway begins a gradual ascent northbound to Broad Pass, the gap in the Alaska Range crossed by both the railroad and highway. Undeveloped parking areas below highway on the creek.

A 179.7 (289.2 km) **F 178.3** (286.9 km) Paved turnout to west by small lake. In early September blueberries are plentiful for the next 25 miles/40 km.

A 180 (289.7 km) **F 178** (286.5 km) Small paved turnout to west by small lake. Short trail to **Mile 180 Lake**, stocked with grayling.

A 183.2 (294.8 km) **F 174.8** (281.3 km) Large paved double-ended turnout to west of highway. Look to the west across the Chulitna River for dramatic view of the Alaska Range.

A 184.5 (296.9 km) **F 173.5** (279.2 km) Paved turnout to west.

A 185 (297.7 km) **F 173** (278.4 km) East Fork DOT/PF highway maintenance station.

A 185.1 (297.9 km) **F 172.9** (278.3 km) Bridge over East Fork Chulitna River.

A 185.6 (298.7 km) **F 172.4** (277.4 km) East Fork rest area (no sign at turnoff) on right northbound. A 0.5-mile/0.8-km paved loop gives access to a gravel picnic area with overnight parking, 23 tables, concrete fireplaces and picnic shelter. The rest area is in a bend of the East Fork Chulitna River amid a healthy growth of Alaskan spruce and birch. Cut wood is often available.

A 186.4 (300 km) **F 171.6** (276.2 km) Small paved turnout to east.

A 187.5 (301.8 km) **F 170.5** (274.4 km) Paved double-ended turnout to west; small paved turnout east side of highway.

A 189.9 (305.6 km) **F 168.1** (270.5 km) Gravel double-ended turnout. Watch for beaver dam to east northbound.

A 191.5 (308.2 km) **F 166.5** (267.9 km) Large paved turnout to west. Look for cotton grass.

A 194.3 (312.7 km) **F 163.7** (263.4 km) *CAUTION: Railroad crossing.*

A 194.5 (313 km) **F 163.5** (263.1 km) Bridge over Middle Fork Chulitna River. Undeveloped parking area southwest of bridge below the highway. *CAUTION: Windy area through Broad Pass.*

A 195 (313.8 km) **F 163** (262.3 km) Entering Broad Pass northbound. Good views of Broad Pass.

A 195.9 (315.3 km) **F 162.1** (260.9 km) Large paved turnout east; mountain views.

A 201.1 (323.6 km) **F 156.9** (252.5 km) Large paved parking area to east with mountain view.

A 201.3 (324 km) **F 156.7** (252.2 km) Summit of Broad Pass (not signed), 2,300 feet/701m. Broad Pass is one of the most beautiful areas on the Parks Highway. A mountain valley, bare in some places, dotted with scrub spruce in others, and surrounded by mountain peaks, it provides a top-of-the-world feeling for the traveler, although it is one of the lowest summits along the North American mountain system. Named in 1898 by George Eldridge and Robert Muldrow, the 2,300-foot/701m pass, sometimes called Caribou Pass, marks the divide between the drainage of rivers and streams that empty into Cook Inlet and those that empty into the Yukon River.

Orange towers of weather service station building west of highway.

A 202.3 (325.6 km) **F 155.7** (250.6 km) Boundary of Matanuska–Susitna and Denali boroughs.

A 203.1 (326.9 km) **F 154.9** (249.3 km) *CAUTION: Railroad crossing.*

A 203.6 (327.7 km) **F 154.4** (248.5 km) Paved parking area with view to east.

A 208 (334.7 km) **F 150** (241.4 km) Turnout to west at end of bridge over Pass Creek; blueberries in season.

A 209.4 (337 km) **F 148.6** (239.1 km) Large gravel parking area to east.

A 209.5 (337.1 km) **F 148.5** (239 km) Bridge over Jack River; paved turnout.

A 209.9 (337.8 km) **F 148.1** (238.3 km) **Junction** of the Parks Highway and the Denali Highway (Alaska Route 8) and turnoff for Cantwell (description follows). Turn west

Flightseeing the Alaska Range and Mount McKinley. (© W. Wright-Diamond Photo)

on the Denali Highway for Cantwell (1.8 miles/2.9 km from junction); turn east for Paxson (see page 517 in the DENALI HIGHWAY section for log).

Cantwell

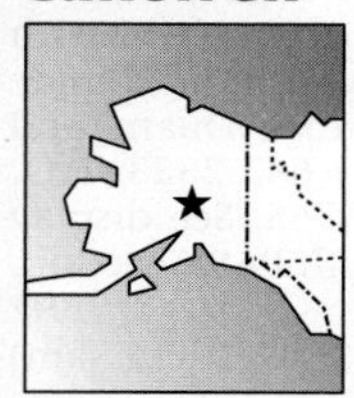

Located 1.8 miles/2.9 km west of Parks Highway, end of the Denali Highway. **Population:** 145. **Emergency Services: Alaska State Troopers,** business phone (907) 768-2202. **Fire Department,** emergency only phone (907) 768-2240. **Ambulance,** phone (907) 768-2982.

Elevation: 2,190 feet/668m. **Private Aircraft:** Cantwell airport, adjacent north; elev. 2,190 feet/668m; length 2,100 feet/640m; gravel, dirt; fuel 100LL.

Cantwell began as a railroad flag stop on the Alaska Railroad. The village was named for the Cantwell River, the original name of the Nenana River, which was named by Lt. Allen in 1885 for Lt. John C. Cantwell of the Revenue-Cutter Service, who explored the Kobuk River region.

Many of Cantwell's businesses are clustered around the intersection of the Denali and Parks highways or on the way into downtown Cantwell. Services include food, gas, lodging and camping. ▲

George Parks Highway Log

(continued)

A 210 (338 km) **F 148** (238.2 km) Cantwell post office (ZIP code 99729).

A 210.2 (338.3 km) **F 147.8** (237.9 km) **Parkway Gift Shop.** See display ad this section.

CANTWELL ADVERTISERS

Atkins Guiding & Flying Service..............Ph. (907) 768-2143
Backwoods Lodge............Ph. (907) 768-2232
Cantwell Lodge.................Ph. (907) 768-2300
Cantwell RV Park..........Mile 209.9 Parks Hwy.

Mount McKinley, also called Denali, is the highest peak in North America at 20,320 feet.

A 210.3 (338.4 km) **F 147.7** (237.7 km) **Cantwell Food Mart.** See display ad this section.

A 210.4 (338.6 km) **F 147.6** (237.5 km) **Cotter's Quality Services.** See display ad this section.

A 211.5 (340.4 km) **F 146.5** (235.8 km) Paved double-ended parking area to west.

A 212.7 (342.3 km) **F 145.3** (233.8 km) Gravel turnout to west by Nenana River. Watch for large beaver dam to west. Slide area northbound.

A 213.9 (344.2 km) **F 144.1** (231.9 km) Paved double-ended turnout to west among tall white spruce and fireweed.

A 215.3 (346.5 km) **F 142.7** (229.6 km) Access road to Nenana River, which parallels the highway northbound.

A 215.7 (347.1 km) **F 142.3** (229 km) First bridge northbound over the Nenana River. Highway narrows northbound.

A 216.2 (347.9 km) **F 141.8** (228.2 km) Entering Game Management Unit 20A and leaving unit 13E northbound.

A 216.3 (348.1 km) **F 141.7** (228 km) Paved double-ended turnout to west. Good spot for photos of Panorama Mountain (elev. 5,778 feet/1,761m), the prominent peak visible to the east.

A 217.6 (350.2 km) **F 140.4** (225.9 km) Small gravel turnout to west.

A 218.6 (351.8 km) **F 139.4** (224.3 km) Paved double-ended turnout to west with beautiful view of Nenana River.

A 219 (352.4 km) **F 139** (223.7 km) Slide area: Watch for rocks next 0.4 mile/0.6 km northbound.

A 219.8 (353.7 km) **F 138.2** (222.4 km) Paved double-ended turnout to west overlooking Nenana River.

A 220 (354 km) **F 138** (222.1 km) Slime Creek.

A 220.2 (354.4 km) **F 137.8** (221.8 km) Wide gravel turnout to west.

A 222.2 (357.6 km) **F 135.8** (218.5 km) Large paved double-ended turnout to west beside Nenana River slough. Snow poles beside roadway guide snowplows in winter.

Parks Highway parallels the Nenana River between Cantwell and Nenana.
(© Lee Foster)

A 223.9 (360.3 km) **F 134.1** (215.8 km) **Carlo Creek Lodge.** Located 12 miles south of Denali Park entrance. 32 wooded acres bordered by beautiful Carlo Creek, the Nenana River and Denali National Park. Cozy creekside log cabins with own bathroom, showers. RV park, dump station, potable water, propane. Clean bathroom, showers. Dishwashing facility. Individual sheltered tent sites each with picnic table and firepit. Unique gift shop. Small store. Information. Pay phone. You won't be disappointed. It's a beautiful place to be. HC 2, Box 1530, Healy, AK 99743. (907) 683-2576, 683-2573. [ADVERTISEMENT] ▲

A 224 (360.5 km) **F 134** (215.7 km) **The Perch.** A beautiful, established restaurant-bar perched on a private hill. Spectacular dining, specializes in freshly baked bread,

seafood and steaks. Also, take-out giant cinnamon rolls. Breakfast 6 A.M. to 11:30 A.M.; lunch 11:30 A.M. to 2 P.M.; dinner 5 P.M. to 10 P.M., open daily mid-May through September; and Friday, Saturday, Sunday October through May. Sleeping cabins with central bath, some with private baths, beside Carlo Creek. Owners/operators, Duane and Leslie Watters. Phone (907) 683-2523. P.O. Box 53, Denali Park, AK 99755. See display ad in the DENALI NATIONAL PARK section. [ADVERTISEMENT] MP

A 224 (360.5 km) **F 134** (215.7 km) Bridge over Carlo Creek.

McKinley Creekside Cabins. Scenic, peaceful setting on the banks of Carlo Creek. Large cabins with private bath; economy cabins with central bath. Home-style cafe and bakery, gourmet espresso bar, tour desk. Reservations: (888) 5-DENALI, or (907) 683-2277. Fax (907) 683-1558. P.O. Box 89, Denali National Park, AK 99755. [ADVERTISEMENT]

A 225 (362.1 km) **F 133** (214 km) Beautiful mountain views southbound.

A 226 (363.7 km) **F 132** (212.4 km) Fang

Mountain (elev. 6,736 feet/2,053m) may be visible to the west through the slash in the mountains.

A 229 (368.5 km) **F 129** (207.6 km) **Denali Backcountry Lodge.** Stop at Denali Cabins (located at **Milepost 229**) and visit the sales office for Denali Backcountry Lodge. The wilderness vacation lodge is for those who want to escape the park's crowded entrance and immerse themselves deep within Denali National Park for a few days. Located at the end of the 97-mile park road, Denali Backcountry Lodge features full-service accommodations, dining room and lounge. One- to 4-night stays include round-trip transportation from the train depot, all meals and lodging, guided hikes, wildlife viewing, bicycling, photography and natural history programs. Many famous naturalists are found staying at the lodge and occasionally they conduct special presentations. Credit cards accepted and discounts are given for last-minute bookings if space is available. P.O. Box 189, Denali National Park, AK 99755. Internet: www.denalilodge.com. Phone (800) 841-0692. [ADVERTISEMENT]

Denali Cabins. Private cabins with bath, outdoor hot tubs, complimentary coffee and extensive information about Denali National Park. Restaurant on premises. Seasonal

service mid-May through mid-September. VISA, MasterCard accepted. (907) 258-0134 (winter) or (907) 683-2643 (summer). Brochure: 200 W. 34th Ave., #362, Anchorage, AK 99503. Fax (907) 243-2062 or summer (907) 683-2595. See display ad in DENALI NATIONAL PARK section. [ADVERTISEMENT]

A 229.2 (368.8 km) **F 128.8** (207.3 km) Private airstrip. Flightseeing service.

Denali Air, Inc. Fly closer to Denali's beauty on our 1-hour aerial tour of Mount McKinley/Denali National Park. Our private airstrip is the closest to Denali Park hotels

and the Alaska Range, offering the best tour and value. A pioneer service with the most experienced pilots. Two person minimum. Reservations: (907) 683-2261. See display ad in the DENALI NATIONAL PARK section. [ADVERTISEMENT]

A 229.7 (369.7 km) **F 128.3** (206.5 km) Paved turnout to west.

A 231.1 (371.9 km) **F 126.9** (204.2 km) **McKinley Village Lodge** is convenient to all Denali National Park activities. Located on a quiet stretch of the Nenana River, the 50-room lodge is complete with a lovely cafe, lounge, gift shop and tour desk to arrange area tour and rafting activities. Phone (800) 276-7234; in Anchorage (907) 276-7234. [ADVERTISEMENT]

Denali Grizzly Bear Cabins & Campground. South boundary Denali National Park. Campground AAA-approved. Drive directly to your individual kitchen, sleeping or tent cabin with its old-time Alaskan atmosphere overlooking scenic Nenana River. Two conveniently located buildings with toilets, sinks, coin-operated hot showers. Advance reservations suggested. Tenting and RV campsite available in peaceful wooded areas. Hookups. Propane, laundromat. Caravans welcome! Hot coffee and rolls, ice cream, snacks, groceries, ice, liquor store, Alaskan gifts, tour desk. VISA, MasterCard, Discover accepted. Owned and operated by pioneer Alaskan family. Reservations (907) 683-2696 (summer); (907) 683-1337 (winter). Internet: www.alaskaone.com/dengrzly/index.htm. See display ad in DENALI NATIONAL PARK section. MP ▲

Denali River Cabins. Located on the banks of the Nenana River, 5 minutes away from the Visitor Center, our cedar cabin resort offers the ideal base for your Denali Park experience. Our cabins are situated both on and off river with an extra large hot tub and riverside sauna. Ask about our free sauna club T-shirts. The new, cozy cedar cabins are fully furnished, all with private bath. Our new Starr Lodge guest center is a cozy place to relax and enjoy the great indoors. We feature works by Alaskan artists represented by the House of Wood Art Gallery. We also feature nightly programs for our guests. There are 3 sun decks right on the riverbank, looking into Denali Park. We also offer exclusive Fairbanks shuttle service and Kantishna tours inside Denali National Park. Phone (907) 683-2500 for reservations year-round or www.denalirivercabins.com. [ADVERTISEMENT] ▲

A 231.3 (372.2 km) **F 126.7** (203.9 km) Crabb's Crossing, second bridge northbound over the Nenana River. Small paved turnout with wide shoulders west side of highway.

At the north end of this bridge is the boundary of Denali National Park and Preserve. From here north for 6.8 miles/10.9 km the Parks Highway is within the boundaries of the park and travelers must abide by park rules. No discharge of firearms permitted.

A 233.1 (375.1 km) **F 124.9** (201 km) Gravel turnout to east.

A 234.1 (376.7 km) **F 123.9** (199.4 km) Double-ended turnout with litter barrels to east; scenic viewpoint. No overnight parking or camping. Mount Fellows (elev. 4,476 feet/

1,364m) to the east. The constantly changing shadows make this an excellent camera subject. Exceptionally beautiful in the evening. To the southeast stands Pyramid Peak (elev. 5,201 feet/1,585m).

A 235.1 (378.4 km) **F 122.9** (197.8 km) *CAUTION: Railroad crossing.* Solar panels and wind generators provide power for crossing signals. Watch for frost heaves and dips.

A 236.7 (380.9 km) **F 121.3** (195.2 km) Alaska Railroad crosses over highway. From this point the highway begins a steep descent northbound to Riley Creek.

A 237.2 (381.7 km) **F 120.8** (194.4 km) Riley Creek bridge.

A 237.3 (381.9 km) **F 120.7** (194.2 km) Entrance to **DENALI NATIONAL PARK AND PRESERVE** (formerly Mount McKinley National Park) to west. Fresh water fill-up hose and dump station 0.2 mile/0.3 km from junction on Park Road; Visitor Center is 0.5 mile/0.8 km from the highway junction. Campsites within the park are available on a first-come, first-served basis; sign up at the visitor center. You may also pick up schedules for the shuttle bus service at the visitor center (private vehicle access to the park is restricted). See DENALI NATIONAL PARK section for details.

Clusters of highway businesses north and south of the park entrance between Cantwell and Healy offer a variety of services to the highway traveler and park visitor. Services include river running, gift shops, accommodations, restaurants and entertainment.

A 238 (383 km) **F 120** (193.4 km) Third bridge northbound over the Nenana River. Era Helicopters office is located here.

The 4.8 miles/7.7 km of road and 7 bridges in the rugged Nenana Canyon cost $7.7 million to build. Sugarloaf Mountain (elev. 4,450 feet/1,356m), to the east, is closed to the hunting of Dall sheep, which are regularly sighted in the early and late summer months. Mount Healy (elev. 5,716 feet/1,742m) is to the west.

Southbound for 6.8 miles/10.9 km the Parks Highway is within the boundaries of Denali National Park and Preserve and travelers must abide by park rules. No discharge of firearms.

A 238.1 (383.2 km) **F 119.9** (193 km) **Denali Raft Adventures.** Come with the original Nenana River rafters! Paddleboats too! Age 5 or older welcome, 7 departures daily. Whitewater or scenic floats. Get away

to untouched wilderness! 2-hour, 4-hour, full-day and overnight trips are available. See display ad in DENALI NATIONAL PARK section. Phone (907) 683-2234. Internet: www.alaskaone.com/denraft. VISA, MasterCard accepted. [ADVERTISEMENT] MP

A 238.3 (383.5 km) **F 119.7** (192.6 km) Kingfisher Creek.

A 238.4 (383.6 km) **F 119.6** (192.5 km) **Denali Bluffs Hotel.** AAA approved. The newest and closest hotel to the Denali National Park and Preserve entrance. 112 rooms; each room features 2 double beds, TVs, phones, refrigerators, in-room coffee. Spectacular views of the Alaska Range. The lodge features a large stone fireplace and cathedral ceilings. There are comfortable sitting areas inside the lodge or outside on the deck to enjoy the panoramic views. Gift shop and coin-operated laundry. Shuttle service to all area facilities. Complete tour and activity desk. Wheelchair accessible. Open mid-May through mid-September. Credit cards accepted. P.O. Box 72460, Fairbanks, AK 99707. Phone (907) 683-7000. Fax (907) 683-7500. E-mail: dbh@polarnet.com. Internet: www2.polarnet.com/~dbh. See display ad in the DENALI NATIONAL PARK section. [ADVERTISEMENT] MP ♿

Denali River View Inn. Beautiful views of the park and sounds of the river. Private bath, attractive rooms, TVs, excellent service and transportation. Pay phone. Conveniently located. Major credit cards. For reservations and information write P.O. Box 49M, Denali Park, AK 99755. Phone (907) 683-2663. Fax (907) 683-7433. See display ad in the DENALI NATIONAL PARK section. [ADVERTISEMENT]

A 238.5 (383.8 km) **F 119.5** (192.3 km) Alaska flag display features a 10-by-15-foot/3-by-5-m state flag and plaques detailing history of flag design and song.

A 238.5 (383.8 km) **F 119.5** (192.3 km) **Denali Princess Lodge.** Riverside lodging near the entrance to Denali National Park featuring spectacular park and Nenana River views, several dining options including Mt. McK's dinner theatre, tour desk, gift shop, complimentary shuttle to rail depot and park activities. Open mid-May through mid-September. Phone (800) 426-0500 year-round. [ADVERTISEMENT]

McKinley/Denali Steakhouse and Salmon Bake. Home-style Alaskan restaurant featuring char-broiled burgers, steaks, sandwiches, chicken, salmon, halibut and beef ribs. Extensive salad bar, homemade

soups. Cocktails. Sourdough breakfasts. Heated indoor seating. Free shuttle from all local hotels. Large selection of T-shirts and sweatshirts in our upstairs gift shop. Open daily 5 A.M. to 11 P.M. in summer. Phone (907) 683-2733. Internet: www.denalipark.com. E-mail: kevin@denalipark.com. See display ad in the DENALI NATIONAL PARK section. [ADVERTISEMENT]

McKinley/Denali Gift Shop. Largest gift shop in park area—upstairs at McKinley/Denali Steakhouse and Salmon Bake. Largest selection of Mount McKinley and Denali National Park T-shirts and sweatshirts. Hundreds of souvenirs and gifts. Photo calendars and postcards. Open 5 A.M. to 11 P.M. Call for free shuttle service. [ADVERTISEMENT]

McKinley/Denali Cabins. Economy tent cabins with electric heat and lights from $65. Beds, linens, blankets. Some cabins with private baths. Pay phone. Closest full-service facility to park entrance, wildlife shuttles. Close to raft trips, store, gift shop, gas. Shuttle to visitor center, railroad depot available. Free visitor information. Reservations: (907) 683-2258 or 683-2733 or write Box 90M, Denali Park, AK 99755. Internet: www.denalipark.com. E-mail: kevin@denalipark.com. See display ad in DENALI NATIONAL PARK section. [ADVERTISEMENT] MP

Denali Crow's Nest Log Cabins and the Overlook Bar & Grill. Open mid-May to mid-September, offering the finest view in area. Close to park entrance. Authentic Alaska log cabins with hotel comforts; all

rooms with private bath. Courtesy transportation. Hot tub, tour bookings. Dine on steaks, seafood, burgers, salmon and halibut indoors or on the deck at The Overlook Bar & Grill. 64 varieties of beer, 9 draft beers; meals 11 A.M. to 11 P.M. Bar open till midnight. For restaurant courtesy shuttle from all local hotels, call (907) 683-2723, fax (907) 683-2323. See display ad in DENALI NATIONAL PARK section. [ADVERTISEMENT] MP

Denali Wilderness Lodge. Alaska's historic fly-in wilderness lodge. We're often called "the most remote hotel in America." Authentic bush homestead nestled in the pristine Wood River Valley just outside Denali National Park. Accessible only by spectacular bush plane flights over the mountains and glaciers of the Alaska Range.

Comfortable accommodations, delicious meals, naturalist programs, flightseeing, horseback riding, nature/photo walks and hikes, bird watching, wildlife museum. Experience all the beauty of wilderness Alaska! Overnight packages and day trips available. Free color brochure. Phone (800) 541-9779. See display ad in DENALI NATIONAL PARK section. [ADVERTISEMENT]

A 238.7 (384.1 km) **F 119.3** (192 km) **Denali Windsong Lodge.** Specialists at serving the highway traveler. 48 clean, modern rooms with full bath, satellite TV and beautiful mountain views from every

room. Located just north of park entrance, near all restaurants and activities. Our friendly staff and reasonable rates make this the place to stay. Phone (800) 208-0200 or (907) 683-1240. See display ad in DENALI NATIONAL PARK section. [ADVERTISEMENT]

A 238.8 (384.3 km) **F 119.2** (191.8 km) **McKinley Raft Tours Inc.** Scenic and whitewater trips on the Nenana River. Several departures daily. Float the eastern boundary of Denali National Park. An exhilarating whitewater adventure you'll remember. Local transportation available. Reservations suggested. MasterCard, VISA, American

Express, Discover accepted. Call (907) 683-2392. See display ad in DENALI NATIONAL PARK section. [ADVERTISEMENT]

Sourdough Cabins. Enjoy the beauty of Denali National Park from your individual cabin set in a spruce forest one mile from the park. The cabins offer comfortable accommodations in a warm atmosphere, all with private bath and within walking distance to all services. Courtesy transportation available. May to September. Phone (907) 683-2773, fax (907) 683-2357. VISA, MasterCard, American Express accepted. See display ad in DENALI NATIONAL PARK section. [ADVERTISEMENT] ▲

A 238.9 (384.5 km) **F 119.1** (191.7 km) **Denali Outdoor Center.** Denali's most diversified river outfitter. Oarboats, paddleboats, inflatable kayak tours and comprehensive whitewater kayak school. Whitewater or scenic wilderness trips daily. 2-hour, 4-hour, 1/2-day guided trips. All gear and custom drysuits provided! Mountain bike rentals. Ages 5 and up. Call for reservations (907) 683-1925. Major credit cards accepted. [ADVERTISEMENT] MP

A 239 (384.6 km) **F 119** (191.5 km) **Northern Lights Theatre and Gift Shop.** Come experience the Northern Lights on a 34-foot screen. This presentation is one-of-a-kind, entertaining and informative. Stop by for show times and tickets. Don't miss Denali's largest gift shop in a beautiful, natural log building, specializing in quality Alaskan gifts. Full mount world-class polar bear on display. Groceries at Denali General

Store. Located 1.5 miles north of park entrance. Large parking area. Don't miss this attraction! P.O. Box 65, Denali Park, AK 99755. Phone (907) 683-4000. Internet: www.akpub.com/akht/lights.html. E-mail: lights@mail.denali.k12.ak.us. [ADVERTISEMENT]

A 239.1 (384.8 km) **F 118.9** (191.3 km) **McKinley Chalet Resort.** Enjoy all the amenities of home at McKinley Chalet Resort. Comfortable mini-suites overlook the beautiful Nenana River. You'll find fine dining, a relaxing lounge, unique gifts, local artist gallery and full-service tour desk. The Chalet Center Cafe specializes in fresh muffins, salads, soup, sandwiches and a specialty drink bar. The Resort is also home to Alaska Cabin Nite Dinner Theater and Alaska Raft Adventures. Phone (800) 276-7234, in Anchorage, 276-7234. [ADVERTISEMENT]

Alaska Cabin Night Dinner Theater has 2 evening shows. Expect an all-you-can-eat dinner featuring salmon and ribs, served family style, followed by a rousing musical revue depicting the exciting gold rush days. Located at McKinley Chalet Resort in a beautiful handcrafted log cabin. For reservations call (800) 276-7234; in Anchorage 276-7234 or stop by the tour desk located in the lobby of the McKinley Chalet Resort. [ADVERTISEMENT]

Alaska Raft Adventures offers 2 wonderful rafting experiences complete with experienced guides and all equipment needed to enjoy a great Nenana River adventure. Our Wilderness Run floats through a glacial valley offering unparalleled scenery. Our Canyon Run offers exciting whitewater action (class III & IV rapids). Both adventures depart 3 times daily, and courtesy transportation is available between area hotels and the Alaska Railroad Depot. Allow for a total of 3 hours. Call (800) 276-7234; in Anchorage (907) 276-7234 or stop by the tour desk at the McKinley Chalet Resort. [ADVERTISEMENT]

A 240.1 (386.4 km) **F 117.9** (189.7 km) Bridge over Ice Worm Gulch. *CAUTION: Rock slide area. Slow down.* High winds in the Nenana Canyon can make this stretch of road dangerous for campers and motorhomes.

WARNING: The highway has many sharp curves. Do not park along the highway. Use the many parking areas provided.

A 240.2 (386.6 km) **F 117.8** (189.6 km) Hornet Creek bridge. Paved double-ended turnout to west beside Nenana River.

A 240.5 (387 km) **F 117.5** (189.1 km) Private RV park. ▲

A 240.7 (387.4 km) **F 117.3** (188.8 km) Paved double-ended turnout to west beside river.

A 241 (387.7 km) **F 117** (188.3 km) Paved turnout to west.

A 241.2 (388.2 km) **F 116.8** (188 km) Bridge over Fox Creek; gravel road to creek. Large gravel turnout to west. Slide area next 0.4 mile/0.6 km northbound.

A 241.7 (389 km) **F 116.3** (187.2 km) Large gravel turnout to west.

A 242.3 (389.9 km) **F 115.7** (186.2 km) Paved double-ended turnout to west.

A 242.4 (390.1 km) **F 115.6** (186 km) Dragonfly Creek bridge; paved double-ended turnout to west.

A 242.8 (390.7 km) **F 115.2** (185.4 km) Paved double-ended turnout to west. *CAUTION: Windy area next mile northbound.*

A 242.9 (390.9 km) **F 115.1** (185.2 km) Moody Bridge. This 4th bridge northbound over the Nenana River measures 174 feet/53m from its deck to the bottom of the canyon. Dall sheep can be spotted from the bridge. Entering Game Management Unit 20A northbound, 20C southbound.

A 243.6 (392 km) **F 114.4** (184.1 km) Bridge over Bison Gulch. Paved viewpoint to east. A steep grade follows northbound, end wind area.

A 244.1 (392.8 km) **F 113.9** (183.3 km) Paved turnout to east. Watch for frost heaves next 1 mile/1.6 km northbound.

A 244.6 (393.6 km) **F 113.4** (182.5 km) Bridge over Antler Creek.

A 245.1 (394.4 km) **F 112.9** (181.7 km) **Denali RV Park & Motel.** 90 full and partial RV hookups, 30-amp electric, laundry, gift shop. Level sites, pull-throughs, easy highway access. Individual restrooms with private showers, flush toilets. Dump station. Caravans welcome! 14 motel rooms: Central bath $49, private bath $69, family units with full kitchen and TVs $99. Outdoor cooking area, covered meeting area, pay phones. 25 percent off extra RV nights. Low season rates for motel ($39 to $79) and RV sites ($10 dry to $14 full hookups) before June 8th and after August 14th. Tour booking and information. Located 8 miles north of park entrance. Close to all park facilities. Beautiful mountain views. Hiking trails. Reasonable rates. VISA/MasterCard/Discover. Box 155, Denali Park, AK 99755. Phone (907) 683-1500, (800) 478-1501. See display ad in the DENALI NATIONAL PARK section. [ADVERTISEMENT] ▲

A 245.6 (395.2 km) **F 112.4** (180.9 km) Watch for rough road, frost heaves and dips 0.4 mile/0.6 km northbound.

A 246.9 (397.3 km) **F 111.1** (178.8 km) Paved turnout to east and beautiful view of Healy area.

A 247 (397.5 km) **F 111** (178.6 km) Side road leads 1 mile/1.6 km to **Otto Lake**, 5 miles/8 km to Black Diamond Coal Mine. Primitive parking area on lakeshore (0.8-mile/1.3-km drive in) with toilet, litter barrels, shallow boat launch. Stocked with rainbow and coho. Denali hostel. Access to bed and breakfasts, golf driving range and RV park. ▲

Homestead Bed and Breakfast, Mile 1.3 Otto Lake Road. Spectacular view overlooking Otto Lake. Old-fashioned comfort and hospitality. Very comfortable beds. Homestyle hearty breakfasts. Smoke-free home. Hiking nearby. Paddle boats and canoes for rent locally. Host Evalyn Morrison. (907) 683-2575. P.O. Box 478, Healy, AK 99743. [ADVERTISEMENT]

Otto Lake Bed & Breakfast. Beautiful lakeside Alaska Range views. Quilt-topped queen, double or twin beds. Private or shared baths. Sitting area with microwave, refrigerator, TV/VCR, library. Open year-round. VISA, MasterCard accepted. Phone (907) 683-2339. Fax (907) 683-2336. Your

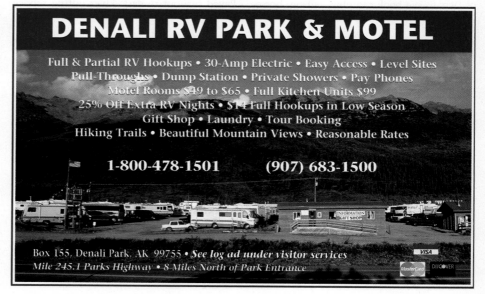

Vivid sunset on Otto Lake. (© Rick Driskell)

hosts, Lyle and Beth Westphal, P.O. Box 45, Healy, AK 99743. [ADVERTISEMENT]

Otto Lake R.V. Park and Campground. Beautiful mountain views from wooded lakeside RV and tent sites, 1/2 mile west of Parks Highway on Otto Lake Road. Spacious and secluded sites with picnic tables, firepits, firewood, potable water, toilets, dump station and pay phone. Boat rentals. Family camping at its best, not a gravel strip. Located 9.7 miles north of Denali National Park entrance. [ADVERTISEMENT] ▲

A 248.3 (399.6 km) **F 109.7** (176.5 km) **Evans Industries Inc.** See display ad this section.

A 248.4 (399.8 km) **F 109.6** (176.4 km) **McKinley RV & Campground.** One of the nicest campgrounds around; 89 sites and utilities available. Come let our family help your family have a great vacation. We will help you experience the sights and sounds of Denali. We book camping, rafting, horseback riding, dinner, flightseeing and shows.

We offer our guests free showers, dump station, wooded landscape, a movie on Alaska, miniature golf, fax service and propane. Caravans/groups welcome. Peaceful setting, spectacular view and beautiful open skies. Come let us make you feel at home. Reservations recommended. Write Box 340MP, Healy, AK 99743. Phone: (907) 683-2379. Fax: (907) 683-2281. National (800) 478-AKOA. See display ad in the DENALI NATIONAL PARK section. [ADVERTISEMENT] ▲

A 248.5 (399.9 km) **F 109.5** (176.2 km) Paved turnout to east. River rafting service office.

Nenana Raft Adventures. Day trips on the Nenana River. Multi-day expeditions on rivers throughout Alaska. We provide full drysuits for all clients. Paddle rafting available. Call (800) 789-RAFT or (907) 683-7238. Write P.O. Box 500, Healy, AK 99743. Office next to McKinley RV & Campground. See display ad, DENALI NATIONAL PARK section. [ADVERTISEMENT]

A 248.7 (400.2 km) **F 109.3** (175.9 km) **Junction** with spur road to community of Healy (see description following **Milepost A 248.8**). Homes and businesses of this Alaska community are dispersed along the highway from here north to **Milepost A 249.6** and in the first mile east along the spur road toward the Nenana River. Hotel and motel accommodations are available at the highway junction, and several bed and breakfasts are located along the spur road.

Totem Inn. Full-service facility year-round. Deluxe, mid-range and economy rooms, restaurant, lounge and gift shop. Satellite TV and laundry facilities for guests. 24-hour access to pay telephones. Good food, reasonable rates, Alaskan hospitality. MasterCard/VISA/Discover. Restaurant (907) 683-2420. Motel/fax (907) 683-2384. [ADVERTISEMENT]

A 248.8 (400.4 km) **F 109.2** (175.7 km) North side of Healy Spur Road intersection.

Denali North Star Inn. Located at Healy intersection, Mile 248.8 Parks Highway. Reasonably priced rooms, finest food and cocktail lounge in Denali Park area. Information and reservations for Denali Park area tours. Shuttle service, Alaskan gifts, beauty salon, barber shop, tanning beds. Recreation and exercise areas, saunas, self-service laundry. 11 miles to Denali Park entrance. (800) 684-1560. See display ad in DENALI NATIONAL PARK section. [ADVERTISEMENT]

Stampede Lodge and Bushmaster Grill. Historic Alaskan lodge and restaurant recently remodeled. Warm, comfortable atmosphere, located 10 minutes from the park entrance. Private baths and phones in all rooms. Free train station pickup. Restaurant open 6 A.M.–10 P.M. Denali's best value—all rooms $79–89. Phone (800) 478-2370, fax (907) 683-2243. [ADVERTISEMENT] MP

Healy

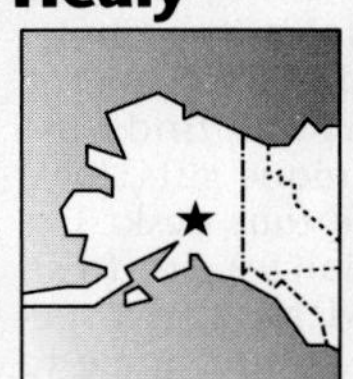

Located on a spur road just east of the Parks Highway **junction. Population:** 605. **Emergency Services: Alaska State Troopers,** phone (907) 683-2232. **Fire Department,** Tri–Valley Volunteer Fire Dept., phone 911 or (907) 683-2223. **Clinic,** Healy Clinic, located on 2nd floor of Tri–Valley Community Center at Mile 0.5 Healy Spur Road, phone (907) 683-2211 or 911 (open 24 hours).

Visitor Information: Available at the Healy Senior Center, located on Healy Spur Road behind the grocery store. Open 11 A.M. to 7 P.M., year-round; phone (907) 683-1317.

Elevation: 1,294 feet/394m. **Radio:** KUAC-FM 101.7. **Private Aircraft:** Healy River airstrip adjacent north; length 2,800 feet/853m; paved; unattended.

Healy's power plant has the distinction of being the largest coal-fired steam plant in Alaska, as well as the only mine-mouth power plant. This plant is part of the Golden Valley Electric Assoc., which furnishes electric power for Fairbanks and vicinity. The Fairbanks–Tanana Valley area uses primarily coal and also oil to meet its electrical needs.

Across the Nenana River lie the mining settlements of Suntrana and Usibelli. Dry Creek, Healy and Nenana river valleys comprise the area referred to as Tri–Valley. Coal mining began here in 1918 and has grown to become Alaska's largest coal mining operation. Usibelli Coal Mine, the state's only commercial coal mine, mines about 800,000 tons of coal a year, supplying South Korea, the University of Alaska, the military and other Fairbanks-area utilities. The Usibelli Coal Mine began a successful reclamation program in 1971; Dall sheep now graze where there was once evidence only of strip mining.

From the highway, you may see a 33-cubic-yard walking dragline (named Ace in the Hole by local schoolchildren in a contest) removing the soil, or overburden, to expose the coal seams. This 4,275,000-lb. machine, erected in 1978, moves an average of 24,000 cubic yards each 24 hours. Private vehicles are not allowed into the mining area and no tours are available.

Denali Suites. Located 15 minutes north of entrance to Denali National Park on Healy Spur Road. Units include 2 or 3 bedrooms, kitchen and dining area, living room with queen-sized hide-a-bed, TV and VCR, and private baths. Coin-operated laundry facilities. Clean, comfortable, affordable. Each unit accommodates up to 6 people, one accommodates 8, with 2 private baths; families welcome. VISA, MasterCard, Discover. Open all year. Call (907) 683-2848 or write Box 393, Healy, AK 99743. E-mail: bharris@mail.denali.k12.ak.us. Internet: www.alaskaone.com/densuites. See display ad in the DENALI NATIONAL PARK section. [ADVERTISEMENT] *MP*

Dry Creek Bed & Breakfast is also home to D & J Kennels. Open year-round. Dogsled rides and demonstrations also available by appointment. Complete breakfast, clean rooms, reasonable rates with Alaskan hospitality. VISA and MasterCard accepted. For reservations phone (907) 683-2386 (also fax) or write Dry Creek B&B, Box 371, Healy, AK 99743. [ADVERTISEMENT]

GrandView Bed & Breakfast. Located 12 miles from the entrance to Denali National Park. Relax and enjoy the spectacular view of the Alaska Range. Deck, barbecue, sitting area. Continental breakfast. Open year-round. VISA/MasterCard. Write GrandView Bed & Breakfast, Box 109, Healy, AK 99743 or call (907) 683-2468. See display ad in the DENALI NATIONAL PARK section. [ADVERTISEMENT]

Greyfox Manor, located at Mile 0.75 Healy Spur Road, is a comfortable, spacious, smoke-free home with a family atmosphere, conveniently situated near Denali National Park. Offering a peaceful respite for weary travelers. Full breakfast served daily. Early continental breakfasts available. Open year-round. Credit cards accepted. Phone (907) 683-2419 for reservations. [ADVERTISEMENT]

Parks Highway Log

(continued)

A 248.8 (400.4 km) **F 109.2** (175.7 km) Healy spur road junction, north side of intersection; food and lodging.

A 249 (400.7 km) **F 109** (175.4 km) Suntrana Road, post office and Tri–Valley School.

A 249.2 (401 km) **F 108.8** (175.1 km) **Larry's Healy Tesoro.** See display ad this section.

A 249.3 (401.2 km) **F 108.7** (174.9 km) Dry Creek Bridge No. 1.

HEALY ADVERTISERS

Denali North Star Inn	Mile 248.8 Parks Hwy.
Denali Suites	Ph. (907) 683-2848
Dry Creek Bed & Breakfast	Ph. (907) 683-2386
GrandView Bed & Breakfast	Ph. (907) 683-2468
Greyfox Manor	Ph. (907) 683-2419
Pat & Windell's Bed and Breakfast	Ph. (907) 683-2472
Stampede Lodge	Mile 248.8 Parks Hwy.
Totem Inn	Ph. (907) 683-2384

A 249.4 (401.4 km) **F 108.6** (174.8 km) Lester Road.

A 249.5 (401.5 km) **F 108.5** (174.6 km) **Motel Nord Haven.** Built in 1994 with your motoring family in mind. West side of highway in the trees. Peaceful and secluded. 12 miles north of Denali National Park entrance. All rooms have queen beds, private bath, television and telephone. Open year-round. MasterCard, VISA, American Express. Phone (907) 683-4500. Fax (907) 683-4503. [ADVERTISEMENT]

A 249.8 (402 km) **F 108.2** (174.1 km) Dry Creek Bridge No. 2. Good berry picking area first part of August.

A 251.1 (404.1 km) **F 106.9** (172 km) Stampede Road to west. Lignite Road to east.

Earth Song Lodge, Denali's natural retreat. Enjoy the Denali Park area without the crowds. Ten charming log cabins with private baths. Evening programs by staff naturalist at comfortable central lodge. Dog sled demonstrations and rides. Continental breakfast available. Located on scenic and historic Stampede Road, just north of the park. Wonderful views of Denali and wildlife. Open year-round. Phone/fax (907) 683-2863. P.O. Box 89-MP, Healy, AK 99743. Internet: www.alaskaone.com/earthsong. E-mail: earthsong@mail.denali.k12.ak.us. See display ad in the DENALI NATIONAL PARK section. [ADVERTISEMENT]

A 251.2 (404.3 km) **F 106.8** (171.9 km) Paved turnout to west. Coal seams visible in bluff to east. Cotton grass and lupine along roadside in June, fireweed in July.

A 252.4 (406.2 km) **F 105.6** (169.9 km) Gravel turnout to west.

A 252.5 (406.4 km) **F 105.5** (169.8 km) Bridge over **Panguingue Creek**; turnout at end. Moderate success fishing for grayling. This stream, which flows 8 miles/13 km to the Nenana River, was named for a Philippine card game.

CAUTION: Watch for frost heaves northbound.

A 253.3 (407.6 km) **F 104.7** (168.5 km) **Ridgetop Cabins.** See display ad this section.

A 259.4 (417.5 km) **F 98.6** (158.7 km) Large paved turnout to east. Views of Rex Dome to the northeast. Walker and Jumbo domes to the east. Liberty Bell mining area lies between the peaks and highway.

A 261.1 (420.2 km) **F 96.9** (155.9 km) Gravel turnout to east. Look for bank swallows, small brown birds that nest in clay and sand banks near streams and along highways. Pond with beaver dam to west.

A 262 (421.6 km) **F 96** (154.5 km) Watch for rough patches in pavement and gravel shoulders, northbound. Watch for frost heaves southbound.

A 263 (423.2 km) **F 95** (152.9 km) Small gravel turnout to east. Wildflowers include sweet pea and oxytrope.

A 264.5 (425.7 km) **F 93.5** (150.5 km) Paved turnout to west.

A 269 (432.9 km) **F 89** (143.2 km) June Creek rest area and picnic spot to east; large gravel parking area. Gravel road leads down to lower parking area on June Creek (trailers and large RVs check turnaround space before driving down). Wooden stairs lead up to the picnic spot and a view of the Nenana River. There are picnic tables, fireplaces, toilets, a litter bin and a sheltered table. Cut wood may be available.

A 269.3 (433.4 km) **F 88.7** (142.8 km) Bridge over Bear Creek. Gravel turnout to east.

A 271.4 (436.8 km) **F 86.6** (139.4 km) Paved turnout to west. Highway northbound leads through boggy area with few turnouts.

A 275.6 (443.5 km) **F 82.4** (132.6 km) Entering Game Management Unit 20A northbound, 20C southbound.

A 275.8 (443.9 km) **F 82.2** (132.3 km) Rex Bridge over Nenana River.

A 276 (444.2 km) **F 82** (132 km) **Tatlanika Trading Co.** Located in a beautiful pristine wilderness setting. Tent sites and RV parking with electricity, water, dump station, showers. 39 miles from Denali National Park on the Nenana River. Our gift shop features a gathering of handmade art/crafts/artifacts from various villages. See the rare Samson fox, along with relics and antiques from Alaska's colorful past in a museum atmosphere. Many historical and educational displays. Nothing sold from overseas. Visitor information. Coffee, pop, juice, snacks. Clean restrooms. This is a must stop. See display ad this section. [ADVERTISEMENT] ▲

A 276.5 (445 km) **F 81.5** (131.2 km) *CAUTION: Railroad crossing.*

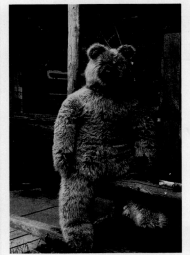

A 280 (450.6 km) **F 78** (125.5 km) Lodge with dining and a cafe/grocery.

Clear Sky Lodge. See display ad this section.

CAUTION: Watch for dips in road next 5 miles/8 km northbound.

A 280.1 (450.8 km) **F 77.9** (125.4 km) **Rochester Lodge.** See display ad this section.

A 280.4 (451.2 km) **F 77.6** (124.9 km) Entering Clear Air Force Station northbound.

A 283.5 (456.2 km) **F 74.5** (119.9 km) Access road west to **ANDERSON** (pop. 1,906) and **CLEAR.** Clear is a military installation (ballistic missile early warning site), and a sign at turnoff states it is unlawful to enter without permission. However, you can drive into Anderson without permission. Located 6 miles/9.7 km northwest of Clear, Anderson has a city campground in a 616-acre park with 40 sites on the Nenana River. RV dump station, toilets, showers. The community also has churches, a restaurant, softball fields and shooting range. For more information call the city office at (907) 582-2500. Emergency aid is available through the Clear Air Force Site Fire Department; phone (907) 585-6321. ▲

Anderson Riverside Park. Come enjoy our city's 616 beautiful acres located along the bank of the Nenana River! Featuring restrooms, showers, RV dump station, electrical hook-ups. Riverside campsites, rustic campsites with barbecue pits, picnic area with covered pavilion, fireplace. Shooting range, bandstand, telephone. Home of the annual Anderson Bluegrass Festival, held the last weekend in July. City of Anderson, P.O. Box 3100, Anderson, AK 99744. Phone (907) 582-2500; fax (907) 582-2496. [ADVERTISEMENT] ▲

Private Aircraft: Clear airstrip, 2.6 miles/4.2 km southeast; elev. 552 feet/168m; length 3,900 feet/1,189m; gravel; unattended. Clear Sky Lodge airstrip, 4.3 miles/6.9 km south; elev. 650 feet/198m; length 2,500 feet/762m; gravel, earth.

A 285.7 (459.8 km) **F 72.3** (116.3 km) Julius Creek bridge.

A 286.3 (460.7 km) **F 71.7** (115.4 km) View of Mount McKinley southbound.

A 286.8 (461.5 km) **F 71.2** (114.6 km) Double-ended paved parking area to east. Watch for frost heaves northbound.

A 288 (463.5 km) **F 70** (112.7 km) Entering Clear Military Reservation southbound.

A 288.2 (463.8 km) **F 69.8** (112.3 km) Denali Borough boundary.

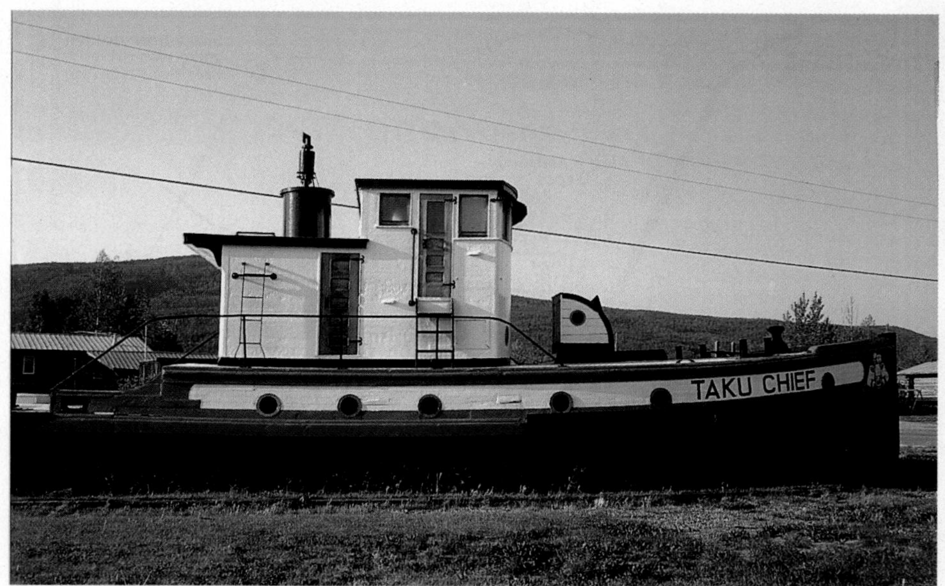

Taku Chief *sternwheeler on display at Nenana.* (Jerrianne Lowther, staff)

A 296.7 (477.5 km) **F 61.3** (98.7 km) Bridge over **Fish Creek.** Small gravel turnout with litter barrels by creek. Access to creek at south end of bridge; moderate success fishing for grayling.

A 302.9 (487.4 km) **F 55.1** (88.7 km) Nenana municipal rifle range.

A 303.7 (488.7 km) **F 54.3** (87.4 km)

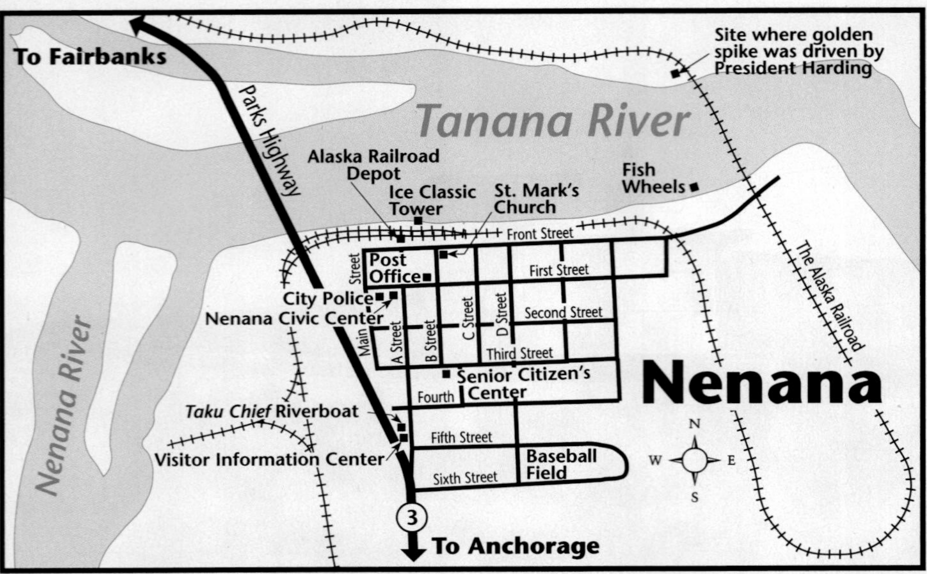

Nenana airport (see Private Aircraft information in Nenana).

A 304.3 (489.7 km) **F 53.7** (86.4 km) **Nenana Tesoro.** See display ad on page 449.

A 304.5 (490 km) **F 53.5** (86.1 km) **A Frame Service.** See display ad this section.

Nenana

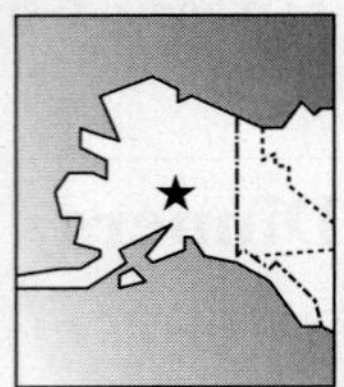

A 304.5 (490 km) **F 53.5** (86.1 km) Located at the confluence of the Tanana and Nenana rivers. **Population: 368. Emergency Services:** Emergency only (fire, police, ambulance), phone 911. **Alaska State Troopers,** phone (907) 832-5554, at **Milepost A 310** Parks Highway. **City Police,** phone (907) 832-5632. **Fire Department,** phone (907) 832-5632.

Visitor Information: In a picturesque log cabin with sod roof at junction of the highway and A Street, phone (907) 832-9953. Open 8 A.M. to 6 P.M., 7 days a week, Memorial Day to Labor Day. Pay phone and ice for sale. Ice Classic tickets may be purchased here.

Marge Anderson Senior Citizen Center, located on 3rd Street between Market and B streets, also welcomes visitors.

Elevation: 400 feet/122m. **Radio:** KIAM 630, KUAC-FM 91.1. **Transportation: Air**—Nenana maintains an FAA-approved airport. **Railroad**—The Alaska Railroad.

Private Aircraft: Nenana Municipal Airport, 0.9 mile/1.4 km south; elev. 362 feet/110m; length 5,000 feet/1,524m; asphalt; fuel 100, Jet B. Floatplane and skiplane strip.

The town got its name from the Indian word *Nenana,* which means "a good place to camp between the rivers." It was first known as Tortella, a white man's interpretation of the Athabascan word *Toghotthele.* In 1902 Jim Duke built a roadhouse and trading post here, trading with Indians and supplying river travelers with goods and lodging.

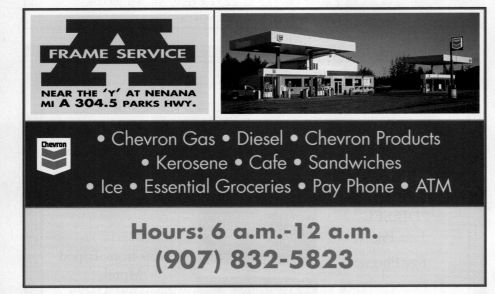

Nenana boomed as a construction base for the Alaska Railroad. Today, Nenana is home port of the tug and barge fleet that in summer carries tons of freight, fuel and supplies to villages along the Tanana and Yukon rivers. Because the Tanana is a wide, shallow, muddy river, the barges move about 12 mph downstream and 5 mph upstream. The dock area is to the right of the highway northbound. Behind the Nenana visitor information center is the *Taku Chief*: This old tug, which has been renovated, once pushed barges on the Tanana.

On July 15, 1923, Pres. Warren G. Harding drove the golden spike at Nenana, signifying completion of the Alaska Railroad. A monument to the event stands east of the depot here. The Nenana Railroad Depot, located at the end of Main Street, is on the National Register of Historic Places. Built in 1923 and renovated in 1988, the depot has a pressed metal ceiling and houses the state's Alaska Railroad Museum; open 9 A.M. to 6 P.M. daily.

One block from the depot is St. Mark's Mission Church. This Episcopal church was built in 1905 upriver from Nenana; it was moved to its present location in the 1930s when riverbank erosion threatened the structure. A school was located next door to the mission until the 1940s, and pupils were brought in by tug from villages along the river. The restored log church has pews with hand-carving and an altar covered with Native beadwork-decorated moosehide.

Nenana is perhaps best known for the Nenana Ice Classic, an annual event that

NENANA ADVERTISERS

A Frame Service ....Mile 304.5 Parks Hwy.
Alaskan Retreat Bed & Breakfast......................Ph. (907) 832-5431
Bed & Maybe Breakfast....Ph. (907) 832-5272
Coghill's General Merchandise......Downtown
Finnish Alaskan Bed and Breakfast......................Ph. (907) 832-5628
King & Queen Size Shoppe..........Behind Tripod Gift Shop
Nenana Valley RV Park.....Ph. (907) 832-5230
Nenana Visitor Center......Ph. (907) 832-9953
Roughwoods Inn..............Ph. (907) 832-5299
Tripod Gift Shop & Mini Mall........Downtown
Two Choice Cafe................................Main St.

Nenana Ice Classic Tripod and line attached to clock. (© Robin Brandt)

offers cash prizes to the lucky winners who can guess the exact minute of the ice breakup on the Tanana River. Ice Classic festivities begin the last weekend in February with the Tripod Raising Festival, and culminate at breakup time (late April or May) when the surging ice on the Tanana River dislodges the tripod. A line attached to the tripod stops a clock, recording the official breakup time.

The Alaska Come-Back Dog Sled Race is held in late March to commemorate the 1925 serum run from Nenana to Nome. Because of a diphtheria outbreak in Nome, serum was brought to Nenana by train and then by dog team to Nome. (The sled dog "Balto"—featured in a popular animated film—led the final relay into Nome.) The Iditarod Trail Sled Dog Race between Anchorage and Nome also commemorates this event. Nenana celebrates River Daze the first weekend in June. The main event is "The Annihilator," the toughest 10-km footrace in Alaska, over Tortella Hill.

Nenana has an auto repair shop, radio station, several churches, restaurants, a laundromat, gift shops, a grocery and general store. Accommodations at motel, inn and bed and breakfast. RV park with hookups. Picnic tables and rest area beside the restored *Taku Chief* are behind the visitor information center. ▲

Bed & Maybe Breakfast. Step back in time and charm yourself in the atmosphere of the old railroad depot built for President Harding's historic visit in 1923. Oak or brass beds, hardwood floors and braided rugs enhance the decor of these rooms. Overlook the hustling loading dock area of the barge lines on the Tanana River. View the Native cemetery and the historic railroad bridge from your window. Credit cards accepted. Reservations: (907) 832-5272 or 832-5556. [ADVERTISEMENT]

Tripod Gift Shop and Mini Mall. "Take time to smell the flowers." Over 19,000 flowers are planted each year to enhance the

beauty of one of the loveliest gift shops in Alaska. A fun stop! Enjoy old-time concertina music played by Joanne Hawkins. Take the boardwalk to our Art Lovers' Gallery; Trapper's Cabin stocked with a wide selection of local furs; king- and queen-sized shop; Bargain Corner with special prices on T-shirts, souvenirs and mugs. Enjoy ice cream or snacks at our Sweets and Treats Shoppe and purchase our fine canned smoked salmon. Also available: ice, worldwide postcard stamps, assorted camera batteries and wildflower seeds. Complimentary gold panning with $5 purchase in any of these shops. The shops are a must, a highlight of any vacation. Interesting displays include record-size moose antlers, Kodiak grizzly bear trap (largest ever manufactured), antique ice saw, working fish wheel, trapper's steam boiler, dog salmon drying rack and authentic 1997 Ice Classic tripod. Be sure to have your picture taken with Sourdough Pete and rub his head for luck. Tour operators may call ahead to reserve a guided tour of Nenana, compliments of Tripod Gift Shop. Joanne Hawkins has hosted tour groups for over 20 years at no charge. Allow 30–45 minutes if the tour is to be included with your rest stop. A little history, a little fact, a little music and a lot of fun are packed into this tour. Have a picture taken of your coach, escort and driver for our display board. Over 15 years of tour operator photos are on display. This tour is a must! Remember, reservations are necessary. Tour operators thinking about lunch can call ahead for reservations at Two Choice Cafe (907) 832-5272. Ask about our soup and sandwich special for groups of 25 or more. Complimentary RV parking for self-contained vehicles. [ADVERTISEMENT]

Parks Highway Log

(continued)

A 305.1 (491 km) **F 52.9** (85.1 km) Tanana River bridge. Large paved turnout to west at north end of bridge. The Tanana is formed by the joining of the Chisana and the Nabesna rivers near Northway and flows 440 miles/708 km westward to the Yukon River. From the bridge, watch for freight-laden river barges bound for the Yukon River. North of this bridge, fish wheels may sometimes be seen in action and occasionally fish may be purchased from the owners of the wheels.

Entering Game Management Unit 20B northbound, 20A southbound.

A 305.5 (491.6 km) **F 52.5** (84.5 km) Paved turnout to west by Tanana River. There is a Native cemetery 0.6 mile/1 km to east on side road.

A 305.6 (491.8 km) **F 52.4** (84.3 km) Paved turnout to west overlooking Tanana River.

A 305.9 (492.3 km) **F 52.1** (83.8 km) Double-ended gravel turnout to east. Paved turnout to west.

A 306.2 (492.8 km) **F 51.8** (83.4 km) RV parking. ▲

A 308.9 (497.1 km) **F 49.1** (79 km) *CAUTION: Railroad crossing.*

A 309 (497.3 km) **F 49** (78.9 km) Restaurant.

A 314.6 (506.3 km) **F 43.4** (69.8 km) Paved double-ended turnout to west.

A 314.8 (506.6 km) **F 43.2** (69.5 km) Bridge over Little Goldstream Creek.

A 315.4 (507.6 km) **F 42.5** (68.6 km) Truck lane next 2.8 miles/4.5 km northbound.

A 318.8 (513 km) **F 39.2** (63.1 km) Paved double-ended turnout to west with scenic view. The view is mostly of bogs, small lakes and creeks, with names like Hard Luck Creek, Fortune Creek, All Hand Help Lake and Wooden Canoe Lake.

Southbound travelers will see the Tanana River on both sides of the highway. It follows a horseshoe-shaped course, the top of the closed end being the bridge at Nenana.

A 321 (516.6 km) **F 37** (59.5 km) Fairbanks-bound traffic: Highway climbs a steep grade with sweeping curves next 1 mile/1.6 km; truck lane next mile northbound. Mount McKinley is visible to the southwest on a clear day.

A 323 (519.8 km) **F 35** (56.3 km) Tanana River visible to east in valley below highway.

A 323.8 (521.1 km) **F 34.2** (55 km) Truck lane next 0.3 mile/0.5 km northbound.

A 324.5 (522.2 km) **F 33.5** (53.9 km) Paved double-ended turnout to east with scenic view to south.

A 325 (523 km) **F 33** (53.1 km) This stretch of highway is often called Skyline Drive; views to west. Downgrade northbound.

A 325.7 (524.1 km) **F 32.3** (52 km) Entering Fairbanks North Star Borough northbound.

A 328.3 (528.3 km) **F 29.7** (47.8 km) Truck lane next 3 miles/4.8 km southbound.

A 331.6 (533.6 km) **F 26.4** (42.5 km) Long paved double-ended turnout to east. Intermittent truck lanes northbound to Fairbanks.

A 338.2 (544.3 km) **F 19.8** (31.9 km) Wide view to east. Look for Murphy Dome (elev. 2,930 feet/893m) with white communication installations on summit to west.

A 339.3 (546 km) **F 19.7** (30.1 km) Viewpoint and sign to east. This is the south end of a 1-mile/1.6-km scenic loop road that rejoins the highway at **Milepost A 339.9.** Highway begins downgrade northbound.

A 339.9 (547 km) **F 18.1** (29.1 km) Turnoff (unmarked) for Bonanza Experimental Forest via 1-mile/1.6-km loop road east; scenic viewpoint.

A 340.9 (548.6 km) **F 17.1** (27.5 km) Long double-ended gravel turnout to west.

A 342.2 (550.7 km) **F 15.8** (25.4 km) Rosie Creek Road.

A 342.4 (551 km) **F 15.6** (25.1 km) Old Nenana Highway.

A 344.2 (553.9 km) **F 13.8** (22.2 km) Monument in honor of George Alexander Parks, former governor of Alaska. Also here is a Blue Star Memorial highway plaque honoring the armed forces. Viewpoint to east. Tanana River can be seen below the Parks monument.

A 349 (561.6 km) **F 9** (14.5 km) Cripple Creek Road to south, Park Ridge Road to north. Truck lane next 4.2 miles/6.8 km southbound.

A 350 (563.3 km) **F 8** (12.9 km) Alder Creek.

A 351.2 (565.2 km) **F 6.8** (10.9 km) Old gold dredges visible to the east.

A 351.7 (566 km) **F 6.3** (10.1 km) Turnoff to west for Ester (description follows).

Ester

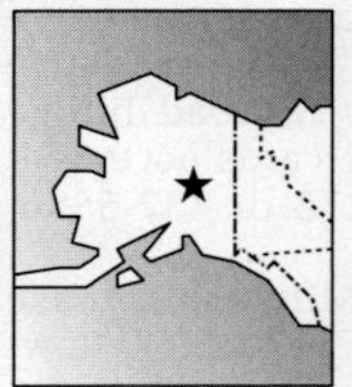

Located 0.6 mile/1 km west of highway. **Population:** 211. **Emergency Services:** Emergency only, phone 911. **Fire Department**, phone (907) 479-6858. A former gold mining camp and current visitor attraction, Ester has a hotel, RV camping, 2 saloons, 3 gift shops and a post office. A village sign on Main Street locates these services.

Ester was a raucous mining camp in 1906, with a population of some 5,000 miners. Today a quiet bedroom community of Fairbanks, Ester's heydays are relived in music, song and dance at the Malemute Saloon. Active gold mining is still under way in the area. One of the best preserved gold dredges from the gold rush days can be seen from **Milepost A 351.2.**

Ester Gold Camp. At the turn of century, discovery of gold in the Ester region drew hundreds of prospectors to seek their fortunes. In 1936, the Fairbanks Exploration Company built Ester Camp to support a large-scale gold dredge operation. After 20 years of operation, the camp was closed. It opened again in 1958, but this time as a summer visitor attraction. Today, Ester Gold Camp, on the National Register of Historic Places, provides services for another kind of prospector: those seeking accommodations, excellent food and a fun-filled night of entertainment. Open late May through early September. See display ad in FAIRBANKS section. [ADVERTISEMENT] ▲

Judie Gumm Designs. Noted for her sculptural interpretations of northern images, her work has been featured in many national publications. Priced moderately; easy to pack—her jewelry makes a perfect remembrance of your adventure North. Follow the signs in Ester. Weekdays 10–6. Saturday 12–5. Catalog available. P.O. Box 169, Ester, AK 99725. Phone: (907) 479-4568. See display ad. [ADVERTISEMENT]

Parks Highway Log

(continued)

A 351.8 (566.2 km) **F 6.2** (10 km) Weigh stations.

A 352.5 (567.3 km) **F 5.5** (8.8 km) Gold Hill Road.

Gold Hill. See display ad this section.

PHTS (Parks Highway Truck Stop). See display ad this section.

Inua Wool Shoppe. Turn on Gold Hill Road, go 0.3 mile left to Henderson, 1 mile to 202 Henderson Road. Inua Wool Shoppe is Interior Alaska's most complete knitting shoppe. Fabulous selection of qiviuq and other fine wool yarns. Large selection of Alaskan, Norwegian and American patterns, needlepoints, buttons, books and needles. Come enjoy a unique knitting shoppe. Open 10–5 Monday–Saturday. (907) 479-5830 (Alaska 1-800-478-9848). VISA and MasterCard welcome. [ADVERTISEMENT]

A 353.5 (568.9 km) **F 4.5** (7.2 km) Gas station and store. Public dumpster.

A 355.8 (572.6 km) **F 2.2** (3.5 km) Sheep Creek Road and Tanana Drive. Road to Murphy Dome (a restricted military site).

A 356.8 (574.2 km) **F 1.2** (1.9 km) Turnoff to University of Alaska, Geist Road, Chena Ridge Loop and Chena Pump Road.

Justa Store. See display ad this section.

A 357.6 (575.5 km) **F 0.4** (0.6 km) Bridge over Chena River.

A 357.7 (575.6 km) **F 0.3** (0.5 km) Fairbanks airport exit.

A 358 (576.1 km) **F 0** Fairbanks exit; Parks Highway (Robert J. Mitchell Expressway) continues to Richardson Highway, bypassing Fairbanks. Take Airport Way exit west for Fairbanks International Airport and Dale Road to Discovery Steamboat Landing. Exit east at Airport Way for: private campground on Boat Street; University Avenue (access to University of Alaska and Chena River state recreation site); Peger Road (access to private campground, flying service and Alaskaland); Cushman Street (access to visitor center and Alaska Railroad depot); and to connect with the Steese Expressway. (See Fairbanks Vicinity map on page 458 in the FAIRBANKS section.)

FAIRBANKS

(See maps, page 458)

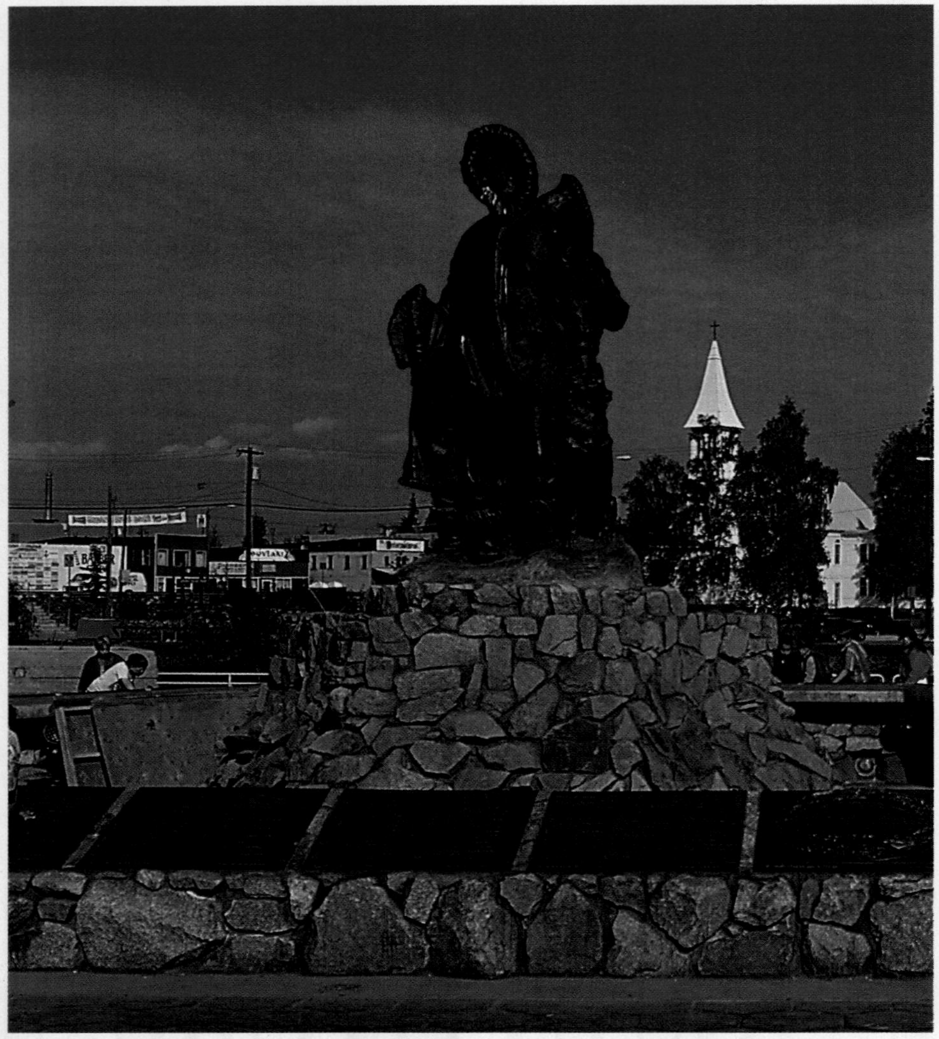

Bronze statue of "Unknown First Family" dominates Golden Heart Park in downtown Fairbanks. (© Harry M. Walker)

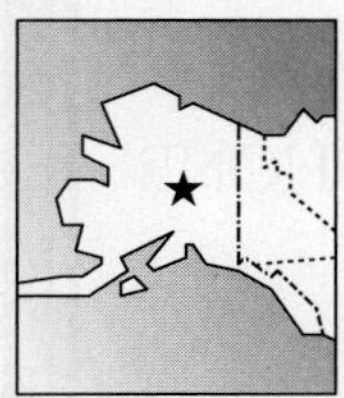

Located in the heart of Alaska's Great Interior country. By highway, it is approximately 1,488 miles/2,395 km north of Dawson Creek, BC, the start of the Alaska Highway (traditional milepost distance is 1,523 miles); 98 miles/158 km from Delta Junction (official end of the Alaska Highway); 358 miles/576 km from Anchorage via the Parks Highway; and 2,305 miles/3,709 km from Seattle.

Population: Fairbanks–North Star Borough, 84,380. **Emergency Services: Alaska State Troopers**, 1979 Peger Road, phone (907) 451-5333; for nonemergencies, (907) 451-5100; and using TTY service, (907) 451-5344. **Fairbanks Police**, 656 7th Ave., phone 911 or, for nonemergencies, phone (907) 459-6500. **Fire Department** and **Ambulance Service**, phone 911. **Hospitals**, Fairbanks Memorial, 1650 Cowles St., phone (907) 452-8181; Bassett Army Hospital, Fort Wainwright, phone (907) 353-5143; Eielson Clinic, Eielson AFB, phone (907) 377-2259. **Women's Crisis Line**, phone (907) 452-2293. **Emergency Management**, phone (907) 459-1481 or (907) 474-7721 (24-hour line). **Borough Information**, phone (907) 459-1000.

Visitor Information: Fairbanks Visitor Information Center at 550 1st Ave. (at Cushman Street, where a riverside marker reads "Mile 1523, Official End of the Alaska Highway"); phone (907) 456-5774 or 1-800-327-5774. In summer, open 8 A.M. to 8 P.M. daily; in winter, open 8 A.M. to 5 P.M. weekdays, closed weekends. Phone (907) 456-INFO for daily recorded information.

Visitor information is also available at Fairbanks International Airport in the baggage claim area, at the Alaska Railroad depot at the University of Alaska Museum and at Alaskaland.

For information on Alaska's state parks, national parks, national forests, wildlife refuges and other outdoor recreational sites, visit the Alaska Public Lands Information Center downstairs in historic Courthouse Square at 250 N. Cushman St. The center is a free museum featuring films on Alaska, interpretive programs, lectures, exhibits, artifacts, photographs and short video programs on each region in the state. The exhibit area and information desk are open 7 days a week in summer; Tuesday through Saturday in winter. Phone (907) 456-0527. For recorded information on Denali National Park, phone (907) 456-0510. TDD information line is (907) 456-0532.

Elevation: 436 feet/133m at Fairbanks International Airport. **Climate:** January temperatures range from -2°F/-19°C to -19°F/-28°C. The lowest temperature ever recorded was -62°F/-52°C in December 1961. July temperatures average 62°F/17°C, with a record high of 99°F/37°C in July 1919. In June and early July daylight lasts 21 hours—and the nights are really only twilight. Annual precipitation is 10.9 inches, with an annual average snowfall of 65 inches. The record for snowfall is 147.3 inches, set the winter of 1990–91. **Radio:** KSUA-FM, KFAR, KCBF, KAKQ, KWLF-FM, KIAK, KIAK-FM, KJNP-AM and FM (North Pole), KUAC-FM 104.7. **Television:** Channels 2, 4, 7, 9, 11, 13 and cable. **Newspapers:** *Fairbanks Daily News–Miner.*

Private Aircraft: Facilities for all types of aircraft. Consult the *Alaska Supplement* for information on the following airports: Eielson AFB, Fairbanks International, Fairbanks International Seaplane, Chena Marina Air Field and Fort Wainwright. For more information phone the Fairbanks Flight Service Station at (907) 474-0137.

HISTORY

In 1901, Captain E.T. Barnette set out from St. Michael on the stern-wheeler *Lavelle Young*, traveling up the Yukon River with supplies for his trading post, which he proposed to set up at Tanana Crossing (Tanacross), the halfway point on the Valdez–Eagle trail. But the stern-wheeler could not navigate the fast-moving, shallow Tanana River beyond the mouth of the Chena River. The stern-wheeler's captain finally dropped off the protesting Barnette on the Chena River, near the present site of 1st Avenue and Cushman Street. A year later, Felix Pedro, an Italian prospector, dis-

(Continues on page 460)

RIVERBOAT DISCOVERY • A most memorable adventure

The Riverboat Discovery is the one adventure you won't want to miss when you travel to Fairbanks. Owned and operated by the Binkley family, whose river boating experience in Alaska spans four generations and almost 100 years, the Riverboat Discovery tour has been rated the top boating attraction in North America in Travel Weekly Magazine. Captain Jim Binkley and his crew of children, grandchildren and native Alaskans takes you back to the heyday of sternwheelers, to an era when prospectors, fur traders and Native people of the Interior relied on rivers as their only link to the outside world.

Passengers relax in the comfort of glass enclosed or open decks as the Discovery III winds its way down the Chena and Tanana Rivers. Drawing on their knowledge of Alaskan history, the Binkley family entertains listeners with witty descriptions of Alaskan life during the four hour narrated cruise. The Discovery makes a brief stop at the river front home of veteran Iditarod Dog Musher Susan Butcher, where visitors hear tales of Susan's Iditarod adventures and are introduced to her champion sled dogs.

One of the highlights of the trip is a stop ashore at the Old Chena Indian Village. Here passengers disembark for a guided tour. Alaskan Natives share their culture as they recount how their ancestors hunted, fished, sewed clothing and built shelters to survive for centuries in the harsh Alaskan wilderness. At the village a dog mushing distance racing team gives passengers a "close-up" view of an actual mushing kennel.

The Discovery departs Steamboat Landing, off Dale Road, daily at 8:45 AM and 2:00 PM mid-May through mid-September. Reservations are required. For further information call 907-479-6673.

Before or after your cruise step into the past at Steamboat Landing, one of the finest gift stores in Alaska. Stroll along the picturesque boardwalk beside the Chena River and enter any of four turn-of-the-century shops. Discovery Trading Post offers unique Alaskan gifts at great low prices. The Susan Butcher Dog Mushing gallery features mementos of the Iditarod champion's lifestyle and an exclusive line of sportswear. Susan's winning Iditarod dogsled and Iditarod trophies are conveniently located so you can take photos you'll always treasure. The Binkley and Barrington Gift Shop offers Alaskan made products, and the Pioneer Hotel is a replica of Fairbanks' first luxury hotel featuring authentic Russian collectibles. Be sure not to miss this cultural treat between Discovery III departures – you'll find an impressive selection of gifts at some of the best prices in Alaska.

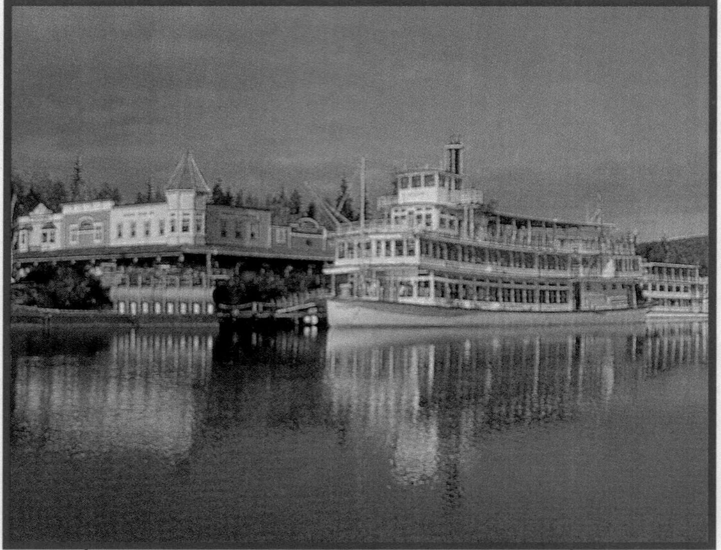

EL DORADO GOLD MINE • Gold Mining History

PAN for GOLD
You're guaranteed to find it!

Pan for gold at the El Dorado Gold Mine. Join the Binkley family for another Alaskan experience that can't be missed! El Dorado Gold Mine is an exciting hands-on adventure for the whole family. Visitors learn about the history of mining in Alaska, experience a modern day mining operation and pan for gold, while enjoying El Dorado Gold Mine's famous Alaskan hospitality.

The two hour tour to a working gold mine begins when passengers board the Tanana Valley Railroad for a narrated trip through the original gold fields of the Interior that were once part of Alaska's richest mining district on record.

Passengers ride the narrow gauge rails through a permaforst tunnel where miners with head lamps and pick-axes seek out the rich gold veins, reminiscent of mining days gone by. Winding through the valley, the train comes to a halt as a prospector crouches down to dip his gold pan into cold, clear waters of Fox Creek in search of the sparkle of gold.

At El Dorado Camp, local miners "Yukon Yonda" and her husband Dexter Clark are on hand to conduct a guided tour through a working gold mine. Visitors gather around to watch the operation of a modern day sluice box and enjoy stories about life in Alaskan mining camps.

A crash course in gold panning is followed by the real thing. Visitors grab a poke filled with pay dirt right from the sluice box and try their hand at panning for gold. And when they strike it rich, they keep the gold!

The next stop is the assay office where visitors, while enjoying complimentary homemade cookies and coffee, weigh their gold and assay its market value. The "all aboard" call gathers everyone onto the train for the short ride back to the station.

Daily tours for the El Dorado Gold Mine depart from the old train station at 1.3 mile Elliott Highway, just past Fox, Alaska, nine miles north of Fairbanks. For reservations call 907-479-7613.

Visit our web site
URL: http://www2.polarnet.com/~discovry
e-Mail: discovery @ ARIInc.com

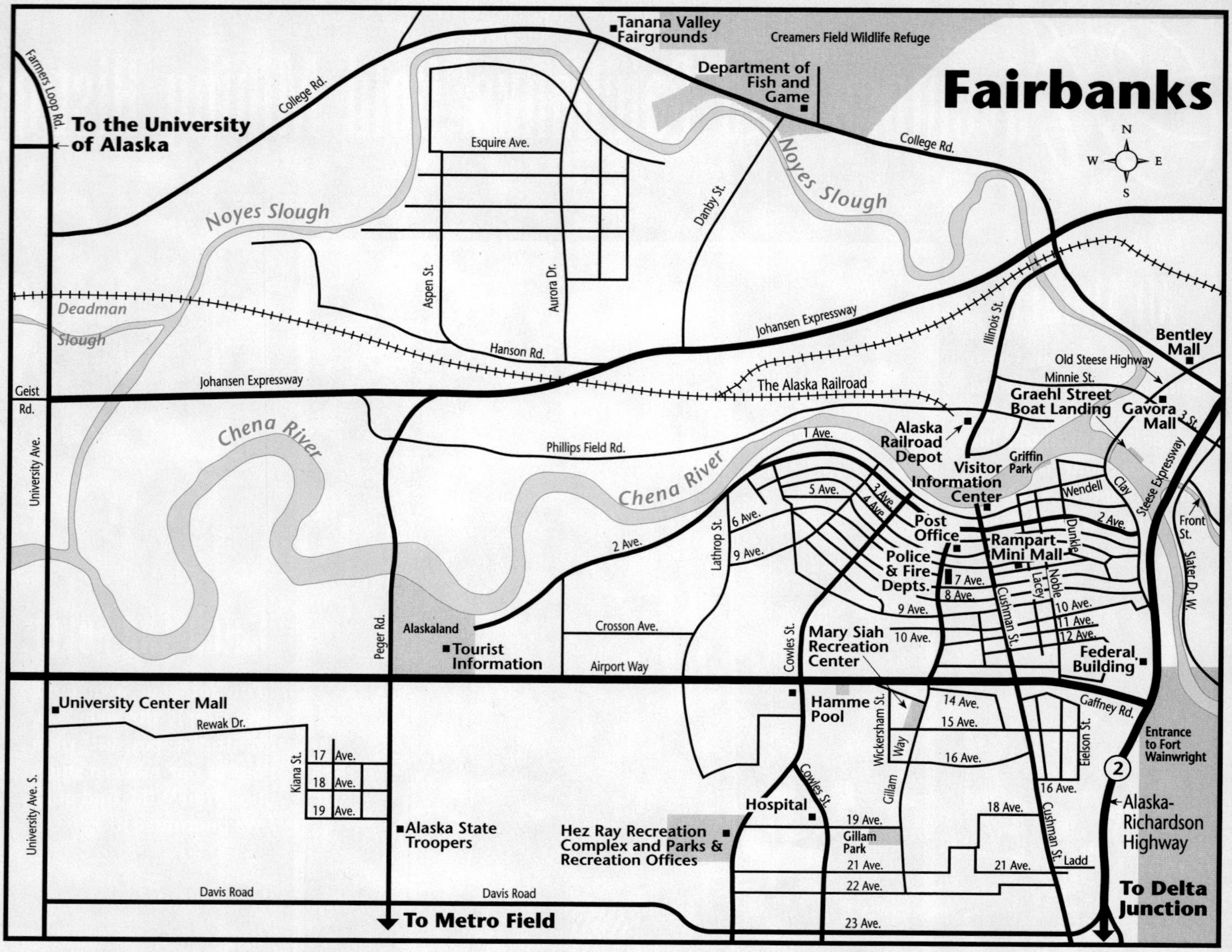

Fairbanks

N
W E
S

Tanana Valley Fairgrounds
Creamers Field Wildlife Refuge
Department of Fish and Game
Farmers Loop Rd.
To the University of Alaska
College Rd.
Esquire Ave.
Noyes Slough
Danby St.
Aspen St.
Aurora Dr.
Deadman Slough
Hanson Rd.
Johansen Expressway
Illinois St.
Bentley Mall
Old Steese Highway
Minnie St.
The Alaska Railroad
Graehl Street Boat Landing
Gavora Mall
3 St.
Geist Rd.
University Ave.
Chena River
Phillips Field Rd.
1 Ave.
Alaska Railroad Depot
Visitor Information Center
Griffin Park
Wendell
Clay
Steese Expressway
5 Ave.
3 Ave.
4 Ave.
6 Ave.
9 Ave.
2 Ave.
Lathrop St.
Post Office
Rampart Mini Mall
Dunkle
Front St.
Slater Dr. W.
Police & Fire Depts.
7 Ave.
8 Ave.
Lacey
Noble
10 Ave.
11 Ave.
12 Ave.
Cushman St.
Peger Rd.
Alaskaland
Tourist Information
Crosson Ave.
Airport Way
Cowles St.
Mary Siah Recreation Center
Federal Building
University Center Mall
Hamme Pool
14 Ave.
15 Ave.
16 Ave.
Gaffney Rd.
Entrance to Fort Wainwright
Rewak Dr.
Kiana St.
17 Ave.
18 Ave.
19 Ave.
Wickersham St.
Way
Gillam
Eielson St.
2
University Ave. S.
Hospital
Alaska-Richardson Highway
Alaska State Troopers
Hez Ray Recreation Complex and Parks & Recreation Offices
19 Ave.
Gillam Park
21 Ave.
22 Ave.
Ladd
Davis Road
To Metro Field
23 Ave.
To Delta Junction

Fairbanks and Vicinity

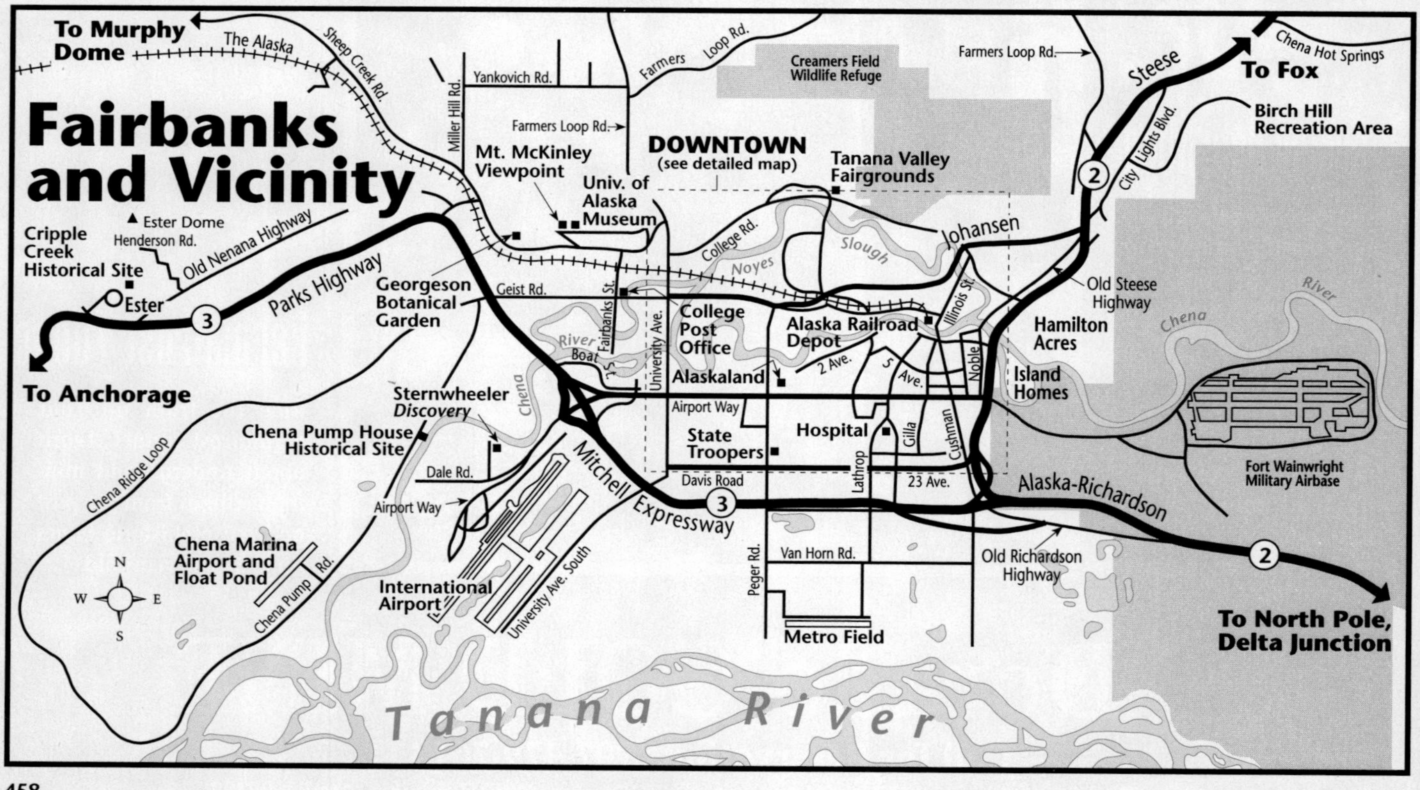

To Murphy Dome
The Alaska
Sheep Creek Rd.
Yankovich Rd.
Miller Hill Rd.
Farmers Loop Rd.
Creamers Field Wildlife Refuge
Steese
To Fox
Chena Hot Springs
Birch Hill Recreation Area
City Lights Blvd.
Mt. McKinley Viewpoint
DOWNTOWN (see detailed map)
Tanana Valley Fairgrounds
Univ. of Alaska Museum
Ester Dome
Henderson Rd.
Old Nenana Highway
Cripple Creek Historical Site
Ester
3
Parks Highway
Georgeson Botanical Garden
Geist Rd.
Fairbanks St.
College Rd.
Noyes
Slough
Johansen
Old Steese Highway
Hamilton Acres
Illinois St.
College Post Office
University Ave.
Alaska Railroad Depot
Alaskaland
2 Ave.
5 Ave.
Noble
Island Homes
Chena River
River
Boat
To Anchorage
Sternwheeler *Discovery*
Airport Way
Chena Pump House Historical Site
State Troopers
Hospital
Gilla
Cushman
Lathrop
Dale Rd.
Chena Ridge Loop
Mitchell Expressway
Davis Road
23 Ave.
Alaska-Richardson
Fort Wainwright Military Airbase
Chena Marina Airport and Float Pond
Chena Pump Rd.
International Airport
University Ave. South
Peger Rd.
Van Horn Rd.
Old Richardson Highway
To North Pole, Delta Junction
Metro Field
Tanana River

RIVER'S EDGE
RV PARK & CAMPGROUND
F A I R B A N K S

"River's Edge is RV heaven!"
Dr. Helen Stover of Richmond, VA

Lynn Nelson

River's Edge RV Park has so much to offer!

- Full and partial hook-ups
- Pull-throughs
- 30-amp electric
- Dump station
- Dry tent sites
- FREE showers
- Laundry
- Gift shop
- Pay phones
- Car/RV wash facility
- Over 160 sites
- Walking distance to major shopping centers and groceries
- FREE shuttle service to Sternwheeler Discovery and Alaska Salmon Bake
- ★ Denali One-Day Tour
- ★ Tour Arrangements: Pt. Barrow & Arctic Circle

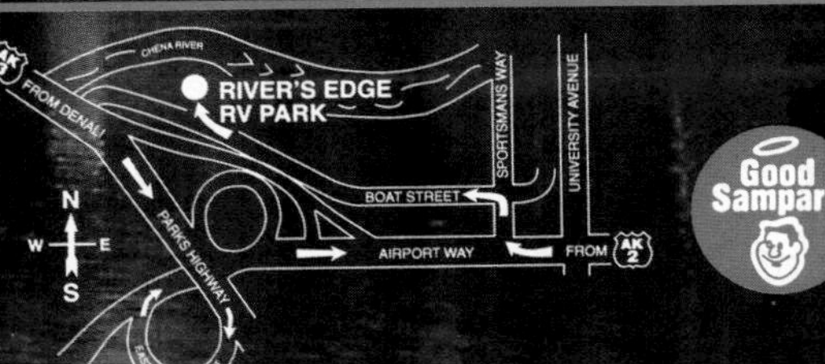

From Anchorage/Denali, AK3: take East Fairbanks exit, left on Sportsmans Way, left on Boat Street.

From Tok/Richardson Hwy., AK2: left on Airport Way, cross University Avenue, right on Sportsmans Way, left on Boat Street.

4140 Boat Street (off Airport Way),
Fairbanks, Alaska 99709 • 1-800-770-3343

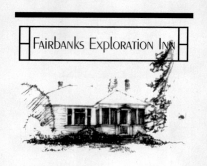

Autumn floral display at Georgeson Botanial Garden, University of Alaska.
(© Ruth Fairall)

(Continued from page 454)
covered gold about 16 miles/26 km north of Barnette's temporary trading post. The opportunistic Barnette quickly abandoned his original plan to continue on to Tanana Crossing.

In September 1902, Barnette convinced the 25 or so miners in the area to use the name "Fairbanks" for the town that he expected would grow up around his trading post. The name had been suggested that summer by Alaska Judge James Wickersham, who admired Charles W. Fairbanks, the senior senator from Indiana. The senator later became vice president of the United States under Theodore Roosevelt.

The town grew, largely due to Barnette's promotion of gold prospects and discoveries in the area, and in 1903 Judge Wickersham moved the headquarters of his Third Judicial District Court (a district which encompassed 300,000 square miles) from Eagle to Fairbanks.

Thanks to Wickersham, the town gained government offices and a jail. Thanks to Barnette, it gained a post office and a branch of the Northern Commercial Company, a large Alaska trading firm based in San Francisco. In addition, after Barnette became the first

ver's Edge Resort presents

BARROW

Land of the Midnight Sun

Don't stop till you reach the top!

Day or Overnight Tours from Fairbanks

eaturing oeing 737 t service on ***laska Airlines*** *d overnight commodations ith* ***Top of the World Hotel.***

One-Day Tour

ver's Edge takes u to the airport in e early morning r your flight on **laska Airlines.**

eceive a certificate ter crossing the ctic Circle.

pend the day in arrow with your n tour guide. cludes an tensive Native ulture Exhibition aturing a Blanket oss and Inupiat skimo Traditional ances.

rive that evening Fairbanks. iver's Edge picks u up.

Overnight Tour

All the excitement of the one-day tour *plus* for a few more dollars:

Stay overnight at the **Top of the World Hotel.**

Return to Fairbanks the next afternoon. River's Edge will meet you.

Barrow is only a 75 minute flight from Fairbanks.

Warm clothing is available.

In-flight breakfast and dinner snack are provided.

Brought to you by: **River's Edge Resort** Cottages & RV Park

Alaska Airlines VACATIONS

For reservations and information, call **River's Edge Resort** **1-800-770-3343**

Busy Second Avenue in downtown Fairbanks. (© Roger Pickenpaugh)

mayor of Fairbanks in 1903, the town acquired telephone service, set up fire protection, passed sanitation ordinances and contracted for electric light and steam heat. In 1904, Barnette started a bank.

The town of "Fairbanks" first appeared in the U.S. Census in 1910 with a population of 3,541. Miners living beside their claims on creeks north of town brought the area population figure to about 11,000.

Barnette stayed in Fairbanks until late 1910, when he resigned the presidency of the Washington–Alaska Bank and moved to California. When the bank collapsed early in 1911, the people of Fairbanks blamed Barnette. The tale of the "most hated man in Fairbanks" is told in *E.T. Barnette, The Strange Story of the Man Who Founded Fairbanks*.

ECONOMY

The city's economy is linked to its role as a service and supply point for Interior and Arctic industrial activities. Fairbanks played a key role during construction of the trans-Alaska pipeline in the 1970s. The Dalton Highway (formerly the North Slope Haul Road) to Prudhoe Bay begins about 75 miles/121 km north of town. Extractive industries such as oil and mining continue to play a major role in the economy.

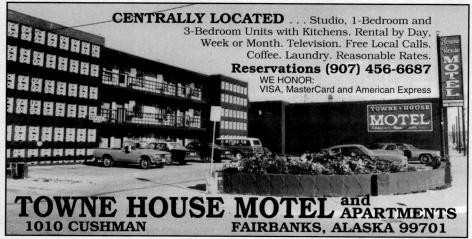

Government employment contributes significantly to the Fairbanks economy. Including military jobs, 50 percent of employment in Fairbanks is through the government. Fort Wainwright (formerly Ladd Field) was the first Army airfield in Alaska, established in 1938. The fort currently employs 4,600 soldiers and 1,600 civilians, and it houses 6,200 family members. Fort Wainwright also provides emergency services by assisting with search and rescue operations. Eielson Air Force Base, located 25 miles/40 km southeast of Fairbanks on the Richardson–Alaska Highway, also has a strong economic impact on the city. Eielson has about 2,700 military personnel and approximately 4,200 family members assigned, with about 1,200 military personnel and family members living off base.

Also boosting the Fairbanks economy are the University of Alaska–Fairbanks, and trade and service industries such as retail sales and tourism.

DESCRIPTION

Alaska's second largest city and the administrative capital of the Interior, Fairbanks lies on the flat valley floor of the Tanana River on the banks of the Chena River. Good views of the valley are available from Chena Ridge Road to the west and Farmers Loop Road to the north.

The city is a blend of old and new: Modern hotels and shopping malls stand beside log cabins and historic wooden buildings.

Fairbanks is bounded to the north, east and west by low rolling hills of birch and white spruce. To the south is the Alaska Range and Denali National Park, about a 2½-hour drive via the Parks Highway. The Steese and Elliott highways lead north to the White Mountains.

Bush plane lands at a private airstrip along the Chena River. (© Michael N. Dill)

ACCOMMODATIONS/VISITOR SERVICES

Fairbanks has more than 100 restaurants, about 2 dozen hotels and motels and more than 100 bed and breakfasts during the summer. Rates vary widely, from a low of about $40 for a single to a high of $150 for a double. Reservations for accommodations are suggested during the busy summer months.

There are several private campgrounds in the Fairbanks area. Chena River recreation site, a state campground, is located on University Avenue by the Chena River bridge. The campground has 57 sites, tables, firepits, toilets, water and a dump station. Camping fee $15/night or annual pass; $3 for use of dump station; and $5 for use of boat launch.

There is overnight camping at Alaskaland for self-contained RVs only with a 4-night limit, $9 fee and use of the Borough dump station on 2nd Avenue. ▲

Ah, Rose Marie Downtown Bed and Breakfast. Historic 1928 Fairbanks home. Very centrally located in downtown neighborhood. Full hearty breakfasts. Friendly cat and dog. Outdoor smoking areas. Singles, couples, triples, families welcomed. Open year-round. Extraordinary hospitality. Single $50 up, doubles $65 up. Wow! John E. Davis, 302 Cowles St., Fairbanks, AK 99701. (907) 456-2040. [ADVERTISEMENT]

Applesauce Inn B&B. Small Alaskan family with 3 friendly cats welcome you! Peaceful, woodsy neighborhood, 5-minute drive to town. Three bedrooms, each with two beds and own bath. Guest living room and screened gazebo. Hearty breakfasts feature reindeer sausage and homemade applesauce. Multi-room and week-long discounts. Brochures. 119 Gruening Way, Fairbanks, Alaska 99712. Phone (907) 457-3392, within Alaska (800) 764-3392. Fax (907) 457-3332. E-mail: appleinn@mosquitonet.com. [ADVERTISEMENT]

Chena Marina RV Park guests speak: "RV having fun? Yes—Thanks to folks like you! ... 'Dankeschon' services really special ... One of the best—location, spacious, landscaped ... First-rate." Extra-wide, long pull-throughs (slide-outs welcome). Free Klondinental breakfast; on floatplane pond (fishing); laundry, free guest showers, electric, water, TV, dump, tour tickets, free RV/car wash. Mile 2.8 Chena Pump Road, watch for signs. (907) 479-GOLD (4653), 1145 Shypoke Dr., Fairbanks, AK 99709. See map in display ad for directions. Open May 1. [ADVERTISEMENT] MP ▲

The Cushman Plaza Laundry appreciates notes from travellers from Florida to Texas, complimenting us as "The nicest laundromat anywhere," "Spotless!" "Just like

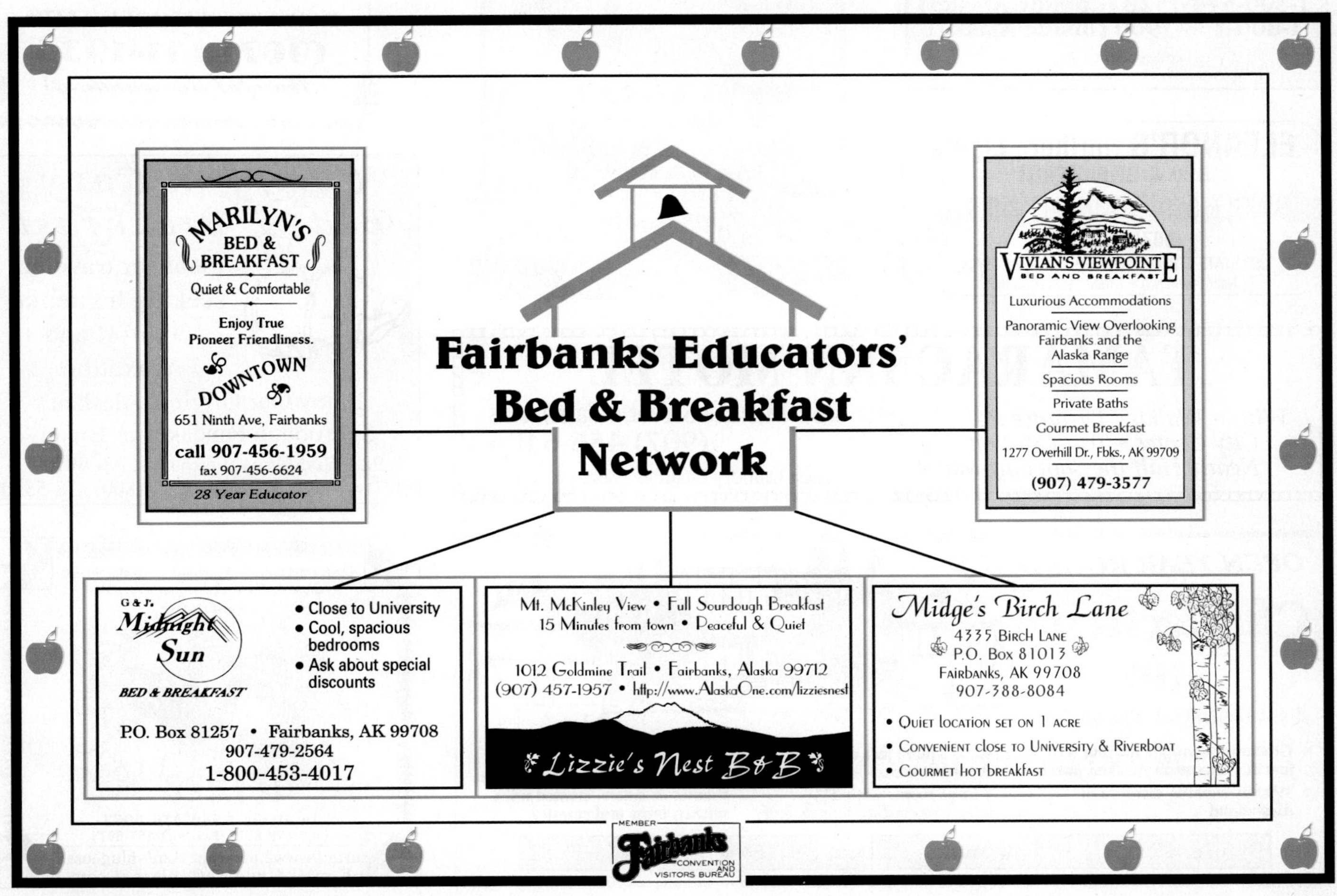

home." "All the machines work!" "So Spacious." On the Alaska/Richardson Highway, adjacent to Tesoro, 7-11, propane and nearby downtown shopping. 23rd and Cushman. (Please see our display ad this section.) Phone (907) 452-4430. [ADVERTISEMENT]

Fairbanks Bed And Breakfast. Barbara Neubauer, hostess and 26-year resident, has many bear and gold mining tales. The quiet historical neighborhood is walking distance to town on bus route. Our home has many interesting ivory artifacts and Alaskan art. Private bath, large yard and deck. Deck smoking. Hearty breakfast and laundry facilities for fee plus ample parking. 902 Kellum St. (907) 452-4967, fax (907) 451-6955. [ADVERTISEMENT]

Fairbanks Princess Hotel. Interior Alaska's finest accommodations located on the Chena River. Featuring an array of dining options, lounge, terraced riverside deck, tour desk, gift shop, health club with steam rooms, complimentary airport shuttle, meeting facilities for groups up to 435. Open year-round. Call 1-800-426-0500 for reservations. [ADVERTISEMENT]

Fairbanks Private Vacation Homes Network. Peaceful, quiet, wooded settings, all within 12 minutes of city center. All have clean and modern kitchens and bathrooms, phones, TV/VCRs and stock breakfast fixings. Smoking outdoors. Reasonable rates. Brochures available. Beth's Vacation Home, 1 bedroom house sleeps four, 1000 Bennett Rd., Fairbanks, AK 99712, (800) 239-2187, pen #4305; Cedar Creek Vacation Home, custom-built 2-story, $2^1/_2$ bedrooms, pets on approval, P.O. Box 10355, Fairbanks, AK 99710, phone (907) 457-3392, within Alaska 1-800-764-3392, fax (907) 457-3332, e-mail appleinn@mosquitonet.com; Gram's Cabin, on 3 riverfront acres, pets on approval, P.O. Box 58034, Fairbanks, AK 99711, phone (907) 488-6513, fax (907) 488-6593. E-mail: Graniff@polarnet.com. [ADVERTISEMENT]

Fountainhead Hotels. Our hotel hotline, (800) 528-4916, gives you access to more than 700 rooms in three of Fairbanks nicest hotels: Sophie Station, Wedgewood Resort and the Bridgewater Hotel. Each hotel varies in her design, layout and amenities, assuring you that

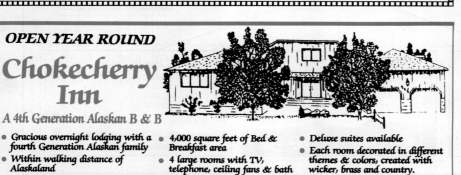

Historic Landmark

Gold Dredge No. 8

A piece of history to experience. A piece of gold to remember it by.

Prospectors used to travel for weeks through ice and snow in hopes of coming across a mere trace of gold. Today, Gray Line of Alaska has made prospecting much easier with tours to Gold Dredge No. 8, the only gold dredge in Alaska still open to the public. Gold Dredge No. 8 offers a truly authentic gold mining experience, including a tour of the site that unearthed millions of ounces of gold, as well as the opportunity to pan for guaranteed gold yourself. Afterwards enjoy the Miner's lunch for an additional $8, and visit the museum or gift shop for a large variety of mining souvenirs.

Open 9 a.m. to 6 p.m. every day from mid May through mid September.
From Fairbanks, take the Steese Highway north to Goldstream Road, then follow the signs.
Gold Dredge No. 8 is approximately 10 minutes from Fairbanks.

GRAY LINE **Gray Line of Alaska**
A DIVISION OF HOLLAND AMERICA LINE-WESTOURS

PHOTO COURTESY OF FAIRBANKS CONVENTION AND VISITORS BUREAU.

View of Fairbanks from a viewpoint on the Steese Highway.
(Jerrianne Lowther, staff)

we have just what you're looking for. Dining, laundry facilities, and free local calls are offered at each property. For additional information phone our hotline, write to us at 1501 Queens Way, Fairbanks, Alaska 99701 or contact us by e-mail at Fountain@mosquitonet.com. [ADVERTISEMENT]

Geni's Bed & Breakfast. Country hospitality May to September. Large bedroom, private bath. Two bedrooms with queen-sized beds, shared full bath. No pets, smoking on deck only. Continental or full country breakfast. Affordable accommodations in woodland setting 15 minutes from Fairbanks at Mile 5.3 Chena Hot Springs Road.

Handmade Alaska crafts available. George and Nila Lyle, P.O. Box 10352, Fairbanks, AK 99710; phone (907) 488-4136. [ADVERTISEMENT]

Norlite Campground, Inc. We've been welcoming guests to Fairbanks for 30 years. We have the usual amenities you find at other campgrounds—showers; 250 full, partial and no hook-up spots; laundry; RV/car wash; tour tickets and information; a small gift and grocery store; VISA/MasterCard; picnic tables and more. What makes us different is our central location and our great Alaskan staff—they are known for making your stay fun. We've won 13 awards for our

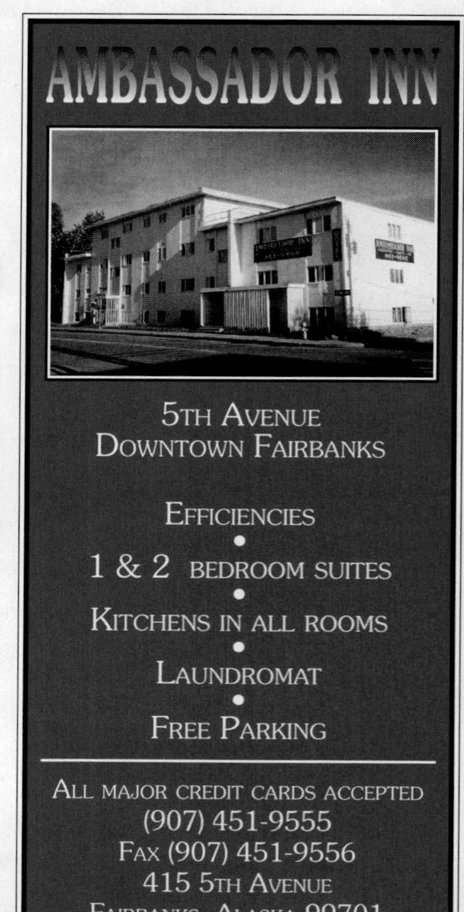

FAIRBANKS
CELEBRATING 50 YEARS OF THE MILEPOST®

FAIRBANKS — END, LOG OF ALASKA HIGHWAY

FAIRBANKS

MILEPOST 1523, Fairbanks, "The Golden Heart of Alaska," has grown rapidly in the past few years, with a present estimated population of 9,000. It is located on the Chena Slough, a channel of the Chena River emptying into the Tanana. Since the discovery of gold by Felix Pedro near here in 1902, the city has become the center of a rich placer-gold region embracing over 1,500 square miles. The present appearance of Fairbanks gives evidence of the effects of the recent boom, with the inevitable housing shortage ensuing. Many ramshackle shelters surround the city, but there is a solid and permanent development manifested in the fine stores, theaters, and homes.

Fairbanks is the northern terminus of the Alaska Railroad, the highways, and the northern crossroads of the airlanes. The seat of Alaska's institute of higher learning at nearby College—The University of Alaska, is noted for the high calibre of its curriculum, its experimental farm, and its museum of native artifacts and fossil remains. A great future is predicted because of the agricultural and mineral potentialities in the region, and because of the very heavy annual tourist traffic.

The climate is typical of interior Alaska, dry and healthful, with temperatures ranging from over 90 degrees in the shade in summer, to an occasional 60 below in winter.

Robinson Studios, Anchorage

Section of Fairbanks Business District

—48—

Frank Whaley–Wien Alaska Airlines

friendliness (we won one so often they stopped giving it out). We specialize in being the perfect host. If the quality of your vacation matters to you, we invite you to stay with us at the Norlite Campground. All discounts honored. Toll free (800) 478-0206; (907) 474-0206; fax (907) 474-0992; e-mail: norlite1@alaska.net; 1660 Peger Road, Fairbanks, Alaska 99709. [ADVERTISEMENT]

River's Edge RV Park & Campground. Beautiful setting on the Chena River and within walking distance of major shopping centers. 180 spacious wooded sites. Wide pull-throughs; 30-amp electric; dump station; full and partial hookups; free showers; gifts; free shuttle to Riverboat *Discovery* and Alaskaland Salmon Bake. Tour arrangements featuring Point Barrow and Arctic Circle. Immaculate facilities. [ADVERTISEMENT] MP ▲

Riverview RV Park & Cookout is one of the top-rated RV parks in Alaska. It is situated on 20 acres adjoining the beautiful Chena River. Total atmosphere and only 10 minutes from downtown Fairbanks. Room for your convenience. It is the only RV park with cable TV in the Fairbanks area. Call Riverview RV Park (888) 488-6392 or (907) 488-6281. Telephones and e-mail. See display ad. [ADVERTISEMENT] ▲

7 Gables Inn. Central to major attractions, this remodeled fraternity house is between the University campus and the airport. The spacious Tudor-style house features a floral solarium, stained-glass foyer with indoor waterfall, cathedral ceilings, banquet/conference facilities. Gourmet breakfast served daily. Cable TV, VCR, phone in each room, laundry, bikes, canoes and skis. Rates $50–$120; 4312 Birch Lane, Fairbanks, AK 99709. Phone (907) 479-0751. [ADVERTISEMENT]

Uebernachtung und Fruehstueck, Bed & Breakfast. English and German speaking with German hospitality. Pets in house. Queen beds, private and shared bath, full breakfast. German TV. Robert and Sylvia Harris, 2402 Cowles St., Fairbanks, Alaska 99701. Phone (907) 455-7958, Fax (907) 452-7958, e-mail: 103707.2401@ Compuserve. [ADVERTISEMENT]

TRANSPORTATION

Air: Several international, interstate and intra-Alaska carriers serve Fairbanks.

Air charter services are available for flightseeing, fly-in fishing and hunting, and trips to bush villages; see ads.

Railroad: Alaska Railroad passenger depot at 280 N. Cushman St. in the downtown area. Daily passenger service in summer between Fairbanks and Anchorage with stop-overs at Denali National Park; less frequent service in winter. For details, phone (800) 544-0552.

Train to Denali (Gray Line of Alaska). Ride the luxurious private-domed railcars of the *McKinley Explorer* to Denali National Park from either Anchorage or Fairbanks. Overnight packages in Denali with round-trip train service are available from only

$285 ppdo. Prices subject to change. Call Gray Line of Alaska at (907) 456-7741 for train and package tour options. [ADVERTISEMENT]

Bus: Scheduled motorcoach service to Anchorage and points south. Local daily bus service by Metropolitan Area Commuter Service (MACS), and regular MACS service is also now available to North Pole weekdays; no service on Sundays and some legal holidays. Drivers do not carry change, and exact change or tokens must be used. Fares: $1.50 or 1 token. All-day passes are $3. Tokens are available at Transit Park, the UAF Woodcenter, Fred Meyer west, Bentley Hall and North Pole Plaza. Information is available via the Transit Hotline, phone (907) 459-1011, or from MACS offices at 3175 Peger Road, phone (907) 459-1002.

Tours: Local and area sightseeing tours are available from several companies; see ads in this section.

Taxi: 9 cab companies.

Car and Camper Rentals: Several companies rent cars, campers and trailers; see ads in this section.

Caribou masks, like these from Anaktuvuk Pass, are one example of Native crafts available in Fairbanks shops. (© Lee Foster)

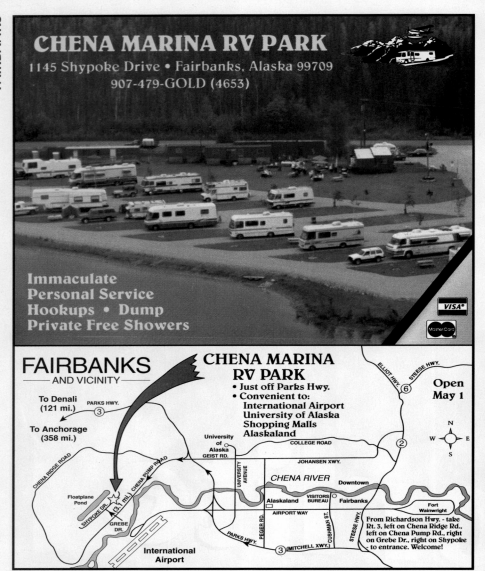

ATTRACTIONS

Get Acquainted: A good place to start is the visitor information center at 550 1st Ave., where you'll find free brochures, maps and tips on what to see and how to get there. Phone (907) 456-5774 or 1-800-327-5774. For a recording of current daily events phone (907) 456-INFO.

Next to the log cabin visitor information center is Golden Heart Park, site of the 18-foot/5-m bronze monument, "Unknown First Family." The statue, by sculptor Malcolm Alexander, and park were dedicated in July 1986 to celebrate Fairbanks' history and heritage.

The Alaska Public Lands Information Center, located in the lower level of historic Courthouse Square at 3rd Avenue and Cushman Street, is a free museum and information center featuring Alaska's natural history, cultural artifacts and recreational opportunities. In addition to detailed information on outdoor recreation in the state, the center offers films, interpretive programs, lectures and a book shop.

Tour the University of Alaska–Fairbanks, situated on a 2,250-acre ridge overlooking the city and Tanana River

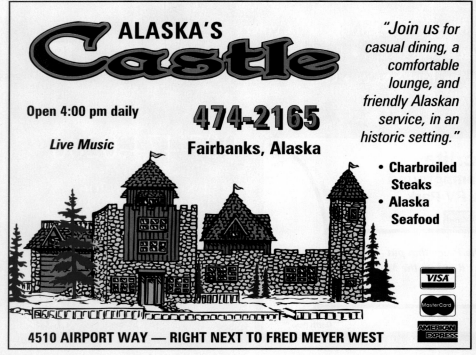

valley. The campus has all the features of a small town, including a fire station, post office, radio and TV stations, medical clinic and a 1,000-seat concert hall.

UAF offers special tours and programs from June through August. Free guided tours of the campus are provided Monday through Friday at 10 A.M.; tours begin at the UA Museum. Also offered are tours of the Large Animal Research Station, Poker Flat Research Range, and a slide show and tour at the Geophysical Institute, where research and study topics range from the center of the earth to the center of the sun. Films on mining in Alaska are also shown. Visitors can take a guided tour or tour on their own at the Agricultural and Forestry Experiment Station's Georgeson Botanical Garden, which is open to the public June through September. Phone (907) 474-7581 for information on any tour.

The University of Alaska Museum is a must stop for Fairbanks visitors. The museum features cultural and natural history displays from all the state's regions. The 5 galleries explore Alaska's history, Native culture, art, natural phenomena, wildlife, birds, geology and prehistoric past. Highlights include a 36,000-year-old Steppe bison mummy, the state's largest gold display, the trans-Alaska pipeline story and a special section on the northern lights. The museum grounds hold sculptures, totem poles, a Russian blockhouse and a nature trail with signs identifying local vegetation. The museum's special summer exhibit in 1998 will be "The Living Tradition of Yup'ik Masks," showing 19th century Eskimo masks from the Arctic Coast. Free summer programs include presentations on natural and cultural history topics and Alaska Native Elders discussing traditional and contemporary lifestyles. Summer shows include "Northern Inua," a 50-minute show of northern athletic games, dance and creation stories produced by the

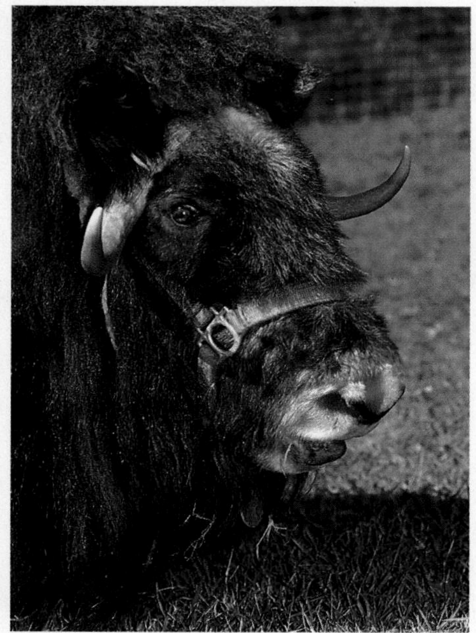

Musk ox may be seen at the University of Alaska. (© Robin Brandt)

World Eskimo-Indian Olympics, and "Dynamic Aurora," a 50-minute show on the scientific and Alaska Native understanding of the northern lights. Admission is charged for these shows; call for times. Hours are: May and September, 9 A.M. to 5 P.M.; June through August, 9 A.M. to 7 P.M.; October through April, weekdays, 9 A.M. to 5 P.M., weekends, noon to 5 P.M. Museum admission fees: adults, $5; seniors, $4.50; youth (12 to 17), $3; children under 12, free. For 24-hour information, call (907) 474-7505.

Take in Some Local Events: Fairbanks has several unique summer celebrations.

Late June is a busy time as Fairbanks celebrates the longest day of the year (summer solstice is June 21). The Midnight Sun Baseball Game will be played at 10:45 P.M. on June 21, 1998, without artificial lights. A Midnight Sun 10K Fun Run begins at 10 P.M. on June 20, 1998.

Golden Days, when Fairbanksans turn out in turn-of-the-century dress and celebrate the gold rush, is July 16-26, 1998. Golden Days starts off with a Felix Pedro look-alike taking his gold to the bank and includes a parade and rededication of the Pedro Monument honoring the man who started it all when he discovered gold in the Tanana Hills. Other events include pancake breakfasts, a dance, canoe and raft races, and free outdoor concerts.

The World Eskimo and Indian Olympics, with Native competition in such events as the high kick, greased pole walk, stick pull, fish cutting, parka contest and muktuk-eating contest will be held July 15-18, 1998.

The annual Tanana Valley State Fair will be held Aug. 7-15, 1998. Alaska's oldest state fair, the Tanana Valley State Fair features agricultural exhibits, arts and crafts, food booths, a rodeo and other entertainment.

Fairbanks Summer Arts Festival, 2 weeks of workshops and concerts including music from jazz to classics, dance, theater and the visual arts, will be held July 24 to Aug. 19, 1998.

Check with the Fairbanks visitor information center for more information on local events.

Besides these special events, summer visitors can take in a semipro baseball game at Growden Park where the Fairbanks Goldpanners take on other Alaska league teams.

The Fairbanks Shakespeare Theatre. 1998 production: "As You Like It" at Birch Hill recreation area. July 14-19, 22-26, and July 29–August 2, 7:30 P.M. nightly except Sunday matinee at 4:00 P.M. Ticket prices: adult $12 door, $10 advance; children and seniors over 60 $8 door, $6 advance. For further information phone (907) 457-7638. [ADVERTISEMENT]

Visit Creamer's Field. Follow the flocks of waterfowl to Creamer's Field Migratory Waterfowl Refuge. Located 1 mile/1.6 km from downtown Fairbanks, this 1,800-acre refuge managed by the Alaska Dept. of Fish and Game offers opportunities to observe large concentrations of ducks, geese, shorebirds and cranes in the spring and fall. Throughout the summer, sandhill cranes eat in the planted barley fields.

Explore the 2-mile/3.2-km self-guided

nature trail and the renovated historic farmhouse that serves as a visitor center. Stop at 1300 College Road to find the trailhead, viewing areas and brochures on Creamer's Field. For more information, phone (907) 452-5162.

Creamer's Field Migratory Waterfowl Refuge—where nature is at its best. Summer visitor center hours, 10–5, closed Sunday and Monday. June–August, guided walks begin at Farmhouse Visitor Center Tuesday and Thursday at 7 P.M.; Wednesday and Saturday at 9 A.M. No charge and the refuge is always open. Phone (907) 452-5162. [ADVERTISEMENT]

Tanana Valley Farmers Market. Visit Alaska's premier Farmers Market, located next to the Fairgrounds on College Road, open from mid-May to mid-September. Vendors offer "thousands of miles fresher" Alaska grown vegetables; blue-ribbon florals; Alaskan meats, fish, honey, jams and syrups; made-in-Alaska handcrafts and baked goods. Look for our brochure at local Visitor's Centers. Market hours are Wednesdays 11 A.M. to 4 P.M. and Saturdays 9 A.M. to 4 P.M.; there's plenty of parking. Stop by the Market and enjoy Alaska made and grown products ... "Meet You At The Market!" [ADVERTISEMENT]

The Alaska Rag Co. A must-see for Fairbanks travelers. This unique Alaskan gift shop manufactures beautiful handwoven rag rugs from 100 percent recycled clothing. The store also features works from 70-plus Alaskan artists. Items include jewelry, pottery, Polarfleece, stained glass, qiviut, dog hair hats, mittens and much more. Stop in, meet our weavers and see their work. 552 2nd Ave., Fairbanks, AK 99701. Phone (907) 451-4401. [ADVERTISEMENT]

The Great Alaskan Bowl Company. One of very few mills in the country still turning out nesting, 1-piece wooden bowls. Watch demonstrations using 1800's ingenuity and 1990's technology as we carve nested sets from a single block. Large viewing area. Close to airport. Open year-round. (907)

474-9663. 1-800-770-4222. P.O. Box 60598, Fairbanks, AK 99706. [ADVERTISEMENT]

Chena Pump House National Historic Site. Built in 1931–33 by the Fairbanks Exploration Co. to pump water from the Chena River to dredging operations at Cripple Creek, the pump house was remodeled in 1978 and now houses a restaurant and saloon. The sheet metal cladding, interior roof and some equipment (such as the intake ditch) are from the original pump house, which shut down in 1958 when the F.E. Co. ceased its Cripple Creek dredging operations. The pump house is located at Mile 1.3 Chena Pump Road.

Sled Dog Racing. The Alaska Dog Mushers' Assoc. hosts a series of dog races beginning in mid-December with preliminary races, and ending in March with the Open North American Championship. The Open is a 3-day event with 3 heats (of 20, 20 and 30 miles) with teams as large as 24 dogs; this race is considered by many to be the "granddaddy of dog races." Fairbanks also hosts the 1,000-mile/1,609-km Yukon Quest Sled Dog Race between Fairbanks and Whitehorse, YT. The Yukon Quest alternates start and finish between the 2 cities. For more information, contact the Alaska Dog Mushers' Assoc. at (907) 457-MUSH, or the Yukon Quest office at (907) 451-8985.

See Bank Displays: The Key Bank, at 1st Avenue and Cushman Street, has a display of gold nuggets and several trophy animals. Mount McKinley Mutual Savings Bank features a display of McKinley prints and the original cannonball safe used when the bank opened. The bank is at 531 3rd Ave.

Visit Historic Churches: St. Matthew's Episcopal, 1029 1st Ave., was originally built in 1905, but burned in 1947 and was rebuilt the following year. Of special interest is the church's intricately carved altar, made in 1906 of Interior Alaska birch and saved from the fire.

Immaculate Conception Church, on the Chena River at Cushman Street bridge,

Maximum summer daylight hours in Fairbanks: 21 hours and 49 minutes.

was drawn by horses to its present location in the winter of 1911 from its original site at 1st Avenue and Dunkel Street.

See the Pipeline: Drive about 10 miles/16 km north from downtown on the Steese Highway to see the trans-Alaska pipeline. Clearly visible are the thermal devices used to keep the permafrost frozen around the pipeline support columns.

View Mount McKinley: The best spot to see Mount McKinley is from the University of Alaska–Fairbanks campus (on Yukon Drive, between Talkeetna and Sheenjek streets) where a turnout and marker define the horizon view of Mount Hayes (elev. 13,832 feet/4,216m); Hess Mountain (elev. 11,940 feet/3,639m); Mount Deborah (elev. 12,339 feet/3,761m); and Mount McKinley (elev. 20,320 feet/6,194m). Distant foothills are part of the Wood River Butte.

Cruise Aboard the Riverboat *Discovery*: Every day at 8:45 A.M. and 2 P.M. in summer, the riverboat *Discovery* departs for a half-day cruise on the Chena and Tanana rivers. Drive out Airport Road, turn south at Dale Road and continue 0.5 mile/0.8 km on Dale to Discovery Drive. Reservations are required, as this is one of the most popular attractions in town. For the first leg of the trip, the *Discovery* winds its way down the meandering Chena River, its banks lined by old homesteads, modern homes and bush planes. The Chena River also joins with Cripple Creek, the Interior's richest gold rush stream. On the Tanana River, fish wheels turn in the swift glacial water, scooping up salmon to be dried and smoked for winter food. Returning up the Tanana River, the boat stops at Old Chena Indian Village, where passengers have the opportunity to see Susan Butcher's Iditarod-champion dog team in action. After the demonstration, passengers disembark for a tour of the village. Guides from the *Discovery*, who are of Indian or Eskimo heritage, are on hand to explain past and present Native culture. For more information on the riverboat *Discovery*, contact Alaska Riverways, Inc., 1975 Discovery Dr., Fairbanks, AK 99709; phone (907) 479-6673, fax 479-4613.

Visit Alaskaland Pioneer Park. Visitors will find a relaxed atmosphere at Alaskaland, a pleasant park with historic buildings, small shops, food, entertainment, playgrounds and 4 covered picnic shelters. The park—

Creamer's Field waterfowl refuge offers guided walks in summer. (© Tom Culkin)

which has no admission fee—is open year-round.

To drive to Alaskaland (at Airport Way and Peger Road), take Airport Way to Wilbur, turn north onto Wilbur, then immediately west onto access road, which leads to Alaskaland enclosure.

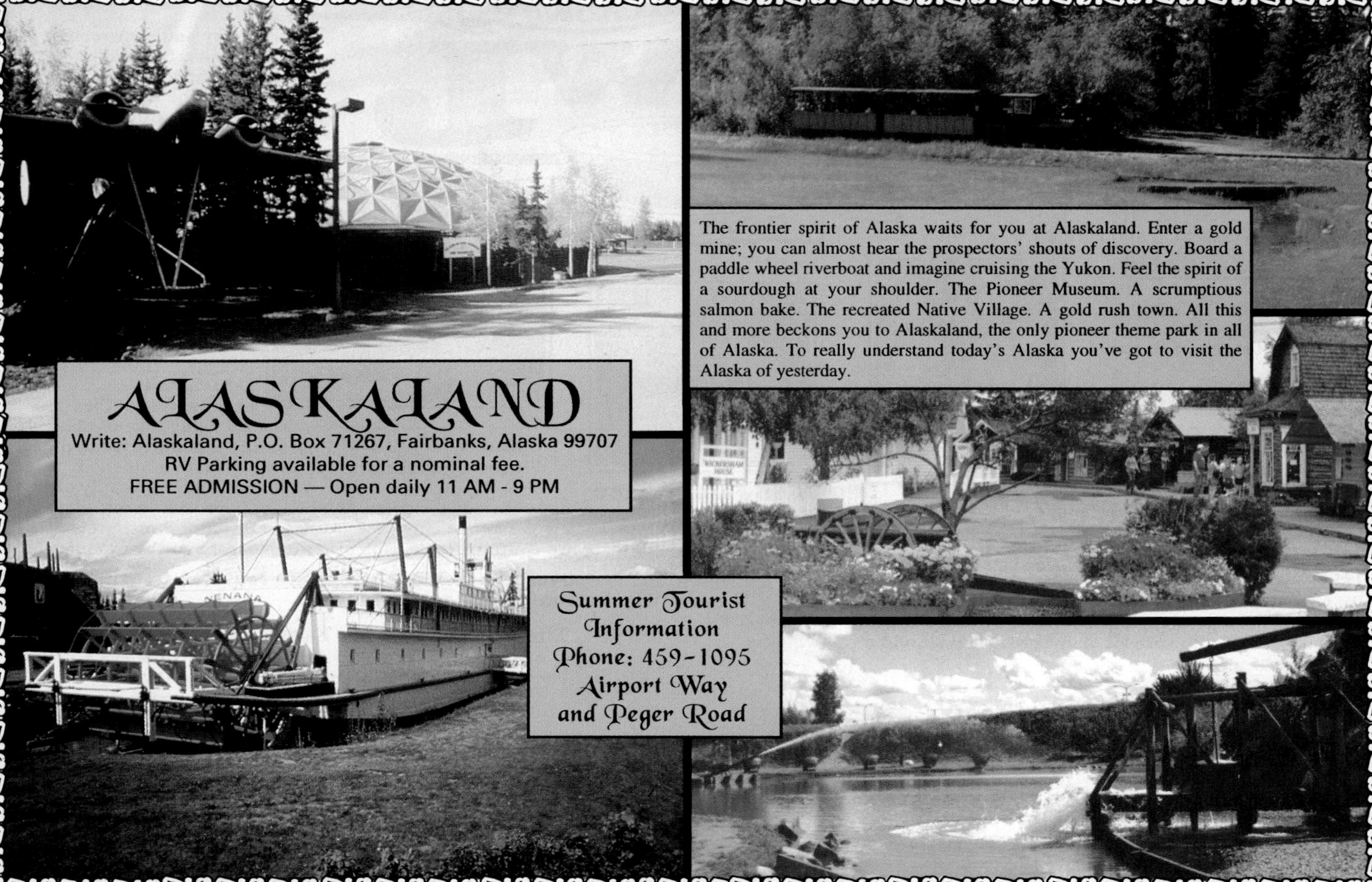

The 44-acre historic park was created in 1967 as the Alaska Centennial Park to commemorate the 100th anniversary of U.S. territorial status and provide a taste of interior Alaska history. Visitors may begin their visit at the information center, which is located just inside the park's main gate. Walk through Gold Rush Town, a narrow, winding street of authentic old buildings that once graced downtown Fairbanks and now house gift shops. Here you will find the Kitty Hensley and Judge Wickersham houses, furnished with turn-of-the-century items; the First Presbyterian Church, constructed in 1906; and the Pioneers of Alaska Museum, dedicated to those who braved frontier life to found Fairbanks. Free guided historical walking tours take place each afternoon.

The park is home to the newly renovated SS *Nenana*, a national landmark. Cared for by the Fairbanks Historical Preservation Foundation, the *Nenana* is the largest sternwheeler ever built west of the Mississippi, and the second largest wooden vessel in existence. The Foundation also displays a 300-foot/91-m diorama of life along the Tanana and Yukon rivers in the early 1900s.

The top level of the Civic Center houses an art gallery featuring rotating contemporary exhibits and paintings; 11 A.M. to 9 P.M. daily, Memorial Day through Labor Day; noon to 8 P.M. daily, except Monday, during the rest of the year.

Behind the Civic Center, you'll find the Pioneer Air Museum, which features antique aircraft and stories of their Alaskan pilots, with displays from 1913–48. Phone (907)

Landmark Immaculate Conception Church at Cushman Street bridge.

(© George Wuerthner)

451-0037, Memorial Day through Labor Day, for information. Admission is $1.

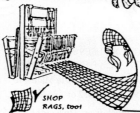

At the rear of the park is the Native Village Museum and Kashims with Native wares, artifacts, crafts and exhibitions of Native dancing. Across from the Native Village is Mining Valley, with displays of gold-mining equipment. The Salmon Bake, with both outdoor and heated indoor seating areas, is also part of Mining Valley. A popular feature, the Salmon Bake is open daily for lunch from noon to 2 P.M. (June 10 to Aug. 15), and for dinner from 5–9 P.M. (end of May to mid-September). Salmon, barbecued ribs, halibut and 18-oz. porterhouse steaks are served, rain or shine.

There's entertainment 7 nights a week starting at 8 P.M. at the Palace Theatre & Saloon, featuring a musical comedy review about life in Fairbanks titled "Golden Heart Review." "Riversong," a musical about Native lifestyles, is performed in the Civic Center Theater at 8 P.M. Thursday through Saturday form mid-June to mid-August. The Big Stampede show in Gold Rush Town is a theater in the round, presenting the paintings of Rusty Heurlin, which depicts the trail of '98; narrative by Ruben Gaines.

The Crooked Creek & Whiskey Island Railroad, a 30-gauge train, takes passengers for a 12-minute ride around the park. Other types of recreational activities available at Alaskaland include miniature golf, an antique carousel and picnicking in covered shelters. A public dock is located on the Chena River at the rear of the park.

Visitors are welcome to take part in square and round dances year-round at the Alaskaland Dance Center. Phone (907) 452-5699 evenings for calendar of events. For more information about Alaskaland, phone (907) 459-1087.

Area Attractions: Fairbanks is a good jumping-off point for many attractions in Alaska's Interior. Head out the Steese Highway for swimming at Chena Hot Springs or Circle Hot Springs. At Fox, 11 miles/17.7 km north of Fairbanks, the Steese Highway intersects with the Elliott Highway, which leads to the start of the Dalton Highway (formerly the North Slope Haul Road). Popular attractions in this area include Gold Dredge

Number 8 (take Goldstream Road exit to Old Steese Highway), a historic 5-deck, 250-foot dredge, and El Dorado Gold Mine at Mile 1.2 Elliott Highway. Both offer gold mining demonstrations and gold panning. See highway sections for details.

Denali National Park is a $2^1/_2$-hour drive, or a $3^1/_2$-hour train trip via the Alaska Railroad, from Fairbanks. Once there, take the shuttle bus or guided tour through the park. For road conditions on the Parks Highway between Fairbanks and Denali, phone the Dept. of Transportation at (907) 451-2226.

Eielson AFB, 25 miles/40 km southeast of Fairbanks on the Richardson–Alaska Highway, was built in 1943. Originally a satellite base to Ladd Field (now Fort Wainwright) and called Mile 26, it served as a storage site

Winter aurora borealis display in the Interior. (© Craig Brandt)

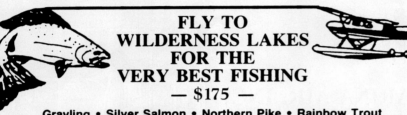

for aircraft on their way to the Soviet Union under the WWII Lend–Lease program. Closed after WWII, the base was reactivated in 1946 and renamed Eielson AFB, after Carl Ben Eielson, the first man to fly from Alaska over the North Pole to Greenland. A tour of the base is offered every Friday during the summer months from 9–10 A.M.; phone the public affairs office at (907) 377-2116 for reservations and more information.

There are 1-day or longer sightseeing trips to Point Barrow, Prudhoe Bay, Fort Yukon and other bush destinations. See ads in this section or consult local travel services.

Historic Gold Dredge No. 8 (Gray Line of Alaska). Gold Dredge No. 8 is a monument to the miners who used the machinery to produce more than 7.5 million ounces of gold, and to the engineers who built it. Visitors tour the only dredge in Alaska open to the public. Gold panning and a "Miner's Buffet" lunch are also available at this national historic site. See advertisement on page 467 in this section. [ADVERTISEMENT]

Play Tennis: There are 6 outdoor asphalt courts at the Mary Siah Recreation Center, 1025 14th Ave. No fees or reservations. For more information phone (907) 459-1070.

Play Golf: Maintaining a scenic 9-hole course with natural greens, the Fairbanks Golf and Country Club (public is invited) is west of the downtown area at 1735 Farmers Loop Road; phone (907) 479-6555 for information and reservations. The 18-hole Chena Bend Golf Course is located on Fort Wainwright; phone (907) 353-6223. North Star Golf Club, located 10 minutes north of downtown on the Old Steese Highway, offers a regulation 9-hole course; phone (907) 457-4653 or (907) 452-2104.

Ride Bikes Around Fairbanks: There are many day-touring choices in Fairbanks. A round-trip tour of the city, the University of Alaska and the college area can be made by leaving town on Airport Way and returning on College Road. The Farmers Loop Road or a ride out the Old Steese Highway toward Fox are easy tours.

Go Skiing: Fairbanks has several downhill ski areas: Cleary Summit, **Milepost F 20.3** Steese Highway; Skiland, **Milepost F 20.9** Steese Highway; Eielson AFB, Fort Wainwright ski hills and Moose Mountain Ski Resort, Spinach Creek Road on Murphy Dome.

Chena Hot Springs Resort at **Milepost J 56.5** Chena Hot Springs Road has over 20 miles of cross-country ski trails, as well as cross-country ski rentals. Other cross-country ski trails are at Birch Hill Recreation Area; drive 2.8 miles/4.5 km north of Fairbanks via Steese Expressway to a well-marked turnoff, then drive in 2.3 miles/

Alyeska pipeline display at Mile 8.4 Steese Highway includes "pig" used for cleaning pipes. (Jerrianne Lowther, staff)

3.7 km. University of Alaska–Fairbanks has 26 miles/42 km of cross-country ski trails. The trail system is quite extensive; you may ski out to Ester Dome.

Go Swimming. Fairbanks North Star Borough Parks and Recreation Dept. offers 3 pools: Mary Siah Recreation Center, 1025 14th Ave., phone (907) 459-1082; Robert Hamme Memorial Pool, 901 Airport Way, phone (907) 459-1086; and Robert Wescott Memorial Pool, 8th Avenue in North Pole, phone (907) 488-9402.

Chena Lakes Recreation Area. This 2,178-acre park, located 17.3 miles/27.8 km southeast of Fairbanks on the Richardson–Alaska Highway, offers a wide assortment of outdoor recreation. There are 86 campsites for both RV and tent camping, including campsites on an island; canoe, sailboat and rowboat rentals; bike paths and trails for nature hikes, skiing, skijoring and dog mushing; and boat ramp access to the nearby Chena River. Admission to the park, maintained by the Fairbanks North Star Borough, is $3 per vehicle between Memorial Day and Labor Day. No admission is charged the rest of the year. For more information, call (907) 488-1655.

Go Fishing: There are several streams

and lakes within driving distance of Fairbanks, and local fishing guides are available. **Chena Lake,** about 20 miles/32 km southeast of the city via the Richardson–Alaska Highway at Chena Lakes Recreation Area, is stocked with rainbow trout, silver salmon and arctic char. The **Chena River** and its tributaries offer fishing for sheefish, whitefish, northern pike and burbot. The Chena River flows through Fairbanks. Grayling fishing in the upper Chena is very good, with some large fish. Grayling fishing in the Chena is restricted to catch-and-release year-round. Chena Hot Springs Road off the Steese Highway provides access to fisheries in the Chena River Recreation Area (see the STEESE HIGHWAY section). The Steese Highway also offers access to the **Chatanika River.** Special regulations apply in these waters for grayling and salmon fishing. Phone the ADF&G Division of Sport Fish office at (907) 459-7207.

Air taxi operators and guides in Fairbanks offer short trips from the city for rainbow trout, grayling, northern pike, lake trout and sheefish in lakes and streams of the Tanana and Yukon river drainages. Some operators have camps set up for overnight trips while others specialize in day trips. The air taxi

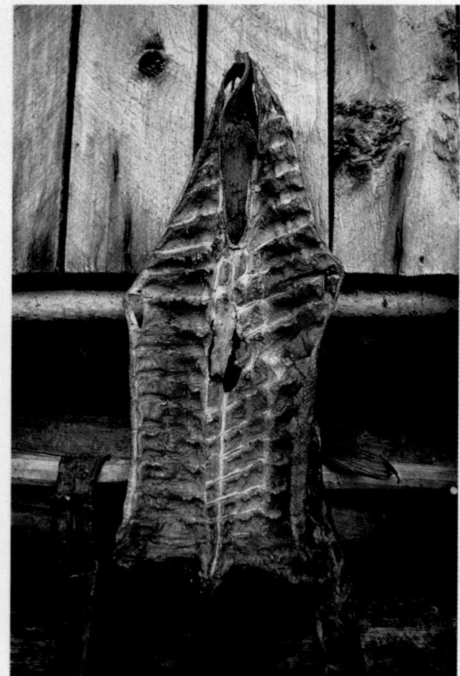

Drying salmon, Interior Alaska.
(© Lee Foster)

operators usually provide a boat and motor for their angling visitors. Rates are reasonable and vary according to the distance from town and type of facilities offered.

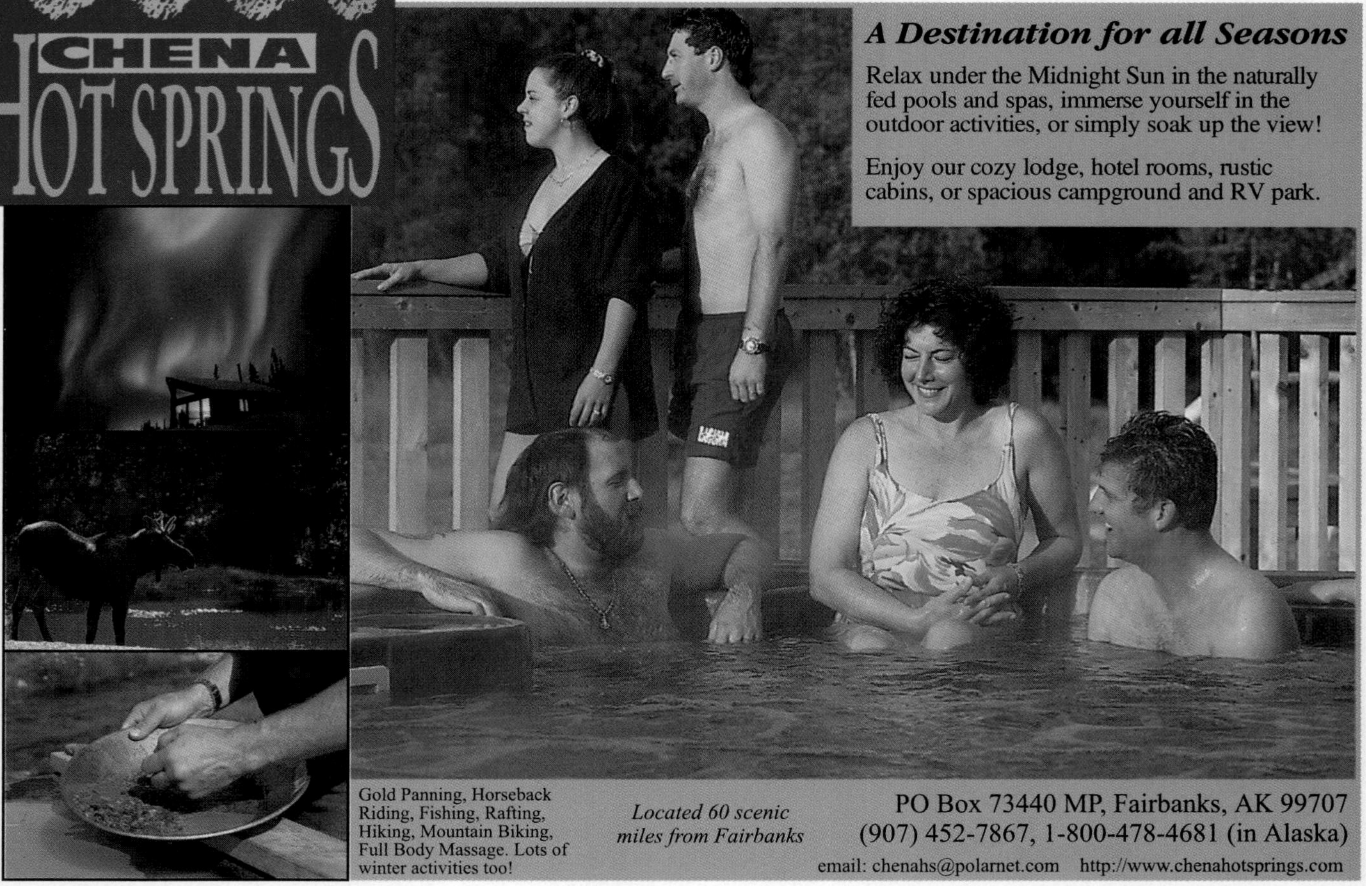

DENALI NATIONAL PARK

(formerly Mount McKinley National Park)
Includes log of Park Road

(See map, page 492)

	Anchorage	Denali Park	Fairbanks
Anchorage		237	358
Denali Park	237		121
Fairbanks	358	121	

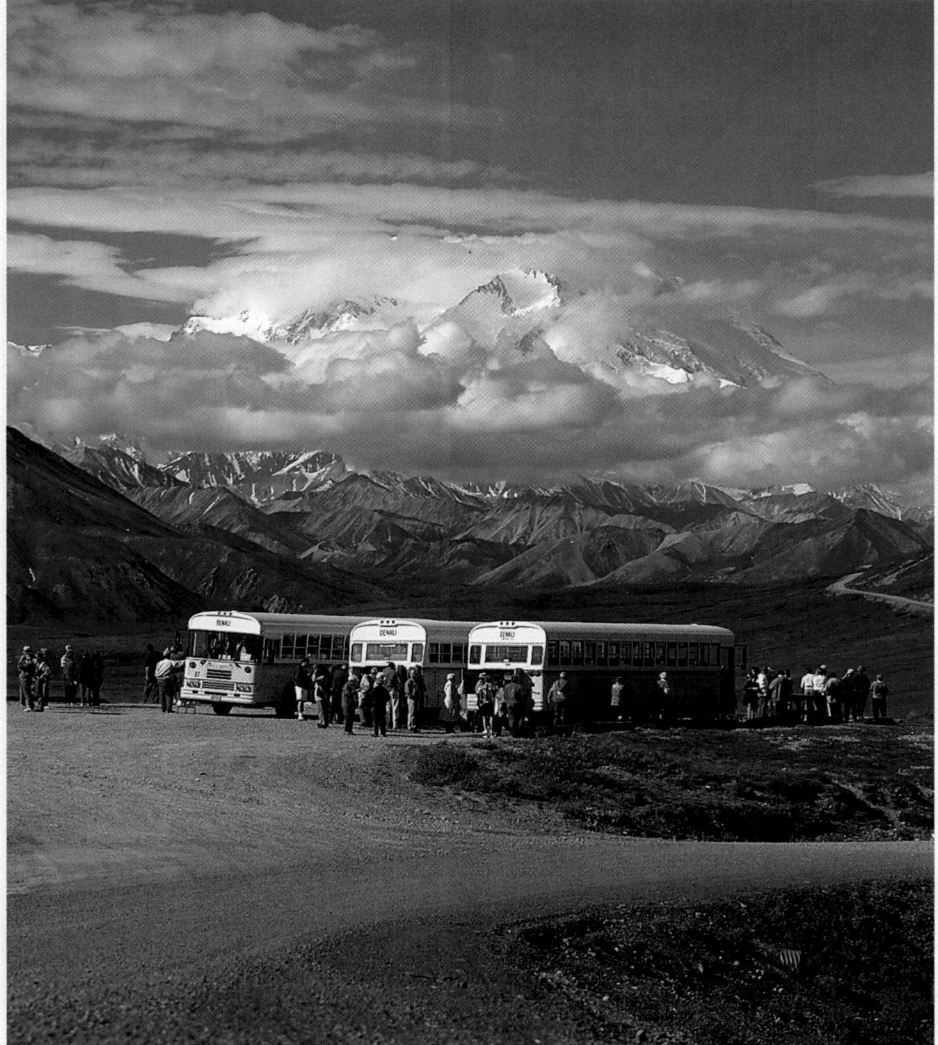

Park tour buses stop at Stony Hill overlook, Milepost J 61 on the Park Road, to view Mount McKinley. (© Craig Brandt)

Denali National Park and Preserve lies on the north flank of the Alaska Range, 250 miles/402 km south of the Arctic Circle. The park entrance, accessible by highway, railroad and aircraft, is 237 highway miles/381 km north of Anchorage, and about half that distance from Fairbanks.

The park is open year-round to visitors, although the hotel, most campgrounds, and food and shuttle bus service within the park are available only from late May or early June to mid-September. (Opening dates for facilities and activities for the summer season are announced in the spring by the Park Service and depend mainly on snow conditions in May.)

When you arrive be sure to stop at the Visitor Center, near the park entrance. The center offers information and limited reservations for campgrounds in the park; maps, brochures and schedules of events; details on ranger talks, hikes, nature walks, sled dog demonstrations and wildlife tours; and shuttle bus schedules and ticket reservations. Also available are National Park entrance passes. The center is open daily in summer, generally from early morning into the evening.

Parking space is limited at the Visitor Center. Day parking is available at Riley Creek Campground (walk or mini-shuttle to Visitor Center).

Lodging and camping are available outside the park on the George Parks Highway, and there are a variety of activities—river rafting, hikes and ranger programs—to enjoy. Check with operators outside the park and with personnel at the Visitor Center about programs and activities.

First-time visitors should be particularly aware of the controlled-access system for Park Road use. Private vehicle traffic on the 92-mile/148-km road into the park is restricted beyond the Savage River check station (**Milepost J 14.8**) to registered campers. Campers may reserve campsites by phone or at the Visitor Center. The shuttle bus system and concessionaire-operated tours are available to allow visitors a means of viewing the park without disturbing the wildlife. See Accommodations/Visitor Services this section for details on the shuttle bus service and campsite reservations system.

There is no policy restricting access by bicycle on the Park Road, although cyclists must stay on the road and overnight at one of the established campgrounds.

In an effort to preserve wildlife viewing opportunities for the public, the National Park Service has set road traffic limits. Traffic will be held to the 1984 averages. Consequently, there are limited bus seats available. When planning trips to the park, visitors should reserve shuttle bus tickets in advance by phone or plan activities in the entrance area—such as attending ranger-led interpretive programs—for the first 1 or 2 days, until bus seats can be obtained.

An admission fee of $5 per person ($10 per vehicle/family) is charged to visitors traveling along the park road. The fee is collected when visitors either obtain shuttle bus tickets, campground permits or stop at the Visitor Center. Persons between the ages of 16 and 62 are charged the entrance fee. U.S. citizens 62 and older may purchase a $10 lifetime Golden Age Passport. 16 years of age or less are exempt from the admission fee. (A $20 annual park pass and the $50 Golden Eagle Pass are valid for admission.)

For information about the park, write Denali National Park and Preserve, Box 9, Denali Park, AK 99755; winter phone (907) 683-2294, summer phone (907) 683-1266 or 1267; Web site www.nps.gov/dena.

One of the park's best-known attractions is Mount McKinley, North America's highest mountain at 20,320 feet/6,194m. On a clear day, Mount McKinley is visible from Anchorage. However, cloudy, rainy summer weather frequently obscures the mountain, and travelers have about a 30 percent chance of seeing it in summer.

First mention of Mount McKinley was in 1794, when English explorer Capt. George Vancouver spotted a "stupendous snow mountain" from Cook Inlet. Early Russian

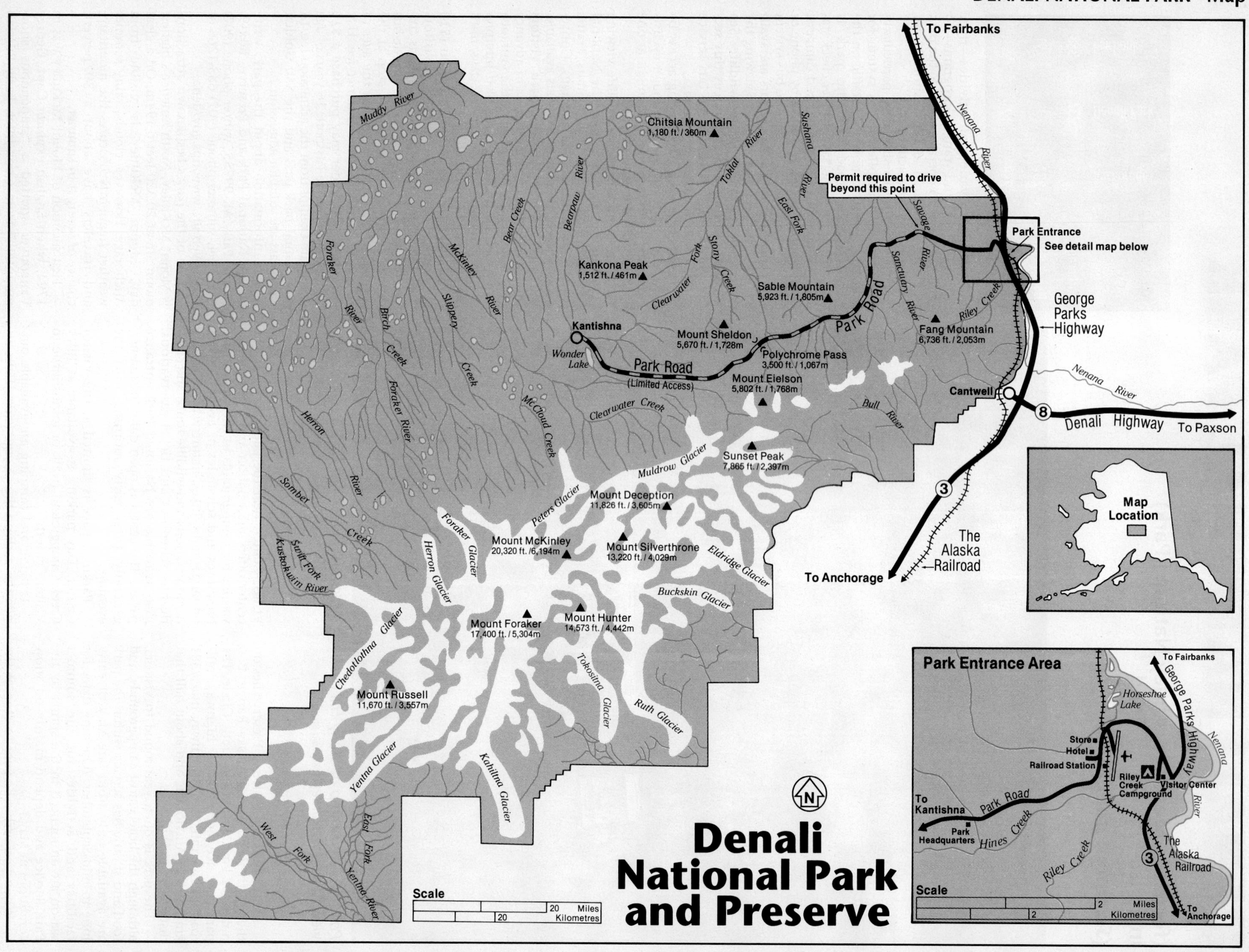
Denali National Park and Preserve
To Fairbanks
Nenana River
Park Entrance
See detail map below
George Parks Highway
Nenana River
Denali Highway
To Paxson
Map Location
Cantwell
The Alaska Railroad
To Anchorage
Permit required to drive beyond this point
Savage River
Riley Creek
Fang Mountain 6,736 ft. / 2,053m
Sanctuary River
Bull River
Park Road
Sable Mountain 5,923 ft. / 1,805m
Polychrome Pass 3,500 ft. / 1,067m
Mount Eielson 5,802 ft. / 1,768m
Sunset Peak 7,865 ft. / 2,397m
Sushana River
East Fork
Toklat River
Stony Creek
Mount Sheldon 5,670 ft. / 1,728m
Chitsia Mountain 1,180 ft. / 360m
Clearwater Fork
Park Road (Limited Access)
Eldridge Glacier
Buckskin Glacier
Muldrow Glacier
Mount Deception 11,826 ft. / 3,605m
Mount Silverthrone 13,220 ft. / 4,029m
Kankona Peak 1,512 ft. / 461m
Kantishna
Wonder Lake
Clearwater Creek
Ruth Glacier
Tokositna Glacier
Mount Hunter 14,573 ft. / 4,442m
Bearpaw River
Peters Glacier
Mount McKinley 20,320 ft. /6,194m
McCloud Creek
Bear Creek
Mount Foraker 17,400 ft. / 5,304m
Kahiltna Glacier
McKinley River
Slippery Creek
Foraker Glacier
Herron Glacier
Muddy River
Birch Creek
Foraker River
Mount Russell 11,670 ft. / 3,557m
Chedotlothna Glacier
Yentna Glacier
East Fork
Yentna River
Foraker River
Herron River
Somber Creek
Swift Fork
Kuskokwim River
West Fork
Scale
20 Miles
20 Kilometres
N
Park Entrance Area
To Fairbanks
George Parks Highway
Nenana River
Horseshoe Lake
Visitor Center
Riley Creek Campground
The Alaska Railroad
To Anchorage
Store
Hotel
Railroad Station
Riley Creek
Hines Creek
Park Road
To Kantishna
Park Headquarters
Scale
2 Miles
2 Kilometres

explorers and traders called the peak *Bolshaia Gora,* or "Big Mountain." The Tanana Indian name for the mountain is *Denali,* said to mean "high one." The mountain was named McKinley in 1896 by a Princeton-educated prospector named William A. Dickey for presidential nominee William McKinley of Ohio. Even today, the mountain has two names: Mount McKinley according to USGS maps, and Denali according to the state Geographic Names Board.

The history of climbs on McKinley is as intriguing as its many names. In 1903, Judge James Wickersham and party climbed to an estimated 8,000 feet/2,438m, while Dr. Frederick A. Cook and party reached the 11,000-foot/3,353m level. In 1906, Cook returned to the mountain and made 2 attempts at the summit—the first unsuccessful, and the second (according to Cook) successful. Cook's vague description of his ascent route and a questionable summit photo led many to doubt his claim. Tom Lloyd, of the 1910 Sourdough Party (which included Charles McGonagall, Pete Anderson and Billy Taylor), claimed they had reached both summits (north and south peaks) but could not provide any photographic evidence. (Much

DENALI PARK AREA ADVERTISERS

Alaska Video Postcards.....Ph. (907) 349-8002
Alaskan Chateau B & B.....Ph. (907) 683-1377
Alpineglow Photo Safaris..............Ph. (800) 770-7275
Alpenglow Tours.............Ph. (800) 770-7275
At Timberline Bed & Breakfast......................Ph. (907) 683-2757
Backwoods Lodge............Ph. (800) 292-2232
Beaver Lake Trail Rides.....Ph. (800) 893-6828
Black Diamond Golf Resort..................Ph. (907) 683-GOLF
Cantwell Lodge............Mile 209.9 Parks Hwy.
Cantwell RV Park.............Ph. (907) 768-2210
Carlo Creek Lodge...........Mile 224 Parks Hwy.
Carlo Heights Bed and Breakfast and Rick Swenson's Sled Dog School.........................Ph. (907) 683-1615
Denali Air..........................Ph. (907) 683-2261
Denali Backcountry Lodge..........................Ph. (800) 841-0692
Denali Bluffs Hotel...........Ph. (907) 683-7000
Denali Cabins Alaska........Ph. (888) 560-2489
Denali Crow's Nest Cabins..............Mile 238.5 Parks Hwy.
Denali Grizzly Bear Cabins & Campground...........Mile 231.1 Parks Hwy.
Denali Hostel....................Ph. (907) 683-1295
Denali Lakeside Lodging..Ph. (907) 683-2511
Denali National Park Hotel...........................Ph. (800) 276-7234
Denali National Park Wilderness Centers–Camp Denali..Ph. (907) 683-2290
Denali National Park Wilderness Centers–North Face Lodge........Ph. (907) 683-2290
Denali North Star Inn.......Ph. (800) 684-1560
Denali Outdoor Center.....Ph. (907) 683-1925
Denali Outlet Store..........Ph. (907) 683-3300
Denali Park Resorts..........Ph. (907) 276-7234
Denali Princess Lodge......Ph. (800) 426-0500
Denali Raft Adventures.....Ph. (907) 683-2234
Denali River Cabins...........Ph. (907) 683-2500
Denali River View Inn.......Ph. (907) 683-2663
Denali Riverside RV Park...Ph. (888) 778-7700
Denali RV Park & Motel...Mile 245.1 Parks Hwy.
Denali Suites.................Mile 248.8 Parks Hwy.
Denali West Lodge...........Ph. (907) 674-3112
Denali Wilderness Lodge..........................Ph. (800) 541-9779
Denali Windsong Lodge...Ph. (907) 683-1240
Denali Wings....................Ph. (907) 683-2245
Destinations in Travel.......Ph. (800) 354-6020
Doug Geeting Aviation.....Ph. (800) 770-2366
Earth Song Lodge............Ph. (907) 683-2863
Era Helicopters.................Ph. (800) 843-1947
Grandview Bed and Breakfast......................Ph. (907) 683-2468
Healy Heights Family Cabins..........................Ph. (907) 683-2639
Hudson Air Service...........Ph. (907) 733-2321
Kantishna Roadhouse.......Ph. (800) 942-7420
Kantishna Wilderness Trails...........................Ph. (800) 942-7420
K2 Aviation......................Ph. (907) 733-2291
Lynx Creek Pizza..........Mile 238.6 Parks Hwy.
McKinley Air Service.........Ph. (800) 564-1765
McKinley Creekside Cabins.........................Ph. (888) 5-DENALI
McKinley/Denali Cabins..........................Ph. (907) 683-2733
McKinley/Denali Gift Shop.................Mile 238.5 Parks Hwy.
McKinley/Denali Salmon Bake...........Mile 238.5 Parks Hwy.
McKinley RV & Campground...........Mile 248.4 Parks Hwy.
McKinley Raft Tours......Mile 238.8 Parks Hwy.
Midnight Sun Express®.....Ph. (800) 835-8907
Motel Nord Haven...........Ph. (907) 683-4500
Mt. McKinley Princess Lodge............Ph. (800) 426-0500
Nenana Raft Adventures..............Mile 248.5 Parks Hwy.
Northern Lights Theater and Gift Shop.....................Ph. (907) 683-4000
Overlook Bar & Grill.........Ph. (907) 683-2723
Otto Lake Bed & Breakfast......................Ph. (907) 683-2339
Otto Lake RV Park...........Mile 247 Parks Hwy.
Perch, The.......................Mile 224 Parks Hwy.
Red Fox Bed & Breakfast, The.............Ph. (907) 683-1227
Rock Creek Country Inn...Mile 261 Parks Hwy.
Sourdough Cabins........Mile 238.8 Parks Hwy.
Stampede Lodge.............Ph. (800) 478-2370
Talkeetna Air Taxi............Ph. (907) 733-2218
Totem Inn........................Ph. (907) 683-2384
Touch of Wilderness Bed & Breakfast..........Ph. (907) 683-2459
Valley Vista Bed & Breakfast..........Ph. (907) 683-2842
Waugamon Village...........Ph. (907) 683-2737
White Moose Lodge.........Ph. (800) 481-1232
Wolf Spirit Expeditions.....Ph. (800) 241-2615

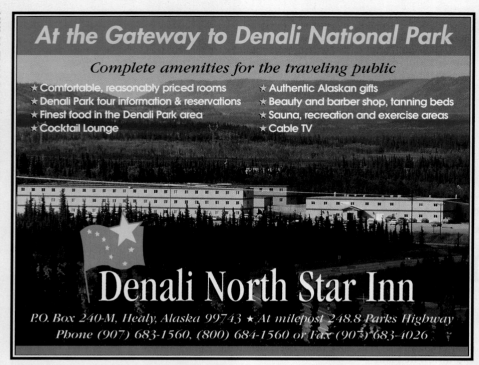

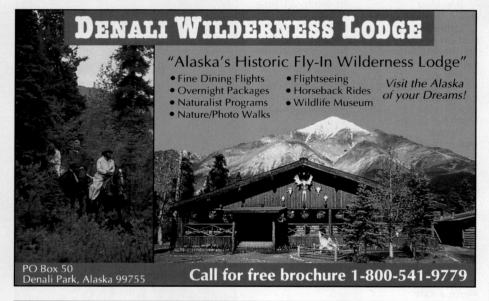

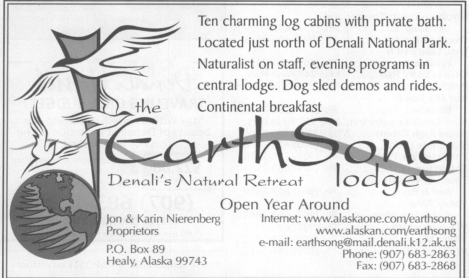

Bull moose in autumn. (© Beth Davidow)

later it was verified that they had reached the summit of the lower north peak.) The first complete ascent of the true summit of Mount McKinley was made in 1913 by Hudson Stuck, Harry Karstens and Walter Harper. Harper, a Native Athabaskan, was the first to set foot on the higher south peak.

Today, more than a thousand people attempt to climb Mount McKinley each year between April and June, most flying in to base camp at 7,000 feet/2134m. (The first airplane landing on the mountain was flown in 1932 by Joe Crosson.) Geographic features of McKinley and its sister peaks bear the names of many early explorers: Eldridge and Muldrow glaciers, after George Eldridge and Robert Muldrow of the U.S. Geographic Service who determined the peak's altitude in 1898; Wickersham Wall; Karstens Ridge; and Mount Carpe and Mount Koven, named for Allen Carpe and Theodore Koven, both killed in a 1932 climb.

The National Park Service maintains a ranger station in Talkeetna that is staffed full time from mid-April through mid-September and intermittently during the winter. Mountaineering rangers provide information on

climbing within the Alaska Range. A reference library and slide/tape program are available for climbers. Mountaineering regulations and information may be obtained from Talkeetna Ranger Station, P.O. Box 588, Talkeetna, AK 99676; phone (907) 733-2231.

Timberline in the park is 2,700 feet/823m. The landscape below timberline in this subarctic wilderness is called taiga, a term of Russian origin that describes the scant growth of trees. Black and white spruce, willow, dwarf birch and aspen grow at lower elevations. The uplands of alpine tundra are carpeted with lichens, mosses, wildflowers and low-growing shrubs. Wildflowers bloom in spring, usually peaking by early July.

Denali National Park represents one of the last intact ecosystems in the world, according to the National Park Service. Here visitors have the opportunity to observe the natural behavior of wild animals. Grizzly bears, caribou, wolves and red foxes freely wander over the tundra. Moose wade through streams and lake shallows. A few lynx pursue snowshoe hare in taiga forests. Marmots, pikas and Dall sheep inhabit high, rocky areas. The arctic ground squirrel's sharp warning call is heard throughout the park.

Migratory bird life encompasses species from 6 continents, including waterfowl, shorebirds, songbirds and birds of prey. Ptarmigan, gray jays and magpies are year-round residents.

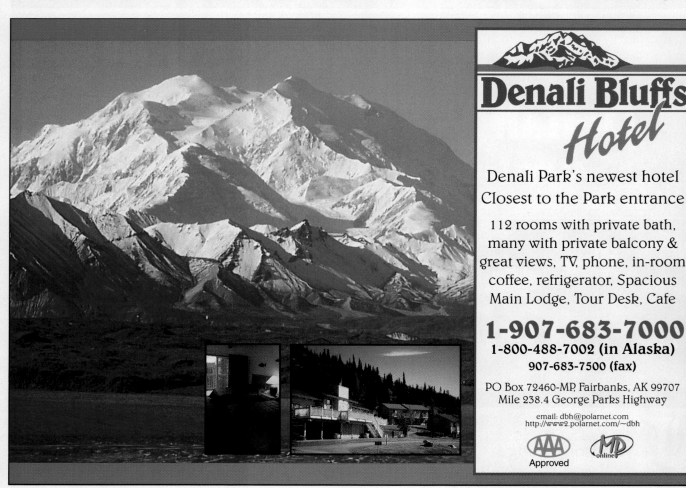

The park's silty glacial rivers are not an angler's delight, but grayling, Dolly Varden and lake trout are occasionally caught in the clear streams and small lakes.

Emergency Services: Within Denali National Park, phone (907) 683-2294 or 911.

ACCOMMODATIONS/VISITOR SERVICES

There is only 1 hotel within the park, but several motels are on the highway, clustered around the park entrance (turn to **Milepost A 237.3** in the PARKS HIGHWAY section). Accommodations are also available in the Kantishna area. *NOTE: Visitors should make reservations for lodging far in advance.* The park hotel and area motels are often filled during the summer. Visitors must book their own accommodations. See ads for accommodations this section.

Visitor services are available from late May to mid-September, depending on weather. The Denali National Park Hotel has a gift shop, restaurant, snack bar and saloon. Limited groceries and showers are available at a small store near the hotel. Gas is no longer available inside the park. Gas service 1 mile/1.6 km north of the Park Road junction, May to mid-September. The post office is near the hotel. There is a dump station near Riley Creek Campground.

NOTE: There are no food services in the park after you leave the headquarters entrance area.

Hoary marmot in Denali National Park. (© Beth Davidow)

Campers should bring a gasoline or propane stove or purchase firewood from concessionaire; a tent or waterproof shelter because of frequent rains; and rain gear.

There are 7 campgrounds in the park along the 92-mile/148.1-km Park Road (see log of Park Road in this section for most locations). Wonder Lake, Sanctuary River and Igloo Creek campgrounds are tent only and accessible only by shuttle bus. Riley Creek, Savage River and Teklanika are available for both RV and tent camping. Morino is for those without vehicles only and is not on the reservation system. ▲

The campgrounds are open from about late May to early September, except for Riley Creek, which is open year-round (snow-covered and no water, flush toilets or dump station in winter). There is a fee and a 14-day limit at all campgrounds in summer. Reservations for campsites at Riley Creek, Teklanika River and Savage River campgrounds are available; see Reservation System following. There is a 3-night minimum stay requirement at Teklanika River Campground, and also a limit of one round-trip to this campground for registered campers with vehicles. Additional travel to and from Teklanika is by shuttle bus. See chart for facilities at each campground. *(NOTE: Campground fees are subject to change!)*

Several private campgrounds are located outside the park along the George Parks Highway. See display ads this section.

For area accommodations, also turn to pages 441–446 in the PARKS HIGHWAY section.

Shuttle bus: The National Park Service concessionaire (Denali Park Resorts) provides

Discover Denali
with the ones who know it best

Denali Park Resorts puts you in touch with Alaska's biggest attraction in ways no one else can match. We offer three comfortable hotels, awe-inspiring wildlife and natural history tours, unique evening entertainment, exciting rafting adventures, excellent restaurants, and a range of activities as big as the Park itself. See Denali the way it was meant to be. Let us make your experience the exciting and memorable adventure you have been dreaming of.

For Information and Reservations:
(800) 276-7234 or (907) 276-7234
Fax (907) 258-3668

We Are Denali!

241 W Ship Creek • Anchorage, AK 99501 • Email: dpr@alaska.net • http://www.denalinationalpark.com
Denali Park Resorts, managed by ARAMARK, is an authorized concessioner of the National Park Service.

shuttle bus service from the Visitor Center to Toklat, Eielson Visitor Center and Wonder Lake. During peak season, bus tickets for the next day's shuttles are generally gone by mid-morning. Up to 8 tickets may be reserved in advance; see Reservation System following. Shuttle buses pick up and drop off passengers along the Park Road on a space-available basis, and stop for scenic and wildlife viewing as schedules permit. The buses generally depart the Visitor Center on the hour and half-hour between 7 A.M. and 2 P.M., May 24 to Sept. 11.

Ticket prices are $12 adult, $6 youth (13–16 years) to Toklat; $20 adult, $10 youth to Eielson; $26 adult, $13 youth to Wonder Lake; and $30 adult, $15 youth to Kantishna. Children 12 and under are free.

A round-trip between the Visitor Center and Eielson Visitor Center takes approximately 8 hours. The round-trip to Wonder Lake takes about 11 hours. Bring a lunch, camera, binoculars, extra film, warm clothes and rain gear. Buses run daily from approximately Memorial Day through Labor Day, weather permitting.

Reservation System: Park shuttle bus tickets and campsites may be reserved through a nationwide, toll-free number, 1-800-622-7275 (PARK). Advance reservations (more than 2 days before departure) are available for 40 percent of the bus tickets and campsites. The remaining 60 percent are available 2 days in advance. Anchorage residents and residents of foreign countries phone (907) 272-7275 for reservations. The phone-in reservation system opens in February. The call center is open 7 A.M. to 5 P.M. (Alaska time), 7 days a week. A maximum of

8 shuttle bus tickets may be requested with each call. Shuttle bus and campsite reservations may also be faxed (907/264-4684) or mailed to Denali Park Resorts, Visitor Transportation System, 241 W. Ship Creek Ave., Anchorage, AK 99501, between Dec. 1 and Sept. 1. Mail-in requests must include a check or credit card number with expiration date, and must be received by Denali Park Resorts 30 days prior to your scheduled departure. Tickets that have been requested and paid for prior to the date of departure can be picked up at a dedicated window at the park visitor center. For travel prior to 7 A.M. each day, unclaimed, prepaid reserved tickets will be in the possession of the bus drivers. During peak season, campgrounds fill up by midmorning for the following day and, on occasion, the day after. *NOTE: This reservation system may be revised in 1998-99.*

At Timberline Bed & Breakfast. The view is simply spectacular. Just minutes from Denali. We have 3 rooms with queen beds. Continental breakfast included. The hospitality is warm and our comfortable rooms are very affordable. Your hosts are Dick and Kim White. Dick was born and raised in Alaska and Kim relocated here in 1987 from Wisconsin. Open year round with fantastic viewing of the Northern Lights from our 16-by-32-foot deck. Reservations strongly suggested, but not required. Box 13 Healy, AK 99743. Phone (907) 683-2757. Fax (907) 683-2767. E-mail: white@mail.denali.k12.ak.us. Internet: www.alaskaone.com/. [ADVERTISEMENT]

Carlo Heights Bed and Breakfast and Rick Swenson's Denali Sled Dog School. Share seclusion and spectacular views. Located on bluff overlooking Nenana River and Alaska Range. Accommodations include 2 double rooms and a private suite, full kitchen and laundry facilities. Ask about our sleeping cabin planned for summer 1998! Open year around, reservations recommended during summertime and required during off season. Sled dog school offers dog mushing courses and tours. Box 86, Denali Park, Alaska 99755. (907) 683-1615. www.mosquitonet.com/~birdsong/sbb.html. [ADVERTISEMENT] MP

Denali Backcountry Lodge. Don't pass up a visit to this lodge if you want to escape the park's crowded east entrance and immerse yourself deep within Denali National Park for a few days. The lodge is located at the end of the 97 mile park road. Full service accommodations feature a comfortable wilderness vacation lodge, cozy cedar cabins, dining room and lounge. One

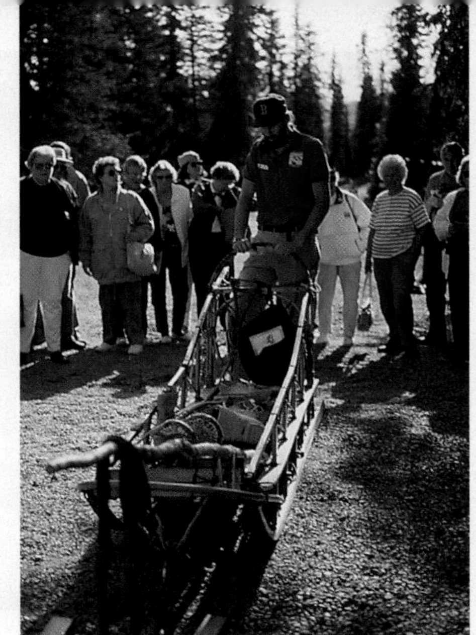

A dog sled demonstration at the park kennels. (© Beth Davidow)

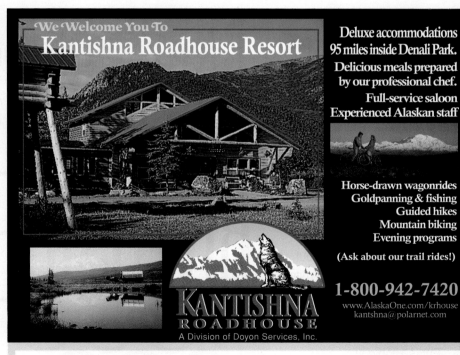

to 4-night stays include round-trip transportation from the train depot, all meals and lodging, guided hikes, wildlife viewing, bicycling, photography and natural history programs. Many famous naturalists are found staying at the lodge and occasionally they conduct special presentations. Credit cards accepted. P.O. Box 189, Denali National Park, Alaska 99755. www.denalilodge.com. Phone (800) 841-0692. [ADVERTISEMENT]

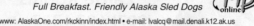

Denali Bluffs Hotel. AAA approved. The newest and closest hotel to the Denali National Park and Preserve entrance. 112 rooms, each room featuring 2 double beds, TVs, phones, refrigerators, in-room coffee. Spectacular views of the Alaska Range. The lodge features a large stone fireplace and cathedral ceilings. There are comfortable sitting areas inside the lodge or outside on the deck to enjoy the panoramic views. Gift shop and coin-operated laundry. Shuttle service to all area facilities. Complete tour and activity desk. Wheelchair accessible. Open mid-May through mid-September. Credit cards accepted. P.O. Box 72460, Fairbanks, AK 99707. Phone (907) 683-7000; or fax (907) 683-7500. E-mail: dbh@polarnet.com. Internet: www2.polarnet.com/~dbh. See display ad this section. [ADVERTISEMENT] ♿ MP

Denali National Park Hotel. Located in park, this 100-room hotel is the bustling center for visitor activities and accommodations. The hotel is a 5 minute walk from the rail depot, provides fine dining, snack shop, gift shop, railcar lounge and grocery store (propane available). The hotel auditorium is the center for national park interpretive services. All accommodations for the hotel, McKinley Chalet (at **Milepost A 238.9** Parks

Highway), McKinley Village Lodge (at **Milepost A 229** Parks Highway), wildlife and history tours, rafting adventures, dinner theater and transportation can be arranged by calling (800) 276-7234; in Anchorage 276-7234. [ADVERTISEMENT]

Denali National Park Wilderness Centers—Camp Denali. Since 1951, Alaska's premier small wilderness lodge and nature center. Log cabin lodging with unparalleled views of Mount McKinley. Natural history emphasis, guided backcountry hiking, wildlife observation, canoeing, biking. Periodic special emphasis sessions and Northern studies credit courses. Three-and four-night stays or longer include lodging, all meals and activities, round-trip transportation from park entrance. Brochure: P.O. Box 67, Denali National Park, AK 99755. (907) 683-2290. E-mail: dupwild@alaska.net. Web site: www.gorp.com/dupwild. [ADVERTISEMENT]

Denali National Park Wilderness Centers—North Face Lodge. Small, well-appointed inn with spectacular Mount McKinley view. Located in the remote heart of the park near the end of the 90-mile park road. Natural history emphasis, guided backcountry hiking, wildlife observation, canoeing, biking. Two- and three-night stays or longer include lodging, all meals and activities, round-trip transportation from park entrance. Brochure: P.O. Box 67, Denali National Park, AK 99755. (907) 683-2290. E-mail: dupwild@alaska.net. [ADVERTISEMENT]

Denali Princess Lodge. Riverside lodging near the entrance to Denali National Park featuring spectacular park and Nenana River

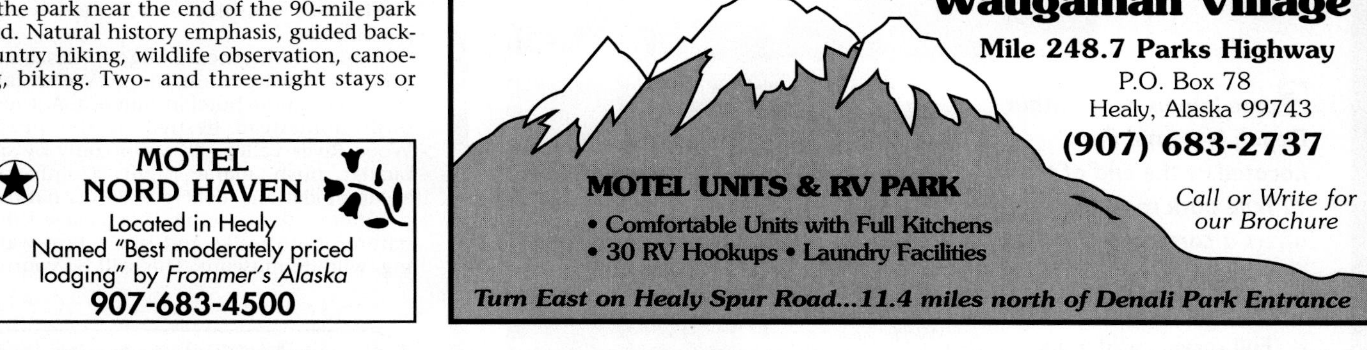

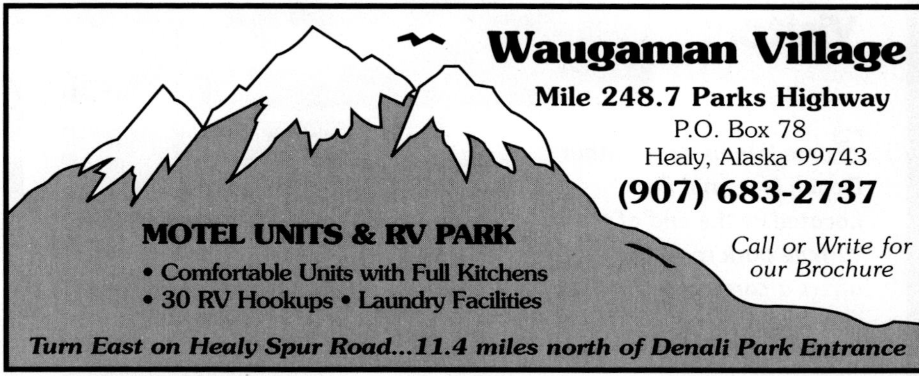

views, several dining options including Mt. McK's dinner theatre, tour desk, gift shop, complimentary shuttle to rail depot and park activities. Open mid-May through mid-September. Phone (800) 426-0500 year-round. [ADVERTISEMENT]

Denali RV Park and Motel. 90 full and partial RV hookups, 30-amp electric. Laundry. Gift Shop. Level sites, pull-throughs, easy highway access. Individual restrooms with private showers, flush toilets. Dump station. Caravans welcome! 14 motel rooms: central bath $49, private bath $69, family units with full kitchens and TVs $99. 25% off extra RV nights. Low season rates for motel ($39 to $79) and RV sites ($10 dry to $14 full hookups) before June 8th and after August 14th. Tour bookings and information. Covered meeting area, outdoor cooking area, pay phones. Close to all park facilities. Beautiful mountain views. Hiking trails. Reasonable rates. VISA/MasterCard/Discover. Box 155, Denali Park, AK 99755. Located 8 miles north of park entrance, Mile 245.1 Parks Highway. (907) 683-1500. 1-800-478-1501. See display ad this section. [ADVERTISEMENT] ▲

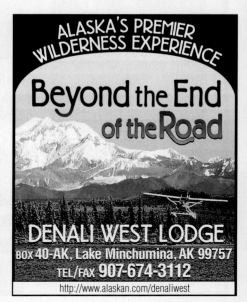

Denali Wilderness Lodge is Alaska's historic fly-in wilderness lodge. We're called the most remote hotel in America. Authentic bush homestead nestled in the pristine Wood River Valley. Accessible only by spectacular bush plane flight. Comfortable accommodations, delicious meals, naturalist programs, flightseeing, horseback riding, nature/photo walks and hikes, bird watching, wildlife museum. This will be your best

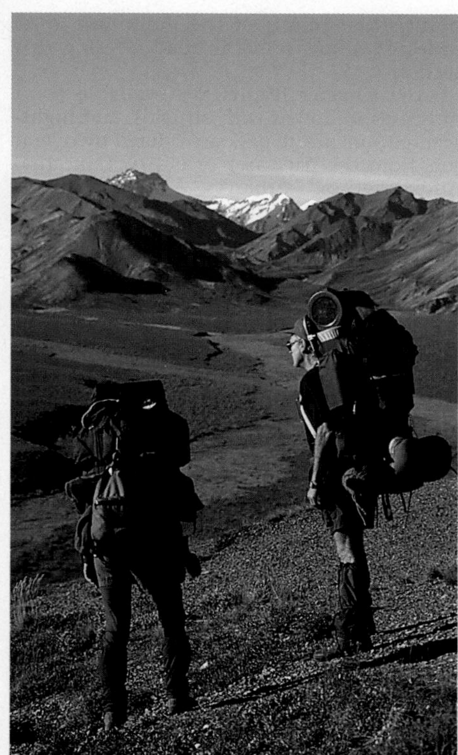

Backpackers in the Polychrome Pass area. (© Beth Davidow)

memory of Alaska! Overnight packages and day trips available. Free brochure. Phone (800) 541-9779. See display ad this section. [ADVERTISEMENT]

Kantishna Roadhouse. Premier wilderness lodge located at the quiet west end of Denali National Park offers opportunities to view, photograph and explore the park. Packages include comfortable log cabins with private baths, guided hiking, gold panning, horses, fishing, fine meals and Alaskan hospitality. P.O. Box 130, Denali Park, AK 99755. Phone (800) 942-7420. E-mail: kantshna@polarnet.com. Internet address: www.alaskaone.com/krhouse/. [ADVERTISEMENT]

Kantishna Wilderness Trails. The ultimate tour through Denali National Park.

95 miles each way with breathtaking mountain vistas and the likelihood of seeing some of Denali's wildlife en route. Arrive at the Kantishna Roadhouse in time for lunch in the dining room, followed by gold panning or an interpretive program. For reservations phone (800) 942-7420; e-mail: kantshna@polarnet.com. [ADVERTISEMENT]

Lynx Creek Pizza. "The Best Pizza in Alaska!" We also offer Mexican specialties, hand-dipped ice cream, espresso, extensive beer/wine selection. In addition, great grocery store. Only 1 mile north of park entrance (Mile 238.6 Parks Highway). In Denali, call (907) 683-2547. [ADVERTISEMENT]

McKinley/Denali Cabins at Denali Steakhouse and Salmon Bake. Economy tent cabins with electric heat and lights from $65. Some cabins with private baths. We have the closest full-service facility to park entrance. Largest T-shirt selection in park. Shuttle to visitor center, railroad depot. Free visitor information. Reservations: (907) 683-2258 or (907) 683-2733 or write P.O. Box 90M, Denali Park, AK 99755. Internet: www.denalipark.com. E-mail: Kevin@denalipark.com. See display ad this section. [ADVERTISEMENT] MP

TRANSPORTATION

Highway: Access via the George Parks Highway and the Denali Highway.

The Park Road runs westward 92 miles/148.1 km from the park's east boundary to Kantishna. The road is paved only to Savage River (**Milepost J 14.7**). Private vehicle travel is restricted beyond the Savage River checkpoint at Mile 14.8. Mount McKinley is first visible at about **Milepost J 9** Park Road, but the best views begin at about **Milepost J 60** and continue with few interruptions to Wonder Lake. At the closest point, the summit of the mountain is 27 miles/43.5 km from the road. See log this section.

Air: Charter flights are available from most nearby towns with airfields, and flightseeing tours of the park are offered by operators from the park area or out of Talkeetna, Anchorage or Fairbanks. A round-trip air tour of the park from Anchorage takes 3 to 4 hours. See ads this section.

Denali Wings. The most comprehensive air tour of Denali National Park. Your 1-hour, 10-minute narrated flight to Mount McKinley overflies both remote and well-known areas of the park. Views of glaciers, mountains and wildlife not seen on ground tours. When you visit Denali, see Denali! Phone (907) 683-2245. Reservation desk at Stampede Lodge, **Mile 248.8** Parks Highway. [ADVERTISEMENT]

Era Helicopters. Enjoy an up close eagle-eye view of the grandeur of Denali National Park. Look for wildlife in the valleys and mountainsides below. Glide by numerous glaciers as Mount McKinley towers on the horizon. Guided heli-hiking tours are also available. Located at Milepost 238. Phone (800) 843-1947 or (907) 683-2574, May to September. [ADVERTISEMENT]

Railroad: The Alaska Railroad offers daily northbound and southbound trains between Anchorage and Fairbanks, with stops at Denali Park Station, during the summer season. For reservations and information, phone (800) 544-0552.

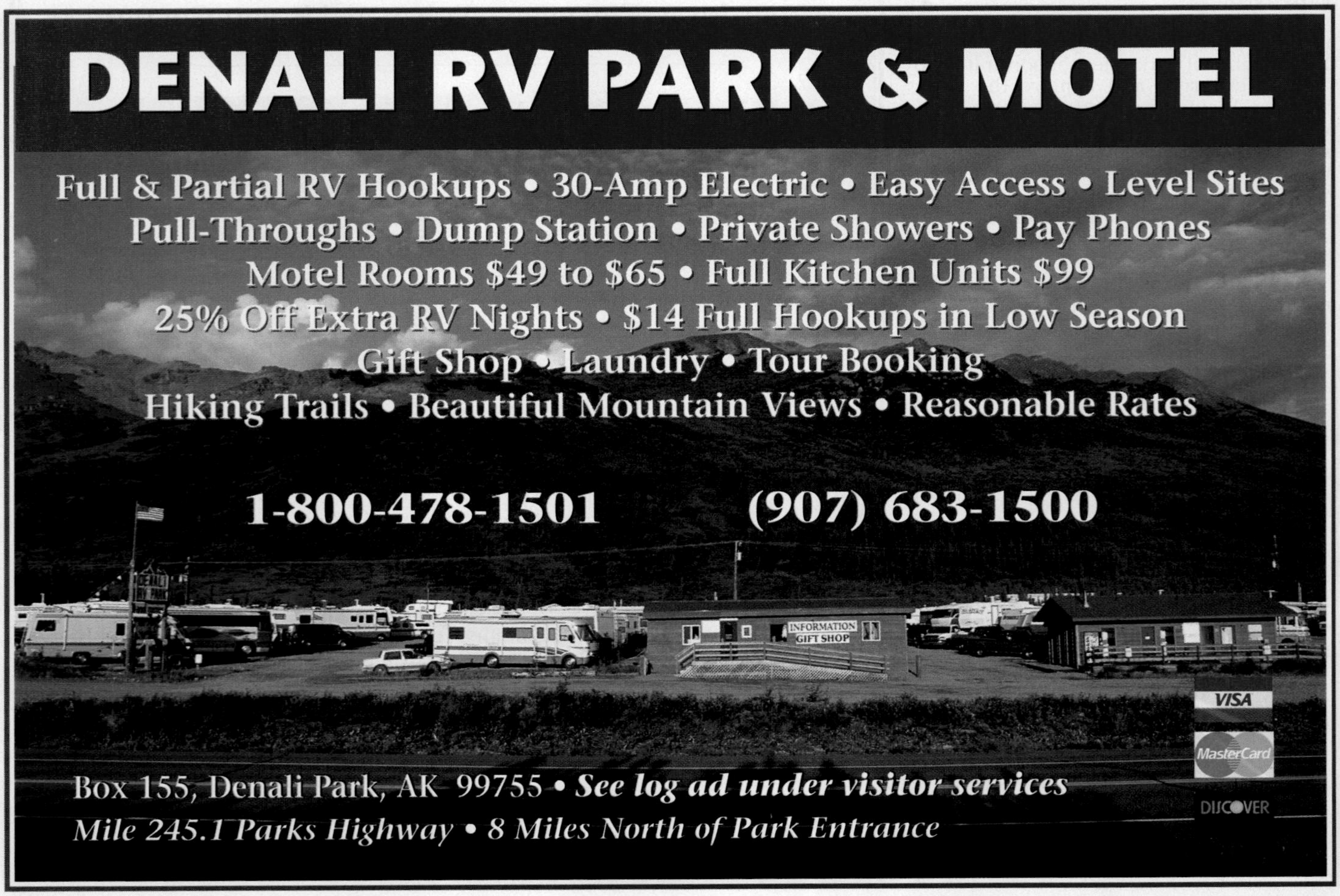

Midnight Sun Express®. Ultra Domes feature glass-domed ceilings, meals freshly prepared by on-board chefs, and exclusive outdoor viewing platforms. Daily service

between Anchorage, Talkeetna, Denali National Park and Fairbanks. Rail packages include overnights at the new Mt. McKinley Princess Lodge and/or Denali Princess Lodge, May to September. Phone (800) 835-8907. [ADVERTISEMENT]

Bus: Daily bus service to the park is available from Anchorage and Fairbanks, and special sightseeing tours are offered throughout the summer months. A 6- to 8-hour guided bus tour of the park is offered by the park concessionaire. Tickets and information are available in the hotel lobby at the front desk tour window. For details on the park shuttle bus system, see Accommodations/Visitor Services this section.

Tours by plane, bus and van are available. See ads this section.

Alpenglow Tours, through Denali National Park in 15-passenger van (not bus) from Fairbanks airport, Nenana, Denali area hotels/RV parks and Cantwell to Mount McKinley Gold Camp in historic Kantishna Mining District. Includes continental breakfast, picnic lunch, snacks and beverages, plenty of rest and photo stops, gold panning. Full- and half-day tours. (800) 770-7275. [ADVERTISEMENT]

ATTRACTIONS

Organized activities put on by the Park Service include ranger-led nature hikes; sled dog demonstrations at park headquarters; campfire programs at Riley Creek, Savage River, Teklanika River and Wonder Lake campgrounds; and interpretive programs at the hotel auditorium.

Private operators in the park offer flightseeing tours, bus tours, raft tours and wintertime dogsled tours. Cross-country skiing and snowshoeing are also popular in winter.

There are few established trails in the park, but there is plenty of terrain for cross-country hiking. Free permits are required for any overnight hikes.

Bear and cubs at Thorofare Pass, Milepost J 64.5 Park Road. (© Robin Brandt)

Avoid surprising bears at close distances; make noise.

A wolf walks across the tundra (© Beth Davidow)

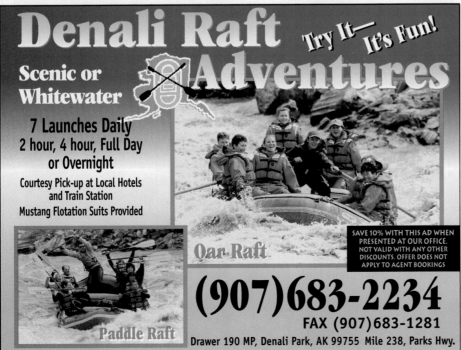

Permits and information on ranger-led hikes and other activities are available at the Visitor Center near the park entrance.

Alpineglow Photo Safaris. Through Denali National Park. Two-day weekend excursion. 10 hours in on Saturday, 10 hours out on Sunday. Overnight wilderness tent cabins. Reservation (800) 770-7275. [ADVERTISEMENT]

Black Diamond Golf. Come visit us on the greens! Golf: 10 holes surrounded by the exceptional beauty of Alaska Mountain Range; or drive a bucket while you enjoy the serenity of Otto Lake. One mile west down the Otto Lake Road. Club rentals available. Phone (907) 683-GOLF (683-4653). [ADVERTISEMENT]

A FEW SPECIAL NOTES FOR VISITORS

The 1980 federal legislation creating a much larger Denali National Park and Preserve also changed some rules and regulations normally followed in most parks. The following list of park rules and regulations apply in the Denali Wilderness Unit—the part of the park that most people visit. Contact the Superintendent at Denali (Box 9, Denali Park, 99755) for more information on regulations governing the use of aircraft, firearms, snow machines and motorboats in the park additions and in the national preserve units.

For those driving: The Park Road was built for scenic enjoyment and not for high speed. Maximum speed is 35 mph/56 kmph except where lower limits are posted.

Your pets and wildlife don't mix. Pets are allowed only on roadways and in campgrounds and must be leashed or in a vehicle at all times. Pets are not allowed on shuttle buses, trails or in the backcountry.

Hikers who stay overnight *must obtain a backcountry permit* and return it when the trip is completed. Backpacking permits must be obtained in person (no phone-ins) up to 1 day in advance at the Visitor Center, **Milepost J 0.5** Park Road. Hikers must pay a fee for the backcountry shuttle bus and park entrance; $15 17 years or older, $7.50 13–16, free under 12.

Mountaineering expeditions are required to acquire a permit and pay a $150 fee before climbing Mount McKinley or Mount Foraker. Permit applications must be received at least 60 days prior to the start of the expedition. Contact the Talkeetna Ranger Station, Box 588, Talkeetna, AK 99676; phone (907) 733-2231.

Natural features: The park was established to protect a natural ecosystem. Destroying, defacing or collecting plants, rocks and other features is prohibited. Capturing, molesting, feeding or killing any animal is prohibited.

Firearms and hunting are not allowed in the wilderness area.

Fishing licenses are not required in the wilderness area; state law is applicable on all other lands. Limits for each person per day are: lake trout—2 fish; grayling and other fish—10 fish or 10 lbs. and 1 fish. Fishing is poor because most rivers are silty and ponds are shallow.

Motor vehicles of any type, including trail bikes, motorcycles and mopeds, may not leave the Park Road.

Feeding wildlife is prohibited. Wild animals need wild food; your food will not help them.

Park Road Log

Distance from the junction (J) with Parks Highway is shown.

J 0 **Junction.** Turn west off the Parks Highway (Alaska Route 3) at **Milepost A 237.3** onto the Park Road. The Park Road is paved to the Savage River bridge.

J **0.2** (0.3 km) Turnoff for Riley Creek Campground and overflow parking area. A dump station is also located here. ▲

J **0.5** (0.8 km) Visitor Center has information on all visitor activities as well as shuttle bus tickets and camping and overnight hiking permits. A park orientation program is available in the theater. The center is open daily. This is also the shuttle bus departure point.

J **1.2** (1.9 km) Alaska Railroad crossing. Horseshoe Lake trailhead.

J **1.4** (2.3 km) Convenience store showers.

J **1.5** (2.4 km) **Denali National Park Hotel.** Located in Denali National Park, this 100-room hotel is the bustling center for visitor activities. The hotel is proud to offer a full-service dining room, snack shop, railcar lounge and grocery store (propane available). The hotel auditorium is the center for national park interpretive services. The hotel is a 5-minute walk from the rail depot. Wilderness activities include wildlife and natural history bus tours, rafting and flightseeing. All arrangements can be made by calling (800) 276-7234; in Anchorage 276-7234, or by contacting the hotel tour desk staff. [ADVERTISEMENT]

J **1.6** (2.6 km) Denali Park Station (elev. 1,730 feet/527m), where visitors can make train connections to Anchorage and Fairbanks; daily service during the summer. Denali National Park Hotel is across from the depot. The post office is located in the

hotel area.

Private Aircraft: McKinley Park airstrip, 1.7 miles/2.7 km northeast of park headquarters; elev. 1,720 feet/524m; length 3,000 feet/914m; gravel; unattended.

J 3.5 (5.6 km) Park headquarters. This is the administration area for Denali National Park and Preserve. In winter, information on all visitor activities can be obtained here. Report accidents and emergencies to the rangers; phone (907) 683-9100 or 911, or outside Alaska (907) 474-7722.

J 5.5 (8.9 km) Paved turnout with litter barrel. Sweeping view of countryside. There are numerous small turnouts along the Park Road.

J 12.8 (20.6 km) Savage River Campground (elev. 2,780 feet/847m). Wildlife in the area includes moose, grizzly bear and fox. ▲

J 14.7 (23.7 km) Bridge over the Savage River. Blacktop pavement ends. Access to river, toilet and picnic tables at east end of bridge.

J 14.8 (23.8 km) Savage River check station. PERMIT OR SHUTTLE/BUS TICKET REQUIRED BEYOND THIS POINT.

NOTE: Road travel permits for access to the Kantishna area are issued at park headquarters only under special conditions. However, the road may be open to all vehicles to Milepost 30 in early May and late September, weather permitting.

J 17.3 (27.8 km) Viewpoint of the Alaska Range and tundra.

J 21.3 (34.3 km) Hogan Creek bridge.

J 22 (35.4 km) Sanctuary River bridge, ranger station and campground (tents only). Wildlife: moose, fox, grizzly bear, wolf. ▲

A bull caribou stops tour buses on the Park Road. (© Loren Taft, Alaskan Images)

J 29.1 (46.8 km) Teklanika River Campground (elev. 2,580 feet/786m). Grizzly bears may sometimes be seen on the gravel bars nearby. ▲

J 30.7 (49.4 km) Rest area with chemical toilets.

J 31.3 (50.4 km) Bridge over Teklanika River.

J 34.1 (54.9 km) Igloo Creek Campground (tents only); accessible by shuttle bus only. Wildlife in the area includes Dall sheep, grizzly bear, moose, fox and wolf. ▲

J 37 (59.5 km) Igloo Creek bridge. *NOTE: The area within 1 mile/1.6 km of each side of the Park Road from **Milepost J 38.3** to **J 42.9** is closed to all off-road foot travel as a special wildlife protection area.* Toklat grizzlies are often seen in the area.

J 39.1 (62.9 km) Sable Pass (elev. 3,900 feet/1,189m).

J 43.4 (69.8 km) Bridge over East Fork Toklat River. Views of Polychrome Mountain, the Alaska Range and several glaciers are visible along the East Fork from open country south of the road.

J 45.9 (73.9 km) Summit of Polychrome Pass (elev. 3,700 feet/1,128m); rest stop with toilets. The broad valley of the Toklat River is visible below to the south. Good hiking in alpine tundra above the road. Wildlife: wolf, grizzly bear, Dall sheep, marmot, pika, golden eagle and caribou.

J 53.1 (85.5 km) Bridge over the Toklat River. The Toklat and all other streams crossed by the Park Road drain into the Tanana River, a tributary of the Yukon River.

J 53.7 (86.4 km) Ranger station.

J 58.3 (93.8 km) Summit of Highway Pass (elev. 3,980 feet/1,213m). This is the highest point on the Park Road.

J 61 (98.2 km) Stony Hill (elev. 4,508 feet/1,374m). A good view of Mount McKinley and the Alaska Range on clear days. Wildlife: grizzly bear, caribou, fox and birds.

J 62 (99.8 km) Viewpoint.

J 64.5 (103.8 km) Thorofare Pass (elev. 3,900 feet/1,189m).

J 66 (106.2 km) Eielson Visitor Center. Ranger-led hikes, nature programs, displays, restrooms and drinking water. Film, maps and natural history publications for sale. Report accidents and emergencies here.

Excellent Mount McKinley viewpoint. On clear days the north and south peaks of Mount McKinley are visible to the southwest. The impressive glacier, which drops from the mountain and spreads out over the valley floor at this point, is the Muldrow. Wildlife: grizzly bear, wolf, caribou.

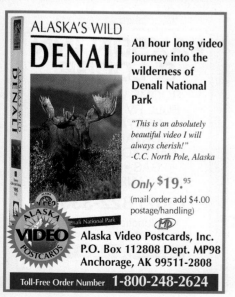

For several miles beyond the visitor center the road cut drops about 300 feet/91m to the valley below, paralleling the McKinley River.

J 84.6 (136.1 km) Access road leads left, westbound, to Wonder Lake Campground (elev. 2,090 feet/637m). Tents only; campground access by shuttle bus only. An excellent Mount McKinley viewpoint. ▲

The road continues to Wonder Lake, where rafting and canoeing are permitted (no rental boats available). Wildlife: grizzly bear, caribou, moose, beaver, waterfowl.

J 85.6 (137.8 km) Reflection Pond, a kettle lake formed by a glacier.

J 86.6 (139.4 km) Wonder Lake ranger station.

J 87.7 (141.1 km) Moose Creek bridge.

J 88 (141.6 km) North Face Lodge.

J 88.2 (141.9 km) Camp Denali.

J 91 (146.4 km) **KANTISHNA** (pop. 2 in winter, 135 in summer; elev. 1,750 feet/533m). Established in 1905 as a mining camp at the junction of Eureka and Moose creeks. Most of the area around Kantishna is private property and there may be active mining on area creeks in summer. Kantishna Roadhouse, which consists of a dozen log guest cabins and a dining hall, comprise the townsite of Kantishna.

Private Aircraft: Kantishna airstrip, 1.3 miles/2.1 km northwest; elev. 1,575 feet/480m; length 1,850 feet/564m; gravel; unattended, no regular maintenance.

J 91.8 (147.7 km) Mt. McKinley Gold Camp.

J 92 (148.1 km) Denali Backcountry Lodge.

DENALI HIGHWAY (8)

Connects: Paxson to Cantwell, AK **Length:** 136 miles
Road Surface: Gravel **Season:** Closed in winter
Highest Summit: Maclaren Summit 4,086 feet
Major Attraction: Tangle Lakes–Delta River Canoe Trail

	Cantwell	Delta Junction	Denali Park	Paxson
Cantwell		217	27	136
Delta Junction	217		244	81
Denali Park	27	244		163
Paxson	136	81	163	

Fall colors along the Denali Highway. The highway is closed in winter. (© Rich Reid)

The Denali Highway extends 135.5 miles/218.1 km from Paxson at Milepost V 185.5 on the Richardson Highway to Cantwell, about 2 miles/3.2 km west of Milepost A 209.9 on the Parks Highway. The first 21 miles/33.8 km from Paxson are paved and the rest is gravel. NOTE: Watch for road construction between Milepost P 21 and P 42 in 1998. The highway is closed from October to mid-May. Do not attempt to drive this highway in the off-season.

The condition of the gravel portion of the highway varies, depending on highway maintenance, weather and the opinion of the driver. The road surface is rough; washboard can develop quickly. Much of the road is in need of gravel, but the roadbed is solid. This can be a dusty and bumpy drive in dry weather. Watch for potholes in wet weather.

There are dozens of primitive campsites and turnouts along the highway (heavily used by hunters in the fall). Excellent fishing in lakes and streams accessible on foot or via designated off-road vehicle trails. Highway access to the Delta River canoe trail through the Tangle Lakes, headwaters of the Delta National Wild, Scenic and Recreational River System, is at **Milepost P 21.5**. The Denali Highway is popular with mountain bikers. There are also many unmarked trails leading off into the Bush. Inquire locally and carry a good topographic map when hiking off the highway.

The Denali Highway has very beautiful scenery and some interesting geography. Glacier-formed features visible from the road include: moraines (drift deposited by glaciers); kames (conical hills or terraces of gravel and sand); kettle lakes (holes formed by blocks of ice melting); and eskers (ridges of gravel formed by streams flowing under glaciers).

Tangle Lakes Archaeological District lies between **Milepost P 17** and **P 35**. Within this 226,000-acre area, more than 400 archaeological sites chronicle man's seasonal exploitation of the local natural resources. For more than 10,000 years, hunter-gatherers have dug roots, picked berries, fished and hunted big game (primarily caribou) in this area. You may hike along the same high, gravel ridges once used by prehistoric people and used today by modern hunters, anglers and berry pickers.

Off-road vehicles are permitted within the district, although some restrictions are in effect spring through fall.

Information on Tangle Lakes Archaeological District and off-road vehicle use is available at the lodges along the Denali Highway and at the Bureau of Land Management office in Glennallen. Write BLM, Box 147, Glennallen, AK 99588; or phone (907) 822-3217.

The Denali Highway was the only road link to Denali National Park and Preserve (formerly Mount McKinley National Park) prior to completion of the Parks Highway in 1972. Before the Denali Highway opened in 1957, Denali National Park was accessible only via the Alaska Railroad.

Emergency medical services: Between Paxson and **Milepost P 77.5** (Susitna Lodge), phone 911 or the state troopers at (907) 822-3263. Between **Milepost P 77.5** and Cantwell, phone the Cantwell ambulance at (907) 768-2982 or the state troopers at (907) 768-2202.

Denali Highway Log

ALASKA ROUTE 8
Distance from Paxson (P) is followed by distance from Cantwell (C).

P 0 C 135.5 (218.1 km) **PAXSON** (pop. 33; elev. 2,650 feet/808m). A lodge with restaurant, gas station, post office and small grocery store is located here. Wildlife often seen near here: grizzly bear, moose and porcupine.

Paxson Inn & Lodge. See display ad this section.

Private Aircraft: Paxson airstrip, adjacent south; elev. 2,653 feet/809m; length

DENALI HIGHWAY *Paxson, AK, to Cantwell, AK*

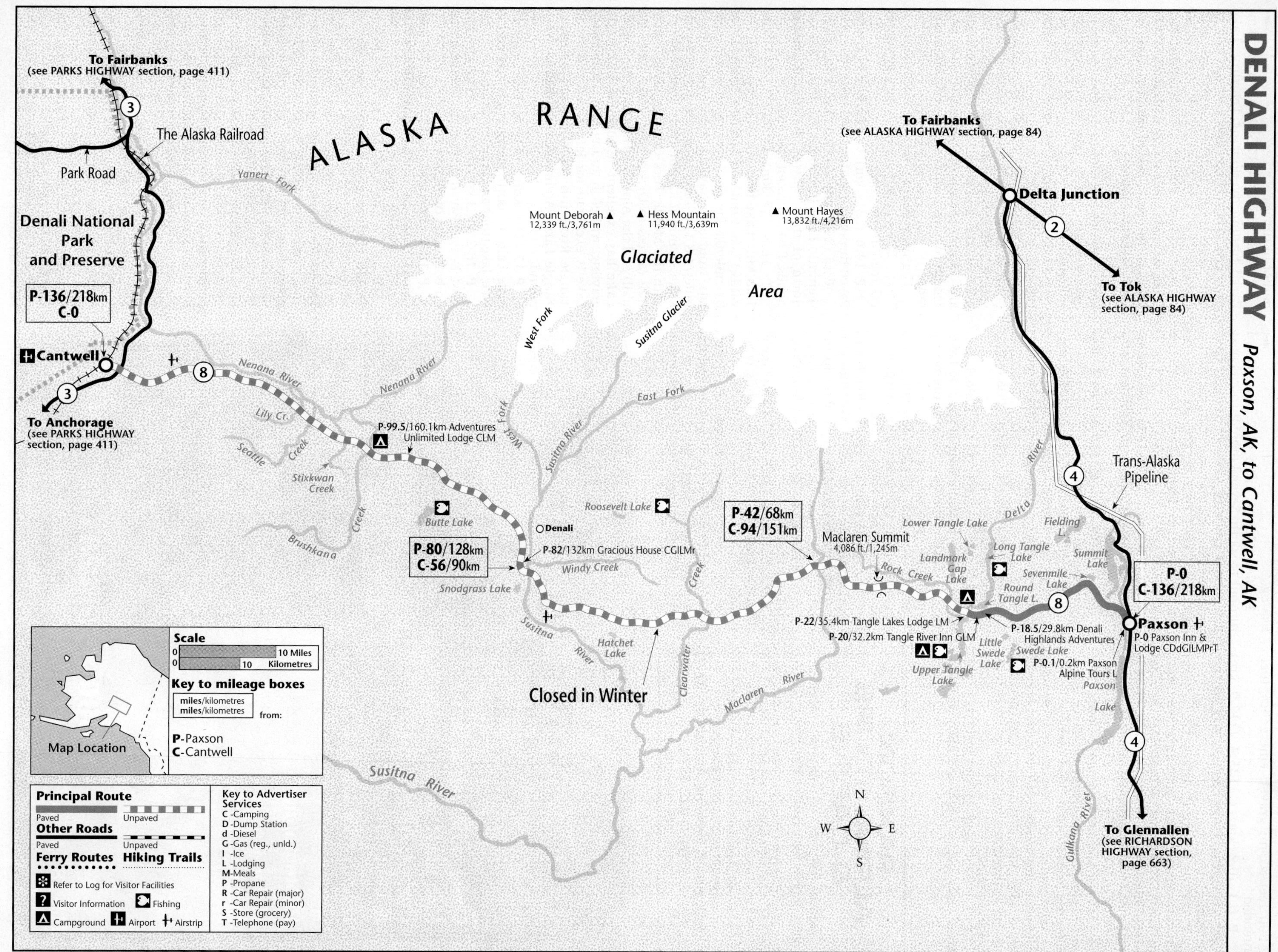

To Fairbanks (see PARKS HIGHWAY section, page 411)
The Alaska Railroad
Park Road
ALASKA RANGE
Denali National Park and Preserve
P-136/218km C-0
Cantwell
To Anchorage (see PARKS HIGHWAY section, page 411)
To Fairbanks (see ALASKA HIGHWAY section, page 84)
Delta Junction
To Tok (see ALASKA HIGHWAY section, page 84)
Mount Deborah 12,339 ft./3,761m
Hess Mountain 11,940 ft./3,639m
Mount Hayes 13,832 ft./4,216m
Glaciated Area
West Fork
Susitna Glacier
East Fork
Susitna River
Yanert Fork
Nenana River
Lily Cr.
Seattle Creek
Stixkwan Creek
Brushkana Creek
P-99.5/160.1km Adventures Unlimited Lodge CLM
Butte Lake
Denali
Roosevelt Lake
P-80/128km C-56/90km
P-82/132km Gracious House CGILMr
Windy Creek
Snodgrass Lake
Hatchet Lake
Clearwater Creek
Closed in Winter
P-42/68km C-94/151km
Maclaren Summit 4,086 ft./1,245m
Rock Creek
Maclaren River
Lower Tangle Lake
Landmark Gap Lake
Long Tangle Lake
Round Tangle L.
Sevenmile Lake
Summit Lake
Fielding L.
Delta River
P-22/35.4km Tangle Lakes Lodge LM
P-20/32.2km Tangle River Inn GLM
P-18.5/29.8km Denali Highlands Adventures
Little Swede Lake
Swede Lake
Upper Tangle Lake
P-0.1/0.2km Paxson Alpine Tours L
Paxson Lake
Trans-Alaska Pipeline
P-0 C-136/218km
Paxson
P-0 Paxson Inn & Lodge CDdGILMPrT
Gulkana River
To Glennallen (see RICHARDSON HIGHWAY section, page 663)
N
E
S
W
Map Location
Scale
0 10 Miles
0 10 Kilometres
Key to mileage boxes
miles/kilometres
miles/kilometres from:
P-Paxson
C-Cantwell
Principal Route Paved Unpaved
Other Roads Paved Unpaved
Ferry Routes
Hiking Trails
Refer to Log for Visitor Facilities
Visitor Information
Fishing
Campground
Airport
Airstrip
Key to Advertiser Services
C -Camping
D -Dump Station
d -Diesel
G -Gas (reg., unld.)
I -Ice
L -Lodging
M-Meals
P -Propane
R -Car Repair (major)
r -Car Repair (minor)
S -Store (grocery)
T -Telephone (pay)

2,800 feet/853m; gravel; emergency fuel; attended.

P 0.1 (0.2 km) C **135.4** (217.9 km) **Paxson Alpine Tours.** See display ad this section.

P 0.2 (0.3 km) C **135.3** (217.7 km) Gulkana River bridge; parking at west end. In season, spawning salmon may be seen here. This portion of the Gulkana River is off-limits to salmon fishing.

P 0.3 (0.5 km) **C 135.2** (217.6 km) Entering Paxson Closed Area westbound. This area is closed to the taking of all big game. Side road leads south to Mud Lake.

Westbound, there are many long steep upgrades and many turnouts the next 21 miles/33.8 km. Wildflowers carpet the tundra in the spring and summer. Watch for nesting swans.

P 1.1 (1.8 km) C **134.4** (216.3 km) **Mud Lake** below highway; early grayling fishing.

P 3.6 (5.8 km) **C 131.9** (212.3 km) Paved turnout to south. Several more turnouts next 2.5 miles/4 km with views of Summit Lake to the north. Gakona Glacier to the northeast and Icefall Peak to the west of the glacier. West of Icefall Peak is Gulkana Glacier.

P 6.1 (9.8 km) **C 129.4** (208.2 km) Paved turnout to north; views of Gulkana and Gakona glaciers.

P 6.7 (10.8 km) C **128.8** (207.3 km) Paved turnout to south.

P 6.8 (10.9 km) C **128.7** (207.1 km) Access to **Sevenmile Lake** 0.8 mile/1.3 km north; excellent fishing for lake trout in summer.

P 7.1 (11.4 km) C **128.4** (206.6 km) Paved turnout to south.

P 7.3 (11.7 km) C **128.2** (206.3 km) Gravel turnout overlooking Sevenmile Lake. Two Bit Lake is the large lake to the north; Summit Lake is to the northeast.

P 7.5 (12.1 km) **C 128** (206 km) Paved turnout to north overlooking Sevenmile Lake. Summit Lake visible to east.

P 8.2 (13.2 km) C **127.3** (204.9 km) Paved turnout to north; small lakes (not visible from highway) in Hungry Hollow to the south.

P 8.7 (14 km) **C 126.8** (204.1 km) Paved turnout to north.

P 9 (14.5 km) **C 126.5** (203.6 km) Gravel turnout. Entering BLM public lands westbound.

P 10.1 (16.3 km) C **125.4** (201.8 km) Paved turnout to south overlooking **Ten Mile Lake**. Short hike downhill to outlet. Fishing for lake trout, grayling and burbot in summer.

P 10.6 (17.1 km) C **124.9** (201 km) Paved turnout overlooking **Teardrop Lake** to south. Short hike down steep hill to lake; lake trout, grayling and burbot in summer.

For the next 4 miles/6.4 km westbound, there are wide-open spaces with magnificent views of the great Denali country. Look for kettle lakes and kames.

P 11.1 (17.9 km) C **124.4** (200.2 km) Paved turnout and trail to **Octopus Lake** 0.3 mile/0.5 km south; lake trout, grayling, whitefish.

P 11.8 (19 km) **C 123.7** (199.1 km) Paved turnout to south.

P 13.1 (21.1 km) **C 122.4** (197 km) Viewpoint at summit; interpretive plaque. In the spring from this spot a traveler can count at least 40 lakes and potholes. To the southeast are Mount Sanford, Mount Drum and Mount Wrangell in the Wrangell Mountain range.

Highway begins descent westbound to Tangle Lakes area. Lupine blooms alongside the road in late June.

P 14.6 (23.5 km) C **120.9** (194.6 km) Paved turnout to south, small lakes to north.

P 15 (24.1 km) **C 120.5** (193.9 km) Fourteenmile Lake lies about 1.5 miles/2.4 km north of the highway, beyond 8 smaller ponds. Paved turnout to north.

P 16.8 (27 km) C **118.7** (191 km) **16.8 Mile Lake** to north (walk up creek 200 yards); lake trout and grayling. **Rusty Lake,** 0.5 mile/0.8 km northwest of 16.8 Mile Lake; lake trout and grayling. Swede Lake trail, 3 miles/4.8 km long, to south; **Little Swede Lake**, 2 miles/3.2 km. This trail connects with the Middle Fork Gulkana River branch trail (access to Dickey Lake and Meier Lake trail) and the Alphabet Hills trail. **Big Swede Lake** has excellent fishing for lake trout, grayling, whitefish and burbot. Little Swede Lake is excellent for lake trout. Inquire at Tangle River Inn for directions. Entering Tangle Lakes Archaeological district westbound.

P 17 (27.4 km) **C 118.5** (190.7 km) **17 Mile Lake** to north, turnout at west end of lake; lake trout and grayling fishing.

P 18.2 (29.3 km) **C 117.3** (188.8 km) Bad frost heave. Paved turnout with lake access on both sides of highway.

P 18.4 (29.6 km) C **117.1** (188.4 km) Gravel turnout by **Denali–Clearwater Creek**; grayling fishing.

P 18.5 (29.8 km) C **117** (188.3 km) **Denali Highlands Adventures.** See display ad this section.

P 20 (32.2 km) C **115.5** (185.9 km) **Tangle River Inn**, known for our cleanliness and warm atmosphere. Restaurant with full menu featuring delicious home-style cooking. Karaoke bar, liquor store, game room. Cozy cabins, log cabin with 5 rooms, 10 beds and private bath—wonderful for groups or families. Newly remodeled rooms with bathrooms. Great fishing, hunting, hiking, berry picking and bird watching. Jack and Naidine Johnson, original owners for over 27 years. Come, meet our friendly crew that's been here for years—a memorable experience. See display ad. [ADVERTISEMENT]

P 20.1 (32.3 km) **C 115.4** (185.7 km) Large paved turnout to north overlooking lake.

P 20.6 (33.2 km) **C 114.9** (184.9 km) Paved parking area with toilets to north.

P 21 (33.8 km) **C 114.5** (184.3 km) The Nelchina caribou herd travels through this

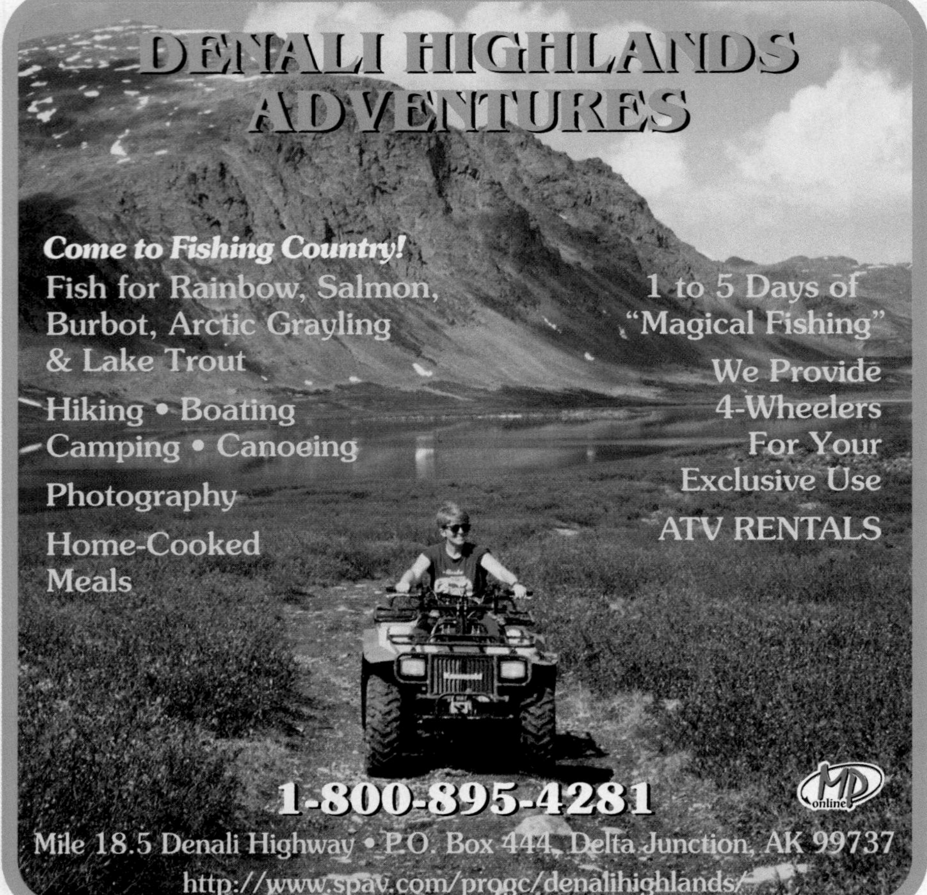

area, usually around the end of August or early in September.

NOTE: Watch for road paving westbound between ***Milepost P 21*** *and* ***P 42.***

P 21.3 (34.3 km) **C 114.2** (183.8 km) Pavement ends westbound.

P 21.4 (34.4 km) **C 114.1** (183.6 km) One-lane bridge over Tangle River.

P 21.5 (34.6 km) **C 114** (183.5 km) Tangle Lakes BLM campground and wayside, 0.7 mile/1.1 km north from highway on shore of Round Tangle Lake; 13 sites, toilets, boat launch, picnicking, hiking (no thick brush, good views). Blueberry picking in August.

Easy access to boat launch for Delta River canoe trail, which goes north through Tangle Lakes to the Delta River. The 2- to 3-day float to the take-out point on the Richardson Highway requires 1 portage. The Delta National Wild, Scenic and Recreational River system is managed by the BLM. For details on this river trail or the Gulkana River trail, contact the BLM, Box 147, Glennallen, AK 99588; phone (907) 822-3217.

Watershed divide. The Gulkana River joins the Copper River, which flows into Prince William Sound. The Delta River joins the Tanana River, which flows into the Yukon River. The Yukon flows into the Bering Sea.

P 21.7 (34.9 km) **C 113.8** (183.1 km) Tangle River BLM campground; toilets, water pump, boat launch. Watch for caribou on surrounding hills. Watch for arctic warblers nesting along the Tangle River.

The name Tangle is a descriptive term for the maze of lakes and feeder streams contained in this drainage system. Access to Upper Tangle Lakes canoe trail, which goes south through Tangle Lakes (portages required) to Dickey Lake, then follows the Middle Fork to the main Gulkana River.

AREA FISHING: Tangle Lakes system north and south of the highway (**Long Tangle, Round Tangle, Upper Tangle** and **Lower Tangle Lake**). Good grayling, burbot and lake trout fishing. Fishing begins as soon as the ice goes out, usually in early June, and continues into September. Good trolling, and some fish are taken from the banks. Early in season, trout are hungry and feed on snails in the shallows at the outlet. Inquire at Tangle Lakes Lodge or Tangle River Inn for information and assistance in getting to where the fish are.

P 22 (35.4 km) **C 113.5** (182.6 km) **Tangle Lakes Lodge,** built in 1952, was the first lodge on the Denali Highway. Owned for the last 8 years by longtime Alaska residents Rich and Linda Homstrom, it has become well known for its fine food and friendly atmosphere. In addition to being the best Arctic grayling fishery you can drive to in Alaska, Tangle Lakes also provides incredible birding opportunities (arctic warbler, Smith's longspur, gyrfalcon, long-tailed jaeger and many more). The Nelchina caribou herd, 50,000 strong, roams throughout the region, which is also a moose calving area, providing excellent wildlife viewing opportunities. Cozy log cabins, canoe rentals, fine food, accurate local information and a friendly lodge staff makes a stop at Tangle Lakes Lodge a most memorable one. Phone: (907) 688-9173 (winter) or (907) 259-7302 (summer). [ADVERTISEMENT] MP

P 22.3 (35.9 km) **C 113.2** (182.2 km) Trail to south along esker.

P 24.8 (39.9 km) **C 110.7** (178.1 km) Landmark Gap BLM trail to north open to ORVs to **Landmark Gap Lake**. Grayling in stream at trail end; trout in main lake. Mountain biking is also popular on this trail. Double-ended turnout to south.

P 24.9 (40.1 km) **C 110.6** (178 km) **Rock Creek** 1-lane bridge; parking and informal campsites at both ends of bridge. Fair grayling fishing. Landmark Gap Lake lies north of highway between the noticeable gap in the mountains (a caribou migration route).

P 28.1 (45.2 km) **C 107.4** (172.8 km) Downwind Lake north side of road.

P 30.6 (49.2 km) **C 104.9** (168.8 km) Cat trail leads 2 miles/3.2 km north to **Glacier Lake**; lake trout, grayling.

P 32 (51.5 km) **C 103.5** (166.6 km) Amphitheater Mountains rise above High Valley to the north. Glacier Lake is visible in the gap in these mountains. Turnout to north.

P 35.2 (56.6 km) **C 100.3** (161.4 km) Turnout at Maclaren Summit (elev. 4,086 feet/1,245m). Highest highway pass in Alaska (not including 4,800-foot/1,463-m Atigun Pass on the Dalton Highway, formerly the North Slope Haul Road). A profusion of flowers—notably the various heaths and frigid shooting star. Dwarf fireweed.

P 36 (57.9 km) **C 99.5** (160.1 km) **36 Mile Lake** 0.5-mile/0.8-km hike north; lake trout and grayling.

P 36.4 (58.6 km) **C 99.1** (159.5 km) Entering Clearwater Creek controlled-use area westbound. Closed to motorized hunting. Small turnouts to north and south.

P 36.6 (58.9 km) **C 98.9** (159.2 km) Osar Lake ORV trail south; 5 miles/8 km.

P 37 (59.5 km) **C 98.5** (158.5 km) Turnout with view of Susitna River valley, Mount Hayes and the Alaska Range. Osar Lake trail leads 5 miles/8 km south toward the Alphabet Hills; Maclaren Summit trail leads 3 miles/4.8 km north to good view of Alaska Range; mountain biking. Osar Lake was first named Asar Lake, the Scandinavian

The Denali Highway is popular with moose hunters in the fall. (© George Wuerthner)

word for esker. (An esker is a ridge of sand and gravel marking the former stream channel of a glacier.) Leaving Tangle Lakes Archaeological district westbound. Expect road construction eastbound to **Mile 21**.

P 39.8 (64.1 km) **C 95.7** (154 km) Sevenmile Lake ORV trail to north; 6.5 miles/10.5 km long, parallels Boulder Creek, crosses peat bog.

P 42 (67.6 km) **C 93.5** (150.5 km) Maclaren River and bridge, a 364-foot/111-m multiple span crossing this tributary of the Susitna River. Parking and litter barrels. Maclaren River Lodge west side. Look for cliff swallows nesting under bridge.

P 43.3 (69.7 km) **C 92.2** (148.4 km) Maclaren River Road leads north 12 miles/19.3 km to Maclaren Glacier; mountain biking. Maclaren River trailhead to south. The Maclaren River rises in the glaciers surrounding Mount Hayes (elev. 13,832 feet/4,216m). For the next 60 miles/96.6 km westbound, the highest peaks of this portion of the mighty Alaska Range are visible, weather permitting, to the north. From east to west: Mount Hayes, Hess Mountain (elev. 11,940 feet/3,639m) and Mount Deborah (elev. 12,339 feet/3,761m). Mount Hayes, first climbed in August 1941, is named after Charles Hayes, an early member of the U.S. Geological Survey. Mount Deborah, first climbed in August 1954, was named in 1907 by Judge Wickersham after his wife.

P 44.1 (71 km) **C 91.4** (147.1 km) Small turnout to south. Beaver lodge and dam.

P 44.6 (71.8 km) **C 90.9** (146.3 km) Highway crosses Crazy Notch gap.

P 46.9 (75.5 km) **C 88.6** (142.6 km) Road north to **46.9 Mile Lake**; fishing for grayling in lake and outlet stream.

P 47 (75.6 km) **C 88.5** (142.4 km) Beaver dam. Excellent grayling fishing in **Crooked Creek**, which parallels the highway.

P 48.6 (78.2 km) **C 86.9** (139.8 km) Informal campsite by small lake.

P 49 (78.8 km) **C 86.5** (139.2 km) The road follows an esker between 4 lakes. Parts of the highway are built on eskers. Watch for ptarmigan, swans, arctic terns, ducks and beaver. Look for a pingo (earth-covered ice hill) at lakeshore.

P 49.7 (80 km) **C 85.8** (138.1 km) Turnout to north overlooks 50 Mile lake. Interpretive plaque on glacial topography and wildlife, including trumpeter swans and loons. Road access to north.

P 51.8 (83.4 km) **C 83.7** (134.7 km) Private hunting camp to south. Trail to north.

P 56.1 (90.3 km) **C 79.4** (127.8 km) **Clearwater Creek** 1-lane bridge and rest area with toilets and litter barrels. Informal camping. Cliff swallows nest under bridge. Grayling fishing in summer.

P 57.5 (92.5 km) **C 78** (125.5 km) Double-ended turnout.

P 58.2 (93.7 km) **C 77.3** (124.4 km) Clearwater Creek walk-in (no motorized vehicles) hunting area north of highway.

P 58.8 (94.6 km) **C 76.7** (123.4 km) Road winds atop an esker flanked by kames and kettle lakes. Watch for moose.

P 64 (103 km) **C 71.5** (115.1 km) Road descends westbound into Susitna Valley. Highest elevation of mountains seen to north is 5,670 feet/1,728m.

P 65.7 (105.7 km) **C 69.8** (112.3 km) Waterfall Creek.

P 68.9 (110.9 km) **C 66.6** (107.2 km) Raft Creek. Hatchet Lake lies about 2 miles/3.2 km south of highway. Inquire at Gracious House, **Milepost P 82**, for directions.

P 71.5 (115.1 km) **C 64** (103 km) Moose often sighted in valley below road.

P 72.2 (116.2 km) **C 63.3** (101.9 km) Nowater Creek.

P 72.8 (117.2 km) **C 62.7** (100.9 km) Swampbuggy Lake.

P 75 (120.7 km) **C 60.5** (97.4 km) Clearwater Mountains to north; watch for bears on slopes. View of Susitna River in valley below.

P 77.5 (124.7 km) **C 58** (93.3 km) Lodge; current status of services unknown.

Private Aircraft: Private airstrip, adjacent west; elev. 2,675 feet/815m; length 2,000 feet/610m; gravel.

P 78.8 (126.8 km) **C 56.7** (91.2 km) Valdez Creek Road. Former mining camp of Denali, about 6 miles/10 km north of the highway via a gravel road, was first established in 1907 after the discovery of gold in 1903. The Valdez Creek Mine operated at this site from 1990 to 1995. The mine pit was converted into a lake in 1996 as part of a reclamation project. Area mining equipment was donated to the Museum of Transportation and Industry (see **Milepost A 47** in the PARKS HIGHWAY section). Do not trespass on private mining claims. Fair fishing reported in **Roosevelt Lake** and area creeks. Watch for bears.

P 79.3 (127.6 km) **C 56.2** (90.4 km) Susitna River 1-lane bridge, a combination multiple span and deck truss, 1,036 feet/316m long. Butte Creek trailhead.

The Susitna River heads at Susitna Glacier in the Alaska Range (between Mounts Hess and Hayes) and flows southwest 260 miles/418 km to Cook Inlet. Downstream through Devil's Canyon it is considered unfloatable. The river's Tanaina Indian name, said to mean "sandy river," first appeared in 1847 on a Russian chart.

Entering Game Management Unit 13E westbound, leaving unit 13B eastbound.

P 81 (130.4 km) **C 54.5** (87.7 km) Snodgrass Lake (elev. 2,493 feet/760m) is about 2 miles/3.2 km south of the highway. Check with Gracious House, **Milepost P 82**, for directions. *CAUTION: Watch for horses.*

P 82 (132 km) **C 53.5** (86.1 km) **Gracious House.** Centrally located on the shortest, most scenic route to Denali National Park. 27 modern cabins or motel units, most with private baths, bar, cafe featuring ice cream and home-baked pies. Tent sites, parking for self-contained RVs overlooking lake. Water, restrooms and showers available at lodge. "Cash" gas, towing, welding, mechanical repairs, tire service. Air taxi, guide service available in a variety of combinations serving the sportsman, tourist, photographer, families with tours and outings to individual desires, from campouts to guided hunts. Winter snowmobiling, ice fishing. Same owners/operators for 40 years. Reasonable rates. For brochure on hunting and fishing trips, write to the Gracious Family. Summer address: P.O. Box 88, Cantwell, AK 99729. Winter address: P.O. Box 21, Anchorage, AK 99521. Message phone (907) 333-3148 or phone (907) 822-7307 (let ring, radio phone). E-mail: crhoa36683@aol.com. Internet: www.alaskaone.com/gracious. [ADVERTISEMENT]

P 83 (133.6 km) **C 52.5** (84.5 km) Visible across the Susitna River is Valdez Creek mining camp at the old Denali townsite.

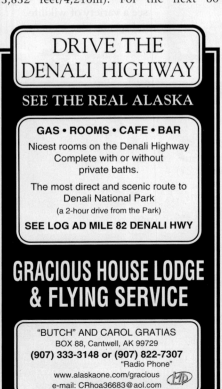

Valdez Creek Mine is operated by Cambior Alaska Inc. *CAUTION: Watch for truck traffic.*

P 84 (135.2 km) **C 51.5** (82.9 km) **Stevenson's Lake** 0.5 mile/0.8 km south; grayling fishing.

P 88.7 (142.7 km) **C 46.8** (75.3 km) Large turnout by pond. Good stop for pictures of the Alaska Range (weather permitting).

P 90.5 (145.6 km) **C 45** (72.4 km) A major water drainage divide occurs near here. East of the divide, the tributary river system of the Susitna flows south to Cook Inlet. West of the divide, the Nenana River system flows north to the Yukon River, which empties into the Bering Sea.

P 91.2 (146.8 km) **C 44.3** (71.3 km) Turnout and access to small lake beside road.

P 93.8 (151 km) **C 41.7** (67.1 km) **Butte Lake,** 5 miles/8 km south of highway. Motorized access by all-terrain vehicle from lodge at **Milepost P 99.5**. Best fishing June through September. Lake trout to 30 lbs., troll with red-and-white spoons or grayling remains; grayling to 20 inches, small flies or spinners; burbot to 12 lbs., use bait on bottom.

P 94.3 (151.8 km) **C 41.2** (66.3 km) Short road leads to parking area above pond. View of Monahan Flat and Alaska Range to the north. Interpretive plaque on earthquakes.

P 94.8 (152.6 km) **C 40.7** (65.5 km) Bridge over Canyon Creek.

P 96.1 (154.7 km) **C 39.4** (63.4 km) Good viewpoint of the West Fork Glacier. Looking north up the face of this glacier, Mount Deborah is to the left and Mount Hess is in the center.

P 97 (156.1 km) **C 38.5** (62 km) Looking at the Alaska Range to the north, Mount Deborah, Mount Hess and Mount Hayes are the highest peaks to your right; to the left are the lower peaks of the Alaska Range and Mount Nenana.

P 99.5 (160.1 km) **C 36** (57.9 km) **Adventures Unlimited Lodge.** Rooms starting at $45. Hiking, mountain biking and fishing. Special packages include Denali Park tour and guided fishing. Remote cabin rental with boat at Butte Lake. Cafe with home cooking and fresh pies. Phone (907) 561-7723, fax (907) 561-2093, e-mail mis@goalaska.com. Visit our web page, www.goalaska.com. See display ad. [ADVERTISEMENT]

P 100 (160.9 km) **C 35.5** (57.1 km) Residents of this area say it is a wonderful place for picking cranberries and blueberries in August. Numerous turnouts and some patches of rough road next 3 miles westbound.

P 103 (165.8 km) **C 32.5** (52.3 km) Highway is built on an esker between kettle lakes.

P 104.6 (168.3 km) **C 30.9** (49.7 km) **Brushkana River** bridge and BLM campground; 12 sites beside river, tables, firepits, toilets, litter barrels and water. Fishing for grayling and Dolly Varden. Watch for moose. ▲

P 106.6 (171.6 km) **C 28.9** (46.5 km) **Canyon Creek,** grayling fishing.

P 107.2 (172.5 km) **C 28.3** (45.5 km) **Stixkwan Creek** flows under highway in culvert. Grayling.

P 111.2 (179 km) **C 24.3** (39.1 km) **Seattle Creek** 1-lane bridge. Fishing for grayling and Dolly Varden.

P 112 (180.2 km) **C 23.5** (37.8 km) Lily Creek. Matanuska–Susitna Borough boundary.

P 113.2 (182.2 km) **C 22.3** (35.9 km) View to east of the Alaska Range and extensive rolling hills grazed by caribou.

The Denali Highway is also popular with bicyclists. (© George Wuerthner)

P 115.7 (186.2 km) **C 19.8** (31.9 km) Large gravel turnout with beautiful view of the Nenana River area.

P 117.1 (188.4 km) **C 18.4** (29.6 km) Log cabin beside Nenana River.

P 117.5 (189.1 km) **C 18** (29 km) Leaving BLM public lands westbound.

P 117.7 (189.4 km) **C 17.8** (28.6 km) Highway parallels the Nenana River, which flows into the Tanana River at the town of Nenana.

P 120 (193.1 km) **C 15.5** (24.9 km) A variety of small water birds, including ducks, snipes and terns, can be observed in the marshy areas along both sides of the road for the next 1 mile/1.6 km westbound.

P 122.3 (196.8 km) **C 11.3** (18.2 km) View (westbound) of Mount McKinley.

P 125.7 (202.3 km) **C 9.8** (15.8 km) **Joe Lake,** about 0.5 mile/0.8 km long (large enough for floatplane), is south of highway. **Jerry Lake** is about 0.2 mile/0.3 km north of the highway. Two small turnouts provide room for campers and fishermen. Both lakes have grayling.

P 128.1 (206.2 km) **C 7.4** (11.9 km) Fish Creek bridge. Access to creek and informal campsite at east end of bridge.

P 128.2 (206.3 km) **C 7.3** (11.7 km) Beautiful view of Talkeetna Mountains to the south.

P 128.6 (207 km) **C 6.9** (11.1 km) Small pond just off highway. Good berry picking in the fall. Fishing for grayling in unnamed creek.

P 130.3 (209.7 km) **C 5.2** (8.4 km) The small town of Cantwell, nestled at the foot of the mountains, can be seen across a long, timbered valley dotted with lakes. Excellent view of Mount McKinley, weather permitting.

P 131.5 (211.6 km) **C 4** (6.4 km) Airstrip; current status unknown.

P 132 (212.4 km) **C 3.5** (5.6 km) Good grayling fishing in stream beside road. Large turnouts in slide area.

P 133 (214 km) **C 2.5** (4 km) Cantwell Station highway maintenance camp.

P 133.1 (214.2 km) **C 2.4** (3.9 km) **Junction** with old Anchorage–Fairbanks Highway; turn right westbound for Alaska State Troopers complex located approximately 0.2 mile/0.3 km north on left side of road.

P 133.7 (215.2 km) **C 1.8** (2.9 km) **Junction** of Denali and Parks highways (Alaska Routes 8 and 3). Cantwell post office and school, a lodge, rental cabins, RV park with hookups, 2 restaurants, mini-grocery, gas stations and gift shop are clustered around this intersection. Continue straight ahead 1.8 miles/2.9 km for the original town of Cantwell. Turn left (south) for Anchorage or right (north) for Denali National Park and Fairbanks. See **Milepost A 209.9** in the PARKS HIGHWAY section for details. ▲

P 134.5 (216.5 km) **C 1** (1.6 km) Jack River bridge.

P 135.5 (218.1 km) **C 0 CANTWELL** (pop. 145), western terminus of the Denali Highway. Cantwell Lodge has rooms, a campground, cafe, bar and liquor store. Flightseeing service available. ▲

Private Aircraft: Cantwell airport, adjacent north; elev. 2,190 feet/668m; length 2,100 feet/640m; gravel, dirt; fuel 100LL.

Cantwell began as a railroad flag stop between Seward on Prince William Sound and Fairbanks on the Chena River. The Alaska Railroad now serves Cantwell several times a week on its Anchorage to Fairbanks run during summer. The village was named for the Cantwell River, which is the former name of the Nenana River.

STEESE HIGHWAY (2) (6)

Connects: Fairbanks to Circle, AK **Length:** 162 miles
Road Surface: 30% paved, 70% gravel **Season:** Open all year
Highest Summit: Eagle Summit, 3,624 feet
Major Attractions: Hot Springs, Gold Dredge No. 8

	Central	Chena Hot Springs	Circle	Circle Hot Springs	Fairbanks
Central		180	35	8	128
Chena Hot Springs	180		214	188	61
Circle	35	214		43	162
Circle Hot Springs	8	188	43		136
Fairbanks	128	61	162	136	

Circle Hot Springs, near Central, is one of 2 hot springs off the Steese Highway. The other is Chena Hot Springs. *(Jerrianne Lowther, staff)*

The Steese Highway connects Fairbanks with Chena Hot Springs (61.4 miles/98.8 km) via Chena Hot Springs Road; the town of Central (127.5 miles/205.2 km); Circle Hot Springs (136.1 miles/219 km) via Circle Hot Springs Road; and with Circle, a small settlement 162 miles/260.7 km to the northeast on the Yukon River and 50 miles/80.5 km south of the Arctic Circle. The scenery alone makes this a worthwhile drive.

The first 44 miles/70.8 km of the Steese Highway are paved. Beyond this it is wide gravel road into Central, where there is a stretch of paved road. From Central to Circle, the highway is a narrow, winding road with gravel surface.

The highway is open year-round; check with the Dept. of Transportation in Fairbanks regarding winter road conditions. The Steese Highway was completed in 1927 and named for Gen. James G. Steese, U.S. Army, former president of the Alaska Road Commission.

Among the attractions along the Steese are Eagle Summit, highest pass on the highway, where there is an unobstructed view of the midnight sun at summer solstice (June 21); the Chatanika River and Chena River recreation areas; and Chena and Circle hot springs.

Emergency medical services: Between Fairbanks and Circle, phone the state troopers at 911 or (907) 452-1313. Use CB Channels 2, 19, 22.

Steese Highway Log

ALASKA ROUTE 2
Distance from Fairbanks (F) is followed by distance from Circle (C).

F 0 C 162 (260.7 km) **FAIRBANKS. Junction** of Airport Way, Richardson–Alaska Highway and the Steese Expressway. Follow the 4-lane Steese Expressway north.

F 0.4 (0.6 km) **C 161.6** (260.1 km) Tenth Avenue exit.

F 0.6 (1 km) **C 161.4** (259.7 km) Expressway crosses Chena River.

F 0.9 (1.4 km) **C 161.1** (259.3 km) Third Street exit.

F 1 (1.6 km) **C 161** (259.1 km) College Road exit to west and access to Bentley Mall and University of Alaska.

F 1.4 (2.3 km) **C 160.6** (258.5 km) Trainer Gate Road; access to Fort Wainright.

F 2 (3.2 km) **C 160** (257.5 km) Johansen Expressway (Old Steese Highway) to west, City Lights Boulevard to east.

F 2.8 (4.5 km) **C 159.2** (256.2 km) Fairhill Road; access to Birch Hill Recreation Area, 2.3 miles/3.7 km from the highway via a paved road. Access to Farmers Loop Road to west; residential areas of Birch Hill, Fairhill, Murray Highlands and View Crest to east. Birch Hill Recreation Area is mainly for winter use as a cross-country ski area; open from 8 A.M. to 10 P.M.; picnic areas, toilets, firepits and hiking trails. Day-use only.

F 4.9 (7.9 km) **C 157.1** (252.8 km) Chena Hot Springs Road underpass, exits both sides of highway. Turn east at exit for Chena Hot Springs Road; see page 520. Turn west for groceries, gas and pay phone at Old Steese Highway.

F 6.4 (10.3 km) **C 155.6** (250.4 km) Steele Creek Road. Exit for Bennett Road, Hagelbarger Road, Old Steese Highway and Gilmore trail. Exit to left northbound for scenic view of Fairbanks.

F 7 (11.3 km) **C 155** (249.4 km) View of pipeline from top of hill.

F 8 (12.9 km) **C 154** (247.8 km) End 4-lane divided highway, begin 2 lanes, northbound. *CAUTION: Watch for moose.*

F 8.4 (13.5 km) **C 153.6** (247.2 km) Trans–Alaska pipeline viewpoint with interpretive displays. Excellent opportunity for pipeline photos. Alyeska Pipeline Service Co. visitor center open May to September, 7 days a week. Free literature and information; phone (907) 456-9391. Highway parallels pipeline.

F 9.5 (15.3 km) **C 152.5** (245.4 km) Goldstream Road exit to Old Steese Highway and Gold Dredge Number 8. The dredge, built in 1928, was added to the list of national historic sites in 1984 and designated a National Historical Mechanical Engineering Landmark in 1986. The 5-deck, 250-foot-long dredge operated until 1959; it is now privately owned and open to the public for tours (admission fee).

F 10.4 (16.7 km) **C 151.6** (244 km) Road to permafrost tunnel to east (research area, not open to public). Excavated in the early 1960s, the tunnel is maintained coopera-

(Continues on page 521)

STEESE HIGHWAY *Fairbanks, AK to Circle, AK*

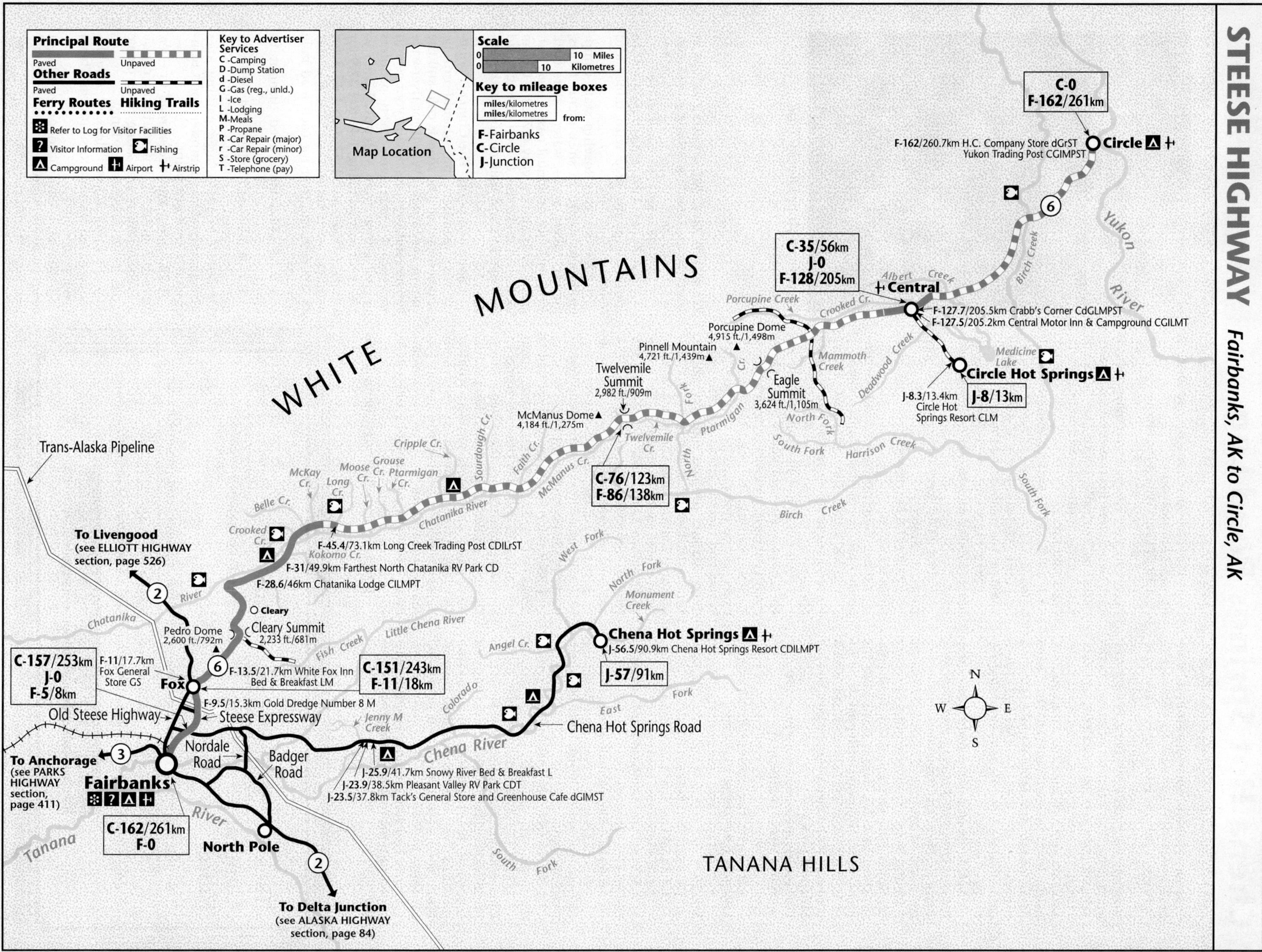

Chena Hot Springs Road Log

This paved road, open year-round, leads 56.5 miles/90.9 km east to Chena Hot Springs, a private resort open daily year-round. Chena Hot Springs Road passes through the middle of Chena River Recreation Area, 254,000 acres of mostly undeveloped river bottom and alpine uplands. This is an exceptional year-round recreation area with picnic sites, campgrounds, hiking trails and easy access to the Chena River, one of the most popular grayling fisheries in the state. *IMPORTANT: Check current ADF&G regulations regarding the taking of any fish.*

NOTE: Watch for paving under way between ***Mileposts J 0*** *and* ***J 7*** *in 1998. Also watch for trucks and crews doing erosion control and flood repair work between* **Mileposts** ***J 28*** and ***J 48.*** (Motorists from Fairbanks or North Pole can avoid the road construction by using Badger Road from the Richardson Highway, **Milepost V 349.5** or **V 357.1**, to access Nordale Road, which connects with Chena Hot Springs Road at **Milepost J 6.4.)**

Distance is measured from junction with the Steese Highway (J).

J 0 Chena Hot Springs Road exit at **Milepost F 4.9** Steese Highway.

J 0.7 (1.1 km) Elementary Drive; School.

J 1.8 (2.9 km) Bennett Road.

J 3.5 (5.6 km) Steele Creek Road.

J 4 (6.4 km) Frost heaves.

J 5.3 (8.5 km) Eberhard Road; access to bed and breakfast.

J 6.4 (10.3 km) Nordale Road.

J 8.3 (13.4 km) Paved double-ended turnout to south. North Pole Borough welcome sign.

J 10.3 (16.6 km) Mini-mart, public dumpster.

J 11.9 (19.2 km) Bridge over Little Chena River. Water gauging station in middle of bridge. This Army Corps of Engineers flood control project, completed in 1979, was designed to prevent floods such as the one which devastated Fairbanks in 1967.

J 14 (22.5 km) Bumpy paved double-ended turnout to south. Dog team crossing.

J 15 (24.1 km) Rough road next 2 miles/3.2 km eastbound.

J 18 (29 km) Watch for moose.

J 18.6 (29.9 km) Two Rivers Road. Access to Two Rivers Elementary School and Two Rivers Recreation Area (maintained by Fairbanks North Star Borough) with cross-country ski and hiking trails. Public dumpster.

J 19.7 (31.7 km) Commercial yak farm.

J 20.1 (32.3 km) Jenny M. Creek. Some 2,000 people reside along the road.

J 20.2 (32.5 km) Large double-ended paved parking area to south; end of new road.

J 23.4 (37.7 km) Grocery with gas; public dumpster.

J 23.5 (37.8 km) Store; Two Rivers post office is in store.

Tacks' General Store and Greenhouse Cafe. See display ad this section.

J 23.8 (38.3 km) Pleasant Valley Plaza; laundry, showers, store, pay phones.

J 23.9 (38.5 km) **Pleasant Valley RV Park** next to Pleasant Valley Plaza. Quiet country setting, gateway to upper Chena Valley. Fishing, hiking, biking, ATV trails, canoe rentals. All pull-throughs. Water and electric hookups, restrooms, dump station, propane and pay phone. Tent sites, firepits, free firewood. Coin-operated laundry and showers available. Convenient to local amenities. P.O. Box 16019, Two Rivers, AK 99716. Phone (907) 488-8198. MasterCard, VISA accepted. [ADVERTISEMENT] ▲

J 25.6 (41.2 km) HIPAS Observatory, UCLA Plasma Physics Lab (Geophysical Institute Chena Radio Facility).

J 25.9 (41.7 km) **Snowy River Bed & Breakfast.** Mile 25.9. Attractive, clean log cabin. 35 minutes from Fairbanks in a private setting on the Chena River. Fishing, guided/unguided, hiking trails, float trips, canoe/raft rentals, wildlife viewing, photography and northern lights viewing. Available year round. No smoking/pets. B&B in a true Alaskan setting. Full breakfast available. (907) 488-7517. [ADVERTISEMENT]

J 26.1 (42 km) Entering **Chena River** Recreation Area. No shooting except at target range. Grayling fishing (check current regulations).

View from Angel Rocks Trail.

(© Rick Reid)

J 26.5 (42.6 km) Flat Creek culvert.

J 26.7 (43 km) Paved turnout to south for picnic area with tables and toilets.

J 27 (43.5 km) Rosehip state campground to south; 25 sites, picnic tables, firepits, toilets, water, water nature trail. $8 nightly fee or annual pass. Large, flat, gravel pads and an easy 0.7-mile/1.1-km loop road make this a good campground for large RVs and trailers. Firewood available, $5. ▲

Canoe exit point. The Chena is popular with paddlers, but should not be underestimated: The river is cold and the current very strong. Watch for river-wide logjams and sweepers. Secure your gear in waterproof containers. Local paddlers suggest a float from **Milepost J 39.5** to **J 37.9** for easy paddling; **J 44** to **J 37.9** for a longer float; and **J 52.3** to **J 47.3** for paddlers with more skill. Allow about an hour on the river for each road mile traveled.

J 27.5 (44.3 km) Paved turnout to south.

J 27.9 (44.9 km) Toilets and access to river via road to south which leads 0.9 mile/1.4 km to large parking area with picnic tables, dumpster, loop turnaround. Canoe exit point.

J 28.8 (46.3 km) Access road to river, drive 0.7 mile/1.1 km south to canoe launch in brushy area along river; picnic table, toilet, dumpster, parking.

J 29.4 (47.3 km) Pleasant double-ended paved turnout to south on Chena River; picnic table.

J 30 (48.3 km) Outdoor education camp (available for rent by groups). Small lake stocked with grayling.

J 31.3 (50.4 km) Bridge over Colorado Creek. River access.

J 31.5 (50.7 km) River access.

J 31.8 (51.2 km) Colorado Creek ATV trail. Toilet, parking, access to Colorado Creek Cabins.

J 33.9 (54.6 km) Fourmile Creek flows under the road.

J 35.8 (57.6 km) Paved turnout to south.

J 36.5 (58.7 km) Target shooting range to north. ORV trails, toilets and picnic tables. Cathedral Bluffs view.

J 37 (59.5 km) Road is subject to flooding after heavy rains.

J 37.9 (61 km) First bridge over the **North Fork Chena River.** Water gauge in center of bridge. There are 3 stream flow meters on the upper Chena. Grayling fishing (check current special regulations).

Side road leaves highway to the south and forks. Left fork is a short road to the river and toilet; right fork leads 0.2 mile/0.3 km to picnic tables by the river. Canoe launch. This road is bordered by dense underbrush which may scratch wide vehicles.

J 39.2 (63.1 km) Paved turnout to south.

J 39.5 (63.6 km) Second bridge over North Fork Chena River. Loop road through Granite Tors trail state campground; 20 large sites among tall spruce trees, parking area, water, toilets, tables, firepits, $8 nightly fee or annual pass. Canoe launch. Picnic area on loop road along river. ▲

Trailhead for Granite Tors trail; follow dike (levee) on west side upstream 0.3 mile/0.5 km to trail sign. It is a 6-mile/9.7-km hike to the nearest tors, 8 miles/12.9 km to the main grouping. Tors are isolated pinnacles of granite jutting up from the tundra.

J 39.7 (63.9 km) A 0.2-mile/0.3-km side road leads south to Chena River picnic area with tables, toilets and a riverbank of flat rocks ideal for sunbathing.

J 39.8 (64.1 km) Campground loop road exit; toilet beside road.

J 42.1 (67.8 km) Large paved turnout south of road. Watch for muskrats and beaver in ponds here.

J 42.8 (68.9 km) Mile 43 Red Squirrel picnic area to north, one of the nicest on this road, with covered tables, firepits, toilets, water and dumpster. Located on edge of small lake stocked with grayling. Watch for moose.

J 43 (69.2 km) Paved double-ended turnout.

J 43.8 (70.5 km) Small lake to north stocked with grayling.

J 44.1 (71 km) Third bridge over North Fork Chena River. Picnic area with tables and toilets to north at east end of bridge. A favorite place to sunbathe and fish. Canoe launch.

J 45.7 (73.5 km) Fourth bridge over North Fork Chena River.

J 46 (74 km) Paved turnout to south.

J 46.8 (75.3 km) **Chena River** flows alongside the road; good access point for fishermen. Paved parking to south opposite river.

J 47.3 (76.1 km) Access to river north side of road.

J 47.9 (77.1 km) Side road leads 0.1 mile/0.2 km south to **48-Mile Pond.** Stocked with grayling; picnic tables, informal campsites.

J 48.8 (78.5 km) Watch for people and horses next mile eastbound.

J 48.9 (78.7 km) Angel Rocks trailhead; table, toilet, dumpster. Angel Rocks trail is a 3.5-mile/5.6-km loop trail to spectacular rock outcroppings; strenuous hike.

J 49 (78.9 km) Fifth bridge over **North Fork Chena River;** parking. Excellent fishing from here.

J 49.1 (79 km) Lower Chena Dome trailhead. Side road leads 0.2 mile/0.3 km north to trailhead, parking, water, dumpster and toilets.

J 49.3 (79.3 km) Cathedral Bluffs, an unusual rock formation to southeast.

J 49.9 (80.3 km) Paved turnout to north. **Angel Creek,** grayling 12 to 17 inches.

J 50.5 (81.3 km) Chena Dome trailhead; this 29-mile/47-km loop trail exits at **Milepost J 49.1.** Angel Creek Cabin ATV trailhead (6 miles/10 km). Parking, toilets. Bring mosquito repellent!

J 50.7 (81.6 km) Chena River Recreation Area boundary.

J 52.3 (84.2 km) Bridge over West Fork Chena River. Gravel side road leads south to parking area along the river. *CAUTION: Abrupt approaches to bridge.*

J 55.3 (89 km) North Fork Chena River bridge. Double-ended paved turnout to south.

J 56.5 (90.9 km) **CHENA HOT SPRINGS:** food, lodging, camping, bar and swimming. There is an airstrip at the lodge. Parking area at end of road, one-lane wooden bridge. ▲

Return to Milepost F 4.9 Steese Highway

Fairyslipper (Calypso bulbosa).
(© Craig Brandt)

(Continued from page 518)
tively by the University of Alaska–Fairbanks and the U.S. Army Cold Regions Research and Engineering Laboratory.

F 11 (17.7 km) **C 151** (243 km) End of Steese Expressway. Weigh station. Check here for current information on Dalton Highway conditions. Turn east at this junction for continuation of Steese Highway, which now becomes Alaska Route 6 (log follows). Continue straight ahead (north) on Alaska Route 2, which now becomes the Elliott Highway, for access to a private RV park, the Dalton Highway and Manley Hot Springs (see ELLIOTT HIGHWAY section for details).

Turn west for Old Steese Highway and for **FOX,** a once-famous mining camp established before 1905 and named for nearby Fox Creek. Gas, food and lodging.

ALASKA ROUTE 6

F 13.5 (21.7 km) **C 148.5** (239 km) **White Fox Inn Bed & Breakfast.** See display ad this section.

F 13.6 (21.9 km) **C 148.4** (238.8 km) Eisele Road; turnoff on right northbound for NOAA/NESDIS Command and Data Acquisition Station at Gilmore Creek. This facility tracks and commands multiple NOAA polar orbiting, environmental satellites. Tours of the satellite tracking station are available 9 A.M. to 4 P.M., Monday through Saturday, from June through August or by appointment September through May. Phone (907) 451-1200 for more information.

F 16.4 (26.4 km) **C 145.6** (234.3 km) Turnout by gold-bearing creek. Now privately claimed; no recreational gold panning permitted.

F 16.5 (26.6 km) **C 145.5** (234.2 km) Gravel turnout to west. Monument to Felix Pedro, the prospector who discovered gold on Pedro Creek in July 1902 and started the rush that resulted in the founding of Fairbanks.

F 17.6 (28.3 km) **C 144.4** (232.4 km) Gravel turnout to east. Winding ascent northbound to Cleary Summit area.

F 19.6 (31.5 km) **C 142.4** (229.2 km) Large gravel turnout to east.

F 20.5 (33 km) **C 141.5** (227.7 km) Cleary Summit (elev. 2,233 feet/681m) has a weekend ski area in winter. Named for early prospector Frank Cleary. On a clear day there are excellent views of the Tanana Valley and Mount McKinley to the south and the White Mountains to the north. Road north to Pedro Dome military site. Fort Knox Gold Mine, privately owned working mine. Pay phone at turnout.

Fairbanks Creek Road to the south leads several miles along a ridge crest; access to Fish Creek Road and dirt roads leading to Solo Creek, Bear Creek and Fairbanks Creek.

Highway descends steep grade northbound. Watch for frost heaves.

F 20.6 (33.2 km) **C 141.4** (227.6 km) View of current mining operation and old buildings from early mining and dredging on Cleary Creek below.

F 21 (33.8 km) **C 141** (226.9 km) Double-ended paved turnout east.

F 23.9 (38.5 km) **C 138.1** (222.2 km) Gravel turnout to east. Watch for frost heaves.

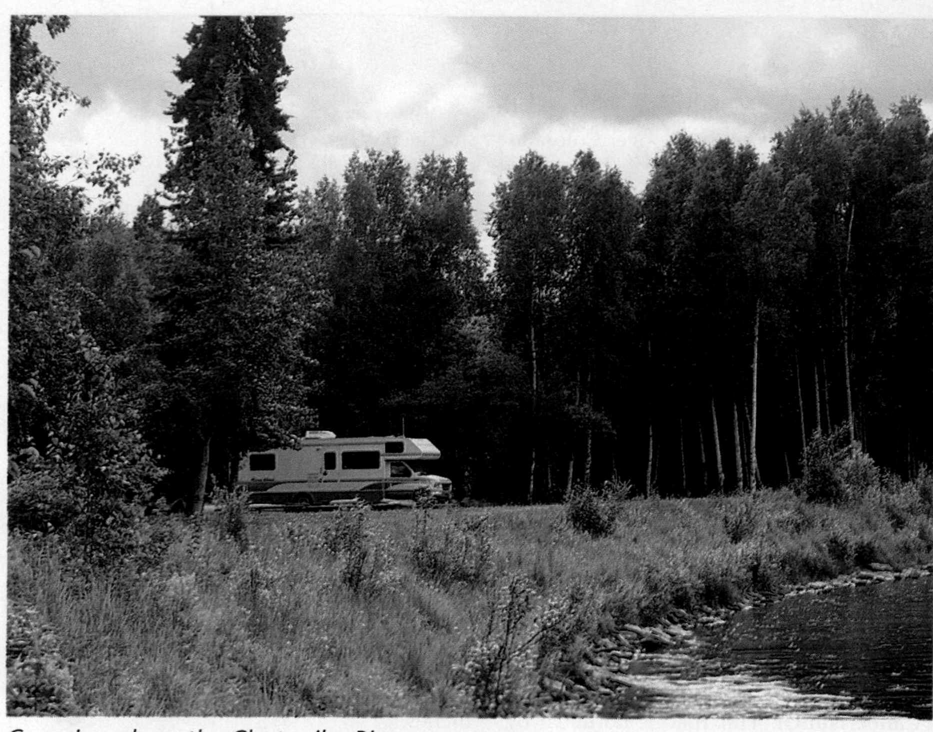

Camping along the Chatanika River. (Jerrianne Lowther, staff)

F 27.6 (44.4 km) **C 134.4** (216.3 km) Tailings (gravel and boulders of dredged streambeds) from early mining activity which yielded millions of dollars in gold. There is quite a bit of mining in the Chatanika area now.

F 27.9 (44.9 km) **C 134.1** (215.8 km) Sharp right turn up hill for historic Fairbanks Exploration Co. gold camp at **CHATANIKA,** built in 1925 to support gold dredging operations in the valley. Between 1926 and 1957 the F.E. Co. removed an estimated $70 million in gold. The gold camp is on the National Register of Historic Places.

F 28.6 (46 km) **C 133.4** (214.7 km) Old gold dredge behind tailing piles to west (private property, *DO NOT TRESPASS*). Lodge to east with meals and lodging.

Chatanika Lodge. Cafe open 9 A.M. daily (year-round). Halibut/catfish fry Friday and Saturday, country-fried chicken on Sunday, served family-style, all you can eat. Diamond Willow Lounge. Rustic atmosphere, Alaska artifacts. Historic Alaska gold dredge across from lodge, plus aurora borealis videos on big-screen TV. Good grayling fishing. Great winter snow machining on groomed trails; snow machine rentals. Rooms available. See display ad this section.

[ADVERTISEMENT]

F 29.5 (47.5 km) **C 132.5** (213.2 km) Neal Brown Road to Poker Flat rocket facility; off-limits except to authorized personnel. The Poker Flat rocket range, operated by the Geophysical Institute, University of Alaska, is dedicated to unclassified auroral and upper atmospheric research. It is the only university-owned sounding rocket range in the world and the only high latitude and auroral zone launch facility on U.S. soil. Tours for interested groups may be arranged by calling (907) 474-7798.

Fishing at gravel pit ponds from here north to **Milepost F 39.5.** Ponds are stocked with grayling. (Watch for green signs at access points.)

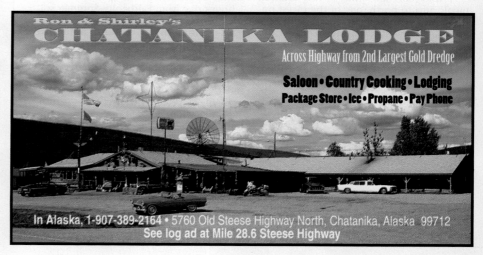

F 31 (49.9 km) **C 131** (210.8 km) **Farthest North Chatanika RV Park.** See display ad this section. ▲

F 31.4 (50.5 km) **C 130.6** (210.2 km) Double-ended gravel turnout to west by pond; stocked with grayling.

F 32.3 (52 km) **C 129.7** (208.7 km) Captain Creek bridge. Watch for frost heaves.

F 32.5 (52.3 km) **C 129.5** (208.4 km) *CAUTION: Severe frost heaves and cracks in pavement next 0.2 mile/0.3 km northbound.*

F 35 (56.3 km) **C 127** (204.4 km) Access to Chatanika River. Double-ended paved turnout to west.

F 36.5 (58.7 km) **C 125.5** (202 km) Gravel turnout alongside ponds to west. Pond stocked with grayling.

F 37.1 (59.7 km) **C 124.9** (201 km) *CAUTION: Severe frost heaves and dips in pavement next 0.1 mile/0.2 km northbound.*

F 37.3 (60 km) **C 124.7** (200.7 km) Kokomo Creek bridge.

F 39 (62.8 km) **C 123** (197.9 km) Chatanika River bridge. Upper Chatanika River State Recreation Site, just north of the bridge, is a beautiful state campground with river access. There are 25 sites with fireplaces and a gravel parking area with toilets and a water pump at the entrance. Firewood is usually available during the summer. Camping fee $8/night or annual pass. Look for wild roses here in June. ▲

Boats can be launched on the gravel bars by the river. Bring your mosquito repellent. This is an access point to the Chatanika River canoe trail. See **Milepost F 60** for more information on canoeing this river.

Chatanika River, grayling 8 to 20 inches, use flies or spinners, May to September.

F 39.5 (63.5 km) **C 122.5** (197.1 km) **39.3 Mile Pond,** to west, is stocked with grayling.

F 40.2 (64.7 km) **C 121.8** (196 km) *CAUTION: Watch for severe dips in highway surface.*

F 40.4 (65 km) **C 121.6** (195.7 km) Bridge over Crooked Creek.

F 41.5 (66.8 km) **C 120.5** (193.9 km) Bridge over Belle Creek. Most homes here are those of permanent residents.

F 42.7 (68.7 km) **C 119.3** (192 km) Bridge over McKay Creek. Gravel turnout to west; McKay Creek trailhead.

F 42.9 (69 km) **C 119.1** (191.7 km) Turnout to east.

F 43.8 (70.5 km) **C 118.2** (190.2 km) Pavement ends; it is good gravel road to Circle with the exception of a short stretch of blacktop at Central. Highway parallels the Chatanika River for the next 10 miles/16 km.

F 45.4 (73.1 km) **C 116.6** (187.6 km) **Long Creek** bridge and trading post. Grayling 8 to 14 inches, use spinners or flies, May to September.

Long Creek Trading Post. See display ad this section. ▲

F 49 (78.9 km) **C 113** (181.9 km) View down Chatanika River valley to east.

F 53.5 (86.1 km) **C 108.5** (174.6 km) Ptarmigan Creek in valley below highway.

F 57.1 (91.9 km) **C 104.9** (168.8 km) White Mountains National Recreation Area (BLM). Access to this area's trails and cabins is from the Elliott Highway.

F 57.3 (92.2 km) **C 104.7** (168.5 km) U.S. Creek to west. The large pipe near U.S. Creek was part of the Davidson Ditch, built in 1925 by the Fairbanks Exploration Co. to carry water to float gold dredges. The 83-mile/133.6-km-long ditch, designed and engineered by J.B. Lippincott, begins near **Milepost F 64** on the Steese Highway and ends near Fox. A system of ditches and inverted siphons, the pipeline was capable of carrying 56,100 gallons per minute. After the dredges closed, the water was used for power until 1967, when a flood destroyed a bridge and flattened almost 1,000 feet/305m of pipe.

All-weather road leads 6 miles/9.7 km west to Nome Creek; recreational gold panning. There are some mining claims on Nome Creek. No dredges allowed. The road to Nome Creek is very steep and not recommended for large or underpowered vehicles. Nome Creek is a historic mining area; additional recreational facilities are under development by the BLM.

F 59 (94.9 km) **C 103** (165.8 km) Wide double-ended gravel parking area to east.

F 60 (96.6 km) **C 102** (164.1 km) Cripple Creek BLM campground (7-day limit), 6 tent, 15 trailer sites; water pumps, fireplaces, toilets, tables, nature trail. Parking for walk-in campers. Firewood is usually available all summer. Recreational gold panning permitted. *Bring mosquito repellent!* ▲

Access to Cripple Creek BLM recreation cabin. Preregister and pay $10 fee at BLM office, 1150 University Ave., Fairbanks, AK 99709; phone (907) 474-2200.

Cripple Creek bridge is the uppermost access point to the Chatanika River canoe trail (follow side road near campground entrance to canoe launch site). *CAUTION: This canoe trail may not be navigable at low water.* The Chatanika River is a clear-water Class II stream. The Steese Highway parallels the river for approximately 28 miles/45 km and there are many access points to the highway downstream from the Cripple Creek bridge. No major obstacles on this canoe trail, but watch for overhanging trees. Downstream pullout points are Perhaps Creek, Long Creek and Chatanika Campground.

F 62.3 (100.3 km) **C 99.7** (160.4 km) Viewpoint to east overlooking Chatanika River.

F 63.4 (102 km) **C 98.6** (158.7 km) View of historic Davidson Ditch pipeline.

F 65 (104.6 km) **C 97** (156.1 km) Side road east to viewpoint. Large parking area.

F 65.6 (105.6 km) **C 96.4** (155.1 km) Sourdough Creek bridge.

F 65.7 (105.7 km) **C 96.3** (155 km) Mile 66. Double-ended turnout to east; Davidson Ditch viewpoint; lodge.

F 66 (106.2 km) **C 96** (154.5 km) Sourdough Creek Road (unmarked) to north.

F 69 (111 km) **C 93** (149.7 km) Faith Creek bridge and road. Creek access to east at north end of bridge. Large parking area to west.

F 72 (115.9 km) **C 90** (144.8 km) View ahead for northbound travelers of highway route along mountains, McManus Creek below.

F 73.8 (118.8 km) **C 88.2** (141.9 km) Faith Creek Road to west.

F 79.1 (127.3 km) **C 82.9** (133.4 km) Road widens for parking next 500 feet/152m.

F 80.1 (128.9 km) **C 81.9** (131.8 km) Montana Creek state highway maintenance station. Montana Creek runs under road and into McManus Creek to the east. McManus Dome (elev. 4,184 feet/1,275m) to west.

F 81.2 (130.7 km) **C 80.8** (130 km) Turnout to east. Spring water (untested) piped to roadside. Wide gravel highway begins ascent to Twelvemile Summit. Avalanche gates.

F 83 (133.6 km) **C 79** (127.1 km) Sharp turn to right northbound. Watch for the hoary marmot and other small mammals.

F 85.5 (137.6 km) **C 76.5** (123.1 km) Large parking area and viewpoint to east at Twelvemile Summit (elev. 2,982 feet/909m) on the divide of the Yukon and Tanana river drainages. Wildflowers carpet the alpine tundra slopes. Entering Game Management Unit 25C, leaving unit 20B, northbound. Fairbanks–North Star Borough limits. This is caribou country; from here to beyond Eagle Summit (**Milepost F 108**) migrating bands of caribou may be seen from late July through mid-September.

Access to Pinnell Mountain national recreation trail (Twelvemile Summit trailhead). The trail is also accessible from **Milepost F 107.1.** Named in honor of Robert Pinnell, who was fatally injured in 1952 while climbing nearby Porcupine Dome. This 27-mile-/43-km-long hiking trail winds through alpine terrain, along mountain ridges and through high passes. Highest elevation point reached is 4,721 feet/1,439m. The trail is marked by rock cairns. Shelter cabins at Mile 10.7 and Mile 17.7. Vantage points along the trail with views of the White Mountains, Tanana Hills, Brooks Range and Alaska Range. Watch for willow ptarmigan, hoary marmot, rock pika, moose, wolf and caribou. Mid-May through July is the prime time for wildflowers, with flowers peaking in mid-June. Carry drinking water and insect repellent at all times. Additional information on this trail is available from the Bureau of Land Management, 1150 University Ave., Fairbanks, AK 99708-3844; phone (907) 474-2350.

F 88 (141.6 km) **C 74** (119.1 km) Twelvemile Creek to east below road.

F 88.7 (142.7 km) **C 73.3** (118 km) Bridge over Reed Creek.

F 90.5 (145.6 km) **C 71.5** (115.1 km) Double-ended turnout to east.

F 93.4 (150.3 km) **C 68.6** (110.4 km) Bridge over the North Fork Twelvemile Creek. Nice picnic spot to west below bridge.

F 94 (151.3 km) **C 68** (109.4 km) Side road leads 0.2 mile/0.3 km down to north fork of Birch Creek; parking area and canoe launch for Birch Creek canoe trail. This is the main put-in point for canoeing Birch Creek, a Wild and Scenic River. Undeveloped campsite by creek. Extensive mining in area. **Birch Creek**, grayling to 12 inches; use flies, June to October.

F 95.8 (154.2 km) **C 66.2** (106.5 km) Bridge over Willow Creek.

Much gold mining activity along this part of the highway. These are private mining claims. *IMPORTANT: Do not trespass. Do not approach mining equipment without permission.*

F 97.6 (157.1 km) **C 64.4** (103.6 km) Bridge over Bear Creek.

F 98 (157.7 km) **C 64** (103 km) Gold mine and settling ponds in creek valley to east.

F 99.7 (160.4 km) **C 62.3** (100.3 km) Bridge over Fish Creek. Privately owned cabins.

F 101.5 (163.3 km) **C 60.5** (97.4 km) Bridge over Ptarmigan Creek (elev. 2,398 feet/731m). Alpine meadows carpeted with wildflowers in spring and summer for next 9 miles/14.5 km. *NOTE: Avalanche gates may be closed if road conditions are hazardous over the summit.*

F 102.3 (164.6 km) **C 59.7** (96.1 km) Ptarmigan Creek access to west.

F 103 (165.8 km) **C 59** (94.9 km) Good view of mining operation next mile northbound.

F 104.6 (168.3 km) **C 57.4** (92.4 km) Snowpoles guide snowplows in winter.

F 105.4 (169.6 km) **C 56.6** (91.1 km) Large gravel parking area to west. Excellent array of arctic wildflowers.

F 107.1 (172.4 km) **C 54.9** (88.4 km) Parking area to west with wheelchair-accessible toilet, trail, bear-proof litter container. Pinnell Mountain trail access (Eagle Summit trailhead); see description at **Milepost F 85.5.**

F 108 (173.8 km) **C 54** (86.9 km) Eagle Summit (elev. 3,624 feet/1,105m) to the east. Steep, narrow, rocky side road leads from the highway 0.8 mile/1.3 km to the summit. This is the third and highest of 3 summits (including Cleary and Twelvemile) along the Steese Highway. *NOTE: Gates at* ***Milepost F 101.5*** *and* ***F 114.2*** *across the highway may be closed in bad weather.* Favorite spot for local residents to observe summer solstice (weather permitting) on June 21. Best wildflower viewing on Alaska highway system.

Scalloped waves of soil on hillsides to west are called solifluction lobes. These are formed when meltwater saturates the thawed surface soil, which then flows slowly downhill.

Wildflowers found here include: dwarf forget-me-nots, alpine rhododendron or rosebay, rock jasmine, alpine azalea, arctic bell heather, mountain avens, Jacob's ladder, anemones, wallflowers, Labrador tea, lupine, oxytropes, gentians and louseworts. The museum in Central has a photographic display of Eagle Summit alpine flowers to help highway travelers identify the wildflowers of this area.

F 109.2 (175.7 km) **C 52.8** (85 km) Large parking area to east with view down into Miller Creek far below. Excellent wildflower display. Highway begins steep descent northbound.

F 114.2 (183.8 km) **C 47.8** (76.9 km) Parking area to east looking down onto the Mastodon, Mammoth, Miller and Independence creeks area. Avalanche gates.

F 114.4 (184.1 km) **C 47.6** (76.6 km) Side road to east leads to Mammoth and Mastodon creeks; active gold placer mining areas.

F 116.2 (187 km) **C 45.8** (73.7 km) Road east to creek.

F 116.4 (187.3 km) **C 45.6** (73.4 km) Bridge over Mammoth Creek. Near here fossil remains of many species of preglacial Alaskan mammals have been excavated and may be seen at the University of Alaska museum in Fairbanks and at the museum in Central.

F 117 (188.3 km) **C 45** (72.4 km) Highway crosses over Stack Pup Creek. From here the highway gradually descends to Central.

F 117.6 (189.3 km) **C 44.4** (71.5 km) Parking area to west.

F 119.1 (191.7 km) **C 42.9** (69 km) Bedrock Creek.

F 119.2 (191.8 km) **C 42.8** (68.9 km) Narrow dirt road leads to site of former Bedrock Creek BLM campground (closed).

F 121 (194.7 km) **C 41** (66 km) Bridge over Sawpit Creek.

F 122.5 (197.1 km) **C 39.5** (63.6 km) Road west to parking space by pond.

F 125.4 (201.8 km) **C 36.6** (58.9 km) Bridge over Boulder Creek. *CAUTION: Road narrows; soft shoulders.*

F 126.8 (204.1 km) **C 35.2** (56.6 km) Paved highway begins and continues through Central.

F 127.1 (204.5 km) **C 34.9** (56.2 km) Central elementary school.

F 127.5 (205.2 km) **C 34.5** (55.5 km) **CENTRAL** (pop. approximately 400 in summer, 130 in winter; elev. 965 feet/294m). **Radio:** KUAC-FM 91.7. This small community, formerly called Central House, is situated on Crooked Creek along the Steese Highway.

Central is the central point in the huge Circle Mining District, one of the oldest and still one of the most active districts in the state. The annual Circle Mining District Picnic for local miners and their families is held in August.

Central has many facilities for the visitor: state airstrip (see **Milepost F 128.3**), cafes and bars, motel, cabins, laundromat, showers, groceries, gas, tire repair, welding, pay phone and post office (ZIP code 99730). Report fires to BLM. Picnic area at Central Park.

The Circle District Historical Society museum has displays covering the history of the Circle Mining District and its people. Also here are a photo display of wildflowers, fossilized remains of preglacial mammals, a minerals display, library and archives, gift shop and visitor information. Admission is $1 for adults, 50¢ for children under 12; members free. Open daily noon to 5 P.M., Memorial Day through Labor Day.

Central Motor Inn and Campground. See display ad this section.

F 127.7 (205.5 km) **C 34.3** (55.2 km) **Crabb's Corner.** Jim and Sandy welcome you to Central with a host of roadhouse services—motel rooms, restaurants, bar, package store, convenience store, gas, diesel,

propane, laundromat, self-contained RV parking, public telephone. As an official checkpoint for the Yukon Quest, we are happy to answer questions on the race, Central and gold panning. Open year-round. Phone (907) 520-5599. [ADVERTISEMENT]

F 127.8 (205.7 km) **C 34.2** (55 km) **Junction** with Circle Hot Springs Road; see CIRCLE HOT SPRINGS ROAD log opposite page.

F 127.9 (205.8 km) **C 34.1** (54.9 km) Bridge over Crooked Creek. Site of Central House roadhouse on north side of bridge.

F 128.1 (206.2 km) **C 33.9** (54.6 km) Central DOT/PF highway maintenance station.

F 128.3 (206.5 km) **C 33.7** (54.2 km) **Private Aircraft**: Central state-maintained airstrip, adjacent north; elev. 932 feet/284m; length 2,700 feet/823m; gravel; unattended.

Pavement ends northbound. Watch for soft spots, curves and little or no shoulder between here and Circle; otherwise, the road

Homemade raft on the Yukon River.
(© Ruth Von Spalding)

Circle Hot Springs Road Log

Distance is measured from junction (J) at Milepost F 127.8 Steese Highway.

J 0 Pavement extends first 0.3 mile/0.5 km of road.

J 0.9 (1.4 km) Graveyard Road, 0.5 mile/0.8 km to cemetery.

J 1.9 (3.1 km) Deadwood Creek Road.

J 2.9 (4.7 km) Bridge over Deadwood Creek.

J 5.7 (9.2 km) Bridge over Ketchem Creek. Primitive camping at site of former Ketchem Creek BLM campground on right before bridge; no facilities.

J 8.3 (13.4 km) **CIRCLE HOT SPRINGS;** year-round swimming, lodging, food and RV parking. A popular spot with Alaskans.

According to research done by Patricia Oakes of Central, the hot springs were used as a gathering place by area Athabascans before the gold rush. Local prospectors probably used the springs as early as the 1890s. Cassius Monohan homesteaded the site in 1905, selling out to Frank Leach in 1909. Leach built the airstrip, on which Noel Wien landed in 1924. (Wien pioneered many flight routes between Alaska communities.)

Private Aircraft: Circle Hot Springs state-maintained airstrip; elev. 956 feet/291m; length 3,600 feet/1,097m; gravel; lighted, unattended.

Return to Milepost F 127.8 Steese Highway

is in good shape. Wildlife is frequently sighted between Central and Circle.

F 130.5 (210 km) **C 31.5** (50.7 km) Pond frequented by a variety of ducks.

F 131.2 (211.1 km) **C 30.8** (49.6 km) Albert Creek bridge. Small parking area with litter barrel at end of bridge.

F 133 (214 km) **C 29** (46.7 km) Repair shop.

F 140.6 (226.3 km) **C 21.4** (34.4 km) Birch Creek access. Toilets, bear-proof litter containers.

F 147.1 (236.7 km) **C 14.9** (24 km) One-lane bridge over Birch Creek; clearance 13 feet, 11 inches. Turnouts, undeveloped campsites, both ends of bridge. Usual take-out point for the Birch Creek canoe trail.

F 147.6 (237.5 km) **C 14.4** (23.2 km) Turnout to east.

F 148.4 (238.8 km) **C 13.6** (21.9 km) Nice stand of quaking aspen.

F 152 (244.6 km) **C 10** (16.1 km) Winding road next 3 miles/4.8 km.

F 155.9 (250.9 km) **C 6.1** (9.8 km) Diamond (Bebb) willow along road. Diamond willow is used to make walking sticks.

F 156.7 (252.2 km) **C 5.3** (8.5 km) Large turnout opposite gravel pit to east. Look for bank swallow nests in cliffs.

F 159.6 (256.8 km) **C 2.4** (3.9 km) Old Indian cemetery to east.

F 161 (259.1 km) **C 1** (1.6 km) Circle post office (ZIP code 99733); airstrip (see **Private Aircraft** in Circle); school.

Circle

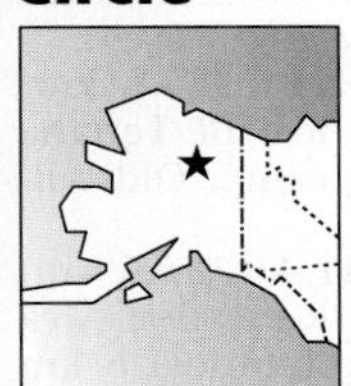

F 162 (260.7 km) **C 0** Located on the banks of the Yukon River, 50 miles/80.5 km south of the Arctic Circle. The Yukon is Alaska's largest river; the 2,000-mile/3,219-km river heads in Canada and flows west into Norton Sound on the Bering Sea. **Population:** 107.

Elevation: 610 feet/186m. **Climate:** Mean monthly temperature in July 61.4°F/16.3°C, in January -10.6°F/-23.7°C. Record high 91°F/32.8°C July 1977, record low -69°F/-56°C in February 1991. Snow from October (8 inches) through April (2 inches). Precipitation in the summer averages 1.45 inches a month.

Private Aircraft: Circle City state-maintained airstrip, adjacent west; elev. 610 feet/186m; length 3,000 feet/914m; gravel; fuel 100LL.

Before the Klondike Gold Rush of 1898, Circle City was the largest gold mining town on the Yukon River. Prospectors discovered gold on Birch Creek in 1893, and the town of Circle City (so named because the early miners thought it was located on the Arctic Circle) grew up as the nearest supply point to the new diggings on the Yukon River.

Today, Circle serves a small local population and visitors coming in by highway or by river. The post office is at **Milepost F 161** just before the airstrip and school. Gas, groceries, snacks and sundries are available at 2 local stores. The trading post houses the post office, cafe and liquor store. Hunting and fishing licenses are also available at the trading post. A motel is located just beyond the trading post. There's a lot of summer river traffic here: canoeists put in and take out.

The old Pioneer Cemetery, with its markers dating back to the 1800s, is an interesting spot to visit. Walk a short way upriver (past the old machinery) on the gravel road to a barricade: You will have to cross through a private front yard (please be respectful of property) to get to the trail. Walk straight ahead on the short trail, which goes through dense underbrush (many mosquitoes), for about 10 minutes. Watch for a path on your left to the graves, which are scattered among the thick trees.

Camping on the banks of the Yukon at the end of the road; tables, toilets, parking area. In 1989, when the Yukon flooded, water covered the bottom of the welcome sign at the campground entrance. From the campground you are looking at one channel of the mighty Yukon. ▲

H.C. Company Store. See display ad this section.

Yukon Trading Post. See display ad this section.

ELLIOTT HIGHWAY ②

Connects: Fox to Manley Hot Springs, AK **Length:** 152 miles
Road Surface: Gravel **Season:** Open all year
Major Attraction: White Mountains National Recreation Area

	Dalton Hwy	Fairbanks	Manley	Minto
Dalton Hwy		84	79	48
Fairbanks	84		163	132
Manley	79	163		53
Minto	48	132	53	

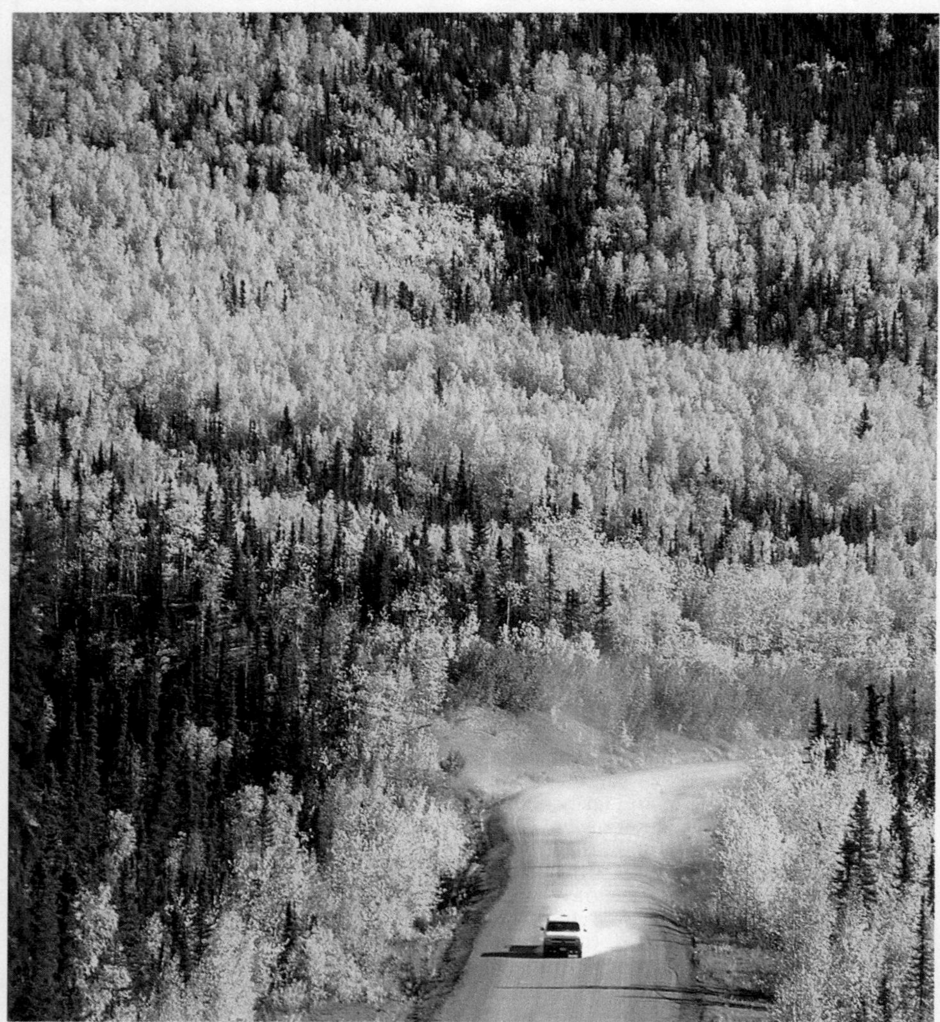

The first 30 miles of the Elliott Highway are paved; the remaining 122 miles are gravel. (© Harry M. Walker Photo)

The Elliott Highway leads 152 miles/244.6 km from its junction with the Steese Highway at Fox (11 miles/17.7 km north of Fairbanks) to Manley Hot Springs, a small settlement with a natural hot springs near the Tanana River. The highway was named for Malcolm Elliott, president of the Alaska Road Commission from 1927 to 1932.

The first 30.4 miles/48.9 km of the Elliott Highway are paved; the remaining 121.6 miles/195.7 km are gravel. The highway is wide, hard-based gravel to the Dalton Highway junction. (The road is treated with calcium chloride for dust control; wash your vehicle after travel to prevent corrosion.) From that junction until Manley, the road is narrower but fairly smooth with some soft spots and a roller-coaster section near Manley. Gas is available at **Milepost F 5.5, F 66** and at Manley on the Elliott Highway and at the Yukon River bridge on the Dalton Highway (see DALTON HIGHWAY section).

Watch for heavy truck traffic. Drivers pulling trailers should be especially cautious when the road is wet. The highway is open year-round; check with the Dept. of Transportation in Fairbanks regarding winter road conditions. *NOTE: Expect road construction between Eureka turnoff (Milepost F 131.3) and Baker Creek (Milepost F 137.4) in 1998.*

The Elliott Highway also provides access to 4 trailheads in the White Mountains National Recreation Area. These hiking trails lead to recreation cabins; the trails and cabins are managed by the BLM in Fairbanks. For more information and cabin registration, contact the BLM office in Fairbanks at 1150 University Ave., Fairbanks, AK 99709; phone (907) 474-2350.

Emergency medical services: Between Fox and Manley Hot Springs, phone the state troopers at 911 or (907) 452-1313. Use CB channels 9, 14, 19.

Elliott Highway Log

ALASKA ROUTE 2
Distance from Fox (F) is followed by distance from Manley Hot Springs (M).

F 0 M 152 (244.6 km) **FOX. Junction** of the Steese Highway with the Elliott Highway. Weigh station.

F 0.2 (0.3 km) **M 151.8** (244.3 km) Private RV park. ▲

F 0.4 (0.6 km) **M 151.6** (244 km) Fox Spring picnic area; 2 tables, spring water.

F 1.2 (1.9 km) **M 150.8** (242.7 km) Turnoff for El Dorado Gold Mine, a commercial gold mine offering tours and gold panning to the public; admission charged.

F 1.8 (2.9 km) **M 150.2** (241.7 km) Fort Knox gold mine.

F 3.4 (5.5 km) **M 148.6** (239.1 km) Rough side road leads west to Murphy Dome, 28 miles/45 km away. Road is signed "restricted military site."

F 5.5 (8.9 km) **M 146.5** (235.8 km) Gas, diesel, phone and food.

F 7.5 (12.1 km) **M 144.5** (232.5 km) Views to the east of Pedro Dome and Dome Creek. Buildings of Dome and Eldorado camps are in the valley below to the east (best view is southbound).

F 8.6 (13.8 km) **M 143.4** (230.8 km) Dome Creek Road to east (right northbound). *CAUTION: Watch for frost heaves.*

F 9.2 (14.8 km) **M 142.8** (229.8 km) Olnes, former railroad station of Tanana Valley Railroad and mining camp. Old tailings and abandoned cabins.

F 10.6 (17.1 km) **M 141.4** (227.6 km) Lower Chatanika River State Recreation Area Olnes Creek Campground, 1 mile/1.6 km west of highway on loop road; 50 campsites, toilets, water, tables, group area with campfire ring and benches. Camping fee $8/night or annual pass. ▲

F 11 (17.7 km) **M 141** (226.9 km) Chatanika River bridge. Lower Chatanika State Recreation Area Whitefish Campground at north end of bridge; picnic area (wheelchair accessible) with covered picnic tables, campsites, toilets, firepits, water, litter barrels, river access and boat launch. Camp-

ELLIOTT HIGHWAY *Fox, AK, to Manley Hot Springs, AK*

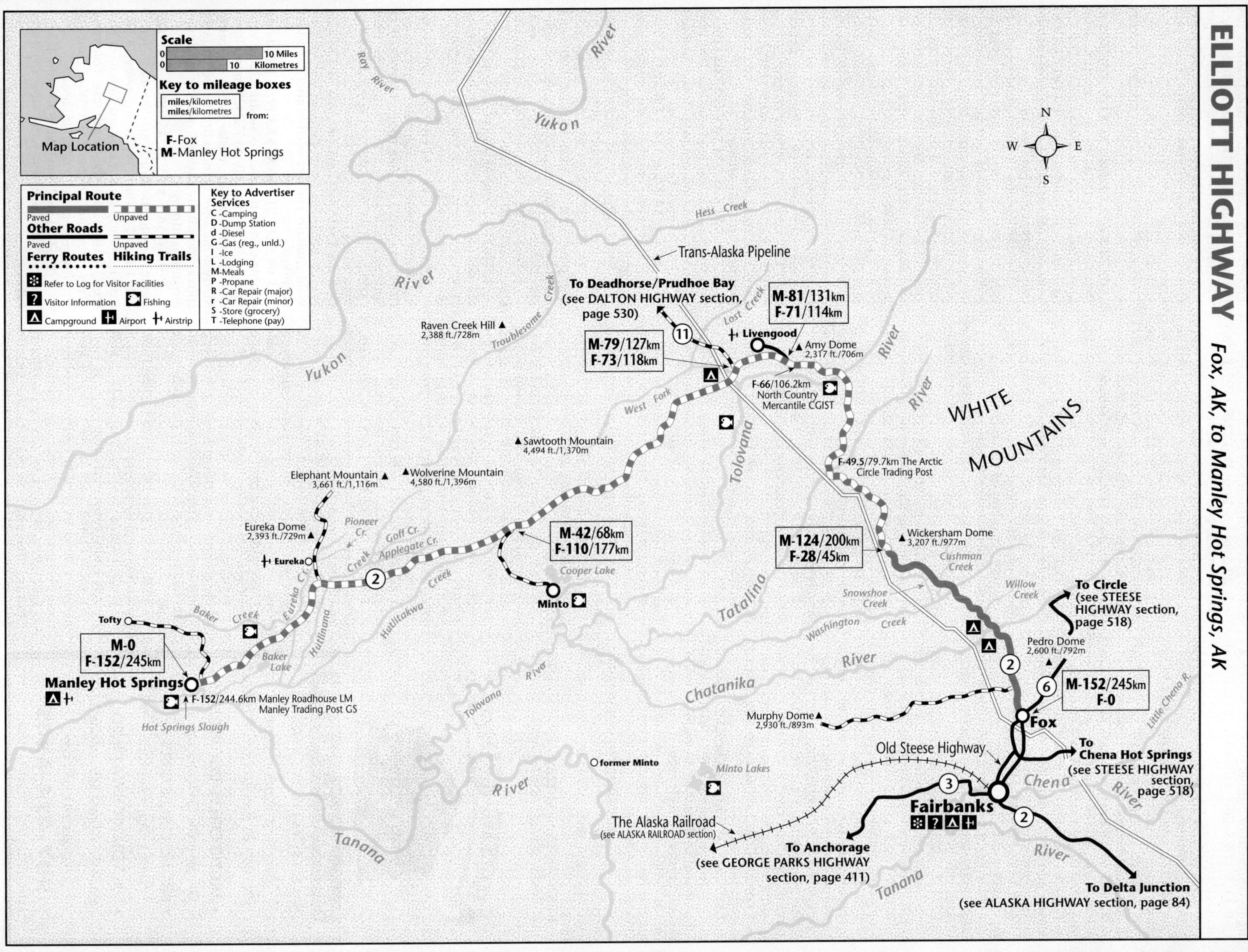

Scale
0 10 Miles
0 10 Kilometres
Key to mileage boxes
miles/kilometres
miles/kilometres
from:
F-Fox
M-Manley Hot Springs
Map Location
Principal Route
Paved
Unpaved
Other Roads
Paved
Unpaved
Ferry Routes
Hiking Trails
Refer to Log for Visitor Facilities
Visitor Information
Fishing
Campground
Airport
Airstrip
Key to Advertiser Services
C -Camping
D -Dump Station
d -Diesel
G -Gas (reg., unld.)
I -Ice
L -Lodging
M -Meals
P -Propane
R -Car Repair (major)
r -Car Repair (minor)
S -Store (grocery)
T -Telephone (pay)
Ray River
Yukon River
Hess Creek
Trans-Alaska Pipeline
To Deadhorse/Prudhoe Bay (see DALTON HIGHWAY section, page 530)
M-81/131km
F-71/114km
Lost Creek
Livengood
Amy Dome 2,317 ft./706m
M-79/127km
F-73/118km
Raven Creek Hill 2,388 ft./728m
Troublesome Creek
F-66/106.2km North Country Mercantile CGIST
West Fork
WHITE MOUNTAINS
Sawtooth Mountain 4,494 ft./1,370m
Elephant Mountain 3,661 ft./1,116m
Wolverine Mountain 4,580 ft./1,396m
F-49.5/79.7km The Arctic Circle Trading Post
Tolovana
Eureka Dome 2,393 ft./729m
Pioneer Cr.
Goff Cr.
Applegate Cr.
Eureka
M-42/68km
F-110/177km
Wickersham Dome 3,207 ft./977m
M-124/200km
F-28/45km
Cushman Creek
Cooper Lake
Minto
Snowshoe Creek
Willow Creek
To Circle (see STEESE HIGHWAY section, page 518)
Tatalina
Washington Creek
Tofty
Baker Creek
Eureka Cr.
Hutlinana
Hutlitakwa Creek
M-0
F-152/245km
Baker Lake
Pedro Dome 2,600 ft./792m
Manley Hot Springs
F-152/244.6km Manley Roadhouse LM Manley Trading Post GS
Hot Springs Slough
Tolovana River
Chatanika River
M-152/245km
F-0
Murphy Dome 2,930 ft./893m
Fox
Little Chena R.
Old Steese Highway
To Chena Hot Springs (see STEESE HIGHWAY section, page 518)
former Minto
Minto Lakes
Chena River
Fairbanks
The Alaska Railroad (see ALASKA RAILROAD section)
To Anchorage (see GEORGE PARKS HIGHWAY section, page 411)
Tanana River
To Delta Junction (see ALASKA HIGHWAY section, page 84)
N
W
E
S

ing fee $8/night or annual pass.

F 11.5 (18.5 km) **M 140.5** (226.1 km) General store.

F 13.1 (21.1 km) **M 138.9** (223.5 km) Willow Creek bridge.

F 13.4 (21.6 km) **M 138.6** (223 km) Landmark old log cabin to west.

F 18.3 (29.5 km) **M 133.7** (215.2 km) Double-ended paved turnout to west.

F 18.5 (29.8 km) **M 133.5** (214.8 km) Washington Creek. Parking area below bridge east of road; undeveloped campsite.

F 20.1 (32.3 km) **M 131.9** (212.3 km) Beaver pond with dam and lodge to east. Paved double-ended turnout.

F 20.3 (32.7 km) **M 131.7** (212 km) Cushman Creek Road.

F 23.5 (37.8 km) **M 128.5** (206.8 km) Large double-ended turnout with view of forested valley to west.

F 24.2 (38.9 km) **M 127.8** (205.7 km) Double-ended gravel turnout to east at top of hill. Snowshoe Creek parallels the road.

F 24.7 (39.7 km) **M 127.3** (204.9 km) Long paved double-ended turnout to east.

F 27.7 (44.6 km) **M 124.3** (200 km) Large double-ended paved turnout to west. Highway winds around the base of Wickersham Dome (elev. 3,207 feet/977m). Views of the White Mountains, a range of white limestone mountains (elev. 5,000 feet/1,524m). Entering Livengood/Tolovana Mining District northbound, Fairbanks Mining District southbound.

Trailhead for White Mountains–Wickersham Creek trail and White Mountains–Summit trail to Borealis–LeFevre BLM cabin. The Wickersham Creek route is 20 miles/32 km in length; ATVs are permitted. The Summit route is 22 miles/35.4 km long and ATVs are prohibited.

Pipeline access restricted to ensure public safety and security, and to protect the reseeding and restoration of construction areas.

F 28.9 (46.5 km) **M 123.1** (198.1 km) Sled Dog Rocks ahead northbound. Double-ended gravel turnout to west.

F 29.5 (47.5 km) **M 122.5** (197.1 km) Double-ended gravel turnout to east.

F 29.8 (48 km) **M 122.2** (196.7 km) Turnouts to west. Spring water piped to road.

F 30.4 (48.9 km) **M 121.6** (195.7 km) Rough double-ended turnout to west. Fairbanks–North Star Borough boundary. Pavement ends, gravel begins, northbound.

F 31 (49.9 km) **M 121** (194.7 km) Long double-ended gravel turnout to east.

F 31.8 (51.2 km) **M 120.2** (193.4 km) Double-ended turnout to west.

F 34 (54.7 km) **M 118** (189.9 km) Good view of pipeline going underground; creek.

F 36.4 (58.6 km) **M 115.6** (186 km) Large double-ended turnout to east.

F 37 (59.5 km) **M 115** (185.1 km) Globe Creek bridge. Steep access road to parking area next to bridge.

F 38 (61.2 km) **M 114** (183.5 km) Highway follows pipeline. View of Globe Creek canyon. Grapefruit Rocks ahead, northbound.

F 39 (62.8 km) **M 113** (181.9 km) Double-ended turnout to east.

F 39.3 (63.2 km) **M 112.7** (181.4 km) Double-ended turnout to west.

F 40.6 (65.3 km) **M 111.4** (179.3 km) Scenic view from double-ended turnout to east at top of hill.

F 41.2 (66.3 km) **M 110.8** (178.3 km) Drive-in parking area to east; no easy turnaround.

F 42.8 (68.9 km) **M 109.2** (175.7 km) Pipeline pump station No. 7 to west.

F 44.8 (72.1 km) **M 107.2** (172.5 km) Tatalina Creek bridge; rest area to east at south end of bridge. The Tatalina is a tributary of the Chatanika.

F 47.1 (75.8 km) **M 104.9** (168.8 km) Turnout to east.

F 49.5 (79.7 km) **M 102.5** (165 km) **The Arctic Circle Trading Post**. See display ad this section.

F 49.9 (80.3 km) **M 102.1** (164.3 km) Northern Lights School. This 2-room public school has an enrollment of 22 students.

F 51.9 (83.5 km) **M 100.1** (161.1 km) Double-ended parking area, water. View of White Mountains to northeast and the Elliott Highway descending slopes of Bridge Creek valley ahead. Bridge Creek flows into the Tolovana River.

F 52 (83.7 km) **M 100** (160.9 km) Watch for grizzly and black bear in this area.

F 57 (91.7 km) **M 95** (152.9) Colorado Creek winter trailhead; wheelchair-accessible toilet; litter container.

F 57.1 (91.9 km) **M 94.9** (152.7 km) **Tolovana River** bridge. Grayling to 11 inches; whitefish 12 to 18 inches; northern pike.

Colorado Creek trail leads to Colorado Creek and Windy Gap BLM cabins.

F 58 (93.3 km) **M 94** (151.3 km) Highway winds around Amy Dome (elev. 2,317 feet/706m) to east. The Tolovana River flows in the valley to the southwest, paralleling the road.

F 59.3 (95.4 km) **M 92.7** (149.2 km) Parking area to west by stream.

F 59.9 (96.4 km) **M 92.1** (148.2 km) Double-ended turnout to west.

F 62.3 (100.3 km) **M 89.7** (144.4 km) Access to Fred Blixt BLM cabin, east side of road. Preregister at BLM office in Fairbanks.

F 66 (106.2 km) **M 86** (138.4 km) **North Country Mercantile** in the beautiful historic Livengood, Tolovana Mining District. Gas, groceries, ice, Alaskan art work, planned pay phone and camping. Have your photo taken as a miner or a Native Alaskan family! Open late for our neighbors traveling to and from! Our coffee is always fresh and hot. [ADVERTISEMENT]

F 70.1 (112.8 km) **M 81.9** (131.8 km) Livengood Creek, 2-lane bridge. Money Knob to northeast.

F 70.8 (113.9 km) **M 81.2** (130.7 km) Double-ended turnout at **junction** with Livengood access road. Drive 2 miles/3.2 km to former mining camp of **LIVENGOOD** (area pop. about 100); state highway maintenance station and EMT squad.

The settlement of Livengood began in July 1914 with the discovery of gold by Nathaniel R. Hudson and Jay Livengood. A lively mining camp until 1920, it yielded some $9.5 million in gold. Large-scale mining was attempted in the late 1930s and again in the 1940s, but both operations were eventually shut down and Livengood became a ghost town.

With the building of the trans-Alaska pipeline and the North Slope Haul Road (now the Dalton Highway) in the 1970s, the town was revitalized as a construction camp. In 1977 a mining corporation acquired much of the gold-rich Livengood Bench. *NO TRESPASSING* on mining claims.

F 71.1 (114.4 km) **M 80.9** (130.2 km) Large double-ended turnout to south. Overnight parking allowed.

F 73.1 (117.6 km) **M 78.9** (127 km) **Junction** with the Dalton Highway (see DALTON HIGHWAY section on page 530); turn left (west) for Manley Hot Springs.

F 74.1 (119.2 km) **M 77.9** (125.4 km) Alyeska pipeline access road (restricted). Pipeline stretches for miles to the east.

F 74.3 (119.6 km) **M 77.7** (125 km) Site of old Livengood pipeline camp.

F 74.7 (120.2 km) **M 77.3** (124.4 km) Camping spot at west end of **Tolovana River** bridge; grayling to 15 inches, use spinners or flies.

F 76.3 (122.8 km) **M 75.7** (121.8 km) Cascaden Ridge (low hills to north).

F 79 (127.1 km) **M 73** (117.5 km) Travelers should appreciate the abundance of dragonflies seen along the Elliott Highway: their main food is mosquitoes.

F 85.5 (137.6 km) **M 66.5** (107 km) Looking south toward the Tolovana River valley, travelers should be able to see Tolovana Hot Springs Dome (elev. 2,386 feet/727m). (Hot springs are on the other side of dome; no road access.)

F 93.7 (150.8 km) **M 58.3** (93.8 km) Watch for foxes from here to top of hill. Wild rhubarb and fireweed border roadsides for miles.

F 94.5 (152.1 km) **M 57.5** (92.5 km) Long double-ended turnout to south. Good vantage point to view Minto Flats, Tanana River and foothills of the Alaska Range to south. Many wildflowers, including arnica, Alaska spirea, mountain harebell, prickly saxifrage, elegant paintbrush.

F 97 (156.1 km) **M 55** (88.5 km) The mountains to the north are Sawtooth (elev. 4,494 feet/1,370m); Wolverine (elev. 4,580 feet/1,396m); and Elephant (elev. 3,661 feet/1,116m). To the south are Tolovana River flats and Cooper Lake. Wild rhubarb and fireweed grow in old burn area.

F 98.3 (158.2 km) **M 53.7** (86.4 km) Turnout to southwest with view of Minto Lakes.

F 106.8 (171.9 km) **M 45.2** (72.7 km)

Turnout with view of Sawtooth Mountains to north.

F 110 (177 km) **M 42** (67.6 km) **Junction** with Minto Road which leads 11 miles/17.7 km to the Indian village of **MINTO** (pop. 233). The village was moved to its present location on the Tolovana River from the east bank of the Tanana River in 1971 because of flooding. Minto has a lodge with accommodations, meals and a general store. Most Minto residents make their living by hunting and fishing. Some local people also work in the arts and crafts center, making birch-bark baskets, beaded skin and fur items. Temperatures here range from 55°F/13°C to 90°F/32°C in summer, and from 32°F/0°C to -50°F/-46°C in winter. Minto Flats is one of the most popular duck hunting spots in Alaska, according to the ADF&G.

Private Aircraft: Minto airstrip 1 mile/1.6 km east; elev. 460 feet/140m; length 2,000 feet/610m; gravel; unattended.

Minto Lakes, name refers to all lakes in this lowland area. Accessible only by plane or boat; best to fly in. Pike to 36 inches; use wobblers, bait, red-and-white spoons, good all summer. Also grayling, sheefish and whitefish.

F 113 (181.9 km) **M 39** (62.8 km) Evidence of 1983 burn.

F 113.5 (182.7 km) **M 38.5** (62 km) West Fork Hutlitakwa Creek.

F 119 (191.5 km) **M 33** (53.1 km) The road travels the ridges and hills, providing a "top of the world" view of hundreds of square miles in all directions.

F 119.5 (192.3 km) **M 32.5** (52.3 km) Eureka Dome (elev. 2,393 feet/729m) to north.

F 121.1 (194.9 km) **M 30.9** (49.7 km) To the north, travelers look down into the draws of Applegate and Goff creeks.

F 123.2 (198.3 km) **M 28.8** (46.3 km) Large turnouts both sides of highway, scenic views to north. Road begins descent into the Eureka area.

F 123.7 (199.1 km) **M 28.3** (45.5 km) Dugan Hills visible to the south at this point.

F 129.3 (208.1 km) **M 22.7** (36.5 km) Hutlinana Creek bridge. *CAUTION: One-lane bridge.*

F 131.3 (211.3 km) **M 20.7** (33.3 km) Eureka Road turnoff; access to private ranch. Active mining is taking place in this area. *NO TRESPASSING* on private claims. A trail leads to the former mining camp of Eureka, at the junction of Pioneer and Eureka creeks, 3 miles/4.8 km south of Eureka Dome. *NOTE: Watch for road construction westbound to Mile 137 in 1998.*

Private Aircraft: Eureka Creek airstrip; elev. 700 feet/213m; length 1,500 feet/457m; turf; unattended.

F 137.4 (221.1 km) **M 14.6** (23.5 km) One-lane bridge over **Baker Creek.** Grayling 5 to 20 inches, use flies, black gnats, mosquitoes, May 15 to Sept. 30.

Winding road with many ups and downs.

F 138.4 (222.7 km) **M 13.6** (21.9 km) Highway goes over Overland Bluff and through a 1968 burn area. Bracket fungus is growing on the dead birch trees.

F 150 (241.4 km) **M 2** (3.2 km) Walter Woods Park to west. *NOTE: This part of the road can be extremely slick after heavy rains. Drive with caution.*

F 151.1 (243.2 km) **M 0.9** (1.4 km) Manley DOT/PF highway maintenance station.

F 151.2 (243.3 km) **M 0.8** (1.3 km) **Junction** with Tofty Road, which leads 16 miles/25.7 km to former mining area of Tofty, founded in 1908 by pioneer prospector A.F. Tofty. Mining activity in area.

Pam and Joee Redington's dog kennel at Manley Hot Springs. (© Rich Reid)

The hot springs are on a hillside on the right before entering the town. One spring runs 35 gallons a minute with a temperature of 136°F/58°C, another runs 110 gallons per minute at 135°F/57°C.

F 151.9 (244.5 km) **M 0.1** (0.2 km) *CAUTION: One-lane bridge over Hot Springs Slough.*

Manley Hot Springs

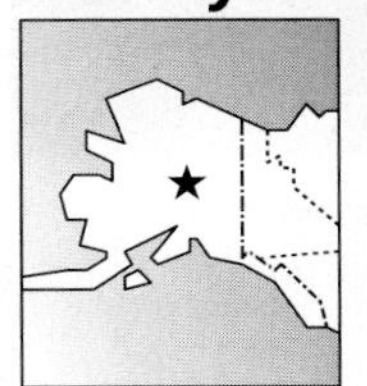

F 152 (244.6 km) **M 0** Located at the end of the Elliott Highway on Hot Springs Slough. **Population:** 88. **Elevation:** 330 feet/101m. **Climate:** Mean temperature in July is 59°F/15°C, in January -10.4°F/-23.6°C. Record high 93°F/33.9°C in June 1969, record low -70°F/-56.7°C in January 1934. Precipitation in summer averages 2.53 inches a month. Snow from October through April, with traces in September and May. Greatest mean monthly snowfall in January (11.1 inches). Record snowfall 49 inches in January 1937.

Private Aircraft: Manley Hot Springs civil airstrip (open year-round), adjacent southwest; elev. 270 feet/82m; length 2,900 feet/884m; gravel; fuel avgas.

A pocket of "Pioneer Alaska." J.F. Karshner homesteaded here in 1902, about the same time the U.S. Army Signal Corps established a telegraph station nearby. The location soon became known as Baker Hot Springs, after nearby Baker Creek. Frank Manley built a 4-story resort hotel here in 1907. The settlement's name was changed to Manley Hot Springs in 1957. Once a busy trading center during peak activity in the nearby Eureka and Tofty mining districts, Manley Hot Springs is now a quiet settlement with a trading post, roadhouse, airfield and hot springs resort. Many residents are enthusiastic gardeners, and visitors may see abundant displays of vegetables and berries growing around homes and businesses. Outstanding display of wild irises at the airstrip in June.

A restaurant, bar and overnight accommodations are at the roadhouse. The post office, gas station and grocery are at the trading post. There is an air taxi service here and scheduled service from Fairbanks.

Manley Trading Post. See display ad this section.

Manley Roadhouse. Come visit one of Alaska's oldest original roadhouses from the gold rush era. See the many prehistoric and Alaskana artifacts on display. New rooms with private baths added 1997. Private cabins. The Manley Roadhouse is a great place to meet local miners, dog mushers, trappers or fishermen. We specialize in traditional Alaska home-style hospitality, fresh-baked pies, giant cinnamon rolls and good food. Largest liquor selection in Alaska. Stop by and see us. See display ad this section. [ADVERTISEMENT] MP

Manley Hot Springs Park Assoc. maintains a public campground near the bridge in town; fee $5 (pay at roadhouse). The hot springs are a short walk from the campground. There's a nice grassy picnic area on the slough near the campground. A boat launch is also nearby.

Manley Hot Springs Slough; pike 18 to 36 inches, use spinning and trolling lures, May through September. Follow the dirt road from the old Northern Commercial Co. store out of town for 2.5 miles/4 km to reach the Tanana River; king, silver and chum salmon from 7 to 40 lbs., June 15 to Sept. 30. Fish wheels and nets are used.

DALTON HIGHWAY (11)

Connects: Elliott Hwy. to Deadhorse, AK **Length:** 414 miles
Road Surface: Gravel **Season:** Open all year
Steepest Grade: 12 percent
Highest Summit: Atigun Pass 4,800 feet
Major Attraction: Trans-Alaska Pipeline

	Coldfoot	Deadhorse	Fairbanks
Coldfoot		239	259
Deadhorse	239		498
Fairbanks	259	498	

Dalton Highway and the trans-Alaska pipeline in Atigun Valley. (© Rich Reid)

The 414-mile/666.3-km Dalton Highway (still referred to as the "Haul Road") begins at **Milepost F 73.1** on the Elliott Highway and ends—for the general public—at Deadhorse, a few miles from Prudhoe Bay and the Arctic Ocean. (Access to Prudhoe Bay, the largest oil field in North America, is available only through commercial tour operators; private vehicles are not permitted on the oil field.) Permits are no longer required to drive the highway to Deadhorse.

The highway is named for James William Dalton, an arctic engineer involved in early oil exploration efforts on the North Slope. It was built as a haul road between the Yukon River and Prudhoe Bay during construction of the trans-Alaska pipeline, and was originally called the North Slope Haul Road. Construction of the road began April 29, 1974, and was completed 5 months later. The road is 28 feet/9m wide with 3 to 6 feet/1 to 2m of gravel surfacing. Some sections of road are underlain with plastic foam insulation to prevent thawing of the permafrost.

Construction of the 800-mile-/1,287-km-long pipeline between Prudhoe Bay and Valdez took place between 1974 and 1977. The 48-inch-diameter pipeline, of which slightly more than half is above ground, has 10 operating pump stations. The control center is in Valdez. Design, construction and operation of the pipeline are managed by Alyeska Pipeline Service Company, a consortium of 7 oil companies (BP, ARCO, Exxon, Mobil, Amerada Hess, Phillips and Unocal). For more information, contact Public Affairs Dept., Alyeska Pipeline Service Co., 1835 S. Bragaw St., Anchorage, AK 99512.

The Bureau of Land Management (BLM) manages 2.1 million acres of public land along the Dalton Highway between the Yukon and Pump Station No. 3. For information on BLM lands, contact Arctic District, BLM, 1150 University Ave., Fairbanks, AK 99709; phone (907) 474-2301.

Services along the Dalton Highway are limited. Shop for groceries before departing Fairbanks. There are no convenience stores or grocery stores along the highway or in Deadhorse. Gas, diesel fuel, tire repair, restaurant, motel, phone and emergency communications are available at **Milepost J 56,** just past the Yukon River bridge, and at Coldfoot, **Milepost J 175.** The last dump station northbound is also located at Coldfoot. (Please do NOT dump holding tanks along the road.) Phones at both locations are for credit card and collect calls only. Public phone at Wiseman. Alyeska pump stations do not provide any public services. Although noted on the map, former pipeline camps have been removed.

There are 4 formal campgrounds on the Dalton, and several informal campsites for self-contained RVs. All are noted in the log. There is overnight parking at the Tesoro in Deadhorse. ▲

IMPORTANT: For emergency services contact the Alaska State Troopers via CB radio, Channel 19, or contact any state highway maintenance camp along the highway. Highway maintenance camps can provide help only in the event of an accident or medical emergency; they cannot fix flat tires nor do they provide gas. Keep in mind that towing fees by private wrecker service can cost $5 a mile, each way.

Road conditions vary depending on weather, maintenance and time of year, but in general the road has a reputation for being rough. Watch for ruts, rocks, dust, soft shoulders and trucks. Calcium chloride is used on the road to control dust; it is corrosive to vehicles and slippery when wet. There are several steep (10 to 12 percent) grades. Drive with your headlights on at all times. Slow down and pull over to the side of the road when meeting oncoming trucks. Stop only at turnouts. Carry spare tires.

*NOTE: Expect road construction between Jim River (**Milepost J 144.1**) and Coldfoot (**Milepost J 175**) in 1998.*

The Dalton Highway is unique in its scenic beauty, wildlife and recreational opportunities. Travelers are requested to stay on the road and to use the formal turnouts

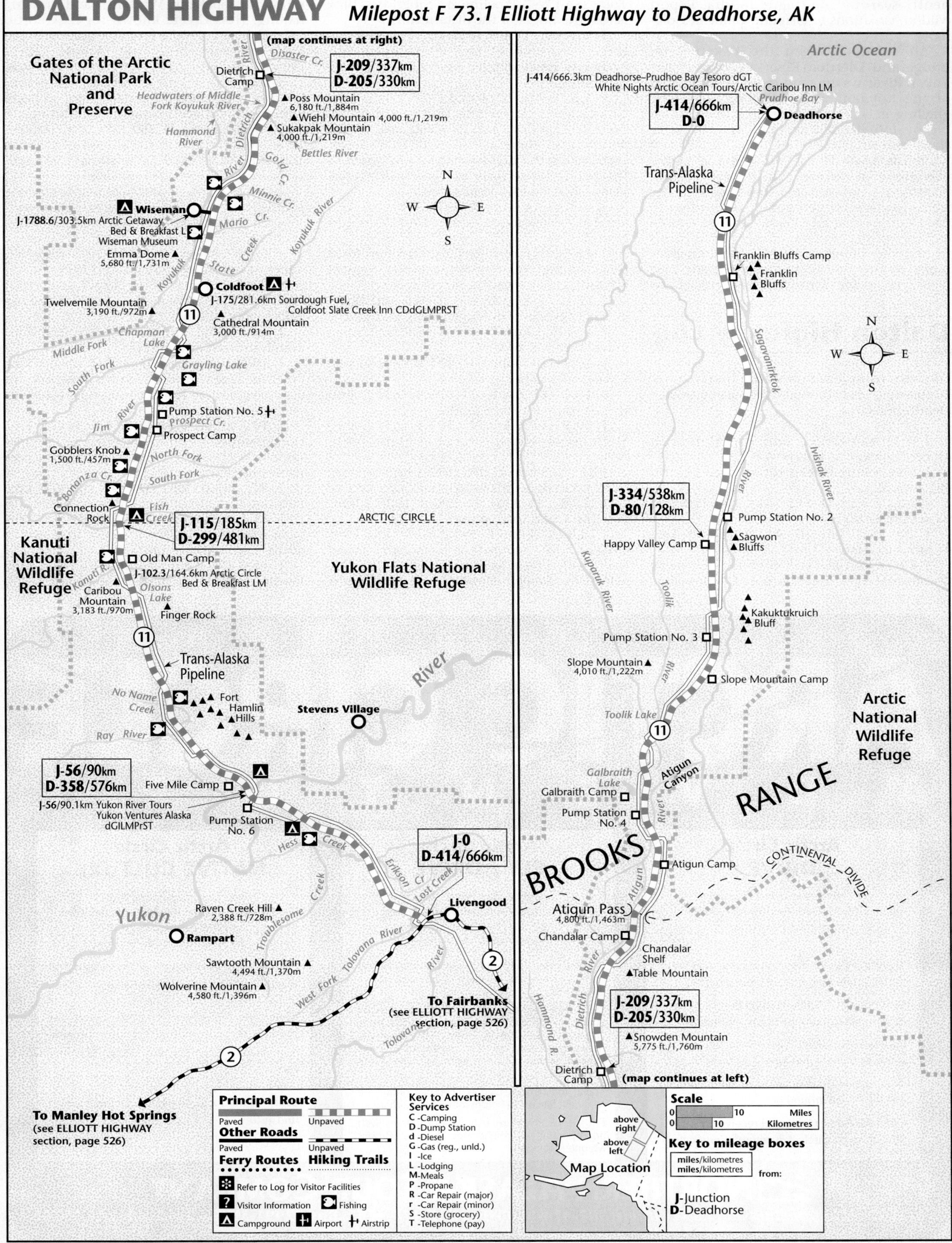
DALTON HIGHWAY
Milepost F 73.1 Elliott Highway to Deadhorse, AK
(map continues at right)
Gates of the Arctic National Park and Preserve
Dietrich Camp
J-209/337km
D-205/330km
Disaster Cr.
Headwaters of Middle Fork Koyukuk River
Poss Mountain 6,180 ft./1,884m
Wiehl Mountain 4,000 ft./1,219m
Sukakpak Mountain 4,000 ft./1,219m
Hammond River
Bettles River
Gold Cr.
Dietrich River
Minnie Cr.
Wiseman
J-1788.6/303.5km Arctic Getaway Bed & Breakfast L
Wiseman Museum
Mario Cr.
Koyukuk River
Emma Dome 5,680 ft./1,731m
State Creek
Coldfoot
J-175/281.6km Sourdough Fuel, Coldfoot Slate Creek Inn CDdGLMPRST
Twelvemile Mountain 3,190 ft./972m
Cathedral Mountain 3,000 ft./914m
Chapman Lake
Middle Fork
Grayling Lake
South Fork
Pump Station No. 5
Jim River
Prospect Cr.
Prospect Camp
Gobblers Knob 1,500 ft./457m
North Fork
South Fork
Bonanza Cr.
Connection Rock
Fish Creek
J-115/185km
D-299/481km
ARCTIC CIRCLE
Kanuti National Wildlife Refuge
Old Man Camp
J-102.3/164.6km Arctic Circle Bed & Breakfast LM
Kanuti R.
Caribou Mountain 3,183 ft./970m
Olsons Lake
Finger Rock
Yukon Flats National Wildlife Refuge
Trans-Alaska Pipeline
No Name Creek
Fort Hamlin Hills
Stevens Village
River
Ray River
J-56/90km
D-358/576km
Five Mile Camp
J-56/90.1km Yukon River Tours Yukon Ventures Alaska dGILMPrST
Pump Station No. 6
Hess Creek
J-0
D-414/666km
Erikson Cr
Lost Creek
Livengood
Yukon
Raven Creek Hill 2,388 ft./728m
Troublesome Creek
Rampart
Tolovana River
Sawtooth Mountain 4,494 ft./1,370m
Wolverine Mountain 4,580 ft./1,396m
West Fork
To Fairbanks (see ELLIOTT HIGHWAY section, page 526)
To Manley Hot Springs (see ELLIOTT HIGHWAY section, page 526)
Arctic Ocean
J-414/666.3km Deadhorse–Prudhoe Bay Tesoro dGT
White Nights Arctic Ocean Tours/Arctic Caribou Inn LM
Prudhoe Bay
J-414/666km
D-0
Deadhorse
Trans-Alaska Pipeline
Franklin Bluffs Camp
Franklin Bluffs
Sagavanirktok River
Ivishak River
J-334/538km
D-80/128km
Pump Station No. 2
Happy Valley Camp
Sagwon Bluffs
Kuparuk River
Toolik River
Kakuktukruich Bluff
Pump Station No. 3
Slope Mountain 4,010 ft./1,222m
Slope Mountain Camp
Arctic National Wildlife Refuge
Toolik Lake
Galbraith Lake
Galbraith Camp
Atigun Canyon
Pump Station No. 4
BROOKS RANGE
Atigun Camp
CONTINENTAL DIVIDE
Atigun Pass 4,800 ft./1,463m
Chandalar Camp
Chandalar Shelf
Table Mountain
Hammond R.
Dietrich River
J-209/337km
D-205/330km
Snowden Mountain 5,775 ft./1,760m
Dietrich Camp
(map continues at left)
Principal Route
Paved
Unpaved
Other Roads
Paved
Unpaved
Ferry Routes
Hiking Trails
Refer to Log for Visitor Facilities
Visitor Information
Fishing
Campground
Airport
Airstrip
Key to Advertiser Services
C -Camping
D -Dump Station
d -Diesel
G -Gas (reg., unld.)
I -Ice
L -Lodging
M -Meals
P -Propane
R -Car Repair (major)
r -Car Repair (minor)
S -Store (grocery)
T -Telephone (pay)
above right
above left
Map Location
Scale
0 10 Miles
0 10 Kilometres
Key to mileage boxes
miles/kilometres
miles/kilometres
from:
J-Junction
D-Deadhorse

and campgrounds provided to avoid permanently scarring the fragile tundra. Report wildlife violations to Fish and Game at Coldfoot.

All waters between the Yukon River bridge and Dietrich River are part of the Yukon River system, and most are tributaries of the Koyukuk River. Fishing for arctic grayling is especially good in rivers accessible by foot from the highway. The large rivers also support burbot, salmon, pike and whitefish. Small Dolly Varden are at higher elevations in streams north of Coldfoot. Fishing for salmon is closed within the trans-Alaska pipeline corridor. According to the Dept. of Fish and Game, anglers should expect high, turbid water conditions throughout much of June as the snowpack melts in the Brooks Range, with the best fishing occurring during July and August.

Dalton Highway Log

Distance from junction with Elliott Highway (J) is followed by distance from Deadhorse (D).

J 0 D 414 (666.3 km) **Junction** with Elliott Highway at **Milepost F 73.1.**

J 1 (1.6 km) **D 413** (664.6 km) Dalton Highway sign.

J 2 (3.2 km) **D 412** (663 km) Pipeline passes under highway.

J 2.9 (4.7 km) **D 411.1** (661.6 km) Turnout to west.

J 4 (6.4 km) **D 410** (659.8 km) Highway descends steeply into the Lost Creek valley. Lost Creek flows into the West Fork Tolovana River. Pipeline is visible stretching across the ridges of the distant hills.

J 5 (8 km) **D 409** (658 km) Yellow numbered signs mark oil spill containment site. Materials are stockpiled here for use in case of an oil spill.

J 5.6 (9 km) **D 408.4** (657.2 km) Lost Creek culvert. Steep hills north- and southbound. Pipeline access road; no public admittance. There are many of these access roads along the highway; most are closed to the public for security and safety concerns. Please do not block road access.

J 8.3 (13.4 km) **D 405.7** (652.9 km) Entering game management unit 20 northbound.

J 9.8 (15.8 km) **D 404.2** (650.5 km) Road follows a high ridge with spectacular view of Erickson Creek area and pipeline.

J 11 (17.7 km) **D 403** (648.5 km) Begin steep (12 percent) downgrade northbound.

J 12 (19.3 km) **D 402** (646.9 km) Small gravel turnouts to west.

J 12.1 (19.5 km) **D 401.9** (646.8 km) Erickson Branch; creek culvert.

J 18.6 (29.9 km) **D 395.4** (636.3 km) Bypass route for steep grade.

J 20.9 (33.6 km) **D 393.1** (632.6 km) Steep double-ended turnout at gravel pit to west.

J 21 (33.8 km) **D 393** (632.5 km) Descent to Hess Creek begins northbound.

J 23.6 (38 km) **D 390.4** (628.3 km) Pipeline access road, pond.

J 23.8 (38.3 km) **D 390.2** (627.9 km) **Hess Creek** bridge. Campsite in trees. Large gravel bar along creek at north end of bridge. *CAUTION: Sandpit at entrance to gravel bar is an easy place to get stuck.* Bring your mosquito repellent. Whitefish and grayling fishing. Hess Creek, known for its colorful mining history, is the largest stream between the junction and the Yukon River bridge.

J 23.9 (38.5 km) **D 390.1** (627.8 km) Road to west leads 0.2 mile/0.3 km to pond with parking space adequate for camping.

J 25 (40.2 km) **D 389** (626 km) Double-ended rough turnout. Good view of pipeline and remote-operated valve site as the highway crosses Hess Creek and valley.

J 26 (41.8 km) **D 388** (624.4 km) Pipeline parallels highway about 250 feet/76m away.

J 26.5 (42.6 km) **D 387.5** (623.6 km) Turnout.

J 27 (43.4 km) **D 387** (622.8 km) Evidence of lightning-caused forest fires.

J 33.7 (54.2 km) **D 380.3** (612 km) Turnout at tributary of Hess Creek. Chiming bells bloom in June.

J 35.5 (57.1 km) **D 378.5** (609.1 km) Rough turnout at gravel pit.

J 38.1 (61.3 km) **D 375.9** (604.9 km) Pipeline goes under road. Evidence of the revegetation project undertaken by the oil companies.

J 40.7 (65.5 km) **D 373.3** (600.7 km) Double-ended turnout. Overview of Troublesome and Hess creeks areas. Brush obscures sweeping views.

J 42 (67.6 km) **D 372** (598.7 km) Turnout; outcrop of dark gabbroic rock.

J 43.1 (69.4 km) **D 370.9** (596.9 km) Isom Creek culvert. Steep ascent from valley north- and southbound.

J 44.6 (71.8 km) **D 369.4** (594.5 km) Turnout with litter barrel at viewpoint.

J 47.5 (76.4 km) **D 366.5** (589.8 km) Yukon radio repeater tower.

J 47.9 (77.1 km) **D 366.1** (589.2 km) Highway begins descent to Yukon River.

J 48.5 (78.1 km) **D 365.5** (588.2 km) Pipeline access road. Goalpost-like structures, called "headache bars," guard against vehicles large enough to run into and damage the pipeline.

J 50.1 (80.6 km) **D 363.9** (585.6 km) Turnout.

J 50.4 (81.1 km) **D 363.6** (585.1 km) Turnout; pond to east.

J 51.1 (82.2 km) **D 362.9** (584 km) Rough side road leads east 5.4 miles/8.7 km to Yukon River.

J 53.2 (85.6 km) **D 360.8** (580.6 km) First view northbound of the Yukon River. As road drops, you can see the pipeline crossing the river. Fort Hamlin Hills are beyond the river.

J 54 (86.9 km) **D 360** (579.3 km) **PUMP STATION NO. 6.** Alyeska pump stations monitor the pipeline's oil flow on its journey from Prudhoe Bay to Valdez. No public facilities.

J 54.3 (87.4 km) **D 359.7** (578.9 km) Highway passes over pipeline.

J 54.5 (87.7 km) **D 359.5** (578.5 km) Turnout to west.

J 55.6 (89.5 km) **D 358.4** (576.8 km) Yukon River bridge (formally the E.L. Patton Bridge, named for the president of the Alyeska Pipeline Service Co. after his death in 1982). This wood-decked bridge, completed in 1975, is 2,290 feet/698m long and has a 6 percent grade. The deck was replaced in 1993.

J 56 (90.1 km) **D 358** (576.1 km) Gas, diesel, tire repair, restaurant, motel, phone and emergency communications available at Yukon Ventures Alaska. Next services northbound: 120 miles/193 km. Tours and charters of the Yukon River include dinner cruise and visit to a working Native fish camp.

Yukon Ventures Alaska. See display ad this section.

Yukon River Tours—Tours and charters on the Yukon River from the Yukon Crossing daily from June 1 to September 1. YRT offers 1 1/2-hour excursions. Explore the natural world that has been our people's home for many generations. Phone (907) 452-7162. 214 2nd Avenue, Fairbanks, AK 99701-4811. [ADVERTISEMENT]

This is the southern boundary of BLM-managed lands. The Yukon Crossing Visitor Contact Station here, managed and staffed by the BLM, is open 7 days a week, June through August. There is also an Alyeska pipeline interpretive display here with information on the Yukon River, pipeline construction and related subjects. Birch forest along river. East of the highway is a camping area with litter barrels. Road closed east of campsite. ▲

J 60.6 (97.5 km) **D 353.4** (568.7 km) Site of **FIVE MILE CAMP**, a former pipeline construction camp. No structures remain at these former construction camps. There is an undeveloped campsite here and a toilet. Water is available from an artesian well. Highway crosses over buried pipeline.

J 60.8 (97.8 km) **D 353.2** (568.4 km) Five Mile airstrip (length 3,500 feet/1,067m); controlled by Alyeska Security. *CAUTION: Be prepared to stop at control gates at both ends of airstrip.*

J 61.3 (98.7 km) **D 352.7** (567.6 km) Airstrip control tower.

J 61.6 (99.1 km) **D 352.4** (567.1 km) View of Fort Hamlin Hills to north, pump station No. 6 to south.

J 61.9 (99.6 km) **D 352.1** (566.6 km) Sevenmile DOT/PF highway maintenance camp.

J 66.8 (107.5 km) **D 347.2** (558.7 km) Turnout to west.

J 68.4 (110.1 km) **D 345.6** (556.2 km) Highway crosses over buried pipeline.

J 69.2 (111.4 km) **D 344.8** (554.9 km) Double-ended turnout at crest of hill overlooking the Ray River to the north. Pipeline goes underground.

J 70 (112.7 km) **D 344** (553.6 km) **Ray River** overlook and double-ended turnout. Scenic view of the Ray Mountains to the west. Burbot, grayling and northern pike fishing.

J 72.5 (116.7 km) **D 341.5** (549.6 km) Fort Hamlin Hills Creek bridge and turnout.

Winter trail scars are visible just beyond the bridge.

J 73.5 (118.3 km) **D 340.5** (548 km) Begin steep 0.5-mile/0.8-km ascent of Sand Hill northbound.

J 74.8 (120.4 km) **D 339.2** (545.9 km) Steep descent northbound followed by steep ascent; dubbed the Roller Coaster. Pipeline to east.

J 79.1 (127.3 km) **D 334.9** (539 km) **No Name Creek** and turnout east side at south end of bridge; burbot, grayling and whitefish.

J 81.6 (131.3 km) **D 332.4** (534.9 km) Fort Hamlin Hills are visible to the southeast. Tree line on surrounding hills is about 2,000 feet/610m.

J 86.5 (139.2 km) **D 327.5** (527 km) Scenic overlook 1 mile/1.6 km west with view of tors to northeast, Yukon Flats Wildlife Refuge to east and Fort Hamlin Hills to southeast. Tors are high, isolated pinnacles of jointed granite jutting up from the tundra and are a residual feature of erosion.

J 88.5 (142.4 km) **D 325.5** (523.8 km) Mackey Hill. Entering Game Management Unit 25D northbound, Unit 20F southbound. The high, unnamed hill east of the road is 2,774 feet/846m in elevation.

J 90.2 (145.2 km) **D 323.8** (521.1 km) Double-ended turnouts both sides of highway. A good photo opportunity of the road and pipeline to the north. The zig-zag design allows the pipeline to flex and accommodate temperature changes. The small green structure over the buried pipe is a radio-controlled valve, allowing the pipeline oil flow to be shut down when necessary.

J 91.1 (146.6 km) **D 322.9** (519.6 km) Culvert directs water from branch of west fork of Dall Creek. Watch for soft spots in road.

J 94 (151.3 km) **D 320** (515 km) Turnout at former gravel pit road to west.

J 96 (154.5 km) **D 318** (511.8 km) The road lies above tree line for about 5 miles/8 km. Good opportunities for photos, berry picking (blueberries, lowbush cranberries), wildflower viewing and hiking. Northbound, the terrain becomes more rugged and scenic.

J 97.5 (156.9 km) **D 316.5** (509.3 km) Finger Rock (signed Finger Mountain), a tor, is visible east of the road and most easily seen to the south. Tors are visible for the next 2 miles/3.2 km. Prehistoric hunting sites are numerous in this region. Please do not collect or disturb artifacts.

J 98.2 (158 km) **D 315.8** (508.2 km) Finger Mountain wayside; toilet, parking, interpretive trail. Caribou Mountain is in the distance to the northwest. Olsens Lake, Kanuti Flats, Kanuti River drainage and site of former Old Man Camp are visible ahead northbound. The road descends and passes through several miles of valley bottom with excellent mountain views.

J 100.7 (162.1 km) **D 313.3** (504.2 km) Pipeline passes under highway.

Arctic Circle display at Milepost J 115.3 is a popular photo stop. (© Bill Sherwonit)

J 102.3 (164.6 km) **D 311.7** (501.6 km) **Arctic Circle Bed & Breakfast.** See display ad this section.

J 105.8 (170.3 km) **D 308.2** (496 km) **Kanuti River**, crossing and turnout; burbot, grayling. Abandoned airstrip to east. Pipeline emerges from underground.

J 107 (172.2 km) **D 307** (494.1 km) Site of **OLD MAN CAMP**, a former pipeline construction camp.

J 108.4 (174.4 km) **D 305.6** (491.8 km) Highway crosses pipeline.

J 109.8 (176.7 km) **D 304.2** (489.5 km) Turnout at Beaver Slide. *CAUTION: Road descends very steeply northbound. Watch for soft spots. Slippery when wet.*

J 110 (177 km) **D 304** (489.2 km) First view of Brooks Range northbound.

J 111.5 (179.4 km) **D 302.5** (486.8 km) View of valley and Fish Creek to the north.

J 112.2 (180.6 km) **D 301.8** (485.7 km) Turnout at pipeline access road. Moose and bear frequent willow thickets here.

J 113.9 (183.3 km) **D 300.1** (483 km) Evidence of old winter trail to Bettles is visible here.

J 114 (183.5 km) **D 300** (482.8 km) **Fish Creek** bridge and turnout; grayling 12 to 18 inches.

J 115.3 (185.5 km) **D 298.7** (480.7 km) The Arctic Circle, north latitude 66°33'. BLM wayside with tables, grills, toilets and interpretive display. Stop and have your picture taken with the sign. This is also a good photo point, with views to the south and to the west. Follow road off turnout 0.6 mile/1 km for primitive campsites (pull-throughs, nice views). If you reach the Alyeska access gate you've gone too far. ▲

J 116.2 (187 km) **D 297.8** (479.2 km) Turnout to east (can be soft).

J 120.7 (194.2 km) **D 293.3** (472 km) Connection Rock; north and south road-building crews linked up here.

J 124.7 (200.7 km) **D 289.3** (465.6 km) Turnout to east at **South Fork Bonanza Creek**; burbot, grayling, whitefish.

J 125.7 (202.3 km) **D 288.3** (464 km) Turnout to east at **North Fork Bonanza Creek**; historic gold mining area; burbot, grayling, whitefish.

J 127.1 (204.5 km) **D 286.9** (461.7 km) Turnout.

J 127.7 (205.5 km) **D 286.3** (460.7 km) Paradise Hill; blueberries and lowbush cranberries in season.

J 128.9 (207.4 km) **D 285.1** (458.8 km) Primitive campsite at gravel pit.

J 129.3 (208.1 km) **D 284.7** (458.2 km) *CAUTION: Long ascent northbound with a short stretch that is very steep. Give trucks plenty of room here!*

J 131.3 (211.3 km) **D 282.7** (454.9 km) Solar-powered communications tower to west.

J 131.5 (211.6 km) **D 282.5** (454.6 km) View of pump station No. 5 to north.

J 132 (212.4 km) **D 282** (453.8 km) Turnout with litter barrels and toilet at Gobblers Knob (elev. 1,500 feet/457m) overlooking the Jack White Range, Pope Creek Dome (the dominant peak to the northwest), Prospect Creek drainage, pump station No. 5, Jim River drainage, South Fork Koyukuk drainage and the Brooks Range on the northern horizon.

J 134.7 (216.8 km) **D 279.3** (449.5 km) Pipeline access road.

J 135.1 (217.4 km) **D 278.9** (448.8 km) **Prospect Creek**; grayling, whitefish and pike. Active gold mining area.

J 135.7 (218.4 km) **D 278.3** (447.9 km) Old winter road goes up creek to mines. Turn left for site of **PROSPECT CAMP**, which holds the record for lowest recorded temperature in Alaska (-80°F/-62°C, Jan. 23, 1971). Rough road leads 0.5 mile/0.8 km to Claja Pond; beaver, ducks. Undeveloped campsite on Jim River. Old winter road to Bettles crosses river here. ▲

J 137.1 (220.6 km) **D 276.9** (445.6 km) **PUMP STATION NO. 5** (signed incorrectly as Prospect Camp). No public access. Side road leads to well. Pump station No. 5 is not actually a pump station, but a "drain down" or pressure relief station to slow the gravity-fed flow of oil descending from Atigun Pass in the Brooks Range. Glacial moraine marks the southern boundary of Brooks Range glaciers during the most recent ice age.

Private Aircraft: Airstrip; length 5,000 feet/1,524m; lighted runway. This airstrip is used as a BLM fire fighting staging area.

J 138.1 (222.2 km) **D 275.9** (444 km) Jim River DOT/PF highway maintenance camp EMT squad. Site of 1988 burn.

J 139 (223.7 km) **D 275** (442.6 km) Road to gravel pit.

J 140.1 (225.5 km) **D 273.9** (440.8 km) **Jim River** Bridge No. 1; narrow bridge, turnouts. Burbot, chum and king salmon, grayling, pike, whitefish. *CAUTION: Bears here for fall salmon run.*

J 141 (226.9 km) **D 273** (439.3 km) **Jim River** Bridge No. 2; narrow bridge, turnouts. See fishing previous milepost.

J 141.8 (228.2 km) **D 272.2** (438.1 km) Douglas Creek; blueberries and lowbush cranberries in season.

J 144.1 (231.9 km) **D 269.9** (434.4 km) **Jim River** Bridge No. 3 (main channel); turnout to east at south end of bridge. See **Milepost J 140.1** for fishing.

*NOTE: Watch for road construction from here to Coldfoot (**Milepost J 175**) in 1998.*

J 145.6 (234.3 km) **D 268.4** (431.9 km) Pipeline passes under road. First views northbound of Brooks Range foothills to the north.

J 150.3 (241.9 km) **D 263.7** (424.4 km) **Grayling Lake** to east has good grayling fishing in open water season.

J 150.8 (242.7 km) **D 263.2** (423.6 km) Turnout on Grayling Lake. The road is passing through the foothills of the Brooks Range. There is an active gold mining area behind the hills to the west.

J 155.2 (249.8 km) **D 258.8** (416.5 km) Overlook for the South Fork Koyukuk River valley.

J 156 (251.1 km) **D 258** (415.2 km) Large turnout with toilet and litter barrels at the **South Fork Koyukuk River** bridge. Self-contained RV camping in turnout. Fishing for grayling, whitefish, chum and king salmon. Active gold mining downstream. ▲

This large river flows past the villages of Bettles, Allakaket, Hughes and Huslia before draining into the Yukon River near Koyukuk.

J 159.1 (256 km) **D 254.9** (410.2 km) Bridge over pipeline; large animal crossing over pipeline.

J 160 (257.5 km) **D 254** (408.8 km) Good view of Chapman Lake 0.5 mile/0.8 km west of road. Old mine trail is visible from the road.

The 2 mountains visible to the north are Twelvemile Mountain (elev. 3,190 feet/972m), left, and Cathedral Mountain (elev. 3,000 feet/914m), on right. The foothills of the Brooks Range are also to the north.

J 161.2 (259.4 km) **D 252.8** (406.8 km) Road to west leads to gold claim.

J 163.3 (262.8 km) **D 250.7** (403.5 km) Turnout to west.

J 164.6 (264.9 km) **D 249.4** (401.3 km) Example of a "sag bend," a short section of buried pipeline that allows large animals to cross.

J 165.1 (265.7 km) **D 248.9** (400.6 km) Turnout to west with view of pipeline.

J 165.7 (266.7 km) **D 248.3** (399.6 km) Turnout on west side of road overlooking Middle Fork Koyukuk River.

J 167.2 (269.1 km) **D 246.8** (397.2 km) Old winter trail to Tramway Bar. "River training structures" in place direct water away from the pipeline and highway during floods.

J 175 (281.6 km) **D 239** (384.6 km) **COLDFOOT**, site of a historic mining camp at the mouth of Slate Creek on the east bank of the Middle Fork Koyukuk River. Coldfoot Services (phone 907/678-5201) offers 3 motels, a 24-hour restaurant, gift shop, general store, trading post, laundromat, fuel facility with gas, diesel and avgas; tire repair, minor vehicle repair; RV park with hookups and dump station; post office, phone and emergency medical service. It is also home of the "farthest North saloon in North America" with "readable walls." Next services northbound: 244 miles/392.7 km. Area tours and guided hunting and fishing trips available. ▲

There is a 3,500-foot/1,067-m runway to west, maintained by the state. An Alaska State Trooper, a Fish and Wildlife officer and BLM field station are located at Coldfoot. A visitor center here, operated by the BLM, USF&WS and National Park Service, offers travel information and nightly presentations on the natural and cultural history of the Arctic. It is open from June 1 through Labor Day. Topographic maps for sale.

Originally named Slate Creek, Coldfoot reportedly got its name in 1900 when gold stampeders got as far up the Koyukuk as this point, then got cold feet, turned and departed. The old cemetery still exists. Emma Dome (elev. 5,680 feet/1,731m) is to the west.

Sourdough Fuel, Coldfoot Slate Creek Inn. See display ad this section. ▲

J 175.7 (282.8 km) **D 238.3** (383.5 km) Radio repeater site on mountains to east.

J 179.9 (289.5 km) **D 234.1** (376.7 km) Marion Creek Campground; 27 sites, $6 camping fee, tables, grills, firepits, water, toilets, bear-proof litter containers, resident campground host, information kiosk, RV parking. Dump station at Coldfoot services. Marion Creek trailhead. ▲

J 184.4 (296.7 km) **D 229.6** (369.5 km) Scenic overlook. Excellent view of Middle Fork Koyukuk River; small slumps and rock slide on adjacent mountain.

J 186 (299.3 km) **D 228** (366.9 km) The historic mining community of Wiseman can be seen across the Koyukuk River to the west. Access to Wiseman from **Milepost J 188.6**.

J 186.7 (300.5 km) **D 227.3** (365.8 km) Turnouts both sides of highway.

J 187.2 (301.3 km) **D 226.8** (365 km) Turnout to west at **Minnie Creek**; burbot, grayling, whitefish.

J 188.5 (303.4 km) **D 225.5** (362.9 km) **Middle Fork Koyukuk River** Bridge No. 1; turnout. Dolly Varden, grayling, whitefish.

J 188.6 (303.5 km) **D 225.4** (362.7 km) Improved access road to **WISEMAN**, a historic mining town. The heyday of Wiseman came in about 1910, after gold seekers abandoned Coldfoot. About 25 residents live here year-round today, and the population increases in the summer with the arrival of miners. (Note that this is an active mining area and all buildings are privately owned.) The Wiseman Museum, located in the historic Carl Frank Cabin, contains old miner's journals, hotel registers and historical photo panels. Limited gift items are for sale. Watch for signs as you enter town. Wiseman has a general store, public phone and campground. ▲

Arctic Getaway Bed & Breakfast. See display ad this section.

Wiseman Museum. See display ad this section.

J 189 (304.2 km) **D 225** (362.1 km) Spur (finger) dikes keep river away from highway and pipeline.

J 190.5 (306.6 km) **D 223.5** (359.7 km)

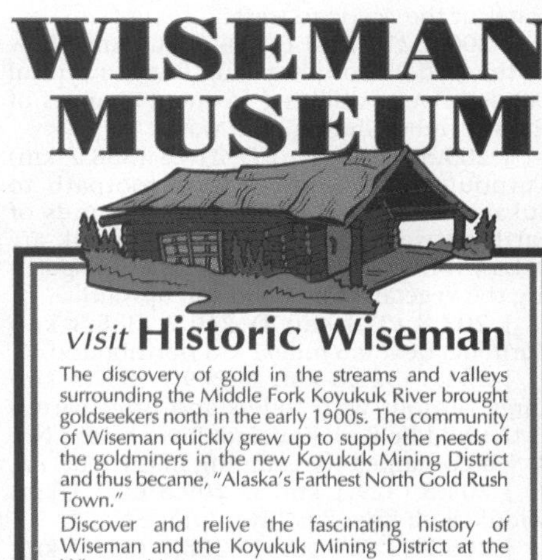

Narrow bridge over Hammond River; gold mining area upstream.

J 190.8 (307.1 km) **D 223.2** (359.2 km) Middle Fork Koyukuk River Bridge No. 2. "Guide banks," another example of river training structures.

J 192.8 (310.3 km) **D 221.2** (356 km) Link Up, where 2 sections of road constructed by different crews were joined.

J 194 (312.2 km) **D 220** (354 km) First view northbound of Sukakpak Mountain (elev. 4,000 feet/1,219m) to north. Sukakpak Mountain is sometimes said to mark a traditional boundary between Eskimo and Athabascan Indian territories. Wiehl Mountain (elev. 4,000 feet/1,219m) is east of Sukakpak. The high mountain just to the west of the road is unnamed.

J 195 (313.8 km) **D 219** (352.4 km) Pipeline close to road is mounted on sliding shoes to allow flexing.

J 197 (317 km) **D 217** (349.2 km) Old cabin just west of road is reported to have been constructed in the early 1900s; private property. Gold Creek bridge.

J 197.3 (317.5 km) **D 216.7** (348.7 km) Cat trail to gold mining area.

J 197.5 (317.8 km) **D 216.5** (348.4 km) Linda Creek in culvert.

J 197.7 (318.2 km) **D 216.3** (348.1 km) Turnout east and view of Wiehl Mountain. Gates of the Arctic to west.

J 200 (321.9 km) **D 214** (344.4 km) View of the Middle Fork Koyukuk River, a typical braided river exhibiting frequent changes of the streambed during high water.

J 203.5 (327.5 km) **D 210.5** (338.7 km) Turnout and 0.5-mile/0.8-km footpath to Sukakpak Mountain. The short mounds of earth between the road and Sukakpak are palsas, formed by ice beneath the soil pushing the vegetative mat and soil upward.

J 203.8 (328 km) **D 210.2** (338.3 km) Turnouts next 0.6 mile/1 km northbound.

J 204.3 (328.8 km) **D 209.7** (337.5 km) Large turnout with toilets and litter barrels at the Middle Fork Koyukuk River bridge No. 3. Self-contained RV camping in turnout. ▲

J 204.5 (329.1 km) **D 209.5** (337.1 km) Middle Fork Koyukuk River bridge No. 4.

J 205.3 (330.4 km) **D 208.7** (335.9 km) Turnout to west. Good view of north side of Sukakpak Mountain.

J 206 (331.5 km) **D 208** (334.7 km) View of Wiehl Mountain.

J 207 (333.1 km) **D 207** (333.1 km) **Dietrich River** bridge, turnout to west at south end; burbot, grayling, whitefish and Dolly Varden.

J 207.5 (333.9 km) **D 206.5** (332.3 km) Small, unnamed lake on east side of road with nice view of Sukakpak Mountain. Dillon Mountain (proposed name) is just to the north.

J 208.2 (335.1 km) **D 205.8** (331.2 km) Unnamed creek in culvert.

J 209.1 (336.5 km) **D 204.9** (329.7 km) Site of **DIETRICH CAMP**, a former pipeline construction camp.

J 211 (339.6 km) **D 203** (326.7 km) Disaster Creek. Turnout with bear-proof litter container to east.

J 216.2 (347.9 km) **D 197.8** (318.3 km) Snowden Creek culvert. Panorama of Dietrich River valley and Brooks Range north and west of the road.

J 217.1 (349.4 km) **D 196.9** (316.9 km) Rock spire to east is Snowden Mountain (elev. 5,775 feet/1,760m). Cirque above highway was carved by a glacier; hike up to waterfall.

J 221.6 (356.6 km) **D 192.4** (309.6 km) Turnout to east is quarry of black marble with white calcite veins.

J 224 (360.5 km) **D 190** (305.8 km) Turnout at gravel pit.

J 225 (362.1 km) **D 189** (304.2 km) River bars; very braided stream.

J 226 (363.7 km) **D 188** (302.5 km) Pipeline remote valve just west of road. The arch-shaped concrete "saddle weights" keep pipeline buried in areas of possible flooding.

J 227.3 (365.8 km) **D 186.7** (300.5 km) Nutirwik Creek culvert.

J 228 (366.9 km) **D 186** (299.3 km) Highway parallels Dietrich River.

J 231.4 (372.4 km) **D 182.6** (293.9 km) Small turnouts both sides of highway. Pipeline is buried under river.

J 234.6 (377.5 km) **D 179.4** (288.7 km) Pipeline emerges from under river.

J 234.9 (378 km) **D 179.1** (288.2 km) Entering North Slope Borough boundary northbound. Borough offices are located in Barrow.

J 235.3 (378.7 km) **D 178.7** (287.6 km) Large turnout with litter barrel at foot of Chandalar Shelf and beginning of a long, steep (10 percent) grade. Truck chain-up area. The farthest north spruce tree along the highway is located just south of the turnout. No trees beyond here.

J 237.1 (381.6 km) **D 176.9** (284.7 km) Turnout at top of Chandalar Shelf; former checkpoint. Headwaters of the Chandalar River are to the east. Table Mountain (elev. 6,425 feet/1,958m) is to the southeast. Dietrich River valley to south.

NOTE: Many mileposts are missing on Atigun Pass. Physical mileposts remaining may not reflect actual driving distance between posts.

J 239 (384.6 km) **D 175** (281.6 km) Brown net structure west of road is called a Wyoming Gage; it is used to measure precipitation. Sponsored by the Natural Resources Conservation Service.

J 239.2 (384.9 km) **D 174.8** (281.3 km) Site of **CHANDALAR CAMP**, a former pipeline construction camp, now used as a BLM field station.

J 239.4 (385.3 km) **D 174.6** (281 km) Chandalar highway maintenance station on west side of highway.

J 240.2 (386.6 km) **D 173.8** (279.7 km) Avalanche gun emplacement; DOT/PF materials storage site.

J 242.2 (389.8 km) **D 171.8** (276.5 km) West Fork Chandalar River bridge.

J 242.5 (390.2 km) **D 171.5** (276 km) Begin long, steep climb northbound toward Atigun Pass. Winter avalanche area. Slide area next 5 miles/8 km northbound.

J 244.7 (393.8 km) **D 169.3** (272.5 km) Turnout at top of Atigun Pass (elev. 4,800 feet/1,463m), highest highway pass in Alaska; Continental Divide. A Wyoming Gage to measure moisture is located here. Nice example of a cirque, an amphitheater-shaped bowl or depression caused by glacier erosion, in mountain east of road. Endicott Mountains are to the west, Phillip Smith Mountains to the east. James Dalton Mountain is to the left ahead northbound.

Highway descends steeply toward the North Slope. Many mountains in the area exceed 7,000 feet/2,134m in elevation. The pipeline is in a buried, insulated concrete cribbing to the east to protect it from rock slides and avalanches, and to keep the ground frozen. Construction in this area was extremely complex, difficult and dangerous.

J 248.4 (399.8 km) **D 165.6** (266.5 km) Turnouts both sides of highway. Good spot to view Dall sheep.

J 250 (402.3 km) **D 164** (263.9 km) Bridge over Spike Camp Creek. Highway crosses buried pipeline.

J 250.2 (402.6 km) **D 163.8** (263.6 km) Site of **ATIGUN CAMP**, a former pipeline construction camp. Turnouts both sides of highway. View of Atigun River valley. Another Wyoming Gage is located here.

J 251.5 (404.7 km) **D 162.5** (261.5 km) Turnouts next 0.3 mile/0.5 km northbound.

J 253.1 (407.3 km) **D 160.9** (258.9 km) Atigun River crossing No. 1. Highway crosses buried pipeline. *CAUTION: Grizzly bears in area.*

J 254 (408.8 km) **D 160** (257.5 km) Mountains to north exhibit extreme folding of sedimentary rock layers.

J 257.6 (414.6 km) **D 156.4** (251.7 km) Check valves on the pipeline keep oil from flowing backwards in the event of a leak.

J 258.4 (415.8 km) **D 155.6** (250.4 km) Trevor Creek bridge.

J 258.6 (416.2 km) **D 155.4** (250.1 km) Turnout.

J 261.4 (420.7 km) **D 152.6** (245.6 km) Turnout.

J 265 (426.5 km) **D 149** (239.8 km) Roche Moutonnee Creek bridge.

J 267.5 (430.5 km) **D 146.5** (235.8 km) Bridge over Holden Creek.

J 268 (431.3 km) **D 146** (235 km) Good view of pump station No. 4.

J 269.3 (433.4 km) **D 144.7** (232.9 km) **PUMP STATION NO. 4**. This station has the highest elevation of all the pipeline stations (2,760 feet/841m), and is also a launching and receiving station for special measuring and cleaning devices called "pigs." A scraper pig consists of spring-mounted scraper blades and/or brushes on a central body which moves through the pipe, cleaning accumulated wax from interior walls and monitoring conditions inside the pipe. There are "dumb" pigs and "smart" pigs. Dumb pigs clean out wax deposits in the line. Smart pigs scan the pipeline to check welds, wall thickness and other properties to help insure the integrity of the piping and identify maintenance needs.

J 269.5 (433.7 km) **D 144.5** (232.5 km) Highway bridge passes over pipeline.

J 270 (434.5 km) **D 144** (231.7 km) Salty rocks attract Dall sheep to slopes above highway.

J 270.5 (435.3 km) **D 143.5** (230.9 km) Small lakes both sides of highway.

J 270.9 (436 km) **D 143.1** (230.3 km) Atigun River crossing No. 2. The Arctic National Wildlife Refuge boundary is located 3 miles/4.8 km east along the Atigun gorge. Galbraith Lake may be seen to the west. There are a large number of archaeological sites in this vicinity.

J 272.9 (439.2 km) **D 141.1** (227.1 km) Look for Dall sheep on mountains to east.

J 274 (440.9 km) **D 140** (225.3 km) View of Galbraith Lake and Galbraith camp.

J 274.7 (442.1 km) **D 139.3** (224.2 km) Road access to **GALBRAITH CAMP**, a construction camp; toilet, litter barrel. Self-contained RV camping available at the public campsite. USF&WS field station. Nice wildflowers in season. ▲

J 276.5 (445 km) **D 137.5** (221.3 km) Island Lake.

J 284.3 (457.5 km) **D 129.7** (208.7 km) Toolik Lake west of road. A former construction camp, it is now the site of Toolik Lake

Research Camp, run by the Institute of Arctic Biology of the University of Alaska–Fairbanks. The field station conducts global warming studies and has no public facilities or services.

J 286.2 (460.6 km) **D 127.8** (205.7 km) Turnout to east at high point in road. View of Brooks Range south and east. Philip Smith Mountains to west; panoramic views; caribou.

J 288.8 (464.8 km) **D 125.2** (201.5 km) Kuparuk River bridge.

J 289.3 (465.6 km) **D 124.7** (200.7 km) Pipeline crossing. Short buried section of pipeline to west is called a sag bend and is to allow for wildlife crossing. Watch for caribou northbound.

J 290.4 (467.3 km) **D 123.6** (198.9 km) Turnout to east; road to materials site.

J 290.6 (467.7 km) **D 123.4** (198.6 km) Toolik Creek.

J 294.4 (473.8 km) **D 119.6** (192.5 km) Second sag bend northbound.

J 297.8 (479.2 km) **D 116.2** (187 km) Oksrukukuyik Creek culvert. Small turnout to east.

J 298.3 (480.1 km) **D 115.7** (186.2 km) Turnout on top of moraine; first view of Sagavanirktok Valley.

J 301 (484.4 km) **D 113** (181.8 km) Turnout. Slope Mountain (elev. 4,010 feet/1,222m) is just west of road. Watch for Dall sheep. This is the northern boundary of BLM-managed land. Land north of here is managed by the state.

J 302 (486 km) **D 112** (180.2 km) "Sag bend" large animal crossing.

J 305.7 (492 km) **D 108.3** (174.3 km) Site of **SLOPE MOUNTAIN CAMP**, a former pipeline construction camp, now Sag River highway maintenance station.

J 306 (492.4 km) **D 108** (173.8 km) Pipeline underground; oil spill containment site.

J 309 (497.3 km) **D 105** (169 km) Highway parallels Sagavanirktok River.

J 311.8 (501.8 km) **D 102.2** (164.5 km) **PUMP STATION NO. 3**; mobile construction camp facility.

J 313.7 (504.8 km) **D 100.3** (161.4 km) Oksrukukuyik Creek in culvert.

J 319.8 (514.7 km) **D 94.2** (151.6 km) Turnout to east at Oil Spill Hill.

J 320 (515 km) **D 94** (151.3 km) The long range of hills east of the road is the Kakuktukruich Bluff.

J 325 (523 km) **D 89** (143.2 km) Large turnout gives public river access from pipeline access road. Self-contained RV parking in turnout. ▲

J 325.1 (523.2 km) **D 88.9** (143.1 km) Jerry Hubbard's "national forest" of willow saplings on revegetated materials site.

J 325.3 (523.5 km) **D 88.7** (142.7 km) Turnout with litter barrel to east at the top of a steep grade called Ice Cut.

J 326.2 (525 km) **D 87.8** (141.3 km) Pipeline crossing on bridge.

J 330.7 (532.2 km) **D 83.3** (134.1 km) Dan Creek bridge.

J 334.4 (538.1 km) **D 79.6** (128.1 km) Site of **HAPPY VALLEY CAMP**, a former pipeline construction camp, now a Fish and Game field station.

J 345.5 (556 km) **D 68.5** (110.2 km) Grant Creek in culvert.

J 347.6 (559.4 km) **D 66.4** (106.9 km) Sagwon airstrip. The airstrip is currently not in use in order to protect nesting peregrine falcons in the area.

J 350.5 (564.1 km) **D 63.5** (102.2 km) View of Sagwon Bluffs to the east. The road passes over several low hills that offer views of the surrounding terrain.

Deadhorse has a plentiful supply of tires for big rigs, but it is suggested visitors bring along 2 mounted spares for conventional vehicles. (© Julie Sprott)

J 353 (568 km) **D 61** (98.2 km) Wyoming Gage west of road on hill.

J 355.1 (571.5 km) **D 58.9** (94.8 km) Turnout with litter barrel to east.

J 358.8 (577.4 km) **D 55.2** (88.8 km) **PUMP STATION NO. 2** to the east.

NOTE: The worst winter weather conditions on the Dalton Highway are experienced the next 38 miles/61 km northbound. Blowing snow may obscure visibility and block road.

J 364 (585.8 km) **D 50** (80.5 km) Low hills to the north are the Franklin Bluffs. East of the road, the Ivishak River empties into the Sagavanirktok River on its journey to the Arctic Ocean.

J 365.1 (587.6 km) **D 48.9** (78.7 km) Turnout by pond to west; watch for nesting waterfowl.

J 366 (589 km) **D 48** (77.2 km) Large animal crossing in pipeline for caribou.

J 376 (605.1 km) **D 38** (61.2 km) The small hill that rises abruptly on the horizon about 5 miles/8 km west of the road is called a pingo. Pingos often form from the bed of a spring-fed lake that has been covered by vegetation. Freezing of the water can raise the surface several hundred feet above the surrounding terrain.

J 377.3 (607.2 km) **D 36.7** (59.1 km) Turnout to east at site of **FRANKLIN BLUFFS CAMP**, a former pipeline construction camp. Winter equipment is stored here in summer. *CAUTION: Watch for loose, coarse gravel on road.*

J 383 (616.4 km) **D 31** (49.9 km) Franklin Bluffs to the east and a pingo to the west.

J 398.7 (641.6 km) **D 15.3** (24.6 km) Underground pipeline crossing.

J 413.3 (665.1 km) **D 0.7** (1.1 km) Turnout with Prudhoe Bay and Deadhorse maps at former highway checkpoint. Oil field activity and equipment become visible along the horizon.

J 414 (666.3 km) **D 0** Northern end of Dalton Highway. Security gate; travel beyond this point is on oil company roads. About 2 miles/3.2 km ahead is the Deadhorse Airport and the public-access portion of the Prudhoe Bay oil field. A number of oil fields make up the Prudhoe Bay industrial area: Kuparuk, Milne Point, Point McIntyre, Prudhoe Bay, Niakuk and Endicott.

Deadhorse

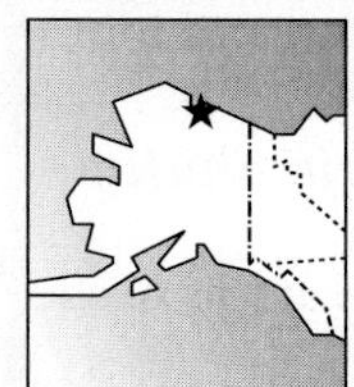

Population: 25; area pop. 2,500. Deadhorse was established to support oil development in the surrounding area; it is not a town in the traditional sense. Deadhorse takes its name from the airport, which was named after

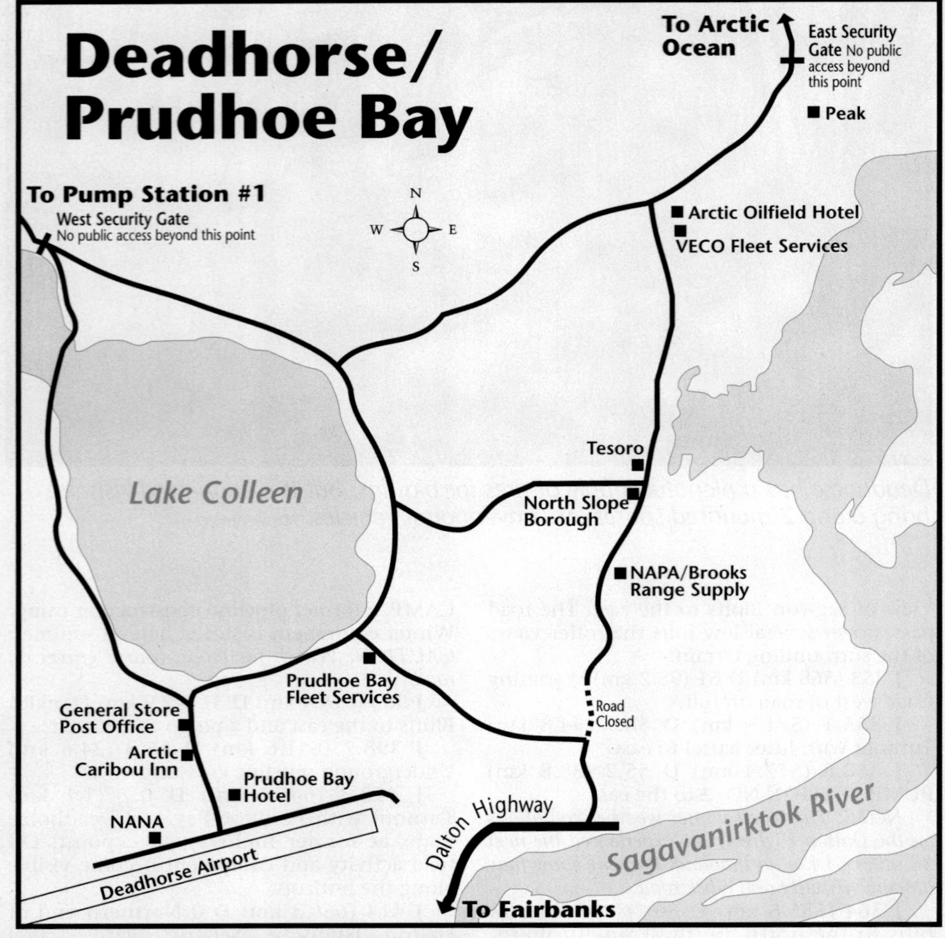

the construction company that built it. Most buildings are modular, pre-fab-type construction, situated on gravel pads on tundra bog. Virtually all the businesses here are engaged in oil field or pipeline support activities, such as drilling, construction, maintenance, telecommunications, warehousing and transportation. Oil field employees work a rotation, such as 2 weeks on the job, then 2 weeks off. While on rotation, workers typically work 7 days a week, 10 to 12 hours each day.

There is scheduled jet service to Deadhorse/Prudhoe Bay from Anchorage (flying time from Anchorage is 1 hour, 35 minutes), Fairbanks and Barrow. Packaged tours of the North Slope area are available from Anchorage and Fairbanks. Air taxi service is available at Deadhorse Airport for sightseeing, hunting or rafting parties, and trips to outlying Native villages.

Accommodations are available at the Arctic Caribou Inn, Arctic Oilfield Hotel (Veco Camp), Peak Base Camp or Prudhoe Bay Hotel. All serve meals; however, only snacks or salad bars may be available at times other than breakfast (5:30–8 A.M.), lunch (noon to 1 P.M.) and dinner (5–8 P.M.). There is a general store, auto parts/hardware store and post office.

Regular unleaded gasoline and No. 1 diesel are available at Nana or the local Tesoro station. Nana is open from 7 A.M. until 5 P.M., with a callout charge after hours. Tesoro is a 24-hour self-serve station; an attendant is available and cash accepted from 7 A.M. until 6 P.M. There are a public phone, toilet and overnight parking with limited services available at Tesoro.

Tire and vehicle repairs are available at either Prudhoe Bay Fleet Shop or the Veco Light Vehicle Shop. Make sure to carry an extra tire, as well as the usual 2 mounted spares, because tire stock is limited. You could wait several days if a tire has to be ordered. The local auto parts store has an assortment of filters, oil, windshield wipers, headlights, etc.

Public access beyond Deadhorse is restricted. For security reasons, travel north of Deadhorse, including visits to the Arctic Ocean, is limited to commercial tours. Tour information is available at either the Arctic Caribou Inn or the Prudhoe Bay Hotel. Aerial tours may be arranged with one of the aircraft or helicopter charter services located at the Deadhorse Airport.

Arctic Caribou Inn invites you to tour Prudhoe Bay, May 25–Sept. 8. Providing guided tours since 1975. Tour includes Milepost 0 at Pump Station 1. See oil rigs and Oilfield Visitor Center, and oil field informative video presentation and exhibits. Walk on the beach at the Arctic Ocean. Arctic Caribou Inn. Clean comfortable rooms. Buffet service, laundry and shower facilities. Summer phone (907) 659-2368. Winter phone (907) 659-2840. Tour Arctic/Arctic Caribou Inn, fax (907) 659-2289. Mailing address: P.O. Box 340112, Prudhoe Bay, AK 99734. [ADVERTISEMENT]

Deadhorse–Prudhoe Bay Tesoro. See display ad this section.

White Nights Arctic Ocean Tours. See display ad this section.

Kenai Peninsula

SEWARD HIGHWAY ① ⑨

Connects: Anchorage to Seward, AK **Length:** 127 miles
Road Surface: Paved **Season:** Open all year
Highest Summit: Turnagain Pass 988 feet
Major Attractions: Mount Alyeska; Portage Glacier; Kenai Fjords National Park

(See map, page 540)

	Alyeska	Anchorage	Hope	Portage Glacier	Seward
Alyeska		42	56	22	95
Anchorage	42		88	54	127
Hope	56	88		46	75
Portage Glacier	22	54	46		85
Seward	95	127	75	85	

The Seward Highway has been designated a National Forest Scenic Byway.
(© Loren Taft, Alaskan Images)

The 127-mile-/204-km-long Seward Highway connects Anchorage with the community of Seward on the east coast of the Kenai Peninsula. It has been called one of the most scenic highways in the country and has been designated a National Forest Scenic Byway. Leaving Anchorage, the Seward Highway follows the north shore of Turnagain Arm through Chugach State Park and Chugach National Forest, permitting a panoramic view of the south shore and the Kenai Mountains.

The Seward Highway provides access to Alyeska ski resort, the Hope Highway, Portage Glacier and Kenai Fjords National Park. There is a bike trail between Anchorage and Girdwood. The bike route is marked by signs. Numerous hiking trails branch off the highway.

The Seward Highway junctions with the other major Kenai Peninsula route, the Sterling Highway (see STERLING HIGHWAY section) at Tern Lake. Both these highways offer hiking, fishing and camping opportunities, and beautiful scenery.

Physical mileposts on the Seward Highway show distance from Seward. The Seward Highway is a paved, 2-lane highway with passing lanes. It is open all year. There are no gas stations on the Seward Highway between **Milepost S 90** (Girdwood turnoff) and **Milepost S 6.6**, just outside Seward. Some sections of the highway are subject to avalanches in winter. Check Anchorage news sources for winter road conditions. In 1998, expect major road construction projects along the Seward Highway between **Milepost S 97** and **S 90** (Girdwood turnoff) and bike trail construction beside the highway between **Milepost S 59** and **S 53** (Hope Highway cutoff).

CAUTION: The Seward Highway from Anchorage to just past Girdwood statistically has one of the highest number of traffic accidents in the state. DRIVE CAREFULLY! Motorists must drive with headlights on at all times.

Emergency medical services: Phone 911 or use CB channels 9, 11 or 19. Cellular phone service is available as far south as Girdwood and is also available in Seward.

Seward Highway Log

ALASKA ROUTE 1
Distance from Seward (S) is followed by distance from Anchorage (A). Physical mileposts show distance from Seward.

S 127 (204.4 km) **A 0** Gambell Street and 10th Avenue in Anchorage. The Seward Highway (Gambell Street) connects with the Glenn Highway in Anchorage via 5th Avenue (westbound) and 6th Avenue (eastbound). (See map in the ANCHORAGE section.) Follow Seward Highway signs south on Gambell.

*NOTE: Expect road construction from here to 36th Avenue (**Milepost S 125.3**) in 1998.*

S 126.7 (203.9 km) **A 0.3** (0.5 km) 15th Avenue (DeBarr Road).

S 126.6 (203.7 km) **A 0.4** (0.6 km) 16th Avenue; access to Sullivan sports arena, ice rinks and baseball stadium.

S 126 (202.8 km) **A 1** (1.6 km) Fireweed Lane.

S 125.8 (202.4 km) **A 1.2** (1.9 km) Northern Lights Boulevard (one-way westbound). Access to shopping centers.

S 125.7 (202.3 km) **A 1.3** (2.1 km) Benson Boulevard (one-way eastbound).

S 125.4 (201.8 km) **A 1.6** (2.6 km) Southbound access only to Old Seward Highway.

S 125.3 (201.6 km) **A 1.7** (2.7 km) 36th Avenue; hospital to east.

*NOTE: Expect road construction from here northbound to 5th Avenue (**Milepost S 127**) in 1998.*

S 125.2 (201.5 km) **A 1.8** (2.9 km) Freeway begins southbound. There are no services or facilities along the new Seward Highway. However, there are several exits in the next 7.5 miles/12.1 km to the Old Seward Highway (which parallels the new Seward Highway) where traveler services are available.

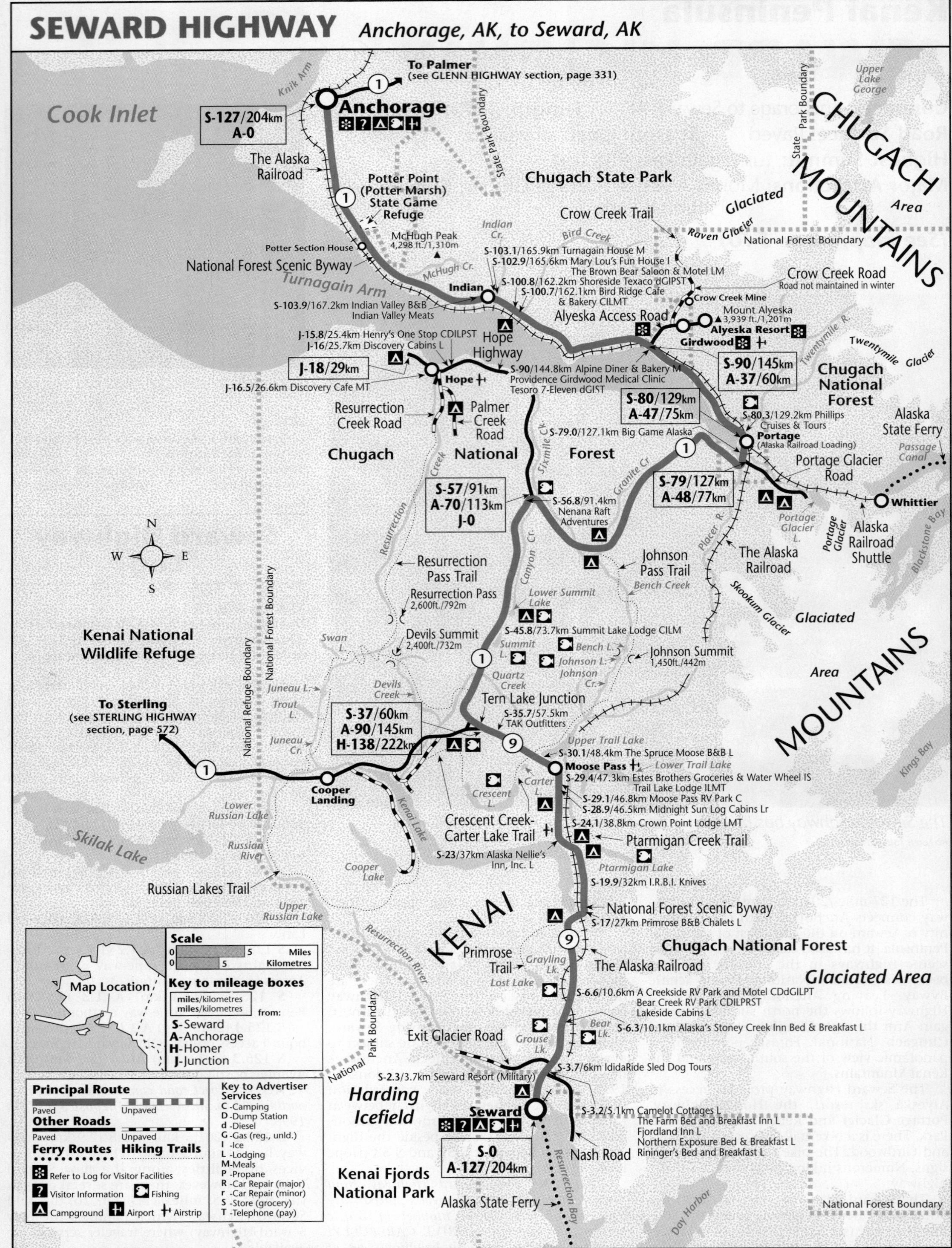
SEWARD HIGHWAY Anchorage, AK, to Seward, AK
To Palmer
(see GLENN HIGHWAY section, page 331)
Cook Inlet
Knik Arm
S-127/204km
A-0
Anchorage
The Alaska Railroad
Potter Point (Potter Marsh) State Game Refuge
State Park Boundary
Chugach State Park
CHUGACH MOUNTAINS
Glaciated Area
Upper Lake George
Crow Creek Trail
Raven Glacier
National Forest Boundary
Indian Cr.
Bird Creek
McHugh Peak
4,298 ft./1,310m
Potter Section House
National Forest Scenic Byway
Turnagain Arm
McHugh Cr.
Indian
S-103.1/165.9km Turnagain House M
S-102.9/165.6km Mary Lou's Fun House I
The Brown Bear Saloon & Motel LM
S-100.8/162.2km Shoreside Texaco dGIPST
S-100.7/162.1km Bird Ridge Cafe
& Bakery CILMT
S-103.9/167.2km Indian Valley B&B
Indian Valley Meats
Crow Creek Road
Road not maintained in winter
Crow Creek Mine
Alyeska Access Road
Mount Alyeska
3,939 ft./1,201m
Alyeska Resort
Girdwood
Twentymile R.
Twentymile Glacier
J-15.8/25.4km Henry's One Stop CDILPST
J-16/25.7km Discovery Cabins L
Hope Highway
J-18/29km
Hope
J-16.5/26.6km Discovery Cafe MT
S-90/144.8km Alpine Diner & Bakery M
Providence Girdwood Medical Clinic
Tesoro 7-Eleven dGIST
S-90/145km
A-37/60km
Chugach National Forest
Resurrection Creek Road
Palmer Creek Road
S-80/129km
A-47/75km
S-80.3/129.2km Phillips Cruises & Tours
Portage
(Alaska Railroad Loading)
Alaska State Ferry
Passage Canal
S-79.0/127.1km Big Game Alaska
Chugach National Forest
Sixmile Ck.
Portage Glacier Road
S-57/91km
A-70/113km
J-0
S-56.8/91.4km Nenana Raft Adventures
Granite Cr.
S-79/127km
A-48/77km
Whittier
Portage Glacier L.
Portage Glacier
Alaska Railroad Shuttle
Blackstone Bay
Resurrection Creek
Canyon Cr.
Placer R.
The Alaska Railroad
Johnson Pass Trail
Bench Creek
Resurrection Pass Trail
Resurrection Pass
2,600ft./792m
Lower Summit Lake
Skookum Glacier
Glaciated Area
Kenai National Wildlife Refuge
Swan L.
Devils Summit
2,400ft./732m
S-45.8/73.7km Summit Lake Lodge CILM
Summit L.
Bench L.
Johnson L.
Johnson Summit
1,450ft./442m
Johnson Cr.
MOUNTAINS
Area
Quartz Creek
Devils Creek
Juneau L.
Trout L.
National Refuge Boundary
National Forest Boundary
To Sterling
(see STERLING HIGHWAY section, page 572)
S-37/60km
A-90/145km
H-138/222km
Tern Lake Junction
S-35.7/57.5km TAK Outfitters
Juneau Cr.
Upper Trail Lake
S-30.1/48.4km The Spruce Moose B&B L
Moose Pass
Lower Trail Lake
S-29.4/47.3km Estes Brothers Groceries & Water Wheel IS
Trail Lake Lodge ILMT
S-29.1/46.8km Moose Pass RV Park C
S-28.9/46.5km Midnight Sun Log Cabins Lr
Kings Bay
Cooper Landing
Crescent L.
Carter L.
Lower Russian Lake
Kenai Lake
Crescent Creek-Carter Lake Trail
S-24.1/38.8km Crown Point Lodge LMT
Ptarmigan Creek Trail
Skilak Lake
Russian River
S-23/37km Alaska Nellie's Inn, Inc. L
Ptarmigan Lake
Cooper Lake
Russian Lakes Trail
S-19.9/32km I.R.B.I. Knives
KENAI
National Forest Scenic Byway
Upper Russian Lake
S-17/27km Primrose B&B Chalets L
Resurrection River
Chugach National Forest
Primrose Trail
Grayling Lk.
The Alaska Railroad
Glaciated Area
Lost Lake
S-6.6/10.6km A Creekside RV Park and Motel CDdGILPT
Bear Creek RV Park CDILPRST
Lakeside Cabins L
Bear Lk.
S-6.3/10.1km Alaska's Stoney Creek Inn Bed & Breakfast L
Exit Glacier Road
Grouse Lk.
National Park Boundary
S-3.7/6km IdidaRide Sled Dog Tours
S-2.3/3.7km Seward Resort (Military)
Harding Icefield
Seward
S-3.2/5.1km Camelot Cottages L
The Farm Bed and Breakfast Inn L
Fjordland Inn L
Northern Exposure Bed & Breakfast L
Rininger's Bed and Breakfast L
S-0
A-127/204km
Nash Road
Kenai Fjords National Park
Alaska State Ferry
Resurrection Bay
Day Harbor
National Forest Boundary
Map Location
Scale
0 5 Miles
0 5 Kilometres
Key to mileage boxes
miles/kilometres
miles/kilometres
from:
S-Seward
A-Anchorage
H-Homer
J-Junction
Principal Route
Paved
Unpaved
Other Roads
Paved
Unpaved
Ferry Routes
Hiking Trails
Refer to Log for Visitor Facilities
Visitor Information
Fishing
Campground
Airport
Airstrip
Key to Advertiser Services
C -Camping
D -Dump Station
d -Diesel
G -Gas (reg., unld.)
I -Ice
L -Lodging
M-Meals
P -Propane
R -Car Repair (major)
r -Car Repair (minor)
S -Store (grocery)
T -Telephone (pay)

S 124.7 (200.7 km) **A 2.3** (3.7 km) Tudor Road overpass; exits both sides of highway. (Tudor Road is used as a bypass route for northbound travelers, connecting them with the Glenn Highway via Muldoon Road.)

S 124.2 (199.8 km) **A 2.8** (4.5 km) Campbell Creek bridge.

S 123.7 (199.1 km) **A 3.3** (5.3 km) Dowling Road underpass; exits on both sides of highway.

S 122.7 (197.5 km) **A 4.3** (6.9 km) 76th Avenue exit, southbound traffic only.

S 122.2 (196.7 km) **A 4.8** (7.7 km) Dimond Boulevard underpass; exits on both sides of highway.

S 120.8 (194.4 km) **A 6.2** (10 km) O'Malley Road underpass; exits on both sides of highway. Turn east on O'Malley Road and drive 2 miles/3.2 km to reach the Alaska Zoo. Turn west for access to Old Seward Highway and major shopping area on Dimond Boulevard. Views of Chugach Mountains along this stretch.

S 119.7 (192.6 km) **A 7.3** (11.7 km) Huffman Road underpass; exits on both sides of highway.

S 118.5 (190.7 km) **A 8.5** (13.7 km) De Armoun Road overpass, exits both sides of highway.

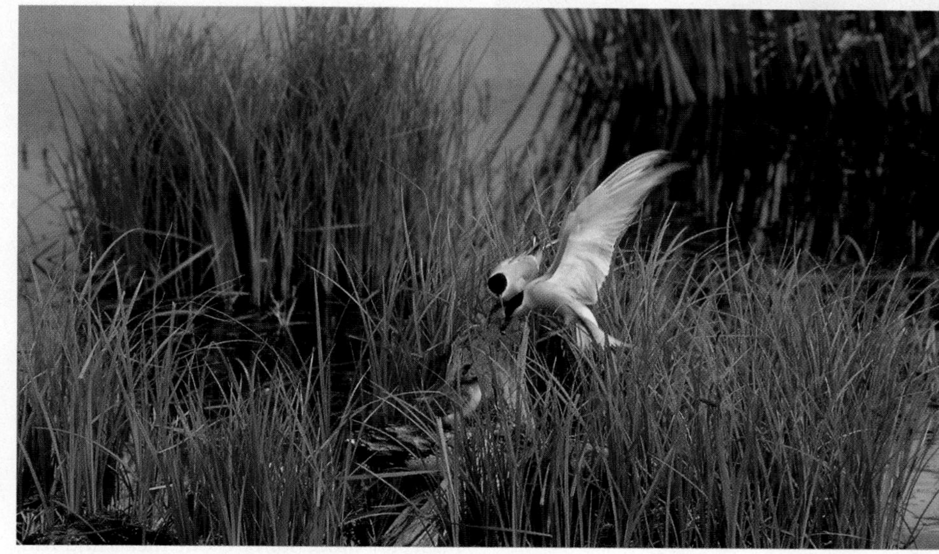

An arctic tern feeds its chick at Potter Point State Game Refuge (Milepost S 117.4). (© James D. Ronan, Jr.)

S 117.8 (189.6 km) **A 9.2** (14.8 km) Overpass: Exits both sides of highway for Old Seward Highway (west); access to Rabbit Creek Road (east). The picturesque Chapel by the Sea overlooks Turnagain Arm. The church is often photographed because of its unique setting and its display of flowers.

S 117.6 (189.3 km) **A 9.4** (15.1 km) View of Turnagain Arm and Mount Spurr.

S 117.4 (188.9 km) **A 9.6** (15.4 km) Rabbit Creek Rifle Range to west. Boardwalk Wildlife Viewing exit leads east to Potter Point State Game Refuge. This is a very popular spot for bird watching. From the parking lot, an extensive boardwalk crosses Potter Marsh, a refuge and nesting area for waterfowl. The marsh was created when railroad construction dammed a small creek in the area. Today, the marsh is visited by arctic terns, Canada geese, trumpeter swans, many species of ducks and other water birds. Bring binoculars.

S 117.3 (188.8 km) **A 9.7** (15.6 km) Highway narrows to 2 lanes southbound.

S 117.2 (188.6 km) **A 9.8** (15.8 km) Small paved turnout at end of boardwalk.

S 116.1 (186.8 km) **A 10.9** (17.5 km) Paved double-ended turnout to east. Highway parallels Alaska Railroad southbound to **Milepost S 90.8.**

S 115.4 (185.7 km) **A 11.6** (18.7 km) **Junction** with Old Seward Highway; access to Potter Valley Road. Old Johnson trail begins 0.5 mile/0.6 km up Potter Valley Road; parking at trailhead. Only the first 10 miles/16 km of this state park trail are cleared. Moderate to difficult hike; watch for bears.

The natural gas pipeline from the Kenai Peninsula emerges from beneath Turnagain Arm here and follows the roadway to Anchorage.

WARNING: When the tide is out, the sand in Turnagain Arm might look inviting. DO NOT go out on it. Some of it is quicksand. You could become trapped in the mud and not be rescued before the tide comes in.

S 115.3 (185.6 km) **A 11.7** (18.8 km) Entering Chugach State Park southbound. Potter Section House, Chugach State Park Headquarters (phone 907/345-5014) to west; pay phone, large parking lot, wheelchair-accessible toilets. Open daily in summer, Monday to Friday 8 A.M. to 4:30 P.M. year-round. The renovated Potter Section House, dedicated in October 1986, was home to a small crew of railroad workers who maintained the Alaska Railroad tracks between Seward and Anchorage in the days of coal- and steam-powered locomotives. Displays here include photographs from the National Archives, a vintage snowblower and working model railroad. ♿

S 115.1 (185.2 km) **A 11.9** (19.2 km) Potter Creek trailhead to east.

S 115 (185 km) **A 12** (19.3 km) Watch for rockfalls. Avalanche area and hazardous driving conditions during winter for the next 25 miles/40.2 km.

From here to **Milepost S 90** there are many turnouts on both sides of the highway, some with scenic views of Turnagain Arm. An easterly extension of Cook Inlet, Turnagain Arm was called Return by the Russians. Captain Cook, seeking the fabled Northwest Passage in 1778, called it Turnagain River, and Captain Vancouver, doing a more thorough job of surveying in 1794, gave it the present name of Turnagain Arm.

S 114.7 (184.6 km) **A 12.3** (19.8 km) Weigh station and pay phone to east.

S 114.5 (184.3 km) **A 12.5** (20.1 km) Double-ended gravel turnout to east. From here to **Milepost S 104**, patches of harebells (Bluebells of Scotland) can be seen in late July and early August.

S 113.3 (182.3 km) **A 13.7** (22.1 km) Large paved turnout for slow vehicles.

S 113.1 (182 km) **A 13.9** (22.4 km) Small gravel turnout to east at McHugh boulder area. Watch for rock climbers practicing on the steep cliffs alongside the highway. The cliffs are part of the base of McHugh Peak (elev. 4,298 feet/1,310m).

S 111.8 (179.9 km) **A 15.2** (24.5 km) McHugh Creek state wayside to east with 30 picnic sites. A stream and waterfall make this a very refreshing place to stop. *CAUTION: Steep but paved road into this picnic site. Be sure you have plenty of power and good brakes for descent, especially if you are towing a trailer.* There is also a parking area beside the highway. Good berry picking in season near the stream for wild currants, blueberries and watermelon berries. A 1-mile portion of the Old Johnson trail here is wheelchair accessible. ♿

S 111.6 (179.6 km) **A 15.4** (24.8 km) Double-ended gravel turnout to east. There are numerous turnouts southbound to Indian.

S 110.3 (177.5 km) **A 16.7** (26.9 km) Beluga Point scenic viewpoint and photo stop has a commanding view of Turnagain Arm. A good place to see bore tides and beluga whales. (The only all-white whale, belugas are easy to identify.) Large paved double-ended turnout to west with tables, benches, telescopes and interpretive signs on orcas, bore tides, mountain goats, etc.

WARNING: Do not go out on the mud flats at low tide. The glacial silt and water can create a dangerous quicksand.

Turnagain Arm is known for having one of the world's remarkably high tides, with a diurnal range of more than 33 feet/10m. A bore tide is an abrupt rise of tidal water just after low tide, moving rapidly landward, formed by a flood tide surging into a constricted inlet such as Turnagain Arm. This foaming wall of water may reach a height of 6 feet/2m and is very dangerous to small craft. To see a bore tide, check the Anchorage-area tide tables for low tide, then add approximately 2 hours and 15 minutes to the Anchorage low tide for the bore to reach points between 32 miles/51.5 km and 37 miles/59.5 km south of Anchorage on the Seward Highway. Visitors should watch for bore tides from Beluga Point south to Girdwood.

S 109.2 (175.7 km) **A 17.8** (28.6 km) Paved turnout to west. Spring water is piped to the highway.

S 108.7 (174.9 km) **A 18.3** (29.5 km) Paved double-ended viewpoint to west.

S 108.5 (174.6 km) **A 18.5** (29.8 km) Rainbow Road to Rainbow Valley.

S 108.4 (174.4 km) **A 18.6** (29.9 km) Rainbow trailhead and parking; access to Old Johnson trail.

S 107.3 (172.7 km) **A 19.7** (31.7 km) Gravel turnout to east. Rock climbers practice on the cliffs here.

S 107 (172.2 km) **A 20** (32.2 km) From here to Girdwood, in summer when snow is

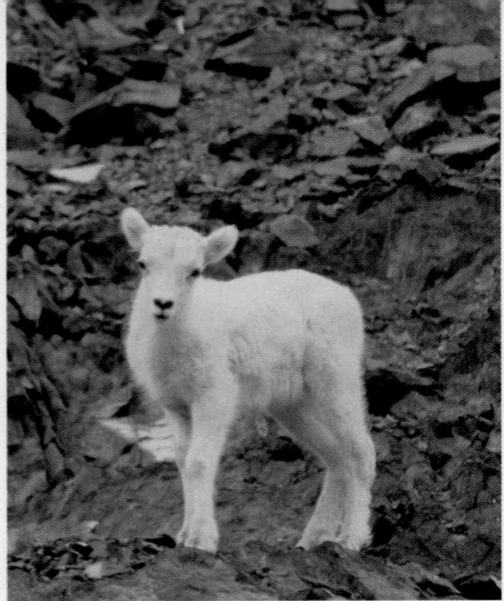

A Dall sheep lamb frolics near the highway. (© Loren Taft, Alaskan Images)

still on the peaks or after heavy rainfall, watch for many small waterfalls tumbling down the mountainsides to Turnagain Arm.

S 106.9 (172 km) **A 20.1** (32.3 km) Scenic viewpoint. Double-ended paved turnout to west; Old Johnson trail access. Watch for Dall sheep near road. *NOTE: DO NOT FEED WILDLIFE.*

S 106.7 (171.7 km) **A 20.3** (32.7 km) Paved turnout to east; Windy trailhead.

S 106.6 (171.5 km) **A 20.4** (32.8 km) Large paved turnout to west; watch for Dall sheep.

S 105.7 (170.1 km) **A 21.3** (34.3 km) Falls Creek trailhead and parking to east; Old Johnson trail access.

S 104 (167.4 km) **A 23** (37 km) Indian Valley Mine National Historic Site.

S 103.9 (167.2 km) **A 23.1** (37.2 km) Indian Road and Indian Valley businesses on east side of highway.

Indian Valley B & B. Clean rooms with private baths. Stunning grounds with live reindeer, exotic birds, pygmy goats, flower gardens, gift shop and a beautiful log hall

with trophy animal mounts. All of this is built on the owner's residential land, creating a beautiful Alaskan setting overlooking Indian Valley and Turnagain Arm. You'll want to stay many nights. Phone (907) 653-7511 for reservation. [ADVERTISEMENT]

Indian Valley Meats. We're a federally inspected processor of exotic meats and fish, including reindeer jerky, buffalo sausage and much more. Let us smoke and ship your salmon, or take home some of ours. We're just 1/2 mile up Indian Road on the left. Please stop in and see the reindeer! Phone (907) 653-7511. [ADVERTISEMENT]

S 103.5 (166.6 km) **A 23.5** (37.8 km) **INDIAN**; current status of services unknown.

S 103.1 (165.9 km) **A 23.9** (38.5 km) Bore Tide Road, also called Ocean View Road. Turnagain House restaurant.

Turnagain House, Milepost 103.1 Seward Highway at Indian, AK. Fresh Alaskan seafood, fine steaks and baby back ribs. Located 16 miles south of Anchorage. Excellent view of Turnagain Arm and bore tides. Rustic and casual atmosphere. The Turnagain House is a year-round favorite of Anchorage residents and is considered one of the finest restaurants in the area. Major credit cards accepted. Reservations: (907) 653-7500. [ADVERTISEMENT]

S 103 (165.8 km) **A 24** (38.6 km) Motel and bar. Bridge over Indian Creek.

Indian Creek, heavily fished! Pink salmon, sea-run Dolly Varden, few coho (silver) salmon and rainbow, June to September; pink salmon run from latter part of July to mid-August in even-numbered years. **Bird Creek**, same fishing as Indian Creek, except heavier run of pink salmon in July and August.

S 102.9 (165.6 km) **A 24.1** (38.8 km) Indian Creek rest area to west; wheelchair accessible toilets and parking. Bar and liquor store to east. Pay phone.

The Brown Bear Saloon & Motel. See display ad this section.

Mary Lou's Fun House. See display ad this section.

S 102.1 (164.3 km) **A 24.9** (40.1 km) Bird Ridge trailhead and parking; Old Johnson trail access.

S 101.5 (163.3 km) **A 25.5** (41 km) Bridge over Bird Creek; parking. Watch for pedestrians next mile southbound.

S 101.2 (162.9 km) **A 25.8** (41.5 km) Bird Creek State Recreation Site with picnic sites and 19 campsites, firepits, pay phone, covered picnic tables, toilets and water. Firewood is sometimes available. Camping fee $10/night or annual pass. A pleasant campground densely wooded but cleared along the high banks of Turnagain Arm. Paved bike trail goes through campground (nice ride along Turnagain Arm). Great spot for sunbathing. This campground is full most weekends in the summer.

WARNING: Do not go out on the mud flats at low tide. The glacial silt and water can create a dangerous quicksand.

S 100.8 (162.2 km) **A 26.2** (42.2 km) **Shoreside Texaco.** See display ad this section.

(Continues on page 546)

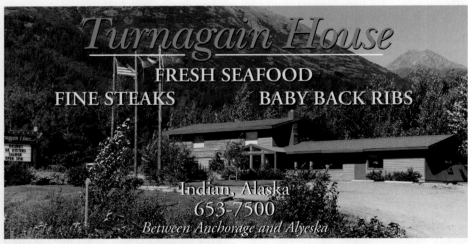

Alyeska Access Road Log

This 3-mile/4.8-km paved spur road provides access to Crow Creek Road, Girdwood, Mount Alyeska ski area and Alyeska Resort. There are many restaurants, gift shops, accommodations and attractions in the Girdwood/Alyeska area. **Distance is measured from junction with Seward Highway (J).**

J 0 Junction with Seward Highway at **Milepost S 90.** Towing service. Girdwood Station Mall: 24-hour convenience store and gas station, medical clinic with emergency services, chiropractic clinic, restaurant and a bakery.

J 0.2 (0.3 km) Bridge over Alaska Railroad tracks. Paved bike trail to Alyeska Resort begins.

J 0.4 (0.6 km) Forest Station Road. Chugach National Forest Glacier Ranger District office (P.O. Box 129, Girdwood, AK 99587; phone 907/783-3242). Open 8 A.M. to 5 P.M. Monday to Friday year-round; also 9 A.M. to 5 P.M. weekends Memorial Day through Labor Day. Maps and information available here.

J 0.5 (0.8 km) **Alaska Candle Factory.** One-half mile off Seward Highway on Alyeska. Home of handcrafted candles made in the form of Alaska wild animals.

Hand-dipped tapers and molded candles made daily. All candles have unique individual designs. Open 7 days a week, 10 A.M. to 6 P.M., in summer until 7 P.M. Visitors welcome. Phone (907) 783-2354. P.O. Box 786, Girdwood, AK 99587. [ADVERTISEMENT]

Fields of lupine line the roadway near the turnoff to Alyeska. (© Tom Culkin)

J 1.6 (2.6 km) **Junction** with Brenner Road.

J 1.9 (3.1 km) **Junction** with Crow Creek Road. Two restaurants and Raven Glacier Lodge are located 0.2 mile/0.3 km up Crow Creek Road. This single-lane dirt road leads 3.1 miles/5 km to Crow Creek Mine, 7 Miles/11.3 km to Crow Pass trailhead. In winter, the road is not maintained past mile 0.6. Crow Creek Mine is a national historic site. The authentic gold mine and 8 other buildings at the mine are open to the public (fee charged).

Crow Creek Mine. Visit this historic 1898 mining camp located in the heart of Chugach National Forest. Drive 3

miles up Crow Creek Road (Old Iditarod trail). Eight original buildings. Pan for gold. Visit our gift shop. Enjoy beautiful grounds, ponds, flowers. Animals and friendly people. Campground for tents and self-contained vehicles. Open May 15–Sept. 15, 9 A.M. to 6 P.M. daily. Phone (907) 278-8060 (mes-

Alyeska Access Road Log

sages). [ADVERTISEMENT] ▲

Crow Pass and Old Iditarod trailhead at Mile 7 Crow Creek Road. Crow Pass trail climbs steeply 3 miles/4.8 km to ruins of an old gold mine and a USFS public-use cabin at Crow Pass near Raven Glacier; hiking time approximately 2½ hours. The Old Iditarod trail extends 22.5 miles/36.2 km north from Crow Pass down Raven Creek drainage to the Chugach State Park Visitor Center on Eagle River Road. All of the hiking trail, from Crow Creek Road trailhead to the state park visitor center, is part of the Iditarod National Historic Trail used in the early 1900s. Trail is usually free of snow by mid-June. Closed to motorized vehicles; horses prohibited during early spring due to soft trail conditions.

J 2 (3.2 km) California Creek bridge.

J 2.1 (3.4 km) **GIRDWOOD** (area pop. 1,500), at the junction of Alyeska access road and Hightower Road. **Emergency Services: Alaska State Troopers, EMS** and **Fire Department**, phone 911 or (907) 783-2704 (message only) or 269-5711. Located here are a post office, restaurants, vacation rental offices, grocery store with gas, a rafting business, small shops and fire hall. Girdwood is a popular resort area for winter sports enthusiasts and for summer activities. There are many fine summer homes here and a substantial year-round community.

Girdwood Community Center offers tennis courts, pay phone, Kinder Park day-care center and picnic area, and is the site of the Girdwood midsummer crafts fair. The town was named after Col. James Girdwood, who established a mining operation near here in 1901.

Alyeska Booking Co. offers free reservation service to travelers. Affordable lodging ranges from bed and breakfasts to luxury condos and chalets. The friendly, knowledgeable staff can also assist you in planning activities. Call them to arrange a glacier cruise from nearby Whittier or Seward, to arrange the flightseeing trip of a lifetime over Prince William Sound or a rafting adventure you'll long remember. Stop at the downtown Girdwood office, next to Chair Five Restaurant, or call (907) 783-4386. [ADVERTISEMENT]

Chair Five Restaurant. A favorite of locals and travelers since 1983, Chair Five offers quality food at affordable prices. Renowned for its famous tundra steak with buffalo and reindeer, always-fresh halibut and pasta dishes. They also offer gourmet fresh-dough pizza that gets rave reviews. Over 60 beer varieties and 30-plus single malt scotch selections round out a great cocktail menu. Open 11–11 daily. MasterCard/VISA/American Express. Phone (907) 783-2500. Mile 2.1 Alyeska Access Road; turn on Hightower Road. [ADVERTISEMENT]

J 2.3 (3.7 km) Glacier Creek bridge.

J 2.6 (4.2 km) Donner access to Airport Road. **Private Aircraft:** Girdwood landing strip; elev. 150 feet/46m; length 2,100 feet/640m; gravel; unattended.

Alpine Air Inc. Scenic flights in spacious, intercom-equipped wheel/ski planes and floatplanes into Prince

William Sound, the Chugach Mountains and Mount McKinley area. Glacier and floatplane landings are our specialty. Guided and unguided fishing trips. Statewide charters available. Federally licensed and fully insured. Visitors welcome year-round to stop in at our hangar/office at the Girdwood airport, last blue hangar on the airport road. Phone (907) 783-2360. Internet address: www.alaska.net/~alpinair; e-mail: alpinair@alaska.net. [ADVERTISEMENT]

Alyeska Air Service. Flightseeing at its best. Minutes away from Alaska's most awe-inspiring sights: Mount McKinley, Prince William Sound and Turnagain Arm. Gaze in amazement at the mighty mountain peaks, massive glaciers and sparkling lakes. Marvel at wildlife in natural habitat and live a full Alaskan experience, starting at $99 per person. Statewide charter and air support year-round. Phone (888) 262-1345 or (907) 783-2163, http://www.alyeskaair.com. [ADVERTISEMENT]

J 2.7 (4.3 km) Timberline Drive. Access to Alyeska View Bed & Breakfast.

J 3 (4.8 km) **ALYESKA** Resort and recreation area at Mount Alyeska (elev. 3,939 feet/1,201m). Road forks: To right are the daylodge and ski lift in the base area. To the left is Alyeska business dis-

GIRDWOOD / ALYESKA ADVERTISERS

Alyeska Access Road Log

trict with jade shop, gift and craft shops, restaurant, ski resort and the Westin Alyeska Prince Hotel.

Alyeska Resort is Alaska's largest ski area and a year-round resort. Owned and operated by Seibu Alaska Inc. since 1980.

Ski season is generally from mid-November through mid-April. Facilities include a high-speed detachable bubble quad, 2 fixed-grip quads, 3 double chair lifts and 2 pony tows. Night skiing available during holiday periods in December, and Friday through Saturday from January through March. Ski school, ski rental shop and sports shops. Wheelchair-accessible mountaintop cafeteria, restaurant and lounge (open year-round) accessed by a 60-passenger tram, see **Milepost J 4.5**. ♿

Winter activities include cross-country skiing, dogsled rides, heli-skiing, ice fishing and snowmachining. Summer activities available are glacier skiing, hiking, mountain biking, flightseeing, canoeing, tennis, gold panning and river rafting.

Alyeska Resort is Alaska's largest ski area. (© Lee Foster)

J 4 (6.4 km) Parking for shuttle to hotel and tram to top of mountain and Glacier Express restaurant.

J 4.5 (7.2 km) Westin Alyeska Prince Hotel and Glacier Terminal (tram). The 307-room hotel has 4 restaurants, 2 lounges and a fitness center with indoor swimming pool. The chalet-style hotel offers deluxe guest rooms. For more information phone (907) 754-1111 or (800) 880-3880.

Return to Milepost S 90 Seward Highway

(Continued from page 542)

S 100.7 (162.1 km) **A 26.3** (42.3 km) **Bird Ridge Cafe & Bakery**. See display ad this section.

S 99.8 (160.6 km) **A 27.2** (43.8 km) Paved turnout to west. Southbound traffic entering avalanche area, northbound traffic leaving avalanche area.

S 99.3 (159.8 km) **A 27.7** (44.6 km) Large gravel turnout to west with view across Turnagain Arm to the cut in the mountains where Sixmile Creek drains into the arm; the old mining settlement of Sunrise was located here. The town of Hope is to the southwest. The peak visible across Turnagain Arm between here and Girdwood is Mount Alpenglow in the Kenai mountain range. Avalanche gates.

S 99.2 (159.6 km) **A 27.8** (44.7 km) Avalanche gun emplacement (motorists will notice several of these along the highway.

S 97.2 (156.4 km) **A 29.8** (48 km) Southbound traffic leaving winter avalanche area, northbound traffic entering avalanche area.

S 96.8 (155.8 km) **A 30.2** (48.6 km) *CAUTION: Watch for road construction next 7 miles/11.3 km southbound in 1998; possible traffic delays.* Winter avalanche area. There are many gravel turnouts the next 5 miles/8 km southbound.

S 95.5 (153.7 km) **A 31.5** (50.7 km) Turnout to west; avalanche gun emplacement. European elder bushes on slopes; white blossoms in spring, red berries (not edible) in fall.

S 94.4 (151.9 km) **A 32.6** (52.5 km) Turnout to west. Avalanche safety zone. Numerous gravel turnouts next 3 miles, west side of highway.

S 90.8 (146.1 km) **A 36.2** (58.3 km) *CAUTION: Railroad crossing and very bad curve.*

S 90.6 (145.8 km) **A 36.4** (58.6 km) Bridge crosses Tidewater Slough. Avalanche gun emplacement at south end of bridge.

S 90.4 (145.5 km) **A 36.6** (58.9 km) Leaving Chugach State Park southbound. The

Dip-netters fish for hooligan and smelt. *(© Loren Taft, Alaskan Images)*

1964 Good Friday earthquake caused land to sink in the Turnagain Arm area, particularly apparent from here to **Milepost S 74.** As a result, many trees had their root systems invaded by salt water, as seen by the stands of dead spruce trees along here. Good bird watching, including bald eagles, arctic terns and sandhill cranes.

S 90.2 (145.2 km) **A 36.8** (59.2 km) Girdwood highway maintenance station. End avalanche area southbound. *NOTE: Major road construction northbound in 1998, next 7 miles/11.3 km.*

S 90 (144.8 km) **A 37** (59.5 km) **Junction** with 3-mile/4.8-km Alyeska (pronounced al-ee-ES-ka) access road to Crow Creek road and mine, Girdwood and Alyeska Recreation Area. Worth the drive! ALYESKA ACCESS ROAD log starts on page 543. This intersection is "old" Girdwood: railroad station, school, towing service and shopping center located here. Girdwood Station Mall houses a 24-hour Tesoro 7–Eleven gas station; medical clinic, restaurant and a bakery. After the 1964 earthquake, Girdwood moved up the access road 2.1 miles/3.4 km.

Alpine Diner & Bakery. See display ad this section.

Providence Girdwood Medical Clinic. See display ad this section.

Tesoro 7–Eleven. See display ad this section.

*NOTE: Next gas available southbound on the Seward Highway is at **Milepost S 6.6**; next gas available westbound on Sterling Highway is at **Milepost S 45** (Sunrise).*

S 89.8 (144.5 km) **A 37.2** (59.9 km) Glacier Creek bridge.

S 89.1 (143.4 km) **A 37.9** (61 km) Virgin Creek bridge. View of 3 glaciers to east.

S 89 (143.2 km) **A 38** (61.2 km) Wide straight highway from here to Portage. The Alaska Railroad parallels the highway.

S 88.2 (141.9 km) **A 38.8** (62.4 km) Turnout to east.

S 87.5 (140.8 km) **A 39.5** (63.6 km) Avalanche gun emplacement.

S 86.1 (138.6 km) **A 40.9** (65.8 km) Small gravel turnout by ocean. Chugach National Forest boundary sign.

S 84.1 (135.3 km) **A 42.9** (69 km) Peterson Creek. View of Blueberry Mountain.

S 82.3 (132.4 km) **A 44.7** (71.9 km) Turnout to east.

S 81 (130.4 km) **A 46** (74 km) BLM observation platform with informative plaques on Twentymile River wetlands and wildlife. Watch for dip-netters in the spring fishing for hooligan (also known as eulachon or candlefish) and smelt. Road access east to Twentymile River.

Twentymile River, good hooligan fishing in May. These smelt are taken with long-handled dip nets. Pink, red and silver (coho) salmon 4 to 10 lbs., use attraction lures, best in August. Dolly Varden 4 to 10 lbs., eggs best, good all summer in clear-water tributaries.

S 80.7 (129.9 km) **A 46.3** (74.5 km) Bridge over Twentymile River, which flows out of the Twentymile Glacier and other glaciers through a long green valley at the edge of the highway. Twentymile Glacier can be seen at the end of the valley to the northeast. Twentymile River is a popular windsurfing area in summer. Gravel turnout west side of highway.

S 80.3 (129.2 km) **A 46.7** (75.2 km) Access to the Alaska Railroad motor vehicle loading area for ferry traffic taking the shuttle train to Whittier. Ticket office and pay phone. Small visitor information center, gift shop and tour boat office. Connections at Whittier with Alaska Marine Highway; regular ferry service is provided across Prince William Sound past the spectacular Columbia Glacier to Valdez.

Philip's Cruises and Tours. Enjoy Alaska's most popular, one-day glacier and wildlife adventure through Prince William

Portage Glacier dwarfs visitors to Portage Lake. (© Barbara Willard)

S 80.1 (128.9 km) **A 46.9** (75.5 km) **PORTAGE.** No facilities here. The 1964 earthquake caused the land to drop between 6 and 12 feet along Turnagain Arm here. High tides then flooded the area, forcing the estimated 50 to 100 residents of Portage to move. Some old buildings are visible; more evidence of trees killed by the invading salt water. Leaving Game Management Unit 14C, entering unit 7, southbound.

S 80 (128.7 km) **A 47** (75.6 km) Second access to motor vehicle loading ramps and passenger parking for Alaska Railroad shuttle train from Portage to Whittier.

S 79.4 (127.8 km) **A 47.6** (76.6 km) Bridge No. 2 southbound over Portage Creek. Parking and interpretive sign to west at south end of bridge. This gray-colored creek carries the silt-laden glacial meltwater from Portage Glacier and Portage Lake to Turnagain Arm. Mud flats in Turnagain Arm are created by silt from the creek settling close to shore.

S 79 (127.1 km) **A 48** (77.2 km) Bridge No. 1 southbound over Portage Creek. Drive-through wildlife park and gift shop.

Big Game Alaska. See display ad this section.

S 78.9 (127 km) **A 48.1** (77.4 km) **Junction** with Portage Glacier access road. Portage Glacier is one of Alaska's most popular attractions. See PORTAGE GLACIER ROAD log this page. *NOTE: There is no gas or lodging available at the glacier.* Tide-water Cafe south side of junction.

S 78.4 (126.1 km) **A 48.6** (78.2 km) Bridge over Placer River; boat launch. Second bridge over Placer River at **Milepost S 77.9.** Turnouts next to both bridges. Between Placer River and Ingram Creek, there is an excellent view on clear days of Skookum Glacier to the northeast. To the north across Turnagain Arm is Twentymile Glacier. Arctic terns and waterfowl are often seen in the slough here.

Placer River has good hooligan fishing in May. These smelt are taken with long-handled dip nets. Silver salmon may be taken in August and September.

Portage Glacier Road Log

Distance is measured from junction with the Seward Highway (J).

J 0 Junction with Seward Highway at **Milepost S 78.9.** *CAUTION: Alaska Railroad tracks, rough crossing.*

J 2 (3.2 km) Portage Glacier Work Center (USFS); no services available.

J 2.4 (3.8 km) Paved turnout. Explorer Glacier viewpoint on right.

J 3.1 (5 km) Bridge. Beaver dam visible from road.

J 3.7 (5.9 km) Black Bear USFS campground; 12 sites (2 will accommodate medium-sized trailers), toilets, water, firepits, dumpsters, tables, $9 fee. Pleasant wooded area. ▲

J 4.1 (6.6 km) Bridge over Williwaw Creek. USFS campground, south of road below Middle Glacier; 38 campsites, toilets, dumpsters, water, firepits, tables, $10 single, $15 double (reservations available, phone 800/280-CAMP). Beautiful campground. Campfire programs in the amphitheater; check bulletin board for schedule. Spawning red salmon and dog salmon can be viewed (from late July to mid-September) from Williwaw Creek observation deck near campground entrance. Self-guided Williwaw nature trail off the campground loop road goes through moose and beaver habitat. ▲

J 5.2 (8.4 km) Paved road forks at Portage Glacier Lodge; left fork leads to visitor center (description follows). Take right fork 0.8 mile/1.3 km to parking lot; 1.2 miles/1.9 km to Byron Glacier overlook; and 1.5 miles/2.4 km to MV *Ptarmigan* sightseeing boat cruise dock and passenger waiting facility.

J 5.5 (8.8 km) Begich, Boggs Visitor Center at Portage Glacier and Portage Lake. Open daily in summer (9 A.M.–6 P.M.); weekends in winter (10 A.M.–4 P.M.). Phone the visitor center at (907) 783-2326 or the U.S. Forest Service district office at (907) 783-3242 for current schedule.

Forest Service naturalists are available to answer questions and provide information about Chugach National Forest resources. There are displays on glaciers and on the natural history of the area. The award-winning film *Voices from the Ice* is shown in the theater hourly. Schedules of hikes and programs led by naturalists are posted at the center. One of the most popular activities is the iceworm safari. (Often regarded as a hoax, iceworms actually exist; the small, black worms thrive at temperatures just above freezing.) A self-guided interpretive trail about glacial landforms begins just south of the visitor center.

Large paved parking area provides views of Portage Lake. There are several excellent spots in the area to observe salmon spawning (August and September) in Portage Creek and its tributaries.

Return to Milepost S 78.9 Seward Highway

S 77.9 (125.4 km) **A 49.1** (79 km) Bridge over Placer River overflow. Paved turnout to south.

S 77 (123.9 km) **A 50** (80.5 km) Boundary of Chugach National Forest.

S 75.5 (121.5 km) **A 51.5** (82.9 km) Paved double-ended scenic viewpoints both sides of highway.

S 75.2 (121 km) **A 51.8** (83.4 km) Bridge over **Ingram Creek**; pink salmon fishing (even years).

S 75 (120.7 km) **A 52** (83.7 km) Paved turnout to west. Welcome to the Kenai Peninsula sign. Highway begins ascent to Turnagain Pass southbound. Passing lane next 5 miles/8 km southbound.

S 74.5 (119.9 km) **A 52.5** (84.5 km) Double-ended paved turnout to east. Several kinds of blueberries, together with false azalea blossoms, are seen along here during summer months.

S 72.5 (116.7 km) **A 54.5** (87.7 km) Double-ended paved turnout to east.

S 71.5 (115.1 km) **A 55.5** (89.3 km) Double-ended paved turnout to west.

S 71.2 (114.6 km) **A 55.8** (89.8 km) Double-ended paved turnout to west.

S 71 (114.3 km) **A 56** (90.1 km) Paved turnout to east. The many flowers seen in surrounding alpine meadows here include yellow and purple violets, mountain heliotrope, lousewort and paintbrush.

S 69.9 (112.5 km) **A 57.1** (91.9 km) Scenic viewpoint with double-ended parking area to west. The highway traverses an area of mountain meadows and parklike stands of spruce, hemlock, birch and aspen interlaced with glacier-fed streams. Lupine and wild geranium grow profusely here in the summer.

S 69.2 (111.4 km) **A 57.8** (93 km) Paved turnout to east.

S 69.1 (111.2 km) **A 57.9** (93.2 km) Passing lane ends southbound.

S 68.9 (110.9 km) **A 58.1** (93.5 km) Divided highway begins southbound, ends northbound.

S 68.5 (110.2 km) **A 58.5** (94.1 km) Turnagain Pass Recreation Area (elev. 988 feet/301m). Parking area, restrooms and dumpster (southbound lane); emergency call box. U-turn. Turnagain Pass Recreation Area is a favorite winter recreation area for snowmobilers (west side of highway) and cross-country skiers (east side of highway). Snow depths here frequently exceed 12 feet/4m.

S 68.1 (109.6 km) **A 58.9** (94.8 km) Parking area, restrooms and dumpster for northbound traffic. U-turn.

S 67.8 (109.1 km) **A 59.2** (95.3 km) Bridge over Lyon Creek.

S 67.6 (108.8 km) **A 59.4** (95.6 km) Divided highway ends southbound, begins northbound.

S 66.8 (107.5 km) **A 60.2** (96.9 km) Paved double-ended turnout with litter container to east.

S 65.3 (105.1 km) **A 61.7** (99.3 km) Bridge over Bertha Creek. Bertha Creek USFS campground; 12 sites, water, toilets, firepits, table, dumpsters and $9 fee.

S 64.8 (104.3 km) **A 62.2** (100.1 km) Bridge over Spokane Creek.

S 63.7 (102.5 km) **A 63.3** (101.9 km) Johnson Pass north trailhead. This 23-mile-/37-km-long trail is a good, fairly level family trail, which follows a portion of the Old Iditarod trail which went from Seward to Nome. See **Milepost S 32.6.**

Johnson Pass trail leads to **Bench Lake,** which has arctic grayling, and **Johnson Lake,** which has rainbow trout. Both lakes are about halfway in on trail.

NOTE: Watch for bike path construction alongside highway in 1998. Exact highway mileages may vary from here to Hope due to road construction.

S 63.3 (101.9 km) **A 63.7** (102.5 km) Bridge over Granite Creek. Traditional halfway point on highway between Anchorage and Seward.

S 63 (101.4 km) **A 64** (103 km) Granite Creek USFS campground, 0.8 mile/1.3 km from main highway; 19 sites (most beside creek), water, toilets, dumpsters, tables, firepits and $9 fee. **Granite Creek,** small Dolly Varden.

S 62 (99.8 km) **A 65** (104.6 km) Bridge over East Fork Sixmile Creek.

S 61 (98.2 km) **A 66** (106.2 km) Bridge over Silvertip Creek.

S 59.7 (96.1 km) **A 67.3** (108.3 km) Gravel turnout next to Granite Creek. Excellent place to photograph this glacial stream. Beaver dam.

S 58.8 (94.6 km) **A 68.2** (109.8 km) Large gravel turnout to west. There are several turnouts along this stretch of highway.

S 57.6 (92.7 km) **A 69.4** (111.7 km) Bridge over Dry Gulch Creek.

S 57.2 (92.1 km) **A 69.8** (112.3 km) Turnout to east with toilets.

S 57 (91.7 km) **A 70** (112.7 km) Bridge over Canyon Creek.

S 56.8 (91.4 km) **A 70.2** (113 km) Staging area for raft trips on Sixmile Creek.

Nenana Raft Adventures, Inc. See display ad this section.

S 56.7 (91.2 km) **A 70.3** (113.1 km) Southbound **junction** with Hope Highway to historic mining community of Hope. See HOPE HIGHWAY log this section.

NOTE: Southbound travelers may find this junction confusing. Hope Highway veers right; Seward Highway veers left.

S 56.6 (91.1 km) **A 70.4** (113.3 km) Northbound **junction** with Hope Highway.

River rafters navigate a canyon on Sixmile Creek. (© Tom Bol)

Numerous gravel turnouts next 6 miles/9.7 km southbound.

S 52.9 (85.1 km) **A 74.1** (119.2 km) Parking area east side of highway.

S 51.5 (82.9 km) **A 75.5** (121.5 km) Paved double-ended turnout to scenic viewpoint.

S 50.1 (80.6 km) **A 76.9** (123.8 km) Begin improved highway southbound with wide shoulders and passing lanes. Winter avalanche area next 1.5 miles/2.4 km southbound.

Truck lane next 2 miles/3.2 km northbound.

S 48 (77.2 km) **A 79** (127.1 km) Fresno Creek bridge; paved double-ended turnout to east at south end of bridge.

S 47.6 (76.6 km) **A 79.4** (127.8 km) Double-ended paved turnout to east on lake.

S 47.2 (76 km) **A 79.8** (128.4 km) Paved double-ended turnout to east next to Lower Summit Lake; a favorite photo stop. Extremely picturesque with lush growth of wildflowers in summer.

Upper and Lower Summit lakes, good spring and fall fishing for landlocked Dolly Varden (goldenfins), ranging in size from 6 to 11 inches, flies and single salmon eggs.

S 46 (74 km) **A 81** (130.4 km) Colorado Creek bridge. Tenderfoot Creek USFS campground 0.6 mile/0.9 km from highway; 28 sites, water, toilets (wheelchair accessible), dumpsters, tables, firepits, boat launch, $9 fee.

S 45.8 (73.7 km) **A 81.2** (130.7 km) Summit Lake Lodge; open year-round. Emergency radio. Winter avalanche area begins

Hope Highway Log

The paved 17.7-mile/28.5-km Hope Highway leads northwest to the historic community of Hope on the south side of Turnagain Arm and provides access to the Resurrection Creek area.

Distance is measured from junction with the Seward Highway (J).

J 0 Junction with Seward Highway at **Milepost S 56.7.**

J 0.1 (0.2 km) Silvertip highway maintenance station.

J 0.7 (1.1 km) Double-ended paved turnout to east; road access to creek.

J 0.9 (1.4 km) Highway parallels Sixmile Creek, a glacial stream. There are many paved turnouts along the Hope Highway, some with views of Turnagain Arm.

J 1.4 (2.3 km) Beaver marsh to east.

J 2.3 (3.7 km) Large paved turnout to east. Moose may often be seen in Sixmile Creek valley below. The old gold mining town of Sunrise City, with a population of 5,000, was founded in 1895 at the mouth of Sixmile Creek. The present community of Sunrise has a population of about 20.

J 3.4 (5.5 km) Large paved turnout to east; trail access to creek.

J 3.9 (6.3 km) Large paved turnout to east; trail access to creek.

J 10 (16.1 km) Double-ended paved turnout to east overlooking Turnagain Arm.

J 11.1 (17.9 km) Large paved turnout to east overlooking Turnagain Arm.

J 11.8 (19 km) Double-ended paved turnout to east overlooking Turnagain Arm.

J 15.8 (25.4 km) **Henry's One Stop.** See display ad this section. ▲

J 15.9 (25.6 km) Bear Creek Lodge.

J 16 (25.7 km) **Discovery Cabins.** See display ad this section.

J 16.2 (26 km) Turn left (south) for Hope airport; USFS Resurrection Pass trailhead, 4 miles/6.4 km south on Resurrection Creek Road; Resurrection Trail Resort, 4.6 miles/7.4 km; and Coeur d'Alene Campground on Palmer Creek Road, 7.6 miles/12.2 km. ▲

The 38-mile-/61-km-long Resurrection Pass USFS trail climbs from an elevation of 400 feet/122m at the trailhead to Resurrection Pass (elev. 2,600 feet/792m) and down to the south trailhead at **Milepost S 53.1** on the Sterling Highway. There are 8 cabins on the trail. Parking area at the trailhead.

Coeur d'Alene, USFS primitive campground has 5 sites (not recommended for large RVs or trailers); toilets, tables, firepits; no water, no garbage service, no camping fee. Palmer Creek Road continues past the campground to alpine country above 1,500 feet/457m elevation, and views of Turnagain Arm and Resurrection Creek valley. The road past the campground is rough and narrow and not recommended for low-clearance vehicles. ▲

J 16.5 (26.6 km) Turn on Hope Road for downtown **HOPE** (pop. 224). Hope Road leads past the post office down to the waterfront, a favorite fishing spot near the ocean; motel, cafe, grocery store and gift shop. **Visitor Information:** Hope Chamber of Commerce, P.O. Box 89, Hope, AK 99605, phone (907) 566-5656.

This historic mining community was founded in 1896 by gold seekers working Resurrection Creek and its tributary streams. Today, many Anchorage residents have vacation homes here.

A rustic Alaskan cabin near Hope.

(© Roy Corral)

Discovery Cafe. See display ad this section.

J 17 (27.3 km) Road to historic Hope townsite. Interpretive sign at intersection. The original townsite of Hope City was founded in 1896. Portions of the town destroyed by the 1964 earthquake are marked with dotted lines on the map sign.

J 17.1 (27.5 km) Resurrection Creek bridge.

J 17.7 (28.4 km) Gas station.

J 17.8 (28.6 km) Hope Highway ends at Porcupine USFS campground; 24 sites, tables, tent spaces, toilets, firepits, dumpster, drinking water and $9 fee. Gull Rock trailhead. ▲

Return to Milepost S 56.7
Seward Highway

southbound.

Summit Lake Lodge. Genuine hospitality on the north shore of Summit Lake in

Alaska's most beautiful log lodge. Located in the heart of Chugach National Forest, it is a landmark for many. The view is spectacular and the food excellent. Complete menu from eye-opening omelettes to mouth-watering steaks. Enjoy our cozy motel and relaxing lounge. Open year-round. Fishing, hiking, photography, cross-country skiing, snowmobiling. It's a must stop for every visitor in the last frontier. See display ad this section. [ADVERTISEMENT] ▲

Summit Lake (Milepost S 47.2) is a favorite photo subject. *(© Loren Taft, Alaskan Images)*

S 45.5 (73.2 km) **A 81.5** (131.2 km) Upper Summit Lake. Paved turnout to east.

S 44.5 (71.6 km) **A 82.5** (132.7 km) Large paved double-ended turnout with interpretive sign to east at end of Upper Summit Lake.

S 44.3 (71.3 km) **A 82.7** (133.1 km) Beaver dams.

S 44 (70.8 km) **A 83** (133.6 km) Gravel turnout to east. Avalanche gun emplacement.

S 43.8 (70.5 km) **A 83.2** (133.9 km) Winter avalanche area begins northbound. Avalanche gates.

S 43.7 (70.3 km) **A 83.3** (134.1 km) Paved double-ended turnout to east.

S 42.6 (68.6 km) **A 84.4** (135.8 km) Summit Creek bridge.

S 42.2 (67.9 km) **A 84.8** (136.5 km) Quartz Creek bridge.

S 41.4 (66.6 km) **A 85.6** (137.8 km) Passing lane next 1 mile/1.6 km northbound.

S 39.6 (63.7 km) **A 87.4** (140.7 km) Avalanche gates.

S 39.4 (63.4 km) **A 87.6** (141 km) Devils Pass trailhead; parking area and toilets to west. This USFS trail starts at an elevation of 1,000 feet/305m and follows Devils Creek to Devils Pass (elev. 2,400 feet/732m), continuing on to Devils Pass Lake and Resurrection Pass trail. Hiking time to Devils Pass is about 5 1/2 hours.

S 39 (62.8 km) **A 88** (141.6 km) Truck lane extends northbound to **Milepost S 39.3**.

S 38.6 (62.1 km) **A 88.4** (142.3 km) Paved turnout to west adjacent **Jerome Lake,** rainbow and Dolly Varden to 22 inches, use salmon egg clusters, year-round, still fish.

S 38.3 (61.6 km) **A 88.7** (142.7 km) Paved double-ended turnout to west overlooking Jerome Lake.

S 38.2 (61.5 km) **A 88.8** (142.9 km) Truck lane ends northbound.

S 37.7 (60.7 km) **A 89.3** (143.7 km) **Junction.** First southbound exit (one-way road) for Sterling Highway (Alaska Route 1) on right. Continue straight ahead on Alaska Route 9 for Seward.

If you are bound for Soldotna, Homer or other Sterling Highway communities and attractions, turn to page 572 in the STERLING HIGHWAY section and begin that log. Continue with this log if you are going to Seward.

ALASKA ROUTE 9

S 37.2 (59.9 km) **A 89.8** (144.5 km) Paved turnout to west overlooking Tern Lake for Seward-bound travelers.

S 37 (59.5 km) **A 90** (144.8 km) **Tern Lake Junction.** Second southbound turnoff on right (2-way road) for Sterling Highway (Alaska Route 1) and access to Tern Lake and Tern Lake USFS Wildlife Viewing Platform. Interpretive signs and ranger talks in summer. This is a good spot to see nesting birds, mountain goats, sheep and occasionally moose and bear. Continue around the lake to the Tern lake picnic area; walk-in picnic sites with water, tables, toilets and firegrates. Salmon-spawning channel with a viewing platform and interpretive signs. Tern Lake is a good spot for bird watching in summer. See STERLING HIGHWAY section. ▲

Continue straight ahead on Alaska Route 9 for Seward.

S 36.7 (59.1 km) **A 90.3** (145.3 km) Truck lane begins northbound.

S 36.4 (58.6 km) **A 90.6** (145.8 km) Avalanche gates.

S 35.7 (57.5 km) **A 91.3** (146.9 km) Outfitter for guided horse pack trips.

TAK Outfitters. See display ad this section.

S 35.3 (56.8 km) **A 91.7** (147.6 km) End

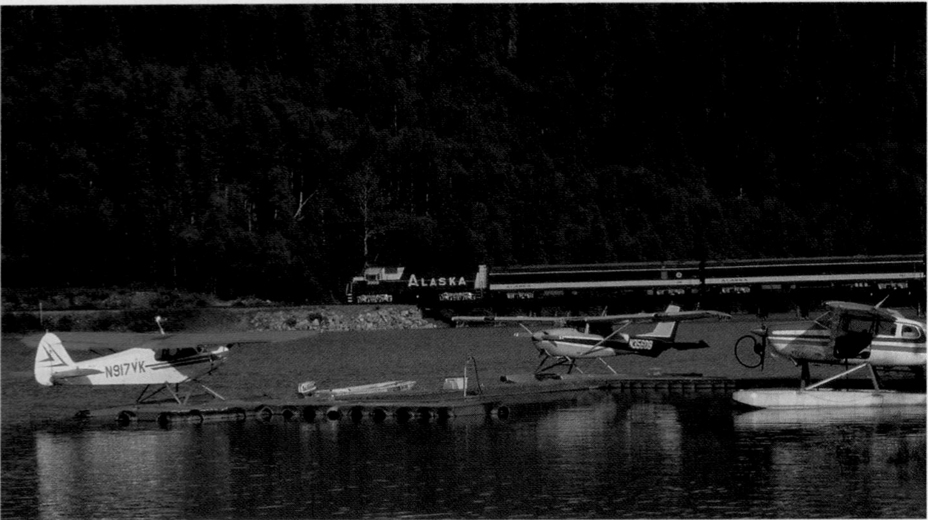

The Alaska Railroad passes float planes on Upper Trail Lake near Moose Pass.
(© Roger Holden)

avalanche area southbound.

S 35 (56.3 km) **A 92** (148 km) For the next 3 miles/4.8 km, many small waterfalls tumble down the brushy slopes. Winter avalanche area between **Milepost S 35.3** and **34.6.** You are driving through the Kenai mountain range.

S 34.1 (54.9 km) **A 92.9** (149.5 km) Turnout to west; large beaver dam.

S 33.1 (53.3 km) **A 93.9** (151.1 km) Carter Lake USFS trailhead No. 4 to west; parking and toilets. Trail starts at an elevation of 500 feet/152m and climbs 986 feet/300m to **Carter Lake** (stocked with rainbow trout). Trail is good, but steep; hiking time about 1½ hours. Good access to sheep and mountain goat country. Excellent snowmobiling area in winter.

S 32.6 (52.5 km) **A 94.4** (151.9 km) Johnson Pass USFS south trailhead with parking area, toilet. North trailhead at **Milepost S 63.7.**

S 32.5 (52.3 km) **A 94.5** (152.1 km) Large paved double-ended turnout; USFS information sign on life cycle of salmon; short trail to observation deck on stream where spawning salmon may be seen in August.

S 32.4 (52.1 km) **A 94.6** (152.2 km) Cook Inlet Aquaculture Association. Trail Lake fish hatchery on Moose Creek; display room. Open 8 A.M. to 5 P.M. daily; phone (907) 288-3688.

S 31.8 (51.1 km) **A 95.2** (153.2 km) Paved double-ended rest area to east on Upper Trail Lake; toilets.

S 30.1 (48.4 km) **A 96.9** (155.9 km) **Spruce Moose Bed and Breakfast.** Two comfortable chalet-style homes are nestled among spruce trees on a 5-acre hillside. Spectacular views of Upper Trail Lake and Lark Mountain. Each spacious chalet, which is yours exclusively, provides everything needed for a relaxing stay for up to 8 people. Available year-round. MasterCard and VISA accepted. Roseann Hetrick, P.O. Box 7, Moose Pass, AK 99631. (907) 288-3667. [ADVERTISEMENT]

S 30 (48.3 km) **A 97** (156.1 km) Short side road to large undeveloped gravel parking area on Upper Trail Lake; boat launch.

S 29.9 (48.1 km) **A 97.1** (156.3 km) Gravel turnout by Trail Lake.

S 29.7 (47.8 km) **A 97.3** (156.6 km) Highway maintenance station.

S 29.4 (47.3 km) **A 97.6** (157.1 km) Large working waterwheel that turns a grindstone, built by the late Ed Estes, on way into Moose Pass. Parking area and sign at waterwheel which reads: "Moose Pass is a peaceful little town. If you have an ax to grind, do it here."

MOOSE PASS (pop. 145) has a motel, bed and breakfast, log cabins for rent, RV park, general store, gift shop, restaurant, salmon bake, post office and highway maintenance station. Pay phone outside GTE building. Alaska State Troopers, emergency only phone 911. This mountain village on Upper Trail Lake was a construction camp on the Alaska Railroad in 1912. Local resident Ed Estes attributed the name Moose Pass to a 1904 observation by Nate White of the first moose recorded in this area. Another version holds that "in 1903, a mail carrier driving a team of dogs had considerable trouble gaining the right-of-way from a giant moose." A post office was established in 1928.

Moose Pass has a 1.3-mile-/2.1-km-long paved bike trail which winds along Trail Lake from the Moose Pass ball diamond to the McFadden house on the south. Gravel turnout by lake.

The main street of town is the site of the Annual Moose Pass Summer Festival, a community-sponsored event which takes place the weekend nearest summer solstice (June 21). The festival features a triathlon, arts and crafts booths, a barbecue, auction and other events.

Estes Brothers Groceries & Water Wheel. See display ad this section.

Trail Lake Lodge. Home cooking, reasonable rates, friendly staff and clean facilities welcome you to this landmark lodge.

Conveniently located in the heart of the Chugach National Forest trail system on the shores of scenic Trail Lake, a short drive to Seward and Kenai Fjords National Park. Phone (800) 208-0200 or (907) 288-3101. See display ad in the Seward section. [ADVERTISEMENT]

S 29.1 (46.8 km) **A 97.9** (157.6 km) **Moose Pass RV Park.** 30 spaces. Electric hookups. Scenic campground-like setting. Close to restaurant, post office, small store, telephone. Rural area in beautiful surroundings. Convenient to Seward, but away from the crowds. Just off main highway. [ADVERTISEMENT]

S 28.9 (46.5 km) **A 98.1** (157.9 km) **Midnight Sun Log Cabins.** See display ad this section.

S 26 (41.8 km) **A 101** (162.5 km) Lower Trail Lake. Timbered slopes of Madson Mountain (elev. 5,269 feet/1,605m) to the west. Crescent Lake lies just west of Madson.

S 25.8 (41.5 km) **A 101.2** (162.9 km) Gravel turnout to west.

S 25.4 (40.9 km) **A 101.6** (163.5 km) Bridge over Trail River. Floatplane base.

S 25 (40.2 km) **A 102** (164.1 km) Bridge over Falls Creek.

S 24.2 (38.9 km) **A 102.8** (165.4 km) Side road leads 1.2 miles/1.9 km to Trail River USFS campground; 64 sites, picnic tables, firepits, dumpsters, toilets, and volleyball and horseshoe area. Day-use group picnic area. Spacious, wooded campsites in tall spruce on shore of Kenai Lake and Lower Trail River. Pull-through sites available. Fee

$9 single, $13 double, reservations available; phone (800) 280-CAMP. Campground host may be in residence during summer, providing fishing and hiking information. Good spot for mushrooming and berry picking in August. ▲

Lower Trail River, lake trout, rainbow and Dolly Varden to 25 inches, July, August and September, use salmon eggs, small spinners. Access via Lower Trail River campground road. **Trail River**, Dolly Varden 12 to 20 inches, spring and fall, and rainbow 12 to 20 inches, spring; use fresh eggs.

S 24.1 (38.8 km) **A 102.9** (165.6 km) **Crown Point Lodge.** Let our staff plan your fishing, hunting, sightseeing or flightseeing while you dine on our true home-cooked meals, pies and breads in an Alaska setting. Clean, comfortable rooms are available at moderate costs. We offer package prices for lodging, meals and charters. Phone (907) 288-3136 or fax (907) 288-3641. Y'all come! [ADVERTISEMENT]

S 23.4 (37.7 km) **A 103.6** (166.7 km) *CAUTION: Railroad crossing.* USFS Kenai Lake work center (no information services available). Report forest fires here.

Private Aircraft: Lawing landing strip; elev. 475 feet/144m; length 2,300 feet/701m; gravel; unattended.

S 23.1 (37.1 km) **A 103.9** (167.2 km) **Ptarmigan Creek** bridge and USFS picnic area and campground with 16 sites, water, toilets, tables, firepits and dumpsters, $9 fee (reservations available, phone 800/280-CAMP). Fair to good fishing in creek and in lake outlets at **Ptarmigan Lake** (hike in) for Dolly Varden. Watch for spawning salmon in Ptarmigan Creek in August. ▲

Ptarmigan Creek USFS trail No. 14 begins at campground (elev. 500 feet/152m) and leads 3.5 miles/5.6 km to Ptarmigan Lake (elev. 755 feet/230m). Trail is steep in spots; round-trip hiking time 5 hours. Good chance of seeing sheep, goats, moose and bears. Carry insect repellent. Trail is poor for winter use due to avalanche hazard.

S 23 (37 km) **A 104** (167.3 km) Turnoff for Alaska Nellie's Homestead. The late Nellie Neal–Lawing arrived in Alaska in 1915. Her colorful life included cooking for the railroad workers and big game hunting and guiding. She converted a roadhouse at Lawing into a museum to house the trophies and souvenirs she and her husband Billie Lawing gathered on their travels.

Alaska Nellie's Inn, Inc. See display ad this section.

S 22.9 (36.9 km) **A 104.1** (167.5 km) Paved viewpoint to west overlooking Kenai Lake. This lake (elev. 436 feet/132m) extends 24 miles/39 km from the head of the Kenai River on the west to the mouth of Snow River on the east. A sign here explains how glacier meltwater gives the lake its distinctive color.

Winter avalanche area next 3 miles/4.8 km southbound.

S 22.5 (36.2 km) **A 104.5** (168.2 km) Rough gravel double-ended turnout to east.

S 21.3 (34.3 km) **A 105.7** (170.1 km) Gravel turnout to east overlooking lake.

S 20.2 (32.5 km) **A 106.8** (171.9 km) Avalanche gun emplacement.

S 20.1 (32.3 km) **A 106.9** (172 km) Gravel turnout. Avalanche area ends southbound.

S 19.9 (32 km) **A 107.1** (172.4 km) **I.R.B.I. Knives.** See display ad this section.

S 19.5 (31.4 km) **A 107.5** (173 km) Victor Creek bridge. Victor Creek USFS trail No. 23 begins here. A 2-mile/3.2-km hike with good view of mountains.

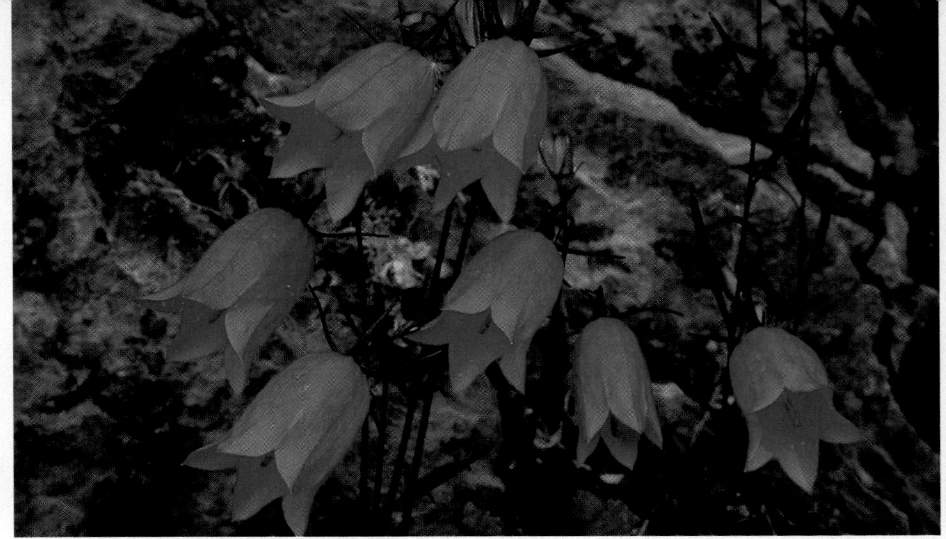

Look for harebells along the highway. (© Loren Taft, Alaskan Images)

S 17.7 (28.5 km) **A 109.3** (175.9 km) Bridge over center channel of Snow River. This river has 2 forks that flow into Kenai Lake.

S 17 (27 km) **A 110** (177 km) Primrose Road. Access to bed and breakfast. Turn west for Primrose USFS campground, 1 mile/1.6 km from the highway. (Campground access road leads past private homes. Drive carefully!) The campground, overlooking Kenai Lake, has 10 sites, toilets, dumpsters, tables, firepits, boat ramp, water, $9 fee. Primrose trail (6.5 miles/10.5 km) starts from the campground and connects with Lost Lake trail (7 miles/11.2 km). High alpine hike, trail is posted. ▲

Primrose B&B Chalets. See display ad this section.

Bridge over south channel of Snow River.

S 16.2 (26.1 km) **A 110.8** (178.3 km) Gravel turnout to east.

S 16 (25.7 km) **A 111** (178.6 km) Snow River hostel.

S 15 (24.1 km) **A 112** (180.2 km) Watch for moose in ponds and meadows.

S 14.9 (24 km) **A 112.1** (180.4 km) Gravel turnout to east.

S 14 (22.5 km) **A 113** (181.9 km) *CAUTION: Railroad crossing.*

S 13.3 (21.4 km) **A 113.7** (183 km)

Grayling Lake USFS trailhead to west, large paved parking area to east. Grayling Lake trail No. 20, 1.6 miles/2.6 km, connects with trails to Meridian and Leech lakes. Good spot for photos of Snow River valley. Watch for moose. **Grayling Lake**, 6- to 12-inch grayling, use flies, May to October.

S 12 (19.3 km) **A 115** (185.1 km) Alaska Railroad crosses under highway.

S 11.6 (18.6 km) **A 115.4** (185.7 km) Gravel parking area to west and trail to **Golden Fin Lake**, Dolly Varden averaging 8 inches. This is a 0.6-mile/1-km hike on a very wet trail: wear rubber footwear. Ski trails in winter.

S 10.8 (17.4 km) **A 116.2** (187 km) Large gravel turnout to east.

S 8.5 (13.6 km) **A 118.5** (190.7 km) Gravel turnout to west.

S 8.3 (13.4 km) **A 118.7** (191 km) Paved turnout by creek to east. Leaving Chugach National Forest land southbound.

S 8 (12.9 km) **A 119** (191.5 km) **Grouse Creek** bridge. Dolly Varden fishing.

S 7.4 (11.9 km) **A 119.6** (192.5 km) **Grouse Lake** access road. Good ice fishing for Dolly Varden in winter.

S 7.1 (11.4 km) **A 119.9** (193 km) Old Mill subdivision.

S 6.6 (10.6 km) **A 120.4** (193.7 km) Bear Creek bridge and Bear Lake Road; access to gas station, 2 private RV parks, bed and breakfast, and a flying service. Drive in 0.7 mile/1.1 km on Bear Lake Road to see a state-operated fish weir. Silver and red (sockeye) salmon are trapped to provide life-cycle data and also eggs for the state's salmon stocking program.

A Creekside RV Park & Motel. See display ad this section. ▲

Bear Creek RV Park, drive 1/2 mile on Bear Lake Road. Good Sam Park has full and partial hookups, dump station, 4 private restrooms with showers, cable TV, travelers lounge, propane, laundry, convenience store, ice, video rentals. 2 free showers per site. Pay phone inside. Excellent water. (907) 224-5725. Fax service available. Bunkhouse for rent. Free shuttle when reservations are booked through our office for glacier and fishing trips. Auto and RV repair and service. RV and boat storage. High pressure wash. Short walk to fish weir. Bear Creek RV Park is not to be mistaken for A Creekside RV Park located at the gas station on the corner of the Seward Highway and Bear Lake Road. Internet: http://www.alaska.net/~bear. See display ad this section. [ADVERTISEMENT] ▲

Lakeside Cabins. See display ad this section.

S 6.3 (10.1 km) **A 120.7** (194.2 km) Lake Drive; access to bed and breakfasts.

Alaska's Stoney Creek Inn Bed & Breakfast. See display ad this section.

S 5.9 (9.4 km) **A 121.1** (194.8 km) **Salmon Creek** bridge. Good fishing in stream for sea-run Dolly Varden averaging 10 inches, use single salmon eggs, begins about Aug. 1.

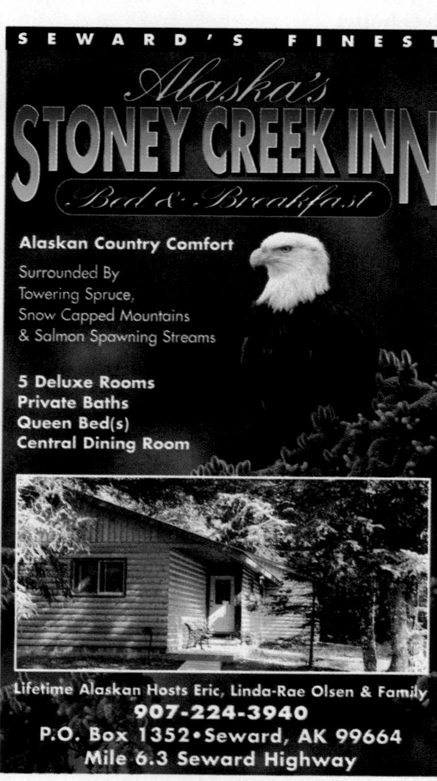

Several loop trails offer spectacular views of Exit Glacier. (© Mike Jones)

S 5.2 (8.4 km) **A 121.8** (196 km) Bear Creek volunteer fire department.

S 3.8 (6.1 km) **A 123.2** (198.3 km) Clear Creek bridge.

S 3.7 (6 km) **A 123.3** (198.4 km) Turnoff for Exit Glacier Road. Access to Seward Windsong Lodge, restaurant, health food store, IdidaRide dogsled rides, and bed and breakfasts; turn right onto loop road (old Exit Glacier Road) immediately after turning off highway.

The 9-mile/14.5-km Exit Glacier Road (maintained by DOT/PF May to September, depending on snow) is paved for the first 4 miles/6.4 km. The road ends at a parking lot with toilets and picnic area next to Exit Glacier ranger station in Kenai Fjords National Park. Look for bears high on the hillside opposite the ranger station. Walk-in campground with 9 sites (no fee, reservations). A public-use cabin is available; access in winter by cross-country skis, dogsled or snow machine; permit required, phone (907) 224-3175. ▲

The National Park Service operates a visitor center at the ranger station (seasonal). The flat, easy 0.8-mile Lower Loop trail leads through alder forest to outwash plain; pick your own route to base of glacier. The longer half-mile Upper Loop trail offers excellent views of the glacier. The first 0.2 mile/0.3 km of this trail is paved and wheelchair accessible. There is also an easy 0.8 mile/1.3 km nature trail loop with 10 interpretive signs on forest succession. A strenuous 3.5-mile/5.6-km trail leads to Harding Icefield from the parking lot (a ranger patrols this trail). Summer activities include ranger-led nature walks at 10 A.M. and 2 P.M. daily. Park Information Line: (907) 224-2132. Worth the drive to see an active glacier up close. *CAUTION: Falling ice at face of glacier, stay behind warning signs.*

The trailhead for Resurrection River trail is located just before crossing the Resurrection River bridge on the access road. The 16-mile/25.7-km USFS trail ties in with the Russian Lakes trail. It is part of the 75-mile/121-km Hope-to-Seward route. *CAUTION: Black and brown bears also use this trail.*

Creekside Cabins Bed & Breakfast. See display ad this section.

IdidaRide Sled Dog Tours. See display ad this section.

S 3.2 (5.1 km) **A 123.8** (199.2 km) Nash Road, access to bed and breakfasts: Camelot Cottages, The Farm, Northern Exposure, Rininger's, Fjordland Inn. It is a scenic 5-mile/8-km drive out Nash Road to Seward's Marine Industrial Center in the Fourth of July Creek valley. Fine views along the way and from Kertulla Point of Resurrection Bay and the city of Seward. At Mile 2.1 Nash Road is the trailhead for the Iditarod Trail, which begins at the ferry terminal in downtown Seward. Hike to Bear Lake; from north end of lake, trail continues to Mile 12 on the Seward Highway.

Camelot Cottages. See display ad this section.

The Farm Bed & Breakfast Inn. Turn off Seward Highway onto Nash Road, cross the railroad tracks, turn left immediately onto Salmon Creek Road, follow signs to "The Farm." Tranquil country setting on acres of trees and lawn. Choose from our main house ... cottages ... economy bungalow ... or kitchenette units. Enjoy cable TV, decks,

barbecue, private baths. Freezer space, laundry facilities. Families welcome. Continental breakfast. Open year-round. VISA, MasterCard, Discover. Long-time Alaskan host Jack Hoogland, Box 305, Seward, AK 99664. Reservations suggested. (907) 224-5691. Fax (907) 224-2300. See display ad in Seward section. [ADVERTISEMENT]

Northern Exposure Bed & Breakfast. See display ad this section.

Rininger's Bed & Breakfast (Mile 1.6 Nash Road) is located on Rabbit Run Road (left at fork). Open year-round. Large, sunny room with skylights and handcrafted furnishings. Private bath and kitchenette; sleeping loft, separate entrance. Breakfast in room at your leisure. Outdoor wood-heated sauna. Hiking and cross-country ski trails nearby. A perfect weekend getaway. Families welcome. Sleeps up to 8. Kent and Lisa Rininger, P.O. Box 548, Seward, AK 99664. (907) 224-5918. [ADVERTISEMENT]

Fjordland Inn. See display ad this section.

S 3 (4.8 km) **A 124** (199.6 km) Resurrection River; 3 channels, 3 bridges. This river flows from the Harding Icefield into Resurrection Bay just northeast of Seward. Seward city limits.

S 2.7 (4.3 km) **A 124.3** (200 km) Turnoff for Seward airport.

S 2.5 (4 km) **A 124.5** (200.4 km) Hemlock Street. Forest Acres municipal campground; water, flush toilets, 14-day limit. No tables.▲

S 2.3 (3.7 km) **A 124.7** (200.7 km) Sea Lion Drive. U.S. Air Force and U.S. Army Seward Recreation Area.

Seward Resort (Military). See display ad this section.

S 2.1 (3.4 km) **A 124.9** (201 km) Dimond Boulevard.

S 2 (3.2 km) **A 125** (201.1 km) Seward Chamber of Commerce–Convention and Visitors Bureau visitor center.

S 1.8 (2.9 km) **A 125.2** (201.5 km) Gas station.

S 1.7 (2.7 km) **A 125.3** (201.6 km) Bear Drive; access to bed and breakfasts.

S 1.5 (2.4 km) **A 125.5** (202 km) Resurrection Blvd., Seward High School.

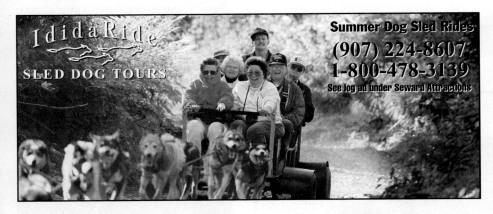

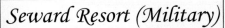

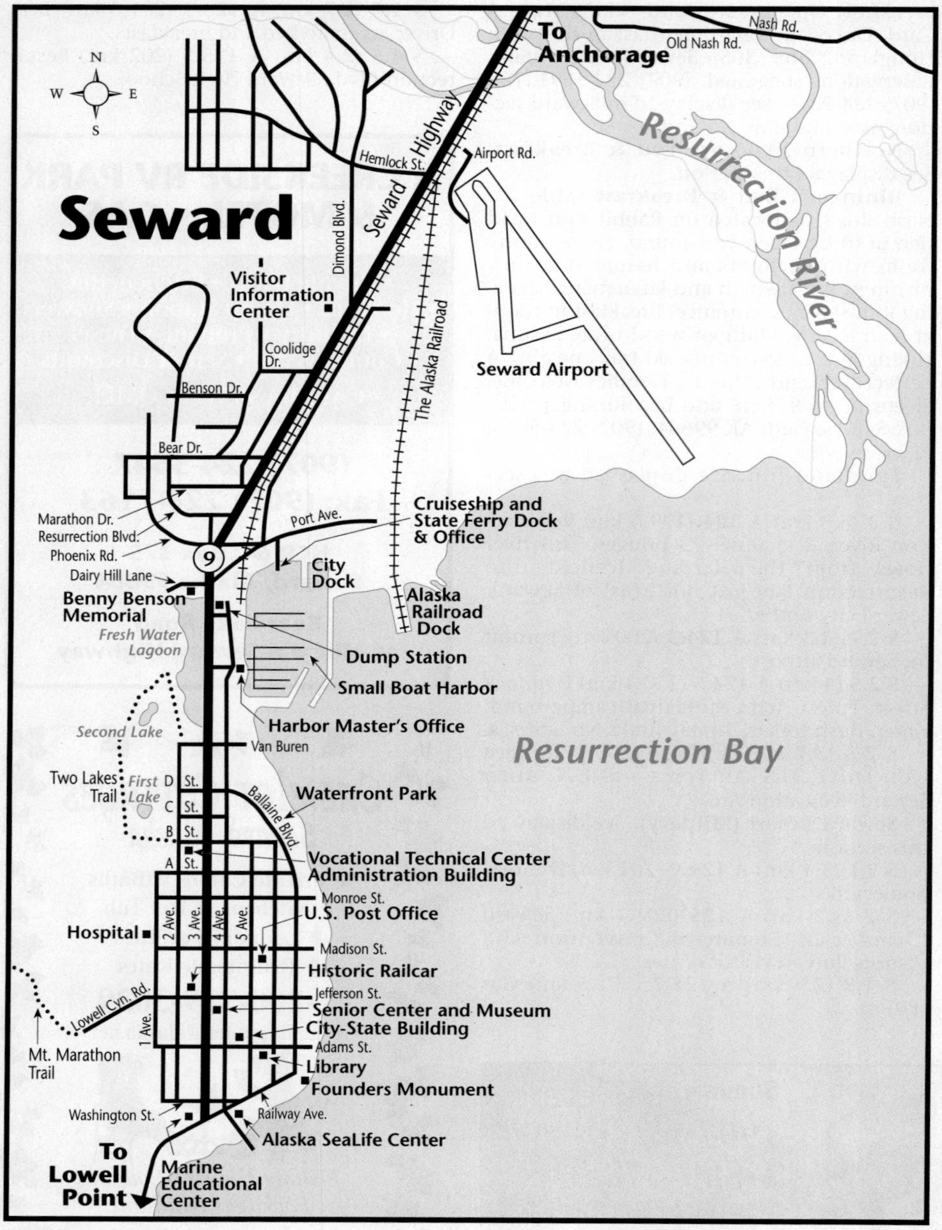

S 1.2 (1.9 km) **A 125.8** (202.4 km) Dairy Hill Lane to west. Large parking area to west with memorial to Benny Benson, who designed the Alaska state flag. Port Avenue to east, access to cruise ship and ferry dock.

S 1 (1.6 km) **A 126** (202.8 km) South Harbor Street and main entrance to boat harbor.

S 0.4 (0.6 km) **A 126.6** (203.7 km) Madison Street. Post office one block east.

S 0.3 (0.5 km) **A 126.7** (203.9 km) Intersection of 3rd Avenue (Seward Highway) and Jefferson. Hospital 2 blocks west. Information Cache railcar at intersection.

S 0 A 127 (204.4 km) Alaska SeaLife Center/Seward Marine Education Center.

Seward

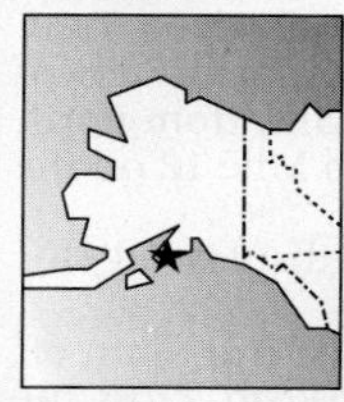

S 0 A 127 (204.4 km) Located on Resurrection Bay, east coast of Kenai Peninsula; 127 miles/204.4 km south of Anchorage by road, or 35 minutes by air. **Population:** 3,500. **Emergency Services: Police, Fire Department** and **Ambulance**, emergency only, phone 911. **State Troopers**, phone (907) 224-3346. **Hospital**, Providence Seward Medical Center, 1st Avenue and Jefferson Street, phone (907) 224-5205. **Maritime Search and Rescue**, phone (800) 478-5555.

Visitor Information: Available at 2 locations, operated by the Seward Chamber of Commerce–Convention and Visitors Bureau. The visitor center at **Milepost S 2** Seward Highway (2001 Seward Highway) is open 7 days a week from Memorial Day through Labor Day, weekdays the rest of the year; phone (907) 224-8051. The Information Cache, located in the historic railroad car *Seward* at 3rd and Jefferson Street, is open daily from 9 A.M. to 5 P.M., June through August; write Box 749, Seward, AK 99664.

Kenai Fjords National Park Visitor Center, 1212 4th Ave. (in the Small Boat Harbor), is open 8 A.M. to 7 P.M. daily, Memorial Day to Labor Day; 8:30 A.M. to 5 P.M. weekdays the remainder of the year. Information on the park, slide show, interpretive programs and bookstore. Phone (907) 224-3175 or the Park Information Line (907) 224-2132. Or write P.O. Box 1727, Seward, AK 99664.

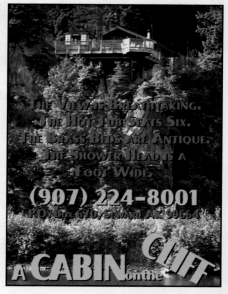

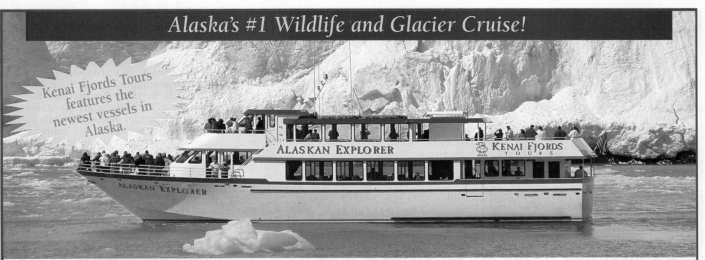

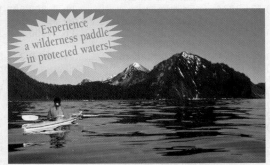

Chugach National Forest, Seward Ranger District office, is located at 334 4th Ave. USFS personnel can provide information on hiking, camping and fishing opportunities on national forest lands. Open weekdays, 8 A.M. to 5 P.M. Mailing address: P.O. Box 390, Seward, AK 99664. Phone (907) 224-3374.

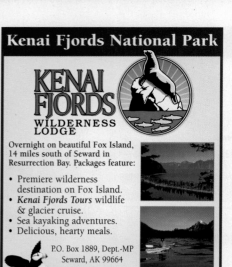

Elevation: Sea level. **Climate:** Average daily maximum temperature in July, 62°F/17°C; average daily minimum in January, 18°F/-7°C. Average annual precipitation, 67 inches; average snowfall, 80 inches. **Radio:** KSKA-FM 92, KWAVE 104.9, KPEN 102.3. **Television:** Several channels by cable. **Newspaper:** *Seward Phoenix Log* (weekly).

Private Aircraft: Seward airport, 1.7 miles/2.7 km northeast; elev. 22 feet/7m; length 4,500 feet/1,371m; asphalt; fuel 80, 100, jet.

Seward—known as the "Gateway to Kenai Fjords National Park"—is a picturesque community nestled between high mountain ranges on a small rise stretching from Resurrection Bay to the foot of Mount Marathon. Thick groves of cottonwood and scattered spruce groves are found in the immediate vicinity of the city, with stands of spruce and alder growing on the surrounding mountainsides.

Downtown Seward (the main street is 4th Avenue) has a frontier-town atmosphere with some homes and buildings dating back to the early 1900s. The town was established in 1903 by railroad surveyors as an ocean terminal and supply center. The 470-mile/756-km railway connecting Fairbanks in the Interior with Seward was completed in 1923.

The city was named for U.S. Secretary of State William H. Seward, who was instrumental in arranging the purchase of Alaska from Russia in 1867. Resurrection Bay was named in 1791 by Russian fur trader and explorer Alexander Baranof. While sailing from Kodiak to Yakutat he found unexpected shelter in this bay from a storm and named the bay Resurrection because it was the Russian Sunday of the Resurrection.

Resurrection Bay is a year-round ice-free harbor, and Seward is an important cargo and fishing port. The Alaska state ferry MV *Tustumena* calls at Seward.

Seward's economic base includes tourism, a coal terminal, marine research, fisheries and government offices. The Alaska Vocational Technical Center is located here. A new (May, 1998) marine educational center—the Alaska SeaLife Center—is located here; see Attractions this section for more details.

ACCOMMODATIONS/VISITOR SERVICES

All visitor facilities, including hotels, motels, bed and breakfasts, cafes and restaurants, post office, grocery stores, drugstore, travel agencies, gift shops, gas stations, bars, laundromats, churches, bowling alley and theater.

The Harbormaster Building has public restrooms and pay showers, mailbox and pay phones. Weather information is available here during the summer. Public restrooms and pay showers on Ballaine Boulevard along the ocean between the boat harbor and town. Dump station and drinking water fill-up at the Small Boat Harbor at the end of 4th Avenue (see city map). There are picnic areas with covered tables along Ballaine Blvd., just south of the harbor, and at Adams Street.

Seward has made a good effort to provide overnight parking for self-contained RVs. There are designated camping areas along the shore south of Van Buren; camping fee charged. RV parking is marked by signs. Restrooms with coin-operated showers; water and electric hookups available at some sites. (Caravans: contact the City Parks and Recreation Dept. for reservations, phone 907/224-3331.) Forest Acres municipal campground is at **Milepost S 2.4** Seward Highway. Private RV parks at Small Boat Harbor, at **Milepost S 6.6** and on Lowell Point Road. Tent camping also available at Exit Glacier (turnoff at **Milepost S 3.7** Seward Highway). ▲

Alaska's Stoney Creek Inn Bed & Breakfast. Alaskan country comfort in a spectacular setting. Surrounded by towering spruce, snow-capped mountains and salmon-spawning streams. Deluxe, smoke-free rooms, private baths, queen beds, handmade comforters. Enjoy Alaskan hospitality with lifetime Alaskans. (907) 224-3940. See display ad at Mile 6.3 Seward Highway. [ADVERTISEMENT]

Alaska's Treehouse Bed and Breakfast. Nestled in the trees at the edge of town. Spectacular views of the Chugach Mountains from the solarium and the hot tub on the new multi-level deck. Hiking and skiing trails at your doorstep, fishing nearby. Relax in the hand-built, wood-fired sauna. Breakfast—hearty Alaskan sourdough pancakes or waffles with local wild berry sauces.

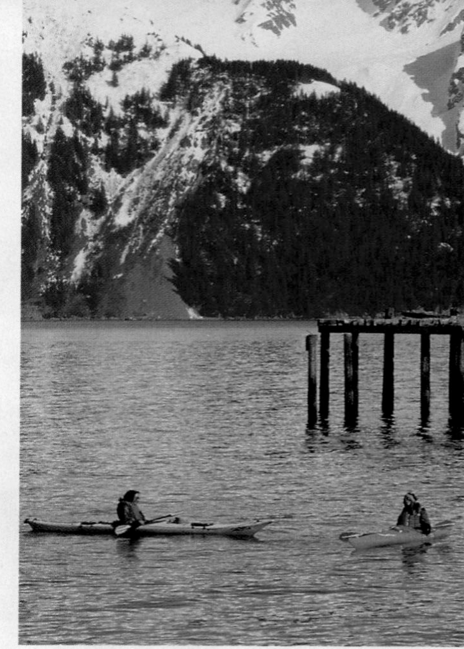

Sea kayaking near the old dock at Caines Head State Recreation Area.
(© Tom Bol)

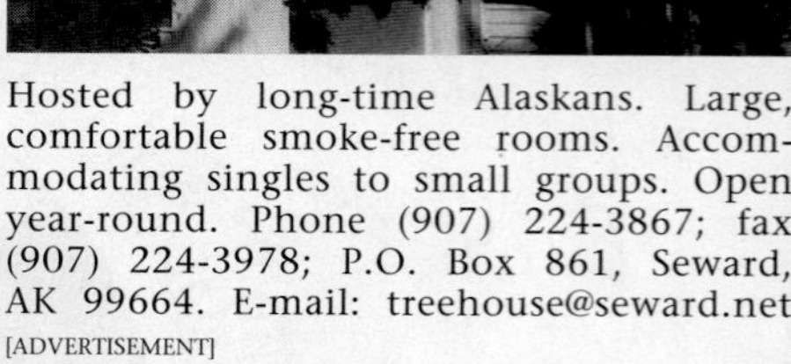

Hosted by long-time Alaskans. Large, comfortable smoke-free rooms. Accommodating singles to small groups. Open year-round. Phone (907) 224-3867; fax (907) 224-3978; P.O. Box 861, Seward, AK 99664. E-mail: treehouse@seward.net [ADVERTISEMENT]

Bear Creek RV Park. Good Sam Park. Full and partial hookups, dump station, 4 private restrooms with showers, cable TV, traveler's lounge, propane, laundry, convenience store, ice, video rentals, pay phone.

Bunkhouse for rent. Shuttle service available. Reservations welcome. Bear Lake Air Service office located at Bear Creek RV Park, Mile 6.6 Seward Highway, drive 1/2 mile on Bear Lake Road. Internet: http://www.alaska.net/~bear. Fax service available. Phone (907) 224-5725. [ADVERTISEMENT] ▲

Benson Bed & Breakfast. Family atmosphere, smoke-free. Queen/double beds, private baths. Full breakfast. Quiet neighborhood near harbor, groceries, bike path, bus, train, visitor center. Hosts: Rich and Sandy Houghton, long-time Alaskans with 8 years experience living and teaching above the Arctic Circle at Kivalina and Noatak. Open year-round. 209 Benson, P.O. Box 3506, Seward, AK 99664. Phone (907) 224-5290. [ADVERTISEMENT]

Best Western Hotel Seward. Enjoy being in the center of activity, yet in a quiet setting overlooking Resurrection Bay. Our extensive 1991 expansion includes breathtaking view rooms with in-room coffee and your own refrigerator. And check this out! For your in-room entertainment, all rooms include (1) remote control TVs with cablevision, (2) remote control VCRs with videotape rental available and (3) 2 channels of free in-room movies featuring the latest hits! Complimentary scheduled shuttle bus service for our guests to boat harbor, train depot and airport. One block to the Alaska SeaLife Center. We accept all major credit cards. Reservations (907) 224-2378 or (800) 811-1191 inside Alaska. Fax (907) 224-3112. See display ad this section. [ADVERTISEMENT]

Camelot Cottages. Affordable, clean, cozy furnished cabins in a natural woodland setting. Beautiful chalet available for families or large groups. The cabins and chalets are heated and have private baths and fully equipped kitchens. Hot tub, laundry facilities and fish freezer available for guest use. Linens and housekeeping services provided. Cabins can sleep 2–8 people. Private, family-friendly, owned and operated by longtime Alaskans. (800) 739-3039 or (907) 346-3039 Anchorage; (907) 224-3039 Seward. Fishing charter information and fishing/lodging packages available. See display ad at Mile 3.2 Seward Highway. [ADVERTISEMENT]

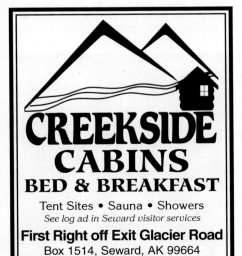

Clear Creek Cottage. Fully furnished smoke-free 2-bedroom cabin, full kitchen. Sleeps up to 8. Clean, comfortable, affordable rates. Perfect hideaway for couples, families, small groups. On the banks of Clear Creek, on Resurrection River Road to Exit Glacier, Mile 3.7 Seward Highway. 7 minutes to downtown Seward. (907) 224-3968. Fax (907) 224-7230. P.O. Box 241, Seward, AK 99664. [ADVERTISEMENT]

Creekside Cabins Bed & Breakfast. Clean, cozy cabins nestled in the trees, along peaceful Clear Creek. Continental breakfast. Central heated restrooms. Toasty log sauna on the creek; tent sites. Peaceful country setting for a relaxing stay. Nonsmoking. Phone (907) 224-3834. See display ad in Seward section. Take first right off Exit Glacier Road, 0.3 mile on right. [ADVERTISEMENT] ▲

Eagle Song Bed & Breakfast is located in a peaceful country setting in the shadow of an active bald eagle's nest, easy 15-minute

commute from Seward. We offer 3 bedrooms with queen-size beds, 1 bedroom with twin beds, 2 shared baths, full country breakfast, smoking outside, no alcohol, adults only. VISA and MasterCard. (907) 224-8755, P.O. Box 2231, Seward, AK 99664. E-mail: eaglesng@ptialaska.net. [ADVERTISEMENT]

Fjordland Inn (formerly The White House B&B), is nestled in a mountain panorama. Country charm, smoke-free. Private baths. Private entrance to guest area. Families and groups welcome. Open year-round. Expanded during recent remodel. Winter rates. (907) 224-3614 or 1-800-785-3614. Fax (907) 224-3615. Owner-hosts Lee and Mary George. Mile 1.7 Nash Road. See display ad at Mile 3.2 Seward Highway. E-mail: lee-mary@fjordland-inn.com. Internet: www.fjordland-inn.com. [ADVERTISEMENT] MP

Harborview Inn. 804 Third Avenue. New: 23 rooms with private entrances, private baths, cable TV in room, telephone, Alaska Native fine art. Just 10-minute walk to tour boats, fishing charters, downtown and laundromat. Also "Seaview," our newly remodeled 2-bedroom apartments on the beachfront, breathtaking view of snow-capped mountains and bay. All nonsmoking. $109. Early reservations advised. Alaska Native hostess. Phone (907) 224-3217; fax (907) 224-3218. P.O. Box 1305MP, Seward, AK 99664. E-mail: harbrinn@ptialaska.net. See display ad. [ADVERTISEMENT]

Harmony Bed & Breakfast, nestled peacefully in Forrest Acres and conveniently close to town and harbor. New rooms, all with private bath and private entrance. $75. VISA/MasterCard accepted. Phone Carol for

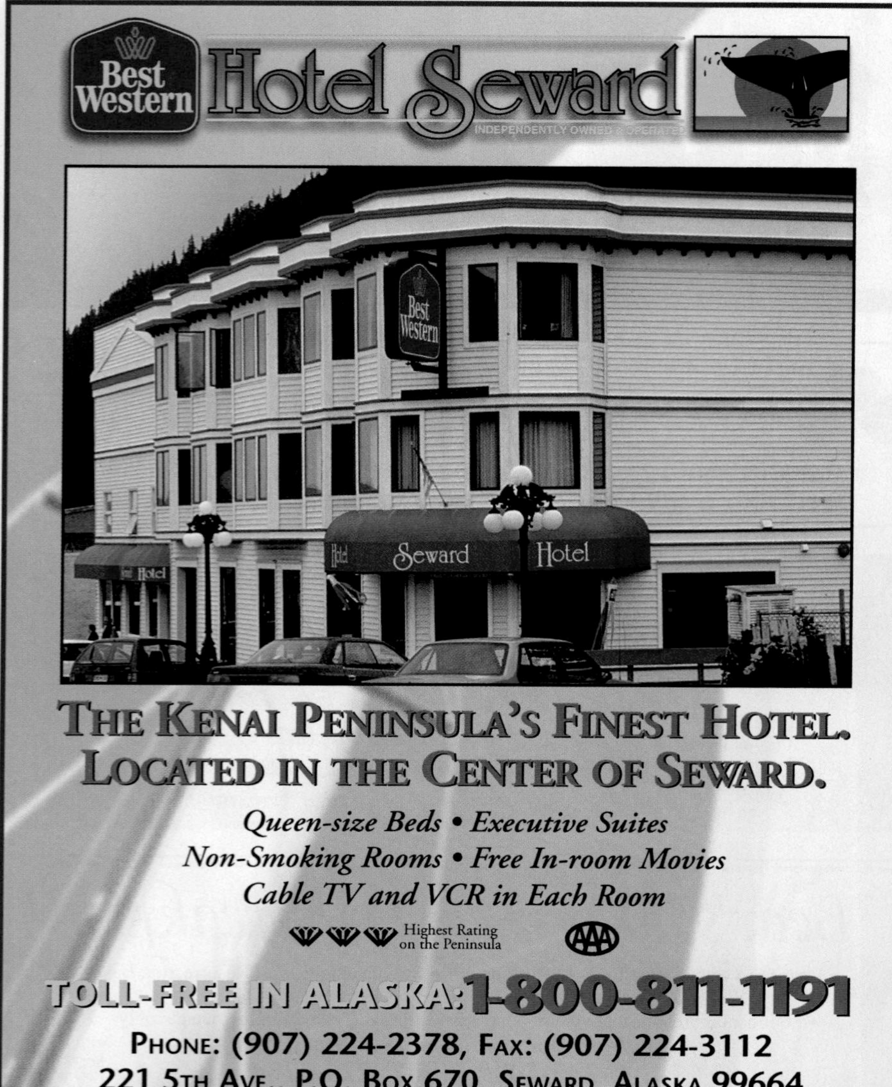

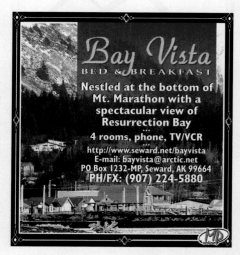

reservations and information, (907) 224-3661. Fax (907) 224-8740. P.O. Box 1606, Seward, AK 99664. [ADVERTISEMENT]

Kenai Fjords Wilderness Lodge. Located 14 miles south of Seward in scenic Resurrection Bay on Fox Island. Enjoy our comfortable wilderness lodging experience, accessible only by boat. Two-day/one-night packages include boat transportation, lodging, wildlife and glacier cruise to Kenai Fjords National Park, and delicious hearty meals. Sea kayaking, hiking available. Phone toll free (800) 478-8068 or (907) 224-8068. [ADVERTISEMENT]

Miller's Landing: Campground, fishing/sightseeing charters, water taxis and boat/kayak rentals. Alaskan owned and operated on family homestead on Resurrection Bay. Scenic campground with beach and forested sites; pull-through electric RV sites 20/30 amp, large tent sites, cozy cabins $30 and up; dry camp $15; electric $20 (hot showers and flush restrooms included). (1997 prices.) Fishing sightseeing charters (full and half day), boat and pole rentals. Water taxi service to remote camping and fishing sites, private boat launch and boat storage available. Kayak rentals and drop-offs to Aialik Glacier, Holgate Arm, Fox Island. Beach fishing for Dolly Varden and salmon, fishing charters for halibut and salmon, bait and tackle provided. Adjacent to Caine's Head State Park and hiking trail. Watch sea otters, eagles, sea lions from private beaches. Down-home Alaskan atmosphere with free coffee. Country store sells bait, tackle, ice, fishing licenses, T-shirts, hats, gifts, wood for campfires, farm-fresh eggs. Mike Miller, an expert on fishing and visitor information, homesteaded here and survived the 1964 earthquake. Fishing advice 5¢, guaranteed effective or your nickel back! Reservations encouraged for guaranteed site. Mile 3 Lowell Point Road, Box 81, Seward, AK 99664. Phone/fax (907) 224-5739. [ADVERTISEMENT] ▲

Morning Calm Bed and Breakfast. A touch of the Orient in Alaska. Quiet residential neighborhood near the visitor center, small boat harbor and railroad depot. Nonsmoking. Two rooms, queen and twin beds,

shared bath. Hot tub. In-room TV/VCR. Open year-round. The Martins, P.O. Box 816, Seward, AK 99664. (907) 224-3049. [ADVERTISEMENT]

New Seward Hotel & Saloon. Centrally located in downtown Seward, one block to Alaska SeaLife Center, within walking distance of shops, ferry, bus terminal, boat harbor; 35 rooms featuring TV, phones, free videos. Some kitchenettes. Salmon and halibut fishing charters or Kenai Fjords tours available. Year-round service. Brochure. All major credit cards accepted. Reservations (907) 224-8001. Fax (907) 224-3112. See display ad this section. [ADVERTISEMENT]

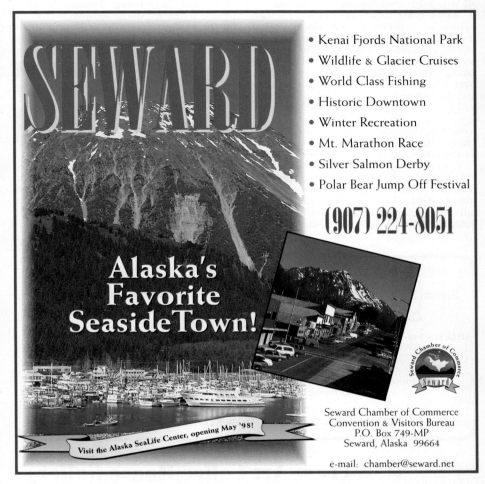

Northern Exposure Bed & Breakfast: 5 minutes from town. Available May–September. Queen and king beds, shared and private baths, cable TV, VCR and phone in common area. Continental breakfast. Smoking permitted outside. Winter room available September–April, full apartment, sleeps 4, has private entrance, bath, phone and TV in room. Phone (907) 224-3211. See display ad **Mile 3.2** Seward Highway. [ADVERTISEMENT]

Ray's Waterfront. Innovative Alaskan cuisine in a spectacular waterfront setting featuring fresh local seafood, steaks and vegetarian selections. Specialties include macadamia nut crusted halibut with Thai curry sauce, cioppino, brandied pepper steak, oven-roasted Tuscan vegetables, king crab and daily specials. Serving lunch and dinner daily. Full bar service with excellent wine selections. Group reservations in advance are welcome. Gourmet box lunches available. Phone (907) 224-5606, fax (907) 224-5631. E-mail: janaska@msn.com. [ADVERTISEMENT]

Seward Resort (Military). Motel, cabins, RV and tent sites. Charter fishing, Resurrection Bay wildlife boat tours. Open year-round. Authorized patrons: active duty military; retirees; National Guard and Reserves; DOD/NAF civilians, families and guests; federal governmental agencies. Phone (800) 770-1858; DSN 384-3474/5463. Internet: 143.213.12.254/mwr/seward.htm. See display ad, **Mile 2.3** Seward Highway. [ADVERTISEMENT] MP ▲

Seward Windsong Lodge. Seward's newest lodge, overlooks Resurrection River, on the road to Kenai Fjords National Park and Exit Glacier. Modern, clean units with full bath, cable, VCRs, phone, and queen

beds in a quiet, forested setting. New for 1998, great casual dining at the Resurrection Roadhouse. One-half mile up Exit Glacier Road. Phone (800) 208-0200 or (907) 224-7116. See display ad in SEWARD section. [ADVERTISEMENT]

Taroka Inn. Why pay more for less? Clean 1- or 2-bedroom units featuring equipped kitchens, private bathrooms and color cable television. Accommodates up to 9 persons. Non-smoking available. Convenient downtown location. One block to shops, restaurants and Marine Education Center. Two blocks to Alaska SeaLife Center, 3/4 mile to boat harbor. (907) 224-8975. E-mail: taroka@arctic.net. Internet: www.alaskaone.com/taroka. See display ad this section. [ADVERTISEMENT] MP

Van Gilder Hotel. Seward's favorite small hotel, built in 1916 and completely renovated for the 1990s. Now a National Historic Site, it retains its original Edwardian charm. Centrally located at 308 Adams Street in downtown Seward within easy walking distance of restaurants and shops. Clean, casual, comfortable rooms for tourists and business travelers. For hotel reservations phone (800) 204-6835. P.O. Box 2, Seward, AK, 99664. Fax (907) 224-3689. E-mail your reservations to: vangilderhotel @onvillage.net. See display ad this section. [ADVERTISEMENT]

Wildflower Bed and Breakfast welcomes you to their spacious country-style home, nestled in a quiet, wooded neighborhood. View majestic mountains, wildflowers and wildlife. Three guest rooms. King/queen/twin beds. A hot, satisfying breakfast. Smoke free. Open year-round. Hosts: Dan and Teresa Campbell, P.O. box

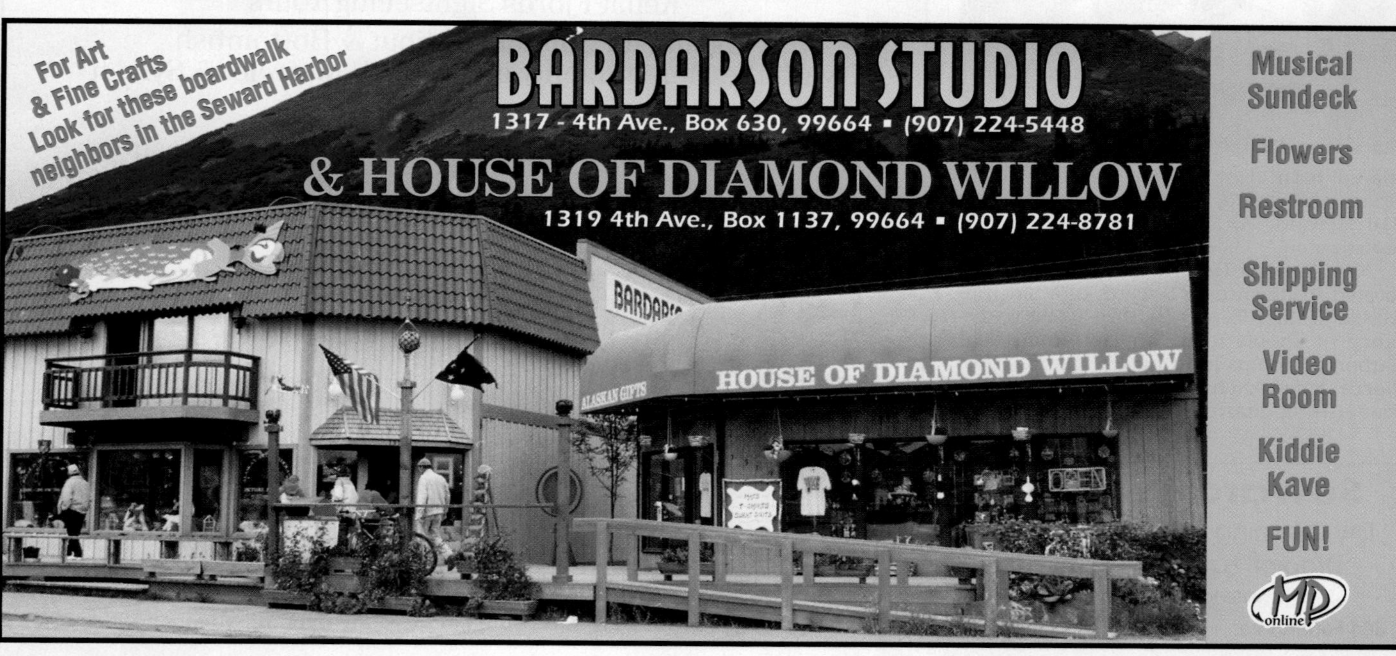

Fourth Avenue in downtown Seward. (© Tom Culkin)

1641, Seward, AK 99664. Phone (907) 224-5764, fax (907) 224-5765. [ADVERTISEMENT]

TRANSPORTATION

Air: Seward airport is reached by turning east on Airport Road at **Milepost S 2.7** on the Seward Highway. Scheduled daily service to Anchorage; charters also available.

Ferry: Alaska Marine Highway office on Cruise Ship Dock; phone (907) 224-5485. The Alaska ferry MV *Tustumena* departs Seward for Kodiak and Valdez.

Railroad: The Alaska Railroad connects Seward to Anchorage and Fairbanks.

Bus: Scheduled service to Anchorage.

Taxi: Service available.

Highway: Seward is reached via the 127-mile/203.2-km Seward Highway from Anchorage.

Tours: Seward Trolley offers city tours 10 A.M. to 7 P.M. daily, Memorial Day through Labor Day.

ATTRACTIONS

The Railcar *Seward* houses the chamber of commerce information center. Located at 3rd and Jefferson Street, this railcar was the Seward observation car on the Alaska Railroad from 1936 until the early 1960s. Information and detailed map of the city are available.

Walking Tour of Seward encompasses more than 30 attractions including homes and businesses that date back to the early 1900s; some are still being used, while others have been restored as historic sites. A brochure containing details on all the attractions of the tour is available at the railcar information center. The complete tour covers about 2 miles/3.2 km and takes about 1 to 2 hours, depending upon how much time you wish to spend browsing.

Marine Educational Center, maintained by the University of Alaska, has laboratories, aquaculture ponds and the vessel *Alpha Helix*, which carries on oceanographic research in Alaskan waters. There is a marine display here. Open 10 A.M. to 4 P.M. Tuesday through Sunday, closed Monday, June through August.

Alaska SeaLife Center. The 7-acre waterfront site next to the Seward Marine Educational Center is the new (May 1998) Alaska SeaLife Center. The center combines research facilities with wildlife rehabilitation and public education. Construction of the SeaLife Center is funded by the Exxon Valdez Oil Spill Restoration fund and private donations.

The Center allows you to come face-to-face with Alaska's exciting marine wildlife, explore their undersea world and experience the wonder of nature in a one-of-a-kind marine science and visitor facility. This $50 million, 115,000-square-foot center opens windows to the sea—above and below the surface. Indoors, view the distinct habitats of marine birds, Steller sea lions, seals, fish and otters. Outdoors, step right to the edge of Resurrection Bay, teeming with Alaska marine wildlife. Open daily 9 A.M.–9:30 P.M. Admission $12.50 adults, $10 youth.

Visit the Small Boat Harbor. This municipal harbor, built after the 1964 earthquake, is home port to fishing boats, charter boats and sightseeing boats. The harbor is also home to sea otters—watch for them! Visitors may notice the great number of sailboats moored here: many are members of the William H. Seward Yacht Club, which sponsors an annual sailboat and yacht show.

Seward Museum, at Jefferson and 3rd

Avenue, is operated by the Resurrection Bay Historical Society (Box 55, Seward 99664). The museum features artifacts and photographs from the 1964 earthquake, WWII, the founding days of Seward and other highlights of Seward's history. Also on display is a collection of Native baskets and ivory carvings. The museum is open daily, 10 A.M. to 5 P.M., May 1 to Sept. 30. Open reduced hours remainder of year; check locally, or phone (907) 224-3902. A modest admission fee is charged.

Seward Community Library, across from the City–State Building, presents (on request) short slide/sound shows on a variety of subjects and has some informative displays. A program on the 1964 earthquake is shown daily at 2 P.M. (except Sunday) from June 15 through the first Saturday in September. Library hours are 1–8 P.M. Monday through Friday, 1–6 P.M. Saturday.

St. Peter's Episcopal Church is 3 blocks west of the museum at the corner of 2nd Avenue and Adams Street. It was built in 1906 and is considered the oldest Protestant church on the Kenai Peninsula. One feature is the unique painting of the Resurrection, for which Alaskans were used as models and Resurrection Bay as the background. Well-known Dutch artist Jan Van Emple was commissioned to paint the picture in 1925 when he was living in Seward. Obtain key to church from the Information Cache in season.

Mountain goat in Kenai Fjords National Park. (© Mike Jones)

Hiking Trails. Two Lakes trail is an easy mile-long loop trail along the base of Mount Marathon. The trail passes through a wooded area and follows what used to be Hemlock Street. Beautiful view of marina below and north end of Resurrection Bay. Start at First Lake, behind the Alaska Vocational and Technical Center Administration Building at 2nd Avenue and B Street.

The **National Historic Iditarod Trail** begins at the ferry terminal and follows a marked course through town, then north on the Seward Highway. At Mile 2.1 Nash Road (turn off at **Milepost S 3.2** Seward Highway), the trail continues from a gravel parking area on the east side of Sawmill Creek north to Bear Lake. The trail eventually rejoins the Seward Highway at **Milepost S 12.**

Caines Head State Recreation Area, 6 miles/9.6 km south of Seward, is accessible by boat or via a 4.5-mile/7.2-km beach trail (low tide only). The trailhead/parking is located about Mile 2 Lowell Point Road. The Caines Head area has bunkers and gun emplacements that were used to guard the entrance to Resurrection Bay during WWII.

Mount Marathon Race™, Seward's annual Fourth of July endurance race to the top of Mount Marathon (elev. 3,022 feet/921m) and back down, is a grueling test for athletes. The race is said to have begun in 1909 with a wager between 2 sourdoughs as to how long it would take to run up and down Mount Marathon. The first year of the official race is uncertain: records indicate either 1912 or 1915. Fastest recorded time is 43 minutes, 23 seconds set in 1981 by Bill Spencer, who broke his own 1974 record. The descent is so steep that it's part run, part jump and part slide. The race attracts competitors from all over, and thousands of spectators line the route each year.

Annual Seward Silver Salmon Derby™ in August is one of the largest sporting events in Alaska. It is held over 9 days, starting the second Saturday in August and continuing through Sunday of the following weekend. 1998 will be the derby's 43rd year. Record derby catch to date is a 20.59-lb. salmon caught off Twin Rocks by John Westlund of Anchorage.

There are more than $225,000 in prizes for the derby, including $10,000 in cash for the largest fish. Also part of the derby are the sought-after tagged silvers worth as much as $100,000. Prizes are sponsored by various merchants and the chamber of commerce.

The town fills up fast during the derby: Make reservations! For more information contact the Seward Chamber of Commerce; phone (907) 224-8051.

Kenai Fjords National Park. Seward is the gateway to this popular 605,000-acre national park. Dominant feature of the park is the Harding Icefield, a 300-square-mile vestige of the last ice age. Harding Icefield can be reached by a strenuous all-day hike from the base of Exit Glacier or by a charter

flightseeing trip out of Seward.

The fjords of the park were formed when glaciers flowed down to the sea from the ice field and then retreated, leaving behind the deep inlets that characterize the coastline here. Substantial populations of marine mammals inhabit or migrate through the park's coastal waters, including sea otters, Steller sea lions, dolphins and whales. Icebergs from calving glaciers provide ideal refuge for harbor seals, and the rugged coastline provides habitat for more than 100,000 nesting birds. The park's spectacular scenery and wildlife may be viewed by daily private tour and charter boats or by charter planes. Four public-use cabins along the coast are available in summer by reservation; phone (907) 271-2737. Kayakers and boaters can also camp on beaches but must be aware ahead of time of land status; 45,000 acres of coastline are owned by Native corporations and are *not* available for public camping. Maps indicating land ownership are available from the park visitor center. *NOTE: Private boaters should consult with local outfitters and charter operators for detailed information on boating conditions.*

Exit Glacier is the most accessible of the park's glaciers. Turn at **Milepost S 3.7** on the Seward Highway and follow Exit Glacier Road to the visitor center parking area. There are several trails through the outwash plain of Exit Glacier that afford excellent views of the ice and surrounding mountains. A 0.2-mile paved trail is wheelchair accessible and leads from the parking lot to an information display. Ranger-led nature walks are available in summer at Exit Glacier, where there is a picnic area and walk-in campground. Visitor information is available at the Exit Glacier ranger station and visitor center; open summer only. Exit Glacier is accessible in winter by skis, dogsled or snow machine. A public-use cabin is available by permit; phone (907) 224-3175 or the Park Information Line (907) 224-2132. *CAUTION: Active glacier with unstable ice. Do not walk past warning signs!* ♿

Slide programs, videos, exhibits and information on Kenai Fjords National Park and organized activities at the park are available at the park visitor center on 4th Avenue in the Small Boat Harbor area next to the Harbormaster's office. The center is open daily from Memorial Day to Labor Day; hours are 9 A.M. to 6 P.M. The remainder of the year hours are 8 A.M. to 5 P.M. (subject to change) weekdays. Phone (907) 224-3175 or write the park superintendent, Box 1727, Seward 99664.

Alaska SeaLife Center. Come face to face with Alaska's exciting marine wildlife and explore their undersea world. Experience the

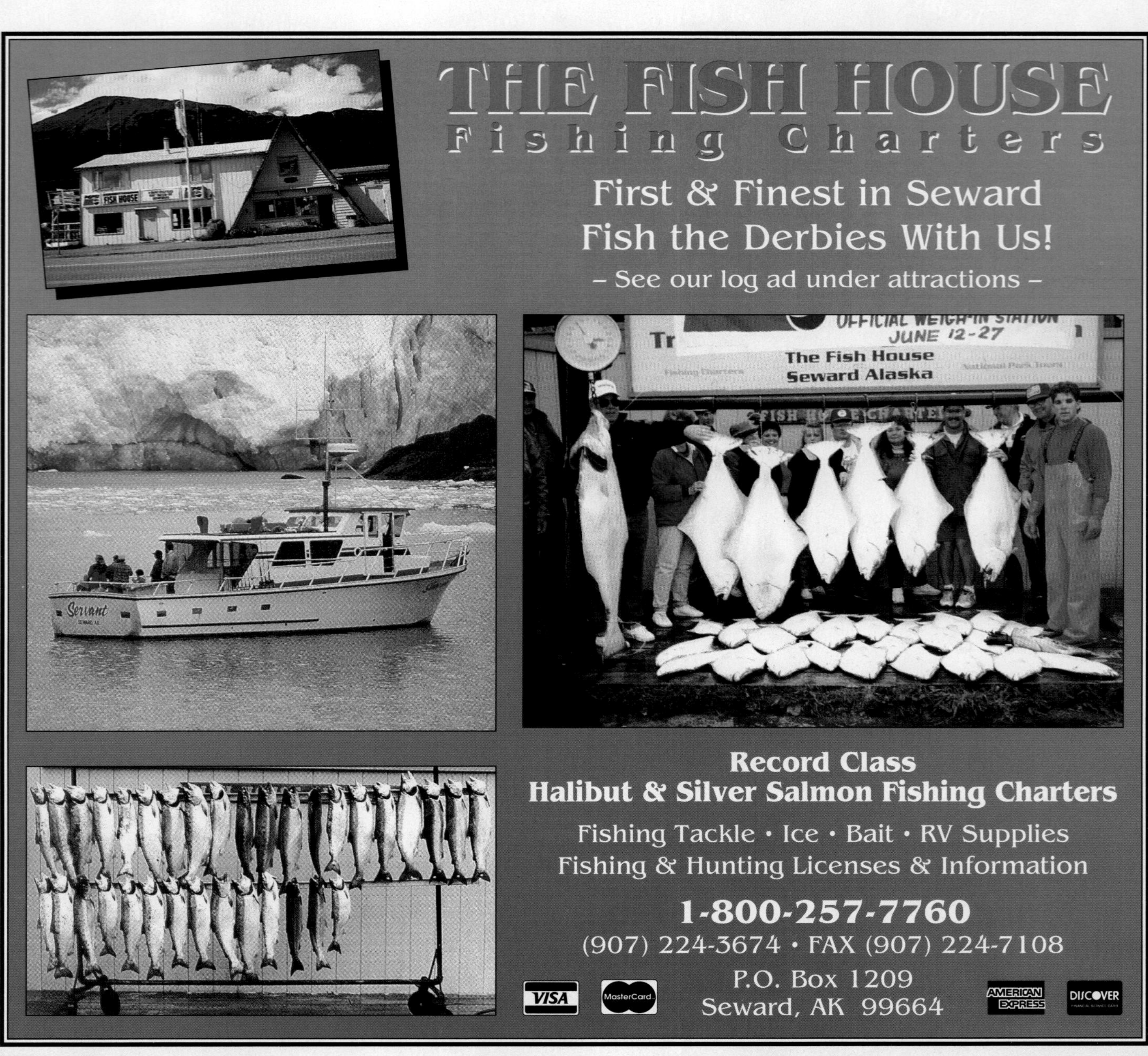

THE FISH HOUSE
Fishing Charters
First & Finest in Seward
Fish the Derbies With Us!
– See our log ad under attractions –
OFFICIAL WEIGH-IN STATION
JUNE 12-27
The Fish House
Seward Alaska
Servant
Record Class
Halibut & Silver Salmon Fishing Charters
Fishing Tackle • Ice • Bait • RV Supplies
Fishing & Hunting Licenses & Information
1-800-257-7760
(907) 224-3674 • FAX (907) 224-7108
P.O. Box 1209
Seward, AK 99664
VISA
MasterCard
AMERICAN EXPRESS
DISCOVER

All Cruises Hosted by National Park Ranger

Kenai Fjords National Park

Experience Otters, Puffins, Whales, Glaciers...and the Great Taste of Alaska Aboard Our Unforgettable Wildlife Cruises

Join Major Marine Tours for an unforgettable wildlife and glacier cruise in Kenai Fjords National Park. On our cruises you'll generally see otters, eagles, puffins, porpoises, whales and the other abundant wildlife in the area. The spectacular scenery includes tidewater and piedmont glaciers and other unforgettable sights. Our boats feature reserved table seating and spacious outside decks for up-close viewing and picture taking. As you cruise, take

advantage of our freshly-prepared all-you-can-eat salmon and chicken buffet with all the trimmings. The boats offer full bar service, heated cabins, restrooms and an attentive crew.

All cruises are hosted by a uniformed National Park Ranger who will narrate the trip and answer questions. Only Major Marine Tours has a ranger on every cruise. Both the half-day and full-day cruises operate daily from May to mid–September.

Whichever cruise you select, we know you'll love the spectacular glaciers and wildlife in the famous Kenai Fjords.

Reservations/Free Brochure
907-274-7300
(Anchorage area)

800-764-7300
(Nationwide, except Anchorage)

411 West 4th Ave. • Anchorage, AK 99501
Visit us at www.majormarine.com.
Ticket offices located in Anchorage and on the boardwalk in Seward's small boat harbor (seasonal phone: 224-8030).
All major credit cards accepted.

wonder of nature in all its grandeur at this new and unique marine science and visitor facility. View the distinct habitats of puffins, sea lions and seals. The Alaska SeaLife Center opens windows to the sea—above and below the surface. [ADVERTISEMENT]

Bardarson Studio. In Seward find Bardarson Studio on the prettiest boardwalk in the boat harbor area, with the best selection of Alaska art and fine crafts set to music. Bardarson Studio recognizes that

shopping is entertainment for travelers, providing a Kiddie-Kave for children, and a video room for your non-shopper. Public restroom and postal service available. 1317 4th Avenue. Phone (800) 354-0141. E-mail: bardasn@ptialaska.net. Internet: www.ptialaska.net/~bardarsn. [ADVERTISEMENT] MP

The Fish House. First and finest fishing charter service in Seward! Record-class halibut and silver salmon fishing charters available now. While fishing, enjoy the scenic beauty of the Kenai Fjords National Park—glaciers, mountains, puffins, whales, sea otters and seals. The Fish House also supplies a complete line of fishing tackle, bait, ice and outboard motor repairs. Call now for reservations or information on fishing the scenic waters surrounding Seward, Alaska. 1-800-257-7760 or (907) 224-3674. Halibut charters: April 1–Oct. 1. Salmon charters: June 1–Sept. 20. P.O. Box 1209, Seward, AK 99664. See display ad this section. [ADVERTISEMENT] MP

Fjordland Gallery exhibits paintings of Alaskan and marine subjects by artist Lee George along with works of invited guest artists. Original paintings and limited edition prints available. The Gallery is wheelchair accessible and expanded in size following recent building remodel. It offers a grand view of Resurrection Bay and is located in the historic "Old Solly's" building at 411 Washington Street, across from the Alaska SeaLife Center. Open year round. Phone (907) 224-6059, fax (907) 224-3615. E-mail: akartist@alaskaartist.com. Internet: www.alaskaartist.com. [ADVERTISEMENT] MP

IdidaRide Sled Dog Tours. Experience dog mushing, summer style, on a 2-mile wilderness dog sled ride at Iditarod racer Mitch Seavey's training location. Informative tour includes 80-husky kennel, cuddly puppies, arctic equipment demonstration. Reservations recommended. P.O. Box 2906, Seward, AK 99664. (907) 224-8607, fax (907) 224-8608. Off Exit Glacier Road. See display ad Mile 3.7 Seward Highway. [ADVERTISEMENT]

Kayak & Custom Adventures Worldwide. Coastal kayakiing excursions in Alaska include unforgettable wilderness experiences. Glaciers calving, whales breaching, icebergs floating, otters frolicking, waterfalls cascading and wildflowers blooming. Take home memories you can't get standing on the shore. Adventures available worldwide. Call now for a free brochure. Toll free (800) 288-3134 or (907) 258-FUNN. In Seward: (907) 224-3960. E-mail: kayak@arctic.net. Internet: www.alaskan.com/kayak. [ADVERTISEMENT]

Kenai Fjords Tours Ltd. The excitement begins the moment you pull away from the Seward boat harbor! You'll be greeted by playful sea otters, view boisterous Steller sea lions, look for whales and porpoises, photograph colorful puffins and bald eagles, and watch a calving glacier. Cruising since 1974, Kenai Fjords Tours is the original Kenai Fjords National Park tour and continues to

Halibut caught in the Gulf of Alaska.
(© Roger Holden)

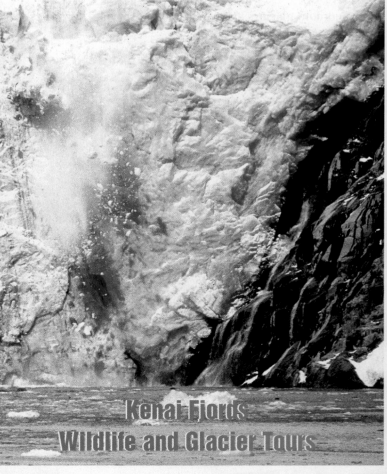

be the most popular. Our new, comfortable boats have walk-around decks so you can easily watch and photograph the magnificent scenery. Our captains are experienced naturalists averaging more than 12 years in Kenai Fjords National Park, so you'll

learn about this coastal wilderness from guides who really know the area. All cruises include a meal and many include a special stop at Fox Island for our delicious all-you-can-eat salmon bake at kenai Fjords Wilderness Lodge. Don't miss it! Call today for reservations. Toll free (800) 748-8068 or (907) 224-8068. Located at the Seward Small Boat Harbor. See display ad this section. [ADVERTISEMENT] MP

Major Marine Kenai Fjords National Park Tours. Join us for Seward's world-class wildlife and glacier cruises of the Kenai Fjords. We offer two wonderful cruise options: 1) a half-day wildlife cruise of the Kenai Fjords, and 2) a full-day wildlife cruise of the Kenai Fjords National Park and Chiswell Islands National Wildlife Refuge. Both cruises are hosted and narrated by a uniformed National Park Ranger. During the cruise you'll generally see otters, sea lions, puffins, eagles, porpoises, whales, giant bird colonies and more. You'll also pull up close to some of Alaska's most awe-inspiring glaciers. The large tour boats feature reserved table seating, inside heated cabins and multiple outside decks. A freshly prepared all-you-can-eat salmon and roasted chicken buffet is available on both cruises for only $10. Both cruises sail from Seward's boat harbor May to late September. The full-day cruise departs at 11:30 A.M. and costs $89. The half-day cruise departs at 1:15 P.M. and 6:00 P.M. and costs $74. For reservations or free brochure, call: (800) 764-7300 or (907) 274-7300. Major Marine Tours, 411 West 4th, Anchorage, Alaska 99501. Ticket office also located on Seward boardwalk: (907) 224-8030 (May to September). Internet: www.majormarine.com. [ADVERTISEMENT]

Mariah Tours. Guided natural history tours in Kenai Fjords and the Chiswell Islands Wildlife Refuge since 1981. Our custom-built 22-passenger ships offer the

small ship alternative to Kenai Fjords National Park, for a more personalized, uncrowded tour. Also featuring tours to spectacular Northwestern Glacier via Granite Passage, the most scenic area within Kenai Fjords National Park. Popular exclusive tours for birding and naturalist groups and other interested parties. Operating mid-May–September. For reservations: (800) 270-1238. In Seward: (907) 223-8623. See display ad this section. [ADVERTISEMENT]

AREA FISHING: Resurrection Bay, coho (silver) salmon to 22 lbs., use herring, troll or cast, July to October; king salmon to 45 lbs., May to August; also bottom fish, flounder, halibut to 300 lbs. and cod, use weighted spoons and large red spinners by jigging, year-round. Charter and rental boats are available.

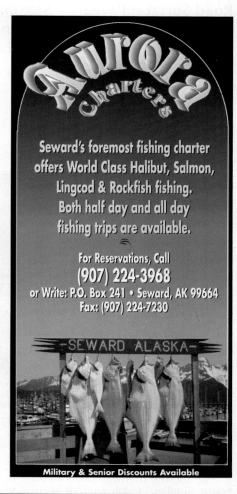

Kenai Peninsula

STERLING HIGHWAY ①

Connects: Seward Highway to Homer, AK **Length:** 143 miles
Road Surface: Paved **Season:** Open all year
Major Attractions: Kenai National Wildlife Refuge, Russian Orthodox Churches, Homer Spit

(See maps, pages 573–574)

	Anchorage	Homer	Kenai	Seward	Soldotna
Anchorage		233	158	127	147
Homer	233		96	180	85
Kenai	158	96		105	11
Seward	127	180	105		94
Soldotna	147	85	11	94	

Boardwalk at Tern Lake picnic area, Milepost S 37.4, has interpretive signs on area wildlife. (© George Wuerthner)

The Sterling Highway (Alaska Route 1) begins 90 miles/145 km south of Anchorage at its junction with the Seward Highway and travels 142.5 miles/229.3 km west and south to the community of Homer. The Sterling Highway junctions with several major Kenai Peninsula side roads (see logs this section): Skilak Lake Loop Road, Swanson River Road, Kenai Spur Highway, Kalifornsky Beach Road, Cohoe Loop Road and Anchor River Beach Road.

From its junction with the Seward Highway at Tern Lake (see SEWARD HIGHWAY section), the Sterling passes through Chugach National Forest and Kenai National Wildlife Refuge. The Kenai Mountains are home to Dall sheep, mountain goats, black and brown bears, and caribou. The many lakes, rivers and streams of the Kenai Peninsula are famous for their sportfishing. The highway also provides access to the Resurrection Pass Trail System.

From Soldotna south, the Sterling Highway follows the west coast of the peninsula along Cook Inlet. There are beautiful views of peaks on the Alaska Peninsula.

Physical mileposts on the Sterling Highway show distance from Seward. The Sterling Highway is a paved 2-lane highway, open year-round.

Emergency medical services: phone 911 or use CB channels 9, 11 or 19.

Sterling Highway Log

Distance from Seward (S) is followed by distance from Anchorage (A) and distance from Homer (H). Physical mileposts show distance from Seward.

S 37.7 (60.7 km) **A 89.3** (143.7 km) **H 141.8** (228.2 km) **Junction** with Seward Highway. First exit southbound (1-way road) for Sterling Highway.

S 37 (59.5 km) **A 90** (144.8 km) **H 142.5** (229.3 km) **Tern Lake Junction.** Second southbound exit (2-way road) for Sterling Highway. This exit provides access to Tern Lake day-use area (see description next milepost). Gravel turnout beside Tern Lake with interpretive boardwalk and viewing platforms. Information signs on area birds and wildlife.

S 37.4 (60.2 km) **A 90.4** (145.5 km) **H 142.1** (228.7 km) USFS Tern Lake day-use picnic area; toilets, water, picnic tables. USFS spawning channel for king salmon on Daves Creek at outlet of Tern Lake. Short viewing trail with information signs illustrating use of log weirs and stream protection techniques.

S 38 (61.1 km) **A 91** (146.4 km) **H 141.5** (227.7 km) Avalanche gates. Gravel turnouts.

S 38.3 (61.6 km) **A 91.3** (146.9 km) **H 141.2** (227.2 km) Gravel turnout. Emergency call box.

S 39 (62.8 km) **A 92** (148 km) **H 140.5** (226.1 km) **Daves Creek,** an unusually beautiful mountain stream which flows west into Quartz Creek. Dolly Varden and rainbow averaging 14 inches, June through September. A good place to view spawning salmon in late July and August.

S 40.5 (65.2 km) **A 93.5** (150.5 km) **H 139** (223.7 km) Double-ended gravel turnout to south.

S 40.9 (65.8 km) **A 93.9** (151.1 km) **H 138.6** (223 km) Bridge over Quartz Creek. This stream empties into Kenai Lake. You are now entering one of Alaska's best-known lake and river fishing regions, across the center of the Kenai Peninsula. The burn on the hillsides to the south was part of a Forest Service moose habitat improvement program.

S 41.1 (66.1 km) **A 94.1** (151.4 km) **H 138.4** (222.7 km) Cooper Landing Closed Area. This area is closed to the hunting of Dall sheep. The ridges to the north are a lambing ground for Dall sheep.

STERLING HIGHWAY *Tern Lake Junction to Soldotna, AK*

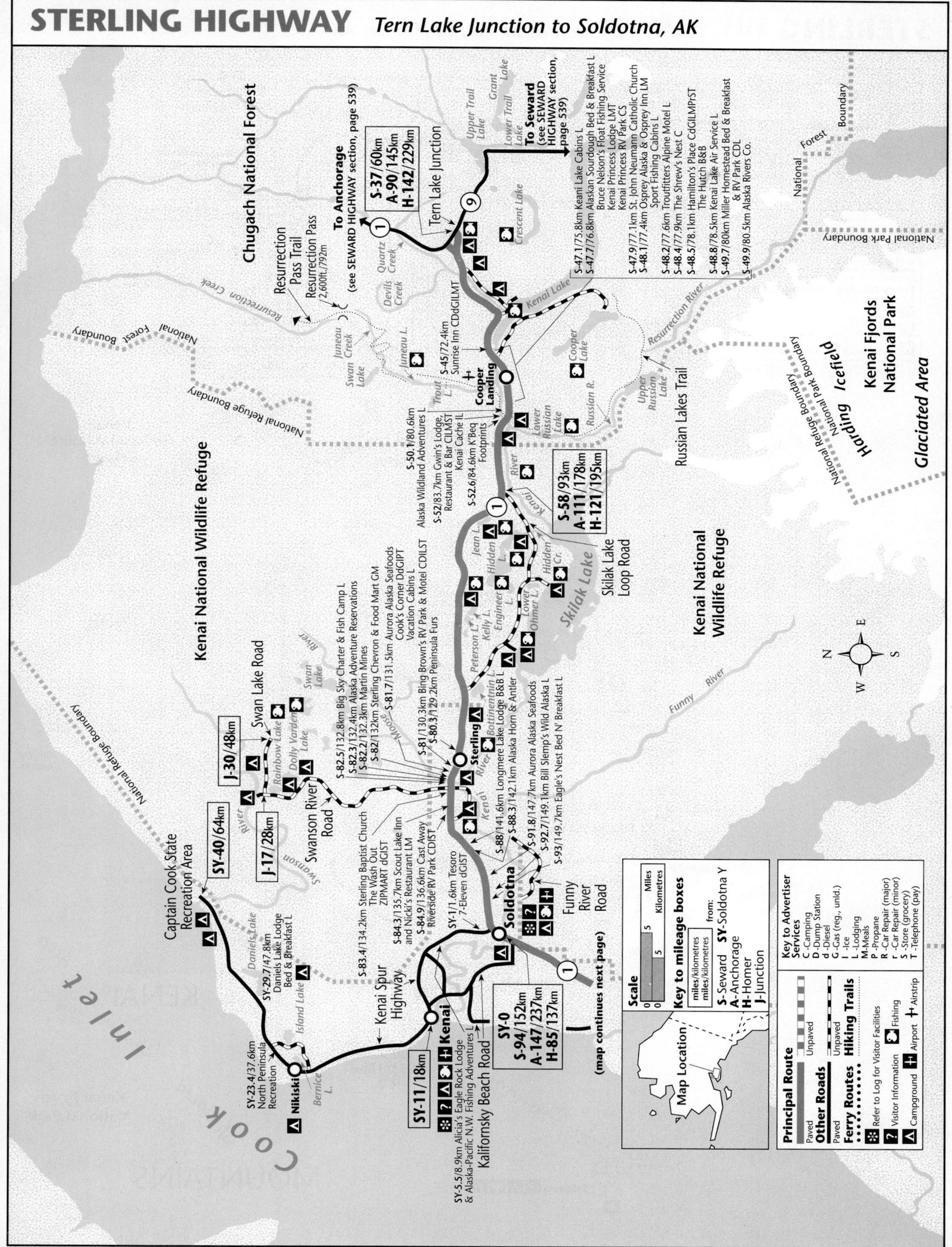

STERLING HIGHWAY *Soldotna, AK, to Homer, AK*

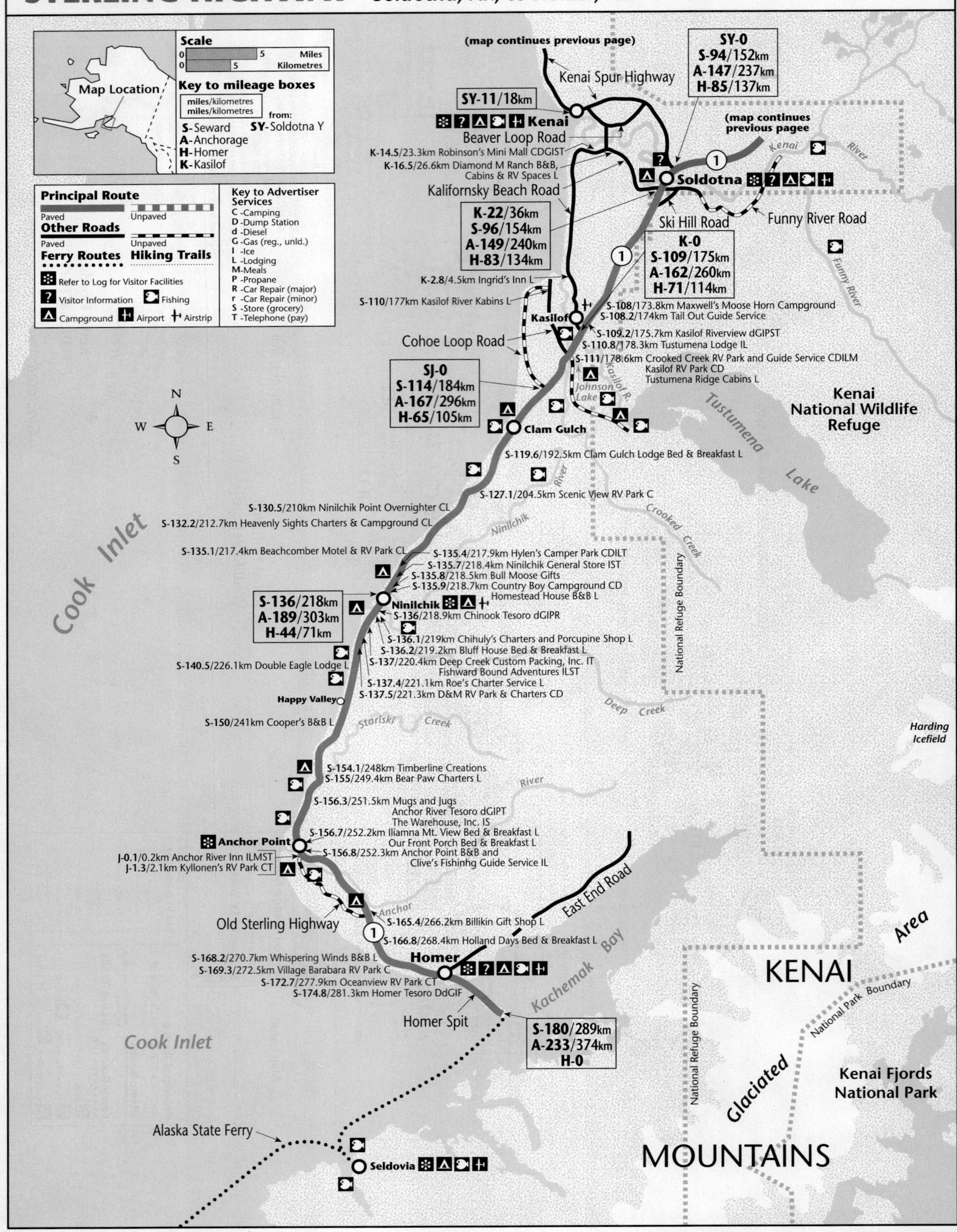

S 42.8 (68.9 km) **A 95.8** (154.2 km) **H 136.7** (220 km) Gravel turnouts on Quartz Creek.

S 43.1 (69.4 km) **A 96.1** (154.6 km) **H 136.4** (219.5 km) Double-ended gravel turnout to east on Quartz Creek.

S 43.5 (70 km) **A 96.5** (155.3 km) **H 136** (218.9 km) Double-ended gravel turnout to east.

S 44 (70.8 km) **A 97** (156.1 km) **H 135.5** (218.1 km) Double-ended, gravel turnout on Quartz Creek.

S 44.3 (71.3 km) **A 97.3** (156.6) **H 135.2** (217.6 km) Solid waste transfer site to east; public dumpsters.

S 45 (72.4 km) **A 98** (157.7 km) **H 134.5** (216.5 km) Quartz Creek Road to Quartz Creek Recreation Area. Quartz Creek Campground, 0.3 mile/0.5 km from the highway, has 31 sites, boat launch, flush toilets, firepits and a $10 camping fee. Crescent Creek Campground, 3 miles/4.8 km from the highway, may be closed in 1998 for renovation. Crescent Creek USFS trail leads 6.2 miles/10 km to the outlet of Crescent Lake. The trailhead is about 1 mile/1.6 km from Crescent Creek Campground. A public-use cabin is located at the lake; permit required for use; not accessible in winter or early spring due to extreme avalanche danger. ▲

The Sterling Highway from the junction with the Seward Highway west to the community of Sterling **(Milepost S 81)** takes the traveler through the heart of some prime fishing country, and provides access to numerous fishing lakes and rivers. *NOTE: The diversity of fishing conditions and frequent regulation changes in all Kenai waters make it advisable to consult locally for fishing news and regulations.*

Beautiful views of Kenai Lake next 3 miles/4.8 km westbound. The lake's unusual color is caused by glacial silt.

Quartz Creek, rainbow, midsummer; Dolly Varden to 25 inches, late May through June. **Crescent Lake**, grayling, July 1 to April 14 (2 grayling daily bag and possession limit). **Kenai Lake**, lake trout, May 15 to Sept. 30; trout, May to September; Dolly Varden, May to September. Kenai Lake and tributaries are closed to salmon fishing.

S 45 (72.4 km) **A 98** (157.7 km) **H 134.5** (216.5 km) **Sunrise Inn**. See display ad this section.

S 45.6 (73.4 km) **A 98.6** (158.7 km) **H 133.9** (215.5 km) Large turnout with toilet. This is an observation point for Dall sheep on Near Mountain and mountain goats on Cecil Rhode Mountain (directly across Kenai Lake); use binoculars.

S 46.3 (74.5 km) **A 99.3** (159.8 km) **H 133.2** (214.4 km) Small gravel turnout to east.

S 47 (75.6 km) **A 100** (160.9 km) **H 132.5** (213.2 km) Turnout to east.

S 47.1 (75.8 km) **A 100.1** (161.1 km) **H 132.4** (213.1 km) **Kenai Lake Cabins.** See display ad this section.

S 47.7 (76.8 km) **A 100.7** (162 km) **H 131.8** (212.1 km) Bean Creek Road, access to a fishing guide service, bed and breakfast and the Kenai Princess Lodge and RV Park on the Kenai River. The lodge's lobby has an interesting chandelier made from antlers. ▲

Alaskan Sourdough Bed & Breakfast. See display ad this section.

Bruce Nelson's Float Fishing Service and Eid's Cabin. See display ad this section.

Kenai Princess Lodge. A wilderness retreat overlooking the salmon-rich Kenai River featuring 70 cozy bungalow-style rooms with sun porches, wood stoves, televisions and telephones. Spacious view deck, fine restaurant, lounge, gift shop, tour desk, hot tubs, exercise room. Meeting facilities. Open March to December. Call (800) 426-0500 year-round. [ADVERTISEMENT]

Kenai Princess RV Park. At Cooper Landing on the salmon-rich Kenai River. Featuring 35 sites with water and power, general store, showers, laundry, septic. Use of facilities at adjacent Kenai Princess Lodge. Open mid-May through mid-September. $20 per night. Phone (907) 595-1425, March through December, for reservations. [ADVERTISEMENT] ▲

S 47.8 (76.9 km) **A 100.8** (162.2 km) **H 131.7** (211.9 km) Kenai River bridge. The new (1997) Cooper Landing boat launch facility, adjacent to the Kenai River Bridge, contains a concrete boat launch, day-use parking, restrooms, viewing decks, informational panels and telescopes. $5 launching fee or $5 parking fee for vehicles not launching boats.

The Kenai River flows directly alongside the highway for the next 10 miles/16 km with several gravel turnouts offering good views. (A proposed plan to reroute this portion of the Sterling Highway away from the Kenai River and into the mountains is under consideration.)

Upper Kenai River, from **Kenai Lake** to **Skilak Lake**, including Skilak Lake within a half mile of the Kenai River inlet, special regulations apply. For current recorded fishing forecast, phone (907) 267-2502. Silver salmon 5 to 15 lbs., August through October; pink salmon 3 to 7 lbs., July and August; red salmon 3 to 12 lbs., June 11 through mid-August; rainbow and Dolly Varden, June 11 through October. *IMPORTANT: Be familiar with current regulations and closures. Dates given here are subject to change!*

S 47.9 (77.1 km) **A 100.9** (162.4 km) **H 131.6** (211.8 km) Snug Harbor Road. This side road leads 12 miles/19.3 km to Cooper Lake and trailhead for 23-mile/37-km USFS trail to Russian River Campground (see **Milepost S 52.6**). A Baptist church and the St. John Neumann Catholic Church, named after one of the first American saints, are on Snug Harbor Road.

St. John Neumann Catholic Church. See display ad this section.

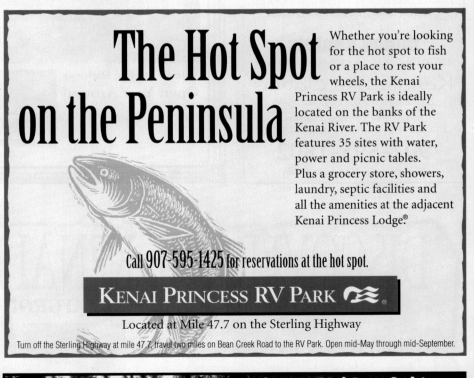

S 48.1 (77.4 km) **A 101.1** (162.7 km) **H 131.4** (211.7 km) **Sport Fishing Cabins.** See display ad this section.

Osprey Alaska. Guided fishing, deluxe motel, restaurant. Day- and week-long touring and fishing packages. Fishing, raft trips and Kenai Canyon dory trips daily. Osprey Inn and Mountain Chalets. Green Door Cafe is a full-service restaurant. Phone (800) 553-5364 or (907) 595-1265. Internet: www.ospreyalaska.com. Box 504, Cooper Landing, AK 99572. Brochure. [ADVERTISEMENT] MP

S 48.2 (77.6 km) **A 101.2** (162.9 km) **H 131.3** (211.3 km) **Troutfitters Alpine Motel.** See display ad this section.

S 48.4 (77.9 km) **A 101.4** (163.2 km) **H 131.1** (211 km) **COOPER LANDING** (pop. 386) stretches along several miles of the highway. All visitor facilities. Cooper Landing ambulance, phone (907) 595-1255.

The Shrew's Nest, Last Resort RV Park and Landing Latté. See display ad this section. ▲

Private Aircraft: Quartz Creek (Cooper Landing) airstrip, 4 miles/6.4 km west; elev. 450 feet/137m; length 2,200 feet/671m; gravel; unattended.

S 48.5 (78.1 km) **A 101.5** (163.3 km) **H 131** (210.8 km) **Hamilton's Place** river resort, only complete stop on the upper

Fishing for salmon on the Kenai River. The Kenai River heads in Kenai Lake and flows 75 miles west to Cook Inlet. (© Loren Taft, Alaskan Images)

Kenai River. Information center for the famous Russian River and surrounding area. Centrally located for day trips to Seward, Soldotna/Kenai, Homer. Make us your Kenai Peninsula headquarters. Tesoro services, 24-hour recovery and transport (flatbed) service, 24-hour locksmith, propane. (All-emergency road service providers.) General store, groceries, licenses, tackle, ice, liquor store. Restaurant, lounge.

Hair salon. RV hookups, modern cabins with cooking facilities, laundromat, phone. Fish freezing, storage, Federal Express shipping. Hamilton's Place, serving the public since 1952, hopes to make your stay enjoyable. Phone (907) 595-1260; fax (907) 595-1530. See display ad this section. [ADVERTISEMENT] ▲

The Hutch B&B. 12 clean rooms, private baths. Twin, queen, king beds. Smoke free. Continental breakfast until 10 A.M. Very reasonable rates. Common area, cable TV each floor. Covered decks. Large parking area accommodates boat trailers, large vehicles. View mountain goats, Dall sheep, Kenai River. "Bunny Trail." Phone (907) 595-1270. See display ad. [ADVERTISEMENT]

S 48.7 (78.4 km) **A 101.7** (163.7 km) **H 130.8** (210.5 km) Cooper Landing post office, located in resort; open 9 A.M. to 5 P.M. weekdays and Saturday morning. Pay phone.

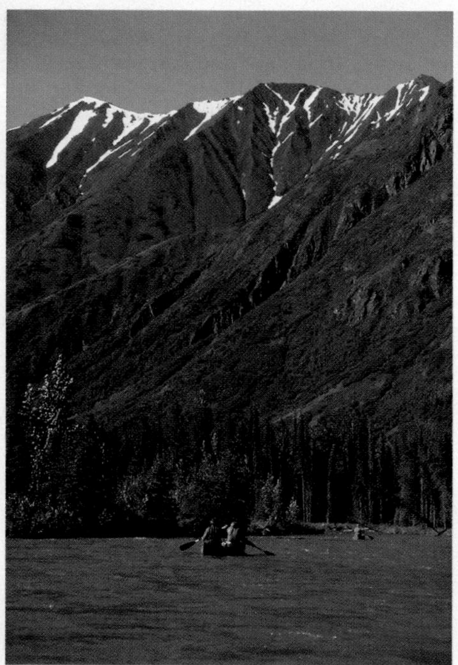

The Kenai Peninsula offers serveral canoe trails. (© Michael DeYoung)

S 48.8 (78.5 km) **A 101.8** (163.8 km) **H 130.7** (210.3 km) **Kenai Lake Air Service.** See display ad this section.

S 49.4 (79.5 km) **A 102.4** (164.8 km) **H 130.1** (209.4 km) Large paved turnout by Kenai River. The highway winds along the Kenai River.

S 49.7 (80 km) **A 102.7** (165.3 km) **H 129.8** (208.9 km) **The Miller Homestead Bed & Breakfast RV Park.** Make us your vacation headquarters for Kenai Peninsula adventures. We can arrange fishing for trophy rainbow trout, Russian River red salmon, Dolly Varden, Kenai River kings, silvers and halibut. Bank fishing River-viewing platform. See display ad this section. [ADVERTISEMENT] ▲

S 49.8 (80.1 km) **A 102.8** (165.4 km) **H 129.7** (208.7 km) Haul road used by loggers removing dead spruce trees. Watch for trucks.

S 49.9 (80.4 km) **A 102.9** (165.7 km) **H 129.6** (208.6 km) **Alaska Rivers Co.,** right side westbound. Rafting daily on the beautiful Kenai River. Half-day scenic float, or full-day canyon trip with white water. Both trips include homemade picnic lunch, excellent viewing of wildlife, professional guides, all

equipment provided. All ages welcome. Personalized guided drift boat fishing for all species of fish. Overnight accommodations available. Family-owned and operated by Cooper Landing residents. Gary Galbraith, owner. (907) 595-1226 for reservations or just stop by. [ADVERTISEMENT]

S 50.1 (80.6 km) **A 103.1** (165.9 km) **H 129.4** (208.2 km) **Alaska Wildland Adventures.** Don't pass up taking a rafting or fishing trip with Alaska Wildland Adventures. You'll enjoy this facility's unique and scenic setting on the Kenai River. They offer daily guided raft trips along with a delicious Alaskan picnic lunch. You can expect to see wildlife and enjoy the scenery of one of the world's most beautiful rivers. If you're seeking a quality fishing experience, ask about their guided fishing trips for salmon and rainbow trout. This company is well known for its professional guides and deluxe boats. All tackle, rods and reels are furnished. Operating since 1977. Phone toll free (800) 478-4100 for more information or reservations. See "Kenai River Trips" display ad. Internet address: www.alaskawildland.com. [ADVERTISEMENT] MP

S 50.4 (81.1 km) **A 103.4** (166.4 km)

H 129.1 (207.8 km) **Juneau Creek**, Dolly Varden and rainbow, mid-June through July.

S 50.5 (81.3 km) **A 103.5** (166.6 km) **H 129** (207.6 km) Bridge over Cooper Creek. USFS Cooper Creek Campground. Camping area on the river side of highway (second entrance westbound) has 7 sites, several on the riverbank. Camping area on the other side of the highway has 23 sites. Both have tables, water and firepits. Fee is $9 single, $13 double. Reservations available, phone (800) 280-CAMP (2267). ▲

S 52 (83.7 km) **A 105** (169 km) **H 127.5** (205.2 km) **Kenai Cache.** See display ad this section.

Gwin's Lodge, Restaurant and Bar, left side southbound. One of Alaska's few remaining traditionally built log roadhouses where Alaskans and visitors alike always stop for food with a homemade touch and

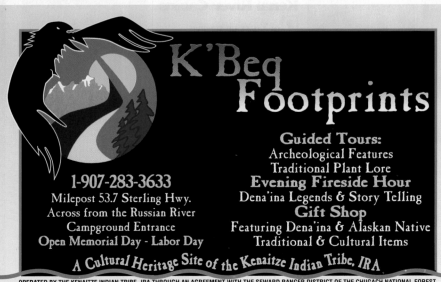

fast, courteous service. At heart of Kenai Peninsula. Closest lodge to nearby Kenai and Russian rivers confluence, Russian Lakes and Resurrection Pass trailheads. World renowned restaurant and bar, package store, modern cabins with private baths, full RV hookups, ice, fishing tackle/licenses, gifts, fish freezing/processing/smoking services. River and saltwater fishing, rafting and booking services. VISA, MasterCard and Discover accepted. (907) 595-1266 (voice); (907) 595-1681 (fax). See display ad. [ADVERTISEMENT] ▲

S 52.6 (84.6 km) **A 105.6** (169.9 km) **H 126.9** (204.2 km) USFS Russian River Campground has 84 sites at the end of a 2-mile/3.2-km road. River access, toilets, water, tables and firepits. Fish cleaning stations and dump station. The Russian River Campground is often full during the summer, particularly during the Russian River red salmon runs. Arrive early! Fees: $11 single RV occupancy, $18 double RV occupancy, $5 12-hour day-use parking, $6 dump station. Concessionaire-operated. For reservations phone (800) 280-CAMP (2267). ▲

Bears attracted by the salmon are frequent visitors to this campground.

Russian Lakes USFS trail, trailhead and parking at Mile 0.9/1.4 km on campground road. Lower Russian Lake at Mile 2.6/4.2 km (elev. 500 feet/152m; hiking time 1½ hours). Good trail to Mile 3/4.8 km. Spur trail to Russian River Falls viewing platform. A good place to view jumping salmon, and a nice family hike. Upper Russian Lake at Mile 12/19.3 km (elev. 690 feet/210m). Trail continues to Cooper Lake at end of Snug Harbor Road (see **Milepost S 47.9**). Public-use cabins along trail. Winter use: good snowmobiling to lower lake only, avalanche danger beyond.

CAUTION: This is brown bear country.

The **Russian River:** Closed to all fishing April 15 through June 10. Bait prohibited at all times in Russian River drainage. Check regulations for limits and other restrictions. Red (sockeye) salmon run starts mid-June. Second run begins July 20–25 and lasts about 3 weeks. Must use flies prior to Aug. 21. Silver (coho) salmon to 15 lbs., run begins mid-August. Catch-and-release only for rainbow trout in lower part of river at all times that season is open.

S 53 (85.3 km) **A 106** (170.6 km) **H 126.5** (203.6 km) Bridge over Kenai River.

S 53.2 (85.6 km) **A 106.2** (170.9 km) **H 126.3** (203.3 km) Well-marked entry point to Resurrection Pass USFS trail; parking at trailhead. This 38-mile-/61-km-long trail climbs to Resurrection Pass (elev. 2,600 feet/792m) and descends to north trailhead near Hope on Turnagain Arm.

S 53.7 (86.4 km) **A 106.7** (171.7 km) **H 125.8** (202.5 km) Cultural heritage site of the Kenaitze Indian tribe; tours, gift shop.

K-Beq Footprints. See display ad this section.

S 54.7 (88 km) **A 107.7** (173.3 km) **H 124.8** (200.8 km) Leaving Chugach National Forest lands westbound. Gravel turnout to east. Many turnouts and access to the Kenai River between here and **Milepost S 58.**

S 55 (88.5 km) **A 108** (173.8 km) **H 124.5** (200.4 km) Kenai–Russian River recreation area, access to Russian River ferry. During salmon season this campground, a favorite with fishermen, is heavily used; toilets, water, dumpsters, interpretive display, pay phone. Fees charged for boat launch, parking or camping. Privately operated 28-person ferry crosses the Kenai River here offering access to good fishing on opposite bank and to the mouth of the Russian River. Ferry fee is $6 adults round-trip, $4 children.

Leaving Game Management Unit 7, entering Unit 15 westbound. Entering Kenai National Wildlife Refuge westbound, administered by the USF&WS; contains more than 1.97 million acres of land set aside to preserve the moose, bear, sheep and other wildlife found here.

S 55.1 (88.7 km) **A 108.1** (174 km) **H 124.4** (200.2 km) Paved turnout.

S 56.4 (90.8 km) **A 109.4** (176.1 km) **H 123.1** (198.1 km) Long, double-ended gravel turnout.

S 57.1 (91.9 km) **A 110.1** (177.2 km) **H 122.4** (197 km) Double-ended turnout to east. Fuller Lake trailhead (well marked), parking. **Lower Fuller Lake**, arctic grayling; **Upper Fuller Lake**, Dolly Varden.

S 58 (93.3 km) **A 111** (178.6 km) **H 121.5** (195.5 km) USF&WS visitor contact station opposite **junction** with Skilak Lake Loop Road. See SKILAK LAKE LOOP ROAD log on page 582. The information cabin is open Memorial Day through Labor Day; brochures and information on Kenai Peninsula attractions including federal, state and local recreation areas, such as Kenai National Wildlife Refuge; restrooms.

S 59 (94.9 km) **A 112** (180.2 km) **H 120.5** (193.9 km) **Milepost S 59.** Actual driving distance between here and **Milepost S 61** is 2.6 miles/4.2 km or 0.6 mile/1 km more than the posts indicate.

S 60.6 (97.5 km) **A 113.6** (182.8 km) **H 118.9** (191.3 km) **Jean Lake**, small campground (3 sites) and picnic area; boat launch, rainbow fishing.

S 61.4 (98.8 km) **A 114.4** (184.1 km) **H 118.1** (190.1 km) Skyline trail to north; double-ended gravel parking area to south.

S 62.3 (100.3 km) **A 115.3** (185.6 km) **H 117.2** (188.6 km) Large gravel turnout to north. Mystery Hills to the north and Hideout Hill to the south.

S 64.5 (103.8 km) **A 117.5** (189.1 km) **H 115** (185.1 km) Gravel turnout to north.

S 68.3 (109.9 km) **A 121.3** (195.2 km) **H 111.2** (179 km) Turnoff to south for Peterson Lake (0.5 mile/0.8 km) and Kelly Lake (1 mile/1.6 km) public campgrounds. Both have tables and firepits for 3 camping parties, water and boat launch, and parking space for self-contained RVs. **Kelly** and **Peterson lakes** have rainbow population. Access to Seven Lakes trail.

S 70.4 (113.3 km) **A 123.4** (198.6 km) **H 109.1** (175.6 km) Egumen wayside with large parking area. East Fork Moose River and Seven Lakes trail. Half-mile marshy trail to **Egumen Lake** (lake not visible from highway); good rainbow population.

S 71.3 (114.7 km) **A 124.3** (200 km) **H 108.2** (174.1 km) Parking area at entrance to Watson Lake public campground; 0.4-mile/0.6-km drive from highway to small campground with 3 sites, toilets, picnic tables, fireplaces, water, dumpsters and steep boat launch (suitable for canoes or hand-carried boats). **Watson Lake**, rainbow.

S 72.8 (117.2 km) **A 125.8** (202.4 km) **H 106.7** (171.7 km) Paved double-ended turnout to south, lake to north.

S 75.2 (121 km) **A 128.2** (206.3 km) **H 104.3** (167.8 km) West **junction** with Skilak Lake Loop Road. See SKILAK LAKE LOOP ROAD log on page 582.

Kenai River from Skilak Lake to Soldotna. Consult regulations for legal tackle,

Skilak Lake Loop Road Log

The 19.1-mile/30.7-km Skilak Lake Loop Road (good gravel) loops south through the Skilak Wildlife Recreation Area to campgrounds, trails and fishing spots. *CAUTION: Do not leave valuables in unattended boats or vehicles.*

Distance from east junction (EJ) with Sterling Highway at Milepost S 58 is followed by distance from west junction (WJ) with Sterling Highway at Milepost S 75.2.

EJ 0 WJ 19.1 (30.7 km) **Junction** with Sterling Highway at **Milepost S 58.**

EJ 0.1 (0.2 km) **WJ 19** (30.5 km) Jim's Landing Day-use area on Kenai River, 0.2 mile/0.3 km from road; toilets, dumpster, tables, firepits, water, boat launch, parking area. Pavement ends westbound.

EJ 0.6 (1 km) **WJ 18.5** (29.7 km) Kenai River trail (6.3-mile/10.1-km hike); parking area.

EJ 2 (3.2 km) **WJ 17.1** (27.5 km) Pothole Lake Overlook turnout overlooks scene of Pothole Lake forest fire of 1991; interpretive sign on fire.

EJ 2.4 (3.9 km) **WJ 16.7** (26.8 km) Kenai River trail (6.3-mile/10.1-km hike); parking area.

EJ 3.6 (5.8 km) **WJ 15.5** (24.9 km) Hidden Lake Campground is an exceptionally nice camping area with 44 sites on paved loop roads. Located 0.5 mile/0.8 km in from the road on the lakeshore, it has picnic pavilions, a dump station, wheelchair-accessible toilets, tables, water, firepits and boat launch. Campfire programs in amphitheater. Observation deck for viewing wildlife. Campground hosts in residence. Camping fee $10 for vehicles. Trailer parking area, interpretive exhibits and kitchen shelter with barbecue. ♿▲

Hidden Lake, lake trout average 16 inches and kokanee 9 inches, year-round, best from May 15 to July 1, use spoon, red-and-white or weighted, by trolling, casting and jigging. This lake is a favorite among local ice fishermen from late December through March.

EJ 4.7 (7.6 km) **WJ 14.4** (23.1 km) Hidden Creek trail (1.5-mile/2.4-km hike); parking area.

EJ 5.3 (8.5 km) **WJ 13.8** (22.2 km) Hidden Creek Overlook double-ended turnout; view of one arm of Skilak Lake; forest fire damage from 1996 fire visible.

View of Kenai River from Jim's Landing on Skilak Lake Loop Road.

(Jerrianne Lowther, staff)

EJ 5.5 (8.9 km) **WJ 13.6** (21.8 km) Skilak Lookout trail (2.6-mile/4.2-km hike); parking area.

EJ 6.2 (10 km) **WJ 12.9** (20.7 km) Bear Mountain trail (1-mile/1.6-km hike); parking area with firepit across from lily pond.

EJ 6.9 (11.1 km) **WJ 12.2** (19.6 km) Scenic viewpoint of Skilak Lake.

EJ 8.5 (13.6 km) **WJ 10.6** (17 km) Upper Skilak Lake Campground, drive 2 miles/3.2 km around Lower Ohmer Lake; 0.2-mile/0.3-km loop road through campground. There are 25 campsites (some sites on lakeshore), boat launch, toilets and tables; similar facilities to Hidden Lake Campground (**Milepost EJ 3.6**). Camping fee $10/vehicle, $6/tent site (walk-in). ▲

Lower Ohmer Lake, rainbow 14 to 16 inches, year-round. **Skilak Lake** offers rainbow and Dolly Varden. Red (sockeye) salmon enter lake in mid-July.

EJ 8.6 (13.8 km) **WJ 10.5** (16.9 km) Lower Ohmer Lake, short side road to parking area on lake; 3 campsites, toilet, boat launch, firepits, tables. ▲

EJ 9.5 (15.2 km) **WJ 9.6** (15.4 km) Short side road to **Engineer Lake,** boat launch and Seven Lakes trail; turnaround and parking area with firepits. Stocked silver salmon to 15 inches, best in July.

EJ 9.6 (15.4 km) **WJ 9.5** (15.3 km) Engineer Lake wayside; gravel turnout.

EJ 11.5 (18.5 km) **WJ 7.6** (12.2 km) Dump station on paved double-ended turnout to east.

EJ 13.8 (22.2 km) **WJ 6.3** (8.5 km) Well-marked 1-mile/1.6-km side road to Lower Skilak Lake Campground; 14 sites, tables, toilets, firepits, boat launch. ▲

CAUTION: Skilak Lake is cold; winds are fierce and unpredictable. Wear life jackets!

EJ 14.2 (22.8 km) **WJ 4.9** (7.8 km) Fire guard station.

EJ 18.7 (30.1 km) **WJ 0.4** (0.6 km) Bottinentnin Lake; well-marked side road leads 0.3 mile/0.5 km to parking area on lakeshore. Shallow lake: No sport fish, but nice area for recreational canoeing.

EJ 19.1 (30.7 km) **WJ 0 Junction** with Sterling Highway at **Milepost S 75.2.**

Return to Milepost S 58 or S 75.2 Sterling Highway

limits and seasons. King salmon 20 to 80 lbs., use spinners, excellent fishing June to August; red salmon 6 to 12 lbs., many, but hard to catch, use flies, best from July 15 to Aug. 10; pink salmon 4 to 8 lbs., abundant fish on even years Aug. 1 to Sept. 1, spoons; silver salmon 6 to 15 lbs., use spoons, Aug. 15 to Nov. 1; rainbow, Dolly Varden 15 to 20 inches, June through September, use spinners, winged bobber, small-weighted spoon.

NOTE: The Kenai River Special Management Area is managed by the Alaska Division of Parks and Outdoor Recreation (DPOR), and includes the waters of Kenai and Skilak lakes and the Kenai River. Motors are limited to maximum 35 horsepower on the river, and prohibited on some sections. For more information, contact DPOR at P.O. Box 1247, Soldotna, AK 99669, phone (907) 262-5581.

S 76.2 (122.6 km) **A 129.2** (207.9 km) **H 103.3** (166.2 km) Large double-ended gravel turnout to east.

Campbell Handmade Knives. See display ad this section.

S 79.2 (127.4 km) **A 132.2** (212.7 km) **H 100.3** (161.4 km) Kenai Keys Road. Divided highway begins southbound.

S 80.3 (129.2 km) **A 133.3** (214.5 km)

H 99.2 (159.6 km) Turnoff for Peninsula Furs and Bing's Landing State Recreation Site with RV and tent camping at 36 sites, picnic area, water, boat launch, toilets (wheelchair accessible), dumpster and access to Kenai River. Camping fee $8/night or annual pass. Boat launch fee $5 or annual boat launch pass. $5 day-use parking fee. ♿▲

Peninsula Furs. See display ad this section.

S 80.6 (129.7 km) **A 133.6** (215 km) **H 98.9** (159.2 km) Double-ended paved turnout to east.

S 81 (130.3 km) **A 134** (215.6 km) **H 98.5** (158.5 km) **STERLING** (pop. 1,732; elev. 150 feet/45m). Traveler services include 2 gas stations, 2 motels, several restaurants and cafes; gift, grocery, hardware, antique, fur and furniture stores, laundromat and several campgrounds. Post office at **Milepost S 81.6.** (Businesses with a Sterling mailing address extend west to **Milepost S 85.**) Nearby recreational opportunities include fishing and the extensive canoe trail system (see description at **Milepost S 82**). Moose River Raft Race and Sterling Days held in July.

Bing Brown's RV Park & Motel. See display ad this section. ▲

S 81.1 (130.5 km) **A 134.1** (215.8 km) **H 98.4** (158.4 km) Gift shop and grocery store.

S 81.6 (131.3 km) **A 134.6** (216.6 km) **H 97.9** (157.6 km) Sterling post office (ZIP code 99672).

S 81.7 (131.5 km) **A 134.7** (216.8 km) **H 97.8** (157.4 km) **Aurora Alaska Seafood.** See display ad this section.

Cook's Corner. See display ad this section. ▲

Vacation Cabins. See display ad this section.

S 82 (132 km) **A 135** (217.3 km) **H 97.5** (156.9 km) Pay phone on highway just

before turnoff for Izaak Walton State Recreation Site, located at the confluence of the Kenai and Moose rivers. Paved access road, 25 campsites, parking, tables, toilets, water and dumpster. Camping fee $10/night or annual pass. Boat launch ($5 fee or annual boat launch pass) and good access to Kenai River. A small log cabin, totem pole and an information sign about Moose River archaeological site. ▲

Sterling Chevron & Food Mart. See display ad this section.

Bridge over Moose River. *CAUTION: Drive carefully during fishing season when fishermen walk along bridge and highway.*

Canoe rentals and shuttle bus service to the head of the canoe trail system are available by the Moose River bridge. This is the terminus of the Swan Lake canoe trail. There are 2 canoe routes in Kenai National Wildlife Refuge: Swan Lake route, a 60-mile/97-km route connecting 30 lakes; and the Swanson River route, an 80-mile/129-km route linking 40 lakes. Guided canoe tours and fishing charters are available. Portions of the canoe system may be traveled, taking anywhere from 1 to 4 days. Contact Kenai National Wildlife Refuge, Box 2139, Soldotna, AK 99669 for details. See SWANSON RIVER/SWAN LAKE ROAD log opposite page.

Moose River, 0.3 mile/0.4 km of fishing down to confluence with Kenai River. Sockeyes here in June. Big summer run of reds follows into August; silvers into October.

Kenai and **Moose rivers** (confluence), Dolly Varden and rainbow trout, salmon (king, red, pink, silver). June 15 through October for trout; year-round for Dolly Varden. King salmon from May through July, pink salmon in August and silver salmon from August through October. This is a fly-fishing-only area from May 15 through Aug. 15; closed to fishing from boats, May 15 until the end of the king salmon season or July 31, whichever is later.

Bald eagle perched near the Kenai River watches for a meal. (© Loren Taft, Alaskan Images)

S 82.2 (132.3 km) **A 135.2** (217.6 km) **H 97.3** (156.6 km) **Martin Mines.** Dawson City atmosphere. Gold nugget jewelry manufactured on site. We have a large selection of Alaska gold nuggets in the gift shop. Economy bunkhouse lodging with showers. RV parking, tackle shop, guide service, fish freezing and fishing pole rental available. Box 261, Sterling, AK 99672. Phone (907) 260-3300 or (907) 262-7570. [ADVERTISEMENT]

S 82.3 (132.4 km) **A 135.3** (217.7 km) **H 97.2** (156.4 km) **Alaska Adventure Reservations.** Charters, fly-ins, bear-viewing camp; 5 or 7 days. Canoe outfitting. Budget camp and fish trips; salmon, halibut and trout. Budget camping trips. We do it all! Phone (800) 544-2261; fax (907) 262-8797; web page: www.greatalaska.com; e-mail: greatalaska@greatalaska.com. See display ad this section. [ADVERTISEMENT]

S 82.5 (132.8 km) **A 135.5** (218.1 km) **H 97** (156.1 km) Keyston Road.

Big Sky Charter & Fish Camp. See display ad this section.

S 82.6 (132.9 km) **A 135.6** (218.2 km) **H 96.9** (155.9 km) Airstrip. Restaurant and bar.

Swanson River/Swan Lake Road Log

Swanson River Road leads north 17.2 miles/27.7 km, where it junctions with Swan Lake Road, which leads east 12.7 miles/20.4 km and dead ends at Paddle Lake. Both roads provide access to fishing, hiking trails and canoe trails. *CAUTION: Do not leave valuables in vehicles at canoe trailheads.*

Distance from junction with the Sterling Highway (J) is shown.

J 0 Junction with Sterling Highway at **Milepost S 83.4.** Swanson River Road is a good gravel road but can be rough in spots; slow speeds are advised. There are numerous turnouts suitable for overnight camping in self-contained RVs.

J 0.7 (1.1 km) Robinson Loop Road; rejoins Sterling Highway at **Milepost S 87.5.**

J 1.3 (2.1 km) Airstrip.

J 4.4 (7.1 km) Entering Kenai National Wildlife Refuge.

J 7.9 (12.7 km) **Mosquito Lake**, turnout; 0.5-mile trail to lake. Rainbow trout.

J 9.1 (14.6 km) **Silver Lake** trailhead and parking: 1-mile/1.6-km hike to lake. Rainbow trout and arctic char.

J 9.8 (15.8 km) **Finger Lake** trailhead: 2.3-mile/3.7-km hike to lake. Good arctic char fishing.

J 10.6 (17.1 km) **Forest Lake** wayside, parking: 0.3-mile/0.5-km trail to lake. Rainbow trout; best fished from canoe or raft.

J 13 (20.9 km) **Weed Lake** wayside: small turnout by lake. Rainbow trout.

J 13.3 (21.4 km) **Drake** and **Skookum lakes** trailhead and parking; 2-mile/3.2-km trail. Rainbow trout and arctic char.

J 14 (22.5 km) Access to Breeze Lake.

J 14.2 (22.9 km) **Dolly Varden Lake** Campground; 15 sites, water, toilets, boat launch. Large RVs and trailers note: 0.5-mile/0.8-km access road to campground is narrow and bumpy; check turnaround space before driving in. Fishing for Dolly Varden and rainbow; best in late August and September. ▲

J 14.9 (24 km) Access road to canoe trails to east. Oil field road to west closed to private vehicles. The Swanson River Road was originally built as an access road to the Swanson River oil field. Chevron operated the field from 1958 to 1986; it is currently operated by Unocal.

J 15.7 (25.2 km) **Rainbow Lake** Campground; small 3-unit camping area on lakeshore with toilets, water and boat launch. Fishing for Dolly Varden and rainbow trout. *CAUTION: Steep road; difficult turnaround. Large RVs: check visually before driving in.* ▲

J 17.2 (27.7 km) **Junction** with Swan Lake Road. Continue north 0.5 mile/0.8 km for Swanson River Landing at end of Swanson River Road; camping area with picnic tables, firepits, water, toilets, boat launch, large gravel parking area. This is the terminus of the Swanson River canoe route, which begins at Paddle Lake at the end of Swan Lake Road. Log now follows Swan Lake Road east. ▲

J 17.3 (27.8 km) Kenai National Wildlife Refuge Outdoor Environmental Education Center. Reservation required. Educational group-use permits obtained at Kenai National Wildlife Refuge Visitor Center in Soldotna.

J 20.2 (32.5 km) **Fish Lake**; 3 sites, tables, firepits, toilets. Fishing for Dolly Varden.

J 21.2 (34 km) **Canoe Lake**, parking. West entrance to Swan Lake canoe route. Fishing for Dolly Varden.

J 21.8 (35.1 km) Sucker Creek wayside; campsite, table, fireplace. **Sucker Lake**, rainbow trout.

J 23.3 (37.5 km) **Merganser Lakes**, 0.5 mile/0.8 km south; rainbow trout.

J 25.4 (40.9 km) Nest Lakes trail, 0.5-mile/0.8-km hike north.

J 26.9 (43.3 km) Large turnout and toilet to west.

J 27 (43.5 km) **Portage Lake**. East entrance to Swan Lake canoe route. Lake is stocked with coho salmon.

J 27.3 (43.9 km) Informal pullout on lake.

J 29.4 (47.3 km) Y in road; bear left.

J 29.9 (48.1 km) End of road. **Paddle Lake** entrance to Swanson River canoe route; parking, picnic table, water and toilet. Fishing for rainbow and Dolly Varden.

Return to Milepost S 83.4 Sterling Highway

S 82.8 (133.3 km) **A 135.8** (218.5 km) **H 96.7** (155.6 km) Truck weigh station; senior center across highway.

Highway narrows to 2 lanes southbound.

S 83.4 (134.2 km) **A 136.4** (219.5 km) **H 96.1** (154.7 km) **Junction** with Swanson River and Scout Lake Loop roads. Swanson River Road turnoff to north (see SWANSON RIVER/SWAN LAKE ROAD log above). Scout Lake Loop Road turns off to south and rejoins the Sterling Highway at **Milepost S 85** (see milepost for description). Sterling elementary school.

Convenience store with gas, church, laundromat and showers located on Swanson River Road, just past intersection.

Sterling Baptist Church. See display ad this section.

The Wash Out Laundromat. See display ad this section.

ZIPMART. See display ad this section.

S 84.3 (135.7 km) **A 137.3** (221 km)

H 95.2 (153.2 km) **Scout Lake Inn and Nicki's Restaurant**, located near the Kenai and Moose rivers. Good fishing June to August 15. Clean, modern rooms with phones, satellite TV, and in-room coffee. Guaranteed lower rates than Soldotna. Nicki's specializes in homemade cinnamon rolls, breads and pies. We have the "locals" stamp of approval for the best food. Visit our Alaskan gift shop. Phone (907) 262-5898. [ADVERTISEMENT]

S 84.9 (136.6km) **A 137.9** (221.9 km) **H 94.6** (152.2 km) Scout Lake State Recreation Site to south on Scout Lake Loop Road; 12 campsites, water, toilets, covered picnic shelter. Camping fee $8/night or annual pass.

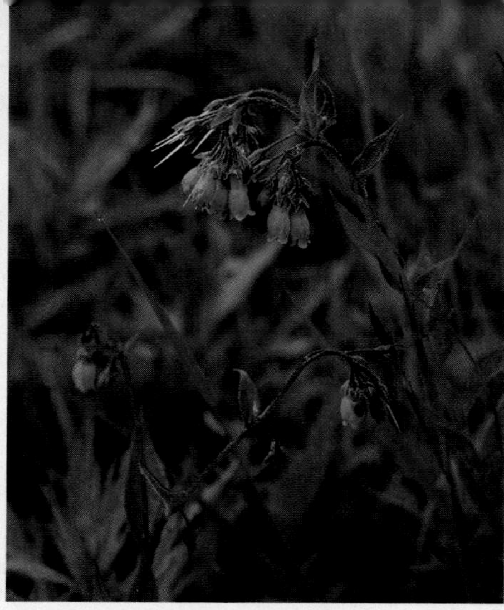

Chiming bells (Mertensia paniculata).
(© Beth Davidow)

Scout Lake Loop Road loops south of the Sterling Highway for 7 miles/11.3 km and rejoins the Sterling Highway at **Milepost S 83.4.** Turn here and drive down Scout Lake Loop Road 1.6 miles/2.6 km to turnoff for Morgan's Landing: follow side road 2.4 miles/3.9 km to reach Morgan's Landing State Recreation Area; $10 nightly fee per vehicle or annual pass, 42 developed campsites with 10 pull-through sites and some double sites, toilets and water. $5 day-use fee or annual pass. Alaska State Parks area headquarters is located here. ▲

Cast Away Riverside RV Park. See display ad this section. ▲

Good access from Morgan's Landing to the **Kenai River**, king salmon from mid-June through July, average 30 lbs. Red (sockeye) salmon average 8 lbs., use flies in July and August; silver (coho) salmon to 15 lbs., August and September, use lure; pink salmon average 4 lbs. with lure, best in July, even-numbered years only; rainbow and Dolly Varden, use lure, June through August.

Divided highway ends southbound.

S 87.5 (140.8 km) **A 140.5** (226.1 km) **H 92** (148.1 km) Robinson Loop Road. Equestrian center.

S 88 (141.6 km) **A 141** (226.9 km) **H 91.5** (147.3 km) St. Theresa's Drive.

Longmere Lake Lodge B&B. Look for blue highway sign. Follow St. Theresa's/Edgington to Ryan. Beautiful lakeside setting. Comfortable, spacious accommodations. Large stone fireplace, Alaskan artifacts. Relax and enjoy the scenery. Master bedrooms

with full private baths, or complete unit with kitchen. Guided salmon, halibut, hiking, bird watching, flightseeing arranged. Longtime Alaskan hosts. P.O. Box 1707, Soldotna, AK 99669. Phone (907) 262-9799. Website: www.bbonline.com/ak/longmere. E-mail: bblodge@ptialaska.net. [ADVERTISEMENT] MP

S 88.3 (142.1 km) **A 141.3** (227.4 km) **H 91.2** (146.8 km) **Alaska Horn & Antler.** See display ad this section.

S 91.3 (146.9 km) **A 144.3** (232.2 km) **H 88.2** (141.9 km) Gas station, convenience store and RV repair.

S 91.8 (147.7 km) **A 144.8** (233 km) **H 87.7** (141.1 km) **Aurora Alaska Premium Smoked Salmon and Seafoods.** Home of the best gourmet-Alaskan smoked salmon and halibut products in the world. We offer a wide variety of products, from refrigerated to non-refrigerated (shelf stable). All our products are low in salt and contain no artificial colors, flavors, or preservatives. They are all-natural. Got your own fish to smoke? We will custom smoke (kipper) or pickle your sport-caught salmon or halibut for you. We will also vacuum pack, freeze, store, box and ship your fish. No luck fishing? Come in and choose from our own specially prepared smoked products. Choose from our world-famous smoked salmon jerky, which is available in 4 delicious flavors, smoked salmon or halibut fillets, canned smoked salmon and halibut, pickled salmon and halibut, smoked salmon and cream cheese spread, or our assorted retort products. Gift packs also available. Remember, whether it is a gift of appreciation or for something grand, we can help in selecting the right gift for that special someone or important client, even if that someone is you. Come in to try our free samples. Two locations to choose from. Box 4085, Soldotna, AK 99669. Phone or fax (907) 262-7007, or dial toll free at (800) 653-FISH (3474). See display ad this section. [ADVERTISEMENT]

S 92 (148 km) **A 145** (233.3 km) **H 87.5** (140.8 km) Public golf course, driving range and cottages.

S 92.4 (148.7 km) **A 145.4** (234 km) **H 87.1** (140.2 km) State Division of Forest, Land and Water Management. Fire danger indicator sign.

S 92.7 (149.1 km) **A 145.7** (234.5 km) **H 86.8** (139.7 km) Mackey Lake Road. Private lodging is available on this side road.

Bill Slemp's Cabin Rentals. See display ad this section.

S 93 (149.7 km) **A 146** (235 km) **H 86.5** (139.2 km) **Eagles' Nest Bed N' Breakfast**. See display ad this section.

S 93.1 (149.8 km) **A 146.1** (235.1 km) **H 86.4** (139 km) Loren Lake.

S 93.7 (150.8 km) **A 146.7** (236.1 km) **H 85.8** (138.1 km) Four-lane highway begins and leads through Soldotna.

Two moose calves browse along the Sterling Highway near Soldotna. (© Barbara Willard)

S 94 (151.2 km) **A 147** (236.6 km) **H 85.5** (137.6 km) Traffic light to shops and gas.

S 94.1 (151.4 km) **A 147.1** (236.7 km) **H 85.4** (137.4 km) Restaurant. Turn on East Redoubt Street and follow the gravel road 0.5 mile/0.8 km for Swiftwater Park municipal campground. The municipal campground has 20 spaces on **Kenai River** (some pull-throughs), some tables, firepits, firewood, phone, dump station, 2-week limit, litter barrels, toilets, boat landing, fee charged, good fishing.

S 94.2 (151.6 km) **A 147.2** (236.9 km) **H 85.3** (137.3 km) **Junction** with Kenai Spur Highway. This junction is called the Soldotna Y.

There are 2 ways to reach the city of Kenai (see description of city on page 602): Turn right (westbound) at the Y, physical **Milepost S 94.2**, and continue 11 miles/17.7 km northwest to Kenai via the Kenai Spur Highway; or continue on the Sterling High-

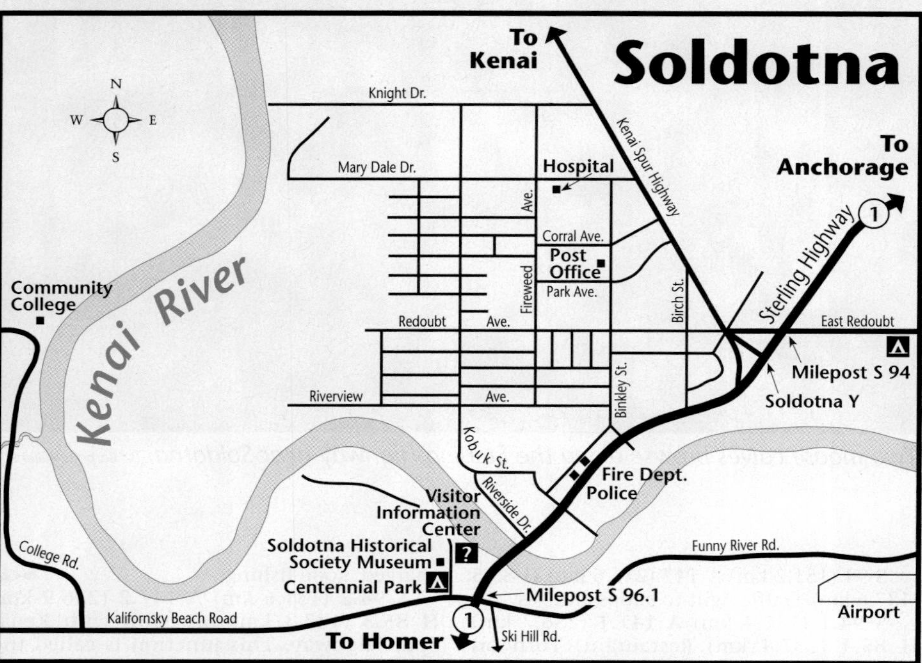

way to **Milepost S 96.1** and turn right (southbound) on the Kalifornsky Beach Road and continue 9.3 miles/14.9 km to Kenai via the Warren Ames Memorial Bridge. For details see KENAI SPUR HIGHWAY log page 599 and KALIFORNSKY BEACH ROAD log page 606. Description of Soldotna follows.

S 94.4 (151.9 km) **A 147.4** (237.2 km) **H 85.1** (137 km) Soldotna DOT/PF highway maintenance station, gas station. Turn east here for access to Soldotna Creek Park (day use only). Follow road behind restaurant.

S 95 (152.9 km) **A 148** (238.2 km) **H 84.5** (136 km) Soldotna city center; Peninsula Center shopping mall. Turn on Binkley Street for access to fire station, police station and post office.

Homer-bound travelers continue south across the Kenai River bridge past visitor center. Turn west on Kalifornsky Beach Road for Centennial Park, the Soldotna city campground, and Soldotna Historical Society Museum. The Slikok Valley School, the last of the Alaska Territory log schools, built in 1958, is one of the attractions at the museum's log village. Turn east off the Sterling Highway on Funny River Road for airport. See description at **Milepost S 96.1**.

Log of the Sterling Highway continues on page 605.

Soldotna

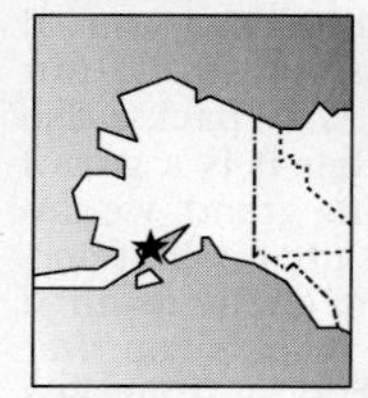

S 95.2 (153.2 km) **A 148.2** (238.5 km) **H 84.3** (135.7 km) On the western Kenai Peninsula, the city stretches over a mile southwest along the Sterling Highway and northwest along the Kenai Spur Highway. **Population:** 4,092; Kenai Peninsula Borough 44,411. **Emergency Services:** Phone 911 for all emergency services. **Alaska State Troopers** at Mile 22 Kalifornsky Beach Road just off Sterling Highway, phone (907) 262-4453. **City Police,** phone (907) 262-4455. **Fire Department,** phone (907) 262-4792. **Ambulance,** phone (907) 262-4500. **Hospital,** Central Peninsula General, 1 mile/1.6 km north of Public Safety Building off Marydale Drive, phone (907) 262-4404.

Visitor Information: The Soldotna Visitor Information Center is located in downtown Soldotna on the Sterling Highway south of the Kenai River bridge. River access to walkway built for bank and fish-habitat protection. The center is open 7 days a week, May through September, 9 A.M. to 7 P.M. The remainder of the year the center is open weekdays from 9 A.M. to 5 P.M. Write: Greater Soldotna Chamber of Commerce, 44790 Sterling Highway, Soldotna, AK 99669; phone (907) 262-1337 or 262-9814, fax (907) 262-3566. E-mail: solchmbr@ptialaska.net.

Elevation: 115 feet/35m. **Climate:** Average daily temperature in July, 63°F to 68°F/17°C to 20°C; January, 19°F to 23°F/ -7°C to -5°C. Annual precipitation, approximately 18 inches. **Radio:** KGTL 620, KFQD 750, KSRM 920, KGTL-FM 100.9/103.5, MBN-FM 95.3/97.7, KWHQ-FM 1001, KPEN-FM 101-7, KZXX 980, KSLP-AM 1140. **Television:** Channels 2, 4, 9, 12 and 13 via booster line from Anchorage, cable and KANG public education channel. **Newspapers:** *Peninsula Clarion* (daily), *The Dispatch* (weekly).

Private Aircraft: Soldotna airstrip, 0.9 mile/1.4 km southeast; elev. 107 feet/32m; length 5,000 feet/1,524m; asphalt; fuel 100LL; unattended.

The town of Soldotna was established in the 1940s because of its strategic location at the Sterling–Kenai Spur Highway junction. (Visitors may see the homestead cabin, which became Soldotna's first post office in 1949, at its original location on the Kenai Spur Highway at Corral Street.) Soldotna was named for a nearby stream; it is a Russian word meaning "soldier," although some believe the name came from an Indian word meaning the "stream fork."

Soldotna was incorporated as a first-class city in 1967. It has a council–manager form of government. Kenai Peninsula Borough headquarters and state offices of the Departments of Highways, Public Safety, Fish and Game, and Forest, Land and Water Management are located here. Soldotna is also headquarters for the Kenai Peninsula Borough school district. There are 3 elementary schools, a junior high school and 2 high schools. University of Alaska–Kenai Peninsula College is also located in Soldotna.

Area terrain is level and forested, with many streams and lakes nearby. Large rivers of the area are the Swanson River, the Moose River and the Kenai River, which empties into Cook Inlet just south of Kenai. The area affords a majestic view of volcanic mountains across Cook Inlet. Always snow-covered, they are Mount Spurr (elev. 11,100 feet/3,383m), which erupted in 1992; Mount Iliamna (elev. 10,016 feet/3,053m), which has 3 smaller peaks to the left of the larger one; and Mount Redoubt (elev. 10,197 feet/3,108m), which was identified by its very regular cone shape until it erupted in December 1989.

ACCOMMODATIONS/VISITOR SERVICES

All modern conveniences and facilities are available, including supermarkets, banks, hotels/motels, restaurants and drive-ins, medical and dental clinics, bowling alley, golf course, veterinarians, churches and a library. Two shopping malls are located on the Sterling Highway near the center of town. Bed-and-breakfasts, cabin rentals and lodges also offer accommodations.

Accommodations and Tours Alaskan Style. When you need help with your vacation plans—call us. We know where the good charters, tours and deals are. We book only vendors that we personally know, and

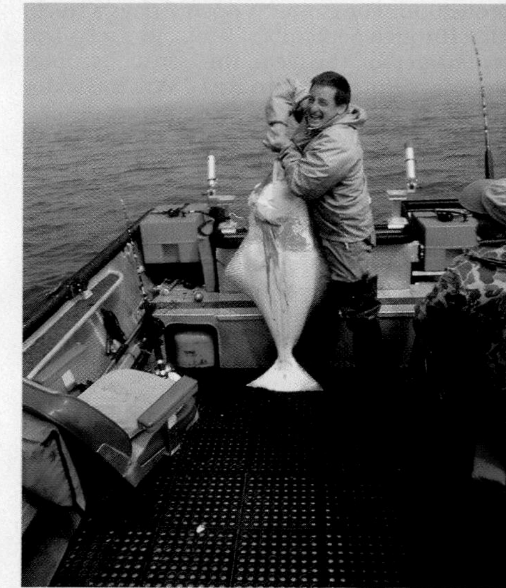

Showing off a 70-lb. halibut caught in Cook Inlet. (© Bill Sherwonit)

SOLDOTNA ADVERTISERS

Accommodations and Tours Alaska Style.................Ph. (800) 262-1421
Accommodations on the Kenai...................Ph. (907) 262-2139
Across The River RV Park......................Ph. (907) 262-0458
Alaska Angler.....................Ph. (907) 262-1416
Alaska Creative Vacations.Ph. (907) 262-5665
Alaska Fishing charters.....Ph. (907) 262-4779
Alaska Recreational Rentals......................Ph. (907) 262-2700
Alaskan Holiday Suites......Ph. (907) 262-9635
Alaskan Hospitality Bed and Breakfast.....................Ph. (907) 260-5388
Beemun's Variety Store.....................35277 Kenai Spur Hwy.
Best Western King Salmon Motel, Restaurant & RV Park.......Kenai Spur Hwy.
Big Eddy Campground.....End of Big Eddy Rd.
Birch Tree Gallery......Mile 0.2 Funny River Rd.
Blazy's B&B.....................Ph. (907) 262-4591
Bo's Fishing Guide Service........................Ph. (800) 699-5154
Centennial Campground..Ph. (907) 262-5299
Custom Seafood Processors..................Ph. (907) 262-9691
Diamond M. Ranch..........Ph. (907) 283-9424
Donna's Country & Victorian Gifts.........................Blazy's Soldotna Mall
Donnie Smith—Kenai River Guide................Ph. (907) 262-7787
Double Eagle RV Park.......Ph. (907) 262-5489
Edgewater RV park..........Ph. (907) 262-7733
EZ Limit Guide Service......Ph. (907) 262-6169
Fenton Bros. Guided Sportfishing................Ph. (907) 262-2502
First Baptist Church.................159 Binkley St.
Frames & Things Gallery West............................Blazy's Soldotna Mall
Fun Fishin' Alaska............Ph. (800) 234-7406
Gold Strike Lanes.............Ph. (907) 262-9065
Gull's Landing B&B...........Ph. (907) 262-6668
Greater Soldotna Chamber of Commerce............................Sterling Hwy.
Hardy's Alaskan Adventures.................Ph. (907) 262-9881
Harry Gaines Kenai River Fishing Guide..............Ph. (907) 262-5097
Irish Lord Charters............Ph. (907) 262-9512
Jim Rusk Fishing Guide.....Ph. (907) 262-4911
Johnson Bros. Guides & Outfitters................................Downtown
Johnson's Landing Lodge.Ph. (907) 262-5965
Kenai Custom Seafoods....Mile 14.4 Kalifornsky Beach Rd.
Kenai Peninsula Condos...Ph. (907) 262-1383
Kenai River Lodge..............Kenai River Bridge
Kenai River Raven Bed & Breakfast..........Ph. (800) 262-5818
Kenai River Retreat..........Ph. (907) 262-1361
Kenai Wash & Dry............Ph. (907) 283-9973
Kings Kitchen Bed & Breakfast..........Ph. (907) 262-2973
King's Budget Charters....Ph. (907) 262-4564
Klondike City..............Mile 95.5 Sterling Hwy.
Knight Manor Bed & Breakfast.................Ph. (907) 262-2438
MACtel.............................Ph. (907) 262-3500
Marydale Manor Apartment Suites.........Ph. (888) 261-9238
Moose Hollow Bed & Breakfast....................Ph. (907) 262-7526
Mykel's Restaurant & Lounge...........Mile 0.2 Kenai Spur Hwy.
Northland Gallery & Wildlife Studio...........................At the 'Y'
Oil Exchange, The............Ph. (907) 262-3954
Orca Lodge......................Ph. (907) 262-5649
Peninsula Center Mall...................Downtown
Poppy Ridge Bed & Breakfast.................Ph. (907) 262-4230
River Quest RV Park..........Ph. (907) 283-4991
River Terrace RV Park.......Ph. (907) 262-5593
Riverside Auto Supply Inc........................Kenai River Bridge
Robin Place Fabrics...........Ph. (907) 262-5438
Rod 'N Real Charters........Ph. (907) 262-6064
Salmon Haus....................Ph. (907) 262-2400
Sal's Klondike Diner....Mile 95.5 Sterling Hwy.
Skyline Bed & Breakfast....Ph. (907) 262-9890
Soldotna Bed & Breakfast Lodge...........Ph. (907) 262-4779
Soldotna Inn............Mile 0.2 Kenai Spur Hwy.
Soldotna Wash & Dry.......................At the 'Y'
Swiftwater Campground..Ph. (907) 262-3151
Tom's Cabins & Guide Service..............Ph. (907) 262-3197
Wildflower Inn.................Ph. (800) 557-WILD

can vouch for the quality of their products. All of our lodging is personally inspected to ensure clean, safe, quality accommodations. Ask about our specially priced packages. P.O. Box 3151, Kenai, AK 99611. Phone (800) 313-3226. Internet: www.ptialaska~ravens/aktours.htm/. [ADVERTISEMENT]

Alaskan Holiday Suites. Two-bedroom, 2-bath suites with fully equipped kitchens. Suites accommodate up to 6. Convenient location, close to all services and just a short walk to the famous Kenai River. Continental breakfast. Free local calls. Cable TV. Guide reservations available. VISA/MasterCard accepted. Reservations: (907) 694-7615 or (907) 262-9635. See display ad. [ADVERTISEMENT]

Best Western King Salmon Motel, Restaurant and RV Park, downtown Soldotna on Kenai Spur Highway. Large rooms, queen beds, some kitchenettes, cable TV, phones. Free in-room coffee. Restaurant serves early fisherman's breakfast, lunch, dinner. Steaks, seafood, salad bar. Beer and wine available. Fishing licenses, ice. Fish processing close by. RV park with 39 pull-through spaces, full hookups, restrooms, coin-operated showers and laundry. Phone (907) 262-5857; fax (907) 262-9441. See display ad this section. [ADVERTISEMENT] ▲

Gulls Landing B&B. Lovely Vermont-style home. Wooded Kenai River setting near Soldotna "Y." River curls around 3 viewing decks. Large fishing/boating dock. Separate entrance, equipped kitchenette, private river-view living room. TV/VCR. Three sizable river-view bedrooms. Queen, twin, king beds. Two bathrooms, one private. Friendly hostess. Delicious breakfasts. VISA, MasterCard. 485 Lingonberry Lane, Soldotna, AK 99669. (907) 262-6668. [ADVERTISEMENT]

Orca Lodge. Beautiful, hand-crafted log cabins on the world-famous Kenai River near Soldotna. Kitchens, outdoor barbecue, dock.

Guided salmon, trout and halibut fishing, raft trips, flightseeing, glacier tours. 3–7 night packages. Box 4653, Soldotna, AK

Kenai River Raven Bed & Breakfast

PO Box 1670, Soldotna, AK 99669 • (907) 262-5818
Fax (907) 260-3972 • email: akrraven@alaska.net

1-888-262-5818

• Elegant new log home . . . located on the Kenai River.
• Four bedrooms . . . private jacuzzi bath and shower .
• Centrally located in Soldotna . . . yet private.
• Continental or full breakfast.
•Fishing charters upon request.
• Opened all year round.

OWNERS/OPERATORS, MOTHER & DAUGHTER : MARY & CHRIS WYNE

SOLDOTNA Bed & Breakfast LODGE & FISH ALASKA with ALASKA FISHING CHARTERS

The finest lodging in Alaska combined with Alaska's top guide service • Fishing, Lodge or Combination Packages Available

Lovely 16-room European Home on the banks of the Kenai River • Tastefully Decorated
Walking distance to Restaurants & Shopping
• Comfortable Beds • Recommended by Alaska Best Places

Checks Accepted • 5% extra for credit cards

399 Lovers Lane, Soldotna, AK 99669

Fish for Kings, Reds & Silver Salmon
Custom Fishing Packages
Professional, Licensed Fishing Guides
Accommodations for up to 50 Guests

(907) 262-4779 • FAX (907) 262-3201
e-mail: akfish@alaska.net
http://www.supershadow.net/akfishandlodge

99669. Phone (907) 262-5649. Web address: http://www.alaskaOne.com/orcalodge; e-mail: fishorca@alaska.net. [ADVERTISEMENT]

For Swiftwater Campground, turn on East Redoubt Street at **Milepost S 94.1** Sterling Highway. Centennial Park Campground is 0.1 mile/0.2 km from the Sterling Highway just south of the Kenai River bridge on Kalifornsky Beach Road; turn west at **Milepost S 96.1**. Both campgrounds are owned by the City of Soldotna. Register for camping at either park; camping fees charged. Wheelchair accessible. Dump station available at Centennial Park Campground. Campsites for both tents and RVs (no hookups). These campgrounds are heavily used; good idea to check in early. There are several private campgrounds located in and near Soldotna; see ads this section and contact the chamber of commerce. ♿▲

Across the River RV Park. Bank fishing for reds, silvers, rainbows. Guided fishing for kings, silvers and halibut. Fly-out fishing charters also available. Public boat launch close by. Fish cleaning tables, ice, DEC approved fresh water, dump station. Electric hookups, laundry, showers, phone. Call 1-800-276-2434, (907) 262-0458. Box 2134, Soldotna, AK 99669. Mile 13.8 Funny River Road. E-mail: acrosstheriver@hotmail.com. See display ad. [ADVERTISEMENT] ▲

Edgewater RV Park on the banks of world famous Kenai River, across from the Soldotna visitors' center. Full and partial hookups, laundry, showers, grassy sites, picnic tables, local guide service and fish cleaning facilities. Bank fishing. Walk to stores, restaurants. Reservations and information: (907) 262-7733. P.O. Box 976, Soldotna, AK 99669. [ADVERTISEMENT] ▲

River Terrace RV Park features 1,100 feet of Kenai River frontage in Soldotna at the bridge. Walking distance to Kenai Peninsula Visitor Center, restaurants, groceries and downtown shopping malls. Full and partial hookups, riverfront sites. Heated

restrooms, showers with unlimited hot water, laundry. World-famous red salmon fishing from the riverbank. 1,004,214 salmon swam by our property in 1994, by Alaska State Fish and Game sonar count. Tackle shop, ice, fish processing and taxidermy available on premises. Let our park resident master guides provide custom king and silver salmon charters on the Kenai and Kasilof rivers. Reserve early to avoid disappointment. Phone (907) 262-5593; fax (907) 262-9229; write P.O. Box 322, Soldotna, AK 99669. [ADVERTISEMENT] ▲

TRANSPORTATION

Air: Charters available. Soldotna airport is south of Soldotna, 2 miles/3.2 km off the Sterling Highway; at **Milepost S 96.1**, just after crossing Kenai River bridge, turn left (east) on Funny River (Airport) Road and continue 2 miles/ 3.2 km.

Local: Taxi service, car rentals, vehicle leasing, boat rentals and charters.

Highway: Accessible via the Sterling Highway (Alaska Route 1), 148.2 miles/ 238.5 km from Anchorage.

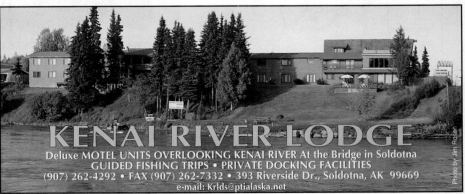

Please support our MILEPOST® advertisers!

ATTRACTIONS

Join in Local Celebrations. July's big event is the annual Soldotna Progress Days, held during the 4th weekend of the month. Activities include a parade, 2 days of rodeo, car show, barbecues, dance, arts and crafts show, and other events.

The Peninsula Winter Games take place in February in Soldotna. Activities include an ice sculpture contest, cross-country ski race, ice bowling and snow volleyball. Games, booths, concessions and demonstrations are held throughout the weekend. The Alaska State Championship Sled Dog Races and Dog Weight Pull Contest take place during the Winter Games.

Donna's Country & Victorian Gifts at Blazy's Soldotna Mall. A shopper's delight, a fisherman's wife's revenge. This is the perfect place to spend an afternoon while your husband goes fishing. Roomfuls of wonderful things, constantly changing. Enjoy our cozy, relaxing atmosphere. Don't miss our Santa room! You'll find things in

our shoppe you never thought you'd find in Alaska! [ADVERTISEMENT]

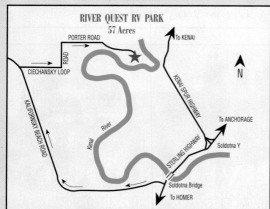

Fish the Kenai River. Soldotna is one of Alaska's best-known sportfishing headquarters, and many claim that some of the world's best fishing is here at the Kenai River, which flows next to town. Many charter boats and fishing guides for Kenai River fishing are located in the Soldotna area. In May 1985, Les Anderson of Soldotna landed a 97-lb., 4-oz. king salmon, a new world's record. The mounted fish is on display at the visitor center.

Soldotna gets very busy during fishing season, and for those fishermen who want a more remote fishing spot—or for visitors who want to see wildlife and glaciers—there are fly-in fishing trips for rainbow, grayling, salmon and Dolly Varden, and flightseeing trips to see Tustumena Lake, the Harding Icefield and wildlife, through local outfitters.

In Soldotna, the early run of kings begins about May 15, with the peak of the run occurring between June 12 and 20. The late run enters the river about July 1, peaking between July 23 and 31; season closes July 31. The first run of red salmon enters the river during early June and is present in small numbers through the month; the second run enters about July 15 and is present through early August. In even years pink salmon are present from early through mid-August. The early silver salmon run arrives in early August, peaks in mid-August, and is over by the end of the month. Late run silver salmon enter the Kenai in early September, peak in mid- to late-September, and continue to enter the river through October. Dolly Varden and rainbow trout can be caught all summer.

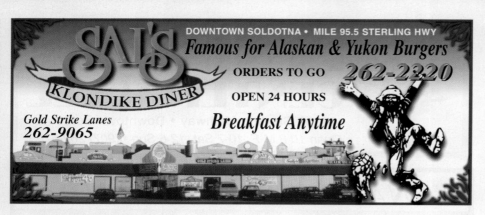

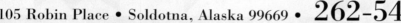

Day-use Parks. Soldotna Creek Park, located off the Sterling Highway on the Kenai River, behind Hutchings Chevrolet at the Y, has covered picnic tables, grills, playground and trails. Facilities include wheelchair-accessible toilets and a boardwalk with wheelchair accessibility for bank fishing. Airport Rotary Park, at Mile 4 Funny River Road, also has a wheelchair-accessible boardwalk with excellent bank fishing during the red salmon run.

Central Peninsula Sports Center, on Kalifornsky Beach (K-Beach) Road, has an Olympic-sized hockey rink, a jogging track, 2 racquetball/volleyball courts, a weight and exercise room, dressing rooms and showers. The Sports Center also has convention facilities and meeting rooms. Phone (907) 262-3150 for more information.

Soldotna Historical Society Museum, located on Centennial Park Road, features a wildlife museum and historic log village. Among the log buildings is the last territorial school (built in 1958). Soldotna's founding settlers arrived in 1947. The "habitable dwellings" that entitled 2 of these first homesteaders to 160 acres from what is now mid-town Soldotna are part of the village. How these latter-day pioneers lived is revealed in a collection of homestead artifacts and photos in the former Soldotna Chamber of Commerce log tourist center.

Food cache displayed at historic log village on Centennial Park Road.
(Courtesy Soldotna Historical Society)

Homes along the Kenai River in Soldotna. (Jerrianne Lowther, staff)

Damon Hall, a large building constructed for the Alaska Centennial, features an outstanding display of wildlife mounts with a background mural of these species' natural habitat. Open 10 A.M. to 4 P.M., Tuesday through Saturday; noon to 4 P.M. Sunday; closed Monday.

Joyce Carver Memorial Library offers temporary cards for visitors; large sunlit reading areas for both adults and children; Alaska videos on summer Saturday afternoons at 2 P.M. Open 9 A.M. to 8 P.M. Monday through Thursday, noon to 6 P.M. Friday, and 9 A.M. to 6 P.M. Saturdays. 235 Binkley St., Soldotna, phone (907) 262-4227.

Kenai National Wildlife Refuge Visitor Center, located at the top of Ski Hill Road (see **Milepost S 97.9**) and also accessible from Funny River Road (see **Milepost S 96.1**), hosts some 25,000 visitors annually. This modern center has dioramas containing lifelike mounts of area wildlife in simulated natural settings. Free wildlife films are shown on the hour daily from noon to 4 P.M. Information available here on canoeing, hiking and camping. There is a 1-mile-/1.6-km-long nature trail with an observation platform and spotting scope on Headquarters Lake. The Alaska Natural History Assoc. has a sales outlet here with books, posters and videos. Pay phone located in center. Open weekdays 8 A.M. to 4:30 P.M., and weekends 10 A.M. to 6 P.M. No admission fee.

The refuge was created in 1941 when President Franklin D. Roosevelt set aside 1,730,000 acres of land (then designated the Kenai National Moose Range) to assure that the large numbers of moose, Dall sheep and other wild game would remain for people to enjoy. With the passage of the Alaska National Interest Lands Conservation Act in 1980, the acreage was increased to 1.97 million acres and redesignated Kenai National Wildlife Refuge. The area is managed by the U.S. Dept. of the Interior's Fish and Wildlife Service. Write: Refuge Manager, Kenai National Wildlife Refuge, P.O. Box 2139, Soldotna, AK 99669-2139; phone (907) 262-7021.

Take a Canoe Trip on one of several routes available in this part of the Kenai Peninsula. Enjoyment of wildlife in their natural habitat, true wilderness scenery, camping, and fishing for trout and salmon are a few highlights of a canoe trip.

Established canoe trails include the Swanson River route (80 miles/129 km) and Swan Lake route (60 miles/97 km). Complete information on Kenai Peninsula canoe trails is available at the USF&WS information cabin at Mile 58 Sterling Highway, the Kenai NWR information center in Soldotna and at chamber of commerce visitor centers in Kenai and Soldotna.

Kenai Spur Highway Log

Snow geese on the Kenai River Flats at Bridge Access Road, Milepost SY 10.5.
(© Bill Sherwonit)

The Kenai Spur Highway branches off the Sterling Highway at the Soldotna Y. **Distance from Soldotna Y (SY) is shown.**

SY 0 Junction with Sterling Highway at **Milepost S 94.2.** *NOTE: Expect road construction from here to* **Mile 2.8** *in 1998.*

SY 0.7 (1.1 km) Hospital, Soldotna High School.

SY 1 (1.6 km) Fishing licenses, tackle, 24-hour gas.

Tesoro 7–Eleven. See display ad this section.

SY 1.8 (2.8 km) Big Eddy Road to west. Access to Big Eddy state recreational site on Kenai River with wheelchair-accessible toilets, fishing guides, private camping, moorage, boat launches and rental facilities. ♿▲

SY 2.2 (3.5 km) Big Eddy second access.

SY 2.5 (4 km) Sport Lake Road; access to bed and breakfast.

SY 4 (6.4 km) Kenai city limits.

SY 5.5 (8.9 km) **Alicia's Eagle Rock Lodge and Alaska–Pacific N.W. Fishing Adventures.** Expert fishing guides on world-famous Kenai River. King salmon, mid-May through July. Silver salmon in

August. Halibut all summer. Excellent lodging, economy units and 2-bedroom family units available. Free RV parking when fishing with us. 5743 Kenai Spur Highway, Kenai, AK 99611. Phone/fax (907) 283-3788. Open May 10–Sept. 5. [ADVERTISEMENT]

SY 5.9 (9.4 km) Dogwood Street.

SY 6.1 (9.8 km) Beaver Creek Park (day use only); parking, toilets, picnic tables, playground, basketball court, covered table, litter barrels.

SY 6.4 (10.3 km) Twin City Raceway. South **junction** with Beaver Loop Road: Drive 2.5 miles/4 km on Beaver Loop Road and turn south (left fork), crossing Warren Ames Memorial Bridge, to connect with Kalifornsky Beach Road. Turn north (right fork) for return to Kenai Spur Highway at Mile 10.9.

SY 8.2 (13.2 km) Begin divided 4-lane highway, 35-mph/56-kmph. Paved bike trails both sides of highway to Kenai.

SY 9.3 (14.9 km) Tinker Lane. Access to Peninsula Oilers baseball park, munici-

Kenai Spur Highway Log (continued)

pal golf course and junior high school.

SY 10.2 (16.4 km) Airport Road (right), Walker Road (left).

SY 10.5 (16.9 km) Bridge Access Road; north **junction** with Beaver Loop Road. Access south to Bridge Access Road and Port of Kenai; public boat launch with parking and toilets available. Road crosses Warren Ames Bridge and junctions with Kalifornsky Beach Road. Kenai River Flats state recreation site south of bridge has toilets and dumpster. Good spot to see migrating waterfowl.

SY 11 (17.7 km) **KENAI** (description of city begins on page 602). Carr's/Kmart shopping complex. Willow Street access to Kenai Municipal Airport 1 mile northeast.

SY 11.8 (19 km) Spruce Street; beach access; toilets.

SY 12.1 (19.5 km) Forest Drive. Scenic viewpoint overlooking Cook Inlet. Municipal day-use park; covered picnic tables; trails.

SY 12.4 (20 km) C Plaza; shopping.

SY 15 (24.1 km) Kenai city limits.

SY 21.3 (34.3 km) Miller Loop Road, connects with Island Lake Road.

SY 22.1 (35.5 km) **NIKISKI** (pop. 5,000). **Emergency Services**, phone 911 for fire and paramedics. Also known as Port Nikiski and Nikishka, this area was homesteaded in the 1940s and grew with the discovery of oil on the Kenai Peninsula in 1957. By 1964, oil-related industries here included Unocal Chemical, Phillips LNG, Chevron and Tesoro. Oil docks serving offshore drilling platforms today include Rigtenders, Standard Oil, Phillips 66 and Unocal Chemical. Commercial fishing is still a source of income for some residents.

Cow parsnip is silhouetted against a Cook Inlet sunset. (© Nancy Faville)

SY 22.5 (36.2 km) Access to Nikiski Rigtenders dock; tankers may be seen next to dock.

SY 23.4 (37.6 km) North Peninsula Recreation and Nikiski elementary school. Dome-shaped building in trees near highway is the Nikiski recreational swimming pool, with indoor slide and hot tub; visitor observation area at pool; wheelchair-access, children's swimming area. Other facilities include an ice rink, hiking and ski trails, a picnic area and ball fields. Phone (907) 776-8800.

North Peninsula Recreation/Nikiski Pool. See display ad this section.

SY 25.8 (41.5 km) Island Lake Road.

SY 26.6 (42.8 km) Nikishka Mall shopping, restaurants, supermarket, gas station and Nikiski branch Kenai post office.

SY 26.7 (43 km) Nikiski Beach Road; views of Nikishka Bay and Cook Inlet. Nikiski Fire Station No. 2. Access to Nikiski High School and Arness Dock, built on a base of WWII Liberty ships (still visible). Scenic view of Mount Spurr, Alaska Range, Nikishka Bay and oil platforms in Cook Inlet.

SY 29.7 (47.8 km) Halbouty Road.

Daniels Lake Lodge Bed & Breakfast. See display ad this section.

SY 30 (48.2 km) Daniels Lake.

SY 32.5 (52.3 km) Turnout west opposite Twin Lakes.

SY 35.6 (57.3 km) Entering Captain Cook State Recreation Area.

SY 35.9 (57.8 km) Bishop Creek State Recreation Site; 15 campsites, parking, toilets, water, picnic area and trail to beach. Camping fee $8/night or annual pass. Watch for spawning red salmon in creek in July and August, silvers August to September. Closed to salmon fishing.

SY 36.5 (58.7 km) Access to **Stormy Lake** swimming area, changehouse, toilet, water, parking, and rainbow and arctic char fishing.

SY 36.7 (59.1 km) Stormy Lake overlook; large paved turnout to east.

SY 36.9 (59.4 km) Stormy Lake picnic area; water, toilets, covered tables.

SY 37.8 (60.8 km) Stormy Lake boat launch; water, toilets, parking.

SY 38.6 (62.1 km) Swanson River canoe landing area; drive 0.6 mile/1 km east to parking and toilets, river access. End of the Swanson River canoe trail system.

SY 38.7 (62.3 km) Clint Starnes Memorial Bridge crosses **Swanson River**; parking next to bridge for fishing access, toilets, view of Mount Spurr. Fishing for silver and red salmon, and rainbow.

SY 39 (62.8 km) Pavement ends at T. Take left fork for Discovery Picnic Area and Campground (Captain Cook SRA); 53 campsites, picnic area, Maggie Yurick Memorial hiking trail, water, beachcombing for agates, campfire circle, scheduled fireside programs in season. Right fork leads to additional parking and toilets. ATV and snowmobile trails. Camping fee $10/night or annual pass.

SY 39.6 (63.7 km) Picnic area with tables and toilets, on bluff overlooking ocean at end of Kenai Spur Highway.

Return to Milepost S 94.2 Sterling Highway

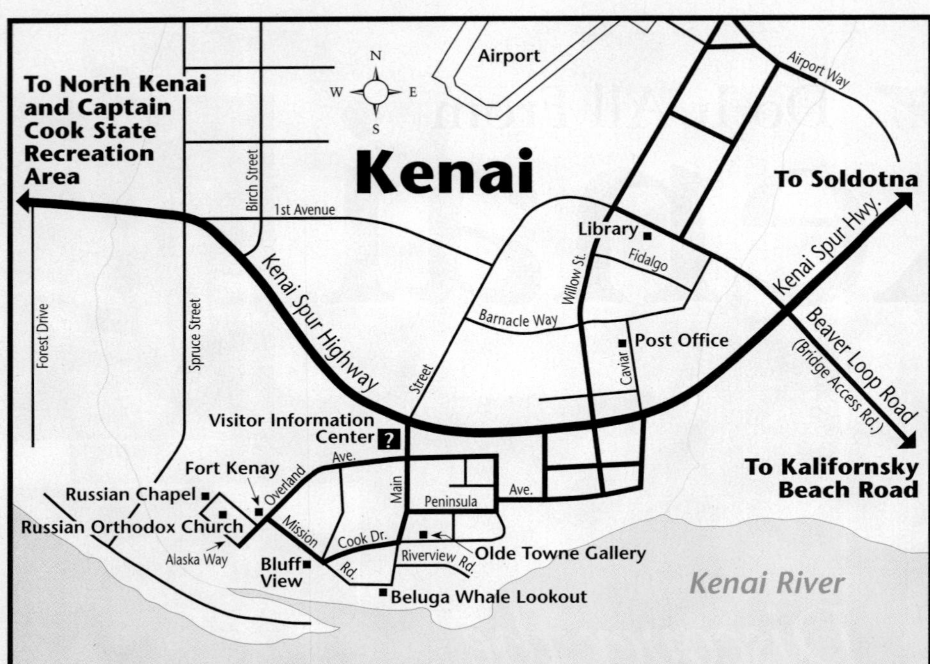

Kenai

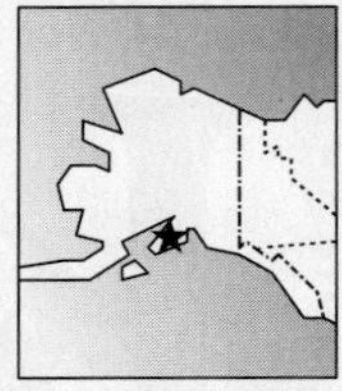

SY 11 (17.7 km). On the western Kenai Peninsula. Reached via the Kenai Spur Highway, or 9.3 miles/14.9 km from Soldotna via the Kalifornsky Beach Road, 158.5 miles/255 km from Anchorage, 89.3 miles/143.7 km from Homer.

Population: 7,000.

Emergency Services: Phone 911 for all emergency services. **Alaska State Troopers** (in Soldotna), phone (907) 262-4453. **Kenai City Police**, phone (907) 283-7879. **Fire Department** and **Ambulance**, phone 911. **Hospital** (in Soldotna), phone (907) 262-4404. **Maritime Search and Rescue**, dial 0 for Zenith 5555, toll free.

Visitor Information: The Kenai Visitors and Cultural Center, located in downtown Kenai, provides brochures and other visitor information. The center features a cultural museum, wildlife displays and movies. For a full list of visitor services available in Kenai, write the Kenai Visitors and Cultural Center, 11471 Kenai Spur Highway, Kenai, AK 99611; phone (907) 283-1991, fax 283-2230. E-mail: kvcb@alaska.net.

Elevation: 93 feet/28m. **Climate:** Average daily maximum temperature in July, 61°F/16°C; January temperatures range from 11° to -19°F/-12° to -28°C. Lowest recorded temperature in Kenai was -48°F/-44°C. Average annual precipitation, 19.9 inches (68.7 inches of snowfall). **Radio:** KCSY 1140, KENI 550, KGTL 620, KSRM 920, KWVV 105, KGTL 100.9/103.5, MBN-FM 95.3/97.7, KENY 980, KWHQ-FM 100.1, KPEN-FM 101.7. **Television:** Several channels and cable. **Newspaper:** *Peninsula Clarion* (daily).

Private Aircraft: Kenai Municipal Airport, adjacent north; elev. 92 feet/28m; length 7,575 feet/2,309m; asphalt; fuel 100LL; attended. Transient tie-down fees $2/day. Adjacent floatplane base offers 3,500-foot/1,067-m basin with 35 slips.

Kenai is situated on a low rise overlooking the mouth of the Kenai River where it empties into Cook Inlet. It is the largest city on the Kenai Peninsula. Prior to Russian Alaska, Kenai was a Dena'ina Native community. The Dena'ina people fished, hunted, trapped, farmed and traded with neighboring tribes here. In 1791 it became the second permanent settlement established by the Russians in Alaska, when a fortified

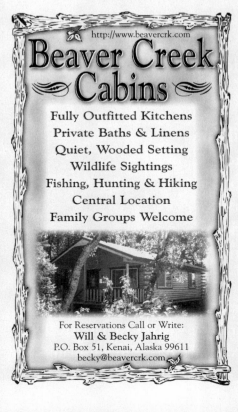

OLD TOWN VILLAGE

Log Cabins Featuring ...

Alaskan Gifts & Specialty Shops

Alaskan Artists with Demonstrations

1000 Mission Avenue • Kenai, Alaska 99611

907-283-4515

Fax: (907) 283-3616 • oldtown@ptialaska.net

Historic Cannery Building Est. 1916

Featuring... Alaskan Seafood
Beer & Wine • Steaks
Daily Specials • Salad Bar
Sourdough Pancakes
(from 50 year old starter)

Gift Shops

Historical Interpretation

Ice Cream & Espresso

Fishing & Sightseeing Charters

Restaurant

Homemade Pies & Cakes

Banquet & conference facilities available.

Historic Alaska

Second Oldest Old Town Kenai Community in Alaska

Map of Old Town Kenai

KENAI SPUR HWY
VISITOR INFORMATION CENTER
OVERLAND
MAIN
Old Town Village
UPLAND
MISSION
COOK
Church
Toyon Villa
Beluga RV Park
COOK INLET
KENAI RIVER

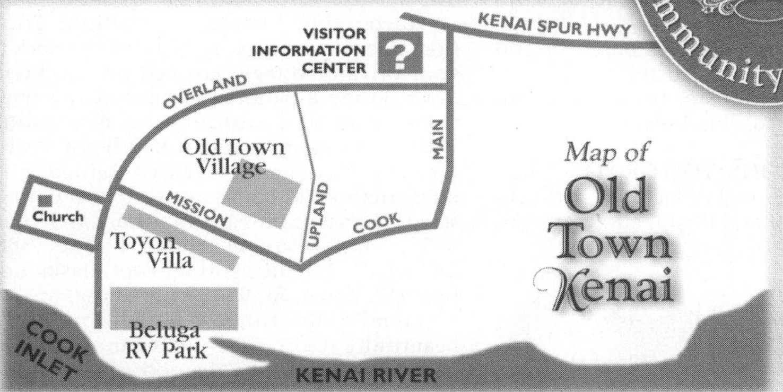

Fantastic Views of

Cook Inlet • Kenai River • Eagles
Beluga Whales • Volcanoes • Fishing

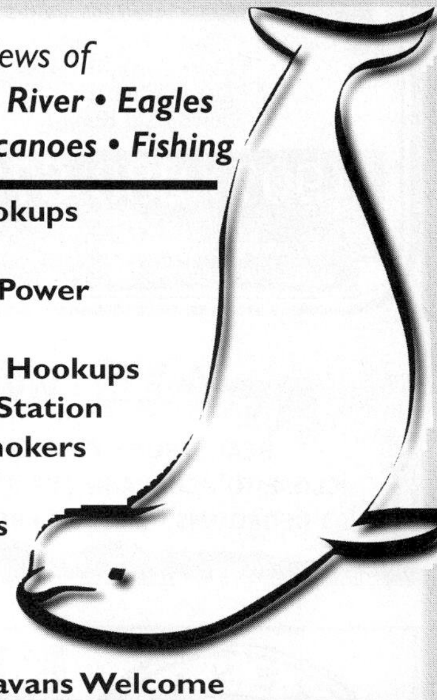

- 75 Full RV Hookups
- Pull Thrus
- 20-30-50 amp Power
- Cable TV
- Private Phone Hookups
- Fish Cleaning Station
- Freezers & Smokers
- Picnic Tables
- Bar-B-Que Pits
- Showers
- Laundry
- Fax
- Groups & Caravans Welcome

BELUGA LOOKOUT RV PARK

929 MISSION AVENUE • KENAI, AK 99611
(907) 283-5999 • AK ONLY 1-800-745-5999
Fax: (907) 283-4939 • belugarv@ptialaska.net

- Microwave & Coffee Maker
- Equipped Kitchens
- Cable TV & Phone
- Spectacular Location
- Maid Service

Fully furnished studio, one and two bedroom APARTMENTS at motel rates.

1001 Mission Ave., Apt. 19
Kenai, Alaska 99611
(907) 283-4221 • Fax 283-4231
tva@alaska.net

TOLL FREE 1-888-283-4221

Kenai Visitors and Cultural Center in downtown Kenai. (Jerrianne Lowther, staff)

post called Fort St. Nicholas, or St. Nicholas Redoubt, was built near here by Russian fur traders. In 1848, the first Alaska gold discovery was made on the Russian River. In 1869 the U.S. Army established Fort Kenai (Kenay); in 1899 a post office was authorized.

Oil exploration began in the mid-1950s, with the first major discovery in this area, the Swanson River oil reserves, 20 miles/32.2 km northeast of Kenai in 1957. Two years later, natural gas was discovered in the Kalifornsky Beach area 6 miles/9.6 km south of the city of Kenai. Extensive exploration offshore in upper Cook Inlet has established that Cook Inlet's middle-ground shoals contain one of the major oil and gas fields in the world.

The industrial complex on the North Kenai Road is the site of Unocal Chemicals, which produces ammonia and urea for fertilizer. Phillips Petroleum operates a liquid natural gas plant. Tesoro has a refinery here.

Offshore in Cook Inlet are 15 drilling platforms, all with underwater pipelines bringing the oil to the shipping docks on both sides of Cook Inlet for loading onto tankers.

Federal and state agencies based in and around Kenai contribute to the local economy. Next to oil, tourism, fishing and fish processing are the leading industries.

ACCOMMODATIONS/VISITOR SERVICES

Kenai has all shopping facilities and conveniences. Medical and dental clinics, banks, laundromats, theaters, pharmacies, supermarkets, and numerous gift and specialty shops are located on and off the highway and in the shopping malls. Several motels and hotels and about a dozen restaurants and drive-ins are located in Kenai. Local artists are featured at the Kenai Fine Arts Center on Cook Street. Showers, sauna, weight room, racquetball courts and gym at Kenai Recreation Center, on Caviar Street. Open 6 A.M. to 10 P.M. Monday through Saturday, Sunday 1 to 10 P.M. Phone (907) 283-3855. For joggers there's the Bernie Huss Memorial Trail, a 0.5-mile jogging and exercise course located just off the Kenai Spur Highway on Main Street Loop. Dump stations located at several local service stations and city dock.

City of Kenai public boat ramp on Boat Launch Road off Bridge Access Road has 24-hour parking, restrooms with flush toilets, pay phone.

Kenai City Park has covered picnic tables and fireplaces. Arrangements for caravan camping may be made in advance through the Kenai Visitors and Cultural Center. Tent camping and private RV parks available in and near shopping areas. Ask at the visitors center for directions. ▲

Drive north of town on the Kenai Spur Highway for more lodging and camping. Municipal park at the end of Forest Drive has wheelchair-accessible trails, firepits, picnic tables and playground. ♿

Beluga Lookout RV Park, 2 blocks from Kenai Visitors Center in historic Old Town, downtown Kenai. Overlooking bluff with fantastic view of beluga whales, Kenai River, Cook Inlet, Mount Redoubt. Historic Russian Orthodox Church, Fort Kenay next door. Log lodge office, private bathrooms, hot showers, laundry. 75 full-hookup spaces, cable TV, picnic tables, instant private phone hookups, pull-throughs, 30–50 amp power. Caravans welcome. VISA, MasterCard. Reservations (800) 745-5999 or (907) 283-5999. E-mail: beluga@ptialaska.net. See display ad. [ADVERTISEMENT] ▲

Harborside Cottages. Location! Location! Spectacular view right from the deck of your private cottage. Located on the Kenai River. Enjoy a panoramic view of the river, Cook Inlet and surrounding mountains. Walk to restaurants, shops, beach and visitor services. Cottages are self-contained with kitchenettes and barbecue area. Each cottage sleeps 2 and groups up to 10 are welcome. VISA, MasterCard accepted. Phone (888) 283-6162. E-mail: cottages@ptialaska.net. Box 942, Kenai, AK 99611. [ADVERTISEMENT]

Kenai's Old Town Village. Dine in the beautifully-refurbished 1918 cannery building, featuring Alaska seafood, steaks, home cooking, beer and wine. Banquet space available for 150. Fantastic view of Kenai River, Cook Inlet and mountains. Visit log shops as they might have been in the early 1900s, featuring local artists and craftspersons. Book charters and sightseeing. Located 2 blocks from visitor center. Phone (907) 283-4515. E-mail: oldtown@ptialaska.net. See display ad. [ADVERTISEMENT]

Tanglewood Bed & Breakfast. Fish king salmon from our backyard, on lower Kenai River. View moose, caribou, bears, wolves, eagles, ducks, seals, beluga whales on regular basis. Rooms $75. Common room with fireplace. Fully equipped private suite with Jacuzzi, $125. Full breakfast. Laundry facilities. (907) 283-6771. Open year-round. Lifelong Alaskans. See display ad. [ADVERTISEMENT]

Toyon Villa. Suites at motel rates; $85 to $125. Studios and one- and 2-bedroom suites. Fully-equipped kitchens, cable TV, private phones, maid service. Located at Kenai River and Cook Inlet, in historic Old Town, across from Old Town Village Restaurant and gift shops. Phone (907) 283-4221. E-mail: tva@alaska.net. See display ad. [ADVERTISEMENT]

TRANSPORTATION

Air: Kenai is served by 3 commuter airlines: Era Aviation, Southcentral Air and Yute Air. Several firms offer charter service out of Kenai. Kenai Municipal Airport (see description under Private Aircraft) is approximately 2 blocks west of the Carr's/Kmart complex on the Kenai Spur Highway.

Local: Limousine and taxi service is available as well as car rentals, vehicle leasing, boat rentals and charters.

Highway: On the Kenai Spur Highway, 11 miles/17.7 km north of Soldotna.

ATTRACTIONS

Get Acquainted. Pick up a brochure at the Kenai Visitors and Cultural Center. The center houses a cultural museum, which has wildlife displays, and information on local activities. The center also shows films on Alaska, daily year-round.

Old Town Kenai self-guided walking tour. Take a leisurely stroll through Old Town and read about the Native and Russian history on informational signs posted along the way. Check with the Kenai Visitors and Cultural Center for information.

Kenai River Flats is a must stop for bird-watchers. Great numbers of Siberian snow geese and other waterfowl stop to feed on this saltwater marsh in the spring. The state recreation site on Bridge Access Road at Warren Ames Bridge has parking and interpretive signs. Boardwalk for wildlife-watchers. Also watch for caribou on the Kenai Flats.

Beluga Whale Watching on the Kenai River beach at the west end of Spruce Street. Beluga whales are the only all-white whale. The beach also offers a good view of Kenai's fish-processing industry and volcanoes.

Watch Baseball or Play Golf. Some fine semipro baseball is played at the Peninsula Oilers ball park on Tinker Lane. Golfers may try the 18-hole Kenai golf course on Lawton Drive.

Fort Kenay was the first American military installation in the area, established in 1868. More than 100 men were stationed here in the 1½ years it officially served to protect American citizens in the area. A replica of the fort's barracks building was built as an Alaskan Purchase Centennial project by Kenai residents in 1967.

Holy Assumption Russian Orthodox Church is across from Fort Kenay. The original church was founded in 1844 by a Russian monk, Igumen Nicholai. The present church was built some 50 years after the original and with its 3 onion-shaped domes is considered one of the finest examples of a Russian Orthodox church built on a vessel or quadrilateral ground plan. It is one of the oldest Russian Orthodox churches in Alaska. In 1971 it was designated a national historic landmark. An 1847 edition of the book of the Holy Gospel of the 4 evangelists—Matthew, Mark, Luke and John—with 5 enameled icons on the cover, is awaiting restoration (not on display). Regular church services are held here, and tours are available; inquire at the church. Donations accepted.

St. Nicholas Chapel, built in 1906, west of the Russian church, marks the burial location of Father Igumen Nicholai and other Russian Orthodox Church workers.

Sterling Highway Log

(continued from page 588)

S 95.9 (154.3 km) **A 148.9** (239.6 km) **H 83.6** (134.5 km) Kenai River bridge.

Entering Soldotna northbound. Description of city begins on page 588.

S 96 (154.5 km) **A 149** (239.8 km) **H 83.5** (134.4 km) Soldotna visitor center at south end of Kenai River bridge.

S 96.1 (154.7 km) **A 149.1** (239.9 km) **H 83.4** (134.2 km) **Junction.** Funny River Road to east, Kalifornsky Beach Road to west. Kalifornsky Beach Road rejoins the Sterling Highway at **Milepost S 108.8.** (See KALIFORNSKY BEACH ROAD log page 606.)

Centennial Park campground, 0.1 mile/0.2 km west, on the banks of the Kenai River. There are 126 campsites (some on river), tables, firepits, firewood provided, water, restrooms, dump station, pay phone, 2-week limit. Boat launch and favorite fishing site at far end of campground. Register at campground entrance. ▲

Funny River (Airport) Road leads east 2 miles/3.2 km to Soldotna airport, 4 miles/6.4 km to Airport Rotary Park (day-use only) and 11.5 miles/18.5 km to Funny River State Recreation Site; 12 campsites, $8 nightly fee per vehicle or annual pass, picnic tables, water, toilets, river access. Salmon and trout fishing at the confluence of the **Kenai** and **Funny rivers** at the recreation area. Turn on Funny River Road and take first right (Ski Hill Loop Road) for USF&WS visitor center. Funny River Road dead ends 17.2 miles/27.7 km from the highway. Private RV park located at Mile 13.8. ▲

S 97.9 (157.6 km) **A 150.9** (242.8 km) **H 81.6** (131.3 km) Sky View High School. Easy-to-miss turnoff for Kenai National Wildlife Refuge headquarters and information center: Turn east off highway and drive 1 mile/1.6 km on Ski Hill Road, which loops back to Funny River Road (see preceding milepost). Nature trail with wildlife observation platform and spotting scope on Headquarters Lake. The center is open 8 A.M. to 4:30 P.M. on weekdays, 10 A.M. to 6 P.M. weekends.

The Tsalteshi Trails System is 7 miles/12 km of loop trails, used in summer for walking, running and mountain biking; groomed in winter for cross-country skiing. Trails start behind the school.

S 108 (173.8 km) **A161** (259.1 km) **H 71.5** (115.1 km) **Maxwell's Moose Horn Campground**. See display ad this section. ▲

S 108.2 (174.1 km) **A 161.2** (259.4 km) **H 71.3** (114.7 km) **Tail Out Guide Service.** See display ad this section.

Kalifornsky Beach Road Log

Also called K–Beach Road, Kalifornsky Beach Road leads west and south from the Sterling Highway at Soldotna, following the shore of Cook Inlet to Kasilof.

Distance from the Sterling Highway junction at Milepost S 96.1 at Soldotna (S) is followed by distance from Sterling Highway junction at Milepost S 108.8 at Kasilof (K). Mileposts run south to north and reflect mileage from Kasilof.

S 0 K 22.2 (35.7 km) **Junction** with Sterling Highway at **Milepost S 96.1**.

S 0.1 (0.2 km) **K 22.1** (35.6 km) Soldotna Alaska Purchase Centennial Park Campground, operated by the city of Soldotna. Kenai River access for bank fishing, boat launch (fee charged).

S 0.2 (0.3 km) **K 22** (35.4 km) Alaska State Troopers.

S 0.4 (0.6 km) **K 21.8** (35.1 km) Rodeo grounds.

S 0.6 (1 km) **K 21.6** (34.8 km) Central Peninsula Sports Center; hockey, ice skating, jogging track and other sports available; phone (907) 262-3150 for more information.

S 1.7 (2.7 km) **K 20.5** (33 km) Kenai Peninsula Community College access road. Also access to Slikok Creek State Recreation Site, 0.7 mile/1.1 km north; day use only with 12-hour parking, wheelchair-accessible toilets, picnic tables, information kiosk and trails. No fires or ATVs.

S 2.9 (4.7 km) **K 19.3** (31.1 km) K–Beach center. ADF&G office; stop in here for current sportfishing information.

S 3.1 (5 km) **K 19.1** (30.7 km) Poppy Lane, access to community college. Grocery and gas.

S 3.5 (5.6 km) **K 18.7** (30.1 km) Red Diamond shopping center, Duck Inn Motel and restaurant. Motor Vehicle Dept. and Fish and Wildlife offices.

S 4.6 (7.4 km) **K 17.6** (28.3 km) Firehouse.

S 4.7 (7.6 km) **K 17.5** (28.2 km) Ciechansky Road leads 2.2 miles/3.5 km to Ciechansky State Recreation Site, a day-use only picnic area with tables, toilets, dumpster and Kenai River access. Also access to private campgrounds with RV hookups on the Kenai River.

S 5.7 (9.2 km) **K 16.5** (26.6 km) **Diamond M Ranch B&B, Cabins & RV Spaces.** Longtime Alaskans, JoAnne and Carrol Martin and family, have expanded their ranch to include a variety of accommodations for Kenai Peninsula visitors. Bed and breakfast features wild berry muffins, guest kitchen, outdoor barbecue, hot tub and sauna, large green lawn, igloo for the kids. New, handcrafted cabins nestled in the trees, rustic or full bath and kitchenette. Variety of RV spaces, including pull-throughs. Central shower, dump station. Magnificent view of Cook Inlet, waterfowl, moose, caribou. Hiking trails. Access to Kenai River. Minutes to airport, shopping, restaurants, churches. VISA, MasterCard, Discover. Phone (907) 283-9424. P.O. Box 1776, Soldotna, 99669. Display ad in Soldotna section. [ADVERTISEMENT]

S 6 (9.7 km) **K 16.2** (26.1 km) Turnoff for city of Kenai, 3.1 miles/5 km north via the Warren Ames Memorial Bridge.

S 6.8 (10.9 km) **K 15.4** (24.8 km) Magnificent beaver dam and lodge, lupine display in June.

S 7.6 (12.2 km) **K 14.6** (23.5 km) **Robinsons Mini-Mall**. See display ad this section.

S 7.8 (12.5 km) **K 14.4** (23.2 km) VIP Drive; Kenai Custom Seafoods.

S 8 (12.9 km) **K 14.2** (22.9 km) Cafe.

S 8.8 (14.2 km) **K 13.4** (21.6 km) K-Beach Fire Station.

S 13 (20.9 km) **K 9.2** (14.8 km) Paved, scenic viewpoint overlooking Cook Inlet.

S 17.4 (28 km) **K 4.8** (7.7 km) Kasilof Beach Road; access to beach, harbor, river.

S 19.4 (31.2 km) **K 2.8** (4.5 km) **Ingrid's Inn Bed & Breakfast**. See display ad this section.

S 20.1 (32.3 km) **K 2.1** (3.4 km) Kasilof Airfield Road.

S 22.1 (35.6 km) **K 0.1** (0.2 km) Kasilof post office.

S 22.2 (35.7 km) **K 0 Junction** with Sterling Highway at **Milepost S 108.8** at Kasilof.

Return to Milepost S 96.1 or S 108.8 Sterling Highway

S 108.8 (175 km) **A 161.8** (260.4 km) **H 70.7** (113.8 km) South **junction** with Kalifornsky Beach Road. (See KALIFORNSKY BEACH ROAD log this page.) Drive west 4.8 miles/7.7 km to Beach Road for access to beach, Kasilof small-boat harbor and Kasilof River. This loop road rejoins Sterling Highway at **Milepost S 96.1.**

KASILOF (kuh-SEE-lawf; pop. 383; elev. 75 feet/23m) was originally a settlement established in 1786 by the Russians as St. George. An Indian fishing village grew up around the site, but no longer exists. Native inhabitants of the peninsula are mostly Kanai Indians, a branch of the great Athabascan family. The population is spread out over the general area which is called Kasilof. The area's income is derived from fishing and fish processing.

Kasilof River. The red salmon dip-net fishery here is open by special announcement for Alaska residents only. Check with the ADF&G for current regulations.

Private Aircraft: Kasilof airstrip, 1.7 miles/2.7 km north; elev. 125 feet/38m; length 2,300 feet/701m; gravel; unattended.

S 109 (175.4 km) **A 162** (260.7 km) **H 70.5** (113.5 km) Grocery store.

S 109.2 (175.7 km) **A 162.2** (261 km) **H 70.3** (113.1 km) **Kasilof Riverview.** See display ad this section.

S 109.4 (176.1 km) **A 162.4** (261.3 km) **H 70.1** (112.8 km) Bridge over Kasilof River, which drains Tustumena Lake, one of the largest lakes on the Kenai Peninsula. Kasilof River State Recreation Site; 10 campsites, $8 nightly fee or annual pass, 5 picnic sites on riverbank, picnic tables, toilets and water are on the south side of the bridge. Boat launch $5 fee or annual pass; $5 day-use fee or annual pass.

Entering Game Management Subunit 15C southbound, 15B northbound.

S 110 (177 km) **A 163** (262.3 km) **H 69.5** (111.8 km) Tustumena Elementary School and north end of Tustumena Lake Road. This is the first turnoff southbound for access to Johnson and Tustumena lakes. Also turn off here for picnic area with covered picnic tables, toilets (wheelchair accessible),

Seward's Day is an Alaska state holiday (March 30, 1998).

firepits, water and dumpster. There is a huge metal T at Tustumena Lake Road, just beyond the picnic area: Turn east at the T for Johnson and Tustumena lakes. **Johnson Lake** is 0.3 mile/0.5 km from the highway. Johnson Lake state campground has 50 sites (some double and some pull-throughs), $10 nightly fee or annual pass, water, toilets, boat launch and firewood. Lake is stocked with rainbow. Watch for beaver, moose and king salmon migrating up Crooked Creek. **Tustumena Lake** is 6.4 miles/10.3 km from the highway; a campground on the Kasilof River near the lake has 10 sites, toilets and boat launch. Fishing for lake trout and salmon. Tustumena Lake is closed to king and sockeye salmon fishing. ♿🐟▲

CAUTION: This lake is 6 miles/10 km wide and 25 miles/40 km long and subject to severe winds.

S 110.5 (177.8 km) **A 163.5** (263.1 km) **H 69** (111 km) Double-ended paved parking by Crooked Creek.

S 110.8 (178.3 km) **A 163.8** (263.6 km) **H 68.7** (110.6 km) **Tustumena Lodge.** Phone (907) 262-4216. E-mail: suziepp@corecom.net. Motel, cocktail lounge, fishing guides. Clean, affordable rooms at half the price of town. Some kitchenettes. Friendly Alaskan atmosphere where a cold drink, light snack and good fish stories are always available. Monday—prime rib, $8. Friday—New York Steak, $7. Saturday—halibut, $8. See the world's largest razor clam. Look for a hat from your hometown among the over 15,000 hats in our pending Guinness record collection. [ADVERTISEMENT]

S 111 (178.6 km) **A 164** (263.9 km) **H 68.5** (110.2 km) Cohoe Loop Road north **junction** (turnoff to west). Crooked Creek State Recreation Site (camping and fishing) 1.8 miles/2.8 km west on Cohoe Loop Road. South end of Tustumena Lake Road (to east) for Johnson and Tustumena lakes (see description at **Milepost S 110**). Cohoe Loop Road rejoins the Sterling Highway at **Milepost S 114.3** (see COHOE LOOP ROAD log page 608).

Just east of the highway on the Johnson and Tustumena lakes access road is Crooked Creek fish hatchery; a sign explains the chinook and sockeye salmon operation here. For further information, contact Cook Inlet Aquaculture Assoc., phone (907) 283-5761. The hatchery-produced salmon create a popular fishery at the confluence of Crooked Creek and the Kasilof River, accessible via the Cohoe Loop Road. Just past the hatchery is Crooked Creek Road, and just beyond is a huge metal T at Tustumena Lake Road. Continue past this monument for a picnic area, and return to Sterling Highway at **Milepost S 110**; turn at the T for lakes and camping. 🐟▲

Crooked Creek RV Park & Guide Service. See display ad this section. ▲

Kasilof RV Park. Clean, modern facilities in a wooded environment make this one of the Kenai Peninsula's cleanest and most popular RV parks. The peaceful setting boasts wildflowers, beavers, moose, eagles, loons and a variety of birds. Enjoy walking, fishing for trout in Johnson Lake, salmon in the nearby Kasilof and Kenai rivers, halibut in Cook Inlet, or clamming on Alaska's most-famous razor-clam beaches. Level gravel sites, electrical hookups, picnic tables, sparkling-fresh well water, spotless restrooms, free private showers, and friendly owners make for "two thumbs up." See our display ad. Phone (907) 262-0418. Internet:

Cohoe Loop Road Log

The Cohoe Loop Road loops south 15.3 miles/24.7 km from **Milepost S 111** on the Sterling Highway. The popular Crooked Creek fishing and camping area is at the top or north end of the loop. The bottom (or south) 10 miles of the Cohoe Loop Road travels through mostly undeveloped parcels of land; no services, views or recreation. Motorists may wish to use the north junction approach.

Distance from north junction with the Sterling Highway (NJ) at Milepost S 111 is followed by distance from south junction (SJ) at Milepost S 114.3. Mileposts run south to north.

NJ 0 SJ 15.3 (24.6 km) **Junction** with Sterling Highway at **Milepost S 111.**

NJ 1.8 (2.9 km) **SJ 13.5** (21.7 km) Crooked Creek/Rilinda Drive; access to private RV park and Crooked Creek State Recreation Site at the confluence of Crooked Creek and the Kasilof River. The recreation site has 83 campsites, 36 day-use sites, toilets and water trails to Kasilof River for fishermen. Camping fee $8/night or annual pass, day-use fee $5/vehicle or annual pass. ▲

Fishing in **Crooked Creek** closed to king salmon fishing and closed to all fishing near hatchery. Fishing access to confluence of Crooked Creek and Kasilof River is through the state recreation site. *NOTE: Fishing access to Crooked Creek frontage above confluence is through a private RV park; fee charged.* Fishing in the **Kasilof River** for king salmon, late May through July, best in mid-June; coho salmon, mid-August to September, use salmon egg clusters, wet flies, assorted spoons and spinners.

NJ 2.4 (3.9 km) **SJ 12.9** (20.7 km) Webb–Ramsell Road. Kasilof River access across private property, fee charged.

NJ 5.3 (8.5 km) **SJ 10** (16 km) Cohoe Spur Road **junction.** A post office was established in 1950 at **COHOE** (area pop. 508), originally an agricultural settlement.

NJ 5.6 (9 km) **SJ 9.7** (15.6 km) T intersection; go west 0.8 mile/1.3 km for beach and boat launch. Private campground on Madsen Road. Cabins for rent on St. Elias Road to right. Cohoe Loop Road continues north. Pavement begins northbound. ▲

Kasilof River Kabins. See display ad this section.

NJ 15.3 (24.6 km) **SJ 0 Junction** with Sterling Highway at **Milepost S 114.3.**

Return to Milepost S 114.3
or Milepost S 111
Sterling Highway

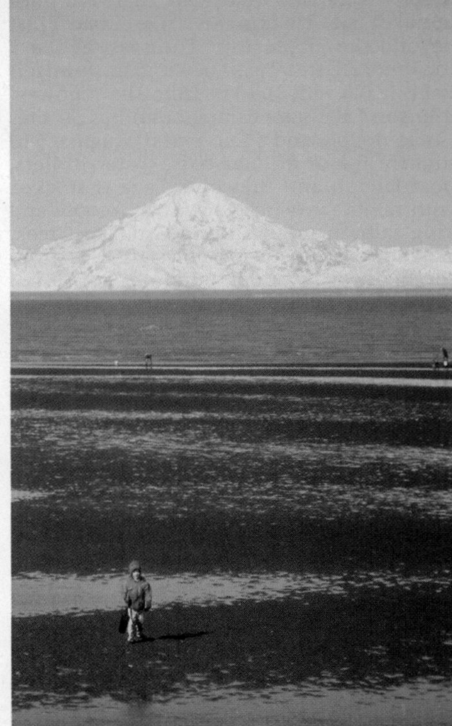
Digging for razor clams near Clam Gulch. (© Barbara Willard)

www.micronet.net/users/~kasilofrv. E-mail: kasilofrv@micronet.net. [ADVERTISEMENT]

Tustumena Ridge Cabins. See display ad this section.

S 114.3 (183.9 km) **A 167.3** (269.2 km) **H 65.2** (104.9 km) Cohoe Loop Road south **junction** with the Sterling Highway. The 13-mile/21-km road loops north to **Milepost S 111.** See COHOE LOOP ROAD log above.

S 117.4 (188.9 km) **A 170.4** (274.2 km) **H 62.1** (99.9 km) Clam Gulch State Recreation Area (watch for easy-to-miss sign) is 0.5 mile/0.8 km from highway; picnic tables, picnic shelter, toilets, water, 116 campsites, $8 nightly fee or annual pass. $5 day-use fee or annual pass. *CAUTION: High ocean bluffs are dangerous.* Short access road to beach (recommended for 4-wheel-drive vehicles only, limited turnaround space). ▲

Clam digging for razor clams on most of the sandy beaches of the western Kenai Peninsula from Kasilof to Anchor Point can be rewarding. Many thousands of clams are dug each year at Clam Gulch. You must have a sportfishing license to dig, and these are available at most sporting goods stores. The bag limit is 60 clams regardless of size (always check current regulations). There is no legally closed season, but quality of the clams varies with month; check locally. Good clamming and fewer people in March and April, although there may still be ice on the beach. Any tide lower than minus 1-foot is enough to dig clams; minus 4- to 5-foot tides are best. The panoramic view of Mount Redoubt, Mount Iliamna and Mount Spurr across Cook Inlet and the expanse of beach are well worth the short side trip even during the off-season.

S 118.2 (190.2 km) **A 171.2** (275.5 km) **H 61.3** (98.7 km) **CLAM GULCH** (pop. 79) post office and lodge.

S 119.6 (192.5 km) **A 172.6** (277.8 km) **H 59.9** (96.4 km) **Clam Gulch Lodge Bed and Breakfast.** Enjoy breakfast buffet with breathtaking mountain views from our fireplace lounge. We guide on the best razor-clam beach in Alaska, and charter for salmon and halibut on fresh and salt water. Call for the best tides. We offer a smoke-free environment, large rooms, twin and king-size beds with private and shared baths. Four RV spots. Box 4999, Clam Gulch, AK 99568. Phone or fax (907) 260-3778, (800) 700-9555. Internet: www.clamgulch.com. See display ad. [ADVERTISEMENT] ▲

S 122.8 (197.6 km) **A 175.8** (282.9 km) **H 56.7** (91.2 km) Paved, double-ended turnout oceanside (no view).

S 124.8 (200.8 km) **A 177.8** (286.1 km) **H 54.7** (88 km) Paved, double-ended turnout oceanside with view of Cook Inlet.

S 126.8 (204.1 km) **A 179.8** (289.4 km) **H 52.7** (84.8 km) Double-ended paved scenic wayside overlooking upper Cook Inlet. Polly Creek, due west across Cook Inlet, is a popular area for clam diggers (fly in). Across the inlet is Mount Iliamna; north of Iliamna is Mount Redoubt.

S 127.1 (204.5 km) **A 180.1** (289.8 km) **H 52.4** (84.3 km) Double-ended paved scenic viewpoint to west with interpretive display on Mount Redoubt and Mount Spurr volcanoes. Private RV park. ▲

Scenic View RV Park. View Mount Redoubt, Cook Inlet. 10 minutes to clamming. Elby fishing charters for halibut and salmon, out of Deep Creek. Visit Homer, Kenai, Soldotna and return to scenic view sunsets. Full hookups, tenting, showers, laundry. Weekly, monthly rates. Pay phone. 27 spaces. Friendly family atmosphere. E-mail: scenicrv@alaska.net. See display ad this section. [ADVERTISEMENT] ▲

S 130.5 (210 km) **A 183.5** (295.3 km) **H 49** (78.9 km) **Ninilchik Point Overnighter.** Spacious, comfortable home-grown log cabins. Scenic getaway. Cook Inlet view. Economy camping, with showers. One cabin self-contained with kitchen. 3-cabins served by shower house. 2-burner electric units. Bedding, linens provided. Outdoor grill. Close to famous fishing, clam beaches. Local charters. (907) 567-3423. See display ad. [ADVERTISEMENT]. ▲

S 132.2 (212.7 km) **A 185.2** (298 km) **H 47.3** (76.1 km) **Heavenly Sights Charters & Camping.** See display ad this section. ▲

S 134.5 (216.4 km) **A 187.5** (301.7 km) **H 45** (72.4 km) Ninilchik State Recreation Area. Ninilchik River Scenic Overlook: $8/camping fee, $5/day-use fee or annual pass. Ninilchik River Campground: $10 camping fee, 43 sites, water, toilets and tables. Trail to **Ninilchik River;** fishing for king and silver salmon, steelhead and Dolly Varden. Ninilchik Beach Campground: $8 camping fee, 35 campsites, toilets, water. $5 day-use fee or annual pass. Popular beach for razor clamming. Access to the clamming beds adjacent to the campgrounds during minus tides.

CAUTION: Drownings have occurred here. Be aware of tide changes when clam digging. Incoming tides can quickly cut you off from the beach. ▲

S 134.7 (216.8 km) **A 187.7** (302 km) **H 44.8** (72.1 km) Coal Street; access west to Ninilchik's historic Russian Orthodox Church at top of hill; plenty of parking and turnaround space; scenic overlook.

S 134.8 (216.9 km) **A 187.8** (302.2 km) **H 44.7** (71.9 km) Large double-ended gravel turnout; scenic overlook.

S 135.1 (217.4 km) **A 188.1** (302.7 km) **H 44.4** (71.4 km) Double-ended gravel turnout and dumpsters at north end of Ninilchik River bridge. Side road leads to **NINILCHIK VILLAGE,** the original village of Ninilchik, and to the beach. Access to mouth of **Ninilchik River;** fishing. A short road branches off this side road and leads into the old village of Ninilchik. Continue straight on side road for motel, beach, overnight RV parking, camping and toilets (follow signs). Sea breezes here keep the beach free of mosquitoes. Historic signs near beach and at village entrance tell about Ninilchik Village, which includes several old dovetailed log buildings. A walking tour brochure is available from businesses in the village and along the highway. Present-day Ninilchik is located at **Milepost S 135.5.** ▲

A beautiful white Russian Orthodox church sits on a hill overlooking the sea above the historic old village. Trail leads up to it from the road into town (watch for sign just past the old village store). The church and cemetery are still in use. You are welcome to walk up to it, but use the well-defined path behind the store (please do not walk through private property), or drive up using the Coal Street access at **Milepost S 134.7.**

Beachcomber Motel & RV Park. See display ad this section. ▲

S 135.3 (217.7 km) **A 188.3** (303 km) **H 44.2** (71.1 km) Gravel turnout to west.

S 135.4 (217.9 km) **A 188.4** (303.2 km)

Photogenic Russian Orthodox church above Ninilchik Village. Access is from Milepost S 134.7. (© Barbara Willard)

H 44.1 (71 km) Kingsley Road; access to Ninilchik post office and 2 private campgrounds. Ninilchik View state campground is across the highway overlooking the village and sea; 12 campsites, water, toilets, litter disposal, 2 dump stations ($5 fee), drinking water fill-up. Camping fee $10/night or annual pass. Foot trail from campground down to beach and village. DOT/PF road maintenance station. ▲

Hylen's Camper Park. 50 full hookups, 19 partial, dry camping with full service for 40-footers to tents. Fish Deep Creek and Ninilchik River for kings, silvers; Afishunt Charters on site to fish Cook Inlet for record halibut, king salmon, May–September. Great clamming. Fish cleaning tables, smoker. Daily, weekly, monthly, seasonal-rated sites. Housekeeping cottages, showers, laundry, storage, social room. Horseshoes. Pay phone. Clean, friendly, reasonable rates. Reservations (907) 567-3393. [ADVERTISEMENT] ▲

Ninilchik

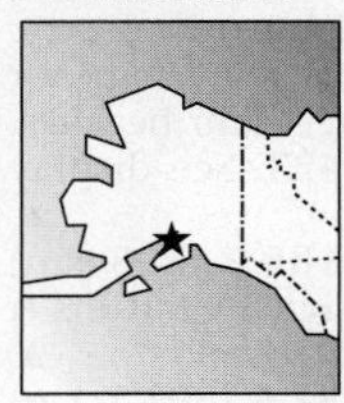

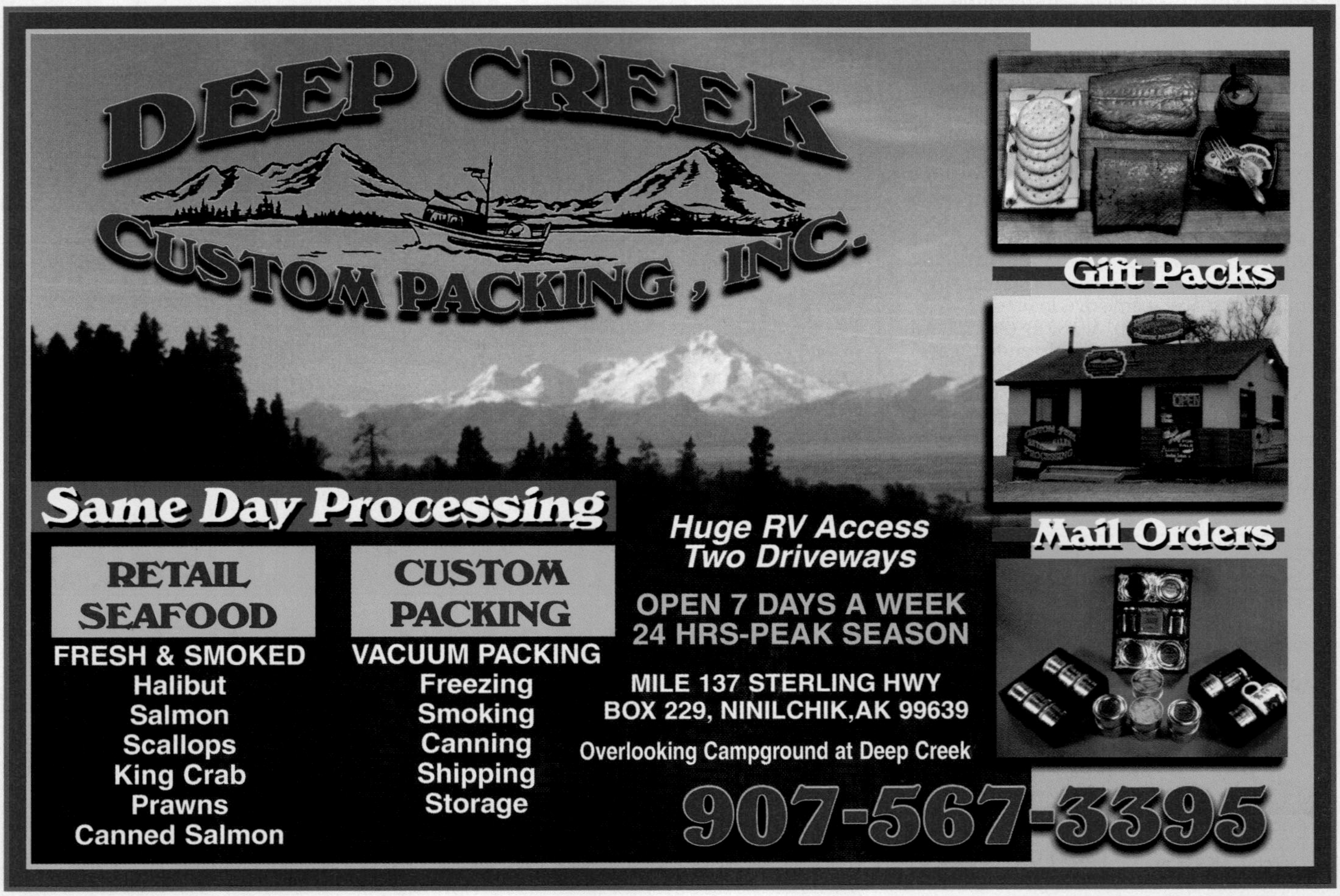

S 135.5 (218 km) **A 188.5** (303.4 km) **H 44** (70.8 km) Pronounced Nin-ILL-chick. **Population:** 456. **Emergency services:** Phone 911. **Clinic and ambulance**, phone (907) 567-3412. **Visitor Information:** At Kiosk, **Milepost S 136.1.** Local businesses are also very helpful. **Private Aircraft:** Ninilchik airstrip, 6.1 miles/9.8 km southeast; elev. 276 feet/84m; length 2,400 feet/732m; dirt; unattended.

Restaurant, lodging and charter service east side of road are part of the community of Ninilchik. Ninilchik extends roughly from Ninilchik State Recreation Area to the north to Deep Creek to the south, with services (grocery stores, gas stations, campgrounds, etc.) located at intervals along the highway. The original village of Ninilchik (signed Ninilchik Village) is reached by a side road from **Milepost S 135.1.**

On Memorial Day weekend, Ninilchik is referred to as the third biggest city in Alaska, as thousands of Alaskans arrive for the fishing (see Area Fishing following). The Kenai

NINILCHIK ADVERTISERS

Chinook Tesoro............Mile 136 Sterling Hwy.
Deep Creek B&B..........Mile 140 Sterling Hwy.
Deep Creek Custom Packing Inc. ....Ph. (907) 567-3395
Hylen's Camper Park and Afishunt Charters.......................Ph. (907) 567-3393
Inlet View Lodge, Inc.........Ph. (907) 567-3330
Key-O's Guide Service......Ph. (800) 478-KEYO
Mary Time Charters..........Ph. (907) 567-3695
Ninilchik Cabins & Fish Camp...........................Ph. (907) 567-3645
Ninilchik Chamber of Commerce..................Ph. (907) 567-3571
Ninilchik Charters............Ph. (907) 248-3507
Ninilchik Saltwater Charters.......................Ph. (907) 567-3611
Ninilchik Village Chache...Ph. (907) 567-1028
O'Fish'ial Charters............Ph. (888) 697-3474
Reel 'Em Inn and Cook Inlet Charters.......................Ph. (800) 567-7335
Roe's Charter Service........Ph. (888) 567-3496

Campers on the beach at Deep Creek State Recreation Area, Milepost S 137.3.
(© Barbara Willard)

Peninsula Fair is held at Ninilchik the third weekend in August. Dubbed the "biggest little fair in Alaska," it features a parade, horse show, livestock competition and exhibits ranging from produce to arts and crafts. Pancake breakfasts, bingo and other events, such as the derby fish fry, are held at the fairgrounds throughout the year. The king salmon derby is held from May to June 15. A halibut derby, sponsored by the Ninilchik Chamber of Commerce, runs from Father's Day through Labor Day. There is an active senior center offering meals and events. Swimming pool at the high school.

AREA FISHING: Well-known area for saltwater king salmon fishing and record halibut fishing. Charter services available. (Combination king salmon and halibut charters are available and popular.) Salt water south of the mouth of **Deep Creek** has produced top king salmon fishing in late May, June and July. Kings 50 lbs. and over are frequently caught. "Lunker" king salmon are available 1 mile/1.6 km south of Deep Creek in **Cook Inlet** from late May through July. Trolling a spinner or a spoon from a boat is the preferred method. Silver, red and pink salmon are available in salt water between Deep Creek and the Ninilchik River during July. A major halibut fishery off Ninilchik has produced some of the largest

BULL MOOSE GIFTS

Mile 135.8 Sterling Highway

"One of the Finest Gift Shops on the Kenai Peninsula"

- Alaskan Dolls
- Framed Art Prints
- Native Arts & Crafts
- Alaskan Gold Nuggets
- Russian Arts & Crafts
- Ivory Carvings and Scrimshaw

- Wide Selection of Jewelry
- Over 50 Shirt Designs
- Souvenirs
- Books
- Stuffed Animals
- Postcards and Notecards

Easy access for large RVs
Open 7 days a week
See log ad at Mile 135.8

Duane & Judith Giarratana, Owners
P.O. Box 39130, Ninilchik, AK 99639
(907) 567-3415

NINILCHIK GENERAL STORE

Mile 135.7 Sterling Highway • (907) 567-3378

See log ad at Mile 135.7

VISA • MasterCard • DISCOVER

All your Fishing & Clamming needs

Licenses • Bait • Tackle • Public Phone • Groceries • Sweatshirts • T-shirts
Gifts • Souvenirs • Postcards • Books • Film • Ice • Hardware • Alaskan Gold Nuggets
Sandwiches • Fountain Soda • Hot Dogs • Hot Coffee

Open Year-round – Easy access for large RVs – Summer Hours 6 a.m. - Midnight

Duane & Judith Giarratana, Owners • P.O. Box 39434, Ninilchik, AK 99639

trophy halibut found in Cook Inlet, including a 466-lb. unofficial world record sport-caught halibut.

Sterling Highway Log

(continued)

S 135.6 (218.2 km) **A 188.6** (303.5 km) **H 43.9** (70.6 km) Ninilchik High School. Ninilchik Library, open 10 A.M. to 4 P.M. daily in the summer.

S 135.7 (218.4 km) **A 188.7** (303.7 km) **H 43.8** (70.5 km) **Ninilchik General Store.** Open every day for all your travel needs. Offering groceries, bait, tackle, licenses, rain gear, ice, film, gifts, books, T-shirts, gold nugget jewelry, hardware and a snack bar. Try our Fisherman's Bag Lunch. Stop in for free information packet on the Ninilchik area. You'll like our prices and service. Ask your friends who have met us. We compete for your business, we don't just wait for it to happen. See display ad this section. [ADVERTISEMENT]

S 135.8 (218.5 km) **A 188.8** (303.7 km) **H 43.7** (70.3 km) **Bull Moose Gifts.** One of the nicest gift shops on the Kenai Peninsula, offering a wide selection of gifts and souvenirs. Alaskan and Russian arts and crafts, fine art prints, jewelry, including Alaskan gold nuggets, caps, postcards, notecards, and over 50 Alaskan designs of T-shirts and sweatshirts. Easy access for large RVs, lots of parking and clean restroom. See display ad this section. [ADVERTISEMENT]

S 135.9 (218.7 km) **A 188.9** (304 km) **H 43.6** (70.2 km) **Country Boy Campground.** See display ad this section.

Homestead House B&B. See display ad this section.

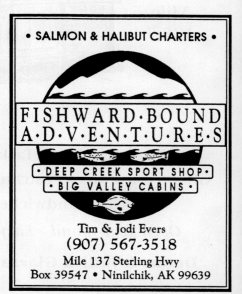

S 136 (218.9 km) **A 189** (304.1 km) **H 43.5** (70 km) **Chinook Tesoro.** Ninilchik. 24-hour card lock. Open year-round. Self-serve gasoline, propane, on-road and dyed diesel. We install quality NAPA Auto Parts. Auto/RV mechanics, tire sales and repair, water/air for RVs. Bait, ice, market items. Free tide books, visitor information on clamming and guided fishing. Tesoro, VISA,

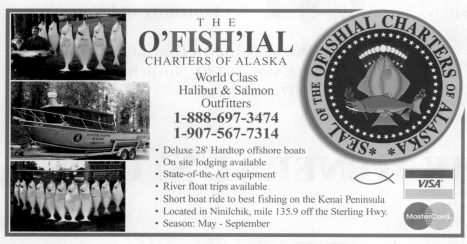

MasterCard, Discover. All major oil company cards welcome. See display ad this section. [ADVERTISEMENT]

S 136.1 (219 km) **A 189.1** (304.3 km) **H 43.4** (69.8 km) **Chihuly's Charters** and **Porcupine Shop.** See display ad this section.

S 136.2 (219.2 km) **A 189.2** (304.5 km) **H 43.3** (69.7 km) Peninsula Fairgrounds. Visitor Information Kiosk opposite the fairgrounds.

Bluff House Bed and Breakfast. See display ad this section.

S 136.7 (219.9 km) **A 189.7** (305.3 km) **H 42.8** (68.9 km) Bridge over Deep Creek. Developed sites on both sides of creek: Deep Creek North Scenic Overlook and Deep Creek South Scenic Overlook. Both have $8/camping fee, $5/day-use fee or annual pass, restrooms, water, interpretive kiosks, tables and fireplaces. Deep Creek South offers camping May and June only, day-use only rest of summer. ▲

Freshwater fishing in **Deep Creek** for king salmon up to 40 lbs., use spinners with red bead lures, Memorial Day weekend and the 4 weekends following; Dolly Varden in July and August; silver salmon to 15 lbs., August and September; steelhead to 15 lbs., late September through October. No bait fishing permitted after Aug. 31. Mouth of Deep Creek access from Deep Creek State Recreation Area turnoff at **Milepost S 137.3.**

S 137 (220.4 km) **A 190** (305.8 km) **H 42.5** (68.4 km) Cannery and sports shop with tackle and clam shovel rentals west side of road.

Fishward Bound Adventures. See display ad this section.

Deep Creek Custom Packing, Inc. Just south of Deep Creek bridge in Ninilchik. Home of the finest gourmet smoked salmon and halibut in the world. Free samples and coffee. Seafood display includes locally caught scallops, razor clams, crab, halibut and salmon. Sport fishermen take their own catch in to be hand-packed, frozen, canned or smoked to their specifications. Mail order service available for gift packs, fresh Alaskan seafood, canned salmon, smoked salmon and halibut. State-of-the-art insulated packaging. Overnight delivery, door-to-door, anywhere in the U.S. Visitor information on the best charters, clam digging and fishing. Stop in and see this truly traditional Alaskan business. See display ad this section. [ADVERTISEMENT]

S 137.3 (220.9 km) **A 190.3** (306.2 km) **H 42.2** (67.9 km) Deep Creek State Recreation Area on the beach at the mouth of Deep Creek; parking for 300 vehicles, overnight camping, water, tables, dumpsters, toilets and fireplaces. Drive 0.5 mile/0.8 km down paved road. Camping fee $10/night per vehicle or annual pass, day-use fee $5 or annual pass. Favorite area for surf fishing and to launch boats. Boat launch $5 fee or annual pass. Private boat launch service here uses tractors to launch boats from beach into Cook Inlet. Seasonal checks by U.S. Coast Guard for personal flotation devices, boating safety. Good bird watching in wetlands behind beach; watch for eagles. Good clamming at low tide. The beaches here are lined with coal, which falls from the exposed seams of high cliffs. ▲

CAUTION: Rapidly changing tides and weather. Although the mouth of Deep Creek affords boaters good protection, low tides may prevent return; check tide tables.

S 137.4 (221.1 km) **A 190.4** (306.4 km) **H 42.1** (67.8 km) **Roe's Charter Service.** Family owned, operated by year-round residents. Halibut, salmon combo charters, April–September. Friendly, personalized service at our quiet location. Circle drive for RV convenience. Fish from custom built 26-foot offshore, heated-cabin boat, or 20-foot open boat. Both boats outfitted with enclosed marine bathroom, comfortable seating, state-of-the-art electronics, custom made rods, top quality gear. Free filleting. Further processing, shipping services nearby. Lodging, etc. available. Phone (888) 567-3496, (907) 567-3496. Internet: www.alaskaone.com/roe. See display ad. [ADVERTISEMENT]

S 137.5 (221.3 km) **A 190.5** (306.7 km) **H 42** (67.5 km) **D & M RV Park & Charters.** Our park is on the bluff, overlooking the beach at Deep Creek. We offer 40 sites, 25 with water and electric. A dump station and fish cleaning facilities are provided. Daily charters are also available. Your hosts, Debbie and Marc, can be reached at: (907) 349-7357 or (800) 479-7357 in winter; (907) 567-4368 in the summer. Located at Mile 137.5 Sterling Highway. Visit our website at: www.alaskaoutdoors.com/DM/. [ADVERTISEMENT] ▲

S 138.6 (223 km) **A 191.6** (308.3 km) **H 40.9** (65.8 km) Solid waste transfer site; public dumpsters.

S 140.3 (225.8 km) **A 193.3** (311.1 km) **H 39.2** (63.1 km) Double-ended turnout with scenic view to west.

S 140.5 (226.1 km) **A 193.5** (311.4 km) **H 39** (62.8 km) **Double Eagle Lodge**. See display ad this section.

S 142.7 (229.6 km) **A 195.7** (314.9 km) **H 36.8** (59.2 km) Double-ended paved turnout with dumpster, view of Mount Iliamna across the inlet.

S 143.8 (231.4 km) **A 196.8** (316.7 km) **H 35.7** (57.4 km) Happy Valley Creek. The area surrounding this creek is known locally as the Happy Valley community.

S 148 (238.1 km) **A 201** (323.5 km) **H 31.5** (50.7 km) Scenic viewpoint. Sign here reads: "Looking westerly across Cook Inlet, Mt. Iliamna and Mt. Redoubt in the Chigmit Mountains of the Aleutian Range can be seen rising over 10,000 feet above sea level. This begins a chain of mountains and islands known as the Aleutian Chain extending west over 1,700 miles to Attu beyond the International Date Line to the Bering Sea, separating the Pacific and Arctic oceans. Mt. Redoubt on the right, and Iliamna on the left, were recorded as active volcanoes in the mid-18th century. Mt. Redoubt had a minor eruption in 1966."

Mount Redoubt had a major eruption in December 1989. The eruptions continued through April 1990, then subsided to steam plumes. Mount Redoubt is still considered active.

S 150 (241 km) **A 203** (326.7 km) **H 29.5** (47.8 km) **Cooper's Bed & Breakfast.** See display ad this section.

S 150.9 (242.8 km) **A 203.9** (328.1 km) **H 28.6** (46 km) Bridge over Stariski Creek.

S 151.9 (244.4 km) **A 204.9** (329.7 km) **H 27.6** (44.4 km) Stariski Creek State Recreation Site on bluff overlooking Cook Inlet; 16 campsites, $10 nightly fee or annual pass, toilets (wheelchair accessible) and well water. ▲

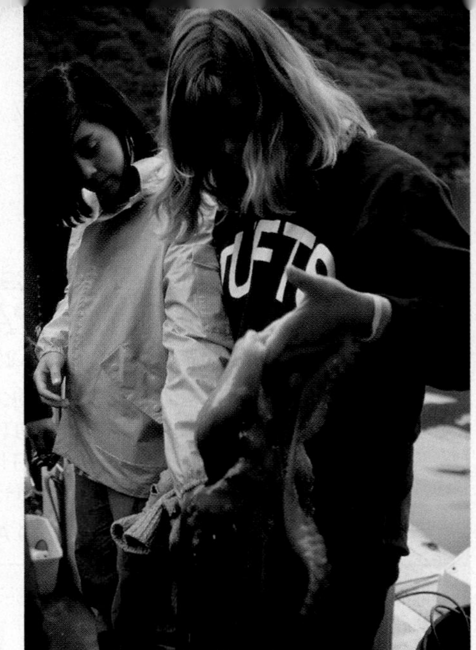

Checking out an octopus found in a shrimp pot. (Jerrianne Lowther, staff)

S 152.7 (245.7 km) **A 205.7** (331 km) **H 26.8** (43.1 km) **Eagle Crest RV Park & Cabins.** See display ad this section. ▲

S 154.1 (248 km) **A 207.1** (333.3 km) **H 25.4** (40.9 km) **Timberline Creations.** See display ad this section.

S 155 (249.4 km) **A 208** (334.7 km) **H 24.5** (39.4 km) **Bear Paw Charters.** This Anchor Point location is only minutes from trophy halibut and salmon fishing. All equipment provided plus free filleting. Small groups and personalized service are the focus of this family-owned and operated business. Lodging also available in private, fully equipped log cabins. You'll like the gift shop. Phone (907) 235-5399. See display ad this section. E-mail: bearpaw@xyz.net; Web address: www.xyz.net\~bearpaw. [ADVERTISEMENT]

EAGLE CREST RV PARK & CABINS

Kenai Peninsula

1-888-235-2905 • Mile 152.7 Sterling Hwy.

FULL HOOKUPS • LAUNDRY • SHOWERS
CABINS WITH PRIVATE BATHS, KITCHENETTES
BEAUTIFUL, QUIET WOODED SETTING
BEACH ACCESS • FISHING CHARTERS

www.xyz.net/~Eagle
e-mail: eagle@xyz.net

P.O. Box 249 Anchor Point, AK 99556 • (907) 235-6851

TIMBERLINE CREATIONS

MP 154.1 STERLING HWY. LARGE CIRCLE DR

STOP IN FOR A FREE PIECE OF ANTLER OR MAMMOTH IVORY

Antler & Fossil Ivory Gifts, Jewelry & Scrimshaw made in our workshop.

Alaskan Mammoth Fossils ~ Antiques Eskimo Artifacts & More!

(907) 235-8288
Michael & Sandra Lettis
HC 67 Box 299, Anchor Point, AK 99556

There are more bald eagles in Alaska than in the Lower 48 combined.

(© Barbara Willard)

S 156.3 (251.5 km) **A 209.3** (336.8 km) **H 23.2** (37.3 km) **Anchor River Tesoro.** See display ad this section.

Mugs and Jugs. See display ad this section.

The Warehouse, Inc. See display ad this section.

S 156.7 (252.2 km) **A 209.7** (337.5 km) **H 22.8** (36.7 km) Anchor Point post office at turnoff for Milo Fritz Road to west and North Fork Road to east, an 18-mile/29-km loop which rejoins the Sterling Highway at **Milepost S 164.3**. Post office is open 9 A.M. to 5 P.M. weekdays, 9 A.M. to noon Saturday.

ANCHOR POINT (pop. 866) has groceries, gas stations with major repair service, motel, restaurant and fast-food stands, liquor store, clinic, sporting goods, gift shops and ceramic studio. Volunteer fire department and ambulance, phone 911. **Visitor Information:** Located in the log cabin just off the Sterling Highway on Old Sterling Highway. Open 10 A.M. to 4 P.M., weekdays, Memorial Day to Labor Day. The center is manned by volunteers from Anchor Point Senior Citizens, Inc.

Iliamna Mt. View B&B. From Anchor Point, from the Sterling Highway, turn west on Milo Fritz Avenue, 0.6 mile to Sand Beach Road, right 0.2 mile. Beautiful log

ANCHOR POINT ADVERTISERS

Bear Paw Charters	Ph. (907) 235-5399
Eagle Crest RV Park and Cabins	Ph. (907) 235-6851
Iliamna Mt. View Bed & Breakfast	Ph. (907) 235-6331
Our Front Porch Bed & Breakfast	Ph. (800) 277-8885

THE WAREHOUSE INC.

Anchor Point Alaska's Little 'super'market

Fresh Produce • Soft Drinks & Snacks
Ice • Bait
Fishing & Hunting Licenses

(907) 235-7999

Mile 156.3 Sterling Highway

home on bluffs above the Anchor River. Guest rooms, patio, sitting rooms have views. Reasonable rates. Phone (907) 235-6331. See display ad. [ADVERTISEMENT]

Our Front Porch Bed and Breakfast. See display ad this section.

S 156.8 (252.3 km) **A 209.8** (337.6 km) **H 22.7** (36.5 km) **Anchor Point B&B, Clive's Fishing Guide Service.** Just off highway on Thurmond Street. Enjoy our quiet clean rooms with private bath and entrance. All new Beautyrest mattresses, central lounge with TV, coffee and phone. Fish for salmon and halibut on the same day, all equipment furnished. U.S. Coast Guard licensed and insured. Call (907) 235-1236. Fax 235-1905. E-mail: clives@ptialaska.net. Hosts: Clive and Marilyn Talkington, Box 97, Anchor Point, AK 99556. [ADVERTISEMENT]

S 156.9 (252.5 km) **A 209.9** (337.8 km) **H 22.6** (36.4 km) **Junction** with Old Sterling Highway; access to Anchor River businesses and Anchor River (Beach) Road. See ANCHOR RIVER (BEACH) ROAD log page 618.

Anchor River Inn. See display ad this section.

S 157.1 (252.8 km) **A 210.1** (338.1 km) **H 22.4** (36 km) Anchor River bridge.

S 160.9 (258.9 km) **A 213.9** (344.2 km) **H 18.6** (29.9 km) Side road to artist Norman Lowell's studio and KWLS radio station.

S 161 (259.1 km) **A 214** (344.4 km) **H 18.5** (29.8 km) Anchor River bridge.

S 162.4 (261.4 km) **A 215.4** (346.6 km) **H 17.1** (27.5 km) Gravel turnout to east by Anchor River.

S 164.3 (264.4 km) **A 217.3** (349.7 km) **H 15.2** (24.5 km) North Fork Loop Road to Anchor River.

S 164.8 (265.2 km) **A 217.8** (350.5 km) **H 14.7** (23.7 km) Old Sterling Highway leads 9.4 miles/15.1 km northwest in a loop to Anchor River (Beach) Road, which provides access to Cook Inlet, Anchor River recreation and Anchor Point businesses. See ANCHOR RIVER (BEACH) ROAD log page 618 and **Milepost S 156.9.**

S 165.4 (266.2 km) **A 218.4** (351.5 km) **H 14.1** (22.7 km) **Billikin Gift Shop.** See display ad this section.

S 166.8 (268.4 km) **A 219.8** (353.7 km) **H 12.7** (20.4 km) Virginia Avenue.

Holland Days Bed & Breakfast Cabins. See display ad this section.

S 167.1 (268.9 km) **A 220.1** (354.2 km) **H 12.4** (20 km) Diamond Ridge Road.

S 168.2 (270.7 km) **A 221.2** (356 km) **H 11.3** (18.2 km) **Whispering Winds Bed & Breakfast.** See display ad this section.

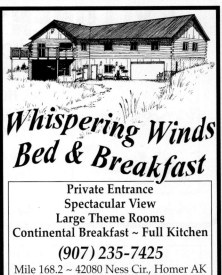

Anchor River (Beach) Road Log

MILEPOST® field editor Jerrianne Lowther on one of her annual treks to the end of Anchor River Road. (Jerrianne Lowther, staff)

Turn off the Sterling Highway at **Milepost S 156.9** on to the Old Sterling Highway and continue past the Anchor River Inn to the Anchor River. Just beyond the bridge is the turnoff for Anchor River (Beach) Road, a 1.2-mile/1.9-km spur road providing access to Anchor River recreation area.

Distance from junction (J) is shown.

J 0 Junction of Old Sterling Highway and Sterling Highway at **Milepost S 156.9.**

J 0.1 (0.2 km) School Road. Anchor Point visitor information center. A plaque across from the visitor center marks the westernmost point on the contiguous North American Highway system.

Anchor River Inn, overlooking beautiful Anchor River and in business for 20 years, has the finest family restaurant on the peninsula, where you can see one of the largest displays of collectible plates in Alaska. Serving breakfast, lunch and dinner. Large cocktail lounge has a wide-screen TV, pool tables, dance floor and video games. 20 modern motel units with phones; 10 spacious units with color TV and 2 queen-sized beds, and 10 smaller units overlooking the river. Our fully stocked liquor, grocery store and gift shop serve the Anchor Point area year-round. Write: Box 154, Anchor Point, AK 99556; phone 1-800-435-8531 in USA, or (907) 235-8531; fax (907) 235-2296. Your hosts: Bob and Simonne Clutts. [ADVERTISEMENT]

J 0.3 (0.5 km) Anchor River bridge, also known as "the erector set bridge."

J 0.4 (0.6 km) Road forks: Old Sterling Highway continues south and rejoins Sterling Highway at **Milepost S 164.8**. Turn right for Anchor River (Beach) Road.

Access to Silverking campground (Anchor River State Recreation Area); RV camping, toilets, dumpster, $8 nightly fee or annual pass. ▲

J 0.6 (1 km) Coho campground (Anchor River SRA); camping, toilets, $8 nightly fee or annual pass. ▲

J 0.7 (1.1 km) Anchor Point Chamber of Commerce Salmon Derby Weigh-in and information. Tackle shop.

J 0.8 (1.3 km) Steelhead campground (Anchor River SRA); camping, toilets, $8 nightly fee or annual pass. ▲

J 1.1 (1.8 km) Slidehole campground (Anchor River SRA); 30 campsites, $10 nightly fee or annual pass, shelter with tables, public water source for campers, special senior/wheelchair camping area, large day-use parking lot, trail access to river. ♿▲

J 1.3 (2.1 km) **Kyllonen's RV Park**, a few steps from famous Anchor River and picturesque Cook Inlet. Providing spring water, electricity and sewer. Additional amenities include fish cleaning station, BBQ pits, free firewood and picnic tables. Showers, restrooms and laundry. Gift shop and Espresso Bar. Fishing licenses. We book fishing charters. May through September. Year-round area information center, phone/fax (907) 235-7762, fax (907) 235-6435. E-mail: susank@xyz.net. See display ad this section. [ADVERTISEMENT] ▲

J 1.5 (2.4 km) Halibut campground (Anchor River SRA); camping, toilets, $8 nightly fee or annual pass. ▲

J 1.6 (2.6 km) Road deadends on shore of Cook Inlet; beach access, 12-hour parking. Private tractor boat launch service. Signs here mark the most westerly point on the North American continent accessible by continuous road system and depict outlines of Cook Inlet volcanoes.

The Anchor Point area is noted for seasonal king and silver salmon, steelhead and rainbow fishing. Saltwater trolling for king salmon to 80 lbs., halibut to 200 lbs., spring through fall. **Anchor River**, king salmon fishing permitted only on 5 consecutive weekends, beginning Memorial Day weekend; trout and steelhead from July to October; closed to all fishing Dec. 31 to June 30, except for king salmon weekends. Excellent fishing for 12- to 24-inch sea-run Dollies in July and late summer. During August silver runs, fish high tides. Anchor River King Salmon Derby is usually held the last weekend in May and the first 4 weekends in June. A silver salmon derby is held in August.

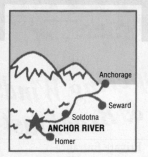

Return to Milepost S 156.9 Sterling Highway

Alaska Day (October 18) is a state holiday commemorating the transfer of Alaska from Russia to the United States.

S 168.5 (271.2 km) **A 221.5** (356.5 km) **H 11** (17.7 km) Alaska State Parks' South District office is located on the bluff here. A small parking lot is adjacent to the log office where visitors may obtain information on Kachemak Bay state park, as well as other southern Kenai Peninsula state park lands.

S 169.3 (272.5 km) **A 222.3** (357.7 km) **H 10.2** (16.4 km) Homer DOT/PF highway maintenance station. RV park.

The Village Barabara RV Park. See display ad this section. ▲

S 169.6 (272.9 km) **A 222.6** (358.2 km) **H 9.9** (15.9 km) Two viewpoints overlooking Kachemak Bay. Double-ended turnout.

S 170 (273.6 km) **A 223** (358.9 km) **H 9.5** (15.3 km) Bay View Inn. Homer demonstration forest.

S 171.2 (275.5 km) **A 224.2** (360.8 km) **H 8.3** (13.4 km) Land fill road.

S 171.9 (276.6 km) **A 224.9** (361.9 km) **H 7.6** (12.2 km) West Hill Road; access to bed and breakfasts. Connects to Skyline Drive and East Hill Road for scenic drive along Homer Bluff.

S 172.5 (277.6 km) **A 225.5** (362.9 km) **H 7** (11.3 km) Hotel.

S 172.6 (277.8 km) **A 225.6** (363 km) **H 6.9** (11.1 km) Homer Junior High School.

S 172.7 (277.9 km) **A 225.7** (363.2 km) **H 6.8** (10.9 km) **Oceanview RV Park.** See display ad this section. ▲

S 172.8 (278.1 km) **A 225.8** (363.4 km) **H 6.7** (10.8 km) Exit onto Pioneer Avenue for downtown **HOMER** (description follows). Drive 0.2 mile/0.3 km on Pioneer Avenue and turn left on Bartlett Avenue for the Pratt Museum (see Attractions in the Homer section) and Homer city campground (follow signs). Pioneer Avenue continues through downtown Homer to Lake Street and to East Hill Road. ▲

S 173.1 (278.6 km) **A 226.1** (363.9 km) **H 6.4** (10.3 km) Homer Chamber of Commerce Visitor Center at Main Street; access to food, lodging, dump station and other services. Bishop's Beach Park.

S 173.5 (279.2 km) **A 226.5** (364.5 km) **H 6** (9.7 km) Eagle Quality Center; shopping, groceries.

S 173.7 (279.5 km) **A 226.7** (364.8 km) **H 5.8** (9.3 km) Heath Street. Post office (ZIP code 99603).

S 173.9 (279.9 km) **A 226.9** (365.2 km) **H 5.6** (9 km) Lake Street. Access to downtown Homer and Lakeside Center. *NOTE: expect road construction on Lake Street in 1998.*

S 174 (280 km) **A 227** (365.3 km) **H 5.5** (8.9 km) Beluga Lake floatplane base.

S 174.4 (280.7 km) **A 227.4** (366 km) **H 5.1** (8.2 km) Lambert Lane, access to floatplane base.

S 174.7 (281.1 km) **A 227.7** (366.4 km) **H 4.8** (7.7 km) Alaska Dept. of Fish and Game office. The ADF&G Division of Sport Fish issues 5 different regulation booklets for each of the 5 different sportfishing regions in Alaska. For a current copy of the Kenai Peninsula–Cook Inlet Salt Water–Susitna–West Cook Inlet regulations, stop by the ADF&G office.

S 174.8 (281.3 km) **A 227.8** (366.6 km) **H 4.7** (7.6 km) **Homer Tesoro.** See display ad this section.

S 175 (281.6 km) **A 228** (366.9 km) **H 4.5** (7.2 km) Airport Road. Sterling Highway crosses onto Homer Spit.

A series of boardwalks along the Spit houses shops, charter services, food outlets, etc. Also on the Spit: a resort hotel, restaurants, seafood markets, private campgrounds, and public camping areas (check in with camping registration office on the Spit); the harbormaster's office, small boat basin, shore fishing for salmon in the Fishing Hole, Alaska Marine Highway ferry terminal and a boat ramp. ▲

S 179.5 (288.9 km) **A 232.5** (374.2 km) **H 0** Sterling Highway ends at Land's End Resort and Campground at the tip of Homer Spit.

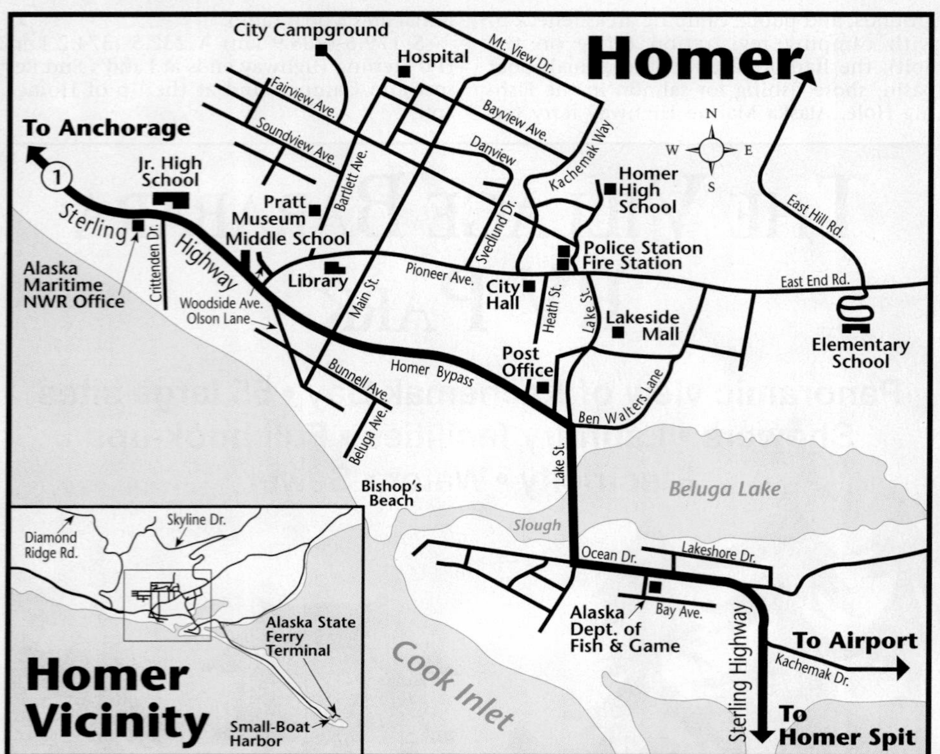

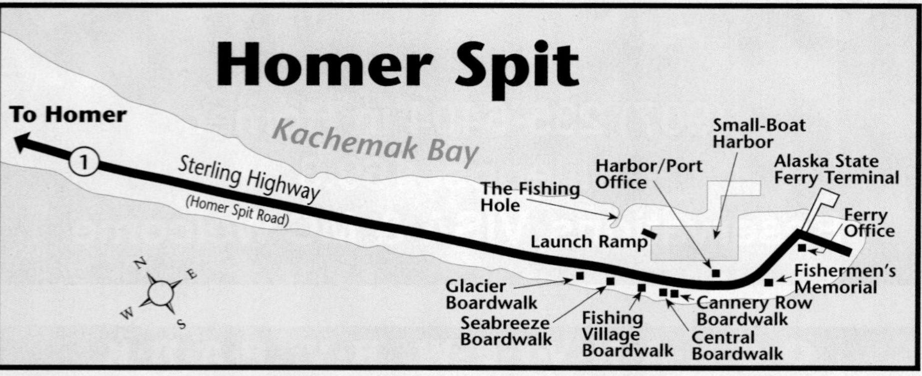

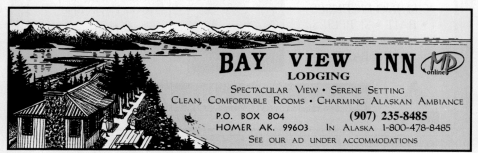

A sailboat on Kachemak Bay.

(© Ruth von Spalding)

Homer

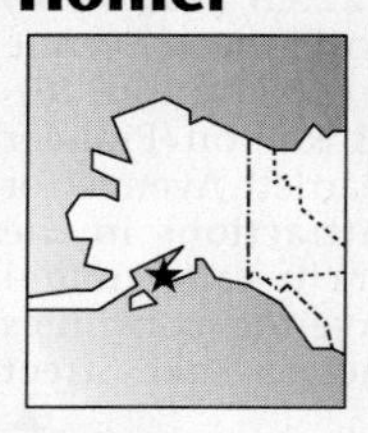

Located on the southwestern Kenai Peninsula on the north shore of Kachemak Bay at the easterly side of the mouth of Cook Inlet; 226 miles/364 km by highway or 40 minutes by jet aircraft from Anchorage. **Population:** 4,064. **Emergency Services:** Phone 911 for all emergency services. **City Police,** phone (907) 235-3150. **Alaska State Troopers,** in the Public Safety Bldg., phone (907) 235-8239. **Fire Department** and **Ambulance**, phone (907) 235-3155. **Coast Guard**, phone Zenith 5555. (Coast Guard Auxiliary, phone (907/235-7277.) **Hospital**, South Peninsula, phone (907) 235-8101. **Veterinary Clinic**, phone (907) 235-8960.

Visitor Information: Chamber of Commerce Visitor Center is located on the Homer Bypass at Main Street. Open year-round. Contact the Homer Chamber of Commerce, Box 541, Homer 99603; phone during business hours (907) 235-7740 or 235-5300.

The Pratt Museum is open daily 10 A.M. to 6 P.M. from May through September; open noon to 5 P.M. Tuesday through Sunday from October through April; closed in January. Contact the Pratt Museum, 3779 Bartlett St., Homer 99603. Phone (907) 235-8635.

Elevation: Sea level to 800 feet/244m. **Climate:** Winter temperatures occasionally fall below zero, but seldom colder. The Kenai Mountains north and east protect Homer from severe cold, and Cook Inlet provides warming air currents. The highest temperature recorded is 81°F/27°C. Average annual precipitation is 27.9 inches. Prevailing winds are from the northeast, averaging 6.5 mph/10.5 kmph. **Radio:** KGTL 620, KWAV 103.5/104.9/106.3, MBN-FM 107.1/96.7/95.3, KBBI 890, KPEN-FM 99.3/100.9/102.3, KWHQ-FM 98.3. **Television:** KTUU, KTBY, KTVA, KAKM, KIMO. **Newspaper:** *Homer News* (weekly), *Homer Tribune* (weekly).

Private Aircraft: Homer airport, 1.7 miles/2.7 km east; elev. 78 feet/24m; length 7,400 feet/2,255m; asphalt; fuel 100LL, Jet A;

attended.

In the late 1800s, a coal mine was operating at Homer's Bluff Point, and a railroad carried the coal out to the end of Homer Spit. (The railroad was abandoned in 1907.) Gold seekers debarked at Homer, bound for the goldfields at Hope and Sunrise. The community of Homer was established about 1896 and named for Homer Pennock.

Coal mining operations ceased around the time of WWI, but settlers continued to trickle into the area, some to homestead, others to work in the canneries built to process Cook Inlet fish.

Today, Homer's picturesque setting, mild climate and great fishing (especially for halibut) attract thousands of visitors each year. In addition to its tourist industry and role as a trade center, Homer's commercial fishing industry is an important part of its economy. Homer calls itself the "Halibut Fishing Capital of the World." Manufacturing and seafood processing, government offices, trades and construction are other key industries.

Homer is host to a large artist community. Potters, sculptors, painters and jewelers practice their craft and sell their goods in local shops and galleries. The local theater group provides live performances year-round.

Rising behind the townsite are the gently sloping bluffs which level off at about 1,200 feet/366m to form the southern rim of the western plateau of the Kenai. These green slopes are tinted in pastel shades by acres of wildflowers from June to September; fireweed predominates among scattered patches of geranium, paintbrush, lupine, rose and many other species. Two main roads (East Hill Road and West Hill Road) lead from the Homer business section to the "Skyline Drive" along the rim of the bluffs,

HOMER ADVERTISERS

Alaska Maritime Tours ....Homer Spit Rd.
Alaska Midnight Sun Charters ....Ph. (800) 438-6257
Alaska Wild Berry Products ....528 E. Pioneer Ave.
Alaska Woodside Lodging ....Ph. (907) 235-8389
Alaska's Pioneer Inn ....244 Pioneer Ave.
All Points North Travel .....Ph. (907) 235-2575
Almost Home B&B Cabins ....Ph. (800) 478-2352
Art Shop Gallery ....Ph. (800) 478-7076
B & C Charters ....Ph. (907) 235-7916
Bald Mountain Air ....Ph. (907) 235-7969
Bay View Inn ....Mile 170 Sterling Hwy.
Beeson's Bed & Breakfast ....Ph. (907) 235-3757
Better Sweater ....Ph. (888) 842-4140
Bob's Trophy Charters......Ph. (907) 235-6544
Bookstore, The................Eagle Quality Center
Brass Ring Bed & Breakfast ....Ph. (907) 235-5450
Bunnell Street Gallery ......Ph. (907) 235-2662
Central Charters Booking Agency, Inc. ....Ph. (907) 235-7847
Chocolate Drop B&B ....Ph. (907) 235-3668
Cloudy Mountain Inn B&B ....Ph. (907) 235-2254
Coal Point Seafood Co......Ph. (800) 325-3877
Coastal Outfitters ....Ph. (907) 235-8492
Copper Helmet B&B ....Ph. (907) 235-5608
Crane's Crest B&B ....Ph. (800) 338-2969
Driftwood Inn & RV Park..Ph. (907) 235-8019
Fireweed Gallery ....Ph. (907) 235-7040
Grizzly Charters ....Ph. (907) 235-4388
Halcyon Heights B&B ....Ph. (907) 235-2148
Halibut Cove Cabins..................Halibut Cove
Head's Rest B&B ....Ph. (907) 235-5188
Heritage Hotel–Lodge ......Ph. (907) 235-7787
Historic B&B.....................Ph. (907) 235-5384
Holland Days Bed and Breakfast.......................Ph. (907) 235-7604
Homer Alaska Referral Agency/Seekins ....Ph. (907) 235-8996
Homer Chamber of Commerce ....Ph. (907) 235-7740
Homer Ocean Charters, Inc.......Cannery Row, Homer Spit
Homer Spit Campground & Lodging.............................Homer Spit
Homer Tesoro ....1554 Homer Spit Rd.
Homer's Finest B&B Network.......................Ph. (800) 764-3211
Inlet Charters ....Ph. (907) 235-6126
Island Watch Bed & Breakfast ....Ph. (907) 235-2265
J.P.'s B&B.........................Ph. (907) 235-7362
Kachemak Air Service, Inc. ....Ph. (907) 235-8924
Kachemak Bay Ferry "Danny J" ....Ph. (907) 296-2223
Kachemak Kiana Bed and Breakfast ....Ph. (907) 235-8824
Kachemak Shores Bed and Breakfast ....Ph. (907) 235-6864
K-Bay Charters ....Ph. (800) 478-8119
Land's End Resort ....End of Homer Spit
Land's End RV Park ....End of Homer Spit
Maria's Majestic View Bed and Breakfast...............Ph. (888) 246-6413
Morning Glory Bed and Breakfast/Charters ......Ph. (907) 235-8084
NOMAR (Northern Marine Canvas Products) ....104 E. Pioneer Ave.
North Country Halibut Charters.............Cannery Row, Homer Spit
NorthStar-Expediton ....Ph. (888) 593-7175
Ocean Shores Motel ....Ph. (907) 235-7775
Oceanview RV Park...........Ph. (907) 235-3951
Picture Alaska...................Ph. (907) 235-2300
Pier One Theatre ....Homer Spit
Pratt Museum ....Ph. (907) 235-8635
Ptarmigan Arts.................Ph. (907) 235-5345
Salty Dawg Saloon.........................Homer Spit
Sarah N Jon's B&B ....Ph. (800) 764-3211
Sea Lion Fine Art Gallery, The ....Ph. (907) 235-3400
Ship to Shore Tours..........Ph. (800) 478-7847
Silver fox Charters ....Homer Spit
Skyline Bed & Breakfast....Ph. (907) 235-3832
Spruce Acres Bed & Breakfast......................Ph. (907) 235-8388
Sun Spin Guest House ......Ph. (907) 235-6677
Tacklebuster Halibut Charters ....Ph. (907) 235-7847
3 Moose Meadow Wilderness B&B ....Ph. (907) 235-0755
Trail's End Horse Adventures ....Ph. (907) 235-6393
Tsimshian Charters ....**Ph. (907) 235-8118**
Washboard, The ....Ph. (907) 235-6781
Wild Rose Bed & Breakfast & Private Cabins ....Ph. (907) 235-8780
Walking River Guide, The ....Ph. (907) 235-7429

Hazy view of Homer Spit, Kachemak Bay and the snowy Kenai Mountains.
(© Corinne Smith/RKI)

and other roads connect with many homesteads on the "Hill."

The name *Kachemak* (in Aleut dialect said to mean "smoky bay") was supposedly derived from the smoke which once rose from the smoldering coal seams jutting from the clay bluffs of the upper north shore of Kachemak Bay and the cliffs near Anchor Point. In the early days many of the exposed coal seams were slowly burning from causes unknown. Today the erosion of these bluffs drops huge fragments of lignite and bituminous coal on the beaches, creating a plentiful supply of winter fuel for the residents. There are an estimated 400,000,000 tons of coal deposit in the immediate vicinity of Homer.

Kachemak is a magnificent deep-water bay that reaches inland from Cook Inlet for 30 miles/48.3 km, with an average width of 7 miles/11.3 km. The bay is rich in marine life. The wild timbered coastline of the south shore, across from Homer, is indented with many fjords and inlets, reaching far into the rugged glacier-capped peaks of the Kenai Mountains.

Jutting out for nearly 5 miles/8 km from the Homer shore is the Homer Spit, a long, narrow bar of gravel. The road along the backbone of the Spit connects with the main road through Homer (all the Sterling Highway). The Spit has had quite a history, and it continues to be a center of activity for the town. In 1964, after the earthquake, the Spit sank 4 to 6 feet, requiring several buildings to be moved to higher ground. Today, the Spit is the site of a major dock facility for boat loading, unloading, servicing and refrigerating. The deep-water dock can accommodate up to 2 340-foot vessels with 30-foot drafts at the same time, making it accessible to cruise and cargo ships. It is also home port to the Alaska Marine Highway ferry MV *Tustumena*. The small-boat harbor on the Spit has a 5-lane load/launch ramp. Also in the small-boat harbor area are the harbormaster's office, canneries, parking/camping areas, charter services, small shops, live theatre, galleries, restaurants, motels and bed and breakfasts.

ACCOMMODATIONS/VISITOR SERVICES

Homer has hundreds of small businesses offering a wide variety of goods and services. There are many hotels, motels, bed and breakfasts, and private campgrounds (reservations advised in summer). Nearly 40 restaurants offer meals ranging from fast food to fine dining. Homer has a post office, library, museum, laundromats, gas stations with propane and dump stations, banks, a hospital and airport terminal. There are many boat charters, boat repair and storage facilities, marine fuel at Homer marina, bait, tackle and sporting goods stores, and also art galleries, gift shops and groceries. City campground accessed via Bartlett Avenue (follow signs).

Homer Spit has both long-term parking and camping. Camping and parking areas are well-marked. Camping fees are $7 per night for RVs and $3 per night for tents. Camping permits are available at the camper registration office on the Spit. There is a 14-day limit; restrooms, water and garbage available. Check with the harbormaster's office or the camper registration office on the Spit if you have questions on rules and regulations pertaining to camping, campfires, long-term parking, boat launching and moorage. ▲

Alaska Woodside Lodging. We will welcome you with hospitality and a wealth of

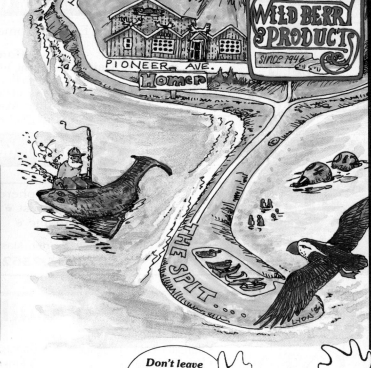

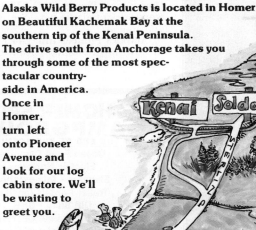

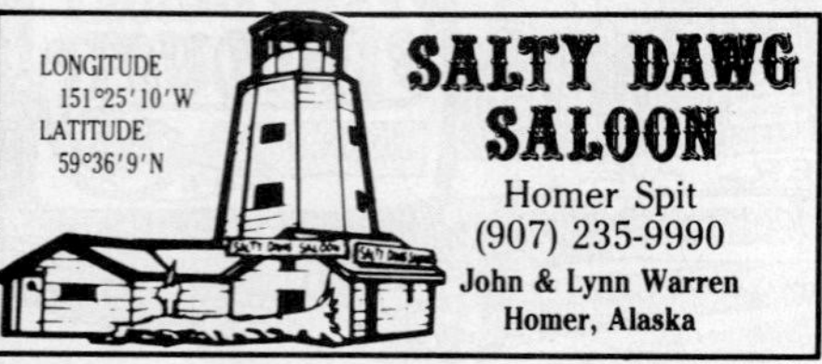

Please support our
MILEPOST® advertisers!

local information. Offering plush, spacious condos for your comfort, with furnished kitchens and bathrooms, linens, phones and TV. Laundry facilities. Conveniently located right in downtown Homer. Bed and breakfast rooms also available. Quiet, reasonable rates. We can make all your reservations for halibut or salmon fishing, lodging, sightseeing or wildlife tours. All you need for your Alaskan adventure. Southbound on Sterling Highway, turn left onto Pioneer Avenue, immediately turn left on Woodside Avenue (behind Intermediate School). See Homer map. Phone: (907) 235-8389. E-mail: woodside@ptialaska.net. See display ad. [ADVERTISEMENT]

Alaska's Pioneer Inn. 244 Pioneer Ave., in downtown Homer. Clean, comfortable 1-bedroom suites with private baths and furnished kitchens. Sleeps up to 4. Compli-

mentary coffee. Single guest rooms available. Year-round. Homer's best value. Credit cards accepted. Brochure: P.O. Box 1430, Homer, AK 99603. (907) 235-5670. Toll free from continental U.S., 1-800-782-9655. In Alaska, 1-800-478-8765. [ADVERTISEMENT]

Almost Home B&B/Cabins. Nestled in the trees overlooking the mountains and the bay. B&B room has private entrance, mini-kitchen, private bath and continental breakfast. Or, choose our cabin with complete kitchen, living room, bath and 2 bedrooms. Clean, comfortable, affordable and friendly!

Halibut fishing packages with hosts, Sorry Charlie Charters. Clean boat with heated cabin and enclosed bathroom. For great fish pictures, see our website. Advance reservations recommended. West Hill Road, $1^1/_2$ miles to Highland, then follow the signs. Phone (907) 235-2553, fax (907) 235-0553. In Alaska: 1-800-478-2352; 1269 Upland Court, Homer, AK 99603. http://www.xyz.net/-sorchart/. [ADVERTISEMENT] MP

Bay View Inn. Spectacular panoramic view from the top of the hill as you enter Homer. Every room overlooks the shimmering waters of Kachemak Bay and the Kenai

358 E Lee • Homer, AK 99603

— Very Affordable —
Quiet, Convenient, Intown Location
Pvt. Suite to Bunk Rooms
Light to Full Breakfast
Charters Available
Secluded Chalet-Sleeps 8

1-800-391-6677

JP's B&B

Homey Atmosphere
Full Breakfast
Affordable

168 East Bayview Homer, Alaska 99603
(907) 235-7362

Manufacturing & Retail Outlet

NOMAR®

- Nomar Fleece Clothing
- Softside 'Laska Luggage®
- Rain Gear/Boots
- Outerwear Fabrics & Patterns
- Upholstery & Emergency Sewing Repairs

MADE IN ALASKA

(See our log ad under Attractions)

Catalog Available

(907) 235-8363 • 104 East Pioneer Ave. • Downtown Homer
www.xyz.net/~nomar • e-mail: nomar@xyz.net

Alaskan Made Products For Alaskan Lifestyles

Mountains. Immaculately clean rooms, non-smoking, firm comfortable beds, color TV, private bathrooms, outside entrances and freshly-brewed morning coffee. Options include kitchenettes, suite with fireplace and separate honeymoon cottage. Serene setting, espresso bar, lawn and picnic tables, Adirondack chairs. Friendly staff, local tour information and activity recommendations. Mile 170 Sterling Highway. P.O. Box 804, Homer, AK 99603. Phone (907) 235-8485. Fax (907) 235-8716. In Alaska only, 1-800-478-8485. See display ad this section. [ADVERTISEMENT] MP

Cloudy Mountain Inn B&B. Hospitality-plus awaits you at our B&B. We have a beautiful panoramic view of the mountains and glaciers from our large deck and hot tub. We offer a two-bedroom apartment with private deck and barbecue. Immaculate rooms with sunshine-fresh linens include a jacuzzi suite or bedrooms with shared and private baths. Fresh baked bread daily, with full breakfasts for all, including early morning fisherfolks. Freezer space available. Located 5 minutes from downtown. Hosts Gary and Treania Stegall, P.O. Box 3801, Homer, AK 99603. Phone (907) 235-2254 or (800) 235-9657, fax (907) 235-6471. [ADVERTISEMENT]

Cranes' Crest B&B. Crandall the Crane and I welcome you to our home. Panoramic view of Kachemak Bay, from 1,200-foot elevation. Sandhill cranes, moose, coyotes visit regularly. Private and shared bath with twin to king beds. Continental breakfast. Ask about wheelchair access. Open year-round. Phone (907) 235-2969, (800) 338-2969. E-mail: crnscrst@xyz.net. See display ad. [ADVERTISEMENT]

Driftwood Inn and RV Park. Charming, historic beachfront inn with 21 rooms and full-hookup RV park. Both have spectacular view overlooking beautiful Kachemak Bay, mountains, glaciers. Quiet in-town location. Immaculately clean, charming rooms. Free coffee, tea, local information. Comfortable common areas with TV, fireplace, library, microwave, refrigerator, barbecue, shellfish cooker, fish cleaning area, freezer, picnic and laundry facilities. Continental breakfast available. We are a smoke-free facility. The RV park has 20-/30-/50-amp electric, water, sewer, clean and comfortable laundry and shower room for RV guests. Phone and cable available. Friendly, knowledgeable staff, specializing in helping make your stay in Homer the best possible. Reasonable, seasonal rates. Open year-round. Write, call for brochure. 135 W. Bunnell Ave., MP, Homer, AK 99603. (907) 235-8019. (800) 478-8019. See our display ad. [ADVERTISEMENT] ▲

Head's Rest B&B (formerly Seekins Homer B&B). Our guests enjoy one of Homer's best views of the Homer Spit, Kachemak Bay and the mountains and glaciers beyond. Our accommodations vary to meet the needs of our guests. Private cabin, private apartments, rooms with shared or private bath, furnished kitchens, cable TV. We serve large, hearty breakfasts every day. Children welcome. Reasonable rates. Nonsmoking. Open year-round. Hosts: Karen and Robin Head. Brochure available. P.O. Box 375, Homer, AK 99603. (907) 235-5188 phone/fax. 2 miles up East Hill Road. [ADVERTISEMENT]

Heritage Hotel-Lodge. One of Alaska's finest log hotels, conveniently located in the heart of Homer. Walking distance to beach, shops, museum. Accommodations: 36 rooms including suite with 2-person Jacuzzi. Reasonable rates. Color TV, movie channels. Phones, free local calls. Courtesy coffee. Restaurants adjacent. Alaskan hospitality. Open year-round. 147 E. Pioneer Ave., phone (907) 235-7787. Reservations 1-800-380-7787. Fax (907) 235-2804. See display ad this section. [ADVERTISEMENT]

Homer Alaska Referral Agency. We do it all with one phone call. Your reservation specialists for bed and breakfasts, lodging, halibut and salmon fishing, wildlife viewing kayaking, bay excursions and adventures, and Kenai Fjords glacier trips. Bookings made at no expense to client for Anchorage, Seward, Homer and all the Kenai Peninsula. For free information, reservations (907) 235-8996 or fax (907) 235-2625. Box 1264, Homer, AK 99603. Established by Seekins, Alaskan residents since 1969. Your reliable source for making Alaskan dreams come true. Call today. E-mail: hara@alaska.net. Internet: www.homer-referral.com. [ADVERTISEMENT]

Homer Spit Campground and Lodging. "Where the land ends and sea begins." Beachfront and ocean-view campsites surrounded by beautiful mountains and bay. Walk to harbor, restaurants and shops. Showers. Dump station, electric, overnight rentals, supplies, gifts. Bookings for halibut charters, boat tours and all recreational needs. Satisfying visitors for over 23 years. P.O. Box 1196, Homer, AK 99603. Phone (907) 235-8206. [ADVERTISEMENT] ▲

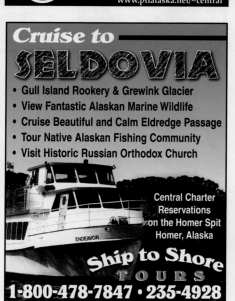

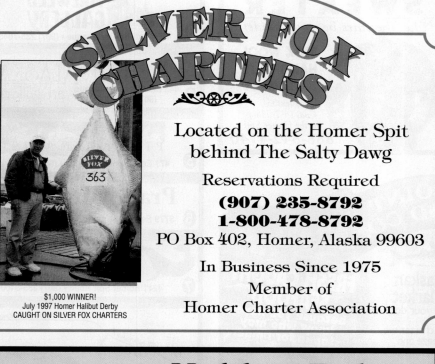

Kachemak Shores Bed and Breakfast. On Kachemak Drive, convenient to airport. Apartment-size units. Kitchenette, satellite TV. Can accommodate parties of 1 to 7 persons. Beach access. Captivating view of Kachemak Bay, romantic harbor lights, glaciers. Watch seals and majestic bald eagles from your window or deck. Reservations: (907) 235-6864 or (907) 235-8234 or 1-800-245-8234. See Kachemak Shores display ad this section. E-mail: nebroke@ptialaska.net. [ADVERTISEMENT]

Land's End Resort. Open year-round! Homer Spit's only hotel, on the water, at the tip of Homer Spit. Breathtaking views! Watch seals, otters, various seabirds and other sea life as you have lunch or cocktails on our spacious outdoor deck. The Chartroom restaurant is famous for its locally caught seafood. The Wheelhouse Lounge provides lighter meals. Truly an Alaskan landmark! (907) 235-2500 or (800) 478-0400 (AK). 4786 Homer Spit Rd., Homer, AK 99603. Internet: http//akms.com/landsend/. [ADVERTISEMENT]

Land's End RV Park. On the water's edge, at the tip of Homer Spit. Truly the most spectacular spot on the Kenai Peninsula. Gorgeous mountain views and sunsets. Minutes from the Spit's boardwalks and small-boat harbor. Electric hookups, laundry. Showers, ice, sundries. Open May through September. (907) 235-2525. P.O. Box 273, Homer, AK 99603. Web page: http://akms.com/landsend/. [ADVERTISEMENT] ▲

Ocean Shores Motel. 22 brand new, spacious seaside rooms located above our beautiful private beach. Each unit has a balcony and 7-foot picture window with spectacular views of the ocean, mountains and glaciers. Cable TV, phones, 5-star queen beds, kitchenette and handicap-accessible rooms. Three blocks to downtown Homer, adjacent to restaurants, quiet location and reasonable rates, all make this the best location in Homer. Highway Frontage #451, Sterling Highway. (907) 235-7775 or (800) 770-7775. E-mail: oceanshs@ptialaska.net. See display ad this section. [ADVERTISEMENT] ♿

Oceanview RV Park just past Best Western Bidarka Inn on your right coming into Homer. Spectacular view of Kachemak Bay, beachfront setting. 85 large pull-through spaces in terraced park. Full/partial hookups, heated restrooms, free showers, laundry, pay phone, free cable TV, picnic area. Walking distance to downtown Homer. Special halibut charter rates for park guests. Phone (907) 235-3951. See display ad at Mile 172.7 Sterling Highway. [ADVERTISEMENT] ▲

3 Moose Meadow Wilderness B&B has taken the bed and breakfast to a new level. Understanding that travelers to Alaska want to experience Alaska, we offer a newly constructed log cabin in a wilderness setting. Your cozy cottage is nestled in the woods and overlooks a meadow with snow-capped mountains beyond. It's very private, with a kitchen and bath, glass-fronted wood stove, large deck and even a porch swing.

Cabin rates are $95/night, $475/week, double occupancy, with breakfast included.

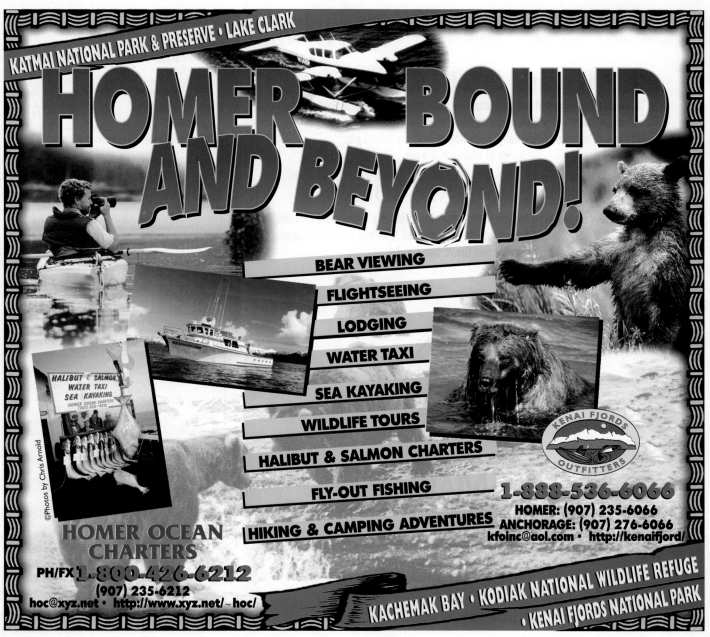

Brochure or reservations phone (907) 235-0755. E-mail: 3moose@xyz.net; webpage: www.xyz.net/~3moose. [ADVERTISEMENT]

TRANSPORTATION

Air: Regularly scheduled air service to Anchorage. Several charter services also operate out of Homer.

Ferry: The Alaska State ferry *Tustumena* serves Seldovia, Kodiak, Seward, Port Lions, Valdez and Cordova from Homer with a limited schedule to Sand Point, King Cove and Dutch Harbor. Natural history programs offered on ferry in summer by Alaska Maritime National Wildlife Refuge naturalists. Contact the offices of the Alaska Marine Highway System at the City Dock, phone (907) 235-8449 for details. Tour boats offer passenger service to Seldovia and Halibut Cove.

Local: 3 rental car agencies and several taxi services.

ATTRACTIONS

The **Pratt Museum**, focusing on the natural and cultural history of southcentral Alaska, is located at 3779 Bartlett St. Exhibits range from artifacts of the area's first Native people, thousands of years ago, to those of homesteaders of the 1930s and 1940s. Excellent aquariums and a tide pool tank feature live Kachemak Bay sea creatures. Also exhibited are Alaskan birds and land and sea mammals, including the complete skeletons of a Bering Sea beaked whale and a beluga whale. Displays also feature local fish industry vessels and the recently restored Harrington homesteader cabin.

Changing exhibits feature Alaskan artwork and other topics of special interest. Beautiful handmade quilts depict local natural history themes. Summer visitors may take a self-guided tour through the botanical garden. This forest trail includes interpretive panels on local wild plants and the homesteader's cabin in the museum yard. The Museum Store features books and Alaskan collectibles.

The Pratt Museum is sponsored by the Homer Society of Natural History. All facilities are wheelchair accessible. $4 admission charged. Summer hours (May through September), 10 A.M. to 6 P.M. daily. Winter hours (October through April), noon to 5 P.M., Tuesday through Sunday. Closed January. Phone (907) 235-8635. ♿

The U.S. Fish and Wildlife Alaska Maritime National Wildlife Refuge protects the habitats of seabirds and marine mammals on 3,500 islands and rocks along the coastline from Ketchikan to Barrow. The visitor center is open in summer from 9 A.M. to 6 P.M. daily. The center has displays focusing on the marine environment, videos and a small shop selling books and pamphlets. Wildlife programs include guided bird walks and beach walks and special slide presentations. Join the naturalists at the visitor center for an informative day. Naturalists are also on board the state ferry runs to Seldovia, Dutch Harbor and Kodiak. Information on the latest bird sightings can be obtained by calling the Bird Hotline at (907) 235-PEEP (7337). The visitor center is located at 451 Sterling Highway, Homer, AK 99603; phone (907) 235-6961.

The Kachemak Bay Shorebird Festival celebrates the arrival of 100,000 migrating shorebirds to the tidal flats of Kachemak Bay. The 6th annual festival is scheduled for May 7–10, 1998. The event promotes awareness of this critical shorebird habitat that provides a feeding and resting place for at

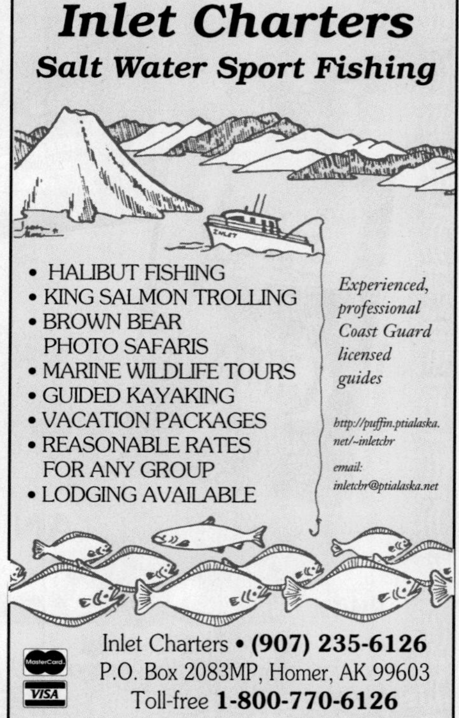

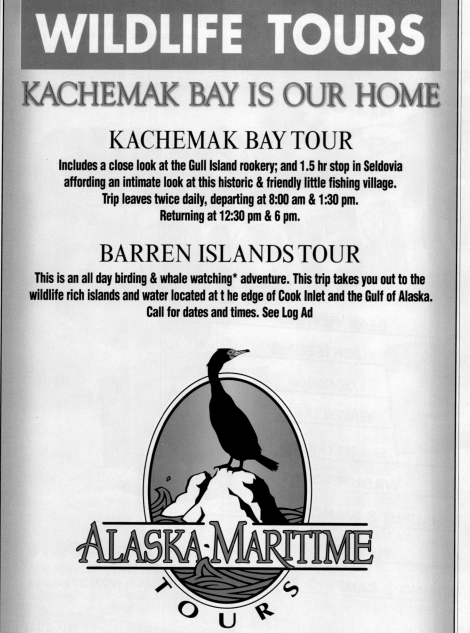

least 20 species of shorebirds on the last leg of their journey from Central and South America to breeding grounds in western and northern Alaska. Festival highlights include guided bird walks, classes for beginning and advanced birders, children's activities and more. Sponsored by the Homer Chamber of Commerce and U.S. Fish & Wildlife Service; phone (907) 235-7740 for more details.

Fish the Homer Halibut Derby. The annual Jackpot Halibut Derby, sponsored by the Homer Chamber of Commerce, runs from May 1 through Labor Day. The state's largest cash halibut derby ($85,000) provides 4 monthly cash prizes, tagged fish and final jackpot prize. Tickets are $7 and available at the Jackpot Halibut Derby headquarters on Homer Spit, visitor center or local charter service offices. Phone (907) 235-7740.

Charter Boats, operating out of the boat harbor on Homer Spit, offer sightseeing and halibut fishing trips. (Charter salmon fishing trips, clamming, crabbing, and sightseeing charters are also available.) These charter operators provide gear, bait and expert knowledge of the area. Homer is one of Alaska's largest charter fishing areas (most charters are for halibut fishing). Charter boats for halibut fishermen cost about $120 to $155 a day. Several sightseeing boats operate off the Homer Spit, taking visitors to view the bird rookery on Gull Island, to Halibut Cove and to Seldovia. (Most sightseeing trips are available Memorial Day to Labor Day). Watch for whales, puffins, sea otters, seals and other marine wildlife.

AREA FISHING: The Kachemak Bay and Cook Inlet area is one of Alaska's most popular spots for halibut fishing, with catches often weighing 100 to 200 lbs. Guides and charters are available locally. Halibut up to 350 lbs. are fished from June through September; fish the bottom with herring. Year-round trolling for king salmon is popular; use small herring. King salmon may also be taken during late May and June in area streams. Pink salmon (4 to 5 lbs.) may be caught in July and August; use winged bobbers, small weighted spoons and spinners. Similar tackle or fresh roe will catch silver salmon weighing 6 to 8 lbs. in August and September. Dolly Varden are taken throughout the area April to October; try single eggs or wet flies. Steelhead/rainbow are available in local streams, but for conservation purposes, must be immediately released unharmed.

Fishermen have had great success in recent years casting from the shore of Homer Spit for king salmon. The Fishing Hole (also referred to as the Fishing Lagoon or Spit Lagoon) on the Homer Spit supports a large run of hatchery-produced kings and silvers beginning in late May and continuing to September. Kings range from 20 to 40 lbs. The fishery is open 7 days a week in season.

Regulations vary depending on species and area fished, and anglers are cautioned to consult nearby tackle shops or Fish and Game before fishing.

Take a Scenic Drive. East Road, a 20-mile/32-km drive from downtown Homer, climbs through hills and forests toward the head of Kachemak Bay; pavement ends at Mile 12.5, beautiful views of the bay. Or turn off East Road on to East Hill Road and drive up the bluffs to Skyline Drive; beautiful views of the bay and glaciers. Return to town via West Hill Road, which intersects the Sterling Highway at **Milepost S 167.1.**

Homer boat harbor is home port to commercial fishermen, pleasure boaters and charter boat operators. (© Corinne Smith/RKI)

The glaciers that spill down from the Harding Icefield straddling the Kenai Mountains across the bay create an ever-changing panorama visible from most points in Homer, particularly from the Skyline Drive. The most spectacular and largest of these glaciers is Grewingk Glacier in Kachemak Bay State Park, visible to the east directly across Kachemak Bay from Homer. The glacier was

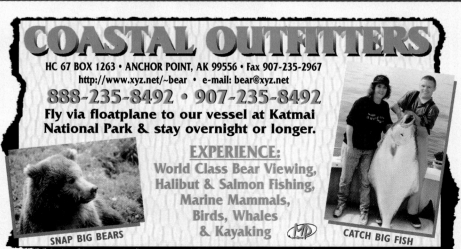

Bear with cubs fishes for salmon at McNeil River, a state game sanctuary accessible from Homer by plane. (© Bill Sherwonit)

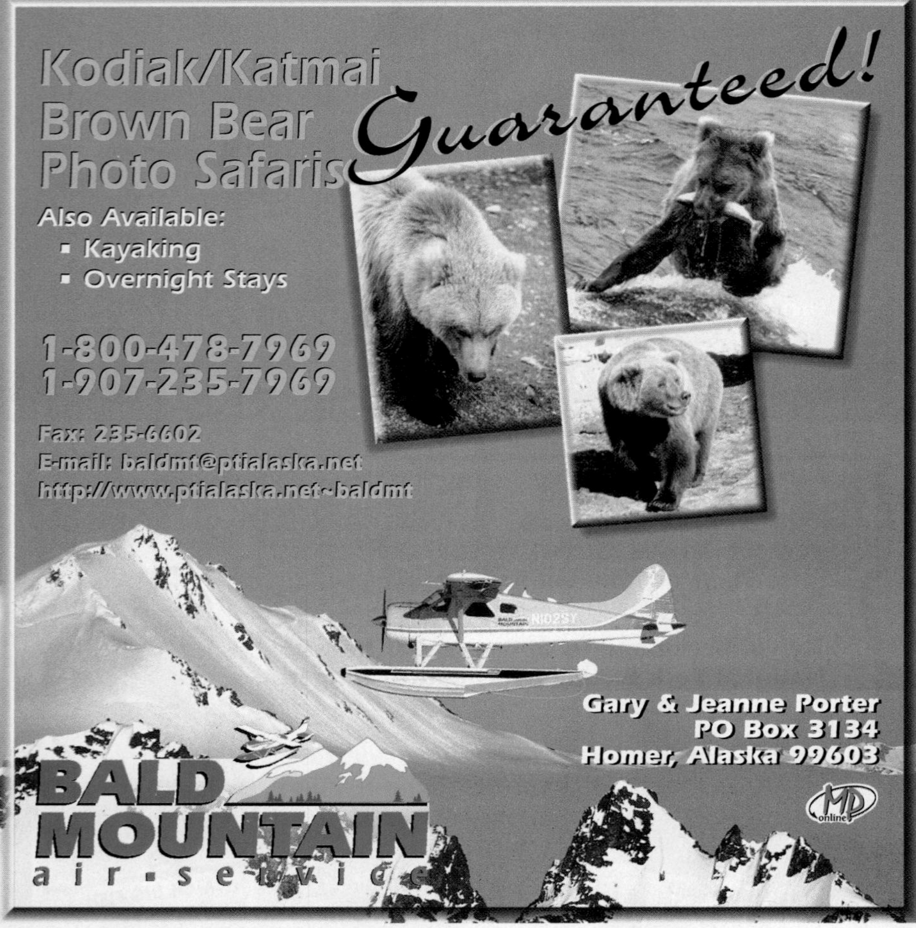

named by Alaska explorer William H. Dall in 1880 for Constantin Grewingk, a German geologist who had published a work on the geology and volcanism of Alaska. The Grewingk Glacier has a long gravel bar at its terminal moraine, behind which the water draining from the ice flows into the bay. This gravel bar, called Glacier Spit, is a popular excursion spot, and may be visited by charter plane or boat. (There are several charter plane operators and charter helicopter services in Homer.) Portlock and Dixon glaciers are also visible directly across from the spit.

Kachemak Bay State Park is located on the south shore of the bay and includes glaciers, alpine tundra, forests, fjords, bays and high-country lakes. Recently the state enlarged this park by the purchase of 23,802 additional acres of land with funds from the settlement of the Exxon Valdez oil spill. The existing trail system offers hiking from Glacier Spit to China Poot Peak. An extensive new trail system is under construction. Campsites are currently available on Glacier Spit, Halibut Cove Lagoon and China Poot Lake. Additional campsites and public-use cabins are planned. Inquire locally about transportation to the park. Daily ferry service and water taxis are available to take you to trailheads. The bay shoreline offers excellent kayaking, clamming, tide pooling and beach combing opportunities. Phone the district office at (907) 235-7024 for more information, or stop by the state park office at **Milepost S 168.5.**

McNeil River State Game Sanctuary/ Katmai National Park. Homer is the main base for visitors flying across Cook Inlet to both locations, where the world's largest concentration of bears in a natural area this size is found. Brown bears congregate near the mouth of the McNeil River, where a falls slows down migrating salmon, making fishing easy for the bears. Visits to the game sanctuary are on a permit basis; a drawing for the limited number of permits is held in March each year. Permit applications

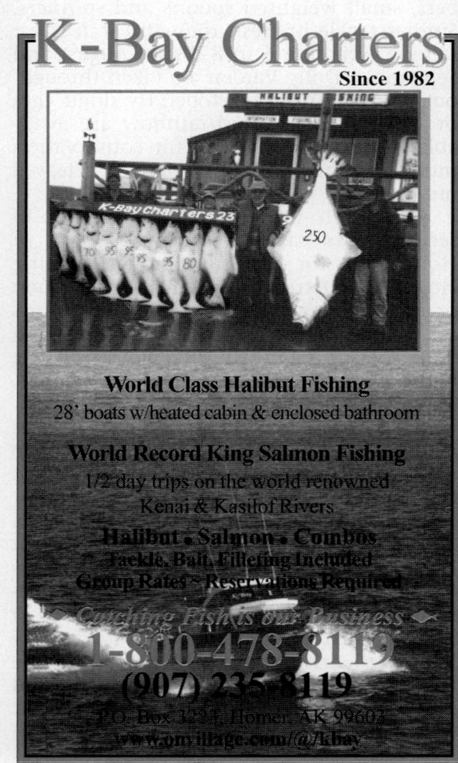

are available from the Alaska Dept. of Fish and Game, Attn: McNeil River, 333 Raspberry Road, Anchorage 99518. Phone (907) 267-2100.

Katmai National Park offers viewing platforms for close (and safe!) brown bear viewing. Several area outfitters provide service, including overnight stays and access to remote areas of the park.

Study Marine Environment. The Center for Alaskan Coastal Studies is located across Kachemak Bay from Homer. Volunteer naturalists lead a day tour which includes Gull Island bird rookery, coastal forest and intertidal areas. Write the Center for Alaskan Coastal Studies, P.O. Box 2225-MP, Homer 99603; phone (907) 235-6667. Reservations, phone (907) 235-7272.

Alaska Maritime Tours. Enjoy the only half-day wildlife tour from Homer to Seldovia which includes Gull Island bird rookery. Top quality, personal service is provided aboard the 50-foot MV *Denaina*. Two daily tours: 8 A.M.–12:30 P.M., and 1:30–6 P.M. All-day birding trips to Barren Islands scheduled June–August, weather dependent. Bring camera, extra film, warm jacket, light rain gear to be prepared to spend time outside on deck for close-up views of puffins, sea otters and occasional whales. Located on Homer Spit Road. Call (907) 235-2490 or in Alaska 1-800-478-2490 for reservations or brochure. See display ad this section. [ADVERTISEMENT]

Alaska Wild Berry Products, celebrating more than 50 years in downtown Homer, invites you to see our wild berry jams, jellies and chocolates handmade the old-fashioned way. Delicious free samples at our taster's stand. Gift shop. Picnic area. Open year-round, 528 East Pioneer Avenue. See display ad this section. [ADVERTISEMENT]

Art Shop Gallery, where Homer shops for art. Open year-round. Original works, prints, posters by local, Alaskan and nationally recognized artists. Alaska Native art, jewelry, dolls, pottery, Christmas tree ornaments by Alaskan artists. Homer's premier gallery. A must see. World-wide shipping. Eagle Quality Center on the bypass. (907) 235-7076 or 1-800-478-7076. [ADVERTISEMENT]

Bald Mountain Air. All-day brown bear photo safari direct from Homer via floatplane landing in Katmai National Park. Let life-long Alaskans Gary and Jeanne Porter take you on an adventure you'll never forget. Scenic wildlife glacier tours. Expect the best from your Alaska vacation. P.O. Box 3134, Homer, AK 99603. (800) 478-7969. See display ad this section. [ADVERTISEMENT] MP

The Bookstore, located in Eagle Quality Center, specializes in Alaskan, nature, cooking, classics and children's books. It is acclaimed as one of the nicest bookstores in the state. Besides a great selection of paperback books, it features the most original card selection on the Peninsula (many by local artists) and a very special kids' corner. While browsing, check out the view. Hours 10 A.M. to 7 P.M. 90 Sterling Highway #8. (907) 235-7496 or in Alaska 1-888-635-BOOK. [ADVERTISEMENT]

Coastal Outfitters: Experience the best wilderness adventure and photographic opportunity for all that Alaska has to offer. Fly from Homer, via floatplane, over ocean, volcanoes, glaciers and coastline en route to our vessel located in the pristine waters along Katmai National Park. Stay overnight or longer aboard our vessel for exclusive bear viewing and halibut or salmon fishing. Sea kayaking is another added feature, guided or unguided. You will thrill to the exposure of the magnificent Alaskan brown bears up close, while surrounded by breath-taking scenery, a multitude of sea birds and marine mammals. See display ad. Phone (907) 235-8492, (888) 235-8492, fax (907) 235-2967. E-mail: bear@xyz.net. Internet: www.xyz.net/~bear. [ADVERTISEMENT] MP

Kachemak Air Service, Inc. offers 2 unique opportunities: Fly over the glaciers across Kachemak Bay with Bill deCreeft in his 1929 Travel Air S6000B floatplane "Limousine of the Air," large, mahogany-framed windows for each passenger; or fly out for the day in Kachemak Air Service, Inc.'s deHavilland Otter floatplane with Chris Day for a day trip viewing brown bears. P.O. Box 1769, Homer, AK 99603. (907) 235-8924. Internet: www.xyz.net/~decreeft/fly1929.htm. [ADVERTISEMENT] MP

NOMAR (Northern Marine Canvas Products) began business the summer of 1978 in a yellow school bus! Today, visit our manufacturing facility and manufacturer's outlet store at 104 E. Pioneer Ave., downtown Homer. NOMAR manufactures a wide variety of products for our Alaskan lifestyles. Warm NOMAR fleece clothing to keep you warm, no matter what the adventure. Soft-sided 'Laska Luggage® that's stuffable and floatplane friendly. Watertight bags for kayak tours or whitewater expeditions, and well-made Homer-made, packable, mailable, useful gifts for everyone on the "list." Park in our spacious, paved parking lot and take a

Seldovia's St. Nicholas Russian Orthodox Church. (© Bill Sherwonit)

walk around our town. We'll gladly ship your purchases for you. See display ad this section. [ADVERTISEMENT]

North Country Charters, on the Homer Spit. Sean and Gerri Martin, original owners since 1979. We have an excellent catch record with prize-winning derby fish, bringing in some of the largest halibut in Homer. Three 6-passenger and one 16-passenger boat for halibut fishing along with a saltwater salmon trolling boat. All vessels are Coast Guard equipped, heated cabins, full restrooms. 1-800-770-7620. See display ad. [ADVERTISEMENT]

NorthStar-Expedition. Start with a spectacular flight over the Harding Ice Fields to secluded Nuka Bay. Relax aboard the *Juliet*, equipped with private cabins, bathroom facilities, and the experience of a skilled local captain. Dine on fresh seafood and enjoy a glacier view while your catch is processed and shipped for you. Phone (888) 593-7175, fax (907) 783-1294; http://www.northstarexpedition.com. [ADVERTISEMENT] MP

Pier One Theatre. Local talent lights up an intimate stage in an Alaskan-friendly waterfront atmosphere halfway out the Homer Spit. Plays, new productions, readings, dance theatre, musicals. Offered summer weekends with some midweek shows. Season information available locally. Phone (907) 235-7333. [ADVERTISEMENT]

Trail's End Horse Adventures. Horses and Alaska are my life. Join me in my 13th season offering trail rides in the Homer hills. Day trips and pack adventures to the head of Kachemak Bay. View mountains and glaciers. Gentle Alaskan horses. Located at **Mile 11.2** East End Road. Write Mark Marette, Box 1771, Homer, AK 99603, or phone (907) 235-6393. [ADVERTISEMENT]

Tsimshian Charters, Judy and Everett Hudson, lifelong Alaskans, truly enjoy showing you where and how to fish for the mighty halibut. All equipment provided and shuttle service to the Homer Spit boat harbor. Our office is conveniently located near downtown Homer. Fish 3 times with us and get a free trip! Our 6-passenger, 32-foot diesel-powered vessel, M/V *Jackpot*, has a fully-enclosed cabin with bathroom facilities. Large deck space provides plenty of elbow room to fish. Phone (907) 235-8118. P.O. Box 577, Homer, AK 99603. E-mail: tsimshian@ptialaska.net. [ADVERTISEMENT]

Seldovia

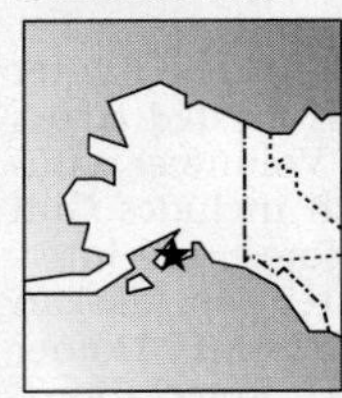

Reached by air, tour boat or ferry. Located on the southwestern Kenai Peninsula on Seldovia Bay, an arm of Kachemak Bay, 16 miles/25.7 km southwest of Homer. **Population:** 403. **Emergency Services: City Police, Ambulance, Fire and Rescue,** emergency only, phone 911, monitor CB Channel 9. **Seldovia Medical Clinic**, phone (907) 234-7825. Seldovia has a resident doctor and visiting dentists.

Visitor Information: Seldovia Chamber of Commerce, Drawer F, Seldovia, AK 99663. Phone (970) 234-7612; Web page: www.xyz.net\~seldovia. Information cache at Synergy Art Works on Main Street, across from the boat harbor. Most Main Street businesses also provide visitor information.

RV parking is restricted along Main Street. Check with the Harbor Master (907/234-7643) for more information on parking.

Elevation: Sea level. **Climate:** Rather mild for Alaska, with a year-round average temperature of about 39°F/4°C. Annual precipitation, 28 inches. Wind is a small factor due to the protecting shield of the Kenai Mountains. **Radio:** Homer stations. **Television:** KENI Channel 2, KTVA Channel 4, KAKM Channel 7, KIMO Channel 13.

Private Aircraft: Seldovia airport, 0.6 mile/1 km east; elev. 29 feet/9m; length 2,000 feet/610m; gravel; unattended.

Seldovia is a small community connected to Homer by the Alaska Marine Highway Southwest ferry system. Because it is removed from Kenai Peninsula highways, Seldovia has retained much of its old Alaska charm and traditions (its historic boardwalk dates from 1931). The St. Nicholas Russian

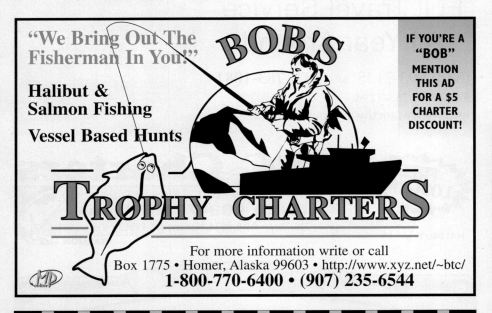

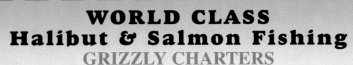

Orthodox Church was built in 1891 and is a national historic site. There are some areas just outside town, accessible by car, that have been called "Alaska's hidden paradises." A good place to observe bald eagles, seabirds, and sea otters, Seldovia is included as a stop on some tour boat cruises out of Homer.

The name Seldovia is derived from Russian *Seldevoy,* meaning "herring bay." Between 1869 and 1882, a trading station was located here. A post office was established in Nov. 1898.

ACCOMMODATIONS/VISITOR SERVICES

Seldovia has most visitor facilities, including 2 hotels, 12 bed and breakfasts, a lodge, general store, 3 restaurants and a variety of shops. The post office is in the center of town. Public restrooms, showers and pay phone in front of the boat harbor near town center. Pay phones are also located at the ferry dock outside ferry office, at the airport, and library.

Fantasy North Halibut Charters and B&B. We are family owned and operated. We believe in quality, personal, professional, friendly services at fair prices. Charters are for 3 to 6 people on our 34-foot Sports Fisherman twin-diesel yacht. Our B&B is a modern, clean, comfortable and spacious 2 bedroom, $1^1/_2$ bath completely private apartment directly across from the Seldovia Boat Harbor. Phone or write for availability and rates (May–September). All travel arrangements can be handled. P.O. Box 211, Seldovia, AK 99663. Phone (907) 234-7557. [ADVERTISEMENT]

Gerry's Place B&B. Bed and breakfast one block from harbor. Convenient for fishermen and families. Freshly-baked continental breakfast. Three bedrooms accommodate 6 people with shared bath. Free airport pickup. Close to shops, hiking trails, bike rentals, beachcombing. Open year-round. Box 33, Seldovia, AK 99663. Phone (907) 234-7471. E-mail: rolpat@xyz.net. [ADVERTISEMENT]

Seldovia Boardwalk Hotel. Waterfront view. 14 lovely rooms with private baths. Large harbor-view deck. In-room phones. Near bike rental and Otterbahn Trail. Free airport or harbor pickup. Friendly service. Romantic getaway. Package prices from Homer. P.O. Box 72, Seldovia, AK 99663. (907) 234-7816. [ADVERTISEMENT]

Undeveloped campground for tent camping only at Outside Beach; picnic tables, litter containers, pit toilet. RV camping at the city-owned Seldovia Wilderness Park located just outside the city. From downtown, drive 1 mile/1.6 km out via Anderson Way to fork in road; turn left and drive 0.9 mile/1.4 km to beach. ▲

TRANSPORTATION

Air: Scheduled and charter service available.

Ferry: Alaska's Southwestern Marine Highway system serves Seldovia, with connections to and from Homer, Port Lions, Kodiak, Valdez, Cordova and Seward.

Charter and Tour Boats: Available for passenger service; inquire locally and in Homer.

ATTRACTIONS

Explore Seldovia. Visitors can learn about Seldovia's cultural and natural history from a series of interpretive signs placed about the town. Guided driving tours of the area are available, and bicycles may be rented to explore the city at one's own pace. Seldovia's sheltered bay is ideal for kayaking. Kayak tours and rentals are available. The Otterbaun, a 1.2-mile hiking trail, is a popular way to get from town to Outside Beach. The trailhead is behind the Susan B. English School. Check the tidal charts before you go; access to the Outside Beach is cut off at high tide.

The community's historical artifacts are housed in 2 museums—the Seldovia Native Association Museum on Main Street and the Seldovia Historical Museum on Anderson Way.

Scenic Drives. Outside Beach, a beautiful spot with undeveloped tent camping, beachcombing, surf fishing, rockhounding, and a view of Kachemak Bay and the volcanoes St. Augustine, Mount Iliamna and Mount Redoubt, is 1.9 miles/3.1 km from town. Drive out Anderson Way from downtown 1 mile/1.6 km to a fork in the road by a gravel pit; turn left and drive 0.9 mile/1.4 km to beach.

Continue on Anderson Way (past the Outside Beach turnoff) to hilly and unpaved Jakolof Bay Road, which offers panoramic views of Kachemak Bay, McDonald Spit, Jakolof Bay and Kasitsna Bay. At Mile 7.5, steps lead down to 1.5-mile-long McDonald Spit, a favorite spot for seabirds and marine life. Spend an afternoon exploring the spit, or continue out to Jakolof Bay, where the road offers many opportunities to get onto the beach. The road becomes impassable to vehicles at Mile 13.

It is a pleasant drive out to Seldovia's refuse dump, with wonderful blueberry picking in the fall. From downtown, cross the bridge over Seldovia Slough; then turn right on North Augustine Avenue, then left on Rocky Street for the dump. This is a 1.4-mile/2.3-km drive.

Special Events. Just about the whole town participates in Seldovia's old-fashioned Fourth of July celebration. The holiday includes food booths, parade, games and contests. Check with the chamber of commerce for details.

Fishing: Kachemak Bay, king salmon January through August; halibut May through October; Dolly Varden June through September; silver salmon in August and September; red salmon July through August. **Seldovia Bay,** king, silver and red salmon, also halibut, May through September. Excellent bottom fishing.

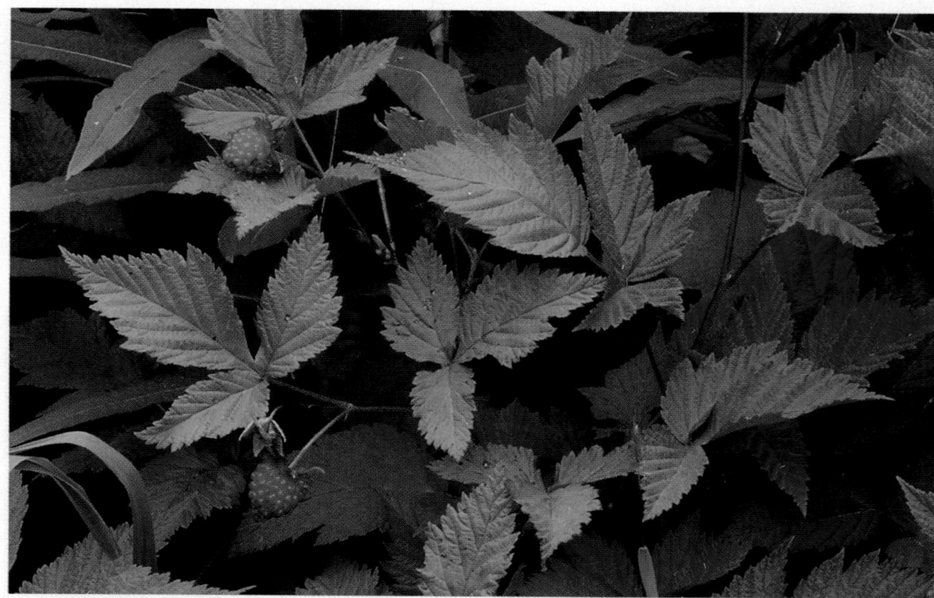

Red raspberries at Jakolof Bay are ripe for picking in late July and August.
(© Tom Culkin)

SELDOVIA ADVERTISERS

KODIAK

(See map, page 641)

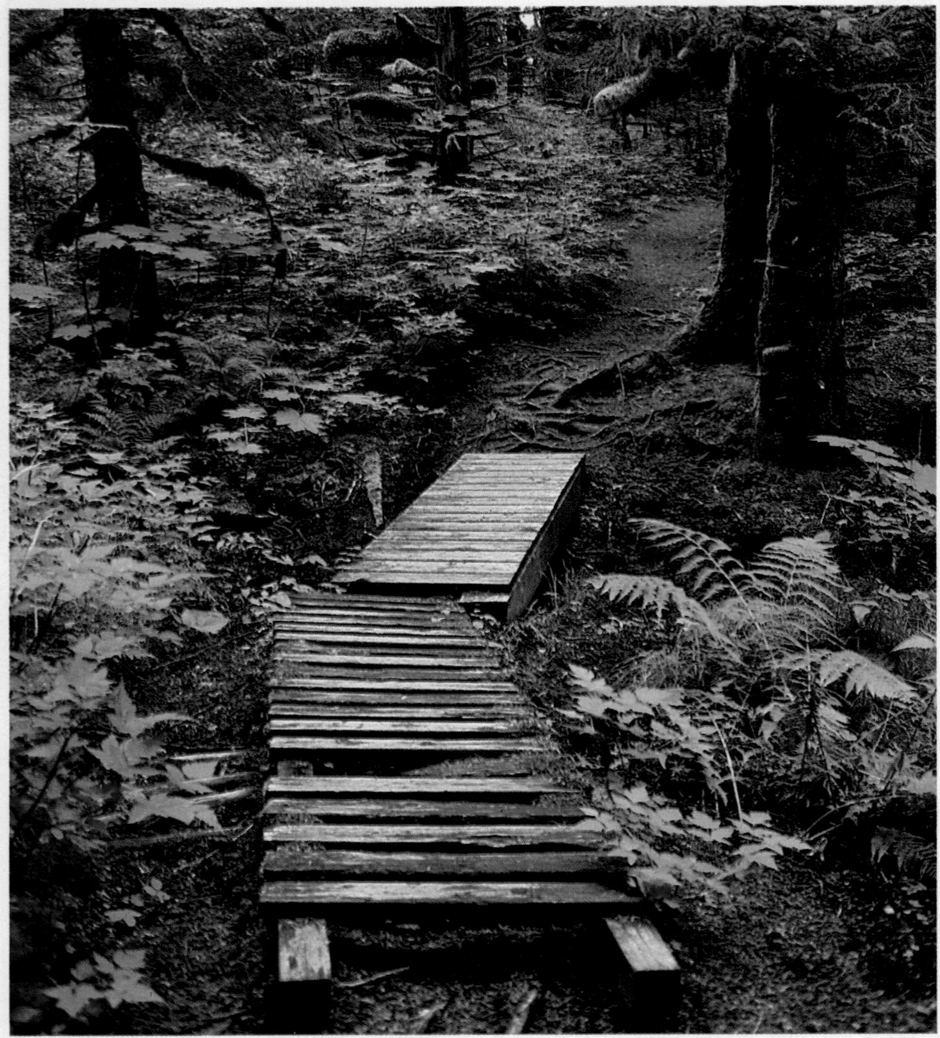

Boardwalk trail leads through lush growth at Fort Abercrombie State Park. (© Rich Reid)

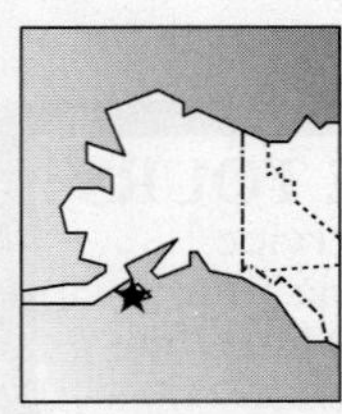

The Kodiak Island group lies in the Gulf of Alaska, southwest of Cook Inlet and the Kenai Peninsula. The city of Kodiak is located near the northeastern tip of Kodiak Island, at the north end of Chiniak Bay. By air it is 1 hour from Anchorage. By ferry from Homer it is 9½ hours.

Population: 14,058 Kodiak Island Borough. **Emergency Services in Kodiak:** Dial 911 for emergencies. **Alaska State Troopers**, phone (907) 486-4121. **Police**, phone (907) 486-8000. **Fire Department**, phone (907) 486-8040. **Hospital**, Providence Kodiak Island Medical Center, Rezanof Drive, phone (907) 486-3281. **Coast Guard**, Public Affairs Officer, phone (907) 487-5542. **Crime Stoppers**, phone (907) 486-3113.

Visitor Information: Located at 100 Marine Way; open year-round. Hours in June, July and August are 8 A.M. to 5 P.M. weekdays, 10 A.M. to 4 P.M. Saturday, 1–5 P.M. Sunday (and later for arriving ferries). Knowledgeable local staff will answer your questions and help arrange tours and charters. Free maps, brochures, hunting and fishing information. For information, contact the Kodiak Island Convention & Visitors Bureau, Dept. MP, 100 Marine Way, Kodiak 99615; phone (907) 486-4782.

Elevation: Sea level. **Climate:** Average daily temperature in July is 58°F/15°C; in January 30°F/-1°C. September, October and January are the wettest months in Kodiak, with each month averaging more than 7 inches of precipitation. **Radio:** KVOK 560, KMXT-FM 100.1, KRXX-FM 101.1, KPEN-FM 102.3, KWVV-FM 105. **Television:** Via cable and satellite. **Newspapers:** *The Kodiak Daily Mirror* (daily except Saturday and Sunday).

Private Aircraft: Kodiak state airport, 4.8 miles/7.7 km southwest; elev. 73 feet/22m; length 7,500 feet/2,286m; asphalt; fuel 100LL, Jet A-1. Kodiak Municipal Airport, 2 miles/3.2 km northeast; elev. 139 feet/42m; length 2,500 feet/762m; paved; unattended. Kodiak (Lilly Lake) seaplane base, 1 mile/1.6 km northeast; elev. 130 feet/40m. Trident Basin seaplane base, on east side of Near Island, unattended, docks; no fuel. Trident Basin has fuel, AVgas, unattended (credit card or pre-pay).

Gravel airstrips at Akhiok, length 3,000 feet/914m; Karluk, length 1,900 feet/579m; Larsen Bay, length 2,400 feet/732m; Old Harbor, length 2,000 feet/610m; Ouzinkie, length 2,500 feet/762m; and Port Lions, length 2,600 feet/792m.

Kodiak Island, home of the oldest permanent European settlement in Alaska, is about 100 miles/161 km long. Known as "Alaska's emerald isle," Kodiak is the largest island in Alaska and the second largest island in the United States (after Hawaii), with an area of 3,588 square miles and about 87 miles/140 km of road (see logs this section). The Kodiak Island Borough includes some 200 islands, the largest being Kodiak, followed in size by Afognak, Sitkalidak, Sitkinak, Raspberry, Tugidak, Shuyak, Uganik, Chirikof, Marmot and Spruce islands. The borough has only one unincorporated townsite, **KARLUK** (pop. 57), located on the west coast of Kodiak Island, 75 air miles/121 km from Kodiak.

The 6 incorporated cities in the Kodiak Island Borough are: **KODIAK** (pop. 6,869) on Chiniak Bay, with all visitor services (see Visitor Services, Transportation and Attractions this section); **AKHIOK** (pop. 84) at Alitak Bay on the south side of Kodiak Island, 80 miles/129 km southwest of Kodiak; **LARSEN BAY** (pop. 127) on the northwest coast of Kodiak Island, 62 miles/100 km southwest of Kodiak; **OLD HARBOR** (pop. 316) on the southeast side of Kodiak Island, 54 miles/87 km from Kodiak; **OUZINKIE** (pop. 259) on the west coast of Spruce Island; and **PORT LIONS** (pop. 264) on Settler Cove on the northeast coast of Kodiak Island.

Kodiak Island was originally inhabited by the Alutiiq people, who were maritime hunters and fishermen. More than 7,000 years later, the Alutiiq still call Kodiak home.

In 1763, the island was discovered by Stephen Glotov, a Russian explorer. The name Kodiak, of which there are several variations, was first used in English by Captain Cook in 1778. Kodiak was Russian Alaska's first capital city, until the capital was moved to Sitka in 1804.

Kodiak's turbulent past includes the 1912 eruption of Novarupta Volcano, on the nearby Alaska Peninsula, and the tidal wave of 1964. The Novarupta eruption covered the island with a black cloud of ash. When the cloud finally dissipated, Kodiak was buried under 18 inches of drifting pumice. On Good Friday in 1964 the greatest earthquake ever recorded in North America (9.2 on the Richter scale) shook the Kodiak area. The tidal wave that followed virtually leveled downtown Kodiak, destroying the fishing fleet, processing plants, canneries and 158 homes.

Because of Kodiak's strategic location for defense, military facilities were constructed on the island in 1939. Fort Abercrombie, now a state park and a national historic landmark, was one of the first secret radar installations in Alaska. Cement bunkers still remain for exploration by the curious.

The Coast Guard occupies the old Kodiak Naval Station. Kodiak is the base for the Coast Guard's North Pacific operations; the U.S. Coast Guard cutters *Storis, Ironwood* and *Firebush* patrol from Kodiak to seize foreign vessels illegally fishing U.S. waters. (The 200-mile/322-km fishing limit went into effect in March 1977.) A 12-foot star, situated halfway up the side of Old Woman Mountain overlooking the base, was rebuilt and rededicated in 1981 in memory of military personnel who have lost their lives while engaged in operations from Kodiak. Originally erected in the 1950s, the star is lit every year between Thanksgiving and Christmas.

Kodiak's St. Paul and St. Herman harbors are home port to 800 local fishing boats and serve about 2,000 outside vessels each year.

Commercial fishing is the backbone of Kodiak's economy. Kodiak is one of the largest commercial fishing ports in the U.S. Some 3,000 commercial fishing vessels use the harbor each year, delivering salmon, shrimp, herring, halibut and whitefish, plus king, tanner and Dungeness crab to the 11 seafood processing companies in Kodiak. Cannery tours are not available. Kodiak's famous seafood is premarketed, with almost all the commercially caught seafood exported. (Kodiak is the only city in Alaska with more tonnage exported than imported.) You can celebrate Kodiak's main industry at the Kodiak Crab Festival, May 21–25, 1998.

View from Near Island of city of Kodiak on Kodiak Island. (© Rich Reid)

KODIAK ADVERTISERS

Adventure Charters & Marine Services Inc. ....Ph. (907) 234-6400
Afognak Wilderness Lodge....Ph. (800) 478-6442
Alaska Marine Highway ...Ph. (800) 526-6731
Baranov Museum....101 Marine Way
Beryl's....202 Center Ave.
Budget....Ph. (907) 487-2220
Cy's Sporting Goods & Outfitters....202 Shelikof
Inlet Guest Rooms....Ph. (907) 486-4004
Kodiak Bed and Breakfast....Ph. (907) 486-5367
Mack's Sport Shop Inc.....117 Lower Mill Bay
Northern Exposure Gallery....103 Center St.
Port Gifts....508 Marine Way
Rent-A-Heap....Ph. (907) 486-5200
Russian Heritage Inn....Ph. (907) 486-5657
Shelikof Lodge....Ph. (907) 486-4141
Uyak Air Service....Ph. (907) 486-3407
Wintel's Bed & Breakfast....Ph. (907) 486-6935

Kodiak is also an important cargo port and transshipment center. Container ships stop here to transfer goods to smaller vessels bound for the Aleutians, the Alaska Peninsula and other destinations.

ACCOMMODATIONS/VISITOR SERVICES

There are 4 hotels/motels in Kodiak and more than 20 bed and breakfasts. A variety of restaurants offers a wide range of menus and prices. Shopping is readily available for gifts, general merchandise and sporting goods. There is a movie theater and 750-seat performing arts center.

There are 3 state campgrounds: Fort Abercrombie, north of town (see Rezanof–Monashka Bay Road log); Buskin River state recreation site, south of town (see Chiniak Road log); and Pasagshak River state recreation site at the end of Pasagshak Bay Road (see log). City campground (established for transient process workers) at Gibson Cove has showers and restrooms, $2 per person/night camping fee. ▲

Dump stations are located at the Petro Express station on Mill Bay Road, at the Union 76 service station in downtown Kodiak, and at Buskin River state recreation site at Mile 4.4 Chiniak Road.

There are 26 remote fly-in hunting and fishing lodges in the Kodiak area; several roadhouses on the island road system; public-use cabins available within Kodiak National Wildlife Refuge, Shuyak Island and Afognak Island state parks; and private wilderness camps and cabin rentals available throughout the Kodiak area.

TRANSPORTATION

Air: Scheduled service via Era Aviation and Alaska Airlines.

Ferry: The Alaska state ferry MV *Tustumena* serves Kodiak from Homer (9½-hour ferry ride) and Seward (13 hours). It also stops at Port Lions. Ferry terminal is downtown; phone (907) 486-3800 or toll free in the U.S. (800) 526-6731.

Highways: There are 4 roads on Kodiak Island (see logs this section). The 11.3-mile/18.2-km Rezanof–Monashka Bay Road leads from downtown Kodiak north to Fort Abercrombie and Monashka Bay. Chiniak Road leads 42.8 miles/68.9 km south from Kodiak along the island's eastern shore to Chiniak Point and Chiniak Creek (it is a beautiful drive!). Anton Larsen Bay Road leads 11.8 miles/19 km from junction with Chiniak Road near Kodiak airport to Anton Larsen Bay. Pasagshak Bay Road branches off Chiniak Road and leads 16.5 miles/26.6 km to Fossil Beach at Pasagshak Point.

IMPORTANT: Most of the land along the road system is privately owned. Using land owned by Leisnoi, Inc. requires a non-fee user permit, available at the Leisnoi office in Kodiak at 202 Center Ave.; phone (907) 486-8191.

Car Rental and Taxi: Available.

ATTRACTIONS

State Fair and Rodeo held Labor Day weekend, at the fairgrounds in Womens Bay, includes all-state competitions in crafts, gardening, 4-H livestock raising and home products. Stock car races are held at the fairgrounds on weekends during the summer.

St. Herman's Day, Aug. 7–9, 1998, is of particular significance to the Kodiak community as Father Herman, the first saint of the Russian Orthodox Church in North America, was canonized in Kodiak in 1970. Father Herman arrived in Kodiak in 1794.

The Baranov Museum (Erskine House), maintained by the Kodiak Historical Society (101 Marine Way, Kodiak 99615; phone 907/486-5920), is open in summer, 10 A.M. to 4 P.M. daily. (Winter hours 11 A.M. to 3 P.M. weekdays, except Thursday and Sunday, and noon to 3 P.M. Saturday. Closed in February.) The building was originally a fur warehouse built in the early 1800s by Alexsandr Baranov. It is one of just 4 Russian-built structures in the United States today. Purchased by the Alaska Commercial Co. around 1867, the building was sold to W.J. Erskine in 1911, who converted it into a residence; it was then referred to as the Erskine House. In 1962 it was declared a national historic landmark. Many items from the Koniag and Russian era are on display. In the gift shop, Russian samovars, Russian Easter eggs, Alaska Native baskets and other items are for sale. Donations accepted, $2 per adult, children under 12 free.

Picnic on the Beach. There are some outstandingly beautiful beaches along Chiniak Road (see log this section). These unpopulated beaches are also good for beachcombing. Watch for Sitka deer and foxes.

Go for a Hike. Hiking trails around the Kodiak area provide access to alpine areas, lakes, coastal rainforests and beaches. Trail guide available for $5 at the visitors center, (907) 486-4782. Pay attention to notes regarding footwear and clothing, tides, bears, trailhead access and weather conditions.

Go Mountain Biking. Kodiak is fast becoming known for its premier mountain biking, attracting racers and enthusiasts from around the country.

Kodiak Tribal Council's Barabara sod house is an authentic Alutiiq dwelling that features presentations of Alutiiq dancing. The Kodiak Alutiiq Dancers form the only Alutiiq dance group in Alaska. The dances have been re-created from stories passed down through generations of the Alutiiq people, who have inhabited Kodiak Island for more than 7,000 years. Dance performances are held in summer, Monday through Saturday at 3:30 P.M., at the barabara located at 713 Rezanof Drive. Phone (907) 486-4449 to confirm performance times.

City Parks and Recreation Department maintains a swimming pool year-round, and the school gyms are available on a year-round basis for community use. The town has 8 parks and playgrounds including the 7-acre Baranof Park with 4 tennis courts, baseball field, track, playgrounds and picnic areas.

Bear Valley Golf Course. The 9-hole Bear Valley Golf Course is located on the Anton Larsen Bay Road. Owned and operated by the U.S. Coast Guard, the course has a driving range, putting green and pro shack. The course is open to the public from approximately June until October, depending on weather. The pro shack carries golf clothing, items and rental equipment, and serves food and beer. Hours of operation vary according to weather and daylight hours. Call (907) 486-7561 or 487-5108.

Fort Abercrombie State Park. Site of a WWII coastal fortification, bunkers and other evidence of the Aleutian campaign. The park is located north of Kodiak on scenic Miller Point. Picnicking and camping in a setting of lush rain forest, wildflowers, seabirds and eagles.

The U.S. Coast Guard Winter Recreation Area is located on the Anton Larsen Bay Road and has a lighted downhill ski slope with rope-tow lift, a separate sledding area and a ski chalet that serves refreshments. Open to the public, depending on weather and snow conditions. Call (907) 487-5108.

Alutiiq Museum Archaeological Repository Center in downtown Kodiak houses artifacts from coastal sites around Kodiak

View of Kupreanof Strait between Raspberry Island and Kupreanof Peninsula on Kodiak Island. (© George Wuerthner)

Island. The Alutiiq are descendants of the Pacific Eskimos, whom Russian explorers encountered and referred to as the Koniag people, many of whom lived in the Karluk area on Kodiak's west coast around 1200 A.D. However, some of the items found date to 3,000 and even 7,000 years ago. The Karluk area is billed as one of the most amazing archaeological finds in Alaska because of the level of preservation of the artifacts and because of the abundance of items used in daily life. Located at 215 Mission Road; phone (907) 486-7004.

Shuyak Island State Park encompasses 47,000 acres and is located 54 air miles north of Kodiak. Access is by boat or by plane only. Hunting, fishing and kayaking are the major recreational activities. Four public-use cabins are available at $30 per night, December through May, and $50 per night, June through November. Cabins are 12 feet by 20 feet and sleep up to 8 people. Reservations accepted up to 6 months in advance with a full nonrefundable payment. Call (907) 486-6339 or 762-2261.

Holy Resurrection Russian Orthodox Church. Orthodox priests, following Russian fur traders from Siberia, arrived in Kodiak and established the first Russian Orthodox Church in North America in September 1794. The original church was built on a bluff overlooking St. Paul Harbor in 1796. A second church was built on the same location. The bluff was leveled during reconstruction following the earthquake and tsunami in 1964.

Three churches have been built on the present site. The first appears on an 1869 map of Fort Kodiak. Another church was begun in 1874 and survived until destroyed by fire in 1943. The present church was built in 1945 and is listed on the National Register of Historic Places.

The church interior provides a visual feast, and the public is invited to attend services. The public may visit Thursday and Saturday at 6:30 P.M.; Sunday service at 8:30 A.M. Phone (907) 486-3854. A $1 donation is encouraged.

A scale replica of the original (1796) church building was completed in May 1994 and is located on the grounds of St. Herman's Theological Seminary on Mission Road.

Arrange a Boat or air charter, or guide for fishing and hunting trips, adventure tours, sightseeing and photography. There are several charter services in Kodiak.

See Kodiak by Kayak. One of the best ways to experience Kodiak's beautiful coastline, and view marine mammals and seabirds, is from a kayak. Day tours around the nearby islands are available for all skill levels, or schedule an extended tour.

Kodiak National Wildlife Refuge encompasses 2,812 square miles on Kodiak Island, Uganik Island, Afognak Island and Ban Island. The refuge was established in 1941 to preserve the natural habitat of the famed Kodiak bear and other wildlife. Biologists estimate that more than 3,000 bears inhabit Kodiak Island. Most bears enter dens by October and remain there until April. Bears are readily observable on the refuge in July and August when they congregate along streams to feed on salmon. At other times they feed on grasses or berries.

Native wildlife within the refuge includes the red fox, river otter, short-tailed weasel, little brown bat and tundra vole. Introduced mammals include the Sitka black-tailed deer, beaver, snowshoe hare and mountain goat. On Afognak Island, an introduced herd of elk share the island with the bears. The coastline of Kodiak refuge shelters a large population of waterfowl and marine mammals. Bald eagles are common nesting birds on the refuge, along with 215 other bird species that have been seen on the island.

Visitors to the refuge typically go to fish, observe/photograph wildlife, backpack, kayak, camp and hunt.

NOTE: The refuge is accessible only by floatplane or boat. There are primitive public-use cabins available; applications must be made in advance to the refuge manager. For more information contact the Kodiak National Wildlife Refuge Manager, 1390 Buskin River Road, Kodiak, AK 99615; phone (907) 487-2600. You may also stop by the U.S. Fish and Wildlife Service Visitor Center on Rezanof Road, a 1/2-mile from the state airport. The center features exhibits and films on Kodiak wildlife, and is open weekdays year-round, and also Saturdays April through September; hours are variable.

Wildlife Watching. The best time to observe animals is when they are most active: at daybreak. Bald eagles can be seen near the city of Kodiak from January through March, and nesting near water in the summer. Peregrine falcons are spotted frequently from the road in October. In the summer, puffins can be seen at Miller Point on calm days. Narrow Cape, Spruce Cape and Miller Point are good stakeout points in the spring for those in search of gray whales. Womens Bay is home to a variety of migrating geese in April.

Kodiak is a gateway to Katmai National Park and Preserve, well-known for its bear-viewing and sportfishing, as well as for an abundance of other wildlife and activities.

There is a National Park Service information office in Kodiak, and local air taxi operators offer direct flights to King Salmon and also to the remote Katmai coast.

Bear-viewing Trips. To see brown bears, it's best to leave the road system and travel to the Bush by plane or boat. Almost all the air charter services offer some sort of bear-viewing excursion, ranging from half-day trips to multiple-day visits in cabins or tent-camps. Many lodge operations and licensed guides/outfitters also provide bear-viewing trips.

AREA FISHING: Kodiak Island is in the center of a fine marine and freshwater fishery and possesses some excellent fishing for rainbow, halibut, Dolly Varden and 5 species of Pacific salmon. Visiting fishermen will have to charter a boat or aircraft to reach remote lakes, rivers and bays, but the island road system offers many good salmon streams in season. Roads access red salmon fisheries in the Buskin and Pasagshak rivers. Pink and silver salmon are also found in the **Buskin** and **Pasagshak rivers**, and **Monashka, Pillar, Russian, Salonie, American, Olds, Roslyn** and **Chiniak creeks.**

Afognak and Raspberry islands, both approximately 30 air miles/48 km northeast of Kodiak, have lodges and offer excellent remote hunting and fishing. Both islands are brown bear country. Hikers and fishermen should make noise as they travel and carry a .30–06 or larger rifle. Stay clear of bears. If you take a dog, make sure he is under control. Dogs can create dangerous situations with bears.

CAUTION: A paralytic-shellfish-poisoning alert is in effect for all Kodiak Island beaches. This toxin is extremely poisonous. There are no approved beaches for clamming on Kodiak Island. For more current information, call the Dept. of Environmental Conservation in Anchorage at (907) 349-7343.

Rezanof–Monashka Bay Road Log

Distance is measured from the junction of Rezanof Drive and Marine Way in downtown Kodiak (K).

K 0.1 (0.2 km) Mill Bay Road access to library, post office and Kodiak businesses.

K 0.4 (0.6 km) Entrance to Near Island bridge to North End Park, a city park with trails and picnic areas; St. Herman Harbor, boat launch ramp, fish-cleaning station; and Fishery Industrial Technology Center (FITC), phone (907) 486-1500 for tours. Also access to Trident Basin seaplane base, located beyond FITC on Trident Way.

K 1.5 (2.4 km) Providence Kodiak Island Medical Center on left.

K 2 (3.2 km) Benny Benson Drive. Turnoff left to Kodiak College and beginning of paved bicycle trail, which parallels main road to Fort Abercrombie State Historic Park. Excellent for walking, jogging and bicycling.

K 3.4 (5.5 km) Turnout and gravel parking area to right for Mill Bay Park. Scenic picnic spot with picnic tables, barbecue grates. Good ocean fishing from beach.

K 3.9 (6.3 km) Road right to Fort Abercrombie State Historic Park. Drive in 0.2 mile/0.3 km to campground; 13 campsites with 7-night limit at $10 per night, water, toilets, fishing, swimming and picnic shelter. Extensive system of scenic hiking trails. No off-road biking. View of bay and beach, WWII fortifications. Miller Point Bunker open Monday, Friday and Sunday at 2:30 P.M. for public viewing. Saturday evening naturalist programs June 1 to Aug. 30. Just beyond the campground entrance is the Alaska State Parks ranger station, open weekdays 8 A.M. to 5 P.M.; pay phone, public restrooms, park information.

K 4.6 (7.4 km) Monashka Bay Park left at junction with Otmeloi Way. Playground equipment, covered picnic area, barbecue grates.

K 6.3 (10.1 km) Kodiak Island Borough baler/landfill facility. Recycling center.

K 6.4 (10.3 km) Pavement ends. Excellent gravel road.

K 6.8 (10.9 km) Gravel turnout to right.

K 6.9 (11.1 km) Good view of Three Sisters mountains.

K 7.1 (11.4 km) Road on right leads to VFW RV park with camping facilities, scenic views, restaurant and lounge, (907) 486-3195; Kodiak Island Sportsman's Association shooting range, (907) 486-8566.

K 7.6 (12.2 km) Pillar Creek bridge and Pillar Creek Hatchery to left.

K 8.3 (13.3 km) Road to right leads to Pillar Beach. Beautiful black-sand beach at mouth of creek. Scenic picnic area. Dolly Varden fishing.

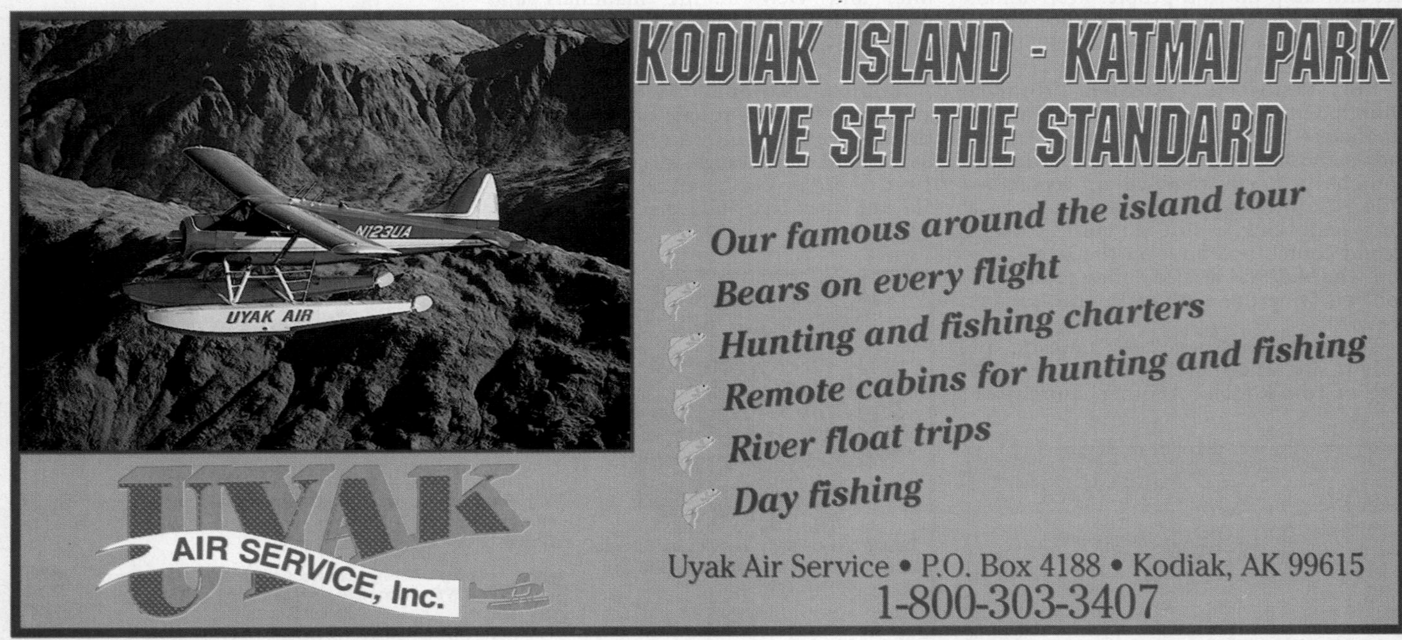

K 9.2 (14.8 km) Pullout to right. Scenic overlook and panoramic views of Monashka Bay and Monashka Mountain.

K 10.1 (16.3 km) Gravel pullout and parking to right. Access to North Sister trailhead directly across road.

K 11.2 (18 km) Bridge over Monashka Creek.

K 11.3 (18.2 km) Road ends. Large turnaround parking area. Paths to right lead through narrow band of trees to secluded Monashka Bay beach. Large, sweeping sandy beach. Excellent for picnics. Fishing off beach for Dolly Varden, pink salmon. To north of parking area is trailhead for Termination Point hike, a beautiful 6-mile loop trail along meadows, ocean bluffs and dense Sitka spruce forest. *NOTE: Leisnoi user-permit required to hike this trail.*

Chiniak Road Log

Distance from Kodiak's U.S. post office building (K).

K 0 Kodiak U.S. post office building.

K 2.2 (3.5 km) Gibson Cove campground, operated by City Parks & Recreation, with showers and restrooms. Fee $2 per person/night; $3/vehicle; $5/trailer.

K 2.4 (3.9 km) Gravel turnout to left with panoramic view of Kodiak, Chiniak Bay and nearby islands.

K 3.8 (6.1 km) **Boy Scout Lake**, stocked; gravel turnout and parking to left.

K 4.4 (7.1 km) U.S. Fish and Wildlife Service Visitor Center and Kodiak National Wildlife Refuge headquarters; open weekdays year-round, 8 A.M. to 4:30 P.M., weekends, noon to 4:30 P.M. Exhibits and films on Kodiak wildlife. Road on left to Buskin River state recreation site; 15 RV campsites with a 14-night limit at $10/night, picnic tables and shelter, water, pit toilets, trails, beach access and dump station. Fishing along **Buskin River** and on beach area at river's mouth for red, silver and pink salmon and trout. Wheelchair-accessible fishing platform. Parking for fishermen.

K 5 (8 km) Unmarked turnoff on right for Anton Larsen Bay Road (see log this section).

K 5.1 (8.2 km) Kodiak airport.

K 5.5 (8.9 km) *CAUTION: Jet blast area at end of runway. Stop here and wait if you see a jet preparing for takeoff. Do not enter or stay in this area if you see a jet.*

K 5.7 (9.2 km) Gravel turnout and limited parking to access Barometer Mountain. Steep, straight, well-trodden trail to 2,500-foot peak. Beautiful panoramic views. To access trailhead, cross paved road and walk halfway back to jet blast area.

K 6.6 (10.6 km) Entrance to U.S. Coast Guard station.

K 7.2 (11.6 km) Road continues around Womens Bay. The drive out to Chiniak affords excellent views of the extremely rugged coastline of the island.

K 9.3 (15 km) Turnoff to right to state fair and rodeo grounds. Excellent bird watching on tideflats to Salonie Creek.

K 10.1 (16.3 km) **Sargent Creek** bridge. Good fishing for pink salmon in August.

K 10.3 (16.6 km) Russian River and Bell Flats Road.

K 10.6 (17.1 km) Pavement ends; gravel begins. *NOTE: Be sure you have a spare tire. It is the law in Alaska to drive with headlights on at all times on the highway.*

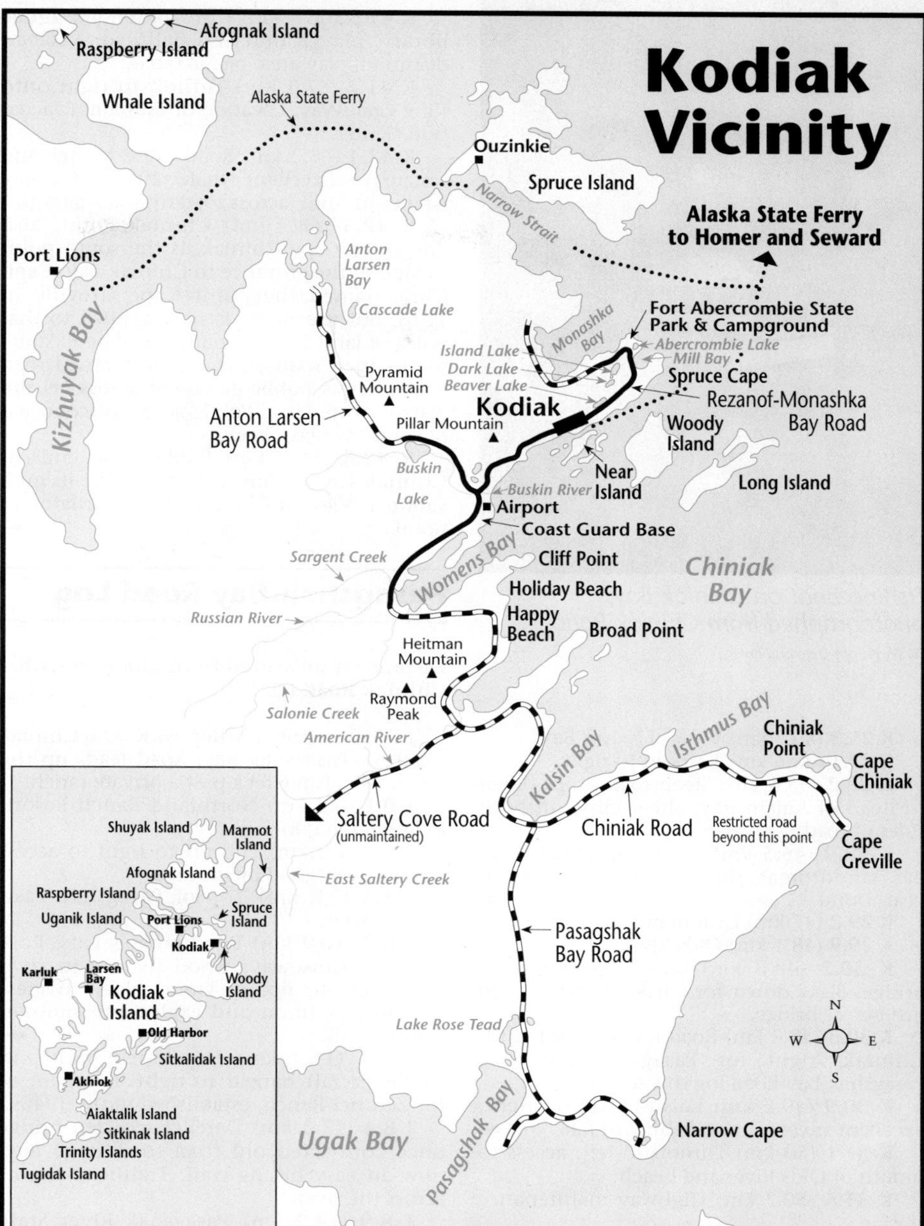

K 10.7 (17.2 km) Grocery and liquor store, diesel and unleaded gas.

K 10.8 (17.4 km) View of Bell Flats.

K 10.9 (17.5 km) Store and gas station (diesel and unleaded), tire repair.

K 12 (19.3 km) Salonie Creek.

K 12.4 (20 km) Kodiak Island Sportsman's Association rifle range turnoff to right.

K 12.6 (20.3 km) Pull off to left; beach access.

K 12.8 (20.6 km) Remnants on beach of WWII submarine dock. Begin climb up Marine Hill.

K 13.6 (21.9 km) Good turnout to left with panoramic view of Mary Island, Womens Bay, Bell Flats, Kodiak. Mountain goats visible with binoculars in spring and fall in mountains behind Bell Flats.

K 14.4 (23.2 km) Pullout and limited parking at **Heitman Lake** trailhead. Beautiful views. Stocked with rainbow trout.

K 15 (24.1 km) View of Long Island.

K 16.2 (26 km) Turnout to left.

K 16.7 (26.9 km) Road east to Holiday Beach. Closed to public. Permission by USCG required for access.

K 17.1 (27.5 km) USCG communication facility; emergency phone.

K 17.8 (28.6 km) View of Middle Bay.

K 19 (30.6 km) Undeveloped picnic area in grove of trees along beach of Middle Bay; easy access to beach. Watch for livestock.

K 19.6 (31.5 km) Small Creek bridge.

K 20 (32.2 km) Salt Creek bridge. Excellent bird watching on tideflats to left.

K 20.8 (33.5 km) American River bridge. River empties into Middle Bay.

K 20.9 (33.6 km) Unimproved road on right, marginal for 4-wheel-drive vehicles, leads toward Saltery Cove. *NOTE: Road is barely passable even for 4-wheel drive vehicles.*

K 21 (33.8 km) Felton Creek Bridge.

K 23.2 (37.3 km) Pullout to left. Foot access to gravel beach; nice picnic site.

K 24.1 (38.8 km) *CAUTION: Steep switchbacks. Slow to 10 mph.*

K 24.5 (39.4 km) Pullout to right, limited parking. Access to Mayflower Lake. Stocked with landlocked silver salmon.

K 24.6 (39.6 km) Mayflower Beach.

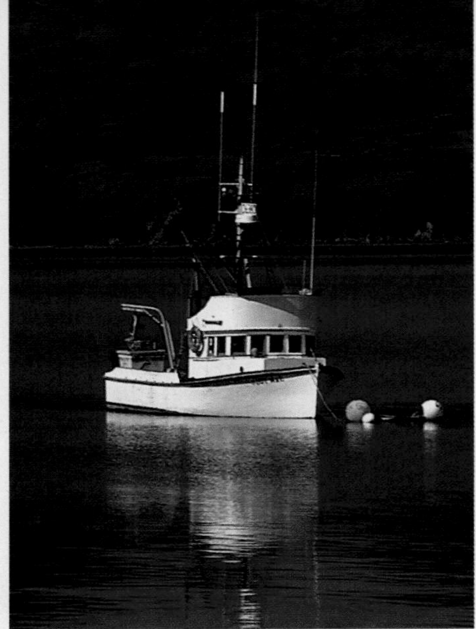

Fishing boat on Chiniak Bay, photographed from Chiniak Road.
(© W. Wright-Diamond Photo)

K 25.3 (40.7 km) View of Kalsin Bay.
K 27.1 (43.6 km) Turnout to right.
K 28.2 (45.4 km) Steep road drops down to head of Kalsin Bay; sheer cliffs on both sides of road.
K 28.9 (46.5 km) Kalsin Bay Inn; food, bar, laundromat, showers, tire repair; open year-round.
K 29.2 (47 km) Deadman Creek Bridge.
K 29.9 (48.1 km) Olds River.
K 30.2 (48.6 km) Kalsin River (creek) bridge. Slow down for cattle guard in road just before bridge.
K 30.6 (49.2 km) Road forks: Turn left for Chiniak, right for Pasagshak Bay. See Pasagshak Bay Road log this section.
K 30.9 (49.7 km) Kalsin Pond on right; excellent silver salmon fishing in fall.
K 31.1 (50 km) Turnoff to left; access to mouth of Olds River and beach.
K 31.5 (50.7 km) Highway maintenance station.
K 32 (51.5 km) Picnic area beside Kalsin Bay.
K 33.2 (53.4 km) Turnoff. Myrtle Creek, picnic site.
K 34.9 (56.2 km) Thumbs Up Cove. Unimproved boat launch ramp.
K 35.1 (56.5 km) Chiniak post office. Window hours Tuesday and Thursday 4 to 6 P.M., Saturday noon to 2 P.M.
K 35.9 (57.8 km) Brookers Lagoon. Access to gravel beach.
K 36.9 (59.4 km) Roslyn River. Access to Roslyn Bay beach, a beautiful area with picnic tables.
K 37.6 (60.5 km) Access to mouth of Roslyn River.
K 39.6 (63.7 km) Access to a beautiful point overlooking the sea; site of WWII installations. Good place for photos.
K 39.9 (64.2 km) Twin Creeks Beach, beautiful dark-sand and rolling breakers. Park in pullout area. Do not drive onto soft beach sand.
K 40.4 (65 km) Twin Creek.
K 40.7 (65.5 km) Silver Beach.
K 40.8 (65.7 km) **Pony Lake** (stocked).
K 41.3 (66.4 km) Chiniak wayside, a borough park; benches, beautiful setting.
K 41.5 (66.8 km) Chiniak school, public library, playground and ballfield. Baseball diamond, play area, picnic tables.
K 41.7 (67.1 km) Turnoff to right onto King Crab Way. Location of Tsunami Evacuation Center.
K 42.4 (68.2 km) Road's End lounge and restaurant. Excellent whalewatching for gray whales in April, across road from restaurant.
K 42.5 (68.4 km) Chiniak Point, also known as Cape Chiniak, is the south point of land at the entrance to Chiniak Bay. Capt. Cook named the point Cape Greville in 1778, but the name is now applied to that point of land 2 miles southeast of here. State-maintained road ends. Unmaintained road continues as public easement across Leisnoi Native Corp. land. Public access discouraged beyond Chiniak Creek.
K 42.8 (68.9 km) Public road ends at **Chiniak Creek.** Pink salmon fishing in midsummer. View of Chiniak Point. Turnaround point.

Pasagshak Bay Road Log

Distance is measured from junction with Chiniak Road (J).

J 0 Turn right at **Milepost K 30.6** Chiniak Road for Pasagshak Bay. Road leads up the valley of Kalsin Creek past a private ranch.
J 0.1 (0.2 km) Northland Ranch Resort; lodging, food, lounge.
J 1.2 (1.9 km) Pull off to right to access Kalsin River, good picnic area.
J 4.5 (7.2 km) Top of Pasagshak Pass; scenic views.
J 6.8 (10.9 km) Road crosses Lake Rose Tead on causeway. Good fishing in river from here to ocean. Good place to view spawning salmon and eagles late summer through fall.
J 7.1 (11.4 km) Combined barn and single aircraft hangar to right. Remnant of Joe Zentner Ranch, established in the 1940s.
J 8.4 (13.5 km) Derelict wooden bridge once connected old road to Portage Bay, now an easy hiking trail. Trailhead begins across the river.
J 8.9 (14.2 km) Pasagshak River State Recreation Site: 7 campsites with a 14-night limit (no fee), toilets, water, picnic sites, fishing and beach access.
J 9.3 (15 km) Mouth of Pasagshak River, view of Pasagshak Bay.
J 9.6 (15.4 km) Turnout at Boat Bay, traditional gravel boat launch ramp and mooring area. Four-wheel drive vehicles required to use launch ramp.
J 10.3 (16.6 km) Turnoff to right takes you to Pasagshak Point, 2 trout lakes, nice vistas.
J 11.1 (17.9 km) Entrance to Kodiak Cattle Co. grazing lease. Public land—hunting, fishing, hiking, but keep vehicle on road.
J 11.4 (18.3 km) Turnout to right provides panoramas of Narrow Cape, Ugak Island, Pasagshak Point, Sitkalidik Island. Good beachcombing on sandy beaches.
J 12.3 (19.8 km) Beach access to the right. *CAUTION: Free-ranging buffalo sometimes block the road. Stop and wait; they will eventually move. Sounding your horn is not advised. Do not approach free-ranging buffalo on foot. They can be dangerous.*
J 14.6 (23.5 km) Entrance to Kodiak Cattle Co. Ranch; guided horseback riding, fishing, camping, hunting.
J 14.9 (24 km) Entrance at right to USCG Narrow Cape Loran Station. No public access. *NOTE: Minimal road maintenance from here to end of road. Drive with caution and have a good spare tire.*
J 16.2 (26.1 km) **Twin Lakes** to the left and right of road. Trout in lake to the left.
J 16.5 (26.6 km) Road ends at Fossil Cliffs. Fossils imbedded in cliffs are visible along Fossil Beach to left and right (low tide only). *CAUTION: Cliffs are extremely unstable. Do not approach cliff face, and watch for falling rocks at all times.* Beautiful vistas and views of WWII observation bunkers on Narrow Cape to the left.

Anton Larsen Bay Road Log

Distance is measured from the turnoff (T) at Milepost K 5 Chiniak Road.

T 0 Unmarked turnoff for Anton Larsen Bay Road at **Milepost K 5** on Chiniak Road immediately before crossing the Buskin River bridge.
T 0.6 (1 km) **Buskin River** bridge No. 6. Parking area to left accessing fishing along river. Road to the right leads to good fishing holes.
T 0.7 (1.1 km) Pavement ends.
T 0.9 (1.4 km) Enter posted restricted-access area in USCG antenna field. Do not leave road for approximately next 1.5 miles.
T 1.5 (2.4 km) **Buskin River** bridge No. 7. Turnoff to left before crossing bridge accesses river and outlet of Buskin Lake. Good fishing for Dolly Varden, salmon.
T 1.6 (2.6 km) Immediately after crossing bridge, paved road to right leads to USCG communications site. Turn on gravel road to left to Anton Larsen Bay. Beautiful drive, berry picking, mountain views, wildflowers, boat launch ramp. Excellent kayaking in bay and around outer islands.
T 2 (3.2 km) High hill on right is Pyramid Mountain (elev. 2,420 feet/738m).
T 2.4 (3.9 km) End restricted access area.
T 2.9 (4.7 km) Bear Valley Golf Course. Driving range, parking on left. Nine-hole course operated by USCG. Open to the public April to October, weather permitting. Phone (907) 486-7561 or 486-4782.
T 3.2 (5.1 km) Turnout to left to unimproved trailhead of Buskin Lake. Watch for bears.
T 4.2 (6.8 km) Steep switchback.
T 5.8 (9.3 km) Buskin Valley Winter Recreation Area. Phone (907) 487-5274 or 486-4782. To right is large parking area and trailhead to top of 2,400-foot Pyramid Mountain. Trail follows ridgeline. Great vistas from top.
T 7.3 (11.7 km) Red Cloud River bridge. Small, unimproved campsite is adjacent to river on right.
T 9 (14.5 km) **Cascade Lake** trail to right. Approximately 5 miles round-trip. Rubber boots recommended to cross tidal areas. Watch for bears. Lake is stocked.
T 9.3 (15 km) Head of Anton Larsen Bay. Fox, land otters and deer can be seen in this area. Good bird watching along tidal flats.
T 10.1 (16.3 km) Public small-boat launch adjacent to road. Road continues on left side of bay for about 1.5 miles/2.4 km.
T 11.8 (19 km) Road ends. A foot-path continues beyond this point. Parking area to right.

PRINCE WILLIAM SOUND

Flightseeing glaciers in the Chugach Mountains along Prince William Sound.
(© Roy Corral)

Southcentral Alaska's Prince William Sound lies at the north extent of the Gulf of Alaska. It is just as spectacular as southeastern Alaska's Inside Passage. The area is also rich in wildlife. Visitors may see Dall sheep, mountain goats, sea lions, sea otters, whales, harbor seals, bald eagles and other birds. The waters carry all species of Pacific salmon; king, Dungeness and tanner crab; halibut; and rockfish.

This section includes: Columbia Glacier; Whittier; Valdez, start of the Richardson Highway; and Cordova, start of the Copper River Highway.

There are several ways to explore Prince William Sound. From Anchorage, drive south on the Seward Highway 47 miles/ 75.6 km to Portage and board the Alaska Railroad shuttle train for a 35-minute ride to Whittier (presently there is no road connection to Whittier). You may also start your trip across Prince William Sound from Valdez. Drive 304 miles/498.2 km from Anchorage to Valdez via the Glenn and Richardson highways (see GLENN HIGHWAY and RICHARDSON HIGHWAY sections).

From Whittier or Valdez, board the ferry or one of the privately operated excursion boats to tour Prince William Sound. Flightseeing trips are also available. Depending on your itinerary and type of transportation, you may see the glacier and return to Anchorage in a day or have to stay overnight along the way. All-inclusive tours of Prince William Sound are available out of Anchorage.

Plan your trip in advance. Reservations for the ferry or cruise boats are necessary. The Alaska Railroad does not take reservations, although passengers with confirmed ferry reservations are given first priority when loading.

Columbia Glacier

Star attraction of Prince William Sound is Columbia Glacier, one of the largest and most magnificent of the tidewater glaciers along the Alaska coast. The Columbia Glacier has an area of about 440 square miles/1144 square km. The glacier is more than 40 miles/64 km long; its tidewater terminus, which visitors to Prince William Sound will see, is about 3 miles/4.8 km across. Columbia Glacier has receded more than 5 miles/8 km since the early 1980s and is expected to leave behind a 26-mile/42-km-long fjord. A bay has formed between its face and terminal moraine (where it rested prior to retreat). This bay has been filled with ice during the retreat, keeping boats away from the glacier's face. In late 1995, the icebergs had cleared enough so that boats were able to approach and visitors could watch ice calving from the face. However, the bay again filled with ice in early 1996, blocking access to the glacier's face.

The face of the glacier varies in height above sea level from 25 to 200 feet/8 to 61m, and reaches 1,000 feet/305m or more below sea level. An abundance of plankton thrives here, attracting great numbers of fish which attract bald eagles, kittiwakes, gulls and harbor seals. Seals can usually be seen resting on ice floes or swimming in the icy waters.

The glacier was named by the Harriman Alaska expedition in 1899 for Columbia University in New York City. The glacier's source is Mount Einstein (elev. 11,552 feet/3,521m) in the Chugach Mountains.

There are daily and weekly charters by yacht or sailboat and flightseeing trips over the glacier. (See the ads in Whittier, Valdez and Cordova in this section for charter boats offering sightseeing trips and flying services offering flightseeing trips.)

Whittier

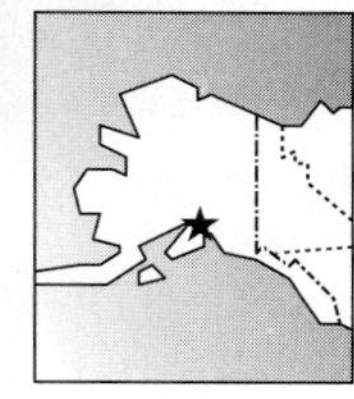

Located at the head of Passage Canal on Prince William Sound, 75 miles/121 km southeast of Anchorage. **Population:** 290. **Emergency Services: Police, Fire and Medical,** phone (907) 472-2340. **Visitor Information:**

Harbor seal mom and pup on an ice floe. Pups weigh approximately 28 lbs. at birth and double their size the first month. (© Robin Brandt)

Information kiosk at the Harbor Triangle.

Elevation: 30 feet/9m. **Climate:** Normal daily temperature for July is 56°F/13°C; for January, 25°F/-4°C. Maximum temperature is 84°F/29°C and minimum is -29°F/-2°C. Mean annual precipitation is 174 inches, including 260 inches of snow. Winter winds can reach 60 mph.

Private Aircraft: Airstrip adjacent northwest; elev. 30 feet/9m; length 1,100 feet/335m; gravel; no fuel; unattended.

Named after the poet John Greenleaf Whittier, the community of Whittier is nestled at the base of mountains that line Passage Canal, a fjord that extends eastward into Prince William Sound. Whittier is connected to the Seward Highway by railroad and to other Prince William Sound communities by ferry and charter air service. No roads lead to Whittier, although a plan for an access road extending the existing Portage Glacier Road to connect with Whittier via the railroad tunnel is under consideration.

Whittier was created by the U.S. Army during WWII as a port and petroleum delivery center tied to bases farther north by the Alaska Railroad and later a pipeline. The railroad spur from Portage was completed in 1943, and Whittier became the primary debarkation point for cargo, troops and dependents of the Alaska Command. Construction of the huge buildings that dominate Whittier began in 1948 and the Port of Whittier, strategically valuable for its ice-free deep-water port, remained activated until 1960, at which time the population was 1,200. The city of Whittier was incorporated in 1969. The government tank farm is still located here.

The 14-story Begich Towers, formerly the Hodge Building, houses more than half of Whittier's population. Now a condominium, the building was used by the U.S. Army for family housing and civilian bachelor quarters. The building was renamed in honor of U.S. Rep. Nick Begich of Alaska, who, along with Rep. Hale Boggs of Louisiana, disappeared in a small plane near here in 1972 while on a campaign tour.

The Buckner Building, completed in 1953, was once the largest building in Alaska and was called the "city under one roof." It is now privately owned and is to be renovated.

Whittier Manor was built in the early 1950s by private developers as rental units for civilian employees and soldiers who were ineligible for family housing elsewhere. In early 1964, the building was bought by another group of developers and became a condominium, which now houses the remainder of Whittier's population.

Since military and government activities ceased, the economy of Whittier rests largely on the fishing industry, the port and

WHITTIER ADVERTISERS

increasingly on tourism.

Annual events in Whittier include a Fourth of July parade, barbecue and fireworks; a Fish Derby, held Memorial Day weekend to Labor Day weekend; and Regatta, at the end of April or beginning of May, when residents boat to Valdez for Game Night and then bus or fly back to Whittier.

Whittier has 2 inns providing accommodations, a bed and breakfast, several restaurants, 2 bars, gift shops, laundry facilities, 2 general stores, video rental, gas station, post office, library and a school (preschool through grade 12), and a camper park for tents and self-contained RVs ($5 nightly fee). Fishing licenses may be purchased locally. There is no bank in Whittier. ▲

Whittier also has a harbor office, marine services and repairs, marine supply store, boat launch and lift, freight services, dry storage and self-storage units.

Valdez

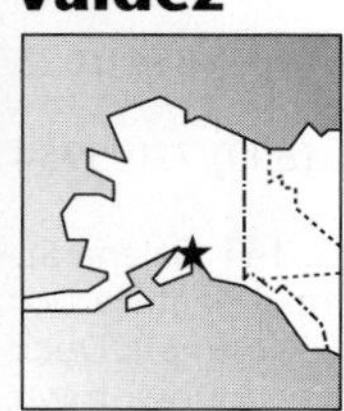

Located on Port Valdez (pronounced val-DEEZ), an estuary off Valdez Arm in Prince William Sound. Valdez is 115 air miles/185 km and 304 highway miles/489 km from Anchorage, 368 highway miles/592 km from Fairbanks. Valdez is the southern terminus of the Richardson Highway and the trans-Alaska pipeline. **Population:** 4,068.

Emergency Services: Alaska State Troopers, phone (907) 835-4359 or 835-4350. **City Police, Fire Department** and

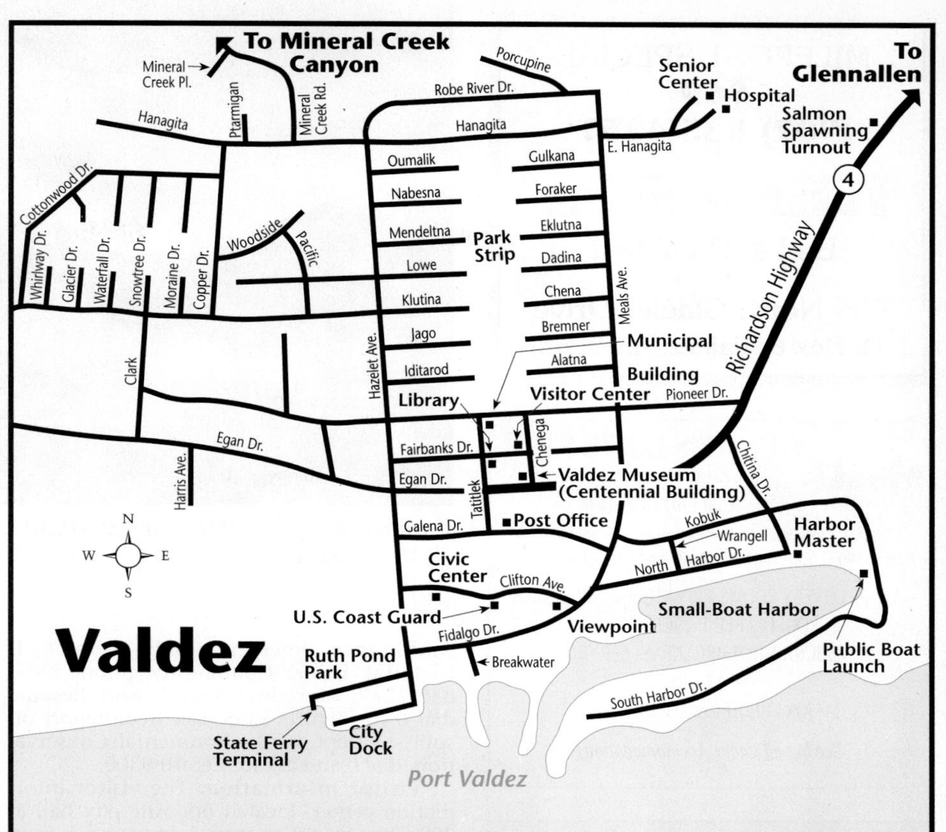

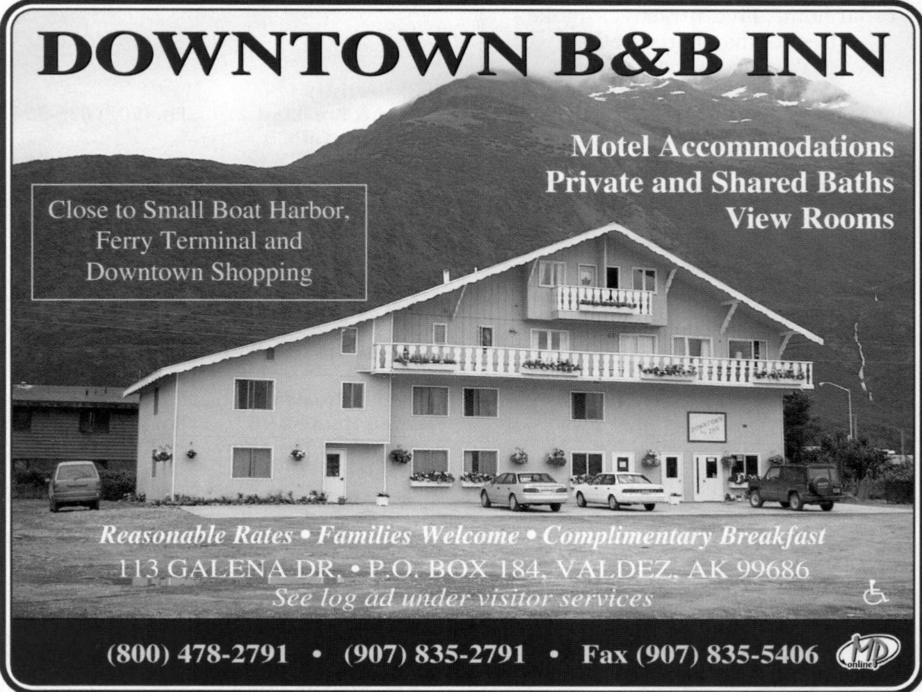

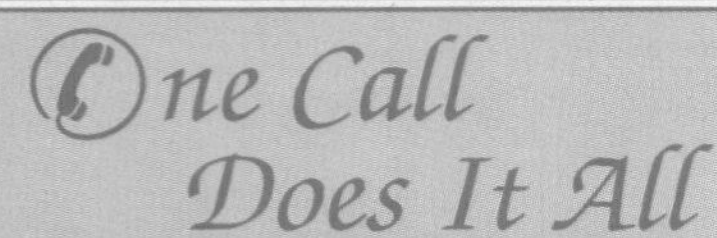

Camper at sunset (that's about 10:30 P.M. in summer) overlooking Port of Valdez. (© Michael DeYoung)

Ambulance, emergency only phone 911. **Hospital**, Valdez Community, phone (907) 835-2249. **Maritime Search and Rescue**, dial 0 for Zenith 5555, toll free. Report oil spills to Dept. of Environmental Conservation, dial 0 and ask for Zenith 9300.

Visitor Information: The visitor information center, located opposite city hall at 200 Chenega St., is open 7 days a week from 8 A.M. to 8 P.M. The visitor center offers a self-guided tour map of homes moved from Old Valdez. Write: Valdez Convention and Visitors Bureau, Box 1603-MP, Valdez 99686; or phone (907) 835-2984, fax 835-4845. E-mail: valdezak@alaska.net. Visitors may also check the community calendar at the Valdez Civic Center by phoning the hotline at (907) 835-3200.

Elevation: Sea level. **Climate:** Record high was 86°F/30°C in June 1997; record low

VALDEZ ADVERTISERS

-20°F/-29°C in January 1972. Normal daily maximum in January, 30°F/-1°C; daily minimum 21°F/-6°C. Normal daily maximum in July, 61°F/16°C; daily minimum 46°F/8°C. Average snowfall in Valdez from October to May is 329.7 inches, or about 25 feet. (By comparison, Anchorage averages about 6 feet in that period.) New snowfall records were set in January 1990, with snowfall for one day at 47½ inches. Record monthly snowfall is 180 inches in February 1996. Windy (40 mph/64 kmph) in late fall. **Radio:** KCHU 770, KVAK 1230. **Television:** Many channels via cable and satellite. **Newspapers:** *Valdez Vanguard* (weekly) and *Valdez Star* (weekly).

Private Aircraft: Valdez, 3 miles/4.8 km east; elev. 120 feet/37m; length 6,500 feet/1,981m; asphalt; fuel 100LL, Jet B; attended.

Situated in a majestic fjord, where the 5,000-foot-tall Chugach Mountains rise from Prince William Sound, Valdez is often called Alaska's "Little Switzerland." The city lies on the north shore of Port Valdez, an estuary named in 1790 by Spanish explorer Don Salvador Fidalgo for Antonio Valdes y Basan, a Spanish naval officer.

Valdez was established in 1897–98 as a port of entry for gold seekers bound for the Klondike goldfields. Thousands of stampeders arrived in Valdez to follow the All American Route to the Eagle mining district in Alaska's Interior, and from there up the Yukon River to Dawson City and the Klondike. The Valdez trail was an especially deadly route, the first part of it leading over Valdez Glacier, where the early stampeders faced dangerous crevasses, snowblindness and exhaustion.

Copper discoveries in the Wrangell Mountains north of Valdez in the early 1900s brought more development to Valdez, and conflict. A proposed railroad from tidewater to the rich Kennicott copper mines at McCarthy began a bitter rivalry between Valdez and Cordova for the railway line. The Copper River & Northwestern Railway eventually went to Cordova, but not before Valdez had started its own railroad north. The Valdez railroad did not get very far: The only trace of its existence is an old hand-drilled railway tunnel at **Milepost V 14.9** on the Richardson Highway.

The old gold rush trail out of Valdez was developed into a sled and wagon road in the early 1900s. It was routed through Thompson Pass (rather than over the Valdez Glacier) by Captain Abercrombie of the U.S. Army, who was commissioned to connect Fort Liscum (a military post established in 1900 near the present-day location of the pipeline terminal) with Fort Egbert in Eagle. Colonel Wilds P. Richardson of the Alaska Road Commission further developed the

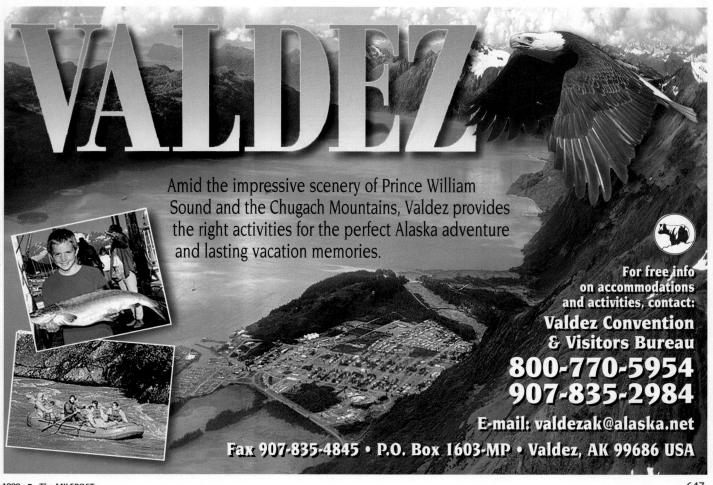

wagon road, building an automobile road from Valdez to Fairbanks which was completed in the early 1920s.

Old photos of Valdez show Valdez Glacier directly behind the town. This is because until 1964 Valdez was located about 4 miles east of its present location, closer to the glacier. The 1964 Good Friday earthquake, the most destructive earthquake ever to hit southcentral Alaska, virtually destroyed Valdez. The quake measured between 8.4 and 8.6 on the Richter scale (since revised to 9.2) and was centered in Prince William Sound. A series of local waves caused by massive underwater landslides swept over Valdez wharf and engulfed the downtown area. Afterward, it was decided that Valdez would be rebuilt at a new townsite. By late August 1964, reconstruction projects had been approved for Valdez and relocation was under way. The last residents remaining at "old" Valdez moved to the new town in 1968.

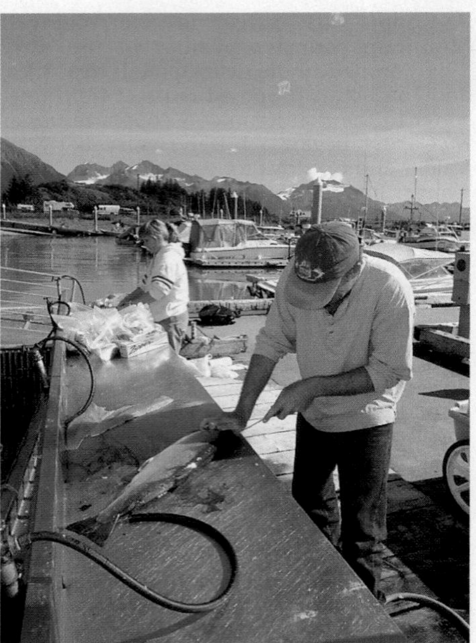

Cleaning silver salmon at Valdez small-boat harbor. (© Michael DeYoung)

Since its days as a port of entry for gold seekers, Valdez has been an important gateway to Interior Alaska. As the most northerly ice-free port in the Western Hemisphere, and connected by the Richardson Highway to the Alaska highway system, Valdez has evolved into a shipping center, offering the shortest link to much of interior Alaska for seaborne cargo.

Construction of the trans-Alaska pipeline was begun in 1974 and completed in 1977 (the first tanker load of oil shipped out of Valdez on Aug. 1, 1977). The 1,000-acre site at Port Valdez was chosen as the pipeline terminus; tours of the marine terminal are available (see Attractions).

From Prudhoe Bay on the Arctic Ocean, the 48-inch-diameter, 800-mile-/1287-km-long pipeline follows the Sagavanirktok River and Atigun Valley, crossing the Brooks Mountain Range at 4,739-foot/1,444m Atigun Pass. South of the Brooks Range it passes through Dietrich and Koyukuk valleys and crosses the hills and muskeg of the Yukon–Tanana uplands to the Yukon River. South of the Yukon, the line passes through more rolling hills 10 miles/16 km east of

Fairbanks, then goes south from Delta Junction to the Alaska Range, where it reaches an elevation of 3,420 feet/1,042m at Isabel Pass before descending into the Copper River basin. It crests the Chugach Mountains at Thompson Pass (elev. 2,812 feet/857m) and descends through the Keystone Canyon to Valdez, where it is fed by gravity into tanks or directly into waiting oil tankers at the marine terminal.

Because of varying soil conditions along its route, the pipeline is both above and below ground. Where the warm oil would cause icy soil to thaw and erode, the pipeline goes above ground to avoid thawing. Where the frozen ground is mostly well-drained gravel or solid rock, and thawing is not a problem, the line is underground.

The line was designed with 12 pump stations (although Pump Station 11 was never built) and numerous large valves to control the flow of oil. Since 1996, 4 pump stations have been placed on standby due to declining North Slope oil production. The entire system can operate on central computer control from Valdez or independent local control at each pump station.

National attention was focused on Valdez and the pipeline when the oil tanker *Exxon Valdez* ran aground in March 1989, causing an 11-million-gallon oil spill.

Valdez's economy depends on the oil industry, the Prince William Sound fishery, government and tourism. The city limits of Valdez comprise an area of 274 square miles and include all surrounding mountains to timberline. Valdez has long been known for its beautiful setting, with the Chugach Mountains rising behind the city, and the small-boat harbor in front. The town has wide streets and open spaces, with the central residential district built around a park strip which runs from the business district almost to the base of the mountains behind town.

ACCOMMODATIONS/VISITOR SERVICES

Services in Valdez include several restaurants and bars, grocery store, sporting goods stores, gift shops, 4 service stations, hardware, hair stylists, 1 drugstore, 2 pharmacies and numerous churches.

Valdez has 7 motel/hotel facilities and numerous bed and breakfasts. You are advised to make reservations well in advance. Summer tourist season is also the peak work season, and accommodations fill up quickly. Expect to pay $100 and up for a double motel room with bath, $55 to $85 for a bed and breakfast.

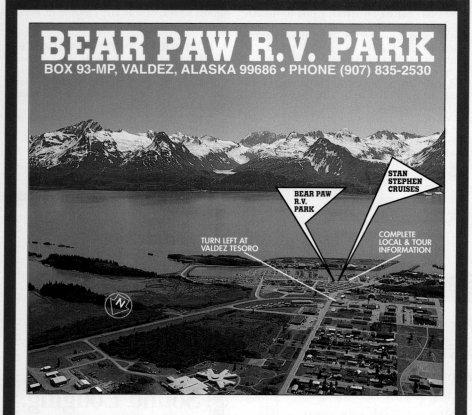

Blessing House B & B. Home-away-from-home. Walk to harbor, museum and shopping. Mountain views! See unique locking caribou horns; play piano or cook. Rates $55–$85. King beds, continental breakfast. Reservations phone (888) 853-5333 (*51 fax); (907) 835-5333, (907) 835-2259; P.O. Box 233, Valdez, AK 99686. Living units also available throughout year; Hursh Realtors, Diann Hursh, Broker. [ADVERTISEMENT]

Downtown B & B Inn. Motel accommodations, 113 Galena Dr. Centrally located near small boat harbor, museum, ferry terminal, downtown shopping. View rooms, private and shared baths, coin-op laundry, TV and phones in rooms. Wheelchair accessible. Complimentary breakfast. Reasonable rates. Single, double, family rooms. Phone (800) 478-2791 or (907) 835-2791. E-mail: brandau@alaska.net. Internet: www.alaskaone.com/downinn/index.htm. See display ad this section. [ADVERTISEMENT] MP ♿

Gussie's Lowe Street Inn. Quiet residential neighborhood a few blocks from downtown and ferry terminal. Clean rooms, queen or twin beds, homey atmosphere. Private or shared baths. In-room phones, cable TV, VCR. No stairs! Delicious hot breakfasts. Longtime Alaskan hosts, Joanne and Bob LaRue, and Gus Too, our lovable family pet. Phone (907) 835-4448. See display ad. [ADVERTISEMENT]

Keystone Hotel. Located downtown (corner of Egan and Hazelet) within walking distance to ferry terminal, shops and restaurants. 107 rooms with private baths, cable TV, phones, nonsmoking or smoking, handicap access, coin-op laundry facilities. Continental breakfast included with room. Comfortable, clean rooms at reasonable rates. (907) 835-3851. See display ad this section. [ADVERTISEMENT] ♿

The Lake House Bed & Breakfast. Comfortable and quiet, this very large home is located only 10 minutes from Valdez's city center. Excellent bird and wildlife viewing and dramatic alpine scenery. Spacious rooms, most with private bath. Continental breakfast. Brochure available. P.O. Box 1499, Valdez, AK 99686; phone (907) 835-4752. Mile 6 Richardson Highway. [ADVERTISEMENT]

One Call Does It All. Free reservation service for Valdez, Kennicott, Cordova and the Greater Copper Valley. Lodging, glacier cruises, extended cruises, fishing charters. Flightseeing, rafting, kayaking, car and RV rentals. VISA, MasterCard accepted. For the spectacular Prince William Sound, One Call Does It All! (907) 835-4988. See display ad

this section. [ADVERTISEMENT]

Totem Inn, completely remodeled restaurant and lounge featuring an Old Town look with a New Town taste. Diners are surrounded by famous works of Alaska art. Restaurant opens at 5 A.M., serving breakfast, lunch and dinner. The lounge offers tall tales and a wide variety of libations. The motel provides deluxe rooms with private baths, satellite TV, phones, handicap access. Ask for rooms or suites in our brand new annex. Motel reservations suggested. Ample parking available. Open year-round. Phone (907) 835-4443, fax (907) 835-5751. See display ad this section. [ADVERTISEMENT]

Valdez Village Inn, downtown Valdez: 100 modern rooms. Cable TV, private baths. Wheelchair access. Fitness center, sauna, Jacuzzi, beauty shop, espresso bar. Casa Valdez Restaurant & Sugarloaf Saloon. Room/Glacier Cruise packages. Phone (907) 835-4445, fax (907) 835-2437. See display ad this section. [ADVERTISEMENT]

There are 6 private RV parks with hookups near the small-boat harbor. Dump station and diesel at Valdez Tesoro. Dump station at Bear Paw R.V. Park for registered guests.

The nearest public campground is Valdez Glacier campground, at the end of the airport road, about 6 miles/9.7 km from town; turn left on Airport Road at **Milepost NV 3.4** Richardson Highway. This city-owned and privately operated campground has 101 sites, tent-camping areas, picnic areas, firepits, tables, litter barrels, water and toilets; 15-day limit, $10 fee charged. ▲

Bear Paw R.V. Park, centrally located on scenic North Harbor Drive overlooking the boat harbor, puts you within easy walking distance of museums, shops, restaurants, entertainment, charter boats—no need to unhook and drive to grocery stores or points

of interest. Full, partial or no hookups; immaculate private restrooms with hot, unmetered showers. Dump station and coin-operated launderette with irons and ironing boards available for guests. Also available, for adults only: waterfront full-hookup RV sites with cable TV, guest lounge, computer modem access line. Very nice, quiet wooded tent sites, some platforms, among the salmonberries on Porcupine Hill. Tables, fire pots and freezer available. Campfire wood

Humpy salmon in snow competes in Valdez Snowman Festival. (© Joe Prax)

for sale. Full discount coupons available. Let us book your glacier tour with Stan Stephens Cruises at the reservations desk in our spacious office lounge. We also book raft trips, flightseeing and pipeline terminal tours. Don't miss the Bear Paw Trading Post Gift Shop. Advance reservations recommended: (907) 835-2530. (Bear Paw does fill up!) The coffee pot is always on at Bear Paw. Let us know if you're coming in on the evening ferry and we'll be there to help you get parked. E-mail: bpawcamp@alaska.net. Internet: www.alaska.net/~bpawcamp/. See our large display ad this section. [ADVERTISEMENT] ▲

Eagle's Rest RV Park, the friendliest RV park in downtown Valdez, offers you Good Sam Park service with a smile. Let Herb, Jeff or Laura take care of all your bookings on

cruises, tours and charters. Enjoy the beautiful panoramic view of our mountains and glaciers right off our front porch! We also can let you know where the hottest fishing spots are or the quietest walking trails! Fish-cleaning table and freezer available. 10-bay golf driving range. Capt'n Joe's Tesoro next door offers gas, diesel, propane; potable water, sewer dump. Parking with us puts you within walking distance of our museum, gift shops, banks and even the largest grocery store on our same block. Shuttle service for glacier cruises. No charge to wash your RV at your site. Phone us for reservations, 1-800-553-7275 or (907) 835-2373. Fax (907) 835-KAMP (835-5267). E-mail: rvpark@alaska.net. Internet: www.alaskaoutdoors.com/eagle/. Stay with us and leave feeling like family. See display ad this section. [ADVERTISEMENT] MP ▲

TRANSPORTATION

Air: Daily scheduled service via Alaska Airlines and Era Aviation. Air taxi and helicopter services available.

Ferry: Scheduled state ferry service to Cordova, Whittier and Seward. Phone (907) 835-4436. Reservations are a must!

Bus: Regularly scheduled service to Anchorage and Fairbanks.

Taxi: One local taxi service.

Car Rental: Two companies offer car rentals; available at airport terminal.

Highway: The Richardson Highway extends north from Valdez to the Glenn Highway and the Alaska Highway. See the RICHARDSON HIGHWAY section.

ATTRACTIONS

Celebrate Gold Rush Days. Held Aug. 5–9, 1998, this celebration includes a parade, contests and a game night. During the celebration cancan girls meet the cruise ships and a jail is pulled through town by "deputies" who arrest citizens without beards, and other suspects.

Visit Valdez Museum, located at 217 Egan Dr. Exhibits depict lifestyles and workplaces from 1898 to present. Displays include a beautifully restored 1907 Ahrens steam fire engine, the original Cape Hinchinbrook lighthouse lens, a Civil War-era field cannon and an illuminated model of the Alyeska Pipeline Marine Terminal. Interpretive exhibits explain the impact of the 1964 earthquake, the construction of the trans-Alaska oil pipeline and the 1989 *Exxon Valdez* oil spill cleanup. Visitors can touch Columbia Glacier ice and feel the luxurious softness of a sea otter pelt. The museum's William A. Egan Commons provides a showcase setting for the Ahrens steam fire engine, models of antique aircraft, and the lighthouse lens. Outside exhibits include displays of local wildflowers, an oil pipeline "pig" and a unique snow tractor. Valdez Museum is open year-round: daily 9 A.M. to 9 P.M. during summer months (May to September); Tuesday through Saturday during off-season (October to April). Children free; $3 for adults (18 and older); $2.50 for seniors. Phone (907) 835-2764 for more information.

Tour the oil pipeline terminus. The marine terminal of the trans-Alaska pipeline is across the bay from the city of Valdez. Bus tours of the pipeline terminal are available daily, from May to September, from Valdez Tours Co.; fee charged, reservations suggested, cameras welcome. Phone (907) 835-2686 for details.

While entry to the terminal is restricted to authorized bus tours only, the drive out to the terminal is worthwhile. From Meals Avenue drive 6.8 miles/10.9 km out the Richardson Highway and turn right on the terminal access road (Dayville exit). The 5.4-mile/8.7-km road leading to the terminal passes Solomon Gulch dam and a spectacular view of Solomon Gulch Falls. There is also excellent fishing in season at Allison Point for pink and silver salmon. Entrance to the pipeline terminal is at the end of the road.

Outside the marine terminal gate is a bronze sculpture commemorating the efforts of men and women who built the trans-Alaska oil pipeline. Dedicated in September 1980, the sculpture was created by Californian Malcolm Alexander. It is composed of 5 figures representing various crafts and skills employed in the construction project. The work is the focal point of a small park from which visitors can watch tankers loading Alaska crude oil at the terminal. A small parking lot accommodates about 30 cars, and a series of signs explains the pipeline and terminal operations.

Take a boat tour to see Columbia Glacier, Shoup Glacier and other Prince William Sound attractions. Columbia Glacier, a tidewater glacier in Columbia Bay 28 miles/45 km southwest of Valdez, has become one of Alaska's best-known attractions. See ads in this section.

Raft and kayak trips of Prince William Sound, Keystone Canyon and surrounding rivers are available.

Go flightseeing and see Columbia Glacier, spectacular Prince William Sound and the surrounding Chugach Mountains from the air. There are several air charter services and 1 helicopter service in Valdez; see ads in this section.

Our Point of View, an observation platform offering views of the original Valdez townsite, pipeline terminal and the town, is located by the Coast Guard office.

Valdez Consortium Library, located on Fairbanks Street, has a magazine and paper-

back exchange for travelers. A trade is appreciated but not required. The library also has music listening booths, public computers, typewriters and a photocopier. Wheelchair accessible. Open Monday and Friday 10 A.M. to 6 P.M., Tuesday through Thursday 10 A.M. to 8 P.M., Saturday noon to 5 P.M. and Sunday 1–5 P.M. when school is session. ♿

Visit Prince William Sound Community College, located at 303 Lowe St. Two huge wooden carvings on campus (1 located in the dorms on Pioneer Street), by artist Peter Toth, are dedicated to the Indians of America. Four Elderhostel programs are held at Prince William Sound Community College in June and July. This educational program (college credit given) is available for people over age 55. Subjects include Alaska history, wildlife and fisheries of Prince William Sound, and Alaska literature. Contact Elderhostel, 80 Boylston St., Suite 400, Boston, MA 02116, for more information on its Alaska programs. The 6th annual Edward Albee Theatre Conference, sponsored by the college, will be held Aug. 10–16, 1998, at the Valdez Convention and Civic Center. Past visiting playwrights at the conference have included Edward Albee and Arthur Miller. For more information contact PWSCC, P.O. Box 97, Valdez, AK 99686.

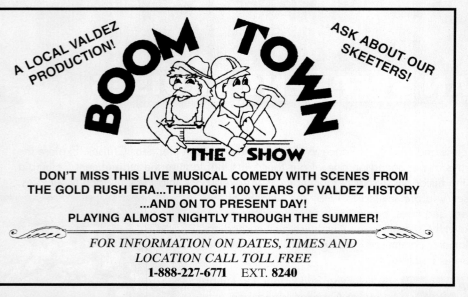

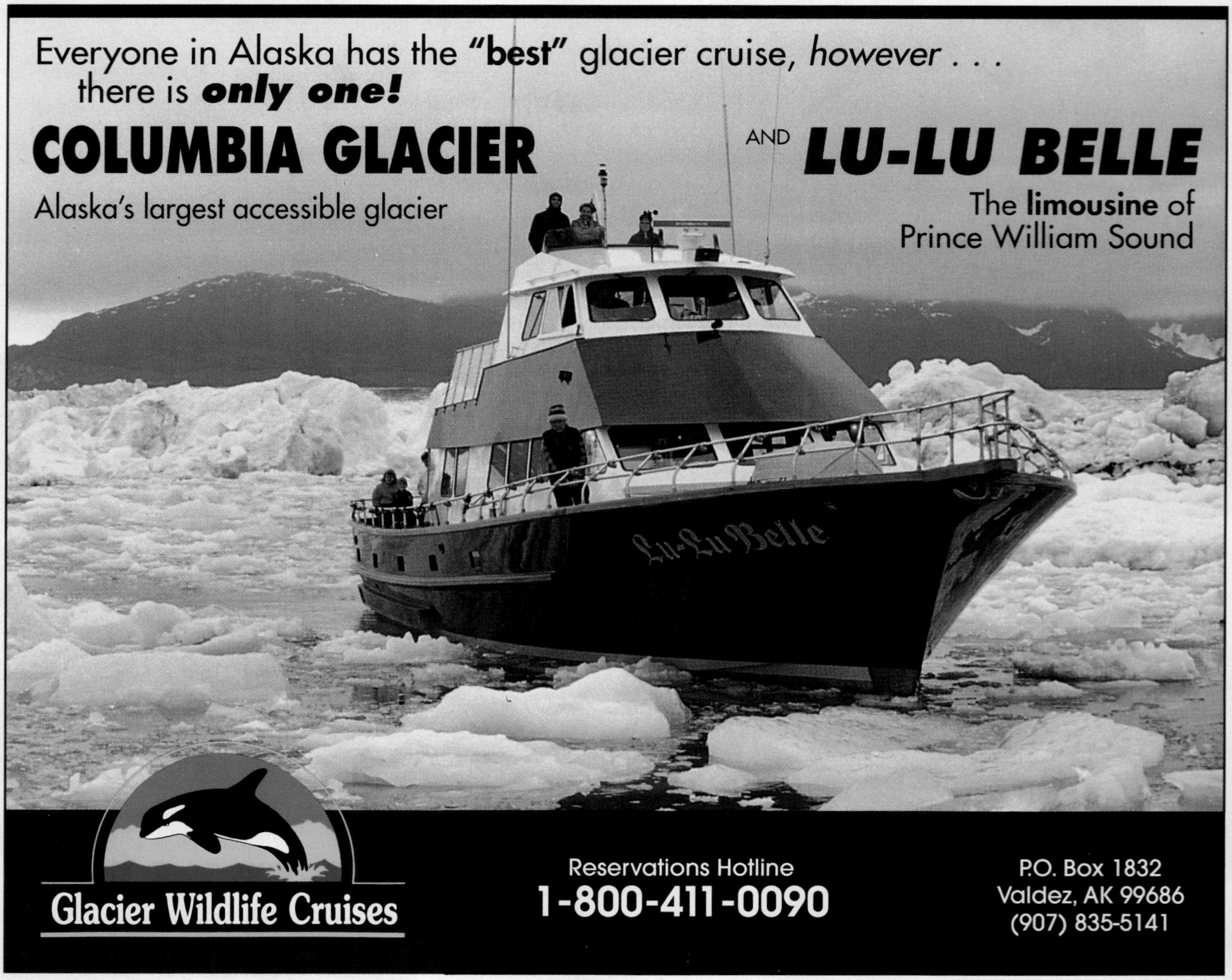

View salmon spawning at Crooked Creek. From Meals Avenue drive 0.9 mile/1.4 km out the Richardson Highway to the Crooked Creek salmon spawning area and hatchery. A U.S. Forest Service information station, open Memorial Day to Labor Day, has interpretive displays and information on cultural history and recreation. An observation platform gives a close-up look at salmon spawning in midsummer and fall. This is also a waterfowl sanctuary and an excellent spot for watching various migrating birds.

Fish a Derby. The Valdez Chamber of Commerce holds a halibut, silver salmon and pink salmon derby every year, with cash prizes awarded to the first through third place winners for all 3 derbies. For further information contact the Valdez Chamber of Commerce at (907) 835-2330.

Drive Mineral Creek Road. A 5.5-mile/8.9-km drive behind town leading northwest through the breathtaking alpine scenery along Mineral Creek. *Drive carefully!* This is a narrow road; conditions depend on weather and how recently the road has been graded. Bears are frequently sighted here. To reach Mineral Creek Road drive to the end of Hazelet Street toward the mountains and turn left on Hanagita then right on Mineral Creek Road. Excellent view of the city from the water tower hill just to the right at the start of Mineral Creek Road.

Valdez Arm supports the largest sport fishery in Prince William Sound. Important species include pink salmon, coho (silver) salmon, halibut, rockfish and Dolly Varden. Charter boats are available in Valdez. A hot fishing spot near Valdez and accessible by road is the **Allison Point** fishery (or "Winnebago Point" as it is known locally) created by the Solomon Gulch Hatchery, which produces major pink and silver salmon returns annually. Turn off the Richardson Highway at **Milepost V 2.9.** It is one of the largest pink salmon fisheries in the state. Pink salmon returns are best in odd years, but with hatchery production good pink runs are anticipated every year. Pinks average 3 to 5 lbs., from late June to early August. Silvers

Sunrise lights up the marine terminal of the trans-Alaska pipeline at Valdez.
(© Tom Culkin)

Spawning pink salmon at Solomon Gulch Hatchery at Milepost V 2.9 Richardson Highway. (© Michael DeYoung)

from 6 to 10 lbs., late July into September.

Bear Paw Trading Post Gift Shop, next to Bear Paw RV Park on Harbor Drive, features fine Alaska Native arts and crafts. Carved walrus ivory, scrimshaw, soapstone carvings, Native masks, fur items. Gold nugget jewelry, jade, hematite. Prints and books by Doug Lindstrand. Film, postcards, souvenirs, Alaska books. VISA, MasterCard accepted. Phone (907) 835-2530. [ADVERTISEMENT]

Boom Town, The Show. Laugh-Out-Loud Productions invites you to experience the history of Valdez in a delightfully clever, live, musical comedy! Join Prospector Pete and friends as they weave their way through the past 100 years of gold seeking, town building and rebuilding, oil shipping and mosquitoes! Great evening family entertainment! For dates, times and location, phone (907) 835-3505. [ADVERTISEMENT]

Era Helicopters. Fly over Valdez and the Prince William Sound with Alaska's most experienced helicopter company. Soar over the breathtaking Columbia Glacier. Land at the face of Shoup Glacier or take a heli-hiking adventure. Phone (800) 843-1947 or (907) 835-2595 locally. Tours also available in Anchorage, Juneau and Mount McKinley. [ADVERTISEMENT]

Ketchum Air Service, Inc. Alaska's outdoor specialists. Floatplane tours/charters into Prince William Sound, Wrangell–St. Elias park. Day fishing/fully equipped. Columbia Glacier tour. Drop-off cabins. Kennecott Mine visit! Floatplane tour office located small-boat harbor, Valdez. Call or write for brochure. VISA, MasterCard. Phone (907) 835-3789 or (800) 433-9114. Box 670, Valdez, AK 99686. [ADVERTISEMENT]

Glacier Wildlife Cruises/*Lu-Lu Belle*. The motor yacht *Lu-Lu Belle* is probably the cleanest, plushest tour vessel you will ever see! We cater to adult travelers. When you come aboard and see all the teak, mahogany and oriental rugs, you will understand why Captain Rodolf asks you to wipe your shoes before boarding. The *Lu-Lu Belle* has wide walk-around decks, thus assuring

everyone ample opportunity for unobstructed viewing and photography, and is equipped with 110-volt outlets for your battery chargers. Captain Rodolf has logged over 2,800 Columbia Glacier cruises since 1979; he will personally guide and narrate every cruise. The Columbia Glacier wildlife cruise of Prince William Sound is awesome. Puffins, sea lions, sea otters, seals and bald eagles are seen on every cruise. Dall porpoise, orca, humpback and minke whale, black bear, Sitka black-tail deer, Dall sheep and mountain goat are often seen as the *Lu-Lu Belle* cruises from Valdez to Columbia Glacier on the calm, protected waters of the sound. We guarantee no sea sickness. Boarding time is 1:45 P.M. each day from Memorial Day to Labor Day. During the busier part of the season, an 8:00 A.M. cruise is added. (No morning cruise on Sunday.) The cost is $65 per person (with a cash discount price of $60). The cruise is approximately 5 hours. During the trip the crew prepares fresh-baked goods in the galley. Friendliness and gracious hospitality on a beautiful yacht with small intimate groups. Come and find out why people refer to the *Lu-Lu Belle* as "the limousine of Prince William Sound." Our best advertisement is our happy guests. Join us for an extra-special day and find out why Captain Rodolf refers to Switzerland as the "Valdez of Europe!" Phone (800) 411-0090 or (907) 835-5141. [ADVERTISEMENT]

Northern Comfort Charters operates 2 boats designed for your fishing comfort and pleasure. For halibut (and a wide variety of other bottom-feeding fish) the 43-ft. Lady Luck features a comfortable warm cabin, full restroom and a 360 degree all-around fishing deck. The 44-ft. Northern Comfort is more suitable for 2-day overnight charters and is an excellent boat for silver salmon fishing featuring a full fishing deck cover, large comfortable cabin and full restroom. Go with us and enjoy the excellent fishing offered by Prince William Sound as well as the abundant sea life, glaciers, majestic mountains and waterfalls. Phone (800) 478-9884 or (907) 835-3070. See our display ad this section. [ADVERTISEMENT]

Northern Magic Charters and Tours—"the small ship alternative"—offers one of the finest personalized tours in Valdez. Enjoy the spacious luxury of our custom-built, 43-foot ship, *The Viking*. The 360-degree, wrap-around deck is ideal for close-up wildlife viewing or fishing, and offers a more relaxed, less crowded tour. One of our more popular sightseeing adventures is the 2 1/2-hour Shoup Glacier and Port of Valdez historic tour. Customized tours and halibut fishing throughout Prince William Sound are available. A maximum of 11 passengers are taken for halibut fishing. For more information, phone toll free (888) 835-4433; or write P.O. Box 1559, Valdez, AK 99686. E-mail: fishtour@alaska.net. Internet: www.alaska.net/~fishtour. [ADVERTISEMENT]

Prince William Sound Cruise. Experience the spectacular beauty of Prince William Sound aboard the *MV Nunatak*. This Gray Line of Alaska tour cruises past Columbia Glacier, the largest glacier in Prince William Sound. Watch for abundant marine life as you travel to picturesque Valdez and Whittier. Two meals are included. This 12-hour tour departs daily from Valdez and costs $114 per person. Prices subject to change. Phone (907) 835-2357. [ADVERTISEMENT]

Raven Sailing Charters. Cruise in comfort aboard our handsome 50-foot ketch on single-day or multi-day trips personalized to fulfill your interests. View wildlife, marine life, glaciers and secluded bays. Involve yourself in wilderness hiking, photography and beachcombing. Hot showers, prepared meals, fresh linens and central heating are some of the amenities offered aboard. Complete safety and navigation equipment. Small group of 1–6 persons. (907) 835-5863, (907) 835-4960 message. See display ad this section. [ADVERTISEMENT]

Stan Stephens Cruises. This Alaskan family-owned business offers a variety of glacier and wildlife cruises in the protected waters of Prince William Sound. Tours departing out of Valdez and Whittier. All of our tours are aboard comfortable, Coast Guard-licensed vessels with heated inner cabins and spacious outer decks. Our experienced and knowledgeable captains and crew will interpret and share the wonders of Prince William Sound with you: the Chugach Mountains, North America's highest coastal mountain range, Columbia Glacier, Meares Glacier, Blackstone Glacier, wildlife and Growler Island Wilderness Camp. Growler Island is unique to Stan Stephens Cruises. We are pleased to share

this pristine Prince William Sound location with visitors to Alaska. Whether you come for the day or spend the night, Growler Island will be one of the highlights of your Alaskan experience. Our 8 1/2 hour and 10 1/2 hour trips stop at Growler Island for an all-you-can-eat Alaskan feast, featur-

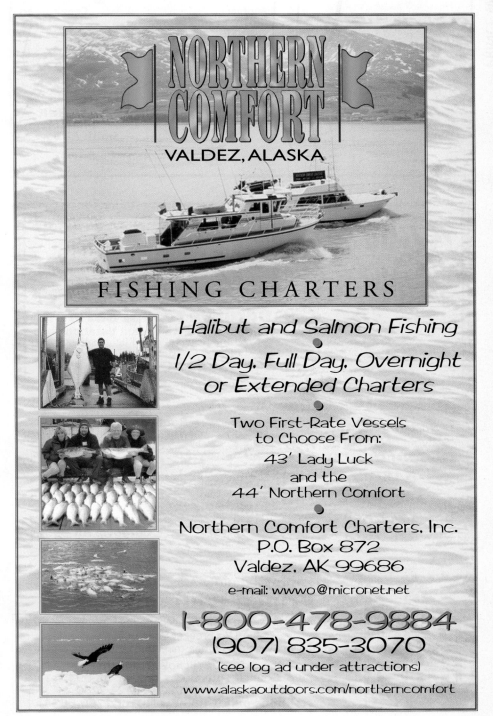

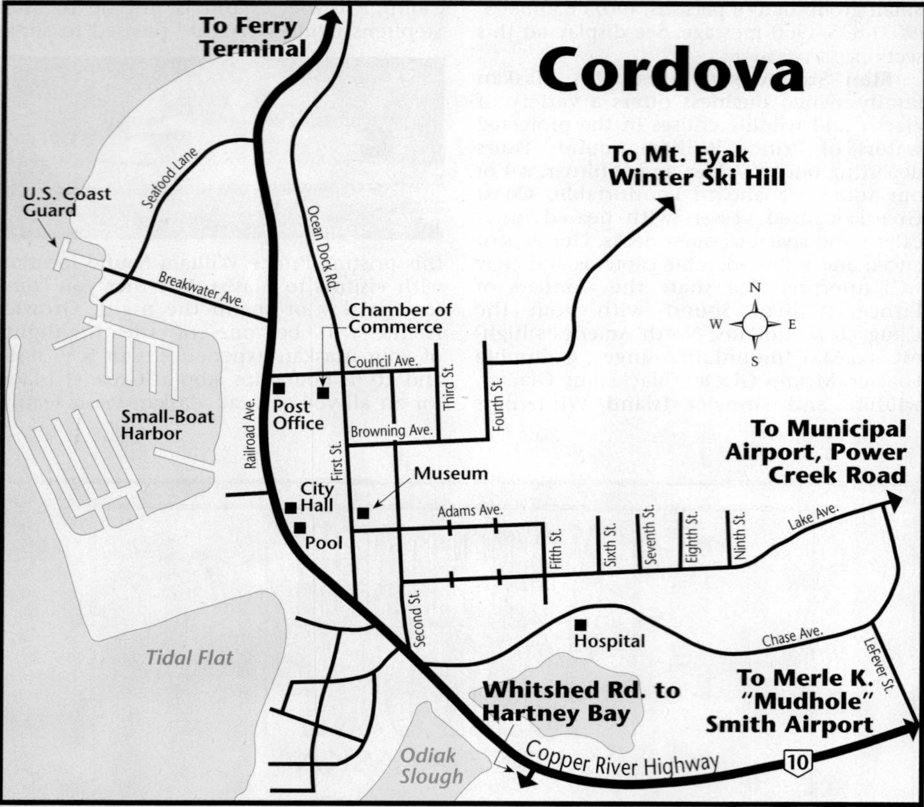

ing salmon, halibut, beef, chicken and a variety of salads and side dishes. Growler Island overnight offers adventure travelers an opportunity to explore the peaceful beauty of Growler and Glacier Islands. Accommodations are in heated tent/cabins. All meals are provided. Overnight space at Growler Island is limited, so reservations are encouraged. Don't miss this opportunity for a truly Alaskan experience. We are successful at accommodating most physically-challenged travelers. Phone toll free or write for schedules, prices and a brochure. P.O. Box 1297, Valdez, AK 99686. Phone (800) 992-1297 or (907) 835-4731; fax (907) 835-3765; Internet: www.alaskaone.com/stanstephens. See our full-page display ad for photos. [ADVERTISEMENT] ♿ MP

Cordova

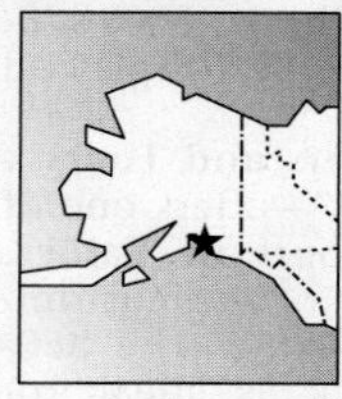

Located on the east side of Prince William Sound on Orca Inlet. **Population:** 2,585. **Emergency Services: Alaska State Troopers**, phone (907) 424-7331, emergency phone 911. **Police, Fire Department, Ambulance**, phone (907) 424-6100, emergency phone 911. **Hospital**, phone (907) 424-8000.

Visitor Information: Chamber of Commerce office on 1st Street inside the Union Hall Building; phone (907) 424-7260 or write Box 99, Cordova, AK 99574. There is also a visitor information center at the museum. A one-hour audio-taped, self-guided walking tour of downtown Cordova is available for rent from the Chamber of Commerce and museum. A self-guided walking tour map of Cordova historic sites, prepared by the Cordova Historical Society, is also available.

Chugach National Forest Cordova Ranger District office is located at 612 2nd St. USFS personnel can provide information on trails,

CORDOVA ADVERTISERS

Cordova Air Service, Inc. ..Ph. (907) 424-3289
Cordova Outboard, Inc. ..211 Breakwater Ave.
Cordova Rose Lodge ....Ph. (907) 424-ROSE
Cordova Travel Service ...Ph. (800) CORDOVA
King's Chamber, The ....Ph. (907) 424-3373
Northern Nights Inn.........Ph. (907) 424-5356
Powder House Bar and Restaurant ....Mile 2.1 Copper River Hwy.
Prince William Motel ....Ph. (907) 424-3201
Prince William Sound Tourism........................Ph. (800) 770-5954
Reluctant Fisherman Inn ..Ph. (800) 770-3272

cabins and other activities on national forest lands. The office is open weekdays from 8 A.M. to 5 P.M. Write P.O. Box 280, Cordova 99574, or phone (907) 424-7661.

Elevation: Sea level to 400 feet/122m. **Climate:** Average temperature in July is 54°F/12°C, in January 21°F/-6°C. Average annual precipitation is 167 inches. Prevailing winds are easterly at about 4 knots. **Radio:** KLAM-AM, KCHU-FM (National Public Radio), KCDV-FM. **Television:** Cable. **Newspaper:** *Cordova Times* (weekly).

Private Aircraft: Merle K. "Mudhole" Smith Airport, 11.3 miles/18.2 km southeast; elev. 42 feet/13m; length 7,500 feet/2,286m; asphalt; attended. Cordova Municipal (city airfield), 0.9 mile/1.4 km east; elev. 12 feet/4m; length 1,900 feet/579m; gravel; fuel 100, 100LL; unattended. Eyak Lake seaplane base, 0.9 mile/1.4 km east.

It was the Spanish explorer Don Salvador Fidalgo who named the adjacent water Puerto Cordoba in 1790. The town was named Cordova by Michael J. Heney, builder of the Copper River & Northwestern Railway. By 1889, the town had grown into a fish camp and cannery site. A post office was established in 1906. Cordova was incorporated in 1909.

One of the first producing oil fields in Alaska was located at Katalla, 47 miles/76 km southeast of Cordova on the Gulf of Alaska. The discovery was made in 1902 and the field produced until 1933.

The town was chosen as the railroad terminus and ocean shipping port for copper ore shipped by rail from the Kennecott mines near Kennicott and McCarthy. The railroad and town prospered until 1938 when the mine closed.

Commercial fishing has now supplanted mining as the basis of the town's economy. The fishing fleet can be seen at Cordova harbor, home port of the MV *Bartlett* and the USCG cutter *Sweetbrier.* Also at the harbor is the Cordova Fishermen's Memorial, *The Southeasterly.*

The fishing and canning season for salmon runs from about May to September, with red, king and silver (coho) salmon taken from the Copper River area, chum, red and pink salmon from Prince William Sound. Black cod, crab and shrimp season runs during winter. Dungeness crab season runs during the summer and early fall months. Razor clams, halibut and scallops are also processed.

ACCOMMODATIONS/VISITOR SERVICES

Cordova has 2 motels and 2 hotels, 10 bed and breakfasts, 12 restaurants, 2 laundromats and a variety of shopping facilities.

Cordova Rose Lodge. Historical 1924 landlocked barge and lighthouse. Former fishtrap setter, cannery, recluse home, machine shop and houseboat. Unique B&B in barge decor; nautical artifacts with a touch of whimsy. Guests from around the world "cruise" on the renovated barge. Alaskan ambiance and hospitality the moment you go on board. (907) 424-7673; 1315 Whitshed Road. See display ad. [ADVERTISEMENT]

Cordova has one campground, Odiak Camper Park, located on Whitshed Road and operated by the city. The camper park has 24 RV sites and a tenting area. Free shower tokens are available for paying campers. Contact Cordova's city hall at (907) 424-6200. ▲

The historic Skater's Cabin on Eyak Lake is available for rent from the city. The rustic cabin has a woodstove and outhouse. The fee is $25 per night. Contact Bidarki Recreation Center, phone (907) 424-7282.

The U.S. Forest Service maintains 17 cabins in the Cordova district. Three are accessible by trail, the rest by boat or plane. Phone (907) 424-7661 for current fees, reservations and information.

Cordova nestles beneath Mount Eyak on Prince William Sound. (Jerrianne Lowther, staff)

TRANSPORTATION

Air: Scheduled service via Alaska Airlines and Era Aviation. Several air taxi services based at the municipal airport, Mile 13 airport, and Eyak Lake offer charter and flightseeing service.

Ferry: The Alaska Marine Highway system ferries connect Cordova with Valdez, Whittier and Seward. Phone (907) 424-7333.

Taxi: Local service available.

Car Rental: Available locally.

Highways: The Alaska state highway system does not connect to Cordova. The Copper River Highway leads 48 miles/77 km east and north of Cordova, ending at the Million Dollar Bridge and Childs Glacier. (See the COPPER RIVER HIGHWAY section.)

Private Boats: Cordova has an 850-slip boat harbor serving recreational boaters as well as the commercial fishing fleet. Berth arrangements may be made by contacting the harbormaster's office at (907) 424-6400 or on VHF Channel 16.

ATTRACTIONS

Cordova's Museum and Library, at 622 1st St., are connected by a central entryway. "Where Cultures Meet" is the theme of the museum. Native artifacts such as stone implements, a dugout canoe and skin bidarka (kayak) represent the rich Native culture. One display tells of early explorers to the area, including Vitus Bering, who claimed Alaska for Russia in 1741. Exhibits of the later mining and railroad era explain the development of the copper mines and of the town. Exhibits include a diorama of a vintage fishing vessel. The museum displays original work by Alaskan artists Sydney Laurence, Eustace Ziegler and Jules Dahlager, who all worked in Cordova. The Cordova Historical Society operates a small gift shop at the museum, featuring books of local interest and Alaskan crafts.

Copper River Delta supports 7 percent of the world's population of breeding trumpeter swans. (© Ruth Fairall)

Admission to the museum is $1. Open Memorial Day to Labor Day, 10 A.M.–6 P.M. Monday through Saturday, 2–4 P.M. on Sunday; Tuesday–Friday, 1–5 P.M. and Saturday 2–4 P.M. the rest of the year. Tours can be arranged. Write P.O. Box 391 or phone (907) 424-6665 for more information. Library hours are 1–8 P.M. Tuesday through Saturday.

Swim in the Bob Korn Memorial Swimming Pool, Cordova's Olympic-sized pool, located on Railroad Avenue below Main Street. Open year-round to the public. Check locally for hours.

Mount Eyak. Ski Hill on Mount Eyak offers summer chair lift rides for sightseeing, June through August. Fee charged: $7 adults, $5 students, under 12 years free. Phone (907) 424-7766 for days and hours of operation. To reach the chair lift from 4th Avenue, take Council Avenue 1 block, then follow Ski Hill Road to top (about 1 mile/1.6 km from Main Street).

The single chair lift rises 880 feet/268m up Mount Eyak and overlooks the town and harbor from 1,600 feet/488km. Walk up, take a cab, take the tour bus or drive your own vehicle.

Ski Hill is usually open for skiing mid-December to the end of April, depending on weather. The winter schedule is Wednesday (adults only), Saturday, Sunday and holidays, 9 A.M. to dusk.

Visit the USFS office on the 3rd floor of the USFS Building at 612 2nd St. Erected in 1925, it is the original federal building for the town of Cordova. Natural history display in 2nd floor Interpretive Center. The USFS office is next to the old courtroom and jail. Open weekdays 8 A.M. to 5 P.M.

Copper River Delta Shorebird Festival, held in May, offers 5 days of birding along the tidal mudflats and wetlands of the Copper River Delta and the rocky shoreline of Prince William Sound. The festival will include workshops, community activities and numerous field trip opportunities. Contact the Chamber of Commerce, Box 99, Cordova 99574, for details; phone (907) 424-7260.

Salmon Derbies. Silver Salmon Derby in August offers cash and merchandise prizes. Contact the Chamber of Commerce, Box 99, Cordova 99574, for details. Tackle, licenses and supplies may be purchased locally. You can fish from the beach (the Fleming Creek area near the ferry terminal is especially popular). The King Salmon Derby will be held in June at Fleming Spit/Orca Inlet.

Attend the Iceworm Festival: Held February 5–7, 1998, this festival offers a parade, art show, dances, craft show, ski events, survival suit race, beard judging and a King and Queen of Iceworm contest. Highlight is the 100-foot-/30-m-long "iceworm" that winds its way through the streets of Cordova. Contact Barbara Beedle at (907) 424-3527 for more information.

Whitshed Road leads out past the lighthouse (Mile 0.4) to a large mudflat at Hartney Bay (Mile 5.5). The lighthouse is privately owned and maintained by the Gleins, who also operate a bed and breakfast in their home: a converted barge. Hartney Bay is part of the 300,000-acre Copper River Delta mudflats. The delta is one of the most important stopover places in the Western Hemisphere for the largest shorebird migration in the world. Birders can view up to 31 different species as millions of shorebirds pass through the delta each spring.

Power Creek Road, from the corner of Lake and Chase avenues, leads out past the municipal airport to Crater Lake trailhead and Skaters Cabin picnic area (Mile 1.2), continues to Hatchery Creek salmon spawning channel (Mile 5.7), and ends at the Power Creek trailhead (Mile 6.9). The Crater Lake trailhead is directly northwest of the Eyak Lake Skaters Cabin. The 2.4-mile/ 3.8-km trail climbs to 1,500 feet/457m. Excellent views, alpine lake with fishing for cutthroat trout. Watch for bears. Visitors may view spawning salmon at the Hatchery Creek channel in July and August. Power Creek trail, 4.2 miles/6.7 km long, accesses both the USFS public-use cabin in Power Creek Basin and a ridge that connects with the Crater Lake trail creating a 12-mile/19.3-km loop. Power Creek trail offers spectacular scenery, with waterfalls, hanging glaciers and views of Power Creek Basin (called "surprise valley" by locals), the Chugach Range and Prince William Sound. Excellent berry picking. Watch for bears.

Drive the Copper River Highway to see the Million Dollar Bridge, Childs Glacier and the Copper River Delta. The 48-mile/77-km highway leads east from Cordova through the Delta to the historic Million Dollar Bridge, built in 1909–10, and Childs Glacier. Viewing platform and picnic area at Childs Glacier. Wildlife seen along the highway includes brown and black bear, moose, beaver, mountain goats, trumpeter swans and numerous other species of birds. See COPPER RIVER HIGHWAY section for log of road.

AREA FISHING: According to the ADF&G, "Saltwater fishing in **Orca Inlet** and adjacent eastern Prince William Sound is accessible from Cordova. Species include halibut, rockfish and 5 species of salmon. Trolling for salmon is best for kings in the winter and spring, and silvers in the summer and fall. Boat charters are available locally. Road-accessible fishing opportunities exist for salmon in salt water at **Fleming Spit/ Lagoon**, near the ferry terminal off Orca Bay Road. Strong runs of hatchery-enhanced kings (in the spring) and silvers (August and September) return to this terminal fishery. Road-accessible freshwater fishing is also good in the Cordova Area. **Eyak River** supports strong returns of sockeye during June and July and silvers in August and September. The area at the outlet of the lake, where the road crosses, is fly-fishing only. Several streams along the **Copper River** Highway between Eyak Lake and the Million Dollar Bridge also support runs of sockeye and coho. These streams include **Clear Creek, Alaganik Slough, Eighteen-mile Creek** and **Twenty-mile Creek.** In addition, cutthroat trout and Dolly Varden are present in most of these streams. Lake fishing for sockeye salmon, Dolly Varden and cutthroat trout is available in **McKinley Lake** and the **Pipeline Lake** system. Fly-out fishing from Cordova is also popular for salmon, Dolly Varden and cutthroat trout. Charter operators are available locally." See also the COPPER RIVER HIGHWAY section for area fishing.

RICHARDSON HIGHWAY (4)

Connects: Valdez to Fairbanks, AK **Length:** 368 miles
Road Surface: Paved **Season:** Open all year
Highest Summit: Isabel Pass 3,000 feet
Major Attractions: Trans-Alaska Pipeline, Worthington Glacier

(See map, page 664)

	Anchorage	Delta Jct.	Glennallen	Paxson	Valdez
Anchorage		340	189	260	308
Delta Jct.	340		151	80	270
Glennallen	189	151		71	119
Paxson	260	80	71		190
Valdez	308	270	119	190	

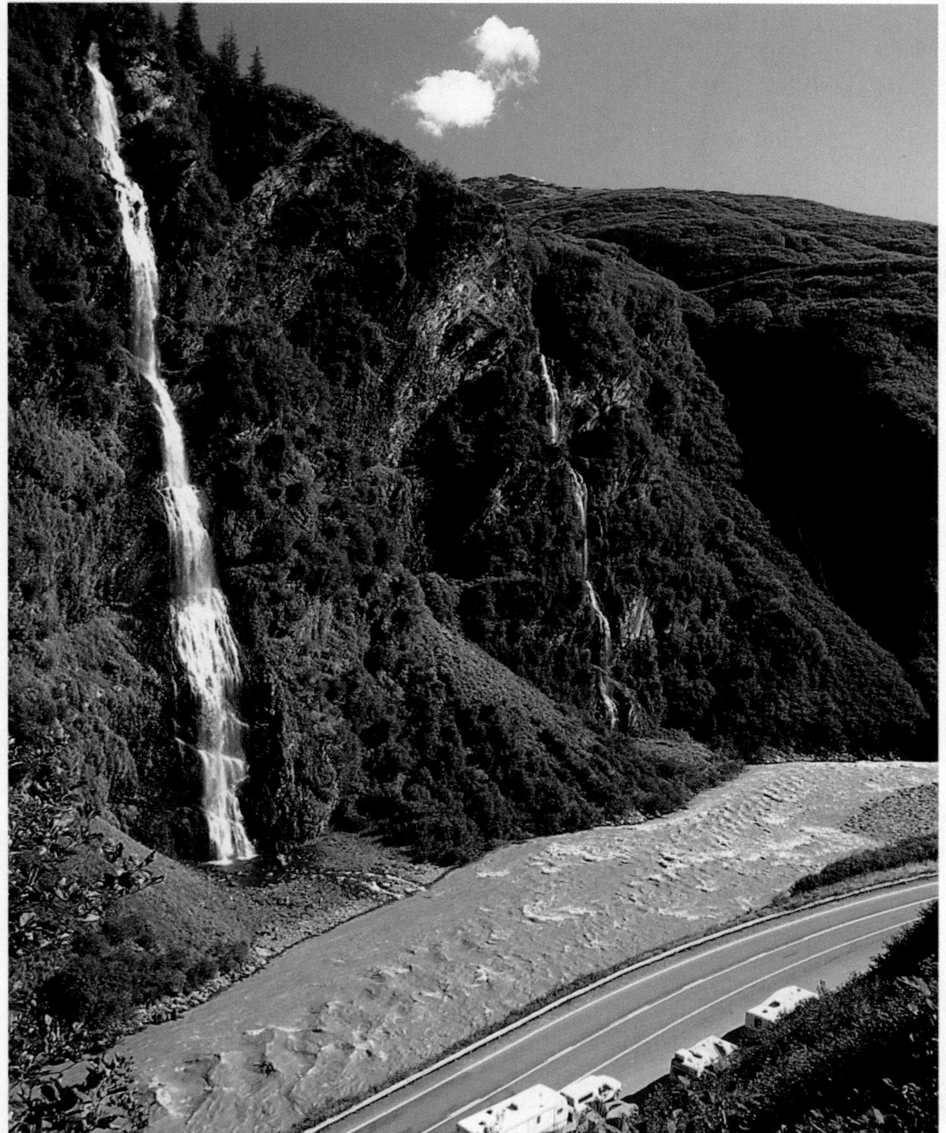

View of Bridal Veil Falls in Keystone Canyon. (© Michael DeYoung)

The Richardson Highway (Alaska Route 4) extends 368 miles/592 km from Valdez to Fairbanks. This section logs the first 270 miles/434.5 km of the Richardson Highway from Valdez to Delta Junction (the remaining 98 miles/157.7 km from Delta Junction to Fairbanks are logged in the ALASKA HIGHWAY section).

The Richardson is a wide paved highway in good condition except for sporadic frost heaving. A section of highway completed in 1989 bypasses the historic community of Copper Center. *The MILEPOST®* logs the old highway through town. The "new" Richardson Highway (bypass route) is of equal distance—6.5 miles/10.5 km—with no notable features. You must exit the highway (watch for signs) to see Copper Center.

The Richardson Highway is a scenic route through the magnificent scenery of the Chugach Mountains and Alaska Range. It passes many fine king salmon streams, including the Gulkana and Tonsina rivers.

*NOTE: Expect road construction on the Richardson Highway between Keystone Canyon (**Milepost V 13.8**) and Thompson Pass (**Milepost V 26**) in 1998.*

The Richardson Highway was Alaska's first road, known to gold seekers in 1898 as the Valdez to Eagle trail. The gold rush trail led over the treacherous Valdez Glacier, then northeast to Eagle and the Yukon River route to the Klondike goldfields. Captain W.R. Abercrombie of the U.S. Army rerouted the trail in 1899 through Keystone Canyon and over Thompson Pass, thus avoiding the glacier. As the Klondike Gold Rush waned, the military kept the trail open to connect Fort Liscum in Valdez with Fort Egbert in Eagle. In 1903, the U.S. Army Signal Corps laid the trans-Alaska telegraph line along this route.

Gold stampeders started up the trail again in 1902, this time headed for Fairbanks, site of a big gold strike. The Valdez to Fairbanks trail became an important route to the Interior, and in 1910 the trail was upgraded to a wagon road under the direction of Gen. Wilds P. Richardson, first president of the Alaska Road Commission. The ARC updated the road to automobile standards in the 1920s. The Richardson Highway was hard-surfaced in 1957.

Emergency medical services: Phone 911 anywhere along the highway.

Richardson Highway Log

Mileposts on the Richardson Highway were erected before the 1964 Good Friday earthquake and therefore begin 4 miles/6.4 km from present-day downtown Valdez near the Old Valdez townsite (destroyed during the earthquake).

Distance from New Valdez (NV) is followed by distance from Old Valdez (OV).

NV 0 OV 4 (6.4 km) Intersection of Meals Avenue and the Richardson Highway.

NV 0.4 (0.6 km) **OV 3.6** (5.8 km) Paved double-ended turnout to north with Valdez information kiosk, maps, brochures, pay phones.

NV 0.5 (0.8 km) **OV 3.5** (5.6 km) DOT/PF district office.

RICHARDSON HIGHWAY *Valdez, AK, to Delta Junction, AK*

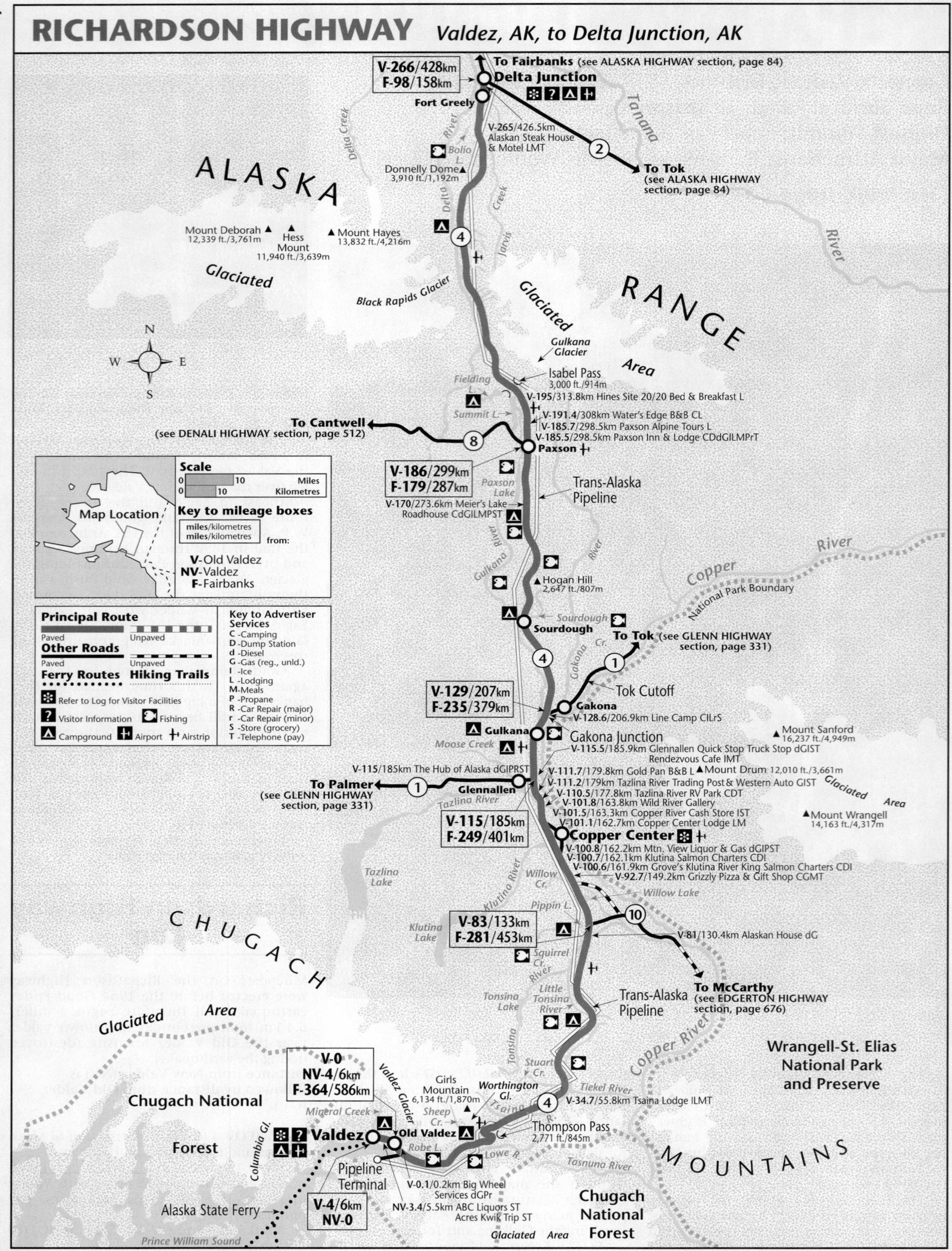
To Fairbanks (see ALASKA HIGHWAY section, page 84)
V-266/428km
F-98/158km
Delta Junction
Fort Greely
V-265/426.5km Alaskan Steak House & Motel LMT
To Tok (see ALASKA HIGHWAY section, page 84)
ALASKA
RANGE
Donnelly Dome 3,910 ft./1,192m
Mount Deborah 12,339 ft./3,761m
Hess Mount 11,940 ft./3,639m
Mount Hayes 13,832 ft./4,216m
Glaciated
Glaciated Area
Black Rapids Glacier
Gulkana Glacier
Isabel Pass 3,000 ft./914m
V-195/313.8km Hines Site 20/20 Bed & Breakfast L
V-191.4/308km Water's Edge B&B CL
V-185.7/298.5km Paxson Alpine Tours L
V-185.5/298.5km Paxson Inn & Lodge CDdGILMPrT
To Cantwell (see DENALI HIGHWAY section, page 512)
Paxson
V-186/299km
F-179/287km
Trans-Alaska Pipeline
V-170/273.6km Meier's Lake Roadhouse CdGILMPST
Hogan Hill 2,647 ft./807m
Sourdough
To Tok (see GLENN HIGHWAY section, page 331)
Copper River
National Park Boundary
Tok Cutoff
V-129/207km
F-235/379km
Gakona
V-128.6/206.9km Line Camp CILrS
Gulkana
Gakona Junction
Mount Sanford 16,237 ft./4,949m
V-115.5/185.9km Glennallen Quick Stop Truck Stop dGIST Rendezvous Cafe IMT
V-115/185km The Hub of Alaska dGIPRST
V-111.7/179.8km Gold Pan B&B L
Mount Drum 12,010 ft./3,661m
V-111.2/179km Tazlina River Trading Post & Western Auto GIST
To Palmer (see GLENN HIGHWAY section, page 331)
Glennallen
V-110.5/177.8km Tazlina River RV Park CDT
V-101.8/163.8km Wild River Gallery
V-101.5/163.3km Copper River Cash Store IST
V-101.1/162.7km Copper Center Lodge LM
Mount Wrangell 14,163 ft./4,317m
V-115/185km
F-249/401km
Copper Center
V-100.8/162.2km Mtn. View Liquor & Gas dGIPST
V-100.7/162.1km Klutina Salmon Charters CDI
V-100.6/161.9km Grove's Klutina River King Salmon Charters CDI
V-92.7/149.2km Grizzly Pizza & Gift Shop CGMT
Tazlina Lake
Klutina Lake
CHUGACH
V-83/133km
F-281/453km
V-81/130.4km Alaskan House dG
To McCarthy (see EDGERTON HIGHWAY section, page 676)
Trans-Alaska Pipeline
Tonsina Lake
Wrangell-St. Elias National Park and Preserve
V-0
NV-4/6km
F-364/586km
Chugach National Forest
Girls Mountain 6,134 ft./1,870m
Worthington Gl.
V-34.7/55.8km Tsaina Lodge ILMT
Thompson Pass 2,771 ft./845m
Valdez
Old Valdez
MOUNTAINS
Pipeline Terminal
V-0.1/0.2km Big Wheel Services dGPr
NV-3.4/5.5km ABC Liquors ST Acres Kwik Trip ST
Alaska State Ferry
V-4/6km
NV-0
Chugach National Forest
Prince William Sound
Map Location
Scale
Miles
Kilometres
Key to mileage boxes
miles/kilometres
miles/kilometres
from:
V-Old Valdez
NV-Valdez
F-Fairbanks
Principal Route
Paved
Unpaved
Other Roads
Paved
Unpaved
Ferry Routes
Hiking Trails
Refer to Log for Visitor Facilities
Visitor Information
Fishing
Campground
Airport
Airstrip
Key to Advertiser Services
C -Camping
D -Dump Station
d -Diesel
G -Gas (reg., unld.)
I -Ice
L -Lodging
M -Meals
P -Propane
R -Car Repair (major)
r -Car Repair (minor)
S -Store (grocery)
T -Telephone (pay)

NV 0.6 (1 km) **OV 3.4** (5.5 km) Valdez highway maintenance station.

NV 0.9 (1.4 km) **OV 3.1** (5 km) Double-ended turnout to north at Crooked Creek salmon spawning area and hatchery. Viewing platform offers close-up look at salmon spawning in midsummer and fall. U.S. Forest Service information station is staffed Memorial Day through Labor Day; interpretive displays, history and recreation. Migrating birds such as Canada geese and various ducks are often here. It is a game sanctuary; no shooting is allowed. Good spot for pictures.

NV 1.3 (2.1 km) **OV 2.7** (4.3 km) Paved turnout to south.

NV 2 (3.2 km) **OV 2** (3.2 km) Paved turnout to south.

NV 2.1 (3.4 km) **OV 1.9** (3.1 km) Mineral Creek Loop Road through business and residential area on outskirts of Old Valdez comes out at **Milepost NV 3.4**. Access to Port of Valdez container terminal and grain elevators.

NV 3.4 (5.5 km) **OV 0.6** (1 km) Airport Road; deli, market, liquor store, laundromat. Turn off to north for Valdez Airport (0.6 mile/1 km), Valdez Glacier campground (2 miles/3.2 km) and Valdez Glacier (3.9 miles/6.3 km). Parking area next to glacial moraine; good views of the glacier area are *not* available from this spot, nor is Valdez Glacier a very spectacular glacier. Valdez Glacier campground has 101 sites, tent camping, covered picnic area, litter barrels, water, toilets and fireplaces; 15-day limit, camping fee. *CAUTION: Beware of bears.* ▲

ABC Liquors. See display ad this section.

Acres Kwik Trip. See display ad this section.

Mineral Creek Loop Road leads south to the original townsite of Valdez, destroyed during the Good Friday earthquake on March 27, 1964. A few homes and businesses are here now; there is little evidence of the earthquake's destruction.

NV 4 (6.4 km) **OV 0** Former access road to Old Valdez, remains of the old dock and memorial for 1964 earthquake. Milepost 0 of the Richardson Highway is located here.

(Southbound travelers note: Physical mileposts end here; it is 4 miles/6.4 km to downtown Valdez.)

Distance from Old Valdez (V) is followed by distance from Fairbanks (F). Physical mileposts begin northbound showing distance from Old Valdez.

V 0 F 364 (585.8 km) **Milepost 0** of the Richardson Highway is located here at the former access road to Old Valdez.

V 0.1 (0.2 km) **F 363.9** (585.6 km) **Big Wheel Services.** See display ad this section.

V 0.9 (1.4 km) **F 363.1** (584.4 km) The highway passes over the terminal moraine of the Valdez Glacier, bridging several channels and streams flowing from the melting ice.

V 1.4 (2.3 km) **F 362.6** (583.5 km) Valdez Trapshooting Range.

V 1.5 (2.4 km) **F 362.5** (583.4 km) City of Valdez Goldfields Recreation Area; trails, ponds, swimming, picnic sites, baseball field.

V 2.2 (3.5 km) **F 361.8** (582.2 km) Dylen Drive.

V 2.4 (3.9 km) **F 361.6** (581.9 km) Paved turnout to west.

V 2.7 (4.3 km) **F 361.3** (581.5 km) River Road. Large paved double-ended turnout to west beside Robe River. During August and early September watch for pink and silver salmon spawning in roadside creeks and sloughs. *DO NOT* attempt to catch or otherwise disturb spawning salmon. *CAUTION: Beware of bears.*

V 2.9 (4.7 km) **F 361.1** (581.1 km) Turnoff for Old Dayville Road to Trans-Alaska Pipeline Valdez Marine Terminal and access to Allison Point fishery. This 5.4-mile/8.7-km paved road (open to the public) crosses the Lowe River 4 times. At Mile 2.4/3.9 km the road parallels the bay, and there is excellent fishing in season at Allison Point, especially for pink and silver salmon; also watch for sea otters and bald eagles along here. At Mile 4.1/6.6 km is the Solomon Gulch water project and a spectacular view of Solomon Gulch Falls; a fish hatchery is located across from the water project. Entrance to the pipeline terminal is at the end of the road. Supertankers load oil pumped from the North Slope to this facility via the trans-Alaska pipeline. Bus tours of the terminal are available; see the VALDEZ section for details.

V 3 (4.8 km) **F 361** (581 km) Weigh station.

V 3.4 (5.5 km) **F 360.6** (580.3 km) A 0.5-mile/0.8-km gravel road to Robe Lake and floatplane base. Watch for cow parsnip and river beauty (dwarf fireweed). Also watch for bears!

V 4.7 (7.5 km) **F 359.3** (578.2 km) Turnout to east. Access to **Robe River**; Dolly Varden, red salmon (fly-fishing only, mid-May to mid-June).

V 5.3 (8.5 km) **F 358.7** (577.3 km) Salmonberry Ridge ski area road to west.

V 7.3 (11.7 km) **F 356.7** (574 km) Lowe River parallels the highway next mile northbound.

V 9.6 (15.4 km) **F 354.4** (570.3 km) Fire station.

V 11.6 (18.7 km) **F 352.4** (567.1 km) Large paved turnout to east.

V 12.8 (20.6 km) **F 351.2** (565.2 km) Here the Lowe River emerges from Keystone Canyon. The canyon was named by Captain William Ralph Abercrombie, presumably for Pennsylvania, the Keystone State. In 1884, Abercrombie had been selected to lead an exploring expedition up the Copper River to the Yukon River. Although unsuccessful in his attempt to ascend the Copper River, he did survey the Copper River Delta and a route to Port Valdez. He returned in 1898 and again in 1899, carrying out further explorations of the area. The Lowe River is named for Lt. Percival Lowe, a member of his expedition. Glacier melt imparts the slate-gray color to the river.

V 13.5 (21.7 km) **F 350.5** (564.1 km) Horsetail Falls; large paved turnout to west.

CAUTION: Watch for pedestrians.

V 13.7 (22 km) **F 350.3** (563.7 km) Goat trail is visible on the west side of the highway; see description of this landmark at **Milepost V 15.2.**

V 13.8 (22.2 km) **F 350.2** (563.6 km) Bridal Veil Falls; large paved turnout to west.

*NOTE: Expect road construction northbound from here to Thompson Pass (**Milepost V 26**) in 1998.*

V 14.9 (24 km) **F 349.1** (561.8 km) Lowe River bridge (first of 3 bridges northbound); view of Riddleston Falls. About 175 yards east of this bridge and adjacent to the highway is an abandoned hand-drilled tunnel. Large paved turnout with historical marker. Sign reads: "This tunnel was hand cut into the solid rock of Keystone Canyon and is all that is left of the railroad era when 9 companies fought to take advantage of the short route from the coast to the copper country. However, a feud interrupted progress. A gun battle was fought and the tunnel was never finished."

V 15.2 (24.5 km) **F 348.8** (561.3 km) Small gravel turnout. On the far side just above the water are the remains of the old sled trail used in the early days. This trail was cut out of the rock just wide enough for 2 horses abreast. 200 feet above, "the old goat trail"can be seen. This road was used until 1945.

V 15.3 (24.6 km) **F 348.7** (561.2 km)

Lowe River bridge No. 2, built in 1980, replaced previous highway route through the long tunnel visible beside highway. Turnout at south end of bridge. Traces of the old trail used by horse-drawn sleds can be seen about 200 feet/61m above the river.

V 15.9 (25.6 km) **F 348.1** (560.2 km) Leaving Keystone Canyon northbound, entering Keystone Canyon southbound. Raft trips of Keystone Canyon are available; check with visitor center in Valdez.

V 16.2 (26.1 km) **F 347.8** (559.7 km) Avalanche gun emplacement.

V 16.3 (26.2 km) **F 347.7** (559.6 km) Lowe River bridge No. 3.

V 18 (29 km) **F 346** (556.8 km) Large paved turnouts both sides of road.

V 18.6 (29.9 km) **F 345.4** (555.8 km) Sheep Creek bridge.

Truck lane begins northbound as highway ascends 7.5 miles/12 km to Thompson Pass. This was one of the most difficult sections of pipeline construction, requiring heavy blasting of solid rock for several miles. The pipeline runs under the cleared strip beside the road. Low-flying helicopters often seen along the Richardson Highway are usually monitoring the pipeline.

V 21.6 (34.8 km) **F 342.4** (551 km) Paved turnout to east.

V 22.2 (35.7 km) **F 341.8** (550.1 km) Snow poles along highway guide snow plows in winter.

V 23 (37 km) **F 341** (548.8 km) Large gravel turnout to east.

V 23.4 (37.7 km) **F 340.6** (548.1 km) Large paved turnout to east with view.

V 23.6 (38 km) **F 340.4** (547.8 km) Loop road past Thompson Lake to Blueberry Lake and state recreation site; see **Milepost V 24.1.**

V 23.8 (38.3 km) **F 340.2** (547.5 km) Small paved turnout to east.

V 24.1 (38.8 km) **F 339.9** (547 km) Loop road to Blueberry Lake State Recreation Site; drive in 1 mile/1.6 km. Tucked into an alpine setting between tall mountain peaks, this is one of Alaska's most beautifully situated campgrounds; 10 campsites, 4 covered picnic tables, toilets, firepits and water. Camping fee $10/night or annual pass. ▲

Blueberry Lake and **Thompson Lake** (formerly Summit No. 1 Lake). Good grayling and rainbow fishing all summer.

V 24.4 (39.3 km) **F 339.6** (546.5 km) Large paved turnout to west. Bare bone peaks of the Chugach Mountains rise above the highway. Thompson Pass ahead; Marshall Pass is to the east.

During the winter of 1907, the A.J. Meals Co. freighted the 70-ton river steamer *Chitina* (or *Chittyna*) from Valdez over Marshall Pass and down the Tasnuna River to the Copper River. The ship was moved piece by piece on huge horse-drawn freight sleds and assembled at the mouth of the Tasnuna. The 110-foot-/34-m-long ship navigated 170 miles/274 km of the Copper and Chitina rivers above Abercrombie Rapids, moving supplies for construction crews of the Copper River & Northwestern Railway. Much of the equipment for the Kennicott mill and tram was moved by this vessel.

V 25.5 (41 km) **F 338.5** (544.7 km) Large paved turnout to west. Entering Game Management Unit 13D, leaving unit 6D, northbound.

V 25.7 (41.4 km) **F 338.3** (544.4 km) Large paved turnout to west with view; Keystone Glacier to the south.

V 26 (41.8 km) **F 338** (543.9 km) Thompson Pass (elev. 2,678 feet/816m) at head of Ptarmigan Creek. Truck lane ends northbound; begin 7.5-mile/12-km descent southbound.

Thompson Pass, named by Captain Abercrombie in 1899, is comparatively low elevation but above timberline. Wildflower lovers will be well repaid for rambling over the rocks in this area: tiny alpine plants may be in bloom, such as Aleutian heather and mountain harebell.

The National Climatic Center credits snowfall extremes in Alaska to the Thompson Pass station, where record measurements are: 974.5 inches for season (1952–53); 298 inches for month (February 1953); and 62 inches for 24-hour period (December 1955). Snow poles along the highway mark the road edge for snow plows.

Private Aircraft: Thompson Pass airstrip; elev. 2,080 feet/634m; length 2,500 feet/762m; turf, gravel; unattended.

V 27 (43.5 km) **F 337** (542.3 km) Thompson Pass highway maintenance station.

V 27.5 (44.3 km) **F 336.5** (541.5 km) Steep turnout to east by **Worthington Lake**; rainbow fishing.

V 27.7 (44.6 km) **F 336.3** (541.2 km) Good viewpoint of 27 Mile Glacier.

V 28 (45.1 km) **F 336** (540.7 km) Paved turnout to east. Entering winter avalanche area southbound.

V 28.6 (46 km) **F 335.4** (539.8 km) Paved turnout to west.

V 28.7 (46.2 km) **F 335.3** (539.6 km) Worthington Glacier State Recreation Site; large viewing shelter, interpretive displays, toilets, picnic sites, parking and pay phone. According to state park rangers, this is the most visited site in the Copper River Basin. The glacier, which heads on Girls Mountain (elev. 6,134 feet/1,870m), is accessible via a short road to the left. It is possible to drive almost to the face of the glacier. Care should be exercised when walking on ice because of numerous crevasses.

NOTE: Watch for road upgrading under way in 1998.

V 30.2 (48.6 km) **F 333.8** (537.2 km) Large paved turnout both sides of highway. Excellent spot for photos of Worthington Glacier.

V 31.1 (50 km) **F 332.9** (535.7 km) Small turnout to east. Avalanche gun emplacement.

V 32 (51.5 km) **F 332** (534.3 km) Highway parallels Tsaina River. Long climb up to Thompson Pass for southbound motorists.

V 33.6 (54.1 km) **F 330.4** (531.7 km) Tsaina River access to west.

V 34.7 (55.8 km) **F 329.3** (529.9 km) **Tsaina Lodge.** Treat yourself to a fine dining experience in the comforting, rustic charm of the hand-hewn log interior. View the spectacular Worthington Glacier surrounded by snow-capped peaks while relaxing in a museum of treasured relics from times long past. Modern gourmet food prepared the old-fashioned way, using fresh local ingredients. Specialties include Alaska seafood, homemade pastas, soups, "supercalifragilisticexpialidocious" desserts and fresh baked goods daily. Full-service bar and wine list. The spring helicopter ski operation attracts the world's finest skiers. Summer activities are many, ranging from berry picking and fishing to rafting and paragliding. Real Alaskan hospitality. New hand-crafted log cabins, yurts and a bunkhouse. (907) 835-3500. See display ad this section. [ADVERTISEMENT]

V 36.5 (58.7 km) **F 327.5** (527 km) Pipeline runs under highway.

V 37 (59.5 km) **F 327** (526.2 km) Entering BLM public lands northbound.

V 37.3 (60 km) **F 326.7** (525.8 km) Tsaina River bridge at Devil's Elbow; paved turnout at south end of bridge.

V 38 (61.2 km) **F 326** (524.6 km) Crest of hill. Beautiful views southbound.

V 40.5 (65.2 km) **F 323.5** (520.6 km) Pipeline passes under highway. Avalanche gun emplacement.

V 40.8 (65.7 km) **F 323.2** (520.1 km) Gravel turnout to west.

V 42 (67.6 km) **F 322** (518.2 km) Gravel turnout to west side. Spruce bark beetles

Camping at Blueberry Lake SRS at Milepost V 24.1. (Jerrianne Lowther, staff)

have killed many of the trees in the forest here. Buried pipeline. View of waterbars (ridges on slope designed to slow runoff and control erosion).

V 43.3 (69.7 km) **F 320.7** (516.1 km) Long double-ended turnout.

V 43.5 (70 km) **F 320.5** (515.8 km) Wide shoulder east side of highway.

V 45.6 (73.4 km) **F 318.4** (512.4 km) Large paved turnout to east at north end of Stuart Creek bridge.

V 45.8 (73.7 km) **F 318.2** (512.1 km) Copper River Valley welcome sign. Watch for moose next 20 miles/32 km northbound.

V 46.9 (75.5 km) **F 317.1** (510.3 km) **Tiekel River** bridge; small Dolly Varden. Small turnout at north end of bridge.

V 47.9 (77.1 km) **F 316.1** (508.7 km) Large paved rest area by Tiekel River; covered picnic sites, toilets, no drinking water. Viewpoint and historical sign for Mount Billy Mitchell.

Lieutenant William "Billy" Mitchell was a member of the U.S. Army Signal Corps, which in 1903 was completing the trans-Alaska telegraph line (Washington–Alaska Military Cable and Telegraph System) to connect all the military posts in Alaska. The 2,000 miles/3,200 km of telegraph wire included the main line between Fort Egbert in Eagle and Fort Liscum at Valdez, and a branch line down the Tanana River to Fort Gibson and on to Fort St. Michael near the mouth of the Yukon and then to Nome. Mitchell was years later to become the "prophet of American military air power."

V 50.7 (81.6 km) **F 313.3** (504.1 km) Bridge over Tiekel River. Dead spruce trees in this area were killed by beetles.

V 53.8 (86.6 km) **F 310.2** (499.2 km) Squaw Creek culvert.

V 54.1 (87.1 km) **F 309.9** (498.7 km) Large paved turnout to east by Tiekel River. Look for lupine in June, dwarf fireweed along river bars in July.

V 54.3 (87.4 km) **F 309.7** (498.4 km) Old beaver lodge. Beaver may inhabit the same site for generations.

V 54.5 (87.7 km) **F 309.5** (498.1 km) Moose often seen here in the evenings.

V 55.1 (88.7 km) **F 308.9** (497.1 km) Large paved turnout to east by Tiekel River.

V 56 (90.1 km) **F 308** (495.7 km) Tiekel River Lodge.

V 56.3 (90.6 km) **F 307.7** (495.2 km) Large paved turnout to east by Tiekel River.

V 57 (91.7 km) **F 307** (494.1 km) Old beaver lodge and dams in pond to east. Tireless and skillful dam builders, beavers construct their houses in the pond created by the dam. Older beaver dams can reach 15 feet in height and may be hundreds of feet long. The largest rodent in North America, beavers range south from the Brooks Range. They eat a variety of vegetation, including aspen, willow, birch and poplar.

V 58.1 (93.5 km) **F 305.9** (492.3 km) Wagon Point Creek culvert.

V 60 (96.6 km) **F 304** (489.2 km) Large paved turnout to east. Highway parallels **Tiekel River**; fishing for small Dolly Varden.

V 62 (99.7 km) **F 302** (486 km) Ernestine Station highway maintenance camp.

V 62.4 (100.4 km) **F 301.6** (485.4 km) Boundary for Sport Fish Management areas. Entering Upper Susitna/Copper River Area N northbound, Prince William Sound southbound.

V 64.7 (104.1 km) **F 299.3** (481.7 km) Pump Station No. 12 to east. Interpretive viewpoint and parking to west. Short walk to viewpoint from parking area.

V 65 (104.6 km) **F 299** (481.2 km) Little Tonsina River.

V 65.1 (104.8 km) **F 298.9** (481 km) **Little Tonsina River** State Recreation Site with 10 campsites, firepits, water, litter barrels and toilets. Camping fee $6/night or annual pass. Dolly Varden fishing. Road to right as you enter wayside dead ends, road to left goes to the river (no turnaround space); follow loop road for easy access. Good berry picking in fall. *CAUTION: Beware of bears!* ▲

Watch for moose next 20 miles/32 km southbound.

V 66.2 (106.5 km) **F 297.8** (479.2 km) Double-ended gravel turnout to west.

V 68.1 (109.6 km) **F 295.9** (476.2 km) Site of former Tonsina Camp (Alyeska Pipeline Service Co.) used during pipeline construction. These camps have been completely removed.

V 70.5 (113.5 km) **F 293.5** (472.3 km) Trans-Alaska pipeline follows base of mountains across valley.

V 71.2 (114.6 km) **F 292.8** (471.2 km) Long double-ended paved turnout to east.

V 72 (115.9 km) **F 292** (469.9 km) Double-ended paved turnout to west. Leaving BLM public lands northbound. View of trans-Alaska pipeline across the valley.

V 74.4 (119.7 km) **F 289.6** (466.1 km) Paved double-ended turnout to west. Vehicle access to Little Tonsina River.

V 78.9 (127 km) **F 285.1** (458.8 km) Bernard Creek trail. According to the BLM, this 15-mile loop road—which was originally part of the WAMCATS line—provides mountain bikers with an uphill ride on hard-packed dirt to near Kimball Pass.

V 79 (127.1 km) **F 285** (458.7 km) Tonsina Lodge. **Private Aircraft:** (Upper) Tonsina airstrip, adjacent south of lodge; elev. 1,500 feet/457m; length 1,400 feet/426m; turf; fuel 80; unattended.

V 79.2 (127.5 km) **F 284.8** (458.3 km) Bridge over Tonsina River, which rises in Tonsina Lake to the southwest.

V 79.6 (128.1 km) **F 284.4** (457.7 km) Bridge and Squirrel Creek state campground. Pleasant campsites on the bank of Squirrel Creek, some pull-through spaces; $10/night or annual pass; dumpster, boat launch, water, toilets and firepits. Rough access road through campground; low-clearance vehicles use caution. Large vehicles note: Limited turnaround on back loop road. ▲

Mouth of **Squirrel Creek** at Tonsina River. Some grayling and salmon; grayling, small, use flies or eggs, all season; salmon, average size, egg clusters and spoons, all season. Also try the gravel pit beside the campground; according to state park rangers, some fishermen have good luck catching rainbow and grayling here using flies, eggs and spinners.

V 79.7 (128.3 km) **F 284.3** (457.5 km) Begin 1.3-mile/2.1-km truck lane northbound up Tonsina Hill. Hill can be slippery in winter. Watch for severe frost heaves.

V 81 (130.4 km) **F 283** (455.4 km) **Alaskan House.** See display ad this section.

View of Wrangell Mountains—Mount Sanford and Mount Drum—from Milepost V 112.6. (Jerrianne Lowther, staff)

V 82.6 (132.9 km) **F 281.4** (452.9 km) **Junction** with the Edgerton Highway east to Chitina and McCarthy Road to McCarthy in Wrangell–St. Elias National Park and Preserve (see EDGERTON HIGHWAY section on page 676).

V 83 (133.6 km) **F 281** (452.2 km) Small paved turnout to west beside Pippin Lake.

V 87.7 (141.1 km) **F 276.3** (444.6 km) Paved double-ended turnout to east at Willow Lake. On a clear day this lake mirrors the Wrangell Mountains which lie within Wrangell–St. Elias National Park and Preserve. The park visitor center is at **Milepost V 105.1**, and there is a good mountain viewpoint at **V 112.6.**

V 88.5 (142.4 km) **F 275.5** (443.4 km) Pipeline parallels road. Interpretive viewpoint to west on pipeline (1 of 3 Alyeska pipeline displays along this highway). National Park Service plaque with schematic diagram of Wrangell Mountains. Loop turnout; pedestrian access.

V 90.8 (146.1 km) **F 273.2** (439.7 km) Large paved turnout to west by Willow Creek culvert; thick patches of diamond willow in woods off highway (and thick clouds of mosquitoes!).

V 91.1 (146.6 km) **F 272.9** (439.2 km) Turnoff to east is an 8-mile/12.9-km gravel cutoff that intersects Edgerton Highway at **Milepost J 7.3.** This is a drive through the rolling hills of homestead country and heavy thickets of birch and spruce.

V 92.7 (149.2 km) **F 271.3** (436.6 km) **Grizzly Pizza & Gift Shop.** See display ad this section.

V 98.1 (157.9 km) **F 265.9** (427.9 km) Microwave tower.

V 100.2 (161.2 km) **F 263.8** (424.5 km) IMPORTANT: South **junction** with Copper Center Bypass (New Richardson Highway). Northbound travelers TURN OFF onto Old Richardson Highway for scenic route through historic Copper Center (log and description follow). *The MILEPOST*® does not log the bypass route (New Richardson Highway), which is the same distance as the old highway (6.5 miles/10.5 km) with no notable features. According to the BLM, however, there is an old 4-wheel-drive road to Klutina Lake (25 miles/40 km) which is appropriate for mountain bikes. Turn west at Brenwick–Craig Road sign on the bypass and cross under pipeline. The old highway rejoins the bypass route at **Milepost V 106.**

V 100.7 (162.1 km) **F 263.3** (423.7 km) Klutina River bridges. Excellent fishing in the **Klutina River** for red (sockeye) and king (chinook) salmon. Also grayling and Dolly Varden. Kings to 50 lbs., average 30 lbs.; from June 15 to Aug. 10, peaking in mid-July. Red's peak run is from late June to early August; fish from either bank downstream from the new bridge to the mouth of the Copper River. *NOTE: Most riverfront property is privately owned. Inquire at the tackle shop about river access.* Two campgrounds and fishing charter services are located here. ▲

Klutina Salmon Charters. See display ad this section. ▲

V 100.8 (162.2 km) **F 263.2** (423.6 km) Copper Center (description follows); loop road opposite gas station provides access to lodge and museum.

Mtn. View Liquor & Gas. See display ad this section.

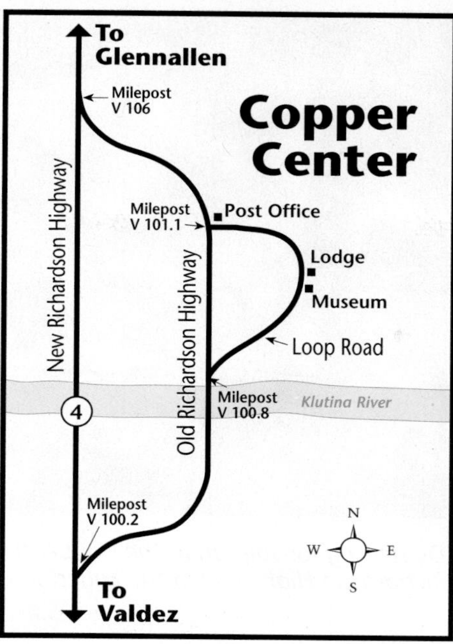

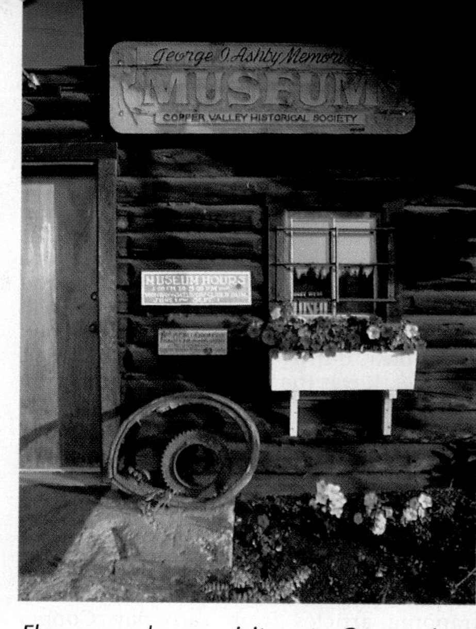

Flowers welcome visitors to George I. Ashby Memorial Museum in Copper Center. (© Harry M. Walker Photo)

Copper Center

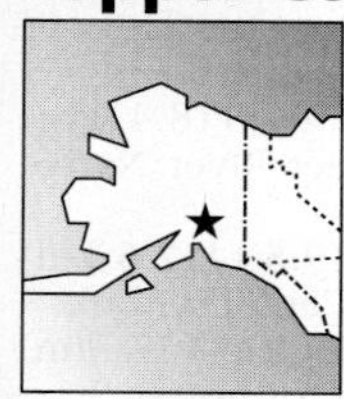

V 100.8 (162.2 km) **F 263.2** (423.6 km) Located on the Klutina River, 1 mile/1.6 km west of its junction with the Copper River; 104.8 miles/168.6 km north of Valdez via Alaska Route 4. An inner loop road leads through Copper Center and rejoins the Richardson Highway at **Milepost V 101.1. Population:** 449. **Emergency Services:** Phone 911. **Ambulance** in Glennallen, phone 911. **Elevation:** 1,000 feet/305m.

Private Aircraft: Copper Center NR 2 airstrip, 1 mile/1.6 km south; elev. 1,150 feet/351m; length 2,500 feet/762m; gravel; unattended.

Facilities include lodging, private campgrounds, meals, groceries, liquor store, gas station, general store, post office, laundromat and gift shops. Fishing charters, tackle, riverboat services and guides available.

With the influx of gold seekers following

COPPER CENTER ADVERTISERS

Copper Center Lodge ....Mile 101.1 Old Richardson Hwy.
Copper River Cash Store.......Mile 101.5 Old Richardson Hwy.
Grove's Klutina River King Salmon Charters..........Ph. (907) 822-5822
Klutina River Bed & Breakfast ....Ph. (907) 822-5858
Klutina Salmon Charters.......................Ph. (907) 822-3991
Mtn. View Liquor & Gas ....Mile 100.8 Old Richardson Hwy.
Wild River Gallery......Mile 101.8 Old Richardson Hwy.

the trail from Valdez to the Klondike, a trading post was established in Copper Center in 1898. A telegraph station and post office were established in 1901, and Copper Center became the principal settlement and supply center in the Nelchina–Susitna region.

Copper Center Lodge on the inner loop road, selected by the Alaska Centennial Commission as a site of historic importance (a plaque is mounted to the right of the lodge's entrance), had its beginning as the Holman Hotel and was known as the Blix Roadhouse during the gold rush days of 1897–98. It was the first lodging place in the Copper River valley and was replaced by the Copper Center Lodge in 1932.

The George I. Ashby Memorial Museum, operated by the Copper Valley Historical Society, is housed in the bunkhouse annex at the Copper Center Lodge. It contains early Russian religious articles, Athabascan baskets, telegraph and mineral displays, copper and gold mining memorabilia, and trapping articles from early-day Copper Valley. Hours vary. Donations appreciated.

Historic buildings in Copper Center are located on private property. Please do not trespass.

The Copper River reportedly carries the highest sediment load of all Alaskan rivers. The river cuts through the Chugach Mountains and connects the interior of southcentral Alaska with the sea; it is the only corridor of its kind between Cook Inlet and the Canadian border.

Dipnetting for salmon in the Copper River at Chitina, 33 miles east of the Richardson Highway via the Edgerton Highway. (© Nancy Faville)

Richardson Highway Log

(continued)

V 101 (162.5 km) **F 263** (423.3 km) A visitor attraction in Copper Center is the log Chapel on the Hill built in 1942 by Rev. Vince Joy with the assistance of U.S. Army volunteers stationed in the area. The chapel is open daily and there is no admission charge. A short slide show on the Copper River area is usually shown to visitors in the chapel during the summer. A highway-level parking lot is connected by stairs to the Chapel on the Hill.

V 101.1 (162.7 km) **F 262.9** (423 km) Inner loop road to historic Copper Center Lodge George I. Ashley Memorial Museum and other businesses.

Copper Center Lodge. Beautifully rustic historic landmark, serving the public since 1898; 21 rooms, private or shared baths. Century-old sourdough starter hotcakes, homemade pies. Restaurant serving breakfast, lunch, dinner. Wine and beer served. Located near the base of the Wrangell–St. Elias National Park and next to the Copper and Klutina rivers. See display ad. [ADVERTISEMENT]

V 101.4 (163.2 km) **F 262.6** (422.6 km) Post office to east; outside mailbox.

V 101.5 (163.3 km) **F 262.5** (422.4 km) **Copper River Cash Store**, established in 1896, sits on part of the first farm started in Alaska. The center of the building is the original structure. Behind the store is the old jail, bars still on windows. Open 6 days a week, all year. Complete line of groceries, general merchandise, RV supplies, video rentals. [ADVERTISEMENT]

V 101.8 (163.8 km) **F 262.2** (422 km) **Wild River Gallery.** All Alaskan handmade art and gifts, paintings, ceramics, beaded and ivory jewelry, furs, paper creations, baskets, beadwork, weaving, dolls, clothing and cards. Open 10 A.M. to 6 P.M. Monday through Saturday in Historic Copper Center, Alaska. Old Richardson Highway Loop Road. Major credit cards accepted. Phone (907) 822-5344. [ADVERTISEMENT]

V 101.9 (164 km) **F 262.1** (421.8 km) Parking area. Historical marker about Copper Center reads: "Founded in 1896 as a government agriculture experiment station, Copper Center was the first white settlement in this area. The Trail of '98 from Valdez over the glaciers came down from the mountains and joined here with the Eagle Trail to Forty Mile and Dawson. 300 miners, destitute and lonely, spent the winter here. Many suffered with scurvy and died. Soon after the turn of the century, the Washington–Alaska Military Cable and Telegraph System, known as WAMCATS, the forerunner of the Alaska communications system, operated telegraph service here between Valdez and Fairbanks."

V 102 (164.1 km) **F 262** (421.6 km) Brenwick–Craig Road. Access to Klutina River Bed & Breakfast.

V 102.2 (164.5 km) **F 261.8** (421.3 km) Copper Center Community Chapel and Indian graveyard.

V 102.5 (165 km) **F 261.5** (420.8 km) Fish wheel may sometimes be seen here operating in Copper River to east. The old school is a local landmark.

V 104 (167.4 km) **F 260** (418.4 km) Ahtna building houses Copper River Native Assoc.

V 104.5 (168.2 km) **F 259.5** (417.6 km) Silver Springs Road. Copper Center school.

V 104.8 (168.7 km) **F 259.2** (417.1 km) Paved turnout to east. Watch for horses.

V 105.1 (169.1 km) **F 258.9** (416.6 km) National Park Service headquarters and visitor center for Wrangell–St. Elias National Park and Preserve. Access to Wrangell–St. Elias National Park and Preserve is via the Edgerton Highway and McCarthy Road (see EDGERTON HIGHWAY section on page 676) and the Nabesna Road off the Tok Cutoff (see page 336 in the GLENN HIGHWAY section). Ranger on duty, general information available. A 10-minute video is shown; additional video programs shown on request. Maps and publications are for sale. Open 8 A.M. to 6 P.M. daily, Memorial Day through Labor Day. Winter hours are 8 A.M. to 5 P.M. weekdays. For more information write P.O. Box 439, Copper Center, AK 99573; or phone (907) 822-5234.

V 106 (170.6 km) **F 258** (415.2 km) IMPORTANT: North **junction** with Copper Center Bypass (New Richardson Highway). Southbound travelers TURN OFF on to Old Richardson Highway for scenic route through historic Copper Center (see description this section). *The MILEPOST®* does not log the bypass route (New Richardson Highway), which is the same distance as the old highway (6.5 miles/10.5 km) but without notable features. The old highway rejoins the bypass route at **Milepost V 100.2.**

V 110 (177 km) **F 254** (408.8 km) Dept. of Highways Tazlina station and Dept. of Natural Resources office. Report forest fires here or phone (907) 822-5533.

V 110.5 (177.8 km) **F 253.5** (408 km) Pipeline storage area. Turn west on pipeline storage area road and take second right for private RV park.

V 110.5 (177.8 km) **F 253.5** (408 km) **Tazlina River RV Park.** See display ad this section. ▲

V 110.6 (178 km) **F 253.4** (407.8 km) Rest area to east on banks of Tazlina River; large paved surface, 2 covered picnic tables, water, toilets.

V 110.7 (178.2 km) **F 253.3** (407.6 km) Tazlina River bridge. *Tazlina* is Indian for "swift water." The river flows east from Tazlina Glacier into the Copper River.

V 111.2 (179 km) **F 252.8** (406.8 km) Community college and trading post; groceries and gas.

Tazlina River Trading Post & Western Auto. See display ad this section.

V 111.7 (179.8 km) **F 252.3** (406 km) Copperville access road. Developed during pipeline construction, this area has a church and private homes. Glennallen fire station.

Gold Pan B&B. See display ad this section.

V 112.3 (180.7 km) **F 251.7** (405 km) Steep grade southbound from Tazlina River to the top of the Copper River bluffs.

V 112.6 (181.2 km) **F 251.4** (404.6 km) Paved parking area with historical information sign on the development of transportation in Alaska. Short (0.1 mile) walk to good viewpoint on bluff with schematic diagram of Wrangell Mountains: Mount Sanford (elev. 16,237 feet/4,949m); Mount Drum (elev. 12,010 feet/3,661m); Mount Wrangell (elev. 14,163 feet/4,317m); and Mount Blackburn (elev. 16,390 feet/4,996m).

Sign at viewpoint reads: "Across the Copper River rise the peaks of the Wrangell Mountains. The 4 major peaks of the range can be seen from this point, with Mount Drum directly in front of you. The Wrangell Mountains, along with the St. Elias Mountains to the east, contain the most spectacular array of glaciers and ice fields outside polar regions. The Wrangell Mountains are part of Wrangell–St. Elias National Park and Preserve, the nation's largest national park. Together with Kluane National Park of Canada, the park has been designated a World Heritage site by the United Nations."

Visitor information for Wrangell–St. Elias National Park is available at **Milepost V 105.1** Old Richardson Highway.

V 114.1 (183.6 km) **F 249.9** (402.2 km) Double-ended turnout to west.

V 115 (185 km) **F 249** (400.7 km) **South junction** of Richardson and Glenn highways at Glennallen. Greater Copper Valley Visitor Information Center at service center at junction, open daily in summer; pay phone, gas, groceries. The town of Glennallen extends west along the Glenn Highway from here, with businesses located at the junction and along the Glenn Highway. Anchorage is 189 miles/304 km, Tok 139 miles/224 km, from here.

Offices of the Alaska State Troopers (phone 907/822-3263), Dept. of Fish and Wildlife, Dept. of Motor Vehicles, Alaska Court and community college located on east side of highway.

For the next 14 miles/22.5 km northbound the Richardson and Glenn highways share a common alignment. They separate at **Milepost V 128.6.**

*NOTE: Anchorage- or Tok-bound travelers turn to **Milepost A 189** in the GLENN HIGHWAY section. Valdez- or Fairbanks-bound travelers continue with this log.*

The Hub of Alaska and Maxi Mart. See display ad this section.

V 115.5 (185.9 km) **F 248.5** (399.9 km) **Rendezvous Cafe.** See display ad this section.

V 115.5 (185.9 km) **F 248.5** (399.9 km) **Glennallen Quick Stop Truck Stop.** Stop for friendly family service. Gas, diesel. Convenience store contains ice, pop, snacks,

postcards, ice cream, specialty items, pay phone and free coffee. Senior citizen, truck and caravan discounts. Several interesting items on display include an authentic Native Alaskan fish wheel. Full-service restaurant adjacent. [ADVERTISEMENT]

V 118 (189.9 km) **F 246** (395.9 km) Dry Creek State Recreation Site; 51 campsites, walk-in tent camping, water, tables, toilets, firepits, 15-day limit. Camping fee $10/night or annual pass. *Bring mosquito repellent!* Old ore car here was once used to haul gravel to Tonsina. ▲

V 118.1 (190.1 km) **F 245.9** (395.7 km) **Private Aircraft**: Gulkana airport; elev. 1,579 feet/481m; length 5,000 feet/1,524m; asphalt; fuel 100.

V 123.2 (198.3 km) **F 240.8** (387.5 km) Large paved turnout to east and well-defined 1.5-mile/2.4-km trail east side of road to the mouth of the **Gulkana River** (see **Milepost V 126.9** for details on access and permits). Excellent fishing mid-June to mid-July for king salmon to 50 lbs. (average is 30 lbs.), and red salmon to 6 lbs. Use bright colored yarn or flies, half-inch hook. Heavy tackle with 25- to 30-lb.-test line recommended for kings. Check special regulations before fishing the Gulkana River.

V 126 (202.8 km) **F 238** (383 km) Paved double-ended turnout to west.

V 126.8 (204.1 km) **F 237.2** (381.7 km) Gulkana River bridge. Entering Game Management Unit 13B, leaving unit 13A, northbound.

V 126.9 (204.2 km) **F 237.1** (381.6 km) Access road to **GULKANA** (pop. 100) on the bank of the Gulkana River. Camping is permitted along the river by the bridge. ▲

NOTE: Gulkana River frontage from 2 miles/3.2 km downstream of Sourdough Campground to the mouth of the Gulkana River is owned by Gulkana Village and managed by Ahtna, Inc. There are public easements along the Richardson Highway between Sourdough Campground and the bridge.

V 128.6 (206.9 km) **F 235.4** (378.8 km) **North junction** (Gakona Junction) of the Richardson Highway and Tok Cutoff (Glenn Highway), known locally as Gulkana Junction. Gas, food and lodging. Tok Cutoff leads east 125 miles/201 km to Tok on the Alaska Highway. The Richardson Highway crosses the Gulkana River bridge and continues straight ahead north.

Line Camp (at junction with Tok Cutoff). Groceries, ice, sporting goods, minor repairs, welding. 2 bed and breakfast units (2 bedrooms and kitchen in each). RV parking. Tourist information, guided king salmon on the Gulkana River. Specialized tours available. Phone (907) 822-3508 or (907) 822-5723; P.O. Box 255, Glennallen, AK 99588. [ADVERTISEMENT]

NOTE: Tok-bound travelers turn to ***Milepost A 203*** *in the GLENN HIGHWAY section. Valdez- or Fairbanks-bound travelers continue with this log.*

V 129.2 (207.9 km) **F 234.8** (377.9 km) Pond with lily pads and occasionally a floatplane.

V 129.4 (208.2 km) **F 234.6** (377.5 km) Paved turnout to west. Sailor's Pit (gravel pit opposite lake to west); BLM trail across to **Gulkana River.** Fishing for rainbow trout, grayling, king and red salmon. Highway follows the Gulkana River.

V 132.1 (212.6 km) **F 231.9** (373.2 km) Paved turnout to west.

V 134.6 (216.6 km) **F 229.4** (369.2 km) Paved double-ended turnout with view of Gulkana River to west.

V 135.5 (218.1 km) **F 228.5** (367.7 km) Watch for caribou.

V 135.8 (218.5 km) **F 228.2** (367.2 km) Paved turnout to east. Old beaver pond; 1 mile/1.6 km winter trail to Gulkana River.

V 136.4 (219.5 km) **F 227.6** (366.3 km) Coleman Creek bridge.

V 136.7 (220 km) **F 227.3** (365.8 km) Side road west to **Gulkana River** fishing access: Poplar Grove/Gulkana River BLM-marked vehicle trail, 1 mile/1.6 km. Informal campsites along river.

V 138.1 (222.2 km) **F 225.9** (363.5 km) **Poplar Grove Creek** bridge; spring grayling fishing. Paved turnout to west at north end of bridge.

V 139 (223.7 km) **F 225** (362.1 km) Watch for frost heaves.

V 139.4 (224.3 km) **F 224.6** (361.4 km) Paved turnout to west with view of Gulkana River.

V 140.6 (226.3 km) **F 223.4** (359.5 km) Paved turnout to east.

V 141.2 (227.2 km) **F 222.8** (358.6 km) Side road west to Gulkana River fishing access. Informal campsites along river.

V 141.4 (227.6 km) **F 222.6** (358.2 km) Paved double-ended scenic viewpoint to west. One-mile/1.6-km trail to Gulkana River.

V 146 (234.9 km) **F 218** (350.8 km) Lakes and potholes next 9 miles/14.5 km northbound; watch for waterfowl and water lilies. Views of Chugach Mountains southbound.

V 146.4 (235.6 km) **F 217.6** (350.2 km) Entering BLM public lands northbound.

V 147.1 (236.7 km) **F 216.9** (349.1 km) Double-ended paved scenic viewpoint. Fishing trail to Gulkana River.

V 147.6 (237.5 km) **F 216.4** (348.3 km) **SOURDOUGH.** BLM Sourdough Creek Campground; 60 sites, good king salmon fishing. Access to **Gulkana River**, marked trail to Sourdough Creek. Across the bridge (load limit 8 tons) and to the right a road leads to parking, toilets and boat launch on river. Watch for potholes in access roads. Native lands; check for restrictions. ▲

The Sourdough Roadhouse, destroyed by fire in December 1992, stood next to the creek. It was established in 1903. A gas station was operating here in 1996. The old Valdez trail runs 150 yards/137m behind the few buildings left standing.

The Gulkana River is part of the National Wild and Scenic Rivers System managed by the BLM. A popular float trip for experienced canoeists begins at Paxson Lake and ends at Sourdough Campground. See description at **Milepost V 175.**

Gulkana River above Sourdough Creek, grayling 9 to 21 inches (same as Sourdough Creek below), rainbow 10 to 24 inches, spinners, June through September; red salmon 8 to 25 lbs. and king salmon up to 62 lbs., use streamer flies or spinners, mid-June through mid-July. **Sourdough Creek**, grayling 10 to 20 inches, use single yellow eggs or corn, fish deep early May through first week in June, use spinners or flies mid-June until freezeup.

Trans-Alaska pipeline. Viewpoint at Milepost V 243.4 is a good pipeline photo stop. (© Bruce M. Herman)

V 150.7 (242.5 km) **F 213.3** (343.3 km) Large gravel turnout to east.

V 151 (243 km) **F 213** (342.8 km) Private gravel driveway to west by large pond; please do not trespass.

V 153.8 (247.5 km) **F 210.2** (338.3 km) Highway passes through boggy terrain; watch for caribou. *CAUTION: No turnouts, little shoulder. Watch for dips and rough patches in highway next 10 miles/16 km northbound.*

V 154.2 (248.2 km) **F 209.8** (337.6 km) Double-ended gravel turnout to east.

V 156.4 (251.7 km) **F 207.6** (334.1 km) As the highway winds through the foothills of the Alaska Range, over a crest called Hogan Hill (elev. 2,647 feet/807m), there are magnificent views of 3 mountain ranges: the Alaska Range through which the highway leads, the Wrangell Mountains to the southeast and the Chugach Mountains to the southwest. To the west is a vast wilderness plateau where the headwaters of the Susitna River converge to flow west and south into Cook Inlet, west of Anchorage.

V 156.7 (252.2 km) **F 207.3** (333.6 km) Good view of pothole lakes to west.

V 157 (252.7 km) **F 207** (333.1 km) Good long-range viewpoints from highway. Moose and other game may be spotted from here (use binoculars).

V 158.9 (255.7 km) **F 205.1** (330.1 km) Sweeping view of the Glennallen area to the south.

V 160.7 (258.6 km) **F 203.3** (327.2 km) **Haggard Creek** BLM-marked trailhead; grayling fishing. Access to Gulkana River 7 miles/11.3 km to west.

V 162.2 (261 km) **F 201.8** (324.8 km) Double-ended gravel turnout to east.

V 166.5 (267.9 km) **F 197.5** (317.8 km) June Lake trail; 1 mile/1.6 km to west. Fishing access 1/4 mile to west.

V 168.1 (270.5 km) **F 195.9** (315.3 km)

Gillespie Lake trailhead and parking to west. Walk up creek 0.3 mile/0.5 km to lake; grayling fishing.

V 169.3 (272.5 km) **F 194.7** (313.3 km) Large gravel pit. Turnout to west.

V 169.4 (272.6 km) **F 194.6** (313.2 km) Middle Fork BLM-marked trail to Meier's Lake and Middle Fork Gulkana River.

V 170 (273.6 km) **F 194** (312.2 km) Roadhouse with gas, food, lodging and camping. **Meier's Lake**; parking area, good grayling fishing.

Meier's Lake Roadhouse. See display ad this section.

V 171.6 (276.2 km) **F 192.4** (309.6 km) Gravel turnout by river to west. Long upgrade begins northbound.

V 172.7 (277.9 km) **F 191.3** (307.9 km) Small turnout to west, view of pipeline to east.

V 173.3 (278.9 km) **F 190.7** (306.9 km) **Dick Lake** to the east via narrow side road (easy to miss); no turnaround space. Good grayling fishing in summer. View of trans-Alaska oil pipeline across the lake. Good spot for photos.

V 175 (281.6 km) **F 189** (304.2 km) BLM Paxson Lake Campground turnoff. Wide gravel road (full of potholes if not recently graded) leads 1.5 miles/2.4 km to large camping area near lakeshore; 50 campsites, some pull-throughs, spaces for all sizes of vehicles but some sites on slope (RVs may need leveling boards); toilets, water, tables, firepits, dump station and concrete boat launch. Parking for 80 vehicles. Bring mosquito repellent. *CAUTION: Watch for bears.* Fishing in **Paxson Lake** for lake trout, grayling and red salmon.

This is the launch site for floating the Gulkana River to Sourdough Campground at **Milepost V 147.6.** Total distance is about 50 miles/80 km and 4 days travel, according to the BLM, which manages this national wild river. While portions of the river are placid, the Gulkana does have Class II and III rapids, with a gradient of 38 feet/mile in one section. Canyon Rapids may be Class IV depending on water levels (there is a portage). Recommended for experienced boaters only. For further information on floating the Gulkana, contact the BLM at Box 147, Glennallen, AK 99588, or phone (907) 822-3217.

V 177.1 (285 km) **F 186.9** (300.8 km) Small gravel turnout to west with view of Paxson Lake.

V 178.7 (287.6 km) **F 185.3** (298.2 km) Small gravel turnout to east.

V 179 (288.1 km) **F 185** (297.7 km) Gravel turnout overlooking Paxson Lake. The lake was named for the former owner of the roadhouse (still Paxson Lodge) about 1906.

V 179.2 (288.4 km) **F 184.8** (297.4 km) Gravel turnout to west overlooking Paxson Lake.

V 182.1 (293 km) **F 181.9** (292.7 km) Large gravel turnout at head of Paxson Lake. Rough gravel trail to lake.

V 183.2 (294.8 km) **F 180.8** (291 km) Entering Paxson Closed Area northbound (closed to taking of all big game).

V 184.4 (296.8 km) **F 179.6** (289 km) Large gravel turnout to west.

V 184.7 (297.2 km) **F 179.3** (288.6 km) One Mile Creek bridge.

V 185.5 (298.5 km) **F 178.5** (287.3 km) **Junction** with Denali Highway (Alaska Route 8) to Denali National Park and Parks Highway. See DENALI HIGHWAY section starting on page 512 for details.

PAXSON (pop. 33), site of a lodge with gas station (open year-round), restaurant and small grocery store. Wilderness tours, inquire at lodge. Sled dog racing first weekend in April. Paxson Mountain (elev. 5,200 feet/1,585m) is 3 miles/4.8 km west-southwest.

Paxson Inn & Lodge. See display ad this section.

Private Aircraft: Paxson airstrip (Hufman Field), adjacent south; elev. 2,653 feet/809m; length 2,800 feet/853m; gravel; emergency fuel; attended.

V 185.7 (298.9 km) **F 178.3** (286.9 km) Site of original Paxson Lodge.

Paxson Alpine Tours. See display ad this section.

V 185.8 (299 km) **F 178.2** (286.8 km) Paxson Station highway maintenance camp.

V 186.4 (300 km) **F 177.6** (285.8 km) Leaving BLM public lands northbound.

V 188.3 (303 km) **F 175.7** (282.8 km) Large paved double-ended rest area to east across from Gulkana River; tables, fireplaces, toilets, dumpster and water. The Gulkana River flows south to the Copper River.

V 189.6 (305.1 km) **F 174.4** (280.7 km) Long paved double-ended turnout to west.

V 190.4 (306.4 km) **F 173.6** (279.4 km) Paved parking area by Gulkana River with picnic tables, dumpster and view of Summit Lake and pipeline. Access to Summit Lake. Interpretive sign about red salmon. Salmon spawning area; fishing for salmon prohibited. Access to **Fish Creek** at north end of turnout; grayling fishing. Access to Fish Lake is via trail paralleling creek for 2 miles/3.2 km, according to the ADF&G.

V 191 (307.4 km) **F 173** (278.4 km) Summit Lake to west; turnout at head of stream.

V 191.4 (308 km) **F 172.6** (277.8 km) **Water's Edge B&B** on Summit Lake. Extra-nice cabins and rooms, some with cooking facilities. Tent and motorhome spaces, showers. Quiet setting, breathtaking view. Good fishing, birding, berry picking, wildflowers, lots of wildlife, unique flower garden. Excellent winter snowmobiling. Hosts are longtime Alaskans. Write P.O. Box 3020, Paxson, AK 99737. Phone/fax (907) 482-9001. [ADVERTISEMENT]

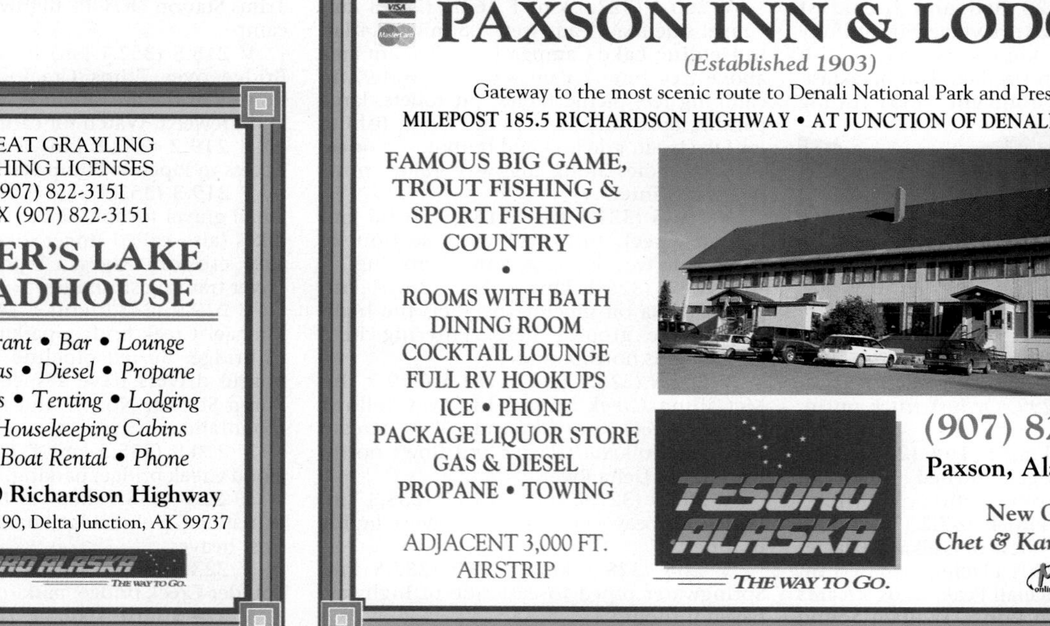

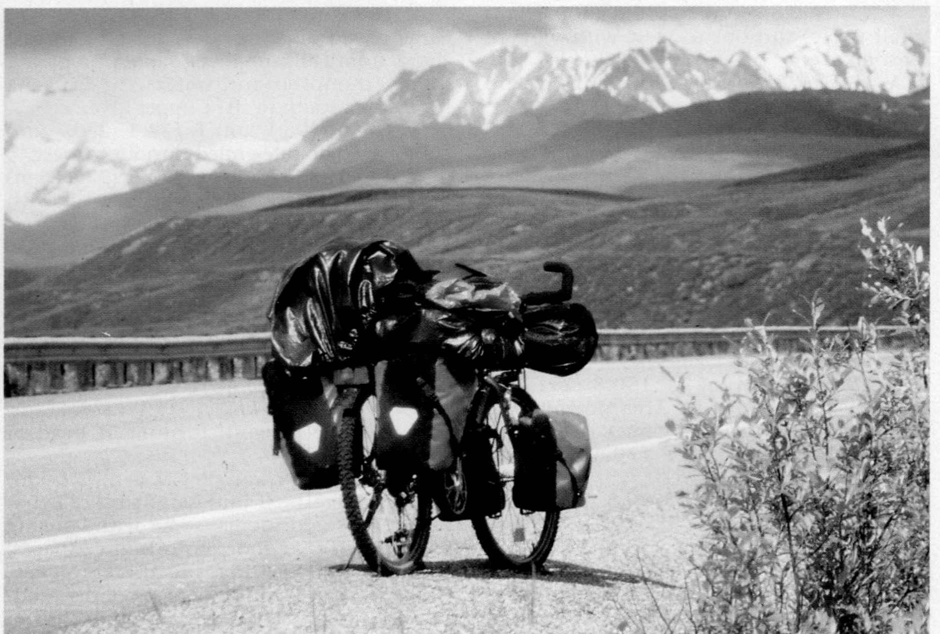

Taking a break on the Richardson Highway, German visitor Herbert Litschke took this photo of his touring bike. (© Herbert Litschke)

V 192.2 (309.3 km) **F 171.8** (276.5 km) Turnout with table and boat launch on **Summit Lake**; lake trout, grayling, burbot and red salmon.

V 192.6 (310 km) **F 171.4** (275.8 km) Large gravel turnout on Summit Lake.

V 193.3 (311.1 km) **F 170.7** (274.7 km) Gravel turnout to west by Summit Lake.

V 194.1 (312.4 km) **F 169.9** (273.4 km) Gravel turnout on Summit Lake.

V 195 (313.8 km) **F 169** (271.9 km) Large gravel turnout at **Summit Lake** (elev. 3,210 feet/978m). Bed and breakfast. This lake, 7 miles/11.3 km long, is named for its location near the water divide between the Delta and Gulkana rivers. The Gulkana River flows into the Copper River, which flows into Prince William Sound. The Delta River is part of the Yukon River drainage. Fishing for lake trout, grayling, red salmon and burbot.

V 195 (313.8 km) **F 169** (271.9 km) Summit Lake Lodge; burned down in November 1993. Current status unknown.

V 196.8 (316.7 km) **F 167.2** (269.1 km) Gunn Creek bridge. View of Gulkana Glacier to the northeast. This glacier, perched on 8,000-foot/2,438m Icefall Peak, feeds streams that drain into both Prince William Sound and the Yukon River.

V 197.6 (318 km) **F 166.4** (267.8 km) Large gravel turnout. Memorial monument honoring Gen. Wilds P. Richardson, for whom the highway is named, at summit of Isabel Pass (elev. 3,000 feet/914m). Sign here reads: "Captain Wilds P. Richardson presented the need for roads to Congress in 1903. His familiarity with Alaska impressed Congress with his knowledge of the country and his ability as an engineer. When the Act of 1905 became a law, he was placed at the head of the Alaska Road Commission in which position he served for more than a decade. The Richardson Highway, from Valdez to Fairbanks, is a fitting monument to the first great road builder of Alaska."

Entering Sport Fish Management Area C southbound.

V 198.5 (319.4 km) **F 165.5** (266.3 km) Gravel turnout to west.

V 200.4 (322.5 km) **F 163.6** (263.3 km) Gravel side road leads west 1.5 miles/2.4 km to **Fielding Lake** Campground. Pleasant area above tree line; 7 campsites, no water, no camping fee, picnic tables, pit toilets, large parking areas and boat ramp. Good fishing for lake trout, grayling and burbot.

Snow poles along highway guide snowplows in winter.

V 201.5 (324.3 km) **F 162.5** (261.5 km) Phelan Creek bridge. Buried section of pipeline to west is a large animal crossing.

V 202 (325.1 km) **F 162** (260.7 km) Trans-Alaska oil pipeline parallels the highway above ground here. Entering BLM public lands northbound.

V 202.5 (325.9 km) **F 161.5** (259.9 km) McCallum Creek bridge, highway follows Phelan Creek northbound. This stream heads in Gulkana Glacier and flows northwest to the Delta River.

V 203.5 (327.5 km) **F 160.5** (258.3 km) Watch for beaver ponds (and beaver); lupine in June.

V 204 (328.3 km) **F 160** (257.5 km) Springwater piped to east side of highway; paved turnout.

V 204.7 (329.4 km) **F 159.3** (256.4 km) Large gravel turnouts both sides of highway.

V 205.3 (330.4 km) **F 158.7** (255.4 km) Small gravel turnout by stream. Good place for pictures of the pipeline climbing a steep hill.

V 206.4 (332.2 km) **F 157.6** (253.6 km) Double-ended turnout with picnic tables, litter barrels and view of mineralized Rainbow Ridge to northeast. Wildflowers include yellow arnica and sweet pea.

V 207 (333.1 km) **F 157** (252.7 km) Good gravel turnout to west. There are frequent turnouts the next 6 miles/9.6 km northbound.

V 207.8 (334.4 km) **F 156.2** (251.4 km) Turnout. Rock slide and avalanche area next mile northbound; watch for rocks on road.

V 208.1 (334.9 km) **F 155.9** (250.9 km) Turnout to west by creek. Look for wild, or Alaskan, rhubarb (*P. alaskanum*), a member of the buckwheat family. Grows to 6 feet with showy clusters of small yellowish-white flowers.

V 208 4 (335.4 km) **F 155.6** (250.4 km) Large gravel turnout to west.

V 211.7 (340.7 km) **F 152.3** (245.1 km) Side roads signed APL are Alyeska pipeline access roads and closed to the public.

V 213.2 (343.1 km) **F 150.8** (242.7 km) Finger dikes to west along Phelan Creek.

V 213.6 (343.7 km) **F 150.4** (242 km) Gravel turnout and road to gravel pit to east. Avalanche area ends northbound.

V 214 (344.4 km) **F 150** (241.4 km) Double-ended paved turnout with picnic tables and litter barrels. Highway follows Delta River northbound, Phelan Creek southbound.

V 215.1 (346.2 km) **F 148.9** (239.6 km) Pipeline crosses Miller Creek right next to bridge. Parking at both ends of bridge, access to creek.

V 215.9 (347.4 km) **F 148.1** (238.3 km) Pipeline interpretive viewpoint with information sign. Gravel turnout to east.

V 216.7 (348.7 km) **F 147.3** (237 km) Lower Miller Creek bridge. Turnouts at both ends of bridge. This is one of the best spots on the highway to photograph the pipeline.

V 217.2 (349.5 km) **F 146.8** (236.2 km) Castner Creek; parking at both ends of bridge, west side of road.

V 218.2 (351.1 km) **F 145.8** (234.6 km) Trims Station DOT/PF highway maintenance camp.

V 218.8 (352.1 km) **F 145.2** (233.7 km) Bridge over Trims Creek, parking. Wildflowers in the area include lupine, sweet pea and fireweed. Watch for caribou on slopes.

V 219.2 (352.8 km) **F 144.8** (233 km) Access to Pipeline Pump Station No. 10.

V 219.3 (352.9 km) **F 144.7** (232.9 km) Small gravel turnout. Note the flood control dikes (also called finger dikes) in stream to slow erosion. Alyeska Pipeline calls these "river training structures."

V 219.9 (353.9 km) **F 144.1** (231.9 km) Michael Creek bridge; parking at both ends of bridge. Buried pipeline to west. Southbound drivers have a spectacular view of Pump Station No. 10 and the surrounding mountains.

V 220.9 (355.5 km) **F 143.1** (230.3 km) Flood Creek bridge; parking.

V 223 (358.9 km) **F 141** (226.9 km) Whistler Creek bridge; parking. Watch for frost heaves.

V 223.8 (360.2 km) **F 140.2** (225.6 km) Boulder Creek bridge; parking.

V 224.5 (361.3 km) **F 139.5** (224.5 km) Lower Suzy Q Creek bridge; parking.

Motorhome along the Richardson Highway at mineralized Rainbow Ridge, Milepost V 206.4. (© Ruth Brandt)

V 224.8 (361.8 km) **F 139.2** (224 km) Suzy Q Creek bridge. Double-ended gravel turnout.

V 225.2 (362.4 km) **F 138.8** (223.4 km) Large gravel turnout to east.

V 225.4 (362.7 km) **F 138.6** (223.1 km) Double-ended paved turnout with picnic table and litter barrels to west. Historical marker here identifies the terminal moraine of Black Rapids Glacier to the west. Currently a retreating glacier with little ice visible, this glacier was nicknamed the Galloping Glacier when it advanced more than 3 miles/4.8 km during the winter of 1936–37.

Black Rapids Lake trail begins across from historical sign (0.3 mile/0.4 km to lake). Look for river beauty and wild sweet pea blooming in June.

Private Aircraft: Black Rapids airstrip, adjacent north; elev. 2,125 feet/648m; length 2,200 feet/671m; gravel.

V 226 (363.7 km) **F 138** (222.1 km) Good gravel turnout by river to west.

V 226.3 (364.2 km) **F 137.7** (221.6 km) Falls Creek bridge.

V 226.7 (364.8 km) **F 137.3** (221 km) Black Rapids U.S. Army training site at Fall Creek. Boundary between Game Management Units 20D and 13.

V 227 (365.3 km) **F 137** (220.5 km) Gunnysack Creek. View of Black Rapids Glacier to west.

V 227.4 (366 km) **F 136.6** (219.8 km) Old Black Rapids Lodge. Dirt airstrip.

V 228.4 (367.6 km) **F 135.6** (218.2 km) Parking beside One Mile Creek bridge.

V 230.4 (370.8 km) **F 133.6** (215 km) Large paved turnout overlooks Delta River.

V 231 (371.7 km) **F 133** (214 km) Darling Creek. Gravel turnout to east.

V 233.3 (375.5 km) **F 130.7** (210.3 km) Bear Creek bridge; turnouts at either end, access to creek. Wildflowers include pale oxytrope, yellow arnica, fireweed, wild rhubarb and cow parsnip.

V 234.2 (376.9 km) **F 129.8** (208.9 km) Double-ended gravel turnout to east.

V 234.5 (377.4 km) **F 129.5** (208.4 km) Paved turnout to west. Pipeline access road. Pipeline comes up out of the ground here and goes through forest.

V 234.8 (377.9 km) **F 129.2** (207.9 km) Ruby Creek bridge; parking to west.

V 237.9 (382.9 km) **F 126.1** (202.9 km) Loop road (watch for potholes) through Donnelly Creek State Recreation Site; 12 campsites, tables, firepits, toilets and water. Camping fee $8/night or annual pass. ▲

V 238.7 (384.1 km) **F 125.3** (201.6 km) Watch for frost heaves northbound.

V 239.1 (384.8 km) **F 124.9** (201 km) Small gravel turnout to east.

V 241.3 (388.3 km) **F 122.7** (197.5 km) Large paved turnout to west.

V 242 (389.5 km) **F 122** (196.3 km) Pipeline parallels highway. Donnelly Dome ahead northbound. Watch for pavement dips.

V 242.1 (389.6 km) **F 121.9** (196.2 km) Coal Mine Road (4-wheel-drive vehicles only) leads east to fishing lakes; **Last Lake,** arctic char; **Coal Mine No. 5 Lake**, lake trout; **Brodie Lake** and **Pauls Pond,** grayling and lake trout. Check with the ADF&G for details.

V 243.1 (391.2 km) **F 120.9** (194.6 km) Weasel Lake trail to west.

V 243.4 (391.7 km) **F 120.6** (194.1 km) Pipeline viewpoint with interpretive signs. Good photo stop.

V 243.9 (392.5 km) **F 120.1** (193.3 km) Paved double-ended turnout to east. The trans-Alaska oil pipeline snakes along the ground and over the horizon. Zigzag design of pipeline converts pipe thermal expansion, as well as movement from other forces (like earthquakes), into a controlled sideways movement. A spectacular view to the southwest of 3 of the highest peaks of the Alaska Range. From west to south they are: Mount Deborah (elev. 12,339 feet/3,761m); Hess Mountain (elev. 11,940 feet/3,639m), center foreground; and Mount Hayes (elev. 13,832 feet/4,216m).

In spring look for wild sweet pea, chiming bells, lupine, lousewort and bluebell for the next 3 miles/4.8 km.

V 244.3 (393.2 km) **F 119.7** (192.6 km) Gravel turnout to east. Trail to **Donnelly Lake**; king and silver salmon, rainbow trout. Donnelly Dome ahead northbound.

V 246 (395.9 km) **F 118** (189.9 km) Donnelly Dome immediately to the west (elev. 3,910 feet/1,192m), was first named Delta Dome. For years the mountain has been used to predict the weather: "The first snow on the top of the Donnelly Dome means snow in Delta Junction within 2 weeks."

V 246.9 (397.3 km) **F 117.1** (188.4 km) Gravel turnout to east.

V 247 (397.5 km) **F 117** (188.3 km) Cutoff to Old Richardson Highway loop to west; access to fishing lakes.

V 247.3 (398 km) **F 116.7** (187.8 km) From here northbound the road extends straight as an arrow for 4.8 miles/7.7 km.

V 249.3 (401.2 km) **F 114.7** (184.6 km) Bear Drop Zone. Military games area. Controlled access road: No trespassing.

V 252.8 (406.8 km) **F 111.2** (179 km) Paved, double-ended and scenic viewpoint to west with picnic tables and litter barrels.

V 253.9 (408.6 km) **F 110.1** (177.2 km) Good view of Pump Station No. 9 if southbound.

V 256 (412 km) **F 108** (173.8 km) Fort Greely Ridge Road to west.

V 257.6 (414.6 km) **F 106.4** (171.2 km) Entrance to U.S. Army Cold Regions Test Center at Fort Greely.

Meadows Road (4-wheel-drive vehicles only) leads west to fishing lakes. Access to **Bolio Lake;** grayling, rainbow, lake trout. Rainbow-producing **Mark Lake** is 4.5 miles/7.2 km along this road. Meadows Road junctions with the Old Richardson Highway loop. Check with the ADF&G for details on fishing lakes.

V 258.3 (415.7 km) **F 105.7** (170.1 km) Pump Station No. 9 access road to east. Tours of Pump Station 9 are offered daily from June to August. Phone (907) 869-3270 or 456-9391 for more information and tour reservations.

V 261.2 (420.3 km) **F 102.8** (165.4 km) **FORT GREELY** (restricted area) main gate. Fort Greely was named for A.W. Greely, arctic explorer and author of *Three Years of Arctic Service*.

V 262.6 (422.6 km) **F 101.4** (163.2 km) Double-ended paved turnout with scenic view. Watch for bison. Wind area next 2 miles/3.2 km northbound.

V 262.7 (422.8 km) **F 101.3** (163 km) FAA buildings. Big Delta.

V 264.9 (426.3 km) **F 99.1** (159.5 km) Jarvis Creek, rises near Butch Lake to the east and flows into the Delta River. Buffalo (bison) may be seen in this area.

V 265.2 (426.8 km) **F 98.8** (159 km) "Welcome to Delta Junction" sign. Bike trail begins northbound.

V 266 (428 km) **F 98** (157.7 km) **Junction** of the Richardson Highway and the Alaska Highway, **Milepost DC 1422,** at Delta Junction. Visitor center is located at junction. Turn to page 195 for description of Delta Junction services and continuation of highway log to Fairbanks (the remaining 98 miles/157.7 km of the Richardson Highway leading into Fairbanks are logged in the ALASKA HIGHWAY section).

EDGERTON HIGHWAY/ McCARTHY ROAD

(10)

Connects: Richardson Highway Junction to McCarthy, AK
Length: 93 miles **Road Surface:** 40% paved, 60% gravel
Season: McCarthy Road not maintained in winter
Major Attraction: Wrangell–St. Elias National Park & Preserve

	Chitina	McCarthy	Richardson Hwy.
Chitina		60	33
McCarthy	60		93
Richardson Hwy.	33	93	

Canoeist paddles through early morning mist on Silver Lake, Milepost J 9.3 McCarthy Road. (© Susan Cole Kelly)

The Edgerton Highway, known locally as the Edgerton Cutoff, is a scenic paved road leading 35.1 miles/56.5 km east from its junction with the Richardson Highway to Chitina, then across the Copper River bridge to the start of the McCarthy Road. The gravel McCarthy Road leads 58.3 miles/93.8 km east and dead ends at the Kennicott River, about 1 mile/1.6 km west of the settlement of McCarthy. Total driving distance from the Richardson Highway turnoff to the end of the McCarthy Road is 93.4 miles/150.3 km.

The Edgerton Highway is paved, with some long, steep grades. From **Milepost R 7.3**, the Edgerton Highway follows the approximate route of the old pack trail that once connected Chitina with Copper Center. The Edgerton Highway is named for U.S. Army Maj. Glenn Edgerton of the Alaska Territorial Road Commission.

NOTE: Expect road construction in the Kenny Lake area, between ***Mileposts R 5 and R 7****, in 1998.*

The McCarthy Road is recommended for the adventurous traveler and only in the summer. Allow 4 hours driving time, with a maximum speed of 20 mph/32 kmph. Maintained by the state Dept. of Transportation, the road is suitable for most vehicles to **Milepost J 13.3** (Strelna Creek). The road is very narrow and may be dusty in dry weather and muddy in wet weather.

The Kennicott River crossing is by 2 foot bridges. There is no vehicle access across the river; see description at **Milepost J 58.2**.

Motorists with large vehicles or trailers should exercise caution, especially in wet weather. Watch for old railroad spikes in roadbed. Unless recently graded, watch for potholes, soft spots and severe washboard. Tire repair and mechanical light-towing service are available at Silver Lake Campground, **Milepost J 9.3**. The National Park Service ranger station in Chitina has information on current road conditions and also on backcountry travel in Wrangell–St. Elias National Park and Preserve. Most land along the McCarthy Road is either privately or publicly held. Local residents have asked that visitors please help protect water sources from contamination.

The McCarthy Road follows the right-of-way of the old Copper River & Northwestern Railway. Begun in 1907, the CR&NW (also referred to as the "can't run and never will") was built to carry copper ore from the Kennecott Mines to Cordova. It took 4 years to complete the railway. The railway and mine ceased operation in 1938.

The solitude and scenery of McCarthy, along with the historic Kennecott Mine and surrounding wilderness of Wrangell–St. Elias National Park and Preserve, have drawn increasing numbers of visitors to this area. It is a 126-mile/202-km drive from Glennallen to McCarthy, 315 miles/507 km from Anchorage.

Emergency medical services: Between the junction of the Richardson and Edgerton highways and McCarthy, contact the Copper River EMS in Glennallen, phone 911 or (907) 822-3203.

Edgerton Highway Log

Distance from junction with Richardson Highway (R) is followed by distance from junction with McCarthy Road (M).

R 0 M 35.1 (56.5 km) **Junction** at **Milepost V 82.6** Richardson Highway. Begin long down-grade eastbound. Watch for horses.

EDGERTON HIGHWAY/McCARTHY ROAD

Richardson Highway to McCarthy, AK

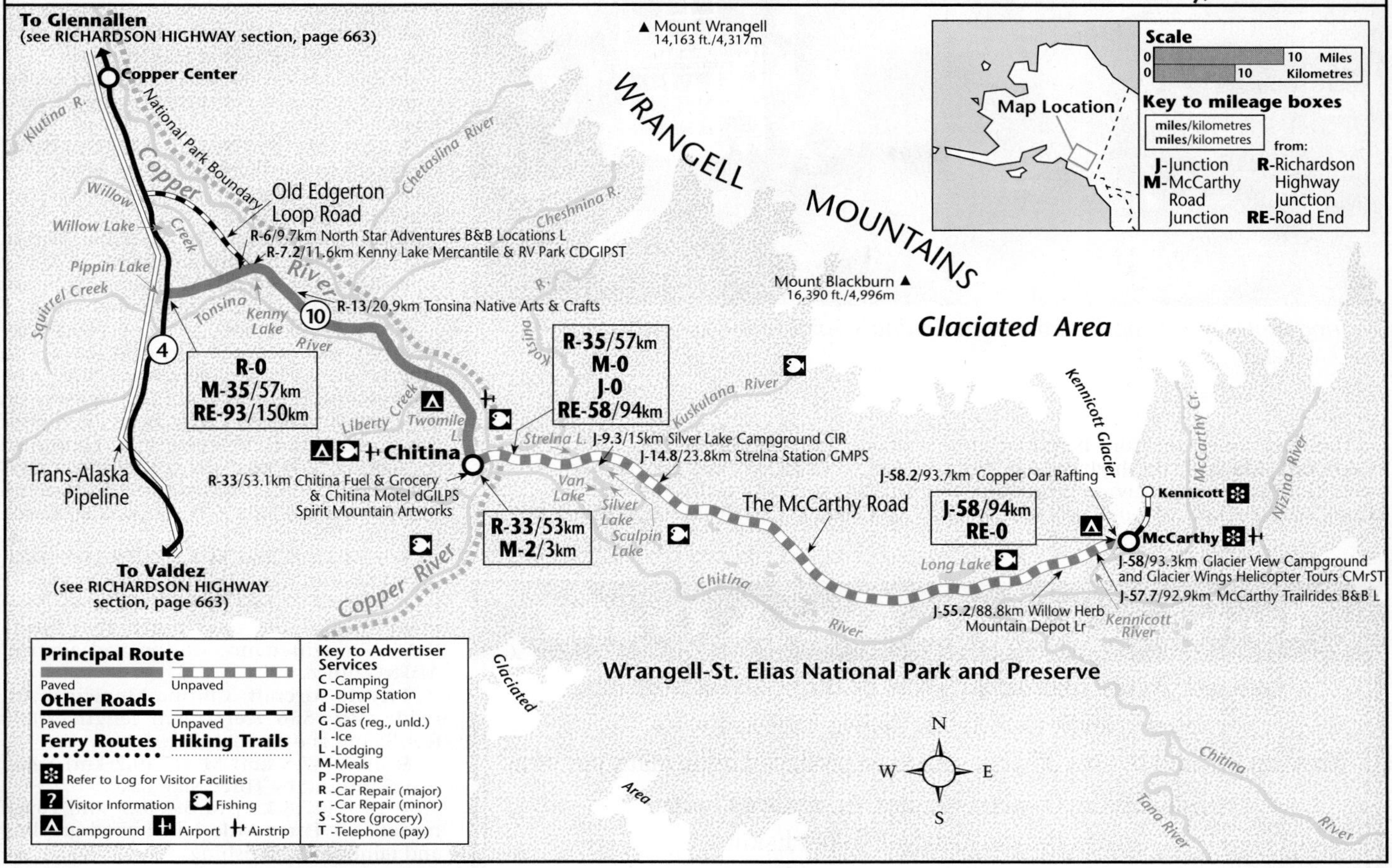

To Glennallen
(see RICHARDSON HIGHWAY section, page 663)
Copper Center
National Park Boundary
Klutina R.
Copper
Willow
Willow Lake
Creek
Pippin Lake
Squirrel Creek
Old Edgerton Loop Road
R-6/9.7km North Star Adventures B&B Locations L
R-7.2/11.6km Kenny Lake Mercantile & RV Park CDGIPST
R-13/20.9km Tonsina Native Arts & Crafts
Tonsina
Kenny Lake
River
Chetaslina River
Cheshnina R.
Mount Wrangell 14,163 ft./4,317m
WRANGELL MOUNTAINS
Mount Blackburn 16,390 ft./4,996m
Glaciated Area
R-0
M-35/57km
RE-93/150km
R-35/57km
M-0
J-0
RE-58/94km
Liberty Creek
Twomile L.
Chitina
Kotsina R.
Kuskulana River
Strelna L.
J-9.3/15km Silver Lake Campground CIR
J-14.8/23.8km Strelna Station GMPS
R-33/53.1km Chitina Fuel & Grocery & Chitina Motel dGILPS
Spirit Mountain Artworks
R-33/53km
M-2/3km
Trans-Alaska Pipeline
To Valdez
(see RICHARDSON HIGHWAY section, page 663)
Van Lake
Silver Lake
Sculpin Lake
The McCarthy Road
J-58.2/93.7km Copper Oar Rafting
J-58/94km
RE-0
Kennicott Glacier
Kennicott
McCarthy
J-58/93.3km Glacier View Campground and Glacier Wings Helicopter Tours CMrST
J-57.7/92.9km McCarthy Trailrides B&B L
J-55.2/88.8km Willow Herb Mountain Depot Lr
Long Lake
Chitina River
Kennicott River
McCarthy Cr.
Nizina River
Copper River
Glaciated Area
Wrangell-St. Elias National Park and Preserve
Chitina River
Tana River
N
W
E
S
Scale
0 10 Miles
0 10 Kilometres
Map Location
Key to mileage boxes
miles/kilometres
miles/kilometres
from:
J-Junction
M-McCarthy Road Junction
R-Richardson Highway Junction
RE-Road End
Principal Route
Paved
Unpaved
Other Roads
Paved
Unpaved
Ferry Routes
Hiking Trails
Refer to Log for Visitor Facilities
Visitor Information
Fishing
Campground
Airport
Airstrip
Key to Advertiser Services
C -Camping
D -Dump Station
d -Diesel
G -Gas (reg., unld.)
I -Ice
L -Lodging
M-Meals
P -Propane
R -Car Repair (major)
r -Car Repair (minor)
S -Store (grocery)
T -Telephone (pay)

Excellent view of Mount Drum (to the northeast), a 12,010-foot/3,661-m peak of the Wrangell Mountains. Mount Wrangell (elev. 14,163 feet/4,317m) and Mount Blackburn (elev. 16,390 feet/4,996m) are visible straight ahead.

R 5.2 (8.4 km) **M 29.9** (48.1 km) Kenny Lake School.

R 5.3 (8.5 km) **M 29.8** (48 km) Paved turnout to north.

R 6 (9.7 km) **M 29** (46.8 km) **North Star Adventures B&B Locations.** See display ad this section.

R 7.2 (11.6 km) **M 27.9** (44.9 km) Grocery store with gas, laundromat, showers, camping, gift shop and pay phone.

Kenny Lake Mercantile & RV Park. See display ad this section. ▲

R 7.3 (11.7 km) **M 27.8** (44.7 km) Old Edgerton Loop Road (gravel) leads from here 8 miles/12.9 km through homestead and farm country to the Richardson Highway at **Milepost V 91.1.**

R 7.5 (12.1 km) **M 27.6** (44.4 km) Kenny Lake community hall, fairgrounds.

R 7.7 (12.4 km) **M 27.4** (44.1 km) Spacious double-ended paved rest area to south with picnic table on shore of Kenny Lake.

R 12.3 (19.8 km) **M 22.8** (36.7 km) Paved turnout to south. Tonsina River BLM trailhead, 2 miles/3.2 km (marked, brushed trail; good hike).

R 12.5 (20.1 km) **M 22.6** (36.4 km) Paved turnout to north. Copper River BLM trailhead, 5 miles/8 km.

R 13 (20.9 km) **M 22.2** (35.7 km) **Tonsina Native Arts & Crafts.** See display ad on page 678.

R 18 (29 km) **M 17.1** (27.5 km) Steep downhill grade eastbound. Views of the Copper River and bluffs.

R 19.3 (31 km) **M 15.8** (25.4 km) Site of the settlement of Lower Tonsina, formerly a roadhouse for travelers using the Copper River (no visible remains). Tonsina and Copper rivers are visible here. Beyond are the Wrangell Mountains.

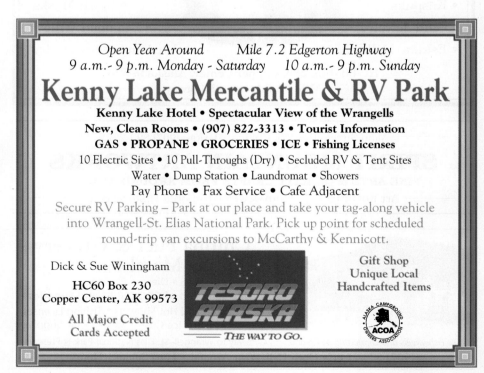

Touring motorcyclists park across from Chitina's Spirit Mountain Artworks.
(© Ruth von Spalding)

The road continues from here east up a steep bluff. Much of the highway has been hewn from solid rock, leaving great cuts on either side. Pockets of pure peat moss are evident in breaks in the rock walls along the road. *CAUTION: Peat fires can be a serious problem; be careful with campfires.*

R 19.4 (31.2 km) **M 15.7** (25.3 km) Tonsina River bridge. Former Lower Tonsina townsite to west of bridge.

R 19.5 (31.4 km) **M 15.6** (25.1 km) Turnout to south.

R 19.6 (31.5 km) **M 15.5** (24.9 km) Double-ended turnout at lake to north.

R 21 (33.8 km) **M 14.2** (22.9 km) Gravel turnout to north overlooking the Copper River.

R 21.6 (34.8 km) **M 13.5** (21.7 km) Paved viewpoint to north above Copper River.

R 21.9 (35.2 km) **M 13.3** (21.4 km) Small gravel turnout to north.

R 22 (35.4 km) **M 13.1** (21.1 km) Top of hill, steep descents both directions.

R 23.5 (37.8 km) **M 11.6** (18.7 km) Liberty Falls Creek BLM trailhead to south.

R 23.7 (38.1 km) **M 11.4** (18.3 km) Liberty Creek bridge (8-ton load limit) and Liberty Falls State Recreation Site. The campground is just south of the highway on the banks of Liberty Creek, near the foot of the thundering falls. Scenic spot. Loop road through campground (large RVs and trailers check road before driving in); 5 sites, no water, no camping fee. Berry picking; watch for bears. ▲

R 28.4 (45.7 km) **M 6.7** (10.8 km) Small gravel turnout to north overlooking river.

R 28.5 (45.9 km) **M 6.6** (10.6 km) Pavement break. Side road north to Chitina DOT/PF maintenance station and airstrip. ADF&G office.

Private Aircraft: Chitina Municipal Airfield; elev. 556 feet/169m; length 2,800 feet/853m; gravel; unattended.

R 29.5 (47.5 km) **M 5.7** (9.2 km) Small gravel turnout by Three Mile Lake.

R 29.7 (47.8 km) **M 5.4** (8.7 km) Paved turnout by **Three Mile Lake;** good grayling and rainbow trout fishing.

R 30.1 (48.4 km) **M 5** (8 km) Small turnout to south by **Two Mile Lake;** good grayling and rainbow trout fishing, canoe launch.

R 30.6 (49.2 km) **M 4.5** (7.2 km) Large paved turnout at end of Two Mile Lake.

R 31.9 (51.3 km) **M 3.2** (5.1 km) One Mile Lake (also called First Lake). Access road to boat launch at east end of lake.

Chitina

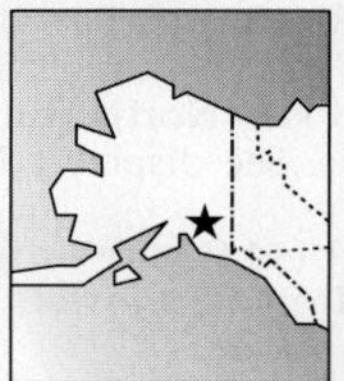

R 33 (53.1 km) **M 2.1** (3.4 km). Located about 120 miles/193 km northeast of Valdez, and about 66 miles/106 km southeast of Glennallen. **Population:** 49. **Emergency Services:** Copper River EMS, phone (907) 822-3203.

Visitor Information: National Park Service ranger station for Wrangell–St. Elias National Park and Preserve in Chitina. Hours were 10 A.M. to 6 P.M., daily, in 1997; hours may vary. Open Memorial Day to Labor Day. A slide show on the McCarthy Road and video programs are available. Write Box 439, Copper Center, AK 99573, or phone (907) 822-5234 (park headquarters); Chitina ranger station, phone (907) 823-2205.

Chitina has a post office, grocery, gas, motel, restaurant, tire repair service and phone service. (The Chitina Saloon, the town's only bar, burned down in December 1996.) The National Park Service ranger station is housed in a historic cabin. Follow signs to public well and toilets. One of the first buildings in Chitina, a hardware and sheet metal shop now on the National Register of Historic Places, houses Spirit

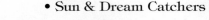

Mountain Artworks. Pay phone next to highway between the ranger station and Town Lake.

Chitina (pronounced CHIT-na) was established about 1908 as a railroad stop on the Copper River & Northwestern Railway and as a supply town for the Kennecott Copper Mines at McCarthy. The mine and railroad were abandoned in 1938. The McCarthy Road east of town follows the old railroad bed, which is listed on the National Register of Historic Places.

Inquire locally about informal camping areas: Much of the land around Chitina is owned by the Chitina Native Corp. and is posted no trespassing. Primitive camping is available along the Edgerton Highway at One Mile and Two Mile lakes. There is an 8-site state campground east of Chitina across the Copper River bridge and a private campground on the McCarthy Road. ▲

A big attraction in Chitina for fishermen and spectators is the seasonal salmon run (reds, kings or silvers), which draws hundreds of dip-netters to the **Copper River.** The dip-net fishery for salmon runs June through September (depending on harvest levels), and it's worth the trip to see fish wheels and dip nets in action. O'Brien Creek Road provides a state right-of-way access to popular fishing areas on large sandbars along the Copper River. This fishery is open only to Alaska residents with a personal-use or subsistence permit. Check with the Chitina ADF&G office for details and current regulations.

Chitina Fuel & Grocery and Chitina Motel. See display ad this section.

Spirit Mountain Artworks. See display ad this section.

Edgerton Highway Log

(continued)

R 33.6 (54.1 km) **M 1.6** (2.6 km) Pavement ends eastbound. No road maintenance east of here between Oct. 15 and May 15.

R 33.8 (54.4 km) **M 1.4** (2.3 km) Turnout overlooking the Copper River.

R 34.1 (54.9 km) **M 1.1** (1.8 km) Turnout overlooking the Copper River. Access to river.

R 34.7 (55.8 km) **M 0.5** (0.8 km) Copper River bridge. Completed in 1971, this 1,378-foot/420-m steel span was designed for year-round use. The $3.5 million bridge reestablished access across the river into the McCarthy–Kennicott area.

R 35.1 (56.5 km) **M 0 Junction** with McCarthy Road (log follows). Dept. of Transportation campground on the **Copper River**; 8 sites, picnic tables, fireplaces, toilets, boat launch, no water. Fishing for red and king salmon. Travelers are now within Wrangell–St. Elias National Park and Preserve. ▲

New (1997) footbridge replaces old hand-pulled cable tram across Kennicott River. *(© Joe Prax)*

McCarthy Road Log

Distance from junction with the Edgerton Highway (J) is followed by distance from road end (RE). Traditional mileposts used by local residents are indicated in the log.

J 0 RE 58.3 (93.8 km) **Junction** with the Edgerton Highway.

J 3.7 (6 km) **RE 54.6** (87.9 km) Turnout overlooking the Chitina River.

J 8.3 (13.4 km) **RE 50** (80.5 km) **Milepost 10.** Physical mileposts indicate distance from Chitina. Trail opposite homestead leads 0.3 mile/0.5 km north to **Strelna Lake;** rainbow trout and silver salmon. (Private property adjacent trail.)

J 9.3 (15 km) **RE 49** (78.9 km) **Milepost 11.** Private campground on **Silver Lake;** rainbow trout fishing, boat and canoe rentals, boat launch, tire repair. Trail access to **Van Lake,** located south of Silver Lake; good rainbow trout fishing. ▲

Silver Lake Campground. Gene and Edith Coppedge invite you to fish for rainbow trout or just relax at beautiful Silver Lake. Bring your camera. RV or tent spaces, motorboat, rowboat and canoe rentals. New tires, tire repairs, fishing tackle, cold pop and candy, ice, bottled drinking water. See display ad. [ADVERTISEMENT] ▲

J 10.8 (17.4 km) **RE 47.5** (76.4 km) **Milepost 12. Sculpin Lake** (also known as Nelson Lake); rainbow trout fishing.

J 13 (20.9 km) **RE 45.3** (72.9 km) Access road leads north 2.5 miles/4 km to trailheads for Dixie Pass, Kotsina and Nugget Creek trails. *NOTE: Access road crosses private homesteads. Please do not trespass.*

J 13.3 (21.4 km) **RE 45** (72.4 km) **Milepost 15. Strelna Creek** (culvert); fair fishing for Dolly Varden.

J 14.8 (23.8 km) **RE 43.5** (70 km) **Strelna Station.** 15 miles past Chitina on the historic McCarthy Road. Groceries, gas, propane, hot food and cold drinks. Located near excellent fishing and Dixie Pass/Nugget Creek trailheads. Local information and maps are available. We sell camping/fishing supplies and firewood bundles. Open 8 A.M.–10 P.M., 7 days a week. Box 97, Chitina, AK 99566. (907) 259-8081. [ADVERTISEMENT]

J 16 (25.7 km) **RE 42.3** (68.1 km) Kuskulana bridge. This old railroad bridge (built in 1910) is approximately 525 feet/160m long and 385 feet/117m above the river. It is a narrow 3-span steel railway bridge with wood decking. Rehabilitated in 1988 for vehicle traffic.

Large gravel turnout at east end of bridge, small turnout at west end.

J 22.3 (35.9 km) **RE 36** (57.9 km) Large gravel turnout to south with view of Wrangell Mountains. There are several turnouts between here and the Kennicott River.

J 22.5 (36.2 km) **RE 35.8** (57.6 km) Boundary between park and preserve lands (unmarked). Wrangell–St. Elias National Park and Preserve allows sport hunting with a valid Alaska state license.

J 23.5 (37.8 km) **RE 34.8** (56 km) **Lou's Lake** to north; silver salmon and grayling fishing.

J 25.5 (41 km) **RE 32.8** (52.8 km) Chokosna River bridge.

J 27.7 (44.6 km) **RE 30.6** (49.2 km) One-lane bridge over Gilahina River. Old railroad trestle and parking.

J 40.3 (64.9 km) **RE 18** (29 km) Crystal Lake.

J 41.4 (66.6 km) **RE 16.9** (27.2 km) Double-ended turnout with view to south.

J 42.9 (69 km) **RE 15.4** (24.8 km) One-lane bridge over Lakina River, access to river at east end.

J 44.1 (71 km) **RE 14.2** (22.9 km) Long Lake Wildlife Refuge next 2.6 miles/4.2 km eastbound.

J 44.2 (71.1 km) **RE 14.1** (22.7 km) Watch for salmon spawning in Long Lake outlet (no fishing at outlet within 300 feet/91m of weir).

J 44.7 (71.9 km) **RE 13.6** (21.9 km) Turnout on **Long Lake;** lake trout, silver salmon, grayling, Dolly Varden, burbot.

J 54.9 (88.4 km) **RE 3.4** (5.5 km) Swift Creek culvert.

J 55.2 (88.8 km) **RE 3.1** (5 km) **Willow Herb Mountain Depot.** Experience Alaskan hospitality at our arts and crafts gallery or stay in our guest cabin. Stop and chat about log building or winter life with year-round McCarthy residents. Our new addition contains a bookstore and card shop. Rent a private, handscribed log cabin with a woodstove and cook-top. Experienced tire repair service. Terry and Dee Frady. MasterCard, VISA. (907) 554-4420. [ADVERTISEMENT]

J 57.7 (92.9 km) RE 0.6 (1.0 km) **McCarthy Trailrides B&B** is conveniently located on the McCarthy Road 1/2 mile from the Kennicott River. Lodging is provided in private cabins. Your host provides you with a hot breakfast in his home and can arrange tours of the area. Contact John Adams, P.O. Box MXY, Glennallen, AK 99588. Phone (907) 554-4433. [ADVERTISEMENT]

J 58 (93.3 km) RE 0.3 (0.5 km) **Glacier View Resort and Glacier Wings Helicopter Tours.** Just 1/2 mile from the bridge, our scenic and private campsites offer breathtaking views of the Root Glacier and surrounding Wrangell Mountains. Take a "thrill-a-minute" helicopter ride over timeless ice or just relax on the sun deck with your favorite beverage and a savory selection from our new barbecue menu. At Glacier View we strive to make your ultimate road trip unforgettable. Phone (907) 554-4490, winter (907) 345-7121. [ADVERTISEMENT] ▲

J 58.1 (93.5 km) RE 0.2 (0.3 km) Local parking lot for Kennicott and McCarthy residents.

J 58.2 (93.7 km) RE 0.1 (0.2 km) Parking lot for visitors crossing Kennicott River; $5/day for parking, $10/day for parking and camping. Two footbridges cross the channels of the Kennicott River. There is no vehicle access across the river. *CAUTION: DO NOT attempt to wade across this glacial river; strong currents and cold water make it extremely treacherous.* ▲

Until the state constructed the new footbridge across the Kennicott River in 1997, travelers had to haul themselves across the river using a hand-pulled, open-platform cable tram.

The Tram Station, constructed from salvaged timbers from the Nizina River railroad bridge, houses the parking concession, tour booking service, snack shop and gift shop. A CB radio at the Tram Station has instructions for calling businesses in McCarthy and Kennicott (they monitor Channel 5 when the Tram Station is closed).

Parking on the riverbank is not recommended in July or early August because of sudden flooding when an ice-dammed lake breaks free upstream.

Copper Oar Rafting. See display ad this section.

J 58.3 (93.8 km) RE 0 McCarthy Road dead ends at Kennicott River. On the east side of the river, follow the road for about 1/2 mile to a fork; the right fork leads to McCarthy (less than a mile) and the left fork goes to Kennicott (about 5 miles/8 km).

McCarthy

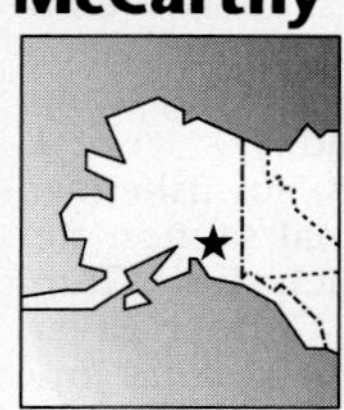
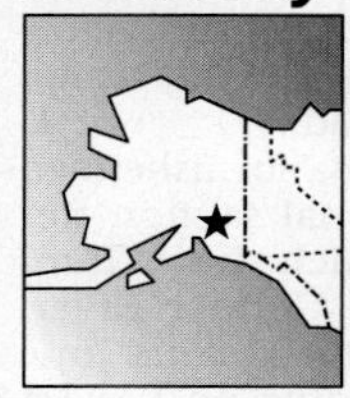

Located across the Kennicott River and about 1.5 miles/2.4 km by road from the end of the McCarthy Road; within Wrangell–St. Elias National Park and Preserve; approximately 60 miles/96.5 km east of Chitina. **Population:** 25.

Transportation: Air—Charter service between Chitina, McCarthy and Kennicott. Van—Scheduled service between Glennallen, McCarthy/Kennicott and Valdez; daily shuttle to Chitina; shuttle service between McCarthy and Kennicott; phone (907) 822-5292. **Radio:** KCAM (Glennallen).

Lodging is available in McCarthy at the McCarthy Lodge, which also offers food service and a bar. The McCarthy area has flightseeing services, a bed and breakfast, a pizza restaurant and an operating gold mine. Check with lodges about activities in the area. Two wilderness guide services operate here. McCarthy has cellular phone service and some businesses can send and receive e-mail and faxes. McCarthy does not have a post office, school or television.

Private Aircraft: McCarthy airstrip, 1 mile/1.6 km south; elev. 1,494 feet/455m; length 1,400 feet/427m; turf, gravel; unattended. McCarthy Nr 2, 1 mile/1.6 km northeast; elev. 1,531 feet/467m; length 3,400 feet/1,036m; gravel; unattended.

The town of McCarthy is in a beautiful area of glaciers and mountains. The Kennicott River flows by the west side of town and joins the Nizina River which flows into the Chitina River. The local museum, located in the railway depot, has historical artifacts and photos from the early mining days.

It is 4.5 miles/7.2 km from McCarthy at the end of the CR&NW railroad bed to the

McCARTHY/KENNICOTT ADVERTISERS

Backcountry Connection	Ph. (907) 822-5292
Historic Kennicott Bed & Breakfast	Ph. (907) 554-4469
Kennicott Cottage	Ph. (907) 345-7961
Kennicott Glacier Lodge	Ph. (800) 582-5128
Kennicott River Lodge and Hostel	Ph. (907) 554-4441
McCarthy Gift Shop & Nugget Liquor Store	Downtown
McCarthy Lodge	Ph. (907) 554-4402
Silk Stocking Air	Ph. (907) 554-4469
Wrangell Mountain Air	Ph. (800) 478-1160

old mining town of **KENNICOTT** (pop. 8 to 15). Perched on the side of a mountain next to Kennicott Glacier, the town was built by Kennecott Copper Corp. between 1910 and 1920. (An early-day misspelling made the mining company Kennecott, while the region and settlement are Kennicott.) The richest copper mine in the world until its closure in 1938, Kennicott processed more than 591,535 tons of copper ore and employed some 800 workers in its heyday. Today, a lodge is located here. The 3 dozen barn-red mine buildings are on private land. Kennecott Copper Mine is a National Historic Site. There are a lodge, bed and breakfast and flightseeing service in Kennicott.

Kennicott Cottage, 16 Silk Stocking. Stay in a newly-renovated 1917 cottage in the National Historic District of this scenic wilderness community and ghost mining town. Charming 3-bedroom cottage has kitchen, propane heat and lights, separate shower house and outhouse. Phone (907) 345-7961 or e-mail kenncott@alaska.net. Visit our webpage at www.alaska.net/~kencott/kcc.htm. [ADVERTISEMENT]

Kennicott Glacier Lodge, located in the ghost town of Kennicott, offers the area's finest accommodations and dining. Built in 1987, this new lodge has 25 clean, delightful guest rooms, 2 living rooms, a spacious dining room, and a 180-foot front porch with a spectacular panoramic view of the Wrangell Mountains, Chugach Mountains and Kennicott Glacier. The homemade food, served family-style, has been called "wilderness gourmet dining." Guest activities at this destination resort include glacier trekking, flightseeing, photography, alpine hiking, historical and nature tours, rafting. May 15 to Sept. 20. (800) 582-5128. See display ad. [ADVERTISEMENT]

Kennicott River Lodge and Hostel. Road accessible. Your choice of accommodations include dormitory-style cabins, wall tents or lodge bunkroom. A 2-story log building provides common area for kitchen and dining. The upstairs sitting lounge with large deck offers views of the Kennicott Glacier. $25 per person. Phone (907) 554-4441. Open May 20–September 20. Internet: www2.polarnet.com/~grosswlr. [ADVERTISEMENT]

McCarthy lies within **WRANGELL–ST. ELIAS NATIONAL PARK AND PRESERVE.** This 13.2 million acre park encompasses the southeast corner of the Alaska mainland, stretching from the Gulf of Alaska to the Copper River basin. Access to the park is by way of the McCarthy Road, the Nabesna Road (off the Tok Cutoff) and out of Yakutat. This vast unspoiled wilderness offers backpacking, mountaineering, river running, hunting and sportfishing. For more information, contact: Superintendent, Wrangell–St. Elias National Park and Preserve, P.O. Box 439, Copper Center, AK 99573; phone (907) 822-5234.

Wrangell Mountain Air provides twice daily, scheduled air service to McCarthy/Kennicott as a time saving alternative to driving the McCarthy Road. Park your car or RV in Chitina at the end of the paved road and enjoy a spectacular flight through the Wrangell–St. Elias Mountains. Affordable fly–drive day trips to Kennicott are also available from Chitina. Wrangell Mountain Air specializes in world-class flightseeing, fly-in alpine hiking, river rafting, glacier trekking. Aircraft are high wing for great viewing and equipped with intercom and headsets for each passenger. Phone free for reservations and information, (800) 478-1160 or (907) 554-4411. Internet: www.AlaskaOne.com/wma. See display ad. [ADVERTISEMENT]

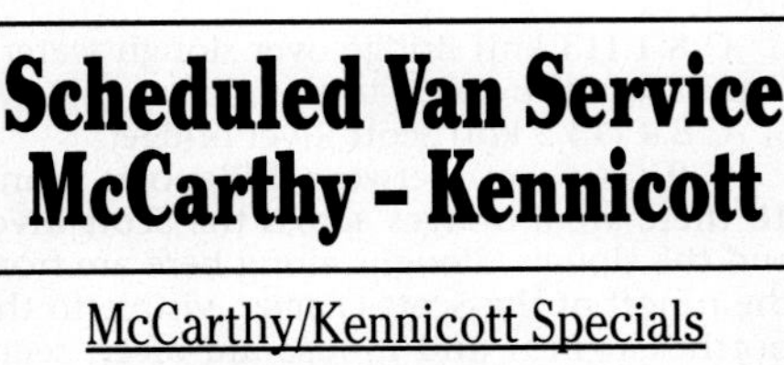

COPPER RIVER HIGHWAY

⑩

Connects: Cordova to Million Dollar Bridge, AK **Length:** 48 miles
Road Surface: 25% paved, 75% gravel
Season: Not maintained in winter
Major Attraction: Childs Glacier

	Cordova	Alaganik Slough	Million Dollar Bridge
Cordova		17	48
Alaganik Slough	17		31
Million Dollar Bridge	48	31	

Driving across the Million Dollar Bridge at the end of the Copper River Highway.
(© Susan Cole Kelly)

The Copper River Highway leads 48.1 miles/77.4 km northeast from Cordova to the Million Dollar Bridge at the Copper River.

Construction of the Copper River Highway began in 1945. Built along the abandoned railbed of the Copper River & Northwestern Railway, the highway was to extend to Chitina (on the Edgerton Highway), thereby linking Cordova to the Richardson Highway.

Construction was halted by the 1964 Good Friday earthquake, which severely damaged the highway's roadbed and bridges. The quake also knocked the north span of the Million Dollar Bridge into the Copper River and distorted the remaining spans. The 48 miles of existing highway have been repaired and upgraded since the earthquake, but repairs to the Million Dollar Bridge remain temporary and travel across the bridge and beyond is not recommended.

Copper River Highway Log

Distance is measured from Cordova (C).

C 0 **CORDOVA.** See description in the PRINCE WILLIAM SOUND section. The Copper River Highway starts at the ferry terminal and leads east through town.

C **1.1** (1.8 km) Council Avenue, Main Street; access to post office and Cordova City Hall.

C **1.3** (2.1 km) Hollis Hendricks Park.

C **1.4** (2.3 km) Whitshed Road on right leads 0.5 mile/0.8 km to Odiak municipal camper park (24 sites, tenting area, obtain shower tokens at City Hall), 5.5 miles/8.9 km to **Hartney Bay.** Fishing from Hartney Bay bridge for Dolly Varden from May; pink and chum salmon, mid-July through August; closed for salmon upstream of bridge. Use small weighted spoons, spinners and eggs. Clam digging at low tide (license required). Shorebird migration in early spring.

C **2.1** (3.4 km) Powder House Bar and Liquor Store (restaurant) overlooking Eyak Lake. Site of CR&NW railway powder house.

C **2.3** (3.7 km) Paved turnout to north by Eyak Lake. Heney Range to the south. Mount Eccles (elev. 2,357 feet/718m) is the first large peak. Pointed peak beyond is Heney Peak (elev. 3,151 feet/960m).

C **3.7** (5.9 km) Large paved turnout Eyak Lake.

C **4.1** (6.6 km) Historical marker on left gives a brief history of the CR&NW railway. Also here is a monument erected by the railroad builder M.J. Heney in memory of those men who lost their lives during construction of the CR&NW. Begun in 1907 and completed in 1911, the CR&NW railway connected the port of Cordova with the Kennecott Copper Mines near Kennicott and McCarthy. The mine and railway ceased operation in 1938.

For the next 2 miles/3.2 km, watch for bears during early morning and late evening (most often seen in June). *CAUTION: Avalanche area.*

C **5.3** (8.5 km) Paved turnout at lake to north.

C **5.6** (9 km) Paved turnout at lake to north.

C **5.7** (9.2 km) Bridge over Eyak River; access to Eyak River trail. This is a good spot to see waterfowl feeding near the outlet of Eyak Lake. An estimated 100 trumpeter swans winter on Eyak Lake.

Eyak River trailhead is on the west bank of the river. The 2.2-mile/3.5-km trail, much of which is boardwalk over muskeg, is popular with fishermen.

C **6** (9.7 km) **Eyak River**, toilet and boat launch. Dolly Varden; red salmon, June–July; silvers, August–September. Also pinks and chums. Use Vibrax spoon, spinner or salmon eggs. Fly-fishing only for salmon within 200 yards of weir.

C **7.4** (11.9 km) Paved turnout. *CAUTION: High winds for next 4 miles/6.4 km.* In January and February, these winds sweep across this flat with such velocity it is safer to pull off and stop.

C **7.6** (12.2 km) Bridge over slough.

C **7.7** (12.4 km) First bridge across Scott River.

C **8.1** (13 km) Bridge over slough waters. Gravel turnout; access to slough.

C **8.4** (13.5 km) Scott River bridge.

C **9** (14.5 km) Between **Mileposts 9** and **10** there are 4 bridges across the Scott River and the slough. Sloughs along here are from the runoff of the Scott Glacier, visible to the northeast. Bear and moose are often seen, especially in July and August. In May and August, thousands of dusky Canada geese nest here. This is the only known nesting area of the dusky geese, which winter in Oregon's Willamette Valley. Also watch for swans.

Moose feed in the willow groves on either side of the highway. Moose are not native to Cordova; the mountains and glaciers prevent them from entering the delta country. Today's herd stems from a transplant of 26 animals made between 1949 and 1959.

C **10.4** (16.7 km) Scott River bridge. Watch for old and new beaver dams and lodges beside the highway.

COPPER RIVER HIGHWAY *Cordova, AK, to Million Dollar Bridge*

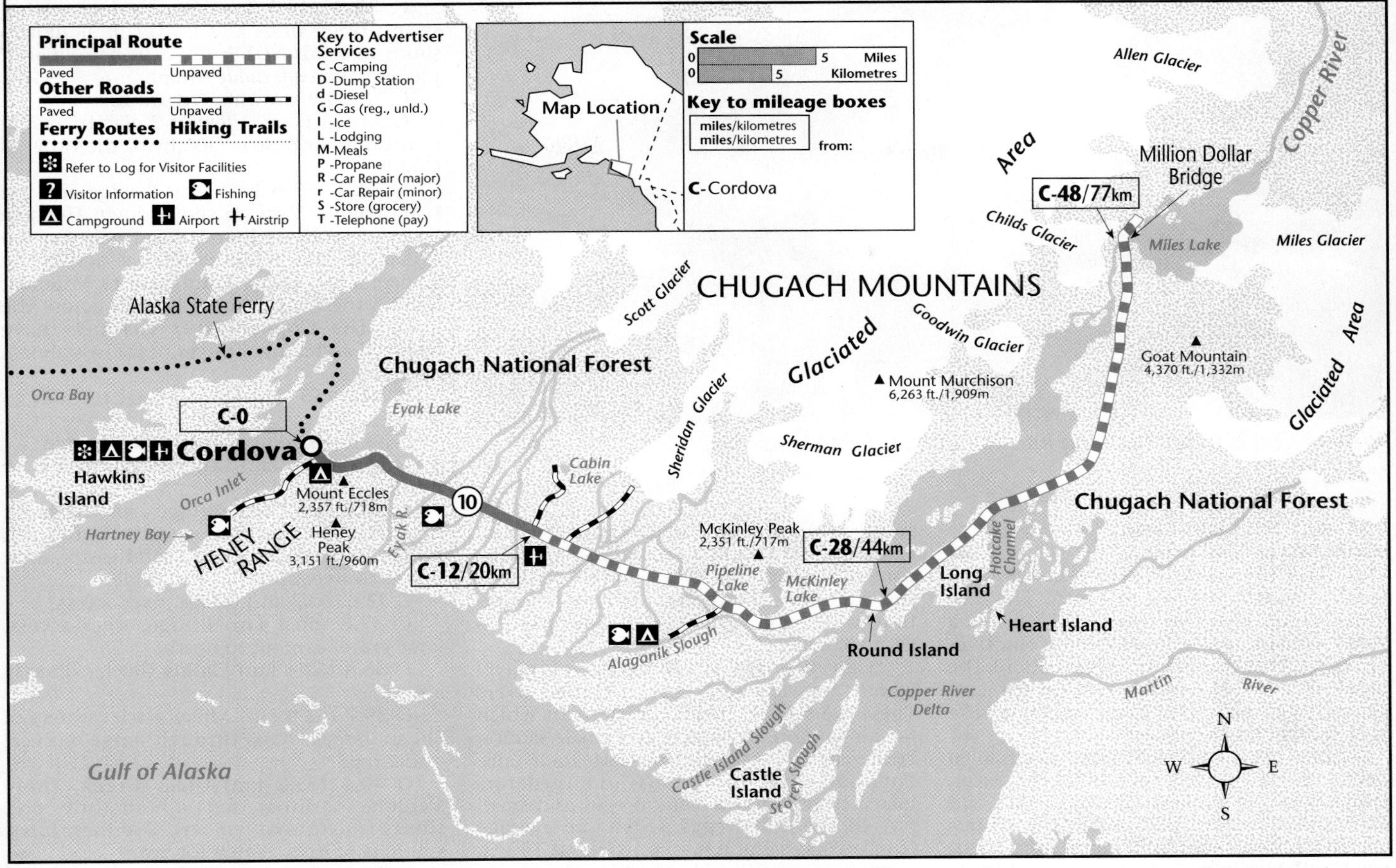

Principal Route
Paved Unpaved
Other Roads
Paved Unpaved
Ferry Routes Hiking Trails
Refer to Log for Visitor Facilities
Visitor Information Fishing
Campground Airport Airstrip

Key to Advertiser Services
C -Camping
D -Dump Station
d -Diesel
G -Gas (reg., unld.)
I -Ice
L -Lodging
M -Meals
P -Propane
R -Car Repair (major)
r -Car Repair (minor)
S -Store (grocery)
T -Telephone (pay)

Map Location

Scale
0 5 Miles
0 5 Kilometres

Key to mileage boxes
miles/kilometres
miles/kilometres
from:
C-Cordova

Allen Glacier
Copper River
Area
Million Dollar Bridge
C-48/77km
Childs Glacier
Miles Lake
Miles Glacier
CHUGACH MOUNTAINS
Scott Glacier
Alaska State Ferry
Goodwin Glacier
Glaciated
Goat Mountain 4,370 ft./1,332m
Glaciated Area
Chugach National Forest
Mount Murchison 6,263 ft./1,909m
Orca Bay
Eyak Lake
Sheridan Glacier
C-0
Sherman Glacier
Cordova
Hawkins Island
Cabin Lake
Orca Inlet
Mount Eccles 2,357 ft./718m
10
Chugach National Forest
Hartney Bay
Heney Peak 3,151 ft./960m
HENEY RANGE
Eyak R.
McKinley Peak 2,351 ft./717m
C-28/44km
Hotcake Channel
C-12/20km
Pipeline Lake
McKinley Lake
Long Island
Heart Island
Alaganik Slough
Round Island
Copper River Delta
Martin River
Gulf of Alaska
Castle Island Slough
Castle Island
Storey Slough
N W E S

C 10.7 (17.2 km) U.S. Forest Service information pavilion (8 interpretive plaques) and large paved turnout with litter barrel to south. Game management area, 330,000 acres. Trumpeter swans and Canada geese. Look for arctic terns.

C 10.8 (17.4 km) Bridge, beaver lodge.

C 11.1 (17.9 km) Elsner River bridge.

C 11.5 (18.5 km) Look for brown bears feeding in the outwash plains of Scott Glacier. Thousands of salmon swim up nearby rivers to spawn. There are numerous beaver lodges on both sides of the highway.

C 11.8 (19 km) State of Alaska Cordova highway maintenance station to northeast. U.S. Coast Guard station.

C 12.1 (19.5 km) Cordova airport and access to Cabin Lake Recreation Area. Drive north 2.8 miles/4.5 km for recreation area (gravel access road forks 0.3 mile/0.5 km in; right fork leads to gravel pit, continue straight ahead for recreation area). *CAUTION: Narrow road, no directional signs, active logging and logging trucks.* Picnic tables, toilet, litter barrel and firepits at **Cabin Lake**; cutthroat fishing.

C 12.4 (20 km) Pavement ends, gravel begins. Watch for potholes.

C 13 (20.9 km) Keep a lookout for snowshoe hare and birds of prey.

C 13.7 (22 km) Sheridan Glacier access road leads 4.3 miles/6.9 km to the terminus of Sheridan Glacier. *CAUTION: Narrow road, watch for logging trucks.* The glacier was named by U.S. Army explorer Capt. Abercrombie for Gen. Philip H. Sheridan of Civil War fame. Sheridan Mountain trailhead, several picnic tables, litter barrels and a partial view of the glacier are available at the end of the access road. It is about a 0.5-mile/0.8-km hike to the dirt-covered glacial moraine.

C 14.8 (23.8 km) Bridge over Sheridan River. Raft takeout point. View of Sheridan Glacier. To the east of Sheridan Glacier is Sherman Glacier.

Winter moose range next 8 miles/13 km eastbound.

C 15 (24.1 km) Silver salmon spawn during September and October in the stream beside the highway.

C 16 (25.7 km) Beautiful view of Sheridan Glacier to the northeast.

C 16.3 (26.2 km) Second bridge over Sheridan River. Large turnout.

C 16.9 (27.2 km) Turnoff for **Alaganik Slough**, Chugach National Forest Recreation Area. Drive south 3 miles/4.8 km via gravel road; picnic tables, firepits, wheelchair-accessible toilets, litter barrel, information kiosk and boat launch. Wheelchair-accessible interpretive boardwalk with viewing blind for watching birds and other wildlife. No water, informal camping. Interpretive plaque on side road reads: "Why are Delta moose the largest and healthiest? This moose herd, first introduced in 1949, maintains its vitality primarily due to its abundant willow supply. As part of a normal cycle, accelerated by the 1964 earthquake, much of the willow is becoming unavailable to moose. As the willow grows tall, the moose can no longer reach the tender new shoots. In the future this could cause a decrease in the numbers of moose on the delta. To slow the cycle down, the Forest Service is experimenting in this area, cutting back the shrubs. This should increase the amount of available willow browse. Biologists will evaluate the response of moose to new willow growth." Fishing for Dolly Varden, sockeye (July) and silver salmon (August and September).

C 17.4 (28 km) Trumpeter swans may be seen in pond beside highway. One of the largest of all North American waterfowl (6 to 8 foot wingspan), it has been almost completely eliminated in the Lower 48 and Canada. Alaska harbors more than 80 percent of breeding trumpeters, and more than 7 percent of the world population breeds in the Copper River Delta.

C 18 (29 km) For the next mile look for silver salmon spawning in streams during September. To the left and on the slopes above timberline mountain goats may be seen. The mountain to the left of the road ahead eastbound is McKinley Peak (elev. 2,351 feet/717m).

C 18.1 (29.1 km) Entering Chugach National Forest eastbound.

C 18.5 (29.8 km) Road narrows. *NOTE: Road not maintained in winter (after Nov. 1) beyond this point.*

C 18.8 (30.3 km) Turnout to north access to Muskeg Meander cross-country ski trailhead; length 2.5 miles/4 km. According to the USFS district office, this trail offers a beautiful view of the Copper River Delta.

C 19.2 (30.9 km) Haystack trailhead to south. Easy 0.8-mile/1.2-km trail leads to delta overlook with interpretive signs. Excellent place to see moose and bear, according to the USFS district office in Cordova. Several small turnouts next mile.

View of Childs Glacier calving into the Copper River. (© Ruth Fairall)

C 20.1 (32.3 km) Large gravel turnout to south; beaver dam, fishing.

C 21.4 (34.4 km) **Pipeline Lakes** trailhead to north, parking to south. The 1.8-mile/2.9-km trail was originally built as a water pipeline route to supply locomotives on the CR&NW railway. Segments of the pipeline are still visible. Fishing for cutthroat, fly or bait. Trail joins McKinley Lake trail. Rubber boots are necessary.

C 21.6 (34.8 km) **McKinley Lake** trail to north; easy 2.1-mile/3.4-km hike with excellent fishing for sockeye, Dolly Varden and cutthroat. Access to USFS public-use cabins: McKinley Trail cabin (100 yards from highway) and McKinley Lake cabin (45-minute walk in from highway; also accessible by boat via Alaganik Slough).

C 22 (35.4 km) Double-ended turnout to north.

C 22.1 (35.5 km) **Alaganik Slough** boat ramp, picnic tables, firepits, toilets, litter barrel, wildflowers, interpretive signs on local cultural history and fishing access to south at west side of Alaganik Slough river bridge. Sockeye (red) and coho (silver) salmon, July to September. Also boat access to McKinley Lake.

C 23.4 (37.7 km) Salmon Creek bridge, parking; creek access.

C 24.6 (39.6 km) One-mile/1.6-km road north leads to Saddlebag Glacier trailhead and parking area; access to canoe route. According to the USFS office in Cordova, this is an easy 3-mile/4.8-km trail to Saddlebag Lake. View of Saddlebag Glacier and icebergs; look for goats on surrounding mountains. *CAUTION: Watch for bears.*

C 24.8 (39.9 km) Channel to beaver pond for spawning salmon. A plaque here reads: "Pathway to salmon rearing grounds. Channel provided access to beaver pond (north side of road) for coho fry. Beaver pond can support up to 25,400 young salmon. Fallen trees and brush provide cover from predators."

C 25.4 (40.9 km) Small gravel turnout by 2 spawning channels with weirs. Interpretive signs along a short trail here explain the project: "Channel built by USDA Forest Service to provide high quality spawning habitat for coho and sockeye salmon. Before construction, the streambed was muddy and the stream dried up during low flow periods. Fish spawned in the streams but few eggs survived. Improved channel is deeper and ensures a consistent flow. Adjustable weirs control water depth. Clean gravels placed in the channel make better spawning conditions while large rip-rap on streambanks prevent erosion.

"Can you see small circles of gravel which appear to have been turned over? These are salmon 'redds,' or nests in which female salmon lay their eggs. Female salmon create the redds by digging with their tails. Environmental conditions and predators take a heavy toll on salmon eggs and small fry. Of the 2,800 eggs which the average female coho salmon lays, only about 14 will survive to adulthood. Most of these will then be caught by commercial, sport or subsistence fishermen. Only 2 salmon from each redd will actually return to spawn and complete their life cycle."

Near here was the cabin of Rex Beach, author of *The Iron Trail,* a classic novel about the building of the CR&NW railway.

C 26.4 (42.5 km) Flag Point. Turnout with view of the Copper River which empties into the Gulf of Alaska. Downriver to the southwest is Castle Island Slough. Storey Slough is visible a little more to the south. Castle Island and a number of small islands lie at the mouth of the Copper River. Monument on the riverbank is dedicated to the men who built these bridges and "especially to the crane crew who lost their lives on July 21, 1971."

CAUTION: Extreme high winds next 10 miles/16 km in fall and winter. Stay in your vehicle.

C 26.7 (43 km) Two bridges cross the Copper River to Round Island, a small island with sand dunes and a good place to picnic.

In midsummer the Copper River has half a million or more red (sockeye) and king salmon migrating 300 miles/483 km upstream to spawn in the river's clear tributaries. There is no sportfishing in this stretch of the Copper River because of glacial silt.

Candlefish (eulachon) also spawn in the Copper River. Candlefish oil was once a significant trade item of the Coastal Indians. These fish are so oily that when dried they can be burned like candles.

C 27.5 (44.3 km) Copper River Bridge No. 3 from Round Island to Long Island. The 6.2 miles/10 km of road on Long Island pass through a sandy landscape dotted with dunes. Long Island is in the middle of the Copper River.

C 28.5 (45.9 km) Lake to south.

C 30.8 (49.5 km) Watch for nesting swans, other birds and beaver in slough to south of road. *NOTE: Use extreme caution if you drive off road: sandy terrain.*

C 31 (49.9 km) Lakes to south.

C 33 (53.1 km) View of 2 glaciers to the northwest; nearest is Goodwin, the other is Childs.

C 33.3 (53.6 km) First bridge leaving Long Island. View to south down Hotcake Channel to Heart Island. Road built on top of a long dike which stretches across the Copper River Delta. From here to **Milepost C 37.7** there are 7 more bridges across the delta. The Copper River channels have changed and many bridges now cross almost dry gulches.

C 34.2 (55 km) Large gravel turnout to north.

C 34.3 (55.2 km) Copper River bridge.

C 35.7 (57.5 km) Large gravel turnout to north.

C 36.8 (59.2 km) Bridge crossing main flow of the Copper River (this is the 5th bridge after leaving Long Island eastbound). Access to river at east end of bridge.

C 37.4 (60.2 km) Bridge, river access.

C 37.8 (60.8 km) Bridge, river access, large gravel turnout to north.

C 38.8 (62.4 km) Childs Glacier directly ahead.

C 39.7 (63.9 km) Milky glacial waters of Sheep Creek pass through large culvert under road.

C 40.5 (65.2 km) **Clear Creek;** Dolly Varden, cutthroat, red salmon (July) and silvers (August–September). Use flies, lures, spinners or eggs. Watch for bears.

C 41.1 (66.1 km) Park on old railroad grade to south for access to Clear Creek.

C 41.7 (67.1 km) Goat Mountain (elev. 4,370 feet/1,332m) rises to the east of the highway. To the west, parts of the Sherman and Goodwin glaciers flow down the sides of Mount Murchison (elev. 6,263 feet/1,909m).

C 42.1 (67.7 km) Side road to gravel pit, pond, informal camping and picnic site by Goat Mountain.

C 48 (77.2 km) Access to Childs Glacier Recreation Area with wheelchair-accessible covered viewing platform, picnic sites, covered tables, toilets and trails. No water. Limited RV parking. U.S. Forest Service hosts on site in summer. Childs Glacier was named by Capt. W.R. Abercrombie (1884 expedition) for George Washington Childs of Philadelphia. The glacier face is approximately 350 feet/107m high and very active. *CAUTION: Calving ice may cause waves to break over the beach and into the viewing area. Be prepared to run to higher ground!*

C 48.1 (77.4 km) The Million Dollar Bridge; viewing platform. The north span collapsed during the 1964 earthquake. Temporary repairs were made and people have been driving across it, but driving across the bridge and beyond is definitely a "drive at your own risk" venture. Primitive road extends only about 10 miles/16 km beyond the bridge to the Allen River. Heavy snow blocks road in winter; road may not be open until June. Proposed extension of the Copper River Highway to Chitina is currently under debate.

From here there is a view of Miles Glacier to the east. This glacier was named by Lieutenant Allen (1885 expedition) for Maj. Gen. Nelson A. Miles.

INSIDE PASSAGE

Southeastern Alaska communities from Ketchikan to Skagway

(See maps, pages 687–691)

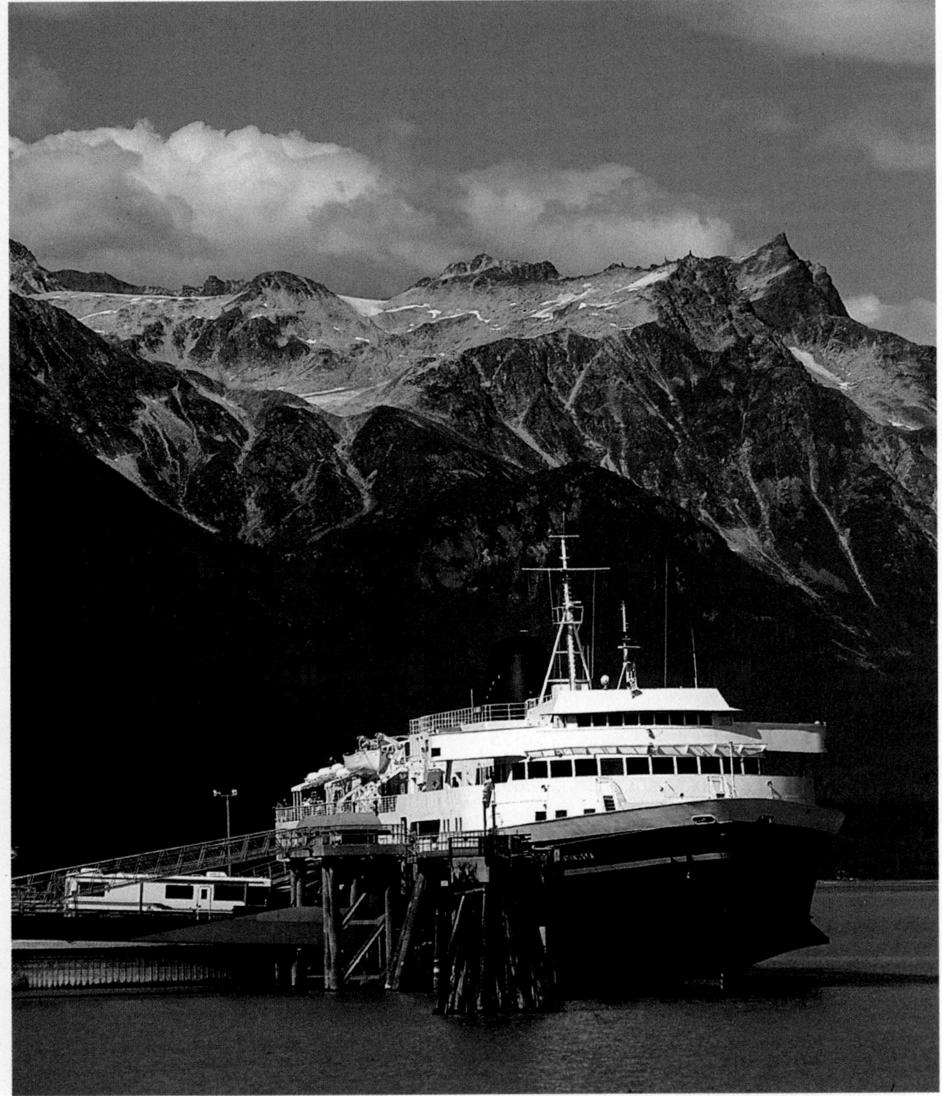

Alaska Marine Highway ferry M/V Matanuska *unloading and loading vehicles at Haines, AK.* *(© Roger Holden)*

Alaska's Inside Passage, located in the southeastern section of the state, is referred to by many of its residents simply as "Southeast." It is a unique region where industry, transportation, recreation and community planning are dictated by spectacular topography.

The region is accessible by air, land or sea. Jet service is available to Juneau, Ketchikan, Wrangell, Petersburg, Sitka and Gustavus. Smaller communities are served by local commuter aircraft. The port communities of Haines and Skagway offer road connections to the Alaska Highway system via the Haines Highway and Klondike Highway 2. The Alaska Marine Highway moves people and vehicles between ports, and connects the Inside Passage with Prince Rupert, BC, and Bellingham, WA. Several cruise ship lines ply the waterways of the Inside Passage and offer a variety of cruising opportunities.

Measuring about 125 by 400 miles/200 by 650 km, 60 percent of the region consists of thousands of islands covered with dense forests of spruce, hemlock and cedar, a result of the mild, moist coastal climate. These islands make up the Alexander Archipelago, and include Prince of Wales Island, the third largest island in the United States (the Big Island of Hawaii is first, followed by Kodiak). The Coast Mountains form the mainland portion of southeastern Alaska.

Southeastern Alaska lies between 54°40′ and 60° north latitude, the same as Scotland, Denmark and southern Sweden. The latitude of Scotland's Loch Ness is slightly north of the latitude at Wrangell Narrows. Stockholm and Skagway share the same latitude, and Ketchikan's latitude is a little south of Copenhagen's.

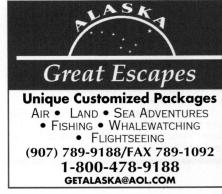

Warmed by ocean currents, this region experiences mild, warm summers, with July temperatures averaging around 60°F/16°C. An occasional heat wave may reach the high 80s. Winters are cool, alternating snow, rain and sunshine; January temperatures average 20° to 40°F/-7° to 4°C. Sub-zero winter temperatures are uncommon. The region receives considerable annual rainfall, from 80 to more than 200 inches (heaviest in late fall, lightest in summer). Populated areas receive 30 to 200 inches of snow annually; the high mountains more than 400 inches a year.

The majority of southeastern Alaska lies within Tongass National Forest, the largest national forest in the United States. (Southeastern Alaska has over 5.6 million acres of wilderness lands.) The forests historically have provided one of the region's major industries; timber harvesting primarily supplies area sawmills.

Commercial fishing and fish processing is another of Southeast's major industries. The numerous rivers and streams, mountains, valleys, melting glaciers and frequent rainfall create ideal spawning grounds for salmon. Local waters harbor an abundance of sea life, including crab, shrimp, halibut, herring and black cod.

Government is a significant employer throughout the region, with federal, state and local government providing the majority of jobs. Juneau serves as the state's capital. Tourism is another major contributor to the region's economy, providing both jobs and revenue.

About 69,000 people live along the Inside Passage, according to 1990 U.S. Census figures. About 70 percent live in the 5 major communities of Juneau (29,755), Ketchikan (15,082), Sitka (9,194), Petersburg (3,350) and Wrangell (2,400). More than 20 percent are Native, mostly Tlingit (KLINK it) Indian, plus Haida (HI duh) and Tsimshian (SHIM shian).

(Continues on page 693)

INSIDE PASSAGE ADVERTISERS

INSIDE PASSAGE *Prince Rupert, BC to Ketchikan, AK*

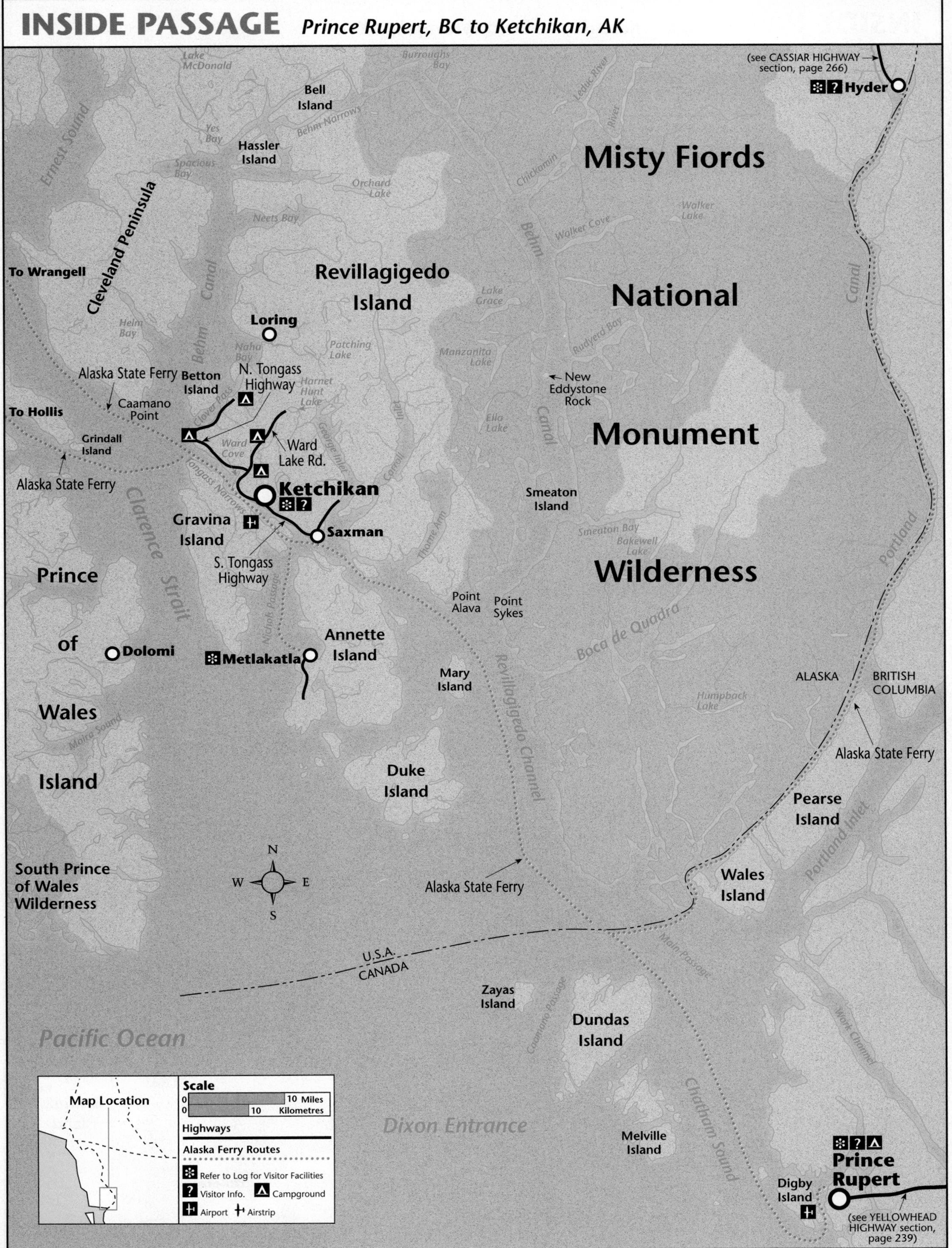

(see CASSIAR HIGHWAY section, page 266)
Hyder
Bell Island
Hassler Island
Misty Fiords
National
Monument
Wilderness
Cleveland Peninsula
To Wrangell
Revillagigedo Island
Loring
Alaska State Ferry
Betton Island
N. Tongass Highway
To Hollis
Caamano Point
Grindall Island
Ward Lake Rd.
Alaska State Ferry
Ketchikan
Gravina Island
Saxman
S. Tongass Highway
New Eddystone Rock
Smeaton Island
Point Alava
Point Sykes
Prince of Wales Island
Dolomi
Metlakatla
Annette Island
Mary Island
ALASKA
BRITISH COLUMBIA
Alaska State Ferry
Duke Island
Pearse Island
South Prince of Wales Wilderness
Alaska State Ferry
Wales Island
U.S.A.
CANADA
Zayas Island
Dundas Island
Pacific Ocean
Dixon Entrance
Melville Island
Digby Island
Prince Rupert
(see YELLOWHEAD HIGHWAY section, page 239)
Map Location
Scale
10 Miles
10 Kilometres
Highways
Alaska Ferry Routes
Refer to Log for Visitor Facilities
Visitor Info.
Campground
Airport
Airstrip

INSIDE PASSAGE *Ketchikan, AK to Wrangell, AK*

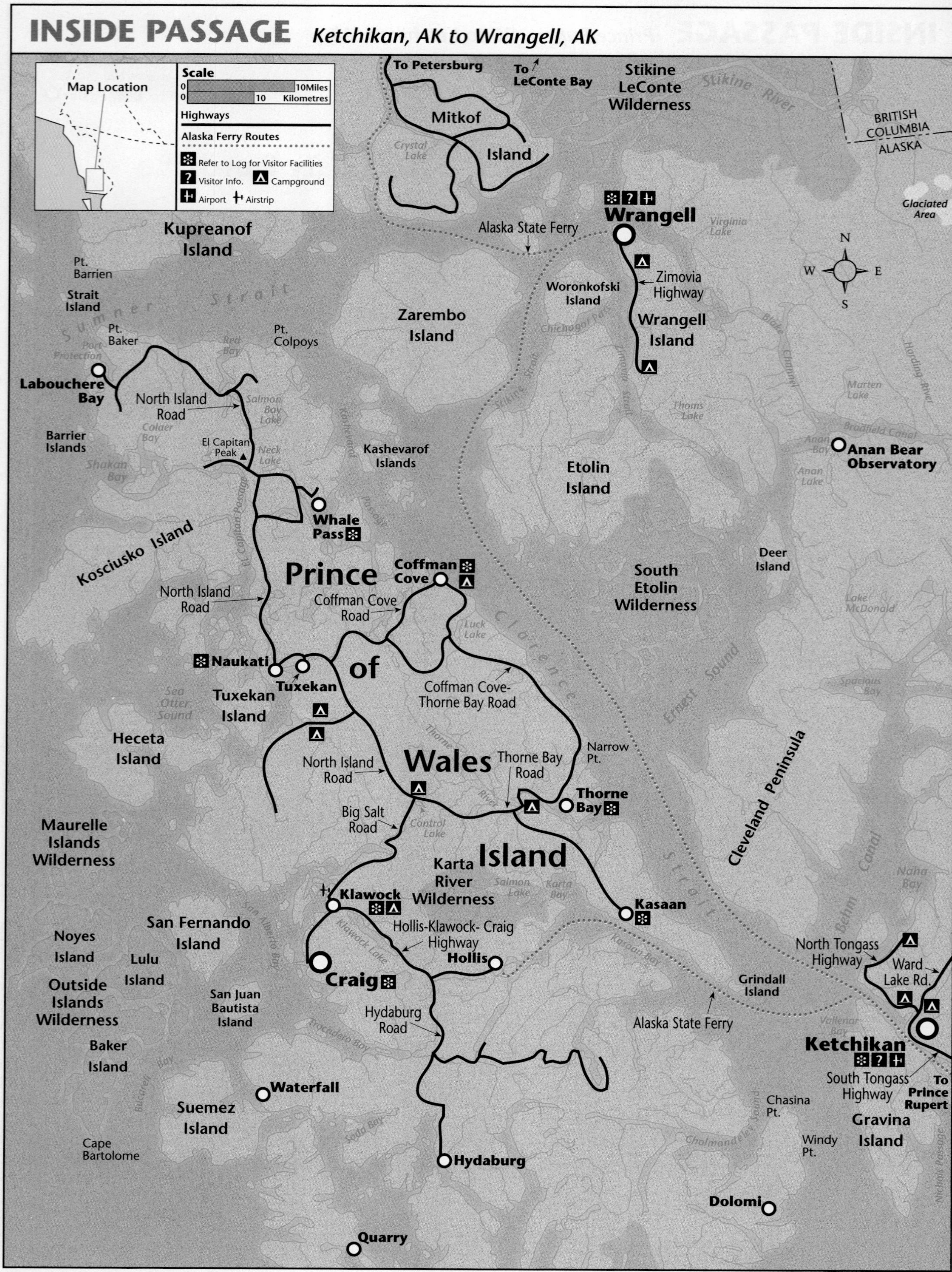
Map Location
Scale
0 10Miles
0 10 Kilometres
Highways
Alaska Ferry Routes
Refer to Log for Visitor Facilities
Visitor Info.
Campground
Airport
Airstrip
To Petersburg
To LeConte Bay
Stikine LeConte Wilderness
Stikine River
BRITISH COLUMBIA
ALASKA
Mitkof Island
Crystal Lake
Wrangell
Virginia Lake
Glaciated Area
Alaska State Ferry
Kupreanof Island
Pt. Barrien
Strait Island
Sumner Strait
Pt. Baker
Port Protection
Red Bay
Pt. Colpoys
Zarembo Island
Woronkofski Island
Zimovia Highway
Wrangell Island
Chichagof Pass
Stikine Strait
Zimovia Strait
Blake Channel
Harding River
Labouchere Bay
North Island Road
Salmon Bay Lake
Coläer Bay
Barrier Islands
El Capitan Peak
Neck Lake
Shakan Bay
Kashevarof Passage
Kashevarof Islands
Thoms Lake
Marten Lake
Bradfield Canal
Anan Bay
Anan Bear Observatory
Anan Lake
Etolin Island
Whale Pass
Kosciusko Island
El Capitan Passage
Prince of Wales Island
Coffman Cove
Coffman Cove Road
Deer Island
South Etolin Wilderness
Lake McDonald
Luck Lake
Clarence Strait
Naukati
Tuxekan
Sea Otter Sound
Tuxekan Island
Coffman Cove-Thorne Bay Road
Ernest Sound
Spacious Bay
Heceta Island
Thorne River
Thorne Bay Road
Narrow Pt.
Cleveland Peninsula
Thorne Bay
Big Salt Road
Control Lake
Maurelle Islands Wilderness
Karta River Wilderness
Salmon Lake
Karta Bay
Behm Canal
Naha Bay
Klawock
San Alberto Bay
Kasaan
Noyes Island
San Fernando Island
Hollis-Klawock- Craig Highway
Klawock Lake
Kasaan Bay
North Tongass Highway
Ward Lake Rd.
Lulu Island
Craig
Hollis
Grindall Island
Outside Islands Wilderness
San Juan Bautista Island
Hydaburg Road
Trocadero Bay
Alaska State Ferry
Vallenar Bay
Ketchikan
Baker Island
Bucareli Bay
Waterfall
South Tongass Highway
To Prince Rupert
Chasina Pt.
Gravina Island
Suemez Island
Soda Bay
Cholmondeley Sound
Windy Pt.
Cape Bartolome
Hydaburg
Nichols Passage
Dolomi
Quarry

INSIDE PASSAGE *Coffman Cove, AK to Sitka, AK*

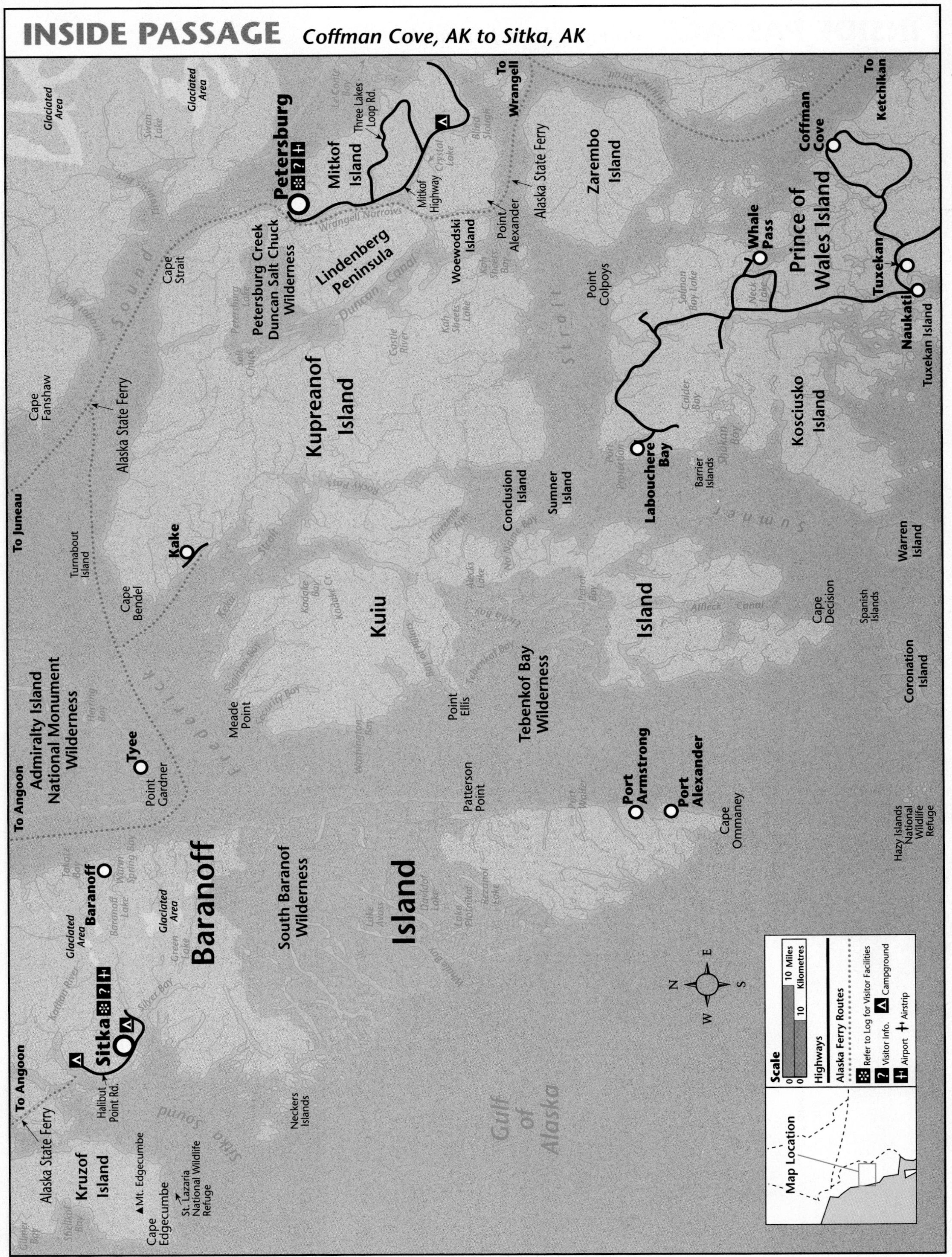

INSIDE PASSAGE *Angoon, AK to Juneau, AK*

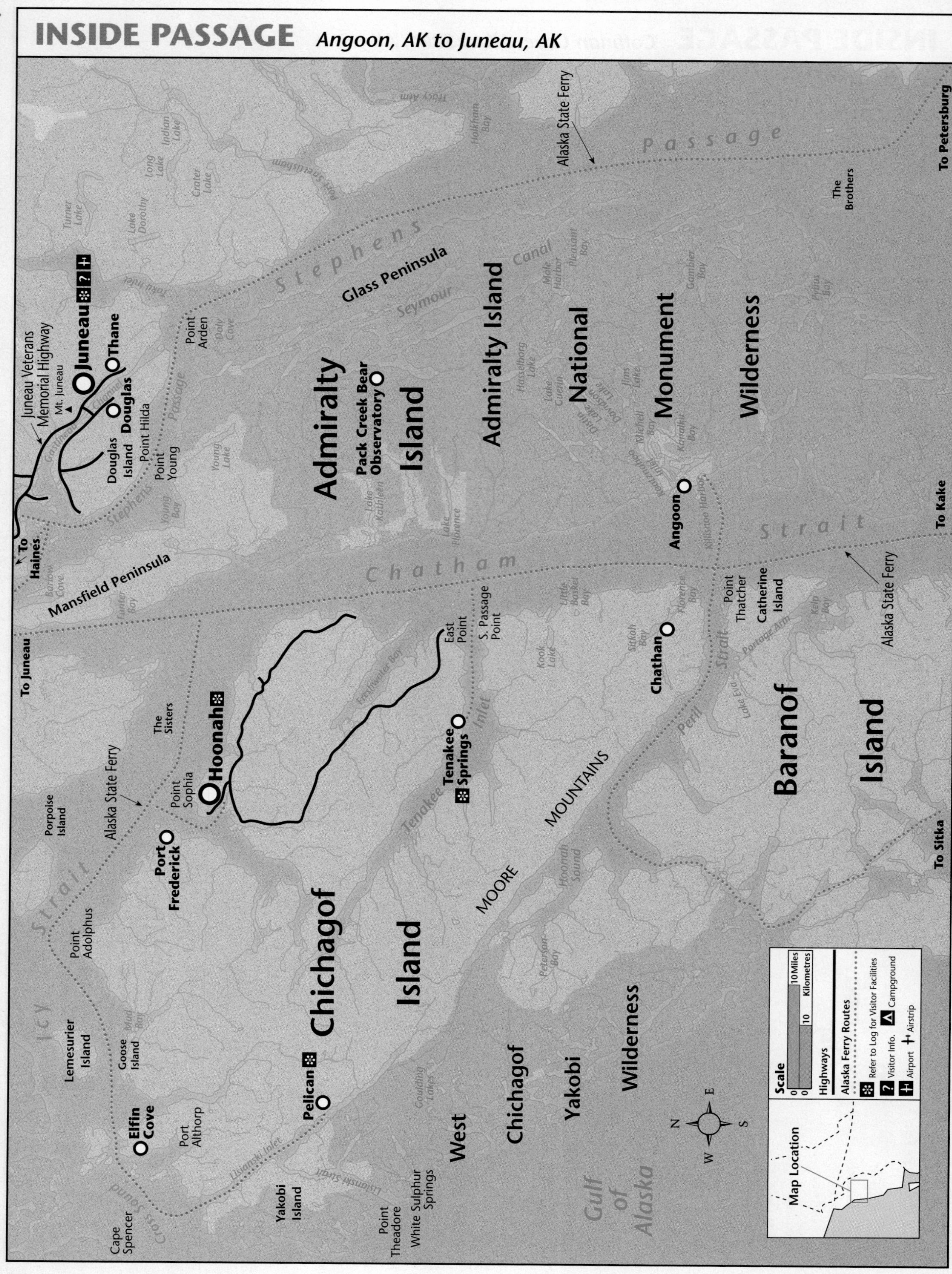
Juneau
Thane
Douglas
Douglas Island
Point Hilda
Point Young
Mt. Juneau
Juneau Veterans Memorial Highway
Gastineau Channel
Stephens Passage
Point Arden
Glass Peninsula
Seymour Canal
Admiralty Island
Pack Creek Bear Observatory
Admiralty Island National Monument Wilderness
Angoon
Killisnoo Harbor
Chatham Strait
Mansfield Peninsula
To Haines
To Juneau
To Kake
To Petersburg
To Sitka
Alaska State Ferry
The Brothers
Point Thatcher
Catherine Island
Chatham
Hoonah
The Sisters
Point Sophia
Port Frederick
Porpoise Island
Icy Strait
Point Adolphus
Tenakee Springs
Tenakee Inlet
East Point
S. Passage Point
Peril Strait
Baranof Island
MOORE MOUNTAINS
Chichagof Island
Lemesurier Island
Goose Island
Elfin Cove
Port Althorp
Pelican
Cape Spencer
Cross Sound
Yakobi Island
Point Theadore
White Sulphur Springs
Lisianski Inlet
Lisianski Strait
West Chichagof Yakobi Wilderness
Gulf of Alaska
Scale
0 10 Miles
0 10 Kilometres
Highways
Alaska Ferry Routes
Refer to Log for Visitor Facilities
Visitor Info.
Campground
Airport
Airstrip
Map Location
N E S W

INSIDE PASSAGE *Juneau, AK to Skagway, AK*

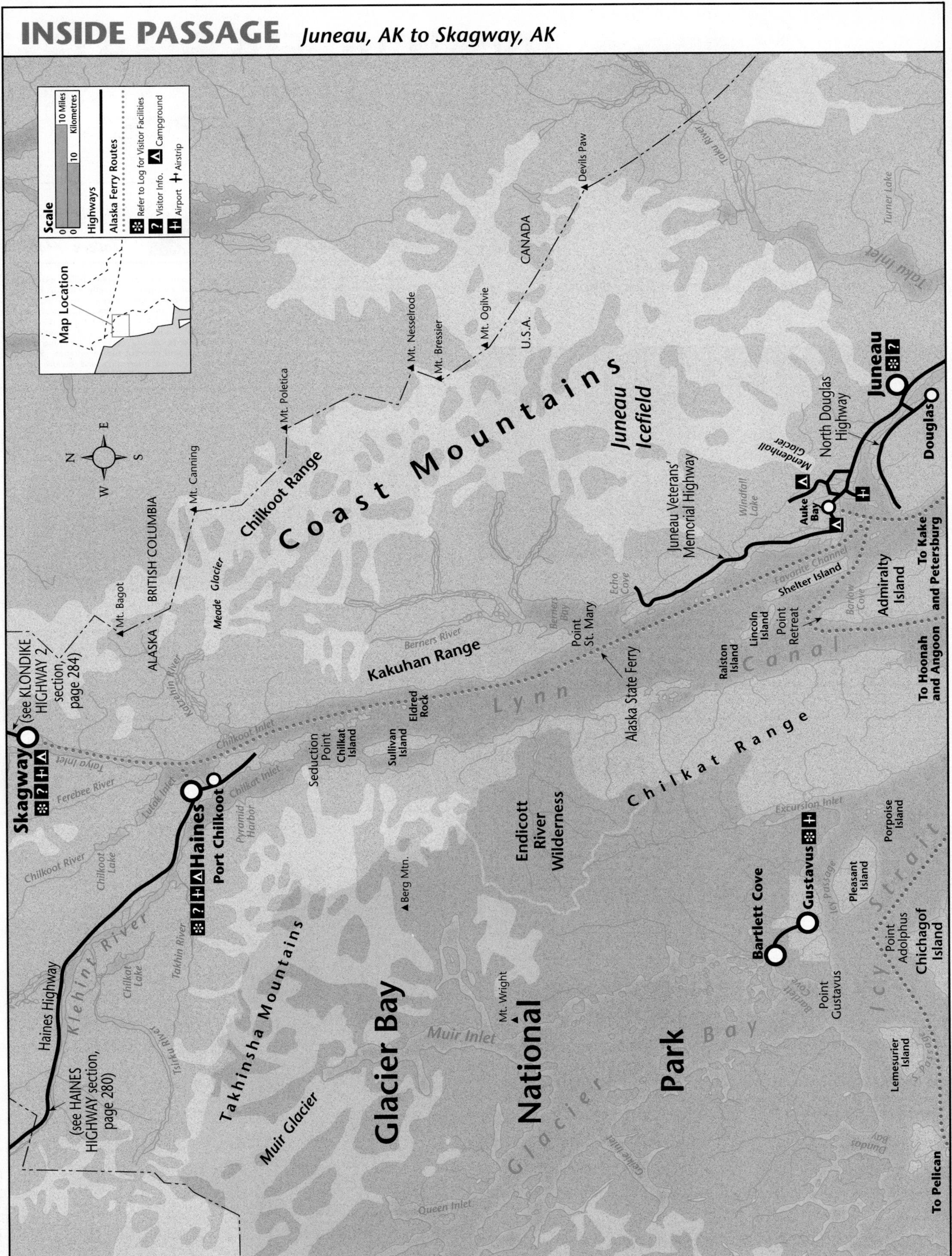
Scale
0 10 Miles
0 10 Kilometres
Highways
Alaska Ferry Routes
Refer to Log for Visitor Facilities
Visitor Info.
Campground
Airport
Airstrip
Map Location
N
E
S
W
CANADA
U.S.A.
BRITISH COLUMBIA
ALASKA
Devils Paw
Mt. Ogilvie
Mt. Bressier
Mt. Nesselrode
Mt. Poletica
Mt. Canning
Mt. Bagot
Coast Mountains
Juneau Icefield
Chilkoot Range
Meade Glacier
Kakuhan Range
Berners River
Berners Bay
Echo Cove
Point St. Mary
Juneau Veterans' Memorial Highway
Windfall Lake
Mendenhall Glacier
North Douglas Highway
Juneau
Douglas
Auke Bay
Taku River
Taku Inlet
Turner Lake
Favorite Channel
Shelter Island
Barlow Cove
Admiralty Island
To Kake and Petersburg
To Hoonah and Angoon
Lincoln Island
Point Retreat
Ralston Island
Lynn Canal
Alaska State Ferry
Eldred Rock
Sullivan Island
Chilkat Island
Seduction Point
Chilkoot Inlet
Taiya Inlet
Chilkat Inlet
Skagway
(see KLONDIKE HIGHWAY 2 section, page 284)
Katzehin River
Ferebee River
Lutak Inlet
Haines
Port Chilkoot
Pyramid Harbor
Chilkoot River
Chilkoot Lake
Klehini River
Takhin River
Chilkat Lake
Haines Highway
(see HAINES HIGHWAY section, page 280)
Tsirku River
Takhinsha Mountains
Muir Glacier
Berg Mtn.
Endicott River Wilderness
Chilkat Range
Excursion Inlet
Gustavus
Bartlett Cove
Icy Passage
Pleasant Island
Porpoise Island
Point Adolphus
Chichagof Island
Icy Strait
Point Gustavus
Lemesurier Island
Dundas Bay
To Pelican
Glacier Bay National Park
Mt. Wright
Muir Inlet
Glacier Bay
Geikie Inlet
Queen Inlet

INSIDE PASSAGE
CELEBRATING 50 YEARS OF THE MILEPOST®

Above (seal)— MV Blue Star. *(Alaska Pictorial Service)*
Below— *Photo of Juneau, AK, from 1959 edition.*
(Juneau Chamber of Commerce)

CRUISE INSIDE PASSAGE—ALASKA, aboard MV "BLUE STAR"
Sightseeing, fishing, camera "hunting" on fabulous Lynn Canal. Salt water excursions to SKAGWAY—JUNEAU—HAINES—GLACIER BAY—TRACY ARM—BARANOF HOT SPRINGS TAKU GLACIER. Staterooms, hot meals, coffee, bait & tackle included in rates. See & photograph whales, sea lions, porpoise, live glaciers, ice bergs, salmon harvest. Picnic & hunt driftwood, berries, wildflowers on secluded beaches & islands. Steady-riding catamaran "BLUE STAR" sleeps 14. For reservations & rates write: MV Blue Star, 65 Willoughby Ave., Juneau, Alaska—or Haines agent, Craft Shop, Box 75, Haines, Alaska.

Alaska Visitors Assoc.

ALASKA FERRIES

This year (1963) is the inaugural year for the State of Alaska's new ferry system from Prince Rupert, B.C. to Haines and Skagway, Alaska on the north through the islands and fjords of Southeast Alaska. Three vessels costing in the neighborhood of $4 million each have been built to provide six days a week service through this long famous "Inside Passage" to provide travelers with an alternate route to the Alaska Highway and Southeast Alaska residents a direct connection to that highway for the first time.

We invite You — Visit Skagway

You'll be greeted when you arrive in Skagway. Some of us always take time to dress up in old-time costumes to meet the boats and ferries—just to give you a warm welcome and a bit of the historic atmosphere of our old town.

Every boat night we stage the "Days of '98" show for you with the "Shooting of Dan McGrew", old-time gambling games with phoney money, skits, dancing and old-fashioned fun.

Visit our '98 museum.
See historic buildings.
Browse in our shops.
Talk with pioneers.
Hike old trails.
Ride the famed White Pass & Yukon R.R.

There are only 700 of us. Each of us invite you to visit Skagway. We love visitors.

THE CITY OF SKAGWAY

Land of the 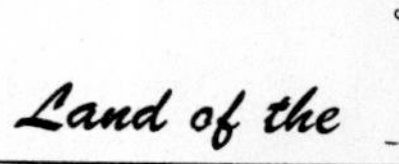  *Totem Pole*

Southeastern Alaska, the "panhandle" and home of the totem pole, extending from Skagway to the Portland Canal to the south of Ketchikan, is justly famous for the gorgeous scenery and protected island waterways of the Inside Passage. From Skagway, scene of the gold rush over the Chilkoot Pass in '98, through modern and prosperous Juneau, the Capital City of Alaska, and on to Ketchikan "Alaska's First City"—(from the south) where lumbering and fisheries are thriving industries, there is a never-ending pageant of forested islands, deep and mysterious fiords, silvery cascades tumbling down from the snow-capped mountains of the Coast Range, and colorful Indian villages. Remote salmon canneries are visited by some steamships, and the interesting and bizarre totem poles may be seen at Sitka, the old Russian capital, Wrangell, and Ketchikan.

Haines and Port Chilkoot
—HOTELS—

The Hotel Halsingland, Port Chilkoot, overlooking Portage Bay, on the Lynn Canal. Spacious steam-heated rooms with convenient bathroom facilities, dining room celebrated for the excellence of its food, and a comfortable lounge room. Special boat excursions arranged to pretty Kochu Island, where you may spend a day or a week in wild surroundings, with splendid views of both the Rainbow and Davidson Glaciers. Hilma and Clarence Mattson, proprietors.

Chilkoot Inn, Port Chilkoot, situated on a beautiful site between the Lynn Canal and the Chilkat River, overlooking the Canal. Rooms, with or without bath, from $3.00 single and $4.00 double. A good night's sleep is insured by "Sealy" innerspring mattresses. Meals served family-style. The Chilkoot Inn is headquarters for Haines, Juneau and Skagway car and passenger ferry service. Owners and operators are Mrs. S. E. Homer & Son.

Skagway, AK. (Hougen's Ltd. photo)

(Continued from page 685)

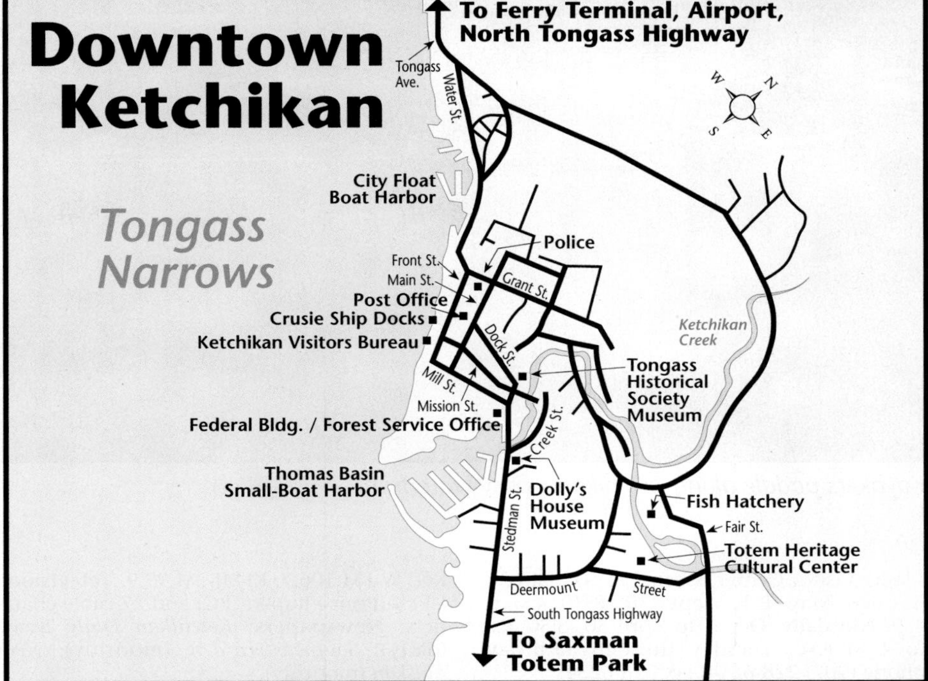

Alaska's Natives, famous for their totem poles, weaving, beading, basketry and dancing, occupied the region long before Vitus Bering discovered Alaska in 1741.

Russia controlled Alaska from the turn of the 19th century until 1867, centering its extensive fur-trading empire in Sitka, the Russian capital of Alaska. Sitka was a port of international trade, controlling trading posts from California to the Aleutians, and was considered cultured because of European influence. At a time when San Francisco was a crude new boom town, Sitka was called the "Paris of the Pacific."

Commercial interest in southeastern Alaska declined with the fur trade, following Alaska's purchase by the United States. Interest in Southeast was rekindled by the salmon industry as canneries were established, the first at Klawock in 1878. Salmon canning peaked in the late 1930s and then declined from overfishing.

But the first significant white populations arrived because of gold. By the time thousands of gold seekers traveled through the Inside Passage in 1898 to Skagway and on to Canada's Klondike (sparking interest in the rest of Alaska), the largest gold ore mine of its day, the Treadwell near Juneau, had been in operation since 1884.

Juneau became Alaska's capital in 1906, and Southeast remained Alaska's dominant region until WWII, when military activity and the Alaska Highway shifted emphasis to Anchorage and Fairbanks.

Additional population growth came to Southeast with new timber harvesting in the 1950s. Increased government activities, as a result of Alaska statehood in 1959, brought even more.

Today, visitors enjoy the many wonders the area offers. Spectacular scenery greets the eye at every turn. Glacier Bay National Park and Preserve, Misty Fiords and Admiralty Island national monuments, Mendenhall Glacier at Juneau, LeConte Glacier near Petersburg and the Stikine River near Wrangell are just a few of the attractions.

The Inside Passage is the last stronghold of the American bald eagle. More than 20,000 eagles reside in the region, and sightings are frequent. Humpback and killer whales, porpoises, sea lions and seals are often observed from ferries, cruise ships and charter boats. Bear viewing opportunities are offered at Pack Creek on Admiralty Island and Anan Creek near Wrangell.

Activities and attractions include Russian and Tlingit dance performances; salmon bakes; historical melodramas; festivals; glaciers and icefield flightseeing; sportfishing and wilderness adventure tours by kayak, canoe and raft. Among other attractions are museums, totem poles, hiking trails, colorful saloons and fine dining.

The following sections describe the communities and attractions of Southeast with the exception of Hyder, which is accessible by highway from British Columbia and is included in the CASSIAR HIGHWAY section.

Ketchikan

(See map, pages 687–688)

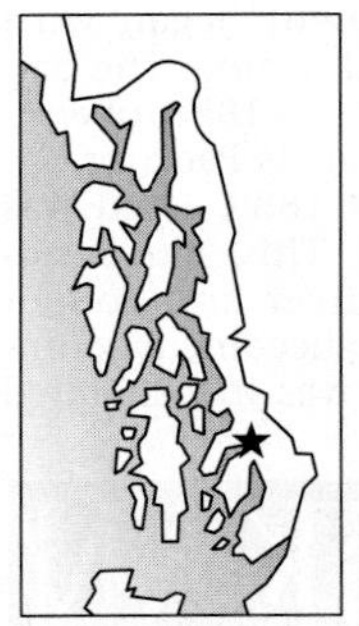

Located on Revillagigedo Island, 235 miles/378 km south of Juneau, 90 miles/145 km north of Prince Rupert, BC. **Population:** Ketchikan Gateway Borough and city, 15,082. **Emergency Services: Alaska State Troopers**, phone (907) 225-5118. **City Police**, phone (907) 225-6631, or 911 for all emergency services. **Fire Department, Ambulance** and **Ketchikan Volunteer Rescue Squad**, phone (907) 225-9616. **Hospital**, Ketchikan General at 3100 Tongass Ave., phone (907) 225-5171. **Maritime Search and Rescue**, call the Coast Guard at (907) 225-5666.

Visitor Information: Ketchikan Visitors Bureau office is located on the downtown dock, open during daily business hours and weekends May through September. Write them at 131M Front St., Ketchikan 99901; phone (907) 225-6166 or (800) 770-2200; fax (907) 225-4250. U.S. Forest Service office for Misty Fiords National Monument and Ketchikan Ranger District is located at 3031 Tongass Ave.; open 8 A.M. to 4:30 P.M. weekdays; phone (907) 225-2148. The Southeast

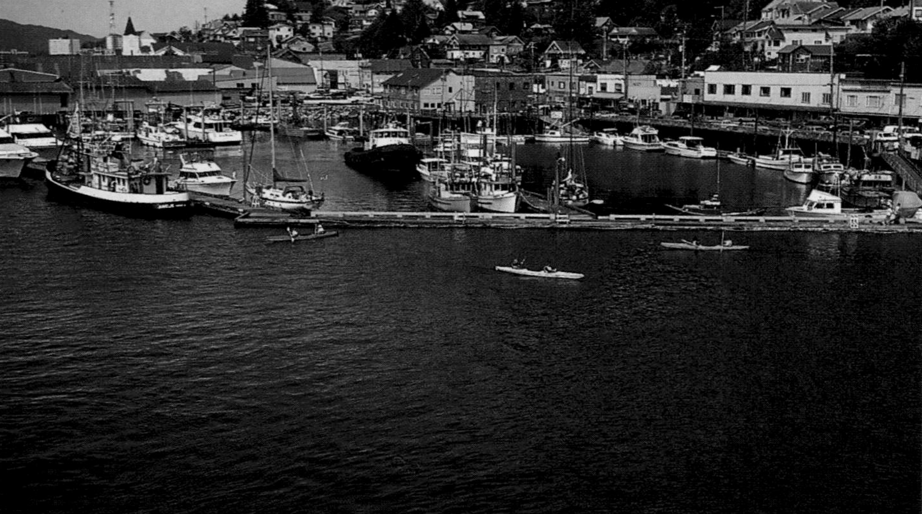

Kayakers paddle along Ketchikan's busy waterfront. (© Michael N. Dill)

Alaska Visitor Center, located at 50 Main St., is open May 1 to Sept. 30, 8:30 A.M to 4:30 P.M. daily; Oct. 1 to April 30, 8:30 A.M. to 4:30 P.M., Tuesday through Saturday; phone (907) 228-6214, fax 228-6234.

Elevation: Sea level. **Climate:** Rainy. Yearly average rainfall is 162 inches and snowfall is 32 inches. Average daily maximum temperature in July 65°F/18°C; daily minimum 51°F/11°C. Daily maximum in January 39°F/4°C; daily minimum 29°F/-2°C. **Radio:** KTKN 930, KRBD-FM 105.9, KGTW-FM 106.7, KFMJ-FM 99.9. **Television:** CFTK (Prince Rupert, BC) and 27 cable channels. **Newspapers:** *Ketchikan Daily News* (daily); *Southeastern Log* (monthly); *New Alaskan* (monthly).

Private Aircraft: Ketchikan International Airport on Gravina Island; elev. 88 feet/27m; length 7,500 feet/2,286m; asphalt; fuel 100LL, A. Ketchikan Harbor seaplane base downtown; fuel 80, 100, A.

Ketchikan is located on the southwest side of Revillagigedo (ruh-vee-uh-guh-GAY-doh) Island, on Tongass Narrows opposite Gravina Island. The name Ketchikan is derived from a Tlingit name, Kitschk-Hin, meaning the creek of the "thundering wings of an eagle." The creek flows through the town, emptying into Tongass Narrows. Before Ketchikan was settled, the area at the mouth of Ketchikan Creek was a Tlingit Indian fish camp. Settlement began with interest in both mining and fishing. The first salmon cannery moved here in 1886, operating under the name of Tongass Packing Co. It burned down in August 1889. Gold was discovered nearby in 1898. This, plus residual effects of the gold, silver and copper mines, caused Ketchikan to become a booming little mining town. It was incorporated in 1901.

As mining waned, the fishing industry began to grow. By the 1930s more than a dozen salmon canneries had been built; during the peak years of the canned salmon industry, Ketchikan earned the title of "Salmon Capital of the World." Overfishing caused a drastic decline in salmon by the 1940s, and today only 4 canneries and a cold storage plant operate. Trident Seafoods Corp., owner of Ketchikan's oldest and largest cannery, provides lodging for 200-plus salmon processors in a floating bunkhouse. An industry under development is the commercial harvest of abalone near Ketchikan.

As fishing reached a low point, the timber industry expanded. The first sawmill was originally built in 1898 at Dolomi on Prince of Wales Island to cut timber for the Dolomi Mine. It was dismantled and moved to Ketchikan and rebuilt in 1903. A large pulp mill was constructed in 1953 at Ward Cove, a few miles northwest of town. It closed in 1997.

Tourism is a very important industry here; Ketchikan is Alaska's first port of call for cruise ships and Alaska Marine Highway vessels.

Ketchikan is Alaska's southernmost major city and the state's fourth largest (after Anchorage, Fairbanks and Juneau). The closest city in British Columbia is Prince Rupert. Ketchikan is a linear waterfront city, with much of its 3-mile/5-km-long business district suspended above water on pilings driven into the bottom of Tongass Narrows. It clings to the steep wooded hillside and has many homes perched on cliffs that are reached by climbing long wooden staircases or narrow winding streets.

The area supports 4 public grade schools, 4 parochial grade schools, a junior high school, 2 high schools and the University of Alaska Southeast campus.

ACCOMMODATIONS/VISITOR SERVICES

Accommodations in Ketchikan include bed and breakfasts (see ads following) and several motels/hotels. Major downtown lodgings include Best Western's The Landing (800/428-8304), Gilmore Hotel (800/275-9423), Ingersoll Hotel (800/478-2124), Super 8 Motel (800/800-8000) and the Westmark Cape Fox Lodge (800/544-0970). The major shopping areas are downtown and the west end.

Blueberry Hill Bed & Breakfast. Experience Ketchikan's historic past by staying in a charming historic home in downtown Ketchikan. Very spacious, comfortable rooms with relaxing ambiance. Super convenient to museums, galleries, shops and restaurants. Treat yourself to scrumptious homemade breads, scones and muffins. 500 Front Street, Ketchikan, AK 99901. Phone (907) 247-BLUE. [ADVERTISEMENT]

Ketchikan AYH hostel is located at the First United Methodist Church, Grant and Main streets; write Box 8515, Ketchikan, AK 99901; phone (907) 225-3319 (summer

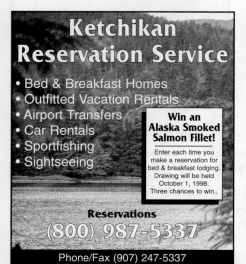

only). Open June 1 to Aug. 31, the hostel has showers, sleeping pads (bring sleeping bag) and kitchen facilities. Check-in time is 6 to 11 P.M. Reservations strongly recommended. Cost is $8 per night for members (AYH membership passes may be purchased at the hostel), $11 for nonmembers.

There are 5 campgrounds (4 public campgrounds and a private resort) north of the city on North Tongass Highway and Ward Lake Road. See highway logs in this section. Dump station located at Ketchikan Public Works office, 2 blocks north of state ferry terminal. Contact the visitors bureau for brochure on RV use and parking. ▲

TRANSPORTATION

Air: Daily scheduled jet service is provided from the Ketchikan International Airport by Alaska Airlines to other Southeast cities, Anchorage and Seattle, WA. Commuter and charter service to other Southeast communities is available via Ketchikan Air, Taquan Air and Promech Air. Taquan Air (800/770-8800) has daily scheduled flights to Prince Rupert, BC.

Airport terminal, across Tongass Narrows on Gravina Island, is reached via shuttle ferry (10-minute ride, $2.50 per person, $5 per vehicle, one way) departing from the ferry terminal on North Tongass Avenue at half-hour intervals. Airport ferry terminal on Revillagigedo Island is 2.7 miles/4.3 km from downtown. Airporter service between downtown and airport is $11 to $12 (includes ferry fare). Shuttle and taxi service is also available between downtown and the airport.

Ferry: Alaska Marine Highway vessels connect Ketchikan with all mainline southeastern Alaska port cities, Prince Rupert, BC, and Bellingham, WA. There are also daily state ferry connections via the MV *Aurora* between Ketchikan and Metlakatla (1 hr. 15 min.), and Ketchikan and Hollis (2 hrs. 45 min.). The *Aurora* also sails between Ketchikan and Stewart/Hyder (11 hrs. 15 min.) 2 to 3 times a month in summer.

Terminal building with waiting room, ticket counter and loading area is on North Tongass Avenue (Highway), 2 miles/3.2 km north of downtown. Phone (907) 225-6181. Foot passengers can walk from the ferry to a post office, restaurant and grocery store if stopover time permits. Taxi service available.

Bus: Daily municipal bus service, stops at every stop within the city limits at half-hour intervals; schedules available at visitors bureau. Fares is $1 one way.

Car Rental: Available at airport and downtown locations from Alaska Car Rental (907) 225-5000 and Payless Car Rental (907) 225-6004.

Taxi: Taxi cabs meet ferry and airport arrivals.

Highways: North Tongass and South Tongass highways and Ward Lake Road (see logs this section).

Cruise Ships: Ketchikan is the first port of call for many cruise ships to Alaska. Cruises depart from U.S. West Coast ports and Vancouver, BC. Two cruise lines depart from Ketchikan.

Private Boats: Two public docks downtown, Thomas Basin and City Float, provide transient moorage. In the West End District, 1 mile/1.6 km from downtown, Bar Harbor has moorage, showers. No gas available. Permits required. Moorage space in Ketchikan is limited; all private boats should contact the harbormaster's office at (907) 225-3610 prior to arrival to secure a spot.

ATTRACTIONS

Ketchikan's waterfront is the center of the city. A narrow city on a mountainside, Ketchikan has a waterfront that runs for several miles and consists of docks, stores on pilings, seaplane floats, 3 picturesque boat harbors, a seaplane base and ferry terminal. There is constant activity here as seaplanes take off and vessels move in and out of the harbor. Walking-tour maps are available at the visitors bureau and at the ferry terminal.

Fish Pirate's Daughter, a well-done local musical-comedy melodrama, portrays Ketchikan's early fishing days, with some of the city's spicier history included. Performed 7 P.M. and 8:45 P.M. Fridays, July through August. Contact First City Players, 338 Main St., phone (907) 225-4792 or 225-2211, for more information. Admission fee.

Tongass Historical Museum, located in the Centennial Building on Dock Street in central downtown, explores the rich culture of the Tlingit, Haida and Tsimshian people, and the history of settlement in this area, in the exhibit "Salmon, Cedar and Gold: The History of Ketchikan." Open in summer from 8 A.M to 5 P.M. daily. Winter (October to mid-May) hours are 1–5 P.M. Wednesday through Friday, 1–4 P.M. Saturday and Sunday. The Raven Stealing the Sun totem stands just outside the entrance. Salmon viewing platforms. Admission fee is $2 for adults; free admission Sunday afternoons. Phone (907) 225-5600 for more information.

Creek Street is Ketchikan's famous "red-light district," where Black Mary, Dolly, Frenchie and others plied their trade for over half a century until 1954. Nearly 20 houses lined the far side of Ketchikan Creek; many have been restored. There are also several art and gift shops. Dolly's House, a former brothel, is open during the summer. Admission charged. Creek Street is a wooden street on pilings that begins just past the bridge on Stedman (South Tongass Highway). Watch for salmon in the creek below the bridge in late August. Also look for the metal sculpture paying tribute to the salmon; it's a local landmark.

Totem Heritage Center, at 601 Deermount St., houses 33 totem poles and fragments retrieved from deserted Tlingit and Haida Indian villages. This national landmark collection comprises the largest exhibit of original totems in the United States. Facilities include craft exhibits, craft classes for children and reference library. Gift shop, craft demonstrations and guided tours during summer months. Summer admission fee $4. No admission charged off-season. Summer hours are 8 A.M. to 5 P.M. daily. Winter hours (October through mid-May) are 1–5 P.M. Tuesday through Friday. Phone (907) 225-5900.

Deer Mountain Hatchery is located in the city park within walking distance of downtown (take the bridge across Ketchikan Creek from the Totem Heritage Center). The hatchery produces about 100,000 king, 150,000 coho, 30,000 rainbow trout and 6,500 steelhead fingerlings annually. Observation platforms and information signs provide education on the life cycles of salmon. Open from 8 A.M. to 4:30 P.M. daily late May to late September.

Ketchikan has a large collection of totems. *(© Lee Foster)*

The Ketchikan Mural on Stedman Street was created by 21 Native artists in 1978. The 125-by-18-foot/38-by-4-m design is collectively entitled *The Return of the Eagle.*

Fourth of July is a major celebration in Ketchikan. The Timber Carnival takes place over the Fourth of July with events such as ax throwing and chopping, power saw bucking and a tug-of-war. There are also fireworks, the Calamity Race (by canoe and kayak, bicycle and on foot), a parade and other events.

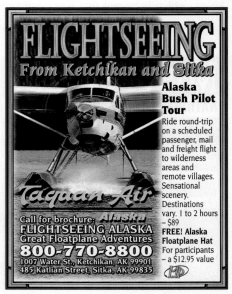

The Blueberry Arts Festival, in August, features arts and crafts, the performing arts and plenty of homemade blueberry pies, blueberry crêpes, blueberry cheesecakes and other culinary delights. Events include a slug race, bed race, pie-eating contest, trivia contest and spelling bee. A juried art show, fun-run and dance are also part of the festival. Sponsored and coordinated by the Ketchikan

Area Arts and Humanities Council, Inc. (338 Main St., Ketchikan 99901; 907/225-2211).

Saxman Totem Park, Milepost 2.5 South Tongass Highway, is included in local sightseeing tours. Open year-round. There is no admission charge, but there is a fee for guided tour (offered May through September). The totem park has 28 totems. The tour includes demonstrations at the Carving Center and performances by the Cape Fox Dancers at the Beaver Tribal House. For more information on hours, tours and events, phone the Cape Fox Tours office at (907) 225-5163, ext. 301 or 304.

Totem Bight community house and totem park, Milepost 9.9 North Tongass Highway, contains an excellent model of a Tlingit community house and a park with 13 totems.

Misty Fiords National Monument/ Ketchikan Ranger District, Tongass National Forest. 3.2 million acres surrounding Ketchikan and nearby communities. Pristine coastal rain forest, glacially carved fjords, waterfalls, wildlife, fishing, spectacular geologic features. Includes 2.3 million acres of the National Monument Wilderness. Forest Service maintains approximately 60 miles of trails. 30 cabins available for public rental—most are accessible by floatplane or boat. Other recreational attractions include Ward Lake Recreation Area (3 campgrounds, day-use area, trails), Naha Dock and Trail, Margaret Bay fish pass and bear viewing. Sea kayaking is a popular means of exploring the coastlines and venturing into remote areas. Cabin reservations, maps, brochures and trip planning assistance available from the Southeast Alaska Visitors Center, 50 Main St., Ketchikan, AK 99901. Phone (907) 228-6214, fax (907) 228-6234. Internet: www.ktn.net/usfs/ketchikan.

Charter boats: About 120 vessels operate out of Ketchikan for half-day, all-day or overnight sightseeing or fishing trips and transport to USFS public-use cabins and outlying communities. See advertisements this section and check with the visitors bureau or at the marinas.

Fishing lodges and resorts in the area offer sportfishing for steelhead, salmon, halibut, trout, lingcod and red snapper. Resorts near Ketchikan include Misty Fiords Lodge, Salmon Falls Resort and Yes Bay Lodge. There are several fishing lodges on Prince of Wales Island, including Waterfall Resort, which is housed in a renovated fish cannery.

Charter planes operate from the airport and from the waterfront on floats and are available for fly-in fishing, flightseeing or service to lodges and smaller communities.

Picnic areas include Settlers Cove by Settlers Cove Campground, **Milepost 18.2** North Tongass Highway; Refuge Cove, **Milepost 8.7** North Tongass Highway; Rotary Beach at **Milepost 3.5** South Tongass Highway; and Grassy Point and Ward Lake, **Milepost 1.1** Ward Lake Road.

Hiking trails include Deer Mountain trail, which begins at the corner of Fair and Deermount streets. The 3-mile/4.8-km, 3,001-foot/915-m ascent gives trekkers an excellent vantage of downtown Ketchikan and Tongass Narrows. Good but steep trail. Access to Deer Mountain cabin, the only USFS public-use cabin accessible by trail from Ketchikan. Cabin reservations are required. Perseverance Lake trail, 2.4 miles/3.8 km from Ward Lake to Perseverance Lake. Connell Lake trail, about 1.5 miles/2.4 km along north shore of Connell Lake, is in poor condition. Silvis Lakes trail, about 2 miles/3.2 km up to Lower Silvis Lake and picnic area. Trail continues to Upper Silvis Lake and Deer Mountain trail, but is very difficult. An easy and informative 1-mile/1.6-km nature trail circles Ward Lake.

Southeast Alaska Visitor Center, 50 Main St., features exhibits on Native cultures, ecosystems, resources and the rainforest in Southeast Alaska. Also 13-minute, award-winning "Mystical Southeast Alaska" audio visual program and Alaska Public Lands trip planning room. Open 8:30 A.M. to 4:30 P.M., daily in summer, Tuesday through Saturday in winter.

AREA FISHING: Check with the Alaska Dept. of Fish and Game at 2030 Sea Level Dr., Suite 215, or phone (907) 225-2859 for details on fishing in the Ketchikan area. Good fishing spots range from Mountain Point, a 5-mile/8-km drive from Ketchikan on South Tongass Highway, to streams, lakes, bays, and inlets 50 miles/80 km away by boat or by air. Half-day and longer charters and skiff rentals available out of Ketchikan. There are fishing resorts at Yes Bay, Clover Pass and at the entrance to Behm Canal (Salmon Falls Resort); and 13 fishing resorts on Prince of Wales Island. Fish include salmon, halibut, steelhead, Dolly Varden, cutthroat and rainbow, arctic grayling, eastern brook trout, lingcod and rockfish; shellfish include dungeness crab and shrimp. Ketchikan has 2 king salmon derbies, a silver salmon derby and a halibut derby in summer.

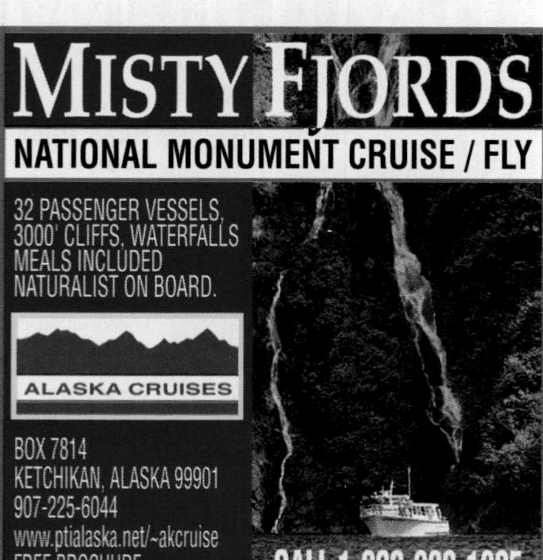

North Tongass Highway Log

The North Tongass Highway is 18.4 miles/29.6 km long with 15.2 miles/24.5 km paved. It begins at the corner of Mill Street and Stedman (at the Federal Bldg.) and proceeds north to Ward Lake Road, Totem Bight, Clover Pass and Settlers Cove Campground.

0 Federal Building on left with area information display. Proceeding on Mill Street.

0.1 (0.2 km) Southeast Alaska visitor center with information on federal lands in Alaska.

0.2 (0.3 km) Turning right onto Front Street, cruise ship dock on left where passengers disembark from major ships.

0.3 (0.5 km) Tunnel. North of this, Front Street becomes Water Street.

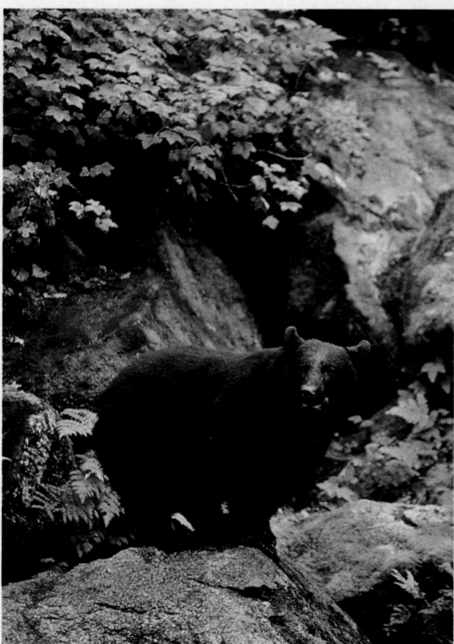

Black bear photographed in Tongass National Forest. (© Bruce M. Herman)

0.5 (0.8 km) City Float on left. Note older vessels.

0.7 (1.1 km) Highway turns left, then right, and becomes Tongass Avenue.

1.2 (1.9 km) West end shopping area begins.

1.7 (2.7 km) Bar Harbor boat basin on left.

2 (3.2 km) Ketchikan General Hospital on right, Ketchikan Ranger Station and Misty Fiords National Monument on left, northbound.

2.3 (3.7 km) Ferry terminals for Alaska Marine Highway.

2.4 (3.9 km) Main branch post office.

2.6 (4.2 km) Carlanna Creek and bridge.

2.7 (4.3 km) Airport shuttle ferry.

3.2 (5.1 km) Almer Wolfe Memorial viewpoint of Tongass Narrows. 24-hour RV parking. Airport terminal is visible across the narrows on Gravina Island.

4 (6.4 km) Hillside on right is a logged area, an example of clear-cut logging method and regrowth.

4.4 (7.1 km) Alaska State Troopers and Highway Dept.

5.5 (8.8 km) Small paved viewpoint overlooking Tongass Narrows and floatplane dock.

6 (9.6 km) Ward Cove Cannery next to road. Cannery Creek and bridge.

6.8 (10.9 km) **Junction** with Ward Lake Road (see log this section).

7 (11.3 km) Ward Creek and bridge; Ketchikan sawmill, owned by Ketchikan Pulp Co.; see **Mile 7.8**.

7.3 (11.7 km) **WARD COVE.** Post office, gas station and grocery.

7.8 (12.5 km) Ketchikan Pulp Co. pulp mill was built in 1953; it closed in 1997.

8.7 (14 km) Refuge Cove state recreation site with 14 picnic sites.

9.4 (15.1 km) Mud Bight; "float houses" rest on mud at low tide and float during high tide.

9.9 (15.9 km) Totem Bight state historical

park; parking area, restrooms and phones. A short trail leads through the woods to Totem Bight community house and totem park. A striking setting. Don't miss this!

10.8 (17.4 km) Grocery store and gas station.

12.9 (20.8 km) Scenic viewpoint overlooking Guard Island Lighthouse built in 1903 and manned until 1969 when finally automated.

14.2 (22.9 km) Clover Pass Resort turnoff. Left, North Point Higgins Road leads 0.6 mile/1 km to turnoff to resort; food, lodging, camping.

Left, then immediately right, is Knudson Cove Road, leading 0.4 mile/0.6 km to Knudson Cove Marina with public float, boat launch and boat rentals. Road rejoins North Tongass Highway at **Milepost 14.8.** ▲

14.8 (23.8 km) Knudson Cove Marina to left 0.5 mile/0.8 km.

15.2 (24.5 km) Pavement ends.

16.6 (26.8 km) Salmon Falls Resort; private fishing lodge with restaurant and boat rentals.

18.2 (29.3 km) Settlers Cove state campground, parking area and picnic area; 13 tent/trailer campsites; 2 covered picnic pavilions flanked by 12 picnic units are along the beach on either side of the campground. Camping fee $6/night. Tables, water, pit toilets. Open year-round. Good gravel beach for kids and boats. To right of beach is **Lunch Creek** (pink salmon in August), falls and trail. ▲

18.4 (29.6 km) Road end.

Ward Lake Road Log

An 8.3-mile/13.4-km road off the North Tongass Highway leading to Ward Lake Recreation Area. (Access to Harriet Hunt Road to Harriet Hunt Lake at **Milepost 7.1**). Motorists and hikers should be aware of private property boundaries, posted by Cape Fox Corp. (CFC), and logging and trucking activities. Campers should be aware of USFS regulations in the Ward Lake Recreation Area: Camping is restricted to developed campgrounds and limited to 7 nights.

0 Right turn northbound from North Tongass Highway at **Milepost 6.8.**

0.1 (0.2 km) Tongass National Forest boundary.

0.4 (0.6 km) Small scenic turnout on right. Pond with lily pads surrounded by pine in muskeg.

0.7 (1.1 km) Signal Creek USFS campground on left; 24 sites with tables, water and pit toilets. Open Memorial Day to Sept. 30. Camping fee charged. Situated among large trees on the shore of Ward Lake. One end of a nature trail around Ward Lake begins here and encircles the lake; it is a 30- to 50-minute easy walk on well-graveled path. Some campsites can be reserved; phone (800) 280-2267 (CAMP) or TDD (800) 879-4496. ▲

0.9 (1.4 km) Beginning of Perseverance Lake trail on right. Trailhead is within 100 feet of CCC Campground with parking across road. Site of WWII Aleut internment camp. The 2.4-mile/3.9-km boardwalk trail leads to **Perseverance Lake** (elev. 518 feet/158m); brook trout fishing.

1 (1.6 km) CCC (or Three C's) USFS campground entrance on right; 4 campsites, camping fee, open mid-May to October. ▲

1.1 (1.8 km) Ward Creek bridge. Grassy Point USFS picnic area. Several walk-in picnic sites with tables and shelters near road. Footbridge across Ward Creek leads to **Ward Lake** trail; good fly-fishing for steelhead, salmon and Dolly Varden.

Ward Creek and **Ward Lake**, cutthroat and Dolly Varden year-round, best March to June; steelhead to 16 lbs.; silver salmon to 18 lbs. and pink salmon to 5 lbs., August to October. (Hatchery-raised coho salmon; bring head of tagged fish to ADF&G.)

1.3 (2.1 km) Ward Lake USFS picnic area; beach, parking area and picnic shelters. One end of nature trail around Ward Lake.

2.9 (4.7 km) Right, Last Chance USFS campground; 19 spaces, tables, pit toilets, water, camping fee. Open mid-June to Sept. 30. ▲

3 (4.8 km) Connell Lake Road, on right, a narrow gravel road extending 0.6 mile/1 km to Connell Lake Reservoir. At Mile 0.4 Connell Lake Road, a bridge passes over large pipe, which carries water from the reservoir to the pulp mill at Ward Cove. Connell Lake trail at reservoir.

3.3 (5.3 km) Turnout.

7.1 (11.4 km) **Junction** with 2.4-mile/3.9-km Harriet Hunt Lake Road. Harriet Hunt Lake Road dead ends at **Harriet Hunt Lake** Recreation Area; parking area, pit toilets; rainbow to 20 inches, May to November. Road is on Cape Fox Corp. lands. Watch for logging trucks.

8.3 (13.4 km) End public highway. Private logging road begins.

South Tongass Highway Log

The 12.9-mile/20.8-km South Tongass Highway leads from the corner of Mill and Stedman streets south to Saxman Totem Park. First 8.5 miles/13.7 km are paved.

0 Federal Building on right.

0.1 (0.2 km) Ketchikan Creek and bridge. Beginning of Creek Street boardwalk on left next to bridge.

0.2 (0.3 km) Thomas Street begins on right, a boardwalk street where old-time businesses are located. Thomas Basin boat harbor.

0.5 (0.8 km) Cannery and cold storage plant.

0.9 (1.4 km) U.S. Coast Guard base.

2.5 (4 km) **SAXMAN** (pop. 389) was founded in 1896 by Tlingit Alaska Natives and named after a Presbyterian missionary who served the Tlingit people. The Native village of Saxman has a gas station and convenience store and is the site of Saxman Totem Park. Developed by Cape Fox Corp., this popular attraction includes a carving center and tribal house. Guided tours available from Cape Fox Tours.

2.7 (4.3 km) Gas station.

3.5 (5.6 km) Rotary Beach, public recreation area, contains a shelter and table.

5 (8.1 km) Mountain Point, suburb of Ketchikan. Parking area and access to good salmon fishing from shore in July and August.

5.6 (9 km) Boat ramp on right.

8.2 (13.2 km) Herring Cove bridge and sawmill. Private hatchery for chum, king and coho salmon on short road to left; no tours.

8.5 (13.7 km) Pavement ends.

8.8 (14.2 km) Whitman Creek and bridge.

9 (14.5 km) Scenic turnout on right. Note different shades of green on trees across the water. Light green are cedar; medium, hemlock; and the darker are spruce. Species grow intermixed.

10.3 (16.6 km) Left, scenic waterfall.

11 (17.7 km) Scenic turnout.

11.8 (19 km) Lodge.

12.9 (20.8 km) Road ends, view of power plant, an experimental sockeye salmon hatchery (no tours) and an abandoned cannery. Two-mile/3.2-km walk up gravel road leads to Lower Silvis Lake picnic area. Trail continues to Upper Silvis Lake and joins Deer Mountain trail, which connects to John Mountain National Recreation trail. Trail between Upper and Lower Silvis lakes is very difficult.

Metlakatla

(See map, page 687)

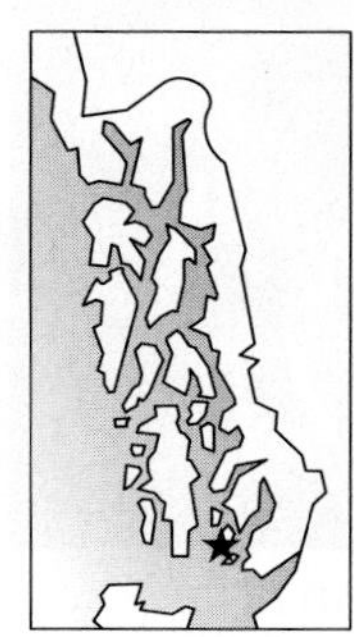

Located on the west coast of Annette Island, 15 miles/24 km south of Ketchikan, Southeastern Alaska's southernmost community. **Population:** 1,673. **Emergency Services: Police, fire** and **ambulance,** emergency only, phone 911. **Visitor Information:** Tours to Metlakatla depart daily from Ketchikan; reservations are required. Contact the Community Tour Office at (800) 643-4898 for scheduling information. The Metlakatla tour and salmon bake operates from early-May to October. A permit from Metlakatla Indian Community is required for long-term visits to Annette Island.

Elevation: Sea level. **Climate:** Mild and moist. Summer temperatures range from 36°F/12°C to 65°F/18°C; winter temperatures from 28°F/-2°C to 44°F/7°C. Average annual precipitation is 115 inches: October is the wettest month with a maximum of 35 inches of rainfall. Annual snowfall averages 61 inches. **Radio:** KTKN 930 (Ketchikan). **Television:** 20 channels via cable.

Private Aircraft: Floatplane services.

Transportation: Air—Charter and scheduled floatplane service. **Ferry**—Daily state ferry service in summer via MV *Aurora* from Ketchikan; crossing time 1 hour 15 minutes.

Overnight accommodations, restaurant, groceries and banking services available.

Metlakatla was founded in 1887 by William Duncan, a Scottish-born lay minister, who moved here with several hundred Tsimshian Indians from a settlement in

Boy poses with eagle totem at Metlakatla, AK. (© Roy Corral)

British Columbia after a falling-out with church authorities. Congress granted reservation status and title to the entire island in 1891, and the new settlement prospered under Duncan, who built a salmon cannery and sawmill.

Today, fishing and lumber continue to be the main economic base of Metlakatla. The community and island also retain the status of a federal Indian reservation, which is why Metlakatla has the only salmon fish traps in Alaska. (Floating fish traps were outlawed by the state shortly after statehood.)

The well-planned community has a town hall, a recreation center with an Olympic-sized swimming pool, a post office, 2 lumber mills and cold storage. The Metlakatla Indian Community is the largest employer in town, with retail and service trades the second largest. Many residents also are commercial fishermen. Subsistence activities remain an important source of food for residents, who harvest seaweed, salmon, halibut, cod, clams, dungeness crab and waterfowl.

There is a replica of the William Duncan Memorial Church here; the original was destroyed by fire in 1948. The Duncan Museum is located in the original cottage occupied by Father William Duncan until his death in 1918.

Alaska has 3 indigenous Native groups—Eskimo, Indian and Aleut. Southeastern Alaska is home to Tlingit, Haida and Tsimshian Indians. — *ALASKA A TO Z*

Prince of Wales Island

(See map, page 688)

Includes Coffman Cove, Craig, Hollis, Hydaburg, Kasaan, Klawock, Naukati,Thorne Bay and Whale Pass

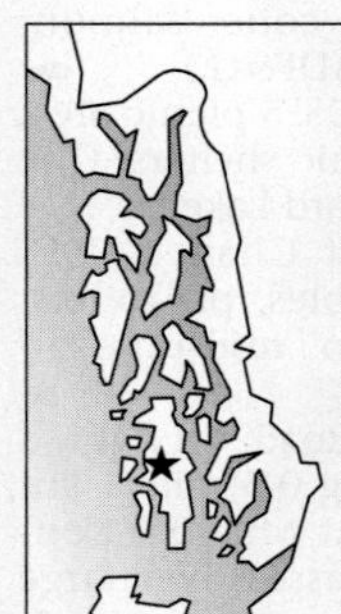

About 15 miles/24.1 km west of Ketchikan. **Population:** Approximately 5,200. **Emergency Services: Alaska State Troopers**, in Klawock, phone (907) 755-2918. **Police**, in Craig, phone (907) 826-3330; in Klawock, phone (907) 755-2777; emergencies only, phone 911; **Village Public Safety Officers** in Thorne Bay, phone (907) 828-3905; in Hydaburg, phone (907) 285-3321; in Klawock, phone (907) 755-2906. **Ambulance**, Hydaburg emergency response team, phone 911. **Health Clinics** for all emergencies, phone 911; in Craig, phone (907) 826-3257; in Klawock, phone (907) 755-4800; in Thorne Bay, phone (907) 828-3906; in Hydaburg, phone (907) 285-3462. **Maritime Search and Rescue**, call the Coast Guard at (800) 478-5555.

Visitor Information: Prince of Wales Island Chamber of Commerce, P.O. Box 497, Craig, AK 99921; phone (907) 826-3870, fax (907) 826-2926.

Elevation: Sea level to 4,000 feet/1,219m. **Climate:** Mild and moist, but variable due to the island's size and topography. Rainfall in excess of 100 inches per year, with modest snowfall in winter at lower elevations. **Radio:** KRSA 580 (Petersburg), KTKN 930 (Ketchikan), KRBD-FM 90.1 (Ketchikan). **Television:** Via satellite. **Newspaper:** *Island News* (Thorne Bay, weekly).

Private Aircraft: Klawock airstrip, 2 miles/3.2 km northeast; elev. 50 feet/15m; length 5,000 feet/1,524m; lighted and paved. Seaplane bases adjacent to all the largest communities and in several bays.

Heavily forested with low mountains, Prince of Wales Island measures roughly 135 miles/217 km north–south by 45 miles/72 km east–west. The third largest island under the American flag (Kodiak is second, the Big Island of Hawaii is first), it is 2,231 square miles/5,778 square km. The 6 communities with city status on the island—Craig (the largest with 1,946 residents), Klawock, Thorne Bay, Hydaburg, Coffman Cove and Kasaan are connected by road, as are the other 3 smaller communities of Hollis, Naukati and Whale Pass. Not connected by road are **PORT PROTECTION** and **POINT BAKER**, both at the northwest tip of the island (see *The ALASKA WILDERNESS GUIDE* for details on these communities).

Prince of Wales Island has been the site of several lumbermills and mining camps since the 1800s. But it was salmon that led to permanent settlement on the island. Klawock was the site of one of Alaska's first canneries, built in 1878. In the following years, some 25 canneries were built on the island to process salmon. Today, logging is prevalent on the island.

Prince of Wales Island offers uncrowded backcountry, fishing for salmon and trout, kayaking and canoeing waters, opportunities for viewing wildlife (black bears, Sitka black-tailed deer, bald eagles), adequate visitor facilities and some historical attractions. Most of the island is national forest land. The Forest Service manages 5 large, designated wilderness areas on Prince of Wales Island. There are also some Native corporation and private land holdings. Respect No Trespassing signs.

There are several roadside fishing spots on Prince of Wales Island. See the road logs in this section for details. Lakes and streams support red, pink and silver salmon, cutthroat, rainbow trout and Dolly Varden.

ACCOMMODATIONS/VISITOR SERVICES

Prince of Wales Island has several hotels, lodges, rental cabins and bed and breakfasts. See community descriptions on pages 701–703.

There are also more than 20 USFS cabins (accessible by plane, boat or on foot) available for public use; reservations and a fee are required. Contact the USFS office in Ketchikan or the local ranger districts at Craig (907/826-3271) and Thorne Bay (907/828-3304).

There are private campgrounds with hookups at Coffman Cove and Klawock. There is one developed USFS campground on the island—Eagle's Nest on Thorne Bay Road ($8 camping fee)—and several undeveloped dispersed camping sites accessible via the island road system. See road logs this section. ▲

TRANSPORTATION

Air: All communities on the island are served by floatplane, most daily. Wheel planes land at Klawock. Daily scheduled service by Taquan Air (800/770-8800) and Pro–Mech Air (800/860-3845) from Ketchikan.

Ferry: Alaska state ferry MV *Aurora* from Ketchikan to Hollis; crossing time 2 hours, 45 minutes. Phone Craig office at (907) 826-3432, Hollis terminal at (907) 530-7115.

Vehicle rental: Car rentals available in Craig at Wilderness Rent-A-Car (phone 800/949-2205); in Coffman Cove from Kingfisher Charters (907/329-2235); in Klawock from Log Cabin RV Park & Resort (800/544-2205); in Thorne Bay from the Thorne Bay Company (907/828-3330). RV rentals from POW Island Getaway in Craig (800/465-7511).

Highways: Prince of Wales Island has the most extensive road network in Southeast Alaska. Over 1,000 miles of road allow access to most areas of the island. The island's 8 main roads are logged in this section. See also the map on page 688.

Rollo Pool Photo

DRIVER CAUTION: Watch for heavily loaded logging trucks while driving; they have the right-of-way. CB radios are helpful. Carry a spare tire and spare gas. (Gas is available in Coffman Cove, Hydaburg, Craig, Klawock, Whale Pass and Thorne Bay.) Use turnouts and approach hills and corners on your side of the road. Spur roads are *NOT* recommended for large RVs or cars with trailers. Some side roads may be closed intermittently during logging operations or highway construction. Watch for signs posted when roads are closed and expect delays.

Taxi: No free public transport meets the ferry at Hollis. Arrangements with taxis can be made. According to the chamber of commerce, the fare ranges from about $25 per person to $50–$60 to charter a taxi (which is usually a van for several people). Available in Klawock from Irish Setter Cab (907/755-2217), Jackson Cab (907/755-2557) and Screaming Eagle (907/755-2699). Available in Craig from Chief Wiah Cab (907/826-3375) and Craig–Klawock Taxi (907/826-3077).

Charters for whale watching may be arranged at Coffman Cove and Klawock on Prince of Wales Island. (© Robin Brandt)

ATTRACTIONS

El Capitan Cave, located just north of Whale Pass off the North Island Road. People have been visiting El Capitan Cave for many years. El Capitan's pit is one of the deepest known in the U.S. Northern Prince of Wales has extensive limestone cave systems. Significant scientific discoveries have been found in these caves, including grizzly bear bones dating back 12,295 years, and black bear bones dating back 11,565 years.

There is a steep trail (more than 365 steps) leading to the cave entrance. Because of damage to cave formations, a gate has been installed to regulate visitation. There is open visitation to the gate some distance within the cave; guided tours beyond the gate. The 2-hour guided tours departed at 8 A.M., 10 A.M., 1 P.M. and 3 P.M., Wednesdays through Sundays, from mid-May to September in 1997; call for 1998 schedule. For guided tours, group size is limited to 6. For reservations write Thorne Bay Ranger District, Box 19001, Thorne Bay 99919; phone (907) 828-3304. There are vault toilets, a government dock and a floatplane and boat tie-up at this U.S. Forest Service-administrated site.

AREA FISHING: Most fish in streams on the island are anadromous (travel upstream to spawn). Try **Klawock Lake** for trout and salmon; **Klawock River** downstream from the hatchery is good for trout, steelhead and salmon; **Thorne River** for Dolly Varden, trout and salmon; and **Sarkar River** for trout, steelhead and salmon. Fresh and saltwater guiding services are available.

World-class saltwater sportfishing abounds immediately offshore and throughout the many smaller islands surrounding Prince of Wales Island. Most communities have boat ramps. For those traveling without a boat, quality half-, full- and multi-day fishing trips are available through many of the local charter operators. Ocean fishing for salmon is best in July and early August for kings (chinook), August and September for coho, July, August and September for pinks, and August and September for chum. 100-lb. halibut, 50-lb. king salmon and 15-lb. coho salmon are not considered uncommon in the sport season, usually May through August due to the weather and fish migration patterns. Abundant bottom fish, including lingcod and red snapper, reside throughout these waters year-round.

COMMUNITY DESCRIPTIONS

COFFMAN COVE (pop. 254), 53 miles/85 km north of Klawock, a 2½-hour drive from Hollis. Formerly one of the largest independent logging camps in Southeast, Coffman Cove is now a small hamlet. Recreation includes hunting (deer and bear), good freshwater and saltwater fishing, boating, hiking. Charters for fishing and whalewatching available. Canoe Lagoon Oyster Co. here is the state's oldest and largest oyster producer; fresh oysters available locally.

Coffman Cove has a general store, liquor and gift shop (both open daily), gas pump, playground and ballfield, showers and laundry facilities, and a campground. Tire repair is available. There is a dock and a small beach with access to salt water for canoes and cartop boats. Oceanview RV Park has 14 full-hookup sites on the beach. Rental cabins are available. EMTs dispatch from Riggin' Shack. ▲

CRAIG (pop. 1,946), 31 miles/50 km from Hollis, is on the western shore of Prince of Wales Island. The original townsite, on Craig Island, is now connected to Prince of Wales by a short causeway. **Visitor information:** Craig City Hall, phone (907) 826-3275, open weekdays 8 A.M. to 5 P.M.; U.S. Forest Service office, open weekdays 8 A.M. to 5 P.M., phone (907) 826-3271; Prince of Wales Chamber of Commerce, phone (907) 826-3870.

Craig has several hotels and lodges, including Haida Way Lodge downtown (800/347-4625); and Sunnahae Lodge (907/826-4000) and Shelter Cove Lodge (888/826-FISH), which specialize in fishing. There are also bed and breakfasts, including Lupine Pens'ion B&B (907/826-3851). Sporting goods, fishing, hunting and camping suppplies, gifts, seafood, grocery and health stores available. There are a laundromat and showers, liquor stores, bars, beauty and barber shops, a library and 2 banks (one with automatic teller machine). Craig has a school, grades K through 12, and an indoor community swimming pool.

Gas, propane, RV supplies, towing and auto repair available. Free RV dump facilities on Cold Storage Road. Contact City Public Works at (907) 826-3405 during business hours for key. Evenings and weekends, contact the police department at (907) 826-3330.

Craig Primary Health Care Facility, commonly known as the Craig clinic, is located just up the hill from the city municipal offices and is currently managed by the Craig Health Corp. The facility is approximately 4,300 square feet and is occupied by a physician and staff, public health nurses and the Craig Native health aide.

Physician services are generally available 24 hours a day except for brief periods of time when the physician is unavailable. An emergency room is provided at the clinic for treatment, minor surgery and stabilization of patients. Medications, emergency pharmaceuticals and medical supplies are available through the clinic (by doctor's prescription only; no retail pharmacies are located on the island). The clinic can take routine X-rays. Clinic hours are 9 A.M. to 5 P.M. Monday through Saturday in the summer; 9 A.M. to 5 P.M. weekdays in winter. Emergency Medical Services are available full-time at 911, or call Craig PD at (907) 826-3330. The Craig Native health aide and public health nurse are available weekdays from 9 A.M. to 4 P.M. Craig also has a chiropractic office and 2 dental clinics.

Craig has 2 modern boat harbors, North Cove and South Cove, located on either side of the causeway, a seaplane float, fuel dock, city dock and float, 2 fish-buying docks and an old cannery dock. The Craig harbormaster's office, with public showers and restrooms, is located on the corner close to South Cove; phone (907) 826-3404, VHF Channel 16.

Craig was once a temporary fish camp for the Tlingit and Haida Natives of the area. In 1907, with the help of local Natives, William D. Craig Millar established a mildcure station known as Fish Egg for nearby Fish Egg Island. The Tlingit name for Fish Egg Island is "Sheenda" and the townsite was "Sheensit," which is now used by the Native Shaan-Seet Corp. Between 1908 and 1911, a permanent saltery and cold storage facility, along with about 2 dozen homes, were built on the city's present location and named for founder Craig Millar. In 1912, the post office

★ Craig (continued) ★

★ Kasaan ★

★ Serving the Island ★

Our Island Neighbor
★ Ketchikan ★

Point Baker
Labouchere Bay
Whale Pass
Coffman Cove
Edna Bay
Naukati
Thorne Bay
Craig
Klawock
Kasaan
Hollis
Hydaburg

Prince of Wales Island

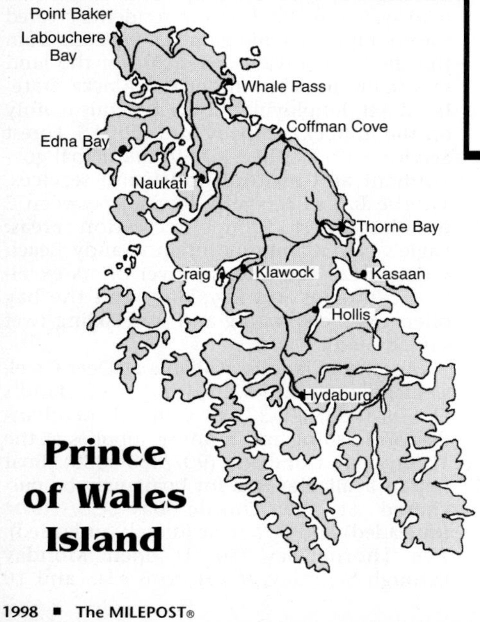

With thousands of miles of graveled byways and uninhabited shoreline, Prince of Wales offers unparalleled opportunity to explore the largest Island of Southeast Alaska.

- ☐ Examine totem poles
- ☐ Spelunk in one of the most extensive cave networks in North America
- ☐ Explore sweeping beaches
- ☐ Kayak unspoiled waterways and watch whales play
- ☐ Hike into remote cabins or view panoramic mountains and pristine glacial lakes
- ☐ Enjoy world class sport fishing both in fresh and salt water
- ☐ Learn how salmon are reared at the hatchery or see them migrate upstream through various fish passes

Whatever your recreation desires, we can accommodate you, so begin *your* Alaska wilderness experience on beautiful Prince of Wales, the island of contrasts.

was established, E.M. Streeter opened a sawmill and Craig constructed a salmon cannery. Both businesses peaked during WWI. Craig was incorporated in 1922, and grew throughout the 1930s, with some families relocating from the Dust Bowl.

Although the salmon industry has both prospered and floundered over the years, fishing and fish processing still account for an important part of area employment. In recent years timber harvesting on the island has contributed many jobs in logging and timber processing. The Viking Lumber Co. mill, located between Craig and Klawock, provides year-round employment, producing moulding, window and door stock for the domestic market, and high-grade cants for export. The mill also produces wood chips for the manufacture of pulp. Despite recent legislation, timber will continue to be a viable though reduced economic influence on the island's economy for many years. Mining, transportation and tourism have the potential to become major employers in the foreseeable future. Construction and government jobs will increase as the island and its economy develop.

Craig is the home port of many commercial fishing and charter sportfishing boats due to its proximity to the fertile fishing grounds off the west coast of the island. Halibut, coho and chinook salmon, lingcod and red snapper (yelloweye) are the primary target species. Craig and Klawock host the annual Craig–Klawock King Salmon Derby from April to July 3, followed by a big Fourth of July parade and celebration. In late July the P.O.W. Chamber of Commerce sponsors its annual fair and logging show with booths, fair entrants and a logging competition.

In 1996 the Healing Heart totem pole was raised in Craig. The totem was carved by Tsimshian master carver Stan Marsden in memory of his son. The totem is 46½ feet/14m tall and is carved from a red cedar tree more than 500 years old.

HOLLIS (pop. 111), 25 road miles/40 km from Klawock, 35 nautical miles/56 km west of Ketchikan. Hollis was a mining town with a population of 1,000 from about 1900 to 1915. In the 1950s, Hollis became the site of Ketchikan Pulp Co.'s logging camp and served as the base for timber operations on Prince of Wales Island until 1962, when the camp was moved to Thorne Bay. Recent state land sales have spurred the growth of a small residential community here.

NOTE: Although Hollis is identified in the state ferry schedules as the port of call on Prince of Wales Island for the MV *Aurora* from Ketchikan, the ferry actually docks at Clark Bay, about 2 miles/3.2 km from Hollis.

HYDABURG (pop. 406), 36 miles/58 km from Hollis, 45 miles/72 km from Craig. Hydaburg was founded in 1911, and combined the populations of 3 Haida villages: Sukkwan, Howkan and Klinkwan. President William Howard Taft established an Indian reservation on the surrounding land in 1912, but, at the residents' request, most of the land was restored to its former status as part of Tongass National Forest in 1926. Hydaburg was incorporated in 1927, 3 years after its people became citizens of the United States.

Most of the residents are commercial fishermen, although there are some jobs in construction and the timber industry. Subsistence is also a traditional and necessary part of life here. Hydaburg has an excellent

Hydaburg is the southernmost road-accessible community on Prince of Wales Island. (© David J. Job)

collection of restored Haida totems. The totem park was developed in the 1930s by the Civilian Conservation Corps, which brought in poles from the three abandoned Haida villages. There is also good salmon fishing here in the fall.

Four boardinghouses provide rooms and meals for visitors. Groceries, hardware and sundry items available locally. There are a gift shop, gas station, public telephones, video store and cafe. Cable television is available.

KASAAN (pop. 41), a small city located at the head of Kasaan Bay, was connected to the road system in 1996. It is approximately 16 miles/25.6 km south of Thorne Bay. There are a bed and breakfast, small cafe, a post office, a school and boat docks.

KLAWOCK (pop. 759), 24 miles/39 km from Hollis. Klawock originally was a Tlingit Indian summer fishing village; a trading post and salmon saltery were established here in 1868. Ten years later a salmon cannery was built—the first cannery in Alaska and the first of several cannery operations in the area. Over the years the population of Klawock, like other Southeast communities, grew and then declined with the salmon harvest. The local economy is still dependent on fishing, along with timber cutting and sawmilling. A fish hatchery operated by Prince of Wales Hatchery Assoc. is located on Klawock Lake, very near the site of a salmon hatchery that operated from 1897 until 1917. Visitors are welcome. Klawock Lake offers good canoeing and boating.

Recreation here includes good fishing for salmon and steelhead in Klawock River, saltwater halibut fishing, and deer and bear hunting. Klawock's totem park contains 21 totems—both replicas and originals—from the abandoned Indian village of Tuxekan (developed by the Civilian Conservation Corps in 1938–40). A 5-year restoration project to restore and replace totems in the park was begun in 1995.

Groceries and gas are available in Klawock. Automatic teller machine located in A&P grocery store. Accommodations available at Columbine Inn (907/755-2287) and Log Cabin Resort (800/544-2205). Log Cabin Resort also offers full-hookup RV sites on the beach. Meals at Dave's Diner. Charters for fishing and whalewatching from lemire Charters (907/826-3007). ▲

NAUKATI (pop. 250). Located 61 miles/97.6 km north of Hollis, Naukati was established as a mining camp, and is currently a logging camp for Ketchikan Pulp Co. Naukati West is privately owned. The Naukati Connection has groceries, gas, propane, liquor, diesel, boat rentals, and tire repair; open daily (phone 907/629-4104). There is a school and a floatplane dock. The EMS squad can be reached on CB channel 16, VHF Channel 16 or phone (907) 629-4283 or 629-4234.

THORNE BAY (pop. 650), 59 miles/95 km from Hollis. Thorne Bay was incorporated in 1982, making it one of Alaska's newest cities. The settlement began as a logging camp in 1962, when Ketchikan Pulp Co. (a subsidiary of Louisiana Pacific Corp.) moved its operations from Hollis. Thorne Bay was connected to the island road system in 1974. Camp residents created the community—and gained city status from the state—as private ownership of the land was made possible under the Alaska Statehood Act. Employment here depends mainly on the lumber company and the U.S. Forest Service, with assorted jobs in municipal government and in local trades and services. Thorne Bay is centrally located between 2 popular Forest Service recreation areas: Eagle's Nest Campground and Sandy Beach picnic area. The Thorne River offers excellent canoeing and kayaking, and the bay offers excellent sailing and waterskiing (wet suit advised).

Accommodations available at Deer Creek Cottage (800/830-3393) and McFarland's Floatel (888/828-3335). General merchandise and fishing and hunting supplies at the Thorne Bay Company (907/828-3330). Boat rentals available. Fuel for boats may be purchased at the Thorne Bay Co. float (unleaded) and JC's float (diesel, unleaded). The Thorne Bay Co. is open Monday through Saturday, 9 A.M. to 6 P.M., and 10

A.M. to 4 P.M. on Sunday. JC's is open daily, 7 A.M. to 6 P.M. Aviation fuel available through Petro Alaska. City-operated RV dump station. Facilities include boat dock (with potable water, power, sewer pumpout station and fish cleaning facilities), cement boat-launch ramp, helicopter landing pad, and floatplane float and parking facility. ▲

WHALE PASS (pop. 92), accessible by 7-mile/11.3-km loop road from **Milepost 39.7** North Island Road, was the site of a floating logging camp on Whale Passage. The camp moved out in the early 1980s, but new residents moved in with a state land sale. The community has a small grocery store and gas pump; cabins and freezer space available. There is also a school, post office and floatplane dock. Accommodations at Northend Cabin (907/846-5315). Good fishing on the loop road into Whale Pass.

Hollis–Klawock–Craig Highway Log

This highway, 31.5 miles/50.7 km long, begins at the ferry landing at Hollis and heads west through Klawock then south to Craig, taking motorists through the temperate rainforest environment typical of Southeast Alaska. It is a wide, paved road. Posted speed is 35 to 50 mph/56 to 80 kmph. Many roads and trails off highway lead to private property; please respect barricades and No Trespassing signs. *CAUTION: Watch for logging trucks.*

Distance from Hollis (H) is followed by distance from Craig (C). Physical mileposts show distance from Craig.

H 0 C 31.5 (50.7 km) Alaska Marine Highway, Hollis ferry terminal at Clark Bay, open during ferry arrivals and departures only (phone 907/530-7115, or in Craig 826-3432). Pay phone; no other services.

H 0.2 (0.3 km) **C 31.3** (50.4 km) Clark Bay subdivision access to right.

H 1.4 (2.3 km) **C 30.1** (48.4 km) Left 0.3 mile to Hollis townsite. School and USFS office, city harbor and float, floatplane dock, post office, telephone; no other services.

H 2 (3.2 km) **C 29.5** (47.5 km) Alaska Power and Telephone power plant and Alascom satellite station to left. Hollis Fire Department and EMS garage to right.

H 2.4 (3.9 km) **C 29.1** (46.8 km) **Maybeso Creek**, cutthroat; Dolly Varden; pink and silver salmon; steelhead run begins in mid-April. Pools offer the best fishing. Walking good along streambed but poor along bank. Watch for bears.

H 4.2 (6.8 km) **C 27.3** (43.9 km) Turnout left, view of mouth of the Harris River.

H 4.8 (7.7 km) **C 26.7** (43 km) Head left for lower Harris subdivision.

H 5.2 (8.4 km) **C 26.3** (42.3 km) Turnout, one of several slide-damaged areas from October 1993 storm that dumped 11 inches of rain in 24 hours.

H 6.4 (10.3 km) **C 25.1** (40.4 km) Entering Tongass National Forest.

H 6.5 (10.5 km) **C 25** (40.2 km) Head left for upper Harris subdivision.

H 7.7 (12.4 km) **C 23.8** (38.3 km) Turnout, slide damage repaired.

H 8.4 (13.5 km) **C 23.1** (37.2 km) USFS hiking trail to **Harris River** fishing: cutthroat; steelhead run mid-April; salmon and Dolly Varden run beginning in mid-July. Easy walking on the gravel bars in the middle of 1.3-mile/2.1-km-long river.

H 8.5 (13.7 km) **C 23** (37 km) Turnout, slide damage repaired.

H 10.5 (16.9 km) **C 21** (33.8 km) **Junction** with Hydaburg Road; see log this section.

H 11.2 (18 km) **C 20.3** (32.7 km) USFS trailhead for 20 Mile Spur Trail (approximately 3 miles/4.8 km long).

H 11.3 (18.2 km) **C 20.2** (32.5 km) Harris River bridge.

H 12.4 (20 km) **C 19.1** (30.7 km) End of Harris River valley. Island divide is here at 500 feet/152m elev.; streams now flow west. Turnout state DOT gravel storage area.

H 12.6 (20.3 km) **C 18.9** (30.4 km) Leaving Tongass National Forest.

H 13.6 (21.9 km) **C 17.9** (28.8 km) East end of Klawock Lake, about 7 miles/11 km long and up to 1 mile/1.6 km wide. Lake borders the road on the left at several places. Private property; contact Klawock–Heenya Corp. in Klawock.

H 16.1 (25.9 km) **C 15.4** (24.8 km) Turnout left, boat launch for Klawock Lake.

H 16.2 (26.1 km) **C 15.3** (24.6 km) 35 mph/56 kmph curve; believe the sign.

H 17.6 (28.3 km) **C 13.9** (22.4 km) Turnout left, view of Klawock Lake.

H 20.1 (32.3 km) **C 11.4** (18.3 km) Turnout right, view of Klawock Lake.

H 22 (33.7 km) **C 9.5** (16.9 km) Klawock Lake Hatchery, operated by the Prince of Wales Assoc. The hatchery produces sockeye, coho and steelhead. Visitors welcome Monday through Friday, 8 A.M. to 4:30 P.M.

H 22.1 (35.6 km) **C 9.4** (15.1 km) Klawock-Heenya Trailer Court to right; turnout left for trail access to Klawock River sportfishing.

H 22.2 (35.7 km) **C 9.3** (15 km) Turnout left, access to Klawock River fishing.

H 22.3 (35.9 km) **C 9.2** (14.8 km) Turnout left, access to Klawock River fishing.

H 22.4 (36 km) **C 9.1** (14.6 km) Turnout left, access to Klawock River fishing.

H 23.3 (37.5 km) **C 8.2** (13.2 km) Belltower Mall, grocery store, liquor store, gift shop and Papa's Pizza.

H 23.4 (37.7 km) **C 8.1** (13 km) **Junction** with Big Salt Road; access to Thorne Bay, Kasaan, Coffman Cove, Naukati, Whale Pass and the north end of the island.

H 23.5 (37.8 km) **C 8** (12.9 km) Turnoff right, services available.

H 23.7 (38.1 km) **C 7.8** (12.6 km) Fireweed Lodge to left, St. John's by the Sea Catholic Church to right. St. John's was designed and built with local lumber and materials by the local church community. The stained-glass designs, representing all known Native tribes, were designed and built by local artists. This is a "must-see" structure. Father Jim Blaney and Sister Tish welcome the opportunity to show the church. Good eagle viewing in Klawock River estuary during salmon season.

H 23.8 (38.3 km) **C 7.7** (12.4 km) Loop road with 21 totem poles.

H 23.9 (38.5 km) **C 7.6** (12.2 km) Klawock-Heenya Corp. offices.

H 24.2 (38.9 km) **C 7.3** (11.7 km) **Klawock River** bridge spans tidal estuary where river meets salt water.

H 24.3 (39.1 km) **C 7.2** (11.6 km) Klawock Fuels (gas and diesel), Alaska State Troopers and Alaska Dept. of Fish and Game to left. Alesha Roberts Center.

H 24.5 (39.4 km) **C 7** (11.3 km) Leaving village of **KLAWOCK.** State troopers in building on left.

Craig is home port for many commercial fishing and charter sportfishing boats. (© David J. Job)

H 24.6 (39.6 km) **C 6.9** (11.1 km) Turnoff right to Phoenix log sort yard, Phoenix shop and Klawock Indian Corp. dock. Ocean-going vessels load locally harvested logs for worldwide transport.

H 25 (40.2 km) **C 6.5** (10.5 km) Viking Lumber Co. mill; produces moulding, window and door stock for the domestic market and high-grade cants for export.

H 26.6 (42.8 km) **C 4.9** (7.9 km) Turnout right, scenic view of Klawock Inlet and San Alberto Bay.

H 27.9 (44.9 km) **C 3.6** (5.8 km) On left is landfill operated by city of Klawock. Bears can usually be seen here.

H 29.1 (46.8 km) **C 2.4** (3.9 km) Crab Creek subdivision.

H 29.3 (47.2 km) **C 2.2** (3.5 km) Crab Creek bridge.

H 29.8 (48 km) **C 1.7** (2.7 km) Shaan-Seet Trailer Court and St. Nicholas Road to left. St. Nicholas Road, which extends 14 miles/22.5 km around Port St. Nicholas, is scenic but in very poor condition.

H 30.1 (48.5 km) **C 1.4** (2.2 km) P.O.W. Chamber of Commerce on right.

H 30.2 (48.6 km) **C 1.3** (2.1 km) Craig schools to left, post office, bank and Thompson House supermarket on right.

H 30.3 (48.8 km) **C 1.2** (1.9 km) Cold Storage Road. Dump station on right, behind supermarket.

H 30.4 (48.9 km) **C 1.1** (1.8 km) North and South Cove Harbors operated by the city of Craig. Turn left for Cemetery Island, ballpark and archaeological dig.

H 30.7 (49.4 km) **C 0.8** (1.3 km) Stop sign, downtown **CRAIG.** Turn left 1 block for Craig municipal offices and city gym. Craig clinic is on left, half block past city office. End of highway is 3 blocks right.

H 31 (49.9 km) **C 0.5** (0.8 km) Road dead ends.

Wildlife on Prince of Wales Island includes Sitka black-tail deer. (© Barbara Willard)

Big Salt Road Log

Big Salt Road begins at **Milepost C 8.1** on the Hollis–Klawock–Craig Highway and extends 17.1 miles/27.5 km, ending at its junction with Thorne Bay Road. It is a gravel road with much logging traffic; scheduled for seal coating. Top speed for much of the road is 25 mph/40 kmph. Good berry picking for blueberries and huckleberries along the road.

Distance is measured from Klawock.

0 Black Bear Quick Stop: grocery store, laundromat and gas station. Dave's Diner/Restaurant.

0.1 (0.2 km) Klawock city trailer park on right with some overnight sites; obtain permits from the city clerk. A camping fee is charged. ▲

0.4 (0.6 km) Log Cabin R.V. Park & Resort: tackle store, skiff rentals, lodging and campground. ▲

0.9 (1.4 km) Airport turnoff. Pavement ends.

8.7 (14 km) Big Salt Lake, actually a saltwater body protected by small islands but permitting tidal flow in and out, is visible to the left from several spots along road. Waterfowl and bald eagles are often observed here. Wreckage of a military aircraft can be seen across lake. The plane crashed in 1969 en route to Vietnam; all on board survived.

8.9 (14.3 km) Boat ramp and canoe launching area on Big Salt Lake. If boating on this tidal lake, be aware of strong currents.

9.7 (15.6 km) **Black Bear Creek**, cutthroat; Dolly Varden; red, pink, dog and silver salmon, run mid-July to mid-September. Except for the lower 2 miles/3.2 km, creek can be fished from the bank. Best at the mouth of stream, 200 yards/183m upstream from the bridge or in large meadow, 1.5 miles/2.4 km from the mouth. Road on right leads to Black Lake. Watch for heavy equipment.

12.6 (20.3 km) **Steelhead Creek**, cutthroat; Dolly Varden; steelhead; pink, dog and silver salmon. Creek can be reached by boat through south entrance to Big Salt Lake. Lake should only be entered during high and low slack tides due to the strong tidal currents. High tide in lake is delayed 2 hours from outside waters. Bank fishing restricted by undergrowth.

15 (24.1 km) Lovely muskeg on right.

16.6 (26.7 km) Short boardwalk on right leads to **Control Lake**, cutthroat; Dolly Varden; pink and silver salmon; good red salmon stream in August. USFS cabin on other side is available for public use. Skiff docked at end of boardwalk is for registered cabin users. Wolf population in area.

17.1 (27.5 km) **Control Lake Junction.** Junction of Big Salt Road (SR 929) with Thorne Bay Road and North Island Road (FR 20). Road to Thorne Bay (log follows) to east. Road to Labouchere Bay, with access to Whale Pass and Coffman Cove, to north; see North Island Road log this section. Turn right for Eagle's Nest Campground. ▲

Thorne Bay Road Log

Thorne Bay Road extends 18 miles/29 km to Thorne Bay logging camp.

Physical mileposts show distance from Thorne Bay post office.

18 (29 km) **Control Lake Junction.** Junction with Big Salt Road and North Island Road.

16.6 (26.7 km) Eagle's Nest USFS campground; 12 sites, tables, water, hand pump, toilet and canoe launch. Camping fee $8. **Balls Lake**, cutthroat; Dolly Varden; red, pink and silver salmon. ▲

13 (20.9 km) Bridge. **Rio Roberts** and **Rio Beaver creeks**, cutthroat; pink and silver salmon. A 0.7-mile/1.1-km cedar-chip and double-plank boardwalk leads to a viewing deck overlooking falls and Rio Roberts Fish Pass.

10.7 (17.2 km) Rio Beaver Creek bridge.

6.7 (10.8 km) **Goose Creek**, cutthroat; pink and silver salmon. Excellent spawning stream. Good run of pink salmon in mid-August. Lake Ellen Road on right leads 4.5 miles/7.2 km south to Lake No. 3 USFS campsite; space to accommodate up to 2 RVs, pit toilet, 2 fire rings and 2 picnic tables. No water or garbage. Road continues beyond campsite to lake and hiking trail to Salt Chuck. Abandoned Salt Chuck Mine is located here. ▲

6.5 (10.5 km) **Thorne River** runs beside road for the next 0.5 mile/0.8 km. Cutthroat; Dolly Varden; steelhead; rainbow; red, pink, dog and silver salmon. Excellent fishing reported from **Milepost 4.9** to **2.1.**

4.9 (7.9 km) Thorne River bridge. Thorne River now follows road on right.

4.1 (6.6 km) Falls Creek.

4 (6.4 km) Gravelly Creek USFS picnic area; walk in to picnic area on the bank of Thorne River at the mouth of Gravelly Creek; 3 tables, fire rings, vault toilet and open-sided shelter. This site was logged in 1918. Note the large stumps with notches. Notches were used by old-time loggers for spring boards to stand on while sawing or chopping.

3.7 (5.9 km) Gravelly Creek.

2.1 (3.4 km) Right, mouth of Thorne River.

1.3 (2.1 km) Log sorting area. Here different species of logs are sorted for rafting and transporting to mills or for export.

1.2 (1.9 km) Log raft holding area. After logs are sorted and tied into bundles, the bundles are chained together into a raft suitable for towing by tugboat.

0.7 (1.1 km) Dump station on Shoreline Drive just past Bayview Tire; $5 charge.

0 THORNE BAY. The road extends about 10 miles/16 km beyond the community to Sandy Beach day-use area with picnic shelter, 6 tables, fire rings, vault toilet and RV parking. Good view of Clarence Strait. Road then continues north to Coffman Cove (see log on page 706).

Kasaan Road Log

This narrow road runs southeast 17.1 miles/27.3 km from Thorne Bay Road to Kasaan. Turnouts, occurring every 1/10 mile, are only noted if some other feature is present. A warning sign says to monitor CB channel 3.

Distance is measured from Thorne Bay Road Mile 6.7.

0 Turn off Thorne Bay Road just past Goose Creek. South to Kasaan.

0.4 (0.6 km) Road splits. Veer north for Kasaan, south for Forest Service campsite. Speed limit 20 mph/32 kmph. ▲

0.5 (0.8 km) Private drive next 1 mile/1.6 km. No hunting. Shake mill to south.

0.6 (1 km) Thorne Bay solid waste facility to north.

0.8 (1.3 km) Sawmill to south.

1.2 (1.9 km) Turnout north. Unnamed lake to north. Informal picnic site.

1.4 (2.2 km) Gravel pit to north.

2.1 (3.4 km) 15 mph/24 kmph curve. Turnout to north at the end of the curve. Slide area.

3.0 (4.8 km) Turnout to north. First view of the waters of Thorne Bay.

4.1 (6.6 km) Road was built around a huge rock. Keep to the right. Note tree growing on top of the rock and splitting it in half.

4.4 (7 km) Water hose to the right.

4.6 (7.4 km) Turnout to south. Informal campsite in old gravel pit.

5.3 (8.5 km) Muskeg to north. Turnout to south.

5.4 (8.6 km) 15 mph/24 kmph curve. No Hunting sign. Road splits; keep north for Kasaan.

5.5 (8.8 km) Turnout to south. Road changes to packed shot-rock Observe sign—"One lane road with pullouts."

5.6 (9 km) Turnouts to north and south. Informal campsite.

6.1 (9.8 km) Turnouts to north and south. Informal tent site.

6.5 (10.4 km) Turnout to north. Setter Lake to east.

6.7 (10.7 km) Turnout to north. View of small lake for next 0.2 mile/0.3 km.

6.9 (11 km) Turnout to south. Informal campsite.

7.1 (11.4 km) Turnout to north. Informal picnic site.

8.8 (14.1 km) Bridge over creek. Turnout to south.

9.2 (14.7 km) Turnout to north. Glimpse of Loon Lake to west.

10.2 (16.3 km) Beaver dam to south. Road crosses over a culvert.

10.5 (16.8 km) Informal picnic site to south.

10.8 (17.3 km) Good view of Tolstoi Bay. Beach access, boat portage. Informal picnic site. 10 mph/16 kmph, one-lane road for next 0.5 mile/0.8 km. Packed shot-rock ends and gravel begins.

11.6 (18.6 km) Bridges with stop signs over creek.

11.7 (18.7 km) Informal campsite to north in the old rock pit.

11.9 (19 km) Informal campsite to north in the old rock pit.

12.5 (20 km) Turnout to north. Informal campsite in the old rock pit.

12.8 (20.5 km) Turnout to north. Sign announces that surrounding forest was harvested in 1973 by Sealaska and thinned in 1993.

13 (20.8 km) Sign on a stump notes trap line 1993–94.

13.1 (21 km) Road splits. Veer south over the bridge for Kasaan. 2000 Road to north.

13.2 (21.1 km) Beaver dams can be seen along creek.

13.9 (22.2 km) Road crosses both north and south.

14.3 (22.9 km) 2300 Road to north.

14.5 (23.2 km) First view of Kasaan Bay and up Twelvemile Arm. Please remember this land is privately owned. Contact Sealaska for permission to camp.

15 (24 km) Turnout to south. Road to north.

15.2 (24.3 km) Road to north.

15.7 (25.1 km) Beautiful viewpoint of Kasaan Bay.

16.1 (25.8 km) Road to south. Note alpine ridge lines.

16.5 (26.4 km) Road to south.

16.9 (27 km) Wide turnout to south.

17.1 (27.4 km) Stop sign. Turn south for Kasaan and totem park, go straight for Dexter Wallace Harbor. To get to the totem park, turn south and head towards the waterfront, driving all the way to the end of the road. At the bed and breakfast ask Annette Thompson for permission to walk down the path and for a personal tour of the totem park.

Hydaburg Road Log

The Hydaburg Road is 24 miles/38.6 km long and begins 11 miles/17.7 km west of the Hollis main ferry terminal on the Hollis–Klawock–Craig Highway. Opened in 1983, the road has been much improved. Road construction may be under way. Some sections of the road are heavily used by logging trucks.

0 Junction with Hollis–Klawock–Craig Highway at **Milepost H 10.5.**

1.1 (1.8 km) Harris River bridge.

2.6 (4.2 km) Trailhead for One Duck 1.3-mile/2.1-km-long trail to alpine area and shelter. Contact the USFS office for more information on all trails along the Hydaburg Road.

4.6 (7.4 km) Bridge over Trocadero Creek.

8.9 (14.3 km) Cable Creek fish pass. Boardwalk to viewing area overlooking stream.

9.3 (15 km) Trocadero trailhead, gravel pullout.

9.5 (15.2 km) Trocadero picnic area. Picnic tables and fire grills; no toilets, trash service or water. Good view of Trocadero Valley.

9.9 (15.9 km) Road on left leads to Twelvemile Arm. This logging road leads to Polk Inlet. Watch for logging and construction activity.

12.3 (19.8 km) Trailhead for Soda Springs trail, 2.5 miles/4 km long.

13.9 (22.4 km) North Pass.

15.6 (25.1 km) Natzuhini logging camp.

15.9 (25.6 km) Natzuhini River bridge.

16.8 (27 km) Road winds along Natzuhini Bay.

21.9 (35.2 km) Hydaburg River bridge.

22.3 (35.9 km) Quarry Road to right.

23.6 (38 km) T-junction: right to Hydaburg, left to Saltery Point. Private land. No trespassing.

24 (38.6 km) **HYDABURG.**

North Island Road Log

Signed as USFS Road No. 20, this narrow 2-lane road leads north 79.5 miles/127.9 km from its junction with Big Salt and Thorne Bay roads near Control Lake to Labouchere Bay on the northwest corner of the island. The road has a fair to excellent gravel surfacing and some steep grades. Slow down for approaching vehicles. Posted speed is 25 mph/40 kmph. Gas is available at Whale Pass and Coffman Cove.

0 Control Lake Junction, junction with Big Salt and Thorne Bay roads near Control Lake.

3.1 (5 km) Drinking water on right (from hose).

4.8 (7.7 km) USFS Road No. 2050 leads west to upper Staney Creek/Horseshoe Hole and loops back to Road No. 20. Access to Staney Bridge campsite. ▲

7.4 (11.9 km) Rock quarry to east.

10.9 (17.5 km) USFS Road No. 2054 leads west to Staney Creek campsite, Staney Creek cabin and access to salt water. ▲

15.5 (24.9 km) **Junction** with Coffman Cove Road (see log this section).

18.4 (29.6 km) Naukati Creek.

19.2 (30.9 km) View to west of Tuxekan Island and Passage.

21 (33.8 km) Logging road leads west to Naukati Bay.

21.4 (34.4 km) Yatuk Creek bridge.

23.3 (37.5 km) **NAUKATI,** established and operating as a mining camp, is 3 miles/4.8 km west. The population has grown due to a state land sale. Liquor, grocery, gas, boat rentals and boat repair available.

CAUTION: Road narrows northbound.

26.5 (42.6 km) **Sarkar Lake** to east. Fishing and boat launch. USFS public-use cabin at east end of lake. Public toilets. Skiff docked at end of dock for registered cabin users only.

27.9 (44.9 km) Bridge over Sarkar Lake outlet to salt water. Good spot to see eagles and sea lions during salmon season.

39.7 (63.9 km) USFS Road No. 25 leads east 7 miles/11.3 km past Neck Lake to small settlement of **WHALE PASS**; groceries and gas available, 4 cabins, floatplane dock, post office and school (1 teacher, 13 grades). Whale Pass Road loops back to the main North Island Road at **Milepost 48.6.**

40 (64.4 km) View of Neck Lake to east.

48.6 (78.2 km) Whale Pass loop road to east. Whale Pass is 8 miles/12.9 km from here; Exchange Cove is 16 miles/25.7 km from here.

50.3 (80.9 km) View of El Capitan Passage and Kosciusko Island to west.

51 (82.1 km) Side road leads west 1 mile/1.6 km to USFS El Cap Work Center; access to El Capitan Cave. Public toilets.

55.6 (89.5 km) Summit of the North Island Road (elev. 907 feet/276m). Keep an eye out for highbush cranberries.

59.5 (95.8 km) Rough road, heavy truck traffic and 1-lane bridges north from here.

60.6 (97.5 km) Red Creek 1-lane bridge.

61.7 (99.3 km) Big Creek 1-lane bridge.

63.9 (102.8 km) View of Red Bay to north; Red Lake is to the south.

67.6 (108.8 km) Buster Creek 1-lane bridge.

68.3 (109.9 km) Shine Creek 1-lane bridge.

72 (115.9 km) Flicker Creek 1-lane bridge.

72.1 (116 km) Memorial Beach picnic area 1.7 miles/2.7 km north; follow signs to parking area. A short trail leads to picnic tables, pit toilet, memorial plaque and beach. Good view of Sumner Strait and Kupreanof Island. This site is a memorial to 12 victims of a 1978 air crash.

79.5 (127.9 km) **LABOUCHERE BAY,** a small logging camp (no facilities) owned and operated by Louisiana Pacific Corp. The road continues several miles and dead ends at the base of Mount Calder.

Coffman Cove Road Log

Coffman Cove Road branches off the North Island Road (No. 20) at **Milepost 15.5** and leads east and north 20.5 miles/33 km to the logging camp of Coffman Cove. Watch for heavy truck traffic; 25 mph/40 kmph. Slow down for approaching vehicles.

0 Junction with North Island Road.

4.4 (7.1 km) Side road on left (USFS Road No. 30) leads 5 miles/8 km through clear-cut and dead ends.

4.5 (7.2 km) **Logjam Creek** bridge; cutthroat and steelhead; Dolly Varden; pink, silver and sockeye salmon.

9.1 (14.6 km) **Hatchery Creek** bridge; fishing same as Logjam Creek. Trailhead for canoe route to Thorne Bay.

9.4 (15.1 km) Bumpy road on right leads 13 miles/20.9 km to USFS parking area and canoe launch (no trailers) on Luck Lake, and junctions with the 3030 Road between Coffman Cove and Thorne Bay.

12.1 (19.5 km) View of Sweetwater Lake to left. USFS access site: parking area for Sweetwater public-use cabin, located 0.5 mile/0.8 km along west shore of lake.

17 (27.4 km) Coffman Creek bridge.

19.5 (31.4 km) Chum Creek bridge.

20.2 (32.5 km) **Junction** with Luck Lake loop road.

20.3 (32.7 km) Chum Creek bridge.

20.5 (33 km) **COFFMAN COVE,** a logging and fishing community; groceries, gas, cafe, rental cabins, gifts and local fresh oysters.

Coffman Cove–Thorne Bay Road Log

The 3030 Road travels 36.1 miles/57.8 km between Coffman Cove and Thorne Bay. Leaving Coffman Cove southbound, cross Dog Creek and begin on the 3030 Road. Turnouts are frequent but are noted here only if some other feature is present. A warning sign says to monitor CB channel 20.

Distance from Coffman Cove (C) is followed by distance from Thorne Bay (T).

C **0.6** (1 km) T **35.5** (56.8 km) End of Muskeg Subdivision. Boardwalk to west is a private residence.

C **1.1** (1.8 km) T **35** (56 km) Road crosses over a small creek.

C **1.7** (2.7 km) T **34.4** (55 km) Rock pit to west. Grassy pullout to east; nice area for a picnic.

C **2.5** (4 km) T **33.6** (53.8 km) Milepost 6. Road crosses over a small creek.

C **3.3** (5.3 km) T **32.8** (52.5 km) Turnout to west. View of Clarence Strait, to the east, begins for next 0.6 mile/1 km.

C **3.6** (5.8 km) T **32.5** (52 km) Turnout to east. Nice informal campsite.

C **3.9** (6.2 km) T **32.2** (51.5 km) Turnout to east. Rock pit to west. Good view of Clarence Strait.

C **4.5** (7.2 km) T **31.6** (50.6 km) Turnout to east. Room for a small camp. Last View of Clarence Strait for 10 miles/16 km.

C **5** (8 km) T **31.1** (49.8 km) Turnout to east. Road veers to west.

C **7** (11.2 km) T **29.1** (46.6 km) Turnout to east. Beginning of Luck Lake trailhead.

C **7.3** (11.7 km) T **28.8** (46.1 km) Turnout to east. View of Luck Lake to east.

C **7.8** (12.5 km) T **28.3** (45.3 km) Turnout to east. Good view of Luck Lake to east.

C **8.5** (13.6 km) T **27.6** (44.2 km) Intersection. Turn east to Thorne Bay and Lick Creek. Turn west to Naukati (29 miles/46.4 km) and Hollis (74 miles/118.4 km). Southbound Forest Service Road 30 continues. Good informal campsite to west.

C **8.9** (14.2 km) T **27.2** (43.5 km) Road crosses over Luck Creek. Turnouts both east and west. Good salmon-watching stream late August/early September.

C **9.2** (14.7 km) T **26.9** (43 km) Milepost 45. Road crosses over creek. Road off to east.

C **9.5** (15.2 km) T **26.6** (42.6 km) Steep, narrow climb begins for next 1.2 miles/1.9 km.

C **9.7** (15.5 km) T **26.4** (42.2 km) Turnout to west. View to east of alder forest, view to west of alpine forest.

C **10.6** (17 km) T **25.5** (40.8 km) Turnout to west. Heed warning sign of 15 mph/24 kmph curves for next 0.3 mile/0.5 km.

C **11.4** (18.2 km) T **24.7** (39.5 km) Steep, narrow road continues to climb up mountainside. Good view to west of alpine forest.

C **11.6** (18.6 km) T **24.5** (39.2 km) Turnout to west. Good informal campsite. Excellent view of mountainside.

C **12.2** (19.5 km) T **23.9** (38.2 km) Turnout to west. Heed 15 mph/24 kmph curves warning.

C **12.5** (20 km) T **23.6** (37.8 km) Turnout to west. Big gravel pit to east. Good view overlooking muskeg and alpine above.

C **13.2** (21.1 km) T **22.9** (36.6) Milepost 41. Road crosses over a little creek. Good berry picking next 0.5 mile/0.8 km in season.

C **13.8** (22.1 km) T **22.3** (35.7 km) Turnout to west. View of Little Lake to the east, next 0.5 mile/0.8 km.

C **14.2** (22.7 km) T **21.9** (35 km) Turnout to east. Milepost 40.

C **14.5** (23.2 km) T **21.6** (34.6 km) Turnout to west. Road leads to gravel pit and through muskeg. Southbound intersection sign: veer west on FS 30 for Sandy Beach (16 miles/25.6 km) and Thorne Bay (22 miles/35.2 km). East is FS 3026.

C **14.6** (23.4 km) T **21.5** (34.4 km) Northbound intersection sign indicates Luck Lake (10 miles/16 km), Coffman Cove (15 miles/24 km) and Hollis (80 miles/128 km). West is FS 3026. First view of Clarence Strait.

C **15.3** (24.5 km) T **20.8** (33.3 km) Turnout to east. View of Clarence strait.

C **15.6** (25 km) T **20.5** (32.8 km) Turnout to east. Descent for next 0.3 mile/0.5 km.

C **16.3** (26.1 km) T **19.8** (31.7 km) Turnouts both east and west. Bridge over small stream. Good salmon viewing in late August and early September.

C **16.4** (26.2 km) T **19.7** (31.5 km) Turnout to east. Bridge over Big Ratz Creek.

C **17.5** (28 km) T **18.6** (29.8 km) Turnout to the east. Road to the west.

C **17.6** (28.2 km) T **18.5** (29.6 km) Turnout to west. Road to west.

C **18.2** (29.1 km) T **17.9** (28.6 km) Turnout to west. First view of Clarence Strait at sea level, continues for next 0.3 mile/0.5 km. Ratz Harbor and beach to east. Road construction 2 miles/3.2 km.

C **18.5** (29.6 km) T **17.6** (28.2 km) Road crosses over culvert. Turnout to east, with beach access. Road to west. Good informal campsite.

C **18.7** (29.9 km) T **17.4** (27.8 km) Road runs through salt marsh estuary next 0.1 mile/ 0.2 km. Turnout to west.

C **20.3** (32.5 km) T **15.8** (25.8 km) Truck crossing.

C **20.7** (33.1 km) T **15.4** (24.6 km) Bridge over small creek. Good salmon-viewing stream in early September.

C **21** (33.6 km) T **15.1** (24.2 km) Road to west. Road narrows next 1 mile/1.6 km.

C **21.6** (34.6 km) T **14.5** (23.2 km) Road to east.

C **21.8** (34.9 km) T **14.3** (22.9 km) Turnout to west. Curves for 2 miles/3.2 km. View of Clarence Strait.

C **22** (35.2 km) T **14.1** (22.6 km) Viewpoint east. Possible to see humpback and orca whales and dall porpoise. Road runs along steep mountainside for next 2 miles/3.2 km.

C **22.4** (35.8 km) T **13.7** (21.9 km) Viewpoint. In kelp beds otters may be visible.

C **24.8** (39.7 km) T **11.3** (18.1 km) Turnouts to east and west. Road narrows next 0.3 mile/0.5 km.

C **25.5** (40.8 km) T **10.6** (17 km) Road to west.

C **25.6** (41 km) T **10.5** (16.8 km) 3020 Road intersects.

C **26.9** (43 km) T **9.2** (14.7 km) Road crosses over a culvert. Turnout to east. Beach and view of Clarence Strait next 0.4 mile/0.6 km.

C **27.3** (43.7 km) T **8.8** (14.1 km) Turnout to east. Beach access.

C **28.2** (45.1 km) T **7.9** (12.6 km) Turnout to east. View of cove and beach access next 0.2 mile/0.3 km.

C **30.2** (48.3 km) T **5.9** (9.4 km) Bridge over Barren Creek. Salmon viewing. Turnout to west after bridge.

C **30.3** (48.5 km) T **5.8** (9.3 km) Turnout to west. Sandy Beach access. Firepit, outhouse, beach access, covered picnic area and trash cans. Parking to east.

C **30.9** (49.4 km) T **5.2** (8.3 km) Bridge over Slide Creek. Salmon viewing. Turnout to east. Informal campsite.

C **32.7** (52.3 km) T **3.4** (5.4 km) Milepost 22. Turnout to east. Informal campsite. Road to west.

C **35.4** (56.6 km) T **0.7**(1.1 km) FS 3018 road to west.

C **35.6** (57 km) T **0.5** (0.8 km) Road crosses over culvert and runs along marsh to the east for next 0.5 mile/0.8 km. Milepost 19. Turnout to east.

C **35.7** (57.1 km) T **0.4** (0.6 km) Creek with natural dams to east. Turnout to west.

C **36** (57.6 km) T **0.1** (0.2 km) No hunting begins southbound. Turnout to east.

C **36.1** (57.8 km) T **0** Turnout to west. Veer east for Thorne Bay. Private land and city limits begin here. See description of Thorne Bay on page 702. Turn to page 704 for log of Thorne Bay Road west to Control Lake Junction (read log backwards from Mile 0).

Wrangell

(See map, page 688)

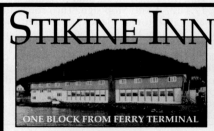

Located at northwest tip of Wrangell Island on Zimovia Strait; 6 miles/9.6 km southwest of the mouth of the Stikine River delta; 3 hours by ferry or 32 air miles/51 km southeast of Petersburg, the closest major community; and 6 hours by ferry or 85 air miles/136 km north of Ketchikan. **Population:** 2,400. **Emergency Services:** Phone 911 for all emergencies. **Police,** phone (907) 874-3304. **Fire Department** and **Ambulance,** phone (907) 874-2000. **Hospital,** Wrangell General, 310 Bennett St. just off Zimovia Highway, phone (907) 874-7000. **Maritime Search and Rescue,** contact the Coast Guard at (800) 478-5555.

Visitor Information: Center located in the Stikine Inn Building at 107 Stikine Ave., near the cruise ship dock; phone (800) 367-9745 or (907) 874-3901, fax (907) 874-3905, Internet: www.wrangell.com, e-mail: wrangell@wrangell.com. Write: Chamber of Commerce, Box 49MP, Wrangell, AK 99929. Information is also available at the Wrangell Museum, 318 Church St.; phone (907) 874-3770.

The U.S. Forest Service maintains several recreation sites and trails along the Wrangell Island road system, as well as remote cabins. Contact the USFS office in Wrangell, 525 Bennett St., phone (907) 874-2323.

Elevation: Sea level. **Climate:** Mild and moist with slightly less rain than other Southeast communities. Mean annual precipitation is 79.2 inches, with 63.9 inches of snow. Record monthly precipitation, 20.43 inches in October 1961. Average daily maximum temperature in June is 61°F/16°C; in July 64°F/18°C. Daily minimum in January is 21°F/-6°C. **Radio:** KSTK-FM 101.7. **Television:** Cable and satellite. **Newspaper:** *Wrangell Sentinel* (weekly).

Private Aircraft: Wrangell airport, adjacent northeast; elev. 44 feet/13m; length 6,000 feet/1,829m; paved; fuel 100LL, A.

Wrangell is the only Alaskan city to have existed under 4 nations and 3 flags—the Stikine Tlingits, the Russians, Great Britain and the United States. Wrangell began in 1834 as a Russian stockade called Redoubt St. Dionysius, built to prevent the Hudson's Bay Co. from fur trading up the rich Stikine River to the northeast. The Russians, in a change of policy, leased the mainland of southeastern Alaska to Hudson's Bay Co. in 1840. Under the British the stockade was called Fort Stikine.

The post remained under the British flag until Alaska was purchased by the United States in 1867. A year later the Americans established a military post here, naming it Fort Wrangell after the island, which was named by the Russians after Baron von Wrangel, a governor of the Russian–American Co.

Its strategic location near the mouth of the Stikine River, the fastest free-flowing navigable river in North America, made Wrangell an important supply point not only for fur traders but also for gold seekers following the river route to the goldfields. Today, the Stikine River is a popular hunting and recreation area. Currently, there is an active hard rock mine on the largest tributary of the Stikine, the Iskut. They are extracting gold, silver, copper and traces of other minerals from the site.

Wrangell serves as a hub for goods, services and transportation for outlying fishing villages, and logging and mining camps. The town depended largely on fishing until Japanese interests arrived in the mid-1950s and established a mill (now closed). A small, locally owned mill is now in operation 2 miles/3.2 km beyond the end of Zimovia Highway, off Forest 6265. Fishing is one of Wrangell's largest industries, with salmon the major catch.

ACCOMMODATIONS/VISITOR SERVICES

Wrangell has several motels including the Stikine Inn (907/874-3388) and Hardings Old Sourdough Lodge (907/874-3613). There are also several bed and breakfasts.

The Wrangell Hostel is located in the Presbyterian church, about 1/4 mile from the ferry terminal, next to the Wrangell Museum. Open from June 9 to Labor Day, 5 P.M. to 9 A.M.; $10/night; phone (907) 874-3534.

There are 4 restaurants downtown, as well as service stations, hardware and appliance stores, banks, drugstore, laundromat, grocery stores (1 with a bakery and deli), a fish market and gift shops. Bed-and-breakfasts are available. Lodges with restaurants are located on Peninsula Street and at **Mile 4.4** Zimovia Highway.

RV camping at Alaska Waters R.V. Park on Berger street. Camping and picnic area at Shoemaker Bay, **Milepost 4.9** Zimovia Highway. Dump stations located at Shoemaker Bay and downtown. City Park, at **Milepost 1.9** Zimovia Highway, has tent sites, camping, picnic area with tables, flush toilets, shelters and playground. ▲

TRANSPORTATION

Air: Daily scheduled jet service is provided by Alaska Airlines to other Southeast cities with through service to Seattle and Anchorage. Scheduled commuter air service to Petersburg, Kake and Ketchikan. Charter service available.

Airport terminal is 1.1 miles/1.8 km from ferry terminal or 1.1 miles/1.8 km from Zimovia Highway on Bennett Street. Hotel courtesy vans are available from the airport to downtown. Taxi service is also available for about $5.

Ferry: Alaska Marine Highway vessels connect Wrangell with all Southeastern Alaska ports plus Prince Rupert, BC, and Bellingham, WA. Ferry terminal is at the north end of town at the end of Zimovia Highway (also named Church or 2nd Street at this point). Walk or take a taxi from terminal to town for approximately $4. Tours for independent travelers are available downtown. Terminal facilities include ticket office, waiting room and vehicle waiting area. Phone (907) 874-3711.

Car Rental: Available from Practical Rent-A-Car (907) 874-3975.

Taxi: Available to/from airport and ferry terminal. Approximate cost is $4 and $5.

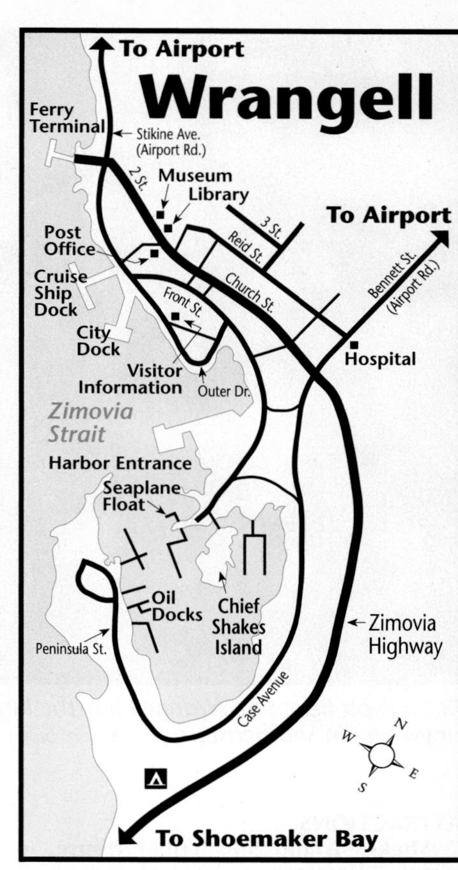

Highways: Zimovia Highway (see log this section). Logging roads have opened up most of Wrangell Island to motorists. Check with the USFS office at 525 Bennett St. for a copy of the Wrangell Island Road Guide map. (Write USDA Forest Service, Wrangell Ranger District, Box 51, Wrangell, AK 99929; phone 907/874-2323.) City maps are also available at the Chamber of Commerce Visitor Center downtown.

Cruise Ships: Wrangell is a regular port of call in summer for several cruise lines.

Private Boats: Transient floats are located downtown and 4.5 miles/7.2 km south of Wrangell on Zimovia Highway at Shoemaker Bay Harbor. Reliance Float is located near Shakes Tribal House.

If you are traveling to Wrangell by boat, radio ahead to the harbor master for tie-up space. Or phone (907) 874-3736 or 874-3051.

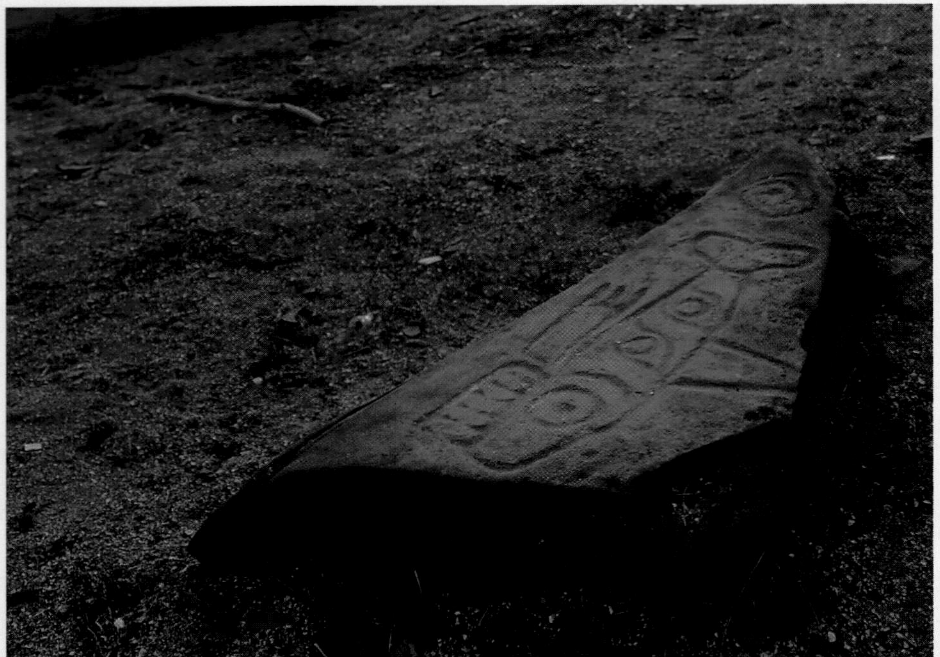

Petroglyph Beach at Wrangell has the largest number of petroglyphs found anywhere in southeastern Alaska. (© David J. Job)

ATTRACTIONS

Shakes Island and Tribal House, in Wrangell Harbor, is reached by boardwalk. It is the site of several excellent totem poles. The replica tribal house contains Indian working tools, an original Chilkat blanket design carved on a house panel and other cultural items. It is listed on the National Register of Historic Places. Open irregular hours when cruise ships are in port during summer (May to September) or by appointment; phone (907) 874-3747 or 874-2023. Admission $1.50.

Totem Poles. The last original totems standing in Wrangell were cut down in November 1981 and removed for preservation. A totem restoration project funded by both state and federal agencies was initiated, and replicas of original totems can be found at Kiksadi Totem Park at the corner of Front and Episcopal streets.

Wrangell Museum, at 318 Church St., features local history and includes displays representing Tlingit, Russian, British, Chinese, Japanese and American influences in Wrangell. Gold rush, trapping, logging and fishing industry exhibits depict Wrangell's boom and bust economy. May to September hours are: 10 A.M. to 5 P.M. weekdays, 1–5 P.M. Saturdays. October to April hours are: 10–11:30 A.M., 12:30–4 P.M. Tuesday through Friday, closed Saturday and Sunday. Open for cruise ships and ferries in port longer than one hour on Saturdays and Sundays when staffing available. Phone (907) 874-3770; fax (907) 874-3785. Admission for adults, $2; children 16 and under, free.

Our Collections Museum, located on Evergreen Avenue, is a private collection of antiques and Alaska memorabilia. Open when cruise ships and ferries are in port and by special request. Phone (907) 874-3646. Donations accepted.

Sightseeing Tours of attractions and fish bakes are available upon request. Sightseeing buses meet some ferries and cruise ships. Inquire at the visitor center or Wrangell Museum. Flightseeing and jetboat excursions available to Stikine River, Stikine Icefield, Anan Wildlife Observatory and other remote locations.

Celebrations in Wrangell include a big Fourth of July celebration which begins with a salmon bake. The annual Tent City Festival, celebrated the first weekend in February, commemorates Wrangell's gold rush days. The Garnet Festival, celebrated the third week of April, marks the arrival of spring and the annual bald eagle migration on the Stikine River. The festival celebrates the arts with family activities, and includes a golf tournament at Muskeg Meadows. A tree-lighting and Christmas celebration takes place on December 4, 1998.

Petroglyphs are ancient designs carved into rock faces, usually found between low and high tide marks on beaches. Petroglyph Beach is located 0.7 mile/1.1 km from the ferry terminal; a boardwalk trail leads to the head of the beach from the left of the road. Turn right as you reach the beach and look for petroglyphs between there and a rock outcrop several hundred feet away. This beach has the largest number of petroglyphs found anywhere in southeastern Alaska; at times as many as 40 can be seen. Petroglyphs are also located on the library lawn and are on display in the museum.

Muskeg Meadows. A new (1998) 9-hole, 36-acre regulation golf course and driving range is open in Wrangell. Annual tournaments have been inaugurated. Contact the Wrangell Golf Assoc., Box 2199, Wrangell, AK 99929, or association president Lloyd Hartshorn, phone (907) 874-3989.

Anan Observatory, managed by the U.S. Forest Service, is located 35 miles/56 km southeast of Wrangell; accessible by boat or plane only. During July and August, visitors can watch bears catch pink salmon headed for the salmon spawning grounds. Bald eagles, ravens, crows and seals are frequently seen feeding on the fish. Contact the visitor center for list of guides permitted to transport visitors to Anan (800/367-9745).

Wrangell Salmon Derby runs from mid-May to Memorial Day weekend. Kings weighing more than 50 lbs. are not unusual.

Garnet Ledge, a rocky outcrop on the right bank of the Stikine River delta at Garnet Creek, is 7.5 miles/12.1 km from Wrangell Harbor, reached at high tide by small boat. Garnet, a semiprecious stone, can be found embedded in the ledge here. The garnet ledge is on land deeded to the Southeast Council of the Boy Scouts of America and the children of Wrangell by the late Fred Hanford (former mayor of Wrangell). The bequest states that the land shall be used for scouting purposes and the children of Wrangell may take garnets in reasonable quantities (garnets are sold by children at the docks when ships and ferries are in port). Contact the Wrangell Museum (Box 1050, Wrangell 99929; phone 907/874-3770) for information on digging for garnets.

The Stikine River delta lies north of Wrangell within the Stikine–LeConte Wilderness. It is accessible by boat or by plane only. The delta is habitat for migrating waterfowl, eagles, bears and moose. During the spring run, the second largest concentration of bald eagles in the world can be seen in the Stikine River delta. Also watch for seals resting on ice floes from LeConte Glacier. The glacier is at the head of LeConte Bay, just north of the delta. It is the southernmost tidewater glacier in North America. It is also an actively calving glacier, known for its prodigious iceberg production.

The Stikine River is the fastest navigable river on North America, and can be rafted, canoed or run by skiff or jet boat from Telegraph Creek, BC, to Wrangell, AK, 165 miles/264 km one way.

USFS trails, cabins and recreation sites on Wrangell Island and in the surrounding area are a major attraction here. Nemo Campsites, for example, only 14 miles/22.5 km south of Wrangell, provides spectacular views of Zimovia Strait and north Etolin Island. No reservations or fees required. Parking areas, picnic tables, fire grills and outhouses at each campsite.

USFS public-use cabins in the Wrangell district are accessible by air or by boat. The 22 USFS cabins are scattered throughout the region.

For details on these sites and others, contact the Forest Service district office at (907) 874-2323, or stop by the USFS office at 525 Bennett St. You may also write the Wrangell Ranger District at Box 51, Wrangell, AK 99929. White courtesy phone located in the ferry terminal building. ▲

AREA FISHING: The Wrangell Island forest road system provides access to several recreation sites and trails with fishing. For more information contact the USFS office in Wrangell at (907) 874-2323.

Fly in to **Thoms Lake, Long Lake, Marten Lake, Salmon Bay, Virginia Lake** and **Eagle Lake.** Thoms Lake and Long Lake are also accessible via road and trail. **Stikine River** near Wrangell (closed to king salmon fishing), Dolly Varden to 22 inches, and cutthroat to 18 inches, best in midsummer to fall; steelhead to 12 lbs., use bait or lures; coho salmon 10 to 15 lbs., use lures, September and October. Saltwater fishing near Wrangell for king salmon, 20 to 40 lbs., best in May and June. Stop by the Dept. of Fish and Game at 215 Front St. for details.

Zimovia Highway Log

Zimovia Highway leads south from the ferry terminal to Pat Creek at Mile 11, where it connects with island logging roads.

0 Alaska Marine Highway ferry terminal, ticket office and waiting area. There is a bike path to Mile 1.9.

0.3 (0.5 km) St. Rose of Lima Catholic Church, the oldest Roman Catholic parish in Alaska, founded May 2, 1879.

0.4 (0.6 km) First Presbyterian Church has a red neon cross, 1 of 2 in the world that serve as navigational aids. This was the first church in Wrangell and is one of the oldest Protestant churches in Alaska (founded in 1877 and built in 1879).

Wrangell Museum interim location situated between the church and Wrangell High School.

0.6 (1 km) Bennett Street (Airport Road) loops north 2.2 miles/3.5 km to the airport and back to the ferry terminal.

0.7 (1.1 km) Public Safety Bldg.

1.9 (3.1 km) City park. Picnic area with shelters, firepits, restrooms, litter barrels. Tent camping only allowed; 24-hour limit. ▲

3.6 (5.8 km) Turnout with beach access. Several turnouts along the highway here offer beach access and good spots for bird watching.

4.4 (7.1 km) Lodge on left with restaurant and lounge.

4.9 (7.9 km) Shoemaker Bay small-boat harbor, boat launch, picnic, camping and parking area. Camping area has tent sites, 29 RV sites ($10 per night, with hookups), water, dump station and restrooms. Tennis court, horseshoe pits and children's playground nearby. Rainbow Falls trailhead; 0.7-mile/1.1-km trail to scenic waterfall. Institute Creek trail intersects with Rainbow Falls trail at Mile 0.6 and leads 2.7 miles/4.3 km to viewpoint and shelter overlooking Shoemaker Bay and Zimovia Strait. ▲

6.5 (10.5 km) Alaska Pulp Corp. (not operating).

7.3 (11.7 km) **Milepost 7**, scenic turnout.

8 (12.9 km) Turnout.

8.5 (13.7 km) Turnout, beach access (8 Mile Beach undeveloped recreation area).

10.8 (17.4 km) Access road west to Pat Creek Log Transfer Facility and small boat launch. Road east (Pat Creek Road) is a 1-lane, maintained, crushed rock road with turnouts. It leads 0.3 mile/0.5 km to Pat's Lake, and continues approximately 6 miles/10 km northeast through both old and active logging areas.

Pat Creek and **Pat's Lake**, cutthroat, Dolly Varden, pink and silver salmon, spinning gear or flies.

11 (17.7 km) Pat Creek camping area (unmaintained, no facilities); parking for self-contained vehicles.

11.1 (17.9 km) State-maintained highway ends. Begin 1-lane Forest Development Road No. 6265 connecting with other Forest Service roads (map showing many island recreation sites and trails available from USFS office in Wrangell). Watch for logging trucks and other heavy equipment.

14 (22.5 km) **Junction** with USFS Road 6267, which leads to the Nemo campsites. Spectacular views of Zimovia Strait and north Etolin Island, parking areas, picnic tables, fire grills and outhouses at each site. No reservations or fees required. ▲

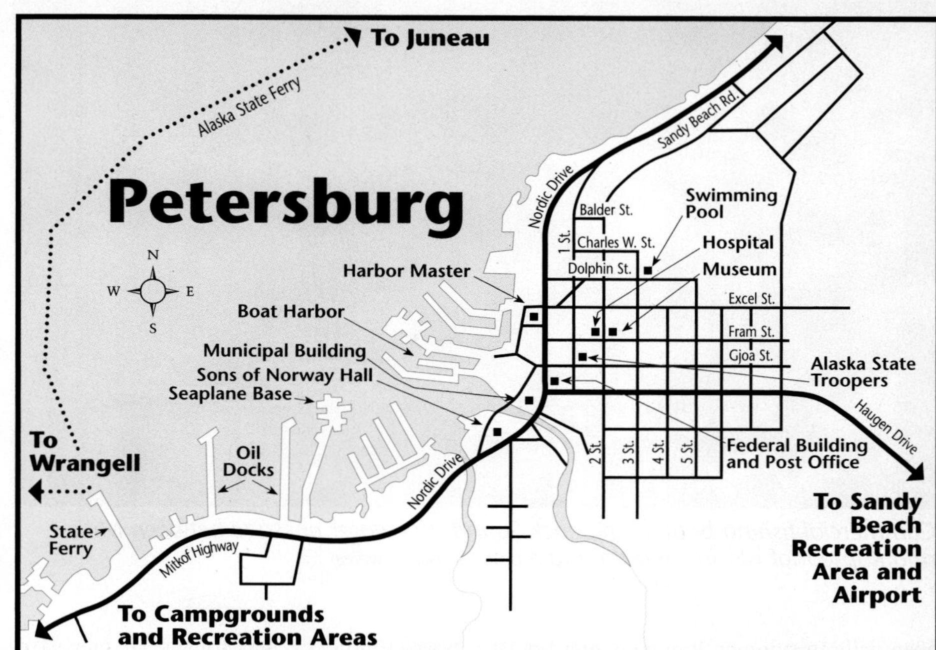

Petersburg

(See map, page 689)

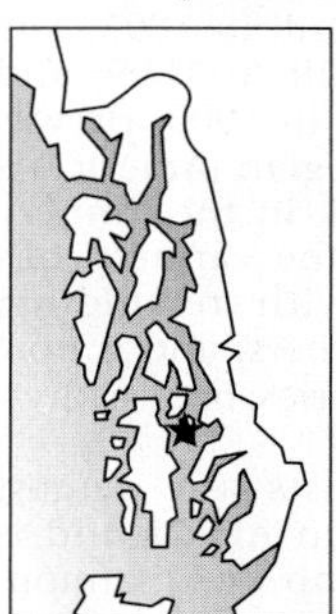

Located on the northwest tip of Mitkof Island at the northern end of Wrangell Narrows, midway between Juneau and Ketchikan. **Population:** 3,350. **Emergency Services:** Phone 911. **Alaska State Troopers,** phone (907) 772-3100. **City Police, Poison Center, Fire Department** and **Ambulance,** phone (907) 772-3838. **Hospital,** Petersburg Medical Center, 2nd and Fram St., phone (907) 772-4291. **Maritime Search and Rescue:** contact the Coast Guard at (800) 478-5555. Harbormaster, phone (907) 772-4688, CB Channel 9, or VHF Channel 16.

Visitor Information: Chamber of Commerce/USFS Information Center located at 1st and Fram streets; open daily from 9 A.M. to 5 P.M. spring and summer, 10 A.M. to 2 P.M. fall and winter. Write: Chamber of Commerce, Box 649MP, Petersburg 99833; phone/fax (907) 772-3646. For national forest information, write Petersburg Visitor Information Center, Box 1328, Petersburg 99833; phone (907) 772-4636. Clausen Memorial Museum, 2nd and Fram streets,

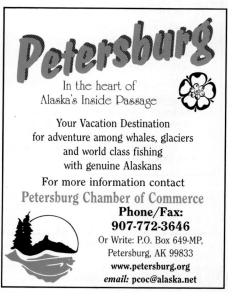

Commercial fishing boat in Frederick Sound, the water passage between Mitkof and Kupreanof islands and the mainland. (© Barbara Willard)

open daily in summer, limited winter hours; phone (907) 772-3598. Alaska Dept. of Fish and Game, State Office Building, Sing Lee Alley; open 8 A.M. to 4:30 P.M., Monday through Friday, phone (907) 772-3801.

Elevation: Sea level. **Climate:** Average daily maximum temperature in July, 64°F/18°C; daily minimum in January, 20°F/-7°C. All-time high, 84°F/29°C in 1933; record low, -19°F/-28°C in 1947. Mean annual precipitation, 105 inches; mean annual snowfall, 119 inches. **Radio:** KRSA-AM 580, KFSK-FM 100.9. **Television:** Alaska Rural Communication Service, Channel 15; KTOO (PBS) Channel 9 and cable channels. **Newspaper:** *Petersburg Pilot* (weekly).

Private Aircraft: James A. Johnson Airport, 1 mile/1.6 km southeast; elev. 107 feet/33m; length 6,000 feet/1,829m; asphalt; fuel 100, A. Seaplane base 0.5 mile/0.8 km from downtown.

Petersburg was named for Peter Buschmann, who selected the present townsite for a salmon cannery and sawmill in 1897. The sawmill and dock were built in 1899, and the cannery was completed in 1900. He was followed by other Norwegian–Americans who came to fish and work in the cannery and sawmill. Since then the cannery has operated continuously (with rebuilding, expansion and different owners) and is now known as Petersburg Fisheries Inc., a division of Icicle Seafoods Inc.

Today, Petersburg boasts the largest home-based halibut fleet in Alaska and is also well known for its shrimp, crab, salmon, herring and other fish products. Most families depend on the fishing industry for livelihood. Sportfishing questions should be directed to the Alaska Dept. of Fish and Game's Division of Sportfishing in Ketchikan, phone (907) 225-2859.

ACCOMMODATIONS/VISITOR SERVICES

Petersburg has a hotel and several motels, including Scandia House (907/772-4301), Tides Inn (907/772-4288) and Narrows Inn. There are also bed and breakfasts, many restaurants and several fast-food outlets downtown. The 5-block-long commercial area on Main Street (Nordic Drive) has grocery stores, marine and fishing supply stores, hardware, a drugstore, travel agency, public showers, banks, gift and variety stores specializing in both Alaskan and Scandinavian items, city hall, post office, gas stations and cocktail bars. A community gym with racquetball courts and a public swimming pool are located a couple of blocks off Nordic Drive. Petersburg has 13 churches.

There are 3 RV parks, dump station, hookups, showers, laundry; fee charged. There is a tent campground (known locally as Tent City) on Haugen Drive; it is often filled to capacity in summer with young cannery workers. Public campgrounds (1 developed, several undeveloped) are located on Mitkof Highway south of town. ▲

TRANSPORTATION

Air: Daily scheduled jet service by Alaska Airlines to major Southeast cities and Seattle, WA, with connections to Anchorage and Fairbanks. Local and charter service available.

The airport is located 1 mile/1.6 km from the Federal Building on Haugen Drive. It has a ticket counter and waiting room. There is no shuttle service to town; hotel courtesy vans and taxis are available for a fee.

Ferry: Alaska Marine Highway vessels connect Petersburg with all Southeastern Alaska cities plus Prince Rupert, BC, and Bellingham, WA. Terminal at **Milepost 0.8** Mitkof Highway, includes dock, ticket office with waiting room, and parking area. Phone (907) 772-3855.

Car Rental: Avis Rent-A-Car at Tides Inn, (907/772-4716), and All Star, Scandia House, (907/772-4281).

Taxi: There are 2 taxi companies. Cab service to and from the airport and ferry terminal.

Highways: Mitkof Highway, Sandy Beach Road and Three Lakes Loop Road (see logs this section).

Cruise Ships: Smaller cruise ships dock 1/4 mile from town. Vans take passengers to town.

Private Boats: Boaters must check with harbormaster for moorage assignment.

ATTRACTIONS

Centennial Celebration. In 1998, Petersburg celebrates its centennial. Special commemorative events occur year-round.

Little Norway Festival is scheduled for May 14–17, 1998, as a celebration for Norwegian Independence Day. Pageantry, old-country dress, contests, Vikings, a Viking ship, dancing and a Norwegian "fish feed" for locals and visitors are featured.

Clausen Memorial Museum, 203 Fram St., features Petersburg area history. On display are artifacts representing the cannery and fisheries, a world-record 126.5-lb. king salmon, the Cape Decision light station lens, a Tlingit canoe and the wall piece "Land, Sea, Sky." Open Wednesday and Saturday, 12:30–4:30 P.M., Oct. 1 to April 30. Open daily, 9:30 A.M. to 4:30 P.M., May 1 to Sept. 21. Phone (907) 772-3598 for programs, updated visitor information and to leave messages. Wheelchair accessible. ♿

The Fisk (Norwegian for fish), a 10-foot/3-m bronze sculpture commemorating Petersburg's fishing tradition, stands in a working fountain in front of the museum. It was completed during the Alaska centennial year of 1967 by sculptor Carson Boysen.

Sons of Norway Hall, on the National Register of Historic Places, was built in 1912. Situated on pilings over Hammer Slough (a favorite photography subject), its window shutters are decorated with rosemaling (Norwegian tole painting).

LeConte Glacier, in LeConte Bay, 25 miles/40 km east of Petersburg, is the continent's southernmost tidewater glacier. Fast-moving, the glacier continually "calves," creating ice falls from its face into the bay. Seals and porpoises are common; whales are often seen. Helicopters, small aircraft and boats may be chartered in Petersburg or Wrangell to see LeConte Glacier.

Salmon migration and spawning are best observed in the Petersburg area July though September. Falls Creek bridge and fish ladder, at **Milepost 10.8** Mitkof Highway, is a good location. The ladder helps migrating salmon bypass difficult falls on the way to spawning grounds in Falls Creek. It can be observed from the creek bank just off the roadside. Other viewing areas include Blind Slough and the Blind River Rapids area, Petersburg Creek and Ohmer Creek.

Crystal Lake Fish Hatchery is at **Milepost 17.5** Mitkof Highway. This hatchery for coho, king and steelhead is operated by the state and used for fish-stocking projects in southeastern Alaska. It is open for visits, and hatchery personnel will explain the operation, though formal guided tours are not available. Best time to visit is between 8 A.M. and 4 P.M., Monday through Friday.

Petersburg King Salmon Derby is scheduled for Memorial Day weekend May 22–25, 1998; $30,000 in prizes are awarded. Check with the chamber of commerce for details.

AREA FISHING: Salmon, steelhead, cutthroat and Dolly Varden at **Falls Creek, Blind Slough** and **Blind River Rapids**; see log of Mitkof Highway this section. Salmon can be caught in the harbor area and **Scow Bay** area. (Rapid tidal currents in front of the town necessitate the use of an outboard motor.) **Petersburg Creek**, directly across Wrangell Narrows from downtown within Petersburg Creek–Duncan Salt Chuck Wilderness Area, also offers good fishing. Blind Slough, located 15 miles/24 km south of the ferry terminal, offers good drive-up fishing for king salmon. Dolly Varden can be caught from the beach north of town and from downtown docks. Sportfishing opportunities for halibut, rockfish, crab and shrimp. Harvest of mussels, clams and the like is not recommended because of the possibility of paralytic shellfish poisoning. Contact the Sport Fish Division of the Alaska Dept. of Fish and Game (907/225-2859) for additional information.

Wrangell Narrows is a 23-mile-/37-km-long channel between Mitkof and Kupreanof islands. The channel was dredged in the 1940s to a depth of 26 feet/7.8m. Extremely narrow in places and filled with rocky reefs, islands and strong currents, the narrows is navigated by ships and ferries with the aid of dozens of markers and flashing lights. The 1½-hour run through Wrangell Narrows begins immediately on ferries departing Petersburg southbound, or about 1½ hours after departing Wrangell northbound.

Cabins, canoe/kayaking routes and hiking trails managed by the U.S. Forest Service are all within reach of Petersburg, which is the administrative center for the Stikine Area of Tongass National Forest. Stop by the USFS office in the Federal Building, or phone (907) 772-3871 for detailed information on cabins and trails. Also consult *The ALASKA WILDERNESS GUIDE* (to order, phone 800/726-4707). Information for canoers and kayakers interested in the Stikine River delta or Tebenkof Bay and Kuiu wilderness areas is also available here or at the USFS office in Wrangell.

Sandy Beach Road Log

From Federal Building, drive north through town; road leads to Sandy Beach Recreation Area.

0 Federal Building and post office.

0.1 (0.2 km) Petersburg boat harbor 1 block to left, contains one of Alaska's finest fishing fleets.

0.2 (0.3 km) Downtown Petersburg.

0.3 (0.5 km) Petersburg Fisheries Inc., the city's largest processing plant.

Eagles Roost Park. Eagles feed on beach at low tide; best viewing in early summer.

1.2 (1.9 km) Eagle observation point. Eagles can be seen nesting nearby and fishing in Wrangell Narrows. To the northeast is Frederick Sound and the mainland.

2 (3.2 km) Bed and breakfast, sightseeing cruises.

2.8 (4.5 km) Sandy Beach Recreation Area on left; picnic tables, playground, volleyball court, shelter, toilets, limited parking, no camping. **Junction** with Haugen Drive, which loops to airport and back to town.

Just past Sandy Beach Recreation Area is the Frederick Point boardwalk, a 1-mile/1.6-km trail that leads through the woods to the beach near Frederick Point. This trail is very popular in summer.

Mitkof Highway Log

The major road on the island, Mitkof Highway leads 33.8 miles/54.4 km south from the Federal Building to the Stikine River delta at the south end of Mitkof Island. The highway is paved to **Milepost 17.5**; good wide gravel to road end.

0 Federal Building and post office.

0.1 (0.2 km) Bridge over Hammer Slough, an intertidal estuary.

0.5 (0.8 km) Harbor parking.

0.6 (1 km) Pier and floatplane base.

0.8 (1.3 km) Alaska Marine Highway ferry terminal, office and waiting area on right.

2.8 (4.5 km) Muskeg meadows on left. Muskeg is a grassy bog, common in Alaska.

2.9 (4.6 km) **Scow Bay**, a wide portion of Wrangell Narrows with king salmon fishing in spring. Scow Bay is noted traditionally as the first election precinct to report its vote in statewide elections. Scow Bay Loop Road rejoins highway at **Milepost 3.1**.

4 (6.4 km) Lodging on right.

4.3 (6.9 km) Turnout on right with view of Wrangell Narrows.

7.5 (12.1 km) Twin Creek RV Park, private campground, small store and phone. ▲

10.7 (17.2 km) North exit to Three Lakes Loop Road (see log this section).

10.8 (17.4 km) **Falls Creek** and fish ladder. Steelhead, April and May; pink salmon below falls in August; coho, August and September; Dolly Varden and cutthroat late summer and fall. No fishing within 300 feet/90m of fish ladder.

11 (17.7 km) Road on right leads 0.5 mile/0.8 km to Papke's Landing; transient boat moorage and boat ramp. USFS Log Transportation Facility.

14.3 (23 km) Entering Tongass National Forest.

14.5 (23.3 km) Blind River Rapids parking area and trail; outhouse. 0.3-mile/0.4-km boardwalk trail through muskeg meadow to **Blind River Rapids**, hatchery steelhead, mid-April to mid-May; king salmon, June to late July; coho, mid-August to October. Also Dolly Varden and cutthroat trout.

16.3 (26.2 km) Blind Slough waterfowl viewing area on right. Covered platform with interpretive sign on area waterfowl. Trumpeter swans winter in this area.

17.5 (28.2 km) Pavement ends; wide, hard-packed gravel to end of road. Short road leads to Crystal Lake Fish Hatchery and **Blind Slough** Recreation Area with picnic tables, shelter and pit toilets; no overnight camping. Hatchery is open for visiting, though no scheduled tours are available. Fishing for steelhead, best in May; cutthroat and Dolly Varden in summer; coho salmon, mid-August to mid-September; king salmon in June and July.

20 (32.2 km) **Manmade Hole** picnic area with tables, firepits, swimming and short trail. Ice skating in winter. Fishing for cutthroat and Dolly Varden year-round; best in summer and fall.

20.6 (33.1 km) Three Lakes Loop Road begins on left leading to Three Lakes on other side of Mitkof Island, looping back to Mitkof Highway at **Milepost 10.7** near Falls Creek bridge.

21.4 (34.4 km) Woodpecker Cove Road (1-lane) leads about 15 miles/24 km along south Mitkof Island to Woodpecker Cove and beyond. Good views of Sumner Strait.

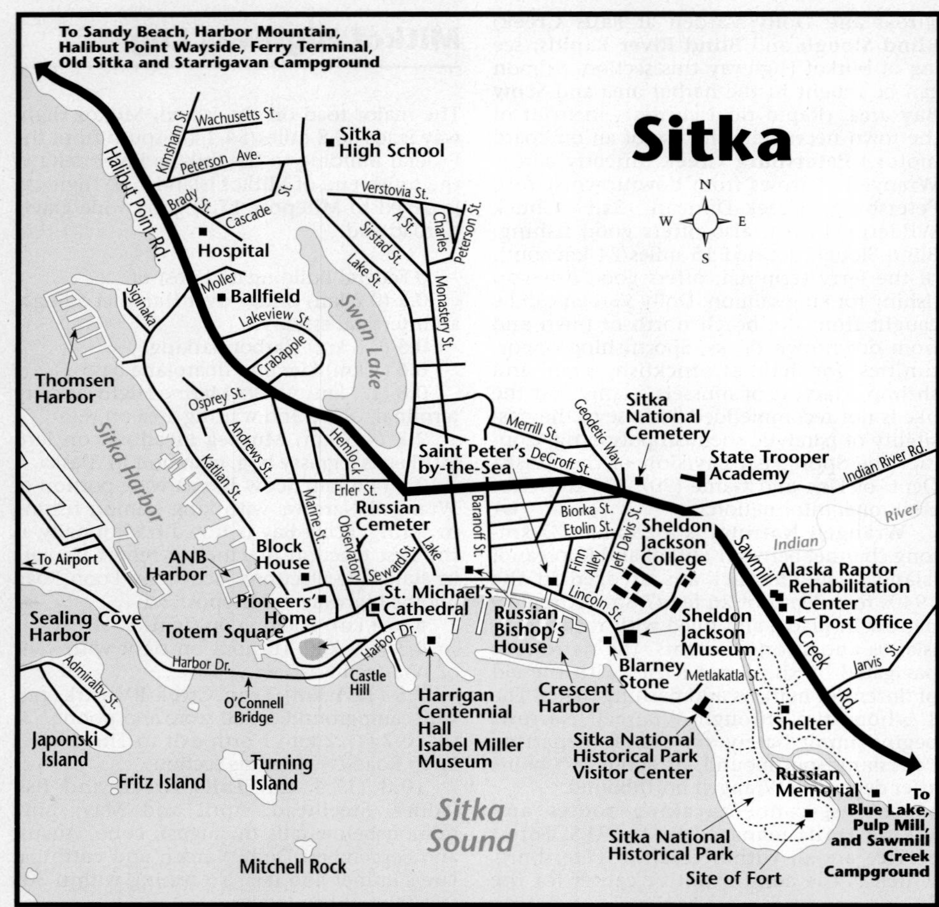

Watch for logging trucks.

21.5 (34.6 km) Ohmer Creek nature trail, 1.5 mile/2.4 km loop; first 0.3 mile/0.5 km is barrier-free. ♿

21.7 (34.9 km) Ohmer Creek Campground, 10 sites (2 are wheelchair accessible), toilets, parking area, picnic tables, drinking water and firepits. Set in meadow area among trees. Open spring to fall; small fee; accommodates RVs to 32 feet/9.6m. ♿▲

24 (38.6 km) **Blind Slough** USFS Log Transportation Facility. Excellent fishing from skiff for king salmon in June and July; coho salmon, mid-August to mid-September.

26.1 (42 km) Narrow 0.7-mile/1.1-km road on right to Sumner Strait Campground, locally called Green's Camp (undeveloped); must walk in, no facilities. May be inaccessible at high tide. ▲

27 (43.4 km) View of city of Wrangell.

28 (45 km) Wilson Creek state recreation area (undeveloped); picnic tables, parking, outhouse. Good view of Sumner Strait.

28.6 (46 km) Banana Point, boat ramp, outhouse.

31 (49.9 km) Stikine River mud flats, visible on right at low tide. Part of the Stikine River delta, this is the area where Dry Strait meets Sumner Strait.

33.8 (54.4 km) Road ends with turnaround.

Three Lakes Loop Road Log

Access to this 21.4-mile-/34.4-km-long, 1-lane loop road is from **Mileposts 10.7** and **20.6** on the Mitkof Highway. *CAUTION: No services; use turnouts.*

0 Junction at **Milepost 10.7** Mitkof Highway; turn east.

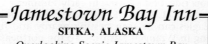

1.4 (2.3 km) View of Wrangell Narrows to west. Older clear-cuts; this area was logged between 1964 and 1968.

4.4 (7.1 km) Falls Creek bridge.

7 (11.3 km) Second-growth stand of spruce–hemlock. First growth was destroyed by fire or wind throw more than 180 years ago. This second-growth stand serves as an example of what a logging unit could look like a century or two after clear-cutting.

9.7 (15.6 km) Directly south is a 384-acre clear-cut logged in 1973 under a contract predating the current policy, which usually limits clear-cut tracts to 100 acres.

10.2 (16.4 km) **Bear Creek**; steelhead in April and May; coho late August and September; cutthroat and Dolly Varden, best late summer and fall.

12.3 (19.8 km) Muskeg; view of Frederick Sound.

12.8 (20.5 km) Turnoff on right to LeConte Glacier Overlook, a picnic site with spectacular view of the mainland. Limited turnaround space.

14.2 (22.8 km) Sand Lake trail. Short boardwalk trail leads to each of the Three Lakes. Tennis shoes are ideal for these short walks, but for areas around the lakes it is advisable to wear rubber boots. A 0.7-mile/1.1-km connecting trail to Hill Lake.

14.7 (23.6 km) Hill Lake trail.

15.1 (24.3 km) Crane Lake trail, 1.3 miles/2.1 km to lake; connecting trail to Hill Lake. USFS skiffs and picnic platforms are located at Sand, Hill and Crane lakes.

Sand, Hill and **Crane lakes,** cutthroat from May through September.

16.4 (26.4 km) Dry Straits Road.

21.4 (34.4 km) Second **junction** with Mitkof Highway, at **Milepost 20.6.**

Sitka

(See map, page 689)

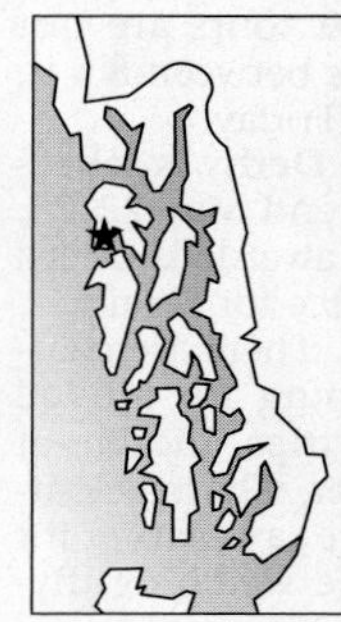

Located on west side of Baranof Island, 95 air miles/153 km southwest of Juneau, 185 air miles/298 km northwest of Ketchikan; 2 hours flying time from Seattle, WA.

Population: City and Borough, 9,194. **Emergency Services: Alaska State Troopers, City Police, Fire Department,** and **Ambulance,** phone 911. **Hospital,** Sitka Community, 209 Moller Ave., phone (907) 747-3241; Mount Edgecumbe, 222 Tongass Dr., phone (907) 966-2411. **Maritime Search and Rescue,** phone the Coast Guard at (800) 478-5555.

Visitor Information: Contact the Sitka Convention and Visitors Bureau at Box 1226-MP, Sitka, AK 99835; phone (907) 747-5940. Also available at the Isabel Miller Museum in Harrigan Centennial Hall on Harbor Drive. Museum hours are 8 A.M. to 5 P.M. in summer, extended hours to accommodate ferry passengers; phone (907) 747-6455. For USDA Forest Service information write the Sitka Ranger District, 201 Katlian, Suite 109, Sitka, AK 99835; phone (907) 747-6671. For information on Sitka National Historical Park, write 106 Metlakatla St., Sitka, AK 99835; phone (907) 747-6281.

Elevation: Sea level. **Climate:** Average daily temperature in July, 55°F/13°C; in January, 33°F/1°C. Annual precipitation, 95 inches. **Radio:** KIFW 1230, KRSA-FM 94.9, KSBZ-FM 103.1, KCAW-FM 104.7. **Television:** Cable channels. **Newspaper:** *Daily Sitka Sentinel.*

Private Aircraft: Sitka airport on Japonski Island; elev. 21 feet/6m; length 6,500 feet/1,981m; asphalt; fuel 100, A1. Sitka seaplane base adjacent west; fuel 80, 100.

One of the most scenic of southeastern Alaska cities, Sitka rests on the ocean shore protected at the west by myriad small islands and Cape Edgecumbe. Mount Edgecumbe, the Fuji-like volcano (dormant), is 3,201 feet/976m high.

The site was originally occupied by Tlingit Indians. Alexander Baranof, chief manager of the Russian–American Co. with headquarters in Kodiak, built a trading post and fort (St. Michael's Redoubt) north of Sitka in 1799. Indians burned down the fort and looted the warehouses. Baranof returned in 1804, and by 1808 Sitka was capital of Russian Alaska. Baranof was governor from 1790 to 1818. A statue of the Russian governor was unveiled in 1989; it is located outside of Centennial Hall. Castle Hill in Sitka is where Alaska changed hands from Russia to the United States in 1867. Salmon was the mainstay of the economy from the late 1800s until the 1950s, when the salmon population decreased. A pulp mill operated at nearby Silver Bay from 1960 to 1993. Today, tourism, commercial fishing, cold storage plants and government provide most jobs.

ACCOMMODATIONS/VISITOR SERVICES

Sitka has several hotels/motels, most with adjacent restaurants, including: Cascade Inn and Boat Charters (907/747-6804), Potlatch Motel (907/747-8611), Sitka Hotel (907/747-3288), Super 8 Hotel (907/747-8804) and Westmark Shee Atika (907/747-6241). Bed and breakfasts are also available; see ads this section.

Alaska Ocean View Bed & Breakfast. You'll enjoy casual elegance at affordable rates at this superior, quality B&B where guests experience a high degree of personal comfort, privacy and friendly, knowledgeable hosts. Open your day with the tantalizing aroma of fresh bread, fresh ground coffee and a delicious, generous breakfast, and close your day with a refreshing soak in the bubbling patio spa. Open year-round, credit cards, smoke-free, on airporter/ferry shuttle route. Business travelers and vacationers rate this lodging a 12 plus! "Delighted beyond our expectations!" Brochure and reservations: 1101 Edgecumbe Drive, Sitka, AK 99835; phone (907) 747-8310. See display ad this section. [ADVERTISEMENT]

Sitka Youth Hostel is located in the United Methodist Church, 303 Kimsham St. (1½ blocks north of McDonald's on Halibut Point Road). Send correspondence to Box 2645, Sitka, AK 99835. Open June 1 to Aug. 31; 20 beds, showers, kitchen facilities, sleeping pads required; $7/member; $10/nonmembers. Phone (907) 747-8661.

An array of businesses cluster in the downtown area, which saw its first traffic light installed in 1992. Services in Sitka's downtown area include restaurants, a laundromat, drugstore, clothing and grocery stores, and gift shops. Shopping and services are also available along Sawmill and Halibut Point roads. Dump stations are located at the Wastewater Treatment Plant on Japonski Island.

Four campgrounds are available in the Sitka area. From the ferry terminal north they are Starrigavan, Sitka Sportsman's, Sealing Cove and Sawmill Creek. Starrigavan Campground (USFS), at **Milepost 7.8** Halibut Point Road, has 32 sites, 2 picnic sites, artesian water, tables, vault toilets, 14-day limit, $8 fee (fee rate subject to change), available first-come, first-served only; phone (907) 747-4216. Sitka Sportsman's Assoc. RV Park, located 1 block south of the ferry terminal on Halibut Point Road, has 16 RV sites, water and electrical hookups, $18.00 fee, reservations accepted; phone (907) 747-6033. Sealing Cove, operated by the City and Borough of Sitka, is located adjacent Sealing Cove Boat Harbor on Japonski Island; overnight parking for 26 RVs, water and electrical hookups, 15-night limit, $16 fee. Sawmill Creek Campground (USFS) is located on Blue Lake Road, which is accessible at **Milepost 5.4** Sawmill Creek Road; 11 tent sites, vault toilet, boil water, no garbage service, no fee, 14-day limit. Phone (907) 747-4216. ▲

TRANSPORTATION

Air: Scheduled jet service by Alaska Airlines. Charter and commuter service also available. The airport is on Japonski Island, across O'Connell Bridge, 1.7 miles/2.7 km from downtown. Airport facilities include ticket counters, rental cars, small gift shop, restaurant and lounge. Van and taxi service to downtown hotels available.

Ferry: Alaska Marine Highway ferry terminal is located at **Milepost 7** Halibut Point

Road; phone (907) 747-8737. Buses for downtown meet all ferries. Van and taxi service also available. Sitka is connected via the Marine Highway to other Southeast ports, Prince Rupert, BC, and Bellingham, WA.

Bus: Available to downtown hotels.

Car Rental: Available from A&A Car Rental–Baranof Motors Inc. (907/747-8228), Advantage Car Rentals (907/747-7557) and Avis Rent-A-Car (907/966-2404).

Taxi: Local service is available.

Highways: Halibut Point Road, 7.9 miles/12.7 km, and Sawmill Creek Road, 7.4 miles/11.9 km; see logs this section.

Cruise Ships: Sitka is a popular port of call for several cruise lines.

Private Boats: Transient moorage available at ANB Harbor, located downtown next to the fuel dock; Thomsen Harbor on Katlian Street, 0.6 mile/1 km from city center; and Sealing Cove on Japonski Island. Moorage is limited during the summer.

ATTRACTIONS

St. Michael's Cathedral is the focal point of Sitka's history as the capital of Russian Alaska. Built in 1844–48 under the direction of Bishop Innocent Veniaminov of the Russian Orthodox Church, one of the finest examples of rural Russian church architecture for 118 years. It was destroyed by fire on Jan. 2, 1966. Priceless icons, some predating 1800, were saved by townspeople and are now back in place in the rebuilt cathedral (an exact replica).

St. Michael's is located in the center of Lincoln Street downtown; a donation is requested when entering to view icons. Open daily June 1 to Sept. 30, 11 A.M. to 3 P.M. St. Michael's currently serves a Russian Orthodox congregation of about 100 families. Visitors are reminded that this is an active parish conducting weekly services.

Castle Hill (Baranof Castle Hill Historic Site) is where Alaska changed hands from Russia to the United States on Oct. 18, 1867. Castle Hill was the site of Baranof's castle. Walkway to site is located on the south side by the bridge (look for sign).

Sitka Pioneers' Home, near the waterfront at Lincoln and Katlian streets, was built in 1934. Pioneers welcome visitors, and handicrafts made by the residents are sold in the gift shop located on the first floor of the west wing.

Native Community House is a northwest coast tribal "longhouse" constructed in traditional Nakaahidi design and aimed at preserving the Tlingit culture. The Community House is a performing arts center offering Tlingit story telling and dance performances. Exhibits on Native culture are also on display. Donations accepted. 200 Katlian St., Sitka, AK 99835; phone (907) 747-7290.

Totem Square is across Katlian Street from the Pioneers' Home and contains a totem, petroglyphs, Russian cannon and 3 large anchors found in Sitka Harbor and believed to be 18th century English.

Russian Blockhouse beside Pioneers' Home is a replica of the blockhouse that separated Russian and Tlingit sections of Sitka after the Tlingits moved back to the area 20 years after the 1804 battle. (See model of early Sitka in Centennial Building.)

New Archangel Russian Dancers, a group of local women, perform authentic Russian dances in authentic costumes. Performances are scheduled to coincide with the arrival of cruise ships. Fee charged.

New Archangel Russian Dancers are a popular Sitka entertainment.

(© Loren Taft, Alaskan Images)

Inquire at the Centennial Building for details.

Old Russian Cemetery is located behind Pioneers' Home and includes graves of such notables as St. Iahov Netsvetov, a recently canonized saint of the Russian Orthodox Church, who was a priest in Russian Alaska for over 40 years.

The Finnish Lutheran Cemetery, dedicated in 1841, is located on Princess Way next to the Russian cemetery. Just a few steps up the hill from Sitka Lutheran Church, it holds the grave of Princess Maskutov, wife of Alaska's last Russian governor, and other important personages.

Sitka National Cemetery, Milepost 0.5 Sawmill Creek Road, is open 8 A.M. to 5 P.M. daily (maintained by the Veterans Administration). It was known locally as Military Cemetery. In 1924 Pres. Calvin Coolidge designated the site as Sitka National Cemetery, and until WWII it was the only national cemetery west of the Rockies. Civil War veterans, veterans of the Aleutian Campaign in WWII and many notable Alaskans are buried here. One gravestone is dated December 1867, 2 months after the U.S. purchase of Alaska from Russia.

Whale Watching. During the summer, whales are often found in Sitka Sound. During the winter, up to 80 whales are near Sitka from mid-September to mid-January. Whale Park, 4.4 miles/7 km from town on Sawmill Creek Road, has stationary binoculars for whale viewing. The 2nd Annual Sitka Whalefest, featuring educational lectures with biologists and guest speakers, takes place November 2–8, 1998.

Alaska Day Celebration, Oct. 14–18, 1998, celebrates the transfer of Alaska from Russia to the United States with a reenactment of the event, complete with Sitka's own 9th (Manchu) Infantry, authentic uniforms and working muskets of the period. Period costumes and beards are the order of the day. Events ranging from pageant to costume ball and parade highlight the affair.

Annual Sitka Summer Music Festival (June 5–26, 1998). Concerts on Tuesday, Friday and some Saturday evenings in Centennial Hall, praised for its excellent acoustics. Emphasizing chamber music, an international group of professional musicians give evening concerts during the festival, plus open rehearsals. Advance tickets are a good idea; the concerts are popular. Dress is informal and concert-goers may have the opportunity to talk with the musicians. Children under 6 years not admitted.

Harrigan Centennial Hall, by the boat harbor on Harbor Drive, is used for Russian dance performances, music festivals, banquets and conventions. Its glass-fronted main hall overlooks Sitka Sound. The Isabel Miller Museum is located here. Nearby is a large hand-carved Tlingit canoe made from a single log.

Sheet'ka Kwaan Naa Kahidi (Sitka's Community House) is a traditional longhouse featuring Native dancing, storytelling and other cultural events. Located on Katlian Street next to the Pioneer's Home. Phone (800) 746-3207 for more information.

Isabel Miller Museum, located in the Centennial Building, has permanent exhibits highlighting the history of Sitka and its people. Russian tools, paintings from all eras, fishing, forestry, tourism, and Alaska Purchase exhibits, and an 8-foot-square scale model of Sitka in 1867 are among the displays. Operated by the Sitka Historical Society; hosts are available to answer questions. Open year-round; free admission. Hours are 9 A.M. to 5 P.M. daily in summer; 10 A.M. to 4 P.M. Tuesday through Saturday during the winter. Phone (907) 747-6455.

Sitka Lutheran Church, downtown on Lincoln Street, has a small historical display. Established in 1840, it was the first Protestant church organized on the west coast of North America.

Sitka National Historical Park reflects both the community's rich Tlingit Indian heritage and its Russian-ruled past. The park consists of 2 units—the Fort Site, located at the end of Lincoln Street, 0.5 mile/0.8 km from town, and the Russian Bishop's House, located on Lincoln Street near Crescent Harbor.

At the Fort Site stood the Tlingit fort, burned to the ground by Russians after the 1804 Battle of Sitka; this was the last major stand by the Tlingits against Russian settlement. For Alexander Baranof, leader of the Russians, the battle was revenge for the 1802 destruction of Redoubt St. Michael by the Tlingits. There is a visitor center here with audiovisual programs and exhibits of Indian artifacts. The Southeast Alaska Indian Cultural Center has contemporary Tlingit artists demonstrate and interpret various traditional arts for visitors.

There is a self-guiding trail through the park to the fort site and battleground of 1804. The National Park Service conducts guided walks; check for schedule. The park's totem pole collection stands near the visitor center and along the trail. The collection includes original pieces collected in 1901–03, and copies of originals lost to time and the elements. The pieces, primarily from Prince of Wales Island, were collected by Alaska Gov. John Brady (now buried in Sitka National Cemetery). The originals were exhibited at the 1904 St. Louis Exposition.

The Russian Bishop's House was built by the Russian–American Co. in 1842 for the first Russian Orthodox Bishop to serve Alaska. It was occupied by the church until 1969, and was added to Sitka National Historical Park in 1972. The house is 1 of 2 Russian log structures remaining in Sitka, and 1 of 4 remaining in North America.

The park's visitor center is open daily, 8 A.M. to 5 P.M., June through September; weekdays, 8 A.M. to 5 P.M., October through May. The park grounds and trails are open daily, 6 A.M. to 10 P.M. in summer; shorter hours in winter. Russian Bishop's House open 9 A.M. to 5 P.M. daily, closed from 1–2 P.M. for lunch; other times by appointment; hours subject to change. The visitor center is closed Thanksgiving, Christmas and New Year's. Admission fee $2 per person and $5 per family. Tours are $3 per person. Students under 18 free with student identification. Phone (907) 747-6281 for more information.

Sheldon Jackson Museum, 104 College Dr., on the Sheldon Jackson College campus, contains some of the finest Native arts and crafts found in Alaska. Much of it was collected by missionary Sheldon Jackson and is now owned by the state of Alaska. Museum shop specializes in Alaska Native arts and crafts: ivory, dolls, masks, silver jewelry, baskets and beadwork. Admission $3, students under 18 free, annual pass $10. Open in summer 8 A.M. to 5 P.M. daily. Winter hours: Tuesday through Saturday, 10 A.M. to 4 P.M. Phone (907) 747-8981.

The Prospector is a 13½-foot/4-m clay and bronze statue in front of the Pioneers' Home. Sculpted by Alonzo Victor Lewis, the statue was dedicated on Alaska Day in 1949. Lewis's model was a genuine pioneer, William "Skagway Bill" Fonda.

Blarney Stone, across from Sheldon Jackson College. Believed to originally have been called Baranof's stone and used as a resting stop by Russian–American Co. chief manager Alexander Baranof.

O'Connell Bridge, 1,225 feet/373m long, connecting Sitka with Japonski Island, was the first cable-stayed, girder-span bridge in the United States. It was dedicated Aug. 19, 1972. You'll get a good view of Sitka and the harbors by walking across this bridge.

Old Sitka, at **Milepost 7.5** Halibut Point Road, is a registered national historic landmark and the site of the first Russian settlement in the area in 1799, known then as Fort Archangel Michael. In 1802, in a surprise attack, the Tlingit Indians of the area destroyed the fort and killed most of its occupants, driving the Russians out until Baranof's successful return in 1804.

Visit the Alaska Raptor Rehabilitation Center, located at 1101 Sawmill Creek Road (**Milepost 0.9**) just across Indian River, within easy walking distance of downtown Sitka. This unique facility treats injured eagles, hawks, owls and other birds. Visitors will have the opportunity to see American bald eagles and other raptors close up, review case histories of birds treated at the center and observe medical care being administered to current patients. From May 15 through September the facility is open daily for tours and educational programs; limited hours October to May 15. Phone (907) 747-8662 or fax 747-8397 for times. Admission charged.

St. Lazaria Island is host to one of the largest seabird colonies in Southeast Alaska. This 65-acre volcanic island was set aside as a wildlife refuge in 1909. A half-million seabirds representing 11 different species breed here. Landing on the island or exploring the island is not advisable because foot traffic damages nesting burrows. Boat charters are available in Sitka for viewing from the water. The best time to visit is May–June. For more information, contact the Refuge Manager, Alaska Maritime National Wildlife Refuge, 2355 Kachemak Bay Dr., Suite 101, Homer, AK 99603; phone (907) 235-6546.

Hiking Trails. Sitka Ranger District office at 201 Katlian, provides information sheets and maps for area trails and remote cabins. Trails accessible from the road include Harbor Mountain Ridge trail; Mount Verstovia trail; the easy 5-mile/8-km Indian River trail; and the short Beaver Lake trail off Sawmill Creek Road on Blue Lake Road.

AREA FISHING: Sitka holds an annual salmon derby Memorial Day weekend and the weekend following. Contact the Sitka Convention and Visitors Bureau for more information; phone (907) 747-5940. Saltwater fishing charters available locally. There are also many lakes and rivers on Baranof Island with good fishing; these range from **Katlian River,** 11 miles/17.7 km northeast of Sitka by boat, to more remote waters such as **Rezanof Lake,** which is 40 air miles/64 km southeast of Sitka. USFS public-use cabins at some lakes. Stop by the Dept. of Fish and Game office at 304 Lake St. for details on fishing.

Sawmill Creek Road Log

Sawmill Creek Road is a 7.4-mile/11.9-km road, paved for the first 5.4 miles/8.7 km, which begins at Lake Street and ends beyond the pulp mill (closed) at Silver Bay.

0 Intersection of Lake Street (Halibut Point Road) and Sawmill Creek Road.

0.5 (0.8 km) Sitka National Cemetery.

0.6 (1 km) Entrance to Sheldon Jackson College.

0.7 (1.1 km) Indian River bridge. Beginning of Indian River trail on left.

0.9 (1.4 km) Alaska Raptor Rehabilitation Center.

1 (1.6 km) Post office.

1.7 (2.7 km) Mount Verstovia trail on left next to supper club. The trail extends 2.5 miles/4 km to summit of Mount Verstovia; strenuous hike, great views.

3.6 (5.8 km) Thimbleberry Creek bridge.

3.7 (6 km) On left past bridge is start of Thimbleberry Lake and Heart Lake trail. Hike in 0.5 mile/0.8 km to **Thimbleberry Lake,** brook trout to 12 inches, May–September. *NOTE: Recent changes in regulations make it illegal to use bait in fresh water, except from Sept. 15–Nov. 15.* Trail continues 1 mile/1.6 km past Thimbleberry Lake to **Heart Lake,** brook trout.

4.4 (7.1 km) Scenic Whale Park viewpoint turnout; stationary binoculars for whale watching.

5.3 (8.5 km) Alaska Pulp Corp. (closed).

5.4 (8.7 km) Blue Lake Road on left. Pavement ends on Sawmill Creek Road. Blue Lake Road (narrow dirt) leads 2.2 miles/3.5 km to small parking area and short downhill trail to Blue Lake (no recreational facilities; check with city for information). At Mile 1.5 on right is Sawmill Creek USFS campground. **Blue Lake,** rainbow, May–September; use flies or lure, do not use bait. Lightweight skiff or rubber boat recommended.

5.7 (9.2 km) Sawmill Creek and bridge. Pavement ends; gravel begins.

7.2 (11.6 km) Public road ends at Herring Cove near mouth of Silver Bay (boat tours of the bay available in Sitka). City road to hydroelectric power plant continues.

7.4 (11.9 km) Gate marking boundary of city road. No vehicles beyond this point; access for hikers and bicyclists only. No guardrails or road signs to road end.

10.5 (16.9 km) Fish hatchery and gate. Steep grades; watch for rocks on road.

13.7 (22 km) Road end. Green Lake Power Plant.

Halibut Point Road Log

Halibut Point Road (paved) leads northwest from the intersection of Harbor Drive and Lincoln Street past Old Sitka to Starrigavan Campground.

0 Harbor Drive and Lincoln Street. Proceed northwest (road is now Lake Street).

0.1 (0.2 km) Fire station. Intersection with Sawmill Creek Road; keep left.

0.3 (0.5 km) **Swan Lake** to right of road, rainbow from 12 to 14 inches.

0.6 (1 km) Katlian Street on left leads to boat ramp and then to downtown. Hospital to the right.

1.8 (2.9 km) Pioneer Park picnic and day-use area with beach access; parking available.

2.2 (3.5 km) Cascade Creek bridge.

2.3 (3.7 km) Tongass National Forest work center.

2.4 (3.9 km) Sandy Beach; good swimming beach, ample parking, view of Mount Edgecumbe. Whales are sometimes sighted.

3.8 (6.1 km) Viewpoint. On a clear day you can see for 50 miles/80 km.

4.2 (6.8 km) Harbor Mountain Road; steep gravel, accessible to cars. Road leads 5 miles/8 km to road end and Harbor Mountain Ridge trail to lookout at 2,300 feet/701m. Great view of Sitka Sound.

4.4 (7.1 km) Granite Creek bridge. Just beyond the bridge on left is Halibut Point state recreation site with swimming beach, shelters, tables, fireplaces and toilets.

7 (11.3 km) Alaska Marine Highway ferry terminal on left.

7.3 (11.7 km) Boat ramp, litter barrel and pit toilet to left.

7.5 (12.1 km) Old Sitka State Historical

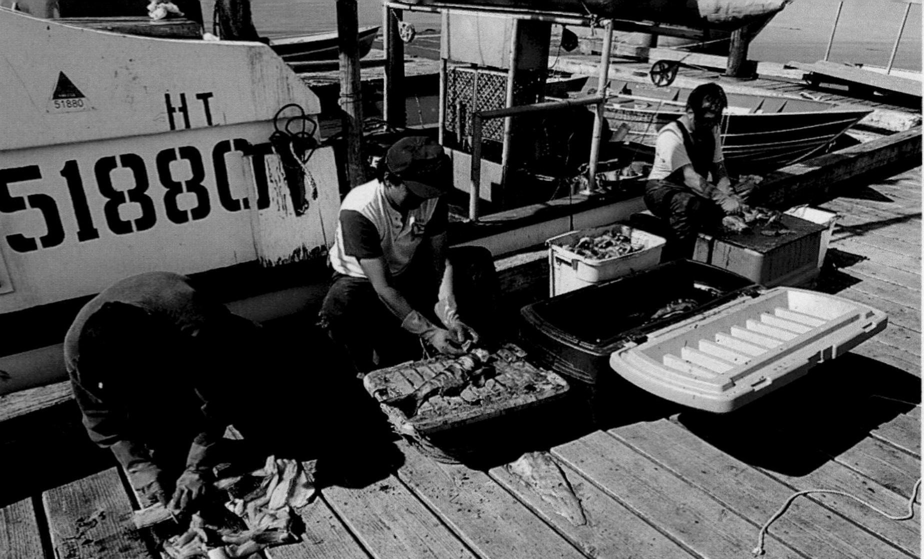

Cleaning a catch of salmon at Kake on Kupreanof Island. (© James D. Ronan, Sr.)

Site at left, and Starrigavan Creek bridge just ahead. Old Sitka was the site of the Russian Fort Archangel Michael, established in 1799. Commemorative plaque and historical markers. The site is a registered national historic landmark.

7.6 (12.2 km) Narrow road on right runs along the bank of Starrigavan Creek, where pink salmon spawn in August and September, and continues several miles through Starrigavan River valley. Off-road vehicles permitted on ATV trail only.

7.7 (12.4 km) USFS estuary life trail, Starrigavan Recreation Area; bird watching. Wheelchair access, vault toilets, trails, parking adjacent.

7.8 (12.6 km) Turnoff for Starrigavan USFS campground and picnic area; artesian well with excellent drinking water. Forest and muskeg nature trail, across from boat ramp, connects with Estuary life trail. Access to beach. **Starrigavan Bay**, Dolly Varden; pink and silver salmon, May to October.

7.9 (12.7 km) Road ends.

Kake

(See map, page 689)

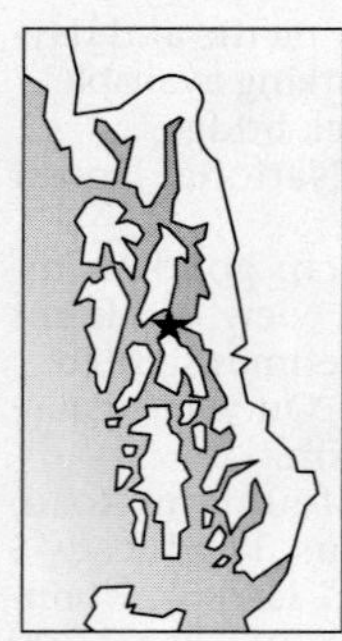

Located on the northwest coast of Kupreanof Island; Petersburg is 40 air miles/64 km or 65 miles/105 km by boat; Juneau is 95 air miles/153 km northeast. **Population:** 820 (approximately 85 percent Native). **Emergency Services:** for all emergencies, 911. **Police,** phone (907) 785-3393. **Public Health Center,** phone (907) 785-3333. **Maritime Search and Rescue,** phone the Coast Guard at (800) 478-5555 or (907) 785-3500.

Visitor Information: City of Kake, Box 500, Kake 99830.

Elevation: Sea level. **Climate:** Less than average rainfall for southeastern Alaska, approximately 50 inches annually. Mild temperatures. January average temperatures are around freezing. Slightly warmer than nearby Petersburg, Kake is noted for being in the "banana belt" of Southeast.

Private Aircraft: Kake seaplane base, located adjacent southeast; fuel 100. Airstrip 1 mile/1.6 km west; elev. 148 feet/45m; length 4,000 feet/1,219m; asphalt; unattended.

Transportation: Air—Scheduled service from Petersburg (15-minute flight), Juneau (45 minutes), Wrangell and Sitka. Scheduled daily charter service provided by Ketchikan Air and L.A.B. Flying Service. **Ferry**—Alaska Marine Highway vessel from Petersburg and Sitka.

Accommodations at local inns and bed and breakfasts. There are general, variety and video stores, a cafe and other services. Church groups include Baptist, Salvation Army, Presbyterian and Assembly of God. Kake has an accredited high school, junior high school and elementary.

The town is a permanent village of the Kake (pronounced cake) tribe of the Tlingit Indians. In a series of incidents in the late 1860s, several white men were killed by Kake warriors in reprisal for the deaths of their clansmen. United States gunboats retaliated by shelling and destroying 3 Kake villages.

The tribe eventually settled at the present-day site of Kake, where the government established a school in 1891. Residents have historically drawn ample subsistence from the sea. However, with the advent of a cash economy, the community has come to depend on commercial fishing, fish processing (there is a cold storage) and logging. In recent years, the fish processing has expanded to include the production of value-added products such as smoked and dried fish, and pet treats made from dried salmon skins. The post office was established in 1904, and the city was incorporated in 1952. The city's claim to fame is its totem, reputedly the world's tallest one-piece pole at 132 feet, 6 inches. It was carved for the 1967 Alaska Purchase Centennial Celebration.

The fourth annual Kake Dog Salmon Festival, July 24–25, 1998, celebrates Tlingit culture and the return of dog salmon, also known as chum salmon. Over 700 people joined the festivities in 1997, which included events such as a Tlingit canoe race called "The Challenge of the Chums," the Chum Run foot race and a dog salmon toss. Contact Kake Tribal Corp. for more information, phone (907) 785-3221.

Other area activities include a guided tour of the local salmon hatchery (907/785-6460) and watching black bear fish for salmon in Gunnuk Creek, which flows through the center of the village.

Angoon

(See map, page 690)

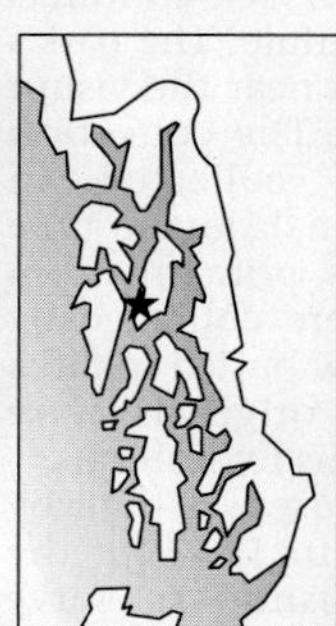

Located on the west coast of Admiralty Island on Chatham Strait, at the mouth of Kootznahoo Inlet. Peril Strait is across Chatham Strait from Angoon. Juneau is 60 air miles/97 km northeast. Sitka is 41 miles/66 km southwest. **Population:** 750. **Emergency Services: Police,** phone (907) 788-3631. **Clinic,** phone (907) 788-3633.

Visitor Information: Local people are happy to help. You may also contact the USFS Admiralty Island National Monument office in Angoon (phone 907/788-3166) or the city of Angoon (phone 907/788-3653).

Elevation: Sea level. **Climate:** Moderate weather with about 40 inches of annual rainfall and mild temperatures.

Private Aircraft: Angoon seaplane base; 0.9 mile/1.4 km southeast; unattended.

Transportation: Air—Scheduled seaplane service from Juneau. **Ferry**—Alaska Marine Highway service.

Accommodations available at a motel and 2 bed and breakfasts. There are 2 general stores. Fuel service available. There are no RV facilities. Canoes and 12 charter boats available. Transient moorage for private boats also available.

Angoon is a long-established Tlingit Indian settlement at the entrance to Kootznahoo Inlet. It is the only permanent community on Admiralty Island. On Killisnoo Island, across the harbor from the state ferry landing, a community of mostly summer homes has grown up along the island beaches. The lifestyle of this primarily Tlingit community is heavily subsistence: fish, clams, seaweed, berries and venison. Fishing, mostly hand trolling for king and coho salmon, is the principal industry.

The scenery of Admiralty Island draws many visitors. All but the northern portion of the island was declared a national monument in December 1980 and is jointly managed by the U.S. Forest Service and Kootznoowoo Inc., the local Native corporation. Kootznahoo Inlet and Mitchell Bay near Angoon offer a network of small wooded islands, reefs and channels for kayaking. Mitchell Bay and Admiralty Lakes Recreational Area are the 2 major recreational attractions within the monument.

Pack Creek, on the east coast of the island, is a well-known bear viewing spot (best mid-July to late August); permit required. Admiralty Island's Indian name, *Kootznoowoo,* means "Fortress of Bears." There are 12 USFS cabins available for public use in the monument; contact the U.S. Forest Service in Angoon.

Local residents can provide directions to the interesting old Killisnoo graveyards, located both on the island and on the Angoon shore of the old Killisnoo settlement, which once was one of the larger communities in southeastern Alaska.

Fishing for salmon is excellent in the Angoon area. (Record kings have been caught in nearby Kelp Bay and in Angoon harbor.) There is also excellent halibut and other bottom fish fishing. Trout (cutthroat and Dolly Varden) fishing in the lakes and streams on Admiralty Island; fair but scattered.

Tenakee Springs

(See map, page 690)

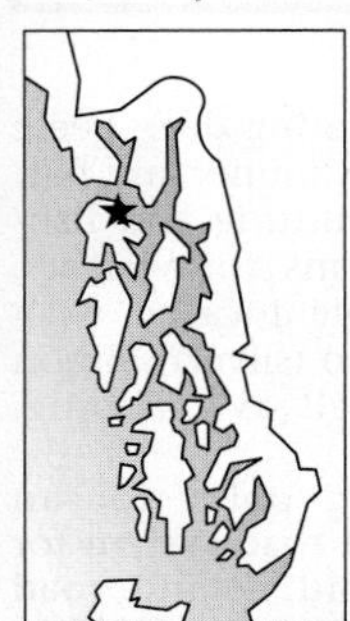

Located on the north shore of Tenakee Inlet on Chichagof Island, 50 miles/81 km northeast of Sitka. **Population:** 107. **Visitor Information:** Can be obtained from city hall, phone (907) 736-2207, or from the town's store, phone (907) 736-2205. **Elevation:** Sea level. **Climate:** Average rainfall 63.2 inches annually, with moderate snowfall. **Private Aircraft:** Seaplane base.

Transportation: Air—Scheduled and charter service available through Wings of Alaska out of Juneau. **Ferry**—Alaska Marine Highway service from Sitka and Juneau.

Tenakee Springs has 1 street—Tenakee Avenue—which is about 1.7 miles/2.7 km long and 4 to 12 feet wide. At each end of town is a foot trail that runs 3 miles/5 km west and 5 miles/8 km east on which no motorized vehicles or bicycles are allowed. Many residents use 3-wheel motor bikes for transportation, some ride bicycles, but most walk the short distances between buildings. There are a store, cafe, clinic, post office, library, sawmill and city hall. Accommodations at 7 rental cabins (bring your sleeping bag) are available at Snyder Mercantile, and Tenakee Hot Springs Lodge offers guided sportfishing and sightseeing; phone (907) 736-2400. Tenakee Springs became a city in 1971 and has a mayor, council and planning commission.

The word Tenakee comes from the Tlingit word *tinaghu,* or "Coppery Shield Bay." This refers to 3 copper shields, highly prized by the Tlingits, which were lost in a storm.

The hot springs (temperatures from 106°F to 108°F/41°C to 42°C) brought people to Tenakee at the turn of the century. A bathhouse, completed in 1940, located on the waterfront posts times of use for men and women. The facility is maintained by contributions from residents and visitors.

The major industry at Tenakee might be described as relaxation, as many retirees have chosen to live here, away from the bustle of other Southeast cities. There are many summer homes along Tenakee Avenue. During the summer, watch for whales in Tenakee Inlet, which are sometimes spotted from town.

Some logging is under way in the area around Tenakee. Tenakee Inlet produces salmon, halibut, Dungeness and king crab, red snapper and cod. A small fleet of fishing vessels is home-ported in Tenakee's harbor, located about 0.5 mile/0.8 km east of the center of town. Although many visitors come to Tenakee to hunt and fish, there are no hunting guides or rental boats available locally. There are 3 fishing and sightseeing charter services.

Pelican

(See map, page 690)

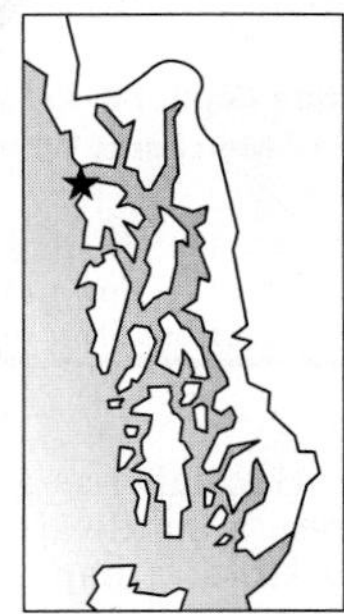

Located on the east shore of Lisianski Inlet on the northwest coast of Chichagof Island; 70 air miles/113 km north of Sitka and 70 air miles/113 km west of Juneau. **Population:** 209. **Emergency Services: Public Safety Officer** and **Fire Department,** phone 911. **Clinic,** phone (907) 735-2250. **Elevation:** Sea level. **Climate:** Average winter temperatures from 21°F/-6°C to 39°F/4°C; summer temperatures from 51°F/11°C to 62°F/17°C. Total average annual precipitation is 127 inches, with 120 inches of snow.

Visitor Information: Contact the Pelican Visitor Assoc., Box 737, Pelican, AK 99832; phone (907) 735-2282 or 735-2259.

Private Aircraft: Seaplane base; fuel 80, 100. **Transportation: Air**—Scheduled air service from Juneau via Alaska Seaplane Services and Taquan Air. Scheduled service from Sitka via Taquan Air. Seaplanes land within walking distance to downtown. **Ferry**—Alaska Marine Highway serves Pelican; terminal is approximately 1/4 mile from downtown boardwalk. There are no cars or taxis in Pelican, which is fine, as the town is not very big. Bring a good pair of walking shoes. Four-wheels are available.

Pelican has 2 bar-and-grills (1 with 4 rooms for rent) and a cafe. Accommodations available at a lodge, 2 seasonal lodges, and bed and breakfast. There are a grocery and dry goods store, laundromat and 2 liquor stores. There are a small-boat harbor, marine repair and a fuel dock.

Established in 1938 by Kalle (Charley) Raataikainen, and named for Raataikainen's fish packer *The Pelican,* Pelican relies on commercial fishing and seafood processing. Pelican Seafoods processes salmon, halibut, crab, herring, black cod, rockfish, sea urchin and sea cucumber, and is the primary year-round employer. Pelican has dubbed itself "closest to the fish," a reference to its close proximity to the rich Fairweather salmon grounds. Salmon trolling season is from about June to mid-September, and the king salmon winter season is from October through April. Pelican's population increases greatly when nonresident fishers work during the salmon seasons. Pelican was incorporated in 1943. Most of Pelican is built on pilings over tidelands. A wooden boardwalk extends the length of the community, and there are about 2 miles/3.2 kmb of gravel road.

Local recreation includes kayaking, hiking, fishing, and watching birds and marine mammals.

Hoonah

(See map, page 690)

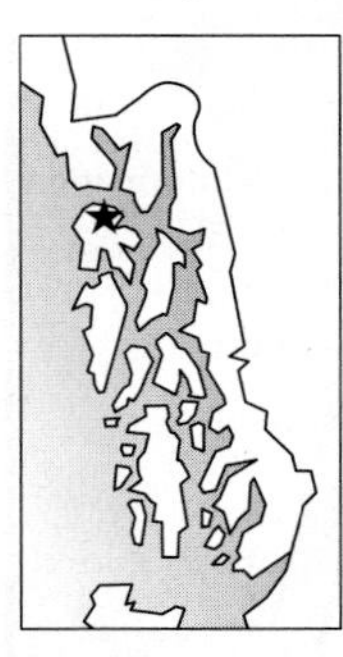

Located on the northeast shore of Chichagof Island, about 40 miles/64 km west of Juneau and 20 miles/32 km south across Icy Strait from the entrance to Glacier Bay. **Population:** 903. **Emergency Services: Alaska State Troopers** and **Hoonah City Police,** phone (907) 945-3655; emergency only phone 911. **Maritime Search and Rescue,** call the Coast Guard at (800) 478-5555.

Visitor Information: Local business people, city office staff (907/945-3663, weekdays 8 A.M. to 4:30 P.M.) and the postmaster are happy to help. The U.S. Forest Service office in Hoonah (Box 135, Hoonah, AK 99829, phone 907/945-3631) also has visitor information, including a $4 Hoonah area road guide showing forest roads on Chichagof Island and a $4 Tongass National Forest map.

Elevation: Sea level. **Climate:** Typical Southeastern Alaska climate, with average annual precipitation of 70 inches. Average daily temperature in July, 57°F/13°C; in January, 35°F/1°C. Prevailing winds are southeasterly.

Private Aircraft: Hoonah airport, adja-

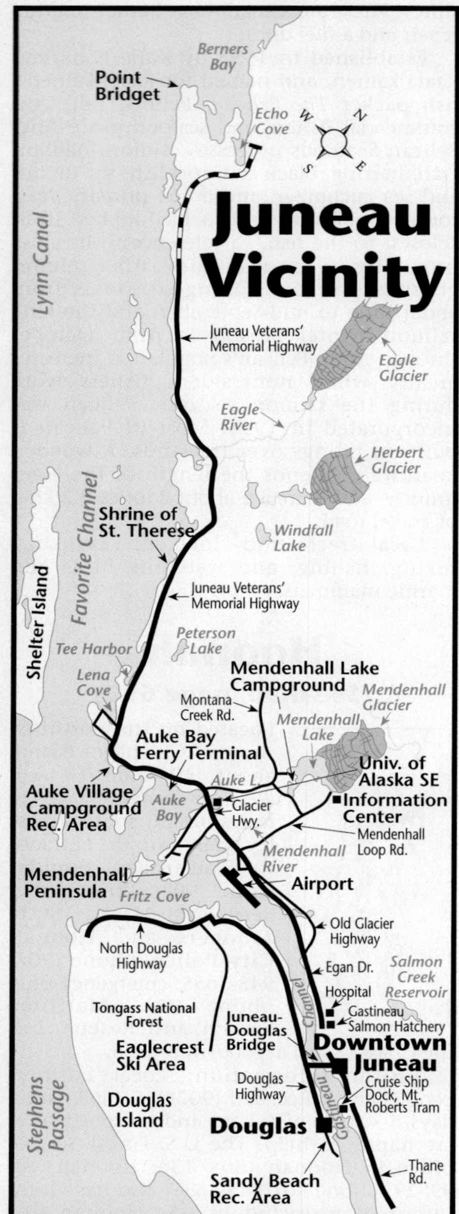

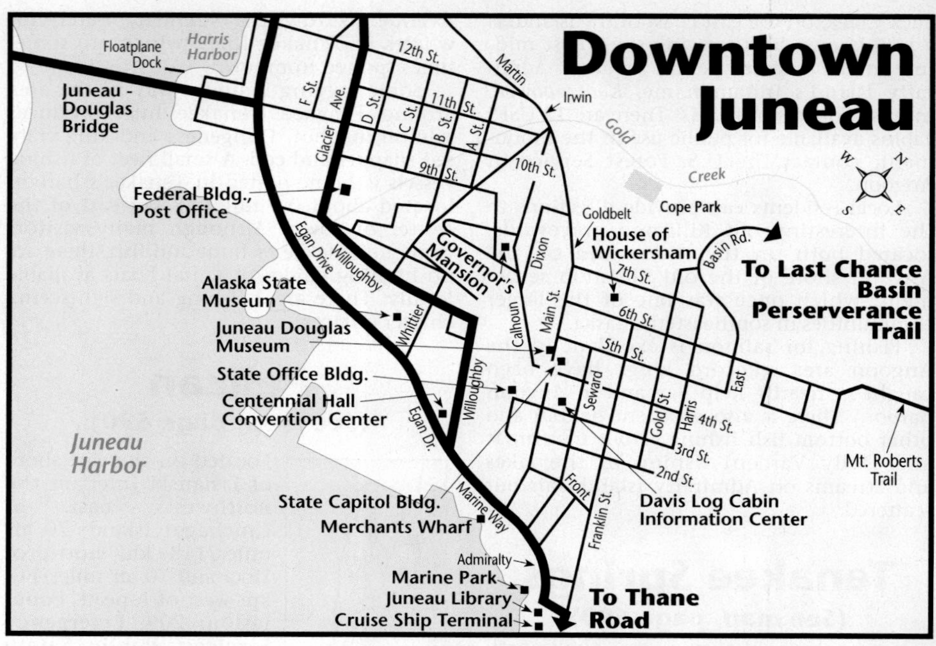

cent southeast; elev. 30 feet/9m; length 3,000 feet/914m; paved. Seaplane base adjacent.

Transportation: Air–Scheduled and charter service from Juneau. Airport is located about 3 miles/5 km from town. **Ferry**–Alaska Marine Highway vessel serves Hoonah.

Bed-and-breakfast lodging at Wind'n Sea Inn (907/945-3438). Accommodations also available at Hoonah Lodge. Hoonah has 2 restaurants, 2 grocery stores, a hardware store, a gift shop, a variety store, a bank, marine fuel docks, a gas pump and 3 flying services. The marina, with showers and a laundromat, is a popular layover for boaters awaiting permits to enter Glacier Bay.

Hoonah is a small coastal community with a quiet harbor for the seining and trolling fleets. The most prominent structures are a cold storage facility, the lodge, bank, post office and the public school. The village has been occupied since prehistory by the Tlingit people. In the late 1800s, missionaries settled here. Canneries established in the area in the early 1900s spurred the growth of commercial fishing, which remains the mainstay of Hoonah's economy. During the summer fishing season, residents work for nearby Excursion Inlet Packing Co. or Hoonah Cold Storage in town. Halibut season begins in May, and salmon season opens in mid-summer and runs through September. Logging also contributes to the economy, with employment loading log ships and other industry-related jobs. Subsistence hunting and fishing remain an important lifestyle here, and many families gather food in the traditional way: catching salmon and halibut in summer, shellfish and bottom fish year-round; hunting deer, geese and ducks; berry picking in summer and fall.

Kayaking, sightseeing, hunting and fishing are the main attractions for visitors. Charter fishing is available locally, with good seasonal king and coho (silver) salmon and halibut fishing as well as crabbing. Guide services are available.

Hoonah is the starting point for an extensive logging and forest road system for northwest Chichagof Island. Island road maps ($3) are available through the USFS in Hoonah, Sitka and Juneau.

Juneau

(See maps, pages 690–691)

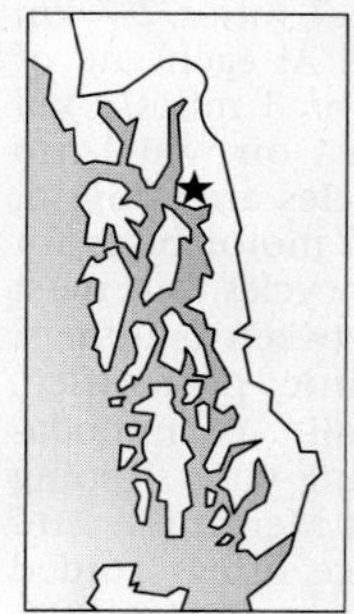

Located on Gastineau Channel; 900 air miles/1,448 km (2 hours, 10 minutes flying time) from Seattle, WA, 650 air miles/1,046 km (1 hour, 25 minutes by jet) from Anchorage. **Population:** Borough 29,755. **Emergency Services:** Phone 911 for all emergencies. **Police,** phone (907) 586-2780. **Fire Department,** phone (907) 586-5245. **Alaska State Troopers,** phone (907) 465-4000. **Poison Center** and **Hospital,** Bartlett Regional, 3260 Hospital Dr., phone (907) 586-2611. **Maritime Search and Rescue,** Coast Guard, phone (907) 463-2000 or (800) 478-5555.

Visitor Information: Juneau Convention & Visitors Bureau, Davis Log Cabin Information Center, 134 3rd St., phone (907) 586-2201 or (888) 581-2201; Internet: www.juneau.com; e-mail: jcub@ptialaska.net. Open year-round 8:30 A.M. to 5 P.M. Monday through Friday; additional hours during the summer, 9 A.M. to 5 P.M. Saturday and Sunday. To find out about current events in Juneau, phone (907) 586-JUNO for a recorded message. Visitor information kiosk located in Marine Park on waterfront near Merchants Wharf, usually open daily 8:30 A.M. to 6 P.M., from about mid-May to mid-September. Information booth at the airport terminal. Visitor information is also available at the cruise ship terminal on S. Franklin Street when cruise ships are in port, and at the Auke Bay ferry terminal. Large groups contact the Davis Log Cabin Information Center in advance for special assistance.

USFS Information Center at Centennial Hall, 101 Egan Dr.; open 8 A.M. to 5 P.M. daily from mid-May to mid-September; 9 A.M. to 5 P.M. Monday through Friday the rest of the year. Phone (907) 586-8751. U.S. Park Service office here open in summer. The center has seasonal features of natural history films. USFS cabins may also be reserved here. The center issues permits for visiting Pack Creek, the bear preserve on Admiralty Island. Juneau Ranger District (USFS), **Milepost 9.4** Glacier Highway (airport area), phone (907) 586-8800; open 8 A.M. to 5 P.M. weekdays. Mendenhall Glacier Visitor Center (USFS), phone (907) 789-0097, open 8:30 A.M. to 5:30 P.M. daily in summer, 9 A.M. to 4 P.M. weekends only in winter.

Elevation: Sea level. **Climate:** Mild and wet. Average daily maximum temperature in July, 63°F/17°C; daily minimum in January, 20°F/-7°C. Highest recorded temperature, 90°F/32°C in July 1975; the lowest -22°F/-30°C in January 1972. Average annual precipitation, 56.5 inches (airport), 92 inches (downtown); 103 inches of snow annually. Snow on ground intermittently from mid-November to mid-April. Prevailing winds are east-southeasterly. **Radio:** KJNO 630, KINY 800, KTOO-FM 104.3, KTKU-FM 105.1, KSUP-FM 106. **Television:** KJUD Channel 8; JATV cable; KTOO (public television). **Newspapers:** *Juneau Empire* (Sunday through Friday) and *Capital City Weekly*.

Private Aircraft: Juneau International Airport, 9 miles/14.5 km northwest; elev. 18 feet/5m; length 8,456 feet/2,577m; asphalt; fuel 100LL, Jet A. Juneau harbor seaplane base, due east; restricted use, no fuel. International seaplane base, 7 miles/11.3 km northwest; 5,000 feet/1,524m by 450 feet/137m, avgas, Jet A. For more information, phone the Juneau Flight Service Station at (907) 789-6124.

HISTORY AND ECONOMY

In 1880, nearly 20 years before the great gold rushes to the Klondike and to Nome, 2 prospectors named Joe Juneau and Dick Harris found "color" in what is now called Gold Creek, a small, clear stream that runs through the center of present-day Juneau. What they found led to the discovery of one of the largest lodes of gold quartz in the world. Juneau (called Harrisburg the first year) quickly boomed into a gold rush town as claims and mines sprang up in the area.

For a time the largest mine was the Treadwell, across Gastineau Channel south of Douglas (which was once a larger town than Juneau), but a cave-in and flood closed the mine in 1917. In 36 years of operation, Treadwell produced $66 million in gold. The Alaska–Gastineau Mine, operated by Bart Thane in 1911, had a 2-mile shaft through Mount Roberts to the Perseverance Mine near Gold Creek. The Alaska–Juneau (A–J) Mine was constructed on a mountain slope south of Juneau and back into the heart of Mount Roberts. It operated until 1944, when it was declared a nonessential wartime activity after producing over $80 million in gold. Post–WWII wage and price inflation and the fixed price of gold prevented its reopening.

In 1900, the decision to move Alaska's capital to Juneau was made because of the city's growth, mining activity and location on the water route to Skagway and the Klondike; the decline of post-Russian Sitka, as whale and fur trading slackened, secured Juneau's new status as Alaska's preeminent city.

Congress first provided civil government for Alaska in 1884. Until statehood in 1959 Alaska was governed by a succession of presidential appointees, first as the District of Alaska, then as the Territory of Alaska. Between 1867 (when the United States purchased Alaska from Russia) and 1884, the military had jurisdiction over the District of Alaska, except for a 3-year period (1877–79) when Alaska was put under control of the U.S. Treasury Dept. and governed by U.S. Collectors of Customs.

With the arrival of Alaska statehood in 1959, Juneau's governmental role increased even further. In 1974, Alaskans voted to move the capital from Juneau to a site between Anchorage and Fairbanks, closer to

Juneau

Call for your **FREE** Juneau Travel Planner
888-581-2201

Juneau Convention & Visitors Bureau • 134 Third Street • Juneau, Alaska 99801
(907) 586-2201 • Fax (907) 586-6304 • e-mail: jcvb@ptialaska.net • visit our web site: http://www.juneau.com

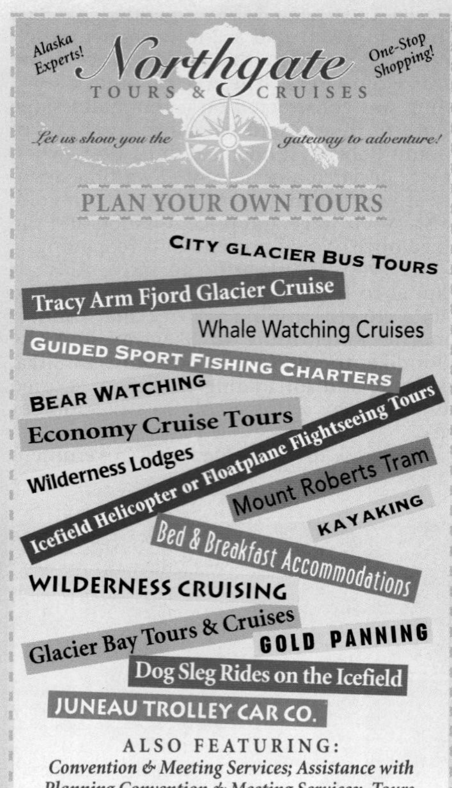

Wings of Alaska Airlines

★ SCHEDULED FLIGHTS ★ CHARTERS ★
★ GLACIER FLIGHTSEEING ★

Wings of Alaska • Juneau Airport • Juneau, AK 99801
(907) 789-0790 • Fax (907) 789-2021
www.wingsofalaska.com

ALASKA STATE MUSEUM STORE

Quality Alaska Native Art & Crafts

395 Whittier St • Juneau, AK 99801 • (907) 465-4845

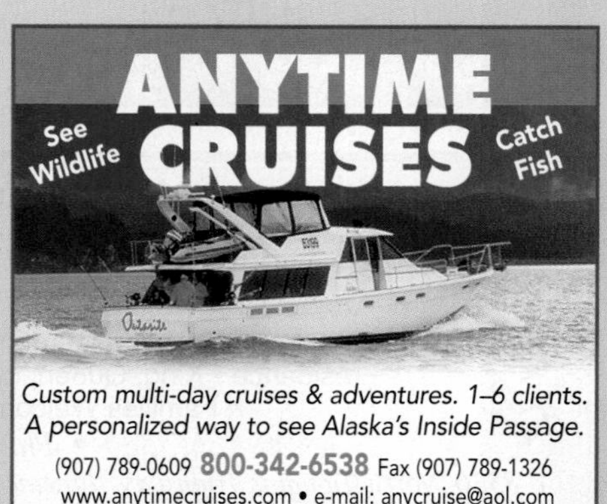

■ Sportfishing for salmon and halibut
■ Sightseeing for whales, wildlife and glaciers
■ Lodging in our comfortable log home
■ Home cooked meals

Whitey and Katy Bloom • (907) 789-0990
P.O. Box 211013 • Auke Bay, Alaska 99821

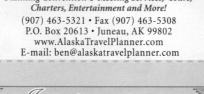

FISH Juneau

SIGHTSEEING
WHALEWATCHING
SPORTFISHING

STATE OF ALASKA, DIV. OF TOURISM

YOUR ADVENTURE INCLUDES:

- Alaskan snacks and beverages.
- Clean, warm cabin cruisers with full facilities.
- Transportation to and from anywhere on the Juneau road system.
- Bait, tackle, and state of the art fishing equipment.
- Fishing licenses may be purchased on board.
- Processing of catch can be arranged with award winning processor.

Remote lodges, overnight charters and custom tours available

Half or full day charters • Boats ranging in size from 22' to 38'

AUKE BAY SPORTFISHING & SIGHTSEEING

1-800-586-6945 • (907) 789-2562

E-mail: simba@ptialaska.net • http://www.nextek.net/aukebay

On National Register of Historic Sites

Antique Oak Bar

Kitchenettes

Hot Tubs

167-MP S. Franklin, Juneau, AK 99801
1-800-327-9347 • Fax (907) 463-3775

Aurora View

INN ON THE MOUNTAIN

• spectacular city views • 144 channel TV •
• private entrances & decks • 3 min. to downtown •
sauna & hot tub • lavish suite & rooms

1-888-580-VIEW • www.ptialaska.net/~auroravu

ABOVE ALL, SEE ALASKA

Come face to face with Alaska's most spectacular scenery. From the massive Juneau icefield to Mt. McKinley's towering peaks. Experience Alaska from above. Era Helicopters. Simply the best way to see Alaska. Tours in Anchorage, Mt. McKinley, Juneau and Valdez.

Call
1-800-843-1947
In Juneau (907) 586-2030

Era Helicopters
Flightseeing Tours
http://www.era-aviation.com/helicoptertours

The Driftwood Lodge

- 24-hour courtesy transportation to/from airport and ferries
- Near Alaska State Museum and Juneau Convention Center
- Restaurant on premises
- Free spacious parking area
- Color TVs and phones in all rooms
- Liquor & grocery store on premises
- 62 units: kitchen units up to two-bedroom suites
- Coffee in rooms
- Baggage storage
- Brochure available
- Rates $68–95

Toll-Free: **1-800-544-2239** • (907) 586-2280 • Fax 907-586-1034
435 Willoughby Ave. W. • Juneau, Alaska 99801

Downtown Juneau is great to explore on foot. (© Robin Brandt)

the state's population center. In 1976, Alaska voters selected a new capital site near Willow, 65 road miles/105 km north of Anchorage on the Parks Highway. However, in November 1982, voters defeated funding for the capital move.

Today, government (federal, state and local) comprises an estimated half of the total basic industry. Tourism is the largest employer in the private sector.

DESCRIPTION

Juneau, often called "a little San Francisco," is nestled at the foot of Mount Juneau (elev. 3,576 feet/1,091m) with Mount Roberts (elev. 3,819 feet/1,164m) rising immediately to the east on the approach up Gastineau Channel. The residential community of Douglas, on Douglas Island, is south of Juneau and connected by a bridge. Neighboring residential areas around the airport, Mendenhall Valley and Auke Bay lie north of Juneau on the mainland.

Shopping is in the downtown area and at suburban malls in the airport and Mendenhall Valley areas.

Juneau's skyline is dominated by several government buildings, including the Federal Building (1962), the massive State Office Building (1974), the State Court Building (1975) and the older brick, and marble-columned Capitol Building (1931). The modern Sealaska Plaza is headquarters for Sealaska Corp., 1 of the 13 regional Native corporations formed after congressional passage of the Alaska Native Claims Settlement Act in 1971.

To explore downtown Juneau, it is best to park and walk; distances are not great. The streets are narrow and congested with pedestrians and traffic (especially rush hours), and on-street parking is scarce. Visitors should check at the Davis Log Cabin and at the police station to see whether parking permits are available. Public parking lots are located across from Merchants Wharf Mall at Main Street and Egan Drive and south of Marine Park at the Marine Park parking garage; fee required.

The Juneau area supports 35 churches, a high school, 2 middle schools, several elementary schools and a University of Alaska Southeast campus at Auke Lake. There are 3 municipal libraries and the state library. The Perseverance Theatre, which was established in 1978, provides Juneau with classical and original works, September through May.

The area is governed by the unified city and borough of Juneau, which encompasses 3,108 square miles/8,060 square km. It is the first unified government in the state, combining the former separate and overlapping jurisdictions of the city of Douglas, city of Juneau and greater Juneau borough.

ACCOMMODATIONS/VISITOR SERVICES

Juneau has several hotels and motels, most of them downtown. These include: Alaska Hotel & Bar (907/586-1000), Best Western Country Lane Inn (907/789-5005), Breakwater Inn (907/586-6303), Driftwood Lodge Motel (907/586-2280), Prospector Hotel (907/586-3737), Super 8 Motel (907/789-4858), Travelodge (907/789-9700), Westmark Baranof (907/586-2660) and Westmark Juneau (907/586-6900). There are also numerous bed and breakfasts as well as wilderness lodges; see ads this section.

The Juneau International Hostel is located at 614 Harris St. (Juneau 99801), 4 blocks northeast of the Capitol Bldg. All ages are welcome. Check-in time is 5–11 P.M. during summer, 5–10:30 P.M. the rest of the year. Showers, cooking, laundry and storage facilities are available. Cost for members is $7, nonmembers $10, children accompanied by parent $5. Groups welcome. Open year-round. Phone (907) 586-9559.

More than 60 restaurants offer a wide variety of dining. Also watch for sidewalk food vendors downtown in summer.

Juneau also has a microbrewery. The Alaskan Brewing Co., located at 5429 Shaune Dr. in the Lemon Creek area, produces Alaskan Amber Beer and Alaskan Pale Ale. Free tours available. Phone (907) 780-5866 for more information.

Fireweed House Bed & Breakfast with spectacular view of the Thomas Glacier on Lemon Creek. Situated in rural setting on Douglas Island, only 8 minutes from downtown Juneau. Ideal base for your Juneau stay. Choose from quality accommodations: 3 well-appointed bedrooms, each with private sitting area; a separate apartment; or executive-style, 2-bedroom guest house. Private and shared baths, some with Jacuzzis. Enjoy resident and migrating birds, regular sightings of small mammals and the occasional bear. On-site blueberry picking in late summer. Regardless of departure time, you will be treated to a delicious full-service breakfast. Arrangements for tours and charters. On-premise freezers. Nonsmoking. Children welcome. Join the family in the open and spacious living room, and enjoy the feel of wood surroundings and the high, 2-story cathedral ceiling. Evening conversation to explore the specialties of Juneau. AAA 3-diamond approved. Toll free (800) 586-3885. Phone (907) 586-3885; fax (907) 586-3385. 8530 North Douglas Highway-MP, Juneau, AK 99801. For reservation information contact us at www.wetpage.com/fireweed. [ADVERTISEMENT]

Pearson's Pond Luxury Inn. Looking for the perfect getaway? You'll find it here, nestled in the rainforest next to the Mendenhall Glacier. You'll be away from the crowds, yet conveniently located, at this breathtaking retreat on the banks of a peaceful pond. Enjoy a relaxing hot tub and massage amid lush gardens and sparkling fountains. Between naps on the dock, bike the adjacent nature trail, photograph wildlife, roast marshmallows, enjoy a workout or winter cross-country ski. Everything, including stocked kitchenettes, is provided for an exceptional value. Year-round, smoke and pet free. Ski, spa and wedding packages. 4541-MP Sawa Circle, Juneau, AK 99801-8723; phone (907) 789-3772, fax 789-6722, e-mail: pearsons.pond@juneau.com. Website: www.juneau.com/pearsons.pond. AAA/ABBA Excellence Awards. Recommended as a "Best B & B" in America (Fodor's/Soule's) and Alaska (Frommer's). Book far ahead, as this place earns its excellent reputation. A definite 10! [ADVERTISEMENT]

The Whale's Eye Lodge is a taste of the Alaskan wilderness in comfort. Located on Shelter Island, a 30-minute boat ride from Juneau. You will find us tucked in the old growth forest on the Inside Passage. Whales, sea lions and eagles can be viewed right from the lodge windows. Private cabins allow you to harmonize with your surroundings. Our charter boat awaits you for excellent salmon and halibut fishing and wildlife excursions. Home-cooked meals with fresh-baked goods and seafood are on the menu daily. We cater to only 4–6 guests at a time for a personal experience. Phone (907) 723-2920. P.O. Box 210166, Auke Bay, AK 99821. E-mail: walseye@pti.net. [ADVERTISEMENT]

The city and borough of Juneau offers limited RV overnight parking spaces at the Juneau Yacht Club (turnoff at **Milepost 1.7** Egan Drive/Glacier Highway) and at Savikko Park/Sandy Beach (**Milepost 2.5** Douglas Highway); $5 per space, per night, paid at the harbormaster's office. For parking at both yacht club and park, sign in at the harbormaster's office (across from high school on Egan Drive). Contact the visitor information center (907/586-2201) for a brochure on RV facilities. Dump stations are located at Mendenhall Lake campground, Valley Tesoro at Mendenhall Center shopping mall in the Mendenhall Valley, and Savikko Park in Douglas.

There are 2 USFS campgrounds and 1 private RV park north of Juneau via the Glacier Highway. The USFS campgrounds are Mendenhall Lake (turn off Glacier Highway at **Milepost 9.4** or **12.2** and continue to Montana Creek Road) and Auke Village (**Milepost 15.4** Glacier Highway). Mendenhall Lake has 60 sites (16 sites accommodate vehicles longer than 20 feet), water, pit toilets, dump station. Ten sites can be reserved; phone (800) 280-CAMP. Auke Village Campground, 1.5 miles/2.4 km west of the ferry terminal, has 12 campsites, flush and pit toilets, water and firewood: first-come, first-served. The private RV park, with hookups, is located at **Milepost 12.3** Glacier Highway; phone (907) 789-9467. ▲

Spruce Meadow RV Park. (Planned to open in spring 1998.) 64 private, unique, full-service spaces located on 10.5 acres of virgin wetlands in spruce, alder and meadows. Services available: 30-amp electric, water, sewer, garbage, phone, cable TV, laundromat, showers, restrooms, recreation hall, gazebos, dump station, on-site management, bicycle rental, tourist information and brochures. Only 5 minutes from Mendenhall Glacier and Auke Bay boat harbor. Reservations strongly recommended. Visit us at 10200 Mendenhall Loop Rd. E-mail: juneauRVer@aol.com. Phone (907) 798-1990. [ADVERTISEMENT]

TRANSPORTATION

Air: Juneau Municipal Airport turnoff is at **Milepost 8.8** Egan Drive (Glacier Highway). Airport terminal contains ticket counters, waiting area, gift shop, rental cars, restaurant, lounge and information booth.

The city express bus stops at the airport weekdays from 8 A.M. to 5 P.M. A shuttle and taxi and van service to downtown are also available. Shuttle service $8 1-way per person, $5 each for groups of 3 or more. Taxi service approximately $15 to $20. Courtesy vans to some hotels.

Alaska Airlines serves Juneau daily from Seattle, WA, Anchorage, Fairbanks, Ketchikan, Sitka, Yakutat, Cordova, Petersburg and Wrangell. Scheduled commuter service to Haines, Skagway, Sitka, Angoon and other points via several air services. Scheduled service by Summit Air between Juneau and Whitehorse, YT, year-round and between Juneau and Atlin, BC, in summer.

Charter air service (wheel and floatplanes and helicopters) for hunting, fishing, sightseeing and transportation to other communities (see ads in this section).

Alaska Seaplane Service provides experienced floatplane service to wilderness cabins, Native villages, and fishing lodges in Southeast Alaska. Thirty years of flying experience guarantees personalized, professional sightseeing and wildlife tours. Visit our ticket counter in the Juneau International Airport or phone (907) 789-3331 for further information. [ADVERTISEMENT]

Ferry: Juneau is served by Alaska Marine Highway ferries.

Alaska state ferries dock at the Auke Bay terminal at **Milepost 13.9** Glacier Highway; phone (907) 465-3941 or 789-7453. Taxi service and private shuttle bus is available from Auke Bay terminal to downtown Juneau. Shuttle service runs mid-May to mid-October; $5 each way. There is also a bus stop 1.5 miles/2.4 km toward town from the ferry terminal (see following).

Bus: Capital Transit city bus system runs from the cruise ship terminal downtown and includes Juneau, Douglas, Lemon Creek, Mendenhall Valley and airport area, Auke Bay (the community, which is about 1.5 miles/2.4 km south of the ferry terminal). Hourly service Monday through Saturday, year-round; limited service on Sundays. Route map and schedule available at the visitor information center. Flag buses at any corner except in downtown Juneau, where bus uses marked stops only. Fare: $1.25 anywhere.

Highways: Longest road is Glacier Highway, which begins in downtown Juneau and leads 40.5 miles/65.3 km north to Echo Cove. Other major roads are Mendenhall Loop Road and Douglas and North Douglas highways. See logs this section.

Taxi: Four companies.

Cruise Ships: Juneau is southeastern Alaska's most frequent port of call. There were 487 port calls by cruise ships in 1996.

Car Rental: Several car rental agencies are available at the airport and vicinity, including All Star/Practical Rent-A-Car (907/790-2414); Avis Rent-A-Car (907/789-9450), Evergreen/Ford–Lincoln–Mercury (907/789-9386), Hertz (907/789-9494), Mendenhall Auto Center (907/789-1386), National Car Rental (907/789-9814) and Rent-A-Wreck (907/789-4111).

There are no car rental agencies downtown, but most rental agencies will take you to their offices (sometimes at an extra charge). Best to reserve ahead of time because of the great demand for cars.

Private Boats: Transient moorage is available downtown at Harris and Douglas floats and at Auke Bay. Most boaters use Auke Bay. For more information call the Juneau harbormaster at (907) 586-5255 or hail on Channel 16 UHF.

ATTRACTIONS

Juneau walking-tour map (in English, French, Spanish, German, Chinese or Japanese) is available from the Davis Log Cabin Information Center at 134 3rd St. and from other visitor information sites and hotels. See Juneau's many attractions—the St. Nicholas Orthodox Church, totems, Capitol Building, Governor's Mansion, historic graves, monuments, state museum, city museum, hatchery and others.

Charter a Boat for salmon and halibut fishing or sightseeing. The visitor information center can provide a list of charter operators; also see ads in this section.

Charter a Plane for fly-in fishing, hunting, transportation to remote lodges and longer flightseeing trips.

Take a Tour. Tours of Juneau and area attractions—by boat, bus, plane and helicopter—can be arranged. These tours range from sightseeing trips out to Mendenhall Glacier to river trips on the Mendenhall River.

Era Helicopters. Soar over the massive Juneau Icefield, viewing 4 unique and distinctive glaciers. Land on a glacier and explore the ancient ice. Fly past historical gold mining areas. Personalized tour with Alaska's most experienced helicopter company. Phone (800) 843-1947 or (907) 586-2030 locally. Tours also available in

Flightseeing the Juneau Icefield is a popular attraction. (© David J. Job)

Anchorage, Mount McKinley and Valdez. [ADVERTISEMENT]

Visit the Juneau Library. Built on top of the 4-story public parking garage in downtown Juneau, this award-winning library designed by Minch Ritter Voelckers Architects is well worth a visit. Take the elevator to the 5th floor and spend a morning or afternoon reading in this well-lit and comfortable space with a wonderful view of Juneau, Douglas and Gastineau Channel. Located at South Franklin and Admiralty Way, between Marine Park and the cruise ship terminal.

Juneau–Douglas City Museum, located in the Veteran's Memorial Building across from the State Capitol Building at 4th and Main streets, offers exhibits and audiovisual presentations on the Juneau–Douglas area, featuring gold mining and local cultural history. Displays include a turn-of-the-century store and kitchen, a large relief map, a hands-on history room that's fun for kids of all ages and a special summer exhibit. Free historical walking-tour maps of Juneau are available. Museum gift shop. Summer hours are 9 A.M. to 5 P.M. weekdays, 10 A.M. to 5 P.M. weekends, mid-May to mid-September Limited hours in winter. Admission $2. Students free. Phone (907) 586-3572 or write Parks and Recreation, Attn: Juneau–Douglas City Museum, 155 S. Seward St., Juneau, AK 99801, for more information.

State Capitol Building, at 4th and Main streets, contains the legislative chambers and the governor's office. Free tours available from capitol lobby; most days in summer on the half-hour from 9 A.M. to 5 P.M. The **State Office Building,** one block west, houses the State Historical Library and Kimball theater organ (free organ concerts at noon Fridays).

Alaska State Museum is a major highlight of Juneau located downtown at 395 Whittier St. Exhibits include dioramas and contain materials from Alaska's Native groups; icons and other artifacts from Russian–America days; and a popular life-size eagle nesting tree surrounded by a mural of a Southeast Alaska scene. A replica of Capt. George Vancouver's ship, *Discovery,* is located in the children's room for kids to explore. During the summer of 1998, there will be an exhibition entitled *Artists for Nature in Alaska's Copper Delta* featuring artists' work from around the world. There will also be an exhibition of glass baskets, based upon Northwest Coast Native baskets, from world-renowned artist Dale Chihuly. The museum store carries Alaska Native crafts and Alaska books and gifts for all ages. Summer hours are 9 A.M. to 6 P.M. Monday through Friday and 10 A.M. to 6 P.M. weekends. Winter hours are 10 A.M. to 4 P.M. Tuesday through Saturday. General admission is $3. Visitors 18 and under, students with current I.D. cards and members of the Friends of the Alaska State Museum are admitted free. A $10 museum pass is also available. Phone (907) 465-2901; Internet: ccl.alaska.edu/local/museum/home.html/. E-mail: bkato@educ.state.ak.us.

The House of Wickersham, 213 7th St., has an important historical collection dating to the days of the late Judge James Wickersham, one of Alaska's first federal judges, who collected Native artifacts and baskets, as well as many photographs and historical documents concerning Native culture, during his extensive travels throughout the territory early in the century. Visiting hours in summer. Phone (907) 586-9001 for more information. (Steep climb up to Seventh Street.)

The Governor's Mansion at 716 Calhoun Ave. has been home to Alaska's chief executives since it was completed in 1913. The 2½-story structure, containing 12,900 square feet of floor space, took nearly a year to build. Tours may be possible by advance arrangement. Phone (907) 465-3500.

The Gastineau Salmon Hatchery, operated by Douglas Island Pink and Chum, Inc., is located on Channel Drive 2.5 miles/4 km from downtown. The hatchery offers visitors a chance to see adult spawning salmon, over 100 species of Southeast Alaska sea-life in saltwater aquariums, aquaculture displays, and other seasonal activities. A variety of salmon products is also available for purchase. Visitor center open in summer 10 A.M. to 6 P.M. Monday through Friday; noon to 5 P.M. Saturday and Sunday. Incubation-room tours available May 15 through June 30; spawning salmon sights and hatchery operations tour July 1 through Oct. 1. Educational tours provided; $2.75 adult; $1 child. Group: 5 adults, $12; 12 children, $12. Phone (907) 463-5114.

See Old Mine Ruins. Remnants from the Treadwell Mine may be seen from a marked trail that starts just south of Sandy Beach on Douglas Island. The impressive remains of the A–J mine mill are located on the hillside along Gastineau Channel just south of downtown Juneau; good views from Douglas Island and from the water. Evidence of the Alaska–Gastineau Mine can be seen south of town along Thane Road. Walking-tour maps of the Treadwell area are available from the city museum.

Marine Park, located at foot of Seward Street, has tables, benches, information kiosk and lighterage facilities for cruise ship launches. The Ed Way bronze sculpture, "Hard Rock Miner," is located at Marine Park. Free concerts on Friday evenings in summer.

Thane Road is a wide, straight paved road beginning just south of downtown Juneau and extending 5.5 miles/8.9 km along Gastineau Channel. Good views of the channel and old mines. Excellent viewpoint for spawning salmon at Sheep Creek bridge and falls, Mile 4.3, in summer.

Mount Juneau Waterfall, scenic but difficult to photograph, descends 3,576 feet/1,091m from Mount Juneau to Gold Creek behind the city. Best view is from Basin Road. The waterfall is also visible from Marine Park.

View of Mendenhall Glacier terminus from Glacier Loop Trail. (© Bruce M. Herman)

Mount Roberts Tramway. Sixty-passenger tram cars depart from base facility on cruise ship dock every 8 to 10 minutes. Passengers are delivered to a 3,500-square-foot observation deck, 2,000 feet/610m above Juneau. There are signed interpretive trails, a restaurant, gift shops and a theater showing "Seeing Daylight." Open to the public from 8 A.M. to 10 P.M. daily, early May through the end of September. Phone (907) 463-3412 for more information on fees and special promotions.

Mount Roberts Trail Observation Point offers an elevated view of Juneau. Though the trail extends to the 3,819-foot/1,164-m summit, an excellent observation point above Juneau is reached by a 20-minute hike from the start of Mount Roberts trail at the top of Starr Hill (6th Street).

Mendenhall Glacier is about 13 miles/21 km from downtown Juneau at the end of Mendenhall Glacier Spur Road. Turn right northbound at **Milepost 9.4** Egan Drive (Glacier Highway), and then drive straight for 3.6 miles/5.8 km to the glacier and visitor center. There is a large parking area, and trails lead down to the edge of the lake (a sign warns visitors to stay back; falling ice can create huge waves). A 0.5-mile/0.8-km nature trail starts behind the visitor center. Trailheads for 2 longer trails—East Glacier and Nugget Creek—are a short walk from the visitor center. Programs and guided hikes with Forest Service interpreters are offered in summer. Ongoing renovations include a new salmon-viewing area and salmon-viewing trail. The visitor center will be closed for renovation until late summer 1998. The new center will feature an exhibit area with a model of a glacier and displays on glacial processes and the rebirth of landscape as a glacier retreats. The new center will also feature an expanded lobby area and a theatre seating 100 people; phone (907) 789-0097 or 586-8800.

Bike Paths. There are designated bike routes to Douglas, to Mendenhall Valley and Glacier, and to Auke Bay. The Mendenhall Glacier route starts at the intersection of 12th Street and Glacier Avenue; total biking distance is 15 miles/24.1 km. Bikes can be rented downtown and in the vicinity of the airport. Bike-route map and hiking information are available at the Davis Log Cabin.

Glacier Bay National Park contains some of the most impressive tidewater glaciers in the world. Juneau is located about 50 miles/80 km east of the bay and is subsequently the main jumping-off point for many Glacier Bay visitors. There are several local businesses offering 1- and 2-day or longer boat and air packages to the park. The state ferries do not service Glacier Bay, but there is a private ferry service available. Contact AUK NU Tours for information on the Glacier Bay Ferry; write 76 Egan Dr., Juneau, AK 99801, or phone 1-800-820-2628, (907) 586-8687, fax (907) 586-1337. See GLACIER BAY NATIONAL PARK and GUSTAVUS sections for more information.

Tracy Arm. Located 50 miles/80 km southeast of Juneau, Tracy Arm and adjoining Endicott Arm are the major features of the Tracy Arm–Fords Terror Wilderness Area. Both Tracy and Endicott arms are long, deep and narrow fjords that extend more than 30 miles/48 km into the heavily glaciated Coast Mountain Range. Active tidewater glaciers at the head of these fjords calve icebergs into the fjords.

Fords Terror, off of Endicott Arm, is an area of sheer rock walls enclosing a narrow entrance into a small fjord. The fjord was named in 1889 for a crew member of a naval vessel who rowed into the narrow canyon at slack tide and was caught in turbulent icy currents for 6 terrifying hours when the tide changed.

Access to this wilderness area is primarily by boat or floatplane from Juneau. Large cruise ships and small cruise ships and charter boats include Tracy Arm and Endicott Arm in their itineraries. It is also a popular destination for sea kayakers.

enclosed and heated cabin, restroom, big windows and plenty of deck space for viewing the majestic scenery and wildlife. For reservations and information, phone (800) 770-3422. 2 Marine Way, Suite 115, Juneau, AK 99801. Phone (907) 463-3422, fax (907) 463-3421. [ADVERTISEMENT]

Juneau Icefield, immediately to the east of Juneau, is a 1,500-square-mile/2,414 km expanse of glaciated mountains that is the source of all the glaciers in the area, including Mendenhall, Taku, Eagle and Herbert. Best way to experience and photograph it is via charter flightseeing. Flights usually take 30 to 60 minutes. Helicopter tours, which land on the glacier, are also available. Helicopter tours last from about 45 minutes to 1½ hours.

Alaska Native Artists Market in Juneau. Located in the Sealaska Cultural Arts Park on the waterfront, the market will feature 150 artists whose work will represent Tlingit, Haida, Tsimshian, Yup'ik, Aleut, Athabascan, Inupiat and other Alaska Native cultures. Takes place May 15 through October 17, 1998. Phone (907) 463-4844.

Ski Eaglecrest, Juneau's downhill and cross-country ski area on Douglas Island. Built and maintained by the city of Juneau, the area features a day-lodge, cafeteria, ski school, ski patrol, ski rental shop, 2 chair lifts, a surface lift and runs for experienced, intermediate and beginning skiers. Three miles/5 km of maintained cross-country trails available. Open 5 days a week, Dec. to mid-April. The view from the top of the chair lift (operating during ski season only) is worth the visit—Mendenhall Glacier, Juneau Icefield, Lynn Canal, Stephens Passage and more. Drive North Douglas Highway to turnoff left at Eaglecrest sign, then 5.3 miles/8.5 km up the Eaglecrest access road to the lodge. For more information, write Eaglecrest Ski Area, 155 S. Seward St., Juneau, AK 99801; phone (907) 586-5284 (790-2000 during ski season), or phone (907) 586-5330 for a recorded message about ski conditions. Internet: www.juneau.lib.ak.us/eaglecrest/eaglcrst.htm.

St. Nicholas Orthodox Church, 5th and Gold streets, a tiny structure built in 1894, is now the oldest original Russian Orthodox church in southeastern Alaska. Visitors are welcome to Sunday services; open daily for summer tours. Phone (907) 586-1023.

Chapel-by-the-Lake (Presbyterian), **Milepost 11.6** Glacier Highway, is a log structure perched above Auke Lake. Its front, made entirely of glass, frames the scenic lake, Mendenhall Glacier and mountains. Popular marriage chapel.

Shrine of St. Therese (Catholic), **Milepost 23.1** Glacier Highway, is a natural stone chapel on its own island, connected to shore by a gravel causeway. A 1 P.M. Sunday mass takes place during the summer.

Golden North Salmon Derby is a 3-day derby in late August.

The Alaskan Brewing Company. Be sure to enjoy our international award-winning beers on your travels throughout Alaska. In Juneau, visit Alaska's oldest and largest opertating brewery for a fascinating tour. Learn about modern and trun-of-the-centruy brewing techniques. Sample our gold-rush recipe Alaskan Amber and other award-winning brews. Tours every half hour. Gift shop and hospitality bar. Phone (907) 780-5866; Internet: www.juneau.com/akbrew. [ADVERTISEMENT]

Glacier Gardens Rainforest Adventures. Nestled along the Inside Passage in picturesque Juneau is one of the world's finest garden tours. Visitors experience the lush tropical feel of an Alaskan rainforest through 100 acres of floral artistry. The gardens dazzle the senses with massive displays of color, fragrance and textures. Gently winding paths link each unique garden and lead to a spectacular view of the world-famous Mendenhall Glacier. Delightful surprises include a tunnel of flowers, unique hanging gardens, wildlife in their natural habitat and beautiful ponds and waterfalls. Educational displays of native plant uses are wheelchair accessible. Electric carts available. Phone (907) 789-5166, fax 789-5598 or write 7600 Old Glacier Hwy., Juneau, AK 99801. Located about ten minutes north of downtown on the city bus line. This is a "must see" for Alaska. [ADVERTISEMENT]

Hiking Trails. *Juneau Trails,* a guidebook of 20-plus area hikes, can be purchased for $4 at Davis Log Cabin Information Center or USFS Information Center in Centennial Hall. Juneau Parks and Recreation Dept. offers free organized hikes Wednesday and Saturday, April through October; phone (907) 586-5226 for information.

AREA FISHING: (Several special sportfishing regulations are in effect in the Juneau area; consult current regulations booklet.) Good Dolly Varden fishing available along most saltwater shorelines in Juneau area; king salmon best from mid-May to mid-June, pink salmon available about mid-July through August, silver salmon best August to mid-September. Good fishing by boat from Juneau, Auke Bay or Tee Harbor in **Favorite** and **Saginaw channels, Chatham Strait** and near mouth of **Taku Inlet** for salmon, Dolly Varden and halibut. USFS public-use cabins available.

For up-to-date angling data in the Juneau area, phone (907) 465-4116 for recorded Alaska Dept. of Fish and Game message (April through Oct.). For specific angling information or for a copy of the local sportfishing guide, contact the ADF&G, Division of Sport Fish, Area Management Biologist, P.O. Box 20, Douglas 99824; phone (907) 465-4270. A list of charter boats is available from the Juneau Convention and Visitors Bureau (phone 907/586-2201). Also see ads this section.

Egan Drive and Glacier Highway/Juneau Veterans' Memorial Highway Log

Egan Drive from downtown Juneau proceeds north to **Milepost 9.4**, then becomes Glacier Highway. Egan Drive is named for William A. Egan (1914–84), first governor of the state of Alaska. From **Milepost 12.2** to road end, Glacier Highway has been renamed the Juneau Veterans' Memorial Highway. The highway ends 40.5 miles/65.3 km north of Juneau near Echo Cove on Berners Bay. It is a scenic drive northward along Favorite Channel.

0 Cruise ship terminal.

0.3 (0.5 km) Parking garage, 3-hour limit.

0.5 (0.8 km) Stoplight. Marine Way and Main Street. Egan Drive begins here.

0.7 (1.1 km) Alaska State Museum, exit east onto Whittier Street.

1.2 (1.9 km) Stoplight. Tenth Street exit east. For access to Douglas Highway and North Douglas Highway, turn west across Juneau–Douglas bridge (see logs this section).

1.3 (2.1 km) Turn west (left northbound) for Harris Harbor for small boats.

1.5 (2.4 km) Juneau–Douglas High School to east (right northbound).

1.7 (2.7 km) Aurora Basin small-boat harbor to west (left northbound). Access to Juneau Yacht Club on Harbor Way Road; 10 RV sites, portable toilet and dumpster. No fee; May 1 through Sept.; sign-in at Harbormaster's office for permit (907/586-5255).

3.9 (6.3 km) Stoplight. Picnic tables at Twin Lakes to east. Also exit east for Bartlett Memorial Hospital and Alaska Native Health Center; access to Old Glacier Highway and residential area. Gastineau salmon hatchery to west.

5.5 (8.9 km) Stoplight. Lemon Creek area.

5.9 (9.5 km) Lemon Creek passes beneath highway.

6.1 (9.8 km) Mendenhall Wetlands viewing area; great place to see eagles and waterfowl.

6.7 (10.7 km) Access to Old Glacier Highway and Switzer Creek; exit east. Department store; service station with gas, propane, dump station.

8.1 (13 km) Airport access road.

8.2 (13.2 km) Fred Meyer shopping center. Access to Glacier Gardens Rainforest Adventures. Turn right on Old Glacier Highway. What began as a project to generate hydro-electricity for commercial greenhouses has emerged as Juneau's newest attraction, scheduled to open in summer of 1998. Rainforest Gardens, natural and domestic, on Thunder Mountain. Guided and self-guided tours. Admission charged.

8.8 (14.2 km) Stoplight; McDonald's. Airport turnoff and access to Nugget Mall and Airport Shopping Center to west. A 0.3-mile/0.5-km loop road (Old Glacier Highway) provides access to malls and to Juneau International Airport. Access to Mendenhall Wetlands State Game Refuge dike trail via Berners Avenue. Loop road rejoins Egan Drive at **Milepost 9.4.**

9.4 (15.1 km) Stoplight. South **junction** with Mendenhall Loop Road. Turn west for airport. Turn east for Mendenhall Center shopping mall and post office (just east of junction), and Mendenhall Glacier and visitor center (3.6 miles/5.8 km from junction).

Mendenhall Loop Road is a paved 6.8-mile/10.9-km loop that rejoins Glacier Highway at **Milepost 12.2.** To reach Mendenhall Glacier from here, drive east 2.2 miles/3.5 km and take spur road another 1.4 miles/2.2 km to the glacier and visitor center. The visitor center is open daily in summer from 8:30 A.M. to 5:30 P.M.; weekends only in winter, 9 A.M. to 4 P.M.

Continue on Mendenhall Loop Road past glacier spur road turnoff for Montana Creek Road (3.7 miles/6 km from junction) and access to Mendenhall Lake USFS campground, at Mile 0.4 Montana Creek Road. The campground has 60 sites, tables, fireplaces, water, pit toilets and dump station. Reservations available for some sites; phone (800) 280-CAMP. $8 fee. Montana Creek Road dead ends 3.5 miles/5.6 km from Mendenhall Loop Road. ▲

9.7 (15.6 km) Airport area access for southbound travelers via Old Glacier Highway.

9.9 (15.9 km) Mendenhall River and Brotherhood Bridge. The bridge was named in honor of the Alaska Native Brotherhood and is lined by bronze plaques symbolizing the Raven and Eagle clans.

10 (16.1 km) Mendenhall Glacier viewpoint to east; parking area with sign about Brotherhood Bridge and short walking trail.

10.5 (16.9 km) State troopers office.

10.8 (17.4 km) The 2.1-mile/3.4-km Mendenhall Peninsula Road, a 2-lane gravel road, to west. About halfway along this road, Engineer's Cutoff leads 0.3 mile/0.5 km to Fritz Cove Road.

11.4 (18.3 km) Auke Lake scenic wayside to east. Good view of Mendenhall Glacier reflected in the lake. This is one of the most photographed spots in Alaska. Red, pink and coho salmon spawn in Auke Lake system July to September (only limited fishing, for coho in September). Chum salmon are primarily from Auke Creek hatchery program.

11.5 (18.5 km) Fritz Cove Road (paved) leads 2.6 miles/4.2 km west and dead ends at Smuggler's Cove; excellent small-boat anchorage. Scenic viewpoint on Fritz Cove Road at Mile 1.2; Engineer's Cutoff at Mile 1.9 extends 0.3 mile/0.5 km to Mendenhall Peninsula Road.

11.6 (18.7 km) Turnoff to east for Chapel-by-the-Lake and to southeastern branch of University of Alaska.

11.8 (19 km) Short road west to National Marine Fisheries Service biological laboratory (self-guided walking tours between 8 A.M. and 4:30 P.M. Monday through Friday).

12.2 (19.6 km) **North junction** with Mendenhall Loop Road to west. Glacier Highway becomes Juneau Veterans' Memorial Highway and curves around Auke Bay to west. A small-boat harbor with snack shop, skiff and tackle rentals, and boat launch located at the head of the bay. Private ferry service (AUK NU) to Glacier Bay departs from here.

The 6.8-mile/10.9-km Mendenhall Loop Road rejoins Glacier Highway at **Milepost 9.4.** Motorists may turn east here and follow loop road 3.1 miles/5 km to Montana Creek Road and access to Mendenhall Lake USFS campground, or drive 4.6 miles/7.4 km and turn off on Mendenhall Glacier spur road, which leads another 1.4 miles/2.2 km to the glacier and visitor center. Parking area at Mendenhall Glacier; short, steep path to visitor center. The center is open daily in summer from 8:30 A.M. to 5:30 P.M. ▲

12.3 (19.8 km) Private RV park.

12.4 (20 km) Auke Bay post office to west.

12.6 (20.3 km) Spaulding trailhead to east; 3.5 miles/5.6 km long. Access to John Muir USFS cabin.

12.8 (20.6 km) Waydelich Creek and bridge.

13.8 (22.2 km) Auke Bay ferry terminal vehicle exit.

13.9 (22.4 km) Auke Bay ferry terminal entrance. *LeConte* ferry passengers use parking area and terminal on right; all others use parking area and large terminal on left. Visitor information counter staffed in summer; open only for ferry arrivals and departures.

15.1 (24.3 km) Auke Village Recreation Area begins northbound; 5 beachside picnic shelters accessible to west of highway (park on highway shoulder).

15.3 (24.6 km) Auke Village totem pole to east.

15.4 (24.8 km) Auke Village USFS campground; 14 picnic units, 12 campsites, tables, fireplaces, water, flush and pit toilets. $8 fee. Open May 1 to Sept. 30. ▲

16.5 (26.6 km) Lena Point Road, south entrance to loop road.

17 (27.3 km) Lena Point Road, north entrance to loop road.

17.4 (28.1 km) Lena Beach picnic area.

18.4 (29.6 km) Tee Harbor–Point Stevens Road (gravel) leads 0.3 mile/0.6 km west to public parking area and a private marina and fuel float.

19.2 (30.9 km) Inspiration Point turnout to west with view of the Chilkat Range, and over Tee Harbor and Shelter Island across Favorite Channel. Once a bread-and-butter commercial fishing area, hence the name "The Breadline" for this stretch of shoreline, it is now a popular sportfishing area.

23.1 (37.3 km) Short road west to Catholic Shrine of St. Terese, located on a small island reached by a causeway.

23.3 (37.5 km) Turnout to west and view of island on which Shrine of St. Terese is situated.

23.9 (38.5 km) Peterson Lake trailhead to east; 4 miles/6.4 km long. Access to Peterson Lake USFS cabin. This trail connects with the Spaulding trail (see **Milepost 12.6**).

24.2 (39 km) **Peterson Creek** bridge. View spawning salmon here in late summer and early fall. Trout fishing. Black and brown bears in area.

24.8 (40 km) Gravel road leads 0.6 mile/1 km west to Amalga Harbor; dock, boat launch, bait-casting area. Fireplace and chimney near end of road are remains of an old trapper's cabin.

27.1 (43.7 km) Windfall Lake trailhead to east; 3 miles/4.8 km long.

27.2 (43.9 km) Herbert River bridge.

27.4 (44.2 km) Herbert Glacier trailhead to east; 5 miles/8 km long.

27.7 (44.7 km) Eagle River bridge. Amalga trailhead just across bridge to east; 4 miles/6.4 km long.

28.4 (45.8 km) Eagle Beach picnic area with beachside picnic shelter and 8 picnic sites. View of Chilkat Range across Lynn Canal. Duck hunting on flats in low tide during open season.

28.7 (46.2 km) Scenic viewpoint to west.

29.3 (47.2 km) Scenic viewpoint to west.

32.7 (52.8 km) Turnout to west with view of Benjamin Island to southwest; just beyond it is Sentinel Island lighthouse. Visible to the northwest is North Island and northwest of it is Vanderbilt Reef, site of a great sea disaster. The SS *Princess Sophia,* carrying 288 passengers and 61 crew, ran aground on the Vanderbilt Reef early in the morning of Oct. 24, 1918. All aboard perished when a combination of stormy seas and a high tide forced the *Sophia* off the reef and she sank early in the evening of Oct. 25. The Vanderbilt Reef is now marked by a navigation light.

32.8 (52.9 km) Pavement ends northbound; 2-lane gravel extension of the Glacier Highway begins.

33 (53.1 km) Scenic viewpoint to west. Yankee Cove and beach below this point.

35.4 (57.1 km) Sunshine Cove public beach access.

37.6 (60.7 km) North Bridget Cove beach access, Point Bridget State Park. The 2,850-acre park offers meadows, forests, rocky beaches, salmon streams and a trail system. Area is popular for cross-country skiing. Fires allowed on beach.

39 (62.8 km) Point Bridget trailhead; 3.5-mile/5.6-km hike to Point Bridget (7 hours round-trip); panoramic view of Lynn Canal and Chilkat Mountains from point.

39.4 (63.5 km) Cowee Creek bridge. Large parking area to west.

40.4 (65 km) Access left to Echo Cove beach. Park area.

40.5 (65.3 km) Road dead ends near Echo Cove on Berners Bay. Berners Bay is a popular destination for Juneau paddlers. It is 3 miles across and 34 miles northwest of Juneau.

Douglas Highway Log

Douglas Highway is a 3-mile/4.8-km paved road beginning on the Juneau side of the Douglas Bridge, crossing to Douglas Island, turning southeast, passing through the city of Douglas to road end and beginning of Treadwell Mine area.

0 Intersection of Egan Drive and Douglas Bridge.

0.5 (0.8 km) Right, Cordova Street leads to Dan Moller trail.

1.5 (2.4 km) Lawson Creek bridge.

2 (3.2 km) Tlingit Indian cemetery and grave houses.

2.5 (4 km) Turn left to boat harbor; dump station and Savikko Park with 4 overnight RV parking spaces without hookups. $5 per night, 3-day limit; obtain permit from Harbormaster's office at 1600 Harbor Way. Short gravel road leads to Juneau Island U.S. Bureau of Mines headquarters. Sandy Beach Recreation Area with water, toilets, play area, tennis courts, track, 2 ball fields, picnic tables, shelters and children's playground. Aptly named, this is one of the few sandy beaches in southeastern Alaska. Highway becomes St. Ann's Avenue.

3 (4.8 km) Road end.

North Douglas Highway Log

North Douglas Highway begins after crossing Douglas Bridge from Juneau and immediately turning right, northwest. **Milepost 1** appears at small bridge on this turn.

0 Douglas Bridge.

0.3 (0.5 km) **Junction** of Douglas Highway and North Douglas Highway.

4.4 (7.1 km) Heliport to right.

6.9 (11.1 km) Eaglecrest Ski Area turnoff on left; drive 5.3 miles/8.5 km on gravel road to ski area. Good blueberry picking in August.

8.3 (13.5 km) Fish Creek bridge. Large parking area on right of bridge. This is a popular roadside fishing spot.

8.6 (13.9 km) Ninemile trail on right; small parking area.

9.5 (15.3 km) Scenic turnout and parking area with excellent view of Mendenhall Glacier; litter barrel. Boat ramp; launch permit required (contact harbormaster before arrival).

10.3 (16.6 km) Small waterfall on left.

11.4 (18.4 km) False Outer Point public beach access. Scenic view of Favorite Channel and Lynn Canal; parking area on right. Near the northern tip of Douglas Island, this is an excellent spot to observe marine activity and eagles.

12.3 (19.8 km) Outer Point trailhead on right.

13.1 (21 km) Road end.

Glacier Bay National Park and Preserve

What Tlingit Indians called "Big Ice-Mountain Bay" in naturalist John Muir's day (1879) is today one of southeastern Alaska's most dramatic attractions, Glacier Bay National Park and Preserve. Muir described Glacier Bay as "a picture of icy wildness unspeakably pure and sublime."

There are no roads to Glacier Bay National Park, except for a 10-mile/16-km stretch of road connecting Bartlett Cove with Gustavus airport. Bartlett Cove is the site of a ranger station and Glacier Bay Lodge. Park naturalists conduct daily hikes and other activities from the visitor center at the lodge, and the excursion boat departs from there. Airlines service Gustavus airport. See Accommodations/Visitor Services and Transportation under Gustavus on page 731.

Visitors should contact the Superintendent, Glacier Bay National Park and Preserve, Gustavus, AK 99826-0140, for more information, or check with Glacier Bay tour operators. The national park's headquarters is at Bartlett Cove; phone (907) 697-2230.

Glacier Bay National Park, at the northwest end of Alexander Archipelago, includes not only tidewater glaciers but also Mount Fairweather in the Fairweather Range of the St. Elias Mountains, the highest peak in southeastern Alaska, and also the U.S. portion of the Alsek River.

With passage of the Alaska National Interest Lands Conservation Act in December 1980, Glacier Bay National Monument, established in 1925 by Pres. Calvin Coolidge, became a national park. Approximately 585,000 acres were added to the park/preserve to protect fish and wildlife habitat and migration routes in Dry Bay and along the lower Alsek River, and to include the northwest slope of Mount Fairweather. Total acreage is 3,328,000 (3,271,000 in park, 57,000 in preserve) with 2,770,000 acres des-

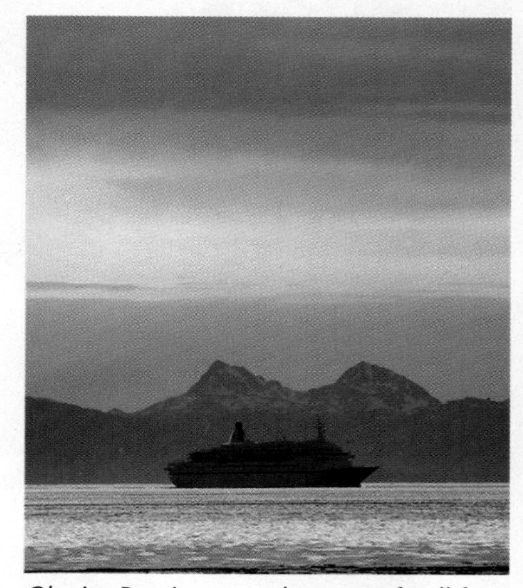

Glacier Bay is a popular port of call for cruise ships. (© David J. Job)

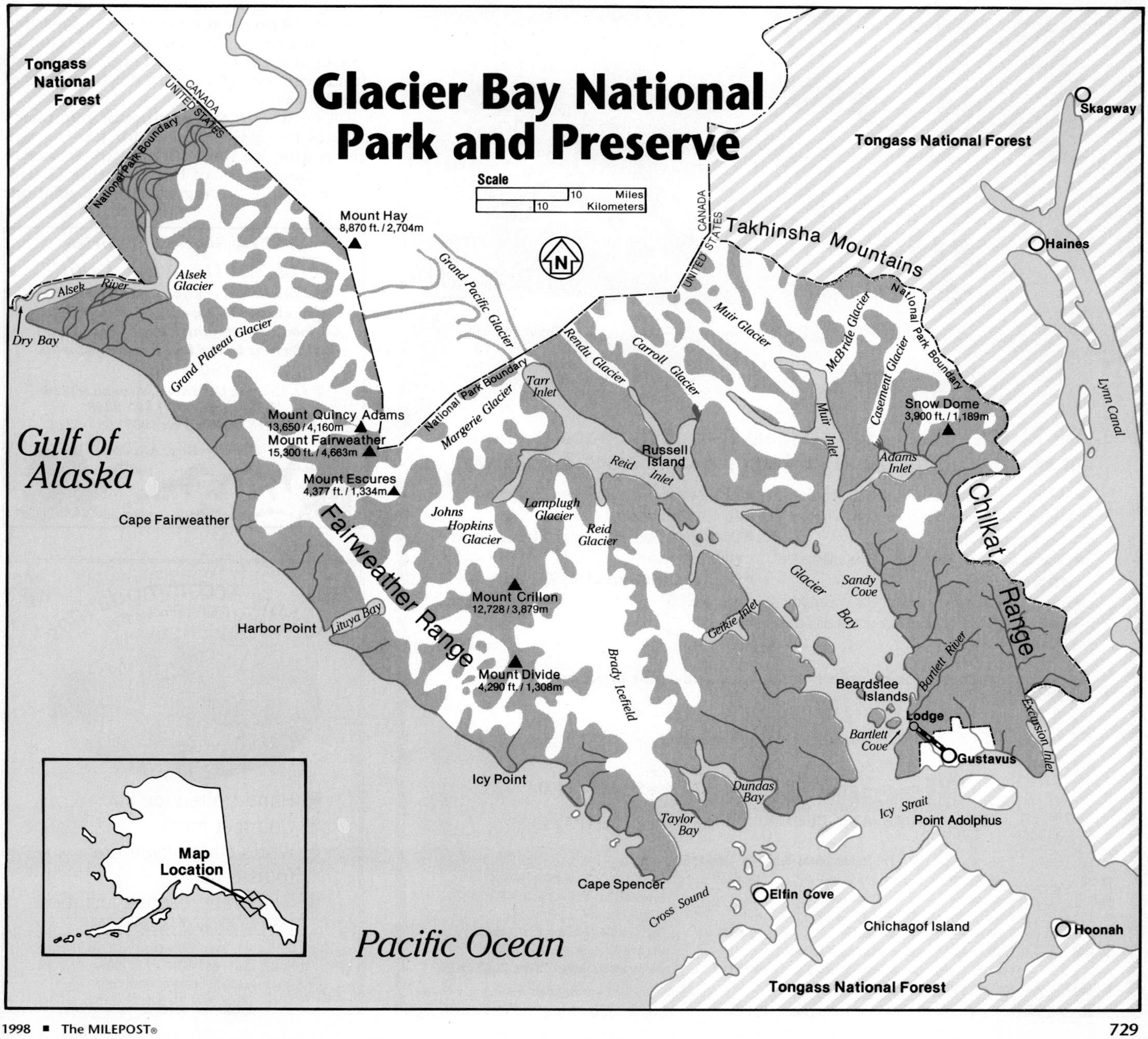

Cruise ship in Icy Strait at entrance to Glacier Bay. (© Harry M. Walker Photo)

ignated wilderness.

When the English naval explorer Capt. George Vancouver sailed through the ice-choked waters of Icy Strait in 1794, Glacier Bay was little more than a dent in the coastline. Across the head of this seemingly minor inlet stood a towering wall of ice marking the seaward terminus of an immense glacier that completely filled the broad, deep basin of what is now Glacier Bay. To the north, ice extended more than 100 miles/160 km into the St. Elias Mountains, covering the intervening valleys with a 4,000-foot-/1,219-m-deep mantle of ice.

During the century following Vancouver's explorations, the glacier retreated some 40 miles/64 km back into the bay, permitting a spruce–hemlock forest to gradually fill the land. By 1916, the Grand Pacific Glacier, which once occupied the entire bay, had receded some 65 miles/105 km from the position observed by Vancouver in 1794. Nowhere else in the world have glaciers been observed to recede at such a rapid pace.

Today, few of the many tributary glaciers that once supplied the huge ice sheet extend to the sea. Glacier Bay National Park encloses 12 active tidewater glaciers, including several on the remote and seldom-visited western edge of the park along the Gulf of Alaska and Lituya Bay. Icebergs, cracked off from near-vertical ice cliffs, dot the waters of Glacier Bay.

A decline in the number of humpback whales using Glacier Bay for feeding and calf-rearing led the National Park Service to limit the number of boats visiting Glacier Bay from June to August. These regulations

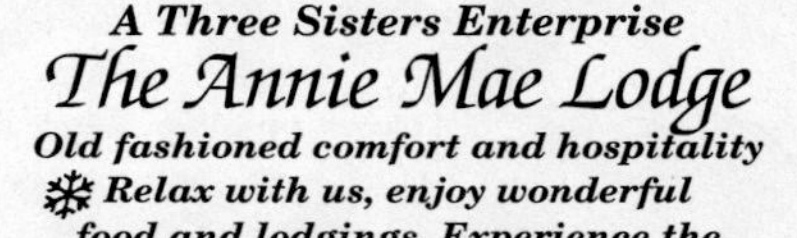

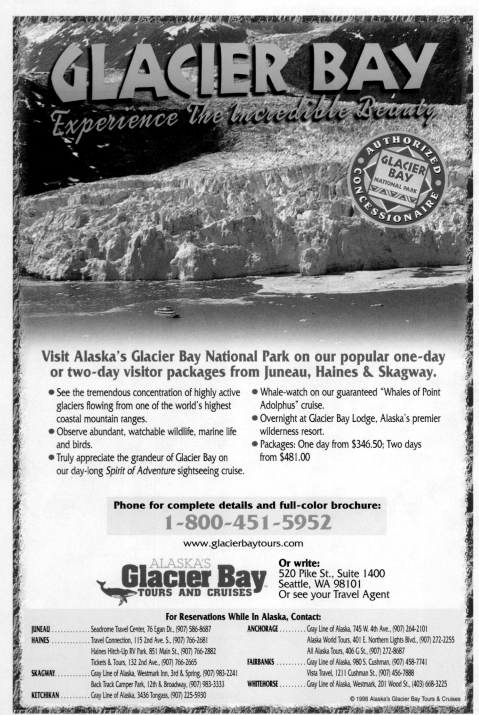

affect all motorized vessels. Check with the National Park Service for current regulations.

Glacier Bay National Park is approximately 100 miles/160 km from Juneau by boat. Park rangers at Bartlett Cove are available to assist in advising visitors who wish to tour Glacier Bay in private boats or by kayak. Guided kayak trips are available through park concessionaire, Alaska Discovery. Permits are required for motorized pleasure boats between June 1 and Aug. 31. The permits are free. A limited number are available, but rarely are boaters turned away. Permits must be obtained prior to entry into Glacier Bay and Bartlett Cove. Request permits no more than 2 months in advance by writing the National Park Service, Gustavus, AK 99826-0140. For more information, phone (907) 697-2627 (May 1 to Sept. 7).

Glacier Bay Lodge is the only accommodation within the national park, although nearby Gustavus (see description this section) has a number of lodges, inns, bed and breakfasts and rental cabins. Contact Glacier Bay Lodge Inc., (800) 451-5952, for more information on the concessionaire-operated Glacier Bay Lodge and excursion boat cruises offered from the lodge.

Gasoline and diesel fuel may be purchased at Bartlett Cove, where a good anchorage is available. There are no other public facilities for boats within park boundaries; Sandy Cove, about 20 miles/32 km from Bartlett Cove, is a popular anchorage. Gustavus has a dock and small-boat harbor.

CAUTION BOATERS: No attempt should be made to navigate Glacier Bay without appropriate charts, tide tables and local knowledge. Floating ice is a special hazard. Because of the danger from waves caused by falling ice, small craft should not approach closer than 0.5 mile/0.8 km from tidewater glacier fronts.

Wildlife in the national park area is protected and hunting is not allowed. Firearms are illegal. *CAUTION: Brown and black bears are present.*

Fishing for silver and king salmon, Dolly Varden and halibut is excellent. A valid Alaska fishing license is required. Charter fishing trips are available.

There is an established campground at Bartlett Cove with 25 sites. Wilderness camping is also available throughout the park. ▲

Gustavus

(See map, page 691)

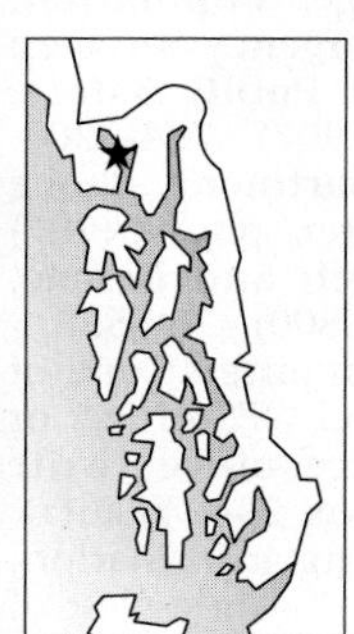

Gateway to Glacier Bay National Park and Preserve, the small community of Gustavus is located just outside the park boundary at the mouth of the Salmon River on the north shore of Icy Passage, 48 miles northwest of Juneau. It is 10 miles/16 km by road from Gustavus to Bartlett Cove within the park. **Population:** 380. **Emergency Services:** Phone 911. **Visitor Information:** Gustavus Visitors Assoc., Box 167, Gustavus 99826.

Private Aircraft: Gustavus airport, adjacent northeast; elev. 36 feet/11m; length 6,700 feet/2,042m; asphalt; fuel 100LL, A. Landing within the park is restricted to salt water (Adams Inlet is closed to aircraft landing).

Gustavus offers great beachwalking.
(Judy Parkin, staff)

Surrounded on 3 sides by the snow-covered peaks of the Chilkat Range and the Fairweather Mountains, Gustavus offers miles of level land with expansive sandy beaches, farmland and forest. Homesteaded in 1914 as a small agricultural community, the area was once named Strawberry Point because of its abundant wild strawberries. Today, most residents maintain gardens and make their living by fishing (commercial and subsistence), fish processing, tourism, arts and crafts, and working for the National Park Service and in various local trades.

Besides its proximity to the national park, Gustavus offers a number of attractions. Local charter boats—sometimes called "6 packs" because they carry about 6 passengers—are available for sportfishing (salmon, halibut), sightseeing Icy Strait and Glacier Bay, and whale watching. Whale sightings are almost guaranteed at Point Adolphous, where there is a resident pod. A paved road in town is great for bike riding.

There are extensive beaches in Gustavus which are great for beachwalking. Flat land walking is possible in the fern wetland environment, which also offers good bird watching for sandhill cranes and other birds. Be sure to bring rubber boots.

ACCOMMODATIONS/VISITOR SERVICES

Accommodations in Gustavus include several inns, lodges, bed and breakfasts, and self-sufficient cabins. There are 2 restaurants. The lodges and inns serve meals for guests;

drop-in customers check for space-available meal reservations.

Businesses in Gustavus include a grocery store, art gallery, cafe, gift shop, hardware/building supply store, gas station, auto repair shop and fish-processing facilities. Fishing supplies and licenses may be purchased locally. A smokehouse is available for fishermen.

Annie Mae Lodge. Old-fashioned good food and good company. Three fine family-style meals using home-baked bread and pastries, fresh caught seafood, berries off the bush, and garden vegetables. We offer beautiful comfortable rooms, peace, quiet, abundant wildlife, wilderness, sportfishing, kayak trips, whale watching. Glacier Bay boat/plane tours. Box 80, Gustavus, AK 99826. Phone (800) 478-2346 or (907) 697-2346, fax (907) 697-2211. [ADVERTISEMENT]

Bear Track Inn. This remarkable luxury inn must be seen to be believed. Offering complete packages—the inn's tour programs include world-class fishing, kayaking, whale watching, glacier viewing, wildlife and more. Enjoy this handcrafted log inn with inspiring views from wrap-around windows in the lobby as you relax beside a roaring fire. Feast on gourmet meals and sleep in large beautifully appointed guest rooms. Special corporate meeting facilities available. It's a worry-free vacation and a trip of a life time. Make tracks to the Bear Track Inn. Phone (907) 697-3017 or e-mail: beartrac@aol.com. [ADVERTISEMENT]

Grand Pacific Charters. Custom boating excursions in and around Glacier Bay. Personalized itinerary may include whale watching; renowned deep sea fishing for halibut and/or salmon. Many excellent angling and fly fishing opportunities in remote areas. P.O. Box 5, Gustavus, AK 99826. Phone (800) 628-0912. E-mail: gbci@thor.he.net. [ADVERTISEMENT]

Gustavus Inn. Country living, family-style gourmet local seafood meals, cozy bar, kitchen garden, bikes, trout fishing poles, courtesy van, afternoon park naturalist trip. Family-run since 1965. Custom fishing and Glacier Bay sightseeing packages arranged. For map, brochures, please write: Gustavus Inn, Box 60-MP, Gustavus, AK 99826 or call (800) 649-5220. [ADVERTISEMENT]

Mystic Sea Charters. Personalized fishing and sightseeing adventures. We are also set up for kayak transfers. Fish for salmon and halibut; watch the famous Point Adolphus humpback whales. Our 27-ft. boat gets you to the hot spots fast and comfortably! We can arrange complete packages for your stay in our remote, yet easily accessible part of Alaska. Aaron and Erin Bohlke. P.O. Box 324, Gustavus, AK 99826. Toll free (888) 699-8422. [ADVERTISEMENT]

The Puffin. See nearby Glacier Bay and Icy Strait. Stay in your own modern, comfortable, attractively decorated cabin with electricity on quiet wooded homestead. New picturesque central lodge. Complete country breakfast. Bicycles included. Children, pets welcome. Reservations for all charters, Glacier Bay tours. Qualified captains guide fishing, sightseeing charters. Friendly, personal attention. (907) 697-2260, fax (907) 697-2258, e-mail 73654.550@compuserve.com. [ADVERTISEMENT]

Spruce Tip Lodge—stay in our handcrafted log lodge and experience this part of Southeast Alaska in comfort and style. Included in our rates are three homecooked meals daily, room with bath and local ground transportation. We can arrange all activities in Gustavus/Glacier Bay. Phone (907) 697-2215, fax (907) 697-2236 or write box 299-MP, Gustavus, AK 99826. [ADVERTISEMENT]

TRI Bed and Breakfast of Glacier Bay. Visit us in our secluded rainforest homesite. Full breakfast with daily fresh eggs, homemade bread/jam. Deluxe and spacious individual cottages with insuite bath. Hiking, kayaking, whale watching, beachcombing, sportfishing, the Glacier Bay day boat or just getting here from Juneau, let us arrange your trip to Glacier Bay/Gustavus. P.O. Box 214MP, Gustavus, AK 99826. Phone (907) 697-2425; fax (907) 697-2450; e-mail trigbay@seaknet.alaska.edu. [ADVERTISEMENT]

Whalesong Lodge. Full-service lodge close to the beach and amenities. B&B accommodation with optional American plan. Also, condominium rental with full meal packages available. Unforgettable day or overnight tours of Glacier Bay, whale watching, sport fishing, kayaking, hiking. Airport transfers. Complimentary bicycles. Box 5-MP, Gustavus, AK 99826. Phone (800) 628-0912, fax (907) 697-2289. [ADVERTISEMENT]

TRANSPORTATION

Ferry: *NOTE: There is no state ferry service to Glacier Bay.* Closest port of call for state ferries is Hoonah. (Kayakers getting off at Hoonah can expect a 2-day paddle across Icy Strait.

Private ferry services Gustavus from Juneau; contact AUK NU Tours, 76 Egan Dr., Juneau, AK 99801; phone (907) 586-8687 or toll free (800) 820-2628, fax (907) 586-1337. One-way fare is $45.

Air: Glacier Bay may be reached by Alaska Airlines daily jet flights from Juneau; summer service begins June 1. Charter service available from Juneau, Sitka, Haines and Skagway to Gustavus airport. Charter air service available in Gustavus. Bus service between the airport and Bartlett Cove is available for arriving jet flights. Taxi service to local facilities and courtesy van service for some lodges are also available.

Many Gustavus bed and breakfasts will make transportation arrangements for guests from Juneau, Haines and Skagway.

Rental Cars: There is one car rental company in Gustavus, BW Rent-A-Car, phone (907) 697-2403.

Boat Service: Excursion boats operated by the park concession depart daily from Bartlett Cove. You may also charter a boat in Gustavus for sightseeing or fishing. Overnight cruise tours are available from Juneau.

Cruise Ships: Several cruise ships include Glacier Bay cruising in their itineraries.

Yakutat

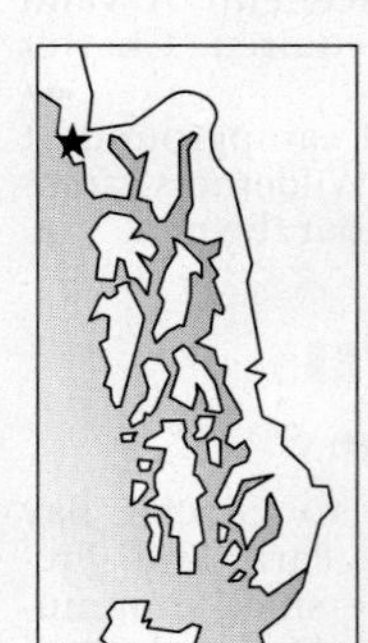

Located on the Gulf of Alaska coast where Southeastern Alaska joins the major body of Alaska to the west; 225 miles/362 km northwest of Juneau, 220 miles/354 km southeast of Cordova and 380 miles/611 km southeast of Anchorage. **Population:** 801. **Emergency Services: Dept. of Public Safety,** phone (907) 784-3206. **Fire Department**, phone 911. **Yakutat Health Center**, phone (907) 784-3275. **Maritime Search and Rescue,** contact the Coast Guard at (800) 478-5555.

Visitor Information: Inquire at one of the lodges, at the USFS and NPS office, or the chamber of commerce office (write Chamber of Commerce, Box 234, Yakutat, AK 99689). For sportfishing information, stop by the ADF&G office, 1/4 mile west of the airport, or write Sport Fish Division, Box 49, Yakutat 99689, phone (907) 784-3222. For information about the National Park Service, contact the visitor center at Box 137, Yakutat, AK 99689; phone (907) 748-3295. Interpretive programs are offered daily at 2 P.M. from June through August.

Elevation: Sea level. **Climate:** Similar to the rest of coastal southeastern Alaska: mild in summer, winters are moderate. Average annual snowfall is 201 inches. Total annual precipitation is about 151 inches. Normal daily maximum in August, 60°F/16°C; minimum in January, 17°F/-8°C. Prevailing winds are southeasterly.

Private Aircraft: Yakutat airport, 5 miles/4.8 km southeast; elev. 33 feet/10m; length 7,700 feet/2,347m; asphalt; fuel 100, A1. Seaplane base 1 mile/1.6 km northwest; float only, no fuel.

Transportation: Air—Daily jet service from Seattle, Juneau, Anchorage and Cordova. Charter air service available.

Yakutat has 4 lodges, 1 inn, 7 bed and breakfasts, a restaurant, cafe, 2 gift shops, bank, 2 grocery stores, 2 hardware stores, ATM, post office, clinic and gas station. Boat rentals, car rentals and cab service are available.

Yakutat Bay is one of the few refuges for vessels along this long stretch of coast in the Gulf of Alaska. The site was originally the principal winter village of the local Tlingit Indian tribe. Sea otter pelts brought Russian to the area in the 19th century. Fur traders were followed by gold seekers, who came to work the black sand beaches. Commercial salmon fishing developed in this century, and the first cannery was built here in 1904. Today's economy is based primarily on fishing and fish processing. Salmon, halibut, crab and black cod make up the fishery. Government and local businesses employ most residents. Subsistence activities are primarily fishing (salmon and shellfish), hunting (moose, bear, goats, ducks and small game), and gathering seaweed and berries. The soil is not suitable for agriculture, and a vegetable garden requires a great deal of preparation to produce small quantities.

While hunting and fishing in particu lar draw visitors to Yakutat, the surge of Hubbard Glacier in June 1986, which sealed off the mouth of Russell Fiord, drew national attention. Malaspina Glacier, largest on the North American continent, is northwest of town. Nearer to town, Cannon Beach has good beachcombing and a picnic area.

AREA FISHING: Yakutat is considered a world-class sportfishing destination. Steelhead fishing is among the finest anywhere. King and silver (coho) salmon run in abundance in Yakutat area, rivers and streams June through September. The area also boasts red and pink salmon and smelt in season. USFS cabins available on some rivers; check with the Forest Service (907/784-3359).

Lost River and **Tawah Creek,** 10 miles/16 km south of Yakutat on Lost River Road, silver (coho) salmon to 20 lbs., mid-August through September. **Situk River,** 12 miles/19.3 km south of Yakutat on the Lost River Road (also accessible by Forest Highway 10), is one of Alaska's top fishing spots spring and fall for steelhead and silver salmon and has one of the best sockeye (red) salmon runs in the state, late June through August; steelhead averaging 10 lbs., April 1 to May 30 for spring run, October and November for fall run; king salmon to 45 lbs., mid-June through July; silver salmon to 23 lbs., mid-August through September; pink salmon run in August, yields Dolly Varden also. **Yakutat Bay,** king salmon 30 to 50 lbs., May through June; silver salmon to 20 lbs., August through September.

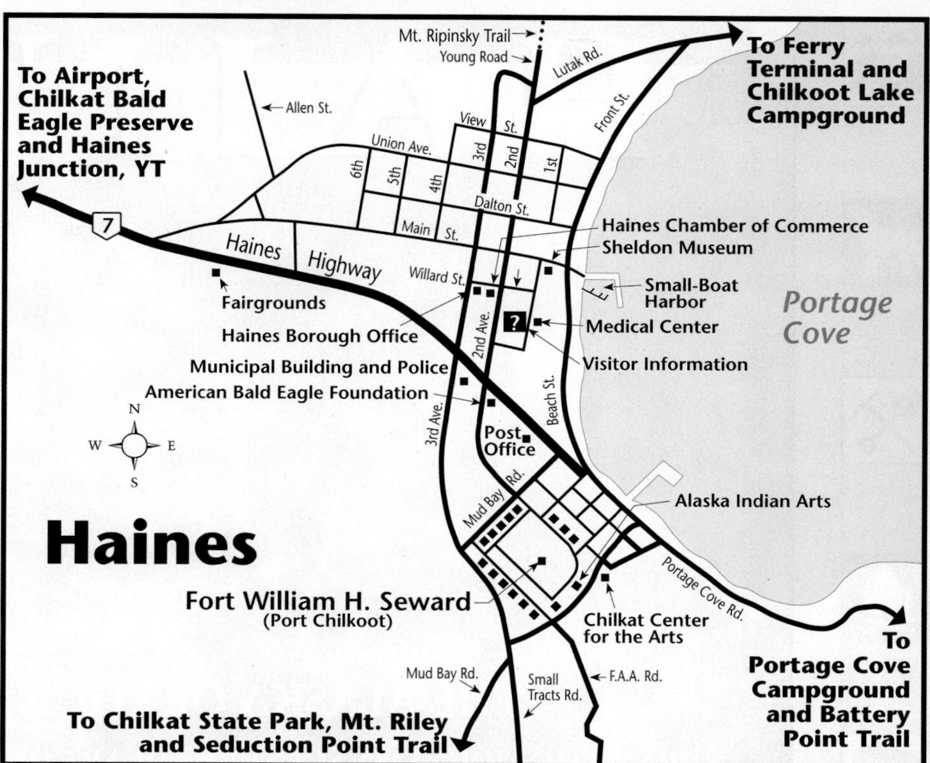

Haines

(See map, page 691)

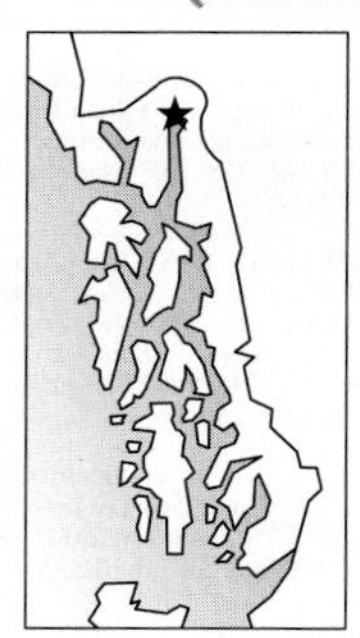

Located on Portage Cove, Chilkoot Inlet, on the upper arm of Lynn Canal, 80 air miles/129 km northwest of Juneau; 151 road miles/243 km southeast of Haines Junction, YT. Southern terminus of the Haines Highway. *NOTE: Although Haines is only 13 miles/21 km by water from Skagway, it is 359 miles/578 km by road!*

Population: Borough, 2,300. **ATMs:** First National Bank of Anchorage and Howser's Supermarket, both on Main Street. **Emergency Services: Alaska State Troopers,** phone (907) 766-2552. **City Police,** phone (907) 766-2121. **Fire Department** and **Ambulance,** emergency only phone 911. **Doctor,** phone (907) 766-2521. **Maritime Search and Rescue,** contact the Coast Guard at 1-800-478-5555.

Visitor Information: At 2nd and Willard streets. There are free brochures for all of Alaska and the Yukon. Open daily, 8 A.M. to 8 P.M., June through August; 8 A.M. to 5 P.M. weekdays, September through May. Phone (907) 766-2234; toll free 1-800-458-3579; Internet: www.haines.ak.us; e-mail: hainesak@wwa.com.. Write the Haines Convention and Visitors Bureau at Box 530, Haines, AK 99827. Phone the Alaska Dept. of Transportation at (907) 766-2340.

Elevation: Sea level. **Climate:** Average daily maximum temperature in July, 66°F/19°C; average daily minimum in January, 17°F/-8°C. Extreme high summer temperature, 90°F/32°C; extreme winter low, -16°F/-27°C; average annual precipitation, 59 inches. **Radio:** KHNS-FM 102.3. **Television:** 24 cable channels. **Newspaper:** *Chilkat Valley News* (weekly), *Eagle Eye.*

HAINES
THE ALASKA OF YOUR DREAMS
DRAMATIC MOUNTAIN SCENERY • HEART OF THE TLINGIT CULTURE
HISTORIC FORT WILLIAM H. SEWARD • VALLEY OF THE EAGLES

© Cynthia L. Jones (CJ)

Sponsored by: Haines Chamber of Commerce 1-800-246-6268
P.O. Box 1449 • Haines, Alaska 99827-1449

ATTRACTIONS & TOURS

1. **ALASKA BALD EAGLE FESTIVAL** November 13-15, 1998. Celebrate the world's largest gathering of bald eagles. Speakers, arts and crafts, family events, and much more. 800-246-6268 or 907-766-2202. P.O. Box 1449, Haines, AK 99827 E-mail: chamber@seaknet.alaska.edu. http://www.haines.ak.us

2. **ALASKA DINNER TOURS** Unique dining and sightseeing cruise. Experience the natural beauty of Alaska's glacier waterfalls and enjoy secluded five star dining. 888-306-7521 or 907-766-2335. 755 Union St., P.O. Box 43, Haines, AK 99827

3. **ALASKA INDIAN ARTS / CHILKAT DANCERS** Traditional Northwest Coast totem carvers, silversmiths & print makers. Home of the Chilkat Dancers performing several times weekly during the summer. Phone/FAX 907-766-2160. Historic Building #13 Fort Seward Dr., P.O. Box 271, Haines, AK 99827

4. **ALASKA MOUNTAIN FLYING & TRAVEL SERVICE** Specializing in Glacier Bay Tours and Cruise Sales. Alaska Ferry Reservations plus Glacier Bay Flightseeing and Statewide TravelServices. 1-800-954-8747. 132 2nd Ave., P.O. Box 1404, Haines, AK 99827 http://www.haines.ak.us/mtnfly/

5. **ALASKA NATURE TOURS** Wildlife viewing in and around the Chilkat Bald Eagle Preserve by experienced local naturalists. Photography. Bus and walking tours & hiking adventures. 907-766-2876 FAX 766-2844.210 Main Street, P.O. Box 491, Haines, AK 99827 E-mail: aknature@kcd.com http://kcd.com/aknature

6. **ALASKA STATE PARKS** Parks include: Chilkat State Park (7 Mile Mud Bay Road), Chilkoot Lake State Recreation Site (10 Mile Lutak Road), Portage Cove State Recreation Site (Beach Road, tent and backpackers only), and Mosquito Lake State Recreation Site (27 Mile Haines Highway) 907-766-2292

7. **CHILKAT GUIDES, LTD.** EAGLES! ! Relaxing, scenic half-day raft trips through the Eagle Preserve. Multi-day adventures on the Tatshenshini and Alsek Rivers also offered. 907-766-2491 FAX 907-766-2409 39 Beach Road, P.O. Box 170, Haines, AK 99827 E-mail: raftalaska@aol.com http://www.haines.ak.us/chilkatguides/

8. **HAINES AIRWAYS INC.** Haines Airways offers Glacier Bay Tours and scheduled flights. We look forward to seeing that your Alaska vacation is unforgettable! ! ! ! 907-766-2646 FAX 766-2780 108 Main St., P.O. Box 470, Haines, AK 99827

9. **HAINES-SKAGWAY WATER TAXI** The Sea Venture through Lynn Canal! See eagles, seals, and waterfalls aboard the Sea Venture II. $32 round-trip, $20 one-way. Phone/FAX 907-766-3395. Small boat harbor, P.O. Box 246, Haines, AK 99827 E-mail: h2Otaxi@kcd.com http://kcd.com/watertaxi

10. **RIVER ADVENTURES** Join us on a wilderness adventure in the heart of the Bald Eagle Preserve in the pristine Chilkat valley 907-766-2050 FAX 766-2051. 1 1/2 mile Haines Hwy., N., P.O. Box 556, Haines, AK E-mail:jetboat@alaskan.com http://www.alaskan.com/riveradventures/

11. **SHELDON MUSEUM & CULTURAL CENTER** Features Native Tlingit Art & Culture/Pioneer History (Ft. Seward, Haines Mission, lighthouse lens, etc.) Featured. Alaskana Book & Gift Store 907-766-2366 FAX 766-2368. 11 Main St., P.O. Box 269, Haines, AK 99827 E-mail:sheldmus@seaknet.alaska.edu

12. **SOCKEYE CYCLE CO.** Daily 1-3 hour guided and multi day fully supported Mountain Bike Tours. Two full service bike shops in Haines & Skagway. Rentals. Phone/FAX 907-766-2869. 24 Portage St., P.O. Box 829, Haines, AK 99827 E-mail: cycleak@ibm.net http://www.haines.ak.us/sockeye/

13. **SOUTHEAST ALASKA STATE FAIR** August 12-16, 1998: Great Music, Parade, Horseshow, Logging Show, Exhibits, Kids Events, Food/Trade booths. For information call 907-766-2476 FAX 766-2478 Fair Drive, P.O. Box 385, Haines, AK 99827

14. **THE TRAVEL CONNECTION** Glacier Bay Headquarters, ferry, local sightseeing, customized tours of Alaska including Denali, the Arctic, Pribilofs, and more. We Know Alaska! 800-572-8006 FAX 907-766-2585 E-mail: randa@alaska4you.com http://www.alaska4you.com

15. **WEEPING TROUT SPORTS RESORT** Day tours & over night accommodations for people seeking paradise. Lake fishing (guided or no), golf, fine food, spectacular scenery. 907-766-2827 FAX 766-2824 Chilkat Lake, P.O. Box 129, Haines, AK 99827 E-Mail: weepingt@aol.com http://www.haines.ak.us/golf/

GALLERIES GIFT SHOPS

16. **BELL'S STORE** Alaskan Seafood at it's Best, Alaskan gifts - Fresh Flowers. Clothing. OPEN ALL YEAR. A unique shopping experience. 907-766-2950 FAX 766-2958 18 Second Ave. N., P.O. Box 1189, Haines, AK 99827

17. **CHILKOOT GARDENS** Utopia for Collectors: Boyds, Bearstones, Snow babies, Harmony Kingdom, Keepsake Ornaments, Alaskan Memoribilia. Great browsing. Open year around. MC/V/AMEX/DIS. FTD Florist 907-766-2226 203 Main St., P.O. Box 662, Haines, AK 99827

18. **THE FAR NORTH** Finest Alaska Native Art. Sculpture in Soapstone, Whalebone & Ivory. Hand carved silver jewelry. Across from Visitor Center. 907-766-3535 FAX 766-3090 2nd Ave., P.O. Box 145, Haines, AK 99827

19. **WHALE RIDER GALLERY** Local artist, Tresham Gregg's gallery featuring woodcarving, jewelry, prints and Alaskan clothing. Phone/FAX 907-766 2540 20 Portage Street, Fort Seward, P.O. Box 776, Haines, AK 99827

LODGING

20. **BEAR CREEK CABINS** Family Cabins ~ $38. Clean, modern kitchen and bath facilities. Campsites, laundry, bike rentals. 907-766-2259. 1 Mile Small Tracts Road, P.O. Box 908, Haines, AK 99827

21. **CAPTAIN'S CHOICE INC MOTEL** Haines' finest & most comfortable lodging. Car rentals; courtesy transfers; centrally located. AAA Approved 907-766-3111 or 800-247-7153 or 800-478-2345 Alaska & Yukon FAX 907 766-3332. 108 2nd Ave., N., P.O. Box 392C, Haines, AK 99827 E-mail: captchoice@usa.net http://kcd.com/captain

22. **CHILKAT EAGLE BED & BREAKFAST** Lovely historic residence, waterfront & mountain views, walk to local services, full breakfast, kitchen facilities, TV lounge. Open Year Round. 907-766-2763 FAX 766-3651. #69 Soap Suds Alley, P.O. Box 387, Haines, AK 99827 E-mail: eaglebb@kcd.com http://kcd.com/eaglebb

23. CHILKAT VALLEY INN BED & BREAKFAST Wilderness Setting. Spectacular Views. 7 1/2 miles from downtown Haines, bordering Chilkat Eagle Preserve. 1959 Homestead overlooks Chilkat River Valley 907-766-3331 800-747-5528. 8 1/2 Mile Haines Highway, P.O. Box 861, Haines, AK 99827

24. EAGLE RV PARK *Free breakfast and fishing lessons for our guests.* 60 spacious full service sites. Tent sites. Immaculate laundromat, showers, and restrooms. Toll Free 888-306-7521 or 907-766-2335. 755 Union St., P.O. Box 43, Haines, AK 99827

25. FORT SEWARD CONDOS Completely furnish 1 & 2 bedroom suites, full kitchen, bath & laundry. 2 day minimum—-no pets. Reasonable. Phone/FAX 907-766-2425. #3 Fort Seward Drive, P.O. Box 75, Haines, AK 99827

26. FORT SEWARD LODGE & RESTAURANT Affordable lodging, oceanview kitchenettes, restaurant, cocktail lounge. Full dinner menu, courtesy transfer, military & senior discounts. See our display ad. 800-478-7772 FAX 907-766 2006. Mile 0 Haines Highway, P.O. Box 307, Haines, AK 99827

27. GLACIER VIEW CABINS AND CAMPING Travel 30 minutes through the scenic glacier fed waters of Lynn Canal to remote ocean view cabins, dining, camping, hiking. Toll Free 888-306-7521 or 907-766-2335. 755 Union St., P.O. Box 43, Haines, AK 99827

28. HAINES HITCH-UP RV PARK 92 Spacious sites. 20 pull-thrus. 24 cable TV sites. Laundromat & gift shop. Tour information & ticket sales. Phone/FAX 907-766-2882. 851 Main Street, P.O. Box 383, Haines, AK 99827 E-mail: hitchuprv@aol.com

29. THE SUMMER INN BED & BREAKFAST Charming, historical house. Open year round. Full homemade breakfast, centrally located, mountain & ocean views. Warm Alaskan hospitality at it's best! Phone/FAX 907-766-2970. 117 2nd Ave., P.O. Box 1198, Haines, AK 99827

RESTAURANTS GROCERIES

30. ALASKAN & PROUD Finest selection of groceries, freshest meats, produce, and dairy products available in Haines. Enjoy our famous Alaskan Hospitality! 907-766-2181 FAX 766-2182. 3rd & Dalton, P.O. Box 1689, Haines, AK 99827

31. BAMBOO ROOM RESTAURANT DOWNTOWN. Famous Halibut Fish 'n' Chips. Breakfast, Lunch, Dinner. Espresso. Senior & Kid's Menu. Pool, Darts, Pull Tabs, Sports Bar. 907-766-2800 FAX 766-2613 11-13 2nd Ave.N., P.O. Box 190, Haines, AK 99827 E-mail: bamboo@kcd.com http://kcd.com/bamboo

32. CHILKAT BAKERY & RESTAURANT Bakery products fresh daily. Breakfast-Lunch-Dinner. 7 a.m.-9 p.m. Plenty of parking. 5th & Dalton Street 907-766-2920 FAX 766-2992, P.O. Box 591, Haines, AK 99827

33. HOWSERS IGA SUPERMARKET One stop shopping. The best values in Haines on Groceries, Fresh Meat, Dairy, Ice, Fresh Sandwiches and Pizzas. ATM Machine 8 a.m. to 9 p.m. Daily. 907-766-2040 FAX 766-2787. 209 Main Street, P.O. Box 1309, Haines, AK 99827

34. KLONDIKE SALOON / RESTAURANT May-October Located in Dalton City - Set of Walt Disney's "White Fang" - Outdoor Seating / Horseshoe Pits. For Information-907-766-2476 FAX 766-2478. Fair Drive, P.O. Box 385, Haines, AK 99827

35. MOUNTAIN MARKET Natural and Organic Foods, Fresh baked goods, and the Best Espresso and Sandwiches in Southeast Alaska. Open Seven Days. Phone/Fax 907-766-3340. 151 3rd Ave. S., P.O. Box 863, Haines, AK 99827

36. THE WILD STRAWBERRY "Quality Food At An Affordable Price" Espresso, Fine Chocolates, Belgian Waffles, Dreyer's Ice Cream, Soups & Sandwiches, Smoothies, Alaskan Seafood 907-766-3608. 138 Second Ave. S., P.O. Box 770, Haines, AK 99827

SERVICES

37. BIGFOOT AUTO SERVICE INC Full service garage - welding - 24 hour towing - Unleaded & Diesel - NAPA Parts - Goodyear Tires 907-766-2458 FAX 766-2460. 987 Haines Hwy., P.O. Box 150, Haines, AK 99827

38. BUSHMASTER AUTO SERVICE Alignment/Brakes/Engines/Transmissions/Electronic Controls. Cars, Light Trucks, RVs. Factory Warranty Service. Professional Workmanship 907-766-3217 FAX 766-2415. 131 4th Ave. North, P.O. Box 1355, Haines, AK 99827

39. CHARLIE'S REPAIR SERVICE Full Service Auto Repair, Marine, Auto, Welding, Fabrication - 24 Hour Gas Cardlock - MC/VISA, Discover, Tesoro - Arctic Cat Dealer 907-766-2494 FAX 766-2794 225. 2nd Ave. N., P.O. Box 389, Haines, AK 99827

40. CHILKAT CRUISES Haines-Skagway Shuttle Ferry. Chilkat Cruises provides Round-Trips Daily (one hour each way) with the Large, Comfortable M/V Fairweather 907-766-2100 FAX 766-2101. 142 Beach Road, P.O. Box 509, Haines, AK 99827 E-mail: chilkat@klukwan.com http://www.chilkatcruises.com

41. DELTA WESTERN Gas and diesel. Free coffee, RV water and dump. Propane. MasterCard/VISA accepted. At intersection of the Haines Hwy./Main Street 907-766-3190 FAX 766-3196. P.O. Box 1369, Haines, AK 99827

42. E. D & D., INC. Electronic Sales and Service. Radio Shack. Cellular One Agent, Video Rental & Sales, Audio CD & Tapes 907-766-2337 FAX 766 2382. 1053 Haines Highway, P.O. Box 1229, Haines, AK 99827

43. HAINES AIRPORT TERMINAL & SERVICES Full Service Terminal for Scheduled Airlines and Flightseeing Tours over Glacier Bay. Jet-A, AV Gas, Film, Snacks, Restrooms and Car Rentals 907-766-3609 FAX 766-3610. P.O. Box 1829, Haines, AK 99827

44. KING'S STORE "Same Day" Photo Center, Film, Cameras, Computer, Color Copier, Laminating, Fax and Notary. Services with a Browsers Paradise Gift Shop. 907-766-2336 FAX 766-2614. 104 Main St., P.O. Box 610, Haines, AK 99827

45. THE PARTS PLACE Auto-RV-Marine If you need it and we don't have it we will get it! 907-766-2940. 104 3rd Avenue S., P.O. Box 9, Haines, AK 99827

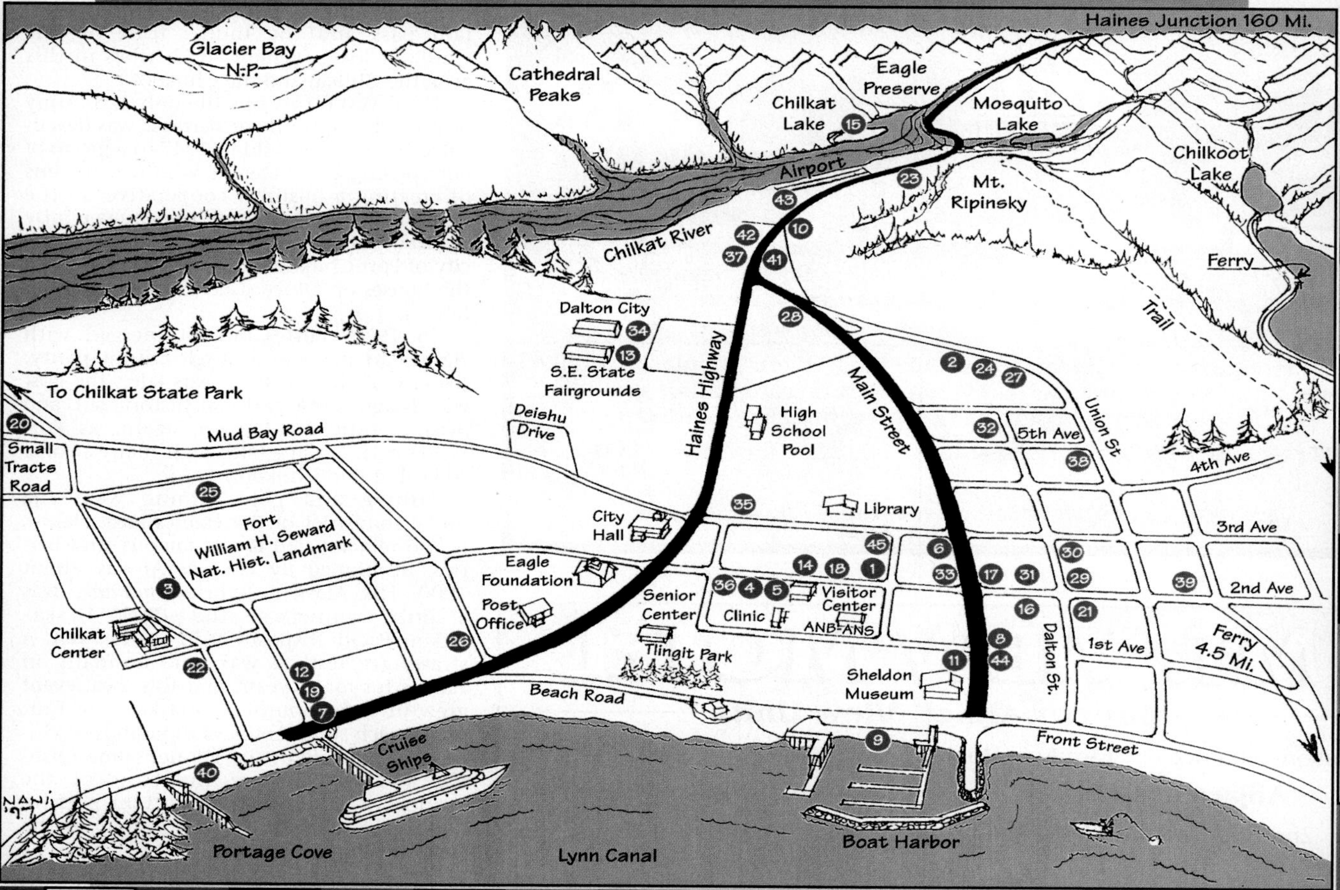

Haines boat harbor and view of Fort Seward. (© Roger Holden)

Private Aircraft: Haines airport, 3 miles/ 4.8 km west;.elev. 16 feet/5m; length 3,000 feet/914m; asphalt; fuel 100; unattended.

The original Indian name for Haines was *Dei Shu,* meaning "end of the trail." It was an area where Chilkat and Chilkoot Indians met and traded with Russian and American ships. It was also their portage route for transporting canoes from the Chilkat River to Portage Cove and Lynn Canal. The first white man to settle here was George Dickinson, who came as an agent for the North West Trading Co.

In 1879 missionary S. Hall Young and naturalist John Muir came to the village of Yen Dustucky (near today's airport) to determine the location of a Presbyterian mission and school. The site chosen, Dei Shu, was on the narrow portage between the Chilkat River and Lynn Canal. The following year, George Dickinson established a trading post for the Northwest Trading Company, next to the mission site. His wife Sarah began a school for Tlingit children. By 1881, Eugene Caroline Willard arrived to establish Chilkat Mission. Later, the mission and eventually the town were named for Francina E. Haines, secretary of the Presbyterian Women's Executive Society of Home Missions, who raised funds for the new mission.

In 1882 the Haines post office was established. The town became an important outlet for the Porcupine Mining District, producing thousands of dollars' worth of placer gold at the turn of the century. The Dalton Trail, which crossed the Chilkat mountain pass to the Klondike goldfields in the Yukon, started at Pyramid Cannery across the Chilkat River from Haines.

Just to the south of Haines city center is Fort Seward.on Portage Cove. Named Fort William H. Seward, in honor of the secretary of state who negotiated the purchase of Alaska from Russia in 1867, this was established as the first permanent Army post in the territory. The first troops arrived in 1904 from Camp Skagway. In 1922, the fort was renamed Chilkoot Barracks, after the mountain pass and the Indian tribe on the Chilkoot River. (There are 2 tribes in this area: the Chilkat and the Chilkoot.)

Until WWII this was the only U.S. Army post in Alaska. Chilkoot Barracks was deactivated in 1946 and sold in 1947 to a group of enterprising U.S. veterans who had designs of creating a business cooperative on the site. Their original plans were never fully realized, but a few stayed on, creating the city of Port Chilkoot and converting some of the houses on Officers' Row into permanent homes.

In 1970, Port Chilkoot merged with Haines to become a single municipality, the city of Haines. Two years later, the post was designated a national historic site and became officially known, again, as Fort William H. Seward (although many people still call it Port Chilkoot).

Fishing and gold mining were the initial industries of the Haines area. Haines is also remembered for its famous strawberries, developed by Charles Anway about 1900. His Alaskan hybrid, *Burbank,* was a prize winner at the 1909 Alaska–Yukon–Pacific Exposition in Seattle, WA. A strawberry festival was held annually in Haines for many years, and this local event grew into the Southeast Alaska State Fair, which each summer draws thousands of visitors. Today, halibut and gill-net salmon fishing and tourism are the basis of the economy. Haines is an important port on the Alaska Marine Highway System as the southern terminus of the Haines Highway, 1 of the 2 year-round roads linking southeastern Alaska with the Interior.

ACCOMMODATIONS/VISITOR SERVICES

Haines offers travelers accommodations

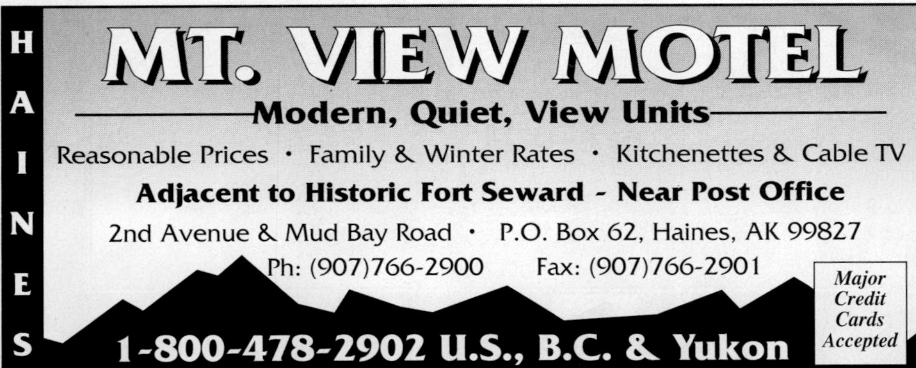

at one hotel and 5 motels, including Captin's Choice Motel (907/766-3111), Eagle's Nest Motel (907/766-2891), Halsingland Hotel (907/766-2000), Mountain View Motel (907/766-2900) and Thunderbird Motel (907/766-2131). There are also 5 bed and breakfasts and 2 apartment/condo rentals. See ads this section.

There is a youth hostel (families welcome) with cabin accommodations on Small Tracts Road.

Haines has all traveler facilities, including hardware and grocery stores, gift shops and art galleries, automotive repair, laundry, post office and bank. Gift shops and galleries feature the work of local artisans. There are several restaurants, cafes and taverns.

Alaskan Sugar Bush, located in Haines, is the only commercial birch syrup production site in Southeast Alaska, one of 7 in the state. The making of syrup from the sap of birch trees is a new and growing cottage industry. Birch Boy Products, a family-owned and operated facility, has produced over 1500 gallons of birch syrup at 18 Mile Haines Highway. Look for Birch Boy Alaskan birch syrup and other Birch Boy gourmet syrups in downtown Haines. [ADVERTISEMENT]

State campgrounds in the area include Portage Cove, Chilkat State Park, Chilkoot Lake and Mosquito Lake. ▲

Portage Cove State Recreation Site offers 9 tent sites, half-mile past Fort Seward on Portage Cove. Water and toilets available. Campers enjoy view of the Coast Range and Lynn Canal. Watch for cruise ships, ferries, eagles, whales and porpoises. *NOTE: This site is for walk-in and bicyclist camping only.* ▲

Chilkat State Park, with 32 RV sites and 3 tent sites, is about 8 miles/13 km from Haines on Mud Bay Road (from the Haines Highway: bear right at the Y by the Welcome to Haines sign; continue straight past the high school and up the hill; turn right on 3rd Ave., which becomes Mud Bay Road at the top of the Hill; then, where the road bends to the right, follow signs from hill to Chilkat State Park). See Mud Bay Road log this section.

Chilkoot Lake Campground (32 sites) is approximately 10 miles/16 km from Haines on Lutak Road (6 miles/10 km past the ferry terminal; turn right when exiting the ferry for Chilkoot Lake); see Lutak Road log this section. There are 5 private campgrounds in Haines. ▲

Mosquito Lake State Recreation Site is located on Mosquito Lake Road, 3 miles/6.5 km north of Mile 27 Haines Highway. It has 6 campsites nestled in a wooded setting around Mosquito Lake. Toilets, drinking water, a picnic shelter, fishing and boat launch are available. Small store and softball diamond at Mile 27. See the HAINES HIGHWAY section. ▲

Eagle RV Park Alaska's finest-full service park offering free breakfast, fishing lessons and an on-site activities director. Good Sam and KOA cards honored. Convenient full- and partial-service RV sites, tent sites, clean restrooms and showers, dump station, laundry and public phones. Gift and bait shop Rod and reel rentals. Crab and shrimp pot rentals. Up to 30 percent discount on area sightseeing and sport-fishing tours. The only RV wash in town. Five star member of the North to Alaska RV Park Association. 755 Union Street, P.O. Box 43, Haines, AK 99827. For reservations and directions to the Eagle, phone toll tree (888) 306-7521 or (907) 766-2335. [ADVERTISEMENT] ▲

Haines Hitch-Up RV Park offers easy access to 92 full hookups (30 amps), spacious, grassy, level sites. 20 pull-throughs. Cable TV sites available. Immaculate restrooms for registered guests only. Gift shop and laundromat. Located at the junction of Haines Highway and Main Street. See map in ad this section. P.O. Box 383, Haines, AK 99827. Phone (907) 766-2882. [ADVERTISEMENT] ▲

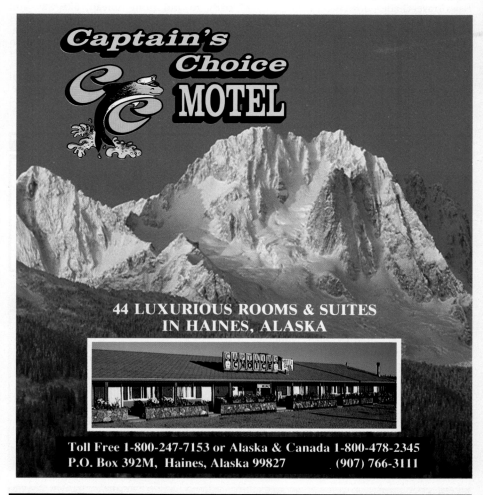

Salmon Run Adventures RV Campground. "A true Alaska experience." Beautiful forested property overlooking Lutak Inlet with superb mountain and water vistas. Depending on season, watch for whales, porpoises, sea lions or eagles. Fish from the beach or book a fishing expedition on the owner's charter boat; guests have preference, but advance bookings are recommended. The facility has attractive private sites appointed with picnic tables, fire rings and firewood. Hot showers and restrooms. On Lutak Road, 1.8 miles north of ferry terminall, 1 mile from city limits. P.O. Box 1122, Haines, AK 99827. Phone (907) 723-4229. Recommended by U.S. News Travel Guide. [ADVERTISEMENT]

A Sheltered Harbor Bed & Breakfast. Waterfront accommodation in Haines, located in historic Fort Seward across from the cruise ship dock providing a panoramic view of the Lynn Canal. Five spacious rooms, each with a private bath, color cable TV with remote, phone and generous hot home-style breakfast. Charter fishing and sightseeing tours available, along with vacuum-packing and freezing of your catch. Browse our gift shop featuring Alaska-made and local arts and crafts. Open year-round. VISA/MasterCard accepted. Reservations: (907) 766-2741. [ADVERTISEMENT]

TRANSPORTATION

Air: L.A.B. Flying Service, Haines Airways and Wings of Alaska offer several flights daily to and from Juneau, Skagway and other southeast Alaska communities. Haines airport is 3.5 miles/5.6 km from downtown. Commercial airlines provide transportation to and from motels, and some motels offer courtesy car pickup.

Bus: Local bus service to ferry terminal and guided sightseeing tours are available. Gray Line of Alaska serves Haines to and from the Alaska interior. Alaska Direct bus line connects the interior with Whitehorse, but does not come down to Haines.

Car Rental: Available at Avis Rent-A-Car, Halsingland Hotel (907/766-2733). Rental Car Service also available at Captain's Choice Motel (907/766-3111), and Eagle's Nest Motel (907/766-2891).

Taxi: 24-hour service to ferry terminal and airport.

Highways: The Haines Highway connects Haines, AK, with Haines Junction, YT. It is maintained year-round. See HAINES HIGHWAY section for details.

Ferry: Alaska Marine Highway vessels serve Haines from southeastern Alaska, Prince Rupert, BC, and Bellingham, WA. Alaska state ferries run year-round; phone (907) 766-2111. Ferries unload at the terminal on Lutak Road, 4.5 miles/7.2 km from downtown Haines. Bus/van service meets all ferries in summer.

Water-taxi: The Haines/Skagway Water Taxi and Chilkat Cruises provide daily water-taxi service to Skagway twice daily during the summer; phone (907) 766-3395.

Cruise Ships: Eleven cruise ships will regularly call in Haines in 1998, with a total of 17 different ships anticipated during the season.

Private Boats: Transient moorage is available at Letnikof Cove and at the small-boat harbor downtown. Contact the harbormaster, phone (907) 766-2448.

ATTRACTIONS

Take the walking tour of historic Fort William H. Seward; details and map are available at the visitor information center and at other businesses. Historic buildings of the post include the former cable office; warehouses and barracks; "Soapsuds Alley," the housing for noncommissioned officers whose wives did washing for the soldiers; the former headquarters building, now a residence, fronted by a cannon and a totem depicting a bear and an eagle; Officers' Row at the "Top O' the Hill," restored homes and apartments; the commanding officers' quarters, now the Halsingland Hotel, where Elinor Dusenbury (who later wrote the music for "Alaska's Flag," which became the state song) once lived; the fire hall; the guard house (jail); the former contractor's office, the plumber's quarters; the post exchange (now a lodge), gymnasium, movie house and the mule stables. Look for historic and interpretive signs.

Visit the Chilkat Center for the Arts at the auditorium. Here, the Chilkat Dancers interpret ancient Tlingit Indian legends. Check with the visitor information center or Alaska Indian Arts Inc. for schedule of

HAINES
ADVENTURE TOURS AND MORE!

performances.

Totem Village, on the former post parade ground, includes a replica of a tribal ceremonial house and a trapper's cabin and cache. There is a salmon bake, the Port Chilkoot Potlatch, held nightly in summer next to the tribal house; reservations recommended.

See the Welcome Totems located at the Y on the Haines Highway. These poles were created by carvers of Alaska Indian Arts Inc. *The Raven* pole is symbolic of Raven, as founder of the world and all his great powers. The second figure is *The Whale,* representing Alaska and its great size. The bottom figure is the head of *The Bear,* which shows great strength. *The Eagle* pole tells of his feeding grounds (the Haines area is noted for its eagles). Top figure is *The Salmon Chief,* who provides the late run of salmon to the feeding grounds. *The Eagle Chief,* head of the Eagle clan, is the third figure, and the bottom figure is *The Brown Bear,* which also feeds on salmon and is a symbol of strength. Inquire at the visitor information center and museum about location of poles.

The Sheldon Museum and Cultural Center is located on the old Haines Mission property at the end of Main Street by the boat harbor. Exhibits present the pioneer history of the Chilkat Valley and the story and culture of the Tlingit Native people. Chilkat blankets, Russian trunks, blue dishes, mounted eagles, Jack Dalton's sawed-off shotgun, photographs and a video on eagles make a fascinating history lesson. Children's "discovery" sheet available. Open daily 1–5 P.M. in summer, plus most mornings and evenings; winter, 1–4 P.M Sunday, Monday and Wednesday, 3–5 P.M. Tuesday, Thursday and Friday. Admission fee $3; children free. Phone (907) 766-2366.

Mountain Flying Service/Tickets & Tours. Located 3 doors south of the visitors' center, specializing in flights over and into Glacier Bay as well as Alaska ferry reservations and all Haines/Glacier Bay tour sales. We provide the highest quality high wing "Bush" aircraft and experienced pilots to give you the best flight in all of Alaska. Mountain Flying Service (907) 766-3007. Tickets & Tours 1-800-954-8747, Box 1404, Haines, AK 99827. [ADVERTISEMENT]

Enjoy the Fourth of July celebration, which includes canoe and kayak races on Chilkoot Lake, logging events, bicycle and foot races, pie-eating and other contests, parades and performances at the Chilkat Center for the Arts.

The Southeast Alaska State Fair, held at the fairgrounds in Haines (Aug. 12–16, 1998), features agriculture, home arts, and fine arts and crafts. A big event at the fair is the Bald Eagle Music Festival. There are exhibits of flowers, livestock, baked goods, beer and wine, needlework, quilting, woodworking and over a dozen other categories. There are also a parade, horse show and other events, including pig racing for cookies. Brochures available from the Fair offices or the visitor information center. Write to Box 385, Haines 99827, or (907) 766-2476.

American Bald Eagle Foundation is Haines' newest attraction. Interpretive center shows visitors how the bald eagle interacts with its environment through exhibits; mounted eagles, a wide variety of mammals, and fish and undersea life. Admission fee $2 for adults; $5 for families. Children under 12 are free. Open daily 10 A.M. to 6 P.M. in summer. Located at the Haines Highway and 2nd Street, just across 2nd Street from the city/municipal building.

Bald Eagle Festival. The festival includes release of wild rehabilitated eagles, live bird presentations, art exhibits, naturalist-guided tours to bald eagle preserve, exhibits and more. The events take place Nov. 13–15, 1998, and coincide with "the gathering," when eagles congregate to feed on late fall run salmon (see following). Contact the chamber of commerce at (800) 246-6268 for more information.

Alaska Chilkat Bald Eagle Preserve, where the world's greatest concentration of American bald eagles takes place October through January on Chilkat River flats below Klukwan. The eagle viewing area begins at **Milepost H 17** on the Haines Highway. The 48,000-acre Alaska Chilkat Bald Eagle Preserve was established in 1982. The Chilkat Valley at Haines is the annual gathering site of more than 3,000 bald eagles, which gather to feed on the late run of chum and coho salmon in the Chilkat River.

Dalton City, opened in 1992, is housed in the "White Fang" Disney film set. It is located at the fairgrounds. The former movie set houses a few businesses and a Klondike restaurant open in summer.

Visit the small-boat harbor at the foot

of Main Street for an interesting afternoon outing. Watch gill-net and crab fishermen setting out from here. Good views from Lookout Park and also from the shoreline between Haines and Portage Cove Campground. Land otters may sometimes be seen cavorting on the floating dock at the northeast corner of the harbor where commercial fishing nets are set out to dry.

Visit State Parks. Chilkoot Lake, at the end of Lutak Road, is worth a visit. Beautiful setting with a picnic area, campground and boat launch. Watch for brown bears in nearby waters in the fall, attracted by spawning salmon. (Private boat tours of Chilkoot Lake are available; check in town.) Chilkat State Park on Mud Bay Road is also a scenic spot with hiking trails, beach access, views of glaciers (Rainbow and Davidson), saltwater fishing (boat required), camping and picnicking. Both parks are within 10 miles/16 km of downtown Haines.

Go Flightseeing. Local air charter operators offer flightseeing trips for spectacular close-up views of glaciers, ice fields, mountain peaks and bald eagles. The heart of Glacier Bay is just west of Haines.

Charter boat operators in Haines offer fishing, sightseeing and photography trips.

Watch totem carvers at the Alaska Indian Arts Inc. workshop, located in the restored hospital at Fort Seward. This nonprofit organization is dedicated to the revival of Tlingit Indian art. Craftsmen also work in silver and stone, and sew blankets. Visitor hours 9 A.M. to noon and 1–5 P.M. weekdays year-round.

Hike Area Trails. Mount Ripinsky trail is a strenuous all-day hike, with spectacular views from the summit of mountains and tidal waters. Start at the north end of Young Road angling right at the top of the hill. Follow the upper road, then turn left at the water tower. Follow the pipeline right-of-way for 0.5 mile/0.3 km to the chain across the road. Turn left onto the trail which climbs 3.5 miles/5.8 km to the 3,610 foot/1,100m summit. Hikers should stop at the visitor information center for updates on wildlife sightings and to pick up a free copy of the pamphlet *Haines is for Hikers*, which contains trail descriptions and maps. *CAUTION: This is an unmaintained trail, recommended for experienced hikers only.*

Battery Point trail starts 1 mile/1.6 km beyond Portage Cove Campground and leads about 1.5 miles/2.4 km to a primitive camping site on Kelgaya Point overlooking Lynn Canal.

Mount Riley (elev. 1,760 feet/536m) has 3 routes to the summit. The steepest and most widely used trail starts at Mile 3 Mud Bay Road and climbs 2.8 miles/4.5 km to the summit. A second route starts at the end of F.A.A. Road and leads 1.7 miles/2.7 km along the city water-supply route to connect with the trail from Mud Bay Road to the summit. A third route follows the Battery Point trail for approximately 0.9 mile/1.4 km, then forks right for a fairly steep climb 3.1 miles/5 km to the summit of Mount Riley.

Seduction Point, at the southern tip of the Chilkat Peninsula, is accessible from Chilkat State Park via a 6-mile/9.7-km trail; a rolling forest and beach walk. Views of Davidson and Rainbow glaciers.

AREA FISHING: Local charter boat operators and freshwater fishing guides offer fishing trips. Sportfishing lodges at Chilkat Lake offer good fishing in a semi-remote setting. Good fishing in the spring for king salmon in **Chilkat Inlet.** Halibut best in summer in **Chilkat, Lutak** and **Chilkoot inlets.** Dolly Varden fishing good in all lakes and rivers, and along marine shorelines from early spring to late fall. Great pink salmon fishing every other year in August along the marine shoreline of **Lutak Inlet** and in the **Chilkoot River.** Sockeye salmon in the **Chilkoot River,** late June through August. Coho salmon in the **Chilkoot** and **Chilkat rivers,** mid-September through October. Cutthroat trout year-round at **Chilkat** and **Mosquito lakes. Herman Lake** is full of hungry grayling stocked there in the mid-1970s. The lake is located off the Sunshine Mountain Road (watch out for logging trucks) accessed from the steel bridge across the Klehini River at **Milepost H 26.3** Haines Highway; get directions locally. For more information, contact the Alaska Dept. of Fish and Game at (907) 766-2625.

Mud Bay Road Log

Mileposts on Mud Bay Road measure distance from its junction with the Haines Highway near Front Street to road end at Mud Bay, a distance of 8 miles/13 km. This road, first paved, then wide gravel, leads to Chilkat State Park, following the shoreline of Chilkat Inlet to Mud Bay on Chilkoot Inlet.
Distance is measured from junction with Haines Highway.

0.1 (0.2 km) Hotel on left, motel and private camper park on right. ▲

0.2 (0.3 km) **Junction** with 3rd Street, which leads back to town.

0.5 (0.8 km) Small Tracts Road on left, a 1.9-mile/3.1-km loop road which rejoins Mud Bay Road at **Milepost 2.3.** Small Tracts Road leads to private residences and to Bear Creek Camp and Youth Hostel (dorms, cabins and tent camping).

Mud Bay Road leads to the right, down Cemetery Hill (the old military cemetery was located here), then follows the shoreline of Chilkat Inlet, with views of Pyramid Island. Excellent area for eagle pictures.

2.3 (3.7 km) Stop sign at T intersection: go right for state park, left to return to town via Small Tracts Road.

3 (4.8 km) Mount Riley trail on left, parking area on right.

3.9 (6.3 km) View of Pyramid Island and Rainbow Glacier across Chilkat Inlet. Rainbow Glacier, is a hanging glacier. The ice field moved out over a cliff rather than moving down a valley to the sea. Davidson Glacier is about 2 miles/3.2 km south of Rainbow Glacier.

4.9 (7.9 km) Boat dock on right for small boats (summer tie-off only), boat ramp.

5.3 (8.5 km) Private road on right to cannery on Letnikof Cove.

6.7 (10.8 km) Pavement ends, gravel begins. Turn right and drive in 1.2 miles/1.9 km to entrance of Chilkat State Park (camping area 0.5 mile/0.8 km beyond entrance): 32 campsites, 3 tent sites on beach, $6 nightly fee or annual pass, picnic sites, pit toilets and boat launch. Access road paved and graveled, grades to 11 percent. Drive carefully. Beach access, view of glaciers and hiking trail to Seduction Point at southern tip of Chilkat Peninsula. ▲

8 (12.9 km) Mud Bay Road turns east and crosses Chilkat Peninsula to Flat Bay (commonly called Mud Bay) off Lynn Canal. Road ends at Mud Bay; short walk to rocky beach. These are private lands. No camping.

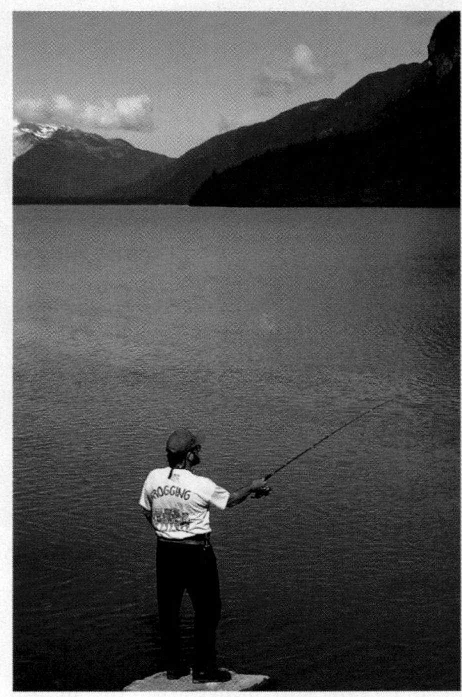

Fishing at Chilkoot Lake, Mile 8.3 Lutak Road. (© Ruth von Spalding)

Lutak Road Log

Lutak Road begins at Front Street, and leads north along Chilkoot and Lutak inlets past the Alaska Marine Highway ferry terminal. Pavement ends at a fork in the road: the left fork leads straight along the Chilkoot River to Chilkoot Lake campground; the right crosses the the Chilkoot River and serves a residential area at the end of Lutak Inlet (no outlet or turnaround).
Distance is measured from the junction of Front Street with Lutak Road.

0 Junction, Front Street and Lutak Road.

0.1 (0.2 km) Turnout on right with view of Fort Seward and Lynn Canal.

1.6 (2.6 km) Turnouts along road from here to Mile 7 allow good view of gill-net fleet, July through September.

2.4 (3.9 km) Government tank farm, petroleum distribution terminal and beginning of an oil pipeline to Fairbanks. No entry.

3.2 (5.1 km) Dock for oil tankers on right.

3.6 (5.8 km) Alaska Marine Highway ferry terminal on right.

3.8 (6.1 km) City dock on right is used for shipping lumber and also for docking barges.

4.4 (7.1 km) Closed and partly dismantled sawmill. A small building for fish processing is also here.

8.3 (13.4 km) Road on left follows a wide stretch of the Chilkoot River for 1 mile/1.6 km to Chilkoot Lake picnic area and boat launch; state campground with 32 sites just beyond picnic area, 7-day limit, $10 nightly

Much of downtown Skagway is part of Klondike Gold Rush National Historic Park.

(© George Wuerthner)

fee or annual pass.

8.4 (13.5 km) Bridge over the mouth of the **Chilkoot River.** Fair salmon fishing June through August. Watch for bears.

In 1983, the Chilkoot tribe dedicated Deer Rock here as a historic reminder of the original location of their village.

Road continues to private homes and dead ends; no turnaround.

Skagway

(See map, page 691)

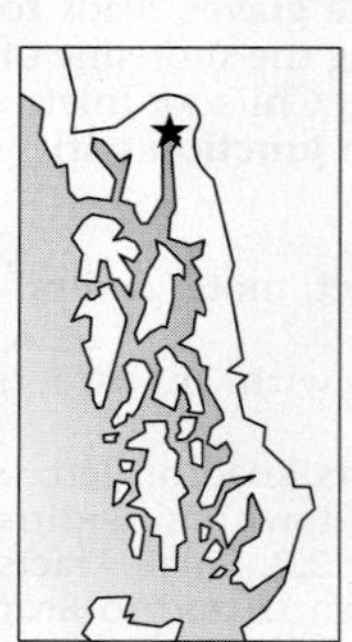

Located on the north end of Taiya Inlet on Lynn Canal, 90 air miles/145 km northwest of Juneau; 108 road miles/174 km south of Whitehorse, YT. The northern terminus of the Alaska Marine Highway Southeast ferry system and southern terminus of Klondike Highway 2 which connects with the Alaska Highway. *NOTE: Although Skagway is only 13 miles/21 km by water from Haines, it is 359 miles/578 km by road!* **Population:** 816. **Emergency Services: Skagway Police Department**, phone (907) 983-2232. **Fire Department** and **Ambulance**, phone 911. **Clinic**, phone (907) 983-2255. **Maritime Search and Rescue**, contact the Coast Guard at (800) 478-5555.

Visitor Information: Write the Skagway Convention and Visitors Bureau, Box 415MP, Skagway, AK 99840. Phone (907) 983-2854, fax 983-3854. Klondike Gold Rush National Historical Park Visitor Center has exhibits and films on the history of the area and information on hiking the Chilkoot Trail; write Box 517, Skagway, AK 99840; phone (907) 983-2921. Located in the restored railroad depot on 2nd Avenue and Broadway, it is open daily in summer.

Elevation: Sea level. **Climate:** Average daily temperature in summer, 57°F/14°C; in winter, 23°F/-5°C. Average annual precipitation is 29.9 inches. **Radio:** KHNS-FM 91.9. **Newspaper:** *Skagway News* (biweekly).

Private Aircraft: Skagway airport, adjacent west; elev. 44 feet/13m; length 3,700 feet/1,128m; asphalt; fuel 100LL; attended.

The name Skagway (originally spelled Skaguay) is said to mean "home of the north wind" in the local Tlingit dialect. It is the oldest incorporated city in Alaska (incorporated in 1900). Skagway is also a year-round port and 1 of the 2 gateway cities to the Alaska Highway in Southeast Alaska: Klondike Highway 2 connects Skagway with the Alaska Highway. (The other gateway city is Haines, connected to the Alaska Highway via the Haines Highway.)

The first white residents were Capt. William Moore and his son, J. Bernard, who settled in 1887 on the east side of the Skagway River valley (a small part of the Moore homesite was sold for construction of a Methodist college, now the city hall).

But Skagway owes its birth to the Klondike Gold Rush. Skagway, and the once-thriving town of Dyea, sprang up as thousands of gold seekers arrived to follow the White Pass and Chilkoot trails to the Yukon goldfields.

In July 1897, the first boatloads of stampeders bound for the Klondike landed at Skagway and Dyea. By October 1897, according to a North West Mounted Police report, Skagway had grown "from a concourse of tents to a fair-sized town, with well-laid-out streets and numerous frame buildings, stores, saloons, gambling houses, dance houses and a population of about 20,000." Less than a year later it was reported that "Skagway was little better than a hell on earth." Customs office records for 1898 show that in the month of February alone 5,000 people landed at Skagway and Dyea.

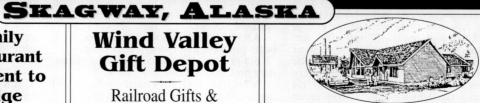

By the summer of 1899 the stampede was all but over. The newly built White Pass & Yukon Route railway reached Lake Bennett, supplanting the Chilkoot Trail from Dyea. Dyea became a ghost town. Its post office closed in 1902, and by 1903 its population consisted of one settler. Skagway's population dwindled to 500. But Skagway persisted, both as a port and as terminus of the White Pass & Yukon Route railway, which connected the town to Whitehorse, YT, in 1900. Cruise ships, and later the Alaska State Ferry System, brought tourism and business to Skagway. Scheduled state ferry service to southeastern Alaska began in 1963.

Today, tourism is Skagway's main economic base, with Klondike Gold Rush National Historical Park Skagway's major visitor attraction. Within Skagway's downtown historical district, false-fronted buildings and boardwalks dating from gold rush times line the streets. The National Park Service, the city of Skagway and local residents have succeeded in retaining Skagway's Klondike atmosphere.

Skagway has modern schools, churches, a clinic, bank and post office. U.S. customs office is located at Mile 6.8 Klondike Highway 2; phone or fax (907) 983-2325. The boat harbor and seaplane base has space for cruisers up to 100 feet/30m. Gas, diesel fuel and water are available.

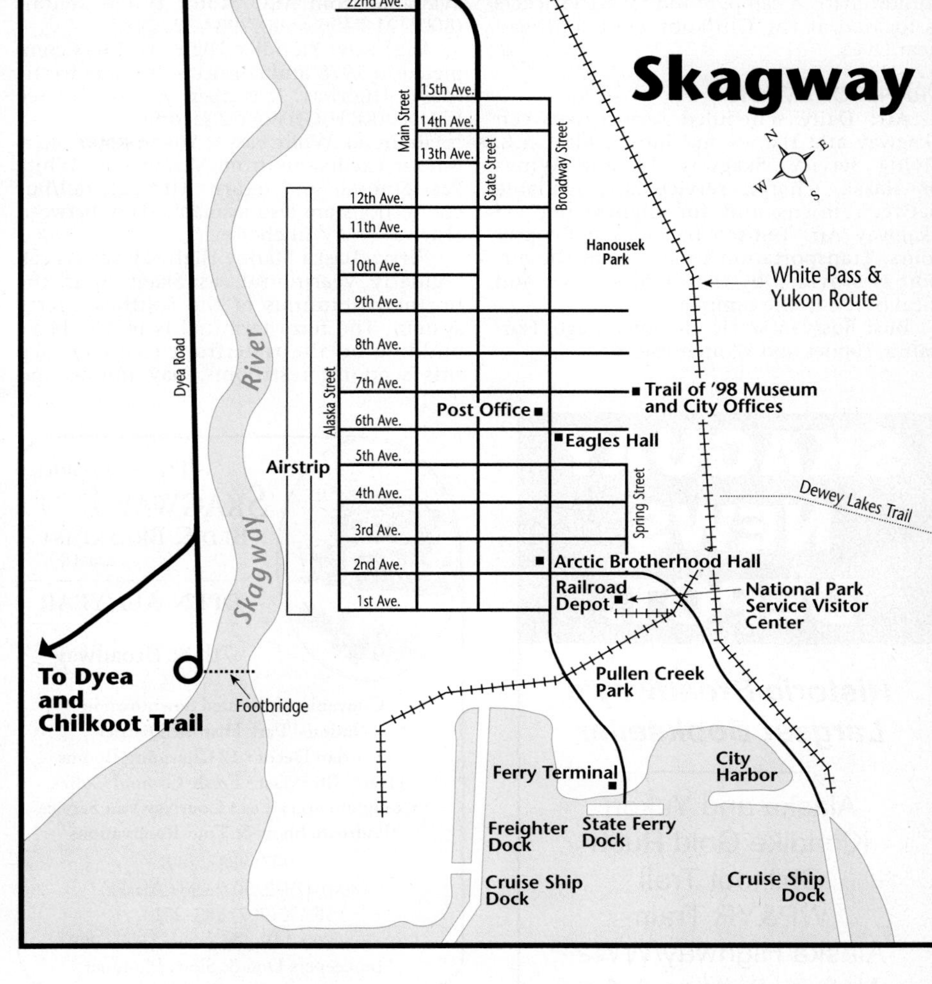

ACCOMMODATIONS/VISITOR SERVICES

Skagway offers a variety of accommodations, including the Gold Rush Lodge (907/983-2831), Golden North Hotel (907/983-2294), Miner's Inn (907/983-3303), Sergeant Preston's Lodge (907/983-2521), Skagway Bed & Breakfast (907/983-2289), Westmark Inn–Skagway (907/983-6000) and Wind Valley Lodge (907/983-2236). See ads this section. Reservations advised in summer.

Historic Skagway Inn Bed & Breakfast, established 1897, located at 7th and Broadway in historic district. Once a gold rush brothel, Victorian-style rooms are comfortable. Hearty breakfast and fresh-ground coffee. Walking distance to shops, museums and trails. Friendly innkeepers can make your reservations for railroad, shows, tours plus arrange transportation to Chilkoot trailhead. Known for fine dining. Phone (907) 983-2289. (800) 478-2290 (inside Alaska), fax (907) 983-2713. [ADVERTISEMENT]

The White House, historic accommodations. Newly renovated 10-room inn features private baths and phones in each room, hand-made quilts on every comfortable bed, original woodwork, family antiques, high ceilings, spacious yard, delicious breakfast and bottomless cookie jar. Owner operated, we're open year-round. 475 8th Avenue, P.O. Box 41-MP, Skagway, AK 99840-0041. Phone (907) 983-9000, fax (907) 983-9010, e-mail: whitehse@ptialaska.net. [ADVERTISEMENT]

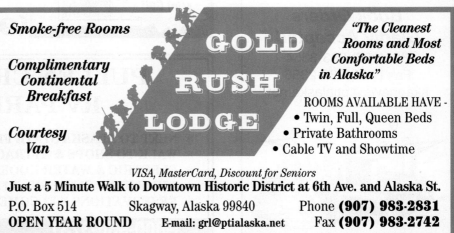

There are several restaurants, cafes and bars, grocery, hardware and clothing stores, and many gift and novelty shops offering Alaska and gold rush souvenirs, photos, books, records, gold nugget jewelry, furs and ivory. Propane, marine and automobile gas are available, as is diesel fuel.

Earth's Past. Experience nature's wonders at Skagway's exclusive prehistoric gallery. Fine fossil walrus and mammoth ivory carvings in Alaska themes. Unique jewelry, handcrafted from prehistoric ivory and rare, fiery, iridescent ammolite. Fine fossils, minerals, geodes, etc. Great gifts for all ages. 7th at Broadway, Skagway, AK 99840. Phone (907) 983-2880. [ADVERTISEMENT]

There is 1 bank in town (National Bank of Alaska), located at 6th and Broadway; open 9:30 A.M. to 5 P.M. Monday through Friday in summer. Automatic teller machines at bank and next to the Trail Bench gift shop on Broadway between 2nd and 3rd avenues.

There are several private campgrounds in Skagway offering hookups, tent sites, restrooms and showers, dump stations and laundromats. A campground for backpackers is located at the Chilkoot Trail trailhead near Dyea. ▲

TRANSPORTATION

Air: Daily scheduled service between Skagway and Haines and Juneau via L.A.B. Flying Service, Skagway Air and Wings of Alaska. Charter service also available between towns and for flightseeing via Skagway Air. Temsco provides helicopter tours. Transportation to and from the airport is provided by the flight services and local hotels in the summer.

Bus: Bus/van service to Anchorage, Fairbanks, Haines and Whitehorse, YT.

Car Rental: Available from Avis Rent-A-Car (907/983-2247) and Sourdough Car & Van Rental (907/983-2523). Motorhomes available from ABC Motor Home Rentals (800/421-7456 or 907/983-3222).

Highway: Klondike Highway 2 was completed in 1978 and connects Skagway to the Alaska Highway. It is open year-round. See KLONDIKE HIGHWAY 2 section.

Railroad: White Pass & Yukon Route offers 3-hour excursions from Skagway to White Pass Summit and return. Through rail/bus connections are also available daily between Skagway and Whitehorse.

Ferry: Alaska Marine Highway vessels call regularly year-round, as Skagway is the northern terminus of the Southeast ferry system. The ferry terminal is in the large building on the waterfront (see city map this section); restrooms, pay phone and lockers inside. Ferry terminal office hours vary: opening hours are usually posted at the front door. Phone (907) 983-2941 or 983-2229. It's an easy walk into town, but hotel and motel vans do meet ferrys.

Water-taxi: Service is available between Haines and Skagway. For schedules and rates, phone (907) 983-2083 in Skagway; (907) 766-3395 in Haines.

Cruise Ships: Skagway is a regular port of call for cruise ships. Downtown is not far from the dock. Tours can be purchased dockside and at downtown offices.

Private Boats: Transient moorage is available at the Skagway small-boat harbor. Contact the harbormaster at (907) 983-2628.

ATTRACTIONS

Trail of '98 Museum is temporarily relocated in the Arctic Brotherhood Hall on

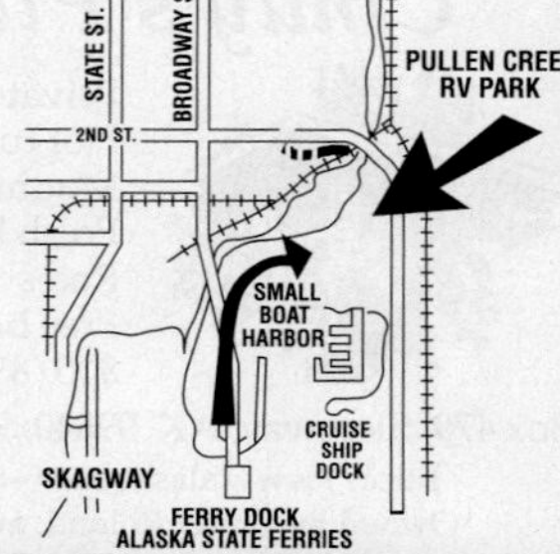

McCabe College Building houses Skagway City Hall. (Judy Parkin, staff)

Broadway Street between 2nd and 3rd avenues, while its original home, McCabe College Building/City Hall, is being renovated. The Arctic Brotherhood Hall's facade has almost 10,000 pieces of driftwood sticks arranged in a mosaic pattern, with the brotherhood's AB letters and symbols, a gold pan with nuggets. The museum's primary interest is to help preserve Alaskan historical material and to display Alaskan pioneer life. The museum is open daily May through October, 9 A.M. to 5 P.M.; contact the museum for winter hours. Phone (907) 983-2420.

McCabe College Building/City Hall is the first granite building constructed in Alaska. It was built by the Methodist Church as a school in 1899–1900 to be known as McCabe College, but public-school laws were passed that made the enterprise impractical, and it was sold to the federal government. For decades it was used as U.S. District Court No. 1 of Alaska, but as the population of the town declined, the court was abandoned, and in 1956 the building was purchased by the city. The main floor is occupied by City of Skagway offices. From the waterfront, walk up Broadway and turn right on 7th Avenue.

See the show *The Days of 1898 Show With Soapy Smith.* This show, produced by Gold Rush Productions, is put on several times a day; summer evening performances (subject to cruise ship arrivals) in Eagles Hall. Check the billboard in front of the hall for show times. The show relates the history of Skagway, from the days of the notorious Soapy Smith. Phone (907) 983-2545.

This show is good family entertainment; bring your camera, gamble with funny money (during evening show only), and enjoy this well-done historical musical comedy. Admission fee charged.

Alaska Wildlife Adventure displays Alaska wildlife mounts and has an extensive and eclectic collection of Alaskana memorabilia. Gift shop and donut shop. Admission fee charged.

Klondike Gold Rush National Historical Park was authorized in 1976 to preserve and interpret the history of the Klondike Gold Rush of 1897–98. The park, managed by the National Park Service, consists of 4 units: a 6-block historical district in Skagway's business area; a 1-mile-/1.6-km-wide, 17-mile-/27.4-km-long corridor of land comprising the Chilkoot Trail; a 1-mile-/1.6-km-wide, 5-mile-/8-km-long corridor of land comprising the White Pass Trail; and a visitor center at 117 S. Main St. in Seattle, WA.

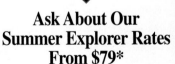

In Skagway, the National Park Service offers a variety of free programs in summer. There are daily, guided walking tours of downtown Skagway and ranger talks on a variety of topics. Films are also shown. Check with the Park Service's visitor center in the restored railroad depot on 2nd Avenue and Broadway. Summer (June through August) hours are 8 A.M. to 6 P.M.

Hike the Chilkoot Trail. This 33-mile/53-km trail begins on Dyea Road (see log this section) and climbs Chilkoot Pass (elev. 3,739 feet/1,140m) to Lake Bennett, following the historic route of the gold seekers of 1897–98. The trail is arduous but offers both spectacular scenery and historical relics. There are several campgrounds and shelters along the route. Hikers planning to take the Chilkoot Trail should check with the Chilkoot Trail Center in Skagway, phone (907) 983-3655. The Trail Center is open daily from 7 A.M. to 7 P.M. May through mid-September. Trail maps, local natural and cultural history guides, bear precaution and safety information, and other materials are available free or for sale. *The ALASKA WILDERNESS GUIDE* also has details on the Chilkoot Trail, and "Chilkoot Pass" by Archie Satterfield is a good hiking and history guide to the trail.

Corrington Museum of Alaska History, located at 5th and Broadway, offers a unique record of events from prehistory to the present. Each of the 40 exhibits at the museum features a scene from Alaska history hand-engraved (scrimshawed) on a walrus tusk. The museum is open in summer. Free admission.

Picnic at Pullen Creek Park. This attractive waterfront park has a covered picnic shelter, 2 footbridges and 2 small docks. It is located between the cruise ship and ferry docks, behind the White Pass & Yukon Route depot. Watch for pink salmon in the intertidal waters in August, silver salmon in September.

Helicopter and airplane tours of Skagway and White Pass are available in summer.

Gold Rush Cemetery is 1.5 miles/2.4 km from downtown and makes a nice walk. Go north on State Street to a sign pointing to the cemetery. Follow dirt road across tracks into railroad yard, follow posted direction signs, then continue about 0.4 mile/0.6 km farther to the cemetery. If you drive in, a circular road around the cemetery eliminates having to back up to get out. A path on left at the end of the road leads to the cemetery where the graves of both "bad guy" Soapy Smith and "good guy" Frank Reid are located (both men died in a gunfight in July 1898). Smith's original gravestone was whittled away by souvenir hunters, and the resting place of the feared boss of Skagway is now marked by a metal marker.

Reid Falls are located near Gold Rush Cemetery, and it is only a short hike from Frank Reid's grave to view them.

AREA FISHING: Local charter boat operators offer fishing trips. The ADF&G Sport Fish Division recommends the following areas and species. Dolly Varden: Fish the shore of **Skagway Harbor**, **Long Bay** and **Taiya Inlet**, May through June. Try the **Taiya River** by the steel bridge in Dyea in early spring or fall; use red and white spoons or salmon eggs. Hatchery-produced king salmon have been returning to the area in good numbers in recent years. Try fishing in salt water during June and July and in **Pullen Creek** in August. Pink salmon are also plentiful at Pullen Creek in August. Coho and chum salmon near the steel bridge on the **Taiya River**, mid-September through October. Trolling in the marine areas is good but often dangerous for small boats. Trout: A steep trail near town will take you to Dewey lakes, which were stocked with Colorado brook trout in the 1920s. **Lower Dewey Lake,** 1/2-hour to 1-hour hike; heavily wooded shoreline, use raft. The brook trout are plentiful and grow to 16 inches but are well fed, so fishing can be frustrating. **Upper Dewey Lake,** a steep 2 1/2-hour to 4-hour hike to above tree line, is full of hungry brook trout to 11 inches. Use salmon eggs or size #10 or #12 artificial flies. **Lost Lake** is reached via a rough trail near Dyea (ask locals for directions). The lake lies at about elev. 1,300 feet/396m and has a good population of rainbow trout. Use small spinners or spoons. For more information, contact the ADF&G office in Haines at (907) 766-2625.

Dyea Road Log

The Dyea Road begins at **Milepost S 2.3** on Klondike Highway 2. It leads southwest toward Yakutania Point, then northwest past Long Bay and the Taiya River to the beginning of the Chilkoot Trail and to a side road leading to the old Dyea townsite and Slide Cemetery. The Dyea Road is a narrow winding gravel road.

Distance is from the junction with Klondike Highway 2.

0 Junction.

0.1 (0.2 km) Old cemetery on right.

0.4 (0.6 km) View of Reid Falls east across the Skagway River.

1.4 (2.3 km) A scenic wayside with platform on left southbound affords view of Skagway, Taiya Inlet and the Skagway River.

1.7 (2.7 km) A steep, primitive road on left southbound descends 0.4 mile/ 0.6 km toward bank of the Skagway River, with a view of the Skagway waterfront and Taiya Inlet.

Drive to parking area and walk 0.2 mile/ 0.3 km to Yakutania Point; horse trail beyond parking area. Bridge at base of hill leads to a short trail back to town. Dyea Road turns northwest along Long Bay at this point.

1.9 (3.1 km) Skyline trailhead (poorly signed). This trail leads to top of AB Mountain (elev. 5,000 feet/1,524m).

2.1 (3.4 km) Head of Long Bay.

4 (6 km) City dump.

4.3 (6.9 km) Taiya Inlet comes into view on left northbound as the road curves away from Long Bay.

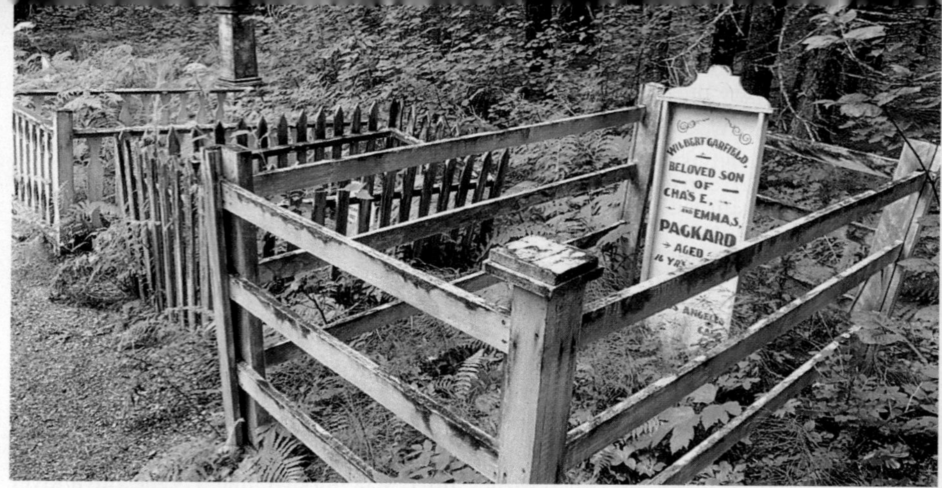

Slide Cemetery on Dyea Road contains graves from 1898 avalanche.
(© Bruce M. Herman)

5.1 (8.2 km) View of the old pilings in Taiya Inlet. The docks of Dyea used to stretch from the trees to beyond the pilings, which are still visible. These long docks were needed to reach deep water because of the great tidal range in this inlet.

5.7 (9.2 km) Hooligan (smelt) run here in the Taiya River in May and early June. Local swimming hole across the road.

6.5 (10.5 km) Dyea information display.

6.7 (10.8 km) Chilkoot Trail trailhead campground, parking area and ranger station.

7.2 (11.6 km) The Chilkoot Trail begins on right northbound. Bridge over Taiya River.

7.4 (11.9 km) A primitive road on left northbound leads southwest to Slide Cemetery (keep right at forks and follow signs) and old Dyea townsite. The cemetery, reached by a short unmarked path through the woods, contains the graves of men killed in the Palm Sunday avalanche, April 3, 1898, on the Chilkoot Trail. At Dyea townsite, covered with fireweed and lupine in summer, hardly a trace remains of the buildings that housed 8,000 people here during the gold rush. About 30 people live in the valley today.

8.4 (13.5 km) Steel bridge across West Creek. Four-wheel drive recommended beyond this point.

ALASKA STATE FERRY SCHEDULES

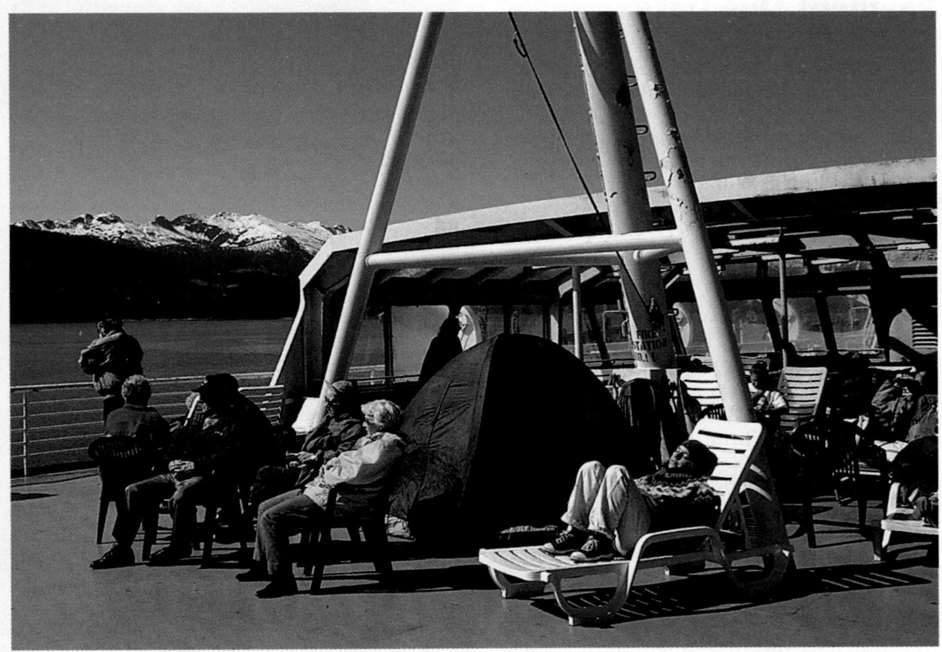

Passengers on the solarium deck of an Alaska state ferrry. (© Ruth von Spalding)

On the following pages are summer schedules and rates—effective May 1 through September 30, 1998—provided by the Alaska Marine Highway office. NOTE: The state reserves the right to revise or cancel schedules and rates without prior notice and assumes no responsibility for delays and/or expenses due to such modifications. On-line updates on the Alaska state ferry system are available on the Internet at: http://www.dot.state.ak.us/external/amhs/home.html. Or phone 1-800-642-0066 for more information. Copies of the Alaska Marine Highway summer schedules are available at all state ferry terminals or from the Alaska Marine Highway, P.O. Box 25535, Juneau, AK 99802-5535.

For additional information on Alaska State ferry travel, see "Ferry Travel" in the TRAVEL PLANNING section.

How to Determine Fares

Fares for passengers, vehicles and staterooms are all calculated separately and must be added together to determine the total cost of your travel. For a breakdown of rates, see the Tariff sections on pages 762–764 and 766.

One-way fares for passage, vehicles and alternate means of conveyance (bicycles, kayaks, and inflatable boats) are charged from the port of embarkation to the port of debarkation.

Stateroom fares are calculated according to the route taken, and may vary from the rates printed here depending on the ship and schedules.

Payments and Cancellations

Payment may be made by mail with certified or cashier's check, or money order in U.S. dollars. Mail payments to: Alaska Marine Highway, P.O. Box 25535, Juneau, AK 99802-5535. Personal checks will not be accepted unless written on an Alaskan bank. No counter checks are accepted. VISA, MasterCard, American Express, Discover and Diners Club credit cards are accepted at all terminals and by phone (some restrictions may apply).

Cancellation charges apply for changes made within 14 days of sailing. Unless other arrangements are made and noted in your itinerary, full payment is required on or before the due date state at the time of reservations. Bookings will be canceled if reservations are not paid for by the payment due date.

Payment Due Date

If reservation is made 55 days or more before sailing, payment is due 30 days after booking.

If reservation is made less than 55 days before sailing, payment is due within 10 days of making the reservation.

If reservation is made 10 days or less before sailing, payment is due at time of booking

Call or Fax Reservations

Reservations are required on all vessels for passengers, vehicles and cabins. For reservations write the Alaska Marine Highway, P.O. Box 25535, Juneau, AK 99802-5535; phone toll free 1-800-642-0066, or fax (907) 277-4829; TDD 1-800-764-3779. Phone local reservation numbers in Juneau (907/465-3941) and Anchorage (907/272-7116).

To make a reservation, you will need to provide the following information: ports of embarkation/debarkation; full names of all travelers, and ages of those under 12 years; width, height and overall length of vehicles (including extensions such as trailer hitches, bike racks, and storage containers); mailing address and phone number; alternate travel dates (cabin or vehicle space may not be available on your first choice of travel dates); and approximate date you will be leaving your home.

If you have passenger space but do not have a confirmed cabin space, you may sign up on the purser's "Standby" list on board. If your vehicle space has not been confirmed, you must sign up on the "Standby" list at the ferry terminal. Standbys literally stand in line until all reserved passengers and vehicles are on board; if there is space, standbys may board. Standbys are subject to off-loading at each port of call.

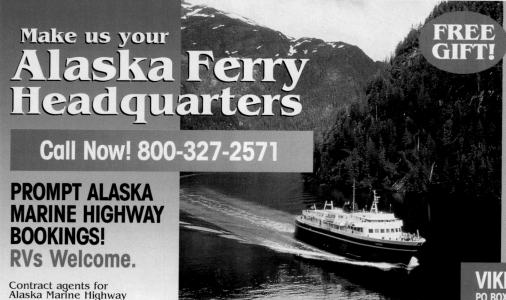

M/V E.L. Bartlett *under way in Prince William Sound.* (© Ruth Fairall)

Getting on our Waitlist

If the desired space is not available, reservation personnel may offer to place your request on a waitlist. A limited number of requests will be added to a waitlist, which is checked on a regular basis. If cancellations occur you will be notified of confirmation of space. If your cabin has not been confirmed, you must sign-up on the purser's "STANDBY" list on board. If your vehicle's waitlist space has not been confirmed, you must sign up on the "STANDBY" list at your boarding terminal. DO NOT SEND PAYMENT FOR WAITLISTED SPACE UNTIL CONFIRMED.

ARRIVAL/DEPARTURE INFORMATION

For recorded arrival/departure information call the specific terminal/office number listed below. Tidal conditions at some cities may cause slight variations in arrival or departure times. Check with the local office on your departure day for exact sailing times.

SOUTHEAST ALASKA OFFICES

	Recorded Arrival/ Departure Information	Locations and distance from city center
Bellingham	(360) 676-8445	1-5 Exit #250
	(360) 676-0212	(24-hour recorded info.)
Prince Rupert	(250) 627-1744	Yellowhead Hwy #16
Ketchikan	(907) 225-6181	2 5 miles north
Wrangell	(907) 874-3711	2.0 blocks north
Petersburg	(907) 772-3855	0.9 miles south
Sitka	(907) 747-3300	7.1 miles north
Juneau	(907) 465-3940	14.0 miles north
Haines	(907) 766-2113	5.0 miles north
Skagway	(907) 983-2229	3.0 blocks south

SOUTHCENTRAL/ SOUTHWEST

Anchorage	(907) 272-4482	Fax (907) 277-4829
Cordova	(907) 424-7333	
Homer	(907) 235 -8449	
Kodiak	(907) 486-3800	
Seldovia	(907) 234-7868	
Seward	(907) 224-5485	
Valdez	(907) 835-4436	

Ferry terminals are located within 1/2 mile of all Southcentral and Southwest city centers.

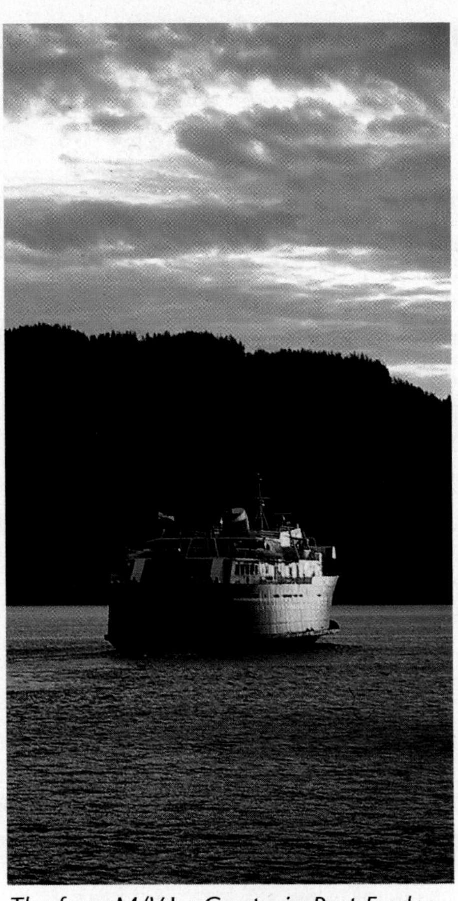

The ferry M/V Le Conte *in Port Frederick near Hoonah, AK.* (© David Job)

HOW TO ESTIMATE ARRIVAL TIMES

Arrival times are not generally listed for interport stops. In-port times vary from 30 minutes to 3 hours. To calculate an approximate unlisted arrival time, add the running time listed in the table to the departure time from the port preceding your arrival city.

Please note that these running times are approximate and are listed for the convenience of those meeting passengers, and for travelers planning stopovers. For more accurate arrival times, please contact the local Marine Highway office on the day of arrival.

Due to traffic demands and tidal conditions, most Marine Highway vessels run continuously, docking at all hours of the day for brief transfers of passengers and vehicles. The passenger wishing to explore a particular community should consider a stopover and continuation on another Marine Highway vessel.

RUNNING TIME TABLE

INSIDE PASSAGE ROUTE:

Bellingham–Ketchikan	37 hrs.
Prince Rupert–Ketchikan	6 hrs.
Ketchikan–Wrangell	6 hrs.
Wrangell–Petersburg	3 hrs.
Petersburg–Juneau	8 hrs.
Petersburg–Sitka	11 hrs.
Sitka–Juneau/Auke Bay	9 hrs.
Juneau/Auke Bay–Haines	4 hrs. 30 min.
Haines–Skagway	1 hr.

SOUTHCENTRAL/SOUTHWEST:

Homer–Kodiak	9 hrs. 30 min.
Homer–Port Lions	10 hrs.
Seward–Kodiak	13 hrs. 15 min.

SOUTHCENTRAL ROUTE:

Whittier–Valdez	6 hrs. 45 min.
Valdez–Cordova	5 hrs. 30 min.
Cordova–Whittier	7 hrs.
Cordova–Seward	11 hrs.
Valdez–Seward	11 hrs.
Homer–Seldovia	1 hr. 30 min.

SOUTHWEST ROUTES:

Kodiak–Port Lions	2 hrs. 30 min.
Kodiak–Chignik	18 hrs. 30 min.
Chignik–Sand Point	9 hrs. 15 min.
Sand Point–King Cove	6 hrs. 30 min.
King Cove–Cold Bay	2 hrs.
Cold Bay–False Pass	4 hrs. 15 min.
False Pass–Akutan	10 hrs. 30 min.
Akutan–Unalaska	3 hrs. 30 min.

ALASKA STATE FERRY SCHEDULES

MAY 1998 NORTHBOUND - INSIDE PASSAGE/SOUTHEAST ALASKA

LEAVE BELLINGHAM	LEAVE PRINCE RUPERT	LEAVE STEWART/HYDER	METLAKATLA	KETCHIKAN	HOLLIS	WRANGELL	PETERSBURG	KAKE	ARRIVE SITKA	ANGOON	TENAKEE	HOONAH	JUNEAU/ AUKE BAY	HAINES	ARRIVE SKAGWAY
	TH3011:15P	NO SAILINGS UNTIL JUNE		F1 6:15A	F1 12:15P	F1 7:15P	F1 11:15P	S2 4:15A	S2 12:15P			SU3 1:30A	SU3 5:30A	SU311:00A	SU3 11:55A
								Lv. Sitka	S2 8:30A	S2 2:45P	S2 6:00P		S2 11:00P		
										Lv. Pelican	SU3 8:30A		SU3 3:00P		
F1 6:00P				SU310:00A		SU3 4:45P	SU3 9:30P								
													M4 6:30A	M4 11:55A	M4 1:00P
			T5 1:00P	T5 3:15P	T5 6:00P										
				T5 1:00A		T5 7:45A	T5 11:30A								
													T5 8:15P	W6 1:45A	W6 2:45A
			W6 12:45A	W6 3:00A	W6 5:45A										
				W6 10:30A			W6 7:00P		TH7 5:00A	TH7 1:30P		TH7 6:30P	TH710:45P	F8 4:15A	F8 5:15A
				TH7 6:15P	F8 12:15A	F8 7:15A	F8 11:15A	F8 4:30P	S9 12:30A			S9 1:45P	S9 6:15P	SU1012:15A	SU10 1:15A
								Lv. Sitka	S9 8:45A	S9 3:00P	S9 6:15P		S9 11:15P		
F8 6:00P				SU1010:00A		SU105:00P	SU1010:00P								
													M11 8:00A	M11 2:00P	M11 3:00P
			T12 6:15A	T12 8:30A	T1211:15A										
			T12 6:00P	T12 8:15P	T1211:00P										
				T12 1:45A		T12 8:45A	T12 12:45P								
													T12 9:30P	W13 3:00A	W13 4:00A
				W13 7:45A			W13 4:45P		TH14 2:45A	TH1411:15A		TH14 4:15P	TH148:30P	F15 2:00A	F15 3:00A
	TH1411:45P			F15 6:45A	F1510:30A	F15 5:30P	F15 9:30P	S16 2:30A	S16 10:30A			S16 11:45P	SU173:45A	SU179:15A	SU1710:15A
								Lv. Sitka	S16 6:30A	S1612:45P	S16 4:00P		S16 9:00P		
F15 6:00P				SU179:30A		SU174:30P	SU17 8:30P								
													M1810:30A	M18 4:30P	M18 5:30P
S1610:00A				SU1711:30P											
	M18 6:15P			T1912:30A		T19 7:30A	T19 12:30P								
													T19 9:30P	W20 3:00A	W20 4:00A
			T19 12:15P	T19 2:30P	T19 5:15P										
	T19 11:00A			T19 5:00P		W2012:15A	W20 4:15A		W20 3:00P						
													TH213:15A		
			T19 11:55P	W20 2:15A	W20 5:00A										
				W20 9:45A			W20 6:00P	W2011:45P	TH21 9:45A	TH216:15P		TH2111:15P	F22 3:30A	F22 9:00A	F22 10:00A
	TH21 9:30P			F22 5:00A		F2211:55A	F22 6:15P		S23 5:30A				S23 5:45P		
								Lv. Sitka	S23 1:45P	S23 8:00P	S2311:15P	SU24 3:30A	SU246:45A		
	S23 8:45A			S23 3:45P		S2310:45P	SU24 2:45A								
													SU2412:15P	SU246:15P	SU24 7:15P
F22 6:00P				SU2411:45A		SU246:45P	SU2410:45P								
													M2510:45A	M25 4:45P	M25 5:45P
	M25 8:30P			T26 2:45A		T26 9:45A	T26 2:45P								
													T2611:45P	W27 5:15A	W27 6:15A
			T26 2:30P	T26 5:00P	T26 7:45P										
	T26 11:45A			T26 5:45P		W2712:45A	W27 4:15A		W27 3:00P				TH283:30A		
			W27 2:30A	W27 4:45A	W27 7:30A										
													F29 7:00A	F2912:30P	F29 1:30P
				W2712:15P			W27 8:30P	TH28 1:30A	TH28 9:30A	TH286:15P		TH2811:15P	F29 2:30A		
													S30 7:00A	S3012:30P	S30 1:30P
	TH2811:15P			F29 5:30A		F2912:30P	F29 5:30P		S30 4:45A				S30 5:15P		
													SU317:00A	SU3112:30P	SU31 1:30P
	S30 10:15A			S30 5:15P		SU3112:15A	SU31 4:00A						SU311:45P	SU317:15P	SU31 8:15P
			SU31 2:15P	SU316:15P	SU319:00P										
F29 6:00P				SU319:30A		SU315:30P	SU31 9:15P						M1 8:30A	M1 2:30P	M1 3:30P

ALL TIMES ARE LOCAL TIMES

HOW TO READ YOUR SCHEDULE

1. Reading across the top of each page, find the month you wish to travel, and refer to either the Northbound or Southbound schedule. (Using the example of traveling from Skagway to Juneau/Auke Bay, you would read the Southbound schedule on the right hand page.)

2. Reading across the top of the schedule, find the city from which you wish to depart. (e.g., Leave Skagway)

3. Read down the column to locate your desired departure date. For example: Leave Skagway T2 (Tuesday, the 2nd) 1:45 A.M.

4. Beginning with the departure date, read horizontally from left to right for dates and times of departure from various ports. For Example: After departing Skagway, the ferry will dock in Haines, and after a short time in port will depart Haines on T2, (Tuesday the 2nd) at 5:15 A.M. for Juneau/Auke Bay.

5. The color of the horizontal bars indicate the vessel on which you will travel.

6. Refer to the Running Time Table on page 20 to calculate approximate arriva l times.

LEAVE SKAGWAY	HAINES	JUNEAU/ AUKE BAY	HOONAH	TENAKEE	ANGOON	ARRIVE SITKA	KAKE	PETERSBURG	WRANGELL	HOLLIS	KETCHIKAN	METLAKATLA	ARRIVE STEWART/HYDER	ARRIVE PRINCE RUPERT	ARRIVE BELLINGHAM
S30 5:30P	S30 8:00P	SU311:30A						SU3110:30A	SU31 3:00P		SU3110:30P			M1 6:00A	
SU318:30P		M1 1:30A													
M1 12:15P	M1 2:45P	M1 8:15P						T2 4:45A			T2 1:15P			T2 8:15P	
T2 1:45A	T2 5:15A	T2 11:45A				T2 8:00P		W3 11:45A	W3 3:45P		W3 10:15P				F5 7:15A
										M1 6:15A	M1 12:15P	M1 1:30P			
		M1 3:00A	M1 7:15A	M1 11:15A	M1 2:30P	M1 7:30P									

Day of Week

Day of Month

AM or PM

Time

VESSEL COLOR CODES: Aurora, Columbia, Le Conte, Malaspina, Matanuska, Taku, Kennicott

MAY 1998 SOUTHBOUND - INSIDE PASSAGE/SOUTHEAST ALASKA

LEAVE SKAGWAY	HAINES	JUNEAU/ AUKE BAY	HOONAH	TENAKEE	ANGOON	ARRIVE SITKA	KAKE	PETERSBURG	WRANGELL	HOLLIS	KETCHIKAN	METLAKATLA	ARRIVE STEWART/HYDER	ARRIVE PRINCE RUPERT	ARRIVE BELLINGHAM
F1 6:00A	F1 8:00A	F1 1:30P	F1 5:45P	F1 9:45P	S2 1:00A	S2 6:00A							NO SAILINGS UNTIL JUNE		
SU3 2:00P	SU3 4:00P	SU3 9:30P					M4 5:45A	M4 10:30A	M4 2:15P	M4 9:15P	M4 11:55P				
		SU312:30A	Ar. Pelican	SU3 7:00A											
		SU3 4:00P	SU3 8:15P	M4 12:15A	M4 3:30A	M4 8:30A		M4 9:45P		T5 7:15A	T5 11:00A	T5 12:15P			
M4 4:00P	M4 6:00P	M4 11:45P				T5 9:30A		W6 12:30A	W6 4:45A		W6 2:15P				F8 6:15A
										T5 7:00P	T5 10:45P	T5 11:55P			
W6 5:30A	W6 7:30A	W6 1:30P						W6 10:15P	TH7 2:15A	TH7 9:30A	TH712:15P				
										W6 6:45A	W6 9:30A				
F8 6:45A	F8 8:45A	F8 2:15P	F8 6:30P	F8 10:30P	S9 1:30A	S9 6:30A									
SU104:15A	SU10 6:15A	SU101:45P					SU1010:15P	M11 3:15A	M11 7:45A	M11 2:45P	M11 5:30P				
		SU109:15A	SU10 1:30P	SU105:30P	SU108:45P	M11 1:45A		M11 3:00P		T1212:30A	T12 4:15A	T12 5:30A			
M11 6:00P	M11 8:15P	T12 4:45A				T12 2:30P		W13 5:00A	W13 9:00A		W13 5:00P				F15 8:00A
										T1212:15P	T12 4:00P	T12 5:15P			
										W1312:15A	W13 3:00A				
W13 7:00A	W13 9:15A	W13 2:45P						W1311:15P	TH14 3:00A	TH1410:00A	TH141:45P			TH148:45P	
F15 4:30A	F15 6:30A	F1511:55A	F15 4:15P	F15 8:15P	F1511:15P	S16 4:15A									
SU171:15P	SU17 3:15P	M18 1:30A						M1810:00A	M18 1:45P	M18 9:45P	T19 1:30A			T19 8:30A	
		SU177:15A	SU1711:30A	SU173:30P	SU176:45P	SU1711:45P	M18 11:45A	M18 4:30P		T19 6:15A	T1910:00A	T19 11:15A			
M18 8:30P	M18 11:00P	T19 5:15A				T19 1:45P		W20 3:30A	W20 7:45A		W20 4:15P				F22 6:15A
											M18 6:15A			M18 1:45P	
W20 7:00A	W20 9:00A	W20 2:30P						W2011:45P	TH21 4:00A		TH2111:00A			TH216:30P	
										T19 6:15P	T1910:00P	T19 11:15P			
		TH2112:15P				TH2110:00P		F22 12:45P	F22 4:45P		F2211:45P			S23 6:45A	
										W20 6:00A	W20 8:45A				
F2211:30A	F22 1:30P	F22 7:00P	F22 11:15P	S23 3:15A	S23 6:30A	S2311:30A									
		S23 8:45P				SU246:30A		SU24 9:15P	M25 1:30A		M25 8:30A			M25 4:00P	
		SU242:45P	SU24 7:00P	SU2411:00P	M25 2:15A	M25 7:15A	M25 6:30P	M2511:15P		T26 8:45A	T2612:30P	T26 1:45P			
SU2410:15P	M25 12:15A	M25 6:15A						M25 2:45P	M25 6:45P		T26 1:45A			T26 8:45A	
M25 8:45P	M25 11:15P	T26 5:45A				T26 2:15P		W27 3:45A	W27 8:00A		W27 4:30P				F29 6:30A
W27 9:15A	W27 11:15A	W27 4:45P						TH28 1:45A	TH28 5:45A		TH2812:45P			TH288:15P	
										T26 8:45P	W271230A	W27 1:45A			
		TH2811:55A				TH289:45P		F29 2:00P	F29 6:15P		S30 1:15A			S30 8:15A	
										W27 8:30A	W2711:15A				
F29 3:30P	F29 5:30P	F2910:00P													
		F29 6:00A	F29 10:15A	F29 2:15P	F29 5:30P	F2910:30P		S30 2:15P		S3011:45P	SU3112:15P	SU31 1:30P			
S30 3:30P	S30 5:30P	S3010:00P													
		S30 7:45P				SU315:30A		SU31 8:30P	M1 1:00A		M1 8:00A			M1 3:30P	
SU313:30P	SU31 5:30P	SU3110:00P													
		SU312:00P	SU31 6:15P	SU3110:15P	M1 1:30A	M1 6:30A	M1 6:30P	M1 10:30P							
SU3111:15P	M1 1:15A	M1 6:45A						M1 3:15P	M1 7:15P		T2 2:15A			T2 9:15A	

ALL TIMES ARE LOCAL TIMES

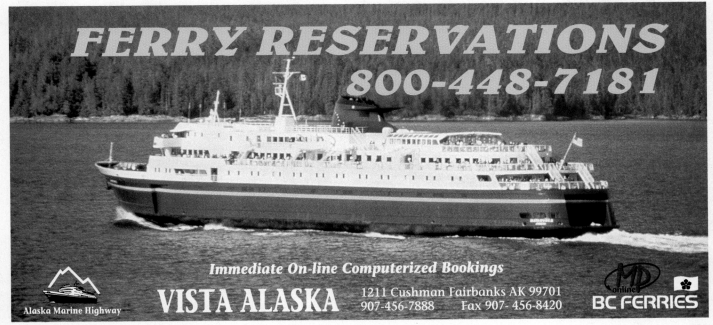

Aurora Columbia Le Conte Malaspina Matanuska Taku Kennicott

JUNE 1998 NORTHBOUND - INSIDE PASSAGE/SOUTHEAST ALASKA

LEAVE BELLINGHAM	LEAVE PRINCE RUPERT	LEAVE STEWART/HYDER	METLAKATLA	KETCHIKAN	HOLLIS	WRANGELL	PETERSBURG	KAKE	ARRIVE SITKA	ANGOON	TENAKEE	HOONAH	JUNEAU/ AUKE BAY	HAINES	ARRIVE SKAGWAY
F29 6:00P		SEE M/V AURORA SCHEDULE BELOW	SEE M/V AURORA SCHEDULE BELOW	SU319:30A	SEE M/V AURORA SCHEDULE BELOW	SU315:30P	SU31 9:15P						M1 8:30A	M1 2:30P	M1 3:30P
	M1 6:30P			T2 12:45A		T2 8:30A	T2 2:15P						T2 11:15P	W3 4:45A	W3 5:45A
T2 6:00P				TH4 8:00A		TH4 2:45P	TH4 6:30P		F5 4:30A				F5 7:00P	S6 1:15A	S6 2:15A
							T2 1:00A	T2 6:00A	T2 2:00P	T2 10:30P		W3 3:30A	W3 6:45A		
	T2 11:15A			T2 5:30P		W3 12:30A	W3 4:15A		W3 3:00P				TH4 3:30A		
							TH4 7:45A	TH4 12:45P		TH4 5:45P	TH4 9:00P	F5 1:15A	F5 4:30A		
	TH4 11:15P			F5 6:00A		F5 1:00P	F5 6:00P		S6 5:15A				S6 5:30P		
								Lv. Sitka	S6 1:45P	S6 8:00P	S6 11:15P	SU7 3:30A	SU7 6:45A		
	S6 9:15A			S6 4:15P		S6 11:15P	SU7 3:15A						SU7 1:00P	SU7 6:30P	SU7 7:30P
F5 6:00P				SU710:00A		SU7 5:30P	SU7 9:15P						M8 8:30A	M8 2:30P	M8 3:30P
	M8 8:00P			T9 2:15A		T9 9:15A	T9 2:15P						T9 11:15P	W10 4:45A	W10 5:45A
T9 6:00P				TH1110:30A		TH116:30P	TH1111:00P		F12 9:00A				F1210:30P	S13 4:30A	S13 5:30A
							T9 5:15A	T9 10:15A	T9 7:30P	W10 4:00A		W10 9:00A	W1012:15P		
	T9 10:15A			T9 4:15P		T9 11:15P	W10 3:15A		W10 2:00P				TH112:30A		
							TH11 1:15P	TH11 6:15P		TH1111:15P	F12 2:30A	F12 6:45A	F1210:00A		
	TH1110:15P			F12 4:30A		F1211:15A	F12 4:00P		S13 3:15A				S13 3:45P		
								Lv. Sitka	S13 11:45A	S13 6:00P	S13 9:15P	SU14 1:30A	SU144:45A		
	S13 8:45A			S13 3:45P		S1310:45P	SU14 2:30A						SU141:00P	SU146:30P	SU14 7:30P
										Lv. Pelican	SU143:30P		SU1410:00P		
F12 6:00P				SU149:30A		SU144:30P	SU14 8:30P						M15 9:15A	M15 3:15P	M15 4:15P
	M15 4:15P			M1510:30P		T16 5:45A	T16 10:30A						T16 7:30P	W17 1:00A	W17 2:00A
T16 6:00P				TH1812:30P									F19 8:30A	** TO SE/ SW INTER-TIE	
							T16 9:45A	T16 3:45P	W17 12:45A	W17 9:15A		W17 2:15P	W17 5:30P		
	T16 10:15A			T16 4:15P		T1611:00P	W17 2:45A		W17 1:30P				TH182:00A		
							TH18 3:00P	TH18 8:00P		F19 1:00A	F19 4:15A	F19 8:30A	F1911:45A		
	TH18 8:30P			F19 4:30A		F1911:55A	F19 5:00P		S20 4:15A				S20 4:30P		
								Lv. Sitka	S20 6:45P	SU211:00A	SU214:15A	SU21 8:30A	SU2111:45A		
	S20 8:45A			S20 3:45P		S2010:45P	SU21 2:45A						SU211:00P	SU216:30P	SU21 7:30P
F19 6:00P				SU219:30A		SU215:00P	SU21 9:00P						M2210:15A	M22 4:15P	M22 5:15P
											**FROM SE/SW INTER-TIE		T23 1:00P	T23 6:30P	T23 7:30P
	M22 6:00P			T2312:15A		T23 8:30A	T23 1:30P						T2310:30P	W24 4:00A	W24 5:00A
							T23 4:45A	T23 10:15A	T23 7:15P	W24 3:45A		W24 8:45A	W2411:55A		
	T23 10:15A			T23 4:15P		T2311:15P	W24 3:00A		W24 1:45P				TH252:15A		
	TH25 1:00P			TH257:45P		F26 2:45A	F26 6:45A						F26 6:00P	F2611:55P	S27 1:00A
							TH25 1:00P	TH25 6:00P		TH2511:00P	F26 2:15A	F26 6:30A	F26 9:45A		
	TH2510:30P			F26 4:45A		F2611:30A	F26 4:15P		S27 3:30A				S27 4:00P		
								Lv. Sitka	S27 11:55A	S27 6:15P	S27 9:30P	SU28 1:45A	SU285:00A		
	S27 9:15A			S27 4:15P		S2711:15P	SU28 3:00A						SU281:00P	SU286:30P	SU28 7:30P
										Lv. Pelican	SU283:30P		SU2810:00P		
F26 9:00P				SU2810:30A		SU286:00P	SU2810:00P						M29 9:15A	M29 3:15P	M29 4:15P
	M29 5:00P			M2911:15P		T30 7:15A	T30 1:15P						T3010:15P	W1 3:45A	W1 4:45A
							T30 10:45A	T30 3:45P	W1 12:45A	W1 9:15A		W1 2:15P	W1 5:30P		
	T30 10:00A			T30 4:00P		T3010:45P	W1 2:30A		W1 1:15P				TH2 1:45A		
T30 6:00P				TH210:30A		TH2 6:30P	TH2 11:00P		F3 9:00A				F3 10:30P	S4 4:30A	S4 5:30A

ALL TIMES ARE LOCALTIMES

M/V MALASPINA NORTH LYNN CANAL TRIPS

The M/V Malaspina operates on a daily schedule as indicated in the following table. To determine the best connection for your trip, use these schedules. Please allow enough time to make appropriate connections with the sailings listed above. (See tables above)

DAILY SCHEDULE MAY 29 - SEPTEMBER 7, 1998

Leave Juneau	7:00AM
Arrive Haines	11:30AM
Leave Haines	12:30PM
Arrive Skagway	1:30PM
Leave Skagway	3:30PM
Arrive Haines	4:30PM
Leave Haines	5:30PM
Arrive Juneau	10:00PM

NOTE: The operation of the M/V Malaspina requires legislative approval and funding. Reservations will be confirmed after February 15, 1998.

M/V KENNICOTT **SOUTHEAST/SOUTHWEST INTER-TIE TRIPS

The M/V Kennicott for the month of June will depart from Juneau as indicated in the following table. To determine the best connection for your trip, use this schedule. Please allow enough time to make appropriate connections with the sailings listed above. (See tables above).

Leave Juneau	Friday	June 19	8:30AM
Arrive Valdez	Saturday	June 20	4:30PM
Leave Valdez	Saturday	June 20	6:30PM
Arrive Seward	Sunday	June 21	6:30AM
Leave Seward	Sunday	June 21	10:30AM
Arrive Valdez	Sunday	June 21	10:30PM
Leave Valdez	Monday	June 22	12:30AM
Arrive Juneau	Tuesday	June 23	8:30AM

The M/V Kennicott is being constructed at the time of publication of this schedule. Please contact any Alaska Marine Highway Office for an update on construction progress.

Aurora Columbia Le Conte Malaspina Matanuska Taku Kennicott

JUNE 1998 SOUTHBOUND - INSIDE PASSAGE/SOUTHEAST ALASKA

LEAVE SKAGWAY	HAINES	JUNEAU/ AUKEBAY	HOONAH	TENAKEE	ANGOON	ARRIVE SITKA	KAKE	PETERSBURG	WRANGELL	HOLLIS	KETCHIKAN	METLAKATLA	ARRIVE STEWART/HYDER	ARRIVE PRINCE RUPERT	ARRIVE BELLINGHAM
		S30 7:45P				SU31 5:30A		SU31 8:30P	M1 1:00A	SEE M/V AURORA SCHEDULE BELOW	M1 8:00A	SEE M/V AURORA SCHEDULE BELOW	SEE M/V AURORA SCHEDULE BELOW	M1 3:30P	
		SU31 2:00P	SU31 6:15P	SU31 10:15P	M1 1:30A	M1 6:30A	M1 6:30P	M1 10:30P							
SU31 11:15P	M1 1:15A	M1 6:45A						M1 3:15P	M1 7:15P		T2 2:15A			T2 9:15A	
M1 6:30P	M1 9:00P	T2 5:30A				T2 1:45P		W3 3:00A	W3 8:00A		W3 4:00P				F5 6:00A
W3 8:45A	W3 10:45A	W3 4:15P						TH4 1:30A	TH4 5:45A		TH4 12:45P			TH4 8:15P	
S6 5:15A	S6 7:45A	S6 4:30P						SU7 1:30A	SU7 5:30A		SU7 4:30P				T9 7:00A
		W3 12:45P	W3 5:00P		W3 10:00P		TH4 3:00A	TH4 7:00A							
		TH4 12:15P				TH4 10:00P		F5 12:30P	F5 4:30P		S6 12:15A			S6 7:15A	
		F5 12:30P	F5 4:45P	F5 8:45P	F5 11:55P	S6 5:00A									
		S6 8:15P				SU7 6:00A		SU7 8:30P	M8 1:00A		M8 8:00A			M8 3:30P	
		SU7 8:00P	M8 12:15A	M8 4:15A	M8 7:30A	M8 12:30P	T9 12:15A	T9 4:15A							
SU7 10:30P	M8 12:30A	M8 6:00A						M8 2:30P	M8 6:15P		T9 1:15A			T9 8:15A	
M8 6:30P	M8 9:00P	T9 5:00A				T9 1:15P		W10 2:15A	W10 7:30A		W10 4:00P				F12 6:00A
W10 8:30A	W10 10:30A	W10 4:00P						TH11 1:00A	TH11 5:00A		TH11 11:55A			TH11 7:30P	
S13 8:30A	S13 11:00A	S13 6:45P						SU14 3:15A	SU14 7:15A		SU14 6:15P				T16 8:45A
		W10 6:15P	W10 10:30P		TH11 3:30A		TH11 8:30A	TH11 12:30P							
		TH11 11:00A				TH11 8:45P		F12 12:45P	F12 4:45P		F12 11:45P			S13 6:45A	
		F12 5:00P	F12 9:15P	S13 1:15A	S13 4:30A	S13 9:30A									
		S13 6:15P				SU14 4:00A		SU14 7:00P	SU14 11:15P		M15 6:15A			M15 1:45P	
		SU14 7:00A	Ar. Pelican	SU14 1:30P											
SU14 10:15P	M15 12:15A	M15 5:45A						M15 2:15P	M15 6:15P		T16 1:15A			T16 8:15A	
		M15 12:45A	M15 5:00A	M15 9:00A	M15 12:15P	M15 5:15P	T16 5:00A	T16 9:00A							
M15 7:15P	M15 9:45P	T16 3:45A				T16 11:55A		W17 1:15A	W17 6:15A		W17 3:45P				F19 6:00A
W17 5:00A	W17 7:00A	W17 12:30P						W17 9:45P	TH18 2:00A		TH18 9:00A			TH18 4:30P	
		W17 7:30P	W17 11:45P		TH18 4:45A		TH18 9:45A	TH18 1:45P							
		TH18 10:45A				TH18 8:30P		F19 11:15A	F19 3:15P		F19 11:15P			S20 6:15A	
		F19 6:00P	F19 10:15P	S20 2:15A	S20 5:30A	S20 10:30A									
		S20 7:30P				SU21 5:15A		SU21 8:00P	M22 12:15A		M22 7:15A			M22 2:45P	
		SU21 8:00P	M22 12:15A	M22 4:15A	M22 7:30A	M22 12:30P	M22 11:55P	T23 4:00A							
SU21 10:15P	M22 12:15A	M22 5:45A						M22 2:15P	M22 6:15P		T23 1:15A			T23 8:15A	
M22 8:15P	M22 10:45P	T23 10:45A				T23 7:00P		W24 11:30A	W24 3:15P		W24 10:45P				F26 1:00P
T23 10:30P	W24 1:00A	W24 7:30A									TH25 3:00A			TH25 10:00A	
W24 8:00A	W24 10:00A	W24 3:30P						TH25 12:45A	TH25 5:00A		TH25 11:55A			TH25 7:30P	
		W24 6:00P	W24 10:15P		TH25 3:15A		TH25 8:15A	TH25 12:15P							
		TH25 11:00A				TH25 8:45P		F26 1:00P	F26 5:00P		S27 12:15A			S27 7:15A	
S27 4:00A	S27 6:30A	S27 4:00P						SU28 1:00A	SU28 5:15A		SU28 4:15P				T30 6:15A
		F26 5:15P	F26 9:30P	S27 1:30A	S27 4:45A	S27 9:45A									
		S27 6:30P				SU28 4:15A		SU28 7:15P	SU28 11:30P		M29 6:30A			M29 2:00P	
		SU28 7:00A	Ar. Pelican	SU28 1:30P											
SU28 10:15P	M29 12:15A	M29 5:45A						M29 2:15P	M29 6:00P		T30 1:00A			T30 8:00A	
		M29 1:00A	M29 5:15A	M29 9:15A	M29 12:30P	M29 5:30P	T30 5:15A	T30 9:15A							
M29 7:15P	M29 9:45P	T30 3:45A				T30 11:55A		W1 1:15A	W1 6:15A		W1 3:45P				F3 6:00A

ALL TIMES ARE LOCALTIMES

M/V AURORA - SOUTHERN PANHANDLE SUMMER 1998
EFFECTIVE JUNE 1, 1998 THROUGH SEPTEMBER 15, 1998

SUN Lv Hollis 6:15AM
Ar Ketchikan 9:00AM
Lv Ketchikan 12:15PM
Ar Metlakatla 1:30PM
Lv Metlakatla 2:15PM
Ar Ketchikan 3:30PM
Lv Ketchikan 6:15PM
Ar Hollis 9:00PM

MON Lv Hollis 6:15AM
Ar Ketchikan 9:00AM
Lv Ketchikan 11:00AM
Ar Metlakatla 12:15PM
Lv Metlakatla 2:45PM
Ar Ketchikan 4:00PM
Lv Ketchikan 6:15PM
Ar Hollis 9:00PM

MON Lv Hollis 10:00PM
TUE Ar Ketchikan 12:45AM
Lv Ketchikan 1:45AM
Ar Hyder 12:30PM
Lv Hyder 3:45PM
WED Ar Ketchikan 12:30AM
Lv Ketchikan 1:30AM
Ar Hollis 4:15AM

WED Lv Hollis 6:15AM
Ar Ketchikan 9:00AM
Lv Ketchikan 12:15PM
Ar Metlakatla 1:30PM
Lv Metlakatla 2:15PM
Ar Ketchikan 3:30PM
Lv Ketchikan 6:15PM
Ar Hollis 9:00PM

***WED** Lv Hollis 10:00PM
THU Ar Ketchikan 12:45AM
Lv Ketchikan 2:00AM
Ar Pr. Rupert 9:30AM
Lv Pr. Rupert 11:30AM
Ar Ketchikan 5:00PM
Lv Ketchikan 6:15PM
Ar Hollis 9:00PM

FRI Lv Hollis 6:15AM
Ar Ketchikan 9:00AM
Lv Ketchikan 12:15PM
Ar Metlakatla 1:30PM
Lv Metlakatla 2:15PM
Ar Ketchikan 3:30PM

FRI Lv Ketchikan 6:15PM
Ar Hollis 9:00PM
Lv Hollis 10:00PM
SAT Ar Ketchikan 12:45AM

SAT Lv Ketchikan 6:15AM
Ar Metlakatla 7:30AM
Lv Metlakatla 8:15AM
Ar Ketchikan 9:30AM
Lv Ketchikan 10:30AM
Ar Hollis 1:15PM
Lv Hollis 2:15PM
Ar Ketchikan 5:00PM
Lv Ketchikan 6:45PM
Ar Metlakatla 8:00PM
Lv Metlakatla 8:45PM
Ar Ketchikan 10:00PM
Lv Ketchikan 11:00PM
SUN Ar Hollis 1:45AM

JUNE 25, 1998

***THU** Lv Hollis 9:15AM
Ar Ketchikan 11:55AM
Lv Ketchikan 6:15PM
Ar Hollis 9:00PM

Aurora | Columbia | Le Conte | Malaspina | Matanuska | Taku | Kennicott

ALASKA STATE FERRY SCHEDULES

JULY 1998 NORTHBOUND - INSIDE PASSAGE/SOUTHEAST ALASKA

LEAVE BELLINGHAM	LEAVE PRINCE RUPERT	LEAVE STEWART/HYDER	METLAKATLA	KETCHIKAN	HOLLIS	WRANGELL	PETERSBURG	KAKE	ARRIVE SITKA	ANGOON	TENAKEE	HOONAH	JUNEAU/ AUKE BAY	HAINES	ARRIVE SKAGWAY
	M29 5:00P	SEE M/V AURORA SCHEDULE BELOW	SEE M/V AURORA SCHEDULE BELOW	M2911:15P	SEE M/V AURORA SCHEDULE BELOW	T30 7:15A	T30 1:15P						T3010:15P	W1 3:45A	W1 4:45A
T30 6:00P				TH210:30A		TH2 6:30P	TH2 11:00P		F3 9:00A				F3 10:30P	S4 4:30A	S4 5:30A
							T30 10:45A	T30 3:45P	W1 12:45A	W1 9:15A		W1 2:15P	W1 5:30P		
	T30 10:00A			T30 4:00P		T3010:45P	W1 2:30A		W1 1:15P				TH2 1:45A		
							TH2 2:45P	TH2 7:45P		F3 12:45A	F3 4:00A	F3 8:15A	F3 11:30A		
	TH2 10:15P			F3 4:30A		F3 11:30A	F3 4:30P		S4 3:45A				S4 4:00P		
								Lv. Sitka	S4 6:15P	SU512:30A	SU5 3:45A	SU5 8:00A	SU511:15A		
	S4 8:15A			S4 2:15P		S4 9:15P	SU5 1:15A						SU5 1:00P	SU5 6:30P	SU5 7:30P
F3 6:00P				SU5 9:30A		SU5 4:30P	SU5 8:30P						M6 9:00A	M6 3:30P	M6 4:30P
	M6 5:30P			M6 11:45P		T7 8:15A	T7 1:15P						T7 10:15P	W8 3:45A	W8 4:45A
							T7 4:30A	T7 9:30A	T7 6:30P	W8 3:00A		W8 8:00A	W8 11:15A		
	T7 10:00A			T7 4:00P		T7 11:00P	W8 2:30A		W8 1:15P				TH9 1:30A		
							TH9 12:15P	TH9 5:15P		TH910:15P	F10 1:30A	F10 5:45A	F10 9:00A		
T7 6:00P				TH9 8:00A		TH9 3:45P	TH9 8:45P		F10 8:00A				F10 9:45P	S11 3:45A	S11 4:45A
	TH9 9:30P			F10 3:45A		F1010:30A	F10 3:15P		S11 2:30A				S11 3:00P		
								Lv. Sitka	S11 11:00A	S11 5:15P	S11 8:30P	SU1212:45A	SU124:00A		
	S11 9:15A			S11 4:00P		S1111:00P	SU12 2:45A						SU121:00P	SU126:30P	SU12 7:30P
										Lv. Pelican	SU123:30P		SU1210:00P		
F10 6:00P				SU129:30A		SU124:30P	SU12 8:30P						M13 8:30A	M13 2:30P	M13 3:30P
	M13 3:15P			M13 9:30P		T14 4:30A	T14 9:15A						T14 6:15P	T1411:45P	W1512:45A
							T14 8:30A	T14 2:00P	T14 11:15P	W15 7:45A		W15 12:45P	W15 4:00P		
	T14 12:15P			T14 7:15P		W15 2:15A	W15 6:15A		W15 6:00P				TH166:30A		
							TH16 3:00P	TH16 8:00P		F17 1:00A	F17 4:15A	F17 8:30A	F1711:45A		
T14 6:00P				TH1610:30A		TH165:45P	TH16 9:45P		F17 7:45A				F17 9:00P	S18 3:00A	S18 4:00A
	TH16 7:00P			F17 3:30A		F1710:30A	F17 3:30P		S18 2:45A				S18 3:00P		
								Lv. Sitka	S18 5:15P	S1811:30P	SU192:45A	SU19 7:00A	SU1910:15A		
	S18 8:15A			S18 3:15P		S1810:15P	SU19 2:15A						SU191:00P	SU196:30P	SU19 7:30P
F17 6:00P				SU199:30A		SU194:30P	SU19 8:30P						M20 9:15A	M20 3:15P	M20 4:15P
	M20 4:30P			M2010:45P		T21 6:15A	T21 12:15P						T21 9:15P	W22 2:45A	W22 3:45A
							T21 3:45A	T21 9:15A	T21 6:15P	W22 2:45A		W22 7:45A	W2211:00A		
	T21 9:45A			T21 3:45P		T2110:30P	W22 2:15A		W22 1:00P				TH231:30A		
T21 6:00P				TH239:45A									F24 8:30A	** TO SE/SW INTER-TIE	
							TH2311:55A	TH23 5:00P		TH2310:00P	F24 1:15A	F24 5:30A	F24 8:45A		
	TH23 9:15P			F24 3:30A		F2410:30A	F24 3:15P		S25 2:30A				S25 3:00P		
								Lv. Sitka	S25 11:15A	S25 5:30P	S25 8:45P	SU26 1:00A	SU264:15A		
	S25 9:15A			S25 4:00P		S2511:00P	SU26 3:00A						SU261:00P	SU266:30P	SU26 7:30P
										Lv. Pelican	SU263:30P		SU2610:00P		
F24 6:00P				SU269:30A		SU264:30P	SU26 8:30P						M2711:00A	M27 4:30P	M27 5:30P
											**FROM SE/SW INTER-TIE		T28 1:00P	T28 6:30P	T28 7:30P
	M27 3:15P			M27 9:30P		T28 4:30A	T28 9:00A						T28 6:15P	T2811:45P	W2912:45A
							T28 8:30A	T28 2:00P	T28 11:00P	W29 7:30A		W29 12:30P	W29 3:45P		
	T28 12:15P			T28 8:15P		W29 3:00A	W29 6:45A		W29 5:30P				TH306:00A		
	TH30 3:30P			TH3010:30P		F31 5:45A	F31 9:30A						F31 8:45P	S1 2:45A	S1 3:45A
							TH3012:45P	TH30 5:45P		TH3010:45P	F31 2:00A	F31 6:15A	F31 9:30A		
	TH30 6:00P			F3112:30A		F31 7:30A	F31 12:30P		S1 1:45A				S1 2:00P		
F31 9:00P				SU210:30A		SU2 5:15P	SU2 9:00P						M3 8:45A	M3 2:45P	M3 3:45P

ALL TIMES ARE LOCALTIMES

M/V MALASPINA NORTH LYNN CANAL TRIPS

The M/V Malaspina operates on a daily schedule as indicated in the following table. To determine the best connection for your trip, use these schedules. Please allow enough time to make appropriate connections with the sailings listed above. (See tables above)

DAILY SCHEDULE MAY 29 - SEPTEMBER 7, 1998

Leave Juneau	7:00AM
Arrive Haines	11:30AM
Leave Haines	12:30PM
Arrive Skagway	1:30PM
Leave Skagway	3:30PM
Arrive Haines	4:30PM
Leave Haines	5:30PM
Arrive Juneau	10:00PM

NOTE: The operation of the M/V Malaspina requires legislative approval and funding. Reservations will be confirmed after February 15, 1998.

M/V KENNICOTT **SOUTHEAST/SOUTHWEST INTER-TIE TRIPS

The M/V Kennicott for the month of July will depart from Juneau as indicated in the following table. To determine the best connection for your trip, use this schedule. Please allow enough time to make appropriate connections with the sailings listed above. (See tables above)

Leave Juneau	Friday	July 24	8:30AM
Arrive Valdez	Saturday	July 25	4:30PM
Leave Valdez	Saturday	July 25	6:30PM
Arrive Seward	Sunday	July 26	6:30AM
Leave Seward	Sunday	July 26	10:30AM
Arrive Valdez	Sunday	July 26	10:30PM
Leave Valdez	Monday	July 27	12:30AM
Arrive Juneau	Tuesday	July 28	8:30AM

The M/V Kennicott is being constructed at the time of publication of this schedule. Please contact any Alaska Marine Highway Office for an update on construction progress.

Aurora Columbia Le Conte Malaspina Matanuska Taku Kennicott

JULY 1998 SOUTHBOUND - INSIDE PASSAGE/SOUTHEAST ALASKA

LEAVE SKAGWAY	HAINES	JUNEAU/ AUKE BAY	HOONAH	TENAKEE	ANGOON	ARRIVE SITKA	KAKE	PETERSBURG	WRANGELL	HOLLIS	KETCHIKAN	METLAKATLA	ARRIVE STEWART/HYDER	ARRIVE PRINCE RUPERT	ARRIVE BELLINGHAM
M29 7:15P	M29 9:45P	T30 3:45A				T3011:55A		W1 1:15A	W1 6:15A	SEE M/V AURORA SCHEDULE BELOW	W1 3:45P	SEE M/V AURORA SCHEDULE BELOW	SEE M/V AURORA SCHEDULE BELOW		F3 6:00A
W1 7:45A	W1 9:45A	W1 3:15P						TH2 12:30A	TH2 4:45A		TH211:45A			TH2 7:15P	
S4 8:30A	S4 11:00A	S4 5:30P						SU5 2:15A	SU5 6:15A		SU5 5:15P				T7 7:45A
		W1 7:45P	W1 11:55P		TH2 5:00A		TH2 10:00A	TH2 2:00P							
		TH210:30A				TH2 8:15P		F3 11:00A	F3 3:00P		F3 11:15P			S4 6:15A	
		F3 5:30P	F3 9:45P	S4 1:45A	S4 5:00A	S4 10:00A									
		S4 7:00P				SU5 4:45A		SU5 7:30P	SU5 11:55P		M6 7:00A			M6 2:30P	
		SU5 7:15P	SU5 11:30P	M6 3:30A	M6 6:45A	M6 11:45A	M6 11:15P	T7 3:15A							
SU510:15P	M6 12:15A	M6 5:45A						M6 2:15P	M6 6:00P		T7 1:00A			T7 8:00A	
M6 7:30P	M6 10:00P	T7 4:00A				T7 12:15P		W8 2:00A	W8 6:30A		W8 4:00P				F10 6:00A
W8 7:45A	W8 9:45A	W8 3:15P						TH9 12:15A	TH9 4:15A		TH911:15A			TH9 6:45P	
		W8 5:15P	W8 9:30P		TH9 2:30A		TH9 7:30A	TH9 11:30A							
		TH910:00A				TH9 7:45P		F10 12:15P	F10 4:15P		S1112:15A			S11 7:15A	
		F10 4:15P	F10 8:30P	S1112:30A	S11 3:45A	S11 8:45A									
S11 7:45A	S11 10:15A	S11 7:00P						SU12 4:00A	SU12 8:00A		SU126:15P				T14 8:45A
		S11 5:15P				SU123:00A		SU12 5:45P	SU12 9:45P		M13 4:45A			M1312:15P	
		SU127:00A	Ar. Pelican	SU121:30P											
SU1210:15P	M13 12:15A	M13 5:45A						M13 2:15P	M13 6:15P		T14 2:15A			T14 9:15A	
		SU1211:00P	M13 4:00A	M13 8:00A	M1311:15A	M13 4:15P	T14 3:45A	T14 7:45A							
M13 6:00P	M13 8:30P	T14 2:30A				T1410:45A		W15 3:00A	W15 7:15A		W15 3:45P				F17 6:00A
W15 3:30A	W15 5:30A	W1511:00A						W15 8:15P	TH1612:30A		TH168:30A			TH164:00P	
		W15 8:00P	TH1612:15A		TH165:15A		TH1610:15A	TH16 2:15P							
		TH169:15A				TH167:00P		F17 9:45A	F17 1:45P		F1711:15P			S18 6:15A	
		F17 4:30P	F17 8:45P	S1812:45A	S18 4:00A	S18 9:00A									
S18 7:00A	S18 9:30A	S18 4:00P						SU1912:45A	SU19 4:45A		SU193:45P				T21 6:15A
		S18 6:00P				SU193:45A		SU19 6:45P	SU1911:00P		M20 6:00A			M20 1:30P	
		SU196:30P	SU1910:45P	M20 2:45A	M20 6:00A	M2011:00A	M20 10:30P	T21 2:30A							
SU1910:00P	SU19 11:55P	M20 5:30A						M20 2:00P	M20 5:45P		T2112:45A			T21 7:45A	
M20 7:15P	M20 9:45P	T21 3:45A				T2111:55A		W22 1:15A	W22 6:15A		W22 4:00P				F24 6:00A
W22 6:45A	W22 8:45A	W22 2:15P						W2211:30P	TH23 3:45A		TH2310:45A			TH236:15P	
		W22 5:00P	W22 9:15P		TH232:15A		TH23 7:15A	TH2311:15A							
		TH2310:00A				TH237:45P		F24 12:15P	F24 4:15P		S2512:15A			S25 7:15A	
		F24 4:30P	F24 8:45P	S2512:45A	S25 4:00A	S25 9:00A									
		S25 5:30P				SU263:15A		SU26 6:00P	SU2610:00P		M27 5:00A			M2712:30P	
		SU267:00A	Ar. Pelican	SU261:30P											
SU2610:15P	M27 12:15A	M27 5:45A						M27 2:15P	M27 6:15P		T28 2:15A			T28 9:15A	
		SU2611:45P	M27 4:00A	M27 8:00A	M2711:15A	M27 4:15P	T28 3:45A	T28 7:45A							
M27 8:30P	T28 1:00A	T2811:30A				T2810:45P		W29 2:45P	W29 6:30P		TH302:00A				F31 1:00P
T2810:45P	W29 1:00A	W29 9:30A									TH305:30A			TH3012:30P	
W29 3:30A	W29 5:30A	W2911:00A						W29 8:15P	TH3012:30A		TH307:30A			TH303:00P	
		W29 5:45P	W29 10:00P		TH303:00A		TH30 8:00A	TH3011:55A							
		TH308:30A				TH306:15P		F31 8:45A	F31 2:15P		F3111:15P			S1 6:15A	
		F31 3:30P	F31 7:45P	F3111:45P	S1 3:00A	S1 8:00A									

ALL TIMES ARE LOCALTIMES

M/V AURORA - SOUTHERN PANHANDLE SUMMER 1998
EFFECTIVE JUNE 1, 1998 THROUGH SEPTEMBER 15, 1998

SUN	Lv Hollis	6:15AM
	Ar Ketchikan	9:00AM
	Lv Ketchikan	12:15PM
	Ar Metlakatla	1:30PM
	Lv Metlakatla	2:15PM
	Ar Ketchikan	3:30PM
	Lv Ketchikan	6:15PM
	Ar Hollis	9:00PM
MON	Lv Hollis	6:15AM
	Ar Ketchikan	9:00AM
	Lv Ketchikan	11:00AM
	Ar Metlakatla	12:15PM
	Lv Metlakatla	2:45PM
	Ar Ketchikan	4:00PM
	Lv Ketchikan	6:15PM
	Ar Hollis	9:00PM

MON	Lv Hollis	10:00PM
TUE	Ar Ketchikan	12:45AM
	Lv Ketchikan	1:45AM
	Ar Hyder	12:30PM
	Lv Hyder	3:45PM
WED	Ar Ketchikan	12:30AM
	Lv Ketchikan	1:30AM
	Ar Hollis	4:15AM
WED	Lv Hollis	6:15AM
	Ar Ketchikan	9:00AM
	Lv Ketchikan	12:15PM
	Ar Metlakatla	1:30PM
	Lv Metlakatla	2:15PM
	Ar Ketchikan	3:30PM
	Lv Ketchikan	6:15PM
	Ar Hollis	9:00PM

***WED**	Lv Hollis	10:00PM
THU	Ar Ketchikan	12:45AM
	Lv Ketchikan	2:00AM
	Ar Pr. Rupert	9:30AM
	Lv Pr. Rupert	11:30AM
	Ar Ketchikan	5:00PM
	Lv Ketchikan	6:15PM
	Ar Hollis	9:00PM
FRI	Lv Hollis	6:15AM
	Ar Ketchikan	9:00AM
	Lv Ketchikan	12:15PM
	Ar Metlakatla	1:30PM
	Lv Metlakatla	2:15PM
	Ar Ketchikan	3:30PM
FRI	Lv Ketchikan	6:15PM
	Ar Hollis	9:00PM
	Lv Hollis	10:00PM
SAT	Ar Ketchikan	12:45AM

SAT	Lv Ketchikan	6:15AM
	Ar Metlakatla	7:30AM
	Lv Metlakatla	8:15AM
	Ar Ketchikan	9:30AM
	Lv Ketchikan	10:30AM
	Ar Hollis	1:15PM
	Lv Hollis	2:15PM
	Ar Ketchikan	5:00PM
	Lv Ketchikan	6:45PM
	Ar Metlakatla	8:00PM
	Lv Metlakatla	8:45PM
	Ar Ketchikan	10:00PM
	Lv Ketchikan	11:00PM
SUN	Ar Hollis	1:45AM

JULY 30, 1998

***THU**	Lv Hollis	9:15AM
	Ar Ketchikan	11:55AM
	Lv Ketchikan	6:15PM
	Ar Hollis	9:00PM

Aurora Columbia Le Conte Malaspina Matanuska Taku Kennicott

AUGUST 1998 NORTHBOUND - INSIDE PASSAGE/SOUTHEAST ALASKA

LEAVE BELLINGHAM	LEAVE PRINCE RUPERT	LEAVE STEWART/HYDER	METLAKATLA	KETCHIKAN	HOLLIS	WRANGELL	PETERSBURG	KAKE	ARRIVE SITKA	ANGOON	TENAKEE	HOONAH	JUNEAU/ AUKE BAY	HAINES	ARRIVE SKAGWAY
	TH30 3:30P	SEE M/V AURORA SCHEDULE BELOW	SEE M/V AURORA SCHEDULE BELOW	TH3010:30P	SEE M/V AURORA SCHEDULE BELOW	F31 5:45A	F31 9:30A						F31 8:45P	S1 2:45A	S1 3:45A
	TH30 6:00P			F3112:30A		F31 7:30A	F31 12:30P		S1 1:45A				S1 2:00P		
								Lv. Sitka	S1 4:15P	S1 10:30P	SU2 1:45A	SU2 6:00A	SU2 9:15A		
	S1 8:15A			S1 3:15P		S1 10:15P	SU2 2:15A						SU2 1:00P	SU2 6:30P	SU2 7:30P
F31 9:00P				SU210:30A		SU2 5:15P	SU2 9:00P						M3 8:45A	M3 2:45P	M3 3:45P
	M3 2:45P			M3 9:00P		T4 4:15A	T4 9:00A						T4 6:00P	T4 11:30P	W5 12:30A
							T4 3:15A	T4 8:15A	T4 5:15P	W5 1:45A		W5 6:45A	W5 10:00A		
	T4 10:45A			T4 5:00P		TH411:55P	W5 4:00A		W5 5:45P				TH6 6:30A		
							TH6 11:00A	TH6 4:00P		TH6 9:00P	F7 12:15A	F7 4:30A	F7 7:45A		
T4 6:00P				TH6 8:15A		TH6 3:00P	TH6 7:45P		F7 7:00A				F7 9:45P	S8 3:45A	S8 4:45A
	TH6 8:15P			F7 2:30A		F7 9:15A	F7 2:15P		S8 1:30A				S8 2:00P		
								Lv. Sitka	S8 10:00A	S8 4:15P	S8 7:30P	S8 11:45P	SU9 3:00A		
	S8 8:15A			S8 3:15P		S8 10:15P	SU9 2:15A						SU9 1:00P	SU9 6:30P	SU9 7:30P
										Lv. Pelican	SU9 3:15P		SU9 9:45P		
F7 6:00P				SU9 8:00A		SU9 3:00P	SU9 7:00P						M10 8:45A	M10 3:15P	M10 4:15P
	M10 2:00P			M10 8:15P		T11 3:00A	T11 7:30A						T11 4:45P	T11 10:15P	T11 11:15P
							T11 8:00A	T11 1:45P	T11 10:15P	W12 6:45A		W12 11:45A	W12 3:00P		
	T11 12:15P			T11 7:15P		W12 2:30A	W12 6:15A		W12 5:00P				TH135:30A		
							TH13 2:00P	TH13 7:00P		TH1311:55P	F14 3:15A	F14 7:30A	F1410:45A		
T11 6:00P				TH139:30A		TH134:30P	TH13 8:15P		F14 6:15A				F14 7:30P	S15 1:30A	S15 2:30A
	TH13 5:45P			F14 1:15A		F14 8:45A	F14 2:00P		S15 1:15A				S15 1:30P		
								Lv. Sitka	S15 4:00P	S1510:15P	SU161:30A	SU16 5:45A	SU169:00A		
	S15 7:15A			S15 2:15P		S15 9:15P	SU16 1:15A						SU161:00P	SU166:30P	SU16 7:30P
F14 6:00P				SU169:00A		SU164:00P	SU16 8:00P						M17 8:45A	M17 3:15P	M17 4:15P
	M17 4:45P			M1711:00P		T18 6:00A	T18 11:00A						T18 8:00P	W19 1:30A	W19 2:30A
							T18 2:45A	T18 7:45A	T18 5:00P	W19 1:30A		W19 6:30A	W19 9:45A		
	T18 10:45A			T18 4:45P		T1811:45P	W19 3:45A		W19 6:00P				TH206:30A		
							TH20 9:45A	TH20 2:45P		TH207:45P	TH2011:00P	F21 3:45A	F21 7:00A		
T18 6:00P				TH2012:30P									F21 8:30A	** TO SE/SW INTER-TIE	
	TH20 8:00P			F21 2:30A		F21 9:30A	F21 2:30P		S22 1:45A				S22 2:00P		
								Lv. Sitka	S22 10:15A	S22 4:30P	S22 7:45P	S22 11:55P	SU233:15A		
	S22 8:15A			S22 3:15P		S2210:15P	SU23 2:15A						SU231:00P	SU236:30P	SU23 7:30P
										Lv. Pelican	SU233:15P		SU239:45P		
F21 6:00P				SU238:00A		SU233:00P	SU23 7:00P						M24 9:00A	M24 3:30P	M24 4:30P
											* FROM SE/SW INTER-TIE		T25 1:00P	T25 6:30P	T25 7:30P
	M24 6:00P			T2512:15A		T25 9:15A	T25 2:15P						T2511:15P	W26 4:45A	W26 5:45A
							T25 7:45A	T25 12:45P	T25 9:45P	W26 6:15A		W26 11:15A	W26 2:30P		
	T25 11:45A			T25 6:30P		W26 1:30A	W26 5:15A		W26 4:00P				TH274:45A		
	TH27 3:30P			TH2710:30P		F28 5:30A	F28 9:30A						F28 8:45P	S29 2:45A	S29 3:45A
							TH2711:15A	TH27 4:15P		TH279:15P	F2812:30A	F28 4:45A	F28 8:00A		
	TH2711:15P			F28 6:15A		F28 1:45P	F28 6:45P		S29 6:00A				S29 6:15P		
								Lv. Sitka	S29 2:15P	S29 8:30P	S2911:45P	SU30 4:00A	SU307:15A		
	S29 8:15A			S29 3:15P		S2910:15P	SU30 2:15A						SU301:00P	SU306:30P	SU30 7:30P
F28 9:00P				SU309:30A		SU304:30P	SU30 8:30P						M31 8:45A	M31 2:45P	M31 3:45P
	M31 9:15P			T1 3:30A		T1 10:30A	T1 3:15P						W2 12:15A	W2 5:45A	W2 6:45A

ALL TIMES ARE LOCAL TIMES

M/V MALASPINA NORTH LYNN CANAL TRIPS

The M/V Malaspina operates on a daily schedule as indicated in the following table. To determine the best connection for your trip, use these schedules. Please allow enough time to make appropriate connections with the sailings listed above. (See tables above)

DAILY SCHEDULE MAY 29 - SEPTEMBER 7, 1998

Leave Juneau	7:00AM
Arrive Haines	11:30AM
Leave Haines	12:30PM
Arrive Skagway	1:30PM
Leave Skagway	3:30PM
Arrive Haines	4:30PM
Leave Haines	5:30PM
Arrive Juneau	10:00PM

NOTE: The operation of the M/V Malaspina requires legislative approval and funding. Reservations will be confirmed after February 15, 1998.

M/V KENNICOTT **SOUTHEAST/SOUTHWEST INTER-TIE TRIPS

The M/V Kennicott for the month of August will depart from Juneau as indicated in the following table. To determine the best connection for your trip, use this schedule. Please allow enough time to make appropriate connections with the sailings listed above. (See tables above)

Leave Juneau	Friday	August 21	8:30AM
Arrive Valdez	Saturday	August 22	4:30PM
Leave Valdez	Saturday	August 22	6:30PM
Arrive Seward	Sunday	August 23	6:30AM
Leave Seward	Sunday	August 23	10:30AM
Arrive Valdez	Sunday	August 23	10:30PM
Leave Valdez	Monday	August 24	12:30AM
Arrive Juneau	Tuesday	August 25	8:30AM

The M/V Kennicott is being constructed at the time of publication of this schedule. Please contact any Alaska Marine Highway Office for an update on construction progress.

Aurora | Columbia | Le Conte | Malaspina | Matanuska | Taku | Kennicott

AUGUST 1998 SOUTHBOUND - INSIDE PASSAGE/SOUTHEAST ALASKA

LEAVE SKAGWAY	HAINES	JUNEAU/ AUKE BAY	HOONAH	TENAKEE	ANGOON	ARRIVE SITKA	KAKE	PETERSBURG	WRANGELL	HOLLIS	KETCHIKAN	METLAKATLA	ARRIVE STEWART/HYDER	ARRIVE PRINCE RUPERT	ARRIVE BELLINGHAM
		TH30 8:30A				TH30 6:15P		F31 8:45A	F31 2:15P	SEE M/V AURORA SCHEDULE BELOW	F31 11:15P	SEE M/V AURORA SCHEDULE BELOW	SEE M/V AURORA SCHEDULE BELOW	S1 6:15A	
		F31 3:30P	F31 7:45P	F31 11:45P	S1 3:00A	S1 8:00A									
S1 6:45A	S1 9:15A	S1 6:15P						SU2 3:15A	SU2 7:15A		SU2 6:15P				T4 8:15A
		S1 4:00P				SU2 2:45A		SU2 5:15P	SU2 9:15P		M3 4:15A			M3 11:45A	
		SU2 5:30P	SU2 9:45P	M3 1:45A	M3 5:00A	M3 10:00A	M3 9:45P	T4 1:45A							
SU2 10:15P	M3 12:15A	M3 5:45A						M3 2:15P	M3 6:15P		T4 1:45A			T4 8:45A	
M3 6:15P	M3 8:45P	T4 2:45A				T4 11:00A		W5 12:15A	W5 5:00A		W5 3:45P				F7 6:00A
W5 3:30A	W5 5:30A	W5 11:00A						W5 8:15P	TH6 2:15A		TH6 9:45A			TH6 5:15P	
		W5 4:00P	W5 8:15P		TH6 1:15A		TH6 6:15A	TH6 10:15A							
		TH6 9:00A				TH6 6:45P		F7 10:45A	F7 2:45P		F7 11:15P			S8 6:15A	
		F7 3:00P	F7 7:15P	F7 11:15P	S8 2:30A	S8 7:30A									
S8 7:45A	S8 10:15A	S8 7:00P						SU9 4:00A	SU9 8:00A		SU9 6:15P				T11 8:45A
		S8 4:30P				SU9 2:15A		SU9 4:45P	SU9 8:45P		M10 3:45A			M10 11:15A	
		SU9 7:00A	Ar. Pelican	SU9 1:30P											
SU9 10:15P	M10 12:15A	M10 5:45A						M10 2:15P	M10 6:15P		T11 2:15A			T11 9:15A	
		SU9 10:45P	M10 3:00A	M10 7:00A	M10 10:15A	M10 3:15P	T11 3:30A	T11 7:30A							
M10 7:15P	M10 10:15P	T11 6:30A				T11 3:45P		W12 5:30A	W12 9:45A		W12 5:15P				F14 7:45A
W12 2:15A	W12 4:15A	W12 9:45A						W12 7:00P	W12 11:15P		TH13 7:15A			TH13 2:45P	
		W12 7:00P	W12 11:15P		TH13 4:15A		TH13 9:15A	TH13 1:15P							
		TH13 8:00A				TH13 5:45P		F14 8:15A	F14 12:15P		F14 10:15P			S15 5:15A	
		F14 3:15P	F14 7:30P	F14 11:30P	S15 2:45A	S15 7:45A									
S15 5:30A	S15 8:00A	S15 2:30P						S15 11:30P	SU16 3:30A		SU16 3:30P				T18 6:00A
		S15 4:30P				SU16 2:15A		SU16 5:30P	SU16 9:45P		M17 4:45A			M17 12:15P	
		SU16 5:15P	SU16 9:30P	M17 1:30A	M17 4:45A	M17 9:45A	M17 9:15P	T18 1:15A							
SU16 10:15P	M17 12:15A	M17 5:45A						M17 2:15P	M17 6:15P		T18 1:15A			T18 8:15A	
M17 8:15P	M17 10:45P	T18 8:30A				T18 4:45P		W19 9:15A	W19 1:00P		W19 8:30P				F21 10:45A
W19 5:30A	W19 7:30A	W19 1:00P						W19 10:15P	TH20 2:30A		TH20 9:30A			TH20 5:00P	
		W19 2:45P	W19 7:00P		W19 11:55P		TH20 5:00A	TH20 9:00A							
		TH20 9:00A				TH20 6:45P		F21 10:45A	F21 2:45P		F21 11:15P			S22 6:15A	
		F21 3:30P	F21 7:45P	F21 11:45P	S22 3:00A	S22 8:00A									
		S22 4:30P				SU23 2:15A		SU23 5:15P	SU23 9:30P		M24 6:00A			M24 1:30P	
		SU23 7:00A	Ar. Pelican	SU23 1:30P											
SU23 10:15P	M24 12:15A	M24 5:45A						M24 2:15P	M24 6:15P		T25 1:45A			T25 8:45A	
		SU23 10:45P	M24 3:00A	M24 7:00A	M24 10:15A	M24 3:15P	T25 2:45A	T25 6:45A							
M24 7:30P	M24 10:30P	T25 10:15A				T25 9:30P		W26 1:00P	W26 4:45P		TH27 12:15A				F28 1:15P
T25 10:30P	W26 1:00A	W26 9:30A									TH27 5:30A			TH27 12:30P	
W26 8:45A	W26 10:45A	W26 4:15P						TH27 1:30A	TH27 5:45A		TH27 12:45P			TH27 8:15P	
		W26 3:45P	W26 8:00P		TH27 1:00A		TH27 6:00A	TH27 10:00A							
		TH27 7:00A				TH27 4:45P		F28 7:30A	F28 12:15P		F28 11:15P			S29 6:15A	
S29 6:45A	S29 9:15A	S29 6:15P						SU30 3:15A	SU30 7:15A		SU30 6:15P				T1 8:15A
		F28 1:30P	F28 5:45P	F28 9:45P	S29 1:00A	S29 6:00A									
		S29 9:15P				SU30 7:00A		SU30 10:00P	M31 2:15A		M31 9:15A			M31 4:45P	
		SU30 3:30P	SU30 7:45P	SU30 11:45P	M31 3:00A	M31 8:00A	M31 8:00P	M31 11:55P							
SU30 10:15P	M31 12:15A	M31 5:45A						M31 2:15P	M31 6:15P		T1 1:15A			T1 8:15A	
M31 6:45P	M31 9:15P	T1 7:15A				T1 3:30P		W2 6:45A	W2 10:45A		W2 6:15P				F4 9:00A

ALL TIMES ARE LOCAL TIMES

M/V AURORA - SOUTHERN PANHANDLE SUMMER 1998
EFFECTIVE JUNE 1, 1998 THROUGH SEPTEMBER 15, 1998

SUN	Lv Hollis	6:15AM
	Ar Ketchikan	9:00AM
	Lv Ketchikan	12:15PM
	Ar Metlakatla	1:30PM
	Lv Metlakatla	2:15PM
	Ar Ketchikan	3:30PM
	Lv Ketchikan	6:15PM
	Ar Hollis	9:00PM
MON	Lv Hollis	6:15AM
	Ar Ketchikan	9:00AM
	Lv Ketchikan	11:00AM
	Ar Metlakatla	12:15PM
	Lv Metlakatla	2:45PM
	Ar Ketchikan	4:00PM
	Lv Ketchikan	6:15PM
	Ar Hollis	9:00PM
MON	Lv Hollis	10:00PM
TUE	Ar Ketchikan	12:45AM
	Lv Ketchikan	1:45AM
	Ar Hyder	12:30PM
	Lv Hyder	3:45PM
WED	Ar Ketchikan	12:30AM
	Lv Ketchikan	1:30AM
	Ar Hollis	4:15AM
WED	Lv Hollis	6:15AM
	Ar Ketchikan	9:00AM
	Lv Ketchikan	12:15PM
	Ar Metlakatla	1:30PM
	Lv Metlakatla	2:15PM
	Ar Ketchikan	3:30PM
	Lv Ketchikan	6:15PM
	Ar Hollis	9:00PM
***WED**	Lv Hollis	10:00PM
THU	Ar Ketchikan	12:45AM
	Lv Ketchikan	2:00AM
	Ar Pr. Rupert	9:30AM
	Lv Pr. Rupert	11:30AM
	Ar Ketchikan	5:00PM
	Lv Ketchikan	6:15PM
	Ar Hollis	9:00PM
FRI	Lv Hollis	6:15AM
	Ar Ketchikan	9:00AM
	Lv Ketchikan	12:15PM
	Ar Metlakatla	1:30PM
	Lv Metlakatla	2:15PM
	Ar Ketchikan	3:30PM
FRI	Lv Ketchikan	6:15PM
	Ar Hollis	9:00PM
	Lv Hollis	10:00PM
SAT	Ar Ketchikan	12:45AM
SAT	Lv Ketchikan	6:15AM
	Ar Metlakatla	7:30AM
	Lv Metlakatla	8:15AM
	Ar Ketchikan	9:30AM
	Lv Ketchikan	10:30AM
	Ar Hollis	1:15PM
	Lv Hollis	2:15PM
	Ar Ketchikan	5:00PM
	Lv Ketchikan	6:45PM
	Ar Metlakatla	8:00PM
	Lv Metlakatla	8:45PM
	Ar Ketchikan	10:00PM
	Lv Ketchikan	11:00PM
SUN	Ar Hollis	1:45AM

AUGUST 27, 1998

***THU**	Lv Hollis	9:15AM
	Ar Ketchikan	11:55AM
	Lv Ketchikan	6:15PM
	Ar Hollis	9:00PM

Aurora · Columbia · Le Conte · Malaspina · Matanuska · Taku · Kennicott

SEPTEMBER 1998 NORTHBOUND - INSIDE PASSAGE/SOUTHEAST ALASKA

LEAVE BELLINGHAM	LEAVE PRINCE RUPERT	LEAVE STEWART/HYDER	METLAKATLA	KETCHIKAN	HOLLIS	WRANGELL	PETERSBURG	KAKE	ARRIVE SITKA	ANGOON	TENAKEE	HOONAH	JUNEAU/ AUKE BAY	HAINES	ARRIVE SKAGWAY
	M31 9:15P	SEE M/V AURORA SCHEDULE BELOW	SEE M/V AURORA SCHEDULE BELOW	T1 3:30A	SEE M/V AURORA SCHEDULE BELOW	T1 10:30A	T1 3:15P						W2 12:15A	W2 5:45A	W2 6:45A
							T1 1:30A	T1 6:30A	T1 3:30P	T1 11:55P		W2 5:00A	W2 8:15A		
	T1 11:00A			T1 5:00P		T1 11:45P	W2 3:30A		W2 4:45P				TH3 5:15A		
							TH3 9:15A	TH3 2:15P		TH3 7:15P	TH3 10:30P	F4 2:45A	F4 6:00A		
T1 6:00P				TH3 9:00A		TH3 4:00P	TH3 8:00P		F4 6:00A				F4 8:30P	S5 2:30A	S5 3:30A
	TH3 11:45P			F4 6:15A		F4 1:45P	F4 7:30P		S5 6:45A				S5 7:00P		
								Lv. Sitka	S5 9:00A	S5 3:15P	S5 6:30P	S5 10:45P	SU6 2:00A		
	S5 8:15A			S5 3:15P		S5 10:15P	SU6 2:00A						SU6 1:00P	SU6 6:30P	SU6 7:30P
										Lv. Pelican	SU6 3:30P		SU6 10:00P		
F4 6:00P				SU6 8:00A		SU6 3:00P	SU6 9:45P						M7 9:15A	M7 3:15P	M7 4:15P
	M7 10:00P			T8 4:15A		T8 11:15A	T8 4:15P						W9 1:15A	W9 6:45A	W9 7:45A
							T8 1:30P	T8 6:30P	W9 3:30A	W9 11:30A		W9 4:30P	W9 7:45P		
	T8 10:45A			T8 5:45P		W9 12:45A	W9 4:45A		W9 3:30P				TH10 4:15A		
								Lv. Sitka	TH10 1:00P	TH10 7:15P	TH10 10:30P	F11 2:45A	F11 7:00A	F11 12:30P	F11 1:30P
T8 6:00P				TH10 12:30P									F11 8:30A	** TO SE/SW INTER-TIE	
	F11 12:45A			F11 7:15A		F11 2:00P	F11 6:45P		S12 6:00A				S12 6:15P		
								Lv. Sitka	S12 8:45P	SU13 3:00A	SU13 6:15A	SU13 10:30A	SU13 1:45P		
	S12 11:15A			S12 6:00P		SU13 1:00A	SU13 5:00A						SU13 2:15P	SU13 8:15P	SU13 9:15P
								Lv. Sitka	M14 10:30A	M14 4:45P	M14 8:00P	T15 12:15A	T15 3:30A		
F11 6:00P				SU13 9:30A		SU13 4:30P	SU13 8:30P						M14 10:30A	M14 4:30P	M14 5:30P
	M14 8:15P			T15 2:30A		T15 10:30A	T15 3:30P						W16 12:30A	W16 6:00A	W16 7:00A
											** FROM SE/SW INTER-TIE		T15 12:30P	T15 6:30P	T15 7:30P
	T15 1:15P			T15 9:15P		W16 5:30A	W16 9:15A		W16 11:00P				TH17 11:45A		
							W16 4:15P	W16 9:15P	TH17 5:15A	TH17 1:45P		TH17 6:45P	TH17 11:00P	F18 4:30A	F18 5:30A
	F18 12:15A			F18 7:00A		F18 2:00P	F18 7:30P		S19 6:45A				S19 7:00P		
								Lv. Sitka	S19 3:15P	S19 9:30P	SU20 12:45A	SU20 5:00A	SU20 8:15A		
	S19 11:15A			S19 4:15P											
										Lv. Pelican	SU20 5:45P		M21 12:15A		
								Lv. Sitka	M21 10:30P	T22 4:45A	T22 8:00A	T22 12:15P	T22 3:30P		
F18 6:00P				SU20 8:00A		SU20 3:00P	SU20 9:30P						M21 9:00A	M21 3:00P	M21 4:00P
	M21 8:15P			T22 2:30A		T22 9:30A	T22 2:30P						T22 11:30P	W23 5:00A	W23 6:00A
							TH24 1:15A	TH24 6:15A	TH24 3:30P	TH24 11:55P		F25 5:00A	F25 9:15A	F25 2:45P	F25 3:45P
	TH24 11:00P			F25 5:30A		F25 12:30P	F25 5:15P		S26 4:30A				S26 4:45P		
								Lv. Sitka	SU27 1:15A	SU27 7:30A	SU27 10:45A	SU27 3:00P	SU27 6:15P		
F25 6:00P				SU27 9:30A		SU27 4:45P	SU27 8:30P						M28 10:30A	M28 4:30P	M28 5:30P
								Lv. Sitka	M28 2:00P	M28 8:15P	M28 11:30P	T29 3:45A	T29 7:00A		
	M28 7:00P			T29 1:15A		T29 8:15A	T29 1:15P						T29 10:15P	W30 3:45A	W30 4:45A

ALL TIMES ARE LOCAL TIMES

M/V MALASPINA NORTH LYNN CANAL TRIPS

The M/V Malaspina operates on a daily schedule as indicated in the following table. To determine the best connection for your trip, use these schedules. Please allow enough time to make appropriate connections with the sailings listed above. (See tables above)

DAILY SCHEDULE MAY 29 - SEPTEMBER 7, 1998

Leave Juneau	7:00AM
Arrive Haines	11:30AM
Leave Haines	12:30PM
Arrive Skagway	1:30PM
Leave Skagway	3:30PM
Arrive Haines	4:30PM
Leave Haines	5:30PM
Arrive Juneau	10:00PM

NOTE: The operation of the M/V Malaspina requires legislative approval and funding. Reservations will be confirmed after February 15, 1998.

M/V KENNICOTT **SOUTHEAST/SOUTHWEST INTER-TIE TRIPS

The M/V Kennicott for the month of September will depart from Juneau as indicated in the following table. To determine the best connection for your trip, use this schedule. Please allow enough time to make appropriate connections with the sailings listed above. (See tables above)

Leave Juneau	Friday	Sept 11	8:30AM
Arrive Valdez	Saturday	Sept 12	4:30PM
Leave Valdez	Saturday	Sept 12	6:30PM
Arrive Seward	Sunday	Sept 13	6:30AM
Leave Seward	Sunday	Sept 13	10:30AM
Arrive Valdez	Sunday	Sept 13	10:30PM
Leave Valdez	Monday	Sept 14	12:30AM
Arrive Juneau	Tuesday	Sept 15	8:30AM

The M/V Kennicott is being constructed at the time of publication of this schedule. Please contact any Alaska Marine Highway Office for an update on construction progress.

Aurora   Columbia   Le Conte   Malaspina   Matanuska   Taku   Kennicott

SEPTEMBER 1998 SOUTHBOUND - INSIDE PASSAGE/SOUTHEAST ALASKA

LEAVE SKAGWAY	HAINES	JUNEAU/ AUKE BAY	HOONAH	TENAKEE	ANGOON	ARRIVE SITKA	KAKE	PETERSBURG	WRANGELL	HOLLIS	KETCHIKAN	METLAKATLA	ARRIVE STEWART/HYDER	ARRIVE PRINCE RUPERT	ARRIVE BELLINGHAM
SU3010:15P	M31 12:15A	M31 5:45A						M31 2:15P	M31 6:15P	SEE M/V AURORA SCHEDULE BELOW	T1 1:15A	SEE M/V AURORA SCHEDULE BELOW	SEE M/V AURORA SCHEDULE BELOW	T1 8:15A	
M31 6:45P	M31 9:15P	T1 7:15A				T1 3:30P		W2 6:45A	W2 10:45A		W2 6:15P				F4 9:00A
W2 9:30A	W2 11:30A	W2 5:15P						TH3 2:15A	TH3 6:15A		TH3 1:15P			TH3 8:45P	
		W2 2:15P	W2 6:30P		W2 11:30P		TH3 4:30A	TH3 8:30A							
		TH3 8:00A				TH3 5:45P		F4 9:15A	F4 1:00P		F4 11:15P			S5 6:15A	
		F4 2:15P	F4 6:30P	F4 10:30P	S5 1:45A	S5 6:45A									
S5 6:30A	S5 9:00A	S5 6:15P						SU6 2:45A	SU6 6:45A		SU6 5:45P				T8 8:15A
		S5 9:45P				SU6 7:30A		SU6 10:45P	M7 3:00A		M7 10:00A			M7 5:30P	
		SU6 7:00A	Ar. Pelican	SU6 1:30P											
SU610:15P	M7 12:15A	M7 5:45A						M7 2:15P	M7 6:15P		T8 1:15A			T8 8:15A	
		M7 4:00A	M7 8:15A	M7 12:15P	M7 3:30P	M7 8:30P	T8 8:00A	T8 11:55A							
M7 7:15P	M7 9:45P	T8 6:15A				T8 2:45P		W9 5:45A	W9 9:45A		W9 5:15P				F11 7:15A
W9 10:45A	W9 12:45P	W9 6:15P						TH10 3:15A	TH10 7:15A		TH102:15P			TH109:45P	
		W9 8:45P	TH10 1:00A		TH105:45A	TH1010:45A									
		TH1012:45P				TH1010:30P		F11 1:15P	F11 5:15P		S12 1:15A			S12 8:15A	
F11 4:00P	F11 6:00P	S12 1:30A	S12 5:45A	S12 9:45A	S12 1:00P	S12 6:00P									
		S12 9:15P				SU137:00A		SU1310:00P	M14 2:15A		M14 9:15A			M14 4:45P	
		SU133:45P	SU13 8:00P	SU1311:55P	M14 3:15A	M14 8:15A									
M1412:15A	M14 2:15A	M14 8:15A						M14 5:15P	M14 9:15P		T15 4:15A			T1511:15A	
		T15 7:30A	T15 11:45A		T15 4:45P	T15 9:45P	W16 9:45A	W16 1:45P							
M14 8:30P	M14 11:00P	T15 7:15A				T15 3:45P		W16 8:30A	W16 12:45P		W16 8:15P				F18 10:15A
W1610:00A	W16 11:55A	W16 5:30P						TH17 2:30A	TH17 6:45A		TH171:45P			TH179:15P	
T1510:30P	W16 1:00A	W16 9:30A									TH175:30A				F18 8:00P
		TH172:00P				TH1711:45P		F18 2:15P	F18 6:15P		S19 1:15A			S19 8:15A	
F18 8:00A	F18 10:00A	F18 8:30P	S19 12:45A	S19 4:45A	S19 8:00A	S19 1:00P									
		S19 9:45P				SU207:30A		SU2010:30P	M21 2:45A		M21 9:45A			M21 5:15P	
		SU209:15A	Ar. Pelican	SU203:45P											
		M21 3:45A	M21 8:00A	M2111:55A	M21 3:15P	M21 8:15P									
		T22 6:45P	T22 11:00P		W23 4:00A	W23 9:00A	W23 8:30P	TH2412:30A							
M21 7:00P	M21 9:30P	T22 5:45A				T22 2:15P		W23 4:30A	W23 8:30A		W23 5:00P				F25 7:00A
W23 9:00A	W23 11:00A	W23 5:00P						TH24 2:00A	TH24 6:00A		TH241:00P			TH248:30P	
F25 6:15P	F25 8:15P	S26 6:30A	S26 10:45A	S26 2:45P	S26 6:00P	S2611:00P									
		S26 7:15P				SU275:00A		SU27 7:45P	SU2711:55P		M28 7:00A			M28 2:30P	
		SU277:15P	SU2711:30P	M28 3:30A	M28 6:45A	M2811:45A									
M28 8:30P	M28 11:00P	T29 5:30A				T29 2:00P		W30 3:30A	W30 7:30A		W30 4:00P				F2 6:00A
		T2911:55A	T29 4:15P		T29 9:15P	W30 2:15A	W30 2:00P	W30 6:00P							
W30 7:45A	W30 9:45A	W30 3:15P						TH1 12:15A	TH1 4:15A		TH111:15A			TH1 6:45P	

ALL TIMES ARE LOCAL TIMES

M/V AURORA - SOUTHERN PANHANDLE SUMMER 1998
EFFECTIVE JUNE 1, 1998 THROUGH SEPTEMBER 30, 1998

SUN Lv Hollis 6:15AM
Ar Ketchikan 9:00AM
Lv Ketchikan 12:15PM
Ar Metlakatla 1:30PM
Lv Metlakatla 2:15PM
Ar Ketchikan 3:30PM
Lv Ketchikan 6:15PM
Ar Hollis 9:00PM

MON Lv Hollis 6:15AM
Ar Ketchikan 9:00AM
Lv Ketchikan 11:00AM
Ar Metlakatla 12:15PM
Lv Metlakatla 2:45PM
Ar Ketchikan 4:00PM
Lv Ketchikan 6:15PM
Ar Hollis 9:00PM

***MON** Lv Hollis 10:00PM
TUE Ar Ketchikan 12:45AM
Lv Ketchikan 1:45AM
Ar Hyder 12:30PM
Lv Hyder 3:45PM
WED Ar Ketchikan 12:30AM
Lv Ketchikan 1:30AM
Ar Hollis 4:15AM

WED Lv Hollis 6:15AM
Ar Ketchikan 9:00AM
Lv Ketchikan 12:15PM
Ar Metlakatla 1:30PM
Lv Metlakatla 2:15PM
Ar Ketchikan 3:30PM
Lv Ketchikan 6:15PM
Ar Hollis 9:00PM

WED Lv Hollis 10:00PM
THU Ar Ketchikan 12:45AM
Lv Ketchikan 2:00AM
Ar Pr. Rupert 9:30AM
Lv Pr. Rupert 11:30AM
Ar Ketchikan 5:00PM
Lv Ketchikan 6:15PM
Ar Hollis 9:00PM

FRI Lv Hollis 6:15AM
Ar Ketchikan 9:00AM
Lv Ketchikan 12:15PM
Ar Metlakatla 1:30PM
Lv Metlakatla 2:15PM
Ar Ketchikan 3:30PM

FRI Lv Ketchikan 6:15PM
Ar Hollis 9:00PM
Lv Hollis 10:00PM
SAT Ar Ketchikan 12:45AM

SAT Lv Ketchikan 6:15AM
Ar Metlakatla 7:30AM
Lv Metlakatla 8:15AM
Ar Ketchikan 9:30AM
Lv Ketchikan 10:30AM
Ar Hollis 1:15PM
Lv Hollis 2:15PM
Ar Ketchikan 5:00PM
Lv Ketchikan 6:45PM
Ar Metlakatla 8:00PM
Lv Metlakatla 8:45PM
Ar Ketchikan 10:00PM
Lv Ketchikan 11:00PM
SUN Ar Hollis 1:45AM

SEP 15 - SEP 30, 1998

***TUE** Lv Hollis 6:15AM
Ar Ketchikan 9:00AM
Lv Ketchikan 6:15PM
Ar Hollis 9:00PM

Aurora Columbia Le Conte Malaspina Matanuska Taku Kennicott

INSIDE PASSAGE/SOUTHEAST ALASKA PASSENGER & VEHICLE TARIFFS

ADULT 12 YEARS OR OVER (Meals and Berth NOT included) — ITEM ADT

BETWEEN / AND	BELLINGHAM	PRINCE RUPERT	STEWART/HYDER	KETCHIKAN	METLAKATLA	HOLLIS	WRANGELL	PETERSBURG	KAKE	SITKA	ANGOON	HOONAH	JUNEAU	HAINES	SKAGWAY	PELICAN
KETCHIKAN	164	38	40													
METLAKATLA	168	42	44	14												
HOLLIS	178	52	54	20	22											
WRANGELL	180	56	58	24	28	24										
PETERSBURG	192	68	70	38	42	38	18									
KAKE	202	80	82	48	52	48	34	22								
SITKA	208	86	88	54	58	54	38	26	24							
ANGOON	222	100	102	68	72	68	52	40	28	22						
HOONAH	226	104	106	74	78	74	56	44	38	24	20					
JUNEAU	226	104	106	74	78	74	56	44	44	26	24	20				
HAINES	240	118	120	88	92	88	70	58	58	40	38	34	20			
SKAGWAY	246	124	126	92	96	92	76	64	64	44	42	40	26	14		
PELICAN	248	126	128	96	100	96	78	66	52	40	38	22	32	46	54	
TENAKEE	226	104	106	74	78	74	56	44	32	22	16	16	22	34	40	32

CHILD 2 THROUGH 11 YEARS (Under 2 Transported Free) — ITEM CHD

BETWEEN / AND	BELLINGHAM	PRINCE RUPERT	STEWART/HYDER	KETCHIKAN	METLAKATLA	HOLLIS	WRANGELL	PETERSBURG	KAKE	SITKA	ANGOON	HOONAH	JUNEAU	HAINES	SKAGWAY	PELICAN
KETCHIKAN	82	18	20													
METLAKATLA	84	20	22	8												
HOLLIS	88	26	28	12	14											
WRANGELL	90	28	30	12	14	12										
PETERSBURG	96	34	36	20	22	20	10									
KAKE	102	40	42	24	26	24	18	12								
SITKA	104	42	44	26	28	26	20	14	12							
ANGOON	110	50	52	34	36	34	26	20	14	12						
HOONAH	114	52	54	38	40	38	28	22	20	12	10					
JUNEAU	114	52	54	38	40	38	28	22	22	12	12	10				
HAINES	120	60	62	44	46	44	36	30	30	20	20	18	10			
SKAGWAY	124	62	64	46	48	46	38	32	32	22	22	20	14	8		
PELICAN	126	64	66	48	50	48	40	34	26	20	20	12	16	24	28	
TENAKEE	114	52	54	38	40	38	28	22	16	12	8	8	12	18	20	16

ALTERNATE MEANS OF CONVEYANCE (Bicycles-Small Boats-Inflatables) — ITEM AMC

BETWEEN / AND	BELLINGHAM	PRINCE RUPERT	STEWART/HYDER	KETCHIKAN	METLAKATLA	HOLLIS	WRANGELL	PETERSBURG	KAKE	SITKA	ANGOON	HOONAH	JUNEAU	HAINES	SKAGWAY	PELICAN
KETCHIKAN	28	10	11													
METLAKATLA	29	11	12	7												
HOLLIS	30	12	13	8	9											
WRANGELL	31	13	14	9	10	9										
PETERSBURG	32	14	15	11	12	11	8									
KAKE	34	16	17	12	13	12	10	8								
SITKA	35	17	18	13	14	13	11	9	8							
ANGOON	37	19	20	15	16	15	13	11	9	7						
HOONAH	38	20	21	16	17	16	14	12	11	8	8					
JUNEAU	38	20	21	16	17	16	14	12	12	9	9	8				
HAINES	39	22	23	18	19	18	16	14	14	11	10	10	8			
SKAGWAY	40	23	24	19	20	19	17	15	15	12	11	11	9	7		
PELICAN	41	23	24	19	20	19	17	15	13	11	10	8	10	12	13	
TENAKEE	38	20	21	16	17	16	14	12	10	8	7	7	9	10	11	10

TWO WHEELED MOTORCYCLES (No Trailers - Driver NOT included) — ITEM 705

BETWEEN / AND	BELLINGHAM	PRINCE RUPERT	STEWART/HYDER	KETCHIKAN	METLAKATLA	HOLLIS	WRANGELL	PETERSBURG	KAKE	SITKA	ANGOON	HOONAH	JUNEAU	HAINES	SKAGWAY	PELICAN
KETCHIKAN	133	28	31													
METLAKATLA	140	32	35	8												
HOLLIS	146	40	44	16	17											
WRANGELL	150	45	47	20	23	20										
PETERSBURG	160	54	58	30	33	30	14									
KAKE	169	66	68	40	44	40	26	17								
SITKA	174	70	72	45	48	45	30	20	18							
ANGOON	186	82	84	56	60	56	43	32	22	16						
HOONAH	191	86	89	61	64	61	46	36	30	18	15					
JUNEAU	191	86	89	61	64	61	46	36	36	20	18	15				
HAINES	204	98	100	72	76	72	58	47	47	31	30	26	15			
SKAGWAY	208	104	105	77	81	77	62	53	53	36	35	31	20	8		
PELICAN	210	106	107	79	83	79	64	53	41	32	30	17	26	38	44	
TENAKEE	191	86	89	61	64	61	46	36	25	17	13	13	17	28	32	26

All motorcycles must be fully secured on the car deck with tie-downs. It is the responsibility of the owner to ensure this is completed properly. Rope may be obtained from car deck personnel for lashing purposes.

VEHICLES UP TO 10 FEET (Driver NOT Included) — ITEM 710

BETWEEN / AND	BELLINGHAM	PRINCE RUPERT	STEWART/HYDER	KETCHIKAN	METLAKATLA	HOLLIS	WRANGELL	PETERSBURG	KAKE	SITKA	ANGOON	HOONAH	JUNEAU	HAINES	SKAGWAY	PELICAN
KETCHIKAN	218	45	50													
METLAKATLA	223	53	56	14												
HOLLIS	238	66	71	26	29											
WRANGELL	243	73	76	31	38	31										
PETERSBURG	259	89	94	49	54	49	23									
KAKE	275	105	110	65	71	65	43	28								
SITKA	284	114	118	73	79	73	49	33	30							
ANGOON	303	133	136	91	98	91	69	53	36	26						
HOONAH	310	140	144	99	105	99	75	59	49	30	25					
JUNEAU	310	140	144	99	105	99	75	59	59	33	30	24				
HAINES	330	160	163	118	124	118	94	76	76	51	49	43	25			
SKAGWAY	338	168	170	125	131	125	101	85	85	59	56	51	33	14		
PELICAN	341	171	174	129	134	129	104	86	68	53	49	29	43	63	71	
TENAKEE	310	140	144	99	105	99	75	59	41	28	20	20	28	45	53	43

ALL TARIFFS AND RATES ARE QUOTED IN U.S. DOLLARS

VEHICLES UP TO 15 FEET (Driver NOT Included) — ITEM 715

BETWEEN / AND	BELLINGHAM	PRINCE RUPERT	STEWART/HYDER	KETCHIKAN	METLAKATLA	HOLLIS	WRANGELL	PETERSBURG	KAKE	SITKA	ANGOON	HOONAH	JUNEAU	HAINES	SKAGWAY
KETCHIKAN	374	75	83												
METLAKATLA	372	84	95	21											
HOLLIS	394	107	119	41	46										
WRANGELL	405	117	129	51	61	51									
PETERSBURG	433	145	158	80	90	80	35								
KAKE	460	174	187	109	119	109	70	44							
SITKA	473	187	200	122	132	122	80	52	49						
ANGOON	505	220	233	155	164	155	116	86	60	41					
HOONAH	534	240	246	168	177	168	126	98	82	49	39				
JUNEAU	534	240	246	168	177	168	126	98	98	52	47	38			
HAINES	568	273	278	200	210	200	158	129	129	85	80	71	39		
SKAGWAY	581	286	291	213	224	213	172	143	143	99	94	85	53	21	
PELICAN	570	285	298	220	228	220	176	147	114	86	80	47	70	104	119
TENAKEE	(Unable to off-load vehicles longer than ten feet)														

VEHICLES UP TO 19 FEET (Driver NOT Included) — ITEM 719

BETWEEN / AND	BELLINGHAM	PRINCE RUPERT	STEWART/HYDER	KETCHIKAN	METLAKATLA	HOLLIS	WRANGELL	PETERSBURG	KAKE	SITKA	ANGOON	HOONAH	JUNEAU	HAINES	SKAGWAY
KETCHIKAN	445	90	99												
METLAKATLA	443	100	113	25											
HOLLIS	470	128	141	49	55										
WRANGELL	482	139	153	61	73	61									
PETERSBURG	515	172	188	95	107	95	42								
KAKE	548	207	223	130	141	130	83	52							
SITKA	563	223	238	145	157	145	96	63	58						
ANGOON	602	261	277	184	196	184	138	103	71	49					
HOONAH	636	285	292	200	211	200	150	117	97	58	47				
JUNEAU	636	285	292	200	211	200	150	117	117	62	56	45			
HAINES	676	325	331	238	250	238	188	154	154	101	95	84	46		
SKAGWAY	692	341	347	254	267	254	205	171	171	117	112	101	63	25	
PELICAN	679	339	354	261	271	261	210	175	136	103	95	56	83	124	141
TENAKEE	(Unable to off-load vehicles longer than ten feet)														

VEHICLES UP TO 21 FEET (Driver NOT Included) — ITEM 721

BETWEEN / AND	BELLINGHAM	PRINCE RUPERT	STEWART/HYDER	KETCHIKAN	METLAKATLA	HOLLIS	WRANGELL	PETERSBURG	KAKE	SITKA	ANGOON	HOONAH	JUNEAU	HAINES	SKAGWAY
KETCHIKAN	557	112	127												
METLAKATLA	572	129	145	31											
HOLLIS	606	164	182	62	70										
WRANGELL	622	179	197	78	93	78									
PETERSBURG	665	222	242	122	137	122	53								
KAKE	707	267	287	167	182	167	107	67							
SITKA	727	287	307	187	202	187	123	80	74						
ANGOON	777	337	357	237	252	237	177	132	91	63					
HOONAH	821	368	377	257	272	257	193	150	125	74	60				
JUNEAU	821	368	377	257	272	257	193	150	150	79	72	57			
HAINES	872	419	427	307	322	307	242	198	198	130	122	108	59		
SKAGWAY	893	440	447	327	344	327	264	220	220	151	144	130	81	31	
PELICAN	877	437	457	337	350	337	270	225	175	132	122	71	107	159	182
TENAKEE	(Unable to off-load vehicles longer than ten feet)														

HOW TO DETERMINE FARES

TARIFFS — All fares are one-way. Fares for passengers, vehicles and staterooms are all calculated separately and must be added together to determine the total cost of your travel.

Passage and vehicle fares are charged from the port of embarkation to the port of debarkation. Stateroom fares are calculated according to the route taken, and may vary from the printed rates depending on the ship and schedules.

PETS - Dogs, cats, and other household pets are charged $25 to/from Bellingham, and $10 to/from Prince Rupert and Stewart/Hyder. There is no charge for a certified service animal traveling with a disabled person.

VEHICLE FARES — Vehicle fares are determined by the vehicle's overall length and width. Vehicles 8-1/2 to 9 feet wide will be charged approximately 125% of the listed fare. Vehicles over 9 feet wide will be charged approximately 150% of the listed fare. If you are towing a vehicle, the overall connected length is used to determine fares.

VEHICLES OVER 21 FEET — Contact any Marine Highway office for fares. Vessels in Southeast Alaska can load vehicles up to 70 feet long with special arrangements. Fares for towed vehicles or trailers are calculated at their combined connected length. Vehicles may not be disconnected for travel at separate rates on the same sailing.

MINIMUM 25' RATE — Vehicles with high centers of gravity (commercial highway vans, loaded flat bed trailers) are charged at the 25 ft. rate unless the vehicle is over 25 ft.in which case the appropriate rate for the vehicle length applies. Contact the commerical booking desk (907) 465-8818 for information and reservations.

INSIDE PASSAGE/SOUTHEAST ALASKA CABIN TARIFFS

FOUR BERTH CABIN/SITTING ROOM - OUTSIDE/COMPLETE FACILITIES **ITEM 4BS**
M/V COLUMBIA - M/V MALASPINA

BETWEEN AND	BELLINGHAM	PRINCE RUPERT	KETCHIKAN	HOLLIS	WRANGELL	PETERSBURG	KAKE	SITKA	JUNEAU	HAINES
PRINCE RUPERT	248									
KETCHIKAN	272	63		N			N			
WRANGELL	300	89	58	O			O			
PETERSBURG	318	103	71		47					
SITKA	351	128	91	S	71	60	S			
JUNEAU	371	145	107	T	91	78	T	54		
HAINES	392	164	129	O	108	97	O	74	51	
SKAGWAY	392	164	129	P	108	97	P	74	51	39

FOUR BERTH CABIN - OUTSIDE/COMPLETE FACILITIES **ITEM 4BF**
M/V COLUMBIA - M/V MALASPINA - M/V MATANUSKA - M/V TAKU - M/V KENNICOTT

BETWEEN AND	BELLINGHAM	PRINCE RUPERT	KETCHIKAN	HOLLIS	WRANGELL	PETERSBURG	KAKE	SITKA	JUNEAU	HAINES
PRINCE RUPERT	226									
KETCHIKAN	248	58								
HOLLIS	266	71	48							
WRANGELL	274	80	53	50						
PETERSBURG	289	92	65	56	41					
KAKE	304	104	75	65	53	48				
SITKA	319	114	84	74	64	55	50			
JUNEAU	337	128	100	90	80	69	63	48		
HAINES	362	152	121	110	100	90	77	67	45	
SKAGWAY	362	152	121	110	100	90	77	67	45	35

FOUR BERTH CABIN - INSIDE/COMPLETE FACILITIES **ITEM 4BI**
M/V COLUMBIA - M/V MALASPINA - M/V MATANUSKA - M/V TAKU - M/V KENNICOTT

BETWEEN AND	BELLINGHAM	PRINCE RUPERT	KETCHIKAN	HOLLIS	WRANGELL	PETERSBURG	KAKE	SITKA	JUNEAU	HAINES
PRINCE RUPERT	191									
KETCHIKAN	210	50								
HOLLIS	229	57	42							
WRANGELL	233	69	48	43						
PETERSBURG	250	80	57	49	39					
KAKE	262	90	64	56	46	40				
SITKA	275	100	75	65	56	48	42			
JUNEAU	292	112	88	78	69	60	55	42		
HAINES	311	131	106	96	88	79	69	59	39	
SKAGWAY	311	131	106	96	88	79	69	59	39	31

TWO BERTH CABIN - OUTSIDE/NO FACILITIES **ITEM 2NO**
M/V KENNICOTT

BETWEEN AND	BELLINGHAM	PRINCE RUPERT	KETCHIKAN	HOLLIS	WRANGELL	PETERSBURG	KAKE	SITKA	JUNEAU	HAINES
KETCHIKAN	142	33		N			N			
WRANGELL	157	46	30	O			O			
PETERSBURG	165	53	37		23					
SITKA	182	65	48	S	37	31	S			
JUNEAU	193	73	57	T	46	39	T	27		
HAINES	207	87	69	O	57	51	O	38	25	
SKAGWAY	207	87	69	P	57	51	P	38	25	20

TWO BERTH - INSIDE/NO FACILITIES **ITEM 2NI**
M/V KENNICOTT

BETWEEN AND	BELLINGHAM	PRINCE RUPERT	KETCHIKAN	HOLLIS	WRANGELL	PETERSBURG	KAKE	SITKA	JUNEAU	HAINES
KETCHIKAN	128	30		N			N			
WRANGELL	141	41	27	O			O			
PETERSBURG	149	47	33		21					
SITKA	164	59	43	S	33	28	S			
JUNEAU	173	66	51	T	41	35	T	25		
HAINES	186	78	62	O	51	46	O	34	23	
SKAGWAY	186	78	62	P	51	46	P	34	23	18

THREE BERTH CABIN - OUTSIDE/COMPLETE FACILITIES **ITEM 3BF**
M/V COLUMBIA - M/V MATANUSKA

BETWEEN AND	BELLINGHAM	PRINCE RUPERT	KETCHIKAN	HOLLIS	WRANGELL	PETERSBURG	KAKE	SITKA	JUNEAU	HAINES
KETCHIKAN	202	45		N			N			
WRANGELL	222	63	44	O			O			
PETERSBURG	232	72	52		35					
SITKA	254	90	67	S	52	45	S			
JUNEAU	271	102	77	T	62	55	T	40		
HAINES	294	119	91	O	74	67	O	53	37	
SKAGWAY	294	119	91	P	74	67	P	53	37	30

TWO BERTH - OUTSIDE/COMPLETE FACILITIES **ITEM 2BF**
M/V COLUMBIA - M/V MALASPINA - M/V MATANUSKA - M/V TAKU - M/V KENNICOTT

BETWEEN AND	BELLINGHAM	PRINCE RUPERT	KETCHIKAN	HOLLIS	WRANGELL	PETERSBURG	KAKE	SITKA	JUNEAU	HAINES
PRINCE RUPERT	162									
KETCHIKAN	177	43								
HOLLIS	188	50	35							
WRANGELL	193	58	37	36						
PETERSBURG	204	67	46	44	33					
KAKE	216	76	54	46	40	34				
SITKA	227	84	61	58	47	40	36			
JUNEAU	243	97	72	70	58	50	45	37		
HAINES	263	113	84	82	69	62	60	48	34	
SKAGWAY	263	113	84	82	69	62	60	48	34	27

TWO BERTH CABIN - INSIDE/COMPLETE FACILITIES **ITEM 2BI**
M/V COLUMBIA - M/V MALASPINA - M/V MATANUSKA - M/V TAKU

BETWEEN AND	BELLINGHAM	PRINCE RUPERT	KETCHIKAN	HOLLIS	WRANGELL	PETERSBURG	KAKE	SITKA	JUNEAU	HAINES
PRINCE RUPERT	142									
KETCHIKAN	156	38								
HOLLIS	164	44	27							
WRANGELL	174	53	34	28						
PETERSBURG	180	60	41	36	29					
KAKE	189	68	48	42	36	30				
SITKA	199	74	53	47	41	35	32			
JUNEAU	211	83	63	60	51	44	40	33		
HAINES	227	98	76	73	63	57	56	44	31	
SKAGWAY	227	98	76	73	63	57	56	44	31	25

TWO BERTH ROOMETTE - OUTSIDE/NO FACILITIES/*NO LINEN **ITEM 2RO**
M/V KENNICOTT

BETWEEN AND	BELLINGHAM	PRINCE RUPERT	KETCHIKAN	HOLLIS	WRANGELL	PETERSBURG	KAKE	SITKA	JUNEAU	HAINES
KETCHIKAN	85	20		N			N			
WRANGELL	94	27	18	O			O			
PETERSBURG	99	32	22		14					
SITKA	109	39	29	S	22	19	S			
JUNEAU	116	44	34	T	27	24	T	16		
HAINES	124	52	41	O	34	31	O	23	15	
SKAGWAY	124	52	41	P	34	31	P	23	15	12

TWO BERTH ROOMETTE - INSIDE/NO FACILITIES/*NO LINEN **ITEM 2RI**
M/V KENNICOTT

BETWEEN AND	BELLINGHAM	PRINCE RUPERT	KETCHIKAN	HOLLIS	WRANGELL	PETERSBURG	KAKE	SITKA	JUNEAU	HAINES
KETCHIKAN	71	17		N			N			
WRANGELL	78	23	15	O			O			
PETERSBURG	83	26	19		12					
SITKA	91	33	24	S	18	16	S			
JUNEAU	96	37	29	T	23	20	T	14		
HAINES	103	43	35	O	29	26	O	19	13	
SKAGWAY	103	43	35	P	29	26	P	19	13	10

SOUTHEAST/SOUTHWEST INTER-TIE TARIFFS

	BELLINGHAM VALDEZ	KETCHIKAN VALDEZ	JUNEAU VALDEZ
Passengers (12 yrs & older)	328	164	90
Child (2 yrs through 11 yrs)	164	82	44
AMC (Bicycles-Kayaks-Inflatables)	56	28	12
2 Wheeled Motorcycles	266	133	72
Vehicles up to 10 feet	436	218	119
Vehicles up to 15 feet	748	374	206
Vehcles up to 19 feet	890	445	245
Vehicles up to 21 feet	1114	557	300
Vehicles up to 23 feet	1396	698	376
Vehicles up to 25 feet	1658	829	447
CABINS			
4 Berth - Outside/complete facilities	496	248	148
4 Berth -Inside/complete facilities	420	210	122
2 Berth - Outside/complete facilities	354	177	105
2 Berth - Outside/no facilities	283	142	85
2 Berth - Inside/no facilities	255	128	72
2 Berth Roomette - Outside/no facilities*	170	85	51
2 Berth Roomette - Inside/no facilities*	142	71	42

*No linen - Linen may be rented separately.

	BELLINGHAM SEWARD	KETCHIKAN SEWARD	JUNEAU SEWARD
Passengers (12 yrs & older)	386	222	148
Child (2 yrs through 11 yrs)	194	112	74
AMC (Bicycles-Kayaks-Inflatables)	66	38	22
2 Wheeled Motorcycles	306	173	112
Vehicles up to 10 feet	504	286	187
Vehicles up to 15 feet	860	486	318
Vehcles up to 19 feet	1024	579	379
Vehicles up to 21 feet	1286	729	472
Vehicles up to 23 feet	1612	914	592
Vehicles up to 25 feet	1914	1085	703
CABINS			
4 Berth - Outside/complete facilities	587	339	239
4 Berth -Inside/complete facilities	496	286	198
2 Berth - Outside/complete facilities	421	244	172
2 Berth Outside/no facilities	337	196	139
2 Berth - Inside/no facilities	304	176	125
2 Berth Roomette - Outside/no facilities*	202	117	83
2 Berth Roomette - Inside/no facilities*	169	98	69

*No linen - Linen may be rented separately.

M/V TUSTUMENA CABIN TARIFFS

FOUR BERTH CABIN - OUTSIDE/COMPLETE FACILITIES — ITEM 4BF

BETWEEN / AND	UNALASKA	AKUTAN	FALSE PASS	COLD BAY	KING COVE	SAND POINT	CHIGNIK	KODIAK	PORT LIONS	SELDOVIA	HOMER	SEWARD
AKUTAN	23											
FALSE PASS	80	57										
COLD BAY	109	86	29									
KING COVE	122	129	72	43								
SAND POINT	152	165	108	79	68							
CHIGNIK	194	210	153	124	113	80						
KODIAK	282	295	238	209	194	166	124					
PORT LIONS	282	295	238	209	194	166	124	43				
SELDOVIA	337	350	293	264	250	216	182	96	96			
HOMER	328	342	285	256	242	209	175	88	88	43		
SEWARD	349	362	305	276	262	228	194	98	98	163	155	
VALDEZ	(NO DIRECT SAILINGS)							164	164	216	209	91

FOUR BERTH CABIN - INSIDE/NO FACILITIES — ITEM 4NO

BETWEEN / AND	UNALASKA	AKUTAN	FALSE PASS	COLD BAY	KING COVE	SAND POINT	CHIGNIK	KODIAK	PORT LIONS	SELDOVIA	HOMER	SEWARD
AKUTAN	19											
FALSE PASS	66	47										
COLD BAY	91	72	25									
KING COVE	102	108	61	36								
SAND POINT	127	138	91	66	57							
CHIGNIK	162	175	128	103	94	67						
KODIAK	235	246	199	174	162	138	103					
PORT LIONS	235	246	199	174	162	138	103	36				
SELDOVIA	281	292	245	220	208	180	152	80	80			
HOMER	274	285	238	213	202	174	146	73	73	36		
SEWARD	291	302	255	230	218	190	162	82	82	136	129	
VALDEZ	(NO DIRECT SAILINGS)							137	137	180	174	76

TWO BERTH CABIN - OUTSIDE/NO FACILITIES — ITEM 2NO

BETWEEN / AND	UNALASKA	AKUTAN	FALSE PASS	COLD BAY	KING COVE	SAND POINT	CHIGNIK	KODIAK	PORT LIONS	SELDOVIA	HOMER	SEWARD
AKUTAN	13											
FALSE PASS	47	33										
COLD BAY	64	51	17									
KING COVE	75	79	45	28								
SAND POINT	100	97	63	46	40							
CHIGNIK	129	129	95	78	68	43						
KODIAK	179	192	158	141	130	110	76					
PORT LIONS	179	192	158	141	130	110	76	28				
SELDOVIA	213	226	192	175	164	140	115	56	56			
HOMER	208	221	187	170	159	136	111	52	52	28		
SEWARD	218	230	196	179	168	144	119	60	60	101	96	
VALDEZ	(NO DIRECT SAILINGS)							103	103	144	140	54

M/V TUSTUMENA ALEUTIAN CHAIN TRIPS

LV KODIAK	WED	4:55 PM	LV UNALASKA	SAT	11:45 AM
LV CHIGNIK	THU	1:00 PM	LV AKUTAN	SAT	4:00 PM
LV SAND POINT	FRI	12:30 AM	LV COLD BAY	SUN	4:45 AM
LV KING COVE	FRI	9:00 AM	LV KING COVE	SUN	7:15 AM
LV COLD BAY	FRI	11:55 AM	LV SAND POINT	SUN	3:00 PM
LV FALSE PASS	FRI	5:30 PM	LV CHIGNIK	MON	1:45 AM
AR UNALASKA	SAT	6:30 AM	AR KODIAK	MON	8:15 PM

REFER TO COLOR CODED BARS ON M/V TUSTUMENA SCHEDULE BEGINNING AND ENDING AT KODIAK

M/V BARTLETT / AK RAILROAD SCHEDULE

Effective May 1, 1998

The M/V BARTLETT serves the port of Whittier using the Alaska Railroad shuttle between Portage and Whittier. In Portage, passengers and their vehicles load on an Alaska Railroad flatcar for a 40 minute sight-filled trip through mountain tunnels to Whittier, a former military town. Ferry service from Whittier is available to Cordova and Valdez.

PORTAGE TO WHITTIER*

LV	PORTAGE	10:15 AM
AR	WHITTIER	10:55 AM
LV	PORTAGE	1:20 PM
AR	WHITTIER	2:00 PM

WHITTIER TO PORTAGE

LV	WHITTIER	3:30 PM
AR	PORTAGE	4:10 PM
LV	WHITTIER	6:15 PM
AR	PORTAGE	6:55 PM

*Check-in time in Portage is one hour earlier than departure.

THE STATE OF ALASKA RESERVES THE RIGHT TO ALTER, REVISE OR CANCEL SCHEDULES AND RATES WITHOUT PRIOR NOTICE AND ASSUMES NO RESPONSIBILITY FOR DELAYS AND/OR EXPENSES DUE TO SUCH MODIFICATIONS.

SOUTHCENTRAL/SOUTHWEST ALASKA - M/V BARTLETT SCHEDULE

EFFECTIVE MAY 1 — MAY 28, 1998 AND AUGUST 28 — SEPTEMBER 13, 1998

MON	LV	CORDOVA	7:00 AM
	AR	WHITTIER	2:00 PM
	LV	WHITTIER	2:45 PM
	AR	CORDOVA	9:45 PM
TUE	LV	CORDOVA	12:30 AM
	AR	VALDEZ	6:15 AM
	LV	VALDEZ	7:15 AM
	AR	WHITTIER	2:00 PM
	LV	WHITTIER	2:45 PM
	AR	VALDEZ	9:30 PM
WED	LV	VALDEZ	6:45 AM **
	AR	CORDOVA	2:30 PM
	LV	CORDOVA	6:30 PM **
THU	AR	VALDEZ	2:15 AM
THU	LV	VALDEZ	7:15 AM
	AR	WHITTIER	2:00 PM
	LV	WHITTIER	2:45 PM
	AR	VALDEZ	9:30 PM
*FRI	LV	VALDEZ	12:15 AM ###
	AR	CORDOVA	6:00 AM
	LV	CORDOVA	7:00 AM
	AR	WHITTIER	2:00 PM
	LV	WHITTIER	2:45 PM
	AR	CORDOVA	9:45PM
SAT	LV	CORDOVA	12:30 AM ***
	AR	VALDEZ	6:15 AM
	LV	VALDEZ	7:15 AM
	AR	WHITTIER	2:00 PM
	LV	WHITTIER	2:45 PM
	AR	VALDEZ	9:30 PM
SUN	LV	VALDEZ	7:15 AM
	AR	WHITTIER	2:00 PM
	LV	WHITTIER	2:45 PM
	AR	VALDEZ	9:30 PM
	LV	VALDEZ	11:45 PM
MON	AR	CORDOVA	5:30 AM

*** PRINCE WILLIAM SOUND GOLD RUSH REGATTA MAY 9, 1998

SAT	LV	CORDOVA	12:30 AM	SAT	LV	WHITTIER	11:00 AM
	AR	WHITTIER	7:30 AM		AR	VALDEZ	6:00 PM

EFFECTIVE MAY 28, 1998 — AUGUST 28, 1998

MON	LV	VALDEZ	7:15 AM
	AR	WHITTIER	2:00 PM
	LV	WHITTIER	2:45 PM
	AR	CORDOVA	9:45 PM
MON	LV	CORDOVA	10:45 PM **
TUE	AR	VALDEZ	6:15 AM
	LV	VALDEZ	7:15 AM
	AR	WHITTIER	2:00 PM
TUE	LV	WHITTIER	2:45 PM
	AR	VALDEZ	9:30 PM
	LV	VALDEZ	11:45 PM
WED	AR	CORDOVA	5:30 AM
WED	LV	CORDOVA	7:00 AM
	AR	WHITTIER	2:00 PM
	LV	WHITTIER	2:45 PM
	AR	VALDEZ	9:30PM
THU	LV	VALDEZ	7:15 AM
	AR	WHITTIER	2:00 PM
	LV	WHITTIER	2:45 PM +++
	AR	VALDEZ	9:30 PM
FRI	LV	VALDEZ	5:00 AM **
	AR	CORDOVA	12:45 PM
	LV	CORDOVA	6:30 PM
SAT	AR	VALDEZ	12:15 AM
SAT	LV	VALDEZ	7:15 AM
	AR	WHITTIER	2:00 PM
	LV	WHITTIER	2:45 PM
	AR	VALDEZ	9:30 PM
SUN	LV	VALDEZ	7:15 AM
	AR	WHITTIER	2:00 PM
	LV	WHITTIER	2:45 PM
	AR	VALDEZ	9:30 PM

* Schedule begins here May 1, 1998.
** Tatitlek Whistle Stops available by notifying Valdez or Cordova terminal.
+++ Switch to this schedule at Whittier, Thursday May 28.
Switch to this schedule at Valdez, Friday August 28.

SOUTHCENTRAL/SOUTHWEST ALASKA M/V TUSTUMENA

MAY EASTBOUND

Leave SELDOVIA	Leave HOMER	PORT LIONS	Arrive KODIAK	Leave SEWARD	Arrive VALDEZ
SU3 6:00A	SU3 9:30A		SU3 7:00P		
	M4 9:30A		M4 7:00P		
T5 6:00P	T5 11:30P		W6 9:00A		
FROM ALEUTIAN CHAIN TRIP			M11 8:15P		
T12 4:00P	T12 7:55P	W13 6:30A	Lv. W13 4:00P	TH14 5:15A	
SU17 6:00A	SU17 9:30A		SU17 7:00P		
	M18 9:30A		M18 7:00P		
*T19 5:00P	W20 1:30A		Lv. W20 4:00P	TH21 9:45A	TH21 11:00P
SU24 5:00A	SU24 8:00A		SU24 5:30P		
	*M25 9:30A		M25 7:00P		
T26 7:00P	T26 9:55P	W27 8:30A	Lv. W27 4:00P	TH28 9:45A	TH28 11:00P
SU31 6:00A	SU31 9:30A		SU31 7:00P		

*** Kodiak King Crab Festival May 20 - 25**

MAY WESTBOUND

Leave VALDEZ	Leave SEWARD	Leave KODIAK	PORT LIONS	Leave HOMER	Arrive SELDOVIA
	F1 9:30P	S2 12:45P	S2 3:45P	SU3 3:30A	SU3 4:55A
		SU3 10:30P		Ar. M4 8:00A	
		M4 10:30P		T5 12:30P	T5 2:00P
		W6 4:55P	***TO ALEUTIAN CHAIN TRIP***		
		M11 10:30P		T12 12:30P	T12 2:00P
	F15 9:30P	S16 12:45P	S16 3:45P	SU17 3:30A	SU17 4:55A
		SU17 10:30P		Ar. M188:00A	
		M18 10:30P		T19 12:30P	T19 2:00P
F22 5:00A	F22 8:00P	S23 11:30A	S23 2:30P	SU24 2:30A	SU24 4:00A
		SU24 10:30P		Ar. M258:00A	
		M25 11:55P		T26 2:00P	T26 3:30P
F29 6:30A	F29 9:30P	S30 12:45P	S30 3:45P	SU31 3:30A	SU31 4:55A
		SU31 10:30P		Ar. M1 8:00A	

JUNE EASTBOUND

Leave SELDOVIA	Leave HOMER	PORT LIONS	Arrive KODIAK	Leave SEWARD	Arrive VALDEZ
	M1 9:30A		M1 7:00P		
T2 4:00P	T2 7:55P	W3 6:30A	Lv. W3 4:00P	TH4 9:45A	TH4 11:00P
SU7 6:00A	SU7 9:30A		SU7 7:00P		
	M8 9:30A		M8 7:00P		
T9 4:00P	T9 11:30P		W10 9:00A		
FROM ALEUTIAN CHAIN TRIP			M15 8:15P		
T16 4:00P	T16 7:55P	W17 6:30A	Lv. W17 4:00P	TH18 9:45A	TH18 11:00P
SU21 6:00A	SU21 9:30A		SU21 7:00P		
	M22 9:30A		M22 7:00P		
T23 4:00P	T23 7:55P	W24 6:30A	Lv. W24 4:00P	TH25 9:45A	TH25 11:00P
SU28 6:00A	SU28 9:30A		SU28 7:00P		
	M29 9:30A		M29 7:00P		
T30 4:00P	T30 7:55P	W1 6:30A	Lv. W1 4:00P	TH2 9:45A	TH2 11:00P

JUNE WESTBOUND

Leave VALDEZ	Leave SEWARD	Leave KODIAK	PORT LIONS	Leave HOMER	Arrive SELDOVIA
		M1 10:30P		T2 12:30P	T2 2:00P
F5 6:30A	F5 9:30P	S6 12:45P	S6 3:45P	SU7 3:30A	SU7 4:55A
		SU7 10:30P		Ar. M8 8:00A	
		M8 10:30P		T9 12:30P	T9 2:00P
		W10 4:55P	***TO ALEUTIAN CHAIN TRIP***		
		M15 10:30P		T16 12:30P	T16 2:00P
F19 6:30A	F19 9:30P	S20 12:45P	S20 3:45P	SU21 3:30A	SU21 4:55A
		SU21 10:30P		Ar. M228:00A	
		M22 10:30P		T23 12:30P	T23 2:00P
F26 6:30A	F26 9:30P	S27 12:45P	S27 3:45P	SU28 3:30A	SU28 4:55A
		SU28 10:30P		Ar. M298:00A	
		M29 10:30P		T30 12:30P	T30 2:00P

JULY EASTBOUND

Leave SELDOVIA	Leave HOMER	PORT LIONS	Arrive KODIAK	Leave SEWARD	Arrive VALDEZ
SU5 6:00A	SU5 9:30A		SU5 7:00P		
	M6 9:30A		M6 7:00P		
T7 4:00P	T7 11:30P		W8 9:00A		
FROM ALEUTIAN CHAIN TRIP			M13 8:15P		
T14 4:00P	T14 7:55P	W15 6:30A	Lv. W15 4:00P	TH16 9:45A	TH16 11:00P
SU19 6:00A	SU19 9:30A		SU19 7:00P		
	M20 9:30A		M20 7:00P		
T21 4:00P	T21 7:55P	W22 6:30A	Lv. W22 4:00P	TH23 9:45A	TH23 11:00P
SU26 6:00A	SU26 9:30A		SU26 7:00P		
	M27 9:30A		M27 7:00P		
T28 4:00P	T28 7:55P	W29 6:30A	Lv. W29 4:00P	TH30 9:45A	TH30 11:00P

JULY WESTBOUND

Leave VALDEZ	Leave SEWARD	Leave KODIAK	PORT LIONS	Leave HOMER	Arrive SELDOVIA
F3 6:30A	F3 9:30P	S4 12:45P	S4 3:45P	SU5 3:30A	SU5 4:55A
		SU5 10:30P		Ar. M6 8:00A	
		M6 10:30P		T7 12:30P	T7 2:00P
		W8 4:55P	***TO ALEUTIAN CHAIN TRIP***		
		M13 10:30P		T14 12:30P	T14 2:00P
F17 6:30A	F17 9:30P	S18 12:45P	S18 3:45P	SU19 3:30A	SU19 4:55A
		SU19 10:30P		Ar. M208:00A	
		M20 10:30P		T21 12:30P	T21 2:00P
F24 6:30A	F24 9:30P	S25 12:45P	S25 3:45P	SU26 3:30A	SU26 4:55A
		SU26 10:30P		Ar. M278:00A	
		M27 10:30P		T28 12:30P	T28 2:00P
F31 6:30A	F31 9:30P	S1 12:45P	S1 3:45P	SU2 3:30A	SU2 4:55A

AUGUST EASTBOUND

Leave SELDOVIA	Leave HOMER	PORT LIONS	Arrive KODIAK	Leave SEWARD	Arrive VALDEZ
SU2 6:00A	SU2 9:30A		SU2 7:00P		
	M3 9:30A		M3 7:00P		
T4 4:00P	T4 11:30P		W5 9:00A		
FROM ALEUTIAN CHAIIN TRIP			M10 8:15P		
T11 4:00P	T11 7:55P	W12 6:30A	Lv. W12 4:00P	TH13 9:45A	TH13 11:00P
SU16 6:00A	SU16 9:30A		SU16 7:00P		
	M17 9:30A		M17 7:00P		
T18 4:00P	T18 7:55P	W19 6:30A	Lv. W19 4:00P	TH20 9:45A	TH20 11:00P
SU23 6:00A	SU23 9:30A		SU23 7:00P		
	M24 9:30A		M24 7:00P		
T25 4:00P	T25 7:55P	W26 6:30A	Lv. W26 4:00P	TH27 9:45A	TH27 11:00P
SU30 6:00A	SU30 9:30A		SU30 7:00P		
	M31 9:30A		M31 7:00P		

AUGUST WESTBOUND

Leave VALDEZ	Leave SEWARD	Leave KODIAK	PORT LIONS	Leave HOMER	Arrive SELDOVIA
		SU2 10:30P		Ar. M3 8:00A	
		M3 10:30P		T4 12:30P	T4 2:00P
		W5 4:55P	***TO ALEUTIAN CHAIN TRIP***		
		M10 10:30P		T11 12:30P	T11 2:00P
F14 6:30A	F14 9:30P	S15 12:45P	S15 3:45P	SU16 3:30A	SU16 4:55A
		SU16 10:30P		Ar. M178:00A	
		M17 10:30P		T18 12:30P	T18 2:00P
F21 6:30A	F21 9:30P	S22 12:45P	S22 3:45P	SU23 3:30A	SU23 4:55A
		SU23 10:30P		Ar. M248:00A	
		M24 10:30P		T25 12:30P	T25 2:00P
F28 6:30A	F28 9:30P	S29 12:45P	S29 3:45P	SU30 3:30A	SU30 4:55A
		SU30 10:30P		Ar. M318:00A	
		M31 10:30P		T1 12:30P	T1 2:00P

SEPTEMBER EASTBOUND

Leave SELDOVIA	Leave HOMER	PORT LIONS	Arrive KODIAK	Leave SEWARD	Leave CORDOVA	Arrive VALDEZ
T1 4:00P	T1 7:55P	W2 6:30A	Lv.W2 4:00P	TH3 9:45A		TH3 11:00P
SU6 6:00A	SU6 9:30A		SU6 7:00P			
	M7 9:30A		M7 7:00P			
T8 4:00P	T8 11:30P		W9 9:00A			
FROM ALEUTIAN CHAIN TRIP			M14 8:15P			
T15 4:00P	T15 7:55P	W16 6:30A	Lv.W16 4:00P	TH17 9:45A	TH17 11:45P	*F18 7:30A
					S19 9:55P	SU20 3:30A
T22 1:00P	T22 7:55P	W23 6:30A	Lv.W23 4:00P	TH24 9:45A	TH24 11:45P	*F25 7:30A
					S26 9:55P	SU27 3:30A
T29 1:00P	T29 7:55P	W30 6:30A	Lv.W30 4:00P	TH1 9:45A	TH1 11:45P	*F2 7:30A

Whistle stops at Chenega Bay are on Thursdays Between Seward and Valdez arriving Chenega Bay at 2:15PM. Vessel will not stop if there are no reservations.

SEPTEMBER WESTBOUND

Leave VALDEZ	Arrive CORDOVA	Leave SEWARD	Leave KODIAK	PORT LIONS	Leave HOMER	Arrive SELDOVIA
F4 6:30A		F4 9:30P	S5 12:45P	S5 3:45P	SU6 3:30A	SU6 4:55A
			SU6 10:30P		Ar.M7 8:00A	
			M7 10:30P		T8 12:30P	T8 2:00P
			W9 4:55P	***TO ALEUTIAN CHAIN TRIP***		
			M14 10:30P		T15 12:30P	T15 2:00P
F18 9:00A	F18 2:30P					
SU20 4:30A	*SU20 1:45P	M21 2:15A	M21 6:00P	M21 9:00P	T22 9:00A	T22 10:30A
F25 9:00A	F25 2:30P					
SU27 4:30A	*SU27 1:45P	M28 2:15A	M28 6:00P	M28 9:00P	T29 9:00A	T29 10:30A

* SEPTEMBER ONLY - Whistle stops at Tatitlek. Vessel will not stop if there are no reservations.

SOUTHCENTRAL/SOUTHWEST ALASKA PASSENGER & VEHICLE TARIFFS

PASSENGER 12 YEARS & OVER (Meals and Berths NOT included) — ITEM ADT

BETWEEN / AND	UNALASKA	AKUTAN	FALSE PASS	COLD BAY	KING COVE	SAND POINT	CHIGNIK	KODIAK	PORT LIONS	SELDOVIA	HOMER	SEWARD	WHITTIER	VALDEZ	TATITLEK
AKUTAN	16														
FALSE PASS	46	34													
COLD BAY	62	50	18												
KING COVE	74	66	34	18											
SAND POINT	98	90	58	42	32										
CHIGNIK	132	124	92	76	66	42									
KODIAK	202	194	162	146	136	112	76								
PORT LIONS	202	194	162	146	136	112	76	20							
SELDOVIA	246	240	208	192	180	156	122	52	52						
HOMER	242	236	204	188	176	152	118	48	48	18					
SEWARD	250	242	210	194	184	160	124	54	54	100	96				
WHITTIER	316	308	276	260	250	226	190	120	120	166	162				
VALDEZ	292	286	254	238	226	202	168	98	98	142	138	58	58		
TATITLEK	292	286	254	238	226	202	168	98	98	142	138	58	58	30	
CORDOVA	292	286	254	238	226	202	168	98	98	142	138	58	58	30	30

CHILDREN 2 THROUGH 11 YEARS OLD (Under 2 Transported Free) — ITEM CHD

BETWEEN / AND	UNALASKA	AKUTAN	FALSE PASS	COLD BAY	KING COVE	SAND POINT	CHIGNIK	KODIAK	PORT LIONS	SELDOVIA	HOMER	SEWARD	WHITTIER	VALDEZ	TATITLEK
AKUTAN	8														
FALSE PASS	24	18													
COLD BAY	32	26	10												
KING COVE	38	34	18	10											
SAND POINT	50	46	30	22	16										
CHIGNIK	66	62	46	38	34	22									
KODIAK	102	98	82	74	68	56	38								
PORT LIONS	102	98	82	74	68	56	38	10							
SELDOVIA	124	120	104	96	90	78	62	26	26						
HOMER	122	118	102	94	88	76	60	24	24	10					
SEWARD	126	122	106	98	92	80	62	28	28	50	48				
WHITTIER	158	154	138	130	126	114	96	60	60	84	82				
VALDEZ	146	144	128	120	114	102	84	50	50	70	70	30	30		
TATITLEK	146	144	128	120	114	102	84	50	50	70	70	30	30	16	
CORDOVA	146	144	128	120	114	102	84	50	50	70	70	30	30	16	16

ALTERNATE MEANS OF CONVEYANCE (Bicycles-Kyaks-Inflatables) — ITEM AMC

BETWEEN / AND	UNALASKA	AKUTAN	FALSE PASS	COLD BAY	KING COVE	SAND POINT	CHIGNIK	KODIAK	PORT LIONS	SELDOVIA	HOMER	SEWARD	WHITTIER	VALDEZ	TATITLEK
AKUTAN	6														
FALSE PASS	10	8													
COLD BAY	12	10	8												
KING COVE	14	12	10	6											
SAND POINT	18	16	12	9	8										
CHIGNIK	23	18	14	15	13	9									
KODIAK	33	23	18	25	23	20	15								
PORT LIONS	33	23	23	25	23	20	15	6							
SELDOVIA	40	33	23	32	30	26	21	11	11						
HOMER	39	40	33	31	29	26	21	10	10	5					
SEWARD	40	39	40	32	30	27	22	11	11	18	17				
WHITTIER	50	44	42	42	40	37	31	21	21	28	27				
VALDEZ	47	54	52	38	37	33	28	18	18	24	24	10	8		
TATITLEK	47	54	52	38	37	33	28	18	18	24	24	10	8	8	
CORDOVA	47	54	52	38	37	33	28	18	18	24	24	10	8	8	8

TWO-WHEELED MOTORCYCLES (No trailers-Driver not included) — ITEM 705

BETWEEN / AND	UNALASKA	AKUTAN	FALSE PASS	COLD BAY	KING COVE	SAND POINT	CHIGNIK	KODIAK	PORT LIONS	SELDOVIA	HOMER	SEWARD	WHITTIER	VALDEZ	TATITLEK
FALSE PASS	38	N													
COLD BAY	52	O	14												
KING COVE	61		28	14											
SAND POINT	197	V	48	35	25										
CHIGNIK	227	E	78	64	55	35									
KODIAK	171	H	139	125	115	209	64								
PORT LIONS	171	I	139	125	115	209	64	15							
SELDOVIA	210	C	176	162	153	132	102	43	43						
HOMER	207	L	174	160	151	130	99	39	39	12					
SEWARD	213	E	178	164	155	135	105	45	45	84	81				
WHITTIER	265	S	232	219	209	189	160	100	100	139	135				
VALDEZ	246		213	199	190	169	139	82	82	121	118	40	29		
TATITLEK	246		213	199	190	169	139	82	82	121	118	40	29	24	
CORDOVA	246		213	199	190	169	139	82	82	121	118	40	29	24	24

All motorcycles must be fully secured on the car deck with tie-downs. It is the responsibility of the owner to ensure this is completed properly. Rope may be obtained from car deck personnel for lashing purposes.

VEHICLES UP TO 10 FEET (Driver NOT included) — ITEM 710

BETWEEN / AND	UNALASKA	AKUTAN	FALSE PASS	COLD BAY	KING COVE	SAND POINT	CHIGNIK	KODIAK	PORT LIONS	SELDOVIA	HOMER	SEWARD	WHITTIER	VALDEZ	TATITLEK
FALSE PASS	61	N													
COLD BAY	84	O	23												
KING COVE	99		45	23											
SAND POINT	133	V	79	56	41										
CHIGNIK	181	E	128	105	90	56									
KODIAK	279	H	225	203	188	154	105								
PORT LIONS	279	I	225	203	188	154	105	25							
SELDOVIA	341	C	286	264	249	215	166	69	69						
HOMER	335	L	281	259	214	210	161	64	64	19					
SEWARD	345	E	290	268	253	219	170	73	76	136	131				
WHITTIER	436	S	383	360	345	311	263	165	165	229	223				
VALDEZ	405		350	328	313	279	230	133	133	196	191	68	49		
TATITLEK	405		350	328	313	279	230	133	133	196	191	68	49	39	
CORDOVA	405		350	328	313	279	230	133	133	196	191	68	49	39	39

VEHICLES UP TO 15 FEET (Driver NOT included) — ITEM 715

BETWEEN / AND	UNALASKA	AKUTAN	FALSE PASS	COLD BAY	KING COVE	SAND POINT	CHIGNIK	KODIAK	PORT LIONS	SELDOVIA	HOMER	SEWARD	WHITTIER	VALDEZ	TATITLEK
FALSE PASS	104	N													
COLD BAY	142	O	38												
KING COVE	168		72	34											
SAND POINT	226	V	131	93	67										
CHIGNIK	311	E	215	177	151	93									
KODIAK	480	H	384	346	320	262	177								
PORT LIONS	480	I	384	346	320	262	177	39							
SELDOVIA	587	C	492	454	428	369	285	116	116						
HOMER	577	L	482	444	418	359	275	106	106	29					
SEWARD	593	E	498	460	434	376	291	122	122	233	223				
WHITTIER	753	S	657	619	593	535	450	281	281	392	382				
VALDEZ	697		602	564	538	480	395	226	226	337	327	112	72		
TATITLEK	697		602	564	538	480	395	226	226	337	327	112	72	64	
CORDOVA	697		602	564	538	480	395	226	226	337	327	112	72	64	64

VEHICLES UP TO 19 FEET (Driver NOT included) — ITEM 719

BETWEEN / AND	UNALASKA	AKUTAN	FALSE PASS	COLD BAY	KING COVE	SAND POINT	CHIGNIK	KODIAK	PORT LIONS	SELDOVIA	HOMER	SEWARD	WHITTIER	VALDEZ	TATITLEK
FALSE PASS	123	N													
COLD BAY	169	O	46												
KING COVE	200		87	41											
SAND POINT	269	V	156	110	80										
CHIGNIK	370	E	257	211	180	110									
KODIAK	571	H	458	412	381	312	211								
PORT LIONS	571	I	458	412	381	312	211	46							
SELDOVIA	699	C	586	540	509	439	339	138	138						
HOMER	687	L	574	528	497	428	327	126	126	35					
SEWARD	706	E	594	548	517	447	347	145	145	277	265				
WHITTIER	896	S	783	737	706	637	536	335	335	467	455				
VALDEZ	830		718	672	641	571	470	269	269	401	389	134	85		
TATITLEK	830		718	672	641	571	470	269	269	401	389	134	85	76	
CORDOVA	830		718	672	641	571	470	269	269	401	389	134	85	76	76

VEHICLES UP TO 21 FEET (Driver NOT included) — ITEM 721

BETWEEN / AND	UNALASKA	AKUTAN	FALSE PASS	COLD BAY	KING COVE	SAND POINT	CHIGNIK	KODIAK	PORT LIONS	SELDOVIA	HOMER	SEWARD	WHITTIER	VALDEZ	TATITLEK
FALSE PASS	158	N													
COLD BAY	217	O	59												
KING COVE	257		111	52											
SAND POINT	347	V	201	142	102										
CHIGNIK	477	E	331	272	232	142									
KODIAK	737	H	591	532	492	402	272								
PORT LIONS	737	I	591	532	492	402	272	59							
SELDOVIA	902	C	756	697	657	567	437	177	177						
HOMER	887	L	741	682	642	552	422	162	162	44					
SEWARD	912	E	766	707	667	577	447	187	187	357	342				
WHITTIER	1157	S	1011	952	912	822	692	432	432	602	587				
VALDEZ	1072		926	867	827	737	607	347	347	517	502	172	110		
TATITLEK	1072		926	867	827	737	607	347	347	517	502	172	110	97	
CORDOVA	1072		926	867	827	737	607	347	347	517	502	172	110	97	97

ALL TARIFFS AND RATES ARE QUOTED IN U.S. DOLLARS

TARIFFS — All fares are one-way. Fares for passengers, vehicles and staterooms are all calculated separately and must be added together to determine the total cost of your travel.

Passage and vehicle fares are charged from the port of embarkation to the port of debarkation. Stateroom fares are calculated according to the route taken, and may vary from the printed rates depending on the ship and schedules.

VEHICLE FARES — Vehicle fares are determined by the vehicle's overall length and width. Vehicles 8-1/2 to 9 feet wide will be charged approximately 125% of the listed fare. Vehicles over 9 feet wide will be charged approximately 150% of the listed fare. If you are towing a vehicle, the overall connected length is used to determine fares.

VEHICLES OVER 21 FEET — Contact any Marine Highway office for fares. The M/V TUSTUMENA can load vehicles to a maximum length of 40 feet. The M/V BARTLETT will accept vehicles up to 60 feet in length. Please notify your reservation agent at the time of booking if your vehicle is over 6 foot 6 inches in height. Fares for towed vehicles or trailers are calculated at their combined connected length. Vehicles may not be disconnected for travel at separate rates on the same sailing.

MINIMUM 25' RATE — Vehicles with high centers of gravity (commercial highway vans, loaded flat bed trailers) are charged at the 25 ft. rate unless the vehicle is over 25 ft.in which case the appropriate rate for the vehicle length applies. Contact the commerical booking desk (907) 465-8816 for information and reservations.

Communities, Highways, National Parks (NP), National Wildlife Refuges (NWR) and other attractions. *(*Detailed map.)*